THE ALMANAC OF AMERICAN POLITICS

THE ALMANAC OF AMERICAN POLITICS 1980

The Senators, the Representatives, the Governors,

—their records, states, and districts

MICHAEL BARONE
GRANT UJIFUSA
DOUGLAS MATTHEWS

Photography by Shepard Sherbell

E.P. DUTTON *New York*

As part of its non-profit educational objectives, the Fund for Constitutional Government assists THE ALMANAC OF AMERICAN POLITICS by co-publishing this edition with E. P. Dutton, providing the authors with research grants, and managing the direct mail marketing of both hard-cover and paperback editions. FCG's address is Room 4242, 515 Madison Avenue, New York, N.Y. 10022 Phone: (212) 421-2155.

Additional photo credits: Dev O'Neill, Chase Ltd., the Seattle *Times.*

Published simultaneously in Canada by
Clarke, Irwin & Company Limited, Toronto and Vancouver

ISBN: 0-525-93074-4 (Cloth)
ISBN: 0-525-93086-8 (Paper)
Library of Congress Catalog Card Number: 70-160417

First Edition
10 9 8 7 6 5 4 3 2 1

Acknowledgments

For the research help provided, the authors would like to thank Jonathan Baum, Audrey K. Burt, David Fischer, Walt Harris, Craig Lalley, Michael P. Leahy, Weston Loegering, Jeffrie Lyons, Sunday Orme, Jonathan Simon, Ann Spaner, David Zimansky, and John Hodgkins.

For their support, enthusiasm, and hard work at E.P. Dutton, the authors are indebted to Constance Schrader, Guido Anderau, and David Zable.

Similarly at Inforonics, many thanks to Gloria Nillson, Elaine Handel, Mike Chievers, and Larry Buckland.

Special thanks to Stewart R. Mott and the Fund for Constitutional Government, and to Daphne Dwyer, Karen Kessler, and Anne Zill.

Contents

Abbreviations

ABS	Absent *or* Abstain
ACA	Americans for Constitutional Action
ADA	Americans for Democratic Action
CFA	Consumer Federation of America
CG	Coast Guard
CHOB	Cannon House Office Building
COPE	Committee on Political Education
D	Democrat
Debt.	Interest on Government Securities
DFL	Democrat-Farmer-Labor Party
DNV	Did not vote
DOC	Department of Commerce
DOD	Department of Defense
DOI	Department of Interior
DOT	Department of Transportation
DSOB	Dirksen Senate Office Building
EPA	Environmental Protection Agency
ERDA	Energy Research & Development Administration
HEW	Department of Health, Education, and Welfare
HUD	Department of Housing and Urban Development
Ind.	Independent
Jt. Com.	Joint Committee
LCV	League of Conservation Voters
LHOB	Longworth House Office Building
L	Liberal Party
NAB	National Association of Businessmen
NASA	National Aeronautics and Space Agency
NE	Not [yet] Elected
NFU	National Farmers' Union
NSI	National Security Index of the American Security Council
NTU	National Taxpayers Union
PC	Public Citizen
R	Republican
Rank. Mbr.	Ranking Member
RevS	Revenue Sharing
RHOB	Rayburn House Office Building
RSOB	Russell Senate Office Building
Sel. Com.	Select Committee
Sp. Com.	Special Committee
Sub.	Subcommittee
USAF	United States Air Force
USAFR	United States Air Force Reserve
USDA	United States Department of Agriculture
USMC	United States Marine Corps
USMCR	United States Marine Corps Reserve
VA	Veterans Administration
ZIP CODES:	Senate—20510 House—20515

Introduction

As the nation enters the political year of 1980, an unmistakable mood of depression and uncertainty lies across the land. Though the country continues to enjoy a broad-based prosperity and finds itself fighting no wars anywhere in the world, an overwhelming number of us have very little confidence in our political system and the government it provides. But we encounter a paradox. A majority of Americans doubt that government can do anything to solve the country's big problems. At the same time, however, that same majority believes that those problems, if they are to be faced at all, can not be faced and solved without government action.

What accounts for our state of psychic depression, uncertainty, and confusion? In the last ten or twelve years, the fundamental sense we have had of ourselves has been jolted by a series of blows that were completely unanticipated. There was first a war we could not win—the experience called Vietnam. Neither did we win in Korea, but with the last veteran of the Civil War long since dead, few Americans were prepared to deal with a war that so split our society and culture.

Second, the confidence we once had in future of our economy and our personal lives has been shaken by rates of inflation we have never before seen. This is something that our present generation of leaders, raised during the deflationary times of the Depression and the controlled economy of World War II, find hard to comprehend. The flush times coupled with the real growth of the early sixties lead many Americans to believe that unemployment and recession, not inflation, should engage the almost complete attention of our policymakers. That has changed with a vengeance, and we are left uncertain as to what the shift in concerns might mean for us.

Finally, there was the experience called Watergate, wherein the legitimacy of our higrest elected official was called into doubt. The upshot was that the American public was forced to admit that, for once, it has failed to choose an honest and fair-minded man president. The issue of legitimacy, however, may go back further than the crimes of Richard Nixon. The assassination of President John Kennedy in 1963 and then of Senator Robert Kennedy in 1968 seems to have led many Americans to feel that they were being led by men not of their own choosing, that the course of history itself had been deceived. In any case, it is clearly evident that voter participation—one index of satisfaction with the political system—reached a zenith in the years 1960 and 1962, and has fallen ever since. Meanwhile, the confidence accorded our national leadership in the fifties and early sixties has not reappeared.

Other advanced industrial democracies have trouble making sense of the black mood that afflicts the world's great military and economic power. That which we may regard as unprecedented and profoundly unnerving, most Europeans and the Japanese have understood to be part of the nature of things. Within living memory, people of these societies have lived through massive inflation as well as deep depression, and they have seen themselves utterly defeated militarily and occupied by foreign powers. Moreover, most Europeans, and the Japanese have endured political leadership which many, if not most, of the citizenry considered illegitimate. To them, matters like Vietnam, Watergate, and inflation are simply political and economic problems that must be faced, and if possible, overcome and solved. To us, however, these issues have induced soul searching, handwringing, and doubt.

Which brings us to a way of looking at the American people of the seventies. They have asked for a president to undo the damage done to us by events of the recent past. To an extent greater than is perceived, much of the damage has in fact been repaired. The country is no longer at war in Vietnam, and if Washington did not get what it wanted there, our society is no longer deeply divided over the issue. Some expected recriminations against war protestors, but that has in no way materialized. In fact, most politicians today take for granted that we cannot intervene militarily in third world conflicts.

Watergate was also resolved. Nixon was forced to quit, and he was replaced by two men, Ford and Carter, who possess qualities Nixon so conspicuously lacked—honesty and an identification with the ordinary person. But given our negative mood, such virtues now don't seem to matter much. In fact, we have seen a resurgence of interest in aggressive and imperious presidential leadership, the kind of leadership practiced by Johnson and Nixon which the public once found so distasteful.

Inflation, and inflation as it is linked to the supply and cost of energy, remains a problem. And it is a problem for which there is no pat solution. This Americans find hard to take. It used to be that people who wanted to stop inflation went Republican and those who wanted to get out of a recession voted Democratic. But for most of the seventies inflation raged under Republican administrations. Meanwhile, the energy issue is not one that can be easily sorted out by traditional New Deal categories, and acted upon by the voter. Instead, the politics of energy breaks down into a conflict between regions, and the issue resists solution because the competing regions are so evenly matched.

So elections are fought in an increasingly negative atmosphere. Voter turnout declines. Job ratings of all public officials, not just the president, tend to decline. Yet there is some evidence that we may be reaching a turning point—a kind of revolution of lowered expectations. Even as we have berated President Ford or President Carter for not being able to deliver what we have wanted, we have begun to think that perhaps no one can; even as we nostalgically long for the kind of leadership provided by Franklin Roosevelt. FDR, however, was president at a time when our economy was in collapse and then when our nation was united in support of a total war. The country's condition was more desperate than it is today, but it was also easier then to persuade people to support a program, or anything that might conceivably help. In our times, when most people are comfortable and many have vested interests in the status quo, it is much harder to produce change.

This negative attitude affects elections for every office, from the presidency to the local county council, but the impact of the attitude varies.

The presidency is of course the focus of our politics. As this is written in mid-1979, it is risky to predict anything about the 1980 presidential race, yet some of the fundamentals already seem clear. Jimmy Carter approaches 1980 as Gerald Ford did 1976—a president with mild personal popularity and a low job rating. Voters are not upset with his issue positions—he is probably closer to the average voter in major issues than any other public figure—but they believe he is ineffective. Carter appears vulnerable to Edward Kennedy and perhaps to Jerry Brown in the Democratic primaries, and he is by no means a certain winner in a general election. Incumbency, in these sour times, may have become a liability rather than an asset.

Yet there may be certain advantages to Carter's position. The 1977 and 1978 gubernatorial elections showed that voters skeptically scrutinize not only incumbents but also their challengers in elections for executive office. Thus governors who were not especially popular were reelected in New York, New Jersey, Connecticut, Ohio, and California. Moreover, it is by no means certain that Edward Kennedy will run or that if he does he can maintain the same level of popularity he has as a non-candidate. Carter is still vulnerable in the Democratic primary setting; not that many primary voters or party activists have strong positive feelings about him. He won the nomination in 1976 as a kind of alternative candidate: less liberal than Udall and the others in New Hampshire, less conservative than Wallace in Florida. While he might be defeated in the primaries and might even choose not to run, he cannot be counted out in 1980.

There is not much point in trying to predict the Republican nominee. The outcome of the general election will depend to some extent on the state of the economy and the energy problem, but many of the old rules of the game no longer hold up. Voters want limits to the size of government, but they did not give Republicans—the traditional less-government party—anything like an overwhelming victory in 1978, and at this writing the voters appear ready to give a majority of their votes in 1980 to the leading advocate of new government programs, Edward Kennedy. The public show no sign of believing that either party or any candidate can solve the inflation or energy problems, and so presumably votes will be cast on other bases: traditional party identification, regional loyalties, cultural antipathy, minor issues. In every presidential election year but one for the last 40 years, the incumbent president has at least tried to win reelection. The outcome as we approach 1980 seems as uncertain as it ever has been.

One of the biggest political stories of the 1978 election year centered on the defeats, sometimes in upsets, of several liberal Democratic senators: Hathaway of Maine, McIntyre of New Hampshire, Clark of Iowa, Anderson of Minnesota, Haskell of Colorado. To some extent this phenomenon, and the generally more conservative mood of the newly elected senators, reflected the concern over the size and cost of government—a matter that also received expression in the California voters' approval of Proposition 13 and the Republicans' endorsement of the Kemp-Roth plan to cut federal income taxes. All of this nicely reflects the general negative mood of voters; who at once want to dismantle our makeshift welfare state we have in America, but who fear that it has become too expensive and gotten out of control. Another factor in the Democrats' defeat were so-called single issues, most prominent of them abortion. Groups concerned about such issues were able to organize opposition to incumbents based on their stands on them, and to persuade significant segments of the electorate—like the normally heavily Democratic Catholics of Iowa—to vote against an incumbent on the basis of that single issue. In some cases, the Republicans elected Jepsen in Iowa, Humphrey in New Hampshire—are not among their party's most attractive candidates, and one wonders if they would have won had attention and media scrutiny had been focused on them from the beginning.

There has been much hand-wringing over the phenomenon of single issue voting, but its real significance is that it shows how incumbent senators (or well known Senate candidates) have become the point men of American politics. Executive officials—governors, perhaps even presidents—are reelected if voters conclude the alternative would be worse. Theer is no way in such elections to vent one's frustrations and anger with what is. House elections are usually contests between familiar, non-controversial incumbents and unknown challengers; there is little room here either for expression of negative attitudes. But in Senate races all the major candidates are fairly well known, with their issue positions evident to most voters. A challenger can comb an incumbent's hundreds of roll call votes and find some that may be obnoxious to a key group of voters. The Senate races are one opportunity for voters in these negative times to vote against somebody, and so it should be no surprise that in 1976 and 1978 most of the senators who had serious challenges lost.

For 1980, this may mean great trouble for the Democrats, who hold 24 of the 34 seats that are up in November. It seems almost certain that the Democrats will lose a few seats. Many of their incumbents have some vulnerability, while only a few of the 10 Republican seats provide good Democratic targets. The trend in the Senate in the late seventies has been decidedly to the right. Democrats in states like Colorado and Iowa have been replaced, in effect, by much more conservative Democrats from states like Nebraska and Oklahoma. Republicans have had particular success in the Rocky Mountain states, which are now represented by more than half a dozen young, dedicated, and very conservative Republicans. The upshot is that the Senate, for much of the sixties and early seventies, the liberal bastion of the federal government, now is distinctly more conservative than the House on many issues.

Meanwhile, the House remains substantially the same body that was elected in 1974, when the reaction to Watergate helped deliver 40-odd to young, ambitious Democrats who grew to political maturity in the years of Vietnam and Richard Nixon. Most of these Democrats have survived politically. Although the major issues that developed in the 1978 congressional elections—controlling the size of government, cutting taxes—seemed initially to favor the Republicans, Democrats were adept enough to turn the issues to their advantage. Few of the 1974 freshman Democrats have been defeated, and Democrats lost no more than 11 seats in 1978; since 1974, the Democratic House majority has slipped from 290 to 276 seats, not a major loss.

Nonetheless, the atmosphere and trend of thinking are very much different in the House than one might have anticipated five years ago. This class of '74 Democrats, along with like minded Democrats elected in the years since remain an important part of the House, were and are liberal on non-economic issues—like Vietnam and Watergate—but they do not automatically plunk for the traditional Democratic line on economic issues. Lobbyists for organized labor, in particular, have learned as much to their sorrow. Organized labor began the 1977 lobbying year by pushing the common situs picketing bill, a measure that would most benefit the building trades. It had passed before in 1976, but was beaten in a stunning upset early in the Carter Administration. Labor lobbyists have never really recovered. Once one of the most powerful lobbies in the House, it saw most of its priority legislation defeated in the 95th Congress. On other measures as well, the younger Democrats were not reliable allies of tradtiional Democratic liberals.

To a surprising extent, the initiative in the House has been seized by the Republicans, badly outnumbered but usually cohesive and led by a group of younger, aggressive, partisan, and solidly conservative members. Unlike the younger Democrats, they have a definite economic program—lower government spending, greater incentives for private enterprise, an end to government controls and much government regulation. That program, they believe, will solve most of the nation's problems. The Republicans have the luxury all minorities enjoy of being able to attack the party in power from many angles without being responsible for the policy adopted in the end, and they have shown the ability as well to attract enough Democratic votes—from many quarters, not just to the South—to prevail on many issues. If the Democrats should lose a substantial number of seats in 1980—that is, more than they have lost since 1974—Republicans will have the potential to take effective control of the House. And out in the 435 congressional districts, first soundings indicate that most of the young, ambitious, well-financed candidates who are seeking to beat incumbents or seize open districts, are—unlike 1974 and 1976—Republicans.

The political perspective for 1980 would not be complete without a look at the increasingly divergent political attitudes found in the various regions of the country. Elections for governor and other state offices—though there are not that many governorships up in 1980—are simply no comprehensible without a regional perspective. The nation is split along regional lines on one of the two major issues before it, energy, and to an increasing extent it is also similarly split on the issue of government spending and taxes. We are a long way from the America of the sixties when there was little difference between California and New Jersey Democrats or between Iowa and Tennessee Republicans. We are moving toward what Kevin Phillips calls "the Balkanization of America."

The East was once the richest part of the nation, the home of its major economic institutions and private capital. Increasingly in the seventies the East has come to see itself as an economically aggrieved region, dependent on support from the federal government. The East produces little energy, but with its air conditioned office buildings and cold winters, it consumes a great deal. Energy costs here are the highest in the nation, and virtually every politician from the region supports controls over the prices of oil and gas. State taxes are higher here than anywhere else, and yet these states, with sluggish economic growth or even population losses, are typically tight-pinched fiscally. So it is no surprise that the East strongly supports federal aid programs. The region also pioneered major government services; now, with its high wage structure driving low skill jobs elsewhere, it finds it hard to pay for them. The East is not monolithically Democratic in presidential elections, though Democrats usually win most of its electoral votes. Against a candidate who is perceived, as Barry Goldwater was in 1964, as a dismantler of federal spending programs, the East will probably be solidly, if unenthusiastically, Democratic.

The West often seems like another country. Here population and economic growth has been most rapid in the seventies. The Rocky Mountain states and of course Alaska are energy exporters, and although environmental issues are important here, these states are, for the most part, boosters of rapid growth and free enterprise. These states have become the most Republican section of the country, and seem particularly antipathetic to Jimmy Carter. Meanwhile, California, Oregon, and Washington, painted a different picture. On cultural issues—Vietnam, Watergate, marijuana, the environment, homosexuality—they are probably the most liberal in the country. Traditional ties of all sorts are weak here; people are affluent and want to be free to indulge a favorite life style. But their affluence has also moved their politics very much to the right on economic issues. California gave the nation Proposition 13, a successful effort to use the meat-axe approach on state and local government by cutting property taxes. Opponents of Proposition 13, including Jerry Brown, charged that it would bring chaos if passed; backers of Proposition 13, including Jerry Brown after the voters spoke, said that there was plenty of fat in government and plenty of the surplus resulting from California's very productive private economy. All of the West except Hawaii went for Gerald Ford in 1976, but the West Coast states—which have most of the region's electoral votes—gave Ford only narrow margins, and will likely be seriously contested in 1980.

The South has developed a politics that is distinctively its own, one based not on race, as it was for so many years, but on economics. Jimmy Carter finally banished the race issue from the South by beating George Wallace in the 1976 primaries and by forging a coalition of poor and working class whites and blacks to carry all of the region except Virginia in the general election. The results in many states were close, howevr, reflecting the large size of the affluent white vote, which is overwhelmingly conservative and usually Republican. And in 1978, when the affluent had more elan, they won some notable victories. The South, especially in Texas, unlike the East or the West Coast, has virtually no radical chic politics, nor does it have very many Archie Bunkers. It is a politics where the people who belong to the country club vote against the people who work in the textile mills, with the blacks staying pretty much solidly with candidates they consider most sympathetic to them.

The South is further split these days by the energy issue. The big oil-producing states, Texas, Louisiana, Oklahoma, and Mississippi, strongly oppose government price controls and regulations over what most voters here seem to regard as *their* industry. So it seems hardly likely that any of these states will vote for a backer of controls, either in the primaries or the general election. But east of the energy states, starting with Arkansas, Tennessee, and Alabama, through to the Carolinas, the balance is different. These are states where blue collar workers tend to outnumber affluent voters. Like the energy states, they have seen substantial population and economic growth in the late sixties and seventies. At the same time, they have not seen the outmigration of the young which was typical of earlier decades, and their take home pay, after basic expenses and taxes, is now competitive with the East. But there is no identification here with the needs of the oil industry, and so a politics based on economics leaves these states very competitive in 1980.

That leaves the Midwest, which, at its fringes, resembles surrounding regions. Cleveland and job-losing cities like Youngstown and Dayton in Ohio have many of the same problems—and the same attitudes toward government programs—as much of the East. Out in North Dakota, one finds the same kind of strip coal mining as one gets in Montana—raising the same kind of issues. Below a line formed by U.S. 40, the old National Road, stretching from Wheeling, West Virginia, through Columbus, Indianapolis, St. Louis, and Kansas City, people speak with a Southern accent and often possess voting patterns to match. Southern Ohio and rural Missouri gave Jimmy Carter the electoral votes of those crucial states in 1976—the only Midwestern votes he won aside from Walter Mondale's Minnesota and neighboring Wisconsin. In general, the region has become the battleground of close presidential elections: Kennedy carried crucial states here in 1960, Humphrey failed to do so in 1968, and Carter was successful in just enough in 1976. For 1980 the Midwest may also be the key. Regional trends seem to give Democrats an edge in the East and Republicans the advantage in the West; the South, despite its seeming monolithic behavior in the past, may well be split. That would leave the outcome of the election in the hands of the closely divided larg and medium sized states of the Midwest.

But American politics cannot be seen only as the product of broad trends. The results of elections are also the product of a detailed, complex electoral system—more complex by far than that of any other major democracy. Jimmy Carter's victory in 1976, for example, can be seen as a product of certain basic desires among American voters. But it could not have occurred without Carter campaign's shrewd strategy in the complicated Democratic delegate selection process. The *Almanac of American Politics* attempts to present for the general reader and the specialist some of the basic facts about American politics and some of the basic trends, state by state and district by district.

I. THE GOVERNOR, THE SENATOR, THE REPRESENTATIVE

A. Biographies and Career

This section lists the date each governor, senator, and representative was first elected, when the governors' and senators' seats are up, their residence, and relevant facts about their personal background. Also listed is a brief outline of the office-holder's career, and his or her capitol and home offices and telephone numbers.

B. Committees

In every legislative body, most of the real work takes place in committees and subcommittees, not on the floor. Such is especially true in the Congress. Issues are framed, compromises are worked out, technical language is drafted in committee or subcommittee; so often all the decisions have really been made by the time a bill reaches the floor. Particularly in the House, committees are so important to the legislative process that you would do well to think of your congressman as a committee member rather than as a member of the House as a whole.

Within recent memory, committees were typically dominated or even controlled by their chairmen. Within the last ten years that has ceased to be the case. In the House, beginning with the Congress elected in 1974, committee chairmen are elected by the members of the majority party; and in the first such election three chairmen were defeated. Since then a number of powerful committee and subcommittee chairmen have been forced out in large part because they knew they could no longer win such elections—Wayne Hays of House Administration, Charles Diggs of the District of Columbia Committee, and Daniel Flood of the Labor-HEW Appropriations Subcommittee. The old seniority system is still generally followed. But it can be ignored when it produces results that make no sense: after the 1978 elections the important Health Subcommittee chair was contested by two talented Democrats neither of whom would have gotten it under the old system. And even when a chairman is selected according to seniority, he knows he holds his chair under the sufferance of the Democratic Caucus and behaves accordingly. The most notable example here is Jamie Whitten, the Mississippian who now chairs the Appropriations Committee, and in just about the way most Democrats would like to see it chaired.

The Senate has not had such reforms, but has perhaps needed them less. Because there are fewer senators than representatives, most senators chair (or are ranking minority members on) more than one subcommittee. With fewer opportunities for one senator to ride roughshod over others, the others usually have the means to retaliate. Because senators have more committee responsibilities, what happens in fact, is that more of the actual legislative work in the Senate is done by staff than is the case in the House, consequently, senators are often at a disadvantage in conference committee fights with their more knowledgeable counterparts from the other side of the Capitol.

We have listed each member's committee and subcommittee assignments and in parentheses his or her seniority on each. Seniority is calculated only with reference to members of the same political party. For Democrats, the first ranking member is the chairman, the second is "2d," and so forth. For Republicans, the most senior member is called "ranking member," the next, "2d," and so forth. In the appendix we have listed the full membership of all standing committees and subcommittees.

The following is a list of committees of both houses, with a short description of the jurisdiction of each. More complete descriptions of important committees and subcommittees will be found in the Political Background sections of their chairmen.

Standing Committees of the Senate

Agriculture, Nutrition, and Forestry—agriculture, meat inspection, forestry, nutrition and anti-hunger programs, farm credit and farm security, rural electrification.

Appropriations—all federal appropriations. Since the Appropriations Committee passes on federal spending for all departments and agencies, any one of the Appropriations subcommittees may have just as much influence over an agency as the corresponding standing committee. However, Appropriations' freedom of action has been limited somewhat by the limits set by the Budget Committee.

Armed Services—defense, Panama Canal, Naval petroleum reserves (except Alaska), military aeronautical and space activities.

Banking, Housing, and Urban Affairs—banking and currency, financial aid to industry, public and private housing, price controls over commodities and services, export controls, urban mass transit.

Budget—sets targets for federal revenues and expenditures.

Commerce, Science, and Transportation—interstate commerce, transportation (railroads, buses, trucks, vessels, pipelines, and civil aviation), communications, civil aeronautics, consumer products and services, merchant marine, navigation (oceans and inland waterways), Coast Guard, Bureau of Standards, sports.

Energy and Natural Resources—policy concerning regulation and conservation of energy including research and development, oil and gas production and distribution (including Alaskan oil reserves), solar energy, nuclear energy development, hydroelectric power, and coal production; public lands and the minerals thereon; national parks and forest reserves; mining; territorial possessions of the U.S.

Environment and Public Works—environmental policy, fisheries and wildlife, air and water pollution, environmental regulation and control of nuclear energy, water resources, flood control, rivers and harbors, bridges and dams, highways, public buildings.

Finance—taxation, customs, tariffs and import quotas—reciprocal trade agreements, Social Security, revenue sharing.

Foreign Relations—foreign affairs, including consideration of all treaties and executive agreements (except reciprocal trade agreements), World Bank, International Monetary Fund.

Governmental Affairs—structure of the federal government, including reorganization; the budgetary process, and intergovernmental relations; District of Columbia, Civil Service, Postal Service, Census Bureau, National Archives.

Human Resources—education, labor, public health, aging, the handicapped, arts and humanities.

Judiciary—constitutional amendments, federal judiciary and penal systems, antitrust, immigration and naturalization, bankruptcy, espionage, counterfeiting, patent, copyrights, trademarks.

Rules and Administration—federal elections, credentials and election of senators, corrupt practices, internal housekeping matters.

Small Business—small business.

Veterans' Affairs—veterans' pensions, compensation, education, and medical benefits; national cemeteries.

Standing Committees of the House

Agriculture—agriculture, meat inspection, forestry, nutrition and anti-hunger programs, rural development.

Appropriations—all federal appropriations. Since the Appropriations Committee passes on federal spending for all departments and agencies, any one of the Appropriations subcommittees may have just as much influence over an agency as the corresponding standing committee. However, Appropriations' freedom of action has been limited somewhat by the limits set by the Budget Committee.

Armed Services—defense, Naval petroleum reserves, international arms control and disarmament.

Banking, Finance, and Urban Affairs—banking and currency, public and private housing, price controls of commodities and services, financial aid to industry, other than transportation, urban development.

Budget—sets targets for federal revenues and expenditures.

District of Columbia—District of Columbia. However, the District now has home rule and does much of its own legislating.

Education and Labor—education, labor, welfare, including the various antipoverty and work programs.

Government Operations—structure of the federal government, including reorganization, the budgetary process, and intergovernmental relations; National Archives.

House Administration—internal housekeeping matters, including laws relating to raising, reporting, and using campaign funds in elections to the House.

Interior and Insular Affairs—public lands and the minerals thereon, forest reserves and national parks, island possessions of the U.S., irrigation and reclamation, mining, oil conservation, Indians, the regulation of the nuclear energy industry.

Foreign Affairs—foreign affairs. This committee changed its name to International Relations in 1975 and changed it back to Foreign Affairs in 1979.

Interstate and Foreign Commerce—interstate and foreign commerce, railroads, communications, securities and power regulation, inland waterways, public health, nuclear energy, consumer affairs.

Judiciary—federal judiciary and penal system, constitutional amendments and revision of statutes, antitrust, immigration and naturalization, bankruptcy, espionage, counterfeiting, patents, copyrights, trademarks.

Merchant Marine and Fisheries—merchant marine, navigation, water-borne common carriers except those under the jurisdiction of the Interstate Commerce Commission, Coast Guard, fisheries and wildlife, Panama Canal, international fishing agreements.

Post Office and Civil Service—Civil Service, Postal Service, Census Bureau.

Public Works—rivers and harbors, bridges and dams, navigation on internal waterways, flood control, water power, water pollution, federal buildings, highways, civil aeronautics, transportation, including buses, trucks, and gas pipelines.

Rules—conduct of House business. The Rules Committee is responsible for setting a "rule" for each bill that comes before the House. The rule sets the terms of debate and amendment, and so can have much influence on the outcome. This power to set rules is what makes this committee so important.

Science and Technology—NASA, National Science Foundation, all non-military research and development, science scholarships, Bureau of Standards, all energy research and development.

Small Business—small business.

Ways and Means—taxation, customs, tariffs, import quotas and restrictions, reciprocal trade agreements, Social Security.

Joint Committees are made up of members from both houses, with the chair rotating between senior House and Senate members of the majority party. The most important of these bodies is the Joint Economic Committee. Since joint committees do not have legislative powers, they are less important than standing committees.

C. Group Ratings

A large number of groups seek to rate the records of members of Congress according to their own lights. We have included the 1976, 1977, and 1978 ratings of all members of the 96th Congress by 11 different organizations. In our judgment, these group ratings represent, in composite, a reasonably accurate picture of the voting records of members. We have arranged the various groups' ratings on a rough spectrum—"liberals" on the left and "conservatives" on the right, with single-issue groups in the middle. We have used the percentage figure supplied by the named organization; where none is supplied, we have calculated the percentage of votes deemed correct by that organization of total votes cast by the member. The groups whose ratings we have used are as follows:

• ADA—Americans for Democratic Action, 1411 K Street NW, Washington DC 20005. This is generally regarded as the premier liberal political organization in the United States, and its ratings reflect explicitly liberal values.

• COPE—AFL-CIO Committee on Political Education, 815 16th Street NW, Washington DC 20006. This rating reflects the point of view of the nation's largest organized labor organization.

• PC—Public Citizen, 133 C Street SE, Washington DC 20003. This is an organization founded by Ralph Nader in 1971, and tends to reflect his views.

• RIPON—The Ripon Society, 800 18th Street NW, Washington DC 20006. This is a group of people who identify themselves as liberal Republicans.

• NFU—National Farmers Union, 1012 14th Street NW, Washington DC 20005. This farmers' organization tends to be closer in views to Democrats than Republicans, in contrast to, inter alia, the American Farm Bureau Federation, which does not issue ratings.

• CFA—Consumers' Federation of America, 1012 14th Street NW, Washington DC 20005. This group describes itself as pro-consumer.

• NAB—National Associated Businessmen, Inc., 1000 Connecticut Avenue NW, Washington DC 20036. This is a group which works for economy in government, concentrating on domestic spending, and which issues regularly a "Watchdog of the Treasury" award.

• NSI—National Security Index of the American Security Council, 499 S. Capitol SW, Washington DC 20003. This index reflects support for or opposition to major defense expenditures and military programs.

• ACA—Americans for Constitutional Action, 955 L'Enfant Plaza SW, Washington DC 20024. This is a group as explicitly conservative as the ADA is liberal.

• NTU—National Taxpayers Union, 1521 Pennsylvania Avenue SE, Washington DC 20003. This group wants to cut government spending and compiles a rating based on every spending vote in Congress during the year.

D. Key Votes

Finally, we have attempted to provide ourselves some indication of how members of Congress have voted on major issues by indicating their stands on each of 15 key votes. The selection of such key votes is necessarily a difficult business. On the one hand, there is the danger of selecting a vote which combines two issues—typically, a procedural and a substantive issue—which allows a member to argue that although he favors substantive program A he voted against it in order to uphold procedural principle B. On the other hand, there is the danger of selecting votes which are so one-sided or on which there was so little question of the outcome that many members could vote differently from the way they would vote if their decision really made a difference to the outcome.

The votes here have been chosen to spotlight members' views on major issues, particularly those which are not readily apparent from their party affiliation of their group ratings. The FOR and AGN notations convey the legislator's attitude toward the basic issue; depending on how the parliamentary question was framed, he might have voted yea or nay in either case. The notation NE means that a member was not a member of that house at the time the vote was taken. Our treatment of paired votes is as follows. When a legislator wants to vote on a bill but finds it inconvenient or impossible to attend the session, he will sometimes call a colleague who takes the opposite position and agree with him to refrain from voting. They form a "pair" on the record, with zero net result. The pairs are recorded, and we have taken them as substantive votes. When there is no pair, and the member does not vote, we have noted ABS for absent.

Here are brief descriptions of each of the 15 Senate and 15 House key votes.

SENATE

(1) Warnke Nom. March 9, 1977. Confirmation of President Carter's nomination of Paul C. Warnke to head the U.S. delegation to the Strategic Arms Limitation (SALT) talks with the Soviet Union. Confirmed 58–40. Yea = FOR Warnke Nom; Nay = AGN Warnke Nom.

(2) Neutron Bomb. H.R. 7553, July 13, 1977. Amendment by Mark Hatfield (R-Oreg) to prohibit production of any enhanced radiation weapon (i.e., the neutron bomb). Rejected 38–58. Yea = AGN Neutron Bomb; Nay = FOR Neutron Bomb.

(3) Waterway User Fee. H.R. 5885, June 22, 1977. Amendment by Adlai Stevenson (D-Ill) to authorize construction of a lock and dam at Alton, Illinois, and to order a study of waterway user charges (rather than institute them). Rejected 44–51. Yea = AGN Waterwy User Fee; Nay = FOR Waterwy User Fee.

(4) Dereg Nat Gas. S. 2104, October 4, 1977. Amendment by James Pearson (R-Kans) and Lloyd Bentsen (D-Texas) to end federal price controls for natural gas found onshore retroactive to January 1, 1977, and to end controls on new offshore gas after December 31, 1982, but to provide certain protections for consumers. Adopted 50–46. Yea = FOR Dereg Nat Gas; Nay = AGN Dereg Nat Gas.

(5) Kemp-Roth. H.R. 13511, October 6, 1978. Amendment by William Roth (R-Del) to cut individual income tax rates by 7% in 1979, 13% in 1980, and 10% in 1981. Rejected 36–60. Yea = FOR Kemp-Roth; Nay = AGN Kemp-Roth.

(6) Egypt-Saudi Arms. S. Con. Res. 86, May 15, 1978. Adoption of resolution to disapprove the sale of $4.5 billion worth of jet fighter planes to Israel, Egypt, and Saudi Arabia. Rejected 44–51. Yea = AGN Egypt-Saudi Arms; Nay = FOR Egypt-Saudi Arms.

(7) Draft Restr Pardon. S. Res. 18, January 25, 1977. Motion by Robert Byrd (D-WVa) to table and thus kill a resolution expressing the sense of the Senate in opposition to President Carter's pardon for Vietnam era draft resisters and evaders. Adopted 48–46. Yea = FOR Draft Restr Pardon; Nay = AGN Draft Restr Pardon.

(8) Wheat Price Support. S. 275, May 24, 1977. Amendment by Edmund Muskie (DMe) to reduce the 1977 target price for wheat from $2.90 to $2.65 a bushel. Rejected 46–50. Yea = AGN Wheat Price Support; Nay = FOR Wheat Price Support.

(9) Panama Canal Treaty. Exec. N. March 16, 1978. Adoption of the resolution of ratification to the neutrality treaty guaranteeing that Panama will be permanently neutral and remain secure and open to vessels of all nations. Adopted 68–32. Yea = FOR Panama Canal Treaty; Nay = AGN Panama Canal Treaty.

(10) Labor Law Rev Clot. H.R. 8410, June 14, 1978. Motion by Robert Byrd (D-WVa) to invoke cloture on his own substitute to the bill to amend the National Labor Relations Act. Rejected 58–41 (60 votes needed to invoke cloture). Yea = FOR Labor Law Rev Clot; Nay = AGN Labor Law Rev Clot.

(11) Hosptl Cost Contnmnt. H.R. 5285, October 12, 1978. Motion by Herman Talmadge (D-Ga) to table and thus kill a substitute amendment by Gaylord Nelson (D-Wis) to authorize prospective reimbursement of hospitals by Medicare and Medicaid, to endorse a voluntary effort by hospitals to cut costs, and to authorize national hospital revenue limits if goals of the voluntary effort were not met. Rejected 42–47. Yea = AGN Hosptl Cost Contnmnt; Nay = FOR Hosptl Cost Contnmnt.

(12) Clinch River Reactr. S. 1811, July 11, 1977. Substitute amendment by Dale Bumpers (D-Ark) to amendment by Frank Church (D-Idaho) to limit spending on the Clinch River breeder reactor project to $33 million in fiscal year 1978 for the purpose of terminating the project. Rejected 38–49. Yea = AGN Clinch River Reactr; Nay = FOR Clinch River Reactr.

(13) Pub Fin Cong Cmpgns. S. 926, August 2, 1977. Motion by Robert Byrd (D-WVa) to invoke cloture on bill to permit use of federal tax revenues to help pay for Senate general election campaigns. Rejected 52–46 (60 votes needed to invoke cloture). Yea = FOR Pub Fin Cong Cmpgns; Nay = AGN Pub Fin Cong Cmpgns.

(14) ERA Ratif Recissn. H.J. Res. 638, October 4, 1978. Amendment by Jake Garn (D-Utah) to allow a state to rescind its ratification of the proposed Equal Rights Amendment. Rejected 44–54. Yea = FOR ERA Ratif Recissn. Nay = AGN ERA Ratif Recissn.

(15) Med Necssy Abrtn H.R. 7555, June 29, 1977. Amendment by Edward Brooke (R-Mass) to prohibit the use of federal funds for abortions except where the life of the mother was endangered, a doctor considered the operation "medically necessary," or pregnancy resulted from rape or incest. Adopted 56–39. Yea = FOR Med Necssy Abrtn; Nay = AGN Med Necssy Abrtn.

HOUSE

(1) Increase Def Spnd. H. Con. Res. 195, April 27, 1977. Substitute amendment by Omar Burleson (D-Texas) to amendment by Otis Pike (D-NY) to increase fiscal 1978 budget authority by $4.1 billion and outlays by $2.3 billion to bring spending for national defense to the levels requested by the President. Adopted 225–184. Yea = FOR Increase Def Spnd; Nay = AGN Increase Def Spnd.

(2) B-1 Bomber. H.R. 9375, February 22, 1978. Motion by George Mahon (D-Texas) that the House recede and concur in the Senate amendment to the Bill rescinding $462 million appropriation in fiscal 1977 for production of three B-1 bombers. Adopted 234–182. Yea = AGN B-1 Bomber; Nay = FOR B-1 Bomber.

(3) Cargo Preference. H.R. 1037, October 19, 1977. Passage of the bill to guarantee U.S. flag ships a 9.5% share of the nation's oil imports. Rejected 165–257. Yea = FOR Cargo Preference; Nay = AGN Cargo Preference.

(4) Dereg Nat Gas. H.R. 8444, August 3, 1977. Amendment by Clarence Brown (R-Ohio) to end federal controls on the price of new onshore natural gas retroactive to April 20, 1977, and on new offshore natural gas beginning April 20, 1982, and to extend the Emergency Natural Gas Act of 1966 for three years. Rejected 199–227. Yea = FOR Dereg Nat Gas; Nay = AGN Dereg Nat Gas.

(5) Kemp-Roth. H.R. 13511, August 10, 1978. Motion by Jack Kemp (R-NY) to recommit the bill to the Ways and Means Committee with instructions to report it back with an amendment to reduce individual income tax rates by one-third over the next three years. Rejected 177–240. Yea = FOR Kemp-Roth, Nay = AGN Kemp-Roth.

(6) Alaska Lands Protect. H.R. 39, May 18, 1978. Amendment by Lloyd Meeds (D-Wash) to reduce from 66 million acres to 33 million acres the land in proposed and existing parks, refuges, and forests that would also be classified as wilderness, a designation that prohibited development. Rejected 119–240. Yea = AGN Alaska Lands Protect; Nay = FOR Alaska Lands Protect.

(7) Water Projects Veto. H.R. 12928, October 5, 1978. Passage over the President's veto of the bill to appropriate $10.2 billion for energy and water development projects of the Army Corps of Engineers and the Interior and Energy Departments. Rejected 223–190 (2/3 majority needed to override veto). Yea = AGN Water Projects Veto; Nay = FOR Water Projects Veto.

(8) Conum Protect Agcy. H.R. 6805, February 8, 1978. Passage of the bill to establish an independent Office of Consumer Representation to represent the interests of consumers before the federal agencies and courts. Rejected 189–227. Yea = FOR Conum Protect Agcy; Nay = AGN Conum Protect Agcy.

(9) Common Situs Picket. H.R. 4250, March 23, 1977. Passage of the bill to permit a labor union with a grievance with one contractor to picket all contractors on the same construction site and to establish a construction industry collective bargaining committee. Rejected 205–217. Yea = FOR Common Situs Picket; Nay = AGN Common Situs Picket.

(10) Labor Law Revision. H.R. 8410, October 6, 1977. Passage of the bill to aid union organizing and bargaining by streamlining regulatory procedures and stiffening penalties against employers who violate labor laws. Passed 257–163. Yea = FOR Labor Law Revision; Nay = AGN Labor Law Revision.

(11) Delay Auto Pol Cntrl. H.R. 6161, May 26, 1977. Substitute amendment by

John Dingell (D-Mich) to delay and relax automobile emissions standards, to reduce the warranties for emissions control devices, and make other changes in existing law regarding mobile sources of air pollution. Adopted 255–139. Yea = FOR Delay Auto Pol Cntrl; Nay = AGN Delay Auto Pol Cntrl.

(12) Sugar Price Escalator. H.R. 13750, October 6, 1978. Amendment by William Steiger (R-Wis) to add an automatic inflation adjustment for the support price for domestic sugar producers. Adopted 194–164. Yea = FOR Sugar Price Escalator; Nay = AGN Sugar Price Escalator.

(13) Pub Fin Cong Cmpgns. H.R. 11983, July 19, 1978. Motion by B. F. Sisk (D-Calif) to end debate on the adoption of the rule providing for House floor consideration of the fiscal 1979 authorization bill for the Federal Election Commission. (Opponents of the motion sought to defeat it in order to permit drafting an alternative rule that would allow a House vote on public financing of House general elecions.) Adopted 213–196. Yea = AGN Pub Fin Cong Cmpgns; Nay = FOR Pub Fin Cong Cmpgns.

(14) ERA Ratif Recissn. H.J. Res. 638, August 15, 1978. Amendment by Tom Railsback (R-Ill) to allow states to rescind their ratification of the proposed Equal Rights Amendment during the proposed 39-month extended period for ratification. Rejected 196–228. Yea = FOR ERA Ratif Recissn; Nay = AGN ERA Ratif Recissn.

(15) Prohibt Govt Abrtns. H.R. 7555, June 17, 1977. Amendment by Henry Hyde (R-Ill) to prohibit use of federal funds to finance or encourage abortions. Adopted 201–155. Yea = FOR Prohibt Govt Abrtns; Nay = AGN Prohibt Govt Abrtns.

E. Election Results

A politician can do little without getting elected. This section of the *Almanac* tells you who got elected, and by how much—and gives you at least a hint as to why. We have included not only the results of the last two general elections, but also the result of the most recent primary since, in many areas, the real decision is made in the primary contest.

Beyond this, the 1980 *Almanac* also provides the facts on how much money each candidate spent in the 1978 general election. In most cases, the spending figures will indicate how seriously the seat was contested. For it is a fact that, with only a few exceptions, you cannot win an election today without spending a lot of money.

The 1980 *Almanac* also presents election results for Gubernatorial races, and for the 1976 presidential primaries.

II. THE DISTRICT

This section presents the political, economic, and social demography of an officeholder's constituency.

A. Census Data

Along with voting figures, census returns are the hardest kind of data available for analysis of states and congressional districts. Fortunately, the 1970 census remains useful today because there has been relatively little population growth in the last half decade. We show not only total population, but the percentage of the population contained in government-designated standard metropolitan statistical areas (SMSAs) and central cities in 1970—a good indication of the urban-suburban-rural breakdown.

Every ten years the Census data requires a reapportionment of the nation's 435 House districts among the states, and during the 1960s the one-person-one-vote doctrine of the Supreme Court required frequent redistrictings. Now they are rare. Between 1972 and 1974 only California and Texas changed their congressional district lines; since the 1974 elections only Tennessee shifted lines slightly.

The census data section also shows the state's percentage of the total U.S. population—a useful figure for comparison with its share of the tax burden and federal expenditures. We show the state's median family income and the percentage of families making under $3,000 and over $15,000 per years; these are in 1970 dollars, but still provide a good index of poverty and affluence. Finally, list the "median years education," which covers everyone over 25. The ranking of the states includes the 50 states only, and excludes the District of Columbia.

B. Federal outlays and tax burden

Politicians like to brag about how much federal money they have brought into their states or districts. We give you the actual figures. We also show how much of the federal tax burden each state bears; the figures are provided by the Tax Foundation, Inc., of New York, a nonprofit, nonpartisan agency whose credentials are beyond reproach. The data on how much money each state gets from Uncle Sam are from the fiscal year 1976 federal outlays published by the Office of Economic Opportunity. The reader should beware of reading too much into the data, since the lion's share of federal spending is fixed by automatic formulas (non-discretionary spending) which cannot be affected by the efforts of a single legislator, or indeed by an entire state delegation.

DOD	Department of Defense
ERDA	Energy Research Development Administration
NASA	National Aeronautics and Space Administration
DOT	Department of Transportation
DOC	Department of Commerce
DOI	Department of the Interior
USDA	Department of Agriculture
HEW	Department of Health, Education, and Welfare
HUD	Department of Housing and Urban Development
VA	Veterans' Administration
EPA	Environmental Protection Agency
RevS	Revenue Sharing
Debt.	Interest paid on government securities

We have not computed federal outlay figures for the congressional district. OEO gives figures only for whole counties, but because the vast majority of congressional districts cut across county lines, the congressional district figures are difficult, if not impossible, to calculate with any precision.

C. Economic base

This listing tells us something about the state's economic health, its prospects for growth, the jobs its citizens and voters hold, and the sources of wealth of its big money men. For that reason, we have computed each state's most important manufacturing, mining, finance, insurance, and real estate activities under the category of Economic Base. The classifications are derived from the Census Bureau's Standard Industrial Code. An effort has been made to be as specific as possible and to indicate by "especially" cases where one type of production is particularly important. Production activity is ranked in importance according to the number of people employed —the obvious classification in a book concerned with voters.

D. Political lineup

This is very simple—the Governor, the Senators, the House delegation, and the state legislatures, by party.

E. The Voters

You don't really know why candidates get elected until you know who votes— and why. We like to think of the American voter as a one person civics class, gravely weighing the issues and measuring the mettle of the competing candidates. But we know this is not so. Voters like to talk about being for the man, not the party; but there are still plenty who agree wih the reasoning process ascribed to Harry Truman: "I vote for the better man. He is the Democratic nominee." And when people actually do "vote for the man," they often mean the only man in the race they've heard of, which in congressional races usually means the incumbent.

Political scientists have shown that, more often than not people inherit their political preferences, and that these preferences remain remarkably constant through the years. Accordingly, it makes some sense to analyze the electorate by blocs. One source of differentiation is economic status. We have provided an "employment profile" for each state and district, showing the percentage of employed persons working in white collar, blue collar, service (which are usually blue collar), and farm jobs. In addition, we have shown the "median family income" for each state and district. This gives you a quick picture of the economic and social nature of the constituency, but does not provide an automatic guide to voting behavior. The richest congressional district in terms of median family income, the 8th of Maryland, rejected the Republican candidacies of Richard Nixon twice and gave him a smaller than average majority the third time; the poorest, the 5th of Kentucky, is inevitably one of the most Republican districts in the nation. Thus conventional wisdom that rich people vote Republican and poor people vote Democratic does not yield a very close understanding of American political preferences.

Another way to look at the electorate is along ethnic lines. We are past the time when Polish-Americans, say, will automatically vote for a Polish-American candidate; that kind of ethnic politics is more and more on the decline. But people who share an ethnic inheritance also tend to share a cultural background—and a political preference. So for every state and district, we have provided racial and ethnic percentages calculated from the 1970 census. The figures require some explanation to be useful. The racial category is obvious; and if blacks in central cities have been undercounted by the Census Bureau, as some have charged, then the kind of people who have avoided the census taker are also the kind least likely to participate in the political process.

The Census also notes which of us were born in foreign countries or had parents who were; these two groups are lumped together as "foreign stock." Obviously, a foreign stock figure will understate the ethnicity of some areas (a lot of Boston Irish are descended from people who left the old country physically in the 1840s but whose hearts are still there) and will overstate the ethnicity of others (what reason is there to suppose that people born in the United Kingdom and living in Santa Barbara will vote any differently from the other people there?). The category "Spanish heritage" represents a variety of different groups: Mexican-Americans mainly in California, Texas, and Illinois; Puerto Ricans in New York and New Jersey; and the ancient Spanish-speaking community in New Mexico, which is older than Plymouth Rock. We have also included the category "French native tongue" in Maine, New Hampshire, Vermont, Massachusetts, Rhode Island, and upstate New York, to indicate people of French Canadian stock, and in Louisiana to indicate the so-called Cajuns; both groups have distinctive voting patterns. No group is shown unless it represents 1% or more of the state's or district's total population.

III. POLITICAL BACKGROUND

This is our interpretation of how things fit together. What kind of men and women are your Governors, Senators, and Representatives? What do they accomplish in office? How do they get elected, and what are their prospects for reelection—or defeat? What are the local issues, and local attitudes on national issues?

These are the questions the Political Background sections seek to answer. They form a kind of mosaic, we think, a picture of political leanings and trends throughout the nation and what they mean for the federal government and federal elections. Read them all, and we think you will get a pretty accurate picture of what is going on politically around the country and on Capitol Hill. But the *Almanac* is designed to be read and used piecemeal; you might want to begin with your home state, or with the member of a committee whose subject matter interests you. We have tried to design the *Almanac* to make it easy to use, whatever your interest.

A. Statewide

American politics, for better or worse, is still the politics of the 50 states. There are signs that the national media have begun to homogenize our politics, to eliminate local peculiarities and to replicate conflicts along the same ideological lines throughout the nation. But even the most contemporary politics is the outgrowth of history, and for 180 years American politics has been a thing of unmatched diversity. Each state has been a little political arena all its own. The Electoral College system—whereby the winner takes all a state's electoral votes—has strengthened this tendency, even in national contests; in most presidential elections, about half the states are not seriously contested by one candidate or the other. Most states have well-developed traditions of political conflict: New York City vs. upstate, Chicago vs. downstate Illinois, east Tennessee vs. middle Tennessee vs. West Tennessee. Some of these are changing; others remain rigidly fixed. We have tried to present them in their historical contexts and to explain what, if anything, these regional conflicts mean today.

Each state also has its own political flavor, an ambiance about its politicians and its voting behavior that is not found elsewhere. Connecticut, with its still strong tradition of straight tickets lies right next to Massachusetts, where voters have been splitting their tickets on a massive scale for years. Illinois is a land of fabled political corruption and cronyism; Wisconsin just to the north, is as clean as a hound's tooth and has nothing resembling the late Richard J. Daley's machine. Political patterns have grown up in response to local ground-rules, pressures, and personal initiatives; the voting public responds in various ways, and a political culture grows. We have attempted to impart the ambiance of the 50 political cultures which make up our Republic.

B. Congressional Districts

There has been a great deal of writing on the politics of the various states, but very little on the politics of individual congressional districts (CDs). One reason for the dearth of information about CDs is that they, unlike the states, usually do not have a political culture of their own. Each one is just a piece of a culture that exists on a statewide basis, and each is often made up of disparate elements of that culture. The trend toward heterogeneity has been increased by the Supreme Court's one-man-one-vote decision, *Wesberry v. Sanders*. Today, the districts are pretty much equal in population, at least according to the 1970 census; but the equal-population requirement makes for some odd political combinations. For example, the 200,000-population, old 4th Texas district, represented for nearly 50 years by Sam Rayburn, was a compact, homogeneous unit; so was the 900,000-population district that existed at the time of Rayburn's death, including all of Dallas County. Now Rayburn's successor has some of Dallas County in his district, and while that is clearly fairer, it makes a description of the current 4th district a more complicated affair. Nevertheless, we have tried to describe and analyze the politics of each district, and to indicate the impact its Congressman makes on Capitol Hill.

What were our sources? Just about everything: interviews with members of Congress and their aides, and with local politicians and political observers in Washington and around the country; newspapers, magazines, books; publicly available data, including the *Congressional Record;* and a lifelong collection of political and historical miscellany. We have paid particular attention to what we consider the hardest of data, the election returns; we taxpayers spend millions of dollars to obtain these figures, and political adversaries have the strongest incentives to make sure they are accurate. We have examined in detail returns going back at least to 1964, and we believe that, intelligently read, the election returns give as good an insight as can be had into what Americans think and believe about the issues of the day. They also provide clues for what we imagine must be one major interest of many of our readers: whether Senator X or Congressman Y can be beaten in the next election.

We've enjoyed writing and putting together the 1980 edition of this book.

—The authors

THE ALMANAC OF AMERICAN POLITICS

ALABAMA

Alabama is no longer George Wallace country. In 1978, for the first time in 20 years, George /allace was not running for governor, in person or by proxy; indeed, Wallace was not even a ignificant factor in the race. Early in 1978, it had been assumed that Wallace would want and win ohn Sparkman's Senate seat; but Wallace wisely declined to make the race and failed to show ny interest in the seat created a short time later by Senator Jim Allen's death. As things turned ut, Alabama was one of two states which produced a clean sweep in its top elective offices in 978 (the other was Minnesota), and with one exception the new faces little resemble the old. The ew governor is Fob James, an Auburn University football star and successful businessman who ever dwells on the racial issues that made Wallace a national figure. Allen—the Senate's last)ixiecrat stickler for parliamentary procedure and the leader of the opposition to the Panama :anal Treaty—has been replaced by Donald Stewart, a 40-year-old lawyer who made his name in ne state Senate as an opponent of utility rate increases. Only John Sparkman, the state's senior enator who retired after 42 years in Congress, has been replaced by a man congenial to his own iews: former State Supreme Court Chief Justice Howell Heflin.

This abrupt change in representation reflects a slower, but equally profound, change in labama racial and political attitudes during the 1970s. There is no better measure of that change nan in attitudes toward George Wallace. In 1968, 67% of Alabama's voters—a group already ncluding the state's blacks—voted for Wallace for president. Ten years later, in 1978, Wallace ould not muster enough votes for a consolation-prize seat in the Senate. Of course his health had eteriorated since he was shot while campaigning in the 1972 Maryland presidential primary. But part from doubts about whether he could handle the job physically, actual antipathy to Wallace ad surfaced by 1978. His time was up, and he knew it.

George Wallace instinctively understood this. From the first, he was a fighter, and if his evotion to the segregationist cause was not always clear (he had run as a moderate once and lost, nd vowed not to be "out-segged" again), he nevertheless had the gift of capturing the nagination. He was the man who stood in the schoolhouse door when integration came to the Jniversity of Alabama—never mind that it accomplished nothing. And unlike other Southern egregationists, Wallace knew how to take a local issue and make it national. In the 1964)emocratic primaries, he ran strong races in Wisconsin and Indiana; and for four presidential lections in succession he was a major national candidate. In 1968 he won 13.6% of the national ote—the best third party showing in the last 50 years. In 1972 he had more actual votes in the rimaries than anyone else. But even as he was winning these votes, it was clear that Wallace vould never win respectability as a national candidate. By 1976, many white Southerners were ired of him, and when Jimmy Carter demonstrated that Wallace could be beaten, Wallace's upport evaporated almost without a trace. Wallace had an undeniable gift for appealing to ertain voters, but he could not overcome the handicaps of how he had risen. Only a segregationist ould rise to the top in the Alabama of the early 1960s, and a segregationist, even one as adroit as Vallace, could not become a successful national candidate in the years that followed.

In the longer view of Alabama's political history, the Wallace era, long as it was, may one day e seen as an unusual episode, an aberration from the norm. It covered a period when intense oncentration on racial issues and reactions to unanticipated changes in racial mores dominated he thinking of white Alabamians. But these have not always been the central issues of Alabama olitics. This is a state which has often been called populistic, and for good reason. Composed rimarily of small farms and hardscrabble land, of steel mills in Birmingham and shipbuilding in Aobile, Alabama has no dominant elite, like the planters of Mississippi or the country lawyers of 'irginia, to run things smoothly, elegantly, and without disturbing the established order. This is a tate of people who work with their hands, who have fierce national and local pride and it has lways liked its politicians to be fighters.

So if it makes sense for Alabama to have produced a George Wallace at a time when white outherners still hoped they could resist desegregation, it also makes sense for the same state to ave produced a string of populist officeholders whose tenure lasted longer than Wallace's. 'erhaps the most famous of these is Hugo Black. Elected to the Senate in 1926 over the opposition f the banks, railroads, and utilities, Black became one of the Senate's leading liberals until he was ppointed to the Supreme Court in 1937. There his career was even more distinguished, although is strong support of civil liberties and civil rights made him unwelcome for some years back in labama.

For 30 years the Alabama congressional delegation was dominated by New Deal populists; they took the obligatory stands against civil rights, but devoted most of their energy to housing, hospital, and highway programs. The state's populist congressmen were mostly defeated in the Goldwater sweep of 1964; but they were represented, until his retirement in 1978, by Senator John Sparkman. Early in his Senate career, Sparkman had been considered liberal enough to be nominated as Adlai Stevenson's running mate in 1952. Later, particularly as Chairman of the Banking Committee, Sparkman came to fit in more comfortably with powers that be; on national issues, he was amenable to appeals from the administration, particularly if it was a Democratic one. During his last four years in the Senate Sparkman was Chairman of the Foreign Relations Committee, a prestigious post for which he seemed, in his late 70s, to have little energy. He loyally supported the administration's Panama Canal Treaty—a position not in line with populistic sentiment in Alabama.

Sparkman's retirement had been a foregone conclusion since 1972, when he had narrowly avoided a runoff in the Democratic primary. For years, it was assumed that George Wallace would take the seat if he wanted it; but that was not what happened. During the last two years of Wallace's governorship, his popularity dropped. He was divorced, after some discord; it became increasingly obvious that his health prevented him from working full time; and voters, dissatisfied with state government, began to blame the man who had been governor, in fact or in effect, for 1[illegible] of the last 16 years. Wallace surprised the nation when he announced in late spring that he would not run for the Senate; he surprised Alabamians less. Although he insisted it was not so, it was clear that he was already beaten.

Wallace's chief rival at that time was Howell Heflin. As the state's Chief Justice, he had pushed through a reorganization of the state's court system, and had tangled with Wallace—and won. Heflin's views on national issues were not far out of line with those of most Alabamians: strong for national defense, a mild populism on economic issues, a strong desire to promote Alabama economically. On racial matters, it was understood that Heflin, like most Alabama politicians these days, supports the civil rights laws and racial desegregation but opposes some types of busing plans. With Wallace out of the race, Heflin's major opponent proved to be Congressman Walter Flowers. Although he began the election with considerable assets—notably his agonized but impressive performance as a member of the House Judiciary Committee voting to impeach Richard Nixon—Flowers managed to run a campaign which destroyed his chances. He stressed his knowledge of and experience in Washington, after 10 years in Congress, though voters increasingly prefer officeholders with experience closer to home. He also opened himself up to charges that he was friendly to South Korea lobbyist Tongsun Park and that he billed the government for auto mileage rather than the less expensive plane fare for some trips back to the district. Heflin made the most of these opportunities, saying that Flowers was part of "the Washington crowd" (a theme Jim Allen used in 1968), and led Flowers by a startling 48%–31% in the initial primary. The runoff was a foregone conclusion: Heflin carried all but five counties, and won with 65%. Faced with such strength, the Republican candidate, Jim Martin, opted for the other Senate race, and Heflin was elected without major party opposition.

He can be expected to be a considerably different kind of Senator from his uncle, "Cotton Tom" Heflin, a fierce segregationist who served from 1920 to 1931. Heflin is a lawyer's lawyer and has a seat on the Judiciary Committee. He is likely to be one of an increasing number of Southern Democrats whose votes can be crucial on all kinds of issues.

The state's other Senate seat had not been expected to be contested this year, until James Allen died suddenly of a heart attack in June. Allen had attracted little attention when first elected to the Senate in 1968, but as the years went on he became one of the body's most powerful members. His weapon was an encyclopedic knowledge of Senate rules and procedures and a willingness to hold up business until his objections were met or the legislation he opposed defeated. Allen's power was particularly great late in the session, when many members urgently want bills passed and the pressure to give in to Allen's demands could become enormous. With courtly politeness, with a bland, seemingly hesitant speaking style, Allen had become a major force in the Senate by 1976; the party leadership had got almost to the point of having to clear all major scheduling decisions with him. Meanwhile, his conservative politics and upright personal character made him popular at home.

Allen was a passionate believer in the causes he espoused, and it was natural that he would be one of the leaders of the fight against the Panama Canal Treaty. It was a fight that seemed doomed from the beginning, but Allen put great energy and passion into it. His kind of politics requires steady attendance on the floor of the Senate, and considerable stamina. The task he took on apparently exhausted him, and on a vacation shortly afterwards he collapsed and died

George Wallace was left with the duty of appointing an interim successor, just after he had ruled himself out of the other Senate race. (He probably could not have appointed himself, since he was feuding with his lieutenant governor.) He made what seemed the obvious decision, appointing the Senator's widow, Maryon Allen, a former newspaperwoman and a person of considerable character in her own right. She was expected to win the remaining two years of her husband's term with little problem.

But one who expected a tougher fight was state Sen. Donald Stewart. He had been running for the full six-year term, but seemed to be trailing behind the two best known candidates, Howell Heflin and the recently entered Walter Flowers; his chances of making the runoff seemed poor. Against Mrs. Allen, who had no creditable opponent, they seemed better. She campaigned by not campaigning, remaining in Washington and voting as she believed James Allen would have. But she became controversial because of quotations from an interview by Sally Quinn in the Washington *Post* (including a story about how she talked with some repairmen one morning while dressed in a nightgown). Censorious Alabamians clucked that this is not what Jim Allen would have wanted. Perhaps more important was the fact that Stewart had raised substantive issues, notably utility rates, which showed him as a fighter, while there was little substantive content whatever to Allen's campaign. Maryon Allen received only 42% in the first primary to Stewart's 35%. He had the momentum, and easily prevailed in the runoff.

But that was not the end. The Republicans, feeling that Stewart was more vulnerable than Mrs. Allen would have been, decided to field a formidable candidate. Jim Martin had nearly beaten Senate veteran Lister Hill in 1962, had been elected Congressman in 1964, and might have done well in the 1966 governor's race except that he was running against George Wallace's wife. He was the Republicans' best proven statewide vote-getter. After the Democratic runoff, he switched from the race against Heflin to the race against Stewart. (Because he ran in two different races, the Republican National Committee contributed double the amount allowed by statute for two Senate candidates—a move of dubious legality.) Martin was able to spend more money in the general election campaign period than Stewart, and of course his theme was that Stewart was some kind of liberal. Stewart stressed his populist record again, and pointed to Martin's high absenteeism during his one term in Congress. The final result pretty well paralleled Alabama's vote in the 1976 presidential race: 57% for Stewart, 43% for Martin. Martin carried Birmingham and did well in the southern part of the state; Stewart carried the Black Belt and the all white working class counties that had once provided such large margins for George Wallace.

Elected at 38, Stewart has the prospect of a long Senate career. But he must first win the full term in 1980—and there are plenty of politicians in Alabama, some of them losers in the crowded 1978 race for governor, who would like his job. Stewart can be expected to be on the spot on issues such as the SALT Treaty and on some spending issues. He will also have to establish a close linkage with the state in a relatively short period of time.

Alabama's new Governor is a man almost wholly unlike George Wallace in his background —not that he is a pointy-headed bureaucrat. Instead, he is a sleek, attractive businessman, a Republican (and member of the state executive committee) as recently as 1976, and a man who had never previously won an election. Fob James attracted public attention first as a football star at Auburn University—an asset, though there are more 'Bama rooters in the state. Thereafter, he went into business and invented a barbell made of high density plastic. Improbably, this revolutionized the weight lifting industry, and James became a very rich man indeed.

James had not been expected to be a heavy competitor in the 1978 gubernatorial race. That was supposed to be a battle of the three Bs: Albert Brewer, the man who had succeeded Lurleen Wallace as Governor in 1968 and had almost beaten George Wallace in 1970; Jere Beasley, Wallace's lieutenant governor; and Bill Baxley, the attorney general whose greatest triumph was to convict the people who bombed the black Birmingham church in 1963. But Beasley faded early, Brewer seemed too close to the business interests, and Baxley admitted that he owed gambling debts in six figures. Meanwhile, James was spending very large sums—no one is just sure how much—on television advertisements portraying him as a new face, above the old politics and mudslinging, who would bring a new era of businesslike government to the state. James finished first in the crowded primary, with 28% of the vote. Baxley gained the number two position, and in the runoff had the support of most black voters and George Wallace (who is said to admire his feistiness). But Alabama voters wanted a change from the past, and James won with 55%. Against his former Republican allies it was no contest at all.

No one can be sure what kind of governor James will be, although his curriculum vitae and campaign advertising suggest certain directions. But it seems pretty clear that he will not be much like George Wallace. There was something plaintive about Wallace's departure; not only was he crippled physically, but as a man who lived totally on politics he seemed broken psychically. But there can be no mistaking that the Wallace exit is what Alabamians wanted: there seems to be less sadness about his retirement here than outside the state. George Wallace leaves behind no movement, only bad memories; and he reminds Alabamians, and all Americans, of what they believed and how they behaved not so very long ago, which they would prefer to forget.

Census Data Pop. 3,444,165; 1.70% of U.S. total, 21st largest; Central city, 26%; suburban, 27%. Median family income, $7,263; 48th highest; families above $15,000: 11%; families below $3,000: 19%. Median years education, 10.8.

1977 Share of Federal Tax Burden $4,283,000,000; 1.24% of U.S. total, 25th largest.

1977 Share of Federal Outlays $6,126,629,000; 1.55% of U.S. total, 21st largest. Per capita federal spending, $1,695.

DOD	$1,397,218,000	20th (1.53%)	HEW	$2,395,499,000	20th (1.62%)
ERDA	$30,015,000	23d (0.51%)	HUD	$11,915,000	19th (0.28%)
NASA	$198,791,000	5th (5.04%)	VA	$381,530,000	16th (1.99%)
DOT	$192,812,000	26th (1.35%)	EPA	$29,189,000	36th (0.36%)
DOC	$78,526,000	27th (0.95%)	RevS	$125,874,000	23d (1.49%)
DOI	$11,915,000	43d (0.26%)	Debt	$104,111,000	32d (0.35%)
USDA	$283,062,000	31st (1.42%)	Other	$886,172,000	

Economic Base Agriculture, notably broilers, cattle, cotton lint and eggs; primary metal industries, especially blast furnaces and basic steel products, and iron and steel foundries; finance, insurance and real estate; apparel and other textile products, especially men's and boys' furnishings; textile mill products, especially cotton weaving mills; food and kindred products, especially meat products; lumber and wood products, especially sawmills and planing mills.

Political Line-up Governor, Fob James (D). Senators, Donald W. Stewart (D) and Howell Heflin (D). Representatives, 7 (4 D and 3 R). State Senate (35 D); State House (100 D, 4 R, 1 vacancy).

The Voters

Registration 1,938,231 Total. No party registration.
Median voting age 42
Employment profile White collar, 41%. Blue collar, 43%. Service, 13%. Farm, 3%.
Ethnic groups Black, 26%. Total foreign stock, 2%.

Presidential vote

1976	Carter (D)	659,171	(57%)
	Ford (R)	504,070	(43%)
1972	Nixon (R)	728,701	(74%)
	McGovern (D)	256,923	(26%)

Sen. Donald W. Stewart (D) Elected 1978, seat up 1980; b. Feb. 8, 1940, Munford; home, Anniston; U. of Ala., B.S. 1962, J.D. 1965; Methodist.

Career Practicing atty.; Ala. House of Reps., 1971–75; Ala. Senate, 1975–78.

Offices 110 RSOB, 202-224-5744. Also Rm. 818, Aronov Bldg., 474 S. Court St., Montgomery 36104, 205-832-7600.

Committees *Agriculture, Nutrition, and Forestry* (8th). Subcommittees: Environment, Soil Conservation, and Forestry; Agricultural Research and General Legislation (Chairman); Rural Development.

Banking, Housing, and Urban Affairs (8th). Subcommittees: Financial Institutions; Rural Housing and Development; Insurance (Chairman).

Select Committee on Small Business (8th).

Group Ratings: Newly Elected

Key Votes: Newly Elected

Election Results

1978 general	Donald Stewart (D)	401,852	(56%)	($816,456)
	James D. Martin (R)	316,170	(44%)	($552,504)
1978 run-off	Donald Stewart (D)	502,346	(57%)	
	Mrs. Jim Allen (D)	375,894	(43%)	($305,498)
1978 primary	Mrs. Jim Allen (D)	334,758	(46%)	
	Donald Stewart (D)	259,795	(35%)	
	Two others (D)	137,583	(19%)	
1974 general	Jim Allen (D)	501,541	(100%)	($37,328)

Sen. Howell Heflin (D) Elected 1978, seat up 1984; b. June 19, 1921, Lovina, Georgia; home, Tuscumbia; Birmingham-Southern College, B.A., U. of Ala., J.D. 1948; Methodist.

Career USMC, WWII; Practicing atty., 1948–71; Pres., Ala. State Bar, 1965–68; Chief Justice, Ala. Supreme Court, 1971–77.

Offices 3203 DSOB, 202-224-4124. Also P.O. Box 3294, Montgomery 36101, 205-832-7287.

Committees *Commerce, Science, and Transportation* (10th). Subcommittees: Consumer; Science, Technology, and Space; Surface Transportation.

Judiciary (10th). Subcommittees: Constitution; Jurisprudence and Governmental Relations (Chairman); Limitations of Contracted and Delegated Authority.

Group Ratings: Newly Elected

Key Votes: Newly Elected

Election Results

1978 general	Howell Heflin (D)	547,054	(94%)	($1,059,113)
	Jerome B. Couch (Proh.)	34,951	(6%)	
1978 run-off	Howell Heflin (D)	556,685	(65%)	
	Walter Flowers (D)	300,654	(35%)	($755,259)
1978 primary	Howell Heflin (D)	369,270	(48%)	
	Walter Flowers (D)	236,894	(31%)	
	John Baker (D)	101,110	(13%)	($179,388)
	Four others (D)	56,179	(8%)	
1972 general	John Sparkman (D)	654,491	(65%)	($702,109)
	Winton M. Blount (R)	347,523	(35%)	($764,961)

Gov. Fob James, Jr. (D) Elected 1978, term expires Jan. 1983; b. Sept. 15, 1934, Lanett; Auburn U., B.S. 1955; Episcopalian.

Career Professional Football Player, Montreal Alouettes, 1956; U.S. Army Corps of Engineers, 1957; Construction Engineer, 1958–59, Superintendent, 1960–61; Pres. and Bd. Chairman, Diversified Products Corp., 1962–78.

Offices Executive Dept., Montgomery 36130, 205-832-3511.

Election Results

1978 general	Forrest James, Jr. (D)	551,886	(74%)
	Guy Hunt (R)	196,963	(26%)
1978 run-off	Forrest James, Jr. (D)	515,520	(55%)
	Bill Baxley (D)	418,932	(45%)
1978 primary	Forrest James, Jr. (D)	256,196	(28%)
	Bill Baxley (D)	210,089	(23%)
	Albert Brewer (D)	193,479	(21%)
	Sid McDonald (D)	143,930	(16%)
	Nine others (D)	96,223	(11%)
1974 general	George C. Wallace (D)	497,574	(85%)
	Elvin McCary (R)	88,381	(15%)

FIRST DISTRICT

The Tombigbee and Alabama Rivers flow south from Alabama's Black Belt—named for the fertility of its black cotton-growing soil—to the port of Mobile and the Gulf of Mexico. Mobile (pop. 190,000) is Alabama's second largest city, and the largest port on the Gulf between New Orleans and Tampa. Dominated by industries sensitive to economic cycles—shipping, shipbuilding, and paper—the Mobile area had little population growth during the 1950s and 1960s. But like most of the South, this area has grown more rapidly during the 1970s, largely because its young people are no longer migrating northward.

Mobile is the most blue collar of Alabama's large cities; and though its proximity to New Orleans and vaguely French name suggest a certain creole gentility, it is in fact a rough town. In the Wallace years this was the most pro-Wallace major city in Alabama—although 35% of its residents are black. Mobile has been one of the last cities in the South where blacks have gained political influence and representation in proportion to their numbers. Curiously, the contiguous industrial suburb of Prichard (pop. 41,000) elected a black Mayor as long ago as 1972, and has reelected him since.

Alabama's 1st congressional district stretches from Mobile north to the Black Belt, and includes one black-majority county (Wilcox). But most of the people here live in and around Mobile, and Mobile County casts almost 60% of the district's votes. The 1st's feelings about national politics can be gauged from its choices in the last four presidential elections: solidly for Goldwater in 1964, Wallace in 1968, Nixon in 1972, and narrowly for the more conservative Ford over fellow Southerner Carter in 1976.

The 1964 election, which showed that this part of the South was discontented enough to go Republican, also pretty well determined that this would be a Republican seat in successive Congresses. It was Barry Goldwater's showing that probably more than anything else accounted for the 1964 victory of Republican Jack Edwards. And it has been Edwards's own attractive personal qualities, as well as his record, which is usually characterized as solidly conservative, which has kept him confortably entrenched ever since. In 1978 Edwards faced his strongest opponent in years, a state Senator and former University of Alabama football star, and still won easily.

In the House, Edwards has become one of the most respected of Southern Republicans. He early won a seat on the Appropriations Committee, on which he is now the 5th ranking Republican. Moreover, he is ranking Republican on the Defense Appropriations Subcommittee, a body which has jurisdiction over a large portion of the federal budget; this position was held, some 16 years ago, by one Gerald Ford. Edwards is also Secretary of the House Republican Conference, a post with no technical powers but which is evidence of the esteem in which he is widely held. While there is no sign that the current House Republican leaders are about to retire, it may be that Edwards will get a position of considerably greater visibility in the next few years; he already has considerable influence.

Census Data Pop. 491,747. Central city, 39%; suburban, 38%. Median family income, $7,305; families above $15,000: 11%; families below $3,000: 18%. Median years education, 10.8.

The Voters

Median voting age 42.
Employment profile White collar, 41%. Blue collar, 42%. Service, 14%. Farm, 3%.
Ethnic groups Black, 33%. Total foreign stock, 2%.

Presidential vote

1976	Carter (D)	81,012	(49%)
	Ford (R)	83,622	(51%)
1972	Nixon (R)	103,842	(76%)
	McGovern (D)	33,276	(24%)

Rep. Jack Edwards (R) Elected 1964; b. Sept. 20, 1928, Birmingham; home, Mobile; U. of Ala., B.S. 1952, LL.B. 1954; Presbyterian.

Career USMC, 1946–48, 1950–51; Instructor in Business Law, U. of Ala., 1954; Practicing atty., 1954–64.

Offices 2369 RHOB, 202-225-4931. Also 8011 Fed. Ofc. Bldg., 109 St. Joseph St., Mobile 36602, 205-690-2811.

Committees *Appropriations* (5th). Subcommittees: Defense; Transportation.

Group Ratings

	ADA	COPE	PC	RPN	NFU	LCV	CFA	NAB	NSI	ACA	NTU
1978	20	11	13	50	30	–	14	100	90	89	–
1977	5	38	10	38	58	18	15	–	–	72	46
1976	0	23	8	63	28	26	9	75	89	81	41

Key Votes

1) Increase Def Spnd	FOR	6) Alaska Lands Protect	AGN	11) Delay Auto Pol Cntrl	FOR
2) B-1 Bomber	AGN	7) Water Projects Veto	AGN	12) Sugar Price Escalator	FOR
3) Cargo Preference	FOR	8) Consum Protect Agcy	AGN	13) Pub Fin Cong Cmpgns	AGN
4) Dereg Nat Gas	FOR	9) Common Situs Picket	AGN	14) ERA Ratif Recissn	FOR
5) Kemp-Roth	FOR	10) Labor Law Revision	AGN	15) Prohibt Govt Abrtns	FOR

Election Results

1978 general	Jack Edwards (R)	71,711	(64%)	($166,456)
	L. W. Noonan (D)	40,500	(36%)	($85,773)
1978 primary	Jack Edwards (R), unopposed			
1976 general	Jack Edwards (R)	98,257	(63%)	($71,310)
	Bill Davenport (D)	58,906	(37%)	($30,016)

SECOND DISTRICT

It was not until some years after Alabama was admitted to the Union that Southern planters, their soil in Virginia and the Carolinas growing tired, discovered the Black Belt of Alabama. The fertile black soil gave the region its name, and almost cried out for the crop that came to characterize the Confederacy: King Cotton. As every schoolchild knows, cotton was a crop that required cheap, abundant labor, and Alabama's Black Belt became slave territory; before the Civil War slaves outnumbered whites as much as 10–1 in some counties. For years after the Civil War the majority of the Black Belt's citizens were the descendants of slaves. But as black migration to the north continued, the black percentage here diminished, and by the time the 1965 Voting Rights Act gave blacks the ballot, only a handful of small, predominantly rural counties were left with black majorities.

On a map Alabama's congressional lines look perfectly regular. Closer inspection, however, shows them to have been carefully crafted to divide the black majority counties among several districts, to prevent black voters from exerting a major influence in any congressional election. The 2d district, for example, contains only one black majority county (Bullock), but just outside the district lines there are three others (Macon, Lowndes, and Wilcox).

So the blacks in the 2d are heavily outnumbered by the white majority in Montgomery, the state's capital, and by those in the nearly all white "piney woods" counties to the south of the Black Belt. Montgomery is a city with a special Deep South heritage. It was the Cradle of the Confederacy, the rebels' capital before Richmond. And it was the site of the 1956 Montgomery bus boycott, which gave national prominence to a young black minister named Martin Luther King, Jr.

This is one of three Alabama districts with a Republican congressman. As in the others, the incumbent first won in 1964, when he had the good fortune to be running as a Republican when Barry Goldwater swept the state. In those straight ticket days, the Republicans won five House seats and wiped out 87 years of Democratic House seniority. The Republicans lost two of the seats in 1966, but they have held on to the other three ever since, helped by the usual advantages of incumbency. But these have not helped 2d district Congressman William Dickinson to win by larger majorities; on the contrary, he seems to find himself in more trouble every two years. In 1976 he was held to 58% by an inept opponent; in 1978, state Sen. "Walking Wendell" Mitchell nearly won, with Dickinson getting only 54%.

Why such weakness in a longtime incumbent? The problem is not Dickinson's voting record, which is not far out of line with opinion in this patriotic, anti-spending district. Rather, Dickinson does not seem to have demonstrated the kind of solid personal character which Jack Edwards of the neighboring 1st district, for one, has. Dickinson has a tendency to shoot from the hip. In his first term in Congress, he charged without documentation that the Selma marchers—who passed through part of the district—engaged in sexual misconduct. In the 95th Congress, he was arguing that the neutron bomb was needed on the theory that the Russians know we cannot otherwise use nuclear weapons without killing West Germans. Another problem for Dickinson: despite his seniority, he was unable to keep the Air University at Montgomery's Maxwell Air Force Base.

The seniority system has elevated Dickinson to a position of some significance: he is the number two Republican on the House Armed Services Committee. Not surprisingly, he is an ardent supporter of a strong defense, as are most members of the Committee. He is expected to look after the interests of his district's two Air Force bases and giant Fort Rucker near Dothan; he is less likely, however, to exert major influence on policy. Dickinson's weak showings in recent elections suggest that in 1980 he may be defeated or may choose, as many similarly threatened incumbents have, to retire.

Census Data Pop. 491,676. Central city, 27%; suburban, 7%. Median family income, $6,749; families above $15,000: 10%; families below $3,000: 21%. Median years education, 11.0.

The Voters

Median voting age 42.
Employment profile White collar, 42%. Blue collar, 39%. Service, 14%. Farm, 5%.
Ethnic groups Black, 30%. Total foreign stock, 2%.

Presidential vote

1976	Carter (D)	88,208	(54%)
	Ford (R)	75,528	(46%)
1972	Nixon (R)	107,702	(78%)
	McGovern (D)	31,190	(22%)

Rep. William L. Dickinson (R) Elected 1964; b. June 5, 1925, Opelika; home, Montgomery; U. of Ala., A.B. 1948, LL.B. 1950; Methodist.

Career Navy, WWII; Practicing atty., 1950–63; Judge, Opelika City Court, Lee Co. Court of Common Pleas and Juvenille Court, Fifth Judicial Circuit; Asst. V.P., Southern Railway System.

Offices 2468 RHOB, 202-225-2901. Also 401 Fed. Court Bldg., Montgomery 36104, 205-832-7292.

Committees *Armed Services* (2d). Subcommittees: Military Installations and Facilities; NATO Standardization, Interoperability, and Readiness; Research and Development.

House Administration (Ranking Member). Subcommittees: Services.

Group Ratings

	ADA	COPE	PC	RPN	NFU	LCV	CFA	NAB	NSI	ACA	NTU
1978	5	16	10	60	30	–	5	100	100	96	–
1977	5	23	10	70	42	3	5	–	–	92	35
1976	0	17	5	47	20	0	9	92	80	96	56

Key Votes

1) Increase Def Spnd	FOR	6) Alaska Lands Protect	AGN	11) Delay Auto Pol Cntrl	FOR
2) B-1 Bomber	FOR	7) Water Projects Veto	AGN	12) Sugar Price Escalator	FOR
3) Cargo Preference	AGN	8) Consum Protect Agcy	AGN	13) Pub Fin Cong Cmpgns	AGN
4) Dereg Nat Gas	FOR	9) Common Situs Picket	AGN	14) ERA Ratif Recissn	FOR
5) Kemp-Roth	FOR	10) Labor Law Revision	AGN	15) Prohibt Govt Abrtns	FOR

Election Results

1978 general	William L. Dickinson (R)	57,924	(54%)	($139,313)
	Wendell Mitchell (D)	49,341	(46%)	($115,372)
1978 primary	William L. Dickinson (R), unopposed			
1976 general	William L. Dickinson (R)	90,069	(58%)	($51,210)
	J. Carole Keahey (D)	66,288	(42%)	($122,265)

THIRD DISTRICT

The 3d district of Alabama extends from the cotton-growing Black Belt in the southern part of the state to the red clay hills of the north. In the south is Tuskegee, a black-majority town in a black-majority county, and the home of Booker T. Washington's Tuskegee Institute. Tuskegee has had an ambitious young black mayor who made headlines by endorsing Richard Nixon (1972) and George Wallace (1974)—a strategy which might have paid more dividends had it been pursued earlier when these men had more political time ahead of them. Also in the southern portion is Phenix City, a onetime Alabama "sin city" across the Chattahoochee River from Georgia's huge Fort Benning. A mid-1950s cleanup of Phenix City propelled a young prosecutor, John Patterson, into the governor's chair; he beat George Wallace in the 1958 Democratic primary, the one time Wallace allowed himself to be "out-segged." In the northern part of the district is the small industrial city of Anniston, home of a distinguished small Southern newspaper and of the Army's Fort McClellan.

Outside of the Black Belt counties in the south, the 3d district is mostly white, and the whites living in the district's small towns and hilly farm country were for years George Wallace's kind of people. The current Congressman, Bill Nichols, was a Wallace floor leader in the Alabama Senate, and his House voting record is what one would expect, assuming one knows that the Wallace line on economic issues was considerably more business-oriented than the populist tone of his rhetoric. In 1966 Nichols was the only Alabama Democrat who beat a Republican elected in the Goldwater landslide two years before. Since then Nichols has been sent back to Washington every two years with more than 75% of the votes; he has not had a Republican opponent since 1972. With a middle level (8th) seniority position on the House Armed Services Committee, Nichols has made little impression on official Washington outside of certain corners of the Pentagon. He chairs a subcommittee on military pay and benefits, and much of his legislative efforts concern veterans' benefits.

Census Data Pop. 493,588. Central city, 0%; suburban, 16%. Median family income, $6,817; families above $15,000: 8%; families below $3,000: 19%. Median years education, 10.2.

The Voters

Median voting age 42.
Employment profile White collar, 34%. Blue collar, 50%. Service, 14%. Farm, 2%.
Ethnic groups Black, 31%. Total foreign stock, 1%.

Presidential vote

1976	Carter (D)	93,766	(60%)
	Ford (R)	63,819	(40%)
1972	Nixon (R)	98,640	(75%)
	McGovern (D)	33,480	(25%)

Rep. Bill Nichols (D) Elected 1966; b. Oct. 16, 1918, near Becker, Miss.; home, Sylacauga; Auburn U., B.S. 1939, M.S. 1941; Methodist.

Career Army, 1942–47; V.P. Parker Fertilizer Co., Pres., Parker Gin Co., 1947–66; Ala. Senate 1963–67.

Offices 2417 RHOB, 202-225-3261. Also Fed. Bldg., P.O. Box 2042, Anniston 36201, 205-236-5655.

Committees *Armed Services* (8th). Subcommittees: Investigations; Military Compensation (Chairman); Military Personnel; NATO Standardization, Interoperability, and Readiness.

Group Ratings

	ADA	COPE	PC	RPN	NFU	LCV	CFA	NAB	NSI	ACA	NTU
1978	5	20	25	50	33	–	9	100	100	83	–
1977	5	26	23	18	–	28	15	–	–	74	38
1976	5	33	13	24	50	20	27	50	90	84	50

Key Votes

1) Increase Def Spnd	FOR	6) Alaska Lands Protect	AGN	11) Delay Auto Pol Cntrl	FOR
2) B-1 Bomber	FOR	7) Water Projects Veto	AGN	12) Sugar Price Escalator	FOR
3) Cargo Preference	FOR	8) Consum Protect Agcy	AGN	13) Pub Fin Cong Cmpgns	AGN
4) Dereg Nat Gas	AGN	9) Common Situs Picket	AGN	14) ERA Ratif Recissn	FOR
5) Kemp-Roth	AGN	10) Labor Law Revision	AGN	15) Prohibt Govt Abrtns	FOR

Election Results

1978 general	Bill Nichols (D), unopposed	($13,212)
1978 primary	Bill Nichols (D), unopposed	
1976 general	Bill Nichols (D), unopposed	($16,569)

FOURTH DISTRICT

Nowhere were the shifting tides of Alabama politics during the time it was dominated by George Wallace more clearly evident than in the 4th congressional district. During the late 1950s and early 1960s, when everyone thought massive desegregation in the South was impossible, this part of northern Alabama, between Birmingham on the south and the Tennessee River valley on the north, was considered a populist stronghold. The local congressman, Carl Elliott, was considered reliable enough by the Kennedy Administration to be entrusted with one of the two new seats created, after bitter struggle, on the Rules Committee in 1961. Organized labor was strong enough here to play some role in the district's politics, and Elliott always had a good labor rating. The workingmen from the industrial towns like Gadsden, Jasper, and Cullman and the leatherhanded farmers of the red clay hills consistently supported economic liberals like Sens. Lister Hill and John Sparkman and Gov. (1947–51, 1955–59) "Kissin' Jim" Folsom against more business-oriented candidates.

Then suddenly race became the major factor in politics here, and everything changed. George Wallace was elected governor by promising to stand in the schoolhouse door to prevent —somehow—desegregation. Barry Goldwater swept the state, and in the process helped elect a Republican Congressman, Jim Martin, from the 4th. Martin, a successful businessman, voted a solid pro-business line in Washington, and could probably have held the seat had he not decided to run for governor in 1966. Meanwhile, the citizens here had stopped thinking of themselves as working people and voted simply as white people. The results show near unanimity: 71% for Wallace in 1968, 78% for Nixon in 1972.

The Republicans were unable to duplicate Martin's victory when he stepped aside in 1966, and Democrat Tom Bevill won the seat. Although it was not clear at the time, Bevill's election meant at least a partial return to the populist tradition of representation—and presaged the change in attitudes that was to come in northern Alabama.

For even as northern Alabama was giving Wallace large majorities in his last race for governor in 1974, race was becoming a less and less important factor in its politics. Integration had proceeded so far (in public accommodations, schools, jobs) and seemed likely to proceed no farther (in bars, churches, private clubs). In any case, it had been more the idea of integration than the fact of it that irritated whites in this 91% white district. And when integration finally came it seemed, if not the best thing that ever happened to the South as Jimmy Carter said, then at least tolerable enough. The 1976 general election showed how things had changed: the last two presidential candidates with black support had had 10% and 22% of the vote here; Carter won with 65%.

Bevill's voting record is better suited to this kind of a constituency than the one he served in the late 1960s. He has generally had a voting record rated at better than 50% by organized labor, with his ratings much lower from liberal groups. He is Chairman of the Public Works Appropriations Subcommittee, in which capacity he has reported out the bills passed by the Congress and vetoed by President Carter. Bevill adheres to the philosophy, shared by many of Alabama's populist Democrats, that the government should spend liberally on public works projects in order to build things people need and to create jobs. That philosophy is a little out of fashion today with liberals, who worry about the environmental effect of the projects, and with conservatives, who don't like to spend public money; but it still commands a majority in the House.

Bevill is also an Assistant Whip, and so technically at least a member of the House leadership. He is also the leadership's most loyal follower on the Alabama delegation. Electorally, he appears to have nothing to worry about. His constituents, no longer concerned about racial issues, seem to have no complaints about his performance.

Census Data Pop. 492,196. Central city, 11%; suburban, 21%. Median family income, $6,350; families above $15,000: 7%; families below $3,000: 22%. Median years education, 9.9.

The Voters

Median voting age 44.
Employment profile White collar, 31%. Blue collar, 53%. Service, 11%. Farm, 5%.
Ethnic groups Black, 9%.

Presidential vote

1976	Carter (D)	124,601	(65%)
	Ford (R)	66,263	(35%)
1972	Nixon (R)	117,823	(78%)
	McGovern (D)	34,059	(22%)

Rep. Tom Bevill (D) Elected 1966; b. Mar. 27, 1921, Townley; home, Jasper; U. of Ala., B.S. 1943, LL.B. 1948; Baptist.

Career Army, WWII; Practicing atty., 1949–67; Ala. House of Reps., 1958–66.

Offices 2305 RHOB, 202-225-4876. Also 600 Broad St., Gadsden 35901, 205-546-0201.

Committees *Appropriations* (17th). Subcommittees: HUD—Independent Agencies; Energy and Water Development (Chairman).

Group Ratings

	ADA	COPE	PC	RPN	NFU	LCV	CFA	NAB	NSI	ACA	NTU
1978	15	40	28	42	40	–	18	75	90	67	–
1977	15	64	25	8	83	19	40	–	–	56	23
1976	25	50	30	29	64	25	45	27	90	64	59

Key Votes

1) Increase Def Spnd	FOR	6) Alaska Lands Protect	FOR	11) Delay Auto Pol Cntrl	FOR
2) B-1 Bomber	AGN	7) Water Projects Veto	AGN	12) Sugar Price Escalator	FOR
3) Cargo Preference	FOR	8) Consum Protect Agcy	AGN	13) Pub Fin Cong Cmpgns	AGN
4) Dereg Nat Gas	AGN	9) Common Situs Picket	AGN	14) ERA Ratif Recissn	FOR
5) Kemp-Roth	AGN	10) Labor Law Revision	AGN	15) Prohibt Govt Abrtns	FOR

Election Results

1978 general	Tom Bevill (D), unopposed			($8,413)
1978 primary	Tom Bevill (D)	112,847	(94%)	
	One other (D)	7,764	(6%)	
1976 general	Tom Bevill (D)	141,490	(80%)	($27,484)
	Leonard Wilson (R)	34,531	(20%)	($8,658)

FIFTH DISTRICT

Fifty years ago the Tennessee River coursed through Alabama's northern counties untamed, and every spring flooded the farm country and small towns along its banks. Then the Tennessee Valley Authority, TVA, was created in the 1930s. The agency dammed the wild river for most of its length, controlled the flooding, and produced cheap public power. This part of Alabama has had a populistic streak since the time of Andrew Jackson, and with the coming of TVA, elected to Congress New Dealers like John Sparkman, who served in the House from what is now the 5th district from 1937 to 1946, and Bob Jones, who succeeded Sparkman and served until his retirement in 1976.

These men helped to bring to the 5th district other benefits from the federal government; and the changes in the district have been striking. In 1950 Huntsville, considered a big place in these parts, was just a sleepy hill town of 14,000. Today its population is ten times that, and still growing. The principal agent of change has been the Redstone Missile Arsenal, the home of hundreds of Army and NASA rocket engineers and technicians. In recent years the Pentagon and

NASA have pumped into the seven counties that make up the 5th district more than half a billion dollars a year, most of it going to Huntsville.

Congressman Jones's career was one of not much interest to the general public—but he was a significant man in the House. He was one of those Southern Democrats who often, though not always, voted with his northern copartisans, and could generally be counted on to do so when his vote was needed; his rating from organized labor was as high as 90% in some sessions. As Chairman of the Public Works Committee, Jones championed New Deal ideas: build lots of roads and dams; even if they aren't strictly needed or damage the environment, they still create lots of jobs.

Jones's successor is Ronnie Flippo. Although considerably younger, he shows signs of embarking on a similar career. Flippo chose in his first term to serve on the Public Works and Science Committees—each of which obviously is of great economic importance to the district. His attitude toward public works projects seems congruent with Jones's. On the floor he is a swing vote, sometimes going along with other Democrats, sometimes voting with Republicans. Flippo beat nine other Democrats in the 1976 primaries, and has had only nominal opposition since. Barring mistakes, he seems likely to win continuously for some time.

Census Data Pop. 489,771. Central city, 28%; suburban, 18%. Median family income, $8,271; families above $15,000: 17%; families below $3,000: 15%. Median years education, 11.8.

The Voters

Median voting age 40.
Employment profile White collar, 47%. Blue collar, 38%. Service, 12%. Farm, 3%.
Ethnic groups Black, 13%. Total foreign stock, 2%.

Presidential vote

1976	Carter (D)	106,191	(68%)
	Ford (R)	50,039	(32%)
1972	Nixon (R)	98,504	(75%)
	McGovern (D)	33,603	(25%)

Rep. Ronnie G. Flippo (D) Elected 1976; b. Aug. 15, 1937, Florence; home, Florence; U. of N. Ala., B.S. 1965, U. of Ala., M.A. 1966; Church of Christ.

Career C.P.A., 1966-77; Ala. House of Reps., 1971-75; Ala. Senate, 1975-77.

Offices 439 CHOB, 202-225-4801. Also 122 Hilton Ct., Florence 35630, 205-766-7692.

Committees *Public Works and Transportation* (21st). Subcommittees: Aviation; Public Buildings and Grounds; Water Resources.

Science and Technology (13th). Subcommittees: Energy Research and Production; Investigations and Oversight; Space Science and Applications.

Group Ratings

	ADA	COPE	PC	RPN	NFU	LCV	CFA	NAB	NSI	ACA	NTU
1978	10	42	33	50	40	–	9	70	88	74	–
1977	5	50	10	22	80	0	10	–	–	38	31

Key Votes

1) Increase Def Spnd	FOR	6) Alaska Lands Protect	FOR	11) Delay Auto Pol Cntrl	FOR
2) B-1 Bomber	AGN	7) Water Projects Veto	AGN	12) Sugar Price Escalator	FOR
3) Cargo Preference	FOR	8) Consum Protect Agcy	AGN	13) Pub Fin Cong Cmpgns	AGN
4) Dereg Nat Gas	DNV	9) Common Situs Picket	AGN	14) ERA Ratif Recissn	FOR
5) Kemp-Roth	AGN	10) Labor Law Revision	FOR	15) Prohibt Govt Abrtns	DNV

Election Results

1978 general	Ronnie G. Flippo (D)	68,985	(100%)	($41,660)
1978 primary	Ronnie G. Flippo (D)	92,359	(91%)	
	One other (D)	8,908	(9%)	
1976 general	Ronnie G. Flippo (D), unopposed			($172,689)

SIXTH DISTRICT

Birmingham is one of the few major Southern cities which did not exist at the time of the Civil War. It was founded a few years later and named, in the hopes of a great industrial future, for the great English manufacturing center. The hopes of the founders have been realized—but only partially. Birmingham is, as it has been for years, the major steel producer in the South. But it is not a city with a particularly robust local economy. A generation ago, it was about equal to Atlanta in terms of size and importance. Since then Atlanta has boomed and Birmingham has stagnated.

Part of the reason is economic. Birmingham is dangerously close to being a one industry town, and in the last generation the steel industry in the United States has been anything but healthy. In an era when business is increasingly dependent on airline travel, Atlanta has the busiest airport in the South, while Birmingham has relatively few flights, except those coming from or going to Atlanta.

But another reason for Birmingham's lack of growth was the city's response to the civil rights revolution. In the days when Atlanta billed itself as the city too busy to hate, Birmingham's police commissioner Bull Connor set dogs and firehoses against civil rights demonstrators. That same year, 1963, Connor seemed unperturbed when someone set off a bomb in a black church and killed four young girls. These events in Birmingham supplied some of the momentum that produced the Civil Rights Act of 1964; and they also damaged the city's economy. Investors, after all, don't like commotion of any kind. During the 1960s, metropolitan Atlanta grew 37% while metropolitan Birmingham grew 3%.

Despite the turmoil of 1963, Birmingham is one part of Alabama which always tended to oppose George Wallace; it voted heavily against him in 1970, his toughest election, against Albert Brewer. This is the only part of Alabama with a substantial high income vote—a vote that produces relatively large Republican votes any time the Republicans come close to contesting a statewide race seriously. The blacks here, of course, always opposed Wallace unanimously; unlike blacks in small towns, they could not be swayed by the urgings or threats of pro-Wallace neighbors. That leaves relatively few votes for Wallace-type Democrats, or even for Jimmy Carter, who did badly here.

Alabama's 6th congressional district includes all of Birmingham and most of its Jefferson County suburbs, excluding only the area to the west in the 7th district. It elects a congressman who in his personal beliefs and affiliations is unique in the Alabama delegation and probably in the whole Congress. John Buchanan is a Republican who was first elected with the Goldwater landslide of 1964. In his first terms in Congress he seemed a conventional Republican conservative.

He is also a Baptist minister, and one who has taken his ministry seriously. In Washington he joined a congregation which included blacks as well as whites—which must have been an unusual experience to someone fresh from the Birmingham of 1963. Into the 1970s, as Buchanan became closer to many black fellow church members, he shifted his positions on some issues. Not only on civil rights, but on some economic issues as well, Buchanan broke with the standard Republican position. Though remaining a strong Republican partisan on some matters, he took a leading role in the legislation giving home rule to the District of Columbia.

Buchanan's politics might seem tempered to his constituency, with something for the country club set and something for the blacks; but in fact it has proved politically very risky. He has suffered significant challenges in each of the last three election years. In 1974 a liberal Birmingham councilwoman held him to 58%; in 1976 a conservative Jefferson County Sheriff held him to 57%. In 1978, he encountered his toughest challenge to date in the Republican primary—a particularly difficult forum since so few people vote in the Republican contest, and most of them who do are strongly conservative. With the help of a campaign to get some Democrats to cross over and vote for Buchanan, he managed to eke out a victory; but again it was not by an especially impressive margin.

How will Buchanan fare in the future? It has been suggested that he might run better as a Democrat, but so far he has resisted the alternative. He may very well attract some kind of competition again in 1980. His main comfort is that he has faced just about every kind of opponent who could possibly run against him, and prevailed.

Census Data Pop. 493,045. Central city, 61%; suburban, 39%. Median family income, $8,683; families above $15,000: 16%; families below $3,000: 13%. Median years education, 11.9.

The Voters

Median voting age 44.
Employment profile White collar, 52%. Blue collar, 34%. Service, 14%. Farm, –%.
Ethnic groups Black, 30%. Total foreign stock, 3%.

Presidential vote

1976	Carter (D)	70,995	(44%)
	Ford (R)	90,928	(56%)
1972	Nixon (R)	108,102	(72%)
	McGovern (D)	41,625	(28%)

Rep. John H. Buchanan (R) Elected 1964; b. Mar. 19, 1928, Paris, Tenn.; home, Birmingham; Samford U., B.A. 1949, U. of Va., Southern Theological Sem.; Baptist.

Career Navy WWII; Pastor of Baptist Churches, 1953–62; Finance Dir., Ala. Repub. Party, 1962–64.

Offices 2263 RHOB, 202-225-4921. Also Suite 105 Fed. Bldg., 1800 5th Ave. N., Birmingham 35203, 205-254-1525.

Committees *Education and Labor* (3d). Subcommittees: Health and Safety; Elementary, Secondary and Vocational Education; Post-secondary Education.

Foreign Affairs (4th). Subcommittees: Africa; International Operations.

Group Ratings

	ADA	COPE	PC	RPN	NFU	LCV	CFA	NAB	NSI	ACA	NTU
1978	30	44	18	58	38	–	9	58	80	67	–
1977	40	57	28	54	50	35	50	–	–	48	27
1976	25	23	20	83	67	58	9	50	80	67	35

Key Votes

1) Increase Def Spnd	FOR	6) Alaska Lands Protect	FOR	11) Delay Auto Pol Cntrl	AGN
2) B-1 Bomber	FOR	7) Water Projects Veto	AGN	12) Sugar Price Escalator	FOR
3) Cargo Preference	FOR	8) Consum Protect Agcy	AGN	13) Pub Fin Cong Cmpgns	AGN
4) Dereg Nat Gas	FOR	9) Common Situs Picket	AGN	14) ERA Ratif Recissn	FOR
5) Kemp-Roth	FOR	10) Labor Law Revision	AGN	15) Prohibt Govt Abrtns	AGN

Election Results

1978 general	John Buchanan (R)	65,700	(62%)	($123,808)
	Don Hawkins (D)	40,771	(38%)	($20,238)
1978 primary	John Buchanan (R)	9,078	(57%)	
	Albert Lee Smith (R)	6,802	(43%)	($196,283)
1976 general	John Buchanan (R)	92,113	(57%)	($92,985)
	Mel Bailey (D)	69,384	(43%)	($81,246)

SEVENTH DISTRICT

The 7th congressional district of Alabama contains almost a cross-section of the state. It includes a substantial part of metropolitan Birmingham, including the steel mill suburb of Bessemer, and Fairfield, site of Mills College—both with black majorities. At the other end of the district are some Black Belt counties with the highest black percentages and lowest incomes in Alabama. They are, however, far less important politically than they would have been if blacks had gotten the vote sooner; their population is less than half that of 50 years ago, as a result of migration to the great cities of the north. In between, the geographical center of the district lies in Tuscaloosa, a reasonably prosperous medium sized city, the proud home of the University of Alabama and of Bear Bryant.

The 7th district lacks a uniform political identity. It has the largest black percentage of any Alabama congressional district—38% in 1970. Yet for years the congressmen elected by this district seemed to have voting records more conservative than the Alabama average. The politicians seemed to think of themselves as representing the well-to-do—culturally and politically conservative folks they knew from the local country club. And of course, in the days when blacks did not vote and many whites didn't keep up their poll tax, this is precisely the kind of people they did represent.

Certainly this seemed to be the view of the 7th district held by Congressman Walter Flowers when he voted for the impeachment of Richard Nixon on the House Judiciary Committee in 1974. Of all the Committee's members, Flowers seemed most wrenched by his decision, and most fearful of its political effect back home. In fact, it hurt him scarcely at all—and not simply because Nixon resigned a short time later. The district's black voters, who had opposed Flowers in 1972 and 1974 primaries, were pleased with his vote; and so were far more whites than he apparently assumed. The heavy anti-Nixon sentiment in the 7th district was an example of opinion among Southerners of both races moving in the same direction—something that has happened increasingly in the years since.

Flowers was first elected to Congress from the 7th district in 1968, and aside from the primary challenges mentioned, won easily every two years. He might easily have won a sixth term in 1978, and was planning on doing so, when George Wallace announced he would not run for the Senate. Flowers, a Wallace supporter in the past though never close to the Governor, decided to make the race. Despite a generally popular voting record, some significant legislative accomplishments, and an attractive character, Flowers was beaten by ex-Chief Justice Howell Heflin, who had started earlier. Flowers made the mistake of stressing his Washington experience and was attacked as part of the "Washington crowd." It was the same epithet applied to his predecessor in the House, Armistead Selden, that helped James Allen defeat Selden in the primary ten years before.

Flowers's sudden Senate candidacy created an opening in the 7th district which had not been expected. The Congressman's Tuscaloosa law partner, Richard Shelby, had been running for lieutenant governor; he switched to the congressional race, and won. In the runoff he was opposed by state Rep. Chris McNair, who had received a respectable percentage; it is symbolic of how far the South has come that not much was made, one way or the other, of the fact that McNair is black. Meanwhile, the Republican candidate expressly conceded the general election. Shelby appears to have a safe seat, and a pretty free hand to be whatever kind of congressman he wants.

Census Data Pop. 492,142. Central city, 14%; suburban, 47%. Median family income, $6,806; families above $15,000: 10%; families below $3,000: 22%. Median years education, 10.4.

The Voters

Median voting age 43.
Employment profile White collar, 38%. Blue collar, 43%. Service, 15%. Farm, 4%.
Ethnic groups Black, 38%. Total foreign stock, 1%.

Presidential vote

1976	Carter (D)	93,693	(57%)
	Ford (R)	71,799	(43%)
1972	Nixon (R)	92,421	(66%)
	McGovern (D)	47,536	(34%)

Rep. Richard C. Shelby (D) Elected 1978; b. May 6, 1934, Fairfield; home, Tuscaloosa; U. of Ala., A.B. 1957, LL.B. 1963; Presbyterian.

Career Practicing atty., 1963–; Ala. Senate, 1971–79.

Offices 1408 LHOB, 202-225-2511. Also P.O. Box 2627, Tuscaloosa 35401, 205-752-3578.

Committees *Interstate and Foreign Commerce* (27th). Subcommittees: Energy and Power; Health and the Environment.

Judiciary (20th). Subcommittees: Immigration, Refugees, and International Law; Criminal Justice.

Veterans' Affairs (16th). Subcommittees: Medical Facilities and Benefits; Housing.

Group Ratings: Newly Elected

Key Votes: Newly Elected

Election Results

1978 general	Richard C. Shelby (D)	77,742	(100%)	($181,405)
1978 run-off	Richard C. Shelby (D)	75,329	(59%)	
	Chris McNair (D)	52,659	(41%)	($19,636)
1978 primary	Richard C. Shelby (D)	46,706	(48%)	
	Chris McNair (D)	36,312	(38%)	
	Goodloe Sutton (D)	13,361	(14%)	($6,722)
1976 general	Walter Flowers (D), unopposed			($27,763)

ALASKA

Alaska is the nation's largest state (586,000 square miles) and also one of its smallest (403,000 in 1978—and one-quarter of that represents growth since 1970). Alaskans live in the land of the midnight sun and of darkness at noon; of winter wind-chill factors that reach 100 below and of muggy, mosquito-filled summers; of the tallest mountains in North America and thousands of miles of rugged seacoast. It is a land where a penniless immigrant like Walter Hickel can make millions in the construction business, and where some Eskimos and Aleuts still live in grinding poverty. Most important these days, Alaska is the land of the great North Slope oil strike, of sudden boom—and the nation's highest unemployment.

It is hard for someone from the "Lower 48" to grasp the size of Alaska. More than twice as large as Texas, the state spans four different time zones. But for all its expanse, Alaska has only one railroad and a few paved highways—the only way to get around is by airplane. Even the most isolated villages in the interior have an airstrip cleared in the bush or on a frozen river. Politicians especially have to fly a lot, and crashes are not uncommon: one killed Congressman Nick Begich and House Majority Leader Hale Boggs in 1972, and another seriously injured Senator Ted Stevens and killed his wife in 1978.

Most of Alaska still belongs to nature; it remains the home of the caribou and perhaps an occasional Eskimo hunter. Most of the population is clustered in a few small urban areas, with more than 40% of the people living in greater Anchorage. Dreams of sudden riches still bring men to Alaska (and this is one state that has many more men than women), but riches are seldom found. Life here can be hard: high wages are eaten up by high prices, and there are fewer people proportionately over 65 than in any other state. After a while, things are just too rough, and people tend to move back south.

For years Alaska longed for statehood, for control of its own affairs and release from the economic thrall of Washington, D.C., and Seattle, Washington. But Alaska remains an economic—and political—dependent. Decisions continue to be made in Washington and in the headquarters of the big oil companies that will shape Alaska's future as much as the Northwest Ordinance did Ohio's or the Homestead Act Nebraska's. For example, only in 1971, when Congress passed the Alaska Native Claims Act, could the most basic issue—ownership of land—begin to be settled. The natives—Eskimos, Aleuts, and Indians—had never surrendered title to the land to anyone, and the law passed in 1971 gave them $962 million and 40 million acres—the money to be administered and the precise acreage selected by 12 regional native corporations. The legislation also ended the freeze on federal lands imposed five years before; this allowed the state to select the 103 million acres promised by the Statehood Act back in 1959, and of course the state proceeded to choose the land with the greatest mineral potential.

Mineral potential in Alaska means, primarily, oil—the huge oil strike in the remote North Slope. It is more than a decade since oil was found here, but it only began flowing to the rest of the country in 1977—and there is not nearly enough of it to solve the energy shortage that no one anticipated in 1968. From the days of initial oil strike, the history of Alaska pivoted around the question of how to get the oil out. Tankers were impractical: the waters off the North Slope are frozen all year. Rail or truck would have been too expensive. So it had to be a pipeline, to be built across land largely uninhabited, much of which white men had never seen. Environmentalists charged that the pipeline would destroy the permafrost (land which remains frozen all year except for a few inches at the top), interfere with caribou migrations, and otherwise irreparably injure Alaska's unique and fragile environment. They went to court and in 1973 got a ruling halting pipeline construction.

The oil companies and Alaska's boomers—people who favor economic development and the creation of jobs—were furious. There was little doubt that their feelings were shared by most Alaskans, and "Sierra Club go home" bumper stickers began to appear. Alaska's congressional delegation, its two Senators, Republican Ted Stevens and Democrat Mike Gravel, and Congressman Don Young, were under intense pressure to do something. They responded in what has become a familiar pattern.

Stevens concentrated on working with the legislative powers that be, in this case Interior Committee Chairman Henry Jackson, on getting through a bill which would comprehensively revise federal pipeline law and which would leave unsettled the adequacy of the Interior Department's environmental impact statement on the pipeline. With Jackson's support, that approach was sure to work; but it would still be some time before the physical work on the pipeline began. Gravel said he supported Stevens and Jackson. But in a surprise mood he moved to exempt the pipeline from the requirement of filing an environmental impact statement altogether. Jackson was furious, because the exemption would threaten the National Environmental Protection Act, which he had sponsored. But Gravel prevailed by a 50–49 margin, with a tie-breaking vote from Spiro Agnew, and the pipeline got the green light.

Gravel badly needed that kind of political victory in 1973, for he was in as much political trouble as an Alaska Senator has ever been in. Alaska expects its senators to work for the state's economic interests, but Gravel's interests had gone farther afield. He had attempted to read into the Senate record massive excerpts from the then-banned Pentagon Papers; foiled by a timely objection, he began crying. In 1972, a year later, he ran for vice president, nominating himself, at the Democratic National Convention. But with the pipeline issue, Gravel managed to avoid tough opposition, and won his second term by beating a member of the John Birch Society.

Now Gravel is up for reelection in 1980, this time having avoided controversial national issues. Again he is concentrating on an Alaska issue, and working at cross-purposes with Stevens and the rest of the Alaska delegation. At stake this time is the amount of land the federal government can protect under wilderness or other designations. Under the Native Claims Act, the Interior Department had withdrawn until December 1978 some 80 million acres from all development, pending a congressional decision as to how much should be protected. Environmentalists wanted more land protected; boomers wanted much less. The House, led by Interior Chairman Morris Udall and John Seiberling of Ohio, passed a bill protecting even more acres—over the loud but ineffective protests of Alaska's Congressman Young. The question, as 1978 drew to a close, was what the Senate would do.

There Gravel and Stevens had considerably more leverage than Young had in the House; traditionally, senators are not going to support laws affecting one state if both that state's senators oppose them. And Stevens and Gravel both opposed the Udall-Seiberling bill. But they disagreed on what to do about it. Stevens worked hard with the Senate leadership and environmentalists to effect a compromise, which would protect considerably less than the 80 million acres, would give the state some degree of control over others, and would free up for development the rest. Personally popular, hard working, conciliatory but firm, Stevens was a fine negotiator, and got a compromise which environmentalists felt gave away far too much. But Gravel would have none of it. Instead of supporting Stevens, he used his prerogative to block home state legislation to prevent any action on the Udall-Seiberling bill at all. The protection on the 80 million acres was left to vanish December 18.

The only problem for Gravel's position is that Interior Secretary Cecil Andrus, who strongly supported major protection, had some other alternatives. Using administrative procedures, the Department created 56 million acres of national monuments, protected another 40 million acres, and had the President designate 6 million more under the Antiquities Act. The end result was that more land was protected from development after Gravel's action than before; and while this freeze could be voided by congressional action, it can remain in force indefinitely, not lapse as the earlier action had. Such was the situation going in the 96th Congress. Stevens can still work to get some form of compromise bill through, but there is less reason now for environmentalists and the Administration to make concessions than in 1978.

Their performances on the pipeline and wilderness issues show the differences between the two senators. Gravel, though a Democrat and probably more in line with the Senate majority on most issues, is very much an outsider in Washington. He has thoroughly antagonized Henry Jackson, Chairman of the Energy Committee which is so important to Alaska, and does not have major allies in the Senate. He is able to articulate the opinions of most Alaskans on issues, particularly those relating to development, and he cannot be considered without political strength at home. But it seems entirely possible that he could be defeated by a strong candidate like former Governor Hickel. Gravel's chances in 1980 may very well depend on whether he is able, as he was in 1974, to avoid drawing a strong opponent.

Stevens, in contrast, is one of the best liked senators personally, on both sides of the aisle. He has risen far though quietly in the Republican leadership, chairing their Campaign Committee in 1975 and being unanimously elected Republican Whip in 1977. His voting record might be described as middle of the road on economic issues and somewhat conservative on other matters. He is probably not conservative enough to succeed to the Minority Leader post if Baker should run for or be elected president, but his chances cannot be ruled out altogether. Stevens was appointed to the Senate by Hickel in 1968 to fill a vacancy. He had to win a seriously contested election in 1970, but won easily in 1972 and beat a nuisance candidate in 1978 with 76% of the vote. As much as any senator, he can be considered to have a safe seat.

The state's single House seat has been held by as many men as both Senate seats taken together. The current incumbent, Don Young, was chosen in a March 1973 special election. In that race, as in 1974 and 1976, Young's opponent was of native background; Young was aided by his vociferous backing of the pipeline as well as lingering resentment of the Native Claims Act. He had a closer race in 1978, when his Democratic opponent charged that he was not an effective opponent of the Udall-Seiberling wilderness act.

Today the oil is finally flowing through the pipeline. Ironically, had it not been for actions taken by OPEC during the embargo, Alaskan oil would not be on the market, for production would not have been profitable at pre-1973–74 prices. The pipeline itself ended up costing $9 billion; original estimates had been $900 million. Naturally, there was great waste and pilferage, and wage rates, set by Alaska's powerful Teamsters, were very high, and unemployment increased substantially when the pipeline was finished. Finally, because the oil is more than the West Coast needs, some is shipped through the Panama Canal and some would be sold to Japan had Congress not expressly forbidden that.

Yet Alaskans seem fairly happy with the direction of their state and certainly do not adhere to the no-growth philosophy of some of their critics. The state's earlier governors—William Egan, elected in 1959, 1962, and 1970, and Walter Hickel, elected in 1966—believe strongly in development. The major newspaper in the state, the Anchorage *Times,* agrees strongly. So does Jess Carr, a major force in the state as head of the Teamsters Union, which has a membership of one-third of all employed Alaskans. Yet the state has elected, not once but twice, a governor who has severe doubts about some kinds of development, and who has fought the boomers on a number of issues.

To be sure, Jay Hammond hasn't won election by much. In the 1974 Republican primary he beat Hickel and Keith Miller, the interim governor who followed him, with less than a majority. In that year's general election, Hammond beat Egan by just 287 votes. In 1978 Hickel ran again. This time the counting was hectic, and the result not approved by the courts until October 20; Hammond's lead was 98 votes. In the general election his main opponent was again Hickel, running a last minute write-in campaign which won an amazing 27% of the vote; a pro-development Independent had 13%, almost as many as the Democrat. So Hammond won a second four-year term with far less than a majority. His adversaries must be enraged at the narrowness of the margins that have placed him in the governor's chair for eight years.

No one seriously claims that Hammond is a no-growth advocate. He joined Stevens and Young in fighting the federal wilderness bill, for instance. But he does favor increasing taxes on the oil companies, and he has expressed doubts as to whether the state government ought to be spending all its oil wealth immediately. Hammond's chief asset is his character. He is just the kind of man you would cast for an Alaska version of Mr. Smith Goes to Washington: a bearded bush pilot (who rescued people from a downed plane in the 1978 campaign), a sometime poet (or doggerel writer), a former trapper, commercial fisherman, and air taxi operator. Hammond is open and informal, and ready to concede the strong points of his adversaries.

In 1976 Alaska gave Gerald Ford one of his largest percentages. This was behavior out of line from the state's performance in the previous close elections of 1968 and 1960, when it came close to mirroring the national result. For Alaskans the major difference between the candidates was on Alaska issues: Ford favored the pipeline, while Carter tended to take environmentalist positions. It appears that Alaskans have come to view national politics from a perspective that is almost colonial, voting not on the great national issues that move voters in other states, but solely on the basis of issues peculiar to Alaska. This suggests a certain selfishness, but it may simply reflect the fact that Alaska has not yet developed a private economy that can support all the people who have come to live here. The natural response, in the America of the 1970s, is to ask the federal government to do something about it.

A final note. Alaska has voted to move its state capital from Juneau to a new site north of Anchorage called Willow. The initial decision, to move, was reached by referendum in 1974; only the residents of the Panhandle area, around Juneau itself, opposed the measure. Willow was picked by referendum over two other sites in 1976, and the architectural plans seem both humanistic and beautiful. Most Alaskans consider Juneau too inaccessible (it's a long plane ride and two time zones from Juneau to Anchorage, where most Alaskans live), and they apparently think the money the state spends on maintaining the seat of government in Juneau is just a wasteful subsidy to the place, which is much dependent on it. In other words, most Alaskans feel about Juneau as most Americans, if they thought much about it, might feel about Alaska. This is a state that has yet to find an identity, or peace of mind.

Census Data Pop. 302,173; 0.15% of U.S. total, 50th largest; Central city, 0%; suburban, 0%. Median family income, $12,441; 1st highest; families above $15,000: 38%; families below $3,000: 7%. Median years education, 12.5.

1977 Share of Federal Tax Burden $1,036,000,000; 0.30% of U.S. total, 47th largest.

1977 Share of Federal Outlays $1,544,854,000; 0.39% of U.S. total, 44th largest. Per capita federal spending, $4,389.

DOD	$505,249,000	35th (0.55%)	HEW	$185,351,000	51st (0.13%)
ERDA	$1,237,000	45th (0.02%)	HUD	$7,194,000	49th (0.17%)
NASA	$836,000	38th (0.02%)	VA	$24,080,000	51st (0.13%)
DOT	$285,044,000	16th (2.00%)	EPA	$13,560,000	46th (0.17%)
DOC	$82,914,000	26th (1.00%)	RevS	$17,977,000	50th (0.21%)
DOI	$146,861,000	10th (3.16%)	Debt	$17,630,000	51st (0.06%)
USDA	$83,351,000	43d (0.42%)	Other	$173,570,000	

Economic Base Finance, insurance and real estate; food and kindred products, especially canned and cured sea foods; agriculture and fishing, notably fish, dairy products, eggs, potatoes and cattle; oil and gas field services, and other oil and gas extraction activity; paper pulp, and other paper and allied products.

Political Line-up Governor, Jay S. Hammond (R). Senators, Ted Stevens (R) and Mike Gravel (D). Representative: 1 R at large. State Senate (11 R and 9 D); State House (25 D, 14 R, and 1 Libertarian).

The Voters

Registration 240,121 Total. 67,629 D (28%); 36,211 R (15%); 129,708 Non-Partisan (54%); 6,573 Others (3%).
Median voting age 34
Employment profile White collar, 55%. Blue collar, 30%. Service, 15%. Farm, 4%.
Ethnic groups Black, 3%. Indian, 16%. Total foreign stock, 11%.

Presidential vote

1976	Carter (D)	44,055	(38%)
	Ford (R)	71,555	(62%)
1972	Nixon (R)	55,349	(63%)
	McGovern (D)	32,967	(37%)

Sen. Ted Stevens (R) Elected Appointed Dec. 23, 1968, elected 1970, seat up 1978; b. Nov. 18, 1923, Indianapolis, Ind.; home, Anchorage; Oreg. St. U., Mont. St. U., UCLA, A.B. 1947, Harvard U. LL.B., 1950; Episcopalian.

Career Air Force, WWII; Practicing atty., 1950–53, 1961–68; U.S. Atty., 1953–56; U.S. Dept. of Interior, Legis. Council, 1956–58, Asst. to the Secy., 1958–60, Solicitor 1960–61; Alaska House of Reps., 1964–68.

Offices 260 RSOB, 202-224-3004. Also 221 Fed. Bldg., Anchorage 99501, 907-272-9561; and 200 Fed. Bldg., Fairbanks 99701, 907-452-5264.

Committees *Minority Whip*

Appropriations (3d). Subcommittees: Defense; Interior and Related Agencies; Legislative Branch; Military Construction; State, Justice, and Commerce, the Judiciary and Related Agencies

Energy and Natural Resources (5th). Subcommittees: Energy Research and Development; Energy Resources and Materials Production; Parks, Recreation, and Renewable Resources.

Governmental Affairs (4th). Subcommittees: Governmental Efficiency and the District of Columbia; Energy, Nuclear Proliferation and Federal Spending; Civil Service and General Services.

Group Ratings

	ADA	COPE	PC	RPN	NFU	LCV	CFA	NAB	NSI	ACA	NTU
1978	10	33	13	78	60	15	20	42	70	61	–
1977	20	47	10	80	75	–	12	–	–	50	22
1976	25	36	14	85	56	22	35	67	90	45	42

Key Votes

1) Warnke Nom	AGN	6) Egypt-Saudi Arms	FOR	11) Hosptl Cost Contnmnt	AGN
2) Neutron Bomb	FOR	7) Draft Restr Pardon	AGN	12) Clinch River Reactor	FOR
3) Waterwy User Fee	AGN	8) Wheat Price Support	FOR	13) Pub Fin Cong Cmpgns	AGN
4) Dereg Nat Gas	FOR	9) Panama Canal Treaty	AGN	14) ERA Ratif Recissn	AGN
5) Kemp-Roth	FOR	10) Labor Law Rev Clot	FOR	15) Med Necssy Abrtns	FOR

Election Results

1978 general	Ted Stevens (R)	92,783	(76%)	($346,837)
	Donald W. Hobbs (D)	29,574	(24%)	($21,234)
1978 primary	Ted Stevens (R), unopposed			
1972 general	Ted Stevens (R)	74,216	(77%)	($195,123)
	Gene Guess (D)	21,791	(23%)	($47,131)

Sen. Mike Gravel (D) Elected 1968, seat up 1980; b. May 13, 1930, Springfield, Mass.; home, Anchorage; Assumption Col., American Internatl. Col., Columbia U., B.S. 1956; Unitarian.

Career Army, 1951–54; Taxi driver 1956; Real estate developer 1956–58; Alaska House of Reps., 1962–66, Speaker 1965; Candidate for Dem. nomination for U.S. House of Reps., 1966.

Offices 3121 DSOB, 202-224-6665. Also P.O. Box 2283, Anchorage 99510, 907-277-4591; and P.O. Box 1480, Fairbanks 99707, 907-452-6228.

Committees *Environment and Public Works* (3d). Subcommittees: Water Resources (Chairman); Regional and Community Development; Resource Protection.

Finance (6th). Subcommittees: International Trade; Taxation and Debt Management Generally; Energy and Foundations (Chairman).

Group Ratings

	ADA	COPE	PC	RPN	NFU	LCV	CFA	NAB	NSI	ACA	NTU
1978	70	81	43	67	71	43	40	25	10	12	–
1977	55	76	35	50	78	–	32	–	–	20	20
1976	45	71	38	53	92	41	28	14	0	16	21

Key Votes

1) Warnke Nom	FOR	6) Egypt-Saudi Arms	FOR	11) Hosptl Cost Contnmnt	FOR
2) Neutron Bomb	AGN	7) Draft Restr Pardon	FOR	12) Clinch River Reactor	DNV
3) Waterwy User Fee	FOR	8) Wheat Price Support	DNV	13) Pub Fin Cong Cmpgns	FOR
4) Dereg Nat Gas	FOR	9) Panama Canal Treaty	FOR	14) ERA Ratif Recissn	FOR
5) Kemp-Roth	FOR	10) Labor Law Rev Clot	FOR	15) Med Necssy Abrtns	DNV

Election Results

1974 general	Mike Gravel (D)	54,361	(58%)	($469,300)
	C. R. Lewis (R)	38,914	(42%)	($353,701)
1974 primary	Mike Gravel (D)	22,834	(54%)	
	Gene Guess (D)	15,090	(36%)	
	Two others (D)	4,123	(10%)	
1968 general	Mike Gravel (D)	36,527	(45%)	
	Elmer Rasmuson (R)	30,286	(37%)	
	Ernest Gruening (write-in)	14,188	(18%)	

Gov. Jay Hammond (R) Elected 1974, term expires Dec. 1978; b. July 21, 1922, Troy, N.Y.; Penn. St. U., 1940–42, U. of Alaska, B.S. 1948.

Career Navy, WWII; Bush pilot, trapper, and guide, 1946–48; Pilot Agent, U.S. Fish and Wildlife Svc., 1948–56; Commercial fisherman and air taxi operator, 1956–74; Alaska House of Reps., 1959–65; Mgr., Bristol Bay Borough, 1965–67; Alaska Senate, 1967–72; Mayor, Bristol Borzough, 1972–74.

Offices Pouch A, State Capitol, Juneau 99811, 907-465-3500.

Election Results

1978 general	Jay S. Hammond (R)	49,580	(40%)
	Walter J. Hickel (write-in)	33,555	(27%)
	Chancy Croft (D)	25,656	(21%)
	Tom Kelly (I)	15,656	(13%)
1978 primary	Jay S. Hammond (R)	31,896	(39%)
	Walter J. Hickel (R)	31,798	(39%)
	Tom Fink (R)	17,487	(22%)
1974 general	Jay S. Hammond (R)	45,840	(50%)
	William A. Egan (D)	45,553	(50%)

Rep. Don Young (R) Elected Mar. 6, 1973; b. June 9, 1933, Meridian, Cal.; home, Fort Yukon; Chico St. Col., B.A. 1956; Episcopalian.

Career Construction work, 1959; Teacher 1960–69; River boat Capt.; Fort Yukon City Cncl., Mayor; Alaska House of Reps., 1966–70; Alaska Senate 1970–73.

Offices 1210 LHOB, 202-225-5765. Also 115 Fed. Bldg., Anchorage 99501, 907-279-1587.

Committees *Interior and Insular Affairs* (4th). Subcommittees: Public Lands; Mines and Mining; Oversight/Special Investigations.

Merchant Marine and Fisheries (6th). Subcommittees: Coast Guard and Navigation; Fish and Wildlife; Maritime Education and Training.

Group Ratings

	ADA	COPE	PC	RPN	NFU	LCV	CFA	NAB	NSI	ACA	NTU
1978	5	53	8	25	40	–	5	89	100	73	–
1977	5	55	13	75	64	0	5	–	–	64	30
1976	0	53	2	44	50	0	0	60	100	75	39

Key Votes

1) Increase Def Spnd	DNV	6) Alaska Lands Protect	AGN	11) Delay Auto Pol Cntrl	DNV
2) B-1 Bomber	FOR	7) Water Projects Veto	AGN	12) Sugar Price Escalator	FOR
3) Cargo Preference	FOR	8) Consum Protect Agcy	AGN	13) Pub Fin Cong Cmpgns	AGN
4) Dereg Nat Gas	FOR	9) Common Situs Picket	AGN	14) ERA Ratif Recissn	DNV
5) Kemp-Roth	FOR	10) Labor Law Revision	FOR	15) Prohibt Govt Abrtns	FOR

Election Results

1978 general	Don Young (R)	68,811	(55%)	($270,359)
	Patrick Rodey (D)	55,176	(45%)	
1978 primary	Don Young (R), unopposed			
1976 general	Don Young (R)	83,722	(71%)	($175,589)
	Eben Hopson (D)	34,194	(29%)	($21,184)

ARIZONA

To most Americans Arizona has meant the Grand Canyon, Navajo hogans, Tombstone and Wyatt Earp, or maybe even London Bridge which, thanks to an imaginative developer, now sits proudly in a patch of Arizona desert. More recently Arizona has become a scene of scandal: the place where investigative reporter Don Bolles, looking into landselling scandals, was murdered; a place where leading citizens have been accused of involvement with organized crime. Behind it all is the reality of rapid growth, probably the most rapid in the country, concentrated in the Phoenix and Tucson metropolitan areas. In effect Arizona consists of two cities—one now major, one middle sized—in the midst of sparsely populated desert, tourist sites, and Indian reservations. Some 56% of the voters live in greater Phoenix, and another 21% in and around Tucson. In 1940 Arizona had a population of 550,000; by 1970 it had reached 1,772,000 and according to Census estimates it reached 2,300,000 in 1977—the fastest rate of growth of any state in the 1970s. Quite literally a new majority has completely transformed the politics of Arizona in the last 25 years.

The change—from an old-fashioned Democratic state to a sleek conservative one—is best illustrated by contrasting the careers of the state's two best known politicians: Congressman (1912–27) and Senator (1927–69) Carl Hayden and Senator (1953–65, 1969–) Barry Goldwater. Hayden began his political career as a councilman in Tempe (formerly Hayden's Crossing) in 1902, when Phoenix was just a hot, sleepy depot on the Southern Pacific Railroad. Hayden was a Democrat, and a fairly conservative one—as were just about all successful Arizona politicians until the early 1950s. The state had a Democratic heritage that came from the Southern origin of many of its early settlers and the Mexican background of many of the rest. Although Arizona occasionally went Republican in national elections (it never supported a losing presidential candidate until 1960), Hayden and his fellow Democrats never had any difficulty with the voters.

The basic Hayden formula was to see that federal money—and water—was pumped into the state. He was especially interested in highways, but the last great legacy of his career was the Central Arizona Project, pushed through in 1968, when he was 91 years old. Interestingly, most of this water goes not to residential Phoenix, but to the agribusiness farms in the otherwise parched Gila River valley nearby. Jimmy Carter tried to phase out the CAP, but Arizona politicians of all stripes—House Interior Committee Chairman Morris Udall as well as Minority Leader John Rhodes and Barry Goldwater—fought successfully for its preservation.

The birth of Arizona's long dominant conservative Republicanism can be dated with some precision to the year 1949, when Barry Goldwater, then proprietor of his family's Phoenix department store, was elected to the Phoenix City Council. The next year Goldwater helped Republican Howard Pyle win the governorship, and in 1952 Republicans swept the state: Eisenhower won its electoral votes, Pyle was reelected, and Goldwater went to the United States Senate. (The man he beat, Sen. Ernest MacFarland, was then Senate Majority Leader, and his defeat set the stage for Lyndon Johnson's ascent to the Senate Democratic leadership.) Goldwater won reelection by a large margin in 1958, again against MacFarland; the Republican directed the thrust of his rhetoric against national union leaders like Walter Reuther—targets with little political clout in Arizona.

The year 1958 was a bad one for conservative Republicans almost everywhere—except Arizona. So Goldwater's victory elevated him to national prominence. His frank, often blunt, and impolitic articulation of his beliefs brought him such devotion and volunteer support all over the country that he won the 1964 Republican presidential nomination despite his malapropisms, his modesty, and his evident distaste for running.

Goldwater's resolute conservatism—he said he wanted to repeal federal programs, not start new ones—struck a chord in booming Arizona. The big influx of population here consists of white collar technicians from the Midwest, South, and southern California—the kind of people who have made metropolitan Phoenix more Republican in the 1972 and 1976 presidential races than Orange County, California. The years 1958 to 1972 were almost entirely Republican years in Arizona. This is the only state which has gone Republican in every presidential election since 1948, where Republicans held the governorship for all but two years of the 1958–74 period, whose congressional delegation was all Republican, except for Morris Udall, during the entire Nixon and Ford Administrations.

Yet all has not gone well for Arizona Republicans. They lost the governorship in 1974 and 1978, and they lost the state's other Senate seat in 1976. They suffered the indignity of having John Rhodes's House seat seriously contested in 1974 and 1976, and they lost the 3d district to a Democrat, albeit a very conservative one, in 1976. It would be going too far to say that this is a Democratic state, or about to become one. It gave Gerald Ford one of his largest percentages in 1976; and Republicans have come close in every significant race they have lost.

Closer examination of the election results shows that Republicans have faced two separate problems. First, in the period between 1970 and 1976 Republicans were under heavy attack in statewide and congressional elections. Incumbent Jack Williams nearly lost the governorship to Democrat Raul Castro in 1970, and Democrat Sam Grossman threw a scare into Sen. Paul Fannin until the Arizona Republic raised questions about Grossman's Arizona residency. In 1972 Democrat Jack Brown made a serious bid for the 4th congressional district. In 1974 Rhodes faced his toughest challenge, Castro was elected Governor, and a young lawyer named Bruce Babbitt, campaigning against corruption and consumer fraud, was elected Attorney General. Two years later, when Senator Fannin retired, Democrat Dennis DeConcini was elected Senator, following a bitter Republican primary between Congressmen Sam Steiger and John Conlan.

Today the Democrats seem in even better shape. Babbitt was elected Governor in 1978 by a margin much larger than Castro's. But in fact 1978 saw a strong trend to the Republicans in Arizona. They retained control of the state Senate and the attorney general's office. Far from being on the defensive in their own congressional districts, they managed to make a serious challenge to Morris Udall. The Republican trend is all the more noteworthy, because the Republican Party has had great difficulty in fielding strong candidates, while the Democratic Party, for once, has the attractive and popular incumbents. Consider what happened in the 1978 governor's race.

It is a rather involved story. Raul Castro, unpopular after three years in office, won appointment as Ambassador to Argentina in October 1977. His successor, Wesley Bolin, had been Secretary of State since 1948—a man with a fine silvery mane who liked to ride horses and wear western clothes. A "pinto" Democrat, to use the Arizona term, Bolin hired conservative Republicans as his chief advisers; meanwhile, he was facing likely primary opposition from Dino DeConcini, a former Castro aide and brother of Senator Dennis DeConcini. Suddenly in March 1978 Bolin died, giving Arizona its third governor in five months—Bruce Babbitt, who had not been running for governor at all. But Babbitt's popularity and achievements as Attorney General made him a strong candidate, and DeConcini dropped out of the race. Babbitt had promised to do something about corruption; as Attorney General, he had cracked the Bolles case and successfully prosecuted Bolles's killers—including some well-connected land developers. He had promised to do something about consumer ripoffs; he successfully sued the bread companies and forced them to rebate cash to every family in Arizona. Babbitt was also personally attractive: he comes from an old Flagstaff family, he goes backpacking with his family in the Grand Canyon, he remains accessible to ordinary citizens despite the death threats he received in the Bolles case.

Against this kind of candidate the Republicans nominated Evan Mecham, a former state Senator and Pontiac dealer. Mecham had run unsuccessfully for office before, against Hayden in the 1962 Senate race and twice without success in the governor's race. He kept his name before the public with advertisements extolling the virtues of less government—and asking people to buy their Pontiacs from him. He was strong enough to win the 1978 primary, beating a candidate whom rumor connected with land fraud practices, but he was not considered a strong candidate in the general election. The Arizona *Republic,* normally strongly conservative, broke with tradition and endorsed Babbitt. His mild liberalism—he favors having Medicaid in Arizona, the only state which has spurned the program—apparently was less unpalatable to them than Mecham.

Yet despite all these advantages, Babbitt was elected with only 54% of the vote—a solid enough victory, but by no means a landslide. Despite all his weaknesses Mecham was able to carry metropolitan Phoenix; Babbitt needed a nearly 2–1 margin in metropolitan Tucson and a solid win in the rest of the state for his victory. Babbitt can be expected to be an innovative and interesting governor. He will probably try to place some environmental controls on the state's growth and to produce some modest increase in state government services. Working against these goals most likely will be the Republican majorities in the legislature. Babbitt is considered by some one of the brightest and most attractive young Democratic politicians in the nation, but he will have to work hard to come up with achievements as dazzling as those he made as Attorney General.

If the Arizona Republican Party's failure to nominate a strong candidate in 1978 helped Bruce Babbitt win, its fielding of two strong candidates in 1976 helped Dennis DeConcini win election as Senator. The incumbent, Paul Fannin, had retired at 69; the two Republican competitors, Congressman Sam Steiger and John Conlan, had the lowest opinions of each other. Conlan is an evangelical Christian many of whose backers share his strong religious beliefs; he called for the election of more Christians in politics—infuriating Steiger, who is Jewish, and causing Barry Goldwater, who is not, to charge Conlan with anti-Semitism. Steiger was no less controversial. He killed Morris Udall's land use bill in 1974, and was nearly defeated that year after being placed on Environmental Action's Dirty Dozen list. His excitable personality evinced itself in many ways: once in Arizona he shot two burros, in self defense he claimed. But an autopsy showed the burros had been shot from behind—and the burros became an issue in the Senate campaign. Steiger won the primary, but by a narrow margin; Conlan sulked and never really endorsed the winner.

The Republican primary fight certainly helped Dennis DeConcini, the Democratic nominee, but he also had assets of his own. He is from a politically prominent family in Tucson, and as Pima County Attorney (the Tucson prosecutor) he made a good record. He stressed his experience in local affairs and closeness to the voters—in contrast to the Republican congressmen—and came out against national Democratic positions which cause trouble in Arizona, like opposition to right to work laws. DeConcini actually won metropolitan Phoenix by a small margin, and got much larger percentages in Tucson and the rest of the state.

Winning an election at age 39, DeConcini had the potential of staying in as long as Carl Hayden, but he favors limiting senators to 12 years of service and announced that he would seek no more than two terms. In the Senate he has proceeded more in the Hayden than the Goldwater tradition, looking after Arizona's interests rather than staking out positions on broad national issues. But there is one notable exception. In the Panama Canal Treaty debate DeConcini suddenly became the center of national attention when he advanced his own understanding that the Treaty did not bar the United States from using military force to keep the Canal open in the future. The Carter Administration had to negotiate carefully with DeConcini, then with Panama's Torrijos, then back with DeConcini again, in order to get the Treaty through. DeConcini's vote turned out to be crucial. It also caused him some problems in Arizona. Treaty opponents seemed to see him, not as a brave young senator wringing a concession out of the national administration, but as a sneaky politician who was seeking excuses for supporting the Treaty. Recall petitions were circulated for a while, and DeConcini's popularity was not helped.

Meanwhile Barry Goldwater continues as the state's senior Senator. He is entitled to take satisfaction from the current trend of public opinion and the direction of public policy. It seems now that politicians of every description are vying to cut down to size the federal programs and federal spending which Goldwater was once so alone in attacking. Higher defense budgets —always a Goldwater priority—now seem to be in vogue. No one now dismisses Goldwater as irresponsible or fatuous.

It seems likely that Goldwater is serving his last term. He turns 71 in 1980, and has said before that he would not run past age 70. He loves living in Arizona, and winter in Phoenix by any measure is more pleasant than winter in Washington. His health has apparently not been the best, and despite the increasing strength of conservative ideas, Goldwater does not necessarily find himself being emulated by the younger, more enthusiastic Republicans recently elected. He was not, for example, a fervent opponent of the Panama Canal Treaty; in fact, he had even supported Gerald Ford's Canal position against Ronald Reagan's. Goldwater wanted to be ranking Republican on the Armed Services Committee, but John Tower, who has more consecutive seniority on the Committee, took the post instead.

Goldwater's likely retirement represents a sort of counterpoint to Hubert Humphrey's removal from the political scene. Both were, for much of the 1950s, 1960s, and 1970s, articulators of sets of political ideas. If Humphrey was more successful in producing legislation, that was partly because his philosophy was naturally expressed that way; Goldwater's goal is for government not to do things. Humphrey expressed the ideas that prevailed in the 1950–75 period; Goldwater expressed ideas that are increasingly accepted as a critique of our system—but which do not yet govern, if they ever will.

A word should be said about Arizona's House delegation. What state with such a small delegation has had two leaders, of different parties, of such brainpower, clout, and integrity? John Rhodes of the 1st district is the House Republican leader; Morris Udall of the 2d is Chairman of the House Interior Committee, and probably the most legislatively productive member of the 95th Congress. Curiously, both men have been seriously challenged in the fierce ideological politics of Arizona in recent years.

Census Data Pop. 1,772,482; 0.88% of U.S. total, 33d largest; Central city, 27%; suburban, 48%. Median family income, $9,186; 24th highest; families above $15,000: 19%; families below $3,000: 11%. Median years education, 12.3.

1977 Share of Federal Tax Burden $3,178,000,000; 0.92% of U.S. total, 31st largest.

1977 Share of Federal Outlays $4,506,249,000; 1.14% of U.S. total, 31st largest. Per capita federal spending, $2,026.

DOD	$1,219,789,000	24th (1.33%)		HEW	$1,406,523,000	34th (0.95%)
ERDA	$5,700,000	33d (0.10%)		HUD	$35,503,000	33d (0.84%)
NASA	$12,486,000	20th (0.32%)		VA	$272,818,000	26th (1.42%)
DOT	$154,984,000	29th (1.09%)		EPA	$22,317,000	39th (0.27%)
DOC	$98,352,000	22d (1.18%)		RevS	$82,043,000	31st (0.97%)
DOI	$391,496,000	2d (8.42%)		Debt	$101,080,000	33d (0.34%)
USDA	$196,780,000	37th (0.99%)		Other	$506,378,000	

Economic Base Finance, insurance and real estate; electrical equipment and supplies, especially electronic components and accessories; agriculture, notably cattle, cotton lint, lettuce and dairy products; metal mining, especially copper ores; machinery, especially office and computing machines; food and kindred products; tourism.

Political Line-up Governor, Bruce Babbitt (D). Senators, Barry Goldwater (R) and Dennis DeConcini (D). Representatives, 4 (2 D and 2 R). State Senate (16 R and 14 D); State House (42 R and 18 D).

The Voters

Registration 969,430 Total. 496,206 D (51%); 404,421 R (42%); 68,803 Other (7%).
Median voting age 42
Employment profile White collar, 51%. Blue collar, 32%. Service, 14%. Farm, 3%.
Ethnic groups Black, 3%. Indian, 5%. Spanish, 19%. Total foreign stock, 17%. Canada, Germany, 1% each.

Presidential vote

1976	Carter (D)	295,602	(41%)
	Ford (R)	418,642	(59%)
1972	Nixon (R)	402,812	(67%)
	McGovern (D)	198,540	(33%)

Sen. Barry Goldwater (R) Elected 1968, seat up 1980; b. Jan. 1, 1909, Phoenix; home, Phoenix; U. of Ariz., 1928; Episcopalian.

Career Maj. Gen., USAFR, 1937–67; Phoenix City Cncl., 1949–51; U.S. Sen., 1952–64; Repub. nominee for Pres., 1964.

Offices 427 RSOB, 202-224-2235. Also 5429 Fed. Bldg., Phoenix 85025, 602-261-4086, and Suite 7-G, Fed. Bldg., Tucson 85701, 602-792-6334.

Committees *Armed Services* (3d). Subcommittees: General Procurement; Research and Development; Procurement Policy and Reprogramming.

Commerce, Science, and Transportation (2d). Subcommittees: Aviation; Communications; Science, Technology, and Space.

Group Ratings

	ADA	COPE	PC	RPN	NFU	LCV	CFA	NAB	NSI	ACA	NTU
1978	10	12	23	33	10	8	15	100	90	95	–
1977	0	13	10	83	10	–	12	–	–	100	36
1976	0	8	3	69	10	0	0	100	100	94	73

Key Votes

1) Warnke Nom	AGN	6) Egypt-Saudi Arms	FOR	11) Hosptl Cost Contnmnt	AGN
2) Neutron Bomb	FOR	7) Draft Restr Pardon	DNV	12) Clinch River Reactor	FOR
3) Waterwy User Fee	FOR	8) Wheat Price Support	FOR	13) Pub Fin Cong Cmpgns	AGN
4) Dereg Nat Gas	FOR	9) Panama Canal Treaty	AGN	14) ERA Ratif Recissn	AGN
5) Kemp-Roth	FOR	10) Labor Law Rev Clot	AGN	15) Med Necssy Abrtns	AGN

Election Results

1974 general	Barry Goldwater (R)	320,396	(58%)	($394,042)
	Jonathan Marshall (D)	229,523	(42%)	($129,260)
1974 primary	Barry Goldwater (R), unopposed			
1968 general	Barry Goldwater (R)	274,607	(57%)	
	Roy Elson (D)	205,338	(43%)	

Sen. Dennis DeConcini (D) Elected 1976, seat up 1982; b. May 8, 1937, Tucson; home, Tucson; U. of Ariz., B.A. 1959, LL.B. 1963; Catholic.

Career Army Adjutant General Corps, 1959–60; Practicing Atty., 1963–65, 1968–73; Special Counsel, Admin. Asst. to Gov. Samuel P. Goddard, 1965–67; Pima Co. Atty., 1973–76.

Offices 4104 DSOB, 202-224-4521. Also Ariz. Bank Bldg., 101 N. 1st St., Suite 1634, Phoenix 85003, 602-261-6756, and 301 W. Congress, Tucson 85701, 602-792-6831.

Committees *Appropriations* (15th). Subcommittees: Energy and Water Development; Foreign Operations; Interior and Related Agencies; State, Justice, and Commerce, the Judiciary and Related Agencies; Treasury, Postal Service, and General Government.

Judiciary (7th). Subcommittees: Constitution; Criminal Justice; Improvements in Judicial Machinery (Chairman).

Roles and Administration (6th).

Select Committee on Indian Affairs.

Group Ratings

	ADA	COPE	PC	RPN	NFU	LCV	CFA	NAB	NSI	ACA	NTU
1978	35	58	55	60	63	43	30	64	40	39	–
1977	40	65	58	44	50	–	52	–	–	36	28

Key Votes

1) Warnke Nom	FOR	6) Egypt-Saudi Arms	AGN	11) Hosptl Cost Contnmnt	AGN
2) Neutron Bomb	AGN	7) Draft Restr Pardon	FOR	12) Clinch River Reactor	FOR
3) Waterwy User Fee	AGN	8) Wheat Price Support	AGN	13) Pub Fin Cong Cmpgns	FOR
4) Dereg Nat Gas	FOR	9) Panama Canal Treaty	FOR	14) ERA Ratif Recissn	FOR
5) Kemp-Roth	AGN	10) Labor Law Rev Clot	FOR	15) Med Necssy Abrtns	AGN

Election Results

1976 general	Dennis DeConcini (D)	400,334	(55%)	($597,405)
	Sam Steiger (R)	321,236	(45%)	($679,384)
1976 primary	Dennis DeConcini (D)	121,423	(53%)	
	Carolyn Warner (D)	71,612	(32%)	
	Wade Church (D)	34,266	(15%)	
1970 general	Paul Fannin (R)	228,284	(56%)	
	Sam Grossman (D)	179,512	(44%)	

Gov. Bruce E. Babbitt (D) Elected 1978, term expires Jan. 1981; b. June 27,1938, Flagstaff; Notre Dame U., B.S., Marshall Scholar, U. of Newcastle, England, M.S. 1963, Harvard U., J.D. 1965.

Career Special Asst. to the Director of VISTA, 1965–67; Practicing atty., 1967–74; Atty. Gen. of Ariz., 1974–78.

Offices Capitol West Wing, 9th floor, Phoenix 85007, 602-255-4331.

Election Results

1978 general	Bruce Babbitt (D)	282,605	(54%)
	Evan Mecham (R)	241,093	(46%)
1978 primary	Bruce Babbitt (D)	108,548	(77%)
	One other (D)	32,785	(23%)
1974 general	Raul H. Castro (D)	278,375	(50%)
	Russ Williams (R)	273,674	(50%)

FIRST DISTRICT

Phoenix is one of those instant cities in what Kevin Phillips named the Sun Belt. It is almost totally the creation of the air-conditioned years after World War II. In 1940 Phoenix had 65,000 residents; by 1970 within the city limits there were 581,000, and the metropolitan population is now well over one million. Once a sleepy stop on the Southern Pacific Railroad, Phoenix is now one of the nation's major metropolitan areas, the headquarters of national corporations like Greyhound and the home of national figures like Barry Goldwater. Major cities have traditionally been Democratic, but that is not the case with Phoenix. Like other Sun Belt cities—Dallas, Houston, Albuquerque, San Diego—it is Republican. Indeed, no other major metropolitan area in the country has consistently voted as heavily Republican as the Arizona capital.

Why? One reason usually given is the retirees. Older people with enough money to afford Del Webb's Sun City (nobody under 50, nobody with schoolchildren, very few blacks) usually cast heavily Republican majorities. But more important, most of the jobs that buttress the boom in

Phoenix are in defense, electronic, and other technical industries. People attracted to such jobs like certainty, order, and discipline, and usually prefer conservative politicians. They are not people who, having moved west, miss the New York *Times*; they are quite content with the late Eugene Pulliam's militantly conservative (and fearlessly muckraking) Arizona *Republic*. Finally there is the state's political culture. The Goldwater movement of the fifties and sixties, consisting mostly of clean-cut, talented, hard-working young men in Phoenix (they were often migrants from the Midwest), hit it off well with the influx of newcomers. The Democrats, most of them cigar-chewing oldtimers from dusty county seats, did not.

One of the crew-cut young men from the early days of the Goldwater movement—he has since let his hair grow out—is 1st district Congressman and House Minority Leader John Rhodes. In 1952, when Goldwater was first elected to the Senate, Rhodes became the first Republican ever elected to the House from Arizona. At the time, Rhodes's seat was all of Maricopa County, including Phoenix and all of its suburbs. But in the last dozen years the district has been pruned by redistricting, leaving Rhodes by 1972 with the bulk of the city's black and chicano populations, as well as with the 30,000 students at Arizona State University at Tempe.

That meant political trouble for Rhodes back home, even as he was gaining power and prestige on Capitol Hill. In 1972, when he was Chairman of the House Republican Policy Committee and number two Republican on Appropriations, Rhodes was held to 57% of the vote—far below his normal level. Two years later a member of the Tempe school board held him to 51%, with 7% diverted by an anti-abortion candidate. In 1976 the same Democrat ran again, but this time Rhodes's percentage ran up to 58%. At that, the Democrats apparently quit; Rhodes received 71% in 1978 against nominal opposition.

Rhodes's succession to the Minority Leadership came suddenly, in 1973, when Gerald Ford had become Vice President. He seemed to be much in Ford's mold. He is not a great orator, although his speaking style is smoother than Ford's and his syntax better. Like Ford, he is not an innovative thinker, and his record betrays few strayings from conventional Republicanism. But the House has changed since Ford left it, and Rhodes has emerged as a different kind of leader. For one thing, the Democrats under Tip O'Neill are not as accommodating to their partisan adversaries as they were under earlier Speakers. Rhodes, who, in any case, was probably less inclined than Ford to cooperate with Democrats, had had little opportunity to do so. The other big change is that increasingly it is Republicans, rather than Democrats, who have been crackling with new ideas and advancing new legislative solutions to the nation's problems. Rhodes has not been an initiator of measures like the Kemp-Roth bill, but he was astute enough to recognize it as a good partisan measure when it came along, and he probably deserves some of the credit for the fact that it was endorsed by every segment of what had previously been a fractious Republican Party. At the end of the 95th Congress the House Republicans, normally a cohesive body, were united as never before.

Another difference between Ford and Rhodes is that Ford operated on a somewhat more personal level, while Rhodes tends to be more cerebral. One cannot imagine Ford writing a book as incisive and frank as Rhodes's *The Futile System*, which is as solid a criticism of the House as has been seen since Richard Bolling's books in the early sixties. Predictably Rhodes assails the Democrats for running the House inefficiently and unfairly—charges for which it is not impossible to find substantiation. And while he may not quite transgress the bounds of congressional courtesy, he does name names. Wayne Hays (then still a power) is a bully, Tip O'Neill is too partisan, and so on.

Rhodes's basic fairness is not in doubt. It so much was widely recognized when Rhodes was chosen chairman of the 1976 Republican National Convention; he was acceptable to both the Ford and Reagan forces. But in Washington he has not been as effective a leader as he would probably like. Initially, his problem seemed to be that there were not enough Republicans to lead. Since the 1974 elections, the party has been outnumbered by about 2-1 in the House, and the policies of the Nixon years helped to make the Democrats cohesive. There was little for the Republicans to do but protest.

But since the Carter Administration came to office, Rhodes's problems have been different. He has not always shared the elan and aggressiveness of Republican House members. In 1977 he initially supported universal voter registration, a measure House Republicans later defeated. Although he supported Kemp-Roth in 1978, he expressed doubts about the wisdom of a constitutional amendment requiring a balanced budget. And in 1979 he unsuccessfully urged House Republicans not to join liberal Democrats in defeating a budget resolution. House

Republicans now seem as likely to follow conservative militants like Robert Bauman as they do to follow Rhodes on some issues; and many of the younger members undoubtedly grumble that he has been in Washington too long and is too comfortable with the way things have always been done. Nonetheless, it seems likely that Rhodes will not be seriously challenged for the minority leadership in the next several years.

Census Data Pop. 442,589. Central city, 52%; suburban, 48%. Median family income, $9,126; families above $15,000: 18%; families below $3,000: 10.1%. Median years education, 12.2.

The Voters

Median voting age 42.
Employment profile White collar, 52%. Blue collar, 32%. Service, 14%. Farm, 2%.
Ethnic groups Black, 6%. Indian, 1%. Spanish, 17%. Total foreign stock, 16%. Canada, Germany, 2% each.

Presidential vote

1976	Carter (D)	62,632	(39%)
	Ford (R)	99,375	(61%)
1972	Nixon (R)	98,436	(68%)
	McGovern (D)	46,573	(32%)

Rep. John J. Rhodes (R) Elected 1952; b. Sept. 18, 1916, Council Grove, Kans.; home, Mesa; Kans. St. U., B.S. 1938, Harvard U., LL.B. 1941; Methodist.

Career Air Force, WWII; Practicing atty., 1949–53; V.P., Farm & Home Like Ins. Co.

Offices 2310 RHOB, 202-225-2635. Also 1930 Valley Ctr., Phoenix 85073, 602-261-3181.

Committees *Minority Leader.*

Group Ratings

	ADA	COPE	PC	RPN	NFU	LCV	CFA	NAB	NSI	ACA	NTU
1978	15	13	13	89	22	–	18	100	100	70	–
1977	5	17	15	75	25	17	10	–	–	88	35
1976	0	9	8	67	8	19	9	100	90	67	35

Key Votes

1) Increase Def Spnd	FOR	6) Alaska Lands Protect	AGN	11) Delay Auto Pol Cntrl	FOR
2) B-1 Bomber	FOR	7) Water Projects Veto	AGN	12) Sugar Price Escalator	DNV
3) Cargo Preference	AGN	8) Consum Protect Agcy	AGN	13) Pub Fin Cong Cmpgns	AGN
4) Dereg Nat Gas	FOR	9) Common Situs Picket	AGN	14) ERA Ratif Recissn	FOR
5) Kemp-Roth	FOR	10) Labor Law Revision	AGN	15) Prohibt Govt Abrtns	FOR

Election Results

1978 general	John J. Rhodes (R)	81,108	(71%)	($201,177)
	Ken Graves (D)	33,178	(29%)	($6,306)
1978 primary	John J. Rhodes (R), unopposed			
1976 general	John J. Rhodes (R)	96,397	(58%)	($202,086)
	Patricia M. Fullinwider(D)	68,404	(42%)	($75,528)

SECOND DISTRICT

There is an unnoted tradition of defeated presidential candidates becoming highly active legislators in the years after the election. Robert Taft, for example, defeated by Eisenhower in 1952, went on to become Senate Majority Leader. Hubert Humphrey, defeated by Kennedy in 1960, became Majority Whip and successfully managed such legislation as the nuclear test ban treaty and the civil rights bill. Morris Udall, defeated by Jimmy Carter in 1976, is in the same tradition. His campaign for the presidency was a disappointment: he finished second in several primaries, but never first, and was never a credible threat to Carter's nomination. But in 1977 and 1978 Udall has emerged as probably the most productive and hardworking legislator on Capitol Hill.

Like Taft and Humphrey, Udall had a strong legislative background long before he ran for president. He was first elected to Congress in 1961, when his brother Stewart resigned his seat to become the Kennedy Administration's Secretary of the Interior. He won seats on the Interior Committee—always important for a Westerner—and on Post Office and Civil Service. He has most of the qualities needed for good legislative work: a legal scholar's concern for dotting i's and crossing t's, a willingness to listen patiently to the points of view of others and strike acceptable compromises, a passionate concern for some goals, and the capacity for hard work. He became involved in a variety of causes, doing the hard work of pushing through reforms of the congressional franking system, the Post Office, and the federal salary system. And of course there was legislation from Interior, most notably the land use regulation bill he championed until it was torpedoed by fellow Arizonan Sam Steiger in 1974.

This was an impressive record, but not the sort that usually produces presidential candidates; but then Udall's candidacy was anything but usual. It was first proposed by two Wisconsin Democrats, David Obey and Henry Reuss, who wondered why House members are never deemed presidential timber; asked to name one who was, they settled on Udall. Udall agreed to run when he got the support of one-tenth of the House Democrats. The Udall strategy was to win two of the first primaries, New Hampshire and Massachusetts, where Udall's liberal policies and flinty character were expected to be appealing. But in both states the support of the kind of Democrats who had come into politics to oppose the Vietnam war was split between Udall (who had opposed the war in 1967) and other candidates like Birch Bayh and Fred Harris. The result: Jimmy Carter, with months of hard personal campaigning, won New Hampshire, and Henry Jackson, running in effect against the whole field of opponents, got a plurality in Massachusetts. Udall was a close second in both cases.

A close second—that was how Udall continued to finish, in Wisconsin (where initial returns put Udall ahead of Carter) and New York, in Michigan, Connecticut, and South Dakota. In retrospect the Udall campaign was in deep trouble after New Hampshire and Massachusetts; the liberal position that Udall occupied there had failed to produce needed victories, and it made Udall (whose voting record is a good deal more moderate than, say, George McGovern's) unable to win in many other states. Udall lacks that steely ambition and unqualified belief in himself that so many politicians have; he has a dry and often self-deprecatory sense of humor and cultivates an appreciation of the admirable qualities of his adversaries.

If Udall had not run for president in 1976, he probably would have run for senator—and if he had, he would have missed the delicious opportunity he had in 1977 to choose between two committee chairmanships. Initially it looked as if he would have the Post Office chair. But Bizz Johnson of California, given the choice of Interior and the pork-barrel-rich Public Works Committee, chose Public Works, thus giving Udall, next in line in seniority, the option of Interior. Udall readily took it. Although he has had considerable legislative achievements on Post Office and Civil Service, he is much more interested in the environmental matters that cover Interior. And, for the first time, Interior has a chairman who is deeply committed to the environmental point of view. As it happened, Udall in effect chaired two committees; the new Post Office Chairman, Robert Nix of Pennsylvania, was so weak that Udall had to take charge of its major legislation.

The 95th Congress is generally regarded as one in which the large Democratic majorities were unable to produce Democratic legislation. But Udall's record is otherwise. Consider his victories:

* Civil service reform. This was one of the few major Carter Administration initiatives which passed in something like its original form. That was due in very large part to Udall, who conducted extensive negotiations on Post Office and Civil Service. Working with ranking Republican Edward Derwinski and William Ford, who informally represented organized labor, Udall was able to fashion a bill which accomplished most of the Administration's goals, met

labor's objections, and could command Republican support. The law passed in much the form Udall crafted it, and represents the first major attempt to make government employees more responsive and the bureaucracy more efficient since civil service was created.

* Strip mining. For years Udall has been sponsoring bills to regulate the strip mining of coal. His efforts have sometimes been sufficient to pass the House, but White House hostility helped to kill them. But Jimmy Carter took a different attitude, and in the 95th Congress Udall was able to shepherd through a comprehensive strip mining law.

* Alaska wilderness. The question here is whether some 100 million acres of Alaska wilderness is to be protected by federal designations. Udall, together with John Seiberling of Ohio, got a large majority in the House for a bill opposed by most Alaska commercial and labor leaders and politicians. That gave the wilderness cause considerable leverage in negotiations with the Senate, where Alaska's two senators were able to influence opinion. As it happened, the bill was blocked from passage by Alaska's Mike Gravel, but the White House set aside almost as much land as Udall's bill protected by administrative action. It is doubtful that the Carter Administration would have chosen to do so if Udall had not demonstrated heavy support in the House for such a move.

Udall has also had his disappointments legislatively. He was unable to persuade the House, despite its heavy Democratic majorities, to favor universal voter registration by post card and other devices. His proposals for public financing of congressional elections have not passed. And he ran into heavy home district opposition on his proposals to reform federal mining laws generally; there were charges that his bill would shut down Arizona's copper industry, which in any case was in bad economic shape at the time. On that issue Udall changed his position.

What is ironic is that even as Udall grows in stature as a legislator he has lost political strength at home, in Arizona's 2d congressional district. In 1976 his percentage in the general election fell—even though his Republican opponent had dropped out of the race. In 1978 he was targeted by national Republican sources, and an expensive campaign waged against him. His opponent was not especially strong: a 58-year-old former state legislator who was not the party's first choice. His campaign featured a spot with a tape showing Udall saying "I am a socialist, because . . ." Actually, Udall had said, "They say I am a socialist, because . . ." and had gone on to refute the charge. The quality of Udall's opposition can be gauged by the fact that when this was pointed out to the Republican, he blandly declined to drop the ad.

Udall won, but with only 54% of the vote—his lowest percentage since his first campaign in 1961. Why this weakness? First, there is probably lingering negative feeling from Udall's presidential campaign—a feeling that he is too liberal and too aligned with politicians from the snow belt. Tucson, the city whose metropolitan area makes up the vast bulk of Udall's 2d district, is traditionally Arizona's Democratic city; but it does not behave politically like a city in Massachusetts. Second, Udall's busy schedule, first as a presidential candidate and then as an extremely active legislator, has probably made it difficult for him to spend time in a district hard to get to. Third, demography is working against him: Tucson's population is rising rapidly, and most of the new voters are the kind of affluent Midwesterners and Southerners who have made Phoenix so heavily Republican. Fourth, there was the strong anti-Democratic trend that was visible everywhere in Arizona in 1978.

At least some of these factors will be operating in 1980, and Udall can probably expect significant opposition again. Nonetheless, he shows little sign of flagging in his legislative interests. And there may even be the possibility of a leadership role one day: he does not possess the capacity to produce divisiveness of some of the other possible contenders. He ran for Speaker quixotically in 1969 to demonstrate his unhappiness with the way things were run in the House and waged a more serious campaign for Majority Leader in 1971, losing again. But for now, without such a post, he is one of the most influential and productive members of the House.

Census Data Pop. 443,117. Central city, 59%; suburban, 20%. Median family income, $8,832; families above $15,000: 17%; families below $3,000: 11%. Median years education, 12.3.

The Voters

Median voting age 42.
Employment profile White collar, 51%. Blue collar, 32%. Service, 15%. Farm, 2%.
Ethnic groups Black, 3%. Indian, 2%. Spanish, 27%. Total foreign stock, 23%. Canada, Germany, 2% each.

Presidential vote

1976	Carter (D)	85,224	(48%)
	Ford (R)	91,113	(52%)
1972	Nixon (R)	89,052	(57%)
	McGovern (D)	65,926	(43%)

Rep. Morris K. Udall (D) Elected May 2, 1961; b. June 15, 1922, St. Johns; home, Tucson; U. of Ariz., J.D. 1949; Church of Latter Day Saints.

Career Air Force, WWII; Pro basketball player, Denver Nuggets, 1948–49; Practicing atty., 1949–61; Pima Co. Atty., 1952–54.

Offices 235 CHOB, 202-225-4065. Also 301 W. Congress, Tucson 85701, 602-792-6404.

Committees *Interior and Insular Affairs* (Chairman). Subcommittees: Energy and the Environment (Chairman); Oversight/Special Investigations; Mines and Mining; National Parks and Insular Affairs; Water and Power Resources; Pacific Affairs; Public Lands.

Post Office and Civil Service (2d). Subcommittees: Civil Service; Postal Operations and Services.

Group Ratings

	ADA	COPE	PC	RPN	NFU	LCV	CFA	NAB	NSI	ACA	NTU
1978	70	79	73	58	70	–	73	0	10	13	–
1977	85	90	73	58	80	84	70	–	–	0	21
1976	45	88	69	43	100	72	73	13	0	0	40

Key Votes

1) Increase Def Spnd	AGN	6) Alaska Lands Protect	FOR	11) Delay Auto Pol Cntrl	AGN
2) B-1 Bomber	AGN	7) Water Projects Veto	AGN	12) Sugar Price Escalator	AGN
3) Cargo Preference	AGN	8) Consum Protect Agcy	FOR	13) Pub Fin Cong Cmpgns	FOR
4) Dereg Nat Gas	AGN	9) Common Situs Picket	FOR	14) ERA Ratif Recissn	AGN
5) Kemp-Roth	AGN	10) Labor Law Revision	FOR	15) Prohibt Govt Abrtns	AGN

Election Results

1978 general	Morris K. Udall (D)	67,878	(54%)	($294,849)
	Tom Richey (R)	58,697	(46%)	($134,130)
1978 primary	Morris K. Udall (D), unopposed			
1976 general	Morris K. Udall (D)	106,054	(60%)	($45,791)
	Laid Guttersen (R)	71,765	(40%)	($31,008)

THIRD DISTRICT

Arizona's 3d and 4th congressional districts are both hybrids: combinations of large parts of heavily Republican Phoenix and of the sparsely populated, traditionally Democratic counties of the northern part of the state. Geographically, the 3d spans the desert expanse from Yuma (pop. 29,000) on the hot Colorado River just north of the Mexican border, past the town of Flagstaff (pop. 30,000)—known for Northern Arizona University and as one of the last places in the United States where one can be confident of finding unpolluted air—up to Glen Canyon Dam and the Navajo and Hopi Reservations near the Utah state line.

Traditionally this is "pinto" Democrat country—closer in spirit, we can say, to Oklahoma than to California. Exceptions are the town of Prescott (pop. 23,000), long a Republican stronghold where Barry Goldwater has begun all his Senate campaigns, and Mohave County, where new developments in Lake Havasu City and Kingman have attracted far more Republicans than Democrats.

But most of the votes in the 3d—61% in 1978—are cast in the heavily Republican Phoenix area. The district includes the west side of Phoenix, and just wings the city's small black and Mexican-American ghettoes. Phoenix is a new city; here on the west side the vacant lots between the small stucco houses and the gaudy roadside establishments grow easily back into small patches of Arizona desert. The 3d does not take in the richest parts of Phoenix; there's less grass here (water is expensive) and fewer palm trees. Yet there is little political difference between the people who live here and their richer neighbors in the northern and eastern parts of the city. Every white Anglo section of Phoenix votes heavily Republican in most elections.

The Congressman from this hybrid district for 10 years was something of a hybrid himself: Sam Steiger, brought up in New York City, a Prescott rancher. Steiger became known best in Congress as an opponent of environmentalists, whom he called "green bigots." As a member of the Interior Committee he torpedoed Morris Udall's land use bill in 1974. Two years later, the flamboyant Steiger ran for the Senate, won the Republican nomination, but lost the general election. He could conceivably run for Barry Goldwater's seat in 1980.

Meanwhile this is one of several districts vacated by ambitious or retiring Republican which went Democratic in 1976—one of the reasons why Democrats increased rather than decreased their number of House seats two years after their landslide victory in 1974. The Republican candidate here was a state Senator of the Goldwaterish stripe, but he was hampered by the Independent candidacy of another Republican state Senator and by the fact that the Democratic candidate, state Senator Bob Stump, spent most of the campaign labelling himself a conservative. He had a record to match, and managed to win by a 48%–42% margin.

Anyone who voted for Stump because of his conservatism has no reason to be disappointed; he has had 100% ratings from conservative groups and near zeroes from liberals and labor. He had only weak primary opposition in 1978, and his Republican opponent withdrew after the primary—more evidence of the weakness of Arizona's Republican organization. Stump can hardly count on a free ride again, but his voting record leaves him with few problems in general elections; if he is vulnerable, it will be in the primary. He has been mentioned as a candidate for the Senate in 1980, and some have suggested that he would run as a Republican.

Census Data Pop. 443,201. Central city, 36%; suburban, 26%. Median family income, $8,964; families above $15,000: 16%; families below $3,000: 10%. Median years education, 12.2.

The Voters

Median voting age 41.
Employment profile White collar, 46%. Blue collar, 36%. Service, 13%. Farm, 5%.
Ethnic groups Black, 2%. Indian, 4%. Spanish, 19%. Total foreign stock, 15%. Canada, Germany, 1% each.

Presidential vote

1976	Carter (D)	74,467	(40%)
	Ford (R)	111,116	(60%)
1972	Nixon (R)	104,197	(72%)
	McGovern (D)	41,012	(28%)

Rep. Bob Stump (D) Elected 1976; b. Apr. 4, 1927, Phoenix; home, Tolleson; Ariz. St. U., B.S. 1951; Seventh Day Adventist.

Career Navy, WWII; Cotton and grain farmer; Ariz. House of Reps., 1958–66; Ariz. Senate, 1967–76, Senate Pres., 1975–76.

Offices 211 CHOB, 202-225-4576. Also Federal Building, Phoenix 85025, 606-261-6923.

Committees *Armed Services* (23d). Subcommittees: Procurement and Military Nuclear Systems; NATO Standardization, Interoperability, and Readiness.

Group Ratings

	ADA	COPE	PC	RPN	NFU	LCV	CFA	NAB	NSI	ACA	NTU
1978	5	10	18	56	10	–	9	100	100	100	–
1977	5	9	13	60	33	5	10	–	–	100	45

Key Votes

1) Increase Def Spnd	FOR	6) Alaska Lands Protect	AGN	11) Delay Auto Pol Cntrl	FOR
2) B-1 Bomber	FOR	7) Water Projects Veto	AGN	12) Sugar Price Escalator	FOR
3) Cargo Preference	AGN	8) Consum Protect Agcy	AGN	13) Pub Fin Cong Cmpgns	AGN
4) Dereg Nat Gas	FOR	9) Common Situs Picket	AGN	14) ERA Ratif Recissn	FOR
5) Kemp-Roth	FOR	10) Labor Law Revision	AGN	15) Prohibt Govt Abrtns	FOR

Election Results

1978 general	Bob Stump (D)	111,850	(85%)	($198,085)
	Kathleen Cooke (L)	19,813	(15%)	
1978 primary	Bob Stump (D)	26,414	(71%)	
	One other (D)	10,860	(29%)	
1976 general	Bob Stump (D)	88,854	(47%)	($113,438)
	Fred Koury, Jr. (R)	79,162	(42%)	($103,383)
	Bill McCune (NPI)	19,149	(10%)	($14,969)

FOURTH DISTRICT

Every tenth year since 1950, with each new Census, Arizona has been awarded a new congressional seat. The 4th district is the latest. Its boundaries were drawn by a Republican legislature and approved by a Republican governor. Although the territory included some Democratic territory—notably old mining towns like Globe and Morenci and the Navajo Reservation in northeast Arizona—the new district appeared certain to be dominated by its share of Maricopa County (Phoenix), which would cast two-thirds of its votes. This part of Maricopa includes almost all of the most Republican areas of heavily Republican metropolitan Phoenix: the posh suburbs of Scottsdale and Paradise Valley and the hilltop homes near the mountains that bisect the northern part of Phoenix itself. This is the part of Arizona where Barry Goldwater lives, and an area that gave Richard Nixon a whopping 76% in 1972.

As it has happened, the 4th has indeed become a Republican district—but not necessarily a safe one. Instead this has been one of the most fiercely—and expensively—contested congressional seats in the nation. It was first won in 1972 by Republican John Conlan, son of major league umpire Jocko Conlan and a proud fundamentalist Christian. The two general election competitors that year spent more than $500,000—more than in any other district in the nation. In 1974 Conlan was reelected somewhat more easily and at a far lower cost. But there was plenty of heat from another source: Conlan's feud with 3d district Congressman Sam Steiger. It became one of the most bitter personal conflicts in recent American politics, as the two faced off in the 1976 Senate campaign. Steiger won the Republican nomination, but lost the general election. Now both Steiger and Conlan may be interested in Goldwater's seat if, as expected, Goldwater chooses to retire in 1980. Indeed, Conlan might even choose to challenge the Senator if he doesn't step down. When Goldwater endorsed Steiger, Conlan wondered out loud, "Maybe it's the pain, maybe it's the drinking he's been doing."

When Conlan relinquished the House seat, the stage was set for another close contest. The favored candidate was Tony Mason, a Democrat and former head of the Phoenix Planning and Zoning Commission. But Mason's opponent, Eldon Rudd, though a wooden speaker, had a solid background: an FBI agent, previous election to the Maricopa County Board of Supervisors, and a reputation as an unblemished Conlan conservative. The campaign again featured some of the heaviest spending in the nation, and Rudd won by less than 1,000 votes. As expected, Rudd has had a solidly conservative record in the House. Like other Arizona Republicans, he benefited from the state Democrats' apparent collapse of strength in 1978, winning with well over 60% of the vote. Rudd is mentioned sometimes as a possible candidate himself for the 1980 Senate seat; if he does vacate the 4th, the question will be whether the Democrats will be able to contest this seat as strongly as they have in the past.

Census Data Pop. 443,575. Central city, 48%; suburban, 9%. Median family income, $9,886; families above $15,000: 23%; families below $3,000: 11%. Median years education, 12.3.

The Voters

Median voting age 42.
Employment profile White collar, 56%. Blue collar, 29%. Service, 12%. Farm, 3%.
Ethnic groups Black, 1%. Indian, 14%. Spanish, 13%. Total foreign stock, 13%. Canada, Germany, 1% each.

Presidential vote

1976	Carter (D)	72,578	(38%)
	Ford (R)	116,475	(62%)
1972	Nixon (R)	111,127	(71%)
	McGovern (D)	45,029	(29%)

Rep. Eldon Rudd (R) Elected 1976; b. July 15, 1920, Camp Verde; home, Scottsdale; Ariz. St. U., B.A. 1947, U. of Ariz., J.D. 1949; Catholic.

Career USMC, WWII; Practicing atty., 1949; Spec. Investigator, FBI, 1950–70; Maricopa Co. Bd. of Supervisors, 1972–76.

Offices 1110 LHOB, 202-225-3361. Also 6009 Fed. Bldg., 230 N. 1st Ave., Phoenix 85025, 602-261-4803.

Committees *Appropriations* (17th). Subcommittees: District of Columbia; Legislative.

Group Ratings

	ADA	COPE	PC	RPN	NFU	LCV	CFA	NAB	NSI	ACA	NTU
1978	0	0	13	67	20	–	5	100	100	96	–
1977	5	17	15	54	25	10	10	–	–	100	50

Key Votes

1) Increase Def Spnd	FOR	6) Alaska Lands Protect	AGN	11) Delay Auto Pol Cntrl	FOR
2) B-1 Bomber	FOR	7) Water Projects Veto	AGN	12) Sugar Price Escalator	DNV
3) Cargo Preference	AGN	8) Consum Protect Agcy	AGN	13) Pub Fin Cong Cmpgns	AGN
4) Dereg Nat Gas	FOR	9) Common Situs Picket	AGN	14) ERA Ratif Recissn	FOR
5) Kemp-Roth	FOR	10) Labor Law Revision	AGN	15) Prohibt Govt Abrtns	FOR

Election Results

1978 general	Eldon Rudd (R)	90,768	(65%)	($178,134)
	Michael McCormick (D)	48,661	(35%)	($23,548)
1978 primary	Eldon Rudd (R)	28,648	(84%)	
	One other (R)	5,379	(16%)	
1976 general	Eldon Rudd(R)	93,154	(50%)	($116,302)
	Tony Mason (D)	92,435	(50%)	($171,629)

ARKANSAS

Fifteen years ago the outlook for Arkansas was pretty bleak. The state had pretty well earned the Dogpatch reputation it held across the nation. Since the days of the Great Depression Arkansas had been losing population, and its young people continued to leave by the thousands, looking for jobs elsewhere. Arkansas's reputation as a relatively tolerant border state was shattered by the machinations of Gov. Orval Faubus, who blocked implementation of a federal court integration order and forced President Eisenhower to send federal troops into Little Rock's Central High. (The Little Rock episode, however, guaranteed political success for Faubus, who was able to break the state's two term tradition and remained Governor through 1966.)

Today the picture has changed dramatically and largely through the efforts of one man, former Gov. (1966–70) Winthrop Rockefeller, who died in early 1973. Rockefeller had come to Arkansas after a notorious (and expensive) divorce, and Faubus recruited him to help attract industry to the state. Once elected Governor, in 1966, Rockefeller worked even harder at it. Aided by a powerful congressional delegation, Rockefeller concentrated on getting small, non-defense industries whose plants could be located out in the country, near the people who needed jobs. Moreover, retirees and others seeking a life of greater tranquillity began to move in large numbers to the hills north and west of Little Rock. The 1970 Census figures showed that northern Arkansas was one of the few non-metropolitan areas to score substantial population increases in the sixties, and in the seventies Arkansas has continued to grow faster than the nation as a whole, though not at a disastrously rapid rate.

Rockefeller also managed to effect a total change in the political atmosphere of the state. Unusual among Southern Republicans for his commitment to civil rights and his appointment of blacks to government positions, Rockefeller managed to beat an outright segregationist in the 1966 gubernatorial race and a Faubus protege in 1968. When he was finally beaten himself in 1970, it was by a young, previously unknown Democrat named Dale Bumpers, who forthrightly declared that segregation was "immoral." Bumpers, for his part, was free to admit that a candidate like himself could not have won except for the example set by Rockefeller.

Having beaten one of the state's moderate and seemingly unbeatable officeholders in 1970, Bumpers went on in 1974 to beat another, Sen. J. William Fulbright. Against any other candidate Fulbright would have won, though he was 69 and a Senate veteran of 30 years. As Chairman of the Senate Foreign Relations Committee, he brought an aura of prestige and urbanity to Arkansas which more than compensated for the unpopularity in official Washington of some of his positions (opposition to the war in Vietnam, coolness toward Israel). Bumpers had few issue differences with Fulbright and refrained from attacking him altogether. He won, by nearly a 2–1 margin, on the basis of his popularity as Governor.

Bumpers came to Washington with a national reputation and, some thought, national ambitions; but the presidential candidate from the South was not to be a U.S. senator, but a former Georgia governor who had stayed home. Bumpers is regarded as a bright and energetic Senator. A member of the Energy and Armed Services Committees, he has developed considerable expertise in their subject areas; but he is not yet regarded as a major leader in the Senate. His voting record is generally liberal, but he did oppose the AFL-CIO's labor law reform. He is up for reelection in 1980, and his seat may be regarded as safe.

Arkansas's senior senator, until his death in November 1977, was John McClellan, first elected in 1942 and long a power in the Senate. McClellan achieved national fame in the 1950s as Chairman of the committee investigating corruption in the Teamsters Union (the committee's counsel was Robert Kennedy). A dour, doleful man, McClellan was one of the bulwarks of the old Southern conservative bloc; generally opposing the measures of the Kennedy and Johnson Administrations and supporting Nixon and Ford. He was nonetheless not shy about sending large sums of federal money to Arkansas, and he is memorialized in the Kerr-McClellan Navigation System, which opened the Arkansas River to seagoing ships as far as Tulsa, Oklahoma. McClellan was not seriously challenged until 1972, when he was 76; he barely beat Congressman David Pryor, in large part by asserting that Pryor was too close to labor unions and liberal groups.

McClellan had announced his retirement before he died, and the governor entitled to fill the vacancy was none other than David Pryor, who had won the office in 1974 and had been easily reelected in 1976. Under Arkansas law, interim appointees to the Senate cannot run for full terms; Pryor's choice was Kaneaster Hodges, a small town lawyer who had backed McClellan in 1972, and who compiled a moderate voting record during his year in the Senate.

Pryor naturally was interested in the McClellan seat, but so were several others. Arkansas has been in the habit of choosing its senators young and reelecting them for years: Fulbright had served 30 years, McClellan 35. Bumpers obviously had a lock on one seat, and so the seat up in 1978 would, in all likelihood, be the only Senate seat available in the political lifetimes of politicians currently active. Accordingly, two of the state's four congressmen got into the Democratic primary: Jim Guy Tucker of Little Rock and Ray Thornton from the southern part of the state. All three major candidates had reputations as progressives. Pryor as a young congressman had voted against seating the regular Mississippi delegation at the 1968 national convention, favored civil rights legislation, and when denied funds to investigate nursing homes, had set up his own volunteer committee and worked in a nursing home incognito to learn of conditions first hand. As Governor, he had a generally progressive record, though he lost the support of organized labor by sending in the National Guard when firemen struck in Pine Bluff. Tucker, though only 35, had been a crusading state Attorney General and in his one term in Congress had the most liberal and pro-labor voting record in the Arkansas delegation. Not far behind was Thornton, whose greatest exposure came during the House Judiciary Committee impeachment hearings; he was one of several Southern Democrats who made a strong case for impeaching Richard Nixon.

With such similar candidates, the voters apparently had a hard time making up their minds; the result of the first primary was practically a dead heat. Pryor was first with 34%. Separated by just 3,473 votes were Tucker and Thornton, with Tucker qualifying for the runoff. In that contest Pryor took the part McClellan had taken against him six years before, accusing Tucker of being the labor candidate. Tucker in turn accused the Governor of delaying until after the runoff a decision on a rate increase for Arkansas Louisiana Gas Company, which is owned by Thornton's uncle. Pryor won with 55% of the vote. The general election, as expected, was not seriously contested.

Pryor is expected to have a voting record similar to Bumpers's. But like Bumpers he enters what appears likely to be a long Senate career relatively unconstrained by home state opinions or expectations. He has won support from both progressives and conservatives; and despite the close margins of the 1978 primary and runoff he seems unlikely to be seriously challenged soon unless he makes a major mistake.

Arkansas currently has the youngest governor in the nation: Bill Clinton, elected in 1978 at the age of 32. Clinton has a background which would hardly seem likely for a successful Southern politician a decade ago. He was a Rhodes scholar and a graduate of Yale Law School. He was a McGovern campaign worker in 1972 and a staff attorney for the House Judiciary Committee before the impeachment hearings. He became a law professor at the University of Arkansas in Fayetteville, nearly beat Republican Congressman John Paul Hammerschmidt in 1974, and was elected Attorney General in 1976. In that office he sued to hold down utility rates, fought the 25¢ pay phone call, and ended bans on liquor and eyeglass advertising. But there are limits on Clinton's liberalism. Although he had the support of ACORN, a liberal grass roots citizens action group, he opposed ACORN's ballot proposal to eliminate the 3% sales tax on food and medicine, for the standard incumbent's reason: it would cut revenues.

Nonetheless Clinton easily beat his Republican opponent, and seems likely to remain Governor for some time if he cares to. (For years Arkansas paid its governors only $10,000 a year—one reason why Bumpers and Pryor ran for the Senate.) Like Tucker and Thornton, he seems unlikely to move to the Senate. The outlook in any case is for continued progressive government in Little Rock.

The scrambling in the 1978 race for Senate cost Arkansas some considerable seniority in the Congress. Going into 1979 four out of its six members of Congress are freshmen, and the state as a whole has only 26 years of seniority. This is quite a change for Arkansas, which used to specialize in electing its members of Congress young and keeping them in forever. Following the 1976 elections, the state had 58 years of seniority; going back a ways farther, after the 1964 elections Arkansas had 138 years of seniority, and none of its members of Congress had been in office for less than 20 years. Fortunately for Arkansas, seniority is not as crucial as it once was, and the state is no longer so dependent on federal largesse and favors.

Census Data Pop. 1,923,295; 0.95% of U.S. total, 32d largest; Central city, 17%; suburban, 14%. Median family income, $6,271; 49th highest; families above $15,000: 8%; families below $3,000: 22%. Median years education, 10.5.

1977 Share of Federal Tax Burden $2,453,000,000; 0.71% of U.S. total, 33d largest.

1977 Share of Federal Outlays $3,288,534,000; 0.83% of U.S. total, 34th largest. Per capita federal spending, $1,554.

DOD	$443,766,000	37th (0.49%)	HEW	$1,474,784,000	31st (1.00%)
ERDA	$2,192,000	40th (0.04%)	HUD	$53,826,000	25th (1.28%)
NASA	$243,000	43d (0.01%)	VA	$260,541,000	28th (1.36%)
DOT	$103,719,000	37th (0.73%)	EPA	$37,798,000	34th (0.46%)
DOC	$54,430,000	37th (0.66%)	RevS	$81,498,000	32d (0.96%)
DOI	$19,275,000	37th (0.41%)	Debt	$116,197,000	31st (0.39%)
USDA	$336,374,000	24th (1.69%)	Other	$303,891,000	

Economic Base Agriculture, notably soybeans, broilers, cattle and cotton lint; food and kindred products, especially meat products; finance, insurance and real estate; lumber and wood products, especially sawmills and planing mills; electrical equipment and supplies, especially electrical industrial apparatus; apparel and other textile products, especially men's and boys' furnishings; furniture and fixtures, especially household furniture.

Political Line-up Governor, Bill Clinton (D). Senators, Dale Bumpers (D) and David H. Pryor (D). Representatives, 4 (2 D and 2 R). State Senate (35 D); State House (94 D and 6 R).

The Voters

Registration 1,047,453 Total. No party registration.
Median voting age 45
Employment profile White collar, 39%. Blue collar, 41%. Service, 13%. Farm, 7%.
Ethnic groups Black, 18%. Total foreign stock, 2%.

Presidential vote

1976	Carter (D)	498,604	(65%)
	Ford (R)	267,903	(35%)
1972	Nixon (R)	448,541	(69%)
	McGovern (D)	199,892	(31%)

1976 Democratic Presidential Primary

Carter	315,543	(63%)
Wallace	81,704	(16%)
Udall	37,661	(8%)
Jackson	9,726	(2%)
No preference	57,507	(11%)

1976 Republican Presidential Primary

Reagan	20,209	(63%)
Ford	11,449	(36%)
No preference	465	(1%)

Sen. Dale Bumpers (D) Elected 1974, seat up 1980; b. Aug. 12, 1925, Charleston; home, Charleston; U. of Ark., Northwestern U., LL.B. 1951; Methodist.

Career USMC, WWII; Practicing atty., 1951–70; Charleston City Atty.; Gov. of Ark., 1970–74.

Offices 6243 DSOB, 202-224-4843. Also 2527 Fed. Bldg., 700 W. Capitol, Little Rock 72201, 501-378-6286.

Committees *Appropriations* (16th). Subcommittees: Defense; District of Columbia; Legislative Branch; State, Justice, and Commerce, the Judiciary, and Related Agencies; Treasury, Postal Service, and General Government.

Energy and Natural Resources (4th). Subcommittees: Energy Regulations; Energy Research and Development; Parks, Recreation, and Renewable Resources (Chairman).

Select Committee on Small Business (5th).

Group Ratings

	ADA	COPE	PC	RPN	NFU	LCV	CFA	NAB	NSI	ACA	NTU
1978	45	26	53	67	60	79	35	82	20	35	–
1977	75	67	68	45	82	–	56	–	–	15	34
1976	70	79	59	47	64	54	64	30	40	19	35

Key Votes

1) Warnke Nom	FOR	6) Egypt-Saudi Arms	FOR	11) Hosptl Cost Contnmnt	FOR
2) Neutron Bomb	AGN	7) Draft Restr Pardon	AGN	12) Clinch River Reactor	AGN
3) Waterwy User Fee	AGN	8) Wheat Price Support	AGN	13) Pub Fin Cong Cmpgns	FOR
4) Dereg Nat Gas	AGN	9) Panama Canal Treaty	FOR	14) ERA Ratif Recissn	FOR
5) Kemp-Roth	AGN	10) Labor Law Rev Clot	AGN	15) Med Necssy Abrtns	FOR

Election Results

1974 general	Dale Bumpers (D)	461,056	(85%)	($335,874)
	John Harris Jones (R)	82,026	(15%)	($18,651)
1974 primary	Dale Bumpers (D)	380,748	(65%)	
	J. William Fulbright (D)	204,630	(35%)	
1968 general	J. William Fulbright (D)	349,965	(59%)	
	Charles T. Bernard (R)	241,731	(41%)	

Sen. David Pryor (D) Elected 1978, seat up 1984; b. Aug. 29, 1934, Camden; home, Camden; U. of Ark., B.A. 1957, LL.B. 1964; Presbyterian.

Career Ed. and Publisher, *Ouachita Citizen,* Camden, 1957–61; Practicing atty., 1964–66; U.S. House of Reps., 1967–72; Candidate for Dem. nomination for U.S. Senate, 1972, Gov. of Ark., 1975–78.

Offices 440 RSOB, 202-224-2353. Also Suite 3030 Fed. Bldg., Little Rock 72201, 501-387-6336.

Committees *Agriculture, Nutrition, and Forestry* (9th). Subcommittees: Agricultural Production, Marketing, and Stabilization of Prices; Rural Development; Foreign Agricultural Policy.

Governmental Affairs (8th). Subcommittees: Federal Spending Practices and Open Government; Civil Service and General Services (Chairman); Oversight of Government Management.

Special Committee on Aging (5th).

Group Ratings: Newly Elected

Key Votes: Newly Elected

Election Results

1978 general	David Pryor (D)	395,506	(76%)	($774,824)
	Thomas Kelly, Jr. (R)	84,308	(16%)	($16,208)
	John G. Black (Ind.)	37,211	(7%)	($32,863)
1978 run-off	David Pryor (D)	265,525	(55%)	
	Jim Guy Tucker (D)	218,026	(45%)	($1,019,659)
1978 primary	David Pryor (D)	198,039	(34%)	
	Jim Guy Tucker (D)	187,568	(32%)	
	Ray Thornton (D)	184,095	(32%)	($1,004,515)
	One other (D)	8,166	(1%)	
1972 general	John L. McClellan (D)	386,398	(61%)	($516,573)
	Wayne H. Babbitt (R)	248,238	(39%)	($72,643)

Gov. Bill Clinton (D) Elected 1978, term expires Jan. 1981; b. 1946, Hope; Georgetown U., B.A. 1968, Rhodes Scholar, Oxford U., 1969–70, Yale U., J.D. 1973.

Career Law Professor, U. of Ark., 1973–76; Dem. Nominee for U.S. House of Reps., 1974; Atty. Gen. of Ark., 1977–78.

Offices 250 State Capitol Bldg., Little Rock 72201, 501-371-2345.

Election Results

1978 general	Bill Clinton (D)	331,611	(63%)
	A. Lynn Lowe (R)	192,256	(37%)
1978 primary	Bill Clinton (D)	341,118	(60%)
	Joe Woodward (D)	123,674	(22%)
	Frank Lady (D)	75,026	(13%)
	Two others (D)	31,994	(6%)
1976 general	David Pryor (D)	605,083	(83%)
	Leon Griffith (R)	121,716	(17%)

FIRST DISTRICT

Eastern Arkansas—the flat, fertile, cotton-growing plains that line the west bank of the Mississippi River—is economically more tied to the state of Mississippi or Memphis, Tennessee, than to the hilly regions of central Arkansas or the Ozark Mountains. Like the Delta in Mississippi, eastern Arkansas is occupied by large farms and even plantations where, until the last 15 years or so, whites made most of the money and cast most of the votes. This part of the state has seldom supported any form of upcountry populism, though it always retained a nominal Democratic allegiance. It has been the part of the state least appreciative of the appeal of progressive governors like Winthrop Rockefeller, Dale Bumpers, and David Pryor, although the difference from the rest of the state is one of degree rather than kind.

Eastern Arkansas is the heart of the state's 1st congressional district. Although population-mandated redistricting has forced the inclusion of several hill counties, the flatlands along the unpredictable Mississippi still dominate the district's balloting. For 30 years the 1st's congressman was Ezekiel C. Gathings, who never won much national recognition but rose diligently on the seniority ladder to become Chairman of Agriculture's Cotton Subcommittee. Gathings retired in 1968 and his successor, Bill Alexander, seems to be a politician in the same mold. First elected at 34, he had ample opportunity to accumulate seniority.

He began by winning a seat on the Agriculture Committee. But in 1975 Alexander switched from Agriculture to Appropriations. To be sure, he sits on the Agriculture Appropriations Subcommittee, a body with considerable leverage over USDA policies. But his best chance for a chairmanship in the near future seems to be on the State, Commerce, and Judiciary Subcommittee, on which the two more senior Democrats are considerably older. This is the subcommittee from which the late John Rooney exercised great control over the State Department for years. Its jurisdiction suggests that Alexander will have considerably broader legislative concerns than the support price of cotton and flood control projects on the Mississippi.

Alexander's moderate voting record—he has low ratings from liberal and conservative groups and about 50% from labor and business—seems to suit his district pretty well, and the best Republicans have been able to do against him is 31% in 1976. In 1978 he had no general election opponent, and like his predecessor he seems likely to go on representing this district for many years.

Census Data Pop. 479,893. Central city, 0%; suburban, 10%. Median family income, $5,381; families above $15,000: 7%; families below $3,000: 29%. Median years education, 8.8.

The Voters

Median voting age 45.
Employment profile White collar, 34%. Blue collar, 40%. Service, 13%. Farm, 13%.
Ethnic groups Black, 23%. Total foreign stock, 1%.

Presidential vote

1976	Carter (D)	120,799	(70%)
	Ford (R)	52,491	(30%)
1972	Nixon (R)	98,979	(69%)
	McGovern (D)	45,355	(31%)

Rep. Bill Alexander (D) Elected 1968; b. Jan 16, 1934, Memphis, Tenn.; home, Osceola; U. of Ark., Southwestern at Memphis, B.A. 1957, Vanderbilt U., LL.B., 1960; Episcopalian.

Career Army, 1951–53; Practicing atty., 1960–69.

Offices 201 CHOB, 202-225-4076. Also Fed. Bldg., Jonesboro 72401, 501-972-1550.

Committees *Appropriations* (20th). Subcommittees: Agriculture and Agencies; State, Justice, Commerce, and the Judiciary.

Group Ratings

	ADA	COPE	PC	RPN	NFU	LCV	CFA	NAB	NSI	ACA	NTU
1978	25	59	30	50	67	–	23	18	60	41	–
1977	25	61	38	45	70	29	35	–	–	24	18
1976	30	59	33	43	73	44	45	18	90	41	16

Key Votes

1) Increase Def Spnd	AGN	6) Alaska Lands Protect	FOR	11) Delay Auto Pol Cntrl	FOR
2) B-1 Bomber	FOR	7) Water Projects Veto	AGN	12) Sugar Price Escalator	DNV
3) Cargo Preference	AGN	8) Consum Protect Agcy	AGN	13) Pub Fin Cong Cmpgns	AGN
4) Dereg Nat Gas	AGN	9) Common Situs Picket	AGN	14) ERA Ratif Recissn	AGN
5) Kemp-Roth	AGN	10) Labor Law Revision	FOR	15) Prohibt Govt Abrtns	DNV

Election Results

1978 general	Bill Alexander (D), unopposed			($37,844)
1978 primary	Bill Alexander (D), unopposed			
1976 general	Bill Alexander (D)	116,217	(69%)	($147,088)
	Harlan Holleman (R)	52,565	(31%)	($194,308)

SECOND DISTRICT

The 2d congressional district of Arkansas is the center of the state—politically as well as geographically. Something more than half its population can be found in Pulaski County, including the state capital of Little Rock. The district also takes in a number of hill counties to the north, and to the southeast part of the flat, cotton-growing Mississippi plain. Little Rock made an international name for itself by forcibly resisting integration of Central High School in 1957; President Eisenhower had to send in federal troops when Gov. Orval Faubus refused to enforce the law. But Little Rock has long since lived down its bad reputation, and has become one of the most politically progressive cities in the South. The city has supported Republican Governor Winthrop Rockefeller and his two Democratic successors, Dale Bumpers and David Pryor; it has elected progressive candidates to office at just about every level. Moreover, it is home base to ACORN, one of the most interesting grass roots lobbying organizations in the United States, and one which has had some considerable effect on public policy.

The 2d district has been a good example in the recent sudden changes in Arkansas's House representation—a shift from the tradition of great seniority which the state had built up over the years. Until 1976 the district was represented by Wilbur Mills, first elected in 1938 and Chairman of the House Ways and Means Committee from 1958 until his downfall in 1974 following the Fanne Fox scandal. Mills's original district had not included Little Rock, but the capital was pleased to support him after redistricting in the 1960s. But the district was not particularly eager to stick with him in adversity, giving him only 59% of its votes against a Republican woman in 1974. Perhaps voters anticipated, correctly, that Mills would lose his committee chairmanship and clout.

After electing and reelecting a congressman who served 38 years, the 2d district has proceeded to elect two new congressmen in each of the past two elections. The first was Jim Guy Tucker, a wunderkind of Arkansas politics, elected at 27 as Prosecuting Attorney in Little Rock, at 29 as state Attorney General, and at 33 to Congress. Tucker had a reputation as a liberal, a consumer activist, a supporter of civil rights. He also won Mills's seat on the House Ways and Means Committee. There he got into some difficulties for having originally supported the Social Security tax increases and then apparently proposing that general revenues be used instead to pay for the increased benefits. That and Tucker's vote against the common situs picketing bill caused some disappointment among liberals, who had expected more support from him.

Nonetheless, Tucker could probably have been reelected without difficulty, except that he decided to run for the Senate. The temptation was obvious: Arkansas Sens. John McClellan and William Fulbright had served 36 and 30 years respectively, Dale Bumpers had already captured the Fulbright seat, and whichever of the young competitors won the McClellan seat could expect a lifetime in the Senate. In the close three-way primary, Tucker ran a strong second. But in the runoff Gov. David Pryor finessed him, making him appear to be the labor- and liberal-dominated candidate; Tucker's percentage was creditable, but not enough. Still young, he has plenty of options left, including returning to run in the 2d district.

For the district was captured, to the surprise of almost everyone, by a Republican in 1978. Ed Bethune, a Searcy lawyer, was a protege of the late Winthrop Rockefeller, the kind of moderate Republican who, aside from Rockefeller, had seldom managed to win office in Arkansas. Bethune himself had tried, in 1972, running even against Tucker within the confines of the 2d district in the race for attorney general, but losing the race elsewhere. In 1978 Bethune had a well organized and financed campaign and a natural geographic base in the hill counties north of Little Rock. His Democratic opponent, Little Rock state Representative Doug Brandon, was unable to win a home town majority. Bethune further demonstrated his political ability by winning election as the head of the 35-member 1978 Republican freshman class. This proved to be a group unusually assertive for Republicans, pressing the leadership for better committee assignments and pushing for tough action against convicted Democrat Charles Diggs. Bethune appears to have the political know-how to hold this district, but it may not be easy. This area was heavily pro-Carter in 1976, and it is possible that Tucker may run against him.

Census Data Pop. 481,120. Central city, 40%; suburban, 27%. Median family income, $7,484; families above $15,000: 12%; families below $3,000: 16%. Median years education, 12.0.

The Voters

Median voting age 43.
Employment profile White collar, 46%. Blue collar, 37%. Service, 13%. Farm, 4%.
Ethnic groups Black, 16%. Total foreign stock, 3%.

Presidential vote

1976	Carter (D)	126,790	(68%)
	Ford (R)	60,457	(32%)
1972	Nixon (R)	100,761	(64%)
	McGovern (D)	56,514	(36%)

Rep. Ed Bethune (R) Elected 1978; b. Dec. 19, 1935, Pocahontas; home, Searcy; Little Rock Jr. Col., 1957–58, U. of Ark., B.S. 1961, J.D. 1963; Methodist.

Career USMC, 1954–57; Randolph Co. Dep. Prosecuting Atty., 1963–64; FBI Agent, 1964–68; Practicing atty., 1968–.

Offices 1330 LHOB, 202-225-2506. Also 1527 New Fed. Ofc. Bldg., Little Rock 72201, 501-378-5941.

Committees *Banking, Finance, and Urban Affairs* (11th). Subcommittees: Housing and Community Development; Financial Institutions Supervision, Regulation and Insurance; International Development Institutions and Finance.

Small Business (12th). Subcommittees: SBA and SBIC Authority and General Small Business Problems; Special Small Business Problems.

Group Ratings: Newly Elected

Key Votes: Newly Elected

Election Results

1978 general	Ed Bethune (R)	65,285	(51%)	($255,098)
	Doug Brandon (D)	62,140	(49%)	($329,590)
1978 primary	Ed Bethune (R), unopposed			
1976 general	Jim Guy Tucker (D)	144,780	(86%)	($122,253)
	James J. Kelly (R)	22,819	(14%)	($2,568)

THIRD DISTRICT

The 3d district of Arkansas is the northwest quadrant of the state. It is a region of green hills rising to mountains, of historic poverty, but recent prosperity. The new economic climate comes in large part from retirees and younger people attracted by the area's mild climate, its scenic mountains and reservoirs, by jobs in its small industries, and by a low-keyed pace of life. The cities of the 3d are medium-sized, the kind that most Americans say they prefer. Among them are such places as Fort Smith (pop. 62,000), on the Oklahoma border and Arkansas's second largest city; Fayetteville (pop. 30,000), site of the University of Arkansas and home of its former president, J. William Fulbright; and Hot Springs (pop. 35,000), the onetime gambling center and still a popular resort town. The district also contains the state's most reliably Republican territory, the mountain counties in the north which opposed the Confederacy and even in the depression thirties remained faithful to the party of the Union.

For the first three-quarters of the 20th century, this has been the only Arkansas district to be the site of real two-party contests, and until 1978 it was the only one represented by a Republican congressman. In 1966 the 3d surprised practically everyone when it ousted longtime Rep. James Trimble, then 72 and a member of the House Rules Committee, and elected in his place then state Republican Chairman John Paul Hammerschmidt. The new Congressman carried the Republican counties in the north by a large margin and generally profited from Winthrop Rockefeller's strong showing in the gubernatorial contest that year.

As a Congressman, Hammerschmidt has been a fairly reliable member of the Republican caucus and on the Public Works Committee has tended to support pork barrel projects and to oppose things like diverting gasoline tax money to mass transit. Back in the district he is known as a friendly Congressman who keeps in touch with his constituents constantly through newsletters and visits back home. That reputation was enough for him to win overwhelming victories against lackluster Democrats in 1968, 1970, and 1972.

But in 1974 he faced a different kind of opponent: 28-year-old Bill Clinton, a law professor at the University of Arkansas, and a veteran (though he didn't mention it much) organizer in the McGovern campaign. Clinton waged an energetic campaign, and his personality was at least as engaging as Hammerschmidt's. He also attacked the Congressman sharply on various issues, particularly in the economic area, and charged that he was working more for business interests than for ordinary people. It turned out to be a close race indeed, with Hammerschmidt squeaking to the narrowest victory of his career with only 52%; he was saved by a strong showing in Fort Smith.

Clinton and other Democrats drew from that race the obvious lesson: that if Hammerschmidt couldn't be beaten in a banner Democratic year by a strong candidate, he couldn't be beaten at all in the foreseeable future. Clinton was elected Attorney General in 1976 and Governor in 1978; Hammerschmidt was reelected unopposed in 1976 and against very weak opposition in 1978. Still, there remains the at least theoretical possibility of a clash between the two some time later, if Clinton should tire of the governorship and the state's two Senate seats remain as tightly held as they now seem likely to be.

Census Data Pop. 481,106. Central city, 13%; suburban, 9%. Median family income, $6,057; families above $15,000: 7%; families below $3,000: 20%. Median years education, 10.8.

The Voters

Median voting age 46.
Employment profile White collar, 38%. Blue collar, 42%. Service, 13%. Farm, 7%.
Ethnic groups Black, 3%. Total foreign stock, 3%.

Presidential vote

1976	Carter (D)	128,322	(56%)
	Ford (R)	99,178	(44%)
1972	Nixon (R)	138,541	(74%)
	McGovern (D)	47,922	(26%)

Rep. John Paul Hammerschmidt (R) Elected 1966; b. May 4, 1922, Harrison; home, Harrison; The Citadel, Okla. A&M Col., U. of Ark.; Presbyterian.

Career Army Air Corps, WWII; Bd. Chm., Hammerschmidt Lumber Co.; Chm., Ark. Repub. State Central Comm., 1964–.

Offices 2160 RHOB, 202-225-4301. Also Fed. Bldg., Fayetteville 72701, 501-442-5215.

Committees *Public Works and Transportation* (5th). Subcommittees: Aviation; Economic Development; Surface Transportation.

Veterans' Affairs (Ranking Member). Subcommittees: Special Investigations; Compensation, Pension and Insurance; Medical Facilities and Benefits.

Group Ratings

	ADA	COPE	PC	RPN	NFU	LCV	CFA	NAB	NSI	ACA	NTU
1978	10	11	13	45	20	–	14	100	100	88	–
1977	5	18	13	54	64	0	5	–	–	89	43
1976	0	26	13	56	42	26	0	50	90	85	56

Key Votes

1) Increase Def Spnd	FOR	6) Alaska Lands Protect	AGN	11) Delay Auto Pol Cntrl	FOR
2) B-1 Bomber	FOR	7) Water Projects Veto	AGN	12) Sugar Price Escalator	FOR
3) Cargo Preference	AGN	8) Consum Protect Agcy	AGN	13) Pub Fin Cong Cmpgns	AGN
4) Dereg Nat Gas	FOR	9) Common Situs Picket	AGN	14) ERA Ratif Recissn	FOR
5) Kemp-Roth	FOR	10) Labor Law Revision	AGN	15) Prohibt Govt Abrtns	FOR

Election Results

1978 general	John Paul Hammerschmidt (R)	130,086	(78%)	($47,521)
	William C. Mears (D)	35,748	(22%)	
1978 primary	John Paul Hammerschmidt (R), unopposed			
1976 general	John Paul Hammerschmidt (R), unopposed			($11,569)

FOURTH DISTRICT

Geographically the 4th congressional district of Arkansas takes in the southern third of the state. It stretches from the flat Delta lands along the Mississippi River, west across rolling hills to Texarkana, a town situated so squarely on the Arkansas-Texas border that the state line runs through City Hall. The principal towns in the district are quiet places like El Dorado (pop. 25,000), Camden (pop. 15,000), Arkadelphia (pop. 9,000), and Pine Bluff (pop. 57,000), the childhood home of the late Martha Mitchell. The chief economic activity is raising chickens.

By many indices the 4th district is more like neighboring Mississippi or northern Louisiana than the rest of Arkansas. It has the largest black population in the state (31%) and produced the largest vote for George Wallace in 1968 (46%). But this resemblance to the Deep South stops when one considers the kind of congressman the 4th has sent to Washington in the last decade.

One was David Pryor, first elected in 1966, who achieved distinction by supporting civil rights legislation and setting up his own subcommittee in a mobile home to investigate nursing homes. Pryor ran for the Senate in 1972, and lost a close race to John McClellan, who said he was too close to labor and liberals.

Pryor's successor, Ray Thornton, had been state Attorney General; he was also known as the nephew of W. R. Stephens, head of Arkansas Louisiana Gas Company, a longtime kingmaker in state politics. Thornton had a moderate voting record and helped to form a Rural Caucus, but his most noteworthy moment in Congress came during the House Judiciary Committee impeachment hearings, in which he was one of several Southern Democratic members to vote to impeach Richard Nixon. Thornton also ran for the Senate, in 1978, against Pryor and 2d district Congressman Jim Guy Tucker. The race was exceedingly close: Pryor came in first in the initial primary with 34%, while Thornton came in third with 32%, just votes away from making the runoff.

Thornton's successor in the House is Beryl Anthony, another Democrat expected to have a moderate voting record. In the initial primary Anthony, a local prosecutor from El Dorado, trailed Secretary of State Winston Bryant, but he managed to win a 52% victory in the runoff. That was tantamount to election in the district: Republicans have not fielded a candidate since 1966. Anthony has a seat on the Agriculture Committee, a body of considerable importance to this district.

Census Data Pop. 481,176. Central city, 16%; suburban, 8%. Median family income, $6,191; families above $15,000: 7%; families below $3,000: 23%. Median years education, 10.4.

The Voters

Median voting age 46.
Employment profile White collar, 36%. Blue collar, 44%. Service, 14%. Farm, 6%.
Ethnic groups Black, 31%. Total foreign stock, 1%.

Presidential vote

1976	Carter (D)	122,693	(69%)
	Ford (R)	55,777	(31%)
1972	Nixon (R)	107,470	(69%)
	McGovern (D)	49,108	(31%)

Rep. Beryl Anthony, Jr. (D) Elected 1978; b. Feb. 21, 1931, El Dorado; home, El Dorado; U. of Ark., B.S., B.A. 1961, J.D. 1963; Episcopalian.

Career Asst. Atty. Gen. of Ark., 1964–65; Deputy, Union Co. Prosecutor, 1966–70; Prosecuting Atty., 13th Judis. Dist., 1971–76; Legal Counsel, Anthony Forest Products Co., 1977; Practicing atty., 1977–.

Offices 506 CHOB, 202-225-3772. Also Fed. Bldg., P.O. Box 2021, El Dorado 71730, 501-863-0121.

Committees *Agriculture* (26th). Subcommittees: Dairy and Poultry; Forests.

Science and Technology (24th). Subcommittees: Energy Research and Production; Energy Development and Applications.

Group Ratings: Newly Elected

Key Votes: Newly Elected

Election Results

1978 general	Beryl F. Anthony Jr. (D), unopposed			($372,652)
1978 runoff	Beryl F. Anthony Jr. (D)	67,380	(52%)	
	Winston Bryant (D)	61,619	(48%)	($173,830)
1978 primary	Winston Bryant (D)	50,835	(33%)	
	Beryl F. Anthony Jr. (D)	40,326	(26%)	
	Bill Elder (D)	23,275	(15%)	($67,010)
	Tom Wynne (D)	19,978	(13%)	($62,143)
	Don Smith (D)	17,952	(12%)	($80,189)
1976 general	Ray Thornton (D), unopposed			

CALIFORNIA

California's reputation as a harbinger of national political trends has been well earned in the 1970s. This is not just a matter of partisan preferences, although one can argue that California's increasing preferences for Democrats in the early 1970s presaged the Democratic congressional victories in 1974 and the election of Jimmy Carter in 1976, and that the state's mild tilt toward Republicans in 1976 presaged the moderate success the Republicans enjoyed nationally in 1978. But California voters, probably more than those in any other state, are regularly called on to vote on issues directly, through initiative or referendum; and the results tell us a good deal about public opinion here—and where it may be headed elsewhere. More than the latest partisan trend or the newest political initiative of Governor Jerry Brown, the votes on ballot propositions give us an idea of where voters in the nation are headed.

Thus the Californians of the early 1970s showed themselves increasingly tolerant of what were once considered deviant lifestyles—up to a point. As long ago as 1972 a substantial minority voted to legalize marijuana, a drug still denounced by then Governor Ronald Reagan; it seems likely that a majority would vote for legalization today, although the issue doesn't arise but for practical purposes there are no restrictions any more. In 1978, a majority of voters rejected an attempt to bar homosexuals from teaching in public schools, the first time in the nation a major anti-gay initiative has been defeated. But Californians' enthusiasm for liberal causes has its limits. This is a state where more than two-thirds of the voters favor capital punishment. And it is a state which defeated a measure advanced by the United Farm Workers which would have allowed union organizers to campaign on farmers' property; opponents argued that this was like allowing unfriendly strangers on the ordinary person's lawn.

But the ballot issue result that is most often remembered and which has had the most profound effect on national politics was California voters' adoption of Proposition 13 in June 1978. The approval for the measure to reduce property taxes was not a foregone conclusion. In 1973 voters had turned down a spending limit proposal pushed heavily by retiring Governor Reagan; apparently at that time they were more eager to receive the benefits of government programs than they were to cut down spending. And in the spring of 1978 many voters seemed inclined to accept the arguments of Proposition 13 opponents—including Governor Jerry Brown and the Los Angeles *Times*—that the measure was irresponsible and would destroy state and local government in California. Then a few weeks before the election the Los Angeles County Assessor sent out new property tax assessments. The increases only reflected California's rapidly rising property values, but the total amount of tax—$4,000 a year on many very middle class houses—seemed onerous to many voters. The more so as middle and upper income people today depend on their homes, as their parents depended on common stocks, to increase their net worth and provide them some assets for a comfortable retirement. The government was taxing at high rates the one kind of asset that keeps up with inflation.

Suddenly the measure, concocted by long unsuccessful anti-tax crusader Howard Jarvis and real estate man Paul Gann, took off in the polls. It brought an unusually high turnout on primary day, and took 65% of the statewide vote. Governor Brown, in a swift about-face, promised to administer the law as the voters intended, and the legislature got down to the difficult work of deciding what would be cut. It turned out that cuts in spending would not have to be nearly as drastic as opponents of 13 had predicted. The state was able to use the $5 billion surplus which Brown and the legislature had allowed to accumulate to take the sting out of 13. The result: the voters got lower property taxes and only slightly reduced public services. It was not so much California's passage of Proposition 13 that stimulated voters all over the nation to seek tax and spending cuts; it was the fact, widely reported, that taxes could be cut with few or no consequences. Those who had been saying that there was plenty of fat in government were apparently right, and the meat axe thay had urged voters to wield on it proved to be the one effective means of trimming it. Of course California may have to cut programs much more if future revenues do not provide as much money as the revenues-plus-surplus of 1978. But the state's progressive income tax, in a time of general prosperity, local boom, and steady inflation, produces an increase in revenues larger than the growth of GNP or inflation.

The conventional wisdom about American politics since the New Deal has been that it is best to be liberal on economic issues and conservative on social issues. This was Roosevelt's formula and Truman's and Kennedy's; it was also the liberal Republican formula of Eisenhower and the Nelson Rockefeller-influenced Richard Nixon of 1960. What California suggests is that the more successful formula in the future will be liberalism on social issues and conservatism on economic issues. This makes sense. We are no longer a nation in or haunted by a depression; we are affluent (Californians more than average) and worried about inflation. Nor are we a nation where Victorian mores are the rule; we allow ourselves all kinds of liberties our grandparents did not possess (Californians are very much in the lead here) and we don't want someone stopping us.

This is the framework in which Jerry Brown's politics makes sense, to the extent it make sense at all. Brown likes to say that he comes from the era of the civil rights revolution; but his own involvement in civil rights activities was limited, and today he is ready to slash programs that black politicians say are necessary for their communities. To be sure, Brown has a better record of appointing blacks, Mexican-Americans, and women to important positions than any other politician in the country. But the voter he speaks for increasingly is the ordinary citizen—not the one who is distinguished by being a member of a minority group.

Brown's other major connection with the liberal politics of the past is his strong stands on environmental issues. He has taken a tough stand against nuclear power—and killed nuclear plants which utilities say are necessary to serve California's increasing population. He backs other environmental measures strongly, and has taken tough measures to reduce air pollution in the Los Angeles basin and other urban areas. But he is also acutely conscious of the need to attract jobs. During the 1978 campaign he liked to brag about the big increase in jobs during his first term, an increase resulting more from the vigorous private economy in the state than the state government. He tells business and labor leaders that he won't let environmental and other laws interfere with economic growth—but no one knows which side he'll come out on in the crunch.

Perhaps the most cynical event in Brown's career was his about-face on Proposition 13. Running for reelection against a candidate who had no dramatic weaknesses, and on the wrong side of issues like nuclear power and capital punishment, Brown needed desperately to get voters to forget that he opposed Proposition 13 and that his opponent, Evelle Younger, favored it. He was able to accomplish as much by taking credit for the legislature's actions to adapt to 13 and with impressive cut-spending rhetoric. Brown reverted to the theme of "the era of limits," which he had employed earlier in his gubernatorial career, although then he had been talking about the need to make do with less squandering of economic resources, and was now talking about leaving more of those resources with the citizen rather than taking them for local government. Brown capped his Proposition 13 metamorphosis by calling in his second inaugural for an amendment to the federal constitution requiring a balanced federal budget—and for a constitutional convention to pass such an amendment if Congress declined to do so. The proposal for a constitutional convention has been raised over the years by backers of various amendments which otherwise seemed unlikely to be adopted; for the most part, the convention has been shunned by responsible politicians. No one is sure how a convention would be chosen or what limits, if any, there would be on its work; it would perhaps repeal the Bill of Rights. Brown's proposal can be seen as a bold initiative to do the people's will or as an irresponsible attempt to advance his presidential candidacy.

Brown's 1978 campaign must be considered some kind of masterpiece. After beginning on the wrong side of most issues, he ended up winning with 61% of the two-party vote—a higher figure than either Ronald Reagan or his father Pat Brown ever got. He was helped by the ineptness and dullness of his opponent: Younger was called by one primary opponent "as dull as a mashed potato sandwich." Nonetheless, Brown managed to attack Younger for his high government pensions and for installing a shower in his Sacramento office—in unstated contrast to Brown's well known austerity. Brown also profited from his liberalism on social issues; he got an overwhelming margin from California's increasingly important young voters. If he had had to appeal only to those eligible to vote in the elections Ronald Reagan won, Brown would have prevailed by only a narrow margin.

Yet it is not clear that Brown's big victory has national implications. A CBS election day poll showed that many of those voting for Brown for governor did not think he should run for president. It is by no means clear that he could win the kind of big victory he had in California's 1976 presidential primary once again in 1980. Brown's flip-flop on Proposition 13 may have been enough to convince voters that he can be trusted to handle state government issues efficiently and intelligently. But it undermines any confidence they might have had that they understand what he really stands for and believes. His forays into presidential politics in early 1979 were not encouraging. Poor planning and advance work forced cancellation of a Brown appearance before the New Hampshire legislature to push the balanced budget amendment. A trip to Africa produced more headlines about his relationship with Linda Ronstadt than about his tête-à-tête with Julius Nyerere. Liberal Democrats unhappy with the Carter Administration were turned off by his willingness to call a constitutional convention and his eagerness to balance the federal budget.

Still there is every reason to believe that Jerry Brown will run for president in 1980, given the slightest opening. He cannot forget that in his 1976 campaign, after starting late, he beat Jimmy Carter in four primaries—in states as diverse and important as Maryland, New Jersey, California, and Nevada—and even as a write-in candidate finished just behind him in Oregon. Of course the very lateness of Brown's entry may have inflated his total; some of his votes might have come from people who, assuming Carter had already won, wished to register a protest vote or simply wanted to signal interest in a new face. Brown avoided being tagged as a left or right candidate in 1976; in 1980, he will almost have to be characterized as a supporter of less spending for government programs—which might hurt him with some constituencies in states where affluence and new attitudes have not proceeded as far as they have in California.

Brown's fiscal stringency has been compared to Ronald Reagan's, and there is some similarity. But the politics that produced Reagan was very different from what produced Brown. In retrospect, Reagan seems to have been the product of a kind of social unrest which occupied only a moment in our history, but which was very powerful when it prevailed. Reagan was elected in 1966, when it was thought that conservative Republicans could not win in major states, just two years after the Goldwater candidacy had been repudiated nationally. What Reagan did to win was to focus on events like the Berkeley student riots of 1964 and the Watts riot of 1965, and to make himself a tribune for the middle class values that seemed to be under attack from angry students and blacks.

The mid-sixties were a time when the parents of the baby boom generation had housefuls of surly adolescents, and were desperately seeking for someone to uphold the old values. Reagan, calm, reassuring, and talking in simple but sometimes impassioned language, was their man. And in his years in office, though he allowed government to grow somewhat, allowed abortions to become in effect legalized (a mistake, he says now), and actually raised payments substantially for welfare recipients (though the number of recipients was lowered), he was careful to take symbolic actions which spoke to his followers' concerns. He spurned compromise and welcomed the opportunity to send state troopers into university towns; he made a point of denying the claims of minority groups; he defended the validity of laws against marijuana and other drugs.

But even as Reagan was standing up for the old order, California was changing. When he left office, in 1974, California had far more long-haired, bearded, dope-smoking people on its streets than it did in 1966. The Vietnam war, supported by the majority in 1966, had become a big mistake for the majority of 1974. Each year, mortality took its toll of Reagan supporters, and the number of Reagan opponents in the electorate grew. Reagan had directed so much of his attacks against the style and mores of California's young people that he should not have been surprised that he was exceedingly—far more than any other Republican except Richard Nixon—unpopular among them. More than any other politician of his time, Reagan polarized his electorate along the lines of age. Although that polarization has diminished somewhat today, it is still a serious question whether Reagan is popular enough to be able to carry California in a presidential election—despite his undoubted high popularity with older voters here.

The devotion of older Californians and registered Republicans to Reagan was shown pretty clearly in the 1976 presidential primary, where he won 65% of the vote against Gerald Ford. Indeed, Reagan's showing in the whole series of presidential primaries and at the Republican National Convention is impressive indeed: here is a 65-year-old former governor nearly unseating an incumbent president of the United States. Can he do it again? One impediment is age, but Reagan, though he turns 69 in 1980, is in good health and seems reasonably vigorous and entirely lucid. Another is his reputation as a right-winger, a problem for him in any general election held in the big industrial states of the Northeast and Great Lakes. But Reagan is taking care to make himself more acceptable to voters in these regions and in official Washington as well—something he began to do when he made Senator Richard Schweiker of Pennsylvania his running mate in 1976.

Reagan's major problem in the primaries is the proliferation of other conservative candidates. There is a danger the votes which went entirely to him in 1976 will be sliced up among several contenders; and that if he fails to get the kind of percentages he won against Ford, he will be perceived as having fallen short of a mark he must achieve. That is one way Reagan's candidacy might be destroyed, long before his likely big victory in California could be reached. Nevertheless, Reagan remains the candidate to beat for the Republicans in 1980, and he must be considered a serious contender in a general election. He could have been elected twice before in years when he just narrowly lost the Republican nomination—1968 and 1976—and he certainly cannot be ruled out this time.

There is another presidential hopeful currently residing in California: Gerald Ford, who moved into a desert condominium after he left the White House. Actually, Ford has little base here: he tried to keep voting in Michigan, but when challenged decided to become a California voter. Ford's involvement in California politics has been limited to a television commercial for Evelle Younger—not an auspicious beginning. Southern California is also the home of two other former national leaders: Richard Nixon in San Clemente and Spiro Agnew in Palm Desert, but neither has been asked to play any role in state politics.

California has had only five governors in the past 35 years; in that same period it has had 11 U.S. senators. Indeed, the state has only reelected a senator once since 1962. It is difficult for a public official to communicate closely with 20 million constituents who are 3,000 miles away from where he works, particularly in an era when most people are not very interested in politics. With little seniority, California senators find it hard to make major accomplishments; without a very well known record, they find it hard to convince their constituents they have done anything. Instead, the electorate seems more likely to fasten on some defect in the incumbent and make its decision on that basis.

That certainly has been the case with the Senate seat currently held by S. I. Hayakawa. And Pierre Salinger was beaten in 1964 because voters resented his appointment to the seat (the incumbent had died) and because he might start a Kennedy empire. George Murphy was beaten in 1970 when it was revealed that he had been collecting $20,000 a year from Technicolor while in the Senate. John Tunney was beaten in 1976 partly because his occasional skiing vacations with Ted Kennedy gave him a playboy image. But Tunney got in trouble whatever he did. At first he failed to focus on a single issue; then when he did, by stopping U.S. intervention in Angola, he was criticized for arcane specialization. Meanwhile, liberals were angry with him because he supported growers as a congressman from Riverside and the Imperial Valley; conservatives were upset with him because he had a generally liberal voting record. Finally, many criticized Tunney for not being in touch with Californians. But when he returned to campaign heavily in 1976, Hayakawa criticized him for missing roll call votes.

So S. I. Hayakawa became a freshman Senator at 70, after a long and varied career. Nearly 40 years ago he coined the term "semantics" and was regarded as something of a liberal. But as president of San Francisco State College in 1968 he led spirited opposition to student rebels, sporting a red tam o'shanter and ripped the wires off the speakers on a sound truck—on television. In 1974, Hayakawa had wanted to run against Senator Alan Cranston, but had not changed his registration early enough. In 1976 he was careful to do that. He beat better known Republicans in the primary (former HEW Secretary Robert Finch, Los Angeles Congressman Alphonzo Bell) and edged Tunney in the general election. Interestingly, Hayakawa was able to win roughly half the votes of young people in the general election—proof of Tunney's special unpopularity among what in California has been a very anti-Republican group. Hayakawa profited from the kind of frankness he brought to the campaigning, saying that "We should keep the Panama Canal, because we stole it fair and square." (Later in the Senate he voted to ratify the Panama Canal Treaty.) That kind of talk seems to have been enough to beat the man on whom the movie "The Candidate" was reportedly based.

Hayakawa has not proved to be a legislatively productive Senator, but no one expected that. He has had some successes, notably in organizing pressure to allow Rhodesia's Ian Smith to visit the United States. On many issues Hayakawa is a Senator who must be lobbied; he has a varied enough political past and set of beliefs that his vote cannot always be predicted.

If Hayakawa is considered something of an accidental Senator, so too was his senior colleague when he was first elected. This is Alan Cranston, who is now Senate Majority Whip—the number two position in the leadership. Cranston came to Washington after a career as a journalist, businessman, and California state controller. But in 1968 he seemed a political has-been: he had been defeated for reelection as controller in the Reagan landslide, and he was running for the Senate against Thomas Kuchel, a moderate Republican who seemed invulnerable in general elections. But this was the high water mark of the Reagan years, and Kuchel was defeated in the primary by Max Rafferty, the conservative superintendent of public instruction. It is a measure of how well right-wing candidates were doing then that even after certain facts about Rafferty's past had come out—he had sat out World War II with an alleged injury and then thrown away his crutches on VJ Day—Cranston still won with only 53%.

Cranston began his political career as a founder of the California Democratic Council, a liberal volunteer group important in the fifties and early sixties. He was expected to gravitate naturally to the articulate, but often powerless, liberal wing of the Senate. Instead he showed an unusual talent for maintaining good relations with conservatives and for becoming a dealmaker when he sensed that compromises could be struck. By 1974, when he sought his second term, Cranston had won the reputation in some quarters as the best liberal vote counter in the Senate. He shows the enthusiasm one expects from a young liberal idealist and the physical energy one expects from a man who holds the world 100 yard dash record for his age group.

In his 1974 campaign Cranston got something of a free ride. Potential opponents who were well known declined to run. So his opponent turned out to be a state senator who had dissented—from the right—from many Reagan programs, and who treated the campaign as an opportunity to educate the voters in his beliefs. Cranston was reelected with 63%, the biggest win any opposed senator of either party has had in California since Hiram Johnson of progressive era fame.

Cranston's ascension to Majority Whip seemed almost as easy. He had never really been in contention for the Majority Leadership; and no competition for the whip post emerged. The position is a job for a hard worker, one with the capacity for careful attention to detail, which is why Russell Long and Edward Kennedy, each of whom went through personal difficulties while holding the post, lost the job. Cranston, like Robert Byrd before him, seems to fill the bill. He also has the opportunity to use his influence on those issues with which he is particularly concerned. He was singlehandedly responsible for passing the $250 million bailout of Lockheed, a major California employer, when he talked an errant colleague into switching his vote at the last minute. For the 96th Congress, probably his first priority will be ratification of any SALT agreement; Cranston has always been a strong backer of disarmament and cares deeply about the issue. At 66 he is up for reelection in 1980—undoubtedly the most effective California senator in years, perhaps ever. The question is whether he will encounter tough opposition and the skeptical, corrosive attitude California voters have brought to examining their senators; or whether he will coast to another victory like the one in 1974.

California's presidential primary has been of critical importance in the past. It was here where Barry Goldwater clinched the Republican nomination in 1964 and George McGovern clinched the Democratic nomination in 1972, and Robert Kennedy's victory here in 1968 might have had great consequences had he not been assassinated. But in 1976 California's primary was dominated by favorite son candidates: Ronald Reagan easily won the Republican primary, and Jerry Brown did even better in the Democratic primary. Coming late in the season, California has the capacity to sew up a nomination for a winning candidate, although that is less the case in the Democratic primary now that the winner does not get all the state's delegate votes. The Republicans still have winner-take-all.

For 1980 the assumption is that Reagan and Brown should be able to carry California if they are still serious candidates when the primary is held; should they fail to win at home, their candidacies, of course, would be seriously hurt. Otherwise, what is necessary to keep in mind about the primary electorates is how very different they are. The Democratic primary electorate, which includes nearly 60% of all of California's voters, tends to be younger and more liberal on issues, especially non-economic issues, than the voting population as a whole. The much smaller Republican electorate is older, more affluent, and solidly conservative on both economic and non-economic issues. About one-third of those who vote in the Republican primary will usually vote for a liberal or moderate candidate, but that candidate cannot hope for much more unless the opposition is weak indeed.

A great deal has been made in the past of the differences between the geographical sections of the state. In particular, people in the San Francisco Bay area and people in southern California are eager to assert that their regions are different, while the Central Valley and other rural areas, which together comprise no more than one-fourth of the population, clearly are different. But too much can be made of regional peculiarities. To be sure, southern California is more Republican than the Bay area, but the difference is not great unless there is a stark liberal-conservative difference on non-economic issues. The Bay area then becomes strikingly more liberal. In 1972, for example, McGovern carried the Bay area while getting only 43% in Los Angeles County and 34% in the rest of southern California. But in 1976 Jimmy Carter—who with his Southern Baptist background was seen by many Californians as culturally more conservative than Gerald Ford—received 52% in the Bay area, 51% in Los Angeles County, and 42% in the rest of the south. When it comes to elections decided on economic issues, whether they involve candidates or ballot measures like Proposition 13, the Bay area is just about as conservative as the rest of the state. After all, the people around San Francisco participate in California's affluence; house prices here in 1978 were the most expensive in the nation.

The typical picture of an American political community since the New Deal has been the factory town, with the poor and working class people voting Democratic and the white collar and affluent people voting Republican. A network of community relations—churches, family, social—has been assumed to guide people's personal lives, restraining them from unusual forms of behavior. That picture still describes life in a Pennsylvania factory town, but it has little to do with most parts of California. This is a state where nearly everyone, or at least nearly everyone who votes, is affluent. It is also a state where the traditional community ties are weak: the cities are too new, the people too mobile, the need for traditional kinds of restraint less apparent. So in California we have a politics which is conservative on economic issues and liberal on non-economic issues—the reverse of the traditionally successful American political formula. This is the politics which Jerry Brown had developed—or stumbled upon—and which accounts for his political success. And it is a politics which may become increasingly common in the America of the eighties and nineties.

Census Data Pop. 19,953,134; 9.86% of U.S. total, 1st largest; Central city, 36%; suburban, 56%. Median family income, $10,729; 9th highest; families above $15,000: 27%; families below $3,000: 8%. Median years education, 12.4.

1977 Share of Federal Tax Burden $38,341,000,000; 11.1% of U.S. total, 1st largest.

1977 Share of Federal Outlays $47,194,857,000; 11.9% of U.S. total, 1st largest. Per capita federal spending, $2,233.

DOD	$16,237,912,000	1st (17.77%)	HEW	$15,182,970,000	2d (10.28%)
ERDA	$718,158,000	2d (12.15%)	HUD	$419,524,000	1st (9.94%)
NASA	$1,779,338,000	1st (45.11%)	VA	$2,005,238,000	1st (10.43%)
DOT	$1,064,234,000	3d (7.45%)	EPA	$817,751,000	2d (9.97%)
DOC	$980,427,000	1st (11.81%)	RevS	$964,017,000	2d (11.40%)
DOI	$419,524,000	1st (9.02%)	Debt	$1,160,453,000	3d (3.86%)
USDA	$1,377,058,000	2d (6.92%)	Other	$4,068,253,000	

Economic Base Finance, insurance and real estate; agriculture, notably cattle, dairy products, grapes and hay; transportation equipment, especially aircraft and parts; electrical equipment and supplies, especially radio and television communication equipment; food and kindred products; machinery, especially office and computing machines; tourism; ordnance and accessories.

Political Line-up Governor, Edmund G. Brown, Jr. (D). Senators, Alan Cranston (D) and S. I. Hayakawa (R). Representatives, 43 (25 D, 17 R, and 1 vacancy). State Senate (25 D and 15 R); State Assembly (50 D and 30 R).

The Voters

Registration 10,129,601 Total. 5,729,755 D (57%); 3,465,279 R (34%); 84,884 AIP (1%); 31,407 Peace and Freedom (–); 28,083 Miscellaneous (–); 790,197 Declined to State (8%).
Median voting age 41
Employment profile White collar, 54%. Blue collar, 36%. Service, 13%. Farm, 2%.
Ethnic groups Black, 7%. Japanese, 1%. Spanish, 16%. Total foreign stock, 25%. Canada, UK, Germany, Italy, 2% each; USSR, 1%.

Presidential vote

1976	Carter (D)	3,742,284	(49%)
	Ford (R)	3,882,244	(51%)
1972	Nixon (R)	4,602,096	(57%)
	McGovern (D)	3,475,847	(43%)

1976 Democratic Presidential Primary

Brown	2,013,210	(59%)
Carter	697,092	(20%)
Church	250,581	(7%)
Udall	171,501	(5%)
Wallace	102,292	(3%)
Others	213,444	(6%)

1976 Republican Presidential Primary

Reagan	1,604,836	(65%)
Ford	845,655	(35%)

Sen. Alan Cranston (D) Elected 1968, seat up 1980; b. June 19, 1914, Palo Alto; home, Los Angeles; Pomona Col., 1932–33, U. of Mexico, 1935, Stanford U., B.A. 1936; Protestant.

Career Foreign Correspondent, Internatl. News. Svc., 1936–38; Lobbyist, Common Cncl. for Amer. Unity, 1939; Army, WWII; Real estate business, 1947–67; Pres., United World Federalists, 1949–52; State Comptroller of Cal., 1958–66.

Offices 229 RSOB, 202-224-3553. Also 10960 Wilshire Blvd., Los Angeles 90024, 213-824-7641, and One Hallidie Plaza, Suite 301, San Francisco 94102, 415-556-8440.

Committees *Majority Whip.*

Banking, Housing, and Urban Affairs (3d). Subcommittees: Housing and Urban Affairs; Financial Institutions (Chairman); International Finance.

Labor and Human Resources (7th). Subcommittees: Health and Scientific Research; Employment, Poverty, and Migratory Labor, Child and Human Development (Chairman).

Veterans' Affairs (Chairman).

Group Ratings

	ADA	COPE	PC	RPN	NFU	LCV	CFA	NAB	NSI	ACA	NTU
1978	85	89	68	60	40	85	55	27	20	8	–
1977	80	79	73	40	73	–	64	–	–	4	27
1976	75	88	79	56	100	84	78	9	10	4	33

Key Votes

1) Warnke Nom	FOR	6) Egypt-Saudi Arms	AGN	11) Hosptl Cost Contnmnt	FOR
2) Neutron Bomb	AGN	7) Draft Restr Pardon	FOR	12) Clinch River Reactor	AGN
3) Waterwy User Fee	FOR	8) Wheat Price Support	FOR	13) Pub Fin Cong Cmpgns	FOR
4) Dereg Nat Gas	AGN	9) Panama Canal Treaty	FOR	14) ERA Ratif Recissn	FOR
5) Kemp-Roth	AGN	10) Labor Law Rev Clot	FOR	15) Med Necssy Abrtns	FOR

Election Results

1974 general	Alan Cranston (D)	3,693,160	(63%)
	H. L. Richardson (R)	2,210,267	(37%)
1974 primary	Alan Cranston (D)	2,262,574	(84%)
	Two others (D)	445,229	(16%)
1968 general	Alan Cranston (D)	3,680,352	(53%)
	Max Rafferty (R)	3,329,148	(47%)

Sen. S. I. Hayakawa (R) Elected 1976, seat up 1982; b. July 18, 1906, Vancouver, B.C., Canada; home, Mill Valley; U. of Manitoba, B.A. 1927, McGill U., M.A. 1928, U. of Wis., Ph.D. 1935; Methodist.

Career Professor, U. of Wis., Illinois Inst. of Tech., U. of Chicago, San Fran. St. Col., 1955–68; Acting Pres. San Fran. St. Col., 1968, Pres., 1969–73.

Offices 6217 DSOB, 202-224-3841. Also Rm. 812, 523 W. 6th St., Los Angeles 90014, 213-688-6081.

Committees *Agriculture, Nutrition, and Forestry* (4th). Subcommittees: Environment, Soil Conservation, and Forestry; Agricultural Credit and Rural Electrification; Nutrition.

Foreign Relations (5th). Subcommittees: African Affairs; East Asian and Pacific Affairs; Western Hemisphere Affairs.

Select Committee on Small Business (4th).

Group Ratings

	ADA	COPE	PC	RPN	NFU	LCV	CFA	NAB	NSI	ACA	NTU
1978	15	18	30	70	30	12	25	82	80	68	–
1977	5	10	8	50	30	–	0	–	–	96	44

Key Votes

1) Warnke Nom	AGN	6) Egypt-Saudi Arms	FOR	11) Hosptl Cost Contnmnt	AGN
2) Neutron Bomb	FOR	7) Draft Restr Pardon	AGN	12) Clinch River Reactor	FOR
3) Waterwy User Fee	FOR	8) Wheat Price Support	AGN	13) Pub Fin Cong Cmpgns	AGN
4) Dereg Nat Gas	FOR	9) Panama Canal Treaty	FOR	14) ERA Ratif Recissn	AGN
5) Kemp-Roth	FOR	10) Labor Law Rev Clot	AGN	15) Med Necssy Abrtns	FOR

Election Results

1976 general	Sam Hayakawa (R)	3,748,973	(52%)	($1,184,624)
	John Tunney (D)	3,502,862	(48%)	($1,940,988)
1976 primary	Sam Hayakawa (R)	886,743	(38%)	
	Bob Finch (R)	614,240	(26%)	
	Alphonzo Bell (R)	532,969	(23%)	
	Seven others (R)	285,822	(12%)	
1970 general	John Tunney (D)	3,496,558	(55%)	
	George Murphy (R)	2,877,617	(45%)	

Gov. Edmund G. Brown, Jr. (D) Elected 1974, term expires Jan. 1983; b. Apr. 7, 1938, San Francisco; U. of Cal., B.A. 1961, Yale U., J.D. 1964, U. of Santa Clara; Catholic.

Career Research atty., Cal. Supreme Ct.; Practicing atty.; Study for the Priesthood, Sacred Heart Novitiate, Los Gatos; Secy. of State of Cal., 1971–75.

Offices State Capitol, Sacramento 95814, 916-445-2841.

Election Results

1978 general	Edmund G. Brown, Jr. (D)	3,878,812	(61%)
	Evelle J. Younger (R)	2,526,534	(39%)
1978 primary	Edmund G. Brown, Jr. (D)	2,567,067	(78%)
	Eight others (D)	743,673	(22%)
1974 general	Edmund G. Brown, Jr. (D)	3,131,648	(51%)
	Houston I. Flourney (R)	2,952,954	(49%)

FIRST DISTRICT

The 1st is physically the largest of California's congressional districts; with 2% of the state's population, the district covers 22% of its terrain. And varied terrain it is: the 1st extends from the Oregon border to a point south of Lake Tahoe. Not taking in any of the state's Pacific coastline, the district's western boundary is the Coast Range, which means it is pretty well insulated from the coastal counties. But the 1st does include most of the Sierra Nevada, much of the upper valley of the Sacramento River, and most of what is called the Mother Lode country. Some of the county names here—Placer, El Dorado—recall the Gold Rush of 1849, and the banks of many streams coming down from the Sierra to the Central Valley may not look much different today from how they did when the first prospectors began to pan for gold in them 130 years ago.

The streams that come down from the Sierra, the Coast Range, and the giant (active or dormant) volcanoes like Mount Shasta and Mount Lassen are important today not for the gold that is in them but for the water that is sometimes not. This is the part of California that provides the lion's share of the state's water. And the state's water plan, begun under the first Governor Brown but still not entirely completed, involves sending it from this part of California down to the southern Central Valley as well as to the Los Angeles Basin. The dependence of southern California's cities and the Central Valley's farms on aqueduct water was shown vividly by the 1976–77 drought, which seriously damaged California's economy. It is a reminder of how dependent Californians are on their state's unusual physical environment.

The voters in the 1st district are not spread out equally over this vast and often hauntingly beautiful country. There are not many left in the Mother Lode country, where some counties had smaller populations in 1970 than in 1850. There are two significant concentrations of people. The first is to be found in the upper Sacramento valley, around towns like Redding, Red Bluff, Chico, and Oroville. This is the northern tip of the Central Valley, the nation's richest agricultural area. About 40% of the 1st's residents live here. Another 20% live in the northeast suburbs of Sacramento, stretched out along Interstate 80 as it heads for the Sierras.

The 1st is historically a Democratic district; its traditional Republican areas (Chico, Oroville) are outnumbered and outpolled by Democratic places (Red Bluff, Redding, the Sacramento suburbs). And the district has not sent a Republican to Congress since 1942. But political preferences are no longer cast in iron here. As statewide and state legislative elections show, candidates of both parties can carry every county here, personal popularity rather than party label being the key. Often the 1st is something of a bellwether: in 1976 it gave small majorities to both Jimmy Carter and S. I. Hayakawa.

Partisan considerations have not yet played a major role in congressional elections here, however. Since 1958 the Congressman has been Harold "Bizz" Johnson, a Democrat of the old school. He was a veteran of the old California Senate, where the disproportionate power of legislators from the rural northern part of the state was used for local advantage; in Washington he has also concentrated on conferring benefits on his district. Johnson is a man who got along by going along, and he has not been particularly sympathetic to the ideas of freshman members. He now has enviable seniority: he was able at the beginning of 1977 to choose between two committee chairmanships. It had looked like he would head Interior, a committee on which he had tended to favor reclamation projects and dams even when they were attacked by environmentalists. But Interior has a majority whose thinking differs somewhat from Johnson's. So when the Public Works chair opened up—Jim Wright, who otherwise would have been

Chairman, was elected House Majority Leader—Johnson snapped up that position. Public Works still has a workable majority that believes in federal spending on big projects.

The next few years must have been a frustrating time for Johnson. Although he cooperated with the Carter Administration on some measures, such as imposing a toll on barge traffic, he must have been dismayed by the Administration's hostility to public works laws and its outright vetoes of public works appropriations. Johnson had worked for years to benefit the Central Valley with two other local legislators, B. F. Sisk of Fresno, who had a crucial seat on Rules, and John McFall of Manteca, Chairman of the Transportation Appropriations Subcommittee. But in 1978 Sisk retired and McFall, touched by Koreagate, was defeated, leaving Johnson as the lone oldtimer from the Valley.

Finally, there are signs that the 1st district's voters no longer appreciate so much all the things Johnson has done for the district. In 1976 he was reelected with 74% of the vote; in 1978, against the same opponent, he won with only 59%. That does not put him in imminent danger of defeat, but it may very well mean that in 1980, at 73, he will have to fight hard if he wants another term. It may be that, after four years as Public Works Chairman, he may choose to retire instead.

Census Data Pop. 464,028. Central city, 0%; suburban, 19%. Median family income, $8,681; families above $15,000: 16%; families below $3,000: 11%. Median years education, 12.3.

The Voters

Median voting age 44.
Employment profile White collar, 45%. Blue collar, 33%. Service, 16%. Farm, 6%.
Ethnic groups Black, 2%. Indian, 1%. Spanish, 6%. Total foreign stock, 13%. Canada, 2%; UK, Germany, Italy, 1% each.

Presidential vote

1976	Carter (D)	110,186	(51%)
	Ford (R)	106,842	(49%)
1972	Nixon (R)	109,546	(55%)
	McGovern (D)	87,914	(45%)

Rep. Harold T. Johnson (D) Elected 1958; b. Dec. 2, 1907, Yolo County; home, Roseville; U. of Nev.; Presbyterian.

Career Supervisor, Pacif. Fruit Express Co.; Dist. Chm., Brotherhood of Railway Clerks; City Cncl., Mayor of Roseville 1941–49, Cal. Senate, 1948–58.

Offices 2347 RHOB, 202-225-3076. Also P.O. Drawer 100, 320 Vernon St., Roseville 95678, 916-782-4411.

Committees *Public Works and Transportation* (Chairman).

Group Ratings

	ADA	COPE	PC	RPN	NFU	LCV	CFA	NAB	NSI	ACA	NTU
1978	45	85	48	17	70	–	50	0	57	15	–
1977	30	95	45	27	70	44	55	–	–	11	16
1976	55	87	64	33	67	39	81	8	80	22	8

Key Votes

1) Increase Def Spnd	AGN	6) Alaska Lands Protect	AGN	11) Delay Auto Pol Cntrl	FOR
2) B-1 Bomber	FOR	7) Water Projects Veto	AGN	12) Sugar Price Escalator	FOR
3) Cargo Preference	FOR	8) Consum Protect Agcy	FOR	13) Pub Fin Cong Cmpgns	FOR
4) Dereg Nat Gas	AGN	9) Common Situs Picket	FOR	14) ERA Ratif Recissn	AGN
5) Kemp-Roth	AGN	10) Labor Law Revision	DNV	15) Prohibt Govt Abrtns	AGN

Election Results

1978 general	Harold T. Johnson (D)	125,122	(59%)	($26,620)
	James E. Taylor (R)	85,690	(41%)	($10,617)
1978 primary	Harold T. Johnson (D)	77,831	(73%)	
	Two others (D)	29,192	(27%)	
1976 general	Harold T. Johnson (D)	160,477	(74%)	($21,539)
	James E. Taylor (R)	56,539	(26%)	($7,713)

SECOND DISTRICT

For 300 miles north out of San Francisco the California coast stands in massive grandeur, and cut off by the Coast Range from the interior, the region is covered with Douglas firs and redwoods. The first white settlers here were Russians, down from Alaska, but little evidence of their activities remains except for a number of place names, like the Russian River and the town of Sebastopol. More enduring is the rocky, foggy coastline and the redwoods; the new Redwoods National Park, a subject of continuing controversy, attracts many tourists. This was lumbering country in the late nineteenth century, and the Victorian mansions in towns like Eureka and Mendocino testify to the riches of the harvest. But today this is not an area of great general prosperity. Any decline in the demand for housing—and there have been many in recent years—depresses the local lumber industry. Meanwhile, proposals to expand the redwoods park, like those advanced by San Francisco's Phillip Burton, excite protest demonstrations by lumbermen. Despite the beauty there has traditionally been outmigration here, as young people leave to look for jobs or to probe the mysteries of San Francisco and Berkeley. They have been replaced to some extent by veterans of the counterculture seeking a quiet, rural life in the hills of Sonoma or Mendocino Counties, but of course their contribution to the local economy is limited.

The Redwood Empire, as it is sometimes called, makes up most of the 2d congressional district of California. It stretches from the Marin County line, just a few miles north of the Golden Gate, to the Oregon border. Metropolitan growth intrudes only in the southern part of Sonoma County, up to Santa Rosa, where Luther Burbank had his laboratory, and the southern edge of wine-growing Napa County. Politically just about the whole area is marginal territory. It went for Carter over Ford by a small margin in 1976, for Nixon over Humphrey by a small margin in 1968.

In congressional races the 2d has followed the pattern of most California districts: regularly reelecting its congressman, regardless of party. In 1958 on the retirement of a five-term incumbent Republican the district sent Democrat Clement Miller to Congress. Miller was the author of *Member of the House,* a collection of letters to friends which is probably the most sensitive account of the House of that period—a time when it functioned very differently from the way it does today. Miller was killed in a plane crash in the 1962 campaign, and although he was reelected posthumously, the winner of the special election to fill the vacancy was his Republican opponent, Del Clausen. With a voting record almost diametrically opposed to Miller's, Clausen has been winning ever since.

Clausen is the ranking Republican on the House Interior Committee and third ranking Republican on Public Works—two committees on which he has seniority almost equivalent to that of the 1st district's Bizz Johnson. Like Johnson, Clausen tends to favor substantial public works projects, even when environmental objections are raised, and has worked to make sure that his local area is favored with its share of projects. Of course as a Republican, Clausen has nothing like Johnson's clout; but his ranking position on Interior makes him one of his party's leading spokesmen on environmental issues of all kinds.

For a veteran, Clausen has not made impressive showings at the polls in recent years. In 1974 and 1976 he managed 55% and 58% against a Democrat who carried his protests against taxes far enough to earn a prison term for failing to file a tax return. In 1978 the Democratic nomination was won by Norma Bork, a speech pathologist and erstwhile Republican who criticized Clausen for failing to open the Klamath River to sports fishing. Bork's underfinanced campaign held Clausen to 52%. Given that showing, he must expect another strong challenge in 1980.

Census Data Pop. 464,028. Central city, 18%; suburban, 42%. Median family income, $9,474; families above $15,000: 19%; families below $3,000: 11%. Median years education, 12.3.

The Voters

Median voting age 45.
Employment profile White collar, 47%. Blue collar, 34%. Service, 15%. Farm, 4%.
Ethnic groups Indian, 2%. Spanish, 6%. Total foreign stock, 18%. Canada, UK, Germany, Italy, 2% each.

Presidential vote

1976	Carter (D)	111,043	(51%)
	Ford (R)	106,197	(49%)
1972	Nixon (R)	119,136	(56%)
	McGovern (D)	92,863	(44%)

Rep. Don H. Clausen (R) Elected Jan. 22, 1963; b. Apr. 27, 1923, Humboldt County; home, Crescent City; San Jose St. Col., Cal. Poly., Weber Col., St. Mary's Col.; Lutheran.

Career Navy, WWII; Banking, insurance, professional aviation; Del Norte Co. Supervisor.

Offices 2336 RHOB, 202-225-3311. Also Rm. 216 Eureka Inn, Eureka 95501, 707-442-0912.

Committees *Interior and Insular Affairs* (Ranking Member). Subcommittees: National Parks and Insular Affairs; Water and Power Resources; Energy and the Environment; Public Lands; Mines and Mining; Oversight/Special Investigations; Pacific Affairs.

Public Works and Transportation (3d). Subcommittees: Economic Development; Investigations and Review; Surface Transportation; Water Resources.

Group Ratings

	ADA	COPE	PC	RPN	NFU	LCV	CFA	NAB	NSI	ACA	NTU
1978	10	24	5	42	22	–	14	100	100	89	–
1977	0	29	18	55	30	7	5	–	–	68	35
1976	10	27	13	75	17	25	9	58	100	79	46

Key Votes

1) Increase Def Spnd	FOR	6) Alaska Lands Protect	AGN	11) Delay Auto Pol Cntrl	FOR
2) B-1 Bomber	FOR	7) Water Projects Veto	AGN	12) Sugar Price Escalator	FOR
3) Cargo Preference	FOR	8) Consum Protect Agcy	AGN	13) Pub Fin Cong Cmpgns	AGN
4) Dereg Nat Gas	FOR	9) Common Situs Picket	FOR	14) ERA Ratif Recissn	AGN
5) Kemp-Roth	FOR	10) Labor Law Revision	AGN	15) Prohibt Govt Abrtns	FOR

Election Results

1978 general	Don H. Clausen (R)	114,451	(53%)	($200,924)
	Norma Bork (D)	99,712	(47%)	($80,437)
1978 primary	Don H. Clausen (R), unopposed			
1976 general	Don H. Clausen (R)	121,290	(58%)	($123,828)
	Oscar Klee (D)	88,829	(42%)	($40,576)

THIRD DISTRICT

The 3d district of California contains most of the city of Sacramento and some of its suburbs. The site of Sutter's Fort, Sacramento has been an important urban center since the Gold Rush of 1849. Today it is the largest city in the Central Valley, the much irrigated and incalculably rich farmland north along the Sacramento River and south along the San Joaquin. Ever since the Gold Rush, Sacramento has been a Democratic stronghold. These days that preference can be seen as a function of the large number of public employees in this capital city, who tend to be more favorably disposed than the ordinary citizen toward the concept of big government. In fact the 3d district has a higher proportion of public employees than all but four others in the nation—three districts in the suburbs of Washington, D.C., and the state of Alaska. Nonetheless there are limits: Sacramento gave a majority of its votes to Proposition 13 in June 1978.

Sacramento is one of the few American cities with staunchly Democratic newspapers—part of the McClatchy chain that also dominates journalism in Modesto and Fresno farther south in the Valley. As a result, Sacramento's Democratic voting habits are strong enough that this middle class, middle income district just missed by a hair going for George McGovern in 1972. At the same time, Sacramento has its problems with Democrats who run against big government: Jimmy Carter got an unimpressive margin in 1976, considering that he was winning nationwide, and Jerry Brown ran behind his statewide percentage here in 1978.

Ordinarily the 3d has been a Democratic district, and for 26 years it sent a very partisan Democrat indeed to Congress, John Moss. Moss has a major piece of legislation to his credit: the Freedom of Information Act, which he conceived, nurtured, and finally managed to pass. He seemed to come into his element as the Watergate scandal broke. He was one of the first congressmen to suggest publicly that the House should prepare for impeachment (in March 1973). Angry and articulate, Moss was a natural leader for the class of freshmen elected in 1974, and they helped make him a major legislative force, by placing him in the chair of the Commerce Investigations Subcommittee over full committee Chairman Harley Staggers. In that capacity Moss investigated such diverse subjects as the world uranium cartel, FBI foreign security activities, accountants' practices, drug costs, college athletics, HEW birth control policy, and pesticide regulation. The legislative results included laws on securities regulation, auto and tire safety standards, product warranty protection, and establishing the Consumer Product Safety Commission. He has been called the man who perfected the legislative oversight process; Ralph Nader called him one of the best members of Congress in the twentieth century. But in 1978, at age 63, he decided to retire and return to California.

For the first time in years Republicans seriously contested this district. Their candidate was Sandy Smoley, who had won two terms on the Sacramento County Board of Supervisors in technically nonpartisan races and presumably had some considerable local popularity. But so did her Democratic opponent, Sacramento Councilman Robert Matsui, who won a crowded primary. Smoley made a strong showing and her high percentage must be considered something of a moral victory. But Matsui won the seat and will be sitting in the House—probably for some years to come.

Census Data Pop. 464,541. Central city, 44%; suburban, 56%. Median family income, $11,019; families above $15,000: 27%; families below $3,000: 7%. Median years education, 12.5.

The Voters

Median voting age 41.
Employment profile White collar, 62%. Blue collar, 25%. Service, 12%. Farm, 1%.
Ethnic groups Black, 5%. Japanese, 2%. Chinese, 2%. Spanish, 9%. Total foreign stock, 20%. Canada, UK, Germany, Italy, 2% each.

Presidential vote

1976	Carter (D)	110,313	(53%)
	Ford (R)	98,706	(47%)
1972	Nixon (R)	103,642	(50%)
	McGovern (D)	101,927	(50%)

Rep. Robert T. Matsui (D) Elected 1978; b. Sept. 17,1941, Sacramento; home, Sacramento; U. of Cal., B.A. 1963, Hastings Col. of Law, J.D. 1966; Methodist.

Career Practicing atty., 1967–; Sacramento City Cncl., 1971–78.

Offices 502 CHOB, 202-225-7163. Also 8058 Fed. Bldg., Sacramento 95814, 916-440-3543.

Committees *Government Operations* (24th). Subcommittees: Commerce, Consumer and Monetary Affairs; Manpower and Housing; Government Activities and Transportation.

Judiciary (17th). Subcommittees: Courts, Civil Liberties, and the Administration of Justice; Civil and Constitutional Rights; Monopolies and Commercial Law.

Group Ratings: Newly Elected

Key Votes: Newly Elected

Election Results

1978 general	Robert T. Matsui (D)	105,537	(53%)	($468,028)
	Sandy Smoley (R)	91,966	(47%)	($329,408)
1978 primary	Robert T. Matsui (D)	37,314	(36%)	
	Eugene T. Gualco (D)	30,159	(29%)	($121,511)
	Phil Isenberg (D)	29,341	(28%)	($145,985)
	Two others (D)	6,862	(7%)	
1976 general	John E. Moss (D)	139,779	(73%)	($50,869)
	George R. Marsh (R)	52,075	(27%)	($1,346)

FOURTH DISTRICT

The low, flat delta lands where the Sacramento and San Joaquin Rivers empty into San Francisco Bay; the rich fruit growing land of the lower Sacramento valley; and some of the fast growing suburbs of Sacramento itself make up the 4th congressional district of California. The southern part of the district—Vallejo and surrounding Solano County—has long been industrial and Democratic. The same inclination is shared by the Sacramento suburbs in Yolo and Sacramento Counties. Only the more sparsely populated northern counties—Colusa, Lake—regularly turn in Republican majorities, and these are, at the very least, balanced by a new center of Democratic strength, the University of California at Davis. Situated on flat delta lands, Davis seems to have the nation's best developed set of bicycle paths and highest population of bicycles.

The 4th district has never been considered especially interesting territory politically, yet it has provided a pivot for several of the most interesting political stories of the 1977–78 period—all stories that tended to hurt the district's dominant Democrats. The first of these is the Bakke case, which concerned admission to Davis's medical school. Bakke spotlighted the injustices and absurdities of many affirmative action programs; and although the Davis campus itself probably was persuaded that the medical school's quota system should have been upheld, relatively few ordinary citizens agreed. Then there was Proposition 13, another blow to liberalism; though the ballot measure passed the entire state, it was prompted by the failure of the governor and legislature in Sacramento, just on the edge of the 4th district, to extend property tax relief.

Finally, there is the Koreagate scandal. The 4th is one of the nation's two major rice growing areas, and many of Tongsun Park's activities were connected with rice. One of the congressmen he befriended was the 4th district's Robert Leggett. But Leggett was never criminally charged in the Koreagate case, nor did the Bakke case or Proposition 13 cause him any problems. His career, at age 52, was already over before these issues came to a head. For in 1976 it had been revealed that Leggett had not only had an affair with a secretary, but had actually had two children by her and was maintaining two households. Leggett beat a weak Republican opponent that year, but with only 51% of the vote. It was clear that he could not win in 1978, and he did not run.

Leggett had run for Congress as a young Assemblyman, after helping to draw the district's boundaries. He has been succeeded by another young Assemblyman, Vic Fazio, who was strong enough to win the four-candidate Democratic primary in this Democratic district with 57% of the vote. In the general election, running against an active and well financed Ronald Reagan protege, Fazio won with a creditable 55%—good enough in a year when Democrats might have had to carry the baggage of Bakke, Proposition 13, and Koreagate. Fazio won a seat on the Armed Services Committee, which is important to the district; the 4th contains an Air Force base as well as the giant Mare Island Shipyard near Vallejo. The district does not seem to have been shaken from its traditional Democratic allegiance, and Fazio has begun what is likely to be a long congressional career.

Census Data Pop. 464,171. Central city, 25%; suburban, 63%. Median family income, $9,556; families above $15,000: 19%; families below $3,000: 9%. Median years education, 12.3.

The Voters

Median voting age 38.
Employment profile White collar, 51%. Blue collar, 30%. Service, 14%. Farm, 5%.
Ethnic groups Black, 6%. Spanish, 11%. Total foreign stock, 18%. Canada, Germany, 2% each; UK, Italy, 1% each.

Presidential vote

1976	Carter (D)	96,028	(56%)
	Ford (R)	76,230	(44%)
1972	Nixon (R)	88,410	(51%)
	McGovern (D)	83,334	(49%)

Rep. Vic Fazio (D) Elected 1978; b. Oct. 11, 1942, Winchester, Mass.; home, Sacramento; Union Col., B.A. 1965; Episcopalian.

Career Aide to U.S. Rep. Ronald Cameron; Consultant, Cal. Assembly, 1967; founder, *The California Journal*; Dir., Office of Assembly Majority Consultants and Asst. to the Assembly Speaker, 1971; Cal. Assembly, 1975–78.

Offices 1709 LHOB, 202-225-5716. Also 823 Marin St., Rm. 8, Vallijo 94590, 707-552-0720.

Committees *Armed Services* (24th). Subcommittees: Seapower and Strategic and Critical Materials; Military Installations and Facilities; Military Compensation.

House Administration (16th). Subcommittees: Libraries and Memorials; Accounts.

Group Ratings: Newly Elected

Key Votes: Newly Elected

Election Results

1978 general	Vic Fazio (D)	87,764	(55%)	($235,600)
	Rex Hime (R)	70,733	(45%)	($138,085)
1978 primary	Vic Fazio (D)	47,319	(57%)	
	David E. Hansen (D)	20,591	(25%)	($52,427)
	Two others (D)	14,961	(18%)	
1976 general	Robert L. Leggett (D)	75,844	(50%)	($73,047)
	Albert Dehr (R)	75,193	(50%)	($10,674)

FIFTH DISTRICT

The 5th congressional district of California takes in the northwest portion of San Francisco and all of Marin County, two of the more prosperous and scenic parts of the cosmopolitan San Francisco Bay area. The San Francisco portion includes the highest income parts of the city: the expensive Pacific Heights, Marina, and Sea Cliff districts. These neighborhoods are on hilltops or near water. In valleys inland are some of San Francisco's poorer neighborhoods: the black Fillmore district, the Western Addition, and the Haight-Ashbury area, famous a decade ago as the center of hippie culture in America and now being revived by young people renovating homes.

But most of this part of San Francisco is solid middle class country. It is not quite suburbia: the houses are older, sitting amidst the unburied telephone and electric wires, and there are not as many young families as in the suburbs. There is a tradition of tolerance typical of San Francisco here, and majorities of even middle class voters never went over to the politics of Richard Nixon or Spiro Agnew. It is not their middle class sensibilities, but their pocketbooks, they worry about. Even before Proposition 13, there was a backlash in San Francisco against the demands of the municipal employees' unions; and while Proposition 13 was beaten in the ghetto and trendy parts of the district, it prevailed in the more middle class areas.

The Marin County portion of the 5th lies just across the Golden Gate Bridge. A series of suburbs nestled between rugged mountains and the Bay, this is the West Coast source of what Tom Wolfe called "The Me Decade." Marin's lifestyle has been captured neatly in Cyra McFadden's spiral-bound book, *The Serial*. If the traditional politics of the standard Middle American has been liberal on economic issues and conservative on social issues, the politics of Marin County has been just the reverse. This is traditionally a Republican area, but its Republicanism is of the Earl Warren variety, to the extent that Gerald Ford was able to beat Ronald Reagan here in the 1976 presidential primary. Marin moved away from Richard Nixon's Republicans the more they waved the flag and attacked unusual lifestyles, and back in 1972, 49% of its voters supported legalization of marijuana in a referendum. At the same time, Marin is a wealthy county, and one that does not believe that it has any particular obligation to give its money away. It voted 62% for Proposition 13 in 1978, just about the state average, and in the same year it ousted a Democratic assemblyman. Marin has never been very warm toward Jimmy Carter, who as a Georgia Baptist seems inherently un-simpatico and as a not-so-trendy Democrat may harbor untoward progressive economic policies.

These unusual attitudes have left the 5th congressional district out of kilter with national trends. In 1972 this district went for George McGovern and in 1976 for Gerald Ford. It is the only congressional district in the nation to back the losers in the last two elections.

The shifting attitudes of San Francisco and Marin have also resulted in a change in the district's congressional representation. For more than 20 years the district was represented by William Mailliard, a Republican from a patrician San Francisco family, who had served as an aide to Earl Warren. Mailliard found himself in a vise: if he did not vote for Nixon policies he would be vulnerable in a primary and, apparently, would be violating his own rather conservative instincts; but if he did not oppose Nixon policies, he would be vulnerable, as he never was before 1970, in general elections. He was nearly beaten in 1970 and 1972, and when in 1974 redistricting added the Democratic Fillmore to his district, he got an Administration foreign policy job and retired from Congress at midterm.

The 5th was the scene of the last of the spring special elections of 1974 which did so much to show Washington how unpopular Nixon was throughout the country. The winner was John Burton, brother of Congressman Phil Burton of the 6th district. Six years younger than his brother, he had succeeded to his Assembly seat in 1964. At that time he was considered a far out liberal, sometimes a lone dissenter from the Assembly consensus. Both Burtons were even then opponents of American military involvement in Vietnam; both spent much of their time on legislation to help poor people. By 1974 when he was elected to Congress John Burton had become part of the California political establishment. A close ally of then Speaker Bob Moretti, he was Chairman of the Assembly Rules Committee; an early McGovern backer, he was Chairman of the California Democratic Party. And he had achieved all this without altering his basic positions or priorities: California politics had come to the Burtons.

John Burton has spent much of his time in the House as a lieutenant for his brother, helping him to put together support in his narrowly unsuccessful fight to become House Majority Leader. For the moment, at least, he lacks the influence and clout he had in the California Assembly. At home he has been reelected with percentages rising from 60% (1974) to 67% (1978), though he has yet to break the 60% barrier in Marin.

Census Data Pop. 463,523. Central city, 54%; suburban, 46%. Median family income, $12,010; families above $15,000: 36%; families below $3,000: 7%. Median years education, 12.8.

The Voters

Median voting age 41.
Employment profile White collar, 69%. Blue collar, 17%. Service, 14%. Farm, –%.
Ethnic groups Black, 10%. Chinese, 5%. Japanese, 2%. Filipino, 2%. Spanish, 7%. Total foreign stock, 34%. UK, Germany, Italy, 3% each; Canada, USSR, Ireland, 2% each.

Presidential vote

1976	Carter (D)	94,329	(50%)
	Ford (R)	95,721	(50%)
1972	Nixon (R)	96,120	(46%)
	McGovern (D)	112,246	(54%)

Rep. John L. Burton (D) Elected June 4, 1974; b. Dec. 15, 1932; home, San Francisco; San Fran. St. Col., B.A. 1954, U. of San Fran., LL.B. 1960.

Career Army 1954–56; Deputy Atty. Gen. of Cal.; Cal. Assembly, 1965–74; Chm., Cal. Dem. Party, 1973–74.

Offices 1714 LHOB, 202-225-5161. Also 450 Golden Gate Ave., Box 36024, San Francisco 94102, 415-556-1333.

Committees *Government Operations* (10th). Subcommittees: Environment, Energy and Natural Resources; Government Activities and Transportation (Chairman).

House Administration (13th). Subcommittees: Accounts; Office Systems.

Group Ratings

	ADA	COPE	PC	RPN	NFU	LCV	CFA	NAB	NSI	ACA	NTU
1978	80	100	80	27	88	–	77	0	0	13	–
1977	100	86	88	45	100	82	75	–	–	20	40
1976	90	86	85	50	91	96	81	9	0	4	25

Key Votes

1) Increase Def Spnd	AGN	6) Alaska Lands Protect	FOR	11) Delay Auto Pol Cntrl	AGN
2) B-1 Bomber	AGN	7) Water Projects Veto	FOR	12) Sugar Price Escalator	FOR
3) Cargo Preference	FOR	8) Consum Protect Agcy	FOR	13) Pub Fin Cong Cmpgns	FOR
4) Dereg Nat Gas	AGN	9) Common Situs Picket	FOR	14) ERA Ratif Recissn	AGN
5) Kemp-Roth	FOR	10) Labor Law Revision	FOR	15) Prohibt Govt Abrtns	AGN

Election Results

1978 general	John L. Burton (D)	106,046	(67%)	($88,923)
	Dolores Skore (R)	52,603	(33%)	
1978 primary	John L. Burton (D), unopposed			
1976 general	John L. Burton (D)	103,746	(62%)	($77,550)
	Branwell Fanning (R)	64,008	(38%)	($56,693)

SIXTH DISTRICT

San Francisco is a special city, named over and over as the city where most Americans would like to live and as the American city most foreigners would like to visit. It has a unique climate, physical beauty, and a special atmosphere spiritually. Yet not all is well in San Francisco. It is the city with the nation's highest suicide rate—partly because it attracts the single, the lonely, and the depressed. And it has had more than its share of tragic events in recent years, from the Patricia Hearst kidnapping and Sara Jane Moore's attempt to assassinate President Ford to the Guyana massacre of the San Francisco-based People's Temple and the murders of Mayor George Moscone and Supervisor Harvey Milk. Is there, some have begun to wonder, something terribly wrong with San Francisco?

San Francisco has always had the reputation of an exotic city, hospitable to political radicals and cultural deviants when most American cities wanted no part of them. Yet the city's economy is based solidly on that most prosaic of commodities: food. It is through San Francisco's port and rail facilities that most of California's incredibly rich harvest of vegetables, fruits, and other agricultural products are transported to the rest of the world. This is the mouth of the Central Valley's cornucopia.

The city had its beginnings as the supply center of gold mining camps—it sprang suddenly into existence in 1849—and it got some of its raffish character in those lawless days. It had its own unique ethnic migrations (many Chinese, many Italians). Instead of standard machine politics it spawned its own breed of radicals, like Denis Kearney, who wanted to prohibit Chinese immigration, and its own kind of political boss, like Abe Ruef, who was finally thrown out by the progressive reformer Hiram Johnson. By the turn of the century San Francisco had developed its own sensibility in the arts and its own literary heroes, like Jack London, Frank Norris, and Ambrose Bierce. It also fostered one of the strongest union movements in the nation, one whose successes were probably made possible by the fact that the city's economy had such a solid base.

San Francisco's political tradition was progressive Republican until the thirties, when it became Democratic. But it was a political tradition that in many ways seemed peculiarly distant from the rest of the country. San Francisco was a place apart, and proud of it. Since that time, changes in transportation and communication have made San Francisco less distinctive; the sheer physical distances which isolated it from other American cities are no longer much of a barrier. Nevertheless, no one would deny that San Francisco has remained unique. Its early reputation as a home for writers and artists has attracted several generations of bohemians here; the climate is pleasant, people are used to unusual neighbors, and the artistic atmosphere is not as exacting or as bitchy as New York's. The economy has remained prosperous—it was not hit as hard by the depression of the thirties as many cities, for people still have to eat—and population has risen and spread from the city to the various lowlands between the Bay and the mountains. The city itself has become increasingly the home of the very rich and the very poor, of the single and the elderly and the homosexual, of the black and the Chinese and the Filipino.

In the early seventies, San Francisco seemed sure of where it was going. Riding on its continuing prosperity and growth, it could afford to become the largest office center in the nation after New York and Chicago—and to conduct campaigns against high rises at the same time. This was a city where the majority was determined to tolerate all of its minorities: San Francisco voted to legalize marijuana in 1972, it favored gay rights, it opposed capital punishment. And it had a group of savvy political leaders who seemed destined for positions of greater power. Foremost among them was Congressman Phillip Burton, who as head of the Democratic Study Group in the early seventies was the major force behind critical reforms in the House. The group also included John Burton, Phil's brother, who was a leading member of the State Assembly and Democratic State Chairman as well, and Willie Brown, Chairman of the Assembly Ways and Means Committee and head of the 1972 California McGovern delegation. Another was George Moscone, a leading state senator who was then widely expected to be the next mayor. All personal friends, these men represented a set of ideas of what government should be. Their first priority was the poor—increasing welfare payments, providing more benefits, instituting national health insurance. They were strong supporters of labor unions. They opposed the Vietnam war, and had opposed it from the beginning. They were always on the side of toleration of minorities. They worked to preserve the environment. They were classic California liberals—and also practical, hard-headed politicians.

By the late seventies they had accomplished much of what they set out to do. But some of their dreams had gone sour. Phil Burton had failed, by one vote, to be elected House Majority Leader after the 1976 elections; his heavy-handed tactics and alliance with Wayne Hays alienated one too many of his Democratic colleagues. Willie Brown had been beaten two years before in a contest for Assembly Speaker by Leo McCarthy, another San Franciscan whose personal style is closer to that of the residential neighborhoods he represents in the southern part of the city. McCarthy, by any measure, was a solid liberal Democrat, and a talented legislator as well; he held the Assembly on a straight course during the first four years of the Brown years, when the Governor couldn't be bothered with legislative lobbying; and he beat Brown's effort to have the California legislature endorse the proposal for a constitutional amendment to prohibit federal deficit spending.

George Moscone, as predicted, was elected Mayor in 1975 to replace Joseph Alioto, who had gotten on well with both the unions and the business community. But even as Moscone won, San Francisco seemed to be changing. Voters had rejected a salary increase for city employees, and nearly elected a budget-cutter over Moscone. It was clear that the majority felt that enough was being done for the unions and the poor—and by most standards they were doing well. The great battles of the early seventies had been won: Vietnam was over, Nixon was out, and under Moscone the city behaved about as tolerantly and nurturingly toward minorities as a city government can. Moscone and his friends who had burned to accomplish things suddenly found themselves in positions of power with most of their goals accomplished.

That was the context in which the Guyana massacre and, weeks later, the Moscone and Milk murders occurred. In Guyana a man who had hovered around the edges of the liberal subculture and had been accepted by the political community turned out to be a homicidal maniac; Moscone and other Democrats who had accepted Jim Jones's support in the past were dismayed at their misjudgment. Dan White, the former supervisor who shot Moscone and Milk, had represented the part of the city least sympathetic to the Mayor's tolerant policies—a kind of Middle America at the edge of San Francisco—and his act was reminiscent of the cultural conflicts of the sixties and early seventies. Ironically, White was found guilty only of manslaughter—leniency which suggested that some San Franciscans considered the killings of a liberal mayor and a gay supervisor not particularly heinous crimes. The street riot by gays that followed suggested a breakdown of the apparent truce between different segments of the city. The new Mayor, Dianne Feinstein, took pains to point out that San Francisco was a city of family people with normal values, not just kooks, even as she appointed a homosexual to Milk's supervisor seat. San Francisco and its politics remain distinctive, but the city which had seemed to reach a liberal consensus became a place of civil discord instead. Its economy, as always, remains strong, and its appeal to outsiders continues, but the political future of San Francisco is far from clear.

The majority of the city of San Francisco is within the 6th congressional district, the seat represented by Phil Burton. It includes all of San Francisco's downtown, and most of its tourist attractions—Chinatown, Telegraph Hill and North Beach, Nob Hill and Union Square. The district includes the middle income Sunset district near the Ocean and St. Francis Wood, home of the conservative Catholic upper class. It includes also the city's docks, the foundation of its prosperity though they look anything but prosperous themselves. The 6th also includes the

Mission district, mostly Mexican but with many gingerbread houses restored by Anglos; the geographically isolated Hunters Point ghetto; the dreary sameness of the subdivisions visible from the Bayshore Freeway. This could be the most polyglot district in the nation: 12% black, 18% Spanish speaking, 8% Chinese, 5% Italian, 4% Filipino, and even a few Samoans. Only about one-quarter of the district's residents are white, English-speaking, third generation Americans. Not surprisingly, this is a solidly Democratic district—one of the most reliably Democratic in California.

Phillip Burton, despite his defeat in the majority leader race in 1976, remains one of the nation's most important congressmen. He is probably more responsible than any other single person for the changes which have made the House of Representatives an open, responsive place today—in stark contrast to what it was a decade ago. Burton's achievements are all the more notable because he seemed so unlikely, when first elected, ever to be a power in Washington. Back in 1964, he was part of the tiny left wing of the House: an opponent of the Vietnam war and an advocate of the abolition of the House Un-American Activities Committee. But he was not just a protestor; he also worked hard on legislation. As a member of the Education and Labor Committee, he became a generally recognized expert on welfare legislation.

Burton is also a kind of instinctive dealmaker, with a taste for unusual alliances. Thus he got labor Democrats to join Southerners in opposition to low limits on farm subsidy payments in return for more money for welfare. He assembled the whole California delegation, Republicans as well as Democrats, to support redistricting plans which would return all incumbents. When he became head of the Democratic Study Group in 1971, he made the organization a real power—perhaps the real power in the House. The DSG rounded up votes on important issues, prepared crucial amendments, and raised campaign money for candidates who Phil Burton thought could win. Burton thus moved into a power vacuum while Carl Albert was Speaker, and although others succeeded to the DSG chair, Burton has remained the driving force behind the organization.

Burton could not have hoped to ascend to the leadership, however, without the support of the 75 freshman Democrats elected in 1974. They helped him beat fellow Californian Bernie Sisk for the Steering Committee chair and seemed likely to elect him Majority Leader. But his alliance with Wayne Hays hurt after the Elizabeth Ray scandal. In December 1976 Burton led on the first ballots as Californian John McFall and then Richard Bolling, considered his toughest rival, were eliminated. But in the final race he was beaten by Jim Wright of Texas by a single vote. It was a defeat that had to be interpreted as a personal rejection of Phil Burton.

Such a setback would effectively end the congressional careers of many men, but this has not happened in Burton's case. He has no leadership role, and the DSG is no longer so responsive to him—nor is its work quite so necessary since Tip O'Neill has become Speaker. He is not one of O'Neill's favorites, and he is a natural rival of Majority Leader Wright, Majority Whip John Brademas, and Rules Committee Chairman Bolling, all of whom might be his competitors for the speakership some day. And Burton is not a full committee chairman. But he remains an active member of Education and Labor and has been particularly effective on the Interior Committee. He took the lead in pushing through a large Redwoods park in northern California, despite the opposition of local lumber workers. With Chairman Morris Udall, he led the fight, successful in the House in 1979, for a large wilderness area in Alaska. He is, in other words, one of the most prolific legislators in a rather inactive House. He has also kept up his ties and alliances with a wide variety of Democrats, and cannot be counted out in any future leadership fight. There is no vacancy at present, and no real prospect of one in the near future. But no one should be too surprised if Phil Burton is Speaker of the House one of these days.

Census Data Pop. 463,521. Central city, 100%; suburban, 0%. Median family income, $10,606; families above $15,000: 27%; families below $3,000: 10%. Median years education, 12.3.

The Voters

Median voting age 45.
Employment profile White collar, 58%. Blue collar, 26%. Service, 16%. Farm, –%.
Ethnic groups Black, 12%. Chinese, 8%. Filipino, 4%. Spanish, 18%. Total foreign stock, 47%. Italy, 5%; Ireland, 3%; Canada, UK, 2% each; USSR, 1%.

Presidential vote

1976	Carter (D)	83,668	(57%)
	Ford (R)	62,223	(43%)
1972	Nixon (R)	73,349	(43%)
	McGovern (D)	96,794	(57%)

Rep. Phillip Burton (D) Elected Feb. 18, 1964; b. June 1, 1926, Cincinnati, Ohio; home, San Francisco; USC, A.B. 1947; Golden Gate Law School, LL.B. 1952; Unitarian.

Career Army, WWII and Korea; Practicing atty.; Cal. Assembly, 1956–64.

Offices 2304 RHOB, 202-225-4965. Also Rm. 11104 Fed. Ofc. Bldg., 450 Golden Gate Ave., San Francisco 94102, 415-556-4862.

Committees *Education and Labor* (6th). Subcommittees: Labor-Management Relations; Labor Standards.

Interior and Insular Affairs (2d). Subcommittees: National Parks and Insular Affairs (Chairman); Public Lands; Pacific Affairs.

Group Ratings

	ADA	COPE	PC	RPN	NFU	LCV	CFA	NAB	NSI	ACA	NTU
1978	95	94	85	45	80	–	86	0	0	4	–
1977	85	87	78	42	92	100	80	–	–	0	37
1976	90	87	85	50	100	96	100	0	0	0	30

Key Votes

1) Increase Def Spnd	AGN	6) Alaska Lands Protect	FOR	11) Delay Auto Pol Cntrl	DNV
2) B-1 Bomber	AGN	7) Water Projects Veto	FOR	12) Sugar Price Escalator	FOR
3) Cargo Preference	FOR	8) Consum Protect Agcy	FOR	13) Pub Fin Cong Cmpgns	FOR
4) Dereg Nat Gas	AGN	9) Common Situs Picket	FOR	14) ERA Ratif Recissn	AGN
5) Kemp-Roth	AGN	10) Labor Law Revision	FOR	15) Prohibt Govt Abrtns	AGN

Election Results

1978 general	Phillip Burton (D)	81,801	(71%)	($96,933)
	Tom Spinosa (R)	33,515	(29%)	
1978 primary	Phillip Burton (D), unopposed			
1976 general	Phillip Burton (D)	86,493	(71%)	($85,149)
	Tom Spinosa (R)	35,359	(29%)	($2,887)

SEVENTH DISTRICT

The 7th congressional district of California is one of the more politically marginal parts of the San Francisco Bay area. Although of apparently regular, rectangular shape and lying wholly within Contra Costa County, the 7th is really a collection of heterogeneous industrial and suburban communities separated by high mountains. Richmond, a working class city facing San Francisco Bay, is the anchor to the west. It supplies large Democratic margins in all elections, in part because of its large (36%) black population. Along the Bay that leads to the Sacramento River Delta are the industrial towns of Martinez, Pittsburg, and Antioch—more Democratic bastions. Republican margins come from the more prosperous, faster growing inland suburbs like middle income Concord (now the 7th's largest city with 85,000 people) and high income Walnut Creek. The increasing importance of these affluent communities has been moving the 7th closer to the

Republican column in statewide elections. But in congressional contests it has remained Democratic.

The 7th's congressman, George Miller, might be called a fairly typical member of the freshman class of 1974. The seat was opened up for him when incumbent Jerome Waldie, an early pro-impeachment voice on the House Judiciary Committee, ran unsuccessfully for governor, and two popular local state legislators decided not to leave Sacramento. That left the field pretty clear for Miller. As the son of a former state Senator, he had a well known name in Contra Costa County, and he won the Democratic primary fairly easily. In the general election he had a significant opponent. But the issues of 1974 favored Democrats, he had a well financed well run campaign, and he won the election with a solid 56%—above Democratic levels in close statewide contests.

In the House Miller was one of the freshmen who supported the 6th district's Phillip Burton for House Majority Leader; he serves on the same committees as Burton, Interior and Education and Labor. While some freshmen have expressed doubts about the efficacy of government spending programs, Miller generally supports them and has high labor and liberal voting records. Like most other freshmen, he has managed to maintain a high profile in his district, using the advantages of incumbency to the maximum. He was reelected with 76% of the vote in 1976 and—something of a drop but still a comfortable percentage—63% in 1978. The key question for the future about the freshman of 1974 is how long people like Miller will be willing to exert all the effort that is needed to keep a district like this safe: regular trips back on weekends, frequent telephoning to key constituents, maintaining efficient constituency service. Miller is only 35 in 1980 and so has the prospect of long service if he wants it; but will he and others like him find the working conditions they have in effect imposed acceptable for the long haul?

Census Data Pop. 464,283. Central city, 0%; suburban, 100%. Median family income, $11,826; families above $15,000: 31%; families below $3,000: 6%. Median years education, 12.4.

The Voters

Median voting age 41.
Employment profile White collar, 52%. Blue collar, 35%. Service, 12%. Farm, 1%.
Ethnic groups Black, 9%. Spanish, 10%. Total foreign stock, 19%. Canada, UK, Germany, Italy, 2% each.

Presidential vote

1976	Carter (D)	104,664	(52%)
	Ford (R)	95,241	(48%)
1972	Nixon (R)	100,894	(53%)
	McGovern (D)	89,056	(47%)

Rep. George Miller (D) Elected 1974; b. Richmond, May 17, 1945; home, Martinez; Diablo Valley Col., San Fran. St. Col., B.A. 1968, U. Cal. at Davis, J.D. 1972.

Career Legis. aide to Cal. Senate Majority Leader, 1969–74.

Offices 1531 LHOB, 202-225-2095. Also 367 Civic Dr., Pleasant Hill 94523, 415-687-3260.

Committees *Education and Labor* (13th). Subcommittees: Select Education; Labor Standards; Elementary, Secondary and Vocational Education; Labor-Management Relations; Labor Standards; Select Subcommittee on Education.

Interior and Insular Affairs (13th). Subcommittees: Water and Power Resources.

Group Ratings

	ADA	COPE	PC	RPN	NFU	LCV	CFA	NAB	NSI	ACA	NTU
1978	85	94	75	25	60	–	59	11	0	6	–
1977	85	83	83	50	67	88	65	–	–	19	38
1976	95	86	95	56	83	91	91	0	0	15	32

Key Votes

1) Increase Def Spnd	AGN	6) Alaska Lands Protect	DNV	11) Delay Auto Pol Cntrl	AGN
2) B-1 Bomber	AGN	7) Water Projects Veto	FOR	12) Sugar Price Escalator	FOR
3) Cargo Preference	AGN	8) Consum Protect Agcy	FOR	13) Pub Fin Cong Cmpgns	FOR
4) Dereg Nat Gas	AGN	9) Common Situs Picket	FOR	14) ERA Ratif Recissn	AGN
5) Kemp-Roth	AGN	10) Labor Law Revision	FOR	15) Prohibt Govt Abrtns	AGN

Election Results

1978 general	George Miller (D)	109,676	(65%)	($65,404)
	Paula Gordon (R)	58,332	(35%)	($57,786)
1978 primary	George Miller (D), unopposed			
1976 general	George Miller (D)	147,064	(76%)	($47,633)
	Robert L. Vickers (R)	45,863	(24%)	($23,582)

EIGHTH DISTRICT

The closest thing we have to a self-consciously radical congressional district in the United States is the 8th district of California. This is where the first great student rebellion of the sixties broke out, the Free Speech Movement of 1964 at the University of California's Berkeley campus. The city itself has a unique sort of politics—one of a few places in the United States where an elected school board imposed a busing program for integration, to mix together black children from the flatlands along San Francisco Bay and affluent whites from the hills above the campus. In the late sixties and early seventies there was one crisis here after another, like the People's Park riots where Ronald Reagan sent in state troopers because students were walking across two vacant blocks owned by the University. In 1971 a slate of self-styled radicals won control of the city government; council meetings for years afterwards were dominated by quarrels between members of the original group.

Berkeley is not the only distinctive part of the 8th. The district also includes the north Oakland ghetto, the Black Panthers' birthplace. The Panthers have gone through several stages, from something like guerrilla warfare to quasimilitary breakfast programs for schoolchildren to the 1973 candidacy of Bobby Seale for mayor of Oakland—a solid campaign that won 36% of the vote. More recently the news about them has concerned the legal problems of Huey Newton. Groups with rhetoric as grandiose as the Panthers but whose membership can be counted on the fingers of one hand spring up from time to time, like the now famous Symbionese Liberation Army, which murdered Oakland School Superintendent Marcus Foster and kidnapped Patricia Hearst.

Today the campus is quieter; toga parties have replaced genuine riots, and student political activism has almost vanished. The ghetto is quiet too, and there are few lurid rebel armies in evidence. But the politics of the 8th congressional district still is rooted in the turbulent period of protest and rebellion, and the district's congressman is as explicit a product of those movements as there is in Congress. He is Ronald Dellums, a former social worker and Berkeley council member, who was first elected in 1970. Dellums won that year by defeating the incumbent, Jeffrey Cohelan, in the Democratic primary. The complaint against Cohelan was not his voting record—it was solidly liberal and antiwar—as it was stylistic. Cohelan had the support of older liberals and organized labor, Dellums of students and blacks; and in the politics of 1970, that was enough for a Dellums victory.

Dellums' explicitly radical stance infuriated California Republicans, who in 1970—the midpoint of Ronald Reagan's service as Governor—and 1972 poured considerable amounts of money into this highly un-Republican district. Dellums has consistently lost some votes which usually go to Democrats. But there are enough Democratic votes to spare in this district, and Dellums has always gotten at least 56% of the vote. He might have a problem with redistricting after the 1980 census; but most likely he, like other California Democrats, will be protected by the legislature.

In the House, Dellums now has nearly a decade of seniority and considerable clout for a member with his beliefs. He became Chairman of the House District of Columbia Committee when his predecessor, Charles Diggs, was barred from the position because of his conviction on payroll-padding charges. The D.C. Committee is not as powerful as it was before the District got home rule; but it still carries some clout, and there is a certain symbolic value to having someone like Dellums chair a House committee. Dellums has also advanced to a fairly high position (15th) on the House Armed Services Committee, a body to which he won assignment over the objections of the then chairman and on which he seldom finds himself in agreement with the majority. Such positions tend to limit Dellums's legislative output, and he is perhaps as active on welfare bills as he is on military matters. For example, he opposed with some passion a move to prescribe the kinds of food recipients of food stamps could purchase with their coupons. Neither is Dellums unafraid to take up exotic causes. He argues, for example, that Puerto Rico should be given some form of independence so that it can vote on whether it wants to be independent—although in perfectly free elections, more than 90% of the Puerto Ricans have rejected independence.

Such stands apparently do not generate controversy in the 8th district. Dellums is disliked by a large number of his constituents, including some who vote for him every November; but he has not attracted primary opposition since 1974 and cannot be beaten in the general. So while it is unlikely that even this district would pick, *ab initio,* this kind of congressman today, he remains in the House as a kind of reminder of the politics of protest which carried all before it in Berkeley just a few years ago.

Census Data Pop. 462,953. Central city, 50%; suburban, 50%. Median family income, $11,401; families above $15,000: 34%; families below $3,000: 9%. Median years education, 12.7.

The Voters

Median voting age 42.
Employment profile White collar, 66%. Blue collar, 22%. Service, 12%. Farm, -%.
Ethnic groups Black, 21%. Japanese, 1%. Chinese, 3%. Spanish, 7%. Total foreign stock, 27%. Canada, UK, Germany, Italy, 2% each.

Presidential vote

1976	Carter (D)	115,361	(59%)
	Ford (R)	79,368	(41%)
1972	Nixon (R)	85,741	(39%)
	McGovern (D)	136,330	(61%)

Rep. Ronald V. Dellums (D) Elected 1970; b. Nov. 24, 1935, Oakland; home, Berkeley; Oakland City Col., A.A. 1958, San Fran. St. Col., B.A. 1960; U. of Cal., M.S.W. 1962; Protestant.

Career USMC, 1954–56; Psychiatric Social Worker, Cal. Dept. of Mental Hygiene, 1962–64; Program Dir., Bayview Community Ctr., 1964–65; Dir., Hunter's Pt. Bayview Youth Opportunity Ctr., 1965–66; Assoc. Dir., San Fran. Econ. Opportunity Council's Concentrated Empl. Program, 1967–68; Berkely City Cncl., 1967–71.

Offices 2464 RHOB, 202-225-2661. Also 2490 Channing Way, Rm. 202, Berkely 94704, 415-548-7767.

Committees *Armed Services* (15th). Subcommittees: Research and Development.

District of Columbia (Chairman). Subcommittees: Fiscal Affairs and Health (Chairman); Government Affairs and Budget.

Group Ratings

	ADA	COPE	PC	RPN	NFU	LCV	CFA	NAB	NSI	ACA	NTU
1978	95	95	95	44	80	–	96	0	0	8	–
1977	95	86	85	54	67	90	95	–	–	19	45
1976	100	87	95	56	83	100	91	17	0	11	33

Key Votes

1) Increase Def Spnd	AGN	6) Alaska Lands Protect	FOR	11) Delay Auto Pol Cntrl	AGN
2) B-1 Bomber	AGN	7) Water Projects Veto	FOR	12) Sugar Price Escalator	FOR
3) Cargo Preference	AGN	8) Consum Protect Agcy	FOR	13) Pub Fin Cong Cmpgns	FOR
4) Dereg Nat Gas	AGN	9) Common Situs Picket	FOR	14) ERA Ratif Recissn	AGN
5) Kemp-Roth	AGN	10) Labor Law Revision	FOR	15) Prohibt Govt Abrtns	AGN

Election Results

1978 general	Ronald V. Dellums (D)	94,824	(57%)	($75,945)
	Charles V. Hughes (R)	70,481	(43%)	($7,933)
1978 primary	Ronald V. Dellums (D), unopposed			
1976 general	Ronald V. Dellums (D)	122,342	(64%)	($44,744)
	Phillip S. Breck, Jr. (R)	68,374	(36%)	($22,025)

NINTH DISTRICT

Not all of the East Bay across from San Francisco was a hotbed of political radicalism during the 1960s. The suburbs south of Oakland—places like San Leandro, San Lorenzo, Castro Valley—can sometimes seem like outposts of Middle America on San Francisco Bay. These are the places where people have always worked at ordinary jobs in the East Bay's and San Francisco's offices and factories, and live in comfortable, well tended neighborhoods. These suburbs, together with the southern part of Oakland, about half black but most of it resolutely middle class, and portions of Alameda and Contra Costa County suburbs over the range, form California's 9th congressional district.

More of the people who live here consider themselves Democrats than Republicans. But the label means something different here from what it does in Berkeley. Thus while Berkeley was 73% opposed to Proposition 13 in June 1978, San Leandro was 72% in favor. Another factor moving the middle class residents of the East Bay in a conservative direction has been the Oakland *Tribune,* still owned by the family of the late William Knowland, former Senator from California and onetime (1953–55) Senate Majority Leader.

The 9th district has sent Democrats to Washington for as long as anyone can remember. For 28 years the congressman was George Miller (no relation to current 7th district incumbent George Miller) who rose silently to become Chairman of the House Space Committee. Miller, in the tradition of many oldtimers, got out of touch with his district. In 1972, at age 81 and against strong competition, Miller could win only a pathetic 22% of the primary vote.

The winner of that primary was Fortney (Pete) Stark, a strong opponent of the Vietnam war and local banker. Stark had combined ideology and financial interest by erecting a large peace symbol over his suburban bank in Walnut Creek; he attracted the accounts of peace activists all over the Bay area by printing checks with the peace symbol on them. Stark spent liberally on his own campaign, and won the general election even though George McGovern failed, though just barely, to carry the 9th.

In his first term, Stark won assignment to the Banking Committee. He reversed the usual pattern: many members have acquired banking interests and voted for them once they got on the Committee; Stark sold his bank stock and often voted against the bank lobbies. In his second term he moved to the Ways and Means Committee, where he is one of the more reliable backers of measures like progressive tax reform and national health insurance. He serves on the committee that handles welfare legislation and has concentrated much of his legislative effort in this area.

Census Data Pop. 464,934. Central city, 28%; suburban, 72%. Median family income, $11,309; families above $15,000: 28%; families below $3,000: 7%. Median years education, 12.3.

The Voters

Median voting age 42.
Employment profile White collar, 52%. Blue collar, 35%. Service, 12%. Farm, 1%.
Ethnic groups Black, 14%. Spanish, 12%. Total foreign stock, 22%. Canada, UK, Germany, Italy, Portugal, 2% each.

Presidential vote

1976	Carter (D)	91,871	(56%)
	Ford (R)	72,063	(44%)
1972	Nixon (R)	92,267	(50%)
	McGovern (D)	91,030	(50%)

Rep. Fortney H. (Pete) **Stark** (D) Elected 1972; b. Nov. 11, 1931, Milwaukee, Wis.; home, Oakland; MIT, B.S. 1953, U. of Cal., M.B.A. 1959; Unitarian.

Career Air Force, 1955–57; Founder, Beacon Savings and Loan Assn., 1961; Founder and Pres., Security Natl. Bank, Walnut Creek, 1963–72.

Offices 1034 LHOB, 202-225-5065. Also 7 Eastmont Mall, Oakland 94605, 415-635-1092.

Committees *District of Columbia* (6th). Subcommittees: Metropolitan Affairs (Chairman).

Ways and Means (9th). Subcommittees: Select Revenue Measures; Public Assistance and Unemployment Compensation.

Group Ratings

	ADA	COPE	PC	RPN	NFU	LCV	CFA	NAB	NSI	ACA	NTU
1978	95	95	90	50	67	–	96	0	0	17	–
1977	80	84	80	45	73	96	90	–	–	0	41
1976	95	87	89	56	91	100	73	9	0	0	25

Key Votes

1) Increase Def Spnd	AGN	6) Alaska Lands Protect	DNV	11) Delay Auto Pol Cntrl	AGN
2) B-1 Bomber	AGN	7) Water Projects Veto	FOR	12) Sugar Price Escalator	AGN
3) Cargo Preference	DNV	8) Consum Protect Agcy	FOR	13) Pub Fin Cong Cmpgns	FOR
4) Dereg Nat Gas	AGN	9) Common Situs Picket	FOR	14) ERA Ratif Recissn	AGN
5) Kemp-Roth	AGN	10) Labor Law Revision	FOR	15) Prohibt Govt Abrtns	AGN

Election Results

1978 general	Fortney H. Stark (D)	88,179	(68%)	($24,697)
	Robert S. Allen (R)	41,138	(32%)	($7,234)
1978 primary	Fortney H. Stark (D)	63,749	(78%)	
	One other (D)	17,589	(22%)	
1976 general	Fortney H. Stark (D)	116,398	(72%)	($20,890)
	James K. Mills (R)	44,607	(28%)	($12,591)

TENTH DISTRICT

During the last decade or two, population growth in the San Francisco metropolitan area has been most rapid near the southern end of San Francisco Bay. The growth has centered around the old farm market town of San Jose—now indistinguishable from its suburban neighbors. Located in the area is much of northern California's defense business, notably the huge Lockheed plant in Sunnyvale, which in some years has been the Defense Department's largest supplier. Many migrants to the area have come from the Southwest and point east, but most are natives of some other part of the Bay area. They are mainly white working class people, many of whom grew up in neighborhoods now dominated by blacks in Oakland or far-out types in San Francisco. Also here are the Mexican-Americans of San Jose, people who have moved up from farm labor camps to middle class respectability.

The working class whites and Mexican-Americans are the two groups which are electorally the most important in the politics of California's 10th congressional district. Its terrain spans the southern edge of the Bay from Hayward in Alameda County, not far south of Oakland, to the edge of the Lockheed Sunnyvale plant, west of San Jose. The district lines in the San Jose area, which are somewhat jagged, take in most of the city's chicano population. The result is a congressional district which does not really constitute a community, but a lumping together of people who usually vote the same way.

With a larger Mexican-American population than all but two other California districts (26%), the 10th was intended to go Democratic, and it has. Since the lines were first drawn in 1962, they have been shifted three times, but the district has continued to reelect Democratic Congressman Don Edwards.

Edwards is one of those relatively senior congressmen who was a prime beneficiary of the tidal wave of Democratic freshmen of 1974. He had the seniority and experience to hold high committee positions, and at the same time he reflected the views of the freshmen well enough that he could, for the first time, be sure of a large number of votes on the floor. Edwards has an odd background for a liberal: he was once an FBI agent, and he got rich as the owner of the only title company in San Jose and Santa Clara County which increased in size from 290,000 in 1950 to 1.1 million in 1970). He is nonetheless one of the most liberal members of the House: an early opponent of the Vietnam war and onetime Chairman of Americans for Democratic Action. He is also the fourth-ranking Democrat on the House Judiciary Committee and chairman of the subcommittee that handles constitutional amendments. This means he must handle such ticklish chores as floor managing the extension of time for ratification of the Equal Rights Amendment; his is also the subcommittee which has kept anti-abortion constitutional amendments from coming to the floor of the House. Edwards was on a special committee investigating the CIA, and his own subcommittee conducted a sensitive and careful ongoing investigation of the FBI.

It is many years since Edwards has had significant opposition; the worst he has done was to slip to 57% in 1968 at the height of Ronald Reagan's popularity in California. But his percentage, like that of other Bay area Democrats, declined somewhat in 1978. This is not a district that is seriously contested for good reason: its Democratic leanings are very strong, going for McGovern as well as Carter.

Census Data Pop. 463,419. Central city, 35%; suburban, 65%. Median family income, $11,095; families above $15,000: 24%; families below $3,000: 7%. Median years education, 12.2.

The Voters

Median voting age 38.
Employment profile White collar, 47%. Blue collar, 40%. Service, 12%. Farm, 1%.
Ethnic groups Black, 2%. Japanese, 1%. Spanish, 26%. Total foreign stock, 26%. Italy, 3%; Canada, Portugal, 2% each; UK, Germany, 1% each.

Presidential vote

1976	Carter (D)	92,239	(59%)
	Ford (R)	65,121	(41%)
1972	Nixon (R)	78,375	(47%)
	McGovern (D)	87,054	(53%)

Rep. Don Edwards (D) Elected 1962; b. Jan. 6, 1915, San Jose; home, San Jose; Stanford U., Stanford U. Law School; Unitarian.

Career FBI Agent, 1940–41; Navy, WWII; Pres., Valley Title Co., San Jose.

Offices 2329 RHOB, 202-225-3072. Also 1625 The Alameda, San Jose 95126, 408-292-0143.

Committees *Judiciary* (4th). Subcommittees: Civil and Constitutional Rights (Chairman); Crime.

Veterans' Affairs (3d). Subcommittees: Housing; Medical Facilities and Benefits.

Group Ratings

	ADA	COPE	PC	RPN	NFU	LCV	CFA	NAB	NSI	ACA	NTU
1978	80	84	75	27	67	–	73	9	10	4	–
1977	95	78	85	54	64	100	70	–	–	12	37
1976	95	87	93	59	82	96	100	8	0	0	18

Key Votes

1) Increase Def Spnd	AGN	6) Alaska Lands Protect	FOR	11) Delay Auto Pol Cntrl	AGN
2) B-1 Bomber	AGN	7) Water Projects Veto	FOR	12) Sugar Price Escalator	AGN
3) Cargo Preference	AGN	8) Consum Protect Agcy	FOR	13) Pub Fin Cong Cmpgns	FOR
4) Dereg Nat Gas	AGN	9) Common Situs Picket	FOR	14) ERA Ratif Recissn	AGN
5) Kemp-Roth	AGN	10) Labor Law Revision	FOR	15) Prohibt Govt Abrtns	AGN

Election Results

1978 general	Don Edwards (D)	84,488	(67%)	($31,740)
	Rudy Hansen (R)	41,374	(33%)	($25,124)
1978 primary	Don Edwards (D), unopposed			
1976 general	Don Edwards (D)	111,992	(75%)	($10,788)
	Herb Smith (R)	38,088	(25%)	($6,625)

ELEVENTH DISTRICT

The Peninsula is the bony finger of land south of San Francisco that connects the city to the rest of California. Almost down the middle of the Peninsula runs the San Andreas Fault, which some experts believe will shift again within the next 20 years or so and produce an earthquake like the one which devastated San Francisco in 1906. To the west of the Fault the land is mountainous enough to have discouraged development, except in the suburb of Pacifica, which clings to the foggy mountainsides above the Ocean, directly south of San Francisco. Most of the Peninsula's population is packed into neat little suburbs between the Fault and the salt flats and industrial areas created by landfill dumped into San Francisco Bay.

The Peninsula suburbs, notably sunnier and warmer than the city, are occupied mainly by white collar people who commute to San Francisco or, more likely, work around San Jose or on the Peninsula itself. Politically these towns behave more like Eastern upper middle class suburbs than like the archconservative wealthy towns around Los Angeles. These are people who trend Democratic when social issues dominate the political dialogue, as they did in the years of the Vietnam war, student rebellion, and the debate over legalization of marijuana. They trend Republican, however, when purely economic issues are at stake, as was the case in 1978 with Proposition 13.

The 11th congressional district includes the northern Peninsula suburbs—Daly City, South San Francisco ("the industrial city," it says in big letters on a mountain near the Bayshore Freeway), and San Bruno, on down to Redwood City. There are really two sets of suburbs here. In the northern part of the Peninsula, just south of San Francisco, are Daly City, Pacifica, and South San Francisco; these are really extensions of the blue collar neighborhoods of the city itself. To the south, starting at the San Francisco Airport, are the traditionally Republican towns—San Bruno, Millbrae, Burlingame, San Mateo, Belmont, San Carlos. Some of these are now Democratic in many elections, but this part of the Peninsula elects a Republican assemblyman and in 1978 defeated an incumbent Democratic state senator. In the hills above is the town of Hillsborough, the home of many of San Francisco's wealthiest and most socially prominent families.

This is the district that elected Leo Ryan, whose death in Jonestown, Guyana, made international news in November 1978. Ryan had gone to Guyana to investigate the People's Temple cult of Jim Jones, which had started in San Francisco and which had attracted, among others, relatives of many of Ryan's constituents. There were allegations that people were tortured and held in Jonestown against their will—allegations that seemed fully verified when several People's Church members attempted to leave Jonestown with Ryan. Just as a plane was being boarded, Ryan and several newsmen were shot. The world knows the rest of the story: how Jones persuaded almost all his followers to kill themselves and their children.

Ryan's expedition to Guyana was unorthodox—which was in line with his usual political pattern. He had come to politics not as an ambitious young lawyer, but as a teacher and principal getting involved on the South San Francisco City Council; he later became Mayor and, in 1962, Assemblyman. Ten years later, when congressional lines were redrawn, Ryan won the 11th district seat without substantial opposition. He set himself apart from the rest of the Bay area delegation by being somewhat less dovish on Vietnam and other international issues; he antagonized organized labor by opposing public employee strikes and backing strong environmental controls over growth. He was reelected easily although, like other Bay area Democrats, by a smaller margin in 1978 than in previous years.

The Peninsula, the bony finger of land south of San Francisco, connects the city with the rest of California. Almost down the middle of the Peninsula runs the San Andreas Fault, which some experts believe will shift again within the next 20 years or so and produce an earthquake like the one which devastated San Francisco in 1906. To the west of the Fault the land is mountainous enough to have discouraged development, except in the suburb of Pacifica, which clings to the foggy mountainsides above the Ocean, directly south of San Francisco. Most of the Peninsula's population is packed into neat little suburbs between the Fault and the salt flats and industrial areas created by landfill dumped into San Francisco Bay.

The Peninsula suburbs, notably sunnier and warmer than the city, are occupied mainly by white collar people who commute to San Francisco or, more likely, work around San Jose or on the Peninsula itself. Politically these towns behave more like Eastern upper middle class suburbs than like the archconservative wealthy towns around Los Angeles. These are people who trend Democratic when social issues dominate the political dialogue, as they did in the years of the Vietnam war, student rebellion, and the debate over legalization of marijuana. They trend Republican, however, when purely economic issues are at stake, as was the case in 1978 with Proposition 13.

The 11th congressional district includes the northern Peninsula suburbs—Daly City, South San Francisco ("the industrial city," it says in big letters on a mountain near the Bayshore Freeway), and San Bruno, on down to Redwood City. There are really two sets of suburbs here. In the northern part of the Peninsula, just south of San Francisco, are Daly City, Pacifica, and South San Francisco; these are really extensions of the blue collar neighborhoods of the city itself. To the south, starting at the San Francisco Airport, are the traditionally Republican towns—San Bruno, Millbrae, Burlingame, San Mateo, Belmont, San Carlos. Some of these are now Democratic in many elections, but this part of the Peninsula elects a Republican assemblyman and in 1978 defeated an incumbent Democratic state senator. In the hills above is the town of Hillsborough, the home of many of San Francisco's wealthiest and most socially prominent families.

This is the district that elected Leo Ryan, whose death in Jonestown, Guyana, made international news in November 1978. Ryan had gone to Guyana to investigate the People's Temple cult of Jim Jones, which had been centered in San Francisco and which had attracted, among others, relatives of many of Ryan's constituents. There were allegations that members were tortured and held in Jonestown against their will—allegations that seemed fully verified when several of them attempted to leave Jonestown with Ryan. Just as a plane was being boarded, Ryan and several newsmen were shot. The world knows the rest of the story: how Jones persuaded almost all his followers to kill their children and themselves.

Ryan's expedition to Guyana was unorthodox—which was in accordance with his usual political pattern. He had come to politics not as an ambitious young lawyer, but as a teacher and principal getting involved on the South San Francisco City Council; he later became Mayor and, in 1962, Assemblyman. Ten years later, when congressional lines were redrawn, Ryan won the 11th district seat without substantial opposition. He set himself apart from the rest of the Bay area delegation by being somewhat less dovish on Vietnam and other international issues; he antagonized organized labor by opposing public employee strikes and backing strong environmental controls over growth. He was reelected easily, but like other Bay area Democrats, by a smaller margin in 1978 than in previous years.

Ryan's successor was chosen in a March 1979 special election, and his political coloration reflects recent changes in attitudes in the Peninsula and the Bay Area generally. For William Royer is a Republican, a local official who sat on the County Board of Supervisors, a moderate whose image was enhanced by strong support from the 12th district's Pete McCloskey (who once represented all the territory within the 11th). Royer's campaign was well financed, and he marshalled his political assets effectively.

The Democrats, in contrast, were in disarray. The best financed of them, who also had the presumed advantage of the support of Governor Jerry Brown, was eliminated in the special primary; that candidate called foul because the successful candidate had pointed to his Arab ancestry in the course of the campaign. The Democratic nominee, Joseph Holsinger, was a former aide to Ryan, but he could neither rise above the hubbub raised by his opponents nor overcome the Republican trend among affluent Bay Area residents. It was the first time since the redistricting of the seventies that any Bay Area district except McCloskey's had elected a Republican, and it suggests that there is at least the possibility of further Republican gains in some other districts should the incumbents not be running.

Census Data Pop. 464,187. Central city, 0%; suburban, 100%. Median family income, $13,062; families above $15,000: 38%; families below $3,000: 4%. Median years education, 12.6.

The Voters

Median voting age 42.
Employment profile White collar, 59%. Blue collar, 29%. Service, 12%. Farm, -%.
Ethnic groups Black, 2%. Japanese, 1%. Filipino, 1%. Spanish, 12%. Total foreign stock, 32%. Italy, 4%; Canada, UK, Germany, 3% each; USSR, Ireland, 1% each.

Presidential vote

1976	Carter (D)	85,027	(47%)
	Ford (R)	94,646	(53%)
1972	Nixon (R)	105,286	(55%)
	McGovern (D)	85,842	(45%)

Group Ratings: Newly Elected

Key Votes: Newly Elected

Election Results

1979 special	Bill Royer (R)	52,585	(58%)	
	Joe Holsinger (D)	37,685	(42%)	
1979 special primary	Bill Royer (r)	19,409	(52%)	
	Les Kelting (R)	6,562	(18%)	
	Bruce Maker (R)	5,980	(16%)	
	Two others (R)	5,189	(14%)	
1978 general	Leo J. Ryan (D)	92,882	(63%)	($40,588)
	Dave Welch (R)	54,621	(37%)	($26,229)
1978 primary	Leo J. Ryan (D)	60,315	(75%)	
	Charles T. Plough III (D)	20,441	(25%)	
1976 general	Leo J. Ryan (D)	130,332	(68%)	($51,864)
	Bob Jones (R)	61,526	(32%)	($110,328)

TWELFTH DISTRICT

The 12th congressional district of California is a part of the Peninsula south of San Francisco. Its northern end lies in Redwood City, in San Mateo County about 10 miles south of the San Francisco city limit; it extends south and east to the boundaries of San Jose. Its central communities are probably Palo Alto and Menlo Park, the former the home of Stanford University and the latter the home of such diverse California lifestyle publications as the *Whole Earth Catalogue* and *Sunset* magazine. The 12th includes the woodsy suburbs of Portola Valley and Woodside and the affluent suburb of Atherton on land between the hills and the Bay. South of Palo Alto, in Santa Clara County, are the more middle class suburbs of Santa Clara, Sunnyvale, and Mountain View.

In Sunnyvale there is a giant Lockheed plant which in some years has absorbed more federal dollars than any other defense plant in the nation. But the district likes to define itself not by its role in defense production but by its attitude toward the environment. This is an area with a disproportionately large number of Sierra Club members; there are bicycle paths everywhere; tennis courts are in constant use. And the feeling for the environment here is not just an academic impulse. From the hilly affluent areas or the valleys below you cannot avoid seeing how fast the available land is being occupied. Nor can you help noticing, as you drive on the Bayshore Freeway that links the communities of the 12th together, how the ugly industrial fill land is gradually eating away at the expanse of San Francisco Bay.

This is the district which has elected, for more than ten years now, Congressman Pete McCloskey. His is a political career more full of pitfalls than the Perils of Pauline, but he has survived and politically seems in better shape than ever. At the heart of McCloskey's appeal has always been the environmental issue. When he first ran for Congress, in a 1967 special election, it was his environmental interests that made this Menlo Park lawyer the winner over Shirley Temple Black. (Mrs. Black may also have been hurt by her movie star background. That was right after the elections of Governor Ronald Reagan and Senator George Murphy—neither of whom had great support in the Peninsula.)

It was only after his first election that McCloskey became known as an ultra-liberal Republican. And that was really only because of his views on the war; on economic issues he has tended to reflect the caution of his upper income constituents and their aversion to organized labor. Even his opposition to the Vietnam war came from an unlikely source: his feelings, as a decorated Marine veteran, that the war was perverting the Corps and the military generally. With a fervor that may only come from experience in battle, McCloskey argued against unnecessary war and bloodshed, and made as strong a case as was made against the Vietnam adventure.

All this was during the years when Ronald Reagan conservatives dominated California's Republican Party. They opposed McCloskey in primary after primary, holding him to 53% in 1968, 60% in 1970, 44% in 1972 (against two opponents) and 50% in 1974. In 1972 McCloskey ran for president against Richard Nixon, receiving microscopically less than his goal of 20% in New Hampshire and dropping out of the race in time to run again in California. In 1973 McCloskey considered switching parties, as his friend Donald Riegle did. But he decided to stay a

Republican, and was helped when then Vice President Gerald Ford came out to campaign for him in the 1974 primary.

McCloskey has reason to feel much more comfortable in the Republican Party today. He believes strongly in the free market economic system, and has no problem supporting Republican positions like deregulation of natural gas or the Kemp-Roth bill. Much of his legislative effort has been concentrated on the Merchant Marine and Fisheries Committee, on which he became ranking Republican in 1979. McCloskey opposes efforts to subsidize the U.S. shipping industry—the primary business of the Committee—and he successfully led efforts in 1977 to kill the bill requiring that 9.5% of oil imported into the U.S. be shipped in U.S. carriers. McCloskey was able to get most Republicans and many younger Democrats on his side; against him was organized labor and the maritime unions and companies. McCloskey gets about 50% voting records from labor and liberal groups—far higher than the average Republican, but low enough to suggest that he is by no means a Democrat-in-disguise.

After all the turbulence and expense of his earlier campaigns, this must seem an easier time for McCloskey. He had no primary opposition in 1976 and beat another Republican easily in 1978. A Democrat spent substantial time and money against him in 1976 and won only 32% of the vote; McCloskey won even more easily in 1978. The 12th is just about evenly split in presidential contests—it gave Richard Nixon in 1972 and Gerald Ford in 1976 the same 53%—but it seems to be utterly safe for McCloskey for the foreseeable future.

Census Data Pop. 463,161. Central city, 3%; suburban, 97%. Median family income, $13,418; families above $15,000: 41%; families below $3,000: 5%. Median years education, 12.8.

The Voters

Median voting age 40.
Employment profile White collar, 65%. Blue collar, 24%. Service, 10%. Farm, 1%.
Ethnic groups Black, 4%. Japanese, 1%. Chinese, 1%. Spanish, 11%. Total foreign stock, 25%. Canada, UK, Germany, Italy, 2% each.

Presidential vote

1976	Carter (D)	89,818	(47%)
	Ford (R)	103,233	(53%)
1972	Nixon (R)	103,806	(53%)
	McGovern (D)	93,176	(47%)

Rep. Paul N. McCloskey, Jr. (R) Elected Dec. 12, 1967; b. Sept. 29, 1927, San Bernardino; home, Portola Valley; Occidental Col., Cal. Inst. of Tech., 1945–46, Stanford U., B.A. 1950, LL.B. 1953; Presbyterian.

Career Navy, 1945–47; USMC, Korea; Deputy Dist. Atty., Alameda Co., 1953–54; Practicing atty., 1955–67.

Offices 205 CHOB, 202-225-5411. Also 305 Grant Ave., Palo Alto 94306, 415-326-7383.

Committees *Government Operations* (5th). Subcommittees: Environment, Energy, and Natural Resources.

Merchant Marine and Fisheries (Ranking Member).

Group Ratings

	ADA	COPE	PC	RPN	NFU	LCV	CFA	NAB	NSI	ACA	NTU
1978	65	58	53	100	50	–	36	56	14	32	–
1977	55	55	58	100	64	74	35	–	–	21	24
1976	45	35	51	94	67	75	27	50	30	27	55

Key Votes

1) Increase Def Spnd	AGN	6) Alaska Lands Protect	DNV	11) Delay Auto Pol Cntrl	AGN
2) B-1 Bomber	AGN	7) Water Projects Veto	FOR	12) Sugar Price Escalator	FOR
3) Cargo Preference	AGN	8) Consum Protect Agcy	FOR	13) Pub Fin Cong Cmpgns	FOR
4) Dereg Nat Gas	FOR	9) Common Situs Picket	FOR	14) ERA Ratif Recissn	AGN
5) Kemp-Roth	FOR	10) Labor Law Revision	FOR	15) Prohibt Govt Abrtns	AGN

Election Results

1978 general	Paul N. McCloskey, Jr. (R)	116,982	(77%)	($56,144)
	Kirsten Olsen (D)	34,472	(23%)	($54,203)
1978 primary	Paul N. McCloskey, Jr. (R)	47,801	(76%)	
	Joseph A. Zingale (R)	14,992	(24%)	
1976 general	Paul N. McCloskey, Jr. (R)	130,332	(68%)	($104,183)
	David Harris (D)	61,526	(32%)	($158,043)

THIRTEENTH DISTRICT

Twenty years ago, what now is the 13th congressional district of California was for the most part acres of vineyards and fruit orchards below the mountains of the Coast Range near San Jose. This was one of the richest agricultural areas in the country, but it was also directly in the path of some of the most explosive suburban growth the nation has ever seen. Santa Clara County, which includes San Jose and the 13th district, grew from 290,000 people in 1950 to 1,064,000 in 1970. In the 1960s alone the 13th district just about doubled in population—a rate of growth exceeded by only four other congressional districts in the United States.

Today the vineyards are almost all gone, their owners having prudently recultivated the grapes in more remote places before selling the land to developers. There is still some agriculture in the southern part of the district, but the 13th is now almost entirely suburban in character. The wealthier suburbs, as usual in California, are those higher up in the hills; here, Cupertino, Saratoga, Monte Sereno, and Los Gatos. Most of the district's population, 60%, lives in San Jose, technically a central city, but about as suburban in aspect as one could want: a vast, prosperous area of shopping centers and stucco homes, virtually all of them built in the last 20 years.

Ironically, the Congressman from this fast growing suburban district is the former Mayor of San Jose, who finally insisted that the process of growth had to take second place to the process of orderly planning. When Norman Mineta was elected Mayor in 1971, San Jose had grown from a small city of 95,000 in 1950 to a sprawling set of subdivisions of 445,000 in 1970. So rapid had been the growth that the city itself had difficulty maintaining, from day to day, a map which showed accurately all the streets that had been carved out by developers. Mineta said, in effect, "Enough," and pushed for zoning which would slow development to a pace that would allow the city to pay for the increased services new residents would require.

Mineta's policy was popular in San Jose, and in 1974, when Republican Congressman Charles Gubser decided to retire, Mineta was an obvious candidate. Gubser had been easily the most conservative member of the San Francisco Bay area delegation, a Republican who enjoyed baiting Pete McCloskey for his apostasy, a member of the Armed Services Committee who believed, and advanced his beliefs with some acerbity, in a large defense budget and most Pentagon policies. The Republicans ran a moderate former assemblyman, but this was the Watergate year, and Mineta won easily.

In Washington Mineta is recognized as one of the more promising members of the freshman class of 1974. He has high ratings from liberal and labor organizations, but he has chosen to concentrate on issues which have not historically attracted the attention of crusading Democrats. One of these is airline deregulation, which he has supported on the Public Works Aviation Subcommittee. Another is sunset legislation, which would require Congress to reauthorize federal programs or to let them die; he is one of the House's leading sponsors of this measure. The esteem in which he is held in Washington is shown by his seats on the Permanent Intelligence Committee and on the Budget Committee. On the latter he has concentrated less on expanding federal spending programs than on controlling them.

Mineta won reelection with more than two-thirds of the vote in 1976, running more than 20% ahead of Jimmy Carter. In 1978, the year of Proposition 13 in California, his percentage fell but is still high enough to keep him out of the marginal class.

Census Data Pop. 466,988. Central city, 58%; suburban, 42%. Median family income, $12,972; families above $15,000: 37%; families below $3,000: 5%. Median years education, 12.7.

The Voters

Median voting age 38.
Employment profile White collar, 60%. Blue collar, 29%. Service, 10%. Farm, 1%.
Ethnic groups Black, 1%. Japanese, 1%. Spanish, 16%. Total foreign stock, 22%. Italy, 3%; Canada, UK, Germany, 2% each.

Presidential vote

1976	Carter (D)	91,620	(46%)
	Ford (R)	108,664	(54%)
1972	Nixon (R)	109,760	(58%)
	McGovern (D)	81,125	(42%)

Rep. Norman Y. Mineta (D) Elected 1974; b. Nov. 12, 1931, San Jose; home, San Jose; U. of Cal., B.S. 1953.

Career Army, 1953–56; Owner/Agent, Mineta Ins. Agency; San Jose City Cncl., 1967–71, Vice Mayor, 1968–71, Mayor, 1971–74.

Offices 313 CHOB, 202-225-2631. Also Golden Pacific Ctr., 1245 S. Winchester Blvd., Suite 310, San Jose 95128, 408-984-6045.

Committees *Budget* (8th). Subcommittees: State and Local Government; Budget Process (Chairman).

Public Works and Transportation (8th). Subcommittees: Aviation; Oversight and Review (Chairman); Surface Transportation.

Group Ratings

	ADA	COPE	PC	RPN	NFU	LCV	CFA	NAB	NSI	ACA	NTU
1978	80	84	65	42	60	–	59	8	20	4	–
1977	80	87	70	46	75	73	65	–	–	4	21
1976	95	82	85	44	75	91	82	0	10	0	31

Key Votes

1) Increase Def Spnd	AGN	6) Alaska Lands Protect	FOR	11) Delay Auto Pol Cntrl	AGN
2) B-1 Bomber	AGN	7) Water Projects Veto	AGN	12) Sugar Price Escalator	FOR
3) Cargo Preference	AGN	8) Consum Protect Agcy	FOR	13) Pub Fin Cong Cmpgns	FOR
4) Dereg Nat Gas	AGN	9) Common Situs Picket	FOR	14) ERA Ratif Recissn	AGN
5) Kemp-Roth	AGN	10) Labor Law Revision	FOR	15) Prohibt Govt Abrtns	AGN

Election Results

1978 general	Norman Y. Mineta (D)	100,809	(59%)	($176,628)
	Dan O'Keefe (R)	69,306	(41%)	($54,741)
1978 primary	Norman Y. Mineta (D), unopposed			
1976 general	Norman Y. Mineta (D)	135,291	(68%)	($187,068)
	Ernest L. Konnyu (R)	63,130	(32%)	($59,413)

FOURTEENTH DISTRICT

The 14th congressional district of California occupies a portion of the state's Central Valley, probably the world's most productive farmland. Only 50 miles from San Francisco Bay, the 14th is cut off from that cosmopolitan influence and, politically at least, the district is almost part of another world. The prosperity of the cities here, the most notable of which is Stockton, is rooted firmly in agriculture. The farms of the area—the district goes as far north in the Valley as the suburbs of Sacramento and as far south as Stanislaus County around Modesto—are not as often in the hands of the huge conglomerates as those in the southern reaches of the Valley. Many rather small, family-owned farms still exist in the 14th, on either side of the string of medium-sized cities along the Route 99 freeway. The district has a fair amount of industry, but agriculture is king.

Above the Valley, sometimes visible in the far distance, rises the Sierra Nevada, and the 14th has its share of the Mother Lode country and the mountains, going as far as Yosemite and Lake Tahoe. This area is underpopulated and of little significance politically; its importance is economic. Ordinarily, except in years of drought, these mountains shed their snows down numerous rivers whose waters, carefully apportioned, irrigate the thirsty farms of the Valley.

The political traditions of the Valley are Democratic—the result of the politics of some of its initial settlers from the South; of the great depression; and, to an unknown extent, of the Democratic politics of the McClatchy newspapers that dominate Valley journalism from Sacramento to Fresno. But while the Valley may be as Democratic as the San Francisco Bay area in partisan elections, it is by no means as liberal in its attitudes on social questions. These are measured with nice precision by the plethora of referenda on the California ballot. In 1978, for example, the Valley was evenly divided on the proposition, which was defeated, to bar homosexuals from teaching in schools; the Bay area, in contrast, voted 65% against. In the past the Valley has been the part of the state strongest for capital punishment, against coastal preservation, and against legalization of marijuana.

The 14th is currently represented by a Republican, as a direct result of the Koreagate scandal. For 22 years this district had been the political property of John McFall. A Democrat of moderate political tendencies, McFall had been Chairman of the Transportation Appropriations Subcommittee and in that capacity had been able to funnel much federal money to the district. McFall had also been appointed House Majority Whip by Speaker Albert and Majority Leader O'Neill after the 1972 elections. But his kind of politics was not what the newer generation of Democrats wanted. When the majority leadership was open after the 1976 elections, McFall ran but was only able to get 31 votes in the caucus.

McFall was hurt in that contest by what helped defeat him in the 1978 campaign: the revelation that in 1974 he had received $3,000 from Tongsun Park, had deposited it in his office account, and had later used it for personal business. In October 1978 the House Ethics Committee recommended that McFall be reprimanded for that, and he was—by the House and the voters as well.

For McFall's problems had attracted strong Republican opposition. The winner of the six-candidate Republican primary, Norman Shumway, had been elected twice to the board of supervisors in San Joaquin County, which includes Stockton and a majority of the 14th district's voters. His campaign was well financed by national Republican sources, who saw a good chance to win a seat they might otherwise never have a shot at. Shumway ran just behind McFall in San Joaquin County. But in the rest of the district he ran ahead and won by a convincing margin. For the 96th Congress Shumway can be counted on to try to use the advantages of incumbency to make this ordinarily Democratic territory into a safe Republican House seat.

Census Data Pop. 464,656. Central city, 23%; suburban, 56%. Median family income, $9,348; families above $15,000: 18%; families below $3,000: 10%. Median years education, 12.1.

The Voters

Median voting age 44.
Employment profile White collar, 44%. Blue collar, 33%. Service, 14%. Farm, 9%.
Ethnic groups Black, 4%. Filipino, 2–. Spanish, 15%. Total foreign stock, 23%. Italy, 2%; Canada, UK, Germany, USSR, 1% each.

Presidential vote

1976	Carter (D)	92,328	(50%)
	Ford (R)	92,163	(50%)
1972	Nixon (R)	103,566	(58%)
	McGovern (D)	75,662	(42%)

Rep. Norman D. Shumway (R) Elected 1978; b. July 28, 1934, Phoenix, Ariz.; home, Stockton; U. of Utah, B.S. 1960, Hastings Col. of Law, J.D. 1963; Church of Latter Day Saints.

Career Practicing atty., 1964–74; San Joaquin Co. Bd. of Supervisors, 1974–78, Chmn., 1978.

Offices 1228 LHOB, 202-225-2511. Also 1045 N. El Dorado, Stockton 95202, 209-464-7612.

Committees *Banking, Finance, and Urban Affairs* (12th). Subcommittees: Economic Stabilization; International Development Institutions and Finance; International Trade, Investment and Monetary Policy.

Group Ratings: Newly Elected

Key Votes: Newly Elected

Election Results

1978 general	Norman D. Shumway (R)	95,962	(56%)	($251,948)
	John J. McFall (D)	76,602	(44%)	($240,114)
1978 primary	Norman D. Shumway (R)	21,508	(37%)	
	James W. Pinkerton, Jr. (R)	12,278	(21%)	($45,132)
	Fred Van Dyke (R)	10,438	(18%)	($8,673)
	Four others (R)	13,286	(23%)	
1976 general	John J. McFall (D)	123,285	(73%)	($91,239)
	Roger A. Blain (R)	46,674	(27%)	($11,909)

FIFTEENTH DISTRICT

The 15th district of California is another Central Valley district, one of two dominated by the city and county of Fresno. Except for Sacramento, this is the part of the Valley that has most steadily maintained Democratic leanings. One reason is the large (21%) Mexican-American population here, the largest in the Valley except for the next door 17th district. The chicanos here are not migrants who pass through; they are often middle class citizens with roots in their communities—and they vote. Moreover, the Fresno area has a more heterogeneous population than many parts of the Valley. There are especially large numbers of Armenian-Americans, like novelist William Saroyan, who grew up and lives in Fresno. Another large group is made up of descendants of the original Okies, the people who left the dried-out fields of Oklahoma, Kansas, and Texas during the 1930s in search of the promised land of California. Here as John Steinbeck chronicled in *The Grapes of Wrath* these poor white people did backbreaking work in steamy hot fields for next to nothing and lived in miserable labor camps. Ironically their sons and daughters are not particularly sympathetic—often are downright hostile—to the very similar plight of Mexican-Americans in the same fields today.

The representation the 15th district has had in the last generation mirrors its sociologic background. From 1954 to 1978 its Congressman was B. F. Sisk, a Democrat who grew up on the dusty plains of central Texas and moved to the Valley in 1937. In Congress Sisk worked closely with the big landowners and pushed farm labor laws opposed by Cesar Chavez's United Farm Workers. With a seat on the Rules Committee, Sisk had considerable influence in the House. He also had leadership ambitions, which were finally squelched when Phil Burton of San Francisco beat him for the chair of the Democratic Steering Committee, 162–111, in 1974. Sisk had the support of most Southerners and many oldtimers, but Burton had most of the votes of the incoming freshmen.

In his last years in the House Sisk seemed to concentrate on the not yet successful campaign to get a major league baseball team back in Washington. But he had one other achievement that few members can boast of: he was able to hand-pick his successor. His choice was his longtime administrative assistant, 36-year-old Tony Coelho. Coelho's own district roots and campaigning ability, combined with Sisk's clout, were enough to give him 79% against a weak primary opponent. In the general election the Democratic label helped Coelho here. The Republican nominee, former Air Force and stunt pilot Chris Patterakis, had enough home town celebrity in the Modesto area for a lead there, but Coelho carried strongly enough elsewhere to get 60% of the vote district-wide. Coelho won a seat on the Agriculture Committee, which is of course of great importance here. He seems likely to have Sisk's long tenure, though he reportedly is closer to the attitudes of the younger Democrats on many issues.

Census Data Pop. 465,631. Central city, 34%; suburban, 33%. Median family income, $7,930; families above $15,000: 14%; families below $3,000: 13%. Median years education, 11.8.

The Voters

Median voting age 43.
Employment profile White collar, 43%. Blue collar, 31%. Service, 14%. Farm, 12%.
Ethnic groups Black, 6%. Spanish, 21%. Total foreign stock, 21%. Germany, 2%; Canada, USSR, 1% each.

Presidential vote

1976	Carter (D)	81,797	(55%)
	Ford (R)	66,972	(45%)
1972	Nixon (R)	77,992	(51%)
	McGovern (D)	76,038	(49%)

Rep. Tony Coelho (D) Elected 1978; b. June 15, 1942, Los Banos; home, Merced; Loyola U., L.A., B.A. 1964; Catholic.

Career Staff of U.S. Rep. B.F. Sisk, 1965–78, Admin. Asst., 1970–78.

Offices 216 LHOB, 202-225-6131. Also Fed. Bldg., 415 W. 18th St., Merced 95340, 209-383-4455.

Committees *Agriculture* (23d). Subcommittees: Cotton; Dairy and Poultry; Forests.

Veterans' Affairs (19th). Subcommittees: Medical Facilities and Benefits; Compensation, Pension, Insurance and Memorial Affairs.

Group Ratings: Newly Elected

Key Votes: Newly Elected

Election Results

1978 general	Tony Coelho (D)	75,212	(60%)	($266,094)
	Chris Patterakis (R)	49,914	(40%)	($104,164)
1978 primary	Tony Coelho (D)	48,253	(79%)	
	One other (D)	12,926	(21%)	
1976 general	B. F. Sisk (D)	92,735	(72%)	($64,099)
	Carol Harner (R)	35,700	(28%)	($4,656)

SIXTEENTH DISTRICT

The 16th congressional district of California boasts some of the nation's most spectacular scenery, from the Monterey cypresses at Carmel's Pebble Beach, through the mountainous wild Big Sur coast, to William Randolph Hearst's San Simeon. Just a few miles from the ocean is some of the nation's richest farmland: the lettuce fields of the Salinas valley, the artichoke fields around Castroville. This is John Steinbeck country: he grew up in Salinas, and the Cannery Row he described in Monterey still exists, even if only as a tourist attraction.

The coastal counties over the years have tended to vote Republican. Landowners around Salinas and retirees in Santa Cruz and the Monterey peninsula tend to be conservative; the district's Mexican-Americans and its sprinklings of artists and writers are far outnumbered. But in the last decade, the 16th has moved noticeably to the left. A large part of the reason is the impact of environmental issues. It can be argued that there is no environment in America more worthy of protection, and people here have the examples of Los Angeles and the San Francisco Bay area to show what can happen. In addition, this district has an unusual number of students, more than 8% of the eligible electorate; those at the University of California's Santa Cruz branch are so liberal (97% for McGovern in 1972) that they have changed the voting balance of the whole county. Finally there seems to have been a notable generational change here, even more pronounced than in the state as a whole. The old electorate that went for Ronald Reagan in 1966 and Richard Nixon in 1968 is to a considerable extent gone, replaced by a group of voters for whom those men and those who followed them represent the enemy.

The movement left has been reflected in the representation of the district. In the sixties this was a safe seat for Republican Burt Talcott, a man so strait-laced that he made a speech chiding his colleagues for wearing sport coats on the House floor—too informal. Talcott was a faithful follower of the Nixon Administration, and his record on environmental issues got him put on the Dirty Dozen list. In 1972 and 1974 he was nearly beaten by a Mexican-American candidate, and in 1976 he was beaten conclusively.

The winner was Leon Panetta, a former Republican who resigned as head of the Office of Civil Rights of HEW in 1970, charging that the Nixon Administration was sacrificing school desegregation to its Southern strategy. Panetta, who had grown up in the district, changed his party registration to Democratic and returned; after the 1974 election he was determined to run. He capitalized ably on the favorable trends in the district, and at the same time avoided antagonizing local agricultural interests and shunned a United Farm Workers initiative that was on the ballot. Panetta has been one of those congressmen who pays incredibly close attention to his district, constantly attending meetings, bringing in disaster relief money, getting rid of a sand drift, and helping local sugar beet farmers.

Panetta has used his seat on the House Agriculture Committee to good advantage. And in 1979 he won a seat on the prestigious Budget Committee—which could very well be a political asset at a time when voters are demanding some control over federal spending and programs.

In 1978, Panetta was opposed by a former John Birch Society member, and won reelection with an impressive 61%. While he probably could not have done so well against a stronger candidate, it was nonetheless a performance that suggests that Panetta should remain in Congress for some time.

Census Data Pop. 465,345. Central city, 18%; suburban, 35%. Median family income, $9,384; families above $15,000: 20%; families below $3,000: 10%. Median years education, 12.4.

The Voters

Median voting age 40.
Employment profile White collar, 47%. Blue collar, 28%. Service, 16%. Farm, 9%.
Ethnic groups Black, 3%. Filipino, 2%. Spanish, 18%. Total foreign stock, 25%. Canada, UK, Germany, Italy, 2% each.

Presidential vote

1976	Carter (D)	95,482	(50%)
	Ford (R)	97,003	(50%)
1972	Nixon (R)	106,134	(56%)
	McGovern (D)	82,492	(44%)

Rep. Leon E. Panetta (D) Elected 1976; b. June 28, 1938, Monterey; home, Carmel Valley; U. of Santa Clara, B.A. 1960, J.D. 1963; Catholic.

Career Army, 1964–66; Legis. Asst. to U.S. Sen. Thomas Kuchel, 1966–69; Dir., U.S. Ofc. of Civil Rights, H.E.W., 1969–70; Exec. Asst. to the Mayor of New York City, 1970–71; Practicing atty., 1971–76.

Offices 431 CHDB, 202-225-2861. Also 380 Alvarado, Monterey 93940, 408-649-3555.

Committees *Agriculture* (17th). Subcommittees: Conservation and Credit; Domestic Marketing, Consumer Relations, and Nutrition; Family Farms, Rural Development, and Special Studies.

Budget (14th). Subcommittees; Legislative Savings Task Force; Regulations and Spending Limitations Task Force.

Group Ratings

	ADA	COPE	PC	RPN	NFU	LCV	CFA	NAB	NSI	ACA	NTU
1978	50	63	75	36	30	–	36	58	10	50	–
1977	75	70	70	58	83	75	45	–	–	36	34

Key Votes

1) Increase Def Spnd	AGN	6) Alaska Lands Protect	FOR	11) Delay Auto Pol Cntrl	AGN
2) B-1 Bomber	AGN	7) Water Projects Veto	FOR	12) Sugar Price Escalator	DNV
3) Cargo Preference	AGN	8) Consum Protect Agcy	AGN	13) Pub Fin Cong Cmpgns	FOR
4) Dereg Nat Gas	AGN	9) Common Situs Picket	FOR	14) ERA Ratif Recissn	AGN
5) Kemp-Roth	AGN	10) Labor Law Revision	FOR	15) Prohibt Govt Abrtns	AGN

Election Results

1978 general	Leon E. Panetta (D)	104,550	(61%)	($219,357)
	Eric Seastrand (R)	65,808	(39%)	($184,169)
1978 primary	Leon E. Panetta (D), unopposed			
1976 general	Leon E. Panetta (D)	104,545	(53%)	($181,410)
	Burt Talcott (R)	91,160	(47%)	($217,053)

SEVENTEENTH DISTRICT

The richest agricultural land in the United States lies in the southern part of California's Central Valley. The variety of crops grown here is impressive: grapes, cotton, alfalfa, cantaloupes, plums, peaches, lima beans, tomatoes, sugar beets, walnuts, olives, poultry, and dairy products. Fresno County each year produces the largest dollar volume of agricultural products in the United States, but other Valley counties are not far behind. This bounteous production is made possible by vast systems of irrigation, for a little more than a century ago nothing was grown here at all.

Agriculture is naturally the central subject of politics in the Central Valley. It was the politicians who built the irrigation systems and still control the critical price of water. Politicians decide on what basis farmworkers can bargain for their wages. And politicians tend to determine the support prices or conditions of sale of many of the products grown in the Valley.

This kind of politics tends to cross party lines, a fact pretty clearly shown by the history of representation of the 17th congressional district of California. In partisan terms, this has proved to be a volatile district. Its current boundaries cross the imaginary line halfway between Fresno and Bakersfield which separates traditional Democratic and traditional Republican territory. Three times in the past 12 years the district has defeated its incumbent congressman—an unusual record in an era when most incumbents are reelected easily. Yet all three followed roughly similar policies on agricultural issues, just as all three made a point of serving on the House Agriculture Committee.

The first of these incumbents to be defeated was Harlan Hagen, who lost in 1966. Hagen worked for the interests of the large growers here, and was anything but a supporter of the United Farm Workers, which began strikes in this area as early as 1965. But he was caught up in the enthusiasm for Ronald Reagan and the strong local following of his Republican opponent. That was Bob Mathias, known internationally as the winner of the Olympic gold medal in the Decathlon in 1948 and 1952. A native of Tulare County, Mathias was affable, attractive, and conservative. Even more than Hagen, he was supportive of the district's major agricultural interests.

Mathias, too, ultimately found himself in political trouble. He suffered particularly from a redistricting, which added much of Democratic Fresno County to the district for the 1974 election. His opponent that year was a member of the Fresno Board of Supervisors, John Krebs. An immigrant from Germany with a Kissingerian accent, Krebs was well known locally as an advocate of planned growth. He beat Mathias by a wide margin, and proceeded to service on the Agriculture Committee himself.

Krebs's tenure in the House lasted only half as long as Mathias's. He was reelected easily in 1976, and seemed to be tending satisfactorily to district interests. But in 1978 he was upset by Republican Chip Pashayan. A native of Fresno of Armenian descent, Pashayan was able to cut Krebs's home town majority to almost nothing, and he won big in Republican Tulare County. Pashayan attacked Krebs as a big spender and for his opposition to the Mineral King resort complex in the nearby Sierras. Krebs may also have been hurt by the fact that it takes a long time to commute by air from Washington to Fresno, and in a day when constituents increasingly expect to see their congressman in person, that can make for higher than average turnover in a district like this. In any case, Pashayan can be expected not to vary substantially from the agricultural policies of his predecessors. The question is whether he can hold on to this increasingly difficult district.

Census Data Pop. 465,492. Central city, 14%; suburban, 35%. Median family income, $8,672; families above $15,000: 17%; families below $3,000: 11%. Median years education, 12.1.

The Voters

Median voting age 41.
Employment profile White collar, 46%. Blue collar, 28%. Service, 12%. Farm, 14%.
Ethnic groups Black, 2%. Japanese, 1%. Spanish, 24%. Total foreign stock, 23%. USSR, 2%; Canada, 1%.

Presidential vote

1976	Carter (D)	75,605	(46%)
	Ford (R)	87,145	(54%)
1972	Nixon (R)	91,629	(58%)
	McGovern (D)	65,907	(42%)

Rep. Charles Pashayan, Jr. (R) Elected 1978; b. Mar. 27, 1941, Fresno; home, Fresno; Pomona Col., B.A. 1963, U. of Cal., J.D. 1968, Oxford U., B. Litt. 1977; Episcopalian.

Career Army, 1968–70; Practicing atty., 1969–; Spec. Asst. to Gen. Counsel, U.S. Dept. of H.E.W., 1973–75.

Offices 1427 LHOB, 202-225-3341. Also 4114 Fed. Bldg., 1130 "O" St., Fresno 93721, 209-487-5487.

Committees *Interior and Insular Affairs* (12th). Subcommittees: Water and Power Resources; Public Lands; National Parks and Insular Affairs.

Post Office and Civil Service (7th). Subcommittees: Civil Service; Census and Population.

Group Ratings: Newly Elected

Key Votes: Newly Elected

Election Results

1978 general	Charles Pashayan, Jr. (R)	81,296	(54%)	($260,412)
	John Krebs (D)	67,885	(46%)	($156,932)
1978 primary	Charles Pashayan, Jr. (R)	32,696	(65%)	
	Lee Mirigian (R)	17,605	(35%)	($10,164)
1976 general	John Krebs (D)	103,898	(66%)	($69,800)
	Henry J. Andreas (R)	54,270	(34%)	($23,585)

EIGHTEENTH DISTRICT

The Central Valley of California stands out clearly on a relief map—a swatch of green down the central part of the state, from up near Oregon to a point only 100 miles north of Los Angeles, the green surrounded by the yellow and brown of the Coast Range and the Sierra Nevada. These flat, vast, heavily irrigated plains are probably the world's most productive farmland. The prosperity of the Central Valley has been built on the drive of agricultural entrepreneurs and the backs of migrant laborers. In the 1930s the workers were Okies forced off their land by swirling dust storms. Today they are mainly Mexican-Americans (including some who have come across the border illegally). Both groups started off with Democratic voting habits—to the extent that migrant workers vote at all. But underlying the common Democratic registration of the thirties migrants and the chicanos is a basic economic question: how shall the profits of the land be distributed?

The descendants of the Okies and others whose ancestors were more fortunate believe that the demands of today's farm workers, especially Cesar Chavez's United Farm Workers, will diminish the Anglos' share of the pie. For everyone in the Valley partakes of the profits of big farming, and nobody in the Valley thinks that the big companies that dominate agribusiness will absorb any losses caused by higher wages or better working conditions. So the politics in much of the Central Valley has come down to a conflict between the growers and the farm laborers, with the vast majority on the side of the growers. You could have seen the same thing in the thirties in towns dominated by the auto or steel industries: the only voters who supported the demands of the workers were the workers themselves.

In California so much was never plainer than in 1976, when the UFW placed Proposition 14 on the ballot. This was a measure to continue fully the compromise agricultural labor relations bill worked out by the UFW, the Teamsters, the growers, and Governor Jerry Brown—with a couple of changes in the rules. One feature of 14 seized upon by opponents was a provision that union organizers could conduct their drives on the property of the growers, which ads likened to the prospect of a homeowner having his property invaded by unwanted demonstrators. The result was unequivocal: Proposition 14 got only one out of three votes statewide, and in the Central Valley south from Sacramento 80% voted against it.

This kind of feeling is especially intense in Kern County around Bakersfield, which forms the heart of California's 18th congressional district. Kern is the southern end of the Valley and also the direct western terminus of the road from Oklahoma. It has an especially large number of descendants of the Dust Bowl migrants of the thirties and more than an average number of Mexican-American farm workers: Kern County is the home of country singer Merle Haggard and the headquarters of Chavez's UFW. It was here that Chavez's first epic strike and boycott took place, against table grape producers in Delano, a dusty town some 25 miles north of Bakersfield, back in 1965. That was happening just as Kern County was trending strongly toward the Republicans, despite Democratic traditions and a heavy Democratic registration.

This area has had several congressmen, all conservative Republicans, in the last dozen years. The first was Bob Mathias, whose territory was gradually shifted north until he lost in 1974, from having too much of Democratic Fresno in his district. The second was William Ketchum, who was originally from Paso Robles near the coast; he was elected here in 1972 and moved his residence to Bakersfield in 1974. He seemed in good shape for reelection when he died suddenly of a heart attack in the summer of 1978.

To replace him on the ticket, the Republicans nominated Bakersfield Assemblyman Bill Thomas, who had won his office as a strong backer of capital punishment. Thomas stressed defense and economy issues and promised to represent the district in Ketchum's tradition. On the district's ethnic balance, he once said that "Kern County has a vested interest in keeping people where they are, especially racially." The Democrat, Bob Sogge, who had managed a nearly successful challenge to Ketchum in 1974, tried also to strike a conservative note. But Thomas, better known and better financed, won easily with 59% of the vote. With a good margin and a seat on the Agriculture Committee, he appears to have a good chance to make the 18th a safe seat.

Census Data Pop. 463,813. Central city, 15%; suburban, 77%. Median family income, $9,300; families above $15,000: 19%; families below $3,000: 11%. Median years education, 12.1.

The Voters

Median voting age 42.
Employment profile White collar, 44%. Blue collar, 32%. Service, 14%. Farm, 10%.
Ethnic groups Black, 5%. Spanish, 15%. Total foreign stock, 15%. Canada, UK, 1% each.

Presidential vote

1976	Carter (D)	70,093	(44%)
	Ford (R)	89,166	(56%)
1972	Nixon (R)	105,941	(66%)
	McGovern (D)	55,207	(34%)

Rep. William M. Thomas (R) Elected 1978; b. Dec. 6, 1941, Wallace, Idaho; home, Bakersfield; Santa Ana Community Col., San Fran. St. U., B.A., M.A. 1965; Conservative Baptist.

Career Prof., Bakersfield Community Col., 1965–74; Cal. Assembly, 1974–78.

Offices 324 CHOB, 202-225-2915. Also 800 Truxtun, Bakersfield 93301, 805-323-8322.

Committees *Agriculture* (15th). Subcommittees: Cotton; Oilseeds and Rice; Family Farms, Rural Development, and Special Studies.

Standards of Official Conduct (4th).

Group Ratings: Newly Elected

Key Votes: Newly Elected

Election Results

1978 general	William Thomas (R)	85,663	(59%)	($166,534)
	Bob Sogge (D)	58,900	(41%)	($142,280)
1978 primary	William M. Ketchum (R), unopposed			($66,359)
1976 general	William M. Ketchum (R)	101,658	(64%)	($104,003)
	Dean Close (D)	56,683	(36%)	($39,971)

NINETEENTH DISTRICT

There are still parts of California which can make you understand what brought so many people—retirees, young families, hoboes, millionaires—out here 30 or 40 years ago: the soft climate, the mountains falling into the sea, the peaceful small towns, and the well-ordered smogless cities. One such area is the part of the state within the bounds of the 19th congressional district, which includes Santa Barbara County, much of Ventura County to the east, and a small part of San Luis Obispo County to the north. The Coast Range is as rugged, the Pacific as blue and warm, the towns—despite recent heavy growth—as pristine as any place on the coast.

This is also, for mystery fans, Ross Macdonald land. Macdonald lives here, in Santa Barbara, and most of his novels are set here or in other thinly disguised towns between here and Los Angeles. In one of the most recent, *Sleeping Beauty,* Macdonald weaves the story around the famous Santa Barbara oil spill of 1969. The Interior Department had been allowing offshore oil drilling in the Santa Barbara Channel; something went wrong with the apparatus; oil gushed out, covering the beaches, destroying the birds, fouling the air. It was an incident which radicalized wealthy retirees and politicized young students—and, it can be argued, permanently shoved the Santa Barbara community at least a couple of notches leftward.

That shift in opinion had little effect at first in local elections. The then Congressman, Republican Charles Teague, a member of the family that started the Sunkist combine, was reelected easily until his death in 1973. But in elections for state Assembly and Senate and in statewide contests Ventura and particularly Santa Barbara Counties were voting increasingly for Democrats—and indeed still are today. And even the Republicans who continue to win make considerable concessions to environmental positions.

Which has been the case with the district's current Congressman, Robert Lagomarsino. To win the seat, he had to win a special election early in the Watergate year of 1974; and as it turned out he was just about the only Republican anywhere in the nation to do so. He had some special advantages. Under California law anyone who wins 50% in a special election primary wins the seat automatically, and in the 19th Lagomarsino was the only significant Republican running, while the Democratic opposition was split between several little known candidates. Lagomarsino had the advantage of having represented the Santa Barbara and Ventura Counties in the state Senate since 1960; he had a reasonably good environmental record; and he made a point of saying that he would not support Richard Nixon and might even vote for impeachment. He won 53% in the primary, enough to win the seat; and he has held it ever since. A member of the Interior and Foreign Affairs Committees, he is more liberal on environmental matters than on either foreign policy or economic issues. These stands seem entirely acceptable to the 19th district, and he has won reelection with increasingly large percentages.

Census Data Pop. 465,095. Central city, 42%; suburban, 52%. Median family income, $10,241; families above $15,000: 24%; families below $3,000: 8%. Median years education, 12.5.

The Voters

Median voting age 40.
Employment profile White collar, 52%. Blue collar, 29%. Service, 14%. Farm, 5%.
Ethnic groups Black, 2%. Spanish, 20%. Total foreign stock, 24%. Canada, UK, Germany, 2% each.

Presidential vote

1976	Carter (D)	95,297	(49%)
	Ford (R)	98,614	(51%)
1972	Nixon (R)	110,267	(58%)
	McGovern (D)	79,671	(42%)

Rep. Robert J. Lagomarsino (R) Elected Mar. 5, 1974; b. Sept. 4, 1926, Ventura; home, Ventura; U. of Cal. at Santa Barbara, B.A. 1950, Santa Clara Law School LL.B. 1953.

Career Navy, WWII; Practicing atty., 1954–74; Ojia City Cncl., 1958, Mayor 1958–61; Calif. Senate, 1961–1974.

Offices 1117 LHOB, 202-225-3601. Also Studio 121, 814 State St., Santa Barbara 93102, 805-963-1708.

Committees *Interior and Insular Affairs* (7th). Subcommittees: National Parks and Insular Affairs;Oversight/Special Investigations; Pacific Affairs.

Foreign Affairs (8th). Subcommittees: Inter-American Affairs; International Economic Policy and Trade.

Group Ratings

	ADA	COPE	PC	RPN	NFU	LCV	CFA	NAB	NSI	ACA	NTU
1978	5	5	13	83	10	–	14	100	100	96	–
1977	0	17	25	62	33	40	10	–	–	85	41
1976	10	17	25	72	0	35	9	83	100	79	56

Key Votes

1) Increase Def Spnd	FOR	6) Alaska Lands Protect	FOR	11) Delay Auto Pol Cntrl	FOR
2) B-1 Bomber	FOR	7) Water Projects Veto	AGN	12) Sugar Price Escalator	FOR
3) Cargo Preference	AGN	8) Consum Protect Agcy	AGN	13) Pub Fin Cong Cmpgns	AGN
4) Dereg Nat Gas	FOR	9) Common Situs Picket	AGN	14) ERA Ratif Recissn	FOR
5) Kemp-Roth	FOR	10) Labor Law Revision	AGN	15) Prohibt Govt Abrtns	FOR

Election Results

1978 general	Robert J. Lagomarsino (R)	123,192	(75%)	($95,044)
	Jerome Zamos (D)	41,672	(25%)	($14,042)
1978 primary	Robert J. Lagomarsino (R), unopposed			
1976 general	Robert J. Lagomarsino (R)	124,201	(64%)	($81,808)
	Don Sisson (D)	68,722	(36%)	($39,155)

TWENTIETH DISTRICT

What is now the 20th district of California is the lineal descendant of a seat which has been redistricted so many times since its initial creation in 1962 that it contains today virtually none of ts original territory. As it is today, the 20th represents an attempt to create a political entity out of he people who have moved west from the San Fernando Valley, people trying to leapfrog the uburban sprawl of Los Angeles. Thus the district includes Malibu Beach and the rustic Topanga anyon area along the ocean beyond the city limits; it includes the towns of Newhall and Saugus bove the mountains which are the northern boundary of the San Fernando Valley; and it ncludes fast growing Ventura County suburbs like Simi Valley and Thousand Oaks (known ocally as T.O.), connected by freeway to Los Angeles, over the mountains to the east.

The 20th also contains the western edge of Los Angeles's San Fernando Valley, where about 0% of its residents live. All these varied areas have in common a political affection for the onservative right; this is the first, numerically, of those suburban California districts which sually provide large margins for conservative candidates. The 20th and its various predecessors ave had a number of different congressmen: a John Birch Society member; a Democratic ssembly veteran who ousted him and who then, disgusted with the pace of things in the House, etired; Ed Reinecke, who campaigned against obscenity, became Lieutenant Governor in 1969, nd was convicted of perjury in 1974 while running for governor; and the present incumbent, the on of Mr. Conservative, Barry Goldwater, Jr.

Young Goldwater won the seat in a 1969 special election, largely because of his name, when he vas just past 30. For a while his name was his only political asset, and he was not regarded highly n the House. But in recent years he has been both active and effective. Goldwater lobbied hard nd effectively to save the Lockheed loan legislation, and with then Congressman Ed Koch of New York worked to develop legislation to protect the privacy of citizens from the computerized ists which have proliferated in government and private business. Since Koch left the House to ecome Mayor of New York, Goldwater has become indisputably the House's leading expert on rivacy matters, and deserves much credit for the bills on these matters passed in the 95th Congress. It is a classically conservative cause; but Goldwater was the first conservative in Congress to really pursue it.

Goldwater was urged to run for the Senate in 1976 and decided not to for personal reasons. In etrospect he might have won; there is no reason to suppose him politically much weaker than S. I. Hayakawa. Some possibility exists that he would run against Sen. Alan Cranston in 1980. But gain he would be forced to give up this very safe Republican seat. His 1976 and 1978 opponent tirred up some interest. She was Patti Lear Corman, daughter of the inventor of the Lear jet and hen wife of 21st district Congressman James Corman. Corman had forbidden his wife to run, and vhen she went ahead anyway, their marriage broke up. In 1978 she ran again, this time simply as Pat Lear. But in both cases Goldwater got two-thirds of the votes.

Census Data Pop. 466,149. Central city, 42%; suburban, 58%. Median family income, $13,583; amilies above $15,000: 42%; families below $3,000: 5%. Median years education, 12.7.

The Voters

Median voting age 39.
Employment profile White collar, 62%. Blue collar, 26%. Service, 10%. Farm, 2%.
Ethnic groups Spanish, 11%. Total foreign stock, 22%. Canada, 3%; UK, Germany, Italy, 2% each; USSR, 1%.

Presidential vote

1976	Carter (D)	86,610	(40%)
	Ford (R)	129,113	(60%)
1972	Nixon (R)	132,965	(68%)
	McGovern (D)	63,588	(32%)

Rep. Barry M. Goldwater, Jr. (R) Elected Apr. 29, 1969; b. July 15, 1938 Los Angeles; home, Woodland Hills; U. of Colo., 1957–60, Ariz. St. U. B.A. 1962; Episcopalian.

Career Stock broker, 1962–69.

Offices 2240 RHOB, 202-225-4461. Also 23241 Ventura Blvd., Suite 119 Woodland Hills 91364, 213-883-1233.

Committees *Public Works and Transportation* (9th). Subcommittees Aviation; Public Buildings and Grounds.

Science and Technology (3d). Subcommittees: Energy Research and Production; Transportation, Aviation, and Communication.

Group Ratings

	ADA	COPE	PC	RPN	NFU	LCV	CFA	NAB	NSI	ACA	NTU
1978	5	0	8	73	0	–	14	100	100	100	–
1977	0	10	18	50	27	7	10	–	–	96	45
1976	5	14	11	67	10	19	9	90	100	88	63

Key Votes

1) Increase Def Spnd	FOR	6) Alaska Lands Protect	AGN	11) Delay Auto Pol Cntrl	FOR
2) B-1 Bomber	FOR	7) Water Projects Veto	AGN	12) Sugar Price Escalator	FOR
3) Cargo Preference	DNV	8) Consum Protect Agcy	AGN	13) Pub Fin Cong Cmpgns	AGN
4) Dereg Nat Gas	FOR	9) Common Situs Picket	AGN	14) ERA Ratif Recissn	FOR
5) Kemp-Roth	FOR	10) Labor Law Revision	AGN	15) Prohibt Govt Abrtns	FOR

Election Results

1978 general	Barry M. Goldwater, Jr. (R)	129,714	(66%)	($122,120)
	Pat Lear (D)	65,695	(34%)	($229,306)
1978 primary	Barry M. Goldwater, Jr. (R), unopposed			
1976 general	Barry M. Goldwater, Jr. (R)	146,158	(67%)	($109,624)
	Patti Lear Corman (D)	71,193	(33%)	($74,079)

TWENTY-FIRST DISTRICT

California's 21st congressional district is the heart of the San Fernando Valley. This vast expanse of land, surrounded on all sides by mountains, is almost entirely within the Los Angeles city limits. Annexed long ago, when it consisted of dusty fields and movie ranches—the movie Chinatown gives the details with fair accuracy—the Valley is now thoroughly filled up, but still suburban in character. The straight streets go on for mile after mile, lined by neat stucco houses or by low rise stores and offices. At major intersections there are great shopping centers. Hanging over all is the Los Angeles smog, a little less dismal here than in downtown L.A., but still a depressing part of life for those who came here looking for the Golden West.

The Valley has seen southern California's boom industries rise and fall—first agriculture, then the movie business, aerospace, and electronics. The boom and bust cycle is a common experience here, with the most notable recent bust in the early seventies, when Lockheed lost some major government contracts. As the layoffs were being announced, the Valley was hit by the earthquake of 1971, which destroyed a veterans' hospital and threatened to crack the Van Norman Dam—a catastrophe that would have destroyed the homes of some 150,000 people. A period of disillusion set in. People began talking about moving back east, and indeed this period is the beginning of the great migrations to the Rocky Mountains states of the seventies. The Valley is a happier, more confident place today: there have been no more major quakes, smog has decreased, and those who were most discontent have moved away. But the euphoric optimism of the years after World War II has not returned.

Some political observers like to use the San Fernando Valley as a kind of synonym for right wing, racist suburbia. This is not accurate: this kind of sneering started with people in the entertainment business, who live in Beverly Hills or Bel Air south of the Santa Monica Mountains when they're making lots of money and in the Valley north of the Mountains when they're not. Actually the Valley is not nearly as Republican as Orange County, nor is it so concerned about racial change as the factory suburbs southeast of Los Angeles (though a city-wide busing plan has aroused much opposition here). The Valley politically is really middle of the road. With the rise of right wing popularity in the middle sixties the Valley moved right—nearly defeating 21st district Congressman James Corman in 1964, for example. But the Valley was one of the first places to move in the other direction too. It gave George McGovern a significantly higher percentage than his national average and went for Jimmy Carter in 1976. The 21st district went handily for Jerry Brown twice and for John Tunney in 1976. The Valley gave a large minority of its votes to Mayor Thomas Bradley, a black, in 1973 and 1977, even though in the latter case his main opponent was an anti-busing Valley legislator.

The 21st district occupies the northeast corner of the Valley and spreads out almost to the Santa Monica Mountains in the south and to within four or five miles of the mountains to the west. It includes Democratic North Hollywood, with its large Jewish population, middle class Van Nuys and Northridge, and Pacoima, with the Valley's small black ghetto. It does not include the Valley's highest income areas—Woodland Hills, Encino, Sherman Oaks—which tend to be more Republican; and there is perhaps some trend to the Democrats here because of outmigration to farther suburbs of the kind of voters who simply dislike being in a central city.

Congressman James Corman of the 21st was first elected in 1960, when he upset a Republican incumbent; he was one of the few Democrats to do so that year (another was New York Governor Hugh Carey). He held on to the seat in tough races in 1964 and 1966 and has a firm lock on it today. Like most California Democrats, he saw his percentage drop in 1978, but it is still at the 60% level.

Corman has a seat and considerable seniority on the House Ways and Means Committee. He is currently the fourth-ranking Democrat and Chairman of the subcommittee on Public Assistance. He is probably the Committee's leading supporter of progressive tax reform, and has been chief sponsor in the House of the national health insurance bill supported by organized labor. He has worked hard on welfare matters, and was the chief sponsor of the Carter Administration's welfare proposals. He has considerable expertise in all these areas; but it was his misfortune that opinion in the House in the 95th Congress was moving away from his positions and toward those he opposes.

Corman was well enough liked and trusted by his fellow Democrats to be chosen in 1976, when Wayne Hays was forced to step down, as Chairman of the Democratic Congressional Campaign Committee, the official body which doles out contributions and assistance to Democratic candidates across the country. He has done a good job of seeing that needy challengers get their share rather than having most of the money go to comfortable incumbents, and he can take some credit for the small number of net losses Democrats suffered in the 1978 House elections.

Census Data Pop. 464,934. Central city, 96%; suburban, 4%. Median family income, $11,440; families above $15,000: 29%; families below $3,000: 6%. Median years education, 12.4.

The Voters

Median voting age 41.
Employment profile White collar, 55%. Blue collar, 34%. Service, 11%. Farm, –%.
Ethnic groups Black, 4%. Spanish, 17%. Total foreign stock, 30%. Canada, Italy, 3% each; UK, Germany, Italy, 2% each; Poland, 1%.

Presidential vote

1976	Carter (D)	80,681	(52%)
	Ford (R)	73,773	(48%)
1972	Nixon (R)	98,207	(56%)
	McGovern (D)	76,271	(44%)

Rep. James C. Corman (D) Elected 1960; b. Oct. 20, 1920, Galena Kans.; home, Van Nuys; UCLA, B.A. 1942, USC LL.B. 1948; Methodist.

Career USMC, WWII and Korea; Practicing atty., 1949–57; L. A. City Cncl., 1957–60; Natl. Advisory Comm. on Civil Disorders, 1967.

Offices 2217 RHOB, 202-225-5811. Also 14545 Friar St., Van Nuys 91411, 213-787-1776.

Committees *Small Business* (4th). Subcommittees: General Oversight and Minority Enterprise.

Ways and Means (4th). Subcommittees: Health; Public Assistance and Unemployment Compensation (Chairman).

Group Ratings

	ADA	COPE	PC	RPN	NFU	LCV	CFA	NAB	NSI	ACA	NTU
1978	70	80	68	36	60	–	68	10	30	4	–
1977	85	81	68	42	83	80	65	–	–	10	17
1976	90	87	75	39	100	57	91	0	0	0	26

Key Votes

1) Increase Def Spnd	AGN	6) Alaska Lands Protect	FOR	11) Delay Auto Pol Cntrl	AGN
2) B-1 Bomber	AGN	7) Water Projects Veto	AGN	12) Sugar Price Escalator	AGN
3) Cargo Preference	FOR	8) Consum Protect Agcy	FOR	13) Pub Fin Cong Cmpgns	FOR
4) Dereg Nat Gas	AGN	9) Common Situs Picket	FOR	14) ERA Ratif Recissn	AGN
5) Kemp-Roth	AGN	10) Labor Law Revision	FOR	15) Prohibt Govt Abrtns	AGN

Election Results

1978 general	James C. Corman (D)	73,869	(62%)	($241,423)
	G. (Rod) Walsh (R)	44,519	(38%)	($25,429)
1978 primary	James C. Corman (D), unopposed			
1976 general	James C. Corman (D)	101,837	(70%)	($142,770)
	Erwin Hogan (R)	44,094	(30%)	($2,581)

TWENTY-SECOND DISTRICT

Pasadena and Glendale, both with more than 100,000 people, are two Los Angeles area towns with well established images. From sources as diverse as the mid-sixties rock song "Little Old Lady from Pasadena" and Raymond Chandler's description of the massive houses of wealthy recluses, one gets a picture that is still fairly accurate. These are towns of large houses, of tree-shaded streets, of older, upper income people whose basic instincts are profoundly conservative. All these adjectives apply also to California's 22d congressional district, of which Glendale and Pasadena and several adjacent suburbs are the major part.

Some discordant notes have been struck in recent years, of a type never mentioned by Jan and Dean nor Chandler. Pasadena has a significant black population, and has also had a controversy over school busing for some time. The older residents have to a considerable extent been replaced by younger, affluent people, who often have what are called liberal attitudes on issues of style, like the Vietnam war or the environment. During the early seventies Republican margins here showed signs of sagging. But as economic issues—like Proposition 13—come to the fore, these newer residents share the conservatism of their elders. In 1978 Glendale and Pasadena delivered Republican margins as high as ever.

This has been good news for the 22d's Congressman, Republican Carlos Moorhead. On his predecessor's retirement, Moorhead was first elected in 1972 with an uninspiring 57%; two years ater, after he voted against the impeachment of Richard Nixon on the House Judiciary Committee, he was reelected with an undistinguished 56%. But with the change of issue focus, Moorhead's percentages rose to 64% in 1978. In the House he is an earnest and faithful follower of conservative policies.

Census Data Pop. 464,760. Central city, 12%; suburban, 88%. Median family income, $11,741; families above $15,000: 33%; families below $3,000: 6%. Median years education, 12.6.

The Voters

Median voting age 46.
Employment profile White collar, 63%. Blue collar, 27%. Service, 11%. Farm, -%.
Ethnic groups Black, 6%. Spanish, 10%. Total foreign stock, 27%. Canada, UK, Germany, 3% each; Italy, 2%.

Presidential vote

1976	Carter (D)	71,648	(38%)
	Ford (R)	115,685	(62%)
1972	Nixon (R)	134,792	(68%)
	McGovern (D)	62,080	(32%)

Rep. Carlos J. Moorhead (R) Elected 1972; b. May 6, 1922, Long Beach; home, Glendale; UCLA, B.A. 1943, USC, J.D. 1949; Presbyterian.

Career Army, WWII; Practicing atty., 1950–72; Cal. Assembly, 1966–72.

Offices 2442 RHOB, 202-225-4176. Also Rm. 404, 420 N. Brand Blvd., Glendale 91203, 213-247-8445.

Committees *Interstate and Foreign Commerce* (8th). Subcommittees: Communications; Energy and Power.

Judiciary (5th). Subcommittees: Administrative Law and Governmental Relations; Courts, Civil Liberties, and the Administration of Justice.

Group Ratings

	ADA	COPE	PC	RPN	NFU	LCV	CFA	NAB	NSI	ACA	NTU
1978	5	0	13	64	0	–	14	100	100	100	–
1977	0	9	25	62	27	24	15	–	–	96	46
1976	5	18	10	61	17	22	9	92	100	89	65

Key Votes

1) Increase Def Spnd	FOR	6) Alaska Lands Protect	AGN	11) Delay Auto Pol Cntrl	FOR
2) B-1 Bomber	FOR	7) Water Projects Veto	FOR	12) Sugar Price Escalator	FOR
3) Cargo Preference	AGN	8) Consum Protect Agcy	AGN	13) Pub Fin Cong Cmpgns	AGN
4) Dereg Nat Gas	FOR	9) Common Situs Picket	AGN	14) ERA Ratif Recissn	FOR
5) Kemp-Roth	FOR	10) Labor Law Revision	AGN	15) Prohibt Govt Abrtns	FOR

Election Results

1978 general	Carlos J. Moorhead (R)	99,502	(65%)	($56,371)
	Robert S. Henry (D)	54,442	(35%)	($13,368)
1978 primary	Carlos J. Moorhead (R)	64,732	(81%)	
	One other (R)	15,438	(19%)	
1976 general	Carlos J. Moorhead (R)	114,769	(63%)	($51,069)
	Robert L. Salley (D)	68,543	(37%)	($41,167)

TWENTY-THIRD DISTRICT

The 23d congressional district of Los Angeles is situated in one of the most prosperous—and most famous—parts of greater Los Angeles. It includes middle class West Los Angeles and well-to-do Westwood, around the UCLA campus, and over the mountains in the San Fernando Valley, the communities of Sherman Oaks, Encino, Tarzana, and Reseda. Far better known is the separate city of Beverly Hills, one of the richest cities in the nation. Beverly Hills is still host every day to busloads of tourists gawking at the homes of the stars and to Mercedes-loads of the rich who shop at Beverly Hills's ultraexpensive and chic stores. There has been a hubbub lately because a wealthy young Arab has painted the statues on his lawn and put plastic flowers in the pots; it is perhaps a measure of the progress of American civilization that most Beverly Hills residents now sternly uphold various canons of good taste. Not far away is glittering Century City, the giant office and apartment development built on the former Twentieth Century Fox backlot. Above in the mountains, in Laurel and Coldwater Canyons, are the overpriced rustic cabins and tree-secluded mansions of the would-be and genuinely rich.

The 23d is possibly the most heavily Jewish congressional district outside New York City, and of course many of its residents were lured here from New York by the entertainment business. It is also one of the most reliably Democratic high income districts in the nation; Beverly Hills, with its large Jewish population, has the distinction of never having voted for Richard Nixon. This is also one of the half dozen or so districts where are concentrated most of the big contributors to national campaigns; even with the current limits on contributions, this is an especially important area for Democrats and for Republicans as well.

Curiously, until 1976 the 23d had never elected a Jewish congressman, though the area has been represented by a series of famous people. One was James Roosevelt (1955–65), son of FDR; the younger Roosevelt was a leading liberal in Congress, but in 1972 endorsed Nixon at a time coinciding with the legal troubles of Bernard Cornfeld's Investors Overseas Service, of which Roosevelt had been vice president. Another was Sam Yorty (1951–55), the three-term Mayor of Los Angeles (1961–73), a hawkish Democrat (in the 1972 New Hampshire presidential primary) turned Republican (after his 1973 loss to Tom Bradley) with a leftish political past. Going back a few more years, there was Helen Gahagan Douglas (1945–51), wife of actor Melvyn Douglas and once an actress herself; she was the target of Richard Nixon's famous 1950 Senate race, when he smeared her as the "pink lady."

The most recent ex-Congressman, Thomas Rees, was less well known at home and in Washington. He decided to quit in 1976, at 51, to practice law—one of many not-so-old congressmen who have been quitting these days. One reason is the redeye, the planes which leave the West Coast around midnight and arrive in Washington at seven in the morning. California congressmen have to ride them all the time, and no life style, even one representing Beverly Hills in Congress, can be entirely pleasant under such circumstances.

Rees's successor is Anthony Beilenson, a Beverly Hills state Senator who won the six-candidate Democratic primary with 58%. His margin in the general election was a little lower than expected, but it rose to a comfortable 66% in 1978, when many other California Democrats were slipping. After two years of service on the Judiciary and Science Committees and a solid liberal record, Beilenson won a seat on the Rules Committee. He seems likely to settle into a long congressional career.

Census Data Pop. 464,026. Central city, 88%; suburban, 12%. Median family income, $14,141; families above $15,000: 46%; families below $3,000: 5%. Median years education, 12.9.

The Voters

Median voting age 44.
Employment profile White collar, 75%. Blue collar, 16%. Service, 9%. Farm, –%.
Ethnic groups Japanese, 1%. Spanish, 7%. Total foreign stock, 39%. USSR, 8%; Canada, 4%; UK, Germany, Poland, 3% each; Italy, Austria, 2% each; Hungary, 1%.

Presidential vote

1976	Carter (D)	119,138	(53%)
	Ford (R)	106,129	(47%)
1972	Nixon (R)	119,617	(50%)
	McGovern (D)	117,663	(50%)

Rep. Anthony C. Beilenson (D) Elected 1976; b. Oct. 26, 1932, New Rochelle, N.Y.; home, Sacramento; Harvard U., B.A. 1954, LL.B. 1957; Jewish.

Career Practicing atty., 1957–59; Counsel, Cal. Assembly Com. on Finance and Insurance, 1960; Staff Atty., Cal. State Comp. and Insurance Fund, 1961–62; Cal. Assembly, 1963–66; Cal. Senate, 1971–77.

Offices 1025 LHOB, 202-225-5911. Also 11000 Wilshire Blvd., Los Angeles 90024, 213-824-7801.

Committees *International Relations* (21st). Subcommittees: Asian and Pacific Affairs; International Security and Scientific Affairs.

Rules (10th). Subcommittees: Legislative Procedures.

Group Ratings

	ADA	COPE	PC	RPN	NFU	LCV	CFA	NAB	NSI	ACA	NTU
1978	80	79	83	45	60	–	68	0	10	8	–
1977	90	78	90	73	75	90	90	–	–	11	35

Key Votes

1) Increase Def Spnd	AGN	6) Alaska Lands Protect	DNV	11) Delay Auto Pol Cntrl	AGN
2) B-1 Bomber	AGN	7) Water Projects Veto	FOR	12) Sugar Price Escalator	AGN
3) Cargo Preference	AGN	8) Consum Protect Agcy	FOR	13) Pub Fin Cong Cmpgns	FOR
4) Dereg Nat Gas	AGN	9) Common Situs Picket	AGN	14) ERA Ratif Recissn	AGN
5) Kemp-Roth	AGN	10) Labor Law Revision	FOR	15) Prohibt Govt Abrtns	AGN

Election Results

1978 general	Anthony C. Beilenson (D)	117,498	(66%)	($47,776)
	Joseph Barbara (R)	61,496	(34%)	($9,170)
1978 primary	Anthony C. Beilenson (D)	81,616	(80%)	
	One other (D)	19,786	(20%)	
1976 general	Anthony C. Beilenson (D)	130,619	(60%)	($102,547)
	Thomas F. Bartman (R)	86,434	(40%)	($99,465)

TWENTY-FOURTH DISTRICT

Despite periodic stories that Hollywood is dying, it keeps going. The entertainment business is more profitable, if also more fragmented, than ever. Records now gross more than movies, though both appeal primarily to a rather narrow audience—the young. Television is closer to a universal medium, but it is not what movies were in the thirties and forties; the young people who are busy going to movies and buying records have little to do with TV. Subteens and over fifties are the heart of the TV market; increasingly industry executives seem to be learning how to develop shows targeted at particular segments of the population—at least those segments advertisers are willing to pay to reach.

The heart of the entertainment business in the United States—of records and television as well as movies—remains where it has been for the last fifty years, on the west side of Los Angeles: from the old Hollywood neighborhood itself (it is not a separate city) down to Beverly Hills and Westwood and, over the mountains, in Universal City and downtown Burbank. Most of this territory, from Hollywood to the still gaudy Sunset Strip, lies within the bounds of the 24th congressional district of California. Here you will find Hollywood itself—a rather disappointing Hollywood Boulevard and tawdry stucco side streets. To the north, their precipitous rise dominating smogless days, are the Santa Monica Mountains; on the face of one of them is the Hollywood sign recently refurbished by show business celebrities. Among the mountains are picturesque houses built in steep canyons or on flat-topped mountains; yet from Hollywood the mountains look surprisingly desolate and wild. North of the mountains the 24th extends into the San Fernando Valley, including part of predominantly Jewish North Hollywood, and stretching to Sherman Oaks on the west and Burbank on the east. Here, within the 24th (or the 23d, just to the west) are the old movie and new TV studios, almost all the agents and production companies, and the homes of most of the stars.

Show business is in many ways a Jewish industry, and the 24th district, like the 23d, has a large Jewish population. Not everyone here lives in the well manicured streets and spacious houses of Hancock Park or nearby Beverly Hills. There are also the middle class streets of the Fairfax district, an older Jewish neighborhood, or of North Hollywood on the other side of the mountains. The southern edge of the district touches on Los Angeles's black ghetto, and there is also a significant Mexican-American population within its bounds. But neither of these groups bulks particularly large in the electorate, and politically the ethnic flavor of the 24th is definitely Jewish.

This district was created quite anew by the court-ordered redistricting of 1973; before that its territory had been divided up between neighboring constituencies. What is odd is that it was not created earlier, in 1972, by the then California Assembly Reapportionment Committee Chairman, Henry Waxman, who now represents it. That someone like Waxman should be a power in the Assembly says something about the fluidity and accessibility of power there and, in contrast, the inaccessibility of power in the Congress of the early seventies. Waxman, elected to the Assembly at 29, had chosen the right side on a speakership fight, and so got control of one of the Assembly's choicest committees. In Congress he continues to maintain close contact with a number of west Los Angeles state legislators, notably Howard Berman, whom Waxman helped elect in a Republican district in 1972 and who in 1975 became Assembly Majority Leader (he, too, picked the right side in a speakership fight).

In Congress power has become much more accessible since Waxman was first elected, as he himself has most vividly demonstrated. A decade ago a member with only two terms' seniority hardly rated a good morning from a committee chairman; but Waxman successfully challenged the Democratic leadership and respected senior members for the chair of one of the House's most important subcommittees. This is the Commerce Committee's Health Subcommittee, which under Paul Rogers of Florida was a model of legislative competence. Rogers retired in 1978. In the past, the chair would have gone to the next senior Democrat, David Satterfield of Virginia; but his record was so reactionary that he was not even considered—a sign of how things have changed in the House. The next senior Democrat, Richardson Preyer, was highly respected and personally well-liked, hard-working and intelligent. Yet Waxman challenged and beat him. Preyer was hurt because he has substantial holdings in a major pharmaceutical company, though no one doubted his integrity; he was also hurt because, as a North Carolina congressman, he supported tobacco subsidies and opposed anti-smoking measures. Waxman was helped because he distributed over $24,000 of his own money in campaign funds to colleagues—a practice that is legal, but one engaged in only by senior House members until recently. Rules Chairman Richard Bolling attacked Waxman for trying to buy the chair, and the House leadership reportedly backed Preyer. But Waxman won among Commerce Committee Democrats 15–12.

This was a striking victory, but also one which put Waxman on the spot. The Health Subcommittee must deal with some important legislation, notably hospital cost care containment, and the pressure is on to see whether Waxman can deliver votes as ably for major legislation as he could for the chairmanship contest.

Census Data Pop. 465,475. Central city, 98%; suburban, 2%. Median family income, $10,137; families above $15,000: 28%; families below $3,000: 9%. Median years education, 12.5.

The Voters

Median voting age 47.
Employment profile White collar, 69%. Blue collar, 20%. Service, 11%. Farm, –%.
Ethnic groups Black, 5%. Japanese, 3%. Chinese, Filipino, 2% each. Spanish, 16%. Total foreign stock, 49%. USSR, 6%; Canada, UK, Germany, Poland, 3% each; Italy, 2%; Austria, Hungary, 1% each.

Presidential vote

1976	Carter (D)	93,650	(56%)
	Ford (R)	74,042	(44%)
1972	Nixon (R)	94,038	(49%)
	McGovern (D)	98,225	(51%)

Rep. Henry A. Waxman (D) Elected 1974; b. Sept. 12, 1939, Los Angeles; home, Los Angeles; UCLA, B.A. 1961, J.D. 1964; Jewish.

Career Practicing atty., 1965–68; Cal. Assembly, 1968–74.

Offices 1721 LHOB, 202-225-3976. Also 8425 W. 3d St., Los Angeles 90048, 213-651-1041.

Committees *Government Operations* (19th). Subcommittees: Government Activities and Transportation; Environment, Energy, and Natural Resources.

Interstate and Foreign Commerce (10th). Subcommittees: Health and Environment (Chairman).

Group Ratings

	ADA	COPE	PC	RPN	NFU	LCV	CFA	NAB	NSI	ACA	NTU
1978	90	90	88	33	67	–	73	0	10	13	–
1977	80	76	88	55	82	92	80	–	–	0	25
1976	80	86	90	56	100	91	81	0	11	0	20

Key Votes

1) Increase Def Spnd	AGN	6) Alaska Lands Protect	FOR	11) Delay Auto Pol Cntrl	AGN
2) B-1 Bomber	AGN	7) Water Projects Veto	FOR	12) Sugar Price Escalator	FOR
3) Cargo Preference	AGN	8) Consum Protect Agcy	FOR	13) Pub Fin Cong Cmpgns	FOR
4) Dereg Nat Gas	AGN	9) Common Situs Picket	FOR	14) ERA Ratif Recissn	AGN
5) Kemp-Roth	AGN	10) Labor Law Revision	FOR	15) Prohibt Govt Abrtns	AGN

Election Results

1978 general	Henry A. Waxman (D)	85,075	(66%)	($26,019)
	Howard G. Schaefer (R)	44,243	(34%)	($48,400)
1978 primary	Henry A. Waxman (D)	58,551	(81%)	
	One other (D)	14,174	(19%)	
1976 general	Henry A. Waxman (D)	108,296	(68%)	($29,505)
	David Irvins Simmons (R)	51,478	(32%)	($8,310)

TWENTY-FIFTH DISTRICT

The 1970 Census tells us that almost 16% of Californians are of "Spanish heritage." The vast majority of these people of course are Mexican-Americans who constitute the largest and, in many respects, the most hidden ethnic group in the state. Mexican-Americans do not always live in well-defined ghettoes; they are found all over the state (no congressional district has less than 5% "Spanish heritage"). Chicanos can merge quite easily into the white Anglo middle class. And then there are illegal immigrants from Mexico, whose numbers are uncertain (they shun contact with officials, including census-takers) but have surely been growing in recent years.

Politically, Mexican-Americans have long been the most under-represented group in the state. California sends three blacks to the House, but only one of its 43 congressmen is of Spanish origin, and no more than six Mexican-Americans sit in the state legislature out of 120. Republicans have charged that Democrats slice up Mexican neighborhoods to add Democratic votes to districts dominated by other groups; there is some truth to that, but Republican plans would result in the election of more chicanos and fewer Democrats, whom chicano voters almost always prefer. But it is a mistake to suppose that Mexican-Americans' votes are as solidly Democratic as blacks'; chicano voting behavior is really closer to what you would have seen in many immigrant neighborhoods fifty years ago: a preference for Democrats, but a willingness to go Republican, particularly when personal economic circumstances become more comfortable.

In 1974, for the first time, the predominantly Mexican-American communities of eastern Los Angeles neighborhoods, like Boyle Heights and Highland Park, have been put together with the suburb of East Los Angeles to form a single congressional district, the 25th. The district also includes downtown Los Angeles—a more vital place than many people suppose—MacArthur Park, and Dodgers Stadium, and reaches west toward the seedy, once elegant Silver Lake district near Hollywood. Not surprisingly the 25th is one of the poorest—and most Democratic—districts in California. Mexican-Americans, as they become better off and more assimilated, tend to move out, generally to the east, to working class and middle class suburbs. Those who cannot get out stay in the barrio.

For more than a decade one or another downtown Los Angeles district has been electing and reelecting Congressman Edward Roybal. Though of Spanish descent, Roybal is not directly from Mexico; he is from Albuquerque, New Mexico, where the Spanish-speaking community dates from before Plymouth Rock, and his ancestors have been living within the geographical bounds of this country probably for as long as those of any member of Congress.

The 95th Congress was not a pleasant session for Roybal. In September 1978, the House Ethics Committee recommended that he be censured for having lied about a $1,000 campaign contribution from Tongsun Park which he converted to his own use. Roybal admitted taking the money but said that he just made an error in judgment; his supporters persuaded the House that he should be only reprimanded, not censured. Some observers believe he would have been censured but for his minority status.

The political damage in this heavily Democratic district was distinctly limited. Roybal's winning percentage dropped from 72% in 1976 to 68% in 1978. Nevertheless one must wonder how pleasant it can be for him to return to Congress. Although he has served 16 years, he is only the 15th ranking Democrat on the Appropriations Committee, to which he did not win appointment till 1971. With a reprimand on his record, he may not be able to get a subcommittee chair even if seniority would otherwise provide it, as might happen on the Treasury-Post Office-General Government Subcommittee. At 64 it is possible that Roybal will choose to retire in 1980. If he does so, there will be several ambitious young Mexican-American politicians vying for this seat.

Census Data Pop. 464,972. Central city, 82%; suburban, 18%. Median family income, $7,804; families above $15,000: 13%; families below $3,000: 13%. Median years education, 10.3.

The Voters

Median voting age 41.
Employment profile White collar, 39%. Blue collar, 48%. Service, 13%. Farm, –%.
Ethnic groups Black, 5%. Japanese, Chinese, 2% each. Spanish, 60%. Total foreign stock, 55%. Canada, Germany, Italy, 1% each.

Presidential vote

1976	Carter (D)	52,234	(63%)
	Ford (R)	30,106	(37%)
1972	Nixon (R)	44,924	(43%)
	McGovern (D)	58,785	(57%)

Rep. Edward R. Roybal (D) Elected 1962; b. Feb. 10, 1916, Albuquerque, N.M.; home, Los Angeles; UCLA, Southwestern U.; Catholic.

Career Army, WWII; Dir. of Health Educ., L.A. Co. Tuberculosis & Health Assn., 1945–49; L.A. City Cncl., 1949–62, Pres. Pro Tempore, 1961–62.

Offices 2211 RHOB, 202-225-6235. Also New Fed. P.O. Bldg., 300 N. Los Angeles St., Los Angeles 90012, 213-688-4870.

Committees *Appropriations* (14th). Subcommittees: Labor-HEW; Treasury, Postal Service, and General Government.

Group Ratings

	ADA	COPE	PC	RPN	NFU	LCV	CFA	NAB	NSI	ACA	NTU
1978	85	79	80	18	70	–	68	0	0	15	–
1977	85	91	68	31	92	80	70	–	–	0	31
1976	100	87	92	39	91	93	91	17	0	7	28

Key Votes

1) Increase Def Spnd	AGN	6) Alaska Lands Protect	FOR	11) Delay Auto Pol Cntrl	AGN
2) B-1 Bomber	AGN	7) Water Projects Veto	FOR	12) Sugar Price Escalator	FOR
3) Cargo Preference	FOR	8) Consum Protect Agcy	FOR	13) Pub Fin Cong Cmpgns	FOR
4) Dereg Nat Gas	AGN	9) Common Situs Picket	FOR	14) ERA Ratif Recissn	AGN
5) Kemp-Roth	AGN	10) Labor Law Revision	FOR	15) Prohibt Govt Abrtns	AGN

Election Results

1978 general	Edward R. Roybal (D)	45,881	(67%)	($41,232)
	Robert K. Watson (R)	22,205	(33%)	
1978 primary	Edward R. Roybal (D), unopposed			
1976 general	Edward R. Roybal (D)	57,966	(77%)	($31,141)
	Jim Madrid (R)	17,737	(23%)	($4,587)

TWENTY-SIXTH DISTRICT

The mountains that encircle the Los Angeles basin are responsible for the area's mild climate; the desert to the north and east is usually 20 to 30 degrees hotter. But the mountains also bottle up the basin's air, allowing the sun to interact with automobile emissions to produce that typically Los Angeles product called photochemical smog. The same mountains provide a neat geographic barrier to dense settlement. North of the mountains there are 133,000 people in Los Angeles County; in the smaller area of land to the south, nearly 7,000,000.

Partly because of the action of the smog, it is considered more pleasant to live on the land, slightly higher up close against the mountains than in the flatter, hotter, smoggier valley below. That is certainly the case in the part of the Los Angeles basin running east from the city toward San Bernardino, the area which 34 years ago first elected Richard Nixon to Congress. Here the lower suburbs are mainly inhabited by people with blue collar backgrounds and nominally Democratic allegiances, while the suburbs through which Foothill Boulevard passes—Sierra Madre, Arcadia, Monrovia, Bradbury, Duarte, Azusa, Glendora—are relatively high income and Republican. These communities form the ideological heart of California's 26th congressional district, which also includes below them the less distinguished suburbs of Temple City and San Gabriel and even working class Baldwin Park. An exception to the rule just cited—not next to the mountains, but the most conservative of all suburbs—is the small community of San Marino, home of Los Angeles's wealthiest WASPs (like the Chandlers of the Los Angeles *Times*), which seldom delivers a Republican vote below 87%.

San Marino also happens to be the home of the 26th district's Congressman, John Rousselot, who is not only a conservative Republican, but also a proud member of that liberal bugbear, the John Birch Society. Membership has given him some trouble in his political career. Rousselot was first elected to Congress in 1960, but was beaten in 1962 after the Democrats went to great pains to draw him a district he couldn't win. (Too great pains, it turned out: the Democrats couldn't hold it either, and lost it in 1966.) Rousselot went back on the JBS payroll for a while and in 1970, when Congressman Glenard Lipscomb died, Rousselot entered the Republican primary and beat a moderate by 127 votes out of 87,000 cast. In the general election he beat Myrlie Evers, widow of the slain Mississippi civil rights leader, by better than a 2–1 margin.

Rousselot has a reputation in some quarters as a hard-eyed fanatic. Actually he is a pleasant, humorous man who will work for his ideas when they seem popular (he opposes the gasoline tax) or not (he opposes federal regulation of debt collectors). He is a man with a strong drive and energy which may come, as it did for Theodore Roosevelt, from having been crippled in childhood. His Birch Society membership still causes some problems; he lost a bid for the chair of the Republican Congressional Campaign Committee in 1975. But in 1979 he won a seat on the Ways and Means Committee; and in his home district he is reelected easily. Rousselot may have wider ambitions, however. He is reported to be considering a race against Senator Alan Cranston in 1980. Although Rousselot's background will make him the underdog, he should not be underestimated. Capable of overcoming initial bad reaction, he could prove to be a formidable candidate.

Census Data Pop. 464,122. Central city, 0%; suburban, 100%. Median family income, $11,668; families above $15,000: 31%; families below $3,000: 6%. Median years education, 12.5.

The Voters

Median voting age 44.
Employment profile White collar, 59%. Blue collar, 31%. Service, 10%. Farm, –%.
Ethnic groups Black, 1%. Spanish, 15%. Total foreign stock, 25%. Canada, 3%; UK, Germany, Italy, 2% each.

Presidential vote

1976	Carter (D)	66,151	(38%)
	Ford (R)	108,532	(62%)
1972	Nixon (R)	132,894	(70%)
	McGovern (D)	56,014	(30%)

Rep. John H. Rousselot (R) Elected June 30, 1970; b. Nov. 1, 1927, Los Angeles; home, San Marino; Principia Col., B.A. 1949; Christian Scientist.

Career Pres. and Owner, John H. Rousselot & Assoc., public relations consultants, 1954–58; Dir. of Public Info., Fed. Housing Admin., 1958–60; U.S. House of Reps., 1961–63; Management consultant, 1967–70.

Offices 2133 RHOB, 202-225-4206. Also 735 W. Duarte Rd., Arcadia 91006, 213-447-8125.

Committees *Banking, Finance and Urban Affairs* (4th). Subcommittees: Financial Institutions Supervision, Regulation and Insurance; General Oversight and Renegotiation; Housing and Community Development.

Ways and Means (11th). Subcommittees: Public Assistance and Unemployment Compensation; Social Security.

Group Ratings

	ADA	COPE	PC	RPN	NFU	LCV	CFA	NAB	NSI	ACA	NTU
1978	5	5	10	67	0	–	14	100	100	100	–
1977	0	9	20	67	10	14	10	–	–	96	56
1976	5	9	7	56	9	12	0	100	100	88	75

Key Votes

1) Increase Def Spnd	FOR	6) Alaska Lands Protect	AGN	11) Delay Auto Pol Cntrl	FOR
2) B-1 Bomber	FOR	7) Water Projects Veto	AGN	12) Sugar Price Escalator	FOR
3) Cargo Preference	AGN	8) Consum Protect Agcy	AGN	13) Pub Fin Cong Cmpgns	AGN
4) Dereg Nat Gas	FOR	9) Common Situs Picket	AGN	14) ERA Ratif Recissn	FOR
5) Kemp-Roth	FOR	10) Labor Law Revision	AGN	15) Prohibt Govt Abrtns	FOR

Election Results

1978 general	John H. Rousselot (R), unopposed			($54,386)
1978 primary	John H. Rousselot (R), unopposed			
1976 general	John H. Rousselot (R)	112,619	(66%)	($86,592)
	Bruce Latta (D)	59,093	(34%)	($6,727)

TWENTY-SEVENTH DISTRICT

The 27th congressional district of California is a long, thin swath of land along the Pacific Ocean, from Pacific Palisades in the north to Palos Verdes in the south. Between these two hilly, high income prominences overlooking the ocean is a whole string of beach towns: sedate Santa Monica, with its own high income areas and black ghetto; seedy Venice, its 1920s canals now in ruins; flashy new Marina del Rey, where many of the apartment complexes allow singles only or ban children; Playa del Rey with Los Angeles International Airport right behind (the only airport referred to generally by its three-letter code, LAX); El Segundo and its oil refineries; Manhattan and Hermosa and Redondo Beaches, with their closely packed little houses and narrow streets.

For many years the beach area was heavily Republican, the voting habits of its towns dominated by the conservatism of elderly Midwestern migrants. But morality and mobility have produced a sharp shift in recent years. The beach towns have filled up with young people—singles, surfers, freaks, whatever—whose political instincts, if they get to the polls at all, lead them to oppose the politics and social values of Ronald Reagan and Richard Nixon. Thus the 27th went for Barry Goldwater in 1964 and delivered a large margin for Nixon over Humphrey in 1968. But there was a marked swing toward the Democrats in 1972 and 1974. It continued through 1976, although Jimmy Carter is not especially attractive to these California young people and Gerald Ford, if only because of his relations with his own children, is not as repellent as Nixon or Reagan. When politics moves from stylistic to economic issues, the district, with its above average income, becomes more Republican. But when stylistic issues become more important, this is a district that can go Democratic.

That seems to be the lesson of recent congressional campaigns. For 16 years the congressman from this district was Alphonzo Bell, heir to an oil and aircraft fortune whose family name is memorialized in the working class suburbs of Bell and Bell Gardens. Bell was a moderate Republican with ambitions for higher office. He ran for mayor of Los Angeles in 1969 and for the U.S. Senate in 1976, and both times was eliminated in the primary. There seems little doubt that he could have kept on winning in the district had he chosen to keep running here.

That does not seem to be the case with the current incumbent, Robert K. Dornan. A conservative television commentator, he won the 1976 Republican primary against two moderates; he was well known for his TV broadsides, and also as inventor of the POW bracelet and for his involvement in a campaign against certain textbooks in Kanawha County, West Virginia. As that last credential suggests, Dornan is a man of considerable enthusiasm and energy who is willing to go where his beliefs lead him. His 1976 race was the most expensive in the nation—he spent $404,000 and his liberal Democratic opponent, $637,000—and one of the most bitterly fought.

Dornan gained a certain notoriety in the House for his willingness to jump up and take on any cause that excited him. But on occasion he was effective. He was one of the first Republicans to challenge Democratic efforts to make voter registration easier—and helped to defeat them. His greatest energies and most histrionic efforts were reserved for the cause of the B-1 bomber. After President Carter announced that the Administration did not want to build the manned bomber, Dornan led the effort in the House to reverse the decision—though he does not sit on the Armed Services Committee. What he lacked in seniority and clout he made up for in passion. Although some snickered at his efforts, and although they were finally unsuccessful, on balance Dornan probably won votes for his cause.

Whether he won votes for himself is another question. The North American Aviation plant that would have manufactured the B-1 is in the 27th district, but not that many of the workers actually live here; most live in working class towns farther inland. Dornan's high emotional pitch and near-perfect conservative ratings gave him a strong ideological identification, which in this district is no advantage. The 27th is repelled by those who take conservative stands on lifestyle issues; and if one includes defense under that definition, Dornan does little else. He faced a serious challenge in 1978 from Carey Peck, a former Capitol Hill aide and son of actor Gregory Peck; Dornan has his own show business background as the nephew of Jack Haley, the tin woodman in The Wizard of Oz. Peck was considered the underdog, but after another expensive campaign he was able to win 49% against Dornan.

This virtually guarantees that Dornan will have tough opposition in 1980. Given the demographic change going on in the district, he might very well be beaten. Certainly there is little chance that he will moderate his views or modulate their expression. Dornan is one of the last true believers on Capitol Hill.

Census Data Pop. 464,100. Central city, 25%; suburban, 75%. Median family income, $13,625; families above $15,000: 43%; families below $3,000: 5%. Median years education, 12.8.

The Voters

Median voting age 41.
Employment profile White collar, 67%. Blue collar, 23%. Service, 10%. Farm, –%.
Ethnic groups Black, 2%. Spanish, 9%. Total foreign stock, 27%. UK, 4%; Canada, 3%; Germany, USSR, 2% each. 1%.

Presidential vote

1976	Carter (D)	82,854	(40%)
	Ford (R)	125,254	(60%)
1972	Nixon (R)	138,282	(64%)
	McGovern (D)	78,853	(36%)

Rep. Robert K. Dornan (R) Elected 1976; b. Apr. 3, 1933, New York, N.Y.; home, Los Angeles; Loyola U., Westchester/Playa Del Ray, 1950–53.

Career Air Force, 1953–58; Freelance traveling journalist; Host, KTLA TV talk show, 1969–73; TV producer and personality.

Offices 419 CHOB, 202-225-6451. Also 11000 Wilshire Blvd., Los Angeles 90024, 213-824-7222.

Committees *Merchant Marine and Fisheries* (10th). Subcommittees: Merchant Marine; Panama Canal.

Science and Technology (11th). Subcommittees: Space Science and Applications; Energy Development and Applications; Transportation, Aviation, and Communication.

Group Ratings

	ADA	COPE	PC	RPN	NFU	LCV	CFA	NAB	NSI	ACA	NTU
1978	5	5	13	58	22	–	9	100	100	92	–
1977	0	9	10	62	42	7	0	–	–	96	56

Key Votes

1) Increase Def Spnd	FOR	6) Alaska Lands Protect	DNV	11) Delay Auto Pol Cntrl	FOR
2) B-1 Bomber	FOR	7) Water Projects Veto	FOR	12) Sugar Price Escalator	FOR
3) Cargo Preference	AGN	8) Consum Protect Agcy	AGN	13) Pub Fin Cong Cmpgns	AGN
4) Dereg Nat Gas	FOR	9) Common Situs Picket	AGN	14) ERA Ratif Recissn	FOR
5) Kemp-Roth	FOR	10) Labor Law Revision	AGN	15) Prohibt Govt Abrtns	FOR

Election Results

1978 general	Robert K. Dornan (R)	89,392	(51%)	($291,762)
	Carey Peck (D)	85,880	(49%)	($308,017)
1978 primary	Robert K. Dornan (R), unopposed			
1976 general	Robert K. Dornan (R)	114,623	(55%)	($403,675)
	Gary Familian (D)	94,988	(45%)	($637,080)

TWENTY-EIGHTH DISTRICT

In 1971 the California legislature decided to create a second black congressional district in Los Angeles County, and drew a peculiarly shaped seat. Two years later the state Supreme Court's redistricting plan smoothed out the district's rough edges, but maintained basically the same political unit. The Los Angeles city limits wander through the 28th district, enclosing the predominantly black area around the University of Southern California and the integrated Crenshaw neighborhood, which is one of several pockets of more or less amiable and stable neighborhood integration, and the home of Los Angeles Mayor Thomas Bradley. The suburban integrated city of Inglewood is also included, as is mostly white Culver City and the well-to-do Palms district near Beverly Hills. The district comprises an area that was mostly white in the early sixties, and into which Los Angeles's middle and upper income blacks have been moving in the years since. Today the 28th is compact, residential (despite a few oil derricks in Ladera Heights), middle class, and middle income. In 1970 the racial balance was 40% black, 12% Spanish, and 48% Anglo white; today the black percentage is probably over 50%.

The 28th district has elected two representatives since its creation. The first, and the intended beneficiary of the district's creation, was Yvonne Brathwaite Burke. In the early seventies she was a member of the California Assembly, a body which has given Congress many talented legislators. When the people running the 1972 Democratic National Convention were looking for a black woman to serve as co-chair of the proceedings, Burke was picked and did a creditable job. Her election to Congress was anticlimactic. While she generally voted with her fellow members of the Black Caucus, she avoided the shrill tones and overblown rhetoric which emanates from some of them; she seems to have been as popular with white as with black constituents. Burke could easily have continued in Congress, but she wanted to return to California and in 1978 ran for attorney general. It is an important post, but one for which many voters apparently felt she did not have proper credentials. After winning the seriously contested Democratic primary, Burke was put on the defensive when her opponent pointed out that she had no prosecutorial experience and opposed the death penalty. Nor does she have a prosecutorial demeanor, and California voters seemed unwilling to entrust the office to one who has repeated the time-worn liberal line that crime can ultimately be stopped only by getting at the root causes of poverty and discrimination. Burke lost to state Senator George Deukmejian, a strong death penalty advocate, by a 53%–43% margin.

Burke's successor in Congress is Assemblyman Julian Dixon, who conclusively beat state Senator Nate Holden in the Democratic primary. Dixon can be expected to vote with other black Democrats. Elected at 44, he has the potential for a long career in Congress. Locally he has been an ally of 24th district Congressman Henry Waxman and Assembly Majority Leader Howard Berman. He appears to share their political shrewdness: in his first term, he won a seat on the Appropriations Committee.

Census Data Pop. 465,182. Central city, 70%; suburban, 30%. Median family income, $9,942; families above $15,000: 23%; families below $3,000: 9%. Median years education, 12.4.

The Voters

Median voting age 41.
Employment profile White collar, 54%. Blue collar, 31%. Service, 15%. Farm, -%.
Ethnic groups Black, 40%. Japanese, 4%. Chinese, 1%. Spanish, 12%. Total foreign stock, 26%. Canada, Germany, 2% each; UK, Italy, USSR, 1% each.

Presidential vote

1976	Carter (D)	104,135	(71%)
	Ford (R)	42,972	(29%)
1972	Nixon (R)	62,037	(37%)
	McGovern (D)	107,019	(63%)

Rep. Julian C. Dixon (D) Elected 1978; b. Aug. 8, 1934, Washington, D.C.; home, Los Angeles; Cal. St. U. at L.A., B.S. 1962, Southwestern U., LL.B. 1967; Episcopalian.

Career Army, 1957–60; Practicing atty.; Cal. Assembly, 1973–78.

Offices 423 CHOB, 202-225-7084. Also One La Brae Ave., Englewood 90301, 213-678-5424.

Committees *Appropriations* (35th). Subcommittees: Energy and Water Development; Foreign Operations.

Group Ratings: Newly Elected

Key Votes: Newly Elected

Election Results

1978 general	Julian C. Dixon (D), unopposed			($231,444)
1978 primary	Julian C. Dixon (D)	42,988	(48%)	
	Nate Holden (D)	30,162	(34%)	($149,482)
	Six others (D)	16,639	(19%)	
1976 general	Yvonne Braithwaite Burke (D)	114,612	(80%)	($50,252)
	Edward S. Skinner (R)	28,303	(20%)	($555)

TWENTY-NINTH DISTRICT

Watts has been a familiar American place name since the 1965 riot there put it in the national headlines. Though no longer in the headlines, Watts remains the heart of Los Angeles's black community, directly south of downtown. And, as official Los Angeles found out after 1965, despite its central location Watts is isolated from the mainstream of Los Angeles—off the principal bus lines, with no hospitals, few parks, and little in the way of municipal facilities. (Indeed, much of the territory around Watts isn't part of the city of Los Angeles at all, and the city has shown no inclination to annex it.) The area's most distinctive feature is the Watts Tower, a weird sculpture of bits of broken glass and scrap metal, assembled over some 30 years by Italian immigrant Simon Rodia. New York journalists sent to Watts in the wake of the riot were quick to write that the place didn't look like a ghetto. Actually more American blacks live in places like Watts—with its small frame double or single family houses along quiet streets—than in places like Harlem, with its five story turn-of-the-century tenements.

Watts is also the heart of California's 29th congressional district, and it is the almost unanimously Democratic voting habits of the black areas which inevitably place the district in the Democratic column. But there is another side to the 29th which is worth noting, across the almost impenetrable racial barrier of Alameda Street, just east of the Rodia tower. Blacks are moving north, west, and south of Watts, but across Alameda the working class white suburbs—places like Huntington Park, Bell, and South Gate, which on first glance look not too much different—are determined to remain all white. This is California backlash country, where politicians like Ronald Reagan and Richard Nixon picked up many erstwhile Democratic votes in the years after the Watts riot.

The 29th district includes these areas, added to keep the black majority district up to the one-person-one-vote population standard. Their inclusion has lowered the Democratic percentage here, but has had no impact on election outcomes. Congressman Augustus Hawkins, first elected in 1962, has not had any trouble winning reelection by overwhelming margins.

Hawkins, now past 70, is probably the most experienced black legislator in American history. For 28 years, from 1934 to 1962, he served in the California Assembly, and for most of that time was its only black member; in 1959 he was nearly elected speaker. But California was apparently not ready for that then, and so Hawkins had to settle for a seat in Congress. His experience has not been of the kind to produce verbal militance, and he has not been a favorite of some of the more voluble members of the Black Caucus.

Hawkins has been as productive a legislator as any current black member. He chairs an Education and Labor subcommittee and was the chief House sponsor of the Humphrey-Hawkins bill. Humphrey-Hawkins was intended to attack what anyone must admit is a severe problem: the persistently high rates of unemployment among blacks and other poor people, particularly young blacks. In its original form, the bill would have required the federal government to create jobs, at prevailing wage rates, until unemployment dropped to a set figure. In the 1976 campaign, Humphrey-Hawkins became a kind of litmus test for Democratic candidates; Jimmy Carter eventually endorsed it, but in lukewarm terms, leaving little doubt he considered it impractical. Opponents of the measure charged that it would be inflationary and would produce make-work jobs, and in the inflation-conscious 95th Congress it was inevitable that the measure would be watered down or defeated. After Hubert Humphrey's death, there was a sentimemtal push to enact something with the Humphrey-Hawkins label on it. But the bill that was passed did not require the government to do anything, and it bears little relation to the measure Hawkins first proposed.

The fate of Humphrey-Hawkins must have been a disappointment to Hawkins, but it cannot have been the first he has suffered in a legislative career of 45 years. He is an authentic trailblazer who has seen much history and made some—and who has the capacity, if he wishes to stay in Congress a while longer, to do more.

Census Data Pop. 464,125. Central city, 57%; suburban, 43%. Median family income, $7,359; families above $15,000: 10%; families below $3,000: 17%. Median years education, 11.1.

The Voters

Median voting age 42.
Employment profile White collar, 36%. Blue collar, 46%. Service, 18%. Farm, –%.
Ethnic groups Black, 59%. Spanish, 15%. Total foreign stock, 15%.

Presidential vote

1976	Carter (D)	83,291	(81%)
	Ford (R)	19,596	(19%)
1972	Nixon (R)	33,571	(26%)
	McGovern (D)	96,415	(74%)

Rep. Augustus F. Hawkins (D) Elected 1962; b. Aug. 31, 1907, Shreveport, La.; home, Los Angeles; UCLA, A.B. 1931; USC Institute of Govt.; Methodist.

Career Real estate business; Cal. Assembly 1935–62.

Offices 2371 RHOB, 202-225-2201. Also 936 W. Manchester St., Los Angeles 90044, 213-750-0260.

Committees *Education and Labor* (4th). Subcommittees: Select Education; Employment Opportunities (Chairman); Elementary, Secondary, and Vocational Education.

House Administration (4th). Subcommittees: Contracts; Printing (Chairman).

Group Ratings

	ADA	COPE	PC	RPN	NFU	LCV	CFA	NAB	NSI	ACA	NTU
1978	75	82	65	30	89	–	59	0	0	16	–
1977	60	86	68	25	91	72	60	–	–	4	21
1976	70	96	85	35	83	76	91	8	20	8	16

Key Votes

1) Increase Def Spnd	AGN	6) Alaska Lands Protect	FOR	11) Delay Auto Pol Cntrl	AGN
2) B-1 Bomber	DNV	7) Water Projects Veto	AGN	12) Sugar Price Escalator	FOR
3) Cargo Preference	FOR	8) Consum Protect Agcy	FOR	13) Pub Fin Cong Cmpgns	AGN
4) Dereg Nat Gas	AGN	9) Common Situs Picket	FOR	14) ERA Ratif Recissn	AGN
5) Kemp-Roth	AGN	10) Labor Law Revision	FOR	15) Prohibt Govt Abrtns	AGN

Election Results

1978 general	Augustus F. Hawkins (D)	65,214	(85%)	($13,887)
	Uriah J. Fields (R)	11,512	(15%)	($6,602)
1978 primary	Augustus F. Hawkins (D), unopposed			
1976 general	Augustus F. Hawkins (D)	82,515	(88%)	($3,873)
	Michael D. Germonprez (R)	10,852	(12%)	($60)

THIRTIETH DISTRICT

The 30th congressional district of California is a string of suburbs in the San Gabriel Valley just east of downtown Los Angeles. While the wealthy and comfortable suburban towns of the next-door 26th district hug the mountains, those of the 30th are in the lower part of the valley, below the San Bernardino Freeway, where the smog fills the air from 7:30 in the morning on, and the Los Angeles and San Gabriel Rivers flow (when any water flows in them at all) through open concrete conduits. What makes these suburbs interesting is not smog or concrete river bottoms, but rather the fact that they are becoming increasingly the home of the Los Angeles area's middle-income Mexican-American population. Places like Monterey Park and Montebello, built as comfortable Anglo suburbs in the forties and fifties, lie only a few miles from the Los Angeles barrio; and it is here that people from the barrio, when they are able, are moving. The residential migration pattern here is not the kind of white flight and wholesale change in neighborhood complexion one sees when a white neighborhood suddenly becomes black; the process is slower, and somewhat more amiable.

But it has political consequences nonetheless. One of them is a reinforcement of the 30th district's traditional Democratic voting habits. The second is the increasing strength of candidates of Mexican descent. The first helps Congressman George Danielson; the second tends to hurt him. Danielson has been a scrambler all his political life. From Los Angeles's once proud, now seedy Silver Lake district, he was elected to the California Assembly in 1962 and 1964 and to the state Senate in 1966 (beating political prankster Dick Tuck in the primary) and finally to Congress in 1970. Danielson has always had some Mexican-American constituents, whom he has wooed in somewhat wooden Spanish. But he never seems to have achieved close rapport with his district—as witness the ease with which he moved his legal residence from Silver Lake when the 1973 redistricting moved his territory entirely to the suburbs.

The 1974 election was Danielson's toughest contest. At first it appeared that he had been thrown in the same district with Chet Holifield, a member of the House since 1942; but Holifield decided to retire. Then he faced primary opposition, in a district in which 42% of the population was of Spanish heritage, from Esteban Torres, head of a local Mexican-American organization. Here Danielson may have been saved by his seat on the House Judiciary Committee—and that body's investigation into the impeachment of Richard Nixon. That president had no popularity left in the heavily Democratic 30th, and Danielson was in a position to act against him.

In the primary, Danielson won an absolute majority (53%) against Torres and another Mexican-American, just before the hearings were opened to television cameras. On TV Danielson's performance was impressive; he proceeded aggressively against Nixon's defenders and made some telling points. Since then he has had no significant electoral opposition—none in primaries and nothing to worry about from Republicans. After a career of political scrambling, he enjoys the unusual luxury of a safe seat. Legislatively, he has been productive, initiating successful bills on temporary special prosecutors, financial disclosure for all branches of government, and lobbying disclosure.

Census Data Pop. 464,892. Central city, 0%; suburban, 100%. Median family income, $10,120; families above $15,000: 20%; families below $3,000: 8%. Median years education, 11.8.

The Voters

Median voting age 40.
Employment profile White collar, 42%. Blue collar, 48%. Service, 10%. Farm, –%.
Ethnic groups Japanese, 2%. Spanish, 42%. Total foreign stock, 34%. Canada, Italy, 2% each; UK, Germany, USSR, 1% each.

Presidential vote

1976	Carter (D)	69,424	(60%)
	Ford (R)	46,152	(40%)
1972	Nixon (R)	74,551	(54%)
	McGovern (D)	64,217	(46%)

Rep. George E. Danielson (D) Elected 1970; b. Feb. 20, 1915, Wausa, Neb.; home, Monterey Park; U. of Neb., B.A. 1937, J.D. 1939; Protestant.

Career Practicing atty.; FBI Agent, 1939–44; Navy, WWII; Asst. U.S. Atty., Southern Dist. of Cal., 1949–51; Cal. Assembly 1962–66; Cal. Senate, 1966–70.

Offices 2202 RHOB, 202-225-5464. Also 8873 E. Valley Blvd., Rosemead 91770, 213-287-1134.

Committees *International Relations* (23d). Subcommittees: Europe and the Middle East.

Judiciary (7th). Subcommittees: Administrative Law and Governmental Relations (Chairman); Courts, Civil Liberties, and the Administration of Justice; Immigration, Refugees, and International Law.

Veterans' Affairs (5th). Subcommittees: Compensation, Pension, Insurance and Memorial Affairs; Medical Facilities and Benefits.

Group Ratings

	ADA	COPE	PC	RPN	NFU	LCV	CFA	NAB	NSI	ACA	NTU
1978	60	85	65	22	71	–	68	0	50	4	–
1977	60	91	60	31	83	60	60	–	–	15	20
1976	75	96	70	41	75	66	73	8	60	19	9

Key Votes

1) Increase Def Spnd	AGN	6) Alaska Lands Protect	FOR	11) Delay Auto Pol Cntrl	AGN
2) B-1 Bomber	FOR	7) Water Projects Veto	AGN	12) Sugar Price Escalator	AGN
3) Cargo Preference	FOR	8) Consum Protect Agcy	FOR	13) Pub Fin Cong Cmpgns	FOR
4) Dereg Nat Gas	AGN	9) Common Situs Picket	FOR	14) ERA Ratif Recissn	AGN
5) Kemp-Roth	AGN	10) Labor Law Revision	FOR	15) Prohibt Govt Abrtns	AGN

Election Results

1978 general	George E. Danielson (D)	66,241	(71%)	($98,834)
	Henry Ares (R)	26,511	(29%)	($50,823)
1978 primary	George E. Danielson (D), unopposed			
1976 general	George E. Danielson (D)	82,767	(74%)	($67,893)
	Harry Couch (R)	28,503	(26%)	($10,915)

THIRTY-FIRST DISTRICT

The 31st district of California is a patch of fairly typical forties and fifties Los Angeles County suburban territory, about 10 to 15 miles south of downtown Los Angeles and Beverly Hills. Most of it is made up of neat single-family pastel stucco houses, often with an above-ground backyard swimming pool and some slightly shabby lawn furniture. There are parcels of still vacant land here and newly laid-out subdivisions, and next to them the overgrown lots of factory workers' widows who are just getting by on Social Security. The 31st also contains sparkling steel and glass shopping centers and the fading pink stucco commercial strips of the late forties. Undergirding the economy are the huge defense and auto assembly plants to the east and west.

One thing about the 31st that is not quite typical—or at least is not thought of as such—is the fact that 28% of its citizens in 1970 were black. Not that the area is integrated; with a few exceptions quite the contrary. Blacks made up 72% of the population of Compton in 1970 and less than 1% of that in Lynwood, which is right next door. What has happened here is that the black ghetto running south of Watts extends right through the center of the 31st district, dividing the white working class suburbs of Lynwood and Paramount on the east from those of Hawthorne, Gardena, and Lennox on the west. Another fact of some demographic import: the western suburbs here, together with those in the adjacent 28th district, have the largest concentration of Japanese-Americans in California.

Some of these suburbs were part of the assembly district which first sent Jess Unruh to the California Assembly in 1954 and served as his ultimate electoral base during his terms as Speaker from 1961 to 1968. (He is now living in semi-retirement as state Treasurer.) Among Unruh's friends and allies who have gone on to the House of Representatives is Congressman Charles Wilson of the 31st. His service in Washington for years attracted little notice. An assignment to the Post Office and Civil Service Committee has produced few headlines, although Wilson has managed major postal reorganization bills. And in his years on the Armed Services Committee he has made few waves. He does, however, have considerable seniority; and he will be in line to chair the Post Office Committee if James Hanley of New York leaves Congress.

But in 1978 Wilson finally succeeded in attracting attention, when he was reprimanded by the House for lying about a $600 wedding gift he had received from Tongsun Park. Wilson admitted receiving the money and said that he had forgotten about the envelope full of cash when the committee had questioned him. In any case, it was no secret that Wilson was one of the House's most steadfast backers of aid to South Korea.

Wilson's reprimand did not cause him much problem in the 1978 general election. Against a weak Republican he won with 68% of the vote, not much less than the 71% he got the last time he was opposed, in 1974. The 31st district is too Democratic for Wilson to have to worry about Republicans. But he may face problems in the Democratic primary. The large black minority in the district provides one base for a challenger; and the white suburbs in the district are split geographically and do not form a cohesive unit. Even before his reprimand, in the 1978 primary, he was held to 40% of the vote by seven challengers. While that was far ahead of the second place candidate's 22%, it was certainly not enough to scare off strong challengers in the future.

Census Data Pop. 463,470. Central city, 7%; suburban, 93%. Median family income, $10,042; families above $15,000: 20%; families below $3,000: 9%. Median years education, 12.1.

The Voters

Median voting age 39.
Employment profile White collar, 44%. Blue collar, 44%. Service, 12%. Farm, –%.
Ethnic groups Black, 28%. Japanese, 3%. Spanesh, 15%. Total foreign stock, 20%. Canada, 2%; UK, Germany, Italy, 1% each.

Presidential vote

1976	Carter (D)	72,775	(66%)
	Ford (R)	38,052	(34%)
1972	Nixon (R)	64,074	(46%)
	McGovern (D)	73,874	(54%)

Rep. Charles H. Wilson (D) Elected 1962; b. Feb. 15, 1917, Magna, Utah; home, Hawthorne.

Career Army, WWII; Founder, Charles H. Wilson Insurance Co., 1945; Cal. Assembly 1954–62.

Offices 2409 RHOB, 202-225-5425. Also 15000 Aviation Blvd., Rm. 2W30, Lawndale 90261, 213-536-6680.

Committees *Armed Services* (6th). Subcommittees: Procurement and Military Nuclear Systems; Military Installations and Facilities.

Post Office and Civil Service (3d). Subcommittees: Postal Operations and Services (Chairman); Postal Personnel and Modernization; Compensation and Employee Benefits.

Group Ratings

	ADA	COPE	PC	RPN	NFU	LCV	CFA	NAB	NSI	ACA	NTU
1978	30	63	43	50	50	–	32	0	71	40	–
1977	45	79	35	36	91	28	35	–	–	29	18
1976	50	80	57	53	75	64	45	9	40	25	11

Key Votes

1) Increase Def Spnd	FOR	6) Alaska Lands Protect	DNV	11) Delay Auto Pol Cntrl	AGN
2) B-1 Bomber	FOR	7) Water Projects Veto	FOR	12) Sugar Price Escalator	AGN
3) Cargo Preference	FOR	8) Consum Protect Agcy	FOR	13) Pub Fin Cong Cmpgns	AGN
4) Dereg Nat Gas	FOR	9) Common Situs Picket	FOR	14) ERA Ratif Recissn	FOR
5) Kemp-Roth	FOR	10) Labor Law Revision	FOR	15) Prohibt Govt Abrtns	AGN

Election Results

1978 general	Charles H. Wilson (D)	55,667	(68%)	($139,728)
	Don Grimshaw (R)	26,490	(32%)	
1978 primary	Charles H. Wilson (D)	23,705	(40%)	
	Donald E. Wilson (D)	12,913	(22%)	($66,845)
	Joe Rice (D)	7,899	(13%)	($31,448)
	Five others (D)	15,153	(25%)	
1976 general	Charles H. Wilson (D), unopposed			($56,987)

THIRTY-SECOND DISTRICT

The 32d is one of 16 congressional districts wholly or partially within Los Angeles County. The focus of the 32d is the busy port area of Los Angeles—San Pedro, Wilmington, and Long Beach—and the nearby suburbs of Carson (blue collar) and Torrance (white collar). This is one of the working class districts of the Los Angeles area; people here tend to work on the docks or in fishing boats, in one of the area's huge aircraft plants, or in the factories found in the industrial corridor to the northeast. There are—or were when the 1970 Census was taken—relatively few blacks, and most of them in Carson and Long Beach; but their numbers are doubtless increasing because of movement from Compton and Watts to the north. The 32d also includes near the port a sizeable Yugoslav-American community—proof that Los Angeles is by no means without ethnic variety.

Most of the residents of the 32d are traditional Democrats, union members who supported the programs of Franklin D. Roosevelt and John F. Kennedy, but who have felt threatened by social trends not to their liking. On a few occasions this district has even gone Republican—for Ronald Reagan in 1966 and Richard Nixon in 1972. In the latter case this was the California district with the greatest defection from normal Democratic allegiance.

For many years this district routinely reelected Democratic Congressman Cecil King, co-sponsor of the original Medicare act. When King retired in 1968, a real battle developed between Democrat Glenn Anderson and Republican Joseph Blatchford. Anderson had been Lieutenant Governor for eight years under Pat Brown and was unlucky enough to have been acting governor when the Watts riot broke out. Afterwards some people accused Anderson of waiting too long before dispatching the National Guard; and in the 1966 election he was badly beaten by Republican Robert Finch. Two years later Anderson just barely squeaked ahead of Blatchford—who later became head of the Peace Corps and in 1976 nearly won the Republican nomination in the next-door 27th district.

In the House Anderson, always strongly supported by labor, received the kind of mundane committee assignments that tend to go to representatives of port areas: Public Works and Merchant Marine and Fisheries. On both he has moved up rapidly in seniority, ranking sixth on Merchant Marine and fourth on Public Works. Anderson has been a rather busy legislator. He floor managed the ultimately successful move to allow some highway funds to be used for mass transit—an idea that was not always popular in Los Angeles—and as Chairman of the Aviation Subcommittee has been a leader on legislation in this field. Since his initial election, Anderson has had few political problems, and this seems to be a completely safe seat for him.

Census Data Pop. 466,639. Central city, 66%; suburban, 34%. Median family income, $9,873; families above $15,000: 22%; families below $3,000: 10%. Median years education, 12.2.

The Voters

Median voting age 40.
Employment profile White collar, 46%. Blue collar, 41%. Service, 13%. Farm, –%.
Ethnic groups Black, 8%. Japanese, 2%. Filipino, 2%. Spanish, 18%. Total foreign stock, 26%. Canada, UK, Germany, Italy, 2% each; Yugoslavia, 1%.

Presidential vote

1976	Carter (D)	72,386	(55%)
	Ford (R)	58,147	(45%)
1972	Nixon (R)	82,921	(56%)
	McGovern (D)	65,507	(44%)

Rep. Glenn M. Anderson (D) Elected 1968; b. Feb. 21, 1913, Hawthorne; home, Harbor City; UCLA, B.A. 1936; Protestant.

Career Mayor of Hawthorne, 1940–43; Cal. Assembly, 1943, 1945–51; Army, WWII; Lt. Gov. of Cal., 1958–67.

Offices 2410 RHOB, 202-225-6676. Also 300 Long Beach Blvd., Long Beach 90801, 213-548-2721.

Committees *Merchant Marine and Fisheries* (6th). Subcommittees: Fish and Wildlife; Panama Canal; Merchant Marine.

Public Works and Transportation (4th). Subcommittees: Aviation (Chairman); Surface Transportation; Water Resources.

Group Ratings

	ADA	COPE	PC	RPN	NFU	LCV	CFA	NAB	NSI	ACA	NTU
1978	60	80	60	18	67	–	55	17	50	41	–
1977	65	77	58	31	67	65	50	–	–	35	28
1976	85	91	67	29	75	71	81	17	30	25	40

Key Votes

1) Increase Def Spnd	AGN	6) Alaska Lands Protect	FOR	11) Delay Auto Pol Cntrl	AGN
2) B-1 Bomber	FOR	7) Water Projects Veto	AGN	12) Sugar Price Escalator	AGN
3) Cargo Preference	FOR	8) Consum Protect Agcy	FOR	13) Pub Fin Cong Cmpgns	FOR
4) Dereg Nat Gas	AGN	9) Common Situs Picket	FOR	14) ERA Ratif Recissn	AGN
5) Kemp-Roth	AGN	10) Labor Law Revision	FOR	15) Prohibt Govt Abrtns	AGN

Election Results

1978 general	Glenn M. Anderson (D)	74,004	(71%)	($109,228)
	Sonya Mathison (R)	23,242	(22%)	
	Ida Bader (AMI)	6,363	(6%)	
1978 primary	Glenn M. Anderson (D), unopposed			
1976 general	Glenn M. Anderson (D)	92,034	(72%)	($66,419)
	Clifford O. Young (R)	35,394	(28%)	($25,420)

THIRTY-THIRD DISTRICT

The 33d district of California, the end result of several redistrictings, centers of the southeast Los Angeles County suburbs of Norwalk, Downey, and Whittier. The last of these of course is the most famous: the boyhood home of Richard Nixon, the place founded by Quakers and named after the New England poet, and the profoundly conservative little town in sunny California. But the image created by the media is not quite right any more, for Whittier has long since been swallowed up—and its own size swollen—by the advancing suburban tide of Los Angeles, and its special qualities have been diluted or lost. The function which Whittier, together with the other suburbs of the 33d, serves is to house factory and lower and middle level white collar workers, people who in just about every way exemplify what we mean by middle class.

On paper this is a Democratic district, and in fact the 33d shows a healthy Democratic registration edge. But numbers often mean far less than many political writers assume, for ordinary voters feel no obligation to vote the way they register. Between 1958 and 1974 the 33d voted solidly Republican in every statewide election—for Barry Goldwater as well as Richard Nixon, for Ronald Reagan as well as Thomas Kuchel. Indeed, right wing Republicanism has more strength here—certainly more enthusiasm and overt support—than the moderate Republicans who are supposed to be the party's strongest candidates in areas like this.

To understand why this should be so, go back to the early sixties, when the smog was getting worse every year, taxes were rising as welfare costs went up, and students and blacks were rioting in Berkeley and Watts. With their values—and perhaps their savings—under attack, the middle class people in places like the 33d felt that things were going sour, and it did not help that Watts was only a few miles away. It was then, after a conservative Democratic congressman died, that conservative Republican Del Clawson won a special election in June 1963 in an area that included much of what is now the 33d. President Kennedy was then preparing his civil rights bill and Martin Luther King Jr. was planning the march on Washington—a time of turmoil and uncertainty, a time when the people of the 33d wanted a politics rooted in old-fashioned values.

And that is what conservatives like Clawson, Goldwater, and, later, Ronald Reagan offered—not so much tax relief as psychological assurance, assurance that their threatened way of life was the right one and that the things they had worked so hard for should not be scorned. Reagan in particular has excelled at soothing and reassuring middle class people that they, not their fashionable detractors, are right about what is good for society.

Through shifting tides of redistricting, Clawson was reelected every two years. His conservative regularity helped him win a seat on the House Rules Committee, where he usually reflected the wishes of the House leadership. He was not a productive legislator, but then he did not go to Washington to pass new laws, but to prevent bad ones from passing. At home his percentages were declining, but he didn't seem in danger of losing. In 1978, at 64, Clawson decided to retire.

No fewer than seven Republicans and ten Democrats competed to represent the 33d in his place. The Democratic nominee was Dennis Kazarian, a 28-year-old former aide to 30th district Congressman George Danielson, who won his primary with 22% after a last minute mailing of potholders to every Democrat in the district. Kazarian, who wore expensive suits and drove a Cadillac, tried to convince voters he was more conservative than Danielson; he also brought in Transportation Secretary Brock Adams to try to get action on the long-stalled Century Freeway. But this razzamatazz was not enough to prevail against the normal voting patterns here and the Republican trend in the year of Proposition 13. The winner was 55-year-old La Mirada Councilman Wayne Grisham, who attacked Kazarian as a carpetbagger and who stressed the need to hold down taxes and government spending. He promised to follow in Clawson's footsteps, and there is no reason to believe he will not.

Census Data Pop. 464,494. Central city, 0%; suburban, 100%. Median family income, $12,340; families above $15,000: 33%; families below $3,000: 4%. Median years education, 12.4.

The Voters

Median voting age 40.
Employment profile White collar, 54%. Blue collar, 36%. Service, 10%. Farm, –%.
Ethnic groups Spanish, 18%. Total foreign stock, 22%. Canada, 3%; UK, Germany, Italy, 2% each.

Presidential vote

1976	Carter (D)	75,709	(43%)
	Ford (R)	99,127	(57%)
1972	Nixon (R)	126,430	(70%)
	McGovern (D)	55,330	(30%)

Rep. Wayne Grisham (R) Elected 1978; b. Jan. 10, 1923, Lamar, Colo.; home, La Mirada; Long Beach City Col., A.A. 1947, Whittier Col., B.A. 1947, U.S.C., 1950–51; Methodist.

Career Army Air Corps;, WWII; Realtor; La Mirada City Cncl., 1970–79, Mayor, 1973–74, 1977–78.

Offices 511 CHOB, 202-225-3576. Also Suite 100, 13601 E. Whittier Blvd., Whittier 90605, 213-945-3061.

Committees *Government Operations* (13th). Subcommittees: Manpower and Housing.

Veterans' Affairs (9th). Subcommittees: Housing; Education, Training and Employment.

Group Ratings: Newly Elected

Key Votes: Newly Elected

Election Results

1978 general	Wayne Grisham (R)	79,533	(56%)	($162,423)
	Dennis S. Kazarian (D)	62,540	(44%)	($109,248)
1978 primary	Wayne Grisham (R)	14,013	(24%)	
	William L. Greene (R)	12,113	(21%)	($21,896)
	Albert C. Zapanta (R)	11,711	(20%)	($60,660)
	John E. Dempsey (R)	9,425	(16%)	($32,261)
	Three others (R)	11,433	(19%)	
1976 general	Del Clawson (R)	95,398	(55%)	($83,115)
	Ted Snyder (D)	77,807	(45%)	($42,630)

THIRTY-FOURTH DISTRICT

Long Beach, with 358,000 people, is one of the few parts of suburban Los Angeles County with an urban character of its own. Long Beach has a man-made harbor competitive with LA's San Pedro next door, which makes it one of the nation's major ports. There is also the beach, which gave the city its name; back in the twenties and thirties it helped to draw thousands of Midwestern migrants to Long Beach, and the city built its own downtown and boardwalk-cum-amusement park. In the thirties the large number of retirees here contributed to California's zany political reputation; they were the strongest supporters of welfare schemes like the Townsend Plan and the Ham 'n' Eggs movement (the latter of which helped to elect Earl Warren Governor in 1942). Oldtimers can still recall when the Iowa picnics of the same period drew more than 50,000 people to Long Beach.

Today the atmosphere of Long Beach is different. Most of the town is filled with ordinary middle class families. Retirees are just as likely to live in developments like the self-contained Rossmoor Leisure World, just across the line in Orange County, as in the stucco walkup apartments a couple of blocks from the ocean. Suburbia has grown out to Long Beach and absorbed it.

This newer Long Beach is still the largest single part, despite several boundary changes, of the 34th congressional district of California. The district now extends into Orange County, including half of Huntington Beach as well as Leisure World; in Los Angeles County the district includes half of Long Beach—generally speaking, the city's more prosperous part—and the middle income suburbs of Lakewood and Bellflower. Overall the 34th is basically a Republican district, delivering solid Republican margins in statewide elections; but in its brief history it has elected a Democratic as well as a Republican congressman.

The Democratic congressman was Mark Hannaford, a professor at Long Beach City College and Mayor of Lakewood. He was first elected in an upset over a Long Beach assemblyman in 1974, the Watergate year. Two years later, he was able to beat Republican Daniel Lungren, a young lawyer whose father was Richard Nixon's personal physician. Hannaford fought hard and did just about everything possible to hold the district. He pushed measures to allow construction of an oil tanker terminal in Long Beach—which is opposed by some environmentalists but strongly backed by local business interests. He led the drive to abolish the Renegotiation Board, a body designed to recoup overcharges on government contracts, which is opposed by the district's aerospace and defense industries. He fought against formulas which would channel more federal aid to the Northeast and Midwest. He compiled ADA and labor ratings below average for a non-Southern Democrat. He used his franked mail extensively to keep in touch with voters.

But none of it was enough. Lungren, at 32, was determined to avoid the mistakes of his 1976 campaign. He also had the advantage on the tax and spending issue since Hannaford, like many local government officials, had opposed Proposition 13. Lungren's conclusive victory here makes it about as clear as can be that this is a district which no Democrat could hold against a competent Republican challenger. Lungren, in contrast, is much less likely to have strong competition in the near future.

Census Data Pop. 464,336. Central city, 42%; suburban, 58%. Median family income, $11,831; families above $15,000: 31%; families below $3,000: 5%. Median years education, 12.5.

The Voters

Median voting age 42.
Employment profile White collar, 57%. Blue collar, 32%. Service, 11%. Farm, –%.
Ethnic groups Spanish, 8%. Total foreign stock, 20%. Canada, 3%; UK, Germany, 2% each; Italy, Netherlands, 1% each.

Presidential vote

1976	Carter (D)	84,977	(43%)
	Ford (R)	112,251	(57%)
1972	Nixon (R)	135,141	(66%)
	McGovern (D)	70,071	(34%)

Rep. Dan Lungren (R) Elected 1978; b. Sept. 22, 1946, Long Beach; home, Long Beach; Notre Dame U., B.A. 1964, U.S.C., Georgetown U., J.D. 1971; Catholic.

Career Staff of U.S. Sen. George Murphy, 1969–70; Staff of U.S. Sen. Bill Brock of Tenn., 1971; Spec. Asst., Repub. Natl. Comm., 1971–72; Practicing atty., 1973–78.

Offices 1313 LHOB, 202-225-2415. Also 5514 Britton Dr., Long Beach 90815, 213-594-9761.

Committees *Judiciary* (10th). Subcommittees: Immigration, Refugees, and International Law; Criminal Justice.

Group Ratings: Newly Elected

Key Votes: Newly Elected

Election Results

1978 general	Daniel E. Lungren (R)	90,554	(55%)	($268,604)
	Mark W. Hannaford (D)	73,608	(45%)	($329,904)
1978 primary	Daniel E. Lungren (R)	42,967	(68%)	
	Art Jacobson (R)	19,828	(32%)	($12,150)
1976 general	Mark W. Hannaford (D)	100,988	(51%)	($167,547)
	Daniel E. Lungren (R)	98,147	(49%)	($152,109)

THIRTY-FIFTH DISTRICT

It is hard to say which suburban Los Angeles County congressional district is the lineal descendant of the one represented by Richard Nixon from 1947 to 1951. There have since been five redistrictings, and the territory included in Nixon's 12th district, much more populous today than it was then, is divided among several seats now. The 26th has a reasonable claim to be the Nixon district, but so do the 33d which contains Whittier, Nixon's home town, and the 35th which probably contains more of the acreage of Nixon's old 12th—plus the home town of Jerry Voorhis, the liberal Democrat Nixon beat—than any of the others.

At any rate the 35th includes the eastern Los Angeles County suburbs of West Covina (which is much larger than neighboring Covina) and Pomona and Claremont which between them contain several high quality small colleges. Also just across the San Bernardino County line it includes some other comfortable suburbs: Ontario (with its own airport, now a major regional field for jets), Montclair, and Upland.

As districted by the California Supreme Court, the 35th had no incumbent congressman and a definite Republican complexion. That attracted Victor Veysey, a Republican incumbent from another southern California district which had been partitioned among its neighbors like Poland in the eighteenth century. This gave the Democrat, West Covina Mayor Jim Lloyd, a natural issue and may very well have made the difference in what was a very close election. Lloyd was also helped by the Democratic trend of that year and perhaps by the fact that he was considered a somewhat conservative Democrat in this not very liberal district.

Lloyd's congressional career has been a good example of how a narrow winner in a critical election can use the advantages of incumbency to make a safe seat of a district which would seem, on paper, likely to go for the other party. He has made a point, when returning to the district, of working one day a week in some ordinary job—to show that he understands the problems of the ordinary person. His voting record, while largely Democratic on economic issues, has been increasingly conservative on non-economic matters. In 1976 against former Covina Mayor Louis Brutucao, Lloyd won reelection with 53%. In 1978, against a weaker and less well-financed opponent but in a more Republican year, he won reelection with 54%. Those are not margins which could incline one to call this an entirely safe seat; a strong Republican might well have a chance in 1980. But Lloyd's electoral achievement is nonetheless impressive.

In the House Lloyd's major impact has been on military matters. A 21-year veteran of the Navy, he is an experienced pilot. On the Armed Services Committee and on the floor his opinion is often sought by members of varying background; Lloyd has actually flown some of the planes under consideration and is presumed to know whereof he speaks. He has also pushed measures like a solar satellite research program which would provide contracts for big companies in his district.

Census Data Pop. 464,185. Central city, 14%; suburban, 86%. Median family income, $11,265; families above $15,000: 28%; families below $3,000: 6%. Median years education, 12.4.

The Voters

Median voting age 40.
Employment profile White collar, 52%. Blue collar, 34%. Service, 12%. Farm, 2%.
Ethnic groups Black, 3%. Spanish, 15%. Total foreign stock, 20%. Canada, 3%; UK, Germany, Italy, 2% each.

Presidential vote

1976	Carter (D)	72,664	(44%)
	Ford (R)	90,929	(56%)
1972	Nixon (R)	107,616	(66%)
	McGovern (D)	55,895	(34%)

Rep. Jim Lloyd (D) Elected 1974; b. Sept. 27, 1922, Helena, Mont.; home, West Covina; U. of Oreg., Tulane U., Stanford U., B.A. 1958, USC, M.A. 1966.

Career Navy, 1942–63; Public Relations Dir., Aerojet General Corp., 1963–65; Founder, Lloyd's Public Relations and Advertising, 1966; West Covina City Cncl., 1968–74, Mayor, 1973; Instructor, Mt. San Antonio Co., 1970–73.

Offices 222 CHOB, 202-225-2305. Also Suite 507, 100 S. Vincent St., West Covina 91790, 213-919-5711.

Committees *Armed Services* (21st). Subcommittees: NATO Standardization, Interoperability, and Readiness; Research and Development.

Science and Technology (8th). Subcommittees: Investigations and Oversight (Chairman); Transportation, Aviation, and Communication.

Group Ratings

	ADA	COPE	PC	RPN	NFU	LCV	CFA	NAB	NSI	ACA	NTU
1978	45	75	44	33	56	–	55	8	80	38	–
1977	35	91	50	31	83	46	50	–	–	35	16
1976	50	83	67	50	75	57	54	17	30	39	32

Key Votes

1) Increase Def Spnd	AGN	6) Alaska Lands Protect	FOR	11) Delay Auto Pol Cntrl	FOR
2) B-1 Bomber	FOR	7) Water Projects Veto	AGN	12) Sugar Price Escalator	AGN
3) Cargo Preference	FOR	8) Consum Protect Agcy	FOR	13) Pub Fin Cong Cmpgns	FOR
4) Dereg Nat Gas	AGN	9) Common Situs Picket	FOR	14) ERA Ratif Recissn	AGN
5) Kemp-Roth	FOR	10) Labor Law Revision	FOR	15) Prohibt Govt Abrtns	AGN

Election Results

1978 general	Jim Lloyd (D)	80,388	(54%)	($147,556)
	David Dreier (R)	68,442	(46%)	($152,315)
1978 primary	Jim Lloyd (D), unopposed			
1976 general	Jim Lloyd (D)	87,472	(53%)	($132,031)
	Louis Brutorgo (R)	76,765	(47%)	($224,853)

THIRTY-SIXTH DISTRICT

Congressman George Brown of the 36th district of California is one of the Horatio Algers of the Congress. In the early fifties Brown was an industrial physicist living in Monterey Park, a middle class suburb east of Los Angeles. With his crew cut and slight paunch, Brown was scarcely distinguishable from tens of thousands of Los Angeles area scientists and engineers—but for his Quaker upbringing, a strong belief in disarmament and peace, and nascent political yearnings. In 1954 he ran for and won a seat on the Monterey Park City Council. His interest in government whetted, he tried for the state legislature and in the very Democratic year of 1958 was elected. Three years later the legislature was charged with drawing the state's congressional district lines and allotting the eight new districts California had gained in the 1960 Census—the largest number of new districts any American legislature has had to deal with. George Brown served on the appropriate committee, and one of the districts came to be centered on Monterey Park. He was elected to Congress in 1962.

The story doesn't end there. In the House, Brown was one of the original peaceniks, even before the big escalation of the Vietnam war in 1965. Because many of his constituents considered his positions on issues far out, he had to fight every two years to win reelection. But he did win and in 1970 decided to make a try for the Senate. It looked like a dubious move at first. But Republican Senator George Murphy got into serious trouble when it was revealed that Technicolor was paying him $20,000 a year while he was serving in the Senate. Then just a month before the primary Richard Nixon invaded Cambodia, and a strong wave of antiwar feeling propelled Brown upward in the polls. His underfinanced campaign brought him nearly even with the favorite, Congressman John Tunney, and a switch of 99,000 votes out of 2.4 million cast would have given the peacenik the nomination and—judging from the size of Tunney's 1970 victory—the Senate seat as well.

There is more. Relatively few former congressmen make it back to Capitol Hill nowadays; it is just too wrenching to return without all that seniority you once had. But Brown, motivated more by a desire for peace than a hunger for power, decided to try anyway. Once again redistricting gave him his chance. In 1971 the legislature created a new district in the eastern end of the Los Angeles basin, at the intersection of Los Angeles, San Bernardino, and Riverside Counties. The district included all the most Democratic parts of San Bernardino and Riverside—the Mexican-American barrio, the local University of California campus, and the working class subdivisions around the Kaiser Steel plant in Fontana. Everyone assumed it would go Democratic in November. In an eight-candidate field Brown won the nomination with 28% of the vote; in the general he won with 56%, although Nixon was carrying the district.

Brown returned to serve on the Science Committee, as he had before, and also got a seat on Agriculture (this district produces a huge farm crop, though most of its residents live in suburban settings). He made relatively few waves this time, and his very liberal voting record was not as distinctive as it had been in the early sixties. He has not had significant opposition since 1972. Thanks to the retirements, deaths, or defeats of more senior (and usually more conservative) Democrats, Brown now has impressive seniority: he is the sixth ranking Democrat on Agriculture and the fourth on Science. He serves as Chairman of the Environment and Atmosphere Subcommittee—an important assignment for a congressman from the 36th which, situated at the east end of the Los Angeles basin, has some of the poorest quality air in the nation.

Census Data Pop. 463,898. Central city, 46%; suburban, 54%. Median family income, $9,407; families above $15,000: 18%; families below $3,000: 10%. Median years education, 12.2.

The Voters

Median voting age 40.
Employment profile White collar, 47%. Blue collar, 37%. Service, 14%. Farm, 2%.
Ethnic groups Black, 7%. Spanish, 18%. Total foreign stock, 19%. Canada, 2%; UK, Germany, 1% each.

Presidential vote

1976	Carter (D)	82,538	(56%)
	Ford (R)	64,801	(44%)
1972	Nixon (R)	80,137	(53%)
	McGovern (D)	69,883	(47%)

Rep. George E. Brown, Jr. (D) Elected 1972; b. Mar. 6, 1920, Holtville; home, Colton; UCLA, B.A. 1946.

Career Army, WWII; Monterey Park City Cncl., Mayor. 1954–58; Personnel, Engineering, and Management Consultant, City of Los Angeles, 1957–61; Cal. Assembly, 1959–62; U.S. House of Reps. 1963–71; Candidate for Dem. nomination for U. S. Senate, 1970

Offices 2342 RHOB, 202-225-6161. Also 552 N. LaCadena St., Colton 92324, 714-825-2472.

Committees *Agriculture* (6th). Subcommittees: Conservation and Credit; Department Investigations, Oversight, and Research.

Science and Technology (4th). Subcommittees: Space Science and Applications; Science, Research and Technology (Chairman); Natural Resources and Environment.

Group Ratings

	ADA	COPE	PC	RPN	NFU	LCV	CFA	NAB	NSI	ACA	NTU
1978	70	79	65	50	44	–	64	10	10	8	–
1977	80	81	78	45	82	80	75	–	–	4	24
1976	80	79	64	59	91	68	81	8	10	19	32

Key Votes

1) Increase Def Spnd	AGN	6) Alaska Lands Protect	FOR	11) Delay Auto Pol Cntrl	AGN
2) B-1 Bomber	FOR	7) Water Projects Veto	FOR	12) Sugar Price Escalator	FOR
3) Cargo Preference	FOR	8) Consum Protect Agcy	FOR	13) Pub Fin Cong Cmpgns	FOR
4) Dereg Nat Gas	AGN	9) Common Situs Picket	FOR	14) ERA Ratif Recissn	AGN
5) Kemp-Roth	AGN	10) Labor Law Revision	FOR	15) Prohibt Govt Abrtns	AGN

Election Results

1978 general	George E. Brown, Jr. (D)	80,448	(63%)	($39,914)
	Dana Warren Carmody (R)	47,417	(37%)	($11,179)
1978 primary	George E. Brown, Jr. (D), unopposed			
1976 general	George E. Brown, Jr. (D)	90,830	(65%)	($38,543)
	Grant Carner (R)	49,368	(35%)	($36,682)

THIRTY-SEVENTH DISTRICT

In the 1920s, when California first became a noted retirement haven, most older people moving out here were looking for homes along the ocean. If they were poor they retired in Long Beach or one of the beach towns near Los Angeles; if they were rich, they might go to Santa Barbara or La Jolla. Retirees were a larger percentage of California's population before World War II than they have been since; the state is now actually younger than the national average. But there are still plenty of retirees, and in the sixties and seventies they have been moving not to the seashore, where it is crowded, smoggy and urban—but to the desert.

This is the land of California's 37th congressional district, a seat that takes in territory from two counties, San Bernardino and Riverside, but covers most of California's desert lands—at least the parts where people live. The district's boundaries begin roughly at the eastern end of the Los Angeles basin: it includes some of San Bernardino and the surrounding area, including the Seventh Day Adventist town of Loma Linda and some of the territory around Riverside. But most of the district lies east of the mountains which stop—or at least hinder—the Los Angeles smog from reaching the desert. Here the days are crystal clear, with the reddish mountains always visible in the distance, and the sky usually blue and cloudless. The desert can be fertile farmland, as it is in the Coachella Valley, but it needs to be irrigated; without daily doses of water almost any plant will wilt and die in the heat. The first white settlers in the desert were prospectors, and some ghost towns still stand. They constitute quite a contrast to Palm Springs and Palm Desert, which are outposts of affluence (Palm Springs is more show business, Palm Desert more WASPy). It is too hot here in the summer for most people, even though the heat is dry, but the winter weather is almost ideal. Two presidents have retired within the confines of the district, Eisenhower in Palm Desert for the winters, Ford in nearby Rancho Mirage—which is also the home of Frank Sinatra, Walter Annenberg, and Spiro Agnew.

There are of course more modest retirement communities sprinkled here and there, all of them basically Republican. People who have enough money to move to a condominium or even a trailer when they are 65 are far more likely to be Republicans than not, and the 37th district, with one of the highest median ages of any California district, is definitely Republican.

That party preference has prevailed in both presidential and congressional elections. Representing the area from 1966 until his death in a plane crash was Jerry Pettis, a self-made millionaire, Seventh Day Adventist (the only one in Congress), and member of the Ways and Means Committee. He was succeeded by his widow Shirley, who won a full term in 1976, but surprised her constituents by declining to run in 1978. Her successor is San Bernardino area Assemblyman Jerry Lewis (no relation to the comedian), who like the Pettises is regarded as an independent-minded conservative. Lewis won the Republican primary without difficulty and had an impressive margin in the general election.

Census Data Pop. 462,640. Central city, 7%; suburban, 93%. Median family income, $8,794; families above $15,000: 19%; families below $3,000: 11%. Median years education, 12.3.

The Voters

Median voting age 46.
Employment profile White collar, 49%. Blue collar, 30%. Service, 16%. Farm, 5%.
Ethnic groups Black, 3%. Spanish, 15%. Total foreign stock, 20%. Canada, UK, Germany, 2% each.

Presidential vote

1976	Carter (D)	84,725	(45%)
	Ford (R)	101,935	(55%)
1972	Nixon (R)	107,237	(66%)
	McGovern (D)	54,835	(34%)

Rep. Jerry Lewis (R) Elected 1978; b. Oct. 21, 1934, Seattle, Washington; home, Highland; U.C.L.A., B.A. 1956; Protestant.

Career Life insurance agent, 1959–78; Field Rep. to U.S. Rep. Jerry Pettis, 1968; Cal. Assembly, 1968–78.

Offices 327 CHOB, 202-225-5861. Also 101 6th St., Redlands 92373, 714-862-6030.

Committees *House Administration* (8th). Subcommittees: Accounts; Services; Information and Computers.

Public Works and Transportation (16th). Subcommittees: Economic Development; Surface Transportation; Water Resources.

Group Ratings: Newly Elected

Key Votes: Newly Elected

Election Results

1978 general	Jerry Lewis (R)	106,581	(64%)	($159,43
	Dan Corcoran (D)	60,463	(36%)	($50,00
1978 primary	Jerry Lewis (R)	40,101	(55%)	
	John J. Joyner (R)	10,619	(15%)	
	Danney E. Ball (R)	8,574	(12%)	($8,39
	A. J. Mathewson (R)	8,557	(12%)	($12,30
	One other (R)	5,314	(7%)	
1976 general	Shirley N. Pettis (R)	133,634	(73%)	($144,15
	Douglas C. Nilson, Jr. (D)	49,021	(27%)	($7,63

THIRTY-EIGHTH DISTRICT

"Orange County" are two words which have become synonymous with "conservative" i political discourse. Twenty years ago Orange County, California, had all the notoriety possesse by a few thousand acres of citrus trees; its 1950 population was 216,000. By 1975 that figure ha grown to 1.7 million, which increased rapidly since. As the population mushroomed, Orang County has consistently turned in the highest Republican percentages of any major Californi county and, in some elections though by no means all, of any major county in the country. Y Orange County is not as monolithically conservative and Republican as is generally suppose Democrats currently hold three out of six Orange County Assembly seats, and since 196 Democrats have held the congressional district currently numbered the 38th.

Roughly speaking, the district includes the central portion of the heavily populated western ha of Orange County, halfway between the ocean and the hills which separate it from the San Gabri Valley in Los Angeles County. In its current borders the 38th includes most of Santa Ana (with i Mexican-American community, about the only conspicuous minority in Orange County), virtuall all of Garden Grove, and the bulk of the factory worker suburbs of Buena Park, Stanton, an Westminster. These are places one could not mistake for high income areas, whether one speeding by at 70 on the freeway or driving down the little cul-de-sacs and curving streets favore by developers in the fifties and sixties for even the squarest tracts of land.

For 12 years the predecessor of the current 38th district was represented by Richard Hanna, genial, joke-telling, and in his later days in Congress, bearded Democrat. Hanna had sever secrets of survival: careful redistricting, a computerized list of 90,000 friendly voters, a goo rapport with (and a seat on the Banking Committee for) local savings and loan magnates, wh were making huge fortunes out of Orange County's fast growth. Hanna also became an inveterat junketeer and friend of South Korean lobbyist Tongsun Park. Hanna retired in 1974. In 1978 h was convicted of engaging in a bribery scheme with Park and sent to jail.

Hanna was succeeded by another Democrat, Jerry Patterson, then Mayor of Santa Ana. Lik many California congressmen, he was able to build a relatively nonpartisan and noncontroversi image in his years in local government. He easily defeated a former prisoner of war—one c several POWs who failed to win congressional elections in 1974 and 1976. Patterson has bee reelected by wide margins, and Republicans seem to have given up on this district. In the Hous he sits on the Banking and Merchant Marine Committees, and has a record not too far out of lin with most non-Southern Democrats.

Census Data Pop. 463,879. Central city, 56%; suburban, 44%. Median family income, $11,367 families above $15,000: 26%; families below $3,000: 5%. Median years education, 12.

The Voters

Median voting age 38.
Employment profile White collar, 48%. Blue collar, 39%. Service, 12%. Farm, 1%.
Ethnic groups Black, 2%. Spanish, 16%. Total foreign stock, 20%. Canada, 3%; UK, 2% Germany, Italy, 1% each.

Presidential vote

1976	Carter (D)	67,994	(44%)
	Ford (R)	85,873	(56%)
1972	Nixon (R)	107,451	(68%)
	McGovern (D)	50,126	(32%)

Rep. Jerry M. Patterson (D) Elected 1974; b. Oct. 25, 1934, El Paso, Tex.; home, Santa Ana; Long Beach St. U., B.A. 1960, UCLA, J.D. 1966; Congregationalist.

Career Coast Guard, 1953–57; Practicing atty., 1967–74; Santa Ana City Cncl., 1969–73, Mayor, 1973–74.

Offices 137 CHOB, 202-225-2965. Also Suite 921, 34 Civic Ctr. Plaza, Santa Ana 92701, 714-835-3811.

Committees *Banking, Finance and Urban Affairs* (12th). Subcommittees: Financial Institutions Supervision, Regulation and Insurance; Housing and Community Development; International Trade, Investment, and Monetary Policy.

Interior and Insular Affairs (26th). Subcommittees: Coast Guard and Navigation; Merchant Marine.

Group Ratings

	ADA	COPE	PC	RPN	NFU	LCV	CFA	NAB	NSI	ACA	NTU
1978	60	94	68	20	63	–	64	10	50	24	–
1977	65	90	73	33	89	66	65	–	–	8	24
1976	60	82	79	41	91	87	81	8	20	14	36

Key Votes

1) Increase Def Spnd	AGN	6) Alaska Lands Protect	FOR	11) Delay Auto Pol Cntrl	AGN
2) B-1 Bomber	FOR	7) Water Projects Veto	FOR	12) Sugar Price Escalator	AGN
3) Cargo Preference	FOR	8) Consum Protect Agcy	FOR	13) Pub Fin Cong Cmpgns	FOR
4) Dereg Nat Gas	AGN	9) Common Situs Picket	FOR	14) ERA Ratif Recissn	AGN
5) Kemp-Roth	AGN	10) Labor Law Revision	FOR	15) Prohibt Govt Abrtns	AGN

Election Results

1978 general	Jerry M. Patterson (D)	75,471	(59%)	($134,557)
	Don Goedeke (R)	53,298	(41%)	($61,319)
1978 primary	Jerry M. Patterson (D), unopposed			
1976 general	Jerry M. Patterson (D)	103,317	(64%)	($104,635)
	James Combs (R)	59,092	(36%)	($50,299)

THIRTY-NINTH DISTRICT

The 39th congressional district of California is the northern section of the heavily populated part of Orange County, one of three districts wholly or primarily within the limits of this jurisdiction whose name has become synonymous with conservatism. It includes some of Orange County's most important landmarks. In Anaheim there is Disneyland, the amusement park whose opening here in 1955 introduced millions to Orange County, and Angels Stadium. In Fullerton there is the headquarters of Norton Simon's business empire—just one of dozens of successful enterprises which have helped to make Orange County so prosperous. And in tiny Yorba Linda, where the subdivisions thin out and the scrubby hills begin, is the birthplace of Richard Nixon, a man whose career has moved back and forth out of Orange County over the past several decades.

The 39th district is pretty solidly Republican territory; most of the Orange County precincts which sometimes go Democratic were placed in the 38th district next door. In presidential elections it has consistently been the second most Republican district in California; in congressional elections it has pretty much followed suit. For several years this was the district which sent Charles Wiggins to Congress. Wiggins's performance at the House Judiciary Committee impeachment hearings will not be forgotten. Although he took the side that history will record as wrong, his defense of Richard Nixon was eloquent without being rhetorical and persuasive without being hortatory. Wiggins talked calmly, reasonably, and with full command of the facts—a fine trial lawyer with the case of his life. His work came as little surprise to those who had watched him in the House: he was a thoughtful, convincing advocate usually, but not always, of conservative causes. By the time the impeachment hearings had ended, he had enough prestige that his assessment of the June 23 tape was enough to get Nixon to resign.

Like many congressmen, Wiggins tired of the pace of congressional work and the need to stay in touch with constituents so far away. In 1978, after 12 years of service, he decided to retire. The succession in the 39th district was determined when Assemblyman William Dannemeyer was left without opposition in the Republican primary. He had 64% in the general election. Dannemeyer has an unusual background for a Republican congressman: he served in the California Assembly in the middle sixties as a Democrat and only switched parties after he lost a race for the state Senate. But one can assume that his Republican credentials are in order today, and he is not expected to be a major dissenter from Republican ranks in the House.

Census Data Pop. 463,836. Central city, 33%; suburban, 67%. Median family income, $12,749; families above $15,000: 37%; families below $3,000: 5%. Median years education, 12.6.

The Voters

Median voting age 40.
Employment profile White collar, 60%. Blue collar, 28%. Service, 11%. Farm, 1%.
Ethnic groups Spanish, 11%. Total foreign stock, 19%. Canada, 3%; UK, Germany, 2% each; Italy, 1%.

Presidential vote

1976	Carter (D)	73,263	(36%)
	Ford (R)	131,577	(64%)
1972	Nixon (R)	142,003	(73%)
	McGovern (D)	53,220	(27%)

Rep. William E. Dannemeyer (R) Elected 1978; b. Sept. 22, 1929, Long Beach; home, Fullerton; Valparaiso U., B.A. 1950, Hastings Col. of Law, J.D. 1952; Lutheran.

Career Army, Korea; Practicing atty.; Dep. Fullerton Dist. Atty.; Cal. Assembly, 1963–66, 1976–78.

Offices 1206 LHOB, 202-225-4111. Also 1370 Brea Blvd., Suite 108, Fullerton 92632, 714-992-0141.

Committees *Interstate and Foreign Commerce* (15th). Subcommittees: Oversight and Investigations; Health and the Environment.

Post Office and Civil Service (8th). Subcommittees: Postal Personnel and Modernization; Human Resources.

Group Ratings: Newly Elected

Key Votes: Newly Elected

Election Results

1978 general	William E. Dannemeyer (R)	112,160	(64%)	($161,151)
	William E. Farris (D)	63,891	(36%)	($47,172)
1978 primary	William E. Dannemeyer (R), unopposed			
1976 general	Charles E. Wiggins (R)	122,657	(59%)	($51,047)
	William E. Farris (D)	86,745	(41%)	($22,676)

FORTIETH DISTRICT

Only four congressional districts in the United States more than doubled their populations during the sixties. The one with by far the greatest growth—up 130% in 10 years—was the 40th district of California, one of three districts wholly or primarily within the boundaries of Orange County. There was a pause here in growth in the early seventies, so that other districts' populations have probably increased faster during this decade. But in the past few years the Orange County boom has begun again, and it has been concentrated in the central and southern part of the County. So great has been the demand for new houses and condominiums that developers have staged lotteries; the people who get the lucky numbers get to buy the house. The boom has shown no signs of abating, even as large parts of the Irvine Ranch—long the largest undeveloped parcel of land adjacent to a major metropolitan area—is subdivided and sold off. Another factor buoying up market prices: not far beyond the Irvine Ranch and just above the coastal communities to the south are the mountains. There is only so much Orange County, and some day there will be no land left to develop.

Long before Watergate, Orange County entered our political vocabulary as a synonym for conservatism. As its population grew in the fifties and sixties, its Republican margins grew even faster. The kind of people Orange County attracted were naturally inclined to favor Republicans, especially candidates like Ronald Reagan and Richard Nixon. These are well-off people, though not usually the richest in the Los Angeles area; many are engineers, technicians, draftsmen —people who tend to be comfortable with technological precision and apprehensive about social change. They believe strongly in the free enterprise system, the work ethic, and traditional social mores.

Orange County, with its geometrically laid-out subdivisions, its clean shopping centers, and its seemingly homogeneous population, seemed to be the kind of place these people were looking for. In the sixties, when blacks in Watts and students in Berkeley rioted and asserted other values, people in Orange County responded at the ballot box with huge margins for the politicians who upheld their own standards.

But as the seventies have gone on, Republican allegiances have become less solid in Orange County and the confidence and esprit of the conservative voters here seems to have been damaged. One reason is that in many ways their adversaries have prevailed: the lifestyle of most Californians today, including residents of Orange County, resembles more closely the counterculture heroes of a dozen years ago than it does the traditional model people here had in mind. Orange County has become younger, and as it has become larger it has become less homogeneous. Also Orange County's values seem to have been betrayed by some of its leaders. This was a county very much touched by Watergate: Richard Nixon was born here and his San Clemente mansion is within the 40th district; a few miles away on the Pacific Coast Highway is the gleaming high-rise on whose top floor Nixon's personal lawyer, Herbert Kalmbach, had his offices and went forth to distribute hush money. Nixon and his aides claimed to be representing the old morality; but they betrayed its most basic tenets. Ronald Reagan claimed that the Watergate defendants were "not criminals at heart." But they were criminals under the law and in the settled judgment of the American people.

Scandals and schisms have also hurt conservative morale in the 40th congressional district. Congressman John Schmitz, a member of the John Birch Society, was defeated in his Republican primary in 1972 and became the presidential candidate of the American Independent Party, once George Wallace's vehicle. He got a negligible number of votes, outside Idaho and a few Rocky Mountain enclaves. But he has made a local comeback and with his puckish good humor was elected to the California Senate in 1978. Schmitz's successor was the Orange County Assessor,

Andrew Hinshaw, a man with a reputation for efficiency and honesty in a demanding job. But in 1976 Hinshaw was convicted of accepting bribes from Radio Shack.

In the primary that year, Assemblyman Robert Badham edged Schmitz by 1%. The 40th, which contains the most Republican parts of Orange County, is still a very Republican district despite the party's sag in fortunes, and Badham was elected with 59% in the general election. In 1978, he increased that to a more customary 66%. His voting record is by any measure solidly conservative.

Census Data Pop. 464,254. Central city, 7%; suburban, 93%. Median family income, $12,093; families above $15,000: 35%; families below $3,000: 6%. Median years education, 12.8.

The Voters

Median voting age 37.
Employment profile White collar, 64%. Blue collar, 23%. Service, 12%. Farm, 1%.
Ethnic groups Black, 1%. Spanish, 8%. Total foreign stock, 19%. Canada, UK, 3% each; Germany, 2%; Italy, 1%.

Presidential vote

1976	Carter (D)	79,649	(32%)
	Ford (R)	167,203	(68%)
1972	Nixon (R)	157,926	(73%)
	McGovern (D)	59,110	(27%)

Rep. Robert E. Badham (R) Elected 1976; b. June 9, 1929, Los Angeles; home, Newport Beach; Occidental Col., 1947–48, Stanford U., B.A. 1951; Lutheran.

Career Navy, Korea; Secy. and V.P., Hoffman Hardware, Los Angeles, 1954–69; Cal. Assembly, 1963–77.

Offices 1108 LHOB, 202-225-5611. Also 1649 Westcliff, Newport Beach 92660, 714-631-0040.

Committees *Armed Services* (13th). Subcommittees: Investigations; Procurement and Military Nuclear Systems.

House Administration (6th). Subcommittees: Accounts; Office Systems.

Group Ratings

	ADA	COPE	PC	RPN	NFU	LCV	CFA	NAB	NSI	ACA	NTU
1978	10	21	10	73	10	–	0	100	100	100	–
1977	0	10	13	67	14	5	10	–	–	96	66

Key Votes

1) Increase Def Spnd	FOR	6) Alaska Lands Protect	DNV	11) Delay Auto Pol Cntrl	DNV
2) B-1 Bomber	FOR	7) Water Projects Veto	AGN	12) Sugar Price Escalator	FOR
3) Cargo Preference	AGN	8) Consum Protect Agcy	AGN	13) Pub Fin Cong Cmpgns	AGN
4) Dereg Nat Gas	FOR	9) Common Situs Picket	AGN	14) ERA Ratif Recissn	AGN
5) Kemp-Roth	FOR	10) Labor Law Revision	AGN	15) Prohibt Govt Abrtns	DNV

Election Results

1978 general	Robert E. Badham (R)	147,882	(66%)	($51,719)
	Jim McGuy (D)	76,358	(34%)	($5,182)
1978 primary	Robert E. Badham (R), unopposed			
1976 general	Robert E. Badham (R)	148,512	(59%)	($124,733)
	Vivian Hall (D)	102,132	(41%)	($27,040)

FORTY-FIRST DISTRICT

Before World War II, San Diego was a sleepy resort town with a fine natural harbor and a few Navy installations. Then the United States fought a war in the Pacific, and San Diego was forever changed. It became the Navy's West Coast headquarters, and Navy installations proliferated. In ater years its pleasant climate—perhaps the most equable in the continental United States—made t a favorite retirement place for Navy officers and for others as well. But San Diego, like most Sun Belt cities, is far more than a collection of retirement villages. It has developed a major ndustrial base, largely on high-skill businesses; its metropolitan area population has reached more han 1.5 million.

Before World War II San Diego was evenly divided politically, split between the well-to-do Republican north side and the more Mexican-American Democratic south side. In the years ollowing the war, the heavy in-migration gave both the city and county of San Diego a very Republican, conservative complexion. Richard Nixon for years regarded this as his "lucky city"—until the unfolding ITT scandal caused him to cancel plans to have the 1972 Republican National Convention here. Since Watergate San Diego seems to have become an area where the wo parties are competitive; Democrats have even managed to capture most of the county's Assembly seats. The city has elected a moderate Republican, Pete Wilson, as Mayor, who has urned around traditional attitudes by stressing that there sould be limits on San Diego's growth.

San Diego has also seen a significant challenge of 41st congressional district Congressman Bob Wilson. The 41st includes most of the city's comfortable neighborhoods, like Mission Bay, and ew of its black and Mexican-American areas; the affluent parts are full of Navy retirees, who often have strong right-wing views. But the 41st also includes a couple of local colleges and ncreasingly a younger population; the newer retirement subdivisions are being built in the hills of the city beyond the district or in the suburbs. Bob Wilson had been peripherally involved in the negotiations in which ITT helped guarantee San Diego's bid for the Republican convention, and he found himself with strong opposition in 1974. He ended up winning with a creditable 56%, in arge part because his opponent clamped a low spending limit on her campaign; Wilson outspent her 3–1.

Since then Wilson has been reelected with accustomed ease, though not with overwhelming margins. He was first elected to Congress in 1952, which makes him tied with John Rhodes as the number one seniority Republican in the House. He used to be Chairman of the House Republican Campaign Committee, until the Nixon people dumped him in 1973. Now he is ranking Republican on the House Armed Services Committee. He is one who would rather risk spending oo much on defense than too little, and presumably he looks after the military needs of San Diego.

Census Data Pop. 464,046. Central city, 89%; suburban, 11%. Median family income, $11,118; amilies above $15,000: 29%; families below $3,000: 7%. Median years education, 12.6.

The Voters

Median voting age 39.
Employment profile White collar, 64%. Blue collar, 23%. Service, 13%. Farm, –%.
Ethnic groups Black, 1%. Spanish, 9%. Total foreign stock, 21%. Canada, 3%; UK, Germany, 2% each; Italy, 1%.

Presidential vote

1976	Carter (D)	90,795	(43%)
	Ford (R)	122,469	(57%)
1972	Nixon (R)	135,629	(63%)
	McGovern (D)	79,660	(37%)

Rep. Bob Wilson (R) Elected 1952; b. April 5, 1916, Calexico; home, San Diego; San Diego St. Col., 1933–35, Otis Art. Inst.; Presbyterian.

Career Advertising, public relations.

Offices 2307 RHOB, 202-225-3201. Also Rm. 6(S)15, Fed. Bldg., 880 Front St., San Diego 92188, 714-231-0957.

Committees *Armed Services* (Ranking Member). Subcommittees: Procurement and Military Nuclear Systems.

Group Ratings

	ADA	COPE	PC	RPN	NFU	LCV	CFA	NAB	NSI	ACA	NTU
1978	15	26	5	60	10	–	14	89	89	73	–
1977	0	35	20	33	27	3	10	–	–	67	29
1976	0	23	5	88	18	24	0	83	100	57	29

Key Votes

1) Increase Def Spnd	FOR	6) Alaska Lands Protect	AGN	11) Delay Auto Pol Cntrl	FOR
2) B-1 Bomber	FOR	7) Water Projects Veto	AGN	12) Sugar Price Escalator	FOR
3) Cargo Preference	FOR	8) Consum Protect Agcy	AGN	13) Pub Fin Cong Cmpgns	AGN
4) Dereg Nat Gas	FOR	9) Common Situs Picket	AGN	14) ERA Ratif Recissn	AGN
5) Kemp-Roth	FOR	10) Labor Law Revision	FOR	15) Prohibt Govt Abrtns	FOR

Election Results

1978 general	Bob Wilson (R)	107,685	(58%)	($118,820)
	King Golden, Jr. (D)	77,540	(42%)	($26,331)
1978 primary	Bob Wilson (R), unopposed			
1976 general	Bob Wilson (R)	128,784	(58%)	($93,238)
	King Golden, Jr. (D)	94,590	(42%)	($28,448)

FORTY-SECOND DISTRICT

To many San Diego evokes images of La Jolla, its shopping streets lined with boutiques and stockbrokers' offices, or Mission Bay, with its comfortable rambling homes of retired Navy officers, or perhaps just a picture of the magnificent Balboa Park Zoo. But there is another San Diego, just a few miles away, down by the docks and on the flat, dusty land going down to Tijuana. It is here that most of the city's blacks and Mexican-Americans live, on the south side of San Diego and in the dockside suburbs of Chula Vista and National City. Together with a few suburbs and some middle class neighborhoods, this poorer, blacker, browner part of San Diego makes up the 42d congressional district of California.

This is the only part of the San Diego area with traditional Democratic voting habits. When it came time after the 1960 Census to create a second district in the area, the Democratic legislature made sure that all the heavily Democratic territory was gathered together in the seat, and it has been ever since. The first and so far only Congressman here has been Democrat Lionel Van Deerlin, a former television newscaster and editorialist. He has had a mostly quiet congressional career, except in early 1967, when he was the first to raise his voice against Adam Clayton Powell and his alleged malpractices. A kind of hysteria swept the House and Powell was barred from taking his seat—an act which the Supreme Court later ruled unconstitutional.

Van Deerlin has sat on the Commerce Committee since he came to Congress and in recent years has succeeded to a position of real power. He became a subcommittee chairman in 1975, but the body he headed then, Consumer Protection and Finance, was not one of the committee's plums; it governs no major regulatory commission or great industry.

But in 1977, after Torbert Macdonald died, Van Deerlin took over the Communications Subcommittee. It must have been a heady moment for a former newscaster; this is the body that writes the laws which govern the heavily regulated broadcasting industry. Macdonald had done little with the subcommittee, but in his first term as Chairman Van Deerlin proposed a major overhaul of the Communications Act. He has pushed some lesser legislation through, notably on public broadcasting, and hopes for action on the major bill in the 96th Congress. Van Deerlin's bill would, at least theoretically, lessen regulation of television and radio and make the duration of broadcast licenses indefinite; it would also ease entry into cable TV and tax broadcasters for use of airwave frequencies. While the major broadcast interests might welcome deregulation, they oppose the latter provisions. It is not clear that there is much of constituency behind Van Deerlin's bill, nor does he appear to have the kind of clout which could get it enacted single-handed. Moreover, he has been quoted as saying that he would compromise any provision to pass the bill—which suggests that any overhaul bill which is finally enacted may not change things very much.

Census Data Pop. 464,208. Central city, 53%; suburban, 47%. Median family income, $8,960; families above $15,000: 16%; families below $3,000: 11%. Median years education, 12.2.

The Voters

Median voting age 35.
Employment profile White collar, 46%. Blue collar, 36%. Service, 17%. Farm, 1%.
Ethnic groups Black, 11%. Filipino, 2%. Spanish, 19%. Total foreign stock, 23%. Canada, 2%; UK, Germany, Italy, 1% each.

Presidential vote

1976	Carter (D)	69,939	(53%)
	Ford (R)	62,460	(47%)
1972	Nixon (R)	76,127	(57%)
	McGovern (D)	58,538	(43%)

Rep. Lionel Van Deerlin (D) Elected 1962; b. July 25, 1914, Los Angeles; home, San Diego; USC, B.A., 1937; Episcopalian.

Career Reporter and desk man, Minneapolis *Tribune*, Baltimore *Evening Sun*; City Ed., San Diego *Journal*; Army, WWII; News Director, San Diego TV Stations KFSD and XETV.

Offices 2408 RHOB, 202-225-5672. Also P.O. Box 729, San Diego 92112, 714-233-8959.

Committees *House Administration* (9th). Subcommittees: Personnel and Police; Printing; Information and Computers.

Interstate and Foreign Commerce (3d). Subcommittees: Communications (Chairman).

Group Ratings

	ADA	COPE	PC	RPN	NFU	LCV	CFA	NAB	NSI	ACA	NTU
1978	60	83	68	67	80	–	55	9	40	0	–
1977	60	90	75	40	58	72	75	–	–	12	22
1976	80	91	80	50	73	93	64	27	50	11	25

Key Votes

1) Increase Def Spnd	AGN	6) Alaska Lands Protect	FOR	11) Delay Auto Pol Cntrl	AGN
2) B-1 Bomber	AGN	7) Water Projects Veto	AGN	12) Sugar Price Escalator	AGN
3) Cargo Preference	FOR	8) Consum Protect Agcy	FOR	13) Pub Fin Cong Cmpgns	FOR
4) Dereg Nat Gas	AGN	9) Common Situs Picket	FOR	14) ERA Ratif Recissn	AGN
5) Kemp-Roth	AGN	10) Labor Law Revision	FOR	15) Prohibt Govt Abrtns	DNV

Election Results

1978 general	Lionel Van Deerlin (D)	85,126	(74%)	($72,903)
	Lawrence C. Mattera (R)	30,319	(26%)	($16,833)
1978 primary	Lionel Van Deerlin (D)	47,730	(82%)	
	One other (D)	10,618	(18%)	
1976 general	Lionel Van Deerlin (D)	103,062	(76%)	($63,764)
	Wes Marden (R)	32,565	(24%)	($3,924)

FORTY-THIRD DISTRICT

The 41st and 42d districts of California include most of the city of San Diego; the 43d includes almost all of the rest of San Diego County, plus Imperial County and a small slice of Riverside County as well. This district has a somewhat complex history: in its present form it includes most of the political base of Congressman Clare Burgener (the San Diego suburbs), plus some territory that used to belong to Congressman Victor Veysey (Imperial and Riverside). Veysey, knowing that Burgener would win any primary between them, moved to the newly created 35th district in 1974, but was beaten.

Most of the population of the 43d district is clustered around San Diego: the beach towns of Del Mar, Leucadia, and Carlsbad along the ocean to the north; inland hill suburbs like Escondido; and the residential middle class enclaves east of the city like El Cajon and Spring Valley. Farther inland one comes to the Indian reservations that dot the interior mountains. Across the mountains is the Imperial Valley, an incredibly rich agricultural area whose large landowners like to think of themselves as the last bastion of free enterprise, but who are actually direct beneficiaries of millions of dollars the federal government has spent on irrigation projects.

Congressman Burgener, first elected in 1972, votes like a standard conservative Republican —which is surely in accord with the wishes of most of his constituents. A former state legislator, he was widely respected in Sacramento for his work on welfare legislation; in Washington, he has attracted little notice but has won seats on the Budget and Appropriations Committees. That Burgener is not a run-of-the-mill legislator, however, is indicated by a proposal he made to bar people from serving in Congress past 70. In his late fifties himself, he has quite a few years ahead; he was reelected with 69% in 1978.

Census Data Pop. 464,325. Central city, 9%; suburban, 75%. Median family income, $9,995; families above $15,000: 23%; families below $3,000: 9%. Median years education, 12.4.

The Voters

Median voting age 44.
Employment profile White collar, 52%. Blue collar, 30%. Service, 13%. Farm, 5%.
Ethnic groups Black, 1%. Spanish, 16%. Total foreign stock, 22%. Canada, UK, Germany, 2% each.

Presidential vote

1976	Carter (D)	106,706	(40%)
	Ford (R)	159,790	(60%)
1972	Nixon (R)	148,139	(68%)
	McGovern (D)	68,647	(32%)

Rep. Clair W. Burgener (R) Elected 1972; b. Dec. 5, 1921, Vernal, Utah; home, Rancho Sante Fe; San Diego St. U., A.B. 1950; Church of Latter Day Saints.

Career Army Air Corps, WWII; Pres. and Owner, Clair W. Burgener Co., Realtors, 1947–72; San Diego City Cncl., 1953–57, Vice-Mayor, 1955–56; Cal. Assembly, 1963–67; Cal. Senate, 1967–73.

Offices 343 CHOB, 202-225-3906. Also Rm. 5(S)35, 880 Front St., San Diego 92188, 714-231-1912

Committees *Appropriations* (14th). Subcommittees: Energy and Water Development; Interior.

Group Ratings

	ADA	COPE	PC	RPN	NFU	LCV	CFA	NAB	NSI	ACA	NTU
1978	10	11	5	60	20	–	9	100	100	88	–
1977	5	19	8	45	36	13	5	–	–	92	43
1976	10	23	5	53	8	12	0	92	100	85	60

Key Votes

1) Increase Def Spnd	FOR	6) Alaska Lands Protect	AGN	11) Delay Auto Pol Cntrl	FOR
2) B-1 Bomber	FOR	7) Water Projects Veto	AGN	12) Sugar Price Escalator	FOR
3) Cargo Preference	FOR	8) Consum Protect Agcy	AGN	13) Pub Fin Cong Cmpgns	AGN
4) Dereg Nat Gas	FOR	9) Common Situs Picket	AGN	14) ERA Ratif Recissn	AGN
5) Kemp-Roth	FOR	10) Labor Law Revision	AGN	15) Prohibt Govt Abrtns	FOR

Election Results

1978 general	Clair W. Burgener (R)	167,150	(69%)	($90,072)
	Ruben B. Brooks (D)	76,308	(31%)	($8,511)
1978 primary	Clair W. Burgener (R)	84,234	(76%)	
	Martin J. Kinkade (R)	27,106	(24%)	
1976 general	Clair W. Burgener (R)	173,576	(65%)	($61,233)
	Pat Kelly (D)	93,475	(35%)	($5,276)

COLORADO

To outsiders Colorado means backpacking in the Rockies, skiing at Aspen or Vail, or wandering through old mining towns like Central City. But the part of Colrado that matters most politically is the thin strip of land at the base of the Rockies' Eastern Slope, where the arid plateau of eastern Colorado yields suddenly to the mountains. Two-thirds of Colorado's voters live on this sliver of land running up and down the state, and the proportion is growing—Eastern Slope population rose 33% during the sixties and another 15% in the first half of the seventies, considerably more than the rest of the state. Attracted by the temperate climate, the proximity of winter and summer recreation, a local economy which has been booming (Denver has become a major energy development center), newcomers continue to arrive, particularly in metropolitan Denver (which has 55% of the state's population) and other Eastern Slope cities like Colorado Springs, Greeley, and Fort Collins.

In the days before the Eastern Slope dominated Colorado, this rather homogeneous state had a politics of bipartisan conservatism. Republicans from the ranching and farming areas of the eastern plains vied against Democrats from the mountains of the Western Slope, with few sharp differences between them. But in the last 15 years Colorado has been swept by two political movements, both notably more ideological than Colorado had been used to, and both given major impetus by newcomers to the state. Both were rooted chiefly in the concerns of the people of the Eastern Slope; both relied heavily on volunteer activity by suburban housewives and even high school students; both reflected the changing concerns of Coloradans and both movements overturned the state's political order. First there were the conservative Republicans, who established their hegemony in 1962, and who ran out of steam in the early seventies. Then there were the liberal Democrats, who swept the state in 1974 and, while they have suffered significant setbacks since, still hold most of the major statewide offices.

First the Republicans. In 1962 a group of young, personable, obscure Republicans got together and planned to unseat the Democratic governor and senator. Their candidates were John Love of Broadmoor (a suburb of Colorado Springs) for governor and Peter Dominick of Englewood (a suburb of Denver) for senator, and they both won handily. They were not the sort of moderate, middle-of-the-road Republicans who were thought to be the only kind who could win statewide elections in those days; they (Dominick especially) were strongminded conservatives, and they showed how much appeal their politics could have in middle class neighborhoods. This was, remember, the early Kennedy years—a time when the young, newly successful suburban migrants of Colorado were resenting the high level of federal taxes and were beginning to believe that the country needed less government interference in their affairs. They were tired of the steel-rimmed oldtime New Dealers who were spending their money to pay off union members and welfare chiselers back east; they were self-reliant Westerners, and they identified with the views and personalities of the well-groomed, well-to-do Love and Dominick. They formed the hard core that reelected Love in 1966 and 1970, Dominick in 1968, and Republican Senator Gordon Allott in 1966.

As the years went on, these Colorado Republicans found themselves under attack by a new breed of Democrats. The source of their initial fervor and energy was opposition to the Vietnam war; and by 1970 they were able to beat the more hawkish oldtime Democrats, including incumbent congressmen, in major primaries. But later the issue became not so much the war as a strong insistence on reforming political procedures and the environment.

In Colorado, as throughout the West, environmental issues became important as the sixties turned into seventies. You only have to visit a place like Denver, not to mention Los Angeles, to see why. Every day metropolitan concentrations have been changing the face of the land—and the quality of the air and quantity of the water as well. In Eastern cities suburbs shade gently into farmland; but beyond the last sidewalk of a suburban Denver subdivision you can see nothing but the arid, virgin land and perhaps the side of a mountain. There is no greater contrast possible between what the land was and what it has become. Environmental issues almost inevitably involve a tradeoff between somebody's economic gain and the general public's interest in environmental purity. Republicans in states like Colorado, with their strong belief in free enterprise and their antipathy to government regulation, are inclined to sympathize with affected business interests; antiwar Democrats by temperament are inclined the other way—which, when the environment first became an important issue, was by far the more popular.

The shift of opinion became clear in 1972. That year a group of environmental activists put on the ballot the issue of state funding of the 1976 Winter Olympics. The businessmen who wanted the Olympics in Colorado could have expected strong public support a few years before. But now voters were ready to listen to arguments that the Olympics would be too expensive and would destroy too much of Colorado's natural environment; and the Olympics were voted out of the state. That same year Senator Gordon Allott, a man given to acerbic statements about environmental and other issues, was defeated by a Republican-turned-Democrat, Floyd Haskell, whose television campaign used Allott's statements against him.

The politician who was the biggest winner in the Olympics referendum was Richard Lamm, a young state legislator and law professor who led the referendum campaign. He had already attracted controversy as the sponsor of Colorado's liberalized abortion law; as an outdoors buff he seemed to symbolize the young newcomers who didn't want to see Colorado "Californicated" in order to make profits for developers. Considered a far-out reformer, Lamm was elected Governor in 1974, beating John Vanderhoof, who had succeeded Love when he took a Ford Administration appointment. Lamm represented a new kind of liberalism—not the kind of New Deal thinking that saw the federal government as the only champion of the common man. Like the conservatism of Colorado Republicans, it owed some of its success to the desires of

Coloradans—many of them newcomers—that some things just be left alone. And like the earlier movement, it made its greatest gains in the politically volatile suburbs of Denver.

Lamm proved something of a disappointment to his backers, particularly in his first two years in office, which have been described as disastrous. He was unable to get his programs through; he feuded with the press; he managed to be abrasive without being effective. In 1976 Republicans won control of both houses of the legislature, and Lamm switched directions. He became more conciliatory and stressed governmental economy. He also took a strong stand against the Carter Administration's policy of cancelling federal water projects in Western states. Environmentalists a few years before had argued that extensive water projects opened the way for overdevelopment and destruction of the environment. But Lamm boasted that he was able to restore some of the projects Carter cancelled.

Lamm was expected to be in trouble in 1978, and would have been but for the mistakes of his opponent, state Senator Ted Strickland. The cultural contrast between the two candidates reflected differences among recent migrants to Colorado: Lamm was educated in Wisconsin and California, calls himself a Unitarian, taught in a university, is a backpacker and mountain climber; Strickland was born in Texas, is a Baptist, has had success in an oil-related business, was a leader in the Reagan for president campaign in 1976, and likes to preach in Baptist churches. Lamm and Strickland got into a heated argument over who had sabotaged efforts to improve Colorado's air quality, but probably more important to the result was Strickland's proposal to phase out Lowry Air Force Base near Denver and to place a solar energy research center in rural Colorado rather than the Denver area. Coloradans who in principle approve of the idea of lower government spending do not always follow it to its logical extreme when it involves projects in Colorado. Lamm was reelected with 60% of the vote, an excellent percentage but one which reflects Strickland's unpopularity more than Lamm's strength. The Republicans continue to have majorities in the legislature.

The other major official chosen in the 1974 campaign was Senator Gary Hart. Two years earlier, this seemed an unlikely result; Hart was campaign manager for George McGovern, who got only 36% in Colorado. Yet Hart beat incumbent Peter Dominick with fully 59% of the vote. And Hart had to win the nomination over opponents with significant backing. In the general, he was aided by Dominick's mistakes: Dominick had said that Watergate was "insignificant," and his personal health was visibly poor. Yet Hart also established a political persona of his own. He stressed that he opposed a lot of federal programs and was wary of government action generally; he promoted himself explicitly as the representative of a new generation ("They've had their turn, now it's our turn"). In the Senate he serves on the Environment Committee (formerly Public Works) and is a respected member of the Armed Services Committee and the special panel that has jurisdiction over intelligence agencies. Though he can be called an environmentalist, Hart has not hesitated to fight the Carter Administration when it tried to cancel Colorado water projects. He is respected by both hawks and doves on Armed Services, and when he takes a position on any issue he is taken seriously.

Hart is sometimes given credit for having one of the best political brains in Washington. He played a large part in fashioning McGovern's 1972 primary strategy, whose brilliance is often forgotten because of the general election campaign that followed. In any case, Hart's 1974 campaign in Colorado was a tour de force. He articulates as well as anyone what might be called post-New Deal liberalism, and legislatively he is well on top of his facts before making a significant move. Hart is up for reelection in 1980, in a state that has just rejected one Democratic senator and seems to be in the midst of at least a mild Republican trend generally. But he seems to have stayed in close touch with opinion in Colorado and to enter the election year in good shape. Hart has begun what appears to be a strong Senate career, and there are those who think he has wider ambitions. He has made little attempt as yet to establish himself as a national figure—he turned 40 only in 1977—but to some he seems a more authentic and persuasive spokesman of his generation of Democrats than his law school classmate (but no special friend), Jerry Brown of California.

The Colorado Republicans' 1962 victories were followed by 12 years of pretty much undisturbed governance; the Democrats' tenure may very well be shorter and in any case has proved more turbulent. The state's economy has suffered some recessions, and some voters are seeing virtues in growth that they had not noticed in more prosperous times. Jimmy Carter has proved to be anything but popular here: Coloradans find fault with his energy policies, his water policies, his economic policies, and generally do not find him a sympathetic figure. And individual Democratic officeholders have their weaknesses.

That certainly was the case with Senator Floyd Haskell, who was soundly defeated in his bid for a second term in 1978. Haskell's problem can be summarized simply: he was elected in a quick, inexpensive campaign aimed at his opponent's weaknesses, and he never did enough to improve his own standing. Haskell is a stand-offish man, not fond of campaigning or promoting himself. He became a Democrat only in 1970, but in the Senate had a strongly liberal record; he worked hard on the Energy and Finance Committees, but had few easy-to-summarize accomplishments he could point to.

The Republican candidate, William Armstrong, had his own vulnerabilities: an ultraconservative voting record, a not particularly good environmental record. But he also had 1978's major issue very much on his side: he is strong for cutting government spending and taxes, and could paint Haskell as a typical Democratic big spender. Armstrong won big in the Denver suburbs, and his victory establishes him at a youthful age—he was born the same year as Hart—as a major political figure here. In the Senate Armstrong is expected to work more or less closely with the informal group of Rocky Mountain conservative Republicans which has formed around Nevada's Paul Laxalt and Utah's Jake Garn.

Colorado's other 1978 election results showed the Democrats on the defensive—although they did not lose much ground. They retained, by varying margins, three of the state's five congressional districts; they lost a little ground in the legislature. Colorado has not repudiated the Democrats who won in 1974, but it has not endorsed them without reservations either. The political direction of this state that many believe has become a pace-setter in the nation is by no means clear.

Census Data Pop. 2,207,259; 1.09% of U.S. total, 30th largest; Central city, 34%; suburban, 38%. Median family income, $9,553; 21st highest; families above $15,000: 20%; families below $3,000: 9%. Median years education, 12.4.

1977 Share of Federal Tax Burden $4,076,000,000; 1.18% of U.S. total, 26th largest.

1977 Share of Federal Outlays $5,227,530,000; 1.32% of U.S. total, 26th largest. Per capita federal spending, $2,063.

DOD	$1,444,537,000	19th (1.58%)	HEW	$1,400,500,000	35th (0.95%)
ERDA	$132,096,000	14th (2.23%)	HUD	$46,613,000	29th (1.10%)
NASA	$56,185,000	11th (1.42%)	VA	$254,581,000	29th (1.32%)
DOT	$266,851,000	17th (1.87%)	EPA	$50,487,000	32d (0.62%)
DOC	$117,037,000	18th (1.41%)	RevS	$82,867,000	30th (0.98%)
DOI	$366,168,000	3d (7.87%)	Debt	$178,346,000	25th (0.59%)
USDA	$280,215,000	32d (1.41%)	Other	$551,047	

Economic Base Finance, insurance and real estate; agriculture, notably cattle, wheat, dairy products and corn; food and kindred products; machinery, especially electronic computing equipment; electrical equipment and supplies, especially electronic measuring instruments; printing and publishing, especially newspapers; tourism.

Political Line-up Governor, Richard D. Lamm (D). Senators Gary Hart (D) and William L. Armstrong (R). Representatives 5 (3 D and 2 R). State Senate (22 R and 13 D); State House (38 R and 27 D).

The Voters

Registration 1,345,006 Total. 470,858 D (35%); 373,270 R (28%); 500,878 Unaffiliated (37%).
Median voting age 40
Employment profile White collar, 54%. Blue collar, 28%. Service, 14%. Farm, 4%.
Ethnic groups Black, 3%. Spanish, 13%. Total foreign stock, 13%. Germany, 2%; UK, USSR, 1% each.

Presidential vote

1976	Carter (D)	460,801	(44%)
	Ford (R)	584,456	(56%)
1972	Nixon (R)	597,189	(64%)
	McGovern (D)	329,980	(36%)

Sen. Gary Hart (D) Elected 1974, seat up 1980; b. Nov. 28, 1937, Ottawa, Kans.; home, Denver; Bethany Col., Yale U., LL.B. 1964.

Career Atty., U.S. Dept. of Justice; Special Asst. to U.S. Secy. of Interior; Practicing atty., 1967–74; Natl. Campaign Dir., McGovern for Pres., 1971–72.

Offices 254 RSOB, 202-224-5852. Also 1748 High St., Denver 80218, 303-837-4421, and 303 Fed. Bldg., Pueblo 81003, 303-544-5277, ext. 355.

Committees *Armed Services* (8th). Subcommittees: Arms Control; General Procurement; Military Construction and Stockpiles (Chairman).

Budget (8th).

Environment and Public Works (7th). Subcommittees: Water Resources; Resource Protection; Nuclear Regulation (Chairman).

Group Ratings

	ADA	COPE	PC	RPN	NFU	LCV	CFA	NAB	NSI	ACA	NTU
1978	65	78	70	67	100	93	55	27	10	17	–
1977	90	75	90	73	83	–	76	–	–	4	18
1976	75	84	86	60	80	72	85	20	0	8	64

Key Votes

1) Warnke Nom	FOR	6) Egypt-Saudi Arms	AGN	11) Hosptl Cost Contnmnt	FOR
2) Neutron Bomb	AGN	7) Draft Restr Pardon	FOR	12) Clinch River Reactor	AGN
3) Waterwy User Fee	FOR	8) Wheat Price Support	FOR	13) Pub Fin Cong Cmpgns	FOR
4) Dereg Nat Gas	AGN	9) Panama Canal Treaty	FOR	14) ERA Ratif Recissn	FOR
5) Kemp-Roth	AGN	10) Labor Law Rev Clot	FOR	15) Med Necssy Abrtns	FOR

Election Results

1974 general	Gary W. Hart (D)	471,691	(59%)	($352,557)
	Peter H. Dominick (R)	325,508	(41%)	($502,343)
1974 primary	Gary W. Hart (D)	81,161	(40%)	
	Herrick S. Roth (D)	66,819	(33%)	
	Marty Miller (D)	55,339	(27%)	
1968 general	Peter H. Dominick (R)	459,952	(59%)	
	Stephen McNichols (D)	325,584	(41%)	

Sen. William L. Armstrong (R) Elected 1978, seat up 1984; b. Mar. 16, 1937, Fremont, Neb.; home, Aurora; Tulane U., U. of Minn.; Lutheran.

Career Pres., Radio Station KOSI, Aurora; Colo. House of Reps., 1963–64; Colo. Senate, 1965–72, Majority Leader 1969–72; U.S. House of Reps. 1973–78.

Offices 452 RSOB, 202-224-5941. Also Suite 736, 1450 S. Havana, Auroro 80012, 303-837-2655.

Committees *Banking, Housing, and Urban Affairs* (4th). Subcommittees: Financial Institutions; International Finance; Consumer Affairs.

Budget (4th).

Labor and Human Resources (5th). Subcommittees: Employment, Poverty, and Migratory Labor; Aging; Child and Human Development.

Group Ratings

	ADA	COPE	PC	RPN	NFU	LCV	CFA	NAB	NSI	ACA	NTU
1978	5	6	8	43	22	–	9	100	90	92	–
1977	0	17	25	58	17	24	10	–	–	100	74
1976	0	13	15	71	0	16	0	100	100	93	71

Key Votes

1) Increase Def Spnd	FOR	6) Alaska Lands Protect	FOR	11) Delay Auto Pol Cntrl	FOR
2) B-1 Bomber	FOR	7) Water Projects Veto	AGN	12) Sugar Price Escalator	FOR
3) Cargo Preference	AGN	8) Consum Protect Agcy	AGN	13) Pub Fin Cong Cmpgns	AGN
4) Dereg Nat Gas	FOR	9) Common Situs Picket	AGN	14) ERA Ratif Recissn	FOR
5) Kemp-Roth	FOR	10) Labor Law Revision	AGN	15) Prohibt Govt Abrtns	FOR

Election Results

1978 general	William L. Armstrong (R)	480,801	(59%)	($1,081,944)
	Floyd K. Haskell (D)	330,148	(41%)	($664,249)
1978 primary	William L. Armstrong (R)	109,021	(73%)	
	Jack Swigert (R)	39,415	(27%)	($321,545)
1972 general	Floyd K. Haskell (D)	457,545	(51%)	($176,234)
	Gordon Allott (R)	447,957	(49%)	($308,305)

Gov. Richard D. Lamm (D) Elected 1974, term expires Jan. 1983; b. Aug. 3, 1935; U. of Wis., B.B.A. 1957, U. of Cal., LL.B. 1961.

Career CPA, 1961–62; Atty., Colo. Anti-Discrimination Comm., 1962–63; Practicing atty., 1963–75; Colo. House of Reps., 1966–75, Asst. Maj. Ldr., 1971–75; Assoc. Prof. of Law, U. of Denver, 1969–75.

Offices Rm. 136, State Capitol, Denver 80203, 303-892-2471.

Election Results

1978 general	Dick Lamm (D)	483,885	(60%)
	Ted Strickland (R)	317,232	(40%)
1978 primary	Dick Lamm (D), unopposed		
1974 general	Dick Lamm (D)	444,199	(54%)
	John D. Vanderhoof (R)	378,907	(46%)

FIRST DISTRICT

Within sight—except on days when the smog is bad—of the Front Range of the Rockies is the mile high city of Denver. It got its start servicing the needs of local gold miners and cattle ranchers; today it is the service and distribution center for the entire Rocky Mountain region and a major regional center for energy exploration and development. Denver is the largest metropolitan area in the Rocky Mountain states, in fact the largest, except for Houston and Dallas-Fort Worth, between the Mississippi River and the West Coast. But Denver does not necessarily resemble an Easterner's idea of a central city. It has its downtown office buildings—more of them, it seems, every month—but it has no manufacturing base. Most of

Denver's neighborhoods are made up of small, carefully tended houses on pleasant streets. It also has one of the nation's most garish strip highways, Colfax Avenue. There are, to be sure, some slummish neighborhoods in Denver, and there are about equal-sized communities of blacks and Mexican-Americans. But, the mountains aside, this is a city that looks very ordinary—which is striking since its residents consider themselves to be living in a rather distinctive and special place.

Of course it is the regional environment, not the residential neighborhoods, that makes Denver unique. People here like to think of themselves as being close to nature; they are weekend backpackers or amateur mountain climbers. Few other major cities have such an interesting hinterland. The attitudes that this environment inspires have been important indeed in Denver politics in recent years.

The 1st congressional district of Colorado includes most, though not quite all, of the city of Denver. It is more Democratic than the state generally, and it was the only Colorado district to go for Jimmy Carter in 1976. In the early seventies the 1st district registered some of the ups and downs of Colorado politics. Represented for 20 years by a traditional Democrat, it elected two new members of Congress in two successive elections.

The veteran Democrat, Byron Rogers, was upset in the 1970 primary by an antiwar, environment-minded young Democrat. But Denver was not quite ready for such representation and so the 1st instead elected the Republican, District Attorney Mike McKevitt. He was aided by the Democrat's ties to a group which had sought to impose a busing plan in the Denver schools. But McKevitt proved unable to hold onto the district. In 1972, the year young Democratic activists were beating the Winter Olympics in a referendum, they nominated for Congress a 32-year-old attorney, Patricia Schroeder. Her slogan—"if she wins, we win"—referred to the aspirations of Denver's young residents who had not felt represented by Rogers or McKevitt. She opposed the Winter Olympics and backed mass transit and, in an upset, beat McKevitt even as Richard Nixon was sweeping the nation.

Schroeder's career on the Hill has been as unconventional as her first campaign. She won assignment to the House Armed Services Committee, over the objection of then Chairman Edward Hebert; she is currently 17th ranking Democrat on that body. She tends to oppose the Committee's hawkish bipartisan majority. Schroeder remains controversial enough in Denver that she has had tough races almost every two years. Only in 1978 did she win with a percentage that suggests that she has really made this a safe seat—and that may simply result from the out-migration to the suburbs of the kind of voters who are inclined to oppose her. She can probably go on winning; the real question is whether she has the ambition and drive to keep running indefinitely.

Census Data Pop. 441,881. Central city, 99%; suburban, 1%. Median family income, $9,977; families above $15,000: 24%; families below $3,000: 9%. Median years education, 12.5.

The Voters

Median voting age 42.
Employment profile White collar, 61%. Blue collar, 24%. Service, 15%. Farm, –%.
Ethnic groups Black, 10%. Spanish, 14%. Total foreign stock, 17%. Germany, USSR, UK, 2% each.

Presidential vote

1976	Carter (D)	93,764	(50%)
	Ford (R)	93,723	(50%)
1972	Nixon (R)	101,950	(55%)
	McGovern (D)	82,403	(45%)

Rep. Patricia Schroeder (D) Elected 1972; b. July 30, 1940, Portland, Oreg.; home, Denver; U. of Minn., B.S. 1961, Harvard U., J.D. 1964.

Career Field Atty., Natl. Labor Relations Bd., 1964–66; Practicing atty.; Lecturer and Law Instructor, Community Col. of Denver, 1969–70, U. of Denver, Denver Ctr., 1969, Regis Col., 1970–72; Hearing Officer, Colo. Dept. of Personnel, 1971–72; Legal Counsel, Colo. Planned Parenthood.

Offices 2437 RHOB, 202-225-4431. Also Denver Fed. Bldg., 1767 High St., Denver 80218, 303-837-2354.

Committees *Armed Services* (17th). Subcommittees: Research and Development; NATO Standardization, Interoperability, and Readiness.

Post Office and Civil Service (6th). Subcommittees: Civil Service (Chairwoman).

Group Ratings

	ADA	COPE	PC	RPN	NFU	LCV	CFA	NAB	NSI	ACA	NTU
1978	85	85	78	50	50	–	55	33	0	37	–
1977	90	65	83	77	58	72	60	–	–	22	51
1976	65	65	77	72	67	93	73	25	10	22	52

Key Votes

1) Increase Def Spnd	AGN	6) Alaska Lands Protect	FOR	11) Delay Auto Pol Cntrl	FOR
2) B-1 Bomber	AGN	7) Water Projects Veto	FOR	12) Sugar Price Escalator	FOR
3) Cargo Preference	AGN	8) Consum Protect Agcy	AGN	13) Pub Fin Cong Cmpgns	FOR
4) Dereg Nat Gas	FOR	9) Common Situs Picket	FOR	14) ERA Ratif Recissn	AGN
5) Kemp-Roth	AGN	10) Labor Law Revision	FOR	15) Prohibt Govt Abrtns	AGN

Election Results

1978 general	Patricia Schroeder (D)	82,742	(62%)	($119,930)
	Gene Hutcheson (R)	49,845	(38%)	($146,210)
1978 primary	Patricia Schroeder (D), unopposed			
1976 general	Patricia Schroeder (D)	103,037	(54%)	($132,679)
	Don Friedman (R)	89,384	(46%)	($150,047)

SECOND DISTRICT

In 1974 many districts which had regularly elected Republican congressmen chose Democrats instead. The vast majority of those 1974 freshmen have been reelected, changing the partisan balance and the tone of the House in the last three Congresses. One such constituency is the 2d district of Colorado which in the past three elections has chosen Congressman Timothy Wirth, who was one of the original leaders of the 1974 freshman class and in many ways personifies it.

The 2d is a varied district, made up of three distinct parts. First there is Jefferson County, just west of Denver and its fastest-growing suburban area, a place where young engineers and accountants and office clerks and assembly line workers and their families have been settling within clear sight (on most days) of the Front Range. Affluent, upwardly mobile, home of the ultraconservative and politically active Coors brewing family, Jefferson County is usually solidly Republican. Second there is Boulder County, with the University of Colorado dominating the neat town just at the base of a mountain. In 1972 the 18-year-old vote produced a mini-revolution here, with Democrats elected to local office; two years later students were more apathetic, and two councilmen who voted for a gay rights ordinance were swept from office. Third there is a small Mexican-American neighborhood on the west side of Denver, which casts only 8% of the district's votes, but produces large enough Democratic margins to make a political difference.

When Tim Wirth decided to run here in 1974, it was apparent that the district was moving in his direction. Environmental issues—like the 1972 referendum on the Winter Olympics—definitely favored the Democrats. With Boulder County suddenly capable of producing Democratic margins, the tenacious Republican incumbent, Donald Brotzman, was in trouble. Wirth, a 35-year-old former White House fellow, was an attractive candidate and managed a 52% win.

Once elected Wirth was one of the leaders of the 1974 Freshman Caucus. Previous freshman class organizations had been social; this one had a real effect. It insisted on better committee assignments and pushed for ouster of some committee chairmen. The effect continues to be felt in the House today: chairmen now know that they are accountable to their fellow members and no longer feel free to act arbitrarily as they did in the past.

Wirth's voting record is not typical of oldtime Democrats. In general he seems, like many of the 1974 freshmen elected in previously Republican districts, to be more liberal than traditional Democrats on non-economic issues and more conservative than traditional Democrats on economic issues. This can have important consequences, since he is a member of the Budget Committee. On specifics he sometimes is found on both sides of an issue; on deregulation of natural gas, for example, he initially lined up with opponents but has later worked for compromises which would provide some deregulation. Overall his record probably is responsive to the thinking of at least large parts of his constituency.

Since 1974 Colorado has been trending in the Republican direction; the environmental ideas which were so attractive in the abstract have proved more controversial when people try to put them into effect. Wirth has been closely pressed in the last two elections by state Senator Ed Scott, who once played Sheriff Scotty on a Denver children's TV show. These have been expensive campaigns and every precinct has been seriously contested. Wirth has won by accumulating substantial margins in Boulder and Denver each time, to overcome Scott's small edge in Jefferson County. A 53% winner in 1978, Wirth still cannot be considered the holder of a safe seat.

Census Data Pop. 439,399. Central city, 17%; suburban, 83%. Median family income, $11,201; families above $15,000: 26%; families below $3,000: 6%. Median years education, 12.6.

The Voters

Median voting age 38.
Employment profile White collar, 60%. Blue collar, 28%. Service, 11%. Farm, 1%.
Ethnic groups Spanish, 10%. Total foreign stock, 12%. Germany, 2%; UK, USSR, 1% each.

Presidential vote

1976	Carter (D)	100,538	(42%)
	Ford (R)	137,501	(58%)
1972	Nixon (R)	142,326	(65%)
	McGovern (D)	76,789	(35%)

Rep. Timothy E. Wirth (D) Elected 1974; b. Sept. 22, 1939, Santa Fe, N.M.; home, Denver; Harvard U., A.B. 1961, M.Ed. 1964, Stanford U., Ph.D. 1973.

Career White House Fellow, Spec. Asst. to Secy. of HEW, 1967–68; Deputy Asst. Secy. of Educ., HEW, 1969–70; Businessman, Great Western United Corp.; Mgr., Rocky Mt. Ofc., Arthur D. Little, Inc., consultants.

Offices 312 CHOB, 202-225-2161. Also 9485 W. Colfax, Lakewood 80215, 303-234-5200.

Committees *Interstate and Foreign Commerce* (11th). Subcommittees: Communications; Energy and Power; Oversight and Investigations.

Budget (13th). Subcommittees: Regulations and Spending Limitations; Budget Process; Legislative Savings.

Group Ratings

	ADA	COPE	PC	RPN	NFU	LCV	CFA	NAB	NSI	ACA	NTU
1978	50	65	73	75	70	–	55	20	22	23	–
1977	70	83	85	67	75	85	55	–	–	12	39
1976	75	78	77	65	83	89	81	17	10	12	19

Key Votes

1) Increase Def Spnd	AGN	6) Alaska Lands Protect	FOR	11) Delay Auto Pol Cntrl	AGN
2) B-1 Bomber	AGN	7) Water Projects Veto	AGN	12) Sugar Price Escalator	FOR
3) Cargo Preference	AGN	8) Consum Protect Agcy	FOR	13) Pub Fin Cong Cmpgns	FOR
4) Dereg Nat Gas	FOR	9) Common Situs Picket	FOR	14) ERA Ratif Recissn	AGN
5) Kemp-Roth	AGN	10) Labor Law Revision	FOR	15) Prohibt Govt Abrtns	AGN

Election Results

1978 general	Timothy E. Wirth (D)	98,889	(53%)	($396,798)
	Ed Scott (R)	88,072	(47%)	($554,538)
1978 primary	Timothy E. Wirth (D), unopposed			
1976 general	Timothy E. Wirth (D)	121,336	(50%)	($183,708)
	Ed Scott (R)	118,936	(50%)	($147,719)

THIRD DISTRICT

The 3d congressional district of Colorado is an odd geographical combination. It looks regular enough on the map, covering roughly the southern half of the state. But anyone who knows anything about Colorado knows that the 3d spans some of the most diverse terrain in the United States. The western half of the district is entirely mountainous. This is an area with its own special needs and inclinations and its own political traditions, the so-called Western Slope of the Rockies, where almost half the district's votes are cast. There is substantial variation here: there are skiing resorts, mining towns, Indian reservations, and places where Spanish is the most commonly spoken language. East of the Front Range the mountains suddenly cease; there begin the flat plains that slope imperceptibly hundreds of miles to the Mississippi River. Most of the voters here are concentrated in Pueblo, one of Colorado's least glamorous cities. Having a major steel plant and relatively little else, it is a blue collar town, with a substantial Spanish-speaking minority. The 3d also includes a small portion of Colorado Springs, a much more affluent and faster-growing town, as well as some ranching country to the east.

The 3d gained its present geographical shape for political reasons that no longer obtain. It was drawn to be a safe district for Democratic Congressman Frank Evans, but no sooner was that done than Evans found himself in political trouble. He was attacked by Democrats for being insufficiently devoted to environmental causes (a primary opponent got 38% in 1974) and by Republicans for not paying close enough attention to the district (a general election opponent got 48% in 1976). First elected in 1964 and with substantial seniority on the Appropriations Committee, Evans nonetheless decided to retire in 1978. He might be counted as a victim of the increasing demands placed on a congressman's time by his colleagues and his constituents.

In partisan terms, the 3d is a fairly evenly divided district; Gerald Ford carried it with just 51% in 1976, and Hubert Humphrey edged Richard Nixon here by 95 votes in 1968. The 1978 congressional race here was expected to be close, and it was. The initial favorite was Ray Kogovsek, a 37-year-old state Senator from Pueblo. The son of a steelworker, Kogovsek had strong union support and a solid base in Pueblo. As Senate Minority Leader, he could claim legislative expertise. But apparently he came to take the election for granted. The Republican, 60-year-old state Senator Harold McCormick, drove thousands of miles over the district and stressed his expertise on water policy—an important issue in Colorado.

Although both candidates opposed Carter Administration water policies, McCormick was apparently able to use the issue to better advantage. The Republican amassed a substantial majority on the Western Slope as well as in Colorado Springs and the plains counties. Only 66%

margins in Pueblo and the Spanish-speaking counties enabled Kogovsek to win a narrow 366-vote victory. It was one of the closest congressional races in the nation in 1978, and the margin suggests that this may again be a seriously contested district in 1980. Kogovsek, as a member of the Interior Committee, will have an opportunity to help himself on local issues, especially those involving water; but he will be watched closely for errors, too.

Census Data Pop. 442,217. Central city, 28%; suburban, 17%. Median family income, $7,578; families above $15,000: 10%; families below $3,000: 13%. Median years education, 12.1.

The Voters

Median voting age 41.
Employment profile White collar, 43%. Blue collar, 33%. Service, 16%. Farm, 8%.
Ethnic groups Black, 2%. Spanish, 23%. Total foreign stock, 11%. Germany, 2%.

Presidential vote

1976	Carter (D)	84,783	(49%)
	Ford (R)	88,106	(51%)
1972	Nixon (R)	102,569	(64%)
	McGovern (D)	57,152	(36%)

Rep. Ray Kogovsek (D) Elected 1978; b. Aug. 19, 1941, Pueblo; home, Pueblo; Pueblo Jr. Col., 1960–62, Adams St. Col., B.S. 1964; Catholic.

Career Pueblo Co. Chief Dep. Clerk, 1964–72; Colo. House of Reps., 1969–71; Colo. Senate, 1971–78, Minor. Ldr., 1973–78.

Offices 501 CHOB, 202-225-4761. Also Rm. 425 United Bank Bldg., Pueblo 81003, 303-544-5277 ext. 313.

Committees *Education and Labor* (23d). Subcommittees: Elementary, Secondary, and Vocational Education; Labor-Management Relations.

Interior and Insular Affairs (27th). Subcommittees: Water and Power Resources; Public Lands.

Group Ratings: Newly Elected

Key Votes

Election Results

1978 general	Ray Kogovsek (D)	69,669	(50%)	($121,323)
	Harold L. McCormick (R)	69,303	(50%)	($81,500)
1978 general	Ray Kogovsek (D)	26,861	(66%)	
	Tom Watkinson (D)	13,769	(34%)	($16,095)
1976 general	Frank E. Evans (D)	89,302	(52%)	($57,990)
	Melvin H. Takaki (R)	82,315	(48%)	($90,499)

FOURTH DISTRICT

The 4th congressional district of Colorado, like the 3d, is a combination of counties on the plains east of the Front Range of the Rockies with counties west of the Front Range—on the Western Slope, as they say here. Only about one in four residents here live in the Western Slope portion, but until 1964 it had a congressional district all its own and until 1972 dominated the politics of the 4th. People on the Western Slope live amid some of the most beautiful scenery in the world, but aside from some who have sought it out—like the entertainers and writers near Aspen—they do not seem to value it too highly. They seem more interested in developing the land, and making some money. That may mean putting up a ski resort where there has been mountain wilderness, or winter condominiums where wild animals lived; or it may mean strip mining for coal or developing some economic way of extracting oil from shale.

People on the Eastern Slope—the majority in the district—have been leery of these things, even as they have continued to enjoy the proximity of the mountains and the money they help generate. The string of suburban towns and small cities running north from Denver has been one of the parts of the state responsive to environmental stands. It was these voters who in 1972 defeated Wayne Aspinall, Chairman of the House Interior Committee for 14 years, a man who knew water law like no one else and whose pro-development stands infuriated environmentalists.

Aspinall's defeat was a major event in Colorado politics, a sign that the old order had changed irrevocably. But subsequent elections in the 4th district have shown that the new order is not precisely what Aspinall's opponents hoped for. The 1972 general election winner was the Republican candidate, Jim Johnson. He has an unusual voting record: he was an opponent of the Vietnam war and continues to question defense spending; he takes stands on environmental issues which cannot be readily classified; he has waged what *Congressional Quarterly* called "a one-man war on the tobacco subsidy program"; and he takes pretty standard Republican positions on economic issues. Elected rather fortuitously, Johnson was seriously challenged in 1974. He has won every two years since by increasing margins, with more than 60% of the vote in 1978.

Census Data Pop. 442,024. Central city, 0%; suburban, 20%. Median family income, $8,992; families above $15,000: 15%; families below $3,000: 10%. Median years education, 12.4.

The Voters

Median voting age 40.
Employment profile White collar, 47%. Blue collar, 30%. Service, 14%. Farm, 9%.
Ethnic groups Spanish, 10%. Total foreign stock, 12%. USSR, 3%; Germany, 2%.

Presidential vote

1976	Carter (D)	93,021	(42%)
	Ford (R)	130,713	(58%)
1972	Nixon (R)	129,253	(67%)
	McGovern (D)	63,181	(33%)

Rep. James P. (Jim) **Johnson** (R) Elected 1972; b. June 2, 1930, Yankton, S.D.; home, Fort Collins; Northwestern U., B.A. 1952, U. of Colo., LL.B. 1959; Presbyterian.

Career USMC, 1952–56; Prosecuting Atty., 8th Jud. Dist. of Colo.; Municipal Judge, Ault and Ft. Collins, 1962–65.

Offices 2242 RHOB, 202-225-4676. Also Fed. Bldg., Fort Collins 80521, 303-493-9132.

Committees *Agriculture* (5th). Subcommittees: Forests; Livestock and Grains.

Interior and Insular Affairs (6th). Subcommittees: Water and Power Resources; Public Lands; National Parks and Insular Affairs.

Group Ratings

	ADA	COPE	PC	RPN	NFU	LCV	CFA	NAB	NSI	ACA	NTU
1978	25	16	20	80	30	–	18	90	50	67	–
1977	20	16	13	85	55	0	0	–	–	73	48
1976	40	19	20	71	28	21	18	100	40	78	29

Key Votes

1) Increase Def Spnd	AGN	6) Alaska Lands Protect	AGN	11) Delay Auto Pol Cntrl	FOR
2) B-1 Bomber	AGN	7) Water Projects Veto	AGN	12) Sugar Price Escalator	FOR
3) Cargo Preference	AGN	8) Consum Protect Agcy	AGN	13) Pub Fin Cong Cmpgns	FOR
4) Dereg Nat Gas	FOR	9) Common Situs Picket	AGN	14) ERA Ratif Recissn	FOR
5) Kemp-Roth	FOR	10) Labor Law Revision	AGN	15) Prohibt Govt Abrtns	AGN

Election Results

1978 general	James P. Johnson (R)	103,121	(61%)	($92,842)
	Morgan Smith (D)	65,421	(39%)	($160,520)
1978 primary	James P. Johnson (R)	22,116	(64%)	
	Richard Davis (R)	12,582	(36%)	($26,586)
1976 general	James P. Johnson (R)	119,458	(55%)	($65,579)
	Don Ogden (D)	76,995	(36%)	($46,431)
	Richard Davis (Ind.)	20,398	(9%)	($58,221)

FIFTH DISTRICT

The 5th congressional district of Colorado is a combination of several disparate communities, designed carefully by a Republican legislature in 1972. The bulk of its people live in the Denver suburbs north, east, and south of the city. As one proceeds clockwise in this manner, one goes from the more Democratic communities (Commerce City plus a chunk of Denver itself) to the middle of the road (Aurora) to the wealthy and heavily Republican (Englewood and Littleton). To the south, after travelling Interstate 25 through some residential sprawl and then the arid, empty, mile-high plateau, there is Colorado Springs. This is a well-to-do, fast-growing city, known for its military installations (the Air Force Academy, Fort Carson) and tourist attractions (Pike's Peak, the Garden of the Gods). Politically Colorado Springs is a kind of Rocky Mountain San Diego, conservative and Republican—though like the Denver suburbs it did go for Democrats in 1974.

The 5th also moves east to the Kansas border. It was out in this vast country that Colorado boomers, in the wake of the Gold Rush of 1858, set the cavalry on defenseless Cheyenne men, women, and children in the Sand Creek massacre. Today this part of Colorado has scarcely changed: it is a region of large cattle ranches, tumbleweed, and gas station stop towns along Interstate 70. It showed signs of an unusual (for Colorado) movement away from the Republicans and toward Jimmy Carter in 1976 and away from Dick Lamm and toward Republican Ted Strickland in the 1978 governor's race; that may be because both Carter and Strickland are of Southern origin, as are many residents here. But this area casts only 6% of the district's votes, as compared to 62% for the Denver suburbs and 32% in the Colorado Springs area.

The first congressman from this district was William Armstrong, then Colorado Senate Minority Leader and today a U.S. Senator. Armstrong is proof that not all Colorado politicians are environment-conscious Democrats. He was a successful businessman and a solidly conservative Republican when he was first elected to Congress in 1972; and his record in the House caused no problems for the Republican leadership or the Nixon or Ford Administrations. Though he has been involved in the heavily regulated business of broadcasting, he wants to reduce the powers and spending of the federal government. Almost from the time he went to the House, Armstrong had been assumed to be aiming at Floyd Haskell's Senate seat; and in 1978, not too much to anyone's surprise, he won it.

His successor, Republican Ken Kramer, is if anything more conservative. A state Representative from Colorado Springs, Kramer just barely beat a more moderate Republican in a hotly contested primary. He was chief sponsor of Colorado's anti-pornography law and unsuccessful backer of a move for a state right-to-work law. Like Armstrong, he enters Congress young and with a district that seems likely to continue reelecting him; and he may very well make a mark as one of the most conservative members of the House. He serves as one of the increasing number of conservative Republicans on the pro-labor and pro-social programs Education and Labor Committee.

Census Data Pop. 441,738. Central city, 26%; suburban, 68%. Median family income, $10,278; families above $15,000: 23%; families below $3,000: 7%. Median years education, 12.5.

The Voters

Median voting age 39.
Employment profile White collar, 55%. Blue collar, 29%. Service, 13%. Farm, 3%.
Ethnic groups Black, 2%. Spanish, 9%. Total foreign stock, 11%. Germany, 2%; UK, 1%.

Presidential vote

1976	Carter (D)	82,313	(40%)
	Ford (R)	124,534	(60%)
1972	Nixon (R)	121,492	(71%)
	McGovern (D)	50,546	(29%)

Rep. Ken Kramer (R) Elected 1978; b. Feb. 19, 1942, Chicago, Ill.; home, Colorado Springs; U. of Ill., B.A. 1963, Harvard U., J.D. 1966; Jewish.

Career Army, 1967–70; Dep. Dist. Atty., 4th Judicial Dist., Colo. Springs, 1970–72; Practicing atty., 1972–78; Colo. House of Reps., 1973–78.

Offices 1724 LHOB, 202-225-4422. Also Suite C & D, 1520 N. Union Blvd., Colorado Springs 80909, 303-632-8555.

Committees *Education and Labor* (8th). Subcommittees: Labor-Management Relations; Select Education.

Science and Technology (10th). Subcommittees: Space Science and Applications; Energy Development and Applications.

Group Ratings: Newly Elected

Key Votes: Newly Elected

Election Results

1978 general	Ken Kramer (R)	91,933	(60%)	($161,413)
	Gerry Frank (D)	52,914	(34%)	($63,325)
	L. W. Dan Bridges (I)	8,933	(6%)	($43,978)
1978 primary	Ken Kramer (R)	19,506	(54%)	
	Robert L. Eckelberry (R)	16,830	(46%)	
1976 general	William L. Armstrong (R)	126,784	(66%)	($143,466)
	Dorothy Hores (D)	64,067	(34%)	($21,334)

CONNECTICUT

Connecticut is a state in political transition. There are still traces left of the "Connecticut Yankee" tradition of Mark Twain's novel. If you drive around the state, you might even think it was dominated by small, neat cities and little salt-box colonial towns, by whaling ships and low green mountains, by old Yankees with slightly dry New England accents. That old Connecticut was characterized by a peculiar contrariness. In the early days of the Republic, it stayed with the Federalists after they had become extinct elsewhere, and in the depression year of 1932 it supported Republican Herbert Hoover over Democrat Franklin Roosevelt.

But Connecticut's Republicanism did not outlast the New Deal. It was not just a matter of the attractiveness of Roosevelt's policies; also the state's demography was changing. The old Yankee Connecticut might still dominate the tourist's view of things, but most of the people lived in the state's medium-sized cities. There—in Hartford, New Haven, Bridgeport, Waterbury, New Britain, New London—in all these cities and their often dreary suburbs most people were descendants of Irish and Italian and Polish immigrants; and most were Democrats. By the 1940s they had made the Democrats competitive in state politics; by the 1960s, dominant. More or less at the same time, members of the Catholic Church came to outnumber Protestants, and registered Democrats came to outnumber Republicans.

Now in the seventies Connecticut's political identity is less certain. In the last two close presidential elections, it has backed the loser both times, giving Hubert Humphrey a solid margin in 1968 and Gerald Ford a comfortable lead in 1976. The state has a Democratic governor, but has reelected its senators of both parties easily; Democrats dominate other offices now, but they did not a few years ago, and cannot be sure of doing so in the future.

These results represent a sharp break from Connecticut's straight ticket tradition and show how weak Connecticut's once mighty political organizations have become. As recently as a dozen years ago, Connecticut had the strongest parties in the nation. The Republicans were controlled by a string of able leaders, the Democrats by John Bailey, state party chairman from 1946 until his death in 1975. These men could deliver their party's delegation in the legislature and commanded huge majorities in the party conventions that nominated candidates for senator, governor, and congressman. Theoretically, candidates who lost on the convention floor could, if they had enough votes there, force a primary; in fact no one did so until 1970.

The straight party lever helped the bosses keep control. To activate the voting machine, you had to pull a straight party lever; then, if you wished, you could split your ticket, but few voters took the trouble to do so. The result was that all politicians had a stake in the success of the top of their tickets—which were determined by the good or bad judgment of the bosses. The power of the straight party lever can be gauged by the fact that in the 1956 Eisenhower landslide, the state elected six Republican congressmen and no Democrats; two years later, when Abe Ribicoff was reelected governor with a record margin, six Democrats and no Republicans were elected.

What has happened to change this system? First, the straight party lever was abolished, and slowly Connecticut voters have learned to split their tickets as voters in most states routinely do. Second, the party organizations have tended to atrophy. Political patronage is not as attractive as it once was, and young people are simply not enlisting in the party ranks. Republicans lost their stranglehold on the lower house of the legislature in a 1965 redistricting decision. Democrats in the late sixties and early seventies were faced with a series of divisive issues like the Vietnam war and crime. In 1970 Bailey's machine seemed to come apart. The governorship was lost, and in the Senate race the party could not cope with the problem of incumbent Thomas Dodd. Censured by the Senate, he did not run as a Democrat—leading to a primary between Bailey's choice, a New Haven rival, and Joseph Duffey, an antiwar activist. Duffey won and ran a strong campaign; but the Democratic vote was split between him and Dodd, running as an Independent.

That was how Lowell Weicker came to the Senate, with 42% of the vote. He remained little known until three years later, when he served on the Senate Watergate Committee. He was the only member with his own personal investigating staff, and if he sometimes acted like the "excitable kid" John Ehrlichman said he was, he also expressed the indignation felt by many citizens, including many of his fellow Republicans. His denunciations of Nixon and his continuing denunciations of what he considers his party's neanderthals have left him unpopular in many party circles. But they have undoubtedly helped him in Connecticut. He was reelected in 1976 over a strong opponent, Secretary of State Gloria Schaffer, with an impressive 58% of the vote.

Weicker is one of many senators who has seen himself as a possible president. In 1979 he announced he was running. It seemed highly unlikely that a Republican with his unorthodox approach and Senate record (he has well above 50% ratings from labor and liberal groups) could win many votes in a Republican primary, and he conceded that he was the longest shot in the race. A few months later, when a poll showed him trailing other candidates among Connecticut Republicans, he bowed out—the first to withdraw from the 1980 contest.

Connecticut's senior senator has no presidential ambitions but considerably more experience in government. He is Abraham Ribicoff, elected to the legislature in 1938, to Congress in 1948 and 1950; he was Governor from 1955 to 1961 and Secretary of HEW for two years after that. In 1962 Ribicoff returned to Connecticut, where he was elected to the Senate by a surprisingly narrow margin. After that he did not take the voters at home for granted. He had to campaign hard in 1968, after he had stood up at the Democratic National Convention to nominate George McGovern and looked directly down at Mayor Daley and accused him of Gestapo-like tactics. Before the 1974 election he returned to the state frequently to help patch up the then-shredded Democratic party. After that race, he decided to retire in 1980, when he turns 70, and announced his intentions early in 1979. The two most likely contenders for his seat are Democratic Congressmen Christopher Dodd and Toby Moffett. Both were first elected in 1974, both have records of considerable accomplishment, and both are widely known throughout the state. The Republicans most often mentioned—Bob Steele, state legislator Lewis Rome—would begin the race with less recognition, but Connecticut is a state which Republicans carried against Jimmy Carter in 1976 and hope to carry again in 1980. This seems likely to be one of the most seriously contested Senate seats of 1980, and the winner has a good chance of holding it for years.

Ribicoff is not the kind of senator who builds coalitions or amasses large numbers of votes on the Senate floor. He does exert considerable influence on occasion by well-timed statements on important issues. He is now Chairman of the Governmental Affairs Committee, a post which gives him jurisdiction over most federal government activities—and also had the duty to hold hearings on matters like Bert Lance's difficulties. In general Ribicoff has strongly supported the Carter Administration's government reorganization plans.

Ribicoff is also the third ranking Democrat on the Senate Finance Committee, behind Chairman Russell Long and Georgia's Herman Talmadge. Sometimes Ribicoff has fought lonely battles against Long, as when he kept the Nixon Administration's family assistance program alive even after Nixon abandoned it. More often recently he has teamed up with Long, as on their proposal for catastrophic health insurance—advanced as a cure for the leading health care finance problem but attacked by some on the theory that it would prevent enactment of broader legislation. Ribicoff on occasion has played an important role on foreign policy issues, as when he supported the Carter Administration's plans to sell jets to Saudi Arabia; he was the only Jewish senator to do so, and his support greatly helped the Administration.

Connecticut's governor is the first woman elected in her own right to that position in American history, Ella Grasso. She has won the governorship twice now, against formidable opponents both times; she has also had a turbulent administration during a period of difficult times for the state. Her career provides a good review of Connecticut politics. She was first elected to the legislature in 1952; she built a reputation as a programmatic liberal, but she owed promotions in the legislature to John Bailey. In 1958 Bailey chose her to run for Secretary of State; her status as a woman and as an Italian-American was important for ticket balancing. (Bailey was a superb ticket-balancer, and also a daring one: he slated the first Jewish governor in Connecticut, Ribicoff, and was the first major politician to line up behind the candidacy of our first Catholic president.) In 1970 she ran for Congress and, running 11% ahead of the ticket, was elected in a Republican year.

Grasso had substantial advantages: a good statewide reputation, her Italian heritage in a state where Italians are the largest ethnic group, backing by both liberals and organization Democrats who had split disastrously in 1970. But she had to prove that a woman could be a creditable governor. Her campaign and her performance in office seem to have done that, not only for Connecticut but for the nation as a whole. In 1974 she showed leadership on the utility rate issue, bringing a lawsuit that resulted in a lowering of rates; that gave her a solid lead over her popular opponent, 2d district Congressman Robert Steele. As Governor, she has had to deal with the hard times facing Connecticut and the need to cut government spending. Connecticut has always resisted an income tax, and Grasso opposes it; her task, then, has been to make painful cuts. This is not what many Democrats expected, and it sparked opposition from Nick Carbone, the Democratic leader in Hartford. Lieutenant Governor Robert Killian challenged her in a primary, and although he got only 33% of the votes and carried few towns outside Hartford, Grasso nonetheless still spent the early part of 1978 on the defensive.

But this kind of primary opposition may also have helped Grasso in the general election by validating her fiscal conservative credentials. Her opponent, 5th district Congressman Ronald Sarasin, charged her with fiscal gimmickry and tried to emphasize his own determination to hold down taxes, but Grasso had already made it clear that she would not allow an income tax. Moreover, Grasso benefited from her performance during the early 1978 blizzard, when she set up a storm center, helicoptered throughout the state, and trudged through snowdrifts when her car got stuck. The "Mother Ella" image stuck and helped her to a 59% vote against Sarasin.

Connecticut had its first presidential primary in 1976, an affair conducted by the Democratic Party in which Jimmy Carter just barely edged Morris Udall. It was held late enough in the primary season to have had minimal impact on the nomination. In 1977 the legislature passed a bill requiring both parties to stage presidential primaries on the first Tuesday in March. This means that Connecticut, together with Massachusetts and Vermont, will have a primary one week after New Hampshire's. The Connecticut primary may well deliver the final word on George Bush's candidacy (if he can't win in his native state, he's in trouble) and could be a good testing ground for a Kennedy or Brown candidacy.

Census Data Pop. 3,032,217; 1.50% of U.S. total, 24th largest; Central city, 35%; suburban, 47%. Median family income, $11,808; 2d highest; families above $15,000: 31%; families below $3,000: 5%. Median years education, 12.2.

1977 Share of Federal Tax Burden $6,321,000,000; 1.83% of U.S. total, 19th largest.

1977 Share of Federal Outlays $5,920,940,000; 1.50% of U.S. total, 23d largest. Per capita federal spending, $1,913.

DOD	$2,170,359,000	12th (2.37%)	HEW	$2,059,224,000	24th (1.39%)
ERDA	$43,155,000	20th (0.73%)	HUD	$83,823,000	17th (1.99%)
NASA	$34,611,000	16th (0.88%)	VA	$213,645,000	33d (1.11%)
DOT	$111,559,000	34th (0.78%)	EPA	$201,638,000	14th (2.46%)
DOC	$139,443,000	15th (1.68%)	RevS	$117,519,000	24th (1.39%)
DOI	$4,889,000	47th (0.11%)	Debt	$491,375,000	9th (1.64%)
USDA	$187,982,000	39th (0.94%)	Other	$61,718,000	

Economic Base Transportation equipment, especially aircraft and parts; finance, insurance and real estate; machinery, especially general industrial machinery; fabricated metal products, especially cutlery, hand tools and hardware; electrical equipment and supplies; primary metal industries, especially nonferrous rolling and drawing; printing and publishing, especially newspapers and commercial publishing.

Political Line-up Governor, Ella T. Grasso (D). Senators, Abraham A. Ribicoff (D) and Lowell P. Weicker, Jr. (R). Representatives, 6 (5 D and 1 R). State Senate (26 D and 10 R); State House (103 D and 48 R).

The Voters

Registration 1,627,571 Total. 620,399 D (38%); 419,589 R (26%); 586,584 Unaffiliated (36%); 999 Other (-).
Median voting age 43
Employment profile White collar, 52%. Blue collar, 36%. Service, 11%. Farm, 1%.
Ethnic groups Black, 6%. Spanish, 2%. Total foreign stock, 32%. Italy, 8%; Canada, 4%; Poland, 3%; UK, Ireland, Germany, USSR, 2% each.

Presidential vote

1976	Carter (D)	647,895	(47%)
	Ford (R)	719,261	(52%)
1972	Nixon (R)	810,763	(59%)
	McGovern (D)	555,498	(41%)

Sen. Abraham Ribicoff (D) Elected 1962, seat up 1980; b. Apr. 9, 1910, New Britain; home, Hartford; New York U., U. of Chicago, LL.B. 1933; Jewish.

Career Conn. Gen. Assembly, 1939–42; Municipal Judge, Hartford, 1941–43; U.S. House of Reps., 1949–1953; Gov. of Conn., 1955–61; Secy. of HEW, 1961–62.

Offices 337 RSOB, 202-224-2823. Also Suite 707, 450 Main St., Hartford 06103, 203-224-3545.

Committees *Finance* (3d). Subcommittees: Health; International Trade (Chairman); Social Security.

Governmental Affairs (Chairman).

Select Committee on Ethics.

Group Ratings

	ADA	COPE	PC	RPN	NFU	LCV	CFA	NAB	NSI	ACA	NTU
1978	55	78	60	86	20	78	50	17	30	14	–
1977	75	78	70	57	64	–	64	–	–	8	20
1976	80	84	82	69	67	81	85	36	40	8	29

Key Votes

1) Warnke Nom	FOR	6) Egypt-Saudi Arms	FOR	11) Hosptl Cost Contnmnt	FOR
2) Neutron Bomb	FOR	7) Draft Restr Pardon	FOR	12) Clinch River Reactor	AGN
3) Waterwy User Fee	AGN	8) Wheat Price Support	AGN	13) Pub Fin Cong Cmpgns	FOR
4) Dereg Nat Gas	AGN	9) Panama Canal Treaty	FOR	14) ERA Ratif Recissn	FOR
5) Kemp-Roth	AGN	10) Labor Law Rev Clot	FOR	15) Med Necssy Abrtns	FOR

Election Results

1974 general	Abraham A. Ribicoff (D)	125,215	(68%)	($435,985)
	James H. Brannen III (R)	60,017	(32%)	($66,162)
1974 primary	Abraham A. Ribicoff (D), nominated by convention			
1968 general	Abraham A. Ribicoff (D)	655,043	(54%)	
	Edwin H. May, Jr. (R)	551,455	(46%)	

Sen. Lowell P. Weicker, Jr. (R) Elected 1970, seat up 1982; b. May 16, 1931, Paris, France; home, Greenwich; Yale U., B.A. 1953, U. of Va., LL.B. 1958; Episcopalian.

Career Army, 1953–55; Practicing atty.; Conn. Gen. Assembly, 1962–68; U.S. House of Reps., 1969–71.

Offices 313 RSOB, 202-224-4041. Also 102 U.S. Court House, 915 Lafayette Blvd., Bridgeport 06603, 203-579-5830.

Committees *Appropriation* (7th). Subcommittees: Defense; HUD-Independent Agencies; Labor and HEW, and Related Agencies; State, Justice, and Commerce, the Judiciary, and Related Agencies; Transportation and Related Agencies.

Energy and Natural Resources (3d). Subcommittees: Energy Conservation and Supply; Energy Resources and Materials Production; Parks, Recreation, and Renewable Resources.

Select Committee on Small Business (Ranking Member).

Group Ratings

	ADA	COPE	PC	RPN	NFU	LCV	CFA	NAB	NSI	ACA	NTU
1978	60	87	50	100	40	72	55	22	33	20	–
1977	60	67	48	67	60	–	48	–	–	39	30
1976	75	65	46	100	73	65	57	8	50	25	38

Key Votes

1) Warnke Nom	AGN	6) Egypt-Saudi Arms	AGN	11) Hosptl Cost Contnmnt	DNV
2) Neutron Bomb	AGN	7) Draft Restr Pardon	AGN	12) Clinch River Reactor	FOR
3) Waterwy User Fee	FOR	8) Wheat Price Support	AGN	13) Pub Fin Cong Cmpgns	AGN
4) Dereg Nat Gas	FOR	9) Panama Canal Treaty	FOR	14) ERA Ratif Recissn	FOR
5) Kemp-Roth	AGN	10) Labor Law Rev Clot	FOR	15) Med Necssy Abrtns	FOR

Election Results

1976 general	Lowell P. Weicker, Jr. (R)	785,683	(58%)	($480,709)
	Gloria Schaffer (D)	561,018	(42%)	($306,104)
1976 primary	Lowell P. Weicker, Jr. (R), nominated by convention			
1970 general	Lowell P. Weicker, Jr. (R)	443,008	(42%)	
	Joseph P. Duffey (D)	360,094	(34%)	
	Thomas J. Dodd (I)	260,264	(24%)	

Gov. Ella T. Grasso (D) Elected 1974, term expires Jan. 1983; b. May 10, 1919, Windsor Locks; Mt. Holyoke Col., B.A. 1940, M.A. 1942.

Career Asst. Research Dir., Conn. War Manpower Comm., WWII; Conn. House of Reps., 1953–59, Floor Leader, 1955; Secy. of State of Conn., 1959–71; U.S. House of Reps., 1971–75.

Offices State of Connecticut, Executive Chambers, Hartford 06115, 203-566-4840.

Election Results

1978 general	Ella T. Grasso (D)	613,109	(59%)
	Ronald A. Sarasin (R)	422,316	(41%)
1978 primary	Ella T. Grasso (D)	137,904	(67%)
	Robert K. Killian (D)	66,924	(33%)
1974 general	Ella T. Grasso (D)	643,490	(59%)
	Robert H. Steele (R)	440,169	(41%)

FIRST DISTRICT

Hartford is Connecticut's largest city, the state capital, and the headquarters of many of the nation's largest insurance companies. Hartford and its suburbs also contain much of Connecticut's defense industry—notably United Technology's big aircraft engine factories. As with most of Connecticut's large cities, people have long since moved out of Hartford into a string of comfortable suburbs. They range from working class areas like East Hartford and Windsor on the Connecticut River to the high income Protestant and Jewish precincts of West Hartford and Bloomfield. Hartford itself, with the bulk of the area's poor and black residents, has many of the typical urban problems. But here in this small city, with its gleaming new office buildings, its ornate state Capitol, and its high white-collar employment, these problems do not seem as overwhelming as they do in New York or Philadelphia. There is a feeling here that problems can be solved, and optimistic city fathers have launched an ambitious and extensive regional development program—the Greater Hartford Process—for Hartford and its environs.

The 1st congressional district, which includes the city and most of its suburbs, has long been the Democratic stronghold of Connecticut. This is in large part due to the efforts of the late John Bailey, longtime state (1946–75) and national (1961–68) Democratic chairman. In year after year turnout and Democratic totals have been higher in the Hartford area than elsewhere in the state. In 1976, when Jimmy Carter did poorly in Connecticut, the 1st was the only congressional district to give him a significant margin.

The 1st has had Democratic congressmen for more than 20 years. The current incumbent, William Cotter, was first elected in 1970, a difficult year for Democrats here, and had a tough primary and a close general election. He has had a rather quiet career in the House. He is the eighth ranking Democrat on the Ways and Means Committee, and serves on the Health and Social Security Subcommittees; but he still does not have a subcommittee chair. He has been reelected every two years by adequate, but not huge percentages. His 1978 opponent, a black who was head of the Connecticut NAACP, attracted some notice and support from national Republican sources, but was not able to crack the Democratic margin in Hartford very much.

Census Data Pop. 505,418. Central city, 35%; suburban, 47%. Median family income, $12,031; families above $15,000: 32%; families below $3,000: 6%. Median years education, 12.2.

The Voters

Median voting age 44.
Employment profile White collar, 58%. Blue collar, 31%. Service, 11%. Farm, –%.
Ethnic groups Black, 10%. Spanish, 3%. Total foreign stock, 34%. Italy, 7%; Canada, 6%; Poland, 4%; Ireland, 3%; USSR, UK, Germany, 2% each.

Presidential vote

1976	Carter (D)	120,874	(53%)
	Ford (R)	108,585	(47%)
1972	Nixon (R)	121,196	(51%)
	McGovern (D)	114,473	(49%)

Rep. William R. Cotter (D) Elected 1970; b. July 18, 1926, Hartford; home, Hartford; Trinity Col., Hartford, B.A. 1949; Catholic.

Career Member, Court of Common Council, Hartford, 1953; Aide to Conn. Gov. Abraham Ribicoff, 1955–57; Deputy Insurance Commissioner of Conn., 1957–64, Commissioner, 1964–70.

Offices 2134 RHOB, 202-225-2265. Also 450 Main St., Hartford 06103, 203-244-2383.

Committees *Ways and Means* (8th). Subcommittees: Trade; Social Security.

Group Ratings

	ADA	COPE	PC	RPN	NFU	LCV	CFA	NAB	NSI	ACA	NTU
1978	50	63	48	27	56	–	32	10	56	28	–
1977	55	86	60	38	83	47	70	–	–	16	16
1976	60	90	70	39	82	48	81	17	40	13	24

Key Votes

1) Increase Def Spnd	AGN	6) Alaska Lands Protect	FOR	11) Delay Auto Pol Cntrl	FOR
2) B-1 Bomber	AGN	7) Water Projects Veto	AGN	12) Sugar Price Escalator	DNV
3) Cargo Preference	AGN	8) Consum Protect Agcy	FOR	13) Pub Fin Cong Cmpgns	AGN
4) Dereg Nat Gas	AGN	9) Common Situs Picket	FOR	14) ERA Ratif Recissn	AGN
5) Kemp-Roth	AGN	10) Labor Law Revision	DNV	15) Prohibt Govt Abrtns	FOR

Election Results

1978 general	William R. Cotter (D)	102,749	(60%)	($96,791)
	Ben F. Andrews Jr. (R)	67,828	(40%)	($54,733)
1978 primary	William R. Cotter (D), nominated by convention			
1976 general	William R. Cotter (D)	128,479	(58%)	($61,594)
	Lucien P. DiFazio, Jr. (R)	94,106	(42%)	($24,023)

SECOND DISTRICT

The 2d district is the eastern half, geographically, of Connecticut. The district has Yankee villages and high income summer and retirement colonies with names like Old Saybrook and Old Lyme. It also has small and middle-sized mill towns like Norwich, Danielson, and Putnam, with heavily Catholic and ethnic populations. Traditional Yankee Republicanism still has some strength here, but the political balance lies in the hands of second- and third-generation ethnics in places like New London and Middletown. This mix makes the 2d a middle of the road, bellwether district in national, statewide, as well as in congressional elections. In 1960, for example, it produced a thin margin for John Kennedy; in 1976, it went 50.1% for Jimmy Carter.

During the 1950s, when the straight party lever was still mandatory and few tickets were split, congressional elections were usually close in the 2d, with party control shifting a couple of times. More recent elections have shown a change to the common national trend: the election of a congressman by a fairly close margin and his reelection by much larger margins as long as he keeps running. Consequently the 2d has had an unusually large number of congressmen over the last 25 years, including a heavyweight like Chester Bowles (1959–61), who was a prime candidate for secretary of state while he served; a Republican with the marvelous WASPy name of Horace Seely-Brown, Jr.; and a Democrat of French Canadian origin named William St. Onge. The most recent ex-congressman, Republican Bob Steele, was a former CIA agent who had the misfortune to run against Ella Grasso in 1974. He put on a stronger gubernatorial campaign than his 41% of the vote suggests, and could have stayed on in the 2d if he had chosen to do so.

The seat is currently held by a young Democrat with the familiar name of Christopher Dodd. He is the son of the former Congressman (1953–57) and Senator (1959–71) Thomas Dodd. The elder Dodd was not just a standard liberal Democrat; he was a vocal anti-Communist and a major force behind gun control legislation. Lyndon Johnson tantalized everyone by considering him at the last minute for the vice presidency in 1964. His last years in the Senate were sad ones: he was attacked by Drew Pearson for misusing government and campaign funds and was censured by the Senate.

The younger Dodd, who served in both the Peace Corps and the Army, seems more in line with the views of the northern Democrats of his time. He was elected with 60% of the vote in 1974 and has raised that to the 70% level in 1978. He is the seventh-ranking Democrat on the House Rules Committee, and a dozen years younger than the next youngest senior member. He also served as one of the most thoughtful and careful members of the House committee investigating assassinations. Dodd has been mentioned as a candidate for the Senate seat being vacated by Abraham Ribicoff. He is one of the most highly respected members of the 1974 freshman class and would likely be a formidable candidate.

Census Data Pop. 505,493. Central city, 33%; suburban, 66%. Median family income, $10,885; families above $15,000: 24%; families below $3,000: 7%. Median years education, 12.1.

The Voters

Median voting age 40.
Employment profile White collar, 48%. Blue collar, 39%. Service, 12%. Farm, 1%.
Ethnic groups Black, 2%. Spanish, 1%. Total foreign stock, 26%. Canada, 6%; Italy, 4%; Poland, 3%; UK, Germany, 2% each; USSR, Ireland, 1% each.

Presidential vote

1976	Carter (D)	111,161	(50%)
	Ford (R)	110,616	(50%)
1972	Nixon (R)	127,923	(60%)
	McGovern (D)	85,382	(40%)

Rep. Christopher J. Dodd (D) Elected 1974; b. May 27, 1944, Willimantic; home, North Stonington; Providence Col., B.A. 1966, U. of Louisville, J.D. 1972.

Career Peace Corps, 1966–68; Army 1969–75.

Offices 224 CHOB, 202-225-2076. Also One Thames Place, Norwich 06360, 203-886-0139.

Committees *Rules* (7th).

Group Ratings

	ADA	COPE	PC	RPN	NFU	LCV	CFA	NAB	NSI	ACA	NTU
1978	80	90	65	42	70	–	59	0	44	8	–
1977	70	89	58	60	71	74	50	–	–	14	22
1976	60	76	80	59	75	72	100	8	10	17	32

Key Votes

1) Increase Def Spnd	DNV	6) Alaska Lands Protect	DNV	11) Delay Auto Pol Cntrl	AGN
2) B-1 Bomber	AGN	7) Water Projects Veto	AGN	12) Sugar Price Escalator	FOR
3) Cargo Preference	DNV	8) Consum Protect Agcy	FOR	13) Pub Fin Cong Cmpgns	FOR
4) Dereg Nat Gas	AGN	9) Common Situs Picket	FOR	14) ERA Ratif Recissn	AGN
5) Kemp-Roth	AGN	10) Labor Law Revision	FOR	15) Prohibt Govt Abrtns	AGN

Election Results

1978 general	Christopher J. Dodd (D)	116,624	(70%)	($125,326)
	Thomas H. Connell (R)	50,167	(30%)	($17,714)
1978 primary	Christopher J. Dodd (D), nominated by convention			
1976 general	Christopher J. Dodd (D)	142,684	(66%)	($98,021)
	Richard M. Jackson (R)	74,743	(34%)	($19,363)

THIRD DISTRICT

The 3d congressional district of Connecticut centers on the city of New Haven, once the state's largest and most industrialized major city and the home of the state's best known institution, Yale University. At the turn of the century, New Haven was one of the most important factory towns in Connecticut, and it attracted thousands of Irish, Italian, and Polish immigrants. Today their ancestors have spread out, from the old neighborhoods of frame houses huddled within walking distance of the factories to suburbs like West Haven, East Haven, and Hamden. Founded by WASPs in the sixteenth century, and still WASP-dominated at the upper reaches of its society, greater New Haven is essentially an ethnic town. Yale, despite its national reputation, is a small university in terms of enrollment, and except for a few blocks near the campus, New Haven is not really a college town.

New Haven's ethnic background might suggest that this is a heavily Democratic area, but the truth is more complicated. As in most American cities of the nineteenth century, an even-odd pattern prevailed. The native Yankees were usually Republican, and the first-arriving immigrant group, here as usual the Irish, were Democrats. The next immigrant group to arrive, slighted by the Irish and on occasion wooed by the WASPs, turned to the Republican Party, and so on. In New Haven, the second ethnic group to arrive was the Italian-Americans, and the very large number of Italian-Americans helped make the Republican Party very competitive with the Democrats. Although New Haven has not had a Republican mayor for a generation, many of the suburbs now have Republican governments. Meanwhile, Gerald Ford carried the 3d district with a solid 54% in 1976.

Robert Giaimo has been Congressman from the 3d district for more than 20 years. He has been one of Connecticut's few congressmen without statewide ambitions, and has served for a record number of years—though not always without serious challenge. For years his thinking on issues seemed to be more in line with traditional big-city Democrats than with the leaders of the Democratic Study Group; but in the post-Watergate years those groups have tended to come together, and Giaimo has become a leader of both. As a member of the Defense Appropriations Subcommittee, he led the fight against American involvement in Cambodia and Vietnam in 1975; and in the same year led the move to oust Lucien Nedzi as chairman of a special committee on intelligence on the grounds that he was not tough enough on the CIA. Giaimo is the eighth-ranking Democrat on the Appropriations Committee—an important position. But even more important, he is Chairman of the House Budget Committee. He first won that position, by a 139–129 margin, over Thomas Ashley of Ohio after the 1976 elections. The House Democrats intentionally made the position temporary, but after the 1978 elections they voted to allow an incumbent to serve another term—an indirect but eloquent vote of confidence in Giaimo. This is a difficult position: House Republicans do not cooperate with Democrats at all on the budget, and Giaimo has to keep his budget limits from being overturned by a combination of those who want more and those who want less federal spending. Such a combination did succeed in voting down the Fiscal Year 1978 budget resolutions; but Giaimo was able to get through the resolutions for Fiscal Year 1979.

Giaimo has also had some difficulty in the 3d district. The underfinanced campaign of Republican John Pucciano held him to 56% of the vote in 1976—not a good percentage for such a veteran. Two years later national Republicans helped fund a second Pucciano challenge. But Giaimo fought harder, too, and increased his percentage. Still it was below 60%—an indication of the continuing Republican heritage that still plays a role in the politics of the New Haven area.

Census Data Pop. 505,293. Central city, 27%; suburban, 62%. Median family income, $11,463; families above $15,000: 29%; families below $3,000: 6%. Median years education, 12.2.

The Voters

Median voting age 43.
Employment profile White collar, 53%. Blue collar, 35%. Service, 11%. Farm, 1%.
Ethnic groups Black, 9%. Spanish, 2%. Total foreign stock, 31%. Italy, 10%; Poland, Ireland, UK, Canada, USSR, Germany, 2% each.

Presidential vote

1976	Carter (D)	105,602	(46%)
	Ford (R)	121,685	(54%)
1972	Nixon (R)	142,56962	
	McGovern (D)	87,766	(38%)

Rep. Robert N. Giamo (D) Elected 1958; b. Oct. 15, 1919, New Haven; home, North Haven; Fordham Col., B.A., 1941, U. of Conn., LL.B. 1943; Catholic.

Career Army, WWII; Practicing atty., 1947–58; Chm., Personal Appeals Bd., North Haven, 1955–58.

Offices 2207 RHOB, 202-225-3661. Also 303 P.O. Bldg., New Haven 06510, 203-432-2043.

Committees *Budget* (Chairman).

Appropriations (8th). Subcommittees: Defense; Legislative; Treasury-Postal Service-General Government.

Group Ratings

	ADA	COPE	PC	RPN	NFU	LCV	CFA	NAB	NSI	ACA	NTU
1978	50	55	35	36	30	–	27	50	40	33	–
1977	60	81	53	58	45	50	40	–	–	24	20
1976	40	84	54	53	67	70	45	8	40	10	20

Key Votes

1) Increase Def Spnd	AGN	6) Alaska Lands Protect	FOR	11) Delay Auto Pol Cntrl	AGN
2) B-1 Bomber	AGN	7) Water Projects Veto	AGN	12) Sugar Price Escalator	DNV
3) Cargo Preference	FOR	8) Consum Protect Agcy	AGN	13) Pub Fin Cong Cmpgns	FOR
4) Dereg Nat Gas	FOR	9) Common Situs Picket	FOR	14) ERA Ratif Recissn	AGN
5) Kemp-Roth	AGN	10) Labor Law Revision	FOR	15) Prohibt Govt Abrtns	AGN

Election Results

1978 general	Robert N. Giaimo (D)	96,830	(59%)	($157,304)
	John G. Pucciano (R)	66,663	(41%)	($102,667)
1978 primary	Robert N. Giaimo (D), nominated by convention			
1976 general	Robert N. Giaimo (D)	121,623	(56%)	($63,188)
	John G. Pucciano (R)	96,714	(44%)	($14,008)

FOURTH DISTRICT

If Hartford County has been the traditional home of Connecticut's Democrats, then Fairfield County has been the bedrock of the state's Republicans. Fairfield is one of the richest counties in the nation, a land of broad well manicured lawns sweeping down to Long Island Sound, of woodsy New Canaan and artsy-craftsy Westport, of commuters driving down to the station to take the bedraggled New Haven Railroad into Manhattan. Unlike the rest of Connecticut, Fairfield County is in many ways an extension of New York City, economically and culturally. People watch New York, not Connecticut, television; they are Mets, not Red Sox, fans; and their political attitudes more than in other parts of this small state are shaped by what is happening in the Big City. Indeed, people here often have little idea at all of what is happening in Connecticut.

Most of the people in Fairfield County live in the 4th congressional district—a string of high-income, traditionally Republican towns along Long Island Sound: Greenwich, Stamford, Darien, Norwalk, Westport, Fairfield. But it would be inaccurate to say that the harried advertising executive on a long commute is the typical 4th district voter. For the 4th also takes in the industrial city of Bridgeport—Connecticut's second largest—as well as the affluent towns. Even in the latter, below the railroad station or around the old downtown, you can see the slightly shabby small houses where the district's poorer voters live. Some 10% of the 4th district's residents are black, and it has a higher proportion of foreign stock residents than any other district in the state.

The two segments of the 4th—Bridgeport and the Republican towns—perform a kind of political counterpoint. Westport, for example, which had gone 36% for Kennedy in 1960, went 41% for McGovern in 1972; Carter, with his Southern background, did no better, also winning 41% there. Far more shiftable were votes in the ethnic wards of Bridgport. The Catholic Kennedy received 61% in the city, while the leftish McGovern got only 45%; Carter recovered, but fell short of the Kennedy figure, with 56%. Bridgeport has swung even farther in state elections, giving fully 71% of its votes to Ella Grasso in 1974.

The 4th has elected a Democratic congressman within recent memory, in 1964 and 1966, who was beaten in 1968, by Lowell Weicker, when the incumbent's pro-Vietnam war stance antagonized the Democratic voters in the well-to-do towns. Since 1970 the district has been represented by Stewart McKinney, a moderate Republican with a background in business and the Connecticut legislature. McKinney's toughest race was in 1974, but he won with 54% and survived. One of his main legislative interests is the affairs of the District of Columbia. He is the ranking Republican on the House D.C. Committee and has gone so far in the District's behalf as to endorse a measure that would allow Washington to tax the incomes of suburbanites who work in the city. (Connecticut commuters who work in New York are taxed there.) That bill will never pass: the suburban Maryland and Virginia congressmen on the House District Committee will never allow it.

McKinney has been criticized for his concern for District matters. His 1978 opponent charged that it constituted a conflict of interest, since McKinney has financed the renovation of a number of houses in Washington. This charge, plus the opponent's base in Stamford, may have helped him hold McKinney's percentage down below what he had in 1976.

Census Data Pop. 505,366. Central city, 68%; suburban, 32%. Median family income, $12,692; families above $15,000: 38%; families below $3,000: 5%. Median years education, 12.3.

The Voters

Median voting age 45.
Employment profile White collar, 56%. Blue collar, 33%. Service, 11%. Farm, -%.
Ethnic groups Black, 10%. Spanish, 5%. Total foreign stock, 35%. Italy, 8%; Poland, UK, 3% each; Canada, Ireland, Germany, USSR, 2% each.

Presidential vote

1976	Carter (D)	91,058	(43%)
	Ford (R)	118,716	(57%)
1972	Nixon (R)	138,496	(63%)
	McGovern (D)	81,802	(37%)

Rep. Stewart B. McKinney (R) Elected 1970; b. Jan. 30, 1931, Pittsburgh, Pa.; home, Fairfield; Princeton U., 1949–51, Yale U., B.A. 1958; Episcopalian.

Career Air Force, 1951–55; Pres., CMF Tires, Inc.; Real Estate Development; Conn. Gen. Assembly, 1967–70.

Offices 106 CHOB, 202-225-5541. Also Fed. Bldg., Lafayette Blvd., Bridgeport 06604, 203-384-2286.

Committees *Banking, Finance and Urban Affairs* (3d). Subcommittees: Economic Stabilization; Housing and Community Development; The City.

District of Columbia (Ranking Member). Subcommittees: Fiscal Affairs and Health; Metropolitan Affairs.

Group Ratings

	ADA	COPE	PC	RPN	NFU	LCV	CFA	NAB	NSI	ACA	NTU
1978	55	55	48	83	40	–	41	20	0	26	–
1977	35	60	35	90	64	64	10	–	–	13	35
1976	50	50	36	94	64	44	36	36	40	23	38

Key Votes

1) Increase Def Spnd	AGN	6) Alaska Lands Protect	FOR	11) Delay Auto Pol Cntrl	AGN
2) B-1 Bomber	AGN	7) Water Projects Veto	AGN	12) Sugar Price Escalator	AGN
3) Cargo Preference	AGN	8) Consum Protect Agcy	FOR	13) Pub Fin Cong Cmpgns	FOR
4) Dereg Nat Gas	DNV	9) Common Situs Picket	FOR	14) ERA Ratif Recissn	AGN
5) Kemp-Roth	FOR	10) Labor Law Revision	FOR	15) Prohibt Govt Abrtns	DNV

Election Results

1978 general	Stewart B. McKinney (R)	83,990	(58%)	($123,628)
	Michael G. Morgan (D)	59,918	(42%)	($51,744)
1978 primary	Stewart B. McKinney (R), nominated by convention			
1976 general	Stewart B. McKinney (R)	126,314	(62%)	($113,344)
	Geoffrey G. Peterson (D)	76,722	(38%)	($49,038)

FIFTH DISTRICT

The 5th district is an amalgam of Connecticut's lesser known cities and towns which are spread out over the hills just north of Long Island Sound. The district includes the industrial city of Waterbury and the decaying mill towns of the Naugatuck Valley; the relatively prosperous working class town of Meriden to the east; and Danbury, the onetime hat manufacturing center in the west. The industrial cities and towns are all traditionally Democratic; found between them are the smaller, Yankee towns which are inevitably more Republican. Included also in the 5th in the 1972 redistricting were the heavily Republican towns of New Canaan, Wilton, and Weston. The result is a district which is finely balanced on the partisan scale. In 1972, 1974, and 1978 this has been a very closely contested district and one which has in the seventies elected congressmen of both parties.

The 1972 result was an upset: Democratic Congressman John Monagan was beaten by Republican state legislator Ronald Sarasin. Sarasin campaigned hard, while Monagan took a trip to Europe in October. Even so Sarasin would not have won without the three new Republican towns added to the district; they provided all of his margin and more. Two years later, in the Watergate year of 1974, Sarasin was hard pressed by former House Speaker William Ratchford, and reelected with a bare 51%. After one easy reelection in 1976, Sarasin again took on a tough task in 1978, running against Ella Grasso. This time he was not so fortunate; though he ran a solid campaign, he was beaten by a large margin, and failed to carry the 5th district.

The Democratic nominee in 1978 was Ratchford, fresh from a stint as the state commissioner on aging. But despite the strength he had shown against Sarasin, Ratchford did not win easily. Republican state Senator George Guidera, once the youngest member of the state legislature, began with a base in Republican Weston. His work on issues like child abuse, divorce, and decriminalization of alcoholism helped give him a moderate image, and he swept most of the district's smaller towns. Ratchford needed big pluralities in Waterbury and his home town of Danbury for a 52% victory.

As an experienced legislator and incumbent, Ratchford should have the edge in keeping this seat in the years ahead. But the district has proved to be volatile before, and after 1980 will have to be redistricted once again, with consequences which cannot now be predicted.

Census Data Pop. 505,316. Central city, 42%; suburban, 39%. Median family income, $12,200; families above $15,000: 33%; families below $3,000: 5%. Median years education, 12.2.

'he Voters

Median voting age 44.
Employment profile White collar, 51%. Blue collar, 39%. Service, 10%. Farm, –%.
Ethnic groups Black, 4%. Spanish, 2%. Total foreign stock, 34%. Italy, 9%; Canada, 4%; Poland, 3%; UK, Ireland, Germany, 2% each; USSR, 1%.

'residential vote

1976	Carter (D)	104,081	(44%)
	Ford (R)	133,654	(56%)
1972	Nixon (R)	144,149	(62%)
	McGovern (D)	87,747	(38%)

Rep. William R. Ratchford (D) Elected 1978; b. May 24, 1934, Danbury; home, Danbury; U. of Conn., B.A. 1956, Georgetown U., LL.B. 1959; Unitarian.

Career Conn. House of Reps., 1962–74, Speaker, 1969–72, Minor. Ldr., 1972–74; Dem. Nominee for U.S. House of Reps., 1974; Chmn., Conn. Blue Ribbon Comm. to Investigate Nursing Home Industry, 1975–76; Commissioner, Conn. Dept. of Aging, 1977–78.

Offices 437 CHOB, 202-225-3822. Also 135 Grand St., Waterbury 06701, 203-573-1418.

Committees *Education and Labor* (22d). Subcommittees: Employment)pportunities; Postsecondary Education.

Iouse Administration (15th). Subcommittees: Libraries and Memorials; Accounts.

;roup Ratings: Newly Elected

Key Votes: Newly Elected

lection Results

978 general	William Ratchford (D)	96,738	(52%)	($139,778)
	George C. Guidera (R)	88,162	(48%)	($245,933)
978 primary	William Ratchford (D), nominated by convention			
976 general	Ronald A. Sarasin (R)	157,007	(67%)	($122,014)
	Michael J. Adanti (D)	77,308	(33%)	($56,272)

;IXTH DISTRICT

Some congressional districts seem to be made up of territory left over after everyone else has onstructed his own constituency. Such a district is the 6th of Connecticut. Its population oncentrations are widely dispersed, at just about the opposite ends of the district. Enfield and Vindsor Locks, in the far northeast corner, are predominantly Italian-American and part of the Iartford-to-Springfield, Massachusetts, industrial corridor. In the southeast corner of the 6th are 3ristol and New Britain, the latter the city with the state's largest concentration of

Polish-Americans. In the north central part of the district, amid the gentle mountains, are the mil towns of Torrington and Winsted, the latter of which is Ralph Nader's home town. In betwee these Democratic areas are the Yankee Republican towns (like Sharon, home of the Buckley clan and some posh Republican suburbs like Farmington, Avon, and Simsbury.

The 1964 legislature, which drew the district's lines (they have been altered only slightly since) expected the 6th to elect a Democrat, and generally it has. But overall the district must b classified as marginal, as it certainly has been in statewide contests. Indeed in its relatively brie history the 6th has had four different representatives—practically a record in this day whe congressmen are reelected routinely. The first congressman here, Bernard Grabowski, was the las beneficiary of the tradition that the state's congressman-at-large be of Polish descent; he wa slated in 1962 when the incumbent rebelled against the leadership of Democratic State Chairma John Bailey. Grabowski did fine while riding the coattails of the state ticket in 1962 and 1964; lef to his own devices in this rather disparate constituency in 1966, he lost. The winner was Thoma Meskill, the brash conservative Republican Mayor of New Britain, who went on to th governorship in 1970; Meskill is now a federal judge, despite considerable feeling that he lack judicial temperament, thanks to the efforts of Senator Lowell Weicker. The same path wa followed by Meskill's successor, Ella Grasso; elected by a narrow margin (1970), reelected easil (1972), then on to Hartford (1974) where she is Governor today.

That left the district up for grabs in 1974. The winner was an unlikely one, at least from th perspective of traditional Connecticut politics: 30-year-old Toby Moffett, once a Nader Raide and director of the Nader-inspired Connecticut Citizens' Action Group. Moffett's strong suit wa constituency service—something 6th district residents were used to; Ella Grasso had a toll-fre telephone number she advertised as the "Ella-phone" to take complaints. Moffett used hi campaign staff even before he was elected to solve constituents' problems and in the proces demolished the Republican candidate by nearly a 2–1 margin.

Moffett has been identified most closely with the energy issue. He is one of the House's mos vocal opponents of deregulation of oil and natural gas prices, and has played an important role i the conference committee handling such issues. In 1979 he defeated three fellow 1974 freshme who had, by luck of the draw, greater seniority for the chairmanship of the Governmen Operations subcommittee on Environment, Energy, and Natural Resources. This gave him forum for his activism and new proposals—such as his 1979 suggestion that every car owne should choose a day of the week on which his car could not get gas. Moffett is considered to be likely candidate for Abraham Ribicoff's Senate seat, although he has said he might like to remai in the House, where he seems more in accord with majority opinion. If he does run, he wil probably have to face in the primary 2d district Congressman Christopher Dodd, another 197 freshman with a solid and similar, though not identical, record.

Census Data Pop. 505,331. Central city, 26%; suburban, 51%. Median family income, $11,898 families above $15,000: 30%; families below $3,000: 5%. Median years education, 12.2

The Voters

Median voting age 43.
Employment profile White collar, 50%. Blue collar, 40%. Service, 9%. Farm, 1%.
Ethnic groups Black, 1%. Spanish, 1%. Total foreign stock, 32%. Italy, 6%; Canada, Poland, 5% each; Germany, UK, 2% each; Ireland, 1%.

Presidential vote

1976	Carter (D)	115,119	(48%)
	Ford (R)	126,005	(52%)
1972	Nixon (R)	136,430	(58%)
	McGovern (D)	98,328	(42%)

Rep. Anthony Toby Moffett (D) Elected 1974; b. Aug. 18, 1944, Holyoke, Mass.; home, Unionville; Syracuse U., A.B. 1966, Boston Col., M.A. 1968.

Career Dir., Ofc. of Students and Youth, Ofc. of the U.S. Commissioner of Educ., 1969–70; Staff aide to U.S. Sen. Walter Mondale of Minn., 1970–71; Dir., Conn. Citizens Action Group, 1971–74.

Offices 127 CHOB, 202-225-4476. Also 160 Farmington Ave., Bristol 06010, 203-589-5750.

Committees *Government Operations* (16th). Subcommittees: Environment, Energy and Natural Resources (Chairman).

nterstate and Foreign Commerce (14th). Subcommittees: Energy and Power; Oversight and nvestigations.

;roup Ratings

	ADA	COPE	PC	RPN	NFU	LCV	CFA	NAB	NSI	ACA	NTU
978	95	89	93	50	80	–	82	0	0	16	–
977	95	83	90	54	67	98	75	–	–	11	35
976	95	86	90	59	83	96	100	18	0	13	48

‹ey Votes

) Increase Def Spnd	AGN	6) Alaska Lands Protect	FOR	11) Delay Auto Pol Cntrl	AGN
:) B-1 Bomber	AGN	7) Water Projects Veto	FOR	12) Sugar Price Escalator	AGN
) Cargo Preference	AGN	8) Consum Protect Agcy	FOR	13) Pub Fin Cong Cmpgns	FOR
) Dereg Nat Gas	AGN	9) Common Situs Picket	FOR	14) ERA Ratif Recissn	AGN
) Kemp-Roth	AGN	10) Labor Law Revision	FOR	15) Prohibt Govt Abrtns	AGN

:lection Results

978 general	Toby Moffett (D)	119,537	(64%)	($162,006)
	Daniel F. MacKinnon (R)	66,664	(36%)	($83,896)
978 primary	Toby Moffett (D), nominated by convention			
976 general	Toby Moffett (D)	134,914	(57%)	($120,987)
	Thomas F. Upson (R)	102,364	(43%)	($84,682)

DELAWARE

Delaware likes to boast that it was the "First State" because it ratified the Constitution before ny other in 1787. But this tiny state's place in our national life depends less on such history than n the fact that, because of its liberal incorporation laws and low taxes, it is the technical home of nost of the nation's large corporations and the fact that it is the physical home of the DuPont :ompany. DuPont, with annual revenues of more than $10 billion, clearly dominates the ninuscule state, whose revenues are around $500 million. Wealthy members of the DuPont amily—there are more than one thousand living DuPonts—and corporate executives have a isproportionate say in what happens here. A few years ago a group of Naderites wrote a book bout Delaware called *The Company State*; while it stumbles over itself in a rush to condemn the)uPonts, its basic point—that the DuPonts tend to run things—is sound. As if to make the

Naderites' point, Delaware voters elected a DuPont as Governor in 1976; but it should be noted that this DuPont has taken care throughout his political career to criticize the company.

The politics of this small state (second smallest in area, fifth smallest in population) has infrequently engaged the attention of writers. Technically Delaware has as much clout in the United States Senate as California or New York; in fact, it has seldom produced important senators. Over the years the state has wavered between Democrats and Republicans, with the DuPonts (the company owned the Wilmington newspapers for years) entrenched in both parties. In the 1960s Republicans seemed to have an edge, in large part because of the increasing importance of fast-growing suburban New Castle County (the Wilmington suburbs). But during the 1970s Delaware has been more up for grabs. It has gone for both parties in both Senate and governor races, and Jimmy Carter carried the state comfortably over Gerald Ford.

Delaware's senior statewide official is Senator William Roth, a Republican first elected to the House in 1966 and to the Senate in 1970. During his first term he was one of the more anonymous senators and could be categorized as a conservative on substantive issues and a reformer on procedural matters (such as holding committee hearings in public). But in the 95th Congress Roth emerged as the leading Senate sponsor of several important pieces of legislation: a case in point for the proposition that Republicans seized the legislative initiative from Democrats in 1977 and 1978. Roth's first major initiative was the tuition tax credit. He has pushed through the Senate a proposal to provide parents with a $250 per student tax credit for college tuitions. The measure has failed to get anywhere in the House, and opponents argue that it would tend to benefit the rich; Roth maintains that it would help the hard-pressed middle class.

Roth's other major legislation was, of course, the Kemp-Roth bill. Although Congressman Jack Kemp received more publicity, Roth was just as enthusiastic a backer of the measure to cut the federal income tax 30% over a three year period. The measure was attacked as being inflationary and defended as a measure to revive the economy by letting private enterprise create jobs. Kemp-Roth became official Republican Party policy and was backed by virtually every Republican member of Congress. Democrats regarded it as an election year gambit and gave it virtually no support, although the Senate did pass a somewhat different version sponsored by Sam Nunn of Georgia.

Despite these measures Roth still cannot be regarded as a real heavyweight in the Senate. But he does seem to speak in the authentic accents of the people who consider themselves the beleaguered middle class, and he is a force to be taken considerably more seriously than he was a few years ago.

Delaware's junior Senator, Joseph Biden, is one of the youngest men ever elected to the Senate. In 1972, when he was just 29, he challenged incumbent Caleb Boggs, who had held statewide office for 26 years without alienating any substantial segment of the electorate. Biden had the advantages of energy, an active campaigning family—and the impression that Boggs really wanted to retire. Biden also handled issues skilfully, attacking the Vietnam war but identifying his own mood with that of people in the hawkish, rural southern part of the state. He won that election narrowly, but shortly thereafter his wife and daughter were killed in an auto accident.

Biden has shunned the traditional rules about a freshman remaining silent, and is usually prepared with a comment on any important concern. He was also the first senator to come out for the presidential candidacy of Jimmy Carter in 1976. Biden's seats on the Foreign Relations and Judiciary Committee give him the opportunity to work on a number of issues. The one on which he has been most visible is one of great importance in Delaware, busing. New Castle County has been under a busing order, which took effect in September 1978, and Biden has introduced several antibusing bills. He has succeeded in limiting the bases on which HEW can issue busing orders. But the bill that he and Roth have backed to prevent the courts from ordering busing unless intentional segregation is shown to exist, did not pass the Senate in the 95th Congress. Some of Biden's critics consider his strongly voiced antibusing stand an example of political opportunism. Others see it as a rational response to a genuine problem: thousands of children are having their education affected, no one is quite sure how, not because of any great public demand for busing, but because a small group of people whom the courts assume speak for all blacks decided to bring a lawsuit.

Biden stressed his busing stand when he was up for reelection in 1978. The Republicans had a primary between an anti-busing activist and a longtime Republican stalwart; the latter, James Baxter, won. Baxter is a chicken farmer—an important business in Delaware—and once worked for Senator John Williams, the Republican who became known as the conscience of the Senate for is investigative work. Baxter tried to attack Biden as a liberal and an opportunist, but the charges id not seem to stick. In this usually evenly divided state, Biden won with a solid margin. Some eople believe he has national political ambitions, and that he may run for president some day. 'hat question till now has been academic: he did not turn 35 until 1977.

Delaware's Governor is Pierre S. DuPont IV, who understandably prefers to be called Pete. He eft the Congress with apparently no place to go but here: as a moderate Republican, he was nlikely to become a power in the House; as for the Senate, Biden seemed too formidable to beat nd the Roth seat was unavailable. DuPont beat a Democratic incumbent much given to nalapropisms. DuPont is a man who is interested in environmental issues, which on occasion may it him against the company; but he is not going to upset the comfortable arrangements Delaware as had with business. Given the close partisan balance of the state, DuPont can probably expect erious competition in 1980.

Delaware's one congressional seat is held by Republican Thomas Evans. A close friend of 1976 ice presidential candidate Robert Dole, with whom he served on the Republican National Committee, Evans had the good fortune to have denounced the Nixon campaign's dirty tricks efore the Watergate scandal broke. He has run now twice against two weak and underfinanced Democrats and won handily both times. His voting record is fairly close to the House Republican orm.

Census Data Pop. 302,173; 0.15% of U.S. total, 46th largest; Central city, 15%; suburban, 56%. Median family income, $12,441; 14th highest; families above $15,000: 22%; families below $3,000: %. Median years education, 12.5.

977 Share of Federal Tax Burden $1,140,000,000; 0.33% of U.S. total, 44th largest.

977 Share of Federal Outlays $890,452,000; 0.23% of U.S. total, 49th largest. Per capita federal pending, $1,538.

DOD	$189,063,000	47th (0.21%)	HEW	$333,628,000	48th (0.23%)
ERDA	$2,323,000	39th (0.04%)	HUD	$11,050,000	47th (0.26%)
NASA	$648,000	40th (0.02%)	VA	$54,393,000	47th (0.28%)
DOT	$27,261,000	50th (0.19%)	EPA	$52,946,000	31st (0.65%)
DOC	$40,842,000	51st (0.49%)	RevS	$28,222,000	44th (0.33%)
DOI	$1,647,000	51st (0.04%)	Debt	$39,369,000	46th (0.13%)
USDA	$23,493,000	51st (0.12%)	Other	$85,567,000	

Economic Base Finance, insurance and real estate; chemicals and allied products, especially plastics materials and synthetics; food and kindred products, especially poultry dressing and canned fruits and vegetables; agriculture, notably broilers, corn, dairy products and soybeans; apparel and other textile products.

Political Line-up Governor, Pierre S. du Pont IV (R). Senators, William V. Roth, Jr. (R) and oseph R. Biden, Jr. (D). Representatives, 1 R at large. State Senate (13 D and 8 R); State House 21 D and 20 R).

The Voters

Registration 278,256 Total. 123,361 D (44%); 90,936 R (33%); 212 AIP (–); 63,747 Others (23%).
Median voting age 41
Employment profile White collar, 51%. Blue collar, 34%. Service, 13%. Farm, 2%.
Ethnic groups Black, 14%. Total foreign stock, 12%.

Presidential vote

1976	Carter (D)	122,559	(53%)
	Ford (R)	109,780	(47%)
1972	Nixon (R)	140,357	(60%)
	McGovern (D)	92,283	(40%)

Sen. William V. Roth, Jr. (R) Elected 1970, seat up 1982; b. July 22, 1921, Great Falls, Mont.; home, Wilmington; U. of Oreg., B.A. 1944, Harvard U., M.B.A. 1947, LL.B. 1947; Episcopalian.

Career Army, WWII; Practicing atty.; Chm., Del. Repub. State Comm., 1961–64; U.S. House of Reps., 1967–71.

Offices 3215 DSOB, 202-224-2441. Also 3021 Fed. Bldg., 844 King St., Wilmington 19801, 302-573-6291, and 200 U.S.P.O. Bldg., Georgetown 19947, 302-856-7690.

Committees *Finance* (3d). Subcommittees: Health; International Trade; Public Assistance.

Governmental Affairs (3d). Subcommittees: Investigations; Intergovernmental Relations; Federal Spending Practices and Open Government.

Group Ratings

	ADA	COPE	PC	RPN	NFU	LCV	CFA	NAB	NSI	ACA	NTU
1978	15	11	25	60	22	44	20	82	78	83	–
1977	20	17	43	80	42	–	32	–	–	88	57
1976	10	26	42	71	33	52	35	100	80	84	69

Key Votes

1) Warnke Nom	AGN	6) Egypt-Saudi Arms	AGN	11) Hosptl Cost Contnmnt	AGN
2) Neutron Bomb	FOR	7) Draft Restr Pardon	AGN	12) Clinch River Reactor	FOR
3) Waterwy User Fee	AGN	8) Wheat Price Support	AGN	13) Pub Fin Cong Cmpgns	AGN
4) Dereg Nat Gas	FOR	9) Panama Canal Treaty	AGN	14) ERA Ratif Recissn	AGN
5) Kemp-Roth	FOR	10) Labor Law Rev Clot	AGN	15) Med Necssy Abrtns	AGN

Election Results

1976 general	William V. Roth, Jr. (R)	125,454	(56%)	($322,080)
	Thomas Maloney (D)	98,042	(44%)	($211,258)
1976 primary	William V. Roth, Jr. (R), nominated by convention			
1970 general	William V. Roth, Jr. (R)	96,021	(60%)	
	Jacob W. Zimmerman (D)	64,835	(40%)	

Sen. Joseph R. Biden, Jr. (D) Elected 1972, seat up 1978; b. Nov. 20, 1942, Scranton, Pa.; home, Wilmington; U. of Del., B.A. 1965, Syracuse U., J.D. 1968; Catholic.

Career Practicing atty., 1968–72; New Castle County Cncl., 1970–72.

Offices 431 RSOB, 202-224-5042. Also Rm. 6021 Fed. Bldg., Wilmington 19801, 302-573-6345.

Committees *Budget* (5th).

Foreign Relations (4th). Subcommittees: International Economic Policy; Arms Control, Oceans, International Operations, and Environment; European Affairs (Chairman).

Judiciary (4th). Subcommittees: Administrative Practice and Procedure; Criminal Justice (Chairman); Jurisprudence and Governmental Relations.

Select Committee on Intelligence (4th).

Group Ratings

	ADA	COPE	PC	RPN	NFU	LCV	CFA	NAB	NSI	ACA	NTU
1978	50	61	70	63	38	92	60	30	0	27	–
1977	70	84	78	20	67	–	68	–	–	13	39
1976	75	82	77	53	70	84	71	36	0	17	50

Key Votes

1) Warnke Nom	FOR	6) Egypt-Saudi Arms	AGN	11) Hosptl Cost Contnmnt	FOR
2) Neutron Bomb	AGN	7) Draft Restr Pardon	AGN	12) Clinch River Reactor	DNV
3) Waterwy User Fee	FOR	8) Wheat Price Support	AGN	13) Pub Fin Cong Cmpgns	FOR
4) Dereg Nat Gas	AGN	9) Panama Canal Treaty	FOR	14) ERA Ratif Recissn	FOR
5) Kemp-Roth	FOR	10) Labor Law Rev Clot	FOR	15) Med Necssy Abrtns	AGN

Election Results

1978 general	Joseph R. Biden, Jr. (D)	93,930	(59%)	($487,504)
	James H. Baxter, Jr. (R)	66,479	(41%)	($206,250)
1978 primary	Joseph R. Biden, Jr. (D), nominated by convention			
1972 general	Joseph R. Biden, Jr. (D)	116,006	(51%)	($260,699)
	J. Caleb Boggs (R)	112,844	(49%)	($167,657)

Gov. Pierre S. du Pont IV (R) Elected 1976, term expires Jan. 1981; b. Jan. 22, 1935, Wilmington; Princeton U., B.S.E. 1956, Harvard U., LL.B 1963, Episcopalian.

Career Navy, 1957–60; Business exec., Photo Products Div., E.I. du Pont Co., 1963–70; Del. House of Reps., 1968–70; U.S. House of Reps., 1971–77.

Offices Legislative Hall, Dover 19001, 302-678-4626.

Election Results

1976 general	Pierre S. du Pont IV (R)	130,531	(57%)
	Sherman W. Tribbitt (D)	97,480	(43%)
1976 primary	Pierre S. du Pont IV (R) nominated by convention		
1972 general	Sherman W. Tribbitt (D)	117,274	(52%)
	Russell W. Peterson (R)	109,583	(48%)

Committees *District of Columbia* (8th). Subcommittees: Metropolitan Affairs.

Rep. Thomas B. Evans, Jr. (R) Elected 1976; b. Nov. 5, 1931, Nashville, Tenn.; home, Wilmington; U. of Va., B.A. 1951, LL.B. 1953; Episcopalian.

Career Pres., Evans and Assoc., Inc., insurance and employee benefits, 1964– ; Partner, Evans, Steffey and Assoc., mortgage brokers; Dir., Del. State Development Dept., 1969–70.

Offices 316 CHOB, 202-225-4165. Also Fed. Ofc. Bldg., Wilmington 19801, 302-571-6181.

Committees *Banking, Finance and Urban Affairs* (8th). Subcommittees: Consumer Affairs; International Development; Institutions and Finance; Housing and Community Development.

Merchant Marine and Fisheries (11th). Subcommittees: Fish and Wildlife. Conservation and the Environment; Oceanography.

Group Ratings

	ADA	COPE	PC	RPN	NFU	LCV	CFA	NAB	NSI	ACA	NTU
1978	15	21	20	70	11	–	23	92	89	76	–
1977	20	27	33	73	36	59	30	–	–	83	33

Key Votes

1) Increase Def Spnd	FOR	6) Alaska Lands Protect	FOR	11) Delay Auto Pol Cntrl	DNV
2) B-1 Bomber	FOR	7) Water Projects Veto	AGN	12) Sugar Price Escalator	AGN
3) Cargo Preference	AGN	8) Consum Protect Agcy	AGN	13) Pub Fin Cong Cmpgns	FOR
4) Dereg Nat Gas	FOR	9) Common Situs Picket	AGN	14) ERA Ratif Recissn	FOR
5) Kemp-Roth	FOR	10) Labor Law Revision	AGN	15) Prohibt Govt Abrtns	DNV

Election Results

1978 general	Thomas B. Evans, Jr. (R)	91,689	(59%)	($241,410)
	Gary E. Hindes (D)	64,863	(41%)	($57,252)
1978 primary	Thomas B. Evans, Jr. (R), nominated by convention			
1976 general	Thomas B. Evans, Jr. (R)	110,637	(52%)	($228,349)
	Samuel Shipley (D)	102,411	(48%)	($72,225)

DISTRICT OF COLUMBIA

In 1974, for the first time in 100 years, the residents of the capital of the United States of America were allowed to vote on who should head their local government. Back in 1874, Congress had taken away the District of Columbia's right to elect its local officials, because of the heavy spending of Governor Alexander Sheppard and out of fear of what was even then the city's large black electorate. Not until 1964 could the residents of the District vote for president; not until 1968 could they elect their own school board; not until 1971 did Washington get a delegate in the House of Representatives. During much of that period, the District's affairs were controlled by Chairman John McMillan and his fellow Dixiecrats on the House District of Columbia Committee—a body implacably hostile to the desires of the District's black majority until Southern domination of the committee ended, with McMillan's defeat and the retirement of several others, in 1972. Within a year, home rule was law.

Why had it been so long coming? The basic reason was Congress's long-standing fear of the city's black majority. Since before the Civil War, Washington has been a special city for blacks; the slave trade was abolished here as part of the Compromise of 1850, and it was a haven for free Negroes, who heavily outnumbered slaves by the time Lincoln became President. Blacks formed more than one-quarter of the electorate that gave power to Governor Sheppard's men; and blacks held high office under Sheppard's Republican government. At the northern edge of the South, Washington always had a larger percentage of blacks than most major cities; and when the city's metropolitan population ballooned in the years of the New Deal and World War II and after, it was inevitable that, with the suburbs restricted to whites, the District would become majority black.

That happened officially in the 1960 census; by 1970, the District was 71% black. Washington is now our only major city without a white working class; its whites live mostly in well-to-do areas west of Rock Creek Park, in redeveloped Capitol Hill, and in neighborhoods like Adams-Morgan and Mount Pleasant which are fast being redeveloped by private owners. The white population is thus highly educated and high income. There are many well-to-do blacks in the District too, though the outmigration of middle income blacks to Prince Georges County, Maryland, has deprived the city of some of the black middle class.

One argument made by opponents of home rule was that District residents were not really much interested in local government; and of course so long as little was at stake, turnout in D.C. elections was low. In presidential contests there has been little point in voting when constituency's electoral votes were obviously going to the Democratic candidate. But even in local contests where something has been at stake, relatively few District residents vote. That was the case in the 1971 Democratic primary which made Walter Fauntroy Washington's congressional Delegate; it was the case in the 1974 primary for mayor between incumbent Walter Washington and Clifford Alexander, who nearly won and later became Secretary of the Army; and it was the case in 1978, when there was a seriously contested primary for mayor between and among Walter Washington, Council President Sterling Tucker, and Councilman-at-Large Marion Barry.

None of these men differed much on their stated positions on issues, but most District voters who follow local politics realized that there were significant differences in temperament which would be reflected in mayoral performance. Walter Washington, a career bureaucrat who was appointed Mayor by Lyndon Johnson and reappointed by Richard Nixon, had walked the streets and cooled the 1968 riots; but he was clearly more comfortable dealing with congressional conservatives and a few close aides.

Washington dextrously got funds out of McMillan and from William Natcher, the conscientious and conservative Chairman of the D.C. Appropriations Subcommittee until 1979. But that skill became less relevant to the District's needs, as Congress became less parsimonious. Then the problem became how to make a bloated bureaucracy actually work and deliver services to citizens. Washington showed less skill here, and spent much of his time defending his close advisers—like Joseph Yeldell, who was convicted of taking bribes (though the conviction was reversed for jury irregularities). In 1974 Washington was almost defeated in an upset by a candidate whose knowledge of District affairs was limited; by 1978 it was obvious that Washington had only minority support and could cling to office only if his opposition was divided.

He almost made it. Sterling Tucker and Marion Barry both had claims on the city's electorate. Tucker, as former head of the city's Urban League, had an activist past and a reputation for knowing how to get things done. Barry, as founder of an organization called Pride, Inc., was known to be close to the black community, and he was the youngest and verbally the most militant of the three contenders. Among black voters, the primary was virtually a dead heat, while the affluent white minority gave Barry a notable edge. His victory in the general election of course was anticlimactic.

Barry's victory has certainly produced a new atmosphere in Washington politics—and has swept some time-servers out of comfortable positions. But there are limitations on what any D.C. mayor can do. Congress still retains some control over the District's budget, because it must appropriate the money to the District in lieu of property taxes on federal buildings. Moreover, Congress prohibits the District from taxing suburbanites who work in the city—something the District would love to do. But not all the constraints are negative. The local economy of Washington is booming, and so are real estate prices. Neighborhoods once considered unsalvageable are now being renovated by young homeowners, many of them black as well as white. The mayor and council have tried to slow down the trend by instituting rent control and trying to prevent apartments from being converted to condominiums, but they might as well compare themselves to King Canute ordering back the sea. The tide of prosperity and affluence in Washington is too great to be stopped. There are still many poor people in the city, but most central cities over the past 25 years would have been happy to have the problems Washington now has. The District government's basic problem is one common to all municipal governments, insuring the delivery of basic services.

The next step in Washington's political maturity would seem to be full representation in Congress. After all, this is a jurisdiction with more people than Montana, more than Alaska and Wyoming put together. And late in the 1978 session, Congress passed a constitutional amendment which would give full voting representation—two senators and probably two representatives—to the District. The problem is that very few states have ratified it, and hard-line conservatives have persuaded some states explicitly to reject it. Such moves may have no constitutional significance, but they do suggest that most Americans do not see the measure as most Washingtonians do, as a matter of simple justice. The amendment seems unlikely ever to be ratified. In the meantime, Delegate Fauntroy has more seniority now than most House members, he is a voting member of the District of Columbia Committee, and he played an important role in preserving the House assassinations investigation after the stormy resignation of Chairman Henry Gonzalez. And it was Fauntroy who played the major role in getting Congress to pass the D.C. representation amendment, and should the District ever get full representation, he would probably become a member of the Senate.

The Voters

Registration 250,750 Total. 197,275 D (78%); 21,169 R (9%); 32,306 Other (13%). Ind. (12%); 1,876 DC Statehood (1%); 1,251 Others (–).
Median voting age 41
Employment profile White collar, 51%. Blue collar, 34%. Service, 13%. Farm, 2%.
Ethnic groups Black, 14%. Total foreign stock, 12%.

Presidential vote

1976	Carter (D)	137,819	(82%)
	Ford (R)	27,873	(18%)
1972	Nixon (R)	35,226	(22%)
	McGovern (D)	127,627	(78%)

1976 Democratic Presidential Primary

Carter	9,281	(40%)
Udal	6,106	(26%)
Fauntroy slate	4,997	(21%)
Washington slate	2,606	(11%)
Harris	370	(2%)

Election Results

1978 general	Marion Barry (D)	69,888	(71%)
	Arthur Fletcher (R)	28,032	(29%)
1978 primary	Marion Barry (D)	32,841	(35%)
	Sterling Tucker (D)	31,277	(33%)
	Walter Washington (D)	29,881	(32%)
	Two others (D)	790	(1%)
1974 general	Walter E. Washington (D)	84,676	(88%)
	Sam Harris (Ind.)	7,514	(8%)
	Jackson Champion (R)	3,703	(4%)

Rep. Walter E. Fauntroy (D) Elected Mar. 23, 1971; b. Feb. 6., 1933, Washington D.C.; Va. Union U., A.B. 1955, Yale U., B.D. 1958; Baptist.

Career Pastor, New Bethel Baptist Church, 1958–; Founder and former Dir., Model Inner City Community Org.; Dir., Washington Bureau, SCLC, 1961–71; Co-Ordinator, Selma to Montgomery March, 1965; Vice Chm., D.C. City Cncl., 1967–69; Natl. Co-Ordinator, Poor Peoples Campaign, 1969; Chm., Bd. of Dirs., Martin Luther King, Jr., Ctr. for Social Change, 1969–.

Offices 2350 RHOB, 202-225-8050. Also 350 G Street NW, Washington DC 20548, 202-275-0171.

Committees *Banking, Finance, and Urban Affairs* (10th). Subcommittees: Housing and Community Development; Financial Institutions Supervision, Regulation and Insurance; General Oversight and Renegotiation; Consumer Affairs.

District of Columbia (3d). Subcommittees: Fiscal Affairs and Health; Government Affairs and Budget (Chairman).

Election Results

1978 general	Walter Fauntroy (D)	76,557	(87%)	($95,668)
	Jackson Champion (R)	11,667	(13%)	
1978 primary	Walter Fauntroy (D), unopposed			
1976 general	Walter Fauntroy (D)	114,615	(85%)	
	Daniel Hall (R)	19,817	(15%)	

FLORIDA

No Southern state has changed more in the last generation than Florida. Even beyond the changes wrought by the civil rights revolution, Florida has been altered by a vast in-migration of a magnitude almost unique in American history. Back in 1950 the state had 2.5 million residents; now its population has swelled past 8 million and by 1980 it will have become our seventh largest state. Just since 1970 Florida's population has grown by 1.5 million—more people than there are in all of Nebraska. They have come from all parts of the nation, in search of sunshine and warmth, of year-round golf and swimming. Many of course are old people who want to spend their last years in a warm climate and to spend their last dollars in a state with no income tax. But too much can be made of the stereotype of Florida retirees. There are also plenty of younger people with families flocking to places like Orlando, with Disney World nearby, and Fort Lauderdale and Jacksonville.

Florida politics has never had much unity; a generation ago V. O. Key described it as "every man for himself." Today the state is much more heterogeneous than it was then, and its voting patterns—both in partisan elections and on issues like casino gambling—reflect the origins of its inhabitants as much as they do any peculiarly Floridian characteristics. The northern part of the state, with the fewest migrants and most of those from rural Southern backgrounds, votes much like adjacent regions of Alabama and Georgia. Miami Beach, full of Jewish former New Yorkers, votes like the Grand Concourse in the Bronx; Sarasota, occupied by well-to-do Midwestern WASPs, is Goldwater Republican, like the wealthy suburbs of Chicago. Some areas change political coloration because of heavy migration. Fort Lauderdale and Broward County have become much more Democratic in recent years as they attract more migrants from the Northeast and from the Miami area just to the south; while Republican margins have been growing vastly in several Gulf Coast counties which have been attracting migrants from middle income Protestant backgrounds.

Like other Southern states, Florida has a Democratic heritage. Even today two-thirds of its voters register as Democrats—a far higher proportion than ever vote Democratic in a seriously contested general election—and only 28% register Republican. A dozen years ago Florida seemed on its way to becoming a Republican state. It elected a Republican governor in 1966 and a Republican senator in 1968. But Democrats had big victories in 1970 and 1974 and today hold virtually all the state's top offices. The only statewide elected Republican is Public Service Commissioner Paula Hawkins, and Republicans hold only three of the state's 15 congressional seats. Part of the reason for Democratic dominance has been strife and scandal among the Republicans. But it also seems to have reflected a more Democratic disposition among the newcomers to the state. Once retirement in Florida was a luxury for the wealthy; today it is within the reach of many factory workers.

In the past, Florida governors did not cut an important figure; limited to one four-year term and surrounded by other state elected officials who were not, they seldom achieved much stature. That is not the case today. Florida now allows its governors two terms. And although the formal powers of the office are limited, in this fast growing, rapidly changing state, the governor has the opportunity to set the public agenda and to shape the future development of the state. That is what Reubin Askew did in the eight years he served as Governor. When he was elected in 1970, he was an unknown state Senator from Pensacola; many voted for him as the only alternative to the erratic incumbent, Claude Kirk. But Askew soon showed Florida that he combined a strict Christian morality (no drinking, smoking, or swearing) with a steely determination to effect major reforms. He got the legislature and the voters to approve a new corporate income tax structure. He pushed through to passage a statewide land use bill. He failed to stop an anti-busing referendum in the 1972 presidential primary, but he did manage to get voters to avow their belief in racial integration. In 1978 he capped his career in the Governor's office by opposing the referendum to allow casino gambling on Miami Beach. It went against Askew's ideas of what the state should permit and he was worried about the possibility of control by organized crime; the proposal was beaten by more than the expected margin, and even failed to carry Dade County.

Since his first years in office Askew has been mentioned as a possible national officeholder. He was nearly on *Time*'s "New South" cover in 1971 (they finally decided on Jimmy Carter instead) and he keynoted the 1972 Democratic National Convention. He is not especially close to Carter (he supported Henry Jackson in the 1976 Florida primary), but he has chaired the Administration's commission on ambassadorial appointments and could probably have a major appointment if he wants it. After the 1978 election, apparently satisfied with his accomplishments as Governor and without the ambition that seems to drive so many politicians, he retired to private life.

The race to succeed Askew was one of the most expensive campaigns of 1978, and one with an unusually large number of candidates of some distinction. The winner had to run quite a gauntlet: first a long campaign that culminated in the September Democratic primary, then a four-week fight that ended in the October Democratic runoff, and then a few more weeks of campaigning for the November general election against the Republican candidate. The man who emerged from the ordeal as Governor of Florida was at first a long shot: state Senator Bob Graham. Not so many years ago it was considered impossible here to elect someone like Graham, a politician from the Miami area who has a reputation as a liberal. But some of his opponents had similar problems, notably Attorney General Robert Shevin. The front-runner in the initial primary, Shevin had an impressive background: he was tough on crime, a fighter for consumer rights, a liberal on many other issues. But Shevin could not seem to build up solid majorities beyond the Miami-to-Palm-Beach Gold Coast, where his Jewish background and Miami identification helped him especially with many Jewish voters. Meanwhile, during the primary, Graham worked at one hundred different jobs throughout the state, as his television advertisements asserted that he was in touch with the ordinary person (though he is a wealthy developer and brother-in-law of the Washington *Post*'s Katharine Graham). Graham's soft-spoken style was an asset, but he also had an aggressive and accomplished record in the state Senate.

In the general election, Graham faced a much wealthier millionaire, Jack Eckerd, founder of the drug store chain that bears his name. Eckerd has spent liberally of his $57 million fortune in Florida elections: he ran for governor in 1970 (losing the primary to Kirk), for senator in 1974 (losing narrowly to Richard Stone), and for governor again in 1978. Eckerd had some problems with other Republicans. Congressman Louis Frey, defeated in the primary, was not a strong supporter. Eckerd ran well in the area covered by Tampa and St. Petersburg television stations, along the Gulf Coast, which contains about one-quarter of the state's voters, and he nearly carried Jacksonville, where he had the support of former Mayor Hans Tanzler, a born-again Christian who lost in the Democratic primary. But Eckerd was not able to carry the northern and panhandle counties; he trailed in the Orlando area which usually goes Republican; and Graham won by huge margins in the Gold Coast.

Graham can be expected to be a Governor much in the Askew mold. Florida, for all its growth and prosperity, faces a variety of serious problems—different in the different parts of the state. The environment is always a serious issue in a state that has experienced so much growth. Moreover, state government services—and the state budget—have had to increase rapidly. And some parts of the state, notably the Miami area, have serious economic problems, though others, notably Orlando, are booming as never before.

Florida has two Democratic senators, both elected during the seventies in upsets. The senior Senator is Lawton Chiles, who was an unknown state Senator from the small city of Lakeland when he ran in 1970. Chiles attracted attention by walking 1,000 miles across the state—the first politician to use that campaign technique. His pleasant personality made a good impression on voters, and they made some impression on him: he switched from Vietnam hawk to dove. He beat a former governor in the Democratic primary runoff and upset the favorite, Republican Congressman William Cramer, in the general election. Cramer had hoped to paint his Democratic opponent as a free-spending Great Society liberal, opposed to capital punishment and the flag. But that picture didn't fit Chiles and he won easily.

In the Senate, Chiles occupies a kind of middle-of-the-road position ideologically. He joins most other Democrats much more often then some of the older generation of Southern senators (like John Stennis and Herman Talmadge), but he joins them notably less often than some other contemporary Southerners (like Dale Bumpers of Arkansas or Jim Sasser of Tennessee). Chiles has seats on key committees like Appropriations and Budget—seats which give him little publicity today but promise great influence in the future. He is known best to the general public as the chairman of committee hearings that helped to expose the GSA scandal in 1978. In other words, Chiles is behaving like a Senator who expects to be a Senator for some time—and he probably will. He did not draw strong opposition in 1976 and was reelected with 63%. It does not now seem especially likely that he will draw strong opposition in 1982.

The other Senator, Richard Stone, is from Miami and is Jewish. He is the first Floridian to overcome these purported handicaps and win major statewide office. Elected Secretary of State in 1970, Stone built an unlikely alliance between condominium dwellers in the Gold Coast and rural Protestants in the northern panhandle, having attracted the latter group by playing the harmonica and spoons on campaign trips in north Florida. Stone squeaked into the runoff against Orlando area Congressman Bill Gunter in 1974, and won by exploiting an unusual issue: Gunter's vote for a law, sponsored by Senator James Eastland of Mississippi, to compensate owners of chickens who had died from a rare disease. The general election was a free-spending race between millionaires Stone and Jack Eckerd, in which the American Party candidate took 16% of the vote, and Stone won again narrowly.

Stone is up for reelection in 1980 and will probably face serious competition once again. He has a voting record which is closer to Chiles's than to what one might expect from a Miami-based politician, and he has worked with Chiles on the so-called sunshine law: measures first passed in Florida requiring all government business to be conducted in public. Stone is a member of the Foreign Relations Committee and Chairman of its Subcommittee on Near Eastern Affairs, where he is a strong supporter of policies to help Israel. He also serves on Agriculture, a committee of more direct importance to many in a state with major agricultural interests.

Florida now has one of the nation's earliest presidential primaries, just two weeks after New Hampshire and one week after Massachusetts, Connecticut, and Vermont. When Florida started this arrangement, in 1972, virtually all the Democratic candidates flocked here, perhaps partly because it is more fun to campaign in the Florida sun than in New Hampshire snow and mud. Henry Jackson, Hubert Humphrey, John Lindsay, and Edmund Muskie were all hoping for major breakthroughs in Florida, and commentators talked of how this was not really a Southern state any more. Then came the busing issue, and George Wallace won the primary with 42%.

It was less than Wallace would get later in Michigan, but it so cooled northern Democrats' interest in Florida that Jimmy Carter and George Wallace had little competition here in 1976, until the last minute when Henry Jackson moved in, apparently afraid that Carter would add Florida to his New Hampshire victory and thereby become a strong national candidate. Although Jackson carried the Gold Coast, Carter was still able to beat Wallace 34%–31%. Carter had seen early that most Florida Democrats didn't really want Wallace in the White House, and were ready to consider a plausible alternative; with his Southern accent, his corps of Georgia supporters, and his strong personal campaigning, Carter made himself that alternative. Wallace's support in other states virtually vanished when it became clear that he couldn't win in Florida; this was truly the end of his national career.

Will the 1980 Democratic primary be seriously contested here? Florida still seems too much of a Southern state for Carter to be vulnerable, and possible challengers may just pass this primary up. But if Carter is beaten in Florida, it would be a smashing blow to his candidacy.

The Republicans also had a presidential primary here in 1976. This is an election in which Florida truly becomes a non-Southern state; most of the state's registered Republicans are transplanted Yankees, concentrated in a few areas—St. Petersburg, Sarasota, Fort Lauderdale, West Palm Beach, Orlando. Accordingly, Gerald Ford's victory over Ronald Reagan was hardly a surprise; it mirrored his success in the suburbs of Chicago, Detroit, Philadelphia, and New York, where most of the voters in the Republican primary come from. In 1980, there may very well be a serious contest here, and much may depend on how many candidates conduct serious campaigns in the state.

Census Data Pop. 6,789,443; 3.35% of U.S. total, 9th largest; Central city, 29%; suburban, 35%. Median family income, $8,261; 35th highest; families above $15,000: 17%; families below $3,000: 13%. Median years education, 12.1.

1977 Share of Federal Tax Burden $12,919,000,000; 3.74% of U.S. total, 9th largest.

1977 Share of Federal Outlays $15,457,169,000; 3.91% of U.S. total, 6th largest. Per capita federal spending, $1,852.

DOD	$3,208,281,000	7th (3.51%)	HEW	$6,911,023,000	5th (4.68%)
ERDA	$36,870,000	21st (0.62%)	HUD	$135,841,000	11th (3.22%)
NASA	$301,929,000	4th (7.65%)	VA	$897,280,000	5th (4.67%)
DOT	$507,137,000	6th (3.55%)	EPA	$217,012,000	12th (2.65%)
DOC	$330,776,000	6th (3.98%)	RevS	$275,544,000	9th (3.26%)
DOI	$101,542,000	15th (2.18%)	Debt	$343,596,000	13th (1.14%)
USDA	$500,559,000	9th (2.52%)	Other	$1,689,779,000	

Economic Base Finance, insurance and real estate; agriculture, notably oranges, cattle, dairy products and grapefruit; food and kindred products, especially canned, cured and frozen foods; tourism; transportation equipment, especially aircraft and parts, and ship and boat building and repairing; electrical equipment and supplies, especially communication equipment.

Political Line-up Governor, Bob Graham (D). Senators, Lawton Chiles (D) and Richard Stone (D). Representatives 15 (12 D and 3 R). State Senate (29 D and 11 R); State House (89 D and 31 R).

The Voters

Registration 4,217,187 Total. 2,812,217 D (67%); 1,178,671 R (28%); 226,299 Other (5%).
Median voting age 46
Employment profile White collar, 50%. Blue collar, 32%. Service, 15%. Farm, 3%.
Ethnic groups Black, 15%. Spanish, 7%. Total foreign stock, 18%. Germany, UK, Canada, 2% each; Italy, USSR, 1% each.

Presidential vote

1976	Carter (D)	1,636,000	(53%)
	Ford (R)	1,469,531	(47%)
1972	Nixon (R)	1,857,759	(72%)
	McGovern (D)	718,117	(28%)

1976 Democratic Presidential Primary

Carter	448,844	(35%)
Wallace	396,820	(31%)
Jackson	310,944	(24%)
Others	143,722	(10%)

1976 Republican Presidential Primary

Ford	321,982	(53%)
Reagan	287,837	(47%)

Sen. Lawton Chiles (D) Elected 1970, seat up 1982; b. Apr. 3, 1930, Lakeland; home, Lakeland; U. of Fla., B.S. 1952, LL.B. 1955; Presbyterian.

Career Army, Korea; Practicing atty., 1955–71; Instructor, Fla. Southern Col., 1955–57; Fla. House of Reps., 1958–66; Fla. Senate 1966–70.

Offices 443 RSOB, 202-224-5274. Also Fed. Bldg., Lakeland 33801, 813-688-6681, and 931 Fed. Bldg., P.O. Box 79, 51 S.W. 1st Ave., Miami 33130, 305-350-4891.

Committees *Appropriations* (9th). Subcommittees: Agriculture and Related Agencies; Defense; Foreign Operations; Labor, HEW, and Related Agencies; Transportation and Related Agencies (Chairman).

Budget (4th).

Governmental Affairs (4th). Subcommittees: Investigations; Intergovernmental Relations; Federal Spending Practices and Open Government (Chairman).

Special Committee on Aging (Chairman).

Group Ratings

	ADA	COPE	PC	RPN	NFU	LCV	CFA	NAB	NSI	ACA	NTU
1978	35	32	30	50	40	51	25	75	50	36	–
1977	35	68	53	64	33	–	40	–	–	50	34
1976	45	84	34	67	82	49	50	58	78	48	31

Key Votes

1) Warnke Nom	AGN	6) Egypt-Saudi Arms	AGN	11) Hosptl Cost Contnmnt	FOR
2) Neutron Bomb	FOR	7) Draft Restr Pardon	AGN	12) Clinch River Reactor	FOR
3) Waterwy User Fee	FOR	8) Wheat Price Support	AGN	13) Pub Fin Cong Cmpgns	FOR
4) Dereg Nat Gas	FOR	9) Panama Canal Treaty	FOR	14) ERA Ratif Recissn	AGN
5) Kemp-Roth	AGN	10) Labor Law Rev Clot	AGN	15) Med Necssy Abrtns	AGN

Election Results

1976 general	Lawton Chiles (D)	1,799,518	(63%)	($362,235)
	John Grady (R)	1,057,886	(37%)	($394,574)
1976 primary	Lawton Chiles (D), unopposed			
1970 general	Lawton Chiles (D)	902,438	(54%)	
	William C. Cramer (R)	772,817	(46%)	

Sen. Richard (Dick) **Stone** (D) Elected 1974, seat up 1980; b. Sept. 22, 1928, New York, N.Y.; home, Tallahassee; Harvard U., A.B. 1949, Columbia U., LL.B. 1954; Jewish.

Career Practicing atty; Miami City Atty., 1966; Fla. Senate, 1967–70; Fla. Secy. of State, 1970–74.

Offices 1327 DSOB, 202-224-3041. Also 2639 N. Monroe, Suite 200-B, Tallahassee 32303, 904-386-2120, and Suite 731, 51 S.W. 1st Ave., Miami 33130, 305-350-4431.

Committees *Agriculture, Nutrition, and Forestry* (4th). Subcommittees: Agricultural Production, Marketing, and Stabilization of Prices; Agricultural Research and General Legislation; Foreign Agricultural Policy (Chairman).

Foreign Relations (6th). Subcommittees: East Asian and Pacific Affairs; Near Eastern and South Asian Affairs (Chairman); Western Hemisphere Affairs.

Veterans' Affairs (4th).

Group Ratings

	ADA	COPE	PC	RPN	NFU	LCV	CFA	NAB	NSI	ACA	NTU
1978	25	50	55	50	70	39	40	36	60	38	–
1977	30	45	40	45	67	–	32	–	–	38	27
1976	50	75	39	29	83	39	35	67	100	48	13

Key Votes

1) Warnke Nom	AGN	6) Egypt-Saudi Arms	AGN	11) Hosptl Cost Contnmnt	FOR
2) Neutron Bomb	FOR	7) Draft Restr Pardon	AGN	12) Clinch River Reactor	FOR
3) Waterwy User Fee	AGN	8) Wheat Price Support	FOR	13) Pub Fin Cong Cmpgns	FOR
4) Dereg Nat Gas	FOR	9) Panama Canal Treaty	FOR	14) ERA Ratif Recissn	FOR
5) Kemp-Roth	AGN	10) Labor Law Rev Clot	AGN	15) Med Necssy Abrtns	AGN

Election Results

1974 general	Richard Stone (D)	781,031	(43%)	($919,787)
	Jack Eckerd (R)	736,674	(41%)	($421,169)
	John Grady (AI)	282,659	(16%)	($148,495)
1974 run-off	Richard Stone (D)	321,683	(51%)	
	Bill Gunter (D)	311,044	(49%)	
1974 primary	Bill Gunter (D)	236,185	(30%)	
	Richard Stone (D)	157,301	(20%)	
	Richard Pettigrew (D)	146,728	(19%)	
	Mallory E. Horne (D)	90,684	(11%)	
	Seven others (D)	161,733	(20%)	
1968 general	Edward J. Gurney (R)	1,131,499	(56%)	
	LeRoy Collins (D)	892,637	(44%)	

Gov. Bob Graham (D) Elected 1978, term expires Jan. 1983; b. Nov. 9, 1936, Miami; U. of Fla., B.A. 1959, Harvard U., J.D. 1962; Congregationalist.

Career Vice Pres., The Graham Co., cattle and dairy production; Chmn. of Bd., Sengra Development Corp., land developers; Fla. House of Reps., 1967–71; Fla. Senate, 1971–78.

Offices The Capitol, Tallahassee 32304, 904-488-1234

Election Results

1978 general	Robert Graham (D)	1,406,580	(56%)
	Jack M. Eckerd (R)	1,123,888	(44%)
1978 run-off	Robert Graham (D)	482,535	(54%)
	Robert L. Shevin (D)	418,636	(46%)
1978 primary	Robert L. Shevin (D)	364,732	(35%)
	Robert Graham (D)	261,972	(25%)
	Hans G. Tanzler (D)	124,706	(12%)
	Jim Williams (D)	124,427	(12%)
	Three others (D)	161,696	(16%)
1974 general	Reubin Askew (D)	1,118,954	(61%)
	Jerry Thomas (R)	709,438	(39%)

FIRST DISTRICT

One of the heaviest concentrations of military bases and installations in the nation can be found in the northern panhandle counties which make up Florida's 1st congressional district. There are many reasons for the concentration. Pensacola, the district's largest city, is an old Gulf of Mexico port, and there has been a naval station there just about as long as the United States has held the territory. There are also more than 100 miles of coastline along the Gulf here, with a good port at Panama City as well as Pensacola. Finally, the climate is mild, the terrain inland flat and, where swampy, reclaimable. Such realities have helped to bring to this area such huge facilities as Eglin Air Force Base, which spreads over the lion's share of three counties. There is one other reason the Defense Department spends more than $500 million yearly around here: the fact that for 12 years, from 1965 to 1977, Bob Sikes, Congressman from the 1st district, was Chairman of the House Appropriations Subcommittee on Military Construction.

Sikes's philosophy and the interests of his district happily coincided. First elected in 1940, he was one of many Southern Democrats who stood with Franklin Roosevelt when he was pushing Lend-Lease and instituting the draft. For his congressional career—the longest in Florida history—Sikes continued to believe that it was better to risk spending too much rather than too little on military preparedness. Naturally a lot of that spending was done in the 1st district. And Sikes also found ways to help himself financially. In 1976 it was revealed that he failed to disclose: that he used his committee position to get the government to allow development on land he owned, that he owned 1,000 shares of Fairchild Industries while voting for a bill granting them a $73 million contract, and that he had an interest in a Florida bank and tried to get a branch approved at the Pensacola Naval Air Station.

Voters in the 1st district had always approved of Sikes's politics. The district is one of the most hawkish in the nation; with few blacks, it delivered some of the nation's largest majorities for George Wallace in 1968 and Richard Nixon in 1972, and went for Gerald Ford over Jimmy Carter in 1976. Even after the House voted to reprimand Sikes by a 381–3 margin, he beat a young Democratic primary opponent with 73% of the vote. But in the next Congress he was stripped of his power; House Democrats voted him out of his subcommittee chair by a 189–93 vote. His ability to help his district severely impaired, his power in the House gone, and at the age of 72, he decided to retire in 1978.

There was a serious contest to succeed him; after all, this seat has not been open for 38 years. The winner was Earl Hutto, a Democratic legislator from Panama City who was formerly a TV newscaster there and in Pensacola as well. Hutto emphasized his religious background and won a surprisingly big victory over the Republican candidate, former Pensacola Mayor Warren Briggs. Hutto's politics are likely to be conservative and hawkish, which experience shows is what the people of the 1st district want.

Census Data Pop. 452,562. Central city, 41%; suburban, 13%. Median family income, $7,621; families above $15,000: 12%; families below $3,000: 15%. Median years education, 12.1.

The Voters

Median voting age 38.
Employment profile White collar, 48%. Blue collar, 36%. Service, 15%. Farm, 1%.
Ethnic groups Black, 14%. Spanish, 2%. Total foreign stock, 5%.

Presidential vote

1976	Carter (D)	89,170	(49%)
	Ford (R)	91,674	(51%)
1972	Nixon (R)	127,607	(84%)
	McGovern (D)	24,860	(16%)

Rep. Earl Dewitt Hutto (D) Elected 1978; b. May 12, 1926, Midland City, Ala.; home, Panama City; Troy St. U., B.S. 1949, Northwestern U., 1951; Baptist.

Career Navy, WWII; Pres., Earl Hutto Advertising Agency; Fla. House of Reps., 1972–78.

Offices 508 CHOB, 202-225-4136. Also Fed. Bldg., Panama City 32401, 904-234-8933.

Committees *Merchant Marine and Fisheries* (23d). Subcommittees: Fish and Wildlife; Oceanography.

Public Works and Transportation (26th). Subcommittees: Economic Development; Public Buildings and Grounds; Water Resources.

Group Ratings: Newly Elected

Key Votes: Newly Elected

Election Results

1978 general	Earl Hutto (D)	85,608	(63%)	($118,847)
	Warren Briggs (R)	49,715	(37%)	($186,711)
1978 run-off	Earl Hutto (D)	58,352	(62%)	
	Curtis Golden (D)	35,721	(38%)	($144,805)
1978 primary	Earl Hutto (D)	39,982	(42%)	
	Curtis Golden (D)	29,692	(31%)	
	Jerry C. Melvin (D)	21,186	(22%)	($44,860)
	One other (D)	3,687	(4%)	
1976 general	Robert Sikes (D), unopposed			($25,917)

SECOND DISTRICT

Like the 1st, the 2d congressional district of Florida in the northern part of the state is part of Dixie—an area politically and sociologically not very different from neighboring south Georgia. For years the area's affection for racial segregation and the Democratic Party determined its politics. In the days before the one-person-one-vote decision, rural legislators from north Florida—known as the Pork Chop Gang—dominated state government. And for some years this part of Florida was overrepresented in the U.S. House of Representatives; the current 2d is basically a consolidation of what were two separate districts before 1966.

There are, however, two significant differences between the 1st and 2d districts—differences which have not yet been decisive in congressional races, but still seem to have had political impact. First, the 2d is Florida's blackest district; some 28% of its residents and 18% of its registered voters are black. Second, the 2d's two largest cities, Gainesville and Tallahassee, contain the state's two largest universities, the University of Florida and Florida State. Both of these schools draw most of their enrollment from south Florida, and these students, far more than those in most Southern universities, tend to support liberal candidates for public office. Altogether 13% of the district's eligible voters are students and, although they do not turn out in proportionate numbers, their impact has been noticeable.

Thus the 2d district contains two sizeable voting blocs inclined to oppose the generally conservative politics of the district's Congressman, Democrat Don Fuqua. Since he was first elected to Congress in 1962, Fuqua has generally voted with the dwindling number of conservative Southern Democrats on the Hill. He is currently Chairman of the Science and Technology Committee—a position from which he can benefit the aerospace industry which is important to Florida, although mainly to parts of the state outside the 2d.

Fuqua has had some close calls at the polls on occasion. In the 1972 Democratic primary he had an opponent who won most of the black and university vote but little more, for a total of 26%. Fuqua may have been disturbed, however, and in the next Congress voted against the bombing of Cambodia. In 1976 he had two primary opponents, education official Jack Armstrong and former Tallahassee Mayor Russell Bevis. The latter spent considerable money on a television campaign, and Fuqua was able to avoid a runoff only after the absentee votes were counted, and then by only 355 votes out of 128,000 cast. Fuqua had carried every county, but he got only 45% in Alachua (Gainesville) and 42% in Leon (Tallahassee). Fuqua had only nominal opposition in the 1974 and 1978 primaries, and the 1978 general election, when he was opposed by a former aide to Edward Gurney and Philip Crane and won with 82%, indicates he is not vulnerable to a Republican. Nonetheless, and despite his new committee chairmanship, Fuqua cannot be considered to have a completely safe seat.

Census Data Pop. 452,633. Central city, 16%; suburban, 30%. Median family income, $7,071; families above $15,000: 13%; families below $3,000: 19%. Median years education, 11.3.

The Voters

Median voting age 39.
Employment profile White collar, 49%. Blue collar, 28%. Service, 16%. Farm, 7%.
Ethnic groups Black, 28%. Spanish, 1%. Total foreign stock, 4%.

Presidential vote

1976	Carter (D)	120,425	(63%)
	Ford (R)	71,806	(37%)
1972	Nixon (R)	111,042	(69%)
	McGovern (D)	50,861	(31%)

Rep. Don Fuqua (D) Elected 1962; b. Aug. 20, 1933, Jacksonville; home, Alta; U. of Fla., B.S. 1957; Presbyterian.

Career Army, Korea; Fla. House of Reps., 1958–62.

Offices 2268 RHOB, 202-225-5235. Also 100 P.O. Bldg., Tallahassee 32302, 904-224-1152.

Committees *Government Operations* (7th). Subcommittees: Legislation and National Security.

Science and Technology (Chairman).

Group Ratings

	ADA	COPE	PC	RPN	NFU	LCV	CFA	NAB	NSI	ACA	NTU
1978	20	30	30	30	30	–	9	100	90	58	–
1977	10	48	20	36	64	29	20	–	–	50	27
1976	20	41	38	40	50	34	36	27	90	58	39

Key Votes

1) Increase Def Spnd	FOR	6) Alaska Lands Protect	DNV	11) Delay Auto Pol Cntrl	FOR
2) B-1 Bomber	FOR	7) Water Projects Veto	AGN	12) Sugar Price Escalator	DNV
3) Cargo Preference	AGN	8) Consum Protect Agcy	AGN	13) Pub Fin Cong Cmpgns	AGN
4) Dereg Nat Gas	FOR	9) Common Situs Picket	AGN	14) ERA Ratif Recissn	FOR
5) Kemp-Roth	AGN	10) Labor Law Revision	AGN	15) Prohibt Govt Abrtns	FOR

Election Results

1978 general	Don Fuqua (D)	112,649	(82%)	($88,381)
	Peter Brathwaite (R)	25,148	(18%)	($19,379)
1978 primary	Don Fuqua (D)	83,308	(86%)	
	One other (D)	14,081	(14%)	
1976 general	Don Fuqua (D), unopposed			($63,434)

THIRD DISTRICT

Jacksonville is a border city—on the border between the Old South and the new boom lands of south Florida. It was long Florida's largest city and, on paper, it has retained that status by annexing most of surrounding Duval County. But in metropolitan population Jacksonville has been eclipsed by Miami, St. Petersburg, Tampa, and even Fort Lauderdale. Jacksonville remains an important port, paper manufacturer, and banking and insurance center; in most other states it would be the premier boom town. Because of its coolish winter climate, Jacksonville has not attracted the retirees or northern migrants who have flocked to Florida cities and condominium villages farther south. But it does have the largest black percentage of any major Florida city and a large population of Southern white origin. It was the largest Florida city to go for George Wallace in 1968, and it delivered a sizeable margin for Jimmy Carter in 1976. A recent Mayor, Hans Tanzler, an enthusiastic born again Christian, had a local following of sufficient fervor that he carried Jacksonville in the 1978 Democratic gubernatorial primary.

The 3d congressional district of Florida includes almost all of Jacksonville and one small county to the north. Its Congressman since 1948, Democrat Charles Bennett, enjoys a reputation for probity and attention to duty which is second to none in the House. He was stricken with polio in the Army during World War II, and in his first campaign it was suggested that he was not physically up to representing the district. Perhaps to refute that, Bennett prided himself on being present for every roll call vote and in the late sixties broke the House record for consecutive attendance. After a while it got to the point that roll calls were sometimes delayed to accommodate Bennett; finally he missed one. The Bennett record as it stands for 1951–72: 3,428 consecutive roll call votes.

Bennett is now one of the most senior members of the House. On the Armed Services Committee he ranks just behind Chairman Mel Price. He chairs a subcommittee on seapower; Jacksonville, as it happens, has major Navy facilities. Bennett generally agrees with the committee majority which favors a strong defense and backs most Pentagon programs, but he is an occasional dissenter from conservative orthodoxy. His most difficult assignment in the 96th Congress is not, however, on Armed Services, but on the Committee officially known as Standards of Official Conduct and unofficially as the Ethics Committee. Bennett has had a seat on this body since the sixties, but he was then passed over for the chair. There was a feeling that he was too much of a stickler for propriety. He opposes unofficial office accounts, outside income for members, and congressional pay raises, which led one colleague to call him "a bit too pious." But in 1978 the two committee members with more seniority than Bennett both retired. With the spate of scandals and criminal trials involving House members, Democrats were in no position to pass over Bennett for the chair. So the Ethics Committee for the first time has a really tough chairman.

Bennett's record is the sort that appeals to Jacksonville, and he has not had any opposition in the last two elections.

Census Data Pop. 452,841. Central city, 0%; suburban, 95%. Median family income, $8,252; families above $15,000: 14%; families below $3,000: 14%. Median years education, 11.8.

The Voters

Median voting age 40.
Employment profile White collar, 50%. Blue collar, 34%. Service, 15%. Farm, 1%.
Ethnic groups Black, 26%. Spanish, 1%. Total foreign stock, 6%.

Presidential vote

1976	Carter (D)	87,760	(64%)
	Ford (R)	48,756	(36%)
1972	Nixon (R)	96,783	(70%)
	McGovern (D)	41,880	(30%)

Rep. Charles E. Bennett (D) Elected 1948; b. Dec. 2, 1910, Canton, N.Y.; home, Jacksonville; U. of Fla., B.A., J.D.; Disciples of Christ.

Career Practicing atty., 1934–42, 1947–48; Fla. House of Reps., 1941–42; Army, WWII.

Offices 2107 RHOB, 202-225-2501. Also Suite 352, Fed. Ofc. Bldg., 400 W. Bay St., Jacksonville 32202, 904-791-2587.

Committees *Armed Services* (2d). Subcommittees: Military Installations and Facilities; Seapower and Strategic and Critical Materials (Chairman).

Standards of Official Conduct (Chairman).

Group Ratings

	ADA	COPE	PC	RPN	NFU	LCV	CFA	NAB	NSI	ACA	NTU
1978	30	25	45	50	10	–	27	100	90	85	–
1977	15	52	45	15	42	55	25	–	–	70	47
1976	25	26	48	56	33	35	27	75	90	86	68

Key Votes

1) Increase Def Spnd	FOR	6) Alaska Lands Protect	FOR	11) Delay Auto Pol Cntrl	FOR
2) B-1 Bomber	FOR	7) Water Projects Veto	FOR	12) Sugar Price Escalator	AGN
3) Cargo Preference	FOR	8) Consum Protect Agcy	AGN	13) Pub Fin Cong Cmpgns	AGN
4) Dereg Nat Gas	AGN	9) Common Situs Picket	FOR	14) ERA Ratif Recissn	FOR
5) Kemp-Roth	AGN	10) Labor Law Revision	FOR	15) Prohibt Govt Abrtns	FOR

Election Results

1978 general	Charles E. Bennett (D), unopposed	
1978 primary	Charles E. Bennett (D), unopposed	
1976 general	Charles E. Bennett (D), unopposed	($2,243)

FOURTH DISTRICT

The 4th congressional district is part of transitional Florida. Occupying territory south of Jacksonville and including some 96,000 residents of the city itself, the 4th sits at the divide of Old Dixie—north Florida—and the boom land to the south. The terrain here is just below the normal reach of wintertime frost—a fact of significance not just to the tourist trade, but also for the area's big orange crop. The 4th district also embodies transitional Florida politics. Its northern counties went for George Wallace in 1968 and stuck with him in the 1972 and 1976 presidential primaries. The southern counties of Lake and Seminole (both partially within the district) near Orlando are solidly Republican. In the middle of the district, both geographically and politically, is Daytona Beach, famous for its rock-hard sand beach. like much of Florida, this is a town of political contradictions: it can elect a black councilman and vote for George Wallace in the same year. The district as a whole went for Jimmy Carter in 1976, but narrowly. The more affluent parts—Jacksonville around the big Mayport Naval Base and next door Clay County—went for Ford.

The 4th's Congressman, Democrat Bill Chappell, may also be described as a transitional figure. Chappell was Speaker of the Florida House of Representatives back in the early sixties when the legislature was still dominated by Old South conservatives—the Pork Chop Gang—from the northern part of the state. In the House he has been a member of the conservative Southern bloc, one of that breed of Democrats who vote more like Republicans. A man with such views would seem well-positioned to win elections in this district, but it was some time before Chappell won by wide margins. He was first elected in 1968, but did not win really solidly until 1974.

One problem Chappell has had is that some of his constituents have had doubts about his honesty. In 1969 he was charged with diverting the salary of one of his employees to a third person—a criminal offense. In October 1972 Chappell was one of six Democrats on the House Banking Committee who voted against investigating the Watergate scandal, and is the only one of the six still in the House today. Writer Marjorie Boyd has suggested that Chappell's vote on this sensitive matter was not unrelated to the fact that the Nixon Administration never prosecuted him. In the last three elections Chappell has not faced significant opposition; not one can be sure what would happen if he did.

Chappell's current committee assignment is a lesson in how some policies get perpetuated on Capitol Hill. A junior member of Appropriations, he was picked over several liberals to be a member of the Defense Subcommittee. Until 1978 that body was dominated by Southern Democrats and Republicans—all basically sympathetic to Pentagon budget requests. With 1978 retirements, the membership has changed, but the presence of members like Chappell mean that this body is tilted more to the bureaucracy it is supposed to oversee than is the House as a whole. This has been demonstrated graphically more than once. Chappell was one of the chief sponsors of both the nuclear aircraft carrier and the B-1 bomber—weapons systems that were approved by the subcommittee but voted down on the House floor.

Census Data Pop. 452,076. Central city, 21%; suburban, 2%. Median family income, $7,719; families above $15,000: 15%; families below $3,000: 15%. Median years education, 12.1.

The Voters

Median voting age 47.
Employment profile White collar, 51%. Blue collar, 30%. Service, 15%. Farm, 4%.
Ethnic groups Black, 15%. Spanish, 1%. Total foreign stock, 11%. UK, Germany, Canada, 2% each.

Presidential vote

1976	Carter (D)	115,332	(53%)
	Ford (R)	100,991	(47%)
1972	Nixon (R)	135,945	(77%)
	McGovern (D)	41,660	(23%)

Rep. Bill Chappell, Jr. (D) Elected 1968; b. Feb. 3, 1922, Kendrick; home, Ocala; U. of Fla., B.A. 1947, LL.B. 1949; Methodist.

Career Navy, WWII; Marion Co. Prosecuting Atty., 1950–54; Fla. House of Reps., 1955–64, 1967–68, Spkr, 1961–63.

Offices 2353 RHOB, 202-225-4035. Also Rm. 258 Fed. Bldg., Ocala 32670, 904-629-0039.

Committees *Appropriations* (18th). Subcommittees: Defense; District of Columbia; Energy and Water Development.

Group Ratings

	ADA	COPE	PC	RPN	NFU	LCV	CFA	NAB	NSI	ACA	NTU
1978	5	25	20	36	20	–	9	100	100	84	–
1977	5	33	13	27	44	18	10	–	–	75	32
1976	5	41	13	31	46	12	0	42	100	91	30

Key Votes

1) Increase Def Spnd	FOR	6) Alaska Lands Protect	AGN	11) Delay Auto Pol Cntrl	FOR
2) B-1 Bomber	FOR	7) Water Projects Veto	AGN	12) Sugar Price Escalator	DNV
3) Cargo Preference	FOR	8) Consum Protect Agcy	AGN	13) Pub Fin Cong Cmpgns	AGN
4) Dereg Nat Gas	FOR	9) Common Situs Picket	AGN	14) ERA Ratif Recissn	FOR
5) Kemp-Roth	FOR	10) Labor Law Revision	AGN	15) Prohibt Govt Abrtns	FOR

Election Results

1978 general	Bill Chappell (D)	113,302	(73%)	($87,346)
	Tom Boney (R)	41,647	(27%)	($9,118)
1978 primary	Bill Chappell (D), unopposed			
1976 general	Bill Chappell (D), unopposed			($90,018)

FIFTH DISTRICT

The 5th congressional district of Florida, with its jigsaw puzzle-like borders, is something of an anomaly: the only congressional district in the United States to elect a non-incumbent Democrat in the Nixon landslide year of 1972 and then to turn around and elect a Republican in the Watergate landslide year of 1974. It is a district which gathers together not a community or two, but some unrelated real estate connecting several thickly populated parts of central Florida. Its genesis was purely political: it was created by the Democratic legislature for state Senator Bill Gunter of Orlando, who won the seat in 1972. But Gunter went on to run unsuccessfully for the Senate in 1974, leaving behind the constituency he had so carefully constructed.

The 5th district includes part of Orlando and part of Sanford in nearby Seminole County. It then sweeps across to the Gulf of Mexico and down the coast, including a part of the city of Clearwater, and terminates at a point near St. Petersburg. Interestingly, the district includes 70% of the black residents of Orlando, Sanford, and Clearwater. Obviously there was an attempt here to edge the district over into the Democratic column; still, much of the territory within its bounds regularly votes Republican.

Since Gunter went on to statewide races (he is now Florida's Insurance Commissioner), the 5th district has been held—precariously—by Republican Richard Kelly. He is from the fast-growing Gulf Coast county of Pasco, which produces increasing Republican majorities as its population of northern migrants rises. Kelly has a colorful political history: as a local judge, he was once impeached. He is an outspoken and voluble conservative, whether he is attacking federal aid to New York City or opposing a bill to regulate debt collectors. In a House where Republicans increasingly have been successful in advancing their ideas, Kelly is not regarded as an adept or effective legislator.

He has also had some political problems at home. Twice he beat Orlando-based Democrat Jo Ann Saunders, but in 1978 Orlando lawyer David Best got 49% of the vote. Best carried the Orlando area, and Kelly was saved only by large margins in Pasco County and the Clearwater area. Kelly must be considered vulnerable in 1980.

Census Data Pop. 452,965. Central city, 52%; suburban, 6%. Median family income, $6,910; families above $15,000: 12%; families below $3,000: 16%. Median years education, 11.7.

The Voters

Median voting age 50.
Employment profile White collar, 44%. Blue collar, 35%. Service, 14%. Farm, 7%.
Ethnic groups Black, 16%. Spanish, 1%. Total foreign stock, 12%. Germany, UK, Canada, 2% each.

Presidential vote

1976	Carter (D)	125,649	(50%)
	Ford (R)	126,229	(50%)
1972	Nixon (R)	143,766	(76%)
	McGovern (D)	44,600	(24%)

Rep. Richard Kelly (R) Elected 1974; b. July 31, 1924, Atlanta, Ga.; home, Zephyrhills; Colo. St. Col. of Ed., A.B. 1949, Vanderbilt Col. of Law, 1949, U. of Fla., J.D. 1952; Presbyterian.

Career USMC, WWII; Zephyrhills City Atty.; Sr. Asst., U.S. Dist. Atty., So. Dist. of Fla., 1956–59; Circuit Judge, 6th. Judicial Circuit of Fla., 1960–74.

Offices 307 CHOB, 202-225-2176. Rm. 203, 1211 North Blvd. W., Leesburg 32750, 904-728-2727.

Committees *Agriculture* (9th). Subcommittees: Conservation and Credit; Dairy and Poultry; Tobacco.

Banking, Finance and Urban Affairs (6th). Subcommittees: Economic Stabilization; Housing and Community Development; The City.

Group Ratings

	ADA	COPE	PC	RPN	NFU	LCV	CFA	NAB	NSI	ACA	NTU
1978	5	0	20	75	0	–	23	100	100	100	–
1977	5	13	23	69	33	15	5	–	–	89	62
1976	0	14	11	56	0	13	9	92	100	100	68

Key Votes

1) Increase Def Spnd	FOR	6) Alaska Lands Protect	AGN	11) Delay Auto Pol Cntrl	FOR
2) B-1 Bomber	FOR	7) Water Projects Veto	AGN	12) Sugar Price Escalator	FOR
3) Cargo Preference	AGN	8) Consum Protect Agcy	AGN	13) Pub Fin Cong Cmpgns	AGN
4) Dereg Nat Gas	FOR	9) Common Situs Picket	AGN	14) ERA Ratif Recissn	FOR
5) Kemp-Roth	FOR	10) Labor Law Revision	AGN	15) Prohibt Govt Abrtns	FOR

Election Results

1978 general	Richard Kelly (R)	106,319	(51%)	($182,597)
	David Best (D)	101,867	(49%)	($149,383)
1978 primary	Richard Kelley (R), unopposed			
1976 general	Richard Kelley (R)	138,371	(59%)	($123,125)
	JoAnn Saunders (D)	96,260	(41%)	($82,642)

SIXTH DISTRICT

When somebody mentions St. Petersburg, almost everyone has an image of elderly retirees sitting on park benches in the Florida sun. The cliché has considerable validity. To be sure, St. Petersburg and its suburbs to the north and west do have some light manufacturing, and there are young families here with children. But this is largely a community of older people. The median age of Florida'a 6th congressional district, which includes St. Petersburg and most of suburban Pinellas County, is the highest of any district in the nation. Some 50% of the 6th's eligible voters are over 58, and fully 39% are 65 or over. In no other congressional district is the median age nearly so high.

Most of these people were not of course born in St. Petersburg. There were not many people here at all 65 years ago. They are immigrants from some other part of the South or, more frequently, from the north. The large Yankee concentration here produced the state's first center of Republican strength. The migrants of the forties and fifties were people of at least modest affluence—blue collar workers of the time didn't get much in the way of a pension—and the new residents continued to vote in St. Petersburg as they had back in Oak Park or Garden City. They carried Pinellas County for Eisenhower, and in 1954 elected a Republican Congressman, William Cramer. A tireless and effective partisan, Cramer built Florida's Republican Party and ultimately ran for the Senate, only to be beaten by Lawton Chiles in 1970.

Former Cramer aide and state Senator Bill Young had no trouble stepping into the seat. But St. Petersburg has been edging more into the Democratic column of late; in 1976 Pinellas County and the 6th district almost went for Jimmy Carter. This is not a matter of affection for a fellow Southerner; most people here are from the north. Rather it seems to reflect the increasing affluence of America's blue collar class. There is inevitably a considerable turnover in the 6th's elderly population, and many of the people who settled here in the late sixties and early seventies were from blue collar—and Democratic—backgrounds.

This trend has not made for any trouble for Bill Young. He is an affable man who provides good constituency services and wins reelection by overwhelming margins. He is a member of the Appropriations Committee, ranking Republican on its Foreign Operations Subcommittee, and a member of its HUD—Independent Agencies Subcommittee. He is a less partisan Republican than Cramer and more inclined to take unusual positions, for example in opposing the cross-Florida barge canal. He has pushed laws to stop international banking agencies from sending funds to countries like Uganda and Cambodia because of human rights violations. But his work on the HUD Subcommittee is probably more important; one of the few successful HUD programs has been housing for senior citizens, for which of course St. Petersburg has a market.

Census Data Pop. 452,615. Central city, 52%; suburban, 48%. Median family income, $7,657; families above $15,000: 14%; families below $3,000: 12%. Median years education, 12.1.

The Voters

Median voting age 58.
Employment profile White collar, 55%. Blue collar, 28%. Service, 17%. Farm, –%.
Ethnic groups Black, 8%. Spanish, 1%. Total foreign stock, 22%. Germany, UK, 4% each; Canada, 3%; Italy, Ireland, Sweden, 1% each.

Presidential vote

1976	Carter (D)	115,795	(49%)
	Ford (R)	118,337	(51%)
1972	Nixon (R)	154,765	(69%)
	McGovern (D)	68,214	(31%)

Rep. C. W. Bill Young (R) Elected 1970; b. Dec. 16, 1930, Harmarville, Pa.; home, Seminole; Methodist.

Career Aide to U.S. Rep. William C. Cramer of Fla., 1957-60; Fla. Senate, 1960–70, Minor. Ldr., 1966–70.

Offices 2453 RHOB, 202-225-5961. Also 627 Fed. Bldg., 144 1st Ave. S., St. Petersburg 33701, 813-893-3191.

Committees *Appropriations* (11th). Subcommittees: Foreign Operations; HUD—Independent Agencies.

Group Ratings

	ADA	COPE	PC	RPN	NFU	LCV	CFA	NAB	NSI	ACA	NTU
1978	10	15	25	58	10	–	23	100	100	93	–
1977	10	17	28	69	25	35	10	–	–	83	48
1976	5	30	30	65	37	17	9	75	100	89	60

Key Votes

1) Increase Def Spnd	FOR	6) Alaska Lands Protect	AGN	11) Delay Auto Pol Cntrl	AGN
2) B-1 Bomber	FOR	7) Water Projects Veto	AGN	12) Sugar Price Escalator	FOR
3) Cargo Preference	AGN	8) Consum Protect Agcy	AGN	13) Pub Fin Cong Cmpgns	AGN
4) Dereg Nat Gas	FOR	9) Common Situs Picket	AGN	14) ERA Ratif Recissn	FOR
5) Kemp-Roth	FOR	10) Labor Law Revision	AGN	15) Prohibt Govt Abrtns	FOR

Election Results

1978 general	C. W. Bill Young (R)	150,694	(79%)	($57,482)
	Jim Christison (D)	40,654	(21%)	($128,579)
1978 primary	C. W. Bill Young (R), unopposed			
1976 general	C. W. Bill Young (R)	151,371	(65%)	($65,050)
	Gabriel Cazales (D)	80,821	(35%)	($26,516)

SEVENTH DISTRICT

Tampa, with 277,000 people, dominates the 7th congressional district of Florida. This is a very different city from St. Petersburg, which is about the same size, shares the same airport, and is just over the bridge across Tampa Bay. If St. Petersburg is known for its many retirees, Tampa is almost as well-known for its large and established Cuban-American community and for being the nation's leading manufacturer of cigars. Tampa's Cuban community dates from long before Castro and is much older than Miami's; it is also different politically. The anti-Castro Cubans of Miami tend toward Nixon Republicanism; the Cuban-Americans of Tampa are traditional Democrats. Beyond the Cuban community in Ybor City, Tampa is as much a white working class city as there is in Florida. The 1968 election returns here suggest the split in the electorate: 35% for Nixon (roughly corresponding to the number of affluent or northern whites); 33% for Humphrey (Cubans, blacks, some union members); 32% for Wallace (Southern-origin whites). Eight years later most of the Wallace group went for Jimmy Carter, giving him a solid 55% victory here.

Until 1962 Tampa was in the same congressional district as St. Petersburg. Then, following the 1960 Census, a Tampa-centered district was created, and its Congressman since that time—the district has been numbered variously the 10th, 6th, and now 7th—has been Democrat Sam Gibbons. Unlike traditional Florida Democrats, Gibbons supported civil rights legislation and voted more often than not with most northern Democrats. In his early career he was one of an outnumbered group of young liberal congressmen pushing for institutional reforms; in recent years the causes he championed have mostly been enacted into law or established as rules.

In the early seventies Gibbons was one of the major rebels in the House. After serving for several years on Education and Labor, he won a seat on Ways and Means, where he championed major tax reform and frequently disagreed with Chairman Wilbur Mills. After the 1972 election he made a brief race for the majority leadership, but withdrew when it was clear that Tip O'Neill had it won. With the influx of freshmen in 1974, it seemed that Gibbons might become an influential leader in causes like tax reform. But his attitudes—and the mood of the House—have changed. Instead of pushing measures to increase the tax bite on the wealthy, in the 95th Congress Gibbons strongly supported the bill to cut the capital gains tax. His voting record on other issues moved to the right as well. He is now the fifth-ranking Democrat on Ways and Means and Chairman of the Oversight Subcommittee. But the direction of his career and the motivating force behind his considerable talents are no longer clear.

Census Data Pop. 452,820. Central city, 39%; suburban, 61%. Median family income, $8,256; families above $15,000: 14%; families below $3,000: 12%. Median years education, 12.

The Voters

Median voting age 43.
Employment profile White collar, 49%. Blue collar, 36%. Service, 13%. Farm, 2%.
Ethnic groups Black, 13%. Spanish, 12%. Total foreign stock, 14%. Italy, 2%; Germany, Canada, UK, 1% each.

Presidential vote

1976	Carter (D)	88,612	(54%)
	Ford (R)	74,570	(46%)
1972	Nixon (R)	99,739	(70%)
	McGovern (D)	43,347	(30%)

Rep. Sam Gibbons (D) Elected 1962; b. Jan. 20, 1920, Tampa; home, Tampa; U. of Fla., LL.B. 1947; Presbyterian.

Career Army, WWII; Practicing atty., 1947–62; Fla. House of Reps., 1952–58; Fla. Senate, 1958–62.

Offices 2206 RHOB, 202-225-3376. Also 510 Fed. Bldg., 500 Zack St., Tampa 33602, 813-228-2101.

Committees *Ways and Means* (5th). Subcommittees: Oversight (Chairman); Trade.

Group Ratings

	ADA	COPE	PC	RPN	NFU	LCV	CFA	NAB	NSI	ACA	NTU
1978	10	26	48	70	11	–	27	91	60	67	–
1977	40	59	63	54	45	70	45	–	–	46	38
1976	45	45	61	44	58	66	45	36	56	48	52

Key Votes

1) Increase Def Spnd	FOR	6) Alaska Lands Protect	FOR	11) Delay Auto Pol Cntrl	AGN
2) B-1 Bomber	AGN	7) Water Projects Veto	FOR	12) Sugar Price Escalator	AGN
3) Cargo Preference	AGN	8) Consum Protect Agcy	AGN	13) Pub Fin Cong Cmpgns	DNV
4) Dereg Nat Gas	AGN	9) Common Situs Picket	AGN	14) ERA Ratif Recissn	FOR
5) Kemp-Roth	AGN	10) Labor Law Revision	FOR	15) Prohibt Govt Abrtns	FOR

Election Results

1978 general	Sam Gibbons (D), unopposed			
1978 primary	Sam Gibbons (D)	49,766	(71%)	($65,558)
	Richard Salem (D)	20,338	(29%)	($151,336)
1976 general	Sam Gibbons (D)	102,739	(66%)	($24,443)
	Dusty Owens (D)	53,599	(34%)	($95,383)

EIGHTH DISTRICT

Florida's 8th congressional district is made up of two distinct areas. Somewhat less than half its population lives along the Gulf Coast in towns like Bradenton and Sarasota. These are well-off, sun-baked communities with lots of migrants and retirees from the north. The voters here, when they are not busy enjoying golf courses and yacht basins and pleasant condominiums, are likely to be reading *Barron's* and muttering about the crazy ways of the federal government. Needless to say this is very Republican territory—Sarasota is often the most Republican part of Florida.

Separated from the Gulf Coast by miles of swampland is the citrus-growing country in and around Polk County. Here the towns are smaller and older, with few of the glittering high rises that tower along the coast. The interior economy is geared more to agriculture than to wealthy tourists. Incongruously set amid the boom cities of central Florida, Polk County remains a part of Old Dixie politically. In 1968 Polk preferred George Wallace to Richard Nixon, while Nixon was carrying Sarasota easily; in 1976 Jimmy Carter carried Polk while he was losing Sarasota. For 30-plus years Polk County has been the home of one of Florida's U.S. senators; Bartow native Spessard Holland, long unbeatable, gave valuable help to Lakeland lawyer Lawton Chiles in his upset victory in 1970.

The 8th is one of those district national Republican strategists have rightly had their eyes on for a long time—and never won. The territory has never gone for any Democratic presidential candidate since the forties, and Carter missed carrying it in 1976. It was one of the few Florida districts that went for Republican gubernatorial candidate Jack Eckerd over Democrat Bob Graham in 1978. But the Republicans have not been able in congressional races to put together a large enough majority in Sarasota and Bradenton to overcome any Democratic edge in Polk. For years they tried to dislodge James Haley, a conservative Democrat and member of the family that owns the Ringling Brothers–Barnum & Bailey Circus, which winters in Sarasota, and in 1968 and 1970 they came close. In 1973 Haley became Chairman of the House Interior Committee, a position he filled without controversy until he decided to retire in 1976.

The Republicans were no more able to beat a non-incumbent than they were an aged veteran. There were six candidates in the Democratic primary, but Andrew Ireland, a Polk County businessman who used professional campaign consultants to good advantage, won without a runoff—a considerable achievement. The Republicans were not so fortunate. Sarasota state Representative Bob Johnson was forced into a runoff with Joe Z. Lovingood, who three times had failed to beat Haley. That must have sapped Johnson's resources, and may also have led him to concentrate unduly on Sarasota, where most of the Republican primary voters are, but which a Republican can take for granted in the general election. Johnson did get 64% in Sarasota in November, but Ireland got 70%—and a margin of 33,000 votes—in Polk County, for a 58% victory overall. In his first term Ireland compiled a rather conservative voting record, which is an advantage in this district. And although Republicans have had their eyes on this district for yesars, in 1978 there was no Republican candidate at all—testimony either to Ireland's strength or to the weakness of the Republicans.

Census Data Pop. 451,776. Central city, 0%; suburban, 8%. Median family income, $7,341; families above $15,000: 13%; families below $3,000: 16%. Median years education, 12.0.

The Voters

Median voting age 50.
Employment profile White collar, 43%. Blue collar, 35%. Service, 14%. Farm, 8%.
Ethnic groups Black, 14%. Spanish, 2%. Total foreign stock, 10%. Germany, Canada, 2% each; UK, 1%.

Presidential vote

1976	Carter (D)	93,597	(48%)
	Ford (R)	103,271	(52%)
1972	Nixon (R)	134,071	(79%)
	McGovern (D)	34,768	(21%)

Rep. Andy Ireland (D) Elected 1976; b. Aug. 23, 1930, Cincinnati, Ohio; home, Winter Haven; Yale U., B.S. 1952, Columbia Business School 1953–54, La. St. U.; Episcopalian.

Career Chm. of the Bd., Barnett Banks of Winter Haven, Cypress Gardens, and Auburndale; Mbr., Winter Haven City Commission, 1966–68.

Offices 115 CHOB, 202-225-5015. Also 519 W. Central Ave., Winter Haven 33880, 813-299-4041.

Committees *Foreign Affairs* (14th). Subcommittees: Inter-American Affairs; International Operations.

Small Business (19th). Subcommittees: Special Small Business Problems; Impact of Energy Programs, Environment and Safety Requirements and Government Research on Small Business.

Group Ratings

	ADA	COPE	PC	RPN	NFU	LCV	CFA	NAB	NSI	ACA	NTU
1978	20	21	20	40	10	–	5	100	67	78	–
1977	15	30	33	69	45	46	15	–	–	61	32

Key Votes

1) Increase Def Spnd	FOR	6) Alaska Lands Protect	FOR	11) Delay Auto Pol Cntrl	FOR
2) B-1 Bomber	AGN	7) Water Projects Veto	AGN	12) Sugar Price Escalator	FOR
3) Cargo Preference	AGN	8) Consum Protect Agcy	AGN	13) Pub Fin Cong Cmpgns	FOR
4) Dereg Nat Gas	FOR	9) Common Situs Picket	AGN	14) ERA Ratif Recissn	FOR
5) Kemp-Roth	FOR	10) Labor Law Revision	AGN	15) Prohibt Govt Abrtns	FOR

Election Results

1978 general	Andy Ireland (D), unopposed			($102,265)
1978 primary	Andy Ireland (D), unopposed			
1976 general	Andy Ireland (D)	103,360	(58%)	($144,362)
	Bob Johnson (R)	74,794	(42%)	($67,881)

NINTH DISTRICT

Probably the fastest-growing part of Florida in the seventies has been the central Florida area around Orlando. This is not an area endowed with great natural advantages, having neither the beaches which first brought so many people to Florida's Gold Coast (much of the beach here, around the Kennedy Space Center, is government property) nor the bays and over-the-water sunsets of the Gulf Coast. Central Florida, hot and muggy in the summer, is not often warm enough for swimming in the winter. There are many small lakes here, but the land is naturally swampy. This is good land for growing oranges, but orange groves usually do not attract large influxes of people.

The appeal of central Florida is not so much natural as man-made. The main attractions are two: the Kennedy Space Center on the coast in Brevard County and Disney World near Orlando in Orange County. They are products of the sixties and seventies, respectively, and have helped to make central Florida perhaps the number one tourist destination in the United States. And they have done more than that. For this is not an area that is overly dependent on tourist dollars or government spending—though both are very important. Central Florida has generated a private metropolitan economy of its own that attracted in-migrants from all over the country. Not a land of retirees thinking about the homes they have left, this is an area dominated by young families looking forward to the future.

As with much of Florida, the initial in-migration here seemed to produce a Republican trend and further in-migration seems to have made it more Democratic. This was one of the first parts of Florida to elect a Republican congressman, when Edward Gurney won in 1962. A transplanted New Englander, handsome, with strong dislike of the big federal programs and the policies of the Kennedy–Johnson Administrations, Gurney was very popular in Orange and Brevard Counties and was reelected by large margins. He dared to run for the Senate in 1968 and became the first Republican senator elected in Florida since Reconstruction. The rest of his career was less happy. He was the strongest Nixon defender on the Senate Watergate Committee. He was later accused of accepting bribes and, although ultimately acquitted, declined to seek reelection in 1974.

Gurney's seat in the House was taken by his former law partner, Louis Frey. After ten years in Congress, he sought the Republican nomination for governor in 1978, but was defeated by drugstore millionaire Jack Eckerd. The Republican candidate to succeed him in the House was none other than Edward Gurney, now 64, but eager for political vindication.

The 9th district seat that Gurney wanted included all of Brevard County and most of Orange; geographically it was almost the same district that elected him in the sixties, and which gave Richard Nixon a big margin in 1972. But its political complexion seems to have changed.

Newcomers were more sympathetic to Democrats, and Democrats, no longer represented by Lyndon Johnson or George McGovern, seemed more sympathetic to central Floridians. The Democratic nominee in the 9th district in 1978 was Bill Nelson, a 36-year-old state Senator from Brevard County. With his personal wealth, Nelson was able to renounce special interest contributions; with his Brevard County base no one could doubt that he would seek the kind of space programs central Florida needs economically.

Gurney failed to get vindication. Nelson carried Orange County cleanly, 55%–45%, and swept to a 68%–32% victory in Brevard. With this kind of majority he would appear not only to have a safe seat but also perhaps to have the kind of regional base needed to seek statewide office. His committee assignments show he has great political savvy and ability: he has seats on the Budget Committee, which is in charge of holding down the federal budget, and on the Science and Technology Committee, which is of great importance to the district that includes Cape Kennedy.

Census Data Pop. 452,923. Central city, 16%; suburban, 34%. Median family income, $10,267; families above $15,000: 24%; families below $3,000: 8%. Median years education, 12.5.

The Voters

Median voting age 41.
Employment profile White collar, 60%. Blue collar, 27%. Service, 12%. Farm, 1%.
Ethnic groups Black, 8%. Spanish, 2%. Total foreign stock, 11%. UK, Germany, Canada, 2% each.

Presidential vote

1976	Carter (D)	82,809	(46%)
	Ford (R)	95,392	(54%)
1972	Nixon (R)	132,323	(81%)
	McGovern (D)	32,041	(19%)

Rep. Bill Nelson (D) Elected 1978; b. Sept. 29, 1942, Miami; home, Melbourne; Yale U., B.A. 1965, U. of Va., J.D. 1968; Episcopalian.

Career Army, 1968–70; Practicing atty.; Fla. House of Reps., 1972–78.

Offices 1513 LHOB, 202-225-3671. Also Suite 202, Goldfield Bldg., 65 E. NASA Blvd., 305-724-1978.

Committees *Budget* (16th). Subcommittees: Inflation; Budget Process; Legislative Savings.

Science and Technology (23d). Subcommittees: Space Science and Applications; Energy Development and Applications; Investigations and Oversight.

Group Ratings: Newly Elected

Key Votes: Newly Elected

Election Results

1978 general	Bill Nelson (D)	89,543	(61%)	($313,325)
	Edward J. Gurney (R)	56,074	(39%)	($212,679)
1978 primary	Bill Nelson (D)	36,565	(86%)	
	One other (D)	5,955	(14%)	
1976 general	Louis Frey, Jr. (R)	130,509	(78%)	($69,349)
	Joseph A. Rosier (D)	36,630	(22%)	($16,055)

TENTH DISTRICT

The 10th is one of three new congressional districts acquired by Florida in the 1970 Census. It is the only one that the Democratic legislature conceded, without a struggle, to the opposition. The shape of the 10th makes little sense except as an agglomeration of all the Republican-leaning territory that south Florida's Democratic congressmen didn't want. The district sweeps across the Florida peninsula, fronting on the Atlantic north of Palm Beach and on the Gulf of Mexico south from Sarasota to Naples. Accordingly, its population centers are widely dispersed. It goes as far north as Disney World near Orlando; it takes in some of the fast-growing suburban territory west of West Palm Beach; it includes the largest town on the Gulf Coast south of Sarasota, Fort Myers. In between there is mostly the remarkable swamp that is the Everglades, the Sebring grand prix race course, and thousands of acres of orange groves and vegetable fields.

The beneficiary of this handiwork, contrived by Democratic politicians, is Republican L. A. (Skip) Bafalis. For Bafalis the creation of the 10th provided the opportunity for a political comeback. After six years in the Florida legislature he had run for governor in 1970 and, despite a campaign that attracted some attention, won only 13% of the Republican primary vote. (In fairness, he was running against a Republican incumbent governor and a man with a net worth over $50 million.) In 1972 Bafalis had it much easier. He won the Republican nomination in the 10th without much fuss and got a landslide 62% in the general election despite a vigorous campaign by a young Democratic opponent.

In the House, Bafalis has been about as quiet as junior members of the minority party have been expected to be. He did join other congressmen of Greek descent in the fight to cut off aid to Turkey. He holds a seat on the Ways and Means Committee, where he favors tax relief for the elderly and incentives to encourage capital formation and investment. He is reelected without difficulty and, in 1978, without any Democratic opposition.

Census Data Pop. 452,848. Central city, 0%; suburban, 6%. Median family income, $7,323; families above $15,000: 14%; families below $3,000: 15%. Median years education, 12.1.

The Voters

Median voting age 52.
Employment profile White collar, 43%. Blue collar, 33%. Service, 15%. Farm, 9%.
Ethnic groups Black, 14%. Spanish, 2%. Total foreign stock, 13%. Germany, UK, Canada, 2% each.

Presidential vote

1976	Carter (D)	122,899	(46%)
	Ford (R)	146,879	(54%)
1972	Nixon (R)	157,854	(79%)
	McGovern (D)	41,504	(21%)

Rep. L. A. (Skip) **Bafalis** (R) Elected 1972; b. Sept. 28, 1929, Boston, Mass.; home, Fort Myers Beach; St. Anselm's Col., A. B. 1952; Protestant.

Career Army, Korea; Banker; Fla. House of Reps., 1964–65; Fla. Senate, 1966–70, Minority Ldr., 1968; Cand. for Gov., 1970.

Offices 2433 RHOB, 202-225-2536. Also Room 106 Fed. Bldg., Ft. Myers 33901, 813-334-4424.

Committees *Ways and Means* (8th). Subcommittees: Trade; Public Assistance and Unemployment Compensation.

Group Ratings

	ADA	COPE	PC	RPN	NFU	LCV	CFA	NAB	NSI	ACA	NTU
1978	10	10	10	64	0	–	18	100	100	100	–
1977	0	19	10	54	36	18	5	–	–	85	44
1976	5	27	10	59	25	24	9	67	100	89	60

Key Votes

1) Increase Def Spnd	FOR	6) Alaska Lands Protect	AGN	11) Delay Auto Pol Cntrl	FOR
2) B-1 Bomber	FOR	7) Water Projects Veto	AGN	12) Sugar Price Escalator	FOR
3) Cargo Preference	AGN	8) Consum Protect Agcy	AGN	13) Pub Fin Cong Cmpgns	AGN
4) Dereg Nat Gas	FOR	9) Common Situs Picket	AGN	14) ERA Ratif Recissn	FOR
5) Kemp-Roth	FOR	10) Labor Law Revision	AGN	15) Prohibt Govt Abrtns	FOR

Election Results

1978 general	L. A. Bafalis (R), unopposed			($22,007)
1978 primary	L. A. Bafalis (R), unopposed			
1976 general	L. A. Bafalis (R)	164,273	(66%)	($100,045)
	Bill Sikes (D)	83,413	(34%)	($25,177)

ELEVENTH DISTRICT

Fifty years ago Palm Beach was already a fashionable resort for the extremely rich. Across Lake Worth, West Palm Beach was a small town, a large percentage of whose residents devoted themselves to ministering to the needs of Palm Beach. There has been little change in Palm Beach since then, but West Palm Beach, near the northern end of the Gold Coast that runs all the way to Miami, has been altered beyond recognition. High rise apartment houses and condominiums practically form a wall that blocks the mainland from the Atlantic. Jai alai frontons vie with gaudy bars for tourists' money, and the small motels of the forties have been replaced with franchised giant motor inns.

The northern end of the Gold Coast—in rough terms from Pompano Beach in Broward County to West Palm Beach in Palm Beach County—is the 11th congressional district of Florida. Like Fort Lauderdale, which is some 40 miles to the south, the 11th during the fifties and sixties became more Republican as more and more people moved here from the WASPy, well-to-do suburbs of the East and Midwest. Now it appears that the migration is becoming more Democratic, with more Jews and people with blue collar backgrounds in the big condominiums that are increasingly important politically here. This is a district that went for Nixon solidly over Humphrey (55%–28%) in 1968 and was 74% for Nixon in 1972. But in 1976 Jimmy Carter got just under 50% of the vote here, and in 1978 Democrat Bob Graham, against formidable competition, carried the area in the race for governor.

For more than 30 years, this district was the political property of the Rogers family, and most of that time (1954–79) it was represented by Paul Rogers. A Democrat with a moderate to conservative voting record, Rogers was one of the premier legislators in the House. His chairing of the Commerce Committee's Health Subcommittee was something of a work of art, and he combined idealistic concern for his subject with a good practical sense of how to get things accomplished. On all sorts of matters relating to health—from hospitals to medical research to clean air protection—Rogers has left a constructive and lasting imprint. Still under 60, he decided to retire in 1978.

If Rogers had quit a few years before, the 11th would almost certainly have gone Republican; in 1978, the district was highly competitive. The Republican candidate, with no serious primary competition, was Bill James, the Republican leader in the state House of Representatives first elected to the legislature in 1967. The Democrats, naturally, had a primary, and the winner, surprisingly in a day when few congressmen can hand on their seats to a candidate of their own choosing, was Dan Mica, a young aide to Rogers. He beat a labor-backed state representative and a circuit court clerk by stressing his experience with Rogers and by winning the support of an association of 21 condominium complexes. In an era when primary turnout is low, organized support in a huge building where voters are concentrated can be crucial in Gold Coast elections.

On paper, James seemed to have the advantages: more time to campaign, Republican background in a year when Republicans seemed on the offensive on the issues, great familiarity in Palm Beach County. Nevertheless Mica was able to win a fairly solid 55% victory. While it is too soon to say that he has a safe district, it does seem that he has demonstrated the Democratic trend in this area.

Census Data Pop. 452,170. Central city, 13%; suburban, 87%. Median family income, $8,995; families above $15,000: 21%; families below $3,000: 11%. Median years education, 12.2.

The Voters

Median voting age 51.
Employment profile White collar, 49%. Blue collar, 31%. Service, 16%. Farm, 4%.
Ethnic groups Black, 18%. Spanish, 3%. Total foreign stock, 21%. Germany, UK, Canada, 3% each; Italy, 2%; Ireland, 1%.

Presidential vote

1976	Carter (D)	128,416	(50%)
	Ford (R)	130,829	(50%)
1972	Nixon (R)	146,024	(74%)
	McGovern (D)	50,733	(26%)

Rep. Dan Mica (D) Elected 1978; b. Feb. 4, 1944, Binghamton, N.Y.; home, West Palm Beach; U. of Fla., 1961–62, Miami Dade Jr. Col., A.A. 1965, Fla. Atlantic U., B.A. 1966; Roman Catholic.

Career Public school teacher, 1966–68; Admin. Asst. to U.S. Rep. Paul Rogers, 1968–78.

Offices 512 CHOB, 202-225-3001. Also 321 Fed. Bldg., W. Palm Beach 33401, 305-832-6424.

Committees *Foreign Affairs* (16th). Subcommittees: International Operations; Asian and Pacific Affairs.

Veterans' Affairs (17th). Subcommittees: Medical Facilities and Benefits; Compensation, Pension, Insurance and Memorial Affairs; Special Investigations.

Group Ratings: Newly Elected

Key Votes: Newly Elected

Election Results

1978 general	Dan Mica (D)	123,346	(55%)	($158,573)
	Bill James (R)	99,757	(45%)	($228,969)
1978 primary	Dan Mica (D)	35,947	(55%)	
	John J. Considine (D)	20,689	(31%)	($44,510)
	One other (D)	9,286	(14%)	
1976 general	Paul G. Rogers (D)	199,031	(91%)	($24,434)
	C. Adams (Amer.)	19,406	(9%)	($4,320)

TWELFTH DISTRICT

For some Fort Lauderdale evokes memories of college sand and beer vacations in the spring (they have made a comeback) or perhaps scenes from an Annette Funicello and Frankie Avalon movie. That is not, however, the impression the town fathers would like you to have; they have long since tried to discourage the influx of college spring vacationers who bring little money and scare away people who do. What they would prefer you to envision is a cosmopolitan, canalled tropical city, with miles of wide beach, lilting palm trees, and cultural attractions and shopping you would expect in a major metropolitan area. For the truth is that Fort Lauderdale, a city with just 172,000 people within its limits, is in the middle of Florida's Gold Coast, a strip of seldom more than six miles wide extending from Miami to north of Palm Beach and with a population of more than 2.5 million. This land dredged from swamp and muck is some of the most valuable real estate in the country.

Fort Lauderdale and most of surrounding Broward County make up Florida's 12th congressional district. Most of the first immigrants here were from the upper income suburbs of the East and Midwest, the Winnetkas and Locust Valleys of America. It was generally felt that the Fort Lauderdale area in the fifties and most of the sixties frowned on potential Jewish residents; this was the WASPy part of Florida. The politics was straight out of the old Chicago *Tribune*: solidly Republican, conservative, unchanging. It was fitting then that when the Fort Lauderdale area got its own congressman in 1966, it elected a Republican brought up in Chicago, a slightly overweight, affable man named J. Herbert Burke.

In the late sixties and early seventies, Fort Lauderdale and Broward County have been changing politically, due largely to a second wave of migration. There has been an increasing number of Jewish voters here, first just across the county border from Miami in Hallandale and Hollywood, and later in Fort Lauderdale itself. Most of the old restrictions have disappeared, and those who want a purely WASPy community have been moving elsewhere, perhaps to the Gulf Coast. The result has been that Broward County and the 12th district have become notably more Democratic. Back in 1964 Broward had gone for Barry Goldwater; by 1970 it gave a majority to Reubin Askew. In 1976 Broward was 52% for Jimmy Carter—the first time it had gone Democratic for president since 1944.

These trends were not good news for Congressman Burke. Held to 51% in 1974, he won in 1976 only because of a major strife in the Democratic primary. Then in May 1978 he was arrested outside a nude go-go club in Fort Lauderdale; in September he pleaded guilty to misdemeanor charges of being disorderly and resisting arrest and was fined $150. An unknown opponent got 41% in the Republican primary, and it was clear that Burke's twelve year congressional career was over.

What was not entirely clear was the identity of the Democrat who would replace him. The leading candidate was Ed Stack, Broward County Sheriff for nine years, who had become a Democrat only in 1975. Indeed, as a Republican Stack nearly beat Burke in the 1966 runoff and had run again in the 1970 primary. As a law and order candidate, Stack had 48% in the first primary in 1978, but in the runoff he could increase his percentage only to 54%. He may have been helped by his strong support for Robert Shevin, the Attorney General who was running for governor and had enthusiastic backers in Broward County's condominiums.

Stack overwhelmed Burke 62%–38% in the general election. But it is not clear that he can hold the seat for a long time. He was elected at the age of 68, making him one of the oldest freshmen and indeed one of the oldest members of the House. And his showings in the 1978 primaries suggest that he could be vulnerable to a challenger more in tune with Broward's new cultural style. Shevin, who lost the 1978 gubernatorial runoff, will be in no position to help him much. This is a district that could change hands once again.

Census Data Pop. 453,053. Central city, 54%; suburban, 46%. Median family income, $9,717; families above $15,000: 22%; families below $3,000: 9%. Median years education, 12.2.

The Voters

Median voting age 48.
Employment profile White collar, 53%. Blue collar, 31%. Service, 15%. Farm, 1%.
Ethnic groups Black, 12%. Spanish, 3%. Total foreign stock, 25%. Italy, 4%; Germany, Canada, UK, 3% each; USSR, 2%; Poland, Ireland, 1% each.

Presidential vote

1976	Carter (D)	112,477	(53%)
	Ford (R)	97,867	(47%)
1972	Nixon (R)	140,157	(72%)
	McGovern (D)	54,394	(28%)

Rep. Edward J. Stack (D) Elected 1978; b. Apr. 29, 1910, Bayonne, N.J.; home, Ft. Lauderdale; Lehigh U., B.A. 1931, U. of Penn., J.D. 1934, Columbia U., M.A. 1938; Roman Catholic.

Career Practicing atty., 1934–42, 1946–56; Coast Guard, WWII; Real estate investor and Banker, 1956–; Commissioner-Mayor of Pompano Beach, 1965–69; Broward Co. Sheriff, 1969–79.

Offices 1440 LHOB, 202-225-3026. Also Suite 408A, 5100 N. Fed. Hwy., Ft. Lauderdale 33308, 305-771-2550.

Committees *Education and Labor* (20th). Subcommittees: Human Resources; Select Education.

Merchant Marine and Fisheries (24th). Subcommittees: Fish and Wildlife; Coast Guard and Navigation.

Group Ratings: Newly Elected

Key Votes: Newly Elected

Election Results

1978 general	Edward J. Stack (D)	107,037	(62%)	($133,351)
	J. Herbert Burke (R)	66,610	(38%)	($74,967)
1978 run-off	Edward J. Stack (D)	25,985	(53%)	
	John Adams (D)	22,816	(47%)	($33,761)
1978 primary	Edward J. Stack (D)	27,923	(48%)	
	John Adams (D)	17,955	(31%)	
	Gerald F. Thompson (D)	12,812	(22%)	($63,155)
1976 general	J. Herbert Burke (R)	107,268	(54%)	($69,423)
	Charles Friedman (D)	91,749	(46%)	($83,264)

THIRTEENTH DISTRICT

Even as cities outwardly stay the same, they change internally, as old residents move out and new groups move in. That is what has happened in Miami and its Dade County suburbs. The numerical population here in the seventies has increased less rapidly than that of most of Florida's metropolitan counties in the seventies, but the demographics have changed considerably. Of the two ethnic groups which seem increasingly to dominate Miami area politics, one was hardly present 20 years ago (the Cuban-Americans) and the other does not comprise much more than 15% of the county's population (the Jews). Yet each seems to dominate the politics of one of Dade County's three congressional districts.

The 13th district, which includes the northern third of Dade County plus the southern edge of Broward County, is the one where Jews are particularly important. That is not because there is a

Jewish majority here; there are no precise figures available, but probably only two districts in the nation, both in Brooklyn, have Jewish majorities. Only 4% of the residents of the 13th have Yiddish as their mother tongue, and there are plenty of other notable ethnic concentrations: WASPs in Miami Shores, blacks on the north side of Miami, white migrants from the Deep South in Hialeah. Jews probably do not comprise more than 15% of the residents of the district. But because they are older and more likely to vote than average, they probably include more than 20% of the voters and more than 30% of the Democratic primary voters. Since the 13th district was created for the 1972 election, all the leading congressional candidates here have been Jewish; and the Jewish voting habits make this Florida's most liberal district and the one most supportive of national Democratic candidates.

This ethnic background makes for a special kind of politics, one familiar to observers of the New York political scene. There is a great deal of king-making and interlocking alliances in Miami politics, much of it at the Tiger Bay Club organized by some politicoes; and there are plenty of state and local offices in Dade County to keep people busy filling slates and making endorsements. Particularly important in primary elections here are condominium associations. The large condominiums have brought together into one easily accessible location many articulate people with a desire to become involved in local politics. Properly organized, a condominium can provide a candidate with an advantage of several hundred votes over his rivals.

Willima Lehman, the 13th's Congressman, has had an interesting—and somewhat unusual—career. Lehman got his start in business as a used car dealer, known widely as "Alabama Bill." He reportedly developed the reputation, unusual in the trade, for reliability and complete honesty. Politics was obviously the next step. Lehman got himself elected to the School Board and, just before his race for Congress in 1972, became its Chairman.

Lehman demonstrated his political acumen by defeating two strong candidates in the Democratic primary and winning the general with 62% over a hard-campaigning Republican. In 1974 he had another tough opponent, but has had few problems since then. Lehman votes like a northern Democrat on most issues, and in 1977 won appointment to the House Budget Committee; he also serves on Appropriations. Lehman is past 65, but this is not a young district, and he seems likely to continue to serve.

Census Data Pop. 452,817. Central city, 9%; suburban, 91%. Median family income, $9,411; families above $15,000: 20%; families below $3,000: 9%. Median years education, 12.0.

The Voters

Median voting age 46.
Employment profile White collar, 49%. Blue collar, 34%. Service, 16%. Farm, 1%.
Ethnic groups Black, 18%. Spanish, 13%. Total foreign stock, 32%. USSR, 4%; Italy, 3%; Canada, Germany, Poland, UK, 2% each; Austria, 1%.

Presidential vote

1976	Carter (D)	130,805	(67%)
	Ford (R)	65,888	(33%)
1972	Nixon (R)	90,997	(56%)
	McGovern (D)	72,957	(44%)

Rep. William Lehman (D) Elected 1972; b. Oct. 5, 1913, Selma, Ala.; home, North Miami Beach; U. of Ala., B.S. 1934, U. of Miami, Teaching Certif., 1963, Additional Studies at Oxford U., Cambridge U., U. of Edinburgh, Harvard U., and Middlebury Col.; Jewish.

Career Auto dealer, 1936–42, 1946–72; Army Air Corps, WWII; Teacher, Pub. Schools, 1963, Miami Dade Jr. col., 1964–66; Dade Co. School Bd., 1964–70, Chm. 1971.

Offices 2440 RHOB, 202-225-4211. Also 2020 N.E. 163rd St., Suite 108, N. Miami Beach 33162, 305-945-7518.

Committees *Appropriations* (31st). Subcommittees: Foreign Operations; Transportation.

Group Ratings

	ADA	COPE	PC	RPN	NFU	LCV	CFA	NAB	NSI	ACA	NTU
978	80	85	69	55	50	–	55	18	30	12	–
977	80	78	73	54	75	89	55	–	–	8	30
976	80	82	85	47	83	89	73	8	10	4	25

Key Votes

) Increase Def Spnd	AGN	6) Alaska Lands Protect	FOR	11) Delay Auto Pol Cntrl	AGN
) B-1 Bomber	AGN	7) Water Projects Veto	FOR	12) Sugar Price Escalator	AGN
) Cargo Preference	AGN	8) Consum Protect Agcy	FOR	13) Pub Fin Cong Cmpgns	FOR
) Dereg Nat Gas	AGN	9) Common Situs Picket	FOR	14) ERA Ratif Recissn	AGN
) Kemp-Roth	AGN	10) Labor Law Revision	FOR	15) Prohibt Govt Abrtns	AGN

Election Results

978 general	William Lehman (D), unopposed			
978 primary	William Lehman (D), unopposed			($70,087)
976 general	William Lehman (D)	127,822	(78%)	($126,640)
	Lee A. Spiegelman (R)	35,357	(22%)	($19,532)

FOURTEENTH DISTRICT

Claude Pepper is the grand old man of Florida politics. Back in 1936 he first went to Capitol Hill as a 36-year-old U.S. Senator. He was known even then for his old fashioned Southern style oratory, and once in the Senate he became a member of the Southern establishment. But when other senators from Dixie began to sour on the New Deal, Pepper remained as loyal to FDR's domestic policies as he did to Roosevelt's conviction that the United States be fully prepared for another war in Europe. For these stands and for his devotion to civil liberties, the young Senator came to be called "Red Pepper." In 1950, during the era of Joe McCarthy, Pepper was defeated in a bitter Senate primary by Congressman George Smathers, and he retired to a Miami law practice.

Today Smathers himself has long since (1968) retired to a lucrative position as a Washington lobbyist, and Claude Pepper is back in Congress. After the 1960 Census, when the Florida legislature was compelled to create a second Miami area House seat, Pepper was the logical choice to fill it. He won a solid majority in the 1962 Democratic primary and has since retained the seat with little difficulty. The Congressman's oratorical style is still out of Dixie, but his record is such that he is a favorite of his black and Jewish constituents.

If Pepper had won the 1950 race against Smathers, he would have become Chairman of the Senate Foreign Relations Committee (and assuming reelection would have held that position from 1958 to this day). As things are, he cuts a lesser figure. But his years of experience on Capitol Hill count for something; only one member of Congress, Senator Jennings Randolph of West Virginia, preceded Pepper to Congress. He holds a seat on the often crucial Rules Committee, where he usually advances the views of the House leadership and House liberals. Pepper has also been something of an aficionado of special committees. He set up a special committee on crime, which finally folded, and a special committee on aging. And he has led the fight for major legislation. It was Claude Pepper who pushed through the bill which raised the mandatory retirement age for most jobs in the United States from 65 to 70; he would like to get rid of mandatory retirement altogether. That law will have a major effect on the nation long after Pepper is no longer with us, particularly when the baby boom generation passes 65; can we be sure that there will be enough jobs for everyone? But one can also argue that with more people available to work, we will have a more productive economy, and that people should have the choice of whether they want to work or retire. Pepper, who has many elderly constituents, passionately supports his law; one reason may be that he himself is the oldest member of the House, and has served almost half his congressional career past the age of 65.

When Pepper was first elected to the House, the most important voting bloc in his district was Jewish. Today, the Cubans are most important—and that is not particularly good news for the Congressman. The central city of Miami has come to have a definite Latin flavor. Spanish is the main spoken language on Southwest 8th and other shopping streets. Miami has become the major center in the United States for Latin American trade and travel; Latins fly up to Miami to shop for consumer goods (most Latin countries have high tariffs), and the clientele of many Miami hotels is mainly Latin. Many American businesses find that Miami, rather than a site in Mexico or South America, is the best location for a Latin American office; it is easier to fly to most parts of Latin America from here than any other place.

The Cuban community in Miami has helped to make the city a major Latin center. There are about 400,000 Cubans in the Miami area; most of them live in Pepper's 14th congressional district, which includes most of Miami and part of Miami Beach and some other suburbs. The Cubans are a diverse group politically, representing all types of opposition to Castro from right wingers who would like a return to a Batista-type dictatorship to mild socialists who oppose Castro's eradication of civil liberties. But on the average the Cubans are much more conservative and much less Democratic than most American immigrant groups. Coming largely out of Cuba's middle class, the migrants eagerly accepted menial jobs upon arrival in Miami and then rapidly worked themselves up to an American version of middle class status. They tend to favor politicians like Richard Nixon who give lip service to the anti-Castro cause; in turn, Miami's Cuban community favored the Vietnam war and produced big margins for Nixon in 1972.

Pepper's Republican opponents in recent elections have come from the Cuban community, and his 1978 opponent, 30-year-old Al Cardenas, put on a formidable campaign. He zeroed in on Pepper's continued participation in the Miami law firm that bears his name—a violation of the American Bar Association's Code of Professional Conduct. Cardenas got only 37% of the vote—not much better than other Pepper rivals—but he got the Miami *Herald* to editorialize that Pepper's current campaign "will be the last of many." Claude Pepper is not, however, a man who relishes retirement, and the 14th could be the scene of a major political battle in 1980.

Census Data Pop. 452,633. Central city, 58%; suburban, 42%. Median family income, $8,203; families above $15,000: 18%; families below $3,000: 13%. Median years education, 11.4.

The Voters

Median voting age 48.
Employment profile White collar, 46%. Blue collar, 37%. Service, 17%. Farm, –%.
Ethnic groups Black, 15%. Spanish, 41%. Total foreign stock, 56%. USSR, 4%; Poland, 2%; Germany, Canada, Italy, Austria, UK, 1% each.

Presidential vote

1976	Carter (D)	76,357	(56%)
	Ford (R)	58,863	(44%)
1972	Nixon (R)	70,005	(58%)
	McGovern (D)	50,458	(42%)

Rep. Claude Pepper (D) Elected 1962; b. Sept. 8, 1900, near Dudleyville, Ala.; home, Miami; U. of Ala, A.B. 1921, Harvard U., LL.B. 1924; Baptist.

Career Instructor in Law, U. of Ark., 1924–25; Practicing atty., 1925–36, 1951–62; Fla. House of Reps., 1929–30; Fla. Bd. of Pub. Welfare, 1931–32; Fla. Bd. of Law Examiners, 1933–34; U.S. Senate, 1937–51; Candidate for Dem. nomination for U.S. Senate, 1950, 1958.

Offices 2239 RHOB, 202-225-3931. Also 823 Fed. Bldg., 51 S.W. 1st Ave., Miami 33130, 305-350-5565.

Committees *Rules* (2d).

Group Ratings

	ADA	COPE	PC	RPN	NFU	LCV	CFA	NAB	NSI	ACA	NTU
1978	50	90	63	50	70	–	36	0	56	12	–
1977	55	86	58	36	100	57	40	–	–	8	9
1976	50	89	64	41	78	76	45	20	50	13	14

Key Votes

1) Increase Def Spnd	FOR	6) Alaska Lands Protect	FOR	11) Delay Auto Pol Cntrl	AGN
2) B-1 Bomber	AGN	7) Water Projects Veto	FOR	12) Sugar Price Escalator	AGN
3) Cargo Preference	DNV	8) Consum Protect Agcy	FOR	13) Pub Fin Cong Cmpgns	AGN
4) Dereg Nat Gas	AGN	9) Common Situs Picket	FOR	14) ERA Ratif Recissn	AGN
5) Kemp-Roth	AGN	10) Labor Law Revision	FOR	15) Prohibt Govt Abrtns	AGN

Election Results

1978 general	Claude Pepper (D)	65,202	(63%)	($239,864)
	Al Cardenas (R)	38,081	(37%)	($242,131)
1978 primary	Claude Pepper (D)	31,597	(81%)	
	Two others (D)	7,414	(19%)	
1976 general	Claude Pepper (D)	82,665	(73%)	($45,650)
	E. S. Estrella (R)	30,774	(27%)	($14,683)

FIFTEENTH DISTRICT

The suburbs south of Dade County are the fastest-growing part of the Miami metropolitan area. With relatively few Latins or blacks, these places lack the special character of Miami, and the area's physical ambiance is not so different from that of Orange County, California. But while the people in California are bounded by ocean and mountains, the people here are hemmed in mainly by a giant swamp, the Everglades, from which their often valuable property was reclaimed. South Dade County is middle class, middle-to-upper income territory which stretches out on both sides as U.S. 1 as it heads toward the Florida Keys.

The bulk of Florida's 15th congressional district lies in these southwest suburbs of Miami. Also in the district are the Keys (Monroe County) and some other territory included obviously for political reasons. For example, the 15th includes the University of Miami in Coral Gables and the nearby Coconut Grove section of Miami, both of them packed with liberal Democratic votes. The district also takes in a couple of blocks of downtown Miami, which connects the mainland with the 15th's section of Miami Beach.

This part of Miami Beach is the older, poorer, and almost entirely Jewish South Beach section, and includes the hall where both parties' 1972 national conventions were held. Those who think the "Jewish vote" is not an important part of Miami politics should consider the role the South Beach plays in the 15th district. In 1972, when the southwest suburbs were going heavily for Nixon, Congressman Dante Fascell had unaccustomed strong opposition. He won that year with 57%; but without the South Beach, he would have been close to 50%—and might have lost.

That was not—and has not been since—Fascell's usual experience. In most elections this is a fairly safe Democratic district, and he wins quite easily. First elected in 1954, Fascell is considered not quite so liberal as the 14th district's Claude Pepper, but he votes far more often with northern Democrats than with conservative Southerners. For many years Fascell chaired a subcommittee on Latin American affairs—an important subject in Miami, which is the nation's leading center for Latin American trade. He now chairs the International Operations Subcommittee, in which capacity he manages sensitive legislation like the State Department authorization bill—sensitive because it attracts mischievous amendments directed at members' pet peeves in foreign policy. Fascell is number three Democrat on the International Relations Committee, behind 68-year-old Clement Zablocki and 67-year-old L. H. Fountain, and has a good chance of becoming Chairman some day.

He is also number three on Government Operations, and while he is not going to overshadow the colorful Chairman, Jack Brooks of Texas, he is not afraid of standing up to Brooks when he disagrees with him. Indeed, Fascell is one of the most fearless members of the House and will not turn away from a fight with even the most formidable opponent. Thus he took on Brooks when Brooks opposed Jimmy Carter's government reorganization authorization bill, just as a few years ago he took on Wayne Hays when Hays opposed various aspects of campaign finance reform. Fascell is considered by some observers of the House to be one of its most competent and sensitive legislative craftsmen—a man who can put together a piece of legislation, explain it, and get it passed without having it watered down in the process. With considerable seniority and still far short of retirement age, he should be in peak form over the next few years.

Census Data Pop. 452,681. Central city, 8%; suburban, 81%. Median family income, $9,909; families above $15,000: 26%; families below $3,000: 11%. Median years education, 12.3.

The Voters

Median voting age 43.
Employment profile White collar, 60%. Blue collar, 24%. Service, 14%. Farm, 2%.
Ethnic groups Black, 11%. Spanish, 14%. Total foreign stock, 31%. USSR, 5%; Poland, UK, Germany, Canada, 2% each; Italy, Austria, 1% each.

Presidential vote

1976	Carter (D)	108,295	(54%)
	Ford (R)	91,053	(46%)
1972	Nixon (R)	104,864	(63%)
	McGovern (D)	60,483	(37%)

Rep. Dante B. Fascell (D) Elected 1954; b. Mar. 9, 1917, Bridgehampton, L.I., N.Y.; home, Miami; U. of Miami, J.D. 1938; Protestant.

Career Practicing atty., 1938–42, 1946–54; Army, WWII; Legal Attache, Dade Co. St. Legislative Del., 1947–50; Fla. House of Reps., 1950–54; Mbr., U.S. Delegation to U.N., 1969.

Offices 2354 RHOB, 202-225-4506. Also 904 Fed. Bldg., 51 S.W. 1st Ave, Miami 33130, 305-350-5301.

Committees *Government Operations* (3d). Subcommittees: Legislation and National Security.

Foreign Affairs (3d). Subcommittees: Inter-American Affairs; International Operations (Chairman).

Group Ratings

	ADA	COPE	PC	RPN	NFU	LCV	CFA	NAB	NSI	ACA	NTU
1978	65	85	70	36	50	–	68	0	33	17	–
1977	80	78	70	54	92	75	60	–	–	8	17
1976	75	77	89	67	83	89	81	10	30	4	32

Key Votes

1) Increase Def Spnd	AGN	6) Alaska Lands Protect	DNV	11) Delay Auto Pol Cntrl	AGN
2) B-1 Bomber	AGN	7) Water Projects Veto	AGN	12) Sugar Price Escalator	AGN
3) Cargo Preference	AGN	8) Consum Protect Agcy	FOR	13) Pub Fin Cong Cmpgns	FOR
4) Dereg Nat Gas	AGN	9) Common Situs Picket	FOR	14) ERA Ratif Recissn	AGN
5) Kemp-Roth	AGN	10) Labor Law Revision	FOR	15) Prohibt Govt Abrtns	AGN

Election Results

1978 general	Dante B. Fascell (D)	108,837	(74%)	($47,724)
	Herbert J. Hoodwin (R)	37,897	(26%)	($69,590)
1978 primary	Dante B. Fascell (D), unopposed			
1976 general	Dante B. Fascell (D)	121,292	(70%)	($28,351)
	P. R. Cobb (R)	50,941	(30%)	($5,242)

GEORGIA

It was one of the few really moving tableaus in recent American politics. Jimmy Carter, his family, all kinds of prominent Democrats stood on the platform as the 1976 Democratic National Convention was ending, their heads bowed, listening to the impassioned oration-in-the-form-of-benediction delivered by the Rev. Martin Luther King, Sr. The father of the greatest symbol of the civil rights movement was giving his blessing to the first white from the Deep South nominated for president in a century. It symbolized the changes that had been achieved in the nation, the South, and, not least, the home state of both Carter and King, Georgia.

For until Jimmy Carter became Governor, Georgia politics—like politics in most Southern states—either revolved entirely around race or threatned to. The great symbol of Southern populism, Georgia's Tom Watson, had ended his political career in the twenties as a raving racist. Georgia's most successful political family, the Talmadges—father Eugene was elected Governor four times, son Herman was Governor himself and has served in the Senate for more than 20 years—gained most of their victories by posing as the champion of rural whites and segregation and the opponents of Atlanta sophisticates and race-mixing. Georgia has had some very distinguished senators: Walter George who served for more than 30 years and chaired Foreign Relations in the fifties, Richard Russell who served 38 years and chaired Armed Services and Appropriations. Both devoted important parts of their careers to opposing civil rights bills, both for political reasons and out of real conviction. And virtually every successful Georgia politician has made the point that he comes from rural Georgia, not cosmopolitan Atlanta. The only major exception to the pattern was the man who most explicitly appealed to rural values, Atlantan Lester Maddox.

Jimmy Carter's home town of Plains (pop. 683) lies in south Georgia, a part of the state where opposition to civil rights was fierce. He represented the area in the state Senate, and when he ran for governor—unsuccessfully in 1966, successfully in 1970—he cast himself as the champion of the small towns and the farms and the opponent of Atlanta. Folks assumed he was against civil rights, and he didn't disabuse them of the idea—until after he was elected. It was rather a surprise in 1971 when, in his inaugural speech, Carter proclaimed that the days of racial segregation were over.

That stance was enough to get Carter national attention and a *Time* cover as an exemplar of the New South. It also infuriated Carter's predecessor and lieutenant governor, Lester Maddox. Elected after a close contest with Howard "Bo" Callaway in 1966, Maddox still articulated many Georgians' dislike of blacks, the federal government, Atlanta, and all things associated with them. But the changes wrought by Carter and the times made Maddox's politics obsolete. Carter deflected the focus of state politics from race to issues like reorganization and efficiency, which were not Maddox's strongest suit, and his support began to erode. Maddox led the 1974 gubernatorial primary with 36%, but could win only 40% in the runoff. The winner was George Busbee, a leader in the state legislature. He narrowly edged Bert Lance, then not nationally famous, for second place in the first primary and then easily beat Maddox.

Busbee has probably turned out to be a more popular and less controversial Governor than Carter. But one may argue that such is so because there is less to be controversial about in Georgia these days. Racial questions are settled, and Busbee, like Carter a product of rural Georgia, stands foresquare for integration. The prosperity of the state—both metropolitan Atlanta and rural Georgia has experienced solid growth and economic development—makes it relatively easy to balance the state budget and hold down taxes. Meanwhile, Busbee was the first Georgia governor eligible for two consecutive four-year terms, and in 1978 he won his second term easily. In the

Democratic primary he won 72% of the vote in a six-candidate field; in the general election he got 81% against the Republican. Busbee's victory was especially impressive because the Republican, Rodney Cook, had impressive credentials of his own: service on the Atlanta council and in the legislature, close races for mayor and Congress, a reputation as a racial moderate and a fiscal conservative. But Cook's campaign was poorly financed, and the candidate could find no dissatisfaction with Busbee to exploit. For his part, Busbee promised not to run against Herman Talmadge in the 1980 Senate race. His statement, however, left open the possibility of running if Talmadge is not a candidate.

Reelected with even bigger margins than Busbee in 1978 was Senator Sam Nunn, another country boy who has made it big. Back in 1972 Nunn was a 34-year-old state Representative, unknown statewide; if anyone were to describe him, it would be as the grandnephew of former Representative (1914–65) Carl Vinson, longtime Chairman of the House Armed Services Committee. Nunn challenged the sitting Senator, David Gambrell, who had been appointed by Carter to fill the vacancy caused by the death of Senator Russell. Like Carter, Nunn was in the enviable position of running as the champion of the rural areas against the city slickers of Atlanta. He beat Gambrell handily in the runoff, and in the general beat Atlanta Congressman Fletcher Thompson, an ultraconservative; Nunn stressed a tough position on crime, and corralled the black vote at the same time.

In the few years since, Nunn has become a major force in American military and foreign policy. He got Russell's seat on Armed Services and impressed Chairman John Stennis and others with his careful preparation and willingness to question old assumptions. This is not to say that he is a dove. On the contrary. If he occasionally finds a way to cut military costs, he is very definitely a believer in a strong defense and one who doubts whether our current defense is strong enough. He was the first member of the Armed Services Committee to direct hostile questions at Paul Warnke, Carter's nominee for arms control negotiator; and his vote may be crucial one way or the other on any strategic arms limitation treaty. He is dubious about cutting American military manpower in Europe or South Korea. He thinks the volunteer army has not worked well and that we should prepare ourselves to return to the draft. Armed Services is a committee with more than its share of heavyweights, and Nunn is as highly regarded and closely listened to as anyone there.

Nunn's political status in Georgia can be gauged by the 1978 election results. He got 80% in a six-candidate Democratic primary, 83% in the general election. Even had he attracted more formidable opposition, it seems clear that he would have won easily. At 40, Nunn can look forward to a long Senate career. He is already the fifth-ranking Democrat on Armed Services, and he is at least 24 years younger than any more senior. He seems almost certain to be Armed Services Chairman for years.

Georgia's senior Senator is Herman Talmadge, who has had a long career in Georgia politics. It began in 1946, when his father died after having been elected governor and the legislature chose the younger (33) Talmadge to take his place. He held office for 67 days until the courts ruled the lieutenant governor-elect was entitled to it. At first opportunity, the voters elected Herman Talmadge as Governor, after which he served six years. In 1956 he eased aside Senator George, and in the next three elections he was returned to office essentially without opposition.

Talmadge has risen to positions of considerable importance in the Senate. He is Chairman of the Senate Agriculture Committee and in that capacity has often managed to weld an unusual group of liberals and conservatives behind a common policy. He is second to Russell Long on the Senate Finance Committee, where he is lukewarm to many proposals for tax reform; Talmadge balances what he sees as business's need for financial incentives and the ordinary person's need for tax relief. Talmadge became best known to the general public for his performance in the Senate Watergate hearings, where his incisive, determined questioning gave the public insight into how his mind works.

But in 1978 Talmadge came under the cloud of scandal himself. A former administrative assistant, himself in trouble, charged that Talmadge ordered him to take some $39,000 of campaign money and deposit it in a personal account for the Senator. Talmadge denied the charges, and said that the aide was acting on his own; in impassioned tones, he told an Atlanta audience in 1978 that he had done no wrong and that he would run for reelection in 1980. Many were not so sure. Talmadge had suffered personal difficulties—the death of a son, an unpleasant divorce followed by his former wife's unsuccessful candidacy for Congress—and the charges put him under great strain. It would surprise few Washington observers if, whatever happens legally,

Talmadge does not run for reelection. If he should, he would risk attracting tough challengers for the first time in years and might have trouble winning.

Interestingly, none of Georgia's top elected officials is a particular admirer of or personally close to Jimmy Carter. Busbee has made a point of denigrating Carter's state government reorganization schemes, and Talmadge and Nunn endorsed his candidacy in 1976 only when it became clear that he would win the nomination. Carter carried Georgia by an overwhelming margin in 1976 and can expect to do so in 1978, but Carter coattails are not very long here. Indeed the Georgia House delegation is one of the less supportive of the President's policies in the South. Carter has tried to help proteges win major office here, but has not been successful. One reason major officeholders may be leery of Carter is that some of them have had to beat Carter-backed opponents.

Census Data Pop. 4,589,575; 2.27% of U.S. total, 15th largest; Central city, 22%; suburban, 27%. Median family income, $8,165; 37th highest; families above $15,000: 15%; families below $3,000: 15%. Median years education, 10.8.

1977 Share of Federal Tax Burden $6,528,000,000; 1.89% of U.S. total, 17th largest.

1977 Share of Federal Outlays $8,767,421,000; 2.22% of U.S. total, 16th largest. Per capita federal spending, $1,780.

DOD	$2,132,474,000	14th (2.33%)	HEW	$2,936,402,000	16th (1.99%)
ERDA	$5,177,000	35th (0.09%)	HUD	$115,440,000	12th (2.74%)
NASA	$5,761,000	25th (0.15%)	VA	$472,397,000	12th (2.46%)
DOT	$792,883,000	4th (5.55%)	EPA	$147,910,000	16th (1.80%)
DOC	$122,573,000	17th (1.48%)	RevS	$168,519,000	14th (1.99%)
DOI	$44,110,000	26th (0.95%)	Debt	$267,543,000	15th (0.89%)
USDA	$497,936,000	10th (2.50%)	Other	$1,058,296	

Economic Base Textile mill products, especially cotton textile mills and floor covering mills; finance, insurance and real estate; agriculture, notably broilers, peanuts, eggs and cattle; apparel and other textile mill products, especially men's and boys' furnishings; food and kindred products; transportation equipment, especially motor vehicles and equipment.

Political Line-up Governor, George Busbee (D). Senators, Herman E. Talmadge (D) and Sam Nunn (D). Representatives, 10 (9 D and 1 R). State Senate (51 D and 5 R); State House (161 D and 19 R).

The Voters

Registration 2,182,938 Total. No party registration.
Median voting age 40
Employment profile White collar, 44%. Blue collar, 40%. Service, 13%. Farm, 3%.
Ethnic groups Black, 26%. Total foreign stock, 2%.

Presidential vote

1976	Carter (D)	979,409	(67%)
	Ford (R)	483,743	(33%)
1972	Nixon (R)	881,490	(75%)
	McGovern (D)	289,529	(25%)

1976 Democratic Presidential Primary

Carter	419,272	(83%)
Wallace	57,594	(12%)
Others	26,605	(5%)

1976 Republican Presidential Primary

Reagan	128,671	(68%)
Ford	59,801	(32%)

Sen. Herman E. Talmadge (D) Elected 1956, seat up 1980; b. Aug. 9, 1913, near McRae; home, Lovejoy; U. of Ga., 1936, Northwestern U., LL.B. 1942; Baptist.

Career Navy, WWII; Practicing atty.; Gov. of Ga., 1949–55.

Offices 109 RSOB, 202-224-3643. Also 275 Peachtree St. N.E., Atlanta 30303, 404-221-6255.

Committees *Agriculture, Nutrition, and Forestry* (Chairman). Subcommittees: Environment, Soil Conservation, and Forestry; Agricultural Research and General Legislation; Foreign Agricultural Policy.

Finance (2d). Subcommittees: Health (Chairman); International Trade; Taxation and Debt Management Generally.

Veterans' Affairs (2d).

Group Ratings

	ADA	COPE	PC	RPN	NFU	LCV	CFA	NAB	NSI	ACA	NTU
1978	40	42	35	33	70	30	35	75	56	39	–
1977	15	44	25	38	58	–	24	–	–	61	35
1976	25	47	10	35	82	26	21	64	88	73	42

Key Votes

1) Warnke Nom	AGN	6) Egypt-Saudi Arms	AGN	11) Hosptl Cost Contnmnt	AGN
2) Neutron Bomb	FOR	7) Draft Restr Pardon	FOR	12) Clinch River Reactor	DNV
3) Waterwy User Fee	FOR	8) Wheat Price Support	FOR	13) Pub Fin Cong Cmpgns	AGN
4) Dereg Nat Gas	AGN	9) Panama Canal Treaty	FOR	14) ERA Ratif Recissn	AGN
5) Kemp-Roth	AGN	10) Labor Law Rev Clot	AGN	15) Med Necssy Abrtns	FOR

Election Results

1974 general	Herman E. Talmadge (D)	627,376	(72%)	($65,207)
	Jerry Johnson (R)	246,866	(28%)	($12,856)
1974 primary	Herman E. Talmadge (D)	523,133	(81%)	
	One other (D)	119,011	(19%)	
1968 general	Herman E. Talmadge (D)	885,093	(78%)	
	E. Earl Patton, Jr. (R)	256,793	(22%)	

Sen. Sam Nunn (D) Elected 1972, seat up 1978; b. Sept. 8, 1938, Perry; home, Perry; Emory U., A.B. 1960, LL.B. 1962; Methodist.

Career Coast Guard, 1959–60; Legal Counsel, U.S. House of Reps. Armed Services Comm., 1962–63; Farmer; Practicing atty., 1963–72; Ga. House of Reps., 1968–72.

Offices 3241 DSOB, 202-224-3521. Also Rm. 430, 275 Peachtree St. N.E., Atlanta 30303, 404-221-4811, and 915B Main St., Perry 31069, 912-987-1458

Committees *Armed Services* (5th). Subcommittees: Manpower and Personnel (Chairman); Research and Development; Military Construction and Stockpiles.

Governmental Affairs (5th). Subcommittees: Investigations (Chairman); Intergovernmental Relations; Federal Spending Practices and Open Government.

Group Ratings

	ADA	COPE	PC	RPN	NFU	LCV	CFA	NAB	NSI	ACA	NTU
1978	25	26	20	70	50	36	20	100	50	67	–
1977	20	37	40	67	55	–	24	–	–	64	37
1976	20	60	20	41	67	29	43	55	100	62	65

Key Votes

1) Warnke Nom	AGN	6) Egypt-Saudi Arms	AGN	11) Hosptl Cost Contnmnt	AGN
2) Neutron Bomb	FOR	7) Draft Restr Pardon	AGN	12) Clinch River Reactor	AGN
3) Waterwy User Fee	FOR	8) Wheat Price Support	AGN	13) Pub Fin Cong Cmpgns	AGN
4) Dereg Nat Gas	AGN	9) Panama Canal Treaty	FOR	14) ERA Ratif Recissn	AGN
5) Kemp-Roth	FOR	10) Labor Law Rev Clot	AGN	15) Med Necssy Abrtns	FOR

Election Results

1978 general	Sam Nunn (D)	536,320	(83%)	($548,814)
	John W. Stokes (R)	108,808	(17%)	
1978 primary	Sam Nunn (D)	525,703	(80%)	
	Five others (D)	131,584	(20%)	
1972 general	Sam Nunn (D)	635,970	(54%)	
	Fletcher Thompson (R)	542,331	(46%)	

Gov. George Busbee (D) Elected 1974, term expires Jan., 1983; b. Aug. 7, 1927, Vienna; Abraham Baldwin Ag. Col., Duke U., U. of Ga., A.B. 1949, LL.B. 1952; Baptist.

Career Navy, WWII; Practicing atty., 1952–75; Ga. House of Reps., 1957–75, Asst. Admin. Floor Ldr., 1963–65, Admin. Floor Ldr., 1966, Maj. Ldr., 1967–75.

Offices State Capitol, Atlanta 30334, 404-656-1776.

1978 general	George Busbee (D)	534,572	(81%)
	Rodney M. Cook (R)	128,139	(19%)
1978 primary	George Busbee (D)	503,875	(72%)
	Roscoe Emory Dean, Jr. (D)	111,901	(16%)
	Four others (D)	80,135	(12%)
1974 general	George Busbee (D)	646,777	(69%)
	Ronnie Thompson (R)	289,113	(31%)

FIRST DISTRICT

The 1st congressional district of Georgia is the southeast part of the state, the portion lying along the Atlantic Ocean and proceeding several counties inland. The major city here is Savannah, the first major city in Georgia. It was laid out carefully in colonial days and contains dozens of parks. Many of the houses in the older section of the city have been restored, and much of Savannah has the sort of tree-shaded elegance that its founders envisaged. South of Savannah are the city of Brunswick and the resorts of St. Simons and Sea Islands. Inland is rural territory: cotton, peanuts, and piney woods.

Georgia, though originally founded as a haven for poor white people, soon became slave territory, and southeast Georgia always had a substantial slave population. Today one-third of the residents of the 1st congressional district are black. They played little role in the politics of the area in the fifties and sixties, but in the seventies their votes have become important in congressional elections.

Black voters provided part of the backing for Bo Ginn, the current Congressman, when he ran against G. Elliott Hagan in 1972. Hagan had been in office for ten years, and Ginn had worked on his staff; but the incumbent was weak in Savannah and among blacks. Apparently the former aide knew his boss's weaknesses well. After winning that primary handily, he has hung onto the district ever since. Ginn has a voting record somewhat more liberal on economic issues than most other rural Georgia congressmen. He held seats on the Merchant Marine and Public Works Committees, which can provide bread-and-butter help for the 1st district, and in 1979 switched to Appropriations, which can serve the same function. His kind of politics seems successful. He has not been seriously challenged since his initial victory in 1972.

Census Data Pop. 456,354. Central city, 26%; suburban, 15%. Median family income, $7,102; families above $15,000: 11%; families below $3,000: 19%. Median years education, 10.6.

The Voters

Median voting age 41.
Employment profile White collar, 39%. Blue collar, 40%. Service, 15%. Farm, 6%.
Ethnic groups Black, 34%. Total foreign stock, 3%.

Presidential vote

1976	Carter (D)	88,992	(64%)
	Ford (R)	49,282	(36%)
1972	Nixon (R)	90,218	(75%)
	McGovern (D)	29,768	(25%)

Rep. Bo Ginn (D) Elected 1972; b. May 31, 1934, Morgan; home, Millen; Abraham Baldwin Ag. Col., 1951–53, Ga. Southern Col., B.S. 1956; Baptist.

Career High school teacher; Asst. Mgr., Planters Electric Membership Corp., 1957–61; Admin. Asst. to U. S. Sen. Herman E. Talmadge, 1961–71; Cattle farmer and businessman, 1971–72.

Offices 317 CHOB, 202-225-5831. Also Rm. 304, Fed. Bldg., Brunswick 31520, 912-264-4040.

Committees *Appropriations* (30th). Subcommittees: Interior; Military Construction.

Group Ratings

	ADA	COPE	PC	RPN	NFU	LCV	CFA	NAB	NSI	ACA	NTU
1978	20	55	23	50	50	–	23	83	90	63	–
1977	20	52	23	8	67	29	25	–	–	62	37
1976	15	43	18	44	42	22	9	25	78	61	29

Key Votes

1) Increase Def Spnd	FOR	6) Alaska Lands Protect	FOR	11) Delay Auto Pol Cntrl	FOR
2) B-1 Bomber	AGN	7) Water Projects Veto	AGN	12) Sugar Price Escalator	AGN
3) Cargo Preference	FOR	8) Consum Protect Agcy	AGN	13) Pub Fin Cong Cmpgns	AGN
4) Dereg Nat Gas	AGN	9) Common Situs Picket	AGN	14) ERA Ratif Recissn	AGN
5) Kemp-Roth	AGN	10) Labor Law Revision	AGN	15) Prohibt Govt Abrtns	AGN

Election Results

1978 general	Bo Ginn (D), unopposed	($58,340)
1978 primary	Bo Ginn (D), unopposed	
1976 general	Bo Ginn (D), unopposed	($13,644)

SECOND DISTRICT

The 2d congressional district is the southwest corner of Georgia. It is the most agricultural, the poorest, and, with the exception of Atlanta's 5th district, the most heavily black congressional district in the state. The 2d has been—at least until its neighbor Jimmy Carter's election as President—part of the still-unreconstructed, economically underdeveloped Old South. The only parts of the district that experienced population growth in the sixties were those around its military bases; the rest of the district seemed to be slowly dying. This was one of George Wallace's banner congressional districts in 1968.

But times are changing here as well as in cosmopolitan Atlanta. Blacks now vote without fear of intimidation, and as Carter has shown that black support is no longer the political kiss of death. Economically the 2d, like many rural areas around the nation, has grown healthier in the seventies, as the job market grows and people decide to enjoy the pleasures of small town life rather than moving to a large, anonymous metropolitan area. The economic upturn here coincides roughly with the time that blacks got full rights of citizenship; and while it may be going too far to say that there is a cause and effect relationship, one cannot help but recall Jimmy Carter's comment that the civil rights revolution was the best thing that has happened to the South.

The young Congressman from the 2d, Democrat Dawson Mathis, is one of several former newscasters in the Congress. This represents a trend that can readily be understood. Local television newscasters are, after all, among the better known people in every community —typically much better known than local state legislators or county officeholders. Mathis after six years of newscasting at an Albany, Georgia, station was about as well known a figure as there was in the 2d district, most of which is served by Albany television. So even without political experience he was able to beat seasoned veterans in the 1970 Democratic primary and general election when the aged incumbent retired.

Mathis embodies the traditional Southern Democrat's view of congressional politics. When asked about his goals in Congress, he replied, "To represent the 2d district as long as I can." As a member of the Agriculture Committee, he has already jumped to the number five position among Democrats and a subcommittee chair (Oilseeds and Rice)—a remarkable rise made possible by a spate of retirements, defeats, and deaths. He also holds a seat on the Interior Committee. And he has had success sponsoring bills in a wide variety of areas: setting limits on the food stamp program, penalizing other counties that expand sugar or citrus production in competition with the U.S., giving cost of living increases to American troops abroad. Mathis has a traditionally conservative voting record, but he has been known to cooperate with other Democrats on procedural and partisan matters, so he is unlikely to have any trouble getting the Democratic Caucus to approve his taking any chair that seniority seems to entitle him to. At home he had no opposition in either primary or general elections from 1970 until the 1978 primary, which he won with 77%.

Census Data Pop. 460,450. Central city, 16%; suburban, 4%. Median family income, $6,238; families above $15,000: 9%; families below $3,000: 23%. Median years education, 9.9.

The Voters

Median voting age 42.
Employment profile White collar, 36%. Blue collar, 38%. Service, 14%. Farm, 12%.
Ethnic groups Black, 37%. Total foreign stock, 1%.

Presidential vote

1976	Carter (D)	88,250	(69%)
	Ford (R)	39,456	(31%)
1972	Nixon (R)	80,769	(80%)
	McGovern (D)	20,745	(20%)

Rep. Dawson Mathis (D) Elected 1970; b. Nov. 30, 1940, Nashville; home, Albany; So. Ga. Col.; Baptist.

Career Radio stations WGNA, Nashville, and WCEH, Hawkinsville, 1959–64; News Dir., WALB-TV, Albany, 1964–70.

Offices 2331 RHOB, 202-225-3631. Also City-County Govt. Bldg., 225 Pine Ave., Rm. 202, Albany 31705, 912-439-8067.

Committees *Agriculture* (5th). Subcommittees: Oilseeds and Rice (Chairman); Tobacco.

Interior and Insular Affairs (15th). Subcommittees: Energy and the Environment; Oversight/Special Investigations; Mines and Mining.

Group Ratings

	ADA	COPE	PC	RPN	NFU	LCV	CFA	NAB	NSI	ACA	NTU
1978	5	29	10	50	63	–	14	89	89	82	–
1977	5	26	20	9	70	23	10	–	–	67	31
1976	15	39	20	33	37	10	18	46	90	84	46

Key Votes

1) Increase Def Spnd	FOR	6) Alaska Lands Protect	AGN	11) Delay Auto Pol Cntrl	DNV
2) B-1 Bomber	AGN	7) Water Projects Veto	AGN	12) Sugar Price Escalator	FOR
3) Cargo Preference	FOR	8) Consum Protect Agcy	AGN	13) Pub Fin Cong Cmpgns	AGN
4) Dereg Nat Gas	AGN	9) Common Situs Picket	AGN	14) ERA Ratif Recissn	FOR
5) Kemp-Roth	FOR	10) Labor Law Revision	AGN	15) Prohibt Govt Abrtns	DNV

Election Results

1978 general	Dawson Mathis (D), unopposed			($100,914)
1978 primary	Dawson Mathis (D)	49,562	(77%)	
	One other (D)	15,036	(23%)	
1976 general	Dawson Mathis (D), unopposed			($24,900)

THIRD DISTRICT

The 3d congressional district is one of several south Georgia districts. It has one good-sized city, Columbus, which in turn is dominated by one of the nation's largest military installations, Fort Benning. Columbus is very much an Army town. Girls grow up here aspiring to marry young officers, and a local hero, Lieutenant William Calley, was confined at Benning during his trial. Fort Benning has a prouder history: it was here in the thirties that Colonel George C. Marshall staged the maneuvers that anticipated so much of the kind of fighting that occurred in World War II—showing a rare knack of being ready to fight the next, rather than the last, war.

Benning is only one major military installation here. Another is Warner Robins Air Materiel Command in the eastern end of the 3d. Both, naturally, are of substantial economic importance of what was, until the seventies, an otherwise economically backward area. Benning may have been placed here initially on the theory that the excruciatingly hot, humid Georgia summers would best condition soldiers for the rigors of combat in the tropics. But it did not hurt that Georgia was represented for years by Richard Russell, Chairman of the Senate Armed Services Committee, and that part of the 3d was represented by Carl Vinson, Chairman of the House Armed Services Committee.

The 3d also has the distinction of being the home district of President Jimmy Carter. You don't have to look very far into the politics of the 3d to find out just how far Jimmy Carter has come—and helped to lead the South—in the last dozen or so years. Back in the middle sixties, when Carter represented part of the 3d in the Georgia Senate, the small city of Americus was one of the parts of the South least hospitable to civil rights workers. Against this background it is not hard to understand how the Carter family's stand against segregation in their church and community was courageous indeed—especially for a politician and businessman who depended on white neighbors for a livelihood. Carter avoided the political fallout from the civil rights revolution; he was elected to the state Senate before it started and campaigned as a rural Georgian rather than a segregationist in his 1966 and 1970 gubernatorial races.

Indeed, Carter probably could have gone to Congress had he wanted to. The 3d district was unique in Georgia outside the Atlanta area for having been represented by a Republican: Howard "Bo" Callaway, the textile heir who was elected in the Goldwater landslide of 1964. Callaway ran for governor in 1966, losing to Lester Maddox; his later career (Secretary of the Army, Ford campaign chairman) was on the national level. In any case, when Callaway vacated the seat, the 1966 Democratic nomination looked to be tantamount to election. Carter decided to run for governor instead, and the winner in the congressional race was state legislator Jack Brinkley. Brinkley's voting record—very conservative on social issues, middle of the road on economic issues—is probably what Carter would have compiled, representing the district and looking towards reelection. And such a record would have disqualified him, in a way that his record as Governor did not, from the 1976 Democratic presidential nomination. For both men things have worked out well. Carter is President, and Brinkley, an obscure member of the Armed Services and Veterans Affairs Committees, has a safe seat in the House.

Census Data Pop. 460,749. Central city, 33%; suburban, 22%. Median family income, $7,550; families above $15,000: 12%; families below $3,000: 16%. Median years education, 10.9.

The Voters

Median voting age 38.
Employment profile White collar, 41%. Blue collar, 40%. Service, 15%. Farm, 4%.
Ethnic groups Black, 32%. Spanish, 1%. Total foreign stock, 4%.

Presidential vote

1976	Carter (D)	82,639	(69%)
	Ford (R)	36,878	(31%)
1972	Nixon (R)	81,300	(78%)
	McGovern (D)	23,534	(22%)

Rep. Jack Brinkley (D) Elected 1966; b. Dec. 22, 1930, Faceville; home, Columbus; Young Harris Col., B. A. 1949, U. of Ga., J.D. 1959; Baptist.

Career Public school teacher, 1949–51; Air Force, 1951–56; Practicing atty., 1959–67; Ga. House of Reps., 1965–66.

Offices 2412 RHOB, 202-225-5901. Also 2429 Norris Rd., Columbus 31907, 404-568-3330.

Committees *Armed Services* (9th). Subcommittees: Intelligence and Military Applications of Nuclear Energy; Military Installations and Facilities.

Veterans' Affairs (7th). Subcommittees: Compensation, Pension, Insurance and Memorial Affairs; Housing (Chairman).

Group Ratings

	ADA	COPE	PC	RPN	NFU	LCV	CFA	NAB	NSI	ACA	NTU
1978	15	35	35	75	60	–	14	92	90	70	–
1977	15	43	23	31	64	30	25	–	–	67	37
1976	10	50	21	39	50	6	18	46	90	67	67

Key Votes

1) Increase Def Spnd	FOR	6) Alaska Lands Protect	FOR	11) Delay Auto Pol Cntrl	FOR
2) B-1 Bomber	AGN	7) Water Projects Veto	AGN	12) Sugar Price Escalator	FOR
3) Cargo Preference	FOR	8) Consum Protect Agcy	AGN	13) Pub Fin Cong Cmpgns	FOR
4) Dereg Nat Gas	FOR	9) Common Situs Picket	AGN	14) ERA Ratif Recissn	FOR
5) Kemp-Roth	FOR	10) Labor Law Revision	AGN	15) Prohibt Govt Abrtns	FOR

Election Results

1978 general	Jack Brinkley (D), unopposed			($14,531)
1978 primary	Jack Brinkley (D), unopposed			
1976 general	Jack Brinkley (D)	93,174	(89%)	($54,628)
	Steve Dugan (R)	11,829	(11%)	($10,831)

FOURTH DISTRICT

Stuck smack in the middle of the Deep South is the booming metropolis of Atlanta—"the city," it liked to boast, "too busy to hate." The slogan grew out of Atlanta's reputation for racial tolerance and moderation, which it earned back in the fifties and sixties. But if Atlanta has practiced little overt segregation and possesses the sophistication of some northern cities, it has also developed some of the problems of urban life. Foremost among them, perhaps, is the white exodus from the central city. As metropolitan Atlanta grew apace—it doubled in population from 1950 to the early seventies—whites have moved increasingly to the suburbs, while blacks have moved out within the city of Atlanta itself. The result: by 1970 a majority of Atlanta's residents were black—the first such major city in the South—while the suburbs formed an almost all-white noose around its perimeter. Children growing up in metropolitan Atlanta, whether black or white, may have less contact with members of the other race than they would have 20 years ago—or than they do now in the integrated schools of the small towns and rural counties of south Georgia.

Just about half of the residents of suburban Atlanta live in DeKalb County, just to the east of the city. With a small part of the city and small, just-suburbanizing Rockdale County, DeKalb makes up the 4th congressional district of Georgia. This area is the home of higher income, better educated Atlanta suburbanites (though the really rich in Atlanta still live in mansions on the city's north side). Statistically the 4th district is far closer to many similar northern areas than to south Georgia. Politically DeKalb and the 4th behave more like a northern constituency than like the non-Atlanta Georgia districts. When it was first created in 1964, the result of a landmark Supreme Court case, the 4th went for Lyndon Johnson and elected a liberal Democratic congressman, while the rest of Georgia switched from its traditional Democratic allegiance to the Republicanism of Barry Goldwater. In 1966, like many northern districts, the 4th elected a Republican congressman, and in the state election gave a big margin to Bo Callaway over Lester Maddox. In the years that followed DeKalb voters generally preferred the Republicans' smooth, neutral-accented candidates to the rural-oriented, Southern-accented candidates nominated by the Democrats. This is the only part of Georgia which has consistently elected a significant number of Republican state legislators.

But suddenly in 1974 the 4th shifted again—and the shift paralleled the movement found outside the South. Republican Congressman Ben Blackburn, who had supported Richard Nixon to the end, was defeated, and Democratic state legislator Elliott Levitas was elected. But Levitas is not a standard Democratic liberal. He shows a deep distrust of government bureaucracy. He opposed the consumer protection agency bill vehemently and helped sponsor deregulation of the airlines. He has been pushing a bill to give Congress a chance to review and reject all rules and regulations issued by government agencies. Critics say the proposal would let Congress meddle in the day-to-day operations of government and might cause it to neglect the work of laying down broad policies; Levitas argues that government agencies should not be able to govern by fiat and should be accountable to the body that gives them power in the first place. Levitas's philosophy appears popular in suburban Atlanta; he has been reelected with amazing percentages (82% in 1978), and in 1976 ran well ahead of fellow Georgian Jimmy Carter here.

Census Data Pop. 459,335. Central city, 16%; suburban, 80%. Median family income, $11,750; families above $15,000: 31%; families below $3,000: 5%. Median years education, 12.4.

The Voters

Median voting age 38.
Employment profile White collar, 66%. Blue collar, 25%. Service, 9%. Farm, –%.
Ethnic groups Black, 15%. Spanish, 1%. Total foreign stock, 5%.

Presidential vote

1976	Carter (D)	94,920	(57%)
	Ford (R)	70,912	(43%)
1972	Nixon (R)	110,574	(77%)
	McGovern (D)	33,043	(23%)

Rep. Elliott H. Levitas (D) Elected 1974; b. Dec. 26, 1930, Atlant; home, Atlanta; Emory U., B.S., LL.B., Rhodes Scholar, Oxford U., M.A., U. of Mich.; Jewish.

Career Practicing atty., 1955–75; Air Force; Ga. House of Reps., 1965–75.

Offices 329 CHOB, 202-225-4272. Also 141 E. Trinity Pl., Decatur 30030, 404-377-1717.

Committees *Government Operations* (14th). Subcommittees: Commerce, Consumer and Monetary Affairs; Intergovernmental Relations and Human Resources.

Public Works and Transportation (9th). Subcommittees: Aviation; Oversight and Review; Public Buildings and Grounds (Chairman).

Group Ratings

	ADA	COPE	PC	RPN	NFU	LCV	CFA	NAB	NSI	ACA	NTU
1978	20	60	38	33	40	–	46	100	70	65	–
1977	30	43	50	38	67	57	35	–	–	63	34
1976	40	52	49	61	67	52	54	55	90	54	24

Key Votes

1) Increase Def Spnd	FOR	6) Alaska Lands Protect	FOR	11) Delay Auto Pol Cntrl	FOR
2) B-1 Bomber	AGN	7) Water Projects Veto	FOR	12) Sugar Price Escalator	AGN
3) Cargo Preference	AGN	8) Consum Protect Agcy	AGN	13) Pub Fin Cong Cmpgns	FOR
4) Dereg Nat Gas	AGN	9) Common Situs Picket	AGN	14) ERA Ratif Recissn	FOR
5) Kemp-Roth	FOR	10) Labor Law Revision	AGN	15) Prohibt Govt Abrtns	AGN

Election Results

1978 general	Elliott H. Levitas (D)	60,284	(81%)	($94,745)
	Homer Cheung (R)	14,221	(19%)	
1978 primary	Elliott H. Levitas (D)	35,942	(84%)	
	One other (D)	6,608	(16%)	
1976 general	Elliott H. Levitas (D)	110,261	(68%)	($113,332)
	George Warren (R)	51,140	(32%)	($34,373)

FIFTH DISTRICT

In the early sixties Atlanta was just one of several Southern cities that people had heard of. In the national consciousness, it was no more important than New Orleans, Miami, Memphis, Birmingham, or Richmond. By the late seventies Atlanta had become the capital of the South—not just the economic capital, but the recognized focal point of a great region. How has this come about? Part of the reason lies in the central role air travel plays today in business communication. Atlanta's airport, with Chicago's O'Hare, is the busiest in the country; the saying is that you can't go anywhere in the South without going through Atlanta first. Naturally businesses tend to locate their Southern headquarters in Atlanta. Then there is the prosperity of Atlanta's big employers: Coca-Cola, Delta Airlines, and so on.

But probably more than anything else the city's response to the civil rights revolution established Atlanta as the capital of the South. The city's two longtime white mayors, William Hartsfield and Ivan Allen, were always far ahead of other Southern leaders in their opposition to massive resistance to integration and support of civil rights; Allen went so far as to testify in support of the Civil Rights Act of 1964, one of the few Southern elected officials to do so. Hartsfield and Allen also got the city's business community together to discourage any violent resistance to civil rights legislation. Atlanta was determined to obey the law, and to obey quietly, so as not to discourage northern investors, who never liked the uncertainty and unpredictability of either civil rights demonstrations or violent white resistance. Atlanta liked to call itself "the city too busy to hate," and to a considerable extent it earned that reputation.

But whites alone did not make Atlanta the capital of the South. There was also black activity. Although Martin Luther King Jr. led his first major civil rights movement in Montgomery, Alabama, his roots were in Atlanta; and although civil rights demonstrations occurred in countless cities and towns all over the South, the organizations and individuals who helped to plan and coordinate them were headquartered, more often than not, in Atlanta. Atlanta has had a strong and vital black community since Reconstruction, and so a set of strong black institutions—colleges, churches, social groups—could play an important part in the civil rights struggle.

The 5th congressional district of Georgia includes most of Atlanta and some of the city's wealthy suburbs to the north. Less than half its residents were black in 1970, but probably more than half its voters are today. It includes most of the black neighborhoods on the west and south sides of the city, as well as the rich white residential neighborhood on the north side. Most of Atlanta's white establishment, as well as most of its black leaders, live in the 5th district.

The 5th congressional district has had a turbulent political history. In 1964 it elected Charles Weltner, a liberal Democrat who backed the Civil Rights Act of 1964, one of the few Southerners to do so. He withdrew his candidacy in 1966 rather than sign a state party loyalty oath pledging to support gubernatorial nominee Lester Maddox. In 1966, 1968, and 1970 the 5th elected Fletcher Thompson, a conservative Republican who was unashamed of saying that he provided no constituency services at all to blacks. In 1970 Thompson beat Andrew Young; he claimed that Young's election would produce the end of Western civilization. Nevertheless in 1972, 1974, and 1976 the 5th district elected Andrew Young to Congress. His background was with Martin Luther King Jr. and the civil rights movement, but Young developed a broader constituency in Congress. His articulateness and political adeptness (which got him a seat on the Rules Committee) set him above some of his more rhetorical, more ideology-bound black counterparts. And the testimony he gave for Jimmy Carter in the 1976 presidential campaign—assuring blacks and white liberals that Carter was a decent person who could be trusted—was probably essential to Carter's success. Despite his controversial statements, Young's position as Ambassador to the United Nations is secure in the Carter Administration.

Young's seat in the House has been taken not by another black but by an ambitious white politician, Wyche Fowler. A former aide to Weltner and head of the Atlanta council, Fowler had solid liberal and civil rights credentials. The principal black candidate, John Lewis, could not prevent Fowler from making inroads in the black community; the Republicans were no longer competitive here. Fowler's strength was shown again when he got 80% of the vote in the 1978 primary against black opposition. His voting record is liberal, though not as liberal as Young's, but his seat seems even safer. In 1979 Fowler demonstrated his political clout in the House by winning a seat on the Ways and Means Committee. He has been mentioned as a possible Senate candidate in 1980.

Census Data Pop. 460,589. Central city, 87%; suburban, 13%. Median family income, $9,050; families above $15,000: 24%; families below $3,000: 3%. Median years education, 12.1.

The Voters

Median voting age 40.
Employment profile White collar, 55%. Blue collar, 28%. Service, 17%. Farm, –%.
Ethnic groups Black, 44%. Spanish, 1%. Total foreign stock, 4%.

Presidential vote

1976	Carter (D)	98,102	(68%)
	Ford (R)	47,204	(32%)
1972	Nixon (R)	69,088	(52%)
	McGovern (D)	63,405	(48%)

Rep. Wyche Fowler, Jr. (D) Elected Apr. 5, 1977; b. Oct. 6, 1940, Atlanta; home, Atlanta; Davidson Col, B.A. 1963; Emory U., Atlanta, LL.B. 1969; Presbyterian.

Career Army, 1963–65; Chief Asst. to U.S. Rep. Charles Weltner, 1965–66; Night Mayor for the City of Atlanta, 1966–69; Mbr., Atlanta Bd. of Aldermen, 1969–73; Pres., Atlanta City Council, 1973–77; Practicing atty., 1970–77.

Offices 1504 LHOB, 202-225-3801. Also Rm. 425, Wm. Oliver Bldg., 32 Peachtree St., Atlanta 30303, 404-688-8207.

Committees *Ways and Means* (22d). Subcommittees: Select Revenue Measures; Public Assistance and Unemployment Compensation.

Group Ratings

	ADA	COPE	PC	RPN	NFU	LCV	CFA	NAB	NSI	ACA	NTU
1978	45	58	55	27	67	–	55	50	86	36	–
1977	63	53	67	40	75	70	55	–	–	43	26

Key Votes

1) Increase Def Spnd	FOR	6) Alaska Lands Protect	FOR	11) Delay Auto Pol Cntrl	AGN
2) B-1 Bomber	AGN	7) Water Projects Veto	FOR	12) Sugar Price Escalator	AGN
3) Cargo Preference	AGN	8) Consum Protect Agcy	FOR	13) Pub Fin Cong Cmpgns	FOR
4) Dereg Nat Gas	AGN	9) Common Situs Picket	NE	14) ERA Ratif Recissn	AGN
5) Kemp-Roth	AGN	10) Labor Law Revision	AGN	15) Prohibt Govt Abrtns	AGN

Election Results

1978 general	Wyche Fowler, Jr. (D)	52,739	(75%)	($142,684)
	Thomas P. Bowles, Jr. (R)	17,132	(25%)	($27,374)
1978 primary	Wyche Fowler, Jr. (D)	45,411	(82%)	
	Clint Deveaux (D)	9,997	(18%)	($42,772)
1977 special runoff	Wyche Fowler, Jr. (D)	54,378	(62%)	
	John Lewis (D)	32,732	(38%)	
1977 special primary	Wyche Fowler, Jr. (D)	29,898	(40%)	
	John Lewis (D)	21,531	(29%)	
	Paul D. Coverdell (R)	16,509	(22%)	
	Ralph D. Abernathy (D)	3,614	(5%)	
	Eight others	3,848	(5%)	
1976 general	Andrew Young (D)	96,056	(67%)	($116,605)
	Ed Gadrix (R)	47,998	(33%)	($21,955)

SIXTH DISTRICT

The 6th congressional district of Georgia presents a nice example of demographic and political change in the South. A dozen years ago the dominant city of the district was Macon; the Atlanta metropolitan area at the district's northern edge had only 10% of its population. But in 1972 redistricting removed Macon and added several south Fulton County suburbs of Atlanta. Today 48% of the 6th's population lives in metropolitan Atlanta, and just over half in the small cities and rural counties that used to comprise almost the whole district. These suburbs—East Point and College Park in south Fulton County and fast-growing adjacent Clayton County—are not the home of Atlanta's ruling elite. They are instead the home of what might be called the uncomfortable middle class, people not quite secure in their apparently pleasant status and fearful of the blacks and poor they have left behind in Atlanta itself. These are areas that have gone Republican in the past, though they have also responded positively to segregationist Democrats like George Wallace and Lester Maddox.

The demographic change has been reflected in political change. Before 1972 the 6th was a safe district for Congressman John Flynt, a courtly Democrat first elected in 1954 and one not inclined to rock the boat. A high ranking member of the Appropriations Committee, Flynt was one of those powerful, usually silent Southern Democrats who for years had influence beyond their numbers. His greatest source of recognition came, however, when he served as Chairman of the Committee on Standards of Official Conduct—generally known as the House Ethics Committee. In that capacity, he found himself on a very hot seat, having to lead the 1977 and 1978 investigations of the Korean lobbying activities of Tongsun Park, as well as of the alleged transgressions of members like Daniel Flood and Joshua Eilberg. Flynt was selected for this position by earlier, complacent Congresses, which had wanted a man who would grant his colleagues a presumption of innocence, and who would not issue a negative verdict without the most convincing and overwhelming evidence. In the 95th Congress a majority—partisan Republicans and angry young Democrats—demanded a tougher attitude, and they forced Speaker O'Neill effectively to remove Flynt from the direction of his committee and to allow Leon Jaworski to control the Koreagate investigation.

Flynt was under attack in the 6th district even before Koreagate. His Republican opponent had pointed out that he rented a farm he owned to one of the auto companies, and at the same time supported easing of the auto emissions requirements. The Republican was Newt Gingrich, a young college professor, who ran against Flynt in 1974 and 1976 and got 49% and 48% of the vote respectively; he felt he lost the first race because of Watergate and the second because of Jimmy Carter's Georgia sweep. Gingrich was already busy running again when Flynt announced that he would retire in 1978. The Democratic primary and runoff produced quite a different opponent for Gingrich: state Senator Virginia Shapard, a strong supporter of the Equal Rights Amendment and leader in a fight to censure a Georgia legislator for filing false travel vouchers. (One of the Democrats Shapard beat was Betty Talmadge, divorced wife of the Senator, who got only 17% of the vote.) Gingrich attacked Shapard for spending her personal wealth in the campaign and adopted an empty shopping cart as his symbol. Shapard carried her home region, but lost the western part of the district, Gingrich's home area, and she was beaten decisively in the Atlanta suburbs. Gingrich becomes the first Republican elected from this district and, given the obstacles he has overcome, it seems likely that he can win again.

Census Data Pop. 455,810. Central city, 5%; suburban, 43%. Median family income, $9,284; families above $15,000: 16%; families below $3,000: 10%. Median years education, 10.9.

The Voters

Median voting age 39.
Employment profile White collar, 44%. Blue collar, 44%. Service, 11%. Farm, 1%.
Ethnic groups Black, 19%. Total foreign stock, 2%.

Presidential vote

1976	Carter (D)	106,430	(68%)
	Ford (R)	51,181	(32%)
1972	Nixon (R)	96,213	(80%)
	McGovern (D)	24,717	(20%)

Rep. Newt Gingrich (R) Elected 1978; b. June 17, 1943, Harrisburg, Pa.; home, Carrollton; Emory U., B.A. 1965, Tulane U., M.A. 1967, Ph.D. 1970; Baptist.

Career Prof., West Ga. Col.; Repub. Nominee for U.S. House of Reps., 1974, 1976.

Offices 417 CHOB, 202-225-4501.

Committees *House Administration* (7th). Subcommittees: Libraries and Memorials; Printing; Personnel and Police.

Public Works and Transportation (13th). Subcommittees: Aviation; Oversight and Review; Water Resources.

Group Ratings: Newly Elected

Key Votes: Newly Elected

Election Results

1978 general	Newt Gingrich (R)	47,078	(54%)	($219,336)
	Virginia Shapard (D)	39,451	(46%)	($313,056)
1978 primary	Newt Gingrich (R)	4,597	(76%)	
	Two others (R)	1,487	(24%)	
1976 general	John J. Flynt, Jr. (D)	77,532	(52%)	($145,793)
	Newt Gingrich (R)	72,400	(48%)	($134,517)

SEVENTH DISTRICT

The 7th congressional district of Georgia covers the northwest corner of the state. On the southeast the district touches the Atlanta city limits; on the northwest it reaches the bounds of Chattanooga, Tennessee. (There is some dispute here about the state line—some Georgians insist that the suburb and battle site of Lookout Mountain is not really in Tennessee.) Most of the 7th's recent population growth has occurred around Marietta, in Cobb County near Atlanta, and in the Georgia suburbs of Chattanooga. Because there are few blacks in this part of north Georgia—no more than 5% of the electorate—racial issues have never played as big a role in politics here as in south Georgia. Nonetheless, George Wallace and Lester Maddox had little trouble carrying the area. For years the economic mainstays of the area have been textiles and carpets, but today its largest employer, and the most significant politically, has been the Lockheed Corporation. Lockheed's huge plant in Marietta, some 30 miles from downtown Atlanta, is where the C-5As were built and massive cost overruns incurred.

The 7th district has had a number of close congressional elections in recent years, due to the weaknesses of its incumbent congressmen. One, Democrat John Davis, was thought to have a drinking problem; after some close calls he was defeated in 1974. The winner was Larry McDonald, a urologist, who is known best in the Congress as a member of the John Birch Society. McDonald is an enthusiastic and tireless proselytizer of his various beliefs. He serves on the Armed Services Committee, where he works for an ever stronger defense, and he has put together some very creative amendments to help his fellow members express their disapproval of abortions and homosexuals.

While none of these beliefs go against the grain in the 7th district, McDonald has nonetheless been a controversial figure. He barely beat both Davis and his Republican opponent in 1974. He got barely enough votes to avoid a runoff in the 1976 primary, and he only got 55% against the self same Republican opponent. In 1978 textile manufacturer Smith Foster held him to 44% in the first primary and forced a runoff which McDonald just barely won. He did well in the general only because of a weak opponent. The charge is made again and again that McDonald is more interested in advancing his right wing views than in serving his constituents. Certainly McDonald seems to be an active idealist, in touch with a few other kindred spirits in Congress, but without clout in the traditional sense. Given his past electoral record, McDonald is almost certain to attract tough competition (one possible candidate: President Carter's son Jack, who lives in the district); and it seems likely that some day he will succumb. In the meantime he makes an original if somewhat eccentric contribution to the Congress.

Census Data Pop. 460,095. Central city, 0%; suburban, 54%. Median family income, $9,223; families above $15,000: 16%; families below $3,000: 10%. Median years education, 10.6.

The Voters

Median voting age 40.
Employment profile White collar, 43%. Blue collar, 47%. Service, 9%. Farm, 1%.
Ethnic groups Black, 7%. Total foreign stock, 2%.

Presidential vote

1976	Carter (D)	102,093	(64%)
	Ford (R)	56,820	(36%)
1972	Nixon (R)	91,477	(83%)
	McGovern (D)	18,726	(17%)

Rep. Larry McDonald (D) Elected 1974; b. Apr. 1, 1935, Atlanta; home, Marietta; Davidson Dol., Emory U., M.D. 1957; Methodist.

Career U.S. Navy Physician and Overseas Flight Surgeon; Residency, Grady Mem. Hosp., Atlanta, and U. of Mich. Hosp., Ann Arbor, Mich.; Jr. Mbr., McDonald Urology Clinic, Atlanta.

Offices 504 CHOB, 202-225-2931. Also 100 Cherokee St., Marietta 30060, 404-422-4480.

Committees *Armed Services* (22d). Subcommittees: NATO Standardization, Interoperability, and Readiness.

Group Ratings

	ADA	COPE	PC	RPN	NFU	LCV	CFA	NAB	NSI	ACA	NTU
1978	15	5	18	70	10	–	18	100	100	100	–
1977	5	9	23	62	17	15	15	–	–	100	65
1976	0	17	11	50	8	1	9	100	100	96	73

Key Votes

1) Increase Def Spnd	FOR	6) Alaska Lands Protect	AGN	11) Delay Auto Pol Cntrl	FOR
2) B-1 Bomber	FOR	7) Water Projects Veto	DNV	12) Sugar Price Escalator	FOR
3) Cargo Preference	AGN	8) Consum Protect Agcy	AGN	13) Pub Fin Cong Cmpgns	AGN
4) Dereg Nat Gas	FOR	9) Common Situs Picket	AGN	14) ERA Ratif Recissn	FOR
5) Kemp-Roth	FOR	10) Labor Law Revision	AGN	15) Prohibt Govt Abrtns	FOR

Election Results

1978 general	Larry McDonald (D)	47,090	(67%)	($331,925)
	Ernie Norsworthy (R)	23,698	(33%)	($9,767)
1978 run-off	Larry McDonald (D)	45,789	(51%)	
	Smith Foster (D)	43,188	(49%)	($208,739)
1978 primary	Larry McDonald (D)	33,323	(44%)	
	Smith Foster (D)	32,440	(43%)	
	Two others (D)	10,229	(13%)	
1976 general	Larry McDonald (D)	84,587	(55%)	($157,651)
	Quincy Collins (R)	68,947	(45%)	($72,638)

EIGHTH DISTRICT

The 8th congressional district is an elongated section of central and south Georgia. With the major exception of Macon—the home of inter alia the Allman Brothers Band—this is mostly a rural area that was once devoted to cotton, but now is mainly in peanuts, tobacco, chickens, and lumber. The once fertile soil here has been exhausted for years, and for years the area exported people—poor blacks and whites who left for the north or Atlanta to make a living. Some of this area once had black majorities, but until the sixties most blacks here did not vote, and they have only recently become a force in local politics.

Like so many parts of the Deep South, the 8th district has had its partisan political leanings reversed by the presidential campaign of Jimmy Carter. Before Carter this was prime conservative territory—it went for Goldwater in 1964, Wallace in 1968, and Nixon in 1972, all by overwhelming margins. Carter carried every county for the Democrats in 1976. That year also saw a change in the district's congressional representation, although one that represented a considerably milder ideological shift.

For ten years before Carter's victory the Congressman from the 8th was W. S. "Bill" Stuckey, a member of the family that started the pecan candy and gift shops that can be seen at interstate highway interchanges in most parts of the country. Stuckey beat an incumbent in the 1966 primary and spent a lot of money when he had to—as when he faced Macon Mayor Ronnie "Machine Gun" Thompson in the 1972 general election. In the House and on the Commerce Committee Stuckey voted as one would expect a major stockholder of a food products conglomerate to vote. At 41, with an apparently safe seat, he retired from Congress in 1976, leaving a prime open seat.

The winner was a man with a country boy name and a capacity for adroit political maneuvers. After serving six years in the legislature as a Republican, Billy Lee Evans found his Macon constituency redistricted in 1974 and promptly became a Democrat. Two years later he won the Democratic congressional primary with a base of support from Maconites and blacks. He turned around and won the general election against a former state senator with heavy margins in the rural counties. With a moderate to conservative voting record, Evans can look forward to a long congressional career.

Census Data Pop. 458,097. Central city, 27%; suburban, 5%. Median family income, $6,836; families above $15,000: 11%; families below $3,000: 20%. Median years education, 9.8.

The Voters

Median voting age 43.
Employment profile White collar, 37%. Blue collar, 42%. Service, 15%. Farm, 6%.
Ethnic groups Black, 31%.

Presidential vote

1976	Carter (D)	110,789	(75%)
	Ford (R)	37,348	(25%)
1972	Nixon (R)	91,338	(78%)
	McGovern (D)	26,033	(22%)

Rep. Billy Lee Evans (D) Elected 1976; b. Nov. 10, 1941, Tifton; home Macon; U. of Ga., B.A. 1963, LL.B. 1965.

Career Practicing atty., 1965–77; Ga. House of Reps., 1969–76.

Offices 113 CHOB, 202-225-6531. Also Rm. 331 Fed. Bldg., Macon 31208, 912-742-5753.

Committees *Small Business* (22d). Subcommittees: SBA and SBIC Authority and General Small Business Problems; Special Small Business Problems.

Public Works and Transportation (20th). Subcommittees: Aviation, Oversight and Review; Economic Development.

Group Ratings

	ADA	COPE	PC	RPN	NFU	LCV	CFA	NAB	NSI	ACA	NTU
1978	15	32	18	45	60	–	9	40	80	65	–
1977	10	30	25	23	73	18	20	–	–	48	28

Key Votes

1) Increase Def Spnd	FOR	6) Alaska Lands Protect	FOR	11) Delay Auto Pol Cntrl	FOR
2) B-1 Bomber	AGN	7) Water Projects Veto	AGN	12) Sugar Price Escalator	FOR
3) Cargo Preference	FOR	8) Consum Protect Agcy	AGN	13) Pub Fin Cong Cmpgns	AGN
4) Dereg Nat Gas	AGN	9) Common Situs Picket	AGN	14) ERA Ratif Recissn	FOR
5) Kemp-Roth	AGN	10) Labor Law Revision	AGN	15) Prohibt Govt Abrtns	FOR

Election Results

1978 general	Billy Evans (D), unopposed			($186,027)
1978 primary	Billy Evans (D), unopposed			
1976 general	Billy Evans (D)	91,351	(70%)	($157,208)
	Billy Adams (R)	39,623	(30%)	($173,763)

NINTH DISTRICT

The northeastern corner of Georgia is hundreds of miles from the cotton, peanut, and tobacco farmlands of Confederate south Georgia. Into this remote part of the state cut the southernmost ridges of the Appalachians, and the culture here is more of the mountains than the Deep South. In some mountain counties a Republican tradition lives on from the days of the Civil War when this area opposed slavery and secession. And other mountain traditions survive: the red clay hills here are reputed to contain more moonshine stills than any other part of the United States.

This bit of Appalachia forms about half of the 9th congressional district of Georgia. The remainder includes, on the west, a few suburbs of Chattanooga, Tennessee, and, to the south, some of the upland Piedmont counties adjoining Interstate 85. This highway might well be called the Textile Route; within a few miles of its interchanges, between Atlanta and Durham, North Carolina, lies perhaps half the textile manufacturing capacity of the nation. Also metropolitan Atlanta is making its way inexorably north out Interstate 85 into the 9th's Gwinnett County, one of the fastest-growing in Georgia. The people moving out are not so much the urban sophisticates Atlanta likes to boast of as they are people who find hilly views from the new subdivisions or apartment complexes of Lliburn or Norcross a suggestion of the rural land they once knew so well.

Overall the Dixie Democrats of the Piedmont and the foothills far outnumber the mountain Republicans in the 9th. Democrats have lost this district only in national elections. In congressional politics there seldom is a significant contest. For 24 years, until 1976, the 9th district was represented by Phil Landrum, a Democrat known as the leading congressional voice of the textile industry. This is one of the least unionized major industries in the nation, and Landrum co-authored the 1959 Landrum-Griffin Act, the last piece of major labor legislation Congress has passed. Landrum was also one of the leading supporters of tariffs and other forms of trade protection for the domestic textile industry.

After experiencing some opposition in the 1974 primary, Landrum decided to retire in 1976. He was able to pass the district along to a former aide, Ed Jenkins. But Jenkins had to win a multi-candidate primary and then a runoff as well as the general election that year. And even two years later, he was still given some trouble in the primary by an opponent who was able to carry Gwinnett County. Jenkins has taken Landrum's seat on the House Ways and Means Committee, but he does not have his predecessor's clout in the House nor yet his unchallenged position in the 9th district.

Census Data Pop. 457,247. Central city, 0%; suburban, 16%. Median family income, $7,657; families above $15,000: 10%; families below $3,000: 14%. Median years education, 9.6.

The Voters

Median voting age 41.
Employment profile White collar, 34%. Blue collar, 53%. Service, 9%. Farm, 4%.
Ethnic groups Black, 6%.

Presidential vote

1976	Carter (D)	117,461	(71%)
	Ford (R)	48,169	(29%)
1972	Nixon (R)	89,299	(82%)
	McGovern (D)	19,544	(18%)

Rep. Ed Jenkins (D) Elected 1976; b. Jan. 4, 1933, Young Harris; home, Jasper; Young Harris Col, A.A. 1951, Emory U., U. of Ga., LL.B. 1959; Baptist.

Career Coast Guard, 1952–55; Admin. Asst. to U.S. Rep. Phil Landrum, 1959–62; Asst. U.S. Atty., North Dist. of Ga., 1962–64; Practicing atty., 1964–76; Jasper City Atty.; Pickens Co. Atty.

Offices 217 CHOB, 202-225-5211. Also P.O. Box 70, Jasper 30143, 404-692-2022.

Committees *Ways and Means* (17th). Subcommittees: Oversight; Trade.

Group Ratings

	ADA	COPE	PC	RPN	NFU	LCV	CFA	NAB	NSI	ACA	NTU
1978	5	18	33	43	56	–	23	80	86	73	–
1977	15	30	30	17	58	35	30	–	–	65	33

Key Votes

1) Increase Def Spnd	FOR	6) Alaska Lands Protect	FOR	11) Delay Auto Pol Cntrl	FOR
2) B-1 Bomber	AGN	7) Water Projects Veto	AGN	12) Sugar Price Escalator	AGN
3) Cargo Preference	AGN	8) Consum Protect Agcy	AGN	13) Pub Fin Cong Cmpgns	AGN
4) Dereg Nat Gas	AGN	9) Common Situs Picket	AGN	14) ERA Ratif Recissn	FOR
5) Kemp-Roth	AGN	10) Labor Law Revision	AGN	15) Prohibt Govt Abrtns	DNV

Election Results

1978 general	Ed Jenkins (D)	47,264	(77%)	($127,124)
	David Ashworth (R)	14,172	(23%)	($16,163)
1978 primary	Ed Jenkins (D)	50,319	(64%)	
	Ray W. Gunnin (D)	27,711	(36%)	($118,344)
1976 general	Ed Jenkins (D)	113,245	(79%)	($142,431)
	Louise Wofford (R)	29,954	(21%)	($8,301)

TENTH DISTRICT

The 10th congressional district of Georgia is a group of 21 counties in the northern part of th state. The district is anchored by the cities of Athens in the northwest and Augusta in the eas Athens, site of the University of Georgia (and home of former Secretary of State Dean Rusk), an Augusta, home of the until recently all white Masters golf tournament, have over the years tende to vote like metropolitan Atlanta, supporting whoever was opposing George Wallace or Leste Maddox. Augusta has one of the state's best organized black communities outside Atlanta, an candidates who are considered moderate or liberal can ordinarily expect majorities there

The rest of the 10th district—primarily rural and small town counties—has a completel different political tradition, akin to what is found in south Georgia. There are a few black majorit counties, and one with a black-controlled local government. But most of this area was in ope rebellion against the national Democratic Party from the passage of the Civil Rights Act of 196 until the nomination of Jimmy Carter in 1976.

As in the 8th and the 9th districts, the year of Carter's election as president also saw the electio of a new congressman. The old incumbent, Robert Stephens, retired. He was a courtly Democra with a proud antebellum name who served on the Banking Committee as a kind of antithesis of it populist Chairman, Wright Patman of Texas. The new Congressman, Doug Barnard, also serve on banking, and indeed his own background in business is as a banker. But he also has a interesting political background. He was a top aide to Carl Sanders, the Governor elected in 196 who was considered a racial moderate in his time; Sanders Jimmy Carter's opponent in the 197 Georgia gubernatorial runoff, carried Atlanta and his home town of Augusta. To win th congressional nomination, Barnard had to beat a former aide of Lester Maddox; he prevailed i the runoff with 52%, with the help of big margins in Augusta and Athens. He was reelecte without difficulty in 1978.

Census Data Pop. 460,829. Central city, 13%; suburban, 22%. Median family income, $7,307 families above $15,000: 11%; families below $3,000: 17%. Median years education, 10.5

The Voters

Median voting age 38.
Employment profile White collar, 39%. Blue collar, 43%. Service, 15%. Farm, 3%.
Ethnic groups Black, 33%. Total foreign stock, 3%.

Presidential vote

1976	Carter (D)	89,733	(66%)
	Ford (R)	46,493	(34%)
1972	Nixon (R)	81,220	(73%)
	McGovern (D)	30,014	(27%)

Rep. Doug Barnard (D) Elected 1976; b. Mar. 20, 1922, Augusta; home Augusta; Augusta Col., Mercer U., B.A. 1943, LL.B. 1948; Baptist

Career Army, WWII; Banker, Ga. Railroad Bank and Trust, 1948–49 1950–62, 1966–76; Fed. Resv. Bank of Atlanta, 1949–50; Exec. Secy. t the Gov. of Ga., 1963–66.

Offices 418 CHOB, 202-225-4101. Also Federal Bldg., Athens 30603 404-546-2194.

Committees *Banking, Finance and Urban Affairs* (25th). Subcommittees: Domestic Monetary Policy; Financial Institutions Supervision, Regulation, and Insurance; General Oversight and Renegotiation; International Trade, Investment and Monetary Policy.

Small Business (23d). Subcommittees: SBA and SBIC Authority and General Small Business Problems.

Group Ratings

	ADA	COPE	PC	RPN	NFU	LCV	CFA	NAB	NSI	ACA	NTU
1978	10	5	18	60	40	–	9	83	90	75	–
1977	20	35	30	46	55	35	20	–	–	69	31

Key Votes

1) Increase Def Spnd	FOR	6) Alaska Lands Protect	FOR	11) Delay Auto Pol Cntrl	FOR
2) B-1 Bomber	AGN	7) Water Projects Veto	AGN	12) Sugar Price Escalator	FOR
3) Cargo Preference	AGN	8) Consum Protect Agcy	AGN	13) Pub Fin Cong Cmpgns	AGN
4) Dereg Nat Gas	FOR	9) Common Situs Picket	AGN	14) ERA Ratif Recissn	FOR
5) Kemp-Roth	FOR	10) Labor Law Revision	AGN	15) Prohibt Govt Abrtns	AGN

Election Results

1978 general	Doug Barnard, Jr. (D), unopposed			($41,709)
1978 primary	Doug Barnard, Jr. (D)	48,096	(72%)	
	Betty Hemenway (D)	18,670	(28%)	($6,203)
1976 general	Doug Barnard, Jr. (D), unopposed			($144,870)

HAWAII

Three thousand miles of Pacific Ocean separate Hawaii from the rest of the United States and, as one might expect, Hawaiian politics differs considerably from the mainland's. Part of the reason is the Islands' unique ethnic and racial composition. The native Polynesians, the people Captain Cook found here in 1778 and whose royal family ruled Hawaii until 1898, are not a small minority, often intermixed with Asian and Caucasian stock. (But the Polynesians have the Islands' highest birth rate, and their percentage will rise in the future.) The Japanese-Americans, who came to Hawaii to work in the pineapple plantations, in 1970 made up 28% of the state's population; there are also many Chinese and Filipino-Americans living here, and even a Portuguese ethnic group. Hawaii is the only state of the fifty where Caucasians—or haoles, as they are called—are a distinct minority.

For the first couple of years after statehood, Hawaii voted Republican; it had become a state during Eisenhower's second term, over the opposition of Southern Democrats. Soon, however, a remarkable Democratic organization took control of the state's politics—and, despite challenges, has never relinquished it. One of its leaders was John Burns, who was elected Governor in 1962 and remained in office until he retired because of illness in 1974. Another was Daniel Inouye, the state's first Congressman-at-Large and Senator since 1962. Inouye was a distinguished member of the group of Japanese-Americans who fought in the Nisei 442d Infantry Regimental Command Team, the most decorated and casualty-ridden American military unit in World War II. Returning to Hawaii after the war, Inouye and other 442d veterans, like Hawaii's other Senator, Spark Matsunaga, moved into the empty ranks of the territorial Democratic Party—and soon came to dominate it. The other major component of Hawaii's Democratic organization is the International Longshoremen's and Warehousemen's Union (ILWU). This is the largest union in ocean-commerce-dependent Hawaii, and an organization with a stormy radical past; its president still is Harry Bridges, who used to be denounced as a Communist and now deals amicably with the big shipowners. The ILWU's clout at the polls in Hawaii is legendary; from 1960 until 1972 no major candidate endorsed by the ILWU lost an election.

Daniel Inouye is now Hawaii's senior elected official, the only person who has held major statewide office in the 20 years since statehood. He is also probably the most popular politician in Hawaii: he won more than 80% of the vote in his last two elections, and he is expected to do well again when his seat is up in 1980. He has also become a national figure of some importance. He keynoted the 1968 Democratic National Convention, but his greatest notice came when he served on the Senate Watergate Committee in 1973. His dignified, well prepared performance contrasted crisply with the performance of some of the witnesses—and with lawyer John J. Wilson's tawdry "little Jap" remark.

Inouye is known in the Senate as a loyal Democrat and a strong believer in the policies the nation has followed in recent years. He steadfastly supported President Johnson's domestic and Vietnam war policies; he would have otherwise hardly been chosen keynoter. As Chairman and member of the special committee on intelligence, he generally took a hard line position, questioning the nomination of Theodore Sorenson to be head of CIA and expressing concern for the security of agency operations. As a member of the Senate Appropriations Committee, Inouye supports federal programs to solve both foreign and domestic problems; while an Appropriations member like William Proxmire is temperamentally inclined to question spending programs, Inouye is temperamentally inclined to accept them. That does not mean that he is not prepared and does not scrutinize the budget thoroughly; he does. But he is one senator who still believes in the basic philosophy behind the New Deal and traditional Democratic programs. Inouye is currently the fifth-ranking Democrat on Appropriations, and stands a good chance of becoming Chairman one day; he also has a high ranking seat on the Commerce Committee. Inouye has been mentioned as a possible vice presidential candidate, but that seems unlikely, though not impossible. But with his strong political standing in Hawaii and his comparatively young age, he is likely to be a power in the Senate for many years to come.

Hawaii's other senator, Spark Matsunaga, is less senior and less well known, although he is actually older than Inouye. Matsunaga sat in the House for 14 years, and he won his Senate seat in a 1976 primary fight with his fellow representative, Patsy Mink. Despite their similar voting records, there was a contrast between them. Mink was something of a rebel—an early opponent of the Vietnam war, for example, a position frowned upon in the land of Pearl Harbor. Matsunaga, on the other hand, was close to the House leadership and not a boat-rocker. Matsunaga won the October primary by a 52%-40% margin, and the general election was anticlimactic. The Republican candidate, the state's first Governor, William Quinn, came out against heavy federal spending; but Hawaii, which receives heavy military spending, federal aid to impacted areas, and so on, was not particularly interested in the theme.

Matsunaga, with seats on the Finance and Energy Committees, has one of the more liberal voting records in the Senate. His seat is not up until 1982, and there is no particular reason to suppose that he would be denied a second term.

For nearly a dozen years after its first big victory in 1962, the Democratic machine built by Burns, Inouye, and the ILWU dominated the state's politics. But since Burns's retirement in 1974 the Democrats have been more fragmented, and there have been pitched battles for control of the state government. One issue is growth. Hawaii has experienced rapid population growth in the sixties and seventies. Most of the population is on the island of Oahu, crowded beneath large mountains and increasingly packed into giant high rises. As Governor, Burns encouraged growth and development. He was challenged by his lieutenant governor on the issue in the 1970 primary and prevailed. More recently, the current of opinion seems to be going the other way. Burns's hand-picked successor, George Ariyoshi, has urged that there should be limits on the number of people who can move to the Islands.

In 1974 and 1978 Hawaii politics has been livened by bitter gubernatorial primaries between Ariyoshi and Honolulu Mayor Frank Fasi. Here there have been stark differences in character as well as on issues. Ariyoshi is not a charismatic figure; "quiet but effective" was his 1978 slogan. His speaking style is such that a half-hour documentary campaign film featured little footage of the Governor talking and employed an actor to play him as a young man. Fasi in contrast is dynamic and flamboyant. He is also, in the opinion of some, something less than honest. In 1977 he was charged with accepting bribes by a prosecutor employed by the Ariyoshi Administration. Eventually the charges were dropped, but the controversy continued. The ethnic differences between the two also are reflected in their constituencies. Ariyoshi has a strong Japanese-American following, while Fasi has strong support from Chinese, Filipinos, and haoles. Ariyoshi has beaten Fasi now twice, but both times by only narrow margins. In both cases the Republican candidates proved weak; the real fight for control of the state government comes in the October Democratic primary.

Hawaii has two congressional districts: the 1st is the city of Honolulu and the 2d includes all of the rest of Oahu and the Neighbor Islands. Hawaii has never elected a Republican to the House, and despite the relinquishments of the seats by Matsunaga and Mink in 1976, it did not do so that year either. The winner in the 1st district was Cecil Heftel, a millionaire broadcaster who had nearly beaten Hiram Fong in the 1970 Senate race. Heftel spent more than $300,000 of his own money in 1976; the question is why someone who could afford as much would want to move from Hawaii to Washington, D.C. Heftel had a bitter primary, supported by Inuoye but strongly opposed by Ariyoshi. The Republican candidate had 45% in the general election, but after two years in office, Heftel was reelected with more than three-quarters of the vote. In the 2d district, the whole contest was determined in the Democratic primary, which was won by Daniel Akaka. Heftel and Akaka have virtually identical voting records in the House, and both seem to hold very safe seats.

On election night in 1976 Hawaii (and Mississippi) gave Jimmy Carter the crucial electoral votes he needed to win, at least on the television networks' projections. But Carter won by only a narrow margin in a state with such a strong Democratic preponderance in state elections. The reason seems to be Hawaii's tilt toward the party in power. In 1972 it was heavily for Nixon, for example, and in 1964 and 1968 heavily for the Democrats; in 1960 and 1976, when Republicans held the White House, it went Democratic but only by small margins. This is a state that takes its patriotism very seriously, in part because the patriotism of some of its citizens was —unjustly—doubted within living memory, and in part because this is the only state whose population center has been under direct foreign attack. This analysis suggests that Jimmy Carter's Democrats should carry Hawaii in 1980, but it also suggests they may have problems if the Republicans can convince Hawaiians that the Democrats are soft on defense issues.

Census Data Pop. 769,913; 0.38% of U.S. total, 40th largest; Central city, 42%; suburban, 40%. Median family income, $11,552; 3d highest; families above $15,000: 33%; families below $3,000: 7%. Median years education, 12.3.

1977 Share of Federal Tax Burden $1,554,000,000; 0.45% of U.S. total, 36th largest.

1977 Share of Federal Outlays $2,065,800,000; 0.52% of U.S. total, 39th largest. Per capita federal spending, $2,338.

DOD	$995,085,000	29th (1.09%)	HEW	$467,998,000	42d (0.32%)
ERDA	$1,923,000	43d (0.03%)	HUD	$18,012,000	40th (0.43%)
NASA	$2,581,000	29th (0.07%)	VA	$60,479,000	46th (0.31%)
DOT	$109,652,000	36th (0.77%)	EPA	$6,974,000	49th (0.09%)
DOC	$50,684,000	41st (0.61%)	RevS	$41,239,000	39th (0.49%)
DOI	$7,787,000	45th (0.17%)	Debt	$44,801,000	43d (0.15%)
USDA	$59,113,000	45th (0.30%)	Other	$199,472,000	

Economic Base Finance, insurance and real estate; agriculture, notably sugarcane, pineapples, cattle and dairy products; food and kindred products; tourism; apparel and other textile products, especially women's and misses' outerwear; printing and publishing, especially newspapers; stone, clay and glass products, especially concrete, gypsum and plaster products.

Political Line-up Governor, George R. Ariyoshi (D). Senators, Daniel K. Inouye (D) and Spark M. Matsunaga (D). Representatives, 2 D. State Senate (18 D and 7 R); State House (42 D and 9 R).

The Voters

Registration 395,262 Total. 241,456 D (61%); 37,663 R (10%); 115,191 Non Affiliated (29%); 952 Other (–).
Median voting age 38
Employment profile White collar, 50%. Blue collar, 31%. Service, 16%. Farm, 3%.
Ethnic groups Japanese, 28%. Chinese, 7%. Filipino, 12%. Total foreign stock, 33%.

Presidential vote

1976	Carter (D)	147,375	(51%)
	Ford (R)	140,003	(49%)
1972	Nixon (R)	168,865	(62%)
	McGovern (D)	101,409	(38%)

Sen. Daniel K. Inouye (D) Elected 1962, seat up 1980; b. Sept. 7, 1924, Honolulu; home, Honolulu; U. of Hawaii, B.A. 1950, Geo. Wash. U., J.D. 1952; Methodist.

Career Army, WWII; Honolulu Asst. Prosecuting Atty., 1953–54; Practicing atty., 1954–59; Hawaii Territorial House of Reps., 1954–58, Majority Ldr.; Hawaii Territorial Senate, 1958–59; U.S. House of Reps., 1959–63.

Offices 105 RSOB, 202-224-3934. Also 300 Ala Moana Blvd., Honolulu 96850, 808-546-7550.

Committees *Appropriations* (5th). Subcommittees: Defense; Foreign Operations (Chairman); Labor, HEW, and Related Agencies; Military Construction; State, Justice, Commerce, the Judiciary, and Related Agencies.

Commerce, Science, and Transportation (5th). Subcommittee: Aviation; Communication; Merchant Marine and Tourism (Chairman).

Select Committee on Intelligence (6th).

Select Committee on Indian Affairs.

Group Ratings

	ADA	COPE	PC	RPN	NFU	LCV	CFA	NAB	NSI	ACA	NTU
1978	60	81	45	50	50	54	25	11	25	19	–
1977	60	86	43	38	89	–	40	–	–	13	16
1976	45	73	48	46	88	49	35	13	43	0	10

Key Votes

1) Warnke Nom	FOR	6) Egypt-Saudi Arms	FOR	11) Hosptl Cost Contnmnt	AGN
2) Neutron Bomb	FOR	7) Draft Restr Pardon	FOR	12) Clinch River Reactor	DNV
3) Waterwy User Fee	AGN	8) Wheat Price Support	FOR	13) Pub Fin Cong Cmpgns	FOR
4) Dereg Nat Gas	AGN	9) Panama Canal Treaty	FOR	14) ERA Ratif Recissn	FOR
5) Kemp-Roth	AGN	10) Labor Law Rev Clot	FOR	15) Med Necssy Abrtns	FOR

Election Results

1974 general	Daniel K. Inouye (D)	207,454	(83%)	($205,265)
	James D. Kimmel (People's Party)	42,767	(17%)	(NA)
1974 primary	Daniel K. Inouye (D), unopposed			
1968 general	Daniel K. Inouye (D)	189,248	(85%)	
	Wayne L. Thiessen (R)	34,008	(15%)	

Sen. Spark M. Matsunaga (D) Elected 1976, seat up 1982; b. Oct. 8, 1916, Kukuiula; home, Honolulu; U. of Hawaii, B.Ed. 1941, Harvard U., J.D. 1951; Episcopalian.

Career Public school teacher, 1941; Army, WWII; Vets. Counsellor, Surplus Prop. Ofc., U.S. Dept. of Interior, 1945–47; Chf., Priority Claimants' Div., War Assets Admin., 1947–48; Honolulu Asst. Public Prosecutor, 1952–54; Practicing atty., 1954–63; Hawaii Territorial House of Reps., 1954–59, majcrity ldr.; U.S. House of Reps., 1963–77.

Offices 362 RSOB, 202-224-6361. Also 300 Ala Moana Blvd., Honolulu 96850, 808-546-7555.

Committees *Energy and Natural Resources* (8th). Subcommittees: Energy Conservation and Supply; Energy Research and Development; Energy Resources and Materials Production.

Finance (8th). Subcommittees: Health; Private Pension Plans and Employee Fringe Benefits; Tourism and Sugar (Chairman).

Veterans' Affairs (6th).

Group Ratings

	ADA	COPE	PC	RPN	NFU	LCV	CFA	NAB	NSI	ACA	NTU
1978	70	89	58	78	63	67	50	0	20	5	–
1977	80	85	48	30	91	–	44	–	–	4	22
1976	65	91	66	53	92	42	91	0	30	9	11

Key Votes

1) Warnke Nom	FOR	6) Egypt-Saudi Arms	AGN	11) Hosptl Cost Contnmnt	FOR
2) Neutron Bomb	AGN	7) Draft Restr Pardon	FOR	12) Clinch River Reactor	AGN
3) Waterwy User Fee	DNV	8) Wheat Price Support	FOR	13) Pub Fin Cong Cmpgns	FOR
4) Dereg Nat Gas	AGN	9) Panama Canal Treaty	FOR	14) ERA Ratif Recissn	FOR
5) Kemp-Roth	AGN	10) Labor Law Rev Clot	FOR	15) Med Necssy Abrtns	FOR

Election Results

1976 general	Spark M. Matsunaga (D)	162,305	(57%)	($435,130)
	William Quinn (R)	122,724	(43%)	($415,138)
1976 primary	Spark M. Matsunaga (D)	109,731	(52%)	
	Patsy Mink (D)	84,732	(40%)	
	Three others (D)	16,697	(8%)	
1970 general	Hiram L. Fong (R)	124,163	(52%)	
	Cecil Heftel (D)	116,597	(48%)	

Gov. George R. Ariyoshi (D) Elected 1974, after serving as Acting Gov. since Oct. 1973, term expires Dec. 1982; b. Mar. 12, 1926, Honolulu; U. of Hawaii, U. of Mich., B.A. 1949, J.D. 1952.

Career Army, WWII; Practicing atty., 1953–70; Hawaii Territorial House of Reps., 1954–58; Hawaii Territorial Senate, 1958–59, State Senate, 1959–70, Maj. Ldr., 1965–66, Maj. Floor Ldr., 1969–70; Lt. Gov. of Hawaii, 1970–74.

Offices Executive Chambers, State Capitol, Honolulu 96813, 808-548-5428.

Election Results

1978 general	George R. Ariyoshi (D)	153,394	(55%)
	John R. Leopold (R)	124,610	(45%)
1978 primary	George R. Ariyoshi (D)	130,527	(51%)
	Frank F. Fasi (D)	126,903	(49%)
1974 general	George R. Ariyoshi (D)	136,262	(55%)
	Randolph Crossley (R)	113,388	(45%)

FIRST DISTRICT

Census Data Pop. 362,119. Central city, 90%; suburban, 10%. Median family income, $12,491; families above $15,000: 38%; families below $3,000: 6%. Median years education, 12.5.

The Voters

Median voting age 38.
Employment profile White collar, 55%. Blue collar, 29%. Service, 16%. Farm, –%.
Ethnic groups Japanese, 31%. Chinese, 10%. Filipino, 9%. Total foreign stock, 35%.

Presidential vote

1976	Carter (D)	65,337	(49%)
	Ford (R)	67,234	(51%)
1972	Nixon (R)	82,729	(62%)
	McGovern (D)	49,994	(38%)

Rep. Cecil Heftel (D) Elected 1976; b. Sept. 30, 1924, Cook Co., Ill.; home, Honolulu; Ariz. St. U., B.S. 1951, U. of Utah, NYU; Church of Jesus Christ of Latter-Day Saints.

Career Army, WWII; Pres., Heftel Broadcasting, 1964– ; Dem. Nominee for U.S. Senate, 1970.

Offices 322 CHOB, 202-225-2726. Also Rm. 4104, 300 Ala Moana Blvd., Honolulu 96850, 808-546-8997.

Committees *Ways and Means* (21st) Subcommittees: Oversight; Health.

Group Ratings

	ADA	COPE	PC	RPN	NFU	LCV	CFA	NAB	NSI	ACA	NTU
1978	35	53	38	50	80	–	36	25	40	15	–
1977	60	86	60	33	83	53	50	–	–	15	21

Key Votes

1) Increase Def Spnd	FOR	6) Alaska Lands Protect	FOR	11) Delay Auto Pol Cntrl	FOR
2) B-1 Bomber	AGN	7) Water Projects Veto	AGN	12) Sugar Price Escalator	FOR
3) Cargo Preference	FOR	8) Consum Protect Agcy	FOR	13) Pub Fin Cong Cmpgns	DNV
4) Dereg Nat Gas	AGN	9) Common Situs Picket	FOR	14) ERA Ratif Recissn	AGN
5) Kemp-Roth	AGN	10) Labor Law Revision	FOR	15) Prohibt Govt Abrtns	AGN

Election Results

1978 general	Cecil Heftel (D)	84,552	(78%)	($174,306)
	William D. Spillane (R)	24,470	(22%)	($18,694)
1978 primary	Cecil Heftel (D)	92,597	(87%)	
	Two others (D)	13,438	(13%)	
1976 general	Cecil Heftel (D)	60,050	(44%)	($555,381)
	Fred Rohlfing (R)	53,745	(39%)	($229,349)
	Kathy Hoshijo (Ind.)	23,807	(17%)	($44,672)

SECOND DISTRICT

Census Data Pop. 407,794. Central city, 0%; suburban, 66%. Median family income, $10,848; families above $15,000: 28%; families below $3,000: 7%. Median years education, 12.2.

The Voters

Median voting age 38.
Employment profile White collar, 44%. Blue collar, 35%. Service, 15%. Farm, 6%.
Ethnic groups Japanese, 25%. Chinese, 4%. Filipino, 16%. Total foreign stock, 32%.

Presidential vote

1976	Carter (D)	82,018	(53%)
	Ford (R)	72,769	(47%)
1972	Nixon (R)	86,136	(63%)
	McGovern (D)	51,415	(37%)

Rep. Daniel K. Akaka (D) Elected 1976; b. Sept. 11, 1924, Honolulu; home, Honolulu; U. of Hawaii, B.Ed. 1952, M.Ed. 1966; Congregationalist.

Career Welder, mechanic and engineer, U.S. Corps of Engineers, 1943–46; Army, WWII; Public school teacher and principal, 1953–71; Dir., Hawaii Ofc. of Econ. Opportunity, 1971–74; Spec. Asst. to the Gov. of Hawaii in Human Resources, 1975–76; Dir., Progressive Neighborhoods Program 1966.

Offices 415 CHOB, 202-225-4906. Also Federal Bldg., Honolulu 96813. Also Rm. 5104 Kuhio, Fed. Bldg., Honolulu 96813, 808-546-8952.

Committees *Agriculture* (21st). Subcommittees: Domestic Marketing, Consumer Relations, and Nutrition; Family Farms, Rural Development, and Special Studies; Dairy and Poultry.

Merchant Marine and Fisheries (19th). Subcommittees: Fish and Wildlife; Maritime Education and Training.

Group Ratings

	ADA	COPE	PC	RPN	NFU	LCV	CFA	NAB	NSI	ACA	NTU
1978	55	80	50	27	70	–	50	9	40	7	–
1977	60	87	63	46	83	60	55	–	–	7	19

Key Votes

1) Increase Def Spnd	FOR	6) Alaska Lands Protect	FOR	11) Delay Auto Pol Cntrl	AGN
2) B-1 Bomber	FOR	7) Water Projects Veto	AGN	12) Sugar Price Escalator	FOR
3) Cargo Preference	FOR	8) Consum Protect Agcy	FOR	13) Pub Fin Cong Cmpgns	FOR
4) Dereg Nat Gas	AGN	9) Common Situs Picket	FOR	14) ERA Ratif Recissn	AGN
5) Kemp-Roth	AGN	10) Labor Law Revision	FOR	15) Prohibt Govt Abrtns	AGN

Election Results

1978 general	Daniel K. Akaka (D)	118,272	(88%)	($208,958)
	Charles Isaak (R)	15,697	(12%)	($7,016)
1978 primary	Daniel K. Akaka (D), unopposed			
1976 general	Daniel K. Akaka (D)	124,116	(84%)	($184,697)
	Hank Inouye (R)	23,917	(16%)	($7,413)

IDAHO

Like most of the other Rocky Mountain states, Idaho had its beginnings as a mining state. But Idaho has followed a different path of development. While most of the other Rocky Mountain states today have their populations concentrated in one or two metropolitan areas, Idaho's people can be found throughout most of the state. For although there is still some mining here, Idaho's principal economic concern today is agriculture. Potatoes, for which Idaho is famous, are grown in the rich farmlands of the panhandle region just east of Spokane, Washington, and along the Snake River valley in the southern part of the state. Idaho's largest city, Boise, with less than 100,000 people, is headquarters of some big national businesses, and has shown some rapid growth in the seventies. But Idahoans seem to want to preserve the character of their state, and do not want to see Boise become a somewhat smaller version of Denver or Phoenix.

Politically Idaho has moved from a populist and New Deal past to a very conservative present. Its populism comes from the days when William Jennings Bryan was urging unlimited coinage of silver; this was a movement of both moneyed silver interests and desperate farmers of the Plains and South. The New Deal had a broader base in Idaho, and it was helped by a suspicion of the Eastern bankers and financiers who were seen as the real leaders of the Republican Party. As late as 1960 John Kennedy was able to win 46% of the state's votes.

Perhaps it was the prominence of Eastern businessmen, professors, and intellectuals in the Kennedy-Johnson Administration which helped to spark the conservative movement here. Certainly there was a resentment over what was seen as intrusive federal policies and a disgust for social programs whose beneficiaries were perceived as distant, alien, and undeserving. Another factor was the increasing political conservatism of the Mormon Church—27% of Idaho's residents are Mormons, and the Church dominates much of the southern part of the state—during a period when political liberalism became identified increasingly with rejection of traditional cultural values.

Few people noticed, but in 1964 Barry Goldwater got 49% in Idaho—his best showing outside the Deep South and Arizona. In that same year, Idaho's 2d congressional district ousted its Democratic congressman for a Republican—the only district outside the South to do so in the year of the LBJ landslide. By 1968 Hubert Humphrey could win only 31% of the vote here; McGovern did even worse and Carter not much better, with 38%. The strength of Idaho's hard core right wing, with roots in many small towns and farming communities, was shown in the 1968 showing of George Wallace (13%, his best west of Texas), and even John Schmitz, the hapless American Party candidate in 1972, got 9%—his best showing in the nation. It was Lester Maddox's best state in 1976—and Gerald Ford's second best.

This is not to say that conservative Republicans have swept everything here. The last time they won the governorship was in 1966. But each of the Democrats' victories has resulted from special circumstances. In 1970 Cecil Andrus, the Democratic candidate, was able to seize on the Republican incumbent's willingness to let a mining company extract molybdenum from the scenic White Clouds area, to win his first term. Andrus combined a calm, conciliatory style with a determination to preserve Idaho's pleasant environment. In a small state, personal character is especially important in elections for governor, and Andrus's character helped him win reelection with 73% of the vote in 1974. He was strong enough to help bring in several Democratic statewide officeholders; and so, when Jimmy Carter made him Secretary of the Interior, Andrus was succeeded by a Democrat, John Evans.

Evans lacked Andrus's political style, but he managed state affairs in a manner satisfactory to voters. On issues, he probably has been more conservative than his predecessor, without dropping environmental matters from the agenda. Evans was blessed in the 1978 general election with an opponent whose strategy backfired. Allan Larsen, the Republican Speaker, is a Mormon, like Evans; but unlike Evans, he believes that the state should legislate Mormon rules of morality. His proposals to restrict liquor sales stirred great opposition in a state where more than 70% of the voters are not Mormons; hurting him even more was a feeling that the Mormon Church was trying to take over the state. Evans won reelection by a solid margin, with especially large margins in the northern panhandle of the state where there are few if any Mormons.

Another Democrat who has fared well in Idaho is Senator Frank Church. He has not only been elected to the Senate four times; he has also provided Idaho with its first presidential candidate since William Borah, the progressive Republican and isolationist who died in 1940. Like Borah, Church is an expert on foreign affairs and, again like Borah, he has not been afraid to dissent from presidents of either party. Church was first elected to the Senate at the age of 32 in 1956, beating a Republican candidate who had personal problems. Building on a friendship with Lyndon Johnson, Church won a seat on the Senate Foreign Relations Committee, but when Johnson was President, Church was one of the first senators to take a stand against the Vietnam war. Church is a strong backer of disarmament measures and one of the most vehement critics of the foreign aid program. He chaired the special Senate committee looking into alleged CIA abuses in 1975 and 1976 and, while critical of the agency (at one point he said it acted "like a rogue elephant"), was careful to recognize its legitimate purposes. Church is almost always well prepared on foreign policy issues; he speaks in a careful, almost schoolmasterish tone that owes something to old-fashioned oratorical styles.

Church is now Chairman of the Senate Foreign Relations Committee, a post he has long looked forward to assuming. It was clear when William Fulbright was defeated in 1974 that Church would have it soon, but he had to wait four years while John Sparkman held the chair before retiring. Church was an important part of the dovish majority of the Committee during the Vietnam war days, but the body he takes over now is different in composition, spirit, and subject matter. The Republicans added in 1979 are strong conservatives, and for the first time the Committee will have a minority staff rather than having all its members served on a bipartisan basis. Inevitably there will be more conflict and clash on the Committee; and while this prevents consensus it will also tend to force the Committee's majority to be better prepared to defend its positions when they reach the floor. Intellectually, Church and others who share his views seem considerably less aggressive and confident than they were a decade ago. They have had to stave off defeat for the Panama Canal Treaty in 1978, and in the 96th Congress they can expect to come to the defense of SALT II against passionate opposition.

Church himself supported the Canal Treaty and can be expected to support the arms agreement with the Russians. Those positions, like his opposition to the Vietnam war, could cause him problems in Idaho: the Canal Treaty was highly unpopular there, and SALT, though less unpopular, could be attacked as a giveaway to the Soviets. In the past Church has been able to invoke the Borah tradition, the idea that Idaho has once before elected a senator of national stature and leadership on foreign policy even though not all Idahoans agreed with each of his stands. Back in the middle sixties, he withstood a movement, of dubious legality, to recall him from the Senate; when it fizzled it made the 1968 race against him anticlimactic, and he won with 60% of the vote. Six years later, running against an unknown Republican, he won with 57%. Now, in 1980, he faces the voters of Idaho again, fresh after Panama and SALT.

Church has other assets besides his work on foreign affairs. He has, for one thing, used his Foreign Relations seat to attack the foreign aid program, and he is probably the best positioned opponent of foreign aid today. He has also steadfastly opposed federal gun control legislation. And he has kept a seat on the Senate Energy and Natural Resources (formerly Interior) Committee, on which he ranks second to Chairman Henry Jackson. He is concerned here less with overall energy policy than with traditional Interior Department matters—notably water. He works well with Jackson, despite their disagreement on foreign policy matters, and he keeps careful watch over Idaho's water needs. (Much of Idaho's farmland would be worthless without irrigation.) For a senator with such international interests, he spends considerable time in Idaho, and his oratorical speaking style does not prevent him from being effective in the personal campaigning which is so important in a state of this size.

Against Church's assets runs the general political trend in the state—and possibly strong opposition. One opponent mentioned is 1st district Congressman Steven Symms, an energetic activist of the far right in Congress. It was his aide who held Church to 57% in 1974; Symms is better known, he would be better financed, and 1980 is likely to be a more Republican year. Indeed, it is by no means impossible that an unknown candidate could give Church trouble. He will be fighting hard, though. He has been waiting 22 years for the Foreign Relations chair, and he will not give it up lightly after two years and at the comparatively youthful age of 56.

Church is one of the many senators who, at one time or another, has run for president. His race came in 1976, after he finished investigating the intelligence agencies. He followed a kind of western strategy, which was surprisingly successful: he beat Carter narrowly in Nebraska and won in Idaho, Montana, and Oregon. One wonders how he might have done in California were Jerry Brown not in the race. Church also competed in Ohio, unsuccessfully, and thereafter turned his efforts to what amounted to a campaign for the vice presidential nomination. Considering how such things usually go, this was no disaster; he apparently was given serious consideration before Carter picked Walter Mondale. Moreover, Church's presidential campaign seems to have hurt him less than it did some of his rivals in their home states. He campaigned, after all, as a westerner, and he tended to solidify rather than reduce his identification with Idaho.

The state's junior Senator is Republican James McClure. First elected to the House, McClure is perhaps the senior, if not the most influential, of the Rocky Mountain conservatives who have become an important force in the Senate. He is an opponent of the Panama Canal Treaty, of voting representation for the District of Columbia, of measures to ban phosphate detergents in the

Great Lakes area, and of banning high emission cars in areas like Idaho. He strongly supports nuclear power, and in 1978 provided a key vote for compromise on the Administration energy bill in return for support of a $417 million energy research project in Idaho. On energy matters McClure of course favors deregulation and maximum leeway for private enterprise.

McClure was first elected to the House in 1966 and won his seat in the Senate in 1972. His campaign that year may be best remembered for his charge that his Democratic opponent favored a potato boycott. Although there was no substantiation whatever for the allegation, it helped McClure in a state where the potato crop is very much number one. In 1978 McClure might very well have had difficulty if Cecil Andrus had run against him, but Andrus was not going to abandon the Interior Secretaryship so short a time after taking it. McClure's opponent was a former television news reporter, who in the midst of the campaign had a novel published by Doubleday. His luck did not run until November and McClure was reelected by better than a 2–1 margin.

When McClure first went to the Senate, he left vacant the 1st congressional district, traditionally the more Democratic of Idaho's two seats. This includes the panhandle, which is connected with the rest of Idaho by just one two-lane highway and no railroads; economically and sociologically the area is part of Spokane, Washington's "Inland Empire." With a large labor vote in Lewiston and Coeur d'Alene and the University of Idaho in Moscow, the panhandle often produces Democratic majorities.

But in 1st district politics these days, the panhandle is outvoted by Boise and nearby Canyon County, both heavily conservative. These votes have been more than enough to produce solid, though not overwhelming, victories for Republican Steven Symms. Elected as a young apple grower and enthusiastic believer in free market economics, Symms has succeeded in having some impact on a House which, initially, regarded his doctrines as exotic. With a few other like-minded members—Robert Bauman of Maryland, Larry McDonald of Georgia—Symms has formed and staffed his own conservative operation; and while he is still considered too extreme by the Republican leadership, he is entitled to some satisfaction with the increasing popularity of free market ideas. Symms is reported to be considering running against Frank Church in the 1980 Senate race. While he will probably encourage a disciple to run in the 1st, this is a district which could be won by anyone, even a Democrat.

The state's 2d congressional district is more of a geographic unit. Most of its people live within a dozen or so miles of the Snake River, in small cities or farmhouses near the irrigation ditches that bring water to the potato fields. The district includes Sun Valley, the Craters of the Moon National Monument, Idaho's small slice of Yellowstone National Park, and the remains of the Teton Dam, which gave way in 1976 and caused great loss of life and property. Much of this area is Mormon country, and except for the small city of Pocatello, usually Republican. It is also the home of Idaho's right wing political subculture. The John Birch Society is strong in the sparsely populated farm counties, and one group, the Posse Comitatus, purports to act as vigilantes, going to the lengths of surrounding and intimidating a policeman about to testify about their activities. It is not hard to see how a few enthusiastic, articulate right wingers can dominate a town's school board and, by assiduous proselytizing and organization, change a small county's voting patterns. The results are clear in the election returns from southern Idaho over the last 15 years. They show up, for example, in the fact that John Schmitz actually outpolled George McGovern in four counties here in 1972.

Additional evidence comes from congressional elections. For this is the district that sends to Congress George Hansen, an ultraconservative Republican with electoral weaknesses which would have been fatal to his career in almost any other district. Hansen has been around a long time now, winning the seat in 1964 and 1966, running unsuccessfully against Frank Church in 1968 and James McClure in 1972, then coming back and beating his far more moderate successor, Congressman Orval Hansen, in the 1974 Republican primary. That race got George Hansen into considerable trouble, since he failed utterly to report some campaign contributions. In 1975 Hansen pleaded guilty to campaign law violations and was sentenced to two months in jail, which was changed to a $42,000 fine. That gave Hansen problems in 1976, when underfinanced Democrat Stan Kress got 49% of the vote. Kress had more money in 1978, but Hansen's problems were farther behind him and the incumbent got 58%. However, he won against a relatively unknown Republican with only 56% in the primary, suggesting that he may be vulnerable to a Republican challenge in the future.

Census Data Pop. 713,008; 0.35% of U.S. total, 42d largest; Central city, 11%; suburban, 5%. Median family income, $8,381; 34th highest; families above $15,000: 13%; families below $3,000: 11%. Median years education, 12.3.

1977 Share of Federal Tax Burden $1,071,000,000; 0.31% of U.S. total, 45th largest.

1977 Share of Federal Outlays $1,689,186,000; 0.43% of U.S. total, 42d largest. Per capita federal spending, $2,057.

DOD	$160,478,000	48th	(0.18%)	HEW	$467,293,000	43d	(0.32%)
ERDA	$172,536,000	12th	(2.92%)	HUD	$13,644,000	44th	(0.32%)
NASA	—			VA	$81,360,000	42d	(0.42%)
DOT	$66,007,000	43d	(0.46%)	EPA	$14,791,000	45th	(0.18%)
DOC	$160,478,000	39th	(1.93%)	RevS	$28,678,000	43d	(0.34%)
DOI	$248,020,000	7th	(5.33%)	Debt	$41,457,000	45th	(0.14%)
USDA	$189,979,000	38th	(0.95%)	Other	$44,465,000		

Economic Base Agriculture, notably cattle, potatoes, dairy products and wheat; food and kindred products, especially canned, cured and frozen foods; lumber and wood products, especially general sawmills and planing mills; finance, insurance and real estate; chemicals and allied products, especially industrial chemicals; trailer coaches and other transportation equipment.

Political Line-up Governor, John V. Evans (D). Senators, Frank Church (D) and James A. McClure (R). Representatives, 2 R. State Senate (19 R and 16 D); State House (50 R and 20 D).

The Voters

Registration 515,260 Total. No party registration.
Median voting age 43
Employment profile White collar, 43%. Blue collar, 33%. Service, 13%. Farm, 11%.
Ethnic groups Total foreign stock, 10%.

Presidential vote

1976	Carter (D)	126,549	(38%)
	Ford (R)	204,151	(62%)
1972	Nixon (R)	199,384	(71%)
	McGovern (D)	80,826	(29%)

1976 Democratic Presidential Primary

Church	58,570	(79%)
Carter	8,818	(12%)
Others	7,017	(9%)

1976 Republican Presidential Primary

Reagan	66,743	(75%)
Ford	22,323	(25%)

Sen. Frank Church (D) Elected 1956, seat up 1980; b. July 25, 1924, Boise; home, Boise; Stanford U., B.A. 1947, LL.B. 1950; Presbyterian.

Career Army, WWII; Practicing atty., 1950–56; Keynote Spkr., Dem. Natl. Conv., 1960; Mbr., U.S. Delegation to U.N., 1966.

Offices 245 RSOB, 202-224-6142. Also 304 Fed. Ofc. Bldg., Boise 83702, 208-384-1700, and 2d Floor, Fed. Bldg., Pocatello 83201, 208-236-6775.

Committees *Energy and Natural Resources* (2d). Subcommittees: Energy Research and Development (Chairman); Energy Resources and Materials Production; Parks, Recreation, and Renewable Resources.

Foreign Relations (Chairman).

Special Committee on Aging (2d).

Group Ratings

	ADA	COPE	PC	RPN	NFU	LCV	CFA	NAB	NSI	ACA	NTU
1978	70	74	58	67	89	64	40	38	20	26	–
1977	65	83	58	55	90	–	64	–	–	21	37
1976	45	92	56	50	88	64	43	22	11	0	30

Key Votes

1) Warnke Nom	FOR	6) Egypt-Saudi Arms	AGN	11) Hosptl Cost Contnmnt	AGN
2) Neutron Bomb	AGN	7) Draft Restr Pardon	FOR	12) Clinch River Reactor	FOR
3) Waterwy User Fee	FOR	8) Wheat Price Support	DNV	13) Pub Fin Cong Cmpgns	FOR
4) Dereg Nat Gas	AGN	9) Panama Canal Treaty	FOR	14) ERA Ratif Recissn	AGN
5) Kemp-Roth	AGN	10) Labor Law Rev Clot	FOR	15) Med Necssy Abrtns	AGN

Election Results

1974 general	Frank Church (D)	145,140	(57%)	($300,300)
	Robert L. Smith (R)	109,072	(43%)	($127,926)
1974 primary	Frank Church (D)	53,659	(86%)	
	One other (D)	8,904	(14%)	
1968 general	Frank Church (D)	173,482	(60%)	
	George V. Hansen (R)	114,394	(40%)	

Sen. James A. McClure (R) Elected 1972, seat up 1978; b. Dec. 27, 1924, Payette; home, Payette; U. of Idaho, J.D. 1950; Methodist.

Career Practicing atty., 1950–66; Payette Co. Atty., 1950–56; Payette City Atty., 1953–66; Idaho Senate 1960–66; U.S. House of Reps., 1967–73.

Offices 5229 DSOB, 202-224-2752. Also 304 N. 8th St., Rm. 434, Boise 83708, 208-384-1560, and 305 Fed. Bldg., Coeur d'Alene 83814, 208-664-3086.

Committees *Appropriations* (8th). Subcommittees: Agriculture and Related Agencies; Defense; Energy and Water Development; Interior and Related Agencies; Transportation and Related Agencies.

Energy and Natural Resources (2d). Subcommittees: Energy Regulation; Parks, Recreation, and Renewable Resources.

Group Ratings

	ADA	COPE	PC	RPN	NFU	LCV	CFA	NAB	NSI	ACA	NTU
1978	0	6	13	40	63	16	5	100	100	91	–
1977	5	11	8	56	25	–	4	–	–	95	44
1976	0	11	6	47	30	3	0	91	100	100	83

Key Votes

1) Warnke Nom	AGN	6) Egypt-Saudi Arms	FOR	11) Hosptl Cost Contnmnt	DNV
2) Neutron Bomb	FOR	7) Draft Restr Pardon	AGN	12) Clinch River Reactor	FOR
3) Waterwy User Fee	FOR	8) Wheat Price Support	FOR	13) Pub Fin Cong Cmpgns	AGN
4) Dereg Nat Gas	FOR	9) Panama Canal Treaty	AGN	14) ERA Ratif Recissn	AGN
5) Kemp-Roth	FOR	10) Labor Law Rev Clot	AGN	15) Med Necssy Abrtns	AGN

Election Results

1978 general	James A. McClure (R)	194,412	(68%)	($385,536)
	Dwight Jensen (D)	89,635	(32%)	($55,163)
1978 primary	James A. McClure (R), unopposed			
1972 general	James A. McClure (R)	161,804	(53%)	
	William E. Davis (D)	140,913	(47%)	

Gov. John V. Evans (D) Elected Succeeded Gov. Cecil D. Andrus, Jan. 24, 1977; term expires Jan. 1981; b. Jan. 18, 1925; Idaho St. U., Stanford U., B.A. 1951.

Career Army, WWII; Rancher and banker; Idaho Senate, 1953–57, 1967–73, Major. Ldr., 1957, Minor. Ldr., 1969–74; Mayor of Malad City, 1960–66.

Offices State House, Boise 83720, 208-384-2100.

Election Results

1978 general	John V. Evans (D)	169,540	(60%)
	Allan E. Larsen (R)	114,149	(40%)
1978 primary	John V. Evans (D), unopposed		
1974 general	Cecil D. Andrus (D)	184,182	(73%)
	Jack M. Murphy (R)	68,731	(27%)

FIRST DISTRICT

Census Data Pop. 356,859. Central city, 15%; suburban, 10%. Median family income, $8,466; families above $15,000: 13%; families below $3,000: 11%. Median years education, 12.2.

The Voters

Median voting age 44.
Employment profile White collar, 43%. Blue collar, 34%. Service, 14%. Farm, 9%.
Ethnic groups Total foreign stock, 11%.

Presidential vote

1976	Carter (D)	68,459	(40%)
	Ford (R)	101,793	(60%)
1972	Nixon (R)	99,087	(69%)
	McGovern (D)	45,309	(31%)

Rep. Steven D. Symms (R) Elected 1972;b. Apr. 23, 1938, Nampa; home, Caldwell; U. of Idaho, B.S. 1960; Protestant.

Career USMC, 1960–63; Personnel and Production Mgr., V.P., Symms Fruit Ranch, Inc., 1963–72, Mbr., Bd. of Dirs., 1967–.

Offices 2244 RHOB, 202-225-6611. Also 304 N. 8th St., Rm. 134, Boise 83701, 208-384-1776.

Committees *Agriculture* (4th). Subcommittees: Domestic Marketing, Consumer Relations, and Nutrition; Forests; Livestock and Grains.

Interior and Insular Affairs (5th). Subcommittees: Energy and the Environment; Mines and Mining.

Group Ratings

	ADA	COPE	PC	RPN	NFU	LCV	CFA	NAB	NSI	ACA	NTU
1978	10	5	13	82	20	–	23	100	100	96	–
1977	5	9	15	58	8	5	10	–	–	100	64
1976	0	9	11	50	0	1	0	100	100	100	71

Key Votes

1) Increase Def Spnd	FOR	6) Alaska Lands Protect	AGN	11) Delay Auto Pol Cntrl	FOR
2) B-1 Bomber	FOR	7) Water Projects Veto	AGN	12) Sugar Price Escalator	FOR
3) Cargo Preference	AGN	8) Consum Protect Agcy	AGN	13) Pub Fin Cong Cmpgns	AGN
4) Dereg Nat Gas	FOR	9) Common Situs Picket	AGN	14) ERA Ratif Recissn	FOR
5) Kemp-Roth	FOR	10) Labor Law Revision	AGN	15) Prohibt Govt Abrtns	FOR

Election Results

1978 general	Steven D. Symms (R)	86,680	(60%)	($278,503)
	Roy Truby (D)	57,972	(40%)	($112,361)
1978 primary	Steven D. Symms (R), unopposed			
1976 general	Steven D. Symms (R)	95,833	(55%)	($135,341)
	Ken Pursley (D)	79,662	(45%)	($107,732)

SECOND DISTRICT

Census Data Pop. 356,149. Central city, 6%; suburban, 1%. Median family income, $8,280; families above $15,000: 13%; families below $3,000: 11%. Median years education, 12.3.

The Voters

Median voting age 42.
Employment profile White collar, 43%. Blue collar, 31%. Service, 12%. Farm, 14%.
Ethnic groups Total foreign stock, 10%.

Presidential vote

1976	Carter (D)	58,090	(36%)
	Ford (R)	102,358	(64%)
1972	Nixon (R)	100,297	(74%)
	McGovern (D)	35,517	(26%)

Rep. George Hansen (R) Elected 1974; b. Sept. 14, 1930, Tetonia; home, Pocatello; Ricks Col., B.A. 1956, Idaho St. U.; Church of Latter Day Saints.

Career Air Force; High school teacher; Insurance and retailing business; Mayor of Alameda, 1961–62; Pocatello City Commissioner, 1962–65; U.S. House of Reps., 1965–69; Repub. nominee for U.S. Senate, 1968; Deputy Under Secy., U.S. Dept. of Agriculture, 1969–71.

Offices 1125 LHOB, 202-225-5531. Also 211 Fed. Bldg., Box 740, Idaho Falls 83401, 208-523-5341.

Committees *Banking, Finance and Urban Affairs* (4th). Subcommittees: Domestic Monetary Policy; Financial Institutions Supervision, Regulation and Insurance; International Trade, Investment and Monetary Policy.

Veterans' Affairs (7th). Subcommittees: Compensation, Pension, Insurance and Memorial Affairs; Medical Facilities and Benefits.

Group Ratings

	ADA	COPE	PC	RPN	NFU	LCV	CFA	NAB	NSI	ACA	NTU
1978	5	6	15	50	22	–	23	100	100	96	–
1977	0	9	13	58	17	9	10	–	–	100	66
1976	0	14	8	59	0	0	0	100	90	100	76

Key Votes

1) Increase Def Spnd	FOR	6) Alaska Lands Protect	AGN	11) Delay Auto Pol Cntrl	FOR
2) B-1 Bomber	DNV	7) Water Projects Veto	AGN	12) Sugar Price Escalator	FOR
3) Cargo Preference	AGN	8) Consum Protect Agcy	AGN	13) Pub Fin Cong Cmpgns	AGN
4) Dereg Nat Gas	FOR	9) Common Situs Picket	AGN	14) ERA Ratif Recissn	FOR
5) Kemp-Roth	FOR	10) Labor Law Revision	AGN	15) Prohibt Govt Abrtns	FOR

Election Results

1978 general	George Hansen (R)	80,591	(57%)	($282,203)
	Stan Kress (D)	60,040	(43%)	($150,956)
1978 primary	George Hansen (R)	35,736	(56%)	
	Jim Jones (R)	28,593	(44%)	($154,502)
1976 general	George Hansen (R)	84,175	(51%)	($122,965)
	Stan Kress (D)	82,237	(49%)	($94,487)

ILLINOIS

As any reader of license plates knows, Illinois is the "Land of Lincoln." Illinois is also a land of tough, patronage-minded politicians—the home of the late Richard J. Daley's Democratic machine and the equally formidable apparatus of the state's conservative Republicans. The grimy realities of everyday politics are hidden to some extent by the blue ribbon candidates both parties run for the top slots. They have given the nation such leaders as Abraham Lincoln and Stephen Douglas in 1858; Adlai Stevenson and Paul Douglas in 1948; and, more recently, Republican Senator Charles Percy, Democratic Senator Adlai Stevenson III, and Republican Governor James Thompson.

But none of these men have been starry-eyed idealists, and politics in Illinois is not an occupation for dreamers. It is a business—and sometimes a very lucrative one. There is outright thievery sometimes: in the fifties a Republican state auditor stole $150,000, and in 1970 the Democratic secretary of state died leaving $800,000 in cash in shoeboxes in his dingy Springfield hotel room. In the early seventies, Republican prosecutors won convictions against such major figures as Chicago City Council President Thomas Keane and former Governor Otto Kerner. Votes are not stolen much any more, however. Forty indictments for vote fraud in 1972 and intensive poll-watching by the Chicago *Tribune* and the Better Government Association have just about eliminated what Republicans claim was systematic vote stealing in Chicago's West Side wards; certainly there were not enough votes to deliver Illinois for Jimmy Carter in the close election of 1976.

It is a mistake to speak of the Chicago machine as a single entity any longer. Even before Daley's death in December 1976 this last patronage-oriented, ward-based political organization was not in the best of shape; in 1975 it could deliver no more than 58% of the primary vote to Mayor Daley over reform Alderman William Singer and two minor opponents. Daley was succeeded as mayor by the man he apparently wanted, 11th ward neighbor Michael Bilandic, who won 51% in a 1977 special primary. But neither Bilandic nor the new Cook County Democratic Chairman George Dunne wielded all that much power by himself.

The machine's weakness became readily apparent in March 1979 when Jane Byrne defeated Bilandic for the nomination for mayor. In fact, Bilandic's 49% was not so far below what Mayor Daley had got four years before. But Bilandic had only a single opponent, and one who—as a high appointee under Daley—could claim that she could run the city better than the incumbent. Probably the difference came several weeks before, when the city government was unable to remove the heavy snows from Chicago's streets. Daley always won in part because people thought he could run city government better than anyone else; Bilandic had lost that advantage. "The city that works doesn't," Byrne said. The machine that controls things doesn't either. Chicago still has a large political culture of ward leaders, patronage employees, and hangers on—and a mayor who is tough as nails and can deal with them. But there is no longer a single, all-powerful machine, and there probably never will be again.

Even at the state level, the machine has been less than successful: it has not supported a winning candidate for governor since 1964. In 1968 the winner was Republican Richard Ogilvie, who got his start as a Daley opponent in Cook County government; he was considered competent but got into political trouble by sponsoring a tax increase. In 1972 the machine supported Lieutenant Governor Paul Simon, a Downstate reformer with strong backing from organized labor and an untarnished reputation. But Simon was too frank for his own good, conceding that tax increases might be necessary; and he was as much hurt as helped by the machine endorsement. The winner that year was Daniel Walker, the former Montgomery Ward executive who had authored the report charging that there was a "police riot" outside the 1968 Democratic National Convention in Chicago and who campaigned by walking 1,000 miles, the length of the state. Walker was a controversial Governor, who managed to cut state spending enough to antagonize both Daley and the liberals but not enough to attract the support of many conservatives. He was beaten in the 1976 primary by Michael Howlett, the Secretary of State whose rotund appearance and Chicago background made him appear the essence of a machine politician. Howlett had done his job by getting rid of Walker; he was a disastrous general election candidate, and lost to Republican James Thompson by a 65%–35% margin.

Thompson came to the governorship with a large reputation and with national notice. His record as United States Attorney in Chicago was outstanding; he jailed some of Illinois' most important politicians, and his conviction rate showed that he did not undertake any cases without strong evidence. As Governor, he has almost inevitably been more controversial, but on the whole successful. He pushed through the legislature a tough anti-crime program; on issues of criminal law he is as aggressive and conservative as the law 'n' order politicians of the early seventies, though Thompson knows what he is talking about. He proved reasonably adept at striking deals with the legislature. His personality—usually very open and engaging, occasionally snappish and petulant—on the whole made a very favorable impression. He built up strong Republican credentials—tough on crime, fiscally conservative—without alienating Democratic voters.

Thompson's major problem in 1978 was the tax issue. His opponent, Democratic Comptroller Michael Bakalis, was underfinanced, but he profited from Thompson's veto of a tax cut bill passed by the Democratic legislature. Thompson recovered by getting enough signatures to put his own tax cut measure on the ballot (though there was some dispute about the validity of the signatures) and won the election by a solid 3–2 margin. In the past Illinois governors have been handicapped by the fact that their terms expired in the presidential election year, but Thompson does not have that problem; the state switched to the non-presidential year in 1978, and he can run for president without giving up the governorship. How far he can go as a presidential candidate is another question. He will be just 44 in 1980 and, though tested in an executive position, he is not exactly a national figure. Moreover, there is plenty of suspicion among the kind of Republicans who dominate the party's national conventions that he is not their kind of man.

Another Illinois Republican who has had presidential ambitions is Senator Charles Percy. He was touted as a presidential candidate even before he was elected Senator in 1966; his success as the young president of Bell & Howell, his performance as head of the 1960 Republican platform-writing committee, and his good looks all made him something of a national figure. But

Percy has never actually run for president. He declined to run in 1968, letting George Romney and Nelson Rockefeller represent the moderate wing of the party, and he supported Richard Nixon in 1972. He might have run in 1976, but when Gerald Ford succeeded to the presidency it was clear that Percy's chances had vanished. The more so, considering Ford's narrow margin; it was clear that anyone with a record as liberal as Percy's could not get a Republican nomination.

In the Senate Percy votes often, but not always, with liberal Democrats. As a successful businessman, he has more faith in the free enterprise system than many Democrats do, and was able to support the Kemp-Roth tax cut. But he has also stayed on good terms with organized labor; though he opposed the proposed labor reform law in 1978, he voted to cut off the filibuster against it. Percy serves on the Foreign Relations Committee and can conceivably play a critical role there; he tended to be dovish on Vietnam, but now may be more concerned about our defense posture. Percy's greatest notice, however, probably came during the 1977 hearings on Bert Lance's affairs. Although he gained some sympathy as the target of attacks from Carter Administration staffers, the fact remained that he and the Committee were asking for Lance's resignation because of facts they had before them when they confirmed his nomination. It was not the sort of performance which is the springboard for a race for national office.

In any case Percy's performance in the 1978 Senate race pretty well demolished any national ambitions he might have. Percy had won the seat in 1966 by beating incumbent Paul Douglas convincingly, and he had won reelection in 1972 with 62% of the vote. But those results apparently told more of the weaknesses of his opponents than of Percy's strength. For in 1978 he was pressed hard by Democrat Alex Seith, a suburban lawyer who combined Democratic Party and foreign policy credentials. Seith confounded Percy by attacking him from both the right and the left. He called for a more aggressive foreign policy and for support for Israel, winning the support of hardliners (including the head of the American Conservative Union) and Jewish voters. He proposed income tax indexing, to prevent income tax rates from rising faster than inflation—a proposal that struck at the taxes and spending issues that were so important in 1978. In late October it became obvious that Seith was gaining, and he even led in a Chicago *Sun-Times* straw poll. Percy's support, which had once seemed so broad, was shown to be very shallow.

Percy counterattacked, seizing on an advertisement Seith had placed on black radio stations. It quoted Percy as supporting former Agriculture Secretary Earl Butz and noted the racial joke that prompted Butz's resignation—neglecting to mention that Percy had called for Butz's ouster. It was the kind of overreaching that plays into the intended victim's hand. Seith was attacked heavily in the Chicago newspapers, and Percy rallied to win reelection with 54%. That gives him six more years in the Senate, but the closeness of the race also assures him tough competition if he chooses to run again in 1984.

Illinois' junior Senator is Adlai Stevenson III, a Democrat who has also been mentioned as a possible national candidate. He made his name in state politics as state Treasurer and in 1970 beat an interim Republican who had been appointed to fill the vacancy caused by the death of Everett Dirksen. That was the year of law 'n' order politics, and Stevenson turned the tide when he appointed the prosecutor of the Chicago Seven as his campaign co-chairman (the other was Daniel Walker) and began wearing an American flag pin in his lapel. Stevenson won a full term in 1974 with a record 63% of the vote, but as in Percy's case that may have resulted more from lack of competition than from strong personal appeal. Stevenson is a quiet senator who can take tough stands when he feels strongly about an issue. His speaking style, at first very hesitant, has improved though he still lacks the homespun polish of his father. Stevenson has made his mark in the Senate less on national issues—his seniority is still unimpressive—than on internal Senate matters. In 1977 he chaired a committee that reorganized the jurisdiction of Senate committees, and in 1978 and 1979 he chaired the Senate Ethics Committee's investigations into the affairs of Edward Brooke and Herman Talmadge. Stevenson found the Ethics Committee work distasteful, and with others tried to leave it.

Stevenson has also expressed discontent with the Carter Administration and its personnel. He has announced he will not seek reelection to the Senate, and has even hinted that he may seek national office in 1980. He begins with a well-known name, but no real constituency and without the force of personality we traditionally associate with—although recently we have not necessarily had in—our presidential candidates. There may be some who will see him as taking the part of Eugene McCarthy against a Kennedy and an unpopular president—although it seems unlikely that that scenario will repeat itself. In the meantime there is naturally great competition for Stevenson's Senate seat; not al Illinois politicians are as negative about serving there as he is. On the Democratic side, Alex Seith may run again; he may be opposed by Secretary of State Alan

Dixon, former Lieutenant Governor Neil Hartigan, and 24th district Congressman Paul Simon. Attorney General William Scott was assumed to have the Republican nomination sewn up until he was indicted; now it may go to someone else. Mentioned as candidates are Congressmen John Anderson and Philip Crane, but they insist they will not abandon their presidential candidacies, and any candidate for the Senate must decide to run by the December 1979 filing date—the earliest in the nation.

Illinois has had a tradition of sending to Washington many congressmen, of both parties, who can best be described as hacks. But today Illinois's House delegation can boast considerable distinction. It has, at this writing, no less than two presidential candidates, moderate Republican John Anderson and conservative Republican Philip Crane; and if their chances initially seemed poor, their credentials are estimable. Illinois also has the House Minority Whip, Robert Michel of Peoria. On the Democratic side, there are thoughtful liberals like Abner Mikva of the North Shore suburbs and Paul Simon from Downstate. And the Chicago delegation has two relatively young members who have excellent chances of chairing major committees in the eighties: Dan Rostenkowski on Ways and Means and Morgan Murphy on Rules.

Illinois over the years has been one of the most evenly divided states politically, with Chicago heavily Democratic, the suburbs heavily Republican, with Downstate Illinois split between a dominant Republican north and a Southern-accented Democratic south. In presidential elections it was one of our major bellwether states until 1976, supporting every winner from Harding to Nixon. Ford's 1976 win here was achieved with just 51%. To a considerable extent that may have resulted from changing demography. Chicago casts fewer votes than it used to, while the suburbs—where Jimmy Carter, as a Democrat and a Southerner, was not at all popular—cast more.

Despite Illinois's size and bellwether status, its presidential primary has never been decisive in choosing either party's nominee. One reason is the early filing date, which scares off a lot of candidates who want more time to make up their minds. Another reason is that the party machines have traditionally had the strength to elect the delegates they select, and no one wants to spend a lot of money on Chicago TV just to win the so-called beauty contest, which gives no delegate votes to the winner. Edmund Muskie won a solid victory here in 1972, but it was only against Eugene McCarthy; the McGovern people somehow got the press to ignore the fact that Muskie delegates had beaten their candidates even in the Chicago suburbs where they were supposed to be strongest. Jimmy Carter won the beauty contest in 1976, and won more delegates than expected in the suburbs and Downstate; he was careful not to run candidates in Mayor Daley's Chicago. On the Republican side, the voters are conservative, less in the ideological sense as in a willingness of going along lockstep with the party leadership. Thus Gerald Ford won one of his biggest percentage victories over Ronald Reagan of the 1976 primaries here. But on the one traditional moderate-conservative battle at the national convention—on delegate selection rules—the Illinois people took the conservative side. For 1980 it seems that Jimmy Carter could be hurt, but not really helped, in the Illinois beauty contest; the national convention delegates will probably go unanimously whichever way the wind is blowing.

As for the Republicans, this is obviously an important primary for Crane and Anderson, who would like to show some home state support; but it could also end up as a critical test for several others. But that may not happen, for other candidates can pass up the race here, with the delegates selected representing orthodox organization Republicans more than any candidate.

Census Data Pop. 11,113,976; 5.49% of U.S. total, 5th largest; Central city, 37%; suburban, 43%. Median family income, $10,957; 7th highest; families above $15,000: 26%; families below $3,000: 8%. Median years education, 12.1.

1977 Share of Federal Tax Burden $21,312,000,000; 6.17% of U.S. total, 3d largest.

1977 Share of Federal Outlays $17,337,302,000; 4.38% of U.S. total, 5th largest. Per capita federal spending, $1,556.

DOD	$1,597,363,000	18th (1.75%)	HEW	$7,374,715,000	4th (4.99%)
ERDA	$274,249,000	7th (4.64%)	HUD	$168,385,000	7th (3.39%)
NASA	$11,264,000	22d (0.29%)	VA	$766,536,000	7th (3.99%)
DOT	$471,377,000	7th (3.30%)	EPA	$392,697,000	5th (4.79%)
DOC	$174,847,000	13th (2.11%)	RevS	$522,818,000	3d (6.18%)
DOI	$22,586,000	34th (0.49%)	Debt	$970,048,000	4th (3.23%)
USDA	$747,528,000	6th (3.76%)	Other	$3,842,889,000	

Economic Base Finance, insurance and real estate; machinery, especially construction and related machinery; electrical equipment and supplies, especially communication equipment; fabricated metal products; agriculture, notably corn, soybeans, hogs and cattle; food and kindred products; printing and publishing, especially commercial printing; primary metal industries, especially blast furnaces and basic steel products.

Political Line-up Governor, James R. Thompson (R). Senators, Charles H. Percy (R) and Adlai E. Stevenson III (D). Representatives, 24 (13 R and 11 D). State Senate (32 D and 27 R); State House (89 D and 88 R).

The Voters

Registration 5,809,045 Total. No party registration.
Median voting age 43
Employment profile White collar, 49%. Blue collar, 37%. Service, 12%. Farm, 2%.
Ethnic groups Black, 13%. Spanish, 3%. Total foreign stock, 20%. Germany, Poland, 3% each; Italy, 2%; UK, 1%.

Presidential vote

1976	Carter (D)	2,271,295	(49%)
	Ford (R)	2,364,269	(51%)
1972	Nixon (R)	2,788,179	(59%)
	McGovern (D)	1,913,472	(41%)

1976 Democratic Presidential Primary

Carter	621,988	(48%)
Wallace	356,676	(28%)
Shriver	207,916	(16%)
Harris	97,183	(8%)

1976 Republican Presidential Primary

Ford	450,812	(59%)
Reagan	307,305	(40%)
Other	7,544	(1%)

Sen. Charles H. Percy (R) Elected 1966, seat up 1978; b. Sept. 27, 1919, Pensacola, Fla.; home, Wilmette; U. of Chi., B.A. 1941; Christian Scientist.

Career Corp. Exec., Bell & Howell, Co., Pres. and Chf. Exec. Officer, 1949–61, Bd. Chm., 1961–66; Navy, WWII; Rep. of Pres. Eisenhower to pres. inaugurations in Peru and Bolivia, 1956; Repub. nominee for Gov., 1964.

Offices 4321 DSOB, 202-224-2152. Also 230 S. Dearborn, Rm. 3859, Chicago 60604, 312-353-4952, and 117 P.O. Bldg., Springfield 62701, 217-515-4442.

Committees *Foreign Relations* (2d). Subcommittees: Arms Control, Oceans, International Operations, and Environment; East Asian and Pacific Affairs; Near Eastern and South Asian Affairs.

Governmental Affairs (Ranking Member). Subcommittee: Investigations.

Special Committee on Aging (2d).

Group Ratings

	ADA	COPE	PC	RPN	NFU	LCV	CFA	NAB	NSI	ACA	NTU
1978	50	47	43	90	33	62	35	57	11	18	–
1977	65	47	45	100	73	–	52	–	–	10	30
1976	45	64	52	100	64	49	50	30	33	19	36

Key Votes

1) Warnke Nom	FOR	6) Egypt-Saudi Arms	FOR	11) Hosptl Cost Contnmnt	AGN
2) Neutron Bomb	AGN	7) Draft Restr Pardon	FOR	12) Clinch River Reactor	AGN
3) Waterwy User Fee	AGN	8) Wheat Price Support	AGN	13) Pub Fin Cong Cmpgns	DNV
4) Dereg Nat Gas	FOR	9) Panama Canal Treaty	FOR	14) ERA Ratif Recissn	FOR
5) Kemp-Roth	FOR	10) Labor Law Rev Clot	FOR	15) Med Necssy Abrtns	FOR

Election Results

1978 general	Charles H. Percy (R)	1,698,711	(54%)	($2,163,555)
	Alex R. Seith (D)	1,448,187	(46%)	($1,371,485)
1978 primary	Charles H. Percy (R)	401,409	(84%)	
	One other	74,739	(16%)	
1972 general	Charles H. Percy (R)	2,867,078	(62%)	($1,408,822)
	Roman Pucinski (D)	1,721,031	(38%)	($335,482)

Sen. Adlai E. Stevenson III (D) Elected Nov. 3, 1970, seat up 1980; b. Oct. 10, 1930, Chicago; home, Chicago; Harvard U., A.B. 1952, LL.B. 1957; Unitarian.

Career USMC, Korea; Clerk to Ill. State Supreme Ct. Justice, 1957–58; Practicing atty.; Ill. House of Reps., 1965–67; State Treasurer of Ill., 1967–70.

Offices 456 RSOB, 202-224-2854. Also Rm. 3960, 230 S. Dearborn St., Chicago 60604, 312-353-5420, and Fed. Bldg., Rm. 108, 6th and Monroe Sts., Springfield 62691, 217-525-4126.

Committees *Banking, Housing, and Urban Affairs* (6th). Subcommittees: Financial Institutions; International Finance (Chairman); Economic Stabilization.

Commerce, Science, and Transportation (6th). Subcommittees: Aviation; Science, Technology and Space (Chairman); Surface Transportation.

Select Committee on Ethics (Chairman).

Select Committee on Intelligence (2d).

Group Ratings

	ADA	COPE	PC	RPN	NFU	LCV	CFA	NAB	NSI	ACA	NTU
1978	65	79	68	44	50	81	50	40	30	13	–
1977	60	74	65	67	80	–	60	–	–	4	36
1976	60	88	69	59	83	56	85	27	0	4	29

Key Votes

1) Warnke Nom	FOR	6) Egypt-Saudi Arms	FOR	11) Hosptl Cost Contnmnt	FOR
2) Neutron Bomb	FOR	7) Draft Restr Pardon	FOR	12) Clinch River Reactor	FOR
3) Waterwy User Fee	AGN	8) Wheat Price Support	AGN	13) Pub Fin Cong Cmpgns	FOR
4) Dereg Nat Gas	AGN	9) Panama Canal Treaty	FOR	14) ERA Ratif Recissn	AGN
5) Kemp-Roth	AGN	10) Labor Law Rev Clot	FOR	15) Med Necssy Abrtns	FOR

Election Results

1974 general	Adlai Stevenson III (D)	1,811,496	(63%)	($757,329)
	George M. Burditt (R)	1,084,884	(37%)	($488,556)
1974 primary	Adlai Stevenson III (D)	822,248	(83%)	
	One other (D)	169,662	(17%)	
1970 general	Adlai Stevenson III (D)	2,065,054	(58%)	
	Ralph Tyler Smith (R)	1,519,718	(42%)	
1968 general	Everett M. Dirksen (R)	2,358,947	(53%)	
	William G. Clark (D)	2,073,242	(47%)	

Gov. James R. Thompson (R) Elected 1976, term expires Jan. 1981; b. May 8, 1936, Chicago; U. of Ill., Chicago, Washington U., St. Louis, Northwestern U., J.D. 1959; Presbyterian.

Career Prosecutor for Cook Co. State Atty., 1959–64; Assoc. Prof., Northwestern Law School, 1964–69; Chief, Dept. of Law Enforcement and Pub. Protection, Ill. Atty. Gen.'s Ofc., 1969; 1st Asst. U.S. Atty., North Dist. of Ill., 1970; U.S. Atty., 1971–75.

Offices State House, Springfield 62706, 217-782-6830.

Election Results

1978 general	James R. Thompson (R)	1,859,684	(60%)
	Michael J. Bakalis (D)	1,263,134	(40%)
1978 primary	James R. Thompson (R), unopposed		
1976 general	James R. Thompson (R)	3,000,395	(65%)
	Michael Howlett (D)	1,610,258	(35%)

FIRST DISTRICT

The most stable and longest lived black community in the United States can be found on Chicago's South Side. Here, as long ago as the turn of the century, was a substantial community of blacks in the vicinity of 63d and Cottage Grove. There have always been poor people in the South Side ghetto, but there have been middle class and prosperous blacks as well; this is the home of the nation's first black bourgeoisie. The South Side has been a center of black culture, since before the jazz age. It is still that today. There have always been more blacks here—at least half a million today—than in New York's Harlem.

The South Side has also furnished political leadership for blacks. Illinois' 1st congressional district, almost entirely black today, includes most of the South Side black community. It first elected a black congressman, Oscar DePriest, in 1928, a Republican. For in those days black voters were still faithful to the party of Lincoln; they even stayed with Herbert Hoover in the depths of the Depression in 1932. But the New Deal and the racial liberalism of Eleanor Roosevelt attracted blacks to the Democratic Party in the thirties. DePriest was beaten by a black Democrat, Arthur Mitchell, in 1934; Mitchell was succeeded in 1942 by another black Democrat, William Dawson.

Dawson was the first black to wield major power in Chicago's Democratic machine. He was consulted by Richard Daley and the bosses before him, just as were ward leaders from other major ethnic groups. Dawson, for his part, was not a boat-rocker. He endorsed civil rights measures, but he was firmly committed to working within the system. His goals were to provide patronage jobs, Democratic nominations, and public services to the South Side's blacks, and generally he delivered. Dawson continued to serve in Congress till long after his health permitted him to be effective. He finally retired in 1970 and died later in the year at 84.

Dawson's black Democratic machine leaders delivered votes as almost no one else in Chicago. The turnout in the 1st district was always high and always pro-machine in the primary and nearly unanimously Democratic in the general. Dawson's black constituency was singlehandedly responsible for keeping Mayor Daley in office in 1963, when he was opposed by a Polish Republican. When Dawson stepped down, it was unthinkable that he would be succeeded by anyone but the machine's choice, and he was. But that new Congressman, Ralph Metcalfe, turned out to behave differently from what Dawson would have expected or, probably, liked.

Metcalfe was well known in the black community for his athletic prowess: as a sprinter he had finished second to Jesse Owens in the 1936 Olympics. And as a member of the Board of Aldermen he had never rebelled. But in 1972 two prominent black dentists were beaten by Chicago police. Metcalfe, outraged, demanded that the Mayor meet him at his, Metcalfe's, office; the Mayor, not in the habit of sitting in other people's waiting rooms, declined. Metcalfe rebelled, and led the South Side in a series of anti-machine votes. He watched benignly while Jesse Jackson led a massive ticket-splitting campaign that carried the usually 90% Democratic South Side for Senator Charles Percy and the Republican candidate for state's attorney in 1972. He endorsed insurgent William Singer for mayor over Daley in 1975. He stood his ground and beat a machine opponent in the 1976 congressional primary by a 71%–29% margin.

But all the while Metcalfe's health was failing. He died in October 1978, which gave the machine just enough time before the election to name another nominee. Alderman Bennett Stewart, a machine loyalist, was ticketed. The Republicans, scenting a possible upset, managed to dump the 27-year-old salesman they had on the ballot and substituted A. A. "Sammy" Rayner, a former alderman and longtime insurgent. Indeed, Rayner had run against Metcalfe in the 1970 Democratic primary, and got only 29% of the vote. The 1st is one of the top two Democratic districts in the country in presidential elections. But even with the Republican label, Rayner was able to win 40% of the vote against Stewart. It now seems fairly clear that Stewart must establish his own political identity if he is not to be very vulnerable indeed in the 1980 Democratic primary. The South Side, once so loyal to the machine, is now an insurgent district and seems unlikely to go back to its old ways.

Census Data Pop. 462,434. Central city, 100%; suburban, 0%. Median family income, $8,373; families above $15,000: 17%; families below $3,000: 14%. Median years education, 11.5.

The Voters

Median voting age 42.
Employment profile White collar, 46%. Blue collar, 35%. Service, 19%. Farm, –%.
Ethnic groups Black, 89%. Spanish, 1%. Total foreign stock, 5%.

Presidential vote

1976	Carter (D)	130,882	(90%)
	Ford (R)	13,817	(10%)
1972	Nixon (R)	16,998	(10%)
	McGovern (D)	145,003	(90%)

Rep. Bennett M. Stewart (D) Elected 1978; b. Aug. 6, 1915, Huntsville, Ala.; home, Chicago; Miles Col., B.A. 1936; Methodist.

Career Asst. High School Principal, 1936; Asst. Prof., Miles Col., 1938; Insurance Exec., Atlanta Life Ins. Co., 1940–68; Inspector, Chi. Bldg. Dept., 1968; Chi. City Alderman, 1971–78.

Offices 503 CHOB, 202-225-4372. Also Suite 3846, 230 S. Dearborn St., Chicago 60604, 312-353-0105.

Committees *Appropriations* (36th). Subcommittees: HUD-Independent Agencies; Transportation.

Group Ratings: Newly Elected

Key Votes: Newly Elected

Election Results

1978 general	Bennett Stewart (D)	47,581	(59%)	($18,471)
	A. A. Rayner (R)	33,540	(41%)	($13,622)
1978 primary	Bennett Stewart (D), chosen by Democratic Party			
	Ralph H. Metcalfe (D), unopposed			($20,397)
1976 general	Ralph H. Metcalfe (D)	126,632	(93%)	($124,236)
	A. A. Rayner (R)	10,147	(7%)	($939)

SECOND DISTRICT

On the far south side of Chicago, where the Calumet River has been deepened to accommodate the huge freighters of the Great Lakes, are the city's giant steel mills, ones that rival those in nearby Gary in size and stark grandeur. This part of Chicago is the heart of the city's heavy industry and has been ever since the Industrial Revolution came to the Midwest. The same area was the site of the Pullman strike of 1893, during which the laissez faire President Cleveland sent in federal troops to uphold the rights of private capital. The Calumet steel mills neatly separate the 2d congressional district of Illinois into two parts. To the east, along the lakefront, are the large apartments and, behind them, the comfortable houses in what used to be a Jewish neighborhood; to the north is the South Side black ghetto. West of the steel mills are middle class neighborhoods, most of them inhabited by members of the various ethnic groups that have for so long contributed most of the labor to keep the mills going.

Both parts of the 2d have one thing in common: they have been the site of Chicago's—and the nation's—most massive neighborhood racial change in recent years. In 1960 less than 20% of the population within the current bounds of the 2d was black; in 1970 it was 40%, and today blacks form a solid majority. Blockbusting tactics have been a way of life here, and the first For Sale sign on a white block can still trigger a spasm of panic selling. Naturally racial change has affected the area's politics. In the late sixties fear of racial change increased the Republican vote in this area. Then, as the whites left, the Democratic percentage has been rising rapidly. Thus Hubert Humphrey had only 56% in this traditionally very Democratic area in 1968; four years later George McGovern had 66%, and in 1976 Jimmy Carter had 77%.

The current Congressman from the 2d is Democrat Morgan Murphy, who first won in 1970. Murphy, the son of the former head of Chicago's Commonwealth Edison, had held a number of offices considered within the gift of Mayor Daley's machine. As a machine loyalist, he beat a black candidate in the 1970 primary and then won the general election easily. In his first term Murphy attracted attention for exposing the wide extent of heroin addiction among American servicemen in Vietnam. In his second term, as a member of the House Rules Committee, he worked more quietly; in tandem with building trades unionists, he helped to kill the federal land use bill in Rules. In his third term, he served on the special House Intelligence Committee, more quietly than many others. In his fourth term he was part of the Rules majority that speeded passage of limits on members' outside income—but very reluctantly, since he had a law practice worth $40,000 a year.

In his fifth term, Murphy advanced to the number three position on the Rules Committee. The Chairman, Richard Bolling, is 16 years older, and the second ranking Democrat, Claude Pepper, 32 years older; Murphy's chances of becoming Chairman some day must be considered excellent. That would represent a victory of considerable importance for old-line big city Democrats in general and the Chicago machine in particular. The increasing black population in the 2d district has so far posed no real threat to Murphy and has helped him in general elections to near-unanimous victories. After the 1980 Census, the legislature is likely to move this district farther out to include some suburban territory, which will reduce the black percentage and make Murphy safer than ever.

Census Data Pop. 464,792. Central city, 100%; suburban, 0%. Median family income, $11,147; families above $15,000: 26%; families below $3,000: 7%. Median years education, 11.8.

The Voters

Median voting age 43.
Employment profile White collar, 48%. Blue collar, 39%. Service, 13%. Farm, –%.
Ethnic groups Black, 40%. Spanish, 5%. Total foreign stock, 25%. Poland, 4%; Italy, Ireland, Germany, 2% each; Yugoslavia, Sweden, 1% each.

Presidential vote

1976	Carter (D)	137,384	(83%)
	Ford (R)	28,498	(17%)
1972	Nixon (R)	60,220	(34%)
	McGovern (D)	116,534	(66%)

Rep. Morgan F. Murphy (D) Elected 1970; b. Apr. 16, 1932, Chicago; home, Chicago; Northwestern U., B.S. 1955, De Paul U., J.D. 1962; Catholic.

Career USMC, 1955–58; Admin. Asst. to Circuit Court Clerk, 1958–61; Practicing atty., 1962–70; Chm., Govt. Div., Crusade of Mercy, 1967–70.

Offices 2436 RHOB. Also Rm. 3976, 230 S. Dearborn St., Chicago 60620, 312-353-5390.

Committees *Standards of Official conduct* (5th).

Rules (3th).

Group Ratings

	ADA	COPE	PC	RPN	NFU	LCV	CFA	NAB	NSI	ACA	NTU
1978	55	70	40	27	80	–	36	20	56	23	–
1977	40	86	48	33	64	35	65	–	–	15	22
1976	55	91	74	31	92	45	91	0	50	20	21

Key Votes

1) Increase Def Spnd	AGN	6) Alaska Lands Protect	AGN	11) Delay Auto Pol Cntrl	FOR
2) B-1 Bomber	AGN	7) Water Projects Veto	AGN	12) Sugar Price Escalator	DNV
3) Cargo Preference	FOR	8) Consum Protect Agcy	FOR	13) Pub Fin Cong Cmpgns	AGN
4) Dereg Nat Gas	FOR	9) Common Situs Picket	FOR	14) ERA Ratif Recissn	FOR
5) Kemp-Roth	AGN	10) Labor Law Revision	FOR	15) Prohibt Govt Abrtns	FOR

Election Results

1978 general	Morgan F. Murphy (D)	80,906	(88%)	($43,328)
	James Wognum (R)	11,104	(12%)	
1978 primary	Morgan F. Murphy (D), unopposed			
1976 general	Morgan F. Murphy (D)	127,297	(85%)	($26,957)
	Spencer Leak (R)	23,037	(15%)	($3,468)

THIRD DISTRICT

The 3d congressional district of Illinois consists of the close-in southwest suburbs of Chicago plus about two wards worth of the city itself. If one had to generalize about the area, one might say that this is the place where the whites from the older ethnic neighborhoods of South Side Chicago have gone, either in flight as blacks have moved into their old neighborhoods, or simply as they grow up and have to move some place to start their own families. There are small black ghettoes here in the towns of Markham and Harvey, but the overall ethnic tone is Irish-American, the group which always dominated southwest Chicago until the blacks moved in. But not everyone is Irish: the area is an ethnic olio with Polish-, Italian-, Lithuanian-, German-, Dutch-, Swedish-, and Czech-Americans represented in significant numbers. The people here are much more likely to hold white collar than blue collar jobs, but one suspects that the situation for their parents was just the opposite. These are people whose hold on middle class status is a little precarious, their recent prosperity notwithstanding.

The 3d district is one of those areas which are crucial to the outcome of Cook County elections which, contrary to outsiders' preconceptions, are not automatically won by the Democratic machine. Indeed, the Chicago suburbs as a whole are more Republican and conservative than those of any major city except Los Angeles. Many times Republicans, with huge suburban majorities, have been able to beat Daley Democrats in races for patronage-rich county offices as well as in statewide elections—with areas like the 3d district making the big difference. Most people here have Democratic backgrounds, but their comparative affluence tends to make Republicans out of them; they are, in short, classic ticket-splitters.

When the 3d district was first created, it was won by a Republican who had proved his mettle in winning a county-wide election. But he was defeated two years later, in 1974, in something of an upset. The winner was Martin Russo, a 30-year-old Democrat. With experience in the Cook County State's Attorney's office, he had organization Democrat credentials. But unlike congressmen from the city of Chicago, he does not run as a machine candidate; he has been unopposed in primaries, and his real contest occurs in the general election.

In the House, Russo is not as liberal on non-economic issues as most 1974 Democratic freshmen. Here he seems definitely to reflect the predilections of his constituents, who are tough on crime and not sympathetic to what they consider trends contrary to traditional morality. On economic issues, he generally votes with other Democrats. For example, he stood with the Carter Administration in opposing total deregulation of natural gas. But he also played a key role in killing the Administration's proposal for hospital cost controls. In 1978, as a member of the Commerce Committee Russo cast some decisive votes against the proposal.

Like most other 1974 freshmen, Russo has raised his winning percentage, from 53% in 1974 to 64% in 1978. As more Democratic voters move out to this district from Chicago, Russo should continue to do well. He will, however, have to watch closely how the Illinois legislature redistricts suburban Cook County after the 1980 elections.

Census Data Pop. 461,180. Central city, 27%; suburban, 73%. Median family income, $12,762; families above $15,000: 34%; families below $3,000: 4%. Median years education, 12.2.

The Voters

Median voting age 44.
Employment profile White collar, 53%. Blue collar, 37%. Service, 10%. Farm, –%.
Ethnic groups Black, 5%. Spanish, 2%. Total foreign stock, 28%. Poland, 4%; Ireland, Germany, Italy, 3% each; Lithuania, UK, 2% each; Netherlands, Sweden, Czechoslovakia, 1% each.

Presidential vote

1976	Carter (D)	88,240	(42%)
	Ford (R)	121,448	(58%)
1972	Nixon (R)	155,092	(70%)
	McGovern (D)	65,226	(30%)

Rep. Marty Russo (D) Elected 1974; b. Jan. 23, 1944, Chicago; home, South Holland; De Paul U., B.S. 1965, J.D. 1967; Catholic.

Career Law Clerk for Ill. Appellate Ct. Judge John V. McCormack, 1967–68; Practicing atty.; Cook Co. Asst. States Atty., 1971–73.

Offices 206 CHOB, 202-225-5736. Also 12526 S. Ashland Ave., Calumet Park 60643, 312-353-0439.

Committees *Interstate and Foreign Commerce* (17th). Subcommittees: Communications; Oversight and Investigations; Transportation and Commerce.

Small Business (13th). Subcommittees: Special Small Business Problems (Chairman).

Group Ratings

	ADA	COPE	PC	RPN	NFU	LCV	CFA	NAB	NSI	ACA	NTU
1978	35	63	40	42	60	–	36	46	56	50	–
1977	45	91	60	23	58	74	50	–	–	38	44
1976	55	74	86	44	67	75	91	25	60	26	44

Key Votes

1) Increase Def Spnd	DNV	6) Alaska Lands Protect	AGN	11) Delay Auto Pol Cntrl	FOR
2) B-1 Bomber	AGN	7) Water Projects Veto	FOR	12) Sugar Price Escalator	AGN
3) Cargo Preference	FOR	8) Consum Protect Agcy	FOR	13) Pub Fin Cong Cmpgns	FOR
4) Dereg Nat Gas	AGN	9) Common Situs Picket	FOR	14) ERA Ratif Recissn	AGN
5) Kemp-Roth	FOR	10) Labor Law Revision	FOR	15) Prohibt Govt Abrtns	FOR

Election Results

1978 general	Martin A. Russo (D)	95,701	(65%)	($219,377)
	Robert L. Dunne (R)	51,098	(35%)	($113,083)
1978 primary	Martin A. Russo (D), unopposed			
1976 general	Martin A. Russo (D)	115,591	(59%)	($169,348)
	Ronald Buikema (R)	79,434	(41%)	($219,156)

FOURTH DISTRICT

The 4th congressional district of Illinois is the southwest corner of Cook County. The district includes some of the most Republican parts of what is supposed to be one of the nation's prime Democratic counties. It really isn't, because the usually Republican suburbs now cast 43% of the County's total votes; and as Chicago's population continues to move from city to suburbs, that percentage will continue to rise. Chicago's suburbs radiate from the city like spokes from the hub of a wheel, and the 4th district contains two widely separated built up areas, one of which extends almost due south from the city, the other directly west. Nevertheless, the 4th is an area of rather homogeneous political complexion. By most social and economic indicators, it resembles the neighboring and closer-in 3d district; the 4th is just a shade richer and a shade less ethnic. People here are several miles and another generation removed from the immigrants who filled up Chicago during its years of explosive growth, 1880–1930. They and their parents worked hard for what they have, and they intend to keep it. They have cut their ties with the city—an increasing number work as well as live in the suburbs—and with the Democratic Party.

As a result, the 4th is a very Republican district—one of about 65 of the current House seats which went for Barry Goldwater in 1964. Its Congressman since 1958, Edward Derwinski, is a conservative proudly in the Goldwater mold. He was a young man when first elected (32), in the crew cut style of the day, and he is one of the few congressmen who still wears the style. His crusty, pungent personality leaves no doubt about where he stands. A proud Polish-American, Derwinski came to Congress when many politicians were talking about rolling the Iron Curtain back in Eastern Europe. He remains a staunch anti-Communist and high ranking member of the Foreign Affairs Committee. In 1977 Derwinski seemed to be in trouble when he was accused of having tipped off the South Korean government about the imminent defection of one of their agents. A strong South Korea supporter, he defended himself successfully.

Much of Derwinski's major legislative work is done in his capacity as the ranking Republican on the House Post Office and Civil Service Committee. As a believer in less government, and as a politician with relatively few federal employees in his district, Derwinski has presumably not been happy with the rapid rise in government pay and benefits. His role on the Committee has not been entirely negative, however. In 1978 he worked closely with the Committee's Chairman, Morris Udall, and pro-labor Democrat William Ford in working out a compromise version of the Carter Administration's civil service reform bill. Without Derwinski's work, this bill—which for the first time moves in the direction of making civil servants more responsible to the elected officials and the public they are supposed to serve—would never have received enough votes to pass. It was one of the major legislative achievements of the 95th Congress, for which Derwinski deserves much credit.

Census Data Pop. 464,452. Central city, 0%; suburban, 100%. Median family income, $13,451; families above $15,000: 39%; families below $3,000: 3%. Median years education, 12.4.

The Voters

Median voting age 42.
Employment profile White collar, 56%. Blue collar, 35%. Service, 9%. Farm, –%.
Ethnic groups Black, 4%. Spanish, 2%. Total foreign stock, 23%. Poland, Germany, Italy, 3% each; Czechoslovakia, 2%; UK, Ireland, Canada, 1% each.

Presidential vote

1976	Carter (D)	80,530	(38%)
	Ford (R)	131,038	(62%)
1972	Nixon (R)	142,635	(71%)
	McGovern (D)	57,082	(29%)

Rep. Edward J. Derwinski (R) Elected 1958; b. Sept. 15, 1926, Chicago; home, Flossmoor; Loyola U., B.S. 1951; Catholic.

Career Ill. House of Reps., 1957–58; Mbr., U.S. Delegation to U.N., 1971.

Offices 1401 LHOB, 202-225-3961. Also 12236 S. Harlem Ave., Palos Heights 60463, 312-448-3500.

Committees *Foreign Affairs* (2d). Subcommittees: International Organizations; International Operations.

Post Office and Civil Service (Ranking Member). Subcommittees: Postal Operations and Services.

Group Ratings

	ADA	COPE	PC	RPN	NFU	LCV	CFA	NAB	NSI	ACA	NTU
1978	20	20	20	50	20	–	14	92	90	78	–
1977	10	17	28	77	25	24	25	–	–	81	46
1976	5	14	26	78	25	25	18	73	90	75	52

Key Votes

1) Increase Def Spnd	AGN	6) Alaska Lands Protect	AGN	11) Delay Auto Pol Cntrl	FOR
2) B-1 Bomber	FOR	7) Water Projects Veto	FOR	12) Sugar Price Escalator	FOR
3) Cargo Preference	AGN	8) Consum Protect Agcy	AGN	13) Pub Fin Cong Cmpgns	AGN
4) Dereg Nat Gas	FOR	9) Common Situs Picket	AGN	14) ERA Ratif Recissn	FOR
5) Kemp-Roth	FOR	10) Labor Law Revision	AGN	15) Prohibt Govt Abrtns	FOR

Election Results

1978 general	Edward J. Derwinski (R)	94,435	(67%)	($72,941)
	Andrew D. Thomas (D)	46,788	(33%)	($73,437)
1978 primary	Edward J. Derwinski (R), unopposed			
1976 general	Edward J. Derwinski (R)	124,847	(66%)	($63,307)
	Ronald A. Roger (D)	64,924	(34%)	($20,563)

FIFTH DISTRICT

In an unpretentious but reportedly comfortable house on the 3500 block of South Lowe Avenue in the 11th ward and 5th congressional district in Chicago lived the most powerful ward committeeman in the United States. He was a man whose advice was routinely sought by presidents and senators and governors. For more than 20 years he held other important offices, like Chairman of the Cook County Democratic Committee and Mayor of the city of Chicago. His name was Richard J. Daley, and no matter how scorned or ridiculed he was elsewhere, he was loved and admired in the 11th ward of Chicago.

Chicago is a city of neighborhoods, and Daley's neighborhood, Bridgeport, is typical both of the 11th ward and the 5th district of which it is a part. More than 30% of the 5th's residents are black, but virtually all of them live at the fringes of the district, in the South Side or West Side ghettoes. The heart of the 5th, neighborhoods like Bridgeport, is all white. The people here live, as Daley did all his life, on these streets with dumpy-looking frame houses and sparkling clean sidewalks. On a nice day a visitor driving down South Lowe can see dozens of children with crisp Irish faces, playing noisily but taking care not to injure the carefully manicured lawns. Blacks moving out from the center of the city have not found neighborhoods like Bridgeport hospitable (to say the least) and have avoided them and moved out farther to places where the whites don't have such deep roots.

This choice urban property, not far from the Loop (Daley was known to ride a bicycle to work on occasion), thus remains the province of tight-knit white communities which, it seems, have always lived here. If there is something insular and anachronistic about these neighborhoods and something intolerant, there is also a vitality and a rootedness unknown in the shopping center land of suburban America.

Very early in life children in Bridgeport are taught their basic loyalties: the United States of America, the Roman Catholic Church, and the Democratic Party. If Bridgeport has not produced a president or a pope, it has produced the last four mayors of Chicago, from Ed Kelly, who took office in 1933, to Martin Kenneally, who was ousted in 1955 by Richard Daley, to Daley's hand-picked successor, Michael Bilandic. No other neighborhood has ever dominated the government of a great city in this way. On occasion some of these loyalties have been called into doubt. The 5th district reacted negatively to blacks and peace demonstrators and gave Republicans unusually high percentages, though never majorities, in the period between 1966 and 1972. But by the Watergate year of 1974, Democratic loyalties had been reestablished.

The congressional succession in this district is a good example of how business is done in Chicago politics. The incumbent Congressman, John Kluczynski, died in February 1975 at age 78. A few days later, state Representative John Fary was called into Mayor Daley's office. At 65, Fary had been a faithful servant of the machine for nearly 25 years; he thought the Mayor was going to tell him it was time to retire. Instead he was told he was going to Congress. The voters of the 5th ratified the choice quickly in a special election. There was some suspicion at the time that in appointing an older man like Fary, Daley was keeping the seat warm for one of his sons. But so far Fary has not chosen—or has not been told—to retire. He has the kind of voting record one would expect from the product of a big city machine, and has been reelected with the kind of margins one would expect as well.

Census Data Pop. 465,990. Central city, 100%; suburban, 0%. Median family income, $9,881; families above $15,000: 20%; families below $3,000: 10%. Median years education, 10.2.

The Voters

Median voting age 44.
Employment profile White collar, 40%. Blue collar, 47%. Service, 13%. Farm, –%.
Ethnic groups Black, 31%. Spanish, 6%. Total foreign stock, 30%. Poland, 10%; Italy, Czechoslovakia, Lithuania, Germany, Ireland, 2% each; Yugoslavia, 1%.

Presidential vote

1976	Carter (D)	113,899	(67%)
	Ford (R)	57,147	(33%)
1972	Nixon (R)	86,644	(47%)
	McGovern (D)	96,012	(53%)

Rep. John G. Fary (D) Elected July 8, 1975; b. April 11, 1911, Chicago; home, Chicago; Loyola U.; Catholic.

Career Businessman, 1931–76; Real Estate Broker; Ill. House of Reps., 1952–75.

Offices 1121 LHOB, 202-225-5701. Also 3968 Fed. Bldg., 230 S. Dearborn, Chicago 60604, 312-353-7251.

Committees *Public Works and Transportation* (15th). Subcommittees: Aviation; Oversight and Review; Surface Transportation.

Group Ratings

	ADA	COPE	PC	RPN	NFU	LCV	CFA	NAB	NSI	ACA	NTU
1978	40	80	50	20	60	–	55	0	50	22	–
1977	50	100	48	17	83	35	60	–	–	15	17
1976	50	91	67	36	92	53	81	0	100	19	8

Key Votes

1) Increase Def Spnd	FOR	6) Alaska Lands Protect	AGN	11) Delay Auto Pol Cntrl	FOR
2) B-1 Bomber	AGN	7) Water Projects Veto	AGN	12) Sugar Price Escalator	FOR
3) Cargo Preference	FOR	8) Consum Protect Agcy	FOR	13) Pub Fin Cong Cmpgns	AGN
4) Dereg Nat Gas	AGN	9) Common Situs Picket	FOR	14) ERA Ratif Recissn	FOR
5) Kemp-Roth	AGN	10) Labor Law Revision	FOR	15) Prohibt Govt Abrtns	FOR

Election Results

1978 general	John G. Fary (D)	98,702	(84%)	($37,315)
	Joseph A. Barracca (R)	18,802	(16%)	
1978 primary	John G. Fary (D), unopposed			
1976 general	John G. Fary (D)	119,336	(77%)	($54,296)
	Vincent S. Krok (R)	35,756	(23%)	($0)

SIXTH DISTRICT

The 6th congressional district of Illinois is a suburban Chicago constituency. These are not the new suburbs, with their gleaming but pasteboardy houses stuck up on treeless lots one after another. The 6th is mostly a series of older, established communities west and northwest of Chicago. Oak Park, for one, was the boyhood home of Ernest Hemingway; it still is a quiet middle class community just across the city limits from the West Side Chicago black ghetto. To the south the very different town of Cicero has scarcely changed since the twenties, when it was a Syndicate stronghold and bedroom community for Czechs and other Eastern European workers. In the middle sixties, Cicero made headlines and TV footage when its citizens forcibly resisted the efforts of Martin Luther King Jr. to integrate the city. Cicero's politics is dominated by an anachronism from the twenties: a working class, ethnic-based Republican machine. In just about every respect Cicero resembles Chicago neighborhoods like Bridgeport, but for some reason—perhaps just because this is a suburb and Bridgeport is part of the city—the partisan political patterns are exactly the opposite.

On the map the remainder of the 6th district looks like a patchwork quilt of towns whose names are various combinations of "Park," "River," and "Forest," sometimes appended to more distinctive names. Most of these communities can claim some special quality. Maywood, for example, has a large black community, and Melrose Park is predominantly Italian-American. (Indeed, this is the most Italian of Illinois's districts. In the East, Italians have tended to stay in the central cities, but here they have long since moved to the suburbs.) Then there is Rosemont, a tiny place 25 years ago situated near a dusty airfield named after someone called O'Hare. Since that time, primarily through the efforts of Richard J. Daley, O'Hare has become the busiest airport in the world, and little Rosemont has sprouted a couple of dozen high rise motels and office buildings. It is the premier example of the kind of businessmen's meeting place culture which has grown up around our major airports.

The 6th district has always been a Republican area, and has always elected a Republican congressman since it was created in 1948. The current incumbent, Henry Hyde, attracted little attention when he was elected in 1974. A respected member of the Illinois legislature, he took seats on the Judiciary and Banking Committees and voted with most other Republicans on most issues. But in the 95th Congress Hyde became one of the House's major legislative forces. For he has been the prime sponsor of a series of Hyde Amendments to prohibit the use of federal funds for abortions. Hyde approaches the issue with a deep conviction that abortion of any kind is morally wrong and amounts to murder; he will not even make exceptions for pregnancies resulting from rape or incest. And he has pursued the issue with great ingenuity and persistence. He sought out not only the obvious targets—abortions financed by Medicaid—but also less obvious ones—abortions for members of the Armed Forces and their dependents.

Hyde has been able to win majorities in the House pretty consistently for his amendments. The majority in the Senate has gone the other way, but even in conference committee Hyde has proved largely victorious—partly because he has made it clear that he will tack his amendments on any conceivable piece of legislation until they are passed. He and his fellow abortion opponents have been less successful in pushing a constitutional amendment to ban all abortions, a move that has not gotten out of Judiciary subcommittee.

It is not clear what the practical effect of Hyde's work has been. No one knows how many women who would have gotten government-financed abortions before now do not have an abortion at all. But its political effect has been clearer. His efforts have helped opponents of abortion to go on the political offensive and, at the least, to get Congress to indicate a disapproval of the practice of abortion.

Census Data Pop. 461,360. Central city, 0%; suburban, 100%. Median family income, $12,700; families above $15,000: 35%; families below $3,000: 4%. Median years education, 12.2.

The Voters

Median voting age 45.
Employment profile White collar, 55%. Blue collar, 36%. Service, 9%. Farm, –%.
Ethnic groups Black, 3%. Spanish, 2%. Total foreign stock, 34%. Italy, 7%; Poland, Germany, Czechoslovakia, 4% each; Ireland, 2%; UK, Canada, Austria, 1% each.

Presidential vote

1976	Carter (D)	78,144	(40%)
	Ford (R)	116,398	(60%)
1972	Nixon (R)	147,633	(69%)
	McGovern (D)	66,815	(31%)

Rep. Henry J. Hyde (R) Elected 1974; b. Apr. 18, 1924, Chicago; home, Park Ridge; Georgetown U., B.S. 1947, Loyola U., J.D. 1949.

Career Navy, WWII; Practicing atty., 1950–75; Ill. House of Reps., 1967–74, Maj. Ldr., 1971–72.

Offices 1203 LHOB, 202-225-4561. Also Rm. 220, Oak Park P.O. Bldg., 901 Lake St., Oak Park 60301, 312-383-6881.

Committees *Banking, Finance and Urban Affairs* (5th). Subcommittees: Financial Institutions Supervision, Regulation and Insurance; International Development Institutions and Finance; International Trade, Investment and Monetary Policy.

Judiciary (7th). Subcommittees: Crime; Civil and Constitutional Rights.

Group Ratings

	ADA	COPE	PC	RPN	NFU	LCV	CFA	NAB	NSI	ACA	NTU
1978	10	5	15	83	10	–	18	75	100	70	–
1977	10	26	23	67	42	25	35	–	–	59	29
1976	0	26	10	78	28	25	9	75	100	70	39

Key Votes

1) Increase Def Spnd	FOR	6) Alaska Lands Protect	AGN	11) Delay Auto Pol Cntrl	FOR
2) B-1 Bomber	FOR	7) Water Projects Veto	FOR	12) Sugar Price Escalator	AGN
3) Cargo Preference	AGN	8) Consum Protect Agcy	AGN	13) Pub Fin Cong Cmpgns	AGN
4) Dereg Nat Gas	FOR	9) Common Situs Picket	AGN	14) ERA Ratif Recissn	FOR
5) Kemp-Roth	FOR	10) Labor Law Revision	AGN	15) Prohibt Govt Abrtns	FOR

Election Results

1978 general	Henry J. Hyde (R)	87,193	(66%)	($153,066)
	Jeanne P. Quinn (D)	44,543	(34%)	($6,834)
1978 primary	Henry J. Hyde (R), unopposed			
1976 general	Henry J. Hyde (R)	106,667	(61%)	($110,215)
	Marilyn D. Clancy (D)	69,359	(39%)	($76,017)

SEVENTH DISTRICT

The Loop is what you think of when you think of Chicago. Here, where high rise construction was pioneered, stand the city's giant skyscrapers, including the new Sears & Roebuck Building, the world's tallest. Chicago also means the Near North Side, with its huge, classically designed high rise apartment buildings along Lake Michigan and, behind them, alternately smart and raunchy shopping streets. This is all part of Illinois' 7th congressional district—the glamorous part, the part best known to the outside world. But beyond the Chicago River and the miles of railroad track—Chicago is still the nation's biggest rail center—lies the grim West Side ghetto. As you go inland from the lakefront, the territory is at first a potpourri: the nation's largest skid row on West Madison, followed by odd settlements of American Indians and Appalachians. Then comes the West Side ghetto, which casts the bulk of the votes here in the 7th district.

The West Side is machine country. The black community here is more newly arrived, less middle class, less well organized—less of a community—than the blacks on the South Side in the 1st district. Some wards here that are virtually 100% black still elect Jewish or Italian ward committeemen—the last vestige of their onetime ethnic composition. When the South Side black wards have broken party lines and voted for Republicans, the West Side has stayed true to the machine, casting huge Democratic majorities for all offices.

Of all of Chicago's 50 wards, the 24th on the far West Side usually turns in the highest Democratic percentages—96% for Jimmy Carter in 1976, for example. (Interestingly, the all-black 24th sits right next to the all-white suburb of Cicero.) This is the part of the city where voting irregularities used to occur regularly when the machine needed votes; it is the West Side wards which Republicans are talking about when they say Richard Daley stole the 1960 election for John Kennedy. Massive vote fraud is now a thing of the past, not because the machine wouldn't like to steal some votes, but because too many people—the State's Attorney, the Better Government Association, the Chicago *Tribune*—are watching.

The 24th ward was the political base for Jacob Arvey, the leading Democratic pol in Illinois during Adlai Stevenson's governorship and first presidential campaign and one of the men who made Richard Daley Mayor; his power declined sharply after Daley took office in 1955. The 24th's more recent history is sometimes violent. One alderman here was murdered, no one is saying by whom, in 1969. The next alderman, George Collins, was elected to Congress in 1970; he was killed in the December 1972 airplane crash that also took the life of Mrs. Howard Hunt. Collins's successor in Congress is his widow, Cardiss Collins, who won a special election in March 1973. Her margin was so large and her opposition so negligible (her Republican opponent was Lar Daly, who used to show up on TV talk shows wearing an Uncle Sam suit) that machine control here must be considered undisputed. A Republican candidate here did well in 1978 to win 13% of the vote.

In the House Collins can be counted on as a solid Democratic vote.

Census Data Pop. 464,283. Central city, 100%; suburban, 0%. Median family income, $7,536; families above $15,000: 13%; families below $3,000: 16%. Median years education, 9.7.

The Voters

Median voting age 39.
Employment profile White collar, 35%. Blue collar, 49%. Service, 16%. Farm, -%.
Ethnic groups Black, 55%. Spanish, 17%. Total foreign stock, 22%. Poland, 4%; Italy, 2%; USSR, 1%.

Presidential vote

1976	Carter (D)	91,956	(81%)
	Ford (R)	21,836	(19%)
1972	Nixon (R)	33,266	(26%)
	McGovern (D)	93,318	(74%)

Rep. Cardiss Collins (D) Elected June 5, 1973; b. Sept. 24, 1931, St. Louis, Mo.; home, Chicago; Northwestern U.; Baptist.

Career Stenographer, Ill. Dept. of Labor; Secy., accountant, and revenue auditor, Ill. Dept. of Revenue.

Offices 2438 RHOB, 202-225-5006. Also 230 S. Dearborn St., Chicago 60604, 312-353-5754.

Committees *Government Operations* (9th). Subcommittees: Manpower and Housing (Chairman).

Foreign Affairs (10th). Subcommittees: Africa; Inter-American Affairs.

Group Ratings

	ADA	COPE	PC	RPN	NFU	LCV	CFA	NAB	NSI	ACA	NTU
1978	65	85	73	38	70	–	59	0	13	14	–
1977	75	95	60	30	90	82	65	–	–	0	24
1976	70	90	87	53	100	82	73	18	20	4	32

Key Votes

1) Increase Def Spnd	AGN	6) Alaska Lands Protect	DNV	11) Delay Auto Pol Cntrl	AGN
2) B-1 Bomber	AGN	7) Water Projects Veto	AGN	12) Sugar Price Escalator	DNV
3) Cargo Preference	FOR	8) Consum Protect Agcy	FOR	13) Pub Fin Cong Cmpgns	AGN
4) Dereg Nat Gas	AGN	9) Common Situs Picket	FOR	14) ERA Ratif Recissn	AGN
5) Kemp-Roth	AGN	10) Labor Law Revision	FOR	15) Prohibt Govt Abrtns	AGN

Election Results

1978 general	Cardiss Collins (D)	64,716	(86%)	($34,857)
	James C. Holt (R)	10,273	(14%)	($13,610)
1978 primary	Cardiss Collins (D)	32,817	(72%)	
	John J. Klich, Jr. (D)	12,910	(28%)	($5,693)
1976 general	Cardiss Collins (D)	88,239	(85%)	($19,957)
	Newell Ward (R)	15,854	(15%)	($0)

EIGHTH DISTRICT

The 8th congressional district of Illinois is part of the North and Northwest Sides of Chicago. This is middle and lower middle class country, some of it in decline, with strip commercial developments and neighborhoods of one and two family houses. The overall impression is rather depressing, though many of the blocks are maintained with meticulous care. Most of the district is resolutely all white, although it does include part of the West Side black ghetto. The atmosphere here is still decidedly ethnic, and the 8th is the heart of Chicago's North Side Polish community. (Altogether, the 8th has the fourth largest Polish-American population of any district in the nation.) Its residents, less prosperous than their cousins in the adjoining 11th district, are closer to old country ways and more dependent on their ward organizations. This is the kind of urban area which many young middle Americans, in their rush to the curved street subdivisions and shopping centers of the suburbs, are leaving behind. But it is still an area of considerable import in Chicago, and one which has not abandoned its ancestral allegiance to the Democratic Party, even in the Republican years of 1966, 1968, and 1972.

Of all the Chicago congressmen who belong to the machine bloc, the clear and undisputed leader is Dan Rostenkowski, Representative from the 8th district. He is something of a prodigy in the organization: he was first elected to the legislature at 24, and when he was first elected to Congress in 1958 he was only 30. That is unusually young for an organization which reveres seniority, and an indication that it was expected that Rostenkowski would accumulate great seniority and become an important congressman.

With a few stumbles along the way, he has done just that. His worst moment came when Tiger Teague ousted him from the caucus chairman post in 1970. It also hurt when reformers led by Phillip Burton took away the Ways and Means Committee Democrats' power to make committee assignments in 1974. But Teague has now retired, and Burton was defeated for the majority leadership in 1976. Dan Rostenkowski, the second ranking Democrat on the House Ways and Means Committee, is still ascending to greater levels of power.

Rostenkowski's positions on major issues before Ways and Means have spotlighted the split which used to be so important between labor-liberals and big city machine Democrats. Rostenkowski is one of the latter. He has not supported the kind of national health insurance backed by Edward Kennedy or organized labor, for example. Nor did he support the Carter Administration's hospital care cost containment bill in 1978—which was important, since he was then Chairman of the Ways and Means Health Subcommittee. But Rostenkowski is not necessarily an adamant opponent of these measures, either. On the contrary, when legislation is actually passed, the chances are that he will have played a major role in crafting it.

In 1979 Chairman Al Ullman persuaded Rostenkowski to move to the chair of the Selected Revenue Measures Subcommittee—a body which could have jurisdiction over major tax cut legislation. His future seems bright—and full of opportunities. He is 14 years younger than Ways and Means Chairman Al Ullman, and has every prospect of succeeding to the chairmanship of Ways and Means. At the same time, he is a by no means implausible candidate for the majority leadership in some future House. Whatever happens, Rostenkowski seems destined to become a major political leader in the early eighties.

Census Data Pop. 459,902. Central city, 100%; suburban, 0%. Median family income, $9,867; families above $15,000: 20%; families below $3,000: 9%. Median years education, 10.1.

The Voters

Median voting age 42.
Employment profile White collar, 39%. Blue collar, 49%. Service, 12%. Farm, -%.
Ethnic groups Black, 18%. Spanish, 13%. Total foreign stock, 35%. Poland, 9%; Italy, 6%; Germany, 3%; Ireland, 2%; Greece, 1%.

Presidential vote

1976	Carter (D)	100,266	(70%)
	Ford (R)	43,152	(30%)
1972	Nixon (R)	71,343	(44%)
	McGovern (D)	90,093	(56%)

Rep. Dan Rostenkowski (D) Elected 1958; b. Jan. 2, 1928, Chicago; home, Chicago; Loyola U., 1948–51; Catholic.

Career Army, Korea; Ill. House of Reps., 1953–55; Ill. Senate, 1955–59.

Offices 2111 RHOB, 202-225-4061. Also 2148 N. Damen Ave., Chicago 60647, 312-431-1111.

Committees *Ways and Means* (2d). Subcommittees: Select Revenue Measures (Chairman); Trade.

Group Ratings

	ADA	COPE	PC	RPN	NFU	LCV	CFA	NAB	NSI	ACA	NTU
1978	50	63	45	44	70	–	41	9	38	21	–
1977	45	95	50	23	83	52	55	–	–	9	20
1976	50	91	69	31	91	45	64	0	60	14	6

Key Votes

1) Increase Def Spnd	DNV	6) Alaska Lands Protect	AGN	11) Delay Auto Pol Cntrl	FOR
2) B-1 Bomber	AGN	7) Water Projects Veto	AGN	12) Sugar Price Escalator	AGN
3) Cargo Preference	FOR	8) Consum Protect Agcy	FOR	13) Pub Fin Cong Cmpgns	FOR
4) Dereg Nat Gas	AGN	9) Common Situs Picket	FOR	14) ERA Ratif Recissn	FOR
5) Kemp-Roth	AGN	10) Labor Law Revision	FOR	15) Prohibt Govt Abrtns	FOR

Election Results

1978 general	Dan Rostenkowski (D)	81,457	(86%)	($150,266)
	Carl C. LoDico (R)	13,302	(14%)	
1978 primary	Dan Rostenkowski (D), unopposed			
1976 general	Dan Rostenkowski (D)	105,595	(81%)	($51,536)
	John F. Urbaszewski (R)	25,512	(19%)	($1,342)

NINTH DISTRICT

Along Chicago's Lake Shore Drive, overlooking Lake Michigan, are some of the nation's architecturally most distinguished high rise apartment buildings. There are more classically modern buildings here, probably, than anywhere else in the world. This is the face the nation's second largest city likes to show the world: affluent, elegant, massive. Behind the apartment towers, however, lies another Chicago—an incredibly varied, sometimes funky, sometimes posh city. There are Appalachians, Italians, Mexicans, American Indians, and blacks—all just a few blocks from the row of high rises. At the northern end of the lakefront, where the big buildings are scaled down to perhaps four or five stories, is Chicago's largest Jewish community, just south of the suburbs of Evanston and Skokie. The lakefront and the territory a mile or two behind it forms Illinois's 9th congressional district, which stretches from the Near North Side to the northern city limits.

So constituted, the 9th includes that part of the city which—along with the Hyde Park area around the University of Chicago—has voted most dependably against the Democratic machine. William Singer, who ran against Daley in the 1975 primary and against Michael Bilandic in 1977, used to be Alderman from this area. It has also produced the longest tenured independent member of the city's congressional delegation, Congressman Sidney Yates.

Yates has represented the Lake Shore area in Congress since 1948—when Richard Daley had not yet been elected Cook County Clerk—with the exception of two years spent in forced retirement following an unsuccessful, but impressive, attempt to unseat Senator Everett Dirksen in 1962. Despite President Kennedy's eagerness to butter up Dirksen, Yates won 47% in that race. With his solid base of support in the liberal and Jewish communities in Chicago, Yates had little trouble winning back his seat in 1964.

Yates serves on the Appropriations Committee. But because of his race for the Senate, his seniority dates only from 1964. Thus he is the 12th ranking Democrat today; had he not given up his House seat, he would now be the number two Democrat, behind Chairman Jamie Whitten. Yates is also Chairman of the Interior Appropriations Subcommittee—a body, like Yates himself, basically in sympathy with environmental goals. As one of the senior liberals on Appropriations, Yates was one of the leaders of various moves to cut American military activity in Southeast Asia. He can likely be reelected for as long as he wishes.

Census Data Pop. 463,991. Central city, 100%; suburban, 0%. Median family income, $10,966; families above $15,000: 29%; families below $3,000: 8%. Median years education, 12.3.

The Voters

Median voting age 44.
Employment profile White collar, 64%. Blue collar, 25%. Service, 11%. Farm, –%.
Ethnic groups Black, 5%. Spanish, 9%. Total foreign stock, 41%. USSR, 6%; Germany, 5%; Poland, 3%; Ireland, Sweden, Italy, UK, 2% each; Austria, Canada, Yugoslavia, Greece, 1% each.

Presidential vote

1976	Carter (D)	105,493	(58%)
	Ford (R)	77,057	(42%)
1972	Nixon (R)	79,997	(42%)
	McGovern (D)	111,512	(58%)

Rep. Sidney R. Yates (D) Elected 1964; b. Aug. 27, 1909, Chicago; home, Chicago; U. of Chi., Ph.B. 1931, J.D. 1933; Jewish.

Career Practicing atty.; Asst. Atty. for Ill. St. Bank Receiver, 1935–37; Asst. Atty. Gen. attached to Ill. Commerce Comm., 1937–40; Navy, WWII; U.S. House of Reps., 1949–63; Dem. nominee for U.S. Senate, 1962.

Offices 2234 RHOB, 202-225-2111. Also 230 S. Dearborn St., Chicago 60604, 312-353-4596.

Committees *Appropriations* (12th). Subcommittees: Foreign Operations; Interior (Chairman); Legislative.

Group Ratings

	ADA	COPE	PC	RPN	NFU	LCV	CFA	NAB	NSI	ACA	NTU
1978	100	85	95	55	60	–	91	9	20	7	–
1977	95	87	85	75	67	80	85	–	–	11	31
1976	90	87	95	59	100	78	100	18	0	11	28

Key Votes

1) Increase Def Spnd	AGN	6) Alaska Lands Protect	FOR	11) Delay Auto Pol Cntrl	AGN
2) B-1 Bomber	AGN	7) Water Projects Veto	AGN	12) Sugar Price Escalator	AGN
3) Cargo Preference	AGN	8) Consum Protect Agcy	FOR	13) Pub Fin Cong Cmpgns	FOR
4) Dereg Nat Gas	AGN	9) Common Situs Picket	FOR	14) ERA Ratif Recissn	AGN
5) Kemp-Roth	AGN	10) Labor Law Revision	FOR	15) Prohibt Govt Abrtns	AGN

Election Results

1978 general	Sidney R. Yates (D)	87,543	(75%)	($14,870)
	John M. Collins (R)	28,673	(25%)	
1978 primary	Sidney R. Yates (D)	40,570	(87%)	
	One other (D)	5,946	(13%)	
1976 general	Sidney R. Yates (D)	121,915	(72%)	($11,749)
	Thomas J. Wajerski (R)	47,054	(28%)	($1474)

TENTH DISTRICT

The 10th district of Illinois is one of two new suburban Chicago districts created by court order in 1971. The district is about as compact and contiguous as possible, and one of socioeconomic homogeneity. Its sameness can be summed up in a single word: rich. According to the 1970 Census this was the district with the second highest median family income in the United States—then over $16,000, now probably over $30,000. That figure was exceeded only in the 8th district of Maryland, where fast-rising federal salaries have inflated the income level. Incomes there depend in large part on taxes which the federal government will exert force, if necessary, to extract from its citizens; the people of the 10th district of Illinois, in contrast, tend to make their money producing goods and services which other people buy voluntarily.

The 10th may be called the North Shore district. Its best known towns include Evanston, home of Northwestern University and for many years home of the Women's Christian Temperance Union. Above Evanston are Winnetka, Wilmette, and Glencoe, whose New Trier Township High School likes to think of itself as (and perhaps is) the most academically distinguished public high school in the country. These suburbs along Lake Michigan were settled long ago, pioneered by commuters using Chicago's efficient railroad lines. The large houses and shady streets of the North Shore have a comfortable, lived-in look, and not a trace of shabbiness. West of the lakefront are newer communities: the predominantly Jewis suburb of Skokie, which grew rapidly in the fifties; and farther inland places like Niles, Des Plaines, Glenview, and Northbrook, situated on the northwest rail lines and freeways, right in the path of the great suburban expansion of the sixties.

Conventional wisdom has long had it that the richer people are, the more Republican they vote. But that is clearly nonsense: if it were true, the 10th would be the second most Republican district in the country, which it is not. To be sure, this is a district which ordinarily goes Republican, and which gives many Republican candidates huge margins. On economic issues it is a district which still believes in the free enterprise system which, after all, has enabled most of its residents to get rich. But it is also a district which, on social issues, may be inclined in a liberal direction. People here do not like to think of themselves as opponents of civil rights, for instance. Many were turned off by the Vietnam war and by Nixon–Agnew appeals to the prejudices of hard-hats and white Southerners. Their opposition to Democrats was long rooted in the notion that the party was rotten with corruption; the Watergate scandal made many of them less enthusiastically Republican. This is a district which refused to go for Barry Goldwater in 1964, and it is one of the few districts where Gerald Ford did about as well as Richard Nixon had in 1972.

It is also a district with a Democratic congressman—and some of the nation's most fiercely contested congressional elections. When created in 1971, the 10th had no incumbent, but it received one by migration: Abner Mikva, a liberal Democrat whose South Side Chicago district had been eliminated. Mikva had some credentials to appeal to the 10th: he was Jewish, a certified (and successful) opponent of the Daley machine, an opponent of the Vietnam war, articulate and possessed a good sense of humor. None of these assets were enough for him to beat conservative Republican Sam Young in 1972; Young won with 52%. But they helped Mikva to a 51% victory over Young in 1974 and a 201-vote win over him in 1976.

Winning congressmen ordinarily go on to increase their margins by using the advantages of incumbency, something Mikva has not been able to do. The district retains a very large number of rock-solid Republican voters. And the economic issues which have been coming increasingly to the fore do not favor Mikva. He is a member of the Ways and Means Committee, and a leading advocate of tax reforms, some of which would increase taxes for just the kind of well-to-do people who live in the 10th district. In the 95th Congress he found himself under particular attack for the increase in Social Security taxes passed by Congress, since the greatest increases fell on owners of small businesses; Mikva introduced a bill to roll back the increases. He also pushed a successful bill to provide business tax credits for a portion of wages paid to new employees—a measure aimed at unemployment which would also help businessmen. But he strongly opposed the Steiger proposal, which eventually passed, to cut capital gains taxes.

The 1978 election was as closely contested as the three preceding. This time the Republicans nominated a moderate, Evanston state legislator John Porter. Both candidates spent liberally and put on highly sophisticated campaigns. Mikva in particular was able to field the kind of volunteer organization which is not often seen these days in Democratic campaigns. His registration and get-out-the-vote drives concentrated on Democratic areas and on students who attend college out of the district. This kind of organizational work probably made the difference, as Mikva won in a comparative landslide, by 650 votes. But Mikva's career as a highly visible, productive member of the Ways and Means Committee in the 96th Congress is coming to an end. In early 1979 it was announced that Mikva would be appointed to the U.S. Court of Appeals in the District of Columbia—one of the nation's most prestigious judgeships and one considered a possible stepping stone to the Supreme Court. He was expected to be confirmed easily. That will probably spare the 10th district the agony of close congressional elections; although Democrats will try to hold the seat, it will almost certainly be taken by a Republican in the special election.

Census Data Pop. 462,121. Central city, 0%; suburban, 100%. Median family income, $16,576; families above $15,000: 55%; families below $3,000: 3%. Median years education, 12.9.

The Voters

Median voting age 44.
Employment profile White collar, 74%. Blue collar, 18%. Service, 8%. Farm, –%.
Ethnic groups Black, 3%. Spanish, 1%. Total foreign stock, 31%. USSR, Germany, Poland, 4% each; Italy, UK, Sweden, Canada, 2% each; Austria, 1%.

Presidential vote

1976	Carter (D)	89,608	(39%)
	Ford (R)	138,449	(61%)
1972	Nixon (R)	147,305	(62%)
	McGovern (D)	89,630	(38%)

Rep. Abner J. Mikva (D) Elected 1974; b. Jan. 21, 1926, Milwaukee, Wis.; home, Evanston; U. of Chi., J.D. 1951.

Career Army Air Corps, WWII; Law Clerk for U.S. Supreme Ct. Justice Sherman Minton, 1951–52; Practicing atty., 1952–68; Ill. House of Reps., 1957–67; Candidate for Dem. nomination for U.S. House of Reps., 1966; U.S. House of Reps., 1969–73; Chm., Ill. Bd. of Ethics, 1973.

Offices 1122 LHOB, 202-225-4835. Also 2100 Ridge Ave., Evanston 60201, 312-864-9595.

Committees *Ways and Means* (12th). Subcommittees: Social Security; Trade.

Group Ratings

	ADA	COPE	PC	RPN	NFU	LCV	CFA	NAB	NSI	ACA	NTU
1978	70	89	83	50	50	–	68	11	0	9	–
1977	85	77	78	54	58	98	75	–	–	17	44
1976	85	83	90	65	83	96	100	17	0	12	39

Key Votes

1) Increase Def Spnd	AGN	6) Alaska Lands Protect	DNV	11) Delay Auto Pol Cntrl	AGN
2) B-1 Bomber	AGN	7) Water Projects Veto	FOR	12) Sugar Price Escalator	DNV
3) Cargo Preference	AGN	8) Consum Protect Agcy	FOR	13) Pub Fin Cong Cmpgns	FOR
4) Dereg Nat Gas	AGN	9) Common Situs Picket	FOR	14) ERA Ratif Recissn	AGN
5) Kemp-Roth	AGN	10) Labor Law Revision	FOR	15) Prohibt Govt Abrtns	AGN

Election Results

1978 general	Abner J. Mikva (D)	89,479	(50%)	($385,007)
	John E. Porter (R)	88,829	(50%)	($536,515)
1978 primary	Abner J. Mikva (D), unopposed			
1976 general	Abner J. Mikva (D)	106,804	(50%)	($248,551)
	Samuel H. Young (R)	106,680	(50%)	($267,255)

ELEVENTH DISTRICT

The 11th congressional district of Illinois is the northwest corner of the city of Chicago. Made up of comfortable middle class neighborhoods, the 11th had the highest percentage of families with incomes over $15,000 in 1970 of any Chicago district. It is also the Chicago district with the lowest percentage of blacks and the highest proportion of people of foreign stock. When second or third generation ethnics can leave their old neighborhoods, they tend to move here to the northwest side. Almost all of Chicago's ethnic groups are well represented in these middle class wards, especially Poles, Germans, Italians, Jews, Irish, and Greeks.

These are not people who are particularly attracted by WASP suburbs; indeed, they seem to consider them cold and unhospitable—and Republican. For these are ancestral Democrats, people who grew up revering Franklin D. Roosevelt and who think of the Chicago machine, not as a group of crooks living off their tax dollars, but as friendly people who can help you out when you need something from the city or county. They are also the kind of Democrats who don't especially like seeing their tax money spent on (black) welfare mothers and antipoverty programs.

Such attitudes have been reflected by the district's representatives for the past 20 years. The first of these was Roman Pucinski. In his early years a supporter of Kennedy and Johnson Administration social programs, he switched after a near-defeat in 1966 to become a kind of gadfly to poverty program administrators. In 1972 he ran for the Senate against Charles Percy and managed to carry only the 11th and three other ethnic congressional districts. Now he is back on the Board of Aldermen, and enough of a maverick, despite long machine support, to have run a quixotic campaign against Mayor Michael Bilandic.

Pucinski's replacement was another incumbent, Frank Annunzio, whose Loop district had been eliminated by redistricting. The transfer was difficult: Annunzio was enjoined from sending franked mail into the 11th, since none of it overlapped with the district he had been representing. Nevertheless Annunzio got 53% against Alderman John Hoellen, who had run the close race against Pucinski six years before. Now Annunzio seems safe. The Republican Party shows signs of imminent collapse here: Hoellen, after his strong race in 1972, ran against Mayor Daley in 1975 and was forced to leave the race because he was defeated as Alderman in the once solidly Republican 45th ward. In the House Annunzio was a favorite of Wayne Hays when they served together on the House Administration Committee. His voting record is solidly liberal on economic issues, much more mixed on social issues. As Chairman of the Consumer Affairs Subcommittee on Banking, Annunzio has successfully sponsored legislation placing tough regulation on debt collectors and has argued against business efforts to revise truth in lending legislation. Consumer advocates who were once skeptical about him have been pleasantly surprised.

Census Data Pop. 461,079. Central city, 100%; suburban, 0%. Median family income, $12,005; families above $15,000: 31%; families below $3,000: 5%. Median years education, 11.5.

The Voters

Median voting age 48.
Employment profile White collar, 53%. Blue collar, 37%. Service, 10%. Farm, -%.
Ethnic groups Spanish, 2%. Total foreign stock, 47%. Poland, 10%; Germany, 7%; Italy, 5%; USSR, 3%; Ireland, Greece, Czechoslovakia, Hungary, 1% each.

Presidential vote

1976	Carter (D)	103,637	(48%)
	Ford (R)	111,064	(52%)
1972	Nixon (R)	144,169	(63%)
	McGovern (D)	85,928	(37%)

Rep. Frank Annunzio (D) Elected 1964; b. Jan. 12, 1915, Chicago; home, Chicago; De Paul U., B.S. 1940; M.A. 1942; Catholic.

Career Public school teacher, 1935–43; Legis. and Ed. Dir., United Steelworkers of Amer., Chicago, Calumet Region Dist. 31, 1943–49; Dir., Ill. Dept. of Labor, 1949–52; Private businessman, 1952–64.

Offices 2303 RHOB, 202-225-6661. Also Suite 201, 4747 W. Peterson Ave., Chicago 60646, 312-736-0700.

Committees *Banking, Finance and Urban Affairs* (7th). Subcommittees: Consumer Affairs (Chairman); Financial Institutions Supervision, Regulation and Insurance; General Oversight and Renegotiation.

House Administration (5th). Services; Personnel and Police (Chairman).

Group Ratings

	ADA	COPE	PC	RPN	NFU	LCV	CFA	NAB	NSI	ACA	NTU
1978	40	79	45	36	60	–	46	17	50	22	–
1977	45	96	55	23	67	40	70	–	–	20	15
1976	55	91	70	19	92	52	91	8	80	15	8

Key Votes

1) Increase Def Spnd	FOR	6) Alaska Lands Protect	AGN	11) Delay Auto Pol Cntrl	FOR
2) B-1 Bomber	AGN	7) Water Projects Veto	AGN	12) Sugar Price Escalator	FOR
3) Cargo Preference	FOR	8) Consum Protect Agcy	FOR	13) Pub Fin Cong Cmpgns	AGN
4) Dereg Nat Gas	AGN	9) Common Situs Picket	FOR	14) ERA Ratif Recissn	FOR
5) Kemp-Roth	AGN	10) Labor Law Revision	FOR	15) Prohibt Govt Abrtns	FOR

Election Results

1978 general	Frank Annunzio (D)	112,365	(74%)	($82,201)
	John Hoeger (R)	40,044	(26%)	($6,164)
1978 primary	Frank Annunzio (D)	54,403	(87%)	
	One other (D)	7,928	(13%)	
1976 general	Frank Annunzio (D)	135,755	(67%)	($77,220)
	Daniel C. Reber (R)	65,680	(33%)	($6,688)

TWELFTH DISTRICT

Only four congressional districts in the United States more than doubled their populations during the sixties. Three were in California, and the other was the 12th district of Illinois. This is not a particularly neatly shaped seat: it includes the six northwestern townships of Cook County and, just to the north, the southern portion of Lake County. The 12th's territory includes the very rich North Shore suburbs of Highland Park and Lake Forest, traditionally Republican, but in 1972 the least pro-Nixon portion of the district. It is not these, but the suburbs farther west, just beyond O'Hare Airport, which have been growing most rapidly. As one drives through Schaumburg on the freeway, one sees the spectacle of one of the nation's largest Sears outlets, which is surrounded by a giant shopping center hard by a cornfield. The corn, one can predict, will not last long; this is prime real estate, the place where young, affluent families in the Chicago area are naturally gravitating. There are fewer old people here, and more children, than in any other Illinois congressional district.

The 12th politically is more or less a descendant of the old 13th district, which also included all of what now is the 10th. For six years, until the Nixon Administration took office, the old district was represented by Donald Rumsfeld, who moved up to become Gerald Ford's Secretary of Defense after performing a variety of chores for the Nixon Administration. As Congressman, Rumsfeld had a reputation in the district for being some kind of liberal Republican, though that seems to have been mainly because he was young and genial; his voting record resembled those of dour, aging Illinois conservatives.

The district is currently represented by a Republican who is also young and genial, and who suddenly has a career with as much national scope as Rumsfeld's. He is Philip Crane, and he is running for president. Crane won the district in a 1969 special election, and his hold was shaky until the North Shore suburbs were excised from the seat; he has had no trouble winning reelection since. But Crane is the kind of person who is not interested in political security. He is a strong conservative, one who seems to take libertarian stands on domestic issues. On foreign policy, he is a strong anti-Communist and favors increased defense spending. He comes from a successful family: his father was a doctor with a radio advice program; one brother was elected to Congress in Downstate Illinois in 1978 and another ran in 1976 and 1978 in Indiana. As the kind of congressman not afraid to cast lone dissenting votes, and as head of the American Conservative Union, he gained the reputation of being far to the right; and in the House he has been less interested in crafting legislation (something which is hard for most Republicans to do) than in asserting his principles.

Crane announced for the presidency in August 1978. His strategy was to knock Ronald Reagan out of the race in New Hampshire and other early primaries and to preempt the conservative majority of Republican primary voters for himself. In late 1978 and early 1979 he seemed to be making progress; many conservative activists in New Hampshire and other states were coming to his side. But in the spring of 1979 his campaign came apart. Top staffers quit, saying that Crane was downplaying his conservative stance on social issues in favor of the conservative stands on economic issues he shared with most other Republican candidates. It seems doubtful whether a little known candidate can survive the publicity. At this writing Crane's campaign continues, but he has until the December 1979 filing date the option of running for the House again.

Census Data Pop. 461,054. Central city, 0%; suburban, 100%. Median family income, $15,173; families above $15,000: 51%; families below $3,000: 2%. Median years education, 12.7.

The Voters

Median voting age 39.
Employment profile White collar, 67%. Blue collar, 25%. Service, 8%. Farm, –%.
Ethnic groups Spanish, 2%. Total foreign stock, 20%. Germany, 4%; Italy, Poland, 2% each; Canada, UK, Sweden, USSR, 1% each.

Presidential vote

1976	Carter (D)	70,460	(31%)
	Ford (R)	157,389	(69%)
1972	Nixon (R)	136,343	(71%)
	McGovern (D)	56,896	(29%)

Rep. Philip M. Crane (R) Elected Nov. 25, 1969; b. Nov. 3, 1930, Chicago; home, Mt. Prospect; De Paul U., Hillsdale Col., B.A., Ind. U., M.A., Ph.D., U. of Mich., U. of Vienna.

Career Instructor, Ind. U., 1960–63; Asst. Prof., Bradley U., 1963–67; Dir. of Schools, Westminster Acad., 1967–68.

Offices 1035 LHOB, 202-225-3711. Also Suite 101, 1450 S. New Wilke Rd., Arlington Heights 60005, 312-394-0790.

Committees *Ways and Means* (5th). Subcommittees: Health; Public Assistance and Unemployment Compensation.

Group Ratings

	ADA	COPE	PC	RPN	NFU	LCV	CFA	NAB	NSI	ACA	NTU
1978	5	6	10	67	0	–	9	100	100	100	–
1977	5	14	20	62	18	19	15	–	–	96	82
1976	5	14	11	50	9	3	9	92	100	96	73

Key Votes

1) Increase Def Spnd	FOR	6) Alaska Lands Protect	AGN	11) Delay Auto Pol Cntrl	FOR
2) B-1 Bomber	FOR	7) Water Projects Veto	DNV	12) Sugar Price Escalator	DNV
3) Cargo Preference	AGN	8) Consum Protect Agcy	AGN	13) Pub Fin Cong Cmpgns	DNV
4) Dereg Nat Gas	FOR	9) Common Situs Picket	AGN	14) ERA Ratif Recissn	FOR
5) Kemp-Roth	FOR	10) Labor Law Revision	AGN	15) Prohibt Govt Abrtns	FOR

Election Results

1978 general	Philip M. Crane (R)	110,503	(80%)	($191,075)
	Gilbert Bogen (D)	28,424	(20%)	
1978 primary	Philip M. Crane (R), unopposed			
1976 general	Philip M. Crane (R)	151,899	(73%)	($118,561)
	Edwin L. Frank (D)	56,644	(27%)	($11,418)

THIRTEENTH DISTRICT

The 13th congressional district of Illinois is part of the Chicago metropolitan area far beyond the reach of the late Mayor Daley's machine, but well within the reach of the Chicago *Tribune*. The district forms a kind of half-circle around the northern and western parts of the metropolitan area, as it stretches from the industrial town of Waukegan on Lake Michigan to a point below the German Catholic town of Aurora, due west of the Chicago Loop. This area is not quite as prosperous as the suburbs closer to Chicago; it contains pockets of urban poverty and rural shabbiness, as well as some working class neighborhoods and middle class towns. The suburban building boom invaded the district's cornfields with real force in the late sixties, but the growth here has not been as explosive—or disruptive—as in the neighboring 12th district.

In 1964 what is now the 13th district was a belt of the suburban Cook County and collar county area that went for Barry Goldwater. Extending around the city at a radius from 20 to 60 miles, this area coincided roughly with the *Tribune*'s major circulation zone, which was notable since the suburbs of other Great Lakes metropolitan areas all went for Johnson. It may seem odd to make this connection between voting behavior and newspaper circulation, but only to those unfamiliar with the old *Tribune*. Today the paper, while conservative editorially, is evenhanded in its choice of columnists and reliable, even authoritative, in its news columns. But in the heyday of its most famous publisher, Colonel Robert McCormick, and for some years afterwards, the *Tribune* was the voice of Midwestern Republicanism and conservatism. In the nineteenth century tradition the entire paper was partisan, designed to persuade its readers of the correctness of its opinions. And it was taken as gospel by hundreds of thousands of suburban Chicago readers, as well as many more in the rural hinterland for miles around. The hard-nosed conservatism of the old *Tribune* still finds expression in Illinois voting behavior today, and nowhere more than in the suburban belt around Chicago.

The tenure of the 13th district's Congressman dates from 1962, when the *Tribune* was becoming more moderate. He is noticeably more of a middle of the road Republican than most of those who represented the state 20 years ago. This is Robert McClory, familiar still to many for his role in the House Judiciary Committee impeachment hearings. McClory was then the second-ranking Republican on the Committee—he lost the top slot by a flip of a coin 12 years before, which gave Edward Hutchinson of Michigan, now retired, more seniority. A thin, nervous-seeming man, McClory was constantly commenting on the evidence, often with disapproval. He finally came out for impeaching Nixon for abuse of power, but not for his complicity in the coverup, for which he felt the evidence was insufficient. McClory was 66 at the time, and while he seemed to have some political problems they turned out to be minimal. He had already won his Republican primary, and though he had a tough challenge in the general, the district's *Tribune* Republicanism helped him to a 55% win. He has won more easily since. In 1976 he became ranking minority member on Judiciary, and despite his age he seems capable of retaining that position for some time.

Census Data Pop. 463,096. Central city, 0%; suburban, 100%. Median family income, $11,994; families above $15,000: 31%; families below $3,000: 5%. Median years education, 12.2.

The Voters

Median voting age 39.
Employment profile White collar, 47%. Blue collar, 40%. Service, 12%. Farm, 1%.
Ethnic groups Black, 5%. Spanish, 3%. Total foreign stock, 18%. Germany, 4%; Poland, UK, Sweden, Canada, 1% each.

Presidential vote

1976	Carter (D)	64,623	(37%)
	Ford (R)	109,215	(63%)
1972	Nixon (R)	112,900	(70%)
	McGovern (D)	49,217	(30%)

Rep. Robert McClory (R) Elected 1962; b. Jan. 31, 1908, Riverside; home, Lake Bluff; Dartmouth Col., 1926–28, Chicago-Kent Col. of Law, LL.B. 1932.

Career Practicing atty.; Ill. House of Reps., 1951–53; Ill. Senate, 1953–63.

Offices 2469 RHOB, 202-225-5221. Also Kane County Municipal Bldg., 150 Dexter Ct., Elgin 60120, 312-697-5005.

Committees *Judiciary* (Ranking Member). Subcommittees: Administrative Law and Governmental Relations; Monopolies and Commercial Law.

Group Ratings

	ADA	COPE	PC	RPN	NFU	LCV	CFA	NAB	NSI	ACA	NTU
1978	45	21	20	91	0	–	18	91	89	73	–
1977	10	17	23	77	18	40	20	–	–	69	24
1976	20	5	20	82	9	34	18	83	70	63	38

Key Votes

1) Increase Def Spnd	FOR	6) Alaska Lands Protect	FOR	11) Delay Auto Pol Cntrl	FOR
2) B-1 Bomber	FOR	7) Water Projects Veto	AGN	12) Sugar Price Escalator	AGN
3) Cargo Preference	AGN	8) Consum Protect Agcy	AGN	13) Pub Fin Cong Cmpgns	AGN
4) Dereg Nat Gas	FOR	9) Common Situs Picket	AGN	14) ERA Ratif Recissn	AGN
5) Kemp-Roth	FOR	10) Labor Law Revision	AGN	15) Prohibt Govt Abrtns	FOR

Election Results

1978 general	Robert McClory (R)	64,060	(61%)	($111,477)
	Frederick J. Steffen (D)	40,675	(39%)	($82,216)
1978 primary	Robert McClory (R)	18,163	(59%)	
	Richard L. Verbic (R)	12,521	(41%)	($74,303)
1976 general	Robert McClory (R)	109,726	(69%)	($53,666)
	James J. Cummings (D)	49,777	(31%)	($6,343)

FOURTEENTH DISTRICT

If you take the 1970 median family income as a standard, three of the nation's five richest congressional districts lie in the suburbs of Chicago. One of them is the 14th. And of all of these rich districts, the 14th is undoubtedly the most heavily Republican and conservative. The district includes practically all of DuPage County, a fast-growing, affluent group of suburbs west of Chicago, which regularly produces higher Republican percentages than Orange County, California. Appropriately, DuPage was the site of the palatial estate of Colonel McCormick, longtime publisher of the Chicago *Tribune*; for almost 50 years McCormick's paper was the house organ for his brand of conservative, isolationist Republicanism. If DuPage County can no longer be counted as isolationist, then it certainly has remained conservative: the Colonel would not be displeased with its voting behavior in the 25 years since his death. In 1964, for example, DuPage went 60% for Barry Goldwater; in 1976, it was 71% for Gerald Ford, giving the Republican a plurality of more than 100,000 votes and wiping out more than half of Jimmy Carter's plurality in Cook County.

The suburbs of Chicago, led by DuPage, have become the heartland of Illinois Republicanism, producing larger percentages and more votes for Republican candidates than historically Republican Downstate Illinois. The suburbs are certainly entitled to credit for Illinois's having gone for Ford over Carter.

The Colonel would also be pleased with the record of the 14th district's Congressman, John Erlenborn. First elected in 1964, he has reached a position of some potential influence in the House: second ranking Republican on both the Education and Labor and the Government Operations Committees. Although he occasionally fails to take orthodox positions—for example, he has opposed restrictions on antipoverty lawyers—he is generally a stalwart and articulate exponent of conservative Republican points of view. His main concentration seems to be on the work of the Education and Labor Committee. For some years this must have been frustrating: this was the body which passed the Great Society legislation and which, because of its liberal composition, kept backing it strongly whatever the opinion of the rest of the House or the general public. But in the 95th Congress those who think like Erlenborn came into their own. He worked against the AFL-CIO's labor law reform bill; it passed the House, but died in the Senate. He worked against the common situs picketing bill, which met a similar fate. Other measures he has worked against have passed nonetheless: liberalized benefits for miners, the ban on mandatory retirement. Nonetheless Erlenborn must have the satisfaction that the point of view he articulates is no longer invariably the loser in the House, although it still does not usually prevail on the Education and Labor Committee.

Census Data Pop. 464,029. Central city, 0%; suburban, 100%. Median family income, $14,527; families above $15,000: 47%; families below $3,000: 2%. Median years education, 12.6.

The Voters

Median voting age 40.
Employment profile White collar, 65%. Blue collar, 27%. Service, 8%. Farm, -%.
Ethnic groups Spanish, 2%. Total foreign stock, 21%. Germany, 4%; Italy, Poland, UK, 2% each; Czechoslovakia, Canada, Sweden, 1% each.

Presidential vote

1976	Carter (D)	68,222	(29%)
	Ford (R)	168,314	(71%)
1972	Nixon (R)	163,652	(75%)
	McGovern (D)	53,631	(25%)

Rep. John N. Erlenborn (R) Elected 1964; b. Feb. 8, 1927, Chicago; home, Elmhurst; U. of Notre Dame, 1944, Ind. St. Teachers Col., 1944–45, U. of Ill., 1945–46, Loyola U., LL.B. 1949; Catholic.

Career Navy, WWII; Practicing atty., 1949–50, 1952–64; Asst. State's Atty., DuPage Co., 1950–52; Ill. House of Reps., 1957–65.

Offices 2265 RHOB, 202-225-3515. Also DuPage Co. Ctr., 421 N. County Farm Rd., Wheaton 60187, 312-668-1417.

Committees *Education and Labor* (2d). Subcommittees: Labor-Management Relations; Labor Standards;

Government Operations (2d). Subcommittees: Government Information and Individual Rights; Legislation and National Security.

Group Ratings

	ADA	COPE	PC	RPN	NFU	LCV	CFA	NAB	NSI	ACA	NTU
1978	30	10	20	90	10	–	18	100	80	69	–
1977	15	22	18	77	25	20	15	–	–	80	49
1976	5	10	15	88	17	21	18	90	70	60	45

Key Votes

1) Increase Def Spnd	FOR	6) Alaska Lands Protect	DNV	11) Delay Auto Pol Cntrl	FOR
2) B-1 Bomber	FOR	7) Water Projects Veto	FOR	12) Sugar Price Escalator	AGN
3) Cargo Preference	AGN	8) Consum Protect Agcy	AGN	13) Pub Fin Cong Cmpgns	AGN
4) Dereg Nat Gas	FOR	9) Common Situs Picket	AGN	14) ERA Ratif Recissn	FOR
5) Kemp-Roth	FOR	10) Labor Law Revision	AGN	15) Prohibt Govt Abrtns	FOR

Election Results

1978 general	John N. Erlenborn (R)	118,741	(75%)	($52,212)
	James A. Romanyak (D)	39,438	(25%)	
1978 primary	John N. Erlenborn (R), unopposed			
1976 general	John N. Erlenborn (R)	176,076	(74%)	($62,489)
	Marie Agnes Fese (D)	60,505	(26%)	($15,286)

FIFTEENTH DISTRICT

The 15th congressional district of Illinois is part of the corn-growing prairie that stretches west from Chicago toward the Rocky Mountains more than a thousand miles away. This is some of the richest farmland in the nation, criss-crossed by railroads and highways which lead to the market town of Chicago. Part of the 15th—the small, conservative city of Aurora—is only 30 miles from Chicago; from there one can proceed to DeKalb, site of Northern Illinois University, or south to small industrial towns, like Ottawa and LaSalle and Streator on the way to Peoria. With its fertile soil and prosperous farmers, the 15th district historically has been one of the most solidly Republican constituencies in the nation; only LaSalle County ordinarily will turn in a Democratic margin. Yet in the last nine years the area has had five different congressmen—and one of them was a Democrat.

Part of the reason for this was redistricting. The old districts represented by Republicans Charlotte Reid (former vocalist on Don McNeill's Breakfast Club) and Leslie Arends were combined; Reid resigned to take a place on the FCC, and her seat was won by Cliffard Carlson, who declined to oppose Arends in the 1972 general election. Arends was one of the grand old men of the Republican Party, first elected to Congress in 1934, House Republican Whip since 1943. With his long white hair curling up under his collar, Arends remained a familiar figure in the House until he was almost 80, eagerly gladhanding his colleagues with the joviality one encounters in a small town Rotary Club. But Arends's performance in the 1972 election was disappointing, and he retired two years later.

The seat was won by Tim Hall, a 49-year-old teacher who had run against Arends in 1972; in the Watergate year he faced former Congressman Carlson, and beat him with 52%. Like most 1974 freshmen, he worked hard to save his seat, but he had a harder task than most and fewer resources. The 1976 Republican candidate, Tom Corcoran, was personable, articulate, and young; as a vice president of the Chicago & Northwestern Railway and a former Washington representative of the state of Illinois, he had good credentials for the job. He lambasted Hall for his liberal record and put the incumbent on the defensive. Corcoran won with a solid 54%; Hall was one of only two 1974 freshman Democrats to be defeated for reelection (the other, Allan Howe of Utah, was involved in a sex scandal). Corcoran compiled a solid conservative record in his first term and used his incumbency to advantage. Against Hall in 1978 he won reelection with a very comfortable 62%. The 15th seems returned to its traditional Republican allegiance.

Census Data Pop. 462,969. Central city, 0%; suburban, 33%. Median family income, $10,619; families above $15,000: 22%; families below $3,000: 6%. Median years education, 12.2.

The Voters

Median voting age 42.
Employment profile White collar, 41%. Blue collar, 42%. Service, 12%. Farm, 5%.
Ethnic groups Black, 2%. Spanish, 2%. Total foreign stock, 14%. Germany, 3%; Italy, UK, Sweden, 1% each.

Presidential vote

1976	Carter (D)	78,766	(60%)
	Ford (R)	115,849	(40%)
1972	Nixon (R)	133,061	(66%)
	McGovern (D)	68,288	(34%)

Rep. Tom Corcoran (R) Elected 1976; b. May 23, 1939, Ottawa; home, Ottawa; U. of Notre Dame, B.A. 1961, U. of Ill., U. of Chi., Northwestern U.; Catholic.

Career Army, 1963–65; Staff Dir. for Ill. Senate Pres. pro tem. W. Russell Arrington, 1966–69; Dir. of the State of Ill. Ofc., Wash., D.C., 1969–72; Admin. Asst. to Ill. Senate Pres. William C. Harris, 1972–74; V.P., Chicago and Northwestern Transportation Co., 1974–76.

Offices 1107 LHOB, 202-225-2976. Also 436 N. Lake St., Aurora 60506, 312-897-2220.

Committees *Interstate and Foreign Commerce* (12th). Subcommittees: Energy and Power; Oversight and Investigations.

Post Office and Civil Service (5th). Subcommittees: Compensation and Employee Benefits; Postal Operations and Services.

Group Ratings

	ADA	COPE	PC	RPN	NFU	LCV	CFA	NAB	NSI	ACA	NTU
1978	25	10	18	70	0	–	23	100	70	88	–
1977	15	9	25	67	25	50	15	–	–	89	52

Key Votes

1) Increase Def Spnd	FOR	6) Alaska Lands Protect	FOR	11) Delay Auto Pol Cntrl	FOR
2) B-1 Bomber	FOR	7) Water Projects Veto	AGN	12) Sugar Price Escalator	AGN
3) Cargo Preference	AGN	8) Consum Protect Agcy	AGN	13) Pub Fin Cong Cmpgns	AGN
4) Dereg Nat Gas	FOR	9) Common Situs Picket	AGN	14) ERA Ratif Recissn	FOR
5) Kemp-Roth	FOR	10) Labor Law Revision	AGN	15) Prohibt Govt Abrtns	FOR

Election Results

1978 general	Tom Corcoran (R)	80,856	(62%)	($180,076)
	Tim L. Hall (D)	48,756	(38%)	($21,368)
1978 primary	Tom Corcoran (R), unopposed			
1976 general	Tom Corcoran (R)	102,555	(54%)	($171,114)
	Tim L. Hall (D)	87,676	(46%)	($77,722)

SIXTEENTH DISTRICT

The northwest corner of Illinois, which forms the state's 16th congressional district, is slightly different politically from the rest of the state. A little like Wisconsin or Iowa, this part of Illinois has a larger number of Scandinavian-Americans and a stronger good government tradition than the patronage-ridden precincts of Chicago or the rest of Downstate Illinois. The largest city here is Rockford, which is actually the state's second largest; but its metropolitan area population of 272,000 is pretty insignificant next to Chicago's nearly seven million. The rest of the 16th is prime agricultural territory. Points of interest include Freeport, site of the most famous Lincoln–Douglas debate; and the home town of President U. S. Grant, Galena, once a thriving commercial center but now a Mississippi River backwater.

John Anderson has been the 16th's Congressman since the 1960 election. He began his House career in a quiet enough fashion, blending in with the conservative Illinois Republican contingent. But over time he has become distinguished from his colleagues. His parliamentary and oratorical skills won him a seat on the House Rules Committee and, in 1969, the position of Chairman of the House Republican Conference. His work on legislation in a wide variety of areas has made him a national leader. He is at this writing considered a likely candidate for president in 1980. Yet he has been a controversial figure in House Republican circles, one considered a traitor to the party by many.

This is not because he has strayed far from the party's position on economic issues. Anderson is a strong believer in the free enterprise system and free market mechanisms. He is skeptical about most Great Society programs and has voted to trim them back. He does not have a good voting record according to organized labor. He favors deregulation of natural gas. Nor has he often gone against Republican foreign policy positions. For years he backed the Nixon and Ford Administrations' policy on Vietnam and Southeast Asia.

Where Anderson has differed with many of his fellow Republicans has been on non-economic issues. For example, with Morris Udall of Arizona he sponsored a bill providing federal matching money for presidential elections; it is basically the mechanism used in 1976 and which will be used again in 1980. With Udall he has pushed to extend the matching funds principle to congressional elections. Although one can argue that these measures would actually help Republicans, few House Republicans have followed Anderson's lead. Anderson has also been a strong supporter of civil rights—a traditional Republican issue, but one not embraced by many conservative Republicans today.

Anderson was one of the first congressmen of either party to speak out against the Nixon Administration's broad view of executive privilege and one of the first Republicans to call for explanations of Watergate. In those difficult years Anderson did not seem to be a team player to many Republicans—although he can argue that his course was better for the party in the long run. He refused to follow the strategy of taking cheap shots against the opposition on issues like marijuana, student demonstrations, abortion, and other social issues. Here again, his stance may have been better for the party in the long run—those students are now voters and, even more important, potential candidates for public office—but in the short run Anderson seemed to be breaking ranks. And perhaps it was a vague sense among more orthodox Republicans that they were indulging in cheap shot politics themselves that made them resent Anderson's strident refusal to follow suit.

In any case, as early as 1971 Anderson was able to keep the Conference Chairman post over Samuel Devine of Ohio by only an 89–81 margin; he did somewhat better in 1975, against Charles Wiggins of California, largely because many old-line conservatives had been beaten in 1974. Antipathy to Anderson also surfaced in his district. In the March 1978 primary he faced opposition from right wing minister Don Lyon, who was considered flaky by some conservative organizations. Nevertheless Anderson was able to win with only 58% of the vote—a good showing in a general election, but not particularly impressive in a primary. Ironically, Anderson's position among House Republicans was growing stronger at the same time; his support of measures like Kemp–Roth and other Republican economic issues was erasing memories of past issues.

After the 1978 primary Anderson decided to consider running for president. His credentials in terms of intellect and command of a wide range of issues are at least as good as Morris Udall's were in 1976. He is an articulate speaker, who can command an audience, although sometimes he seems a little to be lecturing. His first hurdle to overcome is the notion that he is running because he couldn't be reelected; he probably could, but cannot take his district for granted. His next, and probably greater, obstacle is to convince Republican primary voters that he is one of them and that he best represents their views and feelings. Whether that is so is problematical; many of the differences he has had with his House colleagues in the past reflect a very different sense of what is important. To win Republican primary votes, Anderson must concentrate on the economic issues, where he stands in agreement with most Republican voters. But where would that leave him in a general election?

There is little doubt that the 16th district will elect another Republican congressman in 1980. In other years Democrats might have been competitive here. But the emergence of traditional economic issues and the question of the size of the federal government plays to the Republicans' strength in the 16th.

Census Data Pop. 461,719. Central city, 32%; suburban, 36%. Median family income, $10,668; families above $15,000: 21%; families below $3,000: 7%. Median years education, 12.1.

The Voters

Median voting age 43.
Employment profile White collar, 41%. Blue collar, 43%. Service, 11%. Farm, 5%.
Ethnic groups Black, 4%. Spanish, 1%. Total foreign stock, 14%. Germany, Sweden, 3% each; Italy, 2%; UK, 1%.

Presidential vote

1976	Carter (D)	76,448	(41%)
	Ford (R)	108,790	(59%)
1972	Nixon (R)	120,432	(66%)
	McGovern (D)	62,339	(34%)

Rep. John B. Anderson (R) Elected 1960; b. Feb. 15, 1922, Rockford; home, Rockford; U. of Ill., B.A., J.D. 1946, Harvard U. LL.M. 1949; Evangelical Church.

Career Army, WWII; Practicing atty.; U.S. Foreign Svc., Germany, 1952–55; State's Atty., Winnebago Co., 1956–60.

Offices 1101 LHOB, 202-225-5676. Also Fed. Bldg., Rockford 61101, 815-962-8807.

Committees *Rules* (2d).

Group Ratings

	ADA	COPE	PC	RPN	NFU	LCV	CFA	NAB	NSI	ACA	NTU
1978	55	39	50	100	22	–	32	73	63	44	–
1977	40	29	33	100	45	46	25	–	–	38	35
1976	50	28	39	94	33	50	36	80	67	29	24

Key Votes

1) Increase Def Spnd	AGN	6) Alaska Lands Protect	FOR	11) Delay Auto Pol Cntrl	FOR
2) B-1 Bomber	FOR	7) Water Projects Veto	FOR	12) Sugar Price Escalator	AGN
3) Cargo Preference	AGN	8) Consum Protect Agcy	AGN	13) Pub Fin Cong Cmpgns	FOR
4) Dereg Nat Gas	FOR	9) Common Situs Picket	AGN	14) ERA Ratif Recissn	AGN
5) Kemp-Roth	FOR	10) Labor Law Revision	AGN	15) Prohibt Govt Abrtns	AGN

Election Results

1978 general	John B. Anderson (R)	76,752	(65%)	($232,379)
	Ernest W. Dahlin (D)	40,471	(35%)	($17,257)
1978 primary	John B. Anderson (R)	43,055	(58%)	
	Don Lyon (R)	31,266	(42%)	($290,446)
1976 general	John B. Anderson (R)	114,324	(68%)	($47,459)
	Stephen J. Eytalis (D)	54,002	(32%)	($553)

SEVENTEENTH DISTRICT

The 17th is one of the Illinois congressional districts created by a federal court order in 1971. It combines the southern edge of the Chicago metropolitan area with the fertile farmland of the central Illinois prairie. The district's largest city is Joliet, with less than 100,000 people, an economically healthy manufacturing city 50 miles southwest of Chicago. Somewhat less prosperous and considerably smaller is Kankakee, on the river and in the county of the same name, some 80 miles from Chicago and smack in the middle of farmland. Taken together, this territory is politically marginal, normally running about 5% more Republican than the state as a whole. Agricultural Iroquois County, in the southern part of the district, is one of the most Republican in the state (66% for Ford in 1976); Joliet inclines toward the Democrats (but Jimmy Carter and his Southern accent did not do well here); Chicago Heights and Park Forest are swing suburbs, likely to go with (and thus help determine) the winner of any statewide election.

The district's boundaries seem to have been created for a former Illinois House Speaker; but, daunted by criticism, he did not run. Instead the Republican nominee was Joliet state Representative George O'Brien, who beat a Cook County Democrat in 1972 and, with difficulty, in 1974. In 1976 O'Brien seemed to have a tougher opponent, a Kankakee County farmer and businessman named Merlin Karlock, who spent $390,000 in all. But to judge from reports in *Congressional Quarterly*, Karlock's money was not effectively spent. Much of it went for billboards, which do little to influence voters who feel reasonably satisfied with the incumbent, on newspaper ads, and on red, white, and blue station wagons touring rural areas to publicize Karlock. This is the sort of hoopla that some commentators missed in the 1976 presidential campaign, with its limitations on spending. It vanished because campaign managers, able to spend only a limited amount of money, eliminated expenses which did not produce votes. For all the hoopla, Karlock got only 42% of the vote. O'Brien won even more easily in 1978, and serves on the Appropriations Committee. He is generally a reliable Republican vote.

Census Data Pop. 462,943. Central city, 0%; suburban, 72%. Median family income, $11,286; families above $15,000: 26%; families below $3,000: 6%. Median years education, 12.0.

Rep. George M. O'Brien (R) Elected 1972; b. June 17, 1917, Chicago; home, Joliet; Northwestern U., A.B. 1939, Yale U., J.D. 1947; Catholic.

Career Air Force, WWII; Practicing atty.; Will Co. Bd. of Supervisors, 1956–64; Ill. House of Reps., 1971–72.

Offices 2439 RHOB, 202-225-3635. Also 101 N. Joliet St., Joliet 60431, 815-740-2040.

Committees *Appropriations* (15th). Subcommittees: Labor-HEW; State, Justice, Commerce and Judiciary.

Group Ratings

	ADA	COPE	PC	RPN	NFU	LCV	CFA	NAB	NSI	ACA	NTU
1978	25	15	20	70	33	–	23	91	100	77	–
1977	15	18	18	77	50	14	10	–	–	73	34
1976	15	18	15	72	17	34	18	75	86	64	48

Key Votes

1) Increase Def Spnd	FOR	6) Alaska Lands Protect	AGN	11) Delay Auto Pol Cntrl	FOR
2) B-1 Bomber	FOR	7) Water Projects Veto	FOR	12) Sugar Price Escalator	FOR
3) Cargo Preference	AGN	8) Consum Protect Agcy	AGN	13) Pub Fin Cong Cmpgns	AGN
4) Dereg Nat Gas	FOR	9) Common Situs Picket	AGN	14) ERA Ratif Recissn	FOR
5) Kemp-Roth	FOR	10) Labor Law Revision	AGN	15) Prohibt Govt Abrtns	FOR

Election Results

1978 general	George M. O'Brien (R)	94,375	(71%)	($112,346)
	Clifford J. Sinclair (D)	39,260	(29%)	($14,808)
1978 primary	George M. O'Brien (R), unopposed			
1976 general	George M. O'Brien (R)	113,145	(58%)	($118,888)
	Merlin Karlock (D)	81,220	(42%)	($390,266)

EIGHTEENTH DISTRICT

"Will it play in Peoria?" was a favorite question among Nixon White House aides, believing as they did that they had a special and superior understanding of the thinking of Middle America. For them the country was personified by Peoria, a place where market researchers like to test commercial products and one which has always produced comfortable margins for Republicans and Richard Nixon. It can be argued that Peoria is not actually all that typical. After all, most of the country votes for Democrats most of the time. And Peoria is somewhat more heterogeneous than its reputation: it has produced Betty Friedan as well as (his technical home was in Pekin, across the Illinois River) Everett McKinley Dirksen, Senate Minority Leader until his death in 1969.

Nonetheless Peoria, with 127,000 people and another 100,000 in its suburbs, is a reasonably good symbol of Midwestern America. It forms the nucleus of Illinois's 18th congressional district, whose representation over the past 40 years is in line with its conservative Republican reputation. There was Dirksen, who retired from the House in 1948 because he thought he was going blind; he recovered and beat Senate Majority Leader Scott Lucas in the 1950 election. Dirksen, before all the fustian made him a national legend, was a pillar of his party's Taft conservative wing. He was succeeded in the House by Harold Velde, who worked on the old House Un-American Activities Committee in its most un-American days. Velde was succeeded in 1956 by Robert Michel, then his administrative assistant, and now Minority Whip of the House of Representatives. Such steadfast Republican orthodoxy is hard to match.

Michel has moved up in the Republican ranks partly because of seniority. He has served longer now than any other Republican except John Rhodes, the Minority Leader, and Bob Wilson of California; if he were not Whip, he would be ranking Republican on the Appropriations Committee. He also has considerable personal popularity among House Republicans. He was for years a star pitcher on the House Republican softball team, and he has a fine singing voice which he uses at occasional public events.

In 1973 the Nixon White House dumped the Chairman of the House Republican Congressional Campaign Committee and tried to name their own choice. House Republicans rebelled and elected Michel instead. He can hardly be held responsible for Republicans' disastrous showing in the 1974 congressional elections, and his colleagues did not. Instead they elevated him to the Whip post vacated by the retirement of Illinois colleague Les Arends. Working with John Rhodes, Michel at first found his job to be rounding up enough votes to sustain Ford vetoes or the even larger number required to stop Carter programs. But in the 95th Congress Republicans seized the initiative on issues, and Michel played an important role in that process. He is not just affable; he has a talent for framing issues and making arguments, and a solid devotion to the Republican Party. Altogether he seems a clear favorite to succeed Minority Leader John Rhodes some day.

As might be expected, Peoria and the 18th district have generally been willing to reelect Michel with large majorities. The exception was in the Watergate year of 1974, when an underfinanced Democrat held him to only 55% of the vote; a serious challenge might have unseated him. But that ironic footnote to the Nixon years was never written, and Michel's tenure again seems untroubled.

Census Data Pop. 463,155. Central city, 27%; suburban, 40%. Median family income, $10,096; families above $15,000: 20%; families below $3,000: 7%. Median years education, 12.1.

The Voters

Median voting age 44.
Employment profile White collar, 44%. Blue collar, 38%. Service, 13%. Farm, 5%.
Ethnic groups Black, 4%. Total foreign stock, 9%. Germany, 2%; UK, 1%.

Presidential vote

1976	Carter (D)	88,371	(44%)
	Ford (R)	113,592	(56%)
1972	Nixon (R)	128,747	(66%)
	McGovern (D)	67,503	(34%)

Rep. Robert H. Michel (R) Elected 1956; b. Mar. 2, 1923, Peoria; home, Peoria; Bradley U., B.S. 1948; Apostolic Christian.

Career Army, WWII; Admin. Asst., U.S. Rep. Harold Velde, 1949–56.

Offices 2112 RHOB, 202-225-6201. Also 1007 1st Natl. Bank Bldg., Peoria 61602, 309-673-6358.

Committees *Minority Whip*

Appropriations (2d). Subcommittees: Labor-HEW.

Group Ratings

	ADA	COPE	PC	RPN	NFU	LCV	CFA	NAB	NSI	ACA	NTU
1978	15	5	15	92	10	–	14	100	100	75	–
1977	15	9	18	69	17	22	10	–	–	88	35
1976	5	9	8	88	9	10	0	91	90	81	58

Key Votes

1) Increase Def Spnd	FOR	6) Alaska Lands Protect	AGN	11) Delay Auto Pol Cntrl	FOR
2) B-1 Bomber	FOR	7) Water Projects Veto	FOR	12) Sugar Price Escalator	FOR
3) Cargo Preference	AGN	8) Consum Protect Agcy	AGN	13) Pub Fin Cong Cmpgns	AGN
4) Dereg Nat Gas	FOR	9) Common Situs Picket	AGN	14) ERA Ratif Recissn	FOR
5) Kemp-Roth	FOR	10) Labor Law Revision	AGN	15) Prohibt Govt Abrtns	FOR

Election Results

1978 general	Robert H. Michel (R)	85,973	(66%)	($57,439)
	Virgil R. Grunkemeyer (D)	44,527	(34%)	
1978 primary	Robert H. Michel (R), unopposed			
1976 general	Robert H. Michel (R)	108,028	(58%)	($60,317)
	Matthew Ryan (D)	79,102	(42%)	($37,312)

NINETEENTH DISTRICT

Tom Railsback is one of forty-odd Republican congressmen who were elected in previously Democratic districts in 1966—the best Republican congressional year since Eisenhower won his second term. Railsback was then 34, an attorney from Moline who had been in practice for less than ten years, and a four-year veteran of the Illinois legislature. He was the kind of bright young man whom the Republican elders of the area picked as their standard-bearer: a young lawyer who could stay in Congress many years and accumulate seniority and power, and who was noticeably brighter and more personable than the average Illinois small city Republican lawyer. Their hope, of course, was that he would be a solid bulwark of conservative Republicanism, a loyal foot soldier in his first years and some day perhaps a leader in the House Republican ranks. In many respects Tom Railsback has realized these hopes, but in a few respects he must have seriously disappointed some of the oldtimers who first blessed his candidacy.

For Railsback, as most political observers will remember, was part of the minority of Republicans on the House Judiciary Committee which was as responsible as anyone for convincing the Congress and the American people that Richard Nixon ought to be removed from office. Indeed, he may have been the key figure on the Republican side. He became convinced early that he would have to vote for impeachment, and as the hearings went on he began meeting with like-minded Republicans and, later, Southern Democrats to formulate strategy and draw up articles of impeachment they could agree on. In the process Railsback gained an impressive mastery of the facts of the case—and a fervor that gave a certain eloquence to a speaking style that was otherwise rather plain.

Something was made by commentators of Railsback's political predicament, caught between Nixon-loving Republicans and Nixon-hating Democrats and Independents. Actually, it was never as bad as he seemed to think. The Republican primary had taken place in March, long before the hearings, and Railsback had been unopposed. In general he had the support not only of the local Republican Party, but also of the United Auto Workers, with their large membership at agricultural machinery plants in Rock Island and Moline, in and around the area where half the people in Railsback's 19th district live. When he came out for impeachment he destroyed the only issue which could have helped his Democratic opponent and prepared the way for his 65% victory. With Nixon disgraced, he was not even challenged in the 1976 primary.

Railsback is no longer at the center of the national stage. He has been reelected easily, in 1978 with no Democratic opposition whatever. He currently stands behind only 70-year-old Robert McClory, also of Illinois, in seniority among House Judiciary Committee Republicans. Instead of passing on the fate of the presidency, he finds himself making positive contributions on legislation affecting bankruptcy judges, labor law revision, and lobbyist disclosure. It is more in line with what was expected of him when he first ran for office, but it must be nothing like the heady days of 1974.

Census Data Pop. 462,085. Central city, 27%; suburban, 40%. Median family income, $9,579; families above $15,000: 17%; families below $3,000: 9%. Median years education, 12.1.

The Voters

Median voting age 44.
Employment profile White collar, 39%. Blue collar, 39%. Service, 14%. Farm, 8%.
Ethnic groups Black, 2%. Spanish, 2%. Total foreign stock, 11%. Germany, Sweden, 2% each.

Presidential vote

1976	Carter (D)	90,524	(46%)
	Ford (R)	105,234	(54%)
1972	Nixon (R)	124,549	(62%)
	McGovern (D)	77,194	(38%)

Rep. Tom Railsback (R) Elected 1966; b. Jan. 22, 1932, Moline; home, Moline; Grinnell Col., B.A. 1954, Northwestern U., J.D. 1957; Congregationalist.

Career Army, 1957–59; Practicing atty., 1957–67; Ill. House of Reps., 1963–67.

Offices 2104 RHOB, 202-225-5905. Also Rm. 228, Fed. Bldg., 211 19th St., Rock Island 61201, 309-794-1681.

Committees *Judiciary* (2d). Subcommittees: Courts, Civil Liberties, and the Administration of Justice; Monopolies and Commercial Law.

Group Ratings

	ADA	COPE	PC	RPN	NFU	LCV	CFA	NAB	NSI	ACA	NTU
1978	20	25	45	92	30	–	27	100	67	56	–
1977	45	41	40	100	40	41	20	–	–	44	32
1976	25	32	25	73	42	39	18	55	71	50	29

Key Votes

1) Increase Def Spnd	FOR	6) Alaska Lands Protect	FOR	11) Delay Auto Pol Cntrl	AGN
2) B-1 Bomber	FOR	7) Water Projects Veto	FOR	12) Sugar Price Escalator	DNV
3) Cargo Preference	AGN	8) Consum Protect Agcy	AGN	13) Pub Fin Cong Cmpgns	FOR
4) Dereg Nat Gas	FOR	9) Common Situs Picket	AGN	14) ERA Ratif Recissn	FOR
5) Kemp-Roth	FOR	10) Labor Law Revision	FOR	15) Prohibt Govt Abrtns	AGN

Election Results

1978 general	Tom Railsback (R), unopposed			($28,647)
1978 primary	Tom Railsback (R), unopposed			
1976 general	Tom Railsback (R)	132,571	(68%)	($47,499)
	John Craver (D)	60,967	(32%)	($10,515)

TWENTIETH DISTRICT

The 20th district of Illinois is a descendant of the district that sent Abraham Lincoln, then a young Springfield lawyer and Whig politician, to the House of Representatives in 1846. The western part of the district, at least, sometimes seems to have changed little since the nineteenth century. It remains a land of fertile prairies, the bottomlands of the Mississippi and Illinois Rivers, farm marketing towns, and courthouse villages. The river port of Quincy on the Mississippi has not grown much since the turn of the century, nor has the little village of Nauvoo, from which the Mormons were expelled in the 1840s and led by Brigham Young to their promised land in Utah.

The largest city in the 20th district is Springfield, with 90,000 people. It must have been a bustling, perhaps even a gracious town in Abe Lincoln's and Mary Todd's time. Today it is a typical state capital: a middle sized city with an old Capitol building, several not-so-elegant hotels, a small black ghetto, a little bit of industry, and a few shopping centers on the edge of town. Next to state government, the Lincoln tourist business seems to be the mainstay of the local economy.

On paper the 20th is a politically marginal district. It sits right on the traditional boundary separating the Democratic counties to the south and the Republican counties to the north. That division was visible in the returns for the contest between Lincoln and Douglas in 1858; practically the same pattern was visible in the 1976 returns in the contest between Gerald Ford and Jimmy Carter. The division has persisted constantly in local elections, and sometimes in national contests; we are still seeing the basic American split between Yankees and Dixie.

The 1960 Census cost Illinois one congressional seat, and it came out of the rural areas in and near the current 20th. Two incumbents—Republican freshman Paul Findley and Democratic veteran Peter Mack—were forced to fight it out in the new 20th. Findley won that election in 1962 and has had little trouble winning since. As the years have gone by, Findley has moved up in seniority, to the point now that he is third-ranking Republican on both the Agriculture and the Foreign Affairs Committees. But his advancing seniority has not been matched by influence. He makes his positions known in crisply articulated speeches, and he has expertise in a number of areas—on NATO, for example, as well as in Lincoln studies. But some of the fights he takes on are lonely, such as opposing the emergency farm credit bill, and some of his amendments fail, such as his efforts against increased sugar price supports. He has a pretty solidly conservative record on economic issues, but often strays from the position of most Republicans on non-economic issues. He has won reelection in the 20th district by impressive margins, but has not become a major force in the House.

Census Data Pop. 464,551. Central city, 20%; suburban, 31%. Median family income, $9,269; families above $15,000: 17%; families below $3,000: 10%. Median years education, 12.0.

The Voters

Median voting age 46.
Employment profile White collar, 46%. Blue collar, 33%. Service, 14%. Farm, 7%.
Ethnic groups Black, 4%. Total foreign stock, 8%. Germany, 2%; Italy, UK, 1% each.

Presidential vote

1976	Carter (D)	89,300	(47%)
	Ford (R)	99,738	(53%)
1972	Nixon (R)	137,414	(64%)
	McGovern (D)	78,281	(36%)

Rep. Paul Findley (R) Elected 1960; b. June 23, 1921, Jacksonville; home, Pittsfield; Ill. Col., B.A. 1943; Congregationalist.

Career Navy, WWII; Pres., Pike Press, Inc., 1947–60.

Offices 2113 RHOB, 202-225-5271. Also 205 Fed. Bldg., Springfield 62701, 217-525-4062.

Committees *Agriculture* (3d). Subcommittees: Oilseeds and Rice.

Foreign Affairs (3d). Subcommittees: Europe and the Middle East; International Economic Policy and Trade.

Group Ratings

	ADA	COPE	PC	RPN	NFU	LCV	CFA	NAB	NSI	ACA	NTU
1978	35	15	45	80	30	–	32	83	75	79	–
1977	45	27	48	92	42	39	35	–	–	59	44
1976	35	15	21	88	28	33	9	90	44	56	63

Key Votes

1) Increase Def Spnd	FOR	6) Alaska Lands Protect	FOR	11) Delay Auto Pol Cntrl	DNV
2) B-1 Bomber	FOR	7) Water Projects Veto	AGN	12) Sugar Price Escalator	AGN
3) Cargo Preference	AGN	8) Consum Protect Agcy	AGN	13) Pub Fin Cong Cmpgns	AGN
4) Dereg Nat Gas	FOR	9) Common Situs Picket	AGN	14) ERA Ratif Recissn	FOR
5) Kemp-Roth	AGN	10) Labor Law Revision	AGN	15) Prohibt Govt Abrtns	AGN

Election Results

1978 general	Paul Findley (R)	111,054	(70%)	($117,721)
	Victor W. Roberts (D)	48,426	(30%)	($7,318)
1978 primary	Paul Findley (R), unopposed			
1976 general	Paul Findley (R)	137,223	(64%)	($123,422)
	Peter F. Mack (D)	78,634	(36%)	($21,724)

TWENTY-FIRST DISTRICT

Downstate Illinois has always been regarded as overwhelmingly Republican. But that has never really been the case. The largest Republican margins in Illinois come out of the Chicago suburbs, and except for the fertile farmlands in the north and north central part of the state, Downstate Illinois might accurately be described as marginally Republican. Consider the 21st congressional district, located about halfway between Chicago and St. Louis. The 21st lies in flat prairie farm country, but most of its population is clustered in three roughly equal-sized urban areas: Decatur, a farm machine factory town; Champaign-Urbana, home of the University of Illinois; and Bloomington, an insurance town and ancestral home of the Stevenson family. These places are listed in order of their traditional Democratic inclinations, but there have been variations. A large student vote exists here: in 1972 it made Champaign-Urbana the least Republican of these three urban areas, while in 1976 it seems to have gone for Gerald Ford. Decatur, which swung heavily against George McGovern, delivered a fair-sized margin for Jimmy Carter four years later.

In national elections the rural counties usually tip the balance to the Republicans. Local elections tend to be more one-sided; Republicans do better in part because they seem to have a local monopoly on the kind of well-educated, well-spoken candidates whom people prefer to elect to Congress and the legislature.

The current incumbent, Edward Madigan, first won in 1972. He was from one of the smaller counties in the district and had trouble in his first general election, losing Champaign-Urbana and carrying Decatur by only a hair. In the House he won seats on the Agriculture and Commerce

Committees, on the latter of which his predecessor, William Springer, had been ranking Republican. He has generally voted with other Republicans, but not quite always. He seems to excel at the use of the advantages of incumbency, and in 1978 he won reelection by nearly a 4-to-1 margin—one of the best showings of any Republican in the nation. In his early forties, he seems destined for a long House career.

Census Data Pop. 464,693. Central city, 53%; suburban, 31%. Median family income, $10,043; families above $15,000: 21%; families below $3,000: 7%. Median years education, 12.3.

The Voters

Median voting age 38.
Employment profile White collar, 51%. Blue collar, 29%. Service, 15%. Farm, 5%.
Ethnic groups Black, 5%. Total foreign stock, 7%. Germany, 2%.

Presidential vote

1976	Carter (D)	85,545	(45%)
	Ford (R)	106,554	(55%)
1972	Nixon (R)	117,230	(62%)
	McGovern (D)	70,380	(38%)

Rep. Edward R. Madigan (R) Elected 1972; b. Jan. 13, 1936, Lincoln; home, Lincoln; Lincoln Col.; Catholic.

Career Owner, taxi and car leasing co.; Lincoln Bd. of Zoning Appeals; Ill. House of Reps., 1967–72.

Offices 2457 RHOB, 202-225-2371. Also 202 W. Church St., Champaign 61820, 217-398-5516.

Committees *Agriculture* (6th). Subcommittees: Conservation and Credit.

Interstate and Foreign Commerce (7th). Subcommittees: Health and the Environment; Transportation and Commerce.

Group Ratings

	ADA	COPE	PC	RPN	NFU	LCV	CFA	NAB	NSI	ACA	NTU
1978	30	25	30	82	40	–	23	80	89	80	–
1977	15	41	35	77	67	41	30	–	–	52	26
1976	20	18	18	87	17	29	0	75	80	68	48

Key Votes

1) Increase Def Spnd	FOR	6) Alaska Lands Protect	FOR	11) Delay Auto Pol Cntrl	FOR
2) B-1 Bomber	FOR	7) Water Projects Veto	FOR	12) Sugar Price Escalator	FOR
3) Cargo Preference	AGN	8) Consum Protect Agcy	AGN	13) Pub Fin Cong Cmpgns	AGN
4) Dereg Nat Gas	FOR	9) Common Situs Picket	AGN	14) ERA Ratif Recissn	FOR
5) Kemp-Roth	FOR	10) Labor Law Revision	AGN	15) Prohibt Govt Abrtns	FOR

Election Results

1978 general	Edward R. Madigan (R)	97,473	(78%)	($78,219)
	Kenneth E. Baughman (D)	27,054	(22%)	
1978 primary	Edward R. Madigan (R), unopposed			
1976 general	Edward R. Madigan (R)	137,037	(74%)	($54,243)
	Anna Wall Scott (D)	46,996	(26%)	($3,433)

TWENTY-SECOND DISTRICT

The 22d congressional district of Illinois is geographically the largest district in the state, a collection of 20 predominantly rural Downstate counties. Its largest city, Danville, with 42,000 people makes its living manufacturing farm equipment and otherwise serving as a trading center for the rural vicinity. This part of the Illinois prairie is prime agricultural country. The topsoil goes down deeper than just about anywhere else in the world, and the productivity of the farmland here is very high.

This district is, however, not of a piece politically. Across its midsection runs the old National Road—now U.S. 40, paralleled by Interstate 70—which is the approximate boundary of socio-cultural influence in Downstate Illinois. North of this imaginary line is Yankee country, settled originally by farmers from northern Ohio or Indiana or Pennsylvania or Upstate New York. The accents are hard, and the politics has traditionally been Republican. Thus Danville, which is in the northern part of the district, used to elect as its congressman Joseph Cannon, the powerful Speaker against whom the progressives revolted in 1911. South of this imaginary line the land was settled by farmers from Kentucky, Virginia, and Tennessee. The accent here is softer and more drawling, and the politics traditionally more Democratic. Voters here had little use for the national Democratic politics of Hubert Humphrey or George McGovern, but most of them voted for Jimmy Carter. The close division of the 22d between these two segments can be seen in the 1976 presidential election results: Gerald Ford carried this Downstate district, but with only 51% of the vote.

For 20 years the Congressman from this district was George Shipley, a Democrat elected by a narrow margin in 1958 and reelected every two years, usually with percentages just above 50%. Shipley was the kind of Democrat in line with his district's thinking and by no means advanced on social issues. He won a seat on the Appropriations Committee and advanced to the eighth-ranking seniority position and a subcommittee chair. But he was in poor health, and in 1978 he decided at 50 to retire.

Shipley hoped to pass the seat on to his administrative assistant and brother-in-law, Don Watson. But experience on a Capitol Hill staff is not necessarily a good way to learn to run campaigns, and Watson was beaten in the Democratic primary by 34-year-old state Senator Terry Bruce. There was also an upset of sorts in the Republican primary. The early favorite was state legislator Roscoe Cunningham, a middle-aged veteran with an Everett Dirksen manner. But Cunningham was beaten by Daniel Crane, brother of 12th district Congressman Philip Crane and a Danville dentist. What Crane lacked in oratorical ability he made up in the capacity to raise funds and run a shrewd direct mail campaign.

The general election looked like a pretty even contest. But Crane was able to win a solid victory. Again money and organization seem to have made the difference. Philip Crane has access to national fund-raising direct mail lists, and from conservatives all over the country Daniel Crane was able to raise about four times as much money as Bruce. Again Crane relied heavily on direct mail, and again he won by a solid margin. His victory was something of an asset to his brother's presidential campaign, though another Crane brother lost his second straight race in Indiana's 6th district. Daniel Crane can be counted on to join the House's growing conservative bloc.

Census Data Pop. 464,121. Central city, 0%; suburban, 1%. Median family income, $8,350; families above $15,000: 13%; families below $3,000: 12%. Median years education, 11.4.

The Voters

Median voting age 47.
Employment profile White collar, 37%. Blue collar, 40%. Service, 13%. Farm, 10%.
Ethnic groups Black, 1%. Total foreign stock, 4%. Germany, 1%.

Presidential vote

1976	Carter (D)	104,967	(49%)
	Ford (R)	111,465	(51%)
1972	Nixon (R)	141,820	(64%)
	McGovern (D)	80,804	(36%)

Rep. Daniel B. Crane (R) Elected 1978; b. Jan. 10, 1936, Chicago; home, Danville; Hillsdale Col., A.B. 1958, Ind. U., D.D.S. 1963, U. of Mich., 1964–65; Methodist.

Career Army, Vietnam; Dentist, Dir., Crane Clinic, 1963–67.

Offices 509 CHOB, 202-225-5001. Also 426 Whittle Ave., Olney 62450, 618-395-2171.

Committees *Post Office and Civil Service* (9th). Subcommittees: Postal Operations and Services; Compensation and Employee Benefits; Census and Population. *Education and Labor*(11th). Subcommittees: Elementary, Secondary, and Vocational Education; Labor Management Relations; Employment Opportunities; Task Force on Welfare and Pension Plans.

Group Ratings: Newly Elected

Key Votes: Newly Elected

Election Results

1978 general	Daniel B. Crane (R)	86,051	(54%)	($438,764)
	Terry L. Bruce (D)	73,331	(46%)	($107,281)
1978 primary	Daniel B. Crane (R)	15,735	(46%)	
	Roscoe D. Cunningham (R)	12,111	(36%)	($17,168)
	One other	6,183	(18%)	
1976 general	George E. Shipley (D)	129,187	(61%)	($51,571)
	Ralph Y. McGinnis (R)	81,102	(39%)	($5,090)

TWENTY-THIRD DISTRICT

The 23d congressional district of Illinois is the area across from St. Louis's Gateway Arch, where one can see East St. Louis, Belleville, and Granite City through the smog across the Mississippi River. These are not verdant St. Louis suburbs, but grimy industrial towns criss-crossed by miles of railroad tracks. They have all the problems associated with core city areas: air pollution, inadequate housing, crime, and a declining tax base. East St. Louis became a majority black town in the sixties, but when the blacks took over city hall, they found the treasury virtually bare—and the city lacking the resources to fill it. The Illinois side of the St. Louis metropolitan area has a disproportionate share of its poor and low income working class residents; the rich stay on the Missouri side of the River.

The 23d is easily the most Democratic of all the Downstate Illinois congressional districts. It went for Stevenson in both Eisenhower elections, and almost went for McGovern in the 1972 Nixon landslide. Local elections are won only by Democrats. The last time a Republican was elected congressman was in 1942. He was defeated in 1944 by Democrat Mel Price, who has been reelected ever since—by margins of better than 2–1 since 1962.

In Congress Price holds two key positions which, together, give him jurisdiction over a large share of the federal budget. He is a top member of the Joint Committee on Atomic Energy and has served as Chairman of that body. (The chair rotates between Senate and House members.) The Joint Committee has worked especially closely with the agency—now agencies, since the old Atomic Energy Commission has been split in two—it oversees since it was created just after World War II. As an original member of the Joint Committee, Price was a friend of the longtime

Chairman, Chet Holifield of California, and shared his belief in the purposes and practices of the AEC. Price is, for example, a backer of the controversial breeder reactor, and was one of the authors of the Price–Anderson Act, which by providing federal insurance for nuclear disasters tends to encourage the building of nuclear plants.

Even more important, Price is Chairman of the House Armed Services Committee. He did not actively seek the post at first. Following the 1974 election he was in line to be the second-ranking Democrat behind Chairman Edward Hebert of Louisiana. But the newly elected Democratic Caucus dumped the autocratic Hebert and installed Price. He has been more evenhanded than Hebert, but has done a better job of advancing the goals he and his predecessor generally shared. Like so many members who served during or just after World War II, Price learned what he considers the lessons of those years. He believes strongly in military preparedness and does not want to see the United States ever again as weak militarily as it was at the time of Pearl Harbor. He has concurred with the consensus on the Cold War since the forties, and has consistently supported high defense budgets and a strong military posture.

In the years since Price became Chairman, military spending has become more popular among the public and in the House; the days seem past when the Armed Services chairman's programs can be challenged seriously on the floor. At the same time, Price is willing to go along with the Carter Administration on cuts such as the elimination of the B-1 bomber. He is not a man to make waves, nor one to get into serious political trouble. He has been on the Hill since 1933 as an aide or a congressman, and at 72 shows no sign of retiring.

Census Data Pop. 462,960. Central city, 0%; suburban, 100%. Median family income, $9,872; families above $15,000: 18%; families below $3,000: 10%. Median years education, 11.1.

The Voters

Median voting age 43.
Employment profile White collar, 45%. Blue collar, 41%. Service, 13%. Farm, 1%.
Ethnic groups Black, 15%. Spanish, 1%. Total foreign stock, 8%. Germany, 2%.

Presidential vote

1976	Carter (D)	100,616	(59%)
	Ford (R)	69,486	(41%)
1972	Nixon (R)	87,654	(53%)
	McGovern (D)	76,971	(47%)

Rep. Melvin Price (D) Elected 1944; b. Jan. 1, 1905, East St. Louis; home, East St. Louis; St. Louis U., 1923–25; Catholic

Career Newspaper correspondent, E. St. Louis *Journal*, St. Louis *Globe-Democrat*; Sports ed., E. St. Louis *News-Review*; St. Clair Co. Bd. of Supervisors, 1929–31; Secy. to U.S. Rep. Edwin M. Schaefer, 1933–43; Army, WWII.

Offices 2110 RHOB, 202-225-5661; Also Fed. Bldg., 650 Missouri Ave., East St. Louis 62201, 618-274-2200.

Committees *Armed Services* (Chairman). Subcommittees: Procurement and Military Nuclear Systems (Chairman); Investigations.

Group Ratings

	ADA	COPE	PC	RPN	NFU	LCV	CFA	NAB	NSI	ACA	NTU
1978	45	85	60	36	60	–	64	9	38	23	–
1977	45	100	48	18	83	42	60	–	–	12	23
1976	60	96	72	33	92	61	100	0	70	14	8

Key Votes

1) Increase Def Spnd	FOR	6) Alaska Lands Protect	AGN	11) Delay Auto Pol Cntrl	DNV
2) B-1 Bomber	AGN	7) Water Projects Veto	AGN	12) Sugar Price Escalator	FOR
3) Cargo Preference	FOR	8) Consum Protect Agcy	FOR	13) Pub Fin Cong Cmpgns	FOR
4) Dereg Nat Gas	AGN	9) Common Situs Picket	FOR	14) ERA Ratif Recissn	AGN
5) Kemp-Roth	AGN	10) Labor Law Revision	FOR	15) Prohibt Govt Abrtns	FOR

Election Results

1978 general	Melvin Price (D)	74,247	(74%)	($42,416)
	Daniel J. Stack (R)	25,858	(26%)	($12,298)
1978 primary	Melvin Price (D)	37,728	(88%)	
	One other (D)	5,091	(12%)	
1976 general	Melvin Price (D)	128,113	(79%)	($7,430)
	Sam P. Drenovac (R)	34,825	(21%)	($0)

TWENTY-FOURTH DISTRICT

Egypt is the name given the southernmost part of Illinois—the flat, fertile farmland where the Ohio River joins the Mississippi. This is low, alluvial land, subject to floods almost as often as ancient Egypt. The countryside is protected by giant levees, which rise above the fields and hide any view of the rivers. There is more than a touch of Dixie here: the southern tip of Illinois is closer to Jackson, Mississippi, than to Chicago. The unofficial capital of Egypt is Cairo (pronounced KAYroh), a declining town at the exact confluence of the two rivers. Not so many years ago Cairo was the scene of a virtual war between its white majority and its large black minority; it must surely be one of the grimmest small towns in the United States.

There are no official boundaries to Egypt, but it is safe to say that the 24th congressional district goes north considerably beyond them. The district takes in the coal mining area around West Frankfort and Marion—one of the most heavily strip mined areas in the country. It extends to a point near the suburbs of St. Louis, and includes Carbondale, site of Southern Illinois University. Nearly all this territory is Democratic in most elections, because of ancestral Southern allegiance (this is Southern drawl, not Midwestern hard R, territory) or because of coal miners' preferences. The district did not produce a margin for the Catholic John Kennedy, nor did it go for the Great Society's Hubert Humphrey; but it did produce a 54% win for Southerner Jimmy Carter. And in congressional races it has not veered from Democrats for more than 25 years.

For 20 years, until his retirement in 1974, the Congressman here was Kenneth Gray, a flamboyant Democrat and favorite of many lobbyists. His successor is quite another kind of politician: an almost austere liberal named Paul Simon. Formerly the editor of a small newspaper in the town of Troy, near East St. Louis, Simon was elected to the legislature as an independent Democrat and became known not only for his honesty (a quality not to be taken for granted in Springfield), but also for his legislative skill. He was elected Lieutenant Governor in 1968, though a Republican won the governorship, and in 1972 he had the support of organized labor, the Daley machine, and many liberals in the gubernatorial primary. But Simon refused to say that he would repeal an unpopular state income tax, while his opponent, anti-Daley Daniel Walker, hinted that he would. Simon's approach was more honest and less successful; Walker won the primary with heavy Downstate support, though he never managed to get rid of the tax.

Simon was well positioned to run for Congress when Gray retired, and he was elected easily in 1974. He brought to Washington a reputation as a liberal, but not of the knee jerk variety. As a member of the Budget Committee, he does not necessarily push for high spending. And he is concerned enough about controlling spending to make it a habit to drop in on federal offices unannounced, asking employees to explain what work they are doing. On the Education and Labor Committee, he usually supports social programs and pro-labor legislation, but not always. For example, he sponsored a bill to allow workers under 18 to be paid below the minimum wage. Proponents say this would create more jobs for teenagers; opponents fear it would take jobs from older workers. Simon is an interesting and literate man with a safe seat in the House; but it is possible that, though once burned, he might be interested in running for the Senate seat vacated by Adlai Stevenson in 1980.

Census Data Pop. 465,018. Central city, 0%; suburban, 0%. Median family income, $7,501; families above $15,000: 11%; families below $3,000: 17%. Median years education, 10.1.

The Voters

Median voting age 47.
Employment profile White collar, 38%. Blue collar, 40%. Service, 15%. Farm, 7%.
Ethnic groups Black, 4%. Total foreign stock, 5%. Germany, 1%.

Presidential vote

1976	Carter (D)	127,696	(54%)
	Ford (R)	109,391	(46%)
1972	Nixon (R)	138,435	(60%)
	McGovern (D)	92,910	(40%)

Rep. Paul Simon (D) Elected 1974; b. Nov. 29, 1928, Eugene, Oreg.; home, Carbondale; U. of Oreg., 1945–46, Dana Col., 1946–48; Lutheran.

Career Editor-Publisher, Troy *Tribune*, and newspaper weekly chain owner, 1948–66; Army, 1951–53; Ill. House of Reps., 1955–63; Ill. Senate 1963–69; Lt. Gov. of Ill, 1969–73; Candidate for Dem. nomination for Gov., 1972; Instructor, Sangamon St. U., 1973.

Offices 227 CHOB, 202-225-5201. Also 107 Glenview Dr., Carbondale 62901, 618-457-4171.

Committees *Budget* (7th). Subcommittees: Defense and International Affairs.

Education and Labor (11th). Subcommittees: Employment Opportunities; Select Education (Chairman); Post-secondary Education.

Group Ratings

	ADA	COPE	PC	RPN	NFU	LCV	CFA	NAB	NSI	ACA	NTU
1978	65	83	78	63	75	–	73	13	11	10	–
1977	85	72	85	50	92	85	65	–	–	0	21
1976	80	81	85	53	82	87	100	18	20	0	25

Key Votes

1) Increase Def Spnd	AGN	6) Alaska Lands Protect	FOR	11) Delay Auto Pol Cntrl	AGN
2) B-1 Bomber	AGN	7) Water Projects Veto	FOR	12) Sugar Price Escalator	AGN
3) Cargo Preference	AGN	8) Consum Protect Agcy	FOR	13) Pub Fin Cong Cmpgns	FOR
4) Dereg Nat Gas	AGN	9) Common Situs Picket	FOR	14) ERA Ratif Recissn	AGN
5) Kemp-Roth	AGN	10) Labor Law Revision	FOR	15) Prohibt Govt Abrtns	FOR

Election Results

1978 general	Paul Simon (D)	110,298	(66%)	($99,017)
	John T. Anderson (R)	57,763	(34%)	($13,998)
1978 primary	Paul Simon (D), unopposed			
1976 general	Paul Simon (D)	152,344	(67%)	($78,873)
	Peter G. Prineas (R)	73,766	(33%)	($13,109)

The Voters

Median voting age 41.
Employment profile White collar, 42%. Blue collar, 43%. Service, 12%. Farm, 3%.
Ethnic groups Black, 9%. Spanish, 3%. Total foreign stock, 16%. Germany, Italy, 2% each; Poland, 1%.

Presidential vote

1976	Carter (D)	88,241	(44%)
	Ford (R)	110,999	(56%)
1972	Nixon (R)	122,873	(66%)
	McGovern (D)	62,394	(34%)

INDIANA

The most powerful political machines still functioning in the United States are not to be found in the big cities of the East Coast, but rather in the heart of Middle America: in the city of Chicago, at least until recently, and in the state of Indiana. The machine headed for so many years by Mayor Daley is more famous, but the Indiana machines, if less well known, are probably in better shape, as they hum away in Indianapolis, the state's other big cities, and practically all of Indiana's 92 county courthouses. Almost all public offices in Indiana, including judgeships and court clerks, are partisan; and for years nearly every partisan official and each of the employees under him had to kick back 2% of their salaries to the party coffers. The system is not what it once was, and enforcement is not perfect. Nevertheless, the practice of funding political parties through patronage employees is deeply ingrained here, and Indiana today probably has about as many patronage jobs as any state in the country. Republicans currently hold most of the state's major offices, but Democrats are entrenched in many counties; and both parties are better financed here than in most states where they must depend on idealism and zeal for contributions.

Another factor contributed for years to the strength of the parties here. Until 1976 candidates for statewide office were chosen not in primaries, but in party conventions. Primaries have been used for nominees to the U.S. House and state legislative seats, but even in these races party organizations are seldom challenged; and, as 1976 shows, leading candidates for high office receive serious challenges only under unusual circumstances. As a result, unorthodox candidates rarely surface in Indiana politics. The Democrats are moderate-to-liberal and acceptable to organized labor, which plays an important role here. The Republicans, with very few exceptions, are solid conservatives. There is no Indiana equivalent of Illinois' Republican Senator Charles Percy, nor has the Indiana Democratic Party ever found it useful to give a major nomination to such an unpolitical figure as Ohio's Senator John Glenn.

Since a lot is at stake in Indiana elections—not just what policies will be followed, but also cold cash—the Indiana party bosses try hard to slate candidates congenial to Hoosier mores. Elections in Indiana are often very close. Senator Vance Hartke, for example, won his third term in 1970 by just over 4,000 votes out of 1,700,000 cast; Senator Birch Bayh was first elected in 1962 by less than 11,000 votes. Indeed, this is just the reason the nomination system was scrapped in 1975. The Republicans who controlled the legislature and the governorship wanted to win the 1976 Senate race, and they were afraid that a Democratic convention would dump Hartke, who was known to be unpopular. They concluded that Hartke would have a better chance in a primary against an unknown challenger—although even there he almost lost.

Hartke had won before in solid Democratic years—1958, 1964, 1970—but by 1976 he was in deep trouble; many voters had concluded that he wasn't entirely honest. Certainly he had achieved some cozy relationships with companies in industries regulated by the Commerce Committee, of which he was a senior member. His case was all the more hopeless because he had a strong opponent, former Indianapolis Mayor (1968–76) Richard Lugar. A former Rhodes Scholar, first elected at the age of 36, Lugar engineered the consolidation of Indianapolis and surrounding Marion County into something called Unigov (which had the happy effect of adding Republican votes to city elections). Indianapolis, as a result, is more prosperous and less burdened with the problems of aging than many central cities, and Lugar made a point of opposing other big city mayors who constantly called for more federal programs. In 1969 he beat John Lindsay for the vice presidency of the National League of Cities, and the White House let it be known that he was President Nixon's favorite mayor. He even delivered a predictably fulsome seconding speech for Nixon at the 1972 Republican National Convention.

Lugar has the reputation of something of an intellectual. Interested in philosophical questions, he reserves an hour a day for reading and reflection. But those liberals who believe that anyone who reads a lot must share their views will find refutation in Lugar. Whether one is judging by his philosophical principles or by his voting record, he is a solid conservative. In his first two years in the Senate he took a leading role in opposing the AFL-CIO's labor law reform bill. It was a successful effort—labor could not get the 60 votes needed for cloture—and showed Lugar to be a competent legislative tactician. It also showed nicely the sharp contrasts in Indiana politics: the state's other Senator, Democrat Birch Bayh, has long been one of labor's strongest supporters, while Republican Lugar is one of their most effective opponents. This is not a state where politicians try to fudge their records to make themselves acceptable to all local interest groups.

Lugar now has a seat on the Senate Foreign Relations Committee, where he is expected to oppose the strategic arms limitation treaty and generally to stand against the dovish bipartisan consensus that has dominated the Committee in the past. Reportedly the group of Rocky Mountain conservatives consider Lugar to be sympathetic to their views, although he has avoided gaining a far out image. He appears likely to be one of the most effective conservatives in the Senate in the years ahead.

Lugar was escorted down the aisle to take the oath of office by the man who beat him in 1974, Birch Bayh. Although just past 50, Bayh has already had a long Senate and national career. Probably his most lasting achievements lie in Constitutional matters. As a junior senator, he took over Judiciary's Constitutional Amendments Subcommittee, then considered an unimportant assignment. But Bayh shepherded through to passage in the Senate the 25th Amendment, on presidential succession; the 26th Amendment, which established the 18-year-old vote in all elections; and the Equal Rights Amendment, which at this writing has not yet been ratified by the required 38 legislatures. There is a natural reluctance to tamper with a basic document like the Constitution, but the amendments Bayh has helped pass have all been tested and proved useful. The 18-year-old vote helped to cool generational hostility in the wake of the Vietnam war, and has not produced the dire results some predicted. The principles behind the Equal Rights Amendment have been generally accepted even though it has not been ratified. The 25th Amendment has been tested under particularly difficult circumstances. It provided a way to choose a successor when Vice President Agnew was forced to resign—nomination by the president and confirmation by both houses of Congress—and thus was the proximate cause of Gerald Ford, rather than Carl Albert, becoming president when Nixon resigned. It also provides, though few seem to have noticed it, a more democratic way of choosing vice presidents than the traditional method of having a political convention go through the motions of ratifying the choice of one often tired and poorly informed man.

Besides strengthening our organic law, Bayh has also been responsible for strengthening the body which interprets it. When civil rights and labor leaders were looking for a senator to lead the seemingly hopeless fight against Judge Clement Haynsworth in 1969, Bayh volunteered—and managed to convince a majority of the Senate that Haynsworth should not be confirmed. A few months later the Senate was in a mood to confirm anyone Nixon nominated, and Nixon responded by naming the previously unknown Judge Harrold Carswell. Once again Bayh volunteered to lead the fight against the nominee and once again he succeeded in convincing the Senate to turn him down.

But Bayh's work on constitutional amendments and Supreme Court nominations has not always been a political asset. More recently, his work as Chairman of the Constitution Subcommittee has been not to report amendments out, but to prevent them from reaching the floor. He has been attacked, for example, for keeping the old chestnut of an amendment to allow school prayers off the floor. Much more significant politically, he was attacked as long ago as 1974 for not allowing constitutional amendments against abortion to be debated by the full Judiciary Committee or Senate. Today the issue is much hotter; opponents of abortion have built a strong lobby and significant organizations around the country, including Indiana. Bayh may also be on the spot on the proposed constitutional amendment to require a balanced federal budget—a measure which, in the past, he has shown no sign of supporting. Against these emotional issues, Bayh's own initiatives—he has argued, for example, for breaking up the oil companies into smaller units—have not attracted much attention.

Bayh has run for president twice. In 1971 he left the race because of his wife's illness. In 1976 he entered late and finished a disappointing third (16%) in the New Hampshire primary and then a dismal seventh (5%) in Massachusetts, after which he withdrew. In 1980 his Senate seat is up again, and all indications are that he will be hard pressed to keep it, though he has never had easy races. Bayh upset incumbent Homer Capehart in 1962, and got 52% against two strong opponents, William Ruckelshaus in 1968 and Richard Lugar in 1974. In that latter year, Bayh ran behind Democratic House candidates in the state, and no one expects Indiana Democrats to do as well in 1980. He has been helped by the decision of popular Governor Otis Bowen not to run for the Senate; his most likely opponent is 4th district Congressman Dan Quayle. But Bayh's greatest problem may be that the kind of programs he has traditionally supported have relatively little appeal in Indiana these days. In the past he could campaign as the champion of the little guy and the working man; today in Indiana most voters see themselves as prosperous people plagued by inflation. Bayh will need all his campaigning abilities—he remains an engaging and folksy campaigner—in order to win a fourth term.

Governor Bowen is rather quiet and surprisingly undivisive for an Indiana politician. He was elected in 1972 and reelected in 1976—the first Indiana governor eligible for a second four-year term—by record margins. His political success is all the more remarkable in that he sponsored and pushed through a major tax revision. Bowen combines political adroitness (he was Speaker of the Indiana House for six years) with a non-political air (he is an M.D. and proud to remind people of it) and a middle of the road program. He could probably have the Senate nomination if he had wanted it. As for the governorship, there should be plenty of competitors. After all, this is the major prize in a patronage state, and the man who wins it (Indiana is one of the states least likely to elect a woman governor) will likely hold office for eight years.

Indiana has a lingering reputation as a straight ticket state, but voters here, despite the strong political organizations, do seem to be catching up with the rest of the nation in an ability to split tickets. In 1976 Gerald Ford ran behind, not ahead of, the Republican ticket leaders, Bowen and Lugar; at the same time, Indiana elected eight Democrats in its eleven congressional districts. In 1978 the Republicans recaptured the top office on the ballot, secretary of state, but Democrats still won in seven congressional districts. This represents a reversal of historical pattern. In 1958 Democrats had won nine seats, and lost all but four of them to the Republicans in 1960. In the seventies Democratic incumbents have proved more adept at using the advantages of incumbency, and Republicans have not, as they used to, strongly challenged them in every district.

Census Data Pop. 5,193,669; 2.57% of U.S. total, 11th largest; Central city, 34%; suburban, 27%. Median family income, $9,966; 19th highest; families above $15,000: 19%; families below $3,000: 8%. Median years education, 12.1.

1977 Share of Federal Tax Burden $8,221,000,000; 2.38% of U.S. total, 11th largest.

1977 Share of Federal Outlays $6,648,862,000; 1.68% of U.S. total, 19th largest. Per capita federal spending, $1,252.

DOD	$1,301,944,000	22d (1.42%)	HEW	$3,060,539,000	15th (2.07%)
ERDA	$7,050,000	32d (0.12%)	HUD	$70,529,000	21st (1.67%)
NASA	$3,085,000	21st (0.08%)	VA	$335,492,000	20th (1.75%)
DOT	$149,245,000	30th (1.05%)	EPA	$277,489,000	9th (3.38%)
DOC	$103,192,000	21st (1.24%)	RevS	$155,132,000	17th (1.83%)
DOI	$16,662,000	40th (0.36%)	Debt	$450,017,000	10th (1.50%)
USDA	$206,045,000	36th (1.04%)	Other	$512,441,000	

Economic Base Primary metal industries, especially blast furnaces and steel mills; electrical equipment and supplies, radio and television receiving equipment; finance, insurance and real estate; transportation equipment, especially motor vehicles and equipment; agriculture, notably hogs, corn, soybeans and cattle; machinery, especially general industrial machinery; fabricated metal products, especially fabricated structural metal products.

Political Line-up Governor, Otis R. Bowen (R); Senators, Birch Bayh (D) and Richard G. Lugar (R). Representatives, 11 (7 D and 4 R). State Senate (29 R and 21 D); State House (54 R and 46 D).

The Voters

Registration 2,831,876 Total. No party registration.
Median voting age 42
Employment profile White collar, 42%. Blue collar, 43%. Service, 12%. Farm, 3%.
Ethnic groups Black, 7%. Spanish, 1%. Total foreign stock, 7%. Germany, 1%.

Presidential vote

1976	Carter (D)	1,014,714	(46%)
	Ford (R)	1,185,958	(54%)
1972	Nixon (R)	1,405,154	(66%)
	McGovern (D)	708,568	(34%)

1976 Democratic Presidential Primary

Carter	417,480	(68%)
Wallace	93,121	(15%)
Jackson	72,080	(12%)
Other	31,708	(5%)

1976 Republican Presidential Primary

Reagan	323,779	(51%)
Ford	307,513	(49%)

Sen. Birch Bayh (D) Elected 1962, seat up 1980; b. Jan. 22, 1928, Terre Haute; home, Terre Haute; Purdue U., B.S. 1951, Ind. St. Col., 1953–60, Ind. U., J.D. 1960; Lutheran.

Career Army, 1945–46; Farmer; Ind. House of Reps., 1955–63, Min. Ldr., 1957–58, 1961–62, Spkr., 1959–60.

Offices 363 RSOB, 202-224-5623. Also 416 Fed. Bldg., Indianapolis 46204, 317-269-6240.

Committees *Appropriations* (7th). Subcommittees: Agriculture and Related Agencies; HUD-Independent Agencies; Interior and Related Agencies; Labor, HEW, and Related Agencies; Transportation and Related Agencies (Chairman).

Judiciary (2d). Subcommittees: Administrative Practice and Procedure; Antitrust, Monopoly, and Business Rights; Constitution (Chairman).

Select Committee on Intelligence (Chairman).

Group Ratings

	ADA	COPE	PC	RPN	NFU	LCV	CFA	NAB	NSI	ACA	NTU
1978	85	94	75	50	70	75	80	11	11	5	–
1977	75	84	75	55	92	–	88	–	–	0	28
1976	75	94	56	58	100	60	57	0	17	0	42

Key Votes

1) Warnke Nom	FOR	6) Egypt-Saudi Arms	AGN	11) Hosptl Cost Contnmnt	FOR
2) Neutron Bomb	AGN	7) Draft Restr Pardon	FOR	12) Clinch River Reactor	FOR
3) Waterwy User Fee	FOR	8) Wheat Price Support	FOR	13) Pub Fin Cong Cmpgns	FOR
4) Dereg Nat Gas	AGN	9) Panama Canal Treaty	FOR	14) ERA Ratif Recissn	FOR
5) Kemp-Roth	AGN	10) Labor Law Rev Clot	FOR	15) Med Necssy Abrtns	FOR

Election Results

1974 general	Birch E. Bayh, Jr. (D)	889,269	(52%)	($1,024,486)
	Richard G. Lugar (R)	814,117	(48%)	($619,678)
1974 primary	Birch E. Bayh, Jr. (D), nominated by convention			
1968 general	Birch E. Bayh, Jr. (D)	1,060,456	(52%)	
	William D. Ruckelshaus (R)	988,571	(48%)	

Sen. Richard G. Lugar (R) Elected 1976, seat up 1982; b. Apr. 4, 1932, Indianapolis; home, Indianapolis; Denison U., B.A. 1954, Rhodes Scholar, Oxford U., B.A. and M.A. 1956; Methodist.

Career Navy, 1957–60; V.P. and Treasurer, Thomas L. Green & Co. Banking Equip. Co., 1960–67, Pres., 1968–77; Treasurer, Lugar Stock Farms, Inc., 1960–77; Mayor of Indianapolis, 1968–76; Repub. Nominee for U.S. Senate, 1974.

Offices 5109 DSOB, 202-224-4814. Also 447 Fed. Bldg. Indianapolis 46204, 317-269-5555.

Committees *Agriculture, Nutrition, and Human Affairs* (5th). Subcommittees: Agricultural Production, Marketing, and Stabilization of Prices; Agricultural Research and General Legislation; Foreign Agricultural Policy.

Banking, Housing, and Urban Affairs (6th). Subcommittees: Housing and Urban Affairs; Economic Stabilization; Securities.

Foreign Relations (6th). Subcommittees: International Economic Policy; Near Eastern and South Asian Affairs; Western Hemisphere Affairs.

Select Committee on Intelligence (4th).

Group Ratings

	ADA	COPE	PC	RPN	NFU	LCV	CFA	NAB	NSI	ACA	NTU
1978	10	11	30	70	0	24	25	83	100	92	–
1977	10	10	18	73	33	–	20	–	–	81	42

Key Votes

1) Warnke Nom	AGN	6) Egypt-Saudi Arms	FOR	11) Hosptl Cost Contnmnt	AGN
2) Neutron Bomb	FOR	7) Draft Restr Pardon	AGN	12) Clinch River Reactor	FOR
3) Waterwy User Fee	FOR	8) Wheat Price Support	FOR	13) Pub Fin Cong Cmpgns	AGN
4) Dereg Nat Gas	FOR	9) Panama Canal Treaty	AGN	14) ERA Ratif Recissn	AGN
5) Kemp-Roth	FOR	10) Labor Law Rev Clot	AGN	15) Med Necssy Abrtns	AGN

Election Results

1976 general	Richard G. Lugar (R)	1,275,833	(59%)	($727,720)
	Vance Hartke (D)	868,522	(41%)	($654,729)
1976 primary	Richard G. Lugar (R)	393,064	(65%)	
	Edgar Whitcomb (R)	179,203	(30%)	
	One other (R)	28,790	(5%)	
1970 general	Vance Hartke (D)	870,990	(50%)	
	Richard L. Roudebush (R)	866,707	(50%)	

Gov. Otis R. Bowen (R) Elected 1972, term expires 1981; b. Feb. 26, 1918, near Rochester; Ind. U., A.B. 1939, M.D. 1942; Lutheran.

Career Army Medical Corps, WWII; Physician; Marshall Co. Coroner; Ind. House of Reps., 1959–72, Spkr., 1967–72.

Offices Rm. 206 State House, Indianapolis 46204, 317-633-4567.

Election Results

1976 general	Otis R. Bowen (R)	1,236,555	(57%)
	Larry A. Conrad (D)	927,243	(43%)
1976 primary	Otis R. Bowen (R), nominated .... by convention		
1972 general	Otis R. Bowen (R)	1,203,903	(57%)
	Matthew E. Welsh (D)	900,489	(43%)

FIRST DISTRICT

Anyone who has driven west on the Indiana Turnpike toward Chicago has seen it. Between the highway and the invisible shores of Lake Michigan is some of the most impressive and most polluted industrial landscape in the country. These are some of the nation's largest steel mills; from their chimneys and smokestacks come sulphurous fumes by day and the flare of flames at night. This is the heart of the 1st congressional district of Indiana, the northwest corner of Hoosier America.

Without the giant steel mills, there would be no 1st district as we know it. The district's largest city, Gary, was founded in 1906 by J. P. Morgan's colossal United States Steel Corporation and named for one of Morgan's partners, Chicago lawyer and U.S. Steel chairman Elbert Gary. The site chosen was ideal. Iron ore from the Lake Superior ranges could be carried by Great Lakes freighters into the huge man-made port at the southern tip of Lake Michigan. Coal from Pennsylvania and West Virginia could be transported to the mills on the great east-west rail lines, as they pass through Gary, Hammond, and East Chicago on their way to Chicago. Today no less than five of the great steel manufacturers have mills here, and the local economy is totally dominated by steel.

In the last 70 years the steel mills have attracted thousands of immigrants to Gary and vicinity—Irish, Poles, Czechs, Ukrainians, and blacks from the American South. These groups live in uneasy proximity. In 1967 Richard Hatcher, a black, won the Democratic nomination and was elected Mayor of Gary; he was reelected in 1971 and 1975. But his victories were due almost entirely to the fact that Gary had become a black majority city; he won very few white votes. Meanwhile, the Lake County Democratic machinery, as well as most of the county offices, has remained in the control of whites of diverse ethnic origin united in hostility to Hatcher. Lake County has for years been the scene of considerable political corruption, and sometimes of corrupt inertia. The Democrats, elected with the votes of the workers, have always permitted the steel companies to determine the assessed value of their own mills for property tax purposes.

As the seventies have gone on, Gary has become increasingly a black city. Hammond and East Chicago, just to the east, remain heavily white and ethnic. To the south there are newer suburban communities, populated by younger steelworkers and their families. Here the old ethnic traditions and Democratic Party allegiance are much weaker than in the old neighborhoods, and white hostility to blacks has worked somewhat in the Republicans' favor. The 1st congressional district includes all of the older communities of Lake County and some of the newer suburbs.

It is a district of more than ordinary political turbulence, of feuds and battles and sacks full of cash. Yet for 24 years the 1st district sent the same man to Congress, Democrat Ray Madden. For years Madden held his ethnic audiences spellbound by telling how he uncovered the Katyn Forest massacre of 1940. In 1973, at the age of 80, he became Chairman of the House Rules Committee. He was the first pro-labor chairman in 20 years, but he was long past the point of effectiveness. He was also in trouble in the 1st district. In 1972 he was challenged by a young state Senator, Adam Benjamin, and nearly lost.

Four years later Benjamin ran again. Madden again had the support of the Democratic organization, of the big labor unions, and of Mayor Hatcher and his organization—as mutually mistrustful a group of allies as has ever been assembled. They supported Madden to maintain the district's national clout, but the voters didn't seem to care. Benjamin won by a stunning 56%–34% margin; the only other incumbent to lose so badly that year had been convicted of bribery.

Benjamin is considered politically shrewd—innocents don't survive 15 years of Lake County politics and beat all the big powers there. In his first term he gained a seat on the Appropriations Committee, an unusual feat. In his second term he became a subcommittee chairman, something even more unusual. The subcommittee, on Legislative Appropriations, is one which has little direct impact on the ordinary citizen; but it does control the budget of Congress, which makes Benjamin potentially a very influential figure in the House. He is also the second-ranking Democrat on the Transportation Appropriations Subcommittee. At a comparatively youthful age and with a safe seat, he seems destined to be an important member of the House.

Census Data Pop. 471,761. Central city, 70%; suburban, 30%. Median family income, $10,706; families above $15,000: 22%; families below $3,000: 8%. Median years education, 11.6.

The Voters

Median voting age 42.
Employment profile White collar, 37%. Blue collar, 50%. Service, 13%. Farm, –%.
Ethnic groups Black, 24%. Spanish, 7%. Total foreign stock, 20%. Poland, 3%; Germany, 2%.

Presidential vote

1976	Carter (D)	108,388	(61%)
	Ford (R)	68,428	(39%)
1972	Nixon (R)	91,218	(53%)
	McGovern (D)	82,173	(47%)

Rep. Adam Benjamin, Jr. (D) Elected 1976; b. Aug. 6, 1935, Gary; home, Hobart; U.S. Mil. Acad., West Point, B.S. 1958, Valparaiso U., J.D. 1968; Catholic.

Career USMC, Korea; Army, 1958–61; High school teacher, 1961; Computer analyst, 1962–64; Zoning Admin., City of Gary, 1964–65; Exec. Secy. to the Mayor of Gary, 1965–67; Ind. House of Reps., 1967–71; Ind. Senate, 1971–77.

Offices 410 CHOB, 202-225-2461. Also 610 Connecticut St., Gary 46402, 219-886-2411.

Committees *Appropriations* (27th). Subcommittees: Legislative; Transportation.

Group Ratings

	ADA	COPE	PC	RPN	NFU	LCV	CFA	NAB	NSI	ACA	NTU
1978	65	80	65	17	60	–	59	8	50	22	–
1977	50	91	68	38	67	55	70	–	–	26	27

Key Votes

1) Increase Def Spnd	AGN	6) Alaska Lands Protect	FOR	11) Delay Auto Pol Cntrl	FOR
2) B-1 Bomber	AGN	7) Water Projects Veto	AGN	12) Sugar Price Escalator	FOR
3) Cargo Preference	FOR	8) Consum Protect Agcy	FOR	13) Pub Fin Cong Cmpgns	AGN
4) Dereg Nat Gas	AGN	9) Common Situs Picket	FOR	14) ERA Ratif Recissn	AGN
5) Kemp-Roth	AGN	10) Labor Law Revision	FOR	15) Prohibt Govt Abrtns	FOR

Election Results

1978 general	Adam Benjamin, Jr. (D)	72,367	(81%)	($77,483)
	Owen W. Crumpacker (R)	17,419	(19%)	($26,459)
1978 primary	Adam Benjamin, Jr. (D)	65,062	(91%)	
	One other (D)	6,533	(9%)	
1976 general	Adam Benjamin, Jr. (D)	121,155	(71%)	($111,391)
	Robert J. Billings (R)	48,756	(29%)	($78,366)

SECOND DISTRICT

The 2d congressional district covers most of northwest Indiana, except for the industrial zone around Gary which forms the 1st district. This is fertile farmland, rich enough that it has never sprouted populists. For as long as the party has existed, this part of Indiana has been Republican. For 34 years (1935–69) the district was represented in the House by Charles Halleck, a sort of quintessential Midwestern Republican. Halleck was a tough conservative who was House Minority Leader from 1959 to 1965; in that capacity he used to appear on television with his Senate counterpart, Everett McKinley Dirksen, in what became known as the Ev 'n' Charlie Show. Halleck was a hard-working leader, seldom losing key votes, and his ouster as Minority Leader—by a young Michigan congressman named Gerald Ford—came largely as a result of the depletion of Republican ranks in the Johnson landslide of 1964. A few years later Halleck decided to retire, and that set off a chain of events which resulted in the election, in this very Republican district, of a Democratic congressman, and his continuing reelection.

The key here was the victory, with 22% of the vote, of Earl Landgrebe in the 1968 Republican primary. Landgrebe was not just a conservative Republican; he was an authentic small town zany, one of the unintentionally funniest men ever to sit in Congress. From the beginning Landgrebe was in political trouble. He won reelection only narrowly in 1970 and was nearly beaten in the primary in 1972. Watergate did him in. The day before Nixon resigned, Landgrebe said, for attribution, "Don't confuse me with the facts. I've got a closed mind. I will not vote for impeachment. I'm going to stick with my president even if he and I have to be taken out of this building and shot." The end was not so lurid. Landgrebe faced, not a firing squad, but the voters, and got only 39% of the vote.

The winner was Democrat Floyd Fithian, who had lost to Landgrebe in 1972 and never stopped running. If voters here had wanted a solid Republican as their congressman in the Halleck years, now they were most interested in having a hard worker, and Fithian proved he was that. A professor at Purdue University who could also say that he was a farmer, Fithian obtained a seat on the House Agriculture Committee and, like most freshmen these days, began using the perquisites of incumbency to advantage. His voting record has been tilted enough to the right to give him nearly 50% ratings from some conservative groups. A constant flow of mail to the district, regular trips home almost every weekend to meet with constituents, dozens of canned press releases and TV spots sent out to the local media, close attention to constituents' problems with government—these are the ways in which Fithian ended up holding onto a district than which there is none more consistently Republican in national elections.

His 1976 opponent was a serious candidate, a former state legislator and aide to Earl Butz. (It may have hurt him when Butz, a former Purdue professor himself, was forced to resign in October because of his joke about blacks.) Fithian won reelection with a solid 55%. In 1978 he was helped by the third party candidacy of a born again Christian; even so, Fithian had a solid majority by himself.

Census Data Pop. 472,460. Central city, 14%; suburban, 51%. Median family income, $10,377; families above $15,000: 21%; families below $3,000: 7%. Median years education, 12.2.

The Voters

Median voting age 40.
Employment profile White collar, 42%. Blue collar, 41%. Service, 12%. Farm, 5%.
Ethnic groups Spanish, 1%. Total foreign stock, 9%. Germany, 2%.

Presidential vote

1976	Carter (D)	76,951	(39%)
	Ford (R)	118,603	(61%)
1972	Nixon (R)	149,099	(74%)
	McGovern (D)	53,463	(26%)

Rep. Floyd J. Fithian (D) Elected 1974; b. Nov. 3, 1928, Vesta, Neb.; home, Lafayette; Peru St. Col., B.A. 1951, U. of Neb., M.A. 1955, Ph.D. 1964; Methodist.

Career Navy, 1951–54; Farmer; High School Teacher; Assoc. Prof. of History, Purdue U.

Offices 129 CHOB, 202-225-5777. Also 5 N. Earl Ave., Lafayette 47904, 317-447-3181.

Committees *Agriculture* (16th). Subcommittees: Department Investigations, Oversight, and Research; Livestock and Grains.

Government Operations (20th). Subcommittees: Environment, Energy and Natural Resources.

Foreign Affairs (22d). Subcommittees: Africa.

Group Ratings

	ADA	COPE	PC	RPN	NFU	LCV	CFA	NAB	NSI	ACA	NTU
1978	25	50	53	36	50	–	32	55	50	58	–
1977	50	71	60	45	64	66	40	–	–	40	30
1976	40	55	62	39	83	63	45	27	50	23	55

Key Votes

1) Increase Def Spnd	FOR	6) Alaska Lands Protect	FOR	11) Delay Auto Pol Cntrl	FOR
2) B-1 Bomber	AGN	7) Water Projects Veto	FOR	12) Sugar Price Escalator	FOR
3) Cargo Preference	FOR	8) Consum Protect Agcy	AGN	13) Pub Fin Cong Cmpgns	FOR
4) Dereg Nat Gas	AGN	9) Common Situs Picket	FOR	14) ERA Ratif Recissn	AGN
5) Kemp-Roth	AGN	10) Labor Law Revision	FOR	15) Prohibt Govt Abrtns	DNV

Election Results

1978 general	Floyd J. Fithian (D)	82,402	(57%)	($196,945)
	J. Philip Oppenheim (R)	52,842	(37%)	($136,475)
	William Costas (I)	9,368	(6%)	($47,312)
1978 primary	Floyd J. Fithian (D), unopposed			
1976 general	Floyd J. Fithian (D)	117,617	(55%)	($179,309)
	William W. Erwin (R)	95,605	(45%)	($188,118)

THIRD DISTRICT

"Supercongressman" is the way one writer described John Brademas, Democratic Representative from the 3d district of Indiana. Brademas is an important congressman certainly, and a man with a background of contradictions. He is a Methodist of Greek descent whose district includes Notre Dame University; he was until recently a bachelor in a Washington that for most congressmen is a family town; he is a Harvard graduate and Rhodes Scholar who has more than held his own in the rough-hewn field of Indiana politics. In his early fifties, Brademas has been in Congress more than twenty years, he has risen to the number three position on the House Education and Labor Committee, and he is the Majority Whip—the number three position in the House Democratic leadership.

Brademas owes much of his reputation to being articulate. For years he was one of the few members of the House who could speak the language of political science departments and embassy dinners. He is also one of the few members or potential members of the House leadership who speaks with the conversational fluency that is so effective on television. Brademas as yet does not have his name on any really famous piece of legislation, but he has nonetheless been productive. He authored the major higher education aid act, and has played a big role in aid to the arts legislation. He also led the move to cut off military aid to Turkey because of its invasion of Cyprus, a cut off which succeeded for a time over the opposition of Henry Kissinger. On the House Administration Committee, Brademas has helped to write campaign finance legislation, although he has here sometimes taken a partisan approach that has caused him problems.

Brademas's rise to the Majority Whip position came through appointment. Before 1976 he was Chief Deputy Whip, chosen by Speaker Carl Albert, Majority Leader Tip O'Neill, and Whip John McFall. In the past such positions have led to automatic promotion; Albert had become Speaker in 1971 because he had been chosen Whip in 1955. But such is not necessarily the case any longer. While O'Neill was elected Speaker easily, McFall finished fourth out of four in the race for the majority leadership. (In 1978 McFall was defeated for reelection, largely because of his personal use of a contribution from Tongsun Park.)

Can Brademas succeed to a higher position in the leadership when the time comes? Unlike Phil Burton, he probably does not have a large constituency, which would prefer him over any other candidate; but as Burton showed in 1976, you can also have a large constituency which would prefer anyone but you. Brademas is probably an acceptable, if not first choice, candidate to a majority of the Democratic Caucus for any leadership position. He can be expected to run for majority leader if and when Jim Wright steps down or seeks the speakership.

Meanwhile Brademas, like most Indiana congressmen but unlike other members of the leadership, must work hard to make sure he is reelected in his district. The 3d includes the industrial city of South Bend (it used to produce Studebakers), which usually goes Democratic. But its other two counties—affluent Elkhart and industrial-farming LaPorte—are respectively Republican and marginal. Every two years Brademas feels he has to spend significant amounts of money, and his majorities are seldom very great. In 1978 he had a special problem: he had some years before accepted campaign contributions from Tongsun Park, and while there was nothing illegal about Brademas's conduct, it was scarcely an asset. Brademas was able to win with the same percentage he had in 1976 against the same opponent. But that may have been in part because of the Republican candidate's own problems (a drunken driving charge, charging $1,000 worh of personal phone calls to a university credit card). Brandemas still has to expend considerable energy keeping his fences mended in South Bend, even as he continues to work hard on issues in Washington.

Census Data Pop. 471,849. Central city, 27%; suburban, 25%. Median family income, $10,606; families above $15,000: 22%; families below $3,000: 6%. Median years education, 12.1.

The Voters

Median voting age 43.
Employment profile White collar, 44%. Blue collar, 43%. Service, 12%. Farm, 1%.
Ethnic groups Black, 6%. Total foreign stock, 13%. Poland, 3%; Germany, 2%.

Presidential vote

1976	Carter (D)	84,017	(46%)
	Ford (R)	98,139	(54%)
1972	Nixon (R)	120,430	(64%)
	McGovern (D)	66,985	(36%)

Rep. John Brademas (D) Elected 1958; b. Mar. 2, 1927, Mishawaka; home, South Bend; Harvard U., B.A. 1949, Rhodes Scholar, Oxford U. Ph.D. 1954; Methodist.

Career Navy, 1945–46; Asst. Prof., St. Mary's Col., Notre Dame, Legis. Asst. to U.S. Sen. Pat McNamera of Mich., 1955; Admin. Asst. to U.S. Rep. Thomas Ludlow Ashley of Ohio, 1955; Exec. Asst. to Adlai E. Stevenson II, 1955–56.

Offices 1236 LHOB, 202-225-3915. Also Rm. 203, Fed. Bldg., South Bend 46601, 219-233-8203.

Committees *Majority Whip.*

Education and Labor (3d). Subcommittees: Labor-Management Relations; Post-secondary Education; Select Education.

House Administration (3d). Subcommittees: Accounts (Chairman); Library and Memorials.

Group Ratings

	ADA	COPE	PC	RPN	NFU	LCV	CFA	NAB	NSI	ACA	NTU
1978	80	84	80	45	70	–	68	0	30	7	–
1977	75	86	70	54	89	80	55	–	–	4	20
1976	90	87	92	44	100	89	100	8	0	0	24

Key Votes

1) Increase Def Spnd	AGN	6) Alaska Lands Protect	FOR	11) Delay Auto Pol Cntrl	FOR
2) B-1 Bomber	AGN	7) Water Projects Veto	AGN	12) Sugar Price Escalator	AGN
3) Cargo Preference	AGN	8) Consum Protect Agcy	FOR	13) Pub Fin Cong Cmpgns	FOR
4) Dereg Nat Gas	AGN	9) Common Situs Picket	FOR	14) ERA Ratif Recissn	AGN
5) Kemp-Roth	AGN	10) Labor Law Revision	FOR	15) Prohibt Govt Abrtns	AGN

Election Results

1978 general	John Brademas(D)	64,336	(56%)	($251,394)
	Thomas L. Thorson (R)	50,145	(44%)	($102,766)
1978 primary	John Brademas (D), unopposed			
1976 general	John Brademas (D)	101,777	(57%)	($165,905)
	Thomas L. Thorson (R)	77,094	(43%)	($45,214)

FOURTH DISTRICT

The 4th congressional district of Indiana centers on Fort Wayne, the state's second largest city (though it is nowhere near as big as Indianapolis). More than half the district's votes are cast here and in surrounding Allen County. Fort Wayne is a typical medium-sized Midwestern community, with a small black ghetto, nondescript frame houses that belong to the people who work in the factories, and a small neighborhood of imposing houses that belong to the people who own or manage the factories and other local businesses.

The counties around Fort Wayne in the district are mostly agricultural flatland. Those to the south and west of the city have a Democratic tradition, but none went for Jimmy Carter, who did not strike a chord in this hard R, northern-accented part of the state. The counties north and east of Fort Wayne are heavily Republican. Any sophisticated public opinion survey of the area would probably disclose little difference between these two areas on major issues; their differing party identifications are largely a matter of upbringing and tradition, traceable ultimately to differences in attitude toward the Civil War. Altogether the 4th district is politically marginal. Indeed for a period of ten years it was probably the most marginal district in Indiana, with no candidate receiving more than 55% in a general election.

That marginality, however, may only have reflected the weakness of successive incumbents. In the late sixties, Republican Ross Adair, first elected in 1950, was thrown into the same district as Democrat Edward Roush, first elected in 1958. Adair won in 1968, Roush in 1970; then Roush won narrowly in 1972 and 1974. He was finally defeated in 1976.

The winner was a new kind of politician for Indiana, not the kind of lackluster state senator the Republicans had been running in the district before. Running at age 29, J. Danforth Quayle had not had the opportunity to climb the political ladder. But he had other credentials. As the grandson of Indianapolis *Star* and Arizona *Republic* publisher Eugene Pulliam, he had a solid conservative heritage and the capacity to raise a large campaign treasury. Quayle took control of the campaign from the organization—both parties have had weak Fort Wayne machines in the past—developing his own volunteers and controlling his own advertising campaign. He attacked the incumbent for supporting labor-backed measures like the Humphrey-Hawkins bill and won a solid majority in the general election. In his first term in the House, Quayle voted almost always with the conservative bloc. He also apparently used the advantages of incumbency ably: he won reelection by nearly a 2–1 margin, with the highest percentage recorded in the Fort Wayne area for more than a century. He is considered likely to be the Republican candidate for Birch Bayh's Senate seat in 1980. These are two men whose positions on almost every issue are different, and it should be a spirited contest. There are certain parallels with Bayh's first victory in 1962. Now, as then, a challenger in his early thirties is running against an entrenched three-term incumbent; and Quayle hopes to win the kind of upset Bayh did 18 years ago.

Census Data Pop. 472,678. Central city, 38%; suburban, 22%. Median family income, $10,443; families above $15,000: 20%; families below $3,000: 7%. Median years education, 12.2.

The Voters

Median voting age 42.
Employment profile White collar, 44%. Blue collar, 42%. Service, 11%. Farm, 3%.
Ethnic groups Black, 4%. Total foreign stock, 6%. Germany, 2%.

Presidential vote

1976	Carter (D)	79,908	(40%)
	Ford (R)	118,239	(60%)
1972	Nixon (R)	130,321	(67%)
	McGovern (D)	63,938	(33%)

Rep. J. Danforth Quayle (R) Elected 1976; b. Feb. 4, 1947, Indianapolis; home, Huntington; Depauw U., B.A. 1969, Ind. U., J.D. 1974; Grace Bible Church.

Career Admin. Asst. to the Gov. of Ind., 1971–73; Dir., Inheritance Tax Div., State of Indiana, 1973; Practicing atty., Gen. Mgr. and Assoc. Publ. of Huntington *Herald-Press,* 1974–76.

Offices 1407 LHOB, 202-225-4436. Also 326 Fed. Bldg., Ft. Wayne 46803, 219-424-3041.

Committees *Foreign Affairs* (12th). Subcommittees: International Security and Scientific Affairs; International Organizations.

Small Business (6th). Subcommittees: Antitrust and Restraint of Trade Activities Affecting Small Business.

Group Ratings

	ADA	COPE	PC	RPN	NFU	LCV	CFA	NAB	NSI	ACA	NTU
1978	15	11	25	91	22	–	27	100	78	81	–
1977	15	10	33	69	18	40	15	–	–	96	54

Key Votes

1) Increase Def Spnd	FOR	6) Alaska Lands Protect	DNV	11) Delay Auto Pol Cntrl	FOR
2) B-1 Bomber	AGN	7) Water Projects Veto	FOR	12) Sugar Price Escalator	AGN
3) Cargo Preference	AGN	8) Consum Protect Agcy	AGN	13) Pub Fin Cong Cmpgns	AGN
4) Dereg Nat Gas	FOR	9) Common Situs Picket	AGN	14) ERA Ratif Recissn	FOR
5) Kemp-Roth	FOR	10) Labor Law Revision	AGN	15) Prohibt Govt Abrtns	FOR

Election Results

1978 general	J. Danforth Quayle (R)	80,527	(66%)	($142,446)
	John D. Walda (D)	42,238	(34%)	($59,155)
1978 primary	J. Danforth Quayle (R), unopposed			
1976 general	J. Danforth Quayle (R)	107,762	(55%)	($114,888)
	J. Edward Roush (D)	88,361	(45%)	($63,399)

FIFTH DISTRICT

The 5th congressional district lies smack in the middle of Indiana, which is to say in the middle of Middle America. The rich Hoosier farmland here is Farm Bureau country, and politically very conservative. There are also three medium-sized factory towns, Anderson, Kokomo, and Marion, as well as Peru, the boyhood home of Cole Porter. The district also dips south to include a portion of the city of Indianapolis (an integrated Democratic neighborhood, placed in this Republican district to render it politically harmless). Just to the north of the city are the political poles of the district: Hamilton County, high income, exurban Indianapolis, full of people who left this bland, uncrowded city because it was too urban for them, and very Republican; and Anderson, with its huge General Motors plant and thousands of UAW members, which is usually solidly Democratic.

That Anderson was included in this district by a Republican legislature is testimony to the confidence Republican leaders have in the political durability of Congressman Elwood Hillis. First elected in 1970, he has won by comfortable margins ever since, with a slight letdown in the Watergate year of 1974. His voting record makes some bows to Anderson as well as Hamilton County; he has higher ratings from organized labor than most Indiana Republicans. Hillis has never really been targeted by Democrats and has not faced strong opposition. In the House he tends to concentrate on matters military, serving on the Armed Services and Veterans' Affairs Committees.

Census Data Pop. 471,921. Central city, 25%; suburban, 17%. Median family income, $10,314; families above $15,000: 22%; families below $3,000: 7%. Median years education, 12.2.

The Voters

Median voting age 42.
Employment profile White collar, 41%. Blue collar, 44%. Service, 12%. Farm, 3%.
Ethnic groups Black, 6%. Total foreign stock, 4%.

Presidential vote

1976	Carter (D)	89,307	(43%)
	Ford (R)	119,475	(57%)
1972	Nixon (R)	135,915	(70%)
	McGovern (D)	58,893	(30%)

Rep. Elwood Hillis (R) Elected 1970; b. Mar. 6, 1926, Kokomo; home, Kokomo; Ind. U., B.S. 1949, J.D. 1952; Presbyterian.

Career Army, WWII; Practicing atty., 1952–71; Ind. House of Reps., 1967–71.

Offices 2429 RHOB, 202-225-5037. Also 518 N. Main St., Kokomo 46901, 317-457-4411.

Committees *Armed Services* (10th). Subcommittees: Procurement and Military Nuclear Systems; Military Personnel; NATO Standardization, Interoperability, and Readiness.

Veterans' Affairs (4th). Subcommittees: Compensation, Pension, Insurance and Memorial Affairs; Special Investigations.

Group Ratings

	ADA	COPE	PC	RPN	NFU	LCV	CFA	NAB	NSI	ACA	NTU
1978	10	35	13	64	40	–	14	100	78	69	–
1977	25	41	20	91	58	19	20	–	–	62	30
1976	25	36	18	72	17	34	9	55	100	62	21

Key Votes

1) Increase Def Spnd	FOR	6) Alaska Lands Protect	AGN	11) Delay Auto Pol Cntrl	FOR
2) B-1 Bomber	FOR	7) Water Projects Veto	AGN	12) Sugar Price Escalator	DNV
3) Cargo Preference	AGN	8) Consum Protect Agcy	AGN	13) Pub Fin Cong Cmpgns	FOR
4) Dereg Nat Gas	FOR	9) Common Situs Picket	AGN	14) ERA Ratif Recissn	FOR
5) Kemp-Roth	FOR	10) Labor Law Revision	FOR	15) Prohibt Govt Abrtns	AGN

Election Results

1978 general	Elwood Hillis (R)	94,950	(68%)	($72,873)
	Max E. Heiss (D)	45,479	(32%)	
1978 primary	Elwood Hillis (R), unopposed			
1976 general	Elwood Hillis (R)	127,194	(62%)	($61,368)
	William C. Stout (D)	78,807	(38%)	($6,432)

SIXTH DISTRICT

When Washington *Post* political reporter David Broder wrote a column which explained why all but three of the Democratic freshmen elected in 1974 were reelected to the House in 1976, the example he used to illustrate his case was the 6th congressional district of Indiana. It was an example well chosen. A more unlikely place for the election of a Democratic congressman, not to speak of continued reelection, could scarcely be imagined. The 6th takes in about one-third of the geographically sprawling city of Indianapolis, four suburban counties, and a couple of townships in another suburban county. With the exception of part of the Indianapolis black ghetto and a few working class neighborhoods around the Indianapolis Speedway, this is heavily Republican territory in almost every election. The district not only went solidly for Gerald Ford and Richard Nixon, it also, so far as can be determined, provided a good majority to Barry Goldwater in 1964.

Overall, metropolitan Indianapolis has always been one of our most Republican cities. It has never had the really large influxes of Eastern European immigrants who provide so many of the traditional Democratic votes in places like Chicago and Detroit and Cleveland, and its economic base is decidedly white collar, with banks, insurance companies, and state government all major employers. Beyond that there is an ethos here that is profoundly conservative. This is the headquarters of the American Legion, the home town of James Whitcomb Riley and Benjamin Harrison, the base of the Pulliam newspaper chain.

The Congressman here is David Evans, a Democrat who owes his 1974 victory over a 24-year incumbent not to a large budget but to campaign gimmickry, including standing by a highway with a sign asking for votes. After his upset victory he used the advantages of incumbency strenuously. He also compiled a voting record less obnoxious to voters here than the traditional Democrat's; his ratings from conservative organizations have actually been higher than his ratings from liberal organizations in some years. Evans faced strong opposition in 1976 and 1978 from Republican David Crane, a lawyer and physician and brother of Illinois Congressman Philip Crane. The Republican had plenty of money, much raised through conservative direct mailings, and a core of enthusiastic volunteers that was enough to defeat an organization-backed opponent in the 1978 primary. But Crane has been unable to win a majority in the 6th district against Evans.

This is not to say that Evans is invulnerable. His percentage dropped from 1976 to 1978, and it is possible that a less ideological Republican than Crane might win more votes. In the meantime, Evans's career continued in Congress; he is one of the more unpredictable young Democrats on substantive issues and a key swing vote on the Banking and Government Operations Committees.

Census Data Pop. 471,595. Central city, 54%; suburban, 46%. Median family income, $10,497; families above $15,000: 20%; families below $3,000: 6%. Median years education, 12.0.

The Voters

Median voting age 41.
Employment profile White collar, 45%. Blue collar, 42%. Service, 11%. Farm, 2%.
Ethnic groups Black, 4%. Total foreign stock, 4%.

Presidential vote

1976	Carter (D)	80,098	(41%)
	Ford (R)	113,083	(59%)
1972	Nixon (R)	127,566	(74%)
	McGovern (D)	45,691	(26%)

Rep. David W. Evans (D) Elected 1974; b. Aug. 17, 1946, Lafayette; home, Indianapolis; Ind. U., B.A. 1967, 1967–70, Butler U. 1970–72.

Career Parochial school teacher and asst. principal, 1968–74; Dem. nominee for U.S. House of Reps., 1972.

Offices 432 CHOB, 202-225-2276. Also 4th Floor, Administration Bldg., Weir Cook Airport, Indianapolis 46241, 317-269-7364.

Committees *Banking, Finance and Urban Affairs* (18th). Subcommittees: Economic Stabilization; Housing and Community Development; International Trade, Investment and Monetary Policy.

Government Operations (15th). Subcommittees: Government Information and Individual Rights; Government Activities and Transportation.

Group Ratings

	ADA	COPE	PC	RPN	NFU	LCV	CFA	NAB	NSI	ACA	NTU
1978	25	55	45	18	50	–	32	73	78	63	–
1977	40	55	43	50	70	42	35	–	–	56	51
1976	50	55	61	47	64	52	18	36	67	41	75

Key Votes

1) Increase Def Spnd	FOR	6) Alaska Lands Protect	FOR	11) Delay Auto Pol Cntrl	FOR
2) B-1 Bomber	AGN	7) Water Projects Veto	FOR	12) Sugar Price Escalator	FOR
3) Cargo Preference	AGN	8) Consum Protect Agcy	AGN	13) Pub Fin Cong Cmpgns	FOR
4) Dereg Nat Gas	FOR	9) Common Situs Picket	FOR	14) ERA Ratif Recissn	FOR
5) Kemp-Roth	FOR	10) Labor Law Revision	FOR	15) Prohibt Govt Abrtns	FOR

Election Results

1978 general	David W. Evans (D)	66,421	(52%)	($180,870)
	David G. Crane (R)	60,630	(48%)	($431,943)
1978 primary	David W. Evans (D), unopposed			
1976 general	David W. Evans (D)	105,773	(55%)	($99,024)
	David G. Crane (R)	86,854	(45%)	($179,863)

SEVENTH DISTRICT

Like the old Wabash Cannonball—one of the most famous of the vanished passenger trains—the Wabash River flows across the rolling farmland of western Indiana on its way to meet the Ohio and Mississippi Rivers. And in a nearly straight line from Indianapolis to St. Louis runs the old National Road (now U.S. 40), closely paralleled by Interstate 70. The river and the road intersect in Terre Haute, which with fewer than 100,000 people is still the largest city in the 7th congressional district of Indiana. Terre Haute, despite its elegant French name, is a rough and crude town, once known for gambling and vice; it has the look of a rundown factory town. Politically Terre Haute has always had a strong Democratic machine (although it was the home town of the great Socialist Eugene Debs), which more often than not has controlled the Vigo County courthouse.

The Wabash Cannonball traversed, in its day, both Democratic and Republican territory; and the dividing line, roughly, was at Terre Haute and the National Road. To the north the people speak with the hard-edged accent of the Midwest; to the south, they drawl in a manner reminiscent of Dixie. The counties to the north are traditionally Republican; those to the south traditionally Democratic. You can see the same demarcation in maps of the political preferences of the 1860s. And although the preferences were submerged in the politics of the late sixties and early seventies, when all those rural counties went heavily Republican, they emerged again when Jimmy Carter of Plains, Georgia, faced Gerald Ford of Grand Rapids, Michigan, in 1976. Carter carried Terre Haute and the southern counties of the district and, although he didn't carry the 7th, did strikingly better than Hubert Humphrey had in 1968.

The 7th district was created in basically its present form in 1965 by a Democratic legislature, which thought it was creating a Democratic district. It was a classic example of foiled redistricting. The year 1966 was a good one for Republicans and the Republican candidate, a young banker named John Myers, won the seat. And Myers has won ever since. He has often been helped by weak opposition. Eldon Tipton, the man he beat in 1966, ran again in 1968 and 1974; his son was Myers's opponent in 1976. Neither proved to be formidable competition. Probably his toughest opponent was Charlotte Zietlow, a councilwoman from the university town of Bloomington. But she ran in the not very Democratic year of 1978 and though she lowered Myers's percentage, Zietlow didn't come close to unseating him. Myers has a record of Republican regularity on most issues. He sits on the Appropriations Committee, where he serves as the ranking Republican on the Public Works Subcommittee, which parcels out money for post offices, dams, and the like. This was once an important post when congressmen depended on such goodies for reelection; now that they depend more on casework and franked mail it is less important, but not negligible.

Census Data Pop. 472,041. Central city, 15%; suburban, 29%. Median family income, $8,808; families above $15,000: 15%; families below $3,000: 10%. Median years education, 12.1.

The Voters

Median voting age 42.
Employment profile White collar, 42%. Blue collar, 39%. Service, 14%. Farm, 5%.
Ethnic groups Black, 2%. Total foreign stock, 4%.

Presidential vote

1976	Carter (D)	100,362	(47%)
	Ford (R)	111,589	(63%)
1972	Nixon (R)	135,270	(65%)
	McGovern (D)	72,718	(35%)

Rep. John T. Myers (R) Elected 1966; b. Feb. 8, 1927, Covington; home Covington; Ind. St. U., B.S. 1951; Episcopalian.

Career Army, WWII; Cashier and Trust Officer, Foundation Trust Co., 1954–66.

Offices 2301 RHOB, 202-225-5805. Also Fed. Bldg., Terre Haute 47808, 812-238-1619.

Committees *Appropriations* (7th). Subcommittees: Agriculture and Related Agencies; Energy and Water Development.

Group Ratings

	ADA	COPE	PC	RPN	NFU	LCV	CFA	NAB	NSI	ACA	NTU
1978	10	10	15	64	20	–	18	92	100	81	–
1977	5	23	13	54	42	14	10	–	–	85	40
1976	0	14	5	33	8	9	0	83	100	93	64

Key Votes

1) Increase Def Spnd	DNV	6) Alaska Lands Protect	FOR	11) Delay Auto Pol Cntrl	FOR
2) B-1 Bomber	FOR	7) Water Projects Veto	AGN	12) Sugar Price Escalator	FOR
3) Cargo Preference	AGN	8) Consum Protect Agcy	AGN	13) Pub Fin Cong Cmpgns	AGN
4) Dereg Nat Gas	FOR	9) Common Situs Picket	AGN	14) ERA Ratif Recissn	FOR
5) Kemp-Roth	FOR	10) Labor Law Revision	AGN	15) Prohibt Govt Abrtns	FOR

Election Results

1978 general	John T. Myers (R)	86,955	(56%)	($136,796)
	Charlotte Zietlow (D)	67,469	(44%)	($161,992)
1978 primary	John T. Myers (R)	30,680	(79%)	
	One other (R)	8,164	(21%)	
1976 general	John T. Myers (R)	130,005	(63%)	($55,723)
	John Elden Tipton (D)	77,355	(37%)	($1,300)

EIGHTH DISTRICT

The 8th congressional district of Indiana is the southwest corner of the state. It contains the city of Evansville on the Ohio River and several river counties so hilly that they might be considered mountainous by Midwestern standards. This part of Indiana was the first to be settled by white men. Vincennes, now a small town on the Wabash River, was once the metropolis of Indiana, and Robert Owen, the Scottish philanthropist, established the town of New Harmony downstream. (Owen's son was one of the first congressmen from the area, elected in 1842 and 1844.) Today Evansville is a reasonably prosperous city (fourth largest in the state), but much of the rest of the district has suffered ever since the railroads took most of the freight business away from Ohio River steamboats.

Much of southwest Indiana was settled by German Catholics, who have traditionally voted Democratic. During the Civil War most of this area was copperhead country, friendly to the South and hostile to Mr. Lincoln's war. Today, though the issues have changed, the 8th remains generally Democratic. It has gone Democratic in most recent Senate elections and, although it did not cotton to the liberalism of Hubert Humphrey or George McGovern, it went Democratic for Jimmy Carter in 1976, albeit by the narrowest of margins.

With a Democratic tradition and recent shifts toward the Republicans, the 8th has been a marginal district, and it has elected four different congressmen in the last four elections—the only district in the nation to do so. The first was Roger Zion, a Republican first elected in 1966, reelected easily in 1968, with difficulty in 1970, and easily in 1972. A member of the Public Works Committee who favored extensive road-building projects, Zion was slated as one of Environmental Action's Dirty Dozen three times. He lost finally in 1974.

The winner was Democrat Philip Hayes, a state Senator who liked Evansville and Indianapolis better than Washington. Hayes decided that if he had to remain in Washington it might as well be as a senator, and so he ran against Vance Hartke in the 1976 Democratic primary. His almost entirely negative campaign almost beat the unpopular incumbent. He was the only 1974 freshman to give up his seat voluntarily and one of only three who were not reelected in 1976.

Hayes was succeeded by David Cornwell, a Democrat who had been beaten in the 1974 primary. Cornwell had a number of weaknesses: he was from a small rural county, not Evansville, he had a very youthful appearance, and his voting record was not too far from the Democratic mainstream. These handicaps proved too much to overcome, and he was beaten in 1978.

The present incumbent is Joel Deckard, a former state legislator and solar heating contractor and cable television executive. He beat a more moderate Republican in the primary and is expected to join the growing bloc of conservative Republicans in the House. As an incumbent, he will likely have an advantage in 1980; but nothing is for certain in this very changeable district.

Census Data Pop. 472,175. Central city, 29%; suburban, 12%. Median family income, $8,557; families above $15,000: 13%; families below $3,000: 11%. Median years education, 11.8.

The Voters

Median voting age 45.
Employment profile White collar, 38%. Blue collar, 44%. Service, 13%. Farm, 5%.
Ethnic groups Black, 3%. Total foreign stock, 2%. Germany, 1%.

Presidential vote

1976	Carter (D)	110,693	(50%)
	Ford (R)	110,108	(50%)
1972	Nixon (R)	138,545	(65%)
	McGovern (D)	73,835	(35%)

Rep. H. Joel Deckard (R) Elected 1978; b. Mar. 7, 1942, Vandalia, Ill.; home, Evansville; U. of Evansville, 1962–67; Protestant.

Career Radio newscaster, 1961–74; Ind. House of Reps., 1966–74; Div. Mgr., Cable TV Company, 1974–77; Builder, 1977–78.

Offices 507 CHOB, 202-225-4636. Also 210 S.E. 6th St., Evansville 42708, 812-423-4279.

Committees *Government Operations* (14th). Subcommittees: Commerce, Consumer, and Monetary Affairs; Environment, Energy, and Natural Resources.

Veterans' Affairs (10th). Subcommittees: Medical Facilities and Benefits; Special Investigations.

Group Ratings: Newly Elected

Key Votes: Newly Elected

Election Results

1978 general	H. Joel Deckard (R)	83,019	(52%)	($231,632)
	David L. Cornwell (D)	76,654	(48%)	($112,985)
1978 primary	H. Joel Deckard (R)	14,238	(49%)	
	David A. Koehler, Sr. (R)	11,591	(40%)	($14,363)
	One other (R)	3,091	(11%)	
1976 general	David L. Cornwell (D)	109,013	(50%)	($87,163)
	Belden Bell (R)	107,013	(50%)	($134,178)

NINTH DISTRICT

What happens to congressmen carried into office on the strength of a party landslide? Traditionally they have been swept right back out again when there were no more coattails to ride. But that has not been the case in recent years. The change seems to have come to the class of Democrats elected in the LBJ landslide of 1964. Of those Democrats elected that year in previously Republican districts, half survived the 1966 elections, and nearly half still serve in the

House or have retired voluntarily. One of the former is Lee Hamilton of Indiana's 9th district, and his case helps tell us why these members—and increasing numbers of the Republicans elected in 1966 and the Democrats elected in 1974—have survived politically.

In 1964 Hamilton, then president of the Bartholomew County Young Democrats, was a surprisingly big 12,000-vote winner over veteran Republican Congressman Earl Wilson. He was helped by Lyndon Johnson's solid win in the 9th, which is roughly the southeast corner of Indiana. The district is basically Republican territory, from the hills along the Ohio River to the neat small city of Columbus, home of Cummins Engine Company and its scholarly president, J. Irwin Miller. (Esquire in 1967 put liberal Republican Miller on its cover and suggested he should be president of the United States, an idea which unfortunately was not taken seriously by the Republican National Convention that year. Miller later found himself on Richard Nixon's enemies list.)

In his first term Hamilton was successful in getting post office and public works projects for his district which, outside of Columbus, is far from prosperous. By 1966 his sharp campaigning and intelligent use of the advantages of incumbency helped him win reelection over a determined Republican opponent. By 1970 Hamilton was home free, running far ahead of his party's ticket, and by 1972 he was approaching the 2–1 margin level.

In the House Hamilton has had a voting record which bows to the sometimes conservative views of his constituents, but at the same time seldom greatly displeases organized labor or other liberal lobbying groups. His major impact has been in the area of foreign affairs. He is now the sixth-ranking Democrat on the International Relations Committee and Chairman of the Subcommittee on Europe and the Middle East. During the Johnson Administration and most of the Nixon years Hamilton supported the Vietnam war, and moved away from that position only cautiously. When the crunch came in Indochina in 1975, Hamilton's impulse was to compromise on further American aid, but he followed the impulse of the House to permit no aid at all. Hamilton has supported some cuts in defense programs, such as the B-1 bomber, but at the same time stands for strong American commitments.

Hamilton has also moved to cut aid to South Korea if the government there did not cooperate with the investigation of Tongsun Park. Hamilton has been deeply involved in efforts to disclose House members' finances and to limit outside income. Having served on the House Ethics Committee, he is considered as one of the tougher advocates of high ethical standards.

For Hamilton, 1976 was a key political year. By declining to run for the Senate—a race he might well have won—he virtually assured that the balance of his career will be spent in the House. Still comparatively young, with considerable seniority and great popularity at home, he seems capable of being an important congressman in the years ahead.

Census Data Pop. 472,321. Central city, 0%; suburban, 34%. Median family income, $9,001; families above $15,000: 14%; families below $3,000: 9%. Median years education, 11.4.

The Voters

Median voting age 43.
Employment profile White collar, 37%. Blue collar, 47%. Service, 11%. Farm, 5%.
Ethnic groups Black, 2%. Total foreign stock, 2%.

Presidential vote

1976	Carter (D)	105,561	(51%)
	Ford (R)	101,335	(49%)
1972	Nixon (R)	123,569	(64%)
	McGovern (D)	70,613	(36%)

Rep. Lee H. Hamilton (D) Elected 1964; b. Apr. 20, 1931, Daytona Beach, Fla.; home, Columbus; DePauw U., B.A. 1952, Goethe U., Frankfort Germany, 1952–53, Ind. U., J.D. 1956; Methodist.

Career Practicing atty., 1956–64; Instructor, Amer. Banking Inst., 1960–61.

Offices 2470 RHOB, 202-225-5315. Also U.S.P.O., Columbus 47201, 812-372-2571.

Committees *Foreign Affairs* (6th). Subcommittees: Europe and the Middle East (Chairman); International Security and Scientific Affairs.

Standards of Official Conduct (2d).

Group Ratings

	ADA	COPE	PC	RPN	NFU	LCV	CFA	NAB	NSI	ACA	NTU
1978	35	50	65	55	40	–	55	55	70	31	–
1977	60	64	53	46	64	78	35	–	–	15	22
1976	50	52	66	78	58	65	64	33	50	11	59

Key Votes

1) Increase Def Spnd	AGN	6) Alaska Lands Protect	FOR	11) Delay Auto Pol Cntrl	FOR
2) B-1 Bomber	AGN	7) Water Projects Veto	FOR	12) Sugar Price Escalator	AGN
3) Cargo Preference	AGN	8) Consum Protect Agcy	AGN	13) Pub Fin Cong Cmpgns	FOR
4) Dereg Nat Gas	AGN	9) Common Situs Picket	AGN	14) ERA Ratif Recissn	FOR
5) Kemp-Roth	AGN	10) Labor Law Revision	FOR	15) Prohibt Govt Abrtns	FOR

Election Results

1978 general	Lee H. Hamilton, Jr. (D)	99,727	(66%)	($111,793)
	Frank I. Hamilton, Jr. (R)	52,218	(34%)	($48,720)
1978 primary	Lee H. Hamilton, Jr. (D), unopposed			
1976 general	Lee H. Hamilton, Jr. (D), unopposed			($22,614)

TENTH DISTRICT

Before Robert and Helen Lynd published *Middletown* in the thirties, many Americans imagined that small Midwestern cities were tightly knit, homogeneous communities. What the Lynds discovered in Middletown—actually Muncie, Indiana—was something very different: a factory town divided sharply along class lines, with local affairs firmly controlled by a small business elite. Since the thirties the General Motors and other major plants here have been unionized and blue collar wages have risen greatly. But the basic class divisions remain, more pronounced than in just about any other part of the country. Life and death economic power remains in the hands of businessmen, which means faraway GM executives in Detroit and New York as well as the Ball family in Muncie.

Nowhere are the class divisions so clearly expressed as in politics. A New York *Times* article quoted a member of the Muncie elite who thought that everyone in the town was a Republican. That is true of the great majority of the members of the country club, but it is hardly an accurate picture of the city's voting habits. In fact Muncie votes for Democrats as often as for Republicans, and the working class neighborhoods of the city almost always give Democrats big majorities. But there is little contact between people from these different strata and little sense of what the other is like. They know each other better through television programs than from personal experience.

Muncie lies roughly in the middle of Indiana's 10th congressional district, and with less than 100,000 people is still the district's largest city. The only other sizeable town, Richmond, is quite a different kind of place. It has a longstanding Quaker tradition and is the site of the Friends' Earlham College. But the Quakerism of this part of Indiana is closer to that of Richard Nixon's Whittier, California, than to that of Philadelphia's American Friends Service Committee. Richmond has kept strong Republican voting habits from its antislavery days before the Civil War.

The 10th district was the creation of a Republican redistricting; yet today the seat is held by a Democrat, Philip Sharp, a former professor at Ball State University. He is so typical of the 1974 Democratic freshmen that the Washington *Post* chose him as the subject for a series of profiles through the life of the 94th Congress. Sharp's political secret is hard work. He ran for Congress twice, in 1970 and 1972, before winning in 1974; 1980, assuming he runs, will be his sixth congressional campaign. His earlier races laid the groundwork for his 1974 defeat of Republican David Dennis, although it also helped that Dennis, a peppery, combative man, was one of the most visible of Richard Nixon's defenders in the House Judiciary Committee's impeachment hearings. Sharp's attention to constituency service and frequent trips to the district as an incumbent have helped him to win reelection in 1976 and 1978. Certainly Sharp has used the advantages of incumbency more effectively than the Democrat elected here in 1958 who rented his front porch to the government as his district office, and was defeated for reelection.

Sharp is one of the younger Democrats whose service on the Commerce Committee has greatly changed the tone and work product of the committee in the last few years. Before 1974 Commerce tended to be dominated by lobbyists for the business interests the government purports to regulate. Now there is much more volatility: members like Sharp will listen to industry lobbyists as well as spokesmen for consumer groups and government officials, and the results are not always predictable. Sharp was an opponent of deregulation of natural gas, and even as a junior member was chosen by Speaker O'Neill to head an energy task force in 1977. He is respected as a hard-working and thoughtful legislator and could be one of the more important young members of the House in the years ahead.

Census Data Pop. 472,335. Central city, 15%; suburban, 27%. Median family income, $9,635; families above $15,000: 17%; families below $3,000: 8%. Median years education, 12.1.

The Voters

Median voting age 42.
Employment profile White collar, 37%. Blue collar, 47%. Service, 12%. Farm, 4%.
Ethnic groups Black, 3%. Total foreign stock, 3%.

Presidential vote

1976	Carter (D)	86,375	(45%)
	Ford (R)	105,448	(55%)
1972	Nixon (R)	129,455	(69%)
	McGovern (D)	57,073	(31%)

Rep. Philip R. Sharp (D) Elected 1974; b. July 15, 1942, Baltimore, Md.; home, Muncie; DePauw U., Georgetown U. School of Foreign Svc., B.S. 1964, Oxford U., 1966, Georgetown U., Ph.D. 1974; Methodist.

Career Legis. Aide to U.S. Sen. Vance Hartke, 1964–69; Asst. and Assoc. Prof. of Poli. Sci., Ball St. U., 1969–74; Dem. nominee for U.S. House of Reps., 1970, 1972.

Offices 1421 LHOB, 202-225-3021. Also Fed. Bldg., 401 S. High St., Muncie 47305, 317-289-7948.

Committees *Interior and Insular Affairs* (16th). Subcommittees: Energy and the Environment; Water and Power Resources.

Interstate and Foreign Commerce (12th). Subcommittees: Energy and Power; Oversight and Investigations.

Group Ratings

	ADA	COPE	PC	RPN	NFU	LCV	CFA	NAB	NSI	ACA	NTU
1978	50	70	83	58	40	–	64	50	40	26	–
1977	65	70	73	54	58	80	60	–	–	26	30
1976	60	61	74	72	67	70	64	17	20	11	52

Key Votes

1) Increase Def Spnd	AGN	6) Alaska Lands Protect	FOR	11) Delay Auto Pol Cntrl	FOR
2) B-1 Bomber	AGN	7) Water Projects Veto	FOR	12) Sugar Price Escalator	AGN
3) Cargo Preference	AGN	8) Consum Protect Agcy	FOR	13) Pub Fin Cong Cmpgns	FOR
4) Dereg Nat Gas	AGN	9) Common Situs Picket	FOR	14) ERA Ratif Recissn	AGN
5) Kemp-Roth	AGN	10) Labor Law Revision	FOR	15) Prohibt Govt Abrtns	FOR

Election Results

1978 general	Philip R. Sharp (D)	73,343	(57%)	($107,372)
	William G. Frazier (R)	55,999	(43%)	($129,665)
1978 primary	Philip R. Sharp (D)	31,833	(89%)	
	Two others (D)	3,804	(11%)	
1976 general	Philip R. Sharp (D)	114,559	(60%)	($85,620)
	William G. Frazier (R)	76,890	(40%)	($108,653)

ELEVENTH DISTRICT

The 11th district of Indiana includes most of the city of Indianapolis, which several years ago annexed almost all of its Marion County suburbs to provide more rational local government and also to help preserve Republican control of city hall. There are plenty of factories here, but Indianapolis is more of an office town than most major cities in the Midwest, with major banks, insurance companies, and the state government. Like Columbus, the capital of Ohio, it never had the kind of migration of Eastern European ethnics which shaped the politics of the Great Lakes industrial cities; like Columbus, it has prospered and grown in recent years with the expansion of the white collar economy. Cleveland and Detroit and Gary and Chicago are heavily Democratic. Indianapolis remains almost as strongly Republican as it was in the 1920's.

As in all of Indiana, politics is a serious business here. Of the two major banks, for example, one is Republican and the other Democratic; naturally both have an interest in which party wins the state treasurer's office. Patronage is an integral part of politics, and civil servants virtually unheard of. Most state, county, and city employees traditionally have had to "contribute" 2% of their paychecks to the party that got them their jobs. The national headquarters of the American Legion stares down toward the federal building and the state Capitol; this is a serious town, without much sense of humor.

Yet Indianapolis sends to Congress one of its funniest members, 11th district Congressman Andrew Jacobs. Jacobs is a liberal Democrat—though the adjective must be qualified—from a conservative Republican city who approaches politics with an attitude less than stern. He has a fatalistic approach to things: in 1975 he refused to board an Indianapolis-to-Washington plane because only first class seats were available; it crashed, killing all aboard. His fearlessness in flouting tradition was shown in 1975 when he married Congresswoman Martha Keys of Kansas. They had met in that most unromantic of environments, the House Ways and Means Committee; and although their voting records were not identical, they decided to marry. On weekends Jacobs flew to Indianapolis and Keys took the plane on to Kansas City—at least until she was defeated in the 1978 election.

Jacobs has proved to be a durable part of the Indianapolis political scene. He was first elected to Congress in 1964—a Democratic year which coincided with the retirement of a Republican incumbent—and despite redistrictings, he has won reelection three times. In those days he was a strong supporter of Great Society programs and had a standard Democratic voting record. In 1972 Jacobs was beaten by Protestant minister William Hudnut III. Jacobs beat him in turn in 1974, leaving Hudnut to go on to be Richard Lugar's hand-picked successor as Mayor of Indianapolis.

Jacobs was reelected by solid margins in 1976 and 1978. One reason undoubtedly was familiarity and careful use of the advantages of incumbency. Another may have been Jacobs's increasingly independent voting record. On economic issues particularly he has been parting company with his liberal friends. He was one of the first Democrats to oppose the Carter Administration's $50 rebate, and his labor voting record is not much higher than that of 5th district Republican Elwood Hillis. Jacobs is a maverick in another respect. He used to be accompanied by his Great Dane, C-5A, onto the House floor; more recently he has tried to abolish the rule requiring male members of the House to wear coats and ties on the floor. One senses that Indianapolis's only President, Benjamin Harrison, would not have approved.

Census Data Pop. 472,533. Central city, 93%; suburban, 7%. Median family income, $10,785; families above $15,000: 26%; families below $3,000: 7%. Median years education, 12.2.

The Voters

Median voting age 42.
Employment profile White collar, 53%. Blue collar, 34%. Service, 13%. Farm, –%.
Ethnic groups Black, 2%. Total foreign stock, 6%. Germany, 1%.

Presidential vote

1976	Carter (D)	86,916	(45%)
	Ford (R)	104,572	(55%)
1972	Nixon (R)	125,009	(66%)
	McGovern (D)	63,456	(34%)

Rep. Andrew Jacobs, Jr. (D) Elected 1974; b. Feb. 24, 1932, Indianapolis; home, Indianapolis; Ind. U., B.S. 1955, LL.B. 1958; Catholic.

Career USMC, Korea; Practicing atty., 1958–65, 1973–74; Ind. House of Reps. 1959–60; U.S. House of Reps., 1965–73.

Offices 1533 LHOB, 202-225-4011. Also 46 E. Ohio St., 441 A Fed. Bldg., Indianapolis 46204, 317-269-7331.

Committees *Ways and Means* (11th). Subcommittees: Oversight; Social Security.

Group Ratings

	ADA	COPE	PC	RPN	NFU	LCV	CFA	NAB	NSI	ACA	NTU
1978	50	50	58	75	20	–	46	75	40	59	–
1977	75	52	68	69	50	70	55	–	–	41	52
1976	65	55	70	72	55	74	64	50	11	31	68

Key Votes

1) Increase Def Spnd	AGN	6) Alaska Lands Protect	FOR	11) Delay Auto Pol Cntrl	AGN
2) B-1 Bomber	AGN	7) Water Projects Veto	FOR	12) Sugar Price Escalator	AGN
3) Cargo Preference	AGN	8) Consum Protect Agcy	AGN	13) Pub Fin Cong Cmpgns	FOR
4) Dereg Nat Gas	AGN	9) Common Situs Picket	FOR	14) ERA Ratif Recissn	AGN
5) Kemp-Roth	AGN	10) Labor Law Revision	FOR	15) Prohibt Govt Abrtns	AGN

Election Results

1978 general	Andrew Jacobs, Jr. (D)	61,504	(57%)	($18,394)
	Charles F. Bosma (R)	45,809	(43%)	($55,971)
1978 primary	Andrew Jacobs, Jr. (D)	17,138	(95%)	
	One other (D)	918	(5%)	
1976 general	Andrew Jacobs, Jr. (D)	115,895	(61%)	($26,895)
	Lawrence L. Buell (R)	74,829	(39%)	($66,198)

IOWA

Iowa brings to mind the America of the nineteenth century: Grant Wood's American Gothic; Main Street; county fair time; and acres upon acres of rolling cornfields. To this day many aspects of Iowa life seem unaffected by the twentieth century. Most Iowans still live on farms or in small towns, not in large cities or surrounding suburbs. The state has no military installations and virtually no defense industry. Iowa politics, therefore, has not been afflicted with the ills which seem to result from rapid urbanization: the state has never had an equivalent of the Chicago machine or the militant conservatism of southern California.

The economic base of Iowa remains pretty much what it was at the turn of the century. Technology has changed the actual workings of agriculture enormously, vastly increasing the yield of the land and at the same time decreasing the number of actual farmers. But the livelihood of most Iowans still depends, directly or indirectly, on the economics of corn, hogs, and beef cattle. Iowa is part of the vast American heartland that feeds not only this country but much of the rest of the world as well. During most of the seventies this has been a prosperous state. But it remains a nervous one—conscious of the fact that falling commodity prices could put it into a kind of depression. Iowa is a state that watches very closely commodity prices on the Chicago Board of Trade and policy decisions made at the U.S. Department of Agriculture in Washington.

With its nineteenth century atmosphere, its dependence on farming, and its predominantly white Anglo-Saxon Protestant population, Iowa has the reputation of a Republican state. Actually, in recent elections, it has been one of the more closely divided states—as reflected in its current congressional representation, which is evenly divided between the two parties. True, Iowa has voted Republican in the last three presidential elections, but it gave George McGovern a larger than average percentage and came within 13,000 votes out of 1,250,000 cast of going for Jimmy Carter in 1976.

In fact, political cleavages in Iowa are rather deep and long-standing. From its first days as a state, its Protestant majority tended to vote Republican and its Catholic minority tended to vote Democratic. Typically, the small towns, with their bankers, store-owners, and white collar workers, have been the Republican Party's strongholds. People who are actually farmers are somewhat more likely than average to be Democrats. But beyond party labels, there are some shared attitudes here. Iowans are suspicious of the federal government and hostile to large government programs—except those that bolster the prices of agricultural products. They have always been leery of the culture of big cities, particularly of Chicago, the big city which is most important to Iowans. They have disliked its noise and its violence and have been especially averse to its corruption and machine politics. Iowans want their politics, like their small towns and their farms, to be neat, orderly, and clean.

As a result, Iowa is a state which with great consistency has shifted against the party in power. It has typically been discontented with the incumbent administration's farm policies, but, more than that, its basic attitudes predispose it to be suspicious of whoever exercises power and holds office. Thus in the early forties Iowa swung heavily to the Republicans, although an Iowan, Henry Wallace, was Roosevelt's vice president. In the fifties, Iowa was one of those states that gave Eisenhower a lower percentage in 1956 than 1952—and swept in an almost all-Democratic House delegation in 1958. In the sixties, particularly in 1966, Iowa shifted heavily to the Republicans, recoiling from the Great Society and the Vietnam war policies of President Johnson. In the early seventies, Iowa was clearly discontented with the Nixon Administration and was moving toward the Democrats. Watergate seemed to have a special impact here, even in the 1972 election; Iowans were particularly quick to react against the Republicans when they lost the advantage they had long held here as the exemplars of clean government.

In this context the results of the 1978 elections in Iowa make a great deal of sense, for 1978 was about the best year Republicans have had in this state in a decade. They easily reelected Governor Robert Ray—a foregone conclusion—and held all statewide offices except attorney general, which was lost by an unpopular incumbent. They unseated Senator Dick Clark—a major upset which was no more expected here than elsewhere. They defeated an incumbent Democratic congressman in the 2d district, and they seized control of both houses of the legislature. In the early seventies, the Democrats were able to recruit the young, attractive, ambitious candidates who are essential to legislative control these days; in the late seventies, the Republicans were doing it.

Ray is now the senior governor in the nation in terms of continuous service, and he is also one of the most popular. He is open and honest and has an attractive personality; if he is a little stand-offish and reserved, that is probably fine with most Iowans. He has gotten on reasonably well with both Democratic and Republican legislatures, and even in far-off Des Moines has attracted the favorable attention of the national press. After more than a decade his constituents must know him well, and his popularity says much for his character. It also helps that, as a moderate Republican, he is not too far from most voters on most issues. Ray has been mentioned from time to time as a presidential or vice presidential candidate. But he is probably insufficiently conservative to win a Republican nomination, except perhaps as a ticket-balancer, and he has made no move to win support in other states. He would also be a strong contender for a Senate seat. But he declined to run in 1978 against Dick Clark and at this writing seems unlikely to interrupt his four-year term to run against John Culver in 1980. Ray can almost certainly be reelected again in 1982; the question is whether he will want to run.

By any measure Clark was an effective and popular Senator. His chief political liability was thought to be his liberal voting record, which usually earned him 100% ADA ratings. But he had also paid close attention to farm issues as a member of the Agriculture Committee, and his record was highly popular in the state. In Iowa Clark was remembered less for his concentration on Africa policy than for his walk across the state in the 1972 campaign—a move that converted an unknown aide to then Congressman John Culver into a formidable statewide candidate. Clark stayed in closer touch with his constituency than most senators do, and in 1978 the Republicans' strongest candidates declined to run against him.

Clark's opponent, former Lieutenant Governor Roger Jepsen, was generally considered a lightweight. Having feuded with Ray, Jepsen had no effective support from the Governor; Jepsen's campaign financing and volunteers came mainly from the New Right. But Jepsen was able to win, largely by focusing on some aspects of Clark's record and avoiding the spotlight himself. One issue the Republican candidate used was the Panama Canal Treaty, which Clark supported, and which aroused an anger here, as elsewhere, among older, nostalgic voters. Another was abortion. Catholic voters in Iowa are more heavily Democratic than in just about any other state, and they are concentrated in small, insular rural or small town communities. Clark had voted consistently to allow federal benefits to be used for abortions by recipients eligible for the benefits who chose to have abortions. An intensive campaign was waged against him not only by Jepsen's forces but by right-to-life groups, and they cut heavily Clark's margins in Catholic areas. One example of the results is in heavily Catholic Dubuque. George McGovern had won here with a solid 58% in 1972; Clark barely carried the county in 1978. A final factor that hurt Clark was low turnout. Jepsen won no more votes than the Republican who had lost to John Culver in 1974; but the Democratic vote was down sizeably. Republicans, disillusioned by Watergate, had stayed home in 1974. Democrats, disillusioned by a politics of less government and unenthusiastic about the incumbent administration, seemed to stay home disproportionately in 1978.

Much was made after Clark's defeat of the phenomenon of single issue voting. One suspects that many commentators would have been less concerned had they not felt that single issue voting here had replaced one of the best senators with one of the worst. Certainly so far as personal qualities are concerned, this seems to have been the case. Clark is honest, forthright, modest, and hard-working. Jepsen is contentious and appears to some at least to be devious. His dealings with a former state commissioner of the blind led to a series of investigative articles in the Des Moines *Register*, the paper that dominates Iowa journalism; and after the election, there were charges that Jepsen had received money from South African interests.

On issues Jepsen is a forthright member of the New Right, but he has also been unusually petulant, for example in blocking a federal appointment for Clark. Clark's greatest mistake in the campaign may have been in failing to focus attention on Jepsen and his shortcomings. They will not be a secret when his seat comes up again, and given Iowa voters' dispositions, Jepsen may be a one-term Senator.

Iowa's senior Senator, John Culver, presents quite a contrast with Jepsen. He has become one of the Senate's leading Democrats on a number of issues, most notably the strategic arms limitations agreement, and one of its most respected members as well. First elected to the House in 1964, in the Johnson landslide, Culver was the only Iowa Democrat so elected who won reelection in 1966.

In the House he became an influential member and head of the Democratic Study Group. He contemplated running for the Senate in 1972, decided not to, and watched as his former aide Dick Clark won. Culver ran himself in 1974, when Harold Hughes retired, and was elected.

In the Senate Culver sits on the Armed Services Committee, a body with an increasingly intellectually distinguished membership; there he is the leading proponent of arms control and the SALT treaty. An athletic man sometimes given to bursts of temper, Culver was also opposed to the Vietnam war. Often skeptical about the need for new Pentagon hardware, he is known for working hard, for being well informed, and for debating aggressively and ably. He has led successful fights against a number of weapons systems and at this writing appears likely to lead the fight for the SALT treaty. Culver also serves on the Public Works Committee, and led the fight for the current Endangered Species Act. When Elizabeth Drew of the *New Yorker* was looking for a senator who was respected, hard-working, and effective to follow around and chronicle for ten days, she decided on Culver, the result was her book *Senator*.

Nevertheless, Culver is not a heavy favorite for reelection going into 1980. He does not have as high a profile in the state as Clark did, but he does have a similar voting record; and he is attracting strong Republican opposition. Two congressmen, conservative Charles Grassley and moderate James Leach, are considering running, as are businessman Tom Stoner and former Attorney General Richard Turner. Grassley, a vocal opponent of federal spending who has been campaigning hard, is the favorite to win the Republican nomination; and if he does, it should be a spirited general election, with direct clash on important issues of a type not often seen today.

Once every four years, on a frigid day in January, Iowa Democrats and Republicans hold precinct caucuses in school rooms, town halls, and private homes throughout the state—the first definitive step in the nation's presidential delegate selection process. In recent years these Iowa caucuses have attracted increasing attention. No one paid much heed in 1968 when Iowa Democrats picked state convention delegates a large percentage of whom opposed Lyndon Johnson's Vietnam war policy. There was more coverage in 1972, and far more in 1976, when Jimmy Carter put on a major effort here, as he talked with hundreds of small groups and organized industriously. To everyone's surprise Carter had more support (27%) than any other candidate in the caucuses, and his showing here helped give him stature as a serious candidate in other states. As early as 1979 half a dozen Republican presidential candidates began meeting with small groups all over Iowa, hoping to duplicate Carter's coup. Some people argue that it is unwise to have so few people have such a great impact on the presidential election process. But there is a counterargument, that this is one of the few times that ordinary people actually can talk face to face with a possible future president, and size him up. Jimmy Carter has had trouble communicating effectively with the nation en masse, but as the Camp David peace talks and his success in Iowa show, he has a genuine ability to communicate directly with small groups of people.

Census Data Pop. 2,825,041; 1.40% of U.S. total, 25th largest; Central city, 22%; suburban, 13%. Median family income, $9,017; 26th highest; families above $15,000: 16%; families below $3,000: 10%. Median years education, 12.2.

1977 Share of Federal Tax Burden $4,732,000,000; 1.64% of U.S. total, 23d largest.

1977 Share of Federal Outlays $3,671,124,000; 0.93% of U.S. total, 33d largest. Per capita federal spending, $1,279.

DOD	$392,045,000	40th (0.43%)	HEW	$1,827,896,000	26th (1.24%)
ERDA	$11,643,000	26th (0.20%)	HUD	$36,028,000	32d (0.85%)
NASA	$1,790,000	34th (0.05%)	VA	$228,507,000	30th (1.19%)
DOT	$125,434,000	33d (0.88%)	EPA	$47,878,000	33d (0.58%)
DOC	$45,323,000	48th (0.55%)	RevS	$84,695,000	28th (1.00%)
DOI	$12,252,000	42d (0.26%)	Debt	$257,545,000	17th (0.86%)
USDA	$381,462,000	20th (1.92%)	Other	$218,626,000	

Economic Base Agriculture, notably cattle, hogs, corn and soybeans; food and kindred products, especially meat products; finance, insurance and real estate; machinery, especially farm machinery; electrical equipment and supplies, especially household appliances; printing and publishing, especially newspapers; fabricated metal products, especially fabricated structural metal products.

Political Line-up Governor, Robert D. Ray (R). Senators, John C. Culver (D) and Roger W. Jepsen (R). Representatives, 6 (3 D and 3 R). State Senate (28 R and 22 D); State House (56 R and 44 D).

The Voters

Registration 1,587,723 Total. 549,598 D (35%); 477,141 R (30%); 560,984 Ind. (35%).
Median voting age 45
Employment profile White collar, 43%. Blue collar, 31%. Service, 14%. Farm, 12%.
Ethnic groups Black, 1%. Total foreign stock, 11%. Germany, 4%.

Presidential vote

1976	Carter (D)	619,931	(49%)
	Ford (R)	632,863	(51%)
1972	Nixon (R)	706,207	(59%)
	McGovern (D)	496,206	(41%)

Sen. John C. Culver (D) Elected 1974, seat up 1980; b. Aug. 8, 1932, Rochester, Minn.; home, Cedar Rapids; Harvard U., A.B. 1954, LL.B. 1962, Lionel de Jersey Harvard Scholar, Cambridge U., 1954–55; Presbyterian.

Career USMC 1955–58; Dean of Men, Harvard U., 1960; Legis. Asst. to U.S. Sen. Edward M. Kennedy, 1962–63; U.S. House of Reps., 1965–75.

Offices 344 RSOB, 202-224-3744. Also Rm. 721 Fed. Bldg., Des Moines 50309, 515-284-4056, and 206 Fed. Bldg., Cedar Rapids 52401, 319-366-2411.

Committees *Armed Services* (6th). Subcommittees: Manpower and Personnel; Research and Development (Chairman); Procurement Policy and Reprogramming.

Environment and Public Works (6th). Subcommittees: Environmental Pollution; Resource Protection (Chairman); Nuclear Regulation.

Judiciary (5th). Subcommittees: Administrative Practice and Procedure (Chairman); Antitrust, Monopoly, and Business Rights; Criminal Justice.

Select Committee on Small Business (3d).

Group Ratings

	ADA	COPE	PC	RPN	NFU	LCV	CFA	NAB	NSI	ACA	NTU
1978	85	89	83	60	60	96	65	9	20	13	–
1977	85	89	88	50	83	–	88	–	–	4	32
1976	85	90	92	57	91	85	78	0	11	0	31

Key Votes

1) Warnke Nom	FOR	6) Egypt-Saudi Arms	FOR	11) Hosptl Cost Contnmnt	FOR
2) Neutron Bomb	AGN	7) Draft Restr Pardon	FOR	12) Clinch River Reactor	AGN
3) Waterwy User Fee	FOR	8) Wheat Price Support	AGN	13) Pub Fin Cong Cmpgns	FOR
4) Dereg Nat Gas	AGN	9) Panama Canal Treaty	FOR	14) ERA Ratif Recissn	FOR
5) Kemp-Roth	AGN	10) Labor Law Rev Clot	FOR	15) Med Necssy Abrtns	FOR

Election Results

1974 general	John C. Culver (D)	462,947	(52%)	($470,970)
	David M. Stanley (R)	420,546	(48%)	($336,067)
1974 primary	John C. Culver (D), unopposed			
1968 general	Harold E. Hughes (D)	574,884	(50%)	
	David M. Stanley (R)	568,469	(50%)	

Sen. Roger W. Jepsen (R) Elected 1978, seat up 1984; b. Dec. 23, 1928, Cedar Falls; home, Davenport; U. of No. Ia., 1945–46, Ariz. St. U., B.S. 1950, M.A. 1953; Lutheran.

Career Army, 1946–47; Counselor, Ariz. St. U., 1950–53; Farmer and Insurance Agent, 1954–55; Branch Mgr., Conn. General Life Ins. Co., 1956–72; Scott Co. Supervisor, 1962–65; Ia. Senate 1966–68; Lt. Gov. of Ia., 1968–72; Exec. Vice Pres., Agridustrial Electronics Co., 1973–76; Pres. of Marketing Co., 1976–78.

Offices 6313 DSOB, 202-224-3254. Also 1416 W. 16th St., Davenport 52804, 319-322-0120.

Committees *Agriculture, Nutrition, and Forestry* (8th). Subcommittees: Environment, Soil Conservation, and Forestry; Agricultural Credit and Rural Electrification; Rural Development.

Armed Services (7th). Subcommittees: General Procurement; Manpower and Personnel; Procurement Policy and Reprogramming.

Group Ratings: Newly Elected

Key Votes: Newly Elected

Election Results

1978 general	Roger Jepsen (R)	421,598	(52%)	($728,268)
	Dick Clark (D)	395,066	(48%)	($860,774)
1978 primary	Roger Jepsen (R)	87,397	(57%)	
	Maurice Van Nostrand (R)	54,189	(36%)	($68,594)
	One other (R)	10,860	(7%)	
1972 general	Dick Clark (D)	662,637	(56%)	($241,803)
	Jack Miller (R)	530,525	(44%)	($328,263)

Gov. Robert D. Ray (R) Elected 1968, term expires Jan. 1983; b. Sept. 26, 1928, Des Moines; Drake U., B.A., LL.B.; Christian Church.

Career Practicing atty.; Law and Reading Clerk, Iowa Senate; Chm., Iowa Repub. St. Central Comm., 1965–68.

Offices State Capitol, Des Moines 50319, 515-281-5211.

Election Results

1978 general	Robert D. Ray (R)	491,713	(59%)
	Jerome Fitzgerald (D)	345,519	(41%)
1978 primary	Robert D. Ray (R)	136,517	(88%)
	One other (R)	19,486	(12%)
1974 general	Robert D. Ray (R)	534,518	(59%)
	James F. Schaben (D)	377,553	(41%)

FIRST DISTRICT

The 1st congressional district of Iowa is the southeast corner of the state. To a visitor from New York or Los Angeles, this must look like a rather ordinary, sleepy part of the Midwest farm belt. But the 1st does have some distinctive features. The little city of Burlington seems hardly important, but it has given its name to one of the nation's largest railroads (formerly the Chicago, Burlington & Quincy and now the Burlington Northern). Davenport is the home of the Palmer School of Chiropractic, the leading such institution in the nation. Iowa City is the site of the State University of Iowa, among whose programs is a distinguished writers' workshop. Not far away (though in another district) is West Branch, the birthplace of Herbert Hoover.

This is also a district which has had a fiercely contested congressional politics for most of the last 20 years. The partisan balance is relatively even here: Iowa City and Burlington are Democratic, Davenport marginal, and most of the rural counties Republican. And for years the district's congressmen have had difficulty using the advantages of incumbency to full advantage. Failure to do so may have partly resulted from other commitments. Fred Schwengel, a moderate Republican who represented the district in 1955–65 and 1967–73, was president of the National Capital Historical Society and a Lincoln buff. He was beaten in 1964, nearly beaten in both primary and general election in 1970, and beaten again in 1972. His successor, Democrat Edward Mezvinsky, served on the House Judiciary Committee during the impeachment hearings and apparently made a good enough impression to win reelection in 1974, though his motion to impeach for misuse of government funds did not carry. But his marriage to a reporter for one of the local Washington television stations may have kept him from returning to the district very often, and Mezvinsky was defeated in 1976.

The current Congressman, Republican James Leach, does not seem to have such problems. He has a wide ranging background, including stints on the staff of Donald Rumsfeld and in the foreign service. But when he was elected, he was head of the family propane gas business—a down-to-home credential at a time when voters wanted responsiveness more than high level experience in their elected officials. Leach is a kind of Robert Ray Republican. His record on economic issues is in line with his party's tradition of support for free enterprise and suspicion or even hostility to government regulation. But he is considerably more liberal on non-economic issues. It is a combination which seems eminently saleable in Iowa, and Leach finds himself almost as popular in Iowa City—whose liberalism tended to revolve around non-economic issues—as in the well-to-do neighborhoods of Davenport or the rural counties.

In 1978, Leach was reelected by nearly a 2–1 margin—the best showing for any candidate in the district since 1920. The speculation is that Leach may be interested in statewide office, specifically in John Culver's Senate seat which is up in 1980. For that he may have Republican opposition, perhaps from 3d district conservative Charles Grassley; and conservatives have beaten moderates recently in Iowa Republican primaries. Certainly Leach seems in strong shape to retain the 1st district seat should he choose to do so.

Census Data Pop. 471,260. Central city, 21%; suburban, 9%. Median family income, $9,594; families above $15,000: 18%; families below $3,000: 9%. Median years education, 12.3.

The Voters

Median voting age 42.
Employment profile White collar, 45%. Blue collar, 33%. Service, 14%. Farm, 8%.
Ethnic groups Black, 1%. Total foreign stock, 9%. Germany, 3%.

Presidential vote

1976	Carter (D)	104,675	(50%)
	Ford (R)	105,060	(50%)
1972	Nixon (R)	111,577	(56%)
	McGovern (D)	87,448	(44%)

Rep. James A. S. Leach (R) Elected 1976; b. Oct. 15, 1942, Davenport; home, Davenport; Princeton U., B.A. 1964, Johns Hopkins U., M.A. 1966, London Sch. of Econ., 1966–68; Episcopalian.

Career Staff member, U.S. Rep. Donald Rumsfeld of Ill., 1965–66; U.S. Foreign Svc., 1968–69, 1971–72; Admin. Asst. to the Dir. of OEO, 1969–70; Pres., Flamegas Co., Inc., propane gas marketers, 1973– ; Repub. Nominee for U.S. House of Reps., 1974.

Offices 1406 LHOB, 202-225-6576. Also 234 Fed. Bldg., 322 W. Third St., Davenport 52801, 319-326-1841.

Committees *Banking, Finance and Urban Affairs* (7th). Subcommittees: Financial Institutions Supervision, Regulation and Insurance; Housing and Community Development; International Trade, Investment and Monetary Policy.

Post Office and Civil Service (4th). Subcommittees: Investigations; Civil Service.

Group Ratings

	ADA	COPE	PC	RPN	NFU	LCV	CFA	NAB	NSI	ACA	NTU
1978	35	25	40	92	20	–	18	92	50	63	–
1977	50	30	50	77	50	40	30	–	–	59	44

Key Votes

1) Increase Def Spnd	AGN	6) Alaska Lands Protect	FOR	11) Delay Auto Pol Cntrl	FOR
2) B-1 Bomber	AGN	7) Water Projects Veto	FOR	12) Sugar Price Escalator	FOR
3) Cargo Preference	AGN	8) Consum Protect Agcy	AGN	13) Pub Fin Cong Cmpgns	FOR
4) Dereg Nat Gas	AGN	9) Common Situs Picket	AGN	14) ERA Ratif Recissn	AGN
5) Kemp-Roth	FOR	10) Labor Law Revision	AGN	15) Prohibt Govt Abrtns	FOR

Election Results

1978 general	Jim Leach (R)	79,940	(64%)	($241,356)
	Dick Myers (D)	45,037	(36%)	($123,626)
1978 primary	Jim Leach (R), unopposed			
1976 general	Jim Leach (R)	109,694	(52%)	($199,590)
	Edward Mezvinsky (D)	101,024	(48%)	($187,122)

SECOND DISTRICT

The 2d congressional district of Iowa is the northwest corner of the state. The district is dominated by Cedar Rapids, at 163,000 Iowa's second largest city, and by two Mississippi River towns about half that size, Dubuque and Clinton. Cedar Rapids, a major farm machinery manufacturing center, has been politically marginal in recent years—a little more Democratic, usually, than the state as a whole. It is the home base of Senator John Culver and former Senator Dick Clark. Clinton, populated by German Protestants, tends to be Republican; Dubuque, almost entirely German Catholic, is heavily Democratic. The knobby hills that flank the Mississippi are less suitable for corn, hogs, and wheat than the rolling plains farther west; but they provide some of the most beautiful scenery in the Midwest.

The 2d district was the scene of one of the Iowa Republican Party's triumphs in 1978. It must have been very sweet, because this is a district that had not elected a Republican congressman since 1962. Culver after winning in 1964 had put together an efficient precinct organization with the help of Clark, then his administrative assistant. When Culver ran for the Senate in 1974, the Democratic primary was won by Michael Blouin, a 28-year-old state Senator from Dubuque; he was aided by the fact that as much as 40% of the district's Democratic primary votes are cast in

Dubuque County. Blouin proved to be a weak candidate in the general election, however, winning only narrowly in 1974 and 1976.

The current Congressman, Republican Tom Tauke, in many respects resembles his predecessor. He was elected at age 28 after service in the legislature. He is a Catholic from Dubuque and supports anti-abortion measures. But Tauke proved to be a stronger campaigner, and used Dick Clark's tactic of walking across the district to attract attention and show his closeness to the voter. On taking his seat, he was the youngest Republican in the House. It was not clear initially whether he would join the growing bloc of House conservatives or whether he would follow a more moderate course; but he has shown the kind of political ability which suggests he is capable of winning reelection in this closely divided district.

Census Data Pop. 471,933. Central city, 37%; suburban, 17%. Median family income, $9,511; families above $15,000: 17%; families below $3,000: 9%. Median years education, 12.2.

The Voters

Median voting age 43.
Employment profile White collar, 41%. Blue collar, 34%. Service, 13%. Farm, 12%.
Ethnic groups Total foreign stock, 10%. Germany, 4%.

Presidential vote

1976	Carter (D)	101,530	(50%)
	Ford (R)	103,383	(50%)
1972	Nixon (R)	108,517	(56%)
	McGovern (D)	86,714	(44%)

Rep. Thomas J. Tauke (R) Elected 1978; b. Oct. 11, 1950, Dubuque; home, Dubuque; Loras Col., B.A. 1972, U. of Iowa, J.D. 1974; Catholic.

Career Practicing atty.; Iowa House of Reps., 1975–78.

Offices 319 CHOB, 202-225-2911. Also 222 Fed. Bldg., Dubuque 52001, 319-557-7740.

Committees *Education and Labor* (10th). Subcommittees: Employment Opportunities; Postsecondary Education.

Small Business (14th). Subcommittee: Antitrust and Restraint of Trade Activities Affecting Small Business.

Group Ratings: Newly Elected

Key Votes: Newly Elected

Election Results

1978 general	Tom Tauke (R)	72,644	(53%)	($250,432)
	Michael T. Blouin (D)	65,450	(47%)	($141,533)
1978 primary	Tom Tauke (R), unopposed			
1976 general	Michael T. Blouin (D)	102,980	(51%)	($151,389)
	Tom Riley (R)	100,344	(49%)	($150,458)

THIRD DISTRICT

Iowa's 3d congressional district, in the north central part of the state, is almost perfectly square, with a few odd corners where counties were added or removed by redistricting. Its largest city, Waterloo, is a gritty factory town, with big meat packing and farm machinery plants and, next to Des Moines, Iowa's largest black population (6,500). Probably more typical of the district is Marshalltown, home town of Meredith Wilson (*The Music Man*) and Merle Miller (*Plain Speaking*)—a neat, pleasant Republican courthouse town in the middle of an agricultural county. This is in fact rich agricultural country, the kind of land that has made Iowa a symbol of productive fertility. The 3d district's political tradition is Republican, though there are some heavily Catholic counties here which are usually Democratic.

For 26 years the 3d district elected the quintessential Republican Congressman, H. R. Gross. Spending most of his time on the floor, objecting to unanimous consent requests, decrying what he considered wasteful spending, asking for quorum calls, Gross was the undisputed curmudgeon of the House. Many considered him a pain in the neck, but the fact was that the fear of Gross made every bill manager with a request for federal funds prepare a little more carefully—and sometimes modify his proposal to eliminate something Gross might make trouble about. Gross survived the Johnson landslide of 1964 by the barest of margins—the one time he had political trouble—and finally retired in 1974 at the age of 75.

He has been succeeded by a man who shares many of his principles and attitudes, and perhaps even some of his personality, Republican Charles Grassley. The succession was not automatic. Democrats were riding high in Iowa in 1974, and 25-year-old state Representative Steven Rapp held Grassley to 51% of the vote. Grassley, like most of the Democrats elected in the same year, used the perquisites of incumbency to advantage. He also compiled what is easily the most conservative voting record of the Iowa House delegation, showing his dislike of government spending by such symbolic stands as opposing the congressional pay raise. The increasing popularity of Grassley's kind of politics is shown by his percentages in subsequent elections. In a rematch against Rapp in 1976, he won with 56%—a good margin, but not an overwhelming victory. In 1978, admittedly against a very weak opponent, he won three-quarters of the vote—an unprecedented showing.

While no one supposes that Grassley can win that kind of majority against tougher competition, it nevertheless does show the appeal of fiscal conservatism in Iowa in the years of the Carter Administration. It also helps to spotlight Grassley as a possible candidate for the Senate in 1980; he may be further encouraged by the success of conservatives in winning statewide Republican primaries, even when opposed by Robert Ray. Grassley would certainly provide a contrast, on virtually every issue, with Senator John Culver.

Census Data Pop. 471,866. Central city, 16%; suburban, 12%. Median family income, $8,911; families above $15,000: 15%; families below $3,000: 10%. Median years education, 12.2.

The Voters

Median voting age 46.
Employment profile White collar, 40%. Blue collar, 32%. Service, 14%. Farm, 14%.
Ethnic groups Black, 2%. Total foreign stock, 12%. Germany, 5%.

Presidential vote

1976	Carter (D)	101,443	(48%)
	Ford (R)	108,563	(52%)
1972	Nixon (R)	119,372	(60%)
	McGovern (D)	78,687	(40%)

Rep. Charles E. Grassley (R) Elected 1974; b. Sept. 17, 1933, New Hartford; home, New Hartford; U. of No. Ia., B.A. 1955, M.A. 1956, U. of Ia., 1957–58; Baptist.

Career Farmer; Ia. House of Reps., 1959–74.

Offices 1227 LHOB, 202-225-3301. Also 210 Waterloo Bldg., Waterloo 50701, 319-232-6657.

Committees *Agriculture* (10th). Subcommittees: Department Investigations, Oversight and Research; Domestic Marketing, Consumer Relations, and Nutrition; Family Farms, Rural Development, and Special Studies.

Group Ratings

	ADA	COPE	PC	RPN	NFU	LCV	CFA	NAB	NSI	ACA	NTU
1978	5	10	18	50	30	–	18	100	100	93	–
1977	15	17	28	62	42	35	15	–	–	81	49
1976	15	13	23	72	42	17	18	67	80	86	72

Key Votes

1) Increase Def Spnd	FOR	6) Alaska Lands Protect	FOR	11) Delay Auto Pol Cntrl	FOR
2) B-1 Bomber	FOR	7) Water Projects Veto	AGN	12) Sugar Price Escalator	FOR
3) Cargo Preference	AGN	8) Consum Protect Agcy	AGN	13) Pub Fin Cong Cmpgns	AGN
4) Dereg Nat Gas	FOR	9) Common Situs Picket	AGN	14) ERA Ratif Recissn	FOR
5) Kemp-Roth	FOR	10) Labor Law Revision	AGN	15) Prohibt Govt Abrtns	FOR

Election Results

1978 general	Charles E. Grassley (R)	103,659	(75%)	($160,100)
	John Knudson (D)	34,880	(25%)	($11,581)
1978 primary	Charles E. Grassley (R), unopposed			
1976 general	Charles E. Grassley (R)	117,957	(56%)	($131,492)
	Stephen J. Rapp (D)	90,981	(44%)	($95,133)

FOURTH DISTRICT

The 4th congressional district of Iowa is the south central region of the state. More than half its votes are cast in Des Moines and surrounding Polk County, which makes that metropolitan area the dominant, though not the geographically central, part of the district. Des Moines, next to Dubuque, has been Iowa's most Democratic city; it is a major farm machinery manufacturing center, as well as a financial and commercial center for the surrounding farmland. It is also the state capital and the home of the Des Moines *Register*, one of the nation's few newspapers with genuine statewide circulation. South of Des Moines is farm country. The settlers here were primarily Protestant, some from the points east in the Midwest, some from the South. The political map of the area looks something like a quilt, with Democratic and Republican areas alternating with no apparent design. This results from settlement patterns and ancestral preferences, with little change over time at least in relative partisan preference.

Representing the 4th district in the House is Neal Smith, a Democrat first elected in 1958. He seems to have been caught on the wrong side of a political generation gap. He began to enjoy significant seniority just as seniority was being devalued by the 1974 Democratic freshmen. A moderate to liberal Democrat, he finds himself to the right of other Iowa Democrats—after spending most of his political life to the left of most Iowans. In 1975 Smith sought to be the first Chairman of the Budget Committee; he came close, but lost to Brock Adams of Washington, who later became Secretary of Transportation.

Smith is the seventh-ranking Democrat on the Appropriations Committee, but he has not yet become a subcommittee chairman. He is next in line for two: Labor-HEW and State, Commerce, and Judiciary. Instead, he is Chairman of the Small Business Committee. This body had no power to report legislation until recently, and even now its jurisdiction is limited. The Small Business Administration is a small agency, with little impact on most small businesses, while other measures to aid small business tend to fall on other committees' turf. Nevertheless Small Business is a popular committee and has a large membership; it provides members with a forum for doing something for a cause that is, at least rhetorically, popular.

Neal Smith has been popular in Des Moines and the 4th district for years now. He had to fight for his first reelection or two, and in 1972 he had to beat a Republican colleague placed in the same district. Now he is returned to office every two years by about a 2–1 margin. In 1976 Smith won with 69%—the largest percentage ever won by an Iowa Democrat, except for one who had only Socialist opposition and Smith himself in 1964.

Census Data Pop. 468,881. Central city, 43%; suburban, 18%. Median family income, $9,589; families above $15,000: 19%; families below $3,000: 9%. Median years education, 12.3.

The Voters

Median voting age 44.
Employment profile White collar, 51%. Blue collar, 30%. Service, 14%. Farm, 5%.
Ethnic groups Black, 3%. Total foreign stock, 9%. Germany, 1%.

Presidential vote

1976	Carter (D)	116,438	(54%)
	Ford (R)	98,765	(46%)
1972	Nixon (R)	117,283	(56%)
	McGovern (D)	92,752	(44%)

Rep. Neal Smith (D) Elected 1958; b. Mar. 23, 1920, Hendrick; home, Altoona; U. of Mo., 1945–46, Syracuse U., 1946–47, Drake U., LL.B. 1950; Methodist.

Career Farmer; Army Air Corps, WWII; Practicing atty., 1950–58; Chm., Polk Co. Bd. of Social Welfare; Asst. Polk Co. Atty., 1951.

Offices 2373 RHOB, 202-225-4426. Also 544 Insurance Exchange Bldg., Des Moines 50309, 515-284-4634.

Committees *Appropriations* (7th). Subcommittees: Labor-HEW; State, Justice, Commerce, and the Judiciary; Legislative.

Small Business (Chairman). Subcommittees: SBA and SBIC Authority and General Small Business Problems (Chairman).

Group Ratings

	ADA	COPE	PC	RPN	NFU	LCV	CFA	NAB	NSI	ACA	NTU
1978	60	65	53	75	80	–	46	17	40	11	–
1977	55	90	45	60	83	23	60	–	–	8	21
1976	70	82	67	50	100	65	81	0	60	7	26

Key Votes

1) Increase Def Spnd	AGN	6) Alaska Lands Protect	FOR	11) Delay Auto Pol Cntrl	FOR
2) B-1 Bomber	FOR	7) Water Projects Veto	AGN	12) Sugar Price Escalator	FOR
3) Cargo Preference	AGN	8) Consum Protect Agcy	FOR	13) Pub Fin Cong Cmpgns	FOR
4) Dereg Nat Gas	AGN	9) Common Situs Picket	FOR	14) ERA Ratif Recissn	AGN
5) Kemp-Roth	AGN	10) Labor Law Revision	FOR	15) Prohibt Govt Abrtns	DNV

Election Results

1978 general	Neal Smith (D)	88,526	(65%)	($43,447)
	Charles E. Minor (R)	48,308	(35%)	($9,615)
1978 primary	Neal Smith (D), unopposed			
1976 general	Neal Smith (D)	145,343	(69%)	($34,416)
	Charles E. Minor (R)	65,013	(31%)	($19,190)

FIFTH DISTRICT

The 5th congressional district of Iowa is the southwest corner of the state. This is where the plains, as they roll toward the Missouri River, become more brown and less green than they are farther east; the towns become less frequent; the spaces seem to grow more wide open. In eastern Iowa most farmers raise corn and feed grains to fatten their hogs; farther west, you begin to see more cattle and wheat.

There are some slight political differences also between this part of Iowa and the rest of the state. For the 5th district is one of the most Republican parts of Iowa. Its largest city, Council Bluffs, directly across the Missouri from Omaha, Nebraska, is ordinarily Republican and went for Gerald Ford in 1976. Ames, the district's only other city of any size, contains Iowa State University and generally goes Democratic; but it was added to this district only after the 1970 Census. The rural counties are more varied politically than they are agriculturally. The Catholic counties are Democratic, Yankee Protestant counties Republican. The counties along the Missouri border apparently have some affinity for the kind of Southern Democrats rural Missourians favor. They have generally been Republican in recent years, but enough of them went Democratic that Jimmy Carter almost carried the 5th district.

The district also has a Democratic Congressman, Tom Harkin, first elected in 1974. He ran against the conservative Republican in 1972, did well in Ames and got 49% overall, and never stopped campaigning. Harkin was the originator of a campaign technique that has since spread all over the country: work days. In 1974 he set aside one day a week on which he would work at some ordinary, often menial job in the district. The idea was to show voters that Harkin understood the problems they faced in their daily lives—and also to get the candidate on television. The work days provided some good footage for TV commercials, one of which showed Harkin literally shovelling manure.

Harkin has continued to work hard since then, both in the district and in the House. He serves on the Agriculture Committee—obviously a useful post for someone from a district like this. But his legislative activities run far beyond committee jurisdictions. He was the main sponsor of legislation preventing international banks from loaning money to governments which violate human rights. He moved to cut military aid to South Korea by $45 million to show concern about that government's human rights violations. He also strongly opposed the Clinch River breeder reactor. And he argued strongly against a bill that would relax clean air standards in rural areas which now have little pollution.

In his district, evidence of Harkin's hard work is his continuing reelection. He won two-thirds of the votes here in 1976, a stunning achievement. His margin was reduced in 1978 by the Republican trend which was noticeable everywhere in Iowa. But he still won by a comfortable enough margin to suggest that he has made this formerly Republican district into a safe Democratic seat.

Census Data Pop. 470,214. Central city, 0%; suburban, 19%. Median family income, $8,338; families above $15,000: 14%; families below $3,000: 12%. Median years education, 12.2.

The Voters

Median voting age 46.
Employment profile White collar, 40%. Blue collar, 28%. Service, 14%. Farm, 18%.
Ethnic groups Total foreign stock, 9%. Germany, 3%.

Presidential vote

1976	Carter (D)	103,483	(49%)
	Ford (R)	107,605	(51%)
1972	Nixon (R)	125,720	(63%)
	McGovern (D)	74,495	(37%)

Rep. Tom Harkin (D) Elected 1974; b. Nov. 19, 1939, Cumming; home, Ames; Ia. St. U., B.S. 1962, Catholic U., J.D. 1972.

Career Navy, 1962–67; Staff aide to U.S. Rep. Neal Smith, 1969–70; Dem. nominee for U.S. House of Reps., 1972; Atty., Polk Co. Legal Aid Society, 1973–74.

Offices 403 CHOB, 202-225-3806. Also P.O. Box 264, 213 P.O. Bldg., Ames 50010, 515-232-6111.

Committees *Agriculture* (13th). Subcommittees: Conservation and Credit; Family Farms, Rural Development, and Special Studies; Domestic Marketing, Consumer Relations, and Nutrition.

Science and Technology (7th). Subcommittees: Science, Research and Technology; Transportation, Aviation and Communication (Chairman).

Group Ratings

	ADA	COPE	PC	RPN	NFU	LCV	CFA	NAB	NSI	ACA	NTU
1978	60	70	80	42	90	–	77	46	0	26	–
1977	85	71	75	75	92	80	50	–	–	19	43
1976	85	75	87	71	82	81	91	18	0	17	61

Key Votes

1) Increase Def Spnd	DNV	6) Alaska Lands Protect	FOR	11) Delay Auto Pol Cntrl	AGN
2) B-1 Bomber	AGN	7) Water Projects Veto	FOR	12) Sugar Price Escalator	FOR
3) Cargo Preference	AGN	8) Consum Protect Agcy	FOR	13) Pub Fin Cong Cmpgns	FOR
4) Dereg Nat Gas	AGN	9) Common Situs Picket	DNV	14) ERA Ratif Recissn	AGN
5) Kemp-Roth	AGN	10) Labor Law Revision	FOR	15) Prohibt Govt Abrtns	AGN

Election Results

1978 general	Tom Harkin (D)	82,333	(59%)	($144,160)
	Julian B. Garrett (R)	57,377	(41%)	($64,680)
1978 primary	Tom Harkin (D), unopposed			
1976 general	Tom Harkin (D)	135,600	(66%)	($146,642)
	Kenneth R. Fulk (R)	71,377	(34%)	($144,958)

SIXTH DISTRICT

The 6th congressional district of Iowa is the northwest corner of the state where water and trees begin to get scarce and the sky seems to get bigger. Except for Sioux City, an old river town with 85,000 people, the 6th is almost entirely rural in orientation, with small farm market towns and grain elevators towering here and there in the landscape. The district has traditionally been Republican, like most of Iowa, but with some exceptions—the kind of political divergences from normality that dot the maps of all the Great Plains states. These usually stem from their initial settlement by different ethnic or religious groups. A colony of German Catholics or Norwegians, to name only one usually Democratic and one usually Republican group, would send encouraging letters back to the old country, and sometimes would forward steamship passage and railroad fare so that relatives or friends could make their way to new homes in Iowa or Kansas or the Dakotas. Such history makes sense of the Republican sentiments of Sioux County, Iowa (settled by Dutch Protestants and 74% for Gerald Ford in 1976), or the Democratic leanings of Palo Alto County (settled by German Catholics and 55% for Jimmy Carter). Palo Alto has a further distinction: it is one of three American bellwether counties which have never voted for a loser in a presidential election. (The other two are Coos County, New Hampshire, and Crook County, Oregon.)

The 6th district currently has a Democratic congressman, elected in that surge of Democratic strength in Iowa in the early seventies and strong enough to hold onto the seat during the more recent Republican surge. He is Berkley Bedell, an attractive candidate wholly apart from partisan trends. He grew up a fishing enthusiast in the town of Spirit Lake, near the Minnesota border. World War II intervened and he never finished college, but he started his own business manufacturing fishing tackle. This was not ordinary stuff: it was the monofilament line which revolutionized fishing habits, and Bedell became a millionaire. A deeply religious man, he also became a friend of Iowa Governor and Senator Harold Hughes, and Hughes—himself from a small town in the 6th district—convinced him he should enter politics. He became a Democrat, ran for Congress in 1972 and got 48% against Republican incumbent Wiley Mayne. Bedell ran again in 1974. In the meantime, Mayne had voted against impeachment of Richard Nixon, an act of political courage for which he has never received much credit; and Bedell easily won the general election.

Bedell proved to be a popular freshman, though he is older than the median freshman age, and won seats on the Agriculture and Small Business Committees. Both provide him with opportunities to work on issues of great interest to voters in the 6th district. He sponsored the first resolution for the House Ethics Committee to launch an investigation of influence peddling by agents of the South Korean government—certainly a popular act in Iowa, which has always valued integrity in its officeholders. He has also pushed for solar energy development. Bedell has been reelected by impressive margins and seems to have great strength in the district.

Census Data Pop. 470,867. Central city, 18%; suburban, 4%. Median family income, $8,314; families above $15,000: 14%; families below $3,000: 11%. Median years education, 12.2.

The Voters

Median voting age 47.
Employment profile White collar, 40%. Blue collar, 28%. Service, 14%. Farm, 18%.
Ethnic groups Total foreign stock, 16%. Germany, 5%.

Presidential vote

1976	Carter (D)	92,362	(46%)
	Ford (R)	109,482	(54%)
1972	Nixon (R)	123,738	(62%)
	McGovern (D)	76,110	(38%)

Rep. Berkley Bedell (D) Elected 1974; b. Mar. 5, 1921, Spirit Lake; home, Spirit Lake; Ia. St. U., 1940–42; Methodist.

Career Army Air Corps, WWII; Founder and Chm., Berkley & Co., fishing tackle manufacturers; Dem. nominee for U.S. House of Reps., 1972.

Offices 405 CHOB, 202-225-5476. Also 406 Fed. Bldg., Fort Dodge 50501, 515-573-7169.

Committees *Agriculture* (14th). Subcommittees: Conservation and Credit; Family Farms, Rural Development, and Special Studies; Livestock and Grains.

Small Business (11th). Subcommittees: Antitrust and Restraint of Trade Activities Affecting Small Business (Chairman); Access to Equity Capital and Business Opportunities.

Group Ratings

	ADA	COPE	PC	RPN	NFU	LCV	CFA	NAB	NSI	ACA	NTU
1978	70	53	87	67	70	–	77	36	0	22	–
1977	70	65	75	67	75	82	50	–	–	19	48
1976	75	61	72	61	83	78	64	8	10	21	50

Key Votes

1) Increase Def Spnd	AGN	6) Alaska Lands Protect	FOR	11) Delay Auto Pol Cntrl	AGN
2) B-1 Bomber	AGN	7) Water Projects Veto	FOR	12) Sugar Price Escalator	FOR
3) Cargo Preference	AGN	8) Consum Protect Agcy	AGN	13) Pub Fin Cong Cmpgns	FOR
4) Dereg Nat Gas	AGN	9) Common Situs Picket	AGN	14) ERA Ratif Recissn	FOR
5) Kemp-Roth	AGN	10) Labor Law Revision	FOR	15) Prohibt Govt Abrtns	FOR

Election Results

1978 general	Berkley Bedell (D)	87,139	(66%)	($93,188)
	Willis E. Junker (R)	44,320	(34%)	($14,477)
1978 primary	Berkley Bedell (D), unopposed			
1976 general	Berkley Bedell (D)	133,507	(68%)	($88,715)
	Joanne Soper (R)	62,292	(32%)	($58,214)

KANSAS

The political history of Kansas began with a rush in the 1850s, and the outcome of the struggle of that decade has pretty much shaped the state's politics since. The land here was virtually unsettled in 1850, and by the terms of the Kansas-Nebraska Act of 1854 the question of whether Kansas would be a free or slave state would be decided by its voters—a system known to its proponents as popular sovereignty and to its detractors as squatter sovereignty. Everyone assumed that Nebraska would be free soil, but Kansas—just west of slaveholding Missouri—was in doubt. Almost immediately pro-slavery Southerners and abolitionist New Englanders were financing like-minded settlers and moving them to Kansas; soon armed fighting broke out between Democratic "bushwhackers" and free soil "jayhawkers." Pro-slavery raiders from Missouri rode into the territory, and John Brown massacred anti-abolitionists at Pottawatomie Creek. This was "bleeding Kansas"—a major national issue and one of the direct causes of the Civil War. When the South seceded in 1861, Kansas was admitted to the Union as a free state, with the Republican Party in solid control. There it has remained, with just a few exceptions, ever since.

The major exceptions to Republican hegemony came during the depression of the 1890s—the Populist revolt. During the previous decade, years of unusually high rainfall on the plains, Kansas had attracted hundreds of thousands of new settlers. Suddenly the rain all but stopped; and that, together with a worldwide drop in wheat prices, showed that the Kansas plains could not support all who had come to depend on them. The state's boom had gone bust; some Kansas counties have never again reached the population levels recorded in the 1890 Census.

Suddenly Populists were beating Republicans in Kansas. They were politicians like Mary Ellen Lease ("What you farmers need to do is to raise less corn and more hell°) and "Sockless Jerry" Simpson, who served as an impoverished congressman. Lease, Simpson, and the farmers of the Populist Party became advocates of arcane doctrines of free silver and commodity credit programs. William Jennings Bryan, the lion of the prairies, was their man, and he swept Kansas in 1896. The period of Populist dominance—colorful, revivalistic, desperate—was soon over. Around 1900 the nation began to enjoy a decade of agricultural prosperity so great that parity prices are still based on those years. With the small town Republicans back in control, Bryan failed to carry Kansas in 1900 or 1908. William Allen White, the progressive Republican editor of the Emporia *Gazette*, was the closest thing in the state's politics to a radical.

But echoes of the farm revolt of the nineties can still be heard in Kansas politics. Fewer Kansans than ever are actual farmers, but the state's economy still depends heavily on agriculture. For years agriculture has been one of the most heavily regulated and subsidized industries in the nation, the very definition of a special interest; yet there remains an assumption, held not just among farmers, that any government action that will help farmers is by definition in the public interest. When times are bad, farmers and others dependent on agriculture have a hair-trigger readiness to blame the federal government and the administration in power—and to demand immediate government action, whether it is a restoration of parity or an increase in subsidy payments.

These periodic farm revolts occur almost without regard of external conditions. When there is a drought, farmers want help; when the weather is good, there are surpluses, prices are depressed, and farmers want help. The result is that in Kansas, as in other Great Plains states, there tend to be revolts against the party in power in Washington—although the effect is masked here because the state is so Republican in character. Thus while the Nixon and Ford Administrations were in office, Democrats picked up two of the state's House seats, held the governorship for six years, and nearly beat Senator Robert Dole in 1974. Now, with the Carter Administration in, the trend seems to have reversed itself. Republicans have four of the five House seats, and the same man who nearly beat Dole, Bill Roy, made a weaker showing against Nancy Landon Kassebaum in the 1978 Senate race.

The one exception to contrarian rule here would seem to be the election of Democratic Governor John Carlin in 1978, which was not expected. The Republican incumbent, Robert Bennett, had been a reasonably competent executive and had proposed a tax limitation to the state constitution. But Bennett, who comes from the Kansas suburbs of Kansas City, Missouri, did not have roots in the rural part of the state, and he had a personality that some people considered arrogant or stand-offish. Carlin, the 38-year-old House Speaker, was quite a contrast. As a dairy farmer he was hardly citified, and having beaten a more liberal opponent in the primary he could not be depicted as a big spender. The result was a narrow victory and a four-year term for Carlin. He will have a Republican legislature to deal with; the Democrats elected a majority in the lower house in 1976, but lost it in 1978.

The state's leading politician today is undoubtedly Senator Bob Dole. He is a national figure as well, for having been Gerald Ford's vice presidential candidate in 1976; indeed, he was well known to close observers of national politics for some time before that. Dole was first elected to the House in 1960 and to the Senate in 1968, and seemed to be just another conservative Midwestern Republican. But his aggressive partisanship, combined with an acid wit, soon set him apart. While other Senate Republicans were distinguishing themselves by abandoning the Nixon Administration on issues like Haynsworth and Carswell and the ABM and the SST, Dole was a solid Administration vote. Not only that: without being asked, he was constantly rising and defending the president and his programs. So pleased was Richard Nixon with the vigor of Dole's advocacy that he made him Republican National Chairman in 1971. Dole continued in that position throughout 1972, saying what he was told to say (although he could not completely repress his sense of humor) by the White House and the people at the Committee to Reelect the President. Among other things, this included deriding any criticism of the Watergate affair—words he would regret later.

Dole's role in 1972 left him in a great deal of trouble in 1974. Not only was Nixon disgraced, but his assumption of national duties left many Kansans, more used to senators who dealt with Kansas's problems, distressed. He had a strong Democratic opponent: Congressman Bill Roy, a lawyer and doctor from Topeka, with a pleasant manner and a palatable record on issues—the strongest Senate candidate Kansas Democrats had had for 40 years. Dole was behind till he took the offensive in early fall. A series of TV spots showed a poster of Dole being splattered with mud and then, at the end, wiped clean. The message was that Roy and the Democrats by bringing up Watergate were unfairly smearing him. At the same time, Dole attacked Roy for his opposition to bans on abortions, and made the point that Roy as an obstetrician had performed abortions himself. The result was a narrow Dole victory.

Two years later Dole's career was in the best shape ever. Gerald Ford, having already got rid of Nelson Rockefeller, had to find a new vice presidential candidate at the Kansas City convention. The nominee would have to be acceptable to the Reagan forces, who had the votes either to beat or to embarrass a candidate they did not approve. After a process of elimination, the choice fell on Dole. He admitted to being shocked and in this instance, as when he was chosen Republican

National Chairman, he had done little or nothing to achieve national prominence. It was assumed that the Republicans wanted Dole to launch fierce partisan attacks on the Democrats, and he did. But some of them misfired. His reference to "Democrat wars" was counterproductive—a standard practice at Republican fundraising dinners, but not one designed to win the votes of the nominal Democrats Ford needed to win the election. Dole was generally considered the loser in his debate with Walter Mondale. And his sense of humor, or what was left of it as the campaign ended, seemed aimed in a self-deprecating, almost cruel, way against himself.

There is another side to Dole which manifests in the Senate. If he is still capable of clever politics there—such as associating himself with the full parity demands of the farm strikers in the 95th Congress—he is also on occasion a solid and sometimes creative legislator. As ranking Republican on the Agriculture Committee in the 95th Congress, he advanced Republican programs and at the same time worked out with George McGovern a bipartisan revision of the food stamp program. As ranking Republican on the Senate Finance Committee, he has the opportunity to shape Republican policy on the important tax issues. In Dole, more than most public figures, one can see a contrast between two public roles: sometimes he is the competent, thoughtful legislator; sometimes he is the bitter, gut-fighting partisan.

Dole's Senate seat is up in 1980, but he has announced he is running for president. His national candidacy in 1976 gives him the kind of wide notice few others have, and his partisan attacks give him a certain popularity with many Republican primary voters. The problem for Dole is how to pitch his candidacy. If he runs as just a conservative, he risks being lost in a conservative field; if he runs as an aggressive partisan, he risks being seen as a less than effective general election candidate. Others—Reagan, Connally, Bush—have organized their campaigns before Dole has done much of anything.

If Dole runs for reelection to the Senate in 1980, he certainly must be considered the favorite. Nevertheless his recent performances in Kansas have been less than impressive: he nearly lost in 1974 and the Ford–Dole ticket got only a lackluster 54% here in 1976. Kansas is still a Republican state, and he may not attract strong opposition; but his partisan thrusts seem to have made him many enemies as well as enthusiasts. If Dole does not run, look for a wide open race. The Republicans had a nine-candidate primary field in the 1978 Senate race, and the Democrats have some potentially strong candidates: Bill Roy and 4th district Congressman Dan Glickman.

The 1978 Senate race was not expected to be much of a contest; incumbent Republican James Pearson, a moderate, would have been reelected easily if he had run. But he retired, and no less than four serious candidates emerged to succeed him. The race was pretty well decided in the Republican primary, when Nancy Landon Kassebaum suddenly overtook the other candidates and won with 31%. Her credentials by traditional standards were limited: brief service on Pearson's staff, election to a small town school board. A recent divorce had left her free to enter politics. Her main asset, aside from a pleasing personality, was her name. She is the daughter of Alf Landon, the 1936 Republican presidential candidate against Franklin Roosevelt. Landon got only eight electoral votes, but he remains popular in Kansas. He is alive and spry in Topeka, ready to counsel his fellow Republicans or trade stories with local Democrats.

Also Kassebaum was probably helped by the fact that she is a woman. That helped to gain her public attention in a primary where she ran against eight men, and it made it difficult for her general election opponent, Bill Roy, to run an aggressive campaign against her. Roy nevertheless did attack, calling on Kassebaum to release her income tax returns; she lost some ground, but declined to do so. But in the end, the basic Republican trend in Kansas plus the fact that Kassebaum proved to be a competent candidate were enough to give her a solid victory. She brings to the Senate less experience in high level office than many of her colleagues, but she does not seem to be in any way intimidated. Kansas, which does not like to be thought of as old fashioned, is probably pleased to be the only state represented in the Senate by a woman.

Census Data Pop. 2,249,071; 1.11% of U.S. total, 28th largest; Central city, 18%; suburban, 24%. Median family income, $8,690; 30th highest; families above $15,000: 16%; families below $3,000: 11%. Median years education, 12.3.

1977 Share of Federal Tax Burden $3,765,000,000; 1.09% of U.S. total, 28th largest.

1977 Share of Federal Outlays $4,215,055,000; 1.07% of U.S. total, 30th largest. Per capita federal spending, $1,859.

DOD	$875,203,000	30th (0.96%)	HEW	$1,473,959,000	32d (1.00%)
ERDA	$904,000	47th (0.02%)	HUD	$46,582,000	30th (1.10%)
NASA	$2,220,000	30th (0.06%)	VA	$207,372,000	34th (1.08%)
DOT	$161,861,000	38th (1.13%)	EPA	$55,367,000	29th (0.68%)
DOC	$48,465,000	45th (0.58%)	RevS	$60,847,000	34th (0.72%)
DOI	$22,115,000	35th (0.48%)	Debt	$181,701,000	24th (0.61%)
USDA	$768,662,000	5th (3.86%)	Other	$309,797,000	

Economic Base Agriculture, especially cattle, wheat, hogs and sorghum grain; finance, insurance and real estate; transportation equipment, especially aircraft and parts; food and kindred products; machinery; printing and publishing, especially newspapers; oil and gas extraction, especially crude petroleum and natural gas.

Political Line-up Governor, John W. Carlin (D). Senators, Bob Dole (R) and Nancy Landon Kassebaum (R). Representatives, 5 (4 R and 1 D). State Senate (21 R and 19 D); State House (69 R and 56 D).

The Voters

Registration 1,182,032 Total. 283,952 D (24%); 361,736 R (31%); 536,344 Ind., Prohibitionist, and Conservative (45%).
Median voting age 44
Employment profile White collar, 48%. Blue collar, 31%. Service, 13%. Farm, 8%.
Ethnic groups Black, 5%. Spanish, 2%. Total foreign stock, 8%. Germany, 2%.

Presidential vote

1976	Carter (D)	430,421	(46%)
	Ford (R)	502,752	(54%)
1972	Nixon (R)	619,812	(70%)
	McGovern (D)	270,287	(30%)

Sen. Robert Dole (R) Elected 1968, seat up 1980; b. July 22, 1923, Russell; home, Russell; U. of Kans., 1941–43, Washburn Municipal U., B.A. and LL.B. 1952; Methodist.

Career Army, WWII; Kans. House of Reps., 1951–53; Russell Co. Atty., 1953–61; U.S. House of Reps., 1961–69; Chm., Repub. Natl. Comm., 1971–73; Repub. Nominee for V.P., 1976.

Offices 2213 DSOB, 202-224-6521. Also 4601 State Ave., Kansas City 66102, 913-287-4545, and 444 S.E. Quincy St., Topeka 66603, 913-295-2745.

Committees *Agriculture, Nutrition, and Forestry* (3d). Subcommittees: Agricultural Research and General Legislation; Foreign Agricultural Policy; Nutrition.

Finance (Ranking Member). Subcommittees: Health; International Trade; Private Pensions and Employee Fringe Benefits.

Judiciary (5th). Subcommittees: Administrative Practice and Procedure; Improvements in Judicial Machinery; Jurisprudence and Governmental Relations.

Group Ratings

	ADA	COPE	PC	RPN	NFU	LCV	CFA	NAB	NSI	ACA	NTU
1978	20	22	28	50	80	20	25	58	100	58	–
1977	5	11	23	70	55	–	28	–	–	70	35
1976	10	16	8	67	37	11	14	73	89	87	50

Key Votes

1) Warnke Nom	AGN	6) Egypt-Saudi Arms	AGN	11) Hosptl Cost Contnmnt	AGN
2) Neutron Bomb	FOR	7) Draft Restr Pardon	AGN	12) Clinch River Reactor	FOR
3) Waterwy User Fee	FOR	8) Wheat Price Support	FOR	13) Pub Fin Cong Cmpgns	AGN
4) Dereg Nat Gas	FOR	9) Panama Canal Treaty	AGN	14) ERA Ratif Recissn	AGN
5) Kemp-Roth	FOR	10) Labor Law Rev Clot	AGN	15) Med Necssy Abrtns	AGN

Election Results

1974 general	Robert Dole (R)	403,983	(51%)	($1,110,024)
	Bill Roy (D)	390,451	(49%)	($836,927)
1974 primary	Robert Dole (R), unopposed			
1968 general	Robert Dole (R)	490,911	(61%)	
	William I. Robinson (D)	315,911	(39%)	

Sen. Nancy Landon Kassebaum (R) Elected 1978, seat up 1984; b. July 29, 1932, Topeka; home, Wichita; U. of Kans., B.A. 1954, U. of Mich., M.A. 1956; Episcopalian.

Career Staff of Sen. James B. Pearson, 1975.

Offices 304 RSOB, 202-224-4774. Also Fed. Ofc. Bldg. Box 51, 444 S.E. Quincy, Topeka 66683, 913-295-2888.

Committees *Banking, Housing, and Urban Affairs* (5th). Subcommittees: International Finance; Rural Housing and Development; Consumer Affairs.

Budget (5th).

Commerce, Science, and Transportation (5th). Subcommittees: Aviation; Science, Technology, and Space; Surface Transportation.

Special Committee on Aging (3d).

Group Ratings: Newly Elected

Key Votes: Newly Elected

Election Results

1978 general	Nancy Landon Kassebaum (R)	403,354	(56%)	($856,644)
	Bill Roy (D)	317,602	(44%)	($813,754)
1978 primary	Nancy Landon Kassebaum (R)	67,324	(31%)	
	Wayne Angell (R)	54,161	(25%)	($388,334)
	Sam Hardage (R)	30,248	(14%)	($489,983)
	Jan Meyers (R)	20,933	(10%)	($72,307)
	Five others (R)	47,476	(22%)	
1972 general	James B. Pearson (R)	622,591	(76%)	
	Arch O. Tetzlaff (D)	200,764	(24%)	

Gov. John W. Carlin (D) Elected 1978, term expires Jan. 1983; b. Aug. 3, 1940, Salina; Kans. St. U., B.S.; Lutheran.

Career Dairy Farmer and Cattle Sales Mgr.; Kans. House of Reps., 1971–79, Minority Ldr., 1975–77, Speaker, 1977–79.

Offices 2d Floor, State Capitol, Topeka 66612, 913-296-3232.

Election Results

1978 general	John W. Carlin (D)	363,835	(51%)
	Robert F. Bennett (R)	348,015	(49%)
1978 primary	John W. Carlin (D)	71,366	(55%)
	Bert Chaney (D)	34,132	(26%)
	Harry Wiles (D)	23,762	(18%)
1974 general	Robert F. Bennett (R)	387,792	(50%)
	Vern Miller (D)	384,115	(50%)

FIRST DISTRICT

The 1st congressional district of Kansas covers more than half the state's land area. It contains more counties (57) than any other congressional district in the country except the state of North Dakota which elects one congressman-at-large. This fact is not just a bit of trivia; it tells us a good deal about the expectations of the people who first settled this part of Kansas. Most of them came here in the 1880s from states like Illinois and Iowa and Missouri. When they organized counties, as they quickly did, they made them 36 miles square, just as they had in the old Midwest. Deceived by a few years of unusually high rainfall, the settlers expected that the new counties would eventually contain as many people as the old ones back home; hence they were made geographically small. Not just the size of the units, but the grandiosity of the place names (Concordia, Minneapolis, Montezuma) testify to the settlers' hopes, dreams, and ambitions.

But they were never realized. Out here past 98° longitude, rainfall is normally half what it is in Illinois. In the early years of the nineteenth century, this part of the country had been called the Great American Desert—a howling wilderness of arid, treeless land and blowing soil. The early settlers worked hard to prove that image wrong, but they never really succeeded. So the thousands more who were expected to come never arrived; today the average population of the district's 57 counties is a scant 7,800.

Most are far less populous than that because the average is inflated by the district's "urban" concentrations. At 37,000 Salina is the district's largest city; Dodge City, terminus of the old cattle drives and once the home of Wyatt Earp, has just 14,000 people; Holcomb, made famous by Truman Capote's *In Cold Blood*, has just 10,000. Hays, a German Catholic town of 16,000 is one part of the district that goes Democratic; others include the counties along the Arkansas River, first settled by Southerners, which went for Jimmy Carter in 1976. But the real 1st cannot be found in the towns. This is livestock and wheat country, one of the most agricultural districts in the nation. For miles on end you can see nothing but rolling brown fields, sectioned off here and there by barbed wire fence, and in the distance a grain elevator towering over a tiny town.

The 1st is predominantly Republican, but subject to occasional fits of Democratic sentiment during agricultural hard times. In 1956, 1958, and 1960 the western half of the current 1st elected a Democrat to the House. But the district was combined with Bob Dole's after the 1960 Census, and Dole won the 1962 contest. He has been carrying the district ever since, although by varying margins. When he won reelection to the Senate in 1974, he carried the 1st resoundingly; but as Gerald Ford's running mate, he helped the Republican ticket to only 54% in this usually heavily Republican area. Apparently some of the people who know Dole best believe he is better suited to be senator than vice president.

When Dole moved up to the Senate in 1968, he was succeeded by another Republican with a similar voting record, Keith Sebelius. With a background in small town politics, Sebelius has been one of the Republican Party faithful, though he is not as voluble as Dole. At the beginning of the 96th Congress he became ranking Republican on the Agriculture Committee—a position of obvious importance to his district, but one which underlines some problems Republicans face here. For he must reconcile the demands of many of his constituents for government action to help farmers with the less government philosophy which Republicans generally follow and which has become increasingly attractive in the House and among the general public.

Thus Sebelius in the 95th Congress found himself in the uncomfortable position of having President Carter veto his bill to require federal inspection of rabbit meat. Rabbits are a big industry in Kansas, and it is costly for them to be inspected on the local level; but beyond the small group of people who know something about the issue, the bill is easy to lampoon. Sebelius is in a more characteristic posture on the Interior Committee, where he tends to vote against government regulation and control.

Census Data Pop. 447,787. Central city, 0%; suburban, 0%. Median family income, $7,820; families above $15,000: 12%; families below $3,000: 12%. Median years education, 12.2.

The Voters

Median voting age 47.
Employment profile White collar, 40%. Blue collar, 27%. Service, 14%. Farm, 19%.
Ethnic groups Black, 1%. Spanish, 2%. Total foreign stock, 9%. Germany, 3%.

Presidential vote

1976	Carter (D)	91,355	(46%)
	Ford (R)	106,533	(54%)
1972	Nixon (R)	135,605	(72%)
	McGovern (D)	52,842	(28%)

Rep. Keith G. Sebelius (R) Elected 1968; b. Sept. 10, 1916, Almena; home, Norton; Fort Hays Kans. St. Col., A.B., Geo. Wash. U., J.D. 1939; Methodist.

Career Practicing atty.; Army, WWII and Korea; Norton City Cncl., Mayor; Norton Co. Atty.; Kans. Senate, 1962–68.

Offices 1211 LHOB, 202-225-2715. Also P.O. Bldg., Dodge City 67801, 316-227-2244.

Committees *Agriculture* (2d). Subcommittees: Family Farms, Rural Development, and Special Studies; Livestock and Grains; Tobacco.

Interior and Insular Affairs (3d). Subcommittees: National Parks and Insular Affairs; Pacific Affairs.

Group Ratings

	ADA	COPE	PC	RPN	NFU	LCV	CFA	NAB	NSI	ACA	NTU
1978	5	0	10	83	20	–	18	100	90	76	–
1977	5	15	8	73	55	0	0	–	–	91	62
1976	0	17	5	71	8	19	0	91	89	85	58

Key Votes

1) Increase Def Spnd	FOR	6) Alaska Lands Protect	FOR	11) Delay Auto Pol Cntrl	FOR
2) B-1 Bomber	AGN	7) Water Projects Veto	AGN	12) Sugar Price Escalator	FOR
3) Cargo Preference	AGN	8) Consum Protect Agcy	AGN	13) Pub Fin Cong Cmpgns	AGN
4) Dereg Nat Gas	FOR	9) Common Situs Picket	AGN	14) ERA Ratif Recissn	FOR
5) Kemp-Roth	FOR	10) Labor Law Revision	AGN	15) Prohibt Govt Abrtns	FOR

Election Results

1978 general	Keith G. Sebelius (R), unopposed			($52,986)
1978 primary	Keith G. Sebelius (R), unopposed			
1976 general	Keith G. Sebelius (R)	142,311	(73%)	($72,217)
	Randy Yowell (D)	52,459	(27%)	($3,966)

SECOND DISTRICT

Topeka is the capital of Kansas and one of those prosperous, progressive Midwestern cities which have provided much of the dynamism of the region. The economy is based first on state government, but Topeka is also an important agricultural center. There are big, new buildings downtown; clean cut, pleasant neighborhoods in all directions. This is the home town of Alf Landon, the still vigorous and surprisingly progressive Republican who carried Maine and Vermont in the 1936 Roosevelt landslide; and the home as well of the Menninger Clinic. And although Topeka does not like to remember it, this is the city where the lawsuit, Brown vs. Board of Education, was filed which eventually declared segregation in public schools unconstitutional.

Topeka casts about 40% of the votes in the 2d congressional district of Kansas. Other important concentrations of population are Manhattan, site of Kansas State University and not far from the Army's Fort Riley; Leavenworth, where set on the bluffs above the Missouri River is the Army's famous prison; and Kansas City, a small portion of which is included in the district, Otherwise, the district is rural agricultural country. Politically this is basically a Republican area; only Kansas City regularly casts Democratic majorities. But in this era of split tickets, voters' preferences are more volatile than they used to be, and the 2d district today is quite willing to go Democratic on occasion. Indeed, when it elected a Republican congressman in 1978, it was the first time it had done so in ten years.

In fact, the 2d has elected two Democrats to the House. The first was William Roy, the physician and lawyer who won a big upset in 1970 and has run for the Senate in 1974 and 1978. Although he lost both these races, he carried Topeka and the 2d both times. He was succeeded in the House by Martha Keys, who got her start in politics as Kansas coordinator for McGovern in 1972. Despite that beginning, Keys won the race here in 1974; and despite her marriage to fellow Ways and Means Committee member Andrew Jacobs in 1976, she won reelection that year.

But 1978 was a different story. One reason is that the Republican candidate, Jim Jeffries, had much more money. As a 1976 Reagan delegate, Jeffries was able to raise substantial amounts by direct mail appeals to fellow conservatives. He attacked Keys strongly as a supporter of big government in a year in which that reputation was in particular disfavor in Kansas; actually her voting record was more liberal on non-economic than economic issues. Jeffries was also helped, according to Keys's backers, by spying on her campaign and misrepresenting her record. And, curiously, the challenger declined to debate the incumbent. Jeffries's campaign was not able to carry Topeka, Kansas City, or Manhattan. But he won large enough majorities in the rural areas to overcome Keys's margins in the urban areas for a victory. This was one of the bitterest House campaigns in 1978, and in light of the district's shifting preferences it is not possible to predict the outcome of the 1980 race here.

Census Data Pop. 454,028. Central city, 28%; suburban, 14%. Median family income, $8,680; families above $15,000: 15%; families below $3,000: 11%. Median years education, 12.3.

The Voters

Median voting age 40.
Employment profile White collar, 49%. Blue collar, 30%. Service, 14%. Farm, 7%.
Ethnic groups Black, 6%. Spanish, 3%. Total foreign stock, 9%. Germany, 3%.

Presidential vote

1976	Carter (D)	78,881	(45%)
	Ford (R)	97,156	(55%)
1972	Nixon (R)	119,234	(70%)
	McGovern (D)	51,093	(30%)

Rep. Jim Jeffries (R) Elected 1978; b. June 1, 1925, Detroit, Mich.; home, Atchison; Mich. St. U., 1945–47; Presbyterian.

Career Army Air Corps, 1943–45; Farmer, 1947–49; Market research, sales, and investment business, 1949–.

Offices 128 CHOB, 202-225-6601. Also Fed. Ofc. Bldg., Topeka 66683, 913-295-2811.

Committees *District of Columbia* (5th). Subcommittee: Justice, Manpower, and Education.

Government Operations (11th). Subcommittees: Commerce, Consumer and Monetary Affairs; Government Activities and Transportation.

Group Ratings: Newly Elected

Key Votes: Newly Elected

Election Results

1978 general	Jim Jeffries (R)	76,419	(52%)	($332,482)
	Martha Keys (D)	70,460	(48%)	($145,473)
1978 primary	Jim Jeffries (R)	26,826	(58%)	
	Ron Hein (R)	19,063	(42%)	($93,665)
1976 general	Martha Keys (D)	88,645	(52%)	($119,277)
	Ross Freeman (R)	82,946	(48%)	($189,181)

THIRD DISTRICT

The 3d congressional district is a not very typical hunk of Kansas. It lies almost entirely within the Kansas City metropolitan area, and contains most or all of the two counties which regularly produce the state's largest Democratic and Republican majorities. More than 80% of the district's residents live in either Democratic Wyandotte County (Kansas City, much smaller than its more sophisticated Missouri neighbor) or in Republican Johnson County (prosperous Kansas City suburbs, including Overland Park, Prairie Village, and Shawnee Mission). On the Kansas side of the small street that separates Johnson County from Missouri live a disproportionate number of the metropolitan area's richest and most conservative citizens. Wyandotte County—industrial, redolent of meat packing plants—has had little growth lately. Johnson County—a land of new subdivisons and country clubs—is booming. The result is an increasing dominance by Johnson County not only of 3d district but also of Kansas politics. Johnson now casts 60% of the 3d district's votes and, though it is only one of 105 counties, 12% of the state's.

Johnson's growth has made for increasing Republican dominance in the 3d, a district which once was considered within reach by Democrats. About the only thing Wyandotte and Johnson agree on is liquor by the drink; both counties supported it in a recent referendum, but it still lost statewide. Also included in the 3d district is one agricultural county and the county that contains Lawrence, home of the University of Kansas. A few years ago there was a large drug culture here (marijuana grows wild in many Kansas fields) and clashes between students and police; now things are quieter.

If the 3d is not a typical Kansas district sociologically, it is not so politically either. When Kansas City dominated the 3d, Democratic candidates for statewide office used to make strong showings here, and sometimes even carried. Now, in years when Democrats have come close or even won statewide, the 3d is moving to the Republicans. In congressional politics, this has become as safe a Republican seat as any in the state—a circumstance that has developed within the career of Congressman Larry Winn, who was first elected in 1966 and faced a strong challenge as far into his tenure as 1970. Winn won with 70% in 1976 and did not even have a Democratic opponent in 1978. Although he has considerable seniority, he is not yet ranking Republican on any full committee, and he is not as legislatively active as many House Republicans.

Census Data Pop. 449,743. Central city, 0%; suburban, 83%. Median family income, $10,928; families above $15,000: 27%; families below $3,000: 7%. Median years education, 12.5.

The Voters

Median voting age 40.
Employment profile White collar, 58%. Blue collar, 29%. Service, 11%. Farm, 2%.
Ethnic groups Black, 8%. Spanish, 2%. Total foreign stock, 8%. Germany, 1%.

Presidential vote

1976	Carter (D)	79,674	(42%)
	Ford (R)	110,829	(58%)
1972	Nixon (R)	122,474	(67%)
	McGovern (D)	61,367	(33%)

Rep. Larry Winn, Jr. (R) Elected 1966; b. Aug. 22, 1919, Kansas City, Mo; home, Overland Park; U. of Kans., A.B. 1941; Protestant.

Career Radio announcer, WHB, Kansas City, Mo.; North American Aviation; Public Relations Dir., Amer. Red Cross, Kansas City, Mo.; Builder; V.P., Winn-Rau Corp., 1950–.

Offices 2416 RHOB, 202-225-2865. Also 204 Fed. Bldg., Kansas City 66101, 913-621-0832.

Committees *Foreign Affairs* (5th). Subcommittees: Europe and the Middle East; International Security and Scientific Affairs.

Science and Technology (2d). Subcommittees: Transportation, Aviation and Communication; Space Science and Applications.

Group Ratings

	ADA	COPE	PC	RPN	NFU	LCV	CFA	NAB	NSI	ACA	NTU
1978	10	17	10	73	22	–	14	100	90	88	–
1977	10	23	15	64	42	20	15	–	–	85	45
1976	10	23	8	63	28	9	0	58	100	75	34

Key Votes

1) Increase Def Spnd	FOR	6) Alaska Lands Protect	FOR	11) Delay Auto Pol Cntrl	FOR
2) B-1 Bomber	FOR	7) Water Projects Veto	AGN	12) Sugar Price Escalator	FOR
3) Cargo Preference	AGN	8) Consum Protect Agcy	AGN	13) Pub Fin Cong Cmpgns	AGN
4) Dereg Nat Gas	FOR	9) Common Situs Picket	AGN	14) ERA Ratif Recissn	FOR
5) Kemp-Roth	FOR	10) Labor Law Revision	AGN	15) Prohibt Govt Abrtns	DNV

Election Results

1978 general	Larry Winn, Jr. (R), unopposed			($17,691)
1978 primary	Larry Winn, Jr. (R), unopposed			
1976 general	Larry Winn, Jr. (R)	123,578	(70%)	($45,437)
	Philip S. Rhoads(D)	52,110	(30%)	($2,637)

FOURTH DISTRICT

Before World War II, Wichita, Kansas, was a small city, a trading center for farm commodities, depending for its livelihood on the agricultural yield of the surrounding counties. Today Wichita is a substantial city, with a metropolitan area population of nearly half a million; it is, one might say, the Sun Belt city farthest north. Wichita owes much of its prosperity to the aviation industry. During World War II and the years immediately following it, aircraft manufacture caused major growth around the city. Boeing has a big plant here, as does Cessna; and Wichita is far and away the nation's leading center for producing small airplanes. This is a cyclical business. When the kind of businesses which buy most of these planes start to encounter a profit squeeze, one of the easiest ways to economize is not to buy a new company plane; accordingly, Wichita has had some bad times. But since the middle seventies, the demand for small planes has risen. Moreover, this is also an oil center, and the increase in oil prices starting in 1973 has also helped. In recent years Wichita has been as prosperous and booming a city as any in the Sun Belt.

Wichita's politics have reflected two conflicting tendencies. On the one hand, this is a newly prosperous city which believes in free enterprise and economic growth and is suspicious of government regulation; such feelings tend to make Wichita Republican, and that is how it has voted in most statewide and national elections. But at the same time Wichita is a city many of whose residents come from Arkansas, Oklahoma, and southern Kansas; people here often speak with a Southern drawl, and Wichita would just as soon look south to Texas as north to Kansas City. This kind of background tends to make Wichita Democratic. In 1976 Wichita and surrounding Sedgwick County went 48% for Jimmy Carter; the city's best known figure in state politics was a county sheriff and law 'n' order attorney general who was nearly elected governor in 1974.

The 4th congressional district of Kansas includes all of Wichita, most of surrounding Sedgwick County, and several other counties, including the city of Hutchinson; two-thirds of the votes are cast in Wichita and Sedgwick County. The 4th district is represented in the House by a man with a rather unusual background for a Kansas congressman. He is Dan Glickman, a Wichita Democrat, first elected at age 31 in 1976 when he defeated a 16-year Republican incumbent. Glickman was well known locally for his service on the Wichita school board, at a time when voters valued local experience more than years in Washington. Glickman's views were not far out of line with Wichita attitudes. He had once worked for a Republican senator, and he strongly backed the B-1 bomber, part of which would be built in Wichita. He has stressed his skepticism about government programs and his desire to cut federal spending.

Glickman won seats on the Agriculture and Science Committees. The latter has relevance to Wichita's aircraft industry; the former to the major industry of all of Kansas. As an energetic and news-making congressman from Wichita, Glickman has become a possible candidate for statewide office. The Wichita television stations reach the whole western part of the state, so he has become a familiar figure in half of Kansas. His hold on the 4th district is solid—he won more than two-thirds of the votes in 1978—but he must be considered a possible candidate for Bob Dole's Senate seat in 1980.

Census Data Pop. 450,487. Central city, 61%; suburban, 8%. Median family income, $9,097; families above $15,000: 17%; families below $3,000: 9%. Median years education, 12.3.

The Voters

Median voting age 42.
Employment profile White collar, 51%. Blue collar, 32%. Service, 14%. Farm, 3%.
Ethnic groups Black, 7%. Spanish, 2%. Total foreign stock, 7%. Germany, 2%.

Presidential vote

1976	Carter (D)	85,681	(49%)
	Ford (R)	89,201	(51%)
1972	Nixon (R)	110,805	(68%)
	McGovern (D)	52,191	(32%)

Rep. Dan Glickman (D) Elected 1976; b. Nov. 24, 1944, Wichita; home, Wichita; U. of Mich., B.A. 1966; Geo. Wash. U., J.D. 1969; Jewish

Career Trial Atty., SEC, Washington, D.C. 1969–70; Practicing atty., 1970–77.

Offices 1507 LHOB, 202-225-6216. Also Box 403, Wichita 67201, 316-262-8396.

Committees *Agriculture* (20th). Subcommittees: Conservation and Credit; Department Investigations, Oversight and Research; Domestic Marketing, Consumer Relations, and Nutrition.

Science and Technology (14th). Subcommittees: Energy Development and Applications; Transportation, Aviation, and Communication.

Group Ratings

	ADA	COPE	PC	RPN	NFU	LCV	CFA	NAB	NSI	ACA	NTU
1978	50	50	53	67	60	–	32	75	30	48	–
1977	50	65	65	69	67	66	40	–	–	41	37

Key Votes

1) Increase Def Spnd	AGN	6) Alaska Lands Protect	FOR	11) Delay Auto Pol Cntrl	DNV
2) B-1 Bomber	AGN	7) Water Projects Veto	FOR	12) Sugar Price Escalator	FOR
3) Cargo Preference	AGN	8) Consum Protect Agcy	AGN	13) Pub Fin Cong Cmpgns	FOR
4) Dereg Nat Gas	FOR	9) Common Situs Picket	FOR	14) ERA Ratif Recissn	AGN
5) Kemp-Roth	AGN	10) Labor Law Revision	FOR	15) Prohibt Govt Abrtns	AGN

Election Results

1978 general	Dan Glickman (D)	100,139	(70%)	($90,827)
	Jim Litsey (R)	43,854	(30%)	($73,264)
1978 primary	Dan Glickman (D), unopposed			
1976 general	Dan Glickman (D)	90,067	(51%)	($104,924)
	Garner E. Shriver (R)	86,832	(49%)	($135,283)

FIFTH DISTRICT

The southeast corner of Kansas has been nicknamed "the Balkans"—a reference to the Eastern European origin of some of the area's residents and to its low hill country, the outer fringe of the Ozarks. The hills here contain some coal, and the main town was named Pittsburg—another example of the unrealistic optimism of the people who first settled Kansas. This part of the state never became a notable coal or manufacturing center and today it is in unmistakable decline. The southeast corner of Kansas is the heart of the state's 5th congressional district, which stretches north to a point near Kansas City and west toward the Wichita suburbs and beyond.

Emporia is one of the larger towns that dot the district, and the home of William Allen White, the newspaper editor whose name was a household word forty years ago but draws a blank today. White was the voice of progressive Kansas Republicanism. Horrified by Populists in his youth, as were most people in the towns of the Midwest, White was enchanted by Theodore Roosevelt and came to care about the plight of those less fortunate than himself. Though a native of one of the nation's most isolationist regions, White was a leading spokesman for American aid to the British during the ominous days before World War II.

It is hard to say whether White's politics has been embodied in the recent congressman from the 5th district. From 1962 to 1976 the district elected Republican Joe Skubitz, a former Capitol Hill aide who rose to be ranking minority member of the House Interior Committee. In 1974, at age 72,

Skubitz retired. He had been challenged strongly in 1972, and the open seat attracted no less than 11 Republicans and Democrats. The Democratic primary was won by Don Allegrucci, a state Senator from Pittsburg, whose support in the Balkans was enough to overcome his opponents. The Republican nomination was won by a dark horse, optometrist Robert Whittaker. He began campaigning in May 1977, went door to door talking with voters, and worked at various jobs around the district for a day at a time.

Whittaker prevailed rather easily in the general election. The issue he had chosen to emphasize was very much in the public's favor: a constitutional amendment to require a balanced federal budget. Allegrucci was on the defensive for having opposed capital punishment and having supported liquor by the drink. Whittaker would seem to be very much in line with the spirit of the 1978 Republican freshmen, and his performance at the polls suggests that he has a good chance of making this a safe seat.

Census Data Pop. 447,026. Central city, 0%; suburban, 17%. Median family income, $7,450; families above $15,000: 10%; families below $3,000: 15%. Median years education, 12.1.

The Voters

Median voting age 48.
Employment profile White collar, 40%. Blue collar, 36%. Service, 14%. Farm, 10%.
Ethnic groups Black, 2%. Spanish, 1%. Total foreign stock, 6%. Germany, 1%.

Presidential vote

1976	Carter (D)	92,164	(49%)
	Ford (R)	95,763	(51%)
1972	Nixon (R)	124,835	(71%)
	McGovern (D)	50,528	(29%)

Rep. Robert Whittaker (R) Elected 1978; b. Sept. 18, 1939, Eureka; home, Augusta; Ill. Col. of Optometry, B.S. 1961, Dr. of Optometry 1962; Disciples of Christ.

Career Optometrist; Kans. House of Reps., 1975–77.

Offices 516 CHOB, 202-225-3911. Also 109 W. 5th St., Pittsburg 66762, 316-323-2320.

Committees *Interior and Insular Affairs* (13th). Subcommittees: National Parks and Insular Affairs; Mines & Mining.

Group Ratings: Newly Elected

Key Votes: Newly Elected

Election Results

1978 general	Robert Whittaker (R)	86,011	(58%)	($259,120)
	Don Allegrucci (D)	62,402	(42%)	($114,247)
1978 primary	Robert Whittaker (R)	18,329	(39%)	
	Don Johnson (R)	15,537	(33%)	($160,989)
	Pete McGill (R)	8,342	(18%)	($72,515)
	Two others (R)	5,384	(11%)	
1976 general	Joe Skubitz (R)	109,573	(63%)	($57,142)
	Virgil Leon Olson (D)	65,340	(37%)	($9,226)

KENTUCKY

In 1775 Daniel Boone made his way through the Cumberland Gap in the Appalachian Mountains and came upon what we now know as Kentucky—a fertile, virgin land of gently rolling hills. After the Revolutionary War, streams of people from Virginia and other states traveled Boone's Wilderness Road and settled in the hills and countryside around Lexington. This exodus was the new nation's first frontier boom and, up to that time, one of the most extensive mass migrations in Western history. There were no more than a few dozen whites in Kentucky before the War; the 1790 Census counted 73,000; by 1820 there were 564,000 Kentuckians, making this the sixth largest state in the nation. In those days Kentucky was the frontier, its communities full of opportunity and unburdened by the hierarchies that structured the societies of coastal America. Henry Clay, to take the most famous example, came to Kentucky from Virginia as a penniless youth. By the time he was 30 he had done well enough in law and land speculation to build a mansion with silver doorknobs and well enough in politics to become a United States senator.

In some respects Kentucky hasn't changed much since Clay's time. The state is still largely rural: less than 25% of its residents live in greater Louisville and only 8% in the Kentucky suburbs of Cincinnati, the state's only major metropolitan areas. During the fifties and sixties there was continual migration out of the state; Kentuckians looking for jobs left the hills for the industrial cities of the Midwest, California, and Texas. In the seventies there has been a reversal of that migration, but much of it involves people coming home to the somewhat more prosperous rural parts of the state. For the most part, the recent prosperity has not changed the local landscape much; the tobacco fields, the thoroughbred horse country of the Blue Grass, and the cotton fields of western Kentucky are pretty much the same. Coal has caused more changes. Kentucky has always been a major coal producer, with major fields in the eastern mountains and in the western part of the state as well. The seventies have seen a strip mining boom here, and Kentucky is not a state with strict regulation of strip mining. So in many small counties there are new coal millionaires, lots of jobs at high wages, and ugly scars across the hills and valleys.

Politics in Kentucky also seems caught in some kind of time warp. As in many border states, political divisions in Kentucky are still based on the splits caused by the Civil War. Though Kentucky was a slave state, it voted to stay with the Union. There were, to say the least, strong feelings on both sides of the conflict. Most of the hill country was pro-Union and remains Republican today; the major change occurred in counties where coal miners joined the United Mine Workers in the thirties and now favor the Democrats. The Blue Grass region and the western part of the state, sometimes called the Pennyrile, were more likely to be slaveholding territory, and today remain Democratic. Louisville, first settled and influenced by German immigrants, was an antislavery river town, and for years supported a strong Republican organization. These patterns, which have prevailed now for more than 100 years, were never more apparent than in the 1976 presidential election. Carter carried the state with 54%. He lost the county that includes Louisville, and he failed to carry the Kentucky suburbs of Cincinnati. The mountain counties in the southeast went solidly for Ford. Carter's margin came from the mining counties in the east, the Blue Grass, and the Pennyrile.

In most Kentucky elections over the years Democrats outvoted Republicans, though not by the kind of overwhelming margins found farther south. Thus for years major political decisions were made in the Democratic primary. The most famous figure to come out of this era was Alben Barkley, who was Congressman from Paducah (1913–27), U.S. Senator (1927–49), Vice President under Harry Truman, and Senator again until his death in 1956. But by the sixties Kentucky had been moving toward the Republicans, as so many rural-oriented states did during the Kennedy–Johnson Administration, and for one four-year period (1967–71) Republicans held the governorship and both Senate seats.

The first Republican victories were won by moderates from areas of the party's traditional strength, the Cumberland plateau and Louisville. The moderates included Senator John Sherman Cooper who between Senate terms (he kept winning special elections to fill vacancies but for a long time lost the full terms) served as Ambassador to India. An opponent of American involvement in Southeast Asia, Cooper retired voluntarily, still popular, in 1972. Another

Republican moderate was Senator (1957–69) Thruston Morton, onetime Chairman of the Republican National Committee.

But the sixties saw Kentucky's political parties take positions more in line with those of national leaders. Under Governor Bert Combs (1959–63) the Democrats were more attentive to the problems of the black and the poor than was traditional in Kentucky. As if in response, Republicans moved in the direction of Barry Goldwater and Richard Nixon. The key figure here was Louie Nunn, who nearly won the governorship in 1963, did win in 1967, and saw a protege—Kentucky does not allow its governors to serve more than one full term at a time and requires them to swear that they have never participated in a duel—come reasonably close to winning in 1971.

Now that era of competition along national lines seems over. Democrats, with margins almost entirely from the rural areas, have won the governorship and both Senate seats in the seventies. Republicans have shown little strength outside their traditional areas. The governorship has traditionally been the major prize in Kentucky politics; the governor has unusually wide powers and most Kentucky politicoes do not care much about what is happening in Washington. The crucial election was in 1971. Facing Nunn's candidate was Lieutenant Governor Wendell Ford, a Democrat whose economic policies gave him support from teacher groups and organized labor, but whose Owensboro accent and conservative attitude on social issues made him acceptable to traditional rural Democrats who found their party's national candidates objectionable. Nunn had won his election on social issues; Ford's major plank was repeal of the sales tax on food. He was elected by a fair margin, and promptly made good on his promise.

Ford was elected to the Senate in 1974 and was succeeded by Lieutenant Governor Julian Carroll. Like Ford, he had roots in the non-metropolitan part of the state, in his case in Paducah; and though he and Ford were not political allies their support came from the same groups. Carroll was considered a strong Governor indeed, and won a full term in 1975. Carroll has dominated the legislature and presided over a period of economic growth for Kentucky; he could probably have been reelected in 1979 were he eligible to run. Instead there was a large field of serious candidates: Lieutenant Governor Thelma Stovall, Commerce Commissioner Terry McBrayer, Carroll's choice; 1st district Congressman Carroll Hubbard; former Louisville Mayor Harvey Sloane, the only candidate with an urban, rather than rural, base, who has walked across the state to publicize his campaign; John Y. Brown, Jr., who made many millions off Kentucky Fried Chicken and spent about $2 million. Brown won the primary. For the Republicans, former Governor Nunn is trying for a comeback. The odds are against him: voters may remember that there was an unpopular tax increase during his term, and the social issues that carried him into office do not seem pertinent anymore. But he could profit from splits among the Democrats, and if he does win, Kentucky politics in the eighties will be much different from what it has been in the seventies.

Wendell Ford ran for the Senate with some reluctance; in Kentucky one hesitates before giving up one year of a governorship even for what could turn out to be a lifetime Senate seat. Ford also had a tough race that year, against Republican incumbent Marlow Cook. As a freshman Republican, he had cast some important votes against the Nixon Administration on the anti-ballistic missile and the Supreme Court nomination of Judge Harrold Carswell. But during the Watergate period he came increasingly to identify with the Nixon White House and to attack its opponents bitterly. The Democrats claimed he was out of touch with Kentucky, and was enjoying too much the pleasures of Washington. With a head of prematurely white hair and a dignified bearing, Cook certainly looked like a senator; but in an era of walking campaigns and homespum, soft-spoken candidates, he was no longer the kind of senator Kentucky wanted.

Ford won a solid enough victory and went on to Washington. Though he was said to have been discontented with his first months in the Senate, he has proved to be an important Senator. Part of the reason is his service on two committees which handle the economic questions which have been so important in the late seventies: Commerce and Energy. Because he does not invariably vote with liberal or conservative blocs, he has been an important swing vote on many issues. On energy, for example, he has generally opposed deregulation of natural gas and worked with Committee Chairman Henry Jackson. He gets high ratings from organized labor, with much lower ratings from liberal groups more concerned about non-economic issues. He usually supports the Carter Administration, but not always; despite intensive lobbying, he voted against ratification of the Panama Canal Treaty.

Ford has been Chairman of the Senate Democratic Campaign Committee since 1977, and although Democrats lost a majority of Senate races in 1978 he was deemed to have done a good job of raising money. Majority Leader Robert Byrd took the unusual step of asking Ford to take the post another two years, on the theory that he has a special ability to get contributions from business-oriented groups and individuals.

Ford's seat is up in 1980, and whether he has significant opposition probably depends on the outcome of the 1979 gubernatorial race. If a Republican governor is elected, Ford almost certainly will receive a strong challenge; if not, he will probably be reelected without much difficulty. He is unlikely to encounter tough competition in the Democratic primary.

Kentucky's senior Senator is Walter "Dee" Huddleston. To a considerable extent he owes his initial election to Ford: he was the hand-picked choice for the Democratic nomination in 1972, Ford's first year as Governor, and he won the general election narrowly over Louie Nunn. In the Senate he has served quietly on the Agriculture and Appropriations Committees. Huddleston votes more often with northern Democrats than with Republicans, but his vote cannot be taken for granted by liberals or the leadership. His percentage ratings from various organizations are similar to Ford's, but on specific issues the two often vote opposite ways. One example is the Panama Canal Treaty. Huddleston voted for it—an act of political courage, since he was up for reelection in hawkish Kentucky that fall.

Actually, reelection was not that great a problem for Huddleston in 1978. As in 1972, he had no significant primary opposition. His opponent in the general election was a state legislator from Louisville who had little financial support. Huddleston's margin in Louisville was not impressive, but he did exceedingly well in the rural areas and won the highest percentage for any Democratic Senate candidate since Alben Barkley in 1938.

Census Data Pop. 3,219,311; 1.59% of U.S. total, 23d largest; Central city, 17%; suburban, 23%. Median family income, $7,439; 46th highest; families above $15,000: 12%; families below $3,000: 18%. Median years education, 9.9.

1977 Share of Federal Tax Burden $4,352,000,000; 1.26% of U.S. total, 24th largest.

1977 Share of Federal Outlays $5,902,147,000; 1.49% of U.S. total, 24th largest. Per capita federal spending, $1,445.

DOD	$1,121,140,000	26th (1.33%)	HEW	$2,274,630,000	22d (1.54%)
ERDA	$422,585,000	5th (7.15%)	HUD	$53,459,000	26th (1.27%)
NASA	$489,000	41st (0.01%)	VA	$307,330,000	22d (1.60%)
DOT	$210,244,000	24th (1.47%)	EPA	$63,612,000	26th (0.78%)
DOC	$59,910,000	34th (0.72%)	RevS	$125,178,000	21st (1.48%)
DOI	$21,004,000	36th (0.45%)	Debt	$204,090,000	20th (0.68%)
USDA	$296,614,000	30th (1.49%)	Other	$741,862,000	

Economic Base Agriculture, notably tobacco, cattle, dairy products, and hogs; finance, insurance and real estate; electrical equipment and supplies, especially household applicances; machinery; bituminous coal mining; apparel and other textile products, especially men's and boys' furnishings; food and kindred products, especially distilled liquor and other beverages.

Political Line-up Governor, Julian M. Carroll (D). Senators, Walter Huddleston (D) and Wendell H. Ford (D). Representatives, 7 (4 D and 3 R). State Senate (29 D, 8 R, and 1 vacancy); State House (78 D, 21 R, and one vacancy).

The Voters

Registration 1,637,616 Total. 1,121,450 D (68%); 463,946 R (28%); 52,220 No party and others (3%).
Median voting age 43
Employment profile White collar, 40%. Blue collar, 41%. Service, 13%. Farm, 6%.
Ethnic groups Black, 7%. Total foreign stock, 2%.

Presidential vote

1976	Carter (D)	615,717	(54%)
	Ford (R)	531,852	(46%)
1972	Nixon (R)	676,446	(65%)
	McGovern (D)	371,159	(35%)

1976 Democratic Presidential Primary

Carter	181,690	(59%)
Wallace	51,540	(17%)
Udall	33,262	(11%)
Others	39,514	(13%)

1976 Republican Presidential Primary

Ford	67,976	(51%)
Reagan	62,683	(47%)
Other	2,869	(2%)

Sen. Walter Huddleston (D) Elected 1972, seat up 1978; b. Apr. 15, 1926, Cumberland County; home, Elizabethtown; U. of Ky., B.A. 1949; Methodist.

Career Army, WWII; Sports and Program Dir., WKCT Radio, Bowling Green, 1949–52; Gen. Mgr., WIEL Radio, Elizabethtown, 1952–72; Partner and Dir., WLBN Radio, Lebanon, 1957–72; Ky. Senate, 1965–72, Maj. Floor Ldr., 1970, 1972.

Offices 2113 DSOB, 202-224-2541. Also Suite 136C New Fed. Ofc. Bldg., 600 Federal Pl., Louisville 40202, 502-582-6304, and 220 W. Dixie Ave., Elizabethtown 42701, 502-769-6316.

Committees *Agriculture, Nutrition, and Forestry* (3d). Subcommittees: Environment, Soil Conservation, and Forestry; Agricultural Credit and Rural Electrification; Agricultural Production, Marketing, and Stabilization of Prices (Chairman).

Appropriations (11th). Subcommittees: Defense; Energy and Water Development; HUD-Independent Agencies; Interior and Related Agencies; Military Construction (Chairman).

Select Committee on Intelligence (3d).

Select Committee on Small Business (4th).

Group Ratings

	ADA	COPE	PC	RPN	NFU	LCV	CFA	NAB	NSI	ACA	NTU
1978	30	67	35	56	60	41	10	55	50	27	–
1977	45	80	35	22	80	–	28	–	–	19	24
1976	55	84	54	29	83	36	78	18	25	23	18

Key Votes

1) Warnke Nom	AGN	6) Egypt-Saudi Arms	DNV	11) Hosptl Cost Contnmnt	AGN
2) Neutron Bomb	FOR	7) Draft Restr Pardon	FOR	12) Clinch River Reactor	FOR
3) Waterwy User Fee	AGN	8) Wheat Price Support	FOR	13) Pub Fin Cong Cmpgns	FOR
4) Dereg Nat Gas	AGN	9) Panama Canal Treaty	FOR	14) ERA Ratif Recissn	AGN
5) Kemp-Roth	AGN	10) Labor Law Rev Clot	FOR	15) Med Necssy Abrtns	AGN

Election Results

1978 general	Walter Huddleston (D)	290,730	(62%)	($456,432)
	Louie Guenthner, Jr. (R)	175,766	(38%)	($76,445)
1978 primary	Walter Huddleston (D)	89,333	(76%)	
	Three others (D)	28,808	(24%)	
1972 general	Walter Huddleston (D)	528,550	(52%)	($658,590)
	Louis B. Nunn (R)	494,337	(48%)	($603,649)

Sen. Wendell H. Ford (D) Elected 1974, seat up 1980; b. Sept. 8, 1924, Daviess County; home, Owensboro; U. of Ky., Md. School of Insurance; Baptist.

Career Army, WWII; Family insurance business; Chf. Admin. Asst. to Gov. Bert Combs; Ky. Senate, 1965–67; Lt. Gov. of Ky., 1967–71; Gov. of Ky., 1971–74.

Offices 4107 DSOB, 202-224-4343. Also 172-C Fed. Bldg., 600 Federal Pl., Louisville 40202, 502-582-6251.

Committees *Commerce, Science, and Transportation* (7th). Subcommittees: Communications; Consumer (Chairman); Science, Technology, and Space.

Energy and Natural Resources (5th). Subcommittees: Energy Conservation and Supply; Energy Regulation; Energy Resources and Materials Production (Chairman).

Rules and Administration (5th).

Group Ratings

	ADA	COPE	PC	RPN	NFU	LCV	CFA	NAB	NSI	ACA	NTU
1978	45	68	43	60	89	30	25	40	70	42	–
1977	50	68	33	36	83	–	20	–	–	27	24
1976	40	79	34	41	91	32	64	18	20	23	21

Key Votes

1) Warnke Nom	FOR	6) Egypt-Saudi Arms	AGN	11) Hosptl Cost Contnmnt	AGN
2) Neutron Bomb	FOR	7) Draft Restr Pardon	AGN	12) Clinch River Reactor	AGN
3) Waterwy User Fee	AGN	8) Wheat Price Support	FOR	13) Pub Fin Cong Cmpgns	FOR
4) Dereg Nat Gas	FOR	9) Panama Canal Treaty	AGN	14) ERA Ratif Recissn	AGN
5) Kemp-Roth	AGN	10) Labor Law Rev Clot	FOR	15) Med Necssy Abrtns	AGN

Election Results

1974 general	Wendell H. Ford (D)	399,406	(55%)	($1,006,670)
	Marlow W. Cook (R)	328,982	(45%)	($524,569)
1974 primary	Wendell H. Ford (D)	136,458	(85%)	
	One other (D)	24,436	(15%)	
1968 general	Marlow W. Cook (R)	484,260	(52%)	
	Katherine Peder (D)	448,960	(48%)	

Gov. Julian Carroll (D) Elected Succeeded Gov. Wendell H. Ford, Dec. 28, 1974, elected Nov. 1975, term expires Dec. 1979; b. 1931, McCracken County; Paducah Jr. Col., U. of Ky., B.A. 1954, LL.B. 1956; Presbyterian.

Career Air Force; Practicing atty.; Ky. House of Reps., 1961–71, Spkr., 1968–71; Lt. Gov. of Ky., 1971–74.

Offices Frankfort 40601, 502-564-3450.

Election Results

1975 general	Julian M. Carroll (D)	470,159	(63%)
	Robert E. Gable (R)	277,998	(37%)
1975 primary	Julian M. Carroll (D)	263,965	(66%)
	Todd Hollenbach (D)	113,285	(28%)
	Two others (D)	20,739	(5%)
1971 general	Wendell H. Ford (D)	470,720	(53%)
	Tom Emberton (R)	412,653	(47%)

FIRST DISTRICT

The western end of Kentucky, known historically as the Jackson Purchase, almost seems to be part of another state—of west Tennessee or the lowlands of the Bootheel of Missouri or even the Mississippi Delta. This is low-lying land, protected from the great muddy river and cut off from the rest of Kentucky by the dammed-up Tennessee and Cumberland Rivers. Economically and politically, the area resembles the Deep South: it raises cotton, it has some black population (there are few blacks in the rest of Kentucky outside Louisville), it went solidly for Jimmy Carter in 1976 and was carried by George Wallace in 1968.

Just to the east of the rivers is a region called the Pennyrile (after pennyroyal, a prevalent variety of wild mint). Here one finds a land of low hills and small farms. It is also the home of the west Kentucky coal fields, the site of much strip mining in recent years. Like the Jackson Purchase, the Pennyrile is ancestrally Democratic and, with the exception of a few counties, continues to vote that way in almost every election.

These two parts of western Kentucky form the state's 1st congressional district. This is the area that first sent Alben Barkley to Congress, back in 1912. It has elected Democrats ever since. The current incumbent, Carroll Hubbard, was elected in 1974 after he had the foresight to challenge a weak incumbent in the primary. On arrival in Washington, Hubbard was chosen chairman of the Freshman Caucus, the very existence of which was something of an innovation. Actually, Hubbard has turned out to be not very typical of the Democrats first elected that year. His record on non-economic issues is almost uniformly conservative; his record on economic issues is mixed. Hubbard's ambitions, however, are not concentrated on Capitol Hill. He would like to be governor of Kentucky, and if he is not successful in his campaign for that office in 1979, he is likely to try again some time in the future. Meanwhile, the 1st district is sure to continue to have Democratic representation.

Census Data Pop. 460,754. Central city, 0%; suburban, 8%. Median family income, $6,788; families above $15,000: 8%; families below $3,000: 20%. Median years education, 9.9.

The Voters

Median voting age 45.
Employment profile White collar, 33%. Blue collar, 46%. Service, 13%. Farm, 8%.
Ethnic groups Black, 9%. Total foreign stock, 1%.

Presidential vote

1976	Carter (D)	110,686	(67%)
	Ford (R)	55,462	(33%)
1972	Nixon (R)	87,072	(63%)
	McGovern (D)	51,802	(37%)

Rep. Carroll Hubbard, Jr. (D) Elected 1974; b. July 7, 1937, Murray; home, Mayfield; Georgetown Col., Georgetown, Ky., B.A. 1959, U. of Louisville, J.D. 1962; Baptist.

Career Practicing atty., 1962–74; Ky. Senate, 1967–75.

Offices 204 CHOB, 202-225-3115. Also 145 E. Center St., McCoy Bldg., Madisonville 42431, 502-825-1371.

Committees *Banking, Finance and Urban Affairs* (14th). Subcommittees: Economic Stabilization; Financial Institutions Supervision, Regulation and Insurance; General Oversight and Renegotiation.

Merchant Marine and Fisheries (11th). Subcommittees: Merchant Marine; Panama Canal (Chairman).

Group Ratings

	ADA	COPE	PC	RPN	NFU	LCV	CFA	NAB	NSI	ACA	NTU
1978	10	65	30	50	56	–	27	67	100	68	–
1977	15	52	28	15	75	20	30	–	–	65	27
1976	25	65	23	33	58	43	18	25	88	52	38

Key Votes

1) Increase Def Spnd	FOR	6) Alaska Lands Protect	AGN	11) Delay Auto Pol Cntrl	FOR
2) B-1 Bomber	FOR	7) Water Projects Veto	AGN	12) Sugar Price Escalator	FOR
3) Cargo Preference	FOR	8) Consum Protect Agcy	AGN	13) Pub Fin Cong Cmpgns	FOR
4) Dereg Nat Gas	FOR	9) Common Situs Picket	AGN	14) ERA Ratif Recissn	FOR
5) Kemp-Roth	AGN	10) Labor Law Revision	FOR	15) Prohibt Govt Abrtns	FOR

Election Results

1978 general	Carroll Hubbard, Jr. (D), unopposed			($79,097)
1978 primary	Carroll Hubbard, Jr. (D), unopposed			
1976 general	Carrol Hubbard, Jr. (D)	118,886	(82%)	($81,641)
	Bob Bersky (R)	26,089	(18%)	($2,460)

SECOND DISTRICT

The 2d congressional district of Kentucky is a sprawling, largely rural area extending from the Blue Grass country not far from Lexington to the hilly Pennyrile area around Bowling Green. Its largest city is the prosperous factory town of Owensboro on the Ohio River, which has only 50,000 people. The best known features of the district are Fort Knox, where the gold bullion in kept, and Bardstown, where one can find Stephen Collins Foster's "Old Kentucky Home." Bardstown is also a town that suffered disproportionately from the Vietnam war. Sixteen of its sons died there, five of them within two weeks of each other. Also in the district is the birthplace and boyhood home of Abraham Lincoln.

Kentucky was a slave state that was sharply split when the South seceded; for a while it said that it was remaining neutral, but finally sided with the Union. Much of the current 2d district was sympathetic to the South, and most of it still votes Democratic today. An exception to this pattern is a group of Republican counties roughly in the center of this T-shaped district; they are three of the four counties in the district that went for Gerald Ford in 1976.

William H. Natcher, generally considered a conservative Democrat, has represented this district since a special election in 1953. He is now the third-ranking Democrat on the House Appropriations Committee. In Washington, he is known mainly for his service as Chairman of the District of Columbia Subcommittee, in which capacity he effectively controlled the District budget for years. Natcher was considered by some as prejudiced against the District's black majority, but his actions seem to have resulted from different motivations. He is a man who abhors waste, who is meticulous and attentive to detail, and who works very hard. If he sometimes acted autocratically and seemed to substitute his own judgment for that of the people of Washington, he also imposed some discipline on the city government and its budget.

Natcher no longer holds that position. In 1979 he succeeded to the chair of the Labor-HEW Appropriations Subcommittee, a body which passes on the expenditure of far more money than the D.C. Subcommittee. His predecessor, Daniel Flood, had a reputation for generosity toward social programs; Natcher was expected to be more tight-fisted. Certainly he will be conscientious. He is proud that he has never missed a roll call vote or quorum call on the floor of the House since he was elected in 1953—surpassing the old attendance record set by Charles Bennett of Florida. Natcher is one of those old-fashioned congressmen who does his own reading and research and prides himself on being well prepared. Those work habits served him well on the D.C. Subcommittee, where even his adversaries always conceded that he knew what he was talking about. But the larger scope of his new chairmanship may require even the most conscientious of congressmen to rely more on staff, which he is probably reluctant to do.

Natcher's conscientiousness also might not serve him well politically if he should be opposed by a serious challenger. His insistence on perfect attendance in Washington makes it harder for him to appear in the district with the frequency which has become customary in many districts. And he steadfastly refuses to accept any campaign contributions at all; the little he spends on campaigns comes from his own pocket. Most of the time he is unopposed, but a serious challenger held him to 60% in 1976, and there is the possibility of a significant challenge in either the primary or the general election.

Census Data Pop. 459,416. Central city, 11%; suburban, 6%. Median family income, $7,042; families above $15,000: 9%; families below $3,000: 18%. Median years education, 9.8.

The Voters

Median voting age 39.
Employment profile White collar, 35%. Blue collar, 42%. Service, 12%. Farm, 11%.
Ethnic groups Black, 6%. Total foreign stock, 2%.

Presidential vote

1976	Carter (D)	81,529	(55%)
	Ford (R)	65,476	(45%)
1972	Nixon (R)	88,384	(65%)
	McGovern (D)	46,922	(35%)

Rep. William H. Natcher (D) Elected Aug. 1, 1953; b. Sept. 11, 1909, Bowling Green; home, Bowling Green; West. Ky. St. Col., B.A. 1930, Ohio St. U., LL.B. 1933; Baptist.

Career Practicing atty., 1934–53; Fed. Conciliation Commissioner, West. Dist. of Ky., 1936–37; Warren Co. Atty., 1937–49; Navy, WWII; Commonwealth Atty., 8th Judicial Dist. of Ky., 1951–53.

Offices 2333 RHOB, 202-225-3501. Also 414 E. 10th St., Bowling Green 42101, 502-842-7376.

Committees *Appropriations* (3d). Subcommittees: Agriculture, Rural Development, and Related Agencies; District of Columbia; Labor-HEW (Chairman).

Group Ratings

	ADA	COPE	PC	RPN	NFU	LCV	CFA	NAB	NSI	ACA	NTU
1978	35	60	43	33	60	–	41	33	60	26	–
1977	30	61	55	31	75	45	45	–	–	52	23
1976	45	70	52	39	67	48	54	33	70	46	32

Key Votes

1) Increase Def Spnd	FOR	6) Alaska Lands Protect	FOR	11) Delay Auto Pol Cntrl	FOR
2) B-1 Bomber	AGN	7) Water Projects Veto	AGN	12) Sugar Price Escalator	FOR
3) Cargo Preference	AGN	8) Consum Protect Agcy	AGN	13) Pub Fin Cong Cmpgns	AGN
4) Dereg Nat Gas	FOR	9) Common Situs Picket	AGN	14) ERA Ratif Recissn	FOR
5) Kemp-Roth	AGN	10) Labor Law Revision	FOR	15) Prohibt Govt Abrtns	FOR

Election Results

1978 general	William H. Natcher (D), unopposed			
1978 primary	William H. Natcher (D), unopposed			
1976 general	William H. Natcher (D)	79,016	(60%)	($8,162)
	Walter A. Baker (R)	51,900	(40%)	($51,856)

THIRD DISTRICT

The 3d congressional district of Kentucky is made up of the city of Louisville and a few of its suburbs to the south and west. Despite the local pronunciation (LOOuhvul) and Southern traditions—Alistair Cooke calls Kentucky the most self-consciously Southern of states, though it never seceded—Louisville is really less of a Southern town than it likes to think. It is closer in spirit to other old river ports, Cincinnati and St. Louis, which, though larger, sprung up at about the same time in locations which are similar. All three cities, and particularly their large German-American communities, were hostile to the Southern-leaning politics of their slaveholding rural neighbors at the time of the Civil War, and all three had longstanding Republican traditions, among blacks as well as whites. St. Louis turned Democratic in the thirties, Cincinnati is still decidedly Republican, and Louisville moves back and forth.

Thus the sixties were a good decade for Republicans here. They elected a mayor of Louisville and the Jefferson County judge—the administrative head of the county government. Both received promotions—Judge Marlow Cook to the U.S. Senate, Mayor William Cowger to the House—and both were defeated by Democrats in the early seventies. Democrats have held the mayor's office since 1969; as a central city Louisville has become too Democratic for the Republicans to make a strong effort. But the Republicans have come back in Jefferson County as a whole, defeating County Judge Todd Hollenbach in 1978.

One of the beneficiaries of the early seventies' Democratic surge here was 3d district Congressman Romano Mazzoli. He defeated Cowger in 1970 in one of the closest races in the country and held onto the seat with ease in 1972 and 1974. In 1976 he had greater problems. Louisville and Jefferson County were under a federal court busing order, and busing was clearly the most important local issue. There was some feeling that Mazzoli, a member of the Judiciary Committee, had done less than he could have to fight busing. He had to weather tough challenges in both primary and general elections. But by 1978 his problems seemed to have vanished. Busing had become less important to voters, and Mazzoli did not have significant primary opposition. In the general he prevailed by better than 2–1.

Census Data Pop. 460,340. Central city, 79%; suburban, 21%. Median family income, $8,902; families above $15,000: 15%; families below $3,000: 11%. Median years education, 10.9.

The Voters

Median voting age 44.
Employment profile White collar, 44%. Blue collar, 42%. Service, 14%. Farm, –%.
Ethnic groups Black, 20%. Total foreign stock, 4%.

Presidential vote

1976	Carter (D)	79,407	(55%)
	Ford (R)	63,690	(45%)
1972	Nixon (R)	78,143	(55%)
	McGovern (D)	63,796	(45%)

Rep. Romano L. Mazzoli (D) Elected 1970; b. Nov. 2, 1932, Louisville; home, Louisville; Notre Dame U., B.S. 1954, U. of Louisville, J.D. 1960; Catholic.

Career Army, 1954–56; Law Dept., L & N Railroad Co., 1960–62; Practicing atty., 1962–70; Ky. Senate, 1967–71.

Offices 2246 RHOB, 202-225-5401. Also Fed. Bldg., 600 Federal Pl., Louisville 40202, 502-582-5129.

Committees *District of Columbia* (4th). Subcommittees: Judiciary, Manpower, and Education (Chairman).

Judiciary (10th). Subcommittees: Administrative Law and Governmental Relations; Monopolies and Commercial Law; Courts, Civil Liberties, and the Administration of Justice.

Group Ratings

	ADA	COPE	PC	RPN	NFU	LCV	CFA	NAB	NSI	ACA	NTU
1978	40	50	50	82	50	–	32	46	30	31	–
1977	50	86	63	46	45	40	65	–	–	15	23
1976	65	74	66	56	92	62	91	25	40	11	36

Key Votes

1) Increase Def Spnd	AGN	6) Alaska Lands Protect	FOR	11) Delay Auto Pol Cntrl	FOR
2) B-1 Bomber	AGN	7) Water Projects Veto	AGN	12) Sugar Price Escalator	AGN
3) Cargo Preference	AGN	8) Consum Protect Agcy	AGN	13) Pub Fin Cong Cmpgns	FOR
4) Dereg Nat Gas	AGN	9) Common Situs Picket	FOR	14) ERA Ratif Recissn	AGN
5) Kemp-Roth	AGN	10) Labor Law Revision	FOR	15) Prohibt Govt Abrtns	FOR

Election Results

1978 general	Romano L. Mazzoli (D)	37,346	(68%)	($110,638)
	Norbert D. Leveronne (R)	17,785	(32%)	
1978 primary	Romano L. Mazzoli (D)	11,090	(79%)	
	Three others (D) 2,956 (21%)			
1976 general	Romano L. Mazzoli (D)	80,496	(58%)	($95,344)
	Denzil J. Ramsey (R)	58,019	(42%)	($53,274)

FOURTH DISTRICT

The 4th congressional district of Kentucky is a geographical oddity—the result of the state's loss of a congressional district in the 1960 Census and three subsequent redistrictings. The 4th today consists of two nearly equal-sized suburban areas connected by a thin strip of rural counties 120 miles along the Ohio River. The first and larger of the suburban areas is Jefferson County, excluding the city of Louisville and a few adjacent suburbs which make up the 3d district. This part of the 4th is prosperous and growing fairly rapidly; like most affluent suburbs, it tends to vote Republican. This tendency has been fortified of late by the rural and countrified background of Kentucky's leading Democratic politicians, who have won statewide elections easily but who have been unable to carry suburban Jefferson County. The other suburban part of the 4th district lies across the Ohio River from Cincinnati. About half the voters here live in the old, decaying cities of Covington and Newport on the river. Like Cincinnati, they usually go Republican, although they have been known to swing the other way.

The connecting counties along the River are part of an older Kentucky. Bypassed by Interstate 71, these little tobacco towns retain nineteenth century Democratic voting habits, though the few ballots cast here get lost in the district-wide totals.

Since 1966 the congressman from the 4th has been Republican Gene Snyder, who also represented the 3d district one term until he was swept out by the Johnson landslide of 1964. Snyder has had only two tough races since then: the 1966 primary, when he beat onetime Cleveland Browns quarterback George Ratterman, and the 1974 general, when he beat Kyle Hubbard, brother of 1st district Congressman Carroll Hubbard. By any standard, Snyder is probably the most conservative member of the Kentucky delegation. He is one of the leading Republicans on the Merchant Marine and Public Works Committees—odd assignments for a free market conservative, since their job is to supervise the spending of large sums of public monies. Just past 50, he has had a long congressional career, and seems likely to continue in the House for some time to come.

Census Data Pop. 458,896. Central city, 0%; suburban, 93%. Median family income, $10,359; families above $15,000: 21%; families below $3,000: 7%. Median years education, 12.0.

The Voters

Median voting age 41.
Employment profile White collar, 51%. Blue collar, 37%. Service, 10%. Farm, 2%.
Ethnic groups Black, 2%. Total foreign stock, 5%.

Presidential vote

1976	Carter (D)	77,963	(43%)
	Ford (R)	104,266	(57%)
1972	Nixon (R)	112,607	(70%)
	McGovern (D)	47,238	(30%)

Rep. Gene Synder (R) Elected 1966; b. Jan. 26, 1928, Louisville; home, Jefferson County; Jefferson School of Law, LL.B. 1950; Protestant.

Career Practicing atty., 1950–67; Realtor and builder; Jeffersontown City Atty., 1954–58; Jefferson Co. 1st Dist. Magistrate, 1957–65.

Offices 2330 RHOB, 202-225-3465. Also 125 Chenoweth Ln., St. Matthews 40207, 502-895-6949.

Committees *Merchant Marine and Fisheries* (2d). Subcommittees: Fish and Wildlife; Merchant Marine.

Public Works and Transportation (4th) Subcommittees: Aviation; Oversight and Review; Water Resources.

Group Ratings

	ADA	COPE	PC	RPN	NFU	LCV	CFA	NAB	NSI	ACA	NTU
1978	15	20	20	42	20	–	27	83	100	96	–
1977	10	27	15	23	45	0	15	–	–	81	40
1976	5	22	25	47	25	22	9	73	80	89	70

Key Votes

1) Increase Def Spnd	FOR	6) Alaska Lands Protect	AGN	11) Delay Auto Pol Cntrl	FOR
2) B-1 Bomber	FOR	7) Water Projects Veto	AGN	12) Sugar Price Escalator	AGN
3) Cargo Preference	FOR	8) Consum Protect Agcy	AGN	13) Pub Fin Cong Cmpgns	AGN
4) Dereg Nat Gas	AGN	9) Common Situs Picket	AGN	14) ERA Ratif Recissn	FOR
5) Kemp-Roth	FOR	10) Labor Law Revision	AGN	15) Prohibt Govt Abrtns	FOR

Election Results

1978 general	Gene Snyder (R)	62,087	(66%)	($122,834)
	George C. Martin (D)	32,212	(34%)	($30,231)
1978 primary	Gene Snyder (R), unopposed			
1976 general	Gene Snyder (R)	97,493	(56%)	($110,160)
	Edward J. Winterberg (D)	77,009	(44%)	($45,590)

FIFTH DISTRICT

If you are looking for evidence that political preference in the United States is not simply the result of economic status, the results of the 1976 presidential election provide ample proof. For in that election, like those before, the precincts of the richest people in the country—the Upper East Side of Manhattan and Beverly Hills, California—went for the candidate of the Democratic Party. Meanwhile the Republicans, supposedly the party of the rich, were carrying by a 57%–43% margin the 5th congressional district of Kentucky, a district with a median income in 1970 several hundred dollars lower than that of any other in the nation. Very few of the nation's 435 congressional districts produced a higher Republican percentage.

Ford's performance here was, if anything, a little below the usual levels of Republican support. The hills and hollows of the Cumberland Plateau in south central Kentucky have consistently delivered some of the largest Republican percentages in the United States for more than a century. The nomination of a Southerner by the Democrats did not change that. The small farmers here were hostile to the slaveholding South and to the uppity proslavery Blue Grass region to the north in the years around the Civil War. The people here live in one of the most isolated and provincial areas of the United States, and they have had little trouble maintaining their party identification ever since.

Only in places where the United Mine Workers organized successfully in the thirties have the mountain people switched to the Democrats. But there are fewer mines and miners here than in the adjacent 7th district. About the only consistently Democratic county here is "bloody Harlan," where in the thirties the mine owners' men and the UMW members shot and killed each other in pitched battles. For years thereafter Harlan County, like the coal industry, was in decline; its population fell from 64,000 in 1940 to 36,000 in 1970. Now it is up again, and Rolls Royces can be seen in some towns. With the energy crisis of the middle seventies, coal prices have risen and coal production has boomed. And even where there is not enough coal, there has been an upsurge in the local economy and an increase in population. Big metropolitan areas are no longer so attractive to young people anxious to make a living, and Kentucky has enough opportunities for many of them. Older people are returning home after years in the factories of Akron and Detroit.

The 5th district is one part of Southern-accented America where winning the Republican primary is tantamount to winning the general election. In 1964, Republican Tim Lee Carter won 45% of the vote in a 15-candidate primary field; his election in November, even in that Democratic year, was taken for granted. Carter is an original: a small town physician who still practices medicine, a mountain Republican with a populist tinge. He was one of only a few Republicans on the House Commerce Committee who voted against deregulation of natural gas; he voted also for the tough clean air standards opposed by the automobile companies. He is ranking Republican on the important Health Subcommittee, and in the 95th Congress he strongly supported hospital cost containment legislation until the end, when he switched his vote because of allegations that a New Jersey congressman got a veterans' hospital in return for his. Carter has a first-hand knowledge of health problems, which should be hotly debated in 1979 and 1980. He should be an interesting man to watch in the 96th Congress.

Census Data Pop. 459,586. Central city, 0%; suburban, 0%. Median family income, $4,669; families above $15,000: 6%; families below $3,000: 33%. Median years education, 8.5.

The Voters

Median voting age 45.
Employment profile White collar, 33%. Blue collar, 43%. Service, 12%. Farm, 12%.
Ethnic groups Black, 3%.

Presidential vote

1976	Carter (D)	73,330	(43%)
	Ford (R)	97,001	(57%)
1972	Nixon (R)	117,821	(73%)
	McGovern (D)	44,287	(27%)

Rep. Tim Lee Carter (R) Elected 1964; b. Sept. 2, 1910, Tompkinsville; home, Tompkinsville; W. Ky. U., B.A. 1934, U. of Tenn., M.D. 1937; Baptist.

Career Internship, U.S. Marine Hosp. and Chicago Maternity Ctr.; Army, WWII; Practicing physician.

Offices 2267 RHOB, 202-225-4601. Also 203 S. Main St., Somerset 42501, 606-679-2544.

Committees *Interstate and Foreign Commerce* (3d). Subcommittees: Health and Environment.

Small Business (5th). Subcommittees: General Oversight and Minority Enterprise.

Group Ratings

	ADA	COPE	PC	RPN	NFU	LCV	CFA	NAB	NSI	ACA	NTU
1978	20	40	26	45	80	–	36	55	90	65	–
1977	10	36	28	38	73	24	25	–	–	60	24
1976	15	50	16	44	55	18	27	58	100	73	29

Key Votes

1) Increase Def Spnd	FOR	6) Alaska Lands Protect	DNV	11) Delay Auto Pol Cntrl	AGN
2) B-1 Bomber	FOR	7) Water Projects Veto	AGN	12) Sugar Price Escalator	AGN
3) Cargo Preference	AGN	8) Consum Protect Agcy	AGN	13) Pub Fin Cong Cmpgns	AGN
4) Dereg Nat Gas	AGN	9) Common Situs Picket	AGN	14) ERA Ratif Recissn	FOR
5) Kemp-Roth	FOR	10) Labor Law Revision	AGN	15) Prohibt Govt Abrtns	FOR

Election Results

1978 general	Tim Lee Carter (R)	59,743	(79%)	($44,631)
	Jesse M. Ramey (D)	15,714	(21%)	
1978 primary	Tim Lee Carter (R)	17,147	(93%)	
	One other (R)	1,312	(7%)	
1976 general	Tim Lee Carter (R)	100,204	(67%)	($56,999)
	Charles C. Smith (D)	49,128	(33%)	($19,644)

SIXTH DISTRICT

The 6th congressional district of Kentucky, though geographically compact, can be divided into two politically distinct parts. The first may be called the Blue Grass country. This is our traditional picture of Kentucky: the rolling green meadows where, behind white wooden fences, the glistening horses graze; the stately white mansion on the hillock overlooking the fields; the colonel sitting on the mansion's front porch, dressed in a white suit and sipping a mint julep. There actually are places like this in the 6th district, for it contains most of the beautiful horse country around Lexington, and it is the residence of Colonel Harland Sanders himself.

But few of the residents of the Blue Grass are so rich. More typical are the small towns with houses built as long ago as the 1810s—this part of Kentucky was the first part of the United States settled by migrants from across the Appalachians—or the small, poorer farms with their frame houses. The spiritual capital of this part of the 6th district is not Lexington, but Frankfort, the small and surprisingly industrial looking capital city. Frankfort and Franklin County lead the district in Democratic allegiance; the town's usual preference is strengthened by the fact that Kentucky is a patronage state and the Democrats have held the governor's office for most of the seventies. Overall, the traditional Blue Grass part of the 6th district almost always casts Democratic majorities.

The other part of the 6th district is modern Lexington. This is a far bigger town than the city Henry Clay knew, though it retains a few historic structures. Its downtown is hardly picturesque, but it is a place of real prosperity, largely because of the main IBM typewriter plant which is located here. IBM's presence has helped make Lexington a major center for high technology industry and white collar employment. The Lexington area's population has grown an unusually high 10% in the seventies, and most of that growth has been among the kind of affluent people who favor Republicans. They find the rural-oriented Democrats who are usually the party's candidates particularly uncongenial.

With the Lexington area growing considerably faster than the traditional Blue Grass area, it is not surprising that the 6th was one of those districts which ousted a Democratic congressman in 1978 and elected a Republican. What is unusual is how they did it. Democrat John Breckinridge was not especially strong. At 65, his greatest political asset was his name: he was the fifth Kentucky Breckinridge to serve in Congress; his namesakes served as Jefferson's attorney general and Buchanan's vice president. But this particular Breckinridge did not aggressively use the advantages of incumbency nor did he campaign effectively. In 1978 he was upset in the Democratic primary by state Senator Tom Easterly, a former state AFL-CIO staffer who had strong labor support. Easterly won almost entirely because of support in his home town of Frankfort; he carried only two small counties in addition to Franklin.

The general election campaign was an illustration of intelligent strategy by the Republicans and incompetent tactics by Easterly. Easterly could not shake the labor image, even though he endorsed a constitutional amendment to require a balanced budget, and he was unable to get television advertisements on the air until October. The Republicans' initial problem was their candidate: 68-year-old Mary Louise Foust, a former Democratic state Auditor. Foust was persuaded to withdraw from the race, and the Republicans substituted Lexington state Senator Larry Hopkins. His campaign concentrated on calling Easterly a labor-dominated liberal and rallying the faithful in Lexington. Hopkins won with a 2–1 margin in Lexington, more than enough to overcome Easterly's lead in the traditional Blue Grass counties. It is hard to say whether Hopkins has a safe seat, but certainly the demographics of this district are with him, and it should be hard for the Democrats to unseat him in 1980.

Census Data Pop. 460,521. Central city, 24%; suburban, 27%. Median family income, $8,678; families above $15,000: 16%; families below $3,000: 12%. Median years education, 11.7.

The Voters

Median voting age 41.
Employment profile White collar, 46%. Blue collar, 34%. Service, 13%. Farm, 7%.
Ethnic groups Black, 9%. Total foreign stock, 2%.

Presidential vote

1976	Carter (D)	88,195	(53%)
	Ford (R)	77,765	(47%)
1972	Nixon (R)	101,147	(67%)
	McGovern (D)	50,777	(33%)

Rep. Larry J. Hopkins (R) Elected 1978; b. Oct. 25, 1933, Winyo; home, Lexington; Murray St. U., So. Meth. U., Purdue U.; Methodist.

Career USMC, Korea; Stockbroker; Ky. House of Reps., 1972–77; Ky. Senate, 1978.

Offices 514 CHOB, 202-225-4706. Also 400 E. Main, Lexington 40507, 606-233-2848.

Committees *Agriculture* (14th). Subcommittees: Dairy and Poultry; Tobacco; Conservation and Credit.

Group Ratings: Newly Elected

Key Votes

1) Increase Def Spnd	NE	6) Alaska Lands Protect	NE	11) Delay Auto Pol Cntrl	NE
2) B-1 Bomber	NE	7) Water Projects Veto	NE	12) Sugar Price Escalator	NE
3) Cargo Preference	NE	8) Consum Protect Agcy	NE	13) Pub Fin Cong Cmpgns	NE
4) Dereg Nat Gas	NE	9) Common Situs Picket	NE	14) ERA Ratif Recissn	NE
5) Kemp-Roth	NE	10) Labor Law Revision	NE	15) Prohibt Govt Abrtns	NE

Election Results

1978 general	Larry J. Hopkins (R)	52,092	(52%)	($291,920)
	Tom Easterly (D)	47,436	(48%)	($134,770)
1978 primary	Larry J. Hopkins (R), selected by party after nominee withdrew			
1978 primary	Mary Louise Foust (R), unopposed			
1976 general	John B. Breckinridge (D)	90,695	(94%)	
	Anthony A. McCord (Amer.)	5,795	(6%)	

SEVENTH DISTRICT

The 7th congressional district of Kentucky is part—some would say the heart—of Appalachia. Though the 5th district is officially the state's (and the nation's) poorest district, the 7th has been one of the most poverty-stricken and isolated in the entire country. The only city here of any size is Ashland, on the Ohio River near Huntington, West Virginia, and that has only 29,000 people. The rural hills and hollows of the district, however, are some of the most densely populated rural areas in the United States. Coal has been the region's economic mainstay—its sustenance in good years and its scourge in bad. The fifties and sixties were generally bad times for coal: oil was replacing it as a heating and industrial fuel, and machines were replacing miners in the mines that were working. For more than a quarter century, places like the 7th district were exporting their young men and women to the industrial cities of the north. Most of them continued to think of eastern Kentucky as "home."

Now many of these people have returned home for good. Coal is back in demand, and there are suddenly new millionaires and visible prosperity in the Appalachians. But affluence is not yet universal. Employment in mining is far below the forties levels, since so much coal is strip-mined; and many of the new mines do not pay union wages. Still, there is no question that eastern Kentucky is better off today than it was ten years ago, and it may even be in the process of building a self-sustaining local economy that can survive vagaries in the price of coal.

The struggles of the thirties and the New Deal put an end to any Civil War allegiance to the Republican Party in most of the counties of the 7th district. Today the 7th as a whole is staunchly Democratic, with only small patches of Republican sentiment. The district gave Jimmy Carter a solid 61% in 1976. Contrasting election results testify to the long isolation and insularity of the mountain counties. Knott County, for example, was 83% for Carter in 1976, while Jackson County, 20 miles away and quite similar in appearance, was 80% for Gerald Ford.

Knott County is the home of the district's congressman, Carl Perkins, and not surprisingly he is a Democrat. For some years now he has been reelected by better than 2–1 margins. First elected in 1948, Perkins has been, since the ouster of Adam Clayton Powell in 1967, Chairman of the House Education and Labor Committee. At that time Perkins was a firm supporter of Lyndon Johnson's Great Society programs, and Education and Labor was a glamor committee, with jurisdiction over federal aid to education, the anti-poverty programs, and aid to Appalachia.

Education and Labor has since lost its glamor. At the beginning of the 96th Congress, not enough new Democrats applied for membership to fill the Committee's vacant seats, and the leadership had to persuade someone to fill the vacancy. The spending programs over which the Committee has jurisdiction became the object of budget-cutters in the 95th and 96th Congresses; there is a skepticism, among younger Democrats as well as Republicans, as to whether many of these programs are doing anything useful at all. Not that any of these programs are seriously in danger of being beaten in committee. Perkins is an effective chairman, and he works well with his talented subcommittee chairmen. But Education and Labor has lost some of its elan.

It remains nevertheless a liberal—or rather labor—stronghold. Back in 1959, Education and Labor reported out a major labor law which was opposed by the AFL-CIO. Labor's leaders vowed that that would never happen again, and they worked to make sure that only liberal, pro-labor Democrats would get on the Committee. By the time Perkins became Chairman, that goal had been accomplished. Today, all the Committee's Republicans, led by ranking member John Ashbrook, are strongly anti-labor; but almost every one of the Committee's Democrats is a solid labor vote. This has had important consequences—not all of them favorable to organized labor's interests. Thus in 1977 labor was able to get its common situs picketing bill out of committee easily, but it eventually lost the measure in the Senate. The same thing happened to the labor law reform bill that labor wanted. The current balance of power in Education and Labor provides no forecast of when or on what basis a bill will be in trouble on the floor of the House or in the Senate. Like Armed Services, which is tilted toward the Pentagon, Education and Labor does not accurately represent, as committees theoretically should, the body of opinion in the House as a whole.

Census Data Pop. 459,798. Central city, 6%; suburban, 5%. Median family income, $5,528; families above $15,000: 6%; families below $3,000: 28%. Median years education, 8.7.

The Voters

Median voting age 44.
Employment profile White collar, 34%. Blue collar, 47%. Service, 12%. Farm, 7%.
Ethnic groups Black, 1%.

Presidential vote

1976	Carter (D)	104,213	(61%)
	Ford (R)	66,890	(39%)
1972	Nixon (R)	93,088	(58%)
	McGovern (D)	67,062	(42%)

Rep. Carl D. Perkins (D) Elected 1948; b. Oct. 15, 1912, Hindman; home, Hindman; Caney Jr. Col., Lees Jr. Col., U. of Louisville, Jefferson School of Law, LL.B. 1935; Baptist.

Career Practicing atty., 1935–48; Ky. House of Reps., 1940; Knott Co. Atty., 1941–48; Army, WWII.

Offices 2328 RHOB, 202-225-4935. Also P.O. Bldg., Ashland 41101, 606-325-8530.

Committees *Education and Labor* (Chairman). Subcommittees: Elementary, Secondary and Vocational Education (Chairman).

Group Ratings

	ADA	COPE	PC	RPN	NFU	LCV	CFA	NAB	NSI	ACA	NTU
1978	45	67	55	27	70	–	59	17	50	23	–
1977	40	91	55	31	92	45	60	–	–	15	21
1976	60	96	69	41	83	65	91	17	60	11	16

Key Votes

1) Increase Def Spnd	FOR	6) Alaska Lands Protect	FOR	11) Delay Auto Pol Cntrl	FOR
2) B-1 Bomber	AGN	7) Water Projects Veto	AGN	12) Sugar Price Escalator	AGN
3) Cargo Preference	FOR	8) Consum Protect Agcy	AGN	13) Pub Fin Cong Cmpgns	AGN
4) Dereg Nat Gas	AGN	9) Common Situs Picket	FOR	14) ERA Ratif Recissn	FOR
5) Kemp-Roth	AGN	10) Labor Law Revision	FOR	15) Prohibt Govt Abrtns	FOR

Election Results

1978 general	Carl D. Perkins (D)	51,559	(76%)	
	Grandville Thomas (R)	15,861	(24%)	
1978 primary	Carl D. Perkins (D)	19,081	(85%)	
	One other (D)	3,401	(15%)	
1976 general	Carl D. Perkins (D)	110,450	(73%)	($2,032)
	Grandville Thomas (R)	40,381	(27%)	($0)

LOUISIANA

More than forty years ago Huey P. Long was shot and killed in the halls of the Capitol he built in Baton Rouge, but even today he remains an important influence in Louisiana politics. When he was murdered, Long had been a U.S. Senator for less than six years, and before that he had served as Governor for less than a full four-year term. In that short time, however, the Kingfish built monuments to himself and the people of Louisiana: the Capitol, Louisiana State University, a system of badly needed concrete roads, an old age pension system. Long dominated the politics of his state as no other man has done in American history. He was a national figure as well. His nebulous "share the wealth" programgenerated enough pressure to move FDR to support Social Security and the Wagner Act; he feared opposition from Long in 1936. Nor was Roosevelt the only one who believed—and feared—that Huey Long would be president one day.

Huey Long was a brilliant and irreplaceable man. But his political allies and friends have been winning office in Louisiana since the thirties. From 1937 till his death in 1972 Allen Ellender, Huey's Speaker of the Louisiana House, held the Kingfish's old seat in the U.S. Senate; and since 1948, when he reached the constitutional age of 30, the other seat has been held by Huey's son, Russell Long.

If Louisiana politics is remarkable for the influence of a man long dead, it is also remarkable for being conducted in French as well as in a uniquely accented brand of English. New Orleans retains a French or rather Creole ambiance from its original settlers before the Louisiana Purchase which brought in the uncouth Americans; and the city has a kind of lazy tolerance of the unorthodox and the illicit. Surrounded by hundreds of miles of Baptist countryside, Catholic New Orleans is another world—an outpost, as A. J. Liebling once put it, of the Levant along the Gulf of Mexico. An even more pronounced French influence can be found outside New Orleans in the bayou country south of Alexandria and west of the Mississippi River. This is Cajun country, the home of the descendants of the 4,000 Acadians expelled by the British from Nova Scotia in 1755; their story has been known to generations of schoolchildren thanks to Longfellow's "Evangeline." In present day Cajun country almost everyone is Catholic, and a unique dialect of French is spoken. Of course television, radio, and English-speaking teachers have downgraded French. But today there is a strong Cajun pride movement, and it appears that Cajun culture, with its crawfish-based cuisine, will survive.

In Louisiana, elections are sometimes decided along racial lines, as they have been in so many Southern states. But the electorate also sometimes divides along lines of language and religion, and sometimes according to voters' attitudes toward the Longs—which can be summarized by saying that most rich people hate the Longs and most poor people, of whatever race or religion, love them. In addition to all these cross-currents, any observer of Louisiana politics must keep in mind that the game down here is not always played by League of Women Voters rules. Bribery and election fraud have determined election outcomes in the past—Huey Long, for one, was not picky about the means he used to achieve his ends—and no one is surprised to hear politicians accusing each other of such tactics; they may both be right. This is not a civic culture that demands or expects honesty in politics.

One election that was decided along basic economic lines more than anything else was the 1976 presidential contest. Gerald Ford, who had been leading in the polls throughout the campaign, carried all the better off parts of the state. He had a big lead in Jefferson Parish (parish is the Louisiana word for county) outside New Orleans, a nearly all-white, well-to-do suburban area that now casts three-quarters as many votes as the city itself. Ford also carried the oil-rich, heavily Protestant cities of Shreveport and Monroe in northern Louisiana and the oil-rich city of Lafayette, right in the middle of Cajun country. But these were not enough for victory. Jimmy Carter won with virtually unanimous support from blacks and with strong majorities in New Orleans and in the smaller, poorer parishes in both the Catholic South and the Protestant north. It was the same kind of coalition which used to give Long candidates their majorities.

Louisiana's outgoing Governor, Edwin Edwards, was elected with an entirely different coalition. Here religion was the key factor. Edwards, despite his name, is a Cajun. In both the primary against Shreveport state Senator Bennett Johnston and in the general election against Jefferson Parish Congressman David Treen, Edwards won with big margins in the Cajun country, a smaller edge in the New Orleans area, and majorities from black voters. Edwards has been by most criteria a successful Governor. He won reelection easily in November 1975, under a new law he had engineered. (Now for all elections Louisiana has a primary in which all candidates compete, Republicans as well as Democrats; if one candidate has a majority, he wins without a runoff.) Edwards has also dominated the legislature. He has achieved some national notice, in such diverse roles as being a spokesman for the oil industry and nominating Jerry Brown for president in New York in 1976. Edwards has also survived allegations of scandal. It was said that he was a beneficiary, while in Congress, of largesse from agents of the South Korean government, and he admitted that Mrs. Edwards, who served briefly by his appointment in the Senate, had pocketed –10,000 in cash from Tongsun Park without bothering, the Governor said, to tell him about it. There is some feeling in Louisiana that Edwards, who prides himself on his flashily expensive wardrobe and likes to visit Las Vegas, would not survive a complete examination of his personal finances. He leaves office with a handsome pension early in 1980.

The race to succeed him is, at this writing, wide open. Congressman David Treen has been running hard for some time and has a good chance, with his Jefferson Parish and Republican base, of being one of the top two candidates in the November 1979 primary. The Lieutenant Governor, James Fitzmorris, is a veteran of Louisiana politics whose support in the past has tended to come from segregationists. A very different type of politician is House Speaker Bubba Henry, who also is considered a strong competitor. Other candidates include well-financed Democrat Edgar Mouton and Democrats Paul Hardy and Louis Lambert.

Ironically, just as Louisiana got its first Cajun governor in decades, the southern, Catholic part of the state lost its traditional hold on one of the state's Senate seats. This was in 1972, when Allen Ellender died at age 82 in the midst of the primary campaign. Only one candidate had filed against Ellender, Bennett Johnston, and although former Governor John McKeithen made a halfhearted race as an Independent, Johnston was elected easily at the age of 40.

Johnston is a man with that easy charm that so many Southern politicians seem born with. He is popular with his colleagues, who made him Chairman of the Democratic Senatorial Campaign Committee for a two-year term in 1974. His voting record generally has been what one might expect from a man from the comfortable, country club precincts of Shreveport who wants to get on with Senate Democrats. He has a seat on the Appropriations Committee, but he has made his greatest mark so far as a member of the Energy Committee. Louisiana is the second biggest oil producing state, after Texas, and Johnston proved to be an extremely active and competent advocate of positions backed by the oil companies. On the long-stalled conference committee on energy, he was the main advocate of deregulation of natural gas; and he mastered the intricate minutiae of the bill to the point that even those on the other side were almost relying on his expertise.

That performance might have helped him when he sought reelection in 1978—or perhaps it kept him occupied and prevented him from making as strong an effort as he might have. With opposition only from a right wing state legislator from Baton Rouge, Johnston had every reason to be confident. But as it turned out, he won in the initial primary with 59% of the vote—a solid, but not overwhelming, performance. There is a long time before Johnston's seat is up in 1984, but he will have to show more strength in order to deter strong opposition from running against him.

The state's other senator, Russell Long, has held about as safe a seat as there is in Congress. At 60 he had 30 years of seniority and the prospect of continued reelection; he won with only token opposition in 1974 and does not seem likely to attract a strong opponent in 1980. But Long's

Senate career has had its ups and downs. One up was in 1965, when he was elected Majority Whip by an unusual coalition of Southerners and liberals. But after four stormy years and some personal problems since overcome, Long lost that post in an upset to Edward Kennedy, who himself had personal problems and lost it to Robert Byrd in 1971.

Today Long's chief source of power is his position as Chairman of the Senate Finance Committee, a post he has held since 1965. Long no longer monopolizes committee staff resources by refusing to create subcommittees, as he once did, nor is as much of the committee's business conducted in secret session. But Russell Long remains very much the dominant force on Finance, mainly through legislative competence and force of personality. At a committee markup session or conference committee, Long likes to good humoredly josh his colleagues and maintain complete control of the proceedings. Reporters can hear the laughter through the closed doors, and sometimes the bell Long has taken to ringing to signal another billion dollars worth of tax cuts.

Finance has an impressive jurisdiction: all tax measures, including Social Security and Medicare. Under Long the Committee's power to make major financial decisions for the nation has increased. With steady inflation and progressive tax rates, the effective tax rate on individuals tends to rise each year—unless something is done about it. The man who decides what that something is, is Russell Long. In effect, he is redetermining every year the incidence of our taxes and therefore the distribution of income. He doesn't do this singlehandedly, but he certainly has more influence than anyone else in Congress. Of course it looks like Long is cutting taxes—but that is not necessarily the case.

Long has some even more ambitious ideas. He has presided over vast increases in Social Security taxes and nominal cuts of the income tax. Now he is considering a different tax altogether: the value added tax, a major revenue device. This is actually a sales tax levied at every stage of production and distribution; when a consumer buys something, the tax is included in the price, and so is never visible. That and the comparative ease of collection make it attractive; the fact that it would tend to tax the less affluent more than the income tax does makes it less attractive to many. We are probably a long way away from enactment of a value added tax, but no one should underestimate the power of an idea that has Russell Long behind it. He was the first to push the idea of financing federal elections through a $1 checkoff on the income tax, and he keeps pushing a proposal to allow employees to buy shares in their companies. Long can also be a powerful opponent. It was his Finance Committee which killed the Nixon Administration's Family Assistance Program, and his opposition helped to defeat the Carter energy program in the Senate. Long remains on cordial terms with many top Administration officials, but that did not stop him from voting against the Panama Canal Treaty.

Russell Long is not the popular national figure his father was, but his career has lasted much longer now and promises to continue for some time. On some issues, there is little resemblance to Huey Long. The Kingfish was always a big opponent of the oil companies, who were only beginning to be important in the Louisiana of his day. Russell Long, who has major profitable oil investments himself, is one of oil's strongest supporters in the Senate. Nor does Russell Long concentrate only on measures which distribute money directly to the poor; he also wants incentives for investment to be high. But certainly Russell Long has much of his father's brilliance and legislative skill; and he has much of Huey's popularity without being controversial.

Census Data Pop. 3,643,180; 1.80% of U.S. total, 20th largest; Central city, 31%; suburban, 23%. Median family income, $7,527; 43d highest; families above $15,000: 13%; families below $3,000: 19%. Median years education, 10.8.

1977 Share of Federal Tax Burden $4,940,000,000; 1.43% of U.S. total, 22d largest.

1977 Share of Federal Outlays $5,477,699,000; 1.38% of U.S. total, 25th largest. Per capita federal spending, $1,445.

DOD	$1,064,427,000	28th (1.16%)	HEW	$2,225,116,000	23d (1.51%)
ERDA	$2,060,000	41st (0.03%)	HUD	$71,000,000	20th (1.68%)
NASA	$87,376,000	8th (2.21%)	VA	$312,491,000	21st (1.63%)
DOT	$255,659,000	18th (1.79%)	EPA	$68,184,000	25th (0.83%)
DOC	$157,224,000	14th (1.89%)	RevS	$178,273,000	13th (2.11%)
DOI	$18,436,000	39th (0.40%)	Debt	$187,015,000	23d (0.62%)
USDA	$381,953,000	19th (1.92%)	Other	$468,485,000	

Economic Base Finance, insurance and real estate; agriculture, notably cattle, soybeans, rice and dairy products; oil and gas extraction, especially oil and gas field services; food and kindred products; chemicals and allied products, especially industrial chemicals; transportation equipment, especially ship building and repairing.

Political Line-up Governor, Edwin W. Edwards (D). Senators, Russell B. Long (D) and J. Bennett Johnston, Jr. (D). Representatives, 8 (5 D and 3 R). State Senate (38 D); State House(97 D, 8 R).

The Voters

Registration 1,821,494 Total. 1,672,603 D (92%); 80,869 R (4%); 68,022 Other (4%).
Median voting age 41
Employment profile White collar, 45%. Blue collar, 36%. Service, 16%. Farm, 3%.
Ethnic groups Black, 30%. Spanish, 2%. French speaking, 16%. Total foreign stock, 4%.

Presidential vote

1976	Carter (D)	661,365	(53%)
	Ford (R)	587,446	(47%)
1972	Nixon (R)	686,852	(70%)
	McGovern (D)	298,142	(30%)

Sen. Russell B. Long (D) Elected 1948, seat up 1980; b. Nov. 3, 1918, Shreveport; home, Baton Rouge; La. St. U., B.A. 1941, LL.B. 1942; Methodist.

Career Navy, WWII; Practicing atty., 1945–47.

Offices 217 RSOB, 202-224-4623. Also 220 Fed. Bldg., 750 Fla. Blvd., Baton Rouge 70801, 504-387-0181, ext. 445.

Committees *Commerce, Science, and Transportation* (3d). Subcommittees: Merchant Marine and Tourism; Science, Technology, and Space; Surface Transportation (Chairman).

Finance Chairman. Subcommittees: Social Security; Tourism and Sugar; Public Assistance.

Group Ratings

	ADA	COPE	PC	RPN	NFU	LCV	CFA	NAB	NSI	ACA	NTU
1978	25	28	28	40	70	12	35	40	44	47	–
1977	15	59	15	44	58	–	8	–	–	46	23
1976	25	31	13	44	82	25	7	46	90	55	29

Key Votes

1) Warnke Nom	FOR	6) Egypt-Saudi Arms	FOR	11) Hosptl Cost Contnmnt	AGN
2) Neutron Bomb	DNV	7) Draft Restr Pardon	FOR	12) Clinch River Reactor	FOR
3) Waterwy User Fee	AGN	8) Wheat Price Support	FOR	13) Pub Fin Cong Cmpgns	AGN
4) Dereg Nat Gas	FOR	9) Panama Canal Treaty	FOR	14) ERA Ratif Recissn	AGN
5) Kemp-Roth	AGN	10) Labor Law Rev Clot	AGN	15) Med Necssy Abrtns	FOR

Election Results

1974 general	Russell B. Long (D), unopposed			($498,774)
1974 primary	Russell B. Long (D)	520,606	(75%)	
	Two others (D)	175,881	(25%)	
1968 general	Russell B. Long (D), unopposed			

Sen. J. Bennett Johnston, Jr. (D) Elected 1972, seat up 1978; b. June 10, 1932, Shreveport; home, Shreveport; Wash. & Lee U., La. St. U., LL.B. 1956; Baptist.

Career Army, 1956–59; Practicing atty.; La. House of Reps., 1964–68, Floor Ldr.; La. Senate, 1968–72.

Offices 421 RSOB, 202-224-5824. Also Rm. 1010, Hale Boggs Fed. Bldg., 500 Camp St., New Orleans 70130, 504-589-2427, and 7A12 New Fed. Bldg. and Courthouse, 500 Fannin St., Shreveport 71102, 318-226-5085.

Committees *Appropriations* (10th). Subcommittees: Defense; Energy and Water Development (Chairman); Foreign Operations; Interior and Related Agencies; Military Construction.

Budget (6th).

Energy and Natural Resources (3d). Subcommittees: Energy Regulation (Chairman); Energy Research and Development; Parks, Recreation, and Renewable Resources.

Group Ratings

	ADA	COPE	PC	RPN	NFU	LCV	CFA	NAB	NSI	ACA	NTU
1978	15	13	18	20	71	26	15	64	78	60	–
1977	25	58	25	40	33	–	32	–	–	52	25
1976	15	53	15	41	75	22	28	73	75	56	42

Key Votes

1) Warnke Nom	FOR	6) Egypt-Saudi Arms	FOR	11) Hosptl Cost Contnmnt	AGN
2) Neutron Bomb	FOR	7) Draft Restr Pardon	FOR	12) Clinch River Reactor	FOR
3) Waterwy User Fee	AGN	8) Wheat Price Support	AGN	13) Pub Fin Cong Cmpgns	AGN
4) Dereg Nat Gas	FOR	9) Panama Canal Treaty	AGN	14) ERA Ratif Recissn	AGN
5) Kemp-Roth	FOR	10) Labor Law Rev Clot	AGN	15) Med Necssy Abrtns	AGN

Election Results

1978 primary	J. Bennett Johnston, Jr. (D)	498,773	(59%)	($857,860)
	Louis Jenkins (D)	340,896	(41%)	($327,340)
1972 general	J. Bennett Johnson, Jr. (D)	598,987	(57%)	($511,616)
	John J. McKeithen (Ind.)	250,161	(24%)	($394,510)
	Ben C. Toledano (R)	206,846	(20%)	($116,347)

Gov. Edwin W. Edwards (D) Elected Feb. 1, 1972, term expires March, 1980; b. Aug. 7, 1927, Marksville; La. St. U., LL.B. 1949; Catholic.

Career Practicing atty.; Crowley City Cncl., 1954–62; La. Senate, 1964–65; U.S. House of Reps., 1965–72.

Offices P.O. Box 44004, Baton Rouge 70804 504-389-5281.

Election Results

1975 primary	Edwin W. Edwards (D)	750,107	(62%)
	Robert G. Jones (D)	292,220	(24%)
	Wade O. Martin, Jr. (D)	146,368	(12%)
	Three others (D)	14,309	(1%)
1972 general	Edwin W. Edwards (D)	641,146	(57%)
	David C. Treen (R)	480,424	(43%)

FIRST DISTRICT

The 1st congressional district of Louisiana includes the northern and eastern parts of New Orleans, two parishes astride the Mississippi River, and one once rural and now suburbanized parish north of Lake Pontchartrain. This is not the picturesque, tourist's part of New Orleans. The district's boundary passes just north of the French Quarter; it includes most of the city's port facilities and is otherwise almost entirely residential. These are neighborhoods of basementless houses, built on oozy land below sea level, where the ordinary people of New Orleans live. Some, on streets stretching to Lake Pontchartrain, are modern fifties houses, the homes of the city's solid middle class; others are rickety frame homes for poor blacks or whites. (New Orleans has no defined black ghetto; there are blacks in most parts of the city.) Farther east, but still within the city limits, is a swamp that reaches to the Mississippi state border; it is just beginning to be reclaimed, and to be populated with giant apartment complexes and shopping centers.

A more famous part of the 1st are the two small river parishes, St. Bernard and Plaquemines. Much of St. Bernard is now suburbanized, but just downriver in the delta lands of the Mississippi River are insular communities of French-speaking river pilots and shrimp fishermen. Politics is a serious business here. For years Plaquemines was controlled by Leander Perez. Once a Huey Long supporter, Perez was such an ardent segregationist that he was excommunicated by the Catholic Church. But he could still deliver virtually all the votes in Plaquemines. Today his son controls the machine with only slightly reduced effectiveness. Thus in the 1976 general election, Plaquemines went 74% for Republican congressional candidate Robert Livingston; in the June 1977 special election, Livingston received only 23% against a Plaquemines-endorsed Democrat; while in September 1978 Livingston got 95% here.

What is at stake in Plaquemines is no longer segregation. This is rich oil and sulphur country, with large offshore deposits; local landowners, among them the Perezes, are in a position to become very rich indeed. Obviously it is convenient in such circumstances to have iron control of the local government. St. Bernard Parish used to have machine control almost as solid as Plaquemines; but there has been too much suburban growth now, diluting the vote power of the small communities which are the bulwarks of the machine. The people who have moved in are from white working class communities in New Orleans; they are inclined to vote for candidates like Jimmy Carter and George Wallace.

For 36 years the 1st district was represented by F. Edward Hebert, who served for four years (1970–74) as Chairman of the House Armed Services Committee. A hawkish exponent of military spending, Hebert had his pet projects in New Orleans, including a military hospital closed after his retirement for lack of use. After the 1974 elections, he lost his chairmanship and retired in 1976.

There followed one of the most turbulent and expensive series of congressional elections in recent years. The scenario is as follows:

* October 1976: St. Bernard state legislator Richard Tonry upsets New Orleans Councilman James Moreau in the Democratic primary by 352 votes out of nearly 100,000 cast. Tonry's lead comes mostly from his 72% win in St. Bernard Parish. Moreau supporters complain about the validity of the count and about Tonry's campaign practices.

* November 1976: Tonry edges Republican candidate Robert Livingston, again with a huge percentage (70%) in St. Bernard Parish. Former Baton Rouge Congressman John Rarick has nearly 10% of the vote. Again there are allegations of vote fraud.

* Early 1977: Tonry is investigated in the House on charges brought by Moreau of massive vote fraud. Members seem reluctant to expel Tonry: it is hard to gauge the facts from a distance, and this would not be the first time vote counts in Louisiana were not entirely accurate. Apparently under pressure, Tonry resigns in May and announces that he will run for reelection. "Keep my seat warm," he advises Speaker O'Neill, "I'll be back."

* June 1977: Tonry is defeated in the primary by New Orleans state legislator Ron Faucheux. Tonry still carries St. Bernard, but Faucheux has big margins in Plaquemines and New Orleans. Meanwhile in the Republican primary Livingston, who has already put on an extensive and expensive campaign as a Republican, gets 88% of the vote to 12% for James Moreau, who had switched parties in one of the least shrewd political moves of the seventies.

* August 1977: Livingston decisively beats Faucheux in the special election, 51%–37%. Another 12% goes to an Independent with labor support who claims that Faucheux voted with

budget-cutters in the legislature. Rumors are spread that Faucheux, who is very young and looks younger, is a homosexual. But the main reason for the outcome is that Livingston ran a professional, intelligent, and expensive campaign. Altogether in the 1976–78 period he will have spent more than one million dollars.

* April 1978: Tonry is convicted on eleven counts of campaign funds misuse, including an allegation that he received an illegal $5,000 contribution while marching behind Jimmy Carter in a parade. He is sentenced to jail. In years which see scores of hardworking, ambitious, clean-cut candidates, Tonry stands out as a kind of shameless desperado—and a rather foolish one. For if he had not been so greedy and ambitious, he would still presumably be enjoying his tenure in the Louisiana legislature and an undoubtedly successful St. Bernard Parish legal practice.

* September 1978: Livingston, opposed now by the same man who ran as an Independent in August 1977, is reelected with 86% of the vote. Plaquemines, after voting for Faucheux, is back in his corner.

There is not much more to say. Livingston, bearer of a proud old Louisiana name, has generally voted with Republicans in the House and has attended well to local matters. His reelection margin suggests that the hurricane of political turbulence which hit this district has subsided and that Livingston will probably be reelected routinely in future years.

Census Data Pop. 454,873. Central city, 69%; suburban, 25%. Median family income, $8,655; families above $15,000: 18%; families below $3,000: 14%. Median years education, 11.3.

The Voters

Median voting age 42.
Employment profile White collar, 52%. Blue collar, 34%. Service, 14%. Farm, –%.
Ethnic groups Black, 31%. Spanish, 4%. Total foreign stock, 7%. Italy, 2%; French-speaking, 8%.

Presidential vote

1976	Carter (D)	83,061	(51%)
	Ford (R)	78,928	(49%)
1972	Nixon (R)	91,347	(71%)
	McGovern (D)	37,676	(29%)

Rep. Bob Livingston (R) Elected Aug. 27, 1977; b. April 30, 1943, Colorado Springs, Col.; home, New Orleans; Tulane U., B.A. 1967, J.D. 1968; Episcopalian.

Career Practicing atty.; Asst. U.S. Atty., 1970–73; Chief Spec. Prosecutor, Orleans Parish Dist. Atty.'s Ofc., 1974–75; Chief Prosecutor, La. Atty. Gen.'s Ofc. Organized Crime Unit, 1975–76.

Offices 130 CHOB, 202-225-3015. Also 642 F. Edward Hebert Bldg., 610 South St., New Orleans 70130, 504-589-2753.

Committees *Public Works and Transportation* (12th). Subcommittees: Public Buildings and Grounds; Surface Transportation; Water Resources.

Standards of Official Conduct (3d).

Group Ratings

	ADA	COPE	PC	RPN	NFU	LCV	CFA	NAB	NSI	ACA	NTU
1978	10	15	10	60	20	–	23	71	100	92	–
1977	0	29	0	60	75	0	0	–	–	78	0

Key Votes

1) Increase Def Spnd	NE	6) Alaska Lands Protect	AGN	11) Delay Auto Pol Cntrl	NE
2) B-1 Bomber	FOR	7) Water Projects Veto	AGN	12) Sugar Price Escalator	FOR
3) Cargo Preference	FOR	8) Consum Protect Agcy	AGN	13) Pub Fin Cong Cmpgns	AGN
4) Dereg Nat Gas	NE	9) Common Situs Picket	NE	14) ERA Ratif Recissn	FOR
5) Kemp-Roth	FOR	10) Labor Law Revision	AGN	15) Prohibt Govt Abrtns	NE

Election Results

1978 primary	Robert L. Livingston (R)	89,469	(86%)	($347,844)
	Sanford Krasnoff (D)	14,373	(14%)	
1977 special election	Robert L. Livingston (R)	56,121	(51%)	
	Ron Faucheux (D)	40,802	(37%)	
	Sanford Krasnoff (I)	12,665	(12%)	
1977 primary	Robert L. Livingston (R)	5,551	(88%)	
	James A. Moreau (R)	776	(12%)	
1976 general	Richard A. Tonry (D)	61,652	(52%)	($220,495)
	Robert L. Livingston (R)	56,679	(48%)	($154,388)

SECOND DISTRICT

Since New Orleans fell into American hands with the Louisiana Purchase of 1803, it has been one of the nation's most distinctive cities. The heritage of the city's French and Spanish past can still be seen in the French Quarter, where carefully preserved old houses with their iron balconies exist amid the swelter of tourist-packed bars and some of the nation's finest restaurants. New Orleans remains our second busiest port, adding to its historic role as the outlet of the Mississippi Valley and entrepot of Latin American trade the new function of sending out Louisiana's oil and petroleum products in huge tankers.

It is the older, more distinctive parts of New Orleans that make up most of Louisiana's 2d congressional district. It begins at the French Quarter, its nineteenth century houses intact because the Americans built a new downtown west of its boundary at Canal Street, away from the snobbish Creoles. Beyond is the old slum known as the Irish Channel—New Orleans had more European immigrants than any other part of the South—and the Garden District, with its antebellum houses covered with the tangle of vines and Spanish moss. Some of the country's last trolley cars still run out to the Uptown section of large houses near Tulane University. The 2d includes most of New Orleans's richest citizens, but more than half the residents of this part of the city are black; and the blacks here, unlike those in rural Louisiana, have a long, steady tradition of voting on election day. They have provided most of the votes to elect the city's first black mayor, Ernest "Dutch" Morial, as well as his predecessor, Moon Landrieu.

Besides this part of New Orleans, the 2d district takes in part of suburban Jefferson Parish. The parish extends south through the swamps to Barataria Bay, where the pirate Jean Lafitte hung out before he ventured forth to help Andrew Jackson whip the British in 1815. The 2d's portion of Jefferson includes the old, small cities along the banks of the Mississippi River which gave the parish, once upon a time, a reputation for vice and corruption. But the district does not include the prosperous, fast-growing, politically conservative suburb of Metairie just south of Lake Pontchartrain.

From 1941 to 1943 and 1947 to 1972—28 years altogether—the 2d district was represented by Hale Boggs. He won his first race as a rebel against the local machine; and after a spirited struggle, in 1971 became House Majority Leader—just a step away from the Speaker's chair. Boggs's career ended suddenly in October 1972, when he was lost in a plane crash while campaigning with freshman Nick Begich of Alaska. Boggs was a mercurial man: a stirring oldtime orator, a gifted trader of votes, a Southerner who had a strong liberal record and had even dared to support the Civil Rights Acts of 1965 and 1968. Ironically, Boggs died just as the Louisiana legislature had finally drawn a safe district for him. In 1964 and 1968 he had only barely survived strong challenges from Republican David Treen; in the latter year his civil rights votes hurt him so much in the white neighborhoods of New Orleans and Jefferson Parish that he won with only 51%. The current 2d, which was 40% black in 1970, reelected him posthumously in 1972.

The Majority Leader's successor in the 2d district is his widow, Corinne Claiborne Boggs, universally known as Lindy, who won a 1973 special election with 81%. Sometimes when a congressman dies, his widow is elected as a temporary expedient; that is not the case here. For many years Lindy Boggs was rated as one of the most knowledgeable of congressional wives and enjoyed wide respect in Washington and New Orleans. The worst anyone had to say about her was that she seemed sometimes just a little too nice to people. She has the manners of a girl raised on a plantation (which she was) and the political savvy of one who has been campaigning in New Orleans and living in Washington for thirty-odd years (which she has).

Lindy Boggs's talents were on view to the nation when she served as Permanent Chairman of the 1976 Democratic National Convention. She handled her duties gracefully and efficiently, keeping the proceedings moving along at the pace required for television viewers without giving delegates the feelings they were being denied an opportunity to have a say. She showed the capacity to have handled a considerably more acrimonious meeting than the 1976 Convention turned out to be. In the House she does not have great seniority, but does have a seat on the Appropriations Committee. Boggs can be counted as a pretty sure vote for the House leadership.

Census Data Pop. 454,772. Central city, 61%; suburban, 39%. Median family income, $7,611; families above $15,000: 14%; families below $3,000: 18%. Median years education, 10.5.

The Voters

Median voting age 42.
Employment profile White collar, 47%. Blue collar, 35%. Service, 18%. Farm, –%.
Ethnic groups Black, 40%. Spanish, 4%. Total foreign stock, 8%. Italy, 1%; French-speaking, 11%.

Presidential vote

1976	Carter (D)	67,964	(56%)
	Ford (R)	54,014	(44%)
1972	Nixon (R)	65,036	(60%)
	McGovern (D)	43,702	(40%)

Rep. Lindy Boggs (D) Elected Mar. 20, 1973; b. Mar. 13, 1916, Brunswick Plantation; home, New Orleans; Sophie Newcomb Col. of Tulane U., B.A. 1935; Catholic.

Career Public school teacher; Gen. Mgr., campaigns of U.S. Rep. Hale Boggs; Co-Chm., Presidental Inaugural Balls, 1961, 1965.

Offices 1524 LHOB, 202-225-6636. Also 1012 Hale Boggs Bldg., 500 Camp St., New Orleans 70130, 504-589-2274.

Committees *Appropriations* (26th). Subcommittees: HUD-Independent Agencies; Energy and Water Development.

Group Ratings

	ADA	COPE	PC	RPN	NFU	LCV	CFA	NAB	NSI	ACA	NTU
1978	45	65	43	50	60	–	50	0	70	31	–
1977	30	76	40	31	83	33	45	–	–	15	21
1976	30	73	36	50	58	43	36	0	78	31	5

Key Votes

1) Increase Def Spnd	AGN	6) Alaska Lands Protect	FOR	11) Delay Auto Pol Cntrl	FOR
2) B-1 Bomber	FOR	7) Water Projects Veto	AGN	12) Sugar Price Escalator	FOR
3) Cargo Preference	FOR	8) Consum Protect Agcy	FOR	13) Pub Fin Cong Cmpgns	AGN
4) Dereg Nat Gas	FOR	9) Common Situs Picket	DNV	14) ERA Ratif Recissn	AGN
5) Kemp-Roth	AGN	10) Labor Law Revision	FOR	15) Prohibt Govt Abrtns	FOR

Election Results

1978 primary	Lindy Boggs (D)	57,056	(87%)	($60,404)
	Two others (No Party)	8,411	(13%)	
1976 general	Lindy Boggs (D)	85,923	(93%)	($66,850)
	Jules W. Hillery (I)	6,904	(7%)	($163)

THIRD DISTRICT

One of the major phenomena of Louisiana politics in the seventies has been the rise of the Republican Party. As late as 1972 no Republican held a significant public office in Louisiana. Yet by the end of the seventies the Republicans had carried the state for president once and had come close a second time, had elected congressmen in three out of the eight districts, and had competed seriously in two gubernatorial elections. Much of the credit for this development goes to David Treen, a persistent and dedicated Republican; and to his constituents in the 3d congressional district, the electoral base for the Republican Party in Louisiana.

On first glance, the 3d looks like unlikely territory for a Republican. Most of the physical expanse of the district is Cajun country—miles of bayous and swamp giving way from time to time for little roads and crossroad towns where French remains the first language. But this is not an area that looks only to the past. It is also one of the nation's major oil-producing areas, and many of the people here work in local oil production or on offshore wells. Indeed, the oil industry indirectly and inadvertently may have been responsible for preserving much of Cajun culture, for people here, unlike those in many other rural Southern areas, have not found it necessary to migrate to the big cities to make a living.

The Cajun country is Democratic, although the oil-based economy makes it more willing to support a Republican who favors measures supported by the oil industry. But there is another important part of the 3d district, which gives it its unique character. This is the major portion of suburban Jefferson Parish, just west of New Orleans, which casts more than 40% of the district's votes. Here the lowlands between the Mississippi River levees and Lake Pontchartrain have been drained and subdivided and filled with the kind of middle income people who have little use for either the charms or the drawbacks of New Orleans. The 3d's share of the suburb of Metairie is 99% white and pleased to remain that way; it votes as heavily Republican in most elections as Orange County, California.

Metairie is the home and political base of Congressman David Treen. He carried the area back in the sixties, when he ran three times against 2d district Congressman Hale Boggs and almost beat him twice; he carried it solidly when he ran unsuccessfully for governor in 1972. Most important, he got 73% of the vote in Jefferson Parish later in 1972 when he ran for Congress. The incumbent Democrat had retired, the Democratic nominee was from a rural parish far from New Orleans, and Treen took advantage of his opportunity and was finally elected.

Once in office he improved his position to the point that he had no opposition at all in the 1978 election. He serves on the House Armed Services Committee and has had one of the most solidly conservative voting records in Congress. For 1979 Treen's goal is again the governorship. Under Louisiana's unusual system, all candidates run, with their party labels, in a single initial primary; if no one gets 50%, then the top two finishers run in a runoff general election. With his Jefferson Parish support and as the only Republican running against several Democrats, Treen at this writing has an excellent chance of making the runoff and by no means an inconsiderable chance of winning the general election. If elected, he would inject a note of ideological purity into a state government known better for accommodation to vested interest and a relaxed attitude toward ethical questions.

Census Data Pop. 455,575. Central city, 0%; suburban, 35%. Median family income, $9,146; families above $15,000: 16%; families below $3,000: 11%. Median years education, 11.3.

The Voters

Median voting age 38.
Employment profile White collar, 50%. Blue collar, 37%. Service, 11%. Farm, 2%.
Ethnic groups Black, 15%. Spanish, 2%. Total foreign stock, 5%. Italy, 1%; French-speaking, 29%.

Presidential vote

1976	Carter (D)	76,664	(45%)
	Ford (R)	92,277	(55%)
1972	Nixon (R)	102,047	(76%)
	McGovern (D)	31,647	(24%)

Rep. David C. Treen (R) Elected 1972; b. July 16, 1928, Baton Route; home, Metairie; Tulane U., B.A. 1948, LL.B. 1950; Methodist.

Career Practicing atty., 1950–51, 1957–72; Air Force, 1951–52; V.P. and Legal Counsel, Simplex Manufacturing Corp., 1952–57; Repub. nominee for U.S. House of Reps., 1962, 1964, 1968; Repub. nominee for Gov., 1972.

Offices 2404 RHOB, 202-225-4031. Also Fed. Bldg., Suite 107, Houma 70360, 504-876-3033.

Committees *Armed Services* (5th). Subcommittees: Investigations; Military Personnel.

Merchant Marine and Fisheries (4th). Subcommittees: Coast Guard and Navigation; Merchant Marine; Panama Canal.

Group Ratings

	ADA	COPE	PC	RPN	NFU	LCV	CFA	NAB	NSI	ACA	NTU
1978	5	11	13	73	20	–	27	100	100	92	–
1977	0	9	10	58	55	9	0	–	–	85	37
1976	0	14	7	56	18	6	0	92	89	88	64

Key Votes

1) Increase Def Spnd	FOR	6) Alaska Lands Protect	AGN	11) Delay Auto Pol Cntrl	FOR
2) B-1 Bomber	DNV	7) Water Projects Veto	AGN	12) Sugar Price Escalator	FOR
3) Cargo Preference	AGN	8) Consum Protect Agcy	AGN	13) Pub Fin Cong Cmpgns	AGN
4) Dereg Nat Gas	FOR	9) Common Situs Picket	AGN	14) ERA Ratif Recissn	FOR
5) Kemp-Roth	FOR	10) Labor Law Revision	AGN	15) Prohibt Govt Abrtns	FOR

Election Results

1978 general	David C. Treen (R), unopposed			($48,855)
1978 primary	David C. Treen (R), unopposed			
1976 general	David C. Treen (R)	109,135	(73%)	($66,270)
	David H. Schevermann, Sr. (D)	39,728	(27%)	($10,615)

FOURTH DISTRICT

Northern Louisiana is part of the Deep South, with none of the Creole ambiance of New Orleans or the French accents of the Cajun country. For 150 years Baptist farmers have worked the upcountry hills around Shreveport, the commercial center of the area and the largest city in the 4th congressional district. Shreveport and the adjacent suburban areas form almost precisely half of the 4th district, and in recent years they have become rather different in political attitudes from the rest of the district.

For the rural parishes remain wedded to a kind of Deep South attachment to the Democratic Party. To be sure, they were unhappy enough with civil rights and the Great Society to have abandoned candidates like Hubert Humphrey and George McGovern; but they were Democratic enough to have supported George Wallace rather than Richard Nixon and to have voted for Jimmy Carter. (There are blacks here, but not enough to carry any parish for one candidate or another.)

Shreveport started off as part of the same subculture, simply the market town for the adjacent agricultural parishes. But in the forties oil was found here and population grew substantially, and today Shreveport is more like the small oil towns of east Texas than the rural territory that surrounds it. The newly rich are closely acquainted with the virtues of the free enterprise system (little attention is given the subsidies the federal government has given oil industry over the years) and bring a kind of doctrinaire free market philosophy to politics. Traditional labels mean little to them, and they are rather more comfortable supporting Republicans than Democrats. Thus Shreveport was pretty solidly for Gerald Ford in the 1976 election, even as the rural parishes were going for Jimmy Carter.

The differing political preferences of the different parts of the 4th district had little effect on congressional elections so long as Joe Waggoner was running. A Democrat first elected in 1960, Waggoner by dint of talent and hard work had become the unofficial leader of conservative Southern Democrats in the House and of opponents of tax reform and backers of the oil companies' positions on the House Ways and Means Committee. Considered shrewd, candid, and knowledgeable, Waggoner was something of a power in Washington; he did not have significant opposition in the 4th district. But his kind of Democrat was steadily losing power in the House, and in 1978 Waggoner retired.

This set up a battle among four serious candidates, and in effect between the two different parts of the district. The September primary in Louisiana has all the candidates, with their party labels, running against each other. Here there was virtually a three-way tie among Claude "Buddy" Leach, a Democrat, Jimmy Wilson, a Democrat-turned-Republican, and Buddy Roemer, son of an important figure in Governor Edwin Edwards's administration. Roemer was eliminated, setting up a contest between the rural-based Leach and Wilson, whose home base is near Shreveport. Leach had personal wealth to draw on, but a record as a leader in the legislature which included support of tax increases. Wilson had headed a state right-to-work drive, but also hoped to appeal to black voters because he had walked his children across picket lines to integrated schools. But the cleavage turned out to be on rural-urban lines. Wilson carried the two parishes around Shreveport; Leach carried the rest of the district. Leach had led Wilson in September by 169 votes; he led in November by 266. This was one of the most closely contested races in the nation, and obviously nothing definitive can be said about future contests here.

Census Data Pop. 455,272. Central city, 40%; suburban, 25%. Median family income, $7,336; families above $15,000: 11%; families below $3,000: 19%. Median years education, 11.5.

The Voters

Median voting age 41.
Employment profile White collar, 44%. Blue collar, 37%. Service, 17%. Farm, 2%.
Ethnic groups Black, 31%. Spanish, 1%. Total foreign stock, 3%.

Presidential vote

1976	Carter (D)	66,125	(46%)
	Ford (R)	78,365	(54%)
1972	Nixon (R)	89,754	(75%)
	McGovern (D)	29,203	(25%)

Rep. Claude (Buddy) **Leach** (D) Elected 1978; b. Mar. 30, 1933, Leesville; home, Leesville; L.S.U., B.S. 1953, J.D. 1963; Episcopalian.

Career Army; Practicing atty.; La. House of Reps., 1967, 1970–78.

Offices 1229 LHOB, 202-225-2777.

Committees *Armed Services* (25th). Subcommittees: Procurement and Military Nuclear Systems; Military Compensation.

Small Business (24th). Subcommittees: SBA and SBIC Authority and General Small Business Problems; Access to Equity Capital and Business Opportunities.

Group Ratings: Newly Elected

Key Votes: Newly Elected

Election Results

1978 general	Claude Leach (D)	65,583	(50%)	($771,303)
	Jimmy Wilson (R)	65,317	(50%)	($402,713)
1978 primary	Claude Leach (D)	35,010	(27%)	
	Jimmy Wilson (R)	34,841	(27%)	
	Buddy Roemer (D)	33,302	(26%)	($526,618)
	Loy Weaver (D)	17,396	(13%)	($127,225)
	Five others (D)	9,523	(7%)	
1976 general	Joe D. Wagoner, Jr. (D), unopposed			($41,638)

FIFTH DISTRICT

The upcountry 5th congressional district of Louisiana, the state's most rural, is part of the Deep South. Aside from the small city of Monroe, the 5th has no urban center of any consequence. The agricultural establishments in this cotton and piney woods country range from large plantations along the Mississippi River to small, poor hill farms in places like Winn Parish, the boyhood home of Huey P. Long. The 5th has one of the highest black populations (35% in 1970) of any Louisiana congressional district; but unlike the 2d in metropolitan New Orleans, black voters here have played no major role in election outcomes.

For 30 years the 5th district was represented by Congressman Otto Passman, who made a name for himself as long ago as the fifties as the scourge of the foreign aid program. A member of the so-called "college of cardinals," i.e., the chairman of the House Appropriations subcommittee handling foreign aid, Passman was actually playing more complicated games. In 1976 he was indicted for extorting lucrative foreign aid shipping contracts from foreign governments for a favored agent; pleading bad health, he has not been tried at this writing. What is surprising is that Passman's career lasted as long as it did. A challenger came within 11% of forcing him into a runoff in 1972, and when he finally faced a serious primary challenger in 1976 he lost.

The winner was Jerry Huckaby, a dairy farmer and former Western Electric management employee. The Republicans seriously contested this district and in a pattern often seen in the South were able to carry the urban area, Monroe, with its newly affluent and socially mobile population. But Huckaby carried the rural areas, and in the 5th district they outvote the cities. Huckaby's voting record in the House on most issues is strongly conservative; an exception is agriculture, where he tends to support Democratic programs. His hold on the district cannot be considered quite solid yet. He won a majority in the September 1978 initial election here, which gave him a victory; but it was not the kind of overwhelming margin several other Louisiana incumbents had.

Census Data Pop. 455,205. Central city, 12%; suburban, 13%. Median family income, $5,762; families above $15,000: 8%; families below $3,000: 27%. Median years education, 10.1.

The Voters

Median voting age 44.
Employment profile White collar, 40%. Blue collar, 37%. Service, 16%. Farm, 7%.
Ethnic groups Black, 35%. Total foreign stock, 1%.

Presidential vote

1976	Carter (D)	81,204	(49%)
	Ford (R)	84,131	(51%)
1972	Nixon (R)	97,039	(73%)
	McGovern (D)	35,213	(27%)

Rep. Jerry Huckaby (D) Elected 1976; b. July 19, 1941, Jackson Parish; home, Ringgold; La. St. U., B.S. 1963, Ga. St. U., M.B.A. 1968; Methodist.

Career Management position, Western Electric, 1963–73; Dairy farmer, 1963–76.

Offices 228 CHOB, 202-225-2376. Also 1200 N. 18th St., Monroe 71201, 318-387-2244.

Committees *Agriculture* (19th). Subcommittees: Forests; Conservation and Credit.

Interior and Insular Affairs (23d). Subcommittees: Energy and the Environment; Mines and Mining.

Group Ratings

	ADA	COPE	PC	RPN	NFU	LCV	CFA	NAB	NSI	ACA	NTU
1978	25	30	18	69	40	–	23	75	100	88	–
1977	5	27	13	25	58	35	15	–	–	73	28

Key Votes

1) Increase Def Spnd	FOR	6) Alaska Lands Protect	AGN	11) Delay Auto Pol Cntrl	FOR
2) B-1 Bomber	FOR	7) Water Projects Veto	AGN	12) Sugar Price Escalator	FOR
3) Cargo Preference	FOR	8) Consum Protect Agcy	AGN	13) Pub Fin Cong Cmpgns	AGN
4) Dereg Nat Gas	FOR	9) Common Situs Picket	AGN	14) ERA Ratif Recissn	AGN
5) Kemp-Roth	FOR	10) Labor Law Revision	AGN	15) Prohibt Govt Abrtns	FOR

Election Results

1978 primary	Jerry Huckaby (D)	66,276	(52%)	($384,207)
	Jim Brown (D)	38,969	(31%)	($117,800)
	Three others (D)	22,049	(17%)	
1976 general	Jerry Huckaby (D)	83,696	(53%)	($217,031)
	Frank Spooner (R)	75,574	(47%)	($168,762)

SIXTH DISTRICT

When Governor-elect Huey P. Long moved himself and his belongings to Baton Rouge in 1928, the Louisiana capital was a small, sleepy Southern town with a population of 30,000. Today Baton Rouge is a bustling, fast-growing city of 165,000—and the change is thanks to both the Kingfish and his bitterest political enemies. It was Long who built a major university in Baton Rouge (Louisiana State) and who vastly increased the size and scope of state government. And it was his old enemies the oil companies, primarily Standard (now Exxon), who built the big refineries and petrochemical plants, the other basis of Baton Rouge's prosperity. For Exxon, the nation's largest corporation, Baton Rouge is an especially important town; the big Exxon refinery here has produced several of the top executives of the corporation.

Baton Rouge and its suburban fringe make up about half of Louisiana's 6th congressional district and cast about 60% of its votes. The remainder of the district is to the east, in farming and piney woods country; the most notable town here is Bogalusa, a lumber mill town on the Mississippi line and the scene over the years of Ku Klux Klan activity. This area is known as the Florida Parishes, for its acquisition by the United States was accomplished when West Florida was annexed in 1810.

The district is traditionally Democratic, but it currently elects a Republican congressman. He came to office in what seems to be an accidental way, but has won by impressive enough margins to make him a credible statewide candidate. He is Henson Moore, and he profited from the aftermath of the 1974 Democratic primary. Incumbent John Rarick, the most rabid right winger in the House, was defeated by a 29-year-old sportscaster; that gave Moore an opening. Then a voting irregularity in the general election required the whole contest to be rerun; Moore probably would have lost that contest, though no one can be sure. In the next election, Moore attacked his opponent as a liberal and finally won the seat.

Moore is the kind of Republican who receives near-perfect ratings from conservative organizations. He used the advantages of incumbency adeptly enough that in the September 1978 initial election he received 91% of the vote against a single Democrat, a showing unequalled by any other Republican in the nation. In the House he has a seat on the Ways and Means Committee, where he can be expected to work hard to protect Louisiana's oil interests. He is not expected to run for governor in 1979, but with his strong local base he might make a strong candidate for U.S. Senator in some future election.

Census Data Pop. 456,178. Central city, 36%; suburban, 26%. Median family income, $8,230; families above $15,000: 16%; families below $3,000: 17%. Median years education, 12.0.

The Voters

Median voting age 39.
Employment profile White collar, 48%. Blue collar, 34%. Service, 15%. Farm, 3%.
Ethnic groups Black, 30%. Spanish, 1%. Total foreign stock, 3%. French-speaking, 4%.

Presidential vote

1976	Carter (D)	90,224	(55%)
	Ford (R)	74,781	(45%)
1972	Nixon (R)	83,246	(70%)
	McGovern (D)	36,240	(30%)

Rep. W. Henson Moore (R) Elected Jan. 7, 1975; b. Oct. 4, 1939, Lake Charles; home, Baton Rouge; La. St. U., B.A. 1961, J.D. 1965, M.A. 1973; Episcopalian.

Career Army, 1965–67; Practicing atty., 1967–74.

Offices 2444 RHOB, 202-225-3901. Also Rm. 236, Fed. Bldg., 750 Fla. Blvd., Baton Rouge 70801, 504-344-7679.

Committees *Ways and Means* (12th). Subcommittees: Trade; Oversight.

Group Ratings

	ADA	COPE	PC	RPN	NFU	LCV	CFA	NAB	NSI	ACA	NTU
1978	5	0	15	58	30	–	23	100	100	96	–
1977	0	9	15	54	58	20	5	–	–	78	36
1976	0	22	7	53	25	4	0	75	100	82	50

Key Votes

1) Increase Def Spnd	FOR	6) Alaska Lands Protect	AGN	11) Delay Auto Pol Cntrl	FOR
2) B-1 Bomber	FOR	7) Water Projects Veto	AGN	12) Sugar Price Escalator	FOR
3) Cargo Preference	AGN	8) Consum Protect Agcy	AGN	13) Pub Fin Cong Cmpgns	AGN
4) Dereg Nat Gas	FOR	9) Common Situs Picket	AGN	14) ERA Ratif Recissn	FOR
5) Kemp-Roth	FOR	10) Labor Law Revision	AGN	15) Prohibt Govt Abrtns	FOR

Election Results

1978 primary	W. Henson Moore (R)	102,430	(91%)	($78,686)
	Bobby G. Pailette, Sr. (D)	10,256	(9%)	
1976 general	W. Henson Moore (R)	99,780	(65%)	($157,165)
	J. D. De Blieux (D)	53,212	(35%)	($23,000)

SEVENTH DISTRICT

The 7th congressional district of Louisiana is one of the very few in the nation where nearly half the population grew up with a language other than English. Here the language is French, Cajun style, and it is the mother tongue of 44% of the 7th's population. The district hugs the Gulf Coast of Louisiana, as it moves east to west from the swamps of the Atchafalaya River through the medium-sized city of Lafayette across to Lake Charles and the Texas border.

Many rural backwaters like this are now depopulated and their traditions dying; not so the Cajun country in Louisiana. What has kept the people here is petroleum, in plenteous quantity under the swampy soil, with even more below the Gulf a few miles out to sea. Oil and attendant industries have provided jobs here while the rest of the country suffers through recession, and they have provided the money to keep all the Cajuns who want to remain in their homeland. Beyond that the Cajuns themselves increasingly are working to promote the use of French and to hold onto regional traditions.

It was a source of some satisfaction here when 7th district Congressman Edwin Edwards—very much a Cajun, despite his name—was elected Governor in 1972. Edwards's successor is a former member of his staff, John Breaux, also of French origin. Breaux was the youngest freshman in the 93d Congress, in the years before freshmen were a major force for change in the House. And his House career has followed rather traditional lines. He retains membership on two committees of bread-and-butter interest to his district: Public Works and Merchant Marine. They handle legislation to dredge swamps and build levees—the kind of labor-intensive projects traditionally popular in places like southern Louisiana.

The committees also handle legislation on air and water pollution and other environmental issues. And on these Breaux has been very much on the side of those who want to resolve conflicts in favor of economic development. For example, he was the major sponsor of an amendment to relax federal control over landfill and dumping operations in marshes and swamps. He sponsored a successful amendment to relax clean air standards in areas whose air as it exists is reasonably clean; the old law tended to prohibit even tiny increments of pollution, and proponents of Breaux's amendment wanted to allow some economic growth in such areas. Breaux, together with the 3d district's David Treen, also led a fight to change leasing procedures in the continental shelf area in ways favored by the oil industry. And with John Dingell he sponsored the Alaska wilderness proposal supported by development-minded forces in 1979.

This seems to be the kind of politics voters in the 7th district want. In 1978 Breaux faced a serious challenge from a Republican, but he prevailed in the September election by a 60%–33% margin.

Census Data Pop. 455,014. Central city, 32%; suburban, 24%. Median family income, $7,197; families above $15,000: 11%; families below $3,000: 19%. Median years education, 10.2.

The Voters

Median voting age 41.
Employment profile White collar, 42%. Blue collar, 38%. Service, 15%. Farm, 5%.
Ethnic groups Black, 21%. Total foreign stock, 2%. French-speaking, 44%.

Presidential vote

1976	Carter (D)	101,186	(61%)
	Ford (R)	65,387	(39%)
1972	Nixon (R)	85,502	(68%)
	McGovern (D)	41,032	(32%)

Rep. John B. Breaux (D) Elected Sept. 30, 1972; b. Mar. 1, 1944, Crowley; home, Crowley; U. of S.W. La., B.A. 1964, La. St. U., J.D. 1967; Catholic.

Career Practicing atty., 1967–68; Legis. Asst., Dist. Mgr. to U.S. Rep. Edwin W. Edwards, 1968–72.

Offices 2159 RHOB, 202-225-2031. Also 2530 P.O. and Fed. Bldg., Lake Charles 70601, 318-433-1122.

Committees *Merchant Marine and Fisheries* (8th). Subcommittees: Fish and Wildlife (Chairman); Coast Guard and Navigation; Maritime Education and Training; Oceanography.

Public Works and Transportation (7th). Subcommittees: Oversight and Review; Surface Transportation; Water Resources.

Group Ratings

	ADA	COPE	PC	RPN	NFU	LCV	CFA	NAB	NSI	ACA	NTU
1978	5	5	15	30	30	–	18	91	100	86	–
1977	0	45	10	27	73	5	10	–	–	55	26
1976	10	43	11	44	42	25	0	25	100	64	35

Key Votes

1) Increase Def Spnd	FOR	6) Alaska Lands Protect	AGN	11) Delay Auto Pol Cntrl	FOR
2) B-1 Bomber	FOR	7) Water Projects Veto	AGN	12) Sugar Price Escalator	FOR
3) Cargo Preference	AGN	8) Consum Protect Agcy	AGN	13) Pub Fin Cong Cmpgns	AGN
4) Dereg Nat Gas	FOR	9) Common Situs Picket	AGN	14) ERA Ratif Recissn	FOR
5) Kemp-Roth	FOR	10) Labor Law Revision	FOR	15) Prohibt Govt Abrtns	FOR

Election Results

1978 primary	John B. Breaux (D)	78,297	(60%)	($183,424)
	Mike Thompson (R)	42,247	(33%)	($120,978)
	One other (D)	9,126	(7%)	
1976 general	John B. Breaux (D)	117,196	(83%)	($56,433)
	Charles F. Huff (R)	23,414	(17%)	($4,749)

EIGHTH DISTRICT

After the lines for seven of Louisiana's eight congressional districts were drawn, the territory remaining became the steamshovel-shaped 8th district—or so, at least, it seems. This is a seat with no real common sense of identity and which crosses the state's long-acknowledged regional borders; it contains one parish where 96% of the churchgoers are Catholic and another where Catholics are heavily outnumbered by Baptists. Geographically, the 8th is bounded on the east by Lake Pontchartrain; then it moves up along the Mississippi and Red Rivers to a point within 30 miles of the Texas border. Politically, there are three factors which explain its rather unusual political behavior.

The first of these is the large black population—36%, the second highest in the state. In the days before the Civil War, the old sugar and cotton plantations along the Mississippi required hundreds of slaves to do the work; today, blacks form the majority voting blocs in West Feliciana Parish. Second, the district also has a high Cajun population, particularly in the southern parishes of Evangeline and St. Landry. Third, there is the legacy of the Long family. A decade ago, the 8th still contained Huey Long's home parish of Winn; that is now in the 5th district, but this is still very much Kingfish territory.

All three of these factors combine to make the 8th a politically more liberal district than one might expect from a chunk of small city and rural Louisiana. The 8th has a history of willingness to elect congressional liberals—at least if their name is Long. Indeed, an understanding of congressional politics here requires a knowledge of the Long family tree; since 1952, only one Democratic primary has been won by someone outside the family. In 1952, 1954, and 1956 the 8th elected George S. Long, one of Huey's brothers, whose memories of the Kingfish were doubtless fonder after his death than before. George Long died in 1958 and was succeeded by one Harold McSween. But in 1960, Earl Long, another Kingfish brother, won the Democratic primary under circumstances described brilliantly in A. J. Liebling's *The Earl of Louisiana*. But shortly after the primary Earl Long dropped dead, giving McSween a chance to win one more term.

McSween was through in 1962, when he was beaten by Gillis Long, a cousin, who two years later lost to another cousin, Speedy Long. Speedy Long was the most conservative of the 8th district Longs; he served happily on the Armed Services Committee until he decided to retire in 1972. The winner this time once again was Gillis Long.

Gillis Long's return to Congress marks a significant shift in Southern politics. The year he lost, 1964, was the year the civil rights revolution pushed most white Deep South voters into the arms of archconservative candidates like Barry Goldwater; district after district, including the 8th, repudiated one hundred years of history and went Republican. For some years thereafter, when a Southern candidate got tagged as a liberal, that was it—he lost, as Gillis Long lost in 1964. By 1968, when Richard Nixon was elected President, Southern politics seemed perfectly polarized: the majority whites all voting one way, the minority blacks all the other.

By 1972 those days were gone, at least in the 8th district. Against four opponents Gillis Long won his primary without a runoff and won the general election even more easily. George McGovern was doing better than Hubert Humphrey in the 8th, and by 1976 Jimmy Carter was able to win more than 60% of the vote here. Politicians who have the support of blacks can once again win the support of whites in the South.

But Gillis Long is more than an example of a political trend; he is a talented politician and is considered by many to be one of the House's ablest legislators. He is currently the fourth-ranking Democrat on the House Rules Committee and one of the key members of that critical body. Because of the nature of Rules's jurisdiction, Long does not get his name on legislation, but he is one of those who make the legislative process work. On issues, he is that rarity: a genuine, humane Southern populist—and one who stuck with his principles through hard times. Long is very close to Richard Bolling, Chairman of Rules, and he managed the almost successful campaign to make Bolling House Majority Leader after the 1976 elections. Long has political security in the 8th district now, and in 1979 he decided against running for governor.

Census Data Pop. 456,291. Central city, 0%; suburban, 0%. Median family income, $6,092; families above $15,000: 8%; families below $3,000: 26%. Median years education, 9.2.

The Voters

Median voting age 42.
Employment profile White collar, 36%. Blue collar, 39%. Service, 17%. Farm, 8%.
Ethnic groups Black, 36%. Total foreign stock, 2%. French-speaking, 28%.

Presidential vote

1976	Carter (D)	94,900	(62%)
	Ford (R)	59,137	(38%)
1972	Nixon (R)	73,297	(63%)
	McGovern (D)	43,429	(37%)

Rep. Gillis W. Long (D) Elected 1972; b. May 4, 1923, Winnfield; home, Alexandria; La. St. U., B.A. 1949, J.D. 1951; Baptist.

Career Army, WWII; Legal Counsel, U.S. Senate Comm. on Small Business, 1951; Chf. Counsel, U.S. House of Reps. Special Comm. on Campaign Expenditures; U.S. House of Reps., 1963–65; Asst. Dir., U.S. Ofc. of Econ. Opportunity, 1965–66; Legis. Counsel, Natl. Commission of Urban Growth Policy, 1968–69; Practicing atty., 1970–72.

Offices 2445 RHOB, 202-225-4926. Also P.O. Box 410, Alexandria 71301, 318-487-4595.

Committees *Rules* (4th). Subcommittees: Energy; International Economics (Cochairman).

Group Ratings

	ADA	COPE	PC	RPN	NFU	LCV	CFA	NAB	NSI	ACA	NTU
1978	50	63	43	55	67	–	46	25	67	21	–
1977	15	70	28	25	67	24	35	–	–	26	21
1976	30	70	34	56	58	29	45	8	80	32	13

Key Votes

1) Increase Def Spnd	AGN	6) Alaska Lands Protect	DNV	11) Delay Auto Pol Cntrl	FOR
2) B-1 Bomber	AGN	7) Water Projects Veto	AGN	12) Sugar Price Escalator	FOR
3) Cargo Preference	FOR	8) Consum Protect Agcy	FOR	13) Pub Fin Cong Cmpgns	AGN
4) Dereg Nat Gas	FOR	9) Common Situs Picket	FOR	14) ERA Ratif Recissn	AGN
5) Kemp-Roth	AGN	10) Labor Law Revision	FOR	15) Prohibt Govt Abrtns	FOR

Election Results

1978 general	Gillis W. Long (D)	80,666	(80%)	($189,507)
	Robert Mitchell (R)	20,547	(20%)	($7,106)
1976 general	Gillis W. Long (D)	106,285	(94%)	($62,188)
	Kent Courtney (I)	6,526	(6%)	($4,876)

MAINE

It has been known for some time that the slogan, "As Maine goes, so goes the nation," was never accurate—at least since James Farley changed the saying to "As Maine goes, so goes Vermont," after FDR's 1936 landslide. Indeed, the saying got started not because Maine was ever an accurate bellwether, but because up through the fifties the state held its general elections in

September, on the sensible theory that they should not be conducted on a day likely to be snowy and certain to be dark before five o'clock. Today Maine's political behavior is almost countercyclical. It is the only state in the Union which voted for the losers in each of the last four close presidential elections—for Dewey in 1948, Nixon in 1960, Humphrey in 1968, and Ford in 1976. Maine's Democrats captured the governorship and both the state's congressional seats for the first time in 1966, a Republican year elsewhere; and in Democratic 1974, Maine elected two Republican congressmen and the Democrats lost the governorship to a Republican running as an Independent. In 1978 Maine did follow the national pattern and elected a Republican senator, but it also elected a Democratic governor.

The story of Maine politics in recent years centers on the rise and fall of the Democratic Party in this state known for its rock-ribbed Republicanism since the time of the Civil War. Among the reasons for the Democratic ascendancy were intelligent organization, attractive candidates, and the carelessness of Maine Republicans, who had enjoyed too much easy success. Almost exactly the same factors have produced the more recent successes of Maine's Republicans, although the party has failed to win a gubernatorial election since 1962. The appeal of each party seems epitomized in the character of each of the state's senators.

By far the best known is Senator Edmund Muskie, the Democrat who has held statewide office in Maine for more than 25 years. Muskie was elected Governor in 1954 and 1956 and beat an incumbent senator in 1958. During that era Maine was one of several far northern states where a popular leader and competent followers built a strong Democratic Party in a state previously considered Republican; they included the Minnesota of Hubert Humphrey, the Wisconsin of William Proxmire and Gaylord Nelson, the Michigan of Mennen Williams, and the South Dakota of George McGovern. These movements produced half a dozen presidential candidates and most of their original leaders are still active, popular, and productive. All were built on electoral appeal to a traditional Catholic minority—in Maine, the French Canadian and other Catholic voters in the state's mill towns—and candidates with a broad appeal to the larger majority. Muskie, a Catholic of Polish descent, with a taciturn manner and craggy honesty, combined the most appealing characteristics of the state's two traditional religious blocs, and has proven himself unbeatable in Maine elections.

After ten years in the Senate, Muskie was unknown nationally. But he had already made some noteworthy legislative accomplishments. He had turned his seat on the lackluster Public Works Committee into an asset by painstakingly putting together water pollution legislation before environmental causes became fashionable. As a Senator from Maine, Muskie was already aware of possible conflicts between environmental concerns and economic development: this is a poor state, which desperately needs jobs, but also a beautiful state, proud of its particularity, which does not want to be spoiled by pollution or urbanization. Muskie's work on both air and water pollution control has forced him to do more to reconcile these goals than probably any other public figure. At the same time he must fight powerful interests—the auto companies, for example—who think he is going too far. But the fact is that since Muskie became active in the field, both air and water pollution have been reduced in the United States by dint of government action—a striking achievement, for which Muskie deserves much credit.

Muskie's selection as the Democratic vice presidential candidate in 1968 made him a national figure. His quiet Yankee style and his willingness to let opponents speak their piece impressed voters all over the country in a year of political turbulence. Two years later Muskie's low key performance on television just before the 1970 elections, especially in contrast to Richard Nixon's frenzied speech shown just before, made Muskie the Democratic frontrunner for 1972. But in the spring of 1972 the Muskie campaign fell to pieces. There were too many high level advisors, too many prominent endorsements, not enough understanding of the delegate selection process, and not enough first choice votes. Muskie was running as the "center" of a party that consisted almost entirely of two or three hostile "wings." Another reason for Muskie's collapse was systematic sabotage by Nixon campaign operatives: the so-called Canuck letter and other dirty tricks, the reactions to which severely damaged voters' estimate of Muskie's character.

On the whole what defeated Muskie in 1972 is what has otherwise been the strength of his political character. This is a man who likes to reconcile conflicting goals, to reach a workable middle way. That is what he has done on pollution issues, and that is what he is doing on the budget. In 1973, while the Watergate story was breaking, Muskie was working with Sam Ervin drafting the legislation to set up the congressional budget committees. The idea—though no one wanted to put it this way—was to do what the Finance and Appropriations Committees have failed to do, to prepare single target figures for tax revenues and government expenditures and get the Senate to accept them. The hope was to produce a rational congressional fiscal policy, rather than a haphazard pattern resulting from individual decisions to tax or spend.

Muskie became the first and so far only Chairman of the Senate Budget Committee in 1974. His job has been not only to get the Senate to agree to budget revenue and spending targets, but to get it to hold to them when a committee sponsoring one program or another does not. In this enterprise Muskie has had signal assistance from Budget's ranking Republican, Henry Bellmon of Oklahoma; Muskie and Bellmon have gotten bipartisan agreement in the Committee, and then have worked together to enforce it on the floor. They have beaten requests for greater military spending and for greater spending on social issues; for the most part the Budget Committee has done what it set out to do. In the late seventies, as demands for budgetary stringency increased, it seemed to be an idea that had found its time.

Muskie has not always been pleased with the workings of the budget process. He has a temper, and has been known to threaten to quit the committee altogether. But overall the Congress seems to have a more rational idea of what it is doing, and the budget process has imposed some discipline on federal spending. Muskie has another idea for imposing such discipline. He is the Senate's chief sponsor of sunset legislation, which would require all federal programs to be reauthorized every five years by Congress; those that are not would die. Sunset has not yet reached the stage for passage, but like the budget committee proposal, this is an idea that should take some time to grow, time during which its practical difficulties can be anticipated and its potential assessed. Certainly if such legislation is ever passed, Muskie will be more responsible than anyone else.

After the 1980 election, Muskie will have to work without Bellmon, who is retiring; presently the next ranking Republican on Budget is the considerably more partisan Bob Dole. Muskie may choose to retire himself in 1982. He was reelected with a large margin in 1976 and could probably win again; but he will be 68 when his seat is up and will have served nearly 30 years in statewide office.

Maine's other senator, in contrast, is just a freshman, but he has played for the state's Republican Party something of the role Muskie played for the Democrats. When he was first elected to the House in 1972, William Cohen was the only Republican in the state's congressional delegation. His election was the triumph of a pleasant, unusual young mayor of Bangor over a lackluster Democrat. In his first term Cohen became well known both in the district and nationally as a member of the House Judiciary Committee considering the impeachment of Richard Nixon. He was one of the Republicans who supported impeachment, and his able presentation made a good impression. He is carefully spoken, sometimes eloquent (he has written poetry). His voting record in the House was carefully balanced; nearly every group that rates congressmen gave him a mark near 50%. After easy reelection in 1974 and 1976, Cohen decided to challenge Senator William Hathaway in 1978.

Hathaway had won the seat in much the same way. He was Cohen's predecessor as 2d district Congressman, and he ran a vigorous campaign against Senator Margaret Chase Smith in 1972, contrasting his close attention to constituents' problems with her practice of spending virtually all her time in Washington. Once in the Senate, Hathaway himself spent less time in Maine; moreover, with his frank, gruff personality and his rumpled manner he did not make the best case for himself. His record on the Finance and Human Resources Committees did not make headlines locally, and he was not able to identify himself with popular issues or trends of thought in the state.

Cohen spent much of his time exhibiting his energy and youth; he sponsored a 400-mile relay marathon to raise money, and ran the last four miles himself. He constantly attacked Hathaway as a doctrinaire liberal and, although Cohen himself had no military record and had not concentrated on military issues in the House, he charged that Hathaway was not strong enough on defense. The Republican also had some local issues working for him. The first was the Lincoln–Dickey Dam, a proposal that has been around for 20 years to build a hydroelectric power generating facility on the St. Johns River. Democrats and labor have generally supported it because it would advance public power in the East and would provide cheap power and jobs in a chronically depressed area. Hathaway took this position; Cohen agreed with the environmentalists who attacked the project. The latter position in the Maine of 1978 was the more popular.

The other local issue that split the candidates was the Indian land claims. The Passamaquoddy and other tribes have filed lawsuits alleging that they own, altogether, almost half the land area of the state, including some populous areas; it seems that the treaties purporting to take these rights away from the Indians may have been defective. Joseph Brennan, first as state Attorney General and after 1978 as Governor, has fought the Indians' claims without compromise. The state's congressional delegation has pushed for some kind of compromise, with the federal government compensating the Indians for their claims. Hathaway supported a Carter Administration compromise proposal; Cohen attacked it. Opinion in Maine is, to say the least, hostile to the Indians' claims, and Cohen's stand surely helped him.

Cohen won the 1978 election by a margin approaching a landslide. He followed up his campaign emphasis on military matters by joining the Armed Services Committee, and with several other new Republican moderates seemed likely to be a pivotal vote in the Senate.

Cohen's decision to run for the Senate left his seat in the House open, and it was filled by another Republican who seemed to have similar politics and perhaps even more flair. She is Olympia Snowe, a state Senator in her early thirties. The 2d is the northern district, and includes the mill town of Lewiston, heavily Democratic, and Bangor, which is not much less so. Of the two districts it is probably, by a small margin, the more Democratic. Snowe's opponent, Secretary of State Markham Gartley, was well known both for his state office and for his race against Cohen in 1974; he had gotten few votes but much publicity as one of the first Vietnam prisoners of war to run for office. (It says something about the Vietnam war that it was prisoners of war, rather than as in previous wars military heroes, who became political candidates—and that none of the POWs won.) Snowe's attractive personality and superior campaigning ability were enough to produce a solid victory for her.

The race in the 1st district, centered on the state's largest city, Portland, was expected to be close. Congressman David Emery had ousted an unpopular Democrat in 1974 and had been reelected comfortably in 1976; hard work and constituency service rather than strong personal appeal were his biggest assets. The 1978 Democrat had formerly headed the state consumer protection bureau and had gotten favorable publicity; he charged that Emery "gets lost in the crowd." Nevertheless Emery won by nearly a 2–1 margin. He stressed his opponent's liberalism, apparently unpopular in a year of concern about high taxes and spending. Emery himself is not a strong conservative, however; his House voting record has not been too different from Cohen's.

Maine's gubernatorial elections have produced some surprises in recent years, but they seem to have been determined by single issues of great importance in the state. In 1974 James Longley surprised just about everyone by getting elected as an Independent. His campaign featured a charge that the state was unnecessarily spending $23 million a year, and frugal Maine voters gave him a victory over the Democrat in a close race. Longley made at least one other promise which he kept: that he would retire at the end of his first term. He fought often with the legislature, but was popular enough with the voters after four years that every gubernatorial candidate tried to ride his coattails.

There was even another Independent candidate, Herman Frankland, with New Right support. The Republican, Linwood Palmer, was more in the image of the traditional craggy Maine Yankee. But the winner was a Democrat, Attorney General Joseph Brennan. Despite his reputation for fiscal liberalism and his support of the Lincoln–Dickey Dam, Brennan had one strong issue going for him: Indian rights. As Attorney General, he had the major responsibility for defending the state in the lawsuit brought by the Indians, and he stood strongly against negotiated settlements which would cost the state money. Of course there is a risk: if the suit should be decided in favor of the Indians, many Maine voters and the major paper companies would lose a very substantial portion of their land.

Census Data Pop. 993,663; 0.49% of U.S. total, 38th largest; Central city, 13%; suburban, 8%. Median family income, $8,205; 36th highest; families above $15,000: 11%; families below $3,000: 10%. Median years education, 12.1.

1977 Share of Federal Tax Burden $1,347,000,000; 0.39% of U.S. total, 41st largest.

1977 Share of Federal Outlays $1,910,207,000; 0.48% of U.S. total, 40th largest. Per capita federal spending, $1,804.

DOD	$473,171,000	36th (0.52%)	HEW	$767,982,000	37th (0.52%)
ERDA	$422,000	49th (0.01%)	HUD	$19,532,000	39th (0.46%)
NASA	$137,000	46th(—%)	VA	$111,928,000	38th (0.58%)
DOT	$52,836,000	46th (0.37%)	EPA	$17,351,000	44th (0.21%)
DOC	$92,047,000	24th (1.11%)	RevS	$54,971,000	35th (0.65%)
DOI	$6,595,000	46th (0.14%)	Debt	$76,730,000	35th (0.26%)
USDA	$65,986,000	44th (0.33%)	Other	$170,519,000	

Economic Base Leather footwear, and other leather and leather products; paper and allied products, especially paper mills other than building paper; agriculture, notably potatoes, eggs, broilers and dairy products; finance, insurance and real estate; food and kindred products; lumber and wood products.

Political Line-up Governor, Joseph E. Brennan (D). Senators, Edmund S. Muskie (D) and William S. Cohen (R). Representatives, 2 R. State Senate (19 R, 13 D, and 1 nonparty); State House (77 D, 73 R, and 1 nonparty).

The Voters

Registration 691,697 Total. 234,710 D (34%); 223,824 R (32%); 233,092 Not Enrolled (34%).
Median voting age 44
Employment profile White collar, 41%. Blue collar, 44%. Service, 12%. Farm, 3%.
Ethnic groups Total foreign stock, 19%. Canada, 14%.

Presidential vote

1976	Carter (D)	232,279	(50%)
	Ford (R)	236,320	(50%)
1972	Nixon (R)	256,458	(61%)
	McGovern (D)	160,584	(39%)

Sen. Edmund S. Muskie (D) Elected 1958, seat up 1982; b. Mar. 28, 1914, Rumford; home, Waterville; Bates Col., B.A. 1936, Cornell U., LL.B. 1939; Catholic.

Career Practicing atty.; Navy, WWII; Maine House of Reps., 1947–51, Minor. Ldr., 1949–51, Dir., Maine Ofc. of Price Stabilization, 1951–52; Gov. of Maine, 1955–59; Dem. nominee for V.P., 1968.

Offices 145 RSOB, 202-224-5344. Also 112 Main St., Waterville 04901, 207-873-3361, and New Fed. Bldg., 151 Forest Ave., Portland 04101, 207-282-4144.

Committees *Budget* (Chairman).

Environment and Public Works (2d). Subcommittees: Environmental Pollution (Chairman); Regional and Community Development; Resource Protection.

Foreign Relations (8th). Subcommittees: African Affairs; East Asian and Pacific Affairs; Western Hemisphere Affairs.

Group Ratings

	ADA	COPE	PC	RPN	NFU	LCV	CFA	NAB	NSI	ACA	NTU
1978	75	67	85	50	40	76	80	42	10	8	–
1977	90	76	65	22	40	–	48	–	–	13	29
1976	80	79	77	53	83	67	85	30	22	8	31

Key Votes

1) Warnke Nom	FOR	6) Egypt-Saudi Arms	FOR	11) Hosptl Cost Contnmnt	FOR
2) Neutron Bomb	AGN	7) Draft Restr Pardon	FOR	12) Clinch River Reactor	AGN
3) Waterwy User Fee	DNV	8) Wheat Price Support	AGN	13) Pub Fin Cong Cmpgns	FOR
4) Dereg Nat Gas	AGN	9) Panama Canal Treaty	FOR	14) ERA Ratif Recissn	FOR
5) Kemp-Roth	AGN	10) Labor Law Rev Clot	FOR	15) Med Necssy Abrtns	AGN

Election Results

1976 general	Edmund S. Muskie (D)	292,704	(60%)	($320,427)
	Robert A. G. Monks (R)	193,489	(40%)	($598,490)
1976 primary	Edmund S. Muskie (D), unopposed			
1970 general	Edmund S. Muskie (D)	199,954	(62%)	
	Neil S. Bishop (R)	123,906	(38%)	

Sen. William S. Cohen (R) Elected 1978, seat up 1984; b. Aug. 28, 1940, Bangor; home, Bangor; Bowdoin Col., B.A. 1962, Boston U., LL.B. 1965; Unitarian.

Career Practicing atty., 1965–72; Asst. Penobscot Co. Atty., 1968; Instructor, Husson Col., 1968, U. of Maine, 1968–72; Bangor City Cncl., 1969–72, Mayor, 1971–72; U.S. House of Reps., 1973–78.

Offices 1251 DSOB, 202-224-2523. Also Fed. Bldg., Bangor 04401, 207-947-6504.

Committees *Armed Services* (6th). Subcommittees: Arms Control; Manpower and Personnel; Research and Development.

Governmental Affairs (7th). Subcommittees: Investigations; Oversight of Government Management.

Select Committee on Indian Affairs.

Special Committee on Aging (4th).

Group Ratings

	ADA	COPE	PC	RPN	NFU	LCV	CFA	NAB	NSI	ACA	NTU
Group Ratings: Newly Elected											
1978	30	21	35	50	50	–	41	55	78	58	–
1977	65	59	63	83	50	70	65	–	–	48	33
1976	50	52	62	89	75	74	54	50	60	18	24

Key Votes

1) Increase Def Spnd	FOR	6) Alaska Lands Protect	FOR	11) Delay Auto Pol Cntrl	AGN
2) B-1 Bomber	AGN	7) Water Projects Veto	FOR	12) Sugar Price Escalator	DNV
3) Cargo Preference	AGN	8) Consum Protect Agcy	FOR	13) Pub Fin Cong Cmpgns	FOR
4) Dereg Nat Gas	AGN	9) Common Situs Picket	AGN	14) ERA Ratif Recissn	AGN
5) Kemp-Roth	FOR	10) Labor Law Revision	FOR	15) Prohibt Govt Abrtns	AGN

Election Results

1978 general	William S. Cohen (R)	212,294	(58%)	($648,739)
	William D. Hathaway (D)	127,327	(35%)	($423,027)
	Hayes Gahagen (I)	27,824	(8%)	($115,901)
1978 primary	William S. Cohen (R), unopposed			
1972 general	William D. Hathaway (D)	224,270	(53%)	($202,208)
	Margaret Chase Smith (R)	197,040	(47%)	($14,950)

Gov. Joseph E. Brennan (D) Elected 1978, term expires Jan. 1983; b. Nov. 2, 1934, Portland; Boston Col., B.A., U. of Maine, J.D.; Catholic.

Career Practicing atty.; Maine House of Reps., 1965–71; Cumberland Co. Atty., 1971–73; Maine Senate, 1973–75, Dem. Floor Ldr.; Atty. Gen. of Maine, 1975–78.

Offices Augusta 04880, 207-289-3531.

Election Results

1978 general	Joseph E. Brennan (D)	176,493	(48%)
	Linwood E. Palmer, Jr. (R)	126,862	(34%)
	Herman C. Frankland (I)	65,889	(18%)
1978 primary	Joseph E. Brennan (D)	38,361	(52%)
	Philip L. Merrill (D)	26,803	(36%)
	Richard J. Carey (D)	8,588	(12%)
1974 general	James B. Longley (I)	142,464	(40%)
	George J. Mitchell (D)	132,219	(37%)
	James S. Erwin (R)	84,176	(23%)

FIRST DISTRICT

Census Data Pop. 495,681. Central city, 13%; suburban, 15%. Median family income, $8,688; families above $15,000: 13%; families below $3,000: 9%. Median years education, 12.2.

The Voters

Median voting age 45.
Employment profile White collar, 44%. Blue collar, 42%. Service, 12%. Farm, 2%.
Ethnic groups Total foreign stock, 18%. Canada, 11%.

Presidential vote

1976	Carter (D)	123,598	(49%)
	Ford (R)	127,019	(51%)
1972	Nixon (R)	135,388	(61%)
	McGovern (D)	85,028	(39%)

Rep. David F. Emery (R) Elected 1974; b. Sept. 1, 1948, Rockland; home, Rockland; Worcester Polytechnic Inst., B.S. 1970.

Career Maine House of Reps., 1971–74.

Offices 425 CHOB, 202-225-6116. Also 46 Sewall St., Augusta 04330, 207-775-3131.

Committees *Armed Services* (11th). Subcommittees: Military Compensation; Seapower and Strategic and Critical Materials.

Merchant Marine and Fisheries (9th). Subcommittees: Fish and Wildlife; Oceanography; Maritime Education and Training.

Group Ratings

	ADA	COPE	PC	RPN	NFU	LCV	CFA	NAB	NSI	ACA	NTU
1978	25	35	45	45	40	–	32	75	80	69	–
1977	50	48	60	67	50	56	60	–	–	48	32
1976	40	45	49	83	58	65	36	50	70	50	40

Key Votes

1) Increase Def Spnd	FOR	6) Alaska Lands Protect	FOR	11) Delay Auto Pol Cntrl	AGN
2) B-1 Bomber	FOR	7) Water Projects Veto	FOR	12) Sugar Price Escalator	AGN
3) Cargo Preference	FOR	8) Consum Protect Agcy	AGN	13) Pub Fin Cong Cmpgns	FOR
4) Dereg Nat Gas	FOR	9) Common Situs Picket	AGN	14) ERA Ratif Recissn	AGN
5) Kemp-Roth	FOR	10) Labor Law Revision	FOR	15) Prohibt Govt Abrtns	FOR

Election Results

1978 general	David F. Emery (R)	120,791	(63%)	($2,000,480)
	John Quinn (D)	70,348	(37%)	($73,755)
1978 primary	David F. Emery (R), unopposed			
1976 general	David F. Emery (R)	145,523	(57%)	($155,139)
	Frederick Barton (D)	108,105	(43%)	($124,326)

SECOND DISTRICT

Census Data Pop. 497,982. Central city, 13%; suburban, 1%. Median family income, $7,733; families above $15,000: 9%; families below $3,000: 11%. Median years education, 12.0.

The Voters

Median voting age 43.
Employment profile White collar, 37%. Blue collar, 47%. Service, 12%. Farm, 4%.
Ethnic groups Total foreign stock, 20%. Canada, 16%.

Presidential vote

1976	Carter (D)	108,681	(50%)
	Ford (R)	109,301	(50%)
1972	Nixon (R)	121,120	(62%)
	McGovern (D)	75,556	(38%)

Rep. Olympia J. Snowe Elected 1978; b. Feb. 21, 1947, Augusta; home, Auburn; U. of Maine, B.A. 1969; Greek Orthodox.

Career Dist. Ofc. Mgr. for U.S. Rep. William S. Cohen, 1973; Maine House of Reps., 1973–76; Maine Senate 1977–78.

Offices 1729 LHOB, 202-225-6306. Also Rm. 232 Fed. Bldg., Bangor 04401, 207-942-4198.

Committees *Government Operations* (12th). Subcommittees: Intergovernmental Relations and Human Resources; Manpower and Housing.

Small Business (10th). Subcommittees: Antitrust and Restraint of Trade Activities Affecting Small Business.

Group Ratings: Newly Elected

Key Votes: Newly Elected

Election Results

1978 general	Olympia J. Snowe (R)	87,939	(55%)	($220,981)
	Markham L. Gartley (D)	70,691	(45%)	($132,156)
1978 primary	Olympia J. Snowe (R), unopposed			
1976 general	William S. Cohen (R)	169,292	(80%)	
	Leighton Cooney (D)	43,150	(20%)	

MARYLAND

Maryland's attenuated shape reflects the fact that this is one of the most diverse states; although it ranks only 42d in area, you can drive 350 miles wholly within its boundaries. In that distance you move from the south-of-the-Mason–Dixon-Line Eastern Shore, through the booming suburbs of Washington and Baltimore, and up into the Appalachian Mountains. Tiny Maryland has just about all and every kind of people, and in the last few presidential elections the state has been an exemplary statistical mirror of the nation's voting habits. The nuts and bolts of Maryland politics, however, are anything but typical.

The original Mason–Dixon Line was drawn to settle a border dispute between Maryland and Pennsylvania, and Maryland retains even today a touch of the South. Up through World War II the rural part of the state—dominated by Dixie-type Democrats—set the tone for Maryland's politics; its only competition came from the old-fashioned machine politics of Baltimore. Today Baltimore—now almost half black but ruled by a gifted product of machine politics, Mayor Don Schaefer—casts less than 20% of Maryland's votes. The rural areas also cast less than 20%. The remaining 60% are divided about equally between suburban Baltimore and the Maryland suburbs of Washington, D.C.

Just 40 miles apart, these two metropolitan areas could hardly be more different. Baltimore is a major port with big shipbuilding companies and the nation's largest steel mill. Its heavy industries have attracted the kind of ethnic migration common to the big cities of the East Coast, as well as a large black migration from the South. In the sixties, metropolitan Baltimore's growth has continued, while that of other Eastern industrial cities has stopped; but it has not grown as rapidly as metropolitan Washington.

Washington of course is a one company town, and the company is the federal government—for much of the sixties and seventies the nation's fastest growing industry. For the last 20 years, in good economic times and bad, Washington has experienced a major boom. Of all major urban agglomerations, only Houston grew faster than Washington in the sixties, and only a few Sun Belt areas have grown faster in the seventies. Most of that growth has taken place in the Maryland suburbs, where high rise office buildings and apartment complexes stand in what was pasture land a few years ago. The Maryland suburbs of Washington have none of the ethnic-industrial history of Baltimore, nor do they share suburban Baltimore's political tendencies. When the Baltimore suburbs were moving toward the Republicans in 1970 and 1972, for example, the Washington suburbs—especially well-to-do Montgomery County—stuck with the Democrats; there was little positive response here to the law and order campaign of the Nixon years. But in 1976, when the Baltimore area shifted sharply to Jimmy Carter in the general election, suburban Washington, perhaps seeing him as an outsider and anti-Washington candidate, stayed aloof. Carter got a good majority in Prince Georges County, where many residents are whites from the South or blacks from the District of Columbia, but the Democrat barely carried Montgomery County over Gerald Ford.

But what has really given Maryland its national reputation is political corruption. This is a state whose last two elected governors have been convicted of felonies. The first was of course Spiro Agnew, who took bribes from people doing business with the government as Baltimore County Executive, Governor, and Vice President. Agnew has argued that what he did was common practice among Maryland politicians, and convictions of other local and state officials suggest that this is so. This is a state which has seen a lot of growth, construction, and public expenditure; and it has had a civic culture in which officials were not reluctant to take money from businessmen who wanted to influence their decisions. Governor Marvin Mandel, Agnew's successor, was a product of the Maryland legislature and a far shrewder politician. He never took blatant bribes or payoffs, but he was convicted on federal charges of fraud for receiving favors from a few well-placed cronies and doing favors for them in return. There is no question that Mandel's governorship was profitable for these men, but a federal appeals court has overturned his conviction and, at this writing, he seems unlikely to be retried. Ironically, the appeals decision came just before Mandel's term had expired. On his conviction he had been removed from office and his Lieutenant Governor, Blair Lee III, had become Acting Governor for some 14 months.

When the conviction was reversed, Mandel officially reclaimed the office and held it for several days.

Maryland voters had elected Mandel to office in 1970 and 1974 by large margins; apparently they considered his undoubted talent for governing more important than their doubts about his ethics. But in 1978 they opted for change. Blair Lee was the favorite in the Democratic primary. A veteran of Democratic politics in Montgomery County and the bearer of a proud family name—he is related to the Lees of Virginia and the Blairs of Blair House, and his father owned most of what is now downtown Silver Spring—Lee was also the possessor of a candid, crusty personality and an unsmirched reputation for honesty. But he had also been a political ally of Mandel's and the Governor's hand-picked successor. It went against Lee's nature to distance himself too much from the man he had worked with and whom he considered innocent of the charges against him; and during his term as Acting Governor he was unable to define his own goals and accomplishments. The voters were looking for an alternative to Lee; there was a political vacuum to be filled.

The surprise was that it was filled not by a well known political figure but by a man who was hardly known to the public. Lee's foremost rival during most of the primary period was Baltimore County Executive Ted Venetoulis, a former professor and backer of Jerry Brown in his successful run in the 1976 Maryland presidential primary. Venetoulis was well known in the Baltimore area, but he had also made many enemies after four years in local office. Several weeks before the primary the Baltimore *Sun* surprised everyone by endorsing a third candidate, Harry Hughes. He had a competent record in state government, first in the legislature and then as head of Mandel's transportation department—a position he resigned in protest because, he said, of tampering with the process for selecting state contractors. Hughes was from the conservative Eastern Shore, but had put together Maryland's one major tax reform and had supported civil rights measures in the sixties. But all these credentials had meant little before the *Sun* endorsement, for Hughes had virtually no campaign money and had therefore communicated none of this information to the voters.

The *Sun* endorsement changed that. Voters, eager for an alternative, liked what they heard about Hughes, and the *Sun*'s poll showed his support rise rapidly. He ended up defeating Lee by a decisive margin. And that victory pretty much determined the outcome of the general election. Hughes managed to avoid mistakes in the fall campaign, and his Republican opponent, Glenn Beall, was unable to get his campaign off the ground. Beall had served one term as a U.S. Senator, but he actually had little popularity of his own. He had won in 1970 when incumbent Joseph Tydings was attacked by the opponents of gun control and when he received a $250,000 secret campaign contribution from a White House slush fund. When that information came out later, Beall's career was probably over, even though his reputation for personal honesty was not questioned. (He also has a distinguished political family with a reputation for integrity: his father was elected senator in the fifties and his brother George Beall was the U.S. Attorney who prosecuted Spiro Agnew.) Glenn Beall lost badly in the 1976 Senate race to Paul Sarbanes, and he had been prepared to run in 1978 against the sins of Marvin Mandel and his political heir, Blair Lee. When Hughes won the primary, Beall's campaign lost its raison d'etre, and never recovered. Hughes won with as large a percentage as a Maryland governor has had in a century.

The money in Maryland politics is in state and local office; there have been no allegations of corruption or even patronage-oriented politics about the members of the state's congressional delegation. The senior Senator, Charles Mathias, is a model of probity and integrity. He is from an old family in Frederick County, in the hills west of Washington and Baltimore; he served as a liberal Republican Congressman from a district including Montgomery County in the sixties and was elected to the Senate in 1968. Mathias is the old-fashioned kind of Republican for whom one of the party's main attractions is its historic record on civil rights; he was not pleased to see his party dominated by civil rights foes like Barry Goldwater. Ironically, he ranks second on Judiciary to Strom Thurmond; Thurmond specifically took the ranking Republican chair on this committee rather than Judiciary to prevent Mathias from getting it. There was a feeling among conservatives that Mathias was a renegade: he had voted with Judiciary Democrats on Watergate issues; he had opposed the Administration during the Vietnam war; he had resisted the politics of law and order.

It must have rankled the conservatives even more that Mathias was a senator widely respected. He is one of those senators whose views are considered sound, and whose judgment on difficult issues is respected and sought. He is cautious, serious, not eager to take a stand; but when he does, he is listened to. For a while in the middle seventies Mathias was reportedly considering switching to the Democratic Party or running in 1980 as an Independent. As legislative issues switched from style to economic matters, Mathias has apparently abandoned such ideas. He has high ratings from liberal and labor organizations, but he does have a kind of Republican respect for the free market system which Democrats do not seem to share, and he has expressed some doubts about the Carter Administration's foreign policies. In all, he seems a man more temperamentally suited to the role of careful, judicious opposition than to strong advocacy of any establishment's program.

Mathias still could encounter tough primary opposition in 1980, perhaps from House member Robert Bauman. Few people vote in Maryland Republican primaries and many of them are strong conservatives for whom Mathias's stands on many issues are repugnant. A nuisance candidate received one-fourth of the primary vote against Mathias in the 1974 primary. As for the general election, Mathias is the kind of Republican who appeals to Democrats, but he is not the kind of politician who inspires strong feelings on the part of many voters. It is entirely possible that he will face only weak opposition. In 1974 he beat the poorly financed campaign of Barbara Mikulski, now a Baltimore Congresswoman by a solid but not overwhelming margin.

Probably even more secure politically is the state's junior Senator, Democrat Paul Sarbanes. He holds a seat which has changed hands every six years since the fifties, but Sarbanes himself shows no sign of relinquishing it. Indeed, he did not even have much trouble winning it. As a Baltimore Congressman, he easily beat former Senator Joseph Tydings in the primary and Senator Glenn Beall in the general election.

Sarbanes is an even more cautious man than Mathias, and he seldom lets others know what he is thinking until he has made up his mind. In a state where Democratic politicians usually get ahead in a gregarious, back-slapping environment, Sarbanes has always been something of a loner: a rebel against Marvin Mandel in the Assembly, an insurgent who took on an incumbent congressman and committee chairman in the 1970 primary, a Judiciary Committee member who was expected all along to support impeachment but who did not commit himself until he had digested all the evidence. Sarbanes has come out a winner from all these situations not because he has made friends but because he works hard and knows his stuff.

Maryland has a rather odd history of Democratic presidential primaries. (Republican presidential primaries have been unimportant here; far fewer voters register than regularly vote Republican.) George Wallace nearly won the primary here in 1964; the Democrats then abolished it; it was reinstituted in 1972, when Wallace won, but only after he was shot while campaigning in Prince Georges County.

More recently Maryland has been the state which gave Jerry Brown his first primary victory in 1976—and which may provide a basis of comparison for a Carter–Brown faceoff in 1980. Maryland was Brown's first primary because it was the first he could enter when he decided to run. He quickly assembled an odd coalition: young, often teen-aged, volunteers; housewives who believed in change; and practically every machine politician in Maryland (Mandel could not abide Carter). By this time the candidates who represented the ideological strains of the sixties—Wallace, Jackson, Udall—had become also-rans; a vote for Brown was the only way to express doubts about Carter. It may not have been much more; Maryland voters may have realized what was in fact the case—that however they voted, Carter was going to be nominated. In any case Brown had a solid 48%–37% victory. Can he do as well again?

A footnote. Maryland is now the first state of more than minimal size to have a House delegation half of whose members are women. Three of them have fashioned their own careers: 3d district Democrat Barbara Mikulski of Baltimore, 4th district Republican Marjorie Holt of Anne Arundel County, and 5th district Democrat Gladys Spellman of Prince Georges County. The other, 6th district Democrat Beverly Byron, was elected after the sudden death of her husband, Congressman Goodloe Byron, in the fall of 1978.

Census Data Pop. 3,922,399; 1.94% of U.S. total, 18th largest; Central city, 23%; suburban, 61%. Median family income, $11,057; 5th highest; families above $15,000: 29%; families below $3,000: 7%. Median years education, 12.1.

1977 Share of Federal Tax Burden $7,668,000,000; 2.22% of U.S. total, 13th largest.

1977 Share of Federal Outlays $9,874,921,000; 2.50% of U.S. total, 13th largest. Per capita federal spending, $2,410.

DOD	$2,767,090,000	10th (3.03%)	HEW	$3,275,192,000	12th (2.22%)
ERDA	$177,783,000	11th (3.01%)	HUD	$65,587,000	22d (1.55%)
NASA	$317,667,000	3d (8.05%)	VA	$280,475,000	25th (1.46%)
DOT	$444,901,000	9th (3.12%)	EPA	$256,329,000	10th (3.13%)
DOC	$377,299,000	4th (4.54%)	RevS	$157,855,000	15th (1.87%)
DOI	$35,092,000	29th (0.75%)	Debt	$145,057,000	27th (0.48%)
USDA	$256,813,000	33d (1.29%)	Other	$1,347,781,000	

Economic Base Finance, insurance and real estate; primary metal industries, especially blast furnaces and steel mills; food and kindred products; agriculture, notably dairy products, broilers, cattle and corn; electrical equipment and supplies, especially communication equipment; transportation equipment, especially motor vehicles and equipment and ship building and repairing; apparel and other textile products.

Political Line-up Governor, Harry R. Hughes (D). Senators, Charles McC. Mathias, Jr. (R) and Paul S. Sarbanes (D). Representatives 8 (6 D and 2 R). State Senate (40 D, 7 R); House of Delegates (125 D, 16 R)

The Voters

Registration 1,888,313 Total. 1,327,351 D (70%); 435,778 R (23%); 948 AI (–); 124,236 Other (7%).
Median voting age 41
Employment profile White collar, 56%. Blue collar, 31%. Service, 12%. Farm, 1%.
Ethnic groups Black, 18%. Spanish, 1%. Total foreign stock, 12%. Germany, 2%; Italy, USSR, UK, Poland, 1% each.

Presidential vote

1976	Carter (D)	759,612	(53%)
	Ford (R)	672,661	(47%)
1972	Nixon (R)	829,305	(62%)
	McGovern (D)	505,781	(38%)

1976 Democratic Presidential Primary

Brown	286,672	(48%)
Carter	219,404	(37%)
Udall	32,790	(6%)
Wallace	24,176	(4%)
Others	38,704	(5%)

1976 Republican Presidential Primary

Ford	96,291	(58%)
Reagan	69,680	(42%)

Sen. Charles McC. Mathias, Jr. (R) Elected 1968, seat up 1980; b. July 24, 1922, Frederick; home, Frederick; Haverford Col., B.A. 1944, U. of Md., LL.B. 1949; Episcopalian.

Career Navy, WWII; Asst. Atty. Gen. of Md., 1953–54; Frederick City Atty., 1954–59; Md. House of Delegates, 1959–60; U.S. House of Reps., 1961–69.

Offices 358 RSOB, 202-224-4654. Also 1616 Fed. Ofc. Bldg., 31 Hopkins Plaza, Baltimore 21201, 301-962-4850.

Committees *Appropriations* (4th). Subcommittees: District of Columbia; Foreign Operations; HUD-Independent Agencies; Labor, HEW, and Related Agencies; Transportation and Related Agencies.

Governmental Affairs (5th). Subcommittees: Investigations; Governmental Efficiency and the District of Columbia; Federal Spending Practices and Open Government.

Judiciary (2d). Subcommittees: Administrative Practice and Procedure; Antitrust, Monopoly, and Business Rights; Criminal Justice.

Select Committee on Ethics.

Group Ratings

	ADA	COPE	PC	RPN	NFU	LCV	CFA	NAB	NSI	ACA	NTU
1978	50	76	53	100	38	68	30	18	13	22	–
1977	75	79	55	83	33	–	52	–	–	14	28
1976	65	67	62	100	67	76	71	0	0	5	46

Key Votes

1) Warnke Nom	FOR	6) Egypt-Saudi Arms	FOR	11) Hosptl Cost Contnmnt	DNV
2) Neutron Bomb	AGN	7) Draft Restr Pardon	FOR	12) Clinch River Reactor	AGN
3) Waterwy User Fee	FOR	8) Wheat Price Support	AGN	13) Pub Fin Cong Cmpgns	FOR
4) Dereg Nat Gas	FOR	9) Panama Canal Treaty	FOR	14) ERA Ratif Recissn	FOR
5) Kemp-Roth	AGN	10) Labor Law Rev Clot	FOR	15) Med Necssy Abrtns	FOR

Election Results

1974 general	Charles McC. Mathias, Jr. (R)	503,223	(57%)	($329,845)
	Barbara Mikulski (D)	374,563	(43%)	($74,311)
1974 primary	Charles McC. Mathias, Jr. (R)	79,823	(76%)	
	Ross Z. Pierpont (R)	25,512	(24%)	
1968 general	Charles McC. Mathias (R)	541,893	(48%)	
	Daniel B. Brewster (D)	443,667	(39%)	
	George Mahoney (Ind.)	148,467	(13%)	

Sen. Paul S. Sarbanes (D) Elected 1976, seat up 1982; b. Feb. 3, 1933, Salisbury; home, Baltimore; Princeton U., A.B. 1954, Rhodes Scholar, Oxford U., B.A. 1957, Harvard U., LL.B., 1960; Greek Orthodox.

Career Law Clerk to Judge Morris A. Soper, U.S. 4th Circuit Ct. of Appeals, 1960–61; Practicing atty., 1961–62, 1965–71; Admin. Asst. to Chm. Walter W. Heller of the Pres. Cncl. of Econ. Advisers, 1962–63; Exec. Dir., Baltimore Charter Revision Comm., 1963–64; Md. House of Delegates, 1969–70; U.S. House of Reps., 1971–77.

Offices 2327 DSOB, 202-224-4524. Also 1518 Fed. Ofc. Bldg., Baltimore 21201, 301-962-4436, and 344 E. 33d St., Baltimore 21218, 301-962-4436.

Committees *Banking, Housing, and Urban Affairs* (7th). Subcommittees: Housing and Urban Affairs; Securities (Chairman); Consumer Affairs.

Foreign Relations (7th). Subcommittees: International Economic Policy (Chairman); Near Eastern and South Asian Affairs; Western Hemisphere Affairs.

Group Ratings

	ADA	COPE	PC	RPN	NFU	LCV	CFA	NAB	NSI	ACA	NTU
1978	90	95	90	60	60	86	80	8	20	8	–
1977	90	95	90	36	83	–	84	–	–	7	26
1976	80	86	92	56	78	98	81	18	10	0	17

Key Votes

1) Warnke Nom	FOR	6) Egypt-Saudi Arms	AGN	11) Hosptl Cost Contnmnt	FOR
2) Neutron Bomb	AGN	7) Draft Restr Pardon	AGN	12) Clinch River Reactor	AGN
3) Waterwy User Fee	FOR	8) Wheat Price Support	AGN	13) Pub Fin Cong Cmpgns	FOR
4) Dereg Nat Gas	AGN	9) Panama Canal Treaty	FOR	14) ERA Ratif Recissn	FOR
5) Kemp-Roth	AGN	10) Labor Law Rev Clot	FOR	15) Med Necssy Abrtns	FOR

Election Results

1976 general	Paul S. Sarbanes (D)	772,101	(59%)	($891,533)
	J. Glenn Beall, Jr. (R)	530,439	(41%)	($572,016)
1976 primary	Paul S. Sarbanes (D)	302,983	(55%)	
	Joseph D. Tydings (D)	191,875	(35%)	
	Six others (D)	52,896	(10%)	
1970 general	J. Glenn Beall, Jr. (R)	484,960	(51%)	
	Joseph D. Tydings (D)	460,422	(49%)	

Gov. Harry R. Hughes (D) Elected 1978, term expires Jan. 1981; b. Nov. 13, 1926, Easton; U. of Md., B.S. 1949, Geo. Wash. U., LL.B. 1952.

Career Navy Air Corps, WWII; Practicing atty.; Md. House of Delegates, 1955–58; Md. Senate, 1959–70, Major. Ldr., 1965–70; Chmn., Dem. Party of Md., 1969–70; Director, Md. Dept. of Transportation, 1971–77.

Offices Executive Dept., State House, Annapolis 21404, 301-269-3591.

Election Results

1978 general	Harry R. Hughes (D)	718,328	(71%)
	J. Glenn Beall, Jr. (R)	293,635	(29%)
1978 primary	Harry R. Hughes (D)	213,457	(37%)
	Blair Lee (D)	194,236	(34%)
	Ted Venetoulis (D)	140,486	(25%)
	One other (D)	25,200	(4%)
1974 general	Marvin Mandel (D)	602,648	(63%)
	Louise Gore (R)	346,449	(37%)

FIRST DISTRICT

Until the completion of the Chesapeake Bay Bridge in 1952, the Eastern Shore of Maryland was virtually cut off from the rest of the state. The "Eastern" refers to the east shore of the Chesapeake, a part of Maryland that remains almost a world unto itself—a region of Southern drowsiness, chicken farms, and fishing villages. Its history has been told in James Michener's bestseller, *Chesapeake*. Before the Civil War, the Eastern Shore was very much slaveholding country. Up through the sixties, attachment to the mores of the South persisted; until 1964 Maryland had a public accommodations law which explicitly excluded the Eastern Shore counties. Mostly rural, the economy of the area is buoyed by the dollars spent by tourists, summer people, and the rich who have built big estates here.

The Eastern Shore bulks larger than its numbers in Maryland politics. It continues to produce important state legislators and has given the state two of its last four governors—J. Millard Tawes (1959–67) and the current incumbent Harry Hughes. But because its population has not grown much—it only slightly more than doubled between 1790 and 1970—the Shore is less and less important politically. The 1st congressional district is, by reputation, the Eastern Shore district, although only 53% of its residents actually live east of the Bay. The rest are found in two entirely separate areas. The first is Harford County, a northern extension of the Baltimore metropolitan area; the second is Charles, St. Mary's, and Calvert Counties south of Annapolis. The latter are where Lord Baltimore's Catholics first settled Maryland, and there is a substantial rural Catholic population there still. This area is also known for having had until the sixties the East Coast's only legal slot machines.

Both the Eastern Shore and the two western shore parts of the 1st have a Democratic registration which is deceptively high. Although Democrats still hold local and state legislative office, these are areas which for years have preferred Republican candidates, not only for president, but for congressman as well. Fully 19% of the district's population is black—this is the farthest north you will find significant numbers of blacks in rural settings—but their Democratic preferences are ordinarily outweighed by the whites' Republican majorities. The Eastern Shore has gone Democratic in House races only twice since World War II.

The 1st district is currently represented by one of the House's most staunchly conservative Republicans. Robert Bauman was founder of Young Americans for Freedom in the early sixties; he served as a Republican aide on the Hill and in the Maryland Senate. Bauman is as ideologically committed as any Republican in the House; he is also one of the Republican Party's masters of parliamentary procedure. He comes to this role naturally: he objects to what he believes big government is doing to the country, and he interposes objections when he sees advocates of big government trying to get something through on the floor of the House. Bauman forces the majority to play by the rules and to air fully their reasons for doing what they want to do; and sometimes by doing so he forces them to reconsider or stop. His procedural talents won him a seat on the House Rules Committee in 1979. He can be counted on to vote against the wishes of the Democratic leadership almost always and against the wishes of the Republican leadership more often than it would like.

Bauman is not only involved in procedural matters; he has an impact on substantive issues as well. He succeeded in getting a roll call vote on the congressional pay raise and pushed through an amendment cutting most foreign aid across the board by 5%. He got the Hatch Act to provide federal employees from soliciting campaign funds from auditors of federal contracts. Because of his objections the House committee investigating assassinations was delayed from reconvening for one month.

Bauman could continue as an influential figure in the House, or he might run for the Senate in 1980 or 1982. The earlier race would presumably mean a primary race against Senator Charles Mathias. Bauman does not have the widespread respect Mathias enjoys among voters generally, nor is he as well known statewide. If he ran, he would be banking on the conservative leanings of the relatively small number of Marylanders who vote in Republican primaries. That is probably enough to make him a formidable challenger, and maybe a senator. Democrats will probably not have a strong contender for the Mathias seat unless it seems pretty clear that Bauman or someone like him will win the nomination.

Census Data Pop. 489,455. Central city, 0%; suburban, 34%. Median family income, $8,925; families above $15,000: 17%; families below $3,000: 11%. Median years education, 11.1.

The Voters

Median voting age 41.
Employment profile White collar, 42%. Blue collar, 40%. Service, 13%. Farm, 5%.
Ethnic groups Black, 19%. Total foreign stock, 5%. Germany, 1%.

Presidential vote

1976	Carter (D)	85,106	(49%)
	Ford (R)	87,481	(51%)
1972	Nixon (R)	106,539	(72%)
	McGovern (D)	42,257	(28%)

Rep. Robert E. Bauman (R) Elected Aug. 21, 1973; b. Apr. 4, 1937, Easton; home, Easton; Georgetown U., B.S. 1959, J.D. 1964; Catholic.

Career Mbr., Minor. Staff, U.S. House of Reps. Comm. on The Judiciary, 1955–59; Founder and Natl. Chm., Young Americans for Freedom, 1962–65; Repub. Legislative Staff, U.S. House of Reps., 1965–68; Practicing atty., 1968–73; Md. Senate, 1971–73.

Offices 2443 RHOB, 202-225-5311. Also Loyola Fed. Bldg., Goldsborough and Harrison Sts., Easton 21601, 301-822-4300.

Committees *Rules* (5th).

Merchant Marine and Fisheries (7th). Subcommittees: Fish and Wildlife; Panama Canal.

Group Ratings

	ADA	COPE	PC	RPN	NFU	LCV	CFA	NAB	NSI	ACA	NTU
1978	10	15	18	50	30	–	23	100	100	93	–
1977	10	13	15	38	75	25	10	–	–	96	57
1976	5	17	11	56	0	17	0	100	100	93	60

Key Votes

1) Increase Def Spnd	FOR	6) Alaska Lands Protect	AGN	11) Delay Auto Pol Cntrl	FOR
2) B-1 Bomber	FOR	7) Water Projects Veto	FOR	12) Sugar Price Escalator	FOR
3) Cargo Preference	FOR	8) Consum Protect Agcy	AGN	13) Pub Fin Cong Cmpgns	AGN
4) Dereg Nat Gas	FOR	9) Common Situs Picket	AGN	14) ERA Ratif Recissn	FOR
5) Kemp-Roth	FOR	10) Labor Law Revision	AGN	15) Prohibt Govt Abrtns	FOR

Election Results

1978 general	Robert E. Bauman (R)	80,202	(64%)	($220,076)
	Joseph D. Quinn (D)	46,093	(36%)	($88,759)
1978 primary	Robert E. Bauman (R), unopposed			
1976 general	Robert E. Bauman (R)	85,919	(54%)	($192,719)
	Roy Dyson (D)	72,993	(46%)	($58,023)

SECOND DISTRICT

Baltimore County, as anyone who lives there will tell you, is entirely separate from the city of Baltimore. It is, by definition of the Census Bureau, totally suburban. But it is far from homogeneous. In the north of the County are verdant horse farms; just northwest of the city is the predominantly Jewish suburb of Pikesville; due north of downtown Baltimore is WASPy, well-to-do Towson; east of Baltimore are the working class suburbs of Dundalk and Sparrows Point. In one respect, however, Baltimore County is not diverse; while about half the residents of the city are black, only a handful of County residents are.

This is the place that gave us Spiro Agnew. Like most of Maryland, Baltimore County registers and, in local elections, usually votes Democratic. But in 1962 Democrats had scandal problems and, to everyone's surprise, the Republican nominee for county executive—former zoning board member Agnew—actually won. Doubtful of reelection four years later, Agnew got his party's nomination for governor, which became worth something when Democrats chose the eccentric George P. ("your home is your castle") Mahoney as their nominee. From county executive to vice president, Agnew provided mediocre service and was rewarded with immediate advancement —and with a regular series of bribes and payoffs. Agnew's Democratic successor, Dale Anderson, committed the same crimes; unfortunate enough not to have been governor or vice president, he went to jail.

In Congress Baltimore County has been represented during all this time by a professor whose honesty is above reproach. In 1962 the Democrats in the 2d congressional district, which then included all of Baltimore County, nominated Clarence D. Long, Ph.D., professor of economics at Johns Hopkins University, as their candidate for Congress. A blue ribbon candidate in a year of scandals, Long won that election and, through a series of redistrictings, has been reelected ever since. Currently the 2d district includes most of Baltimore County, including such diverse areas as Dundalk, Towson, and Pikesville, plus a small Jewish neighborhood in Baltimore City. The secret of Long's political success has been close attention to his constituents. He returns from Washington every night to his home in the district, and throughout the year rides around in a trailer to meet constituents and handle the problems they bring to him.

In Washington many oldtime members of Congress regard Long—universally referred to as "Doc"—with the suspicion men of the world have traditionally reserved for professors. Younger members, though they respect him more, regard him as part of another generation. After nearly two decades in Congress, seniority and the primary defeat on 76-year-old Otto Passman made Long Chairman of the Foreign Operations Appropriations Subcommittee. This is the body with jurisdiction over the foreign aid program, and one of Long's major jobs in Congress is to steer foreign aid appropriations through to passage. They are perennially unpopular with voters, and they also attract amendments from backers of human rights and upholders of private enterprise, who want to deny aid to nations which offend them. Long himself has favored cutting aid to countries like South Korea and Chile, and has favored cutting military spending. He was one of the few members of Congress with a son who served in Vietnam; he switched from hawk to dove in 1970 and later led the successful amendment cutting off American military spending in Southeast Asia.

Census Data Pop. 491,331. Central city, 5%; suburban, 95%. Median family income, $12,140; families above $15,000: 33%; families below $3,000: 4%. Median years education, 12.1.

The Voters

Median voting age 42.
Employment profile White collar, 59%. Blue collar, 32%. Service, 8%. Farm, 1%.
Ethnic groups Black, 3%. Total foreign stock, 17%. USSR, 4%; Poland, Germany, Italy, 2% each; UK, 1%.

Presidential vote

1976	Carter (D)	101,830	(48%)
	Ford (R)	109,176	(52%)
1972	Nixon (R)	135,329	(68%)
	McGovern (D)	62,755	(32%)

Rep. Clarence D. Long (D) Elected 1962; b. Dec. 11, 1908, South Bend, Ind.; home, Ruxton; Wash. and Jeff. Col., B.A., Princeton U., M.A., Ph.D.; Presbyterian.

Career Navy, WWII; Prof. of Econ., Johns Hopkins U., 1946–64; Sr. Staff Mbr., Pres. Cncl. of Econ. Advisers, 1953–54, 1956–57; Acting Chm., Md. Dem. St. Central Comm., 1961–62.

Offices 2407 RHOB, 202-225-3061. Also Rm. 200, P.O. Bldg., Towson 21204, 301-828-6616.

Committees *Appropriations* (11th). Subcommittees: Foreign Operations (Chairman); Interior; Military Construction.

Group Ratings

	ADA	COPE	PC	RPN	NFU	LCV	CFA	NAB	NSI	ACA	NTU
1978	40	42	65	42	78	–	55	42	67	37	–
1977	55	70	73	50	50	87	65	–	–	30	20
1976	65	55	70	61	73	87	64	33	50	22	28

Key Votes

1) Increase Def Spnd	FOR	6) Alaska Lands Protect	FOR	11) Delay Auto Pol Cntrl	AGN
2) B-1 Bomber	FOR	7) Water Projects Veto	AGN	12) Sugar Price Escalator	AGN
3) Cargo Preference	FOR	8) Consum Protect Agcy	FOR	13) Pub Fin Cong Cmpgns	FOR
4) Dereg Nat Gas	FOR	9) Common Situs Picket	AGN	14) ERA Ratif Recissn	AGN
5) Kemp-Roth	AGN	10) Labor Law Revision	FOR	15) Prohibt Govt Abrtns	AGN

Election Results

1978 general	Clarence D. Long (D)	98,601	(66%)	($61,863)
	Malcolm M. McKnight (R)	49,886	(34%)	($30,777)
1978 primary	Clarence D. Long (D)	70,280	(86%)	
	One other (D)	11,021	(14%)	
1976 general	Clarence D. Long (D)	139,196	(71%)	($77,457)
	John M. Seney (R)	35,258	(18%)	($5,436)
	Ronald A. Meroney (Ind.)	21,849	(11%)	($17,616)

THIRD DISTRICT

East Baltimore is a favorite of political sociologists. It is composed of white ethnic communities—Irish, Italian, German, Greek, and especially Polish—which seem to have changed little since the twenties. The unique Baltimore row houses stand here as carefully maintained as ever, and the streets are spotless and teeming with children. But the politics of east Baltimore has been undergoing constant change. The old machine which once dominated these wards has splintered into a dozen different factions. A newer breed of politician has begun to win elections here, by the old fashioned political methods of door-to-door campaigning and close communication with neighborhood groups.

One such politician is Paul Sarbanes, elected Congressman here in 1970 by beating incumbent George Fallon, Chairman of the House Public Works Committee; Sarbanes went on to the Senate in 1976. Another new style east Baltimore politician is Barbara Mikulski, Baltimore Council member, head of the national Democratic Party's committee on delegate selection, Democratic candidate for the Senate in 1974, and elected as Sarbanes's successor in the House in 1976.

Mikulski's district is centered on east Baltimore and can be described as containing the white majority parts of Baltimore and some adjacent suburbs. The 3d proceeds west from east Baltimore to the city's revitalized downtown and the old neighborhoods near the harbor, including the one which contains Francis Scott Key's Fort McHenry. Still farther west are the middle class suburbs of Catonsville and Arbutus, where the row houses thin out to become detached homes. The 3d also proceeds north from east Baltimore, to take in the predominantly Catholic neighborhoods in the northeast part of the city, Johns Hopkins University, and a small chunk of suburban Baltimore County.

The 3d district is a good place to examine what has happened to the phenomenon of the ethnics—the switch of blue collar ethnics from their traditional Democratic allegiance to the law and order politics exemplified, in their time, by Richard Nixon and Spiro Agnew. This is an area that voted heavily for John Kennedy in 1960, but it went only 41% for Hubert Humphrey in 1968 and a scant 33% for George McGovern in 1972. Jimmy Carter did carry the district in 1976, but with a lackluster 52%. There seems to be a feeling that national Democrats no longer care much for the kind of people who live here—and perhaps that they care more about the blacks on the other side of town. Most Democrats here are young enough or well enough off that they cannot be brought back to the Democratic fold any longer by references to the New Deal; and promises of more social programs are not in any case what they want. There is a feeling that places like east Baltimore have been left behind and that the national Democrats, in their quest for votes in trendier quarters, have forgotten them.

Local Democrats like Mikulski do not have such problems. She has been an important national figure now for half a dozen years, but she remains close to her district—returning there often and listening closely to her constituents. She still speaks their language—and speaks it with a pungent zest that is humorous and at the same time telling. Mikulski is a liberal, but one that believes that many of the Democrats elected with her in 1974 have forgotten the economic needs of the ordinary person. She has not, and she seems solidly entrenched in the 3d district.

Census Data Pop. 490,851. Central city, 80%; suburban, 20%. Median family income, $10,022; families above $15,000: 21%; families below $3,000: 9%. Median years education, 10.6.

The Voters

Median voting age 45.
Employment profile White collar, 54%. Blue collar, 35%. Service, 11%. Farm, –%.
Ethnic groups Black, 13%. Spanish, 1%. Total foreign stock, 15%. Germany, 3%; Italy, Poland, 2% each.

Presidential vote

1976	Carter (D)	83,341	(52%)
	Ford (R)	78,442	(48%)
1972	Nixon (R)	111,007	(67%)
	McGovern (D)	53,981	(33%)

Rep. Barbara A. Mikulski (D) Elected 1976; b. July 20, 1936, Baltimore; home, Baltimore; Mt. St. Agnes Col., Baltimore, B.A. 1958, U. of Md., M.S.W. 1965; Catholic.

Career Administrator, Baltimore Dept. of Soc. Services; Caseworker; Teacher; Adjunct Prof., Loyola Col., 1972–76; Chairwoman, Dem. Natl. Com. Commission on Delegate Selection and Party Structure, 1973; Dem. nominee for U.S. Senate, 1974.

Offices 238 CHOB, 202-225-4016. Also 1414 Fed. Bldg., Baltimore 21201, 301-962-4510.

Committees *Interstate and Foreign Commerce* (22d). Subcommittees: Health and the Environment; Transportation and Commerce.

Merchant Marine and Fisheries (17th). Subcommittees: Coast Guard and Navigation; Merchant Marine; Oceanography.

Group Ratings

	ADA	COPE	PC	RPN	NFU	LCV	CFA	NAB	NSI	ACA	NTU
1978	85	85	83	33	78	–	91	0	11	7	–
1977	90	87	78	38	100	85	70	–	–	7	17

Key Votes

1) Increase Def Spnd	AGN	6) Alaska Lands Protect	FOR	11) Delay Auto Pol Cntrl	AGN
2) B-1 Bomber	AGN	7) Water Projects Veto	AGN	12) Sugar Price Escalator	AGN
3) Cargo Preference	FOR	8) Consum Protect Agcy	FOR	13) Pub Fin Cong Cmpgns	FOR
4) Dereg Nat Gas	AGN	9) Common Situs Picket	FOR	14) ERA Ratif Recissn	AGN
5) Kemp-Roth	AGN	10) Labor Law Revision	FOR	15) Prohibt Govt Abrtns	AGN

Election Results

1978 general	Barbara A. Mikulski (D), unopposed			($38,333)
1978 primary	Barbara A. Mikulski (D)	57,156	(90%)	
	One other (D)	6,271	(10%)	
1976 general	Barbara A. Mikulski (D)	107,014	(75%)	($72,418)
	Samuel A. Culotta (R)	36,447	(25%)	($8,632)

FOURTH DISTRICT

The 4th congressional district of Maryland contains all of Anne Arundel County (Annapolis and Baltimore suburbs) and part of Prince Georges County (near Washington). The creation of the district in 1972 was greeted with cheers in Anne Arundel, which despite its population of nearly 300,000 had never had its own congressman. With two-thirds of the new district's voters, Anne Arundel seemed likely to dominate the 4th's politics, and it has. When the results were in, the new Representative was former Ann Arundel Clerk Marjorie Holt.

The 4th runs from the Baltimore city limits to the District of Columbia line. In between is mostly vacant land, primed for the kind of rapid development that increased the district's population 66% in the sixties. In the middle of the district is Annapolis, the quaint eighteenth century town that contains Maryland's State House—the oldest capitol in the nation still in use—and the United States Naval Academy. Moving inexorably over the lowlying hills and around the wide Chesapeake inlets toward Annapolis are the not-so-fashionable suburbs of Baltimore where most of the 4th district's residents live: Linthicum, Glen Burnie, Severna Park. On the other side of the district, near Washington, are the fast-growing communities of Oxon Hill, Suitland, and Camp Springs. Near Annapolis, but stuck in the middle of the rural countryside is the new townhouse and shopping center suburb of Crofton, where Spiro Agnew first settled after his resignation as Vice President.

This is a district where two-thirds of the voters register Democratic but where a bare plurality supported Jimmy Carter and less than one-third supported either of the two Democratic nominees before him. Mrs. Holt, a Republican generally considered conservative, seems to have found the formula for political success. Twice she has defeated a candidate known as a liberal, and twice she has defeated Democratic moderates. Her constituency service operation is considered good—which is of crucial importance in a district where many of the voters are federal employees. She clearly has a safe seat in the House.

Holt is one of the few women on the House Armed Services Committee, and she has on occasion urged larger defense budgets. She also serves on the House Budget Committee, where she supports and has sponsored major budget cuts.

Census Data Pop. 495,249. Central city, 0%; suburban, 100%. Median family income, $11,892; families above $15,000: 32%; families below $3,000: 5%. Median years education, 12.3.

The Voters

Median voting age 37.
Employment profile White collar, 60%. Blue collar, 28%. Service, 11%. Farm, 1%.
Ethnic groups Black, 10%. Spanish, 2%. Total foreign stock, 10%. Germany, 2%; Italy, UK, 1% each.

Presidential vote

1976	Carter (D)	86,532	(50%)
	Ford (R)	86,352	(50%)
1972	Nixon (R)	107,379	(70%)
	McGovern (D)	44,937	(30%)

Rep. Marjorie S. Holt (R) Elected 1972; b. Sept. 17, 1920, Birmingham, Ala.; home, Severna Park; Jacksonville U., B.A. 1946, U. of Fla., J.D. 1949; Presbyterian.

Career Practicing atty., 1950–66; Anne Arundel Co. Supervisor of Elections, 1963–65; Anne Arundel Co. Clerk of the Circuit Ct., 1966–72.

Offices 2434 RHOB, 202-225-8090. Also 95 Aquahart Rd., Glen Burnie 21061, 301-768-8050.

Committees *Armed Services* (8th). Subcommittees: Procurement and Military Nuclear Systems; Military Personnel.

Budget (4th). Subcommittees: Human and Community Resources; Budget Process; Defense and International Affairs.

Group Ratings

	ADA	COPE	PC	RPN	NFU	LCV	CFA	NAB	NSI	ACA	NTU
1978	5	20	13	45	20	–	14	100	100	85	–
1977	5	23	18	46	25	11	15	–	–	85	40
1976	5	18	10	59	0	18	0	100	100	84	56

Key Votes

1) Increase Def Spnd	FOR	6) Alaska Lands Protect	FOR	11) Delay Auto Pol Cntrl	FOR
2) B-1 Bomber	FOR	7) Water Projects Veto	FOR	12) Sugar Price Escalator	FOR
3) Cargo Preference	AGN	8) Consum Protect Agcy	AGN	13) Pub Fin Cong Cmpgns	AGN
4) Dereg Nat Gas	FOR	9) Common Situs Picket	AGN	14) ERA Ratif Recissn	FOR
5) Kemp-Roth	FOR	10) Labor Law Revision	AGN	15) Prohibt Govt Abrtns	FOR

Election Results

1978 general	Marjorie S. Holt (R)	71,374	(62%)	($107,607)
	Sue F. Ward (D)	43,663	(38%)	($37,478)
1978 primary	Marjorie S. Holt (R), unopposed			
1976 general	Marjorie S. Holt (R)	95,158	(58%)	($110,684)
	Weiner Fornos (D)	69,855	(42%)	($39,989)

FIFTH DISTRICT

The 5th congressional district of Maryland includes most of Prince Georges County, the largest suburban county in the state. Situated just north and east of Washington, D.C., Prince Georges is a little less white collar and less affluent than adjacent Montgomery County. Yet against national averages, Prince Georges does very well indeed. The main reason is the high salaries and wages paid by the federal government. Fully 38% of the work force in the 5th district is employed by Uncle Sam—the highest such figure of any congressional district in the nation. The difference between Prince Georges and Montgomery is not so much money but status; rarely does anyone from Hyattsville or College Park make the gossip columns. The people living here are the bureaucrats who keep all those offices in Washington and the suburbs filled, and the memoes churning out of xerox machines, under Nixon and Ford and Carter, regardless of Vietnam or Watergate or Proposition 13.

The 5th's population shot up 69% in the sixties, making it one of the fastest-growing congressional districts in the nation. The rapid growth began here in the fifties, when metropolitan Washington's population burst outside the District line; the rush to the suburbs was accelerated, though it would have happened anyway, by the integration of the District's schools in 1955. In the seventies this kind of growth has stopped, and a new kind of population movement has taken place. There is little sewer capacity for new subdivisions, so Prince Georges's population has remained at the same figure, but its composition has changed. Now it is blacks, rather than whites, who are streaming out of the District (ironically, in many cases because of poor public schools). Whites, in turn, are moving even farther out, in many cases to the semi-rural Anne Arundel or Charles Counties. The 5th district was 16% black in 1970; the figure may well be double that today.

Back in the fifties, Prince Georges was run by a rural Democratic machine consisting of a few old men, one of them perhaps chewing tobacco, who liked to hang out in the dusty courthouse in tiny Upper Marlboro. These folks were swept out of power by people who understood the new suburban politics, and one of them was Gladys Spellman, onetime County Council member and now Congresswoman from the 5th district. Spellman proved able to work with both the idealistic liberals and the more practical-minded politicians who are so common in Maryland, and she proved adept at taking advantage of opportunities for herself. When Republican Congressman Lawrence Hogan ran for governor in 1974, Spellman was ready. She won the primary and beat a Hogan protege to become the first Democrat elected from this area since 1966.

Spellman has done well in subsequent races. While the local Democratic machine has had its problems—it lost the county executive post to Hogan in 1978 and one of its leading members went down to defeat on Blair Lee's ticket in the 1978 primary—Spellman has built up increasing margins. Of course a congressman's office is a perfect instrument for winning votes in a place like Prince Georges. Federal employees with grievances are particularly common here, and Spellman's office is always glad to help them out. District of Columbia officials want to levy a commuter tax on suburbanites who work in Washington; Spellman is there to make sure it's killed. And federal employees do not want to be the brunt of budget-cutting efforts. Gladys Spellman sits on the Post Office and Civil Service Committee, and there works against any measures which would hold down pay hikes, require productivity increases, or freeze the hiring of new workers. She is concerned about the psychic income of government workers, too. Regularly she issues to a deserving recipient her "Beautiful Bureaucrat" award. It is no surprise that she is reelected by a large margin.

Census Data Pop. 482,721. Central city, 0%; suburban, 100%. Median family income, $12,286; families above $15,000: 33%; families below $3,000: 4%. Median years education, 12.5.

The Voters

Median voting age 34.
Employment profile White collar, 67%. Blue collar, 23%. Service, 10%. Farm, –%.
Ethnic groups Black, 16%. Spanish, 2%. Total foreign stock, 13%. Italy, 2%; Germany, UK, 1% each.

Presidential vote

1976	Carter (D)	82,660	(59%)
	Ford (R)	58,086	(41%)
1972	Nixon (R)	83,579	(57%)
	McGovern (D)	63,821	(43%)

Rep. Gladys Noon Spellman (D) Elected 1974; b. Mar. 2, 1918, New York, N.Y.; home, Laurel; Geo. Wash. U.

Career Public school teacher; Prince Georges Co. Bd. of Commissioners, 1962–74, Chm., Councilor-at-Large.

Offices 308 CHOB, 202-225-4131. Also Rm. 106, 3700 E-W Hwy., Hyattsville 20782, 301-436-8865.

Committees *Banking, Finance and Urban Affairs* (16th). Subcommittees: Consumer Affairs; Housing and Community Development.

Post Office and Civil Service (7th). Subcommittees: Compensation and Employee Benefits (Chairwoman); Human Resources; Investigations.

Group Ratings

	ADA	COPE	PC	RPN	NFU	LCV	CFA	NAB	NSI	ACA	NTU
1978	70	89	78	33	78	–	64	10	40	4	–
1977	75	87	83	50	55	96	70	–	–	16	21
1976	70	83	89	61	82	84	100	17	10	8	52

Key Votes

1) Increase Def Spnd	AGN	6) Alaska Lands Protect	FOR	11) Delay Auto Pol Cntrl	AGN
2) B-1 Bomber	AGN	7) Water Projects Veto	AGN	12) Sugar Price Escalator	AGN
3) Cargo Preference	FOR	8) Consum Protect Agcy	FOR	13) Pub Fin Cong Cmpgns	FOR
4) Dereg Nat Gas	AGN	9) Common Situs Picket	FOR	14) ERA Ratif Recissn	AGN
5) Kemp-Roth	AGN	10) Labor Law Revision	FOR	15) Prohibt Govt Abrtns	AGN

Election Results

1978 general	Gladys Noon Spellman (D)	64,868	(77%)	($72,520)
	Saul J. Harris (R)	19,160	(23%)	($32,209)
1978 primary	Gladys Noon Spellman (D)	34,994	(84%)	
	One other (D)	6,509	(16%)	
1976 general	Gladys Noon Spellman (D)	77,836	(58%)	($148,103)
	John B. Burcham, Jr. (R)	57,057	(42%)	($98,149)

SIXTH DISTRICT

West of Baltimore and Washington a series of gentle Maryland hills rise to the low mountains of the Catoctins and the Appalachian ridges. Here is a land known for its fertile valleys and its antique cities, like Frederick, where Barbara Fritchie supposedly reared her old gray head. Also here are the small industrial cities of Hagerstown and, high in the mountains, Cumberland. The mountain folk and Pennsylvania Dutch who settled western Maryland left behind a Republican heritage, unusual in a state that is Democratic by tradition and custom. Nevertheless, a majority of the voters here, as in the rest of the state, are registered Democrats, simply because the Democratic primary is almost always where the action is. Come November, these "Democrats" are ready to vote Republican once again, as they did in 1976, when Gerald Ford carried western Maryland easily.

The 6th congressional district includes all of western Maryland and a portion of suburban Baltimore County. The only part of the 6th which is markedly out of step with the conservative, rural mores of the district is the much heralded "new town" of Columbia in Howard County. It is a planned, integrated development that had 8,000 people and is supposed to house 110,000 in 1982; Columbia is not as great a departure from other large suburban developments as it would like to think, but its new town rhetoric did have the politically significant effect of attracting a disproportionate number of suburban liberals who otherwise would probably live in Baltimore County.

The dominant figure in congressional politics here was Goodloe Byron, a Democrat first elected to the House in 1970. He was from an old political family; both his father and, when he died in an airplane crash, his mother represented the district in the House. Byron himself was once called the most conservative congressional Democrat from outside the House; he had low ratings from liberal and labor organizations and often voted with Republicans on both economic and non-economic issues. This record made him an exceedingly strong candidate in general elections. But he had some trouble in primaries. In 1976 Dan Rupli, running as a liberal and stressing environmental issues, held Byron to 55%; in 1978 Rupli ran again and made a less impressive showing.

In October 1978, Byron died suddenly while jogging; he was only 49 but had a history of heart trouble. The local Democrats decided without dissent to give the nomination to his wife, Beverly Byron. She had not been active in politics previously, but has an interesting background as the daughter of Captain Harry Butcher, wartime naval aide to President Eisenhower. Newspaper reporters discovered that the Republican nominee lived in the hotel that was the model for the Broadway and television show Hot L Baltimore and had been jailed for assaulting a woman bus driver. When he heard that Byron had died, this man went to the Capitol in Washington and demanded that he be seated. With such opposition Mrs. Byron won with a record majority. The question is whether she will try to keep the seat or will retire from Congress in 1980. In the latter case there will probably be a spirited Democratic primary and possibly a strong Republican candidacy as well.

Census Data Pop. 491,839. Central city, 0%; suburban, 40%. Median family income, $9,749; families above $15,000: 20%; families below $3,000: 8%. Median years education, 11.6.

The Voters

Median voting age 42.
Employment profile White collar, 46%. Blue collar, 39%. Service, 11%. Farm, 4%.
Ethnic groups Black, 4%. Total foreign stock, 5%.

Presidential vote

1976	Carter (D)	92,682	(45%)
	Ford (R)	112,380	(55%)
1972	Nixon (R)	125,878	(71%)
	McGovern (D)	52,346	(29%)

Rep. Beverly B. Byron (D) Elected 1978; b. July 27, 1932, Baltimore; home, Frederick; Hood Col., 1963–64; Episcopalian.

Career Campaign asst., U.S. Rep. Goodloe E. Byron.

Offices 1216 LHOB, 202-225-2721. Also Fredericktown Mall, Frederick 21701, 301-662-8622.

Committees *Armed Services* (26th). Subcommittees: Seapower and Strategic and Critical Materials; Installations and Facilities; Military Compensation.

Group Ratings: Newly Elected

Key Votes: Newly Elected

Election Results

1978 general	Beverly Byron (D)	126,196	(90%)	($1,542)
	Melvin Perkins (R)	14,545	(10%)	
1978 primary	Goodloe Byron (D)	39,523	(62%)	($140,990)
	Dan Rupli (D)	24,606	(38%)	($48,994)
1976 general	Goodloe Byron (D)	126,801	(71%)	($71,015)
	Arthur T. Bond (R)	52,203	(29%)	($13,165)

SEVENTH DISTRICT

Baltimore has always had a large black community. In 1960, 35% of its citizens were black; in 1970, 46%, and today the city probably has a black majority. Yet blacks have never been a really major force in city elections in Baltimore as they have been in such diverse cities as Cleveland and Atlanta and Oakland. The incumbent Mayor, Donald Schaefer, is white and shows no sign of losing office to a black or anyone else. Indeed, Schaefer may be part of a wave of the future—a group of mayors of both races who hold their office regardless of racial constituencies, because their constituents believe they are doing a good job. Schaefer had tough black competition when he was first elected in 1971. But at this writing it seems he will be reelected in 1979 without any significant competition of any kind. A bachelor who lives with his mother in a black neighborhood, Schaefer is devoted to his job and to Baltimore; he has the air of a comfortable old-time politician, but has sponsored some of the most successful housing programs in the country. His style is old-fashioned, but he may well be the best big city mayor in the nation today.

The main focus for political activity for Baltimore's black community is Maryland's 7th congressional district. This seat includes almost all of Baltimore's west side and part of its east side; its boundaries were artfully drawn to include 86% of Baltimore's blacks and only 29% of its whites. The incumbent Congressman, Parren Mitchell, was first elected in 1970 when he beat a white incumbent in the primary by exactly 38 votes; the district then included part of the Baltimore suburbs and had a large Jewish population. Mitchell had one more tough race, a 1972 primary challenge from another black. Otherwise he has won easily.

Mitchell began his career in Congress technically as a political novice. He had been a professor at Morgan State University and had not held public office before. But he is from an important polical family. His older brother, Clarence Mitchell, was for many years the canny Washington lobbyist for the NAACP; his nephew served in the Maryland Senate. Parren Mitchell became the first black member of the Banking Committee, which handles housing programs; and initially he was expected to concentrate in that field. But housing has not been a growth federal activity in the seventies (though Baltimore has some innovative programs), and Mitchell chairs a subcommittee on Domestic and Monetary Policy.

This is not a subject that lends itself very well to militant rhetoric. Mitchell has maintained good working relations with the Federal Reserve and has become knowledgeable about interest rates and monetarism. His solid grounding on the issues helped to make him an effective head of the Congressional Black Caucus and has earned him considerable respect in the House generally.

Census Data Pop. 487,832. Central city, 100%; suburban, 0%. Median family income, $7,841; families above $15,000: 13%; families below $3,000: 16%. Median years education, 9.8.

The Voters

Median voting age 42.
Employment profile White collar, 37%. Blue collar, 40%. Service, 23%. Farm, –%.
Ethnic groups Black, 74%. Total foreign stock, 5%.

Presidential vote

1976	Carter (D)	101,341	(82%)
	Ford (R)	22,795	(18%)
1972	Nixon (R)	32,369	(27%)
	McGovern (D)	89,041	(73%)

Rep. Parren J. Mitchell (D) Elected 1970; b. Apr. 29, 1922, Baltimore; home, Baltimore; Morgan St. Col., B.A. 1950, U. of Md., M.A. 1952, U. of Conn., 1960; Episcopalian.

Career Army, WWII; Prof. and Asst. Dir. of the Urban Studies Institute, Morgan St. Col.; Exec. Secy., Md. Comm. on Interracial Problems and Relations, 1963–65; Exec. Dir., Baltimore Community Action Agency, 1965–68.

Offices 414 CHOB, 202-225-4741. Also Rm. 1018, Geo. Fallon Fed. Ofc. Bldg., 31 Hopkins Plaza, Baltimore 21201, 301-962-3223.

Committees *Banking, Finance and Urban Affairs* (9th). Subcommittees: Domestic Monetary Policy (Chairman); General Oversight and Renegotiation; Consumer Affairs.

Small Business (7th). Subcommittees: General Oversight and Minority Enterprise; Access to Equity Capital and Business Opportunities.

Group Ratings

	ADA	COPE	PC	RPN	NFU	LCV	CFA	NAB	NSI	ACA	NTU
1978	90	95	93	40	80	–	91	0	10	8	–
1977	90	96	78	31	75	93	75	–	–	4	35
1976	95	87	95	41	92	93	100	8	0	0	29

Key Votes

1) Increase Def Spnd	AGN	6) Alaska Lands Protect	FOR	11) Delay Auto Pol Cntrl	AGN
2) B-1 Bomber	AGN	7) Water Projects Veto	AGN	12) Sugar Price Escalator	FOR
3) Cargo Preference	FOR	8) Consum Protect Agcy	FOR	13) Pub Fin Cong Cmpgns	FOR
4) Dereg Nat Gas	AGN	9) Common Situs Picket	FOR	14) ERA Ratif Recissn	AGN
5) Kemp-Roth	AGN	10) Labor Law Revision	FOR	15) Prohibt Govt Abrtns	AGN

Election Results

1978 general	Parren J. Mitchell (D)	51,996	(89%)	($93,693)
	Debra Hanania Freeman (I)	6,626	(11%)	($7,052)
1978 primary	Parren J. Mitchell (D)	36,218	(78%)	
	One other (D)	9,943	(22%)	
1976 general	Parren J. Mitchell (D)	94,991	(94%)	($46,771)
	William Salisbury (Ind.)	5,642	(6%)	($0)

EIGHTH DISTRICT

By most measures one cares to use, the 8th congressional district of Maryland is the wealthiest in the nation. It includes just about all of Maryland's Montgomery County—the hunk of valuable suburban and country real estate immediately northwest of Washington, D.C. Like Prince Georges County to the east, Montgomery experienced vast population increases in the fifties and sixties. The migrants here, however, were of a rather different sort. They tended to have higher incomes and more education, and they were more likely to hold white collar, professional, or executive jobs. The typical resident of the 8th district is a high ranking GS-15 civil servant or perhaps a laywer in private practice; a person as likely as not to have a graduate school degree, and one who professes a vaguely liberal sort of politics. Montgomery voters are usually willing to go with Democrats, but their favorite kind of candidate had been the liberal Republican who cares deeply about the political process, like Senator Charles Mathias.

Radical chic is not the label one would use to describe the 8th district's politics; League of Women Voters liberal is closer. This is one of the few places in the country which, in the year of Proposition 13, turned down a proposal to lower local taxes—because a coalition of county employees and concerned citizens convinced voters the cuts would eliminate needed services. Montgomery was liberal enough to cast 43% of its votes for George McGovern in 1972—better than he did in any other part of Maryland but Baltimore City. But it produced an only average 52% for Jimmy Carter in 1976; this is one part of Maryland that does not identify with born again Southern Baptists.

Montgomery's preference for liberal Republicans was shown during the 1960–76 period, when it voted for Democratic presidential candidates in all three close elections, but also elected Republican congressmen every time: first Mathias, then Gilbert Gude, and in 1976 Newton Steers. Indeed, Steers's campaign in that last year featured endorsements by Mathias and Gude. Yet there was a significant difference in personality. Mathias and Gude are reflective; Steers is brash. And if only because the climate and issue content in the House had changed, Steers seemed to be voting with the Republican leadership more often than his predecessor.

But Steers could surely have stayed in office were it not for the campaign of Democrat Michael Barnes. He had served on the Maryland public service commission and on Senator Edmund Muskie's staff, but he had avoided involvement in the tangled rivalries of Montgomery County politics and so won the nomination with little trouble. Barnes was able to raise the money and motivate the volunteers to get his message across to the voters—a difficult thing in a metropolitan area not overly concerned with local politics. He charged Steers not only with behaving too much like a Republican, but also for conflict of interest and ineffectiveness in getting bills passed. (Steers had spent much time on a spouse abuse bill which did not pass.) Barnes's victory here is a considerable achievement and suggests that he can hold this seat for some time to come.

Census Data Pop. 493,121. Central city, 0%; suburban, 100%. Median family income, $17,102; families above $15,000: 58%; families below $3,000: 3%. Median years education, 13.2.

The Voters

Median voting age 41.
Employment profile White collar, 79%. Blue collar, 13%. Service, 7%. Farm, 1%.
Ethnic groups Black, 4%. Spanish, 3%. Total foreign stock, 21%. USSR, 3%; Germany, UK, 2% each; Canada, Poland, Italy, 1% each.

Presidential vote

1976	Carter (D)	126,116	(52%)
	Ford (R)	117,949	(48%)
1972	Nixon (R)	127,225	(57%)
	McGovern (D)	96,643	(43%)

Rep. Michael D. Barnes (D) Elected 1978; b. Sept. 3, 1943, Washington, D.C.; home, Kensington; U. of No. Carolina, B.A. 1965, Inst. of Higher Internatl. Studies, Geneva, Switz., 1965–66; Geo. Wash. U., J.D. 1972; Protestant.

Career Spec. Asst. to U.S. Sen. Edmund S. Muskie of Maine, 1970–72; Practicing atty., 1972–; Md. Public Service Comm., 1975–78. Vice-Chm., Wash. Metro Area Transit Comm., 1976–78.

Offices 1607 LHOB, 202-225-5341.

Committees *Foreign Affairs* (17th). Subcommittees: Europe and the Middle East; International Economic Policy and Trade.

Judiciary (19th). Subcommittees: Immigration, Refugees, and International Law; Administrative Law and Governmental Relations.

Group Ratings: Newly Elected

Key Votes: Newly Elected

Election Results

1978 general	Michael D. Barnes (D)	81,851	(51%)	($134,588)
	Newton I. Steers, Jr. (R)	77,807	(49%)	($162,980)
1978 primary	Michael D. Barnes (D)	36,540	(72%)	
	Four others (D)	14,270	(28%)	
1976 general	Newton I. Steers, Jr. (R)	111,274	(47%)	($119,707)
	Lanny Davis (D)	100,343	(42%)	($188,555)
	Robin Ficker (Ind.)	26,035	(11%)	($24,505)

MASSACHUSETTS

Massachusetts politics strikes many people as full of paradoxes. This is the state that gives us Edward Kennedy, the leading spokesman for what is known as liberalism today, and the state that elects as its governor a man whose campaign manager said he won the primary by putting all the hate groups in a cauldron and letting them boil. It is the only state that went for George McGovern in 1972, but it is also the only state to go for Henry Jackson in the 1976 presidential primary. There is no explaining these paradoxes on the basis of these results alone. It is necessary to go back into history, to see how Massachusetts politics has developed.

The crucial event which structured electoral politics here is not, as it is in so many states, the Civil War—it was the Irish potato famine of the 1840s. That blight forced hundreds of thousands of Irish to immigrate to the United States, to the point where there are far more people of Irish descent here than in Ireland today, and nowhere did these new Americans make a greater impact than in Boston and Massachusetts. They found a thriving Yankee economic and political culture whose hostility was symbolized by "No Irish need apply" signs. And ever since much of politics in Massachusetts has been a struggle between Yankee and Irish for domination.

That ethnic conflict was very much replicated in partisan identification. The Yankees of the 1840s, not long removed from Federalism, were solid Whigs, who would become one of the bulwarks of the Republican Party when it was formed a decade later. The Whigs and Republicans had policies that appealed to them: promotion of public works to help business (the Yankees were busy building railroads and textile mills all over the country), protective tariffs, sympathy for suitably distant oppressed peoples like the blacks of the South and for uplifting social movements like temperance. The Irish knew from the beginning that they were not going to go very far in the party of the Yankees, and they found the Democrats of the nineteenth century more congenial. We think of the Democrats as a party promoting government action, but in those days more than the Republicans the Democracy represented laissez faire—which was fine with the Irish. They didn't want the government spending money to help the rich, they didn't want it to regulate immigration, they didn't want it to promote the cause of blacks who might compete with them in the labor market, and they didn't want it to prohibit liquor. What they wanted was to get into politics and to beat the Yankees at it.

And that is pretty much the story of a century of Massachusetts politics. Throughout, the Irish share of the population continually rose—and there were other immigrants, who usually became Democrats, too—while the Yankee share of the population declined. Yankees had smaller families, they moved out west; the Irish stayed put and eventually ruled. Massachusetts very slowly moved from being a Republican state to being Democratic. The state gave Republicans majorities in every presidential election from the Civil War to 1924; in 1928, with the Irish Catholic Al Smith running, it went Democratic. In 1918 the state had elected a Democratic senator, but Republicans won as many seats as Democrats in the years ahead. In the twenties, thirties, forties, and fifties there was a pretty close balance between Yankee Republicans and Irish Democrats. The state's preference even in presidential elections shifted relatively little in this period: in Massachusetts it was the balance between Yankee and Irish, not the programs of Roosevelt or the popularity of Eisenhower, that really made the difference.

Thus political conflict in Massachusetts never really fell into the liberal vs. conservative lines of the New Deal. The Republicans here retained a kind of Yankee interventionism, strongly favoring civil rights, an anti-isolationist foreign policy, opposing the excesses of Joe McCarthy. Massachusetts Democrats, on the other hand, like the Republic of Ireland before World War II, were hostile to the British and cheered on McCarthy after World War II as one of their own. (Joseph Kennedy used to invite him to Hyannisport.) The Republicans promised to root out corruption. The Democrats had the more complacent attitude typical of an ethnic group which has only recently been able to aspire to political office.

In the sixties and seventies, for the first time in Massachusetts's history, the Irish Democrats and Yankee Republicans began moving in the same direction. The key figure here is Senator Edward Kennedy. More even than his brother the president, he has by personal example helped to shape attitudes in this state; after all, he has been a major figure here now for nearly twenty years. On a whole series of issues, Kennedy as well as the national Democratic Party took positions which in Massachusetts had been more typical of Yankee interventionists. He strongly supported civil rights. He favored helping people who were impoverished or starving. He opposed the war in Vietnam. He stood against the excesses of Watergate. He was indubitably against corruption. Kennedy's stand made these positions respectable, even mandatory, among the Catholic majority of voters in Massachusetts. And his stand led the Yankee minority to vote more and more often for the Democratic Party. It was no accident then, and not simply the result of local recession, that Massachusetts voted for McGovern in 1972. It represented a kind of reconciliation in this state, which saw the upper crust Yankee suburb of Lincoln and the lower income Irish city of Somerville going for the same candidate.

But that does not mean that Yankee and Irish conflicts have ended. On the contrary, they emerged in classic form in the 1978 gubernatorial election. The incumbent Governor, Michael Dukakis, had been elected in 1974 as a kind of cerebral liberal. He had attracted attention early by his personal austerity (riding to work in the subway) and by cutting the state budget drastically. His actions probably had majority support, but nobody really felt he was their man. The liberals felt betrayed, while Irish and other ethnics found him cold and unwilling to wheel and deal politically. Almost everyone was unhappy that he had raised taxes after promising not to do so. As a result, he was more vulnerable in the Democratic primary than he supposed, and he was beaten by one Edward King.

If Ted Kennedy represents the liberal and humanitarian side of Massachusetts Irish politics, King represents the conservative and resentful side. In his primary campaign he emphasized his support of capital punishment, of mandatory prison sentences for drug dealers, of raising the drinking age to 21, of building nuclear power plants, and of downplaying environmental concerns to spur economic growth. King was opposed by a Republican who was a quintessential Yankee: Francis Hatch, a rich North Shore state legislator, whose wooden manner and generally similar stands would have made him only a sacrificial candidate against Dukakis. Against King, he was suddenly inheriting support from liberals—and was in danger of losing some conservative Republican votes to his opponent.

Some classic themes were sounded in the candidates' advertisements. Hatch forces emphasized King's high living on expense account as director of the Port Authority—the kind of petty chiseling which Yankees have always considered an Irish characteristic. King forces showed aerial photos of Hatch's huge Beverly Farms estate, which sparked Mrs. Hatch into complaining about giving her away to burglars—playing on the resentment of the Irish against the rich Yankees. Kennedy and Speaker Tip O'Neill tried to persuade King to downplay his social issues and to stress that he stood in the basic Democratic economic tradition of helping the little guy. O'Neill had a special interest; his son, Thomas O'Neill III, was the incumbent Lieutenant Governor; he was tied to King's ticket and would lose if King did. It was probably the Speaker more than anyone else who prevented a mass exodus of Democratic politicians from their gubernatorial ticket.

For much of the campaign it looked as if Hatch would win, but King ended up prevailing by a small but decisive margin. Examination of election returns shows that this was little more than the standard triumph of Irish over Yankee. Hatch made big gains in university towns and well-to-do areas where candidates like McGovern had done well; but he could not crack the solidly Catholic middle class suburbs of Boston. The result was not so much a repudiation of Massachusetts's liberalism as it was an extension of the Commonwealth's traditional ethnic politics.

It is not, however, possible to explain the result in the 1978 Senate race in the same way; after all, the two general election candidates were black and Greek-American—neither of which group is very large in Massachusetts. The real story here was the unseating of Edward Brooke, the only black senator elected in the twentieth century and a Republican who had twice won by large margins in this Democratic state. Moreover, Brooke had a number of political assets. He is bright, he is an excellent speaker, he has a magnetic personality which projects well. He also has great political skill. He was the Senate's chief backer of Medicaid abortions, won a majority there, and obtained a better compromise than anyone thought he could from hostile and determined House conferees. His voting record on most issues was not dissimilar from Edward Kennedy's. The major exception was on economic measures like the Kemp–Roth bill——but how much could it hurt him to back a tax cut in 1978?

But Brooke also had his weaknesses. Best known were his personal problems, stemming from a disputed divorce proceeding. There were allegations that Brooke had lied about his financial standing in those proceedings, allegations serious enough to have been considered by the Senate Ethics Committee. There were questions about how Brooke's mother-in-law had received $72,000 in Medicaid payments. But all these charges may not have hurt Brooke as much as first appeared likely, for it became clear that one of his daughters was leaking most of this information to the newspapers; and many thought of Brooke as the victim of a spiteful relative. Probably more damaging to Brooke in the long run was the feeling that he had not been keeping in touch and working hard enough for Massachusetts's interests. People here know that one of their senators, Edward Kennedy, is busy laboring on national issues; they may expect the other senator to concentrate on state matters. In any case, Brooke's vulnerability was obvious to some even before the divorce case stories broke in early 1978.

Those stories were, however, largely responsible for bringing in a field of candidates to oppose him. On the Republican side there was Avi Nelson, an ideological conservative who came within a few percentage points of beating Brooke in the primary. The number of registered Republicans in this state has dwindled to such a point that its relatively few conservatives can come close to controlling its primary. On the Democratic side there was Secretary of State Paul Guzzi, 5th district Congressman Paul Tsongas, and Boston School Committee member Kathleen Sullivan Alioto. The winner of the primary, with clever ads and a good local base, was Tsongas. In the general election he avoided all mention of Brooke's personal problems and concentrated on his differences with him on economic issues and foreign relations (Brooke was not considered a sure vote for a SALT treaty; Tsongas is). Kennedy for the first time associated himself with an opponent of Brooke and campaigned hard for Tsongas. The upshot was a clear Tsongas victory, although with a somewhat different coalition from that which elected King. Brooke's concession and Tsongas's victory statement on election night were classic examples of poise and generosity.

In the Senate Tsongas can be expected to vote for liberal Democrats on just about every issue. He failed to get the seat on Foreign Relations that he wanted; it would have put two Greek-Americans on the committee at a time when the Administration wants to improve relations with the Turks. He sits on the Energy Committee, where he can be expected to be a vote against the oil companies and for environmental causes, and on the Banking Committee. Elected at 37, a Democrat in a Democratic state, he has some reason to expect to be in the Senate for many years. But Massachusetts politics is turbulent, and he should not forget the lesson of Brooke's defeat, which is that voters here want one senator to tend carefully to local interests.

Of course no one in Congress has a safer seat than Ted Kennedy, and very few have done more legislatively than he has. He was considered a lightweight when he was first elected at 30 in 1962; he was considered morally derelict by many in the Chappaquiddick incident of 1969. But no one can deny that he has become one of the most productive and hard working members of the Senate today. Kennedy began in the Senate slowly, and impressed his elders with his willingness to take on mundane chores. But he also had his legislative accomplishments in the sixties and early seventies, notably the strategems that ended the poll tax and produced the 18-year-old vote. He worked hard enough to get himself elected Whip in 1969 over Russell Long, though after Chappaquiddick he was beaten two years later by Robert Byrd.

Today Kennedy seems to be at the center of every legislative issue. He is the leading force for a national health insurance bill both publicly and in the Senate. He pushed through airline deregulation in the 95th Congress and has taken on the politically tougher job of deregulating trucking in the 96th. Though senior, he does not necessarily bow to seniority: he pushed the airline deregulation bill until Senator Howard Cannon, who chaired the aviation subcommittee, came along and worked with him; on trucking deregulation he directly challenged Cannon, now Commerce Committee Chairman.

Kennedy himself of course is Chairman of the Senate Judiciary Committee, a position he inherited on James Eastland's retirement in 1976. To say that there is a difference between their attitudes on issues is to utter a major understatement. Kennedy is expected to push major anti-merger legislation in the committee, and although many of its Republicans are very hostile, he seems to have a working majority there on most issues.

But for all his legislative accomplishments and ability, Edward Kennedy's most important role in our political system is to serve as a sort of alternative—and quite possibly future—president. He explicitly declined to run for president in 1968, 1972, and 1976, though he probably could have had the Democratic nomination if he had wanted it in any of those years. At the midpoint of the Carter Administration, he was running well ahead of the President in polls of likely Democratic primary voters—ahead by nearly a 3–1 margin in the first primary state, New Hampshire. The evidence suggests that Kennedy would be an overwhelming choice among Catholic voters and among ideological liberals, who while far from a majority are not a negligible factor in many states. Among younger voters who find Carter's born again religion an alien life style, Kennedy would lead by a wide margin; among many tradition-minded older voters who remember President Kennedy with affection, he would probably do well also. Blacks would probably give him a wide margin over Carter; so would Jews. Even among white Southerners, evidence is that at the beginning of 1979 Carter would not run much better than even with Kennedy.

What is startling here and in projecting Kennedy as a general election candidate is not so much that he has a large positive constituency, for he has had that for at least ten years; it is that there is apparently a much smaller negative constituency against him. Hatred of the Kennedys and memories of Chappaquiddick seem to have faded. Of course this could simply be the result of Kennedy's current non-candidacy; once people face the idea that he might actually become president, many of the old negative feelings might reemerge. Moreover, Kennedy has made himself, since the death of Hubert Humphrey, the major advocate for a set of programs and ideas which has been losing favor rapidly with the voters. He stands for greater government involvement in health care and more generous budgets for social programs. Kennedy criticized the Carter Administration strongly for cutting social spending in its 1980 budget. (Ironically, he was one of the Administration's most dependable supporters in the 95th Congress and probably will be again, on most issues, in the 96th.) If he became President, Kennedy would be trying to lead the country in a direction it has recently found unappealing. Perhaps he could change people's minds on these issues by force of argument and personal leadership, but if not, there would be a period of acrimonious stalemate on national issues.

There is one other problem Kennedy must face if he should decide to run for president, and that is the problem of high expectations. There is a bright aura to President John Kennedy's Administration and a high regard for Edward Kennedy that suggest that people will expect much more from his administration than others have been able to deliver. There might easily be great exhilaration when a Kennedy takes office, but it could be followed by great disillusion if he does not fulfill the expectations he has raised.

It is highly unusual for so much in a presidential election to hinge on one man's decision to run—the last person in this position was Dwight Eisenhower. Kennedy presumably means it when he says that he expects President Carter to be the Democratic nominee and expects to support him; but he has done most of the things he would need to do if he were to run. Certainly if Carter were in danger of losing to Jerry Brown, for whom Kennedy reportedly has little regard, Kennedy would probably be a candidate; perhaps he would run if he were convinced that his differences with Carter on domestic policy were so great they could no longer be papered over. But it should be remembered that the last time Edward Kennedy dealt with a decision of this sort, when people wanted Robert Kennedy to run against Lyndon Johnson, his was a voice of caution and nobody has yet demonstrated that he has all that strong a desire to be president.

Census Data Pop. 5,689,170; 2.81% of U.S. total, 10th largest; Central city, 30%; suburban, 54%. Median family income, $10,883; 8th highest; families above $15,000: 25%; families below $3,000: 6%. Median years education, 12.3.

1977 Share of Federal Tax Burden $9,844,000,000; 2.85% of U.S. total, 10th largest.

1977 Share of Federal Outlays $11,462,307,000; 2.90% of U.S. total, 11th largest. Per capita federal spending, $1,970.

DOD	$2,917,171,000	9th (3.19%)	HEW	$4,587,546,000	10th (3.11%)
ERDA	$60,946,000	17th (1.03%)	HUD	$140,542,000	10th (3.30%)
NASA	$45,451,000	14th (1.15%)	VA	$602,291,000	8th (3.13%)
DOT	$407,938,000	10th (2.86%)	EPA	$311,399,000	7th (3.80%)
DOC	$302,910,000	9th (3.65%)	RevS	$270,549,000	10th (3.20%)
DOI	$46,391,000	23d (1.00%)	Debt	$439,481,000	11th (1.46%)
USDA	$235,108,000	34th (1.18%)	Other	$1,092,584,000	

Economic Base Finance, insurance and real estate; electrical equipment and supplies, especially communication equipment; machinery, especially special industry machinery; apparel and other textile products, especially women's and misses' outerwear; printing and publishing, especially newspapers and commercial printing; fabricated metal products; food and kindred products.

Political Line-up Governor, Edward J. King (D). Senators, Edward M. Kennedy (D) and Paul Tsongas (D). Representatives, 12 (10 D and 2 R). State Senate (34 D and 6 R); State House (131 D and 29 R).

The Voters

Median voting age 44
Employment profile White collar, 55%. Blue collar, 34%. Service, 13%. Farm, 0%.
Ethnic groups Black 3%. Spanish, 1%. Total foreign stock, 33%. Canada, 8%; Italy, 5%; Ireland, 4%; UK, 3%; Poland, USSR, 2% each; Portugal, 1%.

Presidential vote

1976	Carter (D)	1,030,276	(42%)
	Ford (R)	1,429,475	(58%)
1972	Nixon (R)	1,112,078	(45%)
	McGovern (D)	1,332,540	(55%)

Sen. Edward M. Kennedy (D) Elected 1962, seat up 1982; b. Feb. 22, 1932, Boston; home, Boston; Harvard U., A.B. 1956, Acad. of Internatl. Law, The Hague, Holland, 1958, U. of Va., LL.B. 1959; Catholic.

Career Army, 1951–53; Asst. Dist. Atty., Suffolk Co., 1961–62.

Offices 2241 DSOB, 202-224-4543. Also Rm. 2400A JFK Fed. Bldg., Boston 02203, 617-223-2826.

Committees *Labor and Human Resources* (4th). Subcommittees: Education, Arts, and Humanities; Health and Scientific Research (Chairman); Aging.

Judiciary (Chairman). Subcommittees: Antitrust, Monopoly, and Business Rights; Criminal Justice; Improvements in Judicial Machinery.

Group Ratings

	ADA	COPE	PC	RPN	NFU	LCV	CFA	NAB	NSI	ACA	NTU
1978	95	95	93	56	40	96	80	9	0	4	–
1977	95	89	90	55	80	–	84	–	–	4	26
1976	95	90	89	57	92	87	93	0	10	0	29

Key Votes

1) Warnke Nom	FOR	6) Egypt-Saudi Arms	AGN	11) Hosptl Cost Contnmnt	FOR
2) Neutron Bomb	AGN	7) Draft Restr Pardon	FOR	12) Clinch River Reactor	AGN
3) Waterwy User Fee	FOR	8) Wheat Price Support	FOR	13) Pub Fin Cong Cmpgns	FOR
4) Dereg Nat Gas	AGN	9) Panama Canal Treaty	FOR	14) ERA Ratif Recissn	FOR
5) Kemp-Roth	AGN	10) Labor Law Rev Clot	FOR	15) Med Necssy Abrtns	FOR

Election Results

1976 general	Edward M. Kennedy (D)	1,726,657	(70%)	($896,196)
	Michael S. Robertson (R)	722,641	(30%)	($168,854)
1976 primary	Edward M. Kennedy (D)	534,725	(75%)	
	Two others (D)	176,811	(25%)	
1970 general	Edward M. Kennedy (D)	1,202,856	(63%)	
	Josiah Spaulding (R)	715,978	(37%)	

Sen. Paul E. Tsongas (D) Elected 1978, seat up 1984; b. Feb. 14, 1941, Lowell; home, Lowell; Dartmouth Col., B.A. 1962, Yale U., LL.B. 1967, Harvard U., 1973; Greek Orthodox.

Career Peace Corps, Volunteer, Ethiopia, 1962–64, Training Coord., West Indies, 1967–68; Mbr., Governor's Comm. on Law Enforcement, 1968–69; Mass. Deputy Asst. Atty. Gen., 1969–71; Practicing atty., 1971–74; U.S. House of Reps., 1975–78.

Offices 342 RSOB, 202-224-2742. Also 325 Merrimack St., Lowell 01852, 617-459-0101.

Committees *Banking, Housing, and Urban Affairs* (9th). Subcommittees: International Finance; Insurance; Consumer Affairs (Chairman).

Energy and Natural Resources (10th). Subcommittees: Energy Conservation and Supply; Energy Research and Development; Parks, Recreation, and Renewable Resources.

Group Ratings

	ADA	COPE	PC	RPN	NFU	LCV	CFA	NAB	NSI	ACA	NTU

Group Ratings: Newly Elected

1978	50	88	50	50	40	–	32	0	0	18	–
1977	100	83	93	64	82	100	85	–	–	4	39
1976	85	86	85	56	91	90	91	17	0	4	29

Key Votes

1) Increase Def Spnd	AGN	6) Alaska Lands Protect	DNV	11) Delay Auto Pol Cntrl	AGN
2) B-1 Bomber	AGN	7) Water Projects Veto	FOR	12) Sugar Price Escalator	DNV
3) Cargo Preference	AGN	8) Consum Protect Agcy	FOR	13) Pub Fin Cong Cmpgns	DNV
4) Dereg Nat Gas	AGN	9) Common Situs Picket	FOR	14) ERA Ratif Recissn	AGN
5) Kemp-Roth	AGN	10) Labor Law Revision	FOR	15) Prohibt Govt Abrtns	AGN

Election Results

1978 general	Paul E. Tsongas (D)	1,093,283	(55%)	($768,383)
	Edward W. Brooke (R)	890,584	(45%)	($1,284,855)
1978 primary	Paul E. Tsongas (D)	296,915	(36%)	
	Paul Guzzi (D)	258,960	(31%)	($301,747)
	Kathleen Sullivan Alioto (D)	161,036	(19%)	($143,777)
	Two others (D)	117,861	(14%)	
1972 general	Edward W. Brooke (R)	1,505,932	(65%)	($368,038)
	John J. Droney (D)	823,278	(35%)	($82,888)

Gov. Edward J. King (D) Elected 1978, term expires Jan. 1983; b. May 11, 1925, East Boston; Boston Col., B.A. 1948, Bentley Col., 1951–53; Catholic.

Career Navy, WWII; Pro Football Player, Buffalo Bills 1948–49, Baltimore Colts 1950–51; Accountant, 1953–56; Asst. Dir. and Comptroller, Boston Museum of Science, 1956–59; Mass. Port Authority, Comptroller, 1959, Secy.-Treas., 1960–63, Dir., 1963–74; Pres., New England Cncl., 1975–77.

Offices Rm. 360, State House, Boston 02133, 617-727-3600.

Election Results

1978 general	Edward J. King (D)	1,030,294	(53%)
	Francis W. Hatch, Jr. (R)	926,072	(47%)
1978 primary	Edward J. King (D)	442,174	(51%)
	Michael S. Dukakis (D)	365,417	(42%)
	One other (D)	58,220	(7%)
1974 general	Michael S. Dukakis (D)	992,284	(56%)
	Francis W. Sargent (R)	784,353	(44%)

FIRST DISTRICT

The 1st congressional district of Massachusetts is the western end of the state: the Berkshire Mountains and most of Massachusetts's portion of the Connecticut River valley. The Berkshires are known as a summer resort and for picturesque towns like Lenox, home of the Tanglewood music festival. More important politically are the old mill towns and manufacturing centers nestled in the mountains, like Pittsfield, the district's largest city, and North Adams. The second and third generation immigrants packed into these tiny mill towns almost inevitably outvote the small town and farm Yankee Republicans by substantial margins. The Connecticut valley (called the Pioneer Valley here in Massachusetts) is a similar place politically: small Republican towns which are more than offset by the occasional Democratic mill towns. In the middle of the valley are the college towns of Amherst, with Amherst College and the University of Massachusetts, and Northampton, home of Smith College and of Calvin Coolidge. To the south are industrial and residential suburbs of Springfield: Holyoke, Westfield, and West Springfield.

In national elections, the 1st almost always votes Democratic: it went for McGovern in 1972 and comfortably for Carter in 1976. But in congressional races it is still Republican as it has been since Yankees were a clear majority here. Congressman Silvio Conte has become so entrenched that he seldom has opposition and, when he does, he wins with something like the 64% he received in 1976. Conte's most notable challenge occurred in 1958, his first House race, when he faced Williams College political scientist James MacGregor Burns. The professor got the national publicity but Conte, who had represented Berkshire County in the state Senate for eight years, got the local votes. So Burns went on to finish his Roosevelt biography, and Conte went to Washington.

Conte is considered very affable and politically very shrewd. Early in his House career he won a seat on the Appropriations Committee. His voting record gave him the reputation of being one of the most liberal Republicans in the House, but that is not necessarily because he is always in favor of spending federal money. On the contrary, on many of the issues on which he has dissented from Republican orthodoxy he has favored less spending—the supersonic transport, defense spending, the B-1 bomber. For years he led moves to put ceilings on farm subsidy payments and has succeeded in having a $20,000 ceiling imposed on payments to any one owner. He supported the Carter Administration's proposal to cut spending on federal water projects.

Yet Conte does not hesitate to take care of his district (there have been no cuts in Amtrak lines there, for example) and is not regarded as quixotic. Given his voting record, many conservatives wanted to keep him from becoming ranking Republican on Appropriations in 1979. But Conte had the strong support of Robert Michel, Republican Whip and an Appropriations member himself, and the conservative challenge was overcome with ease. With increasing interest in budget-cutting measures, Conte is likely to be a very important member of the 96th Congress.

Census Data Pop. 469,438. Central city, 23%; suburban, 38%. Median family income, $10,311; families above $15,000: 20%; families below $3,000: 7%. Median years education, 12.2.

The Voters

Median voting age 44.
Employment profile White collar, 49%. Blue collar, 36%. Service, 14%. Farm, 1%.
Ethnic groups Spanish, 1%. Total foreign stock, 27%. Canada, 7%; Poland, 5%; Italy, 3%; Ireland, UK, Germany, 2% each.

Presidential vote

1976	Carter (D)	124,082	(58%)
	Ford (R)	88,051	(42%)
1972	Nixon (R)	102,513	(49%)
	McGovern (D)	107,528	(51%)

Rep. Silvio O. Conte (R) Elected 1958; b. Nov. 9, 1921, Pittsfield; home, Pittsfield; Boston Col., Boston Col. Law School, LL.B. 1949; Catholic.

Career Seabees, SW Pacific, WWII; Practicing atty., 1949–58; Mass. Senate, 1951–59.

Offices 2300 RHOB, 202-225-5335. Also 78 Center St., Pittsfield 01201, 413-442-0946.

Committees *Appropriations* (Ranking Member). Subcommittees: Legislative; Labor-HEW; Transportation.

Small Business (2d). Subcommittees: Energy Programs, Environment and Safety Requirements and Government Research on Small Business.

Group Ratings

	ADA	COPE	PC	RPN	NFU	LCV	CFA	NAB	NSI	ACA	NTU
1978	50	55	55	58	70	–	50	50	50	26	–
1977	65	78	75	85	67	82	75	–	–	12	24
1976	60	57	74	78	58	78	73	42	60	7	24

Key Votes

1) Increase Def Spnd	AGN	6) Alaska Lands Protect	FOR	11) Delay Auto Pol Cntrl	AGN
2) B-1 Bomber	AGN	7) Water Projects Veto	FOR	12) Sugar Price Escalator	AGN
3) Cargo Preference	AGN	8) Consum Protect Agcy	FOR	13) Pub Fin Cong Cmpgns	FOR
4) Dereg Nat Gas	AGN	9) Common Situs Picket	FOR	14) ERA Ratif Recissn	AGN
5) Kemp-Roth	FOR	10) Labor Law Revision	FOR	15) Prohibt Govt Abrtns	FOR

Election Results

1978 general	Silvio O. Conte (R), unopposed			($5,771)
1978 primary	Silvio O. Conte (R), unopposed			
1976 general	Silvio O. Conte (R)	137,652	(64%)	($19,567)
	Edward A. McColgan (D)	78,181	(36%)	($516)

SECOND DISTRICT

The 2d congressional district of Massachusetts includes the city of Springfield, many of its suburbs, and a collection of rural and small industrial towns to the east. Springfield and Chicopee, which together have about one-half of the district's population, are its Democratic bastions, though most of the rest of the 2d often produces Democratic margins as well. The image of the small New England town is of a clapboard village peopled by taciturn Yankees. But in fact many of the old Protestants have died off or long since moved west, and in their place are people more likely to be of Irish, Italian, or Polish descent. The storefronts here may have New England Yankee facades, but hanging above are signs with names of Italian or Polish proprietors.

Springfield is the home town of several famous political pros: Lawrence O'Brien, the Democratic National Chairman whose telephone was the target of the Watergate burglars; the well-known campaign consultant Joseph Napolitan, who still maintains an office here; and Alaska's Senator Mike Gravel. All grew up and learned their first political lessons in Springfield's wards and precincts; their own ethnic origins—Irish, Italian, French Canadian—suggest the variety of this small city.

Another Springfield political pro is 2d district Congressman Edward Boland, a Democrat with more than a quarter century of service in the House. For many years Boland, long a bachelor, roomed with Tip O'Neill, whose wife remained in Cambridge; they have ended that relationship but remain close. Like O'Neill, Boland for years was a politician who could bridge the gap between the senior big city politicians—a group to which he temperamentally belongs—and the younger, more ideological liberals in the Democratic Caucus. Now he is one of the most senior members of the Congress himself, and his career is likely to be much more visible than it has been.

One reason is that Boland chairs the permanent Intelligence Committee in the House. This is a sensitive assignment. Boland has supported some defense budget cuts and questioned some intelligence practices, but he does not share the suspicion of the national security bureaucracies which characterizes many of the liberals coming out of the Vietnam war era. While he is unlikely to neglect his oversight functions, he is not likely to bring things out in public either.

Boland's other major position of power is on the House Appropriations Committee. In the 96th Congress he ranks second among committee Democrats in seniority. At the beginning of the Congress there was a move to elect Boland Chairman. He declined to support it; he has always been a team player, and presumably he and O'Neill had assurances from Jamie Whitten of Mississippi, the most senior member, that he would not use the chair to frustrate the wishes of the Democratic majority. Nonetheless, Boland received 88 votes to Whitten's 157—not quite so much a loss as first appears, since a switch of just 35 votes would have made Boland Chairman.

The difference, in any case, would probably have been less dramatic than the difference between the ADA ratings of the two men. Appropriations has been a committee notably more cautious on domestic spending than the House, and in the anti-spending environment of 1979 Boland would not have tried to make major changes. Moreover, much of the real work is done in subcommittees, and the real powers are the subcommittee chairmen—the so-called college of cardinals. Boland, as a longtime subcommittee chairman, would not have been likely to challenge them directly. He himself chairs the subcommittee on HUD and Independent Agencies, which gives him considerable power over a variety of federal programs.

Census Data Pop. 472,270. Central city, 49%; suburban, 28%. Median family income, $10,268; families above $15,000: 20%; families below $3,000: 7%. Median years education, 12.1.

The Voters

Median voting age 45.
Employment profile White collar, 45%. Blue collar, 42%. Service, 12%. Farm, 1%.
Ethnic groups Black, 5%. Spanish, 2%. Total foreign stock, 31%. Canada, 9%; Poland, 5%; Italy, 3%; Ireland, UK, 2% each; USSR, Germany, 1% each.

Presidential vote

1976	Carter (D)	116,757	(61%)
	Ford (R)	74,953	(39%)
1972	Nixon (R)	88,652	(48%)
	McGovern (D)	95,348	(52%)

Rep. Edward P. Boland (D) Elected 1952; b. Oct. 1, 1911, Springfield; home, Springfield; Boston Col. Law School; Catholic.

Career Mass. House of Reps, 1935–41; Hampton Co. Register of Deeds, 1941–42, 1946–49; Army, WWII; Military Aide to Gov. Paul A. Dever, 1949–52.

Offices 2426 RHOB, 202-225-5601. Also 1883 Main St., Springfield 01103, 413-733-4127.

Committees *Appropriations* (2d). Subcommittees: HUD-Independent Agencies (Chairman); Energy and Water Development; Transportation.

Group Ratings

	ADA	COPE	PC	RPN	NFU	LCV	CFA	NAB	NSI	ACA	NTU
1978	50	75	65	27	60	–	73	9	56	15	–
1977	65	90	75	33	75	66	65	–	–	11	19
1976	75	78	85	50	83	75	81	33	44	4	29

Key Votes

1) Increase Def Spnd	AGN	6) Alaska Lands Protect	DNV	11) Delay Auto Pol Cntrl	AGN
2) B-1 Bomber	AGN	7) Water Projects Veto	AGN	12) Sugar Price Escalator	DNV
3) Cargo Preference	AGN	8) Consum Protect Agcy	FOR	13) Pub Fin Cong Cmpgns	FOR
4) Dereg Nat Gas	AGN	9) Common Situs Picket	FOR	14) ERA Ratif Recissn	FOR
5) Kemp-Roth	AGN	10) Labor Law Revision	FOR	15) Prohibt Govt Abrtns	FOR

Election Results

1978 general	Edward P. Boland (D)	101,570	(73%)	
	Thomas P. Swank (R)	37,881	(27%)	
1978 primary	Edward P. Boland (D), unopposed			
1976 general	Edward P. Boland (D)	134,408	(76%)	($47)
	Thomas P. Swank (R)	41,563	(24%)	($1,729)

THIRD DISTRICT

Worcester, the second largest city in Massachusetts with 176,000 people, is a manufacturing town that lies roughly in the geographical center of the state. Worcester is surrounded by an almost random assortment of comfortable suburbs and tiny mill towns. The thin New England soil only barely covers here, and layers of rock undergird everything. Though there are a number of colleges and universities about, they do not, as in the Boston area, have a major effect on the culture of the entire community. Nor is there here a Yankee upper class moving to the left politically. This is nitty gritty New England, where the Democratic majorities result almost entirely from the all but genetically ingrained voting habits of middle and lower class voters of varied ethnic backgrounds.

In congressional elections, the Worcester-based 3d district has been strongly Democratic for about as long as anyone can remember. From 1946 to 1972 it regularly elected and reelected Democrat Harold Donohue, one of the senior members of the House Judiciary Committee that voted to impeach Richard Nixon. Donohue had had at least one close call at the polls and had stayed in the House after many of his contemporaries had left; he retired in 1974.

There was an unusually serious contest here to replace Donohue. The favorite, Democrat Joseph Early, won, but with only 50%; the energetic Republican had 38%, and an Independent 12%. Early won a seat on the Appropriations Committee once in the House—the kind of reward Tip O'Neill likes to give members of the Massachusetts delegation. On non-economic issues, he is perhaps the most conservative member of the Massachusetts delegation—but by national standards that is not very conservative at all.

Census Data Pop. 469,443. Central city, 38%; suburban, 36%. Median family income, $10,863; families above $15,000: 23%; families below $3,000: 6%. Median years education, 12.2.

The Voters

Median voting age 44.
Employment profile White collar, 49%. Blue collar, 38%. Service, 13%. Farm, –%.
Ethnic groups Total foreign stock, 32%. Canada, 8%; Italy, 5%; Ireland, 3%; UK, Poland, Sweden, 2% each; USSR, Lithuania, 1% each.

Presidential vote

1976	Carter (D)	125,440	(61%)
	Ford (R)	80,584	(39%)
1972	Nixon (R)	83,423	(46%)
	McGovern (D)	98,449	(54%)

Rep. Joseph D. Early (D) Elected 1974; b. Jan. 31, 1933, Worcester; home, Worcester; Col. of the Holy Cross, B.S. 1955; Catholic.

Career Navy, 1955–57; High school teacher and coach, 1959–63; Mass. House of Reps., 1963–74.

Offices 1032 LHOB, 202-225-6101. Also 34 Mechanic St., Rm. 203, Worcester 01608, 617-752-6718.

Committees *Appropriations* (24th). Subcommittees: Labor-HEW; State, Justice, Commerce, and the Judiciary.

Group Ratings

	ADA	COPE	PC	RPN	NFU	LCV	CFA	NAB	NSI	ACA	NTU
1978	70	68	73	36	67	–	68	30	22	23	–
1977	80	81	73	50	60	87	70	–	–	20	43
1976	80	83	90	56	83	87	91	33	20	11	32

Key Votes

1) Increase Def Spnd	AGN	6) Alaska Lands Protect	FOR	11) Delay Auto Pol Cntrl	AGN
2) B-1 Bomber	AGN	7) Water Projects Veto	FOR	12) Sugar Price Escalator	AGN
3) Cargo Preference	AGN	8) Consum Protect Agcy	FOR	13) Pub Fin Cong Cmpgns	AGN
4) Dereg Nat Gas	AGN	9) Common Situs Picket	FOR	14) ERA Ratif Recissn	AGN
5) Kemp-Roth	FOR	10) Labor Law Revision	FOR	15) Prohibt Govt Abrtns	FOR

Election Results

1978 general	Joseph D. Early (D)	119,337	(75%)	($50,609)
	Charles Kevin MacLeod (R)	39,259	(25%)	($8,645)
1978 primary	Joseph D. Early (D), unopposed			
1976 general	Joseph D. Early (D), unopposed			($42,300)

FOURTH DISTRICT

Dozens of Protestant clergymen have served in the House of Representatives, but until 1974 only one Roman Catholic priest had ever been elected congressman: Father Robert Drinan of the 4th congressional district of Massachusetts. From any perspective he is an unusual political figure. With no electoral experience, Drinan beat an incumbent congressman not once but twice in 1970, first in the primary and then in the general, and in the next three general elections prevailed against determined opposition. He was the first congressman to introduce a resolution to impeach Richard Nixon and voted to do just that part of the large majority on the House Judiciary Committee. In an era when most congressmen use the advantages of incumbency to win indefinite reelection, Drinan does not hesitate to antagonize his constituents, or at least a large minority of them, with his views and the ways he expresses them.

The story begins in 1970, when Drinan was finishing 14 years as the highly respected Dean of the Boston College Law School. Living near the school, the priest was a resident of what was then the 3d district—a geographical monstrosity stretching from suburban Newton, just outside Boston, some 100 miles out in a narrow corridor to the town of Fitchburg in central Massachusetts and beyond. For 28 years Congressman Philip Philbin had represented the 3d, combining a liberal record on domestic issues with a strong hawkish point of view as a member of the House Armed Services Committee. In 1968, after redistricting had added Newton and several other Boston suburbs to the district, Philbin won only 49% in a four-candidate Democratic primary and only 48% in a three-candidate general election.

This was obviously a constituency waiting for a candidate. The problem was to put together a majority in a district almost as varied as Massachusetts itself. There is a significant WASPy suburban voting bloc here, but it is outnumbered by Catholic working class voters in the Boston suburb of Waltham and in the area around Fitchburg and Leominster in the western end of the district. Newton and Brookline, the latter added after the 1970 election, have significant Jewish communities. Drinan was first chosen as a candidate in a liberal caucus, and he was one of consultant John Marttila's first clients. A massive grass roots campaign beat Philbin in the primary; he was beaten again, running as an Independent, in the general election, by a 38%–36% margin, with 26% going to a strong Republican.

Drinan's candidacy had its beginnings in opposition to the Vietnam war, and his career has had its greatest intensity in its opposition to Richard Nixon and virtually all his works. Drinan's strong advocacy of his positions, often far ahead of more prudent politicians, plus his status as a priest, have made him very controversial; there is a strong anti-Drinan vote in every election. He has taken one of the strongest stands in Congress in favor of aid to Israel and in support of Soviet Jewry; nevertheless, his general election opponents in 1972, 1974, and 1976, all Jewish, have accused him of being anti-Israel. His status as a priest bothers some Catholics, who have never liked the clergy to meddle in politics. Also troublesome to some is his stand on abortion: he opposes abortion but has written extensively on why government should not impose the beliefs of some on everyone, and therefore has voted against anti-abortion curbs. Now that Vietnam and Watergate are no longer issues, Drinan gets much of his support the way other congressmen do: by working hard to solve constituents' problems. He has been particularly active—and effective—in keeping open the Army's Fort Devens in the western end of the district.

Nevertheless Drinan had four tough general elections in a row—an unusual experience for a congressman these days—and in 1978 primary opposition from a right-to-life advocate. However, there was no Republican nominee that year—a source of considerable irritation to some House Republicans, who dislike Drinan's politics intensely. As the first congressman to advocate impeachment, and as the first priest elected to the House, Drinan already has a couple of footnotes in the history books. He may also be remembered as one of the last members of the

House Un-American Activities Committee (renamed Internal Security before it died). Drinan joined that body to keep a hostile eye on it, and was pleased when it was abolished in 1975.

Census Data Pop. 476,130. Central city, 16%; suburban, 71%. Median family income, $12,409; families above $15,000: 36%; families below $3,000: 5%. Median years education, 12.5.

The Voters

Median voting age 42.
Employment profile White collar, 62%. Blue collar, 27%. Service, 11%. Farm, –%.
Ethnic groups Black, 1%. Spanish, 1%. Total foreign stock, 37%. Canada, 11%; Italy, USSR, 5% each; Ireland, 3%; UK, Poland, 2% each; Germany, 1%.

Presidential vote

1976	Carter (D)	117,919	(57%)
	Ford (R)	88,613	(43%)
1972	Nixon (R)	92,341	(44%)
	McGovern (D)	116,100	(56%)

Rep. Robert F. Drinan (D) Elected 1970; b. Nov. 15, 1920, Boston; home, Newton; Boston Col. A.B., 1942, M.A. 1947, Georgetown U., LL.B. 1949, LL.M. 1950, Gregorian U., Rome, Italy, 1954; Catholic.

Career Ordained Jesuit Priest, 1953–; Dean, Boston Col. Law School, 1956–70.

Offices 2452 RHOB, 202-225-5931. Also 400 Totten Pond Rd., Bldg. 1, Waltham 02154, 617-890-9455.

Committees *Government Operations* (12th). Subcommittees: Manpower and Housing; Government Information and Individual Rights; Environment, Energy, and Natural Resources.

Judiciary (8th). Subcommittees: Civil and Constitutional Rights; Criminal Justice (Chairman).

Group Ratings

	ADA	COPE	PC	RPN	NFU	LCV	CFA	NAB	NSI	ACA	NTU
1978	100	95	98	50	80	–	96	8	11	11	–
1977	100	74	95	62	83	90	100	–	–	7	39
1976	100	86	95	59	92	93	100	17	0	4	33

Key Votes

1) Increase Def Spnd	AGN	6) Alaska Lands Protect	FOR	11) Delay Auto Pol Cntrl	AGN
2) B-1 Bomber	AGN	7) Water Projects Veto	FOR	12) Sugar Price Escalator	AGN
3) Cargo Preference	AGN	8) Consum Protect Agcy	FOR	13) Pub Fin Cong Cmpgns	FOR
4) Dereg Nat Gas	AGN	9) Common Situs Picket	FOR	14) ERA Ratif Recissn	AGN
5) Kemp-Roth	AGN	10) Labor Law Revision	FOR	15) Prohibt Govt Abrtns	AGN

Election Results

1978 general	Robert F. Drinan (D), unopposed			($149,345)
1978 primary	Robert F. Drinan (D)	41,374	(65%)	
	Norman M. Walker (D)	21,919	(35%)	($22,812)
1976 general	Robert F. Drinan (D)	109,268	(52%)	($219,297)
	Arthur D. Mason (R)	100,562	(48%)	($186,262)

FIFTH DISTRICT

The 5th congressional district of Massachusetts centers on two transportation arteries which have, in their times, been vital to the state's economic development. The first is the Merrimack River, whose fall provided the power for the great textile mills built by Boston Brahmins in company towns they named for themselves, Lowell and Lawrence. Back in the mid-nineteenth century, the New England textile business was a boom industry that first employed local farm girls and then went on to hire hundreds of thousands of immigrants from Ireland and French Canada. Virtually all the New England textile firms have long since moved south and even abroad in search of lower wages; and with the mills of Lowell and Lawrence quiet, these cities suffered through a local depression that lasted something like forty years.

In the sixties both cities perked up a bit, largely because of the peripheral influence of the area's other major artery, Route 128, a circumferential highway around greater Boston. Dozens of the nation's leading electronics and defense research firms, drawing brainpower from the area's universities, have located along both sides of the roadway. They have also had their ups and downs. Some defense contractors found the political climate in Massachusetts unfavorable, and the state suffered one-fourth of the nation's military cutbacks in 1973, apparently in retaliation for having voted for McGovern. But since then Route 128 has come back, and Lowell and Lawrence are enjoying a kind of civic rebirth and learning to take pride in their local heritage.

The 5th district has long since become dependably Democratic in national elections, delivering comfortable margins for McGovern in 1972 as well as Carter in 1976. But until 1974 it had never elected a Democratic congressman, electing one genteel Republican lady from 1924 to 1958 and liberal Republican Bradford Morse until he retired in 1972. That year a young Republican captured the district, largely because of the unpopularity of the Democratic candidate, John Kerry. The Republican in turn was beaten by Democrat Paul Tsongas in 1974.

Tsongas was a hard-working local official with roots in Lowell when he was elected; one of his major achievements was getting the old textile mill area in Lowell declared a national historical site. With high ratings from labor and liberal organizations, he seemed likely to be reelected, but not likely to become a national figure. But in 1978 he gambled and ran for the Senate. Commercials playing on the difficulty of pronouncing his last name (the t is silent) helped him win the primary; Edward Brooke's mistakes and the natural Democratic tendencies of Massachusetts helped him win the general.

There was a spirited contest for the 5th district seat in 1978. In the Democratic primary the winner was 26-year-old James Shannon, whose votes came mostly from his local base in Lawrence but who got enough support from the rest of the district to beat a Lowell-based conservative. The Republicans fielded a formidable candidate, Middlesex County Sheriff John Buckley, who had attracted attention by backing decriminalization of marijuana and handgun control. But Buckley dropped emphasis on these stands, which had appeal in the upper income parts of the district, in favor of Republican economic positions like Kemp–Roth, which seemed to have little pull except among hard-core Republicans. Shannon's advocacy of wage and price controls seemed more popular here. The more conservative working class votes went to a state legislator running as an Independent, who got nearly as many votes as Buckley.

As a result Shannon won a solid victory though he had just a little more than half the votes. He became the youngest member of the 96th Congress. He also got one of the better committee assignments for a freshman: a seat on the House Ways and Means Committee. Massachusetts's Speaker Tip O'Neill is known to take care of his home state delegation. The 5th district has now had four congressmen in the seventies. With a young incumbent placed on an important committee, it is possible that the district will now settle down and reelect Shannon for a good long time.

Census Data Pop. 473,154. Central city, 34%; suburban, 57%. Median family income, $11,532; families above $15,000: 29%; families below $3,000: 6%. Median years education, 12.3.

The Voters

Median voting age 43.
Employment profile White collar, 52%. Blue collar, 36%. Service, 11%. Farm, 1%.
Ethnic groups Spanish, 1%. Total foreign stock, 31%. Canada, 10%; Italy, 4%; UK, Ireland, 3% each; Poland, Greece, Germany, 1% each.

Presidential vote

1976	Carter (D)	125,892	(59%)
	Ford (R)	87,340	(41%)
1972	Nixon (R)	106,658	(47%)
	McGovern (D)	120,470	(53%)

Rep. James M. Shannon (D) Elected 1978; b. Apr. 4, 1952, Lawrence; home, Lawrence; Johns Hopkins U., B.A. 1972, Geo. Wash. U., J.D. 1975; Roman Catholic.

Career Aide to U.S. Rep. Michael Harrington; Practicing atty.

Offices 226 CHOB, 202-225-3411. Also 325 Merrimack St., Lowell 01852, 617-459-0101.

Committees *Ways and Means* (24th). Subcommittees: Trade; Health.

Group Ratings: Newly Elected

Key Votes: Newly Elected

Election Results

1978 general	James M. Shannon (D)	90,156	(52%)	($180,667)
	John J. Buckley (R)	48,685	(28%)	($97,637)
	James J. Gaffney III (I)	33,835	(20%)	($17,740)
1978 primary	James M. Shannon (D)	18,529	(22%)	
	Raymond F. Rourke (D)	17,743	(21%)	($54,724)
	Robert F. Hatem (D)	16,359	(20%)	($44,828)
	John K. Markey (D)	14,046	(17%)	($110,186)
	Two others (D)	16,168	(20%)	
1976 general	Paul E. Tsongas (D)	144,217	(67%)	($101,228)
	Roger P. Durkin (R)	70,036	(33%)	($29,124)

SIXTH DISTRICT

The 6th congressional district of Massachusetts is the North Shore district. Along and just back of the rocky coast north of Boston are the estates of some of the Commonwealth's oldest families, including—to name some still important politically—the Saltonstalls, the Lodges, and the Hatches. Only a few miles away are the fishermen of Gloucester, who have suffered in recent years from Russian trawlers until the United States extended its territorial waters to 200 miles. Here also are the textile mill workers in Haverhill and Newburyport on the Merrimack River—or people who used to be textile workers, since most of the mills have closed—and the artists and summer people of Rockport. To the south is Salem, where twenty witches were once hanged and pressed to death, and where Nathaniel Hawthorne's house of seven gables still stands in a neighborhood of neat nineteenth century homes. Also in the southern part of the district is the boating suburb of Marblehead, which Jews now share with WASPs; Lynn, whose troubled shoe industry has been pressing for years for protection against imports; and Peabody, a newer city, inland, with a large shopping center and a middle income population.

The 6th district is the site of the original gerrymander, named for the desire of its perpetrator, Elbridge Gerry, to corral all the area's Federalist voters into one misshapen seat. Since then the North Shore's wealthy towns and Brahmin families have given the area a reputation for Republicanism it has for some time ceased to deserve. Republican domination of the district continued through personal popularity of one William Bates, until his death in 1969.

The result of the special election to replace him showed the way things were going in Massachusetts. Republican William Santonstall was beaten by Democrat Michael Harrington. A hot-tempered opponent of the Vietnam war, Harrington never found a comfortable niche in the House. In the 94th Congress there was a move to censure him for disclosing classified information on American aid to the Chilean junta, although the material was true and government officials were lying about it; Harrington got off on a technicality. He seems to have been the only member of Congress concerned about what this country did in Chile. In 1976 several ballot measures he was strongly backing were defeated in Massachusetts, and his own percentage was sharply reduced. He decided to retire in 1978 and, at 42, to return to Massachusetts.

When he left the race, Harrington was already being challenged by Peabody Mayor Nicholas Mavroules, a more traditional kind of Democrat. A local officeholder for twenty years, Mavroules was no ideologue; he won the three-candidate primary with little difficulty. The Republican candidate, airline pilot Bill Bronson, had run against Harrington in 1976 and was primed to run an anti-Harrington campaign again. Mavroules left him off balance and exposed Bronson's own peculiar views, such as a proposal to return most welfare programs to churches and other private institutions. Nevertheless Bronson got a better percentage against Mavroules than he had against Harrington and ran quite a creditable race. Whether the Republicans will seriously contest this race again, however, is not clear.

Census Data Pop. 475,885. Central city, 10%; suburban, 72%. Median family income, $10,904; families above $15,000: 25%; families below $3,000: 6%. Median years education, 12.3.

The Voters

Median voting age 45.
Employment profile White collar, 52%. Blue collar, 36%. Service, 12%. Farm, –%.
Ethnic groups Total foreign stock, 31%. Canada, 10%; Italy, 4%; Ireland, UK, 3% each; USSR, Poland, Greece, 2% each.

Presidential vote

1976	Carter (D)	119,963	(55%)
	Ford (R)	97,834	(45%)
1972	Nixon (R)	104,027	(47%)
	McGovern (D)	116,157	(53%)

Rep. Nicholas Mavroules (D) Elected 1978; b. Nov. 1, 1929, Peabody; home, Peabody; M.I.T., night courses; Greek Orthodox.

Career Peabody Ward Cncl., 1958–61, Councillor-at-Large, 1964–65, Mayor, 1967–78.

Offices 1204 LHOB, 202-225-8020. Also 99 Washington St., Salem 01970, 617-745-5800.

Committees *Armed Services* (27th). Subcommittees: Procurement and Military Nuclear Systems; Military Compensation.

Science and Technology (22d). Subcommittees: Energy Development and Applications; Transportation, Aviation and Communication.

Group Ratings: Newly Elected

Key Votes: Newly Elected

Election Results

1978 general	Nicholas Mavroules (D)	97,099	(54%)	($290,331)
	William E. Bronson (R)	83,511	(46%)	($185,029)
1978 primary	Nicholas Mavroules (D)	34,511	(44%)	
	James Smith (D)	27,600	(35%)	($75,008)
	One other (D)	16,322	(21%)	
1976 general	Michael J. Harrington (D)	121,562	(57%)	($100,673)
	William E. Bronson (R)	91,655	(43%)	($44,084)

SEVENTH DISTRICT

The 7th congressional district of Massachusetts is a collection of suburbs just north of Boston. Its sociological range extends from Chelsea, where Jewish immigrants first disembarked more than half a century ago, to Melrose, a comfortable and still distinctly Yankee (and Republican) town. Most of the communities here lie somewhere in between those two extremes and contain many descendants of Irish and Italian immigrants who have reached some degree of financial security if not affluence. The political trend in the 7th illustrates the liberalization of Massachusetts politics in the last twenty years. In the fifties the 7th was considered a Republican district, and in 1960 John Kennedy was thought to have done unusually well when he carried the area with 57%. But in 1968 Hubert Humphrey, though not of Boston Irish stock, got 66%; George McGovern, while losing nationally, did as well as Kennedy, with 57%; and Jimmy Carter got 59%.

Obviously those numbers represent a considerable shift of opinion; there are only a handful of districts in the nation where McGovern ran as well as Kennedy. These results reflect a growing belief that voting Republican is no longer required for respectability—indeed, that the opposite may be the case. More than anyone else, Edward Kennedy is responsible for this shift. The positions he takes and the politicians he backs have made great gains here; he has won the respect of the Yankees without losing the affection of the Catholics. So these voters living north of Boston, many of whom—or many of whose parents—supported Joe McCarthy in the fifties, have been voting for years now for candidates who opposed the Vietnam war and favor major new domestic programs.

The Democratic trend here can also be seen in the congressional election results. Until 1954 this was a Republican district with a Republican congressman. That year, two years after John Kennedy was elected to the Senate, one of his college roommates, Torbert Macdonald, was elected to the House as a Democrat in the 7th district. Macdonald was reelected without difficulty until his death in May 1976.

The transformation of the district's politics was reflected in the field of candidates to succeed Macdonald. There were twelve Democrats in the primary and no Republican; 105,000 voters participated in the Democratic primary, 10,000 in the Republican. The winner was 30-year-old state Representative Edward Markey, who beat Macdonald's administrative assistant and ten minor candidates. Markey had a maverick record in the legislature that earned him a legislator of the year award from the bar association; he also had the endorsement of 6th district Congressman Michael Harrington. What he didn't have, in a year when voters didn't want it anyway, was Washington experience. It turned out that he had never been in Washington at all; reporters took to writing "Mr. Smith goes to Washington" stories about him as soon as he came to serve out the rest of Macdonald's term.

Markey has not behaved like a neophyte politically. He won seats on the Commerce and Interior Committees, and won election to a full term over a Republican nominated by write-ins with 81% of the vote. He has the potential to be a senior and powerful congressman before too many years go by.

Census Data Pop. 476,565. Central city, 0%; suburban, 100%. Median family income, $11,406; families above $15,000: 28%; families below $3,000: 5%. Median years education, 12.3.

The Voters

Median voting age 45.
Employment profile White collar, 57%. Blue collar, 32%. Service, 11%. Farm, –%.
Ethnic groups Total foreign stock, 37%. Italy, 12%; Canada, 9%; Ireland, 4%. USSR, UK, 3% each; Poland, 1%.

Presidential vote

1976	Carter (D)	126,935	(59%)
	Ford (R)	86,572	(41%)
1972	Nixon (R)	91,607	(43%)
	McGovern (D)	122,026	(57%)

Rep. Edward J. Markey (D) Elected 1976; b. July 11, 1946, Malden; home, Malden; Boston Col., B.A. 1968, J.D. 1972; Catholic.

Career Mass. House of Reps., 1973–76.

Offices 213 CHOB, 202-225-2836. Also 2100A J.F.K. Bldg., Boston 02203, 617-223-2781.

Committees *Interior and Insular Affairs* (17th). Subcommittees: Energy and the Environment.

Interstate and Foreign Commerce (18th). Subcommittees: Communications; Energy and Power.

Group Ratings

	ADA	COPE	PC	RPN	NFU	LCV	CFA	NAB	NSI	ACA	NTU
1978	90	85	85	42	88	–	96	0	0	7	–
1977	90	78	95	46	92	95	95	–	–	8	41

Key Votes

1) Increase Def Spnd	AGN	6) Alaska Lands Protect	FOR	11) Delay Auto Pol Cntrl	AGN
2) B-1 Bomber	AGN	7) Water Projects Veto	FOR	12) Sugar Price Escalator	AGN
3) Cargo Preference	AGN	8) Consum Protect Agcy	FOR	13) Pub Fin Cong Cmpgns	FOR
4) Dereg Nat Gas	AGN	9) Common Situs Picket	FOR	14) ERA Ratif Recissn	AGN
5) Kemp-Roth	AGN	10) Labor Law Revision	FOR	15) Prohibt Govt Abrtns	FOR

Election Results

1978 general	Edward J. Markey (D)	145,615	(85%)	($60,542)
	James J. Murphy (I)	26,017	(15%)	
1978 primary	Edward J. Markey (D), unopposed			
1976 general	Edward J. Markey (D)	162,126	(81%)	($114,583)
	Richard W. Daly (R)	37,063	(19%)	($3,612)

EIGHTH DISTRICT

The 8th of Massachusetts is a congressional district with a number of distinctive features. It is the home of no less than three major universities—Harvard, MIT, and Boston University—and of dozens of small colleges; in all, the 8th has the second highest proportion of college students (15%

of the potential electorate in 1970) in the nation. The 8th is distinctive physically: it includes most of Boston's downtown, with its twenties buildings alternating with modern architecture and Faneuil Hall and the restored 1820s Quincy Market. It has literally dozens of distinctive neighborhoods, from the Italian quarter in Boston's North End to the insular Irish community of Charlestown, the newer Portuguese community in Cambridge, the Armenians in Watertown, the elderly Jews of Brighton, and the upper income Yankees and professors of Belmont. And it is distinctive in its congressional representation. This heavily Democratic part of heavily Democratic Massachusetts has been represented successively by a president of the United States and a speaker of the House of Representatives—the only district in American history with such a record.

The president of course was John Kennedy, who won this seat in 1946 as a rich young veteran and held it for six years while waiting to run for the Senate; and the speaker is Thomas "Tip" O'Neill, elected here in 1952 after serving as the first Democratic Speaker of the Massachusetts house, and Speaker of the House in Washington since the beginning of 1977.

O'Neill is a man of town, not gown, politics, and he still feels most comfortable in the company of experienced Irish pols. In his first years in the House, he was a man who got along by going along—and got a seat on the Rules Committee out of it. In 1967, however, he took the step—rare at the time—of coming out publicly against Lyndon Johnson's policy in Vietnam. This was long before the university vote was important in the district; O'Neill had been persuaded by his children that the war was wrong. As an Irish big city pol who supported the antiwar position, he was a natural bridge between different segments of the Democratic Caucus in the late sixties and early seventies.

He also knew how to count. In 1971 he supported Hale Boggs's candidacy for majority leader, and brought a number of Eastern votes along with him. Boggs won, and O'Neill was appointed Whip. When Boggs was lost in a plane crash in 1972, O'Neill succeeded to the majority leadership essentially without opposition. The succession to the speakership, after Carl Albert retired in 1976, was even easier.

How has O'Neill stacked up as Speaker? First, he is in fact the functioning leader of the Democratic majority in the House—something that could not really be said of his two predecessors and indeed was seldom true of the fabled Sam Rayburn in his later years. Part of the reason for O'Neill's effectiveness is lack of competing power centers. The Rules Committee, no longer chaired by Southern reactionaries, is responsive to the Speaker's wishes. Committee chairmen like Wilbur Mills of Ways and Means and Wayne Hays of House Administration are gone. Phillip Burton, defeated in 1976 for majority leader by one vote, is not a close O'Neill friend; Jim Wright, the man who did win, does not have as much of a personal power base. If power in the House today is diffused among dozens of subcommittee chairmen and activist members of both parties, it is also concentrated to a greater extent than it used to be at the top, in the hands of the Speaker. Some of those who complain that there are no strong leaders in the House anymore are columnists who used to have good sources on the Hill but who now do not get the inside story and scoop from O'Neill. Instead, the Speaker is candid about his plans and strategies in open press conference.

O'Neill is a highly partisan man, and unlike some of his predecessors, he has no particular affection for his Republican counterparts. Republicans are the enemy, and the Speaker sees his job as getting legislation through with Democratic votes. After all, there are far more than 218 of them available. Perhaps instinctively O'Neill knows that his kind of partisanship is not attractive to most ticket-splitting voters; and so he keeps much of what he is thinking to himself. Moreover, some of his old loyalties have led him to make bad decisions. He stood up for Bob Sikes in his fight to retain a subcommittee chair after he had been reprimanded by the House; Sikes lost badly in the caucus. He fumed when the White House ousted his old Somerville friend Robert Griffin from the number two post at GSA without telling him—not the best way to appeal to the public. And he suffered a number of failures in the 95th Congress, notably on the Consumer Protection Agency, although it should be noted that some of the defeated Democratic bills—labor law reform, deregulation of natural gas—were lost in the Senate, not the House.

On the big issues Tip O'Neill has shown himself to be a legislative strategist of great talent. The best example is the energy bill in the 95th Congress. When the Carter Administration advanced its proposals, O'Neill's impulse was to help get them through the House. But it would be difficult. Various committees had jurisdiction over different parts of the program, and they had different policy preferences; the House had failed to report out anything at all when President Ford submitted an energy bill. So O'Neill set up an ad hoc committee, including members from all the relevant committees which had to pass on the substantive legislation. He chose as its chairman Thomas Ashley of Ohio, a competent worker with few personal enemies and without the sort of ambition that makes other members nervous or jealous. He got the main problems thrashed out in that committee and then got the legislative committees to report out the bill. Most of the points in the program he put into one major bill, which members had to vote up or down; there would be no piece-by-piece dismemberment of the legislation on the floor. Certain particularly important and controversial provisions—notably the question of deregulation of natural gas—were to be voted on separately. Then the bill passed the House. It was quite a contrast with the Senate's approach to the same legislation, which featured lengthy and often frivolous filibustering, endless non-bargaining at conference committee. O'Neill framed the issues, got an up-or-down vote, and passed a major bill. There hasn't been a performance like this in the House for a long, long time.

In the 95th Congress O'Neill generally cooperated with the Carter Administration, and at the beginning of the 96th Congress he seemed to want to do so again. But he is an old-fashioned Democrat, who believes in spending public money to help the poor and disadvantaged, and he has given notice that there may come a parting of the ways between him and the Administration if they push budget-cutting too far. That would set up a major confrontation between the White House and Congress—and no one can say who would be the winner.

Census Data Pop. 474,090. Central city, 35%; suburban, 65%. Median family income, $10,317; families above $15,000: 24%; families below $3,000: 7%. Median years education, 12.3.

The Voters

Median voting age 39.
Employment profile White collar, 63%. Blue collar, 24%. Service, 13%. Farm, -%.
Ethnic groups Black, 2%. Spanish, 1%. Total foreign stock, 41%. Italy, 10%; Canada, 8%; Ireland, 6%. UK, USSR, 2% each; Portugal, Greece, Germany, Poland, 1% each.

Presidential vote

1976	Carter (D)	117,446	(35%)
	Ford (R)	62,247	(35%)
1972	Nixon (R)	65,660	(34%)
	McGovern (D)	127,868	(66%)

Rep. Thomas P. O'Neill, Jr. (D) Elected 1952; b. Dec. 9, 1912, Cambridge; home, Cambridge; Boston Col., A.B. 1936; Catholic.

Career Insurance business; Mass. House of Reps., 1936–52, Minor. Ldr., 1947–48, Spkr., 1948–52; Cambridge School Comm., 1946–47.

Offices 2231 RHOB, 202-225-5111. Also 2200A JFK Fed. Bldg., Boston 02203, 617-223-2784.

Committees *The Speaker of the House.*

Group Ratings: Newly Elected

1976 60 87 79 39 75 69 73 8 30 8 15

Election Results

1978 general	Thomas P. O'Neill, Jr. (D)	102,160	(78%)	($16,274)
	William A. Barnstead (R)	28,566	(22%)	
1978 primary	Thomas P. O'Neill, Jr. (D), unopposed			
1976 general	Thomas P. O'Neill, Jr. (D)	133,131	(80%)	($88,045)
	William A. Barnstead (R)	33,437	(20%)	($6,057)

NINTH DISTRICT

Boston is the most political of cities. Boston malcontents did more than anyone else to start the American Revolution, and Boston was the hotbed of the abolitionist movement which had so much to do with igniting the Civil War. Boston is also, and this is no coincidence, the nation's most Irish city, for the Irish seem to have some magical aptitude for politics. The proportion of Irish-Americans who live here does not really show up in the census figures, which show only the 7% who came themselves or whose parents came from Ireland; the fact is that there has been heavy Irish immigration here since 1845, and that the Boston Irish are remarkably unassimilated. In the old Irish neighborhoods of South Boston and Charlestown, people keep their ethnic identity though their ancestors may have stepped off the boat more than a century ago. This is not a city where Irish identity is forgotten.

The Irish remain the most important ethnic group in Boston; they have held the mayor's office without substantial interruption from 1906 to the present day. Much of the older Boston wealth, it is true, is still in Yankee Protestant hands, controlled by the kind of people who preserve Boston institutions like the Athenaeum and the Somerset Club and live in old town houses in Louisburg Square on Beacon Hill. And much of the attention in Boston in recent years has gone to people who are, in many ways, the spiritual (and sometimes the lineal) descendants of Samuel Adams and his raucous friends: the leftish, recent/former/present students, the young liberated people who make up an increasing percentage of the population here. For Boston is, if you look at it that way, the nation's largest college town, not just because of Harvard and MIT across the river in Cambridge, but because of literally hundreds of other schools of all kinds and all levels of repute. Boston is one of the few American cities where the local media, the big retailers, even the banks cater to a market of this sort.

So we have this arresting paradox. Boston, which by some indications is solidly to the left politically (more than 60% for McGovern in 1972), is also the site of the nation's longest lasting and most bitter antibusing protest (the city went for George Wallace in the 1976 presidential primary). The way to explain the contradiction is to look at just who is upset, and at what. The antiwar movement had its constituency in the post-student generation here; the Irish neighborhoods, after initial hostility and on prompting by Edward Kennedy, concurred. Busing is a problem that troubles almost exclusively the Irish ghettoes, like South Boston, where most of the violence took place. The post-student generation has never been part of the busing controversy.

Moreover, the long term impact of the busing controversy seems limited. The number of people whose children were affected is not all that great. Many of the whites in the city have always sent their children to Catholic schools; many others are too old to have children of school age. The busing orders which began when blacks formed only a minority of the school population have produced enough white flight that relatively few whites are left in the public school system; many have left for the suburbs, where indeed they might have moved in the natural course of things even without busing.

Certainly the evidence of election returns shows that busing is the concern of a minority. Wallace won here in 1976, but with only 25% of the vote. Mayor Kevin White twice beat Louise Day Hicks, the School Committee member closely identified with opposition to busing; and the current School Committee does not have a strong anti-busing majority. Mrs. Hicks was elected to Congress in 1970, but with minorities in both the primary and general election. She had a minority again in the 1972 primary, and lost the general election to a Democratic state senator who was running as an Independent.

That was Joseph Moakley, and he remains the Congressman from the 9th district. After his initial victory, he has had no problem winning reelection. Succeeding to a seat once held by a recent Speaker, John McCormack, who served here from 1928 till his retirement in 1970, he was helped by the current Speaker, Tip O'Neill, to a seat on the House Rules Committee. Predictably his votes are in line with the wishes of the House leadership.

Census Data Pop. 473,680. Central city, 70%; suburban, 30%. Median family income, $10,144; families above $15,000: 25%; families below $3,000: 9%. Median years education, 12.2.

The Voters

Median voting age 43.
Employment profile White collar, 55%. Blue collar, 28%. Service, 17%. Farm, –%.
Ethnic groups Black, 20%. Spanish, 3%. Total foreign stock, 34%. Ireland, 7%; Italy, Canada, 5% each; UK, USSR, 2% each; Poland, Germany, 1% each.

Presidential vote

1976	Carter (D)	90,048	(56%)
	Ford (R)	69,631	(44%)
1972	Nixon (R)	68,748	(41%)
	McGovern (D)	100,720	(59%)

Rep. Joe Moakley (D) Elected 1972, as Independent, seated in Congress as Democrat, Jan. 3, 1973; b. Apr. 27, 1927, Boston; home, Boston; U. of Miami, B.A., Suffolk U., LL.B. 1956; Catholic.

Career Navy, WWII; Mass. House of Reps., 1953–65, Maj.Whip, 1957; Practicing atty., 1957–72; Mass. Senate, 1965–69; Boston City Cncl., 1971.

Offices 221 CHOB, 202-225-8273. Also 1900C JFK Fed. Bldg., Boston 02203, 617-223-5715.

Committees *Rules* (5th).

Group Ratings

	ADA	COPE	PC	RPN	NFU	LCV	CFA	NAB	NSI	ACA	NTU
1978	75	90	70	36	70	–	68	0	10	4	–
1977	80	81	83	38	83	87	75	–	–	8	20
1976	85	87	92	50	83	79	100	8	10	4	20

Key Votes

1) Increase Def Spnd	AGN	6) Alaska Lands Protect	FOR	11) Delay Auto Pol Cntrl	AGN
2) B-1 Bomber	AGN	7) Water Projects Veto	AGN	12) Sugar Price Escalator	AGN
3) Cargo Preference	FOR	8) Consum Protect Agcy	FOR	13) Pub Fin Cong Cmpgns	FOR
4) Dereg Nat Gas	AGN	9) Common Situs Picket	FOR	14) ERA Ratif Recissn	AGN
5) Kemp-Roth	AGN	10) Labor Law Revision	DNV	15) Prohibt Govt Abrtns	FOR

Election Results

1978 general	Joe Moakley (D)	106,805	(94%)	($46,217)
	Brenda Lee M. Franklin (Soc. Workers)	6,794	(6%)	
1978 primary	Joe Moakley (D), unopposed			
1976 general	Joe Moakley (D)	103,901	(75%)	($118,268)
	Robert G. Cunningham (R)	34,547	(25%)	($132)

TENTH DISTRICT

The 10th Congressional district of Massachusetts is one example of a geographical monstrosity tailored to the political needs of one longtime incumbent and now serving those of another in equally good fashion. The 10th is made up of two quite different parts. In the north are the Boston suburbs: posh, WASPy Wellesley and the more middle class Natick next door. This remains one of the most Republican areas in the state. In the south is the city of Fall River, the district's largest city; it is an aging mill town that never really recovered from the southward flight of its 110 cotton mills. The huge granite and brick structures are now occupied, if at all, with marginal dress and curtain sweatshops which pay the French Canadian and Portuguese workers (most of the latter from the Azores) minimal wages. This end of the 10th is dominated politically by voters of Portuguese, French Canadian, and Italian descent who ordinarily vote Democratic. The middle of the 10th, between the two ends of the district, is composed of sparsely populated towns spread out over the rolling hills between Boston and Providence. Among them are Foxboro, home of the New England Patriots, and North Attleboro, home of the district's longtime (1925–67) Congressman, Joseph W. Martin Jr.

For many years the district's boundaries were drawn to provide a safe seat for Martin, who was Speaker of the House following the Republican congressional victories of 1946 and 1952. But by the middle sixties Martin had been ousted from the leadership and, past 80, was no longer capable of campaigning. Challenged in the primary, he was defeated by Margaret Heckler, a Wellesley attorney, who was then the only Republican member of the Governor's Council—an antique institution that survives from colonial days only in Massachusetts, New Hampshire, and Maine.

Heckler has not really had much difficulty winning election since 1966. Her reputation as a liberal Republican helps her in the district, and generally she does score higher ratings from liberal than conservative groups. At the same time, she has been willing to help the Republican leadership when it really needs it. She was part of a solid Republican bloc which voted against Wright Patman's proposed investigation of the Watergate burglary in October 1972 and, with some Democratic votes, killed the probe. She supported the Republican position on the Kemp–Roth bill in 1978. Sometimes she seems torn between her constituency and her party: she often waits till the very end of a roll call before casting her vote.

Census Data Pop. 477,054. Central city, 20%; suburban, 55%. Median family income, $10,747; families above $15,000: 24%; families below $3,000: 6%. Median years education, 12.1.

The Voters

Median voting age 44.
Employment profile White collar, 46%. Blue collar, 41%. Service, 12%. Farm, 1%.
Ethnic groups Total foreign stock, 32%. Canada, 8%; Portugal, 6%; UK, 3%; Italy, Ireland, Poland, 2% each; USSR, 1%.

Presidential vote

1976	Carter (D)	118,890	(56%)
	Ford (R)	95,210	(44%)
1972	Nixon (R)	100,844	(50%)
	McGovern (D)	102,368	(50%)

Rep. Margaret M. Heckler (R) Elected 1966; b. June 21, 1931, Flushing, N.Y.; home, Wellesley; Albertus Magnus Col., A.B. 1953, Boston Col., LL.B. 1956; Catholic.

Career Mbr., Mass. Governors Council, 1962–66.

Offices 2312 RHOB, 202-225-4335. Also One Washington St., Wellesley Hills 02181, 617-235-3350.

Committees *Agriculture* (7th). Subcommittees: Department Investigations, Oversight, and Research; Domestic Marketing, Consumer Relations, and Nutrition; Cotton.

Veterans Affairs (2d). Subcommittees: Education, Training and Employment; Special Investigations; Medical Facilities and Benefits.

Group Ratings

	ADA	COPE	PC	RPN	NFU	LCV	CFA	NAB	NSI	ACA	NTU
1978	55	70	53	40	60	–	64	25	63	22	–
1977	65	65	68	80	83	70	80	–	–	26	31
1976	65	57	67	76	73	72	54	46	40	17	35

Key Votes

1) Increase Def Spnd	AGN	6) Alaska Lands Protect	DNV	11) Delay Auto Pol Cntrl	AGN
2) B-1 Bomber	AGN	7) Water Projects Veto	FOR	12) Sugar Price Escalator	AGN
3) Cargo Preference	AGN	8) Consum Protect Agcy	FOR	13) Pub Fin Cong Cmpgns	FOR
4) Dereg Nat Gas	AGN	9) Common Situs Picket	FOR	14) ERA Ratif Recissn	AGN
5) Kemp-Roth	FOR	10) Labor Law Revision	FOR	15) Prohibt Govt Abrtns	FOR

Election Results

1978 general	Margaret M. Heckler (R)	102,080	(61%)	($210,730)
	John J. Marino (D)	64,868	(39%)	($78,848)
1978 primary	Margaret M. Heckler (R), unopposed			
1976 general	Margaret M. Heckler (R), unopposed			($26,867)

ELEVENTH DISTRICT

The 11th congressional district of Massachusetts includes the southern third of Boston, most of the city's South Shore suburbs, and more suburban territory stretching south to include the shoe manufacturing city of Brockton. With few exceptions, the 11th district's Dorchester and Hyde Park wards of Boston and its suburban towns—Quincy, Braintree (the ancestral home of the Adamses), and the newer Canton, Stoughton, and Randolph, away from the Shore—are filled with sons and daughters of Irish, Italian, and Jewish immigrants. Because most of these residents have remained loyal to their forebears' Democratic voting habits, the 11th has been heavily Democratic in recent years. Its Yankee minority, whose ancestors sent John Quincy Adams to the House for the last years of his life (1831–48), has been steadily abandoning the Republican Party, thus adding to the Republican majorities.

The succession of congressmen from this district points up the changes that have occurred in the last two generations of Massachusetts politics. For 30 years, from 1929 to 1959, the district's congressman was a Brahmin Republican with the imposing name of Richard Wigglesworth. His successor for 20 years, from 1959 to 1979, was James Burke, whose name and visage mirror his Irish descent. A loyal follower of the Democratic leadership, Burke epitomized old-fashioned Boston Irish politics. He was a member of the Ways and Means Committee, and as head of the subcommittee on Social Security, he was always generous about increasing benefits. Concerned about the plight of shoe workers in his district, Burke sponsored a major bill backed by the AFL-CIO to put restrictions on imports. A congressmen with a near-perfect labor record, he joined other Massachusetts Democrats in opposing the Vietnam war. But Burke's approach to politics was always practical rather than idealistic. He is supposed to have advised a young colleague that "you only have to worry about two things around here—Social Security and shoes."

Burke's health deteriorated, and in 1976 he was nearly beaten in the Democratic primary by Patrick McCarthy, who despite his name was a native of California, not Massachusetts. At 68, Burke retired at the end of the term; still bitter about 1976, he and other local politicians backed Brian Donnelly. At 31, he was already a three-term veteran of the state legislature; with deep roots in the district, he easily beat McCarthy and other opponents. The general election was anticlimactic. This district, which had never had a Democratic congressmen before Burke, had no Republican candidate at all. Donnelly has seats on the Public Works and Merchant Marine Committees, suggesting that he, like his predecessor, is more interested in bread-and-butter issues than in starry-eyed causes.

Census Data Pop. 475,789. Central city, 49%; suburban, 51%. Median family income, $11,052; families above $15,000: 25%; families below $3,000: 6%. Median years education, 12.3.

The Voters

Median voting age 45.
Employment profile White collar, 54%. Blue collar, 33%. Service, 13%. Farm, –%.
Ethnic groups Black, 2%. Total foreign stock, 35%. Ireland, Canada, 7% each; Italy, 6%; UK, USSR, 3% each; Poland, Lithuania, 1% each.

Presidential vote

1976	Carter (D)	113,549	(59%)
	Ford (R)	80,004	(41%)
1972	Nixon (R)	86,139	(43%)
	McGovern (D)	112,397	(57%)

Rep. Brian J. Donnelly (D) Elected 1978; b. Mar. 2, 1946, Boston; home, Boston; Boston U., B.S. 1970; Catholic.

Career Dir. of Youth Activities, Dorchester YMCA, 1968–70; High School and Trade School Teacher and Coach, 1969–72; Mass. House of Reps., 1973–79.

Offices 1019 LHOB, 202-225-3215. Also 47 Washington St., Quincy 02169, 617-472-1314.

Committees *Merchant Marine and Fisheries* (25th). Subcommittees: Merchant Marine; Fish and Wildlife.

Public Works and Transportation (25th). Subcommittees: Economic Development; Public Buildings and Grounds; Water Resources.

Group Ratings: Newly Elected

Key Votes: Newly Elected

Election Results

1978 general	Brian J. Donnelly (D)	133,644	(92%)	($184,204)
	H. Graham Lowry (U.S. Labor)	12,044	(8%)	
1978 primary	Brian J. Donnelly (D)	39,236	(43%)	
	Patrick H. McCarthy (D)	18,127	(20%)	($210,070)
	James A. Sheets (D)	15,641	(17%)	($67,305)
	Three others (D)	17,735	(20%)	
1976 general	James A. Burke (D)	131,789	(69%)	($1,270)
	Danielle de Benedictis (I)	59,240	(31%)	($27,160)

TWELFTH DISTRICT

The 12th congressional district of Massachusetts is the closest thing to a Republican district, in national terms, in the overwhelming Democratic commonwealth. It was the only Massachusetts district to deliver a majority, albeit a paper-thin one, to Richard Nixon in 1972; and its 1976 majority percentage for Jimmy Carter was the lowest of any Massachusetts congressional district. Like the 10th, the 12th was originally designed to elect a Republican. The heavily Democratic city of New Bedford, an old whaling port where the hard-pressed fishing industry is still important, was combined with traditionally Republican territory. This includes some of the more well-to-do South Shore suburbs of Boston (Weymouth, Hingham), most of Plymouth County, Cape Cod, and the two resort islands of Martha's Vineyard and Nantucket. The last was the whaling port from which Herman Melville's Captain Ahab sailed in pursuit of Moby Dick; today, like the Vineyard, Nantucket is a place for rich and trendy summer people, with quaint old New England houses carefully restored. Both islands are upset about losing their seat in the Massachusetts legislature, and have been threatening to secede or join New Hampshire or Vermont.

The 12th has now broken with years of Republican tradition and regularly elects a Democratic Congressman, Gerry Studds. (His first name, a reminder that he is distantly related to Elbridge Gerry, Vice President under Madison and drawer of the original gerrymander, is pronounced with a hard g.) Studds first ran in 1970 and nearly beat the Republican incumbent; during the next two years he learned Portuguese and studied the problems of the local fishing industry. Even against a heavy-spending Republican in 1972, he won.

Much of the fervor behind Studds's first two campaigns came from his opposition to the war in Southeast Asia. But his record in the House shows a concentration on the practical problems of the 12th district. He has switched now from Public Works to the International Relations Committee, and he has advanced amendments to prohibit sale of the AWAC weapon system to Iran and to cut military aid to Argentina. But he has also stayed on the Merchant Marine and Fisheries Committee. In his first term he succeeded in pushing through a bill to extend the territorial waters of the United States to 200 miles from shoreline. More recently he has worked on the continental shelf bill, looking out for the interests of small fishermen, and has sponsored a bill to protect local businesses from losses due to oil spills. Concentration on such matters has paid off politically. Since 1972 he has had only nuisance opposition, with no Republican opponents whatever in the last two elections.

Census Data Pop. 475,672. Central city, 21%; suburban, 47%. Median family income, $10,132; families above $15,000: 22%; families below $3,000: 8%. Median years education, 12.2.

The Voters

Median voting age 46.
Employment profile White collar, 48%. Blue collar, 38%. Service, 13%. Farm, 1%.
Ethnic groups Black, 2%. Total foreign stock, 31%. Canada, 7%; Portugal, 5%; UK, 4%; Italy, Ireland, 2% each; Poland, 1%.

Presidential vote

1976	Carter (D)	132,554	(53%)
	Ford (R)	119,237	(47%)
1972	Nixon (R)	121,406	(52%)
	McGovern (D)	113,109	(48%)

Rep. Gerry E. Studds (D) Elected 1972; b. May 12, 1937, Mineola, N.Y.; home, Cohasset; Yale U., B.A. 1959, M.A.T. 1961.

Career U.S. Foreign Service, 1961–63; Exec. Asst. to William R. Anderson, Pres. Consultant for a Domestic Peace Corps, 1963; Legis. Asst. to U.S. Sen. Harrison Williams of N.J., 1964; Prep. School Teacher, 1965–69.

Offices 1501 LHOB, 202-225-3111. Also 243 P.O. Bldg., New Bedford 02740, 617-999-1251.

Committees *Foreign Affairs* (13th). Subcommittees: International Development; International Security and Scientific Affairs.

Merchant Marine and Fisheries (9th). Subcommittees: Coast Guard and Navigation; Fish and Wildlife; Oceanography (Chairman).

Group Ratings

	ADA	COPE	PC	RPN	NFU	LCV	CFA	NAB	NSI	ACA	NTU
1978	95	90	93	42	80	–	86	0	0	7	–
1977	100	83	93	54	83	95	90	–	–	0	42
1976	95	83	97	56	83	96	100	25	10	7	25

Key Votes

1) Increase Def Spnd	AGN	6) Alaska Lands Protect	FOR	11) Delay Auto Pol Cntrl	AGN
2) B-1 Bomber	AGN	7) Water Projects Veto	FOR	12) Sugar Price Escalator	AGN
3) Cargo Preference	AGN	8) Consum Protect Agcy	FOR	13) Pub Fin Cong Cmpgns	FOR
4) Dereg Nat Gas	AGN	9) Common Situs Picket	FOR	14) ERA Ratif Recissn	AGN
5) Kemp-Roth	AGN	10) Labor Law Revision	FOR	15) Prohibt Govt Abrtns	AGN

Election Results

1978 general	Gerry E. Studds (D), unopposed	($20,899)
1978 primary	Gerry E. Studds (D), unopposed	
1976 general	Gerry E. Studds (D), unopposed	($80,458)

MICHIGAN

To understand politics in Michigan, you should think of this as not one, but two states—divided, not between the Lower and Upper Peninsulas (for the Upper Peninsula has only 315,000 people and the Lower 8.7 million), but between the Detroit metropolitan area and outstate Michigan. Not only politically, but also economically these are two quite different regions; and if the boundary between them is not as clear as, the boundary between New York City and upstate New York, it is just as firmly established. Metro Detroit—Wayne, Oakland, and Macomb Counties—was boom country in the 1910–30 era when the growth of the auto industry transformed it from a gadgets and luxury trade to the nation's largest mass production industry and increased metro Detroit's population from 613,000 in 1910 to 2,177,000 in 1930.

In a pattern that is common to one-industry boom towns—Houston may be vulnerable in the future—the bustling growth of Detroit has been matched, a half century later, by sluggish economic growth and population outmigration. In the past there were fits and starts: people used to say during recessions that when the nation caught a cold, Detroit got pneumonia. Unemployment levels were up around 20% here in the 1957–58 recession, for example, when being out of work hurt a lot more than it does today. From such recessions the auto industry seemed to recover; but its long-term outlook is not clear. The high cost of gasoline has made Detroit's staple product, the full-sized car, an expensive luxury; there has been little technological innovation in the business since the thirties, except for anti-pollution and weight-losing devices whose development were forced on the industry by the federal government; there has been a decline in auto factory employment in the Detroit area, due to geographical diversification, since 1953.

Detroit still has a robust local economy. This is a high wage town and even its blue collar areas have median incomes that are among the highest in the country. The central city of Detroit is in better shape than it was, with murder rates down and the new Renaissance Center attracting business downtown; and if Mayor Coleman Young is not loved in the suburbs, he is politically secure in black-majority Detroit. But even so, metro Detroit is not generating enough jobs to keep all its sons and daughters, and many longtime residents have been moving to the quieter surroundings of northern Michigan or central Florida.

Outstate Michigan has few of Detroit's problems. There is some dependence on the auto industry here, too, with major plants in Flint, Lansing, Saginaw, Grand Rapids, and Kalamazoo; but in outstate Michigan as a whole autos are not so dominant an influence. Most of it never experienced the 1910–30 auto boom, and it is not now suffering from the industry's doldrums. Population has risen more than the national average during the seventies; people seem especially eager to move to the quiet towns and evergreened hills of the sparsely settled northern part of the Lower Peninsula. The medium-sized cities and small towns dotting the state are the kind of place most people say they would like to live in. They provide a stable, steady way of life: incomes are high here, if not as high as in the Detroit area; the crime rate is low; recreational facilities are close at hand; and so are virtually all of the state's major universities, which together with the state government have provided a healthy growth industry for outstate. Outstate Michigan's recent growth has made it more important not only economically but politically: its share of the statewide vote rose from 51% in 1964 to 57% in 1976, and will probably be higher in 1980.

Such changes have long term partisan effects. Metro Detroit, filled with auto workers from Poland and Alabama, southern Italy and eastern Kentucky and rural Ontario, and with as politically oriented a union as the United Auto Workers exerting major influence, has been heavily Democratic since the thirties. Outstate, peopled originally by the offspring of Yankee immigrants from the upstate New York of the 1840s, has been Republican since the party was founded; indeed, the Republican Party was founded in Jackson, Michigan. In recent years both areas have moved away from their traditional allegiances. Metro Detroit voters have moved toward the Republicans because of particular issues—aid to parochial schools in 1970, opposition to a busing plan that would have sent suburban pupils into Detroit in 1972, Catholics' doubts about Carter in 1976. At the same time there has been a stronger, more sustained movement in outstate Michigan toward the Democrats. Richard Nixon's Southern strategy seems to have repelled voters throughout the Upper Midwest in the early seventies, from outstate Michigan through the Dakotas. Outstate shifted to its historic balance in 1976, largely because of the personal popularity of outstater Gerald Ford, but in 1978 Democrats here were stronger than ever. While Democrats were losing elections badly in Wisconsin, Iowa, and Minnesota, they were gaining two congressional seats and several seats in the state legislature in outstate Michigan.

This same Democratic surge showed up in the 1976 and 1978 Senate races, both of which were won by Democrats. These were notable victories, for despite the Democratic leanings of the state, the Democratic Party here had been unable to win a seriously contested election for governor or senator between 1960 and 1976. To a considerable extent the Democrats were suffering from their successes in the fifties. Under Governor Mennen Williams, they had won majorities for every statewide office, running on a straight ticket theme. With strong support from the UAW, they framed the issues in state politics as conflicts between labor and management, between the ordinary person and the rich. That won them several elections, but they could not adjust when Republican George Romney, in 1962, changed the terms of discussion. Romney promised to reform state government and to get the state beyond the old labor vs. management quarrels. He used sophisticated polling and sensitive television commercials—methods spurned by the Democrats on the grounds they smacked of selling soap. Romney won in 1962, 1964, and 1966, and was succeeded when he became Richard Nixon's HUD Secretary by his Lieutenant Governor, William Milliken. Using much the same methods as Romney, Milliken won reelection in 1970, 1974, and 1978. By 1982 Republicans will have held the governorship in this Democratic state for twenty consecutive years. Only by applying methods similar to those used by Romney and Milliken were the two Democratic Senators, Donald Riegle and Carl Levin, elected.

Each of these Senate races had its curiosities. Riegle started out the decade not as a Democrat, but as a Republican Congressman from industrial Flint. Elected in 1966, he had become very popular, winning votes from blacks and endorsements from the UAW as well as enjoying the usual management-oriented Republican base. An opponent of the Vietnam war, Riegle campaigned for Pete McCloskey in his 1972 New Hampshire presidential primary effort. After McCloskey lost and Nixon was reelected, Riegle became a Democrat in early 1973. He entered the 1976 Senate primary with a less familiar name than his two competitors—Secretary of State Richard Austin and Congressman James O'Hara—but outcampaigned them and won. The general election turned out to be one of the more bizarre contests of the year. In mid-October 1976 the Detroit *News* reported that Riegle had had sexual relations with a woman on his staff in 1969 and that the sessions had been taped. Not only that, the *News* went on to print transcripts. The paper wanted to beat Riegle in the worst way—but their tactic backfired. Voters who might have thought Riegle indiscreet or ridiculous after the first article were revolted after the transcripts were printed. After all, one of the few things most voters have in common is that they have had intimate sexual experiences, and no one wants transcripts of such experiences printed in the newspaper. Lost in all the commotion was Riegle's opponent, Republican Congressman Marvin Esch, who had been elected the same year as Riegle and had a similar voting record—without the urge toward rebellion. Riegle won the election with 53% of the vote.

Winning the way he did was not likely to make Riegle particularly popular among his new colleagues, and he is not in any case the clubby type. His task was to convince them and Michigan voters that he is a hard-working Senator rather than a character out of the movie "Shampoo." In his first two years he made some progress. He was the Senate's leading advocate of relaxation of clean air standards—a move supported strongly by the automobile companies and the United Auto Workers—and though he was not successful, he was well prepared and presented his case ably. He serves on three committees—Banking, Commerce, and Human Resources—with jurisdiction over basic economic and government regulation matters. Riegle, though his early career lay in management, can be counted as one of the Senate's members most responsive to organized labor and of course in particular to the UAW.

One thing Riegle is not—and neither is anyone else in the Senate—is a public servant in the tradition of his predecessor in the seat, Philip Hart. He was an unusual combination: a man who believed passionately in many liberal causes—regulation of business, antitrust, consumer protection, ending the Vietnam war—and who at the same time could not help having an appreciation of the motives and the arguments of those who took the opposite stands. Hart decided to retire in 1976 and found out later that he had cancer; he died just before his term was about to expire. The Senate in recognition more of his character than his fame named the new Senate office building after him.

Hart's colleague during most of his Senate career was a man different in beliefs, party, and temperament, Robert Griffin. He had served in the House starting in 1956, and as a junior member of the minority party made a major legislative impact: he got the House to substitute his anti-labor racketeering law for that supported by the AFL-CIO even when it had an overwhelming majority, and thus we have the Landrum–Griffin Act of 1959. In 1966 Griffin accepted appointment to the Senate and took on Mennen Williams, and whipped him soundly; in 1972 he ran a stronger anti-busing race than Attorney General Frank Kelley and won a second term. Griffin was the essence of the intelligent, aggressive partisan. It was he who, almost singlehandedly, prevented Abe Fortas from becoming Chief Justice and saving the appointment for the Nixon Administration. From 1969 to 1977 he served as Minority Whip in the Senate, attending to laborious housekeeping chores and never giving an inch of partisan advantage.

But in 1977 everything seemed to go sour for Griffin. Gerald Ford had lost the presidency, and Griffin had lost any chance for a Supreme Court appointment. He had assumed he would be elected Senate Minority Leader, but Howard Baker outcampaigned him among new senators; they were less interested in having someone hard-working and faithful than they were in having someone photogenic and capable of making a good appearance on television. Griffin, articulate but frumpy, did not fill the bill. So in 1977 Griffin announced that he would retire the next year; and this usually diligent senator missed 216 roll call votes. By early 1978 he had reconsidered. Meanwhile, Republican strategists had decided that he was the only candidate who could hold the seat for them, and Griffin himself was once again up for a partisan fight. But he had seriously damaged himself for the general election.

The Democratic nominee was Carl Levin, former president of the Detroit city council and brother of 1970 and 1974 Democratic gubernatorial nominee Sander Levin. Levin had more than a familiar name. His record in Detroit was one of constructive cooperation with, but independence from, Mayor Coleman Young. While Young is very popular with blacks and distrusted by many whites, Levin was one figure who in times of great racial turbulence had earned the trust of both black and white Detroiters. He had an attractive forthrightness and credentials in fighting the federal bureaucracy, plus the Democratic label in a year when the Democrats were not on the defensive on social issues. But Levin's campaign concentrated less on his assets than on Griffin's liabilities, and specifically on his absenteeism in 1977. In a state where 40% of the work force belongs to unions and most working adults have to punch a time clock if they want to get paid, the absenteeism issue worked well. Levin won a victory similar in support levels to Riegle's, with a solid 3–2 edge in metro Detroit and a very respectable 48% in outstate Michigan. He was helped by the increasing migration from the Detroit area to the northern part of the Lower Peninsula; he carried many counties which never used to be Democratic, as well as industrial areas like Flint, Bay City, and Port Huron and the Upper Peninsula.

Levin has rather unusual committee assignments for a Michigan senator: Governmental Affairs and Armed Services. Michigan is a state which receives little defense money and Levin can be expected to be part of an increasing number of Armed Services members skeptical of Pentagon pronouncements and inclined to support the SALT agreement. His voting record on most issues is likely to be similar to Riegle's.

The 1978 elections proved to be almost a clean sweep for the Democrats, except for the gubernatorial contest. Here the key factor was the personality and character of Republican Governor William Milliken. After ten years in office, Milliken had become vulnerable on several issues. He was open to charges that the state was losing jobs and was not diversifying its economic base. In a year in which two tax cut measures were on the Michigan ballot—the less stringent of the two passed, although with less of a margin than expected—he had to take responsibility for the state's high level of taxes. And finally he was vulnerable to charges that he had not acted quickly or aggressively enough to protect the state from PBB contamination. PBB is a flame retardant that was placed in cattle feed by mistake and fed to most of the state's dairy cattle; it is a poison which cannot be expelled from the system, and is present in the bodies of virtually everyone in the state. There has been considerable dispute over whether the state acted fast enough to get infected cattle and dairy products off the market and acted carefully enough when the carcasses of the infected animals were disposed of.

All these issues were raised by state Senator Bill Fitzgerald, who had won the Democratic nomination against two other little known candidates and perennial office-seeker Zolton Ferency. But they were not enough to overcome the basic confidence people had in Milliken. His calm, conciliatory manner and dependability reassured people; they had seen him through ten sometimes difficult years, and on the whole he seemed to be the kind of incumbent they wanted. Fitzgerald, at 36, was not well known and was of course untested in office. Milliken was hurt by some of the issues Fitzgerald raised: the Democrat carried the far northern part of the state, and got 77% in one county where the state had proposed to dump dead cattle. But Milliken made great inroads into the traditionally Democratic Detroit area, winning a fair though not a majority percentage of black votes and doing well in the working class suburbs. The result was another four years of a Republican governor—and increased Democratic margins in the legislature.

In presidential politics Michigan has usually been Democratic except in Republican landslide years and except 1976, when local son Gerald Ford was running. It also has had a presidential primary in May of the last two election years. Voters here do not register by party and can vote in either primary; although defeated candidates are wont to talk of cross-overs, what seems to happen is that voters who in any case have weak partisan preferences tend to be attracted to the primary of the party with the hottest contest. In 1972 that meant the Democrats: busing was a hot issue, and George Wallace got 51% here the day after he was shot in Maryland.

In 1976 it was harder to tell. A tough contest had been expected in the Republican primary between Gerald Ford and Ronald Reagan and a relatively easy sweep by Jimmy Carter was expected among the Democrats. The results were quite the opposite. Ford won by nearly a 2–1 margin, but Carter barely squeaked through to victory. This is the state where Morris Udall ran an anti-Carter campaign, charging in a series of television ads and on a heavy schedule of personal appearances that Carter was fuzzy and inconsistent on the issues. Carter, who was fighting Udall here, Church in Oregon, and Jerry Brown in Maryland at the same time, devoted little attention to Michigan. He was further weakened by his supporters: he appeared together with UAW president Leonard Woodcock, Henry Ford II, and Mayor Coleman Young in what seemed to be a gathering of the powers that be in a year when the little people were fed up with the big guys. In retrospect Michigan did not have the potential to derail the Carter campaign, which even as it barely won was amassing the delegate support it needed; but it did help to spotlight some of the complaints that would be made about Carter in the fall campaign—and later. Certainly Carter in 1980 would do well not to take Michigan for granted.

Census Data Pop. 8,875,083; 4.38% of U.S. total, 7th largest; Central city, 28%; suburban, 49%. Median family income, $11,029; 6th highest; families above $15,000: 27%; families below $3,000: 7%. Median years education, 12.1.

1977 Share of Federal Tax Burden $15,198,000,000; 4.40% of U.S. total, 7th largest.

1977 Share of Federal Outlays $12,307,641,000; 3.11% of U.S. total, 8th largest. Per capita federal spending, $1,344.

DOD	$1,747,052,000	17th (1.91%)	HEW	$6,119,673,000	8th (4.14%)
ERDA	$28,460,000	24th (0.48%)	HUD	$143,248,000	9th (3.39%)
NASA	$8,906,000	23d (0.23%)	VA	$585,587,000	9th (3.05%)
DOT	$325,307,000	14th (2.28%)	EPA	$354,034,000	6th (4.32%)
DOC	$395,953,000	3d (4.77%)	RevS	$387,323,000	8th (4.58%)
DOI	$51,665,000	22d (1.11%)	Debt	$802,738,000	6th (2.67%)
USDA	$334,778,000	26th (1.68%)	Other	$1,022,917,000	

Economic Base Motor vehicles and equipment, and other transportation equipment; machinery, especially metalworking machinery; finance, insurance and real estate; fabricated metal products, especially metal stampings; primary metal industries, especially iron and steel foundries; agriculture, notably dairy products, cattle, dry beans and corn; food and kindred products.

Political Line-up Governor, William G. Milliken (R). Senators, Donald W. Riegle, Jr. (D) and Carl Levin (D). Representatives, 19 (13 D and 6 R). State Senate (24 D and 14 R); State House (70 D and 40 R).

The Voters

Registration 5,230,345 Total. No statewide registration.
Median voting age 40
Employment profile White collar, 45%. Blue collar, 41%. Service, 13%. Farm, 1%.
Ethnic groups Black, 11%. Spanish, 1%. Total foreign stock, 19%. Canada, 4%; Poland, Germany, UK, 2% each; Italy, 1%.

Presidential vote

1976	Carter (D)	1,696,714	(47%)
	Ford (R)	1,893,742	(53%)
1972	Nixon (R)	1,961,721	(57%)
	McGovern (D)	1,459,435	(43%)

1976 Democratic Presidential Primary

Carter	305,997	(43%)
Udall	304,177	(43%)
Wallace	49,227	(7%)
Others	28,616	(4%)
Uncommitted	15,685	(2%)

1976 Republican Presidential Primary

Ford	689,540	(65%)
Reagan	363,797	(34%)
Uncommitted	8,651	(1%)

Sen. Donald W. Riegle, Jr. (D) Elected 1976, seat up 1982; b. Feb. 4, 1938, Flint; home, Flint; Flint Jr. Col., W. Mich. U., U. of Mich., B.A. 1960, Mich. St. U., M.B.A. 1961; Methodist.

Career Consultant, IBM Corp., 1961–64; Faculty Mbr., Mich. St. U., Boston U., Harvard U.; U.S. House of Reps., 1967–77, first elected as Repub., switched to Dem. Party Feb. 27, 1973.

Offices 1207 DSOB, 202-224-4822. Also 477 Michigan Ave., 18th Floor, Detroit 48226, 313-226-3188, and Gennesee Towers, 1st and Harrison Sts., Flint 48502, 313-234-5621.

Committees *Banking, Housing, and Urban Affairs* (6th). Subcommittees: Housing and Urban Affairs; Economic Stabilization (Chairman); Consumer Affairs.

Budget (10th).

Commerce, Science, and Transportation (8th). Subcommittees: Communications; Science, Technology, and Space; Surface Transportation.

Labor and Human Resources (8th). Subcommittees: Handicapped; Child and Human Development; Alcoholism and Drug Abuse (Chairman).

Group Ratings

	ADA	COPE	PC	RPN	NFU	LCV	CFA	NAB	NSI	ACA	NTU
1978	85	89	80	67	80	71	70	11	20	0	–
1977	70	95	69	22	92	–	76	–	–	5	35
1976	30	82	64	44	100	54	36	11	10	0	29

Key Votes

1) Warnke Nom	FOR	6) Egypt-Saudi Arms	AGN	11) Hosptl Cost Contnmnt	FOR
2) Neutron Bomb	AGN	7) Draft Restr Pardon	FOR	12) Clinch River Reactor	DNV
3) Waterwy User Fee	FOR	8) Wheat Price Support	DNV	13) Pub Fin Cong Cmpgns	FOR
4) Dereg Nat Gas	AGN	9) Panama Canal Treaty	FOR	14) ERA Ratif Recissn	FOR
5) Kemp-Roth	AGN	10) Labor Law Rev Clot	FOR	15) Med Necssy Abrtns	FOR

Election Results

1976 general	Donald W. Riegle, Jr. (D)	1,831,031	(53%)	($795,821)
	Marvin L. Esch (R)	1,635,087	(47%)	($809,564)
1976 primary	Donald W. Riegle, Jr. (D)	325,705	(44%)	
	Richard A. Austin (D)	208,310	(28%)	
	James G. O'Hara (D)	170,473	(23%)	
	One other (D)	30,655	(4%)	
1970 general	Philip A. Hart (D)	1,744,672	(67%)	
	Lenore Romney (R)	858,438	(33%)	

Sen. Carl Levin (D) Elected 1978, seat up 1984; b. June 28, 1933, Detroit; home, Detroit; Swarthmore Col., B.A. 1956, Harvard U. J.D.; Jewish.

Career Practicing atty., Asst. Atty. Gen. of Mich. and Gen. Counsel for the Mich. Civil Rights Comm., 1964–67, Spec. Asst. Atty. Gen. of Mich. and Chief Appellate Defender for the City of Detroit, 1968–69; Detroit City Cncl., 1969–78; Pres. 1973–78.

Offices 3327 DSOB, 202-224-6221. Also 18th Floor, McNamara Bldg., Detroit 48226, 313-226-6020.

Committees *Armed Services* (10th). Subcommittees: Arms Control; Research and Development; Procurement Policy and Reprogramming.

Governmental Affairs (9th). Subcommittees: Governmental Efficiency and the District of Columbia; Energy, Nuclear Proliferation, and the District of Columbia; Oversight of Government Management (Chairman).

Select Committee on Small Business (10th).

Group Ratings: Newly Elected

Key Votes: Newly Elected

Election Results

1978 general	Carl Levin (D)	1,484,193	(52%)	($971,775)
	Robert P. Griffin (R)	1,362,165	(48%)	($1,681,550)
1978 primary	Carl Levin (D)	226,584	(39%)	
	Phil Power (D)	115,117	(20%)	($943,500)
	Richard Vander Veen (D)	89,257	(15%)	($264,217)
	Anthony Derezinski (D)	53,696	(9%)	($63,917)
	John Otterbacher (D)	50,860	(9%)	($152,498)
	Paul Rosenbaum (D)	46,896	(8%)	($153,189)
1972 general	Robert P. Griffin (R)	1,781,065	(53%)	($1,394,927)
	Frank J. Kelly (D)	1,577,178	(47%)	($547,819)

Gov. William G. Milliken (R) Elected Appointed 1969, elected 1970, term expires Jan. 1983; b. Mar. 26, 1922; Yale U., B.A.

Career Army Air Corps, WWII; Pres., J.W. Milliken, Inc., Dept. Store Chain; Mich. Senate, 1961–65, Maj. Floor Ldr., 1963; Lt. Gov. of Mich., 1965–69.

Offices State Capitol Box 30013, Lansing 48909

Election Results

1978 general	William G. Milliken (R)	1,628,485	(57%)
	William B. Fitzgerald (D)	1,237,256	(43%)
1978 primary	William G. Milliken (R), unopposed		
1974 general	William G. Milliken (R)	1,365,865	(52%)
	Sander M. Levin (D)	1,242,247	(48%)

FIRST DISTRICT

The 1st congressional district of Michigan includes the north and near northwest sides of Detroit, plus the enclave-suburb of Highland Park. This area is a good example of the pace of neighborhood change in twentieth century America. Sixty-odd years ago the land here was given over completely to Michigan farms; at that time Detroit's growth had not yet reached the southern boundary of the 1st, five miles north of the Detroit River. Then, in 1910, Henry Ford built his first big auto plant in Highland Park. At that time, as now, manufacturers located their factories at the edge of urban settlement, where a labor force is at hand, land prices are cheap, and room to expand is available. In the years that followed mile after mile of closely spaced one- and two-family houses were built, in subdivisions geared to the scale imposed by the automobile. Ethnic neighborhood patterns emerged: Polish in the eastern and southern parts of the current 1st; Jewish in the middle; and a rich WASP section north of Highland Park. During the 1910–30 period population growth here was as rapid as anywhere in the country, and even today most of the 1st's housing units were built in those two decades.

In the years that followed World War II another kind of change took place. In 1945 there were few black enclaves within the lines of the current 1st; even by 1950 less than 5% of the residents of the area were black. By 1970 that figure had risen to 70% and it is higher today. The first white exodus—or, rather, the first black movement in—occurred during the late forties and early fifties. Thousands of blacks who had come to Detroit during the war left the small ghettoes in which they had been confined while whites fled to the outer limits of the city or the FHA-financed suburbs. Whole square miles of Detroit changed racial complexion within a year or two. Then in the wake of the 1967 riot another particularly rapid racial transformation took place. What was previously Detroit's Jewish neighborhood along Seven Mile Road soon became heavily black. Around the same time the city's most affluent area opened up to blacks; today some of the most elegant housing in the Detroit area—the kind they don't build any more—can be found here in black or integrated neighborhoods.

There are still pockets of all white territory in the 1st, particularly in the Polish neighborhoods which resist change of any sort. Generally speaking the blacks in the 1st are more affluent and better educated than those in the nearby 13th district; most people here own their own homes, and they are also more likely to vote. Some analysts have speculated that blacks, as they grow more affluent, will grow more conservative and Republican. Maybe so, but the evidence here is quite to the contrary. In the 1972 and 1976 presidential races this was the second most Democratic congressional district in the country.

The 1st district's Congressman is John Conyers, a Democrat who has always been regarded as outspoken. In 1964, when he was first elected to the House, there were only four other blacks there, and he was by far the most militant. From the beginning, for example, he spoke and voted against the Vietnam war. He was instrumental in setting up the Congressional Black Caucus, in part to get around the mellow ways of the older black members; now, ironically, it is some of the younger blacks who are more prone to work quietly within the system. As a member of the Judiciary Committee, Conyers voted for the impeachment of Richard Nixon; indeed, he had called for Nixon's impeachment in 1972 for what he regarded as his illegal war-making activities.

Conyers seems to regard his job as expressing a point of view, and seems to care less about being effective. Thus in early 1979 he made a point of walking out of a White House meeting with President Carter in disgust. That didn't accomplish much, and it probably reduced Conyers's effectiveness; but as poll evidence showed some weeks later, it did accurately reflect the attitude of many blacks and white liberals toward Carter's proposed budget cuts. Conyers is now fifth-ranking Democrat on the Judiciary Committee and a subcommittee chairman; he has done a competent job of managing legislation on the floor despite his firebrand reputation. His district is safe—he has never received less than 85% in a primary or general election since 1964—and he has at least an outside chance of being Chairman of the Judiciary Committee some day.

Census Data Pop. 467,636. Central city, 92%; suburban, 8%. Median family income, $9,997; families above $15,000: 23%; families below $3,000: 10%. Median years education, 11.5.

The Voters

Median voting age 43.
Employment profile White collar, 41%. Blue collar, 42%. Service, 17%. Farm, –%.
Ethnic groups Black, 70%. Total foreign stock, 15%. Canada, Poland, 2% each; USSR, UK, Germany, 1% each.

Presidential vote

1976	Carter (D)	121,815	(91%)
	Ford (R)	12,618	(9%)
1972	Nixon (R)	22,815	(14%)
	McGovern (D)	137,732	(86%)

Rep. John Conyers, Jr. (D) Elected 1964; b. May 16, 1929, Detroit; home, Detroit; Wayne St. U., B.A. 1957, LL.B. 1958; Baptist.

Career Army, Korea; Legis. Asst. to U.S. Rep. John Dingell, 1958–61; Practicing atty., 1959–61; Referee, Mich. Workman's Comp. Dept., 1961–63.

Offices 2313 RHOB, 202-225-5126. Also 305 Fed. Bldg., 231 W. Lafayette St., Detroit 48226, 313-226-7022.

Committees *Government Operations* (8th). Subcommittees: Commerce, Consumer, and Monetary Affairs; Manpower and Housing.

Judiciary (5th). Subcommittees: Crime (Chairman); Criminal Justice.

Group Ratings

	ADA	COPE	PC	RPN	NFU	LCV	CFA	NAB	NSI	ACA	NTU
1978	45	94	73	25	75	–	64	0	0	11	–
1977	85	83	83	67	73	82	85	–	–	8	46
1976	75	86	85	50	83	80	54	10	0	12	33

Key Votes

1) Increase Def Spnd	AGN	6) Alaska Lands Protect	DNV	11) Delay Auto Pol Cntrl	AGN
2) B-1 Bomber	AGN	7) Water Projects Veto	FOR	12) Sugar Price Escalator	DNV
3) Cargo Preference	AGN	8) Consum Protect Agcy	FOR	13) Pub Fin Cong Cmpgns	FOR
4) Dereg Nat Gas	AGN	9) Common Situs Picket	FOR	14) ERA Ratif Recissn	AGN
5) Kemp-Roth	AGN	10) Labor Law Revision	FOR	15) Prohibt Govt Abrtns	AGN

Election Results

1978 general	John Conyers (D)	89,646	(93%)	($23,759)
	Robert S. Arnold (R)	6,878	(7%)	
1978 primary	John Conyers (D), unopposed			
1976 general	John Conyers (D)	126,161	(93%)	($21,757)
	Isaac Hood (R)	8,927	(7%)	($0)

SECOND DISTRICT

The 2d congressional district of Michigan is an odd amalgam: a mixture of university campuses, burgeoning suburbs, and aging factories. The district takes in the western and southern edges of the Detroit metropolitan area and lies entirely within the Detroit television market. But the 2d's most important city, Ann Arbor, thinks itself no part whatever of what it considers a grimy and industrial Detroit. Ann Arbor, with 99,000 residents, is the home of the University of Michigan, with 43,000 students, one of the nation's largest and most prestigious universities. This institution, along with Eastern Michigan University and its 18,000 students, in nearby Ypsilanti, gives the 2d district the largest proportion of college students among eligible voters—15%—of any congressional district in the nation. Indeed the student vote here is so large than in Ann Arbor it spawned a Human Rights Party which enjoyed some vitality in the partisan and fiercely contested city elections.

Until the early seventies Ann Arbor was a conservative Republican town. Its heritage came from its large German-American population, many of whom are descended from immigrants fleeing from the failures of the revolution of 1848. Democratic strength then lay in the working class wards of Ypsilanti, near the giant Willow Run plant, and in Monroe County, to the south along Lake Erie. Then, with the student vote, things changed sharply. In 1972 Washtenaw County, which includes Ann Arbor and Ypsilanti, was one of four Michigan counties to go for George McGovern. By 1976, with the Vietnam war over and Richard Nixon out of office, Washtenaw went for U of M graduate Gerald Ford; it was the only major county in the country to have favored McGovern and then Ford.

Arrayed consistently against Washtenaw County in the politics of the 2d district is the portion of the district in the Detroit suburbs. The largest town here is Livonia, with more people but fewer votes than Ann Arbor (because more of its residents are children under 18). Despite the presence of a couple of General Motors plants, Livonia is middle income and up, and Republican in national and congressional elections. It is one of those places that ballooned with instant subdivisions; its population rose from 17,000 in 1950 to 110,000 in 1970.

In the early and middle seventies, the 2d district was the scene of pitched congressional battles, both in the Democratic primary—which tended to feature battles between Livonia and Ann Arbor candidates—and in the general election. But the Democrats never won; the district was held by Marvin Esch, a Republican with a voting record acceptable to every rating group and a man adroit enough to appeal to every part of the district. With tough races every two years, he apparently decided that he might as well run for the Senate in 1976; he did so, and almost won. Succeeding him was another Republican, Carl Pursell, who had represented Livonia in the state Senate; by 344 votes Pursell edged out a liberal doctor from Ann Arbor.

In the less turbulent politics of the late seventies Pursell has had less trouble holding onto the district. He won a seat on the Education and Labor Committee, and although his overall voting record was rated better by conservative than liberal groups, his record on committee issues was good enough that he was endorsed for reelection by the United Auto Workers. It helped that no Democrat filed against him; his opponent won the nomination by write-in votes. Nonetheless Pursell seems to have accomplished the considerable feat of pleasing all parts of this various district.

Census Data Pop. 466,852. Central city, 21%; suburban, 79%. Median family income, $12,908; families above $15,000: 37%; families below $3,000: 4%. Median years education, 12.4.

The Voters

Median voting age 36.
Employment profile White collar, 53%. Blue collar, 33%. Service, 13%. Farm, 1%.
Ethnic groups Black, 5%. Spanish, 1%. Total foreign stock, 17%. Canada, 4%; Germany, UK, 2% each; Poland, Italy, 1% each.

Presidential vote

1976	Carter (D)	90,984	(45%)
	Ford (R)	109,460	(55%)
1972	Nixon (R)	106,155	(56%)
	McGovern (D)	85,093	(44%)

Rep. Carl D. Pursell (R) Elected 1976; b. Dec. 19, 1932, Imlay City; home, Plymouth; E. Mich. U., B.A. 1957, M.A. 1962; Protestant.

Career Army, 1957–59; Army Reserve 1959–65; Teacher; Businessman; Mbr., Wayne Co. Bd. of Comm., 1969–70; Mich. Senate 1971–76.

Offices 1414 LHOB, 202-225-4401. Also 15273 Farmington Rd., Livonia 48154, 313-427-1081.

Committees *Appropriations* (18th). Subcommittees: Labor-HEW.

Group Ratings

	ADA	COPE	PC	RPN	NFU	LCV	CFA	NAB	NSI	ACA	NTU
1978	60	56	45	70	50	–	46	46	33	31	–
1977	35	48	45	73	64	52	35	–	–	60	53

Key Votes

1) Increase Def Spnd	AGN	6) Alaska Lands Protect	FOR	11) Delay Auto Pol Cntrl	FOR
2) B-1 Bomber	AGN	7) Water Projects Veto	AGN	12) Sugar Price Escalator	FOR
3) Cargo Preference	AGN	8) Consum Protect Agcy	FOR	13) Pub Fin Cong Cmpgns	FOR
4) Dereg Nat Gas	FOR	9) Common Situs Picket	FOR	14) ERA Ratif Recissn	AGN
5) Kemp-Roth	FOR	10) Labor Law Revision	FOR	15) Prohibt Govt Abrtns	FOR

Election Results

1978 general	Carl D. Pursell (R)	97,503	(68%)	($94,764)
	Earl Greene (D)	45,631	(32%)	($27,212)
1978 primary	Carl D. Pursell (R), unopposed			
1976 general	Carl D. Pursell (R)	95,397	(50%)	($98,778)
	Edward C. Pierce (D)	95,053	(50%)	($99,176)

THIRD DISTRICT

The 3d congressional district of Michigan is in the south central part of the state. Its three major urban areas have a thriving and variegated economy. Battle Creek is known as the cereal city; it was at a tuberculosis sanitarium here that the first cold breakfast cereal was concocted. Both Kellogg's and Post have plants here now. Not far to the west is Kalamazoo, the headquarters of the Upjohn pharmaceutical firm and of the Checker cab manufacturing company. Finally the 3d includes the Eaton County suburbs of Lansing, a city which is the home both of Oldsmobile and of the Michigan state government.

This is a prosperous, stable part of the state, and one which has always been attached to the Republican Party. Indeed, Republicanism got its start in 1854 just east of here, in Jackson. Yet Republicanism is on a definite decline in this area. Both Kalamazoo and Battle Creek have elected some Democratic legislators in the seventies—something that never used to happen. Republican margins in statewide elections have grown smaller. And the 3d district now has a Democratic congressman.

He replaces a Republican elected in 1966—a year when the Republicans gained five Michigan House seats from the Democrats. Garry Brown was a popular and hard-working Congressman here for some years. But as time went on, he seemed busier in Washington defending business interests on the Banking Committee than he was in providing services to people in the district. And active young Democrats were showing that they could do a better job in this regard.

One of them was Howard Wolpe, the first Democrat ever elected to the state legislature from Kalamazoo. Brown's weakness became obvious in 1974, when he won with only 52%, and Wolpe ran in 1976. He fell just short that year, but never stopped running. Wolpe had run poorly in Eaton County; in 1977 Senator Donald Riegle hired him to run his Lansing office, and he moved into Eaton. It paid off: he increased his Eaton County percentage from 40% to 46% and held his own in Kalamazoo and Battle Creek. It was enough to make the difference, and to make the district Democratic. How Wolpe will fare in the future is not clear, of course, but most of the Democrats who have won outstate districts have been able to hold them, and he seems as hard working as any of them.

Census Data Pop. 467,546. Central city, 19%; suburban, 44%. Median family income, $10,913; families above $15,000: 25%; families below $3,000: 7%. Median years education, 12.2.

The Voters

Median voting age 40.
Employment profile White collar, 46%. Blue collar, 39%. Service, 13%. Farm, 2%.
Ethnic groups Black, 5%. Total foreign stock, 10%. Netherlands, Canada, 2% each; Germany, UK, 1% each.

Presidential vote

1976	Carter (D)	80,137	(40%)
	Ford (R)	119,812	(60%)
1972	Nixon (R)	118,023	(62%)
	McGovern (D)	71,608	(38%)

Rep. Howard Wolpe (D) Elected 1978; b. Nov. 2, 1939, Los Angeles, Cal.; home, Lansing; Reed Col., B.A. 1960, M.I.T., Ph.D. 1967.

Career Consultant, U.S. Peace Corps, 1966–67, U.S. State Dept. Foreign Service Inst., 1967–72; Prof., W. Mich. U., 1967–72; Kalamazoo City Cncl., 1969–73; Mich. House of Reps., 1973–76; Dem. Nominee for U.S. House of Reps., 1976; Regional Rep. and State Liaison to U.S. Sen. Donald Riegle, 1977–78.

Offices 416 CHOB, 202-225-5011. Also 142 N. Kalamazoo Mall, Kalamazoo 49007, 616-385-0039.

Committees *Foreign Affairs* (20th). Subcommittees: International Economic Policy and Trade; Africa.

Science and Technology (21st). Subcommittees: Energy Research and Production; Energy Development and Applications.

Group Ratings: Newly Elected

Key Votes: Newly Elected

Election Results

1978 general	Howard Wolpe (D)	83,932	(51%)	($219,397)
	Garry Brown (R)	79,572	(49%)	($242,768)
1978 primary	Howard Wolpe (D), unopposed			
1976 general	Garry Brown (R)	99,231	(51%)	($81,363)
	Howard Wolpe (D)	95,261	(49%)	($116,654)

FOURTH DISTRICT

The 4th congressional district of Michigan is shaped like a very short capital L. It includes Michigan's southwest corner plus a string of counties along the state's border with Indiana and Ohio. The district's main urban concentration is the Benton Harbor–St. Joseph area on Lake Michigan. These two next-door cities could hardly be less alike. Benton Harbor is industrial, with a big Whirlpool plant, and a majority of its citizens are black, while St. Joseph is virtually all white and has the air of a prosperous suburb. Besides Benton Harbor there is also a black community of some size in and near Cassopolis and Dowagiac—descendants of slaves who found their way to these stations on the underground railroad. For the most part the 4th is agricultural and small town, with rolling hills, occasional lakes, and many dairy farms. The district has a relatively large number of German-Americans; in ethnic composition it is more like northern Indiana or Ohio than outstate Michigan. The 4th is also disconnected from Michigan in another way: most of it lies within the Chicago, South Bend, or Toledo media markets.

If you want to understand the political background of this part of America, a good place to visit is the county seat of Hillsdale. Here the courthouse and the local college were built when the Republican Party was young, and the college in particular epitomized the things Republicans then stood for. It believed in absolute honesty and was inclined toward temperance; it was one of the first American colleges to admit women or blacks, and was strongly opposed to slavery. These were the principles that inspired the Republicans of the late nineteenth century. Now, in the late twentieth, things in Hillsdale haven't changed much. This was one of the few Michigan colleges where there was no protest against the Vietnam war; hair always remained short and skirts long; temperance is still encouraged (the longtime Prohibition Party presidential candidate, E. Harold Munn, comes from Hillsdale). College administrators have turned down federal funds and refused to file compliance reports on their admissions or hiring practices; they say that they have been admitting blacks and women for 100 years and don't need the federal government to tell them what to do.

The 4th has always been a Republican district. Its most recent ex-congressman was Edward Hutchinson, the ranking minority member of the House Judiciary Committee during the impeachment hearings, whose support of Richard Nixon illustrated the steadfastness or stubbornness of a small town lawyer. His successor is a man with a similar voting record but a very different temperament. At 29, David Stockman was already a Capitol Hill veteran as director of the House Republican Conference when he ran for Congress. He was a protégé of John Anderson of Illinois, who is considered in some conservative circles a dangerous liberal; but Stockman has provided congressional conservatives with some of their freshest thinking and strongest advocacy in some time. To understand his politics, you have to get away from labels and consider the issues. He is not the kind of Republican who opposes civil rights laws or backed Richard Nixon to the end. But he is suspicious of government regulation and the proliferation of government programs, and he supports a strong defense posture.

Old fashioned Republicans like Hutchinson used to talk about how the federal budget is like a family budget. Stockman is more apt to talk about how Keynesian models do not describe the world today, or how the seemingly endless number of social welfare programs passed by the Education and Labor Committee constitute a "social pork barrel." On the Commerce Committee he has been a strong and effective opponent of new forms of federal regulation and a strong supporter of deregulation of gas and oil prices. He has opposed providing public funds to Amtrak trains and to Gulf Oil for a coal liquefication plant. As he entered the 95th Congress, Stockman must have assumed that he would be in the minority on most votes. Instead, he found himself at the crest of a new wave of thinking which came to dominate the Congress and the nation. Columnist George Will has called Stockman "southern Michigan's contribution to intelligent government," and he could be an important figure in the House in the years ahead. Or he could run for statewide office. Michigan now has two Democratic senators elected by narrow margins, with Donald Riegle's seat coming up in 1982. With his record on regulation issues, Stockman has the potential to raise the kind of campaign funds needed to make him known—and perhaps victorious—statewide.

Census Data Pop. 467,140. Central city, 0%; suburban, 0%. Median family income, $9,693; families above $15,000: 18%; families below $3,000: 10%. Median years education, 12.1.

The Voters

Median voting age 43.
Employment profile White collar, 37%. Blue collar, 47%. Service, 12%. Farm, 4%.
Ethnic groups Black, 6%. Spanish, 1%. Total foreign stock, 10%. Germany, 3%; Canada, 1%.

Presidential vote

1976	Carter (D)	77,086	(41%)
	Ford (R)	111,830	(59%)
1972	Nixon (R)	116,712	(68%)
	McGovern (D)	55,846	(32%)

Rep. David Stockman (R) Elected 1976; b. Nov. 10, 1946, Camp Hood, Tex.; home, St. Joseph; Mich. St. U., B.A. 1968, Harvard U. 1968–70; Methodist.

Career Staff aide to U.S. Rep. John Anderson of Ill., 1970–72; Exec. Dir., U.S. House of Reps. Repub. Conf., 1972–75; Fellow, Harvard U. JFK Sch. of Govt. Inst. of Politics, 1975.

Offices 1502 LHOB, 202-225-3761. Also 2610 Niles Ave., St. Joseph 49085, 616-983-5575.

Committees *House Administration* (5th). Subcommittees: Libraries and Memorials; Office Systems; Policy Group on Information and Computers.

Interstate and Foreign Commerce (10th). Subcommittees: Energy and Power; Health and the Environment.

Group Ratings

	ADA	COPE	PC	RPN	NFU	LCV	CFA	NAB	NSI	ACA	NTU
1978	20	12	30	92	10	–	27	100	88	80	–
1977	25	20	30	92	20	41	20	–	–	83	58

Key Votes

1) Increase Def Spnd	FOR	6) Alaska Lands Protect	AGN	11) Delay Auto Pol Cntrl	FOR
2) B-1 Bomber	FOR	7) Water Projects Veto	FOR	12) Sugar Price Escalator	AGN
3) Cargo Preference	AGN	8) Consum Protect Agcy	AGN	13) Pub Fin Cong Cmpgns	FOR
4) Dereg Nat Gas	FOR	9) Common Situs Picket	AGN	14) ERA Ratif Recissn	FOR
5) Kemp-Roth	FOR	10) Labor Law Revision	AGN	15) Prohibt Govt Abrtns	AGN

Election Results

1978 general	David Stockman (R)	95,440	(71%)	($62,211)
	Morgan L. Hager, Jr. (D)	38,204	(29%)	
1978 primary	David Stockman (R), unopposed			
1976 general	David Stockman (R)	107,881	(61%)	($163,733)
	Richard E. Daugherty (D)	69,655	(39%)	($23,769)

FIFTH DISTRICT

The 5th congressional district of Michigan is the seat which gave us our 40th Vice President, Gerald Ford, and which by electing a member of the opposite party as his successor in the House helped to make Ford our 38th President. The center of the district is Grand Rapids, a medium-sized city which was Ford's boyhood home and the place where he practiced law just before and after World War II. After his election to Congress in 1948 he moved to the Washington area, and after his defeat in 1976 he moved to Rancho Mirage, California. Yet there has always been a warm feeling here for Ford: high schools were named for him while he was still in Congress, and his appearance in downtown Grand Rapids in the last days before the 1976 election was a moment of genuine emotion.

The Grand Rapids that first elected Ford was a solidly Republican town, faithful to the party through all the New Deal years. It had a heritage of Yankee Republicanism and, perhaps more important, of Dutch conservatism. This is the heart of the nation's largest concentration of Dutch-Americans, as a glance at the phone book's list of Vander . . .s will show. The Dutch in Holland may be liberal on many issues; but when Dutch migrate, whether to South Africa or western Michigan, they are rigidly conservative, in personal habits as well as political preference. The Dutch gave us, before Ford, Senator Arthur Vandenberg, the founder of the now abandoned tradition of bipartisan foreign policy. Vandenberg helped Ford win the nomination in 1948 because the local congressman remained an isolationist. Ford's career was helped later on by others when he was a useful instrument to seek their ends, from the group of young Republican congressmen who made him Minority Leader in 1965 to the Richard Nixon who needed a vice presidential nominee who would be confirmed by a Democratic Congress.

As Gerald Ford advanced as a national Republican, the 5th district was slowly moving away from its old party. Ford's seat was safe enough that the slippage didn't need his attention; and he didn't seem concerned when in his last two congressional elections, 1970 and 1972, his percentage declined to 61%—the lowest in his congressional career. This was part of the Democratic trend in the Upper Midwest that occurred even as Nixon was making gains in the South and the Sun Belt. So Ford was stunned when, in the spring 1974 special election to succeed him, the 5th district seat was won by Democrat Richard VanderVeen. The theme of the VanderVeen campaign was simple: Gerald Ford, not Richard Nixon, should be president. For once voters could do something to get rid of an unpopular president, and 53% of them voted for VanderVeen.

VanderVeen had the additional advantage of being a presentable candidate, a successful lawyer of quiet, conservative demeanor. His special election victory was followed by another in the 1974 general election. But 1976 proved too much for him. The Republicans had two advantages: a local hero running for president and a strong congressional candidate. Ford received 68% in Grand Rapids' Kent County and a higher percentage for president than he had ever received for Congress in his old district. Harold Sawyer, the new Congressman, had had a lucrative law practice to become Kent County Prosecutor; in that office he gained a lot of headlines and popularity. He beat VanderVeen by a clean 54%–46% margin.

Sawyer proved to be something of a controversial congressman in Washington, serving on the Ethics Committee and pushing for an investigation of South Korean lobbying. He had been expected to win reelection easily. But like Ford he was surprised by the Democratic trend in the district. Grand Rapids lawyer Dale Sprik came within 1% of winning; indeed, he carried Kent County and lost the election only in the small outlying counties in the district. That assures that there will be a strong Democratic challenge in the 5th district in 1980. The question is whether Sawyer, at 60, will seek a third term.

Census Data Pop. 467,543. Central city, 42%; suburban, 46%. Median family income, $10,550; families above $15,000: 22%; families below $3,000: 7%. Median years education, 12.1.

The Voters

Median voting age 42.
Employment profile White collar, 46%. Blue collar, 40%. Service, 12%. Farm, 2%.
Ethnic groups Black, 5%. Spanish, 1%. Total foreign stock, 17%. Netherlands, 7%; Poland, Canada, Germany, 2% each.

Presidential vote

1976	Carter (D)	67,423	(32%)
	Ford (R)	141,655	(68%)
1972	Nixon (R)	117,832	(61%)
	McGovern (D)	75,224	(39%)

Rep. Harold S. Sawyer (R) Elected 1976; b. Mar. 21, 1920, San Francisco. Cal.; home, Rockford; U. of Cal., LL.B. 1945; Episcopalian.

Career Navy, WWII; Practicing atty., 1945–75; Kent Co. Prosecutor, 1975–77.

Offices 123 CHOB, 202-225-3831. Also Fed. Bldg., 110 Michigan NW, Grand Rapids 49503, 616-451-8383.

Committees *Judiciary* (9th). Subcommittees: Criminal Justice; Courts, Civil Liberties, and the Administration of Justice.

Veterans' Affairs (8th). Subcommittees: Education, Training, and Employment; Medical Facilities and Benefits.

Group Ratings

	ADA	COPE	PC	RPN	NFU	LCV	CFA	NAB	NSI	ACA	NTU
1978	25	11	20	70	0	–	14	86	67	79	–
1977	20	25	27	85	45	55	15	–	–	65	34

Key Votes

1) Increase Def Spnd	FOR	6) Alaska Lands Protect	DNV	11) Delay Auto Pol Cntrl	DNV
2) B-1 Bomber	AGN	7) Water Projects Veto	FOR	12) Sugar Price Escalator	AGN
3) Cargo Preference	AGN	8) Consum Protect Agcy	AGN	13) Pub Fin Cong Cmpgns	AGN
4) Dereg Nat Gas	FOR	9) Common Situs Picket	AGN	14) ERA Ratif Recissn	AGN
5) Kemp-Roth	FOR	10) Labor Law Revision	AGN	15) Prohibt Govt Abrtns	FOR

Election Results

1978 general	Harold S. Sawyer (R)	81,794	(50%)	($134,454)
	Dale R. Sprik (D)	80,622	(50%)	($69,641)
1978 primary	Harold S. Sawyer (R), unopposed			
1976 general	Harold S. Sawyer (R)	109,589	(54%)	($213,718)
	Richard F. Vander Veen (D)	94,973	(46%)	($161,523)

SIXTH DISTRICT

The 6th congressional district of Michigan is yet another Middle America chunk of outstate Michigan, and yet another district which in the past few years has switched from Republican to

Democratic control. The largest city in the district, Lansing, with 130,000 people, is dominated by one growth industry, state government, and by another in reasonably good condition, although with uncertain long-range prospects, automobiles (the big Oldsmobile plant is here). Also in the 6th is Jackson, an older industrial city and site of the state prison, one of the nation's largest; back in 1854, this is where the Republican Party got its start. The other notable presence is East Lansing, until recently known politically as a high income Republican suburbs, but now more significant because it is the home of Michigan State University and its 41,000 students.

Aside from these urban areas, the 6th is a collection of small towns and rural townships. Some, like Stockbridge and Mason, are old towns whose architecture is reminiscent of the Yankee migrants from upstate New York who first settled them. Others, like Howell, are the site of new subdivisions to which former residents of metropolitan Detroit, unhappy with the city's crime rate and large black population, have been moving.

At the beginning of the seventies the 6th had a short-tempered Republican congressman who had served since the fifties; he lobbied actively in Washington for the auto companies but spent little time in the district and was totally out of touch with the newly enfranchised students. Confident of a Republican landslide, he didn't campaign much, but he was nearly beaten by 29-year-old Democrat Bob Carr, an assistant attorney general with a Mark Spitz mustache. Carr kept running After the election, and the Republican retired. Against a conservative Republican his own age, Carr barely won; he beat him by a better margin in 1976.

Carr was an important part of the freshman class of 1974. He got a seat on the House Armed Services Committee, a body usually shunned by young liberals because of its uncongenial membership. But Carr is a qualified pilot himself and seems not to be inhibited by stars or medals. He has worked for the Carter Administration position on some defense bills, notably on the B-1 bomber, which he helped to kill, and the neutron bomb. Probably his greatest achievement in Congress so far was in his first term, in early 1975. President Ford and Secretary of State Kissinger were pressing Congress hard for aid to Cambodia as the Khmer Rouge seemed to be closing in on Phnom Penh. Many congressional veterans had a sort of reflexive instinct to compromise—the same instinct that had got us into the Vietnam war in the first place. Carr felt that was a mistake. At just the right moment he demanded a Democratic Caucus vote on the issue. The result, when people had to be put on record, was a 189–49 vote against the Administration proposal. It was clear Ford could not get approval for any Cambodian intervention from Congress, and the idea was dropped.

In 1978, Carr faced a less ideological but nonetheless conservative Republican opponent who called him a knee-jerk anti-military vote. That issue apparently did not cut very deeply in this not very military district. Carr's reelection percentage rose again, suggesting that despite his sometimes controversial stands on issues he has a pretty safe seat in the House.

Census Data Pop. 467,536. Central city, 38%; suburban, 54%. Median family income, $11,105; families above $15,000: 27%; families below $3,000: 6%. Median years education, 12.3.

The Voters

Median voting age 37.
Employment profile White collar, 50%. Blue collar, 34%. Service, 14%. Farm, 2%.
Ethnic groups Black, 5%. Spanish, 2%. Total foreign stock, 12%. Canada, Germany, 2% each; UK, Poland, 1% each.

Presidential vote

1976	Carter (D)	84,753	(41%)
	Ford (R)	120.079	(59%)
1972	Nixon (R)	115,810	(59%)
	McGovern (D)	80,875	(41%)

Rep. Bob Carr (D) Elected 1974; Mar. 27, 1943, Janesville, Wis.; home, East Lansing; U. of Wis., B.S. 1965, J.D. 1968, U. of Mich., 1968–69.

Career Staff Asst. to U.S. Sen. Gaylord Nelson of Wis., 1967; Staff Mbr., Mich. Senate Minor. Ldr.'s Ofc., 1968–69; Admin. Asst. to Atty. Gen. of Mich., 1969–70; Asst. Atty. Gen. of Mich., 1970–72; Counsel to Mich. Legislature Special Comm. on Legal Educ., 1972; Dem. nominee for U.S. House of Reps., 1972.

Offices 332 CHOB, 202-225-4872. Also Rm. 245 Fed. Bldg., Lansing 48933, 517-489-6517.

Committees *Armed Services* (20th). Subcommittees: Procurement and Military Nuclear Systems; NATO Standardization, Interoperability, and Readiness.

Interior and Insular Affairs (12th). Subcommittees: Energy and the Environment; Water and Power Resources; Public Lands.

Group Ratings

	ADA	COPE	PC	RPN	NFU	LCV	CFA	NAB	NSI	ACA	NTU
1978	80	75	78	42	90	–	55	8	10	26	–
1977	80	83	80	62	75	82	65	–	–	26	44
1976	80	83	85	61	75	75	100	17	20	14	36

Key Votes

1) Increase Def Spnd	AGN	6) Alaska Lands Protect	FOR	11) Delay Auto Pol Cntrl	FOR
2) B-1 Bomber	AGN	7) Water Projects Veto	FOR	12) Sugar Price Escalator	FOR
3) Cargo Preference	AGN	8) Consum Protect Agcy	FOR	13) Pub Fin Cong Cmpgns	FOR
4) Dereg Nat Gas	AGN	9) Common Situs Picket	FOR	14) ERA Ratif Recissn	AGN
5) Kemp-Roth	FOR	10) Labor Law Revision	FOR	15) Prohibt Govt Abrtns	AGN

Election Results

1978 general	Bob Carr (D)	97,971	(57%)	($174,104)
	Mike Conlin (R)	74,718	(43%)	($145,074)
1978 primary	Bob Carr (D), unopposed			
1976 general	Bob Carr (D)	108,909	(53%)	($142,935)
	Clifford W. Taylor (R)	96,008	(47%)	($190,476)

SEVENTH DISTRICT

With five major General Motors plants and a metropolitan population of half a million, Flint is probably the nation's largest company town. Some 60% of metropolitan Flint's wage-earners are on the GM payroll, and although there is some GM white collar employment here, this is mainly the Chevrolet and Buick factory town. Flint has no five o'clock rush hour; its traffic jams come at three thirty when the shifts break. Even those who have profited most handsomely from the auto industry have not taken themselves out of Flint; the plushest residential district here has a panoramic view of a Chevrolet plant. For years civic life in Flint was dominated by Charles Stewart Mott, a member of the General Motors board of directors for 60 years and for most of that time the largest individual shareholder in the corporation; the old man ran his Mott Foundation, one of the nation's largest, out of Flint and concentrated on local projects until his death a few years ago at 97.

Flint owes its present existence to the boom years of the auto industry, the two decades between 1910 and 1930, supplemented by the war and postwar booms of the forties. During both these periods Flint attracted tens of thousands of immigrants from the rural South—whites from the hills of Kentucky and Tennessee and blacks from the cotton fields of Alabama and Mississippi. Since the thirties the politics of the migrants has been Democratic. Oldtimers here can still recall the sitdown strikes of the thirties, led by young unionists Roy, Victor, and Walter Reuther; the United Auto Workers remains a major political and social force here today. In the late sixties racial friction threatened to break the Democratic coalition. In 1968 George Wallace had the support of many white UAW members and a few local presidents; only a concerted union effort held him to 15% of the vote. But unlike Detroit, Flint had no major busing crisis; McGovern actually ran better here than Humphrey, as he did in outstate Michigan generally, and Carter carried the area with a fair majority.

Flint is the nucleus of Michigan's 7th congressional district. The city's metropolitan area and its media market coincide almost perfectly with the district lines. This makes it ideal for an incumbent congressman. It is easy to communicate with voters: the local congressman is a celebrity; he is covered thoroughly by the local newspaper; he can easily get on the local television newscasts. His local staff is as large as that of any public official in the Flint area, and his ability to help citizens solve their problems with government is probably greater. For these reasons it is not surprising that the 7th district has had two extremely strong local congressmen, who at least began as members of different political parties.

The first was Donald Riegle, elected in 1966 at 28 as a Republican; he beat a Democrat who took the district for granted. Riegle worked hard and used all the advantages of incumbency; he established good relations with the black community and by 1970 was able to win the UAW nomination—both unheard of in a town where Republicans spent time only with management and Democrats only with labor. Increasingly he was out of step with Republicans in the House. He opposed the Vietnam war, and in early 1973 switched to the Democratic Party. He was reelected easily as a Democrat and ran successfully for the Senate in 1976.

The current Congressman is Democrat Dale Kildee. First elected to the state House in 1964, he moved to the state Senate in 1974, beating a 26-year incumbent in the primary by a 3–1 margin. In 1976 he won the congressional primary easily over a UAW local president and got 71% in the general; in 1978 he did even better. Where Riegle had relied on expensive television advertising in his first races, Kildee has always relied on old-fashioned door-to-door campaigning; in his career he has probably knocked on every door in Flint.

Kildee, with a background in education and experience in that area in the Michigan legislature, holds a seat on the Education and Labor Committee, where he is part of the committee's liberal majority. In the 95th Congress he was the man who initiated and shepherded through the measure to make the use of children in pornography a federal crime. It was an unusually successful legislative effort by a freshman.

Census Data Pop. 466,287. Central city, 41%; suburban, 57%. Median family income, $11,207; families above $15,000: 27%; families below $3,000: 6%. Median years education, 12.1.

The Voters

Median voting age 40.
Employment profile White collar, 37%. Blue collar, 50%. Service, 12%. Farm, 1%.
Ethnic groups Black, 13%. Spanish, 1%. Total foreign stock, 12%. Canada, 3%; UK, 2%; Germany, 1%.

Presidential vote

1976	Carter (D)	93,377	(52%)
	Ford (R)	84,998	(48%)
1972	Nixon (R)	90,776	(54%)
	McGovern (D)	76,745	(46%)

Rep. Dale E. Kildee (D) Elected 1976; b. Sept. 16, 1929, Flint; home, Flint; Sacred Heart Seminary, Detroit, B.A. 1952, U. of Mich., M.A. 1961, Rotary Fellow, U. of Peshawar, Pakistan; Catholic.

Career High school teacher, 1954–64; Mich. House of Reps., 1965–75; Mich. Senate, 1975–77.

Offices 314 CHOB, 202-225-3611. Also 444 Church St., Flint 48502, 313-239-1437.

Committees *Education and Labor* (18th). Subcommittees: Elementary, Secondary and Vocational Education; Labor-Management Relations; Human Resources.

Small Business (20th). Subcommittees: Impact of Energy Programs; Environment and Safety Requirements and Government Research on Small Business; Special Small Business Problems.

Group Ratings

	ADA	COPE	PC	RPN	NFU	LCV	CFA	NAB	NSI	ACA	NTU
1978	80	95	78	42	100	–	77	0	0	7	–
1977	85	87	90	54	75	85	80	–	–	11	29

Key Votes

1) Increase Def Spnd	AGN	6) Alaska Lands Protect	FOR	11) Delay Auto Pol Cntrl	FOR
2) B-1 Bomber	AGN	7) Water Projects Veto	FOR	12) Sugar Price Escalator	FOR
3) Cargo Preference	AGN	8) Consum Protect Agcy	FOR	13) Pub Fin Cong Cmpgns	FOR
4) Dereg Nat Gas	AGN	9) Common Situs Picket	FOR	14) ERA Ratif Recissn	AGN
5) Kemp-Roth	AGN	10) Labor Law Revision	FOR	15) Prohibt Govt Abrtns	FOR

Election Results

1978 general	Dale E. Kildee (D)	105,402	(78%)	($46,558)
	Gale M. Cronk (R)	29,958	(22%)	($23,487)
1978 primary	Dale E. Kildee (D), unopposed			
1976 general	Dale E. Kildee (D)	124,260	(71%)	($48,595)
	Robin Widgery (R)	50,301	(29%)	($44,300)

EIGHTH DISTRICT

To understand the geography of the 8th congressional district of Michigan, you must know that Michigan's Lower Peninsula is shaped like a mittened hand. The 8th district includes most of the Thumb (as it is called locally) and the bottom part of the index finger. The Thumb is almost entirely agricultural, tilled by descendants of the German and Canadian farmers who first settled the area more than a century ago. During that time the Thumb has been rock-solid Republican territory.

Where the index finger extends from the palm (this is not the local nomenclature) are Saginaw, with nearly 100,000 people, and Bay City, with half as many. Both cities have been important since the nineteenth century when Michigan was the nation's leading lumber producer and the cities were major lumber ports. Today they are sustained in large part by auto plants, notably General Motors's Saginaw Steering, which makes more power steering equipment than any other plant in the world. Unlike most of the rest of outstate Michigan, the 8th district has few institutions of higher learning and has had relatively little growth in recent years.

This is the sort of area that ordinarily remains obscure to followers of national events. Although Bay City has been a Democratic town for many years, Saginaw has not, and the heavy Republican margins in the Thumb have made the area in the 8th district safely Republican for most of the twentieth century. It had little impact on national politics since one of its congressman co-authored the Fordney–McCumber tariff—until 1974. Then, suddenly, the calling of a special election here to replace a retiring Republican congressman made the 8th district the center of national attention. A Democrat had already captured the Gerald Ford seat around Grand Rapids by calling for the impeachment of Richard Nixon, and now the Democrats, in the person of state Representative Bob Traxler, were trying to make the 8th district race another referendum on the unpopular president. The Republican, James Sparling, who had the misfortune of having worked briefly in the Nixon White House, called on Nixon to campaign. That may have backfired; Traxler won, albeit by a narrow margin; and the move for impeachment grew stronger.

When Traxler won that election, he was an important enough national figure to have appeared on Face the Nation. But soon the 8th lapsed into its accustomed obscurity. Traxler eventually won a seat on the House Appropriations, and amassed considerable seniority on the Agriculture and HUD-Independent Agencies Subcommittees. At home he increased his percentages in every election to the point that he was reelected by a 2–1 margin in 1978. He seems to have a safe seat and the potential for a powerful career in the House.

Census Data Pop. 467,206. Central city, 30%; suburban, 45%. Median family income, $10,270; families above $15,000: 21%; families below $3,000: 9%. Median years education, 11.9.

The Voters

Median voting age 42.
Employment profile White collar, 38%. Blue collar, 45%. Service, 13%. Farm, 4%.
Ethnic groups Black, 6%. Spanish, 3%. Total foreign stock, 16%. Canada, 4%; Germany, 3%; Poland, 2%; UK, 1%.

Presidential vote

1976	Carter (D)	84,198	(44%)
	Ford (R)	105,159	(56%)
1972	Nixon (R)	106,524	(62%)
	McGovern (D)	65,442	(38%)

Rep. Bob Traxler (D) Elected April, 1974; b. July 21, 1931, Kawkawlin; home, Bay City; Mich. St. U., B.A. 1953, Detroit Col. of Law, LL.B. 1959.

Career Army, 1953–55; Asst. Bay Co. Prosecutor, 1960–62; Mich. House of Reps., 1963–74, Maj. Floor Ldr., 1965.

Offices 2448 RHOB, 202-225-2806. Also 62 New Fed. Bldg., 100 S. Warren, Saginaw 48606, 517-753-6444.

Committees *Appropriations* (22d). Subcommittees: Agriculture, Rural Development, and Related Agencies; HUD-Independent Agencies.

Group Ratings

	ADA	COPE	PC	RPN	NFU	LCV	CFA	NAB	NSI	ACA	NTU
1978	45	80	50	20	88	–	50	10	67	20	–
1977	60	77	78	45	91	70	65	–	–	22	25
1976	60	78	72	44	67	66	73	8	20	12	27

Key Votes

1) Increase Def Spnd	AGN	6) Alaska Lands Protect	FOR	11) Delay Auto Pol Cntrl	FOR
2) B-1 Bomber	AGN	7) Water Projects Veto	AGN	12) Sugar Price Escalator	FOR
3) Cargo Preference	AGN	8) Consum Protect Agcy	FOR	13) Pub Fin Cong Cmpgns	FOR
4) Dereg Nat Gas	AGN	9) Common Situs Picket	FOR	14) ERA Ratif Recissn	AGN
5) Kemp-Roth	FOR	10) Labor Law Revision	FOR	15) Prohibt Govt Abrtns	FOR

Election Results

1978 general	Bob Traxler (D)	103,346	(67%)	($97,020)
	Norman R. Hughes (R)	51,900	(33%)	($40,795)
1978 primary	Bob Traxler (D), unopposed			
1976 general	Bob Traxler (D)	110,127	(59%)	($140,502)
	E. Brady Denton (R)	75,323	(41%)	($127,238)

NINTH DISTRICT

From Gary, Indiana, up through Chicago and Milwaukee, north to towns like Sheboygan and Manitowoc, Wisconsin, the western shore of Lake Michigan is heavily industrial. Behind the great sand dunes that line the eastern, Michigan side of the lake there are a few grimy industrial towns like Muskegon and old lumber ports like Ludington. But most of the Michigan side of Lake Michigan is given over to farming; despite the northern weather, fruits and vegetables do well here within a few miles of the shore. The area around Traverse City is the chief cherry producing center in the United States.

Michigan's 9th congressional district covers most of the eastern shore of Lake Michigan. The 9th extends from Allegan County in the south to Leelenau in the north—the latter is the extended little finger of Michigan's mitten-shaped Lower Peninsula. Along with Grand Rapids, the southern portion of the district has the nation's largest concentration of Dutch-Americans. One of the cities here, Holland, holds a tulip festival every year, complete with people walking around in wooden shoes.

The Dutch are probably the most conservative and Republican of all identifiable American ethnic groups. Ottawa County, which contains Holland and Zeeland, was one of only three Michigan counties to go for Barry Goldwater in 1964. To the north the country is politically more varied. Muskegon is sometimes Democratic, but Republicans can also carry it. The smaller counties are mostly Republican; those with old lumber ports marginally so. An oddity here is tiny Lake County, a large number of whose residents are black and which always goes Democratic; here one may find one of the nation's first black resort areas, founded at the turn of the century by members of Chicago's black bourgeoisie.

The 9th has always been a Republican district. It was represented for ten years by Robert Griffin, until he went to the Senate in 1966; it has been represented for longer than that by his successor Guy VanderJagt. His background seems ideal for this seat: he comes originally from the northern part of the district, and his Dutch name is a considerable asset in the southern part. VanderJagt has had a number of interesting careers: he was a television newscaster and a practicing attorney, and he holds a divinity degree as well. He has shown an interest in environmental causes not always typical of Republicans and was largely responsible for the creation of the Sleeping Bear Dunes National Lakeshore in the northern part of the district.

VanderJagt currently sits on the House Ways and Means Committee, where he has strongly supported Republican proposals for lower taxation of capital gains. VanderJagt has also spent considerable time as Chairman of the Republican Congressional Campaign Committee. This he has made into a highly professional operation. In 1976 it tried to target many races against Democratic freshmen elected in 1974; this strategy proved almost completely unsuccessful. Learning from their mistakes, VanderJagt and his staff went after open seats, where no incumbent was running, and more senior Democrats who might have gotten lazy and become more vulnerable. This was not much more successful on its face: Republicans gained only 11 House seats in the 1978 elections. But this was partly the result of Republican incumbents losing; VanderJagt can hardly be held responsible if some of his colleagues, despite all the advantages of incumbency, cannot win reelection.

VanderJagt has a strong, if somewhat old-fashioned oratorical style, a pleasant personality, and an ambition for a House leadership post. He is a good bet to go after the Republican Conference chair which will be vacated by John Anderson's retirement from the House in 1980.

Census Data Pop. 467,245. Central city, 13%; suburban, 48%. Median family income, $9,474; families above $15,000: 16%; families below $3,000: 9%. Median years education, 11.8.

The Voters

Median voting age 43.
Employment profile White collar, 37%. Blue collar, 46%. Service, 13%. Farm, 4%.
Ethnic groups Black, 4%. Spanish, 2%. Total foreign stock, 15%. Netherlands, 4%; Germany, Canada, 2% each; Poland, 1%.

Presidential vote

1976	Carter (D)	78,084	(36%)
	Ford (R)	139,170	(64%)
1972	Nixon (R)	130,463	(67%)
	McGovern (D)	64,561	(33%)

Rep. Guy Vander Jagt (R) Elected 1966; b. Aug. 26, 1931, Cadillac; home, Cadillac; Hope Col., B.A. 1953, Yale U., B.D., Rotary Fellow, Bonn U., Germany, 1956, U. of Mich., LL.B. 1960; Presbyterian.

Career Practicing atty., 1960–64; Mich. Senate, 1965–66.

Offices 2334 RHOB, 202-225-3511. Also 950 W. Norton Ave., Muskegon 49441, 616-733-3131.

Committees *Ways and Means* (4th). Subcommittees: Select Revenue Measures; Trade.

Group Ratings

	ADA	COPE	PC	RPN	NFU	LCV	CFA	NAB	NSI	ACA	NTU
1978	10	5	5	70	29	–	9	88	100	79	–
1977	5	16	28	82	42	29	15	–	–	88	35
1976	10	10	13	88	9	29	18	100	89	82	66

Key Votes

1) Increase Def Spnd	FOR	6) Alaska Lands Protect	DNV	11) Delay Auto Pol Cntrl	FOR
2) B-1 Bomber	DNV	7) Water Projects Veto	DNV	12) Sugar Price Escalator	FOR
3) Cargo Preference	AGN	8) Consum Protect Agcy	AGN	13) Pub Fin Cong Cmpgns	AGN
4) Dereg Nat Gas	FOR	9) Common Situs Picket	DNV	14) ERA Ratif Recissn	FOR
5) Kemp-Roth	FOR	10) Labor Law Revision	DNV	15) Prohibt Govt Abrtns	FOR

Election Results

1978 general	Guy Vander Jagt (R)	122,363	(70%)	($197,290)
	Howard M. Leroux (D)	53,450	(30%)	($38,498)
1978 primary	Guy Vander Jagt (R), unopposed			
1976 general	Guy Vander Jagt (R)	146,712	(70%)	($122,513)
	Stephen E. Fawley (D)	61,641	(30%)	($6,840)

TENTH DISTRICT

Draw a line on a map across Michigan's Lower Peninsula from Bay City to Muskegon. South of that line live 90% of the state's residents, almost half in the Detroit metropolitan area and the rest in and around the state's other industrial cities. North of the line, Michigan is covered with forests, and little of it has ever been farmed; the largest city in this part of the Lower Peninsula has a population of only 18,000. The forests here were ravaged by the lumber barons of the turn of the century, and only now are they growing back. More recently there has been another environmental disaster: the feeding of the poisonous flame retardant PBB to cattle. Many of this area's dairy herds have had to be slaughtered, and people in the sparsely populated counties chosen for burial sites have protested loudly. PBB is known to be a poison; it has found its way through the food chain into the bodies of just about everyone in Michigan, and cannot be expelled. But no one knows what its long-term effects are.

For years this northern part of the Lower Peninsula has depended economically on the tourist and recreation business. Every weekend during the summer, and during the hunting season in the fall and the skiing season in the winter, cars jam Interstate 75 as city people flee to cottages on Michigan lakes or resorts in the woods. The fishing here is excellent, as Ernest Hemingway learned as a boy during summer visits; it is even better now that the lakes have been stocked with the huge coho salmon. As the sixties became seventies, many people who had been coming up here for weekends or vacations decided to move to the area permanently. Wages are not as high as in the Detroit area, but neither is the cost of living, and the pace of life is slower and more pleasant. Today these north woods are in the middle of a population boom—something they haven't experienced since the 1890s.

The 10th congressional district spans the line across Lower Michigan. The district dips south to the Lansing city limits, and its lower counties are fairly thickly populated with small towns and farms. The largest city here is Owosso, the boyhood home of Thomas Dewey. Up north, where the farms become woods, the biggest towns are Midland, home of Dow Chemical Company, whose production of napalm once made it controversial; Traverse City, which produced both Governor William Milliken and former Senator Robert Griffin; and Mount Pleasant, home of Central Michigan University.

Most of outstate Michigan has seen a Democratic trend in the seventies, but nowhere has it been more notable—and would it have been more surprising ten years ago—than in the 10th district. This was once the safest of Republican territory. But the recent immigration into the area, much of it from the Democratic Detroit area, has been combined with a general trend toward the Democrats to produce a major change. Certainly among those who would have been most surprised to hear such a trend predicted was Elford Cederberg, for years the 10th district's Congressman. First elected in 1952, he was one of a dwindling number of Republican congressmen who could remember when their party controlled the House. In 1973 he became ranking minority member of the House Appropriations Committee, and generally he was loyal to the Republican leadership.

Beginning in 1974, Cederberg began to experience trouble at home. A poorly financed Democrat held him that year to 54% of the vote. Cederberg showed little zest for returning to the cold of the 10th district, and he was one of those veterans who felt that life in the House was just not as much fun as it used to be. In 1978 he was defeated by Donald Albosta, a farmer who served in the Michigan legislature and had urged strong state government action against PBB. Albosta was not a particularly smooth campaigner; he attacked primary opponent Roger Tilles as a recent migrant "from a Long Island Jewish community." Albosta showed greater energy than Cederberg and won majorities in most of the district's counties, even while failing to carry Midland, Traverse City, and Mount Pleasant. Whether he will be able to win next time is unclear, but certainly the long-term trend in the district seems to favor the Democrats.

Census Data Pop. 467,547. Central city, 0%; suburban, 11%. Median family income, $9,299; families above $15,000: 17%; families below $3,000: 11%. Median years education, 12.1.

The Voters

Median voting age 41.
Employment profile White collar, 41%. Blue collar, 41%. Service, 14%. Farm, 4%.
Ethnic groups Spanish, 1%. Total foreign stock, 11%. Canada, 3%; Germany, 2%.

Presidential vote

1976	Carter (D)	90,223	(41%)
	Ford (R)	129,329	(59%)
1972	Nixon (R)	119,706	(64%)
	McGovern (D)	66,980	(36%)

Rep. Donald Joseph Albosta (D) Elected 1978; b. Dec. 5, 1925, Saginaw Co.; home, St. Charles; Delta Col.; Catholic.

Career Navy, WWII; Farmer; Saginaw Co. Comm., 1970–74; Mich. House of Reps., 1974–76.

Offices 1318 LHOB, 202-225-3561. Also 419 S. Saginaw Rd., Midland 48640, 517-839-0790.

Committees *Post Office and Civil Service* (13th). Subcommittees: Investigation; Postal Operations and Services.

Public Works and Transportation (28th). Subcommittees: Economic Development; Public Buildings and Grounds; Water Resources.

Group Ratings: Newly Elected

Key Votes: Newly Elected

Election Results

1978 general	Don Albosta (D)	94,913	(51%)	($258,244)
	Elford A. Cederberg (R)	89,451	(49%)	($146,993)
1978 primary	Don Albosta (D)	16,266	(59%)	
	Roger Tilles (D)	11,374	(41%)	($134,486)
1976 general	Elford A. Cederberg (R)	118,726	(57%)	($121,518)
	Don Albosta (D)	89,980	(43%)	($78,586)

ELEVENTH DISTRICT

Michigan's Upper Peninsula (or the UP, as it is called here) is a world unto itself. It is isolated most of the year from the rest of the state by the elements, and for years travel here was discouraged by exorbitant ($3.75) tolls on the Mackinac Straits Bridge. The UP was first settled around the turn of the century, when the iron and copper mines were booming, and the place had a Wild West air about it. The population influx here was polyglot: Irish, Italians, Swedes, Norwegians, and Finns, the last of whom remain the largest ethnic group here. While working in the mines, the immigrants picked up some radical social ideas and Democratic voting habits; their descendants still retain the latter.

Some time ago the mines petered out, leaving the UP's stagnant economy dependent on summer tourists and fall hunters. Farming has never been important here; it has been known to snow in July and the growing season is too short for most crops. After World War II the young people of the Upper Peninsula left to move to Detroit, Chicago, and the West Coast. Since the 1940 Census, the UP's population has hovered around 300,000 (it was 332,000 in 1920). In the seventies, as metropolitan areas become more unattractive and job opportunities scarcer there, the UP stopped losing so many people; but there has not been the migration into the area that has been seen in the northern part of the Lower Peninsula. The closest thing to a city here is Marquette, with 22,000 people.

The Upper Peninsula forms about two-thirds of Michigan's 11th congressional district. The 11th altogether is a vast expanse, with 40% of Michigan's land area but only 5% of its population; geographically it is the second largest congressional district east of the Mississippi River. From Tawas City, in the southern part of the 11th in the Lower Peninsula, to Ironwood, at the western tip of the Upper, is a distance of 477 miles. Obviously any serious congressional candidate must travel by airplane.

The Lower Peninsula portion of the 11th, the area below the bridge, has neither the tradition of the mines nor the Democratic voting habits of the UP. It is a more prosperous area, with a big tourist trade and recently significant in-migration. As a whole, the 11th is politically marginal, although oddly the area has elected a Democrat to Congress only once since World War II. From 1966 to 1978 the Congressman was Republican Philip Ruppe, scion of a rich Upper Peninsula brewing family. During that time he compiled a more mixed voting record than most Michigan Republicans and had received fairly high labor ratings. He wanted to run for the Senate in 1978 and announced his candidacy after Robert Griffin announced his withdrawal. When Griffin re-entered the race early in 1978, Ruppe quit running in disgust and ended his political career.

The race to succeed Ruppe was seriously contested. The Republican candidate, state Senator Robert Davis, had a strong base in the Lower Peninsula portion of the district. The Democrat, Keith McLeod, had little political background but was astute enough to beat more experienced primary opponents; his background as a banker and his stands on issues made him seem more like a Republican to many Democratic insiders, however. The race was decided on regional, not economic, lines. This was one district which Republican Governor William Milliken failed to carry, and McLeod carried the Upper Peninsula portion of the district, which casts most of the votes. Davis, however, won 64% of the vote below the bridge, which was enough to give him a decisive victory. He is expected to vote in line with most House Republicans.

Census Data Pop. 467,547. Central city, 0%; suburban, 0%. Median family income, $7,884; families above $15,000: 10%; families below $3,000: 14%. Median years education, 12.0.

The Voters

Median voting age 45.
Employment profile White collar, 41%. Blue collar, 40%. Service, 16%. Farm, 3%.
Ethnic groups Total foreign stock, 23%. Canada, Finland, 5% each; Germany, Sweden, UK, 2% each; Italy, Poland, 1% each.

Presidential vote

1976	Carter (D)	98,653	(49%)
	Ford (R)	103,331	(51%)
1972	Nixon (R)	117,006	(57%)
	McGovern (D)	86,548	(43%)

Rep. Robert W. Davis (R) Elected 1978; b. July 31, 1932, Marquette; home, Gaylord; No. Mich. U., 1950, 1952, Hillsdale Col., 1951–52, Wayne St. U., B.S. 1954.

Career Mortician, 1954–66; St. Ignace City Cncl., 1964–66; Mich. House of Reps., 1966–70; Mich. Senate, 1970–78, Major. Whip, 1970–74, Major. Ldr., 1974–78.

Offices 1223 LHOB, 202-225-4735. Also Rm. 102, Fed. Bldg., Alpena 49707, 517-356-2028.

Committees *Merchant Marine and Fisheries* (13th). Subcommittees: Merchant Marine; Fish and Wildlife; Maritime Education and Training.

Science and Technology (12th). Subcommittees: Science, Research and Technology; Energy Development and Applications.

Group Ratings: Newly Elected

Key Votes: Newly Elected

Election Results

1978 general	Robert W. Davis (R)	96,351	(55%)	($158,755)
	Keith McLeod (D)	79,081	(45%)	($131,304)
1978 primary	Robert W. Davis (R)	18,520	(58%)	
	Edmund Vandette (R)	13,478	(42%)	($80,561)
1976 general	Philip E. Ruppe (R)	118,871	(55%)	($163,887)
	Francis Brouillette (D)	97,325	(45%)	($94,859)

TWELFTH DISTRICT

Macomb County, adjoining Detroit to the northeast, is an area of fast-growing suburban sprawl of the type found in many of the nation's metropolitan reas. In 1950 Macomb had 184,000 people; by 1970, 625,000—more than tripling its population in twenty years. The northern reaches of the county remain rural, but for twenty miles beyond Eight Mile Road, the Detroit city limit, Macomb is an agglomeration of neat suburbs, winding streets, thin-walled garden apartments, and gleaming new shopping centers. Unlike the residents of similar places in southern California, the people here have roots, most of them on the east side of Detroit. The descendants of Polish and Italian immigrants who came to man the east side auto plants have moved in just a generation to suburbs like Warren, East Detroit, Roseville, St. Clair Shores, and Sterling Heights.

Macomb County is mainly a blue collar suburb; most people here earn their living in blue collar or service jobs. Thanks to high UAW wages, Macomb is also one of the highest income counties in the nation, with a median family income of $12,000 in 1970 and much more today. Yet upward mobility has meant more in dollars and comfort than in status: even if you can buy a $75,000 house, it is still less than pleasant to work on an assembly line.

Macomb County residents got their politics from their parents back on the east side, and they were solidly Democratic. President Kennedy won 63% of the vote here in 1960—his best showing in any suburban county in the United States. But as the sixties went, on the Democratic allegiance here faded. In state elections George Romney and then William Milliken carried Macomb. In national elections George Wallace won 14% here in 1968. Then in the early seventies a federal court ordered busing from all of Detroit's suburbs to the city itself. Macomb County was the strongest area opposed: people didn't want their kids to go to school with blacks, to go to school where it might be dangerous, to go to school far away. Richard Nixon won 64% of the vote here, more than double his 1968 percentage. In the seventies Democrats have hoped that Macomb would return to its old voting habits. But, except in local elections, it has not done so. Increasingly its new subdivisions are for the affluent; new immigration is probably more Republican than its earlier residents. But even more important, the Democrats' stands on the social issues of the 1966–72 period seem to have snapped the bonds of an allegiance which, after all, resulted from the struggle between labor and management thirty years ago. People in Macomb County no longer think of themselves as part of the downtrodden half of society; they see themselves as part of a large, comfortable, but put upon middle class.

The 12th congressional district includes most of Macomb County. It has lost some of its most heavily Democratic areas—Warren, East Detroit—to neighboring districts and has added the fair-sized county that includes the old industrial city of Port Huron to the north; but it is still primarily a Macomb district. Given the changes in political attitudes here, it is not surprising that the 12th has experienced close congressional contests in three of the last four elections. The first was in 1972, when veteran Democrat James O'Hara, first elected in 1958, was nearly unseated because of the busing issue, even though he was solidly anti-busing himself; that was how strong opinion was at that time. Once the busing order was overturned by the Supreme Court, the issue vanished, and O'Hara was reelected easily in 1974. But in 1976 he decided to run for the Senate and lost in the primary to 7th district Congressman Donald Riegle. Long a labor ally, O'Hara became a lobbyist for General Motors in Washington—a transformation that was unheard of a generation ago in class-conscious Detroit—and helped to put together the labor-industry alliance to relax the clean air standards.

The new Congressman is Democrat David Bonior, a young veteran of the state legislature who has received high ratings from liberal and labor organizations. In the primary he barely beat a much older legislator who had always catered to the anti-Detroit feelings of many Macomb residents; in the general election he defeated the Republican who had nearly beaten O'Hara on the busing issue. In 1978 Bonior had opposition from a Republican legislator known as a backer of New Right causes. Again he won by a decisive margin, but far from the 3–1 wins O'Hara used to achieve. In the House Bonior is one of the more environment-minded members of the Public Works and Merchant Marine Committees.

Census Data Pop. 467,543. Central city, 0%; suburban, 74%. Median family income, $12,003; families above $15,000: 31%; families below $3,000: 6%. Median years education, 12.1.

The Voters

Median voting age 40.
Employment profile White collar, 46%. Blue collar, 42%. Service, 11%. Farm, 1%.
Ethnic groups Black, 2%. Total foreign stock, 24%. Canada, 7%; Germany, Italy, 3% each; Poland, UK, 2% each.

Presidential vote

1976	Carter (D)	87,787	(46%)
	Ford (R)	104,379	(54%)
1972	Nixon (R)	112,291	(65%)
	McGovern (D)	61,288	(35%)

Rep. David E. Bonior (D) Elected 1976; b. June 6, 1945, Detroit; home, Mount Clemens; U. of Ia., B.A. 1967, Chapman Col., M.A. 1972; Catholic.

Career Probation officer and adoption caseworker, 1967–68; Air Force, 1968–72; Mich. House of Reps., 1973–77.

Offices 1130 LHOB, 202-225-2106. Also 85 N. Gratiot Ave., Mt. Clemens 48043, 313-469-3232.

Committees *Merchant Marine and Fisheries* (18th). Subcommittees: Fish and Wildlife; Maritime Education and Training; Oceanography; Panama Canal.

Public Works and Transportation (18th). Subcommittees: Economic Development; Water Resources.

Group Ratings

	ADA	COPE	PC	RPN	NFU	LCV	CFA	NAB	NSI	ACA	NTU
1978	90	90	93	25	90	–	86	0	0	11	–
1977	90	91	90	54	75	85	90	–	–	15	42

Key Votes

1) Increase Def Spnd	AGN	6) Alaska Lands Protect	FOR	11) Delay Auto Pol Cntrl	FOR
2) B-1 Bomber	AGN	7) Water Projects Veto	FOR	12) Sugar Price Escalator	FOR
3) Cargo Preference	FOR	8) Consum Protect Agcy	FOR	13) Pub Fin Cong Cmpgns	FOR
4) Dereg Nat Gas	AGN	9) Common Situs Picket	FOR	14) ERA Ratif Recissn	AGN
5) Kemp-Roth	AGN	10) Labor Law Revision	FOR	15) Prohibt Govt Abrtns	AGN

Election Results

1978 general	David E. Bonior (D)	82,892	(55%)	($119,682)
	Kirby Holmes (R)	68,063	(45%)	($69,251)
1978 primary	David E. Bonior (D), unopposed			
1976 general	David E. Bonior (D)	94,815	(53%)	($95,986)
	David M. Serotkin (R)	85,326	(47%)	($108,593)

THIRTEENTH DISTRICT

The 13th congressional district of Michigan is Detroit's inner city, the only district completely inside the Detroit city limits. Like the 1st district, the 13th has a majority black population (66% in 1970, probably over 75% today), but unlike the 1st it has only a smattering of middle class blacks. During the sixties the 13th had the largest population loss—19%—of any congressional district. Every indication is that that trend has continued through the seventies. The 13th includes the Renaissance Center, the focal point of Detroit's now resurgent downtown; it includes the city's cultural center, the General Motors Building, Wayne State University, and the impressive headquarters of the United Auto Workers on the Detroit River. It has a set of giant freeways named for Motor City auto magnates: Edsel B. Ford, Walter P. Chrysler, and the Fisher brothers of General Motors.

But inland from the river and behind the major buildings are neighborhoods which, with a few exceptions, are being rapidly abandoned. A generation ago many were filled with large black families; houses were overcrowded because blacks could not buy homes elsewhere in the city. That soon changed, and black outmigration began. In the sixties violent crime became a major problem; after the 1967 riot, gun ownership became universal and Detroit's murder rate was the highest in the country. The outmigration from the inner city continued. There has naturally been a call for saving these neighborhoods. But it is not clear that anybody really wants them saved. The quality of the housing stock is generally low; these are frame houses built at the turn of the century for working people. In the past they were torn down for urban renewal projects, which were built years later; now many are still standing, unoccupied except for occasional vandals.

The 13th is a heavily Democratic district, one of the five or six most Democratic in the country in recent presidential elections. But the most salient fact about its voting history is the sharp decrease in turnout, which parallels the populations loss. Turnout declined here from 125,000 in the 1972 presidential election to 93,000 in 1976; offyear turnout declined from 71,000 in 1974 to 56,000 in 1978. Some have argued that blacks have been seriously undercounted by the Census. That may be, but these figures, showing turnout far below other Michigan districts, indicate that the population of the 13th able and willing to take so minimal a part in civic life as voting is decreasing by about 5% a year.

Charles Diggs was first elected Congressman from the 13th district in 1954, at age 27. His father was one of the richest and politically most astute men in Detroit's black community, and he understood that the 13th district, then with considerably different boundaries, had a black majority and would elect his son over the Irish incumbent in the Democratic primary. Diggs has been reelected easily in every biennial election since. He became Chairman of the House District of Columbia Committee in 1973, after the defeat of South Carolina's John McMillan, and he also served as Chairman of the Africa Subcommittee of Foreign Affairs.

Diggs became best known to the public when he was convicted in October 1978 of diverting $60,000 in staff salaries to pay his personal expenses. On being sentenced to three years in jail, he appealed; as this is written, that appeal is pending. In the House, he was stripped of his committee and subcommittee chairs, despite weak attempts to hold onto the latter, and the question became what was the House going to do about him. There was a move in early 1979 to expel him from the House; by some of the younger members. But more experienced representatives pointed out that Diggs had been reelected (with 81% of the vote) by his constituents after his conviction. Of course the real contest for this seat is in the Democratic primary, and Diggs had not been convicted when he beat several weak opponents in 1978; if he remains in the House, he will have to decide whether to retire or to risk a tougher primary in 1980.

The treatment of Diggs by the House in 1979 contrasts sharply with the treatment of Adam Clayton Powell in 1967. Powell was expelled, though he was never even indicted on criminal charges; his only legal problem was his refusal to pay a judgment on a civil suit. That had been a Congress more ready, even eager, to punish a black colleague, and more heedless of its legal footing (the Supreme Court ruled that Powell was wrongly unseated). There were also sharp contrasts between the two individuals involved. Powell was a strong chairman of an important committee (Education and Labor), and his personal actions had made him nationally well known. Diggs, while bright and knowledgeable, was never particularly aggressive or forceful, and until his conviction was unknown to the public outside Washington and Detroit. Indeed, the personal financial difficulties which led to the acts for which he was convicted suggest not greed or venality but passivity.

Probably by 1980 the 13th district will have elected another congressman, most likely one of the black state legislators or city council members from the area. Diggs's conviction seems unlikely to be reversed, and if he goes to jail he is hardly likely to run—or to be elected. His career is a disappointing one: a man who failed to live up to his potential and ended up by embarrassing his supporters and friends.

Census Data Pop. 465,076. Central city, 100%; suburban, 0%. Median family income, $7,770; families above $15,000: 13%; families below $3,000: 19%. Median years education, 10.0.

The Voters

Median voting age 44.
Employment profile White collar, 32%. Blue collar, 48%. Service, 20%. Farm, -%.
Ethnic groups Black, 66%. Spanish, 2%. Total foreign stock, 12%. Canada, Poland, 2% each; Germany, 1%.

Presidential vote

1976	Carter (D)	82,895	(89%)
	Ford (R)	10,654	(11%)
1972	Nixon (R)	20,561	(16%)
	McGovern (D)	104,556	(84%)

Rep. Charles C. Diggs, Jr. (D) Elected 1954; b. Dec. 2, 1922, Detroit; home, Detroit; U. of Mich., 1940–42, Fisk U., 1942–43, Wayne St. U., B.S. 1946, Detroit Col. of Law, 1950–51; Baptist.

Career Army Air Corps, WWII; Mortician, 1946–50; Mich. Senate, 1951–54.

Offices 2208 RHOB, 202-225-2261. Also 8104 Woodward Ave., Detroit 84207, 313-875-8811.

Committees *District of Columbia* (2d). Subcommittees: Judiciary, Manpower and Education.

Foreign Affairs (4th). Subcommittees: Africa; Asian and Pacific Affairs.

Group Ratings

	ADA	COPE	PC	RPN	NFU	LCV	CFA	NAB	NSI	ACA	NTU
1978	60	88	55	38	90	–	41	0	11	10	–
1977	55	95	68	38	90	65	70	–	–	0	15
1976	60	86	87	46	82	71	36	0	0	0	23

Key Votes

1) Increase Def Spnd	DNV	6) Alaska Lands Protect	DNV	11) Delay Auto Pol Cntrl	FOR
2) B-1 Bomber	AGN	7) Water Projects Veto	FOR	12) Sugar Price Escalator	DNV
3) Cargo Preference	FOR	8) Consum Protect Agcy	FOR	13) Pub Fin Cong Cmpgns	AGN
4) Dereg Nat Gas	AGN	9) Common Situs Picket	FOR	14) ERA Ratif Recissn	AGN
5) Kemp-Roth	AGN	10) Labor Law Revision	FOR	15) Prohibt Govt Abrtns	AGN

Election Results

1978 general	Charles C. Diggs, Jr. (D)	44,771	(79%)	($6,700)
	Dovie T. Pickett (R)	11,749	(21%)	($7,959)
1978 primary	Charles C. Diggs, Jr. (D)	12,837	(62%)	
	Ray Rickman (D)	4,550	(22%)	($8,152)
	Two others (D)	3,297	(16%)	
1976 general	Charles C. Diggs, Jr. (D)	83,387	(90%)	($8,667)
	Richard A. Golden (R)	9,002	(10%)	($1)

FOURTEENTH DISTRICT

The east side of Detroit is the heart of Michigan's 14th congressional district. It is composed of a series of residential neighborhoods of varying degress of affluence, most of them all white and heavily Catholic. Suburban territory nicely brackets and defines the east side. To the east, along Lake St. Clair, are the five Grosse Pointes: wealthy, conservative, snobby. There used to be a "point system" here: potential residents were given points for undesirable characteristics, like swarthy complexions or unusual names, and those with too many points could not buy houses. That is gone now, but the well-to-do Irish and Italian Catholic families who have worked their way here are as eager to maintain the area's exclusivity as the descendants of Michigan's old lumber families.

In the district's southwest corner is the enclave of Hamtramck, an almost entirely Polish-American city surrounded by Detroit. It was here that thousands of immigrants flocked to get jobs in the Dodge Main, Plymouth, and Packard auto plants; during the 1910s Hamtramck was the fastest growing city in the nation. In 1930 as many as 56,000 people lived here. Today the population is down to 27,000, most of whom are old people. Hamtramck has been the butt of dozens of Polish jokes, but anybody who takes the trouble to visit the city will find freshly painted houses and carefully tended lawns—evidence of the pride of ownership that still flourishes here and in so many Polish-American neighborhoods.

To the north of Detroit's east side is yet another suburban part of the district: half of Warren and all of East Detroit, both Macomb County suburbs, which were added to the district in 1972. These are working class suburbs, in which people live in a prosperity that their grandparents in Hamtramck never anticipated. Altogether, the 14th has one of the highest proportions of Polish-Americans of any congressional district, as well as the highest proportion of Belgian-Americans.

The Congressman from the 14th district for nearly two decades has been Lucien Nedzi, a Polish-American who was born in Hamtramck. He was first elected in 1961, and has faced two tough contests after that: in 1964 when he was placed in the same district with another incumbent and in 1972 when emotional opposition to busing almost propelled a Macomb-based candidate past him in the Democratic primary. Nedzi was also opposed to busing, but voters were so incensed at plans—never carried out—to bus suburban children into schools in Detroit that they were ready to throw out anyone; Nedzi was lucky that his opposition was divided.

Nedzi has also had a career of turbulence on occasion in the House. He was assigned early to the House Armed Services Committee—not a body normally of interest to the east side, which contains no military bases. In the late sixties he found himself one of the few doves on the Committee. While his advocacy of antiwar causes was not as strident as, say, Bella Abzug's, he was nonetheless one of the chief sponsors of the Nedzi–Whalen amendment, the House version of the McGovern–Hatfield amendment to end the Vietnam war.

Yet at about the same time Nedzi was considered reliable enough by hawkish Armed Services Chairman Edward Hebert to be named Chairman of the Subcommittee on Intelligence. In that capacity, he heard testimony about the CIA's illegal activity in domestic affairs and involvement in assassination plots. With a subcommittee membership made up of senior Armed Services hawks, Nedzi did not make this testimony public. All that came later, in 1975, just after Nedzi had been named chairman of a special intelligence committee, most of whose members were liberals. Michael Harrington of Massachusetts, among others, was outraged that Nedzi had not disclosed these matters earlier, and demanded that he be deposed as chairman. The leadership stepped in and both Nedzi and Harrington left the committee.

That sort of incident hurts a conscientious congressman, and Nedzi does not seem to have been as important a figure in the House since. He now chairs an Armed Services subcommittee on military installations and facilities; presumably the subject matter is important, but it is not so highly charged with policy implications. He is currently the fifth-ranking Democrat on Armed Services and has a chance of being chairman some day; he is reelected without difficulty every two years.

Census Data Pop. 467,603. Central city, 47%; suburban, 53%. Median family income, $12,394; families above $15,000: 34%; families below $3,000: 5%. Median years education, 11.9.

The Voters

Median voting age 47.
Employment profile White collar, 50%. Blue collar, 39%. Service, 11%. Farm, –%.
Ethnic groups Black, 3%. Total foreign stock, 37%. Poland, 9%; Italy, Canada, 6% each; Germany, 4%; UK, 2%; Austria, Yugoslavia, 1% each.

Presidential vote

1976	Carter (D)	82,896	(49%)
	Ford (R)	87,498	(51%)
1972	Nixon (R)	85,618	(60%)
	McGovern (D)	57,045	(40%)

Rep. Lucien N. Nedzi (D) Elected Nov. 7, 1961; b. May 28, 1925, Hamtramck; home, Detroit; U. of Mich., B.A. 1948, J.D. 1951; Catholic.

Career Army, WWII and Korea; Practicing atty., 1952–61; Wayne Co. Public Administrator, 1955–61.

Offices 2418 RHOB, 202-225-6276. Also 20491 Van Dyke St., Detroit 48234, 313-892-4010.

Committees *Armed Services* (5th). Subcommittees: Military Installations and Facilities (Chairman); Military Personnel.

House Administration (2d). Subcommittees: Libraries and Memorials (Chairman); Accounts.

Group Ratings

	ADA	COPE	PC	RPN	NFU	LCV	CFA	NAB	NSI	ACA	NTU
1978	40	72	48	30	70	–	36	18	40	13	–
1977	55	91	78	46	75	75	65	–	–	23	20
1976	70	83	89	41	83	78	81	8	40	11	22

Key Votes

1) Increase Def Spnd	AGN	6) Alaska Lands Protect	FOR	11) Delay Auto Pol Cntrl	FOR
2) B-1 Bomber	AGN	7) Water Projects Veto	FOR	12) Sugar Price Escalator	FOR
3) Cargo Preference	FOR	8) Consum Protect Agcy	FOR	13) Pub Fin Cong Cmpgns	AGN
4) Dereg Nat Gas	AGN	9) Common Situs Picket	FOR	14) ERA Ratif Recissn	FOR
5) Kemp-Roth	AGN	10) Labor Law Revision	FOR	15) Prohibt Govt Abrtns	FOR

Election Results

1978 general	Lucian N. Nedzi (D)	84,032	(67%)	($23,898)
	John Edward Getz (R)	40,716	(33%)	($6,225)
1978 primary	Lucian N. Nedzi (D)	28,606	(78%)	
	One other (D)	7,928	(22%)	
1976 general	Lucian N. Nedzi (D)	107,503	(67%)	($18,374)
	John E. Getz (R)	52,995	(33%)	($2,159)

FIFTEENTH DISTRICT

The 15th congressional district of Michigan is a collection of suburbs southwest of Detroit. No high income WASPy havens, these are bedroom communities occupied by people who keep the paperwork and assembly lines of the automobile companies moving. The various towns here have atmospheres reminiscent of their decades of greatest growth: Lincoln Park puts you back in the forties, Dearborn Heights recalls the fifties, and Westland—a city named after a shopping center—embodies the sixties. Most of the suburbs here are predominantly blue collar, and one of them, Inkster, has a significant black population. Many of the citizens here grew up in the immigrant neighborhoods of southwest Detroit; many others in the mountains of Kentucky and Tennessee.

The suburbs of most American cities, in the conventional picture, are usually Republican. Not so here; most Detroit suburbs in most elections are Democratic (though not as Democratic as they were 15 years ago). Over the years the 15th district has more often than not turned in 2–1 Democratic margins in most elections. But Democratic margins dropped sharply when a federal court issued a cross-district busing order in 1972; they recovered, but not entirely, when the order was never put into effect. In 1968, the district gave 16% of its vote to George Wallace. With increasing prosperity and decreasing working class consciousness, the 15th went only 53% for Jimmy Carter in 1976.

The district's largest employer is the Ford Motor Company, and its Congressman, coincidentally, is William Ford, a Democrat who is no relation to either Henry or Jerry. When the state legislature split the old 16th district in two in 1964, Ford, a young attorney active in the local politics of Taylor Township, jumped from the state Senate to the U.S. House. There he has remained with little trouble since; he was fortunate in the busing year of 1972 to have had weak opposition.

After a quiet congressional career Ford has become a congressman of considerable importance. He is now the fifth-ranking Democrat on the House Education and Labor Committee, and chairman of its subcommittee on post-secondary education. His rating from organized labor is one of the highest in the House—always at least 90%—and he is counted as one of the most solidly pro-labor votes on a pro-labor committee. Among his recent achievements are an amendment to the labor law reform requiring equal access to workers for employers and unions and a change in the grant formula providing more education funds for the Northeast and Midwest. He is also the fourth-ranking Democrat on Post Office and Civil Service. This committee is generally less important, but in the 95th Congress it handled a major piece of legislation, civil service reform, and Ford played a major role in its enactment. He served, in effect, as organized labor's negotiator and, with Morris Udall (who represented the Administration) and Edward Derwinski (the Republicans), worked out a compromise bill which may prove to be landmark legislation. Ford is not particularly charismatic, but he is one of those hard-working legislators who help put together legislation and make the House work.

Census Data Pop. 466,608. Central city, 0%; suburban, 100%. Median family income, $12,460; families above $15,000: 32%; families below $3,000: 4%. Median years education, 12.1.

The Voters

Median voting age 38.
Employment profile White collar, 42%. Blue collar, 47%. Service, 11%. Farm, –%.
Ethnic groups Black, 5%. Spanish, 1%. Total foreign stock, 19%. Canada, 5%; Poland, 3%; UK, Germany, Italy, 2% each.

Presidential vote

1976	Carter (D)	91,412	(53%)
	Ford (R)	81,619	(47%)
1972	Nixon (R)	94,812	(61%)
	McGovern (D)	61,803	(39%)

Rep. William D. Ford (D) Elected 1964; b. Aug. 6, 1927, Detroit; home, Taylor; Neb. Teachers Col., 1946, Wayne St. U., 1947–48, U. of Denver, B.S. 1949, J.D. 1951; United Church of Christ.

Career Practicing Atty., 1951–64; Taylor Twnshp. J.P., 1955–57; Melvindale City Atty., 1957–59; Mich Senate, 1963–65.

Offices 2368 RHOB, 202-225-6261. Also Wayne Fed. Bldg., Wayne 48184, 313-722-1411.

Committees *Education and Labor* (5th). Subcommittees: Elementary, Secondary and Vocational Education; Labor-Management Relations; Post-secondary Education (Chairman).

Post Office and Civil Service (4th). Subcommittees: Compensation and Employee Benefits; Postal Operations and Services; Postal Personnel and Modernization.

Group Ratings

	ADA	COPE	PC	RPN	NFU	LCV	CFA	NAB	NSI	ACA	NTU
1978	60	100	60	10	90	–	50	9	22	14	–
1977	50	95	70	38	91	68	60	–	–	8	16
1976	60	90	79	33	92	71	91	0	0	7	13

Key Votes

1) Increase Def Spnd	AGN	6) Alaska Lands Protect	FOR	11) Delay Auto Pol Cntrl	FOR
2) B-1 Bomber	AGN	7) Water Projects Veto	AGN	12) Sugar Price Escalator	AGN
3) Cargo Preference	FOR	8) Consum Protect Agcy	FOR	13) Pub Fin Cong Cmpgns	FOR
4) Dereg Nat Gas	AGN	9) Common Situs Picket	FOR	14) ERA Ratif Recissn	AGN
5) Kemp-Roth	AGN	10) Labor Law Revision	FOR	15) Prohibt Govt Abrtns	AGN

Election Results

1978 general	William D. Ford (D)	95,137	(80%)	($61,157)
	Edgar Nieten (R)	23,177	(20%)	
1978 primary	William D. Ford (D), unopposed			
1976 general	William D. Ford (D)	117,313	(75%)	($39,702)
	James D. Walaskay (R)	39,177	(25%)	($0)

SIXTEENTH DISTRICT

Michigan's 16th congressional district is an industrial part of the Detroit metropolitan area made up of three distinct areas of roughly equal population: the Delray section of Detroit, the Downriver suburbs, and the city of Dearborn. Delray, the southwest corner of Detroit, is an old ethnic neighborhood which looks much as it did in the twenties. The Downriver suburbs grow more prosperous and modern as one proceeds south along the Detroit River, though an insular quality remains in places like River Rouge and Ecorse, divided neatly into ethnic and racial sections by the railroad tracks. Dearborn is the district's most famous town. Here the Ford Motor Company has its headquarters and its giant Rouge plant; this is also the place where Henry Ford built his Greenfield Village.

The 16th is one of the nation's most heavily industrial districts. From the Interstate 75 bridge over the Rouge River, you can see the Ford Rouge plant and a couple of refineries on one side and the huge steel mills and chemical plants of the Downriver communities on the other. For the distinction of premier industrial landscape of America, this ranks with the view of Gary from the Indiana Turnpike and the spectacle of northern New Jersey from the Pulaski Skyway. Almost flush up against the industrial plants and well within range of their sulphurous odors are the neat, tightly packed houses of the old ethnic neighborhoods—still mostly Polish, Hungarian, and Italian, but now with considerable numbers of Mexican- and Arab-Americans. The 16th does contain a few high income WASP enclaves in the western part of Dearborn and on the island of Grosse Ile in the Detroit River. Most of the district, however, is working class and vintage Democratic country.

The congressman from this district is John Dingell, a Democrat who has played an important role on major legislation in recent years. He has been a major force in energy legislation. He serves as Chairman of the Commerce Energy Subcommittee, an important post on which he has jurisdiction on much of the energy legislation proposed by the Administration in the 95th Congress; he also served as one of the senior members of the special energy committee convened by Tip O'Neill to pass on the energy bill. Generally Dingell is reckoned as an opponent of positions taken by the oil companies. He was instrumental in getting the House to oppose deregulation of natural gas and to adopt much of the Carter program. Dingell is considered an aggressive advocate and a tough negotiator, and one who comes well prepared to the fray.

Another area in which he has taken a major part is the question of air pollution. As one of the senior members of the Michigan delegation, Dingell has been the leader of moves supported by the auto industry and the United Auto Workers to relax the requirements of the Clean Air Act. Dingell was successful in the House by a narrow margin here as on the energy bill, though in both cases the Senate failed to go along with his position.

One thing which helped Dingell in this fight was his reputation as a conservationist. He comes to such issues from a different route than many environmentalists: he is an enthusiastic hunter (and opponent of gun controls) and avid outdoorsman. On the Merchant Marine and Fisheries Committee and on the floor he has pushed through numerous pieces of conservationist legislation, and his fervor here is just as great as when he opposes the oil companies on pricing matters.

All these accomplishments make Dingell an important congressman, but he could become much more important soon. On the full Commerce Committee he ranks just behind 73-year-old Harley Staggers of West Virginia. He is likely to be chairman soon, and a more forceful, activist—and hot tempered—chairman than the committee has seen for some time. This is the body that writes the laws which regulate most big businesses and which passes on energy and health legislation as well; its potential impact is enormous. The Michigander could become a national force as chairman, if he can control his temper and use his talents fully.

Dingell holds a safe seat in the 16th. His father was first elected to Congress in 1932, and Dingell himself was elected on his father's death in 1955, before he was 30. He has had no trouble winning reelection since, with one exception. That was in 1964, when redistricting placed him in the same district with Congressman John Lesinski. Both were Democrats of Polish descent and both had succeeded fathers who had first been elected in 1932. The major difference was that Dingell had voted for the Civil Rights Act of 1964, while Lesinski was the one northern Democrat to vote against it. With the vigorous support of the United Auto Workers, Dingell won that election, and has had no problems since.

Census Data Pop. 467,168. Central city, 29%; suburban, 71%. Median family income, $11,800; families above $15,000: 31%; families below $3,000: 6%. Median years education, 11.4.

The Voters

Median voting age 45.
Employment profile White collar, 43%. Blue collar, 45%. Service, 12%. Farm, –%.
Ethnic groups Black, 8%. Spanish, 3%. Total foreign stock, 31%. Poland, 7%; Canada, 5%; Italy, 3%; UK, Germany, Hungary, 2% each.

Presidential vote

1976	Carter (D)	93,021	(55%)
	Ford (R)	75,048	(45%)
1972	Nixon (R)	95,564	(54%)
	McGovern (D)	82,219	(46%)

Rep. John D. Dingell (D) Elected Dec. 13, 1955; b. July 8, 1926, Colorado Springs, Colo.; home, Trenton; Georgetown U., B.S. 1949, J.D. 1952; Catholic.

Career Army, WWII; Practicing Atty., 1952–55; Research Asst. to U.S. Dist. Judge Theodore Levin, 1952–53; Wayne Co. Asst. Prosecuting Atty., 1953–55.

Offices 2221 RHOB, 202-225-4071. Also 4917 Schaefer Rd., Dearborn 48126, 313-846-1276.

Committees *Interstate and Foreign Commerce* (2d). Subcommittees: Energy and Power (Chairman).

Merchant Marine and Fisheries (3d). Subcommittees: Fish and Wildlife; Merchant Marine; Panama Canal.

Small Business (3d). Subcommittees: Impact of Energy Programs, Environment and Safety Requirements and Government Research on Small Business.

Group Ratings

	ADA	COPE	PC	RPN	NFU	LCV	CFA	NAB	NSI	ACA	NTU
1978	50	90	65	18	80	–	55	0	50	25	–
1977	70	91	70	27	91	65	70	–	–	16	19
1976	70	91	84	35	92	83	91	0	56	15	24

Key Votes

1) Increase Def Spnd	AGN	6) Alaska Lands Protect	DNV	11) Delay Auto Pol Cntrl	FOR
2) B-1 Bomber	AGN	7) Water Projects Veto	FOR	12) Sugar Price Escalator	AGN
3) Cargo Preference	FOR	8) Consum Protect Agcy	FOR	13) Pub Fin Cong Cmpgns	AGN
4) Dereg Nat Gas	AGN	9) Common Situs Picket	FOR	14) ERA Ratif Recissn	FOR
5) Kemp-Roth	AGN	10) Labor Law Revision	FOR	15) Prohibt Govt Abrtns	AGN

Election Results

1978 general	John D. Dingell (D)	93,387	(78%)	($61,246)
	Melvin E. Heuer (R)	26,827	(22%)	
1978 primary	John D. Dingell (D), unopposed			
1976 general	John D. Dingell (D)	121,682	(77%)	($70,503)
	William E. Rostran (R)	36,378	(23%)	($0)

SEVENTEENTH DISTRICT

Northwest Detroit historically has been the middle class and white collar part of the city. For mile after mile the straight streets here are lined with single-family houses; the factories responsible for their existence are many miles away. This area was almost entirely farmland in 1920; in the years just after World War II it was completely filled with houses. For many years this was the fulcrum of Michigan politics: as it went, so went the state. It was Republican in most elections until the early fifties; then in 1954, as the children of Detroit's first auto workers moved out here, it went solidly Democratic. In the years since, northwest Detroit has sometimes gone

Republican, but never by much; and as migration within the city continues, it has gotten more Democratic. In the seventies increasing numbers of blacks have been moving into northwest Detroit, adding to the Democratic percentages notably.

Northwest Detroit is the heart of the 17th congressional district of Michigan, a district which was once self contained. Now, with population shifting out toward the suburbs, so has the district. It includes Redford Township, politically and sociologically just about indistinguishable from the northwest Detroit neighborhoods it adjoins; Southfield, with a large Jewish population, and with high rise office buildings whose square footage now rivals downtown Detroit's; and Farmington Hills, west of Southfield, generally affluent and Protestant, the only reliably Republican part of the district.

The 1954 election gave the 17th a Democratic representative, Martha Griffiths, who became extremely popular in the district. She served on the Ways and Means Committee, but her most important achievement was persuading the House to pass the Equal Rights Amendment. Griffiths decided to retire in 1974, and the decision on her successor was made in the Democratic primary.

That turned out to be a very close race between very different kinds of Democrats. The second place candidate represented the traditional concerns of white homeowners in northwest Detroit: he was an opponent of busing and was tough on crime. The winner, by 256 votes, was state legislator William Brodhead, whose background was in the kind of politics produced by opponents of the Vietnam war. He had the support of the Liberal Conference, a group of volunteers capable of organizing most precincts in the district and squeezing a few extra votes out of each of them, as well as that of the United Auto Workers, the more traditional force in Democratic politics here.

Brodhead won Griffiths's old seat on Ways and Means and is one of the Committee's strongest backers of tax reform, financing of Social Security out of general revenues, and hospital cost containment. In 1979 he won a seat on the Budget Committee, putting him right at the center of the major issues of taxation and spending. He has had only one serious Republican challenge, in 1976, when he won by nearly a 2–1 margin.

Census Data Pop. 467,544. Central city, 56%; suburban, 44%. Median family income, $13,449; families above $15,000: 41%; families below $3,000: 4%. Median years education, 12.3.

The Voters

Median voting age 45.
Employment profile White collar, 58%. Blue collar, 31%. Service, 11%. Farm, –%.
Ethnic groups Black, 2%. Spanish, 1%. Total foreign stock, 34%. Canada, 8%; Poland, UK, 4% each; Germany, USSR, 3% each; Italy, 2%.

Presidential vote

1976	Carter (D)	87,311	(50%)
	Ford (R)	87,946	(50%)
1972	Nixon (R)	118,347	(60%)
	McGovern (D)	77,659	(40%)

Rep. William M. Brodhead (D) Elected 1974; b. Sept. 12, 1941, Cleveland, Ohio; home, Detroit; John Carroll U., 1959–60, U. of Detroit, 1960–63, Wayne St. U., A.B. 1965, U. of Mich., J.D. 1967.

Career Practicing atty., 1968–71; Mich. House of Reps., 1971–75.

Offices 1410 LHOB, 202-225-4961. Also 24261 Grand River Ave., Detroit 48219, 313-537-1400.

Committees *Ways and Means* (16th). Subcommittees: Public Assistance and Unemployment Compensation.

Budget (12th). Subcommittees: Human and Community Resources; State and Local Governments; Defense and International Affairs; Tax Expenditures and Tax Policy.

Group Ratings

	ADA	COPE	PC	RPN	NFU	LCV	CFA	NAB	NSI	ACA	NTU
1978	85	100	93	45	90	–	82	0	0	7	–
1977	80	91	88	50	75	85	85	–	–	11	37
1976	85	86	89	53	92	100	91	25	0	0	30

Key Votes

1) Increase Def Spnd	AGN	6) Alaska Lands Protect	FOR	11) Delay Auto Pol Cntrl	FOR
2) B-1 Bomber	AGN	7) Water Projects Veto	FOR	12) Sugar Price Escalator	AGN
3) Cargo Preference	FOR	8) Consum Protect Agcy	FOR	13) Pub Fin Cong Cmpgns	FOR
4) Dereg Nat Gas	AGN	9) Common Situs Picket	FOR	14) ERA Ratif Recissn	AGN
5) Kemp-Roth	AGN	10) Labor Law Revision	FOR	15) Prohibt Govt Abrtns	AGN

Election Results

1978 general	William M. Brodhead (D)	106,303	(95%)	($12,158)
	Hector McGregor (AIP)	5,341	(5%)	
1978 primary	William M. Brodhead (D), unopposed			
1976 general	William M. Brodhead (D)	112,746	(65%)	($67,260)
	James W. Burdick (R)	60,476	(35%)	($122,562)

EIGHTEENTH DISTRICT

The 18th congressional district of Michigan combines two areas that until recently have had little in common and had never before been joined in the same constituency: parts of Oakland and Macomb Counties in suburban Detroit. Oakland is a county which traditionally has been as Republican as outstate Michigan. Indeed, it had its beginnings as a farm community, with Royal Oak, the largest city in the 18th district, as a small market town. Then the migration to the suburbs began. Oakland lay adjacent to northwest Detroit, the most affluent part of the city, and it attracted the highest income and best educated people in the metropolitan area. In Detroit, where politics very much resembled class warfare at the time, such people tended to vote heavily Republican. Southern Macomb County, in contrast, had little settlement of any kind and no significant villages. It attracted migrants from the east side of Detroit—factory workers primarily and people of Polish or other Eastern European descent. Their tradition was Democratic. The contrast between the counties can be seen in the 1960 election returns: Macomb was 63% for Kennedy, while Oakland was 54% for Nixon.

In the sixties and seventies the differences between Oakland and Macomb—especially those parts in the 18th district—have tended to fade. The 18th always included some working class suburbs in Oakland, notably Hazel Park and Madison Heights, most of whose residents speak with the accents of the mountains of Kentucky and Tennessee. It also includes the Jewish and heavily Democratic suburb of Oak Park. And in recent years affluent, Republican-leaning voters have tended to move out from suburbs like Royal Oak and Berkley to newer suburbs farther out; the trend is therefore toward the Democrats. In Macomb a different process has taken place. Working class consciousness has been fading, as high auto worker wages have put blue collar workers definitely into the middle income brackets. Now they have summer homes and can afford winter vacations; and they worry, as much as management personnel, about high taxes, inflation, and high levels of government spending. They have stopped thinking of themselves as beneficiaries of government action and have started thinking of themselves as people who finance it. The result is a trend toward the Republicans in Macomb. Consider the results of the 1978 Senate race: Macomb was 54% for the Democrat, Levin; while Oakland was 51% for the Republican, Griffin.

On balance, then, this district leans Democratic. Much of its Oakland territory is Democratic, while its portion of Macomb County—Sterling Heights and half of Warren—has not been trending too strongly to the Republicans. In 1972, when there was no incumbent, the district did elect a Republican congressman; but he won solely because of the busing issue which was then raging. That faded, as the cross-district busing order was overruled, and the Republican lost in

1974. The current incumbent, Democrat James Blanchard, won a tough primary that year and has not had real difficulty in elections since. His voting record is in line with northern Democrats, but his chief legislative goal is not one traditionally associated with them. That is the so-called sunset bill, which would require every federal program to be re-authorized by Congress every five years or else go out of existence. He is the chief House backer of the measure, which is supported in the Senate by Edmund Muskie. While no one knows exactly what its effect would be, it is one attempt to impose some discipline and order on the mass of government programs which exist today without abolishing the best of them.

Census Data Pop. 465,916. Central city, 0%; suburban, 100%. Median family income, $13,627; families above $15,000: 40%; families below $3,000: 3%. Median years education, 12.3.

The Voters

Median voting age 39.
Employment profile White collar, 57%. Blue collar, 34%. Service, 9%. Farm, –%.
Ethnic groups Total foreign stock, 29%. Canada, 7%; Poland, 4%; UK, 3%; Italy, Germany, USSR, 2%.

Presidential vote

1976	Carter (D)	93,705	(46%)
	Ford (R)	109,551	(54%)
1972	Nixon (R)	115,552	(63%)
	McGovern (D)	68,193	(37%)

Rep. James J. Blanchard (D) Elected 1974; b. Aug. 8, 1942, Detroit; home, Pleasant Ridge; Mich. St. U., B.A. 1964, M.B.A. 1965, U. of Minn., J.D. 1968.

Career Practicing atty., 1968–74; Legal Aide, Mich. St. Election Bureau, 1968–69; Admin. Asst. to Mich. Atty. Gen. Frank J. Kelley, 1970–71; Asst. Atty. Gen. of Mich.; Legal Advisor to Mich. Depts. of Licensing and Regulation, Commerce, and Agriculture.

Offices 330 CHOB, 202-225-2101. Also 26111 Woodward, Royal Oak 48070, 313-543-1106.

Committees *Banking, Finance and Urban Affairs* (13th). Subcommittees: Economic Stabilization; Housing and Community Development; International Trade, Investment and Monetary Policy.

Science and Technology (11th). Subcommittees: Natural Resources and Environment; Energy Development and Applications.

Group Ratings

	ADA	COPE	PC	RPN	NFU	LCV	CFA	NAB	NSI	ACA	NTU
1978	65	95	68	42	80	–	59	0	50	15	–
1977	60	87	78	46	83	85	65	–	–	19	20
1976	70	83	92	47	92	80	91	25	30	0	36

Key Votes

1) Increase Def Spnd	AGN	6) Alaska Lands Protect	FOR	11) Delay Auto Pol Cntrl	FOR
2) B-1 Bomber	AGN	7) Water Projects Veto	FOR	12) Sugar Price Escalator	AGN
3) Cargo Preference	FOR	8) Consum Protect Agcy	FOR	13) Pub Fin Cong Cmpgns	FOR
4) Dereg Nat Gas	AGN	9) Common Situs Picket	FOR	14) ERA Ratif Recissn	AGN
5) Kemp-Roth	AGN	10) Labor Law Revision	FOR	15) Prohibt Govt Abrtns	FOR

Election Results

1978 general	James J. Blanchard (D)	113,037	(75%)	($89,842)
	Robert J. Salloum (R)	36,913	(25%)	
1978 primary	James J. Blanchard (D), unopposed			
1976 general	James J. Blanchard (D)	123,113	(67%)	($98,539)
	John E. Olsen (R)	60,995	(33%)	($11,315)

NINETEENTH DISTRICT

Just under half of Oakland County, the second most populous county in Michigan, is in the state's 19th congressional district, which also includes a small portion of Livingston County. Technically, all of the district is in the Detroit metropolitan area; in fact, the picture is a little more complicated. For what is really happening in the 19th is that the most affluent parts of the Detroit metropolitan area are moving out, and when they do, they run into older, working class communities. The most notable of these is Pontiac, an industrial city that produces Pontiac automobiles and GMC trucks. Pontiac has a large population of blacks from the Deep South and whites from the hills of Kentucky and Tennessee. In the early seventies there was great resistance to a busing order here; to a significant extent, many whites responded by moving farther out, to Waterford Township (a suburb which casts as many votes as Pontiac now) or to one of the communities of summer cottages which line the inland lakes or one of the newer subdivisions near a ski resort resting on man-made hills. Scattered throughout northern Oakland County are a number of small working class communities—Wixom, Walled Lake, Lake Orion—which are politically similar to Pontiac and Waterford Township: historically Democratic, but trending to Republicans on social issues.

Not more than a mile south of the Pontiac black ghetto is the Detroit suburb of Bloomfield Hills, which together with nearby Birmingham is the heart of the high income suburban belt in Oakland County. Here most of Detroit's top auto executives live as well as middle management personnel and professionals. While downtown Detroit deteriorated, there was a great boom in both commercial and residential construction in Birmingham, Bloomfield Hills, and the similar communities of Troy, Rochester, and West Bloomfield. The museums and concert halls may remain in Detroit, but the stores and services which service the carriage trade are mostly out here now in Oakland County. These high income suburbs are the heart of the 19th district; they outvote Pontiac, Waterford, and similar areas. And, almost needless to say, these high income areas in this Midwestern industrial community are heavily Republican—often on the order of 3–1 margins. While they have a certain tolerance for social liberalism (Birmingham passed an open housing ordinance by referendum, for example, although few blacks have chosen to move there), on economic issues the voters here have no doubt about which party is on their side.

That makes the 19th the only reliably Republican district in the Detroit metropolitan area and arguably the strongest Republican district in the state. The Congressman is William Broomfield, a Republican who was first elected in the Republican year of 1956. That makes him one of the most senior Republicans in the House, and he is ranking minority member of the Foreign Affairs Committee. On that body he has been a strong supporter of Israel (there is a substantial Jewish population in Oakland County), a backer of Nixon and Ford Administration foreign policies generally, and a man who is inclined now to go along both with the Republican leadership and with the national administration. His voting record, somewhat mixed over the years, is pretty orthodox Republican these days. Broomfield is not a mover and a shaker in the House; he is more a man who likes to go along with opinion generally accepted by the kind of voters who predominate in his district and seldom makes waves.

Back in the fifties Broomfield was one of those young Republican congressmen who pioneered the techniques of using the advantages of incumbency to help him win reelection in a possibly marginal district. He survived the Democratic years of 1958 and 1964 without difficulty. In 1972 he beat another Republican incumbent in the primary when they were thrown in the same district with each other. Still in his fifties, he seems able to continue winning without difficulty for as long as he chooses to run.

Census Data Pop. 467,540. Central city, 0%; suburban, 95%. Median family income, $13,405; families above $15,000: 41%; families below $3,000: 5%. Median years education, 12.4.

The Voters

Median voting age 41.
Employment profile White collar, 53%. Blue collar, 35%. Service, 11%. Farm, 1%.
Ethnic groups Black, 5%. Spanish, 2%. Total foreign stock, 17%. Canada, 5%; UK, Germany, 2% each; Poland, 1%.

Presidential vote

1976	Carter (D)	76,909	(37%)
	Ford (R)	132,349	(63%)
1972	Nixon (R)	122,205	(68%)
	McGovern (D)	57,144	(32%)

Rep. William S. Broomfield (R) Elected 1956; b. Apr. 28, 1922, Royal Oak; home, Birmingham; Mich. St. U., B.A. 1951; Presbyterian.

Career Mich. House of Reps., 1949–55, Spkr. Pro Tem, 1953; Mich. Senate, 1955–57; Mbr. U.S. Delegation to U.N., 1967.

Offices 2306 RHOB, 202-225-6135. Also 430 N. Woodward St., Birmingham 48011, 313-642-3800.

Committees *Foreign Affairs* (Ranking Member). Subcommittees: International Security and Scientific Affairs.

Small Business (4th). Subcommittees: Special Small Business Problems.

Group Ratings

	ADA	COPE	PC	RPN	NFU	LCV	CFA	NAB	NSI	ACA	NTU
1978	10	5	10	92	30	–	18	100	90	76	–
1977	15	26	28	67	33	35	20	–	–	70	33
1976	15	23	15	88	37	34	18	67	89	65	46

Key Votes

1) Increase Def Spnd	FOR	6) Alaska Lands Protect	DNV	11) Delay Auto Pol Cntrl	FOR
2) B-1 Bomber	FOR	7) Water Projects Veto	FOR	12) Sugar Price Escalator	AGN
3) Cargo Preference	AGN	8) Consum Protect Agcy	AGN	13) Pub Fin Cong Cmpgns	AGN
4) Dereg Nat Gas	FOR	9) Common Situs Picket	AGN	14) ERA Ratif Recissn	FOR
5) Kemp-Roth	FOR	10) Labor Law Revision	AGN	15) Prohibt Govt Abrtns	FOR

Election Results

1978 general	William S. Broomfield (R)	117,122	(71%)	($41,916)
	Betty F. Collier (D)	47,165	(29%)	
1978 primary	William S. Broomfield (R), unopposed			
1976 general	William S. Broomfield (R)	131,799	(67%)	($26,078)
	Dorothea Becker (D)	64,337	(33%)	($17,994)

MINNESOTA

Over the years Minnesota has been one of the nation's leading exporters of iron ore, wheat, flour, and political talent. In the past two decades this not especially populous state has given us Hubert Humphrey, Walter Mondale, Eugene McCarthy, Orville Freeman, Warren Burger, and Harry Blackmun. There are still people who remember Minnesota in the thirties when it produced national figures like Harold Stassen (a very real presidential contender in 1940 and 1948) and Floyd Olson, the talented and promising Farmer-Labor governor who died prematurely in 1936. No other state of this size—or of any size—has produced so many presidential candidates in recent years, and few have had congressional delegations of similar distinction.

Nor have any states recently experienced the political upheaval that struck Minnesota in 1978. For most of the seventies the Democratic-Farmer-Labor (DFL) Party here had been supreme, holding all the top offices, a majority of congressional seats, and a large majorities in the state legislature. Recovering quickly from the 1968 division over the Vietnam war, the DFL had become the nation's best organized political party. Yet in 1978 Minnesota's Republicans —officially the Independent-Republicans—won both of the state's Senate seats and the governorship, and made major gains in state legislative seats as well. It was a stunning victory for a party which had had few victories of any kind in the past ten years and a shocking defeat for the party which had just lost its greatest leader, Hubert Humphrey.

To put these developments in context we need to go back to the beginnings of Minnesota. This state was originally far north of the nation's great paths of east-west migration; Minneapolis and St. Paul are at the same latitude as Bangor, Maine, or Vancouver, Washington. In the mid-nineteenth century Yankee immigrants who swelled the populations of Iowa, Nebraska, and Kansas bypassed Minnesota and left it to the Norwegians, Swedes, and Germans who were not deterred by its icy lakes and ferocious winters. They were interested more in setting up communities which would retain at least some of the characteristics of their native lands. The nation was knit together in those days by the great east-west railroads, and the twin cities of Minneapolis and St. Paul sprang up almost at once at the confluence of the Minnesota and Mississippi Rivers as the center of a great agricultural empire stretching west from Minnesota through the Dakotas and eventually into Montana and beyond. The railroad magnates of St. Paul and the giant millers of Minneapolis absolutely governed the economic life of the vast Scandinavian-German province of America.

The various rebellions against this dominance have given the politics of Minnesota an almost Scandinavian ambiance. As in Wisconsin and North Dakota, a strong third party developed here in the years after the Populist era; and that organization, the Farmer-Labor Party, dominated Minnesota politics in the thirties. Its great leader was Floyd Olson, and it was beaten by Harold Stassen in 1938—a year of Republican victory as great as 1978. Even in the forties the Farmer-Labor Party was still at least as important as the state's historically negligible Democrats when they merged to form the Democratic-Farmer-Labor Party in the forties; Hubert Humphrey was one of the architects of that merger. Idealistic, staffed with dozens of talented young men and women, the DFL, led by Humphrey, swept the election of 1948 and since then has been the most important political force in the state. Even when it has lost elections, as in 1966 and 1978, it has been the DFL's mistakes or weaknesses as much as the Republicans' strength that produced the outcome.

In 1976 the DFL was in a position of great strength. Senator Walter Mondale was chosen by Jimmy Carter as his running mate in July and was elected Vice President of the United States in November; the Carter–Mondale ticket won with 57% in Minnesota. Senator Hubert Humphrey was elected to a fifth term with 68% of the vote. The DFL increased its already large margins in the state legislature, and reelected its five congressmen easily.

It was appropriate that Hubert Humphrey led the ticket that year. Just a month before the election, he underwent surgery for cancer, the disease from which he died in January 1978. But Minnesotans were prepared to reelect him whatever the condition of his health. His career here had spanned the entire post-World War II era and existence of the DFL Party. Some of Humphrey's eulogists would concentrate on his failure to become president. But more than any of the presidents of his time, Humphrey influenced the course of government and the thinking of the nation. He first became a national figure in 1948, with his speech before the Democratic National Convention urging a strong civil rights plank. He stayed with that cause, and in 1964, as Senate Majority Whip, floor-managed the landmark Civil Rights Act. He was an early advocate of disarmament, and saw his proposals of the fifties become the policy of the sixties and seventies. He advocated expansionary fiscal policies, which became standard practice in the fifties. More articulately than anyone else, he argued for a government which would be compassionate and try to help the poor, the helpless, and the ordinary person. The very balance between public and private sectors, the size and scope of government activity, the array of government services—all of these today are pretty much what Humphrey had been advocating for thirty years.

Humphrey's career is a good illustration of the fact that achievement does not depend on title or position. He was Senate Majority Whip for four years, but he was never majority leader, though he ran for the office in 1976; he never chaired a standing committee, though he served 23 years in the Senate in all. His four years as Vice President were not his happiest, as he antagonized many of his natural allies by backing the Vietnam war. His races for the presidency were not successful: he was underfinanced in 1960, he was disorganized and facing a disunited party in 1968, and he was late in entering the race in 1972. But over the years he was more successful than any other politician as a purveyor of ideas, a framer of issues. It seemed ironic that in the months after Humphrey died, the quasi-welfare state and big government he had done so much to establish came under increasing attack in Congress and from the voters. But that really is only an example of the American propensity to criticize what is and to idealize what could be; and it is testimony to the extent to which the ideas Humphrey espoused had become the basis of American government.

When Mondale had become Vice President, the vacancy he left in the Senate was filled by Governor Wendell Anderson, who resigned and let his Lieutenant Governor, Rudy Perpich, appoint him. Humphrey's vacancy in the Senate was filled by his widow Muriel Humphrey. In early 1978 the Republicans started making the point that all of Minnesota's top statewide positions were filled by people who had not been elected to them—and all would be up in the 1978 elections. "The DFL is going to face something scary," said a billboard put up by Republican gubernatorial candidate Albert Quie, "an election."

It was not an entirely fair charge. Minnesotans had after all elected DFL candidates to all those posts. They had voted for the Carter–Mondale ticket, knowing that if it won, Mondale would be replaced in the Senate by someone else. They had voted for Hubert Humphrey, although they knew he was ill, though of course they had not expected their governor to procure his own appointment to the Senate. That is what really crippled the DFL in the 1978 elections from the start. Since senators have been elected by popular vote, nine governors have had themselves appointed to the Senate; only one of them has been elected by the voters.

The self-appointment issue, more than anything else, was the determinative factor in the Senate race between Anderson and Republican Rudy Boschwitz. Anderson was by far the better known of the candidates. As governor for six years he was a familiar figure, even if he was surly and uncommunicative with Minnesota reporters. Boschwitz's exposure had come from television ads for his plywood business—enough to give him name identification, but not to persuade people why he should be a senator. Boschwitz tried to campaign as a liberal Republican, downplaying talk of tax cuts and avoiding an appearance with Ronald Reagan. He is a strong backer of Israel and opponent of nuclear power. Boschwitz spent heavily of his own money on the race, and Anderson tried to portray him as the candidate of the rich. But this kind of class warfare politics didn't work in the prosperous Minnesota of 1978. Anderson was far behind in newspaper polls over the summer, and could not rally the DFL faithful. Indeed, the results suggest not so much a partisan race as a general verdict of rejection. Anderson carried only two counties in the state and even lost the heavily DFL 8th congressional district.

But the Anderson-Boschwitz race was overshadowed by late summer by the race for the remainder of Hubert Humphrey's term. Muriel Humphrey had announced early that she would not run, and the early favorite for the seat was Minneapolis Congressman Donald Fraser. He began with the devotion of many DFL liberal activists. His record in Congress and in party affairs was impeccably liberal. He had opposed the Vietnam war, he had headed what was once the McGovern Commission on reforming the Democratic Party structure, he was concluding the House's most energetic and determined investigation into South Korean influence buying. Fraser was a firm believer in a large, compassionate federal government, and a man of strong principle and unflagging devotion to what he believed to be right.

That was enough to give Fraser the endorsement of the DFL convention. In most elections in Minnesota that would have given him the nomination; for Minnesota Democrats and Republicans have an understanding that the party conventions' choices are seldom challenged. But one challenger declined to play by the usual rules. He was Bob Short, a longtime DFL fundraiser who had never before held public office. Short was a rich trucking firm owner, a self-made millionaire whose devotion to the DFL came more from personal regard for Humphrey and from Democratic Party loyalties than from liberal views on public issues. On the contrary, Short was decidedly conservative. In the primary three issues helped him beat Fraser.

The first was the Boundary Waters Canoe Area. This was a proposal for a national park area in the northern lakes of Minnesota. Fraser was its chief backer in the House, and wanted to allow no motorboats or snowmobiles. Local residents felt this would destroy their livelihoods, and Short took their side. This helped him win very one-sided margins in heavily Democratic northern Minnesota. The second issue was abortion. Fraser felt that individuals should be allowed to make their own decisions about the matter; Short favored government action to stop abortions. Fraser was attacked by a right-to-life movement based in small Catholic communities which had traditionally provided many DFL votes in the rural parts of the state. Short carried these areas by very wide margins.

The final big issue in the primary was spending. Short promised to cut $100 billion or 20% out of the federal budget, plus a $50 billion tax rebate. Fraser said that Short sounded like a Republican, and made no concessions to the post-Proposition 13 mood of the voters. In the September primary, Short won a narrow upset victory. Fraser supporters charged that many Republicans voted in the DFL primary and made the difference. There is no party registration in Minnesota, but even if there were, there are not many primaries (the Republicans had none in 1978) and people are allowed to register on election day; a party registration requirement would probably not have made much difference. The problem was that the ideas which Fraser and others have used to motivate liberal activists for so many years seemed to have less force than the ideas Short used to create his coalition of northern power-boaters, rural Catholics, and angry taxpayers.

Fraser backers responded to the result with great bitterness; they felt that Short had lied about Fraser's record and otherwise exceeded the limits of decent campaigning. Fraser declined to endorse Short, and the local Americans for Democratic Action—an organization of which Fraser had been national chairman—endorsed the Republican nominee, David Durenberger. Short's decidedly unsubtle style of campaigning and the increasing awareness that his promises were unrealistic made him less acceptable to voters generally. Those who wanted a real Republican now supported Durenberger. Those who wanted a calmer candidate with more senatorial demeanor did so also. And so did the organized liberals in the Minneapolis-St. Paul area.

With such an array of support, the Republican Durenberger soon became the obvious winner. But what kind of Republican? He had expected to oppose Fraser and to advocate lower government spending and taxes; instead he had an opponent who outbid him, albeit not credibly, on both counts. Durenberger's solution was to run as a thoughtful, careful man who would provide responsible leadership. He won with a huge 64% of the two-party vote, including 71% in the Twin Cities metropolitan area—an unprecedented level which indicated huge DFL defections from Short. Durenberger had not really expected to be a senator; at the beginning of the year, he had been running for governor. His comments after his election suggest that he will indeed be thoughtful, and that he will also be one of the Senate Republicans more inclined to support some Democratic programs; he indicated, for example, that he would very much like to support a SALT treaty. His seat is up again in 1982, so he will have a good opportunity to acquaint Minnesota voters with his thinking.

So Minnesota in 1978 replaced Senators Humphrey and Mondale with two Republicans. But in both cases the victory resulted more from special circumstances—the Anderson appointment, the Fraser–Short primary—than from innate weakness of the DFL. There is every reason to believe the DFL can rebound from these losses, though in the meantime Senators Boschwitz and Durenberger have excellent opportunities to make themselves difficult to beat. In the 1978 elections for state office, however, we see a definite decline of DFL strength—not only in the race for governor, but also in the contests for the lower house of the state legislature, in which Republicans made striking gains and with a 67–67 tie won control. The DFL incumbent, Rudy Perpich, suffered perhaps a little from his role in the Anderson appointment; but he also had assets of his own. A dentist of Croatian descent from the Iron Range of northern Minnesota, he had an irrepressible personality and a propensity for showing up at the oddest places and making a good impression one-on-one. In an era of canned political speeches, Perpich came across as an authentic individual.

But that was not enough in 1978. The Republicans had a presentable candidate in 1st district Congressman Albert Quie, a deeply religious man whose record in Washington was about as acceptable to organized labor as it was to ideological conservatives. Picking up on the popularity of Proposition 13, Quie advocated a 10% across the board tax cut and a constitutional amendment limiting state spending to the growth in personal income. Minnesota is a prosperous state, with one of the nation's lowest unemployment rates; but it is also a high tax state, and voters responded positively to Quie's program. His reputation as a political moderate apparently reassured them that spending would not be cut to the bone.

Quie won the election by a decisive, though not overwhelming, margin, following usual party lines. Perpich carried the Iron Range and Duluth in the 8th congressional district; he did well in many northern and western rural counties. But he failed to carry usually Democratic Ramsey County (St. Paul) as well as usually marginal Hennepin County (Minneapolis), and Quie did extremely well in his old congressional district. No one expects the basic character of Minnesota to change under Quie, but he undoubtedly will put more emphasis on cutting taxes and less on new programs and procedural reforms than his DFL predecessors. Minnesota will have no major statewide elections in 1980—perhaps a welcome breathing spell after 1978—but there will be contests for state legislature. The results there should give us a good idea of the vitality of the state's major parties. Will the Republicans continue to gain, or will the DFL regain its elan and restore the balance to what had come to seem normal?

Minnesota's leading public figure now is a man who hasn't won an election here since 1972, Vice President Walter Mondale. By common consent, he—or, rather, Jimmy Carter—has made the office more useful and active than in any previous administration. Mondale functions as a high-level member of the Administration; he has the confidence of the President and the cooperation of his top staffers; he has prestige and clout around Washington that few holders of his office have enjoyed. Part of that he owes to an amiable character, which has helped him to win promotion after promotion by appointment: he was selected as Attorney General of Minnesota, as Senator, and as Vice President in each case by one man. Yet once in each of the first two offices, he won large margins from the voters. Mondale brings to the Carter Administration credibility among labor and liberal groups and also a reputation. for reliability around Washington. He is a possible candidate for the presidency, but not of course against Jimmy Carter, though he could be a candidate in 1980 if Carter withdrew from the race. He has the problem that Hubert Humphrey faced as a Vice President running for president: he is going to be identified with the Administration's unpopular policies without being able to do anything about them and without being able to take much credit for its successes (though Mondale may be more entitled to them than most vice presidents). He inspires generally warm feelings among Democratic primary voters, but he does not have the strong emotional following Edward Kennedy has. Still, Mondale could be president some day—or he may turn out to be our most useful vice president.

Census Data Pop. 3,805,069; 1.88% of U.S. total, 19th largest; Central city, 24%; suburban, 33%. Median family income, $9,928; 16th highest; families above $15,000: 20%; families below $3,000: 9%. Median years education, 12.2.

1977 Share of Federal Tax Burden $6,148,000,000; 1.78% of U.S. total, 20th largest.

1977 Share of Federal Outlays $6,146,699,000; 1.55% of U.S. total, 20th largest. Per capita federal spending, $1,566.

DOD	$851,319,000	31st (0.93%)	HEW	$2,516,698,000	19th (1.70%)
ERDA	$10,823,000	27th (0.18%)	HUD	$82,930,000	18th (1.97%)
NASA	$8,779,000	24th (0.22%)	VA	$365,195,000	18th (1.90%)
DOT	$209,229,000	25th (1.47%)	EPA	$99,728,000	21st (1.22%)
DOC	$60,658,000	32d (0.73%)	RevS	$148,292,000	18th (1.75%)
DOI	$53,547,000	21st (1.15%)	Debt	$265,015,000	16th (0.88%)
USDA	$897,699,000	4th (4.51%)	Other	$576,787,000	

Economic Base Agriculture, notably cattle, dairy products, corn and hogs; finance, insurance and real estate; machinery, especially electronic computing equipment; food and kindred products, especially meat products; printing and publishing, especially commercial printing; electrical equipment and supplies; fabricated metal products, especially fabricated structural metal products.

Political Line-up Governor, Albert H. Quie (R). Senators, David F. Durenburger (R) and Rudy Boschwitz (R). Representatives, 8 (4 DFL and 4 R). State Senate (47 D and 20 R); State House (67 D and 67 R).

The Voters

Registration 2,511,120 Total. No party registration.
Median voting age 43
Employment profile White collar, 49%. Blue collar, 31%. Service, 13%. Farm, 7%.
Ethnic groups Total foreign stock, 19%. Germany, 4%; Sweden, Norway, 3%; Canada, 2%.

Presidential vote

1976	Carter (D)	1,070,440	(57%)
	Ford (R)	819,395	(43%)
1972	Nixon (R)	898,269	(53%)
	McGovern (D)	802,346	(47%)

Sen. David Durenberger (R) Elected 1978, seat up 1982; b. Aug. 19, 1934, St. Cloud; home, Minneapolis; St. John's U., 1955, U. of Minn., J.D. 1959; Roman Catholic.

Career Army, 1956; Practicing atty., 1959–66; Exec. Secy. to Gov. Harold LeVander, 1969–71; Counsel for Legal & Community Affairs, Corporate Secy., Mgr. Internatl. Licensing Div., H.B. Fuller Co., 1971–78.

Offices 353 RSOB, 202-224-3244. Also 174 Federal Courts Bldg., 110 S. 4th St., Minneapolis 55401, 612-725-6111.

Committees *Finance* (8th). Subcommittees: Health; Energy and Foundations; Revenue Sharing, Intergovernmental Revenue Impact, and Debt Management Generally.

Governmental Affairs (8th). Subcommittees: Intergovernmental Relations; Energy, Nuclear Proliferation, and Federal Services; Oversight of Government Management.

Select Committee on Intelligence (6th).

Group Ratings: Newly Elected

Key Votes: Newly Elected

Election Results

1978 general	Dave Durenburger (I-R)	957,908	(64%)	($1,062,271)
	Bob Short (DFL)	538,675	(36%)	($1,972,060)
1978 primary	Dave Durenburger (I-R)	139,187	(67%)	
	Malcom Moos (I-R)	32,314	(16%)	($25,889)
	Three others (I-R)	35,419	(17%)	
1976 general	Hubert H. Humphrey (DFL)	1,290,736	(73%)	($618,878)
	Jerry Brekke (R)	478,602	(27%)	($43,912)
1976 primary	Hubert H. Humphrey (DFL)	317,632	(91%)	
	One other (DFL)	30,262	(9%)	
1970 general	Hubert H. Humphrey (DFL)	788,256	(58%)	
	Clark MacGregor (R)	568,025	(42%)	

Sen. Rudy Boschwitz (R) Elected 1978, seat up 1984; b. 1930, Berlin, Germany; home, Plymouth; Johns Hopkins U., N.Y.U., B.S. 1950, LL.B. 1953; Jewish.

Career Army, 1953–55; Practicing atty.; Founder and Pres., Plywood Minnesota, 1963–78.

Offices 2107 DSOB, 202-224-5641. Also 210 Bremer Bldg., St. Paul 55101, 612-221-0905.

Committees *Agriculture, Nutrition, and Forestry* (7th). Subcommittees: Agricultural Research and General Legislation; Rural Development; Foreign Agricultural Policy.

Budget (6th).

Select Committee on Small Business (6th).

Group Ratings: Newly Elected

Key Votes: Newly Elected

Election Results

1978 general	Rudy Boschwitz (I-R)	894,092	(58%)	($1,870,163)
	Wendell Anderson (DFL)	638,375	(42%)	($1,154,351)
1978 primary	Rudy Boschwitz (I-R)	185,393	(87%)	
	Harold Stassen (I-R)	28,170	(13%)	($139,230)
1972 general	Walter F. Mondale (DFL)	981,320	(57%)	($536,532)
	Phil Hansen (R)	742,121	(43%)	($304,750)

Gov. Albert H. Quie (R) Elected 1978, term expires Jan. 1983; b. Sept. 18, 1923, near Dennison; St. Olaf Col., B.A. 1950; Lutheran.

Career Navy, WWII; Dairy Farmer; Minn. Senate, 1954–58; U.S. House of Reps., 1958–78.

Offices State Capitol, St. Paul 55155, 612-296-3391.

Election Results

1978 general	Albert H. Quie (I-R)	830,019	(54%)
	Rudy Perpich (DFL)	718,244	(46%)
1978 primary	Albert H. Quie (I-R)	174,799	(84%)
	One other (I-R)	34,406	(16%)
1974 general	Wendell Anderson (DFL)	786,787	(68%)
	John W. Johnson (R)	367,722	(32%)

FIRST DISTRICT

The 1st congressional district of Minnesota, the southeast corner of the state, is a region of farms, grain elevator towns and small, pleasant cities. This is the Minnesota district with the most in common with the rural Midwest farther south. In its ethnic and political traditions, it is more like Iowa—that is, more Yankee and more Republican than Minnesota as a whole. The district's largest city, Rochester, is the home of the Mayo Clinic and, until 1971, of its onetime counsel and now Supreme Court Justice, Harry Blackmun. Rochester is a comparatively rich, idyllic, white collar town; Olmsted County, of which it is a part, is the largest Minnesota county that has consistently gone Republican—not just in 1978, but in 1976 for Ford-Dole over Carter-Mondale.

The northern end of the 1st district is rather different. Here, in Dakota County across the river from St. Paul and in Washington County just to the east of the capital, we pass from the rural and small city atmosphere of southeast Minnesota to the outskirts of the Twin Cities metropolitan area. These are working class suburbs, where newly laid-out subdivisions attract young families who grew up in the straighter streets and smaller houses of St. Paul.

These Dakota and Washington County suburbs tend to vote for DFL candidates, while the other part of the district tends to go Republican. Congressional elections, however, were not close as long as Albert Quie was the Congressman here. First elected in 1958, he was returned to office easily; in the House, he was ranking Republican on the Education and Labor Committee. In 1978 he decided to return to Minnesota and ran for governor. He won a fairly close race, but the regard in which he was held in the 1st district can be gauged from the 66% of the two-party vote he won in the 1st district.

In another year the race to succeed Quie would probably have been very close, but 1978 was a Republican year if there ever was one in Minnesota. The Republican nominee, Arlen Erdahl, although a veteran officeholder, had not been a strong campaigner; he lost the Republican nomination in the 2d district in 1974 and was defeated for reelection as secretary of state later that year. His opponent, 30-year-old Washington County state legislator Gerry Sikorski, was the kind of candidate the DFL Party has been running successfully in other districts. But in 1978 Sikorski was on the defensive on the tax issue and was unable to carry even the suburban counties. He ran far behind in the more rural counties, and Erdahl won a nearly 2–1 margin in the Rochester area. As an incumbent, Erdahl will have every opportunity to hold onto this district and no excuses if he loses it.

Census Data Pop. 473,918. Central city, 11%; suburban, 43%. Median family income, $10,272; families above $15,000: 20%; families below $3,000: 8%. Median years education, 12.3.

The Voters

Median voting age 42.
Employment profile White collar, 46%. Blue collar, 30%. Service, 15%. Farm, 9%.
Ethnic groups Total foreign stock, 14%. Germany, 4%; Norway, 2%; Sweden, Canada, 1% each.

Presidential vote

1976	Carter (D)	125,615	(51%)
	Ford (R)	117,565	(49%)
1972	Nixon (R)	122,634	(60%)
	McGovern (D)	82,155	(40%)

Rep. Arlen Erdahl (R) Elected 1978; b. Feb. 27, 1931, Blue Earth; home, West St. Paul; St. Olaf Col., B.A. 1953, Harvard U., M.P.A. 1966; Lutheran.

Career Minn. House of Reps., 1963–70; Secy. of State of Minn., 1970–74; Minn. Public Service Comm., 1975–78.

Offices 1017 LHOB, 202-225-2271. Also 33 Wentworth Bldg., W. St. Paul 55119, 612-725-7716.

Committees *Education and Labor* (9th). Subcommittees: Elementary, Secondary, and Vocational Education; Select Education.

Small Business (13th). Subcommittee: Impact of Energy Programs, Environment and Safety Requirements and Government Research on Small Business.

Group Ratings: Newly Elected

Key Votes: Newly Elected

Election Results

1978 general	Arlen Erdahl (I-R)	110,090	(57%)	($194,363)
	Gerry Sikorski (DFL)	83,271	(43%)	($149,089)
1978 primary	Arlen Erdahl (I-R)	26,768	(74%)	
	Four others (I-R)	9,482	(26%)	
1976 general	Albert H. Quie (I-R)	158,177	(69%)	($40,063)
	Robert C. Olsen, Jr. (DFL)	70,630	(31%)	($1,330)

SECOND DISTRICT

South central Minnesota, most of which is included in the state's 2d congressional district, is one of the most Republican parts of the state. A majority of the people in the 2d live in the valley of the Minnesota River. The towns here—New Ulm, Mankato, St. Peter—are old and their political allegiances deep rooted and Republican. To the southeast, the district also includes the small industrial and usually DFL city of Austin, near the Iowa border. The 2d also extends well into the Twin Cities metropolitan area to take in the heavily Republican high income territory around Lake Minnetonka and a politically marginal section of Dakota County, just south of St. Paul.

The Democratic tide of 1974 was the acid test of the strength of the 2d district's Republican tradition and, in contrast to many Upper Midwest districts, the tradition prevailed. Incumbent Republican Ancher Nelsen was retiring after 16 years in the House and an uninspiring percentage in 1972. The Republican nominee was 30-year-old Thomas Hagedorn, one of the most conservative members of the Minnesota legislature. Half of Hagedorn's margin came from two small counties he represented in the legislature, but nonetheless he won.

In the House Hagedorn has seats on the Agriculture and Public Works Committees and a voting record far out of line from the Minnesota norm—among Republicans as well as Democrats. He is a strong believer in the free market economy and a skeptic about government programs. He is the House's leading advocate of repeal of the Davis-Bacon Act, which requires the federal government to pay construction workers the prevailing wage in their area. However uncommon in Minnesota, this is getting to be a more important philosophy on Capitol Hill, and Hagedorn is one of its most resolute advocates.

Census Data Pop. 476,647. Central city, 0%; suburban, 19%. Median family income, $9,703; families above $15,000: 19%; families below $3,000: 9%. Median years education, 12.2.

The Voters

Median voting age 43.
Employment profile White collar, 43%. Blue collar, 33%. Service, 12%. Farm, 12%.
Ethnic groups Total foreign stock, 14%. Germany, 5%; Norway, 2%; Sweden, 1%.

Presidential vote

1976	Carter (D)	125,615	(50%)
	Ford (R)	123,435	(50%)
1972	Nixon (R)	129,432	(59%)
	McGovern (D)	88,633	(41%)

Rep. Tom Hagedorn (R) Elected 1974; b. Nov. 27, 1943, Blue Earth; home, Truman; Lutheran.

Career Farmer; Minn. House of Reps., 1970–74.

Offices 440 CHOB, 202-225-2472. Also Box 3148, Mankato 56001, 507-388-4563.

Committees *Agriculture* (11th). Subcommittees: Dairy and Poultry; Livestock and Grains.

Public Works and Transportation (10th). Subcommittees: Public Buildings and Grounds; Surface Transportation; Aviation.

Group Ratings

	ADA	COPE	PC	RPN	NFU	LCV	CFA	NAB	NSI	ACA	NTU
1978	5	0	10	73	30	–	14	92	100	92	–
1977	5	17	25	67	42	14	5	–	–	85	41
1976	0	13	15	71	17	20	0	83	100	89	61

Key Votes

1) Increase Def Spnd	FOR	6) Alaska Lands Protect	AGN	11) Delay Auto Pol Cntrl	FOR
2) B-1 Bomber	FOR	7) Water Projects Veto	AGN	12) Sugar Price Escalator	DNV
3) Cargo Preference	AGN	8) Consum Protect Agcy	AGN	13) Pub Fin Cong Cmpgns	AGN
4) Dereg Nat Gas	FOR	9) Common Situs Picket	AGN	14) ERA Ratif Recissn	FOR
5) Kemp-Roth	FOR	10) Labor Law Revision	AGN	15) Prohibt Govt Abrtns	FOR

Election Results

1978 general	Tom Hagadorn (I-R)	145,415	(70%)	($172,482)
	John F. Considine (DFL)	61,173	(30%)	($22,086)
1978 primary	Tom Hagadorn (I-R), unopposed			
1976 general	Tom Hagadorn (I-R)	148,322	(60%)	($121,010)
	Gloria Griffin (DFL)	97,488	(40%)	($74,283)

THIRD DISTRICT

The natural pattern of urban development in America is for population to spread out from a central city into ever less densely populated rings of suburbs. A good place to observe the phenomenon is in the Minneapolis-St. Paul metropolitan area, which has had substantial population growth and where this pattern of dispersal cannot be attributed to white flight from a black central city. There are very few blacks in the Twin Cities. The economy here is diversified, with many old blue collar industries (the railroads, General Mills, Pillsbury) and many new, predominantly white collar businesses (Honeywell, 3M, Control Data, Investors Diversified Services). Movement has been toward the blue collar suburbs around St. Paul and north and northwest of Minneapolis, around the major railroad lines; and there are signs that many blue collar workers are moving far out beyond the traditional limits of the metropolitan area. With factories in the suburbs and freeways in every direction, it is possible to live 60 or 70 miles from downtown Minneapolis or St. Paul and still work in the metropolitan area.

The white collar suburbs tend to be west and southwest of Minneapolis. Most of them are gathered into the 3d congressional district of Minnesota, which also includes some blue collar territory. At the northern edge of the district, along the Mississippi River as it flows into Minneapolis, are blue collar suburbs like Brooklyn Park and Brooklyn Center. At the far southern end is middle income suburbs like Richfield and Bloomington, settled in the fifties and with populations that are now aging. In the middle of the district are high income WASP retreats like Plymouth, Golden Valley, and Minnetonka, along with Edina, perhaps the state's highest income and most Republican town. Just north of Edina is the predominantly Jewish suburb of St. Louis Park.

This district is mixed enough in its sociological composition to be marginal rather than Republican. Nonetheless the high income Republican suburbs usually overcome the middle income or Jewish DFL suburbs, and the district has elected only Republican congressmen since 1960. The current incumbent, Bill Frenzel, had a close race when he first ran in 1970. He had a reputation in the early seventies as a moderate or even liberal Republican, and he was no lockstep follower of the Nixon Administration. As a member of the House Administration Committee, he worked hard to help put together the campaign finance reform legislation which is still in effect, keeping an eye out for what he considered the legitimate interests of the Republican Party.

More recently the thrust of Frenzel's career seems to have changed. He has always been voluble, but seems increasingly to be acerbic in his denunciations of measures he does not like. His personal image was hurt by revelations that he had been more than a year late in filing his 1972 income tax return. And his voting record seems to have changed. As late as 1974 he had much higher ratings from liberal and labor organizations than from conservative or business organizations. But in 1975 he seems to have shifted, particularly on economic issues, and now his ratings from conservative organizations are much higher than from liberals. He is currently a member of the Ways and Means Committee as well as House Administration, and there he votes mostly with his Republican colleagues.

The shift in Frenzel's voting record does not seem to have affected his popularity. Arguably, it reflects changing opinion in this affluent district. He continues to win reelection by wide margins. But he seems to have missed his chance to run for the Senate. He declined to make the race against Hubert Humphrey in 1976, and in 1978 let two lesser known Republicans have the party's nomination for the two Senate seats up that year. Both won, and both are younger than Frenzel; his future seems to be in the House.

Census Data Pop. 472,662. Central city, 4%; suburban, 96%. Median family income, $13,248; families above $15,000: 38%; families below $3,000: 3%. Median years education, 12.7.

The Voters

Median voting age 39.
Employment profile White collar, 64%. Blue collar, 26%. Service, 10%. Farm, –%.
Ethnic groups Total foreign stock, 16%. Sweden, 3%; Norway, Germany, Canada, 2% each.

Presidential vote

1976	Carter (D)	120,201	(49%)
	Ford (R)	124,439	(51%)
1972	Nixon (R)	129,587	(59%)
	McGovern (D)	89,281	(41%)

Rep. Bill Frenzel (R) Elected 1970; b. July 31, 1928, St. Paul; home, Golden Valley; Dartmouth Col., B.A. 1950, M.B.A. 1951.

Career Navy, Korea; Pres., Minn. Terminal Warehouse Co., Minn. House of Reps., 1962–70.

Offices 1026 LHOB, 202-225-2871. Also 120 Fed. Bldg., 110 S. 4th St., Minneapolis 55401, 612-725-2173.

Committees *House Administration* (4th). Subcommittees: Libraries and Memorials.

Ways and Means (6th). Subcommittees: Trade.

Budget (7th). Subcommittees: Economic Policy, Projections and Productivity; Human and Community Resources; Tax Expenditures and Tax Policy.

Group Ratings

	ADA	COPE	PC	RPN	NFU	LCV	CFA	NAB	NSI	ACA	NTU
1978	35	20	20	89	11	–	14	90	56	64	–
1977	25	27	36	100	56	29	15	–	–	72	43
1976	25	9	28	93	28	48	36	91	50	54	68

Key Votes

1) Increase Def Spnd	FOR	6) Alaska Lands Protect	FOR	11) Delay Auto Pol Cntrl	FOR
2) B-1 Bomber	AGN	7) Water Projects Veto	FOR	12) Sugar Price Escalator	FOR
3) Cargo Preference	AGN	8) Consum Protect Agcy	AGN	13) Pub Fin Cong Cmpgns	AGN
4) Dereg Nat Gas	FOR	9) Common Situs Picket	AGN	14) ERA Ratif Recissn	AGN
5) Kemp-Roth	FOR	10) Labor Law Revision	FOR	15) Prohibt Govt Abrtns	AGN

Election Results

1978 general	Bill Frenzel (I-R)	128,759	(66%)	($179,807)
	Michael O. Freeman (DFL)	67,120	(34%)	($154,738)
1978 primary	Bill Frenzel (I-R), unopposed			
1976 general	Bill Frenzel (I-R)	149,013	(67%)	($57,244)
	Jerome W. Coughlin (DFL)	72,044	(33%)	($8,303)

FOURTH DISTRICT

St. Paul, the smaller of Minnesota's Twin Cities, is an old river town with a history something like that of St. Louis, hundreds of miles farther down the Mississippi River. Settled before Minneapolis, St. Paul was for some years the larger of the two, as well as the state capital. While Minneapolis was attracting Swedes and Yankees, St. Paul got more Irish and German Catholics; while Minneapolis became the nation's largest grain milling center, St. Paul's economic role was that of a transportation hub, a railroad center and river port. Long before the Democratic-Farmer-Labor Party was formed, St. Paul was one of the few places in Minnesota where Democrats sometimes won, and through all the changes that have occurred since, the city and its suburbs have remained staunchly DFL—at least until 1978.

In these days when the one-person-one-vote rule requires intricately drawn congressional district borders, the 4th district of Minnesota is the closest thing in the nation to a district which is totally coincident with a single county: it includes all but the tiniest smidgin of St. Paul's Ramsey County. A solidly Democratic district, the 4th has been represented by Democrats for more than thirty years. Its most prominent congressman was Eugene McCarthy (1949–59), who in those days did not dabble much in poetry. He was a hard-working member of the Ways and Means Committee and one of the founders of the Democratic Study Group. Although he was happy with the pace of life in the House, McCarthy, perhaps eyeing an eventual presidential candidacy, ran for the Senate in 1958.

The succession here has been governed by the DFL convention ever since. Minnesota's political activists believe strongly in the idea of strong political parties, and in an effort to make their party organizations really mean something they tend to respect their decisions on nominations to office. Primaries are unusual, and it is extremely unusual for the party nominee to be defeated (as Congressman Donald Fraser was in the 1978 Senate race). Thus when 4th district Congressman Joseph Karth retired in 1976, the DFL nominating convention was decisive in choosing his successor. On the 13th ballot the nomination went to state legislator Bruce Vento. Later he was challenged in the primary, but got a solid 52%–23% over his nearest opponent.

Vento won his general election by a huge margin and went on to compile a record that earned top marks from labor and liberal ratings organizations. But his percentage dropped to 58% in the 1978 elections. Minnesota's Republican sweep was strong enough to carry Ramsey County out of the DFL column in both Senate races and the contest for governor. That does not put Vento in real jeopardy yet, but he will probably have to work this district harder than anyone expected to keep it safe.

Census Data Pop. 473,902. Central city, 65%; suburban, 35%. Median family income, $11,306; families above $15,000: 26%; families below $3,000: 6%. Median years education, 12.4.

The Voters

Median voting age 41.
Employment profile White collar, 56%. Blue collar, 31%. Service, 13%. Farm, –%.
Ethnic groups Black, 2%. Total foreign stock, 19%. Germany, 3%; Sweden, Canada, 2% each; Norway, 1%.

Presidential vote

1976	Carter (D)	133,051	(61%)
	Ford (R)	85,922	(39%)
1972	Nixon (R)	95,201	(47%)
	McGovern (D)	107,924	(53%)

Rep. Bruce F. Vento (DFL) Elected 1976; b. Oct. 7, 1940, St. Paul; home, St. Paul; U. of Minn., A.A. 1962, Wis. St. U., River Falls, B.S. 1965; Presentation Church.

Career Jr. High school teacher, 1965–76; Minn. House of Reps., 1971–77, Asst. Major. Ldr., 1974–76.

Offices 230 CHOB, 202-225-6631. Also Rm. 544 Fed. Courts Bldg., St. Paul 55101, 612-725-7869.

Committees *Banking, Finance and Urban Affairs* (24th). Subcommittees: Consumer Affairs; Economic Stabilization; Housing and Community Development.

Interior and Insular Affairs (22d). Subcommittees: Energy and the Environment; National Parks and Insular Affairs.

Group Ratings

	ADA	COPE	PC	RPN	NFU	LCV	CFA	NAB	NSI	ACA	NTU
1978	65	95	83	33	90	–	82	0	10	7	–
1977	90	87	93	42	75	87	90	–	–	0	35

Key Votes

1) Increase Def Spnd	AGN	6) Alaska Lands Protect	FOR	11) Delay Auto Pol Cntrl	FOR
2) B-1 Bomber	AGN	7) Water Projects Veto	FOR	12) Sugar Price Escalator	FOR
3) Cargo Preference	FOR	8) Consum Protect Agcy	FOR	13) Pub Fin Cong Cmpgns	FOR
4) Dereg Nat Gas	AGN	9) Common Situs Picket	FOR	14) ERA Ratif Recissn	AGN
5) Kemp-Roth	AGN	10) Labor Law Revision	FOR	15) Prohibt Govt Abrtns	FOR

Election Results

1978 general	Bruce F. Vento (DFL)	95,989	(58%)	($80,225)
	John Berg (I-R)	69,396	(42%)	($76,705)
1978 primary	Bruce F. Vento (DFL), unopposed			
1976 general	Bruce F. Vento (DFL)	133,282	(69%)	($107,510)
	Andrew Engebretson (I-R)	59,767	(31%)	($20,634)

FIFTH DISTRICT

The 5th congressional district of Minnesota is virtually all of the city of Minneapolis and a couple of blue collar suburbs in Anoka County to the north. Minneapolis is known as the nation's leading grain milling center and for its sophisticated white collar industries. But the great business interests of Minneapolis do not account for the city's distinctive political tradition. This comes instead from the Swedish and other Scandinavian immigrants who first came here in the 1880s. They were probably attracted to Minnesota for two reasons: first, from the resemblance of the American north country, with its hilly countryside, thousands of glacier-carved lakes, and long cold winters, to the Scandinavia they had known; and, second, because there were opportunities here which native stock Americans, eager to head straight west out of Illinois and Missouri, failed to pursue. The Scandinavians have given Minneapolis a liberal political tradition, hospitable in turn to the Harold Stassens and David Durenbergers of the Republican Party as well as to the Hubert Humphreys and Walter Mondales of the DFL.

The 5th district has had a succession of congressmen of national stature, whose defeats have hurt the causes they held most dear. The first of these was Walter Judd, the 1960 Republican National Convention keynoter and longtime unofficial head of the China Lobby. His defeat for reelection in 1962 did not destroy the lobby, but it did help to undermine the idea, prevalent in the fifties, that most Americans were deeply devoted to the Nationalist Chinese regime on Taiwan. The second was the man who beat Judd, Donald Fraser. He was always one of the leading liberals in the House, a hard worker who had no impulse to compromise his principles however much it might help him politically. Fraser was national chairman of ADA, and in his last terms investigated Korean lobbying in the Congress and the Sun Myung Moon cult, and sponsored a controversial Boundary Waters Canoe Area which would prohibit motor boats in this northern Minnesota area. All these things, plus his refusal to back anti-abortion laws and indulge in anti-government spending rhetoric, cost him votes when he ran for the Senate in 1978, and he was defeated by the negative primary campaign of Robert Short. That defeat in liberal Minnesota led to national speculation that traditional liberal doctrine simply could not gain public support, at least in the atmosphere of 1978.

Actually, the results in the 5th district could be cited as a refutation of that notion, though not a conclusive one. This is a solidly Democratic district, which delivered a solid majority to George McGovern in 1972. The DFL nominee, Martin Sabo, was Speaker of the Minnesota House; though only 40, he had 18 years of legislative experience. The Republican candidate, a dentist who raised money from his colleagues, actually put on a campaign complete with television advertisements and attacked Sabo's initial reluctance to convert the state's surplus into a tax cut. But he got only 38% of the vote—evidence that this is simply not going to be a Republican district any more. The House leadership has a soft spot in its heart for former speakers—Tip O'Neill himself was Speaker of the Massachusetts House before he came to Congress—and Sabo received a seat on the Appropriations Committee. He was one of only three freshmen to get one, and seems destined for a long career in the House if he wants it.

Census Data Pop. 479,280. Central city, 87%; suburban, 13%. Median family income, $10,323; families above $15,000: 22%; families below $3,000: 8%. Median years education, 12.3.

The Voters

Median voting age 42.
Employment profile White collar, 55%. Blue collar, 30%. Service, 15%. Farm, –%.
Ethnic groups Black, 4%. Total foreign stock, 23%. Sweden, 5%; Norway, 4%; Germany, 3%; Canada, 2%; Poland, 1%.

Presidential vote

1976	Carter (D)	134,503	(64%)
	Ford (R)	76,940	(36%)
1972	Nixon (R)	92,951	(44%)
	McGovern (D)	116,090	(56%)

Rep. Martin Olav Sabo (DFL) Elected 1978; b. Feb. 28, 1938, Crosby, N.D.; home, Minneapolis; Augsburg Col., B.A. 1959, U. of Minn., Lutheran.

Career Minn. House of Reps., 1961–78, Minor. Ldr., 1969–73, Speaker, 1973–78.

Offices 426 CHOB, 202-225-4755. Also Rm. 166, 110 S. 4th St., Minneapolis 55401, 612-725-2081.

Committees *Appropriations* (34th). Subcommittees: HUD-Independent Agencies; Transportation.

Group Ratings: Newly Elected

Key Votes: Newly Elected

Election Results

1978 general	Martin Olav Sabo (DFL)	91,673	(62%)	($84,652)
	Michael Till (I-R)	55,412	(38%)	($129,487)
1978 primary	Martin Olav Sabo (DFL)	47,515	(81%)	
	Two others (DFL)	11,010	(19%)	
1976 general	Donald M. Fraser (DFL)	138,213	(73%)	($71,128)
	Richard M. Erdall (I-R)	50,764	(27%)	($11,630)

SIXTH DISTRICT

The 6th congressional district of Minnesota is farm country, the beginnings of the great wheat fields that sweep across Minnesota into the Dakotas and Montana. Long freight trains move through the landscape, on tracks first laid out by empire builders like James J. Hill of the Great Northern Railway. The groaning diesels pull cars west to the Pacific or east to St. Paul or Chicago; engines and cars whiz through dozens of little crossroads towns, each with its grain elevator and antique depot. The voting patterns of the 6th—long Minnesota's most marginal district—reflect the ethnic groups Hill and other railroad barons attracted to this part of Minnesota: Republican Norwegians and Yankees, Democratic-Farmer-Labor Swedes, ticket-splitting German Catholics.

The German population here is most heavily concentrated in Stearns County, which contains St. Cloud, the largest town in the district, and Sauk Centre, the boyhood home of Sinclair Lewis and the setting for his novel *Main Street*. Until the outbreak of World War I, the Germans who settled here and elsewhere were regarded as the "best" of the nation's immigrants: thrifty and hard-working, just like the old Yankee stock. But when the United States went to war with the Kaiser, these German-Americans found themselves the target of national hatred. The teaching of German was prohibited in many states; sauerkraut became liberty cabbage; the heritage which so many German-Americans had worked hard to protect was suddenly considered subversive.

Not surprisingly, people here were very much against the idea of going to war against Germany in 1917, and twenty years later they again dreaded such a war. This was the part of Minnesota which sent the progressive, antiwar Charles A. Lindbergh, Sr., to Congress during the First World War, and which produced his son, the aviator who became one of the most popular leaders in the fight to keep the United States out of the Second. As Samuel Lubell has pointed out, Stearns County and places like it were the heart of isolationist sentiment in this country, switching wildly from one party to the other in an effort to prevent future wars against Germany or to avenge past ones.

Stearns County continues to play an important role in 6th district elections, although its German heritage is probably less important today than its Catholic religion. Contests in this district have been close: with one exception, no winning candidate has had more than 56% of the vote since 1962. Republican John Zwach, a veteran state legislator, held the seat for eight years, but with Stearns turning against him he was nearly beaten by 28-year-old Rick Nolan in 1972. Nolan kept campaigning and Zwach retired; the Democrat won the seat with 55% in 1974. With two years of incumbency and a seat on the Agriculture Committee, Nolan won reelection with an unusual 60% in 1976. Despite identifying himself closely with farmers' complaints and the family farmer generally, Nolan saw his percentage reduced in 1978 to 55%. This was not so much a result of the Republican trend in the state—that probably cost him only 2%—as it was his Republican opponent's strength in his home county and in Stearns, which is just next door. Nolan's percentage stayed high in the farming counties, but he actually lost Stearns—not a good sign for his future. If the Republicans can sustain their Minnesota surge into 1980, they may very well seriously contest this seat.

Census Data Pop. 476,748. Central city, 0%; suburban, 6%. Median family income, $7,984; families above $15,000: 12%; families below $3,000: 13%. Median years education, 11.5.

The Voters

Median voting age 46.
Employment profile White collar, 38%. Blue collar, 30%. Service, 13%. Farm, 29%.
Ethnic groups Total foreign stock, 18%. Germany, 6%; Norway, Sweden, 3% each.

Presidential vote

1976	Carter (D)	140,420	(57%)
	Ford (R)	104,667	(43%)
1972	Nixon (R)	114,196	(53%)
	McGovern (D)	102,231	(47%)

Rep. Richard Nolan (DFL) Elected 1974; b. Dec. 17, 1943, Brainerd; home, Waite Park; St. John's U., U. of Minn., B.A. 1962, U. of Md., 1967.

Career Laborer, United Parcel Svc., 1964–66; Staff Asst. to U.S. Sen. Walter F. Mondale, 1966–68; Educ. Dir. of Headstart in 3 Minn. Counties, 1968; Curriculum Coord., Adult Basic Educ., Little Falls School Dist., 1968; Teacher, 1968–69; Minn. House of Reps., 1968–72; Fed.-State Coord., Minn. House of Reps., 1973; Admin. Asst. to the Senior V.P. of Fingerhut Corp., 1973–74.

Offices 214 CHOB, 202-225-2331. Also Fed. Bldg., Redwood Falls 56283, 507-637-3565.

Committees *Agriculture* (10th). Subcommittees: Livestock and Grains; Forests; Domestic Marketing, Consumer Relations, and Nutrition; Family Farms, Rural Development, and Special Studies (Chairman).

Small Business (15th). Subcommittees: SBA and SBIC Authority and General Small Business Problems.

Group Ratings

	ADA	COPE	PC	RPN	NFU	LCV	CFA	NAB	NSI	ACA	NTU
1978	80	100	78	27	100	–	64	0	0	4	–
1977	95	91	80	46	82	87	70	–	–	0	24
1976	90	87	92	47	92	89	100	0	10	7	38

Key Votes

1) Increase Def Spnd	AGN	6) Alaska Lands Protect	FOR	11) Delay Auto Pol Cntrl	AGN
2) B-1 Bomber	AGN	7) Water Projects Veto	FOR	12) Sugar Price Escalator	FOR
3) Cargo Preference	FOR	8) Consum Protect Agcy	FOR	13) Pub Fin Cong Cmpgns	FOR
4) Dereg Nat Gas	AGN	9) Common Situs Picket	FOR	14) ERA Ratif Recissn	AGN
5) Kemp-Roth	AGN	10) Labor Law Revision	FOR	15) Prohibt Govt Abrtns	AGN

Election Results

1978 general	Richard Nolan (DFL)	115,880	(55%)	($212,542)
	Russ Bjorhus (I-R)	93,742	(45%)	($138,982)
1978 primary	Richard Nolan (DFL), unopposed			
1976 general	Richard Nolan (DFL)	147,507	(60%)	($189,558)
	James Anderson (I-R)	99,201	(40%)	($110,895)

SEVENTH DISTRICT

The 7th congressional district of Minnesota occupies the northwest quadrant of the state. This is the most sparsely populated part of Minnesota, with 32% of the state's land area but only 12% of its people. Along the Red River of the North, just next to North Dakota, are miles of wheat fields; to the east are acres of lakes, forests, and occasional resort communities. This is the country of the legendary Paul Bunyan and his blue ox Babe, whose statues stand together in Bemidji, a small town on the shores of one of Minnesota's 10,000 lakes. Not far away is Lake Itasca, the headwater of the Mississippi River.

This district was settled by hardy Swedish and Norwegian lumberjacks and farmers. The Republican stronghold is heavily Norwegian Otter Tail County, near the southern end of the district; the strongest DFL territory is in the north, in counties which provided solid support to the old Farmer-Labor Party in the thirties.

The 7th has had a rather colorful political history. It made national headlines in 1958 when Coya Knutson was the DFL Congresswoman here; her husband Andy issued a plaintive statement urging her to come home and, among other things, make his breakfast again. Apparently many voters did not consider the request unreasonable; Knutson was the only Democratic incumbent to lose in the heavily Democratic year of 1958. The man who beat her, an ultraconservative Republican, never demonstrated much popularity, and was finally beaten by DFL candidate Bob Bergland in 1970. Bergland became extremely popular in the district, and made enough of a mark on the Agriculture Committee to be appointed Secretary of Agriculture by President Carter.

That appointment caused a vacancy in the district which was filled, to many people's surprise, by a Republican. It was the Republican Party's first chance nationally to go on the offensive after losing the presidency and the Congress, and they poured in national money and talent. They also selected a better candidate. The DFL nominated a former Bergland and Mondale aide, Mike Sullivan. The Republican candidate, Arlan Stangeland, was a genuine farmer and of Scandinavian descent as well. The result was a smashing Stangeland victory.

Stangeland still declines to attack Bergland's record as Secretary—a clear indication that Bergland remains popular in the district. But the records of the two men on most issues could hardly be more different. Bergland had ratings near 100% from labor and liberal groups; Stangeland has ratings near 100% from business and conservative groups. Despite the Republican tide in Minnesota in 1978, the DFL made a major attempt to recover this seat and, considering the advantages of incumbency, did better than such attempts usually do. This time they ran a young state legislator who is also a farmer, with roots in the southern, more Republican part of the district. He carried several counties and held Stangeland to 54% of the vote. That is the kind of margin which attracts serious competition in future elections, and this cannot be considered a safe seat for anyone.

Census Data Pop. 472,753. Central city, 6%; suburban, 4%. Median family income, $7,089; families above $15,000: 10%; families below $3,000: 17%. Median years education, 10.9.

The Voters

Median voting age 48.
Employment profile White collar, 39%. Blue collar, 28%. Service, 15%. Farm, 18%.
Ethnic groups Total foreign stock, 21%. Norway, 7%; Germany, Sweden, 4% each; Canada, 2%.

Presidential vote

1976	Carter (D)	135,192	(57%)
	Ford (R)	102,502	(43%)
1972	Nixon (R)	118,727	(54%)
	McGovern (D)	100,410	(46%)

Rep. Arlan Stangeland (R) Elected Feb. 22, 1977; b. Feb. 8, 1930, Fargo, N. Dak.; home Barnesville; Lutheran.

Career Farmer; Minn. House of Reps., 1966–74.

Offices 1518 LHOB, 202-225-2165. Also 403 Center Ave., Moorhead 56560, 218-233-8631.

Committees *Government Operations* (8th). Subcommittees: Environment, Energy, and Natural Resources; Legislation and National Security.

Public Works and Transportation (11th). Subcommittees: Oversight and Review; Public Buildings and Grounds; Surface Transportation.

Group Ratings

	ADA	COPE	PC	RPN	NFU	LCV	CFA	NAB	NSI	ACA	NTU
1978	5	0	3	55	30	–	9	91	100	91	–
1977	0	17	20	58	42	2	20	–	–	88	42

Key Votes

1) Increase Def Spnd	FOR	6) Alaska Lands Protect	AGN	11) Delay Auto Pol Cntrl	DNV
2) B-1 Bomber	FOR	7) Water Projects Veto	AGN	12) Sugar Price Escalator	FOR
3) Cargo Preference	AGN	8) Consum Protect Agcy	AGN	13) Pub Fin Cong Cmpgns	AGN
4) Dereg Nat Gas	FOR	9) Common Situs Picket	AGN	14) ERA Ratif Recissn	FOR
5) Kemp-Roth	FOR	10) Labor Law Revision	AGN	15) Prohibt Govt Abrtns	FOR

Election Results

1978 general	Arlan Stangeland (I-R)	109,456	(54%)	($192,034)
	Gene Wenstrom (DFL)	93,055	(46%)	($112,549)
1978 primary	Arlan Stangeland (I-R)	32,470	(97%)	
	One other (I-R)	1,140	(3%)	
1977 special	Arlan Stangeland (I-R)	71,340	(61%)	
	Mike Sulivan (DFL)	45,490	(39%)	
1977 primary	Arlan Stangeland (I-R)	15,382	(97%)	
	One other (I-R)	524	(3%)	
1976 general	Bob Bergland (DFL)	174,080	(73%)	($92,793)
	Bob Leiseth (I-R)	64,333	(27%)	($14,075)

EIGHTH DISTRICT

The 8th congressional district of Minnesota is the northeast corner of the state. Like the 7th, most of the acreage here consists of lakes and forests. But the 8th has far fewer farmers, and most of its population is concentrated in a few essentially urban areas. Because of redistricting, the 8th now reaches down to Anoka County—blue collar, Democratic suburbs of Minneapolis and St. Paul. But the focus of the district—and most of its population—is St. Louis County, in the Lake Superior port of Duluth, which contains almost exactly 100,000 people as it has for 50 years, and the towns of the Mesabi Range. This part of Minnesota has long been the source of most of the nation's iron ore, which is scooped out of the low lying hills of the Mesabi, transported by rail to Duluth, loaded on giant freighters, and shipped to Chicago, Gary, Detroit, Cleveland, and Pittsburgh.

Life has not been gentle here. The entrepreneurs who first began the iron ore operations, around the turn of the century, had little respect for the land, digging it up here and putting a factory or loading dock there, and depositing the waste products of their works wherever they liked. Financial power has always been in the hands of men like these, and the wintry climate brings snow as many as eleven months a year. The men who came to work the Mesabi mines and the Duluth docks were mostly immigrants from Sweden, Finland, Norway, Italy, Poland, and Yugoslavia; they brought with them few illusions. From the beginning they have assumed that just as the Republican Party represents the mine owners, so the Democratic-Farmer-Labor Party represents them, and they have voted accordingly.

This is a politics of perceived self-interest, on both sides; there is little idle contemplation of the environment up here. Several years ago most Minnesotans wanted to stop Armco and Republic Steel from dumping taconite tailings with dangerous asbestos-like fibers into Lake Superior. But the companies said that if ordered to stop they would shut down the plant, and the people in Silver Bay urged that the dumping be continued. More recently there was a controversy over a proposed Boundary Waters Canoe Area park in the northern lakes. The legislation proposed by Minneapolis Congressman Donald Fraser would prohibit motor boats, on the ground that the lakes should be kept pristine; people up here were almost unanimously against it because they were afraid they would lose jobs. In the 1978 DFL Senate primary, candidate Bob Short beat Fraser by huge margins in the 8th district—enough to make the difference in the close statewide contest. Feeling on this issue—and DFL party loyalty—were strong enough that Short carried the 8th district even while he was losing statewide by the biggest margin in DFL history.

The Congressman from this district, Democrat James Oberstar, seems to reflect district opinion closely. He has very high ratings from labor and liberal organizations and a strong Democratic Party support score. But he also stood up strongly against prohibiting motor boats in the Boundary Waters Area. He used to be an aide to John Blatnik, who represented the district for 28 years until his retirement in 1974 and was Chairman of the House Public Works Committee. Oberstar won the seat in an unusual manner for Minnesota. He challenged the DFL convention winner, Tony Perpich (brother of then Lieutenant Governor and later Governor Rudy Perpich) as well as state Senator Florian Chmielewski—names which suggest the ethnic origins of the district. With a big campaign budget, Oberstar won that primary; he has won easily ever since. In the House he sits on the Public Works and Merchant Marine Committees—the kind of prosaic assignments that can mean bread and butter to the 8th district.

Census Data Pop. 479,159. Central city, 21%; suburban, 46%. Median family income, $9,393; families above $15,000: 14%; families below $3,000: 9%. Median years education, 12.1.

The Voters

Median voting age 44.
Employment profile White collar, 41%. Blue collar, 42%. Service, 14%. Farm, 3%.
Ethnic groups Total foreign stock, 24%. Sweden, 5%; Finland, 4%; Norway, 3%; Canada, Germany, 2% each.

Presidential vote

1976	Carter (D)	161,172	(66%)
	Ford (R)	83,325	(34%)
1972	Nixon (R)	95,536	(45%)
	McGovern (D)	115,622	(55%)

Rep. James L. Oberstar (DFL) Elected 1974; b. Sept. 10, 1934, Chisholm; home, Chisholm; Col. of St. Thomas, B.A. 1956, Col. of Europe, Bruges, Belgium, M.A. 1957.

Career Admin. Asst. to U.S. Rep. John A. Blatnik, 1965–74; Administrator, U.S. House of Reps. Comm. on Public Works, 1971–74.

Offices 323 CHOB, 202-225-6211. Also 231 Fed. Bldg., Duluth 55802, 218-727-7474.

Committees *Merchant Marine and Fisheries* (15th). Subcommittees: Coast Guard and Navigation; Fish and Wildlife.

Public Works and Transportation (10th). Subcommittees: Economic Development; Oversight and Review; Water Resources.

Group Ratings

	ADA	COPE	PC	RPN	NFU	LCV	CFA	NAB	NSI	ACA	NTU
1978	70	85	70	25	100	–	68	0	10	7	–
1977	85	96	90	31	83	45	80	–	–	4	32
1976	90	87	92	39	100	74	100	0	10	0	28

Key Votes

1) Increase Def Spnd	AGN	6) Alaska Lands Protect	AGN	11) Delay Auto Pol Cntrl	FOR
2) B-1 Bomber	AGN	7) Water Projects Veto	AGN	12) Sugar Price Escalator	FOR
3) Cargo Preference	FOR	8) Consum Protect Agcy	FOR	13) Pub Fin Cong Cmpgns	FOR
4) Dereg Nat Gas	AGN	9) Common Situs Picket	FOR	14) ERA Ratif Recissn	FOR
5) Kemp-Roth	AGN	10) Labor Law Revision	FOR	15) Prohibt Govt Abrtns	FOR

Election Results

1978 general	James L. Oberstar (DFL)	171,125	(87%)	($64,117)
	John W. Hull (Am.)	25,015	(13%)	
1978 primary	James L. Oberstar (DFL), unopposed			
1976 general	James L. Oberstar (DFL), unopposed			($33,795)

MISSISSIPPI

Mississippi was initially settled in the early 1800s by two different types of white people. Some were land-hungry Jacksonians who poured in from Tennessee and Alabama after the Choctaws and Chickasaws had been driven out of Mississippi. The Jacksonians were ambitious folk, but most became small farmers who owned perhaps a few slaves. Their descendants still people the hillier eastern section of the state. The other immigrants, who had arrived slightly earlier, were the more famous big planters. King Cotton brought the planters and their slaves, upon whom the economy was totally dependent, to the virgin land here. In the flush times that followed, abolitionists charged that Virginia had become a giant slave breeding ground for what was then called the Southwest frontier. The big planters and their property, the slaves, settled primarily in the lower, flatter lands along the Mississippi, in the southern part of the state. The Delta—the northwest edge of Mississippi between the Mississippi and Yazoo Rivers—was not settled heavily till after the Civil War. Its land was too low and swampy, too often flooded by its many rivers to be useful until after levees and flood control dams were built. Once in production, the alluvial land of the Delta proved to be extremely fertile.

At the time of the Civil War, Mississippi had a larger proportion of blacks than any other state, and it still does. As recently as 1940, 49% of the people here were black; in 1970 that figure had dropped to a still high 37%. Note, however, that even if all Mississippi blacks voted, their share of the electorate would still be smaller, for more of them are under 18 than whites.

In any case, the presence of a large number of blacks has shaped Mississippi's history and politics. So has the fact that this state has little of the moderating influence of a large metropolis or of large business firms. Even today, Jackson, the state's capital and by far its largest city, has less than 200,000 people and no substantial suburbs. Economically, Mississippi is just emerging from the status of a colony of the cotton exchanges and banks of Memphis and New Orleans; this is still the poorest state in the union. But if Mississippi's poverty and lack of big business domination left it with little to lose by stubborn and violent resistance to integration, it also leaves it free of the kind of domination by economic interests which is so much a factor in Southern states as diverse as Texas and the Carolinas.

There are two basic themes, two underlying conflicts, that run through all of Mississippi's politics: the conflict between black and white and the conflict between the rich (the big planters, the country club set) and the poor (the small farmers, the textile and paper pulp mill workers). For years there was a consensus in Mississippi politics: the white man must remain indubitably supreme; blacks could not mix in any way with whites, and could possess no political rights whatever. Conflict sometimes became apparent between the economic groups, but when it came to race issues, the quiet aristocrat was beaten by the boisterous upcountry orator. Thus we had Senator Theodore Bilbo, who liked to compare blacks with monkeys, and Ross Barnett, the buffoonish Governor who served when the University of Mississippi was integrated by federal troops in 1963.

During the past decade and a half Mississippi politics has been altered vastly by changes in the racial customs and economic conditions of the state. Racial change is epitomized in the Voting Rights Act of 1965. Before that law was passed, very few blacks voted in Mississippi; it was during a campaign to register blacks that three civil rights workers were murdered in Neshoba County in 1964. Blacks knew that they faced physical reprisals and economic sanctions if they voted; even today black voter participation is significantly lower here than in any other Southern state.

Black participation has tended to erode the unanimity with which Mississippi voters had faced the outside world, and has helped to create a politics where differences on other issues can be resolved on their merits rather than on the vehemence with which different candidates denounced the blacks and integration. For examples of Mississippi's past unanimity all you have to do is to look at the presidential returns. Despite its Democratic heritage, Mississippi cast 87% of its votes for Barry Goldwater in 1964, when virtually no blacks could vote. Four years later, when some blacks were voting, Mississippi was 63% for George Wallace. It was 80% for Richard Nixon in 1972. In no other state did white voters show such solidarity against whatever candidate was supported by most blacks.

But that was not the case in 1976. With Jimmy Carter on the national ticket, white Mississippians failed to respond unanimously, as they had done in every presidential election since 1960. Statewide Carter had a 51% victory. Of course he had overwhelming support from blacks, without whom he would not have won, but he also had the support of a substantial percentage of whites. What is more significant is where the votes came from. Gerald Ford carried relatively few counties, but he got big majorities in urban areas: in Jackson and its suburbs, in small cities like Meridian and Vicksburg and Hattiesburg, in the Biloxi-Gulfport-Pascagoula urban strip on the Gulf of Mexico. Carter carried the eastern hill counties, with their poor white farmers, and the rural Missisipi River counties, with their black majorities.

This represented a clear split along economic lines and illustrated the economic progress Mississippi has made in recent years. Mississippi's cities are growing rapidly, pulsing with economic vitality—part of the vigorous Sun Belt, no longer unreconstructed. And while we think of cities as being filled with poor people and blue collar workers, the kind of economic growth Mississippi is seeking has made its cities increasingly the home of the white collar, the professional and executive and entrepreneur, the upwardly mobile. These are people who are making far more money than they ever imagined, and they appreciate, as sixth generation Ivy League heirs do not, the capitalist system. When conversation turns to politics in antebellum reproduction living rooms or in the country club dining room, they talk of saving the free enterprise system from the bureaucrats and Eastern intellectuals who seem to want to tax everyone into poverty. Their politics is not one of racism, although they tend to oppose civil rights measures; nor is it one of hostility to blue collar workers, for they think free market policies would be better for them, too. This is a classic example of the politics of the new rich; and if the incomes of people in Jackson do not appear, by national standards, very high, they look very good from the perspective of people brought up in the rural South of the thirties and forties.

This kind of conservative politics commands majorities in the upwardly mobile cities; it has fewer adherents in the small towns and rural areas. It is personified by former Mississippi Republican Chairman Clarke Reed, an urbane man who would look at home in any country club in America, and who for ten years was a major force for conservatism in the Republican Party. Recent elections for president, senator, and governor show that Reed's kind of voter amounts to about 40% of the statewide electorate. These are not the old plantation rich, but do represent a clear case of affluent domination, for the blocs of less affluent whites and of blacks amount to only about 30% each.

Those numbers are indeed very close to the results of the 1978 election for U.S. senator—a contest which made national headlines when the state elected its first Republican senator since Reconstruction. He is Thad Cochran, for six years Congressman from Jackson, and in his personal demeanor as well as policy attitudes an excellent representative of the upwardly mobile, affluent voters of Mississippi's cities. He won the election with 45%, with the opposition split—just as he first won his congressional seat with less than a majority. His majorities came primarily from the cities, of which he carried every one. Cochran's Democratic opponent, Maurice Dantin, chosen after an arduous primary and runoff in which he defeated Governor Cliff Finch, carried the eastern hill counties and various rural counties with small black percentages, as well as his home area in the southern part of the state. His total was 32% of the vote. The remaining 23% went to Charles Evers, brother of the slain civil rights leader and mayor of a black-majority hamlet, who carried most of the black vote.

The national press was fascinated by Evers's platform: he was against busing, for cracking down on welfare cheats, against the Panama Canal Treaty. He had backing from businessmen and oil millionaires. This is far different from the issue stances of most northern black politicians, but it was close indeed to the platforms of Cochran and Dantin. In this race there seems to have been little difference on substantive matters among the candidates, with the voters apparently choosing the candidate who came closest to the sociological style they preferred.

Cochran is an engaging, articulate man with a soft-spoken manner and soft drawl reminiscent of Howard Baker. His record in the House was such as to give him very high ratings from conservative and business groups and very low ratings from liberal organizations. He favors market incentives and deregulation of natural gas (Mississippi is a significant oil producer), and he almost always comes out on the side of high defense spending. But he is not likely to be a darling of the New Right. He does not burn with their fervor, and he tends to reach his positions only after some thought. He serves on the Agriculture and Judiciary Committees. In his congressional district Cochran, once elected, was able to win the support of many blacks and won reelection by overwhelming margins, even though his initial election was won with less than an absolute majority. His even-handed manner and evident braininess give him a good chance to do the same statewido.

Mississippi's 1975 gubernatorial race was decided by an electorate divided in the same manner as in 1978, but with an opposite result—because there was no significant independent black candidate. That year the Democratic primary was won by Cliff Finch, a successful country attorney who symbolized his closeness to the people by working at dozens of different jobs; he beat the favorite, William Winter, the Lieutenant Governor who had earned a reputation for racial moderation. The Republican candidate was Gil Carmichael, moderate enough that he backed Gerald Ford over Ronald Reagan without hesitation the next year. Based in Meridian, Carmichael ran a campaign with great appeal in the upwardly mobile areas and got nearly 50%. But Finch was able to win with a coalition of rural whites and blacks—the same coalition that would carry Mississippi for Jimmy Carter a year later.

Finch has not been an entirely successful governor; his bid for a Senate nomination was crushed by a 2–1 margin in the 1978 Democratic runoff. He is in any case ineligible for a second consecutive term. As this is written, the state is preparing for the 1979 gubernatorial election. The initial leaders in the Democratic primary are William Winter and Lieutenant Governor Evelyn Gandy. It is not known whether Evers or another well-known black will run as an Independent; the Republicans will likely nominate Carmichael again. Given the relatively even three-way balance between the three major blocs in Mississippi's electorate, the outcome clearly cannot be predicted.

For 31 years Mississippi had the same two senators, James Eastland and John Stennis, both solidly conservative, both extremely powerful committee chairmen for many years—Eastland of Judiciary from 1955 to 1979 and Stennis of Armed Services from 1969. Eastland will be remembered as the Senate's most implacable and, for a while, most powerful opponent of civil rights; though toward the end, before he decided to retire, he had hired blacks on his staff and was making overtures to black political leaders. He would have had a tough race in 1978, and as soon as one formidable opponent entered, he withdrew.

John Stennis has never had such political problems. In 1976 he was reelected at the age of 75 without significant opposition. That may have resulted partially from the fact that he was shot in Washington in 1973 by a burglar; his valiant recovery increased people's natural sympathy for him. For while Eastland was uncommunicative, Stennis has always seemed a model of sincere concern and devotion to duty. For years he has had a reputation for uprightness and probity. As Chairman of Armed Services, he has always backed a strong defense, remembering this nation's unpreparedness for World War II. He supported the Vietnam war not so much out of enthusiasm for the cause as from a feeling that the Congress must support the flag wherever it is planted. He has been rather skeptical about the proposed SALT Treaty; but the role of informed advocate of high defense spending and skeptic about disarmament has come to be assumed by Sam Nunn of Georgia, a young senator Stennis greatly admires.

Stennis has suffered some rebuffs in recent years. The creation of new committees to oversee the intelligence agencies reflects on him, for he used to chair the Armed Services subcommittee that had that responsibility. He has said that he believed in subjecting the agencies to minimal inspection, while the Senate in the past few years has taken a different view. He has strongly backed the Tennessee-Tombigbee waterway, a barge channel that would connect northern Mississippi directly with the Gulf of Mexico; that too has been subjected to critical scrutiny. Stennis is still respected, but his wishes are not always honored. Back in Mississippi he is also still respected, but this is probably his last term. His son's weak showing in the 4th district House race in 1978 was not a good omen, and he will be 81 when his seat is up in 1982. There will likely be a fiercely contested race to succeed him—and one which is entirely unpredictable at this time.

Mississippi once had one of the House's most senior delegations. Today only one of its five congressmen has great seniority: Jamie Whitten, Chairman of the House Appropriations Committee. But his power is not what it would have been even six years ago, for he holds his chair at the sufferance of the House Democratic Caucus, a majority of which is not going to let him go too far in promoting the traditional Mississippi view of things.

Census Data Pop. 2,216,912; 1.10% of U.S. total, 29th largest; Central city, 11%; suburban, 7%. Median family income, $6,068; 50th highest; families above $15,000: 8%; families below $3,000: 25%. Median years education, 10.7.

1977 Share of Federal Tax Burden $2,349,000,000; 0.68% of U.S. total, 35th largest.

1977 Share of Federal Outlays $4,047,501,000; 1.02% of U.S. total, 31st largest. Per capita federal spending, $1,725.

DOD	$1,073,014,000	27th (1.17%)	HEW	$1,556,791,000	29th (1.05%)
ERDA	$1,024,000	46th (0.02%)	HUD	$49,126,000	28th (1.16%)
NASA	$30,197,000	17th (0.77%)	VA	$228,067,000	31st (1.19%)
DOT	$128,219,000	32d (0.90%)	EPA	$27,952,000	38th (0.34%)
DOC	$61,541,000	31st (0.74%)	RevS	$113,503,000	25th (1.34%)
DOI	$40,926,000	28th (0.88%)	Debt	$121,327,000	29th (0.40%)
USDA	$323,370,000	28th (1.63%)	Other	$292,444,000	

Economic Base Agriculture, notably cattle, cotton lint, soybeans and broilers; apparel and other textile products, especially men's and boys' furnishings; finance, insurance and real estate; lumber and wood products, especially sawmills and planing mills; transportation equipment, especially motor vehicles and equipment and ship building and repairing; food and kindred products.

Political Line-up Governor, Cliff Finch (D). Senators, John C. Stennis (D) and Thad Cochran (R). Representatives 5 (3 D and 2 R). State Senate (50 D, 1 R, and 1 Ind.); State House (145 D, 1 R, and 6 Ind.).

The Voters

Registration 1,200,000 Estimated Total. No party registration.
Median voting age 43
Employment profile White collar, 39%. Blue collar, 41%. Service, 14%. Farm, 6%.
Ethnic groups Black, 37%. Total foreign stock, 1%.

Presidential vote

1976	Carter (D)	381,329	(51%)
	Ford (R)	366,846	(49%)
1972	Nixon (R)	505,125	(80%)
	McGovern (D)	126,782	(20%)

Sen. John C. Stennis (D) Elected Nov. 4, 1947, seat up 1982; b. Aug. 3, 1901, Kemper County; home, De Kalb; Miss. St. U., B.S. 1923, U. of Va., LL.B. 1928; Presbyterian.

Career Miss. House of Reps., 1928–32; Dist. Prosecuting Atty., 16th Judicial Dist., 1931–37; Circuit Judge, 1937–47.

Offices 205 RSOB, 202-224-6253. Also 303 P.O. Bldg., Jackson 39205, 601-353-5494.

Committees *Appropriations* (2d). Subcommittees: Agriculture and Related Agencies; Defense (Chairman); Energy and Water Development; HUD-Independent Agencies; Transportation and Related Agencies.

Armed Services (Chairman).

Group Ratings

	ADA	COPE	PC	RPN	NFU	LCV	CFA	NAB	NSI	ACA	NTU
1978	10	6	28	50	50	23	10	73	80	73	–
1977	5	6	18	38	50	–	20	–	–	78	35
1976	0	28	1	23	37	5	14	78	100	81	50

Key Votes

1) Warnke Nom	AGN	6) Egypt-Saudi Arms	FOR	11) Hosptl Cost Contnmnt	AGN
2) Neutron Bomb	FOR	7) Draft Restr Pardon	AGN	12) Clinch River Reactor	FOR
3) Waterwy User Fee	AGN	8) Wheat Price Support	FOR	13) Pub Fin Cong Cmpgns	AGN
4) Dereg Nat Gas	FOR	9) Panama Canal Treaty	AGN	14) ERA Ratif Recissn	AGN
5) Kemp-Roth	AGN	10) Labor Law Rev Clot	AGN	15) Med Necssy Abrtns	AGN

Election Results

1976 general	John C. Stennis (D), unopposed			($119,852)
1976 primary	John C. Stennis (D)	157,943	(85%)	
	E. Michael Marks (D)	27,016	(15%)	
1970 general	John C. Stennis (D)	286,622	(88%)	
	William R. Thompson (Ind.)	37,593	(12%)	

Sen. Thad Cochran (R) Elected 1978, seat up 1984; b. Dec. 7, 1937, Pontotoc; home, Jackson; U. of Miss., B.A. 1959, J.D. 1965, Rotary Fellow, Trinity Col., Dublin, Ireland, 1963–64; Baptist.

Career Navy, 1959–61; Practicing atty., 1965–72; U.S. House of Reps., 1973–78.

Offices 442 RSOB, 202-224-5054. Also Rm. 316 Fed. Bldg., Jackson 39205, 601-969-1353.

Committees *Agriculture, Nutrition, and Forestry* (6th). Subcommittees: Environment, Soil Conservation, and Forestry; Agricultural Production, Marketing, and Stabilization of Prices; Foreign Agricultural Policy.

Judiciary (6th). Subcommittees: Administrative Practice and Procedure; Criminal Justice; Limitations of Contracted and Delegated Authority.

Group Ratings

Group Ratings: Newly Elected

	ADA	COPE	PC	RPN	NFU	LCV	CFA	NAB	NSI	ACA	NTU
1978	0	7	13	63	25	–	18	100	100	83	–
1977	0	18	13	54	50	0	10	–	–	74	37
1976	5	35	10	59	50	12	18	50	100	77	44

Key Votes

1) Increase Def Spnd	FOR	6) Alaska Lands Protect	DNV	11) Delay Auto Pol Cntrl	FOR
2) B-1 Bomber	FOR	7) Water Projects Veto	AGN	12) Sugar Price Escalator	DNV
3) Cargo Preference	AGN	8) Consum Protect Agcy	AGN	13) Pub Fin Cong Cmpgns	FOR
4) Dereg Nat Gas	FOR	9) Common Situs Picket	AGN	14) ERA Ratif Recissn	FOR
5) Kemp-Roth	FOR	10) Labor Law Revision	AGN	15) Prohibt Govt Abrtns	FOR

Election Results

1978 general	Thad Cochran (R)	263,089	(45%)	($1,052,303)
	Maurice Danton (D)	185,454	(32%)	($873,518)
	Charles Evers (I)	133,646	(23%)	($135,119)
1978 primary	Thad Cochran (R)	50,857	(69%)	
	Charles Pickering (R)	22,880	(31%)	($187,565)
1972 general	James O. Eastland (D)	375,102	(60%)	($410,221)
	Gil Charmichael (R)	249,779	(40%)	($154,913)

Gov. Cliff Finch (D) Elected 1975, term expires Jan. 1980; b. April 4, 1927, Pope; U. of Miss., B.A., LL.B., 1958; Baptist.

Career Army, WWII; Practicing atty., 1958–64, 1972–75; Miss. House of Reps., 1960–64; Dist. Atty., 17th Circuit Court Dist., 1964–72.

Offices The Capitol, Jackson 39205, 601-354-7575.

Election Results

1975 general	Cliff Finch (D)	369,568	(54%)
	Gil Carmichael (R)	319,632	(46%)
1975 runoff	Cliff Finch (D)	442,864	(58%)
	William Winter (D)	324,749	(42%)

1975 primary	William Winter (D)	286,652	(36%)
	Cliff Finch (D)	253,829	(32%)
	Maurice Dantin (D)	179,472	(23%)
	Three others (D)		
	69,941 (9%)		
1971 general	William Waller (D)	601,122	(78%)
	Charles Evers (Ind.)	172,762	(22%)

FIRST DISTRICT

The 1st congressional district of Mississippi occupies the northernmost section of the state. The district spans the gamut of Mississippi's terrain, from the cotton-rich Delta along the Mississippi River to Tishomingo County on the Tennessee River in the state's northeastern corner. The black majorities in some of the Delta counties have been politically active—and in some cases successful—for several years. As one moves east into the hill territory, there are fewer and fewer blacks; instead, one finds poor white farmers whose families have been working the hardscrabble land for more than a century without much luck. In the middle of the district is Oxford, site of Ole Miss and of the racial disorders accompanying the university's integration in 1962. Oxford was also the lifelong home of William Faulkner.

The district boundaries were drawn by a legislature which wanted to make sure that no Mississippi seat would ever have a black majority. When racial divisions dominated the politics of the state, the two sides of the 1st were fundamentally opposed. More recently, they have found common cause. This is one of the least urbanized parts of Mississippi, and the rural blacks and rural whites have tended to support Democrats like Jimmy Carter and Governor Cliff Finch.

The Congressman from this district, first elected a month before Pearl Harbor, is Jamie Whitten. As a Mississippi Democrat, he has always voted for white supremacy and has advanced steadily in seniority. Since 1949 (except for 1953–55 when Republicans had control) he has chaired the Agriculture Subcommittee of the Appropriations Committee. This has made him a kind of permanent secretary of agriculture; the top bureaucrats in the department have long known that Whitten will outlast their titular boss. Whitten has not been afraid to use his influence in departmental affairs. He was a strong force for large subsidy payments to cotton farmers; for years the cotton program has been the most costly of any of Agriculture's crop subsidies. He has backed strongly attempts to increase production and kill vermin with pesticides and been entirely unsympathetic to environmental claims that such practices are damaging and self-defeating. Over thirty years Whitten has developed a network of friends in the state agriculture departments and among county agriculture agents all over the country. A Secretary of Agriculture ignores him at his peril.

In 1979 Whitten succeeded to a position of greater power—but one in which he will probably have considerably less latitude. With the retirement of Texas's George Mahon, Whitten had the most seniority of any Appropriations Committee Democrat, and despite the move of some junior members to pass him over in favor of Massachusetts's Edward Boland he carried the Caucus by a 157–88 vote. Some commentators took that as a signal that little had changed despite the four-year-old requirement that chairmen be elected by the Democratic Caucus. But the facts suggest that much indeed has changed. Whitten's victory margin looks lopsided, until one realizes that a shift of only 35 votes would cost him the chair. It would not be hard to persuade 35 conventional northern Democrats to abandon him if there was evidence that he was using the chairmanship to ramrod through programs which the majority of Democrats didn't want or even if members began to feel he was using his power unfairly.

Whitten had the support of Speaker O'Neill and of Boland, the next most senior member, in his fight for the chair; but one must assume that there were some assurances, explicit or otherwise, as to how he would conduct business on the committee. There is evidence in Whitten's voting record that he will be responsive to the majority of Democrats. In 1975, the year after chairmen started to be selected by Caucus vote, Whitten's rating by organized labor jumped from about the 10% level to about the 40% level, where it has remained since. Obviously he is being a little more generous on federal spending issues. As Agriculture Subcommittee Chairman, he has successfully fought back efforts to cut the food stamp program—not exactly a Whitten favorite in the years before

1975. For the coming years, it seems likely that Whitten will honor the decisions of Appropriations subcommittees and of the Budget Committee's targets for spending—in other words, the major decisions will tend to be in line with the majority of Democrats' wishes. He will retain his power and leverage as Chairman of the Agriculture Subcommittee—which after all handles an area of government policy that most Democrats are not much concerned about.

Whitten has had little trouble winning reelection. He beat another incumbent in the primary when their districts were combined in 1962, and when blacks threatened to get a voting majority in the district the boundaries were changed to their present configuration. If the Democratic Caucus has moved his voting record to the left, they have probably done him a favor; the evidence suggests that against Republican opposition, he is getting solid support from blacks as well as majority support from whites. He was elected to the House young, and although he has been there nearly 40 years he only turns 70 in 1980.

Census Data Pop. 433,825. Central city, 0%; suburban, 0%. Median family income, $5,577; families above $15,000: 6%; families below $3,000: 28%. Median years education, 9.7.

The Voters

Median voting age 44.
Employment profile White collar, 34%. Blue collar, 45%. Service, 12%. Farm, 9%.
Ethnic groups Black, 35%.

Presidential vote

1976	Carter (D)	91,615	(62%)
	Ford (R)	56,974	(38%)
1972	Nixon (R)	92,680	(80%)
	McGovern (D)	23,058	(20%)

Rep. Jamie L. Whitten (D) Elected Nov. 4, 1941; b. Apr. 18, 1910, Cascilla; home, Charleston; U. of Miss.; Presbyterian.

Career Practicing atty.; School principal; Miss. House of Reps., 1931; Dist. Prosecuting Atty., 17th Judicial Dist., 1933–41.

Offices 2314 RHOB, 202-225-4306. Also P.O. Bldg., Charleston 38921, 601-647-2413.

Committees *Appropriations* (Chairman). Subcommittees: Agriculture and Related Agencies (Chairman).

Group Ratings

	ADA	COPE	PC	RPN	NFU	LCV	CFA	NAB	NSI	ACA	NTU
1978	20	39	13	73	56	–	18	60	100	55	–
1977	10	43	13	25	67	14	20	–	–	56	23
1976	15	48	18	18	50	22	27	33	100	71	19

Key Votes

1) Increase Def Spnd	FOR	6) Alaska Lands Protect	DNV	11) Delay Auto Pol Cntrl	FOR
2) B-1 Bomber	FOR	7) Water Projects Veto	AGN	12) Sugar Price Escalator	FOR
3) Cargo Preference	AGN	8) Consum Protect Agcy	DNV	13) Pub Fin Cong Cmpgns	AGN
4) Dereg Nat Gas	AGN	9) Common Situs Picket	AGN	14) ERA Ratif Recissn	AGN
5) Kemp-Roth	AGN	10) Labor Law Revision	AGN	15) Prohibt Govt Abrtns	DNV

Election Results

1978 general	Jamie L. Whitten (D)	57,358	(68%)	($87,331)
	T. K. Moffett (R)	26,734	(32%)	($71,620)
1978 primary	Jamie L. Whitten (D)	62,706	(68%)	
	Gerald Chatham (D)	20,666	(22%)	($38,684)
	One other (D)	8,927	(10%)	
1976 general	Jamie L. Whitten (D), unopposed			($1,525)

SECOND DISTRICT

The 2d congressional district of Mississippi, a belt of counties in the north central part of the state, stretches from the Mississippi River to the hill country along the Alabama border. The flat fertile land along the river is the Delta, an area not fully developed until after the Civil War. This was originally swampy land, often flooded, traversed by many rivers which flow into the Mississippi. In the late nineteenth century the land was drained, the great river lined with levees, and the Illinois Central track laid out from Memphis to New Orleans. It was discovered then that the topsoil here, accumulated over centuries of Mississippi spring floods, reached depths of 25 feet. So the Delta wilderness of northern Mississippi, the destruction of which Faulkner laments in some of his stories, became the region of the state's largest and most productive cotton plantations.

That also meant that the Delta came to have Mississippi's largest concentration of blacks. Though slavery had been abolished, most blacks lived in great poverty at the turn of the century; as sharecroppers or tenant farmers they were essentially outside the cash economy. Serving as low wage labor on the cotton plantations seemed no worse than slavery itself. Many Delta counties still have black majorities. The 2d district includes part of the Delta; it also includes part of mostly white eastern Mississippi, and so does not have a black majority.

The incumbent congressman here retired in 1972 after 30 years in office, which lead to a spirited battle. The winner was David Bowen, a graduate of Harvard and Oxford, who was considered something of a moderate by Mississippi standards. Actually, Bowen's voting record has been in line with traditional conservative Mississippi politics, and his legislative interests are not far afield. He serves on the Merchant Marine and Fisheries Committee and is Chairman of the Agriculture Subcommittee on Cotton.

Bowen has had significant challenges in the last two elections from Republican Roland Byrd, who criticized the incumbent, a bachelor who is a regular at Washington embassy parties, for attending a party given by Tongsun Park and for being named bachelor of the month by Cosmopolitan magazine. These criticisms do not seem to have made much impact, and Bowen has won reelection by large margins. A few years ago, there was speculation that he might run for the Senate some day. But the time for that seems to have gone by. He passed up the 1978 Senate race, and his position in the 2d seems to be too comfortable to give up for the risks of a statewide contest.

Census Data Pop. 440,689. Central city, 0%; suburban, 0%. Median family income, $5,446; families above $15,000: 7%; families below $3,000: 29%. Median years education, 9.9.

The Voters

Median voting age 43.
Employment profile White collar, 37%. Blue collar, 39%. Service, 15%. Farm, 9%.
Ethnic groups Black, 46%. Total foreign stock, 1%.

Presidential vote

1976	Carter (D)	69,152	(53%)
	Ford (R)	61,511	(47%)
1972	Nixon (R)	84,346	(77%)
	McGovern (D)	24,633	(23%)

Rep. David R. Bowen (D) Elected 1972; b. Oct. 21, 1932, Houston; home, Cleveland; Harvard U., A.B. 1954, Oxford U., M.A.; Protestant.

Career Asst. Prof., Miss. Col., 1958–59, Millsaps Col., 1959–64; U.S. Ofc. of Econ. Opportunity, 1966–67; U.S. Chamber of Commerce, 1967–68; Miss. Federal-State Coordinator, 1968–72.

Offices 2421 RHOB, 202-225-5876. Also 101 S. Court St., Cleveland 38732, 601-846-1801.

Committees *Agriculture* (7th). Subcommittees: Cotton (Chairman); Oilseeds and Rice.

Merchant Marine and Fisheries (10th). Subcommittees: Fish and Wildlife; Merchant Marine; Panama Canal.

Foreign Affairs (21st). Subcommittees: International Operations; International Organizations.

Group Ratings

	ADA	COPE	PC	RPN	NFU	LCV	CFA	NAB	NSI	ACA	NTU
1978	15	20	10	60	13	–	5	90	100	88	–
1977	5	39	5	23	55	10	25	–	–	70	23
1976	20	48	15	41	42	20	18	25	100	70	33

Key Votes

1) Increase Def Spnd	FOR	6) Alaska Lands Protect	AGN	11) Delay Auto Pol Cntrl	FOR
2) B-1 Bomber	FOR	7) Water Projects Veto	AGN	12) Sugar Price Escalator	FOR
3) Cargo Preference	FOR	8) Consum Protect Agcy	AGN	13) Pub Fin Cong Cmpgns	AGN
4) Dereg Nat Gas	FOR	9) Common Situs Picket	AGN	14) ERA Ratif Recissn	FOR
5) Kemp-Roth	FOR	10) Labor Law Revision	AGN	15) Prohibt Govt Abrtns	FOR

Election Results

1978 general	David R. Bowen (D)	57,678	(62%)	($90,850)
	Dr. Roland Byrd (R)	35,730	(38%)	($91,580)
1978 primary	David R. Bowen (D)	48,064	(75%)	
	Horace Harned (D)	16,339	(25%)	($23,384)
1976 general	David R. Bowen (D)	75,092	(64%)	($35,349)
	Dr. Roland Byrd (R)	42,601	(36%)	($70,888)

THIRD DISTRICT

The 3d is one of three Mississippi congressional districts that stretch from the heavily black Delta across the hills of central Mississippi to the Alabama border. Like the others, the 3d is so constructed to prevent blacks from controlling the outcome of congressional elections here. Of all of Mississippi's districts, this is the most rural and agricultural. Its only urban areas of any size are the small city of Meridian and the part of Rankin County across the Pearl River from Jackson. More typical—and notorious—are towns like Philadelphia in Neshoba County, where three civil rights workers were murdered in 1964.

The longtime (since 1942) Congressman from the 3d, Philadelphia native W. Arthur Winstead, suffered a rude surprise that same year: he was beaten by a Republican chicken farmer, Prentiss Walker, in the general election. Barry Goldwater was carrying the state by a 7–1 margin, and the unfortunate Winstead was the only incumbent with a Republican opponent; if there had been Republican candidates elsewhere, they probably would have won and wiped out 95 years of Democratic seniority. Walker's later ventures in politics showed that his victory was indeed a fluke. He won just 27% against James Eastland in the 1966 Senate race, 39% in a 1968 congressional try, and a pathetic 2% as an Independent candidate against Eastland in 1972.

When Walker ran for the Senate in 1966, the Democrats promptly recaptured the seat in the person of state Senator Sonny Montgomery. He is an exemplar of the traditional Southern Democrat: devoted to his work, a delightful companion, dedicated to his principles but possessed of a fine sense of humor. A veteran of both World War II and Korea, Montgomery serves on the Armed Services and Veterans Affairs Committees. He is always on the side of urging a stronger defense, and is an unabashed enthusiast for things military. On other issues Montgomery almost inevitably votes with the coalition of Republicans and conservative Southern Democrats—to the extent it still exists.

When Montgomery first came to Congress, there still was a large identifiable bloc of conservative Southern Democrats who thought and voted as he did. In the forties there had been almost 100 of them and even in the late sixties there were about 60. Their numbers were sharply diminished in the next decade. Redistricting eliminated some of their rural districts, Republican competition defeated others, the increasing demand of constituents for greater services and more access to their congressmen persuaded many oldsters to retire. Montgomery was a Nixon loyalist to the end, visiting the beleaguered President on the Sequoia; but Nixon's policies had the effect of cementing most Southern Democrats to their northern co-partisans. Lately there has been a move in the opposite direction, as an increasing number of Democrats are defecting to vote with Republicans on various issues. But this movement is not regionally based, nor is it made up of a large number of reliable conservatives. Sonny Montgomery is a natural leader, ready to take charge of such a bloc, but one that does not really exist.

Montgomery is unlikely to be Chairman of Armed Services ever—he is too far down in seniority—although he may win the Veterans chair; he probably has enough personal popularity to prevent the Democratic Caucus from denying that to him. He suits his district exceedingly well, and in the last election against a Republican opponent received 92% of the vote.

Census Data Pop. 445,713. Central city, 0%; suburban, 10%. Median family income, $5,320; families above $15,000: 6%; families below $3,000: 30%. Median years education, 10.2.

The Voters

Median voting age 45.
Employment profile White collar, 33%. Blue collar, 44%. Service, 13%. Farm, 10%.
Ethnic groups Black, 40%.

Presidential vote

1976	Carter (D)	79,021	(49%)
	Ford (R)	82,515	(51%)
1972	Nixon (R)	110,710	(79%)
	McGovern (D)	28,941	(21%)

Rep. G. V. (Sonny) **Montgomery** (D) Elected 1966; b. Meridian; home, Meridian; Miss St., U., B.S.; Episcopalian.

Career Army, WWII and Korea; Owner, Montgomery Insurance Agency; V.P., Greater Miss. Life Ins. Co.; Miss. Senate, 1956–66.

Offices 2367 RHOB, 202-225-5031. Also P.O. Box 5618, Meridian 39301, 601-693-6681.

Committees *Armed Services* (12th). Subcommittees: Military Personnel.

Veterans' Affairs (4th). Subcommittees: Compensation, Pension, Insurance, and Memorial Affairs (Chairman); Medical Facilities and Benefits.

Group Ratings

	ADA	COPE	PC	RPN	NFU	LCV	CFA	NAB	NSI	ACA	NTU
1978	5	15	10	50	30	–	9	100	89	85	–
1977	0	14	8	27	45	3	10	–	–	92	39
1976	5	13	5	33	17	3	0	83	100	100	60

Key Votes

1) Increase Def Spnd	FOR	6) Alaska Lands Protect	AGN	11) Delay Auto Pol Cntrl	FOR
2) B-1 Bomber	FOR	7) Water Projects Veto	AGN	12) Sugar Price Escalator	FOR
3) Cargo Preference	FOR	8) Consum Protect Agcy	AGN	13) Pub Fin Cong Cmpgns	AGN
4) Dereg Nat Gas	FOR	9) Common Situs Picket	AGN	14) ERA Ratif Recissn	FOR
5) Kemp-Roth	AGN	10) Labor Law Revision	AGN	15) Prohibt Govt Abrtns	FOR

Election Results

1978 general	G. V. Montgomery (D)	101,685	(92%)	($45,478)
	Dorothy Cleveland (R)	8,408	(8%)	
1978 primary	G. V. Montgomery (D)	79,219	(91%)	
	One other (D)	7,499	(9%)	
1976 general	G. V. Montgomery (D)	129,088	(94%)	($9,941)
	Dorothy Cleveland (R)	8,321	(6%)	($0)

FOURTH DISTRICT

Mississippi's capital and largest city, Jackson, is the center of one of the state's two significant urban concentrations. It has experienced considerable growth in the last twenty years—aside from the Gulf Coast, more growth than any other part of the state. Much of Jackson's growth has been accounted for by well-to-do whites; the city has its new subdivisions of pleasant, large houses inhabited by new Mississippi millionaires. Even the less well-to-do—people who grew up poor and now make $18,000 a year, more than they ever dreamed of—tend to think like the nouveaux riches. Both groups share a militant conservatism which is not out of line with old Mississippi political views, except for one thing: these new conservatives are more inclined to vote for Republicans than Democrats.

It is on the votes of such citizens—younger, better educated, upwardly mobile, urban and suburban—that the successes of the Republican Party in the South generally and in Mississippi in particular have been built. Although Republicans don't like to put it that way, their strength is built on the country club South, and those who identify with it. That was where most of the votes came from that elected Thad Cochran the first Republican Senator from Mississippi in a century in 1976, and the votes that first elected him the the House from the 4th district six years before.

Most of the population of the 4th district can be found in Jackson and Hinds County. The rest of the district is the southwest corner of the state, including Vicksburg, site of the great Civil War battle; Natchez, with its well preserved antebellum houses; and several small counties with black majorities. It is these other areas which seem to attract the most attention from political observers. After all, who wants to wander around a 1971 subdivision when you can visit an antebellum mansion in Natchez or wander around the battlefield site in Vicksburg? What reporter is going to write a story on the upwardly mobile young reactionaries of Jackson when he or she can write about blacks seriously contesting elections in counties which were once the state's prime plantation country? Thus much of the coverage of the 4th district's politics has centered on Charles Evers, the black Mayor of Fayette (population 1,725), who ran unsuccessfully for Congress in 1968 and for the Senate in 1978. Evers is an interesting figure, but he does not tell us much about why Republicans are winning elections here recently.

For that explanation, we must look to Jackson. That was where Thad Cochran won the votes he needed for his 1972 victory in the 4th district; he had only a minority of the vote, but a black Independent took 8%. Once in office, Cochran's engaging manner and non-controversial voting record made him extremely popular here; and based on big Jackson margins—36,000 to 8,000 over the Democrat—he built his 1978 Senate victory. Moreover, his kind of politics prevailed in the 1978 congressional race. Many had predicted that the winner would be John Hampton Stennis, son of the Senator and a respected state legislator. But Stennis's Democratic label was no help and his wooden speaking style contrasted poorly with the articulateness of the Republican candidate, John Hinson. A former aide to Cochran, Hinson won a 2–1 margin over Stennis in Jackson and beat him in all the rural counties as well. There was a black Independent again, but this time he was not decisive: Hinton won with 53%. He can be expected to vote—and to win votes—much as Cochran did.

Census Data Pop. 444,704. Central city, 35%; suburban, 14%. Median family income, $6,802; families above $15,000: 12%; families below $3,000: 21%. Median years education, 11.8.

The Voters

Median voting age 43.
Employment profile White collar, 47%. Blue collar, 35%. Service, 15%. Farm, 3%.
Ethnic groups Black, 43%. Total foreign stock, 1%.

Presidential vote

1976	Carter (D)	70,260	(45%)
	Ford (R)	86,002	(55%)
1972	Nixon (R)	101,007	(76%)
	McGovern (D)	32,496	(24%)

Rep. Jon Hinson (R) Elected 1978; b. Mar. 16, 1942, Tylertown; home, Tylertown; U. of Miss., B.A. 1964.

Career USMC, 1964–67; Doorman, U.S. House of Reps., 1967–68; Legis. Asst., Admin. Asst. to U.S. Rep. Charlie Griffin, 1969–73; Admin. Asst. to U.S. Rep. Thad Cochran, 1973–77.

Offices 1512 LHOB, 202-225-5865. Also P.O. Box 22662, Jackson 39205, 601-969-3300.

Committees *Banking, Finance, and Urban Affairs* (15th). Subcommittees: The City; Economic Stabilization; General Oversight and Renegotiation.

Education and Labor (12th). Subcommittees: Elementary, Secondary, and Vocational Education; Labor-Management Relations; Employment Opportunities.

Group Ratings: Newly Elected

Key Votes: Newly Elected

Election Results

1978 general	Jon C. Hinson (R)	68,225	(53%)	($249,548)
	John Stennis (D)	34,837	(27%)	($311,474)
	Evan Doss (I)	25,134	(20%)	($20,564)
1978 primary	Jon C. Hinson (R)	18,895	(70%)	
	Three others (R)	8,264	(30%)	
1976 general	Thad Cochran (R)	101,132	(78%)	($42,053)
	Sterling P. Davis (D)	28,737	(22%)	($1,459)

FIFTH DISTRICT

The 5th congressional district of Mississippi is the state's Gulf Coast district. About half its residents live in and around the Gulf cities of Biloxi, Gulfport, Pascagoula, and Moss Point; together they constitute the only significant urban concentration in Mississippi outside Jackson. The remainder live inland, in farm counties or in the middle-sized cities of Hattiesburg and Laurel. Much of this land is piney woods and paper mill country, and never contained many plantations. As a result there are relatively few blacks here—only 19% of the population, the lowest such figure in Mississippi. That figure has declined in recent years as whites move in from the surrounding countryside or even from the north; for this has been an area of considerable boom.

The vast majority of 5th district residents would be disgusted at the idea that they are beneficiaries of vast subsidies from the federal government. These often newly well-to-do people are fond of thinking of themselves as rugged individualists, people who have worked their way up to a comfortable state in society. This part of Mississippi may be the part of the country most fiercely opposed to government spending for the poor or disadvantaged. But hardly anyone objects here to the annual $500 million the Defense Department pours into the Litton Shipbuilding yards in Pascagoula. Litton was the inexperienced but well connected contractor which got this contract in the Nixon Administration; there were indications later that Litton simply bid low and assumed that it could get the Pentagon to fork over more money later. Certainly performance has been shoddy, and it has been difficult to find qualified labor here. But Mississippi is the home of Armed Services Chairman John Stennis and until 1972 the 5th district was the home of House Rules Chairman William Colmer. It is also the district which gave Richard Nixon his largest percentage in the 1972 general election—a nearly unanimous 87%. And so through most of the seventies the cost overrun payments have been coming into Litton and Gulf Coast Mississippi—a hidden government subsidy if there ever was one.

In Mississippi the Republican trend has been strongest in the urban areas, including the Gulf Coast, and so it is not so surprising that the 5th district has a Republican congressman. He is Trent Lott, first elected in 1972, and he provides some continuity with the past—he used to be William Colmer's administrative assistant. The Republican party affiliation has its advantages here: the district was carried not only by Nixon in 1972, but by Gerald Ford in 1976; and while the Democrats slice themselves up in primaries and runoffs, as ten of them did in 1972, a Republican like Lott can win his nomination with little fuss.

Lott was one of Nixon's strongest defenders in the House Judiciary impeachment hearings in 1974, and he was one congressman who was not hurt in his district by that stand. He has been reelected with huge margins and had no Democratic opponent at all in 1978. Nor did Lott's pro-Nixon stance hurt him among fellow Republicans. In 1975 he received a seat on the House Rules Committee, on which he is now fourth-ranking Republican. He has seen Republicans win elections where they were never supposed to, and it may be that the thought has crossed his mind that some distant day he may be Rules Chairman as was his former boss Colmer.

Census Data Pop. 451,981. Central city, 20%; suburban, 10%. Median family income, $7,053; families above $15,000: 9%; families below $3,000: 18%. Median years education, 11.9.

The Voters

Median voting age 40.
Employment profile White collar, 42%. Blue collar, 43%. Service, 13%. Farm, 2%.
Ethnic groups Black, 19%. Total foreign stock, 3%.

Presidential vote

1976	Carter (D)	71,261	(47%)
	Ford (R)	80,024	(53%)
1972	Nixon (R)	116,382	(87%)
	McGovern (D)	17,654	(13%)

Rep. Trent Lott (R) Elected 1972; b. Oct. 9, 1941, Grenada; home, Pascagoula; U. of Miss., B.A., 1963, J.D. 1967; Baptist.

Career Practicing atty., 1967–68; Admin. Asst. to U.S. Rep. William M. Colmer, 1968–72.

Offices 2400 RHOB, 202-225-5772. Also P.O. Box 1557, Gulfport 39501, 601-864-7670.

Committees *Rules* (4th).

Group Ratings

	ADA	COPE	PC	RPN	NFU	LCV	CFA	NAB	NSI	ACA	NTU
1978	10	25	13	58	30	–	14	100	100	93	–
1977	0	23	5	31	50	0	5	–	–	89	46
1976	0	41	7	47	46	7	9	58	90	85	52

Key Votes

1) Increase Def Spnd	FOR	6) Alaska Lands Protect	AGN	11) Delay Auto Pol Cntrl	FOR
2) B-1 Bomber	FOR	7) Water Projects Veto	AGN	12) Sugar Price Escalator	FOR
3) Cargo Preference	FOR	8) Consum Protect Agcy	AGN	13) Pub Fin Cong Cmpgns	AGN
4) Dereg Nat Gas	FOR	9) Common Situs Picket	AGN	14) ERA Ratif Recissn	FOR
5) Kemp-Roth	FOR	10) Labor Law Revision	DNV	15) Prohibt Govt Abrtns	FOR

Election Results

1978 general	Trent Lott (R), unopposed			($32,708)
1978 primary	Trent Lott (R), unopposed			
1976 general	Trent Lott (R)	104,554	(68%)	($182,585)
	Gerald Blessey (D)	48,724	(32%)	($101,144)

MISSOURI

Missouri is a border state, admitted to the Union in 1821 as part of the compromise that bears its name—a slave state whose boundaries jutted far north into free territory; a state which sent proslavery raiders over the border into Kansas in the 1850s to fight those shipped in by the abolitionists; a state which saw its own civil war, one separated geographically, though not spiritually, from the conflict east of the Mississippi. Missouri was also a gateway to the American West, an avenue for the great Yankee migrations west from Ohio, Indiana, and Illinois, and the eastern terminus of the Pony Express and the Transcontinental Railroad.

Politically Democrats have always dominated Missouri, but there has always been a Republican Party capable of winning some elections. The Democratic edge is the result of Missouri's slave state traditions; Missouri's most famous Democrat, Harry Truman, had a grandfather who fought in the Rebel army, and his mother, who lived to see her son President, remained a Confederate sympathizer all her life. Truman's background—Southern rural and Kansas City urban—typified the tensions within the Missouri Democratic Party and also explains why Truman, who integrated the armed forces, could also react negatively to the civil rights movement of the sixties. Truman's combination of liberalism on economic issues, a mixed response on social question, and an affection for old political friends, still characterizes many Missouri Democratic politicians.

Since 1948 presidential elections in Missouri have been very close. Except for the landslide years of 1964 and 1972, no presidential candidate has carried the state by more than 30,000 votes out of the nearly two million cast, until Jimmy Carter won by 70,000 in 1976; and that was still only a 51% victory. Carter's victory margin here was notable for his rural support. Other Democrats who have won by close margins in Missouri—Governor Joseph Teasdale in 1976, Senator Stuart Symington in his last race in 1970, Senator Thomas Eagleton in his first race in 1968—did it by piling up big margins in the St. Louis and Kansas City metropolitan areas, which together cast slightly more than half the state's votes, and thereby overcoming Republican margins in the rural counties. Carter had only a narrow edge in the St. Louis area (51%), but carried the rural counties as well. It was a resurgence of old Dixie loyalties, which had once existed in even the northern rural counties of Missouri, but which seemed to disappear during the years of the Great Society, the Vietnam war, riots in the cities, and the Nixon Southern strategy.

Carter's victory here was not a big surprise; what was was the failure of Missouri's Republican Party to make major gains. For eight years the Democrats had held nine of Missouri's ten congressional seats. In 1976 five Democrats retired, two to run for the Senate and three simply because they were tired of office, and every one of those districts had given at least one Republican a margin in a major statewide race. Moreover, the state's two strongest Republicans were heading the ticket: Governor Christopher Bond, running for reelection, and Attorney General John Danforth, running for the Senate. Both were young (39 and 42); both are rich and went to Ivy League schools. Both had hired staffs of a caliber not ordinarily found in the sleepy capital of Jefferson City, and both had fashioned political careers out of attacks on the cronyism and old fashioned politics of Missouri Democrats.

Danforth had been elected Attorney General as long before as 1968 and in 1970, campaigning as a champion of the Nixon Administration, had won 49% against Stuart Symington. That same year Bond had upset the longtime state auditor, and in 1972 he ran for governor and won with a solid 55%. Bond had the pleasure of welcoming, as host Governor, the Republican National Convention to Kansas City; and as he spoke, the television commentators assured their audiences that much would be heard from this young man in the future.

Yet Bond was beaten in 1976, in what was one of the most surprising statewide results in the nation; and Republicans did poorly in House races, picking up only one seat. His opponent, Joseph Teasdale, had run for governor before, in 1972, and lost in the Democratic primary; he won the nomination in 1976 against weaker opposition. Bond's major achievements lay in the area of procedural reforms—open meetings, conflict of interest ban—and he had enjoyed much favorable publicity. But Teasdale, a former Jackson County (Kansas City) Prosecutor, retaliated with a major media campaign and an attack on Bond for appointing pro-utility members to the public service commission. That was enough to make Teasdale Governor in 1976; whether it will be enough to keep him Governor in 1980 is not clear. He has been criticized for running an administration less than shipshape, and generally has not projected an image of strength. There may be a Bond-Teasdale rematch in 1980, and this time the Republican will not suffer from overconfidence.

Danforth's victory was a more comfortable one, but it had not been certain all through 1976. He had been expected to face tough competition from Congressman James Symington, son of the retiring senator; but Symington was overtaken in the primary by Congressman Jerry Litton, who featured his background as a farmer and won big majorities in the rural areas. But Litton and his family were killed in a plane crash on primary night; the Democrats, after a period of mourning, nominated the man who edged Symington out of second place in the primary, former Governor Warren Hearnes. He had once been a big vote-getter as Governor, but he left office amid an odor of scandal and seemed to personify the kind of politician Danforth and Bond had been running against. The Republican gained an easy victory.

Danforth, an heir to the Ralston Purina fortune, is one of the richest men in the Senate. He holds not only a law but a divinity degree and approaches politics with a kind of churchy intensity that exudes sincerity. Early in his career Danforth was called a liberal Republican; but his liberalism consisted of opposing traditional corruption and cronyism. His voting record tends to be conventionally Republican on most issues. He tends to favor free market mechanisms over government regulations, he tends to be skeptical of the windom of regulating business, he is not inclined to favor extensions of federal welfare and health programs, and he is skeptical of the SALT treaty. Danforth is typical of the cerebral, cautious young Republicans who seem to be more important in the Senate these days.

Missouri's other Senator is a man whose name became as familiar a household word as Danforth's Rice Chex for a while, at least—Thomas Eagleton. When he was nominated for vice president in 1972, the nation learned of his prodigious career in Missouri: Circuit Attorney in St. Louis at 27, Attorney General at 31, Lieutenant Governor at 35, and U.S. Senator at 39. The last had been the most difficult: he had beaten incumbent Senator Edward Long (under attack for his ties to the Teamsters Union) in the primary and suburban St. Louis Congressman Thomas Curtis in the general election. Voters soon learned much more about Eagleton: how he had been hospitalized and received electroshock treatment for depression. The response to the news was mixed. Many expressed compassion, while others felt that a person subject to such problems should not be a heartbeat away from the presidency. Eagleton took his case to the public and George McGovern said he was behind him 1000%. A few days later McGovern dropped Eagleton from the ticket.

The episode seems to have ended Eagleton's national career, and to have made him more popular than ever in Missouri. While people might worry about instability in a vice president, it is not a matter of compelling concern in a senator; and in any case the last episode of Eagleton's illness occurred in 1960. Both before and after 1972 he was an active and successful Senator. In his first term he chaired the District of Columbia Committee and helped the capital city to achieve home rule in 1973. An original sponsor of the war powers bill, he refused to support it on the grounds that amendments gave the president too much discretion to deploy military troops; he refused to be swept along by conventional wisdom, and still hopes to modify the law. He was the chief Senate sponsor of the move to stop the bombing of Cambodia in 1973 and of the temporarily successful move to cut off aid to Turkey because of its invasion of Cyprus. He is a member of the Senate Appropriations Committee.

Eagleton appears to be widely popular in Missouri. Against the same opponent who nearly beat him six years before, he won reelection with 60% of the vote in 1974. His seat is up in 1980, and he may very well not attract tough opposition at all—although of course no one can be certain. At this point, as he passes 50, this onetime boy wonder seems on his way to becoming one of the powerful insiders in the Senate.

Census Data Pop. 4,677,399; 2.31% of U.S. total, 13th largest; Central city, 30%; suburban, 35%. Median family income, $8,908; 29th highest; families above $15,000: 17%; families below $3,000: 12%. Median years education, 11.8.

1977 Share of Federal Tax Burden $7,081,000,000; 2.03% of U.S. total, 14th largest.

1977 Share of Federal Outlays $9,808,953,000; 2.48% of U.S. total, 14th largest. Per capita federal spending, $2,059.

DOD	$3,330,031,000	6th (3.64%)	HEW	$3,329,661,000	11th (2.25%)
ERDA	$130,171,000	15th (2.20%)	HUD	$94,299,000	15th (2.23%)
NASA	$4,785,000	26th (0.12%)	VA	$444,980,000	14th (2.32%)
DOT	$210,786,000	23d (1.48%)	EPA	$119,268,000	19th (1.45%)
DOC	$76,160,000	28th (0.92%)	RevS	$141,837,000	20th (1.68%)
DOI	$42,015,000	27th (0.90%)	Debt	$306,309,000	14th (1.02%)
USDA	$450,809,000	13th (2.27%)	Other	$1,127,841,000	

Economic Base Agriculture, notably cattle, hogs, soybeans and dairy products; finance, insurance and real estate; transportation equipment, especially motor vehicles and equipment; food and kindred products; printing and publishing; electrical equipment and supplies; apparel and other textile products, especially men's and boys' furnishings, and women's and misses' outerwear.

Political Line-up Governor, Joseph P. Teasdale (D). Senators, Thomas F. Eagleton (D) and John C. Danforth (R). Representatives 10 (8 D and 2 R). State Senate (21 D, 11 R, and 2 vacancies); State House (116 D, 46 R, and 1 vacancy).

The Voters

Registration 2,553,574 Total. No party registration.
Median voting age 44
Employment profile White collar, 47%. Blue collar, 36%. Service, 13%. Farm, 4%.
Ethnic groups Black, 10%. Total foreign stock, 7%. Germany, 2%.

Presidential vote

1976	Carter (D)	999,163	(52%)
	Ford (R)	928,808	(48%)
1972	Nixon (R)	1,153,852	(62%)
	McGovern (D)	697,147	(38%)

Sen. Thomas F. Eagleton (D) Elected 1968, seat up 1980; b. Sept. 4, 1929, St. Louis; home, St. Louis; Amherst Col., B.A. 1950, Harvard U., LL.B. 1953; Catholic.

Career Navy, 1948–49; Practicing atty.; St. Louis Circuit Atty., 1956–60; Atty. Gen. of Mo., 1961–65; Lt. Gov. of Mo., 1965–69.

Offices 1209 DSOB, 202-224-5721. Also 4039 Fed. Ofc. Bldg., St. Louis 63103, 314-425-5067, and Rm. 911, Fed. Bldg., 811 Grand Ave., Kansas City 64106, 816-374-2747.

Committees *Appropriations* (8th). Subcommittees: Agriculture and Related Agencies (Chairman); Defense; Labor, HEW, and Related Agencies; State, Justice, and Commerce, the Judiciary, and Related Agencies; Transportation and Related Agencies.

Governmental Affairs (3d). Subcommittees: Investigations; Governmental Efficiency and the District of Columbia (Chairman); Energy, Nuclear Proliferation, and Federal Services.

Labor and Human Resources (6th). Subcommittees: Handicapped; Education, Arts, and Humanities; Aging (Chairman).

Group Ratings

	ADA	COPE	PC	RPN	NFU	LCV	CFA	NAB	NSI	ACA	NTU
1978	50	79	63	44	50	62	45	42	20	9	–
1977	60	80	70	20	91	–	56	–	–	15	33
1976	60	88	66	38	70	33	85	36	14	8	17

Key Votes

1) Warnke Nom	FOR	6) Egypt-Saudi Arms	FOR	11) Hosptl Cost Contnmnt	FOR
2) Neutron Bomb	FOR	7) Draft Restr Pardon	FOR	12) Clinch River Reactor	FOR
3) Waterwy User Fee	AGN	8) Wheat Price Support	FOR	13) Pub Fin Cong Cmpgns	FOR
4) Dereg Nat Gas	AGN	9) Panama Canal Treaty	FOR	14) ERA Ratif Recissn	DNV
5) Kemp-Roth	AGN	10) Labor Law Rev Clot	FOR	15) Med Necssy Abrtns	AGN

Election Results

1974 general	Thomas F. Eagleton (D)	735,433	(60%)	($647,143)
	Thomas B. Curtis (R)	480,900	(40%)	($362,804)
1974 primary	Thomas F. Eagleton (D)	420,681	(87%)	
	Two others (D)	60,224	(13%)	
1968 general	Thomas F. Eagleton (D)	880,113	(51%)	
	Thomas B. Curtis (R)	845,144	(49%)	

Sen. John C. Danforth (R) Elected 1976, seat up 1982; b. Sept. 5, 1936, St. Louis; home, Flat; Princeton U., A.B. 1958, Yale U., B.D. and LL.B. 1963; Episcopalian.

Career Practicing atty., 1963–69; Atty. Gen. of Mo., 1969–77; Repub. Nominee for U.S. Senate, 1970.

Offices 460 RSOB, 202-224-6154. Also Suite 1867, Railway Exch. Bldg., 611 Olive St., St. Louis 63101, 314-425-6381, and Suites 943–945, U.S. Court House, 811 Grand Ave., Kansas City 64106, 816-374-6101.

Committees *Commerce, Science, and Transportation* (4th). Subcommittees: Communication; Consumer; Surface Transportation.

Finance (4th). Subcommittees: International Trade; Social Security; Revenue Sharing, Intergovernmental Revenue Impact, and Economic Problems.

Governmental Affairs (6th). Subcommittees: Intergovernmental Relations; Federal Spending Practices and Open Government.

Group Ratings

	ADA	COPE	PC	RPN	NFU	LCV	CFA	NAB	NSI	ACA	NTU
1978	25	32	28	70	50	32	25	58	22	38	–
1977	25	30	28	82	50	–	24	–	–	56	38

Key Votes

1) Warnke Nom	AGN	6) Egypt-Saudi Arms	FOR	11) Hosptl Cost Contnmnt	AGN
2) Neutron Bomb	AGN	7) Draft Restr Pardon	FOR	12) Clinch River Reactor	FOR
3) Waterwy User Fee	AGN	8) Wheat Price Support	AGN	13) Pub Fin Cong Cmpgns	AGN
4) Dereg Nat Gas	FOR	9) Panama Canal Treaty	FOR	14) ERA Ratif Recissn	AGN
5) Kemp-Roth	FOR	10) Labor Law Rev Clot	AGN	15) Med Necssy Abrtns	AGN

Election Results

1976 general	John C. Danforth (R)	1,090,067	(57%)	($741,465)
	Warren E. Hearnes (D)	813,571	(43%)	($660,953)
1976 primary	John C. Danforth (R)	284,025	(93%)	
	One other (R)	19,796	(7%)	
1970 general	Stuart Symington (D)	654,831	(51%)	
	John C. Danforth (R)	617,903	(49%)	

Gov. Joseph P. Teasdale (D) Elected 1976, term expires Jan. 1981; b. 1936, Kansas City; Rockhurst Col., B.S., St. Louis U., LL.B.

Career Practicing atty.; Asst. U.S. Atty., Chf. of Organized Crime Section, 1962–66; Jackson Co. Prosecutor, 1966–71.

Offices Exec. Ofc., State Capitol Bldg., Jefferson City 65101, 314-751-3222.

Election Results

1976 general	Joseph P. Teasdale (D)	971,184	(50%)
	Christopher Bond (R)	958,110	(50%)
1976 primary	Joseph P.Teasdale (D)	419,656	(50%)
	William Cason (D)	340,208	(41%)
	Seven others (D)	73,389	(9%)
1972 general	Christopher Bond (R)	1,029,451	(55%)
	Edward L. Dowd (D)	832,751	(45%)

FIRST DISTRICT

The 1st congressional district of Missouri is the northern half of the city of St. Louis and a slice of separate, totally suburban St. Louis County to the west. Because of black migration and the transformation of neighborhoods within the city, the north side of St. Louis is heavily black, and in 1968 the fourth Missouri redistricting of the sixties made blacks a majority districtwide. Because of population loss, suburban areas were added in 1972; but the district overall continues to have a black majority. The suburban part of the district hugs the western city limits of St. Louis, and is mostly white; there are, however, significant and increasing numbers of blacks here in University City, Richmond Heights, and Webster Groves. The socioeconomic makeup of the suburbs in the district varies from blue collar in the north (Normandy, Bel-Ridge) to white collar in the south (Webster Groves, Brentwood). In the middle is Clayton, the St. Louis County seat, which is developing into a center of large high-rise office buildings; it is also the home of Washington University and an adjacent liberal academic community.

The 1st is consistently the most Democratic district in Missouri, by a considerable margin. Since 1968 it has been represented by Bill Clay, who got his political start as a union staffer and civil rights activist. When he was first elected, he was considered one of the most militant black members; only five years before, he had served 105 days in jail for participating in a civil rights demonstration.

Clay's record in the House is somewhat different, however. He is considered one of organized labor's most faithful supporters on the House Education and Labor Committee and on Post Office and Civil Service. From his seat on the latter body, he has been the House's chief sponsor of the measure to repeal the Hatch Act's limitations on the political activities of federal employees. This move has been unsuccessful, in part because members of the committee despite Clay's efforts, were able to attach to it provisions obnoxious to the public employee unions which are its chief backers. Clay also worked hard in behalf of some elements in the public employee unions in opposition to the Carter Administration's civil service reform act. Again he was unsuccessful, with Chairman Morris Udall, pro-labor Democrat William Ford, and Republican Edward Derwinski fashioning a compromise despite the Missourian's efforts.

But such failures to achieve legislative goals are probably less familiar to 1st district residents than some of Clay's peccadilloes. In 1976 it was revealed that he had been billing the government for numerous auto trips home, although he actually was purchasing less expensive airline tickets and, presumably, pocketing the difference. The next year he was under investigation for tax fraud. His administrative asistant was sentenced to jail for falsification of payroll records. All of this inspired considerable opposition to Clay in the last two primaries. In 1976 and 1978, six candidates each time held Clay to just over 60% of the vote. In both cases he got well under a majority in the County—a sign that he excites considerable hostility among his white constituents. He still seems to have the loyalty of the blacks, however; in 1978 he won 79% of the primary vote in the city of St. Louis.

Clay was spared a tougher fight in 1978. His major opponent was expected to be St. Louis Sheriff Benjamin Goins, a black who is well known for wearing a cowboy-type hat with a silver star on it. Unfortunately for his campaign, Goins was indicted shortly after filing, and he got only 4% of the vote. With its current boundaries, this district seems unlikely to elect a white congressman, but it is possible that Clay could be unseated by a black. After the 1980 election, it may be different. The north side of St. Louis has been losing population very rapidly, and the district will probably have to be expanded to include much more suburban territory. That will mean more white voters, and presumably more anti-Clay votes.

Census Data Pop. 468,056. Central city, 66%; suburban, 34%. Median family income, $8,485; families above $15,000: 17%; families below $3,000: 3%. Median years education, 10.7.

The Voters

Median voting age 45.
Employment profile White collar, 46%. Blue collar, 33%. Service, 21%. Farm, –%.
Ethnic groups Black, 54%. Total foreign stock, 8%. Germany, 2%.

Presidential vote

1976	Carter (D)	95,153	(71%)
	Ford (R)	38,903	(29%)
1972	Nixon (R)	45,765	(31%)
	McGovern (D)	101,307	(69%)

Rep. William (Bill) **Clay** (D) Elected 1968; b. Apr. 30, 1931, St. Louis; home, St. Louis; St. Louis U., B.S. 1953; Catholic.

Career Real estate broker; Life insurance business, 1959–61; St. Louis City Alderman, 1959–64; Business Rep., City Employees Union, 1961–64.

Offices 2264 RHOB, 202-225-2406. Also 5980 Delmar Blvd., St. Louis 63112, 314-725-5770.

Committees *Education and Labor* (8th). Subcommittees: Employment Opportunities; Labor-Management Relations.

Post Office and Civil Service (5th). Subcommittees: Civil Service (Chairman); Civil Service; Postal Personnel and Modernization (Chairman); Postal Operations and Services.

Group Ratings

	ADA	COPE	PC	RPN	NFU	LCV	CFA	NAB	NSI	ACA	NTU
1978	85	95	78	33	80	–	82	0	0	12	–
1977	75	95	70	20	91	77	55	–	–	0	39
1976	75	88	80	41	91	87	64	0	0	0	33

Key Votes

1) Increase Def Spnd	AGN	6) Alaska Lands Protect	FOR	11) Delay Auto Pol Cntrl	AGN
2) B-1 Bomber	AGN	7) Water Projects Veto	AGN	12) Sugar Price Escalator	FOR
3) Cargo Preference	FOR	8) Consum Protect Agcy	FOR	13) Pub Fin Cong Cmpgns	AGN
4) Dereg Nat Gas	AGN	9) Common Situs Picket	FOR	14) ERA Ratif Recissn	AGN
5) Kemp-Roth	AGN	10) Labor Law Revision	FOR	15) Prohibt Govt Abrtns	AGN

Election Results

1978 general	William Clay (D)	65,950	(68%)	($91,254)
	Bill White (R)	30,995	(32%)	($40,834)
1978 primary	William Clay (D)	29,780	(62%)	
	Helen L. Gerleman (D)	8,949	(18%)	
	Five others (D)	9,676	(20%)	
1976 general	William Clay (D)			
	87,310 (66%) $32,576			
	Robert L. Witherspoon (R)	45,874	(34%)	($0)

SECOND DISTRICT

The 2d congressional district of Missouri is the heart of St. Louis County, a jurisdiction that is adjacent to, but includes no part of, the city of St. Louis. The county originally set itself apart so that its rural affairs would not get lost in the business of the city; now the city of St. Louis has only about half the population and wealth of St. Louis County. In the northern part of the 2d district, along Interstate 70, are blue collar communities like Jennings, Ferguson, Berkley, and Airport Township. Most of the people who live here grew up on the north side of St. Louis, which is now heavily black; many work in the giant McDonnell-Douglas aircraft plants located on the north side of the County. To the south of the district are WASPY, traditionally Republican suburbs like Kirkwood and Webster Groves, fully occupied by the fifties and placid in their conservatism. To the west the 2d has the bulk of the Jewish population of metropolitan St. Louis in and around University City and the towns north of the Daniel Boone Freeway. Here too is the posh suburb of Ladue, home of most members of the St. Louis establishment (1970 median family income: $32,000).

Altogether the diverse makeup of the 2d district produces election results that are often close to those of the state as a whole—although few other parts of Missouri resemble it much. Its congressmen tend to become well known in the St. Louis area and thus are natural candidates for statewide office. Thus the last two congressmen have run for the Senate and lost: Republican Thomas Curtis in 1968 and Democrat James Symington in 1976.

The current incumbent comes not from the blueblood background of his predecessors but from a blue collar neighborhood in the north side of the district. He is Robert Young, a Democrat elected in a close contest in 1976 and reelected in 1978. Young, a pipefitter, was active in his union; as a young man he was elected to the state legislature, and served 20 years there until he was elected to Congress. His race against Republican Bob Chase, a former St. Louis newscaster, exemplifies his stands on issues. They disagreed on abortion: Young strongly opposes it, Chase would not go along with a constitutional amendment to prohibit it. They disagreed on the Middle East: Young strongly backed Israel, while Chase questioned Israel's stand in the negotiations. They disagreed on taxes: Young said the Kemp-Roth bill was a "kamikaze" plan that would destroy the economy, while Chase backed it. One might say that Young was building a classic Democratic coalition, with stands calculated to appeal to Catholics, Jews, and labor union members; while Chase was appealing to voters generally and not really taking positions on issues that any identifiable bloc cared deeply about. In any case, Young won with a decisive but not overwhelming 56%.

Census Data Pop. 468,808. Central city, 0%; suburban, 100%. Median family income, $12,597; families above $15,000: 35%; families below $3,000: 4%. Median years education, 12.4.

The Voters

Median voting age 42.
Employment profile White collar, 63%. Blue collar, 28%. Service, 9%. Farm, -%.
Ethnic groups Black, 4%. Total foreign stock, 12%. Germany, 2%; Italy, 1%.

Presidential vote

1976	Carter (D)	95,108	(43%)
	Ford (R)	124,204	(57%)
1972	Nixon (R)	127,123	(63%)
	McGovern (D)		(37%)

Rep. Robert A. Young (D) Elected 1976; b. Nov. 22, 1923, St. Louis; home, St. Ann; Catholic.

Career Army, WWII; Pipefitter; Mo. House of Reps., 1957–63; Mo. Senate, 1963–77.

Offices 1317 LHOB, 202-225-2561. Also 4154 Cypress Rd., St. Ann 63074, 314-425-7200.

Committees *Public Works and Transportation* (22d). Subcommittees: Aviation; Oversight and Review; Water Resources.

Science and Technology (17th). Subcommittees: Energy Research and Production; Energy Development and Applications.

Group Ratings

	ADA	COPE	PC	RPN	NFU	LCV	CFA	NAB	NSI	ACA	NTU
1978	25	75	48	25	50	–	41	42	78	48	–
1977	35	91	38	15	83	23	55	–	–	30	17

Key Votes

1) Increase Def Spnd	FOR	6) Alaska Lands Protect	AGN	11) Delay Auto Pol Cntrl	FOR
2) B-1 Bomber	FOR	7) Water Projects Veto	FOR	12) Sugar Price Escalator	AGN
3) Cargo Preference	FOR	8) Consum Protect Agcy	AGN	13) Pub Fin Cong Cmpgns	AGN
4) Dereg Nat Gas	AGN	9) Common Situs Picket	FOR	14) ERA Ratif Recissn	AGN
5) Kemp-Roth	AGN	10) Labor Law Revision	FOR	15) Prohibt Govt Abrtns	FOR

Election Results

1978 general	Robert A. Young (D)	102,911	(56%)	($158,326)
	Bob Chase (R)	79,495	(44%)	($148,440)
1978 primary	Robert A. Young (D)	49,916	(85%)	
	One other (D)	8,765	(15%)	
1976 general	Robert A. Young (D)	111,568	(51%)	($124,793)
	Robert O. Snyder (R)	106,811	(49%)	($165,800)

THIRD DISTRICT

Missouri's 3d congressional district consists of the south side of the city of St. Louis and an adjacent portion of suburban St. Louis County. The line drawn through the middle of St. Louis to separate the 3d from the 1st district also neatly separates the black part of the city from the white. In the seventies, blacks have been moving out from the north side of St. Louis to the suburbs nearby, leaving the south side to whites. Here on the south side there are still signs of the German immigrants who made St. Louis one of the nation's bustling and progressive cities in the late nineteenth century; today, symbolically, an Altenheim (old people's home) still sits on the banks of the Mississippi River. The most famous of the St. Louis Germans was Carl Schurz, a friend of Lincoln, a northern officer in the Civil War, Secretary of the Interior, and U.S. Senator from Missouri.

Schurz was a Republican, and for years St. Louis was a Republican island in a rural Democratic sea. But with the New Deal, St. Louis became one of our most Democratic cities. This is an elderly district (median voting age is 50) and for many of the people here the thirties remain a vivid memory. Most of them retain Democratic voting habits; in some of the traditionally better off wards at the edge of the city, people tend to be Republican. The suburban area is a natural extension of the city. Most of the people living there moved out along the radial avenues extending from the middle of St. Louis. The suburban voters tend to be somewhat more conservative and Republican than their counterparts in the city, and they cast almost half of the district's votes; they are the reason the 3d went for Gerald Ford over Jimmy Carter in 1976.

In 1976 Congresswoman Leonor Sullivan, author of the truth in lending law, retired after 24 years of representing the 3d district. The expectation was that there would be a tough race to determine her successor, and Republicans made a real effort to win the seat. But they were frustrated by the political skills of St. Louis Alderman Richard Gephardt. He ran a strong, well financed campaign, with television advertising as well as precinct work. He won an absolute majority in a four-candidate primary and had nearly a 2–1 margin in the general election over a well known opponent. Gephardt is one of the younger Democrats who does not always go along with the policy views of labor and liberal organizations; his is a vote that must be sought and cannot be taken for granted. In his first term he was assigned to the Ways and Means Committee and in his second to Budget—two indications that he is highly regarded by his colleagues. His electoral performance in the 3d district shows that he is also very highly regarded by his constituents: he received more than 80% in both primary and general election in 1978.

Census Data Pop. 467,544. Central city, 67%; suburban, 33%. Median family income, $10,199; families above $15,000: 20%; families below $3,000: 8%. Median years education, 10.6.

The Voters

Median voting age 47.
Employment profile White collar, 52%. Blue collar, 36%. Service, 12%. Farm, –%.
Ethnic groups Black, 6%. Spanish, 1%. Total foreign stock, 15%. Germany, 4%. Italy, 2%.

Presidential vote

1976	Carter (D)	85,741	(49%)
	Ford (R)	90,574	(51%)
1972	Nixon (R)	102,959	(58%)
	McGovern (D)	73,362	(42%)

Rep. Richard A. Gephardt (D) Elected 1976; b. Jan. 31, 1941, St. Louis; home, St. Louis; Northwestern U., B.S. 1962, U. of Mich., J.D. 1965; Baptist.

Career Practicing atty., 1965–76; St. Louis City Alderman, 1971–76.

Offices 218 CHOB, 202-225-2671. Also 3470 Hampton, St. Louis 63109, 314-351-5100.

Committees *Ways and Means* (18th). Subcommittees: Social Security.

Budget (15th). Subcommittees: Economic Policy, Projections, and Productivity; Budget Process; Tax Expenditures and Tax Policy.

Group Ratings

	ADA	COPE	PC	RPN	NFU	LCV	CFA	NAB	NSI	ACA	NTU
1978	35	75	63	27	40	–	41	50	60	48	–
1977	50	70	78	54	67	65	70	–	–	30	24

Key Votes

1) Increase Def Spnd	AGN	6) Alaska Lands Protect	FOR	11) Delay Auto Pol Cntrl	AGN
2) B-1 Bomber	AGN	7) Water Projects Veto	FOR	12) Sugar Price Escalator	FOR
3) Cargo Preference	AGN	8) Consum Protect Agcy	AGN	13) Pub Fin Cong Cmpgns	FOR
4) Dereg Nat Gas	AGN	9) Common Situs Picket	FOR	14) ERA Ratif Recissn	AGN
5) Kemp-Roth	AGN	10) Labor Law Revision	FOR	15) Prohibt Govt Abrtns	AGN

Election Results

1978 general	Richard A. Gephardt (D)	121,565	(82%)	($113,977)
	Lee Buchschacher (R)	26,881	(18%)	
1978 primary	Richard A. Gephardt (D)	63,933	(91%)	
	One other (D)	6,160	(9%)	
1976 general	Richard A. Gephardt (D)	115,109	(64%)	($168,146)
	Joseph L. Badaracco (R)	65,623	(36%)	($61,862)

FOURTH DISTRICT

The home district of the late Harry Truman was the 4th congressional district of Missouri. Truman's background—he never represented the district in the House, but served in the Senate from 1935 to 1945—tells us a lot about the district, even today. Truman was born in the town of Lamar, in the southern end of the 4th, near the Oklahoma and Arkansas borders. His family was Democratic, which means in his mother's case at least that it cherished a lifelong sympathy for the cause of the Confederacy. The largest city in the 4th district, way at its other end, is Independence.

It is an old courthouse town, where Truman lived on what is now Truman Road in a nineteenth century Victorian house belonging to his wife's family. Just a few blocks away is the Jackson County Courthouse where Truman was County Judge (an administrative position) before his election to the Senate. In those days Independence was a small town, the incongruous seat of a county which included bustling Kansas City. Today the suburban growth emanating from Kansas City has so ballooned the population of Independence that Truman's old Victorian house has nearly been engulfed by subdivisions.

The 4th district is a combination of rural Missouri counties, like the one Truman grew up in, and part of the Kansas City metropolitan area, where he began his political career. Its political history is almost totally Democratic. The rural counties, though to a diminished extent in recent years, have clung to the party more sympathetic to the South—enough so that Jimmy Carter carried this district. Kansas City has been Democratic since the days of Tom Prendergast, the political boss who gave Truman his start and later ended up in jail. Truman himself had no part in Prendergast's graft (the boss was a cement contractor, and under him Kansas City built huge edifices), but Truman was a beneficiary of the fraudulently high number of votes the machine piled up. Jackson County was reported to have cast 295,000 votes in the 1936 election, Prendergast's last—more than it has ever since, despite a subsequent 37% population growth. The 1976 total was 235,000.

The 4th's representation seems to have alternated between Jackson County, which casts 40% of its votes, and the rural areas. In 1976 Congressman William Randall retired after 17 years in office; a Democrat, he had previously been one of Truman's successors as Jackson County Judge. Nine candidates entered the Democratic primary, and the winner, with 40%, was a state senator from a small county not too far from Kansas City, Ike Skelton. There was also a serious Republican effort here, from the Mayor of Independence. But he was unable to carry Jackson County, and Skelton won with big percentages in most of the rural counties. In his first term in the House Skelton obtained a seat on the Agriculture Committee and compiled a voting record fairly liberal on economic but not on social issues. He did not have serious competition for reelection and won by margins reminiscent of the Democratic days of Harry Truman.

Census Data Pop. 466,940. Central city, 2%; suburban, 47%. Median family income, $8,740; families above $15,000: 15%; families below $3,000: 12%. Median years education, 12.1.

The Voters

Median voting age 44.
Employment profile White collar, 42%. Blue collar, 38%. Service, 12%. Farm, 8%.
Ethnic groups Black, 2%. Total foreign stock, 4%. Germany, 1%.

Presidential vote

1976	Carter (D)	108,477	(52%)
	Ford (R)	100,517	(48%)
1972	Nixon (R)	131,874	(69%)
	McGovern (D)	60,472	(31%)

Rep. Ike Skelton (D) Elected 1976; b. Dec. 20, 1931, Lexington; home, Lexington; Wentworth Mil. Acad., U. of Mo., B.A. 1953, LL.B. 1956, U. of Edinburgh, Scotland, 1956; Christian Church.

Career Lafayette Co. Prosecuting Atty., 1957–60; Spec. Asst. Atty. Gen. of Mo., 1961–63; Practicing atty., 1964–71; Mo. Senate, 1971–76.

Offices 1404 LHOB, 202-225-2876. Also 219 Fed. Bldg., 301 W. Lexington, Independence 64050, 816-252-2560.

Committees *Agriculture* (18th). Subcommittees: Department Investigations, Oversight, and Research; Livestock and Grains.

Small Business (21st). Subcommittees: Impact of Energy Programs, Environment and Safety Requirements and Government Research on Small Business; Special Small Business Problems.

Group Ratings

	ADA	COPE	PC	RPN	NFU	LCV	CFA	NAB	NSI	ACA	NTU
1978	20	61	30	56	50	–	14	64	90	68	–
1977	30	71	33	31	75	42	40	–	–	56	30

Key Votes

1) Increase Def Spnd	FOR	6) Alaska Lands Protect	FOR	11) Delay Auto Pol Cntrl	FOR
2) B-1 Bomber	FOR	7) Water Projects Veto	FOR	12) Sugar Price Escalator	DNV
3) Cargo Preference	AGN	8) Consum Protect Agcy	AGN	13) Pub Fin Cong Cmpgns	AGN
4) Dereg Nat Gas	AGN	9) Common Situs Picket	AGN	14) ERA Ratif Recissn	AGN
5) Kemp-Roth	AGN	10) Labor Law Revision	FOR	15) Prohibt Govt Abrtns	FOR

Election Results

1978 general	Ike Skelton (D)	120,748	(73%)	($149,080)
	Bill Baker (R)	45,116	(27%)	
1978 primary	Ike Skelton (D)	61,176	(87%)	
	One other (D)	9,159	(13%)	
1976 general	Ike Skelton (D)	115,955	(56%)	($206,115)
	Richard A. King (R)	91,605	(44%)	($139,279)

FIFTH DISTRICT

The 5th congressional district of Missouri includes the heart of Kansas City—the central portion of the city, including its downtown and most of its industrial area down by the river and the stockyards. This area is the focus of the Kansas City metropolitan area, an important manufacturing and commercial hub for the farmlands of western Missouri and most of Kansas—and a city with the air and assurance of one of the nation's major and growing metropolitan areas. The 5th includes the city's downtown skyscrapers that sit up on the bluffs above the Missouri River and the Kansas City stockyards. Across a valley facing them is the luxurious Crown Center development started by Hallmark, the greeting card company which is headquartered here. Here in the 5th are the city's black ghettoes and some of its white working class neighborhoods. It also includes the high income neighborhoods around the Country Club Plaza—the nation's first shopping center, built in the twenties—just across the state line from the high income suburbs of Johnson County, Kansas.

In 1948 a 32-year-old World War II veteran who had lived in Kansas City only a couple of years, Richard Bolling, was elected Congressman from the 5th district. From the beginning he seemed likely to be an exceptional congressman, and he has been—but his career has had its ups and downs. In his first years he became one of Speaker Sam Rayburn's proteges and won a seat on the Rules Committee. But after Rayburn's death in 1961 he failed to get the leadership post he wanted; Speaker McCormack and Majority Leader Albert picked Hale Boggs to be the Democratic Whip. Frustrated, Bolling wrote two first-rate books analyzing and attacking the way things were done in the House. To the vigorous, activist Bolling the conduct of Rules Committee business must have been excruciating; it did not have a chairman under 74 from 1958 to 1979. In the late sixties Bolling's career seemed at a nadir.

The seventies have been much better for him. He became a trusted adviser to Carl Albert, a weak Speaker, and to Tip O'Neill, a strong one. He became more senior and was able to exert more leadership on the Rules Committee. In 1974 and 1975 he presided over a major effort to reform the House committee structure and although much of it was defeated, because of opposition from labor and the maritime industry, there were some accomplishments, notably the creation of the House Budget Committee. He failed to win the majority leadership after the 1976 elections. On the second ballot in the Democratic Caucus Jim Wright edged him, 95–93, knocking him out of the race; had that ballot gone differently Bolling would undoubtedly have beaten Phil Burton on the next and would now be majority leader. However, Bolling is still a strong contender for the speakership if a vacancy should occur.

But in 1979 Bolling finally became Chairman of the Rules Committee. This is a particularly important position. Every bill that comes before the House must have a rule, that is, a resolution which sets the length of debate and the extent to which the bill can be amended. Rules are obviously a necessity if business is to be conducted efficiently in a legislature with 435 members; but there is obviously the possibility of abuse. Some previous Rules chairmen used their power to defeat measures they didn't like but which could have won majority approval. Under Bolling and his predecessor, James Delaney, Rules has more often performed the function of helping the majority to do its will. Bolling is expected to work in close cooperation with Speaker O'Neill, and while both men are definitely partisan, they are unlikely to repeat some of the abuses of the past.

Bolling's own views are traditionally Democratic in much the same way Senator Henry Jackson's are. He has always had a very high rating from organized labor. He was always a supporter of the Vietnam war and is concerned about the nation's military strength. He is a procedural reformer, but he does not share the liberalism of some younger members on social issues nor their disdain for traditional Democratic economic policies. The 5th district has always been a solidly Democratic district and elects him every two years without fuss. Exactly what his future in the House is no one can say, but he certainly is living up to his promise.

Census Data Pop. 467,457. Central city, 93%; suburban, 7%. Median family income, $9,727; families above $15,000: 20%; families below $3,000: 9%. Median years education, 12.2.

The Voters

Median voting age 44.
Employment profile White collar, 53%. Blue collar, 32%. Service, 15%. Farm, –%.
Ethnic groups Black, 24%. Spanish, 3%. Total foreign stock, 9%. Germany, Italy, 1% each.

Presidential vote

1976	Carter (D)	87,965	(59%)
	Ford (R)	60,538	(41%)
1972	Nixon (R)	80,553	(53%)
	McGovern (D)	71,527	(47%)

Rep. Richard Bolling (D) Elected 1948; b. May 17, 1916, New York, N.Y.; home, Kansas City; U. of the South, B.A. 1937, M.A. 1939, Vanderbilt U., 1939–40; Episcopalian.

Career Army, WWII; Teacher and coach, Sewanee Military Acad.; Vets. Advisor and Dir. of Student Activities, U. of Kansas City.

Offices 2365 RHOB, 202-225-4535. Also 811 Grand Ave., Kansas City 64106, 816-842-4798.

Committees *Rules* (Chairman).

Group Ratings

	ADA	COPE	PC	RPN	NFU	LCV	CFA	NAB	NSI	ACA	NTU
1978	65	94	68	50	67	–	55	0	33	9	–
1977	75	95	53	56	89	73	65	–	–	4	20
1976	75	95	67	40	100	59	73	0	50	7	18

Key Votes

1) Increase Def Spnd	AGN	6) Alaska Lands Protect	DNV	11) Delay Auto Pol Cntrl	AGN
2) B-1 Bomber	AGN	7) Water Projects Veto	FOR	12) Sugar Price Escalator	DNV
3) Cargo Preference	FOR	8) Consum Protect Agcy	FOR	13) Pub Fin Cong Cmpgns	FOR
4) Dereg Nat Gas	AGN	9) Common Situs Picket	FOR	14) ERA Ratif Recissn	AGN
5) Kemp-Roth	AGN	10) Labor Law Revision	FOR	15) Prohibt Govt Abrtns	AGN

Election Results

1978 general	Richard Bolling (D)	82,140	(73%)	($66,241)
	Steven L. Walter (R)	30,360	(27%)	($9,096)
1978 primary	Richard Bolling (D)	36,670	(77%)	
	Two others (D)	10,908	(23%)	
1976 general	Richard Bolling (D)	100,876	(71%)	($44,645)
	JoAnne Collins (R)	41,681	(29%)	($16,925)

SIXTH DISTRICT

Northwest Missouri is mostly farmland, gentle rolling hill country above the bluffs that line the Missouri and other major rivers. In many ways this is a place left behind by the twentieth century. The mechanization of the family farm has thinned out the population here, as young people seek a better way to make a living elsewhere. All the counties of northwest Missouri, except those in the Kansas City metropolitan area, had more people in 1900 than they do today. Perhaps the most poignant story belongs to St. Joseph, once one of the leading ports of entry to the American West: it was here that the Pony Express riders first saddled up for their transcontinental sprints to Sacramento. In 1900 St. Joseph was a solid commercial competitor of Kansas City, with 102,000 people compared to Kansas City's 163,000. Today metropolitan Kansas City has more than a million people, while St. Joseph's population has dwindled to 72,000 and is diminishing still.

The 6th congressional district covers almost precisely the northwest corner of Missouri, the land north and east of the Missouri River, west of a line drawn north and south through the middle of the state. Though most of the expanse of the 6th is given over to agriculture, as it was at the turn of the century, most of its residents now live in metropolitan areas. Some are in St. Joseph, but by far the bulk of its population can be found in Clay and Platte Counties in metropolitan Kansas City. To give itself space to grow, Kansas City has been systematically annexing land in these two counties for the last twenty years; much of it has been bulldozed for subdivisions or to accommodate Kansas City's giant new airport. The Census Bureau considers Clay and Platte Counties as part of the central city, and technically they are; but their character is suburban or even rural. Travellers driving into town from Mid-Continent International, the new airport, pass through miles of dairy grazing land and cornfields—inside the city limits of Kansas City.

The 6th is one of those Missouri districts which in national and statewide election trended Republican during the sixties and early seventies: it didn't like Kennedy's Catholicism, Johnson's Great Society, and Humphrey's and McGovern's liberalism. More recently in national elections it has gone back to its ancestral Democratic habits when the Democrats nominated a Southerner in 1976. Yet in congressional elections, the district's performance has been just the opposite. It was held through the sixties by Democrat W. R. Hull, an old-fashioned rural Missourian who often voted with Southerners, and in the early seventies by Jerry Litton, a rich young farmer who identified himself closely with rural problems, won the Democratic Senate primary in 1976, and was killed in a plane crash on primary night.

The district might still have a Democratic congressman were it not for the problems of Morgan Maxfield, the party's 1976 nominee. Maxfield was a protege of Lamar Hunt, owner of the Kansas City Chiefs, and he spent more than $200,000 on his own campaign. It was going swimmingly until an article about him appeared in the Kansas City *Star* in October. The paper had been doing some digging into Maxfield's background. Reporters found that though he claimed he grew up in poverty, his father was a prosperous doctor; though he said he was a graduate of Harvard Business School, he had actually taken only a six week course there; though he said he was a bachelor, he had a wife and children back in Texas. It would have been interesting to be at the strategy meeting at which the candidate and his advisers decided how to counter these revelations. Many voters were convinced that Maxfield was a fraud, and the Republican candidate, 33-year-old Kansas City state legislator Thomas Coleman, was elected with 59% of the vote.

Coleman's political progress can serve as an object lesson in the intelligent use of incumbency. He did a good job of keeping in touch with his constituents through franked mail and personal appearances. He got a seat on the House Agriculture Committee, and made a major effort to identify himself with agricultural issues in the rural counties, where he was unknown in 1976. In 1978 five Democrats, including Maxfield, considered their chances of winning great enough to make it worthwhile to run in the primary; and the winner, Clay County state Senator Phil Snowden, had good name identification and popularity in the Kansas City area. Nonetheless Coleman was able to win reelection with 56% of the vote. Snowden, a former University of Missouri quarterback, filmed ads with his college coach, Dan Devine, but Coleman was still able to win both the Kansas City suburbs and the rural counties. He may well get tough competition again in the future, but he seems well on his way to making this a safe seat.

Census Data Pop. 469,642. Central city, 30%; suburban, 22%. Median family income, $8,507; families above $15,000: 14%; families below $3,000: 12%. Median years education, 12.1.

The Voters

Median voting age 45.
Employment profile White collar, 43%. Blue collar, 35%. Service, 12%. Farm, 10%.
Ethnic groups Black, 1%. Total foreign stock, 5%. Germany, 1%.

Presidential vote

1976	Carter (D)	107,977	(52%)
	Ford (R)	99,618	(48%)
1972	Nixon (R)	134,977	(67%)
	McGovern (D)	65,754	(33%)

Rep. E. Thomas Coleman (R) Elected 1976; b. May 25, 1943, Kansas City; home, Kansas City; Wm. Jewell Col., B.A. 1965, NYU, M.A. 1969, Washington U., St. Louis, J.D. 1969.

Career Asst. Atty. Gen. of Mo., 1969–72; Mo. House of Reps., 1973–76.

Offices 1527 LHOB, 202-225-7041. Also 2701 Rock Creek Pkwy., Kansas City 64116, 816-474-9035.

Committees *Agriculture* (12th). Subcommittees: Conservation and Credit; Family Farms, Rural Development, and Special Studies; Livestock and Grains.

Education and Labor (7th). Subcommittees: Human Resources; Select Education.

Group Ratings

	ADA	COPE	PC	RPN	NFU	LCV	CFA	NAB	NSI	ACA	NTU
1978	20	11	15	50	40	–	18	92	100	93	–
1977	15	17	33	62	50	45	20	–	–	81	38

Key Votes

1) Increase Def Spnd	FOR	6) Alaska Lands Protect	FOR	11) Delay Auto Pol Cntrl	FOR
2) B-1 Bomber	FOR	7) Water Projects Veto	FOR	12) Sugar Price Escalator	FOR
3) Cargo Preference	AGN	8) Consum Protect Agcy	AGN	13) Pub Fin Cong Cmpgns	AGN
4) Dereg Nat Gas	FOR	9) Common Situs Picket	AGN	14) ERA Ratif Recissn	FOR
5) Kemp-Roth	FOR	10) Labor Law Revision	AGN	15) Prohibt Govt Abrtns	FOR

Election Results

1978 general	Tom Coleman (R)	96,574	(56%)	($274,804)
	Phil Snowden (D)	76,061	(44%)	($280,118)
1978 primary	Tom Coleman (R), unopposed			
1976 general	Tom Coleman (R)	120,969	(59%)	($97,294)
	Morgan Maxfield (D)	83,755	(41%)	($383,277)

SEVENTH DISTRICT

Mention the Ozarks and you evoke an image of rural poverty: people with quaint accents living in hillside shacks, cut off from the current of twentieth century America—a kind of Dogpatch. But for the Ozark Mountains of southwest Missouri, an area roughly coincident with the state's 7th congressional district, the Dogpatch image is far from accurate, and getting less accurate every year. Here you can find sizeable and prosperous cities, like Springfield, third largest in the state, and Joplin. Outside the cities you can see how the landscape has been transformed in recent years, as people from St. Louis and Kansas City and even Chicago build vacation homes or even year-round residences in the pleasant green hills and along the large, often man-made, lakes. Moreover, the climate here is relatively temperate. The Ozarks, long a backwater, are now one of the fastest growing parts of the country.

Many mountain areas—eastern Tennessee and central Kentucky as well as the Ozarks—have developed a politics contrary to that of the lowlands, politics that go back more than a century. Most people here did not share the slaveholding habits or Confederate sympathies of most central Missourians, and during the Civil War period they became staunch Republicans—and have stayed that way. During the sixties the Republican inclination was strengthened by distaste for Democratic social programs and by the urban conservatism of many of the area's new arrivals (one thing many of them liked about the Ozarks is that there are virtually no blacks here). In the close statewide elections of 1968, 1970, and 1972 every county in the 7th went Republican; in 1974, it was the only Missouri congressional district not carried by Senator Thomas Eagleton. Although that Southerner Jimmy Carter did better here than other Democratic presidential candidates, he still did not carry the district.

The 7th also for years was the only Missouri district to send a Republican to Congress. The current incumbent is Gene Taylor, a Sarcoxie auto dealer who was Republican National Committeeman when he first ran for the seat in 1972. His most difficult election was the first Republican primary, in which he narrowly defeated John Ashcroft, now Missouri's Attorney General. Taylor was also pressed in the 1974 general election, but since then has won easily. He serves on the Public Works and Post Office and Civil Service Committees and has a voting record rated near 100% by conservative and business groups.

Census Data Pop. 466,699. Central city, 26%; suburban, 7%. Median family income, $6,832; families above $15,000: 9%; families below $3,000: 18%. Median years education, 11.7.

The Voters

Median voting age 47.
Employment profile White collar, 41%. Blue collar, 39%. Service, 13%. Farm, 7%.
Ethnic groups Total foreign stock, 3%.

Presidential vote

1976	Carter (D)	103,297	(47%)
	Ford (R)	114,881	(53%)
1972	Nixon (R)	153,239	(73%)
	McGovern (D)	57,616	(27%)

Rep. Gene Taylor (R) Elected 1972; b. Feb. 10, 1928, near Sarcoxie; home, Sarcoxie; S.W. Mo. St. Col.; Methodist.

Career Public school teacher; Pres., Gene Taylor Ford Sales, Inc.; Mayor of Sarcoxie, 1954–60.

Offices 2430 RHOB, 202-225-6536. Also 314A Wilhoit Bldg., Springfield 65806, 417-862-4317.

Committees *Post Office and Civil Service* (2d). Subcommittees: Civil Service; Investigations.

Public Works and Transportation (8th). Subcommittees: Aviation; Economic Development; Water Resources.

Group Ratings

	ADA	COPE	PC	RPN	NFU	LCV	CFA	NAB	NSI	ACA	NTU
1978	10	15	18	50	20	–	18	100	100	96	–
1977	0	9	15	54	55	0	0	–	–	89	56
1976	0	13	10	47	25	4	0	83	100	96	71

Key Votes

1) Increase Def Spnd	FOR	6) Alaska Lands Protect	AGN	11) Delay Auto Pol Cntrl	FOR
2) B-1 Bomber	FOR	7) Water Projects Veto	AGN	12) Sugar Price Escalator	FOR
3) Cargo Preference	AGN	8) Consum Protect Agcy	AGN	13) Pub Fin Cong Cmpgns	AGN
4) Dereg Nat Gas	FOR	9) Common Situs Picket	AGN	14) ERA Ratif Recissn	FOR
5) Kemp-Roth	FOR	10) Labor Law Revision	AGN	15) Prohibt Govt Abrtns	FOR

Election Results

1978 general	Gene Taylor (R)	104,566	(61%)	($104,612)
	Jim Thomas (D)	66,351	(39%)	($25,037)
1978 primary	Gene Taylor (R), unopposed			
1976 general	Gene Taylor (R)	133,656	(62%)	($72,750)
	Dolan G. Hawkins (D)	81,848	(38%)	($2,374)

EIGHTH DISTRICT

After five redistrictings in 15 years, the 8th congressional district of Missouri has at last got a fairly regular shape. Before the 1972 redistricting, it looked like a slingshot; today it looks rather like a chocolate rooster with a solid base. The comb includes Columbia, the district's largest city and home of the University of Missouri. At just about where the ears would be if chickens had ears is Jefferson City, the sleepy little state capital. The tail feathers are in the western end of suburban St. Louis County; the feet or leg base is solidly in the Ozarks, extending to the Arkansas border.

These are areas of diverse political leanings. Columbia, with a Dixie Democratic heritage, also has a sizeable university vote. The St. Louis County suburbs in the district are staunchly Republican. Probably the most interesting parts of the district are Jefferson City and the counties to the east, which have been strongly Republican since they were settled by antislavery German '48ers in the middle nineteenth century. Though the Ozark counties are Republican, most of the rural counties in the 8th are traditional Missouri Democratic. The most notable features south of Jefferson City are Fort Leonard Wood, long one of the Army's centers for basic training, and the resort area around Lake of the Ozarks.

All the redistrictings here have not changed the identity of the district's congressman. Since the 1960 election he has been Richard Ichord, a Democrat who receives ratings over 80% from conservative organizations. Ichord has a unique distinction in the House: he is a former committee chairman, whose committee was abolished out from under him. That was the House Internal Security Committee, better known under its previous name as the House Un-American Activities Committee. This was a body that produced virtually no legislation, but concentrated on investigations, mostly of left wing groups but sometimes in its last years of groups like the Ku Klux Klan. Ichord was Chairman from 1969 until 1975. The Committee was unpopular with many of the freshmen elected in 1974 and was abolished by a parliamentary device engineered by Phillip Burton.

Ichord nevertheless has a valuable committee post now: he is fourth-ranking Democrat on the House Armed Services Committee and Chairman of the Subcommittee on Research and Development. His views on military policy can be summarized by noting that he voted for raising the defense budget above what the House had allowed in the 95th Congress. He also has a good chance of becoming Chairman of the full Armed Services Committee. He is ten years younger than the youngest senior member of Armed Services and is only in his early fifties himself. Whether the Democratic Caucus would elect him as chairman is unclear; he is out of line with majority Democratic views on many issues, and while some of his adversaries consider him fair, others find him contentious. Ichord does not seem to have had a great impact on the legislative process, however. An exhaustive, book-length examination of his career by Reid Detchon of the Columbia *Daily Tribune* concluded that aside from getting a national park designation for a wild river in southern Missouri, he has had few legislative accomplishments.

That finding and others in the newspaper series—including charges that he couldn't handle crises well—hurt Ichord in the 1978 election campaign. For the first time he failed to carry Columbia's Boone County, and his active Republican opponent reduced his percentage from 69% in 1976 to 60%. The greatest risk for Ichord in 1980 is if a strong Republican candidate should run and capture his party's normal percentages in Jefferson City and the St. Louis suburbs; one possibility is assistant Attorney General Larry Marshall, a former legislator from a Democratic area. On balance this is not that heavily Democratic a district; it went for Ford over Carter in 1976. Ichord is undoubtedly looking forward to being Armed Services Chairman, but he may first have to win some tougher elections in the 8th district than he has been accustomed to.

Census Data Pop. 467,532. Central city, 13%; suburban, 24%. Median family income, $7,743; families above $15,000: 14%; families below $3,000: 15%. Median years education, 11.2.

The Voters

Median voting age 40.
Employment profile White collar, 46%. Blue collar, 37%. Service, 12%. Farm, 5%.
Ethnic groups Black, 3%. Total foreign stock, 5%. Germany, 2%.

Presidential vote

1976	Carter (D)	93,354	(47%)
	Ford (R)	105,449	(53%)
1972	Nixon (R)	124,585	(68%)
	McGovern (D)	58,036	(32%)

Rep. Richard H. Ichord (D) Elected 1960; b. June 27, 1926, Licking; home, Houston; U. of Mo., B.S. 1949, J.D. 1952; Baptist.

Career Navy, WWII; Practicing atty.; Mo. House of Reps., 1952–60, Spkr. Pro-Tempore, 1957–58, Spkr., 1959–60.

Offices 2302 RHOB, 202-225-5155. Also P.O. Box 298, Jefferson City 65102, 314-634-3510.

Committees *Armed Services* (4th). Subcommittees: Investigations; Research and Development (Chairman); NATO Standardization, Interoperability, and Readiness.

Small Business (16th). Subcommittees: Antitrust, Consumers and Employment; SBA and SBIC Authority and General Small Business Problems; Antitrust and Restraint of Trade Activities Affecting Small Business.

Group Ratings

	ADA	COPE	PC	RPN	NFU	LCV	CFA	NAB	NSI	ACA	NTU
1978	20	30	33	64	30	–	9	92	90	92	–
1977	5	19	23	64	50	4	0	–	–	85	45
1976	5	14	23	24	17	16	27	92	90	96	71

Key Votes

1) Increase Def Spnd	FOR	6) Alaska Lands Protect	FOR	11) Delay Auto Pol Cntrl	FOR
2) B-1 Bomber	FOR	7) Water Projects Veto	AGN	12) Sugar Price Escalator	FOR
3) Cargo Preference	AGN	8) Consum Protect Agcy	AGN	13) Pub Fin Cong Cmpgns	AGN
4) Dereg Nat Gas	FOR	9) Common Situs Picket	FOR	14) ERA Ratif Recissn	FOR
5) Kemp-Roth	AGN	10) Labor Law Revision	AGN	15) Prohibt Govt Abrtns	DNV

Election Results

1978 general	Richard Ichord (D)	96,509	(60%)	($120,482)
	Donald D. Meyer (R)	63,109	(40%)	($78,847)
1978 primary	Richard Ichord (D), unopposed			
1976 general	Richard Ichord (D)	132,386	(69%)	($40,472)
	Charles R. Leick (R)	60,179	(31%)	($12,690)

NINTH DISTRICT

The part of rural Missouri which has most faithfully sustained a Democratic tradition is not the southern part of the state; rather, it is the Little Dixie region, north of the Missouri River and across the Mississippi from Illinois. The land here was settled early in the nineteenth century mainly by immigrants from Kentucky and Tennessee. During the Civil War some citizens of Little Dixie fought on the Confederate side, and at least one county declared itself independent of the unionist state of Missouri. Since then, not much urbanization has come to this part of Missouri—so little that Mark Twain would probably still recognize his native Hannibal, one of Little Dixie's largest towns, were it not for the tourist traps that use Twain himself for bait. Nor have voting habits changed much. This part of the state continues to be more Democratic than Missouri as a whole; it went for Jimmy Carter, and George McGovern even carried one county here.

Little Dixie was once a congressional district unto itself. Now, because of the one-person-one-vote requirements, the region has just a bare majority of residents of Missouri's 9th congressional district. The rest of the 9th is the northern reaches of the St. Louis metropolitan area: fast-growing, increasingly Republican St. Charles County and a northern chunk of St. Louis County, which is predominantly blue collar and Democratic.

This district has had a succession of distinctive congressmen. For forty years it was represented by Clarence Cannon, onetime Parliamentarian of the House and Chairman of the Appropriations Committee for two decades. During his last year he and his Senate counterpart, the late Carl Hayden, got into a monumental battle over which side of the Capitol a conference committee meeting should take place; this battle of the octogenarians held up the whole federal budget for several months. Cannon's successor was William Hungate, a peppery and generally liberal Democrat who was one of the wittier members of the House Judiciary Committee. He retired young in 1976 to get away from the hassles of Congress to the pleasures of private law practice.

This was only the second time in 54 years that the 9th district had a race without an incumbent, and naturally there was considerable competition for the seat. Leading the eleven-candidate Democratic primary with 35% of the vote was Hannibal state legislator Harold Volkmer. He had serious opposition from a Republican state Senator from St. Louis County. Volkmer held this opponent even in the St. Louis metropolitan area and beat him 3–2 in Little Dixie. That race has pretty well determined the succession. Volkmer took Hungate's seat on Judiciary, but his seat on Agriculture has probably been of more political use. His voting record has been middle of the road; he does not vote as often with most northern Democrats as Hungate did, but more often than Cannon had. He had no primary opposition and no serious competition in the general election in 1978, and seems to have a safe seat.

Census Data Pop. 467,990. Central city, 0%; suburban, 49%. Median family income, $9,573; families above $15,000: 18%; families below $3,000: 11%. Median years education, 12.1.

The Voters

Median voting age 43.
Employment profile White collar, 45%. Blue collar, 36%. Service, 11%. Farm, 8%.
Ethnic groups Black, 3%. Total foreign stock, 5%. Germany, 2%.

Presidential vote

1976	Carter (D)	108,189	(50%)
	Ford (R)	109,684	(50%)
1972	Nixon (R)	129,159	(65%)
	McGovern (D)	69,218	(35%)

Rep. Harold L. Volkmer (D) Elected 1976; b. Apr. 4, 1931, Jefferson City; home, Hannibal; Jefferson City Jr. Col., St. Louis U., U. of Mo., LL.B. 1955; Catholic.

Career Army, 1955–57; Practicing atty., 1957–60; Marion Co. Prosecuting Atty., 1960–66; Mo. House of Reps., 1967–77.

Offices 1728 LHOB, 202-225-2956. Also 316 Fed. Bldg., Hannibal 63401, 314-221-1200.

Committees *Science and Technology* (19th). Subcommittees: Energy, Development and Technology; Transportation, Aviation, and Technology.

Judiciary (14th). Subcommittees: Civil and Constitutional Rights; Crime; Monopolies and Commercial Law.

Group Ratings

	ADA	COPE	PC	RPN	NFU	LCV	CFA	NAB	NSI	ACA	NTU
1978	45	65	53	25	40	–	36	75	40	54	–
1977	60	68	58	54	67	45	50	–	–	48	52

Key Votes

1) Increase Def Spnd	AGN	6) Alaska Lands Protect	DNV	11) Delay Auto Pol Cntrl	FOR
2) B-1 Bomber	AGN	7) Water Projects Veto	FOR	12) Sugar Price Escalator	FOR
3) Cargo Preference	AGN	8) Consum Protect Agcy	AGN	13) Pub Fin Cong Cmpgns	FOR
4) Dereg Nat Gas	AGN	9) Common Situs Picket	AGN	14) ERA Ratif Recissn	AGN
5) Kemp-Roth	AGN	10) Labor Law Revision	FOR	15) Prohibt Govt Abrtns	FOR

Election Results

1978 general	Harold Volkmer (D)	135,170	(75%)	($101,375)
	Jerry Dent (R)	45,795	(25%)	
1978 primary	Harold Volkmer (D), unopposed			
1976 general	Harold Volkmer (D)	120,325	(56%)	($109,405)
	J. H. Frappier (R)	94,816	(44%)	($85,829)

TENTH DISTRICT

The 10th congressional district of Missouri is roughly congruent with the southeast corner of the state, known commonly as the Bootheel. This part of the country was first settled by Southerners coming up the Mississippi, looking for more fertile, moist, level land for growing cotton. They found it here, in the late nineteenth and early twentieth centuries, and since then the Bootheel has had more of a Deep South feel to it than any other part of Missouri. One gauge of this is the 19% George Wallace won in the 10th in 1968—a far better showing than he made in any other Missouri congressional district.

Upon the retirement of the incumbent, Democrat Bill Burlison was elected Congressman from the 10th district in 1968. He was formerly prosecutor in Cape Girardeau, the district's largest urban concentration after Jefferson County, which is the southernmost part of the St. Louis metropolitan area. Compiling a middle of the road voting record, Burlison has kept a relatively low profile in the House. His committee choices were made with an eye on district matters. Initially he served on Agriculture; after four years he switched to Appropriations and its Agriculture Subcommittee. That body has been chaired by Jamie Whitten of Mississippi for most of the last thirty years; with the power of the purse Whitten has become known as the "permanent secretary of agriculture."

Today Burlison is the second-ranking Democrat on the Agriculture Subcommittee. Should Whitten, who turns 70 in 1980, leave the chair, he will undoubtedly succeed to it, with all that means. He has generally won reelection without difficulty in the 10th, although rumors that he was having an affair with the wife of a family friend may have lowered his percentage in 1978.

Census Data Pop. 466,731. Central city, 0%; suburban, 23%. Median family income, $7,048; families above $15,000: 9%; families below $3,000: 20%. Median years education, 9.4.

The Voters

Median voting age 45.
Employment profile White collar, 36%. Blue collar, 44%. Service, 13%. Farm, 7%.
Ethnic groups Black, 5%. Total foreign stock, 2%.

Presidential vote

1976	Carter (D)	108,223	(57%)
	Ford (R)	80,655	(43%)
1972	Nixon (R)	111,777	(66%)
	McGovern (D)	57,754	(34%)

Rep. Bill D. Burlison (D) Elected 1968; b. Mar. 15, 1935, Wardell; home, Cape Girardeau; S.E. Mo. St. Col., B.A. 1953, B.S. 1959, U. of Mo., LL.B. 1956, M.Ed. 1964; Baptist.

Career USMC, 1956–59; Practicing atty.; Business Law Instructor, S.E. Mo. St. Col.; Asst. Atty. Gen. of Mo., 1959–62; Cape Giradeau Co. Prosecuting Atty., 1962–68; Pres., Cape Girardeau Co. Bd. of Educ., 1966.

Offices 2346 RHOB, 202-225-4404. Also 246 New Fed. Bldg., Cape Girardeau 63701, 314-335-0101.

Committees *Appropriations* (19th). Subcommittees: Agriculture and Related Agencies; Defense.

Group Ratings

	ADA	COPE	PC	RPN	NFU	LCV	CFA	NAB	NSI	ACA	NTU
1978	45	75	53	27	56	–	41	33	50	22	–
1977	45	91	60	45	58	30	60	–	–	11	21
1976	50	61	62	39	67	48	91	27	70	43	24

Key Votes

1) Increase Def Spnd	FOR	6) Alaska Lands Protect	FOR	11) Delay Auto Pol Cntrl	FOR
2) B-1 Bomber	FOR	7) Water Projects Veto	AGN	12) Sugar Price Escalator	FOR
3) Cargo Preference	AGN	8) Consum Protect Agcy	AGN	13) Pub Fin Cong Cmpgns	FOR
4) Dereg Nat Gas	AGN	9) Common Situs Picket	FOR	14) ERA Ratif Recissn	AGN
5) Kemp-Roth	AGN	10) Labor Law Revision	AGN	15) Prohibt Govt Abrtns	DNV

Election Results

1978 general	Bill Burlison (D)	99,148	(65%)	($51,165)
	James A. Weir (R)	52,687	(35%)	
1978 primary	Bill Burlison (D)	49,539	(64%)	
	Pat McKee (D)	20,649	(27%)	($6,064)
	One other (D)	6,765	(9%)	
1976 general	Bill Burlison (D)	131,675	(72%)	
	Joe Carron (R)	51,024	(28%)	

MONTANA

Montana is the nation's 4th largest state in area, but only 43d in population. To the west in the Big Sky Country are rugged mountains and to the east treeless plains; so vast and underpopulated is this state that you can often drive 40 miles down a road and not see another car. People here love life under the Big Sky, and most seem to prefer weekends of hunting, fishing, camping, and boating to the headier attractions of life in urban America. Montana's urban areas—the biggest, Billings and Great Falls, each have less than 100,000 people—do not loom large on the public consciousness.

Montana's first white settlers were miners, some of whom found large deposits of gold, silver, and copper in the Rockies. Raucous mining towns sprang up, complete with outlaws and vigilantes. The largest mining town, Butte, sitting on "the richest hill on earth," was for many years the state's largest city. Now most of the copper has been dug out, and Butte has lost population; but it still retains some of its funky, sinful ways. Some time after the first miners arrived, cattlemen and dry land wheat farmers moved onto the plains and river valleys of the state. Aside from mining, there has been little industrial development here, indeed little development of any kind. Even the tourist business only began to boom with the opening of the late Chet Huntley's Big Sky development.

For many years Montana politics was a struggle between the mine owners, particularly Anaconda, the power companies, and the cattlemen all on one side, all very much Republican, and the unions, miners, and some smaller farmers on the other, all Democrats. Geographically, this has meant that the eastern plains and Billings usually go Republican and the western mountains and Butte, Great Falls, and Missoula usually go Democratic. But geography is not the real divider here; this is almost class warfare politics, arguably the closest thing we have left to it in the United States. In general the Democrats have won the big elections here, but seldom by very large margins; Montana has only once elected a Republican U.S. senator, but came within a few percentage points of doing so half a dozen times.

For 16 years Montana had the same two senators, Mike Mansfield and Lee Metcalf. Mansfield was of course better known: Lyndon Johnson had made him Senate Democratic Whip, and he was Senate Majority Leader from 1961 to 1977. Mansfield was criticized sometimes for not pushing senators harder, but he saw himself as a kind of moderator, not an arm-twisting dictator. A more aggressive approach probably would not have worked in the Senate of the sixties and seventies. Mansfield also had a strong backbone: he was one of the few to talk back to Lyndon Johnson personally on the Vietnam war—he is an expert on Asian affairs—and he could stand his ground as stubbornly as anyone when he wanted to. He was willing to do that with his constituents too. His Democratic, pro-labor record suited the majority of them fine, but they were not happy that he was the only Rocky Mountain senator to support gun control. Mansfield decided to retire in 1976, but it was not for long; he was soon made Ambassador to Japan. Metcalf was far less visible. In the Montana Democratic tradition he fought the large power companies and the big brokerage firms on Wall Street. First elected in 1960 and reelected narrowly in 1966 and 1972, he decided to retire in 1978; but he died early in the year before his term expired.

There is a certain symmetry to Montana politics. Mansfield and Metcalf were replaced by two Democrats who, like their predecessors, had been congressmen. The succession to the Mansfield seat was nearly automatic; it was won by 2d district Congressman John Melcher. A veterinarian and local officeholder, he had won the seat in the 2d district (the eastern, plains part of the state, including Great Falls and Billings) in a special election in 1969. The 2d is a vast expanse—the fourth largest district in the nation in area—where cattle ranches stretch as far as the eye can see and towering buttes rise over the magnificently eroded high plains. This is the agricultural part of the state, but almost half its votes are cast in the two big urban areas. Melcher soon became a champion vote-getter in this rather unlikely territory; he won 76% in the not very Democratic year of 1972. Two years later, he dipped to 63%, apparently as the result of a drunk driving arrest. But as soon as Mansfield announced his retirement, Melcher entered the race and no other significant Democrat challenged him.

Nor did Melcher have a really significant Republican challenger, either. Stanley Burger won something of an upset in the primary, and he attracted large sums from out of state conservatives—almost all of his vast (for Montana) $563,000 budget. But the money caused him as much trouble as anything else. One fundraiser was held for him in the Capitol Hill office of Senator Jesse Helms; it turns out that it is illegal to raise money for campaigns on federal property. Despite his large media budget, Burger was unable to convince voters that Melcher stood for big brother government; the Democrat won by nearly a 2–1 margin.

Melcher is not likely to be the greatest orator in the Senate, but he should have some influence in two areas which are important for eastern Montana and on which he concentrated in the House. One is agriculture; the plains here are wheat country, and Melcher is on the Agriculture Committee. The other is strip mining. It turns out that Montana has some of the nation's largest coal reserves, all close to the surface; there is continual controversy here over whether the mining companies' efforts at reclamation are satisfactory. Melcher in the House favored tough federal laws, both on general principle and because without them, states with lax enforcement would enjoy an economic advantage. In the Senate he has tended to take the middle ground on the issue. On other issues, Melcher's record is similar to that of most Democrats—but not always. He was, for example, one of the northern Democrats to break ranks and vote against the Panama Canal Treaty.

With Melcher winning the Senate race, the 2d district reverted to the normalcy of a Republican congressman. Ron Marlenee, the Republican, won with a convincing 55% despite the lack of a geographical base and a smaller budget than his opponent. In his first term Marlenee seems to have been a district—oriented rather than ideological congressman. His voting record generally follows Republican lines, but he is not one of the New Right conservatives from the Rocky Mountains. On farm programs he tends to support more generous payments to farmers than many Republicans do. He serves on the Agriculture and Interior Committees—assignments of obvious interest to the district. He was reelected with 57% in 1978. Having declined to run for the Senate in 1978, Marlenee has apparently missed his chance to do so; but he seems comfortable in the 2d district seat.

The succession to Lee Metcalf's Senate seat was not automatic. From the beginning the favorite was Max Baucus, Democratic Congressman from the 1st district, first elected in 1974. But he had to overcome a series of obstacles. First of all, early in 1978 Metcalf died. That gave the appointment to the vacancy to Democratic Governor Thomas Judge, no friend of Baucus. Instead of naming Baucus or a stand-in, and apparently despairing of his own chances to hold the seat, Judge tried to find a formidable candidate and came up with Montana Supreme Court Chief Justice Paul Hatfield, who had just won a partisan race with an impressive majority, but as is so often the case with lesser statewide officials, that reflected less his popularity than his name familiarity and the lack of serious competition. Hatfield was not an accomplished politician, and got little political advantage out of his incumbency. In fact it hurt him. He had to vote on the Panama Canal Treaty, and while his colleague Melcher was opposing it Hatfield became convinced he ought to support it. He did, in one of the more courageous political decisions of 1978, and it broke whatever momentum his campaign had. In the primary he got only 19% of the vote to Baucus's 65%; Hatfield was later in line for an appointment as a federal judge.

What has made Baucus so popular? Largely hard work. Like many incumbents he has returned home often—which with Montana airline schedules is not all that easy. He has helped constituents with their problems with government. He has kept in touch with them frequently with franked mailings. In personal contacts he has the firmness and sincerity Montanans seem to like. He has even gone so far as to ride bucking broncos in a rodeo. His voting record has earned him high ratings from labor and liberal organizations, but he is enough of a penny-pincher to get good ratings from the National Taxpayers' Union.

The Republican nominee, Larry Williams, was largely unknown when he won the primary, but he turned out to be a shrewd and attractive candidate. A successful investment counselor, he poured his own money into the campaign and was adroit enough to use his own problems with the Securities and Exchange Commission as examples of overbearing government interference with private lives. He attacked Baucus for his support of the Panama Canal Treaty and his attitudes toward Southeast Asia; he attacked Baucus as a free spender. Williams's campaign gained momentum in October; Baucus forces slowed it in the last weeks by printing an old promotion picture of Williams, showing him with long curly hair and wearing love beads. Printed next to it was the picture of Baucus on the bronco. Baucus won with 55%. In the Senate he got committee assignments with national scope—Finance and Judiciary. His future potential, assuming he can maintain a good level of popularity in Montana, is great. He was first elected at age 36, and seems to be one of the few senators with a good chance of serving in the twenty-first century.

The 1st district seat Baucus left behind is basically Democratic; Republicans have won it only four times since the twenties. But from 1960 to 1972 it was the scene of constant close elections, largely because of the weakness of Arnold Olsen, a Democrat first elected in 1960 and defeated in 1970 and 1972. The district has some strong Democratic voting blocs: Butte and its miners have been better than 2–1 Democratic for fifty years; Missoula has been increasingly Democratic since students at the University of Montana got the vote; mining and Indian counties at various corners of the state produce big Democratic majorities. The Republican strongholds—the new rich city of Kalispell, Larry Williams's home; the southwest corner of the state near Yellowstone National Park—are not usually enough to overcome the Democrats.

That was the case in 1978. The Democratic nominee, state legislator Pat Williams, lost the primary four years before to Baucus; he is close enough to organized labor that the state AFL-CIO director is godfather to one of his children. The Republican nominee, Missoula County Commissioner Jim Waltermire, surprised everyone by winning the primary over Tippy Huntley, widow of the newscaster. But he was unable to break into the Democrat's strength in Missoula, while Williams carried his home town, the often Republican state capital of Helena. The voting followed almost exactly the same lines as the Baucus-Larry Williams race, and Pat Williams won with 57%. He seems to be in a strong position to hold this district.

Governor Judge won reelection with 63% of the vote in 1976. But this was one of the least edifying races in the country, with charges and countercharges flying wildly—some baseless, some all too true. It began with a scandal in the workmen's compensation department; Attorney General Robert Woodahl, a Republican, said Judge was involved. But Woodahl could not make his charges stand up in court; one case was embarrassingly dismissed. Later Judge revealed that he had failed to disclose $94,000 in contributions to his 1972 campaign—and that he wouldn't reveal them now, either. Further into the campaign, Woodahl was cited for contempt of court in connection with the workmen's compensation cases. The election results, while clearly a personal repudiation of Woodahl, were not necessarily an endorsement of Judge. His chances of winning a third four year term in 1980 may very well depend on his attracting as weak an opponent again.

There is also a positive side to Judge's record. In 1974 he organized a Rocky Mountain governors' association composed, at that time, entirely of Democrats. (Now Nevada has a Republican governor, but all the other Rockies states still have Democrats.) Their goal was to extend state control over use of their lands and to stop both the federal government and big corporations from making basic decisions which affect people's lives and exploit irreplaceable resources. The election of a Democratic president has, if anything, gotten these governors even madder: many worked furiously against Jimmy Carter's decision to stop several federal water projects. Montana has serious problems and great opportunities, with its fertile land, large coal deposits, and great wilderness. It would be good if Montana state politicians addressed themselves more to these problems in the years ahead.

Census Data Pop. 694,409; 0.34% of U.S. total, 43d largest; Central city, 18%; suburban, 7%. Median family income, $8,510; 32d highest; families above $15,000: 14%; families below $3,000: 11%. Median years education, 12.3.

1977 Share of Federal Tax Burden $1,071,000,000; 0.31% of U.S. total, 46th largest.

1977 Share of Federal Outlays $1,690,910,000; 0.43% of U.S. total, 41st largest. Per capita federal spending, $2,261.

DOD	$321,050,000	42d (0.35%)	HEW	$456,872,000	44th (0.31%)
ERDA	$7,423,000	31st (0.13%)	HUD	$15,115,000	42d (0.36%)
NASA	$33,000	49th (—%)	VA	$69,231,000	44th (0.36%)
DOT	$95,714,000	39th (0.67%)	EPA	$12,221,000	47th (0.15%)
DOC	$60,439,000	33d (0.73%)	RevS	$28,755,000	42d (0.34%)
DOI	$107,092,000	14th (2.30%)	Debt	$48,335,000	41st (0.16%)
USDA	$307,492,000	29th (1.55%)	Other	$161,138,000	

Economic Base Agriculture, notably cattle, wheat, barley and dairy products; finance, insurance and real estate; lumber and wood products, especially sawmills and planing mills; primary nonferrous metals, and other primary metal industries; food and kindred products; metal mining.

Political Line-up Governor, Thomas L. Judge (D). Senators, John Melcher (D) and Max Baucus (D). Representatives 2 (1 D and 1 R). State Senate (26 R and 24 D); State House (55 D and 45 R).

The Voters

Registration 410,120 Total. No statewide registration.
Median voting age 43
Employment profile White collar, 45%. Blue collar, 28%. Service, 15%. Farm, 12%.
Ethnic groups Indian, 4%. Total foreign stock, 17%.

Presidential vote

1976	Carter (D)	149,259	(46%)
	Ford (R)	173,703	(54%)
1972	Nixon (R)	183,976	(60%)
	McGovern (D)	120,197	(40%)

1976 Democratic Presidential Primary

Church	63,448	(62%)
Carter	26,329	(26%)
Others	13,244	(12%)

1976 Republican Presidential Primary

Reagan	56,683	(65%)
Ford	31,100	(35%)

Sen. John Melcher (D) Elected 1976, seat up 1982; b. Sept. 6, 1924, Sioux City, Ia.; home, Forsyth; U. of Minn., 1942–43, Ia. St. U., D.V.M. 1950; Catholic.

Career Army, WWII; Veterinarian, 1950–69; Forsyth City Cncl., 1953–55, Mayor, 1955–61; Mont. House of Reps., 1961–63, 1969; Mont. Senate, 1963–67; U.S. House of Reps., 1969–77.

Offices 1123 DSOB, 202-224-2644. Also 1016 Fed. Bldg., Billings 59102, 406-657-6644 and 12 6th St. South, Great Falls 59401, 406-452-9585.

Committees *Agriculture, Nutrition, and Forestry* (7th). Subcommittees: Environment, Soil Conservation, and Forestry (Chairman); Agricultural Production, Marketing, and Stabilization of Prices; Nutrition.

Energy and Natural Resources (9th). Subcommittees: Energy Research and Development; Energy Resources and Materials Production.

Select Committee on Indian Affairs

Special Committee on Aging (4th).

Group Ratings

	ADA	COPE	PC	RPN	NFU	LCV	CFA	NAB	NSI	ACA	NTU
1978	45	63	58	25	78	51	40	17	50	39	–
1977	65	84	40	70	83	–	44	–	–	15	27
1976	75	78	59	40	83	49	54	0	40	15	48

Key Votes

1) Warnke Nom	FOR	6) Egypt-Saudi Arms	AGN	11) Hosptl Cost Contnmnt	AGN
2) Neutron Bomb	AGN	7) Draft Restr Pardon	FOR	12) Clinch River Reactor	FOR
3) Waterwy User Fee	AGN	8) Wheat Price Support	FOR	13) Pub Fin Cong Cmpgns	FOR
4) Dereg Nat Gas	FOR	9) Panama Canal Treaty	AGN	14) ERA Ratif Recissn	FOR
5) Kemp-Roth	AGN	10) Labor Law Rev Clot	FOR	15) Med Necssy Abrtns	AGN

Election Results

1976 general	John Melcher (D)	206,232	(64%)	($311,101)
	Stanley C. Burger (R)	115,213	(36%)	($563,543)
1976 primary	John Melcher (D)	89,413	(89%)	
	One other (D)	11,593	(11%)	
1970 general	Mike Mansfield (D)	150,060	(61%)	
	Harold E. Wallace (R)	97,809	(39%)	

Sen. Max Baucus (D) Elected 1978, seat up 1984; b. Dec. 11, 1941, Helena; home, Missoula; Stanford U., B.A. 1964, LL.B. 1967; Congregational.

Career Staff Atty., Civil Aeronautics Bd., 1967–68; Legal Staff, Securities and Exchange Comm., 1969–71, Legal Asst. to the Chm., 1970–71; Practicing atty., 1971–75; Mont. House of Reps., 1973–75; U.S. House of Reps., 1975–78.

Offices 5327 DSOB, 202-224-2651. Also Fed. Bldg., Helena 59601, 406-443-4041.

Committees *Finance* (10th). Subcommittees: International Trade; Energy and Foundations; Oversight of the Internal Revenue Service (Chairman).

Judiciary (9th). Subcommittees: Antitrust, Monopoly, and Business Rights; Jurisprudence and Governmental Relations; Limitations of Contracted and Delegated Authority (Chairman).

Select Committee on Small Business (9th).

Group Ratings: Newly Elected

	ADA	COPE	PC	RPN	NFU	LCV	CFA	NAB	NSI	ACA	NTU
1978	40	79	68	55	89	–	50	17	40	35	–
1977	65	65	70	64	92	90	45	–	–	23	53
1976	75	74	77	56	92	75	73	17	30	19	48

Key Votes

1) Increase Def Spnd	AGN	6) Alaska Lands Protect	DNV	11) Delay Auto Pol Cntrl	AGN
2) B-1 Bomber	AGN	7) Water Projects Veto	AGN	12) Sugar Price Escalator	FOR
3) Cargo Preference	AGN	8) Consum Protect Agcy	FOR	13) Pub Fin Cong Cmpgns	FOR
4) Dereg Nat Gas	AGN	9) Common Situs Picket	FOR	14) ERA Ratif Recissn	AGN
5) Kemp-Roth	AGN	10) Labor Law Revision	FOR	15) Prohibt Govt Abrtns	AGN

Election Results

1978 general	Max Baucus (D)	160,353	(56%)	($653,756)
	Larry Williams (R)	127,589	(44%)	($346,721)
1978 primary	Max Baucus (D)	87,085	(65%)	
	Paul Hatfield (D)	25,789	(19%)	($124,412)
	John Driscoll (D)	18,184	(14%)	($29,720)
	One other (D)	2,404	(2%)	
1972 general	Lee Metcalf (D)	163,609	(52%)	($136,551)
	Henry S. Hibbard (R)	151,316	(48%)	($286,748)

Gov. Thomas L. Judge (D) Elected 1972, term expires Jan. 1981; b. Oct. 12, 1934, Helena; U. of Notre Dame, B.A., U. of Louisville.

Career Mont. House of Reps., 1961–67; Mont. Senate, 1967–69; Lt. Gov. of Mont., 1969–73.

Offices State Capitol, Helena 59601, 406-449-3111.

Election Results

1976 general	Thomas L. Judge (D)	195,420	(63%)
	Bob Woodahl (R)	115,848	(37%)
1976 primary	Thomas L. Judge (D), unopposed		
1972 general	Thomas L. Judge (D)	172,523	(54%)
	Ed Smith (R)	146,231	(46%)

FIRST DISTRICT

Census Data Pop. 347,447. Central city, 0%; suburban, 0%. Median family income, $8,576; families above $15,000: 13%; families below $3,000: 10%. Median years education, 12.3.

The Voters

Median voting age 43.
Employment profile White collar, 46%. Blue collar, 31%. Service, 15%. Farm, 8%.
Ethnic groups Indian, 3%. Total foreign stock, 16%.

Presidential vote

1976	Carter (D)	77,885	(46%)
	Ford (R)	90,124	(54%)
1972	Nixon (R)	92,166	(58%)
	McGovern (D)	65,384	(42%)

Rep. Pat Williams (D) Elected 1978; b. Oct. 30, 1937, Helena; home, Helena; U. of Mont., Wm. Jewell Col., U. of Denver, B.S. 1961, W. Mont. Col.

Career Public school teacher; Mont. House of Reps., 1966–68; Exec. Asst. to U.S. Rep. John Melcher, 1968–71; Mont. State Coord., Family Educ. Program, 1971–78.

Offices 1233 LHOB, 202-225-3211. Also 306 Steamboat Block, 616 Helena Ave., Helena 59601, 406-443-7878.

Committees *Education and Labor* (21st). Subcommittees: Elementary, Secondary, and Vocational Education; Human Resources; Labor Standards.

Interior and Insular Affairs (28th). Subcommittees: National Parks and Insular Affairs; Oversight/Special Investigations.

Group Ratings: Newly Elected

Key Votes: Newly Elected

Election Results

1978 general	Pat Williams (D)	86,016	(57%)	($177,536)
	Jim Waltermire (R)	64,093	(43%)	($241,888)
1978 primary	Pat Williams (D)	29,966	(41%)	
	Dorothy Bradley (D)	20,381	(28%)	($87,732)
	John Lynch (D)	7,853	(11%)	
	Three others (D)	15,473	(21%)	
1976 general	Max Baucus (D)	111,487	(66%)	($102,148)
	W. D. Diehl (R)	56,297	(34%)	($86,387)

SECOND DISTRICT

Census Data Pop. 346,962. Central city, 35%; suburban, 14%. Median family income, $8,436; families above $15,000: 14%; families below $3,000: 11%. Median years education, 12.3.

The Voters

Median voting age 43.
Employment profile White collar, 45%. Blue collar, 25%. Service, 14%. Farm, 16%.
Ethnic groups Indian, 5%. Total foreign stock, 19%.

Presidential vote

1976	Carter (D)	71,374	(46%)
	Ford (R)	83,579	(54%)
1972	Nixon (R)	91,810	(63%)
	McGovern (D)	54,813	(37%)

Rep. Ron Marlenee (R) Elected 1976; b. Aug. 8, 1935, Scobey; home, Scobey; Mont. St. U., U. of Mont., Reisch Sch. of Auctioneering; Lutheran.

Career Farmer, rancher and businessman.

Offices 126 CHOB, 202-225-1555. Also Fed. Bldg., 310 N. 26th St., Billings 59101, 406-585-6753.

Committees *Agriculture* (13th). Subcommittees: Conservation and Credit; Livestock and Grains.

Interior and Insular Affairs (9th). Subcommittees: Energy and the Environment; Public Lands.

Group Ratings

	ADA	COPE	PC	RPN	NFU	LCV	CFA	NAB	NSI	ACA	NTU
1978	25	26	28	50	50	–	27	91	78	85	–
1977	20	19	30	42	42	20	10	–	–	73	44

Key Votes

1) Increase Def Spnd	FOR	6) Alaska Lands Protect	DNV	11) Delay Auto Pol Cntrl	FOR
2) B-1 Bomber	FOR	7) Water Projects Veto	AGN	12) Sugar Price Escalator	FOR
3) Cargo Preference	AGN	8) Consum Protect Agcy	AGN	13) Pub Fin Cong Cmpgns	AGN
4) Dereg Nat Gas	FOR	9) Common Situs Picket	AGN	14) ERA Ratif Recissn	FOR
5) Kemp-Roth	FOR	10) Labor Law Revision	DNV	15) Prohibt Govt Abrtns	FOR

Election Results

1978 general	Ron Marlenee (R)	75,766	(57%)	($286,863)
	Thomas G. Monahan (D)	57,480	(43%)	($27,019)
1978 primary	Ron Marlenee (R), unopposed			
1976 general	Ron Marlenee (R)	84,149	(55%)	($205,216)
	Thomas E. Towe (D)	68,972	(45%)	($106,254)

NEBRASKA

By almost every measurement—its preference in presidential elections, its congressional delegations over the years, its state politics—Nebraska has usually been the nation's most Republican state. It came by that allegiance in the one decade which made Nebraska politically, economically, and sociologically pretty much what it has since remained. This was the great land rush of the 1880s, when nearly half a million people, most of them from the Republican Midwest, surged into Nebraska. At the beginning of that ten year period, Nebraska had a population of 452,000; in 1890 it reached 1,062,000—not far below the 1970 figure of 1,483,000.

Those were the boom years. As it happened, the 1880s were a time of plentiful rainfall on the high plains west of the Missouri River. The 1890s, sadly, were not. The nineties were a time of drought and depression more severe than any but the 1930s, and hard-hit Nebraska produced the populist prairie radicalism of William Jennings Bryan, "the silver tongued orator of the Platte." Bryan's candidacy swept Nebraska in 1896 and came close to sweeping the nation, but in the next few years—years of prosperity on the farm—even Nebraska returned to its Republican voting habits, favoring McKinley over Bryan in 1900. Since then, Nebraska's only notable lapse from conservatism was the career of George Norris, Congressman (1903–13) and Senator (1913–43). During the progressive era Norris led the House rebellion against Speaker Cannon; during the thirties he pushed through the Norris-LaGuardia Anti-Injunction Act, the first national pro-union legislation, and the Tennessee Valley Authority.

Since 1900 most of Nebraska's growth has occurred in and around the state's two significant cities, Omaha and Lincoln. Between them they now contain about 40% of the state's people. Most of the immigrants to Omaha, a railroad, meatpacking, and manufacturing center, and Lincoln, the state capital and home of the University of Nebraska, come from the rural, Republican hinterland. There is also a sizeable Eastern European community on the south side of Omaha which, like the city's small black ghetto, usually votes Democratic; so too do a few isolated rural counties. But as a whole Nebraska is usually solidly Republican in national elections. In the close elections of 1960, 1968, and 1976, the Republican nominee carries both big cities and lost only three or four counties out of 93.

Yet Nebraska today, for the first time in its history, has two Democratic United States senators. This has resulted not so much from a major shift in opinion as it has from a unique set of circumstances. In 1975 the state had two Republican senators with more than 20 years of experience and records of great party loyalty, Roman Hruska and Carl Curtis. Both had turned 70, and both had nearly lost their last elections. Hruska will be remembered by history for his argument, made in defense of the nomination of Judge Carswell, that mediocre people deserve representation of the Supreme Court. Curtis will be remembered for scurrying around to the morning interview programs after Richard Nixon released the June 23 tape transcript and asserting his continued faith in the President. Obviously both were going to retire and in the normal course of things might have been replaced by the congressman from Omaha and a congressman from the outstate areas, the geographical distribution in accordance with Nebraska tradition. But in neither case did the succession go according to plan.

The problem in 1976, when Hruska retired, was over the Republican nomination. Omaha Congressman John McCollister thought he was entitled to it, and so did Republican leaders and Hruska; Omaha Mayor Edward Zorinsky disagreed. An appliance dealer and tobacco wholesaler who had been elected Mayor in 1973, Zorinsky was a nominal Republican, and he believed he was more popular than McCollister. When told that he had no chance for the Republican nomination, he became a Democrat and in the primary edged state party chairman Hess Dyas. In the general election Zorinsky campaigned like a Republican: he advocated a free market for the nation's farmers with no governmental controls; he was a fiscal conservative who had "the guts to say no" as Mayor. McCollister was depicted as Hruska's hand-picked candidate. It was McCollister's weakness and Zorinsky's strength in their common home town that made the difference. Zorinsky lost the state outside Douglas County. But he got 64% in Omaha—enough for a 53% victory statewide.

Zorinsky is one of the unlikelier Democrats in the Senate. His voting record really resembles that of a Republican moderate—very similar to that of Henry Bellmon of Oklahoma, for example. On critical issues, he feels no need to rally to the Administration; he voted against the Panama Canal Treaty, for example. On the Agriculture Committee he does not really belong to any bloc. On Foreign Relations, which he joined in 1979, he is as likely to line up with some of the committee's conservative Republicans as anyone else. There is speculation that if the Republicans win enough seats in the 1980 elections to get close to control of the House, Zorinsky would be one Democrat who would switch parties and give them control. Probably he would find it a little easier to win reelection in 1982 as a Republican, and perhaps, now that Hruska is gone, the Republican cloakroom would be more congenial.

The way the Curtis seat came to be Democratic was somewhat different. Here it was the strength of the Democratic candidate, Governor James Exon, which was decisive; the outstate Republican congressman who might have run, Charles Thone, sought the governorship instead. The best the Republicans could do for a candidate was Curtis's top aide, Donald Shasteen. Exon first won the governorship in 1970 on a Republican platform—lower taxes and government spending—and capitalized on the unpopularity of his Republican opponent who had raised taxes. Exon's conduct of the office was sufficiently solid to give him nearly a 2–1 margin for reelection; and no one doubts that he could have had a third term if he had been eligible. Instead he ran for the Senate. Shasteen livened up the campaign toward the end by charging that Exon used his influence to benefit his office equipment firm; Exon called the charges "the slime of Shasteen." The Governor carried 92 of 93 counties and won 68% of the vote. Elected at 57, he seems to have a solid political base and can probably remain in the Senate for some time.

A Democrat who has made his name in politics as an economizer is not likely to have a 100% party loyalty record in the Senate. Exon has a seat on Armed Services, where he is likely to be hawkish, and on Commerce, where his stance is hard to predict. He also has a seat on the Budget Committee, where he will be a force for lower federal spending.

The 1978 gubernatorial race represented something like normalcy for Nebraska, although even here special factors came into play. The key was the popularity of 1st district Congressman Charles Thone in his own district, which includes Lincoln and the agricultural counties to the north and south. Both Thone and Democratic Lieutenant Governor Gerald Whalen campaigned as fiscal conservatives; the difference was that Thone said he would get along well with the legislature and Whalen promised to keep the legislators in line. Whalen managed to win a majority in Douglas County and he ran fairly well for a Democrat in his home territory in the western part of the state. But Thone carried Lincoln solidly and won 62% of the vote in the 1st district. That was enough to return the state house to Republican control.

In the 1976 presidential campaign, Nebraska's primary—it comes in early May, in the middle of the primary season—made it the unlikely proving ground for Frank Church's campaign. Jimmy Carter had already won Pennsylvania and seemed to be rolling toward the nomination. But Church spent weeks criss-crossing Nebraska and spent the maximum permissible amount here. He stressed his background as a Westerner and an opponent of federal gun control laws, as well as his work against the war in Vietnam and as chairman of the special committee on intelligence. Church's victory, by the narrowest of margins over Carter, surprised even some of his own staffers; and his campaign went on to other Western states and ultimately Ohio. This is not the first time that Nebraska's Democratic primary has played an important role in the process; Robert Kennedy's win here in 1968 over Eugene McCarthy was significant in that campaign. Curiously the Republicans, who are certain to carry Nebraska in any seriously contested presidential general election, have never had a very important primary here.

Census Data Pop. 1,483,781; 0.73% of U.S. total, 35th largest; Central city, 34%; suburban, 9%. Median family income, $8,562; 31st highest; families above $15,000: 15%; families below $3,000: 11%. Median years education, 12.3.

1977 Share of Federal Tax Burden $2,591,000,000; 0.75% of U.S. total, 32d largest.

1977 Share of Federal Outlays $2,457,569,000; 0.62% of U.S. total, 37th largest. Per capita federal spending, $1,594.

DOD	$403,323,000	39th	(0.44%)	HEW	$939,863,000	36th	(0.64%)
ERDA	$824,000	48th	(0.01%)	HUD	$21,978,000	38th	(0.52%)
NASA	$208,000	44th	(0.01%)	VA	$140,313,000	36th	(0.73%)
DOT	$67,372,000	41st	(0.47%)	EPA	$28,778,000	37th	(0.35%)
DOC	$49,013,000	44th	(0.59%)	RevS	$43,750,000	37th	(0.52%)
DOI	$26,257,000	33d	(0.56%)	Debt	$119,840,000	30th	(0.40%)
USDA	$363,403,000	22d	(1.83%)	Other	$252,647,000		

Economic Base Agriculture, notably cattle, corn, hogs and wheat; finance, insurance and real estate; food and kindred products, especially meat products; electrical equipment and supplies; machinery, especially farm machinery; printing and publishing, especially newspapers; fabricated metal products, especially fabricated structural metal products.

Political Line-up Governor, Charles Thone (R). Senators, Edward Zorinsky (D) and J. James Exon (D). Representatives, 3 (2 R and 1 D). Unicameral Legislature, 49 non-partisan members.

The Voters

Registration 832,628 Total. 382,693 D (46%); 402,097 R (48%); 47,838 Ind. (6%).
Median voting age 44
Employment profile White collar, 45%. Blue collar, 28%. Service, 14%. Farm, 13%.
Ethnic groups Black, 3%. Total foreign stock, 14%. Germany, 4%.

Presidential vote

1976	Carter (D)	233,293	(39%)
	Ford (R)	359,219	(61%)
1972	Nixon (R)	406,298	(71%)
	McGovern (D)	169,991	(29%)

1976 Democratic Presidential Primary

Church	67,097	(40%)
Carter	65,833	(39%)
Humphrey	12,685	(7%)
Others	23,165	(14%)

1976 Republican Presidential Primary

Reagan	113,493	(55%)
Ford	94,542	(45%)

Sen. Edward Zorinsky (D) Elected 1976, seat up 1982; b. Nov. 11, 1928, Omaha; home, Omaha; U. of Neb., B.A., Notre Dame U., Harvard U.; Jewish.

Career Tobacco Wholesaler; Omaha Public Power District, 1969–73; Mayor of Omaha, 1973–77, elected as Repub., switched to Dem. Party Dec. 1975.

Offices 432 RSOB, 202-224-6551. Also 8311 Fed. Bldg., Omaha 68102, 402-221-4381.

Committees *Agriculture, Nutrition, and Forestry* (6th). Subcommittees: Agricultural Credit and Rural Electrification (Chairman); Agricultural Production, Marketing, and Stabilization of Prices; Foreign Agricultural Policy.

Foreign Relations (9th). Subcommittees: Arms Control, Oceans, International Operations, and Environment; East Asian and Pacific Affairs; Western Hemisphere Affairs (Chairman).

Group Ratings

	ADA	COPE	PC	RPN	NFU	LCV	CFA	NAB	NSI	ACA	NTU
1978	25	16	38	40	60	51	45	58	80	74	–
1977	25	40	53	50	45	–	36	–	–	69	45

Key Votes

1) Warnke Nom	AGN	6) Egypt-Saudi Arms	AGN	11) Hosptl Cost Contnmnt	FOR
2) Neutron Bomb	FOR	7) Draft Restr Pardon	AGN	12) Clinch River Reactor	FOR
3) Waterwy User Fee	FOR	8) Wheat Price Support	FOR	13) Pub Fin Cong Cmpgns	FOR
4) Dereg Nat Gas	FOR	9) Panama Canal Treaty	AGN	14) ERA Ratif Recissn	AGN
5) Kemp-Roth	FOR	10) Labor Law Rev Clot	AGN	15) Med Necssy Abrtns	AGN

Election Results

1976 general	Edward Zorinsky (D)	313,805	(53%)	($237,613)
	John V. McCollister (R)	279,284	(47%)	($391,287)
1976 primary	Edward Zorinsky (D)	79,988	(49%)	
	Hess Dyas (D)	77,384	(47%)	
	One other (D)	7,194	(4%)	
1970 general	Roman L. Hruska (R)	240,894	(53%)	
	Frank B. Morrison (D)	217,681	(47%)	

Sen. J. James Exon (D) Elected 1978, seat up 1984; b. Aug. 9, 1921, Geddes, S.D.; home, Lincoln; U. of Omaha; Episcopalian.

Career Army, WWII; Branch Mgr., Universal Finance Co., 1946–54; Pres., Exon's Inc., office equip. business 1954–70; Vice Chm., Neb. St. Dem. Central Comm., 1964–68; Gov. of Neb., 1970–78.

Offices 3229 DSOB, 202-224-4224. Also Fed. Bldg., Omaha 68102, 402-221-4665.

Committees *Armed Services* (9th). Subcommittees: Arms Control; Manpower and Personnel; Research and Development.

Budget (12th).

Commerce, Science, and Transportation (9th). Subcommittees: Aviation; Communication; Surface Transportation.

Group Ratings: Newly Elected

Key Votes: Newly Elected

Election Results

1978 general	J. James Exon (D)	334,096	(68%)	($234,862)
	Don Shasteen (R)	159,706	(32%)	($218,148)
1978 primary	J. James Exon (D), unopposed			
1972 general	Carl T. Curtis (R)	301,841	(53%)	($250,392)
	Terry Carpenter (D)	265,922	(47%)	($38,629)

Gov. Charles Thone (R) Elected 1978, term expires 1983; b. Jan. 4, 1924, Hartington; U. of Neb., J.D. 1950; Presbyterian.

Career Army, WWII; Deputy Secy. of State of Neb., 1950–51; Asst. Atty. Gen. of Neb., 1951–52; Asst. U.S. Dist. Atty., Lincoln Ofc., 1952–54; Admin. Asst. to U.S. Sen. Roman Hruska, 1954–59; Practicing atty., 1959–71; U.S. House of Reps., 1971–79.

Offices State Capitol, Lincoln 68509, 402-471-2244.

Election Results

1978 general	Charles Thone (R)	275,473	(56%)
	Gerald T. Whelan (D)	216,754	(44%)
1978 primary	Charles Thone (R)	89,378	(45%)
	Robert A. Phares (R)	48,402	(25%)
	Stan Juelfs (R)	43,828	(22%)
	Two others (R)	15,546	(8%)
1974 general	J. J. Exon (D)	267,012	(59%)
	Richard D. Marvel (R)	159,780	(35%)
	Ernest Chambers (Ind.)	24,320	(5%)

FIRST DISTRICT

The 1st congressional district of Nebraska is a band of 27 counties in the eastern part of the state. Outside of Lincoln, the district's largest city and state capital, the economy of the 1st is based almost entirely on agriculture. The political inclination of the region is Republican, of course, but there are a couple of counties with large German Catholic communities which have faithfully supported Democrats of such diverse origin as John Kennedy and Jimmy Carter. Lincoln, the capital and—more important to people here—home of the University of Nebraska Cornhuskers, is traditionally Republican. But the city's large number of state employees have sometimes joined members of the university community to swing Lincoln into the Democratic column. But on a number of occasions Lincoln, with all its state government employees, seems to have preferred Republicans to economy-minded Democrats. In 1970 this was one of the few parts of the state that did not favor Governor James Exon, and in 1978 it gave a solid margin to Charles Thone over Exon's Lieutenant Governor, Gerald Whalen.

The 1st district has seen a number of close congressional elections in the sixties and seventies. A Democrat captured the district in 1964 and lost close races in 1966 and 1968; he ran as an Independent in 1970 and split the Democratic vote, helping to elect Thone with a bare majority. Thone had a close contest in 1974 against state Democratic Chairman Hess Dyas, and there was another seriously contested race in 1978, when Thone stepped down to run for governor. Dyas was again the Democratic nominee, while the Republican nomination was won in a tough primary by Douglas Bereuter. He had worked as a top appointee of Governor Norbert Tiemann, the Republican whose tax policies helped elect Exon, and is considered a moderate. The reputation of not being opposed to all government programs helped him carry Lincoln; the Republican Party label helped him carry most of the rural counties in the district. His victory, particularly given the past history of the district, suggests that he should become well established in this district, and might even make him a contender for statewide office.

Census Data Pop. 494,335. Central city, 30%; suburban, 6%. Median family income, $8,203; families above $15,000: 13%; families below $3,000: 12%. Median years education, 12.2.

The Voters

Median voting age 45.
Employment profile White collar, 43%. Blue collar, 27%. Service, 15%. Farm, 15%.
Ethnic groups Total foreign stock, 14%. Germany, 6%.

Presidential vote

1976	Carter (D)	81,590	(41%)
	Ford (R)	116,030	(59%)
1972	Nixon (R)	133,282	(67%)
	McGovern (D)	66,001	(33%)

Rep. Douglas K. Bereuter (R) Elected 1978; b. Oct. 6, 1939, York; home, Utica; U. of Neb., B.A. 1961, Harvard U., M.C.P. 1963, M.P.A. 1973.

Career Army, 1963–65; Residential and Commercial development consultant; Neb. Legislature, 1975–78; Chmn., Urban Development Comm., Natl. Conf. of State Legislatures, 1977–78.

Offices 1314 LHOB, 202-225-4806. Also 1045 K St., Lincoln 68501, 402-471-5400.

Committees *Interior and Insular Affairs* (14th). Subcommittees: Energy and the Environment; Water and Power Resources; National Parks and Insular Affairs.

Small Business (11th). Subcommittees: General Oversight and Minority Enterprise; Impact of Energy Programs, Environment and Safety Requirements and Government Research on Small Business.

Group Ratings: Newly Elected

Key Votes: Newly Elected

Election Results

1978 general	Douglas K. Bereuter (R)	99,013	(58%)	($167,688)
	Hess Dyas (D)	71,311	(42%)	($164,227)
1978 primary	Douglas K. Bereuter (R)	34,790	(52%)	
	Loran Schmit (R)	31,559	(48%)	($60,147)
1976 general	Charles Thone (R)	146,558	(73%)	($102,990)
	Pauline F. Anderson (D)	53,699	(27%)	($24,196)

SECOND DISTRICT

The 2d congressional district of Nebraska is metropolitan Omaha and a couple of rural counties. The latter are politically not very important; metropolitan Omaha (Douglas and Sarpy Counties) casts nine-tenths of the district's votes. Omaha has long been Nebraska's largest city; indeed, with Lincoln, it is the state's only city of any size. In recent years Omaha has shown little growth; its major industries, meatpacking and railroading, have not been growing. Still Omaha remains the commercial and industrial metropolis of much of the Great Plains—the largest city on the Union Pacific and Interstate 80 between Chicago and Denver. Though Omaha contains significant numbers of Democratic Czechs and blacks, it tends to vote Republican in national elections, often by margins not much less than those in rural Nebraska. In 1976, for instance, Douglas County was a solid 60% for Gerald Ford.

The 2d district has usually had Republican congressmen, including one who pushed through a bill requiring people who receive mail from Communist countries to register with the post office.

More recently, Republican John McCollister left his seat in 1976 to run, unsuccessfully, for the Senate. He was beaten by Omaha Mayor Edward Zorinsky, and Omaha made the critical difference. It was a good illustration of the tendency of voters to favor candidates who hold offices close to them over candidates who spend most of their time in distant places like Washington.

The current Congressman is Democrat John Cavanaugh. He won the 1976 election after serving in the legislature. He had additional advantages: a father who had been a Douglas County commissioner for 18 years and the strong support of then Governor Exon. His record in office was more acceptable to liberal ratings groups than to some conservative Omahans. His 1978 opponent attacked him as a liberal and a follower of the Carter Administration; Cavanaugh pointed to his constituency services. In the end Cavanaugh's percentage was reduced and he was reelected with 52% of the vote. He failed to carry the three small rural counties in the district, and his proportion of the vote in Douglas County was only 53%. It was not a particularly impressive showing, and one which suggests that this seat will be seriously contested in 1980.

Census Data Pop. 495,095. Central city, 70%; suburban, 21%. Median family income, $10,163; families above $15,000: 21%; families below $3,000: 7%. Median years education, 12.4.

The Voters

Median voting age 40.
Employment profile White collar, 53%. Blue collar, 31%. Service, 14%. Farm, 2%.
Ethnic groups Black, 7%. Total foreign stock, 14%. Germany, 3%.

Presidential vote

1976	Carter (D)	75,884	(40%)
	Ford (R)	114,991	(60%)
1972	Nixon (R)	124,791	(69%)
	McGovern (D)	56,204	(31%)

Rep. John J. Cavanaugh (D) Elected 1976; b. Aug. 1, 1945, Omaha; home, Omaha; Regis Col. of Denver, B.A. 1967, Creighton U., J.D. 1972; Catholic.

Career Army, 1968–70; Practicing atty., 1972–77; Neb. Legislature, 1972–76.

Offices 1208 LHOB, 202-225-4155. Also Fed. Bldg., 215 N. 17th St., Omaha 68102, 402-221-4117.

Committees *Banking, Finance and Urban Affairs* (21st). Subcommittees: Financial Institutions Supervision, Regulation and Insurance; International Trade, Investment and Monetary Policy; The City; International Development Institutions and Finance; Domestic Monetary Policy.

Group Ratings

	ADA	COPE	PC	RPN	NFU	LCV	CFA	NAB	NSI	ACA	NTU
1978	60	65	58	45	70	–	46	42	10	27	–
1977	80	68	70	67	64	72	60	–	–	23	26

Key Votes

1) Increase Def Spnd	AGN	6) Alaska Lands Protect	FOR	11) Delay Auto Pol Cntrl	AGN
2) B-1 Bomber	AGN	7) Water Projects Veto	AGN	12) Sugar Price Escalator	FOR
3) Cargo Preference	AGN	8) Consum Protect Agcy	AGN	13) Pub Fin Cong Cmpgns	FOR
4) Dereg Nat Gas	AGN	9) Common Situs Picket	AGN	14) ERA Ratif Recissn	AGN
5) Kemp-Roth	AGN	10) Labor Law Revision	FOR	15) Prohibt Govt Abrtns	AGN

Election Results

1978 general	John J. Cavanaugh (D)	77,135	(52%)	($144,071)
	Harold J. Daub (R)	70,309	(48%)	($237,741)
1978 primary	John J. Cavanaugh (D)	34,365	(88%)	
	One other (D)	4,552	(12%)	
1976 general	John J. Cavanaugh (D)	106,296	(55%)	($133,888)
	Lee Terry (R)	88,352	(45%)	($115,666)

THIRD DISTRICT

One-third of Nebraska's population is spread out over the western three-quarters of its land area—the state's 3d congressional district. As one drives west here, the rolling fields of corn and wheat give way to sand hills and cattle country, much of it devoid of signs of human habitation for miles on end. This is the part of Nebraska to which settlers thronged during the unusually moist 1880s and which their descendants have been leaving, often reluctantly, ever since. Today most of the people here live along the Platte River or near towns like Grand Island, Hastings, Kearney, and Scottsbluff—none with more than 31,000 people.

The 3d considers itself conservative on most issues, and has for years. It has had occasional bouts of farm revolt, but they have not been strong enough to elect a Democratic congressman since 1958. The current incumbent, Virginia Smith, was first elected in a year very Democratic elsewhere, 1974. Her Democratic opponent ran a well financed campaign marred (or was it helped?) by an occasional male chauvinist remark. Mrs. Smith is in any case no women's libber. Her organizational career has not been in feminist groups, but on the board of the American Farm Bureau Federation, a group which tends to represent the interests of well-to-do farmers who want less government intervention in their business. She won that election by a 737-vote margin and has become entrenched since: in 1978 she had 80% of the vote. Her first years on Capitol Hill must have been frustrating; she served on the Education and Labor Committee, with its big majority favoring federal spending programs. But she is now on Appropriations, and at a time when congressmen are more interested in cutting than increasing spending; to judge from her record, she finds that atmosphere congenial indeed.

Census Data Pop. 494,361. Central city, 0%; suburban, 0%. Median family income, $7,549; families above $15,000: 11%; families below $3,000: 13%. Median years education, 12.2.

The Voters

Median voting age 47.
Employment profile White collar, 38%. Blue collar, 27%. Service, 14%. Farm, 21%.
Ethnic groups Total foreign stock, 13%. Germany, 4%.

Presidential vote

1976	Carter (D)	75,813	(37%)
	Ford (R)	128,198	(63%)
1972	Nixon (R)	148,142	(76%)
	McGovern (D)	47,750	(24%)

Rep. Virginia Smith (R) Elected 1974; b. June 30, 1911, Randolph, Ia.; home, Chappell; U. of Neb., B.A. 1934; Methodist.

Career Natl. Chm., Amer. Farm Bureau Women, 1955–74; Chm., Pres. Task Force on Rural Development, 1971–72.

Offices 1005 LHOB, 202-225-6435. Also P.O. Bldg., Main Fl., Grand Island 68801, 308-381-0505.

Committees *Appropriations* (16th). Subcommittees: Foreign Operations; Energy and Water Development.

Group Ratings

	ADA	COPE	PC	RPN	NFU	LCV	CFA	NAB	NSI	ACA	NTU
1978	10	5	13	91	40	–	9	92	90	78	–
1977	10	17	23	62	42	19	10	–	–	85	50
1976	0	14	13	67	8	34	0	92	100	82	55

Key Votes

1) Increase Def Spnd	FOR	6) Alaska Lands Protect	FOR	11) Delay Auto Pol Cntrl	FOR
2) B-1 Bomber	FOR	7) Watrr Projects Veto	AGN	12) Sugar Price Escalator	FOR
3) Cargo Preference	AGN	8) Consum Protect Agcy	AGN	13) Pub Fin Cong Cmpgns	AGN
4) Dereg Nat Gas	FOR	9) Common Situs Picket	AGN	14) ERA Ratif Recissn	FOR
5) Kemp-Roth	FOR	10) Labor Law Revision	AGN	15) Prohibt Govt Abrtns	FOR

Election Results

1978 general	Virginia Smith (R)	141,597	(80%)	($66,795)
	Marilyn Fowler (D)	35,371	(20%)	($40,313)
1978 primary	Virginia Smith (R), unopposed			
1976 general	Virginia Smith (R)	150,720	(75%)	($74,642)
	James Thomas Hansen (D)	51,012	(25%)	($9,321)

NEVADA

The history of Nevada dates back to the discovery of the Comstock Lode in 1859—one of those huge mineral finds that triggered a rush of prospectors, speculators, and hangers on. Suddenly there was a large town here, Virginia City, and a territorial government in Carson City; there was even a United States Mint there, to coin some of the silver from the mines. When the Republicans thought they desperately needed electoral votes to reelect Lincoln in 1864, they contrived to make these two towns, plus tens of thousands of square miles of the vacant, arid Great Basin to the north, west, and south, the state of Nevada. Statehood was achieved and the electoral votes cast in time, and Nevada thereby became our third western state.

But soon enough the veins of silver and gold petered out, and the prospectors scattered—to Lead, South Dakota; Bisbee, Arizona; and the Klondike River in the Yukon Territory. Nevada, with fewer than 100,000 residents, was left in economic doldrums for decades. During the depression of the thirties the state government was on the verge of bankruptcy. So the legislature legalized gambling and liberalized its divorce laws at just about the same time the federal government was building Hoover Dam near Las Vegas. Thus were brought to Nevada tourists, water, and big—often tainted—money.

Up through the end of World War II, Nevada's population was still concentrated in the northwest part of the state, in and around Reno and Carson City. But Reno's dominance was challenged starting in 1947, when Bugsy Siegel opened the Flamingo, the first big casino hotel on the Las Vegas Strip. At the same time, just outside Las Vegas, the Atomic Energy Commission established the Nevada Proving Grounds. Today the big casinos and the AEC's successor agency are two of Las Vegas's—and Nevada's—three biggest employers; and the city itself has grown from a small desert gas station crossroads to a major urban center. Today Clark County, which includes Las Vegas, the Strip, and Hoover Dam, has 56% of the state's population. Reno and surrounding Washoe County have 25%, leaving just 19% of the state's people in the so-called Cow Counties.

The vast increases in the state's population in recent decades have naturally had their political effect. Reno, surrounded by pine-clad, snow-capped mountains, remains as it always has been, a strongly Republican town, though it will go for a very popular Democrat. Las Vegas, in a dusty, bowl-like valley surrounded by bone-dry peaks, was Democratic in its early days, primarily because of the Southern origin of its early settlers. With large numbers of blacks and as a big union town (though Nevada is a right-to-work state), Las Vegas remains nominally Democratic; but its Democratic margins have gotten smaller, not larger, over the years as the number of ticket-splitters here has increased. As a result, Nevada seems to be shifting to the Republicans, although it remains very much a two-party state. Its traditional Democrats have been pretty conservative. Nevada senators, for example, have made it a habit to vote against cutting off filibusters, on the theory that they tend to increase the power of the state's two Senate votes, which are of course its main political asset. Nevada has a tradition of powerful conservative Democratic senators that goes back to Key Pittman, Chairman of the Foreign Relations Committee in the thirties, and Pat McCarran, author of the antisubversive act that bears his name (and much of which has proved to be unconstitutional).

This tradition has been continued, in modified form, by the state's senior Senator, Howard Cannon. First elected in 1958, he is one of the more senior Democrats in the Senate. After the death of John McClellan in 1978, Cannon succeeded Warren Magnuson as Chairman of the Senate Commerce Committee. This is a post of great importance. Commerce has jurisdiction over most of the industries heavily regulated by the federal government: the airlines, the broadcasting networks, the maritime industry, the railroads, and trucking. It passes also on most consumer legislation. Naturally, affected industries take care to see that their interests are taken into account in the legislative process. Some members have been known for their close alliances with regulated industries. Magnuson was not, and neither is Cannon, though he is more sympathetic to many industry interests.

There is a tendency to think of Commerce legislation as involving proposed government restrictions on the operation of business, and that is the form much of the committee's work takes. But there are also sets of regulations welcomed by industries. For example, for years the airlines were pleased with the Civil Aeronautics Board control of their rates, because it meant that fares were higher than they would have been if there were free competition. That was exactly what happened when airline deregulation was accomplished during the 95th Congress. Originally Cannon, who had long chaired the Aviation Subcommittee, was wary of that proposal. But when Edward Kennedy began making headway with it, Cannon became interested and took over leadership on the issue from Kennedy. Something rather different happened in the 96th Congress, when Kennedy proposed deregulation of the trucking industry. Entry into trucking is now severely restricted and companies are allowed to agree on set rates—all of which costs consumers hundreds of millions a year. The idea is to protect small companies from going out of business—a legitimate concern in the thirties but hardly a major problem today. Kennedy introduced a bill to repeal the antitrust exemption that allows this price fixing and sought to have it referred to Judiciary, which he chairs; Cannon wanted it sent to Commerce. There is likely to be little agreement here; Cannon seemed pretty strongly opposed to major changes in trucking laws and the trucking interests, together with their allies the Teamsters, have great political clout.

Cannon gave up the chair on Rules to take Commerce, as one might expect, since Rules is a minor committee; but during his chairmanship Rules assumed greater than usual importance. It is the body which passes on nominations to fill vacancies in the vice presidency, which means that Cannon chaired the hearings on Gerald Ford and Nelson Rockefeller. It also handled campaign finance laws. And in 1975 it was faced with the question of who actually had been elected to the Senate from New Hampshire (the election was eventually rerun). Cannon was very much on display in some of these situations, and handled matters fairly and intelligently. Cannon is an airplane buff, a general in the Air Force Reserve who until recently piloted big jets, and generally a backer of the space program. He has a seat on the Armed Services Committee, on which he is behind just John Stennis and Henry Jackson in seniority. While he is generally regarded as hawkish on defense issues, he is sometimes flexible and prepared to hear both sides; he is likely to be a swing vote on SALT, for example.

Cannon's one close call in elections came in 1964 when he beat Paul Laxalt, then Lieutenant Governor, by only 48 votes. Since then he beat the Reno district attorney solidly in 1970 and easily overcame an underfinanced Republican in 1976. He has always had big margins in Clark County. The big question for 1982 is whether voters will think that, at 70, he is too old for another term.

Nevada is a state whose two senators have run against each other—and finished almost in a dead heat. Paul Laxalt went on from that race to the governorship in 1966. His term in office coincided almost exactly with the time Howard Hughes lived in Las Vegas. Hughes's purchase of half the big casinos on the Strip, some of them reportedly owned by organized crime interests, was generally hailed as a good thing in Nevada, and by no one more strongly than Laxalt. When he decided to retire for personal reasons in 1970, Hughes left the state.

After four years out of public life, Laxalt was elected to the Senate in 1974, by a 624 vote margin over Lieutenant Governor Harry Reid. He is a man of pleasant demeanor and strong opinions. He believes that we must strengthen our defense, reduce government spending otherwise, and let the free market make economic decisions. Yet he does not seem to antagonize those who feel he is wrong and he is one of the personally most popular senators. Laxalt was the floor manager of the fight against the Panama Canal Treaties—a fight he pursued with tenacity and good humor. He has been mentioned as a possible Senate Republican leader in the future, but his first priority is presidential politics. He was Ronald Reagan's campaign chairman in 1976 and as of early 1979 seemed likely to hold such a position again in 1980.

Laxalt is up for reelection in 1980, and despite his narrow margin in 1974 seems to be in good shape. Former Governor Mike O'Callaghan left office very popular in 1978 and could probably give him a tough race; but he declined to make the 1974 race and is unlikely to run. Against other candidates, Laxalt's strong character and conservative voting record make him hard to beat. He was one of the few conservative Republicans to win in 1974. Since then, he has been joined in the Senate by many likeminded colleagues, especially from the Rocky Mountain states; the regional trend of opinion seems to be going his way.

A possible but unlikely challenger to Laxalt is Democratic Congressman-at-Large Jim Santini. He was first elected in 1974 when he easily beat a Republican who had won in an upset two years before. His competition since has been weak: in 1976 a Republican who finished second to "none of these candidates"—a ballot choice Nevada provides in every race. Santini has seats on the Interior and Commerce Committees. Like Cannon, he is from Las Vegas, where he was a prosecutor and judge; he might very well run for the Senate if Cannon retires in 1982.

The Nevada governorship followed the recent political trend in the state and went from the Democrats to the Republicans in 1978. Mike O'Callaghan was easily the most popular political figure in Nevada, and could have been elected to a third term if he wanted it; but he honored the apparent intent of an ambiguous provision in the state constitution, and retired. The fight to succeed him was between Lieutenant Governor Robert Rose, a Democrat from Las Vegas, and Robert List, a Republican from Carson City. There were great similarities: both were about 40, both born outside the state (although List attacked Rose as an Easterner), both favored the Equal Rights Amendment in a state that has refused to ratify it. Although Rose tried to identify himself with Las Vegas, the home town factor seemed to matter little in a state made up mostly of two urban areas large enough that people never expect to meet their major officeholders personally. Rose's criticism of the state's foreign gaming law, which prevents Nevada casino owners from setting up branches in other states which legalize gambling unless they meet Nevada standards, may have made him seem overly sympathetic to the owners in a state where voters have often been suspicious of them. In any case, List won a decisive victory and a four year term. He too must be considered a possible contender for the Cannon seat in 1982.

Census Data Pop. 488,738; 0.24% of U.S. total, 47th largest; Central city, 41%; suburban, 40%. Median family income, $10,687; 10th highest; families above $15,000: 25%; families below $3,000: 7%. Median years education, 12.4.

1977 Share of Federal Tax Burden $1,209,000,000; 0.35% of U.S. total, 43d largest.

1977 Share of Federal Outlays $1,184,062,000; 030% of U.S. total, 46th largest. Per capita federal spending, $2,000.

DOD	$251,351,000	45th (0.28%)	HEW	$321,962,000	49th (0.22%)
ERDA	$157,507,000	13th (2.66%)	HUD	$8,439,000	48th (0.20%)
NASA	$1,491,000	35th (0.04%)	VA	$61,095,000	45th (0.32%)
DOT	$62,993,000	44th (0.44%)	EPA	$20,406,000	43d (0.25%)
DOC	$45,990,000	47th (0.55%)	RevS	$21,162,000	48th (0.25%)
DOI	$55,694,000	20th (1.20%)	Debt	$28,432,000	48th (0.09%)
USDA	$26,055,000	50th (0.13%)	Other	$121,485,000	

Economic Base Tourism; finance, insurance and real estate; agriculture, notably cattle, dairy products, hay and sheep; metal mining, especially copper ores; paper and allied products; primary metal industries, especially nonferrous rolling and drawing.

Political Line-up Governor, Robert F. List (R). Senators, Howard W. Cannon (D) and Paul Laxalt (R). Representative, 1 D at large. State Senate (15 D and 5 R); State House (26 D and 14 R).

The Voters

Registration 267,698 Total. 158,576 D (59%); 90,371 R (34%); 17,447 Miscellaneous (7%); 1,047 AIP (–); 257 Libertarian (–).
Median voting age 40
Employment profile White collar, 47%. Blue collar, 26%. Service, 25%. Farm, 2%.
Ethnic groups Black, 6%. Spanish, 6%. Total foreign stock, 14%.

Presidential vote

1976	Carter (D)	92,479	(48%)
	Ford (R)	101,273	(52%)
1972	Nixon (R)	115,750	(64%)
	McGovern (D)	66,016	(36%)

1976 Democratic Presidential Primary

Brown	39,671	(53%)
Carter	17,567	(23%)
Others	18,004	(24%)

1976 Republican Presidential Primary

Reagan	31,637	(71%)
Ford	13,747	(29%)

Sen. Howard W. Cannon (D) Elected 1958, seat up 1982; b. Jan. 26, 1912, St. George, Utah; home, Las Vegas; Dixie Jr. Col.; Ariz. St. Teachers Col., B.E. 1933, U. of Ariz., LL.B. 1937; Church of Latter Day Saints.

Career Reference Atty., Utah Senate, 1938; Washington Co. Atty., 1940–41; Practicing atty., 1938–41, 1946–58; Army Air Corps, WWII; Las Vegas City Atty., 1949–58.

Offices 259 RSOB, 202-224-6244. Also 4602 U.S. Fed. Bldg., 300 Las Vegas Blvd. S., Las Vegas 89101, 702-385-6278, and 4024 Fed. Bldg., 300 Booth St., Reno 89502, 702-784-5544.

Committees *Armed Services* (3d). Subcommittees: General Procurement; Military Construction and Stockpiles; Procurement Policy and Reprogramming.

Commerce, Science, and Transportation (Chairman). Subcommittees: Aviation (Chairman); Communications; Surface Transportation.

Rules and Administration (2d).

Group Ratings

	ADA	COPE	PC	RPN	NFU	LCV	CFA	NAB	NSI	ACA	NTU
1978	30	33	45	60	63	36	45	46	67	43	
	30	61	40	56	45	–	36	–	–	60	19732
1976	40	78	35	44	75	26	57	64	100	38	44

Key Votes

1) Warnke Nom	AGN	6) Egypt-Saudi Arms	FOR	11) Hosptl Cost Contnmnt	FOR
2) Neutron Bomb	FOR	7) Draft Restr Pardon	AGN	12) Clinch River Reactor	FOR
3) Waterwy User Fee	FOR	8) Wheat Price Support	AGN	13) Pub Fin Cong Cmpgns	FOR
4) Dereg Nat Gas	AGN	9) Panama Canal Treaty	FOR	14) ERA Ratif Recissn	AGN
5) Kemp-Roth	AGN	10) Labor Law Rev Clot	AGN	15) Med Necssy Abrtns	AGN

Election Results

1976 general	Howard W. Cannon (D)	127,214	(67%)	($405,380)
	David Towell (R)	63,471	(33%)	($54,842)
1976 primary	Howard W. Cannon (D), unopposed			
1970 general	Howard W. Cannon (D)	85,187	(58%)	
	William J. Raggio (R)	60,838	(42%)	

Sen. Paul Laxalt (R) Elected 1974, seat up 1980; b. Aug. 2, 1922, Reno; home, Carson City; Santa Clara U., 1940–43, U. of Denver, B.S., LL.B. 1949.

Career Army, WWII; Ormsby Co. Dist. Atty., 1951–54; Practicing atty., 1954–66, 1970–74; Lt. Gov. of Nev., 1963–66; Gov. of Nev., 1966–70.

Offices 326 RSOB, 202-224-3542. Also U.S. Fed. Bldg., Rm. 2016, 300 Booth St., Reno 89502, 702-784-5568, and U.S. Fed. Bldg., Rm. 4626, 300 Las Vegas Blvd. S., Las Vegas 89101, 702-385-6547.

Committees *Appropriations* (9th). Subcommittees: HUD-Independent Agencies; Interior and Related Agencies; Military Construction; State, Justice, and Commerce, the Judiciary, and Related Agencies; Treasury, Postal Service, and General Government.

Judiciary (3d). Subcommittees: Administrative Practice and Procedure; Antitrust, Monopoly, and Business Rights; Criminal Justice.

Group Ratings

	ADA	COPE	PC	RPN	NFU	LCV	CFA	NAB	NSI	ACA	NTU
1978	5	18	20	57	44	16	20	75	100	81	–
1977	5	6	15	55	33	–	20	–	–	92	51
1976	5	6	8	53	20	0	0	91	100	95	55

Key Votes

1) Warnke Nom	AGN	6) Egypt-Saudi Arms	DNV	11) Hosptl Cost Contnmnt	AGN
2) Neutron Bomb	FOR	7) Draft Restr Pardon	AGN	12) Clinch River Reactor	DNV
3) Waterwy User Fee	AGN	8) Wheat Price Support	FOR	13) Pub Fin Cong Cmpgns	AGN
4) Dereg Nat Gas	FOR	9) Panama Canal Treaty	AGN	14) ERA Ratif Recissn	AGN
5) Kemp-Roth	FOR	10) Labor Law Rev Clot	AGN	15) Med Necssy Abrtns	AGN

Election Results

1974 general	Paul Laxalt (R)	79,605	(47%)	($385,861)
	Harry Reid (D)	78,981	(47%)	($400,553)
	Jack Doyle (Independent American)	10,887	(6%)	(NA)
1974 primary	Paul Laxalt (R)	33,660	(81%)	
	Two others (R)	7,736	(19%)	
1968 general	Alan Bible (D)	83,622	(55%)	
	Ed Fike (R)	69,083	(45%)	

Gov. Robert F. List (R) Elected 1978, term expires Jan. 1983; b. Sept. 1, 1936, Visalia, Cal.; Utah St. U., B.S. 1959, U. of Cal., J.D. 1962; Presbyterian.

Career Practicing atty., 1962–66; Ormsby Co. Dist. Atty., 1967–70; Atty. Gen. of Nev., 1971–78.

Offices Governors Mansion, Carson City 89701, 702-885-5670.

Election Results

1978 general	Robert F. List (R)	108,097	(59%)
	Robert E. Rose (D)	76,361	(41%)
1978 primary	Robert F. List (R)	40,057	(89%)
	Three others (R)	5,000	(11%)
1974 general	Mike O'Callaghan (D)	114,114	(67%)
	Shirley Crumpler (R)	28,959	(17%)
	James Ray Houston (Ind.)	26,285	(16%)

Rep. Jim Santini (D) Elected 1974; b. Aug. 13, 1937, Reno; home, Las Vegas; U. of Nev., B.S. 1959, Hastings Col. of Law, J.D. 1962.

Career Practicing atty.; Army, 1963–66; Clark Co. Deputy Dist. Atty., 1968–69; Public Defender, 1968–70; Justice of the Peace, 1970–72; Clark Co. Dist. Ct. Judge, 1972–74.

Offices 1007 LHOB, 202-225-5965. Also Suite 4-260 Fed. Bldg., 300 Las Vegas Blvd. S., Las Vegas 89101, 702-385-6575.

Committees *Interstate and Foreign Commerce* (15th). Subcommittees: Oversight and Investigations; Transportation and Commerce.

Interior and Insular Affairs (11th). Subcommittees: Public Lands; Mines and Mining (Chairman); Oversight/Special Investigations.

Group Ratings

	ADA	COPE	PC	RPN	NFU	LCV	CFA	NAB	NSI	ACA	NTU
1978	5	35	40	50	40	–	27	67	78	65	–
1977	25	50	53	40	58	35	35	–	–	44	35
1976	30	43	48	59	55	24	45	42	67	46	41

Key Votes

1) Increase Def Spnd	AGN	6) Alaska Lands Protect	AGN	11) Delay Auto Pol Cntrl	AGN
2) B-1 Bomber	AGN	7) Water Projects Veto	FOR	12) Sugar Price Escalator	AGN
3) Cargo Preference	FOR	8) Consum Protect Agcy	AGN	13) Pub Fin Cong Cmpgns	FOR
4) Dereg Nat Gas	FOR	9) Common Situs Picket	AGN	14) ERA Ratif Recissn	FOR
5) Kemp-Roth	AGN	10) Labor Law Revision	AGN	15) Prohibt Govt Abrtns	FOR

Election Results

1978 general	Jim Santini (D)	132,513	(75%)	($204,389)
	Bill O'Mara (R)	44,425	(25%)	($34,543)
1978 primary	Jim Santini (D)	67,338	(88%)	
	Cal Weston (D)	9,493	(12%)	
1976 general	Jim Santini (D)	153,996	(81%)	($158,510)
	Charles W. Earhardt (R)	24,124	(13%)	($209)
	Janine M. Hansen (IA)	12,038	(6%)	($4,545)

NEW HAMPSHIRE

Once every four years New Hampshire becomes the center of the nation's political attention. Presidential candidates trudge through the melting snow and the gooey mud of the state's industrial cities and small New England towns, wooing the votes of about 100,000 people. New Hampshire's primary is not quite the first event of the presidential campaign season; it is preceded now by the Iowa precinct caucuses and the primary in Puerto Rico. But it is still the first state to have a primary and is determined to remain that way. Thus, far away New Hampshire will periodically continue to attract dozens of candidates, hundreds of journalists, and, sometimes, thousands of idealistic volunteers.

So deluged, New Hampshire voters have a habit of upsetting the confident predictions of the outsiders. In 1964, when Barry Goldwater and Nelson Rockefeller spent gobs of money here, New Hampshire Republicans surprised them both by giving Henry Cabot Lodge a write-in victory, when Lodge was U.S. Ambassador in Saigon. (Write-ins are more difficult now, because more of the state now votes by machine.) Four years later Eugene McCarthy's 42% against Lyndon Johnson destroyed the myth of an incumbent president's vulnerability. In 1972 George McGovern's surprisingly high 37% startled everyone but his own canvassers.

There were more surprises in 1976. While Morris Udall, Birch Bayh, and Fred Harris argued which liberal would be the better nominee, a former Southern governor named Jimmy Carter ran away with the Democratic primary. It made Carter a national rather than a regional candidate, even as he won just 23,000 votes, 28% of the total. The Republican primary, as always in New Hampshire, attracted more voters. But while the Democratic primary produced a Carter victory, the Republican race was a standoff. Gerald Ford had 49%, Ronald Regan 48%—a fairly accurate prefiguring of what would happen later at the Republican National Convention.

The New Hampshire primary is one of the anomalies in our system: it makes and breaks presidential candidates, yet it is an arena for a highly unusual and atypical electorate. For one thing, it is small. About 120,000 people vote in the Republican primary, about 95,000 in the Democratic—about one-quarter of 1% of the number that vote in presidential general elections. This makes particularly important here what is called retail politics. It is possible for a candidate to have personal contact with a significant percentage of the people who will be voting, and the candidate who excells in this format—like Jimmy Carter—has a definite advantage. The importance of personal contact inevitably hurts incumbent presidents, who cannot escape their huge entourages, and frontrunners, who are followed around by reporters and cameramen. It is one advantage Jimmy Carter will not have in 1980. Retail politics also gives an advantage to candidates who can inspire volunteers to make personal contact with voters. Carter sent in brigades of Georgians, McGovern and McCarthy had hundreds of college students. New Hampshire voters who know little else about a candidate will often throw their votes to the one whose volunteer chatted with them for 15 minutes. For 1980 it seems likely that only a right wing candidate—a Philip Crane or perhaps Ronald Reagan—can inspire enough volunteers to really help his campaign.

Another way in which New Hampshire's primary electorate is unusual is that it is more Republican than Democratic; only a few other states have a plurality of registered Republicans. That means that the Republican electorate here covers a broader segment of society, although it is heavily Protestant and Yankee in contrast to the heavily Catholic and French Canadian Democratic electorate. The majority of Republican voters live in small towns and rural areas—the kind of places where most Americans do not live. About half the Democratic voters live in Manchester, Nashua, Portsmouth, and other smaller mill towns—not exactly common in most of the rest of the nation either. The Republican electorate in state and presidential primaries seems increasingly to prefer candidates labelled as conservative or very conservative; the Democratic electorate is not classifiable by ideological label. This is a state where an unusually vociferous conservative newspaper—William Loeb's Manchester *Union Leader*—is thought to have an influence, and sometimes does. But the *Union Leader* apparently has little impact on presidential choices. It endorsed Reagan in 1976, who lost anyway, and Samuel Yorty in the 1972 Democratic primary, who got 6%. The *Union Leader* is more effective when it takes the negative; it was particularly tough—and effective—in tarnishing the image of Edmund Muskie in 1972.

The final problem with the New Hampshire primary is that it is so extensively covered and for so long a period—enterprising political reporters were up there in the summer of 1978—that the results are discounted long in advance. Lyndon Johnson and Edmund Muskie actually had significant pluralities here in 1968 and 1972, but both were generally considered the losers—because they did somewhat poorer than expected and their challengers much better. Jimmy Carter with 28% was a clear winner, because people had expected him to get nothing here. Ronald Reagan, with 48% of the vote against an incumbent, was judged a loser because everyone knew all along he had a chance to win. There is little defense against this sort of thing except a clear head; the intelligent candidate, of course, will poormouth his chances in the hope he exceeds expectations on election day.

New Hampshire's primary now takes place in late February, and by the first of March the politicians and their camps of followers are gone, and New Hampshire, which casts only four electoral votes, often never sees a national candidate again. Politics in the state returns to normal, dominated by fractious politicians and the even more fractious William Loeb (who actually lives in Massachusetts and is a legal resident of Nevada). But that can also have national implications—as happened in 1978. Senator Thomas McIntyre, a Democrat, was up for reelection. He had been around for a long time: he was first elected when Republicans split in 1962 and won full terms in 1966 and 1972. A moderate Democrat, he was a member of the Armed Services Committee and because of his lack of adherence to predictable stands and thoughtful analysis was sometimes influential on important votes. In Washington, McIntyre was regarded as a reflective, moderate senator; but in New Hampshire, he was savaged by the *Union Leader* for his support of the Panama Canal Treaty and other sins. He felt the sting enough to make a speech in the Senate about the "bully boys of the radical new right."

But McIntyre did not seem worried much about the general election. His opponent was Gordon Humphrey, an airplane pilot and right wing activist who was totally unknown and seemed extremist. But Humphrey proved adept at raising money—needed for the expensive Boston television that covers New Hampshire—and attacked McIntyre for supporting the Canal Treaty, food stamps, foreign aid, and federal funding of abortions. The *Union Leader* attacks continued, and seemed to hurt. Humphrey won the election with 51%—one of the stunning upsets of 1978. He made great gains over previous McIntyre opponents in his home area, the southwest corner of the state, but the most striking result was McIntyre's failure to carry Manchester, which has more than a 2–1 Democratic registration edge. Loeb's editorials and news columns seem to have had an impact in this working class city.

Once in office, Humphrey seemed likely to join other new right senators, most of them from the Rocky Mountain states. He started his term by flouting tradition and refusing to be escorted down the aisle to take his oath by his senior colleague, Democrat John Durkin. Durkin himself owes his seat to an upset victory—or perhaps two. He ran in 1974 as a former state insurance commissioner against 1st district Congressman Louis Wyman, long a successful vote-getter. But Wyman had a problem: he had introduced one Ruth Farkas to people at the Committee to Re-elect the President; she had contributed $250,000 after the election, and shortly afterwards had been nominated to be Ambassador to Luxembourg. The election was so close that no one really knows who won. The secretary of state said Durkin was ahead by 10 votes; the Republican ballot commission said Wyman won by 2 votes; the Democratic U.S. Senate was inclined to accept Durkin, but could not end a filibuster led by Republicans. Accordingly, the election was rerun in 1975, and this time Durkin won easily.

As a senator, Durkin has stood up for what he considers the Northeast's interests on energy matters; he has worked generally against industry interests on the Commerce Committee; he has won a seat on the Appropriations Committee. His voting record receives high ratings from labor and liberal groups. What is not clear is whether he will be able to win a second term in 1980. He will undoubtedly have strong opposition and, as McIntyre's defeat shows, many of the basic convictions of the state's voters work against him. But not necessarily all of them; this should be one of the hard fought Senate races of 1980.

New Hampshire voters' choices in their last several governor's races have shown a common basis for decision, although the results have been different. In state politics, voters here have insisted on candidates who will cost them the least money. New Hampshire is the last state without either a sales or an income tax, and it is determined to remain that way. In the late sixties, enlightened opinion was that the state would have to impose one to meet its fiscal needs, and a Republican governor elected in 1968 and 1970 backed the idea. But he was defeated in the 1972 primary by Meldrim Thomson, an authentic political primitive who had Loeb's backing and steadfastly opposed any new tax. He was elected in 1972, 1974, and 1976, despite controversial actions like looking through confidential income tax returns. And his tax policy seemed to help the state. New Hampshire has had the fastest rate of growth of any Eastern state and has attracted much new business—all because of its low taxes. State services are meager, but most people here don't mind; if they really need special help, they can move to Massachusetts.

So in 1978 Thomson's Democratic opponent, Hugh Gallen, promised that he too would not allow a broad-based state tax. And he went on the offensive on another issue: the 17% surcharge for construction work in progress (CWIP) the local utility was charging to build its controversial Seabrook Nuclear Plant. Apparently New Hampshire voters don't share the Clamshell Alliance's opposition to the nuclear facility; they just don't want to pay anything extra for it. Thomson, a strong nuclear backer, vetoed a bill that would have repealed CWIP, because the utility people convinced him they'd stop building the plant if he didn't; and so he ended up sacrificing his office to principle. Gallen rode the issue to victory. The presence of a third candidate, former Republican Governor Wesley Powell, was supposed to have some effect on the outcome, but since analysts cannot agree what effect it was, it can be ignored. Powell is one of several former Republican governors who come out of hiding every four years to endorse various presidential candidates; although why the endorsement of someone who won an election in 1954 should mean anything to a voter who can talk to the candidates himself is unclear.

With only the slightest changes, New Hampshire's two congressional districts have had the same boundaries since 1881. The lines neatly separate the cities of Manchester and Nashua, both mill towns on the Merrimack River, the only two significant urban concentrations in the state. Both have large numbers of Irish, Italian, and especially French Canadian immigrants and their offspring, who form the major Democratic groups in this usually Republican state. The purpose of the 1881 redistricting was to put both districts permanently out of reach of the Democrats, and to an amazing extent it accomplished that end for nearly 100 years.

The 1st district is dominated by Manchester, the state's largest city. There are also significant concentrations of people in the Portsmouth-Rochester area, near Maine, and along the Massachusetts border, where Boston area commuters, in search of life in the country and lower taxes, have been moving in great numbers. Commentators assume these new New Hampshire residents vote like Massachusetts liberals, but that is not always true. They do favor low tax candidates in state elections (but so does everyone else), but many of them reacted negatively to the new right politics of Gordon Humphrey. They are the wild card in the race for the seat of John Durkin, himself a Massachusetts migrant.

When 1st district Congressman Louis Wyman ran for the Senate in 1974, there was a close contest here and the winner, in something of a surprise, was Democrat Norman D'Amours. A rather moderate Democrat, D'Amours is a member of the Banking and Merchant Marine Committees; he has to keep an eye on the Manchester *Union Leader* on the right and some of the local McCarthy/McGovern/Udall activists on the left. He has won his last two elections with more than 60% of the vote, but neither opponent was serious competition; the 1976 Republican was a 61-year-old unemployed man who won only because his name was John Adams.

The 2d district is somewhat less urban than the 1st, although it does include Concord, the state capital, Salem, the most populous town on the Massachusetts border, and Nashua, the state's second largest city. The district has been represented in the House by Republican James Cleveland since 1962. Cleveland's mild-mannered, moderate Republicanism has generally suited his constituents well. He has had one close race, in 1964, and a tough challenge in 1976; he was outraged in the latter year to be named one of Environmental Action's Dirty Dozen, although his record was poor by that organization's lights. Cleveland has had his opportunities to run for the Senate and let them pass by; by now it is a fair guess he would prefer to stay in the House. He is next in line for the ranking minority position on both the Public Works and the House Administration Committees.

Census Data Pop. 737,681; 0.36% of U.S. total, 41st largest; Central city, 19%; suburban, 8%. Median family income, $9,682; 18th highest; families above $15,000: 17%; families below $3,000: 7%. Median years education, 12.2.

1977 Share of Federal Tax Burden $1,244,000,000; 0.36% of U.S. total, 42d largest.

1977 Share of Federal Outlays $1,425,802,000; 0.36% of U.S. total, 47th largest. Per capita federal spending, $1,743.

DOD	$406,108,000	38th (0.44%)	HEW	$521,998,000	41st (0.35%)
ERDA	$2,024,000	42d (0.03%)	HUD	$12,956,000	45th (0.31%)
NASA	$2,212,000	31st (0.06%)	VA	$81,210,000	43d (0.42%)
DOT	$59,295,000	45th (0.42%)	EPA	$62,553,000	27th (0.76%)
DOC	$42,361,00	50th (0.51%)	RevS	$23,015,000	46th (0.27%)
DOI	$3,804,000	48th (0.08%)	Debt	$56,965,000	40th (0.19%)
USDA	$49,168,000	46th (0.25%)	Other	$102,115,000	

Economic Base Leather footwear, and other leather and leather products; tourism; electrical equipment and supplies; finance, insurance and real estate; machinery; textile mill products; rubber and plastics products not otherwise classified, especially miscellaneous plastics products.

Political Line-up Governor, Hugh J. Gallen (D). Senators, John Durkin (D) and Gordon Humphrey (R). Representatives, 2 (1 D and 1 R). State Senate (12 D and 12 R); State House (224 R, 172 D, and 4 vacancies).

The Voters

Registration 324,224 Total. 146,854 D (45%); 177,370 R (55%).
Median voting age 43
Employment profile White collar, 45%. Blue collar, 42%. Service, 12%. Farm, 1%.
Ethnic groups Total foreign stock, 23%. Canada, 13%.

Presidential vote

1976	Carter (D)	147,645	(44%)
	Ford (R)	185,935	(56%)
1972	Nixon (R)	213,724	(65%)
	McGovern (D)	116,435	(35%)

1976 Democratic Presidential Primary

Carter	23,373	(28%)
Udall	18,710	(23%)
Bayh	12,510	(15%)
Harris	8,863	(11%)
Others	18,925	(23%)

1976 Republican Presidential Primary

Ford	55,156	(51%)
Reagan	53,569	(49%)

Sen. John A. Durkin (D) Elected September 16, 1975, seat up 1980; b. Mar. 29, 1936, Brookfield, Mass.; home, Manchester; Holy Cross, B.A. 1959, Georgetown, J.D. 1965; Catholic.

Career Navy, 1960–62; Staff mbr., U.S. Controller of Currency, 1963–66; Staff of N.H. Asst. Atty. Gen., 1966–67; N.H. Asst. Atty. Gen., 1967–68; N.H. Insurance Commissioner, 1968–73.

Offices 3230 DSOB, 202-224-3324. Also Fed. Bldg., Manchester 03101, 603-666-7591, and Fed. Bldg., Portsmouth 03801, 603-431-5900.

Committees *Appropriations* (17th). Subcommittees: District of Columbia; HUD-Independent Agencies; Interior and Related Agencies; Legislative Branch; Transportation and Related Agencies.

Energy and Natural Resources (6th). Subcommittees: Energy Conservation and Supply (Chairman); Energy Regulation; Energy Research and Development.

Veterans' Affairs (5th).

Group Ratings

	ADA	COPE	PC	RPN	NFU	LCV	CFA	NAB	NSI	ACA	NTU
1978	65	95	75	56	60	78	70	9	40	21	–
1977	85	90	75	36	82	–	76	–	–	22	33
1976	80	95	86	40	82	83	100	13	0	0	31

Key Votes

1) Warnke Nom	FOR	6) Egypt-Saudi Arms	AGN	11) Hosptl Cost Contnmnt	FOR
2) Neutron Bomb	FOR	7) Draft Restr Pardon	AGN	12) Clinch River Reactor	AGN
3) Waterwy User Fee	AGN	8) Wheat Price Support	AGN	13) Pub Fin Cong Cmpgns	FOR
4) Dereg Nat Gas	AGN	9) Panama Canal Treaty	FOR	14) ERA Ratif Recissn	FOR
5) Kemp-Roth	AGN	10) Labor Law Rev Clot	FOR	15) Med Necssy Abrtns	AGN

Election Results

1975 special	John A. Durkin (D)	140,778	(55%)
	Louis C. Wyman (R)	113,007	(45%)
1974 general	John A. Durkin (D)	110,924	(50%)
	Louis C. Wyman (R)	110,914	(50%)
1974 primary	John A. Durkin (D)	22,258	(50%)
	Lawrence Radway (D)	14,646	(33%)
	Two others (D)	7,615	(17%)
1968 general	Norris Cotton (R)	170,163	(59%)
	John W. King (D)	116,816	(41%)

Sen. Gordon J. Humphrey (R) Elected 1978, seat up 1984; b. Oct. 9, 1940, Bristol, Conn.; home, Sunapee; Geo. Wash. U., U. of Md., Burnside-Off Aviation Institute Flight Proficiency, Dallas, Tex.; Baptist.

Career Air Force, 1958–62; Civilian ferry pilot, 1964–65; Universal Air Transport, Detroit, Mich., 1966–67; Pilot, Allegheny Airlines, 1967–78.

Offices 6205 DSOB, 202-224-2841. Also Rm. 730, 275 Chestnut St., Manchester 03103, 603-666-7691.

Committees *Armed Services* (5th). Subcommittees: Research and Development; Military Construction and Stockpiles; Procurement Policy and Reprogramming.

Human Resources (6th). Subcommittees: Health and Scientific Research; Child and Human Development; Alcoholism and Drug Abuse.

Veterans' Affairs (4th).

Group Ratings: Newly Elected

Key Votes: Newly Elected

Election Results

1978 general	Gordon J. Humphrey (R)	133,745	(51%)	($357,107)
	Thomas J. McIntyre (D)	127,945	(49%)	($289,628)

1978 primary	Gordon J. Humphrey (R)	35,503	(50%)	
	James Massiello (R)	18,371	(26%)	($75,769)
	Alf E. Jacobson (R)	13,619	(19%)	
	One other (R)	2,885	(5%)	
1972 general	Thomas J. McIntyre (D)	184,495	(57%)	($82,800)
	Wesley Powell (R)	139,852	(43%)	($104,779)

Gov. Hugh Gallen (D) Elected 1978, term expires Jan. 1981; b. July 30, 1924, Portland, Oreg.

Career Minor League Baseball Player; Car Salesman, 1948–, Pres., Hugh J. Gallen, Inc., GM Dealership; Dem. State Chmn., 1971–72.

Offices State House, Concord 03301, 603-271-1110.

Election Results

1978 general	Hugh J. Gallen (D)	133,133	(52%)
	Meldrim Thomson, Jr. (R)	122,464	(48%)
1978 primary	Hugh J. Gallen (D)	26,217	(73%)
	Delbert Downing (D)	9,688	(27%)
1974 general	Meldrim Thomson, Jr. (R)	115,933	(51%)
	Richard W. Leonard (D)	110,591	(49%)

FIRST DISTRICT

Census Data Pop. 367,075. Central city, 24%; suburban, 8%. Median family income, $9,631; families above $15,000: 17%; families below $3,000: 7%. Median years education, 12.2.

The Voters

Median voting age 43.
Employment profile White collar, 45%. Blue collar, 42%. Service, 12%. Farm, 1%.
Ethnic groups Total foreign stock, 23%. Canada, 13%.

Presidential vote

1976	Carter (D)	NA	
	Ford (R)	NA	
1972	Nixon (R)	111,167	(67%)
	McGovern (D)	54,375	(33%)

Rep. Norman E. D'Amours (D) Elected 1974; b. Oct. 14, 1937, Holyoke, Mass.; home, Manchester; Assumption Col., B.A. 1960, Boston U., LL.B. 1963.

Career Practicing atty.; Asst. Atty. Gen. of N.H., 1966–69; Criminal Law Instructor, St. Police Training School, 1967–69; Dir., Manchester Area School for Police Prosecutors, 1970; Manchester City Prosecutor, 1970–72; Instructor, St. Anselm's Col., 1972–73.

Offices 1503 LHOB, 202-225-5456. Also 275 Chestnut St., Manchester 03101, 603-668-6800.

Committees *Banking, Finance and Urban Affairs* (19th). Subcommittees: Domestic Monetary Policy; Financial Institutions Supervision, Regulation and Insurance; Economic Stabilization.

Merchant Marine and Fisheries (14th). Subcommittees: Fish and Wildlife; Maritime Education and Training; Oceanography.

Group Ratings

	ADA	COPE	PC	RPN	NFU	LCV	CFA	NAB	NSI	ACA	NTU
1978	45	80	65	20	60	–	50	25	70	42	–
1977	70	74	80	46	64	55	90	–	–	33	21
1976	75	70	87	44	83	74	91	17	90	14	29

Key Votes

1) Increase Def Spnd	AGN	6) Alaska Lands Protect	FOR	11) Delay Auto Pol Cntrl	FOR
2) B-1 Bomber	AGN	7) Water Projects Veto	FOR	12) Sugar Price Escalator	AGN
3) Cargo Preference	FOR	8) Consum Protect Agcy	FOR	13) Pub Fin Cong Cmpgns	FOR
4) Dereg Nat Gas	AGN	9) Common Situs Picket	AGN	14) ERA Ratif Recissn	FOR
5) Kemp-Roth	AGN	10) Labor Law Revision	FOR	15) Prohibt Govt Abrtns	AGN

Election Results

1978 general	Norman E. D'Amours (D)	82,697	(63%)	($92,791)
	Daniel M. Hughes (R)	49,131	(37%)	($48,897)
1978 primary	Norman E. D'Amours (D), unopposed			
1976 general	Norman D'Amours (D)	107,806	(69%)	($80,126)
	John Adams (R)	48,087	(31%)	($0)

SECOND DISTRICT

Census Data Pop. 370,606. Central city, 15%; suburban, 8%. Median family income, $9,736; families above $15,000: 18%; families below $3,000: 7%. Median years education, 12.2.

The Voters

Median voting age 43.
Employment profile White collar, 45%. Blue collar, 42%. Service, 12%. Farm, 1%.
Ethnic groups Total foreign stock, 23%. Canada, 13%.

Presidential vote

1976	Carter (D)	NA	
	Ford (R)	NA	
1972	Nixon (R)	102,557	(62%)
	McGovern (D)	62,060	(38%)

Rep. James C. Cleveland (R) Elected 1962; b. June 13, 1920, Montclair, N.J.; home, New London; Colgate U., B.A. 1941, Yale U., LL.B. 1948; Protestant.

Career Army, WWII; Practicing atty., 1949–62; N.H. Senate, 1950–62, Maj. Floor Ldr., 1952–55.

Offices 2269 RHOB, 202-225-5206. Also Fed. Bldg.,55 Pleasant St., Concord 03301, 603-228-0315.

Committees *House Administration* (3d). Subcommittees: Accounts; Contracts; Printing.

Public Works and Transportation (2d). Subcommittees: Economic Development; Oversight and Review; Surface Transportation.

Group Ratings

	ADA	COPE	PC	RPN	NFU	LCV	CFA	NAB	NSI	ACA	NTU
1978	10	10	35	73	30	–	23	82	90	80	–
1977	20	35	35	83	45	30	35	–	–	88	44
1976	20	22	34	67	8	52	45	83	100	40	40

Key Votes

1) Increase Def Spnd	FOR	6) Alaska Lands Protect	DNV	11) Delay Auto Pol Cntrl	FOR
2) B-1 Bomber	FOR	7) Water Projects Veto	FOR	12) Sugar Price Escalator	AGN
3) Cargo Preference	AGN	8) Consum Protect Agcy	AGN	13) Pub Fin Cong Cmpgns	FOR
4) Dereg Nat Gas	FOR	9) Common Situs Picket	AGN	14) ERA Ratif Recissn	FOR
5) Kemp-Roth	FOR	10) Labor Law Revision	FOR	15) Prohibt Govt Abrtns	DNV

Election Results

1978 general	James C. Cleveland (R)	84,535	(68%)	($65,961)
	Edgar J. Helms (D)	39,546	(32%)	($22,207)
1978 primary	James C. Cleveland (R), unopposed			
1976 general	James C. Cleveland (R)	100,911	(61%)	($74,914)
	J. Joseph Grandmaison (D)	65,792	(39%)	($83,971)

NEW JERSEY

New Jersey is a much maligned state, an object of derision for New Yorkers and a place little known by almost everyone else. But the state is entitled to some satisfaction with its recent political history. After a decade of turbulence, New Jersey has resolved its two major problems in reasonably satisfactory fashion. It has pretty much ended the high level corruption and government involvement with organized crime which had given it the reputation for being the nation's most corrupt state. And after years of controversy, New Jersey finally has an income tax; it may not like it very much, but the voters have in effect rejected all the alternatives. There remains in the state a nagging dissatisfaction with government and public life, as strong here as anywhere on the East Coast. The dissatisfaction is understandable: reducing corruption constitutes a negative achievement and imposition of a tax, however needed, is not going to please many people.

These problems—and their apparent resolution—are tied up in the career of Governor Brendan Byrne. The corruption issue brought him to office, and the tax issue occupied most of his energies during his first term. It is hard now to recall the impact that corruption had here, but for a time in the late sixties and early seventies it seemed that every top official in the state was being indicted. That happened only because United States attorneys appointed by Republican Senator Clifford Case, who was not beholden to his party's machines, began tough investigations and prosecutions of organized crime figures and public officials. They ended up convicting many of the state's most prominent politicoes, including the Democratic bosses of Hudson County (Jersey City), the mayor of Newark, a respected congressman, the 1970 Republican candidate for U.S. Senate, and leading officials in the administrations of Democratic Governor Richard Hughes (1961–69) and Republican Governor William Cahill (1969–73). New Jersey has an almost unique constitution (Alaska's is modeled after it) under which the governor appoints all major officials; there are no other elective statewide offices. That places the responsibility pretty squarely, and so in 1973 Governor Cahill was defeated for renomination in the Republican primary. Unfortunately for the Republicans, his challenger, Congressman Charles Sandman, did not prove to be a credible candidate; those who remember his performance a year later at the House Judiciary Committee impeachment hearings will understand why. That left the governorship almost by default to the Democratic nominee, Brendan Byrne.

Byrne at that time was almost totally unknown to the New Jersey electorate. It is hard enough for voters to keep up with politics in a state that has few important newspapers and no VHF television stations of its own; many New Jerseyites know more about issues that affect New York or Philadelphia than those at home. Anyway, Byrne was an obscure figure: a former Newark prosecutor and judge who became a candidate after tapes of a Mafia boss's tapped telephone conversations had a don describing him as unbuyable. That was enough to give him a 45% victory in a five-candidate primary and a better than 2–1 victory over Sandman in November.

On corruption Byrne's record, at least so far, has been solid; there have been no significant scandals in his administration. He has a number of other achievements, including a model campaign finance law. But during his first term what attracted most attention was his tax policy. Like Hughes and Cahill before him, he proposed an income tax—without actually having said he would do so in his campaign. Unlike them, he got it through the legislature, after several years of struggle. But by the beginning of 1977, the election year in New Jersey, his popularity was at a record low, and Democrats generally seemed headed for disaster.

Instead Byrne won with a solid majority and Democrats held onto the legislature. Both results were a direct repudiation of Republicans' anti-income tax campaign. There were some extenuating factors. Byrne won the primary with only 30%—because the opposition was split among four other serious candidates. His tax plan included a property tax rebate—which came in October, just weeks before the election. His opponent, Raymond Bateman, proved to be an inept campaigner and a less than credible opponent of the income tax; he had actually voted for it in the legislature. Byrne's campaign focused on his opponent's shortcomings, and showed that even an unpopular executive with an unpopular program—and some achievements—can get reelected.

The lack of New Jersey-oriented media has tended to make the state's U.S. senators less well known than those in almost any other state; it is hard to communicate effectively and continuously with seven million people when New York and Philadelphia television stations and newspapers show little interest in the New Jersey delegation. Certainly Senator Clifford Case seems to have suffered from this phenomenon in 1978. After 24 years in the Senate, he had some significant achievements. He had caused the appointment of the U.S. attorneys who had exposed and punished so much corruption in New Jersey. He had long crusaded for full disclosure of public officials' income and assets. He was ranking minority member on the Senate Foreign Relations Committee. And he was a Republican with liberal credentials on civil liberties and an excellent voting record in the eyes of organized labor.

But Case was also 74, and he was out of touch with Republican primary voters in New Jersey. Turnout in the June primary was low, and Case was defeated by 34-year-old Jeffrey Bell, a one-time aide to Ronald Reagan. In 1976, it was Bell who conceived the disastrous plan, put forward by Reagan, to turn $90 billion of federal spending programs over to the states; in 1978, Bell campaigned hard on the Kemp-Roth plan. His commercials emphasized President Kennedy's support of tax cuts, and took up few other issues. Bell presented his ideas intelligently, but sometimes in language outside the experience of the ordinary person. Local audiences were puzzled when he spoke of "closing the gold window."

The Democratic nominee, Bill Bradley, began the campaign with the advantage of being widely known. He was a basketball star at Princeton and for the New York Knicks. Unlike other professional athletes, he refused to do commercial endorsements but he had written a book about his experiences. Also known for being brainy, Bradley was a Rhodes Scholar, and his command of issues was impressive. Bradley had worked in New Jersey politics for several years, and won the Democratic nomination with ease. In the general election, his ads ridiculed Kemp-Roth as a proposal sponsored by the rich. He won the election with a solid 56%—not quite the landslide some commentators expected, but as well as Senator Harrison Williams did the last time he had serious opposition.

Senators are often suspicious of new colleagues who begin their careers as celebrities. Bradley seems to have disarmed any suspicious lawmaker. In the first weeks he avoided publicity and won choice committee assignments—Energy, Finance—and spent long hours learning the rules. He is one politician who is positioned to command attention in New Jersey and establish some kind of consistent communication with voters. He is settling into what he no doubt hopes is a long senatorial career.

New Jersey's senior Senator, after twenty years of service, is Harrison Williams. Elected in 1958 after one term in the House, he is not a celebrity in the state; he instead has benefited from running in the Democratic years of 1958, 1964, and 1970. In 1976 he had no effective opposition. At one point in the late sixties it appeared that Williams had a drinking problem; but he got that under control before the 1970 election and now, just passing 60, appears to be in good physical shape.

Williams's legislative activity has followed his committee assignments. He has authored at least one major mass transit bill and remains interested in the area, as befits a New Jersey legislator. He has headed the subcommittee that handles securities legislation, which means that his opinions are of great interest to Wall Street. Since the 1970 election he has been Chairman of the Human Resources Committee, whose previous name, Labor and Public Welfare, better describes its functions. The seventies has been a rather quiescent decade for this committee, largely because the Great Society laws it handles were passed in the sixties, and there has been little demand for more ground-breaking legislation of the same sort.

There have, however, been some major controversies over labor legislation, and Williams, as Chairman of the Labor Subcommittee as well as the full committee, has been in the midst of them. On both common situs picketing and labor law reform Williams supported organized labor's position. But neither bill passed the 95th Congress; the former was defeated in the House and the latter filibustered to death in the Senate. Williams had more than 50 votes, but could not get the 60 needed to invoke cloture. On labor and other issues, Williams has a dependable Democratic record, and his reelection will be an important priority for labor in the 1982 campaign, as it was in 1976 and 1970.

New Jersey has featured some close presidential elections, favoring Kennedy in 1960, Nixon in 1968, and Ford in 1976 by small margins. With 17 electoral votes, it is an important state; it is often forgotten that this is our ninth state in population (it was eighth, but Florida has passed it in 1970). New Jersey is also important in presidential politics because it has—or at least in 1976 had—the primary with the latest filing deadline; it was the only race Hubert Humphrey could have entered after Jimmy Carter won the Pennsylvania primary in late April. Oddly, the slate of uncommitted notables who had expected to support Humphrey quickly switched their support to Jerry Brown, transferring their allegiance from the New Deal's greatest booster to a politician who has said that the New Deal is dead. (Some members of that slate, notably Peter Rodino and Kenneth Gibson, withdrew at that point.) After Brown's victories in Maryland and Rhode Island, New Jersey voters gave the uncommitted their pluralities.

On the Republican side, New Jersey has a reputation for Eastern liberal Republicanism. But it hardly lived up to that billing in 1978 when it dumped Clifford Case for Jeffrey Bell. In both parties in New Jersey, county political bosses used to control primary outcomes, but their power has shrunk, and things are pretty much up for grabs.

Though New Jersey has gone Republican in the past three presidential elections, it has a House delegation which is 10–5 Democratic, largely as a result of the 1974 elections. In New Jersey, to a greater extent than in most states, there is little consciousness of congressional district lines, and voters' information about what their representative is doing is available only from the congressman himself. Naturally that information tends to be favorable, and it takes a lot to overcome the advantages of incumbency.

Economic Base Finance, insurance and real estate; chemicals and allied products, especially industrial chemicals and drugs; electrical equipment and supplies, especially communication equipment; apparel and other textile products, especially women's and misses' outerwear; machinery; fabricated metal products; food and kindred products.

Political Line-up Governor, Brendan T. Byrne (D). Senators, Harrison A. Williams, Jr. (D) and Bill Bradley (D). Representatives, 15 (9 D and 6 R). State Senate (27 D, 12 R, and 1 vacancy); State House (53 D, 26 R, and 1 vacancy).

The Voters

Median voting age 44.1
Employment profile White collar, 53%. Blue collar, 36%. Service, 11%. Farm, 0%.
Ethnic groups Black 11%. Spanish, 2%. Total foreign stock, 30%. Italy, 7%; Germany, Poland, 3% each; UK, USSR, Ireland, 2% each; Austria, 1%.

Presidential vote

1976	Carter (D)	1,509,688	(51%)
	Ford (R)	1,444,653	(49%)
1972	Nixon (R)	1,845,502	(63%)
	McGovern (D)	1,102,211	(37%)

Sen. Harrison A. Williams, Jr. (D) Elected 1958, seat up 1982; b. Dec. 10, 1919, Plainfield; home, Bedminster; Oberlin Col., B.A. 1941, Georgetown U. School of Foreign Service, Columbia U., LL.B. 1948; Presbyterian.

Career Navy, WWII; Practicing atty.; U.S. House of Reps., 1953–57.

Offices 352 RSOB, 202-224-4744. Also Rm. 939A Fed. Bldg., 970 Broad St., Newark 07102, 201-645-3030.

Committees *Banking, Housing, and Urban Affairs* (2d). Subcommittees: Housing and Urban Affairs (Chairman); International Finance; Securities.

Labor and Human Resources (Chairman). Subcommittees: Education, Arts, and Humanities; Health and Scientific Research; Alcoholism and Drug Abuse.

Rules and Administration (4th).

Group Ratings

	ADA	COPE	PC	RPN	NFU	LCV	CFA	NAB	NSI	ACA	NTU
1978	80	89	63	70	50	72	55	0	10	9	–
1977	85	85	73	36	73	–	68	–	–	7	23
1976	85	80	77	63	75	81	78	8	10	0	31

Key Votes

1) Warnke Nom	FOR	6) Egypt-Saudi Arms	AGN	11) Hosptl Cost Contnmnt	FOR
2) Neutron Bomb	AGN	7) Draft Restr Pardon	FOR	12) Clinch River Reactor	AGN
3) Waterwy User Fee	AGN	8) Wheat Price Support	AGN	13) Pub Fin Cong Cmpgns	FOR
4) Dereg Nat Gas	AGN	9) Panama Canal Treaty	FOR	14) ERA Ratif Recissn	FOR
5) Kemp-Roth	AGN	10) Labor Law Rev Clot	FOR	15) Med Necssy Abrtns	FOR

Election Results

1976 general	Harrison A. Williams, Jr. (D)	1,681,140	(61%)	($610,090)
	David F. Norcross (R)	1,054,508	(39%)	($73,499)
1976 primary	Harrison A. Williams, Jr. (D)	378,553	(85%)	
	One other (D)	66,178	(15%)	
1970 general	Harrison A. Williams, Jr. (D)	1,157,074	(56%)	
	Nelson G. Gross (R)	903,026	(44%)	

Sen. Bill Bradley (D) Elected 1978, seat up 1984; b. July 28, 1943, Crystal City, Mo.; home, Denville; Princeton U., B.A. 1965, Rhodes Scholar, Oxford U., 1965–68; Protestant.

Career U.S. Olympic Team, 1964; Pro Basketball player, New York Knicks, 1967–77.

Offices 315 RSOB, 202-224-3224. Also 1605 Vauxhall Rd., Union 07083, 201-688-0960.

Committees *Energy and Natural Resources* (11th). Subcommittees: Energy Conservation and Supply; Energy Regulation; Energy Resources and Materials Production.

Finance (12th). Subcommittees: International Trade; Unemployment and Related Problems; Revenue Sharing, Intergovernmental Revenue Impact, and Economic Problems (Chairman).

Special Committee on Aging (6th).

Group Ratings: Newly Elected

Key Votes: Newly Elected

Election Results

1978 general	Bill Bradley (D)	1,082,960	(56%)	($1,688,499)
	Jeffrey Bell (R)	844,200	(44%)	($1,418,931)
1978 primary	Bill Bradley (D)	217,502	(59%)	
	Richard C. Leone (D)	97,667	(26%)	($328,052)
	Alexander Menza (D)	32,386	(9%)	($65,154)
	Three others (D)	21,698	(6%)	
1972 general	Clifford P. Case (R)	1,743,854	(64%)	($145,275)
	Paul J. Krebs (D)	963,573	(36%)	

Gov. Brendan T. Byrne (D) Elected 1973, term expires Jan. 1982; b. Apr. 1, 1924, West Orange; Seton Hall U., Princeton U., A.B. 1949, Harvard U., LL.B. 1951.

Career Army Air Corps, WWII; Practicing atty.; Founder, Bd. Chm., Intercontinental Ins. Co.; Asst. Counsel, Exec. Secy. to Gov. Robert B. Meyner, 1955–58; Deputy Atty. Gen. in charge of Essex Co. Prosecutor's Ofc., 1958–59; Essex Co. Prosecutor, 1959–68; Pres., N.J. St. Bd. of Pub. Utilities, 1968–70; Superior Ct. Judge, 1970–72.

Offices Trenton 08625, 609-292-6000.

Election Results

1977 general	Brendan Byrne (D)	1,184,564	(57%)
	Raymond H. Bateman (R)	888,880	(43%)
1977 primary	Brendan Byrne (D)	175,448	(30%)
	Robert A. Roe (D)	134,116	(23%)
	Ralph C. De Rose (D)	99,948	(17%)
	James J. Florio (D)	87,743	(15%)
	Joseph A. Hoffman (D)	58,835	(10%)
	Six others (D)	22,908	(4%)
1973 general	Brendan Byrne (D)	1,414,613	(68%)
	Charles W. Sandman (R)	676,235	(32%)

FIRST DISTRICT

The 1st congressional district of New Jersey is part of suburban Philadelphia, an area of the state more attuned to the city across the Delaware River than it is to Trenton or certainly Newark. The 1st takes in a cross-section of industrial America. Along the banks of the Delaware are the factories and oil tank farms of cities like Camden, the district's largest and the location of such American institutions as Walt Whitman's last home and the Campbell Soup Company. These are places that are declining in population and suffering from the same ills that afflict much larger central cities—except that here fewer people seem to care. To the east, on the flat plains of south Jersey, are the subdivisions of the forties, fifties, and sixties, that thin out into the truck farming vegetable and fruit country. In general, the suburbs nearest the river vote Democratic, while those farther inland tend to go Republican.

The 1st district is as good a place as any to examine the fluctuations of the voting habits of New Jersey's third and fourth generation ethnics, particularly Italian-Americans, who make up about one-third of the state's and district's populations. Most of these people have their roots in one of the old ethnic neighborhoods across the river in Philadelphia; they got better jobs than their parents, made more money, and moved across the Delaware. As late as the fifties, such people thought of themselves as the beneficiaries of programs like Social Security and unemployment insurance. They supported the New Deal, and their congressman here in south Jersey was William Cahill, a liberal Republican at a time when that term meant a Republican who accepted the New Deal.

Later, as times grew more prosperous, these people became less likely to consider themselves society's underdogs. They thought of themselves instead as hard-working taxpayers and as upholders of traditional standards of morality and order which were under attack from demonstrating students and rioting blacks. In the late sixties, the 1st district in an upset elected a congressman who personified these attitudes, Republican John Hunt. Hunt was a big fan of Philadelphia Mayor Frank Rizzo, and he was the only congressman who chased antiwar lobbyists out of his office. Throughout the Watergate crisis he remained a faithful follower of Richard Nixon.

That snapped the cord which connected the people here to their representative. In a time of inflation Nixon, Hunt, and the Republicans seemed to be doing little for the ordinary person; at a time when traditional morality was under attack, they inflicted the worst wounds. Up and down the East Coast, voters in their middle class suburban neighborhoods flocked back to the Democrats in great numbers. John Hunt was thrown out of office by Democrat James Florio, and by a 60%–40% margin.

Florio typifies the kind of congressman who won that year. He has convictions on issues, and has a voting record that wins high approval from labor and liberal organizations. His Italian origin and his clean-cut appearance suggest he is not some kind of cultural radical. His hard work and constituency service make him popular despite some votes that would probably displease many of his constituents. And the Republican Party, since Watergate, seems to have disappeared from congressional politics after holding this district for so many years. Florio was reelected with 80% of the vote in 1978. He tried to win the governorship in 1977, but could not raise enough money to make a strong statewide race. He won only 15% of the vote statewide, but in the two counties covered by the 1st district he had 73% in an eleven-candidate field. That showing confirmed his local popularity and persuaded him that a statewide race was not prudent: he declined to run for the Senate in 1978.

Census Data Pop. 478,002. Central city, 0%; suburban, 100%. Median family income, $10,314; families above $15,000: 20%; families below $3,000: 7%. Median years education, 11.3.

The Voters

Median voting age 43.
Employment profile White collar, 46%. Blue collar, 42%. Service, 11%. Farm, 1%.
Ethnic groups Black, 13%. Spanish, 2%. Total foreign stock, 18%. Italy, 5%; UK, Germany, Poland, 2% each; Ireland, 1%.

Presidential vote

1976	Carter (D)	112,500	(58%)
	Ford (R)	82,661	(42%)
1972	Nixon (R)	112,632	(60%)
	McGovern (D)	74,821	(40%)

Rep. James J. Florio (D) Elected 1974; b. Aug. 29, 1937, Brooklyn, N.Y.; home, Camden; Trenton St. Col., B.A. 1962, Columbia U., 1962–63, Rutgers U., J.D. 1967.

Career Practicing atty., 1967–74; N.J. Gen. Assembly, 1969–75.

Offices 1726 LHOB, 202-225-6501. Also 23 S. White Horse Pike, Somerdale 08083, 609-627-8222.

Committees *Interior and Insular Affairs* (14th). Subcommittees: National Parks and Insular Affairs; Mines and Mining.

Interstate and Foreign Commerce (13th).Subcommittees: Transportation and Commerce (Chairman).

Group Ratings

	ADA	COPE	PC	RPN	NFU	LCV	CFA	NAB	NSI	ACA	NTU
1978	55	75	73	42	78	–	77	18	57	22	–
1977	50	91	73	25	55	51	55	–	–	32	28
1976	75	83	90	47	82	80	91	9	50	8	17

Key Votes

1) Increase Def Spnd	DNV	6) Alaska Lands Protect	FOR	11) Delay Auto Pol Cntrl	AGN
2) B-1 Bomber	AGN	7) Water Projects Veto	FOR	12) Sugar Price Escalator	AGN
3) Cargo Preference	FOR	8) Consum Protect Agcy	FOR	13) Pub Fin Cong Cmpgns	FOR
4) Dereg Nat Gas	AGN	9) Common Situs Picket	FOR	14) ERA Ratif Recissn	AGN
5) Kemp-Roth	AGN	10) Labor Law Revision	FOR	15) Prohibt Govt Abrtns	DNV

Election Results

1978 general	James J. Florio (D)	106,096	(80%)	($76,026)
	Robert M. Deitch (R)	26,853	(20%)	
1978 primary	James J. Florio (D), unopposed			
1976 general	James J. Florio (D)	136,624	(71%)	($126,455)
	Joseph I. McCullough, Jr. (R)	56,363	(29%)	($46,002)

SECOND DISTRICT

The 2d congressional district of New Jersey takes in Atlantic, Cape May, Cumberland, and Salem Counties, along with parts of Ocean and Burlington Counties. The 2d is the largest and most sparsely populated district in the state. The flat, often swampy lands of south Jersey are one of the premier vegetable farm areas in the country; and along the ocean are the beach resorts of Atlantic City, Wildwood, and Cape May. They span the gamut: Cape May was one of the original beach towns in the United States and has many well preserved Victorian houses; Atlantic City was the nation's leading resort between the two world wars, and its tawdry buildings lately have been spruced up for the influx of visitors enjoying America's first legalized casino gambling outside Nevada. Cumberland and Salem Counties, like neighboring Delaware, have an almost Southern atmosphere and an intermittent Democratic voting tradition that go back to the nineteenth century. Although Jimmy Carter did not carry New Jersey, he did as well here as any Democratic presidential candidate aside from Lyndon Johnson in the last forty years.

Cape May is a Republican bastion. Atlantic City, where most of the district's rather large black population can be found, has been increasingly Democratic, although one still sees signs from time to time of the erstwhile dominance of the county by an old-fashioned Republican machine.

This was the district that elected Charles Sandman, the Republican congressman whose defense of Richard Nixon at the House Judiciary Committee recalled in tone if not in content the manner of the late Joseph McCarthy. That performance ended Sandman's political career; he lost that fall to Democrat William Hughes, who has represented the district ever since. As quiet as Sandman was noisy, Hughes has not attracted much attention in the House. He regularly submits bills to prohibit people working for the government to move immediately into jobs in industries they helped to regulate, and at least one has passed. He has also worked to get a share of revenues for the states from whatever oil is found offshore. Far out at sea from Atlantic City are some of the areas leased to the oil companies for exploration. Hughes's voting record is mixed; he gets almost as high ratings from conservative groups as from liberals. He has in any case proved very popular in the 2d district. Since he first won, he has continually increased his percentage here, even in the not very Democratic year of 1978.

Census Data Pop. 478,126. Central city, 29%; suburban, 47%. Median family income, $9,039; families above $15,000: 17%; families below $3,000: 9%. Median years education, 11.1.

The Voters

Median voting age 48.
Employment profile White collar, 42%. Blue collar, 41%. Service, 15%. Farm, 2%.
Ethnic groups Black, 13%. Spanish, 2%. Total foreign stock, 20%. Italy, 5%; Germany, 3%; UK, USSR, 2% each; Poland, Ireland, 1% each.

Presidential vote

1976	Carter (D)	123,144	(51%)
	Ford (R)	120,914	(49%)
1972	Nixon (R)	138,957	(66%)
	McGovern (D)	73,018	(34%)

Rep. William J. Hughes (D) Elected 1974; b. Oct. 17, 1932, Salem; home, Ocean City; Rutgers U., A.B. 1955, J.D. 1958; Episcopalian.

Career Practicing atty., 1959–74; Cape May Co. Asst. Prosecutor, 1960–70; Ocean City Solicitor, 1970–74.

Offices 436 CHOB, 202-225-6572. Also 2920 Atlantic Ave., Atlantic City 08401, 609-345-4844.

Committees *Judiciary* (11th). Subcommittees: Administrative Law and Governmental Relations; Monopolies and Commercial Law.

Merchant Marine and Fisheries (16th). Subcommittees: Coast Guard and Navigation; Oceanography.

Group Ratings

	ADA	COPE	PC	RPN	NFU	LCV	CFA	NAB	NSI	ACA	NTU
1978	55	68	58	33	60	–	59	36	60	35	–
1977	50	78	65	38	45	56	60	–	–	44	34
1976	60	61	82	56	75	61	81	17	60	36	38

Key Votes

1) Increase Def Spnd	AGN	6) Alaska Lands Protect	FOR	11) Delay Auto Pol Cntrl	FOR
2) B-1 Bomber	AGN	7) Water Projects Veto	FOR	12) Sugar Price Escalator	AGN
3) Cargo Preference	AGN	8) Consum Protect Agcy	FOR	13) Pub Fin Cong Cmpgns	FOR
4) Dereg Nat Gas	AGN	9) Common Situs Picket	AGN	14) ERA Ratif Recissn	AGN
5) Kemp-Roth	AGN	10) Labor Law Revision	FOR	15) Prohibt Govt Abrtns	AGN

Election Results

1978 general	William J. Hughes (D)	112,768	(66%)	($108,703)
	James H. Biggs (R)	56,997	(34%)	
1978 primary	William J. Hughes (D), unopposed			
1976 general	William J. Hughes (D)	141,753	(62%)	($116,671)
	James R. Hurley (R)	87,915	(38%)	($62,703)

THIRD DISTRICT

Monmouth County is a place with a name made notable by a Revolutionary War battle and twentieth century racetrack. Here, around the turn of the century, some of America's first beach resorts were developed, to cater to the increasing number of people with the time and money for summer stays at the seashore. Beach manners have changed a lot since the days of full length swimsuits, but the Monmouth County shore still attracts hundreds of thousands of bathers every year. Its summer home areas, with houses ranging from shacks to mansions, have increasingly become year-round communities, with many residents commuting to jobs in north Jersey and even Manhattan. The flatlands behind the beaches have been the area of greatest growth; here retirement villages and subdivisions attract people from the outer Jersey reaches of the New York metropolitan area.

Virtually all of Monmouth County, plus Lakewood Township and Point Pleasant in Ocean County just to the south, make up New Jersey's 3d congressional district. By tradition Monmouth is a Republican bastion, but its voting patterns have become less predictable with recent growth. This is a swing area: it went for Gerald Ford in 1976 and for Bill Bradley in 1978. In congressional elections, however, it has been fairly steady. It elected the same Republican from 1940 until he retired in 1964, and since that time it has elected Democrat James Howard.

Howard has become a rather important figure in Congress. He chairs the Public Works Subcommittee on Surface Transportation, which means highways primarily; and with the huge amount of money generated by the gasoline tax he is naturally subject to all kinds of arguments as to how that money should be spent. He seems somewhat more open than his predecessors to the idea that our transportation policy should encourage alternatives to the private automobile, but he has not gone so far as to advocate that the gasoline tax money traditionally reserved for highways (although states can now spend some of it on mass transit if they wish) should be used to benefit other modes of transportation. Rather, he has sought other sources of revenue. He once advocated a 2% tax on corporate revenues which would go into a mass transit fund—an idea that predictably got nowhere. He also urged an extra 5¢ per gallon tax on gasoline for mass transit—another idea that evoked less than enthusiasm among House members. More recently, Howard has been working with highway interests to continue the current gasoline tax (which was set up to be used only for building the Interstate system) to repair the Interstate system and perhaps other highways. That would keep highway contractors busy, and would also allow truckers to continue using the heavy rigs which very quickly rip up asphalt and concrete.

With his generally Democratic record on issues, Howard has been targeted by Republicans several times: in 1970, 1972, and 1978. In the most recent attempt, challenger Bruce Coe held Howard to 56% of the vote. That is a far from impressive showing for a 14-year veteran. Howard is the third ranking Democrat on Public Works behind two much older members, but he may have to beat back some tough challenges still before becoming chairman.

Census Data Pop. 475,599. Central city, 0%; suburban, 0%. Median family income, $11,291; families above $15,000: 30%; families below $3,000: 7%. Median years education, 12.3.

The Voters

Median voting age 43.
Employment profile White collar, 56%. Blue collar, 31%. Service, 12%. Farm, 1%.
Ethnic groups Black, 8%. Spanish, 1%. Total foreign stock, 25%. Italy, 5%; Germany, UK, 3% each; USSR, Poland, Ireland, 2% each.

Presidential vote

1976	Carter (D)	93,283	(44%)
	Ford (R)	118,767	(56%)
1972	Nixon (R)	133,272	(67%)
	McGovern (D)	65,028	(33%)

Rep. James J. Howard (D) Elected 1964; b. July 24, 1927, Irvington; home, Wall Township; St. Bonaventure U., B.A. 1952, Rutgers U., M.Ed. 1958; Catholic.

Career Navy, WWII; Teacher and Acting Principal, Wall Twnshp. School Dist., 1952–64.

Offices 2245 RHOB, 202-225-4671. Also 808 Belmar Plaza, Belmar 07719, 201-681-3321.

Committees *Interior and Insular Affairs* (25th). Subcommittees: Energy and the Environment; Pacific Affairs.

Public Works and Transportation (3d). Subcommittees: Oversight and Review; Surface Transportation (Chairman); Water Resources.

Group Ratings

	ADA	COPE	PC	RPN	NFU	LCV	CFA	NAB	NSI	ACA	NTU
1978	60	84	65	17	70	–	68	0	33	9	–
1977	70	95	73	33	82	85	80	–	–	9	16
1976	85	87	87	44	83	77	100	0	0	4	24

Key Votes

1) Increase Def Spnd	FOR	6) Alaska Lands Protect	FOR	11) Delay Auto Pol Cntrl	AGN
2) B-1 Bomber	AGN	7) Water Projects Veto	AGN	12) Sugar Price Escalator	AGN
3) Cargo Preference	FOR	8) Consum Protect Agcy	FOR	13) Pub Fin Cong Cmpgns	FOR
4) Dereg Nat Gas	AGN	9) Common Situs Picket	FOR	14) ERA Ratif Recissn	AGN
5) Kemp-Roth	AGN	10) Labor Law Revision	FOR	15) Prohibt Govt Abrtns	AGN

Election Results

1978 general	James J. Howard (D)	83,349	(56%)	($123,220)
	Bruce G. Coe (R)	64,730	(44%)	($145,048)
1978 primary	James J. Howard (D), unopposed			
1976 general	James J. Howard (D)	127,164	(63%)	($57,627)
	Ralph A. Siciliano (R)	75,934	(37%)	($19,339)

FOURTH DISTRICT

The 4th congressional district of New Jersey occupies a geographically central position in the state. It cuts a swath across New Jersey from the capital in Trenton, along the Delaware River, to Cliffwood Beach, on Raritan Bay, across from Staten Island, New York. The New Jersey Turnpike runs through most of the district, starting in the south about 20 miles from center city Philadelphia, proceeding past industrial suburbs to the south side of Trenton, across flat marshy land to East Brunswick, where it expands to 12 lanes for its final miles, north of the 4th district to New York. All this terrain is essentially Democratic, the kind of place where people who work in New Jersey's factories and hold down jobs in its offices live.

The Congressman here is Frank Thompson, first elected in 1954 and now Chairman of the House Administration Committee. In his early House career, Thompson was something of an outsider, and one of the founders of the liberal Democratic Study Group. Now he is one of the senior Democrats in the House and one of the leading backers of labor and liberal causes. Thompson came to his chairmanship with some difficulty. He ran against Wayne Hays unsuccessfully after the 1974 affair; when Hays resigned the chair after his liaison with Elizabeth Ray was exposed, Thompson took over. He has not tried to exert the kind of tough control over House operations that Hays did, but the committee does maintain authorizing power over the House's own budget.

But the most important issue before House Administration is campaign finance. Unlike Hays, Thompson supports public financing of congressional elections. But he has been unable to get the legislation enacted. In the 95th Congress he sparked a controversy by attaching to the public financing bill a provision limiting contributions by political parties. Republicans saw this as a partisan attempt to change the rules in the middle of the game, for the Republican Party had been much more successful in raising money for the 1978 campaign than had the Democrats. Thompson's move cost the bill the support of some Republicans and of Common Cause, and it led to delays and controversies which finally killed the measure in the Senate.

Thompson's other committee assignment is Education and Labor, where he is second in seniority to 68-year-old Chairman Carl Perkins. Thompson's main interest here has been labor legislation, and he chairs the subcommittee which has jurisdiction over the nation's basic labor-management relations laws. Thompson's ratings from the AFL-CIO have usually been near 100%, and he is considered one of labor's strongest advocates on Capitol Hill. With a Democratic president and a heavily Democratic Congress in 1977, labor and Thompson went on the offensive—and got badly mauled. They began the session by pushing to legalize common situs picketing, a measure which affected only the building trade unions working on construction sites. In retrospect, it seems that no other item on labor's agenda could have been less attractive to most members; there was a feeling among many that the building trades were doing quite well enough and didn't need further advantages. Thompson and labor were shocked when the measure was defeated on the floor; they had had little warning in committee, since Education and Labor is packed with pro-labor members.

That defeat, as it turned out, seriously—perhaps permanently—damaged labor's clout on Capitol Hill. Later in the 95th Congress Thompson was able to persuade the House to pass the labor law reform bill, designed to make it easier for unions to organize employers who use illegal tactics and aimed at resistant industries like textiles. This was a measure much easier to make attractive to a majority of members than common situs picketing. But by the time it reached the Senate, time was short and it was vulnerable to filibustering tactics. Labor could not get enough votes for cloture, and the measure died.

The 95th Congress thus did not turn out nearly as well as Thompson must have anticipated. Nevertheless he remains an important figure in the House and a popular figure in his district. He was reelected against weak opposition with more than 60% of the vote.

Census Data Pop. 478,045. Central city, 22%; suburban, 45%. Median family income, $11,086; families above $15,000: 25%; families below $3,000: 6%. Median years education, 12.1.

The Voters

Median voting age 40.
Employment profile White collar, 49%. Blue collar, 38%. Service, 12%. Farm, 1%.
Ethnic groups Black, 13%. Spanish, 1%. Total foreign stock, 25%. Poland, 4%; Germany, 3%; UK, Hungary, USSR, 2% each; Ireland, Austria, 1% each.

Presidential vote

1976	Carter (D)	97,112	(54%)
	Ford (R)	83,561	(46%)
1972	Nixon (R)	102,645	(58%)
	McGovern (D)	74,902	(42%)

Rep. Frank Thompson, Jr. (D) Elected 1954, b. July 26, 1918, Trenton; home, Trenton; Wake Forest Col., Wake Forest Law School, LL.B.; Catholic.

Career Navy, WWII; Practicing atty., 1948–54; N.J. Gen. Assembly, 1949–53, Asst. Minor. Ldr., 1951, Minor. Ldr., 1953.

Offices 2109 RHOB, 202-225-3765. Also 132 W. State St., Trenton 08608, 609-599-1619.

Committees *Education and Labor* (2d). Subcommittees: Labor-Management Relations (Chairman); Post-secondary Education.

House Administration (Chairman).

Group Ratings

	ADA	COPE	PC	RPN	NFU	LCV	CFA	NAB	NSI	ACA	NTU
1978	75	95	63	27	60	–	46	0	10	4	–
1977	90	91	70	38	92	88	60	–	–	0	48
1976	75	91	85	44	100	94	81	9	0	0	29

Key Votes

1) Increase Def Spnd	AGN	6) Alaska Lands Protect	FOR	11) Delay Auto Pol Cntrl	AGN
2) B-1 Bomber	AGN	7) Water Projects Veto	AGN	12) Sugar Price Escalator	DNV
3) Cargo Preference	FOR	8) Consum Protect Agcy	FOR	13) Pub Fin Cong Cmpgns	FOR
4) Dereg Nat Gas	AGN	9) Common Situs Picket	FOR	14) ERA Ratif Recissn	AGN
5) Kemp-Roth	AGN	10) Labor Law Revision	FOR	15) Prohibt Govt Abrtns	AGN

Election Results

1978 general	Frank Thompson, Jr. (D)	69,259	(62%)	($66,828)
	Christopher H. Smith (R)	41,833	(38%)	($15,717)
1978 primary	Frank Thompson, Jr. (D), unopposed			
1976 general	Frank Thompson, Jr. (D)	113,281	(67%)	($48,181)
	Joseph S. Indyk (R)	54,789	(33%)	($19,114)

FIFTH DISTRICT

Most people's image of New Jersey is the one you get on the drive from Newark Airport to Manhattan: factories spewing smoke into the already smoggy air, swampland pocked with truck terminals and warehouses, grim lines of Jersey City rowhouses, and the docks on the Hudson River. But there is another New Jersey—one which begins 40 or 50 miles outside Manhattan, past the first ridge of mountains west of Newark. Such is the area that is New Jersey's 5th congressional district. Out here the high income suburbs fade into the elegant horse farm country around Morristown and Far Hills, Peapack and Bernardsville and Basking Ridge. The 5th also includes middle class suburbs, places like fast-growing Parsippany-Troy Hills, where subdivisions of tightly grouped houses sell for prices considered modest these days. But most of the 5th district, at least in area, from the horse country of Morris and Somerset Counties to the rich university town of Princeton, is high income territory; in fact, it ranks 11th in median family income of all the nation's 435 congressional districts.

It is appropriate, then, that the 5th district has a line of representatives going back more than fifty years from America's wealthiest and most aristocratic families. There was Charles Eaton, Congressman from 1924 to 1952, a relative of industrialist Cyrus Eaton. He was followed by Peter H. B. Frelinghuysen, descendant of a fire-breathing eighteenth century Dutch preacher and scion of a family which has produced three United States senators, an unsuccessful candidate for vice president, and a secretary of state. A moderate Republican, Frelinghuysen lost a leadership post to Melvin Laird in 1965, but in 1974 became ranking Republican on the Foreign Affairs Committee. His support of Nixon and Ford foreign policies hurt him in the district, and he received stronger than usual competition from a Vietnam war opponent in 1972; perhaps that is why he retired in 1974.

Frelinghuysen's successor is another aristocrat, Millicent Fenwick of Bernardsville. She came to politics late, after such diverse activities as attending the New School for Social Research and working as an editor for Vogue. She is a person of definite and irresistible character. Tall and thin, speaking with the kind of accent heard at the most fashionable girls' schools, at the ends of meetings will take a pipe out of her purse and start puffing away.

Fenwick has had considerable impact on the House, though she is a junior member of the minority party. In her first term she was not afraid to rise on the floor and take on Wayne Hays before his downfall. In her second term she served on the House Ethics Committee and was a major force for a thorough investigation of the Tongsun Park scandal. On a number of issues—campaign finance, committee staffing—she has led strong attacks on the Democratic majority. She is a fervent Republican, with a kind of noblesse oblige liberalism; as a state official in New Jersey, she worked hard to help low income consumers get more value for their money. Her zest for procedural reform is combined with caution on economic issues and some parsimony in spending government money. Of all the groups rating voting records, Americans for Democratic Action usually gives her the highest rating; she receives similar ratings from business and labor groups.

In the 96th Congress Fenwick switched from the Banking and Ethics Committee—the latter was an exhausting and unpleasant assignment, even for this reformer—to Foreign Affairs and the District of Columbia. The latter in particular is an assignment few members want to take on; it can be a lot of work for very little political payoff. Millicent Fenwick seems less interested in accumulating seniority on a committee and less concerned about her popularity in the 5th district than she is determined to go where she can be of service. In fact, her kind of politics is the most popular politics possible in the 5th district, and she has been reelected by overwhelming margins.

Census Data Pop. 478,007. Central city, 0%; suburban, 54%. Median family income, $14,218; families above $15,000: 46%; families below $3,000: 3%. Median years education, 12.6.

The Voters

Median voting age 42.
Employment profile White collar, 65%. Blue collar, 26%. Service, 9%. Farm, –%.
Ethnic groups Black, 3%. Total foreign stock, 29%. Italy, 6%; Germany, UK, Poland, 3% each; USSR, Ireland, 2% each; Austria, Canada, Hungary, 1% each.

Presidential vote

1976	Carter (D)	88,004	(41%)
	Ford (R)	128,276	(59%)
1972	Nixon (R)	139,407	(66%)
	McGovern (D)	73,268	(34%)

Rep. Millicent Fenwick (R) Elected 1974; b. Feb. 25, 1910, New York, N.Y.; home, Bernardsville; Columbia U., 1933, New School for Social Research, 1942.

Career Assoc. Ed., Conde Nast Publications, 1938–52; Mbr., Bernardsville Borough Cncl., 1958–64; N.J. Gen. Assembly, 1969–72; Dir., N.J. Div. of Consumer Affairs, 1972–74.

Offices 1212 LHOB, 202-225-7300. Also 41 N. Bridge St., Somerville 08876, 201-722-8200.

Committees *Foreign Affairs* (11th). Subcommittees: Africa; Europe and the Middle East.

District of Columbia (4th). Subcommittees: Fiscal Affairs and Health; Government Affairs and Budget.

Group Ratings

	ADA	COPE	PC	RPN	NFU	LCV	CFA	NAB	NSI	ACA	NTU
1978	55	35	54	100	50	–	36	58	40	33	–
1977	85	52	80	92	58	85	75	–	–	37	33
1976	65	52	64	87	67	72	54	50	40	19	38

Key Votes

1) Increase Def Spnd	AGN	6) Alaska Lands Protect	FOR	11) Delay Auto Pol Cntrl	AGN
2) B-1 Bomber	AGN	7) Water Projects Veto	FOR	12) Sugar Price Escalator	AGN
3) Cargo Preference	AGN	8) Consum Protect Agcy	FOR	13) Pub Fin Cong Cmpgns	FOR
4) Dereg Nat Gas	AGN	9) Common Situs Picket	AGN	14) ERA Ratif Recissn	AGN
5) Kemp-Roth	AGN	10) Labor Law Revision	FOR	15) Prohibt Govt Abrtns	AGN

Election Results

1978 general	Millicent Fenwick (R)	100,739	(73%)	($61,777)
	John T. Fahy (D)	38,108	(27%)	($43,509)
1978 primary	Millicent Fenwick (R), unopposed			
1976 general	Millicent Fenwick (R)	137,803	(68%)	($59,082)
	Frank R. Nero (D)	64,598	(32%)	($37,339)

SIXTH DISTRICT

The 6th congressional district of New Jersey is a weirdly shaped district, spanning the entire state from the Delaware River to the Atlantic Ocean. It brings into a single constituency people from sociologically diverse and geographically disparate communities. More than 60% of its residents live in the Philadelphia suburbs of Burlington and Camden Counties; important towns here include Cherry Hill and Willingboro (formerly Levittown), both of which more than doubled in population in the sixties. Another 20% of the district's residents live on or near the Jersey shore in Ocean County. This is an area which has had similarly fast population growth in the fifties, much of it retirees from middle class neighborhoods in New York and Philadelphia, fleeing high taxes and crime. Connecting these two regions—which have little in common except for rapid growth and generally Republican voting habits—are the sparsely inhabited swamps and truck farms of south Jersey.

The 6th was created in its present form by the 1966 redistricting, and its first Congressman was Republican William Cahill, who was elected Governor in 1969 and defeated for renomination in 1973. The new Congressman, elected in 1970, was Republican Edwin Forsythe. Despite five terms of service, Forsythe has little seniority. He is a high ranking Republican on the Merchant Marine Committee, which has a limited jurisdiction, and a low ranking Republican on Science and Technology, which he joined in 1977. Perhaps the most interesting aspect of his service is his voting record, which does not follow any of the usual patterns in the House.

Census Data Pop. 478,137. Central city, 0%; suburban, 78%. Median family income, $11,689; families above $15,000: 30%; families below $3,000: 5%. Median years education, 12.3.

The Voters

Median voting age 42.
Employment profile White collar, 59%. Blue collar, 31%. Service, 9%. Farm, 1%.
Ethnic groups Black, 5%. Total foreign stock, 21%. Italy, 5%; Germany, UK, 3% each; Poland, USSR, 2% each; Ireland 1%.

Presidential vote

1976	Carter (D)	108,251	(48%)
	Ford (R)	115,807	(52%)
1972	Nixon (R)	130,276	(66%)
	McGovern (D)	67,191	(34%)

Rep. Edwin B. Forsythe (R) Elected 1970; b. Jan. 17, 1916, Westtown, Pa.; home, Moorestown; Society of Friends.

Career Secy., Moorestown Bd. of Adjustment, 1948–52; Mayor of Moorestown, 1957–62; Chm., Moorestown Twnshp. Planning Bd., 1962–63; N.J. Senate 1963–69, Asst. Minor. Ldr., 1966, Minor. Ldr. 1967, Sen. Pres. and Acting Gov. of N.J., 1968, Pres. Pro Tempore, 1969.

Offices 303 CHOB, 202-225-4765. Also Third and Mill St., Moorestown 08057, 609-235-6622.

Committees *Merchant Marine and Fisheries* (3d). Subcommittees: Fish and Wildlife; Oceanography.

Science and Technology (9th). Subcommittees: Energy Research and Production; Natural Resources and the Environment.

Group Ratings

	ADA	COPE	PC	RPN	NFU	LCV	CFA	NAB	NSI	ACA	NTU
1978	40	16	23	82	20	–	18	80	28	70	–
1977	30	25	33	89	27	36	30	–	–	54	58
1976	25	17	25	93	28	39	9	64	44	48	59

Key Votes

1) Increase Def Spnd	DNV	6) Alaska Lands Protect	AGN	11) Delay Auto Pol Cntrl	DNV
2) B-1 Bomber	AGN	7) Water Projects Veto	FOR	12) Sugar Price Escalator	AGN
3) Cargo Preference	AGN	8) Consum Protect Agcy	AGN	13) Pub Fin Cong Cmpgns	AGN
4) Dereg Nat Gas	FOR	9) Common Situs Picket	AGN	14) ERA Ratif Recissn	AGN
5) Kemp-Roth	FOR	10) Labor Law Revision	AGN	15) Prohibt Govt Abrtns	DNV

Election Results

1978 general	Edwin B. Forsythe (R)	89,446	(61%)	($87,804)
	W. Thomas McGann (D)	56,874	(39%)	($60,647)
1978 primary	Edwin B. Forsythe (R)	17,106	(85%)	
	One other (R)	3,095	(15%)	
1976 general	Edwin B. Forsythe (R)	125,920	(60%)	($63,541)
	Catherine A. Costa (D)	85,053	(40%)	($25,775)

SEVENTH DISTRICT

Bergen County, the northeast corner of New Jersey, is one of the nation's more comfortable and affluent suburban areas. Just across the George Washington Bridge from Manhattan, behind the Palisades that line the Hudson, are some of the nation's wealthiest suburbs, sparsely settled (because of minimum acreage zoning), hilly, and tree-shaded. Most of them have some patina of age; the new, treeless subdivisions are going up farther south in New Jersey or to the north in what used to be called upstate New York. Shopping centers, not skyscrapers, are the most prominent landmarks here, and although there are some out-of-gas industrial towns along the Passaic and Hackensack Rivers, the overall picture here is one of settled affluence and neat prosperity.

Bergen County is divided into two congressional districts; the 7th occupies roughly the western half of it. Republicans drew the slightly irregular lines to split the county's centers of Democratic strength between the two seats: the 7th bulges south to take in industrial Hackensack and Jewish Teaneck to go with the generally Republican suburbs to the north and west. But redistricters' strategies do not always work. Entirely contrary to expectations, both Bergen County districts have shifted parties since their lines were drawn—the 9th went Republican in 1976 and the 7th went Democratic in 1974.

The 1974 race was a classic contest between an elderly Republican with a generally liberal record but unable to campaign vigorously or give constituents the kind of services they have come to expect and a young, vigorous Democrat bent on change and reform. The Democrat, Andrew Maguire, had the kind of classy credentials upper income suburbanites like: a fellowship in England, a Ph.D. from Harvard, a job with the Ford Foundation. Elected in the Watergate year, Maguire was the congressman who forced the House to consider the question of Congressman Bob Sikes's conflicts of interest. Eventually the House reprimanded Sikes, the Democrats took away his Appropriations subcommittee chair, and he retired from office.

But not all of Maguire's initiatives seem to have been in line with feeling in his district. As a member of the Commerce Committee, he has been one of the most vigorous and effective opponents of measures sought by the oil companies. He has also fought for tougher clean air standards, though that might require some sacrifices, and he was the House's most outspoken critic of delaying the ban on saccharin after researchers found it caused cancer in animals.

All of these measures have an appeal; but they are also opposed by many affluent people who believe in less regulation of business—and there are many such people in the 7th district. Maguire won reelection with a solid margin in 1976, but he had a tougher time in 1978 against Republican Margaret Roukema. Roukema won the three-candidate Republican primary with 39%, and with the support of most of the party's old guard faction, not normally the credential that would make a candidate attractive in a general election. But she ran an imaginative campaign, publishing a newspaper for commuters during the New York City newspaper strike. On issues she contrasted with Maguire; locally, she backed a freeway which he opposed because it would cut through a park.

The election ended with a 53% Maguire victory—decisive, but not impressive enough to deter significant competition in 1980. This is a seat Maguire will have to continue to fight for. He has considered running statewide, but declined to enter the 1978 Senate race; he would have had to raise enough money to buy television time in both the New York and Philadelphia media markets, and his prospects for doing that were dim. So he continues as an active and effective member of the House, but he will have to look after his district closely in order to stay there.

Census Data Pop. 479,999. Central city, 0%; suburban, 100%. Median family income, $14,257; families above $15,000: 46%; families below $3,000: 3%. Median years education, 12.4.

The Voters

Median voting age 45.
Employment profile White collar, 65%. Blue collar, 27%. Service, 8%. Farm, -%.
Ethnic groups Black, 3%. Total foreign stock, 36%. Italy, 9%; Germany, 5%; Poland, UK, 3% each; USSR, Ireland, 2% each; Austria, Canada, Netherlands, 1% each.

Presidential vote

1976	Carter (D)	93,764	(42%)
	Ford (R)	129,847	(58%)
1972	Nixon (R)	150,619	(66%)
	McGovern (D)	76,583	(34%)

Rep. Andrew Maguire (D) Elected 1974; b. Mar. 11, 1939, Columbus, Ohio; home, Ridgewood; Oberlin Col., B.A. 1961, Woodrow Wilson and Danforth Fellow, U. of London, England, 1963, Harvard U., Ph.D. 1966.

Career U.N. Advisor on Political and Security Affairs, 1966–69; Dir., multi-development program, Jamaica, N.Y., 1969–72; Consultant, Natl. Affairs Div., Ford Foundation, 1972–74.

Offices 1112 LHOB, 202-225-4465. Also Rm. 100, 277 Forest Ave., Paramus 07652, 201-262-1993.

Committees *Government Operations* (17th). Subcommittees: Environment, Energy and Natural Resources; Manpower and Housing.

Interstate and Foreign Commerce (16th). Subcommittees: Energy and Power; Health and the Environment; Oversight and Investigations.

Group Ratings

	ADA	COPE	PC	RPN	NFU	LCV	CFA	NAB	NSI	ACA	NTU
1978	90	84	90	70	67	–	96	0	0	12	–
1977	95	83	98	73	58	100	100	–	–	15	42
1976	95	83	95	71	83	100	91	17	0	4	56

Key Votes

1) Increase Def Spnd	AGN	6) Alaska Lands Protect	FOR	11) Delay Auto Pol Cntrl	AGN
2) B-1 Bomber	AGN	7) Water Projects Veto	FOR	12) Sugar Price Escalator	AGN
3) Cargo Preference	AGN	8) Consum Protect Agcy	FOR	13) Pub Fin Cong Cmpgns	FOR
4) Dereg Nat Gas	AGN	9) Common Situs Picket	FOR	14) ERA Ratif Recissn	AGN
5) Kemp-Roth	AGN	10) Labor Law Revision	FOR	15) Prohibt Govt Abrtns	AGN

Election Results

1978 general	Andrew Maguire (D)	78,358	(53%)	($202,210)
	Margaret S. Roukema (R)	69,543	(47%)	($142,266)
1978 primary	Andrew Maguire (D), unopposed			
1976 general	Andrew Maguire (D)	120,526	(57%)	($163,715)
	James J. Sheehan (R)	92,624	(43%)	($113,359)

EIGHTH DISTRICT

In the late eighteenth century Alexander Hamilton journeyed to the Great Falls of the Passaic River, some twenty miles west of the Hudson, and predicted major industrial development for the area around it. His prediction made sense: industry then depended on falling water for energy, and the Great Falls were 72 feet high, the highest in the East except for Niagara. Hamilton died—in a duel in nearby Weehawken—before his dream was fulfilled, but in the late nineteenth century Paterson, founded here at the Great Falls, became one of the major manufacturing cities in the United States. It developed major silk and locomotive factories and attracted immigrants from England, Ireland, and, after the turn of the century, Italy and Poland. Paterson was a tough town, and even as its town fathers were erecting impressive public buildings, its narrow streets were buzzing with rumors of anarchist plots. The great silk strike of 1913 here was led by the International Workers of the World.

Today Paterson remains a manufacturing center, though neither silk nor locomotives are its mainstay anymore. Although it is more or less surrounded by suburbs of New York and Newark, it is resolutely non-suburban; it is a small central city which just happens to be an easy freeway ride away from the George Washington Bridge. Paterson is the center of New Jersey's 8th congressional district, which includes most of surrounding Passaic County. To the south there is the old industrial city of Passaic and the larger, more middle class Clifton; to the north and west are upper income suburbs of Paterson, most notably Wayne Township. The political heritage of the 8th district is Democratic, a dim memory perhaps of its more radical past. But as in other blue collar areas there has been a slow shift away from the old party: the 8th went for Kennedy in 1960, Nixon in 1968, and Ford in 1976.

The current Congressman, Democrat Robert Roe, was the victor by only 960 votes in the 1969 special election that first sent him to Washington. Involved in local and state government before that, he serves on the Public Works and Science Committees. It is on the former that he has made his greatest mark. As Chairman of the Economic Development Subcommittee, he has managed the major public works jobs bill; he was particularly eager to provide aid to cities. This kind of legislation has come under attack from some who feel it hurts the environment and from others who feel that it wastes money. Roe maintains the traditional Democratic faith in such programs.

Although he had never been well known outside his district Roe ran for governor in 1977. He raised the kind of substantial sums of money needed to run a media campaign in New Jersey and hoped to capitalize on the unpopularity of incumbent Brendan Byrne. He won fully 86% of the vote in the eleven-candidate race in Passaic County, and did well enough otherwise in north Jersey for 23% of the vote and a respectable second place finish to Byrne. As his local showing suggests, he has had no difficulty in recent years winning reelection in the 8th district.

Census Data Pop. 478,369. Central city, 59%; suburban, 41%. Median family income, $10,783; families above $15,000: 25%; families below $3,000: 7%. Median years education, 10.9.

The Voters

Median voting age 45.
Employment profile White collar, 46%. Blue collar, 44%. Service, 10%. Farm, –%.
Ethnic groups Black, 11%. Spanish, 4%. Total foreign stock, 38%. Italy, 10%; Poland, 5%; Germany, 3%; USSR, UK, Netherlands, Austria, Hungary, 2% each; Czechoslovakia, Ireland, 1% each.

Presidential vote

1976	Carter (D)	79,546	(48%)
	Ford (R)	86,402	(52%)
1972	Nixon (R)	111,671	(63%)
	McGovern (D)	65,125	(37%)

Rep. Robert A. Roe (D) Elected Nov. 4, 1969; b. Feb. 28, 1924, Wayne; home, Wayne; Oreg. St. U., Wash. St. U.; Catholic.

Career Army, WWII; Wayne Twnshp. Committeeman, 1955–56; Mayor, 1956–61; Passaic Co. Bd. of Freeholders, 1959–63, Dir., 1962–63; Commissioner, N.J. Dept. of Conservation and Econ. Development, 1963–69.

Offices 2243 RHOB, 202-225-5751. Also U.S.P.O., 194 Ward St., Paterson 07510, 201-523-5152.

Committees *Public Works and Transportation* (5th). Subcommittees: Economic Development (Chairman); Surface Transportation; Oversight and Review.

Science and Technology (2d). Subcommittees: Energy Research and Production; Energy Development and Applications.

Group Ratings

	ADA	COPE	PC	RPN	NFU	LCV	CFA	NAB	NSI	ACA	NTU
1978	35	85	48	25	67	–	50	9	33	19	–
1977	35	93	53	17	100	40	60	–	–	6	26
1976	70	87	79	44	92	65	91	8	60	14	21

Key Votes

1) Increase Def Spnd	DNV	6) Alaska Lands Protect	FOR	11) Delay Auto Pol Cntrl	DNV
2) B-1 Bomber	FOR	7) Water Projects Veto	AGN	12) Sugar Price Escalator	DNV
3) Cargo Preference	FOR	8) Consum Protect Agcy	FOR	13) Pub Fin Cong Cmpgns	FOR
4) Dereg Nat Gas	AGN	9) Common Situs Picket	FOR	14) ERA Ratif Recissn	AGN
5) Kemp-Roth	AGN	10) Labor Law Revision	FOR	15) Prohibt Govt Abrtns	DNV

Election Results

1978 general	Robert A. Roe (D)	69,496	(74%)	($66,635)
	Thomas Melani (R)	23,842	(26%)	($5,800)
1978 primary	Robert A. Roe (D), unopposed			
1976 general	Robert A. Roe (D)	108,841	(71%)	($69,485)
	Bessie Doty (R)	44,775	(29%)	($6,623)

NINTH DISTRICT

The 9th congressional district of New Jersey is, in rough terms, the eastern half of Bergen County plus a small part of the northern end of Hudson County. North of the George Washington Bridge and west of the Palisades that rise above the Hudson are the wealthy, most heavily Republican parts of Bergen County: Tenafly, Dumont, Closter, Old Tappan. Near the Jersey end of the bridge are several predominantly Jewish and politically liberal suburbs. Atop the Palisades huge apartment towers overlook New York City, occupied by well-to-do people who want to escape the city and its taxes but still want a view of Manhattan. South of the bridge, toward and into Hudson County, are older and less affluent suburbs, where people guard their suburban gentility as if it were their lives and wear as a badge of their social distinction Republican registration.

The Jersey Meadows separate the southern part of the 9th district—a section with about one-fifth of the district's population—from the rest. The Meadows are a swamp for which there have been great plans. The new stadium for the New York (or New Jersey) Giants has been built, and other construction is taking place on this well located land. But much of the Meadows are still pocked with gas stations and their giant signs, oil tank farms, truck terminals, and eight lanes of New Jersey Turnpike. The 9th's southern towns, right next to the Meadows, are peopled with Polish-American and Italian-American citizens who usually vote Democratic. This is the part of the district which has produced its last two congressmen, Democrat Henry Helstoski and Republican Harold Hollenbeck.

Helstoski first won in 1964 and held on through a series of Republican redistrictings and tough challenges for 12 years. Then in 1976 he was indicted for accepting bribes to help aliens stay in the country. He was nearly beaten in the primary—actually, apparently was beaten, but there were enough irregularities to require a rerun which he won—and then lost the general election to Hollenbeck. In his first term Hollenbeck worked the district as assiduously as Helstoski always had, concentrating more on the district than on legislative matters in Washington. It paid off. Helstoski ran as an Independent in 1978 and took 13% of the vote—much of it from the area around the Meadows. The Democratic nominee was from Hudson County, who had won the nomination with a minority vote over two Bergen County candidates. He did predictably poorly in Bergen in the general, winning only 38% district-wide. That left Hollenbeck with a 49% victory.

Anything can happen here in 1980. At this writing, Helstoski has not yet been tried on the 1976 charges. If he is acquitted or vindicated, he may well run again in the Democratic primary or as an Independent; or another Bergen Democrat could give Hollenbeck a tough race.

Census Data Pop. 478,427. Central city, 0%; suburban, 100%. Median family income, $12,428; families above $15,000: 36%; families below $3,000: 5%. Median years education, 12.1.

The Voters

Median voting age 46.
Employment profile White collar, 58%. Blue collar, 34%. Service, 8%. Farm, –%.
Ethnic groups Black, 2%. Spanish, 1%. Total foreign stock, 44%. Italy, 12%; Germany, 5%; Ireland, Poland, 3% each; UK, USSR, 2% each; Austria, 1%.

Presidential vote

1976	Carter (D)	96,933	(46%)
	Ford (R)	116,058	(54%)
1972	Nixon (R)	146,286	(66%)
	McGovern (D)	74,851	(34%)

Rep. Harold C. Hollenbeck (R) Elected 1976; b. Dec. 29, 1938, Passaic; home, East Rutherford; Fairleigh Dickinson U., B.A. 1961, U. of Va., J.D. 1964; Catholic.

Career Practicing atty., 1965–77; Carlstadt Borough Prosecutor, 1966–67; East Rutherford Borough Cncl., 1967–69; N.J. Gen. Assembly, 1968–71; N.J. Senate, 1972–73.

Offices 1526 LHOB, 202-225-5061. Also 1550 Lemoine Ave., Ft. Lee 07024, 201-947-6868.

Committees *Standards of Official Conduct* (2d).

Science and Technology (6th). Subcommittees: Energy Research and Production; Science, Research and Technology.

Group Ratings

	ADA	COPE	PC	RPN	NFU	LCV	CFA	NAB	NSI	ACA	NTU
1978	50	75	53	40	60	–	50	17	56	22	–
1977	55	57	53	62	67	63	55	–	–	56	30

Key Votes

1) Increase Def Spnd	AGN	6) Alaska Lands Protect	FOR	11) Delay Auto Pol Cntrl	AGN
2) B-1 Bomber	FOR	7) Water Projects Veto	FOR	12) Sugar Price Escalator	AGN
3) Cargo Preference	AGN	8) Consum Protect Agcy	FOR	13) Pub Fin Cong Cmpgns	FOR
4) Dereg Nat Gas	AGN	9) Common Situs Picket	AGN	14) ERA Ratif Recissn	AGN
5) Kemp-Roth	FOR	10) Labor Law Revision	FOR	15) Prohibt Govt Abrtns	AGN

Election Results

1978 general	Harold C. Hollenbeck (R)	73,478	(49%)	($84,548)
	Nicholas S. Mastorelli (D)	56,888	(38%)	($121,447)
	Henry Helstoski (Always for People)	19,126	(13%)	($25,622)
1978 primary	Harold C. Hollenbeck (R)	10,083	(82%)	
	One other (R)	2,245	(18%)	
1976 general	Harold C. Hollenbeck (R)	107,454	(54%)	($53,608)
	Henry Helstoski (D)	89,723	(46%)	($69,636)

TENTH DISTRICT

When it became clear that Peter Rodino, Congressman from the 10th district of New Jersey, would chair the hearings on the impeachment of Richard Nixon, some House members were apprehensive. Rodino had only become Chairman of the Judiciary Committee the year before, in 1973, after the defeat of New York's Emanuel Celler; and Celler, though 86 when he lost, was an assertive chairman who let Rodino take little responsibility. But these apprehensions proved ungrounded. Relying on the Judiciary staff assembled by Celler as well as on the more publicized services of impeachment counsel John Doar, Rodino was able to master the factual and legal case against Nixon and to get smoothly past the parliamentary difficulties as well. His chairing of the hearings was even-tempered and fair; he was careful to give the minority every opportunity to advance their views. But there could be little doubt of where Rodino stood in the face of the massive evidence and, to be a bit cynical about it, in light of the overwhelming sentiments of his constituency; he came out solemnly on the side that Richard Nixon should be removed from office.

One strength of the American political system is that it has produced people of extraordinary talent who have happened to find their way into crucial positions at critical times and who have performed far better than their records would have suggested. Such leaders sometimes come from the most unlikely places: a Lincoln from the western hick town of Springfield, Illinois; a Franklin Roosevelt from the aristocratic patroon families of the Hudson Valley. Within that tradition is Peter Rodino from Newark, New Jersey—a place that some, including its mayor, have said will be the first American city to die.

Three decades ago, when Peter Rodino was first elected to Congress, Newark was a fairly prosperous industrial city with a large white collar employment base. With nearly half a million people, it was the financial center of New Jersey, a city proud of its tree-shaded middle class neighborhoods. Today the downtown remains, although Prudential Insurance, the biggest employer there, is rapidly though quietly moving much of its operations to the suburbs. Much of the rest of Newark resembles Berlin after the war. With one notable exception, the middle class has left in search of nicer lawns and safer streets in the suburbs; most of the people remaining in Newark are here because they cannot get out. This is not just a matter of racial change, although Newark is by now two-thirds black, for black middle income people like their white counterparts are abandoning the city for the more comfortable suburbs. Newark suffered through organized crime control of its city government in the sixties and a major riot in 1967. Now with the population declining below the 350,000 mark, it is simply being abandoned.

The one exception to that pattern is the community Peter Rodino comes from, the Italian-Americans who remain in the North Ward. The Jews who once lived in Philip Roth's Weequahic Park have long since moved to places like Maplewood and Short Hills; the Irish have vanished beyond the city limits into Livingston or West Orange; the WASPs, to the extent there ever were any in Newark, are now far away in Morris and Somerset Counties. But many Italians remain, in close-knit neighborhoods where everybody knows everyone else, nobody steals or shoots anyone, and people speak Italian on the streets and in the shops.

The North Ward has steadily resisted black immigration; but within the city as a whole whites have been in the minority for a decade now. Kenneth Gibson, a black engineer with little political background, was first elected Mayor in 1970; there have been black majorities on the council and the school board since 1974. Many blacks are bitter that the city they finally inherited is financially in deep trouble: its tax base is dwindling year by year, and it must go begging to the state and federal governments every year for money for the most basic city services. Newark in 1978 got more than half its budget from the federal government—which is all well and good except when the government threatens, as it did in 1979, to cut spending on those programs.

Newark makes up about three-quarters of the population of the 10th congressional district; the rest lies in East Orange—itself with a black majority—and two tiny suburbs, one industrial and one high income. Back in 1972 Rodino had black opposition, but his strong civil rights record and liberal views on all issues, together with his seniority, helped him win 57% against two black candidates in the Democratic primary. He has not had a serious challenge since. His role in the impeachment hearings seems to have quieted all opposition.

Census Data Pop. 478,217. Central city, 80%; suburban, 20%. Median family income, $8,300; families above $15,000: 15%; families below $3,000: 13%. Median years education, 10.5.

The Voters

Median voting age 41.
Employment profile White collar, 39%. Blue collar, 46%. Service, 15%. Farm, –%.
Ethnic groups Black, 52%. Spanish, 6%. Total foreign stock, 23%. Italy, 7%; Poland, 2%; Ireland, USSR, Germany, UK, 1% each.

Presidential vote

1976	Carter (D)	82,612	(73%)
	Ford (R)	31,267	(27%)
1972	Nixon (R)	46,034	(37%)
	McGovern (D)	78,416	(63%)

Rep. Peter W. Rodino, Jr. (D) Elected 1948; b. June 7, 1909, Newark; home, Newark; Rutgers U., LL.B. 1937; Catholic.

Career Army, WWII; Practicing atty.

Offices 2462 RHOB, 202-225-3436. Also Suite 1435A, Fed. Bldg., 970 Broad St., Newark 07102, 201-645-3213.

Committees *Judiciary* (Chairman). Subcommittees: Monopolies and Commercial Law (Chairman).

Group Ratings

	ADA	COPE	PC	RPN	NFU	LCV	CFA	NAB	NSI	ACA	NTU
1978	35	83	40	0	50	–	27	0	10	0	–
1977	85	91	83	38	75	85	85	–	–	0	23
1976	85	83	89	21	83	82	91	8	0	4	35

Key Votes

1) Increase Def Spnd	AGN	6) Alaska Lands Protect	DNV	11) Delay Auto Pol Cntrl	AGN
2) B-1 Bomber	AGN	7) Water Projects Veto	FOR	12) Sugar Price Escalator	DNV
3) Cargo Preference	FOR	8) Consum Protect Agcy	FOR	13) Pub Fin Cong Cmpgns	DNV
4) Dereg Nat Gas	AGN	9) Common Situs Picket	FOR	14) ERA Ratif Recissn	AGN
5) Kemp-Roth	AGN	10) Labor Law Revision	FOR	15) Prohibt Govt Abrtns	FOR

Election Results

1978 general	Peter W. Rodino, Jr. (D)	55,074	(87%)	($46,110)
	John L. Pelt (R)	8,066	(13%)	
1978 primary	Peter W. Rodino, Jr. (D), unopposed			
1976 general	Peter W. Rodino, Jr. (D)	88,245	(84%)	($26,840)
	Tony Gerandison (R)	17,129	(16%)	($53)

ELEVENTH DISTRICT

The 11th congressional district of New Jersey consists of most of suburban Essex County. This string of suburban towns around Newark is theoretically within commuting distance of New York, but the orientation here is really to northern New Jersey: people here tend to work in downtown Newark or, more frequently lately, in one of the suburban office complexes or factories. The ethnic origins of the different suburbs tend to follow the lines of the radial avenues coming out of the once ethnic neighborhoods of Newark. There is a definite Italian-American flavor to the towns of Belleville, Bloomfield, and Nutley, all adjoining Newark's heavily Italian North Ward. There is a substantial Jewish population in South Orange and Maplewood, adjacent to what was once the Jewish part of Newark. An anomaly is Montclair, situated on a ridge overlooking the Manhattan skyline; part of it is upper income WASP, part middle income black. Farther out are comfortable upper income places like Caldwell, Fairfield, and Essex Fells.

In the sixties, the 11th district included the Central Ward of Newark and the suburb of East Orange, both by the end of the decade with black majorities. But redistricting removed these areas and made the district entirely suburban and, in national elections, much less Democratic; the 11th went for Ford, not Carter, in 1976. But that has posed no political problems for Congressman Joseph Minish. Back in 1962 Minish came out of the labor movement to replace Hugh Addonizio, who became Mayor of Newark because, as he told a friend at the time, you could make a million dollars with the job. However much he made, Addonizio ended up in jail. Minish has seldom been seriously challenged and has had no trouble winning every two years. He is now the sixth ranking Democrat on the Banking Committee and a subcommittee chairman, although not a particularly well known one. His major accomplishment, according to the Nader Congress Project several years ago, was a law setting up credit unions for servicemen living on bases overseas.

Census Data Pop. 475,297. Central city, 0%; suburban, 100%. Median family income, $12,508; families above $15,000: 36%; families below $3,000: 5%. Median years education, 12.2.

The Voters

Median voting age 47.
Employment profile White collar, 60%. Blue collar, 30%. Service, 10%. Farm, –%.
Ethnic groups Black, 7%. Total foreign stock, 38%. Italy, 11%; Poland, USSR, 4% each; Germany, UK, 3% each; Ireland, Austria, 2% each.

Presidential vote

1976	Carter (D)	98,038	(49%)
	Ford (R)	104,088	(51%)
1972	Nixon (R)	128,378	(60%)
	McGovern (D)	84,859	(40%)

Rep. Joseph G. Minish (D) Elected 1962; b. Sept. 1, 1916, Throop, Pa.; home, West Orange; Catholic.

Career Army, WWII; Political Action Dir., AFL-CIO Dist. 4, 1953–54; Exec. Secy., Essex W. Hudwon Labor Cncl., 1954–61, Treas., 1961–62.

Offices 2162 RHOB, 202-225-5035. Also 308 Main St., Orange 07050, 201-645-6363.

Committees *Banking, Finance and Urban Affairs* (6th). Subcommittees: Financial Institutions Supervision, Regulation and Insurance; General Oversight and Renegotiation (Chairman); International Development Institutions and Finance.

House Administration (10th). Subcommittees: Accounts; Personnel and Police.

Group Ratings

	ADA	COPE	PC	RPN	NFU	LCV	CFA	NAB	NSI	ACA	NTU
1978	35	85	75	17	70	–	77	17	44	21	–
1977	55	86	80	45	55	77	80	–	–	16	20
1976	65	87	89	33	92	70	100	17	67	14	12

Key Votes

1) Increase Def Spnd	FOR	6) Alaska Lands Protect	FOR	11) Delay Auto Pol Cntrl	AGN
2) B-1 Bomber	AGN	7) Water Projects Veto	FOR	12) Sugar Price Escalator	AGN
3) Cargo Preference	AGN	8) Consum Protect Agcy	FOR	13) Pub Fin Cong Cmpgns	FOR
4) Dereg Nat Gas	AGN	9) Common Situs Picket	FOR	14) ERA Ratif Recissn	AGN
5) Kemp-Roth	AGN	10) Labor Law Revision	FOR	15) Prohibt Govt Abrtns	FOR

Election Results

1978 general	Joseph G. Minish (D)	88,294	(71%)	($71,900)
	Julius George Feld (R)	35,642	(29%)	
1978 primary	Joseph G. Minish (D)	19,281	(92%)	
	One other (D)	1,710	(8%)	
1976 general	Joseph G. Minish (D)	129,026	(68%)	($62,853)
	Charles A. Poekel, Jr. (R)	59,397	(32%)	($7,870)

TWELFTH DISTRICT

The 12th congressional district of New Jersey consists of all of Union County except for one small city and two townships. For the most part the 12th is classic, if a little timeworn, suburban country. There are a few stereotyped WASP havens like Summit, but more typical of the district are places like Cranford, Westfield, and Union—towns inhabited by the sons and daughters of Italian, Polish, and German immigrants, whose claim on prosperity is now more than a generation old but still, psychologically, a little precarious. Even the district's two most industrial cities, Elizabeth and Plainfield, though they have had crime, riots, and poverty, are not in as bad shape as Newark; Elizabeth indeed has been rejuvenated by a rapidly increasing Hispanic population. The district is bisected by perhaps the most garish strip highway in the East, U.S. 22, which gets less use now than in the sixties. The new Interstate that parallels it gets most of the truck traffic, and the teenagers who used to drag race and gather at the drive-in restaurants have grown up and moved to suburbs.

In Union County political preferences tend to run down the middle of the road. Elizabeth and Plainfield are somewhat Democraric, Summit and Westfield Republican, and usually they cancel each other out. In the close national elections of 1960, 1968, and 1976, this New Jersey district came within a couple of percentage points of duplicating the national results for major party candidates—although it did go for the losers in two out of three. It is also a fairly close predicter of statewide results. In the middle fifties the 12th district produced two of New Jersey's United States senators—Republican Clifford Case who served here from 1945 to 1953 and Democrat Harrison Williams who was elected in 1953 and 1954 and defeated in 1956. The winner of that election was Florence Dwyer, a liberal Republican who won subsequent elections with record margins.

The current Congressman, Republican Matthew Rinaldo, was elected when Dwyer retired in 1972. With experience in local government and the New Jersey Senate, he was well known; his voting record tends to protect him against Democratic challenges. Indeed, on many issues he votes with Democrats; he was one of two Republicans on the Commerce Committee to oppose deregulation of natural gas. The percentages he wins from rating groups are not much different from those for Joseph Minish, the Democrat who represents the next-door 11th district, except that Rinaldo scores higher with the ACA. He has been reelected regularly by impressive margins.

Census Data Pop. 477,887. Central city, 0%; suburban, 100%. Median family income, $12,787; families above $15,000: 37%; families below $3,000: 5%. Median years education, 12.3.

The Voters

Median voting age 46.
Employment profile White collar, 56%. Blue collar, 34%. Service, 10%. Farm, -%.
Ethnic groups Black, 12%. Total foreign stock, 35%. Italy, 7%; Poland, Germany, 4% each; USSR, 3%; UK, Ireland, Austria, 2% each; Canada, 1%.

Presidential vote

1976	Carter (D)	91,007	(46%)
	Ford (R)	106,127	(54%)
1972	Nixon (R)	130,187	(63%)
	McGovern (D)	77,367	(37%)

Rep. Matthew J. Rinaldo (R) Elected 1972; b. Sept. 1, 1931, Elizabeth; home, Union; Rutgers U., B.S. 1953, Seton Hall U., M.B.A. 1959, NYU School of Public Admin., 1969.

Career Pres., Union Twnshp. Zoning Bd. of Adjustment, 1962–63; Union Co. Bd. of Freeholders, 1963–64; N.J. Senate, 1967–72.

Offices 2338 RHOB, 202-225-5361. Also 1961 Morris Ave., Union 07083, 201-687-4235.

Committees *Interstate and Foreign Commerce* (9th). Subcommittees: Oversight and Investigations; Consumer Protection and Finance.

Group Ratings

	ADA	COPE	PC	RPN	NFU	LCV	CFA	NAB	NSI	ACA	NTU
1978	50	80	53	36	70	–	73	18	70	33	–
1977	55	71	68	58	67	72	70	–	–	44	28
1976	60	87	70	60	67	86	91	17	80	19	12

Key Votes

1) Increase Def Spnd	FOR	6) Alaska Lands Protect	FOR	11) Delay Auto Pol Cntrl	AGN
2) B-1 Bomber	FOR	7) Water Projects Veto	AGN	12) Sugar Price Escalator	AGN
3) Cargo Preference	AGN	8) Consum Protect Agcy	FOR	13) Pub Fin Cong Cmpgns	FOR
4) Dereg Nat Gas	AGN	9) Common Situs Picket	FOR	14) ERA Ratif Recissn	AGN
5) Kemp-Roth	FOR	10) Labor Law Revision	FOR	15) Prohibt Govt Abrtns	FOR

Election Results

1978 general	Matthew J. Rinaldo (R)	94,850	(73%)	($192,778)
	Richard McCormack (D)	34,423	(27%)	($13,556)
1978 primary	Matthew J. Rinaldo (R), unopposed			
1976 general	Matthew J. Rinaldo (R)	136,973	(74%)	($156,693)
	Richard A. Buggelli (D)	49,189	(26%)	($17,669)

THIRTEENTH DISTRICT

The 13th congressional district of New Jersey is a new seat, first created in 1972, and in that brief time it has elected three different members of Congress from both major political parties. Geographically, the 13th is the northwestern wedge of New Jersey, from Trenton to the Ramapo Mountains on the New York border. Twenty or thirty years ago this area was almost entirely agricultural, with a few tiny industrial villages, and many more dairy cows than people. But soon enough nearby metropolitan areas began to invade the pastureland. In the southern part of the district people have been pouring out of Trenton into suburban Mercer County, but the really substantial growth has been farther north, in Morris County.

This is not posh horse farm country, like the part of Morris County in the 5th district; the new settlement has been of people in the middle income brackets moving from New York or, more likely, the crowded older suburbs of north Jersey into the townships around the small towns of Boonton and Dover and Netcong. They have brought with them generally conservative voting habits, even if they are often ancestral Democrats; part of the reason they have moved, in many cases, is a dislike of what they believe liberal policies have done to the communities in which they were raised.

The 13th district was originally known as the Maraziti district, for the Republican state senator who designed it for himself and was elected to Congress in 1972. But Joseph Maraziti had the misfortune to serve on the House Judiciary Committee; not only was he a fervent defender of Richard Nixon, he was a particularly ineffective one. He was defeated in 1974 by Helen Stevenson Meyner, a cousin of the Adlai Stevensons and wife of former Governor Robert Meyner. Impeachment was helpful in her first victory; her successful fight to get funds restored for expansion of the Picatinny Arsenal in Morris County helped her win reelection in 1976. But by 1978 the Republican tide in this basically Republican district was too strong.

The current Congressman, Jim Courter, had to win a close primary against Meyner's 1976 opponent and then had a close general election. His prospects for reelection must be considered good—although this district has had an unanticipated history of political instability.

Census Data Pop. 478,164. Central city, 0%; suburban, 69%. Median family income, $11,731; families above $15,000: 30%; families below $3,000: 5%. Median years education, 12.3.

The Voters

Median voting age 42.
Employment profile White collar, 51%. Blue collar, 37%. Service, 10%. Farm, 2%.
Ethnic groups Black, 2%. Total foreign stock, 24%. Italy, Germany, 4% each; UK, 3%; Poland, 2%; Hungary, Ireland, USSR, Austria, 1% each.

Presidential vote

1976	Carter (D)	87,608	(41%)
	Ford (R)	127,723	(59%)
1972	Nixon (R)	141,609	(70%)
	McGovern (D)	61,509	(30%)

Rep. James A. Courter (R) Elected 1978; b. Oct. 14, 1941, Montclair; home, Hackettstown; Colgate U., B.A. 1963, Duke U., J.D. 1966; Methodist.

Career Peace Corps, Venezuela, 1967–69; Practicing atty., 1969–70; Atty., Union Co. Legal Services, 1970–71; 1st Asst. Warren Co. Prosecutor, 1973–77.

Offices 325 CHOB, 202-225-5801.

Committees *Armed Services* (15th). Subcommittees: Research and Development; Military Compensation.

Post Office and Civil Service (6th). Subcommittees: Postal Operations and Services; Civil Service; Census and Population.

Group Ratings: Newly Elected

Key Votes: Newly Elected

Election Results

1978 general	Jim Courter (R)	77,301	(52%)	($330,688)
	Helen S. Meyner (D)	71,808	(48%)	($194,641)
1978 primary	Jim Courter (R)	10,541	(38%)	
	Bill Schluter (R)	10,407	(38%)	($90,224)
	Frank Bell (R)	3,190	(12%)	($4,982)
	Two others (R)	3,379	(12%)	
1976 general	Helen S. Meyner (D)	105,291	(51%)	($114,862)
	Bill Schluter (R)	100,050	(49%)	($99,787)

FOURTEENTH DISTRICT

"I am the law," Frank Hague used to say, and in Hudson County, New Jersey, he was. Back in the thirties, when Hague was at the peak of his powers as boss of the Hudson County Democratic machine, he chose governors and U.S. senators, prosecutors and judges, and even had an influence in the White House of Franklin D. Roosevelt. In Jersey City and other Hudson County towns—then and now the most densely populated part of the United States outside Manhattan—Hague controlled almost every facet of life. He determined who would stay in business and who could not; he controlled tax assessments and the issuance of parking tickets; he had the support of the working man and kept the CIO out of town for years (resulting in a major Supreme Court case). Hague's power was anchored finally in votes. Jersey City and Hudson County had huge payrolls, and every jobholder was expected to produce a certain number of votes on election day. Democratic candidates could expect a 100,000 vote margin in Hudson County, and since they often lost the rest of the state by less than that, they were indebted indeed. Hague's power continued into the forties until some former allies turned on him and took over the machine.

To the naked eye Hudson County has changed little since Frank Hague's golden days. It still consists of the same series of towns on the Palisades ridge between New York harbor and the Jersey Meadows: Jersey City, Bayonne, Weehawken, Union City, and (below the ridge just on the waterfront) Hoboken. To exploit the view of the Manhattan skyline some luxury high rise apartments have gone up in the northern end of the county, but most of Hudson County's residents still live in the same cramped apartments and stone rowhouses that were aging even before the Great Depression.

For years now Hudson County's population has been dropping as young people move out and few people choose to move in. Nearby Newark has shifted from white to black, but most of Hudson County's population has remained Italian, Irish, and Polish, as it has been since the turn of the century. In the seventies there have been some new additions. Union City now has a Spanish-speaking, largely Cuban, majority, and there are Hispanic neighborhoods in Jersey City as well. In Hoboken affluent young people are restoring the old rowhouses, located conveniently near the PATH subway tubes to Manhattan. Still to a considerable extent, Hudson County remains one of the most insular places in the United States. Some people grow up here without ever crossing the river to New York or even meeting anyone from outside Hudson County. The tight-knit neighborhoods, clustered around the parish churches and (until the last decade or so) their Democratic precinct captains are as isolated from the main currents of American life as a tiny community in an Appalachian hollow.

In the seventies there was a kind of political revolution in Hudson County. The group which threw out Hague, led by John V. Kenny, was itself thrown out and most of its leaders sent to jail. The new county leader is Paul Jordan, a young public health physician who became Mayor of Jersey City. But political life continues not too differently from the past. Jordan is considered honest, but there are still many patronage jobs, and an army of political hangers on who expect to be taken care of. Hudson County voters still invariably prefer whatever Democrat the county organization has endorsed on election day. General elections are different, however; the county is not as one-sidedly Democratic as in the past, and like many East Coast blue collar areas will lean to the Republicans on social issues.

The 14th congressional district includes almost all of Hudson County, and it has been some time since it has elected a Republican congressman. For 18 years Democrat Dominick Daniels held the seat; he retired in 1976. The organization choice to replace him was Assembly Speaker Joseph LeFante. But voters here were upset with Governor Brendan Byrne's tax program, and LeFante won the general election with only 52% of the vote. His first term in Congress turned out to be his last, and he was given a state job in consolation. The new Congressman, elected without difficulty in 1978, is former Hudson County Democratic Chairman Frank Guarini. He can be counted as a pretty reliable Democratic vote.

Census Data Pop. 477,939. Central city, 55%; suburban, 45%. Median family income, $9,607; families above $15,000: 19%; families below $3,000: 9%. Median years education, 10.3.

The Voters

Median voting age 45.
Employment profile White collar, 45%. Blue collar, 43%. Service, 12%. Farm, –%.
Ethnic groups Black, 13%. Spanish, 6%. Total foreign stock, 39%. Italy, 10%; Poland, 5%; Ireland, UK, 3% each; Germany, USSR, 2% each; Austria, 1%.

Presidential vote

1976	Carter (D)	91,375	(57%)
	Ford (R)	70,173	(43%)
1972	Nixon (R)	104,907	(60%)
	McGovern (D)	71,098	(40%)

Rep. Frank J. Guarini (D) Elected 1978; b. Aug. 20, 1924, Jersey City; home, Jersey City; Dartmouth Col., Columbia U., N.Y.U., J.D., LL.M., Acad. of Internatl. Law., The Hague, Holland.

Career Navy, WWII; Practicing atty.; N.J. Senate, 1965–72.

Offices 1020 LHOB, 202-225-2765. Also 910 Bergen Ave., Jersey City 07306, 201-659-7700.

Committees *Ways and Means* (23d). Subcommittees: Select Revenue Measures; Trade.

Group Ratings: Newly Elected

Key Votes: Newly Elected

Election Results

1978 general	Frank J. Guarini (D)	67,008	(65%)	($83,325)
	Henry J. Hill (R)	21,355	(21%)	($7,566)
	Thomas E. McDonough (I)	15,015	(15%)	($17,271)
1978 primary	Frank J. Guarini (D)	34,127	(82%)	
	Two others (D)	7,328	(18%)	
1976 general	Joseph A. LeFante (D)	73,174	(52%)	($28,030)
	Anthony L. Compenni (R)	66,319	(48%)	($11,515)

FIFTEENTH DISTRICT

The 15th congressional district takes in most of Middlesex County, the state's fastest-growing Democratic area. The 15th has the largest concentration of Hungarian-Americans of any congressional district in the nation, in and around New Brunswick; it also has sizeable neighborhoods of Poles in Woodbridge and Italians in Perth Amboy. From the old ethnic neighborhoods in these small central cities the children of hyphenated Americans have moved out into places like Edison Township, Piscataway Township, and Sayreville, where they live in what passes for pastoral splendor if you grew up in New Brunswick or Perth Amboy.

These suburban voters have not forgotten their Democratic heritage, but on occasion they are willing to ignore it. John Kennedy got a comfortable 58% in this heavily Catholic county in 1960, but Hubert Humphrey carried it with less than a majority in 1968 and Jimmy Carter carried it with only 52%—one of the reasons he lost New Jersey to Gerald Ford.

Middlesex County and the 15th district have long had a well known Democratic machine, run for many years by David Willentz, who first gained fame in the thirties as the prosecutor of accused Lindbergh kidnapper Bruno Hauptmann and whose Perth Amboy law office in later years somehow always seemed to attract some of the nation's largest businesses as clients. Middlesex acquired its own congressional district in 1962, and the Willentz machine picked Edward Patten as its candidate. Patten was then Secretary of State, an appointive position in New Jersey, usually reserved for a political operator; he was elected to the House in 1962 and has remained there ever since.

Patten's greatest political asset, aside from the organization endorsement, has been his sense of humor; he is the kind of person for whom politics is a joy and campaigning a pleasure. He has had some real challenges over the years: in the 1970 primary from a much publicized peace candidate, in the 1972 general from a Nixon-supporting Republican. But by far his toughest year was 1978. In the June primary a single opponent held him to 59% of the vote. Then in July the House Ethics

Committee charged him with violations relating to Tongsun Park; they said he identified a contribution to a county political organization from Park as having come from him, Patten. He was cleared on that charge October 4, but his Republican opponent kept attacking him for his Korean connection and charging that at his age, 73, he could no longer be effective.

Patten won reelection, but with only 51% of the vote. At the same time, Democratic Senate candidate Bill Bradley was winning 61% in Middlesex County. That leaves Patten in very weak condition if he decides to seek another term: at 75 he will undoubtedly have to face tough competition, both in the primary and the general election. Under those circumstances, he must be considered likely to retire; and he will probably, but not certainly, be replaced by another Democrat.

Census Data Pop. 477,949. Central city, 0%; suburban, 9%. Median family income, $11,793; families above $15,000: 29%; families below $3,000: 4%. Median years education, 12.1.

The Voters

Median voting age 41.
Employment profile White collar, 49%. Blue collar, 41%. Service, 10%. Farm, –%.
Ethnic groups Black, 6%. Spanish, 2%. Total foreign stock, 33%. Italy, Poland, 5% each; Hungary, 4%; Germany, 3%; USSR, UK, Czechoslovakia, Austria, 2% each; Ireland, 1%.

Presidential vote

1976	Carter (D)	101,616	(54%)
	Ford (R)	87,830	(46%)
1972	Nixon (R)	118,439	(61%)
	McGovern (D)	74,752	(39%)

Rep. Edward J. Patten (D) Elected 1962; b. Aug. 22, 1905, Perth Amboy; home, Perth Amboy; Newark St. Col., Rutgers U., LL.B. 1926, B.S.Ed. 1928; Catholic.

Career Practicing atty., 1927–62; Public school teacher, 1927–34; Mayor of Perth Amboy, 1934–40; Middlesex Co. Clerk, 1940–54; Secy. of State of N.J., 1954–62.

Offices 2332 RHOB, 202-225-6301. Also Natl. Bank Bldg., Perth Amboy 08861, 201-826-4610.

Committees *Appropriations* (10th). Subcommittees: Labor-HEW; Treasury, Postal Service, and General Government.

Group Ratings

	ADA	COPE	PC	RPN	NFU	LCV	CFA	NAB	NSI	ACA	NTU
1978	50	90	63	25	78	–	59	0	44	12	–
1977	55	100	55	23	67	50	75	–	–	11	19
1976	60	83	74	39	83	65	73	17	70	11	8

Key Votes

1) Increase Def Spnd	FOR	6) Alaska Lands Protect	AGN	11) Delay Auto Pol Cntrl	AGN
2) B-1 Bomber	AGN	7) Water Projects Veto	FOR	12) Sugar Price Escalator	AGN
3) Cargo Preference	FOR	8) Consum Protect Agcy	FOR	13) Pub Fin Cong Cmpgns	FOR
4) Dereg Nat Gas	AGN	9) Common Situs Picket	FOR	14) ERA Ratif Recissn	AGN
5) Kemp-Roth	AGN	10) Labor Law Revision	FOR	15) Prohibt Govt Abrtns	FOR

Election Results

1978 general	Edward J. Patten (D)	55,944	(51%)	($50,407)
	Charles W. Wiley (R)	53,108	(49%)	($46,314)
1978 primary	Edward J. Patten (D)	20,738	(59%)	
	George A. Spadoro (D)	14,506	(41%)	
1976 general	Edward J. Patten (D)	106,170	(66%)	($24,950)
	Charles W. Wiley (R)	54,487	(34%)	($9,272)

NEW MEXICO

New Mexico is our most unusual state. The culture of every other state is based primarily on what the initial white settlers brought to the land; the original inhabitants (except in Hawaii) have either disappeared or no longer form a substantial part of the population. Not so in New Mexico. The American culture here is superimposed on a society whose written history dates back to 1609, when the first Spaniards established a settlement in Santa Fe, and to centuries long past when the Indians of the various pueblos set up agricultural societies on the sandy, rocky lands of northern New Mexico. A very substantial minority of New Mexicans are descendants of these Indians or the Spanish, or both. Nearly one-third of the people here in the ordinary course of things speak Spanish, and few of them are recent migrants from Mexico. This is the northernmost reach of the Indian civilizations of the Cordillera, which extend south through Mexico, Central America, and down South America as far as Chile.

The Hispanic/Indian culture dominates most of northern and western New Mexico, except for enclaves—usually related to mining or, in the case of Los Alamos, atomic energy—where Anglos have settled. In vivid contrast to the Hispanic part of New Mexico is the area called Little Texas. With small cities, plenty of oil wells, vast cattle ranches, and desolate military bases, this region resembles, economically and culturally, the adjacent high plains of west Texas. Oil is important here, but not as vital as the military presence: a couple of Air Force bases and the Army's White Sands Missile Range, near Alamogordo, where the first atomic bomb was detonated.

In the middle of the state is Albuquerque which, with the coming of the air conditioner, grew from a small desert town into a booming Sun Belt city. Albuquerque is also heavily dependent on the military and on the atomic energy establishment. There are two bases within the city limits and its largest employer is the Bell System's Sandia Laboratories, an atomic energy contractor. Metropolitan Albuquerque now has a little more than one-third of the state's population—about the same percentage as the Hispanic areas and little Texas.

For many years New Mexico politics was a somnolent business. Local bosses—first Republican, then Democratic—controlled the large Hispanic vote. Elections in many counties featured irregularities that would have made a Chicago ward committeeman blush. New Mexico also had for years a balanced ticket: one Spanish and one Anglo senator, with the offices of governor and lieutenant governor split between the groups.

In the last few elections, a new pattern has emerged. The Republicans have pursued a conservative strategy in statewide contests, in effect conceding the Hispanic areas and hoping for compensating margins in Little Texas and Albuquerque. For the most part it has worked, though usually by narrow margins. Gerald Ford carried New Mexico in 1976—the first time in its history the state has voted for a losing candidate for president. New Mexico now has two Republican senators, after electing only Democrats from 1932 to 1970. And while Democrats hold onto the governorship, their margins in the last two elections have totalled 7,530 votes.

Moreover, the elections have produced two very different governors. Jerry Apodaca, elected in 1974, is a Hispanic who was a football star for the University of New Mexico; he was elected with 62% in the Hispanic areas—the best showing any Democrat has made for years. Bruce King, elected in 1970 and 1978, is a rancher from Santa Fe County in the northern part of the state. He too does well in Hispanic areas, but he also runs stronger than Apodaca in Little Texas. The reason for the alternation is that New Mexico does not allow its governors consecutive terms; the two men are not political allies.

New Mexico's senior Senator, Pete Domenici, had been expected to win reelection easily in 1978. A former Albuquerque Mayor, he had won the seat in 1972 with strong home town support. His record seemed well suited to New Mexico. With a seat on the Energy Committee he supported atomic energy—more important in New Mexico than any other state—and generally favored market allocations for oil. A member of the Budget Committee, he tends to want to hold down spending on domestic programs. In the 95th Congress Domenici led a fight to impose tolls on barge traffic, which passes through rivers and canals which cost the federal government millions. This battle, chronicled in depth by the Washington *Post*, is a good example of a principled conservative taking on a cozy special interest group and winning.

Domenici seemed to keep in touch with the state well, and he was fortunate in his opponent, Attorney General Toney Anaya. This is not so much because Anaya was a poor candidate; he had a record of prosecuting well established Democratic politicians and an Hispanic background. But he was never able to get money-givers to take his campaign seriously. New Mexico politicoes stayed out because they disliked him; national Democrats assumed Domenici was a shoo-in. The results suggest that he was not. The incumbent got only 53% in metropolitan Albuquerque—a poor showing that was part of a general Democratic advance in this Sun Belt city. Anaya carried the Hispanic areas, and Domenici was saved only by his large margin in Little Texas. It was a classic example of a senator getting reelected because no one knew how vulnerable he was.

New Mexico's other senator is as unusual as the state, former astronaut Harrison Schmitt. He is by profession a geologist, with degrees from Caltech and Harvard; he got to be an astronaut not because he was an experienced pilot but because he was an expert on rocks. Schmitt grew up in New Mexico, in an out-of-the-way mining town. But he returned only when contemplating his Senate bid; he loaned $90,000 to his own campaign, but he seemed a man of the people when he drove around in his own red pickup truck (which he brought to Washington).

Schmitt's 57% victory was less a measure of his own popularity than of the unpopularity of his opponent, Democratic incumbent Joseph Montoya. People wondered how Montoya accumulated a net worth of $4 million, though he began his public career without means and was seldom off the public payroll. They learned that he was half owner of a building in Santa Fe leased to the Post Office, and that IRS officials had blocked an audit of his tax returns when he chaired an IRS subcommittee. Schmitt's slogan put it succinctly: "Honesty . . . for a change."

More than Domenici, Schmitt is a conservative Republican, part of that group of Rocky Mountain Republicans who have been aggressively and often effectively attacking Democratic programs and precepts. He is undeniably brainy and, if his personality is not exactly magnetic, he seems to have good political instincts. But the circumstances of his own election and the results of the 1978 election—particularly the Democratic trend in Albuquerque—make any conclusion that his seat is safe premature. New Mexico politics is now too volatile to say that either of its senators has a safe seat.

Which is not true in House elections; both the state's congressmen seem firmly entrenched. This is a particularly impressive achievement in the case of 1st district Congressman Manuel Lujan. The 1st district covers the northeastern and north central parts of the state, including Albuquerque and much of the Hispanic area. Santa Fe, the small state capital and a city of distinctive charm, is here, as is Taos, which has attracted artists and hangers on since before D. H. Lawrence came here in the twenties. This is generally the more Democratic part of the state, yet Lujan has been winning election here, and usually by large margins, since 1968. His secret is hard work and a careful cultivation of his constituency. As a Republican with a generally conservative voting record, he appeals to Anglos in Albuquerque; as an Hispanic whose family has been active in politics for decades, he does well in Hispanic areas. He is a high ranking minority member of the Interior Committee—always important in a state like New Mexico—and is also on the Science Committee, which is particularly important in the district which contains Los Alamos and the Sandia Laboratories.

New Mexico's 2d congressional district includes most of Little Texas, the barren Rio Grande Valley, the Navajo country around Gallup, and the Anglo mining town of Farmington in the state's northwest corner. Ancestrally this is a Democratic district, or perhaps a Dixiecrat one—much like west Texas in politics. The current Congressman, Democrat Harold Runnels, who was first elected in 1970, has been described as "a good old boy from Little Texas." He has also been named to New Times magazine's list of the ten dumbest congressmen; in fact, he is one of the few left in Congress. A member of the House Armed Services Committee, he announced in 1973 that he had been purchasing documents from someone in the Pentagon because he could not obtain them through ordinary channels—a bizarre little scandal that has never been resolved. He has not had significant opposition for some time in the district. The last time a Republican captured the 2d was when the incumbent allowed the Pentagon to phase out a military base; that is one thing that even Runnels knows enough to struggle to prevent. Barring that, he is sure of winning reelection.

Census Data Pop. 1,016,000; 0.50% of U.S. total, 37th largest; Central city, 24%; suburban, 7%. Median family income, $7,845; 38th highest; families above $15,000: 15%; families below $3,000: 15%. Median years education, 12.2.

1977 Share of Federal Tax Burden $1,451,000,000; 0.42% of U.S. total, 39th largest.

1977 Share of Federal Outlays $3,068,045,000; 0.76% of U.S. total, 35th largest. Per capita federal spending, $2,675.

DOD	$640,206,000	33d (0.70%)	HEW	$678,718,000	39th (0.46%)
ERDA	$596,356,000	3d (10.09%)	HUD	$32,591,000	35th (0.77%)
NASA	$14,533,000	19th (0.37%)	VA	$123,327,000	37th (0.64%)
DOT	$110,072,000	35th (0.77%)	EPA	$21,194,000	42d (0.26%)
DOC	$71,631,000	29th (0.86%)	RevS	$54,540,000	36th (0.64%)
DOI	$257,860,000	6th (5.54%)	Debt	$71,405,000	37th (0.24%)
USDA	$153,858,000	40th (0.77%)	Other	$241,754,000	

Economic Base Agriculture, notably cattle, dairy products, hay and cotton lint; finance, insurance and real estate; oil and gas extraction, especially oil and gas field services; metal mining, especially uranium-radium-vanadium ores; food and kindred products; tourism.

Political Line-up Governor, Bruce King (D). Senators, Peter V. Domenici (R) and Harrison Schmidt (R). Representatives, 2 (1 D and 1 R). State Senate (33 D and 9 R); State House (41 D and 29 R).

The Voters

Median voting age 40
Employment profile White collar, 51%. Blue collar, 30%. Service, 15%. Farm, 4%.
Ethnic groups Black 2%. Indian, 7%. Spanish, 40%. Total foreign stock, 9%.

Sen. Pete V. Domenici (R) Elected 1972, seat up 1978; b. May 7, 1932, Albuquerque; home, Albuquerque; U. of Albuquerque, 1950–52, U. of N.M., B.S. 1954, Denver U., LL.B. 1958; Catholic.

Career Practicing atty., 1958–72; Mbr., Albuquerque City Commission, 1966–68, Mayor Ex-Officio, 1967–68; Repub. nominee for Gov., 1970.

Offices 405 RSOB, 202-224-6621. Also New Postal Bldg., Santa Fe 87501, 505-988-6511, and New Fed. Bldg. & U.S. Courthouse, Rm. 10013, Albuquerque 87103, 505-766-3481.

Committees *Budget* (2d).

Energy and Natural Resources (4th). Subcommittees: Energy Conservation and Supply; Energy Regulation; Energy Research and Development.

Environment and Public Works (3d). Subcommittees: Water Resources; Regional and Community Development; Nuclear Regulation.

Special Committee on Aging (Ranking Member).

Group Ratings

	ADA	COPE	PC	RPN	NFU	LCV	CFA	NAB	NSI	ACA	NTU
1978	15	47	33	20	80	16	25	91	90	65	–
1977	5	15	15	73	50	–	4	–	–	70	30
1976	5	22	13	80	37	11	7	70	89	87	50

Key Votes

1) Warnke Nom	AGN	6) Egypt-Saudi Arms	AGN	11) Hosptl Cost Contnmnt	DNV
2) Neutron Bomb	FOR	7) Draft Restr Pardon	AGN	12) Clinch River Reactor	FOR
3) Waterwy User Fee	FOR	8) Wheat Price Support	FOR	13) Pub Fin Cong Cmpgns	AGN
4) Dereg Nat Gas	FOR	9) Panama Canal Treaty	AGN	14) ERA Ratif Recissn	AGN
5) Kemp-Roth	FOR	10) Labor Law Rev Clot	AGN	15) Med Necssy Abrtns	AGN

Election Results

1978 general	Pete Domenici (R)	183,442	(53%)	($914,634)
	Toney Anaya (D)	160,045	(47%)	($175,633)
1978 primary	Pete Domenici (R), unopposed			
1972 general	Pete Domenici (R)	204,253	(54%)	($517,310)
	Jack Daniels (D)	173,815	(46%)	($496,980)

Sen. Harrison H. Schmitt (R) Elected 1976, seat up 1982; b. July 3, 1935, Santa Rita; home, Albuquerque; Cal. Tech., B.S. 1957, Fulbright Fellow, U. of Oslo 1957–58, Harvard U., Ph.D. 1964.

Career Consulting geologist; NASA Scientist–Astronaut, 1965–73, Apollo 17 Lunar Module Pilot, 1972; Asst. Administrator for Energy Problems, NASA, 1974.

Offices 248 RSOB, 202-224-5521. Also 9017 New Fed. Bldg., S.W., Albuquerque 87012, 505-766-3636, and U.S. Courthouse, Santa Fe 87501, 505-988-6647.

Committees *Appropriations* (11th). Subcommittees: Agriculture and Related Agencies; District of Columbia; Energy and Water Development; HUD-Independent Agencies; Labor, HEW, and Related Agencies; Treasury, Postal Service; and General Government.

Commerce, Science, and Transportation (3d). Subcommittees: Communications; Science, Technology, and Space; Surface Transportation.

Select Committee on Ethics.

Select Committee on Small Business (5th).

Group Ratings

	ADA	COPE	PC	RPN	NFU	LCV	CFA	NAB	NSI	ACA	NTU
1978	20	24	23	67	70	18	25	92	100	75	–
1977	15	11	10	80	42	–	8	–	–	84	34

Key Votes

1) Warnke Nom	AGN	6) Egypt-Saudi Arms	FOR	11) Hosptl Cost Contnmnt	AGN
2) Neutron Bomb	FOR	7) Draft Restr Pardon	AGN	12) Clinch River Reactor	FOR
3) Waterwy User Fee	FOR	8) Wheat Price Support	FOR	13) Pub Fin Cong Cmpgns	AGN
4) Dereg Nat Gas	FOR	9) Panama Canal Treaty	AGN	14) ERA Ratif Recissn	FOR
5) Kemp-Roth	FOR	10) Labor Law Rev Clot	AGN	15) Med Necssy Abrtns	FOR

Election Results

1976 general	Harrison Schmitt (R)	234,681	(57%)	($441,309)
	Joseph Montoya (D)	176,382	(43%)	($451,111)
1976 primary	Harrison Schmitt (R)	34,074	(72%)	
	Eugene W. Peirce, Jr. (R)	10,965	(23%)	
	One other (R)	2,481	(5%)	
1970 general	Joseph Montoya (D)	151,486	(53%)	
	Anderson Carter (R)	135,004	(47%)	

Gov. Bruce King (D) Elected 1978, term expires Jan. 1983; b. April 6, 1924, Stanley; U. of N.M.

Career Army, WWII; Sante Fe Co. Comm., 1954–58, Chmn., 1957–58; N.M. House of Reps., 1959–69, Speaker, 1963–69; State Dem. Chmn., 1968–69; Pres., N.M. State Constitutional Convention, 1969; Gov. of N.M., 1971–75; Cattle rancher.

Offices Executive Legislative Bldg., Sante Fe 87503, 505-827-4011.

Election Results

1978 general	Bruce King (D)	174,631	(51%)
	Joseph R. Skeen (R)	170,848	(49%)
1978 primary	Bruce King (D)	92,432	(61%)
	Robert E. Ferguson (D)	58,334	(39%)
1974 general	Jerry Apodaca (D)	164,177	(51%)
	Joseph R. Skeen (R)	160,430	(49%)

Census Data Pop. 511,135. Central city, 48%; suburban, 14%. Median family income, $8,187; families above $15,000: 18%; families below $3,000: 15%. Median years education, 12.3.

The Voters

Median voting age 40.
Employment profile White collar, 57%. Blue collar, 26%. Service, 15%. Farm, 2%.
Ethnic groups Black, 1%. Indian, 3%. Spanish, 49%. Total foreign stock, 7%.

Presidential vote

1976	Carter (D)	113,197	(49%)
	Ford (R)	116,334	(51%)
1972	Nixon (R)	125,326	(59%)
	McGovern (D)	85,996	(41%)

Rep. Manuel Lujan, Jr. (R) Elected 1968; b. May 12, 1928, San Ildefonso; home, Albuquerque; St. Mary's Col., San Francisco, Cal., Col. of Santa Fe, B.S. 1950; Catholic.

Career Insurance agent; Vice Chm., N.M. Repub. Party.

Offices 1323 LHOB, 202-225-6316. Also Rm. 10001 Fed. Bldg., 500 Gold Ave., S.W., Albuquerque 87103, 505-766-2538.

Committees *Interior and Insular Affairs* (2d). Subcommittees: Energy and the Environment; Water and Power Resources.

Science and Technology (5th). Subcommittees: Energy Research and Production; Investigations and Oversight.

Group Ratings

	ADA	COPE	PC	RPN	NFU	LCV	CFA	NAB	NSI	ACA	NTU
1978	5	24	18	50	40	–	5	83	90	86	–
1977	15	18	28	60	60	11	25	–	–	81	43
1976	15	20	11	47	25	13	0	73	100	91	63

Key Votes

1) Increase Def Spnd	FOR	6) Alaska Lands Protect	DNV	11) Delay Auto Pol Cntrl	FOR
2) B-1 Bomber	FOR	7) Water Projects Veto	DNV	12) Sugar Price Escalator	FOR
3) Cargo Preference	AGN	8) Consum Protect Agcy	AGN	13) Pub Fin Cong Cmpgns	AGN
4) Dereg Nat Gas	FOR	9) Common Situs Picket	AGN	14) ERA Ratif Recissn	FOR
5) Kemp-Roth	FOR	10) Labor Law Revision	AGN	15) Prohibt Govt Abrtns	FOR

Election Results

1978 general	Manuel Lujan, Jr. (R)	118,075	(63%)	($121,421)
	Robert M. Hawk (D)	70,761	(37%)	($49,707)
1978 primary	Manuel Lujan, Jr. (R), unopposed			
1976 general	Manuel Lujan, Jr. (R)	162,587	(72%)	($77,533)
	Raymond Garcia (D)	61,800	(28%)	($8,825)

Census Data Pop. 504,865. Central city, 0%; suburban, 0%. Median family income, $7,551; families above $15,000: 12%; families below $3,000: 16%. Median years education, 12.0.

The Voters

Median voting age 40.
Employment profile White collar, 45%. Blue collar, 35%. Service, 14%. Farm, 6%.
Ethnic groups Black, 2%. Indian, 11%. Spanish, 31%. Total foreign stock, 10%.

Presidential vote

1976	Carter (D)	87,951	(48%)
	Ford (R)	95,085	(52%)
1972	Nixon (R)	110,280	(67%)
	McGovern (D)	55,088	(33%)

Rep. Harold Runnels (D) Elected 1970; b. Mar. 17, 1924, Dallas, Tex.; home, Lovington; Cameron St. Agric. Col., B.S. 1943; Baptist.

Career Air Force, WWII; Employee of FBI; Mgr., Magnolia Amusement Co.; Partner, Southland Supply Co., 1952; Founder, Runnels Mud Co. and RunCo Acidizing and Fracturing Co.; N.M. Senate, 1960–70.

Offices 1535 LHOB, 202-225-2365. Also Suite A, McCrory Bldg., Lovington 88260, 505-396-2252.

Committees *Armed Services* (13th). Subcommittees: Investigations; Research and Development.

Interior and Insular Affairs (7th). Subcommittees: Public Lands; Mines and Mining; Investigations and Oversight (Chairman).

Group Ratings

	ADA	COPE	PC	RPN	NFU	LCV	CFA	NAB	NSI	ACA	NTU
1978	5	6	15	83	25	–	14	100	80	93	–
1977	5	15	10	25	50	6	10	–	–	88	45
1976	5	24	10	38	33	14	0	75	90	88	67

Key Votes

1) Increase Def Spnd	FOR	6) Alaska Lands Protect	DNV	11) Delay Auto Pol Cntrl	DNV
2) B-1 Bomber	AGN	7) Water Projects Veto	FOR	12) Sugar Price Escalator	FOR
3) Cargo Preference	FOR	8) Consum Protect Agcy	AGN	13) Pub Fin Cong Cmpgns	AGN
4) Dereg Nat Gas	FOR	9) Common Situs Picket	AGN	14) ERA Ratif Recissn	FOR
5) Kemp-Roth	FOR	10) Labor Law Revision	AGN	15) Prohibt Govt Abrtns	FOR

Election Results

1978 general	Harold Runnels (D), unopposed			($69,953)
1978 primary	Harold Runnels (D), unopposed			
1976 general	Harold Runnels (D)	123,563	(70%)	($75,526)
	Donald W. Truby (R)	52,131	(30%)	($18,839)

NEW YORK

In the past, New York, both city and state, was justly proud of having the best and most innovative local and state government in the country. But today, despite evidence of that old pride in the "I Love New York" media campaign, New York City is the basket case of American municipalities, and New York state has serious problems. Since 1975 New York City has been forced to place its affairs in the hands of its creditors, among them the big banks, which had loaned the city money for too long without examining its creditworthiness; another was the state government in Albany. Ultimately the city's most important creditors turned out to be the pension funds of the big municipal unions, which as recipients of generous wages and fringe benefits (especially pension money) from the city, did so much to create the problem in the first place. So it is that New York City officials are periodically forced to go down to Congress to get renewals of the federal loan guarantees (they are called something else, but that is what they are) and to assure everyone that this time is really the last time they'll have to ask anyone for help.

New York state was almost as shaky for a while, but through the efforts of Governor Hugh Carey and both parties in the legislature managed to bail itself out. But budgetary constraints leave the state government with little room for creativity or maneuver.

There is still some feeling in New York that the problems of the city and state are somehow the fault of others, and that it is no more than simple justice that their debts be assumed by the federal government. But it is clear that others are not to blame. New York wanted progressive social policies; politicians, especially city politicians, spent money they didn't have to get the policies they wanted. Later, many New Yorkers felt that others should foot the bill. There was resistance.

It may be said that New York has to bear extraordinary burdens. And it is true that New York City remains, as it has been for more than a century, the nation's leading port of entry for immigrants. Where New York once received immigrants from Ireland, Italy, Germany, and Eastern Europe, it took immigrants from the American South and Puerto Rico until the late sixties when immigration leveled off, and it still receives illegal immigrants from South America and the Caribbean. But New York also has extraordinary resources. It has declined as a manufacturing city, because unions have over the years successfully raised the price of labor, leaving New York no longer able to compete with low wage areas. But office space in Manhattan has more than doubled since the end of World War II, and that borough of New York City remains by far our number one financial, corporate, and media center. New York is also one of the few central cities in the East or Midwest with a population that is a majority white and middle class. Cities like Cleveland and Newark can be excused from the dismal condition of their municipal treasuries. But in New York that conditon represents a failure of political leadership and of the political system of which New Yorkers have been so proud.

As is often the case, such failures proceeded directly from success. A system which had worked well in the past failed to adapt, and for a long time no one noticed. A good place to start is 1910, when the population of immigrant-swollen Manhattan was 2.3 million (as compared to 1.4 million today). Early to middle twentieth century New York politics was shaped in almost every respect by the immigrants in a state where even today one-third of the people were either born abroad or had one parent who was. It was the immigrant population that produced the real strength of New York's political machines: Tammany Hall, the Manhattan machine, was led by Irish-Americans up through the forties and by Italian-Americans thereafter, and the votes that machine and its counterparts in the Bronx and Brooklyn could deliver were mainly those of Irish and Italian immigrants. Other immigrants, especially the Jews, never liked Catholic-dominated Tammany. In the 1910s they were electing Socialists to Congress; and in the thirties and forties the American Labor and Liberal Parties were created so that Jewish immigrants who didn't read much English could vote for Roosevelt and LaGuardia on the same party lever.

New York City was then (and is now) about one-quarter Jewish, and it was this leftish, anti-Tammany vote that became the fulcrum in state elections. In the twenties and thirties the progressive policies of Al Smith, Franklin Roosevelt, and Herbert Lehman helped these Democrats win the governorship for 22 of 24 years. In the forties and fifties, progressive Republican policies—which is to say basic acceptance of the New Deal—helped to win enough Jewish votes for statewide victories for Governors Thomas Dewey (1942, 1946, 1950) and Nelson Rockefeller (1958, 1962, 1966, 1970) and Senators Irving Ives (1946, 1952), Jacob Javits (1956, 1962, 1968, 1974) and Kenneth Keating (1958).

From this basic perception of the New York electorate—machine Democrats and upstate Yankee and wealthy Republicans balanced off evenly, with a decisive, leftish bloc of primarily Jewish immigrants making the choice—grew whole national political strategies. Apparently on the theory that all big states were like New York (though none of the rest have nearly so large a Jewish population), the idea became established that a Republican couldn't win the presidency without appealing to big liberal independent blocs, and that they couldn't lose if they did so successfully. (Unfortunately for this notion, Dewey in 1948 and Nixon in 1960 ran such campaigns and lost, and Nixon won using entirely different strategy in 1968 and 1972.) Liberal Democrats defended the Electoral College on the ground that it gives disproportionate leverage to minority groups in big states; that is to say, the Jewish voters of New York.

Such is the conventional wisdom that developed about New York—and national—politics. It became fully articulated in the fifties, just as the basic demographic conditions that produced it were disappearing. For New York is no longer a state dominated by self-conscious minorities as it was during the New Deal. Immigration was cut off almost completely by law early in the twenties, and as immigrants grew older they became less dependent on—and close to—the political machines. Of the minorities that form a leftish bloc today, blacks and Hispanics, the five boroughs of New York have a smaller percentage than most major cities, and voter participation among them is so low that blacks and Hispanics have become a negligible political factor.

New York no longer has a left wing vote bigger than any other state's, and it no longer has Democratic machines important in determining election outcomes. The machines are now in another business entirely, the business of brokering judicial patronage. Due to rickety old laws (another failure of New York to adapt to new times) machines still control Democratic judicial nominations, which are tantamount to election, and so they have a good deal to say about who gets appointed guardian, who gets the assessor's fee, who writes certain insurance contracts, and so on. These tawdry little matters victimize any innocent unfortunate enough to have dealings with the judicial system, but judicial patronage has nothing to do with Boss Tweed jamming mayors and governors down the public's throat—something the current crop of bosses patently lack the ability to do. In 1974 the bosses endorsed Howard Samuels for governor, and he lost badly; in 1976 they endorsed Henry Jackson for president after he had New York locked up; in 1977 they had no discernible influence on the outcome of the primary for mayor.

The classic business of political bosses has been delivering votes from the ranks of the underprivileged who might not otherwise find their way to the polls. It is a measure of the vitality of New York's Democratic machines that the state's blacks and Spanish-speaking citizens have the lowest level of voter participation in the United States—lower than blacks in the Mississippi Delta or Mexican-Americans in the Lower Rio Grande Valley.

The most recently effective political bosses in New York were in fact not Democrats, but the heads of the Liberal and Republican Parties. The boss of the Republicans was, of course, Nelson Rockefeller, who served as Governor for 15 years (1959–73) and who bankrolled the party personally during much of that period. Although some Republicans always regarded Rockefeller as a dangerous liberal, he always got his way in the state party. His power waned when he left Albany; even while he was vice president, the New York delegation to Kansas City included some Reagan supporters. After being dumped from the vice presidential ticket in 1976—he almost certainly could not have been nominated by a Republican convention—he left politics and in early 1979 suddenly died.

As for the Liberals, their party has long survived its raison d'être: in New York, as elsewhere, people who want to split their tickets are quite capable of doing so without the aid of a separate line on the ballot. The Liberal vote accordingly has declined from 406,000 for Kennedy in 1960 to

145,000 for Carter in 1976. For some years the Liberal line provided a bargaining chip for Alex Rose, the hatters' union leader and undisputed boss of the party until his death in 1976. His most glorious moment probably occurred in 1969, when John Lindsay lost the Republican nomination but was reelected Mayor as a Liberal. The Liberals are very much a generational party, with a base among Jewish needle trade workers born around the turn of the century; the party missed a chance to appeal to a younger generation when it slavishly followed the Johnson line on Vietnam. In 1966 they finished behind and lost their line on the ballot to the Conservatives; in 1978 they finished behind the Right to Life Party.

The Conservative Party for a while seemed the most vital and idealistic political force in the state, but seems also to have passed its peak. Formed in 1962, to decrease the influence of liberal Republicans like Rockefeller and Javits, the Conservatives elected a Senator of their own in James Buckley in 1970, but they have not had such a victory since. Starting with Richard Nixon in 1972, Conservatives have found the top of the Republican ticket worthy of endorsement, and increasingly they have also endorsed the Republicans in congressional and local races. The main mission of the Conservative Party seems largely accomplished—liberal Republicans are doing less well here now than in Pennsylvania or Illinois—but that leaves little for the party to do.

With that introduction to the contending forces, let us review New York statewide politics. The pivot group in the recent past has not been the liberal Jewish voters of the forties and fifties, but the conservative Catholic voters of New York City and its suburbs who came of age in the late sixties and early seventies. Their bête noire was John Lindsay, who was of the wrong party (a Republican, at first), of the wrong religion and ethnic background (a high income WASP and graduate of prep school and Yale), and of the wrong sympathies (directed toward blacks and Puerto Ricans). Indeed, Lindsay appeared to reserve all his liberal instincts for these minorities, to think that all whites were as fortunate and well connected as he. He also vastly raised salaries and pensions for city employees—most of them middle income Catholics—without getting much credit for it. The failure of the city to plow streets in Queens after a major snowfall was seen as an expression of Lindsay's attitude toward the outer boroughs. In fact, he never had a city-wide margin—he was elected against divided opposition both times—and he never got even a plurality outside Manhattan.

Without understanding attitudes toward Lindsay, one cannot understand how James Buckley was elected Senator in 1970 (with a minority in a three-way race himself) or how Nelson Rockefeller who campaigned as a foe of narcotics pushers won a fourth term that year or how New York state gave a majority to Richard Nixon in 1972, and New York City nearly followed suit. Buckley's slogan—"Isn't it time *we* had a Senator?"—said it all. The hard-working people of the outer boroughs and the suburbs, these believers in traditional morality and traditional modes of behavior hated the self-absorbed sophistication and condescending preoccupation with the poor they saw in Lindsay and his followers. As a result, New York, for all its liberal reputation, became a profoundly conservative state.

Sometime between 1972 and 1974 that changed, and the reason was Watergate. Although Archie Bunker may have remained true to Richard Nixon, most of his neighbors did not, and for a very good reason: they didn't think Nixon had been true to them. After all, one of the main appeals of Nixon's style of conservatism is the conviction that middle class life is morally superior to the life of welfare recipients in Harlem or sophisticates on Park Avenue or Greenwich Village. Nixon's denunciation of foul language, marijuana, sex before marriage, and other evils made him seem a champion of traditional morality. The tapes told a different story. He was not only a crook; he was a fraud. The conservative vote has not been the same since.

Evidence of that was clear in the 1974 election. The Republicans had a number of problems. Rockefeller resigned the governorship in December 1973, and his successor, Malcolm Wilson, inherited the unpopularity of Rockefeller's administration without the resources—on the order of $10 million—the Rockefeller campaigns had used to turn opinion around. In addition, Wilson was addicted to polysyllabic Latinisms, procrastination on difficult matters, and an adherence to principle on matters where flexibility would have served his best political interests. His Democratic opponent was Congressman Hugh Carey, a surprise winner in the September Democratic primary. Culturally, Carey seemed traditional: he was a Catholic from a conservative part of Brooklyn, he had twelve children, he looked like a policeman. His record was sufficiently liberal that not even the hair-splittingest writer on the *Village Voice* could find a reason to support Wilson instead. The result was a 58% Carey victory—a landslide as New York gubernatorial elections go.

Then in Carey's first year in office the New York City fiscal crisis struck. Mayor Abraham Beame, the City Controller elected to take Lindsay's place as "the man who knows where the buck is," struggled to keep the city from bankruptcy as the mood swung from crisis to farce and back again. The state government stepped in, nearly got in trouble itself, but managed to help. New York needed, and finally received, guarantees from the federal government which would satisfy its creditors that their money would be repaid, and the first city in the nation became a supplicant. Gerald Ford went along with the plan, but before he did he took a strong rhetorical stand against any aid—which may have been the bargaining tactic needed to force New York officials to make realistic demands. Ford's posture was seen in New York as a cheap political attempt to score points in the hinterland, but it was actually an act of political courage. He gained no electoral votes elsewhere, but he probably lost New York's 41—and therefore the election. There was no forgetting the *Daily News* headline—FORD TO CITY: DROP DEAD—which, though Ford never said it, was stamped indelibly in the minds of New York voters.

For the New York City aid issue seems to have welded the New York metropolitan area electorate together and tied it more strongly to the Democratic Party than anything since the New Deal. So much is true not only in New York City, which casts fewer votes every election, but in the suburbs as well; and together they cast more than 60% of the state's votes. In 1976, for example, Jimmy Carter did poorly in upstate New York, running no better than Hubert Humphrey had in 1968 in a three-way race and well behind John Kennedy's 1960 showing. Upstate New York has a very large Catholic population—about 40%—and Carter was not strong with this group. But in New York City and its suburbs Carter got higher percentages than any Democratic presidential candidate except Lyndon Johnson and Franklin Roosevelt—67% in the City and a near-majority of 47% in the suburbs. That was enough to enable him to carry the state with 52%. His performance in the New York metropolitan area was all the more striking in light of the fact that he was a weak number three in the New York primary; he won in November simply because he was the candidate most favorable to aid to New York City.

That issue also accounted for the result in New York's Senate race that year. Senator Buckley performed in office as a man of conservative principle and no political ambition; he expressed doubts about aid to New York City, which was enough to do him in politically. With just one opponent this time, he carried upstate New York comfortably, but could only break even in the New York suburbs and lost 70%–30% in the City. The shape of the outcome, and the closeness with which it paralleled the results in the presidential race, indicate that Buckley would have lost to any pro-aid to New York City candidate.

As it happened, the winner was Daniel Patrick Moynihan, who had prevailed in the Democratic primary over Bella Abzug by some 10,000 votes. Moynihan was a major political figure long before he ran for the Senate. In the Johnson Administration he wrote the "benign neglect" pamphlet on the black family which enraged so many black intellectuals, but whose conclusions seem borne out by what has happened since. In the Nixon Administration, he put together the Family Assistance Plan, helped sell it to Wilbur Mills and the House, but could not get it through Russell Long's Senate Finance Committee. Moynihan blames its defeat on liberals who were unwilling to accept half a loaf; others say that Moynihan's own strategic mistakes were at fault.

Later Moynihan lobbied for and finally obtained the post of Ambassador to the United Nations. He used the platform, conveniently located in Manhattan, to denounce the third world nations, particularly those with black leadership. He also lambasted the Soviet Union and strongly supported Israel—moves he must have known were wildly popular with Jewish voters and New Yorkers generally. Meanwhile, Moynihan claimed he had no thoughts of seeking electoral office, saying on Face the Nation that it would be "dishonorable" for him to run for Senate after serving at the UN. But he was talked into doing so, without apparent difficulty, by a group of labor, business, and political leaders who were afraid that Abzug might win the primary.

Much of the animus behind Moynihan's politics comes from a quarrel he has sustained with the American liberal community. He does not talk much about the issue that most engaged attention of liberals—Vietnam, a subject on which he is uncharacteristically silent. What he believes he is countering is a set of attitudes that comes out of the Vietnam experience, that this country is not necessarily on the right side of all issues and enjoys little moral superiority over other nations. Moynihan insists that it does, and he believes that it is important for the United States to assert that superiority whatever others might think.

There is so much fustian in Moynihan's rhetoric, so much posturing in his pugnaciousness, that it was hard to take him seriously as a legislator when he was first elected. He has been, and continues to be, a gifted advocate and a spotter of trends and issues before they are seen by others. But he has also proved to be a somewhat more substantial legislator than people anticipated. He sought and won a seat on the same Finance Committee that foiled him in the early seventies, and became an important force there. He has joined Henry Jackson, whom he supported in the 1976 presidential primary in New York, in his opposition to SALT negotiator Paul Warnke, and he has been more outspoken in his opposition to SALT II than Jackson himself.

Moynihan is one of the many senators who seems to have ambitions for higher office. It sometimes seems that he thinks of himself as another Winston Churchill, warning America of the perils others ignore. The question is whether his particular talents make him suitable for the presidency. His apparent eagerness to seek out quarrels, his penchant for seeing himself as an outshouted victim when in fact he speaks from a position of great power and with strong intellectual allies—these are not necessarily qualities which would be good in a president. Should he ever run, Moynihan would begin with much of the constituency Henry Jackson had in 1976; and he has the ability Jackson lacks to express his ideas with force and panache. But whether he has the discipline and self-restraint needed in the long run is not clear.

New York's senior senator, Jacob Javits, has served with six colleagues, some of them, notably Robert Kennedy, much better known. But Javits has been an important senator himself for most of that time. In a poll of Senate aides conducted by Ralph Nader's Congress Watch, Javits was rated the brightest senator and the second most influential. The influence comes not from popularity or a gift for camaraderie; Javits is not considered personally charming by most senators. Nor is it due to leverage from party politics, often assuming minority position within the minority party—or to the importance of his state. Javits's secrets are brains and hard work. He understands complex legislation like the pension reform bill he shepherded through in 1974, and can argue abstruse points almost mechanically on measures like the War Powers Act which he sponsored in 1973. He was the ranking Republican for many years on the Human Resources Committee, which handles education, labor, and welfare legislation; he is ranking Republican now on the Foreign Relations Committee. He is influential in both these areas and was a major force in getting aid to New York City as well. Hard work, solid preparation, analytic ability, excellent staff—these qualities have made Javits a major power in the Senate.

He is not, however, the electoral power in New York he is generally thought to be. He was once an amazing vote-getter: in his younger days he held as a Republican a congressional seat in upper Manhattan, beat Franklin D. Roosevelt, Jr., for New York attorney general in 1954, and beat Mayor Robert Wagner for the Senate in 1956. He was easily reelected in 1962, but in the last two elections—1968 and 1974—he won mainly because the opposition was split between a weak Democrat and the Conservative nominee. In both cases he had less than an absolute majority of the vote. Javits does not seem to have a large core constituency any longer. He remains a favorite of organized labor for his work on social legislation and of big interests in the securities industry for the way he looks after Wall Street's concerns. But he would have great difficulty winning a Republican primary against Jack Kemp in 1980. He turns 76 that year, and although his health is excellent that is not likely to be an advantage. Javits has already taken to writing his memoirs.

The most recent elections for the two important administrative positions in New York, mayor and governor, have been decided not by the old party bosses or new coalitions, but by the vast middle of a shrinking electorate which is reached almost entirely through television advertising. The mood of these voters has been very pessimistic and cynical—an understandable reaction when the government of the richest city in the world nearly goes bankrupt. Thus Mayor Abraham Beame was not only denied a second term in 1977, but received only 18% of the vote in the Democratic primary, just ahead of Bella Abzug, with 17%. She had done much better (35%) the year before against Moynihan in the Senate primary, with voters apparently sharing the view of insiders that her talents are better suited to legislative than executive office. As things turned out, there was a runoff between the two top finishers, Manhattan Congressman Edward Koch and Carey appointee Mario Cuomo. Both departed from the conventional wisdom: Koch for example supported capital punishment, while Queens resident Cuomo opposed it. Koch attacked Cuomo for having Carey's support, and in this era of distrust of politicians it was probably a liability. Perhaps most important, Koch had the assistance of Carey's media advisor, David Garth, whose commercials helped Koch win.

In office Koch has been somewhat less iconoclastic than he was as a candidate. He made up with Carey; and despite some budget trimming his main priority seems to be to extract more money from the federal government. In 1979, for example, Koch was furious when the Board of Estimate refused to approve a plan for a housing project in the South Bronx. Koch's main argument for it seemed to be that the feds were providing the money—even though the project was slated for an area which has undergone huge out-migration and one in which nobody with a choice wants to live. Nonetheless Koch has done more than any previous mayor to change New York's habits and try to get the city government to live only a few hundred million dollars beyond its means. His term expires in 1981.

Like Koch, Governor Hugh Carey is a product of the Democratic Party—the party that in this state practically invented the welfare state as we know it in America. But like Koch, Carey has had to enforce a program of austerity and belt-tightening. Almost as soon as he took office in 1975, Carey saw that the cupboard was bare, and that the days of great Rockefeller projects like the Albany Mall and the Urban Development Corporation (which itself soon went bankrupt) were over. This policy probably produced what people wanted—as minimal a reduction of services as possible with as little increase in taxes as possible. But Carey's approach didn't satisfy anyone. Liberals resented policies like those of making students at New York's City University pay tuition, which is what students at public institutions in the rest of the country in fact do. Meanwhile, conservatives and upstaters resented Carey's unwillingness to crack down harder. Also unpopular was Carey's opposition to capital punishment. And in a state used to politicians with vibrant personalities—Nelson Rockefeller, Robert Kennedy, Bella Abzug, Pat Moynihan—Carey communicated little deep feeling and indeed seemed to spend most of his time with a few close aides.

Carey was blessed in 1978 with even more vulnerable opposition. Perry Duryea had a long record as Republican leader in the state Assembly; he had a local power base in Suffolk County, in eastern Long Island; he had supported some aid to New York City but was trusted by upstaters. But he was also indicted for an election law violation in 1974—which hurt his image even though the law under which he was indicted was declared unconstitutional. Duryea wanted to campaign on the death penalty, but he was dogged by his refusal to make a financial disclosure. In the end Duryea carried upstate and the suburbs only narrowly, and Carey's 2–1 margin in New York City was enough to give him a second term.

New York has customarily played a major role in presidential politics. For years, until 1972, it had more electoral votes than any other state, and for years the state produced far more than its share of presidential candidates. Three times in this century both major parties' candidates have come from New York. But more recently, New York has produced few national contenders. Governors Rockefeller and Harriman ran unsuccessful races for their parties' nominations; Excepting Eisenhower and Nixon, who had legal residences in New York but never made political careers there, the last New Yorker nominated by a major party was Thomas Dewey in 1948. Hugh Carey has been mentioned as a contender for the 1980 presidential nomination, as a Democrat who would favor more compassionate social and fiscal programs than Jimmy Carter. The problem, however, is that Carey's record has perforce been one of austerity and cutbacks. Another New Yorker sometimes mentioned is Senator Moynihan. But neither Carey nor Moynihan, to judge from their most recent primaries, has really overwhelming strength in what must be considered the acid test for any New York candidate, the New York presidential primary.

This is a contest held early enough in the primary season and covering a large enough number of delegates to be of truly major importance. Yet its relevance to the rest of the country seems limited. On the Democratic side, because of higher registration and turnout, Jewish voters comprise a percentage of the electorate larger than their population here—and far larger than their population in any other state. The 1976 contest seemed to be between two generations of Jewish voters, with Henry Jackson representing the older group for whom support of Israel and fierce American patriotism are major causes, and Morris Udall appealing to the younger group who were more concerned about the Vietnam war and incursions on civil liberties. The result proved that there are more of the former than the latter, but little else. Republicans here have not really had primaries before, because Nelson Rockefeller controlled the state delegation. That will not be true in 1980, and there may be a spirited contest. No one should rule conservative candidates out of contention in New York, for the Republican primary electorate is not much different from those in other states. Indeed, one reason Republicans nominated candidates like Rockefeller and Javits for so many years was that there was no primary—Rockefeller himself vetoed primary bills.

As for the general election, there seems less doubt about New York than about most states. As in 1976, the aid to New York City issue is likely to be decisive. Jimmy Carter or any other Democrat except Jerry Brown is likely to be on the right side of the issue for voters here, while the Republican nominee is likely to be on the wrong side. That should guarantee the Democrats New

York's 41 electoral votes to go with Massachusetts's 14 and the District of Columbia's 3. One could almost call this a colonial pattern—voters deciding how to vote on the basis of one issue concerning their relationship to the central government, rather than on the broader range of issues on which most American states base a decision. It is a sign of how far New York's problems—and its weaknesses—have come.

Economic Base Finance, insurance and real estate; apparel and other textile products, especially women's and misses' outerwear; electrical equipment and supplies, especially communication equipment; printing and publishing, especially commercial printing and newspapers; machinery, especially office and computing machines; food and kindred products, especially bakery products and beverages; agriculture, especially dairy products, cattle, eggs, and greenhouse products.

Political Line-up Governor, Hugh L. Carey (D). Senators, Jacob K. Javits (R) and Daniel Patrick Moynihan (D). Representatives, 39 (26 D and 13 R). State Senate (25 D, 35 R); State Assembly (86 D, 64 R).

The Voters

Registration 7,470,770 Total. 3,642,613 D (49%); 2,596,872 R (35%); 114,385 Conservative (2%); 92,894 Liberal (1%); 1,024,006 Blank, Missing, and Void (14%).
Median voting age 44
Employment profile White collar, 55%. Blue collar, 31%. Service, 13%. Farm, 1%.
Ethnic groups Black, 12%. Spanish, 5%. Total foreign stock, 33%. Italy, 7%; USSR, Poland, Germany, 3% each; Ireland, UK, Canada, 2% each; Austria, 1%.

Presidential vote

1976	Carter (D)	3,389,558	(52%)
	Ford (R)	3,100,791	(48%)
1972	Nixon (R)	4,192,778	(59%)
	McGovern (D)	2,951,084	(41%)

Sen. Jacob K. Javits (R) Elected 1956, seat up 1980; b. May 18, 1904, New York City; home, New York City; Columbia U., NYU, LL.B. 1926; Jewish.

Career Practicing atty., 1927–41, 1945–46; Special Asst. to Chf. of U.S. Army Chemical Warfare Svc., 1941–42; Army, WWII; U.S. House of Reps., 1947–55; Atty. Gen. of N.Y. State, 1955–57.

Offices 321 RSOB, 202-224-6542. Also 110 E. 45th St., New York 10017, 212-867-7777, and Leo W. O'Brien Fed. Bldg., Clinton Sq., Albany 12207, 518-472-6182.

Committees *Foreign Relations* (Ranking Member). Subcommittees: International Economic Policy; European Affairs.

Governmental Affairs (2d). Subcommittees: Investigations; Energy, Nuclear Proliferation, and Federal Services.

Labor and Human Resources (2d). Subcommittees: Education, Arts, and Humanities; Health and Scientific Research; Employment, Poverty, and Migratory Labor.

Group Ratings

	ADA	COPE	PC	RPN	NFU	LCV	CFA	NAB	NSI	ACA	NTU
1978	75	95	70	80	14	76	50	9	10	5	–
1977	80	89	60	73	67	–	72	–	–	15	26
1976	85	78	69	87	75	74	71	17	22	0	29

Key Votes

1) Warnke Nom	FOR	6) Egypt-Saudi Arms	AGN	11) Hosptl Cost Contnmnt	FOR
2) Neutron Bomb	AGN	7) Draft Restr Pardon	FOR	12) Clinch River Reactor	DNV
3) Waterwy User Fee	FOR	8) Wheat Price Support	AGN	13) Pub Fin Cong Cmpgns	AGN
4) Dereg Nat Gas	AGN	9) Panama Canal Treaty	FOR	14) ERA Ratif Recissn	FOR
5) Kemp-Roth	AGN	10) Labor Law Rev Clot	FOR	15) Med Necssy Abrtns	FOR

Election Results

1974 general	Jacob K. Javits (R-L)	2,340,188	(46%)	($1,090,437)
	Ramsey Clark (D)	1,973,781	(38%)	($855,576)
	Barbara A. Keating (C)	822,584	(16%)	($192,462)
1974 primary	Jacob K. Javits (R), unopposed			
1968 general	Jacob K. Javits (R-L)	3,269,772	(50%)	
	Paul O'Dwyer (D)	2,150,695	(33%)	
	James L. Buckley (C)	1,139,402	(17%)	

Sen. Daniel Patrick Moynihan (D) Elected 1976, seat up 1982; b. Mar. 16, 1927, Tulsa, Okla.; home, New York City; CCNY, 1943, Tufts U., B.A. 1948, M.A. 1949, Ph.D. 1961; Catholic.

Career University Professor; U.S. Asst. Secy. of Labor, 1963–65; Asst. to the Pres. for Urban Affairs, 1969–70; U.S. Ambassador to India, 1973–74; U.S. Ambassador to the U.N., 1975–76.

Offices 1107 DSOB, 202-224-4451. Also 733 3rd Ave., New York City 10017, 212-661-5150, and Fed. Ofc. Bldg., Buffalo 14202, 716-842-3493.

Committees *Budget* (11th).

Environment and Public Works (8th). Subcommittees: Water Resources; Regional and Community Development; Nuclear Regulation.

Finance (9th). Subcommittees: International Trade; Public Assistance (Chairman); Revenue Sharing, Intergovernmental Revenue Impact, and Economic Problems.

Select Committee on Intelligence (5th).

Group Ratings

	ADA	COPE	PC	RPN	NFU	LCV	CFA	NAB	NSI	ACA	NTU
1978	60	89	60	67	60	65	45	9	30	4	–
1977	70	84	58	40	82	–	48	–	–	17	26

Key Votes

1) Warnke Nom	AGN	6) Egypt-Saudi Arms	AGN	11) Hosptl Cost Contnmnt	FOR
2) Neutron Bomb	FOR	7) Draft Restr Pardon	DNV	12) Clinch River Reactor	AGN
3) Waterwy User Fee	AGN	8) Wheat Price Support	AGN	13) Pub Fin Cong Cmpgns	FOR
4) Dereg Nat Gas	AGN	9) Panama Canal Treaty	FOR	14) ERA Ratif Recissn	FOR
5) Kemp-Roth	AGN	10) Labor Law Rev Clot	FOR	15) Med Necssy Abrtns	FOR

Election Results

1976 general	Daniel P. Moynihan (D)	3,238,511	(56%)	($1,210,796)
	James L. Buckley (R)	2,525,139	(44%)	($2,101,424)
1976 primary	Daniel P. Moynihan (D)	333,697	(36%)	
	Bella S. Abzug (D)	323,705	(35%)	
	Ramsey Clark (D)	94,191	(10%)	
	Paul O'Dwyer (D)	82,689	(9%)	
	Abraham Hirshfeld (D)	82,331	(9%)	

1970 general	James L. Buckley (C)	2,288,190	(39%)
	Richard L. Ottinger (D)	2,171,232	(37%)
	Charles E. Goodell (R-L)	1,434,472	(24%)

Gov. Hugh L. Carey (D) Elected 1974, term expires Jan. 1983; b. Apr. 11, 1919, Brooklyn; St. John's U., J.D. 1951; Catholic.

Career Army, WWII; Family petroleum distrib. business, 1947–51; Practicing atty., 1951–61; U.S. House of Reps., 1961–75.

Offices Executive Chamber, State Capitol, Albany 12224, 518-474-8390.

Election Results

1978 general	Hugh L. Carey (D-L)	2,429,272	(53%)
	Perry B. Duryea (R-C)	2,156,404	(47%)
1978 primary	Hugh L. Carey (D)	376,457	(52%)
	Mary Anne Krupsak (D)	244,252	(34%)
	Jeremiah B. Bloom (D)	103,479	(14%)
1974 general	Hugh L. Carey (D-L)	3,028,503	(58%)
	Malcolm Wilson (R-C)	2,219,667	(42%)

FIRST DISTRICT

The 1st congressional district of New York includes the eastern end of Long Island, from 50 to 100 miles from Manhattan. The best known part of the district is the eastern tip which juts out into the Atlantic Ocean; here rich New Yorkers flock each summer to the fashionable beach resorts of the Hamptons and Montauk. This is a lovely area, settled first by New Englanders, and now maintained in the kind of pristine countrification made possible only from the interest taken by affluent outsiders. Inland and west of the Hamptons is the more typical rural Long Island: acres of potato fields, truck farms, rickety housing occupied by farm workers.

Before World War II virtually all of the current 1st district was agricultural, little changed from the nineteenth century. Today metropolitan New York has moved in inexorably. The 1st district more than doubled in population during the sixties—by far the largest growth of any East Coast congressional district.

As in fast growing parts of the Sun Belt, the mood out here is very conservative. A correlation seems to exist between conservative political attitudes and the desire to move this far away from New York City—a fear of crime, a dislike of blacks and Puerto Ricans, a distaste for the moral tone of cosmopolitan life. There is a desire to leave behind the chaos and the corruption of the city for the supposedly simpler, less hectic pace of life on Long Island. The outcome is seldom so pleasing. The new subdivisions on eastern Long Island have houses larger and farther apart than those back in Brooklyn and Queens, but they also lack the cohesiveness of the old ethnic neighborhoods. Children are no more docile, adolescents no less rebellious out here; there is still juvenile delinquency and lack of respect for elders. The economy here is less diversified than New York's, and sometimes less stable; among the biggest employers are Grumman and Republic Aviation, both of which have had big layoffs.

The high point of political conservatism in the 1st district came in 1970, when Suffolk County (which includes this district, the 2d, and part of the 3d) was one of two New York counties where Conservative Senator James Buckley won an absolute majority. There was a marked change in 1974, the year Watergate had such a major impact. The ancestral preference for Democrats seemed to revive: Hugh Carey carried Suffolk County and Democrats picked up two House seats. Two years later this area was rather close in the presidential election—a startling shift from 1972 or even 1968. That Democratic trend helped Democrat Otis Pike, first elected here in 1960, but pressed hard in 1970 and 1972. Pike was a stylish, witty, sometimes eloquent congressman. He rose to enjoy high seniority on the Armed Services Committee, then switched to Ways and Means; he served also as chairman of the special intelligence committee whose report was ultimately suppressed by the House. Pike decided to retire in 1977, for a number of reasons, including, he said in a speech which attracted a rare standing ovation in the House, the limits on outside income in the new House ethics code. Part of the problem may have been Pike's sources of income—he had shares in a nursing home that was under investigation, though Pike was never charged with wrong doing.

It was no surprise that, with Pike out of the race, the 1st switched from Democrat to Republican. The Democrat, John Randolph, was a local official in a township covering most of the district; he had a reputation as a moderate and Pike's endorsement. But these proved not enough to overcome the advantages of William Carney, a registered Conservative who got Republican organization support as part of a deal between the two parties and who was challenged in the Republican primary. Carney was running as a Republican in a Republican district in a Republican year, and when the Republican ticket was led by a home town boy, Perry Duryea of Montauk. Carney can be expected to be one of the most conservative members of the metropolitan New York delegation; if he does his homework, he should be hard to beat in later elections.

Census Data Pop. 467,742. Central city, 0%; suburban, 100%. Median family income, $11,643; families above $15,000: 30%; families below $3,000: 6%. Median years education, 12.3.

The Voters

Median voting age 41.
Employment profile White collar, 55%. Blue collar, 30%. Service, 14%. Farm, 1%.
Ethnic groups Black, 4%. Spanish, 1%. Total foreign stock, 28%. Italy, 7%; Germany, 4%; UK, Poland, Ireland, 2% each; USSR, 1%.

Presidential vote

1976	Carter (D)	98,409	(46%)
	Ford (R)	117,277	(54%)
1972	Nixon (R)	141,383	(70%)
	McGovern (D)	59,420	(30%)

Rep. William Carney (R) Elected 1972; b. July 1, 1942, Brooklyn; home, Hauppauge; Fla. St. U., 1960–61; Catholic.

Career Army, 1961–64; Salesman, heavy equipment business, 1972–76; Suffolk Co. Legis., 1976–79.

Offices 1113 LHOB, 202-225-3826. Also 180 E. Main St., Smithtown 11787, 516-724-4888.

Committees *Merchant Marine and Fisheries* (14th). Subcommittees: Fish and Wildlife; Panama Canal.

Science and Technology (11th). Subcommittees: Energy Development and Applications; Investigations and Oversight.

Group Ratings: Newly Elected

Key Votes: Newly Elected

Election Results

1978 general	William Carney (R-C)	90,155	(57%)	($130,642)
	John F. Randolph (D)	67,180	(43%)	($76,810)
1978 primary	William Carney (R)	4,939	(31%)	
	James M. Catterson, Jr. (R)	3,203	(20%)	($33,217)
	John J. Hart, Jr. (R)	3,085	(19%)	
	Salvatore C. Nicosia (R)	2,624	(17%)	
	John M. Radway (R)	2,041	(13%)	($101,640)
1976 general	Otis G. Pike (D-L)	135,528	(65%)	($37,066)
	Salvatore C. Nicosia (R)	61,671	(30%)	($19,006)
	Seth C. Morgan (C)	10,269	(5%)	

SECOND DISTRICT

At the end of World War II, Suffolk County, which includes the eastern geographical half of Long Island, was largely given over to potato fields. It was also directly in the path of one of the major suburban migrations of our day. On the highways that Robert Moses built to connect his parks to the middle class parts of New York City came tens of thousands of young veterans and their families, forsaking the rowhouse neighborhoods where they had grown up for the comparatively spacious lots and single family houses of Levittown and other Long Island subdivisions. The first wave of postwar migration moved into Nassau County, and it was a pretty accurate cross-section of all but the poorest New Yorkers: almost half Catholic, about one-quarter Jewish and one-quarter Protestant in background. Then, as Long Island developed an employment base of its own, the next wave of migration started, this time as far out as Suffolk County. This second wave was somewhat more Catholic and less Jewish, more blue collar (aircraft manufacturers were big Suffolk County employers) and less white collar, more Democratic perhaps in ancestral politics but fundamentally more conservative on most issues.

Such was the migration that made Suffolk County the fastest growing part of New York state in the sixties, as its population shot up 69%. This was about the rate of growth in that part of Suffolk County which makes up New York's 2d congressional district, which covers the South Shore suburban communities of Suffolk, including all of the town of Islip and most of Babylon.

Like all of Suffolk, the 2d changed its voting habits sharply between 1972 and 1974, moving rapidly away from the Republicans and toward the Democrats. Nowhere was the change more stark than in the congressional election. Republican James Grover had been reelected with 66% in 1972; in 1974 he was defeated by 25-year-old Thomas Downey. A law student and member of the Suffolk County legislature since 1971, Downey hit hard on Watergate and presented a vigorous contrast to his relaxed opponent.

Downey's election has proved to be more than a fluke; he has shown an impressive political intelligence both in Washington and in the 2d district. In Washington he was a member of the Armed Services Committee for two terms, and in the beginning was regarded as a dovish member of a hawkish committee. As time went on, it became clear that Downey was not a simple ideologue, but studied and mastered issues thoroughly. In 1979, with two reelections behind him, he switched to Ways and Means, where he will likely be an important and well informed vote.

At home Downey has been a kind of model of the constituent-oriented congressman, inviting literally thousands of voters to come over to his parents' house and discuss issues with him. His first year in the House he had a 100% ADA rating, yet he seemed to be able to relate his voting record to his constituents' middle class concerns. Republicans ran a strong candidate with a big budget in 1976, but Downey won reelection with 57% of the vote. Against a weaker candidate in the more Republican year of 1978, he got 55%. He will have to keep working the district hard, but he seems to be the kind of congressman who knows just how to do so.

Census Data Pop. 467,722. Central city, 0%; suburban, 100%. Median family income, $11,938; families above $15,000: 29%; families below $3,000: 4%. Median years education, 12.1.

The Voters

Median voting age 41.
Employment profile White collar, 49%. Blue collar, 37%. Service, 14%. Farm, –%.
Ethnic groups Black, 4%. Spanish, 2%. Total foreign stock, 28%. Italy, 9%; Germany, 3%; Ireland, UK, 2% each; Canada, Poland, 1% each.

Presidential vote

1976	Carter (D)	75,033	(45%)
	Ford (R)	90,243	(55%)
1972	Nixon (R)	123,030	(72%)
	McGovern (D)	46,695	(28%)

Rep. Thomas J. Downey (D) Elected 1974; b. Jan. 28, 1949, Ozone Park; home, West Islip; Cornell U., B.S. 1970, St. John's U. Law School, 1972–74.

Career Personnel management and labor relations, Macy's Dept. Store; Suffolk Co. Legislature, 1971–74.

Offices 1111 LHOB, 202-225-3335. Also 4 Udall Rd., West Islip 11759, 516-661-8777.

Committees *Ways and means* (20th). Subcommittees: Trade; Public Assistance and Unemployment Compensation.

Group Ratings

	ADA	COPE	PC	RPN	NFU	LCV	CFA	NAB	NSI	ACA	NTU
1978	60	100	78	45	80	–	68	18	30	7	–
1977	85	81	78	54	73	92	60	–	–	11	26
1976	75	83	90	56	83	82	100	25	10	15	21

Key Votes

1) Increase Def Spnd	AGN	6) Alaska Lands Protect	FOR	11) Delay Auto Pol Cntrl	AGN
2) B-1 Bomber	AGN	7) Water Projects Veto	FOR	12) Sugar Price Escalator	AGN
3) Cargo Preference	AGN	8) Consum Protect Agcy	FOR	13) Pub Fin Cong Cmpgns	FOR
4) Dereg Nat Gas	AGN	9) Common Situs Picket	FOR	14) ERA Ratif Recissn	AGN
5) Kemp-Roth	AGN	10) Labor Law Revision	FOR	15) Prohibt Govt Abrtns	AGN

Election Results

1978 general	Thomas J. Downey (D)	64,807	(55%)	($149,400)
	Harold J. Withers, Jr. (R-C)	53,322	(45%)	($33,119)
1978 primary	Thomas J. Downey (D), unopposed			
1976 general	Thomas J. Downey (D-I)	91,241	(57%)	($148,913)
	Peter F. Cohalan (R-C)	67,755	(43%)	($137,859)

THIRD DISTRICT

The 3d congressional district of New York was a new seat drawn after the 1970 Census. Its creation recognized the rapid population growth of Long Island in the sixties. As in the case of all New York district lines drawn in the fifties, sixties, and seventies, these boundaries were carefully sculpted by Republican redistricters with the intent of maximizing Republican representation in Congress. Somewhat more than half the 3d district's citizens live in Nassau County, in areas as diverse as fashionable and high income North Shore communities like Locust Valley, less fashionable but nonetheless well-to-do Syosset in the middle of Long Island, and deeply conservative and middle income Massapequa on the South Shore. The remainder of the district is just to the east, in Suffolk County; that portion is dominated by the middle class town of Huntington, but also includes the small black ghetto of Wyandanch.

So far in its brief history the 3d district has had four close congressional races, and it has been carried by a Republican only once. That was in 1972, when Angelo Roncallo was elected. A product of Joseph Margiotta's smooth and competent Nassau County machine, Roncallo seemed to have a safe seat. But he was indicted on conspiracy charges and, though acquitted, was defeated for reelection in 1974.

The winner was Jerome Ambro, Supervisor of Huntington Township. With a Suffolk County base and a corruption issue, Ambro won that election. The Suffolk County base has been decisive in his holding onto the seat; he lost the Nassau County portion by small margins in 1976 and 1978. Ambro has a more moderate voting record than Thomas Downey, another 1974 freshman in the next-door 2d district, but he is not considered to have worked the district as hard. His 1978 margin of only 4,000 votes and the determination of the Margiotta machine insure that he will have tough competition in 1980.

Census Data Pop. 467,894. Central city, 0%; suburban, 100%. Median family income, $14,396; families above $15,000: 47%; families below $3,000: 4%. Median years education, 12.5.

The Voters

Median voting age 42.
Employment profile White collar, 62%. Blue collar, 27%. Service, 11%. Farm, -%.
Ethnic groups Black, 5%. Total foreign stock, 32%. Italy, 9%; Germany, 4%; USSR, 3%; UK, Poland, Ireland, 2% each; Canada, Austria, 1% each.

Presidential vote

1976	Carter (D)	88,901	(46%)
	Ford (R)	105,322	(54%)
1972	Nixon (R)	137,271	(67%)
	McGovern (D)	68,617	(33%)

Rep. Jerome Ambro, Jr. (D) Elected 1974; b. June 27, 1928, Brooklyn; home, East Northport; NYU, B.A.; Catholic.

Career Army, Korea; Huntington Town Supervisor, 1968–74; Suffolk Co. Bd. of Supervisors, 1968–69.

Offices 236 CHOB, 202-225-3865. Also 7600 Jericho Tpk., Woodbury 11797, 516-364-2177.

Committees *Public Works and Transportation* (11th). Subcommittees: Aviation; Surface Transportation; Water Resources.

Science and Technology (9th). Subcommittees: Investigations and Oversight; Natural Resources and Environment (Chairman).

Group Ratings

	ADA	COPE	PC	RPN	NFU	LCV	CFA	NAB	NSI	ACA	NTU
1978	20	53	50	27	60	–	59	42	60	35	–
1977	70	81	85	23	73	87	80	–	–	27	26
1976	50	82	84	39	100	80	91	25	20	22	28

Key Votes

1) Increase Def Spnd	FOR	6) Alaska Lands Protect	FOR	11) Delay Auto Pol Cntrl	AGN
2) B-1 Bomber	AGN	7) Water Projects Veto	FOR	12) Sugar Price Escalator	AGN
3) Cargo Preference	AGN	8) Consum Protect Agcy	FOR	13) Pub Fin Cong Cmpgns	FOR
4) Dereg Nat Gas	AGN	9) Common Situs Picket	FOR	14) ERA Ratif Recissn	FOR
5) Kemp-Roth	FOR	10) Labor Law Revision	FOR	15) Prohibt Govt Abrtns	FOR

Election Results

1978 general	Jerome A. Ambro (D)	70,526	(51%)	($80,256)
	Gregory W. Carman (R-C)	66,458	(49%)	($311,390)
1978 primary	Jerome A. Ambro (D), unopposed			
1976 general	Jerome A. Ambro (D)	94,265	(53%)	($60,230)
	Howard T. Hogan (R-C)	84,824	(47%)	($92,224)

FOURTH DISTRICT

At the end of World War II, Nassau County on Long Island, just beyond the New York City limits, consisted mostly of potato fields. Here and there, in this flat country 30 or 40 miles east of Manhattan, a few subdivisions had been laid out before the war. On the North Shore and in places like Old Westbury sat the Gatsbyesque estates of some of New York's wealthiest families. But the vast center of Nassau County lay undeveloped. It did not stay that way for long. Just after the war, a young builder named William Levitt built an entire town full of small tract houses and named it for himself. Soon Levittown came to symbolize Long Island's vast postwar growth. Young marrieds, after years of war and depression childhoods pent up in the city, flocked out to the Island and created a new lifestyle.

So during the forties and fifties Nassau County filled up, so much so that it has had virtually no growth since the 1960 Census. The population is now aging. The baby boom babies have grown up, and most of them are not staying in Nassau. There aren't many houses for sale here, so some of them head farther out the Island to Suffolk County, some move to Manhattan, and some move outside the New York orbit altogether.

In the fifties there was speculation that the new suburban lifestyle was creating new political attitudes, that when the young postwar marrieds left the New York City limits they dropped their Democratic habits and became Republicans. In retrospect this notion seems clearly wrong. It was not the county line that made the difference; many did register Republican here, but that was because the Republican primary determined who held most local government positions, not because they necessarily thought of themselves as Republicans. But such movement to the Democrats as there was was part of a broader trend, away from the New Deal, and toward the politics of the Eisenhower era. It was a response to times of unanticipated prosperity and affluence, not an attempt to blend into the local landscape.

The 4th congressional district of New York is one of two seats which lies entirely within Nassau County. The 4th includes many areas of the fifties boom, including the original Levittown and next-door Hicksville. Both these places have actually lost population since 1960, as the children of the original settlers grew up and moved away. The district also includes posh Old Westbury and the black ghetto of New Cassel not far away. But the nucleus of the 4th, the part which connects it to predecessor districts, is a string of towns along the South Shore of Long Island. They include Oceanside, Freeport, and Merrick, where most residents come from older Jewish and Catholic neighborhoods in the city; these are marginal politically. Also here are Bellmore, Wantagh, and Seaford, more heavily Catholic and usually much more Republican. These were added in the 1972 redistricting, to help incumbent Republican Congressman Norman Lent.

Lent is the beneficiary of a couple of redistrictings. The first, in 1970, helped him beat Allard Lowenstein, elected two years before with the help of student volunteers after he helped to put together the campaign that ousted Lyndon Johnson from the presidency. The second, in 1972, made the district safely Republican in most contests. Since then, his opposition has gotten weaker and his percentages have grown much higher. In the House Lent is a reliable member of the Republican Party, but is not closely identified with any particular issue.

Census Data Pop. 467,610. Central city, 0%; suburban, 100%. Median family income, $14,376; families above $15,000: 46%; families below $3,000: 3%. Median years education, 12.4.

The Voters

Median voting age 43.
Employment profile White collar, 63%. Blue collar, 26%. Service, 11%. Farm, –%.
Ethnic groups Black, 3%. Total foreign stock, 33%. Italy, 7%; USSR, 5%; Germany, 4%; Poland, Ireland, 3% each; UK, Austria, 2% each; Canada, 1%.

Presidential vote

1976	Carter (D)	98,788	(49%)
	Ford (R)	103,663	(51%)
1972	Nixon (R)	138,983	(64%)
	McGovern (D)	78,124	(36%)

Rep. Norman F. Lent (R) Elected 1970; b. Mar. 23, 1931, Oceanside; home, East Rockaway; Hofstra Col., B.A. 1952, Cornell U., J.D. 1957; Methodist.

Career Navy, Korea; Practicing atty., 1957–70; Asst. East Rockaway Police Justice, 1960–62; N.Y. Senate, 1962–70.

Offices 2228 RHOB, 202-225-7896. Also Rm. 300, 2280 Grand Ave., Baldwin 11510, 516-223-1616.

Committees *Interstate and Foreign Commerce* (6th). Subcommittees: Oversight and Investigations.

Merchant Marine and Fisheries (8th). Subcommittees: Coast Guard and Navigation; Oceanography.

Group Ratings

	ADA	COPE	PC	RPN	NFU	LCV	CFA	NAB	NSI	ACA	NTU
1978	20	20	33	64	30	–	36	56	100	75	–
1977	20	33	38	67	30	53	35	–	–	62	35
1976	20	35	26	88	33	52	9	73	100	54	45

Key Votes

1) Increase Def Spnd	FOR	6) Alaska Lands Protect	DNV	11) Delay Auto Pol Cntrl	AGN
2) B-1 Bomber	FOR	7) Water Projects Veto	FOR	12) Sugar Price Escalator	AGN
3) Cargo Preference	AGN	8) Consum Protect Agcy	AGN	13) Pub Fin Cong Cmpgns	AGN
4) Dereg Nat Gas	FOR	9) Common Situs Picket	AGN	14) ERA Ratif Recissn	FOR
5) Kemp-Roth	FOR	10) Labor Law Revision	FOR	15) Prohibt Govt Abrtns	FOR

Election Results

1978 general	Norman F. Lent (R-C)	94,711	(67%)	($83,658)
	Everett A. Rosenblum (D)	46,508	(33%)	($11,774)
1978 primary	Norman F. Lent (R-C), unopposed			
1976 general	Norman F. Lent (R-C)	106,058	(56%)	($83,008)
	Gerald P. Halpern (D-L)	83,971	(44%)	($45,761)

FIFTH DISTRICT

The 5th congressional district of New York includes most of the older suburban parts of Long Island. In the northern part of the district is Garden City, a WASPy suburb laid out in the twenties; it is, as it always has been, heavily Republican. To the south are places like Hempstead, Rockville Centre, and Valley Stream, towns on the radial highways leading into Queens. These places were developed somewhat later, and each of them has its own, slightly different character. Politically, these towns are a little more Democratic than average in Nassau County and somewhat more Republican than New York state as a whole. At the southern end of the district, below Kennedy Airport and just north of the Atlantic, are Long Beach and the Five Towns—Lawrence, Inwood, Cedarhurst, Hewlett, and Woodmere—all developments that were begun in the twenties, all heavily Jewish, and all solidly Democratic. Each of the towns so far mentioned together make for a marginal constituency; but the New York legislature, then solidly controlled by Republicans, was careful to add to them the heavily Republican suburbs of East Meadow and Uniondale, the latter the home of Nassau County Republican boss Joseph Margiotta.

The current boundaries of the 5th were intended to provide a safe seat for Congressman John Wydler, and for the most part they have. Wydler is part of the generation that came of age in World War II. He was born in Brooklyn and moved to Long Island, and found success in the Nassau County suburbs. He was elected to Congress in 1962, and for the most part has generated little publicity beyond his district. He has risen high on the Government Operations Committee and is ranking Republican on the Science Committee, and is a regional Republican Whip as well. Wydler has a dependably Republican voting record; on Science he is a booster of nuclear energy and of the Clinch River breeder project. He also pays close attention to district matters, and opposed the landing of the Concorde at Kennedy Airport—a move particularly popular in the Five Towns.

Wydler's toughest race came in 1974, when he was opposed by antiwar activist Allard Lowenstein, who had won once in a Long Island district in 1968 and had run in the meantime in Brooklyn and has since run in Manhattan. Wydler won that with 54%; he has done better since, despite the Democratic trend on Long Island in 1974 and 1976.

Census Data Pop. 467,694. Central city, 0%; suburban, 100%. Median family income, $14,102; families above $15,000: 45%; families below $3,000: 5%. Median years education, 12.4.

The Voters

Median voting age 46.
Employment profile White collar, 65%. Blue collar, 24%. Service, 11%. Farm, -%.
Ethnic groups Black, 8%. Total foreign stock, 38%. Italy, 9%; USSR, 5%; Germany, 4%; Poland, Ireland, 3% each; UK, Austria, 2% each.

Presidential vote

1976	Carter (D)	100,782	(48%)
	Ford (R)	107,909	(52%)
1972	Nixon (R)	145,996	(63%)
	McGovern (D)	87,445	(37%)

Rep. John W. Wydler (R) Elected 1962; b. June 9, 1924, Brooklyn; home, Garden City; Brown U., 1941–42, 1945–47, Harvard U., LL.B. 1950; Episcopalian.

Career Air Force, WWII; Practicing atty., 1950–; U.S. Atty's Ofc., 1953–59; Mbr., State Investigation Comm. to probe New York City school construction irregularities.

Offices 2308 RHOB, 202-225-5516. Also 150 Old Country Rd., Mineola 11501, 516-248-7676.

Committees *Government Operations* (3d). Subcommittees: Intergovernmental Relations and Human Resources.

Science and Technology (Ranking Member). Subcommittees: Energy Research and Production; Energy Development and Applications.

Group Ratings

	ADA	COPE	PC	RPN	NFU	LCV	CFA	NAB	NSI	ACA	NTU
1978	10	30	30	55	10	–	32	90	100	68	–
1977	20	35	40	83	27	53	40	–	–	81	48
1976	5	32	36	71	28	48	18	83	100	52	45

Key Votes

1) Increase Def Spnd	FOR	6) Alaska Lands Protect	DNV	11) Delay Auto Pol Cntrl	AGN
2) B-1 Bomber	FOR	7) Water Projects Veto	FOR	12) Sugar Price Escalator	AGN
3) Cargo Preference	AGN	8) Consum Protect Agcy	AGN	13) Pub Fin Cong Cmpgns	AGN
4) Dereg Nat Gas	FOR	9) Common Situs Picket	AGN	14) ERA Ratif Recissn	FOR
5) Kemp-Roth	FOR	10) Labor Law Revision	FOR	15) Prohibt Govt Abrtns	DNV

Election Results

1978 general	John W. Wydler (R-C)	84,882	(58%)	($84,425)
	John W. Matthews (D-L)	60,519	(42%)	($34,334)
1978 primary	John W. Wydler (R-C), unopposed			
1976 general	John W. Wydler (R-C)	110,366	(56%)	($90,568)
	Allard K. Lowenstein (D)	87,868	(44%)	($93,195)

SIXTH DISTRICT

New York's 6th congressional district consists of almost equal parts of the North Shore of Long Island in Nassau County and the Borough of Queens in New York City. The North Shore has long been famous as the home of rich and well-born aristocrats like Theodore Roosevelt as well as nouveaux riches like the fictional Jay Gatsby who tried to imitate the lifestyle. Today huge WASPy estates still sit on peninsulas jutting out into Long Island Sound, as well as in towns like Sands Point and Port Washington. But politically more significant in the 6th district portion of the North Shore are rich, predominantly Jewish suburbs like Great Neck. Despite their wealth, Great Neck and the surrounding communities inevitably produce large Democratic majorities, even for McGovern in 1972. It is inland, to the south, in the less high income, more Protestant suburbs that one finds greater Republican strength in the North Shore.

The boundaries of the Queens portion of the district were drawn by a Republican legislature to include all possible neighborhoods of conservative homeowners and to exclude housing projects and high rise apartment complexes inhabited mainly by Democrats. In the late sixties and early seventies, this was a place where the politics of James Buckley was very popular.

The clear intent of the redistricters was to reelect a Republican Congressman, Seymour Halpern, and defeat a Democrat, Lester Wolff, who were both thrown into this seat. But that intent has been consistently foiled. Halpern, while on the Banking Committee, had gotten $100,000 of loans from various banks without collateral; prudently, he decided to retire in 1972. Wolff managed to defeat the conservative Queens assemblyman that ran only because of his Nassau plurality. Then in 1974, opinion in Queens changed sharply with Watergate. The tradition-minded people who had put their faith in Richard Nixon felt betrayed, and they returned to the party of their fathers, the Democrats. Wolff was a beneficiary of this trend. He was reelected with 67% in 1974, and his percentage has not fallen below 60% since. Now it is the Queens portion of the district where he gets his better percentage. But Wolff has been a beneficiary of luck before: he was one of the Democrats first elected in the Johnson landslide of 1964.

With that kind of seniority, Wolff is now Chairman of the Asia and Pacific Affairs Subcommittee of the Foreign Affairs Committee—a body with an important jurisdiction in these days of openings to China, trade negotiations with Japan, and wars in Vietnam and Cambodia. Wolff has been active in various foreign policy and trade legislative battles; he is also a seasoned traveler, even from before his congressional days, in the Far East.

Census Data Pop. 467,602. Central city, 54%; suburban, 46%. Median family income, $14,483; families above $15,000: 47%; families below $3,000: 4%. Median years education, 12.4.

The Voters

Median voting age 47.
Employment profile White collar, 68%. Blue collar, 22%. Service, 10%. Farm, –%.
Ethnic groups Black, 2%. Total foreign stock, 45%. Italy, 10%; USSR, Germany, 5% each; Poland, Ireland, 4% each; UK, 3%; Austria, 2%, Canada, Greece, 1% each.

Presidential vote

1976	Carter (D)	97,676	(50%)
	Ford (R)	99,497	(50%)
1972	Nixon (R)	140,072	(62%)
	McGovern (D)	84,480	(38%)

Rep. Lester L. Wolff (D) Elected 1964; b. Jan. 4, 1919, New York City; home, Great Neck; NYU, 1939; Jewish.

Career Lecturer, NYU, 1939–41; Army Air Corps, WWII; Head of Marketing Dept., Collegiate Institute, 1945–49; Bd. Chm., Coordinated Marketing Agency, 1945–64; Moderator and Producer, "Between the Lines", TV program, 1948–60; Mgr., U.S. Trade Missions, Philippines, 1962, Malaysia and Hong Kong, 1963.

Offices 2463 RHOB, 202-225-5956. Also 156A Main St., Port Washington 11050, 516-767-4343.

Committees *Foreign Affairs* (7th). Subcommittees: Asia and Pacific Affairs (Chairman); International Security and Scientific Affairs.

Veterans' Affairs (6th). Subcommittees: Special Investigations; Medical Facilities and Benefits.

Group Ratings

	ADA	COPE	PC	RPN	NFU	LCV	CFA	NAB	NSI	ACA	NTU
1978	65	75	58	45	70	–	46	0	44	28	–
1977	70	89	68	67	73	94	60	–	–	24	23
1976	80	87	84	44	92	89	91	18	33	8	30

Key Votes

1) Increase Def Spnd	AGN	6) Alaska Lands Protect	FOR	11) Delay Auto Pol Cntrl	AGN
2) B-1 Bomber	AGN	7) Water Projects Veto	FOR	12) Sugar Price Escalator	AGN
3) Cargo Preference	FOR	8) Consum Protect Agcy	FOR	13) Pub Fin Cong Cmpgns	FOR
4) Dereg Nat Gas	AGN	9) Common Situs Picket	FOR	14) ERA Ratif Recissn	AGN
5) Kemp-Roth	AGN	10) Labor Law Revision	FOR	15) Prohibt Govt Abrtns	AGN

Election Results

1978 general	Lester L. Wolff (D-L)	80,799	(60%)	($39,886)
	Stuart L. Ain (R)	44,304	(33%)	($77,565)
	Howard Horowitz (C)	9,503	(7%)	
1978 primary	Lester L. Wolff (D-L), unopposed			
1976 general	Lester L. Wolff (D-L)	112,422	(65%)	
	Vincent Balletta, Jr. (R)	60,567	(35%)	

SEVENTH DISTRICT

The 7th congressional district of New York in southern Queens takes in a series of middle class neighborhoods of varying ethnic composition. Just north of Kennedy Airport is the two family house neighborhood of Ozone Park, with a large Italian-American population. To the north, along Queens Boulevard, are the high rise apartments of Rego Park, which are predominantly Jewish, though the Forest Hills neighborhood in which they sit, with its old Tudor houses, was originally very WASP. In addition, there are large black neighborhoods here, the slum area of South Jamaica and, overshadowing it, the large middle class areas of Springfield Gardens and St.

Albans. Altogether 37% of the district residents in 1970 were black, which makes them the 7th's largest ethnic group, but Italian-Americans are probably not far behind.

The 7th is a heavily Democratic district, largely because of the Democratic allegiance of its black voters. But the 7th is also, on many issues, conservatively inclined, full of homeowners (not all of them white) who feel oppressed by New York City's high taxes and high cost of living. The whites here were heavily against Mayor John Lindsay and in favor of Senator James Buckley; they switched back to the Democrats in 1974, after Watergate and when the overriding issue in national politics, as perceived here, became whether Washington would bail out New York City.

The 7th district's Congressman, Joseph Addabbo, a Democrat first elected in 1960, has become a very important man in the 96th Congress. With the retirement of George Mahon, first elected in 1934, and Bob Sikes, first elected in 1940, and the political disability of Daniel Flood, first elected in 1944, Addabbo became the Chairman of the Appropriations Subcommittee on Defense. This is the body that handles the Pentagon's appropriations and supplemental appropriations, and its chair is a place of considerable potential influence.

Mahon's instincts on spending generally were parsimonious but his attitude toward the Pentagon was one of friendly cooperation. Addabbo comes from a political background that is very nearly the opposite. He has a solid Democratic voting record on most issues and no particular reputation for penny-pinching. And if he was not marching with peace demonstrators, he was the floor manager of the successful move in 1973 to stop American bombing of Cambodia. Because of turnover, several of the subcommittee's Democrats will be new; but the key question is how forcefully and with what attention to detail Addabbo will wield the chair. Congress at this point is in no particular mood to slash defense expenditures; the question is whether they will be controlled, and the subcommittee is a vital point. Only 53 when he took over the chair, and with a safe seat, Addabbo could be an important figure for many years.

Census Data Pop. 467,449. Central city, 100%; suburban, 0%. Median family income, $11,317; families above $15,000: 30%; families below $3,000: 7%. Median years education, 12.1.

The Voters

Median voting age 45.
Employment profile White collar, 59%. Blue collar, 27%. Service, 14%. Farm, –%.
Ethnic groups Black, 37%. Spanish, 2%. Total foreign stock, 41%. Italy, 7%; USSR, 5%; Poland, Germany, 4% each; Austria, Ireland, 2% each; UK, 1%.

Presidential vote

1976	Carter (D)	98,095	(73%)
	Ford (R)	35,888	(27%)
1972	Nixon (R)	66,305	(41%)
	McGovern (D)	93,806	(59%)

Rep. Joseph P. Addabbo (D) Elected 1960; b. Mar. 17, 1925, Queens; home, Ozone Park; CCNY, 1942–44, St. John's U., LL.B. 1946; Catholic.

Career Practicing atty., 1946–60.

Offices 2256 RHOB, 202-225-3461. Also 96–11 101st Ave., Ozone Park 11416, 212-845-3131.

Committees *Appropriations* (9th). Subcommittees: Defense (Chairman); Military Construction; Treasury, Postal Service, and General Government.

Small Business (5th). Subcommittees: General Oversight and Minority Enterprise; Special Small Business Problems.

Group Ratings

	ADA	COPE	PC	RPN	NFU	LCV	CFA	NAB	NSI	ACA	NTU
1978	70	95	60	18	80	–	64	0	20	12	–
1977	80	91	78	33	82	72	75	–	–	4	20
1976	90	83	97	44	100	90	100	17	10	4	38

Key Votes

1) Increase Def Spnd	AGN	6) Alaska Lands Protect	DNV	11) Delay Auto Pol Cntrl	AGN
2) B-1 Bomber	AGN	7) Water Projects Veto	AGN	12) Sugar Price Escalator	AGN
3) Cargo Preference	FOR	8) Consum Protect Agcy	FOR	13) Pub Fin Cong Cmpgns	FOR
4) Dereg Nat Gas	AGN	9) Common Situs Picket	FOR	14) ERA Ratif Recissn	AGN
5) Kemp-Roth	AGN	10) Labor Law Revision	FOR	15) Prohibt Govt Abrtns	AGN

Election Results

1978 general	Joseph P. Addabbo (D-L-R)	73,066	(95%)	($41,049)
	Mark Elliot Scott (C)	3,935	(5%)	
1978 primary	Joseph P. Addabbo (D-L-R), unopposed			
1976 general	Joseph P. Addabbo (D-L-R), unopposed			($23,342)

EIGHTH DISTRICT

The 8th congressional district of New York encompasses roughly the central part of the borough of Queens. The district's tortuous boundaries were drawn to keep as many conservative and Republican voters as possible within the confines of the adjacent 6th and 9th districts; in effect, the 8th is a district the Republicans conceded to the Democrats. The district radiates in three directions like spokes from a wheel. The hub is Flushing Meadow Park, site of the World's Fairs of 1939–40 and 1964–65, and today the site of Shea Stadium. One of the spokes passes through the middle class, predominantly Jewish neighborhood of Flushing on its way to Long Island Sound. Another proceeds east through Fresh Meadows and a neighborhood with the real estate promoter's name of Utopia, and on toward the Nassau County line. The third spoke moves west from Flushing Meadow to include the high-rise complex of Lefrak City, a small black ghetto in Corona, and the two and four family house neighborhood of lower middle income whites and Hispanics called Jackson Heights.

These seemingly disparate areas all have certain things in common. All have large Jewish populations, as if the redistricters took care to gather together all the major Jewish neighborhoods in Queens. And the district lines, as they writhe about, manage to corral most of the borough's big high rise apartment complexes and many of its public housing projects. Before World War II, most of Queens was given over to neighborhoods of one and two family houses, inhabited by Irish, Italian, and German immigrants. It was a conservative Republican stronghold that happened, technically, to be part of a Democratic central city. But after World War II, most of the growth here has been in high rises, a large percentage of whose occupants are Jewish and liberal Democratic voters. So the 8th district may be said to be postwar Queens—and the reason why this once Republican borough is now almost always Democratic.

The district has lapsed from its Democratic faith occasionally. In the early seventies there were fierce demonstrations here against building low income high rises in Forest Hills; this hurt John Lindsay, George McGovern, and liberal Democrats generally. But the issues of the middle seventies have made voters here, like most New York City area voters, into strong Democrats: Watergate and the question of federal aid to New York City.

Back in 1962, Benjamin Rosenthal was elected to Congress in this district. At that time he looked like another Democratic machine hack: a product of local schools, with a Queens law practice, young enough (38) to be interested in holding the seat for a few terms until a judgeship opened up. But Rosenthal has turned out to be a committed and effective congressman. In the middle sixties he started voting quietly with opponents to the Johnson Administration's war in Vietnam. At the end of the decade he became interested in consumer legislation. By 1970 he became chief sponsor of the bill for a consumer protection agency. That led him into bitter feuds with older members like Chet Holified, Chairman of the Government Operations Committee, and James Delaney of the next-door 9th district, who helped kill the bill. Eventually those feuds were patched up, and the consumer protection agency was passed by both houses, only to be vetoed by President Ford. When Carter reached office, it seemed ripe for passage, but was defeated in the House—one of the first victims of the increasing skepticism toward government programs.

Rosenthal has been more successful in other fields. He was one of the leaders of the original move to cut off arms sales to Turkey in retaliation for its invasion of Cyprus, for example. He was one of the leaders in the House on tough measures to combat the Arab boycott of Israel. Rosenthal is now a subcommittee chairman and a respected, relatively senior member—and still something of a crusader. He is reelected every two years by better than 3–1 margins.

Census Data Pop. 467,691. Central city, 100%; suburban, 0%. Median family income, $12,244; families above $15,000: 35%; families below $3,000: 5%. Median years education, 12.3.

The Voters

Median voting age 45.
Employment profile White collar, 68%. Blue collar, 23%. Service, 9%. Farm, –%.
Ethnic groups Black, 4%. Chinese, 1%. Spanish 2%. Total foreign stock, 59%. Italy, USSR, 8% each; Poland, 6%; Ireland, Germany, 4% each; Austria, 3%; UK, Greece, 2% each; Hungary, Rumania, 1% each.

Presidential vote

1976	Carter (D)	104,158	(67%)
	Ford (R)	52,024	(33%)
1972	Nixon (R)	94,222	(50%)
	McGovern (D)	95,212	(50%)

Rep. Benjamin S. Rosenthal (D) Elected Feb. 20, 1962; b. June 8, 1923, New York City; home, Elmhurst; Long Island U., CCNY, Brooklyn Law School, LL.B. 1949, LL.M. 1952; Jewish.

Career Army, WWII; Practicing atty.

Offices 2372 RHOB, 202-225-2601. Also U.S.P.O. 41–65 Main St., Flushing 11351, 212-939-8200.

Committees *Government Operations* (5th). Subcommittees: Commerce, Consumer and Monetary Affairs (Chairman).

Foreign Affairs (5th). Subcommittees: Europe and the Middle East; Inter-American Relations.

Group Ratings

	ADA	COPE	PC	RPN	NFU	LCV	CFA	NAB	NSI	ACA	NTU
1978	90	94	90	33	67	–	86	0	10	8	–
1977	90	87	78	54	80	93	65	–	–	0	20
1976	100	87	97	56	83	92	81	18	0	0	27

Key Votes

1) Increase Def Spnd	AGN	6) Alaska Lands Protect	FOR	11) Delay Auto Pol Cntrl	AGN
2) B-1 Bomber	AGN	7) Water Projects Veto	AGN	12) Sugar Price Escalator	AGN
3) Cargo Preference	AGN	8) Consum Protect Agcy	FOR	13) Pub Fin Cong Cmpgns	FOR
4) Dereg Nat Gas	AGN	9) Common Situs Picket	FOR	14) ERA Ratif Recissn	AGN
5) Kemp-Roth	AGN	10) Labor Law Revision	FOR	15) Prohibt Govt Abrtns	AGN

Election Results

1978 general	Benjamin S. Rosenthal (D-L)	74,872	(83%)	($30,220)
	Albert Lemishow (R)	15,165	(17%)	
1978 primary	Benjamin S. Rosenthal (D-L), unopposed			
1976 general	Benjamin S. Rosenthal (D-L)	106,935	(78%)	($21,788)
	Albert Lemishow (R-C)	30,191	(22%)	($1,875)

NINTH DISTRICT

It can be said with some certainty that the durable Archie Bunker lives in the 9th congressional district of New York. The aerial shot taken by TV cameramen of Archie's neighborhood shows the kind of aging, though still neatly maintained, one and two family houses that line the streets of Jackson Heights, Long Island City, Ridgewood, or Glendale, Queens. Moreover, Archie's views are a fairly accurate, if stylized, portrayal of attitudes which are often a majority and otherwise a large minority in this district. Geographically, the 9th is the Queens district closest to Manhattan's chic and liberal Upper East Side—but it is far from it in spirit. People here in Queens refer to Manhattan as "the City," as if it were some alien place; to many of them it is.

The boundaries of the 9th district were carefully drawn to include the middle class, heavily Catholic Queens neighborhoods of conservative homeowners—people who live on salaries or wages that make middle class respectability hard to maintain in New York City. It is ironic—or at least a reversal of the conventional wisdom we inherit from the New Deal era—that the wealthy Upper East Side voted 58% for McGovern in 1972, while across the East River, the factory workers and waiters and doormen and clerks living in Long Island City and Sunnyside and Astoria went 73% for Richard Nixon: the rich voting for economic change, the relatively poor for the status quo.

The ethnic composition is important in shaping attitudes here. There are few blacks or Puerto Ricans in the 9th district, though many of its white homeowners live in neighborhoods near the Brooklyn line, on the other side of which there are large ghetto communities. But there have been recent migrants here: Greeks, Arabs, Colombians. Many of these, particularly those from Latin America, are illegal immigrants, and of necessity they are practitioners of the work ethic. All these groups bring from their native culture a taste for enterprise and a sense that effort will be rewarded; they did not come here to get on the welfare rolls.

This part of Queens was not always so enthusiastically Republican as it was in 1972, nor did it maintain its enthusiasm for long. The historic allegiance of at least a large minority of its residents was to the Democratic Party of Franklin Roosevelt and John Kennedy. But during the time the Democrats appeared more interested in ending the Vietnam war and advocating the interests of blacks and Puerto Ricans than they were in the welfare of people like Archie Bunker, the 9th shifted solidly to the Republicans. And in the years the district's new-found political heroes, Richard Nixon and Spiro Agnew, were revealed to be the kind of criminals they loved to denounce, the 9th shifted back toward the Democrats.

For 32 years the Congressman from this district was James Delaney, a Democrat who generally matched his constituents' changes of mood. His most significant legislative achievement is the Delaney Amendment, which prohibits the sale of any drug known to produce cancer in animals. It has been attacked by the drug industry, but probably—for we do not know all the answers here—has saved quite a few lives. In 1977 Delaney became Chairman of the House Rules Committee and, although he had dissented over the years from a number of Democratic positions, worked closely with Speaker O'Neill and made the committee a more effective and rational instrument of majority policy.

Delaney retired in 1978, and the Republicans hoped to pick up the 9th district whose boundaries they had designed for just this eventuality. They had a popular local candidate in Assemblyman Alfred DelliBovi, who despite his youth had served eight years in the legislature. But Democratic nominee Geraldine Ferraro had greater strength. She won her primary with an absolute majority; her experience as a prosecutor gave her good law and order credentials. Her campaign was well financed, and she was able to overcome the handicap of endorsing government-paid abortions for the poor. She won a decisive 55% victory, and appears headed for a long congressional career.

Census Data Pop. 467,207. Central city, 100%; suburban, 0%. Median family income, $10,657; families above $15,000: 24%; families below $3,000: 7%. Median years education, 10.8.

The Voters

Median voting age 48.
Employment profile White collar, 53%. Blue collar, 34%. Service, 13%. Farm, –%.
Ethnic groups Black, 2%. Spanish, 2%. Total foreign stock, 55%. Italy, 14%; Germany, 8%; Poland, USSR, 3% each; Austria, Greece, UK, 2% each; Czechoslovakia, Hungary, 1% each.

Presidential vote

1976	Carter (D)	63,412	(46%)
	Ford (R)	75,415	(54%)
1972	Nixon (R)	128,699	(73%)
	McGovern (D)	46,700	(27%)

Rep. Geraldine A. Ferraro (D) Elected 1978; b. Aug. 26, 1935, Newburgh; home, Forest Hills; Marymount Col., 1956, Fordham U., J.D. 1960; Catholic.

Career Practicing atty., 1961–74; Chief of Special Victims' Bureau and Confidential Unit, Ofc. of N.Y. Dist. Atty., 1974–78.

Offices 1725 LHOB, 202-225-3965. Also 4702 47th St., Woodside 11377, 212-826-5714.

Committees *Post Office and Civil Service* (11th). Subcommittees: Postal Operations and Services; Census and Population.

Public Works and Transportation (24th). Subcommittees: Surface Transportation; Water Resources.

Group Ratings: Newly Elected

Key Votes: Newly Elected

Election Results

1978 general	Geraldine A. Ferraro (D)	51,350	(55%)	($382,074)
	Alfred A. Dellibovi (R-C)	42,108	(45%)	($110,679)
1978 primary	Geraldine A. Ferraro (D)	10,254	(53%)	
	Thomas J. Manton (D)	5,499	(28%)	($23,746)
	One other (D)	3,603	(19%)	
1976 general	James J. Delaney (D-R-C), unopposed			($41,121)

TENTH DISTRICT

The 10th congressional district of New York covers the east Bronx and the northern fringes of Queens. It is the part of New York the Manhattan-bound traveler sees coming in on the taxi from LaGuardia or from the expressways or parkways from Connecticut. Geographically you are not far from Manhattan, but culturally and politically the distance is usually very great. These areas are not poverty-stricken, and few of the streets are run down; people here tend to be homeowners, and they work to keep up their property. But the houses seem to be made in the cheapest way possible, with no regard whatever for appearance: row after row of two- and four-family houses, all occupying the maximum space allowed by the zoning code.

The 10th district does not include the slums of the Bronx; its boundaries are roughly the edge of the borough's black and Puerto Rican ghetto. The ethnic flavor of the district, rather, is Italian-American; this may well be the most heavily Italian congressional district in the United States. Its Congressman has not only an Italian name, Mario Biaggi, but also a background that is typical of many Italian-Americans in New York City. Biaggi was a police officer for 23 years, and when he retired he was the most decorated officer on the New York police force. He was an attorney—he had finished law school at night, like so many ambitious city employees in New York—but his real interest was politics. In 1968 he was elected to Congress from the predecessor of the 10th district, then entirely in the Bronx.

In his first years in the House, Biaggi seemed to be a kind of urban populist with a law and order accent. He voted with Democrats on most issues and went along with the major lobbying groups on the committees on which he served: organized labor on Education and Labor and the maritime industry and unions on Merchant Marine and Fisheries. At home, however, he emphasized the issue of crime, and helped to express the hostility his constituents felt toward the Manhattan-based liberalism of Mayor John Lindsay. Biaggi appeared likely to be elected Mayor himself in 1973. He was a strong contender for the Democratic nomination, and he had the Conservative nomination as well. But in April 1973 newspapers charged that Biaggi had lied when he had said he had not taken the Fifth Amendment before a grand jury. Brazenly Biaggi sued to get some, but not all, of the grand jury records made public; the judge, not to be toyed with, revealed them all. They showed that Biaggi was lying, and his law and order candidacy collapsed.

Even after the rout, Biaggi retained a following, particularly in Italian-American neighborhoods like those which are so important in the 10th district. And he has not had serious opposition in elections since then—though the Conservatives, who bent their principles to endorse him in 1973 and then were stuck with him as their candidate in the general election, have not given him their endorsement since. Biaggi has considerable seniority now, but he is not a particularly important figure in the House. He was caught trying to compete in the big leagues with only minor league talent, and the spark has gone out of his career. The enthusiasm seems to be gone in his district, too; his failings helped convince his constituents that they had no special competence to lead New York City, which is what they thought when they were fighting Lindsay and Manhattan only a few years ago.

Census Data Pop. 474,745. Central city, 100%; suburban, 0%. Median family income, $9,988; families above $15,000: 22%; families below $3,000: 9%. Median years education, 10.7.

The Voters

Median voting age 45.
Employment profile White collar, 52%. Blue collar, 34%. Service, 14%. Farm, -%.
Ethnic groups Black, 13%. Spanish, 9%. Total foreign stock, 47%. Italy, 17%; Ireland, 6%; Germany, 3%; USSR, Poland, Greece, UK, 2% each; Austria, 1%.

Presidential vote

1976	Carter (D)	75,681	(57%)
	Ford (R)	56,741	(43%)
1972	Nixon (R)	103,372	(63%)
	McGovern (D)	60,343	(37%)

Rep. Mario Biaggi (D) Elected 1968; b. Oct. 26, 1917, New York City; home, Bronx; N.Y. Law School, LL.B. 1963; Catholic.

Career Letter carrier, U.S.P.O., 1936–42; N.Y. City Police Dept., 1942–65; Community Relations Specialist, N.Y. State Div. of Housing, 1961–63; Asst. to the N.Y. State Secy. of State, 1961–65; Practicing atty., 1966–; Pres., Natl. Police Officers Assn., 1967.

Offices 2428 RHOB, 202-225-2464. Also 2004 Williamsbridge Rd., Bronx 10461, 212-931-0100.

Committees *Education and Labor* (9th). Subcommittees: Labor-Management Relations; Post-secondary Education; Select Education.

Merchant Marine and Fisheries (5th). Subcommittees: Coast Guard and Navigation (Chairman); Fish and Wildlife; Merchant Marine; Panama Canal.

Group Ratings

	ADA	COPE	PC	RPN	NFU	LCV	CFA	NAB	NSI	ACA	NTU
1978	55	75	55	44	70	–	59	9	78	40	–
1977	70	91	60	15	80	57	80	–	–	8	19
1976	50	83	74	12	82	60	73	17	71	19	23

Key Votes

1) Increase Def Spnd	AGN	6) Alaska Lands Protect	DNV	11) Delay Auto Pol Cntrl	AGN
2) B-1 Bomber	FOR	7) Water Projects Veto	FOR	12) Sugar Price Escalator	AGN
3) Cargo Preference	FOR	8) Consum Protect Agcy	FOR	13) Pub Fin Cong Cmpgns	AGN
4) Dereg Nat Gas	AGN	9) Common Situs Picket	FOR	14) ERA Ratif Recissn	AGN
5) Kemp-Roth	AGN	10) Labor Law Revision	FOR	15) Prohibt Govt Abrtns	FOR

Election Results

1978 general	Mario Biaggi (D-L-R)	77,979	(95%)	($71,493)
	Carmen Ricciardi (C)	4,082	(5%)	
1978 primary	Mario Biaggi (D-L-R), unopposed			
1976 general	Mario Biaggi (D-R)	106,222	(95%)	($66,271)
	Joanne S. Fuchs (C)	5,868	(5%)	($0)

ELEVENTH DISTRICT

The 11th congressional district of New York is the southeastern corner of Brooklyn, the extreme southern and southeastern edges of Queens, and the Rockaway Peninsula. Separated from each other by marshy Jamaica Bay, and circling Kennedy Airport like a donut, these are geographically disparate areas and the neighborhoods contained within them are diverse. East New York in Brooklyn is an aging Italian community, not far from the black ghetto of Brownsville, which is in such miserable condition that it is being rapidly abandoned. To the south, Canarsie and Flatlands are middle class Italian and Jewish communities. These two areas were developed on marshland sometime after the rest of Brooklyn; here in 1970 the borough's first suburban-style shopping center was opened. More recently Canarsie has been embroiled in controversy over a school busing plan. The Rockaway Peninsula, separating Jamaica Bay from the ocean, is largely Jewish, with a black ghetto at one end. North of Kennedy Airport, entirely cut off from the rest of the district, is the middle class black neighborhood of Springfield Gardens.

Historically this seat has been within the gift of the Brooklyn Democratic machine. From 1936 to 1966 it was represented by Eugene Keogh, who retired not because of age but because he wanted to make more money; he left his name on Keogh Plans, which allow self-employed individuals in effect to create their own pension funds. Keogh's successor was Frank Brasco, a young machine stalwart who seemed likely to match his tenure. But in 1974 Brasco was convicted of taking bribes and sentenced to jail.

This time the much overrated Brooklyn organization was unable to hold the seat. The winner was James Scheuer, a former Congressman from the faraway Bronx (1965–73), defeated in his primary in 1972 and now a Rockaway resident. A wealthy real estate developer, Scheuer came to office with a reputation as a liberal, but like so many of his constituents he supported Henry Jackson in the 1976 presidential primary. Scheuer was one of the leaders of the ultimately unsuccessful fight to prevent the Concorde from landing at Kennedy Airport; the problem was that when the plane was finally allowed to land, the sound did not seem so much louder than that of other planes. The fight was popular here, however: most people in the 11th district seldom fly anywhere, much less to London or Paris in a Concorde. Scheuer was one of the 1974 freshmen whose presence did so much to alter the tone and substance of the Commerce Committee; in 1979 he won election as a subcommittee chairman.

Census Data Pop. 469,790. Central city, 100%; suburban, 0%. Median family income, $10,834; families above $15,000: 26%; families below $3,000: 9%. Median years education, 11.7.

The Voters

Median voting age 43.
Employment profile White collar, 58%. Blue collar, 31%. Service, 11%. Farm, –%.
Ethnic groups Black, 17%. Spanish, 6%. Total foreign stock, 41%. Italy, 9%; USSR, 8%; Poland, 6%; Germany, Austria, Ireland, 2% each; UK, 1%.

Presidential vote

1976	Carter (D)	93,240	(70%)
	Ford (R)	39,937	(30%)
1972	Nixon (R)	80,662	(52%)
	McGovern (D)	75,129	(48%)

Rep. James H. Scheuer (D) Elected 1974; b. Feb. 6, 1920, New York City; home, Neponsit; Harvard Business School, 1943, Swarthmore Col., A.B. 1945, Columbia U., LL.B. 1948; Jewish.

Career Army Air Corps, WWII; Economist, U.S. Foreign Economic Admin., 1945–46; Mbr., Legal Staff, Ofc. of Price Stabilization, 1951–52; Pres., N.Y. City Citizens Housing and Planning Cncl.; U.S. House of Reps., 1965–73; Pres., Natl. Housing Conf., 1972–74.

Offices 2402 RHOB, 202-225-5471. Also 1943 Rockaway Parkway, Brooklyn 11236, 212-251-2222.

Committees *Interstate and Foreign Commerce* (8th). Subcommittees: Consumer Protection and Finance (Chairman).

Science and Technology (5th). Subcommittees: Science, Research, and Technology.

Group Ratings

	ADA	COPE	PC	RPN	NFU	LCV	CFA	NAB	NSI	ACA	NTU
1978	70	85	70	45	70	–	73	0	20	12	–
1977	85	91	85	54	75	87	85	–	–	15	33
1976	90	83	85	47	92	87	100	18	0	0	25

Key Votes

1) Increase Def Spnd	AGN	6) Alaska Lands Protect	DNV	11) Delay Auto Pol Cntrl	AGN
2) B-1 Bomber	AGN	7) Water Projects Veto	AGN	12) Sugar Price Escalator	AGN
3) Cargo Preference	AGN	8) Consum Protect Agcy	FOR	13) Pub Fin Cong Cmpgns	FOR
4) Dereg Nat Gas	AGN	9) Common Situs Picket	FOR	14) ERA Ratif Recissn	AGN
5) Kemp-Roth	AGN	10) Labor Law Revision	FOR	15) Prohibt Govt Abrtns	AGN

Election Results

1978 general	James H. Scheuer (D-L)	58,997	(78%)	($24,861)
	Kenneth Huhn (R-C)	16,206	(22%)	
1978 primary	James H. Scheuer (D-L), unopposed			
1976 general	James H. Scheuer (D)	84,770	(77%)	($37,141)
	Arthur Cuccia (R)	19,203	(17%)	($0)
	Bryan F. Levinson (C)	6,316	(6%)	($9,761)

TWELFTH DISTRICT

Celebrity status is fleeting, in politics as in other businesses, and an example is the career of the Congresswoman from the 12th district of New York, Shirley Chisholm. A few years ago she was well known as the obstreperous freshman, rebelling against the powers that be—the image she projected when she entitled her autobiography *Unbought and Unbossed*. Her refusal to knuckle under to male political leaders in her home area of Bedford-Stuyvesant had helped her assemble the group of volunteers which elected her to the New York Assembly in 1964 and to Congress in 1968. In 1972 she became a national figure as the first black woman to run for president. She ran in most of the primaries—and even joined the stop McGovern forces—clean through to the national convention. But it was only a symbolic effort. She failed to win 10% of the vote in any state, and not even her supporters gave much thought to the kind of president she would make. She did, however, get treated on a par with other candidates on television debates and on the convention podium.

During the campaign Chisholm often complained that people were not taking her seriously enough and that she was as qualified as the others. But around Capitol Hill many people sympathetic to her complained that she had done little legislative work, preferring the glamor of the lecture circuit to the hard work of the mark-up session in the committee room. In the years since 1972 Chisholm has become less of a national celebrity and more of a working legislator. She pushed through a law including domestic workers in the coverage of the federal minimum wage law. She won a seat on the House Rules Committee, and there she usually votes with the Democratic leadership.

Chisholm has talked from time to time about retiring; it sounds more like an effort to get people to pay more attention than a serious projection of what she is likely to do. When she was first elected, in 1968, her district included all of the Bedford-Stuyvesant section of Brooklyn; its lines had been drawn specifically to elect Brooklyn's first black member of Congress. For 1974, an ill-advised lawsuit forced the readjustment of the Brooklyn district lines, supposedly to produce two black-and-Puerto Rican majority districts. In that respect the effort was entirely unsuccessful, for minority participation is so low here—lower in New York City than anywhere else in the country—that blacks are easily outvoted by others.

The drawers of the new district lines hoped that Chisholm would run in the 46% black 14th district, but she wisely declined; no more than one-quarter of the actual voters there are black. Instead she picked the new 12th, which includes the eastern half of Bedford-Stuyvesant, the huge Brooklyn ghetto; Bushwick, an old Italian neighborhood which is rapidly becoming majority black; and Williamsburgh and Greenpoint, old ethnic Brooklyn neighborhoods whose aged residents are hostile to whatever they consider the forces for change. The real politics here is in the Democratic primary. Chisholm was challenged in 1976 by Assemblyman Samuel Wright and was hard pressed to win. Wright was later indicted, but Chisholm will have to work her constituency hard in the eighties as she did in the sixties and seventies in order to continue to win.

Census Data Pop. 467,726. Central city, 100%; suburban, 0%. Median family income, $6,432; families above $15,000: 7%; families below $3,000: 19%. Median years education, 9.6.

The Voters

Median voting age 38.
Employment profile White collar, 37%. Blue collar, 45%. Service, 18%. Farm, –%.
Ethnic groups Black, 54%. Spanish, 20%. Total foreign stock, 16%. Italy, 6%; Poland, 2%.

Presidential vote

1976	Carter (D)	49,550	(82%)
	Ford (R)	10,513	(18%)
1972	Nixon (R)	NA	
	McGovern (D)	NA	

Rep. Shirley Chisholm (D) Elected 1968; b. Nov. 30, 1924, Brooklyn; home, Brooklyn; Brooklyn Col., B.A. 1946, Columbia U., M.A. 1952, Methodist.

Career Nursery school teacher and dir., 1946–53; Dir., Hamilton Madison Child Care Ctr., 1954–59; Educ. Consultant, N.Y. City Div. of Day Care, 1959–64; N.Y. State Assembly, 1964–68.

Offices 2182 RHOB, 202-225-6231. Also 1360 Fulton St., Suite 400, Brooklyn 11216, 212-330-7588.

Committees *Rules* (6th).

Group Ratings

	ADA	COPE	PC	RPN	NFU	LCV	CFA	NAB	NSI	ACA	NTU
1978	100	90	80	30	80	–	77	0	0	7	–
1977	95	95	78	45	82	77	70	–	–	0	35
1976	80	86	87	60	92	84	91	9	0	5	33

Key Votes

1) Increase Def Spnd	AGN	6) Alaska Lands Protect	FOR	11) Delay Auto Pol Cntrl	AGN
2) B-1 Bomber	AGN	7) Water Projects Veto	AGN	12) Sugar Price Escalator	FOR
3) Cargo Preference	FOR	8) Consum Protect Agcy	FOR	13) Pub Fin Cong Cmpgns	FOR
4) Dereg Nat Gas	AGN	9) Common Situs Picket	FOR	14) ERA Ratif Recissn	AGN
5) Kemp-Roth	AGN	10) Labor Law Revision	FOR	15) Prohibt Govt Abrtns	AGN

Election Results

1978 general	Shirley Chisholm (D-L)	25,697	(88%)	($14,498)
	Charles Gibbs (R)	3,580	(12%)	
1978 primary	Shirley Chisholm (D-L), unopposed			
1976 general	Shirley Chisholm (D-L)	43,203	(89%)	
	Horance L. Morancie (R)	5,336	(11%)	

THIRTEENTH DISTRICT

The 13th congressional district of New York, in south central Brooklyn, might be called the Ocean Parkway district: it takes in terrain from both sides of that thoroughfare as it makes its way from Prospect Park to Coney Island. There is a large Italian-American community in Bensonhurst, most of which was removed from the district by the 1974 redistricting; still the 13th, according to the Census figures, is one of the most heavily Italian-American districts in the nation. But most of the neighborhoods here, from Midwood in the north, through the streets lined with low-rise apartment buildings along the Parkway, to Sheepshead Bay, Brighton Beach, and Coney Island in the south, are heavily Jewish. With Flatbush, most of which is in the 16th district, the 13th is the heart of Jewish Brooklyn. Though no reliable data exist, the 13th is probably the nation's most heavily Jewish district, and most likely the 13th and the 16th are the only Jewish-majority districts in the nation. It is, of course, overwhelmingly Democratic by tradition and in most, but not all, elections.

As well as being the heart of Jewish Brooklyn, the 13th district has always been one of the bastions of support for the Democratic machine here. With its patronage jobs in the Brooklyn courts and Borough Hall, the machine used to be able to man all the election districts here with faithful—and hungry—precinct workers who would tell their neighbors who it would be good to vote for; and generally they did. For these are not the wealthy, trendy, assimilated Jews of Manhattan's Upper East Side. These are people who own small stores or work for the city or teach school, and who have been struggling to send their children through college and to accumulate enough for a decent retirement for themselves. There has seldom been the time here, or the energy, for a reform politics; elections, like everything else, have been a business—and a tough one.

So from the time the district was created in its present form in 1944 until quite recently the district was represented by machine stalwarts: first Leo Rayfield (1945–47), who became a federal judge; then Abraham Multer (1947–68), who finally got his state judgeship despite talk that he had been engaged in unsavory banking practices in the Bahamas; and then Bertram Podell (1968–75), who ended up before the bench rather than on it. In 1973 Podell was indicted for taking $41,000 to get the Civil Aeronautics Board to award a Bahama route to a Florida airline; after he lost the primary in 1974 he pled guilty.

The winner was 34-year-old Stephen Solarz, elected to the Assembly six years before over a machine candidate and now the victor over the machine again. Solarz became a member of the Foreign Affairs Committee, and of course is one of its strongest supporters of aid to Israel. In 1979 he became Chairman of the Africa Subcommittee—an important assignment in a time when much of Africa is in turmoil. With a liberal voting record and an independent background, Solarz has had no difficulty winning reelection. He also has some credentials for a possible candidacy for the Senate in 1980, and reportedly has some interest in running for Jacob Javits's seat.

Census Data Pop. 468,726. Central city, 100%; suburban, 0%. Median family income, $10,294; families above $15,000: 25%; families below $3,000: 9%. Median years education, 11.2.

The Voters

Median voting age 50.
Employment profile White collar, 64%. Blue collar, 28%. Service, 8%. Farm, –%.
Ethnic groups Black, 2%. Spanish, 2%. Total foreign stock, 61%. Italy, 16%; USSR, 14%; Poland, 9%; Austria, 4%; Germany, Hungary, Rumania, 2% each; Ireland, UK, Czechoslovakia, 1% each.

Presidential vote

1976	Carter (D)	112,044	(72%)
	Ford (R)	44,176	(28%)
1972	Nixon (R)	NA	
	McGovern (D)	NA	

Rep. Stephen J. Solarz (D) Elected 1974; b. Sept. 12, 1940, New York City; home, Brooklyn; Brandeis U., A.B. 1962, Columbia U., M.A. 1967; Jewish.

Career N.Y. State Assembly, 1968–74.

Offices 1530 LHOB, 202-225-2361. Also 1628 Kings Hwy., Brooklyn 11229, 212-965-5100.

Committees *Foreign Affairs* (11th). Subcommittees: Africa (Chairman); Asian and Pacific Affairs.

Budget (11th). Subcommittees: Human and Community Resources; Inflation; Defense and International Affairs.

Group Ratings

	ADA	COPE	PC	RPN	NFU	LCV	CFA	NAB	NSI	ACA	NTU
1978	80	85	78	42	80	–	68	0	20	13	–
1977	90	86	88	46	83	95	90	–	–	4	23
1976	95	87	98	50	83	98	100	9	20	0	25

Key Votes

1) Increase Def Spnd	AGN	6) Alaska Lands Protect	DNV	11) Delay Auto Pol Cntrl	AGN
2) B-1 Bomber	AGN	7) Water Projects Veto	FOR	12) Sugar Price Escalator	AGN
3) Cargo Preference	FOR	8) Consum Protect Agcy	FOR	13) Pub Fin Cong Cmpgns	FOR
4) Dereg Nat Gas	AGN	9) Common Situs Picket	FOR	14) ERA Ratif Recissn	AGN
5) Kemp-Roth	AGN	10) Labor Law Revision	FOR	15) Prohibt Govt Abrtns	AGN

Election Results

1978 general	Stephen J. Solarz (D-L)	68,837	(81%)	($21,565)
	Max Carasso (R-C)	16,002	(19%)	
1978 primary	Stephen J. Solarz (D-L), unopposed			
1976 general	Stephen J. Solarz (D-L)	110,624	(84%)	($23,201)
	Jack Dobosh (R-C)	21,600	(16%)	($914)

FOURTEENTH DISTRICT

The 14th congressional district of New York, in Brooklyn, is about as polyglot an area as you can find in the United States. The district extends along the Brooklyn waterfront from the Italian neighborhood of Red Hook to the Queens border, past the renovated brownstones of Brooklyn Heights and Cobble Hill, with their affluent (and politically liberal) residents. To the east is downtown Brooklyn, with a skyline that would be impressive anywhere but in New York; it is paled here by the vista from Brooklyn Heights of lower Manhattan. Inland the 14th extends far past the transitional Fort Greene area into Bedford-Stuyvesant. North are parts of Greenpoint and Williamsburgh, with large Orthodox and Hasidic Jewish and Puerto Rican communities in uneasy proximity.

If you were to look at the Census statistics about the 14th, you would be seriously mistaken about its political makeup—as were the people who brought the lawsuit to form its present boundaries. In 1970 some 46% of the district's residents were black, 18% were Puerto Rican; but neither of these groups has much clout here, for the simple reason that they scarcely vote at all. In the 14th, the voting blocs which really matter are the Italians in Red Hook and South Brooklyn, some of the old Hasidic Jews, and a relatively few middle class blacks. These are the people who vote in Democratic primaries and who therefore control the congressional representation of the district.

For thirty years the 14th and its predecessors were represented by John Rooney, a crusty Democrat who chaired the Appropriations Subcommittee on State, Commerce, and the Judiciary; for years he terrorized the State Department and coddled the FBI. Rooney had tough primary challenges in 1968, 1970, and 1972, but always withstood them—helped by some questionable tactics. Ill and tired, Rooney retired in 1974.

His successor is Frederick Richmond, who ran against Rooney in 1968 and later supported him. Richmond's secret weapon was money—his own—and he was willing to spend plenty of it. He had spent $200,000 on his 1968 campaign, and later a foundation he controlled poured large sums of money into areas that happened to be within the boundaries of the 14th district. By the time he ran in 1974, he had machine and some reform support, and was an easy winner. Richmond's electoral clout was tested even more in 1978. He was arrested in the summer of that year and charged with soliciting a young man for sex acts. The charges were dropped after he pleaded not guilty and participated in the first offender program of the D.C. courts. In the district his largesse paid off, and he beat a black primary opponent by a solid margin.

Richmond is a member of the Agriculture Committee in the House—one of the few members from urban areas who has stayed on that body. There is a certain amount of good sense in that: Agriculture controls the food stamp program and a variety of policies which affect food prices and thus are of interest to even the most urban of citizens. Richmond himself heads a subcommittee on consumer issues and nutrition, and has gotten much publicity on those subjects.

Census Data Pop. 467,735. Central city, 100%; suburban, 0%. Median family income, $6,874; families above $15,000: 11%; families below $3,000: 17%. Median years education, 10.3.

The Voters

Median voting age 39.
Employment profile White collar, 47%. Blue collar, 37%. Service, 16%. Farm, –%.
Ethnic groups Black, 46%. Spanish, 18%. Total foreign stock, 28%. Italy, 5%; Poland, 2%; USSR, Hungary, 1% each.

Presidential vote

1976	Carter (D)	63,370	(78%)
	Ford (R)	17,735	(22%)
1972	Nixon (R)	NA	
	McGovern (D)	NA	

Rep. Frederick W. Richmond (D) Elected 1974; b. Nov. 15, 1923, Mattapan, Mass., home, Brooklyn; Harvard U., 1942–43, Boston U., B.A. 1945.

Career Navy, WWII; Pres., Greater N.Y. Urban League, 1959–64; Walco Natl. Corp., 1960–74; Bd. Chm., Carnegie Hall Corp., 1960–74; N.Y. City Human Rights Commissioner, 1964–70; Budget Dir., N.Y. State Cncl. on the Arts, 1965–74; N.Y. City Taxi and Limousine Commissioner, 1970–72; N.Y. City Cncl., 1973–74.

Offices 1707 LHOB, 202-225-5936. Also 1368 Fulton St., Brooklyn 11216, 212-636-4707.

Committees *Agriculture* (9th). Subcommittees: Domestic Marketing, Consumer Relations, and Nutrition (Chairman); Family Farms, Rural Development, and Special Studies.

Small Business (12th). Subcommittees: General Oversight and Minority Enterprise; Access to Equity Capital and Business Opportunities.

Group Ratings

	ADA	COPE	PC	RPN	NFU	LCV	CFA	NAB	NSI	ACA	NTU
1978	95	95	90	40	90	–	77	0	0	5	–
1977	95	91	83	31	83	98	75	–	–	0	39
1976	95	87	93	56	92	100	81	17	0	0	30

Key Votes

1) Increase Def Spnd	AGN	6) Alaska Lands Protect	DNV	11) Delay Auto Pol Cntrl	AGN
2) B-1 Bomber	AGN	7) Water Projects Veto	AGN	12) Sugar Price Escalator	AGN
3) Cargo Preference	FOR	8) Consum Protect Agcy	FOR	13) Pub Fin Cong Cmpgns	FOR
4) Dereg Nat Gas	AGN	9) Common Situs Picket	FOR	14) ERA Ratif Recissn	AGN
5) Kemp-Roth	AGN	10) Labor Law Revision	FOR	15) Prohibt Govt Abrtns	AGN

Election Results

1978 general	Frederick W. Richmond (D-L)	31,339	(81%)	($419,663)
	Arthur Bramwell (R)	7,516	(19%)	
1978 primary	Frederick W. Richmond (D)	11,130	(50%)	
	Bernard F. Gifford (D)	7,243	(32%)	($86,089)
	Two others (D)	3,979	(18%)	
1976 general	Frederick W. Richmond (D-L)	55,723	(86%)	($36,991)
	Frank X. Gargiulo (R-C)	8,977	(14%)	($500)

FIFTEENTH DISTRICT

To many who have never seen it, Brooklyn means nonstop slums, the tenement apartment of Ralph and Alice Kramden, and the fear of lurking crime. This is not an accurate, or at least an entirely accurate, picture. Brooklyn has all the diversity one might expect of a city of 2.4 million people. If Brooklyn has some of the nation's most fearsome slums—and it does in Brownsville and parts of Bedford-Stuyvesant—New York's largest borough also has neighborhoods of comfortable, expensive homes. Although its downtown streets are grimy, the parks of Brooklyn are green and its yacht harbors are filled with wind-blown sails and spinnakers. Nothing is dainty about Brooklyn, but in its pleasant middle class neighborhoods, the fear of crime is more academic than residents seem to want to admit. In short, a few trees do grow here.

A disproportionate share of Brooklyn's middle class neighborhoods lie within the boundaries of New York's 15th congressional district. The 15th begins amidst the newly renovated brownstones of Park Slope, a neighborhood just off Prospect Park—one laid out by the architects of Central Park and often considered their masterpiece. To the south is the Sunset Park neighborhood, which has the largest concentration of Norwegian-Americans between Oslo and Minneapolis. In the same area is Borough Park, a middle class Irish and Italian area. Below that, where New York Harbor spills into the Atlantic and the Verrazano Narrows Bridge arches over to Staten Island, is Bay Ridge.

Bay Ridge is a couple of steps up the ladder for middle class Brooklynites of Irish and Italian ancestry. It has some impressive housing, but much of it looks like Tony Manero's neighborhood in *Saturday Night Fever*. Bay Ridge is thus not the highest income neighborhood in Brooklyn, but it is politically the most conservative. People here take their cues from the *Daily News*, not the *Times* or the *Wall Street Journal*. In most elections, this is the most reliably Republican part of New York City. It is also an area whose mores and cultural attitudes have traditionally been conservative and hostile to Manhattan's. Indeed such attitudes were of cardinal importance throughout the 15th district in the late sixties and early seventies, and have moved the entire district closer to the Republican column in many elections.

Until 1960 what is now the 14th was a Republican stronghold in congressional elections. Then the Democrats nominated a Catholic, and a 41-year-old lawyer named Hugh Carey pulled a major upset and was elected to Congress. Despite Republican redistrictings and conservative trends, Carey continued to win here; he was one of the few New York politicians who could win Irish working class votes and at the same time maintain a voting record acceptable to ideological liberals. He switched from hawk to dove, for example, way back in 1966, reportedly from listening to the arguments of several of his twelve children.

Carey always had the ambition—and aptitude and talent, if he could get well known—for higher office. He actually ran for city council president, a mostly honorific post which for some reason gives its holder great publicity, in 1969. Between bouts of city politics, he became something of a power in the House. In 1971 he led the Brooklyn delegation in supporting Hale Boggs for majority leader; as a reward for being on the winning side, he got a seat on Ways and Means. There he was a major pusher behind revenue sharing and also urged, unsuccessfully, tax breaks for parents with children in private schools.

Then in 1974 Carey decided to run for governor—and won. That left his House seat up for grabs and in another year, when a Republican president wasn't being driven from office for criminal conduct, the Republicans might have made a race of it. But in 1974 the most difficult contest was in the Democratic primary, and the winner there was the machine choice, Leo Zeferetti. He had not come up the usual Brooklyn clubhouse ladder; instead, like the Bronx's Mario Biaggi, he was a well-known cop—in his case president of the Correction Officers Benevolent Association—who moved into electoral politics. Zeferetti won that first general election with 58%. He has served on the Education and Labor Committee, where he was a firm vote for organized labor; and on Merchant Marine and Fisheries, where he voted to maintain the elaborate system of subsidies to business and labor which keep the maritime industry comfortable. In 1979, he won a seat on the House Rules Committee, where he can be expected to vote generally with the House Democratic leadership.

Zeferetti is the only member of the Brooklyn delegation who had machine support in his first congressional race. Nonetheless, he has not yet demonstrated political invulnerability. He had an uncomfortably close primary election in 1976 (he beat his major opponent by only 47% to 32%) and has not been seriously challenged since; it is impossible to say whether he could have trouble in a future primary or even general election.

Census Data Pop. 466,741. Central city, 100%; suburban, 0%. Median family income, $9,629; families above $15,000: 21%; families below $3,000: 10%. Median years education, 10.5.

The Voters

Median voting age 46.
Employment profile White collar, 54%. Blue collar, 34%. Service, 12%. Farm, –%.
Ethnic groups Black, 5%. Spanish, 9%. Total foreign stock, 50%. Italy, 21%; Ireland, 4%; Poland, 3%; USSR, UK, 2% each; Germany, Canada, Greece, 1% each.

Presidential vote

1976	Carter (D)	62,332	(50%)
	Ford (R)	62,787	(50%)
1972	Nixon (R)	NA	
	McGovern (D)	NA	

Rep. Leo C. Zeferetti (D) Elected 1974; b. July 15, 1927, Brooklyn; home, Brooklyn; NYU, CUNY.

Career Navy, WWII; Officer, N.Y. City Dept. of Correction, 1957–74; Pres., Correction Officers Benevolent Assn., 1969–74; Mbr., N.Y. State Crime Control Planning Bd., 1973.

Offices 215 CHOB, 202-225-4105. Also 526 86th St., Brooklyn 11209, 212-680-1000.

Committees *Rules* (8th).

Group Ratings

	ADA	COPE	PC	RPN	NFU	LCV	CFA	NAB	NSI	ACA	NTU
1978	35	80	35	20	70	–	36	0	89	36	–
1977	45	95	60	25	75	63	55	–	–	19	16
1976	55	91	84	19	83	62	73	27	90	15	11

Key Votes

1) Increase Def Spnd	FOR	6) Alaska Lands Protect	DNV	11) Delay Auto Pol Cntrl	AGN
2) B-1 Bomber	FOR	7) Water Projects Veto	AGN	12) Sugar Price Escalator	AGN
3) Cargo Preference	FOR	8) Consum Protect Agcy	FOR	13) Pub Fin Cong Cmpgns	AGN
4) Dereg Nat Gas	AGN	9) Common Situs Picket	FOR	14) ERA Ratif Recissn	AGN
5) Kemp-Roth	AGN	10) Labor Law Revision	FOR	15) Prohibt Govt Abrtns	AGN

Election Results

1978 general	Leo C. Zeferetti (D-C)	49,272	(71%)	($67,960)
	Robert Whelan (R)	20,508	(29%)	($15,028)
1978 primary	Leo C. Zeferetti (D)	11,722	(74%)	
	Joseph F. Seminara (D)	4,154	(26%)	
1976 general	Leo C. Zeferetti (D-C)	69,242	(63%)	($107,217)
	Ronald J. D'Angelo (R)	33,611	(31%)	($9,758)
	Arthur J. Paone (L)	6,604	(6%)	($14,350)

SIXTEENTH DISTRICT

Flatbush is the heart of Brooklyn, right in the borough's geographical and psychological center. The name Flatbush has become practically synonymous in the public mind with Brooklyn itself. Probably most of the people in Queens or Long Island have some roots in Brooklyn or Flatbush, but a glance at the map shows how these places differ. Freeways crisscross the suburban terrain and most of Queens as well; but Brooklyn has only one, running along its shore. Proposals for another, cutting across the borough, have been killed. Most of Flatbush and Brooklyn were laid out and occupied before the automobile became a necessity; and you can still live in these one- and two-family houses, walk to shopping streets, take the subway to work, and get on quite as comfortably as most New Yorkers with cars.

During the 1910s and 1920s the then new neighborhoods of Flatbush and East Flatbush were attracting thousands of newly middle income Jews who had grown up on the Lower East Side of Manhattan. They were mostly young people, who raised large families here; many of their children stayed in Flatbush and raised their families there too. Now, as the young people who grew up here increasingly move to Long Island, Westchester, Manhattan, or simply, as many have done, outside the New York metropolitan area altogether, the Jewish population is weighted toward the elderly end of the age scale. Many blacks have been moving into Flatbush from Crown Heights and Bedford-Stuyvesant to the north, and among the older residents there has been much fear of crime.

It is not hard to describe the succession in congressional representation over the last six decades here. In the 1920 Harding landslide the area that is now the 16th congressional district—including most of Flatbush and East Flatbush—elected a Republican congressman. Two years later a 36-year-old Jewish lawyer won the Democratic nomination and unseated the incumbent by a small margin. For the next 24 elections the same man, slowly growing older, was elected again and again: Emanuel Celler, Chairman of the House Judiciary Committee, and co-author of the Celler-Kefauver antitrust law. Celler was always a machine Democrat, and he considered himself invulnerable; he never bothered to provide the kind of constituency services people in other districts had grown accustomed to. So he was more surprised than anyone when he was defeated in the 1972 Democratic primary by Elizabeth Holtzman, a young lawyer and former aide to Mayor John Lindsay.

The Holtzman victory had national significance. If she had lost, it would have been 88-year-old Manny Celler rather than 65-year-old Peter Rodino chairing the Judiciary Committee hearings on the impeachment of Richard Nixon. It also signalled the decline of Democratic machine politics in Flatbush. Numerous machine candidates have been defeated since in Democratic primaries, notably Assembly Speaker Stanley Steingut in 1978.

Holtzman has provided the kind of close attention to constituents which Celler never bothered with. She has also been a hard-working legislator. On the Judiciary Committee, she was well prepared and serious during the impeachment hearings, and she has since been active on a variety of issues—the extension of the Equal Rights Amendment, immigration laws, the federal rules of evidence in rape trials. She made a stir in 1978 when she questioned the presence in this country of the Vietnamese official who had shot a Viet Cong on television film during the Tet offensive. Holtzman has also won a seat on the Budget Committee. The Congresswoman is not a legislator who gets things done through camaraderie; she is deadly serious, and the success she has had is due almost entirely to good preparation and hard work. Holtzman has been mentioned as a possible contender for Jacob Javits's Senate seat in 1980, and would bring to the Senate many of Javits's strengths. The big question facing her campaign is whether she can raise the kind of money needed for a statewide campaign in New York.

Census Data Pop. 466,756. Central city, 100%; suburban, 0%. Median family income, $10,504; families above $15,000: 26%; families below $3,000: 9%. Median years education, 12.0.

The Voters

Median voting age 46.
Employment profile White collar, 64%. Blue collar, 25%. Service, 11%. Farm, –%.
Ethnic groups Black, 22%. Spanish, 4%. Total foreign stock, 49%. USSR, 11%; Poland, 7%; Italy, 6%; Austria, Ireland, 3% each; Germany, UK, 2% each; Rumania, 1%.

Presidential vote

1976	Carter (D)	88,016	(71%)
	Ford (R)	35,378	(29%)
1972	Nixon (R)	74,403	(46%)
	McGovern (D)	86,597	(54%)

Rep. Elizabeth Holtzman (D) Elected 1972; b. Aug. 11, 1941, Brooklyn; home, Brooklyn; Radcliffe Col., B.A. 1962, Harvard U., J.D. 1965; Jewish.

Career Practicing atty., 1965–67, 1970–72; Asst. to the Mayor of N.Y. City, 1967–70.

Offices 2238 RHOB, 202-225-6616. Also 1452 Flatbush Ave., Brooklyn 11210, 212-859-9111.

Committees *Budget* (5th). Subcommittees: Budget Process; Defense and International Affairs.

Judiciary (9th). Subcommittees: Immigration, Refugees, and International Law (Chairwoman); Civil and Constitutional Rights.

Group Ratings

	ADA	COPE	PC	RPN	NFU	LCV	CFA	NAB	NSI	ACA	NTU
1978	100	90	98	42	80	–	100	0	0	7	–
1977	100	87	98	67	58	98	100	–	–	15	41
1976	100	83	100	50	83	96	100	17	0	7	36

Key Votes

1) Increase Def Spnd	AGN	6) Alaska Lands Protect	FOR	11) Delay Auto Pol Cntrl	AGN
2) B-1 Bomber	AGN	7) Water Projects Veto	FOR	12) Sugar Price Escalator	AGN
3) Cargo Preference	AGN	8) Consum Protect Agcy	FOR	13) Pub Fin Cong Cmpgns	FOR
4) Dereg Nat Gas	AGN	9) Common Situs Picket	FOR	14) ERA Ratif Recissn	AGN
5) Kemp-Roth	AGN	10) Labor Law Revision	FOR	15) Prohibt Govt Abrtns	AGN

Election Results

1978 general	Elizabeth Holtzman (D-L)	59,703	(82%)	($44,428)
	Larry Penner (R)	9,405	(13%)	
	John H. Fox (C)	3,782	(5%)	
1978 primary	Elizabeth Holtzman (D-L), unopposed			
1976 general	Elizabeth Holtzman (D-L)	93,995	(83%)	($1,972)
	Gladys Pemberton (R-C)	19,423	(17%)	($134)

SEVENTEENTH DISTRICT

Staten Island is the smallest (pop. 312,000) and least densely populated of the five boroughs of New York City (5,000 people per square mile as against 31,000 for the rest of the city). It is also the most parochial, and most atypical, part of New York. Parts of Staten Island retain a rural character, even after the new development spurred by the opening of the Verrazano Narrows Bridge to Brooklyn in 1965. Before that, Staten Island was even more cut off: the only land route from the rest of New York City was through New Jersey, and the only water route was the Staten Island Ferry from the tip of Lower Manhattan.

Most Staten Islanders are quite happy with their comparative isolation. They are in many ways more suburban than real suburbanites. A large proportion are middle income Italian and Irish

Catholics, brought up often in Brooklyn and happy to leave the city (as they call it) behind. Politically, Staten Islanders are intensely conservative, with Conservative Party candidates sometimes outpolling Democrats. Enough people here are ancestral Democrats to elect Democrats to local office, and when the question in an election seems to be aid to New York City, most Staten Islanders will vote Democratic like their compatriots in other boroughs. Staten Island's most interesting political figure is state Senator John Marchi, an austere Thomistic conservative who was twice (1969, 1973) the Republican candidate for mayor. In the rest of the city, Marchi is considered too conservative; here on Staten Island, the local Conservative Party boycotted him as too liberal, because he supported a modified form of planned development for the island.

Because its population has not merited a full congressional district, Staten Island over the years has been linked politically with various parts of Brooklyn and Manhattan. During the fifties and sixties the island was joined to several different parts of Brooklyn. Today it is joined to the lower part of Manhattan. The conservative homeowners of Staten Island find themselves in the same district with elderly Jewish people living in housing projects and the trendy, artsy folk who are extending Greenwich Village southward into the neighborhood known as SoHo. The utter incompatibility of these two portions of the 17th can be shown by the 1972 presidential returns: the Manhattan portion, with one-third of the district's votes, went 63% for McGovern, while Staten Island was 74% for Nixon.

The Democratic Congressman from Staten Island, John Murphy, has had to hustle to win reelection since he first was sent to the House in 1962. He is probably about the closest thing there could be to a congressman acceptable to both parts of the district: a Democrat but with a not especially liberal record, a West Point graduate with solid roots in Staten Island. Murphy characteristically shows weakness in the primary in Manhattan and in the general election in Staten Island, but overall has managed to win.

Since the 1976 election, Murphy has been Chairman of the Merchant Marine and Fisheries Committee—a body with limited jurisdiction but large membership. This committee has jurisdiction over the series of subsidy arrangements supported by the maritime industry and the maritime unions, and its members—and the heavy majority support the subsidies—tend to receive healthy campaign contributions from the affected interests. Murphy in his first term as Chairman led the fight to require that a certain percentage of U.S. oil imports be carried on U.S. flag ships—a measure which would have benefited the maritime interests greatly. It was supported by organized labor, but was opposed by an odd combination of fiscal conservatives and policy liberals, and was ultimately defeated. Murphy was also a strong opponent of the Panama Canal Treaty, but was not able to get to first base in his drive to require a vote in the House on the Treaty on the grounds that it disposed of American property.

Murphy was more successful in other matters, such as getting the tuna industry to kill fewer porpoises. But the 96th Congress, at least in its first days, has not been good for him. He was resoundingly defeated in his attempt to win a subcommittee chair on the House Commerce Committee. And the new ranking Republican on Merchant Marine and Fisheries, Paul McCloskey of California, is the leading opponent of maritime subsidy measures—thus guaranteeing trouble for Murphy any time such legislation comes up for a vote.

Census Data Pop. 467,656. Central city, 100%; suburban, 0%. Median family income, $10,632; families above $15,000: 26%; families below $3,000: 8%. Median years education, 11.8.

The Voters

Median voting age 41.
Employment profile White collar, 57%. Blue collar, 28%. Service, 15%. Farm, –%.
Ethnic groups Black, 6%. Chinese, 6%. Spanish, 7%. Total foreign stock, 40%. Italy, 12%; Poland, Ireland, USSR, Germany, UK, 2% each; Austria, 1%.

Presidential vote

1976	Carter (D)	83,301	(55%)
	Ford (R)	68,723	(45%)
1972	Nixon (R)	105,543	(62%)
	McGovern (D)	64,601	(38%)

Rep. John M. Murphy (D) Elected 1962; b. Aug. 3, 1926, Staten Island; home, Staten Island; Amherst Col., U.S. Military Acad., B.S. 1950; Catholic.

Career Army, WWII and Korea; Gen. Mgr. and Pres., Cleveland General Transportation Co.; Bd. of Dirs., Empire State Hwy. Transportation Assn., 1960–65.

Offices 2187 RHOB, 202-225-3371. Also Rm. 107, Gen. P.O., 550 Manor Rd., Staten Island 10314, 212-981-9800.

Committees *Interstate and Foreign Commerce* (4th). Subcommittees: Communications; Health and the Environment; Transportation and Commerce.

Merchant Marine and Fisheries (Chairman). Subcommittees: Merchant Marine (Chairman).

Group Ratings

	ADA	COPE	PC	RPN	NFU	LCV	CFA	NAB	NSI	ACA	NTU
1978	35	68	53	27	70	–	50	0	56	30	–
1977	40	95	45	17	90	40	60	–	–	14	12
1976	45	86	62	41	70	53	45	10	71	26	5

Key Votes

1) Increase Def Spnd	FOR	6) Alaska Lands Protect	FOR	11) Delay Auto Pol Cntrl	FOR
2) B-1 Bomber	AGN	7) Water Projects Veto	AGN	12) Sugar Price Escalator	AGN
3) Cargo Preference	FOR	8) Consum Protect Agcy	FOR	13) Pub Fin Cong Cmpgns	AGN
4) Dereg Nat Gas	AGN	9) Common Situs Picket	FOR	14) ERA Ratif Recissn	AGN
5) Kemp-Roth	AGN	10) Labor Law Revision	FOR	15) Prohibt Govt Abrtns	DNV

Election Results

1978 general	John M. Murphy (D)	54,228	(54%)	($190,048)
	John M. Peters (R-C)	33,071	(33%)	($45,525)
	Thomas H. Stokes (L)	12,662	(13%)	
1978 primary	John M. Murphy (D)	11,179	(47%)	
	Thomas H. Stokes (D)	7,565	(32%)	
	Two others (D)	5,109	(21%)	
1976 general	John M. Murphy (D)	89,126	(66%)	($102,580)
	Kenneth J. Grossberger (R)	27,734	(20%)	($15,509)
	John M. Peters (C)	10,399	(8%)	($13,432)
	Ned Schneir (L)	8,656	(6%)	($3,921)

EIGHTEENTH DISTRICT

The 18th congressional district of New York has always been known as the Silk Stocking District. The 18th includes most of the skyscrapers of midtown Manhattan and much of Greenwich Village, whose now inaccurate bohemian reputation dates back to the 1910s. The district also includes the middle income housing developments of Stuyvesant Town and Peter Cooper Village and quaint old squares like Gramercy Park. If one could measure gross national product by congressional district, the 18th would undoubtedly be number one in the country; despite recent publicity about businesses leaving, midtown Manhattan is still the center of commerce and media in the United States and, for that matter, the world. The 18th also includes those parts of Manhattan that make it a world class city, whose only rivals are London and Paris: this is one of the places where the really rich live, shop, and entertain. Indeed, increasing numbers of the very rich are moving to Manhattan, fleeing from political instability elsewhere.

Thousands of writers have struggled to describe this part of New York socially, culturally, even physically. It is easier to describe it politically. For as in all of New York, not everyone here votes, and those who do tend to share a set of attitudes which, though they have changed, can be described without great difficulty. The political, though not geographical, center of the 18th district is the Upper East Side of Manhattan, from 59th to 96th Streets, an area which casts more than half the district's votes. This is an area which we associate with the rich, and most of Manhattan's really rich people live here. But it is also an area with a large number of young, single, trendy people with professional jobs—the kind of articulate, stylish people who make Manhattan the center of the nation's publishing, entertainment, broadcasting, and communications industries. There is considerable turnover in the district's population: people get married and move to the suburbs, they go to another city, they are replaced by younger people with similar background but perhaps quite different attitudes.

Thus it is possible to discern two basic shifts in political attitudes in the Silk Stocking District over the past 15 years. This was once a Republican district, perhaps the most Republican in New York City. From the thirties, when rich people here considered Franklin Roosevelt a traitor to his class, up through the early sixties, when trendy people here considered the Democratic Party as dominated by a bunch of crooked Irish and Italian politicoes, the 18th elected a succession of Republican congressmen. Its best known representative was John Lindsay, elected as a liberal Republican in 1958 and reelected by increasingly wide margins in the next three elections.

Lindsay was exactly the kind of politician Upper East Siders of the time liked. From a WASPy family, a graduate of prep school and Yale, he was obviously the right kind of person. As a Republican, he was not involved in the griminess of Democratic politics; as a procedural reformer and supporter of civil rights, he could be called a liberal. He voted with the Kennedy Administration on many issues, but in city politics he opposed the pitiable remnants of the Democratic machines. When Lindsay ran for mayor in 1965 he swept the East Side and Manhattan by large enough margins to win, even though Abraham Beame had a plurality in the rest of the city.

Over the next ten years the 18th district swung sharply to the left. One reason was the Vietnam war. People here were opposed, particularly the new young people who moved in off the radicalized campuses; and opposition to the war was expressed almost entirely by the Democratic rather than the Republican Party. There was some fear here of crime, but a greater revulsion against its use by people in the outer boroughs—and by the Republican Party of Richard Nixon and Spiro Agnew—to create an apparent code word for capitalizing on racial prejudice against blacks. As Nixon and Agnew kept campaigning against blacks, intellectuals, and students, the Republican allegiance in the Upper East Side quickly vanished. Nor was Mayor Lindsay keeping people in the Republican Party. He lost the Republican nomination for mayor in 1969, was reelected as a Liberal, and switched to become a Democrat in 1971. The demise of the New York *Herald Tribune* in the late sixties finished off the voice that once best articulated the Republicanism of the Upper East Side; the increasingly Democratic editorial columns of the New York *Times* replaced it in influence. And by 1968 the 18th district had elected a Democrat, Edward Koch, as its Congressman. A product of the reform Democratic movement in Greenwich Village, Koch was reelected easily in 1970, 1972, and 1974 in a district which had last elected a Democratic congressman, and then only by a narrow margin, in 1936.

There was more than a touch of snobbery in the liberalism of the Upper East Side. There was always greater concern here for the problems of lettuce workers in California or the Black Panthers—the honorees at the famous "radical chic" party given by Leonard Bernstein—than there was understanding of the problems faced by the cab drivers, doormen, waiters, sanitation workers, policemen, office clerks, janitors, and others whose work makes life in the Upper East Side possible. This kind of snobbery is what did in the Lindsay Administration. His electoral strategy of combining the top and the bottom of the New York (or Manhattan) electorate worked tactically, but as a formula for providing government in whose good faith people have confidence it was a disaster.

In the early seventies, voters on the Upper East Side lost their enthusiasm for Lindsay, but they still backed other liberal Democrats. They were strongly for George McGovern in the 1972 primary and for Morris Udall in 1976, just as they had favored Adlai Stevenson over anyone else in the fifties and Eugene McCarthy over Robert Kennedy in 1968. But now political attitudes here seem to be shifting again—at least enough to permit the election and reelection of a Republican congressman. William Green, an heir to the Grand Union supermarket fortune, had been an Assemblyman from the richest part of the Upper East Side until he ran for another office in 1968; a Democrat was elected in his place, and he was thus the last Republican legislator elected in

Manhattan. But when Edward Koch was elected mayor in 1977, Green decided to put on a real campaign for his 18th district seat in early 1978. He not only won that special election, but he won the 1978 general election as well.

One of Green's assets is his liberal voting record. Like Lindsay and other Republicans who have won elections here, he votes as often with Democrats as Republicans (although he has supported partisan Republican measures like the Kemp-Roth proposal). Another asset is money—he has spent more than $1 million on his campaigns so far. But probably his greatest advantage has been his opposition. In the special election, the Democrats nominated their candidate by party convention, with dozens of delegates. The result was a race so close that it ended up in court, with charges and countercharges of chicanery filling the air and the columns of the *Village Voice*. At first the apparent winner was Carter Burden, a young millionaire who once sat on the city council and who had run unsuccessfully for city-wide office. Burden had also been responsible for selling *New York* magazine and the *Village Voice* to media mogul Rupert Murdoch—a controversial episode which, whatever one's view of the merits of the sale, reflected no credit on Burden.

The other competitor was even more well known: Bella Abzug, former Congresswoman from the 20th district, with her acid tongue and unmistakable style one of the most controversial people in New York politics. Abzug had run for U.S. senator in 1976 and barely lost the primary to Daniel Patrick Moynihan; she ran for mayor in 1977 and ran behind Edward Koch and Mario Cuomo in the primary. By 1978 she seemed to have become a perennial candidate. She had in fact been a hard-working and effective legislator in the House—perhaps more effective than she could have been in the Senate and certainly more effective than she would have been as mayor or in any executive position. But she had accumulated enough enemies to lose the special election to Green by a narrow margin. Carter Burden accumulated enemies too. With Abzug not running, he won the Democratic nomination for the general election, but he too lost to Green.

It may be that Green has beaten the only two Democrats who could not have carried this district. Certainly he does not have a safe seat, and neither his voting record nor the provision of good services to his constituents may be enough to win him a third election in 1980. But he will be fighting hard to win, and in the process turning around the anti-Republican trend that once seemed so strong on the Upper East Side.

Census Data Pop. 467,533. Central city, 100%; suburban, 0%. Median family income, $14,853; families above $15,000: 50%; families below $3,000: 8%. Median years education, 13.0.

The Voters

Median voting age 44.
Employment profile White collar, 79%. Blue collar, 10%. Service, 11%. Farm, –%.
Ethnic groups Black, 4%. Chinese, 1%. Spanish, 7%. Total foreign stock, 44%. USSR, 7%; Germany, Poland, Italy, 4% each; Ireland, UK, Austria, 3% each; Hungary, 2%; Canada, France, Czechoslovakia, 1% each.

Presidential vote

1976	Carter (D)	108,478	(63%)
	Ford (R)	63,441	(37%)
1972	Nixon (R)	82,516	(42%)
	McGovern (D)	114,237	(58%)

Rep. S. William Green (R) Elected Feb. 14, 1978; b. Oct. 16, 1929, New York City; home, New York City; Harvard U., B.A. 1950, J.D. 1953.

Career Army, 1953–55; Law secy., U.S. Court of Appeals for D.C. Circuit, 1955–56; Practicing atty., 1956–70; N.Y. State Assembly, 1965–70; N.Y. Regional Administrator, HUD, 1970–77.

Offices 1118 LHOB, 202-225-2436. Also 137 E. 57th St., New York 10022, 212-826-4466.

Committees *Banking, Finance, and Urban Affairs* (9th). Subcommittees: Housing and Community Development; Economic Stabilization; General Oversight and Renegotiation.

Group Ratings

	ADA	COPE	PC	RPN	NFU	LCV	CFA	NAB	NSI	ACA	NTU
1978	58	61	56	90	78	–	50	20	0	12	–

Key Votes

1) Increase Def Spnd	NE	6) Alaska Lands Protect	FOR	11) Delay Auto Pol Cntrl	NE
2) B-1 Bomber	AGN	7) Water Projects Veto	FOR	12) Sugar Price Escalator	AGN
3) Cargo Preference	NE	8) Consum Protect Agcy	NE	13) Pub Fin Cong Cmpgns	FOR
4) Dereg Nat Gas	NE	9) Common Situs Picket	NE	14) ERA Ratif Recissn	AGN
5) Kemp-Roth	FOR	10) Labor Law Revision	NE	15) Prohibt Govt Abrtns	NE

Election Results

1978 general	S. William Green (R)	60,867	(53%)	($580,463)
	Carter Burden (D-L)	53,434	(47%)	($1,136,112)
1978 primary	S. William Green (R), unopposed			
1978 special	S. William Green (R)	30,332	(51%)	
	Bella S. Abzug (D-L)	29,171	(49%)	
1978 special primary	S. William Green (R), nominated by Republican Party			
1976 general	Edward I. Koch (D-L)	112,187	(79%)	($41,262)
	Sonia Landau (R)	29,728	(21%)	($9,923)

NINETEENTH DISTRICT

In the years following World War I, Harlem, whose tenements had been built just a decade or so earlier for white working class people, became the center of black American culture. The twenties were comparatively good years for Harlem, and not just because many Manhattan sophisticates discovered its night spots and jazz music. But the depression of the thirties hit Harlem hard, and in many ways it has never recovered. A few middle class pockets are still left here, in the apartment complexes built along the Harlem River or at the edge of Morningside Heights. But most of Harlem is very poor, and stricken with the problems of heroin, violent crime, and the kind of attitudes that produced the looting during the summer 1977 blackout. For many years now Harlem has been the kind of place people leave if they can; Harlem's population dropped fully 20% in the sixties and by probably a larger percentage since then. The elan of the twenties has never returned. Black leadership in civil rights battles has dwelled on the handicaps blacks have suffered and the difficulties they have encountered in trying to make progress. One result has been to awaken whites to the injustices they have imposed, but another has been to give a kind of inferiority complex to people who live in places like Harlem.

Harlem has had representation in Congress which cannot be called inferior by any standard—although at times it has been controversial. For a quarter of a century Harlem was represented by one of the best known congressmen in the nation, Adam Clayton Powell, Jr. His career peaked in the early sixties, when he was Chairman of the House Education and Labor Committee, which had jurisdiction over most of the social and antipoverty programs of the Kennedy and Johnson Administrations. Then in 1966 he refused to pay a libel judgment to a plaintiff he had called a "bag woman." Powell's troubles with the New York courts became regular features of national television newscasts. He got into even more trouble when it was learned that he had diverted staff salaries into his own ample bank account. The House ousted him in 1967, refusing even to let him take his seat—an action the Supreme Court two years later ruled unconstitutional. By that time Harlem voters had elected him in a special election and in the 1968 general election. But he had to stay out of New York except on Sundays, to avoid process servers, and increasingly he spent his time at his luxurious home in Bimini.

When Powell was first elected in 1944, his district was just part of Harlem; with redistricting, the district was expanded to include all of Harlem and a part of Manhattan's white liberal Upper West Side. By 1970 Powell's popularity in Harlem had dropped to the point where he could only barely carry the area over Assemblyman Charles Rangel; the West Side produced enough votes to give Rangel the victory.

In the years since, Rangel has shown at least as much political sensitivity as Powell did in his best years. He speaks in street-wise accents rather than Powell's oratorical style; but where Powell got in trouble with the national television audience, Rangel impressed them favorably as a member of the House Judiciary Committee in the Nixon impeachment hearings. His political acumen is shown by the fact that he managed to get Hugh Carey's old seat on Ways and Means. He has been active legislatively on the committee and the floor on welfare issues and on matters affecting New York City's finances.

Electorally Rangel has had no problems. Since Harlem has been losing population, his district has been expanded to include a larger part of the Upper West Side, but he has had no opposition; indeed, he has won the Liberal and Republican nominations in the last three elections.

Census Data Pop. 466,876. Central city, 100%; suburban, 0%. Median family income, $6,712; families above $15,000: 13%; families below $3,000: 18%. Median years education, 10.6.

The Voters

Median voting age 43.
Employment profile White collar, 49%. Blue collar, 27%. Service, 24%. Farm, -%.
Ethnic groups Black, 59%. Spanish, 17%. Total foreign stock, 18%. Italy, 2%; USSR, Germany, 1%.

Presidential vote

1976	Carter (D)	99,111	(87%)
	Ford (R)	14,642	(13%)
1972	Nixon (R)	24,302	(19%)
	McGovern (D)	106,164	(81%)

★ **Rep. Charles B. Rangel** (D) Elected 1970; b. June 11, 1930, New York City; home, New York City; NYU, B.S. 1957, St. John's U., LL.B. 1960; Catholic.

Career Army, 1948–52; Asst. U.S. Atty., So. Dist. of N.Y., 1961; Legal Counsel, N.Y. City Housing and Redevelopment Bd., Neighborhood Conservation Bureau; Gen. Counsel, Natl. Advisory Comm. on Selective Svc., 1966; N.Y. State Assembly, 1966–70.

Offices 2432 RHOB, 202-225-4365. Also 163 W. 125th St., New York City 10027, 212-663-3900.

Committees *Ways and Means* (7th). Subcommittees: Health (Chairman); Public Assistance and Unemployment Compensation.

Group Ratings

	ADA	COPE	PC	RPN	NFU	LCV	CFA	NAB	NSI	ACA	NTU
1978	80	90	88	38	90	–	82	0	0	8	–
1977	100	86	85	38	100	79	85	–	–	0	27
1976	95	87	89	47	83	92	100	9	0	0	32

Key Votes

1) Increase Def Spnd	AGN	6) Alaska Lands Protect	FOR	11) Delay Auto Pol Cntrl	AGN
2) B-1 Bomber	AGN	7) Water Projects Veto	AGN	12) Sugar Price Escalator	AGN
3) Cargo Preference	FOR	8) Consum Protect Agcy	FOR	13) Pub Fin Cong Cmpgns	FOR
4) Dereg Nat Gas	AGN	9) Common Situs Picket	FOR	14) ERA Ratif Recissn	AGN
5) Kemp-Roth	AGN	10) Labor Law Revision	FOR	15) Prohibt Govt Abrtns	AGN

Election Results

1978 general	Charles B. Rangel (D-L-R)	59,731	(100%)	($43,246)
1978 primary	Charles B. Rangel (D-L-R), unopposed			
1976 general	Charles B. Rangel (D-L-R)	91,672	(100%)	($48,970)

TWENTIETH DISTRICT

The West Side of Manhattan, the funkiest part of New York City, is a polyglot area so diverse that it defies accurate description. It's not a long way from Riverside Park and the Hudson River docks to the invisible line that separates the West Side from midtown or Harlem; but nearly every block in this short stretch seems to have its own peculiar character and so, it sometimes seems, does almost every building on the block. New York's 20th congressional district includes most of the West Side. It begins with a geographic salient into hip, expensive Greenwich Village, then moves up through renovated and raffish Chelsea, past apartment complexes and the obscenity palaces of Times Square, north to the Upper West Side. Here the 20th includes the two blocks from Amsterdam Avenue to the Hudson, north all the way along the West Side Highway to the northern tip of Manhattan. Well-known writers and well paid professionals in the West End Avenue apartments live in close and increasingly uneasy proximity to Puerto Ricans and welfare mothers in the side streets; students occupy cheap apartments around Columbia, and elderly ethnics live in even cheaper and definitely more dangerous surroundings in Washington Heights. The 20th goes on to include the expensive apartment units and large single-family houses of the Riverdale section of the Bronx.

Because most of the 20th district's votes are cast on the Upper West Side, its politics is worth some examination. For this is the heartland of much of Manhattan's Democratic reform politics. Back in the late fifties and early sixties, upper-income Stevenson enthusiasts broke the hold of Tammany Hall up here; the aged ethnics whose votes propped up the machine were either dying or moving elsewhere in search of cheaper rents, and the machine people had no rapport with the growing constituency of affluent liberals. The process of neighborhood change has become known since as gentrification, and in many cities now higher income young people are replacing lower income old people (and minority poor) in choice locations near white collar and professional employment and entertainment centers. Much attention and many words were devoted to the Manhattan reform movement because so many writers live in Manhattan; and they, like everyone else, tend to assume that their own experience has instructive value for all. Actually, the clash between gentrification and an old-line political machine is an event not likely to occur in other places, because there are so very few political machines left. In any case, the epic victories the reform groups celebrate were, in retrospect, won rather easily against a machine that had little life left in it.

Today virtually everyone active in Upper West Side politics is a survivor of reform politics. The district has been represented by a succession of reformers. First there was William F. Ryan, the first Manhattan reformer elected to Congress, back in 1960. He was the first congressman to condemn American involvement in Vietnam, and he led the biennial fight against the House Un-American Activities Committee. His views made him an object of derision in the early sixties; they are the conventional wisdom of American politics today. The 20th district, or part of it, also produced Bella Abzug, who was first elected in 1970. She lost an epic primary battle to Ryan in 1972 (they were redistricted together), but Ryan died before the general, and Abzug was nominated in his place and won reelection.

Since then congressional races have been devoid of the kind of acrimony that used to be synonymous with West Side politics; it is almost as if the reform movement, having achieved most of its objectives and the limits of its possible success, has entered a kind of placid and mellow middle age. Abzug was reelected without incident in 1974 and went on to try for the Senate in 1976, the mayoralty in 1977, and the 18th district House seat in 1978. The 20th district was won by Theodore Weiss. At 34 he had been elected as a reformer to the New York City Council, and he served there 15 years, trying for Congress once, in 1968. His position was strong enough on the West Side that he had no opposition whatever in the primary in 1976, and of course he had no trouble at all winning the general election. Weiss has the sort of liberal record one would predict for a member with his background, including 100% rating from the ADA.

Census Data Pop. 468,667. Central city, 100%; suburban, 0%. Median family income, $9,743; families above $15,000: 27%; families below $3,000: 9%. Median years education, 12.2.

The Voters

Median voting age 45.
Employment profile White collar, 64%. Blue collar, 22%. Service, 14%. Farm, –%.
Ethnic groups Black, 15%. Chinese, 1%. Spanish, 9%. Total foreign stock, 52%. USSR, 6%; Germany, 5%; Ireland, 4%; Poland, 3%; Austria, Italy, UK, Greece, 2% each; Hungary, 1%.

Presidential vote

1976	Carter (D)	105,995	(77%)
	Ford (R)	32,250	(23%)
1972	Nixon (R)	57,319	(34%)
	McGovern (D)	109,341	(66%)

Rep. Theodore S. Weiss (D) Elected 1976; b. Sept. 17, 1927, Gava, Hungary; home, New York City; Syracuse U., B.A. 1951, LL.B. 1952; Jewish.

Career Army, 1946–47; Practicing atty., 1953–76; Asst. Dist. Atty., N.Y. County, 1955–59; N.Y. City Cncl., 1961–77; Candidate for Dem. nomination for U.S. House of Reps., 1966, 1968.

Offices 132 LCHOB, 202-225-5635. Also 720 Columbus Ave., New York City 10025, 212-850-1500.

Committees *Education and Labor* (16th). Subcommittees: Post-Secondary Education. Employment Opportunities; Labor-Management Relations.

Government Operations (22d). Subcommittees: Intergovernmental Relations and Human Resources; Government Information and Individual Rights.

Group Ratings

	ADA	COPE	PC	RPN	NFU	LCV	CFA	NAB	NSI	ACA	NTU
1978	100	90	95	36	80	–	96	0	0	8	–
1977	100	86	93	58	92	98	95	–	–	0	40

Key Votes

1) Increase Def Spnd	AGN	6) Alaska Lands Protect	DNV	11) Delay Auto Pol Cntrl	AGN
2) B-1 Bomber	AGN	7) Water Projects Veto	FOR	12) Sugar Price Escalator	AGN
3) Cargo Preference	FOR	8) Consum Protect Agcy	FOR	13) Pub Fin Cong Cmpgns	FOR
4) Dereg Nat Gas	AGN	9) Common Situs Picket	FOR	14) ERA Ratif Recissn	AGN
5) Kemp-Roth	AGN	10) Labor Law Revision	FOR	15) Prohibt Govt Abrtns	AGN

Election Results

1978 general	Theodore S. Weiss (D-L)	64,365	(85%)	($37,859)
	Harry Torczyner (R)	11,661	(15%)	($21,463)
1978 primary	Theodore S. Weiss (D-L), unopposed			
1976 general	Theodore S. Weiss (D-L)	91,977	(87%)	($24,170)
	Denise T. Weiseman (R)	14,114	(13%)	($0)

TWENTY-FIRST DISTRICT

The 21st congressional district of New York is the South Bronx, geographically about a mile from Manhattan's posh Upper East Side, but in fact a world apart. By any measure this is a slum and a picture of social disintegration. Most of its residents are minorities—44% Puerto Rican, 43% black in the 1970 Census—and unlike Harlem or even Bedford-Stuyvesant, there is no history to this community, no set of traditional institutions which might have some ability to handle its problems. Most of the housing here was built between 1906 and 1917, when the newly built subways opened up the Bronx to settlement by the hundreds of thousands of immigrants who were jammed into Manhattan. In the sixties the last of these Italian and Jewish people, now elderly, were dying or moving out, and blacks and Puerto Ricans who could not find housing in more stable communities were moving in. Nearly half (43% in 1970) of the people here are under 18, many of them in large, fatherless families. With no community institutions and little parental supervision, youngsters in their teens commit hundreds of crimes here every day, with relatively little risk of being caught. Arson has become an extremely common crime, committed both by rampaging teenagers and by professional arsonists hired to convert the old buildings here to insurance money cash in the only way that it can be done.

The South Bronx has become a sort of national slum in recent years. Jimmy Carter has toured some rubble-strewn blocks here, and promised a major federal program to help. Mayor Edward Koch and one of his chief deputy mayors, Herman Badillo, who used to be Congressman from the 21st district, have tried to put together programs to rebuild the South Bronx—although they have encountered opposition from other city officials in doing so. The question no one can answer is what should be done. Not surprisingly, most residents of the South Bronx who have been able to leave have done so. It is not clear how much community spirit there is among those who have not. Nor is there any reason to hope that more affluent people are going to move in and redevelop the properties; there are only a few streets of historically interesting buildings. It is not at all clear that anyone wants to live in even a redeveloped South Bronx. Certainly the population has been declining rapidly, and the prospect is for continued decline, particularly among those with very minimal skills for whom there are increasingly fewer jobs in New York City. It may very well be that the South Bronx would better serve New York and its residents if it could become primarily a site for small industry, and that pouring millions of dollars into it for housing is a waste. To put up housing for people for whom there are no jobs makes little sense.

One measure of community cohesion is voter participation, and by that measure the South Bronx is among the least stable communities in the nation. In 1976 only 18% of those eligible to vote in the 21st district did so; in 1974 only 11% did. In both cases this was the lowest voter turnout, on both a numerical and percentage basis, of any congressional district in the country. This is not due to lack of civic proclivities among the ethnic groups represented here: blacks vote in much larger numbers in the Carolinas and Puerto Ricans vote in very much larger numbers in Puerto Rico. Nor is it the result of a large alien population; most of the minorities in this part of New York are American citizens. It does reflect an absence of effective political organizations here and a lack of community infrastructure. It may also reflect simple fear—fear of leaving one's house to go down to the polls after dark.

The 21st district is heavily Democratic; in the 1976 general election it cast the highest Democratic percentage (though far from the largest Democratic majority) of any congressional district in the country. Its first Congressman, elected in 1970, was Herman Badillo, the first full voting member of Congress with a Puerto Rican background. Badillo was elected Bronx Borough President in 1965 over the opposition of the Bronx Democratic organization; he ran for mayor in 1969, 1973, and 1977. His interest has always been in New York City, not congressional, politics, and his attendance record in Washington was never among the best. In 1977, after being eliminated in the first Democratic primary, he supported Edward Koch in the runoff. When Koch was elected, Badillo became one of his chief deputies. Badillo, who lives in middle class Riverdale and whose demeanor is cerebral, provides minority representation as well as a good knowledge of government and political savvy to the Koch Administration. Badillo no longer has the job security he had in Congress, but for a man who wants to be mayor he is probably in just as good a position.

Badillo's successor, Robert Garcia, seems not to share his steely ambition. A state legislator and a Badillo ally, Garcia lost the Democratic nomination to Luis Velez. But as the Republican nominee he managed to prevail in the February 1978 special election—having made it quite clear he would not vote as a Republican in the House. Both contests produced extremely low turnouts. Garcia won a full term in November 1978 without difficulty and has voted as a predictably liberal Democrat in the House.

Census Data Pop. 462,030. Central city, 100%; suburban, 0%. Median family income, $5,613; families above $15,000: 5%; families below $3,000: 23%. Median years education, 9.2.

The Voters

Median voting age 37.
Employment profile White collar, 37%. Blue collar, 42%. Service, 21%. Farm, –%.
Ethnic groups Black, 42%. Spanish, 44%. Total foreign stock, 14%. Italy, USSR, 1% each.

Presidential vote

1976	Carter (D)	45,749	(91%)
	Ford (R)	4,677	(9%)
1972	Nixon (R)	15,293	(20%)
	McGovern (D)	59,375	(80%)

Rep. Robert Garcia (D) Elected Feb. 14, 1978; b. Jan. 9, 1933, New York City; home, Bronx; CCNY.

Career Army, Korea; Computer engineer, 1957–65; N.Y. State Assembly, 1965–67; N.Y. Senate, 1967–78.

Offices 1711 LHOB, 202-225-4361. Also 840 Grand Concourse, Bronx 10451, 212-860-6200.

Committees *Banking, Finance, and Urban Affairs* (27th). Subcommittees: The City; Housing and Community Development; Economic Stabilization.

Post Office and Civil Service (9th). Subcommittees: Census and Population (Chairman); Human Resources.

Group Ratings

	ADA	COPE	PC	RPN	NFU	LCV	CFA	NAB	NSI	ACA	NTU
1978	79	83	75	40	78	–	50	0	0	5	–
1977	–	83	–	–	–	–	–	–	–	–	–

Key Votes

1) Increase Def Spnd	NE	6) Alaska Lands Protect	FOR	11) Delay Auto Pol Cntrl	NE
2) B-1 Bomber	AGN	7) Water Projects Veto	FOR	12) Sugar Price Escalator	AGN
3) Cargo Preference	NE	8) Consum Protect Agcy	NE	13) Pub Fin Cong Cmpgns	FOR
4) Dereg Nat Gas	NE	9) Common Situs Picket	NE	14) ERA Ratif Recissn	AGN
5) Kemp-Roth	AGN	10) Labor Law Revision	NE	15) Prohibt Govt Abrtns	NE

Election Results

1978 general	Robert Garcia (D-L-R)	23,950	(100%)	($45,068)
1978 primary	Robert Garcia (D-L-R), unopposed			
1978 special	Robert Garcia (R-L)	7,959	(58%)	($58,208)
	Louis Nine (D-C)	3,514	(26%)	($17,626)
	Ramon S. Velez (Victory)	2,280	(17%)	($27,749)
1978 special primary	Robert Garcia (R), nominated by Republican Party			
1976 general	Herman Badillo (D-L-R), unopposed			($63,759)

TWENTY-SECOND DISTRICT

The 22d congressional district of New York runs from the Grand Concourse to Co-op City—the heart of the Bronx. Unlike Brooklyn, which has its own history as a city, the Bronx is wholly an offspring of Manhattan. It was largely vacant at the turn of the century, but within ten years the subways had been built which made it an easy commute from Manhattan. The Bronx quickly filled up. From 1900 to 1930 its population increased from 200,000 to 1,265,000—not far from the 1,400,000 of today. Initial settlement followed the subway and el lines, as Jews, Italians, and Irish left the crowded tenements of Manhattan for the comparatively spacious and comfortable apartments of the Bronx. There are several large parks and two major universities (NYU and Fordham) here, but few other amenities. The Bronx has never had much white collar employment, nor for that matter all that many factory jobs either; it remains today basically a residential area.

The Grand Concourse was intended to be the showcase of the Bronx. Laid out as a broad boulevard, it was lined in the twenties with Art Deco apartment houses that were notably more elegant than those on nearby side streets; it was the place you moved when you got that raise or your stock tip paid off. Lately the advancing slums of the South Bronx have shattered the tranquillity—and wrecked the real estate values—of the Concourse. Consequently, the elderly Jews who have been the most numerous residents of the Concourse's buildings are moving out. One place they have headed, assuming they can get in, is Co-op City—a staggeringly vast complex of towering apartment buildings, financed mainly by an offshoot of the Amalgamated Clothing Workers Union. Co-op City is unspeakably ugly, situated on a flat swamp and overlooking a couple of expressways. Like so many buildings in New York—in the posh Upper East Side, as well as out here—it is totally, almost defiantly, lacking in aesthetic merit; it is also miles past the nearest subway stop. But Co-op City has produced clean, safe, relatively inexpensive housing—though not inexpensive enough to suit its tenants, who have conducted a huge rent strike to protest the passing along of increases in the cost of maintaining Co-op City. Like so many New Yorkers, they assume that simple justice requires that other people cough up for things they want and are unwilling to pay for.

Politics and population movements like the one from the Grand Concourse to Co-op City help to explain the convoluted boundaries of the 22d district. The lines threw together in 1972 two reform Democratic congressmen, Jonathan Bingham and James Scheuer, and forced them into a primary fight. Bingham won with Scheuer taking the 11th district seat in Brooklyn and Queens two years later. Bingham has a rather odd background for a Bronx congressman. His father was a wealthy Republican senator from Connecticut; Bingham himself worked for Governor Averell Harriman in the fifties and UN Ambassador Adlai Stevenson in the early sixties. As a resident of the posh Riverdale section, in 1964 he challenged Congressman Charles Buckley, boss of the Bronx Democratic machine and Chairman of the House Public Works Committee. Bingham won that election, but oldtimers in the House were able to keep him off his favored committee (Foreign Affairs) for several terms. But now Bingham is a subcommittee chairman.

But perhaps Bingham's most important moment in Congress came in December 1974 when he moved in the Democratic Steering Committee that all committee chairmen be voted on separately. As a result, two were unseated, and every chairman since has known that he could be ousted if he does not conduct business the way a majority of Democrats want him to. It was a move away from a system of seniority-cum-unaccountability which was indefensible intellectually and not used in any other legislative body in the world. It has done as much as anything else to change the way things are done in the House.

Census Data Pop. 466,931. Central city, 100%; suburban, 0%. Median family income, $8,850; families above $15,000: 18%; families below $3,000: 11%. Median years education, 11.1.

The Voters

Median voting age 47.
Employment profile White collar, 58%. Blue collar, 28%. Service, 14%. Farm, –%.
Ethnic groups Black, 18%. Spanish, 14%. Total foreign stock, 46%. USSR, 9%; Ireland, Poland, 6% each; Italy, 5%; Austria, 3%; Germany, UK, 2% each; Hungary, Rumania, 1% each.

Presidential vote

1976	Carter (D)	96,891	(77%)
	Ford (R)	29,723	(23%)
1972	Nixon (R)	67,371	(40%)
	McGovern (D)	101,683	(60%)

Rep. Jonathan B. Bingham (D) Elected 1964; b. Apr. 24, 1914, New Haven, Conn.; home, Bronx; Yale U., B.A. 1936, LL.B. 1939; United Church of Christ.

Career Correspondent, N.Y. *Herald Tribune,* 1935–38; Practicing atty., 1940–61; Army, WWII; Special Asst. to an Asst. Secy. of State, 1945–46; Asst. Dir., Ofc. of Internatl. Security Affairs, 1951; Secy. to Gov. Averell Harriman, 1955–58; Mbr., U.S. Delegation to U.N., 1961–63; U.S. Rep., U.N. Econ. and Social Cncl., and Chf. Advisor to Amb. Adlai E. Stevenson II, 1963–64.

Offices 2262 RHOB, 202-225-4411. Also Rm. 326 Wagner Bldg., 2488 Grand Concourse, Bronx 10458, 212-933-2310.

Committees *Interior and Insular Affairs* (5th). Subcommittees: Energy and the Environment; National Parks and Insular Affairs; Pacific Affairs.

Foreign Affairs (8th). Subcommittees: International Economic Policy and Trade (Chairman); International Security and Scientific Affairs.

Group Ratings

	ADA	COPE	PC	RPN	NFU	LCV	CFA	NAB	NSI	ACA	NTU
1978	80	83	78	50	80	–	68	0	20	4	–
1977	95	87	90	58	83	100	90	–	–	4	15
1976	90	87	92	50	92	98	91	8	20	0	0

Key Votes

1) Increase Def Spnd	AGN	6) Alaska Lands Protect	FOR	11) Delay Auto Pol Cntrl	AGN
2) B-1 Bomber	AGN	7) Water Projects Veto	FOR	12) Sugar Price Escalator	AGN
3) Cargo Preference	AGN	8) Consum Protect Agcy	FOR	13) Pub Fin Cong Cmpgns	FOR
4) Dereg Nat Gas	AGN	9) Common Situs Picket	FOR	14) ERA Ratif Recissn	AGN
5) Kemp-Roth	AGN	10) Labor Law Revision	FOR	15) Prohibt Govt Abrtns	AGN

Election Results

1978 general	Jonathan B. Bingham (D-L)	58,727	(84%)	($6,040)
	Anthony J. Geidel, Jr. (R-C)	11,110	(16%)	
1978 primary	Jonathan B. Bingham (D-L), unopposed			
1976 general	Jonathan B. Bingham (D-L)	92,044	(89%)	($12,788)
	Paul Slotkin (R)	11,130	(11%)	($2,589)

TWENTY-THIRD DISTRICT

The line that separates the Bronx from Westchester County marks the end of Democratic New York City and, traditionally, the beginning of the Republican suburbs and upstate. Even in these days of ticket-splitting there is still a major contrast here, and there is no better place to look at it than in the 23d congressional district of New York, one-third of which is in the northern Bronx and two-thirds in Westchester.

The Bronx portion of the district, a large middle class residential area, is totally cut off from the rest of the 23d by Van Cortlandt Park. Most of the people here are of Italian descent; as in all of New York City, they are more than normally likely to hold government jobs. The Democratic allegiance of this part of the Bronx springs from an immigrant heritage—the days when the Tammany block captain brought around enough coal for the rest of the winter in return for a couple of votes. The Republicans made some gains here in the sixties, as fear of crime and dislike of the Manhattan-based administration of John Lindsay increased. But in the middle seventies, there has been a return to a kind of machine Democratic allegiance: people here vote for the Democrats because their party tends to favor aid to New York City—aid which will keep their salaries and fringe benefits intact without increasing their taxes.

The tradition in the Westchester portion of the 23d is quite different. This includes most of Yonkers, the towns of Greenburgh and Mount Pleasant, and the suburbs along the Hudson River where Washington Irving once lived. With a few exceptions, Republicans have been in control here for as long as anyone can remember; when Democrat Alfred Del Bello was elected County Executive in 1973, it was the first time in the nearly fifty years the office had existed that it had not been won by a Republican. People here may have ethnic and sociological backgrounds similar to those of people in the middle class parts of the Bronx; but they think of themselves as suburbanites, protecting their property from the taxing demands of the masses in the city. Their chosen instrument in that has always been the Republican Party, and continues to be, in state politics. In federal elections, however, the suburbanites are quite happy to see money from people in other states go to New York City, and so they have voted somewhat more Democratic than usual in 1976 and 1978.

The 23d district was established within its present boundaries for the 1972 election. It has had a series of contests since which read like an intricate call for a square dance. Democrat Richard Ottinger, elected to this seat when it was entirely in Westchester in 1964, 1966, and 1968, and defeated in the 1970 Senate race, ran again in 1972 and lost to Republican Peter Peyser. Peyser won again in 1974, while Ottinger was winning the next-door 24th district. Peyser ran for the Senate in 1976, losing the Republican primary to James Buckley, and the 23d district was won by Republican Bruce Caputo. A brainy and ambitious young man, Caputo was the most aggressive member of the House Ethics Committee and constantly complained that Democrats weren't trying to get to the bottom of the Koreagate scandal; he was predictably unpopular with his colleagues, and decided to run for lieutenant governor in 1978. When Perry Duryea lost the race, so did Caputo. In the 23d, Peyser was running again, this time as a Democrat, and by a narrow margin he defeated Mayor Angelo Martinelli of Yonkers.

Peyser, as his political history suggests, is something of a maverick, with a brash personality and an unpredictable voting record. He won with a big margin in the Bronx and cannot be considered politically safe; but he does know the district, and presumably the district knows him. His career is symbolic of what has happened to the Republican Party here in the late seventies.

Census Data Pop. 467,778. Central city, 34%; suburban, 66%. Median family income, $12,693; families above $15,000: 39%; families below $3,000: 6%. Median years education, 12.3.

The Voters

Median voting age 46.
Employment profile White collar, 62%. Blue collar, 26%. Service, 12%. Farm, -%.
Ethnic groups Black, 13%. Spanish, 2%. Total foreign stock, 42%. Italy, 13%; Ireland, 4%; USSR, Germany, Poland, 3% each; UK, Austria, 2% each; Canada, 1%.

Presidential vote

1976	Carter (D)	90,623	(52%)
	Ford (R)	82,078	(48%)
1972	Nixon (R)	120,690	(61%)
	McGovern (D)	76,152	(39%)

Rep. Peter A. Peyser (D) Elected 1978; b. Sept. 7, 1921, Cedarhurst; home, Irvington; Colgate U., B.A. 1943; Episcopalian.

Career Army, WWII; Life insurance agent; Mgr., Peter A. Peyser Agency, Mutual of N.Y., 1961–70; Mayor of Irvington, 1963–70; U.S. House of Reps., 1971–77; Candidate for Repub. nomination for U.S. Senate, 1976.

Offices 301 CHOB, 202-225-5536. Also 30 S. Broadway, Yonkers 10701, 914-968-8200.

Committees *Education and Labor* (19th). Subcommittees: Higher Education; Labor Management Problems; Task Force on Welfare and Pension Plans.

House Administration (14th). Subcommittees: Libraries and Memorials; Accounts; Personnel and Police.

Group Ratings: Newly Elected

Key Votes: Newly Elected

Election Results

1978 general	Peter A. Peyser (D)	66,354	(53%)	($105,552)
	Angelo R. Martinelli (R-C)	59,455	(47%)	($141,229)
1978 primary	Peter A. Peyser (D)	9,151	(60%)	
	Richard L. Brodsky (D)	6,013	(40%)	($19,301)
1976 general	Bruce F. Caputo (R-C)	93,006	(54%)	($192,520)
	Edward Meyer (D-L)	80,424	(46%)	($177,219)

TWENTY-FOURTH DISTRICT

The conventional wisdom has it that New York's Westchester County is *the* suburb for the wealthy: not only the super-rich like the Rockefellers of Pocantico Hills, but also the ordinary rich, the people who own those large, comfortable houses in Scarsdale and White Plains, with their gently sloping lawns shaded by towering trees; or the glassy contemporary houses in the woodsier hills of Pound Ridge, Armonk, and Briarcliff Manor. All of these places are in New York's 24th congressional district, the only seat entirely within Westchester County. But the conventional image of Westchester and the 24th is not entirely accurate. Plenty of rich people live here—the constituency ranks 18th in median income of the nation's 435 congressional districts. But taken as a whole, the 24th is not uniformly wealthy. More typical of Westchester than WASPy Bedford Village or Jewish Scarsdale are the predominantly Italian-American, middle income neighborhoods of Mount Vernon or Port Chester.

Westchester County and the 24th district are one of the ancestral homes of liberal establishment Republicanism. Upper income voters have set the tone, if they have not provided most of the votes, of Westchester Republican politics; and here you would have found many of the major backers of Thomas E. Dewey, Dwight D. Eisenhower, and Nelson Rockefeller. In the Nixon years, upper income voters began moving to the left—Scarsdale, for example, went for Humphrey in 1968 and nearly for McGovern in 1972—but they were more than counterbalanced numerically by the middle income voters moving toward the Nixon version of the politics of law and order. After Watergate and the emergence of the issue of aid to New York City, these ordinary residents of the 24th have been moving somewhat toward the Democrats, even though some of the richer residents here find the political style of Jimmy Carter unpalatable.

The passage of the 24th district from a preserve of liberal Republicanism to a battleground between liberal Democrats and conservative Republicans is illustrated by the congressional races of the seventies. From 1962 the district was represented by Ogden Reid; as heir to the old New York *Herald Tribune* fortune, as Eisenhower's Ambassador to Israel, and as a Nelson Rockefeller appointee, he was the personification of liberal Republican politics. In Congress Reid's voting record was really more liberal than Republican; his main Republican activity was supporting Rockefeller every time he ran for president.

At general election time Reid's brand of Republicanism made him unbeatable, but as time went on it caused him increasing problems in the primary. In 1970 an unknown conservative challenger got 46% against him—evidence, if any was needed, that conservatively-inclined Republican primary voters were tired of electing someone who stood against them on most major issues. Reid was souring on Republicans, too, and in 1972 he became a Democrat, and survived a Republican challenge financed mainly by his old patron Nelson Rockefeller. In 1974 Reid ran for governor, as he had wanted to for years; he bowed out early, but too late to run for Congress again.

The new congressman from the 24th is a man with a similar background, including a few terms in Congress and a yen for statewide office: Richard Ottinger, former (1965–71) Congressman from the other Westchester district, and Democratic nominee for the U.S. Senate in 1970. Ottinger too comes from a wealthy family with a Republican background (his uncle nearly beat Franklin Roosevelt for governor in 1928), but Ottinger has always run as a Democrat. He was one of the earliest environmentalists in Congress and is an important one today; he has also been a leading opponent of legislation favored by the oil companies on the Energy Subcommittee of the Commerce Committee.

Ottinger, elected with a solid 58% in 1974, fell to 55% in 1976 and 54% in 1978. Such margins, while still decisive, are not sufficiently strong to deter serious Republican opposition in this district.

Census Data Pop. 468,148. Central city, 0%; suburban, 100%. Median family income, $13,577; families above $15,000: 44%; families below $3,000: 5%. Median years education, 12.4.

The Voters

Median voting age 46.
Employment profile White collar, 63%. Blue collar, 24%. Service, 13%. Farm, –%.
Ethnic groups Black, 13%. Total foreign stock, 39%. Italy, 13%; USSR, Germany, Ireland, UK, 3% each; Poland, 2%; Austria, Canada, 1% each.

Presidential vote

1976	Carter (D)	90,302	(47%)
	Ford (R)	101,668	(53%)
1972	Nixon (R)	135,553	(61%)
	McGovern (D)	87,068	(39%)

Rep. Richard L. Ottinger (D) Elected 1974; b. Jan. 27, 1929; home, Pleasantville; Cornell U., B.A. 1950, Harvard U., LL.B. 1953, Internatl. Law Study, Georgetown U., 1960–61.

Career Practicing atty., 1955–60, 1972–74; International corp. contract mgr., 1960-61; Co-Founder, 2nd Staff Mbr. and Dir. of Programs for the West Coast of South America, Peace Corps, 1961–64; U.S. House of Reps., 1965–70; Dem. nominee for U.S. Senate, 1970; Organizer, Grassroots Action, Inc., non-profit consumer and environmental assistance org., 1971–72.

Offices 2241 RHOB, 202-225-6506. Also 10 Fiske Pl., Mt. Vernon 10550, 915-699-2866.

Committees *Interstate and Foreign Commerce* (9th). Subcommittees: Energy and Power; Consumer Protection and Finance.

Science and Technology (6th). Subcommittees: Energy Development and Applications (Chairman); Energy Research and Production.

Group Ratings

	ADA	COPE	PC	RPN	NFU	LCV	CFA	NAB	NSI	ACA	NTU
1978	80	89	90	36	80	–	91	0	0	4	–
1977	100	78	95	54	83	100	100	–	–	0	37
1976	95	74	95	61	83	96	91	8	10	7	29

Key Votes

1) Increase Def Spnd	AGN	6) Alaska Lands Protect	FOR	11) Delay Auto Pol Cntrl	AGN
2) B-1 Bomber	AGN	7) Water Projects Veto	FOR	12) Sugar Price Escalator	AGN
3) Cargo Preference	AGN	8) Consum Protect Agcy	FOR	13) Pub Fin Cong Cmpgns	FOR
4) Dereg Nat Gas	AGN	9) Common Situs Picket	FOR	14) ERA Ratif Recissn	AGN
5) Kemp-Roth	AGN	10) Labor Law Revision	FOR	15) Prohibt Govt Abrtns	AGN

Election Results

1978 general	Richard L. Ottinger (D)	75,397	(57%)	($85,769)
	Michael R. Edelman (R)	57,451	(43%)	($64,314)
1978 primary	Richard L. Ottinger (D), unopposed			
1976 general	Richard L. Ottinger (D)	99,761	(55%)	($61,406)
	David V. Hicks (R-C)	81,111	(45%)	($56,070)

TWENTY-FIFTH DISTRICT

The 25th congressional district of New York occupies the heart of the Hudson River valley, extending from the Bear Mountain Bridge, some 30 miles north of Manhattan, to a point most of the way to Albany. Like most rivers in this country, the Hudson is badly polluted, but its scenery retains much of the grandeur it had when it inspired the painters whose school bears its name in the early nineteenth century. In colonial days, and even after independence, this valley was a place that nurtured one of the few feudal systems in the United States. The Dutch who originally colonized the Hudson gave huge land grants to the patroon families whose names are still well known: Schuyler, van Rensselaer, van Cortlandt, Roosevelt.

Since the middle nineteenth century, the Hudson Valley has been Republican politically, and in the last few years that preference has been strengthened by the arrival of conservative-minded, middle class people from the New York area, who left the city and its close-in suburbs in disgust and anger. Franklin Roosevelt won an upset victory in a state Senate race in the Democratic year of 1910, but during the thirties and forties he was never able to carry his home area. Even more irritating to FDR, the Hudson Valley persisted in reelecting Congressman Hamilton Fish, an isolationist who hated Roosevelt bitterly and whose hatred was returned in kind. The Fish family was perhaps more socially prominent than the Roosevelts; Hamilton Fishes had been representing the Hudson Valley in Congress since 1842, and an earlier Hamilton Fish had been Secretary of State under Grant. Franklin Roosevelt had the pleasure of seeing the Hamilton Fish of his day finally defeated, in the 1944 election.

The Fish dynasty is again in political control of the Hudson Valley congressional district. The present Hamilton Fish won a tough Republican primary in 1968—one opponent was Dutchess County assistant DA G. Gordon Liddy, Jr.—and beat a vigorous and well-financed Democrat in the general election. Unlike his father, Congressman Fish has shown no inclination to roll back the New Deal, though he did share with his father a skepticism about American military involvement in Indochina. Fish has a voting record which works out to about 50% according to most rating groups, and he has proved to be extremely popular in elections. His greatest exposure came in 1974, when he served on the House Judiciary Committee and voted to impeach Richard Nixon—a position his father, nearly 90, publicly opposed.

Census Data Pop. 467,859. Central city, 0%; suburban, 26%. Median family income, $11,885; families above $15,000: 32%; families below $3,000: 6%. Median years education, 12.3.

The Voters

Median voting age 43.
Employment profile White collar, 56%. Blue collar, 30%. Service, 13%. Farm, 1%.
Ethnic groups Black, 5%. Total foreign stock, 25%. Italy, 6%; Germany, 4%; UK, Ireland, 2% each; Canada, Poland, USSR, 1% each.

Presidential vote

1976	Carter (D)	86,387	(42%)
	Ford (R)	118,585	(58%)
1972	Nixon (R)	148,003	(70%)
	McGovern (D)	63,536	(30%)

Rep. Hamilton Fish, Jr. (R) Elected 1968; b. June 3, 1926, Washington, D.C.; home, Millbrook; Harvard U., A.B. 1949, NYU, LL.B. 1957; Episcopalian.

Career Navy, WWII; Practicing atty.; Vice Counsel, U.S. Foreign Svc., Ireland, 1951–53; Counsel, N.Y. State Assembly Judiciary Comm., 1961; Dutchess Co. Civil Defense Dir., 1967–68.

Offices 2227 RHOB, 202-225-5441. Also 82 Washington St., Poughkeepsie 12601, 914-452-4220.

Committees *Judiciary* (3d). Subcommittees: Monopolies and Commercial Law; Immigration, Refugees, and International Law.

Science and Technology (4th). Subcommittees: Energy Development and Applications.

Group Ratings

	ADA	COPE	PC	RPN	NFU	LCV	CFA	NAB	NSI	ACA	NTU
1978	30	35	35	75	44	–	23	64	89	58	–
1977	50	50	45	69	55	70	40	–	–	58	38
1976	35	35	52	83	33	59	36	75	100	48	18

Key Votes

1) Increase Def Spnd	FOR	6) Alaska Lands Protect	FOR	11) Delay Auto Pol Cntrl	AGN
2) B-1 Bomber	FOR	7) Water Projects Veto	FOR	12) Sugar Price Escalator	AGN
3) Cargo Preference	AGN	8) Consum Protect Agcy	AGN	13) Pub Fin Cong Cmpgns	AGN
4) Dereg Nat Gas	FOR	9) Common Situs Picket	AGN	14) ERA Ratif Recissn	AGN
5) Kemp-Roth	FOR	10) Labor Law Revision	FOR	15) Prohibt Govt Abrtns	FOR

Election Results

1978 general	Hamilton Fish, Jr. (R)	114,641	(79%)	($82,983)
	Gunars M. Ozols (D)	31,213	(21%)	
1978 primary	Hamilton Fish, Jr. (R), unopposed			
1976 general	Hamilton Fish, Jr. (R-C)	139,389	(71%)	($57,088)
	Minna Post Peyser (D)	58,216	(29%)	($37,375)

TWENTY-SIXTH DISTRICT

The 26th congressional district of New York is just at the margin between the New York City suburbs and the vast expanse of upstate New York. Fast-growing Rockland County, at the southern end of the district, is definitely within the city's orbit. Though it usually goes Republican, Rockland has a Democratic registration edge and a large Jewish population; many of the county's residents work in the city and commute across the George Washington or Tappan Zee Bridges. North of Rockland and separated from it by a mountain ridge is Orange County, once a largely rural area, with one small stagnant city on the Hudson, Newburgh. In recent years Orange County has been experiencing explosive growth, much of it from an exodus of New York City policemen, firemen, and civil servants; they talk of wanting to protect their children from contact with the horrors of the city even as they congratulate themselves quietly for dealing with them.

By long-standing tradition, Orange County has been Republican; and until 1974, the new migrants here were strongly Republican also. But as throughout the New York metropolitan area, the Watergate affair and the crisis over aid to New York City seem to have brought ancestral Democrats back to their party and to have forgotten their conservative leanings of the early seventies. The one-time Republican stronghold of Orange County nearly went for Hugh Carey in 1974 and 1978 and for Jimmy Carter in 1976.

The 26th has had a history of closely-contested elections, beginning in 1964 when Democrat John Dow unseated conservative Republican Katharine St. George. Dow was a 59-year-old systems analyst and, even then, an opponent of the war in Vietnam. He won again in 1966, lost in 1968 to Martin McKneally, a former national commander of the American Legion, and won again in 1970 when it was revealed that McKneally had neglected to file income tax returns.

But in 1972 Dow's luck ran out. He was beaten by Republican Benjamin Gilman, who has held the district ever since. A veteran of the New York Assembly, Gilman has used the advantages of incumbency adeptly. His voting record is rated more favorably by Democratic- than Republican-oriented rating groups, and so the Conservative Party does not endorse him. But he has been able to win easily anyway. He serves on the Foreign Affairs and Post Office and Civil Service Committees.

Census Data Pop. 467,424. Central city, 0%; suburban, 49%. Median family income, $11,632; families above $15,000: 31%; families below $3,000: 6%. Median years education, 12.3.

The Voters

Median voting age 42.
Employment profile White collar, 53%. Blue collar, 32%. Service, 14%. Farm, 1%.
Ethnic groups Black, 6%. Spanish, 2%. Total foreign stock, 28%. Italy, 6%; Germany, USSR, Ireland, 3% each; Poland, UK, 2% each; Austria, Canada, 1% each.

Presidential vote

1976	Carter (D)	92,098	(46%)
	Ford (R)	106,176	(54%)
1972	Nixon (R)	133,873	(68%)
	McGovern (D)	63,450	(32%)

Rep. Benjamin A. Gilman (R) Elected 1972; b. Dec. 6, 1922, Poughkeepsie; home, Middletown; U. of Penn., B.S. 1946, N.Y. Law School, LL.B. 1950; Jewish.

Career Army Air Corps, WWII; Asst. Atty. Gen. of N.Y. State, 1953; Practicing atty., 1955–72; Atty., N.Y. State Temp. Comm. on the Courts, 1956–57; N.Y. State Assembly, 1967–72.

Offices 2454 RHOB, 202-225-3776. Also P.O. Bldg., 217 Liberty St., Newburgh 12550, 914-565-6400.

Committees *Foreign Affairs* (6th). Subcommittees: Inter-American Affairs; International Economic Policy and Trade.

Post Office and Civil Service (3d). Subcommittees: Postal Personnel and Modernization; Human Resources.

Group Ratings

	ADA	COPE	PC	RPN	NFU	LCV	CFA	NAB	NSI	ACA	NTU
1978	55	75	55	45	80	–	68	18	90	38	–
1977	50	71	63	62	83	72	70	–	–	42	24
1976	45	68	69	72	64	84	64	33	100	33	24

Key Votes

1) Increase Def Spnd	FOR	6) Alaska Lands Protect	FOR	11) Delay Auto Pol Cntrl	FOR
2) B-1 Bomber	FOR	7) Water Projects Veto	AGN	12) Sugar Price Escalator	AGN
3) Cargo Preference	AGN	8) Consum Protect Agcy	FOR	13) Pub Fin Cong Cmpgns	FOR
4) Dereg Nat Gas	AGN	9) Common Situs Picket	FOR	14) ERA Ratif Recissn	AGN
5) Kemp-Roth	FOR	10) Labor Law Revision	FOR	15) Prohibt Govt Abrtns	AGN

Election Results

1978 general	Benjamin A. Gilman (R)	87,059	(62%)	($92,014)
	Charles E. Holbrook (D-L)	41,870	(30%)	($12,588)
	William R. Schaffer, Jr. (C)	10,708	(8%)	
1978 primary	Benjamin A. Gilman (R), unopposed			
1976 general	Benjamin A. Gilman (R)	120,049	(66%)	($42,496)
	John R. Maloney (D)	60,511	(34%)	($8,361)

TWENTY-SEVENTH DISTRICT

New York's 27th congressional district extends along the state's southern border from the Catskills to the Southern Tier. The Catskills are famous for huge Borscht Belt hotels like Grossinger's and the Concord, for Dutch-descended Rip van Winkle, and for the fashionable little town of Woodstock and the rock festival named after it (which actually took place 50 miles away). The low-lying Catskills occupy most of the eastern half of the 27th district; to the west the mountains subside into the Appalachian plateau. There begins the row of counties along New York's boundary with Pennsylvania known as the Southern Tier. Here is Binghamton, an old manufacturing town with new IBM plants nearby, and Ithaca, the home of Cornell University.

With the exception of Sullivan County in the Borscht Belt—one of three counties in the United States where Jews are the largest religious group—most of the 27th is ancestral Republican territory. It did not move as sharply to the right as parts of the New York metropolitan area during the Nixon years, so for a while it was not much more Republican than the state as a whole. Then in 1974 it did not shift back to the Democrats as did the ethnic middle class parts of the New York area. But it did come out of the Watergate years willing enough to vote Democratic to elect—for the first time since 1912—a Democratic congressman.

This was one thing Congressman Howard Robison, who was retiring in 1974, had never expected: to be succeeded by a Democrat. When he was first elected to the House, in 1958, upstate New York was still electing those oldtimers who had been some of the House's most powerful committee chairmen the last time the Republicans had a majority (1953–55): John Taber (Appropriations), Daniel Reed (Ways and Means), and the man Robison succeeded, Sterling Cole (Joint Committee on Atomic Energy). In this conservative company, Robison was a young moderate; by the time he retired, he was the senior Republican in the New York delegation, and all the old conservatives had long since gone.

The new Congressman is Matthew McHugh, who had been District Attorney in Tompkins County, which includes Ithaca. His tenure covered some of the student riot times at Cornell, where black students once marched around with rifles; and he did a good enough job to win a large local following. McHugh started off on the Agriculture and Interior Committees, and won Edward Koch's place on Appropriations when Koch was elected Mayor of New York City. McHugh won reelection with a stunning 67% in 1976, but the district is still Republican enough that a young, self-financed challenger was able to hold him to 56% in 1978.

Census Data Pop. 467,980. Central city, 14%; suburban, 44%. Median family income, $9,904; families above $15,000: 20%; families below $3,000: 8%. Median years education, 12.3.

The Voters

Median voting age 42.
Employment profile White collar, 51%. Blue collar, 32%. Service, 14%. Farm, 3%.
Ethnic groups Black, 2%. Total foreign stock, 19%. Italy, 3%; Germany, UK, Poland, Czechoslovakia, 2% each; USSR, Austria, Canada, 1% each.

Presidential vote

1976	Carter (D)	88,806	(45%)
	Ford (R)	108,821	(55%)
1972	Nixon (R)	141,972	(64%)
	McGovern (D)	81,179	(36%)

Rep. Matthew F. McHugh (D) Elected 1974; b. Dec. 6, 1938, Philadelphia, Pa.; home, Ithaca; Mt. St. Mary's Col., Emmitsburg, Md., B.S. 1960, Villanova U., J.D. 1963; Immaculate Conception Church.

Career Practicing atty., 1964–74; Ithaca City Prosecutor, 1968; Tompkins Co. Dist. Atty., 1969–72.

Offices 336 CHOB, 202-225-6335. Also 201 Fed. Bldg., Binghamton 13902, 607-723-4425.

Committees *Appropriations* (29th). Subcommittees: Agriculture, Rural Development, and Related Agencies; Foreign Operations.

Group Ratings

	ADA	COPE	PC	RPN	NFU	LCV	CFA	NAB	NSI	ACA	NTU
1978	75	80	75	45	80	–	77	8	20	15	–
1977	70	80	88	45	83	76	70	–	–	10	30
1976	80	77	89	50	83	87	100	20	30	4	25

Key Votes

1) Increase Def Spnd	AGN	6) Alaska Lands Protect	AGN	11) Delay Auto Pol Cntrl	AGN
2) B-1 Bomber	AGN	7) Water Projects Veto	FOR	12) Sugar Price Escalator	AGN
3) Cargo Preference	AGN	8) Consum Protect Agcy	FOR	13) Pub Fin Cong Cmpgns	FOR
4) Dereg Nat Gas	AGN	9) Common Situs Picket	FOR	14) ERA Ratif Recissn	AGN
5) Kemp-Roth	AGN	10) Labor Law Revision	FOR	15) Prohibt Govt Abrtns	FOR

Election Results

1978 general	Matthew F. McHugh (D)	83,413	(56%)	($199,786)
	Neil Tyler Wallace (R-C)	66,177	(44%)	($139,043)
1978 primary	Matthew F. McHugh (D), unopposed			
1976 general	Matthew F. McHugh (D-L)	127,048	(67%)	($161,775)
	William H. Harter (R-C)	63,626	(33%)	($99,970)

TWENTY-EIGHTH DISTRICT

The 28th congressional district of New York is the Albany-Schenectady area, where the Mohawk River flows into the Hudson. The district contains virtually all of Albany and Schenectady Counties, plus the aging carpet mill town of Amsterdam in Montgomery County. Of these places, the most interesting and politically significant is Albany, where an old-fashioned Democratic political machine still holds sway over local politics. For fifty years this machine had the same boss, Daniel O'Connell, who operated only from his house much of that time (John Kennedy went there to visit him in 1960); he died finally in 1977 at age 90. Since 1942 the city's mayor has been local aristocrat and machine stalwart Erastus Corning 2d. It remains the practice in Albany for city employees to get clearance from their Democratic ward bosses, who themselves are often blessed with no-show jobs, and there is plenty of favoritism for well-connected contractors. So the antique machine keeps control of the dwindling number of dollars generated by the sagging shopping areas and crumbling brownstone townhouses of Albany; people who can have been moving out of the city to its more spacious—and better governed—suburbs.

For years Albany has produced the largest Democratic majorities between New York City and Buffalo. There have been exceptions. Governor Nelson Rockefeller poured more than $1 billion of bond money into building the giant Albany Mall, which kept the construction industry here busy for years, and Albany obliged by giving him a solid reelection margin in his last race in 1970. For a while Albany also had a Republican congressman, a liberal named Daniel Button who won on the retirement of a machine loyalist in 1966 and was reelected in 1968. But then redistricting put him in the same district with Democrat Samuel Stratton, who is unbeatable in these parts, and Button's tenure came to an end.

Stratton came out of Schenectady, an industrial town dominated economically by General Electric and more sympathetic than Albany to the Republican politics of GE's corporate leadership. Stratton was elected Mayor of Schenectady in 1956, and was a local television news commentator as well; in the 1958 Democratic sweep he was elected to Congress. Twice the Republicans tried to redistrict him out of his seat, and twice failed; his heavy personal campaigning won him 2–1 margins over serious opponents. At one point his district extended most of the way across upstate New York almost to Rochester; by 1970, the legislature gave him Democratic Albany and in effect conceded him victory.

Stratton has served on the Armed Services Committee since he entered Congress, and he had long been known as something of a maverick. But that was not because he differed from the committee's hawkish view of the world, but rather because of his pesky sniping at congressional sacred cows. Stratton has been, for example, the leading opponent for years of the move to increase office space and desecrate the Capitol by tearing down and extending its West Front. Stratton has also always strongly supported financial disclosure. Neither move is popular with senior congressmen who would like a new hideaway Capitol office or who have substantial financial holdings.

Stratton's major interest today is in defense matters. In his first job in public life, Stratton served before Pearl Harbor as an aide to Massachusetts Congressman Thomas Eliot, a supporter of FDR's military preparedness program. Those were the days when aid to Britain was highly controversial, even when Britain seemed likely to be conquered by Hitler, and when the draft passed the House a month before Pearl Harbor by just one vote. Roosevelt himself resorted to some underhanded tactics to aid Britain and to get the United States more involved than most Americans wanted in the fight against Hitler. Those times made a great impression on many young men in Congress then—men like Lyndon Johnson and Henry Jackson. They seem to have made a deep impression on Samuel Stratton as well.

Stratton, like Johnson and Jackson, seems to see himself as continuing FDR's tradition and opposing today's Neville Chamberlains. He strongly backed the Vietnam war, and felt this country should have made a stronger commitment there. He favored the B-1 bomber. He opposed the nomination of Paul Warnke as SALT negotiator and has been worried that the Administration is giving up too much in the arms limitation talks. He favored nuclear aircraft carriers. He opposed cuts in military aid to South Korea. He has proposed unsuccessful amendments to increase the defense budget offered by the Administration.

Many of Stratton's initiatives have been unsuccessful; he is the kind of congressman who does what he thinks is right whether or not he thinks he can carry a majority with him. But he does express the views of many on the Armed Services Committee. He is now the third-ranking Democrat on the committee, behind Mel Price of Illinois and Charles Bennett of Florida; his prospects for becoming chairman are reasonably good. He already heads a potentially important subcommittee. In the 28th district Stratton is regularly reelected by 4–1 margins.

Census Data Pop. 467,219. Central city, 13%; suburban, 47%. Median family income, $10,764; families above $15,000: 25%; families below $3,000: 6%. Median years education, 12.2.

The Voters

Median voting age 46.
Employment profile White collar, 58%. Blue collar, 29%. Service, 12%. Farm, 1%.
Ethnic groups Black, 4%. Total foreign stock, 27%. Italy, 7%; Poland, 4%; Germany, 3%; Canada, UK, Ireland, 2% each; USSR, 1%.

Presidential vote

1976	Carter (D)	107,602	(49%)
	Ford (R)	113,853	(51%)
1972	Nixon (R)	134,123	(57%)
	McGovern (D)	101,128	(43%)

Rep. Samuel S. Stratton (D) Elected 1958; b. Sept. 27, 1916, Yonkers; home, Amsterdam; U. of Rochester, B.A. 1937, Haverford Col., M.A. 1938, Harvard U., M.A. 1940; Presbyterian.

Career Secy. to U.S. Rep. Thomas H. Eliot of Mass., 1940–42; Navy, WWII and Korea; Deputy Secy. Gen., Far Eastern Comm., 1946-48; Radio and TV news commentator; College lecturer; Schenectady City Cncl., 1950–56, Mayor, 1956–59.

Offices 2205 RHOB, 202-225-5076. Also, U.S.P.O., Jay St., Schenectady 12305, 518-374-4547.

Committees *Armed Services* (3d). Subcommittees: Investigations (Chairman); Seapower and Strategic and Critical Materials.

Group Ratings

	ADA	COPE	PC	RPN	NFU	LCV	CFA	NAB	NSI	ACA	NTU
1978	15	50	38	36	30	–	36	42	100	44	–
1977	30	81	43	8	45	30	60	–	–	41	21
1976	25	81	41	63	67	39	45	25	90	38	22

Key Votes

1) Increase Def Spnd	FOR	6) Alaska Lands Protect	FOR	11) Delay Auto Pol Cntrl	FOR
2) B-1 Bomber	FOR	7) Water Projects Veto	FOR	12) Sugar Price Escalator	AGN
3) Cargo Preference	AGN	8) Consum Protect Agcy	AGN	13) Pub Fin Cong Cmpgns	AGN
4) Dereg Nat Gas	AGN	9) Common Situs Picket	FOR	14) ERA Ratif Recissn	AGN
5) Kemp-Roth	AGN	10) Labor Law Revision	FOR	15) Prohibt Govt Abrtns	FOR

Election Results

1978 general	Samuel S. Stratton (D)	139,575	(79%)	($28,057)
	Paul H. Tocker (R-C)	36,017	(21%)	
1978 primary	Samuel S. Stratton (D)	26,508	(81%)	
	One other (D)	6,147	(19%)	
1976 general	Samuel S. Stratton (D)	170,034	(79%)	($12,089)
	Mary A. Bradt (R-C)	44,053	(21%)	($190)

TWENTY-NINTH DISTRICT

The 29th congressional district of New York, once a basically rural area, is now on its way to becoming suburban. Although the district extends from the Dutchess County border in the south to a point near Lake Champlain in the north, more than half of its residents live within 20 miles of Albany, the state capital (though Albany itself is in the 28th district). Almost directly across the Hudson from Albany is Troy, in the early nineteenth century a harbinger of the future as one of the first American cities with an economy based entirely on manufacturing. Troy had major horseshoe and shirt factories; it has been in economic decline for some time, but now young people are renovating some of its old brick mills and stone mansions and townhouses. To the north is Saratoga County, site of the Revolutionary War battle and home of the famous race track, but demographically more significant as the recipient of population spillover from the Albany-Schenectady-Troy metropolitan area. The 29th also includes Columbia County to the south, the home of Martin Van Buren in the nineteenth century and conservative-minded Dutchmen today, and of the headwaters of the Hudson and the area around Lake George and Fort Ticonderoga.

Politically, the 29th district was designed by a Republican legislature to be a Republican district. All its rural counties are Republican, and Troy's Democratic tendencies are mild enough to be outnumbered usually by the Republican votes in rural Rensselaer County. The new residents of Saratoga County may be ancestrally Democratic, but they are also affluent and wary of high taxes—and usually Republican. What is surprising about this district is that it has had close contests in the last three elections, and that a Democrat has won twice.

That occurred in large part because of the weakness of 14-year incumbent Republican Carleton King. Running at 70, in 1974, he was too sick to campaign and too politically insensitive (or loyal) to denounce Richard Nixon. The winner was Rensselaer County Treasurer Edward Pattison. During his next two years in Congress, he worked hard at keeping in touch with the district. But he also had a solidly liberal voting record, making fewer concessions to his constituency than did many 1974 freshman Democrats elected in hitherto Republican districts. In 1976, Pattison was reelected, but with only a minority of the vote; the Republican got 45% of the vote and the Conservative Party candidate 8%.

In 1978 Gerald Solomon, a Republican Assemblyman from the northern part of the district, won both the Republican and the Conservative nominations. He attacked Pattison's liberal voting record strongly, and he may have profited from Pattison's admission that he once smoked marijuana (many congressmen have probably done so, but Pattison is the only one who has publicly admitted it). In November Solomon won with a pretty solid 54% of the vote; Pattison carried little of the district outside Rensselaer County. Solomon's victory has made clear that this is really a Republican district; each of Pattison's two victories, in retrospect, looks like a special case. The likelihood is that Solomon will have a long congressional career.

Census Data Pop. 467,767. Central city, 13%; suburban, 47%. Median family income, $9,621; families above $15,000: 18%; families below $3,000: 8%. Median years education, 12.1.

The Voters

Median voting age 44.
Employment profile White collar, 47%. Blue collar, 38%. Service, 12%. Farm, 3%.
Ethnic groups Black, 2%. Total foreign stock, 18%. Italy, Canada, 3% each; Germany, UK, Ireland, 2% each; Poland, 1%.

Presidential vote

1976	Carter (D)	87,311	(39%)
	Ford (R)	136,099	(61%)
1972	Nixon (R)	156,842	(70%)
	McGovern (D)	67,570	(30%)

Rep. Gerald B. H. Solomon (R) Elected 1978; b. Aug. 14, 1930, Birmingham, Ala.; home, Glens Falls; Siena Col., St. Lawrence U.; Presbyterian.

Career USMC, Korea; Queensbury Town Supervisor; Chmn., Warren Co. Social Services Comm.; N.Y. State Assembly, 1972–78.

Offices 515 CHOB, 202-225-5614. Also 33 2nd St., Troy 12180, 518-274-3121.

Committees *Public Works and Transportation* (15th). Subcommittees: Oversight and Review; Public Buildings and Grounds; Water Resources.

Group Ratings: Newly Elected

Key Votes: Newly Elected

Election Results

1978 general	Gerald B. Solomon (R-C)	99,518	(54%)	($167,723)
	Edward W. Pattison (D-L)	84,705	(46%)	($155,525)
1978 primary	Gerald B. Solomon (R-C), unopposed			
1976 general	Edward W. Pattison (D-L)	100,663	(47%)	($80,441)
	Joseph A. Martino (R)	96,476	(45%)	($61,547)
	James E. DeYoung, Jr. (C)	15,337	(7%)	($31,661)

THIRTIETH DISTRICT

The 30th congressional district of New York covers the northernmost reaches of New York state. It includes the counties across the St. Lawrence River from Canada and the ones at the eastern end of Lake Ontario. The large French Canadian population in Clinton and Franklin Counties, just 100 miles south of Montreal, forms the only Democratic voting bloc in the district; as one moves south and west there are fewer French and more Yankees. Here in the farm country of the St. Lawrence and in the Adirondacks, where it gets bitterly cold in the winter and not very warm in the summer, the voting preference is decidedly Republican—enough so to make the entire district Republican in most elections. Geographically, much of the 30th is taken up with the Adirondack Forest Preserve, a giant state park which the New York Constitution stipulates must remain "forever wild." North of the preserve is Massena, on the St. Lawrence River, which has been blessed with the administrative headquarters of the St. Lawrence Seaway bureaucracy. But the Seaway itself has failed to live up to economic expectations—another blow to this chronically depressed area.

Since the 1964 election the Congressman from the 30th has been Robert McEwen, a quiet conservative Republican who has made few waves in the House. His voting record is predictable and regular. Some time ago he won a seat on the Appropriations Committee. Recently much of his legislative activity has been involved with preparations for the 1980 Winter Olympics at Lake Placid in the Adirondacks.

Surprisingly, McEwen has had significant challenges in recent elections. In 1974 former Truman press secretary Roger Tubby held him to 55%; but for McEwen's large margin in Oswego County, it would have been close indeed. In 1976, Oswego County legislator Norma Bartle held McEwen to 56%, running even in her home territory but unable to win elsewhere. In 1978 Bartle tried again and ran against the conventional wisdom, opposing McEwen proposals to station 15,000 federal troops at Fort Drum and to provide winter navigation on the Seaway. The result was a resounding McEwen victory and the likelihood that this seat will not be seriously contested again for some time.

Census Data Pop. 467,920. Central city, 0%; suburban, 20%. Median family income, $8,584; families above $15,000: 14%; families below $3,000: 10%. Median years education, 12.0.

The Voters

Median voting age 43.
Employment profile White collar, 41%. Blue collar, 37%. Service, 16%. Farm, 6%.
Ethnic groups Total foreign stock, 15%. Canada, 7%; Italy, 2%; UK, 1%.

Presidential vote

1976	Carter (D)	75,006	(42%)
	Ford (R)	104,841	(58%)
1972	Nixon (R)	122,127	(67%)
	McGovern (D)	60,180	(33%)

Rep. Robert C. McEwen (R) Elected 1964; b. Jan. 5, 1920, Ogdensburg; home, Ogdensburg; U. of Vt., U. of Penn., Albany Law School, LL.B. 1947; Presbyterian.

Career Army Air Corps, WWII; N.Y. State Senate, 1954–64.

Offices 2210 RHOB, 202-225-4611. Also 307 Fed. Bldg., Watertown 13601, 315-782-3150.

Committees *Appropriations* (6th). Subcommittees: Military Construction; Treasury, Postal Service, and General Government.

Group Ratings

	ADA	COPE	PC	RPN	NFU	LCV	CFA	NAB	NSI	ACA	NTU
1978	15	5	8	64	22	–	14	91	100	72	–
1977	10	29	15	64	55	6	15	–	–	77	38
1976	5	15	7	78	18	15	18	91	100	70	40

Key Votes

1) Increase Def Spnd	FOR	6) Alaska Lands Protect	DNV	11) Delay Auto Pol Cntrl	DNV
2) B-1 Bomber	FOR	7) Water Projects Veto	AGN	12) Sugar Price Escalator	FOR
3) Cargo Preference	AGN	8) Consum Protect Agcy	AGN	13) Pub Fin Cong Cmpgns	AGN
4) Dereg Nat Gas	FOR	9) Common Situs Picket	AGN	14) ERA Ratif Recissn	FOR
5) Kemp-Roth	FOR	10) Labor Law Revision	FOR	15) Prohibt Govt Abrtns	FOR

Election Results

1978 general	Robert C. McEwen (R-C)	85,478	(61%)	($56,731)
	Norma A. Bartle (D-L)	55,785	(39%)	($50,692)
1978 primary	Robert C. McEwen (R-C), unopposed			
1976 general	Robert C. McEwen (R)	95,564	(56%)	($43,303)
	Norma A. Bartle (D)	75,951	(44%)	($52,106)

THIRTY-FIRST DISTRICT

The 31st congressional district of New York includes most of the Mohawk River Valley, much of the Adirondack Forest Preserve, and a couple of agricultural counties. These other areas add much to its scenic beauty, but most of the people here are concentrated within 30 miles of the Mohawk. During the Revolutionary War, this part of New York was the frontier, where American colonists fought the British and their Iroquois allies, both united in their desire to prevent American penetration of the continent. And this is where they failed as chronicled in, among other places, the movie *Drums Along the Mohawk*.

In the early years of the nineteenth century, the Mohawk Valley became the major route west for migrating New England Yankees, some of whom stayed to settle the valley. When the Erie Canal, which runs parallel to the river, was opened in 1825, the nation had its first major, and for a long time its most important, path from the coast to the interior. The canal was the cheapest way to get bulky agricultural products out of the Old Northwest (Ohio, Indiana, etc.) and finished goods back into the hinterlands. At first the canal, and then the New York Central Railroad which followed this same water-level route, accounted for much of the phenomenal growth of New York City and its port. Boston and Philadelphia, with no similar access inland, were left behind.

As migration slowed and trade increased, the Mohawk Valley became one of the early industrial centers of the nation. The little Oneida County hamlets of Utica and Rome grew to become sizeable industrial centers. First settled by New England Yankees, these towns attracted a new wave of immigration from the Atlantic coast in the early twentieth century. Today they are the most heavily Italian- and Polish-American communities between Albany and Buffalo.

In most parts of the nation, a change in ethnic composition of this magnitude would have moved the area from Republican to Democratic party preference. But not in upstate New York, where suspicion of Democratic New York City has worked to the advantage of the Republican Party since it was founded. Republicans here pay close attention to the sometimes pro-union and pro-abortion, pro-aid to parochial schools sentiments of their blue collar Catholic constituents; theirs is a party which has broadened its base from the all but vanishing white Anglo-Saxon Protestants. Their adaptation has been successful. Only Democrats with the strongest emotional appeal to Catholic voters—like Robert Kennedy in 1964 or Hugh Carey in 1974—have carried Mohawk Valley counties.

In 1972, seven-term incumbent Congressman Alexander Pirnie retired. The winner of the Republican primary was Donald Mitchell, a Herkimer County Assemblyman who also had the Conservative Party nomination. Mitchell has won subsequent elections without difficulty, and has shown sufficient popularity that he had no Democratic opponent at all in 1978. In the House he votes solidly with his fellow Republicans. Like his predecessor, he serves on the House Armed Services Committee, where he is in a good position to protect the interests of Rome's Griffis Air Force Base.

Census Data Pop. 467,717. Central city, 30%; suburban, 44%. Median family income, $9,388; families above $15,000: 17%; families below $3,000: 8%. Median years education, 11.9.

The Voters

Median voting age 46.
Employment profile White collar, 44%. Blue collar, 39%. Service, 13%. Farm, 4%.
Ethnic groups Black, 2%. Total foreign stock, 22%. Italy, 6%; Poland, 3%; Germany, UK, Canada, 2% each.

Presidential vote

1976	Carter (D)	84,661	(44%)
	Ford (R)	107,363	(56%)
1972	Nixon (R)	140,433	(70%)
	McGovern (D)	61,141	(30%)

Rep. Donald J. Mitchell (R) Elected 1972; b. May 8, 1923, Ilion; home, Herkimer; Hobart Col., 1946–47, Columbia U., B.S. 1949, M.A. 1950; Methodist.

Career Navy, WWII; Optometrist, 1950–72; Herkimer Town Cncl., 1954–57, Mayor, 1957–61; Herkimer Town Zoning Bd. of Appeals, 1963; N.Y. State Assembly, 1965–72, Maj. Whip, 1969–72.

Offices 2431 RHOB, 202-225-3665. Also, 319 N. Main St., Herkimer 13350, 315-866-1051.

Committees *Armed Services* (7th). Subcommittees: Military Compensation; Military Installations and Facilities; Research and Development.

Group Ratings

	ADA	COPE	PC	RPN	NFU	LCV	CFA	NAB	NSI	ACA	NTU
1978	25	45	23	58	40	–	27	67	100	70	–
1977	15	41	35	54	67	55	20	–	–	58	23
1976	25	48	26	78	58	48	36	75	100	46	21

Key Votes

1) Increase Def Spnd	FOR	6) Alaska Lands Protect	FOR	11) Delay Auto Pol Cntrl	FOR
2) B-1 Bomber	FOR	7) Water Projects Veto	FOR	12) Sugar Price Escalator	FOR
3) Cargo Preference	AGN	8) Consum Protect Agcy	AGN	13) Pub Fin Cong Cmpgns	FOR
4) Dereg Nat Gas	FOR	9) Common Situs Picket	AGN	14) ERA Ratif Recissn	FOR
5) Kemp-Roth	FOR	10) Labor Law Revision	FOR	15) Prohibt Govt Abrtns	FOR

Election Results

1978 general	Donald J. Mitchell (R-C), unopposed			($44,635)
1978 primary	Donald J. Mitchell (R-C), unopposed			
1976 general	Donald J. Mitchell (R)	115,464	(65%)	($59,607)
	Anita Maxwell (D)	62,032	(35%)	($14,855)

THIRTY-SECOND DISTRICT

From the 1920s until 1974, upstate and suburban Republicans controlled the New York legislature, except after the Democratic landslides of 1936 and 1964. Republican control was founded on the principle of giving New York City far less representation than its population entitled it to, until the Supreme Court prohibited that practice in 1964; and these same Republicans extended their influence into national affairs by drawing with exceeding care the boundaries of New York's congressional districts so as to maximize the number of Republicans elected. The upstate cities of Buffalo and Rochester were traditionally divided between two or three districts, each with plenty of suburban and rural territory to overpower any possible Democratic majority. During the sixties the legislators abandoned this ploy in Buffalo, where one city district became overwhelmingly Democratic, though they retained it in Rochester; in 1970 they applied it to Syracuse.

Until then it had scarcely been necessary. Syracuse and surrounding Onondaga County had been a single district for as long as anyone could remember, and they had the perfect population to continue in that arrangement after the 1970 Census. Syracuse is in many ways upstate New York's most militantly conservative and usually most Republican city (although it voted against Nelson Rockefeller one time because it considered him too big a spender). General Electric, as in much of upstate New York, is the largest employer here, and it has propagated its conservative Republicanism as much as possible. But the real basis for Syracuse's conservatism—and it has been shared for years by the city's large blue collar Italian-American community, which elsewhere might be Democratic—is fear and hostility to New York City. There is a feeling that the city, if it ever got the chance, would tax honest, hard-working upstaters to bankruptcy to support the welfare cheaters and civil service loafers who, in this view, dominate New York City politics.

So Republicans carried Syracuse during the New Deal. Democrats won here only in 1964, when Lyndon Johnson and Robert Kennedy carried Onondaga County, and in 1966, when there was a local uprising against Nelson Rockefeller. In 1964, the Syracuse area also elected a Democratic congressman, James Hanley, and he has in this unlikely territory won reelection ever since. Hanley parlayed the advantages of incumbency into reelection in 1966 and 1968, and so in 1970 the legislature decided to do him in by redistricting. They took half of Syracuse and Onondaga County away from his district and added the rural and small town counties of Madison, Cortland, and Chenango.

Nevertheless Hanley has managed to win. He has often won 2–1 margins in his share of Onondaga County, enough to overcome any deficits in the smaller counties. He has enough seniority that in 1979 he became a committee chairman, of the Post Office and Civil Service Committee. That is not necessarily a plum back in the 32d district, however, particularly at a time when people are questioning whether they have been getting their money's worth out of government bureaucracies and the Postal Service. Indeed, the Senate committee of the same name was abolished after its chairman was defeated in 1976, and Hanley's predecessor lost his primary (though probably for other reasons) in 1978. Hanley's opponent brought up postal rate increases against him in 1978, although Hanley could point out that they are the responsibility of a separate commission.

In the last two elections, Hanley has had some difficulty. He won with 55% in 1976 and 54% in 1978—both well below his previous showings. The major asset of his 1978 opponent, a 30-year-old

Syracuse auto dealer, was an Italian name. It is possible that Hanley could have tough competition indeed in 1980 and perhaps even lose this seat. On the other hand, if he can hold on, Democrats might control the redistricting process or have sufficient leverage over it to give him a more favorable district—one consisting largely if not entirely of Syracuse and Onondaga County—which could give him political security for 1982 and throughout the eighties.

Census Data Pop. 467,826. Central city, 22%; suburban, 47%. Median family income, $10,416; families above $15,000: 22%; families below $3,000: 7%. Median years education, 12.3.

The Voters

Median voting age 41.
Employment profile White collar, 53%. Blue collar, 32%. Service, 12%. Farm, 3%.
Ethnic groups Black, 2%. Total foreign stock, 18%. Italy, 4%; Canada, Germany, UK, 2% each; Poland, 1%.

Presidential vote

1976	Carter (D)	75,658	(39%)
	Ford (R)	117,652	(61%)
1972	Nixon (R)	138,607	(70%)
	McGovern (D)	60,343	(30%)

Rep. James M. Hanley (D) Elected 1964; b. July 19, 1920, Syracuse; home, Syracuse; Catholic.

Career Army, WWII; Funeral home dir.

Offices 239 CHOB, 202-225-3701. Also 1269 Fed. Bldg., Syracuse 13202, 315-423-5657.

Committees *Banking, Finance and Urban Affairs* (8th). Subcommittees: Financial Institutions Supervision, Regulation and Insurance; Housing and Community Development; The City.

Post Office and Civil Service (Chairman). Subcommittees: Investigations (Chairman).

Small Business (9th). Subcommittees: Antitrust and Restraint of Trade Activities Affecting Small Business.

Group Ratings

	ADA	COPE	PC	RPN	NFU	LCV	CFA	NAB	NSI	ACA	NTU
1978	40	70	43	50	33	–	46	25	70	32	–
1977	40	78	68	23	75	61	55	–	–	27	20
1976	65	83	69	33	83	54	81	8	89	14	8

Key Votes

1) Increase Def Spnd	FOR	6) Alaska Lands Protect	FOR	11) Delay Auto Pol Cntrl	FOR
2) B-1 Bomber	AGN	7) Water Projects Veto	FOR	12) Sugar Price Escalator	AGN
3) Cargo Preference	FOR	8) Consum Protect Agcy	AGN	13) Pub Fin Cong Cmpgns	FOR
4) Dereg Nat Gas	AGN	9) Common Situs Picket	FOR	14) ERA Ratif Recissn	AGN
5) Kemp-Roth	AGN	10) Labor Law Revision	FOR	15) Prohibt Govt Abrtns	FOR

Election Results

1978 general	James M. Hanley (D)	76,251	(53%)	($113,595)
	Peter J. DelGiorno (R-C)	67,071	(47%)	($71,961)
1978 primary	James M. Hanley (D), unopposed			
1976 general	James M. Hanley (D)	101,419	(55%)	($95,671)
	George C. Wortley (R-C)	81,597	(45%)	($89,265)

THIRTY-THIRD DISTRICT

The Finger Lakes of upstate New York are long, narrow bodies of water, surrounded by gentle hills. They lie within a triangle, the apexes of which are Syracuse, Rochester, and Elmira. The land above the lakes is dotted with small towns to which some early nineteenth century Yankee, proud of his classical education, gave names: Ovid, Scipio, Romulus, Camillus, Pompey, and many others. The Finger lakes region is pleasant vacation country, and is known also for its vineyards; this is where the New York state wine industry thrives. Just north of the Lakes is the line of the Erie Canal, now replaced by one with a name less euphonious: the New York State Barge Canal. Also here are the small industrial cities of Auburn, Geneva, and Canandaigua. The Finger Lakes country is Republican by tradition; the cities heavily Catholic and sometimes Democratic.

The Finger Lakes region accounts for about half of New York's 33d congressional district. The remainder is the west side of Syracuse and surrounding Onondaga County. In its short existence as a district, the 33d has elected three Republican congressmen. John Terry, elected in 1970, decided to retire in 1972 because he didn't want to move his family to Washington. Former Syracuse Mayor William Walsh, elected in 1972, won reelection twice by very large margins. In 1978, at 66, he decided to retire.

That set up real battles both in the Republican primary and the general election. In the former the winner was Gary Lee, a former director of Cornell University's office of scholarships; he lives in the southern edge of the district, in the Finger Lakes area near Ithaca. His primary opponent, Syracuse-based Robert Byrne, was the Conservative nominee in the general election. The Democrats had a candidate tailor-made for the district: Syracuse City Auditor Roy Bernardi, of Italian descent and a fiscal conservative. Nevertheless Lee won by a comfortable margin and can be expected to represent the district for some time.

Census Data Pop. 467,610. Central city, 20%; suburban, 27%. Median family income, $9,851; families above $15,000: 19%; families below $3,000: 8%. Median years education, 12.1.

The Voters

Median voting age 44.
Employment profile White collar, 46%. Blue collar, 37%. Service, 14%. Farm, 3%.
Ethnic groups Black, 4%. Total foreign stock, 18%. Italy, 5%; Canada, UK, Germany, Poland, 2% each; Ireland, 1%.

Presidential vote

1976	Carter (D)	75,263	(40%)
	Ford (R)	115,166	(60%)
1972	Nixon (R)	135,504	(70%)
	McGovern (D)	59,196	(30%)

Rep. Gary A. Lee (R) Elected 1978; b. Aug. 18, 1933, Buffalo; home, Ithaca; Colgate U., B.A. 1960.

Career Navy, 1952–56; Corning City Alderman, 1961–63; Dryden Town Cncl., 1965–67; Supervisor, 1968–69; Tomkins Co. Supervisor, 1968–69, Bd. of Reps., 1970–74, Chmn. 1974; N.Y. State Assembly, 1974–78.

Offices 513 CHOB, 202-225-3333. Also 1245 Fed. Bldg., Syracuse 13202, 315-423-5333.

Committees *Interstate and Foreign Commerce* (13th). Subcommittees: Health and the Environment; Transportation and Commerce.

Veterans' Affairs (11th). Subcommittees: Medical Facilities and Benefits; Housing.

Group Ratings: Newly Elected

Key Votes: Newly Elected

Election Results

1978 general	Gary A. Lee (R)	82,501	(59%)	($162,725)
	Roy A. Bernardi (D)	58,286	(41%)	($69,614)
1978 primary	Gary A. Lee (R)	17,936	(88%)	
	One other (R)	2,397	(12%)	
1976 general	William F. Walsh (R)	125,163	(72%)	($69,555)
	Charles R. Welch (D)	48,855	(28%)	($11,339)

THIRTY-FOURTH DISTRICT

The 34th congressional district of New York lies along the southern shore of Lake Ontario, and includes the east side of the city of Rochester, the eastern Monroe County, and Wayne County further to the east. Rochester's economy, to an extent greater than those of other upstate New York cities, depends on white collar and highly skilled labor jobs. Major employers here are Eastman Kodak and Xerox, both founded in Rochester; Kodak still has its headquarters here. These high technology companies have given the Rochester area a healthier economy over the years than is found in upstate cities which depend more on heavy industry.

The city of Rochester by itself is almost large enough to constitute a congressional district, and if it were one it would almost certainly elect Democrats. Knowing this, Republican legislators for years have split Rochester into two districts, adding plenty of heavily Republican suburban and rural territory to each. Consequently, both the 34th and 35th congressional districts are considered safely Republican. In the 34th, profoundly conservative Wayne County is a particular Republican stronghold and, incidentally, the birthplace of the Mormon Church.

Since 1963, the 34th's Congressman has been Frank Horton, on most issues upstate New York's most liberal Republican. That political coloration has become traditional in the district; some years ago (1947–59) its Congressman was Kenneth Keating, later U.S. Senator, judge on New York's highest court, and Ambassador to India and Israel. Like Keating, Horton is more in tune with New Deal liberals on economic issues than in step with the dovish Democrats who today control their party's caucus in the House; he is not all that far from the politics of, say, Henry Jackson. However you describe his politics, he has proved very popular in the 34th district. In 1974, despite Watergate and an opponent of substance, he won by a 2–1 margin; despite a drunk driving arrest and a week in jail he did as well in 1976. In 1978 he had no Democratic opponent at all.

Horton is now the ranking Republican on the Government Operations Committee, which has jurisdiction over Jimmy Carter's government reorganization plans; he also served as head of a federal commission on paperwork. On Government Operations, he serves opposite the colorful and partisan Chairman, Jack Brooks, a man who does not let others exercise power if he can help it. Accordingly, Horton's power in the House is considerably less than it might be under other circumstances.

Census Data Pop. 467,461. Central city, 38%; suburban, 62%. Median family income, $12,082; families above $15,000: 34%; families below $3,000: 6%. Median years education, 12.2.

The Voters

Median voting age 44.
Employment profile White collar, 54%. Blue collar, 34%. Service, 11%. Farm, 1%.
Ethnic groups Black, 6%. Spanish, 1%. Total foreign stock, 27%. Italy, 7%; Germany, Canada, 3% each; UK, USSR, Poland, 2% each.

Presidential vote

1976	Carter (D)	87,580	(44%)
	Ford (R)	112,816	(56%)
1972	Nixon (R)	130,757	(63%)
	McGovern (D)	77,699	(37%)

Rep. Frank Horton (R) Elected 1962; b. Dec. 12, 1919, Cuero, Tex.; home, Rochester; La. St. U., B.A., 1941, Cornell U., LL.B. 1947; Presbyterian.

Career Army, WWII; Practicing atty., 1947–62; Rochester City Cncl., 1955–61.

Offices 2229 RHOB, 202-225-4916. Also 314 Fed. Bldg., Rochester 14614, 716-263-6270.

Committees *Government Operations* (Ranking Member). Subcommittees: Legislation and National Security.

Group Ratings

	ADA	COPE	PC	RPN	NFU	LCV	CFA	NAB	NSI	ACA	NTU
1978	55	50	33	55	40	–	32	46	80	33	–
1977	25	72	30	67	64	19	25	–	–	40	23
1976	40	52	36	88	64	48	36	27	60	30	11

Key Votes

1) Increase Def Spnd	FOR	6) Alaska Lands Protect	FOR	11) Delay Auto Pol Cntrl	FOR
2) B-1 Bomber	AGN	7) Water Projects Veto	AGN	12) Sugar Price Escalator	AGN
3) Cargo Preference	AGN	8) Consum Protect Agcy	FOR	13) Pub Fin Cong Cmpgns	AGN
4) Dereg Nat Gas	FOR	9) Common Situs Picket	FOR	14) ERA Ratif Recissn	AGN
5) Kemp-Roth	FOR	10) Labor Law Revision	FOR	15) Prohibt Govt Abrtns	AGN

Election Results

1978 general	Frank Horton (R-D)	122,785	(87%)	($8,262)
	Leo J. Kesselring (C)	18,127	(13%)	
1978 primary	Frank Horton (R-D), unopposed			
1976 general	Frank Horton (R)	126,566	(68%)	($51,532)
	William C. Larsen (D)	58,247	(32%)	($47,998)

THIRTY-FIFTH DISTRICT

The 35th congressional district of New York includes the western half of the city of Rochester, the western Monroe County suburbs, and the adjacent upstate counties of Genesee, Wyoming, Livingston, and part of Ontario. This is fertile, rolling countryside, punctuated by small cities like Batavia, locale of novelist John Gardner's Sunlight Dialogues, and Attica, scene of the 1971 prison riot and tragedy. Some 400 miles from New York City, this part of New York state has an almost Midwestern feeling to it; celebrity city politicians like Nelson Rockefeller or Robert Kennedy seemed as out of place campaigning here as they might have in southern Iowa. As in the case of the 34th district, the Republican voting habits of the smaller counties and Rochester suburbs effectively overwhelm any Democratic margins that might come out of Rochester.

This is the kind of district which, for the past century, has sent so many men to Washington to tend our national affairs: conservative Republicans, most of them, small town lawyers with an aptitude for politics, with perhaps a small family fortune behind them, and a few years in the legislature. Typically they have been elected young, returned to office more or less automatically, and have wound up in important committee positions. They have written tariff laws, led the opposition to new federal programs, put together military budgets, and in many cases —remembering what gave birth to the Republican Party—supporting civil rights laws. They have been cautious, serious men, seldom very stylish or fashionable, but often brighter than sophisticated liberals gave them credit for. Through men like these, the people who run the small towns of upstate New York, central Ohio, outstate Michigan, and downstate Illinois have had a major voice in the way our government has been run.

There are probably fewer such men in the House than there used to be, partly because there are fewer House seats in small town and rural areas and partly because many that do exist are now represented by Democrats. But the tradition does survive in the person of Barber Conable, Republican Congressman from the 35th district of New York. In his first few years he caught the eye of the Republican leadership and won a seat on the Ways and Means Committee. In 1977, when he was only 54, he became ranking Republican on that panel. Conable is respected as a thoughtful, knowledgeable legislator. His voting record is in line with Republican tradition: he likes to balance budgets, to hold down federal spending, to question whether new programs are really necessary. Within that tradition he operates as an intelligent legislative craftsman and compromiser. On procedural issues he was leading successful fights for reform as long ago as 1970. Both because of his committee position and his reputation, he tends to set the Republican position on fiscal and tax issues, and he is listened to with care by many Democrats as well.

These are not the kind of qualities which necessarily make a man a big vote-getter, but in the 35th district Conable does not have to worry overmuch about reelection. His toughest challenge was in 1974, when Rochester Vice Mayor Midge Costanza ran against him and held him to 59%; during that campaign, Costanza met Jimmy Carter and eventually wound up, for a while, on his White House staff.

Census Data Pop. 467,415. Central city, 26%; suburban, 51%. Median family income, $11,528; families above $15,000: 27%; families below $3,000: 5%. Median years education, 12.2.

The Voters

Median voting age 41.
Employment profile White collar, 46%. Blue collar, 40%. Service, 12%. Farm, 2%.
Ethnic groups Black, 6%. Total foreign stock, 20%. Italy, 6%; Canada, Germany, 3% each; UK, 2%; Poland, 1%.

Presidential vote

1976	Carter (D)	85,502	(43%)
	Ford (R)	111,399	(57%)
1972	Nixon (R)	134,216	(66%)
	McGovern (D)	70,126	(34%)

Rep. Barber B. Conable, Jr. (R) Elected 1964; b. Nov. 2, 1922, Warsaw; home, Alexander; Cornell U., B.A. 1942, LL.B. 1948; Methodist.

Career USMC, WWII and Korea; Practicing atty., 1949–64; N.Y. State Senate, 1963–64.

Offices 237 CHOB, 202-225-3615. Also 311 Fed. Ofc. Bldg., 100 State St., Rochester 14614, 716-263-3156.

Committees *Budget* (3d). Subcommittees: Economic Policy, Projections and Productivity; Budget Process; Tax Expenditures and Tax Policy.

Ways and Means (Ranking Member).

Group Ratings

	ADA	COPE	PC	RPN	NFU	LCV	CFA	NAB	NSI	ACA	NTU
1978	30	25	20	100	0	–	18	100	80	56	–
1977	20	19	28	92	27	30	20	–	–	82	49
1976	10	13	13	100	9	29	18	100	80	63	38

Key Votes

1) Increase Def Spnd	FOR	6) Alaska Lands Protect	FOR	11) Delay Auto Pol Cntrl	FOR
2) B-1 Bomber	AGN	7) Water Projects Veto	FOR	12) Sugar Price Escalator	DNV
3) Cargo Preference	AGN	8) Consum Protect Agcy	AGN	13) Pub Fin Cong Cmpgns	FOR
4) Dereg Nat Gas	FOR	9) Common Situs Picket	AGN	14) ERA Ratif Recissn	AGN
5) Kemp-Roth	FOR	10) Labor Law Revision	AGN	15) Prohibt Govt Abrtns	AGN

Election Results

1978 general	Barber B. Conable, Jr. (R)	96,119	(73%)	($59,204)
	Francis C. Repicci (D)	36,428	(27%)	($30,837)
1978 primary	Barber B. Conable, Jr. (R), unopposed			
1976 general	Barber B. Conable, Jr. (R)	120,738	(66%)	($32,575)
	Michael Macaluso, Jr. (D)	61,186	(34%)	($16,183)

THIRTY-SIXTH DISTRICT

The 36th congressional district of New York includes Niagara County, site of the falls; part of suburban Erie County, just outside Buffalo; and the southern shore of Lake Ontario from the Niagara River to within a few miles of Rochester. From the falls, power lines strung on gigantic pylons hum out to the urban Northeast, Midwest, and eastern Canada. The city of Niagara Falls, despite its tourist business, is mostly industrial, with most of its industries doing not especially well of late. Pollution is high—one part of the city had to be abandoned because of it—and the city and its suburbs have been losing population in the sixties and seventies. Niagara Falls has large Italian and Polish communities which lean Democratic; the rest of the county subscribes to upstate New York Republicanism. The Erie County portion of the 36th includes the middle class and politically marginal suburbs of Tonawanda and Grand Island, as well as a few blocks of the city of Buffalo itself.

On paper the 36th is politically marginal, yet until 1974 it was invariably captured by Republicans. One was William Miller, who became famous when he quit Congress in 1964 and was named Barry Goldwater's running mate; he was chosen for his zesty partisan attacks. More recently he has been doing well practicing law and appearing on American Express commercials. Another Republican congressman here was Henry Smith, a frosty former judge who served on the House Judiciary Committee; he threatened to vote for impeachment because of the bombing of Cambodia, but decided not to, and thus missed being a footnote in history. Smith retired voluntarily in that same year, 1974.

Given the Democratic nature of the year and the political leanings of the district, it was almost inevitable that it went Democratic in 1974, and it did in a big way. John LaFalce, a young veteran of both houses of the New York legislature, won the district with a robust 60%. He was one of the new members whose service on the Banking, Housing, and Urban Affairs Committee changed its composition and basic attitudes on a multitude of issues. LaFalce has proved popular in his district, and has won reelection by margins of 2–1 and 3–1.

Census Data Pop. 467,761. Central city, 7%; suburban, 93%. Median family income, $10,702; families above $15,000: 23%; families below $3,000: 6%. Median years education, 12.1.

The Voters

Median voting age 44.
Employment profile White collar, 47%. Blue collar, 40%. Service, 12%. Farm, 1%.
Ethnic groups Black, 3%. Total foreign stock, 27%. Canada, 7%; Italy, 5%; Poland, 4%; UK, Germany, 3% each.

Presidential vote

1976	Carter (D)	88,063	(46%)
	Ford (R)	102,268	(54%)
1972	Nixon (R)	119,213	(60%)
	McGovern (D)	78,931	(40%)

Rep. John J. LaFalce (D) Elected 1974; b. Oct. 6, 1939, Buffalo; home, Tonawanda; Canisius Col., B.S. 1961, Villanova U., J.D. 1964; Catholic.

Career Law Clerk, Ofc. of Gen. Counsel, U.S. Dept. of the Navy, 1963; Practicing atty.; Army, 1965–67; N.Y. State Senate, 1971–72; N.Y. State Assembly, 1973–74.

Offices 225 CHOB, 202-225-3231. Also Fed. Bldg., Buffalo 14202, 716-846-4056.

Committees *Banking, Finance and Urban Affairs* (15th). Subcommittees: Economic Stabilization; Housing and Community Development; International Trade, Investment, and Monetary Policy; International Development Institutions and Finance.

Small Business (10th). Subcommittees: General Oversight and Minority Enterprise (Chairman).

Group Ratings

	ADA	COPE	PC	RPN	NFU	LCV	CFA	NAB	NSI	ACA	NTU
1978	40	60	78	67	50	–	77	36	50	37	–
1977	45	83	60	42	67	56	65	–	–	17	24
1976	50	70	70	53	92	75	81	17	40	15	32

Key Votes

1) Increase Def Spnd	DNV	6) Alaska Lands Protect	AGN	11) Delay Auto Pol Cntrl	FOR
2) B-1 Bomber	AGN	7) Water Projects Veto	FOR	12) Sugar Price Escalator	AGN
3) Cargo Preference	AGN	8) Consum Protect Agcy	FOR	13) Pub Fin Cong Cmpgns	FOR
4) Dereg Nat Gas	AGN	9) Common Situs Picket	FOR	14) ERA Ratif Recissn	AGN
5) Kemp-Roth	AGN	10) Labor Law Revision	FOR	15) Prohibt Govt Abrtns	FOR

Election Results

1978 general	John J. LaFalce (D-L)	99,497	(76%)	($44,407)
	Francina J. Cartonia (R)	31,527	(24%)	($9,476)
1978 primary	John J. LaFalce (D-L), unopposed			
1976 general	John J. LaFalce (D-L)	123,246	(67%)	($90,322)
	Ralph J. Argen (R-C)	61,701	(33%)	($157,047)

THIRTY-SEVENTH DISTRICT

Buffalo is the second largest city in New York and one of the important industrial centers on the Great Lakes. Huge steel mills line the shores of Lake Erie, as the principal east-west rail lines feed into downtown Buffalo and the industrial areas that circle it. This is the easternmost American port on the Great Lakes, and here giant freighters unload iron ore from the Mesabi Range and grain from the western prairies. Buffalo is one of the nation's leading steel producers and rivals Minneapolis as a miller of grain.

At the turn of the century, these basic industries were the fastest growing, most dynamic sector of the economy. There were flush times in Buffalo then. The city sat on the nation's leading transportation lines, and tens of thousands of Italian and Polish immigrants moved here, eager to work in its factories. Today the city's steel mills, grain elevators and docks, along with its downtown and radial avenues, still look like something out of the twenties, only a little rundown and shabby. Buffalo no longer enjoys the advantages it once had. Its basic industries now have sluggish growth or none at all. The major transportation routes have shifted to the south, and the great new mode of transportation, the airplane, scarcely touches down in Buffalo at all. In the early part of the century people were willing to put up with the fact that Buffalo receives an unusually heavy snowfall, because of its position at the extreme eastern end of Lake Erie. Now more and more people are trying to get away, to the Sun Belt; and the snow in Buffalo has become a national joke. All of this does not mean that Buffalo is moribund as a city. But its economy is not generating enough jobs for its current residents' children—much less any new migrants. The downtown is in trouble, and even the local branch of the State University of New York has moved to the suburbs.

Nearly all of Buffalo, together with the industrial city of Lackawanna to the south (home of a giant Bethlehem steel mill) and a few precincts in the suburban town of Cheektowaga, make up New York's 37th congressional district. This is a very heavily Democratic district—indeed the most solidly Democratic of any in upstate New York. Republican voters have died or moved to the suburbs, and Buffalo's relatively depressed economic state has led to desires for the kind of aid programs Democrats tend to favor more than Republicans. The 37th is also the home of a thriving Democratic organization, led by former state Democratic chairman Joseph Crangle. Unlike its counterparts in New York City, this machine is as interested in winning general elections as it is in controlling judicial nomination.

In 1974 the Erie County machine elected two new congressmen, both still in their thirties. One was Assemblyman John LaFalce, who captured the formerly Republican 36th district; the other was Erie County Controller Henry Nowak, elected here in the 37th. Nowak succeeded Thaddeus Dulski, a 16-year veteran who finally became Chairman of the House Post Office and Civil Service Committee, but never left much of a legacy. Nowak's election was a cinch; he was easily nominated, with the imprimatur of the machine, and easily elected in this district which even George McGovern easily carried. Nowak was assigned to the Public Works Committee, traditionally a place for practical-minded politicians who want to help their districts. He is considered easy to get along with and politically astute.

Census Data Pop. 467,759. Central city, 92%; suburban, 8%. Median family income, $8,845; families above $15,000: 14%; families below $3,000: 11%. Median years education, 10.6.

The Voters

Median voting age 46.
Employment profile White collar, 43%. Blue collar, 43%. Service, 14%. Farm, –%.
Ethnic groups Black, 21%. Total foreign stock, 28%. Poland, 8%; Italy, 6%; Germany, Canada, 3% each; UK, Ireland, 1% each.

Presidential vote

1976	Carter (D)	95,413	(63%)
	Ford (R)	55,021	(37%)
1972	Nixon (R)	74,998	(43%)
	McGovern (D)	99,509	(57%)

Rep. Henry J. Nowak (D) Elected 1974; b. Feb. 21, 1935, Buffalo; home, Buffalo; Canisius Col., B.B.A. 1957, Buffalo Law School, J.D. 1961.

Career Army, 1957–58, 1961–62; Practicing atty.; Erie Co. Asst. Dist. Atty., 1964; Confidential Secy. to N.Y. State Supreme Ct. Justice Arthur J. Cosgrove, 1965; Erie Co. Comptroller, 1966–75.

Offices 1514 LHOB, 202-225-3306. Also 212 U.S. Courthouse, Buffalo 14202, 716-853-4131.

Committees *Public Works and Transportation* (12th). Subcommittees: Economic Development; Oversight and Review; Public Buildings and Grounds; Water Resources.

Small Business (17th). Subcommittees: Access to Equity Capital and Business Opportunities (Chairman).

Group Ratings

	ADA	COPE	PC	RPN	NFU	LCV	CFA	NAB	NSI	ACA	NTU
1978	70	95	60	33	70	–	59	0	30	15	–
1977	70	87	70	38	75	60	60	–	–	7	17
1976	85	74	85	44	100	67	100	0	40	7	24

Key Votes

1) Increase Def Spnd	AGN	6) Alaska Lands Protect	FOR	11) Delay Auto Pol Cntrl	FOR
2) B-1 Bomber	AGN	7) Water Projects Veto	AGN	12) Sugar Price Escalator	AGN
3) Cargo Preference	FOR	8) Consum Protect Agcy	FOR	13) Pub Fin Cong Cmpgns	FOR
4) Dereg Nat Gas	AGN	9) Common Situs Picket	FOR	14) ERA Ratif Recissn	AGN
5) Kemp-Roth	AGN	10) Labor Law Revision	FOR	15) Prohibt Govt Abrtns	FOR

Election Results

1978 general	Henry J. Nowak (D-L)	70,911	(80%)	($37,521)
	Charles Poth III (R)	17,585	(20%)	
1978 primary	Henry J. Nowak (D), unopposed			
1976 general	Henry J. Nowak (D-L)	100,042	(81%)	($27,644)
	Calvin Kimbrough (R)	23,660	(19%)	($2,443)

THIRTY-EIGHTH DISTRICT

The 38th congressional district of New York includes most of suburban Erie County, from the Buffalo city limits to the small state Indian reservations at the northern and southern edges of the county. Altogether the district takes in the most prosperous parts of the so-called Niagara Frontier, the heavily industrial Buffalo-Niagara Falls metropolitan area along the Canadian border. Buffalo and its suburbs are the Democratic bastion of upstate New York; in fact, the region often produces higher Democratic percentages than metropolitan New York City, though of course not nearly so many votes. Buffalo is a place much more like Cleveland or Detroit than like New York, and its residents—in large part Polish, Italian, and black—are not as susceptible to either the city's fashionable liberalism or the Archie Bunker reaction to it as are people in the Big Apple.

A totally suburban district, the 38th is the least Democratic part of Erie County, with most of Buffalo's rather scant supply of wealthy suburban enclaves. Much of the district is working class Democratic, particularly the suburbs closest to the Buffalo city limits, like the town of Cheektowaga, which casts about one-quarter of the district's votes. Here are the miles and miles of small tract houses to which people who grew up in immigrant neighborhoods escaped. Overall it is one of the more marginal districts in upstate New York.

The district was held by a Democratic congressman from 1964 to 1970, when he ran for the Senate. It was won that year by Republican Jack Kemp, who has held it ever since. When he first ran, Kemp had retired only recently as quarterback for the Buffalo Bills; never quite a champion, he was nonetheless a talented player and also active in the then new players' associations. His involvement in politics had been limited to a brief period working for Ronald Reagan in his native California and a stint with the Republican National Committee. In his first years in Congress Kemp seemed to be a conventional Republican, strongly supporting the Nixon Administration. At home, he provided the kind of constituency services that got him reelected by wide margins in this otherwise marginal district—winning with as much as 78% in 1976. But he would have been considered one of the members of Congress least likely to prove an intellectual leader in public policy.

Yet that is what he became in the 95th Congress. Kemp had taken to reading economics and talking with economists. He was worried about lowering productivity in the United States and concerned that we were overtaxing the productive (i.e., rich) people in our economy—killing the geese that lay the golden eggs. In his studies Kemp discovered something called the Laffer curve—a theory that at some point taxes get so high that an increase brings in less revenue, because they discourage the activity that is being taxed. With the help of some economist friends, Kemp put together what is known as the Kemp-Roth bill, which would cut taxes 10% a year for each of the next three years. Kemp, claiming that we have reached the high point of the Laffer curve, argues that such a tax cut would bring in more revenue rather than less, because it would encourage economic activity. Accordingly, there would be no need to cut federal spending—a key point for a Buffalo area congressman, since this is one of the relatively few parts of the country where there is no great demand for cutting federal spending.

Kemp used the Kennedy-Johnson tax cut of 1963–64 and the example of President Kennedy as arguing points for his measure. There are some pertinent differences, however: that tax cut was intended to eliminate some of the slack in the economy, while Kemp-Roth was advanced at a time of inflation—and seems likely to do little to stop it. Nevertheless it was adopted as Republican party policy and was supported by almost every Republican in the House. Kemp-Roth was a constructively irresponsible measure—irresponsible because no party in power would ever advance a massive tax cut under such circumstances (the Ford Administration never did) and constructive because it got the country thinking about some problems that are real and which most people want solved. For in a period of constant inflation, progressive tax rates take a larger share of people's real income each year, unless something is done to cut the rates; and while Congress has been cutting rates each year, it has been doing so in an unsystematic and unpredictable manner. Jack Kemp is not the only economic thinker who is concerned about government having an increased share of GNP when most voters want it to have less.

It is still a little difficult to think of Kemp as a major intellectual leader of his party. He is earnest, and seems sure that he has stumbled on some programs which will save the republic; he is hard working, speaking all over the country to concerned Republicans and businessmen; he is honest and good looking and pleasant. But has he demonstrated the intellectual ability, stature, and character to be, as some of his supporters say he could be, a presidential candidate? Irving Kristol, one of his advisors, answers this question in part when he says that you don't have to be all that smart to be president, and that Kemp works hard. The suspicion is certainly alive in Washington that Kemp, for all his earnestness, is something of a lightweight; and that if he has had a major effect on opinion on national policy, that is quite enough to expect from him. A more plausible scenario for Kemp than a presidential campaign in 1980 is a race for the Senate in New York. Incumbent Jacob Javits may want to run again, but he will be 76 years old, and he would not be a strong candidate against Kemp among a primary electorate heavily weighted to conservative ideology and upstate residence. As for the general election, Kemp begins with a strong regional base in the Buffalo area and a fair reputation from Kemp-Roth. His main problem may be the suspicion residents of New York City and its suburbs have that a conservative Republican will not really favor aid to New York City. But if Kemp can overcome that, there is no reason he cannot win a Senate election in New York.

Census Data Pop. 467,761. Central city, 0%; suburban, 100%. Median family income, $11,583; families above $15,000: 27%; families below $3,000: 4%. Median years education, 12.3.

The Voters

Median voting age 43.
Employment profile White collar, 52%. Blue collar, 36%. Service, 11%. Farm, 1%.
Ethnic groups Total foreign stock, 23%. Poland, 5%; Germany, 4%; Italy, Canada, 3% each; UK, 2%.

Presidential vote

1976	Carter (D)	98,494	(45%)
	Ford (R)	122,219	(55%)
1972	Nixon (R)	132,331	(61%)
	McGovern (D)	85,221	(39%)

Rep. Jack F. Kemp (R) Elected 1970; b. July 13, 1935, Los Angeles, Cal.; home, Hamburg; Occidental Col., B.A. 1957, Long Beach St. U., Cal. Western U.; Presbyterian.

Career Pro football quarterback, San Diego Chargers and Buffalo Bills, 1957–70, Co-Founder and Pres., AFL Players Assn., 1965–70, AFL Most Valuable Player, 1965; Army, 1958; TV and Radio Commentator; Special Asst. to Gov. Ronald Reagan of Cal., 1967, and to the Chm., Repub. Natl. Comm., 1969.

Offices 2235 LHOB, 202-225-5265. Also 1101 Fed. Bldg., 111 W. Huron St., Buffalo 14202, 716-846-4123.

Committees *Appropriations* (12th). Subcommittees: Defense; Foreign Operations.

Group Ratings

	ADA	COPE	PC	RPN	NFU	LCV	CFA	NAB	NSI	ACA	NTU
1978	15	15	20	80	0	–	18	100	100	96	–
1977	10	13	20	42	25	14	15	–	–	96	48
1976	5	22	11	63	37	10	9	83	100	85	64

Key Votes

1) Increase Def Spnd	FOR	6) Alaska Lands Protect	AGN	11) Delay Auto Pol Cntrl	FOR
2) B-1 Bomber	FOR	7) Water Projects Veto	AGN	12) Sugar Price Escalator	AGN
3) Cargo Preference	AGN	8) Consum Protect Agcy	AGN	13) Pub Fin Cong Cmpgns	AGN
4) Dereg Nat Gas	FOR	9) Common Situs Picket	AGN	14) ERA Ratif Recissn	FOR
5) Kemp-Roth	FOR	10) Labor Law Revision	AGN	15) Prohibt Govt Abrtns	FOR

Election Results

1978 general	Jack F. Kemp (R-C)	113,928	(95%)	($64,251)
	James A. Peck (L)	6,204	(5%)	($6,418)
1978 primary	Jack F. Kemp (R-C), unopposed			
1976 general	Jack F. Kemp (R-C)	165,702	(78%)	
	Peter J. Geraci (D-L)	46,307	(22%)	

THIRTY-NINTH DISTRICT

The 39th congressional district of New York is the western half of the Southern Tier—that is, the counties on the northern side of the boundary between New York and Pennsylvania. Extending from the small city of Elmira to Lake Erie, the district contains the Corning Glass Works in Steuben County, two small Indian reservations, and a point on the western boundary exactly 496 miles from New York City via the Thomas E. Dewey Thruway. The small cities scattered among the district's valleys—Jamestown, Olean, Hornell, Corning—and on the shores of Lake Erie—Dunkirk, Fredonia—tend to be Democratic or politically marginal, reflecting the preference of the Irish and Italian Catholics who came to this part of upstate New York after it had first been settled by New England Yankees. Outside the towns the Yankee Republicans still predominate and, as in most of upstate New York, control the district politically.

Historically this has always been a Republican district. It was represented by Daniel Reed, the last Republican Chairman of the House Ways and Means Committee; by Charles Goodell, who was appointed to the Senate in 1968 after the death of Robert Kennedy and whose transformation from upstate moderate to Vietnam dove led to his defeat by Conservative James Buckley in 1970; and James Hastings, who resigned in 1976 and was later convicted on salary kickback charges.

Republicans expected to win the seat in the 1976 special election; their candidate, Jack Calkins, longtime head of the Republican Congressional Campaign Committee and a native of the area, seemed like a strong candidate.

But in the middle seventies, voters were especially anxious to have elected officials who understood their problems closely and from first-hand experience. While Calkins had plenty of experience in Washington, he had not lived in the Southern Tier for years and was plainly out of touch with what was going on there. The Democrat, Stanley Lundine, was not. As Mayor of Jamestown, he had made a popular record. He had a strong local base there in Chautauqua County, in the western end of the district, and he was able to make his local experience relevant to people in the eastern counties.

Lundine won that election with a surprising 61%—fully 19% ahead of where Jimmy Carter finished in the 39th later in the year. With an excellent staff and by keeping in touch with his constituents, he has maintained high standing at home. He won again in the 1976 general election and in 1978, the latter time against a hard-campaigning Catholic priest. Lundine was one of the young Democrats who has changed the complexion of the House Banking Committee. He has sponsored legislation in a number of areas, including measures to study employee participation in decision-making at lower level jobs.

Census Data Pop. 467,859. Central city, 0%; suburban, 1%. Median family income, $8,936; families above $15,000: 15%; families below $3,000: 9%. Median years education, 12.2.

The Voters

Median voting age 45.
Employment profile White collar, 43%. Blue collar, 39%. Service, 14%. Farm, 4%.
Ethnic groups Black, 1%. Total foreign stock, 14%. Italy, 3%; Sweden, Germany, Poland, 2% each; UK, Canada, 1% each.

Presidential vote

1976	Carter (D)	77,776	(42%)
	Ford (R)	106,803	(58%)
1972	Nixon (R)	101,792	(66%)
	McGovern (D)	51,963	(34%)

Rep. Stanley N. Lundine (D) Elected March 2, 1976; b. Feb. 4, 1939, Jamestown; home, Jamestown; Duke U., B.A. 1961; NYU, LL.B. 1964; Protestant.

Career Chautauqua Co. Public Defender, 1965–67; Jamestown City Assoc. Corp. Counsel, 1967–69; Mayor, Jamestown, 1969–76.

Offices 430 CHOB, 202-225-3161. Also Fed. Bldg., Jamestown 14702, 716-484-0252.

Committees *Banking, Finance and Urban Affairs* (20th). Subcommittees: Economic Stabilization; Housing and Community Development; International Trade, Investment and Monetary Policy.

Science and Technology (25th). Subcommittees: Energy Research and Production; Natural Resources and Environment.

Group Ratings

	ADA	COPE	PC	RPN	NFU	LCV	CFA	NAB	NSI	ACA	NTU
1978	70	85	63	67	56	–	50	10	40	26	–
1977	75	71	73	73	75	87	45	–	–	15	25
1976	88	82	66	56	78	72	80	25	–	4	40

Key Votes

1) Increase Def Spnd	AGN	6) Alaska Lands Protect	FOR	11) Delay Auto Pol Cntrl	AGN
2) B-1 Bomber	AGN	7) Water Projects Veto	AGN	12) Sugar Price Escalator	AGN
3) Cargo Preference	AGN	8) Consum Protect Agcy	AGN	13) Pub Fin Cong Cmpgns	FOR
4) Dereg Nat Gas	AGN	9) Common Situs Picket	FOR	14) ERA Ratif Recissn	AGN
5) Kemp-Roth	AGN	10) Labor Law Revision	FOR	15) Prohibt Govt Abrtns	AGN

Election Results

1978 general	Stanley N. Lundine (D)	79,385	(58%)	($92,454)
	Crispin M. Maguire (R-C)	56,431	(42%)	($65,508)
1978 primary	Stanley N. Lundine (D), unopposed			
1976 general	Stanley N. Lundine (D)	109,986	(62%)	($158,091)
	Richard A. Snowden (R-C)	68,018	(38%)	($65,622)

NORTH CAROLINA

For more than two centuries, differences between the coastal east and the mountainous west have structured the politics of North Carolina. During the Revolutionary War, the Tidewater towns and plantations in the east were Tory, while the Piedmont to the west was a hotbed of anti-British radicalism. Likewise during the Civil War the east—where most of the state's slaves could be found—was strongly pro-Confederate, while to the west, particularly in the mountains, there was considerable Union sentiment. Overall North Carolina was lukewarm enough about the Rebel cause to have declined to secede until Virginia did, and cut the state off from the north.

Each of North Carolina's regions has its traditional politics, developed largely from this Civil War heritage and from its industrial development. For North Carolina is a prosperous and, it would have you believe, a progressive state, in large part because of the textile, furniture, and tobacco industries. In all three North Carolina ranks first in the nation; the industries have produced some millionaires here and a well-to-do white collar class. But what should not be forgotten, though North Carolina boosters do not dwell on it, is that this is one of the most heavily blue collar states in the nation, and that blue collar wages here, especially in the dominant textile industry, are among the lowest in the nation (as is the level of unionization).

North Carolina is proud of what it considers its progressive tradition of government. For years the state has spent heavily on education; and for years it avoided, for the most part, racial demagoguery. But in the late sixties, North Carolina's record did not seem so glittering. Other Southern states were moving ahead, notably the Georgia of Atlanta skyscrapers. Even South Carolina was attracting industry more aggressively than its larger neighbor. While the most vital and growing sector of the national economy was the white collar sector, North Carolina continued to have a blue collar economy. The state's progressive government, it became clear, rested on an unspoken policy of not disturbing the state's major economic interests—even if that meant not attracting better paying jobs and new industry. The policy of keeping unions and high wages out left North Carolina's textiles increasingly vulnerable to even lower wage competition from Mexico, South Korea, and Taiwan.

In the late seventies that picture seems to have changed, and North Carolina has shared in the growth of the Sun Belt region. The state's lack of a real major metropolitan area, a handicap in the sixties, became an asset in the seventies as more and more Americans moved to the smaller communities they prefer over big cities. Industrial growth was great, and increasingly it occurred in better paying, higher skill jobs. The state government seemed to have strong leadership again. It had drifted under James Holshouser, a mountain Republican elected Governor in an upset in 1972, who had not expected to win and was unprepared to govern.

That was not the case with his successor, Democrat Jim Hunt. He began with what would have been handicaps in the late sixties: a reputation as a liberal and a supporter of civil rights. He backed higher spending on education, but he also supported capital punishment and a tough stance on crime—making it hard to pigeonhole him ideologically. Hunt won the first Democratic primary with an absolute majority over two main rivals, one of them a free-spending millionaire; he won the general election over a Holshouser appointee by a 2–1 margin.

Hunt has a forcefulness and self-confidence reminiscent of John Connally, and though he has been controversial at times he has been a popular governor. He took much criticism outside the state for refusing to exonerate the Wilmington Ten, a group of black activists convicted of fire-bombing a church during a 1968 riot. The charge is that the Ten are political prisoners, convicted for their beliefs not their acts—though there is considerable evidence that they did just what they were charged with; in any case all but one has served his term and been released. Hunt's decision was popular among the state's whites though not among blacks. But he has won black support on his record otherwise; he has high black appointees and engineered the election statewide of a black supreme court justice and state administrative officer—the first times blacks have won statewide elections in the South. Hunt also succeeded in winning voter approval of an amendment allowing governors to seek a second term, despite strong opposition from former Senator Sam Ervin. That makes him the odds on favorite to be reelected Governor in 1980.

The 1972 Republican sweep which made Holshouser Governor also helped elect Jesse Helms to the U.S. Senate. Helms had other assets, though, even then. As a Raleigh TV commentator, he was a familiar face in much of the state; through his hookup on the radio Tobacco Network he had even more exposure in the small towns and farms of eastern and Piedmont North Carolina. He expressed strong right wing views, for example accusing Nixon of "appeasing Red China" by visiting Peking; he expressed the opposition to civil rights and hawkishness on foreign policy issues that were the central beliefs of many North Carolina voters, especially in rural areas. And it was in rural eastern North Carolina—historically very Democratic—that he picked up enough votes to defeat his opponent, Congressman Nick Galifianakis, an opponent of the Vietnam war and civil rights supporter.

Helms came to Washington with the reputation of a right winger, and he has not lost it. He is a stern man of strong views, and is not inclined to mask them with pretty labels. He is invariably hawkish on foreign and military issues and parsimonious on domestic issues; he believes in almost entirely unregulated free enterprise. Helms opposed many of the foreign policies of the Ford Administration; and in 1976 he stationed himself at Kansas City in the week before the Republican convention, and as a sort of one-man lobby forced the adoption of planks that in effect repudiated the policies of the man the convention nominated.

Helms's politics has made him many enemies and many friends. His extremism on many issues and his lack of substantive legislative accomplishments left him vulnerable in 1978 when he ran for reelection. But his steadfast adherence to his principles won him fervent supporters all over the country. Helms used Richard Viguerie's direct mail operation and in 1977 and 1978 raised $6 million for his campaign. His Democratic opponent, John Ingram, dubbed him the "six million dollar man" and called him the captive of the big money interests. This dovetailed well with Ingram's appeal; as the state insurance commissioner, he had opposed rate increases and he had upset wealthy banker Luther Hodges, Jr., in the primary. But Helms's funds came not from moneyed special interests, but from thousands of idealistic citizens; and he used most of the money not for buying votes in North Carolina but for sending out more mailings. In effect Helms was creating a huge mailing list, which he has at his disposal for use in the 1980 elections, to benefit whom he wants. In the process, he spent enough to beat the underfinanced and unsophisticated Ingram, and again showed his strength in the Democratic east. Now he is in a position to play an important role—perhaps even run himself—in the 1980 presidential campaign.

In his first term Helms was not an especially effective Senator; he was always more interested in presenting his views than in reaching some sort of accommodation. But with now many more like-minded senators in Washington than there were in the middle seventies, Helms is in a position to have more impact. He gained a seat on the Foreign Relations Committee in 1979, and along with several other conservatives seems likely to make that once homogeneous body a forum for debate and division. And he has become the ranking Republican on the Agriculture Committee, where he is far less likely than his predecessor, Robert Dole, to work with Democrats on food stamps and nutrition programs. Helms will also be in a good position to defend the interests of North Carolina's tobacco industry.

Between 1972 and 1974 there was almost a political revolution in North Carolina. It was transformed from a competitive two-party state to a solid Democratic bastion. One reason was Watergate, which had a special impact here: for the Chairman of the Senate Watergate Committee was North Carolina's Sam Ervin, who was then 76, in the last two years of what he decided would be his last term. When the hearings began, North Carolinians, like most Southerners, were solidly with their president; by the time the hearings had ended and the special prosecutor fired, a perceptible change had occurred. The result was a Democratic sweep in 1974. Robert Morgan, the Democratic nominee for Ervin's seat, won easily with 63%; two apparently safe Republican congressmen were defeated; the Republican delegation in the state legislature was virtually eliminated (reduced to 3 seats out of 170). In 1976 Democrats again won big; they recaptured the governorship and Jimmy Carter easily carried the state. Even 1978, apart from Helms's victory, was a Democratic year here.

Senator Morgan, like Governor Hunt, combines what have previously been regarded as liberal and conservative positions in one person. He was first prominent in state politics, for example, as campaign manager for I. Beverly Lake, a law professor and segregationist who nearly beat Terry Sanford for the 1960 gubernatorial nomination. But as Attorney General, elected in 1968, Morgan became known as an advocate of consumers' rights. It was perhaps his political past that helped him to the 59% he won in the eastern part of the state in the decisive primary. But it was his more recent record that gave him a creditable 44% in the rest of the state—enough for 50% overall, enough to avoid a runoff. While Helms is one of the most predictable votes in the Senate, Morgan's record defies ideological labels. He tends to favor more defense spending, but his record on the Senate Intelligence Committee was one of careful criticism of some agency abuses. On economic issues his record has been middle of the road. Morgan must seek reelection in 1980, and while it is possible that he might encounter serious opposition in either the primary or the general election, he must be regarded as the favorite.

North Carolina has now had two presidential primaries, and the results show how opinion in the state has changed. In 1972 this was one of George Wallace's victories in the South; he beat former Governor Terry Sanford, a progressive who is now president of Duke University, by a 50%–37% margin. But in 1976 Wallace, fresh from a defeat in Florida, was humiliated here. Jimmy Carter won 85 of 100 counties and beat him 54%–35%. The conservative trend was shown only in the much smaller Republican primary. There Ronald Reagan edged Gerald Ford by a 53%–47% margin. This kept Reagan's candidacy alive; he had lost earlier primaries, albeit by even smaller margins in some cases, and he seemed about ready to quit. Reagan's victory was not just a matter of piling up votes in the east, where there are very few registered Republicans. He carried all the big cities in the Piedmont region—indeed, just about everything except the western mountain counties. The old Republican tradition in North Carolina—based in the mountains, with a touch of populism, and a dislike for the slaveholding flatland counties to the east—today seems to be only a minority even within its own party.

Census Data Pop. 5,082,059; 2.51% of U.S. total, 12th largest; Central city, 19%; suburban, 19%. Median family income, $7,770; 40th highest; families above $15,000: 12%; families below $3,000: 15%. Median years education, 10.6.

1977 Share of Federal Tax Burden $7,012,000,000; 2.03% of U.S. total, 16th largest.

1977 Share of Federal Outlays $7,872,459,000; 1.99% of U.S. total, 18th largest. Per capita federal spending, $1,444.

DOD	$1,848,627,000	16th (2.02%)	HEW	$3,123,575,000	14th (2.11%)
ERDA	$3,360,000	37th (0.06%)	HUD	$104,476,000	13th (2.48%)
NASA	$2,045,000	33d (0.05%)	VA	$489,428,000	10th (2.55%)
DOT	$233,896,000	20th (1.64%)	EPA	$235,419,000	37th (2.87%)
DOC	$104,437,000	20th (1.26%)	RevS	$187,563,000	11th (2.22%)
DOI	$45,362,000	25th (0.98%)	Debt	$233,896,000	18th (0.78%)
USDA	$565,073,000	7th (2.84%)	Other	$695,302,000	

Economic Base Textile mill products, especially knitting mills and yarn and thread mills; agriculture, notably tobacco, broilers, hogs and eggs; apparel and other textile products, especially men's and boys' furnishings; finance, insurance and real estate; household furniture, and other furniture and fixtures; food and kindred products, especially meat products; electrical equipment and supplies, especially communication equipment.

Political Line-up Governor, James B. Hunt, Jr. (D). Senators, Jesse A. Helms (R) and Robert Morgan (D). Representatives, 11 (9 D and 2 R). State Senate (45 D and 5 R); State House (105 D and 15 R).

The Voters

Registration 2,430,306 Total. 1,764,126 D (73%); 567,039 R (23%); 99,045 Unaffiliated (4%); 96 Libertarian (–).
Median voting age 40
Employment profile White collar, 38%. Blue collar, 46%. Service, 11%. Farm, 5%.
Ethnic groups Black, 22%. Total foreign stock, 2%.

Presidential vote

1976	Carter (D)	927,365	(56%)
	Ford (R)	741,960	(44%)
1972	Nixon (R)	1,054,889	(71%)
	McGovern (D)	438,705	(29%)

1976 Democratic Presidential Primary

Carter	324,437	(56%)
Wallace	210,166	(36%)
Others	47,379	(8%)

1976 Republican Presidential Primary

Reagan	101,468	(53%)
Ford	88,897	(47%)

Sen. Jesse A. Helms (R) Elected 1972, seat up 1978; b. Oct. 18, 1921, Monroe; home, Raleigh; Wingate Col., Wake Forest Col; Baptist.

Career Navy, WWII; City Ed., The Raleigh *Times*; Admin. Asst. to U.S. Sens. Willis Smith, 1951–53, and Alton Lennon, 1953; Exec. Dir., N.C. Bankers Assn., 1953–60; Raleigh City Cncl., 1957–61; Exec. V.P., WRAL-TV and Tobacco Radio Network, 1960–72.

Offices 4213 DSOB, 202-224-6342. Also Fed. Bldg., Raleigh 27611, 919-755-4630, and Box 2944, Hickory 28601, 704-322-5170.

Committees *Agriculture, Nutrition, and Forestry* (Ranking Member). Subcommittees: Environment, Soil Conservation, and Forestry; Agricultural Production, Marketing, and Stabilization of Prices; Nutrition.

Foreign Relations (4th). Subcommittees: Arms Control, Oceans, International Operations, and Environment; East Asian and Pacific Affairs; Western Hemisphere Affairs.

Group Ratings

	ADA	COPE	PC	RPN	NFU	LCV	CFA	NAB	NSI	ACA	NTU
1978	5	11	13	75	44	18	5	100	100	96	–
1977	0	10	20	60	9	–	8	–	–	100	56
1976	5	10	6	47	17	10	0	100	90	100	88

Key Votes

1) Warnke Nom	AGN	6) Egypt-Saudi Arms	FOR	11) Hosptl Cost Contnmnt	AGN
2) Neutron Bomb	FOR	7) Draft Restr Pardon	AGN	12) Clinch River Reactor	FOR
3) Waterwy User Fee	FOR	8) Wheat Price Support	FOR	13) Pub Fin Cong Cmpgns	AGN
4) Dereg Nat Gas	FOR	9) Panama Canal Treaty	AGN	14) ERA Ratif Recissn	AGN
5) Kemp-Roth	FOR	10) Labor Law Rev Clot	AGN	15) Med Necssy Abrtns	AGN

Election Results

1978 general	Jesse A. Helms (R)	619,151	(55%)	($7,460,966)
	John R. Ingram (D)	516,663	(45%)	($264,088)
1978 primary	Jesse A. Helms (R), unopposed			
1972 general	Jesse A. Helms (R)	795,248	(54%)	($654,246)
	Nick Galifianakis (D)	677,293	(46%)	($470,093)

Sen. Robert Morgan (D) Elected 1974, seat up 1980; b. Oct. 5, 1925, Lillington; home, Lillington; E. Carolina Col., 1942–44, U. of N.C., 1944–45, E. Carolina Col., B.S. 1947, Wake Forest U., LL.B. 1949; Baptist.

Career Practicing atty., 1950–69; Harnett Co. Clerk of Superior Ct., 1950–54; N.C. Gen. Assembly, 1955–57, 1959–61, 1963–68; Atty. Gen. of N.C., 1969–74.

Offices 5313 DSOB, 202-224-3154. Also Century Post Ofc., P.O. Box 2719, Raleigh 27602, 919-755-4236.

Committees *Armed Services* (8th). Subcommittees: General Procurement; Research and Development; Procurement Policy and Reprogramming (Chairman).

Banking, Housing, and Urban Affairs (5th). Subcommittees: Housing and Urban Affairs; Financial Institutions; Rural Housing and Development (Chairman).

Select Committee on Ethics.

Select Committee on Small Business (6th).

Group Ratings

	ADA	COPE	PC	RPN	NFU	LCV	CFA	NAB	NSI	ACA	NTU
1978	25	33	50	50	67	41	40	67	50	27	–
1977	40	33	53	56	55	–	44	–	–	60	26
1976	25	53	32	36	73	22	43	43	89	41	15

Key Votes

1) Warnke Nom	FOR	6) Egypt-Saudi Arms	FOR	11) Hosptl Cost Contnmnt	AGN
2) Neutron Bomb	FOR	7) Draft Restr Pardon	AGN	12) Clinch River Reactor	AGN
3) Waterwy User Fee	FOR	8) Wheat Price Support	AGN	13) Pub Fin Cong Cmpgns	AGN
4) Dereg Nat Gas	AGN	9) Panama Canal Treaty	FOR	14) ERA Ratif Recissn	AGN
5) Kemp-Roth	AGN	10) Labor Law Rev Clot	DNV	15) Med Necssy Abrtns	FOR

Election Results

1974 general	Robert Morgan (D)	633,775	(63%)	($781,201)
	William E. Stevens (R)	377,618	(37%)	($385,527)
1974 primary	Robert Morgan (D)	294,986	(50%)	
	Nick Galifianakis (D)	189,815	(32%)	
	Henry Hall Wilson (D)	67,247	(11%)	
	Seven others (D)	33,278	(6%)	
1968 general	Sam J. Ervin, Jr. (D)	870,406	(61%)	
	Robert Vance Somers (R)	566,934	(39%)	

Gov. James B. Hunt, Jr. (D) Elected 1976, term expires Jan. 1981; b. May 16, 1937, Greensboro; N.C. St. U., B.S. 1959, M.S. 1962, J.D. 1964.

Career Natl. College Dir., Dem. Natl. Comm., 1962–63; Econ. Adviser 1964–66; Practicing atty., 1966–72; Asst. N.C. Dem. Party Chm., 1969; Lt. Gov. of N.C., 1973–77.

Offices The Capitol, Raleigh 27602, 919-829-5811.

Election Results

1976 general	James B. Hunt, Jr. (D)	1,081,293	(66%)
	David T. Flaherty (R)	564,102	(34%)
1976 primary	James B. Hunt, Jr. (D)	362,102	(53%)
	Ed O'Herron (D)	157,815	(23%)
	George Wood (D)	121,673	(18%)
	Two others (D)	36,341	(5%)
1972 general	James E. Holshouser, Jr. (R)	767,470	(51%)
	Hargrove Bowles (D)	729,104	(49%)

FIRST DISTRICT

Since the end of the draft, eastern North Carolina has produced one of the largest percentages of volunteers for the Army and other military services in the country. Aggressive recruiting may account for some of the enlistments. But the total number of volunteers tells us a great deal about life in the rolling coastal plain east of Raleigh, a region that has no metropolitan area with as many as 100,000 people. Plenty of people here still make their livings on small tobacco farms, but more of them work in textile mills and apparel factories, located in small towns or, increasingly, simply along rural highways. The textile industry is almost entirely non-union, the hours are long, the working conditions poor, and the wages low. Few young men (or women) from eastern North Carolina go to college; book learning is not always prized, and few parents can afford the luxury of more schooling. So the choice comes down to the mills, the bus north to New York, or the Army—and the Army often looks like the best choice.

North Carolina's 1st congressional district lies entirely within the state's eastern coastal zone. It includes the Outer Banks, the string of coastal islands beyond Pamlico and Albemarle Sounds where the Wright brothers flew the first airplane. Also here is Cape Hatteras, where the warm Gulf Stream meets colder currents, creating seas that have sunk countless ships. There is no really good port here (or anywhere else in North Carolina), and most of the people live inland, in small cities like New Bern, Elizabeth City, and Greenville—at 29,000 the district's largest city. Even more live in the countryside, on small farms or in isolated house trailers. Some 36% of the 1st's residents are black, the second largest percentage in North Carolina's eleven districts.

The white voters of the 1st retain from their slaveholding days a Democratic preference. They steadfastly supported Democratic presidential candidates until 1968, when they went for George Wallace, and 1972, when they went for Richard Nixon. Since Watergate, the area has reverted to its historic Democratic voting habits: Senator Robert Morgan received 79% of the vote here in 1974 and Governor James Hunt got 77% in 1976. There is one exception: Senator Jesse Helms has a following here today, going back to his days as a commentator on the radio Tobacco Network, and does very well for a Republican in this area, although he does not quite carry the district.

When Wallace was running in 1968, Congressman Walter Jones of the 1st district was one of several Southern Democrats who announced that, if the election went from the Electoral College to the House of Representatives, he would vote for the candidate who carried the district—which turned out to be Wallace. Jones is one of the more senior Southern conservatives these days. He was first chosen in a 1966 special election, and now ranks high on the Merchant Marine and Fisheries Committee (which his predecessor in the 1st chaired) and on the Agriculture Committee.

On the latter he is Chairman of the Tobacco Subcommittee. Of course he favors strongly the tobacco subsidies which make it possible for farmers here to make a living off as few as 15 acres. Jones has passed 65, but he has never had serious opposition since he first won, and seems likely to remain in the House for some time to come.

Census Data Pop. 459,543. Central city, 0%; suburban, 0%. Median family income, $6,368; families above $15,000: 8%; families below $3,000: 22%. Median years education, 10.2.

The Voters

Median voting age 42.
Employment profile White collar, 36%. Blue collar, 40%. Service, 13%. Farm, 11%.
Ethnic groups Black, 36%. Total foreign stock, 1%.

Presidential vote

1976	Carter (D)	79,503	(60%)
	Ford (R)	52,752	(40%)
1972	Nixon (R)	83,557	(70%)
	McGovern (D)	35,333	(30%)

Rep. Walter B. Jones (D) Elected Feb. 5, 1966; b. Aug. 19, 1913, Fayetteville; home, Farmville; N.C. St. U., B.S. 1934; Baptist.

Career Office supply business, 1934–49; Mayor of Farmville, 1949–53; N.C. Gen. Assembly, 1955–59; N.C. Senate, 1965.

Offices 241 CHOB, 202-225-3101. Also 108 E. Wilson St., Farmville 27828, 919-753-3082.

Committees *Agriculture* (3d). Subcommittees: Dairy and Poultry; Oilseeds and Rice; Tobacco (Chairman).

Merchant Marine and Fisheries (4th). Subcommittees: Coast Guard and Navigation; Panama Canal; Merchant Marine.

Group Ratings

	ADA	COPE	PC	RPN	NFU	LCV	CFA	NAB	NSI	ACA	NTU
1978	25	25	28	64	50	–	9	70	100	78	–
1977	10	45	18	27	50	30	15	–	–	56	23
1976	10	45	21	47	28	19	18	36	70	86	50

Key Votes

1) Increase Def Spnd	DNV	6) Alaska Lands Protect	AGN	11) Delay Auto Pol Cntrl	FOR
2) B-1 Bomber	FOR	7) Water Projects Veto	AGN	12) Sugar Price Escalator	FOR
3) Cargo Preference	FOR	8) Consum Protect Agcy	AGN	13) Pub Fin Cong Cmpgns	AGN
4) Dereg Nat Gas	FOR	9) Common Situs Picket	AGN	14) ERA Ratif Recissn	FOR
5) Kemp-Roth	AGN	10) Labor Law Revision	AGN	15) Prohibt Govt Abrtns	AGN

Election Results

1978 general	Walter B. Jones (D)	67,716	(80%)	($24,067)
	James Newcomb (R)	16,814	(20%)	
1978 primary	Walter B. Jones (D)	62,824	(82%)	
	James J. Bonner (D)	10,527	(14%)	
	One other	3,246	(4%)	
1976 general	Walter B. Jones (D)	98,611	(77%)	($27,780)
	Joseph M. Word (R)	29,295	(23%)	($29,692)

SECOND DISTRICT

North of Raleigh and south of the Virginia line, the 2d congressional district of North Carolina is situated on an inland portion of the coastal plain where it rises to become the Piedmont. This is a predominantly rural and small town district; its largest city, Rocky Mount, has only 34,000 people. Like much of North Carolina, the 2d's economy depends almost entirely on textiles and the tobacco crop. What makes the 2d distinctive politically is the size of its black population—some 40% of its residents (though only 34% of those over 18) are black, the highest percentage in the state, and comparable with what one finds in the Deep South. Black outmigration from this area was great in the decades between World War II and the seventies; it has slowed substantially in the last ten years, as opportunities have been scarcer in northern cities and more plentiful in North Carolina. The prospect, therefore, is for the black percentage of eligible voters to grow slowly in the next decade—the reversal of almost a century-long trend.

The other distinctive feature of the 2d district is the presence here of Orange County. Most of the nation's Orange Counties, in California, Florida, and even New York, are solidly conservative; this one, which contains the University of North Carolina and its beautiful little city of Chapel Hill, is the state's banner liberal county. It was one of two in the state which went for George McGovern in 1972 (the other was Northampton, a black majority area with a liberally inclined white boss, which is also in the 2d).

For nearly three decades the Congressman from the 2d has been a man more akin in spirit to the Old South than to its young blacks or Chapel Hill residents, Democrat L. H. Fountain. He is the kind of politician who wears white linen suits in the summertime and speaks with gentle Southern courtliness the year round. During his years in Congress, Fountain has compiled a solidly conservative record on economic and social issues. But as Chairman of the Intergovernmental Relations and Human Resources Subcommittee, he has been a crusader in one area: drug regulation. For more than a dozen years, Fountain has been holding hearings and arguing that the Food and Drug Administration has been too liberal in allowing possibly dangerous drugs on the market. He has worked to penetrate the layer of secrecy the FDA bureaucracy—convinced that mere laymen cannot understand its workings—puts over its affairs. Fountain's subcommittee has much wider jurisdiction, but apparently he has decided to concentrate on this one area and do a solid job rather than conduct scatter-shot investigations of numerous agencies. He does have other legislative accomplishments, however, notably the writing of a law requiring the setting up of an office of inspector general in each of the Cabinet departments.

For years Fountain had no trouble winning reelection, but he has had some significant challenges in the seventies. They have all come Democratic primary; this is not an area where Republicans have provided any significant competition. In 1972 Fountain was opposed by Howard Lee, the black Mayor of Chapel Hill; Lee got a creditable 41% in the primary, and now serves in a top-level job under Governor James Hunt. It would have been fitting if Lee had won this district: it elected a black, Republican George White, in 1898, whose defeat in 1900 began a 28-year period during which no black person served in Congress. In 1976 Fountain had competition from state Senator Russell Kirby. Kirby fell short of winning, but with two minor candidates he held Fountain to 51%—just above what he needed to avoid a runoff.

Surprisingly, serious competition did not materialize in 1978, and at 65 Fountain won a 14th term. But he may have another tough contest in 1980.

Census Data Pop. 457,601. Central city, 0%; suburban, 13%. Median family income, $6,550; families above $15,000: 9%; families below $3,000: 20%. Median years education, 9.8.

The Voters

Median voting age 42.
Employment profile White collar, 36%. Blue collar, 41%. Service, 13%. Farm, 10%.
Ethnic groups Black, 40%. Total foreign stock, 1%.

Presidential vote

1976	Carter (D)	81,050	(61%)
	Ford (R)	51,543	(39%)
1972	Nixon (R)	86,006	(64%)
	McGovern (D)	47,674	(36%)

Rep. L. H. Fountain (D) Elected 1952; b. Apr. 23, 1913, Leggett; home, Tarboro; U. of N.C., A.B. 1934, J.D. 1936; Presbyterian.

Career Practicing atty., 1936–42, 1946–52, Army, WWII; Reading Clerk, N.C. Senate, 1936–41; N.C. Senate, 1947–52.

Offices 2188 RHOB, 202-225-4531. Also P.O. Bldg., Tarboro 27886, 919-823-4200.

Committees *Government Operations* (2d). Subcommittees: Intergovernmental Relations and Human Resources (Chairman).

Foreign Affairs (2d). Subcommittees: Europe and the Middle East; International Security and Scientific Affairs.

Group Ratings

	ADA	COPE	PC	RPN	NFU	LCV	CFA	NAB	NSI	ACA	NTU
1978	15	10	25	58	50	–	5	92	100	88	–
1977	15	35	20	31	67	20	25	–	–	59	36
1976	0	41	26	41	42	12	9	55	100	74	44

Key Votes

1) Increase Def Spnd	FOR	6) Alaska Lands Protect	AGN	11) Delay Auto Pol Cntrl	FOR
2) B-1 Bomber	FOR	7) Water Projects Veto	FOR	12) Sugar Price Escalator	FOR
3) Cargo Preference	AGN	8) Consum Protect Agcy	AGN	13) Pub Fin Cong Cmpgns	AGN
4) Dereg Nat Gas	AGN	9) Common Situs Picket	AGN	14) ERA Ratif Recissn	FOR
5) Kemp-Roth	AGN	10) Labor Law Revision	AGN	15) Prohibt Govt Abrtns	AGN

Election Results

1978 general	L. H. Fountain (D)	61,851	(79%)	($21,984)
	Barry L. Gardner (R)	15,988	(21%)	($7,335)
1978 primary	L. H. Fountain (D)	51,282	(75%)	
	Elbert Rudasill (D)	17,314	(25%)	
1976 general	L. H. Fountain (D), unopposed			($88,696)

THIRD DISTRICT

The 3d district of North Carolina is one of small farms, small towns, and Atlantic shore seascapes. Lying in the middle of the state's coastal plain, the 3d runs from a point a few miles south of Raleigh and Durham to the Atlantic Ocean near Wilmington. The district's largest city is Goldsboro, with 26,000 people, but an even larger population concentration can be found in Camp Lejeune, the Marine Corps's giant base at the estuary of the New River. One of the Marines' most important installations, Camp Lejeune looms large in the economy of the region, though voters may be disturbed by occasional racial conflict at the base. Also in the 3d is an Air Force base near Goldsboro, with Fort Bragg just over the line in the 7th district.

This is a traditional Democratic area. But with its heavy dependence on the military and its relatively low (27%) black percentage, it was rather conservatively inclined in the late sixties and early seventies. In 1972 the district gave George Wallace his highest percentage of any district in the state's Democratic presidential primary, and in the general election that year it delivered a majority for Senate candidate Jesse Helms. Since Watergate, it has switched back heavily to the Democratic column—except when Helms ran for reelection in 1978.

The 3d district seat in the House of Representatives has been handed down in a kind of succession for more than 40 years. From 1934 to 1960 the seat was held by Graham Barden, a stuffy and bigoted conservative. As Chairman of the House Education and Labor Committee, Barden refused to recognize the number two Democrat, Adam Clayton Powell, because he was black. Barden retired in 1960 and was succeeded by David Henderson, who had served on his staff. After 14 years Henderson became Chairman of the Post Office and Civil Service Committee; in 1976 he decided to retire. His successor was a member of his staff, Charles Whitley.

It would be inaccurate to portray this succession by staffers as automatic. On the contrary, it is becoming more difficult these days for congressional staffers to win House seats. Voters are less impressed with their expertise than they used to be, and are more likely to demand a congressman with experience in local affairs. Whitley wisely made a point of maintaining his actual, not just formal, residence in the 3d district, and concentrated on handling district problems. Thus it was impossible for his main primary opponent, state Representative Jimmy Love, to pin the Washington label on him. It was close, however: Love led the first primary, and Whitley won the runoff with only 54%.

Whitley's committee assignments were choice ones for a congressman with this kind of district—far better, in fact, than Henderson's or Barden's. He won a seat on the Agriculture Committee and, more important, on its Tobacco Subcommittee; like all North Carolina representatives, he is a strong defender of tobacco. And he also got a seat on Armed Services, which gives him some leverage in protecting the district's large military bases. Whitley had one of the lowest party unity scores and most conservative voting records of the 1976 freshmen, though he is not as conservative as many oldtime Southern congressmen. He was reelected easily in 1978.

Census Data Pop. 458,000. Central city, 0%; suburban, 0%. Median family income, $6,193; families above $15,000: 6%; families below $3,000: 21%. Median years education, 10.4.

The Voters

Median voting age 37.
Employment profile White collar, 34%. Blue collar, 43%. Service, 12%. Farm, 11%.
Ethnic groups Black, 27%. Total foreign stock, 2%.

Presidential vote

1976	Carter (D)	68,612	(59%)
	Ford (R)	48,186	(41%)
1972	Nixon (R)	79,431	(74%)
	McGovern (D)	27,878	(26%)

Rep. Charles Whitley (D) Elected 1976; b. Jan. 3, 1927, Silver City; home, Mount Olive; Wake Forest U., B.A. 1949, LL.B. 1950, Geo. Wash. U., M.A. 1974; Baptist.

Career Army, 1944–46; Practicing atty., 1950–60; Mt. Olive Atty., 1961–67; Admin. Asst. to U.S. Rep. David Henderson, 1961–76.

Offices 404 CHOB, 202-225-3415. Also Fed. Bldg., Goldsboro 27530, 919-736-1844.

Committees *Agriculture* (22d). Subcommittees: Oilseeds and Rice; Tobacco; Dairy and Poultry.

Group Ratings

	ADA	COPE	PC	RPN	NFU	LCV	CFA	NAB	NSI	ACA	NTU
1978	25	16	25	50	33	–	9	91	90	95	–
1977	25	52	28	33	67	20	30	–	–	59	30

Key Votes

1) Increase Def Spnd	FOR	6) Alaska Lands Protect	AGN	11) Delay Auto Pol Cntrl	FOR
2) B-1 Bomber	FOR	7) Water Projects Veto	AGN	12) Sugar Price Escalator	FOR
3) Cargo Preference	AGN	8) Consum Protect Agcy	AGN	13) Pub Fin Cong Cmpgns	AGN
4) Dereg Nat Gas	AGN	9) Common Situs Picket	AGN	14) ERA Ratif Recissn	FOR
5) Kemp-Roth	AGN	10) Labor Law Revision	AGN	15) Prohibt Govt Abrtns	AGN

Election Results

1978 general	Charles Whitley (D)	54,452	(71%)	($44,971)
	Willard J. Blanchard (R)	22,150	(29%)	($13,583)
1978 primary	Charles Whitley (D)	54,032	(84%)	
	One other (D)	10,325	(16%)	
1976 general	Charles Whitley (D)	77,193	(69%)	($90,336)
	Willard J. Blanchard (R)	35,089	(31%)	($86,324)

FOURTH DISTRICT

The 4th congressional district of North Carolina consists of four counties in the middle of the state, where the coastal plain rises to meet the Piedmont. Raleigh is the state capital and the district's largest city; it is also a tobacco center and the home of North Carolina State University. Durham, another tobacco center and the home of Duke University, has one of North Carolina's largest and most sophisticated urban black communities. Between these two cities and Chapel Hill, which is just outside the district, is the Research Triangle, a collection of think tanks and research businesses attracted to these pleasant surroundings. The other two counties in the district are far smaller: Randolph, in the west, is traditionally Republican; Chatham, closer to Raleigh and Durham, is traditionally Democratic.

This has been an area of considerable economic growth in the seventies. The Research Triangle, the universities, and Raleigh generally have attracted new white collar migrants; Durham, with an economy based on cigarette factories, has grown more slowly. This kind of growth in the white collar sector has had two effects. On the one hand it makes the area more liberal in Democratic primaries and nonpartisan elections. This was the district most negative to George Wallace in the 1972 and 1976 presidential primaries. Raleigh has elected a black mayor and voted for policies to control its booming growth.

The other political effect has been an increase in Republican strength in general elections. Raleigh and surrounding Wake County went for Gerald Ford for president in 1976, for example, though all the surrounding area and Durham as well were strong for Jimmy Carter. By all odds this should mean that congressional elections here should be contests between liberal Democrats and conservative Republicans, each trying to appeal in his own way to the large and growing white collar vote. That was the case in the late sixties and early seventies when the 4th district was represented by Democrat Nick Galifianakis. But since Galifianakis ran for the Senate unsuccessfully in 1972, it has been another story.

The reason was the victory in the 1972 Democratic primary of Ike Andrews. A state legislator, Andrews was from neither Raleigh nor Durham; his roots are in the town of Siler City in rural Chatham County. His reputation is conservative, like his cultural style, although his voting record is more mixed. He often votes with other Democrats on economic issues and others as well. Andrews sits on the Education and Labor Committee and has been Chairman of the Economic Opportunity Subcommittee; he has been active in the workmanlike business of perfecting legislation. Since his first campaign, Andrews has not really had strong opposition. No strong Democrat has challenged him in the primary—his record has not given either an urban- or a rural-based Democrat an opening—and Republican challenges have fallen flat since Watergate. He had no Republican opponent at all in 1978.

Census Data Pop. 467,046. Central city, 46%; suburban, 47%. Median family income, $8,999; families above $15,000: 16%; families below $3,000: 10%. Median years education, 11.5.

The Voters

Median voting age 39.
Employment profile White collar, 50%. Blue collar, 35%. Service, 12%. Farm, 3%.
Ethnic groups Black, 23%. Total foreign stock, 3%.

Presidential vote

1976	Carter (D)	85,541	(51%)
	Ford (R)	81,852	(49%)
1972	Nixon (R)	107,283	(69%)
	McGovern (D)	47,343	(31%)

Rep. Ike F. Andrews (D) Elected 1972; b. Sept. 2, 1925, Bonlee; home, Siler City; Mars Hill Col., U. of N.C., B.S. 1950, LL.B. 1952; Baptist.

Career Army, WWII; Practicing atty., 1952–72; N.C. Senate, 1959–61; N.C. Gen. Assembly, 1961–63, 1967–72, Maj. Ldr., Spkr. Pro Tempore.

Offices 2446 RHOB, 202-225-1784. Also P.O. Box 12075, Research Triangle Park 27709, 919-541-2981.

Committees *Education and Labor* (10th). Subcommittees: Elementary, Secondary and Vocational Education.

Group Ratings

	ADA	COPE	PC	RPN	NFU	LCV	CFA	NAB	NSI	ACA	NTU
1978	25	37	38	64	44	–	14	82	80	59	–
1977	25	48	33	31	55	29	30	–	–	44	32
1976	35	55	33	44	46	39	9	36	67	52	50

Key Votes

1) Increase Def Spnd	FOR	6) Alaska Lands Protect	FOR	11) Delay Auto Pol Cntrl	FOR
2) B-1 Bomber	AGN	7) Water Projects Veto	AGN	12) Sugar Price Escalator	FOR
3) Cargo Preference	AGN	8) Consum Protect Agcy	AGN	13) Pub Fin Cong Cmpgns	AGN
4) Dereg Nat Gas	AGN	9) Common Situs Picket	AGN	14) ERA Ratif Recissn	FOR
5) Kemp-Roth	AGN	10) Labor Law Revision	AGN	15) Prohibt Govt Abrtns	AGN

Election Results

1978 general	Ike F. Andrews (D), unopposed			($27,970)
1978 primary	Ike F. Andrews (D)	50,893	(83%)	
	One other (D)	10,654	(17%)	
1976 general	Ike F. Andrews (D)	92,165	(61%)	($56,607)
	Johnnie L. Gallemore, Jr. (R)	59,917	(39%)	($20,111)

FIFTH DISTRICT

Perhaps the most scenic part of North Carolina is where the mountains begin to rise from the hilly Piedmont. The land is well watered and green, the weather pleasant most of the year, avoiding the extremes of the snowbound winters of the mountains or the humid, muggy summers of the swampy flatlands to the east. Here before the Revolution a group of Moravians, a religious sect from Pennsylvania and, before that, Germany, made a settlement and called it Salem. Later it joined with the Southern Presbyterian settlement of Winston, and together they became one of North Carolina's largest cities, Winston-Salem. The city has given its names to two brands of cigarettes manufactured here by the R.J. Reynolds Company; it is also the headquarters of the Wachovia Bank (the name comes from the Moravians), long North Carolina's largest and one of the largest in the South.

Winston-Salem shares to some extent the political habits of the hills to the north and west. Here, in hollows surrounded by ridges, there lives a Republicanism that grew up in opposition to the domination of wealthy tobacco farmers on the coastal plain. While recent Republicans in the state, notably Senator Jesse Helms, have styled themselves conservatives, mountain Republicans have been more insurgent in mood. When coastal Republicans talk about law and order, mountain Republicans are likely to think, not entirely with approval, of revenuers driving up into the hills and smashing moonshine stills.

The 5th congressional district of North Carolina extends from Winston-Salem and the furniture manufacturing town of Lexington on the east to the mountains on both sides of the Blue Ridge in the west. The mountain Republican tradition lives on here, particularly in Wilkes County, which only on the most unusual occasions votes Democratic. Winston-Salem shows considerable signs of mountain Republican influence as well. It delivered a respectable 49% for Gerald Ford in 1976 and has produced Republican margins in most other years. Yet it has given no more than average support to the flatland Republicanism of Jesse Helms.

The 5th district was created in roughly its present form in 1968. Since that time it has had two congressmen. The first was Wilmer "Vinegar Bend" Mizell, a major league pitcher for several National League clubs in the fifties and early sixties; he had played for a Winston-Salem club in his minor league days, and when he retired from the game, he moved back to the area, became involved in Republican politics, and ran for Congress. With his local celebrity and appeal to country voters, and in a Republican-leaning constituency, he seemed to have a safe district. He was even touted as a possible candidate for the Senate in 1974.

But Watergate proved fatal for Mizell's political career. His opponent, Stephen Neal, a suburban newspaper publisher, was a respectable candidate, and he brought off one of the most stunning upsets in the nation in 1974, winning with 52%. Neal got a seat on the Banking Committee and had a voting record much different from Mizell's, though he did not invariably vote with northern Democrats. His greatest achievement was preventing the building of a dam on the New River—an important local cause on which all Winston-Salem politicians have been agreed. In 1976 Neal beat the folksy Mizell again. In 1978 he had a very different kind of opponent, former state Senator Hamilton Horton. A scholarly intellectual and almost libertarian conservative, Horton once opposed a bill to require night reflectors on farm equipment because he considered it unnecessary government interference. He ran a strong race, but again lost. Neal has now won three victories, but none by a margin that is certain to deter strong opposition in the future; he cannot yet be considered the holder of a safe seat.

Census Data Pop. 462,401. Central city, 29%; suburban, 18%. Median family income, $8,191; families above $15,000: 12%; families below $3,000: 13%. Median years education, 10.3.

The Voters

Median voting age 41.
Employment profile White collar, 38%. Blue collar, 50%. Service, 9%. Farm, 3%.
Ethnic groups Black, 14%. Total foreign stock, 1%.

Presidential vote

1976	Carter (D)	92,010	(51%)
	Ford (R)	89,368	(49%)
1972	Nixon (R)	109,952	(71%)
	McGovern (D)	45,830	(29%)

Rep. Stephen L. Neal (D) Elected 1974; b. Nov. 7, 1934, Winston-Salem; home, Winston-Salem; U. of Cal. at Santa Barbara, U. of Hawaii, A.B. 1959; Episcopalian.

Career Mortgage banking business, 1959–66; Newspaper business, 1966–74, Pres., Community Press, Inc., Suburban Newspapers, Inc., King Publishing Co., Inc., and Yadkin Printing Co., Inc.

Offices 331 CHOB, 202-225-2071. Also 421 Fed. Bldg., Winston-Salem 27101, 919-761-3125.

Committees *Banking, Finance and Urban Affairs* (11th). Subcommittees: Domestic Monetary Policy; International Trade, Investment and Monetary Policy (Chairman); International Development Institutions and Finance; General Oversight and Renegotiation.

Group Ratings

	ADA	COPE	PC	RPN	NFU	LCV	CFA	NAB	NSI	ACA	NTU
1978	25	25	38	64	20	–	23	82	88	67	–
1977	40	32	66	70	58	79	40	–	–	44	35
1976	45	52	59	56	50	41	45	9	56	46	76

Key Votes

1) Increase Def Spnd	FOR	6) Alaska Lands Protect	FOR	11) Delay Auto Pol Cntrl	AGN
2) B-1 Bomber	AGN	7) Water Projects Veto	FOR	12) Sugar Price Escalator	FOR
3) Cargo Preference	AGN	8) Consum Protect Agcy	AGN	13) Pub Fin Cong Cmpgns	AGN
4) Dereg Nat Gas	FOR	9) Common Situs Picket	AGN	14) ERA Ratif Recissn	FOR
5) Kemp-Roth	AGN	10) Labor Law Revision	AGN	15) Prohibt Govt Abrtns	AGN

Election Results

1978 general	Stephen L. Neal (D)	68,778	(54%)	($166,643)
	Hamilton C. Horton, Jr. (R)	58,161	(46%)	($118,484)
1978 primary	Stephen L. Neal (D), unopposed			
1976 general	Stephen L. Neal (D)	98,789	(54%)	($161,937)
	Wilmer Mizell (R)	83,129	(46%)	($161,338)

SIXTH DISTRICT

The 6th congressional district of North Carolina takes in Greensboro, the state's second largest city, High Point, and Burlington—all in the heart of the Piedmont region. One of the textile giants, Burlington Industries, has its Southern headquarters here, and most of the other big textile firms have mills in the area. High Point is one of the major furniture manufacturing centers in the nation, and there are tobacco factories in the area as well. This area has also moved beyond the traditional North Carolina industries of textiles, tobacco, and furniture; Western Electric, for example, has a big plant here now. An influx of northern managerial and technical talent has been the standard explanation for increasing Republican strength here in the fifties and sixties; but actually most of the new residents are from the South, and their Republican leanings represent a change in local political preference.

In 1968 Congressman Horace Kornegay, a conservative Democrat, decided to retire, perhaps because he had barely won reelection two years before. In most Southern districts, this would have touched off a riproaring Democratic primary fight. But not here. There was no primary in the 6th district at all: L. Richardson Preyer was nominated without opposition. This was all the more remarkable because Preyer was, by North Carolina standards, something of a liberal. He does, however, have impeccable establishment credentials. He is an heir to the Richardson-Merrell drug fortune and a graduate of Princeton and Harvard Law. He became a local judge at 34 and was appointed to the federal bench in 1961. Preyer resigned that position, a lifetime appointment, to run for governor in 1964. He conducted a campaign in the tradition, and with the blessing, of moderate Governor Terry Sanford. But with a conservative tide sweeping North Carolina in response to the civil rights revolution, Preyer lost the runoff primary to Dan Moore, and returned to legal and business circles in Greensboro. There his local prominence made him the logical successor to Kornegay, and he beat a well-known Republican in the general election. He has beaten Republicans since by roughly 2–1 margins.

Preyer has a reputation for great integrity and sound judgment, and the House leadership has called on him to serve in some difficult and unpleasant assignments. He served, for example, as the number two Democrat on the committee investigating assassinations during the imbroglio when Chairman Henry Gonzalez resigned, and he headed the subcommittee investigating the assassination of John Kennedy. He also served on the House Ethics Committee. This was a particularly difficult assignment. The Chairman, John Flynt, was visibly reluctant to investigate the Koreagate scandal; Preyer worked with the House leadership and committee counsel Leon Jaworski to insure a wider investigation. Preyer was also one of the chief advocates of tough financial disclosure for congressmen. And in the process of handling all these matters, he remained active on Paul Rogers's Health Subcommittee, notably in backing clean air legislation against challenges from the automobile companies.

In 1979 Preyer sought the chair of the Health Subcommittee in one of the hottest battles of the opening of the 96th Congress. Strictly speaking, it was not his by seniority; but the senior member of the subcommittee, David Satterfield, was too conservative and had no redeeming popularity among Democrats on the full Commerce Committee, which made the decision. Henry Waxman, a young Californian challenging Preyer, charged correctly that Preyer was not an enthusiast for national health insurance; he also said that Preyer's pharmaceutical holdings would either involve him in conflicts of interest or require him to abstain from too many important issues, and that he supported the tobacco industry. Preyer's backers charged that Waxman's campaign contributions to some Commerce Committee members were an illegitimate tactic; they also argued that Preyer is a man of complete integrity and had the kind of respect in the House which Rogers had enjoyed, and which helps a subcommittee chairman carry important and difficult legislation. Organized labor and some liberals backed Waxman; the House leadership backed Preyer. The committee Democrats favored Waxman by a 15–12 margin which included some last minute switches. Although the result rejected a competent, honest man, this is the kind of fight which is probably salutary to the House; at least all the positive arguments advanced for each candidate were legitimate. The result dictated by the strict seniority system, the elevation of Satterfield, would have made little sense.

After losing the Health chair, Preyer agreed to serve one more term on the Ethics Committee. He seemed to take his defeat with good humor, and he has the potential to be an important and constructive member in future Congresses.

Census Data Pop. 457,354. Central city, 45%; suburban, 18%. Median family income, $9,300; families above $15,000: 17%; families below $3,000: 9%. Median years education, 11.0.

The Voters

Median voting age 41.
Employment profile White collar, 43%. Blue collar, 45%. Service, 10%. Farm, 2%.
Ethnic groups Black, 21%. Total foreign stock, 2%.

Presidential vote

1976	Carter (D)	77,610	(53%)
	Ford (R)	67,483	(47%)
1972	Nixon (R)	97,946	(72%)
	McGovern (D)	38,163	(28%)

Rep. Richardson Preyer (D) Elected 1968; b. Jan. 11, 1919, Greensboro; home, Greensboro; Princeton U., A.B. 1941, Harvard U., LL.B. 1949; Presbyterian.

Career Navy, WWII; Practicing atty., 1950–56; Greensboro City Judge, 1953–54; Judge, N.C. Superior Ct., 1956–61; U.S. Dist. Judge, 1961–63; Candidate for Dem. nomination for Gov., 1964; Sr. V.P. and Trust Officer, N.C. Natl. Bank, 1964; City Exec., 1966.

Offices 2344 RHOB, 202-225-3065. Also 249 Fed. Bldg., Greensboro 27401, 919-272-1161.

Committees *Government Operations* (11th). Subcommittees: Government Information and Individual Rights (Chairman).

Interstate and Foreign Commerce (7th). Subcommittees: Health and Environment; Consumer Protection and Finance.

Standards of Official Conduct (3d).

Group Ratings

	ADA	COPE	PC	RPN	NFU	LCV	CFA	NAB	NSI	ACA	NTU
1978	55	60	60	45	40	–	41	33	60	35	–
1977	45	52	43	38	55	51	35	–	–	27	19
1976	40	61	52	50	67	53	54	0	80	25	13

Key Votes

1) Increase Def Spnd	FOR	6) Alaska Lands Protect	FOR	11) Delay Auto Pol Cntrl	AGN
2) B-1 Bomber	AGN	7) Water Projects Veto	FOR	12) Sugar Price Escalator	FOR
3) Cargo Preference	AGN	8) Consum Protect Agcy	FOR	13) Pub Fin Cong Cmpgns	FOR
4) Dereg Nat Gas	AGN	9) Common Situs Picket	AGN	14) ERA Ratif Recissn	FOR
5) Kemp-Roth	AGN	10) Labor Law Revision	AGN	15) Prohibt Govt Abrtns	AGN

Election Results

1978 general	Richardson Preyer (D)	58,193	(68%)	($18,274)
	George Bemus (R)	26,882	(32%)	($10,386)
1978 primary	Richardson Preyer (D), unopposed			
1976 general	Richardson Preyer (D)	103,851	(100%)	($5,685)

SEVENTH DISTRICT

The 7th congressional district of North Carolina is the southern portion of the state's coastal region, the part of North Carolina most like the Deep South. Wilmington is an old Carolina coastal city that never became a major port—a would-be Charleston or Savannah. It was the site of the 1968 church burnings that led to the arrest and conviction of the Wilmington Ten—a matter of controversy in North Carolina and indeed around the world. Fayetteville, the district's other population center, lies across the rather sparsely settled coastal plain to the west. The city's population exceeds only slightly that of adjacent Fort Bragg, the huge Army base to which Fayetteville owes much of its prosperity. Bragg is the home of the Army's 101st Airborne paratroopers and nearby, along the garish highway with its X-rated drive-in movies and topless night clubs, is one of the nation's largest concentrations of Vietnamese restaurants.

The 7th has a fairly large percentage of blacks (26%), but its most notable minority consists of American Indians (7%). In fact, more Indians live here than in any other congressional district east of the Mississippi. Most of them are the Lumbees of Robeson County, and their place in the traditional caste system of the South was always unclear. Robeson is about one-third white, one-third black, and one-third Indian, and in the days of segregation the county maintained three school systems. Indians have had their own civil rights demonstrations, but they have also objected to having their children bused to go to school with blacks.

The 7th district has gyrated wildly in its preference in the last three presidential races. In 1968 it was a near-even split: Wallace finished first, but Nixon, in third place, was only 6% behind him. In 1972 Nixon carried with 70%; McGovern's dovishness was not popular in this military district. Four years later the district switched back to the Democrats, giving Jimmy Carter 67%.

Congressional elections have had fewer fluctuations, at least since the election of Charles Rose in 1972. Two years before Rose, a former associate in Terry Sanford's law firm, ran against the conservative incumbent in the Democratic primary and nearly beat him; in 1972 the incumbent retired, and Rose won the seat. He got places on the Agriculture and House Administration Committees, neither normally considered prizes, but has made something of both of them. He has become an expert on the use of computers to help the legislative process in the House, and has chaired House Administration's subcommittee on computers. He also became concerned about protecting the privacy of individuals from the knowledge government can get from its computers, and has forced some agencies to change their practices in this area. On Agriculture, Rose has become known as a major critic of the use of additives in food products, and as an expert in such matters as standards of quality for ice cream.

Rose's ambitions do not end with his committee assignments, however. He is one of those natural politicians with an affinity for legislative deal-making and seemingly improbable alliances. He was a notable backer of Phillip Burton in his fight for the majority leadership, for example. Rose himself is a possible candidate for a leadership position in the future. He has a safe district and obvious legislative talents; he is acceptable to both northern Democrats and those from the South. Just past 40, he seems to have a long legislative career ahead of him.

Census Data Pop. 467,476. Central city, 21%; suburban, 47%. Median family income, $6,875; families above $15,000: 9%; families below $3,000: 18%. Median years education, 11.2.

The Voters

Median voting age 35.
Employment profile White collar, 40%. Blue collar, 40%. Service, 13%. Farm, 7%.
Ethnic groups Black, 26%. Indian, 7%. Total foreign stock, 4%.

Presidential vote

1976	Carter (D)	81,207	(67%)
	Ford (R)	40,560	(33%)
1972	Nixon (R)	71,346	(70%)
	McGovern (D)	30,409	(30%)

Rep. Charles Rose (D) Elected 1972; b. Aug. 10, 1939, Fayetteville; home, Fayetteville; Davidson Col., A.B. 1961, U. of N.C., LL.B. 1964; Presbyterian.

Career Practicing atty., 1964–72; Chf. Dist. Ct. Prosecutor, 12th Judicial Dist., 1967–70.

Offices 2435 RHOB, 202-225-2731. Also Rm. 208, P.O. Bldg., Wilmington 28401, 919-343-4959.

Committees *Agriculture* (8th). Subcommittees: Dairy and Poultry Tobacco; Livestock and Grains (Chairman).

House Administration (12th). Subcommittees: Office Systems; Accounts; Policy Group on Information and Computers (Chairman).

Group Ratings

	ADA	COPE	PC	RPN	NFU	LCV	CFA	NAB	NSI	ACA	NTU
1978	50	32	50	40	75	–	27	20	43	43	–
1977	35	57	43	17	73	40	50	–	–	22	23
1976	35	73	41	47	73	49	54	0	100	46	17

Key Votes

1) Increase Def Spnd	FOR	6) Alaska Lands Protect	FOR	11) Delay Auto Pol Cntrl	FOR
2) B-1 Bomber	AGN	7) Water Projects Veto	FOR	12) Sugar Price Escalator	FOR
3) Cargo Preference	FOR	8) Consum Protect Agcy	AGN	13) Pub Fin Cong Cmpgns	DNV
4) Dereg Nat Gas	AGN	9) Common Situs Picket	AGN	14) ERA Ratif Recissn	AGN
5) Kemp-Roth	AGN	10) Labor Law Revision	AGN	15) Prohibt Govt Abrtns	AGN

Election Results

1978 general	Charlie Rose (D)	53,696	(70%)	($57,723)
	Raymond C. Schrump (R)	23,146	(30%)	($47,933)
1978 primary	Charlie Rose (D), unopposed			
1976 general	Charlie Rose (D)	95,463	(81%)	($31,333)
	M. H. Vaughan (R)	21,955	(19%)	($7,332)

EIGHTH DISTRICT

The 8th congressional district of North Carolina consists of two areas: a part of the middle of the Piedmont textile country and the Sand Hills region of the state's coastal plain. The textile counties lie on both sides of Interstate 85 between Charlotte and Greensboro. Along the way the roadway passes through the 8th district towns of Salisbury, Concord, and Kannapolis (a company town, wholly owned by giant Cannon Mills). Here the textile magnates reign supreme. There is no nonsense about unions, or workers' rights—the bosses call the shots. That is true in the mills, it is true in the streets of Kannapolis, and it almost seems to be true at the polls. For whatever reasons, this area is consistently one of the most Republican parts of North Carolina. The textile counties cast two-thirds of the votes in the 8th district; the rest are from the more sparsely populated Sand Hills counties to the east. Here there has always been a traditional Democratic allegiance —expressed for some years as a preference for the politics of George Wallace.

Like the 5th district, the 8th was represented for six years after its creation in 1968 by a Republican and for the six years after that by a Democrat. The Republican was Earl Ruth, a former Democrat and basketball coach and athletic director at a small college in the textile area. Ruth was not only a conservative, but one who could only sputter in outrage that people could oppose the Vietnam war or question the probity of Richard Nixon. He was defeated by a 4–3 margin in 1974 and went on to become, improbably, Governor of American Samoa.

The Democrat who beat him has a different voting record, but his cultural origins are quite similar. Bill Hefner was a country music disc jockey and radio station owner in Kannapolis. His campaigns feature very little liberal oratory and a great deal of country and gospel music. His voting record has been moderate, and he has not been particularly active on the non-controversial committees he sits on. Hefner had opposition from a young protege of Jesse Helms in the 1978 election, but managed to win a third term easily.

Census Data Pop. 454,275. Central city, 0%; suburban, 17%. Median family income, $7,872; families above $15,000: 9%; families below $3,000: 13%. Median years education, 10.0.

The Voters

Median voting age 43.
Employment profile White collar, 30%. Blue collar, 56%. Service, 10%. Farm, 4%.
Ethnic groups Black, 20%.

Presidential vote

1976	Carter (D)	85,084	(55%)
	Ford (R)	69,653	(45%)
1972	Nixon (R)	100,830	(73%)
	McGovern (D)	37,880	(27%)

Rep. W. G. (Bill) **Hefner** (D) Elected 1974; b. Apr. 11, 1930, Elora, Tenn.; home, Concord; Baptist.

Career Pres., WRKB Radio, Kannapolis; Mbr., Harvesters Quartet, with weekly TV show on WXII, Winston-Salem; Promoter, "Carolina Sings", gospel music entertainment.

Offices 328 CHOB, 202-225-3715. Also 2202 S. Cannon Blvd., Kannapolis 28081, 704-933-1615.

Committees *Public Works and Transportation* (16th). Subcommittees: Aviation; Oversight and Review; Surface Transportation.

Veterans' Affairs (9th). Subcommittees: Education, Training and Employment (Chairman); Medical Facilities and Benefits.

Group Ratings

	ADA	COPE	PC	RPN	NFU	LCV	CFA	NAB	NSI	ACA	NTU
1978	25	20	30	67	50	–	18	83	70	63	–
1977	35	43	33	27	64	45	30	–	–	40	30
1976	15	52	21	44	40	19	18	27	67	56	46

Key Votes

1) Increase Def Spnd	FOR	6) Alaska Lands Protect	FOR	11) Delay Auto Pol Cntrl	FOR
2) B-1 Bomber	AGN	7) Water Projects Veto	FOR	12) Sugar Price Escalator	FOR
3) Cargo Preference	AGN	8) Consum Protect Agcy	AGN	13) Pub Fin Cong Cmpgns	AGN
4) Dereg Nat Gas	AGN	9) Common Situs Picket	AGN	14) ERA Ratif Recissn	FOR
5) Kemp-Roth	AGN	10) Labor Law Revision	AGN	15) Prohibt Govt Abrtns	DNV

Election Results

1978 general	W. G. Hefner (D)	63,168	(59%)	($74,546)
	Roger Austin (R)	43,942	(41%)	($22,949)
1978 primary	W. G. Hefner (D), unopposed			
1976 general	W. G. Hefner (D)	99,296	(67%)	($51,985)
	Carl Eagle (R)	49,094	(33%)	($6,764)

NINTH DISTRICT

The name of Charlotte, North Carolina, may be linked by future historians with the political and legal issue we have come to call "busing." For it was here that a federal judge not regarded as a liberal ordered a plan for massive integration of the public schools of Charlotte and surrounding Mecklenburg County. The district court's decision was reversed on appeal, but it was reinstated by a unanimous Supreme Court, led by Chief Justice Warren Burger. The Nixon-appointed jurist declared that transportation—that is, busing—could be ordered when necessary to achieve integration.

When the district court decision was announced, there was consternation in Charlotte. This was never a city known for its liberal social or political attitudes, but it did like to think of itself as a city on the move. It is, after all, the largest city in North Carolina; and while it is not a giant by national or even Southern standards, it is a city with an impressive downtown skyline and prosperous suburban developments. It is predominantly a white collar city and likes to regard itself as a little Atlanta.

With its large white collar population, Charlotte was one of the first Southern cities to go Republican. It went 57% for Eisenhower in 1952, and in that same year elected a Republican Congressman, Charles Jonas. It must have come as a shock that a Republican-appointed judge had issued the busing order; that was not what the party meant here. There was talk back in the early seventies that the order should be defied, but nothing came of it; and as it happened compliance turned out to be less painful than many white parents had imagined. There were some racial fights here and there, and busing never really became popular. But in the South people are used to the proximity of people of other races, and in a city like Charlotte you can't bus children too far away—it's not that big a city. While busing orders were changing the voting patterns of some northern cities, at least temporarily, busing had very little effect on Charlotte's electoral behavior.

That was certainly true in congressional elections. Congressman Jonas, a Democratic target in the fifties, had made his seat safe by the sixties. He became the top Republican on the House Appropriations Committee and then decided to retire in 1972. His 9th district by that time included Charlotte, Mecklenburg County, and two much smaller counties. There was a spirited contest between former Olympic distance runner Jim Beatty, a Democrat, and Davidson College chemistry professor and Mecklenburg County Commissioner Jim Martin, a Republican. With no disagreement on the busing issue, Martin won with 59%—a pretty good indication of the general partisan balance here. In the Democratic surge after Watergate, Martin had close races in 1974 and 1976, but he won by better than 2–1 in 1978. He has a seat on the Ways and Means Committee and a generally conventional Republican voting record.

Census Data Pop. 459,535. Central city, 52%; suburban, 25%. Median family income, $9,594; families above $15,000: 20%; families below $3,000: 9%. Median years education, 11.8.

The Voters

Median voting age 40.
Employment profile White collar, 51%. Blue collar, 37%. Service, 11%. Farm, 1%.
Ethnic groups Black, 22%. Total foreign stock, 3%.

Presidential vote

1976	Carter (D)	85,955	(52%)
	Ford (R)	79,970	(48%)
1972	Nixon (R)	102,879	(81%)
	McGovern (D)	23,918	(19%)

Rep. James G. Martin (R) Elected 1972; b. Dec. 11, 1935, Savannah, Ga.; home, Davidson; Davidson Col., B.S. 1957, Princeton U., Ph.D. 1960; Presbyterian.

Career Asst. Prof. of Chemistry, Davidson Col., 1960–64, Assoc. Prof., 1964–72; Mecklenburg Co. Bd. of Commissioners, 1966–72, Chm., 1967–68, 1970–71; Founder and First Chm., Centralina Regional Cncl. of Govts., 1966–69; V.P., Natl. Assoc. of Regional Cncls., 1970–72.

Offices 341 CHOB, 202-225-1976. Also Rm. 248 Jonas Fed. Bldg., Charlotte 28232, 704-372-1976.

Committees *Ways and Means* (7th). Subcommittees: Health; Trade.

Group Ratings

	ADA	COPE	PC	RPN	NFU	LCV	CFA	NAB	NSI	ACA	NTU
1978	15	10	23	58	10	–	9	100	100	88	–
1977	10	4	20	77	17	24	15	–	–	85	50
1976	20	14	11	78	33	27	9	92	100	96	67

Key Votes

1) Increase Def Spnd	FOR	6) Alaska Lands Protect	AGN	11) Delay Auto Pol Cntrl	FOR
2) B-1 Bomber	FOR	7) Water Projects Veto	FOR	12) Sugar Price Escalator	FOR
3) Cargo Preference	AGN	8) Consum Protect Agcy	AGN	13) Pub Fin Cong Cmpgns	AGN
4) Dereg Nat Gas	FOR	9) Common Situs Picket	AGN	14) ERA Ratif Recissn	FOR
5) Kemp-Roth	FOR	10) Labor Law Revision	AGN	15) Prohibt Govt Abrtns	AGN

Election Results

1978 general	James G. Martin (R)	66,157	(69%)	($252,126)
	Charles Maxwell (D)	29,761	(31%)	($37,657)
1978 primary	James G. Martin (R), unopposed			
1976 general	James G. Martin (R)	82,297	(54%)	($145,751)
	Arthur Goodman, Jr. (D)	70,847	(46%)	($28,818)

TENTH DISTRICT

The 10th congressional district of North Carolina is a collection of seven counties in the western Piedmont and the eastern Appalachian mountains. The southern part of the district, on the South

Carolina border, is dominated by the city of Gastonia and surrounding Gaston County—which may be the single American county with the largest number of textile workers. Gaston County is traditionally Democratic, and has delivered large Wallace margins in the past. North of Gastonia, the hills rise to mountains around towns like Morganton, the home of former Senator Sam Ervin. This is furniture manufacturing country, and the farther one gets into the mountains, the more Republican the territory. The political preferences here reflect Civil War allegiances, ones that have continued to be important in election after election.

The 10th took its current shape in the 1968 redistricting and has had only minor boundary changes since. In 1968 two incumbents were thrown together, with relatively senior Democrat Basil Whitener losing to Republican James Broyhill by a solid margin. Broyhill has had a close race only once since, in 1974, when the Watergate issue and perhaps the local prominence of Sam Ervin helped produce a big Democratic sweep in North Carolina.

Though only in his early fifties, Broyhill has now been in Congress for nearly 20 years. He is not often quoted in the press, but he plays an important part in the legislative process. His family owns a prominent furniture manufacturing company, and he serves as the second ranking Republican on the House Commerce Committee. On that body he is almost invariably a voice for less government regulation. He is an opponent of airbags and he worked with John Dingell of Michigan for more relaxed auto emission standards and longer delays on the clean air act. He has opposed measures to increase government regulation of health care costs. He added a sunset provision to the bill creating the Department of Energy requiring it to go out of existence at the end of 1982 unless Congress reauthorizes it. He has generally been a hard-working advocate of positions espoused by the Chamber of Commerce, the auto industry, the electric utilities, and the nuclear power industry.

Broyhill is also the number two Republican on the Budget Committee. The Republicans on that body, unlike their counterparts in the Senate, have attacked their Democratic colleagues head on and taken their disputes to the floor. Broyhill is one of those Republicans whose support of lower federal spending and less government activity has been getting increasing political and intellectual support in the past few years.

Census Data Pop. 471,777. Central city, 0%; suburban, 0%. Median family income, $8,449; families above $15,000: 11%; families below $3,000: 10%. Median years education, 10.0.

The Voters

Median voting age 40.
Employment profile White collar, 30%. Blue collar, 59%. Service, 9%. Farm, 2%.
Ethnic groups Black, 11%.

Presidential vote

1976	Carter (D)	90,939	(54%)
	Ford (R)	76,532	(46%)
1972	Nixon (R)	105,093	(73%)
	McGovern (D)	38,202	(27%)

Rep. James T. Broyhill (R) Elected 1962; b. Aug. 19, 1927, Lenoir; home, Lenoir; U. of N.C., B.S. 1950; Baptist.

Career Broyhill Furniture Factories of Lenoir, 1945–62.

Offices 2340 RHOB, 202-225-2576. Also 224 Mulberry St., Lenoir 28645, 704-758-4247.

Committees *Budget* (2d). Subcommittees: Economic Policy, Projections and Productivity; Regulations and Spending Limitations; Tax Expenditures and Tax Policy.

Interstate and Foreign Commerce (2d). Subcommittees: Consumer Protection and Finance; Communications.

Group Ratings

	ADA	COPE	PC	RPN	NFU	LCV	CFA	NAB	NSI	ACA	NTU
1978	20	5	23	75	20	–	18	100	100	88	–
1977	15	9	18	69	33	13	10	–	–	85	53
1976	15	13	21	72	18	30	0	92	100	88	65

Key Votes

1) Increase Def Spnd	FOR	6) Alaska Lands Protect	AGN	11) Delay Auto Pol Cntrl	FOR
2) B-1 Bomber	FOR	7) Water Projects Veto	FOR	12) Sugar Price Escalator	FOR
3) Cargo Preference	AGN	8) Consum Protect Agcy	AGN	13) Pub Fin Cong Cmpgns	AGN
4) Dereg Nat Gas	FOR	9) Common Situs Picket	AGN	14) ERA Ratif Recissn	FOR
5) Kemp-Roth	FOR	10) Labor Law Revision	AGN	15) Prohibt Govt Abrtns	AGN

Election Results

1978 general	James T. Broyhill (R), unopposed			($32,586)
1978 primary	James T. Broyhill (R), unopposed			
1976 general	James T. Broyhill (R)	99,882	(60%)	($114,298)
	John J. Hunt (D)	67,190	(40%)	($53,419)

ELEVENTH DISTRICT

The 11th congressional district of North Carolina occupies the western end of the state. Its main features include Asheville, the place to which Thomas Wolfe could not go home again, and the Great Smoky Mountains National Park. The park is the nation's most heavily visited: its roads have become so crowded that the Park Service was forced to install traffic lights—the first ever within a national park. During the summer it is 20° cooler in the mountains than in the lowland towns not far away; the climate and the forested, green, fog-wisped mountains attract some seven million people to the Smokies each year. Over the years the same elements—the mountains, the cool climate—have made western North Carolina a separate unit from the rest of the state. During the Civil War, it was the part of the state most reluctant to secede. With few slaves (only 6% of the people here today are black), many of the small farmers in the hollows remained loyal to the Union, and those who took up the Confederate cause did so largely because of the efforts of Governor Zebulon Vance, an Asheville native and a reluctant secessionist himself.

So there are some ancestral party loyalties here to contend with, Democratic as well as Republican, though this is not monolithically Republican territory like eastern Tennessee on the other side of the mountains. And there is some hostility here to the segregationist Republicanism of eastern North Carolina; Senator Jesse Helms barely carried the district in 1972 and in 1978.

The strength of party loyalties was made clear in 1976. The incumbent, Congressman, Democrat Roy Taylor, retired after 16 years in the House and as the number two Democrat on the House Interior Committee. The Democratic primary was closely contested; the runoff was won with 51% by state Senator Lamar Gudger of Asheville. The general election was also seriously contested. While Carter was getting 54% in the district, and gubernatorial candidate James Hunt was carrying it by a much larger margin, Gudger got only 51% over Republican Bruce Briggs. In 1978 Gudger again had tough and well financed opposition from Buncombe County (Asheville) Commissioner Curtis Ratcliff. Serving on the Judiciary and Interior Committees, Gudger could point to no major legislative accomplishments; at 59, he was not a strong personal campaigner and had suffered from high staff turnover. But at the last minute Jimmy Carter, still popular from the Camp David agreement earlier in the fall, visited Asheville and stumped for Gudger and other local Democrats. The result was a 54% Gudger victory.

Political analysts used to talk about the coattails of presidential candidates and presidents as a major force in our politics. But in recent congressional elections, candidates have increasingly won on their own, totally without regard to the top of the ticket. The 11th congressional district seems an exception to that trend. It is the one district in the country where one can say, with some assurance, that Jimmy Carter has pulled a congressman in on his coattails—not once, but twice. Probably the outcome here in 1980 will depend on the strength of the Carter candidacy.

Census Data Pop. 467,051. Central city, 12%; suburban, 19%. Median family income, $6,857; families above $15,000: 8%; families below $3,000: 18%. Median years education, 10.5.

The Voters

Median voting age 44.
Employment profile White collar, 35%. Blue collar, 51%. Service, 11%. Farm, 3%.
Ethnic groups Black, 6%. Total foreign stock, 2%.

Presidential vote

1976	Carter (D)	99,854	(54%)
	Ford (R)	84,061	(46%)
1972	Nixon (R)	110,566	(71%)
	McGovern (D)	46,095	(29%)

Rep. Lamar Gudger (D) Elected 1976; b. Apr. 30, 1919, Asheville; home, Asheville; U. of N.C., B.A. 1940, LL.B., 1942; Methodist.

Career Air Force, WWII; Practicing atty., 1945–77; N.C. House of Reps., 1951–52; 19th Dist. Solicitor, 1952–54; Secy., N.C. Dem. Party, 1961–62; N.C. Senate, 1971–77.

Offices 428 CHOB, 202-225-6401. Also P.O. Box 7035, Asheville 28801, 704-253-0766.

Committees *Interior and Insular Affairs* (24th). Subcommittees: National Parks and Insular Affairs; Public Lands.

Judiciary (13th). Subcommittees: Crime; Courts, Civil Liberties, and The Administration of Justice.

Group Ratings

	ADA	COPE	PC	RPN	NFU	LCV	CFA	NAB	NSI	ACA	NTU
1978	25	30	35	33	20	–	18	67	80	92	–
1977	35	43	38	31	67	45	25	–	–	48	36

Key Votes

1) Increase Def Spnd	FOR	6) Alaska Lands Protect	FOR	11) Delay Auto Pol Cntrl	FOR
2) B-1 Bomber	FOR	7) Water Projects Veto	FOR	12) Sugar Price Escalator	FOR
3) Cargo Preference	AGN	8) Consum Protect Agcy	AGN	13) Pub Fin Cong Cmpgns	FOR
4) Dereg Nat Gas	AGN	9) Common Situs Picket	AGN	14) ERA Ratif Recissn	FOR
5) Kemp-Roth	AGN	10) Labor Law Revision	AGN	15) Prohibt Govt Abrtns	AGN

Election Results

1978 general	Lamar Gudger (D)	75,460	(53%)	($156,790)
	R. Curtis Ratcliff (R)	65,832	(47%)	($62,579)
1978 primary	Lamar Gudger (D)	36,066	(51%)	
	R. P. (Bo) Thomas (D)	34,633	(49%)	
1976 general	Lamar Gudger (D)	93,857	(51%)	($103,648)
	Bruce Briggs (R)	88,752	(49%)	($107,792)

NORTH DAKOTA

North Dakota occupies the northern section of our Great Plains—the world's largest expanse of arable land. Most of North Dakota is wheat country: the state produces about one-sixth of the nation's crop, with only Kansas growing more. As the North Dakota plains become more arid toward the west, ranching and livestock raising tend to replace wheat. But both forms of agricultural endeavor are demanding and discouraging. North Dakota is a hard, treeless land; its winters ae cold with plains open to Arctic blasts from Canada, and its summers are often too short and too dry. Some 50 years ago, the state had 632,000 people; by 1970, only 617,000. Although the population has since risen, it is not so much because of North Dakota's prosperity as it is the gloomy economic picture in the big states where young North Dakotans used to move. By the late seventies North Dakota had a lower per capita income than several states in the South.

About 25% of all North Dakotans still live on farms and ranches, the highest percentage in any state. Because the economy of the state depends on the farmers who exert little control over the fluctuations of the commodity markets (or the weather), North Dakota over the years has seen raging dissatisfaction with the farm programs of the federal government. By tradition the most common topics of the state's political discourse are the minutiae of wheat and feed grain legislation. And agricultural discontent was the driving force behind the most interesting feature of the state's politics, its time of radicalism in the years around World War I.

Most of North Dakota's settlement occurred between 1890 and 1910. A large portion of the settlers were of immigrant stock: Norwegians to the east, Canadians along the northern border, Volga Germans to the west, and native Germans throughout the state. (Volga Germans were people who had migrated to Russia in the early 1880s, but who retained their German language and character. They are recorded in U.S. Census figures as Russians.) The new North Dakotans lived on lonely, often marginal farms, cut off in many cases from the wider currents of American culture by the barrier of language. Their economic fate seemed to be at the mercy of the grain millers of Minneapolis, the railroads, the banks, and the commodity traders.

These circumstances led A. C. Townley and William Lemke to organize the North Dakota Non-Partisan League (NPL) in 1915. Its program was frankly socialist—government ownership of the railroads and grain elevators—and, like many North Dakota ethnics, the League opposed going to war with Germany. The positions taken by the NPL won it many adherents in North Dakota, and the League spread to neighboring states. But North Dakota was its bastion; the NPL often determined the outcome of the usually decisive Republican primary, and sometimes swung its support to the otherwise heavily outnumbered Democrats. A particular favorite of the NPL was "Wild Bill" Langer, who served intermittently as Governor during the thirties. He was elected to the Senate in 1940, but was allowed to take his seat only after a lengthy investigation of alleged campaign irregularities. His subsequent career was fully as controversial; Langer was the Senate's most unpredictable maverick until his death in 1959. One of his projects was to get a North Dakotan on the Supreme Court; he filibustered every nomination from 1954 till his death in an unsuccessful attempt to achieve that goal.

Another NPL favorite was Congressman Usher Burdick, who served from 1935 to 1945 and then again from 1949 to 1959. Burdick, like Langer, was a nominal Republican, but usually voted with New Deal liberals on economic issues. Burdick's son, Quentin, a Democrat, was a member of the House when Langer died, and won a special election to fill the Senate seat after waging a campaign against the allegedly iniquitous policies of Agriculture Secretary Ezra Taft Benson. The Non-Partisan League of course supported the younger Burdick. By the sixties its very name had become misleading, as it tended to support Democrats in every election.

North Dakota is historically Republican, but in recent elections—including the 1976 presidential contest, which Ford won here with only 53%—this has become a competitive two-party state. It has a Republican senator and a Democratic senator, a Democratic governor and a Republican congressman, a Republican state Senate and a Democratic state House.

The state's willingness to accept Democrats is attested to by the long career of Senator Burdick. He has had strong opposition only once, in 1970, when Congressman Thomas Kleppe ran one of the Nixon–Agnew law and order campaigns against him. Kleppe spent the then unheard of sum of

$300,000 on his campaign, but Burdick won with 62%. In 1976, when other sixtyish senators from not distant states (McGee of Wyoming, Moss of Utah) were defeated, the 68-year-old Burdick was returned almost without a contest. His Republican opponent was an unknown with little money who carried only three counties. Burdick won with 67%.

Burdick is not, despite his long incumbency, a real power in the Senate. He has switched committees a number of times, leaving Judiciary and having had the Post Office and Civil Service Committee abolished just as he would have become Chairman. (That seat was no plum, however; McGee had held it and the chairmanship was used against him in his bid for reelection.) Burdick now has a seat on Appropriations, but he ranks only twelfth in seniority among Democrats; he is the fifth ranking Democrat on Environment and Public Works Committee. Burdick used to be a reliable Democratic vote on issues; now he has been known to stray, notably on the Panama Canal Treaty, which he opposed. Rumpled, past 70, Burdick seems likely to retire when his seat comes up in 1982. But North Dakota has refused to reelect an incumbent senator only once—the isolationist Gerald Nye in 1944—and has not yet shown any discontent with Burdick.

North Dakota's senior Senator is Milton Young, a man not much known outside North Dakota, even within Washington political circles. Yet this quiet man has been a U.S. Senator since 1945, and is the senior Republican in the Senate and indeed in the whole Congress; in the Senate only Warren Magnuson has more seniority. Young is the ranking Republican on the Senate Appropriations Committee and an important voice on the Agriculture Committee. Like a good North Dakotan, he has devoted most of his attention to agricultural issues, and is the architect of the target wheat price legislation, which was intended to provide better and more stable incomes for the farmers of North Dakota and other wheat growing states.

Though not well known nationally, Young like Burdick has a solid following in North Dakota. In the Democratic year of 1974, when he was about to turn 77, Young managed to win reelection, even if by only 177 votes, over former Governor William Guy. And Guy was a formidable opponent, a four term Governor (1961–72) who enjoyed great popularity and, at 55, was comparatively youthful. But Young managed to neutralize the age issue. A karate practitioner, he ran TV ads showing him chopping a block of wood in two with his bare hand; he also took care to remind voters that his halting speech was the result not of age but of a difficulty he has always had. Despite performance in 1974, he is not expected to run for another term in 1980. Young is now the only member of Congress to have been born in the nineteenth century.

The election for Young's seat now appears to be one of the most predictable Senate contests of 1980. The likely winner is Congressman-at-large Mark Andrews. A Republican who nearly beat Guy for the governorship in 1962 and won his House seat in a 1963 special election, Andrews has become very popular. He won his last race statewide with 68% of the vote. Andrews is a farmer who serves on the Agriculture Appropriations Subcommittee. Like Young, he is ready to desert Republican orthodoxy if he thinks it runs contrary to the interests of North Dakota's farmers. Although there are strong Democratic candidates—Guy and current Governor Arthur Link—Andrews must be rated the odds on favorite.

Governor Link is a former Congressman, elected in 1970 to a seat only to see it abolished as North Dakota lost one of its two seats as a result of the 1970 Census. Rather than run against the apparently unbeatable Andrews, Link ran for governor and, to the surprise of many, won. The biggest issue here, certainly from a national perspective, is strip mining; North Dakota sits on top of great veins of coal that can be strip mined and the question is how stringent should be the regulations under which that is done. Link won a second four-year term in 1976. He will be 66 in 1980, which suggests he will not run for the Senate and may not run again for governor. Possible Democratic successors include Lieutenant Governor Wayne Sanstead and Tax Commissioner Byron Dorgan. But Democrats will have held the governorship of this once Republican state for twenty straight years, and it seems hard to believe they can keep it for four more.

Census Data Pop. 617,761; 0.31% of U.S. total, 45th largest; Central city, 9%; suburban, 3%. Median family income, $7,836; 39th highest; families above $15,000: 13%; families below $3,000: 12%. Median years education, 12.0.

1977 Share of Federal Tax Burden $967,000,000; 0.28% of U.S. total, 48th largest.

1977 Share of Federal Outlays $1,476,483,000; 0.37% of U.S. total, 45th largest. Per capita federal spending, $2,318.

DOD	$225,047,000	44th (0.25%)	HEW	$405,135,000	46th (0.27%)
ERDA	$4,204,000	36th (0.07%)	HUD	$12,138,000	46th (0.29%)
NASA	—		VA	$51,540,000	48th (0.27%)
DOT	$41,920,000	48th (0.29%)	EPA	$5,735,000	50th (0.07%)
DOC	$47,624,000	46th (0.57%)	RevS	$18,702,000	49th (0.22%)
DOI	$60,202,000	19th (1.29%)	Debt	$43,044,000	44th (0.14%)
USDA	$421,987,000	14th (2.12%)	Other	$139,205,000	

Economic Base Agriculture, notably wheat, cattle, barley and dairy products; finance, insurance and real estate; food and kindred products, especially dairy products; printing and publishing, especially newspapers; tourism; machinery, especially farm machinery.

Political Line-up Governor, Arthur A. Link (D). Senators, Milton R. Young (R) and Quentin N. Burdick (D). Representative, 1 R at large. State Senate (35 R and 15 D); State House (71 R and 29 D).

The Voters

Registration No statewide registration.
Median voting age 44
Employment profile White collar, 42%. Blue collar, 21%. Service, 16%. Farm, 21%.
Ethnic groups Total foreign stock, 24%. Norway, 6%; USSR, 5%.

Presidential vote

1976	Carter (D)	136,078	(47%)
	Ford (R)	153,470	(53%)
1972	Nixon (R)	174,109	(63%)
	McGovern (D)	100,384	(37%)

Sen. Milton R. Young (R) Elected Appointed Mar. 12, 1945, elected June 25, 1946, seat up 1980; b. Dec. 6, 1897, Berlin; home, La Moure; N.D. St. Ag. Col., Graceland Col.; Church of Latter Day Saints.

Career Farmer; N.D. House of Reps., 1932–34; N.D. Senate, 1934–45, Pres. Pro Tempore, 1941–43, Maj. Floor Ldr., 1943.

Offices 5205 DSOB, 202-224-2043. Also Box 1036, Bismarck 58501, 701-223-3312.

Committees *Agriculture, Nutrition, and Forestry* (2d). Subcommittees: Agricultural Production, Marketing, and Stabilization of Prices; Agricultural Research and General Legislation; Rural Development.

Appropriations (Ranking Member). Subcommittees: Agriculture and Related Agencies; Defense; Energy and Water Development; Interior and Related Agencies.

Group Ratings

	ADA	COPE	PC	RPN	NFU	LCV	CFA	NAB	NSI	ACA	NTU
1978	5	18	10	50	56	11	0	91	70	73	–
1977	5	20	8	44	67	–	0	–	–	79	40
1976	5	8	4	50	33	10	7	73	100	83	69

Key Votes

1) Warnke Nom	FOR	6) Egypt-Saudi Arms	FOR	11) Hosptl Cost Contnmnt	AGN
2) Neutron Bomb	FOR	7) Draft Restr Pardon	AGN	12) Clinch River Reactor	FOR
3) Waterwy User Fee	AGN	8) Wheat Price Support	FOR	13) Pub Fin Cong Cmpgns	AGN
4) Dereg Nat Gas	FOR	9) Panama Canal Treaty	AGN	14) ERA Ratif Recissn	AGN
5) Kemp-Roth	FOR	10) Labor Law Rev Clot	AGN	15) Med Necssy Abrtns	AGN

Election Results

1974 general	Milton R. Young (R)	114,852	(50%)	($300,121)
	William L. "Bill" Guy (D)	114,675	(50%)	($115,561)
1974 primary	Milton R. Young (R), unopposed			
1968 general	Milton R. Young (R)	154,968	(66%)	
	Herschel Lasohkowitz (D)	80,815	(34%)	

Sen. Quentin N. Burdick (D) Elected June 28, 1960, seat up 1982; b. June 19, 1908, Munich; home, Fargo; U. of Minn., B.A. 1931, LL.B. 1932; Congregationalist.

Career Practicing atty., 1932–58; Dem. nominee for Gov., 1946; U.S. House of Reps., 1959–60.

Offices 451 RSOB, 202-224-2551. Also Fed. Bldg., Fargo 58102, 701-237-4000, and Fed. Bldg., Bismarck 58501, 701-255-2553.

Committees *Appropriations* (12th). Subcommittees: Agriculture and Related Agencies; Energy and Water Development, Interior and Related Agencies; Labor, HEW, and Related Agencies; State, Justice, Commerce, the Judiciary, and Related Agencies.

Environment and Public Works (5th). Subcommittees: Environmental Pollution; Transportation; Regional and Community Development (Chairman).

Group Ratings

	ADA	COPE	PC	RPN	NFU	LCV	CFA	NAB	NSI	ACA	NTU
1978	55	74	65	30	90	45	55	18	60	23	–
1977	50	85	45	64	83	–	48	–	–	26	33
1976	65	84	51	56	92	50	78	27	20	19	20

Key Votes

1) Warnke Nom	FOR	6) Egypt-Saudi Arms	AGN	11) Hosptl Cost Contnmnt	FOR
2) Neutron Bomb	FOR	7) Draft Restr Pardon	FOR	12) Clinch River Reactor	FOR
3) Waterwy User Fee	AGN	8) Wheat Price Support	FOR	13) Pub Fin Cong Cmpgns	FOR
4) Dereg Nat Gas	FOR	9) Panama Canal Treaty	AGN	14) ERA Ratif Recissn	FOR
5) Kemp-Roth	AGN	10) Labor Law Rev Clot	FOR	15) Med Necssy Abrtns	FOR

Election Results

1976 general	Quentin Burdick (D)	175,772	(63%)	($117,514)
	Robert Stroup (R)	103,466	(37%)	($136,748)
1976 primary	Quentin Burdick (D), unopposed			
1970 general	Quentin Burdick (D)	134,519	(62%)	
	Thomas S. Kleppe (R)	82,996	(38%)	

Gov. Arthur A. Link (D) Elected 1972, term expires Jan. 1981; b. May 24, 1914, McKenzie County; N.D. Agric. Col.; Lutheran.

Career Farmer; N.D. House of Reps., 1947–71, Minor. Floor Ldr., Spkr.; U.S. House of Reps., 1971–73.

Offices State Capitol Bldg., Bismarck 58505, 701-224-2200.

Election Results

1976 general	Arthur A. Link (D)	153,309	(53%)
	Richard Elkin (R)	138,321	(47%)
1976 primary	Arthur A. Link (D), unopposed		
1972 general	Arthur A. Link (D)	143,899	(51%)
	Richard Larsen (R)	138,032	(49%)

Rep. Mark Andrews (R) Elected Oct. 22, 1963; b. May 19, 1926, Fargo; home, Mapleton; U.S. Military Acad., 1944–46, N.D. St. U., B.S. 1949; Episcopalian.

Career Farmer; Repub. nominee for Gov., 1962.

Offices 2186 RHOB, 202-225-2611. Also Fed. Bldg., Fargo 58102, 701-232-8030.

Committees *Appropriations* (4th). Subcommittees: Agriculture and Related Agencies; State, Justice, Commerce, and the Judiciary.

Group Ratings

	ADA	COPE	PC	RPN	NFU	LCV	CFA	NAB	NSI	ACA	NTU
1978	5	5	15	50	50	–	14	83	100	73	–
1977	20	24	18	30	67	20	20	–	–	67	36
1976	10	36	25	65	46	21	18	67	90	62	52

Key Votes

1) Increase Def Spnd	FOR	6) Alaska Lands Protect	DNV	11) Delay Auto Pol Cntrl	FOR
2) B-1 Bomber	FOR	7) Water Projects Veto	AGN	12) Sugar Price Escalator	FOR
3) Cargo Preference	FOR	8) Consum Protect Agcy	AGN	13) Pub Fin Cong Cmpgns	AGN
4) Dereg Nat Gas	FOR	9) Common Situs Picket	AGN	14) ERA Ratif Recissn	FOR
5) Kemp-Roth	FOR	10) Labor Law Revision	AGN	15) Prohibt Govt Abrtns	FOR

Election Results

1978 general	Mark Andrews (R)	147,746	(68%)	
	Bruce Hagen (D)	68,016	(32%)	
1978 primary	Mark Andrews (R), unopposed			
1976 general	Mark Andrews (R)	181,018	(63%)	($103,803)
	Lloyd B. Omdahl (D)	104,263	(37%)	($26,541)

OHIO

Ohio is the epitome of Middle America: a land of carefully tended farms, God-fearing small towns, and sprawling industrial cities. In 1803, Ohio became the first state from the old Northwest Territory to be admitted to the Union, and within 25 years it was the fourth largest state in population. Its patterns of settlement were not what one might think. The first white people here moved up through Kentucky or down the Ohio River to the southwest corner of the state around Cincinnati. The old stock Americans were followed by Germans, who were fleeing the consequences of the failed European revolutions of 1848. By the time of the Civil War, Cincinnati was heavily German and pro-Union and was the fourth largest city in the country. Meanwhile, the northeast corner of Ohio remained placid farmland, settled by Yankee migrants from New England and upstate New York. Not until the growth of the steel industry in the late nineteenth century did the huge industrial complexes of Cleveland, Akron, and Youngstown come into being. But they grew rapidly, and by 1910 Cleveland was larger than Cincinnati which was itself the nation's fourth largest city.

In politics Ohio has a reputation as a profoundly Republican state, and though that is an exaggeration perhaps resulting from the Republican presidents it has produced (Hayes, Garfield, McKinley, Taft, Harding), the reputation is not entirely undeserved. One factor which has helped Republicans over the years is the decentralization of the state's urban population. Ohio has six metropolitan areas with populations over 500,000; consequently, no one city can provide a solid Democratic base, which is what Chicago has done in Illinois or Detroit in Michigan. Moreover, some Ohio cities—notably Cincinnati and Columbus—are themselves basically Republican. And Ohio has a tradition of brilliant Republican politicians, like the first Senator Robert Taft (1939–53) and the nonideological technician Ray Bliss who served as his party's state chairman during most of the fifties and sixties.

But it would be more accurate today to regard Ohio as a marginal state politically—indeed, with its 25 electoral votes, one of the prime marginal states in the country. Small town Ohio remains heavily Republican, and this is a state where the small town population—in places like Wapakoneta, the home of astronaut Neil Armstrong—remains demographically important. However, in the southern part of the state, in sparsely populated rural counties, remain vestiges of a Democratic tradition that goes back to the Civil War when southern Ohio was copperhead country. These counties, below U.S. 40, the old National Road, provided critical votes for Jimmy Carter in 1976, after most of them went Republican during most of the sixties and seventies. Democratic strength in Ohio is concentrated in the industrial cities—in Cleveland, though the number of voters in metropolitan Cleveland has been dropping sharply in recent years. Democratic cities also include Akron, Youngstown, Toledo, and Dayton. But Ohio's leading white collar city, Columbus, is generally Republican, while Cincinnati, a Republican city since the middle nineteenth century, remains one still. Altogether, these varying political preferences add up to a pretty even balance. They also come fairly close to approximating the national political average.

It was perhaps fitting that Ohio provided crucial electoral votes for Jimmy Carter's election over Gerald Ford—and that Carter carried the state by exactly 11,116 votes out of more than four million cast. Ohio's presidential primary, scheduled in 1976 as the last such election, also played a key part in the races for both parties' nominations. Jimmy Carter's solid victory in the Democratic race gave him a clear majority at the convention; as the results came in, George Wallace and Mayor Daley quickly phoned in congratulations. On the Republican side, what was important was what didn't happen. Ronald Reagan had a solid 45% in the statewide race. But his operatives, apparently sure they couldn't win here, failed to file delegate candidates in eight of Ohio's 23 congressional districts and also failed to make the extra effort which could have won in eight other districts where Reagan delegates got more than 45%. If Reagan had won all those delegates and a few more, he would have been nominated for president at Kansas City.

On the same day Ohioans gave Carter their electoral votes by a narrow margin, they were electing as U.S. senator a man they had twice rejected by narrow margins. Howard Metzenbaum lost the 1970 general election to Robert Taft, Jr., and the 1974 Democratic primary to John Glenn. But in 1976 he beat Cleveland Congressman James Stanton in the primary and reversed the result against Taft in the general. In fact, Metzenbaum had been involved in senatorial politics for a long time. He was campaign manager for Democrat Stephen Young, a salty sometime Congressman who at 69 beat veteran Republican Senator John Bricker and at 75, in 1964, withstood the challenge of the same Taft whom Metzenbaum would face twice. He has the advantages of having made a lot of money in business—airport parking lots—and of enjoying strong support from organized labor.

In 1976 Metzenbaum ran strongly on economic issues, stressing his support of measures to help the little man. In the Senate, he serves on the Energy Committee, where he strongly opposed policies backed by the oil companies and favored strict regulation of oil and gas prices. Together with James Abourezk of South Dakota, Metzenbaum led a filibuster against the compromise natural gas bill; they felt it allowed prices to rise too high. Metzenbaum also serves on Judiciary and in 1979 got a seat on the Budget Committee. He is considered a senator who misses few chances to promote his views to his constituents, and as one who is hard working and generally well prepared. Appointed to fill a Senate vacancy in 1974 and then defeated in the primary by John Glenn, he had the drive and determination to come back and win in 1976—although he and Glenn remain on distant terms personally.

Glenn, like Metzenbaum, had to persevere to win his Senate seat. He won national fame as the first astronaut to venture into space, but he was forced out of a Senate race in 1964 by an injury and was defeated in the 1970 primary by Metzenbaum. Then in 1974 Glenn won. He was helped by a Watergate-type issue: Metzenbaum had paid no income tax in 1969 and was arguing with the IRS about it, while Glenn seemed the picture of integrity. Their voting records also appear different. While Metzenbaum lines up closely with labor and liberal Democrats, Glenn often dissents from them fairly. He is, as one would expect of a former astronaut, a strong backer of the space program. He is also, as a former Marine colonel, less likely to advocate defense spending cuts.

Glenn serves on the Governmental Affairs and Foreign Relations Committees, and more than most senators he has devoted his attention to matters of broad national and global policy. He is considered a hard worker and one who does not speak up on an issue until he has done his homework. He has been concerned about matters like nuclear proliferation and the strategic arms limitation treaty. On the latter, he is considered an important influence; he has been studying especially hard the question of verifiability, and many other senators will examine his conclusions closely.

Glenn's careful approach and moderate image have helped to make him popular. He is from central Ohio—he grew up in a small town and after retirement from the space program lived in Columbus—and he is popular far beyond traditional Democratic industrial counties in Ohio. In the 1974 general election he received 65% of the vote, carrying almost every county in the state. For 1980 the question is the strength of the opposition.

In 1976, Glenn was considered for the vice presidency by Jimmy Carter. He was in the unfortunate position of co-keynoting the national convention with Barbara Jordan, who inevitably got more applause and acclaim; the convention, dominated by activists and antiwar crusaders, did not care for Glenn's moderation or his calm speaking style. He is still sometimes mentioned as a candidate for national office, but he does not seem possessed of the ambition usually necessary and has concentrated heavily on Senate work rather than trying to establish a national image.

An Ohio officeholder with no national image but considerable local success is Governor James Rhodes. He turns 70 in 1979, the oldest governor in the nation, and he has been the Republican nominee for the office every election in the last twenty years but one (when he was barred from running by a two term limit). He was elected in 1962 and 1966 by wide margins, and his policies—low taxes, low services, attract industry to Ohio—were very popular in the prosperous sixties. In 1970, when he couldn't run, Democrat John Gilligan was elected—in reaction to a Republican scandal (which didn't involve Rhodes) and the state's low level of services. Gilligan pushed through a major tax increase, got the voters to ratify it in a referendum, and got big Democratic majorities elected in the legislature. But Gilligan's sharp tongue made too many enemies, and he lost to Rhodes in 1974 by 11,488 votes.

Rhodes's policies have not been so successful in the seventies. Even with favorable taxes, business has not come running to Ohio; it tends to seek sunnier weather and lower cost labor in the Sun Belt. Big plant closings have also hurt Youngstown, Dayton, and other cities. And services have suffered, as schools have closed for extended periods in Youngstown and other industrial cities. Nonetheless, Rhodes was able to win a fourth term in 1978. His opponent, Lieutenant Governor Richard Celeste, was a well prepared, but had some weaknesses. At 40, he was far younger than the age Ohio voters are used to in their governors, and he seemed likely to favor higher taxes to solve some of the state's problems. As in 1974 against Gilligan, Rhodes closed the campaign with a strong negative blitz against his opponent, hoping to demoralize Democrats into providing lower turnout in the industrial northeast. Again he was successful, winning with just 51%. One thing is sure: Rhodes will not run again in 1982, when he will be 73, for the Ohio constitution prohibits consecutive third terms. But he could conceivably be a candidate in 1986.

Rhodes's victory was a personal—and negative—one. Democrats in 1978 won every one of the other statewide offices. They will have complete control of the redistricting of the legislature, as they did after the 1970 Census; and the legislature, nearly 2–1 Democratic, will have strong leverage over congressional redistricting. That in turn could affect a couple of congressional seats, for in the past Republicans have redistricted Ohio's House seats quite carefully. If Democrats can pass their plan over Rhodes's veto or reach a compromise with him, they could consolidate their hold on a Cincinnati district they now have and pick up a seat in the Columbus area—giving them a good chance to gain a majority in the state's House delegation for the first time since 1948. As it is today, Ohio remains the only large state in the nation with a majority Republican delegation in the House.

Census Data Pop. 10,652,017; 5.26% of U.S. total, 6th largest; Central city, 32%; suburban, 45%. Median family income, $10,309; 13th highest; families above $15,000: 22%; families below $3,000: 8%. Median years education, 12.1.

1977 Share of Federal Tax Burden $17,064,000,000; 4.94% of U.S. total, 6th largest.

1977 Share of Federal Outlays $14,641,073,000; 3.70% of U.S. total, 7th largest. Per capita federal spending, $1,361.

DOD	$2,469,374,000	11th (2.70%)	HEW	$6,525,778,000	7th (4.42%)
ERDA	$412,393,000	6th (6.98%)	HUD	$177,326,000	6th (4.20%)
NASA	$131,881,000	7th (3.34%)	VA	$770,441,000	6th (4.01%)
DOT	$406,079,000	11th (2.84%)	EPA	$532,071,000	3d (6.49%)
DOC	$230,055,000	10th (2.77%)	RevS	$333,395,000	6th (3.94%)
DOI	$26,849,000	32d (0.58%)	Debt	$718,933,000	7th (2.39%)
USDA	$483,217,000	11th (2.43%)	Other	$1,433,281,000	

Economic Base Machinery, especially metalworking machinery; transportation equipment, especially motor vehicles and equipment; finance, insurance and real estate; primary metal industries, especially blast furnaces and basic steel products; fabricated metal products, especially metal stampings and fabricated structural metal products; electrical equipment and supplies, especially household appliances and electrical industrial apparatus; agriculture, especially dairy products, cattle, soybeans and corn.

Political Line-up Governor, James A. Rhodes (R). Senators, John Glenn (D) and Howard M. Metzenbaum (D). Representatives, 23 (13 R and 10 D). State Senate (18 D and 15 R); State House (62 D and 37 R).

The Voters

Registration 5,222,041 Estimated Total. No party registration.
Median voting age 42
Employment profile White collar, 45%. Blue collar, 41%. Service, 12%. Farm, 2%.
Ethnic groups Black, 9%. Total foreign stock, 12%. Germany, Italy, 2% each; Poland, UK, 1% each.

Presidential vote

1976	Carter (D)	2,011,621	(50%)
	Ford (R)	2,000,505	(50%)
1972	Nixon (R)	2,441,827	(61%)
	McGovern (D)	1,558,889	(39%)

1976 Democratic Presidential Primary

Carter	458,580	(47%)
Udall	214,677	(22%)
Church	147,759	(15%)
Others	149,982	(16%)

1976 Republican Presidential Primary

Ford	516,111	(55%)
Reagan	419,646	(45%)

Sen. John Glenn (D) Elected 1974, seat up 1980; b. July 18, 1921, Cambridge; home, Columbus; Muskingum Col., B.S. 1939; Presbyterian.

Career USMC, 1942–65; NASA Astronaut, 1959–65, First American to orbit the Earth, 1962; Candidate for Dem. nomination for U.S. Senate, 1964, 1970; V.P., Royal Crown Cola Co., 1966–68, Pres., Royal Crown Internatl., 1967–69.

Offices 204 RSOB, 202-224-3353. Also Suite 600, 200 N. High St., Columbus 43215, 614-469-6697, and Rm. 104, Fed. Court House, Cleveland 44114, 216-522-7095.

Committees *Foreign Relations* (5th). Subcommittees: Arms Control, Oceans, International Operations, and Environment; European Affairs; East Asian and Pacific Affairs (Chairman).

Governmental Affairs (6th). Subcommittees: Investigations; Intergovernmental Relations; Energy, Nuclear Proliferation and Federal Services (Chairman).

Special Committee on Aging (3d).

Group Ratings

	ADA	COPE	PC	RPN	NFU	LCV	CFA	NAB	NSI	ACA	NTU
1978	65	74	58	60	10	76	45	33	40	25	–
1977	60	79	58	45	64	–	60	–	–	19	24
1976	55	83	58	50	92	43	78	18	60	15	25

Key Votes

1) Warnke Nom	FOR	6) Egypt-Saudi Arms	FOR	11) Hosptl Cost Contnmnt	FOR
2) Neutron Bomb	FOR	7) Draft Restr Pardon	FOR	12) Clinch River Reactor	AGN
3) Waterwy User Fee	FOR	8) Wheat Price Support	AGN	13) Pub Fin Cong Cmpgns	FOR
4) Dereg Nat Gas	AGN	9) Panama Canal Treaty	FOR	14) ERA Ratif Recissn	FOR
5) Kemp-Roth	AGN	10) Labor Law Rev Clot	FOR	15) Med Necssy Abrtns	FOR

Election Results

1974 general	John H. Glenn, Jr. (D)	1,930,670	(68%)	($1,149,130)
	Ralph J. Perk (R)	918,133	(32%)	($292,838)
1974 primary	John H. Glenn, Jr. (D)	571,871	(54%)	
	Howard M. Metzenbaum (D) 480,123 (46%)			
1968 general	William B. Saxbe (R)	1,928,964	(52%)	
	John J. Gilligan (D)	1,814,152	(48%)	

Sen. Howard Metzenbaum (D) Elected 1976, seat up 1982; b. June 4, 1917, Cleveland; home, Shaker Heights; Ohio St. U., B.A. 1939, LL.B. 1941; Jewish.

Career Practicing atty.; Co-founder, Airport Parking Co. of America, ComCorp Communications Corp.; Chm. of the Bd., ITT Consumer Services Corp.; Ohio House of Reps., 1943–46; Ohio Senate, 1947–50; Campaign Mgr., Sen. Stephen M. Young, 1958 and 1964; Dem. nominee for U.S. Senate, 1970; U.S. Senate, 1973–74.

Offices 347 RSOB, 202-224-2315. Also Rm. 442, 121 E. State St., Columbus 43215, 614-469-6774.

Committees *Budget* (9th).

Energy and Natural Resources (7th). Subcommittees: Energy Conservation and Supply; Energy Regulation; Parks, Recreation, and Renewable Resources.

Labor and Human Resources (9th). Subcommittees: Health and Scientific Research; Employment, Poverty and Migratory Labor; Alcoholism and Drug Abuse.

Judiciary (6th). Subcommittees: Administrative Practice and Procedure; Antitrust, Monopoly, and Business Rights (Chairman); Constitution.

Group Ratings

	ADA	COPE	PC	RPN	NFU	LCV	CFA	NAB	NSI	ACA	NTU
1978	100	84	98	60	44	78	90	25	10	13	–
1977	90	85	78	55	67	–	84	–	–	7	30

Key Votes

1) Warnke Nom	FOR	6) Egypt-Saudi Arms	AGN	11) Hosptl Cost Contnmnt	FOR
2) Neutron Bomb	AGN	7) Draft Restr Pardon	FOR	12) Clinch River Reactor	AGN
3) Waterwy User Fee	FOR	8) Wheat Price Support	AGN	13) Pub Fin Cong Cmpgns	FOR
4) Dereg Nat Gas	AGN	9) Panama Canal Treaty	FOR	14) ERA Ratif Recissn	FOR
5) Kemp-Roth	AGN	10) Labor Law Rev Clot	FOR	15) Med Necssy Abrtns	FOR

Election Results

1976 general	Howard M. Metzenbaum (D)	1,925,163	(52%)	($1,092,053)
	Robert Taft, Jr. (R)	1,809,283	(48%)	($1,304,207)
1976 primary	Howard M. Metzenbaum (D)	576,124	(54%)	
	James V. Stanton (D)	400,552	(37%)	
	Two others (D)	98,501	(9%)	
1970 general	Robert Taft, Jr. (R)	1,565,682	(51%)	
	Howard M. Metzenbaum (D)	1,495,262	(49%)	

Gov. James A. Rhodes (R) Elected 1974, term expires Jan. 1983; b. Sept. 13, 1909, Coalton; Ohio St. U.

Career Mayor of Columbus, 1943–53; Ohio St. Auditor, 1953–63; Gov. of Ohio, 1963–70; Writer and novelist; Chm., Natl. Council for Vocational Educ.

Offices Columbus 43215, 614-466-3526.

Election Results

1978 general	James A. Rhodes (R)	1,402,167	(51%)
	Richard Celeste (D)	1,354,631	(49%)
1978 primary	James A. Rhodes (R)	393,632	(68%)
	Charles Kurfess (R)	187,544	(32%)
1974 general	James A. Rhodes (R)	1,493,679	(50%)
	John J. Gilligan (D)	1,482,191	(50%)

FIRST DISTRICT

The 1st district of Ohio is the eastern half of Cincinnati and suburban Hamilton County. This is, by and large, the more prosperous half of the old river city, which was the cultural and commercial capital of the Midwest even before the Tafts arrived. In some neighborhoods within Cincinnati and in the hills beyond the city limits are the fashionable estates of the city's elite.

Probably the most prestigious is the suburb of Indian Hill, home of former Senator Robert Taft, Jr. To the north, one finds a mix of shopping centers and high income suburban terrain. Within the city itself are the formerly Jewish sections of Avondale and Walnut Hills, now predominantly black. Many neighborhoods, like Norwood, a suburban enclave surrounded by Cincinnati, are inhabited mainly by migrants from the hills of Kentucky and Tennessee. The 1st has most of the city's Jewish population; from its early days as a German river town, Cincinnati has had an important German Jewish community. Politically, it is more conservative and Republican than Jewish communities in other major cities.

Cincinnati has a well-deserved reputation for being a Republican city. Of the nation's 25 largest metropolitan areas, only Dallas-Fort Worth and San Diego turn in Republican margins with greater regularity. That has been the case since before the Civil War, when Cincinnati was a German, pro-Union, and Republican island in a sea of Southern Democratic sentiment. Later Cincinnati never attracted large numbers of the ethnic groups which have traditionally voted for Democrats. There are fewer blacks here than in Cleveland, Detroit, or Buffalo, and very few people of Eastern or Southern European origin. Many of the city's Appalachians come from solid Republican mountain counties, and bring their politics to the big city here.

Out of Cincinnati have come several prominent Republicans, including Chief Justice Salmon P. Chase, President and Chief Justice William Howard Taft, Speaker of the House Nicholas Longworth (whose nonagenarian widow, Alice Roosevelt Longworth, still thrives in Washington), and of course the late Senator Robert Taft. In more recent years the 1st has produced a series of congressmen of both parties who, for some reason or another, have achieved national prominence. That started in 1964, when John Gilligan, then a Cincinnati Council member and later Governor of Ohio, was elected in an upset; two years later he was beaten by Robert Taft, Jr., later U.S. Senator. When Taft moved up to the Senate he was succeeded by William Keating, who in 1974 became president of the Cincinnati *Enquirer,* resigning and thus avoiding service on the Judiciary Committee during the impeachment hearings.

Keating's resignation provided some guidance, however, for Judiciary Committee members, for it required a special election—one of that series in 1974 which showed the vast unpopularity of Richard Nixon. The contenders were two members of the Cincinnati Council, Democrat Thomas Luken and Republican Willis Gradison. Although there was some disagreement on other issues—Luken was against legalized abortion, Gradison wasn't—the main issue was Nixon, and Luken won. This was the only special election that year whose result was overturned in November. With Nixon gone, Gradison captured the seat; two years later, Luken won in the next-door 2d district.

Gradison has held the seat easily ever since. He is a member of the Ways and Means Committee and is considered one of its brighter and better informed members. He is the kind of congressman who asks basic questions about programs: If we have food stamps, why don't we have energy stamps or housing stamps? If inflation is continuing, why not index our progressive tax rates so that taxes on real incomes don't rise every year? Gradison's answers usually lead him in the direction of less federal regulation and activity; he is for indexing the income tax and for scrapping the food stamp program, for example. He has emerged as one of the intellectual and legislative leaders of the resurgent Republican minority.

Census Data Pop. 462,725. Central city, 48%; suburban, 52%. Median family income, $10,535; families above $15,000: 26%; families below $3,000: 8%. Median years education, 12.1.

The Voters

Median voting age 43.
Employment profile White collar, 53%. Blue collar, 33%. Service, 14%. Farm, –%.
Ethnic groups Black, 20%. Total foreign stock, 9%. Germany, 2%.

Presidential vote

1976	Carter (D)	69,422	(41%)
	Ford (R)	98,225	(59%)
1972	Nixon (R)	111,925	(66%)
	McGovern (D)	57,516	(34%)

Rep. Willis D. Gradison, Jr. (R) Elected 1974; b. Dec. 28, 1928, Cincinnati; home, Cincinnati; Yale U., B.A. 1948, Harvard U., M.B.A. 1951, D.C.S. 1954.

Career Investment broker; Asst. to U.S. Under Secy. of the Treasury, 1953–55; Asst. to U.S. Secy. of HEW, 1955–57; Cincinnati City Cncl., 1961–74, Vice Mayor, 1967–71, Mayor, 1971.

Offices 1519 LHOB, 202-225-3164. Also 8008 Fed. Ofc. Bldg., 550 Main St., Cincinnati 45202, 513-684-2456.

Committees *Ways and Means* (10th). Subcommittees: Oversight; Social Security.

Group Ratings

	ADA	COPE	PC	RPN	NFU	LCV	CFA	NAB	NSI	ACA	NTU
1978	20	15	28	91	10	–	27	100	89	70	–
1977	15	32	28	85	27	24	20	–	–	74	44
1976	15	19	26	88	18	43	27	100	90	72	61

Key Votes

1) Increase Def Spnd	FOR	6) Alaska Lands Protect	FOR	11) Delay Auto Pol Cntrl	FOR
2) B-1 Bomber	FOR	7) Water Projects Veto	FOR	12) Sugar Price Escalator	AGN
3) Cargo Preference	AGN	8) Consum Protect Agcy	AGN	13) Pub Fin Cong Cmpgns	AGN
4) Dereg Nat Gas	FOR	9) Common Situs Picket	AGN	14) ERA Ratif Recissn	FOR
5) Kemp-Roth	FOR	10) Labor Law Revision	FOR	15) Prohibt Govt Abrtns	FOR

Election Results

1978 general	Bill Gradison, Jr. (R)	73,593	(66%)	($84,745)
	Timothy M. Burke (D)	38,669	(34%)	($12,710)
1978 primary	Bill Gradison, Jr. (R), unopposed			
1976 general	Bill Gradison, Jr. (R)	109,674	(66%)	($111,945)
	William F. Bowen (D)	56,936	(34%)	($37,053)

SECOND DISTRICT

The 2d congressional district of Ohio is the western half of Cincinnati and Hamilton County. On the whole, this is the less fashionable half of Cincinnati, though the 2d does have plenty of comfortable neighborhoods, mostly in the suburbs. For the most part, the district consists of middle and lower middle class neighborhoods spread out over Cincinnati's hills. The 2d also includes some of the older and poorer sections of the city, like the Appalachian Over the Rhine area (a name that recalls Cincinnati's German heritage). At the eastern end of the district winds Mill Creek, and next to it lies Cincinnati's industrial corridor. Here are the great Procter and Gamble soap factories and many of the city's machine tool makers; Cincinnati is a leader in both industries. Here also is the General Electric plant that produces many of the nation's aircraft engines.

Like the 1st district, this is one which has always been strongly Republican. In recent years, Cincinnati itself has become more Democratic, because many of its more affluent citizens have moved to the suburbs; but the suburbs are very heavily Republican. This district has elected Republican congressmen for many years, but now it is represented by a Democrat. One reason is that his Republican predecessor, Donald Clancy, became tired of providing all the serivces that constituents have come to expect. Instead of returning frequently to the district, he took to spending more time in Florida. First elected in 1960, he had a tough challenge in 1970, and did poorly against a weak opponent in 1974. He was defeated finally in 1976, when Thomas Luken, a veteran of the Cincinnati Council who had won a special election in the 1st district in the spring of 1974 and then lost the district in the 1974 general election, decided to run in the 2d instead.

Luken was a candidate of considerable strength; he had lost in the 1st district to Willis Gradison, a bright and energetic campaigner. Luken beat Clancy despite the latter's long incumbency, and despite the fact that the district was giving 62% of its votes to Gerald Ford. In 1978 he had stronger competition from state Senator Stanley Aronoff, but managed to win again by a small margin. Luken's greatest strength is in Cincinnati's middle class Catholic neighborhoods. He is a strong foe of abortions and a strong supporter of tuition tax credits. On other issues he has a record which is a few shades more conservative than those of most northern Democrats. He can expect tough competition again in 1980.

Census Data Pop. 463,260. Central city, 49%; suburban, 51%. Median family income, $10,439; families above $15,000: 23%; families below $3,000: 8%. Median years education, 11.9.

The Voters

Median voting age 43.
Employment profile White collar, 53%. Blue collar, 34%. Service, 13%. Farm, –%.
Ethnic groups Black, 11%. Total foreign stock, 9%. Germany, 3%.

Presidential vote

1976	Carter (D)	62,649	(38%)
	Ford (R)	103,650	(62%)
1972	Nixon (R)	127,655	(67%)
	McGovern (D)	61,676	(33%)

Rep. Thomas A. Luken (D) Elected 1976; b. July 9, 1925, Cincinnati; home, Cincinnati; Bowling Green U., 1933–34, Xavier U., B.A. 1947, Salmon P. Chase Law Sch., LL.B. 1950; Catholic.

Career USMC, WWII; Practicing atty.; Deer Park City Solicitor, 1955–61; U.S. Dist. Atty. for South. Dist. of Ohio, 1961–64; Cincinnati City Cncl., 1964–67, 1969–74, Mayor, 1971–72; U.S. House of Reps., 1974.

Offices 1131 LHOB, 202-225-2216. Also Rm. 3409 Fed. Bldg., Cincinnati 45202, 513-684-2723.

Committees *Interstate and Foreign Commerce* (19th). Subcommittees: Communications; Consumer Protection and Finance; Health and the Environment.

Small Business (18th). Subcommittees: Impact of Energy Programs, Environment and Safety Requirements and Government Research on Small Business (Chairman).

Group Ratings

	ADA	COPE	PC	RPN	NFU	LCV	CFA	NAB	NSI	ACA	NTU
1978	25	65	40	40	40	–	46	50	80	60	–
1977	40	68	60	54	75	45	60	–	–	37	27

Key Votes

1) Increase Def Spnd	AGN	6) Alaska Lands Protect	FOR	11) Delay Auto Pol Cntrl	FOR
2) B-1 Bomber	FOR	7) Water Projects Veto	FOR	12) Sugar Price Escalator	AGN
3) Cargo Preference	AGN	8) Consum Protect Agcy	AGN	13) Pub Fin Cong Cmpgns	FOR
4) Dereg Nat Gas	AGN	9) Common Situs Picket	FOR	14) ERA Ratif Recissn	FOR
5) Kemp-Roth	FOR	10) Labor Law Revision	FOR	15) Prohibt Govt Abrtns	FOR

Election Results

1978 general	Thomas A. Luken (D)	64,522	(52%)	($230,690)
	Stanley J. Aronoff (R)	58,716	(48%)	($275,400)
1978 primary	Thomas A. Luken (D), unopposed			
1976 general	Thomas A. Luken (D)	87,876	(51%)	($91,047)
	Donald D. Clancy (R)	83,218	(49%)	($141,991)

THIRD DISTRICT

In many ways Dayton, Ohio, is a typical American city. It sits on the old National Road that spans the middle of the Midwest; it is middle sized (metropolitan area population 850,000) and predominantly middle class. It has given birth to such American phenomena as the Wright brothers and the Phil Donahue Show. Like most central cities, Dayton itself is losing population; it is now about 30% black and has even elected a black mayor. As in most metropolitan areas, the most substantial growth here lately has been in the suburbs, as in middle class Kettering just south of the city. Dayton—or one of its suburbs—is the home of Richard Scammon and Ben Wattenberg's typical American voter: a housewife whose husband works in a factory and whose brother-in-law is a policeman.

The voting behavior of Dayton and surrounding Montgomery County, however, has not always been typical of middle America—although it is responsive to the same issues and conditions as most communities. The law and order politics of Richard Nixon and Spiro Agnew made some impact on the middle class voters here—but not as much as in many other metropolitan areas, particularly on the East Coast, where middle income whites' fears of blacks were joined with dislike of the attitudes of upper income whites. There just isn't very much radical chic in Dayton. And in the seventies, the Dayton area has been getting more and more Democratic. This is one of Ohio's industrial cities which has been losing large numbers of jobs, and unemployment is a very real problem here—not just for teenagers who are looking casually for jobs, but for adult breadwinners who are wondering whether they are going to have to move somewhere else.

Dayton's congressional representation has reflected this trend. The 3d congressional district includes Dayton, Kettering, and most of the Montgomery County suburbs. For a dozen years after the 1966 election it was represented by Charles Whalen, a liberal Republican who won great popularity in the district. Whalen's voting record, unlike that of most Ohio Republicans, was always acceptable to organized labor. He was one of the House's leading Republican opponents of the Vietnam war. A genial and pleasant man, he was popular in the House as well as back home; but increasingly he seemed more comfortable and at home with Democrats than Republicans. In 1978 he decided not to seek reelection.

His successor, as expected, was Tony Hall, a young state Senator with strong local roots (his father was once mayor of Dayton). At first Hall seemed likely to coast to victory on the basis of name identification and party label. But his Republican opponent, Dudley Kircher, grabbed hold of the jobs issue and spotlighted his efforts to save several hundred Defense Department jobs in Dayton. Hall seized the initiative by attacking Kircher as a tool of big business and for his support of deregulation of natural gas—both unpopular positions here. Hall won with 55% of the vote, but Kircher's comparatively good showing illustrates the importance of jobs issues in Dayton's troubled economy. Hall, a veteran of the Peace Corps, seems to share many of Whalen's attitudes and much of his idealism, and his record is expected to be similar to his predecessor's, despite the difference in party identification. With the advantages of incumbency he should win reelection easily, though probably not by as great a margin.

Census Data Pop. 463,140. Central city, 53%; suburban, 47%. Median family income, $11,481; families above $15,000: 29%; families below $3,000: 7%. Median years education, 12.2.

The Voters

Median voting age 41.
Employment profile White collar, 51%. Blue collar, 37%. Service, 12%. Farm, –%.
Ethnic groups Black, 16%. Total foreign stock, 7%. Germany, 2%.

Presidential vote

1976	Carter (D)	78,920	(52%)
	Ford (R)	74,128	(48%)
1972	Nixon (R)	88,701	(58%)
	McGovern (D)	63,890	(42%)

Rep. Tony P. Hall (D) Elected 1978; b. Jan. 16, 1942, Dayton; home, Dayton; Dennison U., B.A. 1964; Presbyterian.

Career Peace Corps, Thailand, 1964–66; Real Estate Broker 1966–; Ohio House of Reps., 1969–73; Ohio Senate, 1973–79.

Offices 1009 LHOB, 202-225-6465. Also 501 Fed. Bldg., 200 W. 2nd St., Dayton 45402, 513-225-2843.

Committees *Foreign Affairs* (19th). Subcommittees: Asian and Pacific Affairs; International Organizations.

Small Business (25th). Subcommittees: SBA and SBIC Authority and General Small Business Problems; Antitrust and Restraint of Trade Activities Affecting Small Business.

Group Ratings: Newly Elected

Key Votes: Newly Elected

Election Results

1978 general	Tony P. Hall (D)	62,849	(55%)	($216,117)
	Dudley P. Kircher (R)	51,833	(45%)	($346,193)
1978 primary	Tony P. Hall (D)	19,780	(80%)	
	Two others (D)	4,930	(20%)	
1976 general	Charles W. Whalen, Jr. (R)	100,812	(75%)	($32,422)
	Leonard E. Stubbs (D)	34,008	(25%)	($1,606)

FOURTH DISTRICT

The 4th congressional district of Ohio is a group of counties, mostly rural but usually with small cities, in the western part of the state. This is a deeply conservative part of the nation, a sort of Grant Woodish enclave set in industrial middle America. It is somehow fitting that the town of Wapakoneta here in the 4th produced the first man to walk on the moon—the strait-laced and taciturn Neil Armstrong. The conservatism of the 4th runs so deep that it is often the most Republican district in Ohio. The district's urban centers, to the extent they can be called that, are as heavily Republican as the countryside, in some cases more so. Findlay is an old Republican town, made newly prosperous as the headquarters of Marathon Oil. Allen County, which contains the district's largest city, Lima, was the largest county east of Chicago and north of Richmond, Virginia, to support the candidacy of Barry Goldwater in 1964. Then there are smaller Republican towns like Bucyrus, Piqua, and Upper Sandusky (which is nowhere near Sandusky).

For 25 years Republican William McCulloch represented the 4th district. When he retired in 1972, McCulloch was the dean of the Ohio delegation and the ranking Republican on the House Judiciary Committee, which has jurisdiction over civil rights legislation. McCulloch was a cautious, conservative man who shared the passion of some of the founders of the Republican Party for the principle of racial equality. He supported strongly the civil rights bills of the fifties and sixties, and his example helped to swing many more dubious Republicans behind the civil rights cause. He is entitled to a great deal of credit for the enactment of the Civil Rights Acts of 1964, 1965, and 1968.

By 1972 McCulloch was 71 and seriously ill, and he retired. His successor, and still the district's Congressman, is Tennyson Guyer, who served for many years before in the state Senate. With a background in public relations for a tire company, Guyer's attitudes are more similar to those of most contemporary Ohio Republicans than were McCulloch's. His voting record is rated very positively by business-oriented groups and very negatively by labor-oriented groups, and he has no special interest in civil rights. To the extent he has a specialty, it is in East Asian affairs, but on most issues he can best be described as a loyal follower of the Republican leadership.

Census Data Pop. 463,143. Central city, 12%; suburban, 31%. Median family income, $9,710; families above $15,000: 17%; families below $3,000: 8%. Median years education, 12.1.

The Voters

Median voting age 43.
Employment profile White collar, 38%. Blue collar, 46%. Service, 12%. Farm, 4%.
Ethnic groups Black, 3%. Total foreign stock, 4%. Germany, 1%.

Presidential vote

1976	Carter (D)	70,588	(40%)
	Ford (R)	104,313	(60%)
1972	Nixon (R)	120,089	(71%)
	McGovern (D)	49,780	(29%)

Rep. Tennyson Guyer (R) Elected 1972; b. Nov. 29, 1913, Findlay; home, Findlay; Findlay Col., B.S. 1934; Church of God.

Career Pastor, Celina Church of God; Mayor of Celina and Pres. of City Cncl., 1940–44; Dir. of Public Affairs, Cooper Tire & Rubber Co., 1950–72; Mbr., Exec. Comm., Ohio Repub. St. Comm., 1954–66; Ohio Senate, 1959–72.

Offices 114 CHOB, 202-225-2676. Also 401 W. North St., Lima 45801, 419-227-6845.

Committees *Foreign Affairs* (7th). Subcommittees: Asian and Pacific Affairs; Inter-American Affairs.

Veterans' Affairs (6th). Subcommittees: Compensation, Pension, Insurance and Memorial Affairs; Medical Facilities and Benefits.

Group Ratings

	ADA	COPE	PC	RPN	NFU	LCV	CFA	NAB	NSI	ACA	NTU
1978	10	85	15	58	44	–	18	89	100	78	–
1977	0	19	13	64	50	14	20	–	–	79	29
1976	10	24	13	64	37	25	9	75	100	71	52

Key Votes

1) Increase Def Spnd	FOR	6) Alaska Lands Protect	AGN	11) Delay Auto Pol Cntrl	FOR
2) B-1 Bomber	FOR	7) Water Projects Veto	FOR	12) Sugar Price Escalator	FOR
3) Cargo Preference	AGN	8) Consum Protect Agcy	AGN	13) Pub Fin Cong Cmpgns	AGN
4) Dereg Nat Gas	FOR	9) Common Situs Picket	AGN	14) ERA Ratif Recissn	FOR
5) Kemp-Roth	FOR	10) Labor Law Revision	AGN	15) Prohibt Govt Abrtns	FOR

Election Results

1978 general	Tennyson Guyer (R)	85,575	(68%)	($23,696)
	John W. Griffin (D)	39,360	(32%)	
1978 primary	Tennyson Guyer (R), unopposed			
1976 general	Tennyson Guyer (R)	119,974	(70%)	($22,789)
	Clinton G. Dorsey (D)	51,757	(30%)	($1,256)

FIFTH DISTRICT

Some 150 years ago, New England Yankee farmers settled the flat lands in the northwest corner of Ohio, together with recently immigrated German Protestants. The land here is more fertile and easier to work than the knobby hills of southern Ohio; its flatness and fertility must have amazed the early settlers. It is the beginning of the great corn and hog belt that stretches into Illinois and Iowa, and it is also one of the heartlands of the Republican Party since it was founded in the 1850s.

Unlike so much of rural America, northwest Ohio was not in economic decline in the decades after World War II. The fertility of its soil, the industry of its farmers, and, most important, its strategic location prevented the kind of outmigration seen elsewhere. This area is encircled by the giant industrial cities of the Midwest and lies on both sides of the nation's major east-west railroads and Interstate highways. Taking advantage of the proximity of these major markets, small factories have sprung up in most of the towns and much of the countryside of northwest Ohio. They have provided jobs for young people here, who otherwise would probably have migrated to a large city.

The 5th congressional district covers most of northwest Ohio. Not included here is the city of Toledo and most of its suburbs, which make up the 9th district. The 5th, as one might expect, is a solidly Republican district which since 1958 has elected and reelected Congressman Delbert Latta. (His name, incidentally, is Welsh, not Italian.) Latta is one of those congressmen who labored for years without much public notice. As a member of the Rules Committee, he was often part, or even the architect, of the coalition of conservative Republicans and Southern Democrats who would kill liberal legislation by refusing to schedule it for debate. Always a fierce and aggressive partisan, Latta could be trusted to follow the wishes of the Republican leadership; and within the leadership he was usually an advocate of hard-line opposition to the Democrats.

In the seventies, Latta has become much more prominent, but his basic orientation has not changed. His well deserved reputation got him a seat on the Judiciary Committee in 1974; he filled a vacancy just for the hearings on the impeachment of Richard Nixon. Apparently the hope was that Latta would provide a no holds barred defense of Richard Nixon, and he did. Again and again he mentioned how much the hearings were costing and he attacked committee counsel Albert Jenner, a Republican favoring impeachment, for having been a member of a committee which recommended the decriminalization of prostitution. Latta's tactics were not particularly effective. These side issues did not bring the angry popular reaction they once might have; the more effective defenses of Nixon, made by Charles Wiggins and others, stuck closer to the facts of the case.

When the congressional budget process was established in 1975, Latta again got a key role. He was named the ranking Republican on the House Budget Committee. The Senate committee has been characterized by cooperation between Chairman Edmund Muskie and ranking Republican Henry Bellmon; the opposite has been the case in the House. Latta has fought the Democrats every step of the way, arguing constantly in committee and then on the floor for lower spending targets in non-defense areas. On occasion he has defeated the budget limits set by the Democrats, although for the most part they have had the votes to prevail. Most commentators compare Latta's stance unfavorably with Bellmon's. But there is something to be said for an adversary process, and for requiring the majority to justify their actions against strenuous opposition. Latta is a man who believes that the Democrats are invariably up to mischief, and who will take any steps he can to stop them. He has been reelected easily every two years.

Census Data Pop. 463,727. Central city, 0%; suburban, 37%. Median family income, $9,945; families above $15,000: 18%; families below $3,000: 8%. Median years education, 12.1.

The Voters

Median voting age 42.
Employment profile White collar, 37%. Blue collar, 46%. Service, 12%. Farm, 5%.
Ethnic groups Total foreign stock, 7%. Germany, 2%.

Presidential vote

1976	Carter (D)	83,692	(45%)
	Ford (R)	104,089	(55%)
1972	Nixon (R)	188,678	(66%)
	McGovern (D)	62,332	(34%)

Rep. Delbert L. Latta (R) Elected 1958; b. Mar. 5, 1920, Weston; home, Bowling Green; Ohio Northern U., A.B., LL.B.; Church of Christ.

Career Practicing atty.; Ohio Senate.

Offices 2309 RHOB, 202-225-6405. Also 100 Fed. Bldg., 280 S. Main St., Bowling Green 43402, 419-353-8871.

Committees *Budget* (Ranking Member). Subcommittees: State and Local Governments; Regulations and Spending Limitations; Defense and International Affairs; Legislative Savings.

Rules (3d).

Group Ratings

	ADA	COPE	PC	RPN	NFU	LCV	CFA	NAB	NSI	ACA	NTU
1978	5	5	18	55	30	–	18	100	100	89	–
1977	10	18	23	75	55	29	20	–	–	88	56
1976	0	13	8	56	8	22	9	92	90	100	71

Key Votes

1) Increase Def Spnd	FOR	6) Alaska Lands Protect	FOR	11) Delay Auto Pol Cntrl	DNV
2) B-1 Bomber	FOR	7) Water Projects Veto	FOR	12) Sugar Price Escalator	FOR
3) Cargo Preference	AGN	8) Consum Protect Agcy	AGN	13) Pub Fin Cong Cmpgns	AGN
4) Dereg Nat Gas	FOR	9) Common Situs Picket	AGN	14) ERA Ratif Recissn	FOR
5) Kemp-Roth	FOR	10) Labor Law Revision	AGN	15) Prohibt Govt Abrtns	FOR

Election Results

1978 general	Delbert L. Latta (R)	85,547	(63%)	($45,705)
	James R. Sherck (D)	51,071	(37%)	($40,249)
1978 primary	Delbert L. Latta (R), unopposed			
1976 general	Delbert L. Latta (R)	89,161	(63%)	($25,134)
	Bruce Edwards (D)	53,391	(37%)	($2,802)

SIXTH DISTRICT

The 6th district of Ohio is a rural district in the southern part of the state. Though the 6th touches the metropolitan areas of Cincinnati to the west and Columbus to the north, little in the 6th partakes of anything metropolitan. From the outer edges of urban Cincinnati and Columbus to the gritty industrial city of Portsmouth on the Ohio River, the district has a Southern-accented, small town feeling. The rolling hill country of the valley of the Scioto River, which runs through Columbus, Chillicothe, and Portsmouth, was once Democratic terrain, reflecting the Southern origin of the valley's first settlers. In the fifties and sixties, this part of Ohio, like much of the South, became more conservative and much more Republican; only tiny Pike County still delivers Democratic majorities reliably in statewide races. In the western part of the district, some Cincinnati exurban growth spilling into Clermont County has contributed to the Republican trend in the 6th.

Until the late fifties this district, in line with tradition, sent a Democrat to the House. After his death in 1959, the Ohio Republican organization of Ray Bliss carefully selected the party nominee, William Harsha, the former local prosecutor in Portsmouth, still in his thirties. Harsha won a special election in 1960 and has represented the district ever since.

In the House Harsha has been a pretty reliable Republican, though he has a somewhat higher rating from organized labor than do most Ohio Republicans. For several terms now he has been ranking Republican on the Public Works Committee. This is a body that has traditionally supervised the pork barrell—highway construction projects, dams, post offices, and federal buildings. For years, particularly depression years when jobs were scarce, congressmen felt they could get reelected if they got enough such projects in their districts; others, mostly Democrats, thought it was a good idea to fund any job-creating project, no matter how much it cost. Harsha is not a purist who has tried to crack down hard on this kind of spending; he has good relations with the lobbies, such as the highway lobby, which follow the committee's activities closely. The pork barrel has become less and less important to most congressmen electorally, but Public Works has remained an important committee because it handles much of the air and water pollution legislation. On these matters, Harsha tends to resolve conflicts between environmental concerns and economic activity in favor of the latter. Back in the 6th district he is reelected easily every two years.

Census Data Pop. 463,067. Central city, 0%; suburban, 37%. Median family income, $8,595; families above $15,000: 13%; families below $3,000: 13%. Median years education, 11.2.

The Voters

Median voting age 43.
Employment profile White collar, 37%. Blue collar, 46%. Service, 12%. Farm, 5%.
Ethnic groups Black, 2%. Total foreign stock, 2%.

Presidential vote

1976	Carter (D)	86,984	(49%)
	Ford (R)	91,352	(51%)
1972	Nixon (R)	118,484	(70%)
	McGovern (D)	49,892	(30%)

Rep. William H. Harsha (R) Elected 1960; b. Jan. 1, 1921, Portsmouth; home, Portsmouth; Kenyon Col., A.B. 1943, Western Reserve U., LL.B. 1947; Presbyterian.

Career USMC, WWII; Practicing atty., 1947–61; Portsmouth Asst. City Solicitor, 1947–51; Scioto Co. Prosecutor, 1951–55.

Offices 2185 RHOB, 202-225-5705. Also 285 Main St., Batavia 45103, 513-732-2247.

Committees *Public Works and Transportation* (Ranking Member).

Group Ratings

	ADA	COPE	PC	RPN	NFU	LCV	CFA	NAB	NSI	ACA	NTU
1978	15	26	13	27	50	–	18	92	90	85	–
1977	15	35	33	33	82	6	35	–	–	65	34
1976	5	29	25	47	40	16	18	64	90	76	50

Key Votes

1) Increase Def Spnd	FOR	6) Alaska Lands Protect	FOR	11) Delay Auto Pol Cntrl	FOR
2) B-1 Bomber	FOR	7) Water Projects Veto	AGN	12) Sugar Price Escalator	AGN
3) Cargo Preference	AGN	8) Consum Protect Agcy	AGN	13) Pub Fin Cong Cmpgns	AGN
4) Dereg Nat Gas	AGN	9) Common Situs Picket	AGN	14) ERA Ratif Recissn	FOR
5) Kemp-Roth	FOR	10) Labor Law Revision	DNV	15) Prohibt Govt Abrtns	FOR

Election Results

1978 general	William H. Harsha (R)	85,592	(65%)	($107,252)
	Ted Strickland (D)	46,318	(35%)	($32,950)
1978 primary	William H. Harsha (R)	26,224	(90%)	
	One other (R)	2,979	(10%)	
1976 general	William H. Harsha (R)	107,770	(62%)	($31,029)
	Ted Strickland (D)	66,998	(38%)	($20,692)

SEVENTH DISTRICT

Bellefontaine, Ohio, is the site of the first concrete street in the United States. It is still there in the downtown part of the town, with the old courthouse looming up on one side and a row of stores on the other. Bellefontaine is part of Ohio's 7th congressional district, most of which has enjoyed a similarly stable existence since the turn of the century. It is true that the suburbs of Dayton have begun to encroach on the southwest corner of the district, where Wright-Patterson Air Force Base is located. But the industrial city of Springfield, the district's largest urban concentration, has neither grown nor changed much in the last fifty years. Neither has the city of Marion, where young Socialist-to-be Norman Thomas delivered newspapers edited by President-to-be Warren Harding.

From 1938 to 1965, the 7th was represented by Republican Clarence Brown, a small town newspaper editor. He was a man who seemed out of an earlier Republican era, from the days of Harding or even McKinley. For some years he was ranking Republican on the House Rules Committee, and as a strong believer in the free enterprise system he would join Chairman Smith of Virginia and other conservatives in killing or delaying liberal legislation. Brown also followed the venerable Republican tradition of strongly backing civil rights measures. After his death in 1965, he was succeeded by his son, Clarence (Bud) Brown, also a small town newspaper editor and publisher. The younger Brown also stands solidly in the Republican tradition and has generally followed the majority Republican position on most issues.

In his years in the House Brown has risen to become fourth-ranking Republican on the Commerce Committee and ranking Republican on its Energy and Power Subcommittee. That latter position, plus his own strong beliefs, have made Brown a major Republican leader on the energy issue. Pitted against acerbic subcommittee Chairman John Dingell, Brown has argued strongly for deregulation of natural gas and against controls and taxes on the oil industry. He believes that free markets will allocate energy supplies more rationally and economically than will federal bureaucrats, and he has likened the tasks the Carter energy bills set for government to the labor of Sisyphus. For the most part Brown's positions have not prevailed in the House, but the battles on these issues have been very close and the House outcomes have often been reversed in the Senate and in conference committee.

On other issues Brown has attacked higher Social Security taxes and opposed subsidies for Amtrak. He has been very popular in his district, and in 1978 won reelection without Democratic opposition.

Census Data Pop. 463,217. Central city, 18%; suburban, 52%. Median family income, $10,132; families above $15,000: 20%; families below $3,000: 7%. Median years education, 12.1.

The Voters

Median voting age 41.
Employment profile White collar, 44%. Blue collar, 42%. Service, 11%. Farm, 3%.
Ethnic groups Black, 6%. Total foreign stock, 5%. Germany, 1%.

Presidential vote

1976	Carter (D)	75,152	(46%)
	Ford (R)	86,785	(54%)
1972	Nixon (R)	106,807	(67%)
	McGovern (D)	52,240	(33%)

Rep. Clarence J. Brown (R) Elected Nov. 2, 1965; b. June 18, 1927, Columbus; home, Urbana; Duke U., B.A. 1947, Harvard U., M.B.A. 1949; Presbyterian.

Career Navy, WWII and Korea; Ed., Blanchester *Star Republican*, 1948–53; Ed. and Co-Owner, Franklin *Cronicle*, 1953–57; Ed., Urbana *Daily Citizen*, 1957–62, Publisher, 1959–70; Founder and Mgr., Radio WCOM-FM; Pres., Brown Publishing Co., 1955-.

Offices 1135 LHOB, 202-225-4324; Also 220 P.O. Bldg., 150 N. Limestone St., Springfield 45501, 513-325-0474.

Committees *Government Operations* (4th). Subcommittees: Government Activities and Transportation; Intergovernmental Relations and Human Resources.

Interstate and Foreign Commerce (4th). Subcommittees: Energy and Power.

Group Ratings

	ADA	COPE	PC	RPN	NFU	LCV	CFA	NAB	NSI	ACA	NTU
1978	15	5	15	67	30	–	23	92	100	80	–
1977	25	22	25	67	45	15	30	–	–	77	33
1976	15	13	7	94	9	29	0	100	80	76	52

Key Votes

1) Increase Def Spnd	FOR	6) Alaska Lands Protect	AGN	11) Delay Auto Pol Cntrl	FOR
2) B-1 Bomber	DNV	7) Water Projects Veto	FOR	12) Sugar Price Escalator	AGN
3) Cargo Preference	AGN	8) Consum Protect Agcy	AGN	13) Pub Fin Cong Cmpgns	AGN
4) Dereg Nat Gas	FOR	9) Common Situs Picket	AGN	14) ERA Ratif Recissn	AGN
5) Kemp-Roth	FOR	10) Labor Law Revision	AGN	15) Prohibt Govt Abrtns	FOR

Election Results

1978 general	Clarence J. Brown (R), unopposed			($33,877)
1978 primary	Clarence J. Brown (R), unopposed			
1976 general	Clarence J. Brown (R)	100,833	(65%)	($50,512)
	Dorothy Franke (D)	54,665	(35%)	($2,428)

EIGHTH DISTRICT

Along the Indiana border, just north of Cincinnati and just west of Dayton, is the 8th congressional district of Ohio. Though the suburban sprawl of both Cincinnati and Dayton spills into the 8th, the district is dominated by two manufacturing cities in Butler County, Hamilton and Middletown. In the 8th the hilly Ohio River country slides into the flatter land of the northern part of the state. Over the years, the district has taken most of its settlers from around the Ohio River and farther south, a fact which shows up in the election returns. In most elections these days, the 8th is heavily Republican and conservative. But a Southern Democratic heritage also exists here, one that surfaced in the hefty 18% of the vote cast for George Wallace in the 1968 general election. That was the highest percentage the Alabamian got in any Ohio district that year, and outside Oklahoma the best he did in any district that did not allow slavery at the time of the Civil War.

The current Congressman, Republican Thomas Kindness, was elected in an unusual three-cornered race in 1974. The seat had been Republican since its creation ten years before, but one incumbent had left to run for statewide office and another never managed to win a convincing majority. Although 1974 was a Democratic year, Kindness was elected with 42% to 38% for the Democrat and 20% for a Wallace-oriented Independent. The results paralleled almost exactly the standings in the 1968 presidential race in the district.

Kindness has proved more popular than his immediate predecessor and less interested in state politics than the one before him. He has been reelected by extremely large margins in 1976 and 1978. In the House he ran against John Anderson for the position of chairman of the House Republican Conference in 1979, and lost by a decisive margin. He was considered the candidate of the conservative wing of the party at a time when Republicans, united around economic issues, are in no mood for internal arguments.

Census Data Pop. 462,915. Central city, 25%; suburban, 64%. Median family income, $10,455; families above $15,000: 21%; families below $3,000: 7%. Median years education, 11.8.

The Voters

Median voting age 40.
Employment profile White collar, 41%. Blue collar, 45%. Service, 11%. Farm, 3%.
Ethnic groups Black, 4%. Total foreign stock, 4%. Germany, 1%.

Presidential vote

1976	Carter (D)	77,534	(46%)
	Ford (R)	92,736	(54%)
1972	Nixon (R)	104,889	(69%)
	McGovern (D)	47,638	(31%)

Rep. Thomas N. Kindness (R) Elected 1974; b. Aug 26, 1929, Knoxville, Tenn.; home, Hamilton; U. of Md., A.B. 1951, Geo. Wash. U., LL.B. 1953; Presbyterian.

Career Practicing atty., 1954–57; Asst. Counsel, Legal Dept., Champion Internatl. Corp., 1957–73; Hamilton City Cncl., 1964–69, Mayor, 1964–67; Ohio House of Reps., 1971–74.

Offices 1124 LHOB, 202-225-6205. Also 202-225-6205. Also 801 High St., Hamilton 45013, 513-895-5656.

Committees *Government Operations* (6th). Subcommittees: Government Information and Individual Rights.

Judiciary (8th). Subcommittees: Administrative Law and Governmental Relations; Criminal Justice.

Group Ratings

	ADA	COPE	PC	RPN	NFU	LCV	CFA	NAB	NSI	ACA	NTU
1978	5	5	15	50	20	–	14	92	90	93	–
1977	10	26	23	50	36	10	15	–	–	88	57
1976	0	11	10	71	6	6	9	100	100	65	62

Key Votes

1) Increase Def Spnd	FOR	6) Alaska Lands Protect	AGN	11) Delay Auto Pol Cntrl	FOR
2) B-1 Bomber	FOR	7) Water Projects Veto	FOR	12) Sugar Price Escalator	FOR
3) Cargo Preference	AGN	8) Consum Protect Agcy	AGN	13) Pub Fin Cong Cmpgns	AGN
4) Dereg Nat Gas	FOR	9) Common Situs Picket	AGN	14) ERA Ratif Recissn	FOR
5) Kemp-Roth	FOR	10) Labor Law Revision	FOR	15) Prohibt Govt Abrtns	FOR

Election Results

1978 general	Thomas N. Kindness (R)	81,156	(71%)	($64,077)
	Lou Schroeder (D)	32,493	(29%)	($15,430)
1978 primary	Thomas N. Kindness (R), unopposed			
1976 general	Thomas N. Kindness (R)	108,402	(70%)	($54,451)
	John W. Griffin (D)	45,937	(30%)	($2,257)

NINTH DISTRICT

The city of Toledo rises incongruously from the flat plains of northwest Ohio; it is different from the surrounding countryside in just about every respect. Situated in the middle of rich agricultural country, Toledo is heavily industrial; set among Anglo-Saxon farmers and small town residents, Toledo is heavily ethnic, with many Polish-Americans; surrounded by one of the nation's staunchest Republican areas, Toledo is solidly Democratic. Toledo is an important factory town: it produces automobile glass, Willys Jeeps, and other bulky products. It is a major Great Lakes port and sits on some of the major east-west railroad lines. Like Detroit, just 60 miles to the north, Toledo experienced its greatest growth between 1910 and 1930, during the initial expansion of the automobile industry. Much of Toledo's industry is directly related to the auto industry, but it has too much diversity to be a one-industry town.

Lucas County, which contains Toledo, is one of two in Ohio that went for George McGovern in 1972. Except for a few suburban and rural townships, all of Lucas County makes up Ohio's 9th congressional district. The 9th is a Democratic stronghold; indeed, it is the only district in northwest Ohio that elects a Democratic congressman. The current incumbent is Thomas Ludlow Ashley, first elected in 1954. He comes to the seat almost by inheritance. His great-grandfather, a radical Republican, was Toledo's Congressman during the Civil War years; as Chairman of the Committee on Territories, he left his imprint on the nation by choosing the names for Montana and Wyoming and possibly for other states as well. The present Congressman Ashley has served on committees with jurisdiction more mundane: Merchant Marine and Fisheries and Banking, Housing, and Urban Affairs. As a subcommittee chairman on the latter, Ashley has been something of an expert on housing legislation and a promoter of a national urban growth policy.

But Ashley's greatest celebrity in the House has come on another issue entirely, energy. In 1977 Speaker O'Neill made him Chairman of a special committee charged with putting together an energy program. Under Ashley's leadership, the committee discarded some of the Carter Administration's program and modified some of the rest. Then the separate parts of the program had to go to the standing committees with jurisdiction over them; appropriate members of these committees had been included on Ashley's ad hoc committee and, as contemplated, most of the arrangements made on the ad hoc committee were followed on standing committees. Ashley has a plodding, uninspiring speaking style and little flair in public appearances. But he also has the capacity to work hard and hammer out agreement on complicated matters, and this is what he did on the energy issue. The bill which his ad hoc committee crafted is substantially what the House passed; and it seems unlikely that it could have been put together without this kind of arrangement and leadership.

Ashley has had some problems in recent elections. Following a drunk driving arrest in 1973, he won only 53% in 1974 and 55% in 1976 against the same Republican opponent. But in 1978, after his work on the energy issue, he won reelection by a solid 2–1 margin and seems to have a safe seat again.

Census Data Pop. 463,286. Central city, 83%; suburban, 17%. Median family income, $10,786; families above $15,000: 24%; families below $3,000: 7%. Median years education, 12.1.

The Voters

Median voting age 44.
Employment profile White collar, 48%. Blue collar, 39%. Service, 13%. Farm, –%.
Ethnic groups Black, 12%. Spanish, 2%. Total foreign stock, 15%. Poland, Germany, 3% each; Canada, UK, 1% each.

Presidential vote

1976	Carter (D)	96,812	(59%)
	Ford (R)	68,409	(41%)
1972	Nixon (R)	83,768	(49%)
	McGovern (D)	87,151	(51%)

Rep. Thomas L. Ashley (D) Elected 1954; b. Jan. 11, 1923, Toledo; home, Maumee; Yale U., B.A. 1948, U. of Toledo Law School, Ohio St. U., LL.B. 1951; Episcopalian.

Career Army, WWII; Practicing atty., 1951–52; Co-Dir, Press Section, and Asst. Dir. of Special Projects, Radio Free Europe, 1952–54.

Offices 2406 RHOB, 202-225-4146. Also 234 Summit St., Fed. Ofc. Bldg., Toledo 43604, 419-243-0050.

Committees *Banking, Finance and Urban Affairs* (2d). Subcommittees: Economic Stabilization; Financial Institutions, Supervision, Regulation and Insurance; Housing and Community Development (Chairman); International Development Institutions and Finance.

Budget (3d). Subcommittees: Economic Policy, Projections and Productivity (Chairman).

Merchant Marine and Fisheries (2d). Subcommittees: Merchant Marine.

Group Ratings

	ADA	COPE	PC	RPN	NFU	LCV	CFA	NAB	NSI	ACA	NTU
1978	65	74	53	22	56	–	55	25	38	20	–
1977	55	90	53	42	70	68	60	–	–	15	21
1976	55	85	61	47	83	53	54	18	60	13	27

Key Votes

1) Increase Def Spnd	AGN	6) Alaska Lands Protect	FOR	11) Delay Auto Pol Cntrl	FOR
2) B-1 Bomber	AGN	7) Water Projects Veto	DNV	12) Sugar Price Escalator	DNV
3) Cargo Preference	FOR	8) Consum Protect Agcy	FOR	13) Pub Fin Cong Cmpgns	FOR
4) Dereg Nat Gas	AGN	9) Common Situs Picket	FOR	14) ERA Ratif Recissn	AGN
5) Kemp-Roth	AGN	10) Labor Law Revision	FOR	15) Prohibt Govt Abrtns	AGN

Election Results

1978 general	Thomas L. Ashley (D)	71,709	(68%)	($100,223)
	John C. Hoyt (R)	34,326	(32%)	($37,320)
1978 primary	Thomas L. Ashley (D), unopposed			
1976 general	Thomas L. Ashley (D)	91,042	(55%)	($150,693)
	Carleton S. Finkbeiner (R)	73,857	(45%)	($141,314)

TENTH DISTRICT

The 10th district of Ohio is the state's southeast corner, a hilly, sparsely populated area. Though the district covers 14% of Ohio's land area, it contains only 4% of the state's residents. Marietta, on the Ohio River here, was the site of the first (1788) permanent American settlement in the Northwest Territory, ceded to the new nation by the British following the Revolutionary War. The town's Republican leanings are evidence of the Yankee origin of its first settlers. Most of the 10th district, however, resembles West Virginia, across the Ohio River. The voters tend to think of themselves as Democrats and vote for Republicans or conservative Southern Democrats. This is a district that gave only 39% of its votes to Hubert Humphrey in 1968, but which went 49% for Southerner Jimmy Carter in 1976—one reason Carter carried Ohio's crucial electoral votes.

The 10th's Democratic-conservative tradition produced some frequent changes in the district's representation in the fifties and sixties. It ousted a Republican in 1958, a Democrat in 1962, a Republican in 1964, and a Democrat in 1966. Since then it has been represented by Republican Clarence Miller. He has worked to solidify his position in the district and has succeeded in winning reelection by margins around 70% in the seventies.

Miller is an engineer and seems to approach political problems with a desire for precise, orderly solutions. He established a record of never missing a House roll call since he was elected—an example of stern precision and discipline. As a member of the Appropriations Committee he has introduced numerous amendments to make across-the-board cuts in departmental appropriations—usually 2%, but sometimes 5% or even 8%. On occasion Miller's cuts have passed the House: on unpopular programs, like foreign aid, or when the vote occurred just after California adopted Proposition 13 in June 1978. The argument made against Miller's motions is that it is irresponsible to order cuts without determining just how and where they should be made. Miller's best argument is that bureaucracies are going to resist cuts until it is absolutely clear that they must be made, and that the only way to do as much is by a meat-axe approach.

Census Data Pop. 463,353. Central city, 0%; suburban, 12%. Median family income, $7,894; families above $15,000: 10%; families below $3,000: 14%. Median years education, 11.8.

The Voters

Median voting age 43.
Employment profile White collar, 39%. Blue collar, 45%. Service, 13%. Farm, 3%.
Ethnic groups Black, 2%. Total foreign stock, 35.

Presidential vote

1976	Carter (D)	92,461	(49%)
	Ford (R)	96,410	(51%)
1972	Nixon (R)	119,083	(67%)
	McGovern (D)	58,831	(33%)

Rep. Clarence E. Miller (R) Elected 1966; b. Nov. 1, 1917, Lancaster; home, Lancaster; Internatl. Correspondence School; Methodist.

Career Electrician; Lancaster City Cncl., 1957–63, Mayor 1964–66.

Offices 2135 RHOB, 202-225-5131. Also 212 S. Broad St., Lancaster 43130, 614-654-5149.

Committees *Appropriations* (9th). Subcommittees: Transportation; Treasury, Postal Service, and General Government.

Group Ratings

	ADA	COPE	PC	RPN	NFU	LCV	CFA	NAB	NSI	ACA	NTU
1978	20	15	25	50	30	–	27	92	90	92	–
1977	15	13	30	62	25	35	20	–	–	93	66
1976	5	13	16	50	0	26	0	92	90	93	80

Key Votes

1) Increase Def Spnd	AGN	6) Alaska Lands Protect	AGN	11) Delay Auto Pol Cntrl	FOR
2) B-1 Bomber	FOR	7) Water Projects Veto	FOR	12) Sugar Price Escalator	FOR
3) Cargo Preference	AGN	8) Consum Protect Agcy	AGN	13) Pub Fin Cong Cmpgns	AGN
4) Dereg Nat Gas	FOR	9) Common Situs Picket	AGN	14) ERA Ratif Recissn	FOR
5) Kemp-Roth	FOR	10) Labor Law Revision	AGN	15) Prohibt Govt Abrtns	FOR

Election Results

1978 general	Clarence E. Miller (R)	99,329	(74%)	($22,957)
	James A. Plummer (D)	35,039	(26%)	
1978 primary	Clarence E. Miller (R), unopposed			
1976 general	Clarence E. Miller (R)	115,365	(68%)	($19,920)
	James A. Plummer (D)	54,650	(32%)	($4,080)

ELEVENTH DISTRICT

The 11th congressional district of Ohio is the northeast corner of the state, a district whose lines were drawn by a Republican legislature to include the more heavily Republican parts of heavily industrial and Democratic northeast Ohio. It carefully avoids such Democratic areas as the industrial city of Warren, near Youngstown; the close-in suburbs of Lake County, near Cleveland (though farther out Lake County, which is more Republican, is included); and Kent, site of Kent State University. Much of the area is still rural, and some of it is wealthy suburban, as in Geauga County; the only decidedly Democratic portion is Ashtabula, which could hardly be excluded, since it lies in the northeast corner of the state.

The current boundaries of the district were drawn to aid 11th district Congressman William Stanton and the Democrats who then held the seats all around him. But on the evidence, Stanton didn't really need the help. Campaigning as a conventional Republican, he was able to capture this district in 1964, a heavily Democratic year, even though it then included all of Lake County, Warren, and Kent, and even though it had elected a Democratic congressman as recently as 1960. In succeeding elections Stanton won easily; in the seventies, after redistricting, his margins have generally been better than 2–1.

One of Stanton's political secrets is a voting record which makes concessions to the opposition. Rather than becoming more conservative since he entered Congress, in his first ten years or so at least he seemed to become more liberal. His ratings from organized labor—an important force in the politics of northeast Ohio—have been unusually high for an Ohio Republican. Stanton nonetheless has an excellent voting record from the point of view of business interests. As ranking Republican on the Banking, Housing, and Urban Affairs Committee, he has generally been sympathetic to the arguments of banking interests and has been skeptical about some federal spending programs, notably aid to New York City.

Census Data Pop. 462,701. Central city, 0%; suburban, 79%. Median family income, $11,142; families above $15,000: 25%; families below $3,000: 6%. Median years education, 12.2.

The Voters

Median voting age 41.
Employment profile White collar, 41%. Blue collar, 47%. Service, 10%. Farm, 2%.
Ethnic groups Black, 2%. Total foreign stock, 15%. Italy, UK, 2% each; Germany, Hungary, Czechoslovakia, 1% each.

Presidential vote

1976	Carter (D)	92,298	(52%)
	Ford (R)	83,674	(48%)
1972	Nixon (R)	104,236	(62%)
	McGovern (D)	63,864	(38%)

Rep. J. William Stanton (R) Elected 1964; b. Feb. 20, 1924, Painesville; home, Painesville; Georgetown U., B.S. 1949; Catholic.

Career Army, WWII; Lake Co. Commissioner, 1956–64.

Offices 2466 RHOB, 202-225-5306. Also 170 N. St. Clair St., Painesville 44077, 216-352-6167.

Committees *Banking, Finance and Urban Affairs* (Ranking Member). Subcommittees: International Development Institutions and Finance; Housing and Community Development; International Trade, Investment and Monetary Policy.

Small Business (3d). Subcommittees: Capital, Investment and Business Opportunities.

Group Ratings

	ADA	COPE	PC	RPN	NFU	LCV	CFA	NAB	NSI	ACA	NTU
1978	15	15	15	67	30	–	27	92	89	52	–
1977	15	48	33	83	50	35	35	–	–	56	23
1976	15	30	16	94	17	39	18	91	71	46	32

Key Votes

1) Increase Def Spnd	FOR	6) Alaska Lands Protect	FOR	11) Delay Auto Pol Cntrl	FOR
2) B-1 Bomber	FOR	7) Water Projects Veto	AGN	12) Sugar Price Escalator	AGN
3) Cargo Preference	AGN	8) Consum Protect Agcy	AGN	13) Pub Fin Cong Cmpgns	AGN
4) Dereg Nat Gas	FOR	9) Common Situs Picket	AGN	14) ERA Ratif Recissn	FOR
5) Kemp-Roth	FOR	10) Labor Law Revision	AGN	15) Prohibt Govt Abrtns	FOR

Election Results

1978 general	J. William Stanton (R)	89,327	(71%)	($24,816)
	Patrick J. Donlin (D)	37,131	(29%)	($11,671)
1978 primary	J. William Stanton (R), unopposed			
1976 general	J. William Stanton (R)	119,301	(72%)	($15,010)
	Thomas R. West, Jr. (D)	47,367	(28%)	($7,417)

TWELFTH DISTRICT

In 1960, while campaigning in Columbus, Ohio, John F. Kennedy was greeted by a tumultuous crowd; he was moved to remark that Columbus was the city where he got the loudest cheers and the fewest votes. He was not far off the mark, at least about the votes. Columbus, like Cincinnati, is an urban Republican stronghold. Of all major urban counties in Ohio, Barry Goldwater made his best showing (46%) in Franklin County, which contains Columbus; it is not quite so heavily Republican now, after the enfranchisement of students at Ohio State University, but it certainly has not become Democratic. Columbus's Republicanism can be explained by many of the factors that produce a similar political inclination in the rather similar city of Indianapolis. Like Indianapolis, Columbus does have a significant (18%) black population, but it has few residents of Eastern or Southern European stock. These people who have provided the Democratic base in the big industrial cities of the Midwest are largely absent here. The economy of Columbus is much more white collar than those of most Great Lakes area cities. Major employers here include the state government, Ohio State University, and several big banks and insurance companies. This is a city with a vibrant and growing private economy, in vivid contrast with Cleveland, Youngstown, and Dayton, which are losing jobs and looking for government aid. Columbus is in the midst of an almost Sun Belt-like boom, and it does not want the government taking any more of its money.

Columbus is divided into two congressional districts, the 12th and the 15th, by a line that runs right through the middle of the city. It was carefully drawn by Republican redistricters to keep the city's students and blacks in the district (15th) where they can do the least harm. The 12th district takes in the east side of Columbus and its suburbs, along with two heavily Republican rural and small town counties.

Yet despite the careful redistricting, and despite Columbus's Republican heritage, 12th district Congressman Samuel Devine was nearly defeated for reelection in 1974 and 1976 and has failed to win as much as 60% of the vote throughout the sixties. In 1970 and 1972, public relations man James Goodrich held Devine to 58% and 56% of the vote respectively. In 1974 Columbus Councilwoman Fran Ryan came within 2,500 votes of beating him and in 1976 she came within less than 2,000. In both instances, all of Devine's margin came from the rural counties; he lost Franklin County to Ryan. Moreover, in the latter election an Independent black candidate got 8% of the vote—which almost certainly would have gone to Ryan otherwise. In the much more Republican year of 1978, against weaker opposition from state Representative James Baumann, Devine was still able to win with only 55%.

Devine's problem is not lack of recognition. He has been representing the Columbus area in the House since 1958, and this is the size and kind of metropolitan area which gives its local congressmen plenty of publicity. Devine's Republican affiliation is an asset, not a liability, and his identification with some conservative causes—he ran as the conservative candidate against John Anderson for Chairman of the House Republican Conference in 1971, for example—is not a particular disadvantage in the Columbus area. More damaging was Devine's to-the-last-ditch support of Spiro Agnew and Richard Nixon, but those are not really live issues any longer.

Devine also has the distinct advantage of having been, since the 1972 election, the ranking Republican on the House Commerce Committee. His voting record has always been responsive to the concerns and arguments of business interests; he tends to oppose federal regulation and to trust market forces to produce results in the public interest. Such stands may be of some help in the Columbus area. But of even more help are the kind of campaign contributions anyone in Devine's position and with his voting record should be able to raise. Commerce has jurisdiction over practically every federally regulated industry, and most of them are quite sensitive to the political problems of congressmen who may be in a position to help them.

Devine's basic political problem is that he isn't very effective. He was hurt in 1976 when the Wolfe newspapers, usually solidly Republican, endorsed Fran Ryan; he was hurt in 1978 when they printed a series of articles about his lack of effort and influence in Washington. Though Devine has the genial smile of the small town Rotarian and a conventional, conservative record, he can point to few legislative accomplishments—even in the form of killing obnoxious programs. After twenty years in Congress, he seems in as much political trouble as ever, even in Republican Columbus. He will be in especially bad shape if the legislature, now Democratic, manages to redraw the district lines in Columbus to create something like a majority-Democratic district here in 1982.

Census Data Pop. 463,120. Central city, 55%; suburban, 41%. Median family income, $10,710; families above $15,000: 23%; families below $3,000: 6%. Median years education, 12.3.

The Voters

Median voting age 39.
Employment profile White collar, 54%. Blue collar, 34%. Service, 11%. Farm, 1%.
Ethnic groups Black, 10%. Total foreign stock, 7%. Germany, Italy, 1% each.

Presidential vote

1976	Carter (D)	84,624	(44%)
	Ford (R)	106,103	(56%)
1972	Nixon (R)	128,129	(68%)
	McGovern (D)	61,644	(32%)

Rep. Samuel L. Devine (R) Elected 1958; b. Dec. 21, 1915, South Bend, Ind., home, Columbus; Colgate U., 1933–34, Ohio St. U., 1934–37, U. of Notre Dame, J.D. 1940; Methodist.

Career FBI Agent, 1940–45; Practicing atty., 1945–55; Ohio House of Reps., 1951–55; Franklin Co. Prosecuting Atty., 1955–58.

Offices 2204 RHOB, 202-225-5355. Also Suite 400, 200 N. High St., Columbus 43215, 614-221-3533.

Committees *House Administration* (2d). Subcommittees: Accounts; Personnel and Police.

Interstate and Foreign Commerce (Ranking member).

Group Ratings

	ADA	COPE	PC	RPN	NFU	LCV	CFA	NAB	NSI	ACA	NTU
1978	5	5	18	67	20	–	23	100	100	93	–
1977	15	17	15	69	17	13	10	–	–	96	57
1976	5	13	8	56	8	3	0	100	90	93	65

Key Votes

1) Increase Def Spnd	FOR	6) Alaska Lands Protect	AGN	11) Delay Auto Pol Cntrl	FOR
2) B-1 Bomber	FOR	7) Water Projects Veto	FOR	12) Sugar Price Escalator	FOR
3) Cargo Preference	AGN	8) Consum Protect Agcy	AGN	13) Pub Fin Cong Cmpgns	AGN
4) Dereg Nat Gas	FOR	9) Common Situs Picket	AGN	14) ERA Ratif Recissn	FOR
5) Kemp-Roth	FOR	10) Labor Law Revision	AGN	15) Prohibt Govt Abrtns	FOR

Election Results

1978 general	Samuel L. Devine (R)	81,573	(57%)	($132,634)
	James L. Baumann (D)	61,698	(43%)	($162,162)
1978 primary	Samuel L. Devine (R), unopposed			
1976 general	Samuel L. Devine (R)	91,181	(46%)	($134,680)
	Fran Ryan (D)	89,271	(45%)	($112,903)
	William R. Moss (Ind.)	15,790	(8%)	($2,232)

THIRTEENTH DISTRICT

The 13th congressional district of Ohio occupies the north central part of the state. It sits between Ohio's industrial, Democratic northeast and its rural, Republican northwest and central areas. The nucleus of the district, with about half its population, is Lorain County, an industrial area just west of metropolitan Cleveland. The dominant places here are the industrial cities of Lorain and Elyria, the latter the only slightly disguised subject of Sherwood Anderson's Winesburg, Ohio. Lorain County also contains Oberlin, home of Oberlin College, founded by abolitionists and the first college in the nation to admit both blacks and women, way back in 1833. To the west of Lorain County is the small industrial town of Sandusky in Erie County; to the east are the Akron working class suburbs of Barberton and Norton. The district has only one traditionally Republican rural county, Medina, and that is fast being transformed by migrants from the Cleveland and Akron areas. While these people are less Democratic than many of the neighbors they left behind, they are more Democratic than their new neighbors, and Medina has been going 50%–50% in recent statewide elections.

Overall, the 13th district is slightly more Democratic than the state as a whole. For example, when Jimmy Carter barely carried Ohio in 1976, the 13th district was 54% for him. In congressional elections the district has had a history of representation similar to the 3d district's. For many years, from 1958 to 1974, it elected a Republican, Charles Mosher, whose record became increasingly liberal. Mosher was an opponent of the Vietnam war, and on a variety of other issues began voting more often with Democrats than Republicans. He decided at age 70 to retire in 1976. His successor is a Democrat, but one with a similar background and similar views. Donald Pease was editor of the Oberlin newspaper, as Mosher had once been, and he was a member of the state legislature. He was elected in 1976 with more than 60% of the votes in both primary and general elections.

Like Mosher, Pease is particularly interested in foreign policy. He serves on the Foreign Affairs Committee, and has been one of the leading supporters of applying the concept of human rights to foreign policy decisions. Pease is also the originator of the proposal to boycott Uganda while it was under the rule of Idi Amin, and has worked to promote a boycott of the sale of Ugandan coffee by American food companies.

Census Data Pop. 464,056. Central city, 28%; suburban, 55%. Median family income, $10,795; families above $15,000: 22%; families below $3,000: 6%. Median years education, 12.1.

The Voters

Median voting age 41.
Employment profile White collar, 40%. Blue collar, 46%. Service, 12%. Farm, 2%.
Ethnic groups Black, 5%. Spanish, 2%. Total foreign stock, 15%. Germany, Hungary, 2% each; Poland, UK, Italy, Czechoslovakia, Yugoslavia, 1% each.

Presidential vote

1976	Carter (D)	94,309	(54%)
	Ford (R)	79,351	(46%)
1972	Nixon (R)	98,505	(59%)
	McGovern (D)	68,481	(41%)

Rep. Donald J. Pease (D) Elected 1976; b. Sept. 26, 1931, Toledo; home, Oberlin; Ohio U., B.S. 1953, M.A. 1955, Fulbright Scholar, U. of Durham, England, 1954–55; Protestant.

Career Army, 1955–57; Co-editor-publisher, Oberlin *News-Tribune*, 1957–68, Editor, 1968–77; Oberlin City Cncl., 1961–64; Ohio Senate, 1965–67, 1975–77; Ohio House of Reps., 1969–75.

Offices 1641 LHOB, 202-225-3401. Also 1936 Cooper Park Rd., Lorain 44053, 216-282-5003.

Committees *Foreign Affairs* (15th). Subcommittees: Europe and the Middle East; International Economic Policy and Trade.

Science and Technology (20th). Subcommittees: Science, Research and Technology.

Group Ratings

	ADA	COPE	PC	RPN	NFU	LCV	CFA	NAB	NSI	ACA	NTU
1978	65	80	73	50	70	–	64	25	20	15	–
1977	80	78	78	85	75	80	70	–	–	11	26

Key Votes

1) Increase Def Spnd	AGN	6) Alaska Lands Protect	FOR	11) Delay Auto Pol Cntrl	FOR
2) B-1 Bomber	AGN	7) Water Projects Veto	FOR	12) Sugar Price Escalator	AGN
3) Cargo Preference	AGN	8) Consum Protect Agcy	FOR	13) Pub Fin Cong Cmpgns	FOR
4) Dereg Nat Gas	FOR	9) Common Situs Picket	FOR	14) ERA Ratif Recissn	AGN
5) Kemp-Roth	AGN	10) Labor Law Revision	FOR	15) Prohibt Govt Abrtns	AGN

Election Results

1978 general	Don J. Pease (D)	80,875	(65%)	($44,919)
	Mark W. Whitfield (R)	43,269	(35%)	($81,502)
1978 primary	Don J. Pease (D)	23,429	(78%)	
	One other (D)	6,543	(22%)	
1976 general	Don J. Pease (D)	105,084	(68%)	($57,758)
	Woodrow W. Mathna (R)	49,219	(32%)	($13,211)

FOURTEENTH DISTRICT

Akron is the rubber capital of America, the place where most of our millions of automobile and truck tires are produced—and a city totally dependent on that one industry. It was an industry that developed relatively late. At the turn of the century Cleveland was one of the nation's biggest cities and Canton, the home of President McKinley, was a bigger urban center than Akron, which lies between them. Akron's growth came in the 1910–30 period, and most of its migrants came not from Europe, but from the hills of West Virginia, giving the city a Southern-accented atmosphere it retains to this day. The newly booming city liked to cultivate a reputation as an all-American place by doing things like sponsoring the Soapbox Derby (although it turns out that for years leading entrants cheated). But in reality Akron was one of America's most class-bound cities. It was a giant factory town where management lived as a privileged minority, quite out of contact—except possibly on the job—with the working class majority.

So it should not be surprising that Akron had a politics of something like class warfare for many years, from the thirties when the United Rubber Workers organized the tire plants up through the sixties. In statewide and presidential elections, working class Akron and surrounding Summit County usually went Democratic. But in local races, and in the race for the 14th congressional district, which for years included all or most of Summit County, Republicans often used their management skills to win. This was the home town of Ray Bliss, longtime Ohio and sometime National Republican Chairman; he made sure that the Republicans had more money in elections and more technical skill. He was also adroit in choosing candidates. One of his first projects in Akron was to rescue the 14th district from the Democrats who had controlled it, with one exception, since New Deal days. His candidate was not a stuffy management type, but a garrulous plumber named William Ayres; he won in 1950 and served in Congress for twenty years. Ayres threw just enough votes to labor and the Democrats to keep himself invulnerable here; but as ranking Republican on the Education and Labor Committee, his bottom line commitment was to management. He was finally defeated in 1970 more for his personal than his political shortcomings.

The breakdown of class warfare politics was signalled by the election of a working class Republican; it was completed by the election in his place of a management class Democrat. John Seiberling bears the name of one of the smaller rubber companies; his grandfather was one of the founders of Goodyear as well. When he ran for Congress in 1970, he was a lawyer for Goodyear; he avoided crossing the United Rubber Workers picket lines during a strike by taking a leave of absence. Seiberling was also known as as ecology buff—a credential normally of greater interest to upper income voters—and had worked for some years to keep power lines and highways out of the Cuyahoga River valley. He was respected enough to win the support to the Akron *Beacon Journal,* the flagship paper of the chain founded by John S. Knight, which had backed Ayres for twenty years; his opposition to the Vietnam war and to the Kent State shootings gave him student support.

Seiberling won that election with a solid 56%, and he has been winning since with much larger percentages. He has played some important legislative roles in the years since. He was part of the Judiciary Committee majority that voted to impeach Richard Nixon. In the 95th Congress, as a member of the Interior Committee, he served as a chief sponsor of several bills covering matters of great complexity and importance: the strip mining of coal, the Boundary Waters Canoe Area in Minnesota (a controversial local issue there), and the Alaskan lands bill. The strip mining bill was successful; the Alaskan lands bill died in the Senate, but many of its goals were accomplished by administrative action. Seiberling proceeded in each instance in a careful, lawyer-like manner, listening to the arguments of all parties; but he also proceeded with a strong commitment to preserving the environment which is reflected in the final terms of the legislation. He is not a politically ambitious or particularly aggressive man, but by dint of commitment and hard work he has managed to have a significant effect on the legislative process.

Census Data Pop. 464,578. Central city, 59%; suburban, 41%. Median family income, $10,876; families above $15,000: 24%; families below $3,000: 7%. Median years education, 12.2.

The Voters

Median voting age 42.
Employment profile White collar, 49%. Blue collar, 38%. Service, 13%. Farm, –%.
Ethnic groups Black, 11%. Total foreign stock, 14%. Italy, 2%; Germany, UK, Yugoslavia, Hungary, 1% each.

Presidential vote

1976	Carter (D)	103,094	(63%)
	Ford (R)	61,167	(37%)
1972	Nixon (R)	88,384	(48%)
	McGovern (D)	94,320	(52%)

Rep. John F. Seiberling (D) Elected 1970; b. Sept. 8, 1918, Akron; home, Akron; Harvard U., B.A. 1941, Columbia U., LL.B. 1949; Protestant.

Career Army, WWII; Practicing atty., 1949–53; Atty., Goodyear Tire and Rubber Co., 1954–70.

Offices 1225 LHOB, 202-225-5231. Also Fed. Bldg., 2 S. Main St., Akron 44308, 216-375-5710.

Committees *Interior and Insular Affairs* (6th). Subcommittees: National Parks and Insular Affairs; Pacific Affairs.

Judiciary (6th). Subcommittees: Civil and Constitutional Rights; Monopolies and Commercial Law.

Group Ratings

	ADA	COPE	PC	RPN	NFU	LCV	CFA	NAB	NSI	ACA	NTU
1978	95	16	83	25	50	–	86	0	0	4	–
1977	95	87	78	62	67	98	75	–	–	0	25
1976	95	86	93	56	91	96	91	9	0	4	33

Key Votes

1) Increase Def Spnd	AGN	6) Alaska Lands Protect	FOR	11) Delay Auto Pol Cntrl	AGN
2) B-1 Bomber	AGN	7) Water Projects Veto	FOR	12) Sugar Price Escalator	AGN
3) Cargo Preference	AGN	8) Consum Protect Agcy	FOR	13) Pub Fin Cong Cmpgns	FOR
4) Dereg Nat Gas	AGN	9) Common Situs Picket	FOR	14) ERA Ratif Recissn	AGN
5) Kemp-Roth	AGN	10) Labor Law Revision	FOR	15) Prohibt Govt Abrtns	AGN

Election Results

1978 general	John F. Seiberling (D)	82,356	(72%)	($20,438)
	Walter J. Vogel (R)	31,311	(28%)	($12,352)
1978 primary	John F. Seiberling (D), unopposed			
1976 general	John F. Seiberling (D)	118,684	(75%)	($21,635)
	James E. Houston (R)	39,129	(25%)	($12,391)

FIFTEENTH DISTRICT

The 15th congressional district of Ohio includes the west side of Columbus, its Franklin County suburbs, and Pickaway County to the south. Next to Cincinnati, Columbus is Ohio's most Republican metropolitan area; it is also the state's fastest growing and most economically buoyant urban area. The 15th district is, marginally, the more Republican of Columbus's two congressional districts, in large part of Upper Arlington. This suburb, just across the Olentangy River from the Ohio State University campus, is the largest in the Columbus area and one of the most Republican (76% for Gerald Ford in 1976).

The 15th district was created by redistricting in the middle sixties, and its first and only Congressman has been Chalmers Wylie, a former state legislator and Columbus city attorney (an elective post). Wylie has compiled a generally conservative legislative record in Washington. He is best known among his colleagues for his work on the school prayer issue; Wylie has perennially introduced and pushed an amendment to overturn the Supreme Court decision that prevents state-sponsored prayers in public schools.

Wylie has been less controversial in Columbus than his colleague Samuel Devine, and in the early seventies the Republican legislature gave him a somewhat more Democratic part of the city of Columbus, including most of its black and student populations. But substantial opposition has never materialized, and he has won reelection easily every two years. The only political problem looming for Wylie is redistricting after the 1980 Census. Democrats may change the boundaries between the two Columbus districts in such a way as to create a Democratic district, and perhaps by pitting Wylie against Devine in the Republican primary. But any such problems cannot occur until the 1982 elections.

Census Data Pop. 462,703. Central city, 52%; suburban, 32%. Median family income, $10,074; families above $15,000: 23%; families below $3,000: 9%. Median years education, 12.3.

The Voters

Median voting age 39.
Employment profile White collar, 57%. Blue collar, 29%. Service, 13%. Farm, 1%.
Ethnic groups Black, 13%. Total foreign stock, 7%. Germany, 1%.

Presidential vote

1976	Carter (D)	68,995	(41%)
	Ford (R)	99,460	(59%)
1972	Nixon (R)	119,846	(65%)
	McGovern (D)	65,381	(35%)

Rep. Chalmers P. Wylie (R) Elected 1966; b. Nov. 23, 1920, NOrwich; home, Columbus; Otterbein Col., Ohio St. U., B.A., Harvard U., J.D.; Methodist.

Career Army, WWII; Asst Atty. Gen. of Ohio, 1948, 1951–54; Asst. Columbus City Atty., 1949–50, City Atty., 1953–56; Administrator, Ohio Bureau of Workmen's Comp., 1957; First Asst. to the Gov. of Ohio, 1957–58; Practicing atty., 1959–66; Ohio House of Reps., 1961–67.

Offices 2335 RHOB, 202-225-2015. Also Fed. Bldg., Suite 500, 200 N. High St., Columbus 43215, 614-469-5614.

Committees *Banking, Finance and Urban Affairs* (2d). Subcommittees: Consumer Affairs; Financial Institutions Supervision, Regulation and Insurance; Housing and Community Development.

Veterans' Affairs (3d). Subcommittees: Medical Facilities and Benefits; Compensation, Pension, Insurance and Memorial Affairs; Education, Training and Employment.

Group Ratings

	ADA	COPE	PC	RPN	NFU	LCV	CFA	NAB	NSI	ACA	NTU
1978	25	30	40	67	30	–	41	75	90	65	–
1977	35	27	60	77	58	50	45	–	–	56	41
1976	10	27	34	78	20	39	18	92	100	76	63

Key Votes

1) Increase Def Spnd	AGN	6) Alaska Lands Protect	FOR	11) Delay Auto Pol Cntrl	FOR
2) B-1 Bomber	FOR	7) Water Projects Veto	FOR	12) Sugar Price Escalator	AGN
3) Cargo Preference	AGN	8) Consum Protect Agcy	FOR	13) Pub Fin Cong Cmpgns	AGN
4) Dereg Nat Gas	FOR	9) Common Situs Picket	AGN	14) ERA Ratif Recissn	FOR
5) Kemp-Roth	FOR	10) Labor Law Revision	AGN	15) Prohibt Govt Abrtns	FOR

Election Results

1978 general	Chalmers P. Wylie (R)	91,023	(71%)	($87,741)
	Henry W. Eckhardt (D)	37,000	(29%)	
1978 primary	Chalmers P. Wylie (R), unopposed			
1976 general	Chalmers P. Wylie (R)	109,103	(65%)	($69,601)
	Manly L. McGee (D)	57,677	(35%)	($11,776)

SIXTEENTH DISTRICT

Canton, Ohio, is known, to the extent it is known at all today, as the home of the Pro Football Hall of Fame. But to American historians, Canton is most memorable as the home of President William McKinley. It was here that McKinley sat on his famous front porch in 1896 and received delegations of voters carefully selected by Republican organizations throughout the country. And it was also here that he received the news that he had been elected president over William Jennings Bryan. Some historians still cling to the notion that factory workers provided McKinley with the votes he needed to win only because their bosses threatened to fire them if they didn't. No more evidence of such coercion exists for this election than for any other in our history. The fact, however unlikely or unwelcome it may seem today, is that McKinley was the heavy choice of northern industrial workers, and that they believed that the Republican Party would produce the full dinner pail he promised.

The case can be made further that McKinley delivered admirably on that promise. In any case, a period of protracted prosperity and expansion followed his election. Much has happened since, and political allegiances all over the country have changed. But in Canton, which has not had explosive growth in the twentieth century, there is still a significant working class Republican vote. This muscular city and the nearby towns of Massillon and Alliance, where some of our current National Football League teams got their start, still retain a basic preference for the Republican Party. So does the 16th congressional district of Ohio, which includes Canton, Massillon, and Alliance in Stark County, plus Wayne County, a rural and small town area to the west.

McKinley was elected to the House six times in the predessor of today's 16th district. In those more volatile times, he lost the seat twice to Democrats—which didn't prevent him, in those days before the seniority system, from becoming Chairman of the House Ways and Means Committee. He is not the only House leader the Canton area has produced. More recently, 16th district Congressman Frank Bow, first elected in 1950, became ranking Republican on the House Appropriations Committee; he decided to retire in 1972 and died just weeks before his last term expired.

The current Congressman is Ralph Regula, a former state Senator who is, appropriately, a graduate of the William McKinley School of Law; in the 95th Congress Regula helped maintain the name Mount McKinley for the mountain in Alaska against proposals to change it to an Alaskan native alternative. Regula is considered a political moderate and has a fairly high rating from organized labor as well as a very high rating from the Chamber of Commerce. He serves on the Appropriations and Budget Committees.

Census Data Pop. 463,699. Central city, 24%; suburban, 57%. Median family income, $10,197; families above $15,000: 19%; families below $3,000: 6%. Median years education, 12.1.

The Voters

Median voting age 43.
Employment profile White collar, 41%. Blue collar, 45%. Service, 12%. Farm, 2%.
Ethnic groups Black, 5%. Total foreign stock, 11%. Italy, 2%; Germany, UK, 1% each.

Presidential vote

1976	Carter (D)	83,776	(48%)
	Ford (R)	90,463	(52%)
1972	Nixon (R)	113,402	(65%)
	McGovern (D)	61,173	(35%)

Rep. Ralph S. Regula (R) Elected 1972; b. Dec. 3, 1924, Beach City; home, Navarre; Mt. Union Col., B.A. 1948, Wm. McKinley School of Law, LL.B. 1952.

Career Navy, WWII; Practicing atty., 1952–73; Ohio Bd. of Educ., 1960–64; Ohio House of Reps., 1965–66; Ohio Senate, 1967–72.

Offices 401 CHOB, 202-225-3876. Also 4150 Belden Village St., Canton 44718, 216-456-2869.

Committees *Appropriations* (13th). Subcommittees: Interior; Military Construction.

Budget (5th).Subcommittees: State and Local Governments; Defense and International Affairs; Tax Expenditures and Tax Policy.

Group Ratings

	ADA	COPE	PC	RPN	NFU	LCV	CFA	NAB	NSI	ACA	NTU
1978	20	25	25	58	30	–	23	83	100	63	–
1977	15	43	35	69	25	30	25	–	–	74	39
1976	10	30	23	78	17	39	18	92	90	54	38

Key Votes

1) Increase Def Spnd	FOR	6) Alaska Lands Protect	FOR	11) Delay Auto Pol Cntrl	FOR
2) B-1 Bomber	FOR	7) Water Projects Veto	FOR	12) Sugar Price Escalator	AGN
3) Cargo Preference	AGN	8) Consum Protect Agcy	AGN	13) Pub Fin Cong Cmpgns	AGN
4) Dereg Nat Gas	FOR	9) Common Situs Picket	AGN	14) ERA Ratif Recissn	AGN
5) Kemp-Roth	FOR	10) Labor Law Revision	AGN	15) Prohibt Govt Abrtns	FOR

Election Results

1978 general	Ralph S. Regula (R)	105,152	(78%)	($55,300)
	Owen S. Hand, Jr. (D)	29,640	(22%)	($5,309)
1978 primary	Ralph S. Regula (R), unopposed			
1976 general	Ralph S. Regula (R)	115,579	(68%)	($59,954)
	John G. Freedom (D)	55,312	(32%)	($8,716)

SEVENTEENTH DISTRICT

Most congressmen find their way onto committees with whose majorities they are in basic sympathy. They get involved in legislative matters on sides where they have many allies and comrades; they look for fights they can win. Not so John Ashbrook, Republican Congressman from the 17th district of Ohio. Ashbrook's political and congressional career is almost a catalogue of lost causes. He is by any measure one of the most conservative members of the House. Yet he serves on its most liberal committees. He managed to take little part in the tax cut offensive of the Republican Party in 1978. Yet he has been fighting hard for lower government spending in less favorable times. Ashbrook's record is a continual triumph of idealism over practicality, of principle over effectiveness.

No better example exists than his now nearly forgotten 1972 campaign for president. He fielded no campaign organization; he failed to raise significant amounts of money, despite the large number of committed and affluent conservatives across the country; he failed to win as much as 10% of the vote in any presidential primary and did not get a single delegate vote at the Republican National Convention. Yet Ashbrook's intentions were deadly serious. He believed that the Nixon Administration had done the wrong thing in opening relations with mainland China and in imposing wage and price controls. He decided he had to raise those issues against Nixon and did so in his campaign. But his very lack of success helped to prove the lack of popularity his policies had. He showed conclusively that there was no significant bloc of voters deeply concerned about Nationalist China. He showed conclusively that no significant bloc of voters was opposed to the controls. He proved the opposite of what he intended.

Ashbrook survived these defeats, though his candidacy helped lower his percentage in his heavily Republican district in central Ohio in the fall of 1972, and it was not until 1978 that he was able to get more than 57% of the vote there. In the House he saw the Committee on Internal Security (formerly Un-American Activities) abolished out from under him. He serves now on the Education and Labor Committee, a body dominated by labor and liberal Democrats, as its ranking Republican member. In that position, he will attempt to harass, if not defeat, measures sought by its Democratic majority. He serves also on Judiciary, where he ineffectively urges more attention to the dangers of subversion by outside powers. Ashbrook is one of the most active members in forcing roll call votes on the floor of the House; he is constantly prepared with amendments and proposals to change legislation the majority is proposing. Sometimes he even wins. But this intelligent, dedicated man spends most of his time as a kind of gadfly, and seems likely to continue doing so.

Census Data Pop. 462,846. Central city, 12%; suburban, 16%. Median family income, $9,460; families above $15,000: 16%; families below $3,000: 9%. Median years education, 12.1.

The Voters

Median voting age 42.
Employment profile White collar, 38%. Blue collar, 46%. Service, 12%. Farm, 4%.
Ethnic groups Black, 3%. Total foreign stock, 6%. Germany, 1%.

Presidential vote

1976	Carter (D)	78,041	(46%)
	Ford (R)	92,350	(54%)
1972	Nixon (R)	111,545	(69%)
	McGovern (D)	50,374	(31%)

Rep. John M. Ashbrook (R) Elected 1960; b. Sept. 21, 1928, Johnstown; home, Johnstown; Harvard U., A.B. 1952, Ohio St. U., J.D. 1955; Baptist.

Career Navy, 1946–48; Publisher, Johnstown *Independent*, 1953–60; Practicing atty., 1955–60; Ohio House of Reps., 1956–60.

Offices 1436 LHOB, 202-225-6431. Also 53 S. Main St., Johnstown 43031, 614-967-5941.

Committees *Education and Labor* (Ranking Member). Subcommittees: Labor-Management Relations.

Judiciary (6th). Subcommittees: Crime; Civil and Constitutional Rights.

Group Ratings

	ADA	COPE	PC	RPN	NFU	LCV	CFA	NAB	NSI	ACA	NTU
1978	5	11	23	55	0	–	27	100	100	100	–
1977	15	13	18	69	25	12	5	–	–	96	60
1976	5	14	9	53	0	7	0	92	90	93	65

Key Votes

1) Increase Def Spnd	FOR	6) Alaska Lands Protect	AGN	11) Delay Auto Pol Cntrl	FOR
2) B-1 Bomber	DNV	7) Water Projects Veto	FOR	12) Sugar Price Escalator	FOR
3) Cargo Preference	AGN	8) Consum Protect Agcy	AGN	13) Pub Fin Cong Cmpgns	DNV
4) Dereg Nat Gas	FOR	9) Common Situs Picket	AGN	14) ERA Ratif Recissn	FOR
5) Kemp-Roth	FOR	10) Labor Law Revision	AGN	15) Prohibt Govt Abrtns	FOR

Election Results

1978 general	John M. Ashbrook (R)	87,010	(67%)	($158,543)
	Kenneth R. Grier (D)	42,117	(33%)	
1978 primary	John M. Ashbrook (R), unopposed			
1976 general	John M. Ashbrook (R)	94,860	(57%)	($173,078)
	John C. McDonald (D)	72,131	(43%)	($96,406)

EIGHTEENTH DISTRICT

The 18th congressional district of Ohio, just across the Ohio River from West Virginia, is a land of marginal farms and hills pockmarked by strip mines—a kind of rural industrial slum. There are no big cities here, just small towns like Steubenville, a place which has had the distinction of having the dirtiest air in the United States. The people of the 18th are the kind of working class Americans who work hard, get little for it, and pay taxes with few complaints. They are ancestrally Democratic, and seldom—the 1972 presidential race was an exception—vote Republican.

This is the district that, for nearly 30 years, sent Wayne Hays to the U.S. House of Representatives. Long before Hays's name was a household word elsewhere, the people of the 18th not only elected him to Congress; in the 1972 presidential primary, heatedly contested in Ohio between George McGovern and Hubert Humphrey, they cast 61% of their votes for Hays for president.

Everyone knows now about the Wayne Hays scandal, about how it was revealed in the spring of 1976 that Hays, Chairman of the House Administration Committee (which helps to write the election laws) and of the House Democratic Campaign Committee (which distributes money to Democratic candidates), kept Elizabeth Ray on the public payroll, in effect as his mistress. The outcome is equally familiar. As Hays retreated to his farm in Ohio, House Democrats, especially freshmen worried about reelection, insisted he be stripped of his campaign committee chair; in the June Ohio primary, a nuisance candidate who had got only 20% against Hays before got 39%; finally, Hays resigned from Congress and left Washington, a ruined man. What made this story inevitable and perhaps poignant was that this was a man who risked everything. With his acid tongue, sharp wit, and willingness not only to fight but to humiliate anyone he took a dislike to, Hays was the most hated and most feared member of the House. With the power to sign all House employees' paychecks, he refused to let elevator operators sit on the job and terrorized the kitchen help. He also set up a House computer system and ran things efficiently, Elizabeth Ray to the contrary notwithstanding. But when he got into trouble, Wayne Hays had very few friends—and a House full of enemies.

Hays might well have been reelected in 1976; two years later he won, by a small majority, a seat in the Ohio legislature. But what could he have done in the House? His withdrawal from the 1976 race allowed local Democrats to nominate Douglas Applegate, a state Senator who had been waiting for years to replace Hays. Applegate won that election and reelection in 1978 by solid margins. He has a conventional record for a Democrat who favors big public works programs and has a solid record with organized labor.

Census Data Pop. 462,797. Central city, 7%; suburban, 32%. Median family income, $8,701; families above $15,000: 11%; families below $3,000: 11%. Median years education, 11.5.

The Voters

Median voting age 46.
Employment profile White collar, 34%. Blue collar, 51%. Service, 12%. Farm, 3%.
Ethnic groups Black, 2%. Total foreign stock, 12%. Italy, 3%; UK, 2%; Poland, Czechoslovakia, Germany, 1% each.

Presidential vote

1976	Carter (D)	106,448	(55%)
	Ford (R)	86,513	(45%)
1972	Nixon (R)	111,800	(61%)
	McGovern (D)	72,581	(39%)

Rep. Douglas Applegate (D) Elected 1976; b. Mar. 27, 1928, Steubenville; home, Steubenville; Presbyterian.

Career Real estate salesman, 1950–56, broker, 1956–76; Ohio House of Reps., 1961–69; Ohio Senate, 1969–77.

Offices 435 CHOB, 202-225-6265. Also 150 W. Main St., St. Clairsville 43950, 614-695-4600.

Committees *District of Columbia* (12th). Subcommittees: Fiscal and Government Affairs; Judiciary.

Public Works and Transportation (23d). Subcommittees: Economic Development; Aviation; Surface Transportation.

Veterans' Affairs (12th). Subcommittees: Cemeteries and Burial Benefits; Education and Training; Medical Facilities and Benefits.

Group Ratings

	ADA	COPE	PC	RPN	NFU	LCV	CFA	NAB	NSI	ACA	NTU
1978	20	55	40	36	70	–	41	42	80	46	–
1977	30	91	40	15	78	35	45	–	–	37	20

Key Votes

1) Increase Def Spnd	AGN	6) Alaska Lands Protect	FOR	11) Delay Auto Pol Cntrl	FOR
2) B-1 Bomber	FOR	7) Water Projects Veto	AGN	12) Sugar Price Escalator	AGN
3) Cargo Preference	FOR	8) Consum Protect Agcy	FOR	13) Pub Fin Cong Cmpgns	AGN
4) Dereg Nat Gas	AGN	9) Common Situs Picket	FOR	14) ERA Ratif Recissn	FOR
5) Kemp-Roth	FOR	10) Labor Law Revision	FOR	15) Prohibt Govt Abrtns	FOR

Election Results

1978 general	Douglas Applegate (D)	71,894	(60%)	($75,802)
	Bill Ress (R)	48,931	(40%)	($69,217)
1978 primary	Douglas Applegate (D)	42,442	(82%)	
	William McKenna (D)	5,968	(12%)	
	Two others (D)	3,263	(6%)	
1976 general	Douglas Applegate (D)	116,768	(64%)	($27,394)
	Ralph R. McCoy (R)	45,524	(25%)	($12,219)
	William Crabbe (Ind.)	21,541	(12%)	($7,335)

NINETEENTH DISTRICT

The 19th congressional district of Ohio is one of the most heavily industrial districts in the nation. Both Youngstown and Warren, the district's two major cities, are important steel manufacturing centers. Situated about halfway between Cleveland and Pittsburgh, these two cities are also halfway between the docks that unload iron ore from the Great Lakes ranges and the coal fields of western Pennsylvania and West Virginia. This was an area of rapid growth at the turn of the century, when the American steel industry was growing rapidly and using the latest technological developments. Now times have changed. Steel has been anything but a growth industry over the last twenty years. Producers in Japan and West Germany have used newer technology, and in some cases can ship steel cheaper to the American Midwest than can Youngstown manufacturers. The steel industry has concentrated on getting presidential permission for price rises (which price it out of foreign markets) and governmental protection for imports (which encourage further inefficiency) rather than improving their product or trying to produce it more cheaply.

The result has been economic disaster for the Youngstown-Warren area. There has been no population growth and considerable outmigration here since 1960. But the late seventies have been especially rough. Several large steel plants have closed down altogether, putting as many as 5,000 employees out of work at a single time. Local officials have tried to attract new business here, and the area has gotten some new plants, such as General Motors's Lordstown assembly plant, which is not far away—and which served as the model for the Fernwood of the Mary Hartman series. Local tax revenues have fallen, voters have refused new taxes, and Youngstown schools have had to close for weeks at a time.

About the only thing left undisturbed about life in the Youngstown-Warren area have been people's Democratic voting habits in most elections. This is classic Democratic country: an industrial area with many immigrants from Eastern and Southern Europe and many from the American South. It has gone for Democrats in almost every election in the last 40 years; it did go for Nixon over McGovern in 1972, but only barely. Yet in 1978 the 19th district, after more than 40 years of Democratic representation, elected a Republican congressman.

This result reflected less the economic climate of Youngstown, dismal as it is, than the weakness of the incumbent Democrat, Charles Carney. It takes a great deal for a Democrat to lose a district like this, but Carney managed. The danger signs were certainly there. He was reelected in 1976 with only 51% of the vote—while Jimmy Carter was carrying 62% here. He won his 1978 primary with only about one-third of the vote, and by just 76 votes over his nearest opponent. He was accused of campaign conduct violations and was called a labor hack. But most of all Carney was in trouble for inaction. Like some Democratic congressman swept into office in a New Deal year, he seemed content to claim his paycheck and show up on the floor every day. He did nothing to help attract new industry to his district as it was losing thousands of jobs. He provided few of the services that most congressmen use to keep constituents familiar with their names. But he did take the trouble to acquire more than 60,000 surplus books from the Library of Congress, many of which he kept or gave to relatives.

Even with such a whimsical note, Carney almost managed to win; the Republican, Trumbull County Commissioner Lyle Williams, took just 51% of the vote. He is considered a moderate and presumably during his term will do his best to win labor support. But he has an extremely difficult task ahead of him if he wishes to win in 1980. This is still a Democratic district, and if Democrats nominate a candidate stronger than Carney, he will probably be the favorite, the advantages of incumbency to the contrary notwithstanding.

Census Data Pop. 463,625. Central city, 44%; suburban, 56%. Median family income, $10,311; families above $15,000: 21%; families below $3,000: 7%. Median years education, 12.1.

The Voters

Median voting age 44.
Employment profile White collar, 41%. Blue collar, 46%. Service, 12%. Farm, 1%.
Ethnic groups Black, 11%. Spanish, 1%. Total foreign stock, 23%. Italy, 6%; Czechoslovakia, 3%; UK, Poland, 2% each; Yugoslavia, Austria, Germany, Hungary, 1% each.

Presidential vote

1976	Carter (D)	112,185	(62%)
	Ford (R)	69,063	(38%)
1972	Nixon (R)	96,607	(52%)
	McGovern (D)	88,500	(48%)

Rep. Lyle Williams (R) Elected 1978; b. Aug. 23, 1942, Philippi, W. Va.; home, North Bloomfield; Church of Christ.

Career Army, 1960–61; Barber; Trumbull Co. Commissioner, 1972–78.

Offices 1004 LHOB, 202-225-5261. Also Suite 204, 4076 Youngstown Rd., S.E., Warren 44484, 216-369-4378.

Committees *Government Operations* (10th). Subcommittees: Commerce, Consumer and Monetary Affairs.

Small Business (9th). Subcommittees: General Oversight and Minority Enterprise; Access to Equity Capital and Business Opportunities.

Group Ratings: Newly Elected

Key Votes: Newly Elected

Election Results

1978 general	Lyle Williams (R)	71,890	(51%)	($101,551)
	Charles J. Carney (D)	69,977	(49%)	($168,257)
1978 primary	Lyle Williams (R)	10,516	(54%)	
	John Hay (R)	5,742	(29%)	($5,611)
	Two others (R)	3,330	(17%)	
1976 general	Charles J. Carney (D)	90,495	(51%)	($85,906)
	Jack C. Hunter (R)	86,113	(49%)	($76,044)

TWENTIETH DISTRICT

Down the center of Cleveland flows the Cuyahoga River, a waterway so polluted with industrial wastes that it once caught fire. On both sides of the Cuyahoga are Cleveland's giant steel mills and other factories—many of the same operations that made Cleveland the nation's fourth largest city in 1910. In the years that followed, Cleveland lost the auto industry to Detroit and otherwise failed to match the growth rate of other big metropolitan areas; today the Cleveland area is only the twelfth largest in the nation. The central city of Cleveland, as is well known, has more than its share of urban problems. Some of them are the result of simple mismanagement: Cleveland has many taxable resources and its budget could have been trimmed in many places to avoid the 1978 and 1979 fiscal crises. And some of them are rooted in cultural differences, symbolized by the Cuyahoga, which divides the races in Cleveland.

East of the Cuyahoga, most of Cleveland is black. Here and there are remnants of ethnic neighborhoods, called cosmo wards in Cleveland, which absorbed the Poles, Czechs, Hungarians, and Italians who came over to work in the grimy steel mills along the Cuyahoga. But the vast majority of Clevelanders living east of the river are black, and some of the neighborhoods are so forbidding that Carl Stokes, the city's first and, so far, only black Mayor (1967–71), lived in a Cleveland house that sat on the line separating the city from the posh suburb of Shaker Heights.

By glaring contrast, Cleveland west of the Cuyahoga is just about 100% white. Here, in this largely working class area, are the city's remaining cosmo wards. This is the political homeland of Mayor Dennis Kucinich, though he gets some black support also. The population west of the river is weighted toward the elderly end of the age scale, as younger people have moved to suburbs like Parma or Brook Park.

Almost all of the west side of Cleveland, plus a couple of cosmo wards in the east, and a few suburbs to the south (Brook Park, Brooklyn, part of Parma, and Garfield Heights among them), make up the 20th congressional district of Ohio. This is a Democratic district by tradition, but not always in practice. In 1967 and 1969, Carl Stokes's Democratic party label gave him only about 20% of the vote here against white Republicans. George Wallace got a surprising 17% here in 1968, and in 1972 Richard Nixon carried the district. Lately the 20th has been more Democratic, but with sharply declining turnout. The older residents, who once believed strongly in the New Deal and in their later days worried about blacks and crime, do not turn out as much any longer; and in many cases the younger people who have replaced them are not voting at all. On the west side, voters see little to attract them from the Republicans, but no strong reasons to support Democrats either. Neither the cerebral humor of former Governor John Gilligan nor the Southern drawl of Jimmy Carter were particularly attractive to voters here.

In congressional elections, this has been a Democratic district for many, many years. Its last two representatives have come from the Cleveland city council. James Stanton, first elected in 1968, was an opponent of Carl Stokes; he served until he ran unsuccessfully for the Senate in 1976. His successor, the 24% winner in a 12-candidate Democratic primary, was Mary Rose Oakar. She in turn is an opponent of her contemporary, Mayor Dennis Kucinich, although like Kucinich she has deep roots in the west side cosmo wards. She appears to be an articulate and competent member, and she was reelected without difficulty in 1978.

Census Data Pop. 462,480. Central city, 65%; suburban, 35%. Median family income, $10,550; families above $15,000: 20%; families below $3,000: 7%. Median years education, 11.1.

The Voters

Median voting age 44.
Employment profile White collar, 41%. Blue collar, 47%. Service, 12%. Farm, -%.
Ethnic groups Black, 3%. Spanish, 2%. Total foreign stock, 32%. Poland, 6%; Czechoslovakia, Italy, 4% each; Germany, 3%; Hungary, Austria, Yugoslavia, 2% each; USSR, UK, Ireland, 1% each.

Presidential vote

1976	Carter (D)	83,949	(62%)
	Ford (R)	50,457	(38%)
1972	Nixon (R)	79,056	(52%)
	McGovern (D)	74,041	(48%)

Rep. Mary Rose Oakar (D) Elected 1976; b. Mar. 5, 1940, Cleveland; home, Cleveland; Ursuline Col., B.A. 1962, John Carroll U., M.A. 1966; Catholic.

Career Clerk, the Higbee Co., 1956–58; Operator, Ohio Bell Telephone Co., 1957–62; Instructor, Lourdes Acad., 1963–70; Asst. Prof., Cuyahoga Comm. Col., 1968–75; Cleveland City Cncl., 1973–77.

Offices 107 CHOB, 202-225-5871. Also 116 Fed. Court Bldg., 215 Superior Ave., Cleveland 44114, 216-522-4927.

Committees *Banking, Finance and Urban Affairs* (22d). Subcommittees: Housing and Community Development; Economic Stabilization; International Development Institutions and Finance; International Trade, Investment and Monetary Policy; The City.

Group Ratings

	ADA	COPE	PC	RPN	NFU	LCV	CFA	NAB	NSI	ACA	NTU
1978	60	95	80	40	80	–	77	0	20	20	–
1977	65	91	73	33	92	65	75	–	–	19	23

Key Votes

1) Increase Def Spnd	AGN	6) Alaska Lands Protect	FOR	11) Delay Auto Pol Cntrl	FOR
2) B-1 Bomber	FOR	7) Water Projects Veto	AGN	12) Sugar Price Escalator	FOR
3) Cargo Preference	FOR	8) Consum Protect Agcy	FOR	13) Pub Fin Cong Cmpgns	FOR
4) Dereg Nat Gas	AGN	9) Common Situs Picket	FOR	14) ERA Ratif Recissn	AGN
5) Kemp-Roth	AGN	10) Labor Law Revision	FOR	15) Prohibt Govt Abrtns	FOR

Election Results

1978 general	Mary Rose Oakar (D), unopposed			($77,081)
1978 primary	Mary Rose Oakar (D)	31,773	(81%)	
	Two others (D)	7,495	(19%)	
1976 general	Mary Rose Oakar (D)	98,128	(83%)	($101,949)
	Raymond J. Grabow (Ind.)	20,450	(17%)	($64,063)

TWENTY-FIRST DISTRICT

The 21st congressional district of Ohio is the east side of Cleveland, plus a couple of adjacent suburbs. This area was once a checkerboard of Polish, Czech, Hungarian, and Italian neighborhoods, but today it is heavily black (66% district-wide in 1970, more like 75% today). The central part of the 21st includes some of the poorest black ghettoes in the nation, while the black neighborhoods to the north and south are more middle class. There are still a few ethnic ("cosmo" in Cleveland) enclaves left in the 21st, populated mainly by old people who cannot afford to move out of the city. The suburban cities in the district are either already majority black (East Cleveland) or in the process of becoming so (Warrensville Heights). Ironically, some of Cleveland's wealthiest suburbs, like Shaker Heights and Cleveland Heights, are no more than a mile or two from some of the city's most dilapidated slums.

The representation of this district in Congress has reflected the ethnic changes here. For a decade and a half, until the 1968 election, the district was represented by Charles Vanik, a Democrat with an Eastern European ethnic background. In 1968 Vanik left to run in the suburban 22d district where he ousted the Republican incumbent, and the new Congressman in the 21st was Louis Stokes. He is the brother of then Cleveland Mayor (and later New York newscaster) Carl Stokes. Like his brother, Congressman Stokes grew up in poverty and was able to attend college and law school only after serving in the Army during World War II.

Stokes's election was a clear reflection of his brother's popularity on the east side. After the congressional victory of 1968, the two brothers put together their own political machine, the 21st District Caucus. It has suffered some defeats, particularly in elections for mayor, but was the only really effective black political organization in Cleveland during the years in which the city's politics revolved entirely around race and racially-oriented issues. Now that has changed. The question of whether to sell the city's municipal light service or the question of whether to recall Mayor Dennis Kucinich are not issues which split either blacks or whites on racial lines; there are divisions here within the black electorate. As a result, an organization like the 21st District Caucus has lost some of its raison d'être. It cannot always expect to express and rally near-unanimous feeling in the black community when unanimity no longer exists.

The Congressman is the older Stokes brother, and although he began his political career later, it has lasted far longer. Carl Stokes has not won an election for ten years, while Louis Stokes has won reelection easily every two years. When he first took office in 1969, Stokes was classified as a militant black Congressman; in the years since he has become known as a skilled and intelligent legislator. He was the first black member of the Appropriations Committee, and now ranks 15th in seniority among its Democrats; he will likely jump a few more slots after 1980 because of pending retirements. Stokes won a reputation in the House for being smart and also for being lazy. But he has worked hard and performed well when faced with a difficult challenge. He was called on to head the special Committee on Assassinations in 1977, after Chairman Henry Gonzalez and Chief Counsel Richard Sprague had been forced to quit. Stokes was able to persuade the House to keep the committee alive, and he was able to guide the committee to constructive deliberations. Not everyone agreed with the committee's conclusions. But it never degenerated into farce, and often performed real services, such as allowing James Earl Ray to discredit himself. Stokes came out of this assignment with increased respect for both his political ability and his capacity for hard work. He was active on other matters during the 95th Congress as well; notably, he was a leading opponent of the Hyde Amendment to prohibit federal spending on abortions.

Census Data Pop. 462,584. Central city, 87%; suburban, 13%. Median family income, $8,573; families above $15,000: 14%; families below $3,000: 16%. Median years education, 10.9.

The Voters

Median voting age 42.
Employment profile White collar, 37%. Blue collar, 44%. Service, 19%. Farm, –%.
Ethnic groups Black, 66%. Total foreign stock, 14%. Yugoslavia, Italy, Hungary, 2% each; Czechoslovakia, Poland, Germany, 1% each.

Presidential vote

1976	Carter (D)	107,813	(86%)
	Ford (R)	17,904	(14%)
1972	Nixon (R)	27,661	(21%)
	McGovern (D)	101,276	(79%)

Rep. Louis Stokes (D) Elected 1968; b. Feb. 23, 1925, Cleveland; home, Cleveland; Western Reserve U., 1946–48, Cleveland-Marshall Law School, J.D. 1953; Methodist.

Career Practicing atty., 1954–68.

Offices 2465 RHOB, 202-225-7032. Also Rm. 2947, New Fed. Ofc. Bldg., 1240 E. 9th St., Cleveland 44199, 216-522-4900.

Committees *Appropriations* (15th). Subcommittees: District of Columbia; HUD-Independent Agencies; Labor-HEW.

Budget (4th). Subcommittees: Human and Community Resources (Chairman).

Group Ratings

	ADA	COPE	PC	RPN	NFU	LCV	CFA	NAB	NSI	ACA	NTU
1978	85	100	95	36	78	–	77	0	10	10	–
1977	90	90	80	38	92	93	80	–	–	0	35
1976	85	87	89	39	100	81	100	9	0	0	29

Key Votes

1) Increase Def Spnd	AGN	6) Alaska Lands Protect	FOR	11) Delay Auto Pol Cntrl	AGN
2) B-1 Bomber	AGN	7) Water Projects Veto	AGN	12) Sugar Price Escalator	FOR
3) Cargo Preference	FOR	8) Consum Protect Agcy	FOR	13) Pub Fin Cong Cmpgns	FOR
4) Dereg Nat Gas	AGN	9) Common Situs Picket	FOR	14) ERA Ratif Recissn	AGN
5) Kemp-Roth	AGN	10) Labor Law Revision	DNV	15) Prohibt Govt Abrtns	AGN

Election Results

1978 general	Louis Stokes (D)	58,934	(86%)	($47,176)
	Bill Mack (R)	9,533	(14%)	
1978 primary	Louis Stokes (D), unopposed			
1976 general	Louis Stokes (D)	91,303	(88%)	($45,452)
	Barbara Sparks (R)	12,443	(12%)	($1,063)

TWENTY-SECOND DISTRICT

The 22d district of Ohio is the eastern half of the ring of suburbs around Cleveland, plus a very small part (12,000 residents) of the city itself. The various suburbs have been settled by people of varying ethnic stock, who have moved here following the radial avenues out of the central city of Cleveland. There are suburbs that are heavily Italian (Mayfield Heights), Serbian (Solon), Hungarian (Euclid), Jewish (University Heights, Beachwood), and high income WASP (Gates Mills, Pepper Pike). The most well known of the 22d's communities is one of its most ethnically varied, Shaker Heights. There is little trace of the Shaker group after whom it was named; this close-in suburb instead contains the estate-like homes of some of the city's wealthiest WASPs and Jews, and of some blacks and ethnics as well.

Following Cleveland's suburban migrations, the 22d extends beyond the Cuyahoga County line into adjacent Lake, Geauga, and Summit Counties. The suburbs in Lake (Wickliffe, Willowick, Willoughby) are basically Democratic; those in Geauga, including the high income community of Chagrin Falls, are solidly Republican. Overall, this is a district most of whose residents have a Democratic tradition, but it is not necessarily that solidly Democratic. Turnout in the older, ethnic areas has been down, and it has been increasing in the Republican areas. As a result, Gerald Ford was able to win this district in 1976, although by less than 1,000 votes.

The current Congressman from the 22d, Charles Vanik, was first elected to the House in 1954, and was first elected from this district in 1968. Previously he had represented the closer-in 21st district; but in 1968 that seat got a black majority, and Vanik moved out and defeated 30-year Republican veteran Frances Bolton. Mrs. Bolton was from one of Cleveland's richest families, but she was not able to compete with this Democrat with his Eastern European ethnic background and his strong support of Israel. Vanik has been reelected without difficulty since; one year he announced he would spend nothing on his campaign, and won with a margin bigger than ever.

Vanik is the third-ranking member of the House Ways and Means Committee now. For years he was chafing under the domination of Chairman Wilbur Mills; now he is a power in his own right. Vanik was one of the committee's leading champions of progressive tax reform for years. But his greatest influence is in the area of trade. He is Chairman of the Trade Subcommittee and has had some important influence here. The Jackson-Vanik Amendment he sponsored in the House prevents the granting of most favored nation status to nations which restrict emigration; it has had the effect of barring close trade relations with the Soviet Union, which refused to let Jews and others emigrate freely. Northeastern Ohio has been a region favoring high tariffs and trade restrictions since the days of William McKinley. Vanik, like most historical Democrats, tends to want freer trade, but has supported restrictions sought by the ailing and locally important steel industry. He will continue to be an important figure in the ongoing trade negotiations with other major industrial countries.

Census Data Pop. 462,271. Central city, 3%; suburban, 97%. Median family income, $13,427; families above $15,000: 41%; families below $3,000: 3%. Median years education, 12.5.

The Voters

Median voting age 45.
Employment profile White collar, 63%. Blue collar, 29%. Service, 8%. Farm, -%.
Ethnic groups Black, 2%. Total foreign stock, 32%. Italy, 5%. USSR, Poland, Germany, Yugoslavia, 3% each; Hungary, UK, Czechoslovakia, Austria, 2% each; Canada, 1%.

Presidential vote

1976	Carter (D)	99,195	(50%)
	Ford (R)	100,076	(50%)
1972	Nixon (R)	119,412	(57%)
	McGovern (D)	90,689	(43%)

Rep. Charles A. Vanik (D) Elected 1954; b. Apr. 7, 1913, Cleveland; home, Euclid; Western Reserve U., B.A. 1933, LL.B. 1936; Catholic.

Career Practicing atty.; Cleveland City Cncl., 1938–39; Ohio Senate, 1940–41; Cleveland Bd. of Educ., 1941–42; Navy, WWII; Cleveland Library Bd., 1946; Judge, Cleveland Municipal Ct., 1947–54.

Offices 2108 RHOB, 202-225-6331. Also U.S. Courthouse, Cleveland 44114, 216-522-4253.

Committees *Ways and Means* (3d). Subcommittees: Health; Trade (Chairman).

Group Ratings

	ADA	COPE	PC	RPN	NFU	LCV	CFA	NAB	NSI	ACA	NTU
1978	70	82	88	58	40	–	96	0	0	12	–
1977	70	85	93	50	60	90	80	–	–	13	23
1976	70	86	90	56	100	86	73	17	20	4	30

Key Votes

1) Increase Def Spnd	AGN	6) Alaska Lands Protect	FOR	11) Delay Auto Pol Cntrl	AGN
2) B-1 Bomber	AGN	7) Water Projects Veto	FOR	12) Sugar Price Escalator	AGN
3) Cargo Preference	AGN	8) Consum Protect Agcy	FOR	13) Pub Fin Cong Cmpgns	FOR
4) Dereg Nat Gas	AGN	9) Common Situs Picket	FOR	14) ERA Ratif Recissn	AGN
5) Kemp-Roth	AGN	10) Labor Law Revision	FOR	15) Prohibt Govt Abrtns	FOR

Election Results

1978 general	Charles A. Vanik (D)	87,551	(74%)	
	Richard W. Sander (R)	30,935	(26%)	($26,715)
1978 primary	Charles A. Vanik (D), unopposed			
1976 general	Charles A. Vanik (D)	128,372	(75%)	($65)
	Harry A. Hanna (R)	42,715	(25%)	($7,189)

TWENTY-THIRD DISTRICT

The 23d congressional district of Ohio includes most of the suburbs south and west of Cleveland. These can be divided into two parts. The suburbs to the west are upper middle income Protestant towns like Lakewood, Rocky River, and Bay Village—all front on Lake Erie and all cast heavy Republican margins. As one moves further from the lake, Republican percentages tend to fall; the suburbs to the south are basically Democratic. These were settled more recently, in the fifties and sixties, generally by people of Slavic and Hungarian descent who grew up in the smoggier, less spacious streets of the west side of Cleveland.

The largest and best known of these suburbs is Parma, with a population of 100,000; most of which is in the 23d district. It is a town of subdivisions spread out between major avenues; its many bowling alleys are closely monitored by national political reporters for signs of change in public opinion. Parma is heavily Polish, Ukrainian, and Slavic; it is ancestrally Democratic, but when it switches to the Republicans, they usually win. This is what happened in 1968, when George Wallace took 14% of Parma's votes. More recently, voters here seem less likely to trust Republicans—not after Watergate—as to not trust any politicians at all. Voter turnout has been down, as a result of which the last two Democratic gubernatorial candidates were narrowly defeated, and the younger generation of potential voters here seems to be refusing to join the electorate.

In the sixties voters in areas like the 23d disliked the Democrats' heavy emphasis on civil rights and concentration on the disadvantaged, which mostly meant blacks. They still felt that New Deal economic programs basically worked to their benefit; they did not want to stop government action altogether, but to see that its benefits went to ordinary people like them. Now these people have less of a sense that government can solve problems. The decade-long failure to stop inflation—a failure as unique in American history as the failure to prevent military defeat in Vietnam—has dried up confidence in the efficacy of government action among people who, for thirty years, saw government action as the way to solve social and economic problems. The result is a sour skepticism toward all politicians and toward most government programs.

From the fifties until the early seventies the 23d district was represented in Congress by a Republican, William Minshall. This was, after all, a basically Republican district before all the migration from the cosmo wards of Cleveland to the suburbs. Its transformation to a Democratic district was delayed by the political antics of Dennis Kucinich, now Mayor of Cleveland. In 1972, at the age of 25, he came close to Minshall but was unable to defeat him. Two years later Kucinich, whose home ward in Cleveland is in the 23d district, ran as an Independent, and nearly managed to defeat the Democrat, state Senator Ronald Mottl of Parma. It was nearly an evenly divided electorate: 37% for Mottl, 32% for the Republican, a creditable 31% for Kucinich.

Mottl's record in the House has reflected many of his constituents' preoccupations. He spends little if any time promoting new federal programs. He has been one of the members most often requesting roll calls, usually on some favorite proposal; it is as if he were reflecting the feeling many of his constituents have that they have been left behind, and that they want recognition. He has devised a number of antibusing amendments, some of which have been adopted, although most of the Cleveland suburbs are not threatened with a busing order. He has sponsored a bill to provide national minimum education standards—reflecting a concern that many parents have that the quality of education today is not high. Mottl has been less productive—relatively few of his proposals are adopted—than he has been articulate, expressing the dissatisfactions of an important and often key group in the American electorate whose attitudes have helped to set the tone for our times.

Census Data Pop. 462,724. Central city, 9%; suburban, 91%. Median family income, $13,101; families above $15,000: 37%; families below $3,000: 3%. Median years education, 12.4.

The Voters

Median voting age 44.
Employment profile White collar, 61%. Blue collar, 30%. Service, 9%. Farm, –%.
Ethnic groups Total foreign stock, 28%. Czechoslovakia, 4%; Germany, Poland, Italy, 3% each; UK, Hungary, Austria, 2% each; Yugoslavia, Canada, Ireland, 1% each.

Presidential vote

1976	Carter (D)	84,525	(43%)
	Ford (R)	110,590	(57%)
1972	Nixon (R)	131,709	(65%)
	McGovern (D)	71,361	(35%)

Rep. Ronald M. Mottl (D) Elected 1974; b. Feb. 6, 1934, Cleveland; home, Parma; U. of Notre Dame, B.S., 1956, LL.B. 1957.

Career Army, 1957–58; Practicing atty., 1958–74; Cleveland Asst. Law Dir., 1958–60; Parma City Cncl., 1960–67, Pres., 1962–67; Ohio House of Reps., 1967–69; Ohio Senate, 1969–74.

Offices 1232 LHOB, 202-225-5731. Also 2951 Fed. Ofc. Bldg., 1240 E. 9th St., Cleveland 44199, 216-522-4382.

Committees *Interstate and Foreign Commerce* (23d). Subcommittees: Communications; Oversight and Investigations.

Veterans' Affairs (8th). Subcommittees: Special Investigations (Chairman); Medical Facilities and Benefits.

Group Ratings

	ADA	COPE	PC	RPN	NFU	LCV	CFA	NAB	NSI	ACA	NTU
1978	30	60	70	36	50	–	46	42	90	58	–
1977	55	71	70	17	50	70	65	–	–	44	55
1976	55	74	85	50	92	87	81	33	40	37	67

Key Votes

1) Increase Def Spnd	AGN	6) Alaska Lands Protect	FOR	11) Delay Auto Pol Cntrl	AGN
2) B-1 Bomber	AGN	7) Water Projects Veto	FOR	12) Sugar Price Escalator	AGN
3) Cargo Preference	FOR	8) Consum Protect Agcy	FOR	13) Pub Fin Cong Cmpgns	FOR
4) Dereg Nat Gas	AGN	9) Common Situs Picket	FOR	14) ERA Ratif Recissn	FOR
5) Kemp-Roth	FOR	10) Labor Law Revision	FOR	15) Prohibt Govt Abrtns	FOR

Election Results

1978 general	Ronald M. Mottl (D)	99,975	(75%)	($40,630)
	Homer S. Taft (R)	33,372	(25%)	($11,197)
1978 primary	Ronald M. Mottl (D)	24,995	(84%)	
	One other (D)	4,719	(16%)	
1976 general	Ronald M. Mottl (D)	130,591	(73%)	($17,238)
	Michael T. Scanlon (R)	47,764	(27%)	($22,836)

OKLAHOMA

Oklahoma has one of the odder and more distinctive state histories, memorialized in the Rogers and Hammerstein musical, an Edna Ferber novel, and half a dozen Hollywood movies. It was at first a land set apart by the federal government for Indians; the Cherokees and the other Civilized Tribes (as they were called) were herded from their ancestral lands in the South and Midwest and sent here over the Trail of Tears. In 1889 the federal government decided to open what is now Oklahoma to white settlement (there were some areas then still reserved for the Indians). On the morning of the great land rush, thousands of would-be homesteaders drove their wagons across the territorial line in a moment captured many times since on film.

The "sooners," as they were called (for those who crossed the line sooner than they were supposed to), quickly came to outnumber the Indians. Nonetheless, Oklahoma today has the largest Indian population of any state (97,000), but there are no reservations left, and the Indians are about as well assimilated with the rest of the population as they are anywhere in the country. During its first years, Oklahoma held out great promise to its settlers, most of whom were from the South. But for many of the white settlers the promise of Oklahoma turned sour as it had for the transplanted Indians. The depression and drought of the thirties drove thousands of Okies, as they were called, to the greener fields of California. As it stands, the population of Oklahoma is about 2.6 million; at statehood in 1907, it was not much lower, 1.5 million, with the 1930 figure at 2.4 million. In 1970, 42 of the state's 77 counties contained fewer people than they did in 1907; so almost all of Oklahoma's growth in the fifties and sixties occurred in and around its two large cities, Oklahoma City and Tulsa.

Yoked to the rise of Oklahoma City and Tulsa has been the rise in political strength of the Republican Party. Traditionally Oklahoma was a Democratic state, since most of its original settlers came from the South. But Oklahoma has always had a Republican minority, especially in the northwest and north central parts of the state, which were settled largely by people from Republican Kansas. The fast-growing, oil-rich cities of Oklahoma City and Tulsa are now new rich, conservative strongholds, much like Dallas-Fort Worth in Texas or Phoenix in Arizona. In 1964 both Oklahoma City and Tulsa went for Barry Goldwater, and together they cast 36% of the state's votes. In 1976 they both went for Gerald Ford, and this time they cast 43% of the state's votes—enough to put Oklahoma in the Republican column. Indeed, the state has gone

Democratic in a presidential election only once since 1948. And in 1972 only one state, Mississippi, gave a higher percentage to Richard Nixon.

Republicans have been competitive in state elections since the early sixties. The first breakthrough was in 1962, when Henry Bellmon was elected Governor. In 1966, Republicans elected another Governor, and a Princeton-educated Catholic at that, Tulsa oil man Dewey Bartlett. Both men went onto the Senate, Bellmon in 1968 and Bartlett in 1972. Although Republicans lost the governorship in 1970 and the Bartlett seat in 1978, they have remained very competitive for statewide office and cannot be counted out in the future.

Henry Bellmon has been the leading Republican figure in the state since he was elected Governor in 1962. After brief service as Richard Nixon's campaign chairman, he ran for the Senate in 1968 and easily beat Democratic incumbent Mike Monroney. For 18 years Monroney had concentrated on things like bringing the Federal Aviation Administration's huge Aeronautical Center to Oklahoma City; but he had also supported most Great Society programs. Monroney was out of touch with the state, and Bellmon swept the cities and made solid inroads in the traditionally Democratic rural areas.

In the Senate Bellmon at first concentrated on his seat on the Agriculture Committee. He is a farmer himself, and Oklahoma is an important agricultural state. In his second term he became ranking Republican on the Senate Budget Committee. His fiscal instincts had always been conservative, but he found it possible to work closely with Chairman Edmund Muskie. Together they labored to set budget limits for federal departments and agencies and to enforce them on the floor. That tends to get them into conflicts with other committees—Armed Services, for example, or Human Resources—which have their own priorities. Muskie has had to get his fellow Democrats to hold down spending on domestic programs; Bellmon has had to get his fellow Republicans to hold down spending on defense. By and large, they have been successful, and Bellmon has won great credit for helping to make the budget process work.

As Bellmon has become a more important figure in Washington, he has seemed to become less interested in maintaining his political standing in Oklahoma. In 1974, when he ran for reelection, he was strangely insensitive to Watergate, and in the spring of 1974 said he would ask Richard Nixon to come in and campaign for him. He ended up beating former Congressman Ed Edmondson by only 3,000 votes. And in 1979 he announced that he would not run for reelection in 1980, although he will be only 59 when his term expires. Bellmon has done great service to his party and in the Senate, but he seems to lack the driving ambition that keeps so many other politicians active.

The state's other Senate seat has not had such a stable history. In the past two decades it has been held by no less than five men. The first was Robert Kerr, uncrowned king of the Senate when he died on New Year's Day 1963. Kerr unabashedly used his great political talents to make himself rich; he also pushed through an Arkansas River project that has made Tulsa a seaport. Kerr was succeeded by J. Howard Edmondson, a lame duck governor who had himself appointed to the seat and was predictably defeated. The winner of that election was Fred Harris, once a Kerr loyalist who became Democratic National Chairman, a member of the Kerner Commission, and finally an underfinanced populist candidate for president in 1972 and 1976; Harris did not run for reelection in 1972 and now lives in New Mexico. His successor was Dewey Bartlett, a vigorous supporter of measures favored by oil companies and of stronger military preparedness; he made a major contribution to American fortifications in the Indian Ocean, but did not run for reelection in 1978 for health reasons.

The new Senator is David Boren, elected at 37 after serving four years as Governor. Boren owes his political career to an astute reading of the temper of the times in 1974. Not only was that the year of Watergate; Oklahoma also had its scandal in the conduct of Governor David Hall, who after leaving office was convicted of bribery and extortion. Boren's symbol was a broom: it symbolized his promise to clean up the mess and make reforms without committing himself to anything specific. That was enough to give him a victory over Hall and a relative of Will Rogers in the Democratic primary and runoff and to beat a Tulsa-based Republican by nearly 2–1 in the general election.

In office Boren ran a clean and fiscally austere administration. He was an early supporter of Jimmy Carter, although he apparently believed that Carter was much more favorable to deregulation of gas and oil prices than he turned out to be, and has kept his distance from the Carter White House. After four reasonably popular years as Governor, it seemed natural for Boren to seek the Senate vacancy, and he would have won easily but for charges made by a minor candidate that he was a homosexual; he eventually swore on a Bible that they were not true. That helped hold him below 50% in the first primary, leaving him in a runoff with Ed Edmondson. Narrowly defeated in both 1972 and 1974 Senate races, Edmondson had not participated in these charges at all, but based his campaign rather against Boren's economic conservatism; he supported Kemp-Roth and a one-third cut in federal spending. But that was enough only to carry his old 2d congressional district; outside the 2d and nearby Tulsa, Boren won by better than 2–1. Boren's Republican-like platform plus his general popularity as Governor were enough to give him a 2–1 victory in the general election. He can be expected to be one of the more conservative Democratic senators, and a strong spokesman for the oil industry; he had enough political savvy to win a seat on the Finance Committee.

The race to succeed Boren was a more humdrum affair, with fewer national implications. The eventual winner was Lieutenant Governor George Nigh, who travelled over the state in a "white hat brigade"—an apparent attempt to imitate Boren's brooms. With 24 years in state office, Nigh beat a younger, more venturesome Democrat, Attorney General Larry Derryberry, in the primary; Nigh had statewide recognition while Derryberry had just a regional base in the southwest part of the state. In the general election 32-year-old former University of Oklahoma football star Ron Shotts promised to cut taxes by $84 million and to amend the constitution to require a two-thirds vote in the legislature to increase taxes. Despite his inexperience, Shotts carried Oklahoma City, Tulsa, and most of the northwest part of the state, and ended up with 48% of the vote. Although Republicans have not won a statewide race now since 1974, they clearly have residual strength, and should not be counted out of the 1980 race for Bellmon's seat.

Census Data Pop. 2,559,253; 1.26% of U.S. total, 27th largest; Central city, 30%; suburban, 20%. Median family income, $7,720; 41st highest; families above $15,000: 13%; families below $3,000: 16%. Median years education, 12.1.

1977 Share of Federal Tax Burden $3,903,000,000; 1.13% of U.S. total, 27th largest.

1977 Share of Federal Outlays $5,155,762,000; 1.30% of U.S. total, 27th largest. Per capita federal spending, $1,901.

DOD	$1,328,550,000	21st (1.45%)	HEW	$1,841,601,000	25th (1.25%)
ERDA	$10,183,000	28th (0.17%)	HUD	$64,713,000	24th (1.53%)
NASA	$734,000	39th (0.02%)	VA	$300,165,000	23d (1.56%)
DOT	$238,269,000	19th (1.67%)	EPA	$80,159,000	28th (0.98%)
DOC	$97,638,000	23d (1.18%)	RevS	$84,066,000	29th (0.99%)
DOI	$86,326,000	17th (1.86%)	Debt	$203,784,000	21st (0.68%)
USDA	$361,817,000	23d (1.82%)	Other	$457,757,000	

Economic Base Agriculture, notably cattle, wheat, dairy products and peanuts; finance, insurance and real estate; oil and gas extraction, especially oil and gas field services and crude petroleum and natural gas; machinery, especially construction and related machinery; fabricated metal products, especially fabricated structural metal products; food and kindred products; electrical equipment and supplies, especially communication equipment.

Political Line-up Governor, George Nigh (D). Senators, Henry Bellmon (R) and David L. Boren (D). Representatives, 6 (5 D and 1 R). State Senate (39 D and 9 R); State House (75 D and 26 R).

The Voters

Registration 1,361,194 Total. 1,022,228 D (75%); 314,621 R (23%); 24,345 Ind. (2%).
Median voting age 44
Employment profile White collar, 48%. Blue collar, 33%. Service, 14%. Farm, 5%.
Ethnic groups Black, 7%. Indian, 4%. Spanish, 1%. Total foreign stock, 4%.

Presidential vote

1976	Carter (D)	532,442	(49%)
	Ford (R)	545,708	(51%)
1972	Nixon (R)	759,025	(75%)
	McGovern (D)	247,147	(25%)

Sen. Henry Bellmon (R) Elected 1968, seat up 1980; b. Sept. 3, 1921, Tonakawa; home, Billings; Okla. St. U., B.S. 1942; Presbyterian.

Career USMC, WWII: Wheat and cattle farmer; Okla. House of Reps., 1946–48; Okla. St. Repub. Chm., 1960–62; Gov. of Okla., 1963–67; Natl. Chm., Nixon-for-Pres. Comm., 1967–68.

Offices 125 RSOB, 202-224-5754. Also 820 Old P.O. Bldg., Oklahoma City 73102, 405-231-4941, and 3003 Fed. Bldg., Tulsa 74103, 918-581-7651.

Committees *Appropriations* (6th). Subcommittees: Agriculture and Related Agencies; Defense; Energy and Water Development; HUD-Independent Agencies; Interior and Related Agencies.

Budget (Ranking Member).

Energy and Natural Resources (6th). Subcommittees: Energy Conservation and Supply; Energy Regulation; Energy Resources and Materials Production.

Group Ratings

	ADA	COPE	PC	RPN	NFU	LCV	CFA	NAB	NSI	ACA	NTU
1978	25	21	38	80	11	16	35	64	40	52	–
1977	20	20	18	89	27	–	20	–	–	64	31
1976	10	18	11	64	37	19	7	82	80	76	59

Key Votes

1) Warnke Nom	AGN	6) Egypt-Saudi Arms	FOR	11) Hosptl Cost Contnmnt	FOR
2) Neutron Bomb	FOR	7) Draft Restr Pardon	AGN	12) Clinch River Reactor	FOR
3) Waterwy User Fee	FOR	8) Wheat Price Support	AGN	13) Pub Fin Cong Cmpgns	AGN
4) Dereg Nat Gas	FOR	9) Panama Canal Treaty	FOR	14) ERA Ratif Recissn	AGN
5) Kemp-Roth	FOR	10) Labor Law Rev Clot	AGN	15) Med Necssy Abrtns	FOR

Election Results

1974 general	Henry Bellmon (R)	390,997	(50%)	($622,480)
	Ed Edmondson (D)	387,162	(50%)	($195,429)
1974 primary	Henry Bellmon (R)	132,888	(87%)	
	One other (R)	19,733	(13%)	
1968 general	Henry Bellmon (R)	470,120	(53%)	
	A. S. Mike Monroney (D)	419,658	(47%)	

Sen. David L. Boren (D) Elected 1978, seat up 1984; b. April 21, 1941, Washington, D.C.; home, Seminole; Yale U., B.A., Rhodes Scholar, Oxford U., U. of Okla., LL.B. 1968; Methodist.

Career Okla. House of Reps., 1966–74; Practicing atty.; Gov. of Okla., 1975–78.

Offices 140 RSOB, 202-224-4721. Also Suite 350, 621 N. Robinson, Oklahoma City 73102, 405-231-4381.

Committees *Agriculture, Nutrition and Forestry* (10th). Subcommittees: Agricultural Production, Marketing, and Stabilization of Prices; Rural Development; Foreign Agricultural Policy.

Finance (11th). Subcommittees: Energy and Foundations; Public Assistance; Unemployment and Related Problems (Chairman).

Group Ratings: Newly Elected

Key Votes: Newly Elected

Election Results

1978 general	David L. Boren (D)	493,953	(67%)	($751,286)
	Robert B. Kamm (R)	247,857	(33%)	($443,712)
1978 runoff	David L. Boren (D)	281,587	(60%)	
	Ed Edmondson (D)	184,175	(40%)	($129,369)
1978 primary	David L. Boren (D)	252,560	(46%)	
	Ed Edmondson (D)	155,626	(28%)	
	Gene Stipe (D)	114,423	(21%)	($370,869)
	Four others (D)	28,409	(5%)	
1972 general	Dewey F. Bartlett (R)	516,934	(52%)	($625,095)
	Ed Edmondson (D)	478,212	(48%)	($512,058)

Gov. George P. Nigh (D) Elected 1978, term expires Jan. 1983; b. June 9, 1927, McAlester; Eastern A & M Jr. Col., E. Central St. Teachers Col., B.A. 1950; Baptist.

Career High School Teacher and Grocer; Okla. House of Reps., 1951–59; Lt. Gov. of Okla., 1959–63, 1967–79; Gov. of Okla., 1963, 1969.

Offices 212 State Capitol Bldg., Oklahoma City 73105, 405-521-2342.

Election Results

1978 general	George Nigh (D)	402,240	(52%)
	Ron Shotts (R)	367,055	(48%)
1978 runoff	George Nigh (D)	269,681	(58%)
	Larry Derryberry (D)	197,457	(42%)
1978 primary	George Nigh (D)	276,910	(50%)
	Larry Derryberry (D)	208,055	(38%)
	Bob Funston (D)	69,475	(13%)
1974 general	David Lyle Boren (D)	514,389	(64%)
	Jim Inhofe (R)	290,459	(36%)

FIRST DISTRICT

Tulsa is a major city that oil built. It has been a major regional center of the oil industry almost since Oklahoma gained statehood in 1907. Even today, years after oil was first discovered in these parts, Tulsa is still growing rapidly. Although its winters are sometimes frigid, Tulsa is very much a part of the Sun Belt in its economic base and in its basic attitudes. For like other oil cities, this is a very conservative place. People here don't resent the big companies and the new rich; they identify with them. They see government as only interfering with corporate efforts to produce goods that people want and are ready to pay for. Tulsa residents also regard some aspects of government policy as antithetical to basic moral values. It is not just an oil town, but the home of Oral Roberts University and a center of fundamentalist religion. Tulsa lacks the new-found sophistication of Dallas or Houston; it is closer in spirit to smaller boom towns like Odessa or Tyler, Texas. That is true politically as well. In national politics Tulsa is distinctly Republican. In 1972, for example, it cast a higher percentage of its votes for Richard Nixon (79%) than any other big metropolitan area outside the Deep South.

Tulsa makes up the bulk of Oklahoma's 1st congressional district. The rest consists of parts of neighboring counties, and much of that is suburban. The 1st also includes a part of the city of

Bartlesville, a prosperous town that is the headquarters of Phillips Petroleum. The boundaries of the district here and elsewhere in Oklahoma are carefully drawn to maximize the number of Democratic votes, but the 1st remains a solidly Republican district. Jimmy Carter could win only 38% of the vote here in 1976.

Nevertheless the 1st has elected and reelected a Democratic congressman four times now. He is James Jones, who even when he ran for the seat for the first time, unsuccessfully, in 1970 at the age of 31, was no political neophyte. He had served four years on Lyndon Johnson's White House staff. Jones has won against tough opposition and under difficult circumstances. In 1970, he came close to beating Republican Page Belcher, who had held the seat for 20 years, and probably prompted Belcher's retirement two years later. In 1972, he beat a former mayor of Tulsa. In January 1976 he pleaded guilty to a misdemeanor charge for failing to report a 1972 campaign contribution from the Gulf Oil company. His challenger that fall, state Senator James Imhofe, had carried the district in 1974 when he ran for governor. Still Jones was able to win with 54%. In 1978 he had tough opposition from former state Republican Chairman Paula Unruh. This time he won with more than 60%.

Jones's political adroitness in the House has probably helped him in his district. He has a seat on the Ways and Means Committee, a key post for protecting the interests of the oil industry. Naturally Jones can be counted as a solid oil vote. He has also become one of the more influential members of the House, a kind of unofficial leader of a group of Democrats, mostly but not all Southerners, who have many doubts about big government programs. He has shown his clout in a number of ways. In 1979 Jones sought a seat on the Budget Committee, but the Democratic Steering Committee gave the vacancies to more liberal members instead. Jones took his case to the floor and argued that in the climate of Proposition 13, House Democrats should put some fiscal conservatives on Budget. That argument apparently prevailed, as he won the seat in the Democratic Caucus—although most caucus members do not share Jones's views on most issues. He now seems to have a solid career in the House, although like most Oklahoma congressmen he may be interested in the Senate vacancy in 1980.

Census Data Pop. 425,620. Central city, 78%; suburban, 18%. Median family income, $7,720; families above $15,000: 13%; families below $3,000: 9%. Median years education, 12.1.

The Voters

Median voting age 42.
Employment profile White collar, 55%. Blue collar, 31%. Service, 13%. Farm, 1%.
Ethnic groups Black, 9%. Indian, 3%. Spanish, 1%. Total foreign stock, 4%.

Presidential vote

1976	Carter (D)	71,288	(38%)
	Ford (R)	114,485	(62%)
1972	Nixon (R)	133,381	(79%)
	McGovern (D)	35,199	(21%)

Rep. James R. Jones (D) Elected 1972; b. May 5, 1939, Muskogee; home, Tulsa; U. of Okla., A.B. 1961, Georgetown U., LL.B. 1964; Catholic.

Career Legis. Asst. to U.S. Rep. Ed Edmondson, 1961–64; Army, 1964–65; White House Staff Asst. to Pres. Lyndon B. Johnson, 1965–69; Practicing atty.

Offices 203 CHOB, 202-225-2211. Also 4536 Fed. Bldg., Tulsa 74103, 918-581-7111.

Committees *Ways and Means* (10th). Subcommittees: Trade.

Budget (10th). Subcommittees: Inflation; Budget Process; Defense and International Affairs; Tax Expenditures and Tax Policy (Chairman).

Group Ratings

	ADA	COPE	PC	RPN	NFU	LCV	CFA	NAB	NSI	ACA	NTU
1978	25	25	33	58	30	–	23	92	100	92	–
1977	5	38	20	58	58	15	5	–	–	72	44
1976	30	41	21	39	33	18	9	50	90	71	65

Key Votes

1) Increase Def Spnd	FOR	6) Alaska Lands Protect	FOR	11) Delay Auto Pol Cntrl	FOR
2) B-1 Bomber	FOR	7) Water Projects Veto	AGN	12) Sugar Price Escalator	AGN
3) Cargo Preference	AGN	8) Consum Protect Agcy	AGN	13) Pub Fin Cong Cmpgns	AGN
4) Dereg Nat Gas	FOR	9) Common Situs Picket	AGN	14) ERA Ratif Recissn	AGN
5) Kemp-Roth	AGN	10) Labor Law Revision	FOR	15) Prohibt Govt Abrtns	FOR

Election Results

1978 general	James R. Jones (D)	73,886	(60%) ✓	($210,179)
	Paula Unruh (R)	49,404	(40%)	($236,437)
1978 primary	James R. Jones (D), unopposed			
1976 general	James R. Jones (D)	100,945	(54%)	($184,250)
	James M. Inhofe (R)	84,374	(46%)	($145,572)

SECOND DISTRICT

The 2d congressional district of Oklahoma takes in all the northeast quadrant of the state, except for the Tulsa area which makes up the 1st district. The 2d is the place where most of Oklahoma's Indians live. Their ancestors were forcibly relocated here from their ancestral lands in the South and Midwest, as early as the 1830s, over the Trail of Tears. This part of Oklahoma remained Indian Territory until it was opened up to white settlement in 1889. Today 8% of the population of the 2d district is Indian, and a larger percentage claim some Indian blood. Even the county names recall the Civilized Tribes: Cherokee, Delaware, Ottawa, Osage, Creek. In 1889, white settlers from the Democratic Deep South and the Republican Ozarks began moving in. As a result, the 2d today is something of a political borderland between Republican and Democratic territory. The Indians, meanwhile, unlike those in the northern plains or Rocky Mountain states, do not vote in any way markedly different from the rest of the population.

The 2d district's largest city is Muskogee, a rather rundown Oklahoma rural center. Anyone who has heard Merle Haggard's "Okie from Muskogee" has a fair idea of the cultural and political attitudes here. There was never much of an establishment in Oklahoma to rebel against (although there was a big Socialist vote in the early years, reflecting hatred of Eastern money interests), and people here have been very positive about traditional American values even as they have been questioned elsewhere. The residents of the district are not a particularly solemn folk, however. This part of Oklahoma produced Will Rogers, who is remembered here with favor—and to Woody Guthrie, who generally is not.

For 20 years the 2d district was represented by the same Democratic Congressman, Ed Edmondson, until he decided to make his first race for the Senate in 1972. Since then, the district has had three different Democratic congressmen, who have differed more in personality than in political attitude. Edmondson represented the changing views of the district accurately. He began as a supporter of Democratic economic programs and ended his House career as a critic of Democratic social attitudes. He was nearly elected to the Senate in both 1972 and 1974 and got 40% against David Boren in the 1978 Senate runoff. Edmondson was succeeded by Clem Rogers McSpadden, a grandnephew of Will Rogers and rodeo impresario; McSpadden ran for governor in 1974 and lost in the runoff to Boren. The next Congressman, Ted Risenhoover, had a flamboyant personality. He won the 1974 runoff in something of an upset and was nearly beaten in the 1976 primary by Ed Edmondson's nephew, while doing poorly in both general elections. In the 1978 primary Risenhoover was ridiculed for possessing a heart-shaped waterbed—a charge he denied.

Risenhoover was beaten in the 1978 runoff by 27-year-old Mike Synar. Like his predecessor, Synar won by an uninspiring margin in the general election, given the basic Democratic leanings of the district. Whether he will be able to hold onto the district any better than Risenhoover is unclear.

Census Data Pop. 426,778. Central city, 0%; suburban, 22%. Median family income, $9,527; families above $15,000: 19%; families below $3,000: 21%. Median years education, 12.3.

The Voters

Median voting age 47.
Employment profile White collar, 41%. Blue collar, 39%. Service, 15%. Farm, 5%.
Ethnic groups Black, 6%. Indian, 8%. Total foreign stock, 2%.

Presidential vote

1976	Carter (D)	101,406	(54%)
	Ford (R)	86,067	(46%)
1972	Nixon (R)	126,446	(73%)
	McGovern (D)	46,648	(27%)

Rep. Michael Lynn Synar (D) Elected 1978; b. Oct. 17, 1950, Vinita; home, Muskogee; U. of Okla., B.A. 1972, J.D. 1977, Northwestern U., M.B.A. 1973.

Career Rancher and real estate broker.

Offices 1338 LHOB, 202-225-2701. Also Rm. 2B22 Fed. Bldg., 125 S. Main, Muskogee 74401, 918-681-2533.

Committees *Government Operations* (23d). Subcommittees: Intergovernmental Relations and Human Resources; Government Activities and Transportation.

Judiciary (16th). Subcommittees: Crime; Criminal Justice.

Group Ratings: Newly Elected

Key Votes: Newly Elected

Election Results

1978 general	Mike Synar (D)	72,583	(55%)	($190,050)
	Gary Richardson (R)	59,853	(45%)	($130,530)
1978 primary	Mike Synar (D)	58,397	(54%)	
	Theodore M. Risenhoover (D)	50,597	(46%)	($134,260)
1976 general	Theodore M. Risenhoover (D)	102,402	(54%)	($123,109)
	Bud Stewart (R)	87,341	(46%)	($102,736)

THIRD DISTRICT

The southern part of Oklahoma is known as Little Dixie. It was first settled, in the period between 1889 and 1907, by white Southerners—some of the county names here were taken directly from Mississippi. Ever since statehood Little Dixie has been the most Democratic part of Oklahoma. "Republicans occasionally travel through the district," says a *Congressional Quarterly* writer, "but they seldom settle there." The 3d congressional district of Oklahoma includes most of the Little Dixie counties, and juts up into the center of the state north of Oklahoma City, to include enough people to meet the equal population standard.

This is the district which for 30 years elected Carl Albert to the House of Representatives. Albert was part of the class of World War II veterans first elected in 1946. Others include John Kennedy and Richard Nixon; none is left in the House today. In his early years, as a loyal Democrat from a Southern-oriented district, Albert attracted the attention of Speaker Sam Rayburn. He was made Majority Whip in 1955, and after that his succession to the Speakership was, literally, automatic. For eight years, from 1971 to 1977, Albert served as Speaker of the House.

Albert's performance as Speaker was a disappointment to those who remembered him as a hard-fighting vote counter in the late fifties and early sixties. A decade and a half of waiting had only made him cautious, and he deferred to every committee chairman and every hoary tradition. He established no legislative priorities, had little to say about scheduling, essentially provided little leadership of any kind. Those were years in which it was difficult to lead. But it was clear that the time had passed when Albert would have been an effective Speaker. His retirement in 1976 spared Democrats the question of whether they wanted to replace him.

Little Dixie had always seemed proud of Albert, and reelected him without difficulty. But he proved unable to hand the 3d district seat on to his administrative assistant, Charles Ward. Instead state Senator Wes Watkins won the Democratic primary and captured the district. Watkins has had a solidly conservative voting record—practically as conservative as that of Oklahoma City's Republican Congressman, Mickey Edwards. He is considered likely to run for the Senate in 1980. His Little Dixie base will probably turn out heavily in the Democratic primary, and his local celebrity gives him a good chance of making the runoff. If he does run statewide, the succession in the 3d district will be determined, as it was in 1976, in the Democratic primary.

Census Data Pop. 426,596. Central city, 0%; suburban, 8%. Median family income, $6,567; families above $15,000: 9%; families below $3,000: 24%. Median years education, 10.9.

The Voters

Median voting age 49.
Employment profile White collar, 39%. Blue collar, 40%. Service, 15%. Farm, 6%.
Ethnic groups Black, 6%. Indian, 5%. Total foreign stock, 2%.

Presidential vote

1976	Carter (D)	117,459	(64%)
	Ford (R)	66,439	(36%)
1972	Nixon (R)	113,281	(70%)
	McGovern (D)	47,962	(30%)

Rep. Wes Watkins (D) Elected 1976; b. Dec. 15, 1938, DeQueen, Ark.; home, Ada; Okla. St. U., B.S. 1960, M.S. 1961, U. of Md., 1961–63; Presbyterian.

Career USDA, 1961–63; Asst. Dir. of Admissions, Okla. St. U., 1963–66; Exec. Dir., Kiamichi Econ. Development Dist. of Okla., 1966–68; Realtor and homebuilder, 1968– ; Okla. Senate, 1975–76.

Offices 424 CHOB, 202-225-4565. Also P.O. Box 1607, Ada 74820, 405-436-1980.

Committees *Banking, Finance and Urban Affairs* (26th). Subcommittees: Housing and Community Development; Economic Stabilization.

Science and Technology (16th). Subcommittees: Space Science and Technology; Science, Research and Technology; Natural Resources and Environment.

Group Ratings

	ADA	COPE	PC	RPN	NFU	LCV	CFA	NAB	NSI	ACA	NTU
1978	20	37	23	58	30	–	14	92	89	84	–
1977	5	18	20	42	50	7	20	–	–	74	36

Key Votes

1) Increase Def Spnd	FOR	6) Alaska Lands Protect	DNV	11) Delay Auto Pol Cntrl	DNV
2) B-1 Bomber	FOR	7) Water Projects Veto	AGN	12) Sugar Price Escalator	FOR
3) Cargo Preference	AGN	8) Consum Protect Agcy	AGN	13) Pub Fin Cong Cmpgns	AGN
4) Dereg Nat Gas	FOR	9) Common Situs Picket	AGN	14) ERA Ratif Recissn	AGN
5) Kemp-Roth	FOR	10) Labor Law Revision	AGN	15) Prohibt Govt Abrtns	DNV

Election Results

1978 general	Wes Watkins (D), unopposed			($23,999)
1978 primary	Wes Watkins (D), unopposed			
1976 general	Wes Watkins (D)	151,271	(83%)	($138,124)
	Gerald Beasley, Jr. (R)	31,732	(17%)	($23,677)

FOURTH DISTRICT

The 4th congressional district of Oklahoma includes most of southwestern Oklahoma and part of metropolitan Oklahoma City. The counties along the Red River, the state's southern border, resemble areas in adjacent Texas—cotton-growing Democratic strongholds. But as one moves north, the district becomes politically more marginal. The 4th's portion of Oklahoma City and its suburbs usually goes Republican, and so more often than not does Cleveland County, which contains Norman and the University of Oklahoma.

The Congressman from this district is Tom Steed, a onetime newspaper reporter and congressional aide who was first elected to the House in 1948. He is one of those moderate Southwestern Democrats who used to be a bigger power in the House than he is now. He joins the majority of Democrats on many votes, and is responsive to the leadership. But he also maintains a record which can legitimately be called conservative.

Steed has seen the system work for a long time, and he is anything but a boat-rocker. As a senior member of the Appropriations Committee, he chairs the subcommittee which handles the budgets of the Treasury, the Postal Service, and the White House. His work came under some scrutiny in 1974, when attention came to rest on the imperial presidency of Richard Nixon, and it turned out that he had been quite indulgent with the Republican president. Steed's experience had been in years when Americans wanted to pamper their presidents, and he said he would do nothing that anyone might think would endanger the chief executive's safety. He had the unpleasant experience of watching his subcommittee's work being ridiculed on the floor of the House.

Steed is now one of the most senior members of the House, but he has not always won reelection easily. In 1966, during a surge of strength for Republicans in Oklahoma, he won reelection by only 364 votes, and in 1968 he had to beat a Republican incumbent when they had been thrown in the same district together. In 1978 he had his first significant challenge in a while, from an aggressive Republican who cut his percentage down to just over 60%. Steed was 74 during that campaign, and while he probably can continue to win here, he may decide to retire instead in 1980.

Census Data Pop. 426,330. Central city, 20%; suburban, 41%. Median family income, $5,846; families above $15,000: 7%; families below $3,000: 15%. Median years education, 10.2.

The Voters

Median voting age 38.
Employment profile White collar, 49%. Blue collar, 32%. Service, 14%. Farm, 5%.
Ethnic groups Black, 6%. Indian, 3%. Spanish, 3%. Total foreign stock, 5%.

Presidential vote

1976	Carter (D)	NA	
	Ford (R)	NA	
1972	Nixon (R)	107,548	(74%)
	McGovern (D)	37,542	(26%)

Rep. Tom Steed (D) Elected 1948; b. Mar. 2, 1904, near Rising Star, Tex.; home, Shawnee; Methodist.

Career Admin. Asst. to U.S. Reps. P.L. Gassaway, R.L. Hill, and Gomer Smith; Reporter, Bartlesville *Examiner,* McAlester *News Capital, Daily Oklahoman,* and Shawnee *News-Star*; Army, WWII; Ofc. of War Info., 1944–45; Automobile dealer, 1945–48.

Offices 2405 RHOB, 202-225-6165. Also 124 E. Main St., P.O. Box 1265, Norman 73069, 405-329-6500.

Committees *Appropriations* (5th). Subcommittees: Transportation; Military Construction; Treasury, Postal Service and General Government (Chairman).

Small Business (2d). Subcommittees: Antitrust and Restraint of Trade Activities Affecting Small Business; Access to Equity Capital and Business Opportunities.

Group Ratings

	ADA	COPE	PC	RPN	NFU	LCV	CFA	NAB	NSI	ACA	NTU
1978	20	45	38	50	40	–	27	50	80	41	–
1977	25	68	28	25	60	14	30	–	–	28	21
1976	35	70	26	24	46	23	36	8	75	44	14

Key Votes

1) Increase Def Spnd	FOR	6) Alaska Lands Protect	FOR	11) Delay Auto Pol Cntrl	FOR
2) B-1 Bomber	FOR	7) Water Projects Veto	AGN	12) Sugar Price Escalator	FOR
3) Cargo Preference	FOR	8) Consum Protect Agcy	AGN	13) Pub Fin Cong Cmpgns	AGN
4) Dereg Nat Gas	FOR	9) Common Situs Picket	AGN	14) ERA Ratif Recissn	FOR
5) Kemp-Roth	AGN	10) Labor Law Revision	FOR	15) Prohibt Govt Abrtns	AGN

Election Results

1978 general	Tom Steed (D)	62,993	(60%)	($55,854)
	Scotty Robb (R)	41,421	(40%)	($150,420)
1978 primary	Tom Steed (D)	55,641	(65%)	
	M. E. Waid, Jr. (D)	29,341	(35%)	($25,654)
1976 general	Tom Steed (D)	116,425	(77%)	($20,273)
	M. C. Stanley (R)	34,170	(23%)	($7,134)

FIFTH DISTRICT

Oklahoma City is the capital of Oklahoma and its largest city, with a metropolitan population of more than half a million. During the sixties the city fathers decided that they would not let the old city limits become a straitjacket, cutting off Oklahoma City from the prosperity and growth of the suburbs. So they annexed so much territory that Oklahoma City now spills over into five counties and three congressional districts. Even without these annexed areas—most of them are still vacant—Oklahoma City is a sprawling and unplanned metropolis. Towering above the dusty plains are a few skyscrapers and, right beside them, huge parking lots. As in the case of Tulsa, the wealth of Oklahoma City comes mainly from oil; on the grounds of the state Capitol there are still a few oil wells pumping away. Like most cities in the Southwest, especially oil cities, Oklahoma City is basically conservative and Republican, though notably less so than Tulsa.

The 5th congressional district, which includes most of Oklahoma City, has had only three different congressmen over the last forty years. The first was Mike Monroney, who as Representative from the 5th from 1939 to 1951 and as U.S. Senator for three terms helped get an Air Force base and the FAA Aeronautical Center located here. The second, first elected in 1950, was Democrat John Jarman, a distinguished looking Ivy League graduate who had the support of E. K. Gaylord's conservative Oklahoma City newspapers. His lackluster record in Congress—though he was chairman of an important subcommittee, he let the number two Democrat run it—became a liability when more voters made more demands on government. Moreover, his lack of ideological identification hurt him with both conservatives and the few liberals here, and his longtime ally, Gaylord, died in 1974 at 101. Jarman made poor showings in both the 1974 primary and general election, decided to retire, and switched to the Republican Party for his last term.

The current congressman is the man who nearly beat Jarman in 1974, Republican Mickey Edwards. He did not get the seat uncontested, however. Edwards had a tough Republican primary with a former Oklahoma attorney general and a close general election against a young Democrat. In the House Edwards quickly became known as one of the most steadfast ideological conservatives, and took seats on two of the most uncongenial committees, Education and Labor and Interior. He seems to be the sort of person who enjoys a good political fight. Edwards has worked the 5th district harder than it has been worked at least since Monroney's time, and against a weak Democrat won by an overwhelming margin in 1978. For 1980 he may very well try to succeed Henry Bellmon in the Senate. Any appearances he makes on Oklahoma City television will expose him to half the state, and he should have no difficulty raising large sums of money by direct mail. Whether Oklahoma is ready for such an ideological, urban-based conservative senator is not clear; but Edwards appears to have the ambition and drive to give the question a good test.

Census Data Pop. 426,484. Central city, 79%; suburban, 21%. Median family income, $7,569; families above $15,000: 12%; families below $3,000: 9%. Median years education, 12.1.

The Voters

Median voting age 42.
Employment profile White collar, 56%. Blue collar, 30%. Service, 13%. Farm, 1%.
Ethnic groups Black, 11%. Indian, 2%. Spanish, 2%. Total foreign stock, 4%.

Presidential vote

1976	Carter (D)	NA	
	Ford (R)	NA	
1972	Nixon (R)	126,859	(76%)
	McGovern (D)	39,955	(24%)

Rep. Mickey Edwards (R) Elected 1976; b. July 12, 1937, Oklahoma City; home, Oklahoma City; U. of Okla., B.S. 1958, Okla. City U., J.D. 1969; Episcopalian.

Career Practicing atty., reporter and editor; Ed., *Private Practice* magazine; Public relations exec., 1973–76.

Offices 413 LHOB, 202-225-2132. Also 215 3rd St., N.W., Oklahoma City 73102, 405-231-4541.

Committees *Education and Labor* (6th). Subcommittees: Health and Safety; Postsecondary Education; Labor Standards.

Interior and Insular Affairs (10th). Subcommittees: Energy and the Environment; National Parks and Insular Affairs.

Group Ratings

	ADA	COPE	PC	RPN	NFU	LCV	CFA	NAB	NSI	ACA	NTU
1978	10	5	18	58	30	–	18	100	100	92	–
1977	5	13	18	54	42	10	5	–	–	93	48

Key Votes

1) Increase Def Spnd	FOR	6) Alaska Lands Protect	AGN	11) Delay Auto Pol Cntrl	FOR
2) B-1 Bomber	DNV	7) Water Projects Veto	AGN	12) Sugar Price Escalator	FOR
3) Cargo Preference	AGN	8) Consum Protect Agcy	AGN	13) Pub Fin Cong Cmpgns	AGN
4) Dereg Nat Gas	FOR	9) Common Situs Picket	AGN	14) ERA Ratif Recissn	FOR
5) Kemp-Roth	FOR	10) Labor Law Revision	AGN	15) Prohibt Govt Abrtns	FOR

Election Results

1978 general	Mickey Edwards (R)	71,451	(80%)	($247,380)
	Jesse Dennis Knipp (D)	17,978	(20%)	($5,637)
1978 primary	Mickey Edwards (R), unopposed			
1976 general	Mickey Edwards (R)	78,651	(51%)	($16,843)
	Tom Dunlap (D)	74,752	(49%)	($705)

SIXTH DISTRICT

The 6th congressional district of Oklahoma occupies the northwest and north central parts of the state. It includes the thin panhandle that goes west to touch the borders of Colorado and New Mexico. Aside from a small portion of Oklahoma City and its suburbs, the 6th is almost entirely small town and rural. Around the turn of the century, the plains west of Tulsa and Oklahoma City attracted thousands of migrants—probably a majority of them from nearby Kansas. Like so many settlers of the Great Plains, these people mistakenly assumed that the land was more fertile and the rainfall more reliable than was actually the case. The Dust Bowl of the thirties hit already arid northwest Oklahoma hard, and in many ways it has yet to recover. In 1907, when Oklahoma was admitted to the Union, there were 401,000 people living in the counties now wholly contained in the 6th district. By 1970 that number was down to 390,000.

Due probably to the Kansas origin of its first settlers, the 6th has always been the most Republican part of non-urban Oklahoma. In the late sixties and early seventies, when the conservative trend in the state was shifting ancestral Democrats to the party of Richard Nixon and Spiro Agnew, the 6th became for a moment one of the most Republican districts in the nation. In 1972 Nixon won a larger percentage of the vote here (79%) than in any other congressional district outside the Deep South.

But that trend was short-lived, as Watergate had impact out here in Middle America as much as anywhere else. Not only did the traditionally Democratic counties in the southern part of the state switch back to Democrats in statewide races, so too, to a considerable extent, did the traditionally Republican counties of the north central region around Enid and Ponca City. The 6th was still Republican, but narrowly, in the 1976 presidential race; but since 1974 it has been represented in the House by a Democrat.

He is Glenn English, once an aide to liberal Democrats in the California Assembly, but a native of this area who in 1974 had been serving as director of the Oklahoma Democratic Party. Running against a Republican twice his age, English simply outcampaigned him and won handily. Since then he has deterred strong opposition and won by overwhelming margins. His voting record is tailored to the district's conservative instincts; and in 1977 he was successful in raising wheat price supports above what the Administration wanted. Like some other members of the Oklahoma House delegation, English is eying the Senate seat Henry Bellmon is vacating in 1980. This will probably be the last Oklahoma Senate seat easily available in this generation—David Boren seems to have a solid lock on the other one—and though he will not be 40 by election day, English is likely to run.

Census Data Pop. 427,445. Central city, 5%; suburban, 10%. Median family income, $9,305; families above $15,000: 19%; families below $3,000: 15%. Median years education, 12.3.

The Voters

Median voting age 45.
Employment profile White collar, 45%. Blue collar, 29%. Service, 15%. Farm, 11%.
Ethnic groups Black, 2%. Indian, 2%. Spanish, 1%. Total foreign stock, 5%.

Presidential vote

1976	Carter (D)	NA	
	Ford (R)	NA	
1972	Nixon (R)	150,998	(79%)
	McGovern (D)	39,712	(21%)

Rep. Glenn English (D) Elected 1974; b. Nov. 30, 1940, Cordell; home, Cordell; Southwestern St. Col., B.A. 1964.

Career Chf. Asst. to Majority Caucus, Cal. State Assembly; Exec. Dir., Okla. Dem. Party, 1969–73; Petroleum leasing business.

Offices 109 CHOB, 202-225-5565. Also 410 Maple St., Yukon 73099, 405-354-8638.

Committees *Agriculture* (15th). Subcommittees: Conservation and Credit; Department Investigations, Oversight and Research; Livestock and Grains.

Government Operations (13th). Subcommittees: Government Information and Individual Rights; Intergovernmental Relations and Human Resources.

Group Ratings

	ADA	COPE	PC	RPN	NFU	LCV	CFA	NAB	NSI	ACA	NTU
1978	15	16	25	67	30	–	9	100	90	88	–
1977	10	17	23	23	50	15	20	–	–	89	45
1976	25	39	23	33	33	20	27	50	90	79	56

Key Votes

1) Increase Def Spnd	FOR	6) Alaska Lands Protect	FOR	11) Delay Auto Pol Cntrl	FOR
2) B-1 Bomber	FOR	7) Water Projects Veto	FOR	12) Sugar Price Escalator	FOR
3) Cargo Preference	AGN	8) Consum Protect Agcy	AGN	13) Pub Fin Cong Cmpgns	AGN
4) Dereg Nat Gas	FOR	9) Common Situs Picket	AGN	14) ERA Ratif Recissn	FOR
5) Kemp-Roth	FOR	10) Labor Law Revision	AGN	15) Prohibt Govt Abrtns	FOR

Election Results

1978 general	Glenn English (D)	103,512	(74%)	($109,668)
	Harold Hunter (R)	36,031	(26%)	($65,053)
1978 primary	Glenn English (D), unopposed			
1976 general	Glenn English (D)	137,498	(71%)	($102,235)
	Carol McCurley (R)	55,953	(29%)	($36,006)

OREGON

Oregon in the seventies seems almost a progressive commonwealth, separated by thousands of miles of mountains and desert from the rest of the United States. The problems and fears that afflict the rest of the country seem far away, and the state is open to new ideas and new solutions. Oregon was one of the first states to show that you could decriminalize marijuana without any serious repercussions, and that you can outlaw throwaway bottles and cans without destroying the glass and brewing industries. In a nation which has always equated population growth with prosperity, Oregon is a state whose former Governor, Tom McCall, urged people to come to visit, "but for heaven's sake don't come to live here!"

Despite McCall's plea, Oregon's clean air and uncrowded spaces have been attracting people from the smog of California and the rigors of the East Coast. The state's population rose 18% during the sixties and another 17% from 1970 to 1978—both rates well above the national average. And for all its natural wonders, Oregon's people, like those in most western states, are still concentrated: more than 80% live in the Portland metropolitan area or in the Willamette valley directly to the south.

But enough of the current clichés about Oregon are true to merit asking just how this state came to be what it is. A substantial part of the answer lies in the economic history of the West Coast in the years following World War II. Those were the days when California and, to a lesser extent, Washington were ballooning in population, and a major reason was the fast expansion of the aerospace and defense industries. Oregon experienced little of this postwar boom; even in recent years the Defense Department spends less here per capita than in almost any other state. The economy of Oregon has continued to depend on a much more old-fashioned commodity—lumber. The wood business does not provide the state with an entirely steady economy. When housing starts are down, usually because of high interest rates, the lumber industry suffers. But in the inflationary seventies, when housing values are about the only kind of asset the ordinary person has which stay ahead of inflation, even record interest rates have not dampened the demand for housing. The result has been a consistently strong lumber market. Unlike a defense plant, lumber has always been an industry which never shuts down completely; now it seems to have a considerable upside potential as well. Moreover, if demand in the United States slackens, demand for West Coast lumber in Japan seems always on the rise.

If the economy of Oregon has a certain long-term stability, despite some short-term fluctuations, so too does its politics. Unlike most states, there are no longstanding political divisions between different regions. It is true that the coastal areas and the lower Columbia River valley are marginally more Democratic than the rest of the state; and that Salem, the state capital, is usually more Republican than Eugene, site of the University of Oregon. Also, the low-lying, less affluent sections of Portland east of the Willamette River are usually Democratic, while the more affluent city neighborhoods and suburbs in the hills to the west tend to be Republican. But there is not all that much difference between these areas—nothing like the difference in outlook between San Francisco and Orange County.

The results of the 1978 election—specifically, the victory of Governor Victor Atiyeh—seemed to indicate a sharp shift in Oregon's politics; but actually it marked little difference at all. This still remains a state concerned to an extraordinary degree with its environment and its own special progressive character. This tradition was really established during the governorship of Tom McCall (1967–74), whose pungent candor and bluff forcefulness made him the state's most popular political figure. He could have won a third term easily in 1974 had he been eligible to run. His successor was state Treasurer Robert Straub, a Democrat who supported similar policies though without the panache; he beat Atiyeh, a state Senator with a conservative reputation who had won the Republican primary in an upset and did not have McCall's strong support.

Yet four years later Atiyeh beat both of his predecessors—McCall in the primary, Straub in the general election. But in each case Atiyeh was careful to campaign as a supporter, not an opponent, of environmental measures; and he benefited as well from the post-Proposition 13 climate. McCall was handicapped by the composition of the Republican primary electorate, which increasingly favors candidates of the right; that electorate just barely preferred Gerald Ford over Ronald Reagan in 1976. McCall also sacrificed some of the aura of respect he had built up over the years when he re-entered the partisan fray; he seemed to become just another politician, rather than a state hero. Atiyeh, in contrast, increased his stature and made himself appear far more in line with Oregon tradition.

In the general election, there was great dispute over taxes, with Atiyeh favoring one ballot measure and Straub getting another—ultimately successful—one on the ballot himself. The difference between the two candidates was as much one of style as substance. Straub was criticized for not providing leadership in the McCall style, while Atiyeh was able to project a forceful image without being under the actual pressures of office. The result was a decisive, but not overwhelming, victory for Atiyeh. In national politics, he may still be counted as a conservative; but in Oregon, he seems unlikely to try—and less likely to succeed in—changing Oregon's special type of government.

Oregon continues to have a Democratic legislature, as well as a Democratic registration edge, and it sends four Democrats to the House of Representatives from its four congressional districts. But Republicans have the top spots, not only the governorship, but the state's two Senate seats. This is a change from the sixties, during most of which Oregon elected two Democratic senators; but both seats went Republican when Democrats quarreled over the Vietnam war, and both Republican beneficiaries of those quarrels, Mark Hatfield and Bob Packwood, have held on since.

Hatfield, the senior Senator was an established figure—and boy wonder—when first elected: he had been elected a state legislator at age 28, Governor at 34 in 1958, and Senator at 42 in 1966. A deeply religious man, Hatfield was a strong and early opponent of the Vietnam war; when he ran in 1966, he got the support of Democratic Senator Wayne Morse, also an early dove, over his opponent, Congressman Bob Duncan. In his first term in the Senate, Hatfield became best known for his position on the war; in 1970 and 1971 he was spending most of his efforts trying to pass the McGovern-Hatfield amendment to end it. But Hatfield is not one who would leave the Republican Party on the war or any other issue. He is enough of a regular Republican to have nominated Richard Nixon at the 1960 national convention and to have strongly advocated party line positions as ranking minority member of the Senate Rules Committee.

Hatfield is now ranking Republican on the Energy Committee, and in the 95th Congress he cast key votes for deregulation of natural gas—the position which prevailed in the Senate. On that committee, which used to be called Interior, Hatfield has also been careful to look out for the interests of Oregon's lumber industry, and he has often supported the lumber companies in disputes with environmentalists. Hatfield is also second-ranking Republican on the Senate Appropriations Committee, immediately behind North Dakota's Milton Young, who turns 83 in 1980 when he is expected to retire. That will put Hatfield into a potentially important position, particularly if the Republicans manage to win control of the Senate. On spending issues, Hatfield is a middle of the roader: neither a really big spender, nor a penny-pincher. He retains his interest in foreign policy and arms control issues, and threatened to vote against the SALT Treaty if the Administration makes too may concessions to its hawkish critics.

Hatfield's opponent in 1972 was the same man who had supported him in 1966, Wayne Morse; having been unseated in 1968, Morse ran again, beat Duncan in the primary, and got 46% in the general. (Morse also won the 1974 Democratic Senate nomination, but died before the general election was held.) In 1978 Hatfield did not attract serious competition; his opponent, Vernon Cook, was an embarrassment to serious Democrats. Hatfield won that election by a 2–1 margin. He seems to be a reasonably safe senator, but Oregon is a difficult state to stay in close touch with (there are no nonstop flights from Washington), and as Hatfield becomes more entrenched in Washington he risks becoming less firmly supported at home. Hatfield is becoming a powerful senator, but he is no longer a boy wonder and may have to fight hard if he gets tough competition.

Oregon's junior Senator, Bob Packwood, also carries the label liberal Republican, but his record is quite different from Hatfield's. Packwood is more of an environmentalist. In the early seventies he became known as the Senate's leading proponent of zero population growth, and he has been a strong advocate of making abortions available to all regardless of means. He dissented less often than Hatfield from Nixon and Ford Administration foreign policies, and if he criticizes the Carter foreign policy it is on the grounds that it is not aggressive enough. On economic issues Packwood is not easily classified. He has had a good enough recent labor record that the unions have said they might support him for reelection in 1980, yet he by no means favors unlimited spending or income redistribution. Packwood has made some innovative proposals to make the free enterprise system work better, but he generally does not take on business interests. Though his abortion position earned him strong opposition from Catholics (who are few in Oregon), he has worked with Daniel Patrick Moynihan as the chief sponsor of a measure to provide tax credits for private school tuition—a measure which would greatly help Catholic schools.

Packwood's victory over Wayne Morse in 1968 was a stunning upset, caused as much by the enemies Morse made as by Packwood's own efforts. He won reelection in 1974 by winning 55% of the vote against Betty Roberts, a state Senator whose own controversial statements got her into trouble. He could certainly be reelected easily in 1980 over weak opposition, but he may have a tough opponent. Portland Mayor Neil Goldschmidt, with a strong local constituency, and 1st district Congressman Les AuCoin, who won in a previously Republican district by nearly a 2–1 margin in 1978, are mentioned as possible candidates. Either could be formidable.

Oregon had one of the nation's first presidential primaries, and in some years it has been a critical one. Back in 1948 Oregon eliminated Harold Stassen from any serious consideration as a presidential candidate. Sixteen years later Oregon kept Nelson Rockefeller in the race against Barry Goldwater, and in 1968 Oregon Democrats chose Eugene McCarthy over Robert Kennedy—the only defeat any of the Kennedy brothers has ever suffered at the polls. One may argue about how decisive these results were: a week or two later both Goldwater and Kennedy won their parties' California primaries. In 1972 neither primary was seriously contested here; in 1976 there were contests but not important ones. This was the only western state where Gerald Ford could compete against Ronald Reagan; and Jerry Brown stirred a flurry of excitement by running a write-in campaign, only to finish second to Frank Church. Oregon's primary may have more significance as the first to impose the requirement, now widely copied, that all candidates recognized as such by the national media be listed on the ballot. But instead of insuring a real contest, this has only enabled the handicappers to pick a likely winner—at which point no one else actively campaigns. The fact is that Oregon is just too remote and too small and too idiosyncratic—the isolated Pacific commonwealth—to name a national presidential nominee. It may forecast the future, but it cannot by any means determine it.

Census Data Pop. 2,091,385; 1.03% of U.S. total, 31st largest; Central city, 25%; suburban, 36%. Median family income, $9,487; 22d highest; families above $15,000: 18%; families below $3,000: 9%. Median years education, 12.3.

1977 Share of Federal Tax Burden $3,696,000,000; 1.07% of U.S. total, 29th largest.

1977 Share of Federal Outlays $3,835,768,000; 0.97% of U.S. total, 32d largest. Per capita federal spending, $1,676.

DOD	$286,904,000	43d (0.31%)	HEW	$1,631,647,000	28th (1.10%)
ERDA	$3,315,000	38th (0.06%)	HUD	$27,459,000	37th (0.65%)
NASA	$2,132,000	32d (0.05%)	VA	$225,568,000	32d (1.17%)
DOT	$172,514,000	27th (1.21%)	EPA	$54,074,000	30th (0.66%)
DOC	$105,984,000	19th (1.28%)	RevS	$97,796,000	27th (1.16%)
DOI	$207,472,000	8th (4.46%)	Debt	$121,571,000	28th (0.40%)
USDA	$418,181,000	15th (2.10%)	Other	$481,151,000	

Economic Base Lumber and wood products, especially millwork, plywood and related products, and sawmills and planing mills; agriculture, notably cattle, dairy products, wheat and greenhouses; finance, insurance and real estate; food and kindred products, especially canned, cured and frozen foods; machinery, especially construction and related machinery; paper and allied products, especially paper mills other than building paper; transportation equipment.

Political Line-up Governor, Victor G. Atiyeh (R). Senators, Mark O. Hatfield (R) and Bob Packwood (R). Representatives, 4 D. State Senate (23 D and 7 R); State House (34 D and 26 R).

The Voters

Median voting age 44
Employment profile White collar, 48%. Blue collar, 34%. Service, 14%. Farm, 4%.
Ethnic groups Black 1%. Spanish, 2%. Total foreign stock, 14%. Canada, 3%; Germany 2%; UK, 1%.

Presidential vote

1976	Carter (D)	492,120	(50%)
	Ford (R)	490,407	(50%)
1972	Nixon (R)	486,686	(55%)
	McGovern (D)	392,760	(45%)

Sen. Mark O. Hatfield (R) Elected 1966, seat up 1978; b. July 12, 1922, Dallas; home, Newport; Willamette U., B.A. 1943, Stanford U., A.M. 1948; Baptist.

Career Navy, WWII; Assoc. Prof. of Poli. Sci., Willamette U., 1949–56, Dean of Students, 1950–56; Oreg. House of Reps., 1950–54; Oreg. Senate, 1954–56; Secy. of State of Oreg., 1956–58; Gov. of Oreg., 1958–66.

Offices 463 RSOB, 202-224-3753. Also 475 Cottage St. N.E., Salem 97301, 503-399-5731, and 105 Pioneer Courthouse, Portland 97204, 503-221-3386.

Committees *Appropriations* (2d). Subcommittees: Energy and Water Development; Foreign Operations; Interior and Related Agencies; Labor, HEW, and Related Agencies; State, Justice, Commerce, the Judiciary, and Related Agencies.

Energy and Natural Resources (Ranking Member). Subcommittees: Energy Regulation; Energy Research and Development; Parks, Recreation, and Renewable Resources.

Rules and Administration (Ranking Member).

Select Committee on Indian Affairs.

Group Ratings

	ADA	COPE	PC	RPN	NFU	LCV	CFA	NAB	NSI	ACA	NTU
1978	50	86	48	63	80	61	35	27	0	22	–
1977	60	37	30	91	83	–	24	–	–	36	45
1976	65	53	51	77	75	51	43	27	0	21	43

Key Votes

1) Warnke Nom	FOR	6) Egypt-Saudi Arms	AGN	11) Hosptl Cost Contnmnt	AGN
2) Neutron Bomb	AGN	7) Draft Restr Pardon	FOR	12) Clinch River Reactor	AGN
3) Waterwy User Fee	AGN	8) Wheat Price Support	FOR	13) Pub Fin Cong Cmpgns	AGN
4) Dereg Nat Gas	FOR	9) Panama Canal Treaty	FOR	14) ERA Ratif Recissn	FOR
5) Kemp-Roth	AGN	10) Labor Law Rev Clot	FOR	15) Med Necssy Abrtns	AGN

Election Results

1978 general	Mark O. Hatfield (R)	550,165	(62%)	($223,874)
	Vernon Cook (D)	341,616	(38%)	($38,976)
1978 primary	Mark O. Hatfield (R)	159,617	(66%)	
	Bert W. Hawkins (R)	43,350	(18%)	($64,574)
	Two others (R)	39,922	(16%)	
1972 general	Mark O. Hatfield (R)	494,671	(54%)	($299,626)
	Wayne L. Morse (D)	425,036	(46%)	($251,904)

Sen. Bob Packwood (R) Elected 1968, seat up 1980; b. Sept. 11, 1932, Portland; home, Portland; Willamette U., B.S. 1954, New York U. LL.B. 1957; Unitarian.

Career Practicing atty., 1958–68; Oreg. House of Reps., 1962–68.

Offices 1321 DSOB, 202-224-5244. Also 1002 N.E. Holladay St., P.O. Box 3621, Portland 97208, 503-233-4471.

Committees *Budget* (3d).

Commerce, Science, and Transportation (Ranking Member). Subcommittee: Merchant Marine and Tourism.

Finance (2d). Subcommittees: Taxation and Debt Management Generally; Social Security; Revenue Sharing, Intergovernmental Revenue Impact, and Economic Problems.

Select Committee on Small Business (2d).

Group Ratings

	ADA	COPE	PC	RPN	NFU	LCV	CFA	NAB	NSI	ACA	NTU
1978	45	69	25	88	70	41	20	33	30	41	–
1977	45	63	20	91	73	–	28	–	–	42	29
1976	45	25	46	100	75	65	35	50	30	40	54

Key Votes

1) Warnke Nom	AGN	6) Egypt-Saudi Arms	AGN	11) Hosptl Cost Contnmnt	AGN
2) Neutron Bomb	FOR	7) Draft Restr Pardon	AGN	12) Clinch River Reactor	FOR
3) Waterwy User Fee	AGN	8) Wheat Price Support	FOR	13) Pub Fin Cong Cmpgns	AGN
4) Dereg Nat Gas	FOR	9) Panama Canal Treaty	FOR	14) ERA Ratif Recissn	FOR
5) Kemp-Roth	FOR	10) Labor Law Rev Clot	FOR	15) Med Necssy Abrtns	FOR

Election Results

1974 general	Robert W. Packwood (R)	420,984	(55%)	($333,004)
	Betty Roberts (D)	338,591	(45%)	($80,193)
1974 primary	Robert W. Packwood (R), unopposed			
1968 general	Robert W. Packwood (R)	408,825	(50%)	
	Wayne L. Morse (D)	405,380	(50%)	

Gov. Victor G. Atiyeh (R) Elected 1978, term expires Jan. 1983; b. Feb. 20, 1923, Portland; U. of Oreg.

Career Pres., Atiyeh Bros. Rug business; Oreg. House of Reps., 1959–65; Oreg. Senate, 1965–69.

Offices 207 State Capitol, Salem 97310, 503-378-3100.

Election Results

1978 general	Victor Atiyeh (R)	498,452	(55%)
	Robert W. Straub (D)	409,411	(45%)
1978 primary	Victor Atiyeh (R)	115,593	(47%)
	Tom McCall (R)	83,568	(34%)
	Three others (R)	48,850	(20%)
1974 general	Robert W. Straub (D)	444,812	(58%)
	Victor Atiyeh (R)	324,751	(42%)

FIRST DISTRICT

The 1st congressional district of Oregon occupies the northwest corner of the state. It includes the area around the mouth of the Columbia River and the coastal counties of Clatsop, Tillamook, and Lincoln. The countryside here still has frontier ambience to it: rain falls constantly on the weathered frame houses, and men in plaid flannel jackets work in lumber mills or on docks. The towns have an unfinished look to them—a part of Oregon which would still like some economic development. The 1st also includes part of the Willamette Valley south of Portland. This is mostly farm land, and it is more staid, settled looking territory, and has been since this area was settled by New England Yankees more than a century ago.

That is the historical 1st district. More recently, most of the population could be found in the metropolitan Portland area. The district includes the part of the city of Portland west of the Willamette River. Geographically it is the smaller part of the city; there is only a little flat land before the hills start to rise. But the district includes both the downtown business section and the affluent neighborhoods in the hills overlooking it. About one-quarter of the district's population is in Washington County, the suburban area directly west of Portland. This is an affluent area where the hills move into the Coast Range; its population increased rapidly during the sixties and seventies. It is the sort of place where people resent both despoliation of the environment and high property taxes.

The district was created in almost its present form in 1892, and for 82 years thereafter it always elected Republican congressmen. The progressive era, the depression of the thirties, the Goldwater debacle—through all these events the 1st district stayed with the Republicans. Time after time the Yankee-descended Republicans of the Willamette Valley outvoted the lumbermen of the coastal area.

That changed in 1974. The district had been moving toward the Democrats in most non-congressional elections. The environmental and Vietnam war issues worked for Democrats in the highly educated parts of Portland and Washington County. The enfranchisement of the 14,000 students at Oregon State University in Corvallis in the early seventies initially benefited the Democrats. Watergate hurt the Republicans in this state which has never seen major political scandal. And in 1974 the Republican who represented the district for ten years decided to retire.

The new Democratic Congressman, Les AuCoin, seems tailor made for the district. At 28 he had been elected to the legislature from Washington County, and after one term had become House Majority Leader. So he had home base appeal in the affluent suburbs which might otherwise go Republican. He had good credentials on environmental issues. He was against the Vietnam war. And he backed traditional Democratic positions on economic issues without alienating traditional Republicans.

AuCoin has seemed to grow more popular since he was first elected. His service on the Banking, Housing, and Urban Affairs Committee is significant for the district, for the state of the housing market is the key variable for Oregon's important lumber industry. On the Merchant Marine and Fisheries Committee he supports subsidies to Oregon's maritime industry and unions, and he has been promoting increased trade between the Pacific Northwest and mainland China. He has emphasized environmental issues which continue to be very important in this part of Oregon. AuCoin has been reelected with increasing margins every two years, even though his 1978 opponent launched a major campaign. He seems to be in strong shape for continued tenure in the 1st district—or possibly for a statewide post, such as Robert Packwood's Senate seat, which is up in 1980.

Census Data Pop. 523,428. Central city, 15%; suburban, 48%. Median family income, $10,430; families above $15,000: 24%; families below $3,000: 8%. Median years education, 12.5.

The Voters

Median voting age 43.
Employment profile White collar, 54%. Blue collar, 30%. Service, 13%. Farm, 3%.
Ethnic groups Spanish, 2%. Total foreign stock, 16%. Canada, 3%; Germany, UK, 2% each.

Presidential vote

1976	Carter (D)	127,470	(45%)
	Ford (R)	156,920	(55%)
1972	Nixon (R)	137,345	(57%)
	McGovern (D)	101,616	(43%)

Rep. Les AuCoin (D) Elected 1974; b. Oct. 21, 1942, Portland; home, Forest Grove; Pacific U., B.A. 1969.

Career Army, 1961–64; Newsman, Portland *Oregonian*, 1965–66; Dir, of Public Info. and Publications, Pacific U., 1966–73; Oreg. House of Reps., 1971–75, Maj. Ldr., 1973–75; Administrator, Skidmore, Owings, and Merrill, engineering firm, 1973–74.

Offices 231 CHOB, 202-225-0855. Also 1716 Fed. Bldg., 1220 SW 3rd Ave., Portland 97204, 503-221-2901.

Committees *Banking, Finance and Urban Affairs* (17th). Subcommittees: Housing and Community Development; International Trade, Investment and Monetary Policy; International Development Institutions and Finance.

Merchant Marine and Fisheries (13th). Subcommittees: Fish and Wildlife; Maritime Education and Training (Chairman). Oceanography.

Group Ratings

	ADA	COPE	PC	RPN	NFU	LCV	CFA	NAB	NSI	ACA	NTU
1978	40	60	58	50	40	–	41	17	38	40	–
1977	65	90	65	45	50	65	65	–	–	35	45
1976	70	61	64	65	64	64	45	33	30	22	40

Key Votes

1) Increase Def Spnd	AGN	6) Alaska Lands Protect	DNV	11) Delay Auto Pol Cntrl	AGN
2) B-1 Bomber	AGN	7) Water Projects Veto	AGN	12) Sugar Price Escalator	AGN
3) Cargo Preference	FOR	8) Consum Protect Agcy	FOR	13) Pub Fin Cong Cmpgns	FOR
4) Dereg Nat Gas	FOR	9) Common Situs Picket	FOR	14) ERA Ratif Recissn	AGN
5) Kemp-Roth	AGN	10) Labor Law Revision	FOR	15) Prohibt Govt Abrtns	AGN

Election Results

1978 general	Les AuCoin (D)	158,706	(63%)	($236,313)
	Nick Bunick (R)	93,640	(37%)	($297,719)
1978 primary	Les AuCoin (D), unopposed			
1976 general	Les AuCoin (D)	154,844	(59%)	($132,330)
	Phil Bladine (R)	109,140	(41%)	($94,547)

SECOND DISTRICT

The 2d congressional district of Oregon contains 73% of the state's land area and 25% of its population. Most of the land lies east of the Cascade Mountains. To the south, the terrain is desert-like; to the north, where rain falls in more generous amounts, one finds much of Oregon's vast forests and timber industry. Oregon east of the Cascades is a sparsely populated region, with some 270,000 people in an area the size of New England. Before 1965, the 2d district was entirely east of the Cascades; it was therefore far short of the equal population requirement. So redistricting added the counties of Marion (Salem) and Linn (Albany) west of the mountains. After the 1970 Census, redistricting also added a few suburbs of Portland.

All of this line drawing failed to change the political complexion of the 2d very much. East Oregon is marginal political territory, where traditional Rocky Mountain populism on economic issues—the area was long keen on public power development—has been overcome in recent years by the mountain country's dislike for the intrusive federal government and for some extreme environmental enthusiasts. It is an area which has been trending Republican. The portion of the district west of the mountains, originally settled by New England Yankees, has been traditionally Republican. But on issues like the environment and the Vietnam war, it has been trending toward the Democrats during the seventies. Overall the two trends tend to cancel each other out.

The 2d district elects one of the major committee chairmen in the House, Al Ullman of Ways and Means. First elected in 1956, he came to the House as a fiery liberal; since then, like his constituents in east Oregon, he has become considerably more conservative. During the sixties, as a representative of a lumber district, he was suspicious of much of the environmental movement; as a loyal Democrat, he was slow to oppose American involvement in Vietnam; as one who accumulated considerable seniority, he was not particularly sympathetic to procedural reforms.

Ullman is inevitably compared with the man from whom he inherited the Ways and Means chair after the 1974 election, Wilbur Mills. Washington had been convinced for a long time that Ways and Means handled such complicated stuff that only a wizard like Mills could understand it, and that its subject matter was so sensitive that the economy would suffer if anyone less subtle should head the committee. Ullman has put these fears to rest. Of course he does not have the near-dictatorial powers that Mills once enjoyed. Ways and Means now has working subcommittees with knowledgeable chairmen who command respect in their own right. Committee bills are no longer automatically protected from amendment on the floor as they were during Mills's day. Of course the chairman can no longer delay action by simply refusing to convene the committee. Finally, Ullman does not have the cozy relationships with newspaper columnists which, in retrospect, seem to have been one secret of Mills's mystique.

Nevertheless Ullman is still criticized for having been less than universally successful in securing the passage of legislation he favors. But it is not clear that any chairman could do much better. Ways and Means continues to handle difficult and controversial legislation—tax cuts, Social Security (which includes rises in taxes), health care financing. No consensus exists in the House. While some members push for progressive tax reform (i.e., closing loopholes, taxing the rich at higher rates), others push for greater incentives and lower capital gains taxes (which fall primarily on the rich). During the 95th Congress majorities seemed to favor both of these proposals. Social Security taxes were increased in 1977 to keep the system fiscally sound; as soon as that was done, however, many who had voted for the measure turned around and tried to repeal it.

It is little wonder then that Ullman sometimes appears nervous and uncertain in public appearances. He is accountable to colleagues who are not always predictable or consistent. He cooperates sometimes with the Carter Administration, but does not hesitate on occasion to oppose it, as for example on its proposal for a wage insurance as part of its anti-inflation program. For all his difficult problems, Ullman is in no danger of losing the Ways and Means chair, nor does he appear to face any significant political difficulty in his home district. He is solidly entrenched in east Oregon, and the 2d district as a whole seems pleased to have such an important congressman.

Census Data Pop. 522,898. Central city, 12%; suburban, 29%. Median family income, $8,821; families above $15,000: 14%; families below $3,000: 11%. Median years education, 12.2.

The Voters

Median voting age 45.
Employment profile White collar, 43%. Blue collar, 34%. Service, 14%. Farm, 9%.
Ethnic groups Spanish, 2%. Total foreign stock, 12%. Canada, Germany, 2% each; UK, 1%.

Presidential vote

1976	Carter (D)	118,067	(49%)
	Ford (R)	124,596	(51%)
1972	Nixon (R)	123,857	(60%)
	McGovern (D)	81,195	(40%)

Rep. Al Ullman (D) Elected 1956; b. Mar. 9, 1914, Great Falls, Mont.; home, Baker; Whitman Col., A.B. 1935, Columbia U., M.A. 1939; Presbyterian.

Career Navy, WWII; Real estate broker and builder, 1945–56.

Offices 1136 LHOB, 202-225-5711. Also P.O. Box 247, Salem, 97308, 503-399-5724.

Committees *Ways and Means* (Chairman).

Group Ratings

	ADA	COPE	PC	RPN	NFU	LCV	CFA	NAB	NSI	ACA	NTU
1978	30	39	35	60	70	–	32	27	56	25	–
1977	65	82	55	36	75	60	45	–	–	12	16
1976	70	57	49	63	75	48	64	9	44	19	22

Key Votes

1) Increase Def Spnd	FOR	6) Alaska Lands Protect	DNV	11) Delay Auto Pol Cntrl	FOR
2) B-1 Bomber	AGN	7) Water Projects Veto	AGN	12) Sugar Price Escalator	AGN
3) Cargo Preference	DNV	8) Consum Protect Agcy	AGN	13) Pub Fin Cong Cmpgns	AGN
4) Dereg Nat Gas	AGN	9) Common Situs Picket	AGN	14) ERA Ratif Recissn	FOR
5) Kemp-Roth	AGN	10) Labor Law Revision	FOR	15) Prohibt Govt Abrtns	AGN

Election Results

1978 general	Al Ullman (D)	152,099	(69%)	($55,401)
	Terry L. Hicks (R)	67,547	(31%)	
1978 primary	Al Ullman (D), unopposed			
1976 general	Al Ullman (D)	173,313	(72%)	($20,854)
	Thomas H. Mercer (R)	67,431	(28%)	($366)

THIRD DISTRICT

Portland is Oregon's big city. Almost half of the people in the state live within its metropolitan area, and far more than half live within 60 miles of its downtown. The 3d congressional district of Oregon takes in most of Portland—the four-fifths of the city east of the Willamette River. The district also includes most of the Portland suburbs along the Willamette and Columbia Rivers. The 3d's eastern borders stretch to a point near the snow-covered peak of Mount Hood, which at 11,000 feet looks down on Portland's green streets and its famous roses.

Portland was founded by New England Yankees (it was nearly called Boston) and had its beginnings as a muscular blue collar town—the place where Oregon unloaded its supplies from the east, on the docks or in the railroad yards, and where it shipped out Oregon's products—lumber, fruit. Portland has gained the reputation of being an almost avant garde city, a place where ecology-minded young marrieds jog together in the mornings, eat health food for dinner, and pray at night that no one else moves to their city. There is some truth to this picture, but it tends to apply to suburbanites and Portland residents west of the Willamette, in the affluent hill areas. On the flat lands east of the river to Mount Hood live Portland's middle class, blue collar majority. They too have a positive feeling about Oregon's unique environment, but not to the exclusion of more conventional sentiments. The people here tend to be traditional Democrats, and the 3d district went for George McGovern in 1972 and Jimmy Carter in 1976.

The 3d district is ordinarily the most Democratic in Oregon. For 20 years, until her retirement in 1974, it was represented by Edith Green, originally an Adlai Stevenson Democrat. Her views on education and general cultural issues helped move her from supporting Robert Kennedy in 1968 to Henry Jackson in 1972 and Gerald Ford in 1976. Her successor is Robert Duncan, who had some previous experience in Congress. He had been elected in the 4th district in 1962 and 1964, and had run close Senate races in 1966 and 1972. These had been attended by great controversy because of his strong support of Lyndon Johnson's Vietnam war policies. But by 1974 the war had vanished as an issue, and Duncan was elected here without difficulty. With a seniority advantage over other freshmen, he won a seat on the Appropriations Committee. There he has attended closely to the needs of his district, sponsoring bills on the Mount Hood National Forest and seeking a veterans' hospital for Portland. In 1979 he became Chairman of the Transportation Subcommittee, an important post with national policy implications. Duncan seems politically secure; he has not had a Republican opponent in the last two elections.

Census Data Pop. 522,258. Central city, 59%; suburban, 41%. Median family income, $10,001; families above $15,000: 19%; families below $3,000: 8%. Median years education, 12.3.

The Voters

Median voting age 45.
Employment profile White collar, 51%. Blue collar, 34%. Service, 14%. Farm, 1%.
Ethnic groups Black, 4%. Spanish, 2%. Total foreign stock, 18%. Canada, 3%; Germany, UK, 2% each.

Presidential vote

1976	Carter (D)	115,564	(55%)
	Ford (R)	93,855	(45%)
1972	Nixon (R)	106,955	(48%)
	McGovern (D)	115,283	(52%)

Rep. Robert Duncan (D) Elected 1974; b. Dec. 4, 1920, Normal, Ill.; home, Gresham; U. of Alaska, 1939–40, Ill. Wesleyan U., B.A. 1942; U. of Mich., LL.B. 1948; Methodist.

Career Navy Air Force, WWII; Practicing atty., 1948–63, 1967–74; Oreg. House of Reps., 1957–63; U.S. House of Reps., 1963–67.

Offices 2458 RHOB, 202-225-4811. Also 1616 Fed. Bldg., 1220 S.W. Third, Portland 97204, 503-221-2123.

Committees *Appropriations* (23d). Subcommittees: Interior; Transportation (Chairman).

Group Ratings

	ADA	COPE	PC	RPN	NFU	LCV	CFA	NAB	NSI	ACA	NTU
1978	35	42	33	50	44	–	27	56	60	41	–
1977	50	86	43	33	64	35	40	–	–	25	20
1976	60	67	51	47	73	39	45	25	67	12	17

Key Votes

1) Increase Def Spnd	AGN	6) Alaska Lands Protect	AGN	11) Delay Auto Pol Cntrl	FOR
2) B-1 Bomber	FOR	7) Water Projects Veto	AGN	12) Sugar Price Escalator	AGN
3) Cargo Preference	FOR	8) Consum Protect Agcy	AGN	13) Pub Fin Cong Cmpgns	AGN
4) Dereg Nat Gas	AGN	9) Common Situs Picket	FOR	14) ERA Ratif Recissn	FOR
5) Kemp-Roth	AGN	10) Labor Law Revision	FOR	15) Prohibt Govt Abrtns	DNV

Election Results

1978 general	Robert B. Duncan (D)	151,895	(85%)	($38,318)
	Martin Simon (N-P)	27,120	(15%)	
1978 primary	Robert B. Duncan (D), unopposed			
1976 general	Robert B. Duncan (D)	148,503	(84%)	($7,232)
	Martin Simon (Ind.)	28,245	(16%)	($0)

FOURTH DISTRICT

The 4th congressional district of Oregon occupies the southwest corner of the state. Though the district contains about half of Oregon's rocky and picturesque Pacific coastline, most of its people can be found inland, in the southern end of the Willamette River valley between the Coast Range and the Cascade Mountains. As in most of the West, relatively few people actually live on farms here, though the area produces much of Oregon's famed fruit crop. Instead, most of the people live in small, well ordered cities like Medford, Grant's Pass, Roseburg, Coos Bay, and Springfield. The largest city here, with 76,000 people, is Eugene, the home of the University of Oregon.

As is the case throughout Oregon, the 4th district has no sharp extremes of political allegiance.

Eugene is more Democratic than the rest, particularly since students got the vote in 1972; the southern counties are somewhat more Republican. Overall, the political balance is close enough that party control of the district has changed six times in the last 25 years. In 1956 the district elected Charles Porter, a Democrat who was a strong peace advocate; he was retired by Republican Edwin Durno in 1960, who in turn lost to Democrat Robert Duncan in 1962. Duncan, now Congressman from the 3d district, ran for the Senate in 1966 and was succeeded in the House by John Dellenback, who was in turn beaten by Democrat James Weaver in 1974. Dellenback's defeat was a particular surprise, and points up a special difficulty incumbents have in holding this seat in an era when constituents expect their congressman to return home almost every weekend: there are no direct flights from Washington, and the quickest route involves eight hours of flying and connection time.

In his first term, Weaver won a seat on the Agriculture Committee, one of special importance to the district, because the Agriculture Department includes the Forestry Service, and this is one of the major lumber-producing districts in the nation. In 1977 Weaver became Chairman of the Forests Subcommittee—a position that makes him kind of a czar to the lumber industry.

Many congressmen, given an opportunity to endear themselves to a strong local economic interest, would have seized it gladly. Weaver, on the other hand, has not hesitated to antagonize the big lumber companies. He pushed through a timber bill that provides for sustained yields—less than many lumbermen wanted, because of restrictions on cutting to meet environmental concerns. He has worked to protect large wilderness areas. In a matter less controversial, he has moved to cut timber exports to Japan, so that American rather than Japanese mills can convert the logs into lumber.

These positions have guaranteed strong opposition to Weaver from major lumber companies. They have also given him a vehement opponent in Jerry Lausmann, a Medford plywood company owner who ran against him in 1976 and 1978. Lausmann charged that Weaver's lumber policies hurt the major industry in the district, but Weaver's environmental emphasis seems more popular, particularly in Eugene. Lausmann's strong conservative views on other issues did not help his cause much. Weaver won decisive victories in both reelection contests. But due to the nature of the district—and its distance from Washington—no future election here can be taken for granted.

Census Data Pop. 522,801. Central city, 15%; suburban, 26%. Median family income, $8,854; families above $15,000: 14%; families below $3,000: 10%. Median years education, 12.2.

The Voters

Median voting age 43.
Employment profile White collar, 43%. Blue collar, 40%. Service, 13%. Farm, 4%.
Ethnic groups Spanish, 1%. Total foreign stock, 11%. Canada, Germany, 2% each; UK, 1%.

Presidential vote

1976	Carter (D)	129,306	(58%)
	Ford (R)	116,717	(42%)
1972	Nixon (R)	117,977	(57%)
	McGovern (D)	94,456	(44%)

Rep. James Weaver (D) Elected 1974; b. Aug. 8, 1927, Brookings, S.D.; home, Eugene; U. of Oreg., B.S. 1952.

Career Navy, WWII; Publisher's Rep., Prentice-Hall Co., 1954–58; Staff Dir., Oreg. Legislative Interim Comm. on Agriculture, 1959–60; Builder and apartment complex developer, 1960–75.

Offices 1226 LHOB, 202-225-6416. Also Fed. Bldg., 211 E. 7th Ave., Eugene 97401, 503-687-6732.

Committees *Agriculture* (11th). Subcommittees:Conservation and Credit; Forests (Chairman).

Interior and Insular Affairs (11th). Subcommittees: Energy and the Environment; Public Lands; Oversight/Special Investigations; Water and Power Resources.

Group Ratings

	ADA	COPE	PC	RPN	NFU	LCV	CFA	NAB	NSI	ACA	NTU
1978	75	89	80	45	63	–	55	30	11	32	–
1977	85	95	73	33	82	70	70	–	–	8	43
1976	95	86	85	53	82	93	81	18	10	8	37

Key Votes

1) Increase Def Spnd	AGN	6) Alaska Lands Protect	FOR	11) Delay Auto Pol Cntrl	AGN
2) B-1 Bomber	AGN	7) Water Projects Veto	FOR	12) Sugar Price Escalator	DNV
3) Cargo Preference	FOR	8) Consum Protect Agcy	FOR	13) Pub Fin Cong Cmpgns	FOR
4) Dereg Nat Gas	AGN	9) Common Situs Picket	FOR	14) ERA Ratif Recissn	AGN
5) Kemp-Roth	AGN	10) Labor Law Revision	FOR	15) Prohibt Govt Abrtns	AGN

Election Results

1978 general	James Weaver (D)	124,745	(56%)	($178,950)
	Jerry S. Lausmann (R)	96,953	(44%)	($206,613)
1978 primary	James Weaver (D)	45,997	(60%)	
	Robert Earl Wood (D)	17,124	(22%)	($33,586)
	One other (D)	13,962	(18%)	
1976 general	James Weaver (D)	122,475	(50%)	($73,589)
	Jerry S. Lausmann (R)	85,943	(35%)	($112,483)
	Jim Howard (Ind.)	22,104	(9%)	($14,399)
	Theodore Nathan (Ind.)	14,307	(6%)	($9,968)

PENNSYLVANIA

Pennsylvania is called the Keystone State, and it is an apt nickname: the commonwealth connects New York and New England with the rest of the nation. Two hundred years ago, the geography of Pennsylvania promised to make it the commercial and transportation hub of the country, and it was the most populous state of the new nation. But the rugged mountains of central Pennsylvania stalled the early development of transportation arteries west. It was New York City, rather than Philadelphia, which mushroomed in the middle nineteenth century, thanks to the building of the Erie Canal and the first water level railroad line. In 1776 Philadelphia was the nation's capital and largest city. Within fifty years it was eclipsed by Washington in government and by New York in commerce, and rivalled by Boston in culture. Philadelphia is still the nation's fourth metropolitan area in size and Pittsburgh is tenth, but neither looms as large in the national consciousness as seemed likely when the Declaration of Independence was signed.

During the nineteenth century, Pennsylvania had remarkable growth—but for reasons not anticipated by the founders. It became the energy capital of the United States, much as Texas is today, and the industrial center as well. The key to all this was coal—Pennsylvania probably has enough coal to supply all the nation's needs even today. Northeastern Pennsylvania was the nation's primary source of anthracite, the hard coal used for home heating; and western Pennsylvania was the major source for bituminous coal, the soft coal used in producing steel and other industrial products. As a result, the area around Pittsburgh had become the center of the steel industry by 1890. Immigrants poured into the state to work the mines and the factories, and the very name Pittsburgh became synonymous with industrial prosperity. During this period Pennsylvania was the nation's second largest state, and growing rapidly.

The boom ended conclusively with the depression of the thirties, and in much of Pennsylvania good times have never returned. The coal industry collapsed after World War II, as both home heating and industry switched to oil. Today, while coal has become more important, its mining is far less labor-intensive; and the population of coal mining communities continues its downward trend. Pennsylvania steel is no longer a growth industry. Steelmakers here chose to ignore technological advances after World War II, and the state's ancient steel mills are far less efficient than those built in postwar Germany or Japan or even the new mills that have been constructed in some parts of the United States. By the early seventies the industry seemed to have thrown in the towel, joining with the United Steelworkers to push for import restrictions on foreign steel. A century ago, the steel producers made Pennsylvania the classic high tariff state, arguing for protection for its "infant" industries; now, by backing trade restrictions; they seem to be conceding that their industry has grown senile.

These economic developments have left Pennsylvania in rather sorry shape. People growing up here have been as likely to leave the state as stay, while out-of-staters show little inclination to move in. Compared to the growth areas of the Sun Belt, the cities and small towns of Pennsylvania give the traveler a sense of having gone back thirty or forty years in time; one can see here both the suburb where John Updike lived as a boy and the gritty coal town where John O'Hara grew up, little changed. In 1930, after its last decade of prosperity, Pennsylvania recorded 9.5 million residents; today the number stands at 11.8 million—by far the smallest growth rate of the nation's biggest states. So once the nation's second largest state, by the middle seventies, Pennsylvania has slipped behind California, New York, and the new energy capital of Texas. This sluggish growth has had important political consequences. As recently as 1950, Pennsylvania had 32 seats in the House of Representatives; today it has only 25.

Traditionally Pennsylvania was heavily Republican, the most Republican of all big states. It was for Lincoln and Union, for the steel industry and the high tariff, and in 1932 it was the only big state that went for Herbert Hoover over Franklin Roosevelt. For years Philadelphia was governed not by a Democratic, but by a Republican machine, which held onto the mayor's office until reformer (and later Senator) Joseph Clark won it in 1951. In the industrial cities of northeast and western Pennsylvania, it was the Republicans, not the Democrats, who organized and won the votes of the workingmen, both immigrant and native. This was not class politics—though there were some primary fights between progressives and conservatives—so much as it was consensus politics, all elements of Pennsylvania standing under the same party banner.

All that changed with the depression and the New Deal. Since then Pennsylvania has been a classically marginal state. The central part of the state—the Welsh railroad workers in Altoona and the Pennsylvania Dutch farmers around Lancaster—remains the strongest Republican voting bloc in the East, and if metropolitan Philadelphia has become Democratic in most elections, Republicans are still definitely competitive there. Pennsylvania's great blue collar enclaves—greater Pittsburgh and the whole western end of the state and the northeast region around Scranton, Wilkes-Barre, Allentown, Bethlehem, and Reading—are now Democratic bulwarks. These are the places that organized labor, especially the United Steelworkers, exerts most of its political influence.

Pennsylvania had always been a political machine state, and to some extent it remains one. Fifteen years ago the state government still had 50,000 patronage employees, appointed for the most part by county political parties. That number was whittled down under recent governors, from Republican William Scranton (1963-67) to Democrat Milton Shapp (1971-79), who had little use for such largesse. But Pennsylvania politics still has a crass, practical tone to it. It has also had more than its share of corruption, notably under Milton Shapp. A self-made millionaire who won the Democratic nomination with his own money, Shapp did not owe his party's leaders anything. Nonetheless he had a weakness for reposing trust in people who did not deserve it. Shapp had some undoubted achievements. He increased taxes when that needed to be done in the early seventies, he appointed some strong consumer champions, and he helped to attract Volkswagen to build a plant in western Pennsylvania—the state's first auto assembly plant. He won a second term in 1974, even if his 1976 presidential campaign got little support. But when his last term expired—he could not seek a third—Pennsylvania voters were mainly interested in ridding the state of corruption and political cronyism.

Both parties' 1978 nominees had good credentials for that. Democrat Peter Flaherty had served eight years as Pittsburgh's Mayor as an opponent of the party leadership and a ruthless cutter of expenses. He seemed the perfect candidate for 1978, and he was the early leader. But his own pledge to accept no special interest contributions left him with only a small campaign budget and a makeshift campaign (his wife was his scheduler). Much better financed was Republican Richard Thornburgh, a former Pittsburgh federal prosecutor and U.S. Deputy Attorney General. Thornburgh was a tough prosecutor who concentrated much of his efforts on Democrats. He began the campaign little known, but he got large contributions from Senator John Heinz and his family, and beat Philadelphia-based Arlen Specter in the primary. In the general, one tactic that helped him win were TV ads attacking Flaherty's record as mayor; but because of Flaherty's home town popularity, he wisely avoided running them in the Pittsburgh media market. Flaherty had enough strength in the area covered by the Pittsburgh television stations to make a race of it, although he did rather poorly in the high income suburbs around Pittsburgh itself. Meanwhile, Thornburgh carried almost all the rest of the state, losing Philadelphia but capturing its suburbs by a larger margin, and winning in most of the industrial areas of the east and northeast.

In Thornburgh, Pennsylvanians have a Governor who is both a strong partisan and impeccably honest. And he seems to have the strength of character and determination necessary to run a clean administration. How he will do on other fronts is less clear. This is a state that needs economic rejuvenation. Its plethora of small towns and mountain ridges may be more of an advantage today now that people are leaving our major metropolitan areas; and its location is still central for the part of the country where most people still live.

Thornburgh's election completed a Republican sweep of the state's top offices, as Republicans have held both of Pennsylvania's Senate seats for more than ten years now. Both senators are comparatively young, both are generally regarded as liberal Republicans, and each has an entirely different political base. The better known of the two is the senior Senator, Richard Schweiker—who, however, was entirely unknown outside of Pennsylvania until he was named as Ronald Reagan's choice for the vice presidency shortly before the 1976 Republican National Convention. Schweiker's selection was part of a Reagan plan to force Ford to come up with his own VP choice, and presumably to antagonize some part of his fragile coalition in the process. Instead it was the Reagan coalition that was affected. Schweiker's 100% labor voting record—an advantage when he ran for a second Senate term in 1974—enraged many Reagan supporters and lost him some delegates in the South. At the same time, the aloof Schweiker could not move a significant number of Pennsylvania delegates to Reagan.

Schweiker insisted that his decision to support Reagan involved no surrender of his own principles—and in one sense he was right. For this is a politician who had made a sharp shift once before. As a suburban Philadelphia Congressman in the sixties, he had a conventional Republican record. He ran for the Senate in 1968 and won, profitting from Joseph Clark's problems with gun owners and Italian-Americans. With a statewide constituency, Schweiker blossomed into a Republican liberal, with strong COPE and ADA records. In the same spirit, he worked hard for the interests of the coal and steel industries. Suddenly given the possibility of a national constituency, Schweiker adapted again and embraced Reagan—the only way he could ever get a nomination from a Republican national convention.

After 1976 Schweiker's voting record in the Senate veered to the right, leaving his labor record around 50%. But his latest ideological switch, made in the national spotlight, failed to impress conservative Republicans nationally and undermined his position in Pennsylvania with his former allies. Schweiker had national ambitions, with no means of fulfilling them; and in early 1979 he declared that he would not run for reelection to the Senate in 1980. His decision leaves his seat very much up for grabs. Among the Republicans who might be interested are Arlen Specter, former Philadelphia District Attorney who has twice lost close statewide primaries, Congressman Marc Marks, and possibly David Marston, the former U.S. Attorney whose firing by Jimmy Carter was a cause celebre; among the Democrats are Peter Flaherty, who lost to Schweiker in 1974 and Thornburgh in 1978; Robert Casey, the former state Auditor; and two 1974 freshman Congressmen, Peter Kostmayer and Robert Edgar. Unlikely to run is former Congressman William Green, who nearly beat John Heinz in the 1976 Senate race and who, at this writing, seems likely to succeed Frank Rizzo as Mayor of Philadelphia in 1979. Green lost to Rizzo in

1971, ushering in a period of name-calling, brawling politics. Green's election would represent a triumph not only of liberalism, but of civility.

Looking at the returns from several of Pennsylvania's statewide general elections and primaries, you might be excused for supposing that all the real battles were not so much between Republicans and Democrats, liberals and conservatives, as they were between Philadelphia and Pittsburgh. It is almost as if the question is whether the Phillies or the Pirates were to represent the state in the World Series. In the 1974 Senate race the Republican was from the Philadelphia area (Schweiker) and the Democrat from Pittsburgh (Flaherty); in 1976 it was the other way around, with Philadelphia's William Green facing Pittsburgh's John Heinz. But in both cases the winners won largely because of unusually large margins in their home areas—and despite large margins for their opponents in their home areas.

Heinz and Green had a number of superficial similarities. Both were the sons of famous fathers: Heinz is from the 57 Varieties family, and Green's father was Democratic City Chairman in Philadelphia as well as Congressman until his death in 1964. Both had inherited valuable political assets: Green was elected to Congress at 25 after his father's death, while Heinz had a personal fortune of $12 million which, after the Supreme Court decision on the campaign finance law in 1976, he was free to spend on his own campaign. Both were 38, tall, dark, handsome, and both had attractive wives and three children; and while Green's voting record ranked higher on liberal indexes, Heinz could not be characterized fairly as anything but a liberal Republican. It was a closely fought election in which Heinz's earlier and bigger media buy—made possible by his personal money—probably made the difference.

Heinz seems to be specializing in money matters. In his first two years in the Senate he sat on the Budget Committee, and in the second he won a seat on the Finance Committee; he sits as well on the Banking Committee. His voting record has been as expected—slightly more acceptable to the liberal than the conservative-oriented groups. However, more than most Democrats he believes in the market mechanism and has doubts about the place of government in it. Heinz's name is not connected with any major piece of legislation, but he has floor managed his share of bills. He is said to have some ambition for national office, but that seems to lie rather far ahead—at least until after he faces the voters in Pennsylvania again in 1982.

Pennsylvania was one of the key states in the 1976 presidential election, when Jimmy Carter carried it with 51%. He had a 2-1 edge in Philadelphia and small margins in metro Pittsburgh, the west, and the northeast—the standard Democratic areas. It can be noted that without Pennsylvania's 27 electoral votes, Carter would have had 270—precisely the number needed to win.

But even more important to Carter was his victory in Pennsylvania's presidential primary. This contest, coming in late April after the first round of primaries and before the bunch in May and early June, was a shootout between the three Democrats who had survived the early contests: Carter, Henry Jackson, and Morris Udall. Pennsylvania was not Udall's kind of state—there are few of the well-to-do suburbs and university towns where he won his biggest percentages—but it was thought to be Jackson's. He had the support of organized labor, although it was expressed in such ham-handed terms that it may have hurt more than it helped. And he had the endorsement of Mayor Rizzo and the Philadelphia machine—which carried him Philadelphia and nothing else. Carter, through his advertisements and television reports of his campaigning, was able to speak over the heads of the putative bosses and to win enough votes for a solid victory. It was decisive, as it turned out. Carter did not do especially well after Pennsylvania, but he was able to accumulate enough delegates to give him a majority at the National Convention in July.

Census Data Pop. 11,793,909; 5.83% of U.S. total, 3d largest; Central city, 29%; suburban, 51%. Median family income, $9,554; 20th highest; families above $15,000: 18%; families below $3,000: 8%. Median years education, 12.0.

1977 Share of Federal Tax Burden $19,447,000,000; 5.63% of U.S. total, 4th largest.

1977 Share of Federal Outlays $19,204,998,000; 4.86% of U.S. total, 4th largest. Per capita federal spending, $1,624.

DOD	$3,515,223,000	5th (3.85%)	HEW	$8,959,374,000	3d (6.06%)
ERDA	$250,322,000	10th (4.24%)	HUD	$284,706,000	3d (6.75%)
NASA	$58,649,000	10th (1.49%)	VA	$911,934,000	4th (4.75%)
DOT	$399,944,000	12th (2.80%)	EPA	$490,968,000	4th (5.99%)
DOC	$320,438,000	8th (3.86%)	RevS	$457,293,000	4th (5.41%)
DOI	$90,970,000	16th (1.96%)	Debt	$831,074,000	5th (2.77%)
USDA	$479,256,000	12th (2.41%)	Other	$2,154,847,000	

Economic Base Primary metal industries, especially blast furnaces and steel mills; finance, insurance and real estate; apparel and other textile products, especially women's and misses' outerwear; machinery; electrical equipment and supplies, especially electronic components and accessories; fabricated metal products, especially fabricated structural metal products; food and kindred products, especially bakery products.

Political Line-up Governor, Richard L. Thornburgh (R). Senators, Richard S. Schweiker (R) and H. John Heinz III (R). Representatives, 25 (15 D and 10 R). State Senate (27 D, 22 R, and 1 vacancy); State House (103 R and 100 D).

The Voters

Registration 5,796,510 Total. 3,224,953 D (56%); 2,321,807 R (40%); 249,750 Constitutional and Other (%).
Median voting age 45
Employment profile White collar, 45%. Blue collar, 42%. Service, 12%. Farm, 1%.
Ethnic groups Black, 9%. Total foreign stock, 18%. Italy, 4%; Poland, Germany, UK, 2% each; USSR, Austria, Czechoslovakia, Ireland, 1% each.

Presidential vote

1976	Carter (D)	2,328,677	(51%)
	Ford (R)	2,205,604	(49%)
1972	Nixon (R)	2,714,521	(60%)
	McGovern (D)	1,796,951	(40%)

1976 Democratic Presidential Primary

Carter	511,905	(37%)
Jackson	340,340	(25%)
Udall	259,166	(19%)
Others	268,599	(19%)

1976 Republican Presidential Primary

Ford	733,472	(95%)
Reagan	40,510	(5%)

Sen. Richard S. Schweiker (R) Elected 1968, seat up 1980; b. June 1, 1926, Norristown; home, Worcester; Penn St. U., B.A. 1950; Central Schwenkfelder Church.

Career Navy, WWII; Business Exec., 1950–60; U.S. House of Reps., 1961–69.

Offices 253 RSOB, 202-224-4254. Also 2001 Fed. Bldg., Pittsburgh 15222, 412-644-3499, and 600 Arch St., Philadelphia 19106, 215-597-7200.

Committees *Appropriations* (5th). Subcommittees: Defense; Energy and Water Development; Foreign Operations; Labor, HEW, and Related Agencies; Legislative Branch.

Labor and Human Resources (Ranking Member). Subcommittees: Handicapped; Education, Arts, and Humanities; Health and Scientific Research.

Rules and Administration (4th).

Group Ratings

	ADA	COPE	PC	RPN	NFU	LCV	CFA	NAB	NSI	ACA	NTU
1978	20	63	38	70	50	35	35	50	90	59	–
1977	15	47	35	82	50	–	52	–	–	56	35
1976	80	91	75	71	88	74	93	8	22	16	41

Key Votes

1) Warnke Nom	AGN	6) Egypt-Saudi Arms	AGN	11) Hosptl Cost Contnmnt	AGN
2) Neutron Bomb	FOR	7) Draft Restr Pardon	AGN	12) Clinch River Reactor	FOR
3) Waterwy User Fee	AGN	8) Wheat Price Support	AGN	13) Pub Fin Cong Cmpgns	AGN
4) Dereg Nat Gas	FOR	9) Panama Canal Treaty	AGN	14) ERA Ratif Recissn	AGN
5) Kemp-Roth	FOR	10) Labor Law Rev Clot	FOR	15) Med Necssy Abrtns	AGN

Election Results

1974 general	Richard S. Schweiker (R)	1,843,317	(54%)	($799,499)
	Pete Flaherty (D)	1,596,121	(46%)	($256,483)
1974 primary	Richard S. Schweiker (R), unopposed			
1968 general	Richard S. Schweiker (R)	2,399,762	(53%)	
	Joseph S. Clark (D)	2,117,662	(47%)	

Sen. H. John Heinz III (R) Elected 1976, seat up 1982; b. Oct. 23, 1938, Pittsburgh; home, Pittsburgh; Yale U., B.A., Harvard U., M.B.A. 1963; Episcopalian.

Career Marketing, H.J. Heinz Co., Pittsburgh, 1965–70; Sales Rep., Internatl. Harvester, Australia; Special Asst. to U.S. Sen. Hugh Scott, 1964; U.S. House of Reps., 1971–77.

Offices 4327 DSOB, 202-224-6324. Also 9456 Wm. J. Green, Jr. Fed. Bldg., 4th and Arch Sts., Philadelphia 19106, 215-925-8750, and 2031 Fed. Bldg., Pittsburgh 15222, 412-562-0533.

Committees *Banking, Housing, and Urban Affairs* (3d). Subcommittees: Housing and Urban Affairs; Financial Institutions; International Finance.

Finance (6th). Subcommittees: International Trade; Public Assistance; Oversight of the Internal Revenue Service.

Group Ratings

	ADA	COPE	PC	RPN	NFU	LCV	CFA	NAB	NSI	ACA	NTU
1978	60	78	50	80	38	66	40	8	40	18	–
1977	50	65	55	80	50	–	64	–	–	31	37
1976	30	67	56	79	56	53	45	27	80	79	29

Key Votes

1) Warnke Nom	AGN	6) Egypt-Saudi Arms	AGN	11) Hosptl Cost Contnmnt	AGN
2) Neutron Bomb	AGN	7) Draft Restr Pardon	FOR	12) Clinch River Reactor	FOR
3) Waterwy User Fee	AGN	8) Wheat Price Support	AGN	13) Pub Fin Cong Cmpgns	AGN
4) Dereg Nat Gas	FOR	9) Panama Canal Treaty	FOR	14) ERA Ratif Recissn	FOR
5) Kemp-Roth	FOR	10) Labor Law Rev Clot	FOR	15) Med Necssy Abrtns	FOR

Election Results

1976 general	John Heinz III (R)	2,381,891	(53%)	($3,004,814)
	William Green (D)	2,126,977	(47%)	($1,269,409)
1976 primary	John Heinz III (R)	358,715	(42%)	
	Arlen Specter (R)	332,513	(39%)	
	George Packard (R)	160,379	(19%)	
1970 general	Hugh Scott (R)	1,874,106	(53%)	
	William G. Sesler (D)	1,653,774	(47%)	

Gov. Richard L. Thornburgh (R) Elected 1978, term expires 1983; b. July 16, 1932, Pittsburgh; Yale U., B.S. 1954, U. of Pitt., LL.B. 1957; Episcopalian.

Career Atty., and advisor, ALCOA, 1957–59; Practicing atty., 1959–69; U.S. Atty. for Western Pa., 1969–75; Asst. U.S. Atty. Gen., U.S. Dept. of Justice, 1975–77.

Offices Main Capitol, Harrisburg 17120, 717-787-2121.

Election Results

1978 general	Richard Thornburgh (R)	1,966,042	(53%)
	Pete Flaherty (D)	1,737,888	(47%)
1978 primary	Richard Thornburgh (R)	323,349	(32%)
	Arlen Specter (R)	206,802	(21%)
	Bob Butera (R)	190,653	(19%)
	David W. Marston (R)	161,813	(16%)
	Three others (R)	113,373	(11%)
1974 general	Milton Shapp (D)	1,878,252	(54%)
	Andrew L. Lewis (R)	1,578,917	(46%)

FIRST DISTRICT

The 1st district of Pennsylvania is the southern end of the city of Philadelphia. The Schuylkill River divides the district into two just about equal parts. On the west bank is the University of Pennsylvania and, beyond the campus, the West Philadelphia black ghetto. On the east side of the river is the heavily Italian-American neighborhood of South Philadelphia, the probable home of "Rocky," the fantasy heavyweight fighter. This has always been the stronghold of Mayor Frank Rizzo, the first politician of Italian descent in Philadelphia to achieve prominence and a kind of folk hero in these parts for his spirited opposition to blacks and intellectual liberals.

Back during the Kennedy years of the early sixties, both South and West Philadelphia voted heavily Democratic. But in the late sixties and early seventies, as black areas were voting Democratic with near unanimity, South Philadelphia shifted to the right. Rizzo began his police career here and achieved considerable prominence; he rose enough in society to attend events in black tie, but he was still proud enough of his background as a tough cop to wear a billy club in his cummerbund. Rizzo was elected Mayor in 1971 and reelected over weak opposition in 1975. Long before his second term ended, Rizzo was besmirched with scandal; and though he kept South Philadelphia's loyalty to the end, he could not get the city's voters to change the charter to allow him to run for a third term.

The 1st district was represented from 1949 until his death in 1976 by William Barrett. He cut an unobtrusive figure in Washington, though he became a high ranking member of the Banking Committee. He was best known for his red hairpiece and for his practice of returning home to Philadelphia every night and holding office hours from 9 to 1. Here, as he told one reporter, he tried to solve problems "on marital matters, child welfare, foreclosures, evictions—everything that affects the human person."

Barrett was renominated after his death in 1976, which gave the Philadelphia Democratic organization the right to name the nominee. That meant that Frank Rizzo made the new congressman, and the man he chose was South Philadelphia legislator Ozzie Myers. A former cargo checker on the Philadelphia waterfront, he was a solid Rizzo loyalist. It is not clear yet, however, whether Myers has a solid hold on the seat. In the 1978 primary six candidates ran against him and held him to less than 50% of the vote; none came close, but if this were the South, he would have had a runoff. Whether he will have strong opposition in 1980 is unclear; Philadelphia politics is in flux with Rizzo's departure. Myers got some unfavorable publicity in early 1979 when he got into a dispute in a Washington area restaurant and defiantly asserted his congressional status; but that is hardly enough to really hurt him. He sits on the Education and Labor and Merchant Marine Committees, on which he may be counted as a solid labor vote.

Census Data Pop. 478,310. Central city, 100%; suburban, 0%. Median family income, $8,690; families above $15,000: 15%; families below $3,000: 12%. Median years education, 10.4.

The Voters

Median voting age 44.
Employment profile White collar, 43%. Blue collar, 40%. Service, 17%. Farm, –%.
Ethnic groups Black, 39%. Total foreign stock, 23%. Italy, 13%; USSR, Ireland, 2% each; UK, 1%.

Presidential vote

1976	Carter (D)	122,695	(71%)
	Ford (R)	50,923	(29%)
1972	Nixon (R)	77,078	(42%)
	McGovern (D)	107,549	(58%)

Rep. Michael O. Myers (D) Elected 1976; b. May 4, 1943, Philadelphia; home, Philadelphia; Catholic.

Career Longshoreman; Penn. House of Reps., 1971–76.

Offices 1217 LHOB, 202-225-4731. Also Wm. J. Green Fed. Bldg., 600 Arch St., Philadelphia 19106, 215-925-6840.

Committees *Education and Labor* (14th). Subcommittees: Health and Safety; Elementary, Secondary and Vocational Education; Labor Standards.

Merchant Marine and Fisheries (20th). Subcommittees: Merchant Marine; Coast Guard and Navigation.

Group Ratings

	ADA	COPE	PC	RPN	NFU	LCV	CFA	NAB	NSI	ACA	NTU
1978	50	78	53	10	56	–	59	0	43	24	–
1977	60	91	48	10	83	45	65	–	–	23	22

Key Votes

1) Increase Def Spnd	AGN	6) Alaska Lands Protect	FOR	11) Delay Auto Pol Cntrl	AGN
2) B-1 Bomber	AGN	7) Water Projects Veto	AGN	12) Sugar Price Escalator	AGN
3) Cargo Preference	FOR	8) Consum Protect Agcy	FOR	13) Pub Fin Cong Cmpgns	AGN
4) Dereg Nat Gas	AGN	9) Common Situs Picket	FOR	14) ERA Ratif Recissn	AGN
5) Kemp-Roth	AGN	10) Labor Law Revision	FOR	15) Prohibt Govt Abrtns	FOR

Election Results

1978 general	Michael Myers (D)	104,412	(73%)	($50,069)
	Samuel N. Fanelli (R)	37,913	(27%)	
1978 primary	Michael Myers (D)	26,013	(50%)	
	Andrew Diantonio (D)	9,540	(18%)	
	Five others (D)	16,640	(32%)	
1976 general	Michael Myers (D)	117,087	(74%)	($21,500)
	Samuel N. Fanelli (R)	40,191	(26%)	($2,990)

SECOND DISTRICT

The 2d district of Pennsylvania is an oddly-shaped chunk of Philadelphia. Though the 2d was designed as the city's black district, it does not center on one of the city's two large black neighborhoods. Instead, the district takes in part of West Philadelphia and then moves across Fairmount Park and the Schuylkill River to encompass part of the North Philadelphia community. The 2d proceeds north to include some of the more middle class integrated areas of Germantown, which at the time of the Revolution was a town separate from Philadelphia altogether. The district then goes all the way out to the WASP upper income precincts of Chestnut Hill, where some of Philadelphia's most prominent families have lived for generations. Chestnut Hill usually goes Republican, but its votes are swamped in the 2d by the huge Democratic majorities coming out of the black neighborhoods to the south and east. Altogether, the 2d consistently reports the largest Democratic percentages in Pennsylvania.

For 20 years the 2d district was represented by Robert Nix, a politician who made few waves of any kind. Although in his last term he inherited the chair of the Post Office and Civil Service Committee, he was one of the least active congressmen. It was no surprise when he was defeated in the 1978 Democratic primary; indeed, he had nearly lost in every primary since 1970.

The man who beat Nix is William Gray, a young Baptist minister who had nearly won in 1976. Almost as soon as he got sworn in, Gray was being hailed as one of the most politically astute freshman members. He won a seat on the Budget Committee and also took a seat on Foreign Affairs, generally considered less desirable; but he collected some chits from others whom he helped to win a committee seat he might have had himself. Gray's voting record seems likely to be solidly liberal, but he seems, like many of the younger black members, to be somewhat more pragmatic and less militant in approach than some of the black congressmen elected in the late sixties and early seventies.

Census Data Pop. 470,267. Central city, 100%; suburban, 0%. Median family income, $8,670; families above $15,000: 19%; families below $3,000: 14%. Median years education, 11.4.

The Voters

Median voting age 45.
Employment profile White collar, 49%. Blue collar, 33%. Service, 18%. Farm, –%.
Ethnic groups Black, 65%. Total foreign stock, 15%. USSR, 4%; Italy, 2%; Ireland, UK, Germany, 1% each.

Presidential vote

1976	Carter (D)	128,921	(80%)
	Ford (R)	31,264	(20%)
1972	Nixon (R)	29,889	(25%)
	McGovern (D)	121,786	(75%)

Rep. William H. Gray III (D) Elected 1978; b. Aug. 20, 1942, Baton Rouge, La.; home, Philadelphia; Franklin and Marshall Col., B.A. 1963, Drew Theological Seminary, M.A. 1966, 1972, Princeton U., M.A. 1970; Baptist.

Career Minister and church history professor.

Offices 429 CHOB, 202-225-4001. Also 6753 Germantown Ave., Philadelphia 19119, 215-438-6070.

Committees *Budget* (17th). Subcommittees: Economic Policy, Projections and Productivity; Human and Community Resources; Defense and International Affairs.

District of Columbia (9th). Subcommittees: Fiscal Affairs and Health.

Foreign Affairs (18th). Subcommittees: International Operations; Africa.

Group Ratings: Newly Elected

Key Votes: Newly Elected

Election Results

1978 general	William H. Gray III (D)	132,594	(84%)	($225,887)
	Roland Atkins (R)	25,785	(16%)	($24,877)
1978 primary	William H. Gray III (D)	36,506	(58%)	
	Robert N. C. Nix, Sr. (D)	24,855	(40%)	($101,832)
	One other (D)	1,482	(2%)	
1976 general	Robert N. C. Nix, Sr. (D)	109,855	(74%)	($24,620)
	Jesse W. Woods, Jr. (R)	37,907	(26%)	($4,072)

THIRD DISTRICT

Whatever the opinion of W.C. Fields, Center City Philadelphia is one of the more amenable of American downtowns. The height of buildings here was kept to a reasonable 38 stories for years by an old ordinance that allowed nothing higher than the spire on Philadelphia's ornate City Hall. A large urban renewal project has gone up on the site of old Penn Central tracks, long known as the Chinese wall. Not far from the office buildings are the elegant Victorian neighborhoods around Rittenhouse Square and the restored eighteenth century townhouses of Society Hill. But as one moves north a few blocks out of Center City, there are nineteenth century suburbs which have long since become slums. Some of these areas along with much of Center City and Society Hill are part of Pennsylvania's 3d congressional district.

At its western fringes, the 3d also takes in part of the black neighborhood of North Philadelphia. But most of the district is made up of white neighborhoods where levels of income and education are little higher than in black ghettoes. An example is Kensington, north of Center City, which seems to have been transported intact from the thirties. Here, in the red brick Philadelphia rowhouses, live the Irish and Italians left behind after the postwar exodus to the suburbs. Most of these people own their own houses—Philadelphia is a city of homeowners, not renters. But the value of this real estate is pathetically low, since there is little demand for it. According to the Census Bureau, the median value of a homeowner's house here in 1970 was $7,800—lower than in any other Philadelphia district. Kensington and neighborhoods like it are traditionally Democratic; they also tended to favor Frank Rizzo during his years of prominence in Philadelphia politics.

This is the area that was the power base for William Green, Jr., Congressman and Democratic boss of Philadelphia until his death in 1964, and his son, William Green III, elected Congressman at 25 to replace his father and later candidate for mayor and U.S. senator. Young Green split with the Democratic machine over 1968 presidential politics and when he ran for mayor against Frank Rizzo in 1971. He lost that primary decisively because of Rizzo's popularity in white lower income, especially Italian, wards. The next year the machine redistricted him in with another incumbent, but Green fought back and kept his seat. In the next few years he concentrated on the House and his seat on the Ways and Means Committee. He became something of an expert in trade matters, and persuaded the House to repeal the oil depletion allowance in 1975. In 1976 Green ran for the Senate, and might well have won, but for the heavy personal spending of Republican John Heinz; Green's campaign was well financed, but not in Heinz's league. After that election Green returned to Philadelphia, and at this writing appears likely to be elected Mayor in 1979—a victory that would sharply change the tone and substance of Philadelphia politics.

Green's successor in the House is a former state legislator and probation department director, Raymond Lederer, who as a Philadelphia ward leader was wise enough to back Frank Rizzo against his enemies. In the decisive 1976 Democratic primary, Lederer got 57% against five opponents. He is a member of the Ways and Means Committee and legislatively has made his biggest mark as an opponent of sugar subsidies.

Census Data Pop. 472,041. Central city, 100%; suburban, 0%. Median family income, $8,368; families above $15,000: 14%; families below $3,000: 13%. Median years education, 9.9.

The Voters

Median voting age 46.
Employment profile White collar, 40%. Blue collar, 45%. Service, 15%. Farm, –%.
Ethnic groups Black, 28%. Spanish, 5%. Total foreign stock, 22%. Poland, 4%; Italy, USSR, 3% each; Germany, UK, Ireland, 2% each.

Presidential vote

1976	Carter (D)	101,997	(68%)
	Ford (R)	47,471	(32%)
1972	Nixon (R)	74,829	(46%)
	McGovern (D)	86,379	(54%)

Rep. Raymond F. Lederer (D) Elected 1976; b. May 19, 1938, Philadelphia; home, Philadelphia; Phila. Comm. Col., St. Joseph's Col., Philadelphia, Penn St. U.; Catholic.

Career Public school football coach and commissioner; Phila. probation officer; Penn. House of Reps., 1974–77.

Offices 119 CHOB, 202-225-6271. Also 600 Arch St., Philadelphia 19106, 215-597-8670.

Committees *Ways and Means* (19th). Subcommittees: Select Revenue Measures; Trade.

Group Ratings

	ADA	COPE	PC	RPN	NFU	LCV	CFA	NAB	NSI	ACA	NTU
1978	50	80	60	18	80	–	59	0	60	15	–
1977	55	95	58	15	64	56	80	–	–	17	22

Key Votes

1) Increase Def Spnd	AGN	6) Alaska Lands Protect	FOR	11) Delay Auto Pol Cntrl	AGN
2) B-1 Bomber	AGN	7) Water Projects Veto	AGN	12) Sugar Price Escalator	AGN
3) Cargo Preference	FOR	8) Consum Protect Agcy	FOR	13) Pub Fin Cong Cmpgns	FOR
4) Dereg Nat Gas	AGN	9) Common Situs Picket	FOR	14) ERA Ratif Recissn	AGN
5) Kemp-Roth	AGN	10) Labor Law Revision	FOR	15) Prohibt Govt Abrtns	FOR

Election Results

1978 general	Raymond F. Lederer (D)	86,015	(71%)	($106,284)
	Raymond S. Kauffman (R)	33,750	(29%)	($6,850)
1978 primary	Raymond F. Lederer (D), unopposed			
1976 general	Raymond F. Lederer (D)	98,627	(74%)	($45,430)
	Terrence J. Schade (R)	35,491	(26%)	($10,571)

FOURTH DISTRICT

The 4th congressional district of Pennsylvania is northeast Philadelphia, the most middle class and prosperous part of the city. In fact, it is still growing. Geographically, most of the 4th is farther from Center City than the Main Line suburbs. Out here, some 10 to 20 miles from Independence Hall, middle income suburban tract housing was still going up during the sixties. In fact, more than half the housing units in northeast Philadelphia were built after 1950; in the rest of the city, more than 80% went up before that. Most of the 4th's residents once lived in more crowded areas closer to Center City, and the district has a fair ethnic mixture, one representing the outward movement of various groups. Of these, the Jews have been most important politically, with more than half the city's Jewish residents living in this district. There are also plenty of Irish and other Catholics out here and a few blacks; but the 4th does not include many old-line Italian or other ethnic communities.

The 4th is the only one of Philadelphia's districts to be represented by a Republican, indeed the only district in the city which has elected a Republican congressman since 1956. Republicans made serious efforts to win the district in 1966 and 1972, but they succeeded in 1978 only because of the legal problems of Congressman Joshua Eilberg. A product of machine Democratic politics, Eilberg was first elected in 1966 and served on the Judiciary Committee, where he was one of the votes there to impeach Richard Nixon. He also chaired the Immigration Subcommittee, an area of increasing controversy with rising illegal immigration. Eilberg made the headlines in November 1977 when he called President Carter and complained of the investigating tactics of Philadelphia's holdover U.S. Attorney, David Marston; the call got Carter as well as Eilberg into considerable political trouble.

Republicans smelled opportunity and in 1978 ran a strong candidate: Charles Daugherty, who represented a substantial part of the district in the Pennsylvania Senate. In September Eilberg was charged by the House Ethics Committee with accepting more than $100,000 from his law firm and two affiliated firms which were helping a Philadelphia hospital get a federal grant. Just before the election he was indicted. The result was a 56% victory for Daugherty. After the election Eilberg a pleaded guilty and was given five years probation.

Daugherty's 56% is about the upper limit a Republican can expect here in most circumstances—in fact, the percentage Richard Nixon received in the 4th district in 1972. It is possible that by assiduous cultivation of the district Daugherty may do better, but he can expect serious Democratic competition in 1980. The new Congressman seems unlikely to be part of the growing group of New Right Republicans; the voters of the 4th resent high taxes, but this is still an area that essentially believes in government as a solver of problems. The district may have a suburban air about it, but it is still Philadelphia.

Census Data Pop. 474,684. Central city, 100%; suburban, 0%. Median family income, $11,069; families above $15,000: 24%; families below $3,000: 5%. Median years education, 11.9.

The Voters

Median voting age 45.
Employment profile White collar, 57%. Blue collar, 33%. Service, 10%. Farm, -%.
Ethnic groups Black, 5%. Total foreign stock, 32%. USSR, 8%; Italy, Germany, 4% each; Poland, Ireland, UK, 3% each; Austria, 1%.

Presidential vote

1976	Carter (D)	129,639	(57%)
	Ford (R)	96,820	(43%)
1972	Nixon (R)	131,066	(56%)
	McGovern (D)	100,940	(44%)

Rep. Charles F. Dougherty (R) Elected 1978; b. June 26, 1937, Philadelphia; home, Philadelphia; St. Joseph's Col., B.S. 1959, U. of Penn., Temple U.; Catholic.

Career USMC, 1959–62; College instructor, 1962–65; Ofc. of Naval Intelligence, 1965–66; Asst. Dean of Students, Comm. Col. of Phila., 1966–70; High School Principal, 1970–72; Dir. of Finance and Development, Phila. Counseling or Referral Assistance Program, 1972; Penn. Senate, 1972–78.

Offices 1428 LHOB, 202-225-8251. Also 6800 Rising Sun Ave., Philadelphia 19111, 215-742-4479.

Committees *Armed Services* (14th). Subcommittees: Seapower and Strategic and Critical Materials; Military Compensation.

Group Ratings: Newly Elected

Key Votes: Newly Elected

Election Results

1978 general	Charles F. Dougherty (R)	110,445	(56%)	($130,837)
	Joshua Eilberg (D)	87,555	(44%)	($159,904)
1978 primary	Charles F. Dougherty (R), unopposed			
1976 general	Joshua Eilberg (D)	144,890	(68%)	($38,439)
	James E. Mugford, Sr. (R)	69,700	(32%)	($5,489)

FIFTH DISTRICT

The 5th congressional district of Pennsylvania can be called an exurban Philadelphia district. It takes in the outer edges of suburban Delaware and Montgomery Counties, along with most of Chester County farther out. Though technically all within the Philadelphia metropolitan area, the 5th is really a kind of borderland where the influence of Philadelphia wanes and that of the Pennsylvania Dutch country begins. It is the kind of country John O'Hara described: grimy small industrial towns surrounded by large suburban estates, and the perfectly tended farms of the Chadds Ford area, where the Wyeth family lives and paints. Not far away is the sleepy town of Oxford, home of Lincoln University, one of the nation's oldest black colleges—and a symbol of the area's Lincoln Republican heritage. The 5th also contains many of the famed Main Line suburbs of Philadelphia, so named because they lay on the main line of what was once the prosperous Pennsylvania Railroad. The 5th is a Republican district, very Republican. The only time it has been known to go Democratic was in the 1964 presidential election, and then by a very narrow margin.

The current Congressman, Republican Richard Schulze, easily won his party's primary in 1974 after serving three terms in the Pennsylvania legislature. Schulze's predecessors had been conservatives in their sixties; he was first elected at age 45. His record in the House has been in line with conventional Republican philosophy. He is a member of the House Ways and Means Committee, where he has objected to proposed limits on business expense deductions. He was also one of the key votes in ending the Turkish arms embargo.

Census Data Pop. 474,435. Central city, 0%; suburban, 100%. Median family income, $12,148; families above $15,000: 33%; families below $3,000: 4%. Median years education, 12.4.

The Voters

Median voting age 42.
Employment profile White collar, 54%. Blue collar, 35%. Service, 9%. Farm, 2%.
Ethnic groups Black, 4%. Total foreign stock, 15%. Italy, 3%; UK, Germany, 2% each; Ireland, 1%.

Presidential vote

1976	Carter (D)	77,048	(39%)
	Ford (R)	121,190	(61%)
1972	Nixon (R)	131,393	(69%)
	McGovern (D)	58,454	(31%)

Rep. Richard T. Schulze (R) Elected 1974; b. Aug. 7, 1929, Philadelphia; home, Malvern; U. of Houston, 1949–50, Villanova U., 1952; Presbyterian.

Career Army, 1951-53; Proprietor, Home Appliance Ctr., Paoli; Chester Co. Register of Wills and Clerk of Orphans Ct., 1967–69; Penn. House of Reps., 1969–74.

Offices 432 CHOB, 202-225-5761. Also 2 W. Lancaster Ave., Paoli 19301, 215-648-0555.

Committees *Ways and Means* (9th). Subcommittees: Select Revenue Measures; Trade.

Group Ratings

	ADA	COPE	PC	RPN	NFU	LCV	CFA	NAB	NSI	ACA	NTU
1978	10	16	20	64	10	–	23	83	100	88	–
1977	20	23	28	69	25	30	15	–	–	85	43
1976	5	18	16	78	33	15	9	75	100	86	56

Key Votes

1) Increase Def Spnd	FOR	6) Alaska Lands Protect	AGN	11) Delay Auto Pol Cntrl	FOR
2) B-1 Bomber	FOR	7) Water Projects Veto	AGN	12) Sugar Price Escalator	AGN
3) Cargo Preference	AGN	8) Consum Protect Agcy	AGN	13) Pub Fin Cong Cmpgns	AGN
4) Dereg Nat Gas	FOR	9) Common Situs Picket	AGN	14) ERA Ratif Recissn	FOR
5) Kemp-Roth	FOR	10) Labor Law Revision	AGN	15) Prohibt Govt Abrtns	FOR

Election Results

1978 general	Richard T. Schulze (R)	110,565	(75%)	($124,390)
	Murray P. Zealor (D)	36,704	(25%)	($5,354)
1978 primary	Richard T. Schulze (R)	54,371	(93%)	
	One other (R)	4,235	(7%)	
1976 general	Richard T. Schulze (R)	119,682	(60%)	($73,960)
	Anthony Campolo, Jr. (D)	81,299	(40%)	($25,850)

SIXTH DISTRICT

The 6th congressional district of Pennsylvania includes Berks and Schuylkill Counties and a small portion of Northumberland County. This is a region of both industry and agriculture, on the margin between the industrial Northeast and the Pennsylvania Dutch country. Schuylkill County is anthracite country: on rugged hills, a collection of small towns first set up to scrape the hard coal from under ground, now scrambling for whatever industry they can attract. Reading, in Berks County, is a factory town, famous in the nineteenth century for its black broad-brimmed hats and in the early twentieth century for its ironware manufactures. The Reading Railroad once made this one of the major rail centers in the country. It is now a center for light, not heavy, industry, and its old brick factories are used for factory outlet stores which attract buyers from all over the East.

The Dutch country obtrudes into Berks County, but politically the 6th district is more industrial than Dutch. The factory workers of Reading and the anthracite miners, or former miners, of Schuylkill County towns like Tamaqua and Mahanoy City and Pottsville vote Democratic in most elections. Their votes are usually about evenly matched by Republican margins cast in the southern, more agricultural part of the district. The hard-pressed conditions of local industry have, if anything, strengthened the 6th's Democratic leanings. Even so, the district is more Democratic in local than national elections; it barely went for Jimmy Carter in 1976.

The current Congressman, Gus Yatron, was first elected in 1968. Owner of a local ice cream business in Reading, he was a 12-year veteran of the state legislature. In the House he serves on the Foreign Affairs Committee; he was part of the group of Greek-American congressmen who led the fight to cut off arms sales to Turkey because of its invasion of Cyprus. Yatron has voted generally with his fellow Democrats on the floor and receives good ratings from organized labor. Despite the marginal nature of this district in statewide elections, he has been reelected recently with 3-1 margins.

Census Data Pop. 473,574. Central city, 19%; suburban, 44%. Median family income, $9,009; families above $15,000: 13%; families below $3,000: 8%. Median years education, 11.0.

The Voters

Median voting age 47.
Employment profile White collar, 35%. Blue collar, 53%. Service, 10%. Farm, 2%.
Ethnic groups Black, 1%. Total foreign stock, 14%. Poland, 3%; Italy, Germany, 2% each; Austria, Lithuania, 1% each.

Presidential vote

1976	Carter (D)	90,203	(50%)
	Ford (R)	89,194	(50%)
1972	Nixon (R)	114,537	(63%)
	McGovern (D)	66,807	(37%)

Rep. Gus Yatron (D) Elected 1968; b. Oct. 16, 1927, Reading; home, Reading; Kutztown St. Teachers Col., 1950; Greek Orthodox.

Career Pro. heavyweight boxer; Proprietor, Yatron's Ice Cream, 1950–69; Mbr., Reading School Bd., 1955–60; Penn. House of Reps., 1956-60; Penn. Senate, 1960–68.

Offices 2400 RHOB, 202-225-5546. Also U.S.P.O. Bldg., 5th and Washington Sts., Reading 19603, 215-375-4573.

Committees *Foreign Affairs* (9th). Subcommittees: Asian and Pacific Affairs; Inter-American Affairs (Chairman).

Group Ratings

	ADA	COPE	PC	RPN	NFU	LCV	CFA	NAB	NSI	ACA	NTU
1978	40	60	28	42	70	–	41	33	78	44	–
1977	30	83	43	31	82	40	45	–	–	36	22
1976	40	83	67	39	83	48	64	36	71	21	21

Key Votes

1) Increase Def Spnd	AGN	6) Alaska Lands Protect	FOR	11) Delay Auto Pol Cntrl	FOR
2) B-1 Bomber	FOR	7) Water Projects Veto	AGN	12) Sugar Price Escalator	FOR
3) Cargo Preference	AGN	8) Consum Protect Agcy	FOR	13) Pub Fin Cong Cmpgns	AGN
4) Dereg Nat Gas	AGN	9) Common Situs Picket	FOR	14) ERA Ratif Recissn	AGN
5) Kemp-Roth	FOR	10) Labor Law Revision	FOR	15) Prohibt Govt Abrtns	FOR

Election Results

1978 general	Gus Yatron (D)	106,431	(74%)	($55,589)
	Stephen Mazur (R)	37,746	(26%)	
1978 primary	Gus Yatron (D), unopposed			
1976 general	Gus Yatron (D)	133,624	(74%)	($53,124)
	Stephen Postupack (R)	46,103	(26%)	($8,222)

SEVENTH DISTRICT

The 7th congressional district of Pennsylvania contains the larger part of Delaware County, a unit that for years has contained more people than the entire state of Delaware just to the south. This is, indeed since the turn of the century has been, a suburban area southwest of Philadelphia, but for the most part not an exclusive one. The towns here are strung out, not on the main line of the old Pennsylvania Railroad, but along less fashionable tracks and radial roads. There are leafy, WASPy suburbs here, like Swarthmore, around the distinguished college of that name. But the more typical suburb is a place like Upper Darby, where the grandchildren of immigrants who lived in South or West Philadelphia have moved out from the crowded rowhouse neighborhoods to the relatively spacious and middle class streets of Delaware County.

The dominant political institution here for years was the Delaware County War Board, a Republican machine which rivals in age the old Republican machine that for so many years ruled Philadelphia. The War Board's initial strength was among the county's Anglo-Saxon Protestants, but it adapted well to new tides of suburban immigration and won strong support from the Irish- and Italian- and Polish-Americans who moved here over the past four or five decades. But the War Board's power seems to have diminished in the seventies. In congressional elections, it decided to purge the incumbent in the 1974 primary, and was only barely able to do so; it was then unable to elect its candidate in the general election.

The winner of that election was 31-year-old Methodist minister Robert Edgar, and despite the district's Republican background he is still the Congressman today. He has taken a number of initiatives to build up his local popularity. As a member of the Public Works Committee, he has pushed for mass transit legislation—this district is still served by commuter rail and public transit lines—and helped organize a "snow belt" caucus of representatives from Northeastern and Midwest states. He called for formal investigations of Pennsylvania Democrats Daniel Flood and Joshua Eilberg—a notable break with party solidarity and undoubtedly a popular move in white collar precincts. Yet Edgar has won reelection with diminishing percentages, and prevailed by only some 1,300 votes in 1978. The apparent reason is his very liberal voting record. He makes few concessions to his district, and his ADA rating has been 100% as often as not. His support of defense cuts was attacked when large defense contracts here were not renewed. This is not a district that is heavily Republican in national politics, with Jimmy Carter getting 46% of its votes. But many of these Democrats are culturally conservative and hostile to many of the things Edgar has supported. Edgar has been mentioned as a possible candidate for the Senate in 1980; whether he runs for that or for the House, he is probably in for a tough race.

Census Data Pop. 470,714. Central city, 0%; suburban, 100%. Median family income, $11,383; families above $15,000: 27%; families below $3,000: 5%. Median years education, 12.2.

The Voters

Median voting age 45.
Employment profile White collar, 57%. Blue collar, 33%. Service, 10%. Farm, -%.
Ethnic groups Black, 8%. Total foreign stock, 21%. Italy, 6%; Ireland, UK, 3% each; Germany, Poland, USSR, 1% each.

Presidential vote

1976	Carter (D)	93,411	(46%)
	Ford (R)	109,441	(54%)
1972	Nixon (R)	133,151	(64%)
	McGovern (D)	73,432	(36%)

Rep. Robert W. Edgar (D) Elected 1974; b. May 29, 1943, Philadelphia; home, Broomall; Lycoming Col., B.A. 1965, Drew U., M.Div. 1968; Methodist.

Career Minister; Utd. Protestant Chaplin, Drexel U., 1968–71; Co-Dir., People's Emergency Ctr., 1971–75.

Offices 407 CHOB, 202-225-2011. Also 204 Long Lane, Upper Darby 19082, 215-352-0790.

Committees *Public Works and Transportation* (13th). Subcommittees: Economic Development; Public Buildings and Grounds; Surface Transportation.

Veterans' Affairs (10th). Subcommittees: Compensation, Pension, Insurance and Memorial Affairs; Medical Facilities and Benefits.

Group Ratings

	ADA	COPE	PC	RPN	NFU	LCV	CFA	NAB	NSI	ACA	NTU
1978	80	89	90	42	70	–	91	0	11	11	–
1977	100	86	95	54	75	100	95	–	–	11	27
1976	95	77	90	59	83	89	100	17	0	0	37

Key Votes

1) Increase Def Spnd	AGN	6) Alaska Lands Protect	FOR	11) Delay Auto Pol Cntrl	AGN
2) B-1 Bomber	AGN	7) Water Projects Veto	FOR	12) Sugar Price Escalator	AGN
3) Cargo Preference	FOR	8) Consum Protect Agcy	FOR	13) Pub Fin Cong Cmpgns	FOR
4) Dereg Nat Gas	AGN	9) Common Situs Picket	AGN	14) ERA Ratif Recissn	AGN
5) Kemp-Roth	AGN	10) Labor Law Revision	FOR	15) Prohibt Govt Abrtns	AGN

Election Results

1978 general	Robert W. Edgar (D)	79,771	(50%)	($142,238)
	Eugene D. Kane (R)	78,403	(50%)	($216,347)
1978 primary	Robert W. Edgar (D)	15,844	(82%)	
	One other (D)	3,377	(18%)	
1976 general	Robert W. Edgar (D)	109,456	(54%)	($129,172)
	John N. Kenney (R)	92,788	(46%)	($170,508)

EIGHTH DISTRICT

The 8th congressional district of Pennsylvania is one of four suburban Philadelphia districts. It includes a small part of Montgomery County, just about directly north of Philadelphia's Center City, and all of Bucks County, which has seven-eighths of its population. Bucks County is one of those geographical names which has entered our literary imagination. The northwestern or upper part of the county is rolling farmland, easily reachable by train from New York as well as Philadelphia. It has long been the residence of well-known writers and artists, who live in stone Quaker farmhouses near villages like New Hope and Lumberville. Their neighbors are, sometimes, Pennsylvania Dutch farmers or, more often, comfortably off people with jobs somewhere closer-in in the Philadelphia metropolitan area.

But this is not the whole story of Bucks County; indeed, upper Bucks has only about half the county's population. Lower Bucks County is an entirely different place—predominantly industrial and blue collar. Here is U.S. Steel's giant Fairless works; here also is one of the original Levittowns. In the other suburban Philadelphia counties, most of the blue collar immigration took place long ago, when Philadelphia itself was solidly Republican and the suburban county machines adept at enrolling new residents in their parties. But in Bucks, the blue collar migration came late, in the fifties and sixties, and there is a strong Democratic voting base here in Levittown and Bristol. The Republican tendencies of upper Bucks and Montgomery Counties still dominate; this was a Ford, not a Carter, district. But there is a sizeable Democratic base here, too—though it never became apparent in congressional elections until 1976, when moderate Republican Congressman Edward Biester decided to retire.

The general election that year was one of the closest in the country. The Republicans nominated a solid conservative, John Renninger, while the Democrats nominated Peter Kostmayer, a young (30) press aide to Governor Milton Shapp. Kostmayer prevailed, but by only some 1,300 votes. Kostmayer immediately became a leader among the 1976 freshmen, pushing for procedural reforms. He shocked experienced Pennsylvania Democrats by calling for investigations of his state colleagues Joshua Eilberg and Daniel Flood; Kostmayer was obviously less interested in Capitol Hill camaraderie than in asking for high ethical standards. He was one of the early advocates of a full investigation of South Korean bribery of members of Congress. He has returned to his district frequently and generally used the advantages of incumbency well to increase his popularity.

As a result, Kostmayer was rather easily reelected in 1978. He had no difficulty with an anti-abortion primary candidate, and won more than 60% of the vote against his Republican opponent. His opposition was not as strong as, say, Robert Edgar's in the 7th district; but his margins were still impressive. Kostmayer has been mentioned as a possible candidate for the Senate seat up in 1980. He would have the advantages of a record showing considerable independence of party ties, though on substantive issues he has generally voted with most Democrats.

Census Data Pop. 475,406. Central city, 0%; suburban, 100%. Median family income, $11,807; families above $15,000: 29%; families below $3,000: 4%. Median years education, 12.3.

The Voters

Median voting age 41.
Employment profile White collar, 52%. Blue collar, 38%. Service, 9%. Farm, 1%.
Ethnic groups Black, 2%. Total foreign stock, 18%. Germany, Italy, 3% each; UK, 2%; Poland, Ireland, USSR, 1% each.

Presidential vote

1976	Carter (D)	89,991	(47%)
	Ford (R)	101,845	(53%)
1972	Nixon (R)	118,601	(65%)
	McGovern (D)	64,330	(35%)

Rep. Peter H. Kostmayer (D) Elected 1976; b. Sept. 27, 1946, New York, N.Y.; home, Solebury; Columbia U., B.A. 1971; Episcopalian.

Career Reporter, *The Trentonian*, 1971–72; Press Secy. to the Atty. Gen. of Penn., 1972–73; Depy. Press Secy. to Penn. Gov. Milton Shapp, 1973–76.

Offices 125 CHOB, 202-225-4276. Also 1 Oxford Valley Mall, Rm. 803, Langhorne 19047, 215-757-8181.

Committees *Government Operations* (21st). Subcommittees: Government Information and Individual Rights; Environment, Energy and Natural Resources.

Interior and Insular Affairs (18th). Subcommittees: Energy and the Environment; Public Lands; National Parks and Insular Affairs.

Group Ratings

	ADA	COPE	PC	RPN	NFU	LCV	CFA	NAB	NSI	ACA	NTU
1978	70	79	88	55	50	–	96	33	0	26	–
1977	85	87	93	75	67	90	90	–	–	22	52

Key Votes

1) Increase Def Spnd	AGN	6) Alaska Lands Protect	FOR	11) Delay Auto Pol Cntrl	AGN
2) B-1 Bomber	AGN	7) Water Projects Veto	FOR	12) Sugar Price Escalator	AGN
3) Cargo Preference	AGN	8) Consum Protect Agcy	FOR	13) Pub Fin Cong Cmpgns	FOR
4) Dereg Nat Gas	AGN	9) Common Situs Picket	FOR	14) ERA Ratif Recissn	AGN
5) Kemp-Roth	AGN	10) Labor Law Revision	FOR	15) Prohibt Govt Abrtns	AGN

Election Results

1978 general	Peter H. Kostmayer (D)	89,276	(61%)	($131,010)
	G. Roger Bowers (R)	56,776	(39%)	($52,584)
1978 primary	Peter H. Kostmayer (D)	25,755	(85%)	
	One other (D)	4,461	(15%)	
1976 general	Peter H. Kostmayer (D)	93,855	(50%)	($58,481)
	John S. Renninger (R)	92,543	(50%)	($80,612)

NINTH DISTRICT

The Appalachian Mountain chains run like a series of backbones through central Pennsylvania. Throughout the state's history, the mountains have constituted a formidable barrier, not so much because of their height, which is unspectacular, but because of their persistence: one rugged chain right after another for 50 to 100 miles. During the eighteenth century, the mountains provided eastern Pennsylvania with a kind of rampart against Indian attacks, but in the nineteenth century they proved less useful. The mountains prevented Pennsylvania from ever digging a satisfactory statewide canal system—the boom mode of transportation in the early nineteenth century. They also delayed, until other states had them, the building of an east-west railroad. Only the aggressive policy of the Pennsylvania Railroad, a relative latecomer to the business, saved the state from branch line status.

The 9th is the only one of Pennsylvania's congressional districts to lie wholly within these mountains. This part of the Alleghenies (the term is often used interchangeably with Appalachians in Pennsylvania) was first settled by poor Scottish and Ulster Irish farmers just after the Revolutionary War. They were a people of fierce independence and pride, as the Whiskey Rebellion demonstrated. They worked their hardscrabble farms and built their little towns; sometimes coal was found nearby, and their communities changed. But for the most part the 9th is not really coal country, and the area was spared the boom-bust cycles of northeastern Pennsylvania and West Virginia. This was an important area for the Pennsylvania Railroad, however. Near Altoona was the railroad's famous Horseshoe Curve, and in Altoona itself the railroad built the nation's largest car yards. As the railroad has become less important and its financial condition changed from prosperity to bankruptcy, Altoona's population declined from 82,000 at the end of the twenties to 62,000 in 1970.

This part of Pennsylvania has been solidly Republican since the election of 1860, and it has not come close to electing a Democrat to Congress in years. The current incumbent, E.G. (Bud) Shuster, is an entrepreneur who made a fortune building up a business and selling it to IBM. He decided to settle in the southern Pennsylvania mountains, became interested in local affairs, decided to run for Congress, and beat the favorite, a local state senator, in the 1972 Republican primary. Shuster has won easily since. He has a solidly conservative voting record, rivalled in that regard in the Pennsylvania delegation only by the 19th district's William Goodling. Shuster has also had some impact on a number of issues. He is the House's leading opponent of the air bag, for example. Shuster's zeal and conservatism have helped him to a leading role in the House Republican leadership, and he is now Chairman of the Republican Policy Committee. In the current political climate of the House, Shuster seems to be an increasingly important member.

Census Data Pop. 468,008. Central city, 13%; suburban, 26%. Median family income, $8,124; families above $15,000: 10%; families below $3,000: 10%. Median years education, 11.4.

The Voters

Median voting age 44.
Employment profile White collar, 34%. Blue collar, 50%. Service, 12%. Farm, 4%.
Ethnic groups Total foreign stock, 4%. Italy, 1%.

Presidential vote

1976	Carter (D)	66,499	(41%)
	Ford (R)	96,867	(59%)
1972	Nixon (R)	114,144	(74%)
	McGovern (D)	40,131	(26%)

Rep. Bud Shuster (R) Elected 1972; b. Jan. 23, 1932, Glassport; home, West Providence Township; U. of Pitt., B.S. 1954, Duquesne U., M.B.A., 1960, American U., Ph.D. 1967.

Career V.P., Radio Corp. of Amer.; Operator, Shuster Farms.

Offices 2455 RHOB, 202-225-2431. Also Suite M, Penn Alto Hotel, Altoona 16603, 814-946-1653.

Committees *Budget* (6th). Subcommittees: Economic Policy, Projections and Productivity; Defense and International Affairs; Inflation.

Public Works and Transportation (6th). Subcommittees: Aviation; Economic Development; Surface Transportation.

Group Ratings

	ADA	COPE	PC	RPN	NFU	LCV	CFA	NAB	NSI	ACA	NTU
1978	5	16	10	50	20	–	18	100	90	96	–
1977	15	17	18	62	8	5	10	–	–	96	55
1976	0	13	11	50	17	13	0	92	90	86	72

Key Votes

1) Increase Def Spnd	FOR	6) Alaska Lands Protect	AGN	11) Delay Auto Pol Cntrl	FOR
2) B-1 Bomber	FOR	7) Water Projects Veto	AGN	12) Sugar Price Escalator	FOR
3) Cargo Preference	AGN	8) Consum Protect Agcy	AGN	13) Pub Fin Cong Cmpgns	AGN
4) Dereg Nat Gas	FOR	9) Common Situs Picket	AGN	14) ERA Ratif Recissn	FOR
5) Kemp-Roth	FOR	10) Labor Law Revision	AGN	15) Prohibt Govt Abrtns	FOR

Election Results

1978 general	E. G. Shuster (R)	101,151	(75%)	($146,318)
	Blaine L. Havice, Jr. (D)	33,882	(25%)	($16,809)
1978 primary	E. G. Shuster (R), unopposed			
1976 general	E. G. Shuster (R), unopposed			($88,297)

TENTH DISTRICT

Scranton is the anthracite town par excellence. Back around the turn of the century, anthracite or hard coal was much in demand: it was the fuel used to heat most homes, in furnaces or pot-bellied stoves. Because the only major deposits of anthracite in the United States lie in the Scranton-Wilkes-Barre region of northeast Pennsylvania, these two cities suddenly came on flush times. Immigrants from Italy, Poland, Austria-Hungary, and Ireland poured in to join the Scots and Welsh already working the mines. Scranton became the third largest city in Pennsylvania, and the region around Scranton and Wilkes-Barre held more than 750,000 people by the end of the twenties.

Then came the depression of the thirties and World War II. Scranton and the anthracite area never really recovered. As the economy began to boom again, Americans were switching from coal to oil or gas furnaces. Demand for anthracite diminished greatly, and the number of miners employed was low. In the sixties and seventies there has been some development: textile and apparel mills, mostly bringing low-wage jobs. But the city of Scranton, isolated in the mountains, can no longer support the numbers it once could. Its population has declined from 143,000 in 1930 to 103,000 in 1970. Just a look at the edges of Scranton shows what happened. On one block stand some large houses, maintained with care, but obviously built in the twenties—the city's last prosperous decade. On the next block, one finds no new suburban tract housing or shopping centers, only trees and hills. In few parts of the country is such a sudden halt in urban development so apparent.

Scranton and the industrial towns around it make up about half of Pennsylvania's 10th congressional district. The 10th consists of a rather anomalous mix: the heavily ethnic city and surrounding Lackawanna County, combined with several Scots-Irish-Welsh counties in the Pocono Mountains (a favorite resort of many middle class New Yorkers), along with some of the counties in the state's northern tier. The partisan balance in this area has remained the same over the years. The number of votes in Democratic Scranton has declined, but the rural counties are becoming slightly less Republican. As a result, the district has given Republicans a slight margin in every close presidential election since World War II, including 1976.

The district's best known Congressman, William Scranton, served only two years. He is from the aristocratic family whose name the city bears, and he has been active in efforts to revitalize it economically. He ran for Congress in 1960 to dislodge a Democrat elected in the 1958 landslide, and went on to be elected Governor in 1962. Scranton has had an active career in national affairs since, running for president in 1964 and serving on important commissions and in critical posts under various presidents. He continues to maintain his residence in Scranton and is an important presence in the area; his son and namesake was elected Lieutenant Governor in 1978.

Scranton's successor in the House is Joseph McDade, a Republican in the Scranton mold. The difference is that McDade does not have statewide aspirations; he has represented the 10th district for almost two decades with no apparent intentions to run for anything else. McDade is generally described as a liberal Republican, and usually he has had voting records rated higher by organized labor than by business interests. On the Appropriations Committee he ranks behind only Silvio Conte, who holds the ranking Republican status, and Robert Michel, the House Republican Whip; still under 50, he should be an important member of that committee for years. He has proved to be very popular in the 10th district, and in 1978 won reelection by a 3-1 margin.

Census Data Pop. 472,007. Central city, 22%; suburban, 36%. Median family income, $8,318; families above $15,000: 12%; families below $3,000: 10%. Median years education, 12.0.

The Voters

Median voting age 46.
Employment profile White collar, 38%. Blue collar, 47%. Service, 11%. Farm, 4%.
Ethnic groups Total foreign stock, 20%. Italy, Poland, 4% each; UK, Austria, Germany, 2% each; Ireland, 1%.

Presidential vote

1976	Carter (D)	97,659	(49%)
	Ford (R)	100,938	(51%)
1972	Nixon (R)	125,686	(64%)
	McGovern (D)	71,105	(36%)

Rep. Joseph M. McDade (R) Elected 1962; b. Sept. 29, 1931, Scranton; home, Scranton; U. of Notre Dame, B.A. 1953, U. of Penn, LL.B. 1956; Catholic.

Career Clerk to Chf. Fed. Judge John W. Murphy, 1956–57; Practicing atty., 1957–62; Scranton City Solicitor, 1962.

Offices 2370 RHOB, 202-225-3731. Also 1223 Northeastern Natl. Bank Bldg., Scranton 18503, 717-346-3834.

Committees *Appropriations* (3d). Subcommittees: HUD-Independent Agencies; Interior.

Small Business (Ranking Member). Subcommittees: SBA and SBIC Authority and General Small Business Problems.

Group Ratings

	ADA	COPE	PC	RPN	NFU	LCV	CFA	NAB	NSI	ACA	NTU
1978	30	45	40	40	63	–	32	46	70	54	–
1977	40	87	55	54	83	51	60	–	–	42	31
1976	40	62	48	63	55	63	45	50	70	26	21

Key Votes

1) Increase Def Spnd	FOR	6) Alaska Lands Protect	FOR	11) Delay Auto Pol Cntrl	FOR
2) B-1 Bomber	FOR	7) Water Projects Veto	AGN	12) Sugar Price Escalator	AGN
3) Cargo Preference	AGN	8) Consum Protect Agcy	AGN	13) Pub Fin Cong Cmpgns	AGN
4) Dereg Nat Gas	AGN	9) Common Situs Picket	FOR	14) ERA Ratif Recissn	AGN
5) Kemp-Roth	FOR	10) Labor Law Revision	FOR	15) Prohibt Govt Abrtns	FOR

Election Results

1978 general	Joseph M. McDade (R)	116,003	(76%)	($66,769)
	Gene Basalyga (D)	35,721	(24%)	
1978 primary	Joseph M. McDade (R), unopposed			
1976 general	Joseph M. McDade (R)	125,218	(63%)	($61,225)
	Edward Mitchell (D)	74,925	(37%)	($87,635)

ELEVENTH DISTRICT

The 11th congressional district of Pennsylvania is centered on Wilkes-Barre and Luzerne County in northeast Pennsylvania. This is part of America's great anthracite coal district, which was of great importance to the nation in the days when most houses were heated by coal. There was a kind of boom here, and immigrants were attracted to Wilkes-Barre and the string of communities in the narrow flood plain on both sides of the Susquehanna River. There were almost half a million people in Luzerne County in 1930, most of them in this valley, but some scattered in mining and manufacturing towns in the hills. But the demand for anthracite dropped with the depression and the conversion to oil and gas heating. Prosperity has never entirely returned to the Wilkes-Barre area. Population has declined, as young people leave to make their livings elsewhere; the new industries that have come in, notably textiles and apparel, pay low wages. This is the kind of congressional district that wants a congressman who will bring federal money and aid to the district and who will do all he can to promote its economy. And that is why the 11th district has elected, and in the face of his legal troubles in 1978 reelected, Congressman Daniel Flood.

Flood has long been a favorite of aficionados of the House. With his waxed mustache, his flowing cape, and his staccato oratory which owes something to his years as a Shakespearean actor—all these contributed to Flood's distinctive style. He was also powerful. He was first elected to the House in 1944, and has risen in seniority until he is now the fourth ranking Democrat on the House Appropriations Committee. For years he chaired the Labor-HEW Subcommittee, which appropriated money for most social programs; not surprisingly, the Wilkes-Barre area usually got more than its share. He was also the number two man on the Defense Subcommittee, and had plenty of friends in the Pentagon. Flood was always working to aid his district. But the high point of his congressional career came in 1972, when Hurricane Agnes and the floods it started devastated the Susquehanna valley. Flood stepped in and took command. Using his Pentagon connections, at one point he even had a fireboat flown in from Boston harbor in a C5-A transport. For such activities Flood was reelected easily every two years.

But he was never known nationally until 1978, when he suddenly found himself in deep trouble. His former administrative assistant, Stephen Elko, accused him of soliciting payments from people for whom he interceded with people in the executive branch; in effect, Flood was accused of selling his clout. To some, the charges seemed dubious. Flood still lived in an old house in Wilkes-Barre and did not spend money lavishly. If he had put a lot of money away, he might have used it to retire; in 1978 he was 75 and had been in poor health. The tendency in Wilkes-Barre was to rally around the Congressman. As the best known public figure in the area, he was a kind of local hero; and he had strong support from local business leaders and the newspaper, which did not print many of the allegations against him. Even when Flood was indicted in October, on ten counts of bribery in Washington and on three counts of perjury in Los Angeles, he was still hailed as a hero in the 11th district. He was renominated in the April primary and reelected over an active Republican in November.

But Flood had already lost much clout in Washington. Younger and some older Democratic members, unwilling to be attacked in their campaigns for condoning corruption in the House, in effect forced Flood to leave his subcommittee chairmanship. Even though reelected, he is no longer likely to have much influence in the House. Executive branch personnel who used to quake at the mention of his name are unlikely to return his calls. Flood was tried in Washington in early 1979 and avoided conviction because one juror steadfastly held out; afterwards, there was an investigation of possible jury tampering. At this writing he seems likely to be tried again in Washington if his health permits and in Los Angeles as well.

It seems likely that this is Flood's last term in Congress, whatever subsequent juries say. Although he won reelection in 1978, his margins were not what he was used to. A weak primary opponent was able to get one-quarter of the vote against him, and in the general election the Republican held him to 58%. The voters of the 11th district have now thanked Flood for all that he has done for them, but they can see that there is little he can do for them in the future.

Census Data Pop. 470,457. Central city, 19%; suburban, 54%. Median family income, $8,161; families above $15,000: 10%; families below $3,000: 9%. Median years education, 11.6.

The Voters

Median voting age 47.
Employment profile White collar, 35%. Blue collar, 53%. Service, 11%. Farm, 1%.
Ethnic groups Total foreign stock, 25%. Poland, 6%; Italy, 4%; Austria, 3%; Czechoslovakia, UK, 2% each; Lithuania, Germany, 1% each.

Presidential vote

1976	Carter (D)	101,571	(54%)
	Ford (R)	85,292	(46%)
1972	Nixon (R)	113,556	(62%)
	McGovern (D)	68,764	(38%)

Rep. Daniel J. Flood (D) Elected 1954; b. Nov. 26, 1903, Hazleton; home, Wilkes-Barre; Syracuse U., B.A., M.A., Harvard Law School, 1925–26, Dickinson U., LL.B. 1929; Catholic.

Career Practicing atty., 1930–54; Atty., Home Owners' Loan Corp., 1934–35; Deputy Atty. Gen. of Penn. and Counsel for Penn. Liquor Control Bd., 1935–39; Dir., Penn. St. Treasury Bureau of Public Assistance Disbursements and Exec. Asst. to the St. Treasurer, 1941–44; U.S. House of Reps., 1945–47, 1949–53.

Offices 108 CHOB, 202-225-6511; Also Rm. 1015 Utd. Penn Bank Bldg., Wilkes-Barre 18701, 717-829-3443.

Committees *Appropriations* (4th). Subcommittees: Defense; Labor-HEW.

Group Ratings

	ADA	COPE	PC	RPN	NFU	LCV	CFA	NAB	NSI	ACA	NTU
1978	40	74	58	10	70	–	46	0	70	21	–
1977	40	100	48	8	82	29	65	–	–	16	11
1976	55	91	67	28	75	61	81	25	90	21	8

Key Votes

1) Increase Def Spnd	AGN	6) Alaska Lands Protect	DNV	11) Delay Auto Pol Cntrl	FOR
2) B-1 Bomber	AGN	7) Water Projects Veto	AGN	12) Sugar Price Escalator	FOR
3) Cargo Preference	FOR	8) Consum Protect Agcy	FOR	13) Pub Fin Cong Cmpgns	AGN
4) Dereg Nat Gas	AGN	9) Common Situs Picket	FOR	14) ERA Ratif Recissn	AGN
5) Kemp-Roth	AGN	10) Labor Law Revision	FOR	15) Prohibt Govt Abrtns	FOR

Election Results

1978 general	Daniel J. Flood (D)	61,433	(58%)	($25,794)
	Robert P. Hudock (R)	45,335	(42%)	($19,149)
1978 primary	Daniel J. Flood (D)	42,823	(74%)	
	Samuel W. Daley (D)	14,904	(26%)	
1976 general	Daniel J. Flood (D)	130,175	(71%)	($41,276)
	Howard G. Williams (R)	53,621	(29%)	($0)

TWELFTH DISTRICT

The hills of western Pennsylvania, eastern Ohio, and northern West Virginia that encircle the Pittsburgh metropolitan area constitute one of the largest industrial sections of the country without a major city. The easternmost part of these industrial mountains forms Pennsylvania's 12th congressional district: five counties and part of another, the largest city of which is Johnstown, with 42,000 people. More typical of the district are small towns like Kittanning and Punxsutawney. This area was first settled by Scots-Irish farmers when it was still the frontier in the 1790s, and in the nineteenth century it became part of the bituminous coal belt. Today coal is still important to the district's economy, but despite the recently improving fortunes of the fuel, the industry employs far fewer people than it did 30 years ago.

In statewide elections, the 12th is as marginal as any district in Pennsylvania; it usually comes in a couple of points more Republican than the state as a whole, although Democrats have a small registration advantage. In congressional elections it has stayed with its incumbents regardless of party. From 1950 to 1972 it elected Republican John Saylor, one of the leading conservationists in the House. After Saylor's death, the district chose Democrat John Murtha in a special election and has reelected him ever since. This was the first of that series of 1974 special elections that demonstrated the unpopularity of Richard Nixon during the Watergate crisis; Murtha did not want to use the Watergate issue, but nonetheless it seems to have hurt his Republican opponent.

Murtha is one of only a few Vietnam veterans in the Congress—a stark contrast from the years after World War II, when almost all new members were veterans—and was the first to be elected. He has worked his district hard and built up larger majorities in each election. He serves on the Appropriations Committee, a body whose junior members, even the hardest working, are seldom very visible. His most notable action in the House has been his fervent discussion of the needs of the Vietnam veterans, and his strong pleas that the government do more for them.

Census Data Pop. 469,999. Central city, 9%; suburban, 47%. Median family income, $8,030; families above $15,000: 10%; families below $3,000: 11%. Median years education, 11.2.

The Voters

Median voting age 46.
Employment profile White collar, 35%. Blue collar, 50%. Service, 12%. Farm, 3%.
Ethnic groups Black, 1%. Total foreign stock, 15%. Italy, 3%; Czechoslovakia, Poland, Austria, 2% each; UK, Germany, 1% each.

Presidential vote

1976	Carter (D)	91,237	(51%)
	Ford (R)	88,382	(49%)
1972	Nixon (R)	112,694	(64%)
	McGovern (D)	64,049	(36%)

Rep. John P. Murtha (D) Elected Feb. 5, 1974; b. June 17, 1932, New Martinsville, W. Va; Home, Johnstown; U. of Pitt., B.A., Ind. U. of Penn.

Career USMC, Vietnam; Owner, Johnstown Minute Car Wash; Penn. House of Reps., 1969–74.

Offices 2423 RHOB, 202-225-2065. Also 226 Fed. Bldg., Johnstown 15901, 814-535-2642.

Committees *Appropriations* (21st). Subcommittees: Interior; Defense.

Standards of Official Conduct (6th).

Group Ratings

	ADA	COPE	PC	RPN	NFU	LCV	CFA	NAB	NSI	ACA	NTU
1978	25	65	35	25	60	–	27	58	90	30	–
1977	20	86	30	0	67	24	30	–	–	27	20
1976	45	91	54	41	75	34	45	17	75	36	16

Key Votes

1) Increase Def Spnd	FOR	6) Alaska Lands Protect	FOR	11) Delay Auto Pol Cntrl	FOR
2) B-1 Bomber	FOR	7) Water Projects Veto	AGN	12) Sugar Price Escalator	AGN
3) Cargo Preference	FOR	8) Consum Protect Agcy	AGN	13) Pub Fin Cong Cmpgns	AGN
4) Dereg Nat Gas	DNV	9) Common Situs Picket	FOR	14) ERA Ratif Recissn	AGN
5) Kemp-Roth	AGN	10) Labor Law Revision	FOR	15) Prohibt Govt Abrtns	FOR

Election Results

1978 general	John P. Murtha, Jr. (D)	104,216	(69%)	($33,377)
	Luther V. Elkin (R)	47,442	(31%)	($15,175)
1978 primary	John P. Murtha, Jr. (D), unopposed			
1976 general	John P. Murtha, Jr. (D)	122,504	(68%)	($36,961)
	Ted Humes (R)	58,489	(32%)	($49,562)

THIRTEENTH DISTRICT

The 13th congressional district of Pennsylvania, part of Montgomery County, is a fair cross-section of the upper income Philadelphia suburbs. Along with the 5th district, the 13th contains the posh Main Line suburbs, places like Haverford, Bryn Mawr, and Ardmore—some of them with famous colleges and all with the patina of wealth and social standing and the dignity of age. The 13th also contains the 21st ward of Philadelphia, a well-to-do, Republican part of the city adjacent to the posh Chestnut Hill neighborhood. On the other side of Philadelphia are predominantly Jewish suburbs like Cheltenham Township, which were built up mostly in the fifties. As one moves away from the city limits, the land becomes hillier and more sparsely settled, with the exception of old industrial towns like Norristown and Conshocken, right on the banks of the Schuylkill River. Not far away is the growing area around King of Prussia and Valley Forge. Overall, the 13th is increasingly the residence of Pennsylvania's elite. It is also the home of some of the state's leading politicians, like Senator Richard Schweiker and former Governor Milton Shapp.

The 13th is today, as it always has been, a solidly Republican district. Up through the fifties it was fiercely conservative, and so were its congressmen; since then, they have been more moderate Republicans. Richard Schweiker was elected here from 1960 until he ran for the Senate in 1968; his successor, chosen then and still serving, is Lawrence Coughlin. He is not well known nationally, although he might have become so had he not switched off the House Judiciary Committee in 1973, just a year before the hearings on Richard Nixon's impeachment. Coughlin is an active member of the Appropriations Committee, and has been mentioned as a possible candidate to succeed Schweiker in the Senate in 1980.

Census Data Pop. 473,179. Central city, 11%; suburban, 89%. Median family income, $13,251; families above $15,000: 41%; families below $3,000: 4%. Median years education, 12.4.

The Voters

Median voting age 45.
Employment profile White collar, 64%. Blue collar, 27%. Service, 9%. Farm, –%.
Ethnic groups Black, 4%. Total foreign stock, 25%. Italy, 6%; USSR, UK, Germany, 3% each; Poland, Ireland, 2% each.

Presidential vote

1976	Carter (D)	89,823	(43%)
	Ford (R)	120,746	(57%)
1972	Nixon (R)	135,464	(64%)
	McGovern (D)	77,715	(36%)

Rep. Lawrence Coughlin (R) Elected 1968; b. Apr. 11, 1929, Wilkes-Barre; home, Villanova; Yale U., B.A. 1950, Harvard U., M.B.A. 1954, Temple U., LL.B. 1958; Episcopalian.

Career USMC, Korea; Practicing atty., 1958–69; Penn. House of Reps., 1965–66; Penn. Senate, 1967–68.

Offices 306 CHOB, 202-225-6111. Also 700 One Montgomery Plaza, Norristown 19401, 215-277-4040.

Committees *Appropriations* (10th). Subcommittees: HUD-Independent Agencies; Transportation.

Group Ratings

	ADA	COPE	PC	RPN	NFU	LCV	CFA	NAB	NSI	ACA	NTU
1978	25	21	38	82	10	–	23	92	60	56	–
1977	35	26	53	92	27	77	35	–	–	67	34
1976	35	35	54	78	42	65	18	58	70	35	56

Key Votes

1) Increase Def Spnd	AGN	6) Alaska Lands Protect	FOR	11) Delay Auto Pol Cntrl	AGN
2) B-1 Bomber	FOR	7) Water Projects Veto	FOR	12) Sugar Price Escalator	AGN
3) Cargo Preference	AGN	8) Consum Protect Agcy	AGN	13) Pub Fin Cong Cmpgns	AGN
4) Dereg Nat Gas	FOR	9) Common Situs Picket	AGN	14) ERA Ratif Recissn	FOR
5) Kemp-Roth	FOR	10) Labor Law Revision	AGN	15) Prohibt Govt Abrtns	FOR

Election Results

1978 general	Lawrence Coughlin (R)	112,711	(71%)	($105,534)
	Alan Bendix Rubenstein (D)	47,151	(29%)	($32,279)
1978 primary	Lawrence Coughlin (R)	51,644	(89%)	
	One other (R)	6,086	(11%)	
1976 general	Lawrence Coughlin (R)	130,705	(63%)	($69,920)
	Gertrude Strick (D)	75,435	(37%)	($35,565)

FOURTEENTH DISTRICT

Pittsburgh, Pennsylvania's second largest city, was the first urban center in the American interior. Pittsburgh grew because of its propitious site; here the Allegheny and Monongahela Rivers join to form the Ohio. The place where that happens—the Golden Triangle—remains the city's focal point: it is now filled with high rise buildings, products of a downtown renaissance. When most of the nation's commerce moved over water, Pittsburgh's location was ideal; and when traffic switched to the railroads, the city adapted nicely. By the turn of the century, Pittsburgh, with large deposits of coal nearby, was the center of the steel industry, then the nation's largest and also one of the fastest growing segments of the economy.

Today Pittsburgh remains the headquarters of many of the nation's largest corporations: U.S. Steel and several other steel companies, Westinghouse, Heinz, and the giant concerns associated with the Mellon family, Alcoa, Gulf Oil, and Koppers. But in spite of the city's recent progress—its program of downtown renewal and its relatively successful campaign against air pollution—Pittsburgh has been unable to keep pace with other major metropolitan areas. Its major industry, steel, has not shown much dynamism lately. And it does not have the advantage of being a great center of air transportation, like Chicago or Atlanta. Its climate is cold. For these and other reasons, Pittsburgh's economy has not grown very rapidly. As a result, the population not only of the central city but of the entire metropolitan area has been declining since 1960—the only major metropolitan area of which this is true.

The 14th congressional district of Pennsylvania includes most of the city of Pittsburgh, including almost all of the central part of the city between the Allegheny and the Monongahela, plus a few suburbs. The district takes in most of the city's landmarks: the Golden Triangle, the University of Pittsburgh and its skyscraper campus, and Carnegie Mellon University. Though few of the city's steel mills lie within the 14th, many of the steel workers do live here, mostly in ethnic neighborhoods nestled between the Pittsburgh hills. The district also includes the Shady Side neighborhood, newly renovated with new shops near some of Pittsburgh's old mansions, and the predominantly Jewish Squirrel Hill neighborhood. Farther out is the main black neighborhood of Pittsburgh. Only 21% of the residents of this district, however, are black, a smaller figure than in most industrial cities because employment opportunities in Pittsburgh peaked before the big waves of black migration from the South. Since the New Deal, the 14th has been solidly Democratic; in 1972, for example, it was one of only four districts in Pennsylvania (the other three were in Philadelphia) which gave George McGovern a majority.

The district's Congressman is Democrat William Moorhead. After 20 years in the House, he is third-ranking Democrat on the Banking, Finance, and Urban Affairs Committee and fourth-ranking Democrat on Government Operations. Moorhead is Chairman of the Economic Stabilization Subcommittee, in which capacity he has managed legislation for aid to New York City and to authorize the President's Council on Wage and Price Stability. This is also the subcommittee which would handle the delicate question of authorizing wage and price controls; though at this writing, neither the Congress nor the Administration will say it wants such legislation. Moorhead has managed important bills successfully, but he is not one of those members whose name and endorsement carry great weight and authority in the House.

Moorhead has seldom had serious political challenges at home. He was selected for the seat in 1958 by then Pittsburgh Mayor David Lawrence. He has been criticized for having close ties to the Mellons, and until 1971 owned considerable stock in the Mellon bank, one of the nation's largest, while serving on the Banking Committee. The Congressman is well known in social circles in Washington, with his wife having recently written a book on entertaining in the nation's capital. But these are not particularly strong credentials back in Pittsburgh these days: Lawrence is dead, the Mellons have little direct electoral clout, and most steel workers are not interested in how much help you need in order to entertain Henry Kissinger properly. Moorhead saw his first serious Republican challenge in years in 1978, and his percentage dropped to 58%—nearly 20% below what he received in the Democratic year of 1974. It is hard to imagine a Democratic congressman losing this district, but it seems likely that Moorhead will have to emulate some of his younger colleagues and work the district hard if he wishes to make it as safe as people used to think it was for him.

Census Data Pop. 470,537. Central city, 83%; suburban, 17%. Median family income, $8,952; families above $15,000: 18%; families below $3,000: 11%. Median years education, 11.9.

The Voters

Median voting age 47.
Employment profile White collar, 53%. Blue collar, 29%. Service, 18%. Farm, –%.
Ethnic groups Black, 21%. Total foreign stock, 25%. Italy, 5%; Poland, Germany, 3% each; USSR, UK, Ireland, 2% each; Austria, 1%.

Presidential vote

1976	Carter (D)	98,609	(59%)
	Ford (R)	68,088	(41%)
1972	Nixon (R)	85,912	(48%)
	McGovern (D)	95,687	(52%)

Rep. William S. Moorhead (D) Elected 1958; b. Apr. 8, 1923, Pittsburgh; home, Pittsburgh; Yale U., B.A. 1944, Harvard U., J.D. 1949; Episcopalian.

Career Navy, WWII; Practicing atty., 1949–59; Pittsburgh Asst. City Solicitor, 1954–57; Mbr., Allegheny Co. Housing Auth., 1956–58; Mbr., Pittsburgh Art Commission, 1958.

Offices 2442 RHOB, 202-225-2301. Also 2007 Fed. Bldg., Pittsburgh 15222, 412-644-2870.

Committees *Banking, Finance and Urban Affairs* (3d). Subcommittees: Economic Stabilization (Chairman); Housing and Community Development; International Development Institutions and Finance.

Government Operations (4th). Subcommittees: Intergovernmental Relations and Human Resources; Legislation and National Security.

Group Ratings

	ADA	COPE	PC	RPN	NFU	LCV	CFA	NAB	NSI	ACA	NTU
1978	65	85	70	50	70	–	59	0	30	11	–
1977	70	96	60	42	83	65	60	–	–	4	20
1976	80	83	80	53	92	71	73	8	30	8	23

Key Votes

1) Increase Def Spnd	AGN	6) Alaska Lands Protect	FOR	11) Delay Auto Pol Cntrl	FOR
2) B-1 Bomber	AGN	7) Water Projects Veto	FOR	12) Sugar Price Escalator	AGN
3) Cargo Preference	FOR	8) Consum Protect Agcy	FOR	13) Pub Fin Cong Cmpgns	FOR
4) Dereg Nat Gas	AGN	9) Common Situs Picket	FOR	14) ERA Ratif Recissn	AGN
5) Kemp-Roth	AGN	10) Labor Law Revision	FOR	15) Prohibt Govt Abrtns	AGN

Election Results

1978 general	William S. Moorhead (D)	68,004$114,623		((58%))
	Stan Thomas (R)	49,992	(42%)	($119,799)
1978 primary	William S. Moorhead (D)	44,603	(76%)	
	Kenneth K. McNulty, Sr. (D)	14,074	(24%)	
1976 general	William S. Moorhead (D)	114,472	(73%)	($46,635)
	John F. Bradley (R)	43,308	(27%)	($779)

FIFTEENTH DISTRICT

The 15th congressional district of Pennsylvania is the industrial Lehigh Valley in the eastern part of the state. It is one of only two congressional districts in the country which consist of two and only two whole counties (the other is the 4th of South Carolina). Here in Northampton and Lehigh Counties are the adjoining, but quite different, cities of Allentown and Bethlehem and, to the east, the smaller city of Easton. Allentown is a diversified industrial town, one of the nation's leading cement centers (because of local limestone deposits) and the home of Mack Trucks; drawing its labor force from the Pennsylvania Dutch country around it and to the south, it has grown steadily in the twentieth century. Bethlehem has a more complex history. It was founded by the Moravian sect in 1741 (the same people who started the Salem of Winston-Salem, North Carolina) and retains many eighteenth century buildings. Across the Lehigh River there was an iron works in the nineteenth century, which grew eventually to be the central plant for Bethlehem Steel.

Allentown with its steady growth tends to be Republican or about evenly divided between the parties; Bethlehem, with its steel worker population, tends to be Democratic. Overall, the 15th should probably be considered a Democratic district, and it has gone Democratic in close presidential elections in recent years. It has been even more reliably Democratic in congressional elections—until 1978. Then the district was the scene of one of the bigger upsets of the congressional elections that year.

It was one of only two really seriously contested elections in this district in the last 15 years. The other was the July 1963 special election to replace Francis Walter, Chairman of the House Un-American Activities Committee and author of the McCarran-Walter anti-subversive act, who died after more than 30 years in Congress. The winner of that election was Democrat Fred Rooney, and for years thereafter he seemed to have a safe seat. He had a solid labor voting record and good relations with local union leaders, and he rose in seniority on the Commerce Committee until he became Chairman of the Transportation Subcommittee, which has jurisdiction over railroads and trucking—both of great importance to this district. But in 1978 Republicans looked hard for experienced Democrats who seemed to have some hidden vulnerability—hidden, because they had not been seriously challenged in years. One of them turned out to be Rooney. The Republican candidate was Donald Ritter, an engineer and administrator at Lehigh University. He attacked Rooney's handling of railroad problems, arguing that the Conrail freight system should be decentralized and that railroads generally should be less regulated and freer to make profits in ways they chose. Those may not have been central issues to most voters, but apparently they helped diminish confidence in Rooney; or perhaps the people here felt he was not paying enough attention to the district. In any case Rooney, who had no opposition in 1974 and won 65% of the vote in 1976 got only 47% in 1978 and was defeated.

That means that 1980 will be a key year for Ritter. He must work hard to establish a strong identity here, because he can be reasonably sure that in this Democratic district some strong Democrat will run against him.

Census Data Pop. 469,672. Central city, 45%; suburban, 55%. Median family income, $10,171; families above $15,000: 19%; families below $3,000: 6%. Median years education, 11.7.

The Voters

Median voting age 45.
Employment profile White collar, 41%. Blue collar, 47%. Service, 11%. Farm, 1%.
Ethnic groups Black, 1%. Total foreign stock, 19%. Italy, Austria, 3% each; Hungary, Germany, Czechoslovakia, 2% each; Poland, UK, 1% each.

Presidential vote

1976	Carter (D)	89,134	(53%)
	Ford (R)	79,821	(47%)
1972	Nixon (R)	99,664	(60%)
	McGovern (D)	65,557	(40%)

Rep. Don Ritter (R) Elected 1978; b. Oct. 21, 1940, Bronx, N.Y.; home, Coopersburg; Lehigh U., B.S. 1961, M.I.T., M.S. 1963, SC.D. 1966; Unitarian.

Career Scientific Exchange Fellow, Moscow, USSR, 1967–78; Asst. Prof., Cal. Poly. U., 1968–76; Mgr., Research Program Development, Lehigh U., 1976–78.

Offices 124 CHOB, 202-225-6411. Also P.O. Bldg., Rm. 212, Allentown 18101, 215-439-8861.

Committees *Banking, Finance and Urban Affairs* (14th). Subcommittees: Housing and Community Development; Consumer Affairs; Domestic Monetary Policy.

Science and Technology (14th). Subcommittees: Science, Research and Technology; Energy Development and Applications; Natural Resources and Environment.

Group Ratings: Newly Elected

Key Votes: Newly Elected

Election Results

1978 general	Donald L. Ritter (R)	65,986	(53%)	($63,205)
	Fred B. Rooney (D)	58,077	(47%)	($131,005)
1978 primary	Donald L. Ritter (R)	11,057	(47%)	
	James R. Feather (R)	3,590	(15%)	
	John Thomas Weaver (R)	3,147	(13%)	
	Three others (R)	5,955	(25%)	
1976 general	Fred B. Rooney (D)	108,844	(65%)	($44,605)
	Alice B. Sivulich (R)	57,616	(35%)	($3,149)

SIXTEENTH DISTRICT

Millions of people know about Pennsylvania Dutch country: farms scrupulously tended and set out among rolling hills, barns decorated with hex signs, and Amish families clad in black, clattering along in horse-drawn carriages. Fewer Americans know that the Pennsylvania Dutch are actually German in origin ("Dutch" is a corruption of "Deutsch"). They are descended from members of Amish, Mennonite, and other pietistic sects who left the principalities of eighteenth century Germany for the religious freedom of the Quaker-dominated colony of Pennsylvania. The Quakers were happy to welcome the Germans, but they were not eager to have them in Philadelphia. So they were sent to Germantown, a few miles away, until they could move out to what was then the frontier, where they might help protect the pacifist Quakers against the Indians. Thus the Dutch came to the rolling green hills of Lancaster and York Counties. The land was naturally fertile, and careful cultivation by the Dutch vastly increased its productivity. Today farms in Lancaster County continue to produce some of the highest per acre yields on earth.

The Pennsylvania Dutch are perhaps the most conservative people in America. They are not like so many residents of the Sun Belt, who seek the reassurance of cultural continuity even as they pursue the economic change inevitably wrought by free market capitalism. The people here see little need for change of any kind; they believe that they live in a real and present paradise, and aside from the less than pleasant tourists much evidence exists to support their belief. Of course most of the Pennsylvania Dutch are not plain people. But the heritage is important: most people here are of German descent, and possess a strong work ethic. Small industries have settled here because of the skills and hard work of the labor force, and agriculture continues to be important economically. The brick townhouses of Lancaster, like the frame farmhouses of the Amish, are sparklingly well kept, and seem little changed from what they must have looked like fifty years ago.

The Pennsylvania Dutch country has produced one president, James Buchanan, and housed another in his retirement, Dwight Eisenhower. In Buchanan's time the politics of this area was Jeffersonian Democratic. But in the 1850s the Dutch became Republican, a preference they have retained to this day. The laissez faire of the Jeffersonians seemed less attractive than the antislavery activism of the Republicans; later the Republicans came to exemplify laissez faire themselves. Today the heart of the Dutch country, Lancaster County, regularly returns Republican majorities on the order of 3-1—usually the largest of any area of similar size in the East.

The most Dutch of all the Pennsylvania congressional districts is the 16th, which includes all of Lancaster County and parts of Chester and Lebanon Counties. Of all the congressional districts in the East, it has cast the highest Republican percentages in the last three presidential elections. The district's Congressman is Robert Walker, a young Republican first elected in 1976, who had been a staff aide to his predecessor, Edwin Eshleman. Walker is one of the more articulate and aggressive proponents of the philosophy that government is too big and ought to be cut back.

Census Data Pop. 467,811. Central city, 12%; suburban, 72%. Median family income, $9,905; families above $15,000: 18%; families below $3,000: 6%. Median years education, 11.4.

The Voters

Median voting age 43.
Employment profile White collar, 38%. Blue collar, 46%. Service, 12%. Farm, 4%.
Ethnic groups Black, 3%. Total foreign stock, 7%. Germany, Italy, 1% each.

Presidential vote

1976	Carter (D)	56,814	(36%)
	Ford (R)	101,642	(64%)
1972	Nixon (R)	115,651	(76%)
	McGovern (D)	37,223	(24%)

Rep. Robert S. Walker (R) Elected 1976; b. Dec. 23, 1942, Bradford; home, East Petersburg; Wm. and Mary Col., 1960–61, Millersville St. Col., B.S. 1964, U. of Del., M.A. 1968; Presbyterian.

Career Teacher, 1964–67; Admin. Asst. to U.S. Rep. Edwin D. Eshleman, 1967–77.

Offices 1028 LHOB, 202-225-2411. Also Lancaster Co. Courthouse, Lancaster 17601, 717-393-0666.

Committees *Government Operations* (7th). Subcommittees: Government Activities and Transportation.

Science and Technology (8th). Subcommittees: Energy Development and Applications; Natural Resources and Environment.

Group Ratings

	ADA	COPE	PC	RPN	NFU	LCV	CFA	NAB	NSI	ACA	NTU
1978	15	20	23	73	11	–	23	73	100	96	–
1977	20	18	28	62	25	35	40	–	–	93	49

Key Votes

1) Increase Def Spnd	FOR	6) Alaska Lands Protect	AGN	11) Delay Auto Pol Cntrl	FOR
2) B-1 Bomber	FOR	7) Water Projects Veto	FOR	12) Sugar Price Escalator	AGN
3) Cargo Preference	AGN	8) Consum Protect Agcy	AGN	13) Pub Fin Cong Cmpgns	AGN
4) Dereg Nat Gas	FOR	9) Common Situs Picket	AGN	14) ERA Ratif Recissn	FOR
5) Kemp-Roth	FOR	10) Labor Law Revision	AGN	15) Prohibt Govt Abrtns	FOR

Election Results

1978 general	Robert S. Walker (R)	91,910	(77%)	($40,289)
	Charles W. Boohar (D)	27,386	(23%)	
1978 primary	Robert S. Walker (R)	35,976	(76%)	
	Norman O. Aamodt (R)	11,299	(24%)	($47,943)
1976 general	Robert S. Walker (R)	97,527	(63%)	($29,241)
	Michael J. Minney (D)	57,836	(37%)	($13,409)

SEVENTEENTH DISTRICT

The 17th congressional district of Pennsylvania lies at just about the center of the state, taking in a collection of counties along the Susquehanna River. The southern end of the district, around Harrisburg, contains nearly two-thirds of its population. The main industry here, of course, is state government. The 17th also takes in the site of the now famous Three Mile Island nuclear power plant. Farther up the Susquehanna is Northumberland County, the waist, as it were, of the district. Here seams of anthracite once drew ethnics to towns like Sunbury and Shamokin. Right across the river are the Lewisburg and Allenwood Federal prisons, where so many veterans of the Nixon White House, as well as dignitaries like Jimmy Hoffa and Carmine DeSapio, did time. To the north is Williamsport, a small manufacturing town on the upper Susquehanna. Its all-American character makes it an appropriate host for the annual Little League World Series.

From the Civil War to the depression of the thirties, Pennsylvania was a solidly Republican state. The big capitalists who owned its plants and the workers who toiled in them, the big city machine bosses and the small farmers—virtually everyone voted Republican. The 17th district retains much of that heritage. Harrisburg, a gritty, population-losing state capital, remains heavily Republican in most elections (can that result from the fact that the governorship in this patronage-oriented state was held by Republicans for years?). In Northumberland County, the miners became Democrats in the thirties, but Williamsport remained true to its ancestral party. Overall, the district remains heavily Republican; Gerald Ford, for example, carried it easily in 1976.

Nevertheless the 17th has elected a Democrat to the House in the last three elections. He is Allen Ertel, and he ran in 1974 when incumbent Herman Schneebeli, ranking minority member of the House Ways and Means Committee, retired. Ertel's greatest assets that time were the national issues working for Democrats in that Watergate year and his own local popularity in the Williamsport area, where he was District Attorney. They were enough to get him elected with 51% of the vote. Since then, he has used his seat on the House Public Works Committee to fight for more flood control for this district, which has little in common except the oft-flooding Susquehanna. He has returned constantly to the district, and overall has had enough strength to repel significant challenges. His 1978 Republican opponent had the distinction of holding degrees from both Columbia University Law School and McDonald's Hamburger University; nonetheless Ertel was reelected with 60% of the vote.

Census Data Pop. 476,141. Central city, 14%; suburban, 33%. Median family income, $8,933; families above $15,000: 14%; families below $3,000: 8%. Median years education, 12.1.

The Voters

Median voting age 45.
Employment profile White collar, 44%. Blue collar, 42%. Service, 12%. Farm, 2%.
Ethnic groups Black, 6%. Total foreign stock, 8%. Italy, 1%.

Presidential vote

1976	Carter (D)	73,061	(42%)
	Ford (R)	98,920	(58%)
1972	Nixon (R)	119,178	(71%)
	McGovern (D)	48,205	(29%)

Rep. Allen E. Ertel (D) Elected 1976; b. Nov. 7, 1936, Williamsport; home, Montoursville; Dartmouth Col, B.A. 1958, Thayer Sch. of Engr., Dickenson U., 1962–63, Yale U., LL.B. 1965; Lutheran.

Career Navy, 1959–62; Practicing atty.; Lycoming Co. Dist. Atty., 1968–77.

Offices 1030 LHOB, 202-225-4315. Also Rm. 230, 240 W. Third St. Williamsport 17701, 717-326-2814.

Committees *Science and Technology* (26th). Subcommittees: Science, Research, and Technology; Energy Development and Applications.

Public Works and Transportation (19th). Subcommittees: Aviation; Surface Transportation; Water Resources.

Group Ratings

	ADA	COPE	PC	RPN	NFU	LCV	CFA	NAB	NSI	ACA	NTU
1978	30	56	35	33	40	–	32	50	60	50	–
1977	40	82	65	69	64	50	45	–	–	44	27

Key Votes

1) Increase Def Spnd	FOR	6) Alaska Lands Protect	FOR	11) Delay Auto Pol Cntrl	FOR
2) B-1 Bomber	AGN	7) Water Projects Veto	AGN	12) Sugar Price Escalator	AGN
3) Cargo Preference	AGN	8) Consum Protect Agcy	AGN	13) Pub Fin Cong Cmpgns	AGN
4) Dereg Nat Gas	AGN	9) Common Situs Picket	AGN	14) ERA Ratif Recissn	FOR
5) Kemp-Roth	AGN	10) Labor Law Revision	FOR	15) Prohibt Govt Abrtns	AGN

Election Results

1978 general	Allen E. Ertel (D)	79,234	(60%)	($149,236)
	Thomas Rippon (R)	53,613	(40%)	($138,223)
1978 primary	Allen E. Ertel (D), unopposed			
1976 general	Allen E. Ertel (D)	86,158	(51%)	($105,394)
	H. Joseph Hepford (R)	82,370	(49%)	($87,162)

EIGHTEENTH DISTRICT

The 18th congressional district of Pennsylvania is the suburban Pittsburgh district. It covers territory on several sides of downtown Pittsburgh, but does not extend farther out into the surrounding counties which, while the Census defines them as suburban, are essentially industrial in character. The district does include some closer-in towns along the Allegheny and Ohio Rivers, which include some of the Pittsburgh area's smaller steel mills, and are industrial, blue collar, and Democratic. They are also too numerous to list: at last count Pittsburgh's Allegheny County contained 129 cities, boroughs, and townships, almost half of them in the 18th district. In the hills that rise above both rivers and all the smokestacks are the more comfortable, affluent, and Republican neighborhoods where management personnel live. These include places like Fox Chapel in the north and Mount Lebanon in the south, as well as many less eminent Republican-leaning places. All in all, the 18th is a little more Republican than Democratic in most elections; certainly it is the least Democratic district in western Pennsylvania.

For many years there were two suburban Pittsburgh districts, represented by two pro-labor Republicans since the early forties—James Fulton and Robert Corbett. Both men died in 1971 and their districts were in effect combined, and in that form won by H. John Heinz III of the Heinz "57 Varieties" family. In his four years in Congress, Heinz became exceedingly popular in the Pittsburgh area—so popular that he was able to win election in 1976 to the U.S. Senate in large part because of his strong local base.

But one thing Heinz was not able to accomplish was to turn the 18th district over to a like-minded liberal Republican. Instead the district was captured by Douglas Walgren, who had lost badly in races for the seat in 1970 and 1972. Walgren had the good fortune to face in the 1976 general election an ultraconservative Republican named Robert Casey. The Casey name is familiar—another Robert Casey had been a popular state auditor, and still another one embarrassed Democrats by winning their lieutenant governor nomination in 1978—but in this instance voters learned that this was not the Casey they wanted. Walgren won that race easily; even more easily he beat the same Robert Casey in 1978, that time in the Democratic primary. His 1978 general election opponent proved somewhat more difficult; Republican Ted Jacob had money to spend and it was after all a good year for Republicans. Nevertheless, Walgren with his solid labor record won convincingly, and seems to have made this a pretty safe seat.

Census Data Pop. 472,074. Central city, 13%; suburban, 87%. Median family income, $10,770; families above $15,000: 25%; families below $3,000: 6%. Median years education, 12.2.

The Voters

Median voting age 46.
Employment profile White collar, 57%. Blue collar, 32%. Service, 11%. Farm, –%.
Ethnic groups Black, 2%. Total foreign stock, 24%. Italy, 5%; Germany, Poland, 3% each; UK, Austria, Czechoslovakia, 2% each; Yugoslavia, Ireland, 1% each.

Presidential vote

1976	Carter (D)	90,062	(45%)
	Ford (R)	108,001	(55%)
1972	Nixon (R)	125,938	(63%)
	McGovern (D)	74,949	(37%)

Rep. Douglas Walgren (D) Elected 1976; b. Dec. 28, 1940, Rochester, N.Y.; home, Pittsburgh; Dartmouth Col., B.A. 1963, Stanford U., LL.B. 1966; Catholic.

Career Practicing atty.; Asst. Allegheny Co. Solicitor, 1971–72; Dem. nominee for U.S. House of Reps., 1972.

Offices 117 CHOB, 202-225-2135. Also 2117 Fed. Bldg., 1000 Liberty Ave., Pittsburgh 15222, 412-391-4016.

Committees *Interstate and Foreign Commerce* (20th). Subcommittees: Health and the Environment; Oversight and Investigations.

Science and Technology (12th). Subcommittees: Energy Development and Applications; Transportation, Aviation and Communication.

Group Ratings

	ADA	COPE	PC	RPN	NFU	LCV	CFA	NAB	NSI	ACA	NTU
1978	55	80	65	58	40	–	55	0	10	26	–
1977	70	86	68	50	64	55	75	–	–	11	20

Key Votes

1) Increase Def Spnd	AGN	6) Alaska Lands Protect	FOR	11) Delay Auto Pol Cntrl	FOR
2) B-1 Bomber	AGN	7) Water Projects Veto	FOR	12) Sugar Price Escalator	AGN
3) Cargo Preference	FOR	8) Consum Protect Agcy	FOR	13) Pub Fin Cong Cmpgns	FOR
4) Dereg Nat Gas	AGN	9) Common Situs Picket	FOR	14) ERA Ratif Recissn	AGN
5) Kemp-Roth	AGN	10) Labor Law Revision	FOR	15) Prohibt Govt Abrtns	FOR

Election Results

1978 general	Doug Walgren (D)	88,299	(58%)	($171,756)
	Ted Jacob (R)	65,088	(42%)	($187,926)
1978 primary	Doug Walgren (D)	46,240	(77%)	
	Robert J. Casey (D)	13,626	(23%)	($20,175)
1976 general	Doug Walgren (D)	113,787	(59%)	($87,335)
	Robert J. Casey (R)	77,594	(41%)	($145,708)

NINETEENTH DISTRICT

The 19th congressional district of Pennsylvania—Adams and York Counties and most of Cumberland—sits at the western edge of the deeply conservative Pennsylvania Dutch country. This is a land of rolling green farmland extending up to the base of the Appalachian ridges that begin to rise at the district's western boundary. The most famous part of this district is also the most sparsely populated, at least by permanent residents: Gettysburg, the tourist-thronged site of the Civil War's northernmost slaughter. Outside the town itself is the retirement home of President Eisenhower, who was of Pennsylvania Dutch stock himself; his father migrated in the late nineteenth century with a group of Mennonite brethren out into Kansas and Texas.

The largest city in the district is York, with 50,000 people, which, from September 1777 to June 1778, was the capital of the young nation. When the Continental Congress met at York, it passed the Articles of Confederation, received word from Benjamin Franklin in Paris that the French would help with money and ships, and issued the first proclamation calling for a national day of thanksgiving. Today York is less Republican than other cities in the Pennsylvania Dutch area, perhaps because of the lingering influence of the old York *Gazette*, which until a recent change in ownership, was one of the most liberal newspapers in the United States.

The other large population center in the 19th district is the fastest growing. This is Cumberland County around Camp Hill, Mechanicsburg, and Carlisle—just across the Susquehanna River from Harrisburg. During the last two decades, Cumberland has absorbed most of the white exodus from the small capital city. The county, already very Republican, is growing more so.

As a result of York's Democratic tendencies, this is a district that was very competitive for years. Democrats won here in 1954, 1958, and 1964; Republicans won narrow victories in 1952, 1956, 1960, and 1966. The last close contest was in 1974. Incumbent George Goodling was retiring at 78. The Republican nominee was his son William, a teacher and school administrator, and he just squeaked by with 52% over Democrat Arthur Berger. In the House, William Goodling has not been particularly effective. He sits on the Education and Labor Committee, where he tries to cut government spending, but there are almost never enough votes on this liberal-packed body. Overall, he has one of the most conservative records in the Pennsylvania delegation. Nevertheless the younger Goodling has become extremely popular at home. In 1976 he won reelection with 71%—the best any candidate has done in this district in more than 100 years. In 1978 no Democrat filed against him, and the nomination went on write-ins to 61-year-old lawyer Rajeshwar Kumar. Goodling had a rousing 79% in the general election.

Census Data Pop. 467,999. Central city, 11%; suburban, 89%. Median family income, $10,107; families above $15,000: 19%; families below $3,000: 6%. Median years education, 12.0.

The Voters

Median voting age 43.
Employment profile White collar, 44%. Blue collar, 43%. Service, 10%. Farm, –%.
Ethnic groups Black, 2%. Total foreign stock, 5%.

Presidential vote

1976	Carter (D)	70,417	(40%)
	Ford (R)	105,544	(60%)
1972	Nixon (R)	115,528	(72%)
	McGovern (D)	45,769	(28%)

Rep. William F. Goodling (R) Elected 1974; b. Dec. 5, 1927, Loganville; home, Jacobus; U. of Md., B.S. 1953, West. Md. Col., M.Ed. 1957, Penn St. U., 1958–62; Methodist.

Career Army, 1946–48; Public school teacher and administrator.

Offices 1713 LHOB, 202-225-5836. Also, Fed. Bldg., 200 S. George St., York 17403, 717-843-8887.

Committees *Education and Labor* (5th). Subcommittees: Human Resources; Elementary, Secondary and Vocational Education.

Foreign Affairs (9th). Subcommittees: Africa; Asian and Pacific Affairs.

Group Ratings

	ADA	COPE	PC	RPN	NFU	LCV	CFA	NAB	NSI	ACA	NTU
1978	20	21	25	60	10	–	23	82	75	87	–
1977	10	29	33	75	17	37	30	–	–	81	61
1976	5	27	13	82	33	25	9	67	90	79	63

Key Votes

1) Increase Def Spnd	AGN	6) Alaska Lands Protect	AGN	11) Delay Auto Pol Cntrl	FOR
2) B-1 Bomber	FOR	7) Water Projects Veto	FOR	12) Sugar Price Escalator	AGN
3) Cargo Preference	AGN	8) Consum Protect Agcy	AGN	13) Pub Fin Cong Cmpgns	AGN
4) Dereg Nat Gas	FOR	9) Common Situs Picket	AGN	14) ERA Ratif Recissn	FOR
5) Kemp-Roth	FOR	10) Labor Law Revision	AGN	15) Prohibt Govt Abrtns	FOR

Election Results

1978 general	William F. Goodling (R)	105,424	(79%)	($37,067)
	Raj Kumar (D)	28,577	(21%)	
1978 primary	William F. Goodling (R), unopposed			
1976 general	William F. Goodling (R)	124,098	(71%)	
	Richard P. Noll (D)	51,686	(29%)	

TWENTIETH DISTRICT

The 20th congressional district of Pennsylvania could be called the Monongahela district. Most of its residents live in a string of industrial communities along the heavily polluted Monongahela and a tributary, the Youghiogheny. "Monongahela," Walt Whitman once wrote, "it rolls off the tongue like venison." But during the last 100 years residents of the area have spotted few deer and eaten little venison. What is more common here is steel. The 20th district probably makes as much steel as any congressional district in the nation. Here are the operations of Jones & Laughlin and no less than four mills of U.S. Steel. They are found along the banks of the Monongahela, which provide just about the only level land available in the Pittsburgh metropolitan area. Most of these mills are ancient and technologically backward; the best known of them is the Homestead Works, site of a great and bloody strike in 1892 when it was owned by Andrew Carnegie.

Not many blacks live in the district, only 7% of the total population, and these live scattered in various Pittsburgh neighborhoods and the smaller towns of McKeesport, Clairton, and Duquesne. Most residents of the 20th are members of the white working class—the children and grandchildren of people who came here from Slovakia, southern Italy, Poland, Wales, and the mountains of West Virginia and Pennsylvania to work in the steel mills. Many of them lived through the twenties, when the prosperity of the great steel corporations failed to trickle down to its sweat-covered workers, through the deprivations of the thirties and the exhilaration of the United Steel Workers' organizing drives in the mills, and finally through the slow decline of the industry in the years after World War II. Today these steel workers live in the same small frame houses found up and down the hills of Braddock, Swissvale, Homestead, and the Hazelwood and St. Clair neighborhoods of Pittsburgh. The populations of all these areas have declined; the children who grew up here have in many cases moved out to find better jobs, sometimes to the outer suburbs, but in many cases away from the Pittsburgh area altogether. As a result, this is an old district, one where an unusual percentage of voters still remember the timbre of Franklin D. Roosevelt's voice.

The image of the melting pot comes to us from the steel-making process. In one respect, at least, the communities of the 20th district, though separated from one another by hills, have melted into a unit, which is that they all share the same preference for the Democratic Party. There are a few white collar suburbs in the 20th, and there has been some dissatisfaction with national Democrats on occasion, as in 1968 when George Wallace got 13% of the vote here. But in most elections, and certainly in local elections, this is a strong Democratic district.

Since the New Deal, the 20th has sent only Democrats to the House of Representatives, and it shows every sign of continuing to do so. The current Congressman is Joseph Gaydos, a former state Senator and attorney for United Mine Workers District 5. Gaydos had Democratic organization and union backing when he first won the seat in 1968. In Washington his record is what one might expect: solidly liberal on economic issues, more conservative on non-economic matters. His record with organized labor has often been 100%. Gaydos has been reelected easily every two years; his percentage was down slightly in 1978, but was still an exceedingly strong 72%.

Census Data Pop. 468,959. Central city, 14%; suburban, 86%. Median family income, $9,937; families above $15,000: 19%; families below $3,000: 7%. Median years education, 12.1.

The Voters

Median voting age 46.
Employment profile White collar, 50%. Blue collar, 38%. Service, 12%. Farm, –%.
Ethnic groups Black, 7%. Total foreign stock, 26%. Italy, Czechoslovakia, 4% each; Poland, UK, 3% each; Germany, Austria, Hungary, Yugoslavia, 2% each; Ireland, 1%.

Presidential vote

1976	Carter (D)	102,730	(55%)
	Ford (R)	83,713	(45%)
1972	Nixon (R)	108,506	(56%)
	McGovern (D)	83,576	(44%)

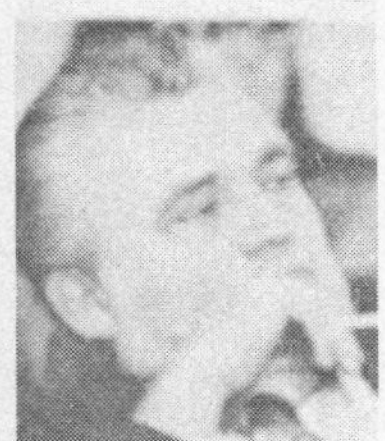

Rep. Joseph M. Gaydos (D) Elected 1968; b. July 3, 1926, Braddock; home, McKeesport; Duquesne U., U. of Notre Dame, LL.B. 1951; Catholic.

Career Navy, WWII; Deputy Atty. Gen. of Penn.; Asst. Allegheny Co. Solicitor; Gen. Counsel, Utd. Mine Workers of Amer., Dist. 5; Penn. Senate, 1967–68.

Offices 2201 RHOB, 202-225-4631. Also Rm. 207, 224 5th Ave. Bldg., McKeesport 15132, 412-673-7756.

Committees *Education and Health and* (7th). Subcommittees: Health and Safety (Chairman); Postsecondary Education.

House Administration (6th). Subcommittees: Contracts (Chairman); Printing.

Group Ratings

	ADA	COPE	PC	RPN	NFU	LCV	CFA	NAB	NSI	ACA	NTU
1978	35	75	40	27	60	–	46	0	33	26	–
1977	55	100	50	17	83	35	60	–	–	19	21
1976	65	96	67	24	92	48	73	18	50	14	20

Key Votes

1) Increase Def Spnd	AGN	6) Alaska Lands Protect	FOR	11) Delay Auto Pol Cntrl	FOR
2) B-1 Bomber	AGN	7) Water Projects Veto	AGN	12) Sugar Price Escalator	AGN
3) Cargo Preference	FOR	8) Consum Protect Agcy	FOR	13) Pub Fin Cong Cmpgns	AGN
4) Dereg Nat Gas	AGN	9) Common Situs Picket	FOR	14) ERA Ratif Recissn	FOR
5) Kemp-Roth	AGN	10) Labor Law Revision	FOR	15) Prohibt Govt Abrtns	FOR

Election Results

1978 general	Joseph M. Gaydos (D)	97,745	(72%)	($67,339)
	Kathleen M. Meyer (R)	37,745	(28%)	
1978 primary	Joseph M. Gaydos (D)	56,939	(82%)	
	One other (D)	12,847	(18%)	
1976 general	Joseph M. Gaydos (D)	134,961	(75%)	($73,549)
	John P. Kostelac (R)	44,432	(25%)	($3,306)

TWENTY-FIRST DISTRICT

The 21st congressional district of Pennsylvania is Westmoreland County, just to the east of Pittsburgh, plus a small portion of suburban Allegheny County. It is a mixed area: there are a few wealthy enclaves here, like Ligonier, but most of Westmoreland is industrial—small factory towns that lie between the hills or along the Allegheny and Monongahela Rivers at the county's western edge. The district contains an especially large number of Italian-Americans, with other ethnic groups present in smaller numbers. The 21st is part of western Pennsylvania's "black country," so named for the region's bituminous coal deposits. Steel is the major industry here, as it is all over western Pennsylvania; the coal, of course, is a major reason why the steel industry grew here in the first place. Politically, western Pennsylvania in general and the 21st district in particular are heavily Democratic.

Although no one knows for sure, the 21st is probably one of not very many—perhaps 30—congressional districts in which a majority of the employed persons are members of labor unions. Union membership is taken for granted in these parts; and politicians are expected to vote the union line. That does not mean, however, that particular local labor bosses are all-powerful politically. On the contrary, union members have little sense of being besieged here, where they are in the majority, and generally do not vote together as a bloc. The Congressman from the 21st for 20 years before his retirement in 1978, John Dent, illustrated the way politicians here vote the labor line; he was probably the surest AFL-CIO and United Steel Workers vote on the House Education and Labor Committee. But the race to succeed him shows how politics here is not controlled by a single labor machine.

For when Dent retired, there were no fewer than 11 candidates competing in the Democratic primary. One candidate was the Westmoreland County Democratic Chairman; he had Dent's support but lost anyway. Another loser was the state House Majority Leader. The winner was 33-year-old attorney Don Bailey, who spent his own money, assembled his own volunteer force, and won with 23% of the vote. But did Bailey get a free ride in the general elections? Besides having to soothe disgruntled organization Democrats—a time-consuming ordeal which does not necessarily produce many voters—he had to face a well-financed and determined Republican opponent. Robert Miller had received 41% of the vote against Dent in 1976, and probably helped to assure the old Democrat's retirement; Miller talked in 1978 about tax cuts and brought in prominent national Republicans. It is not clear that these were winning tactics. Bailey seemed more on the track when he promised aid to the steel industry, support of nuclear power construction (Westinghouse is a big employer around here), and opposition to unnecessary environmental restrictions. Still, Bailey won with only 53% in this basically Democratic district. With that performance, this former University of Michigan and Rose Bowl football player can probably count on tough competition in 1980, in the primary or general election, or possibly both.

Census Data Pop. 473,040. Central city, 0%; suburban, 100%. Median family income, $9,645; families above $15,000: 16%; families below $3,000: 7%. Median years education, 12.1.

The Voters

Median voting age 45.
Employment profile White collar, 45%. Blue collar, 43%. Service, 11%. Farm, 1%.
Ethnic groups Black, 2%. Total foreign stock, 21%. Italy, 6%; Poland, Czechoslovakia, Austria, UK, 2% each; Germany, Yugoslavia, 1% each.

Presidential vote

1976	Carter (D)	92,450	(54%)
	Ford (R)	78,965	(46%)
1972	Nixon (R)	99,366	(58%)
	McGovern (D)	73,049	(42%)

Rep. Don Bailey (D) Elected 1978; b. July 21, 1945, Pittsburgh; home, Greensburg; U. of Mich., B.A. 1967, Duquesne U., J.D. 1976.

Career Army, Vietnam; Practicing atty., 1976–.

Offices 116 CHOB, 202-225-5631. Also 206 N. Main St., Greensburg 15601, 412-837-6420.

Committees *Armed Services* (29th). Subcommittees: Procurement and Military Nuclear Systems.

Education and Labor (24th). Subcommittees: Employment Opportunities; Health and Safety.

Group Ratings: Newly Elected

Key Votes: Newly Elected

Election Results

1978 general	Don Bailey (D)	73,712	(53%)	($125,146)
	Robert H. Miller (R)	65,622	(47%)	($113,186)
1978 primary	Don Bailey (D)	16,671	(23%)	
	Bernard F. Scherer (D)	16,558	(22%)	($64,350)
	John A. Cicco, Jr. (D)	11,355	(15%)	($18,469)
	Eight others (D)	29,187	(40%)	
1976 general	John H. Dent (D)	99,160	(59%)	($82,277)
	Robert H. Miller (R)	67,763	(41%)	($33,704)

TWENTY-SECOND DISTRICT

The 22nd congressional district of Pennsylvania is the northern tip of Appalachia—the southwest corner of the state between West Virginia and the Pittsburgh suburbs. The region is one of rugged hills and polluted rivers, lined with steel mills and blast furnaces. The operations here are smaller than those in the 20th district, which contains the really big mills; this is an area of small industrial towns, huddled around a small factory by a river. Residents of Irish, Polish, and Czech descent are found in great numbers, as well as people from West Virginia and the mountain south. This is rough country: it was in a small town here that Joseph Yablonski, the insurgent candidate for president of the United Mine Workers, was found shot to death with his wife and daughter in 1969.

The 22nd remains one of Pennsylvania's safest Democratic districts. The Democratic leanings of its various ethnic groups are joined with the Democratic tradition of the very large number of union members. From 1944 until his retirement in 1976, the 22nd elected Thomas Morgan, a small town physician, to Congress. He was Chairman of the House Foreign Affairs Committee, criticized by some for not opposing the Vietnam war; he had been brought up in a tradition of bipartisan cooperation on foreign policy, and did not deviate from it until it was clear a majority in the House wanted him to.

Morgan's successor was chosen in the 12-candidate 1976 Democratic primary; the winner was state Senator Austin Murphy, with 29%. He won that fall against a Republican with a less than spectacular 56%. In 1978 one of Murphy's close competitors ran against him again in the primary; this time the incumbent prevailed by a 69%-31% margin. Such are the advantages of incumbency. Murphy won the general election easily this time. As a member of the Education and Labor and Interior Committees, he can be counted on to vote along the lines desired by organized labor and coal interests.

Census Data Pop. 469,778. Central city, 0%; suburban, 59%. Median family income, $8,396; families above $15,000: 13%; families below $3,000: 12%. Median years education, 11.7.

The Voters

Median voting age 46.
Employment profile White collar, 40%. Blue collar, 47%. Service, 12%. Farm, 1%.
Ethnic groups Black, 4%. Total foreign stock, 20%. Italy, 5%; Czechoslovakia, 3%; Poland, Austria, UK, 2% each; Germany, Yugoslavia, 1% each.

Presidential vote

1976	Carter (D)	103,041	(58%)
	Ford (R)	75,161	(42%)
1972	Nixon (R)	95,927	(57%)
	McGovern (D)	72,151	(43%)

Rep. Austin J. Murphy (D) Elected 1976; b. June 17, 1927, North Charleroi; home, Charleroi; Duquesne U., B.A. 1949, U. of Pitt., J.D. 1952; Catholic.

Career USMC, 1944–46; Practicing atty.; Washington Co. Asst. Dist. Atty., 1956–57; Penn. House of Reps., 1959–71; Penn. Senate, 1971–77.

Offices 212 CHOB, 202-225-4665. Also 308 Fallowfield Ave., Charleroi 15022, 412-489-4217.

Committees *Education and Labor* (15th). Subcommittees: Health and Safety; Elementary, Secondary and Vocational Education; Post-secondary Education.

Interior and Insular Affairs (20th). Subcommittees: Energy and the Environment; Mines and Mining; National Parks and Insular Affairs.

Group Ratings

	ADA	COPE	PC	RPN	NFU	LCV	CFA	NAB	NSI	ACA	NTU
1978	40	72	50	27	70	–	59	8	60	40	–
1977	50	91	55	33	75	70	65	–	–	30	24

Key Votes

1) Increase Def Spnd	FOR	6) Alaska Lands Protect	FOR	11) Delay Auto Pol Cntrl	FOR
2) B-1 Bomber	FOR	7) Water Projects Veto	FOR	12) Sugar Price Escalator	AGN
3) Cargo Preference	FOR	8) Consum Protect Agcy	FOR	13) Pub Fin Cong Cmpgns	FOR
4) Dereg Nat Gas	AGN	9) Common Situs Picket	FOR	14) ERA Ratif Recissn	AGN
5) Kemp-Roth	AGN	10) Labor Law Revision	FOR	15) Prohibt Govt Abrtns	FOR

Election Results

1978 general	Austin J. Murphy (D)	99,559	(72%)	($144,228)
	Marilyn Coyle Ecoff (R)	39,518	(28%)	
1978 primary	Austin J. Murphy (D)	57,083	(69%)	
	John Hook (D)	25,534	(31%)	($72,991)
1976 general	Austin J. Murphy (D)	97,036	(56%)	($111,297)
	Roger Raymond Fischer, Jr. (R)	77,030	(44%)	($31,220)

TWENTY-THIRD DISTRICT

The 23rd congressional district of Pennsylvania is the rural north central part of the state. The region is not only the most sparsely populated in Pennsylvania, but in the entire East. The district's terrain is mountainous, and its valleys have only a few small towns here and there. The only significant concentrations of people are found in the Nittany Valley in the southern part of the district and around Oil City in the extreme west. The Nittany Valley is the home of Pennsylvania State University, commonly called Penn State, long known for its powerful football teams. Oil City is near the site of the nation's first oil well, sunk in 1859. Today Pennsylvania crude—a relatively scarce but higher quality oil than that found in the Southwest—continues to occupy an important place in the region's economy.

The isolation of this part of Pennsylvania was ended by the opening in the early seventies of the Keystone Shortway, a superhighway that has replaced the Pennsylvania Turnpike as the main road between New York and Chicago. Some people hoped that the Shortway would bring light industrial development to the area; all it seems to have attracted, at least up to now, are gas stations with 60-foot signs and Holiday Inns. So the 23d remains a rural and small town district, dominated by old-stock farmers.

The area currently covered by the 23d district has a long tradition of electing Republican congressmen, a tradition that goes back to the Civil War. But in the seventies, it seems to be behaving like most other congressional districts in the nation—it's willing to go for one party or the other, depending on the circumstances. Republican Congressman Albert Johnson, despite diminishing margins, declined to retire and was beaten in 1976 by Democratic state Senator Joseph Ammerman. Ammerman's victory looked solid, and he seemed to have the political acumen to hold the district. But in August 1978 Ammerman sustained a broken hip in an automobile accident and was hospitalized for six weeks. He had a strong Republican opponent, William Clinger, who had held a middle level appointment in the Ford Administration and then returned home to Warren, in the northern part of the district. Clinger attacked Ammerman for his support of a consumer protection agency and his high ADA record; the incumbent was unable to show the kind of vigor and willingness to meet constituents which is so important in so many congressional elections. The result was a 54% Clinger victory. With a relatively young, vigorous Republican incumbent, this district seems unlikely to be seriously contested again in 1980, but recent history shows that such may not be the case.

Census Data Pop. 469,717. Central city, 0%; suburban, 0%. Median family income, $8,272; families above $15,000: 11%; families below $3,000: 10%. Median years education, 12.1.

The Voters

Median voting age 42.
Employment profile White collar, 41%. Blue collar, 44%. Service, 13%. Farm, 2%.
Ethnic groups Total foreign stock, 10%. Italy, 2%; UK, Germany, 1% each.

Presidential vote

1976	Carter (D)	77,474	(46%)
	Ford (R)	91,276	(54%)
1972	Nixon (R)	105,463	(66%)
	McGovern (D)	54,138	(34%)

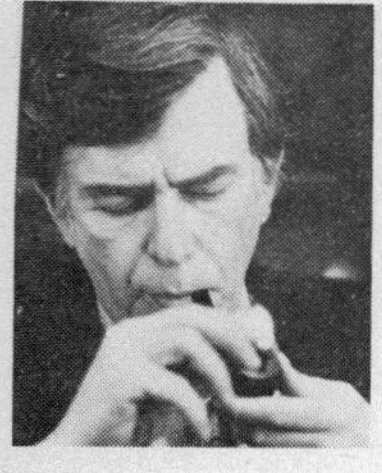

Rep. William F. Clinger, Jr. (R) Elected 1978; b. April 4, 1929, Warren; home, Warren; Johns Hopkins U., B.A. 1951, U. of Va., LL.B. 1965; Presbyterian.

Career Advertising Dept., New Process Co., 1955–62; Practicing atty., 1965–75, 1977–78; Chief Counsel, U.S. Dept. of Commerce Econ. Development Admin., 1975–77.

Offices 1221 LHOB, 202-225-5121. Also 111 S. Allen, State College 16801, 814-238-1776.

Committees *Public Works and Transportation* (14th). Subcommittees: Economic Development; Oversight and Review; Public Buildings and Grounds.

Group Ratings: Newly Elected

Key Votes: Newly Elected

Election Results

1978 general	William F. Clinger, Jr. (R)	73,194	(54%)	($250,697)
	Joseph S. Ammerman (D)	61,657	(46%)	($174,587)
1978 primary	William F. Clinger, Jr. (R)	28,025	(63%)	
	Two others (R)	16,460	(37%)	
1976 general	Joseph S. Ammerman (D)	95,821	(57%)	($95,118)
	Albert W. Johnson (R)	73,641	(43%)	($123,488)

TWENTY-FOURTH DISTRICT

Situated in the northwest corner of the state, the 24th congressional district of Pennsylvania is part of the industrial Great Lakes region. It is a long way overland to the East Coast, and the district has none of metropolitan Philadelphia's seaboard ambiance. The city of Erie, with 129,000 people, is the largest in the 24th district. Like most industrial cities on this polluted lake, Erie is a Democratic stronghold. As one goes inland, the territory becomes more Republican. An exception to this pattern is the steel town of Sharon, just a few miles from Youngstown, Ohio; like most towns dependent on steel mills, Sharon votes Democratic. Overall, the political balance in the 24th makes it one of the state's most marginal districts. In the close presidential elections of 1968 and 1976, its percentages for the various candidates virtually mirrored the state's results—despite its anything but central geographical position.

This was a marginal district for many years, until it was won by Joseph Vigorito in 1964. Through the use of the advantages of incumbency, he won reelection by increasingly safe margins, until in 1973 he was named as one of the "ten dumbest congressmen" by *New Times* magazine. That label—and the nickname of "Jumping Joe" which the article used to describe him—seems to have ended his congressional career. His percentage declined in the Democratic year of 1974 and he was beaten in 1976 by Republican Marc Marks. In 1978 he ran against Marks again and got only 36% of the vote.

Marks has been a smoother candidate and a more articulate Congressman. He is adroit enough to receive ratings above 60% from both organized labor and organized business interests. Along with several other Pennsylvania congressmen, he has been mentioned as a possible candidate for the Senate in 1980—in which case there is no predicting whom the 24th district will elect to the House.

Census Data Pop. 472,171. Central city, 27%; suburban, 28%. Median family income, $9,215; families above $15,000: 15%; families below $3,000: 8%. Median years education, 12.2.

The Voters

Median voting age 44.
Employment profile White collar, 42%. Blue collar, 45%. Service, 11%. Farm, 2%.
Ethnic groups Black, 3%. Total foreign stock, 16%. Italy, Poland, 3% each; Germany, 2%; Czechoslovakia, 1%.

Presidential vote

1976	Carter (D)	95,138	(52%)
	Ford (R)	87,411	(48%)
1972	Nixon (R)	107,785	(61%)
	McGovern (D)	69,394	(39%)

Rep. Marc L. Marks (R) Elected 1976; b. Feb. 12, 1927, Farrell; home, Sharon; U. of Alabama, B.A. 1949, U. of Va., LL.B. 1954; Jewish.

Career Army Air Corps, WWII; Practicing atty., 1955–76; Mercer Co. Solicitor, 1960–66.

Offices 1529 LHOB, 212-225-5406. Also 108 U.S. Courthouse, Erie 16501, 814-455-1313.

Committees *District of Columbia* (3d). Subcommittees: Judiciary, Manpower and Education; Metropolitan Affairs.

Interstate and Foreign Commerce (11th). Subcommittees: Communications; Oversight and Investigations.

Group Ratings

	ADA	COPE	PC	RPN	NFU	LCV	CFA	NAB	NSI	ACA	NTU
1978	50	55	40	42	44	–	50	67	80	38	–
1977	60	70	43	85	55	40	55	–	–	46	27

Key Votes

1) Increase Def Spnd	FOR	6) Alaska Lands Protect	FOR	11) Delay Auto Pol Cntrl	FOR
2) B-1 Bomber	AGN	7) Water Projects Veto	FOR	12) Sugar Price Escalator	AGN
3) Cargo Preference	AGN	8) Consum Protect Agcy	AGN	13) Pub Fin Cong Cmpgns	FOR
4) Dereg Nat Gas	AGN	9) Common Situs Picket	AGN	14) ERA Ratif Recissn	AGN
5) Kemp-Roth	FOR	10) Labor Law Revision	FOR	15) Prohibt Govt Abrtns	AGN

Election Results

1978 general	Marc Lincoln Marks (R)	87,041	(64%)	($171,653)
	Joseph P. Vigorito (D)	48,894	(36%)	($35,220)
1978 primary	Marc Lincoln Marks (R)	29,491	(83%)	
	One other (R)	5,927	(17%)	
1976 general	Marc Lincoln Marks (R)	101,048	(56%)	($141,915)
	Joseph P. Vigorito (D)	79,937	(44%)	($61,021)

TWENTY-FIFTH DISTRICT

The 25th congressional district is part of industrial western Pennsylvania. The district adjoins Ohio and the northern tip of the West Virginia panhandle. Almost half the people of the 25th live in Beaver County, where the steel mills sit in little grimy towns along the banks of the Ohio and Beaver Rivers; the best known of these towns is Beaver Falls, the boyhood home of Joe Namath. Like all of western Pennsylvania within a 100-mile radius of Pittsburgh, Beaver County is rich in ethnic diversity, with especially large numbers of Italian-Americans. The county is ordinarily a Democratic bulwark, though it has occasionally gone Republican.

The other two counties in the district are politically more marginal. Lawrence, dominated by the industrial city of New Castle, was Pennsylvania's bellwether county, until the 1974 and 1976 elections when regional loyalties played as much part as partisan labels. Butler County, a few miles north of the industrial concentrations along the rivers, is less thickly settled and tends toward Republicanism. The 25th also includes the northern tier of townships in Pittsburgh's Allegheny County, which usually go Republican.

Altogether, this is about as good an example of a Democratic district as you can find. Yet it has had four close elections in the seventies, and two of them have been won by a Republican. One reason is the weakness of Congressman Frank Clark. First elected in 1954, he had become one of the House's most inveterate junketeers, but he apparently had not been tending to matters in the 25th district. His percentage was lowered sharply in 1972 by Republican Gary Myers, a young mechanical engineer and steel plant foreman, and he was defeated by Myers in 1974. One issue Myers used was Clark's bill to require oil to be shipped in American flag vessels, which would benefit maritime interests which in turn were big contributors to Clark's campaign. But personal factors were also at work. Clark was obviously not greatly respected: when, after his defeat, he ran for Doorkeeper of the House, only 34 of his 244 Democratic former colleagues voted for him.

Although he voted with organized labor fairly often, Myers was really a management-oriented Congressman. But apparently he was not happy in Congress. In 1976 he won a second term, beating Beaver County Commissioner Eugene Atkinson. But in 1978 he decided to retire, and to return to being a foreman in the steel mill—a decision no one in Washington could understand.

There was a real contest—or contests—to succeed him. Atkinson was the winner in an 11-candidate Democratic primary, but with only 25% of the vote. The Republican, Butler County Solicitor Tim Shaffer, put on a creditable campaign; and there was an Independent candidate as well, who ended up with 8% of the vote. Atkinson was the winner, but with less than an absolute majority—an indication that this seemingly safe Democratic district may be contested seriously again in 1980.

Census Data Pop. 472,929. Central city, 0%; suburban, 50%. Median family income, $9,208; families above $15,000: 14%; families below $3,000: 8%. Median years education, 12.1.

The Voters

Median voting age 44.
Employment profile White collar, 39%. Blue collar, 48%. Service, 12%. Farm, 1%.
Ethnic groups Black, 3%. Total foreign stock, 19%. Italy, 5%; Poland, Yugoslavia, 2% each; UK, Germany, Czechoslovakia, Austria, 1% each.

Presidential vote

1976	Carter (D)	97,466	(54%)
	Ford (R)	84,138	(46%)
1972	Nixon (R)	103,715	(60%)
	McGovern (D)	67,926	(40%)

Rep. Eugene V. Atkinson (D) Elected 1978; b. April 5, 1927, Aliquippa; home, Aliquippa; U. of Pitt.

Career Navy, WWII; Owner, Atkinson Insurance Agency; Dir. of Customs, Port of Pitt., 1962–69; Beaver Co. Comm., 1972–78.

Offices 412 CHOB, 202-225-2565. Also 408 Beaver Valley Mall, Monaca 15061, 412-775-5940.

Committees *Government Operations* (25th). Subcommittees: Commerce, Consumer and Monetary Affairs; Manpower and Housing.

Public Works and Transportation (27th). Subcommittees: Economic Development; Public Buildings and Grounds; Surface Transportation.

Group Ratings: Newly Elected

Key Votes: Newly Elected

Election Results

1978 general	Eugene V. Atkinson (D)	68,293	(48%)	($106,521)
	Tim Shaffer (R)	62,160	(44%)	($91,294)
	John W. Cook (I)	10,588	(8%)	($8,699)
1978 primary	Eugene V. Atkinson (D)	17,044	(25%)	
	Nick Colafella (D)	9,966	(15%)	($31,421)
	Jim Ross (D)	8,606	(13%)	($18,891)
	Eight others (D)	31,837	(47%)	
1976 general	Gary A. Myers (R)	103,632	(57%)	($42,658)
	Eugene V. Atkinson (D)	78,857	(43%)	($77,516)

RHODE ISLAND

The state of Rhode Island and Providence Plantations—the full official name—owes its existence to a religious schism in the Massachusetts Bay Colony. Roger Williams, as most schoolchildren know, founded Providence in 1636 as a haven for dissident Calvinists fleeing the regime to the north. Williams had a profound—and for that day unusual—belief in religious and political freedom; he was the New World's first civil libertarian. Williams's colony soon attracted a motley gathering of Baptists, Antinomians, and even some Papists (Roman Catholics), along with a few American Indians. Williams, unlike many of his contemporaries and Americans to follow, was kindly disposed to the native Americans and became a scholar of their languages and customs.

Rhode Island's later history has been almost as idiosyncratic. The descendants of Williams's colonists began to prosper and, as people do, grew more conservative. The "triangle trade" out of Newport—rum, sugar, and slaves—was especially lucrative. After the Revolutionary War Rhode Island was the last of the thirteen colonies to ratify the Constitution. It had declined to send delegates to the Convention for fear that any proposed union could impose tariffs inimical to ocean-dependent trade. Only after the new nation threatened to sever commercial relations with Rhode Island did it agree to become the thirteenth state. As late as 1840, when most other states had given the franchise to free white males, Rhode Island still allowed only large property owners to vote. This situation led to open revolt, the Dorr Rebellion, during which Rhode Island had two separate state governments, each claiming sovereignty.

In the state's economic history the key event occurred in 1793, when Samuel Slater, a British emigre, built the nation's first water-powered cotton mill in Pawtucket and launched America's industrial revolution. During the nineteenth century the textile industry in Rhode Island boomed, and the tiny state attracted immigrants eager to work the looms and toil on the cutting floor. They came from French Canada, Ireland, and especially from Italy. So by the turn of the century this erstwhile colony of dissident Protestants had become the most heavily Catholic state in the nation. Today 64% of the citizens of Rhode Island are adherents of that faith.

The Protestants and Catholics did not get along very well in politics. Long after they had become a minority numerically, the Protestants, through the Republican Party, were able to maintain control of Rhode Island. The big switch came in 1928, when thousands of immigrants, especially women, who had never before voted, streamed to the polls and carried the state for Al

Smith. From that time on Rhode Island has been one of our most Democratic states. It has gone Republican for president only three times in the last fifty years, twice for Eisenhower and once for Nixon; it has elected only one Republican to the U.S. Senate since 1930; and it has elected no Republicans to the House of Representatives since 1938.

The Republicans have done better in gubernatorial elections. They won in 1958, 1962, 1964, and 1966, and have been competitive in four of the last six elections—Rhode Island is one of the last states with a two-year term for governors. But for most races the decisive battle, when there is one, occurs in the Democratic Party. And the outcome of that contest has, until very recently, almost always been determined by the endorsement of the state Democratic machine. But there are signs that the Democratic machine is losing its omnipotence; in fact, both senators came to office initially over the opposition of the Democratic machine, as did one of the two congressmen. Perhaps not incidentally, both of these senators from ethnic Rhode Island are blue blood aristocrats.

The first is Claiborne deB. Pell, first elected in 1960, from Bellevue Avenue in Newport, where one finds the Vanderbilt and Auchincloss "cottages." Pell's father was congressman from New York for a term, a friend of Franklin Roosevelt, and Minister to Portugal and Hungary during the period around the outbreak of World War II. Pell himself served as a Foreign Service Officer for several years. But such service hardly explains how he was able to beat former Governor (1951-59) Dennis Roberts and former Governor (1941-45), Senator (1947-49), and U.S. Attorney General (1949-52) J. Howard McGrath in the 1960 Democratic primary. (All of them were running for the seat first won by Theodore F. Green in 1936 when he was 69. An entire generation of Rhode Island politicians made plans on the assumption that Green's seat would soon become available. Green, once Chairman of the Foreign Relations Committee, finally decided to retire when he reached 93.) Part of the reason for Pell's victory was the odor of scandal which attached itself to both of his rivals. But the win was also attributable to his quiet, aloof, but still vigorous style of campaigning.

That style was one reason Pell was challenged in 1972 by Rhode Island's strongest Republican, John Chafee. Returning from a stint as Secretary of the Navy in the Nixon Administration, Chafee was still popular from three terms as Governor, and he believed he could attack some of Pell's preoccupations as esoteric (e.g., oceanography and the law of the sea, aid to the arts). But Chafee failed to account for the steel backbone beneath Pell's sometimes halting aristocratic demeanor. Pell had gained attention as an early dove on the Foreign Relations Committee, but he gained support, from teachers, for steering the higher education bill through the Senate.

Since then, Chafee has won Rhode Island's other Senate seat, and Pell did not have serious competition in 1978. He is now the second ranking Democrat on Foreign Relations, and would take over the chair if Frank Church is defeated in 1980. He is also the third-ranking Democrat on the Human Resources Committee, which handles education and labor issues. Here he ranks behind Chairman Harrison Williams and Jennings Randolph of West Virginia; there is a possibility Pell could succeed to this chair, too.

For 16 years Pell's colleague was John Pastore, Rhode Island's most successful Italian-American politician, longtime Chairman of the Commerce Subcommittee on Communications (and in that capacity overseer of the broadcast industry) and quondam Chairman of the Joint Committee on Atomic Energy. In 1976, at 69, Pastore decided to retire, although he could have won another term easily. At first the likely successor seemed to be Governor Philip Noel. He is half French Canadian and half Italian in descent—a good combination for Rhode Island—and had responded aggressively and successfully when the Nixon Administration transferred the state's entire Atlantic fleet to politically more congenial locations like Norfolk, Charleston, and Mayport, Florida, in 1973. Noel had won reelection in 1974 with 78%, carrying every precinct in the state. But in his second term he got into trouble, and was upset in the primary by a Cadillac dealer who spent hundreds of thousands of his own money on a media campaign. The Cadillac dealer in turn was outspent in the general by John Chafee.

Perhaps surprisingly, Chafee was not hurt by the Navy closings, though as Navy Secretary he presumably knew they were coming and said nothing about them when he ran in 1972. He was still popular from his time as governor and enjoyed the reputation as a liberal Republican. In the Senate he has tended to stand with Eastern Republicans like Javits of New York or Mathias of Maryland—though he sticks to the party line more often than they do. In 1979 he won a seat on the Senate Finance Committee. He is not up for reelection until 1982, and he seems reasonably likely to win another term.

For the years the Democratic machine solidly controlled Rhode Island politics, the state's congressional delegation kept the kind of ethnic balance one expects from a well-disciplined organization in a very ethnic state. One senator was Italian-American, another a blue blood WASP; one congressman was of French Canadian descent, the other had an unmistakeably Irish name. All were politically safe. Now all that has changed. Both senators today are WASPs, and both of the state's congressmen seem a little shaky in their holds on their districts.

The more senior of the congressmen is Fernand St. Germain of the 1st district. Appropriately, this is the more French Canadian of the two seats; French is still spoken on the streets of Woonsocket and Central Falls, two textile mill towns in the district. The 1st also takes in the wealthier precincts of Providence, including Brown University, all of Pawtucket, and the east side of Narragansett Bay, including Newport. That old city, hit hard in the seventies by Navy cutbacks, has a large section of restored eighteenth century townhouses as well as the robber barons' cottages of the nineteenth century.

St. Germain, first elected in 1960 at the age of 32, has always had machine support and has seldom had significant opposition. He has become the number four Democrat on the House Banking and Urban Affairs Committee and Chairman of the Subcommittee on Financial Institutions. He has used his committee position to see that the 1st district gets a record amount of housing projects for senior citizens, but he does not necessarily work the district as hard as many younger congressmen. St. Germain is not in any political trouble, but he has not established the kind of strength which would make him a strong contender for statewide office.

The congressman from the 2d district has had a more mercurial career. The 2d includes part of Providence, Rhode Island's larger suburbs of Cranston and Warwick, and the comparatively rural Washington County in the southern part of the state. The Congressman is Edward Beard, who upset incumbent Robert Tiernan in the 1974 primary. Beard was a housepainter then who had served one term in the legislature. He boasted that he had never made more than $9,000 a year, and he claimed that he understood the problems of ordinary people as Tiernan did not.

For a time Beard became the most popular politician in the state. He beat the organization again in the 1976 primary, winning 75% of the vote; he secured the resignation of the Democratic state chairman and the appointment of an acceptable replacement. But now Beard himself seems to be in political trouble. His 1978 Republican opponent, Claudine Schneider, accused him of having succumbed to the blandishments of life in Washington; he may have founded the Blue Collar Caucus, but he also was enjoying the $57,500 salary and junkets abroad. Such charges made a strong impression, and Beard won with only 53% of the vote—a real rebuke in Democratic Rhode Island, and an indication that he is likely to attract strong opposition, in the primary as well as the general election, next time.

Rhode Island is the closest thing we have to a city-state. It includes nearly all of metropolitan Providence, with its population of almost one million, and very little else—just a little strip of rural territory along Long Island Sound. The local media—the Providence *Journal*, the Providence television stations—naturally cover state politics and state government closely, and people get a close picture of the ups and downs of the leading personalities. This sometimes produces great fluctuations in election results over a short period of time—the change in Edward Beard's fortunes, for example, or in those of former Governor Philip Noel. Noel's successor, Joseph Garrahy, seems to have done well by these lights. He was a somewhat familiar figure from eight years as Lieutenant Governor when he was elected Governor in 1976; in the governorship he won sufficient popularity to be reelected by a large margin. The second term, however, is perhaps the toughest time for Rhode Island governors—it is when Noel got into trouble—and the last time the state gave a governor a third term was in 1966. Garrahy seems to have the steadiness and staying power as well as the popular programs. But much could happen before 1980, and whatever does will be well known to the voters of this little state.

Census Data Pop. 949,723; 0.47% of U.S. total, 39th largest; Central city, 36%; suburban, 49%. Median family income, $9,734; 17th highest; families above $15,000: 19%; families below $3,000: 9%. Median years education, 11.5.

1977 Share of Federal Tax Burden $1,520,000,000; 0.44% of U.S. total, 38th largest.

1977 Share of Federal Outlays $1,629,380,000; 0.41% of U.S. total, 43d largest. Per capita federal spending, $1,758.

DOD	$326,859,000	41st (0.38%)		HEW	$742,466,000	38th (0.50%)
ERDA	$1,709,000	44th (0.03%)		HUD	$29,890,000	36th (0.71%)
NASA	$947,000	37th (0.02%)		VA	$100,210,000	40th (0.52%)
DOT	$23,118,000	51st (0.16%)		EPA	$34,627,000	35th (0.42%)
DOC	$58,195,000	36th (0.70%)		RevS	$38,943,000	40th (0.46%)
DOI	$3,706,000	49th (0.45%)		Debt	$73,342,000	36th (0.24%)
USDA	$35,906,000	49th (0.18%)		Other	$159,462,000	

Economic Base Miscellaneous manufacturing industries, especially jewelry, silverware and plated ware; textile mill products, especially narrow fabric mills; finance, insurance and real estate; primary metal industries, especially nonferrous rolling and drawing; fabricated metal products; electrical equipment and supplies; machinery, especially metalworking machinery.

Political Line-up Governor, J. Joseph Garrahy (D). Senators, Claiborne Pell (D) and John H. Chafee (R). Representatives, 2 D. State Senate (45 D and 5 R); State House (84 D and 16 R).

The Voters

Registration 535,778 Total. No party registration.
Median voting age 44
Employment profile White collar, 45%. Blue collar, 42%. Service, 12%. Farm, 1%.
Ethnic groups Black, 3%. Total foreign stock, 33%. Italy, 8%; Canada, 7%; UK, 4%; Portugal, 3%.

Presidential vote

1976	Carter (D)	227,636	(56%)
	Ford (R)	181,249	(44%)
1972	Nixon (R)	220,383	(53%)
	McGovern (D)	194,645	(47%)

1976 Democratic Presidential Primary

Uncommitted	19,066	(31%)
Carter	18,171	(30%)
Church	16,767	(28%)
Others	6,670	(11%)

1976 Republican Presidential Primary

Ford	9,341	(66%)
Reagan	4,419	(31%)
Uncommitted	498	(3%)

Sen. Claiborne Pell (D) Elected 1960, seat up 1984; b. Nov. 22, 1918, New York, N.Y.; home, Newport; Princeton U., A.B. 1940, Columbia U., A.M., 1946; Episcopalian.

Career Coast Guard, WWII; U.S. Foreign Svc. and State Dept., Czechoslovakia and Italy, 1945–52; Exec. Asst. to R.I. Dem. St. Chm., 1952, 1954; Consultant, Dem. Natl. Comm., 1953–60; Dir., Internatl. Rescue Comm.; Mbr., U.S. Delegation to U.N., 1970.

Offices 325 RSOB, 202-224-4642. Also 418 Fed. Bldg., Providence 02903, 401-528-4547.

Committees *Foreign Relations* (2d). Subcommittees: Arms Control, Oceans, International Operations, and Environment (Chairman); European Affairs.

Labor and Human Resources (3d). Subcommittees: Education, Arts, and Humanities (Chairman); Health and Scientific Research; Employment, Poverty, and Migratory Labor.

Rules and Administration (Chairman).

Group Ratings

	ADA	COPE	PC	RPN	NFU	LCV	CFA	NAB	NSI	ACA	NTU
1978	75	89	83	60	30	90	70	9	10	4	–
1977	80	80	85	50	64	–	80	–	–	8	35
1976	90	83	70	67	82	74	78	17	0	0	25

Key Votes

1) Warnke Nom	FOR	6) Egypt-Saudi Arms	AGN	11) Hosptl Cost Contnmnt	FOR
2) Neutron Bomb	AGN	7) Draft Restr Pardon	FOR	12) Clinch River Reactor	AGN
3) Waterwy User Fee	FOR	8) Wheat Price Support	AGN	13) Pub Fin Cong Cmpgns	FOR
4) Dereg Nat Gas	AGN	9) Panama Canal Treaty	FOR	14) ERA Ratif Recissn	FOR
5) Kemp-Roth	AGN	10) Labor Law Rev Clot	FOR	15) Med Necssy Abrtns	AGN

Election Results

1978 general	Claiborne Pell (D)	229,557	(75%)	($373,077)
	James G. Reynolds (R)	76,061	(25%)	($85,614)
1978 primary	Claiborne Pell (D)	69,729	(87%)	
	Two others (D)	10,406	(13%)	
1972 general	Claiborne Pell (D)	221,942	(54%)	($528,347)
	John Chafee (R)	188,990	(46%)	($457,409)

Sen. John H. Chafee (R) Elected 1976, seat up 1982; b. Oct. 22, 1922, Providence; home, East Greenwich; Yale U., B.A. 1947, Harvard U., LL.B. 1950; Episcopalian.

Career USMC, 1942–46, 1950–52; R.I. House of Reps., 1957–63; Governor of R.I., 1963–69; Secy. of the Navy, 1969–72; Repub. Nominee for U.S. Senate, 1974.

Offices 3105 DSOB, 202-224-2921. Also 302 Pastore Bldg., Providence 02903, 401-528-5294.

Committees *Environment and Public Works* (4th). Subcommittees: Environmental Pollution; Regional and Community Development; Resource Protection.

Finance (5th). Subcommittees: International Trade; Taxation and Debt Management Generally; Unemployment and Related Problems.

Select Committee on Intelligence (3d).

Group Ratings

	ADA	COPE	PC	RPN	NFU	LCV	CFA	NAB	NSI	ACA	NTU
1978	55	63	53	100	30	62	35	30	11	26	–
1977	45	44	55	100	42	–	48	–	–	24	33

Key Votes

1) Warnke Nom	FOR	6) Egypt-Saudi Arms	FOR	11) Hosptl Cost Contnmnt	FOR
2) Neutron Bomb	AGN	7) Draft Restr Pardon	FOR	12) Clinch River Reactor	AGN
3) Waterwy User Fee	FOR	8) Wheat Price Support	AGN	13) Pub Fin Cong Cmpgns	AGN
4) Dereg Nat Gas	FOR	9) Panama Canal Treaty	FOR	14) ERA Ratif Recissn	FOR
5) Kemp-Roth	FOR	10) Labor Law Rev Clot	FOR	15) Med Necssy Abrtns	FOR

Election Results

1976 general	John Chafee (R)	230,329	(58%)	($415,651)
	Richard Lorber (D)	167,665	(42%)	($782,931)
1976 primary	John Chafee (R), unopposed			
1970 general	John O. Pastore (D)	230,469	(68%)	
	John McLaughlin (R)	107,351	(32%)	

Gov. J. Joseph Garrahy (D) Elected 1976, term expires Jan. 1981; b. Nov. 26, 1930, Providence; U. of R.I., U. of Buffalo;

Career Air Force, Korea; Sales rep., Narragansett Brewing Co., 1956–62; R.I. State Senate, 1963–69, Depy. Major. Ldr., 1967–68; Dem. State Chmn., 1967–68; R.I. Lt. Gov. 1968–76.

Offices State House, Providence 02903, 401-277-2397.

Election Results

1978 general	J. Joseph Garrahy (D)	197,386	(63%)
	Lincoln C. Almond (R)	96,596	(31%)
	Joseph A. Doorley, Jr. (I)	20,381	(6%)
1978 primary	J. Joseph Garrahy (D), unopposed		
1976 general	J. Joseph Garrahy (D)	218,561	(55%)
	James Taft (R)	178,254	(45%)

FIRST DISTRICT

Census Data Pop. 475,441. Central city, 28%; suburban, 56%. Median family income, $9,713; families above $15,000: 19%; families below $3,000: 9%. Median years education, 11.4.

The Voters

Median voting age 43.
Employment profile White collar, 46%. Blue collar, 42%. Service, 12%. Farm, –%.
Ethnic groups Black, 3%. Total foreign stock, 35%. Canada, 9%; Portugal, Italy, 5% each; UK, 4%.

Presidential vote

1976	Carter (D)	113,522	(57%)
	Ford (R)	85,061	(43%)
1972	Nixon (R)	107,156	(52%)
	McGovern (D)	98,881	(48%)

Rep. Fernand J. St Germain (D) Elected 1960; b. Jan. 9, 1928, Blackstone, Mass; home, Woonsocket; Providence Col., Ph.B. 1948, Boston U., LL.B. 1955; Catholic.

Career Army, 1949–52; R.I. House of Reps., 1952–60; Practicing atty., 1956–.

Offices 2136 RHOB, 202-225-4911. Also 200 John E. Fogarty Bldg., Providence 02903, 401-528-4323.

Committees *Banking, Finance and Urban Affairs* (4th). Subcommittees: Financial Institutions Supervision, Regulation and Insurance (Chairman); Housing and Community Development.

Government Operations (6th). Subcommittees: Commerce, Consumer, and Monetary Affairs; Legislation and National Security.

Small Business (6th). Subcommittees: Capital, SBA and SBIC Authority and General Small Business Problems.

Group Ratings

	ADA	COPE	PC	RPN	NFU	LCV	CFA	NAB	NSI	ACA	NTU
1978	65	85	75	10	70	–	68	0	30	15	–
1977	75	75	78	50	64	70	75	–	–	8	23
1976	90	82	90	39	82	50	91	17	20	4	23

Key Votes

1) Increase Def Spnd	AGN	6) Alaska Lands Protect	FOR	11) Delay Auto Pol Cntrl	AGN
2) B-1 Bomber	AGN	7) Water Projects Veto	FOR	12) Sugar Price Escalator	AGN
3) Cargo Preference	AGN	8) Consum Protect Agcy	FOR	13) Pub Fin Cong Cmpgns	FOR
4) Dereg Nat Gas	AGN	9) Common Situs Picket	FOR	14) ERA Ratif Recissn	FOR
5) Kemp-Roth	AGN	10) Labor Law Revision	FOR	15) Prohibt Govt Abrtns	FOR

Election Results

1978 general	Fernand St Germain (D)	86,768	(61%)	($125,013)
	John J. Slocum, Jr. (R)	54,912	(39%)	($98,082)
1978 primary	Fernand St Germain (D)	23,862	(68%)	
	Norman Jacques (D)	6,324	(18%)	($8,605)
	One other (D)	4,782	(14%)	
1976 general	Fernand St Germain (D)	116,674	(63%)	($85,248)
	John J. Slocum, Jr. (R)	68,080	(37%)	($106,114)

SECOND DISTRICT

Census Data Pop. 474,282. Central city, 44%; suburban, 42%. Median family income, $9,755; families above $15,000: 19%; families below $3,000: 9%. Median years education, 11.6.

The Voters

Median voting age 44.
Employment profile White collar, 45%. Blue collar, 42%. Service, 13%. Farm, –%.
Ethnic groups Black, 3%. Total foreign stock, 31%. Italy, 10%; Canada, 5%; UK, 3%; Portugal, 1%.

Presidential vote

1976	Carter (D)	112,877	(54%)
	Ford (R)	95,702	(46%)
1972	Nixon (R)	113,072	(54%)
	McGovern (D)	94,935	(46%)

Rep. Edward P. Beard (D) Elected 1974; b. Jan. 20, 1940, Providence; home, Cranston; Catholic.

Career Housepainter; R.I. Natl. Guard, 1960–66; R.I. House of Reps., 1973–75.

Offices 131 CHOB, 202-225-2735. Also 307 P.O. Annex, Providence 02903, 401-528-4861.

Committees *Education and Labor* (12th). Subcommittees: Labor Standards (Chairman); Select Education.

Veterans' Affairs (10th).

Group Ratings

	ADA	COPE	PC	RPN	NFU	LCV	CFA	NAB	NSI	ACA	NTU
1978	45	95	65	27	70	–	55	10	40	12	–
1977	60	83	78	50	83	75	65	–	–	11	22
1976	80	83	46	40	83	59	73	8	20	7	22

Key Votes

1) Increase Def Spnd	AGN	6) Alaska Lands Protect	FOR	11) Delay Auto Pol Cntrl	FOR
2) B-1 Bomber	AGN	7) Water Projects Veto	AGN	12) Sugar Price Escalator	AGN
3) Cargo Preference	AGN	8) Consum Protect Agcy	FOR	13) Pub Fin Cong Cmpgns	FOR
4) Dereg Nat Gas	AGN	9) Common Situs Picket	FOR	14) ERA Ratif Recissn	AGN
5) Kemp-Roth	AGN	10) Labor Law Revision	FOR	15) Prohibt Govt Abrtns	FOR

Election Results

1978 general	Edward P. Beard (D)	87,397	(53%)	($84,688)
	Claudine Schneider (R)	78,725	(47%)	($53,879)
1978 primary	Edward P. Beard (D)	35,229	(80%)	
	One other (D)	8,747	(20%)	
1976 general	Edward P. Beard (D)	154,453	(77%)	($61,619)
	Thomas V. Iannitti (R)	45,438	(23%)	($42,336)

SOUTH CAROLINA

South Carolina has one of the most distinctive histories of any state, and to understand it one has to go back to the very beginning. While the other Atlantic seaboard colonies were modelled on life in England or some religious ideal, the model which the first South Carolinians used was Barbados, a sugar-producing island in the West Indies where life for most people was less than completely idyllic. During the colonial period, South Carolina was the only colony where blacks outnumbered whites massively, for the settlers here were almost all large landholders who could grow their main crops—sugar, rice, indigo—only with the labor of vast numbers of slaves. South Carolina produced a planter elite whose most memorable legacy were men like the Pinckneys and John C. Calhoun, and whose gravest fears were that their slaves would revolt, as they did in the Denmark Vesey uprising of 1822. And South Carolinians were responsible for the direct cause of the Civil War. The young aristocrats who dominated political life here were hotheaded opponents of any action which in any way restricted slavery. In early 1861 these rebels opened fire on Fort Sumter in Charleston harbor, and so began the Civil War.

It is not hard to understand why, after the war, the state's white minority was enraged to see blacks take political power. For a time during the 1870s blacks controlled the South Carolina legislature and the state's congressional delegation. Such "outrages" of Reconstruction were soon ended, and the blacks—and most poor whites—lost the vote and all political rights. Meanwhile, as the nineteenth century went on, the once booming port of Charleston settled into economic stagnation, as did the rest of the state. For most of the twentieth century South Carolina has been among the lowest ranking states in per capita income, education levels, and health services. It has also had one of the lowest levels of electoral participation; as late as 1948 only 142,000 South Carolinians voted in the presidential election, in a state with more than two million people.

South Carolina no longer has the same economic base or racial mix that it did in the nineteenth century. Charleston lives today not on its earnings as a port but largely on the wealth poured in by numerous military bases, and the economic strength of the state has moved inland. Textiles are now the major industry here, with the biggest concentration of mills in the Piedmont region, along Interstate 85 which passes through Greenville and Spartanburg. As in other Southern states, there has been substantial black migration from the lowlands to the big cities of the North, and substantial increase in the white population, particularly around Columbia and in the Piedmont.

As a result, South Carolina no longer has a black majority; about 30% of its residents are black—still, a larger percentage than in any other state but Mississippi.

From the days when the Democrats were the party of the South that stood against civil rights, white South Carolinians were Democrats; up through 1944, this was the single most Democratic state, casting more than 88% of its votes for Franklin Roosevelt. That changed, abruptly, when Hubert Humphrey persuaded the 1948 Democratic National Convention to adopt a strong civil rights plank. Strom Thurmond, then South Carolina's Governor, ran as the "Dixiecrat" candidate, and though he won only 1% of the national vote, carried 39 electoral votes. Since then South Carolina has been a marginal state in presidential elections. Democrats nearly lost it in 1952 and 1960, and Barry Goldwater carried it easily in 1964. And though the Voting Rights Act of 1965 enfranchised hundreds of thousands of South Carolina blacks, Richard Nixon was able to carry the state in a close three-way race in 1968. In 1976 South Carolina gave 57% of its vote to fellow Southerner Jimmy Carter, but the electorate was fluid enough that both parties sent their candidates into the state during the last ten days of the campaign.

The Voting Rights Act effected as great a change in politics here as in any state of the Union. Today there are three basic voting groups in South Carolina, of roughly equal size. First there are what one might call the country club whites—well-to-do white people in the suburbs or suburban-style neighborhoods of South Carolina's medium and large cities. Their preferences can be gauged best in the returns for Lexington County, a predominantly suburban area outside Columbia; Lexington was 86% for Nixon in 1972 and 60% for Ford in 1976. Among the affluent in South Carolina, there is no radical chic or sense of noblesse. They believe in the free enterprise system which has helped bring them in many cases to an economic status they never thought they'd achieve, and they believe just as strongly in a strong and aggressive defense posture. The country club whites have been going Republican since the fifties, and their heroes have been Goldwater and Reagan, Strom Thurmond and former Governor James Edwards.

At the other end of the South Carolina electorate are the blacks, who were not a significant political factor until 1965. They now cast more than one-third of the votes in some parts of the state, and all politicians—including Thurmond—seek their support. With few exceptions, however, the blacks prefer Democrats, by overwhelming margins. That leaves as the key element in the electorate what we might call the textile mill whites. These are blue collar workers and farmers; they are found in the mill towns and rural counties and the working class neighborhoods of large cities. In 1960 enough of them were still Democrats to carry the state for Kennedy; when the Democrats put through the Civil Rights Act, they went for Goldwater in 1964. In 1968 they went solidly for George Wallace, who almost carried the state, and in 1972 they were solidly for Nixon. Then in 1976 a majority of them returned to the Democrats and helped elect Carter. This has been the pattern in most statewide elections, with textile mill whites giving crucial votes to Senator Ernest Hollings in 1966, Governor Robert McNair that same year, and Governor John West in 1970.

The one constant factor in South Carolina politics for more than thirty years now has been Strom Thurmond. He has a reputation for firmness and steadfastness, yet he has adjusted adroitly enough to remain popular with the vastly expanded and changed South Carolina electorate. Thurmond was elected Governor in 1946 as a segregationist, and one of the strongest in the South; he was the Dixiecrat candidate in 1948, and in 1954 he was elected to the Senate in a stunning victory as a write-in candidate. In 1964 Thurmond switched from the Democratic Party to the Republicans out of enthusiasm for Barry Goldwater, and in 1968 he lobbied effectively among Southern Republican convention delegations for Richard Nixon, preventing any Reagan breakthrough and getting Nixon his majority on the first ballot.

In the seventies, Thurmond has moved even more adroitly. Noting the increased number of black voters, he hired black staffers early in the decade, and took care to make his constituency services available to black South Carolinians. Those moves have never really paid off in large numbers of black votes for him, but they have tended to prevent a large black turnout against him. When the Nixon Administration seemed weak on stopping textile imports, Thurmond attacked the White House strongly and got action. Though born in 1902, he has remained energetic; widowed, he married a young beauty queen and fathered the first of his three children when he was nearly 70.

In the Senate Thurmond now has more seniority as a Republican than he ever had as a Democrat. Before 1977, he was ranking minority member on the Armed Services Committee, a position he enjoyed; he is temperamentally one of the strongest hawks in the Senate. He is a retired general in the Army, an unabashed enthusiast for things military, a supporter of armed intervention anywhere it is conceivable, and a diehard opponent of the Panama Canal Treaty. But Thurmond left the Armed Services post to become ranking Republican on Judiciary—and incidentally to keep Charles Mathias of Maryland out of that position. Thurmond is not noted for his legislative expertise or for his grasp of detail on issues; what legislative force he has comes from determination and hard work. He will fight hard for his position every step of the way; he once held the record for the longest filibuster in the Senate.

In South Carolina Thurmond has remained a solid favorite of the country club whites, a beloved elder statesman among textile mill whites, and something considerably less than an ogre among blacks. He was able to scare off tough competition in 1972 and won with 63%. When he got tough competition, in the person of Charles "Pug" Ravenel, in 1978 he was still able to win with 56%.

Ravenel and Thurmond provided one of the most vivid contrasts in a 1978 election. Thurmond was 75, Ravenel 40. Thurmond was an old segregationist, in office for 28 of the last 32 years. Ravenel was a Harvard quarterback who returned home to South Carolina to enter business, then ran for governor as a reform candidate in 1974 and upset Lieutenant Governor Earle Morris and Congressman William Jennings Bryan Dorn in the primary. He seemed headed for victory until the courts reversed a ruling and said that he did not meet a constitutional residency requirement; he was stricken off the ballot in November, and the Republican won over Dorn. Ravenel was a fount of new ideas in both that race and his contest against Thurmond, and he also took some politically difficult positions (such as support of the Panama Canal Treaty). He won solid support from blacks and considerable support from textile mill whites; country club whites, however, reacted very negatively to him.

South Carolina's junior Senator is Ernest Hollings, like Thurmond a former Governor but with a rather different sort of career. Hollings won the governorship as a moderate in 1958, and eight years later he beat former Governor Donald Russell in the 1966 primary for the seat vacated by the death of Senator Olin Johnston. That year was the crest of Republican partisan strength in the state, although no one knew it at the time, and Hollings won with only 51%. He has improved his showing substantially since: to 62% in 1968 and 71% in 1974.

Hollings is one of the key insiders in the Senate, a man who seldom makes headlines but often makes things happen. One indication of this was the fact that in 1976 he was a very serious candidate for the majority leadership, although he withdrew from the race when it became clear that Robert Byrd had the votes to win. Hollings did not get as far as he has solely from his voting record, which tends to be somewhat to the right of the average Senate Democrat. He is generally strong for defense, and he tends to be a swing vote on economic issues. He works, of course, for the interests of South Carolina's textile industry, but he did shock state boosters a few years ago by spotlighting the malnutrition and even starvation that existed in some very poor coastal areas in South Carolina. Hollings also led the successful battle to end the oil depletion allowance for large producers.

Hollings is one of the more senior members of the Senate Appropriations Committee, and he is fourth-ranking and next in line for the chair on Commerce. He now chairs the Communications Subcommittee, which has jurisdiction over the broadcast industry. Hollings looks more like a senator than almost any other member, and he has the demeanor—with a deep, commanding voice—to match. He must run for reelection in 1980 and could conceivably face a tough opponent in former Governor James Edwards; but he must be considered the favorite to win.

Edwards won his term as Governor in 1974 in something of a surprise; he was the Republican nominee when Charles Ravenel was stricken from the ballot and Bryan Dorn substituted. The ruckus gave Edwards, till then a dentist who once ran a losing race for Congress, a chance he had never expected. And to the surprise of many, he turned out to be a popular governor. Nevertheless, South Carolina in 1978 was ready for reform. This is a state where a coterie of aged state legislators has run things for years, and as Ravenel's 1974 primary victory showed people were hungry for change.

That was the undoing of the initial favorite in 1978, Lieutenant Governor Brantley Harvey, who tended to embody things as they were. So did Bryan Dorn, a relative progressive despite his many years in Congress and old-fashioned personal style. The most unusual candidate was Tom Turnipseed, a former Wallace backer who claimed to have undergone a conversion on racial issues and campaigned as the people's champion against the big money interests. But Turnipseed's campaign collapsed abruptly and he withdrew. Much of his support went to a fourth candidate, state Senator Richard Riley.

Riley could not come close to imitating Turnipseed's flamboyant personal style. But in his 14 years in the legislature he became known as the leader of the reform elements; he had sponsored aid to the elderly and criticized the makeup of the commission regulating utilities. Riley started out the campaign unknown, but he was able to get his message across. He got Turnipseed's endorsement, edged out Dorn in the initial primary, and then, having attacked Harvey all along, overtook him in the runoff. The general election, against former Congressman Ed Young, was anticlimactic.

In fact, aside from Thurmond, Republicans have had little success in South Carolina. They have elected one congressman for some years and elected another in 1978; but that is not a particularly impressive record considering how well the party has done here in national elections. The closest the Republicans have come to the non-Thurmond Senate seat occurred back in 1966. Edwards's victory as Governor was largely accidental, and he was not able to leave an heir in the office. All this may change, if Jimmy Carter gets in trouble here (or if the Democrats reject him for a Yankee). But for the moment, at least two out of the three blocs of the South Carolina electorate seem pretty clearly committed to the Democrats.

Census Data Pop. 2,590,516; 1.28% of U.S. total, 26th largest; Central city, 9%; suburban, 30%. Median family income, $7,620; 42d highest; families above $15,000: 11%; families below $3,000: 16%. Median years education, 10.5.

1977 Share of Federal Tax Burden $3,351,000,000; 0.97% of U.S. total, 30th largest.

1977 Share of Federal Outlays $4,498,009,000; 1.14% of U.S. total, 29th largest. Per capita federal spending, $1,596.

DOD	$1,294,941,000	23d (1.42%)	HEW	$1,542,215,000	30th (1.04%)
ERDA	$264,377,000	8th (4.47%)	HUD	$38,561,000	31st (0.91%)
NASA	$203,000	45th (0.01%)	VA	$264,675,000	27th (1.38%)
DOT	$98,517,000	38th (0.69%)	EPA	$97,765,000	22d (1.19%)
DOC	$54,083,000	38th (0.65%)	RevS	$104,955,000	26th (1.24%)
DOI	$9,968,000	44th (0.21%)	Debt	$95,856,000	34th (0.32%)
USDA	$233,938,000	35th (1.18%)	Other	$397,955,000	

Economic Base Textile mill products, especially cotton weaving mills; apparel and other textile products, especially women's and misses' outerwear; agriculture, notably tobacco, soybeans, cattle and cotton lint; finance, insurance and real estate; chemicals and allied products, especially plastics materials and synthetics; machinery, especially special industry machinery; food and kindred products.

Political Line-up Governor, Richard W. Riley (D). Senators, Strom Thurmond (R) and Ernest F. Hollings (D). Representatives 6 (4 D and 2 R). State Senate (43 D, 3 R); State House (108 D, 16 R).

The Voters

Registration 1,097,726 Total. No party registration.
Median voting age 40
Employment profile White collar, 37%. Blue collar, 47%. Service, 12%. Farm, 4%.
Ethnic groups Black, 30%. Total foreign stock, 2%.

Presidential vote

1976	Carter (D)	450,807	(57%)
	Ford (R)	346,149	(43%)
1972	Nixon (R)	477,044	(72%)
	McGovern (D)	186,824	(28%)

Sen. Strom Thurmond (R) Elected 1956 as Democrat, changed party affiliation to Repub. Sept. 16, 1964, seat up 1984; b. Dec. 5, 1903, Edgefield; home, Aiken; Clemson Col., B.S. 1923, studied law at night; Baptist.

Career Teacher and coach, 1923–29; Edgefield Co. Supt. of Educ., 1929–33; Practicing atty., 1930–38, 1951–55; S.C. Senate, 1933–38; Circuit Judge, 1938–42; Army, WWII; Gov. of S.C., 1947–51; States Rights candidate for President of U.S., 1948; U.S. Senate, 1954–56.

Offices 209 RSOB, 202-224-5972. Also 1310 Lady St., Columbia 29201, 803-765-5496, and P.O. Drawer O, Charleston 29402, 803-722-3196.

Committees *Armed Services* (2d). Subcommittees: Arms Control; General Procurement; Military Construction and Stockpiles.

Judiciary (Ranking Member). Subcommittees: Antitrust, Monopoly, and Business Rights; Constitution.

Veterans' Affairs (2d).

Group Ratings

	ADA	COPE	PC	RPN	NFU	LCV	CFA	NAB	NSI	ACA	NTU
1978	10	21	23	56	70	11	20	80	100	87	–
1977	5	21	18	60	58	–	24	–	–	85	39
1976	0	10	0	53	17	6	0	91	100	100	71

Key Votes

1) Warnke Nom	AGN	6) Egypt-Saudi Arms	FOR	11) Hosptl Cost Contnmnt	AGN
2) Neutron Bomb	FOR	7) Draft Restr Pardon	AGN	12) Clinch River Reactor	FOR
3) Waterwy User Fee	AGN	8) Wheat Price Support	FOR	13) Pub Fin Cong Cmpgns	AGN
4) Dereg Nat Gas	FOR	9) Panama Canal Treaty	AGN	14) ERA Ratif Recissn	AGN
5) Kemp-Roth	FOR	10) Labor Law Rev Clot	AGN	15) Med Necssy Abrtns	AGN

Election Results

1978 general	Strom Thurmond (R)	351,733	(56%)	($2,013,431)
	Charles D. Ravenel (D)	281,119	(44%)	($1,134,168)
1978 primary	Strom Thurmond (R), unopposed			
1972 general	Strom Thurmond (R)	415,806	(63%)	($666,372)
	Eugene N. Zeigler (D)	241,056	(37%)	($167,750)

Sen. Ernest F. Hollings (D) Elected 1966, seat up 1980; b. Jan. 1, 1922, Charleston; home, Charleston; The Citadel, B.A. 1942, U. of So. Carolina, LL.B. 1947; Lutheran.

Career Practicing atty., 1947–58, 1963–66; S.C. House of Reps., 1949–55, Spkr. Pro Tem., 1951–55; Lt. Gov. of S.C., 1955–59; Gov. of S.C. 1959–63.

Offices 115 RSOB, 202-224-6121. Also 306 Fed. Bldg., Columbia 29201, 803-765-5731, and 103 Fed. Bldg., Spartanburg 29301, 803-585-3702.

Committees *Appropriations* (6th). Subcommittees: Defense; Energy and Water Development; Interior and Related Agencies; Labor, HEW, and Related Agencies; State, Justice, Commerce, the Judiciary, and Related Agencies (Chairman).

Budget (3d).

Commerce, Science, and Transportation (4th). Subcommittee: Communications (Chairman).

Group Ratings

	ADA	COPE	PC	RPN	NFU	LCV	CFA	NAB	NSI	ACA	NTU
1978	30	39	58	44	70	57	60	58	56	52	–
1977	30	50	45	50	58	–	48	–	–	52	25
1976	40	80	58	56	67	42	71	30	67	28	35

Key Votes

1) Warnke Nom	FOR	6) Egypt-Saudi Arms	FOR	11) Hosptl Cost Contnmnt	AGN
2) Neutron Bomb	FOR	7) Draft Restr Pardon	AGN	12) Clinch River Reactor	FOR
3) Waterwy User Fee	AGN	8) Wheat Price Support	AGN	13) Pub Fin Cong Cmpgns	AGN
4) Dereg Nat Gas	AGN	9) Panama Canal Treaty	FOR	14) ERA Ratif Recissn	AGN
5) Kemp-Roth	AGN	10) Labor Law Rev Clot	AGN	15) Med Necssy Abrtns	FOR

Election Results

1974 general	Ernest F. Hollings (D)	356,126	(71%)	($225,678)
	Gwen Bush (R)	146,645	(29%)	($6,754)
1974 primary	Ernest F. Hollings (D), unopposed			
1968 general	Ernest F. Hollings (D)	404,060	(62%)	
	Marshall Parker (R)	248,780	(38%)	

Gov. Richard W. Riley (D) Elected 1978, term expires Jan. 1983; b. Jan. 2, 1932, Greenville; Furman U., B.A.; U. of S.C., LL.B. 1960; Methodist.

Career Legal Counsel to U.S. Sen. Olin D. Johnston, 1960–61; Practicing atty., 1961–; S.C. House of Reps., 1963–67; S.C. Senate, 1967–77.

Offices State House, 1st Floor West Wing, Box 11450, Columbia 29211, 803-758-3261.

Election Results

1978 general	Richard W. Riley (D)	385,016	(62%)
	Edward L. Young (R)	236,946	(38%)
1978 runoff	Richard W. Riley (D)	180,882	(53%)
	Brantley Harvey (D)	158,655	(47%)
1978 primary	Brantley Harvey (D)	142,785	(37%)
	Richard W. Riley (D)	125,185	(33%)
	Bryan Dorn (D)	112,793	(30%)
1974 general	James B. Edwards (R)	266,109	(52%)
	Bryan Dorn (D)	248,938	(48%)

FIRST DISTRICT

In the spring the pastel row houses of Charleston are wreathed with flowers of the blossoming trees. There are few, if any, more beautiful urban scenes in America. Charleston, founded in 1670 and blessed with one of the finest harbors on the Atlantic, was one of the South's leading cities up to the Civil War. Across its docks went cargoes of rice, indigo, cotton—all crops cultivated by black slaves and designed to enrich the white planters and merchants who dominated the state's economic and political life. In the years following the Civil War, Charleston became an economic backwater. Today the old part of the city, beautifully preserved and still the home of the city's elite, houses fewer people than it did in 1860.

In the middle of the twentieth century Charleston found a benefactor who restored some of its old majesty and much of its old power. His name was L. Mendel Rivers, and he was Congressman from the 1st district of South Carolina for 30 years. He was also Chairman of the House Armed Services Committee from 1965 until his death in December 1970. Rivers was as proud of the Defense Department money he funneled into the Charleston area as he was of his superpatriotism (although he himself never served in the military). It was largely because of Rivers that 35% of the payrolls in the 1st district come either from military installations or defense industries. The 1st district, which includes Charleston and several coastal, heavily black, and rural counties, contains no less than 11 major Navy installations.

With his long-flowing white locks and thick accent, Rivers looked and talked the part of a Southern congressman. He was bellicose, self-righteous and too often drunk (though he stopped drinking toward the end). He was ardently pro-Pentagon, but he often joined northern Democrats in supporting bread and butter legislation; he had begun life not as a Charleston aristocrat, but as a poor country boy. There is a monument to Rivers in the elegant old section of Charleston, but his real monument is the line of middle income suburbs along Rivers Boulevard in North Charleston, near the big naval base.

Rivers has been succeeded by a man with a similar background, his godson, Mendel Davis, but the succession was not automatic. Davis only barely edged James Edwards, later Governor, in the 1971 special election, and he had strong Republican competition in 1972. Davis joined the Armed Services Committee, naturally, and almost always supports higher defense spending. He once voted against the B-1 bomber, but that after all is an Air Force, not a Navy, project. Davis also survived some embarrassment in 1976 when it was revealed that he headed the subcommittee of Wayne Hays's House Administration Committee which had kept Elizabeth Ray on its payroll. He won reelection twice after that, but decided not to run again in 1980.

Even more than Rivers, Davis has often voted with northern Democrats on economic issues. But this is a district which has changed greatly from the time when Rivers represented it. Blacks make up about one-third of the vote, and many blue collar whites support Democrats out of economic reasons. The increasing middle class communities in Charleston County provide a solid base for any significant Republican candidacy, and with Davis not running, almost any kind of candidate could win here in 1980.

Census Data Pop. 442,646. Central city, 15%; suburban, 54%. Median family income, $7,355; families above $15,000: 12%; families below $3,000: 18%. Median years education, 11.4.

The Voters

Median voting age 36.
Employment profile White collar, 34%. Blue collar, 39%. Service, 15%. Farm, 2%.
Ethnic groups Black, 34%. Total foreign stock, 4%.

Presidential vote

1976	Carter (D)	70,124	(54%)
	Ford (R)	59,939	(46%)
1972	Nixon (R)	73,480	(69%)
	McGovern (D)	33,488	(31%)

Rep. Mendel J. Davis (D) Elected Apr. 27, 1971; b. Oct. 23, 1942, North Charleston; home, North Charleston; Col. of Charleston, B.S. 1966, U. of So. Carolina, J.D. 1970; Methodist.

Career Practicing atty., 1970–71.

Offices 2161 RHOB, 202-225-3176. Also 640 Fed. Bldg., 334 Meeting St., Charleston 29403, 803-577-4171.

Committees *Armed Services* (16th). Subcommittees: NATO Standardization, Interoperability, and Readiness; Military Compensation; Military Installations and Facilities.

House Administration (11th). Subcommittees: Accounts; Personnel and Police.

Group Ratings

	ADA	COPE	PC	RPN	NFU	LCV	CFA	NAB	NSI	ACA	NTU
1978	45	55	43	36	63	–	46	50	80	58	–
1977	30	62	25	31	64	29	25	–	–	50	23
1976	35	70	43	33	73	35	36	9	90	59	21

Key Votes

1) Increase Def Spnd	FOR	6) Alaska Lands Protect	FOR	11) Delay Auto Pol Cntrl	FOR
2) B-1 Bomber	AGN	7) Water Projects Veto	FOR	12) Sugar Price Escalator	DNV
3) Cargo Preference	FOR	8) Consum Protect Agcy	FOR	13) Pub Fin Cong Cmpgns	AGN
4) Dereg Nat Gas	FOR	9) Common Situs Picket	DNV	14) ERA Ratif Recissn	FOR
5) Kemp-Roth	FOR	10) Labor Law Revision	AGN	15) Prohibt Govt Abrtns	AGN

Election Results

1978 general	Mendel J. Davis (D)	65,832	(61%)	($124,943)
	C. C. Wannamaker (R)	42,811	(39%)	($49,079)
1978 primary	Mendel J. Davis (D)	48,541	(86%)	
	One other (D)	7,631	(14%)	
1976 general	Mendel J. Davis (D)	89,891	(69%)	($59,442)
	Lonnie Rowell (R)	40,598	(31%)	($1,751)

SECOND DISTRICT

Between the coastal swamps and the industrialized Piedmont of South Carolina, square in the middle of the state, is the capital, Columbia. This is South Carolina's largest city, its only one with a population over 100,000, and its fastest growing. Like so many other cities in the South during the sixties and early seventies, Columbia was trending Republican. Some observers attributed this to an influx of northerners; but this is surely wrong, for there are fewer people from out of state here than in just about any other place in the nation.

The Republican trend was something indigenous, the result of upwardly mobile people from smaller towns and rural areas of the state, moving here to white collar jobs in the growing private sector—insurance agents, computer salesmen, production managers, etc. Uprooted from their traditionally Democratic rural environment, and thrust up several notches in social class, these migrants have found the state's Republicans younger, more modern, and generally more congenial than old style Southern Democrats. Raised in the tradition of Franklin D. Roosevelt, they have learned about the glories of the free market and the virtues of the free enterprise system. So most of the white portions of Columbia and its suburbs, particularly those in Lexington County, had by the early seventies become the bulwark of South Carolina Republicanism.

Columbia, with its suburbs in Richland and Lexington Counties, casts more than 70% of the votes in the state's 2d congressional district. The remainder come from an older part of South Carolina: the black majority counties closer to the coast. The largest town here is Orangeburg, with only 13,000 people, where white highway patrolmen massacred several black students at South Carolina State College in 1968. These lower counties usually go Democratic, but in many elections have been heavily outvoted by the Columbia area.

This seat has been in Republican hands since 1965, when Congressman Albert Watson was stripped of his seniority for backing Barry Goldwater, and decided to join the Republican Party. Watson gave up the seat when he ran for governor and lost in 1970, and he was succeeded by Floyd Spence, by then a Republican, but who had lost the 1962 Democratic primary to Watson. A genial man of the good old boy type, Spence won a seat on the Armed Services Committee—a good spot to tend to the needs of Columbia's Fort Jackson—and was also assigned to the Ethics Committee, on which he has served as ranking Republican. Spence is the kind of man whom congressmen have liked to name to ethics posts: personally honest, but not ready to believe anything bad about his colleagues unless he is forced to. Spence is well liked but not quite as well respected; he was named to New Times's list of the ten dumbest congressmen in 1973.

Spence was unopposed for renomination and reelection, but since the Watergate scandal broke he has not had such an easy time. The disgrace of Richard Nixon moved many rural and blue collar whites in South Carolina back to their ancestral Democratic Party, and put politicians like Spence on the defensive. In the three elections since, he has had significant Democratic opposition and has not won with more than 58%. Indeed, some of his opponents have had interesting credentials. Matthew Perry, a black Columbia lawyer who ran in 1974, has since been named to the federal bench on the recommendation of, among others, Strom Thurmond. Jack Bass, the Democratic nominee in 1978, is a top newspaper reporter and writer, and the author of the definitive work on the Orangeburg massacre. But none of them could really crack the newly affluent Republican vote in the Columbia area; Bass, for example, could get no better than 26% in Lexington County. One must conclude from Spence's victories over such candidates that he has reasonable safety in this district.

Census Data Pop. 446,267. Central city, 25%; suburban, 47%. Median family income, $7,900; families above $15,000: 14%; families below $3,000: 15%. Median years education, 11.4.

The Voters

Median voting age 37.
Employment profile White collar, 47%. Blue collar, 36%. Service, 14%. Farm, 3%.
Ethnic groups Black, 34%. Total foreign stock, 3%.

Presidential vote

1976	Carter (D)	76,948	(52%)
	Ford (R)	69,827	(48%)
1972	Nixon (R)	85,637	(69%)
	McGovern (D)	37,756	(31%)

Rep. Floyd Spence (R) Elected 1970; b. Apr. 9, 1928, Columbia; home, Lexington; U. of So. Carolina, B.A. 1952, LL.B. 1956; Lutheran.

Career Navy, Korea; Practicing atty.; S.C. House of Reps., 1956–62; S.C. Senate, 1966–70, Minor. Ldr.

Offices 2351 RHOB, 202-225-2452. Also Rm. 104, 2001 Assembly St., Columbia 29201, 803-765-5871.

Committees *Armed Services* (4th). Subcommittees: Investigations; NATO Standardization, Interoperability, and Readiness; Seapower and Strategic and Critical Materials.

Standards of Official Conduct (Ranking Member).

Group Ratings

	ADA	COPE	PC	RPN	NFU	LCV	CFA	NAB	NSI	ACA	NTU
1978	15	20	15	50	30	–	14	100	100	89	–
1977	0	17	10	42	42	18	15	–	–	88	45
1976	5	22	13	39	25	13	0	67	100	93	58

Key Votes

1) Increase Def Spnd	FOR	6) Alaska Lands Protect	FOR	11) Delay Auto Pol Cntrl	DNV
2) B-1 Bomber	FOR	7) Water Projects Veto	AGN	12) Sugar Price Escalator	FOR
3) Cargo Preference	FOR	8) Consum Protect Agcy	AGN	13) Pub Fin Cong Cmpgns	AGN
4) Dereg Nat Gas	FOR	9) Common Situs Picket	AGN	14) ERA Ratif Recissn	FOR
5) Kemp-Roth	FOR	10) Labor Law Revision	AGN	15) Prohibt Govt Abrtns	FOR

Election Results

1978 general	Floyd Spence (R)	71,208	(57%)	($182,995)
	Jack Bass (D)	53,021	(43%)	($136,959)
1978 primary	Floyd Spence (R), unopposed			
1976 general	Floyd Spence (R)	83,426	(58%)	($59,672)
	Clyde B. Livingston (D)	60,602	(42%)	($0)

THIRD DISTRICT

As you move inland from the South Carolina coast, you see fewer and fewer black people. It is a matter of history and economics. The land along the coast is ideal for growing crops like rice and cotton, which are labor-intensive; so early planters kept thousands of slaves. Inland the terrain is hilly, the rainfall less plentiful, and the soil less fertile; the tradition here is of single family farms, few of which could afford to support slaves. So while many rural counties along the coast have black majorities today, the population of the Piedmont country of the 3d congressional district is 77% white.

The 3d is an upcountry district, lying mostly along the Savannah River, the boundary with Georgia. The southern part of the district is Strom Thurmond country: he grew up in Edgefield and maintains his residence in Aiken, a prosperous nuclear energy city halfway between Columbia and Augusta, Georgia. Like Thurmond, Aiken moved Republican in the sixties, while the counties further upriver remained traditionally Southern Democratic by backing George Wallace in 1968. Anderson, a heavily white textile mill town and the most populous city in the district with 27,000 people, was the largest South Carolina city carried by Wallace that year. But by 1976 the textile mill whites had gone back to the Democrats; Jimmy Carter took Anderson County with 67%.

For a quarter of a century, the 3d district was represented in the House by William Jennings Bryan Dorn. He looked the part of a Southern politician, with a deep drawl and a white linen suit draped over his paunch. Dorn had a more progressive record than many suppose, but he was beaten in the 1974 gubernatorial runoff by Charles Ravenel and then lost the general election after Ravenel was taken off the ballot.

In the Nixon years, Republican strategists had targeted the 3d district. But by the time of the Watergate year of 1974, it was solidly Democratic again. The winner of the Democratic primary, Butler Derrick, took 62% in the general election against a man who had once carried the district in a statewide race. Derrick has attracted some attention in Washington for taking positions not normally associated with Southern congressmen. He was the leadoff speaker in the drive to oust Florida's Bob Sikes from the chair of the Military Construction Subcommittee in 1977. He supported Jimmy Carter's plan to cut funds for water projects, and when Carter announced cancellation of a dam in the 3d district Derrick, instead of squawking, said he agreed. Derrick also got adopted an amendment to the Humphrey-Hawkins bill calling for reductions in the federal deficit. And he has argued for detailed congressional oversight of federal programs with periodic assessment of whether they are meeting their goals. Derrick seems to be a stickler for major procedural reforms, and without being reactionary, is clearly in line with the feeling that the federal budget deficit ought to be reduced. He has been reelected easily, and there is speculation that he may seek statewide office, perhaps when Strom Thurmond's seat comes up again in 1984.

Census Data Pop. 434,427. Central city, 0%; suburban, 35%. Median family income, $8,002; families above $15,000: 10%; families below $3,000: 13%. Median years education, 10.1.

The Voters

Median voting age 42.
Employment profile White collar, 32%. Blue collar, 56%. Service, 10%. Farm, 2%.
Ethnic groups Black, 23%. Total foreign stock, 1%.

Presidential vote

1976	Carter (D)	78,296	(59%)
	Ford (R)	54,640	(41%)
1972	Nixon (R)	84,401	(77%)
	McGovern (D)	24,723	(23%)

Rep. Butler Derrick (D) Elected 1974; b. Sept. 30, 1936, Johnston; home, Edgefield; U. of So. Carolina, B.A. 1958, U. of Ga., LL.B. 1965; Episcopalian.

Career Practicing atty., 1965–74; S.C. House of Reps., 1969–75.

Offices 133 CHOB, 202-225-5301. Also 315 S. McDuffie St., Anderson 29621, 803-224-7401.

Committees *Rules* (9th).

Group Ratings

	ADA	COPE	PC	RPN	NFU	LCV	CFA	NAB	NSI	ACA	NTU
1978	45	68	58	36	40	–	46	46	80	44	–
1977	35	57	55	31	64	62	55	–	–	32	34
1976	40	45	46	47	33	64	54	33	100	57	38

Key Votes

1) Increase Def Spnd	DNV	6) Alaska Lands Protect	FOR	11) Delay Auto Pol Cntrl	FOR
2) B-1 Bomber	AGN	7) Water Projects Veto	FOR	12) Sugar Price Escalator	FOR
3) Cargo Preference	AGN	8) Consum Protect Agcy	AGN	13) Pub Fin Cong Cmpgns	FOR
4) Dereg Nat Gas	FOR	9) Common Situs Picket	AGN	14) ERA Ratif Recissn	AGN
5) Kemp-Roth	AGN	10) Labor Law Revision	AGN	15) Prohibt Govt Abrtns	AGN

Election Results

1978 general	Butler Derrick (D)	81,638	(82%)	✓	($84,641)
	Anthony Panuccio (R)	17,973	(18%)		
1978 primary	Butler Derrick (D), unopposed				
1976 general	Butler Derrick (D), unopposed				($21,504)

FOURTH DISTRICT

The major textile producing area in the United States is a strip of land along Interstate 85 in North and South Carolina. Two of the biggest textile centers here are Greenville and Spartanburg, South Carolina—the two cities which, with the counties that surround them, make up South Carolina's 4th congressional district. It will probably come as a surprise to many readers that this is one of the most industrialized and most blue collar parts of the nation; the fact surprises even tourists who drive through the South Carolina Piedmont on their way south. For the mills are not concentrated in a few big factories, like giant steel plants, in the inner part of grimy cities. They are all over, in small towns and suburbs, at interchanges on the Interstate as well as in Greenville and Spartanburg themselves. Few blacks live here—only 18% district-wide, the lowest percentage in South Carolina. And there are even fewer union members: South Carolina has just about the least unionized work force of any state in the nation, and a major reason is the intransigent opposition of the mill owners to unionization. These conditions—low wages, no unions, large work force—have helped South Carolina attract new industry, and many German and French companies now have major installations not far from Interstate 85. It is one of the boom parts of the country.

Politically Greenville and Spartanburg have different traditions. Greenville is the state's premier Republican city; there are lots of textile management types, and also a local establishment of considerable distinction, including federal Judge and onetime Supreme Court nominee Clement Haynsworth and former Governor and Senator Donald Russell, himself now a federal judge. Spartanburg is a rougher, more blue collar town, traditionally Democratic. Its most famous citizens were the late Senator (1931-41), Supreme Court Justice (1941-42), Secretary of State (1945-47), and Governor (1951-55) James Byrnes and the late Governor (1935-39, 1943-45) and Senator (1945-65) Olin Johnston, who was something of an oldtime Southern populist.

But the dominant fact of political life here for many years was low turnout. In 1972, it cast fewer votes than any other district in the nation except a couple in the New York slums, and 80% of its ballots were for Richard Nixon. The Deering-Milliken executives, the bankers and insurance agents, the country club members were all voting; many white textile workers, with low wages and perhaps no roots in the community other than a lease on a trailer park space, did not. Local population growth and the sudden identification of the Democratic Party, when it nominated Jimmy Carter, with the white South, increased turnout vastly. Between 1972 and 1976, the Republican vote was down 16,000, but the Democratic presidential vote rose by 44,000; Carter carried the district, albeit with only 52%. White lower income people here now seem willing to support candidates supported by blacks and white liberals, but will they be more receptive than they have in the past to labor unions? That is a key question for this area in the future. The betting, however, has to be that the status quo will be maintained.

Traditionally, the 4th district has been represented in the House by a member of the Greenville establishment. That was the case with James Mann, Democratic Congressman for ten years before his retirement in 1978. He will be remembered for his stirring speech at the House Judiciary Committee hearings more than for the personal financial problems which probably impelled his retirement. Two quite different candidates vied for the right to succeed him. One was Max Heller, the Democratic Mayor of Greenville. He had come to the city 40 years before as a refugee from Austria when it was occupied by the Nazis. Starting off as a stock boy, he built his own shirt manufacturing firm; elected Mayor, he put together a successful downtown redevelopment program. But Heller was unable to turn his home town popularity into votes in the congressional race; one reason may have been his Jewish religion in a part of the country where many voters want Christian officeholders.

The winner of the election was the Republican, Carroll Campbell. A generation younger than Heller, he had run for lieutenant governor in 1974 and had been elected to the state Senate in 1976. In both his politics and his personal characteristics he is typical of the young, newly affluent urban voters of states like South Carolina. He believes in the free enterprise system, he believes taxes are too high, and he believes that government is too big. His party label helped him win a majority in Greenville and he was able to prevent Heller from winning a majority in Spartanburg. This is the South Carolina district which is, by most measurements, the most Republican, and if Campbell uses the advantages of incumbency adroitly, he should be the favorite to win reelection in 1980.

Census Data Pop. 414,270. Central city, 15%; suburban, 43%. Median family income, $8,416; families above $15,000: 13%; families below $3,000: 11%. Median years education, 10.8.

The Voters

Median voting age 41.
Employment profile White collar, 39%. Blue collar, 49%. Service, 11%. Farm, 1%.
Ethnic groups Black, 18%. Total foreign stock, 2%.

Presidential vote

1976	Carter (D)	63,848	(52%)
	Ford (R)	59,555	(48%)
1972	Nixon (R)	77,547	(80%)
	McGovern (D)	19,702	(20%)

Rep. Carroll A. Campbell, Jr. (R) Elected 1978; b. July 24, 1940, Greenville; home, Greenville; U. of S.C.; Episcopalian.

Career Real estate and farming; S.C. House of Reps., 1970–74; Exec. Asst. to Gov. James B. Edwards, 1975–76; S.C. Senate, 1976–78.

Offices 1723 LHOB, 202-225-6030. Also P.O. Box 10011, Greenville 29603, 803-232-1411.

Committees *Banking, Finance and Urban Affairs* (13th). Subcommittees: Financial Institutions Supervision, Regulation and Insurance; General Oversight and Renegotiation; International Trade, Investment and Monetary Policy.

House Administration (9th). Subcommittees: Accounts; Personnel and Police; Contracts.

Group Ratings: Newly Elected

Key Votes: Newly Elected

Election Results

1978 general	Carroll A. Campbell, Jr. (R)	51,377	(53%)	($182,461)
	Max M. Heller (D)	45,484	(47%)	($240,150)
1978 primary	Carroll A. Campbell, Jr. (R)	6,808	(88%)	
	One other (R)	899	(12%)	
1976 general	James R. Mann (D)	91,721	(74%)	($46,071)
	Robert L. Watkins (R)	32,983	(26%)	($3,798)

FIFTH DISTRICT

Stock car racing, one of the nation's most popular sports, thrives most today in places like the 5th congressional district of South Carolina. After World War II, textile companies fled from the Northeast to shiny new factories on the outskirts of small towns like Rock Hill and Gaffney in South Carolina. Here plenty of people were eager to work long hours for low wages under poor conditions, and few of them had any funny ideas about joining a union. In the 5th district's textile towns and their outskirts, whites heavily outnumber blacks; though in some smaller, less developed counties, blacks still have a near-majority. But the political spirit prevailing in the 5th is best symbolized by the fan at the stock car races—the yahooing white Southerner whom W.J. Cash called "a hell of a fellow."

The 5th is a traditionally Democratic district, but it was one of two South Carolina districts to go for George Wallace in 1968 and went heavily for Richard Nixon in 1972. But the Democratic allegiance returned after the Watergate scandal was exposed and after the Democrats nominated Jimmy Carter. On Labor Day in 1976 Carter appeared at the Southern 500 stock car race, held just next door to the 5th district, on the same day as Republican vice presidential candidate Bob Dole. Dole got only a tepid welcome, while Carter got big cheers. It was a preview of how the two tickets would run in stock car country; the Georgian took 61% of the votes in the 5th district.

Carter's margin was a political asset for Democratic Congressman Ken Holland. First elected in 1974, he was facing formidable opposition in the person of Bobby Richardson, the longtime scrambling second baseman for the New York Yankees. Richardson was raised in South Carolina, and was known locally for his participation in sports programs for youth and for his strong religious beliefs; he represented the evangelical strain in Southern culture. Holland, who had been divorced in his first term, represented the hell of a fellow strain. With some help from Carter, Holland was able to win with 52%; this is one of the few districts in the country where coattails may have made the difference in 1976.

Since that election, Holland has gained another political asset: a seat on the House Ways and Means Committee. This is not just a matter of academic interest. Ways and Means has jurisdiction over foreign trade restrictions, and the textile industry is desperately eager to prevent or lessen imports of textiles from low wage countries, particularly those in East Asia. Holland is very much textile's man on Ways and Means. He is the senior Democrat on the committee from a textile district and is a member of the Trade Subcommittee. He has won a number of victories for the industry and continually applies pressure for restrictions. After his tough election in 1976, Holland did not have Republican opposition at all in 1978—a fact which tells us something about the depth of the South Carolina Republican Party. His importance to the textile industry should help him make this seat safe if he faces any future significant challenges.

Census Data Pop. 441,907. Central city, 0%; suburban, 0%. Median family income, $7,623; families above $15,000: 9%; families below $3,000: 15%. Median years education, 9.8.

The Voters

Median voting age 41.
Employment profile White collar, 30%. Blue collar, 56%. Service, 12%. Farm, 2%.
Ethnic groups Black, 32%. Total foreign stock, 1%.

Presidential vote

1976	Carter (D)	77,715	(61%)
	Ford (R)	50,328	(39%)
1972	Nixon (R)	78,994	(71%)
	McGovern (D)	32,044	(29%)

Rep. Kenneth L. Holland (D) Elected 1974; b. Nov. 24, 1934, Hickory, N.C.; home, Camden; U. of So. Carolina, A.B. 1960, LL.B. 1963; Methodist.

Career Employee, S.C. State Hwy. Comm., 1953–55; Instrumentman, Daniel Construction Co., 1956; Practicing atty., 1963–74; Legal Counsel, S.C. Dem. Party.

Offices 103 CHOB, 202-225-5501. Also P.O. Box 272, CSS, Rock Hill 29730, 803-327-1114.

Committees *Ways and Means* (15th). Subcommittees: Select Revenue Measures; Trade.

Group Ratings

	ADA	COPE	PC	RPN	NFU	LCV	CFA	NAB	NSI	ACA	NTU
1978	35	61	33	57	50	–	18	67	67	46	–
1977	15	56	33	44	56	67	20	–	–	48	20
1976	35	52	38	33	73	29	27	9	40	57	40

Key Votes

1) Increase Def Spnd	AGN	6) Alaska Lands Protect	AGN	11) Delay Auto Pol Cntrl	DNV
2) B-1 Bomber	AGN	7) Water Projects Veto	FOR	12) Sugar Price Escalator	FOR
3) Cargo Preference	FOR	8) Consum Protect Agcy	AGN	13) Pub Fin Cong Cmpgns	AGN
4) Dereg Nat Gas	FOR	9) Common Situs Picket	AGN	14) ERA Ratif Recissn	AGN
5) Kemp-Roth	AGN	10) Labor Law Revision	AGN	15) Prohibt Govt Abrtns	DNV

Election Results

1978 general	Ken Holland (D), unopposed			($91,690)
1978 primary	Ken Holland (D)	46,247	(65%)	
	Colleen Yates (D)	24,853	(35%)	($24,583)
1976 general	Ken Holland (D)	66,073	(52%)	($129,560)
	Bobby Richardson (R)	62,095	(48%)	($177,384)

SIXTH DISTRICT

The 6th district of South Carolina takes in the northeastern corner of the state, where the Pee Dee and Santee Rivers flow. It is a region of tobacco farms, textile mills, and ocean beaches. Most of the 6th's residents and voters live in and around textile mill towns like Florence and Darlington, the latter the site of the Southern 500 stock car race. But the district is not nearly so white as the state's other textile districts. Some of the lowland counties have black majorities, even among registered voters. Altogether in 1970 42% of the people in the 6th, and 36% of those over 18, were black.

The fact that blacks constitute more than one-third of the electorate of this district has revolutionized its politics within the last 15 years. In 1965, before passage of the Voting Rights Act, few blacks voted here; the informal sanctions against it in rural communities were just too great. In the next presidential race, the 6th was carried by Hubert Humphrey, largely on the strength of black votes; it was the only district in South Carolina, indeed the only nonmetropolitan district in the entire South, which Humphrey won. In 1970 there was a strong challenge in the Democratic primary to John McMillan, who had represented the district since 1938 and had been Chairman of the House District of Columbia Committee since 1948.

McMillan had never paid much attention to the district's blacks, and he was known as an adversary to the District's black majority. His main selling point to his constituents was his seat on the Agriculture Committee and its importance for local tobacco farmers. In 1970 McMillan was lucky that the opponent who made it into the runoff was black; he defeated him fairly easily. But in 1972 he faced a white with a reputation as a liberal, John Jenrette, and lost. Jenrette failed to win the general election that year; the seat was won by Republican Ed Young who was probably helped by the popularity of the Nixon-Agnew ticket. But Young could not hold on in 1974, and Jenrette was finally elected.

He has had a rather tempestuous House career. He was hurt by a series of stories about his amatory exploits; he had been divorced, an attractive young woman had been fired by the Republican National Committee for dating him, and he had married her, two months before the 1976 general election. Nonetheless he beat Young again. In the next two years he tended more visibly to business and his seat on the Agriculture Committee. In 1978 he had no opposition in the general election at all, and in 1979 he won a seat on the Appropriations Committee. After nearly ten years of turbulence, the congressional politics of the 6th district seems to have quieted down.

Census Data Pop. 410,999. Central city, 0%; suburban, 0%. Median family income, $6,203; families above $15,000: 9%; families below $3,000: 23%. Median years education, 9.7.

The Voters

Median voting age 42.
Employment profile White collar, 33%. Blue collar, 43%. Service, 13%. Farm, 11%.
Ethnic groups Black, 42%. Total foreign stock, 1%.

Presidential vote

1976	Carter (D)	83,876	(62%)
	Ford (R)	51,860	(38%)
1972	Nixon (R)	76,985	(68%)
	McGovern (D)	36,846	(32%)

Rep. John W. Jenrette (D) Elected 1974; b. May 19, 1936, Conway; home, North Myrtle Beach; Wofford Col., B.A. 1958, U. of So. Carolina, LL.B. 1962; Methodist.

Career Army, 1958–59; Practicing atty., 1962–74; S.C. House of Reps., 1964–72.

Offices 240 CHOB, 202-225-3315. Also 233 MacMillan Fed. Bldg., Florence 29501, 803-665-0341.

Committees *Appropriations* (33d). Subcommittees: Agriculture, Rural Development and Related Agencies; Energy and Water Development.

Group Ratings

	ADA	COPE	PC	RPN	NFU	LCV	CFA	NAB	NSI	ACA	NTU
1978	40	74	53	44	89	–	41	22	70	43	–
1977	35	65	38	17	73	36	30	–	–	27	16
1976	45	70	48	41	50	52	36	18	60	54	33

Key Votes

1) Increase Def Spnd	FOR	6) Alaska Lands Protect	AGN	11) Delay Auto Pol Cntrl	FOR
2) B-1 Bomber	AGN	7) Water Projects Veto	AGN	12) Sugar Price Escalator	FOR
3) Cargo Preference	FOR	8) Consum Protect Agcy	FOR	13) Pub Fin Cong Cmpgns	FOR
4) Dereg Nat Gas	AGN	9) Common Situs Picket	AGN	14) ERA Ratif Recissn	FOR
5) Kemp-Roth	AGN	10) Labor Law Revision	AGN	15) Prohibt Govt Abrtns	AGN

Election Results

1978 general	John W. Jenrette, Jr. (D), unopposed			($100,829)
1978 primary	John W. Jenrette, Jr. (D)	58,320	(77%)	
	One other (D)	17,541	(23%)	
1976 general	John W. Jenrette, Jr. (D)	75,916	(56%)	($278,457)
	Ed L. Young (R)	60,288	(44%)	($291,153)

SOUTH DAKOTA

South Dakota was once the heartland of the Sioux Indians, who roamed the plains hunting buffalo. Then the white man came and exterminated the buffalo and, in places like Wounded Knee, many Indians as well. Those who survived were herded onto reservations. Today South Dakota still has one of the highest Indian populations in the nation; one out of twenty South Dakotans is a native American. Accordingly one of the constants in the life of South Dakota has been enmity between Indians and the whites. Sometimes the enmity flares up, as in the 1973 occupation of Wounded Knee by Indian militants, and it is particularly important politically in the western part of the state, where most of the Indians live.

For the Indians, South Dakota was good hunting ground because the buffalo could graze and flourish on the semi-arid grass land. But for the white man the region was long considered worthless. The first white settlers decided to come to the state only when gold was found in the Black Hills. Men like Wild Bill Hickok, America's first dime novel hero, made legends in mining towns like Deadwood, Lead, and Spearfish; and then, as the rich veins petered out, they moved on. They left behind the plains which, as farming methods improved and land became more crowded to the east, were slowly being peopled by homesteaders. Some of them were Scandinavians moving from Wisconsin or Minnesota; but most were White Anglo-Saxon Protestants from Nebraska, Iowa, and points east. South Dakota thereby experienced most of its population growth during two decades of agricultural prosperity, 1880-90 and 1900-10. The decade between, the 1890s, was a period of drought and depression and farm rebellion. By 1910 the population of the state had reached seven-eighths of the current figure—which is to say that there has been much outmigration and little in-migration during the last sixty-odd years.

By 1910 the political character of South Dakota had been pretty well set. During the 1890s the state flirted briefly with the Populists and William Jennings Bryan; but by the 1920s, South Dakota had become almost as monolithically Republican as Nebraska. Voters in South Dakota never had much use for the socialist ideas of the Non-Partisan League, which caught on in the more Scandinavian soil of North Dakota, and there was never anything here comparable to the Farmer-Labor Party of Minnesota. As in most other Great Plains states, voters in South Dakota have sometimes been dissatisfied with the farm programs of national administrations. Farming is not only of indirect economic importance here; even today nearly one-quarter of the state's residents actually live on farms. But until the seventies, such dissatisfaction had little effect on election outcomes. Between 1936 and 1970 South Dakota had a Democratic governor for only two years and elected only one Democrat to Congress—George McGovern.

Suddenly in 1970 there was a sharp shift in the state's voting patterns. Democrats were elected to the governorship and to both of South Dakota's two congressional seats. In 1972 McGovern failed to carry the state, but he did get 46% here, better than almost everywhere else; and it otherwise was the best year ever for South Dakota Democrats. Congressman James Abourezk was elected to the Senate, Governor Richard Kneip easily won a second term, Democrats took majorities in both houses of the state legislature, and won five of seven statewide offices.

The Democratic tide has now ebbed somewhat. Democrats had lost both congressional seats by 1974; though they gained one back in 1978, they lost Abourezk's Senate seat. Republican William Janklow was elected to replace Kneip, Republicans control the legislature, and they hold most of the statewide offices. Nevertheless, this is no longer a one-party state. Jimmy Carter won 49% of the vote here in 1976, and Senator Larry Pressler's 1978 victory was more a personal than a partisan triumph. The Democrats' biggest test will come in 1980, when we will see whether they can carry the state in the presidential election and whether George McGovern can win a fourth term in the Senate.

For the story of the Democrats' initial rise here is to a great extent the story of how George McGovern built a party. Like Hubert Humphrey in Minnesota, Edmund Muskie in Maine, Gaylord Nelson and William Proxmire in Wisconsin, and Mennen Williams in Michigan, McGovern took a moribund state party and made it a competitive political force—and made himself a presidential candidate in the process. He was helped locally by feuds between Republicans, who fielded weak candidates in the late sixties and early seventies, and nationally by reaction against the war in Vietnam. The Republicans in turn have benefited from the Democrats' overconfidence and schisms and from the impact of both national and local issues. On the former, South Dakota is still a state suspicious of government spending—except on farm programs—and fond of balanced budgets; on the latter, there has been a backlash against the Indians since the Wounded Knee incident in 1973. Democrats have always been identified, by Indians and whites, as being more sympathetic to the Indians; Republicans were characterized by William Janklow, then the gun-toting Attorney General and now Governor, who made a great political asset out of vehement opposition to Indian claims.

McGovern's story became familiar for a while, to observers of national politics: how the preacher's son drove his beat-up car over back roads to set up Democratic county organizations, how he ran for Congress himself in 1956 and beat an overconfident incumbent, how he lost a Senate race in 1960 but, blessed with an opponent named Joe Bottum, won in 1962 by 597 votes. By 1968 McGovern was running for president at the Democratic convention as a sort of stand-in for Robert Kennedy; by 1971, having distinguished himself as a leading opponent of the Vietnam war, he was running in his own right.

Despite efforts to use other issues—some of which turned out to be disastrous—McGovern was really a one-issue candidate. He had been one of the first senators to speak out against the war ("right from the start") and was a co-sponsor of the McGovern-Hatfield Amendments to end the war in 1970 and 1971. It was the war issue that brought him the volunteers that were so essential to his early primary victories; it was the war that allowed him to argue that he had shown better judgment than Muskie or Humphrey. Unfortunately for McGovern, by the time he won the nomination, most voters had decided that Nixon was about to end the war anyway, and Vietnam had evaporated as an issue—to be replaced by the Eagleton question, the $1,000 a year plan, and so on.

If McGovern's national standing depended initially on Vietnam, his standing in South Dakota has always depended on the farm issue. He ran against Agriculture Secretary Ezra Taft Benson in the fifties and against Agriculture Secretary Earl Butz in the seventies. McGovern has always stood for high price supports and subsidies, if necessary, to maintain high prices for farm commodities, particularly beef and wheat, which people raise in great quantities here. Such stands have benefited him in past campaigns. In 1968 he was able to come back after his foray into presidential politics and beat Republican Archie Gubbrud with 57% of the vote. In 1974 he faced an emotional and well-financed challenge from former Vietnam prisoner of war Leo Thorsness and won with 53%.

In addition to his stands on agriculture issues, McGovern has always done well in the person-to-person campaigning which remains important in a small state made up of small towns and rural areas like South Dakota. That of course requires a grueling schedule, which is difficult for a senator with increasing committee responsibilities in Washington. McGovern can count on having tough, well-financed opposition in 1980, and he will have to fight hard for reelection. He may, however, have a strong asset in hand by that time. He ranks just behind Chairman Herman Talmadge on the Senate Agriculture Committee, and if Talmadge should choose not to run for reelection or were to be eliminated in the Georgia primary, McGovern could tell South Dakotans that he would chair that committee. It would be the first time in years that South Dakota has had an important committee chairman—and one on a subject of such great importance to the state.

McGovern is a Senator who has always been identified with important issues, and he has had some significant legislative accomplishments—particularly in reforming the food stamp program and on the issue of nutrition generally. Less legislative activity comes out of South Dakota's new junior Senator, Larry Pressler. So far Pressler has had a dazzling career, if one were to judge from his vote totals. He upset a Democratic congressman in the Democratic year of 1974, he was reelected in 1976 with 80% of the vote, and he was the early favorite for the 1978 Senate race. James Abourezk, a popular Senator himself whose sometimes audacious stands on foreign policy and the Indians were more than compensated for by his strong constituent relations, seemed unlikely to win against Pressler, though he could have beaten anyone else. But as the Senate's only Arab-American and a backer of Arab causes in the Middle East, he had the prospect of a lucrative Washington lobbying practice. He decided to retire, and Pressler was elected over former Rapid City Mayor Donald Barnett with 67% of the vote.

One of the things that makes Pressler so popular is his extensive cultivation of constituents. He is constantly in the state, and sends out as many press releases as any member of Congress. The definitive work on Pressler's service in the House was written by Albert Hunt of the *Wall Street Journal*, who cited him as a prime example of a congressional show horse (as opposed to work horse). Pressler's contributions to the legislative process were nonexistent; a Republican member of Education and Labor, the committee he served on, said he never took part in its deliberations. Nor does his record disclose any central core of belief. Pressler's ADA rating dropped from 65% in 1975 to 35% in 1977. He shifted positions within a few days on a constitutional amendment to prohibit abortions and switched within minutes on deregulation of natural gas—both issues of major importance. Pressler is undeniably bright and certainly seems ambitious; as one colleague put it, "Larry will go a long way. But I don't have the slightest idea what he'll do when he gets there." Perhaps in the Senate Pressler will buckle down and apply his talents to some problem affecting the public—although there are signs that he is developing a reputation on the embassy party scene.

Pressler's 1st district House seat was expected to stay Republican. The party's candidate was Leo Thorsness, the POW who had run against McGovern in 1974. He was well financed and well known, and it was presumed that his military credentials would impress people (although why it should impress people that a man was captured is unclear; it says something, perhaps, about the American experience in the Vietnam war). Thorsness had bitterly denounced McGovern in 1974; he felt the Senator was responsible for prolonging the war and his own stay in the prison camps. But in 1978 he was less forceful, and hare-like he was overtaken by the tortoise-like campaign of Abourezk aide Thomas Daschle. At 30 Daschle looked no more than his age, but he ran an intensive door-to-door campaign for a year before the election. South Dakotans are still used to meeting their officeholders, and apparently they liked what they saw. This was the nation's closest congressional election of 1978. At first it appeared that Thorsness had won, but when the final votes were counted, Daschle prevailed by 14 votes. The Democratic Caucus gave him a seat on the Agriculture Committee, which should prove a political asset; and he seems to have shown already the talents which have helped so many narrowly elected young congressmen to hold onto their seats in later elections.

The 1st district occupies the eastern quarter of the state; the more sparsely populated western three-quarters makes up the 2d district. The 1st includes Sioux Falls, the 2d Rapid City; the 1st is more devoted to wheat and other crops; the 2d has more cattle raising, as well as the mountains that are misnamed the Black Hills. Technically, the 2d is the more Republican of the districts, but since both have elected members of both parties in the seventies, the partisan differences are not terribly significant.

The current Congressman from the 2d is Republican James Abdnor, first elected in 1972 when Abourezk was running for the Senate. Both men are of Arab descent, but there the resemblance ends. Abourezk was one of the most liberal members of Congress; Abdnor is among the most conservative. Abdnor has developed considerable popularity in the district, and he won reelection by large margins in 1974 and 1976. He did not apparently feel that he had enough strength in 1978, however, to challenge Larry Pressler in the Republican primary for the Senate. He is reportedly waiting for 1980. But he did not do particularly well in 1978. His percentage fell sharply, and although it was still a respectable 57%, his opponent was inexperienced and not expected to do so well. Abdnor could still be a formidable candidate against McGovern in 1980, and he can probably get the nomination if he wants it. But he appears to begin from a position of less strength than he seemed to have before 1978.

It probably matters very little to Americans outside South Dakota who the governor of the state is, but it can be very important here—particularly when there is the possibility of armed confrontations between Indians and whites. The current incumbent, Republican William Janklow, made his reputation out of such confrontations, and it is one which is apparently popular in South Dakota. He has been accused of shooting from the hip, figuratively; literally, he has appeared as Attorney General of the state at the scene of a crime armed and ready to help. He argued strongly against the demands of the American Indian Movement, and became known as the premier anti-Indian politician in the state. Janklow had the advantage of discord among the Democrats: Governor Kneip resigned to become Ambassador to Singapore, and the succeeding Lieutenant Governor, Harvey Wollman, had already been beaten by state Senator Roger McKellips in the primary. McKellips also got into an argument with his party's platform on the Oahe Irrigation Project, a once popular program endorsed by many Democrats but now apparently opposed by most South Dakota voters. In any case, Janklow won the election with a solid 57%. Outsiders will know, by the absence or presence of jarring headlines, whether he has toned down his act.

Census Data Pop. 666,257; 0.33% of U.S. total, 44th largest; Central city, 11%; suburban, 3%. Median family income, $7,490; 44th highest; families above $15,000: 12%; families below $3,000: 15%. Median years education, 12.1.

1977 Share of Federal Tax Burden $898,000,000; 0.26% of U.S. total, 49th largest.

1977 Share of Federal Outlays $1,428,827,000; 0.36% of U.S. total, 46th largest. Per capita federal spending, $2,092.

DOD	$145,262,000	50th (0.16%)	HEW	$441,577,000	45th (2.99%)
ERDA	$343,000	50th (0.01%)	HUD	$15,503,000	41st (0.37%)
NASA	$250,000	42d (0.01%)	VA	$90,917,000	41st (0.47%)
DOT	$66,079,000	42d (0.46%)	EPA	$10,189,000	48th (0.12%)
DOC	$51,060,000	40th (0.61%)	RevS	$21,704,000	47th (0.26%)
DOI	$108,660,000	13th (2.34%)	Debt	$46,383,000	42d (0.15%)
USDA	$333,148,000	27th (1.67%)	Other	$97,752,000	

Economic Base Agriculture, notably cattle, hogs, wheat and dairy products; finance, insurance and real estate; food and kindred products, especially meat packing plants; printing and publishing, especially newspapers; metal mining, especially lode gold; tourism.

Political Line-up Governor, William J. Janklow (R). Senators, George S. McGovern (D) and Larry Pressler (R). Representatives, 2 (1 D and 1 R). State Senate (24 R and 11 D); State House (48 R and 22 D).

The Voters

Registration 420,818 Total. 193,345 D (46%); 191,776 R (46%); 35,707 Other (8%).
Median voting age 45
Employment profile White collar, 41%. Blue collar, 22%. Service, 15%. Farm, 22%.
Ethnic groups Indian, 5%. Total foreign stock, 16%. Germany, 4%.

Presidential vote

1976	Carter (D)	147,068	(49%)
	Ford (R)	151,505	(51%)
1972	Nixon (R)	166,476	(54%)
	McGovern (D)	139,945	(46%)

1976 Democratic Presidential Primary

Carter	24,186	(41%)
Udall	19,510	(33%)
Others	14,975	(26%)

1976 Republican Presidential Primary

Reagan	43,068	(54%)
Ford	36,976	(46%)

Sen. George McGovern (D) Elected 1962, seat up 1980; b. July 19, 1922, Avon; home, Mitchell; Dakota Wesleyan U., B.A. 1945, Northwestern U., M.A. 1949, Ph.D. 1953; Methodist.

Career Army Air Corps, WWII; Prof. of History, Dakota Wesleyan U., 1949–53; Exec. Secy., S.D. Dem. Party, 1953–56; U.S. House of Reps., 1957–61; Dem. nominee for U.S. Senate, 1960; Special Asst. to Pres. John F. Kennedy and Dir. of Food for Peace, 1961–62; Chm., Dem. Comm. on Party Structure and Delegate Selection, 1969–70; Dem. nominee for President, 1972.

Offices 4239 DSOB, 202-224-2321. Also P.O. Box Z, Sioux Falls 57102, 605-339-2880, and 108 E. 3rd St., Mitchell 57301, 605-996-7563.

Committees *Agriculture, Nutrition, and Forestry* (2d). Subcommittees: Agricultural Credit and Rural Electrification; Agricultural Production, Marketing, and Stabilization of Prices; Nutrition (Chairman).

Foreign Relations (3d). Subcommittees: International Economic Policy; African Affairs (Chairman); Near Eastern and South Asian Affairs.

Group Ratings

	ADA	COPE	PC	RPN	NFU	LCV	CFA	NAB	NSI	ACA	NTU
1978	75	88	58	57	90	83	70	22	0	19	–
1977	80	94	65	40	91	–	76	–	–	0	23
1976	70	88	72	73	100	76	78	0	0	0	38

Key Votes

1) Warnke Nom	FOR	6) Egypt-Saudi Arms	FOR	11) Hosptl Cost Contnmnt	FOR
2) Neutron Bomb	AGN	7) Draft Restr Pardon	FOR	12) Clinch River Reactor	AGN
3) Waterwy User Fee	FOR	8) Wheat Price Support	FOR	13) Pub Fin Cong Cmpgns	FOR
4) Dereg Nat Gas	AGN	9) Panama Canal Treaty	FOR	14) ERA Ratif Recissn	FOR
5) Kemp-Roth	AGN	10) Labor Law Rev Clot	FOR	15) Med Necssy Abrtns	FOR

Election Results

1974 general	George McGovern (D)	147,929	(53%)	($1,172,831)
	Leo K. Thorsness (R)	130,955	(47%)	($528,817)
1974 primary	George McGovern (D), unopposed			
1968 general	George McGovern (D)	158,961	(57%)	
	Archie Gubbrud (R)	120,951	(43%)	

Sen. Larry Pressler (R) Elected 1978, seat up 1984; b. Mar. 29, 1942, Humboldt; home, Humboldt; U. of S.D., B.A. 1964, Rhodes Scholar, Oxford U., 1966, Harvard U., M.A., J.D. 1971; Roman Catholic.

Career Army, Vietnam; Aide to U.S. Sen. Francis Case; Ofc. of Legal Advisor of U.S. Secy. of State, 1971–74; U.S. House of Reps., 1975–78.

Offices 3321 DSOB, 202-224-5842. Also 334 S. Phillips Ave., Sioux Falls 57102, 605-336-2980, ext. 433.

Committees *Budget* (8th).

Commerce, Science and Transportation (6th). Subcommittees: Aviation; Communications; Surface Transportation.

Environment and Public Works (6th). Subcommittees: Water Resources; Transportation; Resource Protection.

Select Committee on Small Business (7th).

Group Ratings: Newly Elected

	ADA	COPE	PC	RPN	NFU	LCV	CFA	NAB	NSI	ACA	NTU
1978	25	44	33	45	80	–	32	75	80	37	–
1977	35	23	40	62	64	17	25	–	–	64	42
1976	30	61	44	67	83	39	45	33	75	52	46

Key Votes

1) Increase Def Spnd	AGN	6) Alaska Lands Protect	DNV	11) Delay Auto Pol Cntrl	DNV
2) B-1 Bomber	AGN	7) Water Projects Veto	AGN	12) Sugar Price Escalator	FOR
3) Cargo Preference	AGN	8) Consum Protect Agcy	AGN	13) Pub Fin Cong Cmpgns	AGN
4) Dereg Nat Gas	FOR	9) Common Situs Picket	AGN	14) ERA Ratif Recissn	AGN
5) Kemp-Roth	FOR	10) Labor Law Revision	AGN	15) Prohibt Govt Abrtns	FOR

Election Results

1978 general	Larry Pressler (R)	170,832	(67%)	($449,541)
	Don Barnett (D)	84,767	(33%)	($152,006)
1978 primary	Larry Pressler (R)	66,893	(74%)	
	Ronald F. Williamson (R)	23,646	(26%)	($24,188)
1972 general	James Abourezk (D)	174,773	(57%)	($427,063)
	Robert Hirsch (R)	131,613	(43%)	($300,800)

Gov. William J. Janklow (R) Elected 1978, term expires Jan. 1983; b. Sept. 13, 1939, Chicago, Ill.; U. of S.D., B.S. 1964, J.D. 1966; Lutheran.

Career Staff Atty., Dir. Atty. and Chief Officer, S.D. Legal Services System, Rosebud Indian Reservation, 1966–73; Chief Prosecutor, Office of the Atty. Gen. of S.D., 1973–74; Atty. Gen. of S.D., 1975–78.

Offices State Capitol Bldg., Pierre 57501, 605-773-3212.

Election Results

1978 general	William J. Janklow (R)	147,116	(57%)
	Roger D. McKellips (D)	112,679	(43%)
1978 primary	William J. Janklow (R)	46,423	(51%)
	LeRoy G. Hoffman (R)	30,026	(33%)
	Clint Roberts (R)	14,774	(16%)

1974 general	Richard F. Kneip (D)	149,151	(54%)
	John E. Olson (R)	129,077	(46%)

FIRST DISTRICT

Census Data Pop. 333,107. Central city, 22%; suburban, 7%. Median family income, $7,695; families above $15,000: 12%; families below $3,000: 14%. Median years education, 12.1.

The Voters

Median voting age 45.
Employment profile White collar, 42%. Blue collar, 23%. Service, 16%. Farm, 19%.
Ethnic groups Indian, 1%. Total foreign stock, 18%. Germany, 4%.

Presidential vote

1976	Carter (D)	78,680	(51%)
	Ford (R)	76,758	(49%)
1972	Nixon (R)	80,576	(51%)
	McGovern (D)	76,932	(49%)

Rep. Thomas A. Daschle (D) Elected 1978; b. Dec. 9, 1947, Aberdeen; home, Aberdeen; So. Dak. St. U., B.A. 1969; Catholic.

Career Air Force, 1969–72; Legis. Asst. to U.S. Sen. James Abourezk, 1973–76, District aide, 1976–78.

Offices 510 LHOB, 202-225-2801. Also Box 1274, Sioux Falls 57101, 605-334-9596.

Committees *Agriculture* (24th). Subcommittees: Livestock and Grains; Departmental Investigations, Oversight, and Research; Family Farms, Rural Development, and Special Studies.

Veterans' Affairs (18th). Subcommittees: Medical Facilities and Benefits; Education, Training, and Employment.

Group Ratings: Newly Elected

Key Votes: Newly Elected

Election Results

1978 general	Thomas A. Daschle (D)	64,683	(50%)	($223,221)
	Leo K. Thorsness (R)	64,544	(50%)	($270,366)
1978 primary	Thomas A. Daschle (D)	21,491	(59%)	
	Frank E. Denholm	14,760	(41%)	($42,313)
1976 general	Larry Pressler (R)	121,587	(80%)	($106,680)
	James V. Guffey (D)	29,533	(20%)	($40,021)

SECOND DISTRICT

Census Data Pop. 333,150. Central city, 0%; suburban, 0%. Median family income, $7,283; families above $15,000: 11%; families below $3,000: 16%. Median years education, 12.1.

The Voters

Median voting age 45.
Employment profile White collar, 40%. Blue collar, 21%. Service, 15%. Farm, 24%.
Ethnic groups Indian, 8%. Total foreign stock, 15%. Germany, 4%.

Presidential vote

1976	Carter (D)	68,384	(48%)
	Ford (R)	74,747	(52%)
1972	Nixon (R)	85,900	(58%)
	McGovern (D)	62,013	(42%)

Rep. James Abdnor (R) Elected 1972; b. Feb. 13, 1923, Kennebec; home, Kennebec; U. of Neb., B.S. 1945; Methodist.

Career Army, WWII; School teacher and coach; Farmer and rancher; S.D. Senate, 1956–68, Pres. Pro Tem, 1967–68; Lt. Gov. of S.D., 1969–71.

Offices 1224 LHOB, 202-225-5165. Also 439 Fed. Bldg., Pierre 57501, 605-224-2891.

Committees *Public Works and Transportation* (7th). Subcommittees: Aviation; Public Buildings and Grounds; Water Resources.

Veterans' Affairs (5th). Subcommittees: Housing; Medical Facilities and Benefits.

Group Ratings

	ADA	COPE	PC	RPN	NFU	LCV	CFA	NAB	NSI	ACA	NTU
1978	20	22	18	73	44	–	18	100	100	91	–
1977	10	18	10	58	55	0	5	–	–	88	42
1976	0	26	11	61	28	16	9	75	100	74	52

Key Votes

1) Increase Def Spnd	FOR	6) Alaska Lands Protect	FOR	11) Delay Auto Pol Cntrl	DNV
2) B-1 Bomber	FOR	7) Water Projects Veto	AGN	12) Sugar Price Escalator	FOR
3) Cargo Preference	AGN	8) Consum Protect Agcy	AGN	13) Pub Fin Cong Cmpgns	AGN
4) Dereg Nat Gas	FOR	9) Common Situs Picket	AGN	14) ERA Ratif Recissn	AGN
5) Kemp-Roth	FOR	10) Labor Law Revision	AGN	15) Prohibt Govt Abrtns	FOR

Election Results

1978 general	James Abdnor (R)	70,780	(56%)	($160,804)
	Bob Samuelson (D)	55,516	(44%)	($329,425)
1978 primary	James Abdnor (R), unopposed			
1976 general	James Abdnor (R)	99,601	(70%)	($108,896)
	Grace Mickelson (D)	42,968	(30%)	($48,481)

TENNESSEE

To a remarkable extent, ordinary Tennesseeans are familiar with the political leanings of the various parts of their state, and know that any study of Tennessee politics begins with geography. The state is divisible into three distinct sections, each with its own political history and inclination. East Tennessee is part of the Appalachian chain, an area populated almost completely by white mountaineers. Against secession, it was the political base of Andrew Johnson, Lincoln's vice presidential choice and successor. Over the years it has remained one of the most dependably Republican areas in the entire nation. Even in 1976, with a Southerner on the Democratic ticket, east Tennessee went for Gerald Ford.

The Republicanism of the mountains has usually been matched by the Democratic leanings of middle Tennessee. This is a region of hilly farmland which, in rough terms, lies between the lower Tennessee River and the mountains. Middle Tennessee was the home of Andrew Jackson, the first president to call himself a Democrat, and since Jackson's time the area has remained Democratic in practically every election. West Tennessee, the flat cotton lands along the Mississippi River, was the part of the state with the largest slave-tended plantations. Like middle Tennessee it is Democratic by tradition; but like the Deep South it has been ready to abandon the Democrats for Republicans (Goldwater, Nixon) or third party candidates (Wallace) who are more palatable to its white residents' traditional views on racial issues.

Urban-rural differences have not been nearly as important in Tennessee as elsewhere. The state's four large cities vote more like the rural territory around them than like each other. Recently Memphis, with its large black vote, has been less conservative than the rest of west Tennessee, while Chattanooga, on the Georgia border, is traditionally less Republican than east Tennessee. Meanwhile, the political behavior of Knoxville and Nashville is virtually indistinguishable from the rural counties around them.

So long as middle and west Tennessee remained strongly Democratic, the Republicans were unable to win a statewide election, no matter how many votes the party of Lincoln piled up in east Tennessee. Between Reconstruction and the sixties the allegiances created by the Civil War were forsaken only twice: once in the 1920 Harding landslide, when a Republican governor was elected, and again in 1928 when Protestant Tennessee rejected Catholic Al Smith for Herbert Hoover. The civil rights revolution touched Tennessee, but it did not affect it as it did other Southern states. Its two senators in the fifties, Estes Kefauver and Albert Gore, refused to sign the Southern Manifesto and were reelected anyway. Tennessee, like the rest of the nation, moved toward the Republicans at times. But it gave Eisenhower margins of less than 10,000 both times, and went for Nixon over Kennedy probably more because of religion than politics. In 1964 Tennessee went comfortably for Johnson over Goldwater.

But in the years since, Tennessee has become increasingly a Republican state. Not exclusively—Tennessee went for Carter in 1976, elected a Democratic senator the same year, and elected a Democratic governor in 1974. The legislature is still Democratic (though Republicans had an even split in one house for a while), and so is party registration. But in the last decade it is clear that, at least at the top levels of statewide politics, the Republicans have had greater vitality and stronger candidates. And at least one major reason for the Republican success has been the example set by Tennessee's senior Senator, Howard Baker.

Baker entered statewide politics at a time when the best exemplars of Tennessee politics were liberal Democrats, men such as Senators Estes Kefauver and Albert Gore and Governor Frank Clement. Their style was often old-fashioned—Gore and Clement were tub-thumping orators, trained in the art of arousing a courthouse crowd in a Democratic county to fever pitch—but their politics was surprisingly modern. In the fifties they backed civil rights, took liberal stands on economic issues, and, in Kefauver's case, nearly won the Democratic presidential nomination over the objections of most of the party's big city bosses. But in the sixties their politics was becoming outmoded. Kefauver died in 1963, and Gore had a surprisingly close race in 1964. Clement won his last term as Governor in 1962. Young, affluent Tennesseeans found their political style alien and their support of Great Society policies repugnant. The state was ready for another kind of politics.

And that was the kind of politics provided by Howard Baker. He came from a traditional east Tennessee Republican background; his father and his stepmother had served in the House before him. But instead of running for a safe Knoxville area House seat in 1964, Baker chose to make a risky statewide race for the Senate that year—and lost. He did not run the typical Goldwater-coattail race of Southern Republicans that year, however; he did not oppose the Civil Rights Act of 1964, even though his Democratic opponent, Ross Bass, had voted for it in the House. Nor was Baker a typical old-time orator. Rather, he had a kind of conversational style well adapted to the increasingly important medium of television. He relied for campaign help not on old courthouse regulars, but on well-dressed young men who applied the latest campaigning techniques.

Baker's loss in 1964 did not prevent him from running in 1966, and this time, facing Frank Clement, he won. It was the last time Baker had electoral problems in Tennessee. Well established as a statewide figure, he beat Ray Blanton with 62% of the vote in 1972, with Baker getting a substantial percentage of the black vote that year. In 1978, his main problem at home was his support of the Panama Canal Treaty, which Democrat Jane Eskind dwelled on. Still, Baker carried every congressional district but the black-majority 8th, winning even in middle Tennessee; his overall percentage was a slightly reduced 58%.

However important Baker has been in Tennessee, he is now a national political figure—and one of great importance. He has been Republican Minority Leader in the Senate since 1977—although he sought the job as long ago as 1969, after the death of his father-in-law, Everett Dirksen. Baker won a surprising last-minute victory over Robert Griffin, and probably the decisive factor was his impressive appearance on television. For Baker had become a national figure in his role as the ranking Republican on the Senate Watergate Committee in 1973. Without breaking all ties with the Nixon White House, Baker was able to project himself as a fair-minded and intelligent investigator, whose intention was to determine, he said, what the president knew and when he knew it. As Minority Leader, Baker again has been impressive—calm, ready to listen to other points of view and to appreciate their strong points, persuasive in explaining his own position.

Baker's prominence has naturally made him a contender for national office. He wanted the Republican vice presidential nomination in 1976, and delivered an uncharacteristically partisan and aggressive speech before the Republican National Convention. He was obviously disappointed when Gerald Ford picked Robert Dole instead. For 1980 Baker might very well be the Republicans' strongest general election candidate. His Southern origin might make him competitive against Carter there (or a favorite to carry the South over anyone who beat Carter for the nomination) and, more important, his general demeanor might make him a very strong candidate practically anywhere. But first he must win the nomination. And that will not be easy. Conservative Republicans—the kind who have had big majorities at every national convention since 1964—suspect that Baker is not one of them. His efforts to put together compromises on environmental issues put them off, and in some cases they still resent his refusal to defend Nixon all out. On foreign policy they resent deeply his support of the Panama Canal Treaty—support which was crucial for passage—and they will be watching closely his moves on the Strategic Arms Limitation Treaty.

In fact Baker is pretty solidly hawkish on most foreign policy matters: he has never opposed big defense budgets, he stood behind the U.S. policy in Vietnam, he has never trusted the Russians, and he has criticized many Carter Administration policies. But he does not seem to burn with the same fervor as many conservatives do; his conclusions are more cerebral than emotional, and sometimes he can be convinced to come out on the other side, as on Panama. To get the Republican nomination, Baker will have to win it in primaries; the delegates are not going to give it to him, especially if he supports SALT, if they don't have to. And seeking the nomination will require that he give up, formally or informally, the duties of Senate Minority Leader. Baker is one of the best political strategists around, but in 1980 he will need all his talents if he is to get what he wants.

For six years Tennessee had two Republican senators, from 1970 when Bill Brock beat Albert Gore until 1976 when he lost to James Sasser. Brock's campaign against Gore was one of the classics of the Nixon-Agnew Southern strategy; Gore was denounced for opposing the Vietnam war as if he supported the Viet Cong and was called a radiclib by none other than Spiro Agnew in person. What was surprising was not that Brock won but that he came so close to losing. Gore fought back gamely and almost turned the tide. For some reason Brock was touted almost immediately as a possible presidential candidate, but he was never able, as Baker was, to consolidate his standing back home. A man whose political rise owed more to his personal fortune than to driving ambition and whose soft-spoken delivery seems more halting than Baker's, Brock could not overcome the handicaps of some of his identification with the wealthy and the big corporations. After his defeat he became Republican National Chairman, a nice testimonial to his reputation for thoughtfulness and energy in some circles. He has made a big point of including blacks in Republican ranks, perhaps because he received virtually no black votes in 1976; but he had campaigned as an opponent of civil rights in the past without apparent discomfort. One must conclude that Brock opposed civil rights when there was political gain to be made from it among Southern whites, and when this was no longer the case he started courting blacks.

Tennessee's junior Senator, James Sasser, was one of the few newly elected Democrats that year to run behind Jimmy Carter. He attacked Brock for not disclosing his personal finances, and then attacked him for not paying income tax one year. He was able to appeal to Democratic loyalties not only in middle Tennessee, but in the western part of the state. In the Senate Sasser has voted much more often with his fellow Democrats than Republicans. He does not seek out controversial stands as Gore or Kefauver used to do, but he essentially seems to be following in their political tradition. He is not a boat-rocker, and has managed to win seats on both the Appropriations and Budget Committees.

For nearly 20 years (1952-70) the governorship of Tennessee was batted back and forth between two Democrats, Frank Clement and Buford Ellington. In 1970 it was captured by a Memphis dentist, Winfield Dunn; this was the great year of Republican triumph in Tennessee. Watergate changed that in 1974. The Democratic nominee, former Congressman Ray Blanton, was a demonstrated political weakling; he had only got 38% against Howard Baker two years before. But he won the Democratic nomination in a 12-candidate field with 23%, and he was able to beat the Republican, 34-year-old former baker and Nixon White House aide Lamar Alexander, by a significant, standard partisan margin.

Blanton's performance in office seems to have soured Tennessee on Democrats. He was criticized for expensive travels in the state executive jet and for taking from jail and putting on his staff the son of a former aide who had shot and killed his former wife and her lover. Alexander this time ran a strong campaign against Blanton as if he were a candidate—which he wisely declined to be—and virtually apologized to the people of the state for not having campaigned harder in 1974 to keep him out of office. Alexander's walk across the state made him seem more in line with Tennessee mores; his opponent was a Knoxville banker, Jake Butcher, who had had dealings with Bert Lance and whose campaign was largely self-financed. Butcher could not shake off his party's connection with Blanton, and Alexander won by a decisive margin. After the election Blanton began pardoning literally dozens of state prisoners. The U.S. attorney's office was investigating charges that Blanton had been selling pardons, and several days before the planned inauguration day Democrats were able to persuade Alexander to take the oath of office. Nashville country musicians put out a record called "Pardon Me, Ray," and the outgoing Governor became national news; his conduct in office was about as disgraceful as Tennessee had ever seen. The contrast with the brainy, articulate, honest Alexander could not have been greater. So while Democrats still have the numbers in Tennessee, Republicans seem to have most of the best known and most respected public figures, and they have the potential to frame the issues in the years ahead.

Census Data Pop. 3,924,164; 1.94% of U.S. total, 17th largest; Central city, 35%; suburban, 14%. Median family income, $7,447; 45th highest; families above $15,000: 12%; families below $3,000: 17%. Median years education, 10.7.

1977 Share of Federal Tax Burden $5,734,000,000; 1.66% of U.S. total, 21st largest.

1977 Share of Federal Outlays $8,217,930,000; 2.08% of U.S. total, 17th largest. Per capita federal spending, $1,962.

DOD	$1,141,420,000	25th (1.25%)	HEW	$2,659,936,000	17th (1.80%)
ERDA	$915,855,000	1st (15.50%)	HUD	$92,759,000	16th (2.20%)
NASA	$3,715,000	27th (0.09%)	VA	$425,622,000	15th (2.21%)
DOT	$221,466,000	22d (1.55%)	EPA	$126,098,000	18th (1.54%)
DOC	$69,948,000	30th (0.82%)	RevS	$142,255,000	19th (1.68%)
DOI	$14,101,000	41st (0.30%)	Debt	$210,286,000	19th (0.70%)
USDA	$503,183,000	8th (2.53%)	Other	$1,691,259,000	

Economic Base Apparel and other textile products, especially men's and boys' furnishings; agriculture, notably cattle, dairy products, soybeans and tobacco; finance, insurance and real estate; chemicals and allied products, especially plastics materials and synthetics; electrical equipment and supplies, especially household appliances; food and kindred products; textile mill products, especially knitting mills.

Political Line-up Governor, Lamar Alexander (R). Senators, Howard H. Baker, Jr. (R) and James R. Sasser (D). Representatives, 8 (5 D and 3 R). State Senate (20 D, 12 R, and 1 Ind.); State House (60 D, 38 R, and 1 Ind.).

The Voters

Registration 2,137,789 Total. No party registration.
Median voting age 42
Employment profile White collar, 41%. Blue collar, 42%. Service, 13%. Farm, 4%.
Ethnic groups Black, 16%. Total foreign stock, 2%.

Presidential vote

1976	Carter (D)	825,879	(57%)
	Ford (R)	633,969	(43%)
1972	Nixon (R)	813,147	(69%)
	McGovern (D)	357,293	(31%)

1976 Democratic Presidential Primary

Carter	259,243	(78%)
Others	74,411	(22%)

1976 Republican Presidential Primary

Ford	120,685	(50%)
Reagan	118,997	(50%)

Sen. Howard H. Baker, Jr. (R) Elected 1966, seat up 1984; b. Nov. 15, 1925, Huntsville; home, Huntsville; Tulane U., U. of the South, U. of Tenn., LL.B. 1949; Presbyterian.

Career Navy, WWII; Practicing atty., 1949–66.

Offices 4123 DSOB, 202-224-4944. Also 716 U.S. Courthouse, 801 Broadway, Nashville 37203, 615-749-5129, and 313 P.O. Bldg., Knoxville 37901, 615-546-5486.

Committees *Minority Leader.*

Environment and Public Works (2d). Subcommittees: Regional and Community Development; Resource Protection; Nuclear Reaction.

Foreign Relations (3d).

Rules and Administration (2d).

Group Ratings

	ADA	COPE	PC	RPN	NFU	LCV	CFA	NAB	NSI	ACA	NTU
1978	25	37	30	100	67	32	20	67	63	79	–
1977	15	26	15	82	42	–	8	–	–	52	27
1976	5	14	10	81	28	26	28	70	100	80	64

Key Votes

1) Warnke Nom	AGN	6) Egypt-Saudi Arms	FOR	11) Hosptl Cost Contnmnt	AGN
2) Neutron Bomb	FOR	7) Draft Restr Pardon	AGN	12) Clinch River Reactor	FOR
3) Waterwy User Fee	FOR	8) Wheat Price Support	FOR	13) Pub Fin Cong Cmpgns	AGN
4) Dereg Nat Gas	FOR	9) Panama Canal Treaty	FOR	14) ERA Ratif Recissn	AGN
5) Kemp-Roth	FOR	10) Labor Law Rev Clot	AGN	15) Med Necssy Abrtns	FOR

Election Results

1978 general	Howard H. Baker, Jr. (R)	642,644	(58%)	($1,922,573)
	Jane Eskind (D)	466,228	(42%)	($1,903,532)
1978 primary	Howard H. Baker, Jr. (R)	205,680	(83%)	
	Five others (R)	40,819	(17%)	
1972 general	Howard H. Baker, Jr. (R)	716,539	(62%)	($830,769)
	Ray Blanton (D)	440,599	(38%)	($224,653)

Sen. James R. Sasser (D) Elected 1976, seat up 1982; b. Sept. 30, 1936, Memphis; home, Nashville; Vanderbilt, B.A. 1958, J.D. 1961; Methodist.

Career Practicing atty.; Chm., Tenn. State Dem. Comm., 1973–76.

Offices 2104 DSOB, 202-224-3344. Also U.S. Courthouse, Nashville 37203, 615-251-7353.

Committees *Appropriations* (14th).

Budget (7th).

Governmental Affairs (7th). Subcommittees: Investigations; Intergovernmental Relations; Civil Service and General Services.

Select Committee on Small Business (7th).

Group Ratings

	ADA	COPE	PC	RPN	NFU	LCV	CFA	NAB	NSI	ACA	NTU
1978	55	74	53	60	40	47	30	27	50	57	–
1977	60	89	60	40	67	–	72	–	–	8	20

Key Votes

1) Warnke Nom	FOR	6) Egypt-Saudi Arms	AGN	11) Hosptl Cost Contnmnt	FOR
2) Neutron Bomb	FOR	7) Draft Restr Pardon	FOR	12) Clinch River Reactor	FOR
3) Waterwy User Fee	AGN	8) Wheat Price Support	AGN	13) Pub Fin Cong Cmpgns	FOR
4) Dereg Nat Gas	AGN	9) Panama Canal Treaty	FOR	14) ERA Ratif Recissn	AGN
5) Kemp-Roth	AGN	10) Labor Law Rev Clot	FOR	15) Med Necssy Abrtns	FOR

Election Results

1976 general	James R. Sasser (D)	751,180	(53%)	($839,379)
	Bill Brock (R)	673,231	(47%)	($1,301,033)
1976 primary	James R. Sasser (D)	244,930	(44%)	
	John J. Hooker, Jr. (D)	171,716	(31%)	
	Five others (D)	137,201	(25%)	
1970 general	Bill Brock (R)	562,645	(52%)	
	Albert Gore (D)	519,858	(48%)	

Gov. Lamar Alexander (R) Elected 1978, term expires Jan. 1983; b. July 3, 1940, Maryville; Vanderbilt U., B.A. 1962, N.Y.U., J.D. 1965; Presbyterian.

Career Newspaper reporter, Knoxville *News-Sentinel,* Nashville *Banner,* Maryville *Alcoa Daily Times;* Practicing atty., 1965, 1971–; Law Clerk, U.S. Circuit Court of Appeals, 5th Dist., New Orleans 1965–66; Legis. Asst. to U.S. Sen. Howard Baker, 1967–69; Exec. Asst. to Bryce Harlow, Counselor in charge of Cong. relations, 1969; Rep. nominee for Gov. of Tenn., 1974.

Offices State Capitol Bldg., Nashville 37219, 615-741-2001

Election Results

1978 general	Lamar Alexander (R)	661,959	(56%)
	Jake Butcher (D)	523,495	(44%)
1978 primary	Lamar Alexander (R)	230,922	(86%)
	Three others (R)	37,696	(14%)
1974 general	Ray Blanton (D)	575,205	(56%)
	Lamar Alexander (R)	457,095	(44%)

FIRST DISTRICT

The 1st district of Tennessee is the far northeast corner of the state. Most of it is an extension of the Shenandoah Valley of Virginia and the Blue Ridge Mountains of the Appalachian chain. In fact, the district is closer to Richmond, Virginia, than to Memphis, Tennessee. Though the 1st is part of the Appalachian region, it has not suffered anything like the poverty that recently afflicted the hollows of West Virginia or hills of eastern Kentucky. Because coal has never been very important here, northeast Tennessee has not gone through the various booms and busts of coal country. Instead, the small towns of the region—Johnson City, Kingsport, Bristol—have been quietly attracting new industries. The region has low taxes and lots of low wage labor, and its valleys provide reasonably level east-west transportation routes.

The changing economy of the district has not, however, produced much shift in its political inclinations. For more than a century, the 1st has remained solidly Republican, as Republican as any district in Kansas or Nebraska. People up here in the mountains never had many slaves, and they had little use for secession in 1861. They stayed loyal to the Union and continued to send congressmen to Washington. Abraham Lincoln picked a local boy, Andrew Johnson, to be his second Vice President in 1864. To this day voters in the 1st continue to support the party of the Union. Even in 1976, after Watergate and with a Southerner as the Democratic candidate, the 1st went for Gerald Ford.

For 40 years the congressional politics of this area was dominated by B. Carroll Reece, a Republican who represented the district for most of the period between 1921 and 1961. Reece's successor, first elected in 1962, is Republican Jimmy Quillen. He is one of the quieter senior members of the House. He has a seat on the Rules Committee and is the ranking Republican on that body. His voting record is solidly Republican. Legislatively, he has spoken up to try to repeal limits on members' outside incomes, and has attacked the decision holding up the building of the Tellico Dam.

Census Data Pop. 490,518. Central city, 0%; suburban, 0%. Median family income, $6,820; families above $15,000: 8%; families below $3,000: 18%. Median years education, 9.8.

The Voters

Median voting age 42.
Employment profile White collar, 36%. Blue collar, 49%. Service, 10%. Farm, 5%.
Ethnic groups Black, 2%.

Presidential vote

1976	Carter (D)	83,151	(46%)
	Ford (R)	96,233	(54%)
1972	Nixon (R)	113,840	(78%)
	McGovern (D)	31,200	(22%)

Rep. James J. (Jimmy) **Quillen** (R) Elected 1962; b. Jan. 11, 1916, near Gate City, Va.; home, Kingsport; Methodist.

Career Founder and Publisher, Kingsport *Mirror*, 1936–39, Johnson City *Times*, 1939–44; Navy, WWII; Pres. and Bd. Chm., real estate and insurance businesses, 1946–; Dir., 1st Tenn. Bank, Kingsport; Tenn. House of Reps., 1955–62, Minor. Ldr., 1959–60.

Offices 102 CHOB, 202-225-6356. Also Rm. 157, 1st Floor, Fed. Bldg., Kingsport 37662, 615-247-8161.

Committees *Rules* (Ranking Member).

Group Ratings

	ADA	COPE	PC	RPN	NFU	LCV	CFA	NAB	NSI	ACA	NTU
1978	15	25	15	58	30	–	18	100	89	85	–
1977	5	19	8	55	55	19	15	–	–	79	32
1976	10	13	7	41	18	24	0	100	100	88	50

Key Votes

1) Increase Def Spnd	FOR	6) Alaska Lands Protect	FOR	11) Delay Auto Pol Cntrl	FOR
2) B-1 Bomber	AGN	7) Water Projects Veto	AGN	12) Sugar Price Escalator	AGN
3) Cargo Preference	AGN	8) Consum Protect Agcy	AGN	13) Pub Fin Cong Cmpgns	AGN
4) Dereg Nat Gas	FOR	9) Common Situs Picket	AGN	14) ERA Ratif Recissn	FOR
5) Kemp-Roth	FOR	10) Labor Law Revision	AGN	15) Prohibt Govt Abrtns	FOR

Election Results

1978 general	James H. Quillen (R)	92,143	(65%)	($218,151)
	Gordon Ball (D)	50,694	(35%)	($46,199)
1978 primary	James H. Quillen (R), unopposed			
1976 general	James H. Quillen (R)	97,781	(58%)	($55,915)
	Lloyd Blevins (D)	69,507	(42%)	($74,582)

SECOND DISTRICT

John Gunther called Knoxville, the largest city in east Tennessee, "the ugliest city I ever saw in America." It is indeed an undistinguished looking place, sitting in a hot valley flanked by nondescript hills that do not seem to anticipate the cool green Smokies 40 miles away. Knoxville has a solid blue collar economy and is the home as well of the University of Tennessee. It is also the headquarters of the Tennessee Valley Authority, the federal project which has brought low cost power, recreational lakes, and plenty of jobs to Knoxville. All of these facts would lead one to believe that Knoxville is a Democratic town. Yet for all its factories, despite the university, and despite having one of the most successful examples of government enterprise in the country in TVA, Knoxville is still one of the most heavily Republican cities in the United States.

Knoxville is the center of Tennessee's 2d congressional district, a safe Republican seat if there ever was one. The district has not elected a Democratic congressman since 1853. The 2d is also the home base of Senator Howard Baker, who has a house in the hills and keeps an office in Knoxville. Baker's father represented the district from 1951 until his death in 1963; he was succeeded for the remainder of his term by his widow. Baker, Jr., could have had the seat for the asking, but he decided to run for the Senate instead—with results that have already made a little history.

So the Republican nomination in 1964 went to Knoxville Mayor John Duncan. He won by a comfortable margin in that Democratic year and has represented the district ever since. Duncan does not make much noise around the Capitol, blending quietly into the conservative folds of the

Republican Conference. But he does hold a position of potential power, as second-ranking Republican on the Ways and Means Committee and ranking minority member of its Health Subcommittee. Duncan has a faithful Republican record, and can be counted on to favor lower taxes and greater incentives for business and to oppose further federal roles in health care financing. His own legislative output seems limited to technical matters, perfecting sloppy pieces of legislation and preventing unintended application of new laws.

Census Data Pop. 492,539. Central city, 35%; suburban, 34%. Median family income, $7,285; families above $15,000: 11%; families below $3,000: 17%. Median years education, 10.8.

The Voters

Median voting age 42.
Employment profile White collar, 43%. Blue collar, 42%. Service, 13%. Farm, 2%.
Ethnic groups Black, 6%. Total foreign stock, 1%.

Presidential vote

1976	Carter (D)	94,759	(49%)
	Ford (R)	98,032	(51%)
1972	Nixon (R)	112,505	(73%)
	McGovern (D)	40,799	(27%)

Rep. John J. Duncan (R) Elected 1964; b. Mar. 24, 1919, Scott County; home, Knoxville; Presbyterian.

Career Army, WWII; Asst. Atty. Gen. of Tenn., 1947–56; Knoxville Law Dir., 1956–59; Pres., Knoxville Pro Baseball Club, 1956–59; Mayor of Knoxville, 1959–64.

Offices 2458 RHOB, 202-225-5435. Also 318 P.O. Bldg., Knoxville 37902, 615-546-5686.

Committees *Ways and Means* (2d). Subcommittees: Health; Oversight; Select Revenue Measures.

Group Ratings

	ADA	COPE	PC	RPN	NFU	LCV	CFA	NAB	NSI	ACA	NTU
1978	20	20	20	55	30	–	23	83	80	85	–
1977	0	17	18	54	58	20	25	–	–	67	28
1976	15	22	8	56	33	34	9	75	90	89	56

Key Votes

1) Increase Def Spnd	FOR	6) Alaska Lands Protect	FOR	11) Delay Auto Pol Cntrl	FOR
2) B-1 Bomber	AGN	7) Water Projects Veto	AGN	12) Sugar Price Escalator	AGN
3) Cargo Preference	AGN	8) Consum Protect Agcy	AGN	13) Pub Fin Cong Cmpgns	AGN
4) Dereg Nat Gas	FOR	9) Common Situs Picket	AGN	14) ERA Ratif Recissn	FOR
5) Kemp-Roth	FOR	10) Labor Law Revision	AGN	15) Prohibt Govt Abrtns	FOR

Election Results

1978 general	John J. Duncan (R)	125,082	(82%)	($139,956)
	Margaret Francis (D)	27,745	(18%)	
1978 primary	John J. Duncan (R), unopposed			
1976 general	John J. Duncan (R)	117,256	(63%)	($155,990)
	Mike Rowland (D)	69,449	(37%)	($90,798)

THIRD DISTRICT

The 3d congressional district of Tennessee is dominated by the city of Chattanooga. East of the city is rugged hill country, solidly Republican since the Civil War, except for Polk County, where the boundaries of Tennessee, North Carolina, and Georgia meet. This is a place with a political history as violent as any in the United States; three people were killed during the 1948 election. The 3d also includes Dayton, the site of the Scopes trial of 1925, where William Jennings Bryan and Clarence Darrow debated whether the state of Tennessee could prohibit the teaching of Darwin's theory of evolution. Chattanooga itself was the focus of several Civil War battles (Lookout Mountain, Chickamauga), but it was then only a village; it is one of those Southern cities which, like Birmingham and Atlanta, grew into an industrial town during the New South years after the Civil War. Chattanooga therefore does not have a politics rooted as deeply in Civil War sentiments as do most parts of Tennessee. It has been traditionally Democratic, in contrast to the hill counties to the east, but during the sixties and seventies it was inclined to the Republicanism of Howard Baker and William Brock.

Indeed, Chattanooga and the 3d district have been the political home base for key important figures in postwar Tennessee politics, Estes Kefauver and Bill Brock. Kefauver was first elected to Congress here in 1938, moving on to the Senate—and national fame—in 1948. Brock first won election to the House in 1962, campaigning against the Kennedys, creeping socialism, and civil rights laws. He won election to the Senate in 1970, in a victory which seemed to herald a sleek, articulate Republican future for Tennessee. But not for Brock; he was defeated for reelection in 1976. His successor in the House was a Republican, LaMar Baker, but one with limited political savvy. He barely won in 1970 and 1972 and was defeated in 1974.

The winner that year had not expected to go to Congress. Marilyn Lloyd was the wife of Chattanooga TV personality Mort Lloyd when he won the Democratic congressional nomination in 1974; when he was killed in a plane crash in August, she was given the nomination by local Democrats. The Democratic tide was running strong, Baker was weak, and she was elected with 52%.

Marilyn Lloyd provides a good example of how a member of the House with a pleasing personality, hard work, and shrewd use of the advantages of incumbency can make a marginal district safe. She rapidly achieved the kind of popularity matched by none of her predecessors since Kefauver. She had the advantage of being a Democrat at a time when that label did not require decisions which would be unpopular in this kind of constituency, and she could please most whites and almost all blacks at the same time. By election day 1976, Lloyd was reelected over LaMar Baker by better than a 2-1 margin; by 1978 she had no Republican opposition whatever in a district which had been held by Republicans for 12 years. After that election, she remarried, and is now known officially as Marilyn Lloyd Bouquard.

Census Data Pop. 486,363. Central city, 25%; suburban, 40%. Median family income, $7,940; families above $15,000: 13%; families below $3,000: 15%. Median years education, 11.2.

The Voters

Median voting age 42.
Employment profile White collar, 42%. Blue collar, 45%. Service, 12%. Farm, 1%.
Ethnic groups Black, 11%. Total foreign stock, 2%.

Presidential vote

1976	Carter (D)	96,126	(52%)
	Ford (R)	88,578	(48%)
1972	Nixon (R)	108,187	(72%)
	McGovern (D)	41,430	(28%)

Rep. Marilyn Lloyd Bouquard (D) Elected 1974; b. Jan. 3, 1929, Fort Smith, Ark.; home, Chattanooga; Shorter Col., 1967–70; Church of Christ.

Career Co-Owner and Mgr., WTTI Radio, Dalton, Ga.; Family agriculture flight service business.

Offices 208 CHOB, 202-225-3271. Also 230 P.O. Bldg., Chattanooga 37401, 615-483-8611.

Committees *Public Works and Transportation* (14th). Subcommittees: Economic Development; Aviation; Oversight and Review.

Science and Technology (10th). Subcommittees: Space Science and Applications; Energy Research and Production.

Group Ratings

	ADA	COPE	PC	RPN	NFU	LCV	CFA	NAB	NSI	ACA	NTU
1978	15	53	20	30	60	–	9	73	90	68	–
1977	10	52	20	23	67	30	35	–	–	63	30
1976	10	65	34	22	67	17	27	25	80	61	44

Key Votes

1) Increase Def Spnd	FOR	6) Alaska Lands Protect	FOR	11) Delay Auto Pol Cntrl	FOR
2) B-1 Bomber	AGN	7) Water Projects Veto	AGN	12) Sugar Price Escalator	AGN
3) Cargo Preference	AGN	8) Consum Protect Agcy	AGN	13) Pub Fin Cong Cmpgns	AGN
4) Dereg Nat Gas	FOR	9) Common Situs Picket	AGN	14) ERA Ratif Recissn	FOR
5) Kemp-Roth	FOR	10) Labor Law Revision	FOR	15) Prohibt Govt Abrtns	FOR

Election Results

1978 general	Marilyn Lloyd (D)	108,282	(89%)	($75,923)
	Dan East (Ind.)	13,535	(11%)	
1978 primary	Marilyn Lloyd (D), unopposed			
1976 general	Marilyn Lloyd (D)	123,872	(68%)	($100,187)
	LaMar Baker (R)	57,116	(32%)	($69,715)

FOURTH DISTRICT

The Tennessee River crosses the state that bears its name twice. The first time the river heads south from its headwaters to Chattanooga; the second time, after turning around in Alabama and Mississippi, the river moves lazily north to its confluence with the Ohio River in Kentucky. Along most of its route the Tennessee is made amenable to the needs of man by the operation of TVA dams. Between the two lengths of the river lies middle Tennessee, with most of its geographical expanse making up the state's 4th congressional district. To the east the district is mountain country, but most of the 4th is part of the hilly farmlands of the Cumberland Plateau, which is known in some quarters as "the dimple of the universe."

For 150 years the Cumberland Plateau has been a region of small and medium sized farms and small county seat towns. The 4th district's largest city is Murfreesboro, with a population of 26,000. The first local hero in these parts was Andrew Jackson, victor at the Battle of New Orleans and seventh President of the United States. With the exception of a couple of mountain counties, the 4th has remained loyal to Jackson's party ever since. Indeed, it has produced a number of the party's national leaders, including Congressman (1907-21, 1923-31), Senator (1931-33), and Secretary of State (1933-44) Cordell Hull and Congressman (1939-53) and Senator (1953-71) Albert Gore.

The race issue in the 4th has seldom been the burning issue it has been in other parts of the Deep South. This has always been a region of white small farmers, and only 6% of the district's residents are black. The farmers almost always vote Democratic. Even in 1972 George McGovern got 35% of the vote here—a low figure, but one showing as much support from whites as he had anywhere in the South. In 1976 Jimmy Carter carried the 4th with 68% of the vote—one of his best congressional district percentages in the nation—and got as much as 83% in some counties. Ordinarily this is the most heavily Democratic district in Tennessee.

It also has had a tradition of congressmen who vote with other national Democrats. This was certainly true of Albert Gore in his years in both the House and Senate, and it was true of his successor in the House, Joe Evins. During his 24 years in the House Evins rose to become Chairman of the Public Works Appropriations Subcommittee, the body which decides how much money is to be spent on various dams, highways, and other public works projects. This was obviously a crucial post in the days when most congressmen depended on such projects for reelection; it was less important when Evins retired in 1976.

His successor, naturally, was chosen in the Democratic primary. And although the contest was close, the winner was very much in the 4th district tradition: Albert Gore, Jr. Like his father, he has voted mainly with northern Democrats. But he has not yet shown—in these more placid times has not really had occasion to show—the kind of daring and even defiance that characterized the elder Gore's last Senate term, when he opposed the Vietnam war and both of Nixon's Southern Supreme Court nominations. Gore is unusual for being one of the few Vietnam veterans in Congress; he is considered a knowledgeable and politically adept member. On the Commerce Committee, for example, he supported hospital cost containment but on the floor opposed labor's common situs picketing bill. Gore may very well have a future in statewide politics: he has a well known name in a state with few obvious Democratic statewide contenders. But any such effort must wait for some time; in the meantime he seems sure to win reelection to the House, if indeed he has any opposition at all.

Census Data Pop. 492,124. Central city, 0%; suburban, 19%. Median family income, $6,451; families above $15,000: 8%; families below $3,000: 20%. Median years education, 9.2.

The Voters

Median voting age 43.
Employment profile White collar, 34%. Blue collar, 47%. Service, 11%. Farm, 8%.
Ethnic groups Black, 6%.

Presidential vote

1976	Carter (D)	124,267	(65%)
	Ford (R)	58,441	(32%)
1972	Nixon (R)	82,879	(65%)
	McGovern (D)	44,719	(35%)

Rep. Albert Gore, Jr. (D) Elected 1976; b. Mar. 31, 1948, Washington, D.C.; home, Carthage; Harvard U., B.A. 1969, Vanderbilt U.; Baptist.

Career Army, Vietnam; Home building and subdivision business operator, 1971–76.

Offices 1417 LHOB, 202-225-4231. Also U.S. Courthouse, Carthage 37030, 615-735-0173.

Committees *Interstate and Foreign Commerce* (21st). Subcommittees: Communications; Oversight and Investigations; Energy and Power.

Science and Technology (15th). Subcommittees: Investigations and Oversight; Energy Development and Applications.

Group Ratings

	ADA	COPE	PC	RPN	NFU	LCV	CFA	NAB	NSI	ACA	NTU
1978	65	70	68	50	80	–	77	33	50	15	–
1977	45	78	65	46	83	66	60	–	–	30	30

Key Votes

1) Increase Def Spnd	AGN	6) Alaska Lands Protect	FOR	11) Delay Auto Pol Cntrl	AGN
2) B-1 Bomber	AGN	7) Water Projects Veto	AGN	12) Sugar Price Escalator	FOR
3) Cargo Preference	AGN	8) Consum Protect Agcy	FOR	13) Pub Fin Cong Cmpgns	FOR
4) Dereg Nat Gas	AGN	9) Common Situs Picket	AGN	14) ERA Ratif Recissn	AGN
5) Kemp-Roth	AGN	10) Labor Law Revision	FOR	15) Prohibt Govt Abrtns	AGN

Election Results

1978 general	Albert Gore, Jr. (D), unopposed			($47,097)
1978 primary	Albert Gore, Jr. (D), unopposed			
1976 general	Albert Gore, Jr. (D)	115,392	(94%)	($188,560)
	William H. McGlanery (Ind.)	7,320	(6%)	($0)

FIFTH DISTRICT

Nashville is Tennessee's capital and second largest city; after its consolidation with surrounding Davidson County in the sixties, it had the impressive population of 447,000. Because of its location near the center of the state, Nashville is in many ways—especially politically—more important to Tennessee than is its larger rival, Memphis. The two newspapers in Nashville reflect neatly the state's two-party politics: the *Banner* is as resolutely Republican as the *Tennesseean* is determinedly Democratic. The city is also a major center for industries like printing and insurance. Nashville is best known, however, for country music. It has been the home of the Grand Ole Opry since the twenties, and today it is the undisputed country and western music capital of the world. It has several major recording studios, and many of the big stars live here or in fabled mansions outside of town. The country music scene is not all that different from that shown in Los Angeles-based Robert Altman's film *Nashville*.

Nashville can claim other cultural ornaments besides country music. The city contains several colleges, including Vanderbilt and Fisk Universities. Also here, not far from the old state Capitol, is the famous replica of the Parthenon. But Nashville's favorite shrine—and the one most significant politically—is the Hermitage, the home of Andrew Jackson. Old Hickory moved to Nashville from the Carolinas when Tennessee was still very much the frontier. He made a small fortune, won election to the House while George Washington was still President, and was elected to the Senate, where he served briefly just after he turned 30; for a few years after that, he served on the state Supreme Court. It was only after this youthful political career, and after some financial setbacks, that Jackson made his national reputation as a merciless Indian fighter, the scourge of the British at the Battle of New Orleans, and the common man's candidate for president. But he had already set Nashville's political preferences. Jackson was a Democrat, and Nashville has remained, with only the most occasional exceptions, Democratic ever since.

The 5th congressional district includes all of Nashville and two small rural counties which are becoming partly suburban. The 5th is usually a reliably Democratic district in statewide elections (though it went once for George Wallace, once for Richard Nixon, and twice for Howard Baker), and it always elects Democrats to Congress. The real contests here are between Democrats. Thus in 1962 liberal Democrat Richard Fulton ousted the reactionary incumbent. Fulton was popular locally and had a seat on the Ways and Means Committee, but in 1975, at age 48, he ran for Mayor of Nashville and won easily. Fulton's successor, elected in November 1975, was 63-year-old Tax Assessor Clifford Allen, who had won great popularity by fighting high utility rates. Allen had a national Democratic voting record and was unbeatable locally. But he died in the summer of 1976, after the filing deadline and before the primary election.

The primary winner was state Senator Bill Boner, the only well-known candidate in the field. He had a controversial reputation from some personal problems and for alleged close ties to business. In the general election he faced a former aide to Senator Bill Brock and a former aide to Senator Albert Gore, the latter running as an Independent. The outcome, with Boner barely winning an absolute majority, suggests that the succession in this district cannot be considered settled until after the 1980 election. Boner will certainly have an advantage from his incumbency, but he is also likely to have strong competition for this seat.

Census Data Pop. 490,178. Central city, 100%; suburban, 0%. Median family income, $9,231; families above $15,000: 18%; families below $3,000: 10%. Median years education, 11.9.

The Voters

Median voting age 41.
Employment profile White collar, 53%. Blue collar, 33%. Service, 13%. Farm, 1%.
Ethnic groups Black, 19%. Total foreign stock, 3%.

Presidential vote

1976	Carter (D)	110,779	(53%)
	Ford (R)	64,543	(37%)
1972	Nixon (R)	89,046	(63%)
	McGovern (D)	53,175	(37%)

Rep. William Hill Boner (D) Elected 1978; b. Feb. 14, 1945, Nashville; home, Nashville; Middle Tenn. St. U., B.S. 1967, Peabody Col., M.A. 1969; YMCA Night Law School, Nashville, J.D. 1978; Methodist.

Career College basketball coach, 1969–71; Tenn. House of Reps., 1970–72, 1974–76; Senior Staff Asst., Nashville Mayors Ofc., 1971–72; Asst. V.P. and Dir. of Public Relations, First Amer. Natl. Bank, Nashville; Law Clerk, 1976–77; Tenn. Senate, 1976–78.

Offices 118 CHOB, 202-225-4311. Also 552 U.S. Courthouse, Nashville 37203, 615-251-5296.

Committees *Public Works and Transportation* (30th). Subcommittees: Aviation; Public Buildings and Grounds; Surface Transportation.

Veterans' Affairs (14th). Subcommittees: Medical Facilities and Benefits; Education, Training, and Employment.

Group Ratings: Newly Elected

Key Votes: Newly Elected

Election Results

1978 general	Bill Boner (D)	68,608	(51%)	($192,960)
	Bill Goodwin (R)	47,288	(35%)	($40,494)
	Henry Haile (I)	17,674	(13%)	($5,838)
1978 primary	Bill Boner (D)	50,987	(58%)	
	Charles Galbreath (D)	25,768	(29%)	($32,923)
	Four others (D)	10,695	(12%)	
1976 general	Clifford Allen (D)	125,830	(92%)	($96,684)
	Roger E. Bissell (Ind.)	10,292	(8%)	($0)

SIXTH DISTRICT

The 6th congressional district of Tennessee is a rather odd amalgam, stretching from the Nashville city limits in the heart of middle Tennessee to the city of Memphis on the Mississippi River in the southwest corner of the state. Its shape is the result of the settlement of a redistricting problem which arose when Tennessee lost one of its nine congressional districts after the 1970 Census. The Democratic legislature chose essentially to consolidate two districts: the middle Tennessee district represented by William Anderson and the west Tennessee district represented by Ray Blanton. Both were Democrats, but Blanton was running for Howard Baker's Senate seat that year (he lost, but was later elected Governor), and Anderson seemed to be strong enough to win.

But the Democrats failed to anticipate the weakness of their party that year or the strength of Republican Robin Beard. Anderson, the captain of the first nuclear submarine to sail under the North Pole, had a liberal voting record and opposed the war in Vietnam; his constituents in 1972 had different opinions. Particularly critical were the residents of the portion of Shelby County added to the district, a 99% white portion of Memphis and its suburbs. Beard, in contrast, was young, articulate, and aggressively conservative. His identity with the district was tenuous—he was an east Tennessee native and lived in a Nashville suburb just over the Williamson County line. But he strongly opposed busing and strongly backed the Vietnam war. He got 80% in Shelby County; his 20,000-vote edge there wiped out the 3,000-vote edge Anderson had in the rest of the district.

Beard has proved to be a combative Congressman. He serves on the Armed Services Committee where his views are generally shared by the majority. He was the man who brought charges against Massachusetts's Michael Harrington for allegedly leaking secret testimony about American efforts to subvert the elected government of Chile (they were dismissed on what amounted to a technicality). Fiercely conservative on other issues, Beard is a kind of young Strom Thurmond.

Since he was first elected he has strengthened his hold on the district. He was aided slightly by a court-ordered redistricting—the only one in any state between the 1974 and 1976 elections—which shifted six all-white precincts in Memphis from the 8th to the 6th district. He has campaigned hard throughout the year and in 1978 was able to carry every one of the rural counties as well as an overwhelming margin in Shelby.

Census Data Pop. 472,341. Central city, 15%; suburban, 3%. Median family income, $7,151; families above $15,000: 12%; families below $3,000: 19%. Median years education, 10.3.

The Voters

Median voting age 42.
Employment profile White collar, 39%. Blue collar, 45%. Service, 11%. Farm, 5%.
Ethnic groups Black, 14%. Total foreign stock, 2%.

Presidential vote

1976	Carter (D)	104,815	(53%)
	Ford (R)	94,314	(47%)
1972	Nixon (R)	104,742	(72%)
	McGovern (D)	39,799	(28%)

Rep. Robin L. Beard (R) Elected 1972; b. Aug. 21, 1939, Knoxville; home, Franklin; Vanderbilt U., B.A. 1961; Methodist.

Career USMC, 1962–66; Assoc. Dir. of Alumni Development, Vanderbilt U., 1966–68; Tenn. State Personnel Commissioner, 1970–72.

Offices 229 CHOB, 202-225-2811. Also 22 Public Sq., Columbia 38401, 615-388-2133.

Committees *Armed Services* (6th). Subcommittees: Investigations; NATO Standardization, Interoperability, and Readiness; Military Installations and Facilities.

Group Ratings

	ADA	COPE	PC	RPN	NFU	LCV	CFA	NAB	NSI	ACA	NTU
1978	5	0	13	64	40	–	9	100	100	96	–
1977	0	14	8	64	55	9	10	–	–	85	42
1976	5	14	3	56	9	17	0	92	100	93	58

Key Votes

1) Increase Def Spnd	FOR	6) Alaska Lands Protect	AGN	11) Delay Auto Pol Cntrl	FOR
2) B-1 Bomber	FOR	7) Water Projects Veto	AGN	12) Sugar Price Escalator	FOR
3) Cargo Preference	AGN	8) Consum Protect Agcy	AGN	13) Pub Fin Cong Cmpgns	AGN
4) Dereg Nat Gas	FOR	9) Common Situs Picket	AGN	14) ERA Ratif Recissn	FOR
5) Kemp-Roth	FOR	10) Labor Law Revision	AGN	15) Prohibt Govt Abrtns	FOR

Election Results

1978 general	Robin L. Beard, Jr. (R)	114,630	(75%)	($156,405)
	Ron Arline (D)	38,954	(25%)	($10,175)
1978 primary	Robin L. Beard, Jr. (R), unopposed			
1976 general	Robin L. Beard, Jr. (R)	116,905	(64%)	($222,656)
	Ross Bass (D)	64,462	(36%)	($83,368)

SEVENTH DISTRICT

The 7th congressional district of Tennessee is the northwest part of the state. The district extends from the TVA lakes of the Tennessee and Cumberland Rivers at the Kentucky state line to the city of Memphis. Physically and politically the 7th resembles the Mississippi Delta or east Arkansas: flat cotton lands and soybean fields, occasional small towns, and a fairly large (19%), mostly rural black population. Outside of Memphis and Shelby County, the district's largest city is Jackson, with a population of 39,000.

Most of the counties here are traditionally Democratic, but only those around the Tennessee River gave statewide Democratic candidates majorities in the years from 1968 to 1972. Indeed, this has been the pivotal part of the state in recent close elections. When it went for Bill Brock in the 1970 Senate election, he won; when it switched and backed Democrat Jim Sasser in 1976, Brock lost. The Shelby County portion of the district, with one-quarter of the 7th's population, is 98% white, relatively high income, and heavily conservative—almost as devoted to the Republican Party as the 6th district's share of Shelby County.

This is a district which has had only one substantial general election contest in the past 20 years. That happened in 1969, in a special election after the incumbent died. Republicans, hoping for new victories for their Southern strategy, made a major effort here; so did George Wallace, who came in to campaign for the American Party candidate. But the winner, with 51%, was Democrat Ed Jones. A former state Agriculture Commissioner, he did without national endorsements and ran as a folksy local Democrat.

In Congress Jones received a seat on the Agriculture Committee and its Cotton and Conservation and Credit Subcommittees. With several surprise retirements and defeats, Jones is now the third-ranking Democrat on the full committee. He has chaired the Cotton Subcommittee, and now chairs Conservation and Credit.

Nevertheless he has had some problems at home. In 1976 a 31-year-old banker held him to 59% in the Democratic primary—not a high percentage for a longtime veteran. In 1978 he had no primary opposition and won the general election easily. Jones is in good health and has a record that suits his district, but he turns 68 in 1980 and may attract a serious challenger—or may simply decide that it is time to retire.

Census Data Pop. 487,097. Central city, 10%; suburban, 16%. Median family income, $7,030; families above $15,000: 10%; families below $3,000: 19%. Median years education, 10.2.

The Voters

Median voting age 43.
Employment profile White collar, 37%. Blue collar, 44%. Service, 12%. Farm, 7%.
Ethnic groups Black, 19%. Total foreign stock, 2%.

Presidential vote

1976	Carter (D)	100,751	(58%)
	Ford (R)	73,714	(42%)
1972	Nixon (R)	105,072	(75%)
	McGovern (D)	34,241	(25%)

Rep. Ed Jones (D) Elected Mar. 25, 1969; b. Apr. 20, 1912, Yorkville; home, Yorkville; U. of Tenn., B.S. 1934; Presbyterian.

Career Inspector, Tenn. Dept. of Agric., 1934–41; Supervisor, Tenn. Dairy Products Assn., 1941–43; Agric. Rep., Ill. Central R.R., 1943–48, 1952–69; Tenn. Commissioner of Agric., 1949–52.

Offices 104 CHOB, 202-225-4714. Also P.O. Box 27190, 3179 N. Watkins St., Memphis 38127, 901-358-4094.

Committees *Agriculture* (4th). Subcommittees: Conservation and Credit (Chairman); Cotton; Livestock and Grains.

House Administration (7th). Subcommittees: Contracts; Services (Chairman).

Group Ratings

	ADA	COPE	PC	RPN	NFU	LCV	CFA	NAB	NSI	ACA	NTU
1978	20	42	18	45	60	–	9	46	60	56	–
1977	25	73	40	46	58	24	50	–	–	52	18
1976	15	64	28	29	67	29	18	33	70	59	29

Key Votes

1) Increase Def Spnd	FOR	6) Alaska Lands Protect	FOR	11) Delay Auto Pol Cntrl	FOR
2) B-1 Bomber	AGN	7) Water Projects Veto	AGN	12) Sugar Price Escalator	FOR
3) Cargo Preference	AGN	8) Consum Protect Agcy	AGN	13) Pub Fin Cong Cmpgns	AGN
4) Dereg Nat Gas	AGN	9) Common Situs Picket	AGN	14) ERA Ratif Recissn	FOR
5) Kemp-Roth	FOR	10) Labor Law Revision	FOR	15) Prohibt Govt Abrtns	AGN

Election Results

1978 general	Ed Jones (D)	96,863	(73%)	($124,445)
	Ross Cook (R)	36,003	(27%)	($49,769)
1978 primary	Ed Jones (D), unopposed			
1976 general	Ed Jones (D), unopposed			($164,859)

EIGHTH DISTRICT

Memphis, Tennessee's largest city with more than 600,000 people, is set in the far southwest corner of the state. The city is the major financial and commercial center for much of the lower Mississippi Valley. As such, Memphis looks as much south to Mississippi and west to Arkansas as it does east and north to the rest of Tennessee. In recent years Memphis has grown rapidly, doubling its population since World War II. Most of the newcomers are from the Deep South, especially Mississippi. Blacks have found more economic opportunity here, and more political power; for a decade now Memphis has elected black state legislators and even a black judge—Benjamin Hooks, now executive director of the national NAACP.

Memphis is the home of many quintessentially American institutions. Beale Street here gave birth to jazz in the twenties, and in the thirties the first supermarket—a Piggly Wiggly—opened in Memphis. In the fifties Memphis gave us Elvis Presley and the Holiday Inn (the first of which is no longer operated under that aegis, but sports a memorial plaque). Memphis, or at least the white majority here, likes to think of itself as a plain Middle American city, but the fact is that the prevailing community opinion, like the accent, remains basically Southern.

The city as a whole is dominated by its middle class whites. Many of these are people from the small town South, who are now making more money than they ever imagined. They live comfortable lives in the vast suburban tracts that have sprung up inside and outside the expanding city limits in the last 20 years. Their political traditions are Democratic, but they now use their ballots to protect their new-found prosperity—and the whiteness of their neighborhoods—by voting Republican. They are attracted particularly to youngish, lightly accented candidates like Howard Baker, Bill Brock, and Lamar Alexander, whose sometimes cerebral conservatism and thoughtful articulation symbolize what they hope they have become rather than what they were.

There is one other fact that any political analyst should know about Memphis: this is one of the most segregated cities in the country. There is little of that phenomenon, once so common in Atlanta and still the case in New Orleans, of blacks and whites living in close proximity. The blacks are concentrated entirely in the central portion of the city, while the whites have long since moved to the newer subdivisions. Thirty-odd years ago there were no differences between the voting habits of Memphis blacks and Memphis whites: they both went down the line for candidates endorsed by Boss Ed Crump's machine, which is to say Democrats. But long ago the white neighborhoods started moving toward the Republicans, while the blacks became more Democratic than ever. The result is voting patterns more racially polarized than in any other major American city. In 1976 Jimmy Carter carried Memphis's Shelby County, because of virtually unanimous black support; but more than 60% of the whites voted against him. In the suburban and city areas that are in the 6th congressional district, fully 70% went for Gerald Ford.

Most of Memphis and virtually none of its suburbs make up Tennessee's 8th congressional district. For some years Tennessee legislators drew the lines to prevent a black-majority district, but in 1972, to maximize Democratic chances, they made a district 47% of whose residents and 41% of whose residents over 18 were black. The percentages have risen since, both because of racial change in some neighborhoods and because of a 1976 redistricting. The latter removed from the 8th seven precincts which had gone 90%, with a margin of nearly 6,000 votes, for the Republican candidate in 1974.

Back in 1972 the 8th still had a white Republican congressman, but it was only a matter of time before he would lose to a black Democrat. The time came earlier than expected, probably because of Watergate, in 1974, when state Representative Harold Ford won by 744 votes.

Ford is part of a local political family; his older brother is a state legislator. With the Black Caucus accommodating an increasingly diverse group of legislators from around the nation, Ford comes closest to projecting the Superfly image: a young, brash man who drives an Olds 98 and who enjoys the fact that he is becoming well-to-do as well as politically powerful. Ford makes as few concessions to the sensibilities of white voters (though he does provide them with constituent services) as his predecessor did to blacks, and voting in the 8th district still breaks largely along racial lines. Ford's percentage has risen precipitously, as the district's black population has grown and the Republicans have ceased to contest the seat seriously. Ford is a member of the Ways and Means Committee, with the prospect of winning great seniority.

Census Data Pop. 513,004. Central city, 99%; suburban, 1%. Median family income, $7,874; families above $15,000: 14%; families below $3,000: 15%. Median years education, 11.4.

The Voters

Median voting age 42.
Employment profile White collar, 47%. Blue collar, 36%. Service, 17%. Farm, –%.
Ethnic groups Black, 47%. Total foreign stock, 3%.

Presidential vote

1976	Carter (D)	111,229	(65%)
	Ford (R)	60,114	(35%)
1972	Nixon (R)	96,876	(57%)
	McGovern (D)	71,930	(43%)

Rep. Harold E. Ford (D) Elected 1974; b. May 20, 1945, Memphis; home, Memphis; Tenn. St. U., B.S. 1967, John Gupten Col., L.F.D., L.E.D. 1969; Baptist.

Career Mortician, 1969–75; Tenn. House of Reps., 1971–74.

Offices 1230 LHOB, 202-225-3265. Also 369 Fed. Bldg., Memphis 38103, 901-521-4131.

Committees *Ways and Means* (14th). Subcommittees: Health; Oversight.

Group Ratings

	ADA	COPE	PC	RPN	NFU	LCV	CFA	NAB	NSI	ACA	NTU
1978	70	90	70	36	89	–	46	0	10	12	–
1977	75	78	73	50	75	55	75	–	–	7	49
1976	80	91	83	50	83	64	81	25	20	21	36

Key Votes

1) Increase Def Spnd	AGN	6) Alaska Lands Protect	FOR	11) Delay Auto Pol Cntrl	FOR
2) B-1 Bomber	AGN	7) Water Projects Veto	FOR	12) Sugar Price Escalator	FOR
3) Cargo Preference	AGN	8) Consum Protect Agcy	FOR	13) Pub Fin Cong Cmpgns	FOR
4) Dereg Nat Gas	AGN	9) Common Situs Picket	AGN	14) ERA Ratif Recissn	AGN
5) Kemp-Roth	AGN	10) Labor Law Revision	FOR	15) Prohibt Govt Abrtns	AGN

Election Results

1978 general	Harold E. Ford (D)	80,776	(71%)	($179,244)
	Duncan Ragsdale (R)	33,679	(29%)	($12,372)
1978 primary	Harold E. Ford (D)	54,235	(81%)	
	One other (D)	13,093	(19%)	
1976 general	Harold E. Ford (D)	100,683	(61%)	($147,288)
	A.D. Alissandratos (R)	63,819	(39%)	($126,154)

TEXAS

Texas is the only state in the Union which was an independent nation for a significant length of time, and today it probably possesses the most distinctive image of any state. Although its border areas are not much different from those of its neighbors—east Texas resembles southern Arkansas, west Texas resembles the Little Texas area of New Mexico—the state as a whole evokes for outsiders and residents a set of pictures and ideas generally consistent and not wholly divorced from reality. Texas's distinctive history is well known, and everyone automatically remembers the Alamo—even if it is John Wayne defending it. From the movie *Giant* we have the dusty plains of west Texas cattle ranches and the sudden wealth of oil. By the forties Texas jokes—featuring boisterous millionaires and braggarts—were a staple of American humor.

But Texas has always been a more complex and diverse place than cartoon images suggest. We think of the typical Texan as a drawling white Anglo, but at least 18% of the state's residents are of Mexican origin (no one is sure how many, because of heavy illegal immigration) and another 12% are black. And certainly not every Texan has become an oil millionaire. On the contrary, vast differences in income and wealth are especially obvious in fast-growing cities like Houston—in the same way and for the same reasons that disparities in income have always been most obvious in places with rapid economic development. Those who own or start the successful businesses become rich fast; the growth they help to generate attracts poor people from the rural hinterland to better opportunities in the city.

Texas has been growing more rapidly economically in the seventies than ever before. The multiplication in oil prices in 1973-74 and after has meant huge prosperity for Texas. This is not so much because of the state's own oil and gas production. It is still the leading oil producer among the states, but of course the U.S. is now an importer, not an exporter, of oil; and it is still prevented from selling its natural gas beyond its borders at the free market price. Texas prospers because it has become the corporate center of the world oil and gas business. Many of the giants—Exxon, Shell, Gulf—have moved headquarters operations here in the seventies. Even more important, Texas has literally thousands of specialized companies which can produce oil drill bits or put out oil well fires or construct oil pipelines. In the thirties and forties, Texas benefited from the good geological luck of having big oil deposits; it now is benefiting from its skill at getting its own and others' oil and gas out of the ground. In the late nineteenth century Pennsylvania, with its hard and soft coal deposits, was the nation's energy capital, and on that base built the nation's largest mass production industry, steel. In the late twentieth century Texas has become the nation's energy capital, and its potential for future growth seems great indeed.

That potential seems especially great because attitudes—at least among the affluent minority that dominates the business community and the media here—are strongly positive about growth. These Texans have the kind of confidence in the future and in their own goodness and fairness and efficiency that most affluent Americans had in the fifties but lost in the next decade. There is no apology or guilt about wealth here, no notion that it is evil unless it is given away to foundations. The feeling is that it is the God-given reward for building productive businesses and creating a thriving economy where none existed before. So there is very little radical chic or sense of noblesse in Texas. The wealthy west side of Houston and north side of Dallas are strongly Republican; in 1976 the two congressional districts there were the most heavily Republican districts in the nation, even as the state as a whole was going for Jimmy Carter. The affluent parts of the state are where the growth has been fastest and the elan is most vibrant. They believe that they represent the Texas of the future.

But despite their appreciation for Texas history, at least politically the rich do not really represent the Texas of the past. Before the oil strikes of the turn of the century, this was a state made up almost entirely of dirt farmers, most of them white Anglos, with some blacks and Mexicans. It was also one of the nation's poorest, least educated, and most strongly Democratic states. As the oil industry grew and some Texans made really big money, there was no immediate move to the Republicans; rather the new rich Texans became Democrats. Their prototype was Jesse Jones, the Houston banker who was Franklin Roosevelt's Secretary of Commerce, but never much of a New Dealer. Sam Rayburn and Lyndon Johnson, when they ran the Congress in the fifties, were in close touch with these men, but did not always share their views; more in line were so-called Tory Democrats, like Governor and Senator Price Daniel and Governor John Connally. These politicians were not necessarily enemies of big government—particularly when it could subsidize Texas's cotton farmers, irrigate its Lower Rio Grande Valley, or provide a large depletion allowance for its oil. But they believed firmly that the best interests of the state were to serve the best interests of its richest and most successful citizens—to keep taxes and public services low, to provide incentives and low wage labor to business. Texas is the only one of our really major states with a right to work law, and among the big states, its labor unions are the weakest; Texas also has, amid its boom, the lowest wage levels (and lowest costs of living) of the major states. Services recently have been increased while taxes have been cut: the prosperity here has been so great as to generate embarrassingly large revenues.

The Tory Democrats were for years the dominant force in Texas politics. They held onto the governorship for 40 solid years, from 1938 to 1978, and seldom lost effective control of the legislature. They carried the state for the Democratic presidential nominee in close elections like 1960, 1968, and 1976, despite major differences on policy. Their large and usually senior delegations in the House provided crucial aid to Democratic administrations on occasion and protected Texas's interests throughout. Their influential senators, notably Lyndon Johnson, combined liberalism on some issues with a canny appreciation for the Texas power structure and its needs.

The instrument of control was the open Democratic primary. Anyone could vote in the primary, although for years Texas discouraged registration by the poor, first by poll tax and then by onerous requirements. With no contested Republican primaries, conservative voters could participate in Democratic contests; and the mood of a majority of Texas voters in most contests was conservative. Meanwhile, insurgents could never raise the money necessary for sophisticated media campaigns; insiders always could. In general elections, the Tory Democrats won with the help of the liberal vote, mostly from minorities and in working class sections of the big cities, and with the large rural vote—still more than one-third of the total. Most of the people in the small towns and rural counties of east and central Texas retain Baptist religious and Democratic political affiliation; the loyalty to the party was so strong that even George Wallace failed to crack it in 1968. Tradition-oriented rural Texas provided the key votes for Texas Democrats from Lyndon Johnson through Connally to Senator Lloyd Bentsen and Governor Dolph Briscoe in the seventies.

Now the pattern of Tory Democratic domination seems to have changed—at least temporarily, quite possibly permanently. The victors have not been the liberal Democrats who had hoped to build a populist coalition of blue collar workers, blacks, and chicanos, but the Republicans. In 1978 they won two smashing victories, electing William Clements Governor and reelecting John Tower Senator. In both cases they prevailed over strong Democratic opposition and, in Clements's case, their win was a tremendous upset. To be sure, in both cases the victories were by narrow margins—less than 17,000 votes out of more than two million cast. They were, however, the product of vast differences in turnout. In affluent urban Republican areas, turnout was high, and that is where Clements and Tower were elected; in rural east Texas and in the poorer neighborhoods of Houston, Dallas, Fort Worth, and San Antonio, turnout was low. Both traditional and liberal Democrats seemed to have little elan, little sense that they had the answers for society's problems; the Republicans did.

It is important to note the differences between the Republicans and the Tory Democrats—and indeed the differences between most Texas Republicans and the two members of the party, John Connally and George Bush, who have entered the 1980 presidential race. For Texas Republicans, as shown by Ronald Reagan's smashing victory over Gerald Ford here in the 1976 primary, believe strongly in an aggressive foreign policy—Reagan's opposition to a Panama Canal Treaty was a big asset—and in untrammelled free enterprise. They believe that private investment has made Texas prosperous and vibrant, while welfare state measures have impoverished the Northeast. They do not believe as many rural Democratic voters do in some traditional values; residents of west Houston and north Dallas are proud of their cultural achievements, their knowledge of foreign wines and gourmet food and tasteful decoration, and they have little use for the evangelical religion and prohibitionism of rural Baptists. At the same time, they do not have the tolerance for the weird cultural styles one sees in affluent Californians. So they do not worry much about civil liberties or civil rights, or pay lip service to causes which are fashionable among affluent Northeasterners. When Bill Clements was asked to express some concern about problems of Mexican-Americans, he replied gruffly that he was not running for Governor of Mexico. Texas Republicans are not defensive about what they believe.

John Connally shares, indeed exemplifies, much of the confidence these people have; and he played a major role in the Clements campaign. But as Nixon's Treasury Secretary he put through wage and price controls and backed the opening to China. George Bush, originally from the Northeast, has a somewhat different attitude. He stresses that his own beliefs on foreign and domestic policies are not significantly different from Ronald Reagan's. But his record as a two-term congressman from Houston showed him supporting the antipoverty program and the federal open housing law. In any case, neither man has been much of a success in Republican politics here. Connally of course was elected Governor as a Democrat, not a Republican; Bush failed twice to be elected senator here, once against a moderate Democrat and once against a liberal. Indeed, both men would seem to have major disqualifications. Connally, though acquitted on bribery charges, has much of the remoteness from the ordinary person people disliked in Nixon and the penchant for wheeling and dealing they disliked in Johnson. Bush was Republican National Chairman during the Watergate era and director of the CIA when it was accused of covering up its various dirty tricks. But both men must be taken seriously. Connally's self-assurance and crisp speaking style provides a contrast to the last two presidents, and Bush's assiduous courting of grass roots Republicans may make him a serious candidate. It will be interesting to see what happens if they both survive to the Texas presidential primary.

The 1978 gubernatorial race gave Texans a choice they have never really had before: between a rather liberal Democrat, Attorney General John Hill, and a laissez-faire Republican, Bill Clements. Hill had won an upset victory in the primary over incumbent Dolph Briscoe, whose six years in office were characterized by ennui. While most Texans may not want an activist government, Briscoe carried inaction too far; and in the national perspective, he let other petroleum-producing state governors, David Boren of Oklahoma and Edwin Edwards of Louisiana, emerge as spokesmen for the region. Hill led in the polls throughout the fall campaign, since he was the Democratic nominee and few voters had ever heard of Clements. But apparently commitment to him was weak, and overcome by Clements's money. There was plenty of that. Clements founded an extremely successful oil drilling company, and after returning home to Dallas after four years as Deputy Secretary of Defense—one of the top jobs in Washington—decided to run for governor and spend what it takes to win. It turned out to take about $7 million, and Clements was not a bit bashful or apologetic about spending it.

Clements's victory was very much a victory for the west side of Houston, the north side of Dallas, and other affluent parts of Texas. He carried significant margins in only six of the state's 24 congressional districts and ran virtually even with Hill in three others; the other 15 gave Hill margins. But turnout was higher and margins larger in the Republican districts, and Texas now has its first Republican in more than 100 years. The affluent parts of Texas have always liked to imagine that they represent the consensus thinking of the state; that has not been so in the past, but it was in 1978. Now they look forward to exerting their influence over the whole country. Clements, unlike Briscoe, will be a national figure, forcefully, even pungently, advocating policies to encourage free enterprise and to cut down the size of government.

Another major force in national policy is Senator John Tower. No one would have suspected that that would be so when he was first elected in 1961. He had a reputation as a kind of gadfly candidate, running against Lyndon Johnson when LBJ ran for both vice president and senator in 1960. Tower got a respectable 41% in that race, and in the 1961 special election outpolled an ultra-reactionary Democrat who had been appointed to the seat. Tower again beat a Tory Democrat in 1966, with the help of some liberal voters who figured he might not last as long—they seem to have been proved wrong. Against moderate Democrat Barefoot Sanders he won 55% in 1972, running better than a Republican ever had before in rural counties. His toughest race was in 1978, against Congressman Bob Krueger. A former English professor at Duke who quoted Shakespeare copiously on the campaign trail, Krueger had a tailored-to-Texas voting record. His major achievement was coming as close as anyone ever has to getting the House to vote for deregulating natural gas. His well-financed primary campaign beat an underfinanced liberal, and with his west Texas roots and acceptability to liberal Democrats he was a strong contender. Toward the end the campaign was marred by smear tactics. Krueger forces accused the twice-married Tower of being a womanizer. Others accused the never married Krueger of being a homosexual. Tower refused to shake Krueger's hand in October when their paths crossed; and for once the Senator's sour personality seems to have worked to his benefit. The result was extremely close, almost an exact duplicate of the gubernatorial race; turnout again was the key factor.

Tower was considered somewhat lazy in his first years in the Senate; he apparently did not expect to stay there long and decided to enjoy his tenure. But now he has served in the Senate about as long as any Texan ever has, and he has long since buckled down and used his considerable brainpower to advance the causes he believes in. He is now ranking Republican on the Senate Armed Services Committee and inevitably a backer of strong defense measures and high expenditures. On economic issues he takes the side almost inevitably which is favored by business interests. Tower is not a star orator or a persuasive arm-twister, but he is a thoroughly competent, often effective senator.

So, in a different way, is Texas's leading Democratic officeholder, Senator Lloyd Bentsen. His roots are very much in the Tory Democrat tradition. He is from a big landowning family in the Lower Rio Grande Valley, and was first elected to the House in 1946 at the age of 27. He left Congress after eight years to make money in business, and returned to electoral politics in 1970. That year he upset Senator Ralph Yarborough, Texas's leading liberal, by running commercials featuring the riots outside the Chicago Democratic National Convention of 1968. For the general election, against George Bush, Bentsen cultivated the support of Barbara Jordan, Congressman Henry Gonzalez, and the state AFL-CIO; he combined rural traditional Democrats and urban minorities in sufficient numbers to win.

As a Senator Bentsen has stayed fairly close to mainstream Democrats. He is brainy and has the ability to deal effectively with complex legislative problems. His expertise was essential to passage of the 1974 pension reform bill, with the support of both organized labor and business interests. His expertise helped him to get enacted a law cutting off the oil depletion allowance for the major oil companies and retaining it for smaller producers. This had the effect of placing him in public opposition to what had been a major Texas interest group and at the same time placating the small producers, many of whom are Texas multimillionaires in the habit of making campaign contributions.

Bentsen's major failure was his presidential candidacy, which raised a lot of money in 1975 but won little support in 1976. Bentsen thought it would be a good idea if the Democrats nominated someone with a business background, from a Southern state, who was not involved deeply in the party's past struggles. They did, but the winner was Jimmy Carter, not Bentsen, whose campaign in retrospect seems too cerebral. Bentsen's reelection campaign that year worked better. His opponent was Alan Steelman, a young Dallas Congressman with a rather unusual record for a Republican: he was predictably conservative on economic issues, but he showed a strong concern for the environment. His career in Dallas had been boosted by his opposition to the Trinity River canal project ("Why make Dallas a seaport?") But environmental qualms are not very common in booming Texas, and Steelman was never able to raise enough money to make himself known outside his home media market. Bentsen won comfortably with 57%. How would Bentsen do against a more ideological Republican, someone like Clements or Tower? No one can be sure, but we may find out when his seat comes up in 1982.

Texas has traditionally had a powerful House delegation. Two Texas Democrats have served as Speakers of the House—John Nance Garner (1931-33) and Sam Rayburn (1940-47, 1949-53, 1955-61)—and today a Texan, Jim Wright of Fort Worth, is House Majority Leader. But in 1978 Texas saw the retirement of a record number, six, of its congressmen and the defeat of three others. Included in the retirees were committee chairmen or ex-chairmen George Mahon (Appropriations), Olin "Tiger" Teague (Science), Bob Poage (ex-Agriculture), and Omar Burleson (ex-House Administration), as well as the nationally famous Barbara Jordan and Senate candidate Bob Krueger. Altogether Texas lost 190 years of House seniority. Still Texas retains considerable clout in the House, with Wright and a strong committee chairman, Jack Brooks (Government Operations), as well as three intelligent and politically adept subcommittee chairmen, Jake Pickle, Bob Eckhardt, and Charles Wilson, and a leading Republican, Bill Archer.

The Texas delegation does not have the cohesion it had under Rayburn, but its partisan composition does show the narrow geographic and demographic base from which the state's Republicans made their 1978 triumphs: of its 24 members, 20 are Democrats and four Republicans. There had been hopes that Republicans would pick up more open districts, but they failed to win any except two which include large affluent sections of major cities. For the first time the Republicans have a real opportunity to frame the issues in this state and to make their point of view prevail with the great majority. But they begin with a narrow base, and it is not clear whether they will be able to win the kind of victory they want.

Census Data Pop. 11,196,730; 5.53% of U.S. total, 4th largest; Central city, 48%; suburban, 25%. Median family income, $8,486; 33d highest; families above $15,000: 17%; families below $3,000: 13%. Median years education, 11.7.

1977 Share of Federal Tax Burden $18,963,000,000; 5.49% of U.S. total, 5th largest.

1977 Share of Federal Outlays $20,196,082,000; 5.10% of U.S. total, 3d largest. Per capita federal spending, $1,651.

DOD	$6,353,241,000	2d (6.96%)	HEW	$6,827,904,000	6th (4.62%)
ERDA	$58,621,000	18th (0.99%)	HUD	$245,803,000	4th (5.83%)
NASA	$349,623,000	2d (8.86%)	VA	$1,024,353,000	3d (5.33%)
DOT	$575,944,000	5th (4.03%)	EPA	$171,738,000	15th (2.09%)
DOC	$185,016,000	12th (2.23%)	RevS	$364,162,000	5th (4.31%)
DOI	$65,687,000	18th (1.41%)	Debt	$601,298,000	8th (2.00%)
USDA	$1,248,979,000	3d (6.28%)	Other	$2,123,713,000	

Economic Base Finance, insurance and real estate; agriculture, notably cattle, sorghum grain, cotton lint and dairy products; transportation equipment, especially aircraft; food and kindred products, especially meat products; oil and gas extraction, especially oil and gas field services; boys' furnishings; machinery, especially construction and related machinery.

Political Line-up Governor, Bill Clements (R). Senators, John G. Tower (R) and Lloyd M. Bentsen (D). Representatives, 24 (20 D and 4 R). State Senate (28 D and 3 R); State House (130 D and 20 R).

The Voters

Registration 5,681,875 Total. No party registration.
Median voting age 41
Employment profile White collar, 49%. Blue collar, 34%. Service, 13%. Farm, 4%.
Ethnic groups Black, 12%. Spanish, 18%. Total foreign stock, 11%.

Presidential vote

1976	Carter (D)	2,082,319	(52%)
	Ford (R)	1,953,300	(48%)
1972	Nixon (R)	2,298,896	(67%)
	McGovern (D)	1,154,289	(33%)

1976 Democratic Presidential Primary

Carter slate	(48%)
Bentsen slate	(22%)
Wallace slate	(17%)
Other	(13%)

1976 Republican Presidential Primary

Reagan slate	(66%)
Ford slate	(34%)

Sen. John Tower (R) Elected May 27, 1961, seat up 1984; b. Sept. 29, 1925, Houston; home, Wichita Falls; Southwestern U., B.A. 1948, U. of London, 1952, SMU, M.A., 1953; Methodist.

Career Navy, WWII; Prof. of Government, Midwestern U., 1951–61.

Offices 142 RSOB, 202-224-2934. Also 961 Fed. Ofc. Bldg., 300 E. 8th St., Austin 78701, 512-397-5933, and Fed. Bldg., 1114 Commerce St., Dallas 75202, 214-749-7525.

Committees *Armed Services* (Ranking Member). Subcommittees: Arms Control; General Procurement; Military Construction and Stockpiles.

Banking, Housing, and Urban Affairs (2d). Subcommittees: Housing and Urban Affairs; Financial Institutions; Economic Stabilization.

Rules and Administration (3d).

Select Committee on Ethics.

Group Ratings

	ADA	COPE	PC	RPN	NFU	LCV	CFA	NAB	NSI	ACA	NTU
1978	10	6	13	75	67	0	15	60	100	86	–
1977	15	11	5	64	55	–	4	–	–	96	34
1976	5	11	1	53	25	4	0	83	100	92	67

Key Votes

1) Warnke Nom	AGN	6) Egypt-Saudi Arms	FOR	11) Hosptl Cost Contnmnt	AGN
2) Neutron Bomb	FOR	7) Draft Restr Pardon	AGN	12) Clinch River Reactor	FOR
3) Waterwy User Fee	AGN	8) Wheat Price Support	FOR	13) Pub Fin Cong Cmpgns	AGN
4) Dereg Nat Gas	FOR	9) Panama Canal Treaty	AGN	14) ERA Ratif Recissn	AGN
5) Kemp-Roth	FOR	10) Labor Law Rev Clot	AGN	15) Med Necssy Abrtns	FOR

Election Results

1978 general	John G. Tower (R)	1,151,376	(50%)
	Robert Krueger (D)	1,139,149	(50%)
1978 primary	John G. Tower (R)	142,202	(100%)
1972 general	John G. Tower (R)	1,822,877	(55%)
	Barefoot Sanders (D)	1,511,985	(45%)

Sen. Lloyd Bentsen (D) Elected 1970, seat up 1982; b. Feb. 11, 1921, Mission; home, Houston; U. of Tex., LL.B. 1942; Presbyterian.

Career Army Air Corps, WWII; Judge, Hidalgo Co., 1946; U.S. House of Reps., 1949–55; Pres., Lincoln Consolidated, financial holding co.

Offices 240 RSOB, 202-224-5922. Also Fed. Bldg., Rm. 912, Austin 78701, 512-397-5834, and Fed. Bldg., Houston 77002, 713-226-5496.

Committees *Environment and Public Works* (4th).

Finance (7th). Subcommittees: Taxation and Debt Management Generally; Pension Plans and Employee Fringe Benefits (Chairman); Revenue Sharing, Intergovernmental Revenue Impact, and Economic Problems.

Group Ratings

	ADA	COPE	PC	RPN	NFU	LCV	CFA	NAB	NSI	ACA	NTU
1978	35	26	25	56	67	41	30	67	50	57	–
1977	30	60	23	56	55	–	24	–	–	48	29
1976	15	40	18	36	82	18	7	40	75	47	46

Key Votes

1) Warnke Nom	FOR	6) Egypt-Saudi Arms	FOR	11) Hosptl Cost Contnmnt	AGN
2) Neutron Bomb	FOR	7) Draft Restr Pardon	AGN	12) Clinch River Reactor	FOR
3) Waterwy User Fee	DNV	8) Wheat Price Support	FOR	13) Pub Fin Cong Cmpgns	AGN
4) Dereg Nat Gas	FOR	9) Panama Canal Treaty	FOR	14) ERA Ratif Recissn	AGN
5) Kemp-Roth	AGN	10) Labor Law Rev Clot	AGN	15) Med Necssy Abrtns	FOR

Election Results

1976 general	Lloyd Bentsen (D)	2,199,956	(57%)	($1,237,910)
	Alan Steelman (R)	1,636,370	(43%)	($665,058)
1976 primary	Lloyd Bentsen (D), unopposed			
1970 general	Lloyd Bentsen (D)	1,226,568	(53%)	
	George Bush (R)	1,071,234	(47%)	

Gov. Bill Clements (R) Elected 1978, term expires Jan. 1983; b. April 13, 1917, Dallas; S.M.U.; Episcopalian.

Career Oil driller, 1937–47; Founder, Chmn. of Bd., Chief Exec. Officer, SEDCO, Inc., 1947–.

Offices Austin 78711, 512-475-2731.

Election Results

1978 general	Bill Clements (R)	1,183,839	(50%)
	John L. Hill (D)	1,166,979	(50%)
1978 primary	Bill Clements (R)	115,345	(73%)
	Ray Hutchison (R)	38,268	(24%)
	One other (R)	4,790	(3%)
1974 general	Dolph Briscoe (D)	1,016,334	(63%)
	Jim Granberry (R)	514,725	(32%)
	Ramsey Muniz (La Raza Unida)	93,295	(6%)

FIRST DISTRICT

The 1st district of Texas is the northeast corner of the state. This is not part of the gleaming new urban Texas; the cities here are places like Marshall, Paris, and the Texas half of Texarkana, with 30,000 people the largest city in the district. The character of this part of Texas has remained agricultural. It is the part of the state geographically closest to the Deep South, and one of the parts of the state spiritually closest also: it nearly gave a plurality of its votes to George Wallace in 1968. This is also a part of the South where the populist tradition retains at least a little validity. Like Jim Hogg, the populist Governor of Texas in the 1890s, the farmers and townspeople of the 1st are suspicious of bankers, insurance companies, oil men, and Republicans.

Those feelings were exemplified in the congressional career of Wright Patman, who was the 1st's Congressman for nearly 50 years. Elected in 1928, he soon made history by moving for the impeachment of Treasury Secretary Andrew Mellon; toward the end of his career, in 1972, he tried to launch an investigation of Watergate just before the election. Both efforts failed, though their ultimate goals were achieved. Patman was Chairman of the House Banking Committee for many years, and irritated big bankers greatly; but he did not change their business practices as much as he would have liked to.

Patman was ousted from his chairmanship after the 1974 election by the Democratic Caucus; younger members didn't mind his politics, but they felt he was too old to run the committee effectively and would not be an effective spokesman for them on national television. He died in June 1976, and his successor had been chosen effectively in the runoff that had just been held. The winner was Sam Hall, a Democrat who had run against Patman in 1972 and had a local following around his home town of Marshall. Hall's voting record shows little trace of Patman's kind of populism; indeed, he tends to vote as often with Republicans as with his fellow Democrats. He was reelected without difficulty in 1978.

Census Data Pop. 466,545. Central city, 7%; suburban, 8%. Median family income, $6,543; families above $15,000: 8%; families below $3,000: 21%. Median years education, 10.6.

The Voters

Median voting age 49.
Employment profile White collar, 37%. Blue collar, 44%. Service, 13%. Farm, 6%.
Ethnic groups Black, 22%. Spanish, 1%. Total foreign stock, 1%.

Presidential vote

1976	Carter (D)	104,400	(60%)
	Ford (R)	69,297	(40%)
1972	Nixon (R)	100,495	(70%)
	McGovern (D)	42,139	(30%)

Rep. Sam B. Hall, Jr. (D) Elected June 19, 1976; b. Jan. 11, 1924, Marshall; home, Marshall; E. Tex. Baptist Col., B.A. 1942, U. of Tex., 1942–43, Baylor U., LL.B. 1948; Church of Christ.

Career Air Force, WWII; Practicing atty., 1948–76.

Offices 318 CHOB, 202-225-3035. Also P.O. Box 1349, Marshall 75670, 214-938-8386.

Committees *Judiciary* (12th). Subcommittees: Criminal Justice; Immigration, Refugees, and International Law.

Veterans' Affairs (11th). Subcommittees: Compensation, Pension, Insurance, and Memorial Affairs; Medical Facilities and Benefits.

Group Ratings

	ADA	COPE	PC	RPN	NFU	LCV	CFA	NAB	NSI	ACA	NTU
1978	20	15	20	55	30	–	27	91	80	92	–
1977	5	19	8	17	50	5	15	–	–	85	52
1976	0	29	15	0	0	14	20	50	–	100	100

Key Votes

1) Increase Def Spnd	FOR	6) Alaska Lands Protect	AGN	11) Delay Auto Pol Cntrl	FOR
2) B-1 Bomber	FOR	7) Water Projects Veto	AGN	12) Sugar Price Escalator	FOR
3) Cargo Preference	FOR	8) Consum Protect Agcy	AGN	13) Pub Fin Cong Cmpgns	AGN
4) Dereg Nat Gas	FOR	9) Common Situs Picket	AGN	14) ERA Ratif Recissn	FOR
5) Kemp-Roth	AGN	10) Labor Law Revision	AGN	15) Prohibt Govt Abrtns	FOR

Election Results

1978 general	Sam B. Hall, Jr. (D)	73,708	(78%)	($44,229)
	Fred Hudson (R)	20,700	(22%)	($76,520)
1978 primary	Sam B. Hall, Jr. (D), unopposed			
1976 general	Sam B. Hall, Jr. (D)	135,384	(84%)	($216,184)
	James Hogan (R)	26,334	(16%)	($12,881)

SECOND DISTRICT

The 2d congressional district of Texas is an almost entirely rural and small town part of east Texas; the largest cities here are Orange and Lufkin, neither with more than 25,000 people. More than any other Texas district, the 2d is an extension of the Deep South. Farmers from that region first settled this none too fertile land; their lot was a hard one, and residents of this part of east Texas retain a streak of populism. During the thirties, it was here in the 2d district that the first really big Texas oil strikes were made. But for the most part the money seems to have gone elsewhere, to Houston and Dallas and to small east Texas oil cities like Tyler and Longview. Farming and lumber—the kind of scrubby pine that grows rapidly in the humid South—remain the important industries here.

The 2d district elects one of the politically canniest members of the traditionally shrewd Texas delegation, Congressman Charles Wilson. Wilson has been known since his days in the state Senate as some kind of liberal; his voting record on economic issues generally is in accord with northern Democrats. On oil matters he is, of course, a loyal Texan. He has gotten away with this voting record in even the most conservative years with a personal hell of a fellow style which has always been effective in east Texas campaigns. He first won the seat in 1972, when the incumbent, John Dowdy had been indicted and convicted on bribery charges; Wilson easily beat Dowdy's wife, who was running as a stand-in.

Wilson is an aggressive and ambitious Congressman. He elbowed the more senior Richard White of the 16th district aside to win a seat on the Appropriations Committee. He has looked after interests in his district carefully, and has been active on national energy legislation. Wilson is a savvy political operator, and has been mentioned as a possible candidate for the Senate. More likely, with his increasing seniority and with the increasing difficulty Democrats are having winning statewide elections in Texas, he will stay in the House.

Census Data Pop. 466,565. Central city, 5%; suburban, 28%. Median family income, $7,259; families above $15,000: 10%; families below $3,000: 19%. Median years education, 10.5.

The Voters

Median voting age 44.
Employment profile White collar, 38%. Blue collar, 44%. Service, 14%. Farm, 4%.
Ethnic groups Black, 20%. Spanish, 3%. Total foreign stock, 2%.

Presidential vote

1976	Carter (D)	105,487	(58%)
	Ford (R)	76,438	(42%)
1972	Nixon (R)	96,398	(68%)
	McGovern (D)	46,325	(32%)

Rep. Charles Wilson (D) Elected 1972; b. June 1, 1933, Trinity; home, Lufkin; Sam Houston St. U., U.S. Naval Acad., B.S. 1956; Methodist.

Career Navy, 1956–60; Mgr., retail lumber store; Tex. House of Reps., 1961–66; Tex. Senate, 1967–72.

Offices 1214 LHOB, 202-225-2401. Also Fed. Bldg., Lufkin 75901, 713-634-8247.

Committees *Appropriations* (25th). Subcommittees: District of Columbia (Chairman); Foreign Operations.

Group Ratings

	ADA	COPE	PC	RPN	NFU	LCV	CFA	NAB	NSI	ACA	NTU
1978	35	68	30	75	40	–	9	36	75	50	–
1977	25	75	28	33	82	47	25	–	–	26	34
1976	20	71	43	50	56	34	45	0	60	40	28

Key Votes

1) Increase Def Spnd	FOR	6) Alaska Lands Protect	AGN	11) Delay Auto Pol Cntrl	FOR
2) B-1 Bomber	FOR	7) Water Projects Veto	AGN	12) Sugar Price Escalator	DNV
3) Cargo Preference	FOR	8) Consum Protect Agcy	AGN	13) Pub Fin Cong Cmpgns	AGN
4) Dereg Nat Gas	AGN	9) Common Situs Picket	FOR	14) ERA Ratif Recissn	AGN
5) Kemp-Roth	AGN	10) Labor Law Revision	FOR	15) Prohibt Govt Abrtns	AGN

Election Results

1978 general	Charles Wilson (D)	66,986	(70%)	($218,901)
	James Dillon (R)	28,584	(30%)	($7,091)
1978 primary	Charles Wilson (D), unopposed			
1976 general	Charles Wilson (D)	133,910	(95%)	($106,983)
	James William Doyle III (A)	6,992	(5%)	($2,110)

THIRD DISTRICT

The rich Texan in all the old rich Texan jokes probably lives on the north side of Dallas. This is where the late right wing oilman H.L. Hunt lived in his larger than life copy of Mount Vernon, and where other millionaires live in mansions or in pleasant colonial houses on tree-shaded streets. The north side is also the fastest growing part of the Dallas-Fort Worth metroplex. Affluence has pushed the boundaries of development northward, past the Dallas city limits through suburbs like Irving, Farmers Branch, and Richardson, and on into the southern edges of Collin and Denton Counties. Along with most of north Dallas, these suburban areas form the 3d congressional district of Texas.

Dallas is the older and probably the more conservative of Texas's two largest cities. Its initial wealth was based not on oil, which was not discovered in Texas till the turn of the century, but on cotton; indeed, Texas is today one of the major cotton-producing states. By 1900 Dallas was already the banking, financial, and insurance center for the cotton business in Texas; nearby Fort Worth was the urban center of the state's other major industry, cattle. Dallas has continued to be the financial center of Texas and much of the Southwest, though it has strong competition from Houston; it has also continued to be an entrepreneurial center of some note. Of course many of the hugely successful new businesses here are oil-related, like William Clements's oil drilling company; but there are also diverse Dallas-based businesses from giants like Texas Instruments to the well-known retailer Neiman Marcus.

The north side of Dallas and the west side of Houston—basically the areas within the 3d and 7th congressional districts—are not only the most prosperous parts of the state, they seem increasingly to be the most intellectually influential. The old traditions of Texas populism—the farmers' distrust of banks and insurance companies—seem increasingly to be a thing of the past. Unlike wealthy people in the Northeast, rich people in north Dallas do not feel that they have done something bad because they have gotten rich. People here still believe in free markets and that success goes to those who earn it. And unlike much of the rest of affluent America, these are people who believe that things are getting better, that a strong and vibrant future for America is more than a distinct possibility, and that technology and economic growth can produce a better life for all. They do not see the world through Malthusian or Marxist eyes, and they seem to be convincing at least the majority of Texans who do not share all their affluence that their view is the correct one.

Dallas is a free enterprise city, which has little use for big government; and obviously a career in government is not a major aspiration here. This becomes clear when one contrasts the number of bright, articulate people who must live within the 3d district with the congressional representation the seat has had. In the fifties it was represented by a Republican best known for shoving Lyndon and Lady Bird Johnson in a Dallas hotel in the 1960 campaign. Later it was represented by an old-style—rotund, garrulous, bibulous—Democrat named Joe Pool. Since the 1968 election the Congressman has been James Collins, a Republican and successful businessman. He votes a predictably conservative line, and has taken some leadership role in recent years. He is routinely reelected every two years, if indeed he has any opposition at all.

Census Data Pop. 466,266. Central city, 54%; suburban, 46%. Median family income, $13,395; families above $15,000: 41%; families below $3,000: 4%. Median years education, 12.9.

The Voters

Median voting age 39.
Employment profile White collar, 74%. Blue collar, 19%. Service, 7%. Farm, –%.
Ethnic groups Black, 1%. Spanish, 5%. Total foreign stock, 8%. Germany, 1%.

Presidential vote

1976	Carter (D)	NA	
	Ford (R)	NA	
1972	Nixon (R)	174,319	(80%)
	McGovern (D)	43,972	(20%)

Rep. James M. Collins (R) Elected Aug. 24, 1968; b. Apr. 29, 1916, Hallsville; home, Dallas; SMU, B.S.C., 1937, Northwestern U., M.B.A. 1938, American Col., C.L.U., 1940, Harvard U., M.B.A. 1943; Baptist.

Career Army, WWII; Pres., Consolidated Industries, Inc., and Internatl. Industries, Inc.; Pres., Fidelity Union Life Ins. Co., 1954–65.

Offices 2419 RHOB, 202-225-4201. Also 12900 Preston Rd., Dallas 75230, 214-767-4848.

Committees *Interstate and Foreign Commerce* (5th). Subcommittees: Energy and Power; Communications.

Group Ratings

	ADA	COPE	PC	RPN	NFU	LCV	CFA	NAB	NSI	ACA	NTU
1978	10	5	23	83	0	–	23	100	90	96	–
1977	5	4	23	69	17	30	15	–	–	100	72
1976	0	13	8	53	8	9	0	100	90	96	75

Key Votes

1) Increase Def Spnd	FOR	6) Alaska Lands Protect	AGN	11) Delay Auto Pol Cntrl	FOR
2) B-1 Bomber	FOR	7) Water Projects Veto	FOR	12) Sugar Price Escalator	FOR
3) Cargo Preference	AGN	8) Consum Protect Agcy	AGN	13) Pub Fin Cong Cmpgns	AGN
4) Dereg Nat Gas	FOR	9) Common Situs Picket	AGN	14) ERA Ratif Recissn	FOR
5) Kemp-Roth	FOR	10) Labor Law Revision	AGN	15) Prohibt Govt Abrtns	FOR

Election Results

1978 general	James M. Collins (R), unopposed			($80,442)
1978 primary	James M. Collins (R), unopposed			
1976 general	James M. Collins (R)	171,343	(74%)	($137,306)
	Lee E. Shackelford (D)	60,070	(26%)	($8,736)

FOURTH DISTRICT

The 4th congressional district of Texas is part of the Red River Valley. This land was settled, on the Texas side, more than a century ago, and soon became thickly populated; it has some of the best farm land in the state. The district remains largely agricultural today, except to the extent that the Dallas-Fort Worth metroplex is growing and reaching out to take over farming acreage. This is the part of Texas where the Deep South turns into the Southwest. The 1st district, just to the east, is 22% black; the 4th is 15% black; the 13th district, to the west, is 5% black. For the most part the 4th is still peopled by small farmers and the residents of the small towns.

From the days of its first settlement, with only the most minor of exceptions, the Red River Valley has been staunchly Democratic. It has also produced some of the nation's leading Democratic politicians. From the Oklahoma side of the river came Carl Albert, Speaker of the House from 1971 to 1977, and from the Texas side came Sam Rayburn, Speaker except during periods of Republican control from 1940 to 1961 and Congressman from the 4th district from 1913 to 1961. Rayburn's career spans most of our modern political history. When the young Texan was first elected, Henry Adams still lived on Lafayette Park across from the White House. Rayburn saw Washington grow from the provincial outpost disdained by the Boston Brahmin into the most powerful city in the world.

Rayburn entered the House just after it had freed itself from the iron rule of Speaker Joseph Cannon. In 1961, Rayburn went home to die just a few months after he had led and won a struggle to increase the membership of the Rules Committee—an attempt to restore power to the Speaker and to take it away from a reactionary committee chairman. During Rayburn's first term in the House, President Wilson, working with Speaker Champ Clark and Majority Leader Oscar Underwood, enacted the entire Democratic legislative program with automatic votes from the Democratic Caucus. A half century later, the Rules Committee fight exposed all the cracks and fissures that had developed within the caucus since Wilson's time.

"To get along, you have to go along," Mister Sam often said and, in so saying, he admitted that the Democratic Party, split by civil rights and other issues, could no longer operate as a cohesive unit. Members of the party would simply have to take account of the differences among them, and not exacerbate them. Rayburn was Speaker for longer than anyone else in American history. Critics said that he did not use his power often or forcefully enough; Rayburn would have replied that a heavy hand would only have led to irrevocable splits within the Democratic Party.

Sam Rayburn also witnessed nearly all the modern political history of Texas. Back in 1912, Texas was still a state of populist farmers, and big oil money was not yet a factor in its politics. Fifty years later, oil dominated the state in every conceivable way. Rayburn, as much as anyone, built the politics of oil into the congressional establishment. He made certain that the Ways and Means Committee had a solid majority for the oil depletion allowance, for instance. Rayburn was also largely responsible for the cohesion of the Texas delegation, whether the issue was oil, cotton, or military installations. Texas often elected more Democratic congressmen than any other state, and many of them had great seniority; the result was that Texas usually got what it wanted from the federal government.

Oil changed Sam Rayburn's Texas, and so did shifts in population. In 1912, towns like Rayburn's Bonham (1970 pop. 7,698) were typical of the state—small, dusty agricultural market centers. By 1961, Houston and Dallas-Fort Worth were increasingly important, and in that year they helped elect the first Republican senator here since Reconstruction. Today, Bonham is no longer part of Rayburn's 4th district; it was moved to the 1st to satisfy the equal population requirement. As it stands now, two-thirds of the 4th is classified as metropolitan, most of it part of the Dallas-Fort Worth metropolitan area. Since Rayburn's death, the 4th has also come to include the archconservative, heavily Republican oil towns of Tyler and Longview.

Rayburn's successor in the 4th district is Ray Roberts, who was born three weeks after Rayburn was first sworn in. In terms of attitudes, Roberts is similar to the kind of Democrat most rural Texas districts elected in the fifties and sixties: not generally disposed to support national Democratic programs, but willing to be persuaded to do so on occasion. Roberts, now past 65 himself, is Chairman of the Veterans Affairs Committee, but is not considered a legislative power. A senior member of Public Works, he has an encyclopedic knowledge of Texas dams. The increasingly metropolitan nature of this district makes it a natural target for Texas Republicans; although Jimmy Carter carried it narrowly in 1976, it went solidly for William Clements and John Tower in 1978. But so far Republicans have not made a really strong effort here; they will likely do so, however, if Roberts retires.

Census Data Pop. 466,234. Central city, 24%; suburban, 44%. Median family income, $8,032; families above $15,000: 13%; families below $3,000: 14%. Median years education, 11.6.

The Voters

Median voting age 43.
Employment profile White collar, 44%. Blue collar, 38%. Service, 14%. Farm, 4%.
Ethnic groups Black, 15%. Spanish, 3%. Total foreign stock, 3%.

Presidential vote

1976	Carter (D)	87,394	(51%)
	Ford (R)	84,734	(49%)
1972	Nixon (R)	105,236	(72%)
	McGovern (D)	41,471	(28%)

Rep. Ray Roberts (D) Elected Jan. 30, 1962; b. Mar. 28, 1913, Collin County; home, McKinney; Tex. A&M, N. Tex. St., U. of Tex.: Methodist.

Career Dir., Natl. Youth Admin., 1935–40; Staff of U.S. House of Reps. Spkr. Sam Rayburn, 1940–42; Navy, WWII and Korea; Tex. Senate, 1955–62.

Offices 2184 RHOB, 202-225-6673. Also A 105 Fed. Bldg., McKinney 75069, 214-542-2617.

Committees *Veterans' Affairs* (Chairman). Subcommittees: Housing; Education, Training and Employment.

Public Works and Transportation (2d). Subcommittees: Oversight and Review; Surface Transportation; Water Resources (Chairman).

Group Ratings

	ADA	COPE	PC	RPN	NFU	LCV	CFA	NAB	NSI	ACA	NTU
1978	15	22	18	55	30	–	14	75	100	79	–
1977	0	19	18	42	58	9	10	–	–	70	31
1976	15	45	8	24	55	20	18	20	100	80	40

Key Votes

1) Increase Def Spnd	FOR	6) Alaska Lands Protect	DNV	11) Delay Auto Pol Cntrl	FOR
2) B-1 Bomber	FOR	7) Water Projects Veto	AGN	12) Sugar Price Escalator	DNV
3) Cargo Preference	AGN	8) Consum Protect Agcy	AGN	13) Pub Fin Cong Cmpgns	AGN
4) Dereg Nat Gas	FOR	9) Common Situs Picket	AGN	14) ERA Ratif Recissn	FOR
5) Kemp-Roth	AGN	10) Labor Law Revision	AGN	15) Prohibt Govt Abrtns	FOR

Election Results

1978 general	Ray Roberts (D)	58,336	(61%)	($125,814)
	Frank S. Glenn (R)	36,582	(39%)	($80,606)
1978 primary	Ray Roberts (D)	53,540	(68%)	
	Rudy Dockray (D)	14,190	(18%)	($34,610)
	One other (D)	11,420	(14%)	
1976 general	Ray Roberts (D)	105,394	(63%)	($76,102)
	Frank S. Glenn (R)	62,641	(37%)	($87,578)

FIFTH DISTRICT

The 5th congressional district of Texas includes much of the southern and eastern parts of Dallas and its adjacent suburbs. It includes a significant part of Dallas's black population and its relatively small community of Mexican-Americans; but overall the atmosphere is working class white. This is not the glittering north Dallas with its millionaires and swimming pools. It is neighborhoods of frame houses where people who grew up in the country live in air-conditioned comfort. The 5th district contains just about any political strain you can find in Texas. There are ideological liberals, nouveaux riches free market enthusiasts, smug Dallas boosters, black militants, upwardly mobile management types, and union shop stewards. And during the past 20 years just about every strain has been personified by one of the district's congressmen.

The 5th, when it included all of Dallas County, elected Republican Bruce Alger as long ago as 1954; a noisy and sometimes raucous reactionary, he was defeated in 1964 in a wave of remorse over the assassination of President Kennedy. The new Congressman was Earle Cabell, a conservative Democrat and Mayor of Dallas; he had been installed in the latter post by the city's business leaders who for years successfully guided its politics. Cabell was defeated in 1972 by Alan Steelman, a young Republican with experience in private sector business and the Nixon Administration. He personified many young management types: a free enterpriser on economic policy, but an opponent on environmental grounds of a proposal to build a canal from Dallas to the Gulf of Mexico. That latter position was not popular with big money interests in Texas, however; and when Steelman ran for the Senate in 1976 against Lloyd Bentsen, his campaign fizzled when he could not raise enough money.

The current Congressman, Jim Mattox, is a Democrat, who worked summers during college as a dock worker; he has been known in Dallas as a sort of liberal Democrat. On economic issues, he receives better ratings from labor than business groups—though his labor ratings are not nearly as high as those of some other urban Texas Democrats. In the House Mattox has shown considerable political acumen, winning a seat on the Budget Committee as a freshman and emerging as one of the organizers of the 1976 freshman caucus. He has had more political difficulties at home, however. He denounced his 1978 Republican opponent, Tom Pauken, as a "young Nazi," and was caught misquoting Vice President Mondale in a press release. Turnout was not heavy in the 5th. The Republicans profited from the great enthusiasm among upper income voters for the Clements candidacy, and in the Republican neighborhoods of the district turnout was high. But there was little motivating the lower income voters, and so few of them came to the polls that Mattox came very close to being defeated. Accordingly, he can expect tough competition again in 1980, and the outcome may very well depend on the relative enthusiasm the two parties' presidential candidates inspire in their natural constituencies here.

Census Data Pop. 466,620. Central city, 63%; suburban, 37%. Median family income, $9,480; families above $15,000: 17%; families below $3,000: 9%. Median years education, 11.6.

The Voters

Median voting age 38.
Employment profile White collar, 48%. Blue collar, 38%. Service, 14%. Farm, –%.
Ethnic groups Black, 20%. Spanish, 7%. Total foreign stock, 5%.

Presidential vote

1976	Carter (D)	NA	
	Ford (R)	NA	
1972	Nixon (R)	78,522	(64%)
	McGovern (D)	43,354	(36%)

Rep. Jim Mattox (D) Elected 1976; b. Aug. 29, 1943, Dallas; home, Dallas; Baylor U., B.B.A. 1965, S.M.U., J.D. 1968; Baptist.

Career Summer dock worker, 1964–66; Intern for U.S. Rep. Earle Cable, 1967; Asst. Dallas Co. Dist. Atty., 1968–70; Practicing atty., 1970–76; Tex. House of Reps., 1973–77.

Offices 1127 LHOB, 202-225-2231. Also Fed. Bldg., Dallas 75201, 214-749-1771.

Committees *Banking, Finance and Urban Affairs* (23d). Subcommittees: Financial Institutions Supervision, Regulation and Insurance; Domestic Monetary Policy; International Trade, Investment and Monetary Policy.

Budget (9th). Subcommittees: State and Local Government; Inflation; Defense and International Affairs (Chairman).

Group Ratings

	ADA	COPE	PC	RPN	NFU	LCV	CFA	NAB	NSI	ACA	NTU
1978	40	79	68	67	44	–	46	36	60	50	–
1977	60	65	70	54	67	80	45	–	–	30	42

Key Votes

1) Increase Def Spnd	AGN	6) Alaska Lands Protect	FOR	11) Delay Auto Pol Cntrl	AGN
2) B-1 Bomber	AGN	7) Water Projects Veto	FOR	12) Sugar Price Escalator	AGN
3) Cargo Preference	FOR	8) Consum Protect Agcy	FOR	13) Pub Fin Cong Cmpgns	FOR
4) Dereg Nat Gas	FOR	9) Common Situs Picket	FOR	14) ERA Ratif Recissn	AGN
5) Kemp-Roth	AGN	10) Labor Law Revision	FOR	15) Prohibt Govt Abrtns	AGN

Election Results

1978 general	Jim Mattox (D)	35,524	(51%)	($269,015)
	Tom Pauken (R)	34,672	(49%)	($252,047)
1978 primary	Jim Mattox (D), unopposed			
1976 general	Jim Mattox (D)	67,871	(55%)	($257,744)
	Nancy Judy (R)	56,056	(45%)	($145,764)

SIXTH DISTRICT

On the map, the 6th district of Texas looks like a basically rural and small town district. As it stretches south of Dallas and Fort Worth to a point near Houston, the district moves through Waxahachie and Hillsboro to Bryan and College Station, home of Texas A&M. Some blacks live in the rural counties here (they are 10% of the population in the district), as do a few Mexican-Americans (5%). But overall, poor white farmers and their children who have moved to town dominate this part of the 6th. Raised as staunch Democrats, they still vote Democratic from congressman on down. In recent statewide and national elections, however, they have given at least some of their votes to Republicans.

The map of the 6th district is misleading, however. For the majority of the 6th district's population lives in metropolitan areas, and almost precisely half live in either Dallas or Tarrant (Fort Worth) Counties. The shape of the 6th represents the typical response of the Texas legislature to the equal-population rule: rather than eliminate an underpopulated rural district, tack on enough metropolitan territory to preserve the seat for the incumbent.

The incumbent in this case was Olin (Tiger) Teague, a Democrat first elected in a 1946 special election. He was a much decorated and severely wounded combat veteran of World War II; from 1963 to 1973 he was Chairman of the House Veterans Affairs Committee. In 1973 Teague, a strong backer of the space program, moved to the chair of the Science and Aeronautics Committee. After 32 years in Congress, and after a bout of bad health, Teague retired in 1978.

This was one of several Texas districts that were seriously contested following the retirement of incumbents that year. Here the Democratic primary victory went to Phil Gramm, an economics professor at A&M. Gramm had run two years before in the Senate primary against Lloyd Bentsen, without great success; he is an ardent free market man, opposed to practically all forms of government interference. Politically, his backing was in the traditionally Democratic southern counties of the 6th. His opponent, Fort Worth rancher Wes Mowery, had run a weak race against Teague two years before. This time he hoped to win big majorities in the urban areas of the district, but Gramm managed to hold him even there and win by a nearly 2-1 margin overall. Gramm appears to have won himself a safe seat, at least for the foreseeable future. His greatest problem may come in the Democratic primary, in which Gramm might conceivably have tough opposition from a liberal opponent.

Census Data Pop. 466,285. Central city, 44%; suburban, 36%. Median family income, $9,417; families above $15,000: 20%; families below $3,000: 12%. Median years education, 12.0.

The Voters

Median voting age 42.
Employment profile White collar, 53%. Blue collar, 32%. Service, 11%. Farm, 4%.
Ethnic groups Black, 10%. Spanish, 5%. Total foreign stock, 5%.

Presidential vote

1976	Carter (D)	NA	
	Ford (R)	NA	
1972	Nixon (R)	114,865	(72%)
	McGovern (D)	43,610	(28%)

Rep. Phil Gramm (D) Elected 1978; b. July 8, 1942, Ft. Benning, Ga.; home, College Station; U. of Ga., B.B.A. 1964, Ph.D. 1967; Episcopalian.

Career Prof., Tex. A.&M. U., 1967–78.

Offices 1609 LHOB, 202-225-2002. Also Suite 102, 5001 S. Hulen, Ft. Worth 76132, 817-294-2040.

Committees *Interstate and Foreign Commerce* (24th). Subcommittees: Energy and Power; Health and the Environment.

Veterans' Affairs (15th). Subcommittees: Medical Facilities and Benefits; Compensation, Pension, Insurance and Memorial Affairs; Education, Training and Employment.

Group Ratings: Newly Elected

Key Votes

1) Increase Def Spnd	NE	6) Alaska Lands Protect	NE	11) Delay Auto Pol Cntrl	NE
2) B-1 Bomber	NE	7) Water Projects Veto	NE	12) Sugar Price Escalator	NE
3) Cargo Preference	NE	8) Consum Protect Agcy	NE	13) Pub Fin Cong Cmpgns	NE
4) Dereg Nat Gas	NE	9) Common Situs Picket	NE	14) ERA Ratif Recissn	NE
5) Kemp-Roth	NE	10) Labor Law Revision	NE	15) Prohibt Govt Abrtns	NE

Election Results

1978 general	Phil Gramm (D)	66,025	(65%)	($480,778)
	Wesley H. Mowery (R)	35,393	(35%)	($116,386)
1978 run-off	Phil Gramm (D)	23,712	(53%)	
	Ron Godbey (D)	21,169	(47%)	($56,830)
1978 primary	Ron Godbey (D)	23,536	(29%)	
	Phil Gramm (D)	22,271	(27%)	
	Chet Edwards (D)	22,156	(27%)	($85,982)
	Three others (D)	13,038	(16%)	
1976 general	Olin E. Teague (D)	119,025	(66%)	($250,330)
	Wesley H. Mowery (R)	60,316	(34%)	($44,547)

SEVENTH DISTRICT

In the past few years Houston has become widely known as the nation's leading boom city. It is indubitably the center of the American oil industry, and not just because some of the big giants have moved their headquarters there. More important, Houston is the home of hundreds of businesses that service and aid the production, transportation, and refining of oil—as well as the lawyers who try to interpret the government regulations covering it. The signs of Houston's prosperity are instantly and readily apparent to any visitor. There are new skyscrapers, both downtown and on the well-to-do west side, new hotels, new apartment buildings, and countless new residential subdivisions. Houston is proud that it is attracting some of the world's luxury trade—at the Galleria shopping mall you can find Tiffany's, Gucci, etc.—but even more impressive is the wide range of upper and upper middle income stores and services that are thriving here. The big question for the future is whether Houston is fated to be a one-industry town, another Detroit or Pittsburgh, or whether it will build on this decade of growth the way Los Angeles did on the fifties or Chicago on the 1880s and become a true world city.

Most of the visible boom in Houston has occurred on the west side of the city. The downtown sits separately, amid a kind of marginal area, and to the east are the great refineries and the Houston Ship Channel. The west and southwest sides are where virtually all of the upper income people in Houston live. The commercial streets here do not look special: Houston has no zoning laws, and next to a pleasant garden apartment can be a little U-Totem shopping center or a drive-in restaurant. But the neighborhoods behind the main streets preserve their character through protective covenants, and use the lush greenery that thrives in humid Houston to compensate for the uninteresting flatness of the land. The visitor may marvel at the high prices commanded by the mansions of River Oaks or the Memorial Drive area. But there are literally hundreds of newly built subdivisions on the west side of Houston—the city has been expanding its city limits to take part in the growth—where the prices are, by the standards of other large metropolitan areas, quite reasonable.

The 7th congressional district covers most of the west side of Houston, with just a little of the area lying in the neighboring 22d district. This is an area that doubled its population in the sixties and seems to have doubled it again in the seventies. In other words, there were about 250,000 people on the west side of Houston and in adjacent suburban areas in 1960 and there are about 900,000 today. If this is one of the nation's fastest growing districts, it is also one of the highest status: in 1970 a higher percentage of the workers here held white collar jobs than in all but two of the nation's 434 other congressional districts. It is also a very high income district, though it does not rank extraordinarily high by national standards; but then the cost of living is much lower in Texas than in the Northeast or California.

The 7th district has one other superlative: it has become the most Republican congressional district in the United States. Fully 74% of its votes went to Gerald Ford in 1976—more than in any other district. Moreover, it is the home of no less than two competitors for the Republican presidential nomination. One is John Connally, who moved here after serving as Governor of Texas and whose personal style as well as political philosophy expresses the confidence and sense of command affluent Texans have today. The other is George Bush, the transplanted Yankee who served as Republican National Chairman, as Ambassador to the United Nations and chief envoy to Peking, and who was elected the 7th district's Congressman in 1966 and 1968. Bush's father was a partner in the New York investment banking firm of Brown Brothers Harriman, but the son made his money in oil in Texas. He also enunciates the themes one hears again and again from affluent Houstonians. But Bush has never been entirely successful in Texas politics: he was defeated in races for the Senate by liberal Ralph Yarborough in 1964 and moderate Lloyd Bentsen in 1970.

Bush's successor in Congress, Bill Archer, was born and grew up in Texas; he was a successful businessman who was elected to the legislature as a Democrat and then became a Republican. Archer became a member of the Ways and Means Committee after the 1972 election, and there he has been an articulate and effective spokesman for positions backed by the oil industry. On issues generally he seems to represent well the free market ideology that is shared by a large majority of residents of the 7th district. He has been reelected regularly with some of the largest margins in the nation.

Census Data Pop. 466,336. Central city, 77%; suburban, 23%. Median family income, $13,561; families above $15,000: 41%; families below $3,000: 3%. Median years education, 13.0.

The Voters

Median voting age 38.
Employment profile White collar, 77%. Blue collar, 16%. Service, 6%. Farm, 1%.
Ethnic groups Black, 2%. Spanish, 6%. Total foreign stock, 10%. Germany, UK, 1% each.

Presidential vote

1976	Carter (D)	66,790	(26%)
	Ford (R)	186,190	(74%)
1972	Nixon (R)	161,078	(81%)
	McGovern (D)	37,172	(19%)

Rep. Bill Archer (R) Elected 1970; b. Mar. 22, 1928, Houston; home, Houston; Rice U., 1946–46, U. of Tex., B.B.A., LL.B. 1951; Catholic.

Career Air Force, Korea; Pres., Uncle Johnny Mills, Inc., 1953–61; Hunters Creek Village Cncl. and Mayor Pro Tem, 1955–62; Tex. House of Reps., 1966–70; Dir., Heights State Bank, Houston, 1967–70; Practicing atty., 1968–71.

Offices 1024 LHOB, 202-225-2571. Also Suite 5108 Fed. Bldg., 515 Rusk St., Houston 77002, 713-226-4941.

Committees *Ways and Means* (3d). Subcommittees: Social Security; Trade.

Group Ratings

	ADA	COPE	PC	RPN	NFU	LCV	CFA	NAB	NSI	ACA	NTU
1978	10	0	13	83	0	–	4	100	100	100	–
1977	5	4	8	69	25	30	15	–	–	96	51
1976	0	13	8	59	8	3	0	91	90	92	70

Key Votes

1) Increase Def Spnd	FOR	6) Alaska Lands Protect	AGN	11) Delay Auto Pol Cntrl	FOR
2) B-1 Bomber	FOR	7) Water Projects Veto	FOR	12) Sugar Price Escalator	FOR
3) Cargo Preference	AGN	8) Consum Protect Agcy	AGN	13) Pub Fin Cong Cmpgns	AGN
4) Dereg Nat Gas	FOR	9) Common Situs Picket	AGN	14) ERA Ratif Recissn	FOR
5) Kemp-Roth	FOR	10) Labor Law Revision	AGN	15) Prohibt Govt Abrtns	FOR

Election Results

1978 general	Bill Archer (R)	128,214	(85%)	($120,720)
	Robert L. Hutchings (D)	22,415	(15%)	
1978 primary	Bill Archer (R), unopposed			
1976 general	Bill Archer (R), unopposed			($10,751)

EIGHTH DISTRICT

When visitors come to Houston, the home folks like to show the out-of-towners the sights of the city: the gleaming new skyscrapers downtown, the River Oaks mansion of Ima Hogg (daughter of 1890s populist Governor Jim Hogg), Rice University and the vast expanse of the Texas Medical Center, and of course the Astrodome. The drive takes the visitor southwest from downtown; seldom is an outsider escorted to the east and northeast parts of the city. Here are the industrial and working class sections of Houston that make up Texas's 8th congressional district. Here the tremendous growth of petrochemical and oil industries has produced some of the nation's worst air pollution. From a downtown high rise, you can look out across the flat Texas plains, but the view of east Houston is obscured by a smoggy haze. Below the smog flows the sluggish Houston

Ship Channel, a marvel of engineering that made this inland city a major American port. The waterway is so full of sludge and effluent from the chemical plants and refineries that the Ship Channel is something of a fire hazard.

The 8th district is mostly white working class, though some 19% of its residents are black. This part of Houston has not experienced the kind of growth that has hit the west side of town. There are no shopping centers with kicky boutiques and expensive chocolate stores. The houses here often do not have air conditioning, and they are often within sight (or smell) of chemical plants and refineries. Most people in the 8th are natives of the Texas countryside or some other part of the rural South. Their politics combines populism and racial fears—neither evident in the politics of the west side 7th district—as demonstrated in the 1968 presidential election: 46% for Humphrey, 28% for Wallace, and only 26% for Nixon.

The 8th district once included all of Houston's Harris County and was represented by Albert Thomas, a savvy Democrat who chaired the subcommittee controlling appropriations for the space program. More than anyone else, Thomas brought the space program to the Houston area. The current Congressman, Bob Eckhardt, has quite different interests. He is one of that hardy and always endangered breed, the Texas liberal. Before coming to Congress, he spent eight years in the Texas legislature, where he fought valiantly, though usually without success, for what he believed. He continues to do so in Congress. Liberals from other parts of the country tend to get discouraged during a losing streak, and even drop out of politics; Texas liberals, who never expect to win anything anyway, fight on—and keep their sense of humor, too. Traditionally, Texas congressmen have preferred to work in the cloakrooms, whispering quietly to each other. Eckhardt, sporting a bow tie and a brightly colored shirt, does most of his work in committee sessions and on the floor. He is a longtime trial lawyer and the possessor of one of the rare eloquences in the House; he has the gift, too, of being able to explain arcane legal matters lucidly and persuasively.

Eckhardt was first elected in 1966, and now he is one of the higher ranking members of the House Commerce Committee. He used to chair the Consumer Protection Subcommittee; now he heads the Oversight and Investigations Subcommittee—potentially one of the most important panels in Congress. Despite his high rank and considerable talents, Eckhardt has not been all that successful legislatively, although he was able to extend the life of the Consumer Product Safety Commission. The problem for Eckhardt was that in the 95th Congress opinion was moving away from him; not only were many members not ready to support the kind of measures he backed, it seemed that fewer were prepared to do so than in previous years. Eckhardt is not likely to be discouraged, however. He is a man whose politics is bottomed on a strong philosophy and much scholarship, and when he feels compelled to he will go against the crowd. He is the only Texas congressman who votes consistently against the oil companies, he is one of the few House liberals who voted against the extension for the Equal Rights Amendment, and he is a trial lawyer who supports no fault insurance.

Eckhardt used to be reelected without difficulty; this is, after all, a district that went 63% for Carter while the 7th district, across town, was 74% for Ford. A well financed Republican opponent in 1976 and 1978 did not get very far. However, a conservative primary opponent held Eckhardt to 53% of the vote in 1978—a perilously low level of support for a long-time incumbent. Eckhardt is not one of those young congressmen who spends all his time returning to the district and sending out mail to his constituents; and he turns 67 in 1980. He may have a difficult election that year.

Census Data Pop. 466,704. Central city, 48%; suburban, 52%. Median family income, $9,555; families above $15,000: 15%; families below $3,000: 9%. Median years education, 10.9.

The Voters

Median voting age 39.
Employment profile White collar, 40%. Blue collar, 47%. Service, 13%. Farm, –%.
Ethnic groups Black, 19%. Spanish, 10%. Total foreign stock, 7%.

Presidential vote

1976	Carter (D)	89,254	(63%)
	Ford (R)	52,248	(37%)
1972	Nixon (R)	66,870	(55%)
	McGovern (D)	54,313	(45%)

Rep. Bob Eckhardt (D) Elected 1966; b. July 16, 1913, Austin; home, Harris County; U. of Tex., B.A. 1935, LL.B. 1939; Presbyterian.

Career Practicing atty., 1939–42, 1944–67; Army Air Corps, WWII; Tex. House of Reps., 1958–66.

Offices 1741 LHOB, 202-225-4901. Also 8632 Fed. Bldg., 515 Rusk St., Houston 77002, 713-226-4931.

Committees *Interior and Insular Affairs* (9th). Subcommittees: Energy and the Environment; Public Lands; Water and Power Resources; National Parks and Insular Affairs.

Interstate and Foreign Commerce (6th). Subcommittees: Oversight and Investigations (Chairman).

Group Ratings

	ADA	COPE	PC	RPN	NFU	LCV	CFA	NAB	NSI	ACA	NTU
1978	75	89	83	40	78	–	59	0	11	4	–
1977	90	91	75	46	92	87	75	–	–	0	45
1976	75	87	87	47	100	84	81	0	10	4	30

Key Votes

1) Increase Def Spnd	AGN	6) Alaska Lands Protect	FOR	11) Delay Auto Pol Cntrl	AGN
2) B-1 Bomber	AGN	7) Water Projects Veto	FOR	12) Sugar Price Escalator	AGN
3) Cargo Preference	FOR	8) Consum Protect Agcy	FOR	13) Pub Fin Cong Cmpgns	FOR
4) Dereg Nat Gas	AGN	9) Common Situs Picket	FOR	14) ERA Ratif Recissn	FOR
5) Kemp-Roth	AGN	10) Labor Law Revision	FOR	15) Prohibt Govt Abrtns	AGN

Election Results

1978 general	Bob Eckhardt (D)	39,429	(62%)	✓	($285,214)
	Nick Gearhart (R)	24,673	(38%)		($139,102)
1978 primary	Bob Eckhardt (D)	20,719	(54%)		
	Joe Archer (D)	17,962	(46%)		($175,049)
1976 general	Bob Eckhardt (D)	84,404	(61%)		($125,587)
	Nick Gearhart (R)	54,566	(39%)		($302,587)

NINTH DISTRICT

The 9th congressional district of Texas is the eastern segment of the state's Gulf Coast—an area of big refineries, petrochemical plants, and other factories. It is, in other words, an area dominated by heavy, oil-related industry, and it has one of the highest concentrations of blue collar workers in Texas. It is dominated by two urban centers of roughly equal size. On Galveston Bay, which leads into the Houston Ship Channel, are the cities of Galveston and Texas City. Galveston, one of the oldest cities in Texas, is situated on a sand bar where the bay empties into the Gulf of Mexico. It was the state's first port, but now handles far less tonnage than Houston or Texas City. The other major population center in the 9th is around the oil and petrochemical cities of Beaumont and Port Arthur. These are in the southeastern corner of the state, where there is a little Louisiana Cajun influence.

Most of the residents of this district are migrants, recent or otherwise, from the rural South. Some 22% are black, and another 6% are Cajun. To a surprising extent people here have retained populistic Democratic voting habits. This is probably the most unionized part of generally non-union Texas, and the labor movement here inspires much more loyalty among its members than it does in large industrial states with large union membership. The 9th has stayed Democratic in statewide races, even in 1978, and Jimmy Carter won a solid 59% here in 1976.

The district's Congressman is Democrat Jack Brooks. He has served in the House since the 1952 election, and for the most part he has a voting record in line with the Democratic leadership. He is not always a liberal on non-economic issues, but he has always been a supporter of civil rights measures; he voted for the 1964 Civil Rights Act when his district included some east Texas counties with attitudes very similar to the Deep South. On policy matters and in personality also, Jack Brooks is probably more similar to Lyndon Johnson than any other current member of Congress.

Brooks is extremely partisan, profane, knowledgeable, witty, effective—all qualities he shares with Johnson. They all came out in the House Judiciary Committee hearings on the impeachment of Richard Nixon. Brooks was then the third-ranking Democrat on the committee, and is now second behind Chairman Peter Rodino. But his most important post today is the chair of the Government Operations Committee. This is the body which has jurisdiction over the Carter Administration's government reorganization plans. Brooks opposed Carter's bill which allows the president to institute changes unless one house of Congress votes them down within 30 days; the Chairman felt it was unconstitutional, and of course it would deprive his committee of much clout. But Brooks carried few votes with him, and it is not at all clear that he wants to stop any specific reorganization programs.

The larger question for Brooks is what he will do with Government Operations. This is a committee with broad jurisdiction to look into the workings of just about any agency of government; if its legislative power is limited, its investigative power has the capacity to make it the center of national attention. It was Government Operations subcommittees in the Senate which held the McCarthy hearings and the McClellan hearings on the Teamsters in the fifties. But it is harder to get the press to notice the House, and recent Government Operations chairmen have not used the committee to its full potential. It is not clear that Brooks has ambitious plans for the committee; he is a man who likes to get things done, but is not by temperament a reformer. In the 9th district he is reelected every two years without much fuss.

Census Data Pop. 466,678. Central city, 60%; suburban, 38%. Median family income, $9,344; families above $15,000: 17%; families below $3,000: 11%. Median years education, 11.5.

The Voters

Median voting age 42.
Employment profile White collar, 45%. Blue collar, 40%. Service, 14%. Farm, 1%.
Ethnic groups Black, 22%. Spanish, 7%. Total foreign stock, 7%.

Presidential vote

1976	Carter (D)	97,800	(59%)
	Ford (R)	67,280	(41%)
1972	Nixon (R)	86,079	(60%)
	McGovern (D)	58,117	(40%)

Rep. Jack Brooks (D) Elected 1952; b. Dec. 18, 1922, Crowley, La; home, Beaumont; Lamar Jr. Col., 1939–41, U. of Tex., B.J. 1943, J.D. 1949; Methodist.

Career USMC, WWII; Tex. House of Reps., 1946–50; Practicing atty., 1949–52.

Offices 2449 RHOB, 202-225-6565. Also 230 Fed. Bldg., Beaumont 77701, 713-838-0271.

Committees *Government Operations* (Chairman). Subcommittees: Legislation and National Security (Chairman).

Judiciary (2d). Subcommittees: Monopolies and Commercial Law.

Group Ratings

	ADA	COPE	PC	RPN	NFU	LCV	CFA	NAB	NSI	ACA	NTU
1978	30	45	38	45	50	–	36	58	80	40	–
1977	15	68	33	31	64	21	50	–	–	31	28
1976	30	77	41	44	58	43	45	8	88	33	14

Key Votes

1) Increase Def Spnd	AGN	6) Alaska Lands Protect	FOR	11) Delay Auto Pol Cntrl	DNV
2) B-1 Bomber	AGN	7) Water Projects Veto	AGN	12) Sugar Price Escalator	AGN
3) Cargo Preference	FOR	8) Consum Protect Agcy	FOR	13) Pub Fin Cong Cmpgns	AGN
4) Dereg Nat Gas	FOR	9) Common Situs Picket	FOR	14) ERA Ratif Recissn	FOR
5) Kemp-Roth	AGN	10) Labor Law Revision	FOR	15) Prohibt Govt Abrtns	AGN

Election Results

1978 general	Jack Brooks (D)	50,792	(63%)	($80,171)
	Randy Evans (R)	29,473	(37%)	
1978 primary	Jack Brooks (D)	39,470	(70%)	
	Alan Verret (D)	17,178	(30%)	
1976 general	Jack Brooks (D), unopposed			($32,689)

TENTH DISTRICT

The 10th district of Texas is the LBJ congressional district. Here in central Texas the towns are farther apart and the trees less common than in east Texas; the land is less fertile, and there is much less rain. Lyndon Johnson was born and raised and began his political career amid the rolling hills of central Texas, which yield a living only to those who work hard. The 10th district left its mark on Johnson. The comparative poverty of its people—especially back in the thirties, when Johnson was a young man—helped to shape his populistic impulses. And the comparatively good relations here between the Anglo white majority and the black (now 14%) and Mexican-American (also 14%) minorities helped shape the Johnson who would push Congress into passing the Civil Rights Acts of 1964 and 1965.

Johnson in turn has certainly left his imprint on the 10th district. Though its boundaries have changed, the district still includes Johnson City and the LBJ Ranch in Blanco County; Southwest Texas State Teachers College in San Marcos, where Johnson got his degree; and Austin, the state capital, home of the University of Texas, and site of the Lyndon B. Johnson Library. Also in Austin is television station KLBJ—the initial cornerstone of the Johnson family fortune.

Austin has grown substantially since Johnson represented the 10th district. It is now a city of nearly 300,000 people—large enough to dominate a congressional district, but a small town next to Houston or the Dallas-Fort Worth area. Austin is not an oil town or an industrial town or even an agricultural marketing town; economically, its mainstays are state government and higher education. Austin is the home of the state's almost always successful business and oil-oriented lobbyists, but it is also the home of two diverse publications, the very successful *Texas Monthly* and the very liberal *Texas Observer*, which together provide an interesting and continuous view of life in the state.

Unlike Texas's bigger cities, Austin is usually Democratic and liberal in elections. The growing affluent population of the city is Republican, as in most Texas cities, but not by as large a margin. But on the other side is the electorate provided by the University of Texas's 39,000 students. In the early seventies they were solidly liberal; now they seem more into toga parties and afraid that they might not get a job with Exxon. Nevertheless, the students are more likely than their parents to consider voting against a Republican—if they end up voting at all.

Since Lyndon Johnson won this seat in a 1937 special election there have been only three congressmen in this district, all of them Democrats who usually voted with their party's majority in the House and who also were adept at getting things done. When Johnson ran for the Senate in 1948, he was succeeded by Homer Thornberry, who was appointed to the federal bench in 1963. Thornberry's successor in the House is a member in good standing both of the state's Tory Democratic establishment and of the House Democratic Caucus. Congressman Jake Pickle seems sympathetic to the economic interests of Texans, whether they are rich or poor, and like LBJ does not see why there should be any conflict between the two. He is an able and influential member of the Ways and Means Committee. Locally he has never been close to the liberals, who may have worried him by winning local elections in Austin; but he has had no trouble winning reelection easily.

Census Data Pop. 466,313. Central city, 54%; suburban, 9%. Median family income, $7,825; families above $15,000: 16%; families below $3,000: 16%. Median years education, 11.8.

The Voters

Median voting age 39.
Employment profile White collar, 53%. Blue collar, 26%. Service, 16%. Farm, 5%.
Ethnic groups Black, 14%. Spanish, 14%. Total foreign stock, 10%. Germany, 2%; Czech, 1%.

Presidential vote

1976	Carter (D)	115,946	(54%)
	Ford (R)	97,640	(46%)
1972	Nixon (R)	104,400	(59%)
	McGovern (D)	71,161	(41%)

Rep. J. J. Pickle (D) Elected Dec. 17, 1963; b. Oct. 11, 1913, Big Spring; home, Austin; U. of Tex., B.A. 1938; Methodist.

Career Area Dir., Natl. Youth Admin., 1938–41; Navy, WWII; Co-Organizer, KVET radio, Austin; Advertising and public relations business; Dir., Texas State Dem. Exec. Comm., 1957–60; Mbr., Texas Employment Commission, 1961–63.

Offices 242 CHOB, 202-225-4865. Also 763 Fed. Bldg., Austin 78701. 512-397-5921.

Committees *Ways and Means* (6th). Subcommittees: Oversight; Social Security (Chairman).

Group Ratings

	ADA	COPE	PC	RPN	NFU	LCV	CFA	NAB	NSI	ACA	NTU
1978	45	50	35	55	40	–	32	67	70	65	–
1977	10	50	8	25	43	40	15	–	–	58	23
1976	25	57	28	35	25	29	45	42	100	42	32

Key Votes

1) Increase Def Spnd	FOR	6) Alaska Lands Protect	FOR	11) Delay Auto Pol Cntrl	FOR
2) B-1 Bomber	FOR	7) Water Projects Veto	AGN	12) Sugar Price Escalator	AGN
3) Cargo Preference	FOR	8) Consum Protect Agcy	FOR	13) Pub Fin Cong Cmpgns	AGN
4) Dereg Nat Gas	FOR	9) Common Situs Picket	AGN	14) ERA Ratif Recissn	AGN
5) Kemp-Roth	AGN	10) Labor Law Revision	AGN	15) Prohibt Govt Abrtns	DNV

Election Results

1978 general	J. J. Pickle (D)	94,529	(76%)	($46,726)
	Emmett L. Hudspeth (R)	29,328	(24%)	($19,263)
1978 primary	J. J. Pickle (D), unopposed			
1976 general	J. J. Pickle (D)	160,683	(77%)	($45,721)
	Paul McClure (R)	48,482	(23%)	($13,882)

ELEVENTH DISTRICT

The 11th congressional district is deep in the heart of Texas. Made up of all or part of 19 counties, the district sits slightly off the geographical center of the state, but at just about its center of population. The 11th includes two good-sized cities, Waco and Temple, and a huge Army base, Fort Hood. The rest of the district is classic Texas agricultural country, given over to cotton, livestock, and occasional small towns. People here are descended from settlers who came from the Deep South in the nineteenth century; they brought Democratic Party identification with them, and the area has remained Democratic ever since. In 1968, even with George Wallace on the ballot, the 11th gave an absolute majority of its votes to Hubert Humphrey; it left the Democrats over the McGovern candidacy in 1972, but returned with a solid 57% for Jimmy Carter in 1976. This was not a part of the state which went for John Tower and William Clements in 1978.

This is a district that was represented for 42 years by the same Congressman: W.R. (Bob) Poage. Elected at the age of 36, he became Chairman of the House Agriculture Committee; he generally backed the programs of subsidies to major crops, including most notably cotton. Poage was also, in an unsung crusade, the chief advocate in Congress for the humane slaughter of animals. His record on non-agricultural issues in the sixties and seventies was more in line with the Republican leadership than the Democratic. That was one reason the Democratic Caucus stripped him of his chairmanship after the 1974 elections.

In 1976 Republican Jack Burgess won 43% of the vote, and Poage decided to retire two years later. The 11th became one of the Republicans' favorite targets in 1978; unfortunately for them, of all the rural-based Texas districts they were looking at, this was the one with the strongest Democratic tradition. Burgess had hoped to face former Waco state Representative Lane Denton in the general. But Denton's reputation as a liberal already proved fatal to him in the Democratic runoff, in which he lost decisively to businessman Marvin Leath. Once a campaign manager for Poage, Leath was solidly conservative on the issues; the best the Republicans could do was charge him with having voted for Barry Goldwater in 1964. Nevertheless Burgess made this a very close race indeed; in a somewhat more hospitable district, he surely would have won it.

Leath seems like just the kind of congressman this district wants: a non-liberal Democrat. The question for 1980 is whether he will be able to build up sufficient strength to deter strong opposition in the primary and the general election. He could be hurt if the presidential and congressional primaries are held on the same day, because many of his likely supporters will probably take part in the Republican primary for president.

Census Data Pop. 466,258. Central city, 20%; suburban, 11%. Median family income, $6,755; families above $15,000: 10%; families below $3,000: 18%. Median years education, 11.2.

The Voters

Median voting age 43.
Employment profile White collar, 44%. Blue collar, 33%. Service, 15%. Farm, 8%.
Ethnic groups Black, 12%. Spanish, 9%. Total foreign stock, 8%. Germany, 2%.

Presidential vote

1976	Carter (D)	94,548	(57%)
	Ford (R)	71,096	(43%)
1972	Nixon (R)	91,162	(70%)
	McGovern (D)	39,753	(30%)

Rep. Marvin Leath (D) Elected 1978; b. May 6, 1931, Rusk County; home, Marlin; U. of Tex., B.A. 1954; Presbyterian.

Career Army, 1954–56; High School Teacher and Coach, 1956–58; Banker, 1962–72, 1975–78; Spec. Asst. to U.S. Rep. Bob Poage, 1972–75.

Offices 1331 LHOB, 202-225-6105. Also 205 Fed. Bldg., Waco 76701, 817-752-9609.

Committees *Public Works and Transportation* (29th). Subcommittees: Economic Development; Public Buildings and Grounds; Water Resources.

Veterans' Affairs (13th). Subcommittees: Medical Facilities and Benefits; Education, Training and Employment.

Group Ratings: Newly Elected

Key Votes: Newly Elected

Election Results

1978 general	J. Marvin Leath (D)	53,354	(52%)	($588,492)
	Jack Burgess (R)	49,965	(48%)	($320,084)
1978 run-off	J. Marvin Leath (D)	40,261	(55%)	
	Lane Denton (D)	33,029	(45%)	($164,558)
1978 primary	Lane Denton (D)	38,984	(40%)	
	J. Marvin Leath (D)	29,523	(30%)	
	Lyndon Olson, Jr. (D)	22,929	(23%)	($157,139)
	Two others (D)	7,223	(7%)	
1976 general	W. R. Poage (D)	92,142	(57%)	($42,967)
	Jack Burgess (R)	68,373	(43%)	($69,547)

TWELFTH DISTRICT

Between Fort Worth and Dallas, through the new Dallas-Fort Worth Regional Airport and near the Freeway Stadium and Six Flags Over Texas park in the suburb of Arlington, runs an invisible line marking the geological divide known as the Balcones Escarpment. It divides dry west Texas from humid east Texas; it separates the treeless grazing lands that run west from Fort Worth from the green croplands that run east from Dallas. Fort Worth and Dallas are only 30 miles apart, but they are very different cities, from their geology to their recent development and their politics. As the old saying has it, Dallas is the end of the East and Fort Worth is the beginning of the West.

Fort Worth got its start as a cattle town. It was once the western end of the railroad here, and cowboys drove their stock into Fort Worth to have them shipped east. Then Fort Worth built its own railroad, the Texas Pacific, and its own stockyards, the largest in Texas. While Dallas was concentrating on cotton and banking, Fort Worth was concentrating on railroads and meat-packing. Fort Worth developed more as a blue collar town, though of course it had its management class and town fathers; Dallas of course also had its factories, but became more white collar. The differences even extend to recent defense contracts. Dallas tends to produce high technology items; Fort Worth has the General Dynamics assembly plant that produces many of the nation's military aircraft. Dallas residents sometimes look down on Fort Worth and call it Cowtown. But Fort Worth has its own strong civic culture and a set of art museums far superior to any others in Texas. Among them is the Amon Carter Museum of Western Art, the premier collection of its kind; looking west from one of Fort Worth's hills, toward the treeless skyline in the distance, you can almost see some of those scenes come to life again on the high plains.

As the differences between Fort Worth and Dallas suggest, Fort Worth tends to be more Democratic and Dallas more Republican. The difference is a matter of degree. For example, in 1976 Dallas County went 57% for Gerald Ford, while Fort Worth's Tarrant County was almost dead even—50.4% Republican. The results were similar in the close statewide races of 1978. The 12th congressional district, which includes most of Fort Worth and the Tarrant County suburbs to the north, is somewhat more Democratic than the county as a whole. Although it includes Fort Worth's affluent west side neighborhoods, it has generally supported Democrats who in Texas are considered liberal, and that has certainly been true in congressional races.

This is the district which elects Congressman Jim Wright, the House Majority Leader. He was first elected in 1954, and in the fifties he was considered the most liberal member of the Texas delegation. He has remained a strong supporter of national Democratic policies on most economic issues, and has generally had a good labor voting record. But on other issues, he has often parted company with other Democrats. A strong supporter of American policy in Vietnam, he has also been skeptical about many environmental causes. These stances have undoubtedly been in line with majority opinion in his district, and have helped make him more accepted in the Texas delegation. Since his election as Majority Leader, however, his ratings from national liberal groups have increased, as he has gotten more in line with his new constituency in the House Democratic Caucus.

Wright has proven himself again and again as a skilled legislative tactician. He is an adroit and sometimes eloquent speaker, he does his homework, he is pleasant and ingratiating—and he usually wins on issues he concentrates on. He had less luck early in his congressional career when he ran for the Senate. In 1961 he ran for the seat vacated by Lyndon Johnson and just missed making the runoff; if he had he might very well have won, and by now would surely have become an important senator. In 1966 he wanted to run again. But he was unable to raise money from the state's big economic interests. He went on television and asked for $10 contributions, and got a lot of them—but not enough for a Senate race in Texas.

After the 1976 elections, Wright expected to become Chairman of the House Public Works Committee; he was in line for the post under the seniority system and would not have been seriously opposed. He decided also to run for the majority leadership, and at first his chances looked dim. He had the support of the Texas delegation and of some, but by no means all, Southerners, but not much beyond that. But on the second ballot he edged Richard Bolling of Missouri for second place by two votes; on the third he beat Phillip Burton of California, 148-147. Suddenly he was a national figure, summoned regularly to the White House, speaking regularly on national television.

Can Wright become Speaker? Part of his appeal in his present post is the argument that there should be at least one moderate in the Democratic leadership; but that argument is less persuasive if Wright wants to run for the Speakership. Wright's problem is to convince a Democratic Caucus that does not share his views on a number of important issues to trust him to provide the kind of leadership they want. He is sure to have strong opposition—either from Burton and Bolling or from some younger members. In any case, Speaker O'Neill shows no sign of stepping down, and Wright was not challenged for the post after the 1978 elections. He has performed creditably helping O'Neill round up crucial votes, and represents House Democrats forcefully, if grandiloquently, on the national media. He has been reelected every two years in the 12th district without difficulty.

Census Data Pop. 466,930. Central city, 61%; suburban, 39%. Median family income, $9,441; families above $15,000: 18%; families below $3,000: 9%. Median years education, 11.6.

The Voters

Median voting age 41.
Employment profile White collar, 47%. Blue collar, 39%. Service, 13%. Farm, 1%.
Ethnic groups Black, 16%. Spanish, 7%. Total foreign stock, 6%.

Presidential vote

1976	Carter (D)	74,381	(56%)
	Ford (R)	58,562	(44%)
1972	Nixon (R)	75,156	(62%)
	McGovern (D)	45,508	(38%)

Rep. Jim Wright (D) Elected 1954; b. Dec. 22, 1922, Fort Worth; home, Fort Worth; Weatherford Col., U. of Tex.; Presbyterian.

Career Army Air Corps, WWII; Partner, trade extension and advertising firm; Tex. House of Reps.; Mayor of Weatherford; Pres., Tex. League of Municipalities, 1953.

Offices 2459 RHOB, 202-225-5071. Also 1 Fed. Bldg., 819 Taylor St., Fort Worth 76102, 817-334-3212.

Committees *Majority Leader.*

Budget (2d).

Group Ratings

	ADA	COPE	PC	RPN	NFU	LCV	CFA	NAB	NSI	ACA	NTU
1978	35	83	55	40	60	–	36	0	50	29	–
1977	45	95	43	33	80	45	45	–	–	4	31
1976	30	86	39	47	70	25	54	0	90	19	17

Key Votes

1) Increase Def Spnd	FOR	6) Alaska Lands Protect	DNV	11) Delay Auto Pol Cntrl	FOR
2) B-1 Bomber	AGN	7) Water Projects Veto	AGN	12) Sugar Price Escalator	FOR
3) Cargo Preference	FOR	8) Consum Protect Agcy	FOR	13) Pub Fin Cong Cmpgns	FOR
4) Dereg Nat Gas	AGN	9) Common Situs Picket	FOR	14) ERA Ratif Recissn	FOR
5) Kemp-Roth	AGN	10) Labor Law Revision	FOR	15) Prohibt Govt Abrtns	AGN

Election Results

1978 general	Jim Wright (D)	46,456	(68%)	($283,125)
	Claude K. Brown (R)	21,364	(32%)	($12,571)
1978 primary	Jim Wright (D), unopposed			
1976 general	Jim Wright (D)	101,814	(76%)	($49,004)
	W. R. Durham (R)	31,941	(24%)	($2,159)

THIRTEENTH DISTRICT

The 13th congressional district of Texas is an entity which is totally the creation of politics, an amalgam of two old congressional districts which, because of the equal population rule, had to be combined, but which had always been separate and rather different regions. The old 13th district, which forms the eastern part of the current seat, is part of the agricultural land of the Red River Valley; like all of that valley, it is traditionally and heavily Democratic. Typical of the rural territory here is Archer County, where *The Last Picture Show* was filmed. It is dusty land, with empty skylines; it only grudgingly yields a living. Virtually all the people here are white Anglos; few blacks got this far west and few Mexican-Americans this far north. Population has been declining here not only in the rural counties, but also in the district's second largest city, Wichita Falls, whose population has fallen below 100,000.

The other half of the 13th district is the old 18th, situated on the high plains of the Texas panhandle, drier and less fertile land than the Red River Valley. West of the 100th meridian, the land is full of dry gullies that swell to floods when it rains. But it seldom does; instead, the wind blows as hard and unremittingly as anywhere in the United States. Over the years, most of the panhandle farmers and ranchers seem to have moved into Amarillo, the district's largest city with 127,000 people, and smaller towns like Pampa and Borger. First settled by people from neighboring northwest Oklahoma and western Kansas, the panhandle has always been one of the most Republican parts of Texas. In recent years the heavily conservative leanings of Amarillo, the helium capital of the world, have strengthened the area's traditional Republicanism.

The two parts of the district result in a pretty even balance; the 13th was nearly evenly split in the 1976 presidential election. At the beginning of the seventies it combined the seats of two incumbents, Democrat Graham Purcell and Republican Bob Price. They lost in successive elections, Purcell in 1972 and Price in 1974.

The current Congressman is Democrat Jack Hightower. He was helped in 1974 by low turnout in the traditionally Republican panhandle part of the district; evidently voters there were dispirited after the Watergate scandal and the resignation of Richard Nixon. After serving on the Agriculture and Small Business Committees for two terms, he has moved to the Appropriations Committee. His voting record is rated higher by conservative than liberal groups. He was reelected without any great difficulty in 1976 and by a 3-1 margin in 1978.

Census Data Pop. 466,663. Central city, 48%; suburban, 10%. Median family income, $8,182; families above $15,000: 14%; families below $3,000: 11%. Median years education, 12.1.

The Voters

Median voting age 43.
Employment profile White collar, 46%. Blue collar, 32%. Service, 14%. Farm, 8%.
Ethnic groups Black, 5%. Spanish, 6%. Total foreign stock, 4%.

Presidential vote

1976	Carter (D)	85,220	(49%)
	Ford (R)	87,302	(51%)
1972	Nixon (R)	115,660	(76%)
	McGovern (D)	36,339	(24%)

Rep. Jack Hightower (D) Elected 1974; b. Sept. 6 1926, Memphis; home, Vernon; Baylor U., B.A. 1949, LL.B. 1951; Baptist.

Career Navy, WWII; Practicing atty., 1951–74; Tex. House of Reps., 1953–54; Dist. Atty., 1955–61; Tex. Senate, 1965–74.

Offices 120 CHOB, 202-225-3706. Also Rm. 109 Fed. Bldg., Amarillo 79101, 806-376-2381.

Committees *Appropriation* (32d). Subcommittees: Agriculture, Rural Development and Related Agencies; State, Justice, Commerce and Judiciary.

Group Ratings

	ADA	COPE	PC	RPN	NFU	LCV	CFA	NAB	NSI	ACA	NTU
1978	30	35	30	64	50	–	32	67	90	67	–
1977	15	30	18	15	58	11	20	–	–	56	29
1976	15	35	16	33	33	35	27	36	100	64	36

Key Votes

1) Increase Def Spnd	FOR	6) Alaska Lands Protect	AGN	11) Delay Auto Pol Cntrl	FOR
2) B-1 Bomber	AGN	7) Water Projects Veto	AGN	12) Sugar Price Escalator	FOR
3) Cargo Preference	AGN	8) Consum Protect Agcy	AGN	13) Pub Fin Cong Cmpgns	AGN
4) Dereg Nat Gas	FOR	9) Common Situs Picket	AGN	14) ERA Ratif Recissn	AGN
5) Kemp-Roth	AGN	10) Labor Law Revision	AGN	15) Prohibt Govt Abrtns	FOR

Election Results

1978 general	Jack Hightower (D)	75,271	(75%)	($44,551)
	Clifford A. Jones (R)	25,275	(25%)	($30,086)
1978 primary	Jack Hightower (D), unopposed			
1976 general	Jack Hightower (D)	101,798	(59%)	($112,418)
	Robert Price (R)	69,328	(41%)	($85,364)

FOURTEENTH DISTRICT

The 14th congressional district of Texas moves along the state's steamy Gulf Coast from the Brazosport area just south of Houston all the way to Padre Island, the National Seashore below Corpus Christi. Behind the sand bars that protect the harbors from the Gulf are some of the largest oil refineries and chemical plants in Texas, in places like Brazosport, Port Lavaca, Victoria, and Corpus Christi. The latter, with more than 200,000 people, is by far the district's largest city, and has a large Mexican-American population.

The 14th is sweaty, heavy industry country. It is one of the few parts of Texas where the state's labor unions have much influence. Few blacks live this far south and west in Texas, but there is a large Mexican-American minority here (37% of the district's population). On economic issues, this is one of the state's more liberal districts, although it is hardly similar in attitude to places in New York or Massachusetts.

For 22 years the district seemed to have a congressman whose views pretty well reflected those attitudes. John Young entered Congress in the fifties when Sam Rayburn was Speaker and leader of the Texas delegation; he got a seat on the Rules Committee and was a key vote for much of the legislation of the Kennedy and Johnson Administrations. Even in the seventies Young remained responsive to the Democratic leadership and had a good record with organized labor.

But Young also had political troubles. In 1976 a woman who used to serve on his staff charged him with sexual improprieties, and while no one found cause for action against him, he was damaged politically. In 1978 he attracted strong opposition from state Representative Joe Wyatt. Despite labor support Young lost the runoff; he carried Corpus Christi but lost the rest of the district. Republican efforts to make a fight of it in the general election came to nothing, and Wyatt was elected easily. He now serves on the Armed Services and Merchant Marine Committees, and can be expected to look after local interests and to vote as often as not with the bipartisan conservative coalition.

Census Data Pop. 466,437. Central city, 44%; suburban, 17%. Median family income, $7,683; families above $15,000: 13%; families below $3,000: 16%. Median years education, 11.1.

The Voters

Median voting age 42.
Employment profile White collar, 44%. Blue collar, 36%. Service, 15%. Farm, 5%.
Ethnic groups Black, 7%. Spanish, 37%. Total foreign stock, 13%. Germany, 1%.

Presidential vote

1976	Carter (D)	95,485	(58%)
	Ford (R)	68,780	(42%)
1972	Nixon (R)	84,574	(61%)
	McGovern (D)	54,815	(39%)

Rep. Joe Wyatt, Jr. (D) Elected 1978; b. Oct. 12, 1941, Victoria Co.; home, Bloomington; Victoria Col., U. of the Americas, Mexico City, U. of Tex., B.A. 1969; Catholic.

Career Auditor; Tex. House of Reps., 1971–78.

Offices 1730 LHOB, 202-225-2831. Also Rm. 307, U.S. Courthouse, Corpus Christi 78401, 512-888-3381.

Committees *Armed Services* (28th). Subcommittees: Seapower and Strategic and Critical Materials; Military Compensation.

Merchant Marine and Fisheries (21st). Subcommittees: Fish and Wildlife; Oceanography.

Group Ratings: Newly Elected

Key Votes: Newly Elected

Election Results

1978 general	Joe Wyatt (D)	63,953	(72%)	($310,890)
	Jay Yates (R)	24,325	(28%)	($10,766)
1978 run-off	Joe Wyatt (D)	36,409	(56%)	
	John Young (D)	28,905	(44%)	($164,374)
1978 primary	Joe Wyatt (D)	34,812	(42%)	
	John Young (D)	30,871	(38%)	
	Jason Luby (D)	16,383	(20%)	($8,554)
1976 general	John Young (D)	93,589	(61%)	($16,835)
	L. Dean Holford (R)	58,788	(39%)	($44,612)

FIFTEENTH DISTRICT

South Texas lives closer to the feudal ages than any other region of the United States. Here are the fabled Texas ranches: the King Ranch covers more acreage than the state of Rhode Island, and produces an annual income of $25 million—mostly from oil, not cattle. Just down the road (which is to say, in the next county) is a spread, not too much smaller, belonging to former White House Counselor Anne Armstrong and her husband, who is now a top aide to Governor Clements. Farther south is the Lower Rio Grande Valley. Here, thanks to irrigation water and the semitropical climate, are fields of cotton, fruits, and vegetables tended by Mexican farm hands. The United Farm Workers have tried to do some organizing here, but with little success. Inevitably, many of the workers are Mexican nationals, and many of those are illegal immigrants; they are interested in receiving what are, by their standards, generous wages and are not interested in making trouble.

This is the land of Texas's 15th congressional district. It includes not only the Lower Rio Grande, but also some of the interior counties between Corpus Christi and Laredo, though it contains neither of these two cities. Though 75% of the residents of the district are of Mexican stock, virtually all the important decisions here are made by Anglo ranchers, bankers, lawyers, and farmers. Evidence of Anglo power is apparent in the election returns. Richard Kleberg, owner of the King Ranch, represented this part of Texas in the House from 1931 to 1945; a young poor boy from the hills around Austin named Lyndon Johnson got his first government job in Kleberg's office.

Another Lower Rio Grande Valley congressman was Lloyd Bentsen. His father had made a fortune in land in the Valley (and was accused of selling parcels to northern retirees without water or sewers); young Lloyd was elected County Judge at 25 and Congressman at 27, in 1946. Bentsen retired from the House in 1954 to make a fortune of his own in Houston; his successor was Joe M. Kilgore, a pillar of the Connally Tory Democratic establishment. Kilgore wanted to run against Ralph Yarborough in the 1964 Senate primary; LBJ persuaded him not to, and six years later Yarborough was beaten by Bentsen.

In the smaller counties of the district, the votes are easy to manipulate. Almost all of them are cast by Mexican-American field hands whose jobs depend on a single landowner. The evidence is plain from the election returns: Jim Hogg County, for example, went 82% for Humphrey in 1968 and 47% for Nixon in 1972. Most interesting is the voting history of Duval County, long the fiefdom of the Parr family. Its most famous performance came in the 1948 Senate runoff. After some delay, Duval reported 4,622 votes for Lyndon Johnson and 40 for his opponent. Inasmuch as the county had gone the other way a few weeks before, people were suspicious of the result; but it was certified, and "Landslide Lyndon" carried the state by 87 votes. George Parr, the last "Duke of Duval," was sentenced to jail on an income tax charge and killed himself in 1974. But the same kind of power is now being exerted by a Mexican-American family which used to be allied with the Parrs.

When Kilgore retired from the House in 1964, someone apparently decided that it was time the 15th had a Mexican-American congressman. Accordingly Eligio de la Garza was elected. He had shown his reliability through 12 years in the legislature; he is by no means a favorite of the militant chicanos, and generally votes like other Texas rural Democrats. The seniority system has been kind to de la Garza. He is chairman of an Agriculture subcommittee and second-ranking Democrat on the full Committee; if Chairman Thomas Foley, who has had political trouble at home lately, should not return de la Garza will become committee chairman. The few times he has had opponents in the 15th he has won easily.

Census Data Pop. 466,359. Central city, 37%; suburban, 32%. Median family income, $5.059; families above $15,000: 8%; families below $3,000: 29%. Median years education, 8.3.

The Voters

Median voting age 41.
Employment profile White collar, 40%. Blue collar, 34%. Service, 13%. Farm, 13%.
Ethnic groups Spanish, 75%. Total foreign stock, 36%.

Presidential vote

1976	Carter (D)	94,926	(66%)
	Ford (R)	49,873	(34%)
1972	Nixon (R)	65,696	(55%)
	McGovern (D)	53,967	(45%)

Rep. E de la Garza (D) Elected 1964; b. Sept. 22, 1927, Mercedes; home, Mission; Edinburg Jr. Col., St. Mary's U., San Antonio, LL.B. 1952; Catholic.

Career Navy, WWII; Army, Korea; Practicing atty., 1952–64; Tex. House of Reps., 1952–64.

Offices 1434 LHOB, 202-225-2531. Also 1418 Beach St., La Posada Village, McAllen 78501, 512-682-5545.

Committees *Agriculture* (2d). Subcommittees: Department Investigations, Oversight, and Research (Chairman); Livestock and Grains.

Merchant Marine and Fisheries (7th). Subcommittees: Coast Guard and Navigation; Fish and Wildlife; Merchant Marine.

Group Ratings

	ADA	COPE	PC	RPN	NFU	LCV	CFA	NAB	NSI	ACA	NTU
1978	10	39	15	50	60	–	27	60	90	83	–
1977	5	43	20	31	50	15	40	–	–	52	25
1976	25	71	26	35	60	39	36	27	100	57	29

Key Votes

1) Increase Def Spnd	FOR	6) Alaska Lands Protect	AGN	11) Delay Auto Pol Cntrl	FOR
2) B-1 Bomber	FOR	7) Water Projects Veto	AGN	12) Sugar Price Escalator	FOR
3) Cargo Preference	FOR	8) Consum Protect Agcy	AGN	13) Pub Fin Cong Cmpgns	AGN
4) Dereg Nat Gas	FOR	9) Common Situs Picket	AGN	14) ERA Ratif Recissn	FOR
5) Kemp-Roth	FOR	10) Labor Law Revision	AGN	15) Prohibt Govt Abrtns	FOR

Election Results

1978 general	E. (Kika) de la Garza (D)	54,560	(66%)	($85,184)
	Robert L. McDonald (R)	27,853	(34%)	($30,535)
1978 primary	E. (Kika) de la Garza (D), unopposed			
1976 general	E. (Kika) de la Garza (D)	102,837	(74%)	($70,626)
	R. L. Lendy McDonald (R)	35,446	(26%)	($14,118)

SIXTEENTH DISTRICT

"West of the Pecos" is a phrase associated with the frontier justice of Judge Roy Bean, but it is also a pretty fair description of the location of the 16th congressional district of Texas. When Bean held his court in his barroom in the town of Langtry, there was precious little of anything except uninhabited desert west of the Pecos. Today there is not much more—except for the city of El Paso. With 359,000 residents, El Paso dominates the 16th district. Aside from the little town of Pecos and the 49,000 residents of the oil drilling and mechanics' town of Odessa, El Paso is the only significant population center of the 16th. Typical of the landscape beyond is the harsh desert of Loving County, which in 1970 had a population of 164 people—the lowest population of any county in the nation.

El Paso is a Sun Belt city that mushroomed after World War II. Its economy was fueled by the nearby presence of giant military installations like Fort Bliss and the White Sands Proving Ground. But its chief economic asset is low wage labor. Just across the Rio Grande from El Paso is the city of Juarez, which has a population considerably larger than El Paso's and is separated from any other concentration of population in Mexico by as great a distance as El Paso is in the United States. This is the part of the Mexican border that gave us the word "wetback," the forties synonym for illegal immigrant; and the fact is that you don't even have to get very wet to cross the Rio Grande, which is just a trickle most of the year. A majority of El Paso's residents are Mexican in origin, and no one knows for sure how many are U.S. citizens. As befits the border between two free countries, hundreds or even thousands of people cross the line every day, and many live on one side and work on the other.

Even subminimum wages in the United States look good to people brought up in rural Mexico, and so thousands of Mexicans have moved to Juarez, looking for jobs in El Paso. The Texas city has become a center for the apparel business and for other low wage, low skill industries; if wages are low enough, it pays to ship raw materials into El Paso and finished goods out. A few years ago there was a long and bitter strike at the Farah pants plant, and Catholic bishops backed the strikers. But basic conditions haven't changed and aren't likely to in the future.

Although El Paso has a Mexican majority, most of its voters are Anglos—in part because many of the Mexicans are not American citizens at all. Accordingly, the 16th is not all that liberal a district; in 1976, with the help of Republican Odessa, it gave Gerald Ford a narrow margin over Jimmy Carter. In congressional races, except for the two-year tenure of a Republican congressman after the Billie Sol Estes scandal, the 16th has gone Democratic. The current Congressman, Richard White, was first elected in 1964. He has made a variety of concessions in his voting record to the Mexican-Americans; he supported civil rights, and he has sometimes had high ratings from organized labor. But his basic instincts seem to be more in the traditional Texas Tory Democratic mold. Currently he chairs the Democratic Research Organization, founded by Southerners as a kind of counterweight to the liberal Democratic Study Group.

White has not been a particularly forceful Congressman. Several years ago he lost an Appropriations seat to the more junior and more aggressive Charles Wilson of east Texas. Now a relatively senior member of Armed Services, White had liberal primary opposition in 1976 and managed to win 57%-35%. That year he won the general election with only 58%. But in most elections he does not have such opposition; in 1978 he won easily.

Census Data Pop. 466,663. Central city, 81%; suburban, 9%. Median family income, $7,936; families above $15,000: 14%; families below $3,000: 12%. Median years education, 12.0.

The Voters

Median voting age 38.
Employment profile White collar, 49%. Blue collar, 36%. Service, 13%. Farm, 2%.
Ethnic groups Black, 3%. Spanish, 50%. Total foreign stock, 34%. Germany, 2%.

Presidential vote

1976	Carter (D)	NA	
	Ford (R)	NA	
1972	Nixon (R)	69,211	(64%)
	McGovern (D)	39,749	(36%)

Rep. Richard C. White (D) Elected 1964; b. Apr. 29, 1923, El Paso; home, El Paso; U. of Tex. at El Paso, U. of Tex., B.A. 1946, LL.B. 1949; Episcopalian.

Career USMC, WWII; Practicing atty., 1949–64; Tex. House of Reps., 1955–58.

Offices 2266 RHOB, 202-225-4831. Also Rm. 146 U.S. Courthouse, El Paso 79901, 915-543-7650.

Committees *Armed Services* (7th). Subcommittees: Military Personnel (Chairman); Military Installations and Facilities.

Science and Technology (18th). Subcommittees: Energy Research and Production; Energy Development and Application.

Group Ratings

	ADA	COPE	PC	RPN	NFU	LCV	CFA	NAB	NSI	ACA	NTU
1978	25	20	28	58	56	–	23	70	100	80	–
1977	10	39	15	23	67	20	15	–	–	44	24
1976	15	59	28	27	46	30	27	9	90	53	17

Key Votes

1) Increase Def Spnd	FOR	6) Alaska Lands Protect	DNV	11) Delay Auto Pol Cntrl	FOR
2) B-1 Bomber	FOR	7) Water Projects Veto	AGN	12) Sugar Price Escalator	FOR
3) Cargo Preference	FOR	8) Consum Protect Agcy	AGN	13) Pub Fin Cong Cmpgns	AGN
4) Dereg Nat Gas	FOR	9) Common Situs Picket	AGN	14) ERA Ratif Recissn	FOR
5) Kemp-Roth	AGN	10) Labor Law Revision	AGN	15) Prohibt Govt Abrtns	FOR

Election Results

1978 general	Richard C. White (D)	53,090	(70%)	($107,976)
	Michael Giere (R)	22,743	(30%)	($34,881)
1978 primary	Richard C. White (D)	48,493	(80%)	
	One other (D)	12,185	(20%)	
1976 general	Richard C. White (D)	71,876	(58%)	($161,473)
	Vic Shackilford (R)	52,488	(42%)	($80,872)

SEVENTEENTH DISTRICT

The 17th congressional district is the geographical heart of Texas. Here there are thousands and thousands of acres of arid farming and grazing land stretching west from Fort Worth to the horizon. The 17th is primarily cattle grazing country, though there is some oil here and some raising of cotton and grain. Its largest city is Abilene, with 89,000 people. As is often the case on the plains, the town is more conservative than the countryside; all the bankers, lawyers, and professionals are concentrated there, who form the bulk of the conservative vote. Like most of central Texas, this area was settled originally by Southerners who brought their Democratic politics with them, and it has remained pretty solidly Democratic, even in the turbulent political years of the seventies.

The 17th was one of eight Texas districts which Republicans targeted in 1978—and one of the six that they had lost. For 32 years it had elected a Congressman, Omar Burleson, who to judge from his voting record really belonged in the Republican Party. For years he had 0% ADA ratings and not much higher from organized labor; yet occasionally he would give the Democratic leadership a little help, usually on a procedural vote. Quiet and gentlemanly, Burleson gave up the Chairmanship of the House Administration Committee to serve as the Texas member of Ways and Means, to protect oil's tax advantages. He seems seldom to have irritated anyone. In any case, since 1964 he was reelected without primary or general election opposition—the longest free ride of any contemporary member of Congress. He retired at 72 when he finally became eligible for the maximum congressional pension.

Naturally there was a fierce battle for this district. The winner of the Democratic runoff was Charles Stenholm, a rancher from the town of Stamford, where White House power and former Democratic National Chairman Robert Strauss grew up. Stenholm had been active in the state Agriculture Stabilization and Conservation Board; he built a strong political organization county by county. His Republican opponent, Billy Lee Fisher, tried to put on a serious campaign, but was not able to get off the ground. Stenholm won by better than 2-1. In the House he won a seat on the Agriculture Committee, and presumably can expect to use his positions on farming issues as a source of political strength for the future. Stenholm won his first election at the same age that Burleson won his, and there is nothing to indicate that Stenholm cannot last as long in the House.

Census Data Pop. 466,432. Central city, 19%; suburban, 5%. Median family income, $7,144; families above $15,000: 11%; families below $3,000: 16%. Median years education, 11.2.

The Voters

Median voting age 46.
Employment profile White collar, 40%. Blue collar, 34%. Service, 15%. Farm, 11%.
Ethnic groups Black, 4%. Spanish, 9%. Total foreign stock, 4%.

Presidential vote

1976	Carter (D)	95,482	(57%)
	Ford (R)	71,103	(43%)
1972	Nixon (R)	97,197	(73%)
	McGovern (D)	36,122	(27%)

Rep. Charles W. Stenholm (D) Elected 1978; b. Oct. 26, 1938, Stamford; home, Stamford; Tarleton St. Jr. Col., 1959, Tex. Tech. U., B.S. 1961, M.S. 1962; Lutheran.

Career Vocational Agriculture teacher, 1962–64; Farm manager, 1961–.

Offices 1610 LHOB, 202-225-6605. Also 903 E. Hamilton, Stamford 79553, 915-773-3623.

Committees *Agriculture* (27th). Subcommittees: Cotton; Dairy and Poultry; Oilseeds and Rice.

Post Office and Civil Service (12th). Subcommittees: Investigations.

Group Ratings: Newly Elected

Key Votes: Newly Elected

Election Results

1978 general	Charles W. Stenholm (D)	69,030	(68%)	($331,516)
	Billy Lee Fisher (R)	32,302	(32%)	($149,705)
1978 run-off	Charles W. Stenholm (D)	46,599	(67%)	
	A. L. "Dusty" Rhodes (D)	22,865	(33%)	($604,484)
1978 primary	Charles W. Stenholm (D)	36,527	(36%)	
	A. L. "Dusty" Rhodes (D)	34,172	(34%)	
	Jim Baum (D)	16,622	(16%)	($29,604)
	Four others (D)	14,091	(14%)	
1976 general	Omar Burleson (D), unopposed			($10,131)

EIGHTEENTH DISTRICT

The 18th congressional district of Texas covers the central part of the city of Houston. It includes within its boundaries most of the city's blacks and many of its Mexican-Americans. In 1970, 44% of its residents were black and 19% of Spanish origin; with the explosive growth of Houston, those percentages have undoubtedly risen since, leaving relatively few white Anglos. This is a very different part of Houston from the gleaming west side. Like many rapidly growing cities in developing countries, Houston seems to have unusually great disparities of income and wealth. While entrepreneurs are getting rich in the oil business and living in $500,000 houses near the Galleria, many black and Mexican-American residents live east and south of downtown in unpainted frame houses complete with cracks wide enough to let in Houston's humid, smoggy air. Of course, there is no air conditioning in this part of town. The Houston slums look like something out of the sharecropper thirties, and they remind us that although this is one of our fastest growing cities, its growth is based in large part on cheap labor. Houston has a strong developing economy, and eventually perhaps everyone will benefit, perhaps is benefiting already; but in the meantime, it is a fact that some people are getting rich a lot faster than others.

Houston's black neighborhoods cast higher Democratic percentages—on the order of 98%—than any other part of the United States. The voting habits here in the 18th district are thus a considerable contrast from the 7th district, immediately to the west, which is the most Republican district in the country. The real question in Houston politics is, who will outvote whom? In 1976, there were enough votes cast in the 18th—nearly half as many as in the 7th—to help carry Texas for Jimmy Carter. But in 1978 enthusiasm and elan belonged entirely to the Republicans. More than four times as many people voted in the 7th district as in the 18th. If the ratio of turnout had been the same as in 1976, the statewide results would have been different: Senator John Tower would have been defeated, and William Clements would not have been elected Texas's first Republican Governor in more than 100 years.

The black part of Houston is the place which gave political birth to Barbara Jordan. She is a familiar figure now, from her stirring speech at the House Judiciary Committee impeachment hearings and even more from her tumultuously greeted keynote speech at the 1976 Democratic National Convention. Jordan was the first black state Senator in Texas; and a powerful state Senator at that, one who could get the ear of the ruling powers and who could get herself chosen Acting Governor. She also demonstrated clout by constructing a congressional district, the 18th, tailored to her ambitions. Although it did not have a black voting majority in 1972, she was elected easily—and never had any electoral problems after, until she decided to retire in 1978.

Jordan's retirement puzzled many observers. Some attributed it to health; she does have a painful condition in her knee, but she otherwise seems to be in fine health in Austin, where she works at the Lyndon Johnson School. Others have said Jordan just got tired of Congress. She had been legislatively active on several issues, notably on getting Texas covered by the Voting Rights Act; but her gifts for oratory and political horse-trading were seldom seriously engaged. Without great seniority, she did not have a committee position commensurate with her celebrity; and she remains a celebrity without holding public office. Jordan has indicated an interest in running for statewide office in Texas, but apparently has concluded she could not be elected. And so, having achieved so much, so very much more than anyone could have expected, she has turned to something else.

Jordan's successor in the House, Mickey Leland, seems likely to be more comfortable in the Congressional Black Caucus. He does not have Jordan's taste for getting along with powerful conservatives nor her disdain for militant speech-making. He is a pharmacist, and in the Texas legislature and in the House he has advocated replacing name brand with generic brand drugs. He was chosen in a fierce primary and runoff in 1978, but if the usual pattern holds he will not be faced with serious competition in the years ahead.

Census Data Pop. 466,520. Central city, 100%; suburban, 0%. Median family income, $7,288; families above $15,000: 10%; families below $3,000: 15%. Median years education, 10.4.

The Voters

Median voting age 39.
Employment profile White collar, 40%. Blue collar, 40%. Service, 20%. Farm, –%.
Ethnic groups Black, 44%. Spanish, 19%. Total foreign stock, 12%.

Presidential vote

1976	Carter (D)	82,608	(76%)
	Ford (R)	26,606	(24%)
1972	Nixon (R)	34,355	(31%)
	McGovern (D)	75,243	(69%)

Rep. Mickey Leland (D) Elected 1978; b. Nov. 27, 1944, Lubbock; home, Houston; Texas So. U., B.S. 1970; Catholic.

Career Instructor, Texas So. U., 1970–71; Dir. of Special Development Projects, Hermann Hospital, 1971–78; Tex. House of Reps., 1972–79.

Offices 1207 LHOB, 202-225-3816. Also Suite 101, 4101 San Jacinto Ctr., Houston 77004, 713-527-9692.

Committees *District of Columbia* (7th). Subcommittees: Judiciary, Manpower, and Education.

Interstate and Foreign Commerce (26th). Subcommittees: Energy and Power; Oversight and Investigations; Health and the Environment.

Post Office and Civil Service (10th). Subcommittees: Postal Personnel and Modernization; Census and Population.

Group Ratings: Newly Elected

Key Votes: Newly Elected

Election Results

1978 general	Mickey Leland (D), unopposed			($258,366)
1978 run-off	Mickey Leland (D)	15,587	(57%)	
	Anthony Hall (D)	11,821	(43%)	($145,022)
1978 primary	Mickey Leland (D)	17,946	(48%)	
	Anthony Hall (D)	9,003	(24%)	
	Judson Robinson (D)	6,091	(16%)	($124,487)
	Four others (D)	4,592	(12%)	
1976 general	Barbara H. Jordan (D)	93,953	(86%)	($36,585)
	Sam H. Wright (R)	15,381	(14%)	($4,459)

NINETEENTH DISTRICT

The 19th congressional district of Texas takes in part of the flat, dusty plains and the distant, treeless skyline of west Texas. This is the high plains, land of little rainfall and giant gullies, of parching hot summers, snowbound winters, and tremendous winds. There is relatively little farming here; the land is used primarily for grazing—and for oil. For this is also the center of the Permian Basin, one of the greatest areas for oil exploration and development in the decades after World War II. Even as the agricultural communities here were declining in population, their young people going off to cities to find jobs, two significant urban centers were growing as the Permian Basin was being explored. One was Lubbock, which has always been the main commercial center for farming and grazing in the area, and the home of Texas Tech as well; it is a sort of regional capital of west Texas. The other is Midland, a much smaller town created almost entirely by the Permian Basin boom. This is a rich man's town, a part of north Dallas or west Houston transplanted to the desert, with expensive stores and restaurants and all the accoutrements of cultured living that affluent Texans are growing used to.

Politically, this is a part of Texas which is ancestrally Democratic, but which increasingly has been going Republican in recent elections. Lubbock, like many fast-growing cities in the Southwest, is considerably more Republican than the rural area around it, particularly in national elections. Midland is as heavily Republican as the rich neighborhoods in the big cities it resembles. The result is a district solidly Republican in national and now in statewide contests, but one which has remained Democratic in congressional elections.

The main reason has been the strength of the Democratic candidates. This is the district which for 34 years was represented by George Mahon. First elected in 1934, he chaired the House Appropriations Committee from 1964 until his retirement in 1978. For even longer Mahon chaired the Defense Appropriations Subcommittee, which handled a large chunk of the federal budget. Mahon was a fiscal conservative except on defense matters, and even there he tried to keep the Pentagon in check as he did his best to provide for an ample defense. He was basically out of step with the thinking of most congressional Democrats, but there was no significant move to oust him from his chairmanship. His austere personality and sense of fairness made him invulnerable.

Naturally Mahon did not work his district the way junior congressmen do and in 1976, when he was 76 years old, he must have been somewhat surprised when Republican Jim Reese, a Lubbock stockbroker with no previous electoral experience, held him to 55% of the vote. Mahon's decision to retire followed, and most Republican strategists eagerly awaited picking up the district. But their plans fell victim to intraparty competition. Reese ran again, but he was challenged in the primary by George Bush, the 32-year-old son of the former Houston Congressman and 1980 Republican presidential candidate. The elder Bush had participated in the Permian boom and had lived in Midland for some years, and the younger Bush had a solid electoral base there. Not many people vote in Texas Republican primaries, and in the 19th district enough people voted in Midland to give Bush a large enough majority to win the nomination even though he failed to carry another county in the district.

Bush had plenty of money in the general election, but he also had a shrewd and competent opponent, state Senator Kent Hance. Hance's base was in Lubbock; he had grown up in the area and graduated from Texas Tech. The contrast with Bush—a graduate of an Eastern prep school who attended Harvard and Yale—was obvious. Hance's policies were basically in line with district opinion, and he ended up winning the election with almost the same percentage Mahon had had two years before. It is too early to say that Hance has a safe seat. He may have to face Reese or some other Lubbock-based candidate in 1980. But he has demonstrated considerable political savvy, and if he continues to do so seems likely to keep the 19th in Democratic hands.

Census Data Pop. 466,649. Central city, 50%; suburban, 9%. Median family income, $8315; families above $15,000: 16%; families below $3,000: 12%. Median years education, 12.1.

The Voters

Median voting age 40.
Employment profile White collar, 47%. Blue collar, 29%. Service, 13%. Farm, 11%.
Ethnic groups Black, 6%. Spanish, 19%. Total foreign stock, 7%.

Presidential vote

1976	Carter (D)	68,836	(42%)
	Ford (R)	93,985	(58%)
1972	Nixon (R)	108,282	(76%)
	McGovern (D)	33,494	(24%)

Rep. Kent Hance (D) Elected 1978; b. 1942, Dimmitt; home, Lubbock; Tex. Tech. U., B.B.A. 1965, U. of Tex. LL.B. 1968; Baptist.

Career Practicing atty., 1968–; Tex. Senate, 1974–78.

Offices 1039 LHOB, 202-225-4005. Also 611 Fed. Ofc. Bldg., 1205 Texas Ave., Lubbock 79401, 806-763-1611.

Committees *Agriculture* (25th). Subcommittees: Cotton; Livestock and Grains.

Science and Technology (27th). Subcommittees: Science, Research and Technology; Energy Development and Applications.

Group Ratings: Newly Elected

Key Votes: Newly Elected

Election Results

1978 general	Kent Hance (D)	54,729	(53%)	($314,110)
	George W. Bush (R)	48,070	(47%)	($434,909)
1978 primary	Kent Hance (D)	46,505	(64%)	
	Morris Sheats (D)	25,791	(36%)	($142,729)
1976 general	George H. Mahon (D)	87,908	(55%)	($124,855)
	Jim Reese (R)	72,991	(45%)	($164,794)

TWENTIETH DISTRICT

San Antonio was the most important town in Texas when the state was part of Mexico. It was here, of course, that Santa Ana and his troops wiped out Davy Crockett, Jim Bowie, and 184 others at the Alamo in 1836. (Crockett was a Tennessee Congressman in 1827-31 and 1833-35; if he had not lost his bid for reelection in 1835, he would never have left Tennessee for Texas.) Today San Antonio is Texas's third largest city, with 650,000 people and a metropolitan population approaching one million. Because it has never been a center of the Texas boom industries of oil, electronics, or cattle, San Antonio has not been growing as fast as Houston or Dallas-Fort Worth. But this is not a withering city, either. It also has its own special atmosphere, particularly along the banks of the San Antonio River as it wanders through the center of town. The Alamo is nearby, thronged with tourists—a monument to patriotism, though it represents a defeat nearly unparalleled in our history.

Only 130 miles from the Mexican border, San Antonio has a Mexican-American majority within its city limits; it is, in fact, the most Hispanic major city in the country. That is the single demographic fact one needs to understand most of the electoral politics here. The other thing that is politically important about San Antonio is that this is a city heavily dependent on government, primarily military, payrolls. San Antonio has Fort Sam Houston, with 10,000 men; the Brooks Aero Medical Center, the major medical facility of the Air Force; and no less than three Air Force bases either within the city limits or just outside them. San Antonio politics has always been a struggle between liberals, who depend on Mexican-Americans for most of their votes, and conservatives, whose constituency is the well-to-do Anglo middle class which is sympathetic with and often dependent on the military establishment here.

Control has oscillated between the two groups. In the thirties San Antonio's Congressman was a witty liberal named Maury Maverick. He was beaten in the 1938 Democratic primary by Paul Kilday, and power changed hands; Kilday was a conservative and a powerful member of the Armed Services Committee. Power changed hands again in 1961, when Kilday was named Judge of the Court of Military Appeals. He was succeeded by a young Mexican-American lawyer and state Senator, Henry B. Gonzalez—the first Mexican-American Congressman from the district, which at that time included all of San Antonio and surrounding Bexar County.

During the early part of his career Gonzalez was hailed as the patron saint of Texas liberals; later they became displeased with some of his stands. But he could reply that he had never shifted ground. He backed Lyndon Johnson's conduct of the Vietnam war; he had never claimed to be a dove. And he had little but scorn for the younger generation of chicano militants who preached various kinds of political separatism. Gonzalez always believed in working with others with similar interests, and in recent years he has even found himself comfortable in meetings of the Texas delegation, where he was once not altogether welcome.

Gonzalez is a senior member of the Banking Committee, but he achieved his greatest notice in 1977 when he served, briefly, as Chairman of the special committee on assassinations. Gonzalez was riding in the procession in Dallas in 1963, and he was the main force behind setting up the inquiry. But he got into a fight with committee counsel Richard Sprague, and when he tried to fire him, found that the rest of the committee wasn't backing him. He went back to San Antonio and, after remaining incommunicado for a while, resigned the chairmanship.

Since Gonzalez was first elected, the equal population rule has required a reduction in the size of his 20th district. It has lost most of the suburban areas as well as the Anglo north side of San Antonio. Now it includes the central portion of the city, and has a large Mexican-American majority. No one knows exactly how large, or how many residents are actually U.S. citizens; but there are enough Mexican-Americans for voting control. For all his feuds with young chicano militants and his troubles with the assassination committee, Gonzalez has had no problems winning reelection and has no particular reason to expect any.

Census Data Pop. 466,514. Central city, 92%; suburban, 8%. Median family income, $6,566; families above $15,000: 7%; families below $3,000: 18%. Median years education, 9.4.

The Voters

Median voting age 40.
Employment profile White collar, 42%. Blue collar, 40%. Service, 18%. Farm, –%.
Ethnic groups Black, 11%. Spanish, 60%. Total foreign stock, 25%. Germany, 1%.

Presidential vote

1976	Carter (D)	77,691	(74%)
	Ford (R)	26,711	(26%)
1972	Nixon (R)	37,021	(40%)
	McGovern (D)	56,470	(60%)

Rep. Henry B. Gonzalez (D) Elected Nov. 4, 1961; b. May 3, 1916, San Antonio; home, San Antonio; San Antonio Col., U. of Tex., St. Mary's U., San Antonio, LL.B.; Catholic

Career Army WWII; Bexar Co. Chf. Probation Officer, 1946; Work with bilingual publications; Teacher, San Antonio Night School; San Antonio City Cncl., 1953–56, Mayor Pro Tem., 1955–56; Tex. Senate, 1956–61.

Offices 2252 RHOB, 202-225-3236. Also Rm. B-124 Fed. Bldg., 727 E. Durango, 512-229-6199.

Committees *Banking, Finance, and Urban Affairs* (5th). Subcommittees: International Development Institutions and Finance (Chairman); General Oversight and Renegotiation; Housing and Community Development.

Small Business (8th). Subcommittees: General Oversight and Minority Enterprise; Antitrust and Restraint of Trade Activities Affecting Small Business.

Group Ratings

	ADA	COPE	PC	RPN	NFU	LCV	CFA	NAB	NSI	ACA	NTU
1978	70	95	63	42	70	–	64	9	88	26	–
1977	30	90	35	18	83	30	50	–	–	36	20
1976	50	90	48	25	67	35	54	8	71	37	4

Key Votes

1) Increase Def Spnd	FOR	6) Alaska Lands Protect	FOR	11) Delay Auto Pol Cntrl	FOR
2) B-1 Bomber	FOR	7) Water Projects Veto	AGN	12) Sugar Price Escalator	AGN
3) Cargo Preference	FOR	8) Consum Protect Agcy	FOR	13) Pub Fin Cong Cmpgns	AGN
4) Dereg Nat Gas	AGN	9) Common Situs Picket	FOR	14) ERA Ratif Recissn	AGN
5) Kemp-Roth	AGN	10) Labor Law Revision	FOR	15) Prohibt Govt Abrtns	AGN

Election Results

1978 general	Henry B. Gonzalez (D), unopposed	($28,703)
1978 primary	Henry B. Gonzalez (D), unopposed	
1976 general	Henry B. Gonzalez (D), unopposed	($18,214)

TWENTY-FIRST DISTRICT

Most of the physical expanse of the 21st congressional district of Texas is unpopulated—a vast near-desert given over to the raising of cattle and cotton, the pumping of oil, and the extraction of natural gas. In the middle of this vast expanse is the small city of San Angelo, a place less picturesque than its name, which shares the conservative Democratic political tradition and inclination of much of rural Texas. In the eastern part of the district is a noteworthy area, the Texas German district around (but not including) San Antonio. Towns like New Braunfels and Fredericksburg (where Lyndon Johnson used to go to church) were founded by '48ers—liberal Germans who left Europe after the failure of the revolutions of 1848 and settled on the frontier of southern Texas. Because the Germans considered slaveholding barbarous, they soon became attracted to the then radical Republican Party, and their opposition to secession solidified their allegiance to the party of Lincoln. To this day, the counties in which the descendants of the '48ers are still a majority—Comal, Kendall, Gillespie, Kerr—cast huge Republican margins in almost every election.

But the most significant part of the 21st district is the small geographical segment in Bexar County which casts two-thirds of the district's votes. This is the north side of San Antonio and its suburbs. Although a majority of San Antonio's residents are of Mexican background, there are few here; most are in the central city 20th district, and the affluent neighborhoods of the north are solidly white Anglo. These places are not as affluent as the booming west side of Houston and north side of Dallas; there is not the profusion of fancy shops, restaurants, and other signs of sudden wealth and sophistication. But the north side of San Antonio is just about as heavily Republican as these richer neighborhoods. Whether it is in reaction to the rest of San Antonio or simply out of general principles, this area regularly delivers huge Republican majorities.

Yet until 1978 this district had never elected a Republican congressman. From 1942 until 1972 it elected O.C. Fisher, as conservative a Democrat as ever sat in the House, a quiet man who stayed in till he qualified for the maximum pension. His successor, elected in 1974 and 1976, was Robert Krueger, a young Shakespearean scholar and hosiery mill heir from New Braunfels, by way of Duke and Oxford Universities. Krueger spent huge sums of money (more than $350,000 in 1974), beat a strong Republican candidate, and made a name for himself in the House by nearly persuading that body to deregulate natural gas. It was a bravura performance, and Krueger seemed to have a fine legislative future, but he decided he wanted it to be in the Senate. In 1978 he came heartbreakingly close to beating Senator John Tower; perhaps he will run again.

The 1978 Democratic candidate was a man Krueger had beaten in the primary four years before, former state Senator Nelson Wolff; the Republican was a young former aide to John Tower and Ford Administration official, Tom Loeffler, He showed a sturdy loyalty to conservative principles, expressing reservations about bilingual education in a district with a significant Spanish minority and questioning federal aid to schools in areas impacted by federal installations in an area loaded with military bases. Nevertheless Loeffler was able to win a large enough margin in Bexar County to overcome Wolff's edges in many of the rural counties. This was a year in which Texas's statewide ticket, led by William Clements, inspired genuine enthusiasm among affluent, market-oriented, urban voters, while the Democrats were unable to bestir their constituency. It is fitting, therefore, that one of the few Republican gains in the Texas delegation should come in this district which, despite its geographical shape, is basically urban and affluent.

Census Data Pop. 466,753. Central city, 42%; suburban, 17%. Median family income, $8,789; families above $15,000: 20%; families below $3,000: 11%. Median years education, 12.2.

The Voters

Median voting age 43.
Employment profile White collar, 57%. Blue collar, 26%. Service, 11%. Farm, 6%.
Ethnic groups Black, 2%. Spanish, 24%. Total foreign stock, 14%. Germany, 2%.

Presidential vote

1976	Carter (D)	NA	
	Ford (R)	NA	
1972	Nixon (R)	120,737	(76%)
	McGovern (D)	38,623	(24%)

Rep. Thomas G. Loeffler (R) Elected 1978; b. Aug. 1, 1946, Fredericksburgh; home, Hunt; U. of Tex., B.B.A., 1968, J.D. 1971.

Career Practicing atty. and Rancher; Chief Legis. Consul to U.S. Sen. John Tower, 1972–74; Spec. Asst. for Legis. Affairs, Fed. Energy Admin., 1974–75; Spec. Asst. for Legis. Affairs to Pres. Gerald Ford, 1975.

Offices 1213 LHOB, 202-225-4236. Also Rm. B-209, 727 E. Durango, San Antonio 78205, 512-229-5880.

Committees *Interstate and Foreign Commerce* (14th). Subcommittees: Energy and Power.

Group Ratings: Newly Elected

Key Votes: Newly Elected

Election Results

1978 general	Tom Loeffler (R)	84,336	(57%)	($402,299)
	Nelson W. Wolff (D)	63,501	(43%)	($438,013)
1978 primary	Tom Loeffler (R)	8,779	(59%)	
	Wallace R. Larson (R)	2,558	(17%)	($67,351)
	Neil Calnan (R)	2,007	(14%)	($31,022)
	Bobby Locke (R)	1,433	(10%)	
1976 general	Robert Krueger (D)	149,395	(73%)	($104,175)
	Bobby A. Locke (R)	56,211	(27%)	($2,577)

TWENTY-SECOND DISTRICT

The 22d district of Texas moves from the south side of Houston across the coastal plain to the Brazosport area on the Gulf of Mexico. This territory was almost vacant 20 years ago. Like so many other Sun Belt boom areas, its development was dependent on the technology of the air conditioner. Life here goes on inside: in air conditioned houses, air conditioned shopping malls, and in the air conditioned Houston Astrodome. Outside, at least during the summer, is the shimmering heat and almost eerie silence.

The 22d takes in the prosperous, middle income, and rapidly growing suburban tracts of the south side of Houston. It includes the cultural complex around Rice University and the vast and impressive Houston Medical Center. In the eastern parts of the district are the suburbs of Pasadena and Baytown, places where people who grew up in rural surroundings have moved to find good jobs and during the evenings in bars like Gilley's live the lives of urban cowboys. There are some blacks here, 13% of the population in 1970, but the overall complexion is basically white and the accent east Texas. Down the Gulf Freeway the 22d stretches toward Galveston, and includes the NASA Manned Spacecraft Center. Beyond to the southwest are Fort Bend and Brazoria Counties, which are experiencing now the phenomenal growth that has shaped the south and west sides of Houston.

The 22d has been the scene of some of the closest congressional races in the country since the resignation of Congressman Bob Casey in 1975. Casey was a rather conservative Democrat, the kind who used to dominate the Texas delegation but found it increasingly difficult to survive in this urban district. Since he left Congress there have been three successive races between two very different politicians, all decided by narrow margins. Ron Paul can be called a right wing Republican; he is the kind of conservative who is concerned about the government closing the gold window. Bob Gammage is a Democrat with a liberal reputation and some cautious instincts; he has had a pretty good labor voting record, but doesn't particularly want to advertise that in this affluent district. In the 1976 special election, Paul and his enthusiastic supporters were better organized and got out their vote, and he won by some 8,000 votes. In the 1976 general, the outcome was reversed: Gammage won by the narrow margin of 236 votes. In 1978, with turnout again lower, Paul reversed this result and prevailed by a little more than 1,000 votes. It seems likely that the 1980 result will depend on turnout and on the comparative enthusiasm of the two blocs who support these very different candidates. Neither seems likely to accumulate much seniority.

Census Data Pop. 466,707. Central city, 38%; suburban, 61%. Median family income, $11,022; families above $15,000: 25%; families below $3,000: 6%. Median years education, 12.3.

The Voters

Median voting age 38.
Employment profile White collar, 54%. Blue collar, 34%. Service, 11%. Farm, 1%.
Ethnic groups Black, 13%. Spanish, 10%. Total foreign stock, 9%.

Presidential vote

1976	Carter (D)	95,479	(50%)
	Ford (R)	95,998	(50%)
1972	Nixon (R)	100,489	(65%)
	McGovern (D)	53,818	(35%)

Rep. Ron Paul (R) Elected April 6, 1976; b. Aug. 20, 1935, Pittsburgh, Pa.; home, Lake Jackson; Gettysburgh Col., B.A. 1957, Duke U., M.D. 1961; Episcopalian.

Career Flight surgeon, U.S. Air Force, 1963–65; Practicing physician.

Offices 1234 LHOB, 202-225-5951. Also Suite 406, 1110 NASA Road One, Houston 77058, 713-333-2566.

Committees *Banking, Finance, and Urban Affairs* (10th). Subcommittees: Economic Stabilization; General Oversight and Renegotiation; Domestic Monetary Policy.

Group Ratings: Newly Elected

Key Votes: Newly Elected

Election Results

1978 general	Ron Paul (R)	54,643	(51%)	($322,156)
	Bob Gammage (D)	53,443	(49%)	($476,852)
1978 primary	Ron Paul (R), unopposed			
1976 general	Bob Gammage (D)	96,433	(50%)	($249,956)
	Ron Paul (R)	96,197	(50%)	($554,358)

TWENTY-THIRD DISTRICT

From San Antonio south, Texas is majority Mexican-American. Much of the territory can be called feudal: desert-like rural counties where big landowners effectively run the lives of their Mexican field hands. This is one part of the United States where there is a stark disparity between the power conferred by money and the power at least theoretically conferred by numbers and votes. In general, money wins. There have been so-called "brown power" movements in some of the small towns and counties here, and one in Zavala County has taken over the local government. But the problem remains of how to finance services and provide jobs when the wherewithal lies in the hands of the people who have been defined as the enemy. The future for most Mexican-Americans, at least to judge from their own behavior, seems to be in the larger urban centers where there are jobs, not in the parched reaches of south Texas which posess little economic activity of any kind.

The 23d congressional district of Texas covers much of the Mexican-American rural counties of south Texas. It also includes about 100,000 people in Bexar County—the south side of San Antonio and its suburbs, also a predominantly Mexican-American area. The rest of the district is a group of counties east and southeast of San Antonio. The area contains some Texas Germans and a fairly large Mexican-American minority; but the political preferences tend to fall more along the lines of John Connally, who comes from Wilson County in the 23d.

The 23d district has existed in basically its present form since the middle sixties and has had only one congressman. He is Abraham Kazen, who is of Lebanese rather than Mexican descent, but who has always had Mexican-American support in elections. Kazen spent 20 years in the Texas legislature before being elected to Congress, and he seems to have developed a Lyndon Johnson-like knack for pleasing both the powerful and the minorites in his district. He has not had major legislative accomplishments, but neither has he had significant electoral opposition in years

Census Data Pop. 466,424. Central city, 35%; suburban, 22%. Median family income, $6,512; families above $15,000: 9%; families below $3,000: 20%. Median years education, 9.8

The Voters

Median voting age 41.
Employment profile White collar, 43%. Blue collar, 35%. Service, 13%. Farm, 9%.
Ethnic groups Black, 3%. Spanish, 49%. Total foreign stock, 23%. Germany, 2%.

Presidential vote

1976	Carter (D)	83,251	(59%)
	Ford (R)	57,139	(41%)
1972	Nixon (R)	72,629	(62%)
	McGovern (D)	44,843	(38%)

Rep. Abraham Kazan, Jr. (D) Elected 1966; b. Jan. 17, 1919, Laredo; home, Laredo; U. of Tex., 1937–40, Cumberland U. Law School, 1941; Catholic.

Career Air Force, WWII; Practicing atty., 1945–66; Tex. House of Reps., 1947–53; Tex. Senate, 1953–66, Pres. Pro Tempore, 1959.

Offices 2411 RHOB, 202-225-4511. Also Rm. 201 Fed. Bldg., Laredo 78040, 512-723-4336.

Committees *Armed Services* (18th). Subcommittees: Investigations; Military Personnel.

Interior and Insular Affairs (4th). Subcommittees: Energy and the Environment; Mines and Mining; Water and Power Resources (Chairman).

Group Ratings

	ADA	COPE	PC	RPN	NFU	LCV	CFA	NAB	NSI	ACA	NTU
1978	10	33	18	42	56	–	18	46	100	64	–
1977	5	48	13	23	75	20	25	–	–	59	19
1976	15	61	16	44	58	17	36	18	100	68	26

Key Votes

1) Increase Def Spnd	FOR	6) Alaska Lands Protect	AGN	11) Delay Auto Pol Cntrl	FOR
2) B-1 Bomber	FOR	7) Water Projects Veto	AGN	12) Sugar Price Escalator	FOR
3) Cargo Preference	FOR	8) Consum Protect Agcy	AGN	13) Pub Fin Cong Cmpgns	AGN
4) Dereg Nat Gas	FOR	9) Common Situs Picket	AGN	14) ERA Ratif Recissn	FOR
5) Kemp-Roth	AGN	10) Labor Law Revision	AGN	15) Prohibt Govt Abrtns	FOR

Election Results

1978 general	Abraham Kazen, Jr. (D)	62,649	(90%)	($55,734)
	Augustin Mata (La Raza Unida)	7,185	(10%)	($5,337)
1978 primary	Abraham Kazen, Jr. (D)	63,847	(80%)	
	Martin Ross (D)	15,597	(20%)	
1976 general	Abraham Kazen, Jr. (D), unopposed			($5,968)

TWENTY-FOURTH DISTRICT

The 24th congressional district of Texas is known as the mid-cities district. It sits between Fort Worth and Dallas and contains parts of both. Geographically the district appears to consist of two tentacles emanating from the Dallas-Fort Worth Regional Airport—a Texas-sized establishment where everything (telephones and an ingenious but confusing mass transit system) costs a quarter and where the dollar changing machines return 95 cents. One tentacle reaches into Dallas, which contains precisely half the district's population. This is not the wealthy, Republican north side of Dallas, however; that is in the 3d district to the north. Rather, this is part of the city south of the Trinity River, an old neighborhood with funky Victorian houses and an interesting history called Oak Cliff. This is becoming increasingly a black neighborhood, and more than half of the 24th district's portion of Dallas is black. Thus in this district, if not in statewide elections, Dallas is a liberal force; it has supported the liberal candidate in primaries and has voted heavily Democratic in the general election. The Dallas tentacle also contains the suburb of Grand Prairie, a prosperous place many of whose residents grew up in rural Texas, and Irving, which stands a little higher on the socioeconomic scale.

The Fort Worth tentacle moves south and west from the Airport. It includes the western edge of Fort Worth and the suburbs of Euless and Arlington. The latter shows what has happened to this area in recent years. This was a town of 7,000 in 1950 and has more than 100,000 people today. Situated on the Dallas-Fort Worth Turnpike, it attracts thousands each year to the Six Flags Over Texas park and is the smallest city with a major league baseball team, the Texas Rangers who play in Turnpike Stadium. This Tarrant County part of the district, with its many middle income and upwardly mobile residents, is several shades to the right of the Dallas County portion of the 24th; it tends to favor conservative candidates in the Democratic primary and Republicans in the general election.

Since its creation in 1972, the 24th district has been the scene of more tough political battles than there have been election years. Its first Congressman was Dale Milford, a meteorologist and weathercaster on Dallas's WFAA-TV. Milford beat outspokenly liberal and conservative candidates in the 1972 Democratic primary, and overcame serious competition in the general election. Milford, a pilot, specialized in aviation matters, which are of considerable importance here, what with the Airport and the big General Dynamics and Bell aircraft factories in the Fort Worth area. But his generally conservative voting record attracted primary opposition. He had a difficult time beating liberal Dallas attorney Martin Frost in 1974, and in the 1976 general election he had significant competition from a retired Air Force officer, Leo Berman.

In 1978 Frost ran again. This time he had a strong base in Dallas, not just among blacks but among whites in the Oak Cliff area as well. He accused Milford of junketeering at taxpayers' expense, and he may have profited from the fact that Milford had suffered a heart attack since the last election. In any case, Frost won the primary. In the general, Berman was running again, and made a real effort of it, for Frost was a better target for him than Milford. But with the large black vote in this district, Frost was able to win a small but decisive victory. If he showed political acumen in his campaigning, he showed the same in the House, where he won assignment to the Rules Committee. The question for 1980 is whether this congressional district will see another tough contest again, or whether it is ready to settle down with its new congressman.

Census Data Pop. 466,875. Central city, 54%; suburban, 46%. Median family income, $9,583; families above $15,000: 18%; families below $3,000: 9%. Median years education, 11.9.

The Voters

Median voting age 37.
Employment profile White collar, 48%. Blue collar, 38%. Service, 14%. Farm, -%.
Ethnic groups Black, 26%. Spanish, 7%. Total foreign stock, 5%.

Presidential vote

1976	Carter (D)	NA	
	Ford (R)	NA	
1972	Nixon (R)	70,819	(60%)
	McGovern (D)	47,374	(40%)

Rep. Martin Frost (D) Elected 1978; b. Jan. 1, 1942, Glendale, Cal.; home, Dallas; U. of Mo., B.A., B.J. 1964, Georgetown U., LL.B. 1970.

Career Practicing atty., 1970–.

Offices 1123 LHOB, 202-225-3605. Also Suite 1319, Oakcliff Bank Tower, Dallas 75208, 214-941-6032.

Committees *Rules* (11th). Subcommittee: Legislative Procedures.

Group Ratings: Newly Elected

Key Votes: Newly Elected

Election Results

1978 general	Martin Frost (D)	39,201	(54%)	($347,177)
	Leo Berman (R)	33,314	(46%)	($228,740)
1978 primary	Martin Frost (D)	22,791	(55%)	
	Dale Milford (D)	18,595	(45%)	($121,638)
1976 general	Dale Milford (D)	82,743	(64%)	($76,031)
	Leo Berman (R)	47,075	(36%)	($55,677)

UTAH

In 1827 Joseph Smith, a young Palmyra, New York, farmer, experienced a vision in which the Angel Moroni appeared to him. Moroni was a prophet of the lost tribe of Israel (the American Indians) which had presumably found its way to the New World some 600 years before the birth of Christ. Moroni told Smith where to unearth several golden tablets inscribed with hieroglyphic writings. With the aid of magical spectacles, Smith translated the tablets and published them as the Book of Mormon in 1830. He then declared himself a prophet and founded a religious group he called the Church of Jesus Christ of Latter Day Saints.

The group was just one wave in a wash of religious revivalism, prophecy, and utopianism that swept across upstate New York—Palmyra is just east of Rochester—during the 1820s and 1830s; the region was so alive with religious enthusiasm that it was known as the "burned-over district." Very quickly the prophet's new sect attracted hundreds of converts. Persecuted for their beliefs, these Mormons, as they were called, moved west to Ohio, Missouri, and then Illinois. In 1844 the Mormon colony at Nauvoo, Illinois, had some 15,000 members, all living under the strict theocratic rule of Joseph Smith. In secular Illinois politics Nauvoo—then the largest city in the state—held the balance of power between contending Democrats and Whigs. It was here that

Smith received a revelation sanctioning the practice of polygamy, which led to his death at the hands of a mob in 1844.

After the murder, the new president of the church, Brigham Young, decided to move the faithful, "the saints," farther west into territory that was still part of Mexico and far beyond the pale of white settlement. Young led a well-organized migration across the Great Plains and into the Rocky Mountains. In 1847 the prophet and his followers stopped along the western slope of the Wasatch Range, and as Brigham Young viewed the valley of the Great Salt Lake spread out below, he uttered the now famous words "This is the place."

The place was Utah. And it is the only state that continues to live by the teachings of the church responsible for its founding. Throughout the nineteenth century "Zion" attracted thousands of converts from the Midwest, the north of England, and Scandinavia. The object of religious fear, prejudice, and perhaps some envy, Utah was not granted statehood until 1896, after the church renounced polygamy. Presently more than 70% of all Utah citizens are members of the Church of Jesus Christ of Latter Day Saints (LDS).

The distinctive features of the LDS Church dominate Utah politics. Leaders of the church have always exerted great political influence. For one thing, Utah has sent very few Gentiles (non-Mormons) to Congress during 80 years of statehood. Today the church owns one of the two leading Salt Lake City newspapers and a statewide television station. It has holdings in an insurance company, various banks, and real estate, and runs the largest department store in Salt Lake City. The Mormon hierarchy confidently takes stands on secular matters, economic and political. For example, it strongly supports Utah's right to work law as well as Anita Bryant's crusade against homosexual rights.

One church doctrine in particular has embarrassed many Mormons—the faith denied blacks, supposedly cursed in the Bible, the "priesthood," i.e., full church membership. All Mormons are lay persons, as the church does not employ a professional clergy; but laymen may be called to service, and seldom refuse. (That is what happened to former Congressman Wayne Owens, a Democrat who lost the 1974 Senate race. He was sent by the church to eastern Canada in 1975 and effectively removed from Utah politics.) The church doctrine towards blacks was finally changed in 1978, when LDS president Spencer Kimball received a revelation. The president is the most senior member of the church's ruling body, and from 1964 through the seventies the post was held by men over 90. The man next in line for the post is Ezra Taft Benson, Eisenhower's Secretary of Agriculture in the fifties, a member of the board of the John Birch Society (referred to matter-of-factly as the JBS in Utah newspapers), and a man whose view of the boundaries between religion and politics is not clear.

LDS doctrine carries the virtues of nineteenth century upstate New York to their logical ends. Even today Mormons are forbidden to consume alcohol, tobacco, coffee, or tea; apparently as a result incidence of cancer is lower than average among them. Mormons are strong upholders of traditional sexual morality, as millions have learned from the most famous Mormon entertainers, the Osmond family. Many young Mormons give two years of their lives to "missions" at home and in some of the unlikeliest places overseas, in which they attempt to win new converts to the faith. And members are required to pledge a 10% tithe of their income to the church.

That income is often substantial, for Mormons have a well-deserved reputation for hard work and tend to do well in business and the professions. And it seems that their very traditional cultural attitudes together with their general affluence (there is little poverty in Utah) that has made Mormons generally and Utah voters in particular increasingly conservative and Republican in the sixties and seventies. Utahns in the thirties had voted for Franklin Roosevelt and elected New Deal senators and congressmen. But with the coming of the Kennedy Administration, as national Democrats became increasingly identified with the causes of racial minorities and with detractors of traditional morality, Utah moved hard to the right. As late as 1960 John Kennedy got a respectable, if losing, 45% here. Barry Goldwater won 45% himself four years later—one of his best showings in the nation. In 1972 Richard Nixon carried the state with a record 72%. This was the trend of the future; Utah's young people, at least those who stay close to the church, are probably more conservative than their parents. At Brigham Young University, a Mormon institution known for its conservatism, Nixon took 79%, Schmitz 15%, and McGovern 6% in 1972. In 1976 Utah gave Gerald Ford 65% of its vote—his largest percentage in any state in the nation. It was the first time, but probably not the last, that Utah would be the most Republican of states. The mood here is sharply hostile to the federal government and fiercely defensive of the free enterprise system and of traditional moral standards. Utahns believe they have found the way to run a society successfully—and there is much in life in Utah to support that contention. They see no reason to change; to paraphrase Lincoln Steffens, their contention might be: "I have seen the past—and it works."

This is not to say that Democrats cannot win elections here. In fact Utah has had Democratic governors since 1964. But they have been Democrats very much in the Utah style. Calvin Rampton, Governor for 12 years, was a hard-line defender of the Vietnam war and a fiscal conservative. His successor, Scott Matheson, was a Salt Lake City lawyer whose clients included the Union Pacific Railroad and Anaconda, and who advocates a "preparedness growth plan." Matheson's term expires in 1980.

But it is the Republicans who hold both of Utah's Senate seats—and the Republicans who hold them are among the Senate's leading conservatives. Jake Garn was elected in a close race against Wayne Owens in 1974, and Orrin Hatch upset three-term incumbent Democrat Frank Moss in 1976. But both have now become well established in the state and in the Senate. Garn indeed may be the intellectual leader of the group of Rocky Mountain "New Right" senators who have become so influential in 1977 and 1978. Garn is bright and has a good sense of humor; he is also aggressive and strongly committed. As a member of the Armed Services Committee, he is a well informed backer of strong defense measures and one who believes that the nation is not doing enough in the world to protect its interests. He was a strong opponent of the Panama Canal Treaty. Garn is also ranking Republican now on the Senate Banking, Housing, and Urban Affairs Committee. Previously that position had been held by backers of big housing programs. Garn, a former Mayor of Salt Lake City, is skeptical about federal domestic programs, and may be able to use his committee position to cut housing programs down even further. Garn is up for reelection in 1980; young, vigorous, in tune with the current of thought in his state, he seems in excellent political shape.

Orrin Hatch's politics are very similar to Garn's, but his personal approach and style differ. Where Garn is almost urbane and intellectual in his conservatism, Hatch is fervent and almost feverish. While Garn had deep roots in Utah, Hatch moved there from Pittsburgh only a few years ago. He was head of the Reagan delegate forces in 1976, and ran for the Senate only at the last minute. He won the Republican nomination by campaigning with Reagan's picture. In the general, his comparative youth contrasted with Moss's age (65) and his conservative politics contrasted with Moss's support of most Democratic programs. Hatch brings the kind of passion to politics of a man who believes that if his advice is not taken, disaster will soon follow. Although he works hard and has helped less than conservative Republicans in some elections, he seems to be considered something of a fanatic by some senators. In early 1979 he ran against John Heinz for the chair of the Republican Senatorial Campaign Committee; and although his politics is closer to most Senate Republicans' than Heinz's, he still lost by a one-vote margin. Hatch is the ranking Republican on the Human Resources Committee and spearhead of the effort to defeat the AFL-CIO's labor law reform. He has been an influential senator on occasion because of sheer energy and determination, and he is apparently popular in Utah. It is not clear what path his career will follow.

Utah has two congressional districts, and though they both stretch far from the Wasatch Front—the land between the mountains and the Great Salt Lake where 88% of the state's people live—that is where the battles are really fought. The 1st district covers geographically the eastern half of the state, but its two main population concentrations are separated by Salt Lake City, which is in the 2d district. To the north are the well-to-do suburbs of Davis County and the working class town of Ogden, near which the Golden Spike was pounded linking the nation by transcontinental railroad in 1869. To the south is Utah County, whose main town is Provo, the home of Brigham Young University and of the Osmonds.

Politically the 1st is the more conservative and Republican of the two districts, and yet it has elected a Democratic congressman since 1970. He is Gunn McKay, nephew of the late LDS president David McKay and a former aide to Governor Rampton. McKay does not always line up with northern Democrats, being more in the Rampton tradition than in that of the House Democratic leadership. He has won reelection by margins recently which suggest that he is politically invulnerable. Several years ago he got a seat on the Appropriations Committee, and when Bob Sikes was ousted as Chairman of the Military Construction Subcommittee, McKay inherited the post.

The 2d district includes several of the state's western counties, but for all practical purposes it is the Salt Lake City district; 86% of the vote is cast in Salt Lake County. It is also something of a jinx seat: in the last five elections, it has elected four different congressmen—one of the few districts in the nation with such high turnover. Republican Sherman Lloyd, the winner in 1970, was defeated in 1972 by Wayne Owens, who in turn ran for the Senate and lost in 1974, at which point the 2d district seat was won by Democrat Allan Howe. Howe might have won again had he not had the misfortune, shortly after Wayne Hays's downfall, to have been accused of soliciting an undercover policewoman for an act of prostitution on a notorious Salt Lake City street, West Second South. Howe was convicted, but refused to get off the ticket; predictably, he lost. A Brooklyn congressman can win reelection after soliciting a teen-age boy, but in Salt Lake City soliciting an adult woman is political ruin.

The winner in 1976 was Republican Dan Marriott, a solid conservative who has not made as much of an impression in the House as Garn and Hatch have in the Senate. Nonetheless Marriott was reelected with a very satisfactory margin in 1978.

Census Data Pop. 1,059,273; 0.52% of U.S. total, 36th largest; Central city, 31%; suburban, 47%. Median family income, $9,320; 23d highest; families above $15,000: 17%; families below $3,000: 9%. Median years education, 12.5.

1977 Share of Federal Tax Burden $1,554,000,000; 0.45% of U.S. total, 37th largest.

1977 Share of Federal Outlays $2,382,914,000; 0.60% of U.S. total, 38th largest. Per capita federal spending, $1,976.

DOD	$752,795,000	32d (0.82%)	HEW	$606,239,000	40th (0.41%)
ERDA	$8,406,000	30th (0.14%)	HUD	$15,030,000	43d (0.36%)
NASA	$52,062,000	12th (1.32%)	VA	$103,562,000	39th (0.54%)
DOT	$90,195,000	40th (0.63%)	EPA	$22,257,000	40th (0.27%)
DOC	$49,222,000	43d (0.59%)	RevS	$41,394,000	38th (0.49%)
DOI	$158,753,000	9th (3.41%)	Debt	$61,591,000	39th (0.21%)
USDA	$98,852,000	42d (0.50%)	Other	$322,556,000	

Economic Base Finance, insurance and real estate; agriculture, notably cattle, dairy products, turkeys and sheep; primary metal industries; metal mining; food and kindred products; transportation equipment, especially aircraft and parts; apparel and other textile products, especially women's and misses' outerwear.

Political Line-up Governor, Scott M. Matheson (D). Senators, Jake Garn (R) and Orrin G. Hatch (R). Representatives, 2 (1 D and 1 R). State Senate (40 D, 19 R); State House (24 D, 51 R).

The Voters

Registration 666,451 Total. No party registration.
Median voting age 39
Employment profile White collar, 52%. Blue collar, 32%. Service, 13%. Farm, 3%.
Ethnic groups Spanish, 4%. Total foreign stock, 12%. UK, 3%.

Presidential vote

1976	Carter (D)	182,110	(35%)
	Ford (R)	337,908	(65%)
1972	Nixon (R)	323,643	(72%)
	McGovern (D)	126,284	(28%)

Sen. Jake Garn (R) Elected 1974, seat up 1980; b. Oct. 12, 1932, Richfield; home, Salt Lake City; U. of Utah, B.S. 1955; Church of Latter Day Saints.

Career Navy, 1956–60; Asst. Mgr., Salt Lake Ofc., Home Life Insurance Co. of New York, 1961–66; Salt Lake City Commission, 1967–71; Mayor of Salt Lake City, 1971–74.

Offices 4203 DSOB, 202-224-5444. Also 4225 Fed. Bldg., Salt Lake City 84138, 801-524-5933, and Fed. Bldg., Ogden 84401, 801-399-6208.

Committees *Appropriations* (10th). Subcommittees: Agriculture and Related Agencies; Defense; Energy and Water Development; Foreign Operations; State, Justice, and Commerce, the Judiciary, and Related Agencies.

Banking, Housing, and Urban Affairs (Ranking Member). Subcommittees: Housing and Urban Affairs; Financial Institutions; Insurance.

Group Ratings

	ADA	COPE	PC	RPN	NFU	LCV	CFA	NAB	NSI	ACA	NTU
1978	5	5	18	60	30	11	20	75	100	95	–
1977	10	5	13	64	9	–	12	–	–	100	48
1976	0	10	6	75	33	3	0	100	88	96	75

Key Votes

1) Warnke Nom	AGN	6) Egypt-Saudi Arms	FOR	11) Hosptl Cost Contnmnt	AGN
2) Neutron Bomb	FOR	7) Draft Restr Pardon	AGN	12) Clinch River Reactor	FOR
3) Waterwy User Fee	AGN	8) Wheat Price Support	AGN	13) Pub Fin Cong Cmpgns	AGN
4) Dereg Nat Gas	FOR	9) Panama Canal Treaty	AGN	14) ERA Ratif Recissn	AGN
5) Kemp-Roth	FOR	10) Labor Law Rev Clot	AGN	15) Med Necssy Abrtns	AGN

Election Results

1974 general	Jacob Garn (R)	210,299	(50%)	✓	($363,162)
	Wayne Owens (D)	185,377	(44%)		($445,400)
	Bruce Bangerter (A)	24,966	(6%)		($1,488)
1974 primary	Jacob Garn (R), unopposed				
1968 general	Wallace F. Bennett (R)	225,075	(54%)		
	Milton Weilenmann (D)	192,168	(46%)		

Sen. Orrin G. Hatch (R) Elected 1976, seat up 1982; b. Mar. 22, 1934, Pittsburgh, Pa.; home, Salt Lake City; Brigham Young U., B.S. 1959, U. of Pittsburgh, J.D. 1962; Church of Jesus Christ of Latter Day Saints.

Career Practicing atty., 1962–77.

Offices 411 RSOB, 202-224-5251. Also Fed. Bldg., 125 S. State, Salt Lake City 84138, 801-524-4380.

Committees *Budget* (7th).

Labor and Human Resources (4th). Subcommittees: Health and Scientific Research; Employment, Poverty, and Migratory Labor; Alcoholism and Drug Abuse.

Judiciary (4th). Subcommittees: Antitrust, Monopoly, and Business Rights; Constitution; Criminal Justice.

Group Ratings

	ADA	COPE	PC	RPN	NFU	LCV	CFA	NAB	NSI	ACA	NTU
1978	5	11	15	50	67	7	15	92	100	96	–
1977	0	12	13	67	20	–	12	–	–	92	50

Key Votes

1) Warnke Nom	AGN	6) Egypt-Saudi Arms	FOR	11) Hosptl Cost Contnmnt	AGN
2) Neutron Bomb	FOR	7) Draft Restr Pardon	AGN	12) Clinch River Reactor	FOR
3) Waterwy User Fee	AGN	8) Wheat Price Support	AGN	13) Pub Fin Cong Cmpgns	AGN
4) Dereg Nat Gas	FOR	9) Panama Canal Treaty	AGN	14) ERA Ratif Recissn	AGN
5) Kemp-Roth	FOR	10) Labor Law Rev Clot	AGN	15) Med Necssy Abrtns	AGN

Election Results

1976 general	Orrin J. Hatch (R)	290,221	(56%)	($370,517)
	Frank E. Moss (D)	223,948	(44%)	($343,598)
1976 primary	Orrin J. Hatch (R)	104,490	(65%)	
	Jack Carlson (R)	57,249	(35%)	
1970 general	Frank E. Moss (D)	210,207	(57%)	
	Laurence J. Burton (R)	159,004	(43%)	

Gov. Scott M. Matheson (D) Elected 1976, term expires Jan. 1981; b. Jan. 8, 1929; U. of Utah, B.S. 1950, Stanford U., J.D. 1952.

Career Practicing atty., 1953–54, 1956–68; Parowan City Atty. and Depy. Iron Co. Atty., 1953–54; Law Clerk for U.S. Dist. Judge, Salt Lake City, 1954–56; Depy. Salt Lake Co. Atty., 1956–57; Atty., Union Pacific R.R., 1958–69, Gen. Solicitor, 1972–76; Counsel, Anaconda Co., 1969–70, Asst. Gen. Counsel, 1970–1972.

Offices 210 State Capitol, Salt Lake City 84114, 801-328-5231.

Election Results

1976 general	Scott M. Matheson (D)	280,606	(53%)
	Vernon B. Romney (R)	248,027	(47%)
1976 primary	Scott M. Matheson (D)	50,505	(59%)
	Jack Preston Creer (D)	35,154	(41%)
1972 general	Calvin L. Rampton (D)	331,988	(70%)
	Nicholas L. Strike (R)	144,449	(30%)

FIRST DISTRICT

Census Data Pop. 529,688. Central city, 28%; suburban, 41%. Median family income, $9,080; families above $15,000: 16%; families below $3,000: 9%. Median years education, 12.5.

The Voters

Median voting age 38.
Employment profile White collar, 50%. Blue collar, 33%. Service, 13%. Farm, 4%.
Ethnic groups Spanish, 4%. Total foreign stock, 10%. UK, 2%.

Presidential vote

1976	Carter (D)	82,741	(33%)
	Ford (R)	170,399	(67%)
1972	Nixon (R)	166,517	(77%)
	McGovern (D)	50,225	(23%)

Rep. K. Gunn McKay (D) Elected 1970; b. Feb. 23, 1925, Ogden; home, Huntsville; Weber St. Col., 1958–60, Utah St. U., B.S. 1962; Church of Latter Day Saints.

Career Coast Guard, WWII; small business and teaching; Utah House of Reps., 1962–66; Admin. Asst. to Gov. Calvin L. Rampton, 1967–70.

Offices 2209 RHOB, 202-225-0453. Also Suite 206, 1st Security Bank, 92 N. University Ave., Provo 84601, 801-373-4150.

Committees *Appropriations* (16th). Subcommittees: District of Columbia; Interior; Military Construction (Chairman).

Group Ratings

	ADA	COPE	PC	RPN	NFU	LCV	CFA	NAB	NSI	ACA	NTU
1978	15	37	38	42	40	–	14	67	70	60	–
1977	25	62	30	50	55	37	15	–	–	41	37
1976	40	50	39	44	60	39	27	27	60	38	27

Key Votes

1) Increase Def Spnd	AGN	6) Alaska Lands Protect	AGN	11) Delay Auto Pol Cntrl	FOR
2) B-1 Bomber	FOR	7) Water Projects Veto	AGN	12) Sugar Price Escalator	DNV
3) Cargo Preference	AGN	8) Consum Protect Agcy	AGN	13) Pub Fin Cong Cmpgns	AGN
4) Dereg Nat Gas	FOR	9) Common Situs Picket	AGN	14) ERA Ratif Recissn	FOR
5) Kemp-Roth	AGN	10) Labor Law Revision	FOR	15) Prohibt Govt Abrtns	FOR

Election Results

1978 general	Gunn McKay (D)	93,892	(52%)	($149,143)
	Jed J. Richardson (R)	85,028	(48%)	($147,556)
1978 primary	Gunn McKay (D), unopposed			
1976 general	Gunn McKay (D)	155,631	(59%)	($52,142)
	Joe H. Ferguson (R)	106,542	(41%)	($28,197)

SECOND DISTRICT

Census Data Pop. 529,585. Central city, 33%; suburban, 53%. Median family income, $9,537; families above $15,000: 18%; families below $3,000: 8%. Median years education, 12.5.

The Voters

Median voting age 40.
Employment profile White collar, 53%. Blue collar, 32%. Service, 13%. Farm, 2%.
Ethnic groups Spanish, 5%. Total foreign stock, 14%. UK, 3%.

Presidential vote

1976	Carter (D)	99,369	(37%)
	Ford (R)	167,509	(63%)
1972	Nixon (R)	157,126	(67%)
	McGovern (D)	76,059	(33%)

Rep. Dan Marriott (R) Elected 1976; b. Nov. 2, 1939, Bingham; home, Salt Lake City; U. of Utah, B.S. 1967, Amer. Col. of Life Underwriters, C.L.U.; Church of Latter Day Saints.

Career Pres., Marriott Associates, corp. benefit planners and business consultants, 1967–77.

Offices 1133 LHOB, 202-225-3011. Also 2311 Fed. Bldg., Salt Lake City 84138, 801-524-4394.

Committees *Interior and Insular Affairs* (8th). Subcommittees: Energy and the Environment; Mines and Mining.

Small Business (7th). Subcommittees: SBA and SBIC Authority and General Small Business Problems; Special Small Business Problems.

Group Ratings

	ADA	COPE	PC	RPN	NFU	LCV	CFA	NAB	NSI	ACA	NTU
1978	5	15	10	64	0	–	14	100	100	100	–
1977	5	13	18	54	9	15	10	–	–	96	38

Key Votes

1) Increase Def Spnd	FOR	6) Alaska Lands Protect	AGN	11) Delay Auto Pol Cntrl	FOR
2) B-1 Bomber	DNV	7) Water Projects Veto	AGN	12) Sugar Price Escalator	FOR
3) Cargo Preference	AGN	8) Consum Protect Agcy	AGN	13) Pub Fin Cong Cmpgns	AGN
4) Dereg Nat Gas	FOR	9) Common Situs Picket	AGN	14) ERA Ratif Recissn	FOR
5) Kemp-Roth	FOR	10) Labor Law Revision	AGN	15) Prohibt Govt Abrtns	FOR

Election Results

1978 general	Dan Marriott (R)	121,492	(64%)	($353,520)
	Edwin B. Firmage (D)	68,899	(36%)	($230,760)
1978 primary	Dan Marriott (R), unopposed			
1976 general	Dan Marriott (R)	144,861	(57%)	($119,349)
	Allan T. Howe (D)	110,931	(43%)	($64,696)

VERMONT

In many ways Vermont still seems part of the nineteenth century. The classic New England town squares still stand here; the cows still graze on the hillsides; the taciturn Yankee farmers still tap sugar maple trees in early spring; and the autumn foliage is perhaps the most magnificent in the world. Vermont remains, by Census definition, our most rural state, with two-thirds of the population living outside urban areas. But even so the sixties and seventies have brought change here. There are now large IBM and General Electric complexes around Burlington, the state's largest city, whose metropolitan population has passed 100,000. The ski resort and summer home industries have boomed so much that the price of rural land has skyrocketed and led many farmers to sell. And so, the very things which attract people to Vermont threaten to vanish. From 1850 to 1960 Vermont's population hovered between 300,000 and 400,000; only in 1963 were there finally more people than cows in the state. But in 1970 there were 444,000 people living in Vermont, and today there are more than 487,000.

There have also been massive political changes here—massive enough that this state, long the most Republican in the nation, today has a Democratic senator and for most of the sixties and seventies has had Democratic governors. Before 1960 the only areas of Democratic strength were the small Irish and French Canadian communities in Burlington and other towns near the Canadian border; it was almost as if all the Catholic minority were Democrats and all the Protestant majority Republicans. But in 1962 Democrat Philip Hoff was elected Governor, and he was reelected easily in 1964 and 1966.

That, however, did not usher in an era of Democratic dominance. Hoff himself was defeated for the Senate in 1970, as the coalition of Yankees attracted to his environmentalist record and traditional Catholic Democrats fell apart over the Vietnam war and related cultural issues. But Hoff's successors as governor—Republican Deane Davis (1968–72), Democrat Thomas Salmon (1972–76), and Republican Richard Snelling (1976–)—have not veered sharply from his basic policies. Salmon in particular was associated with the idea of preserving Vermont's way of life and its physical environment. Unlike most Eastern states and like many states in the West, Vermont is facing fundamental issues about the kind of place it wants to be, issues which are made urgent by rapid growth and considerable prosperity.

Vermont's senior public official now is Senator Robert Stafford, who has held statewide elective office since 1954. A moderate Republican with a serious demeanor, he has never antagonized a significant group of voters. His record in the House from 1960 to 1971 was liberal enough that he never attracted serious opposition and conservative enough that his early appointment was urged by the Nixon Administration when Senator Winston Prouty died in 1971. Stafford is the ranking Republican on the Environment and Public Works Committee.

Stafford has been considered politically invulnerable in Vermont, but in his most recent election, in 1976, he had a serious challenge. His opponent was Governor Thomas Salmon, who had his own problems: he had sponsored an unpopular sales tax increase and he was nearly beaten in the primary by a little known candidate. Nevertheless the brash Salmon made great inroads against the bland Stafford in most parts of the state. Salmon had 48% of the vote, and he would have won if he had gotten normal Democratic pluralities in the Burlington area.

Vermont's junior Senator is a Democrat—the only Democrat the state has ever sent to the Senate. Patrick Leahy won the seat in 1974, when the quintessential Vermont Yankee, George Aiken, retired after 34 years in the Senate. Born the year Aiken went to Washington, Leahy had made a name for himself in Vermont as the Burlington area prosecutor who tried all major felony cases personally and attacked the big oil companies during the gasoline crisis of 1974. Leahy had a solid base in Democratic Burlington together with the kind of quiet, thoughtful temperament Yankee Vermonters like in their public officials. He was able to outpoll Republican Congressman-at-Large Richard Mallary by a narrow margin.

On many issues Leahy's voting record is in line with most national Democrats. Yet at the same time there is very much a Vermont emphasis in his record. He serves on the Agriculture Committee, a useful post for a senator whose state is a major dairy producer and possesses major forest resources. And after a term on the Armed Services Committee, where he questioned some military programs, he won a seat on the Appropriations Committee. There he has a reputation for parsimoniousness that undoubtedly accords with the state's instincts. He has chaired the Subcommittee on the District of Columbia and held up some big spending programs even while being subjected to considerable pressure.

However well Leahy's record fits Vermont, he cannot count on a free ride when his seat comes up in 1980; no Democrat can be considered safe in Vermont. One possible competitor is Governor Snelling; another is Congressman-at-Large James Jeffords. In his three terms in the House, he has cultivated a liberal image and an environmental profile, although as a moderate Republican his legislative productivity has been limited. Jeffords has had only weak opposition in elections, and won in 1976 and 1978 by overwhelming margins.

Census Data Pop. 444,732; 0.22% of U.S. total, 48th largest; Central city, 0%; suburban, 0%. Median family income, $8,928; 28th highest; families above $15,000: 16%; families below $3,000: 9%. Median years education, 12.2.

1977 Share of Federal Tax Burden $622,000,000; 0.18% of U.S. total, 51st largest.

1977 Share of Federal Outlays $871,808,000; 0.22% of U.S. total, 50th largest. Per capita federal spending, $1,851.

DOD	$152,726,000	49th (0.17%)	HEW	$354,925,000	47th (0.24%)
ERDA	$43,000	51st (—%)	HUD	$5,807,000	50th (0.14%)
NASA	$87,000	47th (—%)	VA	$47,189,000	50th (0.25%)
DOT	$39,910,000	49th (0.28%)	EPA	$21,857,000	41st (0.27%)
DOC	$59,674,000	35th (0.72%)	RevS	$25,016,000	45th (0.30%)
DOI	$2,723,000	50th (0.06%)	Debt	$34,350,000	47th (0.11%)
USDA	$37,339,000	48th (0.19%)	Other	$90,162,000	

Economic Base Agriculture, notably dairy products, cattle, eggs and forest products; finance, insurance and real estate; electrical equipment and supplies, especially electronic components and accessories; machinery, especially metal working machinery; printing and publishing, especially book printing; lumber and wood products; cut stone and stone products, and other stone, clay and glass products.

Political Line-up Governor, Richard A. Snelling (R). Senators, Robert T. Stafford (R) and Patrick J. Leahy (D). Representative, 1 R at large. State Senate (20 R and 10 D); State House (81 R, 68 D, and 1 Ind.).

The Voters

Registration 286,275 Total. No party registration.
Median voting age 42
Employment profile White collar, 46%. Blue collar, 35%. Service, 14%. Farm, 5%.
Ethnic groups Total foreign stock, 18%. Canada, 10%.

Presidential vote

1976	Carter (D)	78,789	(44%)
	Ford (R)	100,387	(56%)
1972	Nixon (R)	117,149	(63%)
	McGovern (D)	68,174	(37%)

1976 Democratic Presidential Primary

Carter	16,335	(46%)
Shriver	10,699	(30%)
Others	8,217	(23%)

1976 Republican Presidential Primary

Ford	27,014	(85%)
Reagan	4,892	(15%)

Sen. Robert T. Stafford (R) Elected Appointed Sept. 16, 1971, elected Jan. 7, 1972, seat up 1982; b. Aug. 8, 1913, Rutland; home, Rutland; Middlebury Col., B.S. 1935, U. of Mich., Boston U., LL.B. 1938; Congregationalist.

Career Rutland City Prosecuting Atty., 1938–42; Navy, WWII and Korea; Rutland Co. State's Atty., 1947–51; Deputy Atty. Gen. of Vt., 1953–55, Atty. Gen. of Vt., 1955–57; Lt. Gov. of Vt., 1957–59; Gov. of Vt., 1959–61; U.S. House of Reps., 1961–71.

Offices 5219 DSOB, 202-224-5141. Also 501 Fed. Bldg., Burlington 05401, 802-951-6707, and 27 S. Main St., Rutland 05701, 802-775-5446.

Committees *Environment and Public Works* (Ranking Member). Subcommittees: Environmental Pollution; Transportation; Regional and Community Development.

Labor and Human Resources (3d). Subcommittees: Handicapped; Education, Arts, and Humanities; Aging.

Veterans' Affairs (Ranking Member).

Group Ratings

	ADA	COPE	PC	RPN	NFU	LCV	CFA	NAB	NSI	ACA	NTU
1978	55	58	55	88	50	74	35	17	44	29	–
1977	45	68	48	56	55	–	48	–	–	22	24
1976	60	71	70	73	75	59	57	11	80	20	13

Key Votes

1) Warnke Nom	FOR	6) Egypt-Saudi Arms	FOR	11) Hosptl Cost Contnmnt	FOR
2) Neutron Bomb	FOR	7) Draft Restr Pardon	AGN	12) Clinch River Reactor	DNV
3) Waterwy User Fee	FOR	8) Wheat Price Support	AGN	13) Pub Fin Cong Cmpgns	FOR
4) Dereg Nat Gas	FOR	9) Panama Canal Treaty	FOR	14) ERA Ratif Recissn	FOR
5) Kemp-Roth	AGN	10) Labor Law Rev Clot	FOR	15) Med Necssy Abrtns	FOR

Election Results

1976 general	Robert T. Stafford (R)	94,481	(52%)	($157,927)
	Thomas P. Salmon (D)	85,682	(48%)	($169,296)
1976 primary	Robert T. Stafford (R), unopposed			
1972 special	Robert T. Stafford (R)	45,888	(66%)	
	Randolph T. Major (D)	23,842	(34%)	
1972 special primary	Robert T. Stafford (R), unopposed			
1970 general	Winston L. Prouty (R)	91,198	(59%)	
	Phillip H. Hoff (D)	62,271	(41%)	

Sen. Patrick J. Leahy (D) Elected 1974, seat up 1980; b. Mar. 31, 1940, Montpelier; home, Burlington; St. Michael's Col., Winooski, B.A. 1961, Georgetown U., J.D. 1964; Catholic.

Career Practicing atty., 1964–74; Chittenden Co. State's Atty., 1966–74.

Offices 232 RSOB, 202-224-4242. Also Box 2, Burlington 05401, 802-863-2525.

Committees *Agriculture, Nutrition, and Forestry* (5th). Subcommittees: Agricultural Research and General Legislation; Rural Development (Chairman); Nutrition.

Appropriations (13th). Subcommittees: Defense; District of Columbia (Chairman); Foreign Operations; HUD-Independent Agencies; Interior and Related Agencies.

Judiciary (8th).

Group Ratings

	ADA	COPE	PC	RPN	NFU	LCV	CFA	NAB	NSI	ACA	NTU
1978	65	79	80	60	70	94	55	8	22	21	–
1977	80	80	83	55	80	–	68	–	–	15	32
1976	85	85	90	47	92	79	85	20	0	8	33

Key Votes

1) Warnke Nom	FOR	6) Egypt-Saudi Arms	FOR	11) Hosptl Cost Contnmnt	FOR
2) Neutron Bomb	AGN	7) Draft Restr Pardon	FOR	12) Clinch River Reactor	AGN
3) Waterwy User Fee	FOR	8) Wheat Price Support	FOR	13) Pub Fin Cong Cmpgns	FOR
4) Dereg Nat Gas	AGN	9) Panama Canal Treaty	FOR	14) ERA Ratif Recissn	FOR
5) Kemp-Roth	AGN	10) Labor Law Rev Clot	FOR	15) Med Necssy Abrtns	AGN

Election Results

1974 general	Patrick J. Leahy (D)	70,629	(52%)	($152,817)
	Richard W. Mallary (R)	66,223	(48%)	($90,617)
1974 primary	Patrick J. Leahy (D)	19,801	(84%)	
	One other (D)	3,703	(16%)	
1968 general	George D. Aiken (R-D), unopposed			

Gov. Richard A. Snelling (R) Elected 1976, term expires Jan. 1981; b. Feb. 18, 1927; U. of Havana, Cuba, Lehigh U., Harvard U., A.B. 1948; Unitarian.

Career Army, WWII; Founder and Chm., Shelburne Industries, Inc.; Vt. House of Reps., 1959–60, 1973–76, Major. Ldr., 1975–76.

Offices Governor's Office, Montpelier 05602, 802-828-3333.

Election Results

1978 general	Richard A. Snelling (R)	78,181	(65%)
	Edwin C. Granai (D)	42,482	(35%)
1978 primary	Richard A. Snelling (R) unopposed		
1976 general	Richard A. Snelling (R)	98,206	(54%)
	Stella B. Hackel (D)	72,761	(40%)
	Bernard Sanders (LU)	11,317	(6%)

Rep. James M. Jeffords (R) Elected 1974; b. May 11, 1934, Rutland; home, Montpelier; Yale U., B.S. 1956, Harvard U., LL.B. 1962.

Career Navy, 1956–59; Law Clerk to U.S. Dist. Ct. Judge Ernest W. Gibson, 1962; Practicing atty., 1963–75; Chm., Rutland Co. Bd. of Property Tax Appeals, 1964–66; Vt. Senate, 1967–68; Atty. Gen. of Vt., 1969–73.

Offices 1510 LHOB, 202-225-4115. Also P.O. Box 676, Fed. Bldg., Montpelier 05602, 802-223-5274.

Committees *Agriculture* (8th). Subcommittees: Conservation and Credit; Dairy and Poultry.

Education and Labor (4th). Subcommittees: Employment Opportunities; Postsecondary Education.

Group Ratings

	ADA	COPE	PC	RPN	NFU	LCV	CFA	NAB	NSI	ACA	NTU
1978	40	30	58	82	90	–	64	36	67	25	–
1977	75	62	75	85	83	85	65	–	–	42	28
1976	55	48	61	83	58	70	54	50	70	33	17

Key Votes

1) Increase Def Spnd	FOR	6) Alaska Lands Protect	FOR	11) Delay Auto Pol Cntrl	AGN
2) B-1 Bomber	AGN	7) Water Projects Veto	FOR	12) Sugar Price Escalator	AGN
3) Cargo Preference	AGN	8) Consum Protect Agcy	FOR	13) Pub Fin Cong Cmpgns	FOR
4) Dereg Nat Gas	AGN	9) Common Situs Picket	AGN	14) ERA Ratif Recissn	FOR
5) Kemp-Roth	FOR	10) Labor Law Revision	FOR	15) Prohibt Govt Abrtns	AGN

Election Results

1978 general	James M. Jeffords (R)	90,688	(75%)	($66,589)
	S. Marie Dietz (D)	23,228	(19%)	($8,768)
	Peter Isaac Diamondstone (LU)	6,505	(5%)	
1978 primary	James M. Jeffords (R), unopposed			
1976 general	James M. Jeffords (R)	124,458	(69%)	($62,770)
	John A. Burgess (D)	57,053	(31%)	($46,574)

VIRGINIA

Fifteen years ago any analysis of Virginia politics began and ended with the Byrd machine, the unique group of conservative Democrats who utterly dominated the politics of this large and variegated state. Today, after a decade of political turmoil and uncertainty, the Byrd machine in its old form is gone. It has been replaced, however, in such a way that its basic objectives continue to be fulfilled. At the statewide level, Virginia's Republican Party serves the function fulfilled by the Byrd Democrats. The party carries the state for Republicans in presidential elections (it has gone Democratic only once since 1952), and it holds onto the governorship (Republicans won in 1969, 1973, 1977). The Republicans have the Senate seat not held by Harry Byrd, Jr., a man who runs as an Independent, votes to organize the Senate as a Democrat, and might switch to be a Republican if that would make them the majority party in the Senate. Finally, the Virginia congressional delegation is perhaps the most conservative in the nation. On the local level, Byrd-type Democrats continue to dominate the politics of most of Virginia's small county courthouses, but face more turbulence and competition in some of the state's urban and suburban areas.

The replacement of the Byrd machine by this somewhat untidy but congenial arrangement has been a major political accomplishment. For fifteen years ago the Byrd machine and the ideas it represented seemed in very serious trouble indeed. The Massive Resistance that the machine had sponsored against school integration in the fifties had failed; the strategy had first disgraced Virginia by closing public schools, and then had to be ignominiously abandoned. The bulwark of the machine—small town lawyers, bankers, businessmen, and gentleman farmers, who dominated life in the small towns of Southside Virginia or the Shenandoah Valley—were increasingly unable to deliver votes as the electorate increased vastly in size. Areas which had never been friendly to the Byrd machine were growing in importance: the Washington suburbs were 5% of the state in 1940 and 21% in 1970; the Tidewater area was 13% of the state in 1940 and 22% in 1970. Massive Resistance was the Byrd machine's one appeal to a mass vote—otherwise they had worked to keep the electorate small—and combined with the impact of the Voting Rights Act, it seemed to produce a body of voters too big for the old-time Byrd leaders to control. Senator Harry Byrd, Sr., himself, after forty years of dominance of state public life, resigned in 1965.

Into this vacuum sprang a number of talented Republican politicians, of which the most notable was the party's state chairman, Richard Obenshain. Republicans began as a regional party in Virginia, with a base in the western mountains where they were competitive with anti-Byrd Democrats and in the valley area around Roanoke. These traditional Republicans came from a background that was antislavery, and they had opposed the Byrd machine both in policy and politics. This traditional base was the origin of Linwood Holton, the party's gubernatorial candidate in 1965, when he was beaten by the last Byrd Democrat Governor, Mills Godwin, and in 1969, when he won following a divisive Democratic primary and runoff. The Obenshain Republicans, together with the Nixon Administration, wanted to use the famous Southern strategy in Virginia, identifying their party with resistance to integration. But Holton made a point of accompanying his young daughter to the majority-black elementary school to which a court order assigned her. That essentially finished Holton in the new style of Virginia Republican politics; he was not considered for a gubernatorial nomination again, and ran third among three major candidates in the race for the 1978 Senate nomination.

The transformation of Virginia politics was signalled by the gubernatorial election of 1973. The Republicans nominated Mills Godwin, until then a stalwart of the Byrd machine though as a governor one who abandoned some of its segregationist policies. The Democrats had no candidate at all—a sorry state which resulted from the vogue for independent candidacies here in the early seventies. Running against Godwin was Henry Howell, a self-styled populist from Norfolk who had managed to get himself elected Lieutenant Governor in a three-way race. Howell had a vision of a new kind of Virginia politics. As a folksy personal injury lawyer, he was accustomed to make stirring pleas to juries; he combined country cornpone and generous social policy into what he hoped would become a new populism. The end of the Byrd machine, Howell thought, would turn the state's politics over to the little people, white and black, and to him as their representative. With his Norfolk base, he had run a respectable third-place race for governor in the 1969 primary. Against a Godwin who was visibly ailing and less than eager to run, and in the Watergate year, he looked like a formidable candidate in 1973.

Howell nevertheless managed to lose. Godwin and state Chairman Obenshain raised the school busing issue and capitalized on a statement Howell made which seemed to endorse court-ordered busing plans. Instead of re-emphasizing his populist refrain, Howell went on the defensive and concentrated on busing in the last few weeks. It was enough to defeat him by one of the narrowest margins in Virginia history—and to destroy any chances of success for the kind of politics he represented. Four years later Howell ran again, and had enough support to win an upset victory over Attorney General Andrew Miller in the primary; Miller came from an old anti-Byrd family and had a progressive record of his own, but did not match Howell's fiery advocacy. In the 1977 general election, however, Howell ran out of steam. The Republican candidate, Lieutenant Governor John Dalton, came from the mountain branch of the party; his father, like Miller's father, had run against Senator Byrd himself. But Dalton was a loyal follower of Godwin and the new Virginia Republicans. He ran a campaign almost totally devoid of content except to point out that there was a candidate running against Henry Howell. The strategy worked. Dalton carried not only the mountains and the Byrd strongholds, but the Washington suburbs as well, and he held down Howell's edge in the Tidewater to a pittance.

The next governor seems likely to be one of the two young men who won Virginia's other statewide offices in 1977. One of them, Lieutenant Governor Charles Robb, has a national reputation because he married Lynda Bird Johnson; he also has Virginia roots and had worked diligently in the vineyards of state politics. With a reputation as a moderate, he was one of the few Democrats who have been able to carry the state. The other, Attorney General Marshall Coleman, was an upset winner. A mountain Republican, he beat a Byrd Democrat associated with segregationist policies; he did particularly well in the Washington suburbs where the old-fashioned Byrd machine has never been popular. Both men are likely to be running in 1981.

One of the new Virginia Republicans' greatest triumphs was the election in 1972 of Senator William Scott. A Washington area Congressman, he had seemed likely to lose to scholarly Democratic incumbent William Spong; but Scott got a last-minute injection of money and ran a series of controversial ads attacking Spong as a liberal. They said little about Scott, and you will hear little about him from Virginia Republicans today. For shortly into his term he was named the dumbest member of Congress by *New Times* magazine—in response to which he called a press conference. His efforts at refutation were generally considered unsuccessful. An inveterate junketeer, Scott was able to sum up his insights succinctly; he understood the Panama Canal, he said, because he had seen ships going both ways. Scott's shrewdest political move was his decision not to run for reelection in 1978.

The Democratic nomination that year went to Andrew Miller; after his narrow defeat in the gubernatorial primary the year before and Howell's defeat afterwards, he had no opposition. The Republicans, however—and this is a sign of the vitality of their party—had a spirited race. It was conducted not in a primary, but in a state party convention with some 9,000 delegates—a bigger convention, as far as anyone can remember, than any American political party has ever conducted. Running were former Governor Holton, who finished third, and former Navy Secretary and Bicentennial Commission Chairman John Warner, who finished second. The winner was Richard Obenshain, the architect of Virginia's Republican Party. He had been more successful in his party work than in his own candidacies—he lost the 3d district Congress seat in 1964 and the attorney generalship in 1969, both narrowly—but he looked like at least an even bet in 1978. Then one August night he was killed in a plane crash outside Richmond.

The Obenshain forces were not particularly happy with replacing him with the convention's number two candidate, Warner, but they had little choice. Warner was widely regarded as a lukewarm conservative, though he had served the Nixon Administration faithfully enough; he had few roots in state politics, and his campaign had been helped by the money of his first wife (a Mellon) and the celebrity of his second (Elizabeth Taylor). Many Virginia ladies cringed at the thought of a candidate whose wife had had seven husbands. But Warner seemed as strong a candidate as the party had (Godwin refused to run), and he had quietly offered to help Obenshain after he had lost the nomination himself (when he seemed to have nothing to gain from such an offer).

Warner proved to be a candidate of the slightly malapropish variety. He told one television interview program that as Navy Secretary he had worked to slow integration—and then tried desperately to have the tape edited. He admitted that some of his campaign literature may have included misleading information on the lobbying that got him the Navy secretary job. He endorsed President Ford for 1980 just days before Ronald Reagan—the favorite of most Virginia Republicans—was coming in to campaign for him. Nevertheless Warner had plenty of money and inherited a strong, vibrant Republican organization. Miller had neither advantage. In the end Miller carried the traditional anti-Byrd areas: the Washington suburbs, Tidewater, the mountains—but only by the narrowest of margins. Warner won big in the Valley, in Southside, and most of all in the Richmond area. He brings his celebrity and his enthusiasm to the Armed Services and Commerce Committees.

Virginia's senior Senator is Harry Byrd, Jr., who was destined for the Senate from the beginning of his career, and who was appointed to the seat when his father resigned. With a distinguished appearance and white hair, he looks like a senator; with his slow-paced, careful tones, he talks like one. He has had somewhat more trouble in Virginia elections than he must have anticipated, but he has found a winning formula. Byrd had tough competition for the Democratic nomination in 1966, and in 1970, when it appeared that the Democratic primary electorate might reject him, he decided to run as an Independent instead. He had the covert support of many Republican activists, although Governor Holton insisted the party run a candidate, and from the Nixon Administration as well; he won an absolute majority of the vote and easily outclassed his liberal Democratic opponent. Against Democrat Elmo Zumwalt, former Chief of Naval Operations, he increased his percentage somewhat in 1976.

Byrd continues to vote with Democrats to organize the Senate, though he does not often vote with them on substantive issues. This gives him high-ranking seats on the Senate Armed Services and Finance Committees. It is unlikely that he will ever be in line for those chairs; but if so it is by no means clear whether Senate Democrats will let him have one.

Like his father, Byrd is parsimonious and concerned about saving the government money. Unlike his father, who chaired the Finance Committee for years, he does not have an impact on major national policies. He seems more interested in matters like his successful bill to restore posthumously Robert E. Lee's citizenship. He is punctilious and attentive to duty but like some other sons of famous father he lacks the drive and ambition so evident in so many politicians. He is a kind of survivor of an earlier style and if he has the tacit support of Virginia's new Republican Party he personally is a reminder of the Byrd machine which was its predecessor.

Census Data Pop. 4,648,494; 2.30% of U.S. total, 14th largest; Central city, 24%; suburban, 37%. Median family income, $9,045; 25th highest; families above $15,000: 20%; families below $3,000: 11%. Median years education, 11.7.

1977 Share of Federal Tax Burden $7,806,000,000; 2.26% of U.S. total, 12th largest.

1977 Share of Federal Outlays $11,783,159,000; 2.98% of U.S. total, 9th largest. Per capita federal spending, $2,373.

DOD	$5,387,606,000	3d (5.90%)	HEW	$2,607,782,000	18th (1.77%)
ERDA	$34,823,000	22d (0.59%)	HUD	$96,548,000	14th (2.29%)
NASA	$180,091,000	6th (4.57%)	VA	$449,081,000	13th (2.34%)
DOT	$466,194,000	8th (3.26%)	EPA	$74,827,000	24th (0.91%)
DOC	$136,639,000	16th (1.65%)	RevS	$156,650,000	16th (1.85%)
DOI	$112,402,000	12th (2.42%)	Debt	$172,038,000	26th (0.57%)
USDA	$413,190,000	16th (2.08%)	Other	$1,495,288,000	

Economic Base Finance, insurance and real estate; agriculture, notably dairy products, tobacco, cattle and broilers; textile mills products, especially cotton weaving mills; apparel and other textile products, especially men's and boys' furnishings, and women's and misses' outerwear; chemical and synthetics; food and kindred products; electrical equipment and supplies.

Political Line-up Governor, John N. Dalton (R). Senators, Harry F. Byrd, Jr. (Ind.) and John W. Warner (R). Representatives, 10 (6 R and 4 D). State Senate (34 D and 6 R); State House (77 D, 22 R, 1 other).

The Voters

Registration 1,965,338 Total. No party registration.
Median voting age 40
Employment profile White collar, 49%. Blue collar, 36%. Service, 12%. Farm, 3%.
Ethnic groups Black, 19%. Spanish, 1%. Total foreign stock, 5%.

Presidential vote

1976	Carter (D)	813,896	(49%)
	Ford (R)	836,554	(51%)
1972	Nixon (R)	988,493	(69%)
	McGovern (D)	438,887	(31%)

Sen. Harry F. Byrd, Jr. (I) Elected Appointed Nov. 12, 1965, elected 1966 as Democrat, re-elected 1970 as Independent, seat up 1982; b. Dec. 20, 1914, Winchester; home, Winchester; Va. Military Inst., 1931–33, U. of Va., 1933–35; Episcopalian.

Career Newspaper editor; Orchardist; Navy, WWII; Va. Senate, 1948–65.

Offices 417 RSOB, 202-224-4024. Also Winchester 22601, 703-662-7745.

Committees *Armed Services* (4th). Subcommittees: General Procurement (Chairman); Manpower and Personnel; Military Construction and Stockpiles.

Finance (4th). Subcommittees: International Trade; Taxation and Debt Management Generally (Chairman); Oversight of the Internal Revenue Service.

Group Ratings

	ADA	COPE	PC	RPN	NFU	LCV	CFA	NAB	NSI	ACA	NTU
1978	10	11	25	40	10	35	20	100	90	100	–
1977	5	5	20	45	8	–	12	–	–	96	58
1976	5	15	10	41	18	32	7	100	100	96	71

Key Votes

1) Warnke Nom	AGN	6) Egypt-Saudi Arms	FOR	11) Hosptl Cost Contnmnt	AGN
2) Neutron Bomb	FOR	7) Draft Restr Pardon	AGN	12) Clinch River Reactor	FOR
3) Waterwy User Fee	FOR	8) Wheat Price Support	AGN	13) Pub Fin Cong Cmpgns	AGN
4) Dereg Nat Gas	FOR	9) Panama Canal Treaty	AGN	14) ERA Ratif Recissn	AGN
5) Kemp-Roth	AGN	10) Labor Law Rev Clot	AGN	15) Med Necssy Abrtns	AGN

Election Results

1976 general	Harry F. Byrd, Jr. (Ind.)	890,778	(57%)	($802,928)
	E.R. (Bud) Zumwalt (D)	596,009	(38%)	($443,107)
	Martin H. Perper (Ind.)	70,559	(5%)	
1976 primary	Harry F. Byrd, Jr. (Ind.)	(noprimary)		
1970 general	Harry F. Byrd, Jr. (Ind.)	506,327	(54%)	
	George C. Rawlings, Jr. (D)	294,582	(31%)	
	Ray Garland (R)	144,765	(15%)	

Sen. John W. Warner (R) Elected 1978, seat up 1984; b. Feb. 18, 1927, Washington, D.C.; home, Middleburg; Wash. & Lee U., B.S., U. of Va., LL.B. 1953; Episcopalian.

Career Navy, WWII; Law Clerk, U.S. Court of Appeals Chief Judge E. Barrett Prettyman, 1953–54; Practicing atty., 1954–56, 1960–69; Asst. U.S. Atty., 1956–60; Cattle farm owner and operator, 1961–.

Offices 2313 DSOB, 202-224-2023. Also Rm. 8000 Fed. Bldg., Richmond 23240, 804-782-2579.

Committees *Armed Services* (4th). Subcommittees: Manpower and Personnel; Research and Development; Military Construction and Stockpiles.

Commerce, Science, and Transportation (7th). Subcommittees: Communications; Consumer; Merchant Marine and Tourism.

Group Ratings: Newly Elected

Key Votes: Newly Elected

Election Results

1978 general	John W. Warner (R)	613,232	(50%)	($2,897,237)
	Andrew P. Miller (D)	608,511	(50%)	($832,773)
1978 primary	John W. Warner (R), nominated by Republican party			
	Richard Obenshain (R), nominated by convention			
1972 general	William Lloyd Scott (R)	718,337	(53%)	($619,908)
	William B. Spong, Jr. (D)	643,963	(47%)	($380,921)

Gov. John N. Dalton (R) Elected 1977, term expires Jan. 1982; b. July 11, 1931, Emporia; Col. of Wm. and Mary, B.A. 1953, U. of Va., J.D. 1957; Baptist.

Career Army, 1953–54; Practicing atty., 1957–; Va. House of Delegates, 1965–73; Va. Senate, 1973–74; Lt. Gov. of Va., 1974–78.

Offices State Capitol, Richmond 23219, 804-786-2211.

Election Results

1977 general	John N. Dalton (R)	699,302	(56%)
	Henry Howell (D)	541,319	(44%)
1977 primary	John N. Dalton (R), nominated by convention		
1973 general	Mills E. Godwin, Jr. (R)	525,075	(51%)
	Henry Howell (Ind.)	510,103	(49%)

FIRST DISTRICT

The 1st congressional district is part of Tidewater Virginia, the lowlands by the wide tidal marshes of the Atlantic Ocean and Chesapeake Bay. The district includes the southern tip of the Delmarva Peninsula, site of the annual roundup of wild Chincoteague ponies, and the rural Northern Neck counties that have changed little since George Washington's time—when they produced such worthies as Washington himself and the various Lees. But the district's population is concentrated not in these essentially rural areas, but in the Hampton Roads area, where 62% of the 1st district's residents live, most of them in Newport News and Hampton, which have more than 120,000 residents each.

This has been a fast-growing, industrialized area which owes much of its prosperity to the federal government. Hampton Roads—the strait that separates Newport News and Hampton on the north from Norfolk and Portsmouth on the south—is one of the best natural harbors on the Atlantic seaboard, and is now the headquarters of the Navy's Atlantic Fleet. Most of the naval bases are on the south side of the Roads, but here in the 1st is Tenneco's Newport News Shipbuilding and Dry Dock Company, which for years has been one of the nation's largest shipbuilders, and one heavily dependent on Navy business. Altogether the Defense Department has regularly spent more than $1 billion a year in this district—obviously the basis of its current economy.

Naturally any successful congressman from this district is going to have to pay close attention to the federal spending which is so important here. Thomas Downing, a Democrat who represented the district for 18 years until his retirement in 1976, chaired a NASA oversight committee—there is a big NASA facility in Hampton—and as a member of the Merchant Marine and Fisheries Committee favored the subsidies which flow to shipbuilders, shippers, and members of the maritime unions. Only in his last term did Downing indulge more esoteric interests, by helping to set up and briefly chairing the special House committee on assassinations.

Downing's successor is, to many people's surprise, a Republican; Virginia is one state where Republicans have shown much more aptitude for congressional elections than Democrats. The 1976 Democratic nominee, a state legislator from the Hampton Roads area, apparently assumed he couldn't lose; the Republican, Paul Trible, knew he would have to fight hard to win. He managed to carry Newport News and most of the Northern Neck counties, none of which have a Republican tradition, and to win a narrow victory. Once in the House he won seats on the two committees of crucial economic importance to the district—Armed Services and Merchant Marine and Fisheries. This was no mean feat: there are already two Virginia Republicans from the Hampton Roads area on Armed Services. Moreover, Trible was able to wage an apparently effective campaign for his constituency. The Carter Administration announced early in 1978 that it would transfer overhaul work on the aircraft carrier Saratoga from Newport News to Philadelphia.

Ordinarily there would not be much that a freshman Republican could do about such a decision. But Trible yelled long and hard that it was the result of politics, that the Administration wanted to pay off Philadelphia (Carter had carried Pennsylvania in both primary and general election) which had been promised and denied other defense work and to punish Virginia (the only Southern state which went for Ford). And he managed to secure a year's delay of the decision, until after the 1978 election—a major victory. Apparently it was so recognized by 1st district voters. Trible had a well-known opponent in 1978: Lew Puller, son of a famous Marine general and himself a double amputee Vietnam veteran. Puller attacked Trible for not doing more to save the Newport News jobs, and despite Trible's symbolic gestures to blacks he won the endorsement of black political groups. But Trible won the election by better than a 2–1 margin. First elected when he was not yet 30, he seems to have a long congressional career ahead of him.

Census Data Pop. 465,981. Central city, 56%; suburban, 7%. Median family income, $8,490; families above $15,000: 16%; families below $3,000: 13%. Median years education, 11.5.

The Voters

Median voting age 40.
Employment profile White collar, 45%. Blue collar, 38%. Service, 14%. Farm, 3%.
Ethnic groups Black, 30%. Spanish, 1%. Total foreign stock, 5%.

Presidential vote

1976	Carter (D)	80,485	(52%)
	Ford (R)	75,601	(48%)
1972	Nixon (R)	95,400	(69%)
	McGovern (D)	43,069	(31%)

Rep. Paul S. Trible, Jr. (R) Elected 1976; b. Dec. 29, 1946, Baltimore, Md.; home, Tappahannock; Hampden-Sydney Col., B.A. 1968, Wash. and Lee U., J.D. 1971; Episcopalian.

Career Law clerk, U.S. Dist. Judge Albert Bryan, Jr., 1971–72; Asst. U.S. Atty. for East. Dist. of Va., 1972–74; Essex Co. Commonwealth's Atty., 1974–76.

Offices 326 CHOB, 202-225-4261. Also Tower Box 59, Exec. Tower, 2101 Executive Dr., Hampton 23666, 804-838-3287.

Committees *Armed Services* (12th). Subcommittees: Military Installations and Facilities; Seapower and Strategic and Critical Materials.

Merchant Marine and Fisheries (12th). Subcommittees: Fish and Wildlife; Merchant Marine.

Group Ratings

	ADA	COPE	PC	RPN	NFU	LCV	CFA	NAB	NSI	ACA	NTU
1978	20	21	28	50	33	–	18	92	100	88	–
1977	5	13	13	38	58	25	5	–	–	85	39

Key Votes

1) Increase Def Spnd	FOR	6) Alaska Lands Protect	FOR	11) Delay Auto Pol Cntrl	FOR
2) B-1 Bomber	FOR	7) Water Projects Veto	AGN	12) Sugar Price Escalator	FOR
3) Cargo Preference	FOR	8) Consum Protect Agcy	AGN	13) Pub Fin Cong Cmpgns	AGN
4) Dereg Nat Gas	FOR	9) Common Situs Picket	AGN	14) ERA Ratif Recissn	FOR
5) Kemp-Roth	FOR	10) Labor Law Revision	AGN	15) Prohibt Govt Abrtns	FOR

Election Results

1978 general	Paul S. Trible, Jr. (R)	89,158	(72%)	($257,257)
	Lew Puller (D)	34,578	(28%)	($134,051)
1978 primary	Paul S. Trible, Jr. (R), nominated by convention			
1976 general	Paul S. Trible, Jr. (R)	71,789	(51%)	($125,626)
	Robert E. Quinn (D)	70,159	(49%)	($175,843)

SECOND DISTRICT

Norfolk, Virginia, is the headquarters of the Navy's Atlantic Fleet. Within its city limits is one of the world's largest naval bases and more than half a dozen other naval installations, not to mention the dozen or so military facilities in nearby Portsmouth, Virginia Beach, or Hampton and Newport News across Hampton Roads. The naval buildup during and after World War II made Norfolk what it is today. Before the war it was a city of 144,000 with perhaps another 100,000 in adjacent areas; today Norfolk is the center of an urban area of nearly a million people. Suburban homes have been built in the low-lying land near the wide inlets off the bay, and shopping centers have sprouted up at freeway interchanges. During the sixties and seventies the area of fastest growth has been in the east, in the relatively high income suburb of Virginia Beach.

Politically Norfolk is a working class town. For the most part Navy personnel do not vote here, and their absence from the electorate shows up in low turnout figures. The Norfolk voter is more likely to be a blue collar worker, who moved here from a small town in Southside Virginia or eastern North Carolina looking for a job. This is a definitely segregated city, and the large black minority is reliably Democratic in most elections. The whites are a swing vote: they have gone for George Wallace and Richard Nixon, but they have also given big margins to Jimmy Carter and Henry Howell.

Howell has put together a kind of populist coalition here of blacks and blue collar whites, but it has never had much impact in congressional elections. The 2d congressional district, which includes all of Norfolk and virtually all of Virginia Beach, elected conservative Democrats to the House until 1968 and since then has elected a basically conservative Republican. The Republican victory, in 1968, was something of an upset. But his continued reelection has been less surprising.

William Whitehurst was a professor at a local college and commentator on a local television station when he was first elected. His major political assets are a willingness to return to the district almost every weekend and his seat on the Armed Services Committee. He is now the third-ranking Republican on that body, which is important when the Pentagon spends several hundred million dollars a year in your district. The fast growth of Virginia Beach and its increasing share of the district's vote are helpful to him. His toughest challenge came in 1974, and he won easily; in 1978 he was reelected without opposition.

Census Data Pop. 464,692. Central city, 66%; suburban, 34%. Median family income, $8,733; families above $15,000: 18%; families below $3,000: 12%. Median years education, 12.1.

The Voters

Median voting age 34.
Employment profile White collar, 55%. Blue collar, 30%. Service, 15%. Farm, –%.
Ethnic groups Black, 22%. Spanish, 2%. Total foreign stock, 8%. UK, 1%.

Presidential vote

1976	Carter (D)	62,494	(51%)
	Ford (R)	60,261	(49%)
1972	Nixon (R)	73,728	(68%)
	McGovern (D)	35,107	(32%)

Rep. G. William Whitehurst (R) Elected 1968; b. Mar. 12, 1925, Norfolk; home, Virginia Beach; Washington & Lee U., B.A. 1950, U. of Va., M.A. 1951, W.Va. U., Ph.D. 1962; Methodist.

Career Navy, WWII; Prof. of History, Old Dominion Col., 1950–68, Dean of Students, 1963–68; News analyst, WTAR-TV, Norfolk, 1962–68.

Offices 2427 RHOB, 202-225-4215. Also Rm. 815 Fed. Bldg., Norfolk 23510, 804-441-3340.

Committees *Armed Services* (3d). Subcommittees: Military Installations and Facilities; Research and Development; NATO Standardization, Interoperability and Readiness.

Group Ratings

	ADA	COPE	PC	RPN	NFU	LCV	CFA	NAB	NSI	ACA	NTU
1978	15	25	23	55	10	–	14	100	100	89	–
1977	0	14	10	31	60	15	10	–	–	75	37
1976	5	19	11	59	18	12	0	80	100	84	48

Key Votes

1) Increase Def Spnd	FOR	6) Alaska Lands Protect	FOR	11) Delay Auto Pol Cntrl	DNV
2) B-1 Bomber	FOR	7) Water Projects Veto	AGN	12) Sugar Price Escalator	DNV
3) Cargo Preference	FOR	8) Consum Protect Agcy	AGN	13) Pub Fin Cong Cmpgns	AGN
4) Dereg Nat Gas	FOR	9) Common Situs Picket	AGN	14) ERA Ratif Recissn	FOR
5) Kemp-Roth	FOR	10) Labor Law Revision	AGN	15) Prohibt Govt Abrtns	FOR

Election Results

1978 general	G. William Whitehurst (R), unopposed ..			($37,796)
1978 primary	G. William Whitehurst (R), nominated by convention			
1976 general	G. William Whitehurst (R)	79,381	(66%)	($104,659)
	Robert E. Washington (D)	41,464	(34%)	($54,341)

THIRD DISTRICT

Richmond, the capital of the Confederacy, remains the capital of Virginia and a major tobacco producing center. In many ways Richmond is Virginia's most important city, although it is eclipsed in size by the Washington suburbs and the Tidewater area around Norfolk. But Richmond is not only the state capital, it is also its ideological center and the headquarters of its major economic interests. The state government continues in the hands of men sympathetic to friends who run the Virginia Electric and Power Company and the big Richmond banks. The Richmond newspapers provide a sometimes stylishly articulated defense of the status quo and of free enterprise; during the fifties, they provided the most intellectually phrased defense of racial segregation. In the words of political analyst Mark Shields, Richmond is a famous center of social rest.

Virginia's 3d congressional district consists of Richmond and virtually all of its two principal suburban counties, Henrico and Chesterfield. This was the area covered by the Richmond school busing case in the early seventies, a decision which was ultimately reversed to the great relief of Richmond area whites. There is a large black minority in the city—which now controls the city council because members are elected by district—and sometimes the city goes for liberal candidates; Jimmy Carter carried it with 55%. But the Richmond suburbs, nearly all white, are among the most conservative areas in the United States. Carter was beaten 2–1 here, and some Democrats have lost the suburban counties by margins like 7–1.

The current Congressman, David Satterfield, is a Democrat whose father once (1937–45) represented the same district. He won it in 1964 in a three-cornered race with a liberal Independent and Republican Richard Obenshain, who as the 1978 Republican Senate nominee was killed in a plane crash. Satterfield has not had a really significant challenge since, and in the last three elections has won over an Independent.

In the Congress Satterfield's voting record is what one would expect from a conservative Republican. Under the old seniority system, he would have become Chairman of the Health Subcommittee of the Commerce Committee in 1979—one of the most important subcommittee chairs in the House. But Satterfield's views are far out of line with those of most House Democrats, and he has no particular flair or personal following which might compensate for that. There was a contest for the Health chair, but it was between two less senior Democrats, Richardson Preyer and Henry Waxman; no one even seemed to think it worthy of comment that Satterfield was passed over. He can of course continue to serve in the House, but he cannot hope to achieve a position of real power or legislative leadership.

Census Data Pop. 465,289. Central city, 54%; suburban, 46%. Median family income, $9,945; families above $15,000: 21%; families below $3,000: 8%. Median years education, 11.7.

The Voters

Median voting age 42.
Employment profile White collar, 55%. Blue collar, 32%. Service, 13%. Farm, –%.
Ethnic groups Black, 26%. Total foreign stock, 5%.

Presidential vote

1976	Carter (D)	77,387	(43%)
	Ford (R)	101,624	(57%)
1972	Nixon (R)	117,472	(72%)
	McGovern (D)	44,566	(28%)

Rep. David E. Satterfield III (D) Elected 1964; b. Dec. 2, 1920, Richmond; home, Richmond; U. of Richmond, U. of Va.; Episcopalian.

Career Navy, WWII; Practicing atty., 1948–50, 1953–65; Asst. U.S. Atty., 1950–53; Richmond City Cncl., 1954–56; Va. House of Delegates, 1960–64.

Offices 2348 RHOB, 202-225-2815. Also Fed. Ofc. Bldg., Richmond 23240, 804-782-2809.

Committees *Interstate and Foreign Commerce* (5th). Subcommittees: Energy and Power; Health and Environment; Consumer Protection and Finance.

Veterans' Affairs (2d). Subcommittees: Special Investigations; Medical Facilities and Benefits (Chairman).

Group Ratings

	ADA	COPE	PC	RPN	NFU	LCV	CFA	NAB	NSI	ACA	NTU
1978	10	5	20	42	20	–	18	100	100	100	–
1977	0	9	8	31	33	15	5	–	–	96	41
1976	0	13	7	44	17	6	0	92	100	96	56

Key Votes

1) Increase Def Spnd	FOR	6) Alaska Lands Protect	AGN	11) Delay Auto Pol Cntrl	FOR
2) B-1 Bomber	FOR	7) Water Projects Veto	AGN	12) Sugar Price Escalator	FOR
3) Cargo Preference	AGN	8) Consum Protect Agcy	AGN	13) Pub Fin Cong Cmpgns	AGN
4) Dereg Nat Gas	FOR	9) Common Situs Picket	AGN	14) ERA Ratif Recissn	FOR
5) Kemp-Roth	FOR	10) Labor Law Revision	AGN	15) Prohibt Govt Abrtns	FOR

Election Results

1978 general	David E. Satterfield III (D)	104,550	(88%)	($5,626)
	Alan R. Ogden (Ind.)	14,453	(12%)	
1978 primary	David E. Satterfield III (D), nominated by convention			
1976 general	David E. Satterfield III (D)	129,066	(88%)	($1,599)
	Alan R. Ogden (Ind.)	17,503	(12%)	($75)

FOURTH DISTRICT

The 4th congressional district of Virginia presents a good example of the demographic changes wrought in Virginia in the past decades—and the limited effect they have had on political results. In the past 15 years the 4th district has shifted from an almost entirely rural, small county district to a predominantly urban one. In the middle sixties the 4th took in most of Southside Virginia, tobacco growing country south of Richmond, with small courthouse towns and the continuing dominance of a large black population by white landowners. Today the district's boundaries have been moved sharply to the east, and more than two-thirds of its population is in the Tidewater area: the industrial, 40% black city of Portsmouth, blue collar suburban Chesapeake, and the smaller city of Suffolk. The 4th also includes the old city of Petersburg, a major center when it was the focus of several Civil War battles and not much bigger now, with a substantial black minority; and Hopewell, made famous in the middle seventies as the site of the plant that produced kepone—which poisoned many workers and, dumped into the James River, produced fishing bans in Chesapeake Bay.

The 1972 redistricting eliminated from the 4th the symbolic town of Appomattox Court House, where Lee surrendered to Grant; it was also the home of then Congressman Watkins Abbitt, an old style Byrd Democrat. Abbitt retired in 1972 and, finally free to express himself, supported the reelection of Richard Nixon. Abbitt's retirement left the 4th a scene of major political conflict. There were no fewer than three Independent candidates that year (one a write-in who got 5%) as well as the Democratic and Republican nominees. The winner, with 47%, was Republican Robert Daniel, a former CIA agent and local farmer and businessman.

Daniel's hold on the seat seemed tenuous for some time. He failed to win absolute majorities in 1972 and 1974, and in 1976 beat a Democrat with just 53%. Yet he always came out on top. As in so many contests in Virginia, the Republicans seem to have the political skills when they are needed, and so this seat, with its large urban black vote and its electorate which gave Jimmy Carter 59% of the vote, has stayed in Republican hands through most of the seventies. In 1978 there was no Democratic candidate at all. Daniel serves on the Armed Services and District of Columbia Committees, and has a predictably conservative record.

Census Data Pop. 465,738. Central city, 35%; suburban, 39%. Median family income, $8,294; families above $15,000: 13%; families below $3,000: 12%. Median years education, 10.4.

The Voters

Median voting age 41.
Employment profile White collar, 39%. Blue collar, 43%. Service, 15%. Farm, 3%.
Ethnic groups Black, 37%. Total foreign stock, 3%.

Presidential vote

1976	Carter (D)	89,112	(59%)
	Ford (R)	62,961	(41%)
1972	Nixon (R)	85,780	(65%)
	McGovern (D)	45,346	(35%)

Rep. Robert W. Daniel, Jr. (R) Elected 1972; b. Mar. 17, 1936, Richmond; home, Spring Grove; U. of Va., B.A. 1958, Columbia U., M.B.A. 1961; Episcopalian.

Career Practicing financial analyst, 1961–62; Instructor of Economics, U. of Richmond Business School, 1963; CIA, 1964–68; Owner and operator, Brandon agricultural enterprise.

Offices 2236 RHOB, 202-225-6365. Also 209 P.O. Bldg., Petersburg 23803, 804-732-2544.

Committees *Armed Services* (9th). Subcommittees: Procurement and Military Nuclear Systems; Investigations.

District of Columbia (2d). Subcommittees: Government Affairs and Budget.

Group Ratings

	ADA	COPE	PC	RPN	NFU	LCV	CFA	NAB	NSI	ACA	NTU
1978	10	11	13	58	40	–	18	100	100	93	–
1977	5	13	8	38	58	15	10	–	–	93	36
1976	0	17	8	61	17	13	0	90	100	93	56

Key Votes

1) Increase Def Spnd	FOR	6) Alaska Lands Protect	AGN	11) Delay Auto Pol Cntrl	FOR
2) B-1 Bomber	FOR	7) Water Projects Veto	AGN	12) Sugar Price Escalator	FOR
3) Cargo Preference	FOR	8) Consum Protect Agcy	AGN	13) Pub Fin Cong Cmpgns	AGN
4) Dereg Nat Gas	FOR	9) Common Situs Picket	AGN	14) ERA Ratif Recissn	FOR
5) Kemp-Roth	FOR	10) Labor Law Revision	AGN	15) Prohibt Govt Abrtns	AGN

Election Results

1978 general	Robert W. Daniel, Jr. (R), unopposed			($31,644)
1978 primary	Robert W. Daniel, Jr. (R), nominated by convention			
1976 general	Robert W. Daniel, Jr. (R)	74,495	(53%)	($93,836)
	J. W. O'Brien (D)	65,982	(47%)	($93,734)

FIFTH DISTRICT

The 5th congressional district of Virginia covers most of Southside Virginia, from the Richmond city limits out to the Blue Ridge near Roanoke. The eastern counties are flat and humid, and the most heavily black part of the district. Slowly, as the land gets hillier, it rises into the Piedmont, and moves past the textile and furniture manufacturing centers like Danville and Martinsville. As one goes west, there is more livestock and less tobacco, more whites with mountain accents and fewer blacks. Altogether the 5th is 29% black—significantly less than the figure for the 4th district, which takes in Southside and Tidewater counties just to the east.

Southside Virginia was always a stronghold for Byrd Democrats, with its politics firmly in the hands of prosperous bankers and planters who still remember the Civil War. More recently Southside has fallen into the racially polarized patterns that characterize the Deep South. This is one of two Virginia districts which went for George Wallace in 1968 and the one which gave him his largest percentage here. Since then, at least some of the Wallace vote has been trending Republican. In the close presidential race of 1976 and the close Senate race of 1978, the Republican candidates won small margins in the 5th district—and were able to carry the state.

For more than ten years the 5th district has been represented by one of the last survivors in the Virginia delegation of the Byrd Democratic tradition. Dan Daniel, a former executive at Danville's Dan River Mills, was first elected in 1968 over spirited Republican and Independent competition; since then he has won easily or has been unopposed. Daniel is a member of the Armed Services and District of Columbia Committees, where his voting record may be confused with that of fellow committee member Robert Daniel, the Republican congressman from the 4th district.

Census Data Pop. 462,807. Central city, 0%; suburban, 13%. Median family income, $7,471; families above $15,000: 10%; families below $3,000: 15%. Median years education, 9.4.

The Voters

Median voting age 43.
Employment profile White collar, 32%. Blue collar, 52%. Service, 10%. Farm, 6%.
Ethnic groups Black, 29%. Total foreign stock, 1%.

Presidential vote

1976	Carter (D)	75,894	(48%)
	Ford (R)	82,011	(52%)
1972	Nixon (R)	101,546	(72%)
	McGovern (D)	39,194	(28%)

Rep. Dan Daniel (D) Elected 1968; b. May 12, 1914, Chatham; home, Danville; Baptist.

Career Asst. to Bd. Chm., Dan River Mills, Inc., and various other business positions, 1939–68; Va. House of Delegates, 1959–68.

Offices 1705 LHOB, 202-225-4711. Also 315 P.O. Bldg., Danville 24541, 804-792-1280.

Committees *Armed Services* (11th). Subcommittees: Investigations; Procurement and Military Nuclear Systems; NATO Standardization, Interoperability and Readiness (Chairman).

Group Ratings

	ADA	COPE	PC	RPN	NFU	LCV	CFA	NAB	NSI	ACA	NTU
1978	0	5	13	50	20	–	9	100	100	96	–
1977	0	9	10	23	58	15	10	–	–	93	37
1976	5	13	5	29	17	9	0	92	100	96	56

Key Votes

1) Increase Def Spnd	FOR	6) Alaska Lands Protect	AGN	11) Delay Auto Pol Cntrl	FOR
2) B-1 Bomber	FOR	7) Water Projects Veto	AGN	12) Sugar Price Escalator	FOR
3) Cargo Preference	AGN	8) Consum Protect Agcy	AGN	13) Pub Fin Cong Cmpgns	AGN
4) Dereg Nat Gas	FOR	9) Common Situs Picket	AGN	14) ERA Ratif Recissn	DNV
5) Kemp-Roth	FOR	10) Labor Law Revision	AGN	15) Prohibt Govt Abrtns	FOR

Election Results

1978 general	Dan Daniel (D), unopposed	($4,991)
1978 primary	Dan Daniel (D), nominated by convention	
1976 general	Dan Daniel (D), unopposed	($1,373)

SIXTH DISTRICT

Traditionally the most Republican parts of Virginia are in the great valley west of the Blue Ridge around Roanoke. Because this fertile land was never given over to slave-tended plantations, the hardy farmers here were not especially sympathetic to the Confederacy. In the hundred years that followed the Civil War, the Roanoke area was usually the most Republican—or least Democratic—part of the state. Unlike places farther north in the valley, this area was always suspicious of the Byrd machine and, to some extent, of its alliance with Virginia's largest and most powerful economic interests. There has always been a tinge of populism, of insurgency to the Republicanism of these hills; it os not the political faith of a comfortable majority, as it was in the rich farmlands of the Midwest, but of people who believe they have been excluded from power.

The 6th congressional district is centered on Roanoke and this vestigially Republican part of Virginia. Its traditional Republicanism can be seen by its presidential performance in 1968, when it was the only Virginia district to give Richard Nixon an absolute majority. In more recent elections, as the state's Republicans have made alliances with former Byrd Democrats, the 6th is no longer the most Republican part of the state. There are some traces of insurgency left.

That is true too of the congressional career of 6th district Congressman Caldwell Butler. First elected in 1972 to replace a Republican who had been elected in the first Eisenhower year and who had made the district safely Republican, Butler came from the mountain tradition; he was the law partner of Governor Linwood Holton, who earned the enduring wrath of many Virginia Republicans by escorting his daughter to a school integrated by court order. On most issues Butler is a conventional Republican. He favors free enterprise and market mechanisms over government decision-making, he is cautious about new federal spending programs, he tends to favor tough measures against crime. But he is also a careful lawyer. As a member of the Judiciary Committee during the impeachment hearings, he studied the evidence thoroughly, reportedly aided by his wife, who read *All the President's Men* to him in the evening. Butler came to the conclusion that Nixon should be impeached, and he was one of the Republicans and Southern Democrats who worked to draw up articles of impeachment they could agree on. In the public hearings his rapid-fire delivery, his peppery voice, his occasional sense of humor, and his lawyer's instinct for the main issue helped to cinch the case against the president.

As a matter of strict politics, Butler was probably the least likely impeachment vote on the committee. He was a Republican in a Republican district in the South, where Nixon's popularity sagged least. Faced as he had been in 1972 with an Independent as well as a Democratic opponent, Butler saw his share of the vote drop from 55% to 46%. Since then, he has not been presented with such grave issues, and on most matters has voted with most Republicans. He was reelected comfortably in 1976 and without opposition in 1978.

Census Data Pop. 464,356. Central city, 31%; suburban, 25%. Median family income, $8,594; families above $15,000: 14%; families below $3,000: 10%. Median years education, 11.3.

The Voters

Median voting age 43.
Employment profile White collar, 43%. Blue collar, 42%. Service, 13%. Farm, 2%.
Ethnic groups Black, 12%. Total foreign stock, 2%.

Presidential vote

1976	Carter (D)	82,077	(49%)
	Ford (R)	85,448	(51%)
1972	Nixon (R)	104,443	(75%)
	McGovern (D)	35,356	(25%)

Rep. M. Caldwell Butler (R) Elected 1972; b. June 22, 1925, Roanoke; home, Roanoke; U. of Richmond, A.B. 1948, U. of Va., LL.B. 1950; Episcopalian.

Career Practicing atty., 1950–72; Va. House of Delegates, 1962–71, Minor. Ldr., 1966–71.

Offices 409 CHOB, 202-225-5431. Also 313 U.S.P.O. and Courthouse Bldg., 900 Church St., Lynchburg 24505, 804-845-1378.

Committees *Judiciary* (4th). Subcommittees: Immigration, Refugees, and International Law; Monopolies and Commercial Law.

Government Operations (9th). Subcommittees: Manpower and Housing; Government Information and Individual Rights.

Group Ratings

	ADA	COPE	PC	RPN	NFU	LCV	CFA	NAB	NSI	ACA	NTU
1978	10	0	18	91	11	–	14	100	90	96	–
1977	5	9	10	69	25	14	10	–	–	85	39
1976	10	14	8	67	17	7	0	92	100	84	56

Key Votes

1) Increase Def Spnd	FOR	6) Alaska Lands Protect	DNV	11) Delay Auto Pol Cntrl	FOR
2) B-1 Bomber	FOR	7) Water Projects Veto	AGN	12) Sugar Price Escalator	FOR
3) Cargo Preference	AGN	8) Consum Protect Agcy	AGN	13) Pub Fin Cong Cmpgns	AGN
4) Dereg Nat Gas	FOR	9) Common Situs Picket	AGN	14) ERA Ratif Recissn	FOR
5) Kemp-Roth	FOR	10) Labor Law Revision	AGN	15) Prohibt Govt Abrtns	AGN

Election Results

1978 general	M. Caldwell Butler (R), unopposed			($16,307)
1978 primary	M. Caldwell Butler (R), nominated by convention			
1976 general	M. Caldwell Butler (R)	90,830	(62%)	($59,453)
	Warren D. Saunders (Ind.)	55,115	(38%)	($53,833)

SEVENTH DISTRICT

East and west of the Blue Ridge Mountains in northern Virginia is some of the most beautiful countryside in the United States. Away from the tidal flatlands, the climate is cool and salubrious; the flowering bushes and trees in the spring provide an even greater riot of color than the turning leaves in the fall; the mountains to the west protect against icy blasts. The Piedmont, on the eastern side of the Blue Ridge, was once the property of large landowners, like Lord Fairfax, George Washington's patron; much of the land here now is the property of some of the nation's wealthiest families, who spend their winters riding in the hunt. West of the Blue Ridge is the Shenandoah Valley, once the granary of the Confederacy and still marvelously fertile land, though now more often given over to orchards than to grain. The region's major towns—Winchester and Harrisonburg in the Valley, Charlottesville and Fredericksburg in the Piedmont, none with a population over 38,000—still retain an old-fashioned air at least in the narrow streets of their downtowns, though a McDonald's culture has developed on the bypass roads on their outskirts.

This is the land of the 7th congressional district of Virginia—the northern part of the state beyond the Washington metropolitan area. It was the home of three presidents (Jefferson, Madison, and Monroe) and the scene of more carnage and killing in the Civil War than any other area of comparable size in the nation. The district is also the home turf of the twentieth century Byrd dynasty. The late Senator Harry Byrd, Sr., developed one of the world's largest and most productive apple orchards in the Shenandoah Valley and also acquired newspapers in Winchester and Harrisonburg; his son, the current Senator, retains these interests. The 7th continues today to be solid Byrd country in most elections—which means that it has long since shifted from its traditional Democratic preference to conservative Republicanism in most presidential and statewide races. This was a solid district for Gerald Ford in 1976, John Dalton in 1977, and John Warner (a resident of the hunt country) in 1978.

Nowhere has the trend from Byrd Democrat to Ford Republican been better illustrated than in the 7th district's congressional representation. From 1963 to 1971 the Congressman here was John Marsh, a nominal Democrat who became a top White House aide to President Ford. Marsh declined to seek renomination in 1970—the year Byrd first ran as an Independent—because it appeared that liberals had got control of the Democratic primary. The Byrd imprimatur—unofficial, but not open to doubt—went to the Republican nominee, state Senator Kenneth Robinson. Back in 1962 he had nearly defeated Marsh; later he had been elected to the state Senate vacancy caused by the elevation of Harry Byrd, Jr., to the United States Senate. The Byrd machine, driven out of the Democratic Party, thus reappeared in Republican guise.

A solid conservative, Robinson serves on the Appropriations Committee and on its Agriculture and Defense Subcommittees. His one tough general election was in 1974, when a Democrat held him to 53%. Some observers expected him to have trouble in 1978, but his opponent carried only Fredericksburg, and Robinson won by nearly a 2–1 margin.

Census Data Pop. 465,342. Central city, 0%; suburban, 8%. Median family income, $7,952; families above $15,000: 13%; families below $3,000: 12%. Median years education, 10.5.

The Voters

Median voting age 42.
Employment profile White collar, 40%. Blue collar, 42%. Service, 13%. Farm, 5%.
Ethnic groups Black, 15%. Total foreign stock, 3%.

Presidential vote

1976	Carter (D)	79,319	(45%)
	Ford (R)	96,884	(55%)
1972	Nixon (R)	104,720	(73%)
	McGovern (D)	39,691	(27%)

Rep. J. Kenneth Robinson (R) Elected 1970; b. May 14, 1916, Winchester; home, Winchester; Va. Polytechnic Inst., B.S. 1937; Society of Friends.

Career Family fruit growing and packing business, 1937–42; Army, WWII; Dir., Winchester Cold Storage, R & T Packing Corp., Inc., Winchester Apple Growers Assn., and Green Chemical Co.; Va. Senate, 1965–70.

Offices 2233 RHOB, 202-225-6561. Also 112 N. Cameron St., P.O. Box 136, Winchester 22601, 703-667-0990.

Committees *Appropriations* (8th). Subcommittees: Agriculture, Rural Development and Related Agencies.

Group Ratings

	ADA	COPE	PC	RPN	NFU	LCV	CFA	NAB	NSI	ACA	NTU
1978	10	10	18	67	30	–	18	100	100	93	–
1977	0	9	8	54	42	10	5	–	–	93	40
1976	0	13	7	56	17	9	0	92	100	96	60

Key Votes

1) Increase Def Spnd	FOR	6) Alaska Lands Protect	AGN	11) Delay Auto Pol Cntrl	FOR
2) B-1 Bomber	FOR	7) Water Projects Veto	AGN	12) Sugar Price Escalator	FOR
3) Cargo Preference	AGN	8) Consum Protect Agcy	AGN	13) Pub Fin Cong Cmpgns	AGN
4) Dereg Nat Gas	FOR	9) Common Situs Picket	AGN	14) ERA Ratif Recissn	FOR
5) Kemp-Roth	FOR	10) Labor Law Revision	AGN	15) Prohibt Govt Abrtns	FOR

Election Results

1978 general	J. Kenneth Robinson (R)	84,517	(64%)	($87,087)
	Lewis Fickett (D)	46,950	(36%)	($58,493)
1978 primary	J. Kenneth Robinson (R), nominated by convention			
1976 general	J. Kenneth Robinson (R)	115,508	(82%)	($42,724)
	James B. Holt, Jr. (Ind.)	25,731	(18%)	($9,040)

EIGHTH DISTRICT

The 8th congressional district covers the southern portion of the Virginia suburbs of Washington, D.C. Just across the Potomac from Washington is Alexandria, whose old town section recalls the tobacco port George Washington once frequented. Today, it is more significant politically that Alexandria has its own little black ghetto and that about two-thirds of its residents live in multifamily units, usually high rise apartments. These two groups make Alexandria the most Democratic part of northern Virginia. Beyond Alexandria, in Fairfax County, are the suburbs of Springfield, Annandale, and Mount Vernon. These are affluent places, with large colonial or, occasionally, contemporary houses built for large families; voters here are wary both of new developments and higher taxes, and they have the cautious and sometimes reactionary feelings you find in parents of teenage children. South of Fairfax is Prince William County. Here zoning requirements are less stringent and there are fewer minimum acreage requirements. You could not call this a poor area, but it is where the blue collar and lower-paid federal employees are moving; the cheapest new housing in metropolitan Washington is in places like this, 30 miles from the White House.

The 8th district was one of the fastest growing congressional districts in the nation in the sixties; and despite the efforts of some Fairfax County officials it is still one of the fastest growing areas on the eastern seaboard. The primary reason for this growth is of course the federal government. Federal paychecks have more than doubled since 1960, and here in the 8th 29% of all wage earners have such checks to cash every two weeks.

In the sixties, the 8th district spread far into the Virginia countryside. But its fast-growing suburban areas made a political revolution when in 1966 they ousted Congressman Howard Smith in the Democratic primary. Smith was Chairman of the House Rules Committee, a reactionary who could often control the pace and substance of House debate by commanding a committee majority—or simply by refusing to convene the committee at all. Smith's political demise was followed by a period of political instability, which continues to this day. The Democrat who beat him in 1966 was beaten in turn by the Republican in the general election—William Scott, later elevated to the Senate and named as the dumbest member of Congress. Scott was succeeded in 1972 in the district by Republican Stanford Parris, who in turn lost to Democrat Herb Harris in 1974.

Harris had come up through the often turbulent politics of the Fairfax County Board of Supervisors. He favored limits on growth and supported construction of the Metro subway system. In the House, he serves on three committees: Judiciary, Post Office and Civil Service, and District of Columbia. The latter two seats give him great opportunity to protect the interests of the district. He is a staunch supporter of measures to increase the pay and fringe benefits of federal employees, and an opponent of measures to make them more accountable to the elected officials and the public they are supposed to serve. He has favored home rule for the District of Columbia, but absolutely opposes allowing the District to levy taxes on suburbanites who work there.

On other issues, Harris tends to vote with most northern Democrats. It was on such matters that his 1978 Republican opponent, Jack Herrity, concentrated. He attacked Harris as a big spender—curiously, since many 8th district residents are direct beneficiaries of such spending. Herrity was well known as Chairman of the Fairfax County Board of Supervisors, but that position may have hurt rather than helped him. The Board is narrowly divided on many issues, and voters may have decided that they could have their cake and eat it too by keeping Harris in Congress and Herrity on the Board. It was, however, a closely contested election, and promises another close contest in the 8th in 1980.

Census Data Pop. 464,038. Central city, 0%; suburban, 98%. Median family income, $13,146; families above $15,000: 40%; families below $3,000: 4%. Median years education, 12.7.

The Voters

Median voting age 36.
Employment profile White collar, 68%. Blue collar, 21%. Service, 10%. Farm, 1%.
Ethnic groups Black, 7%. Spanish, 2%. Total foreign stock, 11%. Germany, UK, 1% each.

Presidential vote

1976	Carter (D)	78,914	(48%)
	Ford (R)	83,943	(52%)
1972	Nixon (R)	94,715	(67%)
	McGovern (D)	46,870	(33%)

Rep. Herbert E. Harris II (D) Elected 1974; b. Apr. 14, 1926, Kansas City, Mo.; home, Mount Vernon; Mo. Valley Col., U. of Notre Dame, Rockhurst Col., B.A., Georgetown U., J.D.; Catholic.

Career Navy, WWII; Internatl. trade atty.; Fairfax Co. Bd. of Supervisors, 1968–74, Vice Chm., 1971–74, Chm., 1974; Commissioner, No. Va. Transportation Comm., 1968–74; Vice Chm., Washington Metropolitan Area Transit Auth., 1971–74.

Offices 1114 LHOB, 202-225-4376. Also 9256 Mosby Street, Manassas 22110, 703-368-1331.

Committees *District of Columbia* (5th). Subcommittees: Government Affairs and Budget; Metropolitan Affairs.

Judiciary (15th). Subcommittees: Administrative Law and Governmental Relations; Immigration, Refugees, and International Law; Monopolies and Commercial Law.

Post Office and Civil Service (8th). Subcommittees: Civil Service.

Group Ratings

	ADA	COPE	PC	RPN	NFU	LCV	CFA	NAB	NSI	ACA	NTU
1978	70	90	85	42	40	–	73	0	56	7	–
1977	70	65	83	46	83	95	75	–	–	15	26
1976	80	83	93	56	83	96	81	17	20	11	29

Key Votes

1) Increase Def Spnd	AGN	6) Alaska Lands Protect	FOR	11) Delay Auto Pol Cntrl	AGN
2) B-1 Bomber	AGN	7) Water Projects Veto	FOR	12) Sugar Price Escalator	AGN
3) Cargo Preference	AGN	8) Consum Protect Agcy	FOR	13) Pub Fin Cong Cmpgns	FOR
4) Dereg Nat Gas	AGN	9) Common Situs Picket	FOR	14) ERA Ratif Recissn	AGN
5) Kemp-Roth	AGN	10) Labor Law Revision	FOR	15) Prohibt Govt Abrtns	AGN

Election Results

1978 general	Herbert E. Harris II (D)	56,137	(52%)	($164,352)
	John F. Herrity (R)	52,396	(48%)	($223,973)
1978 primary	Herbert E. Harris II (D), nominated by convention			
1976 general	Herbert E. Harris II (D)	83,245	(52%)	($86,339)
	James R. Tate (R)	68,729	(43%)	($127,105)
	Michael D. Cannon (Ind.)	9,292	(6%)	($513)

NINTH DISTRICT

The southwest corner of Virginia is perhaps the only part of the nation sometimes known in ordinary discourse by the number of its congressional district: the Fighting Ninth. Part of the Appalachian mountain country, the 9th probably has more in common with neighboring eastern Kentucky or Tennessee than with the rest of Virginia. It is not, however, one of the poorest regions of Appalachia. Except for a few counties, the area has never been as dependent on coal as southern West Virginia; and it has benefited recently from economic development in the valley that reaches from the Shenandoah to Knoxville, Tennessee, along Interstate 81. The mountain area of southwest Virginia is a place with its own cultural traditions, where the federal government can still mean the hated revenuers, and where the kind of music most favored is still what is heard from fiddlers and guitar, banjo, and mandolin pickers at the annual Galax Old Time Fiddlers' Convention.

The Fighting Ninth never did cotton much to the Byrd organization. In fact, its Republican tradition goes back to the days of the Civil War, when the virtually all white mountains had little use for slavery and the Confederacy. The local breed of Democrats date mostly from New Deal days, and a devotion to Franklin D. Roosevelt was quite exclusive with a devotion to Harry Byrd, Sr. The political alignments here are really closer to those of West Virginia than those of most of Virginia. This was the only part of the state which Harry Byrd did not carry in his 1970 Senate race, and he nearly lost it again in 1976. The Fighting Ninth has a taste for raucous, noisy politics: it has favored the loud conservatism of William Scott, the yahooing populism of Henry Howell, and the Southern accents of Jimmy Carter.

The current Congressman from the Fighting Ninth is Republican William Wampler. First elected in 1952, when he was only 26, Wampler was defeated in 1954 and 1956 by liberal Democrat Pat Jennings. For a while Wampler returned to his furniture and carpet business, but by 1966 he apparently sensed the public's disenchantment with Lyndon Johnson's Great Society and Vietnam war. Wampler ran once again, and this time defeated Jennings, who has not run again and instead serves comfortably as Clerk of the House.

Wampler is one of only three Republican congressmen who can remember serving in a House in which his party had the majority. He is also the ranking minority member on the House Agriculture Committee and, incidentally, the brother-in-law of Senator Howard Baker of Tennessee. Wampler had tough opposition from the same candidate in 1974 and 1976 and has won more easily since then.

Census Data Pop. 465,136. Central city, 0%; suburban, 0%. Median family income, $6,608; families above $15,000: 7%; families below $3,000: 19%. Median years education, 8.8.

The Voters

Median voting age 42.
Employment profile White collar, 32%. Blue collar, 52%. Service, 11%. Farm, 5%.
Ethnic groups Black, 2%. Total foreign stock, 1%.

Presidential vote

1976	Carter (D)	90,065	(53%)
	Ford (R)	79,376	(47%)
1972	Nixon (R)	95,065	(68%)
	McGovern (D)	44,540	(32%)

Rep. William C. Wampler (R) Elected 1966; b. Apr. 21, 1926, Pennington Gap; home, Bristol; Va. Polytechnic Inst., B.S. 1948, U. of Va. Law School, 1949–50; Presbyterian.

Career Navy, WWII; Newspaperman, Bristol *Herald Courier* and *Virginia-Tennessean;* U.S. House of Reps., 1953–55; Repub. nominee for U.S. House of Reps., 1954, 1956; Special Asst. to the Gen. Mgr., Atomic Energy Comm., 1955; Furniture and carpet business, 1955–66; Bristol Utilities Bd. and Redevelopment and Housing Auth., 1965–66.

Offices 2422 RHOB, 202-225-3861. Also Reynolds Arcade Bldg., Bristol 24201, 703-466-9451.

Committees *Agriculture* (Ranking Member). Subcommittees: Department Investigations, Oversight and Research.

Group Ratings

	ADA	COPE	PC	RPN	NFU	LCV	CFA	NAB	NSI	ACA	NTU
1978	10	20	18	58	40	–	23	92	100	85	–
1977	5	13	8	46	50	12	15	–	–	65	31
1976	5	22	2	35	37	16	0	67	100	82	56

Key Votes

1) Increase Def Spnd	FOR	6) Alaska Lands Protect	AGN	11) Delay Auto Pol Cntrl	FOR
2) B-1 Bomber	FOR	7) Water Projects Veto	AGN	12) Sugar Price Escalator	FOR
3) Cargo Preference	AGN	8) Consum Protect Agcy	AGN	13) Pub Fin Cong Cmpgns	AGN
4) Dereg Nat Gas	FOR	9) Common Situs Picket	AGN	14) ERA Ratif Recissn	FOR
5) Kemp-Roth	FOR	10) Labor Law Revision	AGN	15) Prohibt Govt Abrtns	FOR

Election Results

1978 general	William C. Wampler (R)	76,877	(62%)	($112,016)
	Champ Clark (D)	47,367	(38%)	($56,121)
1978 primary	William C. Wampler (R), nominated by convention			
1976 general	William C. Wampler (R)	96,052	(57%)	($126,354)
	Charles J. Horne (D)	71,439	(43%)	($86,045)

TENTH DISTRICT

The 10th congressional district of Virginia—a portion of the commonwealth's suburbs of Washington, D.C.—is one of those places whose recent history can be told through the perspective of its congressional representation. This is a district that was famous, in the Washington area at least, for returning to Congress Joel Broyhill, a conservative Republican who was first elected in 1952 and who survived, despite bitter opposition, until 1974. Now it has a very different kind of congressman, a cerebral liberal Democrat with a considerably different set of interests and priorities.

Back in 1952, Broyhill was the beneficiary of external factors: the Eisenhower coattails and the creation of the first suburban Washington congressional district. As a young man in the real estate business, Broyhill seemed almost to symbolize the young families who after World War II left the central cities and poured into suburbs like Arlington and Fairfax Counties in Virginia. In their pleasant houses, over their well-tended lawns, they cultivated the lifestyle that characterized the Eisenhower years. Though they were its beneficiaries in many ways, they were skeptical of the New Deal; they were more concerned about issues like property taxes and the schools. They did not like to think of themselves as opposed to blacks, but they wanted little to do with the District of Columbia, then becoming America's first major majority-black city; they were afraid what might happen if blacks in the District got political power. They crossed over the Potomac as seldom as possible, fleeing at 4:00 or 5:00 if they worked in a government bureaucracy.

These were people on the road to security and affluence. Although many of them were against big government, a very large number of them worked for it. With the rise of federal salaries in the sixties, the 10th district has the seventh highest median family income of all the 435 congressional districts by the end of the decade. Joel Broyhill suited these new suburbanites perfectly. He voted a conservative Republican line on the House floor, to keep their taxes low. On the District of Columbia Committee, he worked hard to stop self-government in the District and to prevent the District from taxing suburbanites. He was one of the first congressmen to grasp the notion that the best way to get reelected was not to wait around for your party label to become popular, but to go to bat for your constituents when they have problems with the government—federal, state, or local. In his 22 years in Congress, Broyhill resolved more than 100,000 constituent complaints; there were few offices that took care of constituents' needs and problems with greater efficiency.

For most congressmen that would have been the end of the matter. To run such an office and to avoid irritating any significant number of constituents would have guaranteed reelection for years. But Broyhill should be credited with voting his conscience and advancing his views so strongly that few constituents could avoid knowing where he stood. And that is what ultimately defeated him.

For change has been coming slowly to the Virginia suburbs. The children who jammed the schools of Arlington in the fifties have grown up, gone to college, and moved away—if not physically, at least in attitude. About half the Fairfax and Arlington electorates, to judge from local elections, are now dubious about further population growth and against building a new Interstate highway. Nor is the District so disliked any more. By the seventies, solid majorities of Virginia suburbanites were backing, rather than opposing, District home rule. Northern Virginia is now a place of fewer children and more secure affluence—a place where people have experimented with liberal ideas on the environment, foreign policy, and race. But Joel Broyhill didn't change.

Broyhill never got more than 60% of the vote in the 10th district; there was always a large minority solidly against him. The conditions of 1974 added enough voters to the opposition to defeat him. Watergate hurt him, like most pro-Nixon Republicans, and he had a solid opponent in Arlington County Supervisor Joseph Fisher. A professional economist of some repute, with the backing of a seasoned precinct organization, Fisher won with a solid 54%. The Eisenhower years in northern Virginia were over.

In his first term Fisher got a seat on the House Ways and Means Committee, on which Broyhill had also sat. The new Congressman played an important role on some tax and energy matters, and in the post-1974 House won a respect that would not have been accorded a freshman in the past. But it may be that the Fisher era in the 10th will be much briefer than the Broyhill era. In local government elections, the liberals have been losing ground since 1976. And in the 1978 election Fisher had a surprisingly close race against Republican Frank Wolf. Like his predecessor, Fisher is not afraid to take controversial positions—he backed a gasoline tax, for example—and he does not seem interested in hiding his views from his constituents in order to become noncontroversial. The prospect, therefore, is for continued close races in the 10th district in the years ahead.

Census Data Pop. 465,115. Central city, 0%; suburban, 100%. Median family income, $14,457; families above $15,000: 47%; families below $3,000: 4%. Median years education, 12.9.

The Voters

Median voting age 40.
Employment profile White collar, 75%. Blue collar, 15%. Service, 9%. Farm, 1%.
Ethnic groups Black, 5%. Spanish, 3%. Total foreign stock, 15%. UK, Germany, 2% each.

Presidential vote

1976	Carter (D)	92,341	(48%)
	Ford (R)	100,521	(52%)
1972	Nixon (R)	115,664	(64%)
	McGovern (D)	65,148	(36%)

Rep. Joseph L. Fisher (D) Elected 1974; b. Jan. 11, 1914, Pawtucket R.I.; home, Arlington; Bowdoin Col., B.S. 1935, Harvard U., Ph.D. 1947, Geo. Wash. U., M.A. 1951; Unitarian.

Career Planner, Natl. Resources Planning Bd., 1939–42; Economist, U.S. State Dept., 1942–43; Army, WWII; Exec. Officer and Sr. Economist, Cncl. of Econ. Advisors, 1947–53; Assoc. Dir., Resources for the Future, Inc., private research foundation, 1953–59, Pres., 1959–74.

Offices 223 CHOB, 202-225-5136. Also 450 W. Broad St., Falls Church 22046, 703-534-2888.

Committees *Ways and Means* (13th). Subcommittees: Trade; Social Security.

Group Ratings

	ADA	COPE	PC	RPN	NFU	LCV	CFA	NAB	NSI	ACA	NTU
1978	60	65	78	50	30	–	64	33	60	22	–
1977	75	83	85	62	58	95	70	–	–	19	29
1976	70	65	87	67	58	87	91	8	22	22	17

Key Votes

1) Increase Def Spnd	AGN	6) Alaska Lands Protect	FOR	11) Delay Auto Pol Cntrl	AGN
2) B-1 Bomber	AGN	7) Water Projects Veto	FOR	12) Sugar Price Escalator	AGN
3) Cargo Preference	AGN	8) Consum Protect Agcy	FOR	13) Pub Fin Cong Cmpgns	FOR
4) Dereg Nat Gas	AGN	9) Common Situs Picket	FOR	14) ERA Ratif Recissn	AGN
5) Kemp-Roth	AGN	10) Labor Law Revision	FOR	15) Prohibt Govt Abrtns	AGN

Election Results

1978 general	Joseph L. Fisher (D)	70,892	(53%)	($147,340)
	Frank Wolf (R)	61,981	(47%)	($232,286)
1978 primary	Joseph L. Fisher (D), nominated by convention			
1976 general	Joseph L. Fisher (D)	103,689	(55%)	($130,126)
	Vincent F. Callahan, Jr. (R)	73,616	(39%)	($128,752)
	E. Stanley Rittenhouse (Ind.)	12,124	(6%)	($1,552)

WASHINGTON

In the far northwest corner of the continental United States is the state of Washington, which the massive Cascade Range separates into two topographical and economic regions. To the east is the so-called Inland Empire. Here the Columbia River winds through plateau country, its waters backed up into giant reservoirs by dams and distributed through irrigation canals to many of the area's farms. There are some urban areas here—Spokane, the smaller city of Yakima, the complex around the nuclear Hanford Works—but the Inland Empire is primarily agricultural. Wheat is the biggest crop here, and apples and hops are also important—Washington is a big exporter of apples and beer. Like most of rural America, this area had outmigration in the fifties and sixties, but has had some population growth in the seventies.

The more populous region of Washington is the land west of the mountains, around Puget Sound. Here there is a strip of continuous urban development for more than fifty miles, from Everett south through Seattle and beyond Tacoma; in this area nearly two-thirds of the people of Washington live. The physical environment here is unique in the United States. The Olympic Mountains west of Puget Sound are the rainiest part of the nation, and the Sound itself is bathed in what sometimes seems a constant drizzle. The result are hills that were covered with green firs when the first white men arrived, and to a considerable extent they still are, for this is prime lumber country. The hills of Seattle and its suburbs, covered now with often colorful houses, dive down toward the Sound or the inland lakes not far away; ferries ply from Seattle and other harbors across the Sound. The valleys are dense with factories, warehouses, railroad yards; for railroads made the Puget Sound what it is. This is the closest continental U.S. port to Alaska and the Orient, a major point for exports (wheat from the Northwest and Great Plains) and imports (Japanese goods, Alaskan oil) as well as a major fishing center (salmon). The railroads did not reach the Sound until the 1880s, and it was not clear which port—Seattle, Tacoma, Everett—would emerge dominant until Seattle grew, in a flash, with the 1898 Alaska gold strike. It quickly became and has remained the major city of the Northwest.

In that booming, young, lusty Seattle there developed a turbulent politics. This was the major center of the International Workers of the World (the IWW or Wobblies) in the years before World War I; Seattle's business and civic leaders decided to exterminate the movement and in brutal fashion did so. Adding to the distinctiveness of the area were its large numbers of Scandinavian immigrants. They rode the Great Northern or Northern Pacific west from Minneapolis after the long trip from Bergen or Goteborg. The Scandinavians brought with them attitudes favorable to cooperative enterprises (Washington has more businesses owned by workers than any other part of the country). They had no suspicions of public power development, and Washington, blessed with the hydroelectric resources of the Columbia, became the leader in public power in the United States in the thirties. Also, despite the experience of the IWW, Washington proved hospitable to the trade union movement from the thirties on; today it has one of the largest percentages of workers in unions of any state (less than West Virginia, roughly equal with Michigan and Pennsylvania).

All of these factors led Washington voters to support the New Deal, and the state—especially the Puget Sound counties—piled up large margins for Franklin Roosevelt and his fellow Democrats. With only one exception since the New Deal, Washington has elected only Democrats to the Senate. But since World War II this has become a two-party state in just about every other respect. Republicans have held the governorship more often than not, probably because their almost always rather liberal candidates have been personally more attractive than the intensely political Democratic nominees they have beaten. In the fifties the Republicans controlled the state's House delegation; since 1964 it has been heavily Democratic. The legislature is usually closely divided. Seattle, once a Democratic stronghold, as it has grown more prosperous and white collar has also grown more Republican in many elections. It is the smaller cities in the Puget Sound area—Tacoma, Everett, Bremerton—that ordinarily deliver the largest Democratic percentages. The result is that in the last three close presidential elections, Washington's electoral votes have been determined by very small margins—and have gone to the losing candidate each time. This is a state far from the rest of America—the nearest big city to Seattle is Vancouver, British Columbia—and Washington's political rhythms are not necessarily those of the rest of the country.

With World War II there came to be another major force in Washington's economy, the aircraft industry. The giant here is Boeing, and its prosperity helped Washington achieve substantial growth in the fifties and sixties. But building airplanes is anything but a steady business: there are few potential customers and demand can vanish suddenly, even for an accomplished manufacturer like Boeing. That is what happened here in 1970. The year before Boeing employed 101,000 people in Washington—8% of the state's total work force. By the end of 1970 Boeing's payroll had shrunk to 38,000. Unemployment lines were jammed, 55,000 people left the state, and the Seattle area real estate market went into depression. Now Boeing tries not to hire as many people here as it did in the sixties boom and to keep its business steadier. By the late seventies the Seattle area and Washington generally have seen some of the kind of growth that has been the common experience of most of the West throughout the seventies.

Washington has the nation's pair of senators with the most seniority and the most clout—Warren Magnuson and Henry Jackson. They know their way around Capitol Hill: Magnuson was first elected to the House in 1936 and was elected to the Senate in 1944; Jackson was first elected to the House in 1940 and was elected to the Senate in 1952. By the end of 1980 they will have 64 years of seniority in the Senate and 84 years of experience in Congress. Both have been committee chairmen for many years now. Magnuson chaired the Commerce Committee for years—an important body since it covers almost all direct federal regulation of industry—and now is Chairman of Appropriations and, as senior Senate Democrat, President Pro Tempore as well. Jackson is Chairman of the Energy and Natural Resources Committee, which used to be called Interior, and is a major force on and next in line for the chair of Armed Services. Both men were sons of Scandinavian immigrants, grew up poor, and achieved success early; both have passed the tests of character that long service and great responsibility impose.

The state's senior Senator, Warren Magnuson, is less well known nationally than Jackson, but he retains as much clout in the Senate. Magnuson has never been an accomplished orator, and he is now past 70, but he still knows how to use the levers of legislative power. With his seniority and experience he has the operating style of one of those Southern senators of yore, but he uses it to far different purposes. Magnuson has always seen himself as the champion of the little guy, and despite the close relations one in his position inevitably has with business lobbyists, he has remained true to that vision. Long before Ralph Nader he was effectively pushing consumer legislation on the Commerce Committee. As Chairman of the HEW and Labor Appropriations Subcommittee, he has always favored generous budgets for domestic programs. His committee jurisdictions have given him a major voice in almost any area of domestic policy when he chooses to exercise it; bureaucrats and even Cabinet secretaries will return phone calls from Maggie's office very quickly. He also has a reputation in the Senate for practicality and sound judgment. When he puts his name on a bill and attaches his imprimatur to a cause, that is a sign to others that practical, pragmatic men had better give it serious consideration.

Magnuson has seldom been in political trouble at home, though he did have a close call back in 1962. In 1968 and 1974 he was reelected against the same weak opponent with more than 60% of the vote. The question for 1980 is whether he will seek another term. He turns 75 that year and is probably not eager for a vigorous campaign. But that is a year younger than Strom Thurmond and Jennings Randolph were in 1978 when they were reelected, and both had tough opposition. Magnuson can argue that he is still in a good position to get things done for the little guy in the Senate. One question is whether one of the state's top Republicans, like Attorney General Slade Gorton or Secretary of State Bruce Chapman, will make the race against him.

At the peak of his Washington career is Senator Henry "Scoop" Jackson. He has been disappointed in presidential elections: he was an also ran in 1972 and his seemingly strong campaign collapsed in 1976. But he remains a hard-working legislator with mastery over many subjects—a living refutation of the charge that the Senate no longer has leaders of broad interests and deep knowledge and experience. As Chairman of Interior, Jackson showed concern for environmental matters long before they became fashionable. He sponsored the Environmental Protection Act, which set up EPA and required the filing of environmental impact statements before most government projects can proceed. In the old days Jackson warned against over-exploitation of resources; now he warns against over-regulation. He appeals to businessmen and labor leaders as a politician affirmatively interested in economic growth and development but still committed to some environmental safeguards.

Probably Jackson's major impact is on military and foreign policy. He has been a member of the Armed Services Committee since the fifties, and during most of that time has been concerned over whether this country is strong enough to prevail against its potential adversaries. In the fifties he joined John Kennedy and Lyndon Johnson in charging that the Eisenhower Administration was spending too little on defense. In the sixties he felt that the Johnson and Nixon Administrations were not trying hard enough for victory in Vietnam. In the seventies he believed Henry Kissinger was conceding too much to the Russians in arms limitations agreements and was not doing enough to protect human rights. Jackson detests the Soviets and has always been strongly anti-Communist (though he was an opponent of Joe McCarthy as well), and he is deeply suspicious of any agreement with the Russians.

During Jimmy Carter's tenure, Jackson has again been a major figure in foreign policy issues. His staff keeps well informed of the substance of the SALT negotiations, and in effect Jackson has become a party to them; the Administration knows and the Russians should know that any SALT agreement is unlikely to get through the Senate without Jackson's approval. He was fiercely opposed to the appointment of former SALT negotiator Paul Warnke, and he may get the Senate. At this writing his position is unclear. If he follows the pattern he took in SALT I, he will extract concessions perhaps in the form of reservations from the Administration and then help muster the two-thirds needed for approval.

Jackson is a major force in other policy areas. He has become known as the Senate's leading backer of aid to Israel, in large part because of his role in enacting the Jackson-Vanik Amendment. This law, enacted over Kissinger's protest, requires the Soviets to provide free emigration for Jews and others before the Soviet Union can be granted most favored nation treatment by the United States. The Soviets found it so unpalatable that they scuttled the trade agreement altogether and actually lowered emigration for a while; now the numbers of Jews leaving the Soviet Union and arriving in Israel, which needs the manpower, have increased. And of course on energy Jackson, as Energy Chairman, is a major figure. Generally, he has supported efforts to control the prices of oil and natural gas and to regulate the internal market in them. Jackson remains a disciple here, as in other areas, of the New Deal, with its penchant for exerting control over chaotic situations. At the same time, he was one of the conference committee members willing to compromise in order to enact some version of the Administration's energy bill; he is not a man who likes to sit out on a lonely limb.

A superb legislator, Jackson turned out to be less than a brilliant presidential candidate. Jackson brought great experience to the 1976 race, at a time when voters were sick of experienced candidates after Nixon. He was a Washington insider when voters were looking for someone close to the problems of the ordinary person. Much of the impetus and elan behind his candidacy came from people concerned about Israel—a concern of a small minority of voters outside the New York Democratic primary—and about attitudes spawned by protesters against the Vietnam war. Jackson's backers wanted him very much to stand for the old ways of doing things in the Democratic Party. But they found out that the old power structures had crumbled. In the

Pennsylvania primary Jackson had the support of all the big labor leaders and of all the big city politicoes, but he lost anyway to Jimmy Carter. His campaign did have a big victory in New York and an especially sweet one in Massachusetts, but by the end of April it was all over.

At 68, and not likely to run for president again, Jackson has not been mentioned as a challenger to Jimmy Carter in 1980. After his presidential campaign ended, he ran for reelection in Washington and won a fifth term with 75% of the vote. He is in excellent health and is likely to continue to be a power in the Senate for a long time.

Washington's current Governor is an unusual political figure. Dixy Lee Ray had never run for public office before 1976. A scientist and oceanographer, she had been appointed to the Atomic Energy Commission during the Nixon Administration. She left Washington state in her camper with her Irish wolfhound to take the appointment, and became known not only for her lifestyle but for her strong advocacy of atomic power. In 1975 she returned with camper and wolfhound, ran for governor, won the Democratic primary by a small margin over then Seattle Mayor Wes Uhlman, and then won the general election, with large support from rural areas, over her moderate Republican opponent, King County (Seattle) Executive John Spellman. She is anything but an orthodox Democrat or an orthodox politician. She got a highly favorable cover story in *Time* magazine, but local press coverage has been far more critical—partly because she has gotten in furious feuds with the press. Her advocacy of nuclear power and her battle with Senator Magnuson over oil tankers in Puget Sound—he wants them out, she wants them in—have made her some detractors in this environment-minded state.

For 1980, she has going for her not only her unique and obviously genuine style, but the general improvement in the state's economic condition. But she may also face tough opposition, from Republicans like Spellman, Gorton, or Chapman, and quite possibly in the Democratic primary as well.

Census Data Pop. 3,409,169; 1.68% of U.S. total, 22d largest; Central city, 27%; suburban, 39%. Median family income, $10,404; 12th highest; families above $15,000: 23%; families below $3,000: 8%. Median years education, 12.4.

1977 Share of Federal Tax Burden $6,321,000,000; 1.83% of U.S. total, 18th largest.

1977 Share of Federal Outlays $8,878,833,000; 2.24% of U.S. total, 15th largest. Per capita federal spending, $2,503.

DOD	$3,086,765,000	8th (3.38%)	HEW	$2,377,025,000	21st (1.61%)
ERDA	$431,539,000	4th (7.30%)	HUD	$65,548,000	23d (1.55%)
NASA	$27,502,000	18th (0.70%)	VA	$370,166,000	17th (1.93%)
DOT	$304,734,000	15th (2.13%)	EPA	$105,288,000	20th (1.28%)
DOC	$205,192,000	11th (2.47%)	RevS	$132,343,000	22d (1.57%)
DOI	$334,788,000	4th (7.20%)	Debt	$198,218,000	22d (0.66%)
USDA	$391,018,000	18th (1.97%)	Other	$848,707,000	

Economic Base Finance, insurance and real estate; transportation equipment, especially aircraft and parts; agriculture, notably wheat, dairy products, cattle and apples; lumber and wood products, especially sawmills and planing mills; food and kindred products, especially canned, cured and frozen foods; paper and allied products; primary metal industries, especially primary nonferrous metals.

Political Line-up Governor, Dixy Lee Ray (D). Senators, Warren G. Magnuson (D) and Henry M. Jackson (D). Representatives 7 (6 D and 1 R). State Senate (30 D and 19 R); State House (49 D and 49 R).

The Voters

Registration 1,960,900 Total. No party registration.
Median voting age 42
Employment profile White collar, 51%. Blue collar, 33%. Service, 13%. Farm, 3%.
Ethnic groups Black, 2%. Spanish, 2%. Total foreign stock, 19%. Canada, 4%; Germany, UK, Norway, 2% each; Sweden, 1%.

Presidential vote

1976	Carter (D)	717,323	(48%)
	Ford (R)	777,732	(52%)
1972	Nixon (R)	837,135	(60%)
	McGovern (D)	568,334	(40%)

Sen. Warren G. Magnuson (D) Elected 1944, seat up 1980; b. Apr. 12, 1905, Moorhead, Minn.; home, Seattle; U. of N.D., 1923, N.D. St. U., 1924, U. of Wash., J.D. 1929; Lutheran.

Career Practicing atty.; Wash. House of Reps. 1933–34, Asst. U.S. Dist. Atty., West Dist. of Wash., 1934; King Co. Prosecuting Atty., 1934–36; U.S. House of Reps., 1937–44.

Offices 127 RSOB, 202-224-2621. Also 1010 5th Ave., Rm. 900, Seattle 98104, 206-442-5545, and W. 290 Riverside Ave., Rm. 576, Spokane 99201, 509-456-4654.

Committees *Appropriations* (Chairman). Subcommittees: Defense; Energy and Water Development; Labor, HEW, Related Agencies (Chairman); State, Justice, and Commerce, the Judiciary, and Related Agencies; Transportation and Related Agencies.

Budget (2d).

Commerce, Science, and Transportation (2d). Subcommittees: Communications; Consumer; Merchant Marine and Tourism.

Group Ratings

	ADA	COPE	PC	RPN	NFU	LCV	CFA	NAB	NSI	ACA	NTU
1978	45	75	63	44	89	65	55	17	50	13	–
1977	75	90	65	45	92	–	60	–	–	15	26
1976	70	79	59	41	83	49	64	25	50	9	14

Key Votes

1) Warnke Nom	AGN	6) Egypt-Saudi Arms	FOR	11) Hosptl Cost Contnmnt	FOR
2) Neutron Bomb	FOR	7) Draft Restr Pardon	AGN	12) Clinch River Reactor	FOR
3) Waterwy User Fee	AGN	8) Wheat Price Support	FOR	13) Pub Fin Cong Cmpgns	FOR
4) Dereg Nat Gas	AGN	9) Panama Canal Treaty	FOR	14) ERA Ratif Recissn	FOR
5) Kemp-Roth	AGN	10) Labor Law Rev Clot	FOR	15) Med Necssy Abrtns	FOR

Election Results

1974 general	Warren G. Magnuson (D)	611,811	(63%)	($463,116)
	Jack Metcalf (R)	363,626	(37%)	($63,153)
1974 primary	Warren G. Magnuson (D)	228,038	(91%)	
	One other (D)	23,438	(9%)	
1968 general	Warren G. Magnuson (D)	796,183	(65%)	
	Jack Metcalf (R)	435,894	(35%)	

Sen. Henry M. Jackson (D) Elected 1952, seat up 1982; b. May 31, 1912, Everett; home, Everett; U. of Wash., LL.B. 1935; Presbyterian.

Career Practicing atty., 1936–38; Snohomish Co. Prosecuting Atty., 1938–40; U.S. House of Reps., 1941–53.

Offices 137 RSOB, 202-224-3441. Also 802 U.S. Courthouse, Seattle 98104, 206-442-7476.

Committees *Armed Services* (2d). Subcommittees: Arms Control (Chairman); General Procurement; Military Construction and Stockpiles.

Energy and Natural Resources (Chairman). Subcommittee: Energy Resources and Materials Production.

Governmental Affairs (2d). Subcommittees: Investigations; Federal Spending Practices and Open Government; Energy, Nuclear Proliferation, and Federal Services.

Select Committee on Intelligence (7th).

Group Ratings

	ADA	COPE	PC	RPN	NFU	LCV	CFA	NAB	NSI	ACA	NTU
1978	55	84	55	40	80	71	45	8	50	8	–
1977	80	95	70	36	92	–	68	–	–	22	24
1976	50	95	72	54	83	53	57	13	90	13	7

Key Votes

1) Warnke Nom	AGN	6) Egypt-Saudi Arms	AGN	11) Hosptl Cost Contnmnt	FOR
2) Neutron Bomb	FOR	7) Draft Restr Pardon	AGN	12) Clinch River Reactor	FOR
3) Waterwy User Fee	AGN	8) Wheat Price Support	FOR	13) Pub Fin Cong Cmpgns	FOR
4) Dereg Nat Gas	AGN	9) Panama Canal Treaty	FOR	14) ERA Ratif Recissn	AGN
5) Kemp-Roth	AGN	10) Labor Law Rev Clot	FOR	15) Med Necssy Abrtns	FOR

Election Results

1976 general	Henry M. Jackson (D)	1,071,219	(75%)	($198,375)
	George M. Brown (R)	361,546	(25%)	($10,841)
1976 primary	Henry M. Jackson (D)	549,974	(87%)	
	Two others (D)	79,029	(13%)	
1970 general	Henry M. Jackson (D)	879,385	(84%)	
	Charles W. Elicker (R)	170,790	(16%)	

Gov. Dixy Lee Ray (D) Elected 1976, term expires Jan. 1981; b. Sept. 3, 1914, Tacoma; Mills Col., B.A. 1937, M.A. 1938, Stanford U., Ph.D. 1945.

Career Public School Teacher, 1939–42; Prof. of Zoology, U. of Wash., 1945–76; Spec. Consultant in Bio. Oceanography, Nat. Sci. Found., 1960–63; Dir., Pacific Science Ctr., 1963–72; Mbr., A.E.C., 1972, Chairwoman, 1973–75; Asst. Secy. of State, Dept. of Oceans, Internatl. Environ. and Scientific Affairs, 1975.

Offices Legislative Bldg., Olympia 98504, 202-753-6780.

Election Results

1976 general	Dixy Lee Ray (D)	821,797	(54%)
	John D. Spellman (R)	687,039	(46%)
1976 primary	Dixy Lee Ray (D)	205,232	(38%)
	Wes Uhlman (D)	198,336	(37%)
	Marvin Durning (D)	136,290	(25%)
1972 general	Daniel J. Evans (R)	747,825	(51%)
	Albert D. Rosellini (D)	630,613	(43%)
	Vick Gould (Taxpayers PCT)	86,843	(6%)

FIRST DISTRICT

Like most large American cities, Seattle has its own personality. If its high rise downtown buildings are not that dissimilar to those of many cities elsewhere—though they are impressive for a metropolitan area with less than two million people—then a few blocks below them is the city's funky waterfront, with stands where you can get salmon and dungenesse crab. Nearby is the Pioneer Square area, where stores and warehouses from the turn of the century have been restored and renovated. Some have compared Seattle to San Francisco, and there is some similarity in the topography; Seattle too has steep hills, with picturesque views overlooking a bay and other bodies of water.

There are other similarities. Seattle's upper class, like San Francisco's, continues to be anchored downtown and has kept residential quarters not so far away; it favors conservative clothes and outdoor recreation. Seattle's working class, like San Francisco's, has maintained many comfortable neighborhoods of frame houses on steep hillsides. The ethnic groups here are less distinctive, however—partly because so many are of Scandinavian background, and to all outward appearances have assimilated with the Yankee Protestants.

Like every city, Seattle is divided into distinct neighborhoods, mostly by voluntary residential choices. Generally blue collar workers live on the south side of the city, near the factories, warehouses, and railroad yards in the valley near Puget Sound. The wealthier, more white collar, better educated people tend to live on the north side of the city, in neighborhoods like Broadmoor and Magnolia Bluff that sit on the hills between Puget Sound and Lake Washington. There are less wealthy neighborhoods here too, like the Scandinavian Ballard section, but overall the north side is the more affluent area. The north side of Seattle is also the heart of Washington's 1st congressional district—the only part of the state (except for the 7th district in one special election) to send a Republican to Congress in the seventies.

The 1st takes in the north side, extends farther north to a working class suburb in Snohomish County, and then bends west to Lake Washington to take in the affluent suburbs of Bellevue and Mercer Island. There are plenty of Democratic votes in the 1st—it has gone Democratic in many statewide races—but there is also a large Republican base here, which is not true in many other parts of the Puget Sound area.

The Congressman from this district is Joel Pritchard, a Republican who has gotten high ratings from the Ripon Society, a group which has several important Republican members in the state. Pritchard served in the Washington legislature for 12 years when he challenged incumbent Thomas Pelly in the Republican primary in 1970; Pelly, though high ranking on an important committee, returned to the district seldom because he refused to fly, and he was weaker than had been expected. He retired in 1972. Pritchard did not win automatically, however; he had to beat strong challenges from a member of the Boeing family in the primary and from an aide to Henry Jackson in the general election. Since then he has had little difficulty winning; even with a strong opponent he won 66% in 1978. As a Ripon-type Republican, Pritchard has been increasingly in line with his party's majority in recent years, as it has shifted its focus from social to economic issues. He is on record to the effect that no member of Congress should serve more than 12 years—which means he probably will retire in 1984.

Census Data Pop. 465,810. Central city, 68%; suburban, 32%. Median family income, $12,084; families above $15,000: 33%; families below $3,000: 5%. Median years education, 12.7.

The Voters

Median voting age 42.
Employment profile White collar, 65%. Blue collar, 23%. Service, 12%. Farm, –%.
Ethnic groups Spanish, 2%. Total foreign stock, 25%. Canada, 6%; Norway, UK, 3% each; Germany, Sweden, 2% each.

Presidential vote

1976	Carter (D)	NA	
	Ford (R)	NA	
1972	Nixon (R)	137,563	(58%)
	McGovern (D)	97,967	(42%)

Rep. Joel Pritchard (R) Elected 1972; b. May 5, 1925, Seattle; home, Seattle; Marietta Col., 1946–48; Presbyterian.

Career Army, WWII; Griffin Envelope Co., 1948–72, Pres., 1970–72; Wash. House of Reps., 1958–66; Wash. Senate, 1966–70.

Offices 2349 RHOB, 202-225-6311. Also 2888 Fed. Bldg., 915 2nd Ave., Seattle 98174, 206-442-4220.

Committees *Foreign Affairs* (10th). Subcommittees: Asian and Pacific Affairs; International Operations.

Merchant Marine and Fisheries (5th). Subcommittees: Fish and Wildlife; Oceanography.

Group Ratings

	ADA	COPE	PC	RPN	NFU	LCV	CFA	NAB	NSI	ACA	NTU
1978	40	32	50	100	38	–	36	60	38	39	–
1977	50	41	35	85	55	45	35	–	–	54	34
1976	45	35	26	89	64	52	27	50	57	46	68

Key Votes

1) Increase Def Spnd	AGN	6) Alaska Lands Protect	AGN	11) Delay Auto Pol Cntrl	FOR
2) B-1 Bomber	AGN	7) Water Projects Veto	FOR	12) Sugar Price Escalator	FOR
3) Cargo Preference	FOR	8) Consum Protect Agcy	FOR	13) Pub Fin Cong Cmpgns	FOR
4) Dereg Nat Gas	FOR	9) Common Situs Picket	AGN	14) ERA Ratif Recissn	AGN
5) Kemp-Roth	FOR	10) Labor Law Revision	FOR	15) Prohibt Govt Abrtns	AGN

Election Results

1978 general	Joel Pritchard (R)	99,942	(65%)	($125,399)
	Janice Niemi (D)	52,706	(35%)	($60,121)
1978 primary	Joel Pritchard (R), unopposed			
1976 general	Joel Pritchard (R)	161,354	(74%)	($70,204)
	Dave Wood (D)	58,006	(26%)	($13,725)

SECOND DISTRICT

The 2d congressional district of Washington constitutes the far northwest corner of the continental United States. This is a region of green mountains, of heavily wooded inlets, and of gentle rain and fog. The 2d takes in sparsely populated islands in the Puget Sound and the Strait of Juan de Fuca, along with the counties just east of the Sound from Seattle to the Canadian border. Most of the population of the district is concentrated in a narrow strip of land between the

Sound and the Cascade Mountains, in or near cities like Bellingham, Everett, and several suburbs of Seattle. Mostly this is blue collar country; affluent people in Seattle have stayed in the city or moved east, across Lake Washington, rather than north into the 2d; Everett and Bellingham are rather grim paper mill towns. This is an area where people work hard, and favor strenuous forms of outdoor recreation, like hiking, boating, hunting, and fishing.

The 2d is a district that tends toward Democrats in state elections. It was represented for 12 years (1941–53) by Henry Jackson. But the most important issue here in recent congressional elections has been one virtually unheard of in the rest of the United States: Indian fishing rights. Several years ago a federal court in Washington recognized the treaty right of some Indian tribes to half the salmon catch in some of the state's major waterways. Sports fishermen, of whom there are plenty in the 2d district, worried that some fish might be depleted; commercial fishermen were faced with the prospect of going bankrupt. Liberal Democrats, like Lloyd Meeds who had represented the district since 1964, had a natural tendency to identify with the Indians; after all, they had suffered for years from broken promises and racial discrimination in what was once their own land.

But few residents of the 2d felt much sympathy. Meeds was Chairman of the Interior subcommittee with jurisdiction on the matter; he proposed a federal-state commission to deal with the problem. He was faced in 1976 with a Republican opponent named John Nance Garner—a grandnephew of Franklin Roosevelt's first Vice President—who opposed the federal court decision and would allow Indians no greater fishing rights than whites. This put him on the majority side of public opinion, and put him within 542 votes of upsetting Meeds in 1976.

After that near-defeat Meeds apparently gave up on the seat. He abandoned his seniority on the Education and Labor Committee and moved to Rules, where he supported the leadership; he also stayed on Interior and did some work on the fishing rights issue, but did not change his position greatly. Garner ran again in 1978, but this time the Democratic nominee, former Bellingham newscaster Al Swift, did not have the fishing rights issue working against him. He attacked Garner for having out-of-state financing and support, and apparently unnerved the Republican enough that he fired his Florida-based campaign manager. Swift won the race narrowly, but he will have the advantages of incumbency; he is not a member of Interior, where he might have to deal with the fishing rights issue in detail.

Census Data Pop. 472,289. Central city, 11%; suburban, 54%. Median family income, $10,563; families above $15,000: 22%; families below $3,000: 8%. Median years education, 12.4.

The Voters

Median voting age 41.
Employment profile White collar, 48%. Blue collar, 37%. Service, 12%. Farm, 3%.
Ethnic groups Spanish, 1%. Total foreign stock, 20%. Canada, 5%; Norway, UK, Germany, Sweden, 2% each.

Presidential vote

1976	Carter (D)	NA	
	Ford (R)	NA	
1972	Nixon (R)	121,349	(62%)
	McGovern (D)	75,728	(38%)

Rep. Al Swift (D) Elected 1978; b. Sept. 12, Tacoma; home, Bellingham; Whitman Col., 1953–55, Cent. Wash. U., B.A. 1957.

Career Broadcaster and Dir. of Public Affairs, KVOS-TV, Bellingham, 1957–62, 1969–77; Admin. Asst. to U.S. Rep. Lloyd Meeds, 1965–69, 1977.

Offices 1511 LHOB, 202-225-2605. Also Fed. Bldg., 3002 Colby, Everett 98201, 206-252-3188.

Committees *Interstate and Foreign Commerce* (25th). Subcommittees: Energy and Power; Communications.

Group Ratings: Newly Elected

Key Votes: Newly Elected

Election Results

1978 general	Al Swift (D)	70,620	(51%)	($150,435)
	John Nance Garner (R)	66,793	(49%)	($324,456)
1978 primary	Al Swift (D)	19,057	(44%)	
	Brian Corcoran (D)	15,176	(35%)	($117,972)
	Three others (D)	8,700	(20%)	
1976 general	Lloyd Meeds (D)	107,328	(50%)	($157,259)
	John Nance Garner (R)	106,786	(50%)	($111,013)

THIRD DISTRICT

Lumber is one of Washington's most important industries. And nowhere in the state is lumber a more important part of the economy than in the damp, mountainous region along the Pacific coast and the lower Columbia River. This is Washington's 3d congressional district, which encircles the Seattle and Tacoma metropolitan areas and just fails to include the industrial town of Vancouver, right across the Columbia from Portland, Oregon. This is not an urban district: the largest cities are Longview, with 28,000 people, and the state capital of Olympia, with 23,000; the largest concentration of population, in the Army's Fort Lewis (38,000), which sits at the district's edge, near Tacoma, is not part of the 3d's electoral politics.

The political atmosphere in the 3d has not changed too much since the turn of the century, when the lumberjacks first attacked the firs and the sawmill towns grew up on the bays off the Pacific and Puget Sound. It is an atmosphere that retains a kind of rough-hewn populism, reminiscent of the days when the International Workers of the World were trying to organize the lumber camps. People usually vote Democratic here, and have since the New Deal, for basic economic reasons; they think the Democrats are on the side of the little guy. Politics here has sometimes been radical, but it has never been chic.

The importance of lumber here apparently helped the current Congressman, Democrat Don Bonker, to win the seat in 1974. Bonker's Republican opponent, Secretary of State Ludlow Kramer, backed unlimited exports of timber to Japan. Bonker opposed them, arguing that the timber should be milled into lumber first in the United States, or should otherwise be left standing in American forests. Bonker won that election with a solid 62%. He is a member of the Merchant Marine and Fisheries Committee—of obvious local import—and of the Foreign Affairs Committee. On the latter, he is Chairman of the International Organizations Subcommittee. Bonker is considered bright and politically astute. Nevertheless, his winning percentage dropped noticeably in 1978, although his opponent had not been conceded much chance. This district seems unlikely to go Republican, but it is one which will require close attention from its incumbent.

Census Data Pop. 506,840. Central city, 0%; suburban, 36%. Median family income, $9,736; families above $15,000: 18%; families below $3,000: 9%. Median years education, 12.2.

The Voters

Median voting age 40.
Employment profile White collar, 42%. Blue collar, 42%. Service, 13%. Farm, 3%.
Ethnic groups Black, 1%. Spanish, 2%. Total foreign stock, 15%. Canada, 3%; Germany, 2%; UK, Norway, Sweden, 1% each.

Presidential vote

1976	Carter (D)	NA	
	Ford (R)	NA	
1972	Nixon (R)	112,130	(58%)
	McGovern (D)	82,747	(42%)

Rep. Don Bonker (D) Elected 1974; b. Mar. 7, 1937, Denver, Colo.; home, Olympia; Clark Col., Vancouver, Wash., A.A. 1962, Lewis & Clark Col., B.A. 1964, American U., 1964–66.

Career Coast Guard, 1955–59; Research asst. to U.S. Sen. Maurine B. Neuberger of Oreg., 1964–66; Clark Co. Auditor, 1966–74; Candidate for Secy. of State of Wash., 1972.

Offices 434 CHOB, 202-225-3536. Also 209 Federal Bldg., Olympia 98501, 206-753-9528.

Committees *Foreign Affairs* (12th). Subcommittees: Africa; International Development.

Merchant Marine and Fisheries (12th). Subcommittees: Coast Guard and Navigation; Fish and Wildlife; Maritime Education and Training.

Group Ratings

	ADA	COPE	PC	RPN	NFU	LCV	CFA	NAB	NSI	ACA	NTU
1978	65	89	50	50	60	–	46	17	13	21	–
1977	75	86	70	50	80	74	70	–	–	8	36
1976	75	68	77	53	82	84	81	25	20	12	35

Key Votes

1) Increase Def Spnd	AGN	6) Alaska Lands Protect	FOR	11) Delay Auto Pol Cntrl	FOR
2) B-1 Bomber	AGN	7) Water Projects Veto	AGN	12) Sugar Price Escalator	FOR
3) Cargo Preference	FOR	8) Consum Protect Agcy	AGN	13) Pub Fin Cong Cmpgns	FOR
4) Dereg Nat Gas	AGN	9) Common Situs Picket	FOR	14) ERA Ratif Recissn	AGN
5) Kemp-Roth	AGN	10) Labor Law Revision	FOR	15) Prohibt Govt Abrtns	DNV

Election Results

1978 general	Don Bonker (D)	82,607	(59%)	($43,324)
	Rick Bennett (R)	58,270	(41%)	($51,753)
1978 primary	Don Bonker (R), unopposed			
1976 general	Don Bonker (D)	145,198	(72%)	($36,125)
	Chuck Elhart (R)	57,517	(28%)	($8,680)

FOURTH DISTRICT

For most of its length in Washington, the Columbia River flows either within or along the borders of the 4th congressional district. To the west the district expands to the city of Vancouver, an industrial town across the Columbia from Portland, Oregon. Upriver the 4th cuts through the Cascade Mountains at Bonneville Dam, past McNary Dam to the town of Richland near ERDA's Hanford Works, one of the government's major nuclear facilities, and still farther upriver past Wenatchee to the Grand Coulee Dam. In area the 4th is the state's largest congressional district, and most of its area is taken up with the Cascade and its ridges, blessed with picturesque names like Horse Heaven Hills. The district's largest center of population is not along the Columbia at all, but instead in the fertile Yakima valley, which contains the district's largest city of Yakima.

The valley produces a great share of the state's agricultural yield, not just wheat, but also apples, hops, and other vegetables and fruits.

The current incumbent here, Democrat Mike McCormack, upset his predecessor Catherine May in the 1970 election. This kind of surprise result is always possible in a district like this, which is very far in flying time from Washington, D.C.; a member who loses his or her yen for returning to the district risks possible defeat.

McCormack benefited that year also from the strong support of Senator Henry Jackson, and on most issues he is a Jackson Democrat. He is also a man who has stirred great controversy. As Chairman now of the Science Committee's Energy, Research Development and Demonstration Committee, he has a lot to say about how energy research money is allocated. His background is in nuclear power, and he is a strong backer of increased reliance on nuclear energy; he regards it as cheap, efficient, and safe. That and an abrasive personality have brought him vigorous opposition from many environmentalists. McCormack has used his expertise in nuclear energy and his background as a scientist to convince other congressmen to agree with his judgments in these difficult policy areas. The environmentalists claim that he was just a public relations man in Hanford, and they have tried to defeat him in practically every election this decade. He has argued for more support for solar energy, but his opponents charge that he does not back enough.

That has not been easy. McCormack apparently works the district well and has developed considerable popularity. His views on nuclear energy probably help him win especially big margins in the Hanford area. And in 1978 his opponent was a person whom the environmentalists could not support: a housewife who formed a group that blocked creation of a state women's commission. Nevertheless, this is the kind of district, with its geographical isolation and Republican voting tendencies, that a congressman like McCormack will have to keep working hard in order to be assured of reelection.

Census Data Pop. 467,171. Central city, 0%; suburban, 25%. Median family income, $9,206; families above $15,000: 17%; families below $3,000: 11%. Median years education, 12.2.

The Voters

Median voting age 44.
Employment profile White collar, 44%. Blue collar, 34%. Service, 12%. Farm, 10%.
Ethnic groups Spanish, 4%. Total foreign stock, 14%. Canada, 3%; Germany, 2%. UK, 1%.

Presidential vote

1976	Carter (D)	NA	
	Ford (R)	NA	
1972	Nixon (R)	112,728	(59%)
	McGovern (D)	77,042	(41%)

Rep. Mike McCormack (D) Elected 1970; b. Dec. 14, 1921, Basil, Ohio; home, Richland; U. of Toledo, 1949–53, Wash. St. U., B.S. 1948, M.S. 1949, Gonzaga U. Law School.

Career Army, WWII; Research scientist, Atomic Energy Comm. Hanford Project, 1950–70; Wash. House of Reps., 1956–60; Wash. Senate 1960–70.

Offices 2352 RHOB, 202-225-5816. Also Fed. Bldg., Richland 99352, 509-942-7243.

Committees *Public Works and Transportation* (6th). Subcommittees: Public Buildings and Grounds; Surface Transportation; Water Resources.

Science and Technology (3d). Subcommittees: Energy Research and Production (Chairman); Energy Development and Applications.

Group Ratings

	ADA	COPE	PC	RPN	NFU	LCV	CFA	NAB	NSI	ACA	NTU
1978	30	70	48	42	70	–	32	42	33	30	–
1977	45	81	33	60	67	29	30	–	–	19	29
1976	35	77	49	59	67	49	45	8	50	19	20

Key Votes

1) Increase Def Spnd	AGN	6) Alaska Lands Protect	AGN	11) Delay Auto Pol Cntrl	FOR
2) B-1 Bomber	AGN	7) Water Projects Veto	AGN	12) Sugar Price Escalator	FOR
3) Cargo Preference	FOR	8) Consum Protect Agcy	AGN	13) Pub Fin Cong Cmpgns	FOR
4) Dereg Nat Gas	FOR	9) Common Situs Picket	AGN	14) ERA Ratif Recissn	AGN
5) Kemp-Roth	AGN	10) Labor Law Revision	FOR	15) Prohibt Govt Abrtns	AGN

Election Results

1978 general	Mike McCormack (D)	85,602	(61%)	($132,190)
	Susan Roylance (R)	54,389	(39%)	($65,371)
1978 primary	Mike McCormack (D)	50,434	(89%)	
	One other	6,397	(11%)	
1976 general	Mike McCormack (D)	115,364	(59%)	($103,123)
	Dick Granger (R)	81,813	(41%)	($100,015)

FIFTH DISTRICT

The 5th congressional district is the western part of Washington state. It is the heart of the Inland Empire and centers on Spokane, with 170,000 people the state's second largest city. Lying between the Cascades and the Rockies, the land here was originally arid plateau, but with the help of irrigation it has become one of the major wheat-growing areas of the United States. Much of the water is provided by the Grand Coulee Dam, the engineering marvel of the New Deal; the reclamation project also furnishes cheap public power. Washington, blessed with the nation's greatest hydroelectric resources, has always been a big backer of public power development.

In the intermountain West, Spokane is the largest city north of Salt Lake City. Spokane County, which contains the city and its suburbs, has about 60% of the 5th district's people and voters. Spokane is more Republican than the Puget Sound area in national races; the 1976 race Carter ran even in the Puget Sound area, but Ford carried Spokane solidly. Strengthening the Republican tendencies of the 5th are small counties and towns like Walla Walla near the Idaho and Oregon borders.

This is a district which has elected only two congressmen in the last 38 years: Republican Walt Horan, who served from 1943 to 1965, and Democrat Thomas Foley, who defeated him in 1964 and has won reelection ever since. Nevertheless, the seat has been closely contested in the last two elections and probably will be again in 1980. And that has happened despite the congressional eminence of its incumbent congressman.

For Foley has been very lucky in seniority. As a freshman, he was assigned to the Agriculture and Interior Committees, both important posts for a congressman from this district. He gave up the seat on Interior after rising to sixth position in seniority; but on Agriculture he became Chairman just after the 1974 election, at the age of 45. His rise was rapid: in 1970, he had been only eighth among the committee's 20 Democrats. But a series of retirements and defeats, plus the rejection of incumbent Chairman Bob Poage by the Democratic Caucus in December 1974 placed Foley in the chair, just as he was finishing a term as head of the liberal Democratic Study Group.

The chairmanship of a full committee is the sort of plum most traditional congressmen would have been delighted to have brought home to their constituents. But Foley has had nothing but political trouble in the 5th district since he got the post. Apparently it has only spotlighted his generally Democratic voting record on most issues—a record not particularly popular in this essentially Republican district. And his powers over agricultural policy, even his support for wheat support prices, has not been a great political asset. Instead he seems to have been caught between those demonstrating farmers who want huge subsidies from the federal government and angry right wingers who want no government involvement in agriculture at all.

As late as the fall of 1976 it seemed that Foley had no problems at home. The Republican candidate had died in a plane crash, and his replacement, ultraconservative tire dealer Duane Alton, decided not to campaign hard. Nevertheless Alton held Foley to 59% of the vote—a notable drop from his previous percentages. In 1978 Alton ran again, and this time ran a serious, well financed campaign. He criticized Foley as an ultraliberal out of touch with the district. Alton did not even seem hurt by his extreme stands—an end to food stamps and farm price supports. Foley was hurt also by the candidacy of Mel Tonasket, an Indian tribe official, who got 9% of the vote district-wide. Alton had 43% of the vote, leaving Foley with less than a majority, 48%. That obviously means trouble for Foley. Although one can argue that the large percentage of Tonasket's votes would have gone to him if the Indian had not run, it remains true that the incumbent got less than an absolute majority. The New Right movement which has proved so popular in much of the Rocky Mountain area also seems to have considerable appeal here. Neither Foley's chairmanship nor his opponent's position against all farm subsidies was enough to prevent Foley from winning an absolute majority in Spokane County.

Foley is respected as a knowledgeable and sensitive Congressman in the capital, but he can look forward to tough electoral opposition again—unless he decides to run for Warren Magnuson's Senate seat. But the latter alternative depends on Magnuson's intentions and its chances of success are not enhanced by Foley's recent showing in his home seat.

Census Data Pop. 471,144. Central city, 35%; suburban, 24%. Median family income, $9,164; families above $15,000: 17%; families below $3,000: 10%. Median years education, 12.4.

The Voters

Median voting age 43.
Employment profile White collar, 49%. Blue collar, 28%. Service, 16%. Farm, 7%.
Ethnic groups Black, 1%. Spanish, 2%. Total foreign stock, 16%. Canada, 4%; Germany, 2%; UK, Norway, Sweden, 1% each.

Presidential vote

1976	Carter (D)	NA	
	Ford (R)	NA	
1972	Nixon (R)	126,627	(63%)
	McGovern (D)	72,966	(37%)

Rep. Thomas S. Foley (D) Elected 1964; b. Mar. 6, 1929, Spokane; home, Spokane; U. of Wash., B.A. 1951, LL.B. 1957; Catholic.

Career Practicing atty.; Spokane Co. Deputy Prosecuting Atty., 1958–60; Instructor, Gonzaga U. Law School, 1958–60; Asst. Atty. Gen. of Wash., 1960–61; Asst. Chf. Clerk and Special Counsel, U.S. Senate Comm. on Interior and Insular Affairs, 1961–63.

Offices 1201 LHOB, 202-225-2006; Also 574 U.S. Courthouse, Spokane 99201, 509-456-4680.

Committees *Agriculture* (Chairman).

Group Ratings

	ADA	COPE	PC	RPN	NFU	LCV	CFA	NAB	NSI	ACA	NTU
1978	30	65	48	42	70	–	41	42	40	22	–
1977	45	96	53	38	67	45	50	–	–	15	39
1976	55	65	51	65	75	65	64	8	67	14	26

Key Votes

1) Increase Def Spnd	AGN	6) Alaska Lands Protect	AGN	11) Delay Auto Pol Cntrl	FOR
2) B-1 Bomber	AGN	7) Water Projects Veto	AGN	12) Sugar Price Escalator	FOR
3) Cargo Preference	AGN	8) Consum Protect Agcy	AGN	13) Pub Fin Cong Cmpgns	FOR
4) Dereg Nat Gas	AGN	9) Common Situs Picket	FOR	14) ERA Ratif Recissn	AGN
5) Kemp-Roth	AGN	10) Labor Law Revision	FOR	15) Prohibt Govt Abrtns	AGN

Election Results

1978 general	Thomas S. Foley (D)	77,201	(48%)	($347,573)
	Duane Alton (R)	68,761	(43%)	($174,978)
	Mel Tonasket (Ind.)	14,887	(9%)	($18,141)
1978 primary	Thomas S. Foley (D)	36,697	(90%)	
	One other (D)	3,910	(10%)	
1976 general	Thomas S. Foley (D)	120,415	(59%)	($46,418)
	Duane Alton (R)	84,262	(41%)	($12,582)

SIXTH DISTRICT

Tacoma, the second largest city on Puget Sound, has always lived in the shadow of its larger neighbor, Seattle. Back in 1900, just before the state's most explosive decade of growth, Tacoma was still a credible rival—it had 37,000 people to Seattle's 80,000. But in the years that followed, Seattle's growth continued, while Tacoma got itself embroiled in an unsuccessful attempt to rewrite history and change the name of Mount Rainier (which is in Pierce County like the city) to Mount Tacoma. Seattle was diversifying, adding white collar employment to its basic industries of shipping, fishing, lumber, and railroading. Tacoma remained primarily a lumber town, headquarters of the giant Weyerhauser firm, with only about one-quarter the population of its larger neighbor. Tacoma sits today on the hills rising from Commencement Bay, not as grim an environment as many mill towns, but not the city it once hoped it would become.

Tacoma is the heart of Washington's 6th congressional district, which includes the city and virtually all of its suburbs. The 6th also crosses the Puget Sound Narrows (where the Tacoma Straits Bridge collapsed in 1940) to include Kitsap County and its major city, Bremerton, a naval repair port, which lies across the Sound from Seattle. The 6th is a Democratic area in most elections—blue collar territory which is often the most Democratic part of the state. Even so, a Republican represented the district for 20 years, a politician with the asset of an unmistakably Scandinavian name, Thor Tollefson. In the 1964 Democratic landslide, he was unseated by Democrat Floyd Hicks, a local judge whose greatest desire was always to return to the bench. It was arranged for him to be nominated and elected to the Washington Supreme Court in 1976, and he returned to Tacoma after an honorable but rather quiet congressional career.

The succession was determined in the Democratic primary, and the winner in a five-candidate race was Norman Dicks. He had spent most of his adult years as a member of Senator Warren Magnuson's staff, but he kept enough roots in the area to beat several candidates who held local office. He has the reputation for political savvy which has always surrounded Magnuson, and in his first term in the House he won a seat on the Appropriations Committee. Dicks's general election majority was reduced in 1978, but he still won easily, and he must be considered to have a safe seat. He is one of the people who is mentioned as a possible Democratic candidate for Magnuson's seat if Magnuson should decide to retire in 1980.

Census Data Pop. 454,793. Central city, 32%; suburban, 47%. Median family income, $10,481; families above $15,000: 22%; families below $3,000: 8%. Median years education, 12.3.

The Voters

Median voting age 42.
Employment profile White collar, 50%. Blue collar, 36%. Service, 13%. Farm, 1%.
Ethnic groups Black, 3%. Spanish, 1%. Total foreign stock, 19%. Canada, Germany, 3% each; Norway, UK, 2% each; Sweden, 1%.

Presidential vote

1976	Carter (D)	NA	
	Ford (R)	NA	
1972	Nixon (R)	115,377	(60%)
	McGovern (D)	75,698	(40%)

Rep. Norman D. Dicks (D) Elected 1976; b. Dec. 16, 1940, Bremerton; home, Port Orchard; U. of Wash., B.A. 1963, J.D. 1968; Lutheran.

Career Staff mbr., ofc. of U.S. Sen. Warren G. Magnuson, Legis. Asst., 1968–73, Admin. Asst., 1973–76.

Offices 1508 LHOB, 202-225-5916. Also Security Bldg., Tacoma 98402, 206-593-6536.

Committees *Appropriations* (28th). Subcommittees: Interior; Defense.

Group Ratings

	ADA	COPE	PC	RPN	NFU	LCV	CFA	NAB	NSI	ACA	NTU
1978	45	90	58	50	70	–	59	27	33	19	–
1977	50	90	55	31	92	40	55	–	–	9	31

Key Votes

1) Increase Def Spnd	FOR	6) Alaska Lands Protect	AGN	11) Delay Auto Pol Cntrl	FOR
2) B-1 Bomber	AGN	7) Water Projects Veto	AGN	12) Sugar Price Escalator	DNV
3) Cargo Preference	FOR	8) Consum Protect Agcy	FOR	13) Pub Fin Cong Cmpgns	FOR
4) Dereg Nat Gas	AGN	9) Common Situs Picket	FOR	14) ERA Ratif Recissn	AGN
5) Kemp-Roth	AGN	10) Labor Law Revision	FOR	15) Prohibt Govt Abrtns	AGN

Election Results

1978 general	Norman D. Dicks (D)	71,057	(62%)	($166,731)
	James E. Beaver (R)	43,640	(38%)	($19,308)
1978 primary	Norman D. Dicks (D)	44,822	(84%)	
	One other (D)	8,329	(16%)	
1976 general	Norman D. Dicks (D)	137,964	(74%)	($140,816)
	Robert M. Reynolds (R)	47,539	(26%)	($5,301)

SEVENTH DISTRICT

The 7th congressional district of Washington is the south side of Seattle and most of its southern suburbs, from Lake Washington and downtown Seattle about halfway down to Tacoma. This is the more blue collar side of Seattle. The city's industrial area is concentrated in a flat plain that slides into Puget Sound; here the railroads and freeways come in from the south and east and service the factories and warehouses that are everywhere. At the southern end of this valley are the major Boeing plants, built some years after the initial industrial boom, but for some years—from the forties through 1969, when Boeing employment plummeted, and now again in the late seventies—the biggest industry in town.

Seattle's blue collar workers live in hilly neighborhoods on either side of the industrial flatlands. And if their houses are architecturally undistinguished, their streets look out often on pleasant views of Lake Washington or Puget Sound. Farther south of the city, one comes on newer and newer suburbs—Renton, Burien, Kent—which have filled up with the sons and daughters of those who settled the working class neighborhoods of Seattle itself. There is a small black community in the 7th, which includes nearly half the state's black population, but it still amounts to only 7% of the district's population; there are also small Mexican-American and Asian communities. But overall, racial differences have been less important to people than economic status; and that has meant that most of the people here over the years have been voting Democratic.

The 7th district has had three congressmen during the Carter Administration. The first was Brock Adams, who resigned when he was named Secretary of Transportation by the President. Adams, a Democrat, had attracted notice in the House when he worked on the legislation to set up Conrail, the government-sponsored entity which took over the northeastern railroads, and when he chaired the House Budget Committee. Although Adams had been reelected easily since his first victory in 1964, this was not all that Democratic a district in national elections; Jimmy Carter barely carried it in 1976. In May 1977 a special election was held to replace Adams, and in an upset the Republican, Jack Cunningham, won.

In retrospect it is easy to understand Cunningham's victory—and his failure to hold the seat in 1978. In the special election his Democratic opponent was Marvin Durning, an environmentalist and advocate of low growth. Cunningham, well funded by national mailings and with intelligent Republican advisors, argued that Durning's philosophy would prevent creation of new jobs. In this blue collar district he seized control of the jobs issue and held on for victory. This strategy did not work again in 1978, however. This time the Democrat was Mike Lowry, who called himself a Humphrey Democrat and criticized Cunningham for voting against the Humphrey-Hawkins bill and against raising the minimum wage. He had the additional advantage that Cunningham had been abrupt and even rude in dealing with constituents in circumstances that could not be controlled by campaign advisors. Cunningham's strong opposition to Indian land claims, while an issue all over Washington, was not a strong enough factor here to prevent Lowry from winning a small but decisive victory. With the advantages of incumbency, he should be the favorite to hold the district in 1980.

Census Data Pop. 420,058. Central city, 43%; suburban, 57%. Median family income, $11,706; families above $15,000: 30%; families below $3,000: 6%. Median years education, 12.4.

The Voters

Median voting age 41.
Employment profile White collar, 54%. Blue collar, 33%. Service, 13%. Farm, –%.
Ethnic groups Black, 7%. Spanish, 2%. Total foreign stock, 22%. Canada, 4%; UK, Germany, Norway, 2% each; Sweden, 1%.

Presidential vote

1976	Carter (D)	NA	
	Ford (R)	NA	
1972	Nixon (R)	111,127	(56%)
	McGovern (D)	85,891	(44%)

Rep. Michael E. Lowry (D) Elected 1978; b. Mar. 8, 1939, St. John; home, Mercer Island; Wash. St. U., B.A. 1962; Baptist.

Career Chief Fiscal Analyst and Staff Dir., 1969–73; Govt. Affairs Dir., Puget Sound Group Health Coop., 1974–75; King Co. Cncl., 1975–78, Chmn., 1977.

Offices 1205 LHOB, 202-225-3106. Also 3400 Rainier Ave. S., Seattle 98118, 206-442-7170.

Committees *Banking, Finance, and Urban Affairs* (28th). Subcommittees: The City; Housing and Community Affairs; International Trade, Investment, and Monetary Policy.

Merchant Marine and Fisheries (22d). Subcommittees: Fish and Wildlife; Panama Canal.

Group Ratings: Newly Elected

Key Votes: Newly Elected

Election Results

1978 general	Michael Lowry (D)	67,450	(53%)	($214,609)
	John E. Cunningham (R)	59,052	(47%)	($523,905)
1978 primary	Michael Lowry (D)	19,601	(74%)	
	One other (D)	6,713	(26%)	
1977 special	John E. Cunningham (R)	42,650	(55%)	
	Marvin Durning (D)	35,525	(45%)	
1977 special primary	John E. Cunningham (R)	11,293	(65%)	
	Norwood J. Brooks (R)	4,278	(25%)	
	Three others (R)	1,870	(10%)	
1976 general	Brock Adams (D)	133,637	(74%)	($81,874)
	Raymond Pritchard (R)	46,448	(26%)	

WEST VIRGINIA

West Virginia lies in the middle of the Appalachian chain that separates the East Coast from the vast Mississippi Valley of middle America. This is a state with scarcely a square mile of level ground, and it has been said that if all the mountains were ironed out, the resulting surface area would cover the entire nation. Maybe so, but in any case, the mountains and the narrow twisting roads that wind through them give West Virginia an isolation and a sense of distance from the rest of the country. This is not a state that thinks of itself as part of the East or Midwest or even the South; the term Appalachian (with a hard "ch" sometimes) is heard occasionally, but people here really think of themselves as West Virginians.

It is an identity hard won. Until 1863 the mountain counties were part, a misfit part, of the commonwealth of Virginia. There were few slaves here; in the last 1820s legislators from the mountain counties teamed up with Jeffersonian aristocrats and almost abolished slavery in Virginia. But the spectre of slave rebellions and the increasing profitability of breeding slaves for sale in the cotton belts of the Deep South strengthened the peculiar institution east of the Blue Ridge, and the mountain counties went their own way. They opposed secession, they stayed part of the Union and continued to send congressmen to Washington. In 1863, after a dispute over the name (it was nearly called Kanawha), West Virginia was admitted to the Union as a separate state.

The new state contained about one-quarter of the residents of old Virginia. But in the years that followed the Civil War, West Virginia grew much more rapidly than its parent. The reason was simple: coal. Under virtually all the mountains here and often near the surface are rich veins of bituminous coal, the essential fuel for industry and home heating in the late nineteenth and early twentieth centuries. West Virginia was then a kind of frontier. Men from all over the Appalachian region and even some immigrants from southern and eastern Europe came to work the booming mines.

The working conditions in the mines were never very good and were sometimes deadly. Lovers of country music know something of life in the coal company towns and the credit practices of company stores, where workers and their families had to buy everything. Immigrant communities in the big cities of the time had some geographical proximity and exposure to other kinds of American life. The coal mining communities of West Virginia, often literally up a creek or in a hollow, were effectively cut off from the rest of the world. Conditions were bad enough that a union movement developed, and during the thirties John L. Lewis's United Mine Workers organized most of West Virginia's mines—so successfully that West Virginia is now the most heavily unionized state in the nation. But just as unionization was complete, the coal industry entered a decades-long decline. The railroads switched from coal-powered steam engines to oil-powered diesels. Homes switched from messy coal to clean oil or gas. After World War II Lewis worked with the companies to encourage mechanization of the industry and to reduce the work force. The program was a vast success—but something of a disaster for West Virginia. In 1950 the state's population exceeded two million; by 1970, as thousands left to look for work elsewhere, it was down to 1.7 million. Almost a whole generation of young people had found themselves forced to leave the state.

Recently the coal industry has come on better times. As other fuels—oil and gas—become more expensive, coal becomes more attractive. And there is plenty of it: West Virginia alone has enough coal to supply the nation for hundreds of years. But the new prosperity has a price. Now that labor is relatively expensive, companies look for capital-intensive ways to mine the coal. One solution is strip mining: much of the coal is near the surface and can be scooped up with giant steam shovels. But strip mining often leaves ugly, sometimes irreparable scars on the landscape. The big companies have claimed they use sound reclamation methods, which are sometimes clearly less than successful. Many of the smaller operators do not bother. Nor are federal or state regulations automatically an answer. The Buffalo Creek disaster of 1972—when a company-constructed dam burst and flood waters destroyed a small town—shows how negligent or corrupt regulators can be. Companies are also careless about wastes, and hundreds of the narrow valleys and hollows of West Virginia suffer from serious air and water pollution. This is a state that operates very near the margin and the incentive for profit is often desperate.

The proliferation of small operators in the coal business has helped to create a few local millionaires, but it has also helped change the conditions of West Virginia life: the big companies were easier to regulate and easier to unionize. The United Mine Workers represents a smaller percentage of the mine work force than it used to, and it appears in danger of breaking up as well. Lewis's successor, Tony Boyle, who ran a cozy and corrupt operation, has been convicted of murdering a rival who ran against him in the 1968 union election. In 1972 Boyle was beaten by Arnold Miller, a former miner with black lung disease who was backed by a group called Miners for Democracy. Miller was opposed from the beginning by Boyle loyalists; he has been only partially successful in shutting off massive wildcat strikes, which in turn have diminished the union's bargaining ability. Miller was challenged by an erstwhile ally in the 1977 union election. The UMW, once so centralized under Lewis, seems now to be drifting in a dozen different directions—and losing control of the coal labor force.

Politics in West Virginia is a rough—and often corrupt—business. Many state jobs are filled by patronage, and bribery is not uncommon. One recent former governor, W. W. Barron (1961–64) has gone to jail, and another, Arch Moore, was tried and acquitted on charges of taking $25,000 from a savings and loan executive seeking a bank charter. Vote fraud has been so much a matter of course that returns from Mingo County, to take the most flagrant example, have traditionally been interpreted as indicating whom the county leaders were paid off by rather than which candidate the voters actually preferred. As in underdeveloped nations, so in this impoverished state, idealism and altruism are scarce in politics. In a state where most of the executive positions are held by outsiders in companies headquartered elsewhere, the best local avenues to riches are through public and union office.

Yet the state's governorship is currently held by a man against whom charges of greed have no credibility: John D. Rockefeller IV, universally called Jay. He first moved to West Virginia in 1964 to work in an antipoverty program, at the time an expert in East Asian affairs. He decided to stay and enter politics, as a Democrat rather than a Republican like his uncles the governors of New York and Arkansas. He was elected to the legislature in 1966 and to statewide office in 1968. His one setback occurred in 1972, when he ran against Arch Moore, the first West Virginia governor eligible for a second consecutive term. Moore was running in good times and was able to point to rising employment, rising population, and new roads; he called Rockefeller a carpetbagger (one ad showed people on a New York street being asked whether they would elect an outsider from West Virginia as governor). Moore won that race with 55%, and Rockefeller spent several years as president of a small West Virginia college.

In 1976 Rockefeller ran again. In a strong primary field, including 1968 nominee James Sprouse and 4th district Congressman Ken Hechler, Rockefeller won 50% of the vote. Against former Governor Cecil Underwood in the general he won overwhelmingly. His time in office has been more turbulent. He did push through a strip mining control bill, but in 1977 he could not persuade the legislature to remove the sales tax on food. He excelled at providing emergency services when severe flooding hit the state, but he was able to do little about the wildcat strikes and internal UMW strife which has hurt the state. Rockefeller, sometimes mentioned as a candidate for national office, will be seeking reelection in 1980. He is unlikely to have strong primary competition, but he may have serious Republican opposition—particularly if Arch Moore runs again.

If Rockefeller is West Virginia's best known and most glamorous public figure, its most powerful officeholder, at least in national affairs, is Senator Robert Byrd. If you look back to 1958, when Byrd was first elected to the Senate, you could not have picked a less likely candidate for the position of Senate Majority Leader. If he was from a border state, like other Democratic leaders (Johnson, Barkley, Robinson), he also had severe handicaps. He had quit the Ku Klux Klan as late as 1945, just a year before his election to the West Virginia House of Delegates; he had voted as a Congressman and would vote as a Senator against civil rights legislation; he would become known as a vindictive campaigner against alleged welfare abuses in the District of Columbia—a stance that might help him in West Virginia, but not among liberal Democratic senators.

Nevertheless this same Robert Byrd was elected by the most liberal group of Senate Democrats in history as their Majority Leader in 1977. He even beat the Senate's classic liberal, Hubert Humphrey, in the process. Byrd won the majority leadership in the same way he had won other positions: the House of Representatives in 1952, the Senate in 1958, the Senate majority whip position in 1971. His success owes nothing to gladhanding or charm or even patronage, but owes everything to hard work.

For Byrd is a charmless, dour, deadly serious man. He courts senators with the same assiduity that prompts him to keep card files on thousands of West Virginians, so he can write and telephone them constantly, asking their opinions on issues. In 1969 and 1970, when Edward Kennedy was Majority Whip (the number two leadership position), Byrd was Secretary of the Senate Democratic Conference. Here he paid meticulous attention to the petty details that can make the lives of senators easier: keeping them informed of the pace of floor debate and the scheduling of upcoming votes, helping them to get amendments before the Senate, arranging pairs, and even getting taxicabs. He showed his colleagues elaborate courtesy, writing them thank you notes on the slightest pretext. It all paid off in 1971, when Byrd suddenly challenged Kennedy for the whip post. The West Virginian did not announce his candidacy until he was sure he had a majority, which included Richard Russell's deathbed proxy.

When Byrd began rounding up votes for majority leader in 1976—although he really had many of them in hand much earlier—no one challenged his efficiency, and few challenged his fairness. The contest between him and Humphrey was also between two conceptions of the post. Humphrey would have been an inspirational leader, but one not necessarily strong on details; Byrd promised to be quite the opposite. Byrd, to be sure, is not the solid conservative he once was. His voting record is close to that of most Senate Democrats, and he has backed the national Democratic position on such closely contested matters as the energy bill and the Panama Canal Treaty. His attention to detail gave him a critical role in uncovering the Watergate scandal: it was Byrd who got L. Patrick Gray to admit that John Dean "probably lied" about the affair, an admission that sparked Dean's determination to tell the truth. Byrd has run a fairly orderly ship in the Senate, but the body's rules still allow an extremely dilatory pace on occasions; Byrd has attempted to tighten the rules somewhat, but there are limits to the extent to which he can speed things up. He insists that he does not use his position to advance his personal views, and in fact does seem more the servant than the master of the Senate's Democrats—which is how he says he sees his role.

Byrd's careful cultivation of West Virginia voters has not stopped, despite his high position in Washington. Though he is an accomplished country fiddle player, Byrd is not part of any old boy network in the state, but he is West Virginia's champion vote-getter nonetheless. In 1970 he whipped a liberal primary challenger with 88%; in the general election that year he became the first candidate in history to carry all 55 of West Virginia's counties. In 1976 he was prepared to do that all over again, but no one filed to run against him.

West Virginia's other Senator, Jennings Randolph, is one of the most experienced war horses on Capitol Hill. He first came to Congress in 1932, as a 30-year-old freshman New Deal congressman. Defeated in the Republican year of 1946, he became a Hill lobbyist, but he kept a hand in West Virginia politics. In 1958 he won election to the Senate, and he had little trouble winning full terms in 1960, 1966, and 1972.

Randolph is now Chairman of the Environment and Public Works Committee. Under its old name, Public Works, this was the key pork barrel committee, and its chairman had a great deal of clout from doling out dams and post offices and other federal building projects to his colleagues. This was a role Randolph found congenial. Naturally a generous and amiable man, he was pleased to help his friends. And he remains an old-fashioned New Dealer, convinced that public works projects create jobs and help the little people of the nation. More recently the committee has taken on matters suggested by the first half of its new name; it is the body which passes on most air and water pollution legislation. On such matters the legislative workload has usually been hefted by Edmund Muskie, now the number two Democrat on the Committee, who early became knowledgeable about such matters. A cautious man, Muskie has tended to clear his work with Randolph, who in turn of course attends to the interests of West Virginia—which means coal. They split on the question of whether highway trust fund money could be used for mass transit (Randolph said no, and Muskie won), but on sensitive matters like the question of automobile emissions they have tended to cooperate. Most of Randolph's legislative work has been with this committee, but he does have other interests. Since the thirties he has been the Senate's leading backer of projects to help the handicapped; it was he, for example, who wrote the law requiring candy stands in federal buildings to be run by blind persons.

Many people expected Randolph to retire in 1978, when he turned 76 years old—and when the irrepressible Arch Moore was the Republican candidate. But he decided to run just one more time. Moore naturally contrasted their ages and argued that he as Governor, not Randolph as Senator, built the roads West Virginia needed and got its economy moving again. Randolph for the first time used professional television advertisements and public opinion polling, and emphasized his own strengths. He argued that he had done more for West Virginia, that he was still vigorous and powerful, and some of his commercials—though not featuring the polite Randolph himself—went so far as to attack Moore. Robert Byrd made a very strong endorsement of Randolph and campaigned extensively for him—a rare example of colleagues of the same party from the same state working closely for each other. It was one of the closest Senate elections in the country, but Randolph won by some 4,000 votes. Assuming his continued good health, he can expect to celebrate his 80th birthday and the 50th anniversary of his first election to Congress in 1982.

Census Data Pop. 1,744,237; 0.86% of U.S. total, 34th largest; Central city, 13%; suburban, 19%. Median family income, $7,414; 47th highest; families above $15,000: 10%; families below $3,000: 17%. Median years education, 10.6.

1977 Share of Federal Tax Burden $2,349,000,000; 0.68% of U.S. total, 34th largest.

1977 Share of Federal Outlays $2,941,936,000; 0.74% of U.S. total, 36th largest. Per capita federal spending, $2,942.

DOD	$197,402,000	46th (0.22%)	HEW	$1,465,648,000	33d (0.99%)
ERDA	$15,278,000	25th (0.26%)	HUD	$33,415,000	34th (0.79%)
NASA	$59,000	48th (—%)	VA	$202,090,000	35th (1.05%)
DOT	$233,358,000	21st (1.63%)	EPA	$56,310,000	28th (0.69%)
DOC	$50,137,000	42d (0.60%)	RevS	$72,997,000	33d (0.86%)
DOI	$30,058,000	31st (0.65%)	Debt	$70,712,000	38th (0.24%)
USDA	$125,768,000	41st (0.63%)	Other	$388,704,000	

Economic Base Bituminous coal mining; chemicals and allied products, especially industrial chemicals; primary metal industries, especially blast furnaces and basic steel products; stone, clay and glass products, especially glassware, pressed or blown; finance, insurance and real estate; agriculture, especially cattle, dairy products, apples and eggs.

Political Line-up Governor, John D. Rockefeller IV (D). Senators, Jennings Randolph (D) and Robert C. Byrd (D). Representatives, 4 D. State Senate (26 D and 8 R); State House (74 D and 26 R).

The Voters

Registration 1,020,892 Total. 687,584 D (67%); 310,968 R (30%); 22,340 Other (2%).
Median voting age 45
Employment profile White collar, 40%. Blue collar, 45%. Service, 13%. Farm, 2%.
Ethnic groups Black, 4%. Total foreign stock, 4%.

Presidential vote

1976	Carter (D)	435,864	(58%)
	Ford (R)	314,726	(42%)
1972	Nixon (R)	484,964	(64%)
	McGovern (D)	277,435	(36%)

1976 Democratic Presidential Primary

Byrd	284,819	(89%)
Wallace	36,882	(11%)

1976 Republican Presidential Primary

Ford	82,281	(57%)
Reagan	62,975	(43%)

Sen. Jennings Randolph (D) Elected 1958, seat up 1984; b. Mar. 8, 1902, Salem; home, Elkins; Salem Col., B.A. 1924; Baptist.

Career Ed. Staff, Clarksburg *Daily Telegram*, 1924–25; Assoc. Ed., W. Va. *Review*, 1925–26; Prof. and Athletic Dir., Davis & Elkins Col., 1926–32; Instructor and Business Col. Dean, Southeastern U.; U.S. House of Reps., 1933–47; Asst. to the Pres. and Dir. of Public Rel., Capital Airlines, 1947–58.

Offices 5121 DSOB, 202-244-6472. Also 328–329 Fed. Bldg., 300 3d St., Elkins 26241, 304-636-5100.

Committees *Environment and Public Works* (Chairman). Subcommittees: Transportation; Regional and Community Development; Nuclear Regulation.

Labor and Human Resources (2d). Subcommittees: Handicapped (Chairman); Education, Arts, and Humanities; Aging.

Veterans' Affairs (3d).

Group Ratings

	ADA	COPE	PC	RPN	NFU	LCV	CFA	NAB	NSI	ACA	NTU
1978	30	68	43	11	60	51	50	45	70	38	–
1977	40	72	50	36	50	–	36	–	–	43	25
1976	45	60	42	44	75	39	64	25	30	16	38

Key Votes

1) Warnke Nom	FOR	6) Egypt-Saudi Arms	FOR	11) Hosptl Cost Contnmnt	FOR
2) Neutron Bomb	AGN	7) Draft Restr Pardon	FOR	12) Clinch River Reactor	AGN
3) Waterwy User Fee	FOR	8) Wheat Price Support	AGN	13) Pub Fin Cong Cmpgns	FOR
4) Dereg Nat Gas	FOR	9) Panama Canal Treaty	AGN	14) ERA Ratif Recissn	FOR
5) Kemp-Roth	AGN	10) Labor Law Rev Clot	FOR	15) Med Necssy Abrtns	AGN

Election Results

1978 general	Jennings Randolph (D)	249,034	(50%)	($684,605)
	Arch A. Moore, Jr. (R)	244,317	(50%)	($458,823)
1978 primary	Jennings Randolph (D), unopposed			
1972 general	Jennings Randolph (D)	486,310	(66%)	($133,670)
	Louise Leonard (R)	245,531	(34%)	($45,513)

Sen. Robert C. Byrd (D) Elected 1958, seat up 1982; b. Jan. 15, 1918, North Wilkesboro, N.C.; home, Sophia; Beckley Col., Concord Col., Morris Harvey Col., Marshall Col.; Baptist.

Career W. Va. House of Reps., 1946–50; W. Va. Senate, 1950–52; U.S. House of Reps., 1953–59; U.S. Senate Majority Whip, 1971–.

Offices 133 RSOB, 202-224-3954.

Committees *Majority Leader.*

Appropriations (3d). Subcommittees: Agriculture, and Related Agencies; Energy and Water Development, Interior and Related Agencies (Chairman); Labor, HEW, and Related Agencies; Transportation and Related Agencies.

Judiciary (3d). Subcommittee: Improvements in Judicial Machinery.

Rules and Administration (3d).

Group Ratings

	ADA	COPE	PC	RPN	NFU	LCV	CFA	NAB	NSI	ACA	NTU
1978	45	78	63	40	50	56	40	50	50	29	–
1977	50	60	55	27	50	–	40	–	–	37	32
1976	45	79	45	47	92	39	85	50	90	31	47

Key Votes

1) Warnke Nom	FOR	6) Egypt-Saudi Arms	FOR	11) Hosptl Cost Contnmnt	FOR
2) Neutron Bomb	FOR	7) Draft Restr Pardon	FOR	12) Clinch River Reactor	AGN
3) Waterwy User Fee	FOR	8) Wheat Price Support	AGN	13) Pub Fin Cong Cmpgns	FOR
4) Dereg Nat Gas	AGN	9) Panama Canal Treaty	FOR	14) ERA Ratif Recissn	FOR
5) Kemp-Roth	AGN	10) Labor Law Rev Clot	FOR	15) Med Necssy Abrtns	FOR

Election Results

1976 general	Robert C. Byrd (D)	338,444	(100%)	($94,335)
1976 primary	Robert C. Byrd (D), unopposed			
1970 general	Robert C. Byrd (D)	345,965	(78%)	
	Elmer H. Dodson (R)	99,663	(22%)	

Gov. John D. Rockefeller IV (D) Elected 1976, term expires Jan. 1981; b. June 18, 1937; International Christian University, Tokyo, 1957–60, Harvard, B.A. 1961; Presbyterian.

Career Natl. Advisory Cncl. of the Peace Corps, 1961; Asst. to Peace Corps Dir. R. Sargent Shriver, 1962; Staff mbr., President's Comm. on Juvenile Delinquency and Youth Crime, 1964–66; W. Va. House of Delegates, 1966–68; Sec. of State for W. Va., 1968–72; Pres., W. Va. Wesleyan Col., 1972–76.

Offices Charleston, 25305, 304-348-2000.

Election Results

1976 general	John D. Rockefeller IV (D)	495,600	(66%)
	Cecil H. Underwood (R)	253;398	(34%)

1976 primary	John D. Rockefeller IV (D)	206,732	(50%)
	James M. Sprouse (D)	118,707	(29%)
	Ken Hechler (D)	52,791	(13%)
	John G. Hutchinson (D)	26,222	(6%)
	Four others (D)	11,711	(3%)
1972 general	Arch A. Moore, Jr. (R)	423,817	(55%)
	John D. Rockefeller IV (D)	350,462	(45%)

FIRST DISTRICT

West Virginia's northern panhandle is the least isolated part of the state. The terrain here is hilly, not mountainous, and the panhandle is in steel country that sits along the Ohio River just west of Pittsburgh and south of Youngstown, Ohio. Along the river are giant blast furnaces in Wheeling, the home town of Walter Reuther, and Weirton. With the Pittsburgh area, the panhandle is one of the leading glassmaking areas of the country as well. Not surprisingly, industrial pollution here has been a big problem. The Ohio River valley around Wheeling has some of the most polluted air in the United States, and the Ohio itself is not clean. Another problem is the periodically sagging and seldom surging economy. Steel was once America's leading industry; its performance now is lackluster.

The industrial towns of Clarksburg and Fairmont in the Monongahela River valley south of Pittsburgh, the northern panhandle, and the Ohio River counties as far south as Parkersburg make up West Virginia's 1st congressional district. Aside from a few rural counties and Parkersburg, which tend to go Republican, the 1st district is Democratic territory in most elections. But that has not always been the case in congressional elections, thanks to the vote-getting prowess of Arch Moore, who was elected to Congress here from 1956 to 1966 and was elected Governor in 1968 and 1972.

Moore's successor in Congress is also his predecessor: Democrat Robert Mollohan. A veteran of West Virginia political wars, Mollohan was elected here in 1952 and 1954 and then ran unsuccessfully for governor in 1956, when Moore won in the House. Mollohan tried to beat Moore, but even in the Democratic year of 1958 he could not do so; he went into the insurance business and ran for the House when Moore ran for governor in 1968. A member of the Armed Services and House Administration Committees, he has a voting record which wins approval both in the Pentagon and in the halls of organized labor.

He has not always shown great prowess as a vote-getter, however. His margins in 1974 and 1976 were not particularly impressive. Although he did somewhat better in 1978, he turns 70 in 1979, and he must be considered a possible candidate for retirement soon.

Census Data Pop. 436,337. Central city, 17%; suburban, 22%. Median family income, $8,457; families above $15,000: 12%; families below $3,000: 12%. Median years education, 11.6.

The Voters

Median voting age 45.
Employment profile White collar, 39%. Blue collar, 47%. Service, 13%. Farm, 1%.
Ethnic groups Black, 2%. Total foreign stock, 9%.

Presidential vote

1976	Carter (D)	105,377	(56%)
	Ford (R)	84,374	(44%)
1972	Nixon (R)	126,902	(64%)
	McGovern (D)	70,735	(36%)

Rep. Robert H. Mollohan (D) Elected 1968; b. Sept. 18, 1909, Gransville; home, Fairmont; Glenville Co., Shepherd Col.; Baptist.

Career W. Va. Chf., Misc. Tax Div., and cashier, IRS, 1933–36; Dist. Mgr. and State Personnel Dir., Works Projects Admin., 1937–40; State Dir., U.S. Census, 1940; Supt., W. Va. Industrial School for Boys, 1945–49; U.S. Marshall, North. Dist. of W. Va., 1949–51; Clerk, U.S. Senate Comm. on the Dist. of Columbia.

Offices 339 CHOB, 202-225-4172. Also Rm. 603, Deveny Bldg., Fairmont 26554, 304-363-3356.

Committees *Armed Services* (10th). Subcommittees: Investigations; Seapower and Strategic and Critical Materials; Military Compensation.

House Administration (8th). Subcommittees: Services; Office Systems (Chairman).

Group Ratings

	ADA	COPE	PC	RPN	NFU	LCV	CFA	NAB	NSI	ACA	NTU
1978	30	55	45	25	60	–	27	50	80	48	–
1977	25	87	33	27	58	33	40	–	–	41	17
1976	45	83	39	25	73	35	27	20	75	14	8

Key Votes

1) Increase Def Spnd	FOR	6) Alaska Lands Protect	FOR	11) Delay Auto Pol Cntrl	FOR
2) B-1 Bomber	FOR	7) Water Projects Veto	AGN	12) Sugar Price Escalator	AGN
3) Cargo Preference	FOR	8) Consum Protect Agcy	AGN	13) Pub Fin Cong Cmpgns	AGN
4) Dereg Nat Gas	FOR	9) Common Situs Picket	FOR	14) ERA Ratif Recissn	FOR
5) Kemp-Roth	AGN	10) Labor Law Revision	FOR	15) Prohibt Govt Abrtns	FOR

Election Results

1978 general	Robert H. Mollohan (D)	76,372	(63%)	($37,680)
	Gene A. Haynes (R)	44,062	(37%)	($14,129)
1978 primary	Robert H. Mollohan (D), unopposed			
1976 general	Robert H. Mollohan (D)	108,055	(58%)	($36,188)
	John F. McCuskey (R)	78,134	(42%)	($56,623)

SECOND DISTRICT

The 2d congressional district of West Virginia occupies the eastern part of the state, and contains the most mountainous and most sparsely populated counties of West Virginia. The district extends from Harpers Ferry, not far from Washington, D.C., where John Brown's raiders seized the arsenal and tried to free the slaves in 1859, south and west to Fayette County, near the state capital of Charleston, and not far from the Kentucky line. In the northwest part of the district, not far from Pittsburgh, is the 2d's only significant city, Morgantown, with a population of only 29,000—part of the industrial Monongahela River valley and home of West Virginia University.

The problems of the 2d are typical of the entire Appalachian region. For years there have been virtually no four-lane highways in the district, and the existing roads, twisting around the mountains, make the rural counties here effectively more remote from the East Coast than the geographically more distant Great Lakes cities. The beauty of the West Virginia hills has been spoiled by emissions from coal mines and paper mills and by the ugly scars left by strip mining. For years jobs have been leaving the district—although there may have been some change with the revival of coal prices in recent years—and so have young people who might otherwise have decided to stay.

The political map of the 2d district is an odd-looking patchwork of Democratic industrial and mining areas and Republican mountain strongholds. In most statewide elections the district has been marginal, but in congressional elections it has been solidly Democratic. Congressman Harley Staggers has represented the 2d in Congress since the 1948 election. For more than a decade Staggers has chaired the House Interstate and Foreign Commerce Committee, which has jurisdiction over most federally regulated industries and commissions and passes on most consumer and much health legislation.

Despite the length of his tenure, Staggers is not one of the House's powerful committee chairmen. In 1971 he was rebuked when the House voted against citing CBS for contempt for refusing to turn over outtakes to his committee, and in 1975 he was ousted from the chair of the Investigations Subcommittee, which under his leadership had a large budget but was largely inactive. Staggers is a pleasant man with good intentions, but he lacks the force and command needed to be a strong chairman. Moreover, the Commerce Committee's relatively few subcommittees have diverse jurisdiction and often have had strong chairmen. Staggers has exerted little control over Paul Rogers, the longtime Chairman of the Health Subcommittee, now retired; John Dingell, the fiery Chairman of the Energy and Power Subcommittee; Bob Eckhardt, the scholarly Chairman of Oversight and former Chairman of the Consumer Protection Subcommittee; John Moss, the determined former Chairman of Oversight.

For years Staggers was reelected routinely by large margins. But in 1978 he had strong competition from Republican Cleve Benedict, a close associate of former Governor Arch Moore, who attacked Staggers for being overage and uninterested in local matters. Staggers was held to only 56% of the vote—a sharp change from the past. At the end of the 96th Congress he will be 73 years old and will have served the number of years required for the maximum congressional pension. It would not be too surprising if he decided to retire.

Census Data Pop. 436,140. Central city, 0%; suburban, 0%. Median family income, $6,437; families above $15,000: 7%; families below $3,000: 20%. Median years education, 9.9.

The Voters

Median voting age 45.
Employment profile White collar, 37%. Blue collar, 45%. Service, 14%. Farm, 4%.
Ethnic groups Black, 4%. Total foreign stock, 3%.

Presidential vote

1976	Carter (D)	105,377	(56%)
	Ford (R)	84,374	(44%)
1972	Nixon (R)	124,917	(65%)
	McGovern (D)	66,597	(35%)

Rep. Harley O. Staggers (D) Elected 1948; b. Aug. 3, 1907, Keyser; home, Keyser; Emory & Henry Col., A.B. 1931; Methodist.

Career High school teacher and coach; Head Coach, Potomac St. Col.; Mineral Co. Sheriff, 1937–41; Right-of-Way Agent, W. Va. Road Comm., 1941–42; Dir., W. Va. Ofc. of Govt. Reports, 1942; Navy, WWII.

Offices 2366 RHOB, 202-225-4331. Also 116 N. Court St., Lewisburg 24901, 304-645-1278.

Committees *Interstate and Foreign Commerce* (Chairman).

Group Ratings

	ADA	COPE	PC	RPN	NFU	LCV	CFA	NAB	NSI	ACA	NTU
1978	50	85	70	27	80	–	64	10	78	30	–
1977	45	91	60	17	100	52	60	–	–	33	28
1976	65	91	69	33	83	59	45	8	80	22	17

Key Votes

1) Increase Def Spnd	AGN	6) Alaska Lands Protect	FOR	11) Delay Auto Pol Cntrl	AGN
2) B-1 Bomber	FOR	7) Water Projects Veto	FOR	12) Sugar Price Escalator	DNV
3) Cargo Preference	FOR	8) Consum Protect Agcy	FOR	13) Pub Fin Cong Cmpgns	AGN
4) Dereg Nat Gas	AGN	9) Common Situs Picket	FOR	14) ERA Ratif Recissn	AGN
5) Kemp-Roth	AGN	10) Labor Law Revision	DNV	15) Prohibt Govt Abrtns	FOR

Election Results

1978 general	Harley O. Staggers (D)	69,683	(55%)	($37,481)
	Cleveland K. Benedict (R)	56,272	(45%)	($168,782)
1978 primary	Harley O. Staggers (D), unopposed			
1976 general	Harley O. Staggers (D)	145,405	(74%)	($10,346)
	Jim Sloan (R)	52,230	(26%)	($6,656)

THIRD DISTRICT

Charleston is West Virginia's capital, the center of its largest metropolitan area, and, until the 1970 Census, the state's largest city (that distinction now belongs to Huntington). Along the banks of the Kanawha River (pronounced kan-AW locally) stands the Capitol building, one of the largest and most beautiful in the country. But a little more typical of Charleston are the large Union Carbide plants a little farther downriver. Like most West Virginia cities, Charleston is situated in a narrow river valley, hemmed in by mountains; so situated, the city is a victim to a smog which can rival that of Los Angeles. It is primarily an industrial city, with large chemical plants. Though there are a few skyscrapers here, the country atmosphere still prevails; this is where irate fundamentalist parents literally started riots over the allegedly liberal and pornographic contents of school textbooks in 1974.

Charleston and surrounding Kanawha County are the population center and political pivot of West Virginia's 3d congressional district. Upriver in the mountains is coal mining country, the kind of destitute hollows where Jay Rockefeller lived when he first came to the state as an antipoverty worker. The territory below Charleston, down to the Ohio River, is less mountainous and also less densely populated. The coal counties are usually heavily Democratic; the Ohio River counties seem to retain a Republicanism that goes back to the days when West Virginia first became a state during the Civil War. Charleston itself, perhaps surprisingly for an industrial city, often leans a little more to the Republicans than the Democrats. In 1976, for example, Kanawha County was 56% for Carter—a solid carry, but a lower percentage than in the state as a whole.

Just as Jay Rockefeller exemplifies the younger, more idealistic West Virginia politicians, the 3d district's Congressman, John Slack, is typical of the older, more patronage-oriented, go-along-to-get-along breed of West Virginia Democrats. Slack, a former real estate man, made his way to Congress via the Kanawha County assessor's office. His politics are fairly conservative. He votes with other Democrats often enough to have a good record with organized labor, but not often enough to satisfy other liberal groups. His presence and that of other, similarly inclined non-Southern Democrats is one of the reasons why the House Appropriations Committee has been much more conservative than the House as a whole for many years. He is Chairman of the State, Commerce, and Judiciary Subcommittee, a place that gives him great influence in the Justice Department and in the State Department—should he choose to exercise it. A longtime predecessor, John Rooney, was a kind of tyrant over these departments; Slack apparently holds the reins a lot looser.

Slack has never had much trouble in elections since he first won. Primary challenges against him recently have come to nothing, but a Republican held his percentage down to 60% in 1978. That is not enough to put his seat in jeopardy, but it suggests that his high percentage results more from lack of strong opposition than from overwhelming strength.

Census Data Pop. 434,165. Central city, 16%; suburban, 36%. Median family income, $7,574; families above $15,000: 11%; families below $3,000: 18%. Median years education, 10.8.

The Voters

Median voting age 44.
Employment profile White collar, 44%. Blue collar, 43%. Service, 12%. Farm, 1%.
Ethnic groups Black, 3%. Total foreign stock, 2%.

Presidential vote

1976	Carter (D)	111,688	(58%)
	Ford (R)	81,613	(42%)
1972	Nixon (R)	122,907	(62%)
	McGovern (D)	74,219	(38%)

Rep. John M. Slack (D) Elected 1958; b. Mar. 18, 1915, Charleston; home, Charleston; Va. Military Inst.; Presbyterian.

Career Armed Forces, WWII; Mbr., Kanawha Co. Court, 1948–52; Kahawa Co. Assessor, 1952–58.

Offices 1536 LHOB, 202-225-2711. Also New Fed. Ofc. Bldg., 500 Quarrier St., Charleston 25301, 304-343-8923.

Committees *Appropriations* (6th). Subcommittees: Energy and Water Development; State, Justice, Commerce and the Judiciary (Chairman).

Standards of Official Conduct (4th).

Group Ratings

	ADA	COPE	PC	RPN	NFU	LCV	CFA	NAB	NSI	ACA	NTU
1978	25	42	35	25	63	–	9	42	78	67	–
1977	30	78	33	31	73	30	40	–	–	40	24
1976	25	73	36	29	67	27	36	18	80	36	12

Key Votes

1) Increase Def Spnd	FOR	6) Alaska Lands Protect	AGN	11) Delay Auto Pol Cntrl	FOR
2) B-1 Bomber	FOR	7) Water Projects Veto	AGN	12) Sugar Price Escalator	FOR
3) Cargo Preference	FOR	8) Consum Protect Agcy	AGN	13) Pub Fin Cong Cmpgns	AGN
4) Dereg Nat Gas	FOR	9) Common Situs Picket	FOR	14) ERA Ratif Recissn	FOR
5) Kemp-Roth	AGN	10) Labor Law Revision	FOR	15) Prohibt Govt Abrtns	AGN

Election Results

1978 general	John M. Slack (D)	74,837	(59%)	($34,433)
	David M. Staton (R)	51,584	(41%)	($14,878)
1978 primary	John M. Slack (D), unopposed			
1976 general	John M. Slack (D), unopposed			($16,641)

FOURTH DISTRICT

The 4th district of West Virginia is the southern part of the state. This is coal country. The eight counties of the 4th probably have produced more bituminous coal over the years than any other single congressional district in the United States. Not quite all the district is mining country, however; it also contains the state's largest city, Huntington, with 74,000 people, a manufacturing and railroad junction town on the Ohio River. But from the banks of the Ohio the mountains rise steeply, and the heart of the 4th is in the small coal towns sitting between the mountainsides. This was a boom area around the turn of the century, with lots of in-migration, mostly from the South.

But after World War II employment in the mines declined drastically, and the decline continued through the fifties and sixties. The population of the counties now in the 4th declined from 579,000 in 1950 to 437,000 in 1970. Recently the economy of this area has bounced back somewhat, as coal prices rose and mining—or at least strip mining—activity increased. But the number of coal mining jobs is still far from its old peak, and many of the jobs are now non-union. The United Mine Workers has split into several factions, and this has been the site of major wildcat strikes, of varying effectiveness.

The politics of this sometimes poverty-stricken area has little of the altruism that some liberal reformers expect to find among the poor. In places like southern West Virginia there are few ways for a bright young man to make money except by owning a coal mine or winning public or union office. Public office is often more lucrative than published salaries suggest; corruption is common, and there are counties where one is still supposed to be able to buy votes. Under such circumstances maximum feasible participation of the poor amounts to the survival of the fittest—not necessarily of the one who does the most for the ordinary person. In the struggle to get ahead, the ordinary politician has little concern for matters like unsafe mine conditions, black lung disease, or air and water pollution. People are inclined to get what they can and not to worry about others.

The district's last two congressmen, in very different ways, have provided contrasts with this kind of political background. Ken Hechler was first elected here in 1958, shortly after he came to West Virginia as a professor at Huntington's Marshall University; he had a background as a speech writer for Adlai Stevenson. A resourceful campaigner, Hechler opposed the UMW leadership of Tony Boyle when it was physically dangerous to do so and advocate a complete ban on strip mining. Without organized backing, and against all the local politicoes, he beat another incumbent with whom he had been redistricted in 1972. Hechler's congressional career ended abruptly in 1976. He announced early that he would run for governor and for Congress as well—an entirely legal procedure here. Later he opted out of the House race, even as it was becoming clear that he had no chance against front-runner Jay Rockefeller in the gubernatorial primary. Defeated then, he ran as a write-in in the general, and won a phenomenal 37%—not enough to win. In 1978 he ran in the Democratic House primary, and when he was solidly beaten, announced that he would not try again.

If Hechler's advantage was idealism and real empathy with people, his successor's real strength has been hard work and hard cash. Nick Joe Rahall comes from a family that owns broadcasting stations in West Virginia and Florida. In 1976, at 27, he ran in the Democratic primary. With Hechler out of the race, and after spending more than $100,000 of his own money, he won with 37% in a five-candidate field. That fall Rahall had to spend again to repel Hechler's effort, though this time he had the aid of labor, Democratic politicoes, and Rockefeller. During his first two years in the House, Rahall provided the kind of constituency services and attention to district matters that enabled him to overcome Hechler in the Democratic primary. That is testimony again to his strength. Still under 30, he seemed to have vanquished all the tough opposition, and a long congressional career opened up ahead of him. Rahall is a member of the Public Works and Interior Committees, bread-and-butter assignments for a congressman from a coal mining district like the 4th.

Census Data Pop. 437,595. Central city, 17%; suburban, 16%. Median family income, $7,039; families above $15,000: 9%; families below $3,000: 19%. Median years education, 10.1.

The Voters

Median voting age 45.
Employment profile White collar, 42%. Blue collar, 46%. Service, 12%. Farm, -%.
Ethnic groups Black, 7%. Total foreign stock, 2%.

Presidential vote

1976	Carter (D)	105,407	(63%)
	Ford (R)	62,505	(37%)
1972	Nixon (R)	110,238	(63%)
	McGovern (D)	65,884	(37%)

Rep. Nick J. Rahall II (D) Elected 1976; b. May 20, 1949, Beckley; home, Beckley; Duke U., B.A. 1971, Geo. Wash. U., 1973; Presbyterian.

Career Sales rep. and Mbr. of the Bd., Rahall Communications Corp.; Pres., Mountaineer Tour and Travel Agency.

Offices 408 CHOB, 202-225-3452. Also Bair Bldg., Main and N. Fayette Sts., Beckley 25801, 304-252-5000.

Committees *Interior and Insular Affairs* (21st). Subcommittees: Energy and the Environment; Mines and Mining;

Public Works and Transportation (22d). Subcommittees: Aviation; Economic Development; Surface Transportation.

Group Ratings

	ADA	COPE	PC	RPN	NFU	LCV	CFA	NAB	NSI	ACA	NTU
1978	60	79	58	18	70	–	36	25	60	29	–
1977	55	78	55	27	92	45	65	–	–	30	23

Key Votes

1) Increase Def Spnd	AGN	6) Alaska Lands Protect	AGN	11) Delay Auto Pol Cntrl	FOR
2) B-1 Bomber	FOR	7) Water Projects Veto	AGN	12) Sugar Price Escalator	FOR
3) Cargo Preference	AGN	8) Consum Protect Agcy	AGN	13) Pub Fin Cong Cmpgns	AGN
4) Dereg Nat Gas	AGN	9) Common Situs Picket	FOR	14) ERA Ratif Recissn	AGN
5) Kemp-Roth	AGN	10) Labor Law Revision	FOR	15) Prohibt Govt Abrtns	FOR

Election Results

1978 general	Nick J. Rahall (D), unopposed			($242,298)
1978 primary	Nick J. Rahall (D)	41,926	(56%)	
	Ken Hechler (D)	32,746	(44%)	($91,684)
1976 general	Nick J. Rahall (D)	73,626	(46%)	($336,301)
	Ken Hechler (write-in)	59,067	(37%)	($273,487)
	E. S. Goodman (R)	28,825	(18%)	($13,518)

WISCONSIN

Wisconsin is a state of political anomalies. It spawned Bob LaFollette and the Progressive movement and Joe McCarthy and his campaign against Communism in high places. Richard Nixon carried Wisconsin, the state where the Republican Party was founded, three times; yet the state in the seventies has become one of the most Democratic at all levels except the governorship, and it provided 11 crucial electoral votes for Jimmy Carter in 1976. Wisconsin is heavily industrial, though it is also the nation's leading producer of dairy products; a heavily urban state, yet filled with lakes and forests.

Wisconsin owes much of its unique politics to the German and Scandinavian immigrants who formed such a large percentage of its original settlers. Here, as in Minnesota and North Dakota, the immigrants left a distinctive political stamp. In all three states there developed—against the background of an overwhelming preference for the Republican Party—a politics of almost radical economic reform and an isolationist foreign policy. The term "progressive" was coined in Wisconsin, and it was personified by Robert "Fighting Bob" LaFollette. Elected Governor in 1900, he completely revamped the state government before going onto the Senate in 1906. There LaFollette supported other insurgent reformers and voted against American entry into World War I. In 1924 he ran for president under the banner of the Progressive Party and won 18% of the nation's votes—the best third party showing in the last 60 years. LaFollette's sons maintained the tradition of Wisconsin progressivism. Robert LaFollette, Jr., served in the Senate from 1925 to 1947, and Philip LaFollette was Governor of Wisconsin from 1935 to 1939. During the thirties the LaFollettes ran on the Progressive Party line in Wisconsin and dreamed of forming a national third party. But the onset of World War II destroyed the plans of the isolationist reformers. In 1946 Senator LaFollette, busy with congressional reorganization in Washington, was upset in the Republican primary by one Joseph R. McCarthy.

How did the state produce politicians as different as LaFollette and McCarthy at roughly the same time? Part of the answer lies in the leanings of Wisconsin's ethnic groups, particularly the largest—the German-Americans. As Samuel Lubell pointed out, much of the impetus behind postwar anticommunism came from those who had believed that we should not have fought a war allied with the Communists against Germany. In any case, McCarthy proved to be less typical of Wisconsin in the long run than the LaFollettes. "Tail gunner Joe" won his first primary in an upset; his two victories in the general elections of 1946 and 1952 occurred in heavily Republican years, and only the first did he win by a large margin. If McCarthy had not died a broken man in 1957, after his censure by the Senate in 1954, he would probably have been defeated in the 1958 election.

During the McCarthy years Republicans dominated Wisconsin elections more or less by default. The party's progressive side was dormant, and the Democrats had usually been not much of a factor in the state's politics. But in the early fifties a group of liberal Democrats—none of whom had held major office—assumed control over the husk of the party and laid plans to become a majority force. A simple recitation of their names gives evidence of their success: Senator William Proxmire, Senator Gaylord Nelson, former Governor Patrick Lucey, Congressman Henry Reuss, and Congressman Robert Kastenmeier. The group's first victory occurred in the 1957 special election to fill McCarthy's Senate vacancy. The Republican nominee was former Governor Walter Kohler; the Democrat was Proxmire, fresh from three defeats in three consecutive gubernatorial campaigns. But by the summer of 1957 the booming economy of the middle Eisenhower years had begun to turn sour: factories were laying off workers and farm income was declining because of government surpluses. Proxmire's years of campaigning finally paid off, and he beat Kohler by a 56%–41% margin. Since then, Democrats have won every Wisconsin Senate election, and they seem likely to do so for another decade or so.

Proxmire was an unorthodox senator from the start. He is the only senator who runs four miles from his home to the Capitol every morning, the only one to stand rather than sit at his desk, and the first to have hair transplants. Almost as soon as he walked into the Senate chamber he managed to irritate the then all-powerful Lyndon Johnson; sage insiders wrote Proxmire off as an unreliable maverick and a political accident. During the sixties he seemed to specialize in hopeless causes: in 1964, for example, he began an attack on Boeing's supersonic transport. But in the years that followed the Senate was undergoing more change than aficionados of its once unchanging ways noticed. By 1971 Proxmire had finished off the SST once and for all—defeating the Nixon Administration, the nation's most reliable aircraft contractor, and the two powerful senators from the state of Washington, Warren Magnuson and Henry Jackson.

Proxmire did not stop with the SST. He has also proved nettlesome to big defense contractors, the Pentagon, social scientists, and HEW. Proxmire was the senator who brought A. Ernest Fitzgerald before a congressional hearing where the later fired Pentagon aide revealed Lockheed's huge cost overruns on the C5-A. In recent years Proxmire has taken to issuing a monthly "golden fleece" award for federally financed studies of such phenomenon as romantic love. He loves to attack bureaucrats and stuffed shirts, and long before Jimmy Carter came to town he engaged in an ultimately successful crusade to cut down the number of government limousines.

Proxmire's voting record at first sight looks confusing. Usually described as a liberal, he receives respectable ratings from conservative organizations as well. But the record does make sense when you think of him as perhaps the Senate's leading penny-pincher. When in doubt, Proxmire has always been inclined to cut government spending; he is suspicious of both the government-financed sociologist and the Pentagon general. Businessmen sometimes consider Proxmire anti-business when he attacks big companies for charging the government too much or for bribing foreign officials. Actually he believes strongly in the free enterprise system. He just hates to see money wasted.

In 1975, after the defeat of William Fulbright, John Sparkman gave up the Banking Committee chair for Foreign Relations, and Proxmire became Chairman of the Banking, Housing, and Urban Affairs Committee. The big bankers blanched at the prospect, and contributed lots of money to Fulbright to prevent it from occurring. Today they are probably not at all displeased—unless they have something to hide. The committee handles government loans and bail-outs. This gave Proxmire the leverage to force the long overdue ouster of Lockheed's top management in 1976 and to insist on some pretty tough conditions for federal aid to New York City. If the government is going to lend money, he wants to make sure it gets it back. He has shown no unreasonable bias against big banks, but has pushed for consolidation of the three federal agencies which now regulate banks. In the housing field, he has uncharacteristically argued that only so-called housing experts can be trusted to run HUD, and for that reason voted against confirmation of Secretary Patricia Roberts Harris. But housing seems to be a decreasing part of the committee's business.

In 1964 Proxmire won reelection by a smaller margin than expected; he had apparently been taking Wisconsin voters for granted. With typical Proxmire energy he turned that around. A hard worker in Washington throughout the week, he is a fixture in Wisconsin, standing in front of football stadiums or factory gates, shaking hands and asking questions. In 1970 he beat a weak candidate with 71% of the vote; in 1976 he beat a stronger candidate with 73%. Though he turns 65 in 1980, Proxmire looks much younger, and there seems little doubt that he can continue to win for some time.

Aside from Proxmire, the state's top vote-getter is Senator Gaylord Nelson. Nelson grew up in a small town in northern Wisconsin and has always loved to hunt and fish. When he became Governor in 1959, he launched an attack on industrial polluters and sponsored programs to protect the environment. He thus anticipated by a good decade the politics of the environment—back when it was hunters in plaid flannel jackets rather than students in ski parkas who were most concerned. Nelson was reelected in 1960 and two years later unseated four-term, 78-year-old Republican Alexander Wiley.

Nelson has not sought or attracted as much publicity as Proxmire, nor has he emerged as a maverick quite so often. Nevertheless he was one of the first senators to speak and vote against the Vietnam war. He led a fight to cut drug prices and require the use of generic, rather than trade, names on drugs. As a member of the Human Resources Committee he has a near-perfect labor voting record; as a member of the Finance Committee he has always supported liberal tax reform causes.

What has distinguished Nelson from so many of his colleagues is lack of ambition. There are some who believe that he would be just as happy practicing a little law and doing a lot of fishing back in Clear Lake. Nelson is one of the most popular senators among his colleagues, and they seldom take offense when he opposes them. They know he acts solely out of conviction, and without posturing; and they know that however passionately he is committed to a cause, he never loses his sense of humor. He gets on well with Finance Committee Chairman Russell Long and with many conservative Republicans as well as with other liberal Democrats. Other senators seek national exposure. Nelson shuns it. He stubbornly refused when George McGovern tried to make him his running mate in 1972. But the sunniness of his disposition does seem to get across to Wisconsin voters. He won reelection with 62% in 1968 and 1974, and he enters the 1980 election year as a definite favorite. It is possible that Wisconsin's resurgent Republican Party will find a good candidate to challenge him, but it will be a major surprise indeed if Nelson is defeated.

Between 1976 and 1978 Democrats controlled just about every Wisconsin office they could control. They had the governorship, other statewide offices, and big margins in both houses of the legislature. Now that has changed. Republicans made only minor gains in legislative seats, but they have captured the governorship. They did so with an unorthodox candidate whose chances were heavily discounted before the Republican primary, Lee Dreyfus. As chancellor of the Wisconsin State University campus at Stevens Point, he had made a reputation as an opponent of campus rebels and of stuffed shirts at the same time. Dreyfus's zest for campaigning and his hard-hitting speaking style—he is a professor of speech—attracted favorable attention and enabled him to upset the primary favorite, Congressman Robert Kasten of suburban Milwaukee. The Democratic candidate was Martin Schreiber, who had inherited the governorship when Patrick Lucey became Ambassador to Mexico in 1977. The Democrat had taken some of the state's surplus revenue and given it back to voters as property tax relief and retained some of the rest against a rainy day. Schreiber had planned to run against Kasten as a candidate of the wealthy and the well-placed; instead he had to run against a small town professor who simply asked that the state refrain from collecting any more withholding tax in order to cut the surplus. Dreyfus's spirited attacks, his trademark red vest, and the momentum from the primary gave him control of the dialogue of the campaign. He made big inroads among upper income liberals in both the Milwaukee area and in Madison's Dane County, which he actually carried over Schreiber. The Democrat was able to carry only a few industrial enclaves and the north woods counties which receive Minnesota television—where Dreyfus had accordingly made little impression. The result was a solid 55% victory.

The course of a Dreyfus governorship is no easier to predict than was the 1978 campaign. He will be dealing with a Democratic legislature, and he is not even that close to organization Republicans. He seems to have captured the voters' spirit for a moment; the question is how he will wear over the long run. Wisconsin's Republicans have been overdue for a resurgence, and Dreyfus's victory obviously was a big one for them. But it will be harder to capture either of the state's Senate seats, and the Republicans have shown little of the depth in good candidates which is necessary for major gains in the long run. This state which helped start the Republican Party remains basically Democratic today.

Census Data Pop. 4,417,933; 2.18% of U.S. total, 16th largest; Central city, 27%; suburban, 30%. Median family income, $10,065; 15th highest; families above $15,000: 20%; families below $3,000: 8%. Median years education, 12.1.

1977 Share of Federal Tax Burden $7,047,000,000; 2.04% of U.S. total, 15th largest.

1977 Share of Federal Outlays $6,027,420,000; 1.52% of U.S. total, 22d largest. Per capita federal spending, $1,309.

DOD	$566,948,000	34th	(0.62%)	HEW	$3,224,282,000	13th	(2.18%)
ERDA	$5,405,000	34th	(0.09%)	HUD	$50,387,000	27th	(1.19%)
NASA	$3,621,000	28th	(0.09%)	VA	$352,730,000	19th	(1.84%)
DOT	$141,972,000	31st	(0.99%)	EPA	$141,148,000	17th	(1.72%)
DOC	$88,290,000	25th	(1.06%)	RevS	$180,159,000	12th	(2.13%)
DOI	$31,082,000	30th	(0.67%)	Debt	$389,615,000	12th	(1.30%)
USDA	$395,414,000	17th	(1.99%)	Other	$456,367,000		

Economic Base Agriculture, notably dairy products, cattle, hogs and corn; machinery, especially engines and turbines; finance, insurance and real estate; food and kindred products, especially dairy products, and beverages; electrical equipment and supplies, especially electrical industrial apparatus; fabricated metal products; paper and allied products, especially paper mills, other than building paper.

Political Line-up Governor, Lee Sherman Dreyfus (R). Senators, William Proxmire (D) and Gaylord Nelson (D). Representatives, 9 (6 D and 3 R). State Senate (21 D, 11 R); State Assembly (60 D, 37 R, 2 vac.).

The Voters

Median voting age 43
Employment profile White collar, 43%. Blue collar, 37%. Service, 14%. Farm, 6%.
Ethnic groups Black 3%. Total foreign stock, 17%. Germany, 5%; Poland, 2%; Norway, 1%.

Presidential vote

1976	Carter (D)	1,004,987	(49%)
	Ford (R)	1,040,232	(51%)

Sen. William Proxmire (D) Elected Aug. 1957, seat up 1982; b. Nov. 11, 1915, Lake Forest, Ill.; home, Madison; Yale U., B.A. 1938, Harvard U., M.B.A. 1940, M.P.A. 1948; Episcopalian.

Career Wis. House of Reps., 1951; Dem. nominee for Gov., 1952, 1954, 1956; Pres., Artcraft Press, 1953–57.

Offices 5241 DSOB, 202-224-5653. Also Rm. 301, 30 W. Mifflin St., Madison 53703, 608-252-5338, and Fed. Court Bldg., 517 E. Wisconsin Ave., Milwaukee 53202, 414-272-0388.

Committees *Appropriations* (4th). Subcommittees: Agriculture and Related Agencies; Defense; Foreign Operations; HUD-Independent Agencies; Labor, HEW, and Related Agencies.

Banking, Housing, and Urban Affairs (Chairman). Subcommittees: Housing and Urban Affairs; Financial Institutions; Economic Stabilization.

Group Ratings

	ADA	COPE	PC	RPN	NFU	LCV	CFA	NAB	NSI	ACA	NTU
1978	60	63	70	60	20	91	70	83	10	46	–
1977	70	75	88	45	58	–	88	–	–	37	53
1976	65	70	92	41	67	87	93	92	10	30	76

Key Votes

1) Warnke Nom	FOR	6) Egypt-Saudi Arms	AGN	11) Hosptl Cost Contnmnt	FOR
2) Neutron Bomb	AGN	7) Draft Restr Pardon	FOR	12) Clinch River Reactor	AGN
3) Waterwy User Fee	FOR	8) Wheat Price Support	AGN	13) Pub Fin Cong Cmpgns	FOR
4) Dereg Nat Gas	AGN	9) Panama Canal Treaty	FOR	14) ERA Ratif Recissn	FOR
5) Kemp-Roth	FOR	10) Labor Law Rev Clot	FOR	15) Med Necssy Abrtns	AGN

Election Results

1976 general	William Proxmire (D)	1,396,970	(73%)	($697)
	Stanley York (R)	521,902	(27%)	($62,210)
1976 primary	William Proxmire (D), unopposed			
1970 general	William Proxmire (D)	948,445	(71%)	
	John E. Erickson (R)	381,297	(29%)	

Sen. Gaylord Nelson (D) Elected 1962, seat up 1980; b. June 4, 1916, Clear Lake; home, Madison; San Jose St. Col., B.A. 1939, U. of Wis., LL.B. 1942; Methodist.

Career Army, WWII; Practicing atty., 1946–58; Wis. Senate, 1948–58; Gov. of Wis., 1958–62.

Offices 221 RSOB, 202-224-5323. Also 517 E. Wisconsin Ave., Rm. 596, Milwaukee 53202, 414-291-3965.

Committees *Finance* (5th). Subcommittees: Health; Social Security (Chairman); Revenue Sharing, Intergovernmental Revenue Impact, and Economic Problems.

Labor and Human Resources (4th). Subcommittees: Health and Scientific Research; Employment, Poverty, and Migratory Labor (Chairman); Child and Human Development.

Group Ratings

	ADA	COPE	PC	RPN	NFU	LCV	CFA	NAB	NSI	ACA	NTU
1978	70	89	80	67	50	84	80	36	10	13	–
1977	90	80	88	60	92	–	84	–	–	4	41
1976	85	90	80	56	100	87	93	17	0	0	33

Key Votes

1) Warnke Nom	FOR	6) Egypt-Saudi Arms	AGN	11) Hosptl Cost Contnmnt	FOR
2) Neutron Bomb	AGN	7) Draft Restr Pardon	FOR	12) Clinch River Reactor	AGN
3) Waterwy User Fee	FOR	8) Wheat Price Support	FOR	13) Pub Fin Cong Cmpgns	FOR
4) Dereg Nat Gas	AGN	9) Panama Canal Treaty	FOR	14) ERA Ratif Recissn	FOR
5) Kemp-Roth	AGN	10) Labor Law Rev Clot	FOR	15) Med Necssy Abrtns	FOR

Election Results

1974 general	Gaylord A. Nelson (D)	740,700	(63%)	($247,555)
	Thomas E. Petri (R)	429,327	(37%)	($80,590)
1974 primary	Gaylord A. Nelson (D), unopposed			
1968 general	Gaylord A. Nelson (D)	1,020,931	(62%)	
	Jerris Leonard (R)	633,910	(38%)	

Gov. Lee Sherman Dreyfus (R) Elected 1978, term expires Jan. 1981; b. June 20, 1926, Milwaukee; U. of Wis., B.A. 1949, M.A. 1952, Ph.D. 1957; Episcopalian.

Career Navy, WWII; Instructor, Asst. Prof., Assoc. Prof., and Gen. Mgr. of Radio Station WDET, Wayne St. U., 1952–62; Chmn., Wis. Educ. TV Comm., 1962–65; Prof. and Gen. Mgr. of WHA-TV, U. of Wis., 1962–67; Pres., Wis. St. U.—Stevens Point, 1967–72, Chancellor, 1972–78.

Offices State Capitol, Madison 53702, 608-266-1212.

Election Results

1978 general	Lee S. Dreyfus (R)	816,056	(55%)
	Martin J. Schreiber (D)	673,813	(45%)
1978 primary	Lee S. Dreyfus (R)	197,279	(58%)
	Robert W. Kasten (R)	143,361	(42%)
1974 general	Patrick J. Lucey (D)	628,639	(56%)
	William D. Dyke (R)	497,195	(44%)

FIRST DISTRICT

The 1st congressional district of Wisconsin is the southeast corner of the state. The district contains a fairly good microcosm of Wisconsin as a whole. In the eastern part of the 1st, along Lake Michigan, are the industrial cities of Racine and Kenosha, the homes of companies like Johnson's Wax and American Motors. These tend to be Democratic areas, particularly Kenosha. Farther inland is Walworth County, an area of small farms around the posh resort town of Lake Geneva. This is one of the most heavily Republican parts of the state. To the west are the cities of Janesville and Beloit. Like Racine and Kenosha they are industrial. But the workers here are less ethnic and more likely to be Anglo-Saxon Protestants. Unions are not so heavily entrenched, and the dairy farming country around includes a significant percentage of the area's total population. This area, like so much of small city Wisconsin, is basically Republican.

All of this produces a congressional district with a pretty even partisan balance. In the past two presidential elections, it has differed less than 2% from the statewide percentage. During the sixties this was one of the most marginal congressional districts in the country, election after election. That has not been true in the seventies, but the pattern could reemerge in the eighties.

The 1st district's Congressman is Les Aspin, who on occasion has had considerable impact on some of the nation's most important policies. He was first elected in 1970, when he beat Douglas LaFollette in the Democratic primary by 20 votes and overwhelmed a conservative Republican in the general. During two years in the Army, Aspin served as an aide to Secretary of Defense Robert McNamara; in the House, he sought and got a seat on the House Armed Services Committee. He was a Vietnam dove and an advocate of substantial cuts in the defense budget. From some considerable expertise, he felt that there was much waste in the Pentagon budget, and he may have felt that overlarge budgets made possible the adventure in Vietnam.

Aspin of course had no hope of carrying a majority on the Armed Services Committee on any issue; and he did not really try. His forums were the floor of the House and the press. On the floor he was successful in 1973 in getting $950 million cut from the defense budget—a direct rebuke to Armed Services Chairman Edward Hebert. And in the press he got constant coverage because of his habit of sending out numerous press releases. Aspin's secret was that his press releases contained hard news, which was difficult if not impossible for the press to get elsewhere: stories of Pentagon waste, of mismanaged weapons systems, of overlarge military pensions. Moreover, Aspin's information generally checked out; he knew his stuff. On other issues, Aspin has generally voted with most northern Democrats, although he shows a certain parsimoniousness when it comes to federal spending of all kinds—something he may have picked up from a former boss, Senator William Proxmire.

Aspin's influence in the House was definitely greater in the middle seventies than it is today. Voters and congressmen then were suspicious of military spending, and ready to cut it when a strong case was made. Today most voters and congressmen fear that we are spending too little, not too much, and Aspin's views do not often command a majority. He has also experienced unusual difficulty in the 1st district. William Petrie, a local professor, ran a weak race against Aspin in 1976, but in 1978 he increased his percentage 11% and held Aspin to 55%—by far the weakest showing of his career. Aspin's campaign seemed ragged, and in all likelihood he will have to face a tough challenge from Petrie again in 1980. For the first time in a decade, Republicans seem on the offensive in Wisconsin, and this district may see a tough contest this time.

Census Data Pop. 490,817. Central city, 35%; suburban, 23%. Median family income, $10,478; families above $15,000: 20%; families below $3,000: 6%. Median years education, 12.1.

The Voters

Median voting age 42.
Employment profile White collar, 41%. Blue collar, 42%. Service, 14%. Farm, 3%.
Ethnic groups Black, 3%. Spanish, 2%. Total foreign stock, 18%. Germany, 4%; Italy, 2%; Poland, 1%.

Presidential vote

1976	Carter (D)	106,274	(50%)
	Ford (R)	107,457	(50%)
1972	Nixon (R)	111,281	(59%)
	McGovern (D)	77,321	(41%)

Rep. Les Aspin (D) Elected 1970; b. July 21, 1938, Milwaukee; home, Racine; Yale U., B.A. 1960, Oxford U., M.A. 1962, MIT, Ph.D., 1965; United Church of Christ.

Career Staff Asst. to U.S. Sen. William Proxmire, 1960; Staff Asst. to Chm. Walter Heller, Pres. Cncl. of Econ. Advisers, 1963; Army, 1966–68; Asst. Prof. of Economics, Marquette U., 1969–70.

Offices 442 CHOB, 202-225-3031. Also Rm. 200, 603 Main St., Racine 52403, 414-632-4446.

Committees *Armed Services* (14th). Subcommittees: Military Compensation; Research and Development.

Government Operations (18th). Subcommittees: Government Activities and Transportation; Intergovernmental Relations and Human Resources.

Group Ratings

	ADA	COPE	PC	RPN	NFU	LCV	CFA	NAB	NSI	ACA	NTU
1978	60	85	83	50	70	–	68	8	33	12	–
1977	70	71	70	58	82	76	70	–	–	4	23
1976	75	81	79	31	100	80	91	18	30	23	42

Key Votes

1) Increase Def Spnd	AGN	6) Alaska Lands Protect	FOR	11) Delay Auto Pol Cntrl	FOR
2) B-1 Bomber	AGN	7) Water Projects Veto	FOR	12) Sugar Price Escalator	AGN
3) Cargo Preference	AGN	8) Consum Protect Agcy	FOR	13) Pub Fin Cong Cmpgns	FOR
4) Dereg Nat Gas	AGN	9) Common Situs Picket	FOR	14) ERA Ratif Recissn	AGN
5) Kemp-Roth	AGN	10) Labor Law Revision	FOR	15) Prohibt Govt Abrtns	FOR

Election Results

1978 general	Les Aspin (D)	77,146	(54%)	($73,570)
	William W. Petrie (R)	64,437	(46%)	($102,205)
1978 primary	Les Aspin (D), unopposed			
1976 general	Les Aspin (D)	136,162	(66%)	($33,280)
	William W. Petrie (R)	71,427	(34%)	($20,004)

SECOND DISTRICT

Madison is Wisconsin's second largest city, with nearly 200,000 people, and the state capital. Madison is also one of the nation's most important university communities—home of the University of Wisconsin and its 30,000 students. The University was a factor in Wisconsin politics long before the 18-year-old vote of the early seventies. Back in 1900, Robert LaFollette, a Madison native, was elected Governor. Once in office, he called on professors from the University to set up the Wisconsin Tax Commission and to draft a workmen's compensation law—both the first in the nation. Wisconsin's progressive movement, including the *Progressive* magazine which is published in Madison, has always relied heavily on the University community. As a result, Madison, not the much bigger city of Milwaukee, has always been the major center of Wisconsin liberalism.

In the early fifties, when LaFollette progressives had completely lost control of the Republican Party here, Madison became the center of a new liberal movement in the minority and moribund Democratic Party. Today the city remains the home base of Senators William Proxmire and Gaylord Nelson as well as of Patrick Lucey, who served as Governor for six years. Madison is also, as a result of the early seventies, the home of a city politics where students have been exceedingly important. In 1973 they elected 28-year-old Paul Soglin, a one-time campus radical, as Mayor. In the years since, students here have become apathetic, and Soglin continues in power, attacked sometimes by radicals, but retaining the support of his age cohort which remains an important political factor.

Madison is the center of Wisconsin's 2d congressional district, with Madison and surrounding Dane County casting 63% of the district's votes. Since the 1958 election the 2d has been represented by Robert Kastenmeier, one of the youngest members of the group of Madison liberals of the fifties. With a rural background, Kastenmeier was nonetheless one of the most liberal members of Congress in the early sixties; he was not able to win reelection by a wide margin until after the redistricting of 1964.

Until 1974 Kastenmeier was little known outside his district, climbing slowly to a high seniority position on the House Judiciary Committee. Suddenly the impeachment hearings focused national attention on the committee and its members. Kastenmeier, as fourth ranking Democrat, was considered the most senior member absolutely sure for impeachment. Kastenmeier's rather languid speaking style may have bothered some of those most strongly partial to his position; he does not look like a fiery liberal. He made one important contribution to the proceedings, by insisting that each article of impeachment be voted on separately, after evidence pertaining to it was discussed. Some of the Republicans and conservative Democrats favoring impeachment wanted to wait and hold all the roll calls at the end, as if then people would somehow not notice. Kastenmeier's firm stance ensured an orderly procedure and enabled the public to make an easy connection between members' interpretations of the facts and their decisions. Judiciary has not been such an exciting place since, of course. Kastenmeier has concentrated on matters like shepherding through the copyright reform of 1976—the first major revision since 1909.

Kastenmeier experienced little trouble or even visible opposition in elections between 1964 and 1976. But in 1978 Republican James Wright, a Baraboo yo-yo manufacturer, waged a strenuous campaign. Kastenmeier had been accustomed to winning by nearly 2–1 margins; Wright reduced his share of the vote to 59%. The Democrat had been used to carrying the rural dairy counties as well as the Madison area, but Wright carried every county but Dane. Nevertheless, it is unlikely that Republicans can carry this district. Kastenmeier got 65% of the vote in Dane County in 1978, and that percentage seems unlikely to fall greatly; George McGovern got 59% in the county in 1972. Accordingly, a Republican would have to win by better than a 2–1 margin in the rural counties to carry the district—an eventuality that doesn't seem likely.

Census Data Pop. 490,941. Central city, 35%; suburban, 24%. Median family income, $10,397; families above $15,000: 23%; families below $3,000: 7%. Median years education, 12.4.

The Voters

Median voting age 40.
Employment profile White collar, 49%. Blue collar, 28%. Service, 14%. Farm, 9%.
Ethnic groups Total foreign stock, 13%. Germany, 4%; Norway, 2%.

Presidential vote

1976	Carter (D)	125,639	(53%)
	Ford (R)	113,143	(47%)
1972	Nixon (R)	108,506	(49%)
	McGovern (D)	111,508	(51%)

Rep. Robert W. Kastenmeier (D) Elected 1958; b. Jan. 24, 1924, Beaver Dam; home, Sun Prairie; U. of Wis., LL.B. 1952.

Career Practicing atty., 1952–58.

Offices 2232 RHOB, 202-225-2906. Also 119 Monona Ave., Madison 53703, 608-252-5206.

Committees *Interior and Insular Affairs* (3d). Subcommittees: National Parks and Insular Affairs; Public Lands.

Judiciary (3d). Subcommittees: Courts, Civil Liberties, and the Administration of Justice (Chairman); Crime.

Group Ratings

	ADA	COPE	PC	RPN	NFU	LCV	CFA	NAB	NSI	ACA	NTU
1978	95	95	95	50	90	–	96	8	0	4	–
1977	100	74	90	69	83	90	90	–	–	15	42
1976	90	83	92	61	92	96	91	17	0	11	36

Key Votes

1) Increase Def Spnd	AGN	6) Alaska Lands Protect	FOR	11) Delay Auto Pol Cntrl	AGN
2) B-1 Bomber	AGN	7) Water Projects Veto	AGN	12) Sugar Price Escalator	AGN
3) Cargo Preference	AGN	8) Consum Protect Agcy	FOR	13) Pub Fin Cong Cmpgns	FOR
4) Dereg Nat Gas	AGN	9) Common Situs Picket	FOR	14) ERA Ratif Recissn	AGN
5) Kemp-Roth	AGN	10) Labor Law Revision	FOR	15) Prohibt Govt Abrtns	AGN

Election Results

1978 general	Robert W. Kastenmeier (D)	99,631	(58%)	($43,643)
	James A. Wright (R)	71,412	(42%)	($86,041)
1978 primary	Robert W. Kastenmeier (D), unopposed			
1976 general	Robert W. Kastenmeier (D)	155,158	(66%)	($25,762)
	Elizabeth T. Miller (R)	81,350	(34%)	($13,779)

THIRD DISTRICT

The 3d district of Wisconsin occupies the western and southwestern parts of the state. This is rolling farmland, stretching some 200 miles along the Mississippi and St. Croix Rivers. The countryside here probably looks little different from when it first attracted white settlers in the 1840s and 1850s—in the south is gentle, hilly dairy land; in the north, more forests. The district has only two significant urban centers, LaCrosse and Eau Claire, both with names that recall the French chevaliers who came paddling down the Mississippi and St. Croix in the seventeenth century. The 3d of Wisconsin is one of the nation's premier dairy districts; there are more dairy cows in this district than in any other in the nation. Its congressman inevitably finds himself concerned with the arcane details of milk marketing regulations and import restrictions on Dutch and Swiss cheese.

The 3d is one of those Upper Midwest districts that trended Democratic even in the 1972 presidential election, ousted a Republican congressman in 1974, and then reelected its freshman Democrat in 1976—in this case, against very strong opposition—and reelected him again in 1978. This area was once one of the heartlands of the Republican Party. But as the sixties turned into seventies, that was changing. Unemployment was making new Democrats in places like LaCrosse, as industry left for the Sun Belt; and the 23,000 students on the four campuses of Wisconsin State University in the district who were enfranchised in 1972 were strongly against the Vietnam war and Richard Nixon. To people up here, the Nixon Administration seemed too interested in currying favor with its new-found constituency in the South and the Sun Belt, opposing busing (there are no blacks here, but a tradition of supporting civil rights), and pouring money into Sun Belt defense contractors (there is virtually no defense money spent in Wisconsin). Wisconsin voters, accustomed to clean government, were especially upset about Watergate—particularly, one might guess, with the fetid Caribbean aroma left by the Cuban burglars and the Mexican laundry.

The Republican incumbent Congressman, Vernon Thomson, had once served a term as Governor, but he could not win in the atmosphere of 1974. He was beaten by Al Baldus, a leader of the Democratic majority in the Wisconsin legislature. Baldus won a seat on the Agriculture Committee and its Dairy and Poultry Subcommittee—of great value here—and compiled a generally Democratic voting record. His 1976 opponent, Adolf Gundersen, was one of the names Republicans trotted out when asked who was going to beat the 1974 freshman Democrats; but Baldus got 58% of the vote against him. In 1978 the Republicans did not even try to field a serious candidate, despite the Republican tide in other elections in Wisconsin, and Baldus won by a nearly 2–1 margin. The question for 1980 is whether he will have serious opposition again.

Census Data Pop. 491,034. Central city, 10%; suburban, 6%. Median family income, $8,485; families above $15,000: 14%; families below $3,000: 12%. Median years education, 12.1.

The Voters

Median voting age 45.
Employment profile White collar, 37%. Blue collar, 33%. Service, 15%. Farm, 15%.
Ethnic groups Total foreign stock, 13%. Norway, Germany, 4% each; Sweden, 1%.

Presidential vote

1976	Carter (D)	121,904	(50%)
	Ford (R)	119,607	(50%)
1972	Nixon (R)	122,445	(59%)
	McGovern (D)	85,348	(41%)

Rep. Alvin Baldus (D) Elected 1974; b. Apr. 27, 1927, Hancock County, Ia.; home, Menomonie; Austin Jr. Col., A.A. 1958.

Career Merchant Marine, WWII; Army, Korea; Farm machinery salesman, 1953–63; Investment broker, Investors Diversified Services, 1963–74; Wis. House of Reps., 1966–74, Asst. Maj. Floor Ldr., 1972.

Offices 1424 LHOB, 202-225-5506. Also 510 S. Barstow St., Fed. Bldg., Rm. 16, Eau Claire 54701, 715-835-4671.

Committees *Agriculture* (12th). Subcommittees: Conservation and Credit; Livestock and Grains; Tobacco.

Small Business (14th). Subcommittees: Impact of Energy Programs, Environment and Safety Requirements and Government Research on Small Business.

Group Ratings

	ADA	COPE	PC	RPN	NFU	LCV	CFA	NAB	NSI	ACA	NTU
1978	60	85	78	45	100	–	73	0	20	8	–
1977	55	85	78	36	92	57	80	–	–	5	43
1976	50	74	82	50	92	71	91	17	30	15	20

Key Votes

1) Increase Def Spnd	AGN	6) Alaska Lands Protect	FOR	11) Delay Auto Pol Cntrl	FOR
2) B-1 Bomber	AGN	7) Water Projects Veto	AGN	12) Sugar Price Escalator	FOR
3) Cargo Preference	AGN	8) Consum Protect Agcy	FOR	13) Pub Fin Cong Cmpgns	FOR
4) Dereg Nat Gas	AGN	9) Common Situs Picket	FOR	14) ERA Ratif Recissn	AGN
5) Kemp-Roth	AGN	10) Labor Law Revision	FOR	15) Prohibt Govt Abrtns	FOR

Election Results

1978 general	Alvin Baldus (D)	96,326	(63%)	($75,983)
	Michael S. Ellis (R)	57,060	(37%)	($5,414)
1978 primary	Alvin Baldus (D), unopposed			
1976 general	Alvin Baldus (D)	139,038	(58%)	($131,399)
	Adolf L. Gunderson (R)	100,218	(42%)	($200,882)

FOURTH DISTRICT

The 4th district of Wisconsin is the south side of Milwaukee and the Milwaukee County suburbs to the south and west. The Milwaukee River splits the city into two different sections. Traditionally the north side has been German; today, it includes all of Milwaukee's medium-sized black community. Like all of Wisconsin, the south side has large numbers of German-Americans, but since the days of industrial growth at the turn of the century, south side Milwaukee has been known as the Polish part of town. Today the south remains all white and has a large Polish community, while the suburbs to the south are filled mainly with the newly prosperous blue and white collar descendants of the original Polish and German immigrants. The western suburbs, Wauwatosa and West Allis, are more German and white collar.

Milwaukee's south side has attracted national attention in many presidential election years. Because Wisconsin has had one of the nation's earliest presidential primaries, Milwaukee has often been the first large city to participate in the process. So observers come to the south side to see how the Polish and other ethnics are voting this year. In 1964 they found many supporting George Wallace—but the percentage was about the same as in the rest of the state and was due more to a state tax revolt than to racial issues. In 1972 the 4th actually went for George McGovern—a result clearly out of line with the ethnic stereotype reached for by the press. That stereotype has now come to television, in the series Laverne and Shirley, but it does not have great validity.

The south side had a Democratic tradition before the rest of Wisconsin developed one. Its current Congressman, Clement Zablocki, was first elected more than 30 years ago, in 1948. Most of Zabłocki's attitudes seem closer to those of machine Democrats from Chicago or Philadelphia than to those of the ideological liberals in the rest of the Wisconsin delegation. He was the only Wisconsin Democrat to support the Vietnam war policies of the Johnson and Nixon Administrations, and he was considerably more conservative on social issues than his state colleagues.

Zablocki is now Chairman of the House Foreign Affairs Committee. He owes this position mainly to seniority; there is little likelihood that he would have been elected to it de novo, although the caucus declined to take it away from him. The bulk of House Democrats, after all, were elected in the seventies, and campaigned as opponents of the Vietnam war. Zablocki came to office at a time when many of his constituents were convinced, unrealistically but understandably, that the United States could liberate Poland and other Eastern European countries from Soviet domination. Zablocki has been flexible enough to do a workmanlike job of shepherding the war powers act through the House in the seventies. But he has made enemies by being at best a lukewarm supporter of aid to Israel.

In the old days when committee chairmen got their positions automatically and were effectively accountable to no one, such views might have had important consequences. But in this case they have not. When committee Chairman Thomas Morgan retired in 1976, it was made clear to Zablocki that he would have to expedite aid to Israel if he wanted the chair. He agreed. There was a challenge in the Democratic Caucus, from New York's Benjamin Rosenthal, but he got only 72 votes; nevertheless, Zablocki knows that he holds his chairmanship on sufferance. He has an utterly safe seat electorally, but by the 1980 election he will be 68 and eligible for the maximum congressional pension and may choose to retire.

Census Data Pop. 490,690. Central city, 46%; suburban, 54%. Median family income, $11,285; families above $15,000: 24%; families below $3,000: 5%. Median years education, 12.1.

The Voters

Median voting age 44.
Employment profile White collar, 47%. Blue collar, 40%. Service, 13%. Farm, –%.
Ethnic groups Spanish, 2%. Total foreign stock, 24%. Germany, Poland, 6% each; Austria, 1%.

Presidential vote

1976	Carter (D)	119,386	(55%)
	Ford (R)	97,686	(45%)
1972	Nixon (R)	96,755	(49%)
	McGovern (D)	99,537	(51%)

Rep. Clement J. Zablocki (D) Elected 1948; b. Nov. 18, 1912, Milwaukee; home, Milwaukee; Marquette U., Ph.B. 1936; Catholic.

Career Organist and choir dir., 1932–48; High school teacher, 1938–40; Wis. Senate, 1942–48.

Offices 2183 RHOB, 202-225-4572. Also 1401 W. Lincoln Ave., Milwaukee 53215, 414-383-4000.

Committees *Foreign Affairs* (Chairman). Subcommittees: International Security and Scientific Affairs (Chairman).

Group Ratings

	ADA	COPE	PC	RPN	NFU	LCV	CFA	NAB	NSI	ACA	NTU
1978	40	65	48	42	80	–	50	8	60	33	–
1977	40	95	53	23	83	40	70	–	–	23	17
1976	50	96	70	35	83	57	100	8	90	19	8

Key Votes

1) Increase Def Spnd	FOR	6) Alaska Lands Protect	AGN	11) Delay Auto Pol Cntrl	FOR
2) B-1 Bomber	FOR	7) Water Projects Veto	AGN	12) Sugar Price Escalator	FOR
3) Cargo Preference	FOR	8) Consum Protect Agcy	FOR	13) Pub Fin Cong Cmpgns	AGN
4) Dereg Nat Gas	AGN	9) Common Situs Picket	FOR	14) ERA Ratif Recissn	FOR
5) Kemp-Roth	AGN	10) Labor Law Revision	FOR	15) Prohibt Govt Abrtns	FOR

Election Results

1978 general	Clement J. Zablocki (D)	101,575	(66%)	($10,398)
	Elroy C. Honadel (R)	52,125	(34%)	($14,665)
1978 primary	Clement J. Zablocki (D), unopposed			
1976 general	Clement J. Zablocki (D), unopposed			($6,153)

FIFTH DISTRICT

The 5th congressional district of Wisconsin is made up of the north side of Milwaukee, from the center of town to the city limits. The north side is the traditionally German half of Milwaukee; the gemutlichkeit atmosphere of old Milwaukee is now part of our common heritage, thanks to beer advertisements. For years Milwaukee has been famous for its beer, and it is still the home of Schlitz, Miller's, Pabst, Blatz, and others. Not as well known is that for years Milwaukee had its own unique politics, with roots deep in the German tradition. During the years Robert LaFollette and his progressive Republicans were governing the rest of Wisconsin, Milwaukee was electing a series of Socialist mayors and congressmen. The most notable of them was Victor Berger, who served in the House from 1911 to 1913 and again from 1923 to 1929.

After the 1918 and 1920 elections Berger was denied his seat because of his opposition to American entry into World War I. For those who think the prosecution of antiwar dissenters is a phenomenon only of the sixties, it should be recalled that Berger was sentenced in 1919 to 20 years in prison for having written antiwar articles. The prosecution was brought by the Wilson Administration and, after the conviction was reversed by the Supreme Court, all charges were dropped by the "return to normalcy" Harding Administration. It is a measure of the strength of German Milwaukee's opposition to World War I that Berger was reelected to Congress while his case was on appeal and after he had been denied his seat.

Today many descendants of the first German immigrants have left the north side for the suburbs to the north and west, and some of them have been replaced by blacks from the rural South. In 1970, some 21% of the 5th's population was black, which may not seem an especially high figure for a big city district; but it includes 82% of the black population of the entire state.

Since the 1954 election the 5th district has been represented in the House by Henry Reuss, member of an aristocratic Milwaukee German family. Reuss is now one of the most senior and intellectually distinguished liberals in the House, and since the 1974 election has been Chairman of the Banking, Housing, and Urban Affairs Committee. He brought to this position a record of some accomplishment as chairman of two subcommittees. In the field of international finance, he had been for some time the leading congressional expert on such mysterious matters as the gold markets, the ups and downs of various currencies, and the development of the Eurodollar. As head of the Government Operations Subcommittee on Conservation and Natural Resources, he unearthed the 1899 Refuse Act, which baldly prohibits the dumping of pollutants in interstate waterways. The ancient statute had been completely forgotten, but Reuss persuaded the executive branch to revive it, and the law became a major weapon against industrial polluters.

Reuss got the Banking Committee chair when he was only the number four Democrat in seniority. But the House freshmen elected in 1974 apparently considered Chairman Wright Patman too old at 81, and the next two members were disinclined to challenge the seniority system. Reuss was willing to do so. On policy matters, he is if anything to the right of Patman, an old-fashioned populist who never got over his distrust of bankers and businessmen. Reuss is a Keynesian, a veteran of the Office of Price Administration of World War II, a firm believer that government should exert some controls over private economic institutions. Patman had never really had a working majority on his committee; Reuss, with many new freshman members, seemed likely to assemble one. But no real landmark legislation has resulted.

This results partly from the fact that banking has always been one of our most regulated businesses; you can tinker with the mechanisms, but you can't control them much more unless you pass the kind of credit controls Reuss has championed—which would require bankers to extend certain loans they would otherwise find uneconomic. The committee has jurisdiction over wage and price controls, and passed a law authorizing them in 1971 in order to embarrass the Nixon Administration; Nixon surprised the Democrats by using the law and slapping on controls in August 1971. Now the control authorization law has lapsed, and the Carter Administration has opposed reenactment, on the grounds that it would signal everyone that the Administration was going to use the power mandated. The committee also controls housing legislation; but during the seventies there has been a general consensus that government does not do a very good job at meeting most housing needs, and housing programs have not grown or been created. Reuss himself created a subcommittee called simply The City, to study urban problems, but no major legislation has resulted. The committee has passed, rather routinely, legislation to bail out New York City.

At home Reuss has not been seriously challenged for reelection for years and has had no trouble winning in what has become a very Democratic district. He does, however, turn 68 in 1980 and conceivably might retire.

Census Data Pop. 490,708. Central city, 100%; suburban, 0%. Median family income, $10,067; families above $15,000: 19%; families below $3,000: 9%. Median years education, 12.0.

The Voters

Median voting age 42.
Employment profile White collar, 47%. Blue collar, 38%. Service, 15%. Farm, –%.
Ethnic groups Black, 21%. Spanish, 2%. Total foreign stock, 21%. Germany, 7%; Poland, 2%; Italy, Austria, 1% each.

Presidential vote

1976	Carter (D)	116,332	(63%)
	Ford (R)	68,240	(37%)
1972	Nixon (R)	71,196	(42%)
	McGovern (D)	97,596	(58%)

Rep. Henry S. Reuss (D) Elected 1954; b. Feb. 22, 1912, Milwaukee; home, Milwaukee; Cornell U., A.B. 1933, Harvard U., LL.B. 1936; Episcopalian.

Career Practicing atty.; Asst. Corp. Counsel, Milwaukee Co., 1939–40; Asst. Gen. Counsel, OPA, 1941–42; Army, WWII; Chf., Price Control Branch, Ofc. of Military Govt. for Germany, 1945; Deputy Gen. Counsel, Marshall Plan, 1949; Milwaukee Co. Grand Jury Special Prosecutor, 1950.

Offices 2413 RHOB, 202-225-3571. Also 400 Fed. Bldg., Milwaukee 53202, 414-291-1331.

Committees *Banking, Finance and Urban Affairs* (Chairman). Subcommittees: The City (Chairman); International Development Institutions and Finance.

Group Ratings

	ADA	COPE	PC	RPN	NFU	LCV	CFA	NAB	NSI	ACA	NTU
1978	80	90	83	45	80	–	82	17	0	8	–
1977	90	81	88	54	58	75	90	–	–	7	43
1976	90	87	92	56	100	96	100	17	20	0	24

Key Votes

1) Increase Def Spnd	AGN	6) Alaska Lands Protect	FOR	11) Delay Auto Pol Cntrl	FOR
2) B-1 Bomber	AGN	7) Water Projects Veto	FOR	12) Sugar Price Escalator	AGN
3) Cargo Preference	AGN	8) Consum Protect Agcy	FOR	13) Pub Fin Cong Cmpgns	FOR
4) Dereg Nat Gas	AGN	9) Common Situs Picket	FOR	14) ERA Ratif Recissn	AGN
5) Kemp-Roth	AGN	10) Labor Law Revision	FOR	15) Prohibt Govt Abrtns	AGN

Election Results

1978 general	Henry S. Reuss (D)	85,067	(74%)	($68,092)
	James R. Medina (R)	30,185	(26%)	($4,952)
1978 primary	Henry S. Reuss (D), unopposed			
1976 general	Henry S. Reuss (D)	134,935	(79%)	($55,442)
	Robert L. Hicks (R)	36,413	(21%)	($2,463)

SIXTH DISTRICT

The 6th district of Wisconsin is an almost perfectly rectangular slice of the central part of the state, which extends from Lake Michigan west to a point near the Mississippi River. On the lake are the small industrial cities of Manitowoc and Sheboygan, both of which lean Democratic. During the fifties Sheboygan was the scene of a bitter, eight-year-long UAW strike against the Kohler Company. To the west are the quiet, more Republican cities of Oshkosh and Fond du Lac, both on Lake Winnebago, the state's largest inland lake. All around is dairy country, with small paper mill towns here and there. The 6th district also includes the small town of Ripon, where the Republican Party is said to have been founded in 1854. (Jackson, Michigan, also claims this distinction.) The 6th has consistently been one of Wisconsin's most Republican districts, but it has been known to elect Democrats on occasion.

This is the district which was represented for 12 years by Republican William Steiger. First elected in 1966, he was only 28, the youngest member of the House; he then looked so young he was often mistaken for a page. But even as a junior member of the minority party, he played important roles in legislation and party affairs. Steiger was probably the House's leading proponent of ending the military draft—a policy where traditional Republican voluntarism and opposition to the Vietnam war came together. Steiger was head of the Republican Party's Rule 29 Committee on the delegate selection process. Regarded as dangerously moderate by many Republicans, Steiger managed to come up with rules that were widely accepted; his sense of fairness and skillful advocacy were critical to the process. But for all his reputation as a liberal, Steiger was a firm believer in free enterprise over government control. During the 95th Congress he led a movement in the Ways and Means Committee to lower the capital gains tax—this in a body that had been mulling the idea of raising taxes paid by the rich. But Steiger was able to persuade Ways and Means and the House to lower them for the rich—capital gains taxes are paid almost exclusively by the well-to-do. This was a considerable accomplishment, and probably a key step in the movement of Congress and the nation toward the idea of providing greater incentives for investment capital and risk-taking. Steiger seemed in late 1978 to be looking forward to a long House career; he was reelected easily in November. But shortly after the election he died of a heart attack at age 40—already one of the most accomplished legislators in the House.

In the normal course of things the district would be conceded to the Republicans, and one would have thought particularly so in the political climate of early 1979, with its emphasis on less government spending and lower taxes. But that is not exactly what happened in the special election in the 6th—although the Republican finally won. Democrat Gary Goyke, a state Senator from Fond du Lac, seized the government spending issue, campaigned vigorously, and came within about 1,000 votes of winning. The Republican, Thomas Petri, was thought to have good credentials as a state Senator himself and the 1974 opponent of Senator Gaylord Nelson; Petri, however, only squeaked by. Given the advantages of incumbency, he must be considered the favorite here in 1980, but the special election suggests that the result should not be taken for granted.

Census Data Pop. 490,934. Central city, 12%; suburban, 21%. Median family income, $9,727; families above $15,000: 17%; families below $3,000: 8%. Median years education, 12.1.

The Voters

Median voting age 44.
Employment profile White collar, 38%. Blue collar, 41%. Service, 13%. Farm, 8%.
Ethnic groups Total foreign stock, 14%. Germany, 6%.

Presidential vote

1976	Carter (D)	108,920	(48%)
	Ford (R)	118,126	(52%)
1972	Nixon (R)	114,461	(57%)
	McGovern (D)	85,778	(43%)

Rep. Thomas E. Petrie (R) Elected April 9, 1979; b. May 28, 1940, Marinette; home, Fond du Lac; Harvard Col., A.B. 1962; Harvard Law Sch., J.D. 1965; Lutheran.

Career Instructor, Kennedy School; Peace Corps, 1966–67; Practicing atty., 1972–.

Offices 1020 LHOB, 202-225-2476. Also 20 Forest Avenue, Fond du Lac 54935, 414-922-1180.

Committees *Education and Labor* (13th). Subcommittees: Labor-Management Relations.

Group Ratings: Newly Elected

Election Results

1979 special	Thomas Petri (R)	71,715	(50%)	
	Gary R. Goyke (D)	70,492	(50%)	
1979 special primary	Thomas Petri (R)	22,293	(35%)	
	Tommy Thompson (R)	11,850	(19%)	
	Jack D. Steinhilber (R)	11,810	(19%)	
	Kenneth B. Benson (R)	10,965	(17%)	
	Three others (R)	6,316	(10%)	
1978 general	William A. Steiger (R)	114,742	(70%)	($67,664)
	Robert J. Steffes (D)	48,785	(30%)	
1978 primary	William A. Steiger (R), unopposed			
1976 general	William A. Steiger (R)	139,541	(63%)	($79,659)
	Joseph C. Smith (D)	80,715	(37%)	($27,620)

SEVENTH DISTRICT

Northern Wisconsin is a land of forests and lakes and mines. Two natural resources are of key importance here, the dairy cow and the tree; without them, there would be few people here at all. This is the land of Wisconsin's 7th congressional district, which stretches from a point near Green Bay in the south up to the city limits of Duluth, Minnesota. Superior, the Wisconsin town directly next to Duluth, is like its neighbor an iron ore port, with scarcely any other reason to exist there on the icy fastness of Lake Superior. In contrast, most of the jobs in towns like Wausau, Stevens Point, and Wisconsin Rapids, in the southern part of the district, depend on the lumber and paper mills. All these places were off the beaten track of east-west migration; they attracted their own unusual ethnic groups, like the Finns of Superior and the Poles of Stevens Point. The politics of northern Wisconsin and the 7th district has always had a rough-hewn quality about it, a certain populist flavor; although this is an ancestrally Republican area, it is also part of the state that always favored the progressivism of the LaFollettes.

The current Congressman from the 7th, however, is a Democrat, and probably one of the most important young members of the House. He is David Obey, who though he just turned 40 in 1978 has already spent more than ten years in the House. He was elected in something of an upset in a 1969 special election, in the seat vacated by Defense Secretary Melvin Laird. Obey showed signs of political talent early. He won election to the Wisconsin legislature when he was 24. He used issues shrewdly in his special election campaign. Once in office, he behaved like a textbook model for the young congressmen of the seventies: working hard on constituent problems, keeping in touch with the voters and returning to the district regularly, voting solidly with the majority of his party but avoiding ridiculous positions. In 1972 redistricting placed him in the same district with an aging Republican incumbent first elected 30 years before; Obey won that election with 63% of the vote.

Obey owes some of his importance in Congress to his committee position. In his first full term he was appointed to the House Appropriations Committee, and now he is the 13th ranking Democrat out of 36, and is 13 years younger than the youngest more senior Democrat. He is reasonably likely to be Chairman some day; already he is number two on the Foreign Operations Subcommittee. Obey is also one of those members who is singled out by the leadership and asked to undertake difficult jobs. In the 95th Congress he was chairman of a special committee on ethics and came up with a new ethics code. With help from the Speaker, Obey got that passed by the House in 1977, although it included restrictions on outside earnings. Obey lacks the self-righteousness of many traditional liberals, and the bleeding heart quality. He takes positions that he thinks make sense, and he backs them with a fierceness and intensity which is sometimes irritating but is usually effective. Sometimes his temper is short, but he has shown all the qualities of a first class legislator, and has some significant accomplishments to his credit. In 1979 he ran for head of the liberal Democratic Study Group, and was elected by a wide margin. In 1979 he took the lead in challenging the Budget Committee and pushing for more spending on domestic programs. In the 7th district, Obey has been reelected without difficulty, although his percentage fell notably in 1978.

Census Data Pop. 491,030. Central city, 7%; suburban, 3%. Median family income, $8,424; families above $15,000: 12%; families below $3,000: 12%. Median years education, 11.8.

The Voters

Median voting age 46.
Employment profile White collar, 38%. Blue collar, 38%. Service, 14%. Farm, 10%.
Ethnic groups Total foreign stock, 19%; Germany, 6%; Poland, Sweden, Norway, 2% each; Canada, 1%.

Presidential vote

1976	Carter (D)	134,210	(56%)
	Ford (R)	105,666	(44%)
1972	Nixon (R)	110,826	(53%)
	McGovern (D)	98,230	(47%)

Rep. David R. Obey (D) Elected Apr. 1, 1969; b. Oct. 3, 1938, Okmulgee, Okla.; home, Wausau; U. of Wis., Marathon, U. of Wis., Madison, M.A. 1960.

Career Wis. House of Reps., 1962–68.

Offices 2230 RHOB, 202-225-3365. Also Fed. Bldg., Wausau 54401, 715-842-5606.

Committees *Appropriations* (13th). Subcommittees: Foreign Operations; Labor-HEW.

Budget (6th). Subcommittees: Regulations and Spending Limitations (Chairman).

Group Ratings

	ADA	COPE	PC	RPN	NFU	LCV	CFA	NAB	NSI	ACA	NTU
1978	60	80	83	50	70	–	73	18	20	22	–
1977	85	76	73	62	82	90	70	–	–	0	37
1976	90	77	95	53	100	91	91	25	20	12	32

Key Votes

1) Increase Def Spnd	AGN	6) Alaska Lands Protect	FOR	11) Delay Auto Pol Cntrl	AGN
2) B-1 Bomber	AGN	7) Water Projects Veto	FOR	12) Sugar Price Escalator	FOR
3) Cargo Preference	AGN	8) Consum Protect Agcy	AGN	13) Pub Fin Cong Cmpgns	FOR
4) Dereg Nat Gas	AGN	9) Common Situs Picket	FOR	14) ERA Ratif Recissn	AGN
5) Kemp-Roth	AGN	10) Labor Law Revision	FOR	15) Prohibt Govt Abrtns	AGN

Election Results

1978 general	David R. Obey (D)	110,874	(63%)	($53,463)
	Vinton A. Vesta (R)	65,750	(37%)	($13,403)
1978 primary	David R. Obey (D), unopposed			
1976 general	David R. Obey (D)	171,366	(74%)	($46,038)
	Frank A. Savino (R)	60,952	(26%)	($20,689)

EIGHTH DISTRICT

The 8th of Wisconsin might be called the Packers' district. Centered on the Midwest metropolis of Green Bay, with less than 100,000 people, it is the home of the Green Bay Packers and the smallest city with any kind of bigtime athletic franchise in the United States. That the team is here is a reminder of the early days of pro football, when the National Football League included teams from a number of towns like Green Bay and Canton, Ohio. During the late sixties "the Pack" under Vince Lombardi were the first team to dominate the NFL during the Super Bowl era. The Packers in the swirling snows of Lambeau Field are the aspect of the 8th district best known to the outside world, though this 13-county district in northeast Wisconsin has other features of note. It includes the city of Appleton, somewhat smaller than Green Bay, which was Joe McCarthy's home town. As in all of Wisconsin there is good dairy country here, and in the north, near the Upper Peninsula of Michigan, are forests and prime vacation country. The 8th also contains the only recently formed county in the United States, Menominee, which was created when the Menominee Indian Reservation was abolished under the termination policy of the Eisenhower Administration.

Though the 8th is generally considered a solid Republican district, that is not quite right. Green Bay, which usually goes Republican, is a German Catholic town which went for John Kennedy in 1960 and came fairly close to going for Jimmy Carter in 1976. There are some heavily Republican counties here (Shawano, Waupaca), but also some that usually go Democratic (Forest, Florence). The balance, and more than half the votes, are cast in Brown and Outgamie Counties, which contain Green Bay and Appleton.

For nearly three decades the 8th had a very stable congressional representation, but during the seventies it has been the scene of one close race after another. The steady years were when John Byrnes, a Republican, represented the district. First elected in 1944, he was for years ranking Republican on the House Ways and Means Committee, and worked closely with Chairman Wilbur Mills in fashioning legislation. In 1970 Byrnes was held to 55% of the vote by Jesuit priest Robert Cornell; in 1972 Byrnes retired.

Since then Cornell has run four more times, and the district has gone Democratic twice and Republican twice. Republican Harold Forehlich was elected in 1972 and got a seat on the House Judiciary Committee. That turned out to be a hot spot for him. He seemed visibly reluctant to support impeachment of Richard Nixon, but in fact voted for the first two articles; his apparent ambivalence probably hurt him more than any position he took. Cornell won in 1974 with 54%. That was his high mark. He managed to hold on in 1976 with 52%, but he apparently did not use the advantages of incumbency as effectively as many of his colleagues in the Democratic freshman class of 1974.

There was a spiritedly contested Republican primary in 1978, with the winner, Toby Roth, considered the more conservative. But that identification proved to be no particular detriment. Roth won with a solid 58%, with a narrow edge in Brown County and a 2–1 margin in Outgamie. With that kind of showing Roth must be considered the favorite for 1980, although it is too early to say that the 8th has returned to the stability of the fifties and sixties.

Census Data Pop. 490,974. Central city, 29%; suburban, 27%. Median family income, $9,190; families above $15,000: 15%; families below $3,000: 9%. Median years education, 12.1.

The Voters

Median voting age 45.
Employment profile White collar, 39%. Blue collar, 40%. Service, 13%. Farm, 8%.
Ethnic groups Total foreign stock, 14%. Germany, 5%; Poland, Canada, 1% each.

Presidential vote

1976	Carter (D)	105,904	(46%)
	Ford (R)	122,174	(54%)
1972	Nixon (R)	122,672	(61%)
	McGovern (D)	76,912	(39%)

Rep. Toby Roth (R) Elected 1978; b. Oct. 10, 1938; home, Appleton; Marquette U., B.A. 1961; Roman Catholic.

Career Realtor; Wis. House of Reps., 1972–78.

Offices 1008 LHOB, 202-225-5665. Also Rm. 202, 325 E. Walnut, Green Bay 54305, 414-465-3931.

Committees *Science and Technology* (13th). Subcommittees: Energy Research and Production; Investigations and Oversight.

Small Business (8th). Subcommittees: SBA and SBIC Authority and General Small Business Problems; Access to Equity Capital and Business Opportunities.

Group Ratings: Newly Elected

Key Votes: Newly Elected

Election Results

1978 general	Toby Roth (R)	101,856	(58%)	($202,021)
	Robert J. Cornell (D)	73,925	(42%)	($72,202)
1978 primary	Toby Roth (R)	29,782	(69%)	
	Donald Hoeft (R)	13,280	(31%)	($12,430)
1976 general	Robert J. Cornell (D)	115,996	(52%)	($75,024)
	Harold V. Froehlich (R)	107,048	(48%)	($99,732)

NINTH DISTRICT

The 9th is Wisconsin's only predominantly suburban congressional district. It was first created in 1963 when population changes and the Supreme Court's one-person-one-vote decision required the elimination of a rural district and full recognition of the growth of Milwaukee's suburbs. Today—the district lines were redrawn after the 1970 Census—the 9th forms a kind of arc north and west of Milwaukee. The district includes the wealthy, long established suburbs of Shorewood and Whitefish Bay, just north of downtown Milwaukee on Lake Michigan, and a ring of suburbs around Milwaukee in Ozaukee, Washington, and Waukesha Counties: Mequon, Germantown, Menomonee Falls, Brookfield, and New Berlin. The territory combines country clubs, tree-shaded streets, shopping centers, and starkly new suburban housing. Though the 9th also includes some of the dairy country between Milwaukee and Madison, most of its residents live in suburban Waukesha County.

The district was originally designed to remove Republican voters from Robert Kastenmeier's 2d and Henry Reuss's 5th districts. The job was done so well that the 9th is the state's most heavily Republican district. It has always elected Republican congressmen, and except for 1964 has delivered solid Republican margins in presidential elections.

The 9th has nonetheless had three different congressmen in its not too lengthy history. The first, Glenn Davis, was a veteran of the McCarthy era, during which he had represented the 2d district and run for the Senate; but in the seventies he had various problems, and was beaten by Robert Kasten in the 1974 primary. That victory gave Kasten a great reputation as a grass roots

Republican organizer—a reputation that survived until he was beaten by Lee Dreyfus in the 1978 gubernatorial primary. Meanwhile, there was an exceedingly close primary in the 9th between young moderate Susan Engeleiter and conservative James Sensenbrenner. Sensenbrenner won that contest by 589 votes, and his victory in the general election followed anticlimactically. The Democrat, Matthew Flynn, tried to make a race of it, but Sensenbrenner won 61% of the votes. Presumably he will be a strong candidate for reelection in 1980.

Census Data Pop. 490,805. Central city, 0%; suburban, 86%. Median family income, $12,479; families above $15,000: 34%; families below $3,000: 4%. Median years education, 12.4.

The Voters

Median voting age 42.
Employment profile White collar, 51%. Blue collar, 35%. Service, 11%. Farm, 3%.
Ethnic groups Spanish, 1%. Total foreign stock, 16%. Germany, 6%.

Presidential vote

1976	Carter (D)	101,663	(40%)
	Ford (R)	152,888	(60%)
1972	Nixon (R)	131,288	(63%)
	McGovern (D)	77,944	(37%)

Rep. F. James Sensenbrenner, Jr. (R) Elected 1978; b. June 14, 1943, Chicago, Ill.; home, Shorewood; Stanford U., A.B. 1965, U. of Wis., J.D. 1968; Episcopalian.

Career Staff of U.S. Rep. Arthur Younger of Cal., 1965; Asst. to Wis. Senate Minor. Ldr., 1967; Practicing atty., 1968–; Wis. Assembly, 1968–76.

Offices 315 CHOB, 202-225-5101. Also 333 Bishops Way, Brookfield 53005, 414-784-1111.

Committees *Judiciary* (11th). Subcommittees: Civil and Constitutional Rights; Crime.

Standards of Official Conduct (5th).

Group Ratings: Newly Elected

Key Votes

1) Increase Def Spnd	NE	6) Alaska Lands Protect	NE	11) Delay Auto Pol Cntrl	NE
2) B-1 Bomber	NE	7) Water Projects Veto	NE	12) Sugar Price Escalator	NE
3) Cargo Preference	NE	8) Consum Protect Agcy	NE	13) Pub Fin Cong Cmpgns	NE
4) Dereg Nat Gas	NE	9) Common Situs Picket	NE	14) ERA Ratif Recissn	NE
5) Kemp-Roth	NE	10) Labor Law Revision	NE	15) Prohibt Govt Abrtns	NE

Election Results

1978 general	F. James Sensenbrenner (R)	118,386	(61%)	($197,749)
	Matthew J. Flynn (D)	75,207	(39%)	($41,028)
1978 primary	F. James Sensenbrenner (R)	29,584	(43%)	
	Susan Engeleiter (R)	28,995	(42%)	($93,320)
	One other (R)	9,746	(14%)	
1976 general	Robert W. Kasten (R)	163,791	(66%)	($97,591)
	Lynn M. McDonald (D)	84,706	(34%)	($17,446)

WYOMING

Wyoming is the closest thing we have left to the old Wild West. It is one of the few states where ranchers, through the Wyoming Stock Growers' Association, and a railroad, the Union Pacific, remain major political powers. The ranchers were the first white settlers here; the railroad's power comes from the land grants it received for building the transcontinental railroad through the southern part of the state in the 1860s. Politically, the ranchers, the small businessmen, and the farmers who work the irrigated land in the north have usually voted Republican. The people who came to build the UP, along the state's southern edge, have usually been staunch Democrats. This is the basic partisan split in the state. There are no big urban concentrations, and only five "cities" with populations over 10,000, the largest of which is Cheyenne, with 41,000. More common are places like Ten Sleep (320) or Medicine Bow (455). Between the Wyoming settlements, for stretches of 50 or 100 miles, are the high, desolate, serene plateau country; to the north and west are the Rockies.

Wyoming is one of the few Western states whose history did not begin with a gold rush or other mining episodes. There was little gold or silver or copper discovered here. Yet today Wyoming is in the middle of a mining boom of significant proportions—and one which threatens to change the way of life in this sparsely populated state. The mineral boom first struck in the early seventies in Campbell County, in the northern part of the state. It spread through Casper—always an oil town, not far from the original Teapot Dome—to the area around Rock Springs in the south. New oil wells have been drilled, new natural gas deposits discovered, and there is coal. Wyoming is one of those Western and Plains states that sits on huge seams of low sulphur coal near the surface of the land. Once this coal was considered too low grade and too far from any market to be worth the cost of extraction. Now, with the energy crisis and the price of coal following the price of oil up, it is well worth exploiting commercially. Wyoming could become one of the nation's major strip mining states.

Until 1970 Wyoming was a state of stagnant growth and a sagging local economy. But the mineral boom provided it with sudden injections of money—and of people, who in turn needed government services. There was never a strong movement in Wyoming against further growth and development, as there was in Colorado. There is simply too much vacant land here, and it seems hard to believe that all that much of Wyoming will be changed. Nevertheless, while many in the state welcome any kind of growth, among others there is uneasiness. Under Republican Governor (1967–74) Stanley Hathaway, the state government tended to favor growth and to minimize controls. It was an attitude popular in Wyoming at the time, but one which provoked some harsh questions when Hathaway sought confirmation as Gerald Ford's Secretary of the Interior.

In the last two gubernatorial elections Wyoming has had to face issues which will have a major bearing on the fundamental quality of life in the state. And each time they have opted for the candidate who favors at least some limits or controls, Democrat Ed Herschler. In 1974 a major issue was whether Wyoming should have a slurry pipeline—a device to mix coal with water and pipe it out of the state to market. Herschler opposed it, claiming that it would tend to deplete Wyoming's slender water resources. That was a position popular not only with idealistic environmentalists but, more important, with farmers in the northern part of the state who feared a rise in the price of water; they provided Herschler with crucial votes in his victory.

In 1978 other fundamental issues were at stake. On the one hand Herschler had a major scandal problem. Rock Springs, one of the major mineral boom towns of the state, is Democratic territory; it was also the site of much prostitution and gambling, some of it apparently controlled by organized crime interests. One of the state's leading investigators was fired and in 1978 went on CBS's Sixty Minutes to charge that Herschler was involved. A grand jury investigating Rock Springs indicted Attorney General Frank Mendicino, a Herschler appointee. There were charges that Don Anselmi, a Rock Springs hotel owner and state Democratic chairman, was involved in corruption. In 1978 the Rock Springs police chief shot and killed an undercover agent who was looking into crime in the area. Not surprisingly, the Republican candidate for governor, John Ostlund, charged that Herschler was slow to do anything about the mess in Rock Springs. Few voters thought the governor was dishonest, but many considered him dilatory.

After the primary, Herschler responded by firing Mendicino, obtaining Anselmi's resignation, and promised to do something about Rock Springs. He also shifted the focus of the campaign to his proposal to increase Wyoming's severance tax on minerals by 5%—and use the proceeds to reduce property taxes. Ostlund opposed the proposal; Herschler charged him with being a mouthpiece for the big mining companies. It came out that Ostlund had had profitable business dealings with at least one of the companies. Herschler's proposal might tend to reduce mineral production in Wyoming somewhat, but that argument has been made for years by oil companies, and the proposal was apparently popular. Despite a low margin in usually very heavily Democratic Rock Springs, Herschler won a second term in usually Republican Wyoming.

In national politics, Wyoming has become a reliably Republican state. This was not always so; it was Democratic during the New Deal and had two Democratic senators as recently as 1962. But in 1976 Wyoming was one of Gerald Ford's best states, and currently it has an all-Republican, all-freshman congressional delegation. One reason for Republican success here is distrust of the federal government. Out here on the frontier, people—especially well-to-do people—think of themselves as self-sufficient pioneers. The dominant political rhetoric is a hostility to the federal government and all its works. Yet sparsely populated Wyoming, even with its mineral boom, would be even more vacant and economically dependent without the feds. The federal contributions have been many: the oil depletion allowance, still a boon to small producers; national parks, forests, and other lands (some of which are leased to sheep and cattle raisers at bargain rates); the Bureau of Reclamation, which provides cheap water; federal subsidies to feeder airlines, to agriculture, to highway construction. Over the years Wyoming has received $4 million for every $3 it sends to Washington in taxes.

But Wyomingites still chafe at the idea of outsiders making decisions for them—whether they are federal bureaucrats or coal company executives. This is a state where the state Senate voted to abolish the 55 mile per hour speed limit, even though that would cut off vital highway funds. It is a state which feels it is being held down and prevented from achieving its potential by outsiders ignorant of the conditions of life here. Bellicose in foreign affairs, at least verbally committed to traditional morality (despite the vice of Rock Springs and other boom towns), angry at federal interference and high taxes, Wyoming is a natural stronghold of the New Right. The only surprise here is that its congressional delegation is not more stridently conservative than it is.

Perhaps the key event here was the victory of Republican Malcolm Wallop over Senator Gale McGee. A Democrat and former college professor, McGee was skilled enough in the personal campaigning which is still essential in this state to win election to the Senate; he was helped by running in the Democratic years of 1958 and 1964 as well as the not very Republican year of 1970. McGee was a domestic liberal and had solid support from organized labor; he was also a Vietnam and foreign policy hawk. As a member of the Appropriations and Foreign Relations Committees, he could claim to be a Senate insider, in a good position to help Wyoming; he was also Chairman of the Post Office and Civil Service Committee. But in 1976 Wyomingites were less interested than they had been in the past in a senator who could bring federal projects to the state. McGee's chairmanship was converted into a liability by Republicans, who asked voters just how efficient they thought the postal service was.

Wallop attacked McGee on these grounds and for backing congressional pay increases. The challenger also attacked the Occupational Safety and Health Administration for issuing regulations like the one requiring a certain number of portable toilets for farm workers. Such positions come naturally to a rancher, as does Wallop's opposition to non-reclaimed strip mining (you can't graze sheep on a denuded slope); and Wallop used his ranching background and his macho name well in the campaign. (He emphasized less that his parents were born in England and that he went to Yale.) McGee was caught unprepared: on election day he had $120,000 in contributions he had not yet spent.

Wallop is not a down the line New Right senator. He is more sympathetic to environmental concerns than are most Rocky Mountain Republicans, and he opposes federal bans on abortions. But on military and foreign policy positions, he is a solid hawk. On domestic economic questions he tends to favor market rather than regulatory solutions. Wallop is a member of the Energy and Finance Committees, where he can generally be expected to favor measures supported by the oil companies.

Wyoming's other two members of Congress retired in 1978. Senator Clifford Hansen, a Republican, decided to return to his Jackson Hole ranch although he could have won a third term easily. Congressman Teno Roncalio, a Democrat whose father was a Union Pacific Railroad worker, had won reelection with 56% in 1976 and faced a continuing prospect of close elections stretching as far as the Wyoming horizon. After five terms in the House, he called it quits.

The succession to Hansen's Senate seat was about as automatic as in any open seat in the nation. Hansen's predecessor had been Milward Simpson, a conservative Republican who also served as Governor; his successor is Alan Simpson, Milward's son, who also served in the state legislature. Like Wallop, Simpson is from the northern part of the state; like Wallop, he is considered a little soft by some conservatives because he has favored some state control of land use decisions. Simpson's name was familiar, but his most important asset was his personal campaigning. He is tall, balding, friendly, ready to listen to people, and he personally covered practically every corner of the state. He easily won a four-candidate Republican primary and just as easily beat an underfinanced perennial candidate in the general election. Simpson sits on the Environment and Judiciary Committees—the same assignments Wallop had in his first term. He can be expected to have a similar voting record.

Wyoming's one and only congressman is Richard Cheney, who brings to the office an unusual credential: he was White House chief of staff under Gerald Ford. Cheney achieved that position in his middle thirties as a protege of Donald Rumsfeld. In the ordinary course of things, he could have been expected to live a comfortable life in Washington, earning a good living as a lobbyist. Instead he returned to Wyoming and ran for the House of Representatives. Cheney had a mild heart attack during the primary campaign, and his old chief Ford is certainly not as popular among Republicans here as Ronald Reagan. Nevertheless Cheney beat state Treasurer Ed Witzenburger in the primary and a former Roncalio aide in the general. Cheney could hardly have moved from a more powerful position to a less powerful one; being a freshman member of the minority party in the House does not usually give one much potential to accomplish anything. Nor are Cheney's possibilities of promotion to the Senate good, with two young Republicans from Wyoming already firmly entrenched. Nevertheless Cheney is bright enough and politically adept enough to make a mark even under such difficult circumstances, and he has shown in his campaign the determination to make a career in the House. It does not seem likely that he will have difficulty winning reelection.

Census Data Pop. 332,416; 0.16% of U.S. total, 49th largest; Central city, 0%; suburban, 0%. Median family income, $8,944; 27th highest; families above $15,000: 16%; families below $3,000: 9%. Median years education, 12.4.

1977 Share of Federal Tax Burden $691,000,000; 0.20% of U.S. total, 50th largest.

1977 Share of Federal Outlays $729,033,000; 0.18% of U.S. total, 51st largest. Per capita federal spending, $1,949.

DOD	$109,004,000	51st (0.12%)	HEW	$185,611,000	50th (0.13%)
ERDA	$10,145,000	29th (0.17%)	HUD	$4,572,000	51st (0.11%)
NASA	$982,000	36th (0.02%)	VA	$48,040,000	49th (0.25%)
DOT	$43,393,000	47th (0.30%)	EPA	$4,496,000	51st (0.05%)
DOC	$42,447,000	49th (0.51%)	RevS	$10,899,000	51st (0.13%)
DOI	$114,228,000	11th (2.46%)	Debt	$26,817,000	50th (0.09%)
USDA	$47,710,000	47th (0.24%)	Other	$80,689,000	

Economic Base Agriculture, notably cattle, sheep, sugar beets and dairy products; oil and gas extraction, especially oil and gas field services; finance, insurance and real estate; metal mining, especially uranium-radium-vanadium ores; petroleum refining and other petroleum and coal products; food and kindred products.

Political Line-up Governor, Ed Herschler (D). Senators, Malcolm Wallop (R) and Alan K. Simpson (R). Representative, 1 at large (R). State Senate (19 R and 11 D); State House (42 R and 20 D).

The Voters

Registration 200,951 Total. 78,605 D (39%); 97,849 R (49%); 24,497 Unclassified (12%).
Median voting age 42
Employment profile White collar, 47%. Blue collar, 30%. Service, 14%. Farm, 9%.
Ethnic groups Total foreign stock, 11%.

Presidential vote

1976	Carter (D)	62,239	(40%)
	Ford (R)	92,717	(60%)
1972	Nixon (R)	100,464	(69%)
	McGovern (D)	44,358	(31%)

Sen. Malcolm Wallop (R) Elected 1976, seat up 1982; b. Feb. 27, 1933, New York, N.Y.; home, Big Horn; Yale U., B.A. 1954; Episcopalian.

Career Rancher; Army, 1955–57; Wyo. House of Reps., 1969–73; Wyo. Senate 1973–77; Candidate for Repub. nomination for Gov., 1974.

Offices 6327 DSOB, 202-224-6441. Also 2201 Fed. Bldg., Casper 82601, 307-266-3240, and 2009 Fed. Ctr., Cheyenne 82001, 307-634-0626.

Committees *Energy and Natural Resources* (7th). Subcommittees: Energy Conservation and Supply; Energy Research and Development; Energy Resources and Materials Production.

Finance (7th). Subcommittees: Taxation and Debt Management Generally; Energy and Foundations; Tourism and Sugar.

Select Committee on Intelligence (5th).

Group Ratings

	ADA	COPE	PC	RPN	NFU	LCV	CFA	NAB	NSI	ACA	NTU
1978	10	11	15	63	43	21	15	92	100	78	–
1977	0	20	5	73	27	–	8	–	–	96	45

Key Votes

1) Warnke Nom	AGN	6) Egypt-Saudi Arms	FOR	11) Hosptl Cost Contnmnt	AGN
2) Neutron Bomb	FOR	7) Draft Restr Pardon	AGN	12) Clinch River Reactor	FOR
3) Waterwy User Fee	FOR	8) Wheat Price Support	FOR	13) Pub Fin Cong Cmpgns	AGN
4) Dereg Nat Gas	FOR	9) Panama Canal Treaty	AGN	14) ERA Ratif Recissn	AGN
5) Kemp-Roth	FOR	10) Labor Law Rev Clot	AGN	15) Med Necssy Abrtns	FOR

Election Results

1976 general	Malcolm Wallop (R)	84,810	(55%)	($301,595)
	Gale McGee (D)	70,558	(45%)	($181,028)
1976 primary	Malcolm Wallop (R)	41,445	(77%)	
	Two others (R)	12,696	(23%)	
1970 general	Gale McGee (D)	67,207	(56%)	
	John S. Wold (R)	53,279	(44%)	

Sen. Alan K. Simpson (R) Elected 1978, seat up 1984; b. Sept. 2, 1931, Denver, Colorado; home, Cody; U. of Wyo., B.S. 1954, J.D. 1958; Episcopalian.

Career Practicing atty., 1958; Cody City Atty., 1959–69; Wyo. House of Reps., 1964–78, Maj. Whip 1973–75, Maj. Leader 1975–77, Speaker Pro Tempore 1977.

Offices 1513 RSOB, 202-224-3424. Also 1731 Sheridan Ave., Cody 82414, 307-587-5323.

Committees *Environment and Public Works* (5th). Subcommittees: Environmental Pollution; Water Resources; Nuclear Regulation.

Judiciary (7th). Subcommittees: Constitution; Improvements in Judicial Machinery; Jurisprudence and Governmental Relations.

Veterans Affairs (3d).

Group Ratings: Newly Elected

Key Votes: Newly Elected

Election Results

1978 general	Alan K. Simpson (R)	82,908	(62%)	($439,805)
	Raymond B. Whitaker (D)	50,456	(38%)	($142,749)
1978 primary	Alan K. Simpson (R)	37,332	(55%)	
	Hugh Binford (R)	20,768	(30%)	($245,064)
	Two others (R)	10,203	(15%)	
1972 general	Clifford P. Hansen (R)	101,314	(71%)	($169,878)
	Mike M. Vinich (D)	40,753	(29%)	($10,411)

Gov. Ed Herschler (D) Elected 1974, term expires Jan. 1983; b. Oct. 27, 1918, Lincoln County; U. of Colo., B.A., U. of Wyo., LL.B. 1949; Episcopalian.

Career USMC, WWII; Practicing atty., 1949–74; Kemmerer Town Atty., 1949–74; Lincoln Co. Prosecuting Atty.; Wyo. House of Reps., 1960–69.

Offices Capitol Bldg., Cheyenne 82002, 307-777-7434.

Election Results

1978 general	Ed Herschler (D)	69,972	(51%)
	John C. Ostlund (R)	67,595	(49%)
1978 primary	Ed Herschler (D)	28,406	(65%)
	Margaret McKinstry (D)	15,111	(35%)
1974 general	Ed Herschler (D)	71,741	(56%)
	Dick Jones (R)	56,645	(44%)

Rep. Richard Bruce Cheney (R) Elected 1978; b. Jan. 30, 1941, Lincoln, Neb.; home, Casper; U. of Wyo., B.A. 1965, M.A. 1966, U. of Wis., 1968.

Career Spec. Asst. to the Dir. of OEO; Deputy to White House Pres. Counsellor Donald Rumsfeld; Asst. Dir. for Operations, Cost of Living Cncl.; V.P., Bradley, Woods & Co., Inc., investment advisors, 1973–74, 1976–78; Asst. to Pres. Gerald Ford, 1974–76.

Offices 427 CHOB, 202-225-2311. Also Rm. 4005 Fed. Bldg., Casper 82601, 307-265-5550.

Committees *Interior and Insular Affairs* (11th). Subcommittees: Energy and the Environment; Public Lands.

Standards of Official Conduct (6th).

Group Ratings: Newly Elected

Key Votes: Newly Elected

Election Results

1978 general	Richard Cheney (R)	75,855	(59%)	($209,064)
	Bill Bagley (D)	53,522	(41%)	($175,297)
1978 primary	Richard Cheney (R)	28,568	(42%)	
	Ed Witzenburger (R)	20,863	(31%)	($84,365)
	Jack Gage (R)	18,075	(27%)	($49,292)
1976 general	Teno Roncalio (D)	85,721	(56%)	($116,024)
	Larry Hart (R)	66,147	(44%)	($31,824)

Senate Committees

AGRICULTURE, NUTRITION, AND FORESTRY

Herman Talmadge (Ga.), Chairman

Democratic Majority (10 D): Talmadge, McGovern (S. Dak.), Huddleston (Ky.), Stone (Fla.), Leahy (Ver.), Zorinsky (Neb.), Melcher (Mont.), Stewart (Ala.), Pryor (Ark.), Boren (Okla.).
Republican Minority: Helms (N.C.), Young (N. Dak.), Dole (Kan.), Hayakawa (Calif.), Lugar (Ind.), Cochran (Miss.), Boschwitz (Minn.), Jepsen (Iowa).

Subcommittees

AGRICULTURAL CREDIT AND RURAL ELECTRIFICATION

Zorinsky, Chairman

Majority (3 D): Zorinsky, McGovern, Huddleston.
Minority (2 R): Hayakawa, Jepsen.

AGRICULTURAL PRODUCTION, MARKETING, AND STABILIZATION OF PRICES

Huddleston, Chairman

Majority (7 D): Huddleston, McGovern, Stone, Zorinsky, Melcher, Pryor, Boren.
Minority (4 R): Young, Helms, Lugar, Cochran.

AGRICULTURAL RESEARCH AND GENERAL LEGISLATION

Stewart, Chairman

Majority (4 D): Stewart, Leahy, Stone, Talmadge.
Minority (4 R): Lugar, Dole, Young, Boschwitz.

ENVIRONMENT, SOIL CONSERVATION, AND FORESTRY

Melcher, Chairman

Majority (4 D): Melcher, Huddleston, Stewart, Talmadge.
Minority (4 R): Jepsen, Hayakawa, Cochran, Helms.

FOREIGN AGRICULTURAL POLICY

Stone, Chairman

Majority (5 D): Stone, Zorinsky, Talmadge, Boren, Pryor.
Minority (4 R): Cochran, Lugar, Dole, Boschwitz.

NUTRITION

McGovern, Chairman

Majority (3 D): McGovern, Leahy, Melcher.
Minority (3 R): Dole, Helms, Hayakawa.

RURAL DEVELOPMENT

Leahy, Chairman

Majority (4 D): Leahy, Stewart, Pryor, Boren.
Minority (3 R): Boschwitz, Young, Jepsen.

APPROPRIATIONS
Warren Magnuson (Wash.), Chairman

Democratic Majority (17 D): Magnuson, Stennis (Miss.), Byrd (W. Va.), Proxmire (Wis.), Inouye (Hawaii), Hollings (S.C.), Bayh (Ind.), Eagleton (Mo.), Chiles (Fla.), Johnston (La.), Huddleston (Ky.), Burdick (N.Dak.), Leahy (Ver.), Sasser (Tenn.), DeConcini (Ari.), Bumpers (Ark.), Durkin (N.H.).
Republican Minority (11 R): Young (N.D.), Hatfield (Ore.), Stevens (Alaska), Mathias (Maryland), Schweiker (Penn.), Bellmon (Okla.), Weicker (Conn.), McClure (Ida.), Laxalt (Nev.), Garn (Utah), Schmitt (N.M.).

Subcommittees

AGRICULTURE AND RELATED AGENCIES
Eagleton, Chairman

Majority (9 D): Eagleton, Stennis, Proxmire, Byrd, Bayh, Chiles, Burdick, Sasser.
Minority (5 R): Bellmon, Young, McClure, Garn, Schmitt.

DEFENSE
Stennis, Chairman

Majority (11 D): Stennis, Magnuson, Proxmire, Inouye, Hollings, Eagleton, Chiles, Johnston ,Huddleston, Leahy, Bumpers.
Minority (7 R): Young, Stevens, Schweiker, Bellmon, Weicker, Garn, McClure.

DISTRICT OF COLUMBIA
Leahy, Chairman

Majority (3 D): Leahy, Bumpers, Dirkin.
Minority (2 R): Mathias, Schmitt.

ENERGY AND WATER DEVELOPMENT
Johnston, Chairman

Majority (9 D): Johnston, Stennis, Magnuson, Byrd, Hollings, Huddleston, Burdick, Sasser, DeConcini.
Minority (7 R): Hatfield, Young, Schweiker, Bellmon, McClure, Garn, Schmitt.

FOREIGN OPERATIONS
Inouye, Chairman

Majority (6 D): Inouye, Proxmire, Chiles, Johnston, Leahy, DeConcini.
Minority (4 R): Garn, Hatfield, Mathias, Schweiker.

HUD-INDEPENDENT AGENCIES
Proxmire, Chairman

Majority (7 D): Proxmire, Stennis, Bayh, Huddleston, Leahy, Sasser, Durkin.
Minority (5 R): Mathias, Bellmon, Weicker, Laxalt, Schmitt.

INTERIOR
Byrd, Chairman

Majority (9 D): Byrd, Hollings, Bayh, Johnston, Huddleston, Leahy, DeConcini, Burdick, Durkin.
Minority (6 D): Stevens, Young, Hatfield, Bellmon, McClure, Laxalt.

LABOR, HEALTH, EDUCATION, AND WELFARE
Magnuson, Chairman

Majority (9 D): Magnuson, Byrd, Proxmire, Hollings, Eagleton, Bayh, Chiles, Burdick, Inouye.
Minority (5 R): Schweiker, Mathias, Hatfield, Weicker, Schmitt.

LEGISLATIVE BRANCH
Sasser, Chairman

Majority (3 D): Sasser, Bumpers, Durkin.
Minority (2 R): Stevens, Schweiker.

MILITARY CONSTRUCTION
Huddleston, Chairman

Majority (4 D): Huddleston, Johnston, Inouye, Sasser.
Minority (2 R): Laxalt, Stevens.

STATE, JUSTICE, COMMERCE, THE JUDICIARY
Hollings, Chairman

Majority (7 D): Hollings, Magnuson, Eagleton, Inouye, Burdick, DeConcini, Bumpers.
Minority (5 R): Weicker, Hatfield, Stevens, Laxalt, Garn.

TRANSPORTATION
Bayh, Chairman

Majority (6 D): Bayh, Byrd, Stennis, Magnuson, Eagleton, Durkin.
Minority (3 R): McClure, Mathias, Weicker.

TREASURY, POSTAL SERVICE, AND GENERAL GOVERNMENT
Chiles, Chairman

Majority (3 D): Chiles, DeConcini, Bumpers.
Minority (2 R): Schmitt, Laxalt.

ARMED SERVICES
John Stennis (Miss.), Chairman

Democratic Majority (10 D): Stennis, Jackson (Wash.), Cannon (Nev.), Byrd (Vir), Nunn (Ga.), Culver (Iowa, Hart (Colo.), Morgan (N.C.), Exon (Neb.), Levin Mich).
Republican Minority (7 R): Tower (Teas), Thurmond (S.C.), Goldwater (Ariz.), Warner (Va.), Humphrey (N.H.), Cohen (Ma.), Jepsen (Iowa).

Subcommittees

ARMS CONTROL
Jackson, Chairman

Majority (4 D): Jackson, Hart, Exon, Levin.
Minority (3 R): Cohen, Tower, Thurmond.

GENERAL PROCUREMENT
Byrd, Chairman

Majority (5 D): Byrd, Jackson, Cannon, Hart, Morgan.
Minority (4 R): Goldwater, Tower, Thurmond, Jepsen.

MANPOWER AND PERSONNEL
Nunn, Chairman

Majority (4 D): Nunn, Byrd, Culver, Exon.
Minority (3 R): Jepsen, Warner, Cohen.

RESEARCH AND DEVELOPMENT
Culver, Chairman

Majority (5 D): Culver, Nunn, Morgan, Exon, Levin.
Minority (4 R): Warner, Goldwater, Humphrey, Cohen.

MILITARY CONSTRUCTION AND STOCKPILES
Hart, Chairman

Majority (5 D): Hart, Jackson, Cannon, Byrd, Nunn.
Minority (4 D): Thurmond, Tower, Warner, Humphrey.

PROCUREMENT POLICY AND REPROGRAMING
Morgan, Chairman

Majority (4 D): Morgan, Cannon, Culver, Levin.
Minority (3 R): Humphrey, Goldwater, Jepsen.

BANKING, HOUSING, AND URBAN AFFAIRS
William Proxmire (Wis.), Chairman

Democratic Majority (9 D): Proxmire, Williams (N.J.), Cranston (Calif.), Stevenson (Ill.), Morgan (N.C.), Riegle (Mich.), Sarbanes (My.), Stewart (Ala.), Tsongas (Mass.).
Republican Minority (6 R): Garn (Utah), Tower (Texas), Heinz (Penn.), Armstrong (Colo.), Kassebaum (Kan.), Lugar (Ind.).

Subcommittees

HOUSING AND URBAN AFFAIRS
Williams, Chairman

Majority (6 D): Williams, Proxmire, Cranston, Morgan, Riegle, Sarbanes.
Minority (4 R): Garn, Tower, Heinz, Lugar.

SECURITIES
Sarbanes, Chairman

Majority (2 D): Sarbanes, Williams.
Minority (1 R): Lugar.

FINANCIAL INSTITUTIONS
Cranston, Chairman

Majority (4 D): Cranston, Stevenson, Proximire, Morgan.
Minority (3 R): Tower, Garn, Armstrong.

ECONOMIC STABILIZATION
Riegle, Chairman

Majority (3 D): Riegle, Proxmire, Stevenson.
Minority (2 R): Armstrong, Tower.

INTERNATIONAL FINANCE
Stevenson, Chairman

Majority (4 D): Stevenson, Williams, Cranston, Tsongas.
Minority (3 R): Heinz, Kassebaum, Armstrong.

RURAL HOUSING
Morgan, Chairman

Majority (2 D): Morgan, Stewart.
Minority (2 R): Kassebaum, Garn.

CONSUMER AFFAIRS
Tsongas, Chairman

Majority (3 D): Tsongas, Riegle, Sarbanes.
Minority (2 R): Heinz, Kassebaum.

INSURANCE
Stewart, Chairman

Majority (2 D): Stewart, Tsongas.
Minority (1 R): Lugar.

BUDGET
Edmund Muskie (Me.), Chairman

Democratic Majority (12 D): Muskie, Magnuson (Wash.), Hollings (S.C.), Chiles (Florida), Biden (Del.), Johnston (La.), Sasser (Tenn.), Hart (Colo.), Metzenbaum (Ohio), Riegle (Mich.), Moynihan (N.Y.), Exon (Neb.).
Republican Minority (8 R): Bellmon (Okla.), Domenici (N.M.), Packwood (Ore.), Armstrong (Colo.), Kassebaum (Kan.), Boschwitz (Minn.), Hatch (Utah), Pressler (S.D.).

No Subcommittees

COMMERCE, SCIENCE, AND TRANSPORTATION
Howard Cannon (Nev.), Chairman

Democratic Majority (10 D): Cannon, Magnuson (Wash.), Long (La.), Hollings (S.C.), Inouye (Hawaii), Stevenson (Ill.), Ford (Ken.), Riegle (Mich.), Exon (Neb.), Heflin (Ala.).
Republican Minority (7 R): Packwood (Ore.), Goldwater (Ariz.), Schmitt (N.M.), Danforth (Mo.), Kassebaum (Kan.), Pressler (S.D.), Warner (Va.).

Subcommittees

AVIATION
Cannon, Chairman

Majority (4 D): Cannon, Inouye, Stevenson, Exon.
Minority (3 R): Kassebaum, Goldwater, Pressler.

COMMUNICATIONS
Hollings, Chairman

Majority (7 D): Hollings, Magnuson, Cannon, Inouye, Ford, Riegle, Exon.
Minority (5 R): Goldwater, Schmitt, Danforth, Pressler, Warner.

CONSUMER
Ford, Chairman

Majority (3 D): Ford, Magnuson, Heflin.
Minority (2 R): Danforth, Warner.

MERCHANT MARINE AND TOURISM
Inouye, Chairman

Majority (3 D): Inouye, Magnuson, Long.
Minority (2 R): Warner, Packwood.

SCIENCE, TECHNOLOGY, AND SPACE
Stevenson, Chairman

Majority (6 D): Stevenson, Ford, Long, Hollings, Riegle, Heflin.
Minority (3 R): Schmitt, Goldwater, Kassebaum.

SURFACE TRANSPORTATION
Long, Chairman

Majority (7 D): Long, Cannon, Hollings, Stevenson, Riegle, Exon, Heflin.
Minority (4 R): Pressler, Danforth, Schmitt, Kassebaum.

ENERGY AND NATURAL RESOURCES
Henry Jackson (Wash.), Chairman

Democratic Majority (11 D): Jackson, Church (Idaho), Johnston (La.), Bumpers (Ark.), Ford (Kent.), Durkin (N.H.), Metzenbaum (Ohio), Matsunaga (Hawaii), Melcher (Mont.), Tsongas (Mass.), Bradley (N.J.).
Republican Minority (7 R); Hatfield (Ore.), McClure (Idaho), Weicker (Conn.), Domenici (N.M.), Stevens (Alaska), Bellmon (Okla.), Wallop (Wyo.).

Subcommittees

ENERGY RESEARCH AND DEVELOPMENT
Church, Chairman

Majority (7 D): Church, Matsunaga (Vice Chairman), Johnston, Bumpers, Durkin, Melcher, Tsongas.
Minority (5 R): McClure, Hatfield, Domenici, Stevens, Wallop.

ENERGY REGULATION
Johnston, Chairman

Majority (6 D): Johnston, Metzenbaum (Vice Chairman), Bumpers, Ford, Durkin, Bradley.
Minority (4 R): Domnici, Bellmon, Hatfield, McClure.

ENERGY COUSERVATION AND SUPPLY
Durkin, Chairman

Majority (6 D): Durkin, Tsongas (Vice Chairman), Ford, Metzenbaum, Matsunaga, Bradley.
Minority (4 R): Wallop, Domenici, Weicker, Bellmon.

ENERGY RESOURCES AND MATERIALS PRODUCTION
Ford, Chairman

Majority (6 D): Ford, Bradley (Vice Chairman), Jackson, Church, Matsunaga, Melcher.
Minority (4 R): Weicker, Stevens, Bellmon, Wallop.

PARKS, RECREATION, AND RENEWABLE RESOURCES
Bumpers, Chairman

Majority (6 D): Bumpers, Melcher (Vice Chairman), Church, Johnston, Metzenbaum, Tsongas.
Minority (4 R): Hatfield, Stevens, McClure, Weicker.

ENIRONMENT AND PUBLIC WORKS
Jennings Randolph (W.Va.), Chairman

Democratic Majority (8 D): Randolph, Muskie (Me.), Gravel (Alaska), Bentsen (Texas), Burdick (N.D.), Culver (Iowa), Hart (Colo.), Moynihan (N.Y.).
Republican Minority (6 R): Stafford (Vt.), Baker (Tenn.), Domenici (N.M.), Chaffee (R.I.), Simpson (Wyo.), Pressler (S.D.).

Subcommittees

ENVIRONMENTAL POLLUTION
Muskie, Chairman

Majority (4 D): Muskie, Bentsen, Burdick, Culver.
Minority (3 R): Stafford, Chafee, Simpson.

WATER RESOURCES
Gravel, Chairman

Majority (4 D): Gravel, Bentsen, Hart, Moynihan.
Minority (3 R): Domenici, Simpson, Pressler.

TRANSPORTATION
Bentsen, Chairman

Majority (3 D): Bentsen, Randolph, Burdick.
Minority (2 R): Pressler, Stafford.

REGIONAL AND COMMUNITY DEVELOPMENT
Burdick, Chairman

Majority (5 D): Burdick, Randolph, Muskie, Gravel, Moynihan.
Minority (4 R): Chaffee, Stafford, Baker, Domenici.

RESOURCES PROTECTION
Culver, Chairman

Majority (4 D): Culver, Muskie, Gravel, Hart.
Minority (3 R): Baker, Chafee, Pressler.

NUCLEAR REGULATION
Hart, Chairman

Majority (4 D): Hart, Randolph, Culver, Moynihan.
Minority (3 R): Simpson, Baker, Domenici.

FINANCE

Russell Long (La.), Chairman

Democratic Majority (12 D): Long, Talmadge (Ga.), Ribicoff (Conn.), Byrd (Va), Nelson (Wis.), Gravel (Alaska), Bentsen (Texas), Matsunaga (Hawaii), Moynihan (N.Y.), Baucus (Mont.), Moren (Okla.), Bradley (N.J.).
Republican Minority (8 R): Dole (Kan.), Packwood (Ore.), Roth (Del.), Danforth (Mo.), Chaffee (R.I.), Heinz (Penn.), Wallop (Wyo.), Durenberger (Minn.).

Subcommittees

HEALTH

Talmadge, Chairman

Majority (4 D): Talmadge, Ribicoff, Nelson, Matsunaga.
Minority (3 R): Dole, Durenberger, Roth.

INTERNATIONAL TRADE

Ribicoff, Chairman

Majority (7 D): Ribicoff, Talmadge, Byrd, Gravel, Moynihan, Baucus, Bradley.
Minority (5 R): Roth, Danforth, Heinz, Dole, Chaffee.

TAXATION AND DEBT MANAGEMENT GENERALLY

Byrd, Chairman

Majority (4 D): Byrd, Bentsen, Talmadge, Gravel.
Minority (3 R): Packwood, Chaffee, Wallop.

SOCIAL SECURITY

Nelson, Chairman

Majority (3 D): Nelson, Long, Ribicoff.
Minority (2 R): Danforth, Packwood.

ENERGY AND FOUNDATIONS

Gravel, Chairman

Majority (3 D): Gravel, Boren, Baucus.
Minority (2 R): Wallop, Durenberger.

PRIVATE PENSION PLANS AND EMPLOYEE FRINGE BENEFITS

Bentsen, Chairman

Majority (2 D): Bentsen, Matsunaga.
Minority (1 R): Dole.

TOURISM AND SUGAR

Matsunaga, Chairman

Majority (2 D): Matsunaga, Long.
Minority (1 R): Wallop.

PUBLIC ASSISTANCE

Moynihan, Chairman

Majority (3 D): Moynihan, Long, Boren.
Minority (2 R): Heinz, Roth.

OVERSIGHT OF THE INTERNAL REVENUE SERVICE
Baucus, Chairman

Majority (2 D): Baucus, Byrd.
Minority (1 R): Heinz.

UNEMPLOYMENT AND RELATED PROBLEMS
Boren, Chairman

Majority (2 D): Boren, Bradley.
Minority (1 R): Chafee.

REVENUE SHARING, INTERGOVERNMENT REVENUE IMPACT, AND ECONOMIC PROBLEMS
Bradley, Chairman

Majority (4 D): Bradley, Moynihan, Nelson, Bentsen.
Minority (3 R): Durenberger, Packwood, Danforth.

FOREIGN RELATIONS
Frank Church (Idaho), Chairman

Democratic Majority (9 D): Church, Pell (R.I.), McGovern (S.D.), Biden (Del.), Glenn (Ohio), Stone (Fla.), Sarbanes (My.), Muskie (Me.), Zorinsky (Neb.). Republican Minority (6 R): Javits (N.Y.), Percy (Ill.), Baker (Tenn.), Helms (N.C.), Hayakawa (Calif.), Lugar (Ind.).

Subcommittees

INTERNATIONAL ECONOMIC POLICY
Sarbanes, Chairman

Majority (3 D): Sarbanes, McGovern, Biden.
Minority (2 R): Javits, Lugar.

ARMS CONTROL, OCEANS AND INTERNATIONAL OPERATIONS, AND ENVIRONMENT
Pell, Chairman

Majority (4 D): Pell, Biden, Glenn, Zorinsky.
Minority (3 R): Percy, Baker, Helms.

AFRICAN AFFAIRS
McGovern, Chairman

Majority (2 D): McGovern, Muskie.
Minority (1 R): Hayakawa.

EUROPEAN AFFAIRS
Biden, Chairman

Majority (3 D): Biden, Pell, Glenn.
Minority (2 R): Javits, Baker.

EAST ASIAN AND PACIFIC AFFAIRS
Glenn, Chairman

Majority (4 D): Glenn, Stone, Muskie, Zorinsky.
Minority (3 R): Helms, Percy, Hayakawa.

NEAR EASTERN AND SOUTH ASIAN AFFAIRS
Stone, Chairman

Majority (3 D): Stone, McGovern, Sarbanes.
Minority (2 R): Percy, Lugar.

WESTERN HEMISPHERE AFFAIRS
Zorinsky, Chairman

Majority (4 D): Zorinsky, Stone, Sarbanes, Muskie.
Minority (3 R): Lugar, Hayakawa, Helms.

GOVERNMENTAL AFFAIRS
Abraham Ribicoff (Conn.), Chairman

Democratic Majority (9 D): Ribicoff, Jackson (Wash.), Eagleton (Mo.), Chiles (Fla.), Nunn (Ga.), Glenn (Ohio), Sasser (Tenn.), Pryor (Ark.), Levin (Mich.).
Republican Minority (8 R): Percy (Ill.), Javits (N.Y.), Roth (Del.), Stevens (Alaska), Mathias (My.), Danforth (Mo.), Cohen (Me.), Durenberger (Minn.).

Subcommittees

PERMANENT INVESTIGATIONS
Nunn, Chairman

Majority (6 D): Nunn, Jackson (Vice Chairman), Eagleton, Chiles, Glenn, Sasser.
Minority (5 R): Percey, Javits, Roth, Mathias, Cohen.

INTERGOVERNMENTAL RELATIONS
Sasser, Chairman

Majority (4 D): Sasser, Chiles, Glenn, Nunn.
Minority (3 R): Roth, Durenberger, Danforth.

GOVERNMENTAL EFFICIENCY AND THE DISTRICT OF COLUMBIA
Eagleton, Chairman

Majority (2 D): Eagleton, Levin.
Minority (2 R): Mathias, Stevens.

FEDERAL SPENDING PRACTICES AND OPEN GOVERNMENT
Chiles, Chairman

Majority (4 D): Chiles, Nunn, Jackson, Pryor.
Minority (3 R): Danforth, Roth, Mathias.

ENERGY, NUCLEAR PROLIFERATION, AND FEDERAL SERVICES
Glenn, Chairman

Majority (4 D): Glenn, Eagleton, Jackson, Levin.
Minority (3 R): Javits, Stevens, Durenberger.

CIVIL SERVICE AND GENERAL SERVICES
Pryor, Chairman

Majority (2 D): Pryor, Sasser.
Minority (1 R): Stevens.

OVERSIGHT OF GOVERNMENT MANAGEMENT
Levin, Chairman

Majority (2 D): Levin, Pryor.
Minority (2 R): Cohen, Durenberger.

JUDICIARY

Edward Kennedy (Mass.), Chairman

Democratic Majority (10 D): Kennedy, Bayh (Ind.), Byrd (W.Va.), Biden (Del.), Culver (Iowa), Metzenbaum (Ohio), DeConcini (Ariz.), Leahy (Vt.), Baucus (Mont.), Heflin (Ala.).
Republican Minority (7 R): Thurmond (S.C.), Mathias (My.), Laxalt (Nev.), Hatch (Utah), Dole (Kan., Cochran (Miss.), Simpson (Wyo.).

Subcommittees

ADMINISTRATIVE PRACTICE AND PROCEDURE

Culver, Chairman

Majority (5 D): Culver, Leahy, Biden, Metzenbaum, Bayh.
Minority (4 R): Laxalt, Dole, Mathias, Cochran.

ANTITRUST, MONOPOLY AND BUSINESS RIGHTS

Metzenbaum, Chairman

Majority (6 D): Metzenbaum, Kennedy, Bayh, Culver, Leahy, Baucus.
Minority (4 R): Thurmond, Mathias, Laxalt, Hatch.

CONSTITUTION

Bayh, Chairman

Majority (4 D): Bayh, Metzenbaum, DeConcini, Heflin.
Minority (3 R): Hatch, Thurmond, Simpson.

CRIMINAL JUSTICE

Biden, Chairman

Majority (5 D): Biden, Kennedy, Culver, DeConcini, Leahy.
Minority (4 R): Mathias, Cochran, Laxalt, Hatch.

IMPROVEMENTS IN JUDICIAL MACHINERY

DeConcini, Chairman

Majority (3 D): DeConcini, Byrd, Kennedy.
Minority (2 R): Dole, Simpson.

JURISPRUDENCE AND GOVERNMENTAL RELATIONS

Heflin, Chairman

Majority (3 D): Heflin, Baucus, Biden.
Minority (2 R): Simpson, Dole.

LIMITATIONS OF CONTRACTED AND DELEGATED AUTHORITY

Baucus, Chairman

Majority (2 D): Baucus, Heflin.
Minority (1 R): Cochran.

LABOR AND HUMAN RESOURCES

Harrison Williams (N.J.), Chairman

Democratic Majority (9 D): Williams, Randolph (W. Va.), Pell (R.I.), Kennedy (Mass.), Nelson (Wis.), Eagleton (Mo.), Cranston (Calif.), Riegle (Mich.), Metzenbaum (Ohio.)
Republican Minority (6 R): Schweiker (Penn.), Javits (N.Y.), Stafford (Vt.), Hatch (Utah), Armstrong (Colo.), Humphrey (N.H.)

Subcommittees

HANDICAPPED
Randolph, Chairman

Majority (3 D): Randolph, Eagleton, Riegle.
Minority (2 R): Stafford, Schweiker.

EDUCATION, ARTS, AND HUMANITIES
Pell, Chairman

Majority (5 D): Pell, Williams, Randolph, Kennedy, Eagleton.
Minority (3 R): Stafford, Schweiker, Javits.

HEALTH AND SCIENTIFIC RESEARCH
Kennedy, Chairman

Majority (6 D): Kennedy, Williams, Pell, Nelson, Cranston, Metzenbaum.
Minority (4 R): Schweiker, Javits, Hatch, Humphrey.

EMPLOYMENT, POVERTY, AND MIGRATORY LABOR
Nelson, Chairman

Majority (4 D): Nelson, Pell, Cranston, Metzenbaum.
Minority (3 R): Javits, Hatch, Armstrong.

CHILD AND HUMAN DEVELOPMENT
Cranston, Chairman

Majority (3 D): Cranston, Nelson, Riegle.
Minority (2 R): Humphrey, Armstrong.

AGING
Eagleton, Chairman

Majority (3 D): Eagleton Randolph Kennedy.
Minority (2 R): Armstrong, Stafford.

ALCOHOLISM AND DRUG ABUSE
Riegle, Chairman

Majority (3 D): Riegle, Williams, Metzenbaum.
Minority (2 R): Hatch, Humphrey.

RULES AND ADMINISTRATION
Claiborne Pell (R.I.), Chairman

Democratic Majority (6 D): Pell, Cannon (Nev.), Byrd (W. Va.), Williams (N.J.), Ford (Kent.), DeConcini (Ariz.).
Republican Minority (4 R): Hatfield (Ore.), Baker (Tenn.), Tower (Texas), Schweiker (Penn).

No Subcommittees

VETERANS AFFAIRS
Cranston (Calif.), Chairman

Democratic Majority (6 D): Cranston, Talmadge (Ga.), Randolph (W. Va.), Stone (Fla.), Durkin (N.H.), Matsunaga (Hawaii).
Republican Minority (4 R): Simpson (Wyo.), Thurmond (S.C.), Stafford (Vt.), Humphrey (N.H.).

No Subcommittees

JOINT ECONOMIC COMMITTEE

Lloyd Bentsen (Texas), Chairman
Richard Bolling (*Missouri*), *Vice Chairman*

Senators: Bentsen, Proxmire (Wis.), Ribicoff (Conn.), Kennedy (Mass.), McGovern (S.D.), Sarbanes (My.), Javits (N.Y.), Roth (Del.), McClure (Idaho), Jepsen (Iowa).
Representatives: Reuss (Wis.), Moorhead (Penn.), Hamilton (Ind.), Long (La.), Mitchell (My.), Brown (Ohio), Heckler (Mass.), Rousselot (Calif.), Wylie (Ohio).

FISCAL AND INTERGOVERNMENTAL POLICY

Moorhead, Chairman

Representatives: Moorhead, Bolling, Wylie.
Senators: Sarbanes, McClure.

ECONOMIC GROWTH AND STABILIZATION

Bentsen, Chairman

Senators: Bentsen, Ribicoff, McGovern, Sarbanes, Javits, Roth.
Representatives: Hamilton, Heckler, Rousselot.

INTERNATIONAL ECONOMICS

Reuss and Long, Co-chairmen

Representatives: Reuss, Moorhead, Hamilton, Mitchell, Brown.
Senators: Long, Ribicoff, Proxmire, Roth, Jepsen.

PRIORITIES AND ECONOMY IN GOVERNMENT

Proxmire, Chairman

Senators: Proxmire, Bentsen, Kennedy, Jepsen.
Representatives: Mitchell, Rousselot, Wylie.

ENERGY

Kennedy, Chairman

Senators: Kennedy, McGovern, Javits, McClure.
Representatives: Bolling, Hamilton, Long, Brown, Heckler.

House Committees

AGRICULTURE

Thomas Foley (Wash.), Chairman

Democratic Majority (27 D): Foley, de la Garza (Texas), Jones (N.C.), Jones (Tenn.), Mathis (Ga.), Brown (Calif.), Bowen (Miss.), Rose (N.C.), Richmond (N.Y.), Nolan (Minn.), Weaver (Ore.), Baldus (Wis.), Harkin (Iowa), Bedell (Iowa), English (Okla.), Fithian (Ind.), Panetta (Calif.), Skelton (Mo.), Huckaby (La.), Glickman (Kan.), Akaka (Hawaii), Whitley (N.C.), Coelho (Calif.), Daschle (S.D.), Hance (Texas), Anthony (Ark.), Stenholm (Texas).
Republican Minority (15 R): Wampler (Va.), Sebelius (Kan.), Findley (Ill.), Symms (Ida.), Johnson (Colo.), Madigan (Ill.), Heckler (Mass.), Jeffords (Vt.), Kelly (Fla.), Grassley (Iowa), Hagedorn (Minn.), Coleman (Mo.), Marlenee (Mont.), Hopkins (Ky.), Thomas (Calif.).

Subcommittees

CONSERVATION AND CREDIT

Ed Jones, Chairman

Majority (12 D): Jones, Harkin, Huckaby, Glickman, Hance, Brown, Richmond, Baldus, Bedell, English, Panetta, Daschle.
Minority (6 R): Madigan, Jeffords, Kelly, Coleman, Marlenee, Hopkins.

COTTON

Bowen, Chairman

Majority (5 D): Bowen, Coelho, Jones (Tenn.), Hance, Stenholm.
Minority (2 R): Heckler, Thomas.

DAIRY AND POULTRY

Baldus, Chairman

Majority (8 D): Baldus, Rose, Akaka, Coelho, Jones (N.C.), Whitley, Anthony, Stenholm.
Minority (4 R). Jeffords, Kelly, Hagedorn, Hopkins.

DEPARTMENT INVESTIGATIONS, OVERSIGHT, AND RESEARCH

de la Garza, Chairman

Majority (6 D): Garza, Brown, Fithian, Skelton, Glickman, English.
Minority (3 R): Wampler, Heckler, Grassley.

DOMESTIC MARKETING, CONSUMER RELATIONS, AND NUTRITION

Richmond, Chairman

Majority (6 D): Richmond, Panetta, Nolan, Glickman, Akaka, Harkin.
Minority (3 R): Symms, Heckler, Grassley.

FAMILY FARMS, RURAL DEVELOPMENT, AND SPECIAL STUDIES

Nolan, Chairman

Majority (8 D): Nolan, Akaka, Harkin, Daschle, Anthony, Richmond, Iowa, Panetta.
Minority (4 R): Grassley, Sebelius, Coleman, Thomas.

FORESTS
Weaver, Chairman

Majority (5 D): Weaver, Anthony, Huckaby, Coelho, Nolan.
Minority (2 R): Johnson, Symms.

LIVESTOCK AND GRAINS
Rose, Chairman

Majority (12 D): Rose, Bedell, English, Daschle, Stenholm, de la Garza, Fithian, Skelton, Jones, Nolan, Baldus, Hance.
Minority (6 R): Sebelius, Johnson, Hagedorn, Coleman, Symms, Marlenee.

OILSEEDS AND RICE
Mathis, Chairman

Majority (5 D): Mathis, Jones (N.C.), Bowen, Whitley, Stenholm.
Minority (2 R): Findley, Thomas.

TOBACCO
Walter Jones, Chairman

Majority (5 D): Jones (Tenn.), Whitley, Mathis, Rose, Baldus.
Minority (2 R): Kelly, Hopkins.

APPROPRIATIONS
Jamie L. Whitten (Miss.), Chairman

Democratic Majority (36 D): Whitten, Boland (Mass.), Natcher (Ky.), Flood (Penn.), Steed (Okla.), Slack (W. Va.), Smith (Iowa), Giaimo (Conn.), Addabbo (N.Y.), Patten (N.J.), Long (Md.), Yates (Ill.), Obey (Wis.), Roybal (Calif.), Stokes (Ohio), McKay (Utah), Bevill (Ala.), Chappell (Fla.), Burlison (Mo.), Alexander (Ark.), Murtha (Penn.), Traxler (Mich.), Duncan (Ore.), Early (Mass.), Wilson (Texas), Boggs (La.), Benjamin (Ind.), Dicks (Wash.), McHugh (N.Y.), Ginn (Ga.), Lehman (Fla.), Hightower (Texas), Jenrette (S.C.), Sabo (Minn.), Dixon (Calif.), Stewart (Ill.).
Republican Minority (18 R): Conte (Mass.), Michel (Ill.), McDade (Penn.), Mark Andrews (N.D.), Edwards (Ala.), McEwen (N.Y.), Myers (Ind.), Robinson (Va.), Miller (Ohio), Coughlin (Penn.), Young (Fla.), Kemp (N.Y.), Regula (Ohio), Burgener (Calif.), O'Brien (Ill.), Smith (Neb.), Rudd (Ariz.), Pursell (Mich.).

Subcommittees

AGRICULTURE, RURAL DEVELOPMENT AND RELATED AGENCIES
Whitten, Chairman

Majority (8 D): Whitten, Burlison, Traxler, Alexander, McHugh, Natcher, Hightower, Jenrette.
Minority (3 R): Andrews, Robinson, Myers.

DEFENSE
Addabbo, Chairman

Majority (7 D): Addabbo, Flood, Giaimo, Chappell, Burlison, Murtha, Dicks.
Minority (3 R): Edwards, Robinson, Kemp.

DISTRICT OF COLUMBIA
Wilson, Chairman

Majority (5 D): Wilson, Natcher, Stokes, McKay, Chappell.
Minority (2 R): Pursell, Rudd.

ENERGY AND WATER DEVELOPMENT
Bevill, Chairman

Majority (7 D): Bevill, Boland, Slack, Boggs, Chappell, Jenrette, Dixon.
Minority (3 R): Myers, Burgener, Smith.

FOREIGN OPERATIONS
Long, Chairman

Majority (7 D): Long, Obey, Wilson, Yates, McHugh, Lehman, Dixon.
Minority (3 R): Young, Smith, Kemp.

HUD–INDEPENDENT AGENCIES
Boland, Chairman

Majority (7 D): Boland, Traxler, Stokes, Bevill, Boggs, Sabo, Stewart.
Minority (3 R): Coughlin, McDade, Young.

INTERIOR
Yates, Chairman

Majority (7 D): Yates, McKay, Long ,Duncan, Murtha, Dicks, Ginn.
Minority (3 R): McDade, Regula, Burgener.

LABOR–HEALTH, EDUCATION, AND WELFARE
Natcher, Chairman

Majority (8 D): Natcher, Flood, Smith, Patten, Obey, Roybal, Stokes, Early.
Minority (4 R): Michel, Conte, O'Brien, Pursell.

LEGISLATIVE
Benjamin, Chairman

Majority (5 D): Benjamin, Slack, Smith, Giaimo, Yates.
Minority (3 R): Michel, Conte, Rudd.

MILITARY CONSTRUCTION
McKay, Chairman

Majority (5 D): McKay, Ginn, Steed, Addabbo, Long.
Minority (2 R): McEwen, Regula.

STATE, JUSTICE, COMMERCE, AND JUDICIARY
Slack, Chairman

Majority (5 D): Slack, Smith, Alexander, Early, Hightower.
Minority (2 R): O'Brien, Andrews.

TRANSPORTATION
Duncan, Chairman

Majority (7 D): Duncan, Steed, Benjamin, Lehman, Sabo, Stewart, Boland.
Minority (4 R): Conte, Edwards, Miller, Coughlin.

TREASURY–POSTAL SERVICE–GENERAL GOVERNMENT
Steed, Chairman

Majority (6 D): Steed, Addabbo, Roybal, Patten, Diaimo.
Minority (2 R): Miller, McEwen.

ARMED SERVICES
Melvin Price (Ill.), Chairman

Democratic Majority (28 D): Price, Bennett (Fla.), Stratton (N.Y.), Ichord (Mo.), Nedzi (Mich.), Wilson (Calif.), White (Texas), Nichols (Ala.), Brinkley (Ga.), Mollohan (W. Va.), Daniel (Va.), Montgomery (Miss.), Runnels (N.M.), Aspin (Wis.), Dellums (Calif.), Davis (S.C.), Schroeder (Colo.), Kazen (Texas), Won Pat (Guam), Carr (Mich.), Lloyd (Calif.), McDonald (Ga.), Stump (Ariz.), Fazio (Calif.), Leach (La.), Byron (Md.), Mavroules (Mass.), Wyatt (Texas), Bailey (Penn.).
Republican Minority (15 R): Wilson (Calif.), Dickinson (Ala.), Whitehurst (Va.), Spence (S.C.), Treen (La.), Beard (Tenn.), Mitchell (N.Y.), Holt (Md.), R. W. Daniel (Va.), Hillis (Ind.), Emery (Me.), Trible (Va.), Badham (Calif.), Dougherty (Penn.), Courier (N.J.), Evans (Virgin Islands).

Subcommittees

INVESTIGATIONS
Stratton, Chairman

Majority (9 D): Stratton, Mollohan, Daniel, Runnels, Kazen, Won Pat, Price, Ichord, Nichols.
Minority (5 R): Beard, Treen, Daniel, Badham, Spence.

MILITARY COMPENSATION
Nichols, Chairman

Majority (9 D): Nichols, Mollohan, Aspin, Davis, Fazio, Leach, Byron, Mavroules, Wyatt.
Minority (5 R): Mitchell, Emery, Dougherty, Courter, Evans.

MILITARY INSTALLATIONS AND FACILITIES
Nedzi, Chairman

Majority (9 D): Nedzi, Wilson, Brinkley, Davis, Won Pat, Fazio, Byron, Bennett, White.
Minority (5 R): Whitehurst, Beard, Mitchell, Trible, Dickinson.

MILITARY PERSONNEL
White, Chairman

Majority (6 D): White, Montgomery, Kazen, Won Pat, Nedzi, Nichols.
Minority (3 R): Holt, Treen, Hillis.

PROCUREMENT AND MILITARY NUCLEAR SYSTEMS
Price, Chairman

Majority (8 D): Price, Wilson, Daniel Carr, Stump, Leach, Mavroules, Bailey.
Minority (5 R): Wilson, Holt, Daniel, Hillis, Badham.

RESEARCH AND DEVELOPMENT
Ichord, Chairman

Majority (7 D): Ichord, Runnels, Aspin, Dellums, Schroeder, Lloyd, McDonald.
Minority (4 R): Dickinson, Whitehurst, Mitchell, Courter.

SEAPOWER AND STRATEGIC AND CRITICAL MATERIALS
Bennett, Chairman

Majority (7 D): Bennett, Brinkley, Mollohan, Fazio, Byron, Wyatt, Stratton.
Minority (4 R): Spence, Emery, Trible, Dougherty.

BANKING, FINANCE AND URBAN AFFAIRS
Henry Reuss (Wis.), Chairman

Democratic Majority (27 D): Reuss, Ashley (Ohio), Moorhead (Penn.), St Germain (R.I.), Gonzales (Texas), Minish (N.J.), Annunzio (Ill.), Hanley (N.Y.), Mitchell (Md.), Fauntroy (D.C.), Neal (N.C.), Patterson (Calif.), Blanchard (Mich.), Hubbard (Ky.), LaFalce (N.Y.), Spellman (Md.), AuCoin (Ore.), Evans (Ind.), D'Amours (N.H.), Lundine (N.Y.), Cavanaugh (Neb.), Oakar (Ohio), Mattox (Texas), Vento (Minn.), Barnard (Ga.), Watkins (Okla.), Garcia (N.Y.), Lowry (Wash.).
Republican Minority (15 R): Stanton (Ohio), Wylie (Ohio), McKenny (Conn.), Hansen (Idaho), Hyde (Ill.), Kelly (Fla.), Leach (Iowa), Evans (Del.), Green (N.Y.), Paul (Texas), Bethune (Ark.), Shumway (Calif.), Campbell (S.C.), Ritter (Penn.), Hinson (Miss.).

Subcommittees

CONSUMER AFFAIRS
Annunzio, Chairman

Majority (5 D): Annunzio, Spellman, Vento, Fauntroy, Mitchell.
Minority (4 R): Evans, Wylie, Ritter.

DOMESTIC MONETARY POLICY
Mitchell, Chairman

Majority (6 D): Mitchell, Neal, D'Amours, Barnard, Mattox, Cavanaugh.
Minority (3 R): Hansen, Paul, Ritter.

ECONOMIC STABILIZATION
Moorhead, Chairman

Majority (12 D): Moorhead, Blanchard, Lundine, Vento, Watkins, Ashley, Hubbard, LaFalce, Evans, D'Amours, Oakar, Garcia.
Minority (6 R): McKenney, Kelly, Green, Shumway, Hinson, Paul.

FINANCIAL INSTITUTIONS SUPERVISION, REGULATION AND INSURANCE
St Germain, Chairman

Majority (12 D): St Germain, Annunzio, Hanley, Hubbard, Patterson, Ashley, D'Amours, Cavanaugh, Mattox, Minish, Fauntroy, Barnard.
Minority (6 R): Wylie, Hyde, Hansen, Leach, Campbell, Bethune.

GENERAL OVERSIGHT AND RENEGOTIATION
Minish, Chairman

Majority (8 D): Minish, Gonzalez, Annunzio, Hubbard, Mitchell, Neal, Barnard, Fauntroy.
Minority (4 R): Green, Paul, Campbell, Hinson.

HOUSING AND COMMUNITY DEVELOPMENT
Ashley, Chairman

Majority (18 D): Ashley, Moorhead, St Germain, Gonzalez, Hanley, Fauntroy, Patterson, LaFalce, AuCoin, Spellman, Blanchard, Evans, Lundine, Oakar, Vento, Watkins, Garcia, Lowry.
Minority (9 R): Stanton, Wylie, McKennery, Kelly, Evans, Green, Leach, Bethune, Ritter.

INTERNATIONAL DEVELOPMENT INSTITUTIONS AND FINANCE
Gonzalez, Chairman

Majority (10 D): Gonzalez, Minish, Moorhead, LaFalce, Oakar, Ashley, Neal, AuCoin, Cavanaugh, Reuss.
Minority (5 R): Hyde, Evans, Bethune, Shumway, Stanton.

INTERNATIONAL TRADE, INVESTMENT AND MONETARY POLICY
Neal, Chairman

Majority (12 D): Neal, AuCoin, Cavanaugh, Blanchard, Evans, Lundine, Barnard, Oakar, Patterson, LaFalce, Mattox, Lowry.
Minority (6 R): Leach, Hyde, Hansen, Campbell, Shumway, Stanton.

THE CITY
Reuss, Chairman

Majority (6 D): Reuss, Oakar, Hanley, Cavanaugh, Garcia, Lowry.
Minority (3 R): Kelly, McKinney, Hinson.

BUDGET
Robert Giaimo (Conn.), Chairman

Democratic Majority (17 D): Giaimo, Wright (Texas), Ashley (Ohio), Stokes (Ohio), Holtzman (N.Y.), Obey (Wis.), Simon (Ill.), Mineta (Calif.), Mattox (Texas), Jones (Okla.), Solarz (N.Y.), Brodhead (Mich.), Wirth (Colo.), Panetta (Calif.), Gephardt (Mo.), Nelson (Fla.), Gray (Penn.).
Republican Minority (8 R): Latta (Ohio), Broyhill (N.C.), Conable (N.Y.), Holt, (Md.), Regula (Ohio), Shuster (Penn.), Frenzel (Minn.), Rudd (Ariz.).

.... Task Forces .... 8 Cal Bold u&lc ....

BUDGET PROCESS
Mineta, Chairman

Majority (9 D): Mineta, Giaimo, Wright, Holtzman, Jones, Wirth, Panetta, Gephardt.
Minority (2 R): Conable, Holt.

DEFENSE AND INTERNATIONAL AFFAIRS
Mattox, Chairman

Majority (9 D): Mattox, Giaimo, Wright, Holtzman, Simon, Jones, Brodhead, Solarz, Gray.
Minority (5 R): Latta, Holt, Regula, Shuster, Rudd.

ECONOMIC POLICY, PROJECTIONS AND PRODUCTIVITY

Majority (5 D): Ashley, Giaimo, Wright, Gephardt, Gray.
Minority (4 R): Broyhill, Conable, Shuster, Frenzel.

HUMAN AND COMMUNITY RESOURCES
Stokes, Chairman

Majority (5 D): Stokes, Giaimo, Wright, Solarz, Gray.
Minority (2 R): Holt, Frenzel.

INFLATION
Simon, Chairman

Majority (7 D): Simon, Giaimo, Wright, Mattox, Jones, Solarz, Nelson.
Minority (2 R): Shuster, Rudd.

LEGISLATIVE SAVINGS
Panetta, Chairman

Majority (5 D): Panetta, Giaimo, Wright, Wirth, Nelson.
Minority (2 R): Latta, Rudd.

REGULATIONS AND SPENDING LIMITATIONS

Majority (6 D): Obey, Giaimo, Wright, Brodhead, Wirth, Panetta.
Minority (2 R): Latta, Broyhill.

STATE AND LOCAL GOVERNMENTS
Holtzman, Chairwoman

Majority (6 D): Holtzman, Giaimo, Wright, Mineta, Mattox, Brodhead.
Minority (2 R): Latta, Regula.

TAX EXPENDITURES AND TAX POLICY
Jones, Chairman

Majority (5 D): Jones, Giaimo, Wright, Brodhead, Gephardt.
Minority (4 R): Broyhill, Conable, Regula, Frenzel.

DISTRICT OF COLUMBIA
Ronald Dellums (Calif.), Chairman

Democratic Majority (9 D): Dellums, Diggs (Mich.), Fauntroy (D.C.), Mazzoli (Ky.), Harris (Va.), Stark (Calif.), Leland (Texas), Moffett (Conn.), Gray (Penn.).
Republican Minority (5 R): McKinney (Conn.), R. W. Daniel (Va.), Marks (Penn.), Fenwick (N.J.), Jeffries (Kan.).

Subcommittees

FISCAL AFFAIRS AND HEALTH
Dellums, Chairman

Majority (3 D): Dellums, Gray, Fauntroy.
Minority (2 R): McKinney, Fenwick.

GOVERNMENT AFFAIRS AND BUDGET
Fauntroy, Chairman

Majority (3 D): Fauntroy, Harris, Dellums.
Minority (2 R): Daniel, Fenwick.

JUDICIARY, MANPOWER, AND EDUCATION
Mazzoli, Chairman

Majority (3 D): Mazzoli, Diggs, Leland.
Minority (2 R): Marks, Jeffries.

METROPOLITAN AFFAIRS
Stark, Chairman

Majority (3 D): Stark, Harris, Moffett.
Minority (2 R): McKinney, Marks.

EDUCATION AND LABOR
Carl Perkins (Ky.), Chairman

Democratic Majority (23 D): Perkins, Thompson (N.J.), Brademas (Ind.), Hawkins (Calif.), Ford (Mich.), Burton (Calif.), Gaydos (Penn.), Clay (Mo.), Biaggi (N.Y.), Andrews (N.C.), Simon (Ill.), Beard (R.I.), Miller (Calif.), Myers (Penn.), Murphy (Penn.), Weiss (N.Y.), Corrada (P.R.), Kildee (Mich.), Peyser (N.Y.), Stack (Fla.), Williams (Mont.), Ratchford (Conn.), Kogovsek (Colo.), Bailey (Penn.).
Republican Minority (13 R): Ashbrook (Ohio), Erlenborn (Ill.), Buchanan (Ala.), Jeffords (Vt.), Goodling (Penn.), Edwards (Okla.), Coleman (Mo.), Kramer (Colo.), Erdahl (Minn.), Tauke (Iowa), Crane (Ill.), Hinson (Miss.), Petri (Wis.).

Subcommittees

ELEMENTARY, SECONDARY, AND VOCATIONAL EDUCATION
Perkins, Chairman

Majority (10 D): Perkins, Ford, Andrews, Miller, Murphy, Corrada, Kildee, Williams, Hawkins, Myers, Kogovsek.
Minority (5 R): Goodling, Buchanan, Erdahl, Crane, Hinson.

EMPLOYMENT OPPORTUNITIES
Hawkins, Chairman

Majority (6 D): Hawkins, Clay, Weiss, Ratchford, Bailey, Simon.
Minority (3 R): Jeffords, Tauke, Crane.

HEALTH AND SAFETY
Gaydos, Chairman

Majority (4 D): Gaydos, Murphy, Myers, Bailey.
Minority (2 R): Edwards, Buchanan.

HUMAN RESOURCES
Andrews, Chairman

Majority (4 D): Andrews, Corrada, Kildee, Stack, Williams.
Minority (2 R): Coleman, Goodling.

LABOR-MANAGEMENT RELATIONS
Thompson, Chairman

Majority (11 D): Thompson, Clay, Brademas, Ford, Miller, Burton, Kildee, Weiss, Kogovsek, Biaggi, Peyser.
Minority (5 R): Ashbrook, Erlenborn, Kramer, Crane, Hinson.

LABOR STANDARDS
Beard, Chairman

Majority (5 D): Beard, Burton, Miller, Williams, Myers.
Minority (2 R): Erlenborn, Edwards.

POSTSECONDARY EDUCATION
Ford, Chairman

Majority (10 D): Ford, Brademas, Thomson, Biaggi, Simon, Peyser, Gaydos, Murphy, Weiss, Ratchford.
Minority (4 R): Buchanan, Jeffords, Edwards, Tauke.

SELECT EDUCATION
Simon, Chairman

Majority (7 D): Simon, Brademas, Beard, Miller, Hawkins, Biaggi, Stack.
Minority (3 R): Kramer, Coleman, Erdahl.

FOREIGN AFFAIRS
Celment J. Zablocki (Wis.), Chairman

Democratic Majority (22 D): Zablocki, Fountain (N.C.), Fascell (Fla.), Diggs (Mich.), Rosenthal (N.Y.), Hamilton (Ind.), Wolff (N.Y.), Bingham (N.Y.), Yatron (Penn.), Collins (Ill.), Solarz (N.Y.), Bonker (Wash.), Studds (Mass.), Ireland (Fla.), Pease (Ohio), Mica (Fla.), Barnes (Md.), Gray (Penn.), Hall (Ohio), Wolpe (Mich.), Bowen (Miss.), Fithian (Ind.).
Republican Minority (12 R): Broomfield (Mich.), Derwinski (Ill.), Findley (Ill.), Buchanan (Ala.), Winn (Kan.), Gilman (N.Y.), Guyer (Ohio), Lagomarsino (Calif.), Goodling (Penn.), Pritchard (Wash.), Fenwick (N.J.), Quayle (Ind.).

Subcommittees

AFRICA
Solarz, Chairman

Majority (6 D): Solarz, Diggs, Collins, Gray, Wolpe, Fithian.
Minority (3 R): Goodling, Buchanan, Fenwick.

ASIAN AND PACIFIC AFFAIRS
Wolff, Chairman

Majority (6 D): Wolff Mica, Hall, Diggs, Yatron, Solarz.
Minority (3 R): Guyer, Pritchard, Goodling.

EUROPE AND THE MIDDLE EAST
Hamilton, Chairman

Majority (6 D): Hamilton, Rosenthal, Pease, Studds, Barnes, Fountain.
Minority (3 R): Findley, Fenwick, Winn.

INTER-AMERICAN AFFAIRS
Yatron, Chairman

Majority (6 D): Yatron, Fascell, Rosenthal, Collins, Studds, Ireland.
Minority (3 R): Gilman, Guyer, Lagomarsino.

INTERNATIONAL ECONOMIC POLICY AND TRADE
Bingham, Chairman

Majority (5 D): Bingham, Bonker, Pease, Barnes, Wolpe.
Minority (3 D): Lagomarsino, Findley, Gilman.

INTERNATIONAL OPERATIONS
Fascell, Chairman

Majority (5 D): Fascell, Ireland, Mica, Gray, Bowen.
Minority (3 R): Buchanan, Derwinski, Pritchard.

INTERNATIONAL ORGANIZATIONS
Bonker, Chairman

Majority (4 D): Bonker, Hall, Fithian, Bowen.
Minority (2 R): Derwinski, Quayle.

INTERNATIONAL SECURITY AND SCIENTIFIC AFFAIRS
Zablocki, Chairman

Majority (5 D): Zablocki, Fountain, Hamilton, Wolff, Bingham.
Minority (3 R): Broomfield, Winn, Quayle.

GOVERNMENT OPERATIONS
Jack Brooks (Texas), Chairman

Democratic Majority (25 D): Brooks, Fountain (N.C.), Fascell (Fla.), Moorhead (Penn.), Rosenthal (N.Y.), St Germain (R.I.), Fuqua (Fla.), Conyers (Mich.), Collins (Ill.), Burton (Calif.), Preyer (N.C.), Drinan (Mass.), English (Okla.), Levitas (Ga.), Evans (Ind.), Moffett (Conn.), Maguire (N.J.), Aspin (Wis.), Waxman (Calif.), Fithian (Ind.), Kostmayer (Penn.), Weiss (N.Y.), Synar (Okla.), Matsui (Calif.), Atkinson (Penn.).
Republican Minority (14 R): Horton (N.Y.), Erlenborn (Ill.), Wydler (N.Y.), Brown (Ohio), McCloskey (Calif.), Kindness (Ohio), Walker (Penn.), Stangeland (Minn.), Butler (Va.), Williams (Ohio), Jeffries (Kan.), Snowe (Me.), Grisham (Calif.), Deckard (Ind.).

Subcommittees

COMMERCE, CONSUMER, AND MONETARY AFFAIRS
Rosenthal, Chairman

Majority (6 D): Rosenthal, Matsui, Atkinson, St Germain, Conyers, Levitas.
Minority (3 R): Williams, Jeffries, Deckard.

ENVIRONMENT, ENERGY, AND NATURAL RESOURCES
Moffett, Chairman

Majority (6 D): Moffett, Drinan, Fithian, Maguire, Kostmayer, Synar.
Minority (3 R): McCloskey, Deckard, Stangeland.

GOVERNMENT ACTIVITIES AND TRANSPORTATION
J. L. Burton, Chairman

Majority (6 D): Burton, Evans, Aspin, Waxman, Synar, Matsui.
Minority (3 R): Walker, Jeffries, Brown.

GOVERNMENT INFORMATION AND INDIVIDUAL RIGHTS
Preyer, Chairman

Majority (6 D): Preyer, Drinan, English, Evans, Kostmayer, Weiss.
Minority (3 R): Kindness, Butler, Erlenborn.

INTERGOVERNMENTAL RELATIONS AND HUMAN RESOURCES
Fountain, Chairman

Majority (6 D): Fountain, English, Aspin, Weiss, Synar, Moorhead.
Minority (3 R): Wydler, Brown, Snowe.

LEGISLATION AND NATIONAL SECURITY
Brooks, Chairman

Majority (6 D): Brooks, Fuqua, Moorhead, Fascell, St Germain, Levitas.
Minority (3 R): Horton, Erlenborn, Stangeland.

MANPOWER AND HOUSING
Collins, Chairwoman

Majority (5 D): Collins, Conyers, Maguire, Atkinson, Drinan.
Minority (3 R): Grisham, Butler, Snowe.

HOUSE ADMINISTRATION
Frank Thompson (N.J.), Chairman

Democratic Majority (16 D): Thompson, Nedzi (Mich.), Brademas (Ind.), Hawkins (Calif.), Annunzio (Ill.), Gaydos (Penn.), Jones (Tenn.), Mollohan (W. Va.), Van Deerlin (Calif.), Minish (N.J.), Davis (S.C.), Rose (N.C.), J. L. Burton (Calif.), Peyser (N.Y., Ratchford (Conn.), Fazio (Calif.).
Republican Minority (9 R): Dickinson, Devine, Cleveland, Frenzel, Stockman, Badham, Gingrich, Lewis, Campbell.

Subcommittees

ACCOUNTS
Brademas, Chairman

Majority (9 D): Brademas, Minish, Davis, Rose, J. L. Burton, Peyser, Ratchford, Fazio, Nedzi.
Minority (5 R): Devine, Cleveland, Badham, Lewis, Campbell.

CONTRACTS
Gaydos, Chairman

Majority (3 D): Gaydos, Hawkins, Jones.
Minority (3 R): Cleveland, Campbell.

LIBRARIES AND MEMORIALS
Nedzi, Chairman

Majority (5 D): Nedzi, Brademas, Ratchford, Fazio, Peyser.
Minority (3 R): Frenzel, Stockman, Gingrich.

OFFICE SYSTEMS
Mollohan, Chairman

Majority (3 D): Mollohan, Rose, J. L. Burton.
Minority (2 R): Stockman, Badham.

PERSONNEL AND POLICE
Annunzio, Chairman

Majority (5 D): Annunzio, Van Deerlin, Minish, Davis, Peyser.
Minority (3 R): Devine, Gingrich, Campbell.

PRINTING
Hawkins, Chairman

Majority (3 D): Hawkins, Gaydos, Van Deerlin.
Minority (2 R): Cleveland, Gingrich.

SERVICES
Jones, Chairman

Majority (3 D): Jones, Annunzio, Mollohan.
Minority (2 R): Dickinson, Lewis.

POLICY GROUP ON INFORMATION AND COMPUTERS
Rose, Chairman

Majority (3 D): Rose, Van Deerlin, J. L. Burton.
Minority (2 R): Stockman, Lewis.

INTERIOR AND INSULAR AFFAIRS
Morris Udall (Ariz.), Chairman

Democratic Majority (26 D): Udall, P. Burton (Calif.), Kastenmeier (Wis.), Kazen (Texas), Bingham (N.Y.), Seiberling (Ohio), Runnels (N.M.), Won Pat (Guam), Eckhardt (Texas), Santini (Nev.), Weaver (Ore.), Carr (Mich.), Miller (Calif.), Florio (N.J.), Mathis (Ga.), Sharp (Ind.), Markey (Mass.), Kostmayer (Penn.), Corrada (P.R.), Murphy (Penn.), Rahall (W. Va.), Vento (Minn.), Huckaby (La.), Gudger (N.C.), Howard (N.J.), Patterson (Calif.), Kogovsek (Colo.), Williams (Mont.).
Republican Minority (14 R): Clausen (Calif.), Lujan (N.M.), Sebelius (Kan.), Young (Alaska), Symms (Idaho), Johnson (Colo.), Lagomarsino (Calif.), Marriott (Utah), Marlenee (Mont.), Edwards (Okla.), Cheney (Wyo.), Pashayan (Calif.), Whittaker (Kan.), Bereuter (Neb.), Evans (V.I.)

Subcommittees

ENERGY AND THE ENVIRONMENT
Udall, Chairman

Majority (14 D): Udall, Bingham, Eckhardt, Weaver, Carr, Mathis, Sharp, Markey, Kostmayer, Murphy, Rahal, Vento, Huckaby, Howard, Corrada.
Minority (7 R): Symms, Lujan, Marriott, Marlenee, Edwards, Cheney, Bereuter, Evans.

MINES AND MINING
Santini, Chairman

Majority (8 D): Santini, Florio, Mathis, Rahall, Huckaby, Kazen, Runnels, Murphy.
Minority (4 R): Young, Symms, Marriott, Whittaker.

NATIONAL PARKS AND INSULAR AFFAIRS
P. Burton, Chairman

Majority (14 D): P. Burton, Kastenmeier, Florio, Corrada, Gudger, Williams, Won Pat, Kazen, Bingham, Seiberling, Murphy, Vento, Patterson, Eckhardt, Kostmayer, Udall.
Minority (8 R): Sebelius, Clausen, Johnson, Lagomarsino, Edwards, Pashayan, Whittaker, Bereuter, Evans.

OVERSIGHT/SPECIAL INVESTIGATIONS
Runnels, Chairman

Majority (6 D): Runnels, Williams, Santini, Weaver, Mathis, Udall.
Minority (3 R): Clausen, Young, Lagomarsino.

PACIFIC AFFAIRS
Won Pat, Chairman

Majority (5 D): Won Pat, Howard, Seiberling, Bingham, P. Burton, Udall.
Minority (3 R): Lagomarsino, Clausen, Sebelius.

PUBLIC LANDS
Seiberling, Chairman

Majority (12 R): Seiberling, P. Burton, Runnels, Santini, Kostmayer, Gudger, Kogovsek, Eckhardt, Weaver, Kastenmeier, Carr, Udall.
Minority (6 R): Johnson, Clausen, Young, Marlenee, Cheney, Pashayan.

WATER AND POWER RESOURCES
Kazen, Chairman

Majority (8 D): Kazen, Weaver, Miller, Patterson, Kogovsek, Eckhardt, Carr, Sharp, Won Pat.
Minority (4 R): Lujan, Johnson, Pashayan, Bereuter.

INTERSTATE AND FOREIGN COMMERCE
Harley Staggers (W.Va.), Chairman

Democratic Majority (27 D): Staggers, Dingell (Mich.), Van Deerlin (Calif.), Murphy (N.Y.), Satterfield (Va.), Eckhardt (Texas), Preyer (N.C.), Scheuer (N.Y.), Ottinger (N.Y.), Waxman (Calif.), Wirth (Colo.), Sharp (Ind.), Florio (N.J.), Moffett (Conn.), Santini (Nev.), Maguire (N.J.), Russo (Ill.), Markey (Mass.), Luken (Ohio), Walgren (Penn.), Gore (Tenn.), Mikulski (Md.), Mottl (Ohio), Gramm (Texas), Swift (Wash.), Leland (Texas), Shelby (Ala.).
Republican Minority (15 R): Devine (Ohio), Broyhill (N.C.), Carter (Ky.), Brown (Ohio), Collins (Texas), Lent (N.Y.), Madigan (Ill.), Moorhead (Calif.), Rinaldo (N.J.), Stockman (Mich.), Marks (Penn.), Corcoran (Ill.), Lee (N.Y.), Loeffler (Texas), Dannemeyer (Calif.).

Subcommittees

COMMUNICATIONS
Van Deerlin, Chairman

Majority (9 D): Van Deerlin, Murphy, Wirth, Russo, Markey, Mottl, Swift, Luken, Gore.
Minority (4 R): Collins, Broyhill, Moorhead, Marks.

CONSUMER PROTECTION AND FINANCE
Scheuer, Chairman

Majority (5 D): Scheuer, Preyer, Ottinger, Satterfield, Luken.
Minority (2 R): Broyhill, Rinaldo.

ENERGY AND POWER
Dingell, Chairman

Majority (13 D): Dingell, Ottinger, Sharp, Moffett, Satterfield, Wirth, Markey, Gramm, Swift, Shelby, Maguire, Gore, Leland.
Minority (6 R): Brown, Moorhead, Collins, Stockman, Corcoran, Loeffler.

HEALTH AND THE ENVIRONMENT
Waxman, Chairman

Majority (11 D): Waxman, Satterfield, Preyer, Maguire, Luken, Walgren, Mikulski, Gramm, Leland, Shelby, Murphy.
Minority (5 R): Carter, Madigan, Stockman, Dannemeyer, Lee.

OVERSIGHT AND INVESTIGATIONS
Eckhardt, Chairman

Majority (11 D): Eckhardt, Santini, Gore, Sharp, Moffett, Maguire, Russo, Walgren, Mottl, Leland, Wirth.
Minority (5 R): Lent, Rinaldo, Marks, Corcoran, Dannemeyer.

TRANSPORTATION AND COMMERCE
Florio, Chairman

Majority (5 D): Florio, Santini, Mikulski, Murphy, Russo.
Minority (2 R): Madigan, Lee.

JUDICIARY
Peter Rodino (N.J.), Chairman

Democratic Majority (20 D): Rodino, Brooks (Texas), Kastenmeier (Wis.), Edwards (Calif.), Conyers (Mich.), Seiberling (Ohio), Danielson (Calif.), Drinan (Mass.), Holtzman (N.Y.), Mazzoli (Ky.), Hughes (N.J.), Hall (Texas), Gudger (N.C.), Volkmer (Mo.), Harris (Va.), Synar (Okla.), Matsui (Calif.), Mikva (Ill.), Barnes (Md., Shelby (Ala.).
Republican Minority (11 R): McClory (Ill.), Railsback (Ill.), Fish (N.Y.), Butler (Va.), Moorhead (Calif.), Ashbrook (Ohio), Hyde (Ill.), Kindness (Ohio), Sawyer (Mich.), Lungren (Calif.), Sensenbrenner (Wis.).

Subcommittees

ADMINISTRATIVE LAW AND GOVERNMENTAL RELATIONS
Danielson, Chairman

Majority (6 D): Danielson, Mazzoli, Hughes, Harris, Mikva, Barnes.
Minority (3 R): Moorhead, McClory, Kindness.

CIVIL AND CONSTITUTIONAL RIGHTS
Edwards, Chairman

Majority (6 D): Edwards, Seiberling, Drinan, Holtzman, Volkmer, Matsui.
Minority (3 R): Hyde, Ashbrook, Sensenbrenner.

COURTS, CIVIL LIBERTIES, AND THE ADMINISTRATION OF JUSTICE
Kastenmeier, Chairman

Majority (6 D): Kastenmeier, Danielson, Mazzoli, Gudger, Matsui, Mikva.
Minority (3 R): Railsback, Moorhead, Sawyer.

CRIME
Conyers, Chairman

Majority (6 D): Conyers, Kastenmeier, Edwards, Gudger, Volkmer, Synar.
Minority (3 R): Ashbrook, Hyde, Sensenbrenner.

CRIMINAL JUSTICE
Drinan, Chairman

Majority (6 D): Drinan, Conyers, Hall, Synar, Mikva, Shelby.
Minority (3 R): Kindness, Sawyer, Lungren.

IMMIGRATION, REFUGEES, AND INTERNATIONAL LAW
Holtzman, Chairwoman

Majority (6 D): Holtzman, Danielson, Hall, Harris, Barnes, Shelby.
Minority (3 R): Fish, Butler, Lungren.

MONOPOLIES AND COMMERCIAL LAW
Rodino, Chairman

Majority (8 D): Rodino, Brooks, Seiberling, Mazzoli, Hughes, Volkmer, Harris, Matsui.
Minority (4 R): McClory, Railsback, Fish, Butler.

MERCHANT MARINE AND FISHERIES
John Murphy (N.Y.), Chairman

Democratic Majority (25 D): Murphy, Ashley (Ohio), Dingell (Mich.), Jones (N.C.), Biaggi (N.Y.), Anderson (Calif.), de la Garza (Texas), Breaux (La.), Studds (Mass.), Bowen (Miss), Hubbard (Ky.), Bonker (Wash.), AuCoin (Ore.), D'Amours (N.H.), Oberstar (Minn.), Hughes (N.J.), Mikulski (Md.), Bonior (Mich.), Akaka (Hawaii), Myers (Penn.), Wyatt (Texas), Lowry (Wash.), Hutto (Fla.), Stack (Fla.), Donnelly (Mass.).
Republican Minority (14 R): McCloskey (Calif.), Snyder (Ky.), Forsythe (N.J.), Treen (La.), Pritchard (Wash.), Young (Alaska), Bauman (Md.), Lent (N.Y.), Emery (Me.), Dornan (Calif.), Evans (Del.), Trible (Va.), Davis (Mich.), Carney (N.Y.), Evans (V.I.).

Subcommittees

COAST GUARD AND NAVIGATION
Biaggi, Chairman

Majority (11 D): Biaggi, Jones, de la Garza, Stack, Bonker, Oberstar, Mikulski, Myers, Breaux, Studds, Hughes.
Minority (5 R): Treen, Synder, Young, Lent, Evans (V.I.).

FISHERIES AND WILDLIFE CONSERVATION AND THE ENVIRONMENT
Breaux, Chairman

Majority (18 D): Breaux, Dingell, Bowen, Bonker, Oberstar, Hughes, Boior, Lowry, Hutto, Anderson, de la Graza, Studds, AuCoin, D'Amours, Akaka, Wyatt, Stack, Donnelly.
Minority (9 R): Forsythe, Pritchard, Young, Bauman, Emery, Evans, Trible, Davis, Carney, Evans (V.I.).

MERCHANT MARINE
Murphy, Chairman

Majority (12 D): Murphy, Ashley, Anderson, Mikulski, Myers, Donnelly, Dingell, Biaggi, Bowen, Hubbard, Jones, Wyatt.
Minority (6 R): Synder, Treen, Dornan, Trible, Davis, Evans (V.I.).

OCEANOGRAPHY
Studds, Chairman

Majority (12 D): Studds, AuCoin, D'Amours, Akaka, Wyatt, Breaux, Hughes, Boior, Lowry, Hutto, Mikulski, Stack.
Minority (6 R): Pritchard, Forsythe, Lent, Emery, Dornan, Carney.

PANAMA CANAL
Hubbard, Chairman

Majority (8 D): Hubbard, Bowen, Bonior, Dingell, Jones, Biaggi, Anderson, Lowry.
Minority (4 R): Bauman, Treen, Dornan, Carney.

POST OFFICE AND CIVIL SERVICE

Hanley (N.Y.), Chairman

Democratic Majority (13 D): Hanley, Udall (Ariz.), Wilson (Calif.), Ford (Mich.), Clay (Mo.), Schroeder (Colo.), Spellman (Md.), Harris (Va.), Garcia (N.Y.), Leland (Texas), Ferraro (N.Y.), Stenholm (Texas), Albosta (Mich.).
Republican Minority (9 R): Derwinski (Ill.), Taylor (Mo.), Gilman (N.Y.), Leach (Iowa), Corcoran (Ill.), Courter (N.J.), Pashayan (Calif.), Dannemeyer (Calif.), D. Crane (Ill.).

Subcommittees

CENSUS AND POPULATION

Garcia, Chairman

Majority (3 D): Garcia, Leland, Ferraro.
Minority (3 R): Courter, Pashayan, Crane.

CIVIL SERVICE

Schroeder, Chairwoman

Majority (4 D): Schroeder, Udall, Harris, Clay.
Minority (4 R): Leach, Taylor, Pashayan, Courter.

COMPENSATION AND EMPLOYEE BENEFITS

Spellman, Chairwoman

Majority (3 D): Spellman, Wilson, Ford.
Minority (2 R): Corcoran, Crane.

HUMAN RESOURCES

Harris, Chairman

Majority (3 D): Harris, Spellman, Garcia.
Minority (2 R): Dannemeyer, Gilman.

INVESTIGATIONS

Hanley, Chairman

Majority (4 D): Hanley, Stenholm, Spellman, Albosta.
Minority (2 R): Taylor, Leach.

POSTAL OPERATIONS AND SERVICES

Wilson, Chairman

Majority (6 D): Wilson, Ford, Ferraro, Albosta, Udall, Clay.
Minority (4 R): Derwinski, Corcoran, Crane, Courter.

POSTAL PERSONNEL AND MODERNIZATION

Clay, Chairman

Majority (4 D): Clay, Wilson, Ford, Leland.
Minority (2 R): Gilman, Dannemeyer.

PUBLIC WORKS AND TRANSPORATION
H. T. Johnson (Calif.), Chairman

Democratic Majority (31 D): Johnson, Roberts (Texas), Howard (N.J.), Anderson (Calif.), Roe (N.J.), McCormack (Wash.), Breaux (La.), Mineta (Calif.), Levitas (Ga.), Oberstar (Minn.), Ambro (N.Y.), Nowak (N.Y.), Edgar (Penn.), Bouquard (Tenn.), Fary (Ill.), Hefner (N.C.), Young (Mo.), Bonior (Mich.), Ertel (Penn.), Evans (Ga.), Flippo (Ala.), Rahall (W. Va.), Applegate (Ohio), Ferraro (N.Y.), Donnelly (Mass.), Hutto (Fla.), Atkinson (Penn.), Albosta (Mich.), Leath (Texas), Boner (Tenn.).
Republican Minority (17 R): Harsha (Ohio), Cleveland (N.H.), Clausen (Calif.), Snyder (Ky.), Hammerschmidt (Ark.), Shuster (Penn.), Abdnor (S.D.), Taylor (Mo.), Goldwater (Calif.), Hagedorn (Minn.), Stangeland (Minn.), Livingston (La.), Gingrich (Ga.), Clinger (Penn.), Solomon (N.Y.), Lewis (Calif.), Royer (Calif.)

Subcommittees

AVIATION
Anderson, Chairman

Majority (15 D): Anderson, Levitas, Fary, Hefner, Young, Flippo, Boner, Mineta, Ambro, Bouquard, Ertel, Evans, Rahall, Applegate, Ferraro.
Minority (8 R): Snyder, Hammerschmidt, Shuster, Abdnor, Taylor, Goldwater, Hagedorn, Gingrich.

ECONOMIC DEVELOPMENT
Roe, Chairman

Majority (14 D): Roe, Oberstar, Nowak, Bouquard, Evans, Donnelly, Edgar, Bonior, Rahall, Applegate, Hutto, Atkinson, Albosta, Leath.
Minority (7 R): Hammerschmidt, Cleveland, Clausen, Shuster, Taylor, Clinger, Lewis.

OVERSIGHT AND REVIEW
Mineta, Chairman

Majority (13 D): Mineta, Bouquard, Evans, Roberts, Howard, Roe, Breaux, Levitas, Oberstar, Nowak, Fary, Hefner, Young.
Minority (7 R): Cleveland, Goldwater, Stangeland, Gingrich, Clinger, Solomon, Royer.

PUBLIC BUILDING AND GROUNDS
Levitas, Chairman

Majority (11 D): Levitas, McCormack, Edgar, Flippo, Donnelly, Hutto, Albosta, Leath, Boner, Nowak, Atkinson.
Minority (7 R): Abdnor, Goldwater, Hagedorn, Stangeland, Livingston, Clinger, Solomon.

SURFACE TRANSPORTATION
Howard, Chairman

Majority (17 D): Roberts, McCormack, Breaux, Ambro, Young, Bonior, Flippo, Atkinson, Boner, Roberts, Anderson, Roe, McCormack, Breaux, Mineta, Ambro.
Minority (8 R): Shuster, Cleveland, Clausen, Hagedorn, Stangeland, Livingston, Lewis, Royer.

WATER RESOURCES
Roberts, Chairman

Majority 17 D): Roberts, McCormack, Breaux, Ambro, Young, Bonior, Flippo, Hutto, Albosta, Leath, Howard, Oberstar, Nowak, Ertel, Ferraro, Donnelly, Anderson.
Minority (8 R): Clausen, Synder, Abdnor, Taylor, Livingston, Gingrich, Solomon, Lewis.

RULES
Bolling (Mo.), Chairman

Democratic Majority (11 D): Bolling, Pepper (Fla.), Murphy (Ill.), Long (La.), Moakley (Mass.), Chisholm (N.Y.), Dodd (Conn.), Zeferetti (N.Y.), Derrick (S.C.), Beilenson (Calif.), Frost (Texas).
Republican Minority (5 R): Qullen (Tenn.), Anderson (Ill.), Latta (Ohio), Lott (Miss.), Bauman (Md.).

Subcommittees

RULES OF THE HOUSE
Moakley, Chairman

Majority (4 D): Moakley, Dodd, Beilenson, Frost.
Minority (2 R): Anderson, Bauman.

THE LEGISLATIVE PROCESS
Long, Chairman

Majority (4 D): Long, Chisholm, Zeferetti, Derrick.
Minority (1 R): Lott.

SCIENCE AND TECHNOLOGY
Fuqua (Fla.), Chairman

Democratic Majority (27 D): Fuqua, Roe (N.J.), McCormack (Wash.), Brown (Calif.), Scheuer (N.Y.), Ottinger (N.Y.), Harkin (Iowa), Lloyd (Calif.), Ambro (N.Y.), Bouquard (Tenn.), Blanchard (Mich.), Walgren (Penn.), Flippo (Ala.), Glickman (Kan.), Gore (Tenn.), Watkins (Okla.), Young (Mo.), White (Texas), Volkmer (Mo.), Pease (Ohio), Wolpe (Mich.), Mavroules (Mass.), Nelson (Fla.), Anthony (Ark.), Lundine (N.Y.), Ertel (Penn.), Hance (Texas).
Republican Minority (15 R): Wydler (N.Y.), Winn (Kan.), Goldwater (Calif.), Fish (N.Y.), Lujan (N.M.), Hollenbeck (N.J.), Dornan (Calif.), Walker (Penn.), Forsythe (N.J.), Kramer (Colo.), Carney (N.Y.), Davis (Mich.), Roth (Wis.), Ritter (Penn.).

Subcommittees

ENERGY DEVELOPMENT AND APPLICATIONS
Ottinger, Chairman

Majority (16 D): Ottinger, Blanchard, Walgren, Glickman, Gore, Young, White, Volkmer, Wolpe, Mavroules, Nelson, Anthony, Ertel, Hance, Roe, McCormack.
Minority (8 R): Fish, Kramer, Carney, Ritter, Davis, Wydler, Dornan, Walker.

ENERGY RESEARCH AND PRODUCTION
McCormack. Chairman

Majority (11 D): McCormack, Bouquard, Roe, Lundine, Young, White, Wolpe, Flippo, Mavroules, Ottinger, Anthony.
Minority (6 R): Wydler, Forsythe, Roth, Goldwater, Lujan, Hollenbeck.

INVESTIGATIONS AND OVERSIGHT
Lloyd, Chairman

Majority (5 D): Lloyd, Ambro, Flippo, Gore, Nelson.
Minority (3 R): Lujan, Carney, Roth.

NATURAL RESOURCES AND ENVIRONMENT
Ambro, Chairman

Majority (5 D): Ambro, Brown, Blanchard, Watkins, Lundine.
Minority (3 R): Walker, Ritter, Forsythe.

SCIENCE, RESEARCH AND TECHNOLOGY
Brown, Chairman

Majority (7 D): Brown, Scheuer, Pease, Harkin, Ertel, Hance, Watkins.
Minority (3 R): Hollenbeck, Davis, Ritter.

SPACE SCIENCE AND APPLICATIONS
Fuqua, Chairman

Majority (6 D): Fuqua, Flippo, Watkins, Bouquard, Nelson, Brown.
Minority (3 R): Winn, Dornan, Kramer.

TRANSPORTATION, AVIATION AND COMMUNICATION
Harkin, Chairman

Majority (6 D): Harkin, Lloyd, Walgren, Glickman, Mavroules, Volkmer.
Minority (3 R): Goldwater, Dornan, Winn.

SMALL BUSINESS
Neal Smith (Iowa), Chairman

Democratic Majority (25 D): Smith, Steed (Okla.), Dingell (Mich.), Corman (Calif.), Addabbo (N.Y.), St Germain (R.I.), Mitchell (Md.), Gonzalez (Texas), Hanley (N.Y.), LaFalce (N.Y.), Bedell (Iowa), Richmond (N.Y.), Russo (Ill.), Baldus (Wis.), Nolan (Minn.), Ichord (Mo.), Nowak (N.Y.), Luken (Ohio), Ireland (Fla.), Kildee (Mich.), Skelton (Mo.), Evans (Ga.), Barnard (Ga.), Leach (La.), Hall (Ohio).
Republican Minority (14 R): McDade (Penn.), Conte (Mass.), Stanton (Ohio), Broomfield (Mich.), Carter (Ky.), Quayle (Ind.), Marriott (Utah), Roth (Wis.), Williams (Ohio), Snowe (Me.), Bereuter (Neb.), Bethune (Ark.), Erdahl (Minn.), Tauke (Iowa).

Subcommittees

ACCESS TO EQUITY CAPITAL AND BUSINESS OPPORTUNITIES
Nowak, Chairman

Majority (6 D): Nowak, Steed, Mitchell, Richmond, Bedel, Leach.
Minority (3 R): Stanton, Roth, Williams.

ANTITRUST AND RESTRAINT OF TRADE ACTIVITIES AFFECTING SMALL BUSINESS
Bedell, Chairman

Majority (6 D): Bedell, Hanley, Gonzalez, Ichord, Hall, Steed.
Minority (3 R): Quayle, Snowe, Tauke.

GENERAL OVERSIGHT AND MINORITY ENTERPRISE
LaFalce, Chairman

Majority (6 D): LaFalce, Corman, Addabbo, Mitchell, Gonzalez, Richmond.
Minority (3 R): Carter, Williams, Bereuter.

IMPACT OF ENERGY PROGRAMS, ENVIRONMENT AND SAFETY REQUIREMENTS AND GOVERNMENT RESEARCH ON SMALL BUSINESS
Luken, Chairman

Majority (6 D): Luken, Dingell, Baldus, Kildee, Ireland, Skelton.
Minority (3 R): Conte, Bereuter, Erdahl.

SBA AND SBIC AUTHORITY AND GENERAL SMALL BUSINESS PROBLEMS
Smith, Chairman

Majority (8 D): Smith, St Germain, Nolan, Ichord, Evans, Barnard, Leach, Hall.
Minority (4 R): McDade, Marriott, Roth, Bethune.

SPECIAL SMALL BUSINESS PROBLEMS
Russo, Chairman

Majority (6 D): Russo, Ireland, Skelton, Addabbo, Kildee, Evans.
Minority (3 R): Broomfield, Marriott, Bethune.

STANDARDS OF OFFICIAL CONDUCT
Charles Bennett (Fla.), Chairman

Democratic Majority (6 D): Bennett, Hamilton (Ind.), Preyer (N.C.), Slack (W. Va.), Murphy (Ill.), Murtha (Penn.).
Republican Minority (6 R): Spence (S.C.), Hollenbeck (N.J.), Livingston (La.), Thomas (Calif.), Sensenbrenner (Wis.), Cheney (Wyo.).

No Subcommittees

VETERANS' AFFAIRS
Ray Roberts (Texas), Chairman

Democratic Majority (21 D): Roberts, Satterfield (Va.), Edwards (Calif.), Montgomery (Miss.), Danielson (Calif.), Wolff (N.Y.), Brinkley (Ga.), Mottl (Ohio), Hefner (N.C.), Edgar (Penn.), Hall (Texas), Applegate (Ohio), Leath (Texas), Boner (Tenn.), Gramm (Texas), Shelby (Ala.), Mica (Fla.), Daschle (S.D.), Coelho (Calif.).
Republican Minority (11 R): Hammerschmidt (Ark.), Heckler (Mass.), Wylie (Ohio), Hillis (Ind.), Abdnor (S.D.), Guyer (Ohio). Hansen (Idaho), Sawyer (Mich.), Grisham (Calif.), Deckard (Ind.), Lee (N.Y.).

Subcommittees

COMPENSATION, PENSION, INSURANCE, AND MEMORIAL AFFAIRS
Montgomery, Chairman

Majority (9 D): Montgomery, Danielson, Brinkley, Edgar, Hall, Applegate, Gramm, Mica, Coelho.
Minority (5 R): Wylie, Hammerschmidt, Guyer, Hillis, Hansen.

EDUCATION, TRAINING AND EMPLOYMENT
Hefner, Chairman

Majority (6 D): Hefner, Roberts, Leath, Boner, Gramm, Daschle.
Minority (4 R): Heckler, Wylie, Sawyer, Grisham.

HOUSING
Brinkley, Chairman

Majority (4 D): Brinkley, Roberts, Edwards, Shelby.
Minority (3 R): Abdnor, Grisham, Lee.

MEDICAL FACILITIES AND BENEFITS
Satterfield, Chairman

Majority (16 D): Satterfield, Edwards, Montgomery, Danielson, Wolff, Mottl, Hefner, Edgar, Hall, Leath, Boner, Gramm, Shelby, Mica, Daschle, Coelho.
Minority (9 R): Hammerschmidt, Heckler, Abdnor, Guyer, Hansen, Sawyer, Wylie, Lee, Deckard.

SPECIAL INVESTIGATIONS
Mottl, Chairman

Majority (5 D): Mottle, Satterfield, Woff, Mica, Applegate.
Minority (4 R): Hillis, Hammerschmidt, Heckler, Deckard.

WAYS AND MEANS
Al Ullman (Ore.), Chairman

Democratic Majority (24 D): Ullman, Rostenkowski (Ill.), Vanik (Ohio), Corman (Calif.), Gibbons (Fla.), Pickle (Texas), Rangel (N.Y.), Cotter (Conn.), Stark (Calif.), Jones (Okla.), Jacobs (Ind.), Mikva (Ill.), Fisher (Va.), Ford (Tenn.), Holland (S.C.), Brodhead (Mich.), Jenkins (Ga.), Gephardt (Mo.), Lederer (Penn.), Downey (N.Y.), Heftel (Hawaii), Fowler (Ga.), Guarini (N.J.), Shannon (Mass.).
Republican Minority (12 R): Conable (N.Y.), Duncan (Tenn.), Archer (Texas), Vander Jagt (Mich.), P. Crane (Ill.), Frenzel (Minn.), Martin (N.C.), Bafalis (Fla.), Schulze (Penn.), Gradison (Ohio), Rousselot (Calif.), Moore (La.).

Subcommittees

HEALTH
Rangel, Chairman

Majority (6 D): Rangel, Corman, Vanik, Ford, Heftel, Shannon.
Minority (3 R): Crane, Duncan, Martin.

OVERSIGHT
Gibbons, Chairman

Majority (6 D): Gibbons, Pickle, Ford, Jacobs, Jenkins, Heftel.
Minority (3 R): Gradison, Moore, Duncan.

PUBLIC ASSISTANCE AND UNEMPLOYMENT COMPENSATION
Corman, Chairman

Majority (6 D): Corman, Rangel, Stark, Brodhead, Downey, Fowler.
Minority (3 R): Rousselot, Bafalis, Crane.

SELECT REVENUE MEASURES
Rostenkowski, Chairman

Majority (6 D): Rostenkowski, Lederer, Holland, Stark, Fowler, Guarini.
Minority (3 R): Duncan, Schulze, Vander Jagt.

SOCIAL SECURITY
Pickle, Chairman

Majority (6 D): Pickle, Jacobs, Cotter, Mikva, Gephardt, Fisher.
Minority (3 R): Archer, Gradison, Rousselot.

TRADE
Vanik, Chairman

Majority (14 D): Vanik, Gibbons, Rostenkowski, Jones, Mikva, Fisher, Holland, Jenkins, Downey, Cotter, Lederer, Guarini, Shannon, Ullman.
Minority (7 R): Vander Jagt, Archer, Frenzel, Martin, Bafalis, Schulze, Moore.

Maps

ALABAMA
(7 districts)

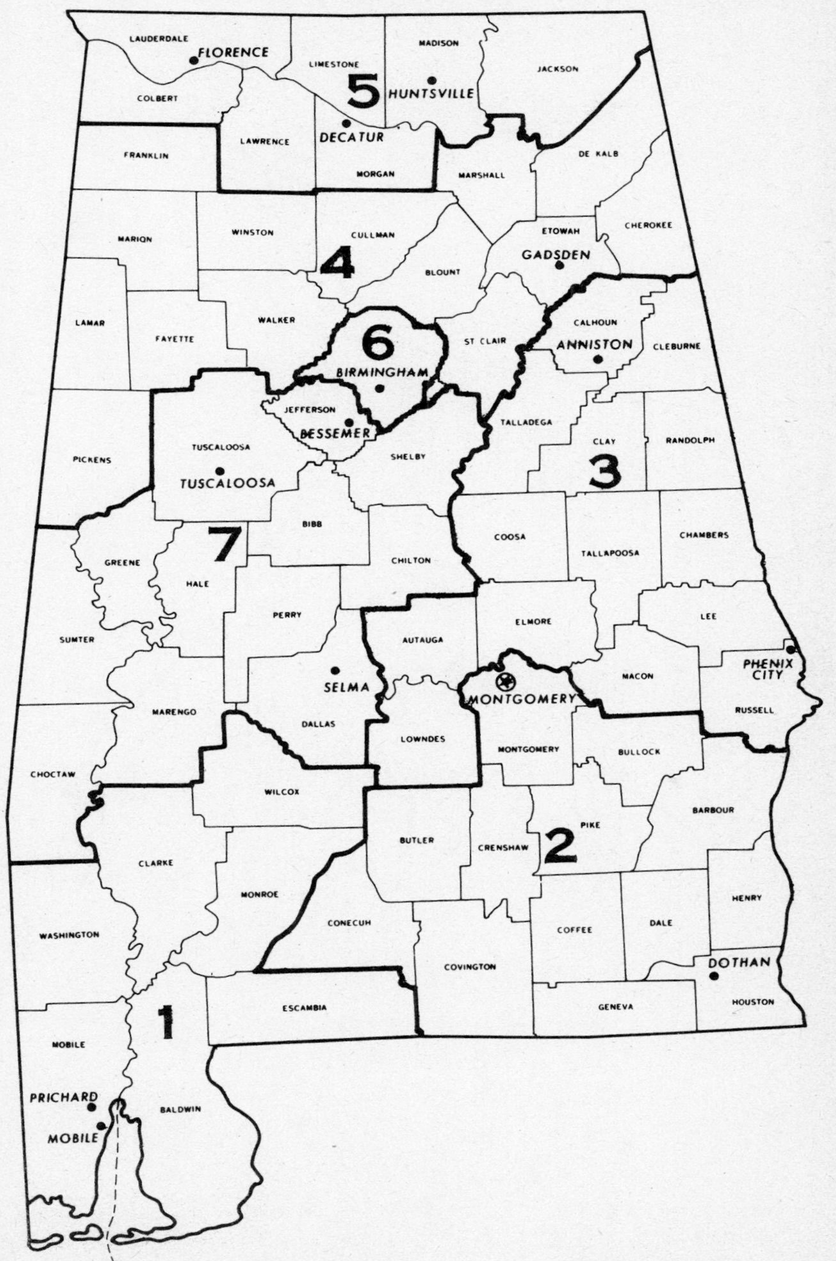

ALASKA

(1 at large)

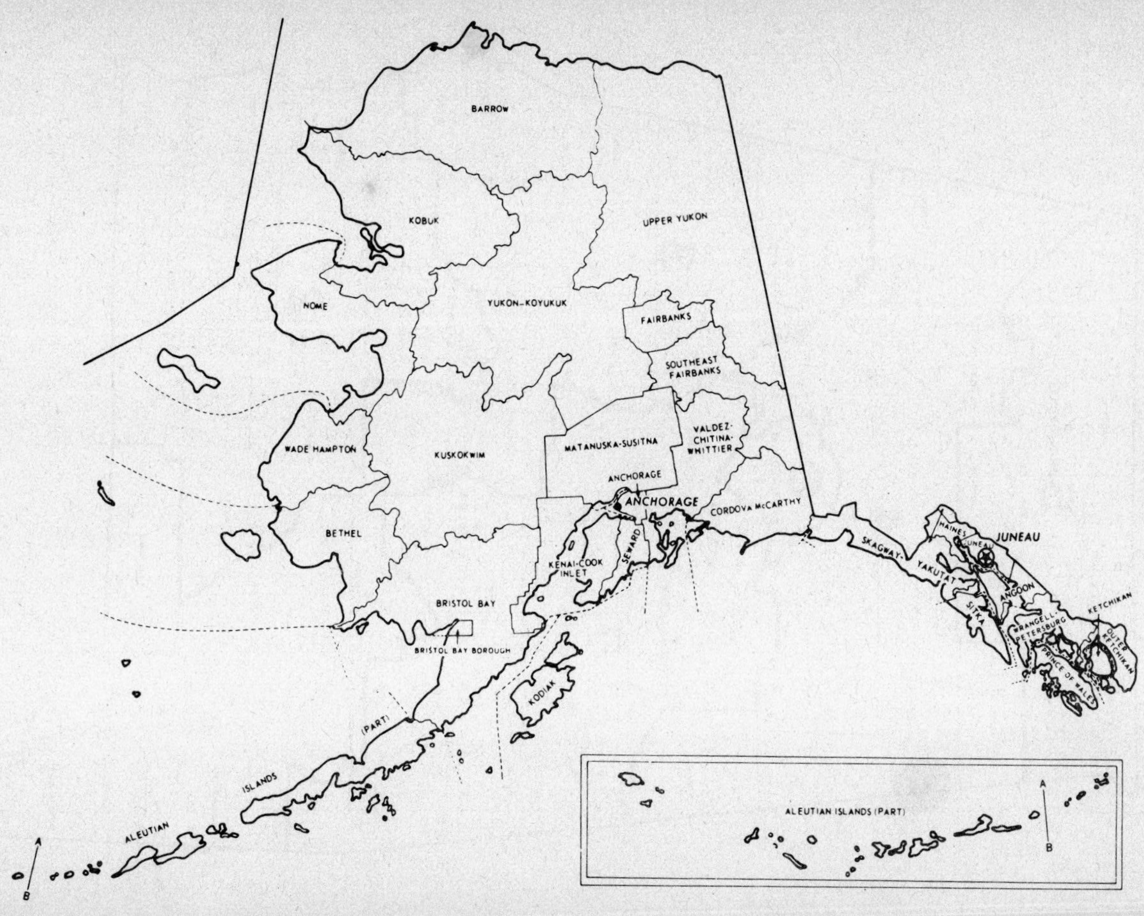

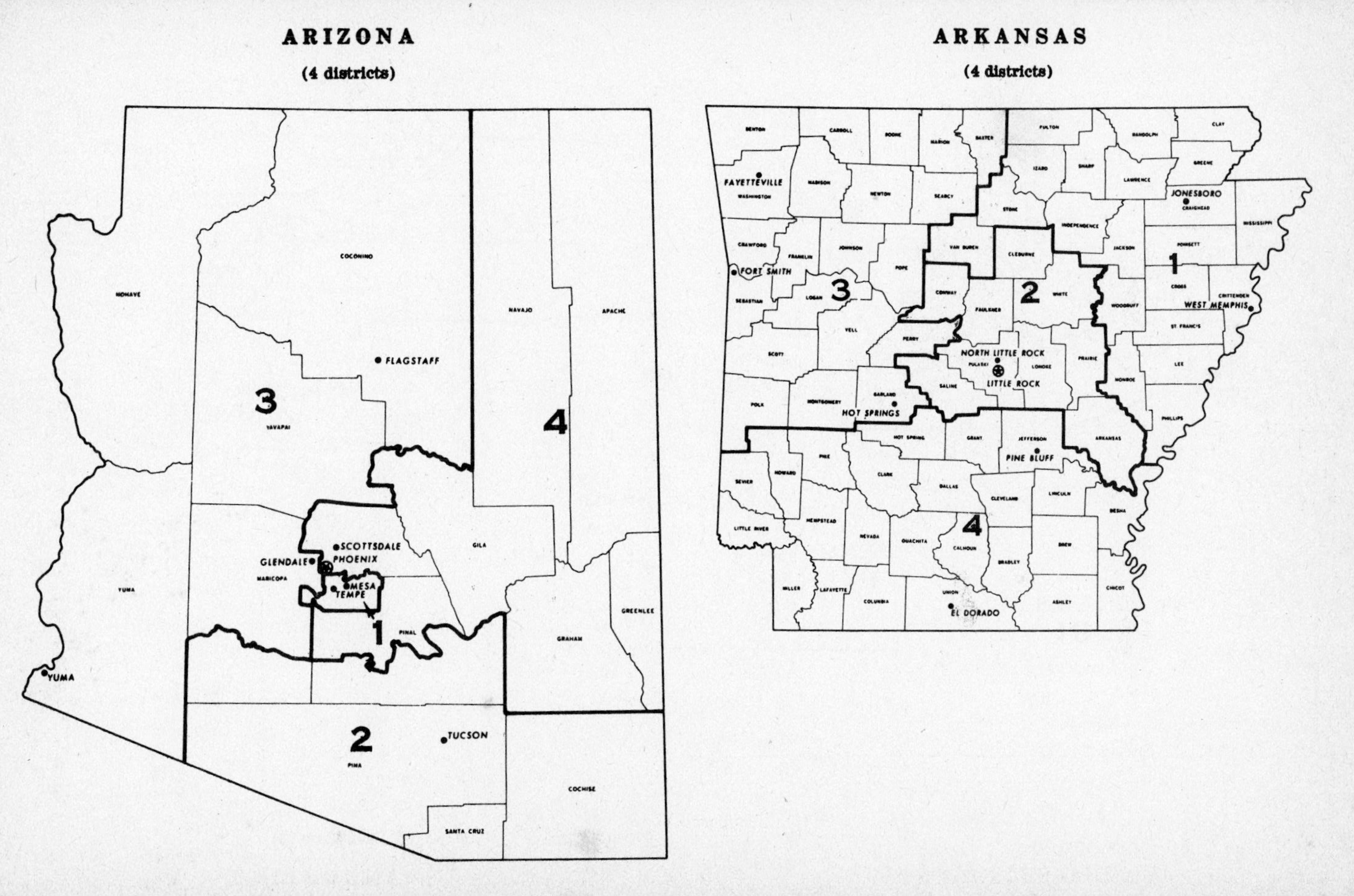
ARIZONA
(4 districts)
1
2
3
4
MOHAVE
COCONINO
NAVAJO
APACHE
YAVAPAI
GILA
MARICOPA
YUMA
PINAL
GRAHAM
GREENLEE
PIMA
COCHISE
SANTA CRUZ
FLAGSTAFF
SCOTTSDALE
GLENDALE
PHOENIX
MESA
TEMPE
TUCSON
YUMA
ARKANSAS
(4 districts)
1
2
3
4
BENTON
CARROLL
BOONE
MARION
BAXTER
FULTON
RANDOLPH
CLAY
GREENE
IZARD
SHARP
LAWRENCE
WASHINGTON
MADISON
NEWTON
SEARCY
STONE
INDEPENDENCE
CRAIGHEAD
MISSISSIPPI
CRAWFORD
FRANKLIN
JOHNSON
POPE
VAN BUREN
CLEBURNE
JACKSON
POINSETT
SEBASTIAN
LOGAN
CONWAY
FAULKNER
WHITE
WOODRUFF
CROSS
CRITTENDEN
YELL
PERRY
ST. FRANCIS
SCOTT
PULASKI
LONOKE
PRAIRIE
LEE
SALINE
MONROE
POLK
MONTGOMERY
GARLAND
PHILLIPS
HOT SPRING
GRANT
JEFFERSON
ARKANSAS
SEVIER
HOWARD
PIKE
CLARK
DALLAS
CLEVELAND
LINCOLN
DESHA
LITTLE RIVER
HEMPSTEAD
NEVADA
OUACHITA
CALHOUN
BRADLEY
DREW
MILLER
LAFAYETTE
COLUMBIA
UNION
ASHLEY
CHICOT
FAYETTEVILLE
FORT SMITH
JONESBORO
WEST MEMPHIS
NORTH LITTLE ROCK
LITTLE ROCK
HOT SPRINGS
PINE BLUFF
EL DORADO

CALIFORNIA

(48 districts)

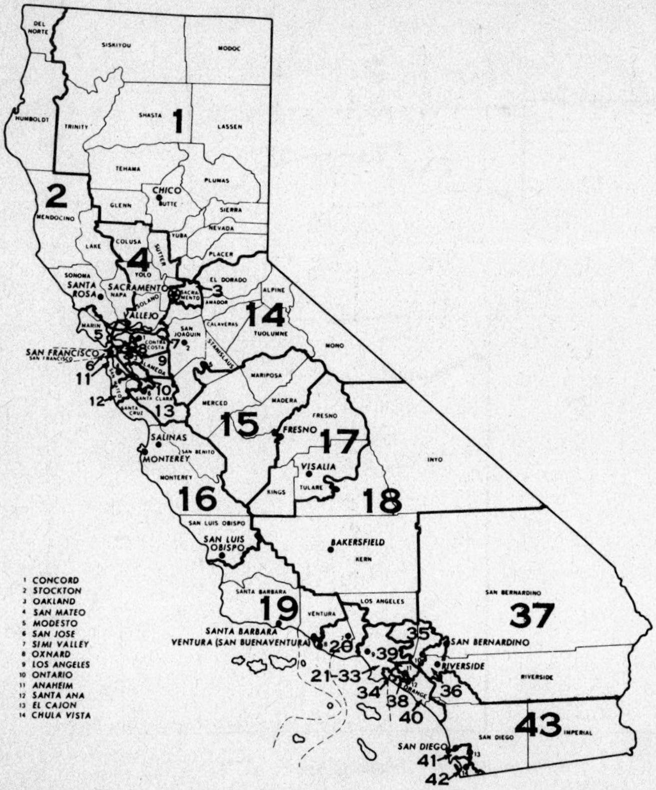

1 CONCORD
2 STOCKTON
3 OAKLAND
4 SAN MATEO
5 MODESTO
6 SAN JOSE
7 SIMI VALLEY
8 OXNARD
9 LOS ANGELES
10 ONTARIO
11 ANAHEIM
12 SANTA ANA
13 EL CAJON
14 CHULA VISTA

LOS ANGELES COUNTY

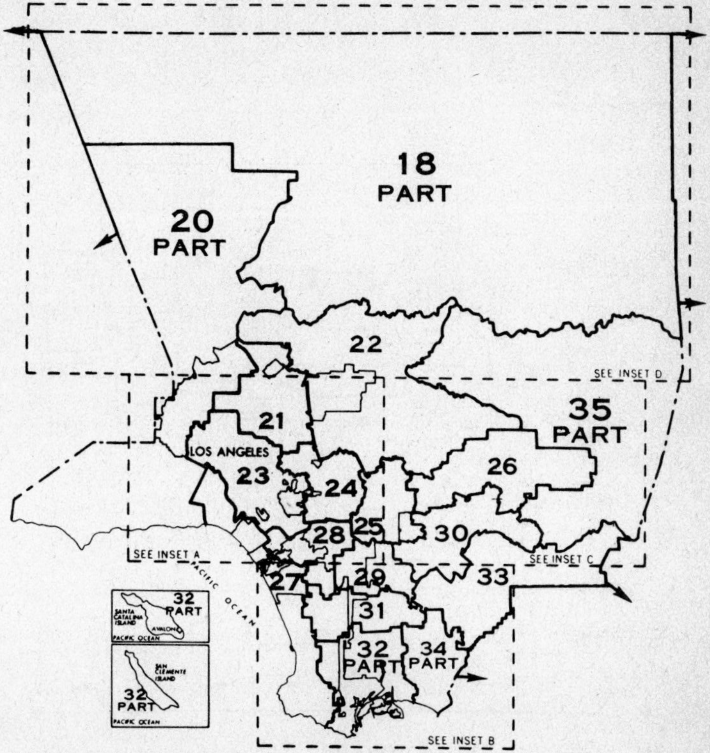

Districts established November 28, 1973

CONNECTICUT
(6 districts)

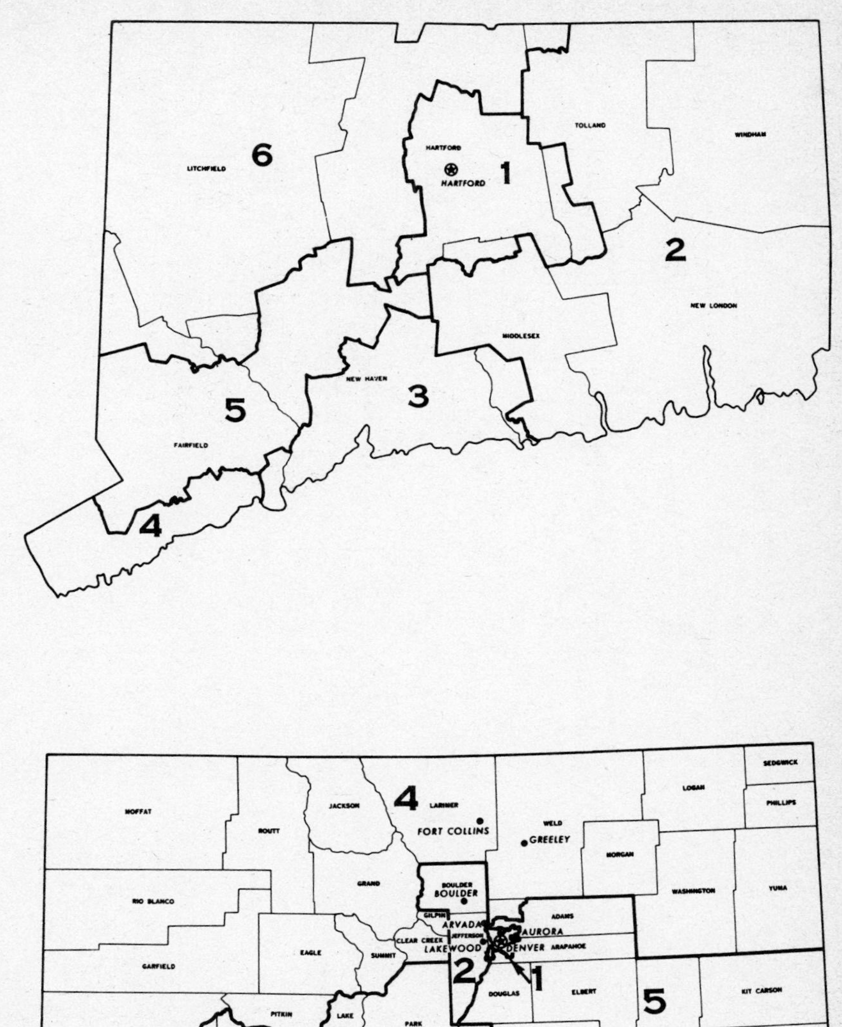

COLORADO
(5 districts)

DELAWARE

(1 at large)

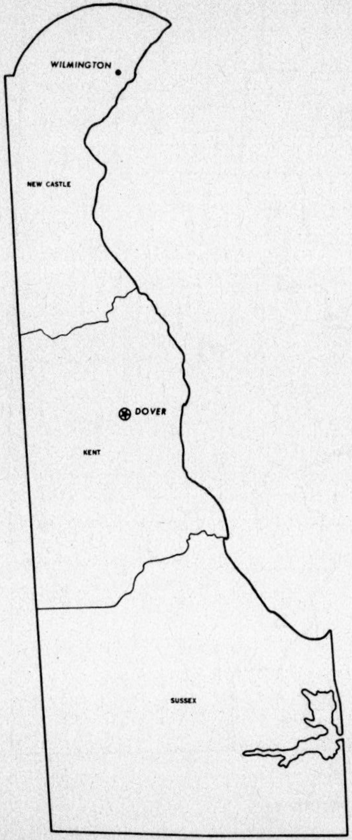

WILMINGTON
NEW CASTLE
DOVER
KENT
SUSSEX

FLORIDA

(15 districts)

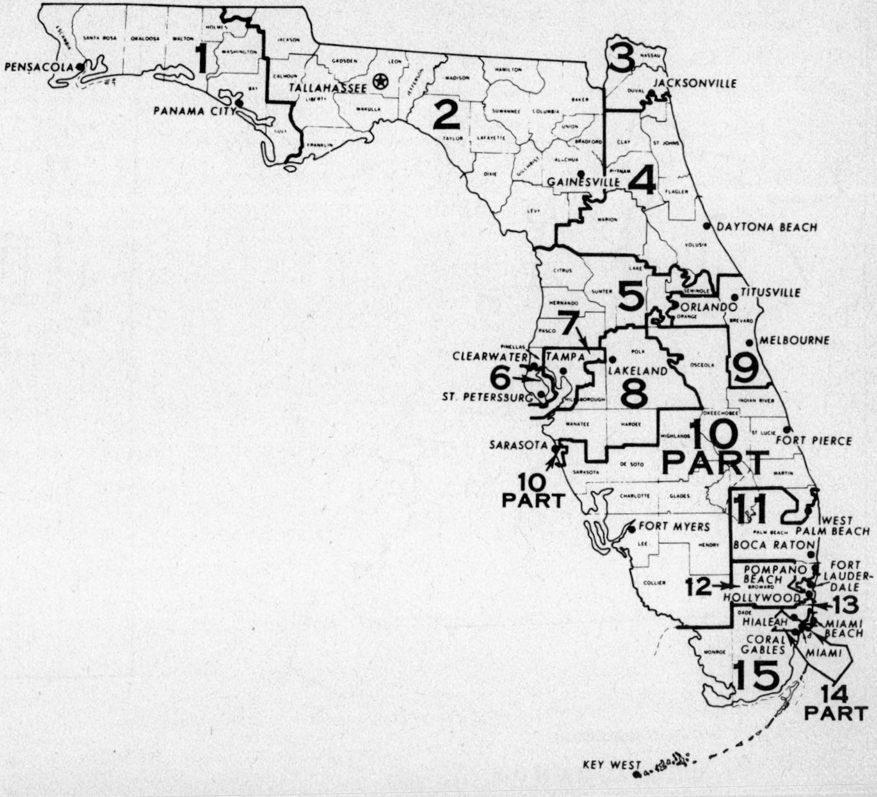

PENSACOLA
PANAMA CITY
TALLAHASSEE
JACKSONVILLE
GAINESVILLE
DAYTONA BEACH
TITUSVILLE
ORLANDO
MELBOURNE
CLEARWATER
TAMPA
LAKELAND
ST. PETERSBURG
SARASOTA
FORT PIERCE
FORT MYERS
WEST PALM BEACH
BOCA RATON
POMPANO BEACH
FORT LAUDERDALE
HOLLYWOOD
HIALEAH
MIAMI BEACH
CORAL GABLES
MIAMI
KEY WEST
1
2
3
4
5
6
7
8
9
10 PART
10 PART
11
12
13
14 PART
15

GEORGIA

(10 districts)

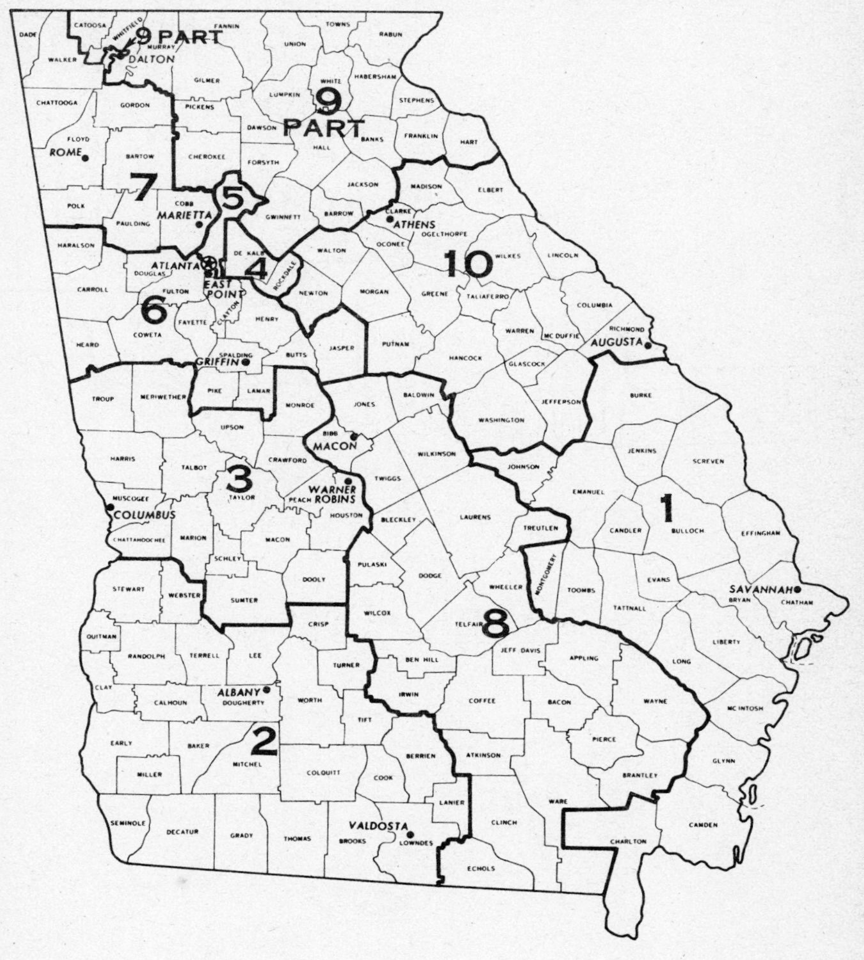

HAWAII

(2 districts)

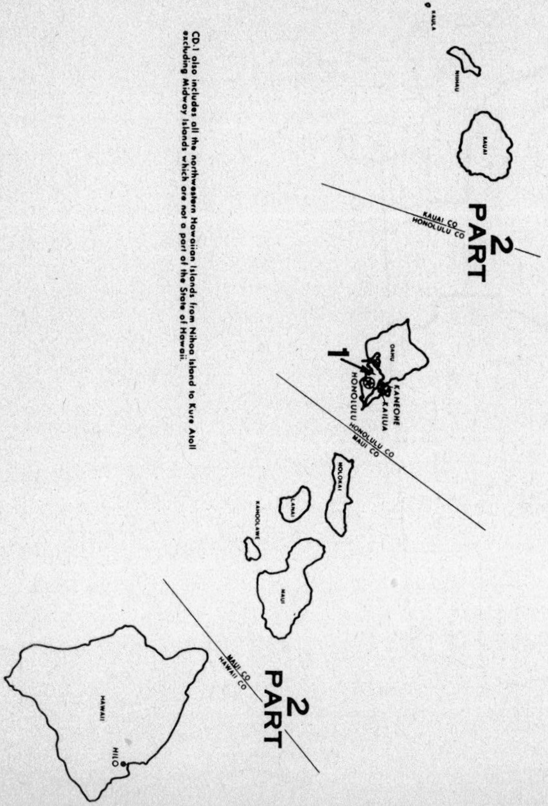

CD-1 also includes all the northwestern Hawaiian Islands from Nihoa Island to Kure Atoll excluding Midway Islands which are not a part of the State of Hawaii.

KAULA
NIIHAU
KAUAI
2 PART
KAUAI CO
HONOLULU CO
OAHU
1
HONOLULU
KANEOHE
KAILUA
HONOLULU CO
MAUI CO
MOLOKAI
LANAI
KAHOOLAWE
MAUI
2 PART
MAUI CO
HAWAII CO
HAWAII
HILO

IDAHO

(2 districts)

BOUNDARY
BONNER
KOOTENAI
SHOSHONE
BENEWAH
LATAH
CLEARWATER
NEZ PERCE
LEWISTOWN
LEWIS
IDAHO
1
ADAMS
VALLEY
WASHINGTON
PAYETTE
GEM
BOISE
CANYON
BOISE CITY
ADA
ELMORE
OWYHEE
LEMHI
CUSTER
CAMAS
BLAINE
BUTTE
2
CLARK
FREMONT
JEFFERSON
MADISON
TETON
IDAHO FALLS
BONNEVILLE
BINGHAM
GOODING
LINCOLN
JEROME
MINIDOKA
TWIN FALLS
CASSIA
POWER
POCATELLO
BANNOCK
CARIBOU
ONEIDA
FRANKLIN
BEAR LAKE

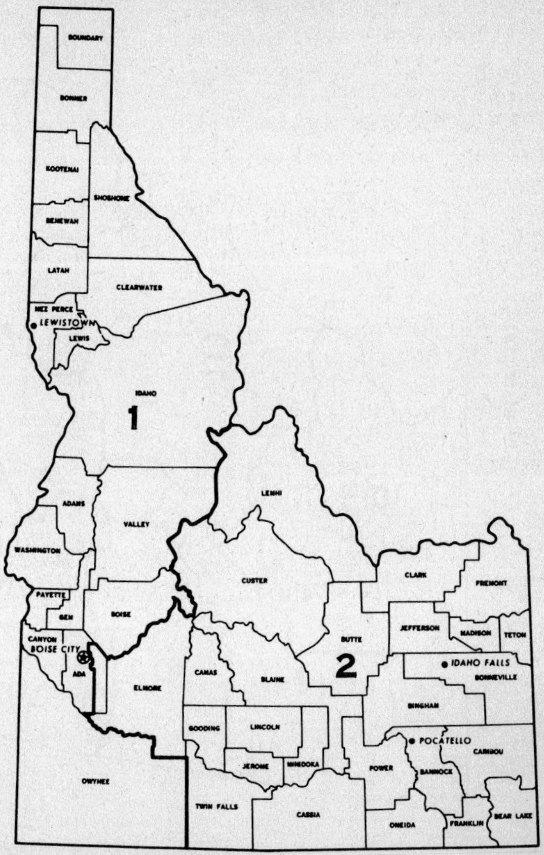

ILLINOIS

(24 districts)

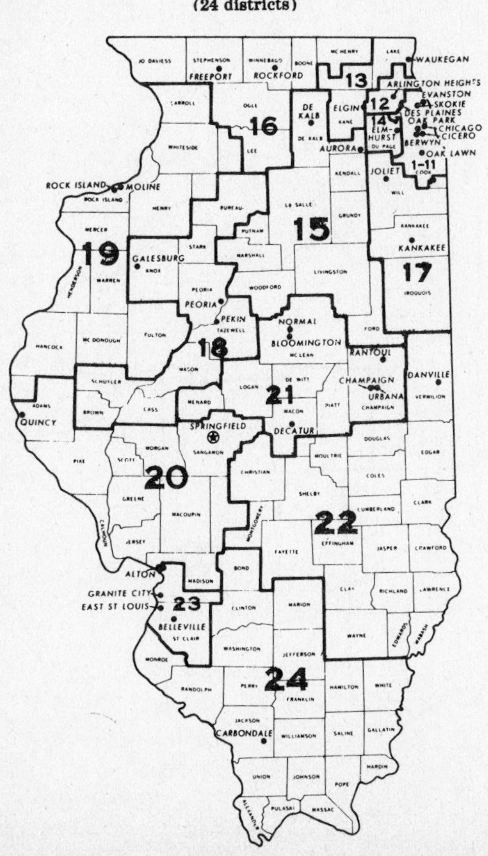

COOK AND DU PAGE COUNTIES

INDIANA

(11 districts)

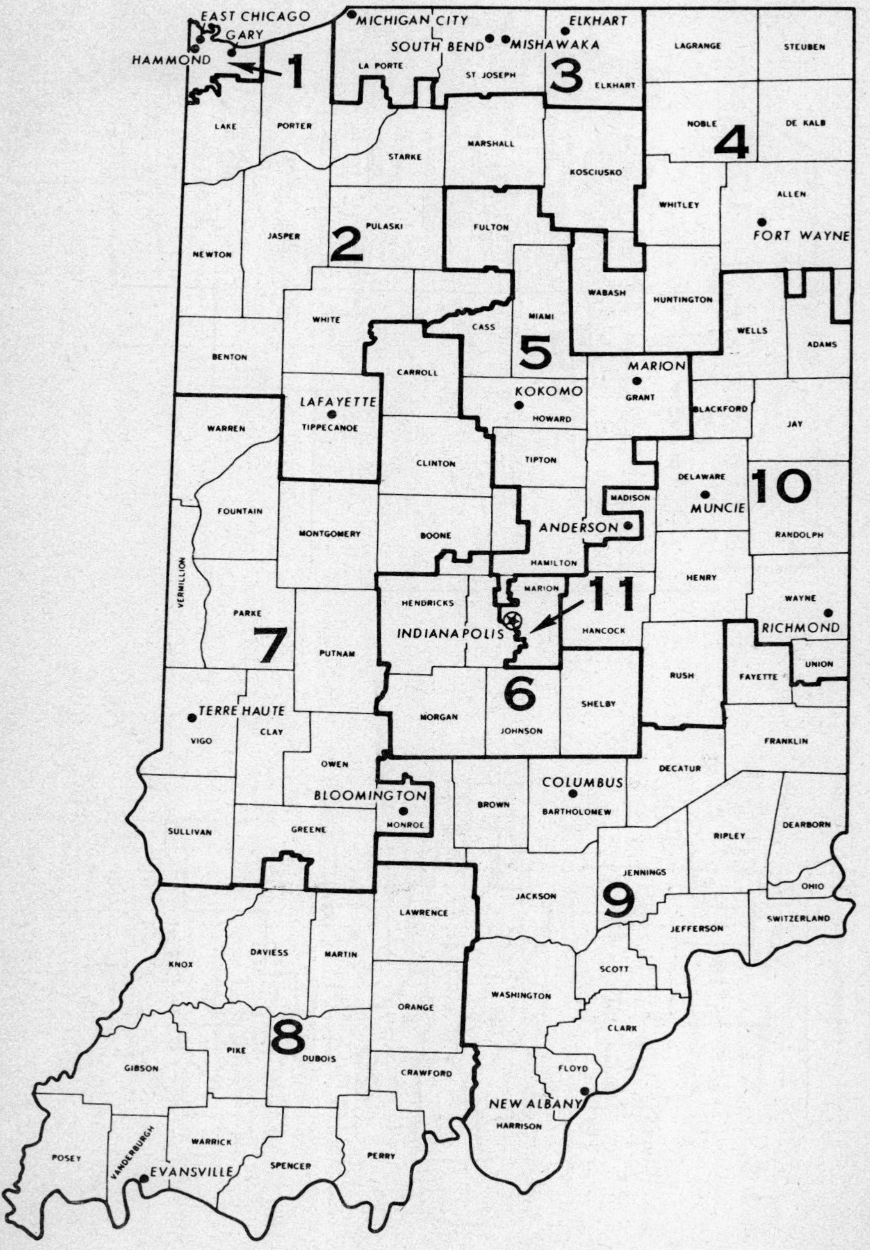

KANSAS
(5 districts)

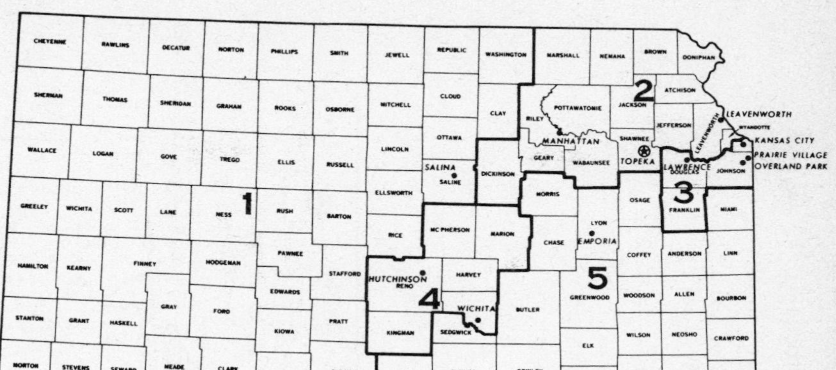

IOWA
(6 districts)

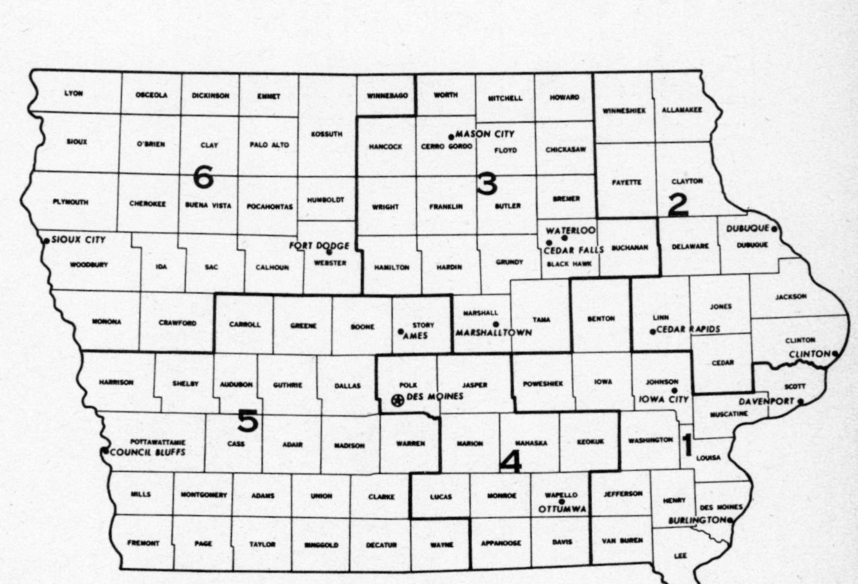

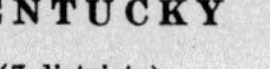

KENTUCKY

(7 districts)

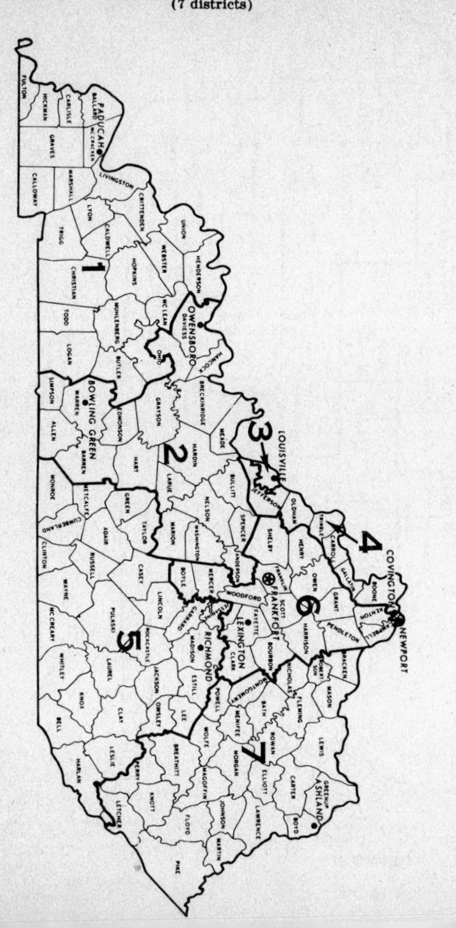

LOUISIANA

(8 districts)

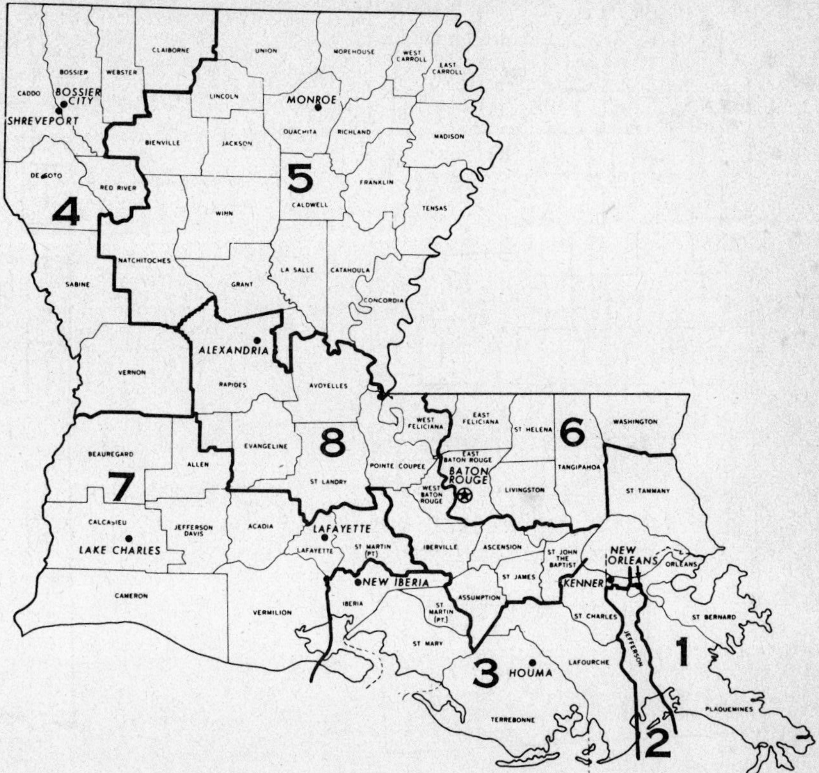

MAINE

(2 districts)

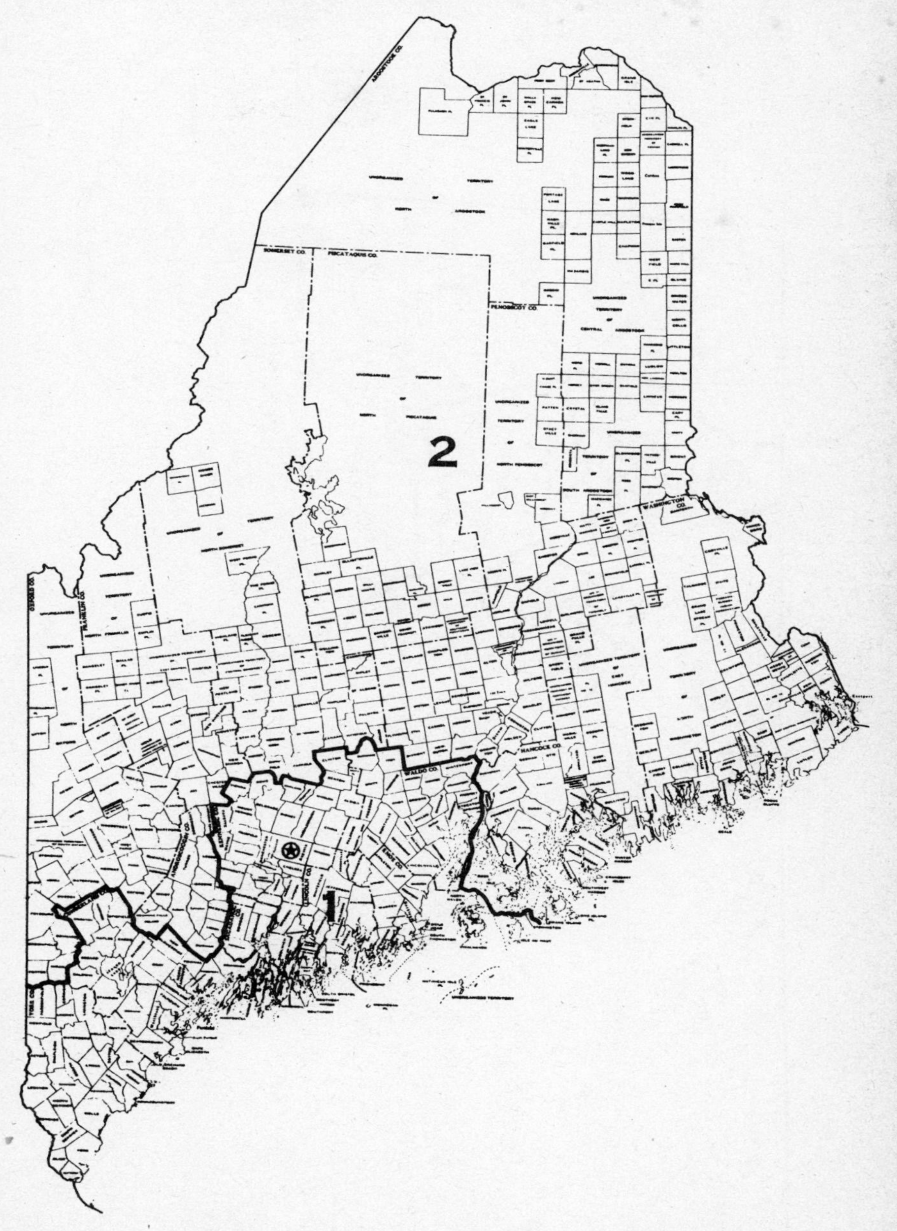

MARYLAND

(8 districts)

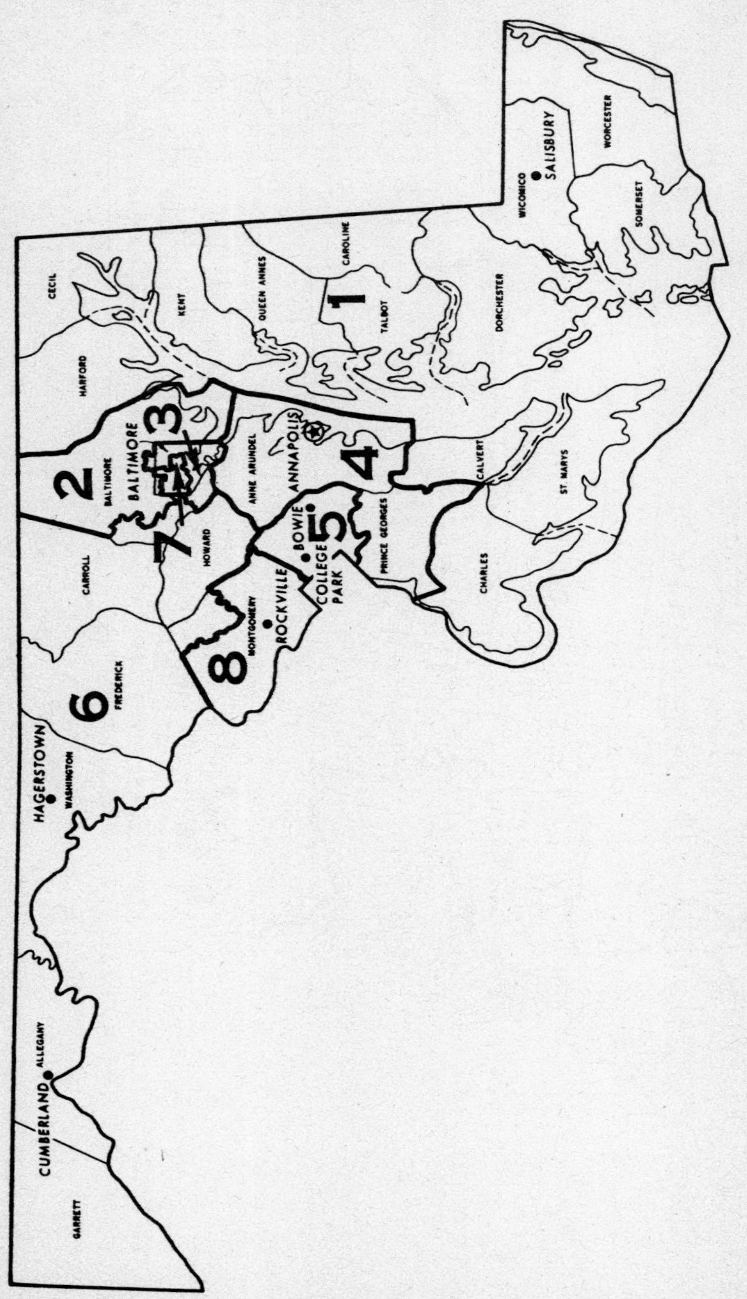

MASSACHUSETTS

(12 districts)

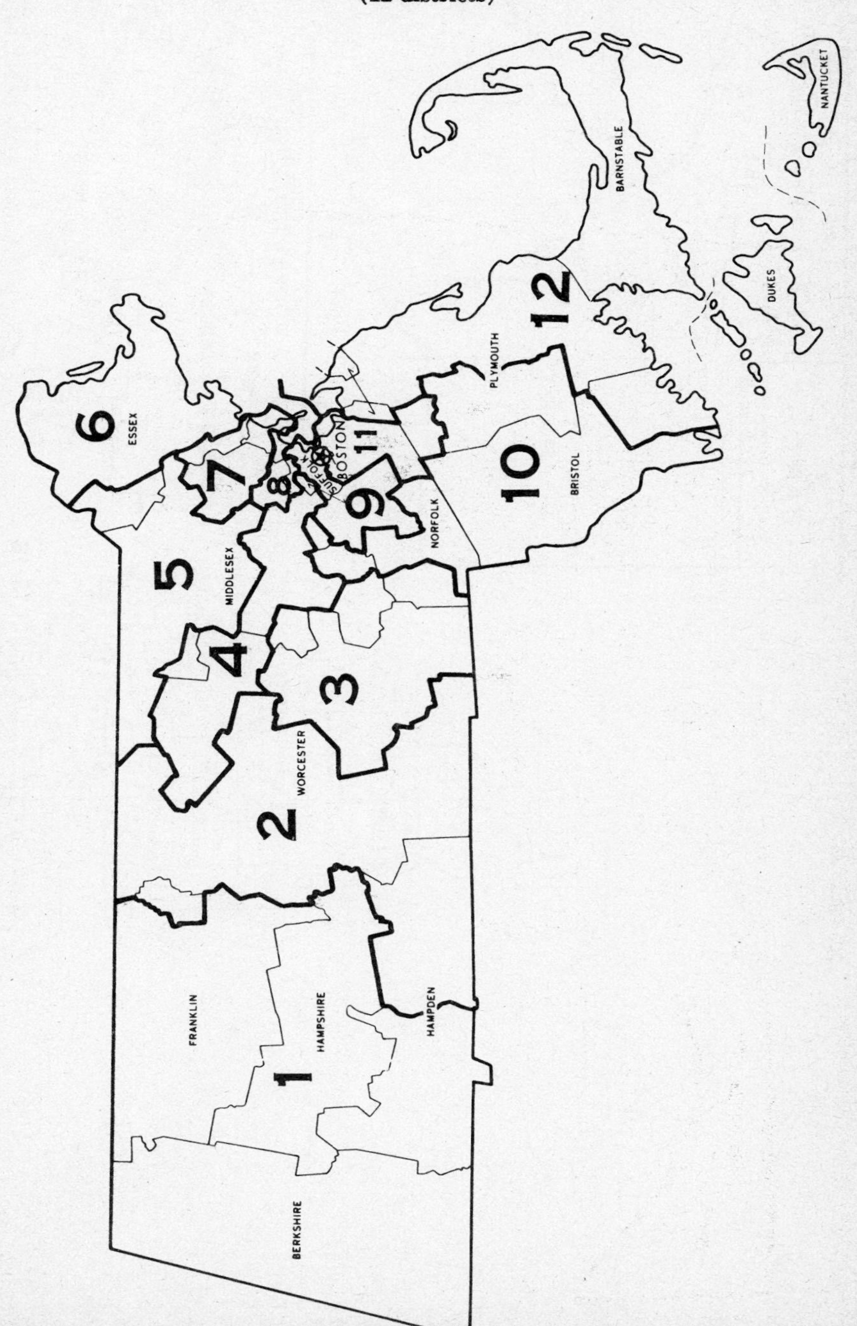

MICHIGAN

(19 districts)

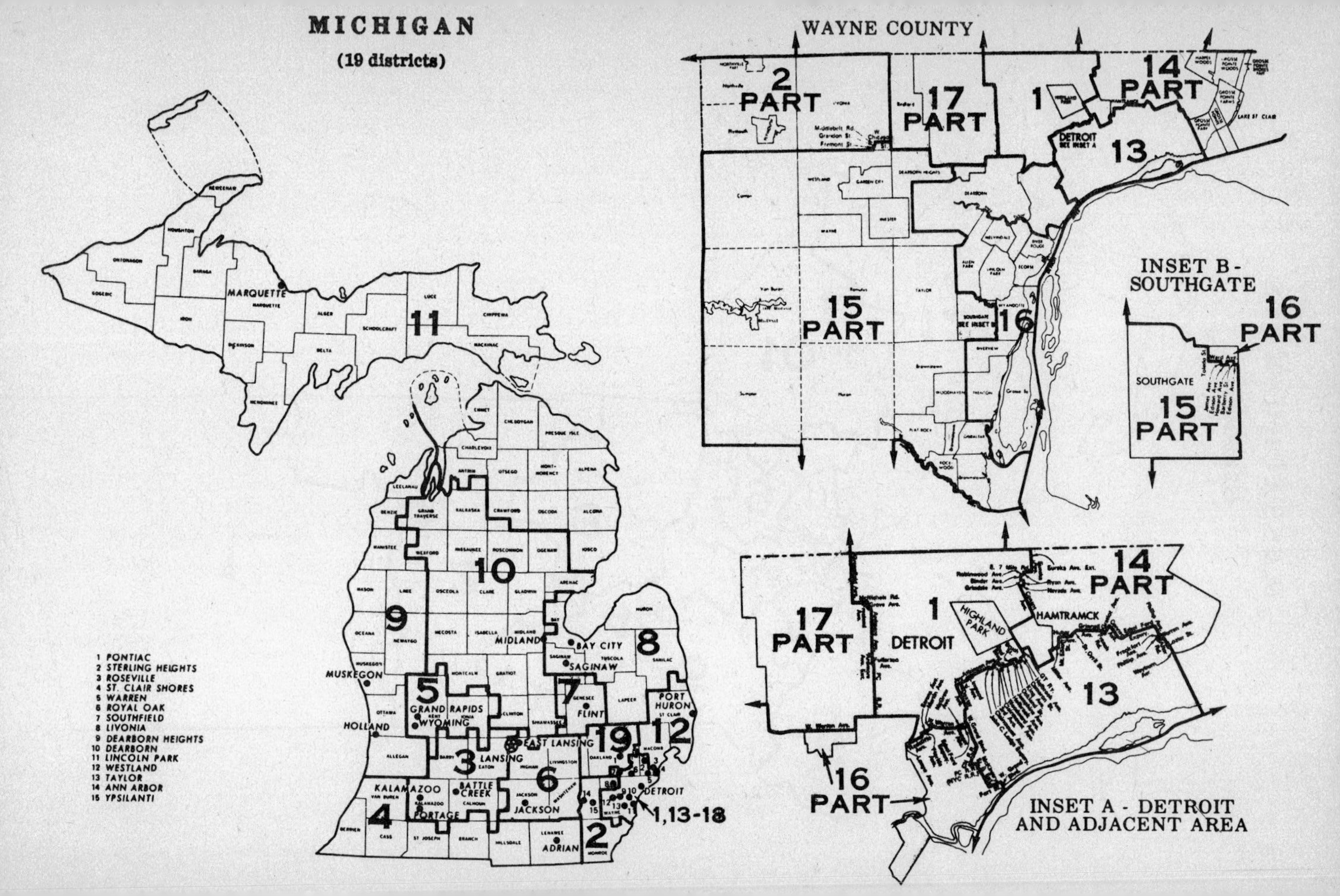

MINNESOTA

(8 districts)

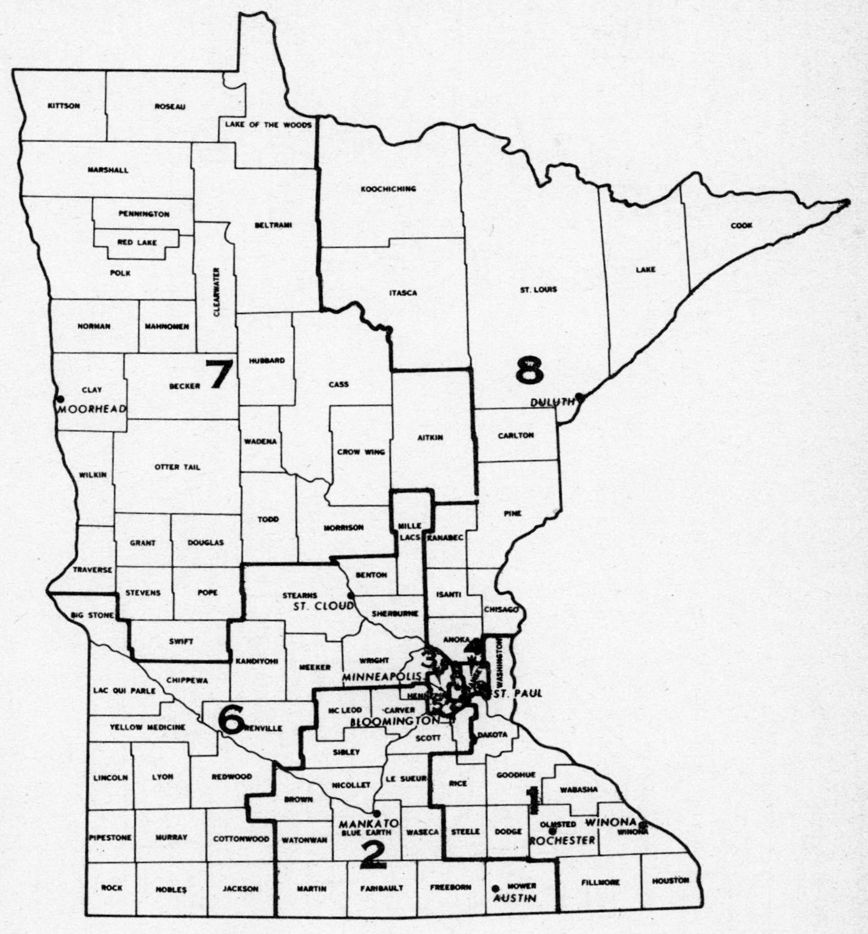

MISSOURI

(10 districts)

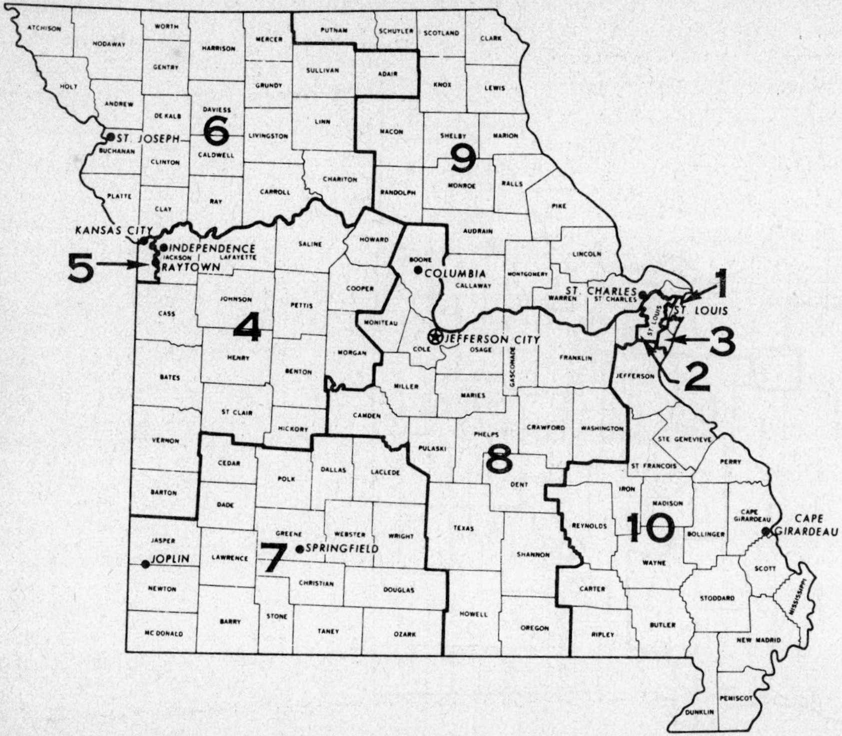

ATCHISON
NODAWAY
WORTH
HARRISON
MERCER
PUTNAM
SCHUYLER
SCOTLAND
CLARK
HOLT
ANDREW
GENTRY
GRUNDY
SULLIVAN
ADAIR
KNOX
LEWIS
DE KALB
DAVIESS
LIVINGSTON
LINN
MACON
SHELBY
MARION
ST. JOSEPH
BUCHANAN
CLINTON
CALDWELL
CHARITON
RANDOLPH
MONROE
RALLS
PIKE
PLATTE
CLAY
RAY
CARROLL
AUDRAIN
LINCOLN
KANSAS CITY
INDEPENDENCE
JACKSON
LAFAYETTE
RAYTOWN
SALINE
HOWARD
BOONE
COLUMBIA
CALLAWAY
MONTGOMERY
ST. CHARLES
WARREN
ST CHARLES
ST. LOUIS
ST LOUIS
CASS
JOHNSON
PETTIS
COOPER
MONITEAU
JEFFERSON CITY
COLE
OSAGE
GASCONADE
FRANKLIN
JEFFERSON
BATES
HENRY
BENTON
MORGAN
MILLER
MARIES
ST CLAIR
HICKORY
CAMDEN
PHELPS
CRAWFORD
WASHINGTON
STE GENEVIEVE
VERNON
CEDAR
POLK
DALLAS
LACLEDE
PULASKI
DENT
ST FRANCOIS
PERRY
IRON
MADISON
BARTON
DADE
REYNOLDS
CAPE GIRARDEAU
BOLLINGER
JASPER
GREENE
WEBSTER
WRIGHT
TEXAS
SHANNON
JOPLIN
LAWRENCE
SPRINGFIELD
WAYNE
SCOTT
NEWTON
CHRISTIAN
DOUGLAS
CARTER
STODDARD
MISSISSIPPI
MC DONALD
BARRY
STONE
TANEY
OZARK
HOWELL
OREGON
RIPLEY
BUTLER
NEW MADRID
PEMISCOT
DUNKLIN
1
2
3
4
5
6
7
8
9
10

MISSISSIPPI

(5 districts)

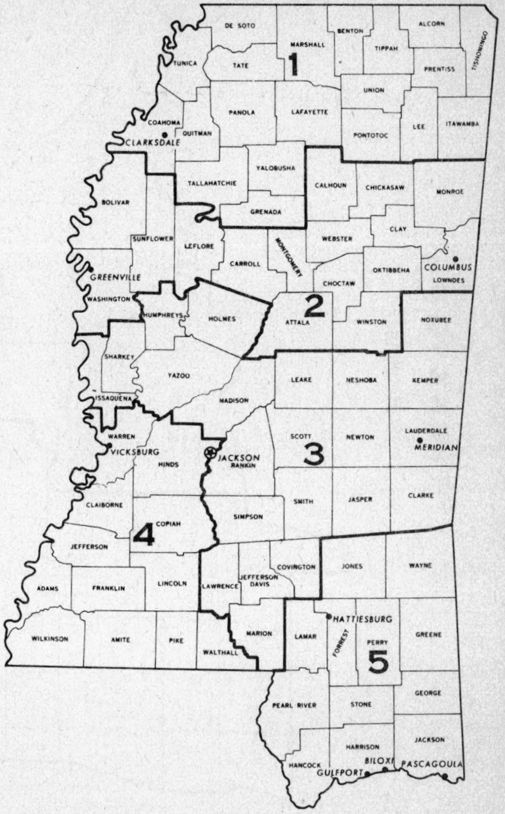

DE SOTO
MARSHALL
BENTON
TIPPAH
ALCORN
TISHOMINGO
PRENTISS
TUNICA
TATE
UNION
COAHOMA
CLARKSDALE
QUITMAN
PANOLA
LAFAYETTE
PONTOTOC
LEE
ITAWAMBA
TALLAHATCHIE
YALOBUSHA
CALHOUN
CHICKASAW
MONROE
BOLIVAR
GRENADA
SUNFLOWER
LEFLORE
CARROLL
MONTGOMERY
WEBSTER
CLAY
GREENVILLE
WASHINGTON
CHOCTAW
OKTIBBEHA
COLUMBUS
LOWNDES
HUMPHREYS
HOLMES
ATTALA
WINSTON
NOXUBEE
SHARKEY
YAZOO
LEAKE
NESHOBA
KEMPER
ISSAQUENA
MADISON
SCOTT
NEWTON
LAUDERDALE
MERIDIAN
WARREN
VICKSBURG
HINDS
JACKSON
RANKIN
CLAIBORNE
COPIAH
SIMPSON
SMITH
JASPER
CLARKE
JEFFERSON
COVINGTON
JONES
WAYNE
ADAMS
FRANKLIN
LINCOLN
LAWRENCE
JEFFERSON DAVIS
WILKINSON
AMITE
PIKE
WALTHALL
MARION
LAMAR
FORREST
HATTIESBURG
PERRY
GREENE
PEARL RIVER
STONE
GEORGE
HARRISON
JACKSON
HANCOCK
GULFPORT
BILOXI
PASCAGOULA
1
2
3
4
5

MONTANA

(2 discricts)

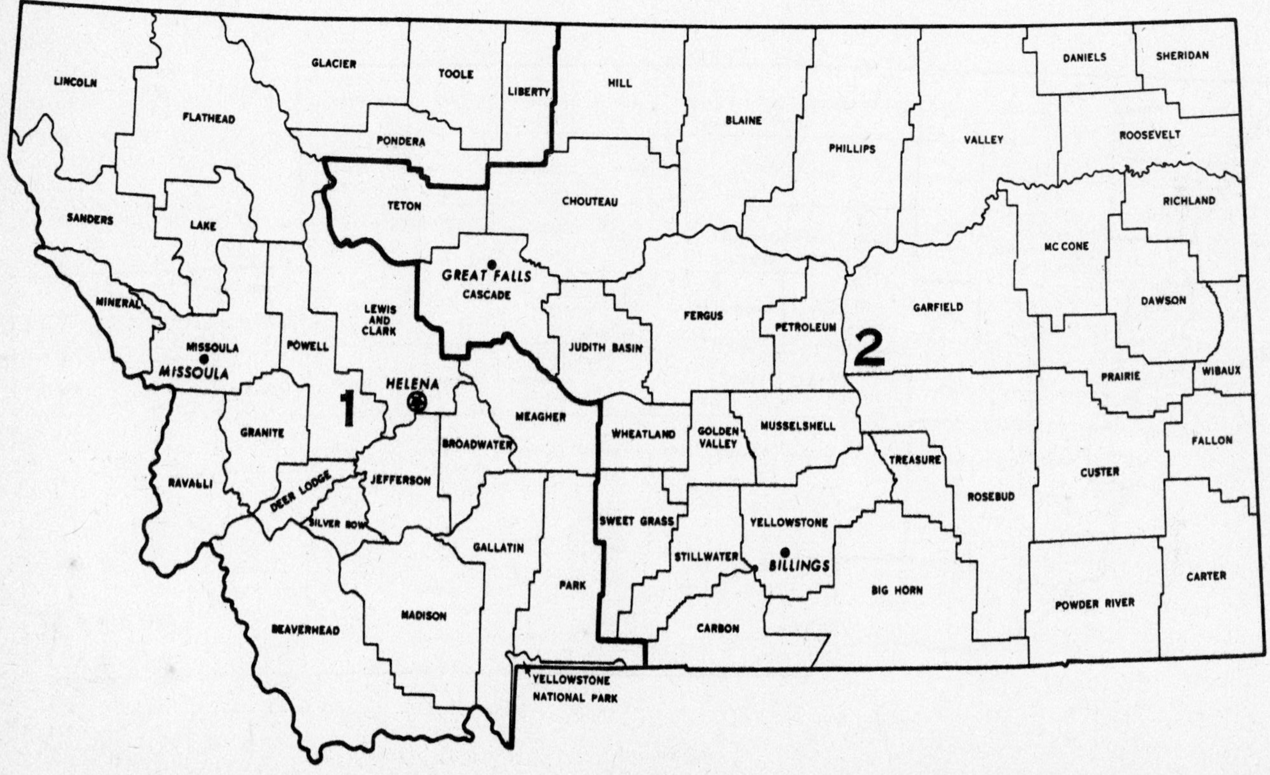

NEBRASKA

(3 districts)

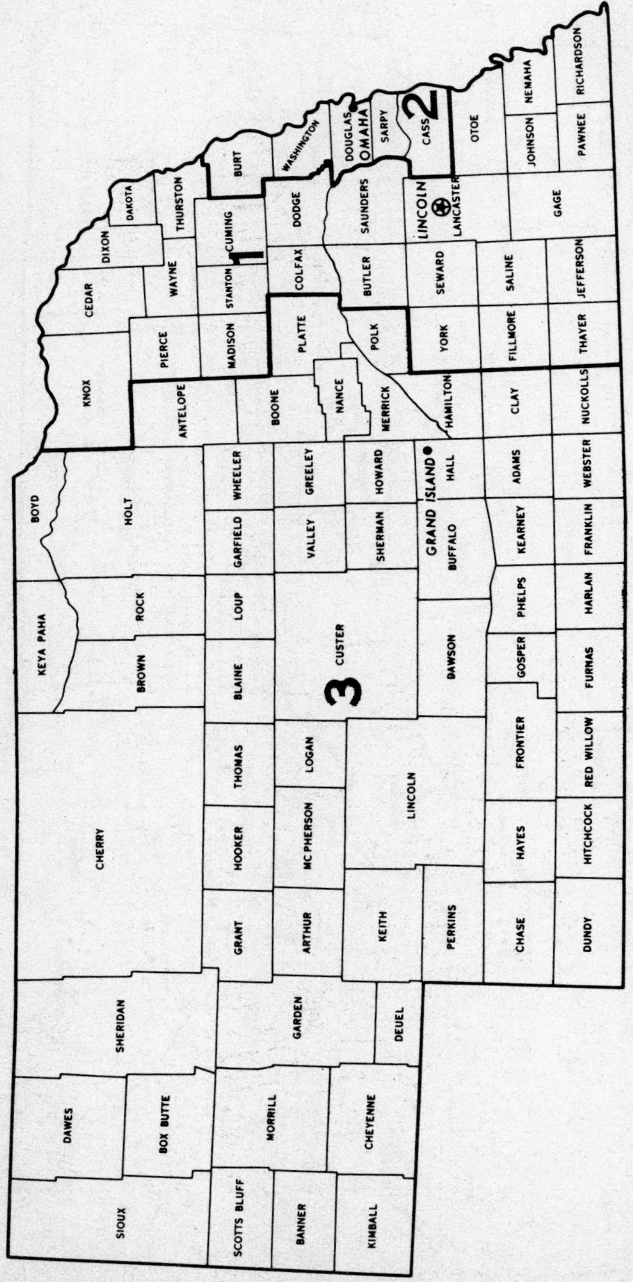

NEW HAMPSHIRE

(2 districts)

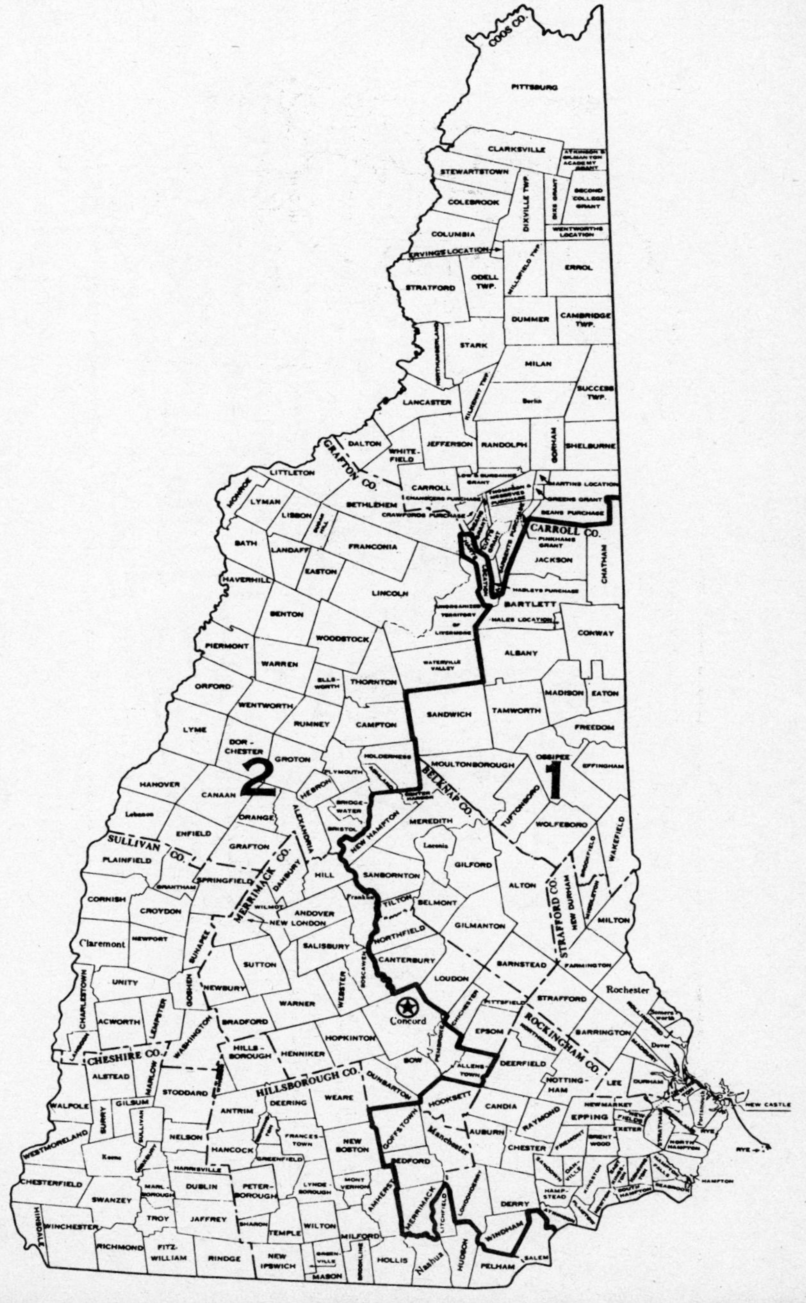

NEW JERSEY

(15 districts)

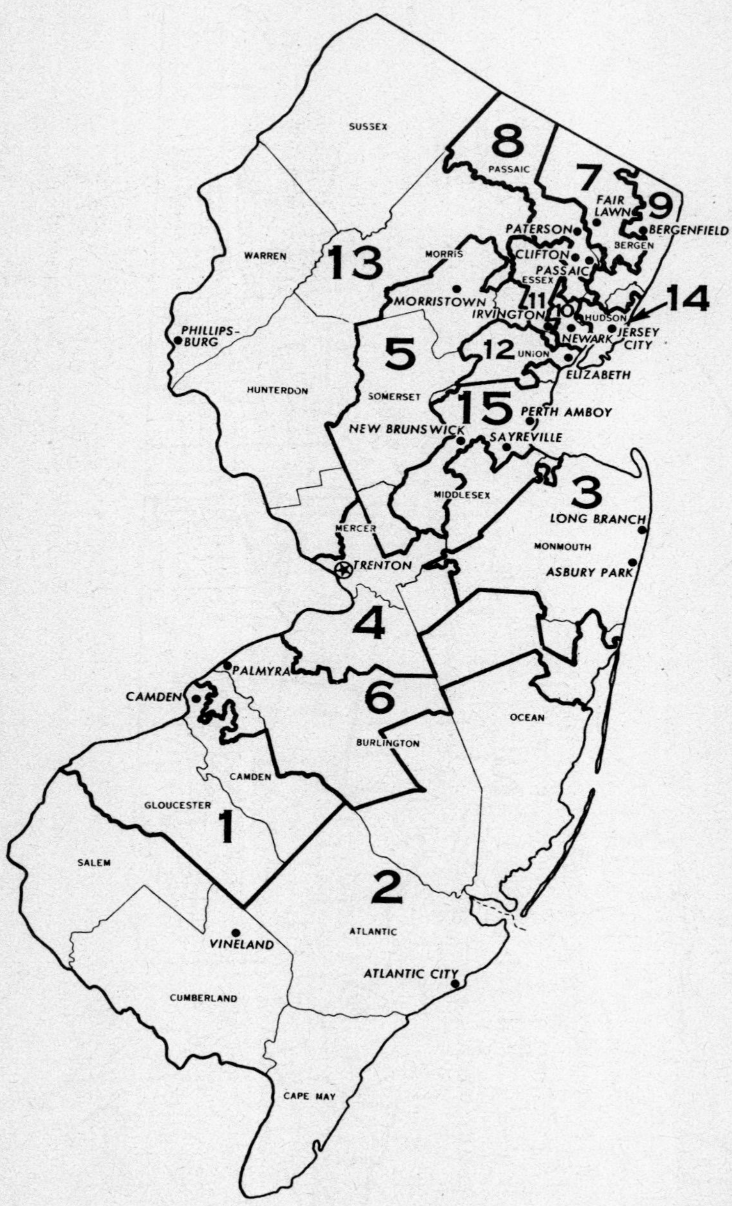

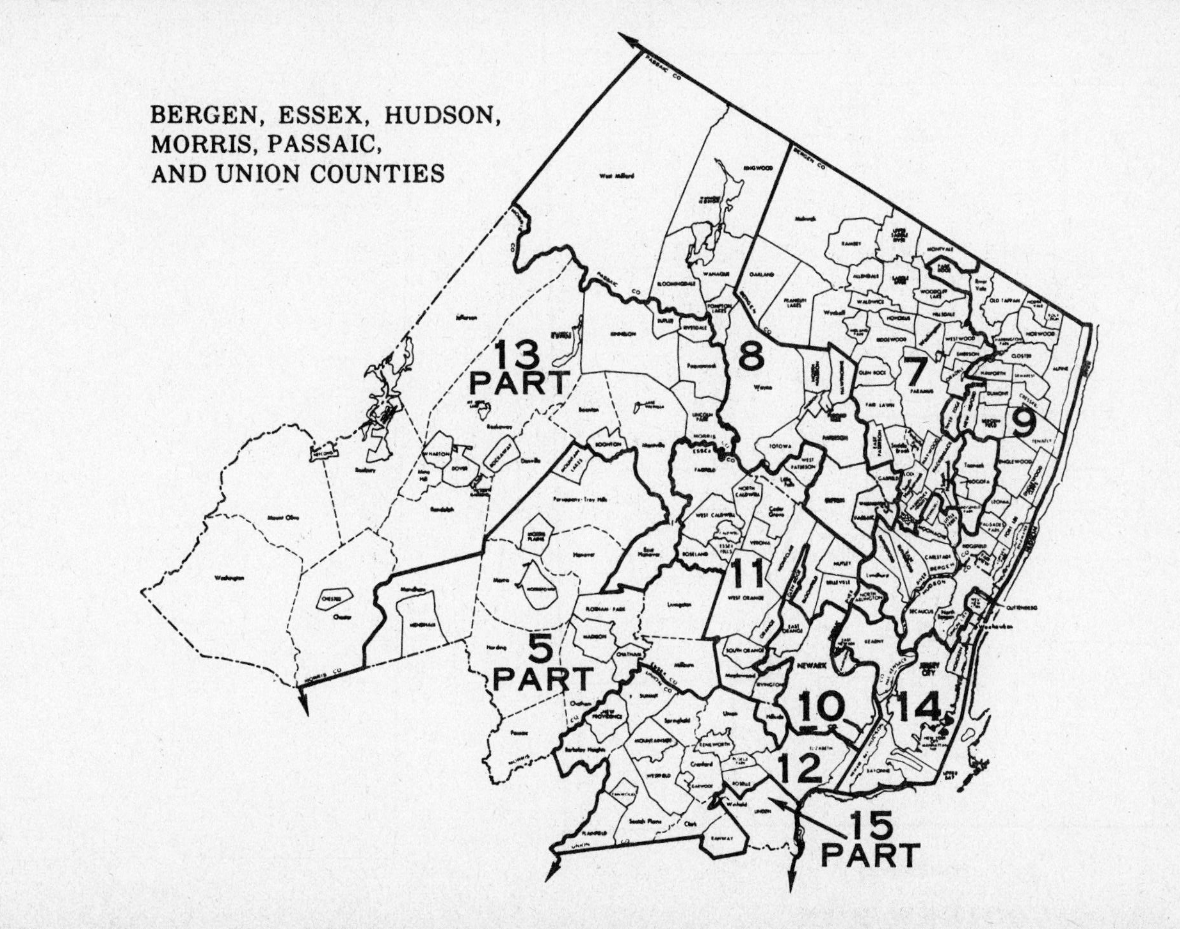
BERGEN, ESSEX, HUDSON,
MORRIS, PASSAIC,
AND UNION COUNTIES
13
PART
8
7
9
11
5
PART
10
14
12
15
PART
West Milford
Ringwood
Mahwah
Wayne
Fair Lawn
Paramus
Totowa
West Caldwell
West Orange
South Orange
Newark
Kearny
Jersey City
Bayonne
Elizabeth
Union
Springfield
Cranford
Westfield
Rahway
Linden
Roselle
Clark
Scotch Plains
Berkeley Heights
Madison
Chatham
Millburn
Livingston
Florham Park
Morristown
Hanover
Parsippany-Troy Hills
Boonton
Montville
Denville
Dover
Wharton
Randolph
Roxbury
Mount Olive
Washington
Chester
Mendham
Harding
Jefferson
Rockaway
Englewood
Tenafly
Closter
Alpine
Norwood
Old Tappan
Montvale
Ramsey
Allendale
Ridgewood
Glen Rock
Oakland
Wanaque
Bloomingdale
Riverdale
Pequannock
Lincoln Park
Fairfield
Verona
Montclair
Bloomfield
Belleville
Nutley
Lyndhurst
Secaucus
Weehawken
Guttenberg
Hoboken
Irvington
Hillside
Kenilworth
Garwood
Plainfield
Summit
New Providence
Mountainside
Bergen Co
Passaic Co
Morris Co
Essex Co
Union Co

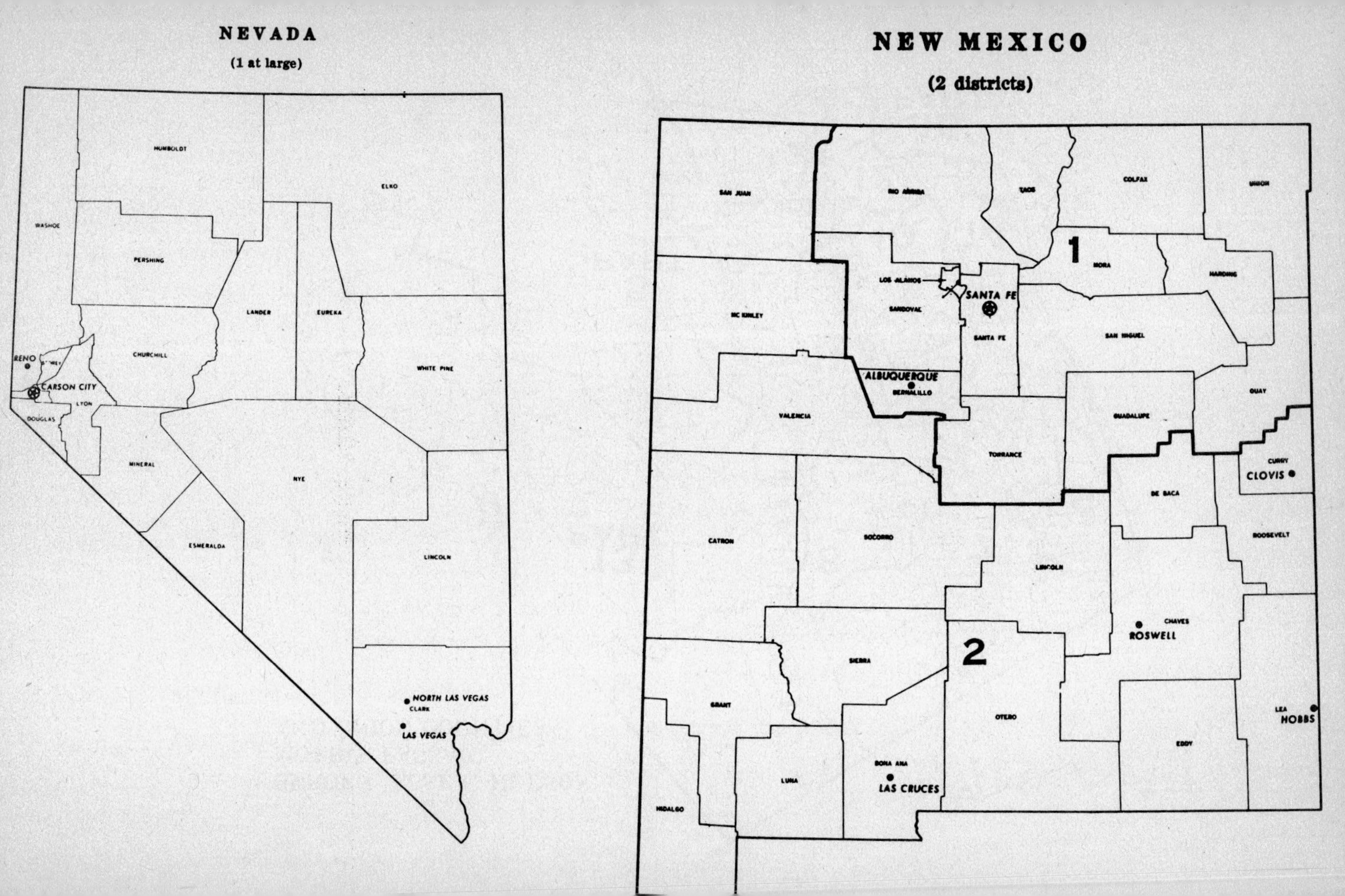
NEVADA
(1 at large)
HUMBOLDT
ELKO
WASHOE
PERSHING
LANDER
EUREKA
CHURCHILL
WHITE PINE
RENO
CARSON CITY
LYON
DOUGLAS
MINERAL
NYE
ESMERALDA
LINCOLN
NORTH LAS VEGAS
CLARK
LAS VEGAS
NEW MEXICO
(2 districts)
SAN JUAN
RIO ARRIBA
TAOS
COLFAX
UNION
1
MORA
HARDING
LOS ALAMOS
SANTA FE
SANDOVAL
MC KINLEY
SANTA FE
SAN MIGUEL
ALBUQUERQUE
BERNALILLO
QUAY
VALENCIA
GUADALUPE
TORRANCE
CURRY
CLOVIS
DE BACA
CATRON
SOCORRO
ROOSEVELT
LINCOLN
CHAVES
ROSWELL
SIERRA
2
GRANT
OTERO
LEA
HOBBS
EDDY
DONA ANA
LUNA
LAS CRUCES
HIDALGO

NEW YORK

(39 districts)

Districts 6-11 and 16-23 established March 28, 1972.
Districts 12-15 established May 30, 1974.
Preliminary map, subject to correction

INSET A - BRONX AND NEW YORK (MANHATTAN) COUNTIES

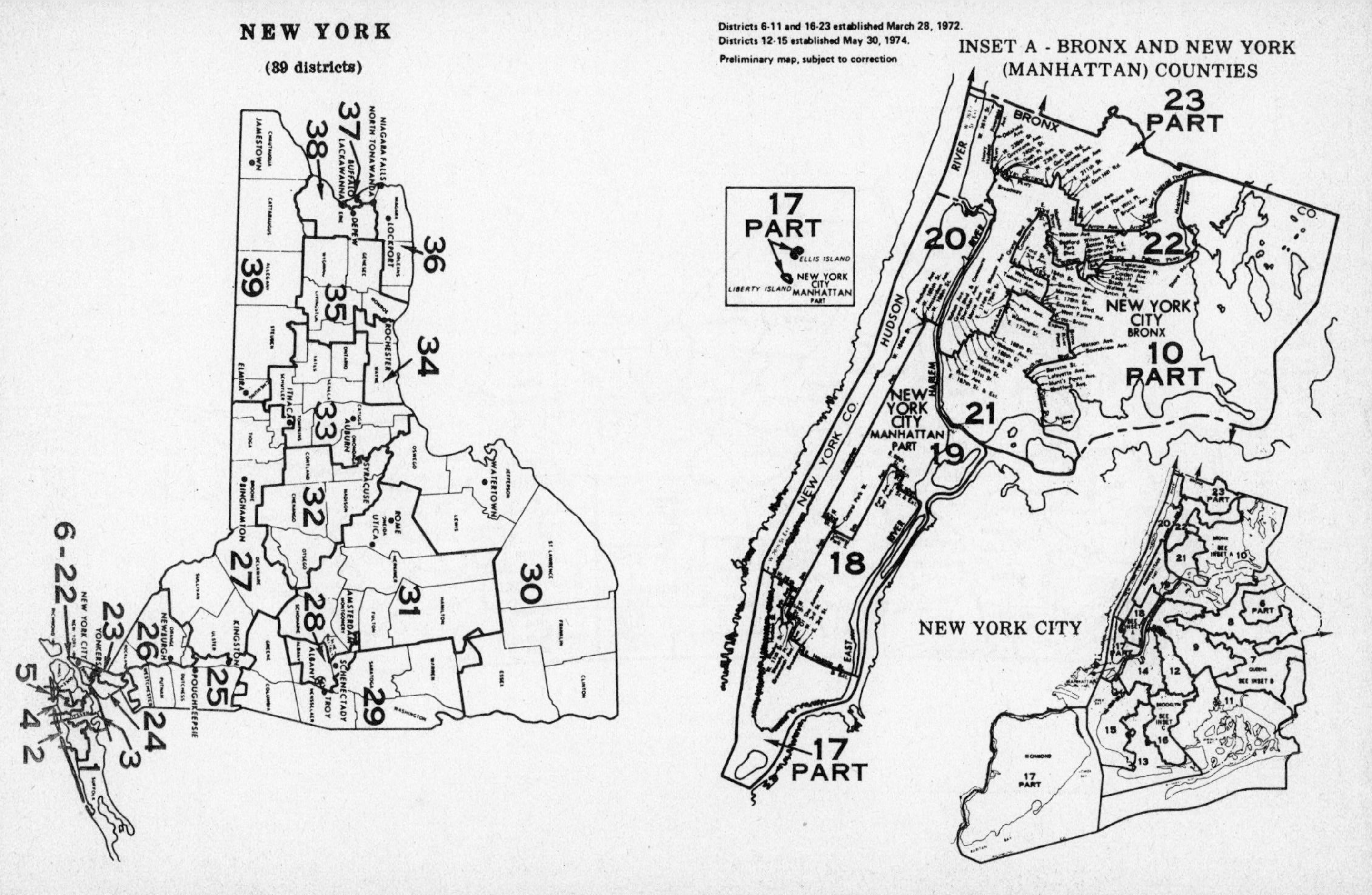

NORTH CAROLINA

(11 districts)

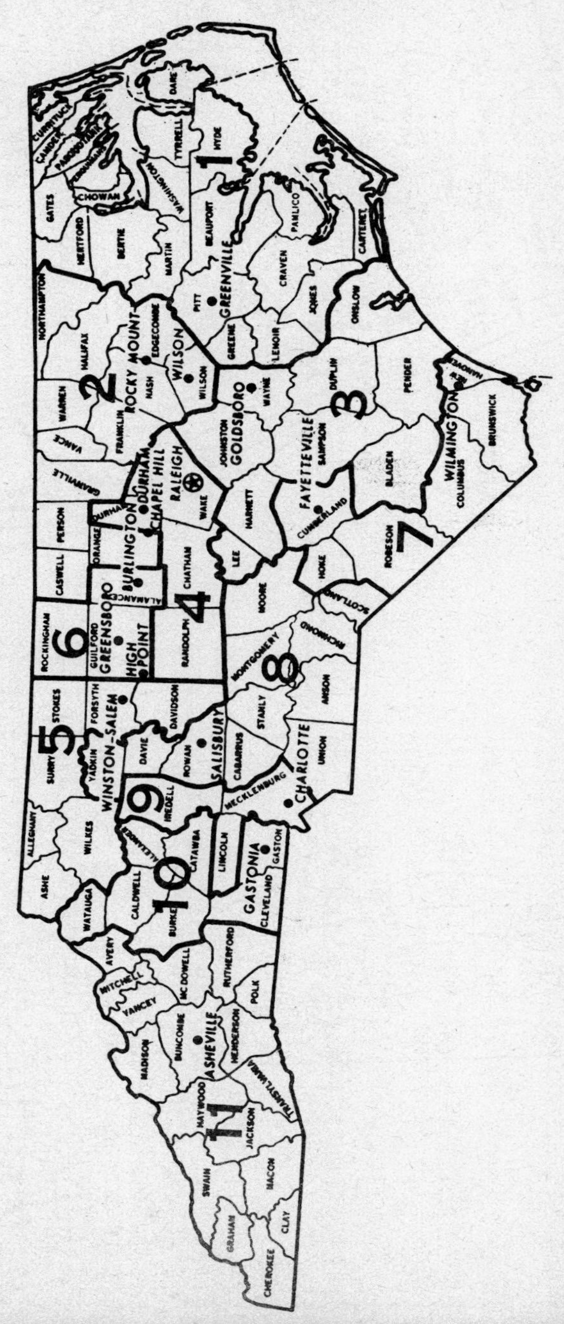

NORTH DAKOTA

(1 at large)

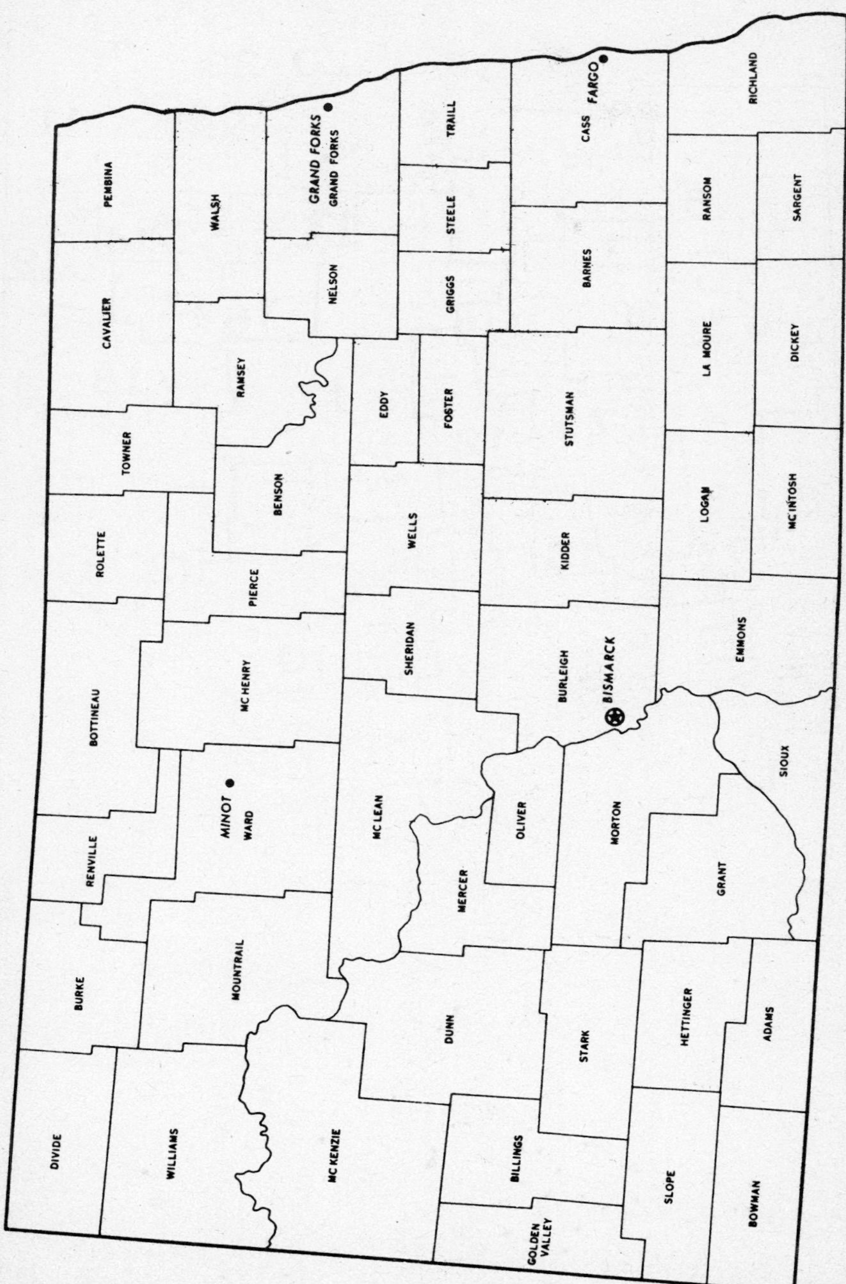

OHIO

(23 districts)

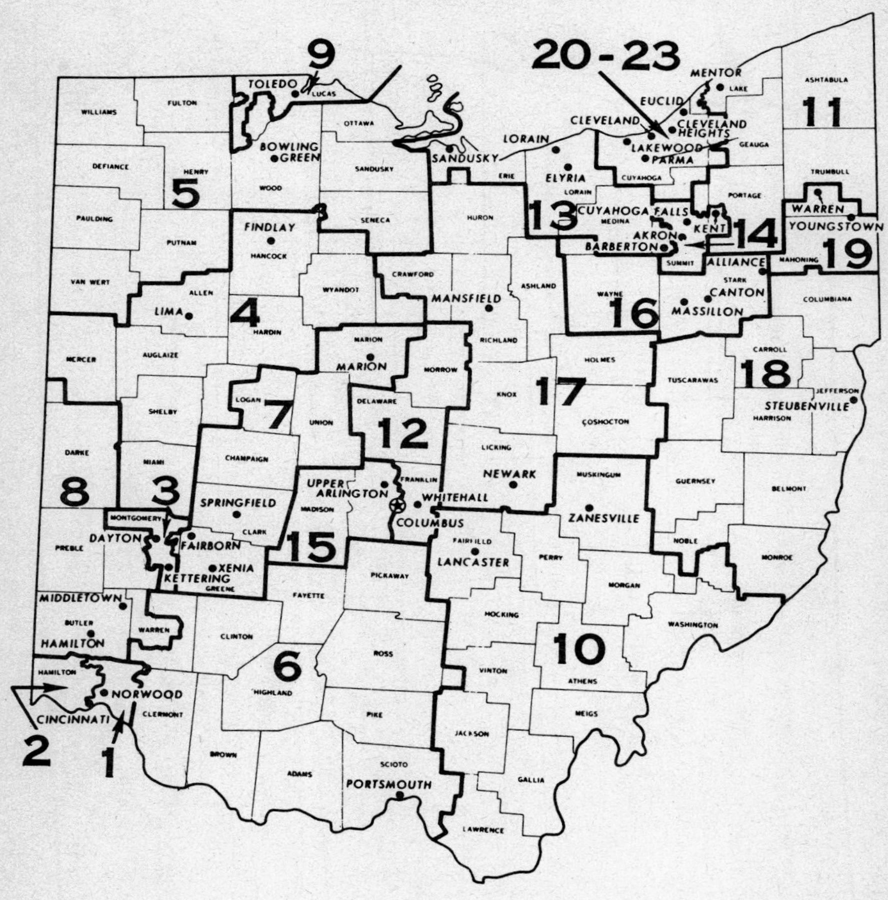

CUYAHOGA, MEDINA, AND SUMMIT COUNTIES

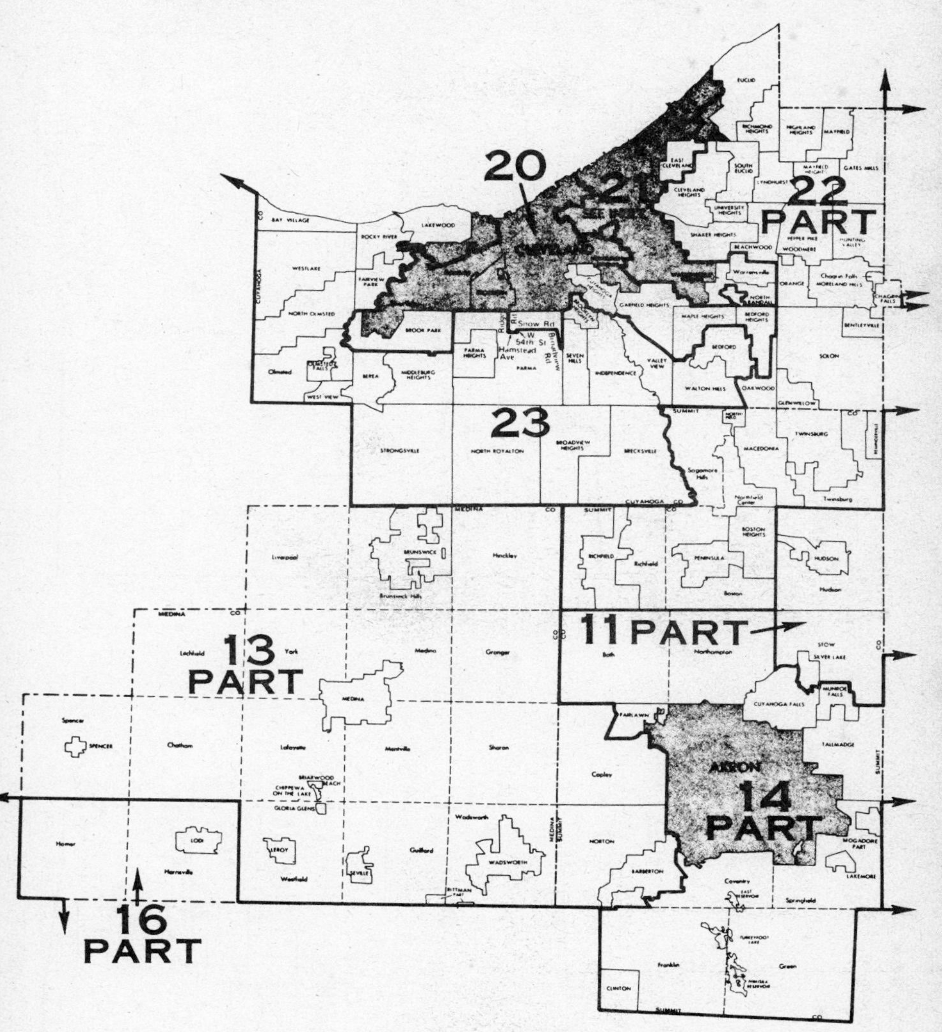

OKLAHOMA

(6 districts)

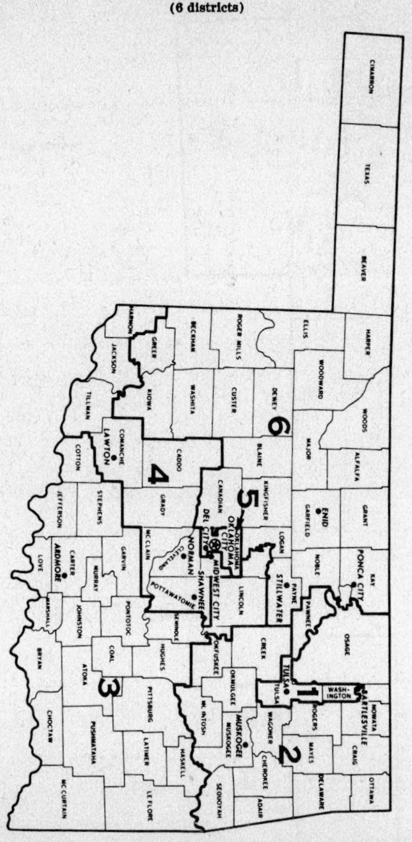

OREGON

(4 districts)

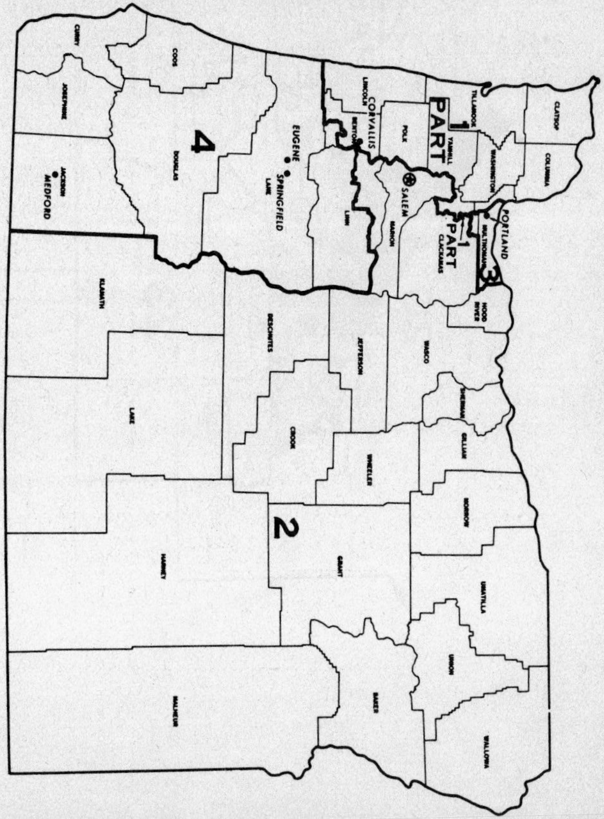

PENNSYLVANIA

(25 districts)

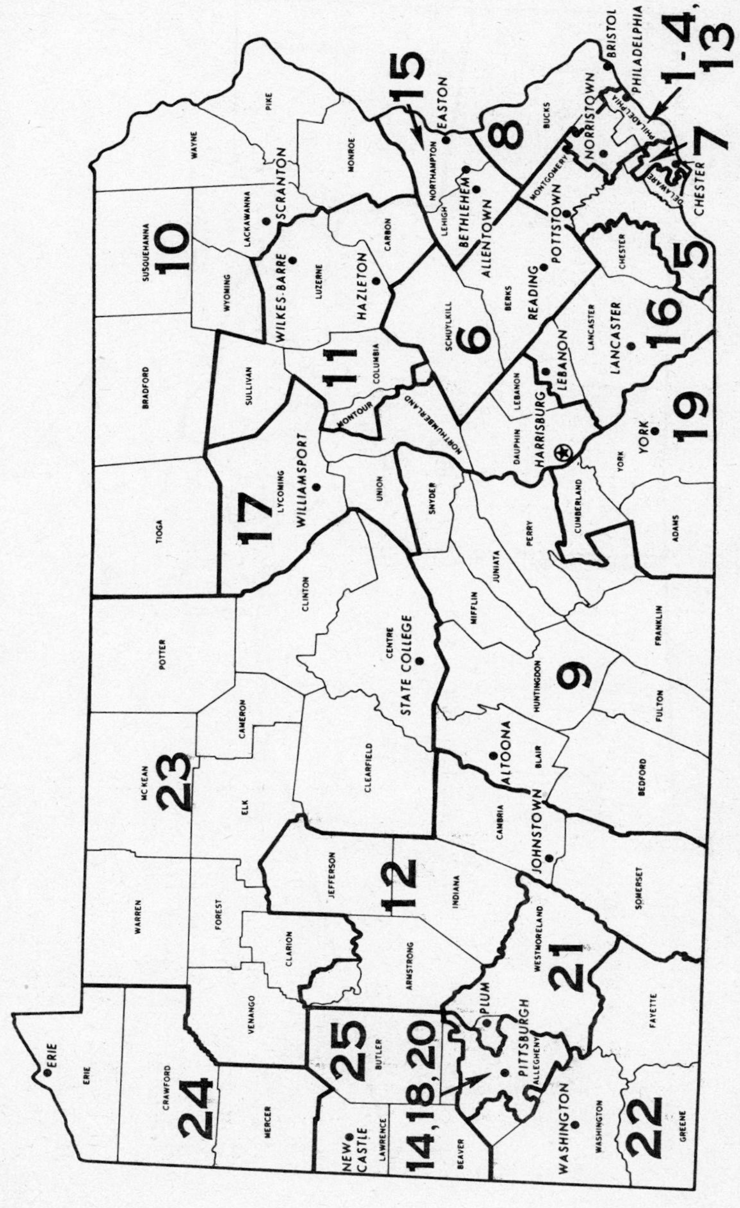

RHODE ISLAND

(2 districts)

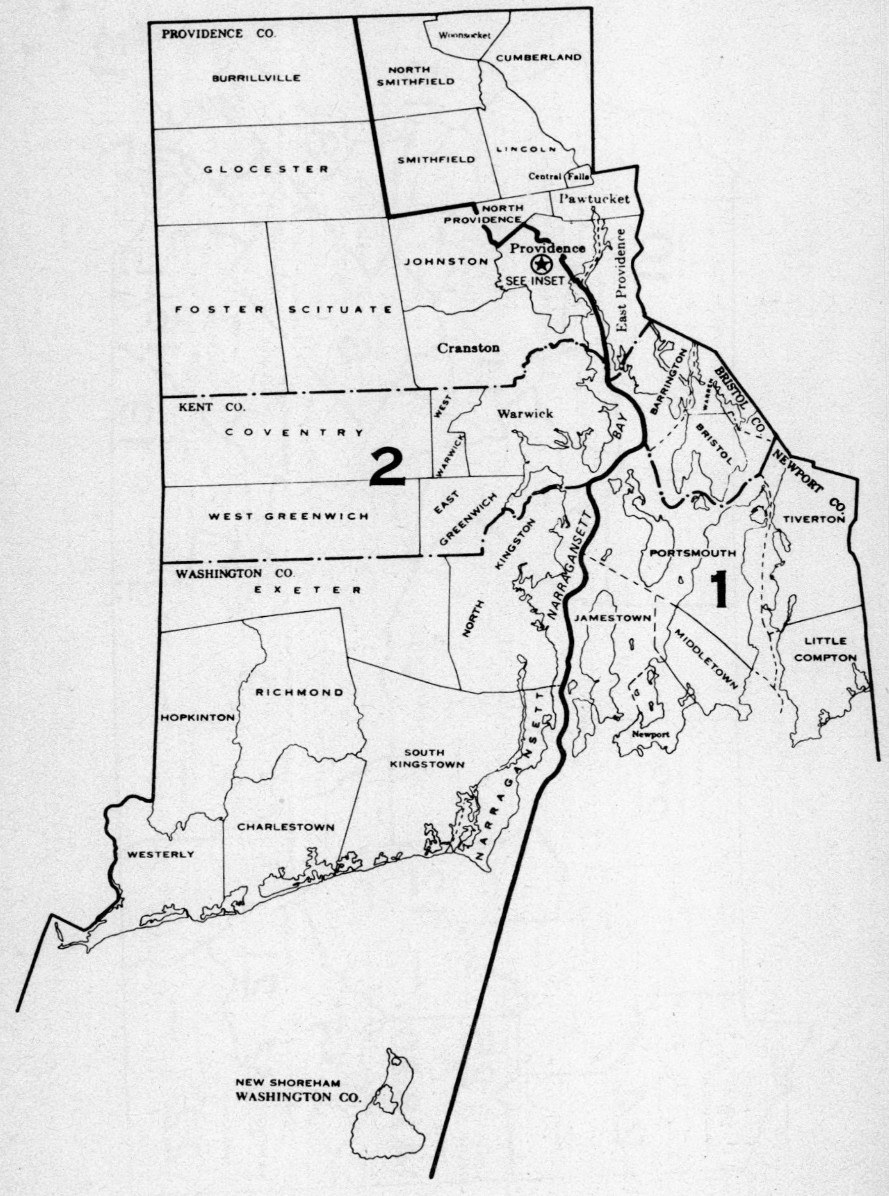

SOUTH CAROLINA

(6 districts)

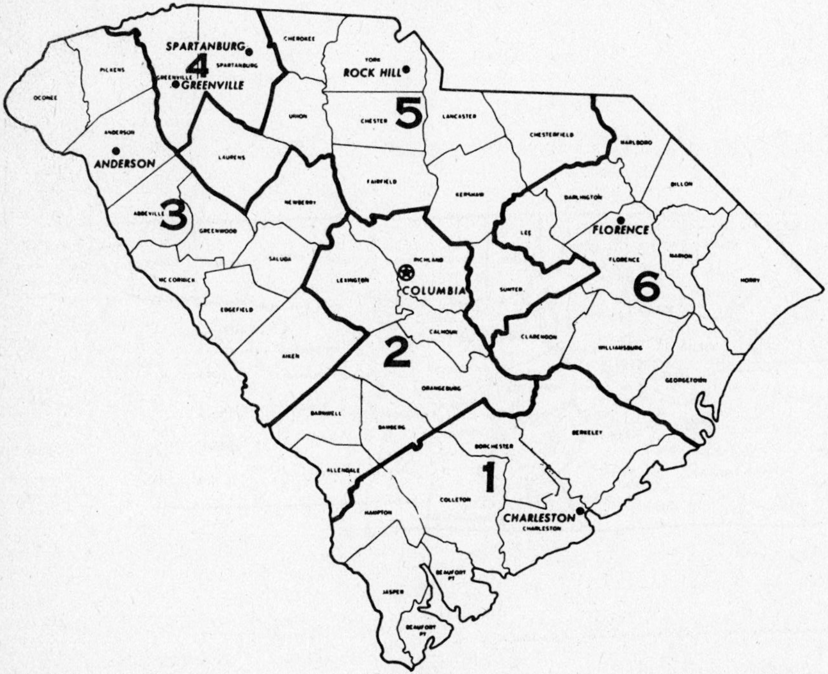

SPARTANBURG
4
GREENVILLE
ROCK HILL
5
ANDERSON
3
FLORENCE
6
COLUMBIA
2
1
CHARLESTON

SOUTH DAKOTA

(2 districts)

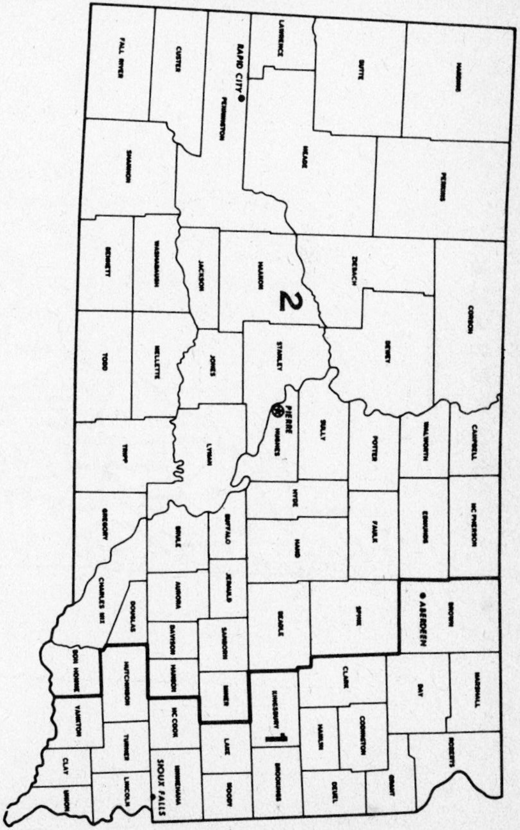

RAPID CITY
2
PIERRE
ABERDEEN
1
SIOUX FALLS

TENNESSEE

(8 districts)

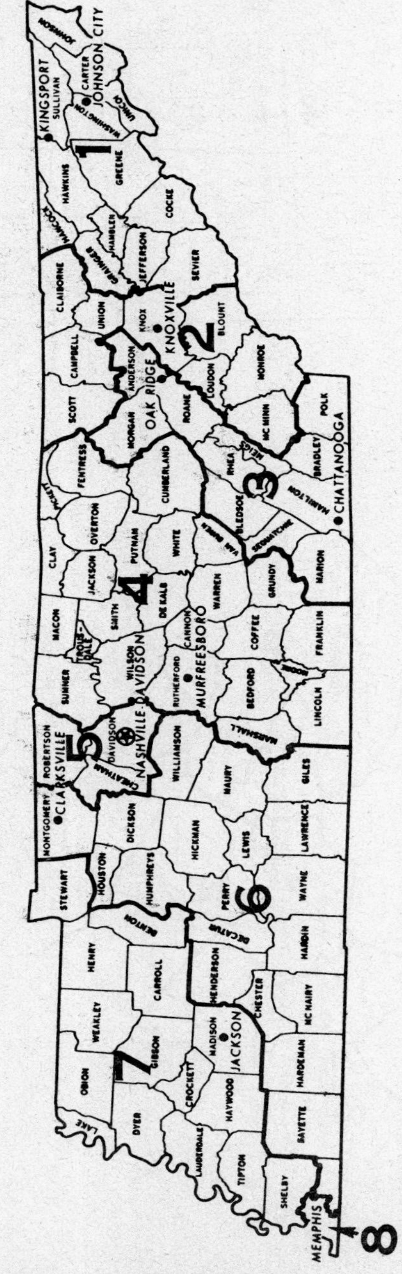

TEXAS

(24 districts)

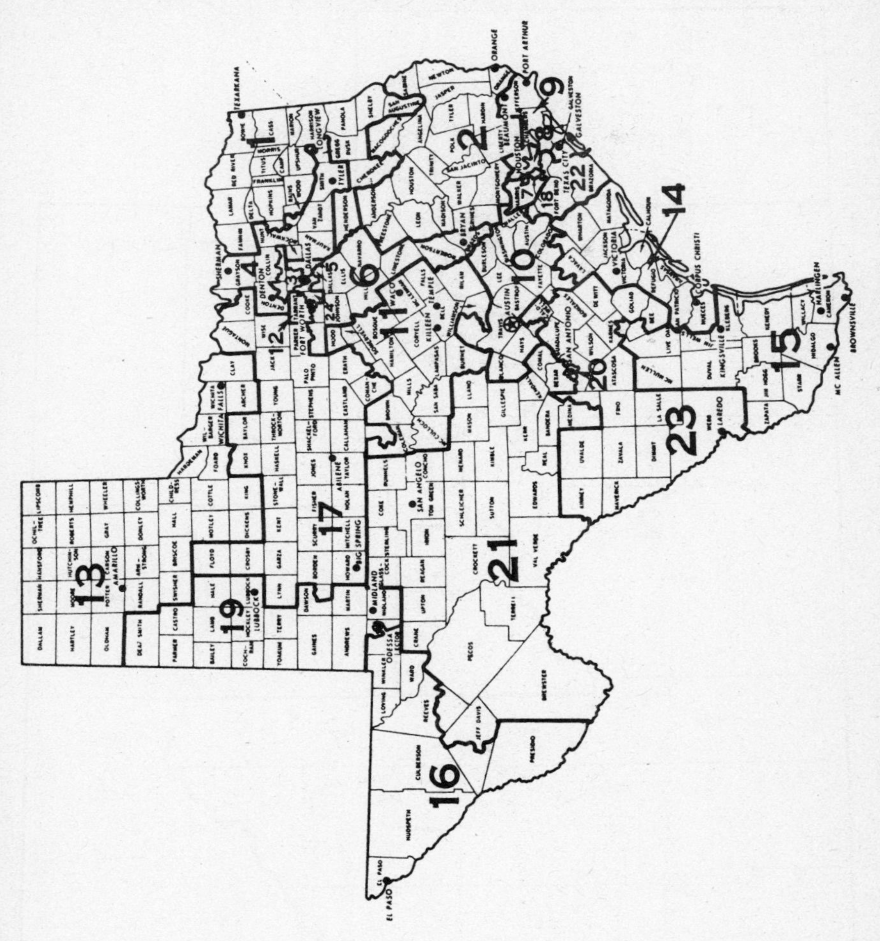

UTAH

(2 districts)

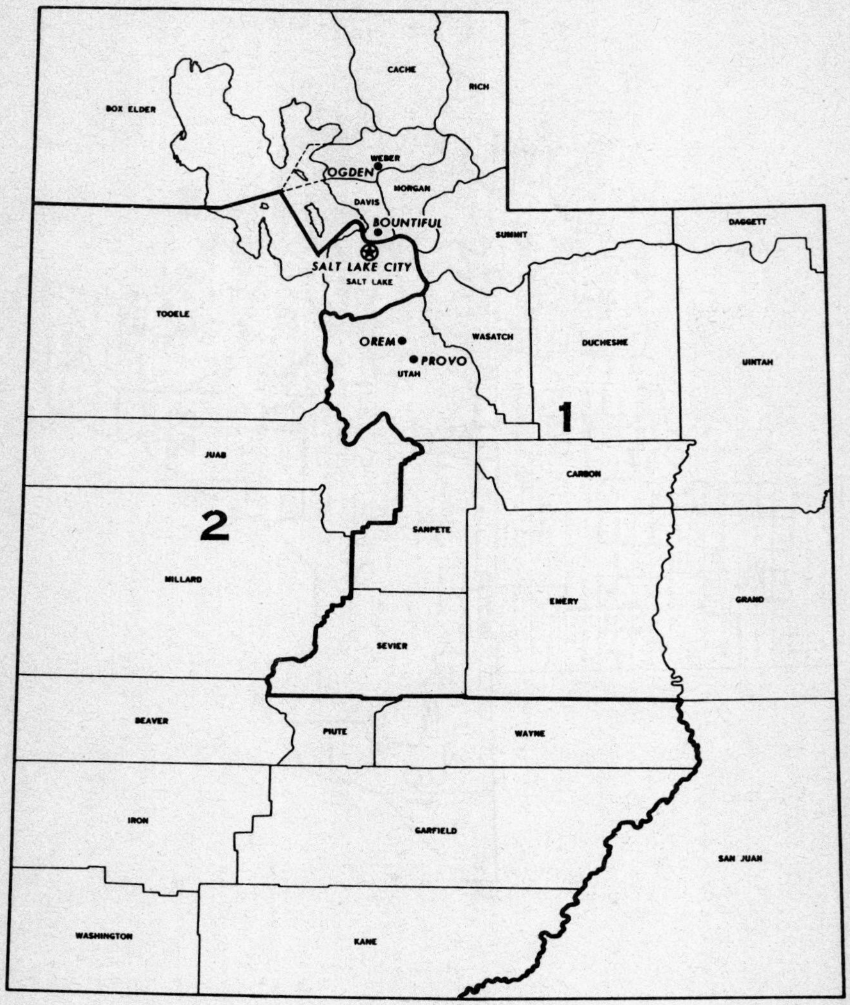

VERMONT

(1 at large)

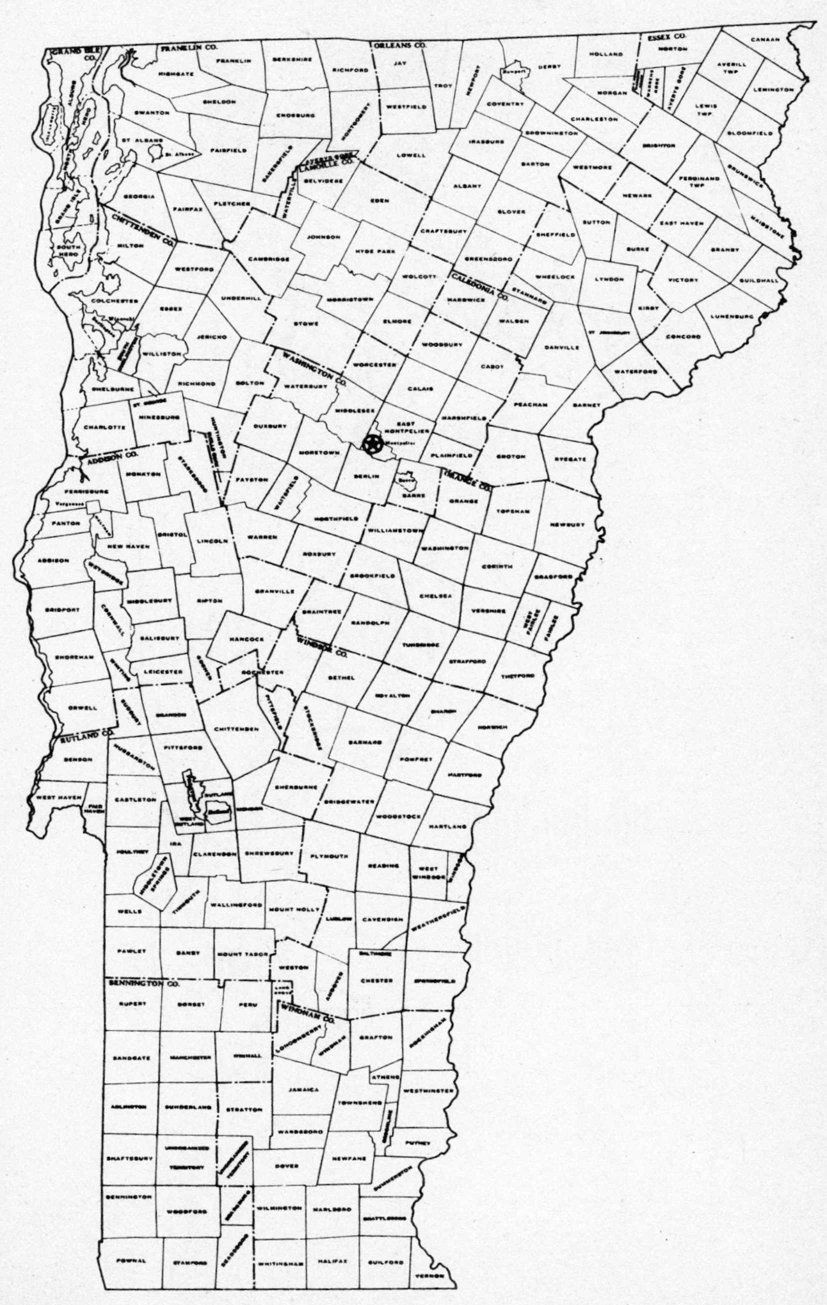

VIRGINIA

(10 districts)

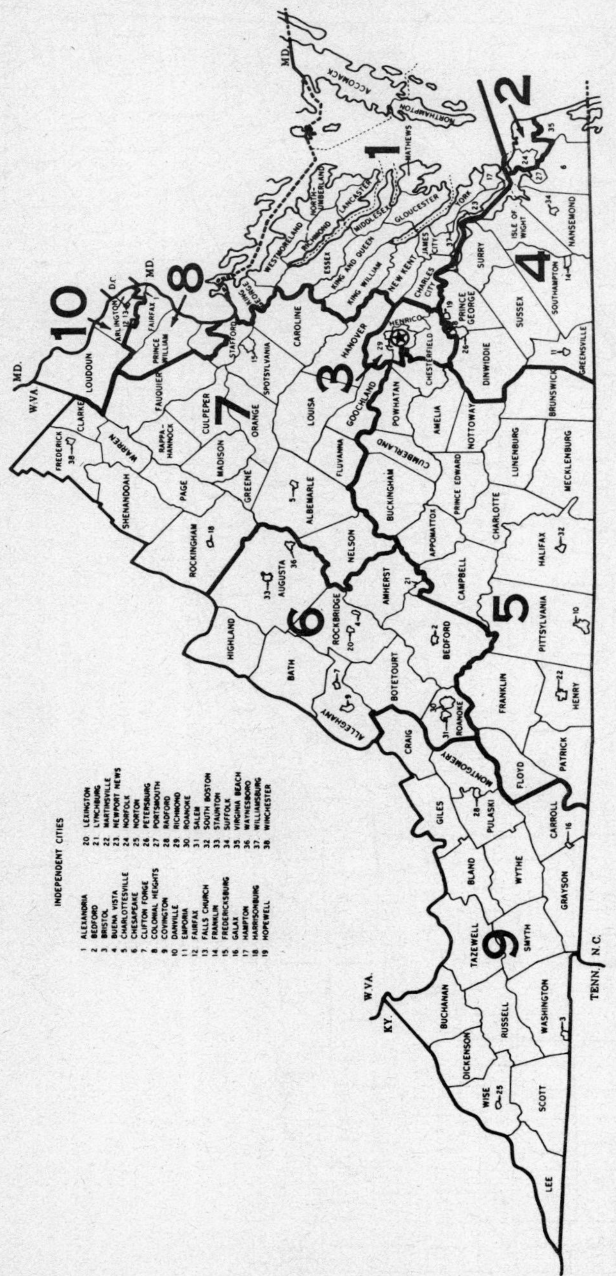

WASHINGTON

(7 districts)

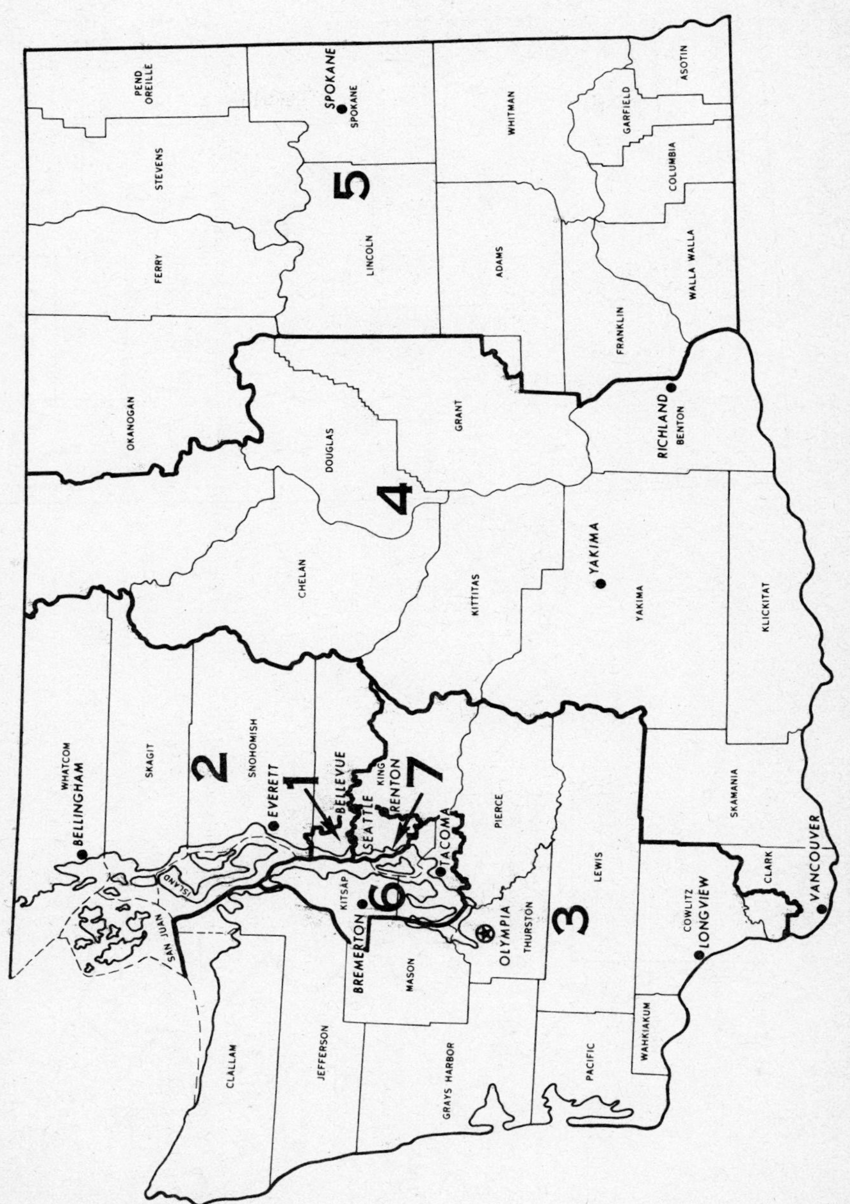

WEST VIRGINIA

(4 districts)

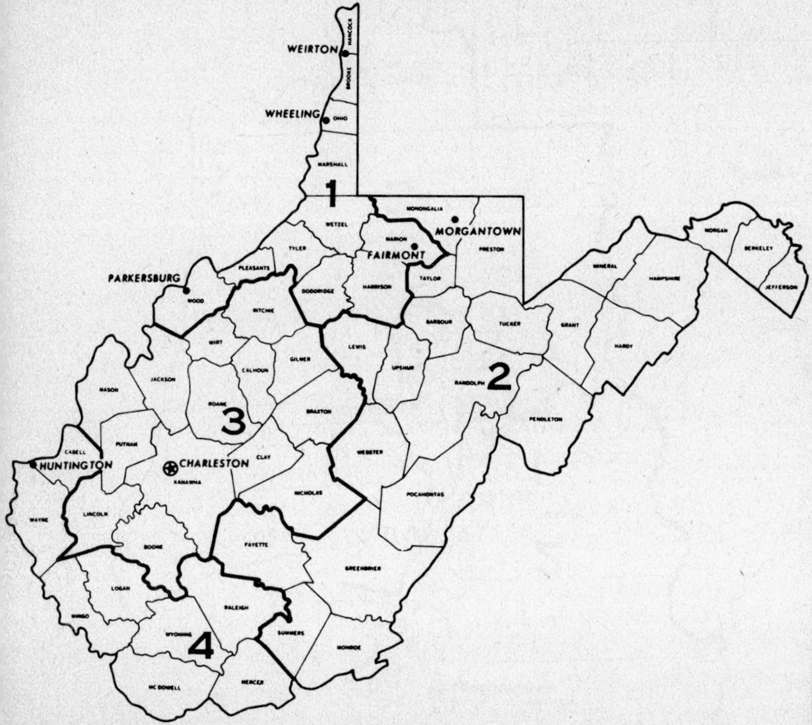

1
2
3
4
WEIRTON
WHEELING
PARKERSBURG
MORGANTOWN
FAIRMONT
CHARLESTON
HUNTINGTON
HANCOCK
BROOKE
OHIO
MARSHALL
WETZEL
MONONGALIA
MARION
PRESTON
TYLER
PLEASANTS
WOOD
DODDRIDGE
HARRISON
TAYLOR
RITCHIE
BARBOUR
TUCKER
GRANT
MINERAL
HAMPSHIRE
MORGAN
BERKELEY
JEFFERSON
HARDY
WIRT
CALHOUN
GILMER
LEWIS
UPSHUR
RANDOLPH
PENDLETON
JACKSON
ROANE
BRAXTON
WEBSTER
MASON
PUTNAM
CABELL
KANAWHA
CLAY
NICHOLAS
POCAHONTAS
WAYNE
LINCOLN
BOONE
FAYETTE
GREENBRIER
LOGAN
MINGO
WYOMING
RALEIGH
SUMMERS
MONROE
MC DOWELL
MERCER

WYOMING

(1 at large)

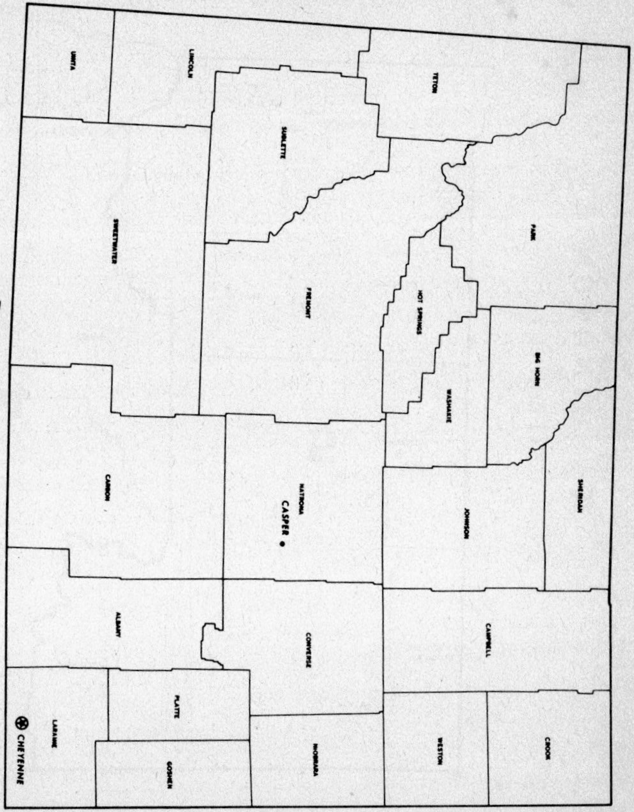

UINTA
LINCOLN
TETON
SUBLETTE
PARK
SWEETWATER
FREMONT
HOT SPRINGS
BIG HORN
WASHAKIE
SHERIDAN
CARBON
NATRONA
CASPER
JOHNSON
ALBANY
CONVERSE
CAMPBELL
LARAMIE
CHEYENNE
PLATTE
GOSHEN
NIOBRARA
WESTON
CROOK

WISCONSIN

(9 districts)

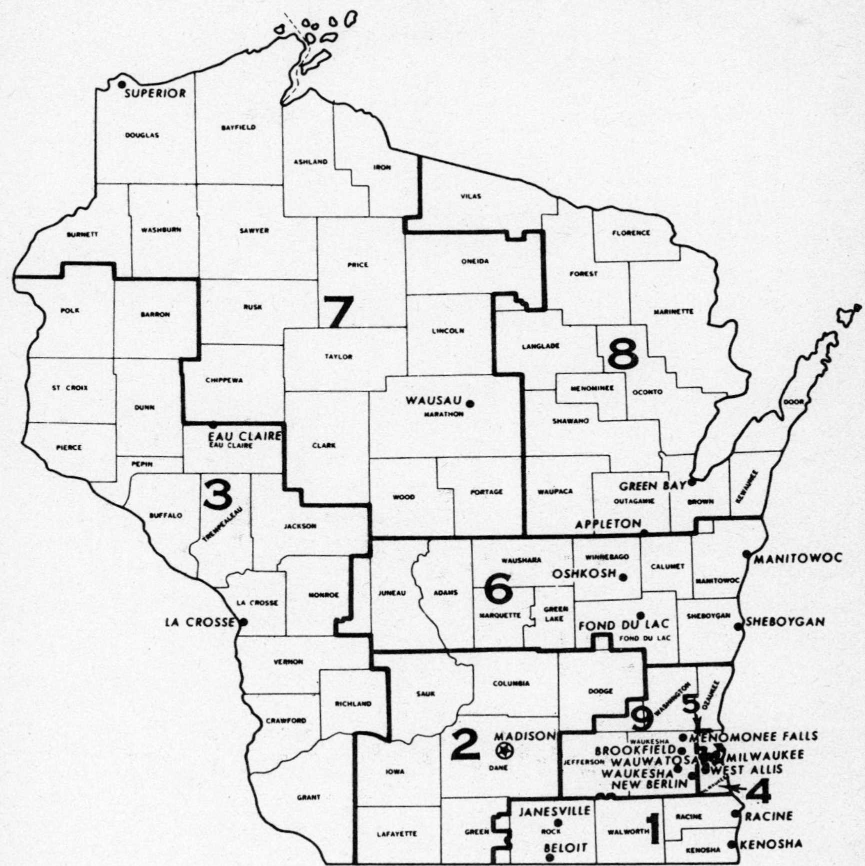

Names Index

The Authors

Michael Barone is a native of the Detroit area and a graduate of Harvard College and Yale Law School. He is now vice president of Peter D. Hart Research Associates, Inc., a public opinion research firm in Washington, D.C. He has served also as a consultant to CBS News. *(Photo: Maxwell Mackenzie.)*

Grant Ujifusa lives with his wife Amy and his son Steven in Manhattan, and works for Random House as an editor of general interest books. *(Photo: Lilian Kemp.)*

Douglas Matthews practices law on his own in Boston. *(Photo: Diana Mara Henry.)*